D MAP PAGES

52

SWEDEN
FINLAND
ESTONIA
LATVIA

TO EUROPE AND
COUNTRY INDEX
EAR ENDPAPER

NY
Slovak Rep.
UKRAINE
AUSTRIA
HUNGARY MOLDOVA
SLOV.
CROATIA BOS.
HERZ.
ITALY SERBIA
& MONT.
BULG.
ROMANIA
MAC.
GREECE

72
GEORGIA
TURKEY
ARM. AZER.
70
SYRIA
74
IRAQ
JORDAN
80
EGYPT
LIBYA

RUSSIA

KAZAKHSTAN

TURKMENISTAN UZBEKISTAN
KYRGYZSTAN
TAJIK.

66 AFGHAN.
68
PAKISTAN
KUWAIT
QATAR
U.A.E.
SAUDI
ARABIA
OMAN

NEPAL
66

INDIA

60

MONGOLIA

56

58

CHINA

BANGLA-
DESH
BURMA

TAIWAN

54
NORTH
KOREA
SOUTH
KOREA
JAPAN

100

Tropic of Cancer

PACIFIC
OCEAN
96

CHAD

SUDAN
ERITREA
YEMEN
DJIBOUTI
ETHIOPIA
SOMALI
REP.
75

64
LAOS
62 THAILAND
CAMB.
65
VIETNAM
65
61
PHILIPPINES

SRI
LANKA

International Dateline

CENTRAL
AFRICAN
REP.
86
UGANDA KENYA
RWANDA
BURUNDI
CONGO
(DEM. REP. OF THE)
TANZANIA
EROON
CONGO
GON

65 MALAYSIA

INDONESIA

63

PAPUA
NEW GUINEA
E. TIMOR

Equator

91

ANGOLA
88
ZAMBIA MALAWI
MOZAMBIQUE
ZIMBABWE
NAMIBIA
BOTSWANA
MADAGASCAR

SWAZILAND

SOUTH
AFRICA LESOTHO

92
94

94

AUSTRALIA

91

91

Tropic of Capricorn

91
NEW
ZEALAND

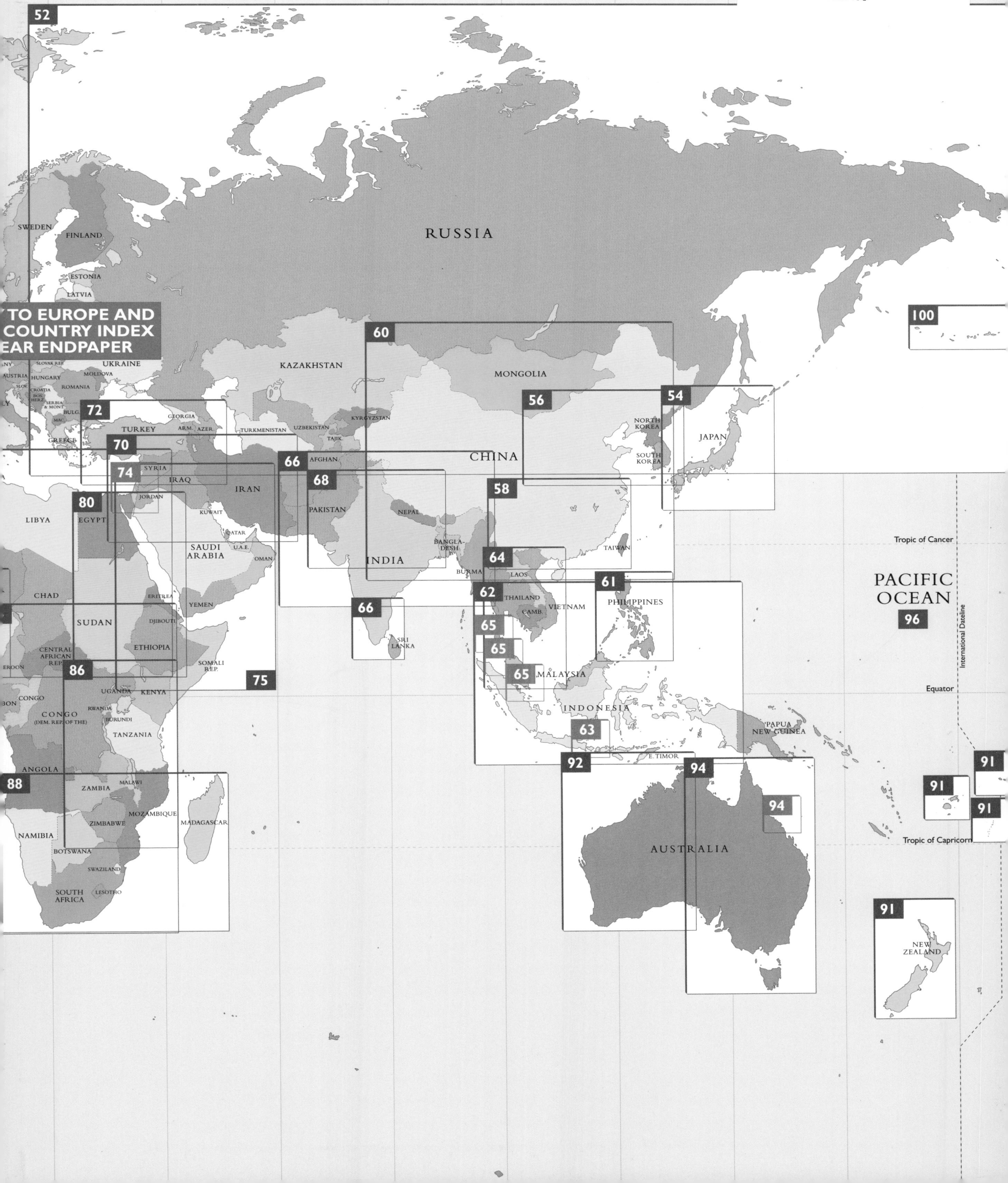

PHILIP'S

WORLD TRAVELLER'S ATLAS

PHILIP'S
WORLD TRAVELLER'S ATLAS

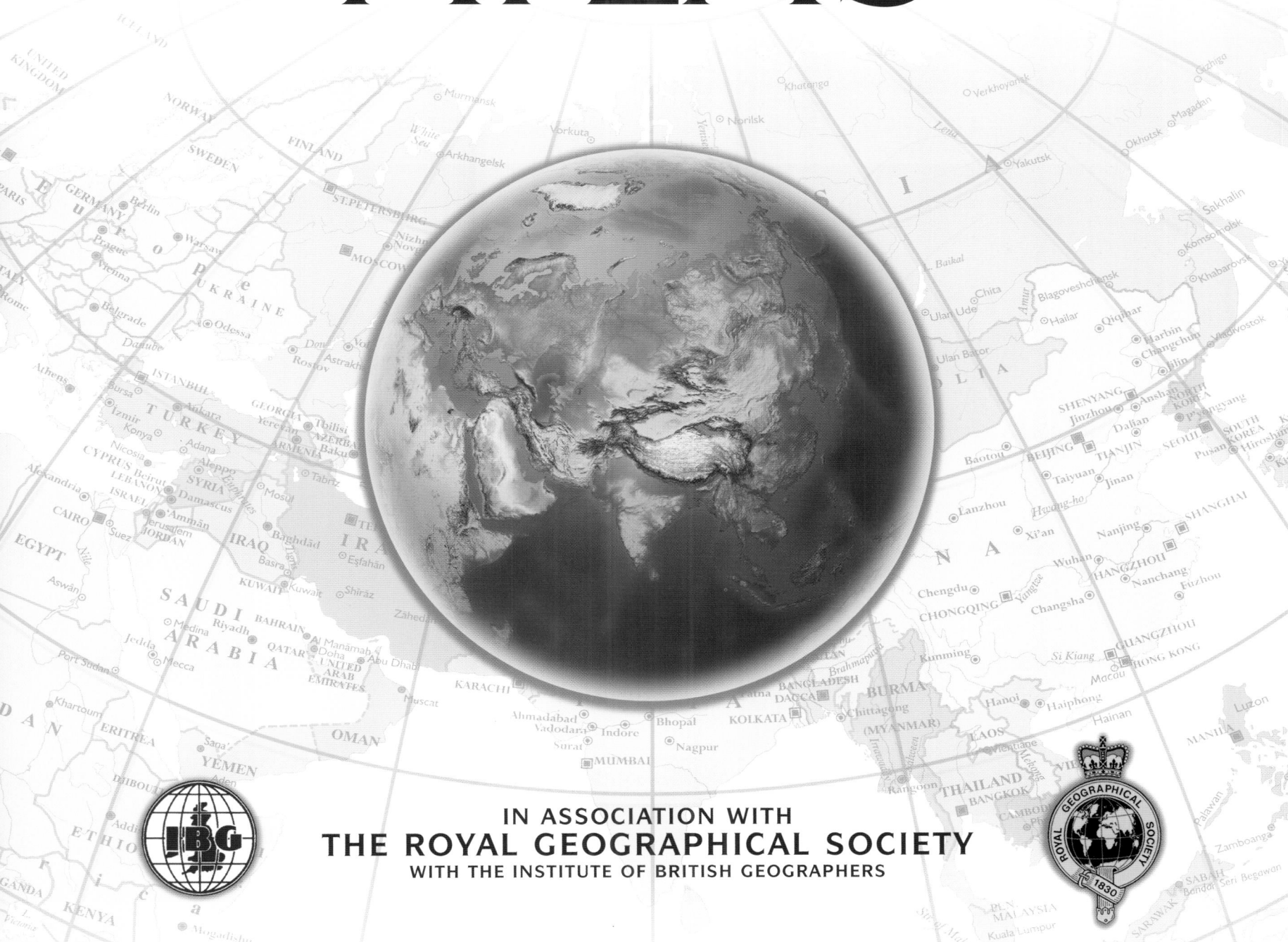

IN ASSOCIATION WITH
THE ROYAL GEOGRAPHICAL SOCIETY
WITH THE INSTITUTE OF BRITISH GEOGRAPHERS

PICTURE ACKNOWLEDGEMENTS

WORLD EXPLORER:
© *CORBIS* 26 bottom, 27 bottom, /Adam Woolfitt 5 centre right, 30 centre left, /AFP 24 top, 25 bottom, /Angelo Hornak 29 centre left, /Australian Picture Library 13 top, /Bob Krist 14 top, /Bob Winsett 20 top, /Brandon D. Cole 11 bottom, /Buddy Mays 26 centre, 22 bottom, /Catherine Karnow 19 bottom, /Charles and Josette Lenars 30 bottom right, /Charles O'Rear 23 left, /Clem Haagner; Gallo Images 10 centre, /Dave G. Houser 30 top, /David Muench 4 left, /Dean Conger 15 bottom, /Derek Hall; Frank Lane Picture Agency 3 centre, /Douglas Peebles 32 bottom, /Duomo 20 right, /Enzo and Paolo Ragazzini 16 bottom, /Galen Rowell 2 left, 9 bottom, 21 top, /George H. H. Huey 4 top, /George Lepp 12 bottom, /Hans Georg Roth 5 top, /Inge Yspeert 10 bottom right, /James Marshall 6 centre right, /John Dakers; Eye Ubiquitous 25 right, /Kevin Schafer 13 bottom, /Marc Muench 20 left, /Michael and Patricia Fogden 8 /Michael Busselle 3 top, /Michael S. Yamashita 22 top, /Milepost 92½ 15 top, /Mimmo Jodice 29 bottom, /Morton Beebe, S. F. 24 centre right, /Nik Wheeler 19 top, /O. Alamany and E. Vicens 5 bottom, /Patrick Ward 7 bottom, 16 centre right, /Peter Johnson 10 top, /Peter Wilson 28 bottom, /Premium Stock 28 top, /Quadrillion 31 bottom, /Raymond Gehman 2 top, 6 top, /Rick Doyle 23 bottom, /Robert Holmes 16 top, /Roger Ressmeyer 3 bottom, /Roger Tidman 9 left, /Stephanie Maze 24 bottom, /Stephen Frink 12 top, 13 centre, /Steve Kaufman 6 bottom, /Tim Thompson 14 centre right, 14 bottom, /Tiziana and Gianni Baldizzone 7 centre right, /Tom Bean 8 bottom, /Tom Brakefield 11 top, /Tom Nebbia 17 right, /Tony Arruza 23 top, /Vanni Archive 29 top, /W. Cody 18 right, 27 top, /Wild Country 26 top, /Wolfgang Kaehler 17 top, 18 top and bottom, 8 top.
© *ALTON TOWERS* 32 left.

CITY GAZETTEER:
© *CORBIS* /Bettmann 41 bottom right, /Carmen Redondo 44 centre left, /Charles E. Rotkin 40 top right, /Chris Lisle 47 centre top, /Hubert Stadler 41 centre top, /John Heseltine 42 top right, /Larry Lee 46 bottom right, /Lindsay Hebberd 42 left, /Patrick Ward 44 bottom right, /Paul A. Souders 47 bottom right, /Richard T. Nowitz 43 bottom centre, /Tim Thompson 41 left, /Todd Gipstein 44 centre top, /Wolfgang Kaehler 45 top right, /Yann Arthus-Bertrand 46 top left.
© *MIKE MOULE* 40 left, 43 top left and centre right, 45 left, 46 centre, 48 centre and right.

CITY MAPS
Cartography by Philip's

PAGE 11, DUBLIN: The town plan of Dublin is based on Ordnance Survey Ireland by permission of the Government Permit Number 7978. © Ordnance Survey Ireland and Government of Ireland.

PAGE 11, EDINBURGH, and PAGE 15, LONDON:
This product includes mapping data licensed from Ordnance Survey® with the permission of the Controller of Her Majesty's Stationery Office. © Crown copyright 2005. All rights reserved. Licence number 100011710.

VECTOR DATA: Courtesy of Gräfe and Unser Verlag GmbH, München, Germany (city centre maps of Bangkok, Beijing, Cape Town, Jerusalem, Mexico City, Moscow, Singapore, Sydney, Tokyo and Washington D.C.)

> **NOTE:**
> For reasons of safety or politics, there may be times when it is not advisable, or desirable, to visit one or more of the places described in the World Explorer and City Gazetteer sections. If in doubt, please check with the Foreign Office.

Published in Great Britain in 2005 by Philip's,
a division of Octopus Publishing Group Limited,
2–4 Heron Quays, London E14 4JP

Copyright © 2005 Philip's

Cartography by Philip's

ISBN-13 978-0-540-08824-9
ISBN-10 0-540-08824-2

A CIP catalogue record for this book is available from the British Library.

Printed in Hong Kong

Details of other Philip's titles and services can be found on our website at:
www.philips-maps.co.uk

Philip's World Atlases are published in association with The Royal Geographical Society (with The Institute of British Geographers).

The Society was founded in 1830 and given a Royal Charter in 1859 for 'the advancement of geographical science'. It holds historical collections of national and international importance, many of which relate to the Society's association with and support for scientific exploration and research from the 19th century onwards. It was pivotal in establishing geography as a teaching and research discipline in British universities close to the turn of the century, and has played a key role in geographical and environmental education ever since.

Today the Society is a leading world centre for geographical learning – supporting education, teaching, research and expeditions, and promoting public understanding of the subject.

The Society welcomes those interested in geography as members. For further information, please visit the website at: www.rgs.org

Philip's World Maps

The reference maps which form the main body of this atlas have been prepared in accordance with the highest standards of international cartography to provide an accurate and detailed representation of the Earth. The scales and projections used have been carefully chosen to give balanced coverage of the world, while emphasizing the most densely populated and economically significant regions. A hallmark of Philip's mapping is the use of hill shading and relief colouring to create a graphic impression of landforms: this makes the maps exceptionally easy to read. However, knowledge of the key features employed in the construction and presentation of the maps will enable the reader to derive the fullest benefit from the atlas.

MAP SEQUENCE

The atlas covers the Earth continent by continent: first Europe; then its land neighbour Asia (mapped north before south, in a clockwise sequence), then Africa, Australia and Oceania, North America and South America. This is the classic arrangement adopted by most cartographers since the 16th century. For each continent, there are maps at a variety of scales. First, physical relief and political maps

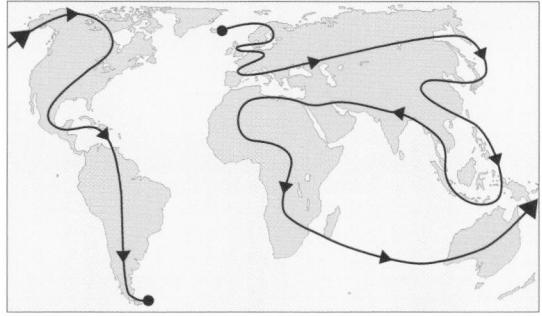

of the whole continent; then a series of larger-scale maps of the regions within the continent, each followed, where required, by still larger-scale maps of the most important or densely populated areas. The governing principle is that by turning the pages of the atlas, the reader moves steadily from north to south through each continent, with each map overlapping its neighbours.

MAP PRESENTATION

With very few exceptions (e.g. for the Arctic and Antarctica), the maps are drawn with north at the top, regardless of whether they are presented upright or sideways on the page. In the borders will be found the map title; a locator diagram showing the area covered; continuation arrows showing the page numbers for maps of adjacent areas; the scale; the projection used; the degrees of latitude and longitude; and the letters and figures used in the index for locating place names and geographical features. Physical relief maps also have a height reference panel identifying the colours used for each layer of contouring.

MAP SYMBOLS

Each map contains a vast amount of detail which can only be conveyed clearly and accurately by the use of symbols. Points and circles of varying sizes locate and identify the relative importance of towns and cities; different styles of type are employed for administrative, geographical and regional place names to aid identification. A variety of pictorial symbols denote landscape features such as glaciers, marshes and coral reefs, and man-made structures including roads, railways, airports, canals and dams. International borders are shown by red lines. Where neighbouring countries are in dispute, for example in parts of the Middle East, the maps show the *de facto* boundary between nations, regardless of the legal or historical situation. The symbols are explained on the first page of the *World Maps* section of the atlas.

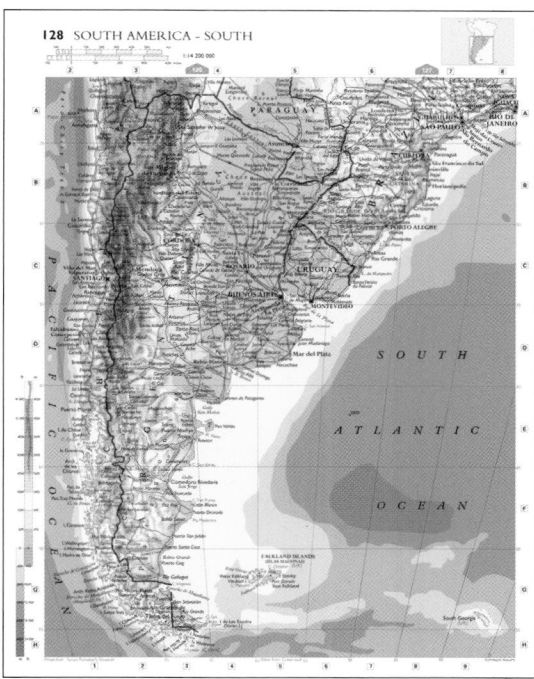

MAP SCALES

1:16 000 000
1 inch = 252 statute miles

The scale of each map is given in the numerical form known as the 'representative fraction'. The first figure is always one, signifying one unit of distance on the map; the second figure, usually in millions, is the number by which the map unit must be multiplied to give the equivalent distance on the Earth's surface. Calculations can easily be made in centimetres and kilometres, by dividing the Earth units figure by 100 000 (i.e. deleting the last five 0s). Thus 1:1 000 000 means 1 cm = 10 km. The calculation for inches and miles is more laborious, but 1 000 000 divided by 63 360 (the number of inches in a mile) shows that 1:1 000 000 means approximately 1 inch = 16 miles. The table below provides distance equivalents for scales down to 1:50 000 000.

LARGE SCALE		
1:1 000 000	1 cm = 10 km	1 inch = 16 miles
1:2 500 000	1 cm = 25 km	1 inch = 39.5 miles
1:5 000 000	1 cm = 50 km	1 inch = 79 miles
1:6 000 000	1 cm = 60 km	1 inch = 95 miles
1:8 000 000	1 cm = 80 km	1 inch = 126 miles
1:10 000 000	1 cm = 100 km	1 inch = 158 miles
1:15 000 000	1 cm = 150 km	1 inch = 237 miles
1:20 000 000	1 cm = 200 km	1 inch = 316 miles
1:50 000 000	1 cm = 500 km	1 inch = 790 miles
SMALL SCALE		

MEASURING DISTANCES

Although each map is accompanied by a scale bar, distances cannot always be measured with confidence because of the distortions involved in portraying the curved surface of the Earth on a flat page. As a general rule, the larger the map scale (i.e. the lower the number of Earth units in the representative fraction), the more accurate and reliable will be the distance measured. On small-scale maps such as those of the world and of entire continents, measurement may only

be accurate along the 'standard parallels', or central axes, and should not be attempted without considering the map projection.

MAP PROJECTIONS

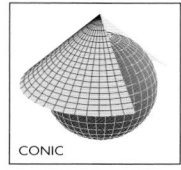  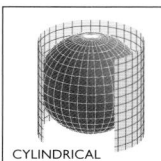

Unlike a globe, no flat map can give a true scale representation of the world in terms of area, shape and position of every region. Each of the numerous systems that have been devised for projecting the curved surface of the Earth on to a flat page involves the sacrifice of accuracy in one or more of these elements. The variations in shape and position of landmasses such as Alaska, Greenland and Australia, for example, can be quite dramatic when different projections are compared.

For this atlas, the guiding principle has been to select projections that involve the least distortion of size and distance. The projection used for each map is noted in the border. Most fall into one of three categories – conic, azimuthal or cylindrical – whose basic concepts are shown above. Each involves plotting the forms of the Earth's surface on a grid of latitude and longitude lines, which may be shown as parallels, curves or radiating spokes.

LATITUDE AND LONGITUDE

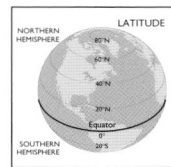 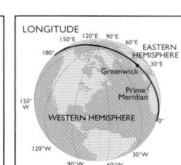 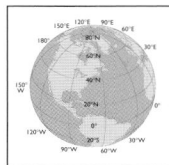

Accurate positioning of individual points on the Earth's surface is made possible by reference to the geometrical system of latitude and longitude. Latitude *parallels* are drawn west–east around the Earth and numbered by degrees north and south of the Equator, which is designated 0° of latitude. Longitude *meridians* are drawn north–south and numbered by degrees east and west of the *prime meridian*, 0° of longitude, which passes through Greenwich in England. By referring to these co-ordinates and their subdivisions of minutes (1/60th of a degree) and seconds (1/60th of a minute), any place on Earth can be located to within a few hundred metres. Latitude and longitude are indicated by blue lines on the maps; they are straight or curved according to the projection employed. Reference to these lines is the easiest way of determining the relative positions of places on different maps, and for plotting compass directions.

NAME FORMS

For ease of reference, both English and local name forms appear in the atlas. Oceans, seas and countries are shown in English throughout the atlas; country names may be abbreviated to their commonly accepted form (e.g. Germany, not The Federal Republic of Germany). Conventional English forms are also used for place names on the smaller-scale maps of the continents. However, local name forms are used on all large-scale and regional maps, with the English form given in brackets only for important cities – the large-scale map of Russia and Central Asia thus shows Moskva (Moscow). For countries which do not use a Roman script, place names have been transcribed according to the systems adopted by the British and US Geographic Names Authorities. For China, the Pin Yin system has been used, with some more widely known forms appearing in brackets, as with Beijing (Peking). Both English and local names appear in the index, the English form being cross-referenced to the local form.

Contents

WORLD STATISTICS

Countries   x
Cities   xi
Distances   xii
Climate   xiii
Physical Dimensions   xiv–xv
Regions in the News   xvi

WORLD EXPLORER

Mountains and volcanoes   2–3
Deserts and canyons   4–5
Lakes and waterfalls   6–7
Wildlife in the Americas
  and Europe   8–9
Wildlife in Africa, Asia
  and Australasia   10–11
Marine wildlife   12–13
Great railway journeys   14–15
River and canal journeys   16–17
Sea and ocean cruises   18–19
Winter sports   20–21
Great beaches   22–23
Festivals   24–25
Historic sites in the
  Americas   26–27
Historic sites in Europe   28–29
Historic sites in Africa,
  Asia and Australasia   30–31
Theme parks   32

WORLD CITIES

CITY MAPS

Amsterdam   2
Athens   2
Atlanta   3
Baghdad   3
Bangkok   3
Barcelona   4
Beijing   4
Berlin   5
Boston   6
Brussels   6
Budapest   7
Buenos Aires   7
Cairo   7
Calcutta (Kolkata)   8

Canton (Guangzhou)   8
Cape Town   8
Chicago   9
Copenhagen   10
Delhi   10
Dublin   11
Edinburgh   11
Helsinki   12
Hong Kong   12
Istanbul   12
Jakarta   13
Jerusalem   13
Johannesburg   13
Karachi   14
Lagos   14
Lisbon   14
London   15
Lima   16
Los Angeles   16
Madrid   17
Manila   17
Melbourne   17
Mexico City   18
Miami   18
Milan   18
Montréal   19
Moscow   19
Mumbai (Bombay)   20
Munich   20
New York   21
Osaka   22
Oslo   22
Paris   23
Prague   24
Rio de Janeiro   24
Rome   25
San Francisco   25
St Petersburg   26
Santiago   26
São Paulo   26
Seoul   26
Shanghai   27
Singapore   27
Stockholm   28
Sydney   28
Tokyo   29
Tehran   30
Tianjin   30
Toronto   30
Vienna   31
Warsaw   31
Washington   32
Wellington   32

INDEX TO CITY MAPS   33–39

CITY GAZETTEER

Accra, Ghana   40
Agra, India   40
Amsterdam, The Netherlands   40
Antwerp, Belgium   40
Athens, Greece   40
Atlanta, Georgia, USA   40
Auckland, New Zealand   40
Bangkok, Thailand   40
Barcelona, Spain   40
Beijing, China   40
Berlin, Germany   40
Boston, Massachusetts, USA   41
Brisbane, Queensland,
  Australia   41
Brussels, Belgium   41
Budapest, Hungary   41
Buenos Aires, Argentina   41
Cairo, Egypt   41
Calcutta (Kolkata), India   41
Canton (Guangzhou), China   41
Cape Town, South Africa   41
Cartagena, Colombia   41
Chicago, Illinois, USA   41
Cologne, Germany   42
Copenhagen, Denmark   42
Delhi, India   42
Dublin, Ireland   42
Edinburgh, Scotland   42
Esfahan, Iran   42
Fès, Morocco   42
Florence, Italy   42
Geneva, Switzerland   42
Hamburg, Germany   42
Hanoi, Vietnam   42
Havana, Cuba   42
Helsinki, Finland   43
Hong Kong, China   43
Istanbul, Turkey   43
Jaipur, India   43
Jakarta, Indonesia   43
Jerusalem, Israel   43
Johannesburg, South Africa   43
Kairouan, Tunisia   43
Karachi, Pakistan   43
Katmandu, Nepal   43
Kraków, Poland   43
Kuala Lumpur, Malaysia   44
Kyoto, Japan   44
Lagos, Nigeria   44
Lahore, Pakistan   44
Las Vegas, Nevada, USA   44
Lima, Peru   44
Lisbon, Portugal   44
London, England   44

Los Angeles, California, USA   44
Luxembourg City, Luxembourg   44
Madrid, Spain   44
Manila, Philippines   45
Marrakech, Morocco   45
Melbourne, Victoria,
  Australia   45
Mexico City, Mexico   45
Miami, Florida, USA   45
Milan, Italy   45
Montréal, Québec, Canada   45
Moscow, Russia   45
Mumbai (Bombay), India   45
Munich, Germany   45
Nairobi, Kenya   45
New Orleans, Louisiana, USA   45
New York, NY, USA   46
Osaka, Japan   46
Oslo, Norway   46
Panama City, Panama   46
Paris, France   46
Perth, Western Australia,
  Australia   46
Prague, Czech Republic   46
Quito, Ecuador   46
Reykjavik, Iceland   46
Riga, Latvia   46
Rio de Janeiro, Brazil   46
Rome, Italy   46
St Petersburg, Russia   47
San Francisco, California, USA   47
Santiago, Chile   47
São Paulo, Brazil   47
Seattle, Washington, USA   47
Seoul, South Korea   47
Shanghai, China   47
Singapore City, Singapore   47
Stockholm, Sweden   47
Sydney, New South Wales,
  Australia   47
Tehran, Iran   47
Tianjin, China   48
Tokyo, Japan   48
Toronto, Ontario, Canada   48
Vancouver, British Columbia,
  Canada   48
Varanasi, India   48
Venice, Italy   48
Vienna, Austria   48
Warsaw, Poland   48
Washington DC, USA   48
Wellington, New Zealand   48
Xi'an, China   48
Yangon (Rangoon), Burma
  (Myanmar)   48

WORLD MAPS

Map Symbols   1

The World: Political
1:71 100 000   2–3

Arctic Ocean
1:31 100 000   4

Antarctica
1:31 100 000   5

Europe

Europe: Physical
1:17 800 000   6

Europe: Political
1:17 800 000   7

Scandinavia
1:4 400 000
Iceland 1:4 400 000
     8–9

Denmark and Southern Sweden
1:2 200 000
     10–11

Ireland
1:1 800 000
     12

Scotland
1:1 800 000
     13

England and Wales
1:1 800 000
     14–15

British Isles
1:4 400 000
     16

Netherlands, Belgium and Luxembourg
1:2 200 000
     17

Northern France
1:2 200 000
     18–19

Southern France
1:2 200 000
     20–21

Central Europe
1:4 400 000
     22–23

Germany and Switzerland
1:2 200 000
     24–25

Austria, Czech Republic and Slovak Republic
1:2 200 000
     26–27

Hungary, Romania and the Lower Danube
1:2 200 000
     28–29

Poland and the Southern Baltic
1:2 200 000
     30–31

Baltic States, Belarus and Ukraine
1:4 400 000
     32–33

The Volga Basin and the Caucasus
1:4 400 000
     34–35

Western Spain and Portugal
1:2 200 000
     36–37

Eastern Spain
1:2 200 000
     38–39

Northern Italy, Slovenia and Croatia
1:2 200 000
     40–41

Southern Italy
1:2 200 000
     42–43

Serbia and Montenegro, Bulgaria and Northern Greece
1:2 200 000
     44–45

Southern Greece and Western Turkey
1:2 200 000

46–47

The Balearics, the Canaries and Madeira
1:900 000 / 1:1 800 000

48

Malta, Crete, Corfu, Rhodes and Cyprus
1:900 000 / 1:1 200 000

49

Asia

Asia: Physical
1:44 400 000

50

Asia: Political
1:44 400 000

51

Russia and Central Asia
1:17 800 000

52–53

Japan
1:4 400 000

54–55

Northern China and Korea
1:5 300 000

56–57

Southern China
1:5 300 000

58–59

China
1:17 800 000

60

The Philippines
1:6 700 000

61

Indonesia and the Philippines
1:11 100 000
Java and Madura 1:6 700 000
Bali 1:1 800 000

62–63

Mainland South-east Asia
1:5 300 000
Ko Phuket 1:900 000
Ko Samui 1:900 000
Pinang 1:900 000
Singapore 1:900 000

64–65

South Asia
1:8 900 000

66–67

Northern India and Nepal
1:5 300 000
Jammu and Kashmir 1:5 300 000

68–69

The Middle East
1:6 200 000

70–71

Turkey and Transcaucasia
1:4 400 000

72–73

The Near East
1:2 200 000

74

Arabia and the Horn of Africa
1:13 300 000

75

Africa

Africa: Physical
1:37 300 000

76

Africa: Political
1: 37 300 000

77

Northern Africa
1:13 300 000

78–79

The Nile Valley
1:7 100 000
The Nile Delta 1:3 600 000

80–81

West Africa
1:7 100 000

82–83

Central and Southern Africa
1:13 300 000

84–85

East Africa
1:7 100 000

86–87

Southern Africa
1:7 100 000
Madagascar 1:7 100 000

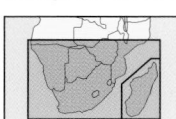

88–89

Australia and Oceania

Australia and Oceania:
 Physical and Political
1:44 400 000   **90**

New Zealand
1:5 300 000
Samoan Islands 1:10 700 000
Fiji and Tonga 1:10 700 000

91

Western Australia
1:7 100 000

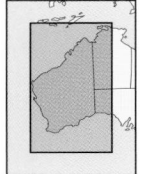

92–93

Eastern Australia
1:7 100 000
Whitsunday Islands 1:2 200 000
Tasmania 1:7 100 000

94–95

Pacific Ocean
1:48 000 000   96–97

North America

North America: Physical
1:31 100 000   **98**

North America: Political
1:31 100 000   **99**

Canada
1:13 300 000
Alaska 1:26 700 000

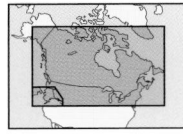

100–101

Western Canada
1:6 200 000

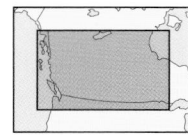

102–103

Eastern Canada
1:6 200 000

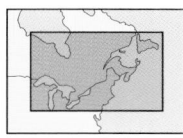

104–105

United States
1:10 700 000
Hawaii 1:8 900 000

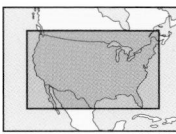

106–107

Western United States
1:5 300 000

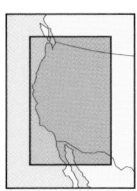

108–109

Central and Southern California
 and Western Washington
1:2 200 000

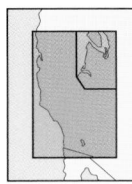

110–111

Middle United States
1:5 300 000

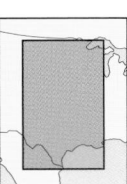

112–113

Eastern United States
1:5 300 000

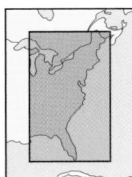

114–115

North-eastern United States
1:2 200 000

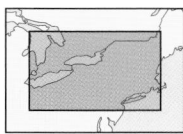

116–117

Mexico
1:7 100 000

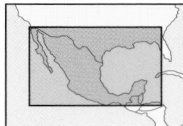

118–119

Central America and the West Indies
1:7 100 000
Jamaica 1:2 700 000
Guadeloupe 1:1 800 000
Martinique 1:1 800 000
Puerto Rico 1:2 700 000
Virgin Islands 1:1 800 000
St Lucia 1:890 000
Barbados 1:890 000

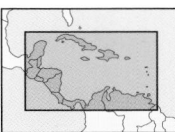

120–121

South America

South America: Physical
1:31 100 000   **122**

South America: Political
1:31 100 000   **123**

South America – North
1:14 200 000
Trinidad and Tobago 1:2 200 000

124–125

Central South America
1:7 100 000

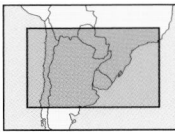

126–127

South America – South
1:14 200 000

128

INDEX TO WORLD MAPS
129–224

World Statistics: Countries

This alphabetical list includes all the countries and territories of the world. If a territory is not completely independent, the country it is associated with is named. The area figures give the total area of land, inland water and ice.

The population figures are 2004 estimates. The annual income is the Gross Domestic Product per capita† in US dollars. The figures are the latest available, usually 2002 estimates.

Country/Territory	Area km^2 *Thousands*	Area $miles^2$ *Thousands*	Population *Thousands*	Capital	Annual Income US $
Afghanistan	652	252	28,514	Kabul	700
Albania	28.7	11.1	3,545	Tirana	4,400
Algeria	2,382	920	32,129	Algiers	5,400
American Samoa (US)	0.20	0.08	58	Pago Pago	8,000
Andorra	0.47	0.18	70	Andorra La Vella	19,000
Angola	1,247	481	10,979	Luanda	1,700
Anguilla (UK)	0.10	0.04	13	The Valley	8,600
Antigua & Barbuda	0.44	0.17	68	St John's	11,000
Argentina	2,780	1,074	39,145	Buenos Aires	10,500
Armenia	29.8	11.5	2,991	Yerevan	3,600
Aruba (Netherlands)	0.19	0.07	71	Oranjestad	28,000
Australia	7,741	2,989	19,913	Canberra	26,900
Austria	83.9	32.4	8,175	Vienna	27,900
Azerbaijan	86.6	33.4	7,868	Baku	3,700
Azores (Portugal)	2.2	0.86	236	Ponta Delgada	15,000
Bahamas	13.9	5.4	300	Nassau	15,300
Bahrain	0.69	0.27	678	Manama	15,100
Bangladesh	144	55.6	141,340	Dhaka	1,800
Barbados	0.43	0.17	278	Bridgetown	15,000
Belarus	208	80.2	10,311	Minsk	8,700
Belgium	30.5	11.8	10,348	Brussels	29,200
Belize	23.0	8.9	273	Belmopan	4,900
Benin	113	43.5	7,250	Porto-Novo	1,100
Bermuda (UK)	0.05	0.02	65	Hamilton	35,200
Bhutan	47.0	18.1	2,186	Thimphu	1,300
Bolivia	1,099	424	8,724	La Paz/Sucre	2,500
Bosnia-Herzegovina	51.2	19.8	4,008	Sarajevo	1,900
Botswana	582	225	1,562	Gaborone	8,500
Brazil	8,514	3,287	184,101	Brasília	7,600
Brunei	5.8	2.2	365	Bandar Seri Begawan	18,600
Bulgaria	111	42.8	7,518	Sofia	6,500
Burkina Faso	274	106	13,575	Ouagadougou	1,100
Burma (= Myanmar)	677	261	42,720	Rangoon	1,700
Burundi	27.8	10.7	6,231	Bujumbura	500
Cambodia	181	69.9	13,363	Phnom Penh	1,600
Cameroon	475	184	16,064	Yaoundé	1,700
Canada	9,971	3,850	32,508	Ottawa	29,300
Canary Is. (Spain)	7.2	2.8	1,682	Las Palmas/Santa Cruz	19,900
Cape Verde Is.	4.0	1.6	415	Praia	1,400
Cayman Is. (UK)	0.26	0.10	43	George Town	35,000
Central African Republic	623	241	3,742	Bangui	1,200
Chad	1,284	496	9,539	Ndjaména	1,000
Chile	757	292	15,824	Santiago	10,100
China	9,597	3,705	1,298,848	Beijing	4,700
Colombia	1,139	440	42,311	Bogotá	6,100
Comoros	2.2	0.86	652	Moroni	700
Congo	342	132	2,998	Brazzaville	900
Congo (Dem. Rep. of the)	2,345	905	58,318	Kinshasa	600
Cook Is. (NZ)	0.24	0.09	21	Avarua	5,000
Costa Rica	51.1	19.7	3,957	San José	8,300
Croatia	56.5	21.8	4,497	Zagreb	9,800
Cuba	111	42.8	11,309	Havana	2,700
Cyprus	9.3	3.6	776	Nicosia	13,200
Czech Republic	78.9	30.5	10,246	Prague	15,300
Denmark	43.1	16.6	5,413	Copenhagen	28,900
Djibouti	23.2	9.0	467	Djibouti	1,300
Dominica	0.75	0.29	69	Roseau	5,400
Dominican Republic	48.5	18.7	8,834	Santo Domingo	6,300
East Timor	14.9	5.7	1,019	Dili	500
Ecuador	284	109	13,213	Quito	3,200
Egypt	1,001	387	76,117	Cairo	4,000
El Salvador	21.0	8.1	6,588	San Salvador	4,600
Equatorial Guinea	28.1	10.8	523	Malabo	2,700
Eritrea	118	45.4	4,447	Asmara	700
Estonia	45.1	17.4	1,342	Tallinn	11,000
Ethiopia	1,104	426	67,851	Addis Ababa	700
Faroe Is. (Denmark)	1.4	0.54	47	Tórshavn	22,000
Fiji	18.3	7.1	881	Suva	5,600
Finland	338	131	5,215	Helsinki	25,800
France	552	213	60,424	Paris	26,000
French Guiana (France)	90.0	34.7	191	Cayenne	14,400
French Polynesia (France)	4.0	1.5	266	Papeete	5,000
Gabon	268	103	1,355	Libreville	6,500
Gambia, The	11.3	4.4	1,547	Banjul	1,800
Gaza Strip (OPT)*	0.36	0.14	1,325	–	600
Georgia	69.7	26.9	4,694	Tbilisi	3,200
Germany	357	138	82,425	Berlin	26,200
Ghana	239	92.1	20,757	Accra	2,000
Gibraltar (UK)	0.006	0.002	28	Gibraltar Town	17,500
Greece	132	50.9	10,648	Athens	19,100
Greenland (Denmark)	2,176	840	56	Nuuk (Godthåb)	20,000
Grenada	0.34	0.13	89	St George's	5,000
Guadeloupe (France)	1.7	0.66	445	Basse-Terre	9,000
Guam (US)	0.55	0.21	166	Agana	21,000
Guatemala	109	42.0	14,281	Guatemala City	3,900
Guinea	246	94.9	9,246	Conakry	2,100
Guinea-Bissau	36.1	13.9	1,388	Bissau	700
Guyana	215	83.0	706	Georgetown	3,800
Haiti	27.8	10.7	7,656	Port-au-Prince	1,400
Honduras	112	43.3	6,824	Tegucigalpa	2,500
Hong Kong (China)	1.1	0.42	6,855	–	27,200
Hungary	93.0	35.9	10,032	Budapest	13,300
Iceland	103	39.8	294	Reykjavik	30,200
India	3,287	1,269	1,065,071	New Delhi	2,600
Indonesia	1,905	735	238,453	Jakarta	3,100
Iran	1,648	636	69,019	Tehran	6,800
Iraq	438	169	25,375	Baghdad	2,400
Ireland	70.3	27.1	3,970	Dublin	29,300
Israel	20.6	8.0	6,199	Jerusalem	19,500
Italy	301	116	58,057	Rome	25,100
Ivory Coast (= Côte d'Ivoire)	322	125	17,328	Yamoussoukro	1,400
Jamaica	11.0	4.2	2,713	Kingston	3,800
Japan	378	146	127,333	Tokyo	28,700
Jordan	89.3	34.5	5,611	Amman	4,300
Kazakhstan	2,725	1,052	15,144	Astana	7,200
Kenya	580	224	32,022	Nairobi	1,100
Kiribati	0.73	0.28	101	Tarawa	800
Korea, North	121	46.5	22,698	Pyŏngyang	1,000
Korea, South	99.3	38.3	48,598	Seoul	19,600
Kuwait	17.8	6.9	2,258	Kuwait City	17,500
Kyrgyzstan	200	77.2	5,081	Bishkek	2,900
Laos	237	91.4	6,068	Vientiane	1,800
Latvia	64.6	24.9	2,306	Riga	8,900

*OPT = Occupied Palestinian Territory   N/A = Not Available

Country/Territory	Area km^2 *Thousands*	Area $miles^2$ *Thousands*	Population *Thousands*	Capital	Annual Income US $
Lebanon	10.4	4.0	3,777	Beirut	4,800
Lesotho	30.4	11.7	1,865	Maseru	2,700
Liberia	111	43.0	3,391	Monrovia	1,000
Libya	1,760	679	5,632	Tripoli	6,200
Liechtenstein	0.16	0.06	33	Vaduz	25,000
Lithuania	65.2	25.2	3,608	Vilnius	8,400
Luxembourg	2.6	1.0	463	Luxembourg	48,900
Macau (China)	0.02	0.007	445	–	18,500
Macedonia (FYROM)	25.7	9.9	2,071	Skopje	5,100
Madagascar	587	227	17,502	Antananarivo	800
Madeira (Portugal)	0.78	0.30	241	Funchal	22,700
Malawi	118	45.7	11,907	Lilongwe	600
Malaysia	330	127	23,522	Kuala Lumpur/Putrajaya	8,800
Maldives	0.30	0.12	339	Malé	3,900
Mali	1,240	479	11,957	Bamako	900
Malta	0.32	0.12	397	Valletta	17,200
Marshall Is.	0.18	0.07	58	Majuro	1,600
Martinique (France)	1.1	0.43	430	Fort-de-France	10,700
Mauritania	1,026	396	2,999	Nouakchott	1,700
Mauritius	2.0	0.79	1,220	Port Louis	10,100
Mayotte (France)	0.37	0.14	186	Mamoundzou	600
Mexico	1,958	756	104,960	Mexico City	8,900
Micronesia, Fed. States of	0.70	0.27	108	Palikir	2,000
Moldova	33.9	13.1	4,446	Chişinău	2,600
Monaco	0.001	0.0004	32	Monaco	27,000
Mongolia	1,567	605	2,751	Ulan Bator	1,900
Montserrat (UK)	0.10	0.04	9	Plymouth	3,400
Morocco	447	172	32,209	Rabat	3,900
Mozambique	802	309	18,812	Maputo	1,100
Namibia	824	318	1,954	Windhoek	6,900
Nauru	0.02	0.008	13	Yaren District	5,000
Nepal	147	56.8	27,071	Katmandu	1,400
Netherlands	41.5	16.0	16,318	Amsterdam/The Hague	27,200
Netherlands Antilles (Neths)	0.80	0.31	218	Willemstad	11,400
New Caledonia (France)	18.6	7.2	214	Nouméa	14,000
New Zealand	271	104	3,994	Wellington	20,100
Nicaragua	130	50.2	5,360	Managua	2,200
Niger	1,267	489	11,361	Niamey	800
Nigeria	924	357	137,253	Abuja	900
Northern Mariana Is. (US)	0.46	0.18	78	Saipan	12,500
Norway	324	125	4,575	Oslo	33,000
Oman	310	119	2,903	Muscat	8,300
Pakistan	796	307	159,196	Islamabad	2,000
Palau	0.46	0.18	20	Koror	9,000
Panama	75.5	29.2	3,000	Panamá	6,200
Papua New Guinea	463	179	5,420	Port Moresby	2,100
Paraguay	407	157	6,191	Asunción	4,300
Peru	1,285	496	27,544	Lima	5,000
Philippines	300	116	86,242	Manila	4,600
Poland	323	125	38,626	Warsaw	9,700
Portugal	88.8	34.3	10,524	Lisbon	19,400
Puerto Rico (US)	8.9	3.4	3,898	San Juan	11,100
Qatar	11.0	4.2	840	Doha	20,100
Réunion (France)	2.5	0.97	766	St-Denis	5,600
Romania	238	92.0	22,356	Bucharest	7,600
Russia	17,075	6,593	143,782	Moscow	9,700
Rwanda	26.3	10.2	7,954	Kigali	1,200
St Kitts & Nevis	0.26	0.10	39	Basseterre	8,800
St Lucia	0.54	0.21	164	Castries	5,400
St Vincent & Grenadines	0.39	0.15	117	Kingstown	2,900
Samoa	2.8	1.1	178	Apia	5,600
San Marino	0.06	0.02	29	San Marino	34,600
São Tomé & Príncipe	0.96	0.37	182	São Tomé	1,200
Saudi Arabia	2,150	830	25,796	Riyadh	11,400
Senegal	197	76.0	10,852	Dakar	1,500
Serbia & Montenegro	102	39.4	10,826	Belgrade	2,200
Seychelles	0.46	0.18	81	Victoria	7,800
Sierra Leone	71.7	27.7	5,884	Freetown	500
Singapore	0.68	0.26	4,354	Singapore City	25,200
Slovak Republic	49.0	18.9	5,424	Bratislava	12,400
Slovenia	20.3	7.8	2,011	Ljubljana	19,200
Solomon Is.	28.9	11.2	524	Honiara	1,700
Somalia	638	246	8,305	Mogadishu	600
South Africa	1,221	471	42,719	C. Town/Pretoria/Bloem.	10,000
Spain	498	192	40,281	Madrid	21,200
Sri Lanka	65.6	25.3	19,905	Colombo	3,700
Sudan	2,506	967	39,148	Khartoum	1,400
Suriname	163	63.0	437	Paramaribo	3,400
Swaziland	17.4	6.7	1,169	Mbabane	4,800
Sweden	450	174	8,986	Stockholm	26,000
Switzerland	41.3	15.9	7,451	Bern	32,000
Syria	185	71.5	18,017	Damascus	3,700
Taiwan	36.0	13.9	22,750	Taipei	18,000
Tajikistan	143	55.3	7,012	Dushanbe	1,300
Tanzania	945	365	36,588	Dodoma	600
Thailand	513	198	64,866	Bangkok	7,000
Togo	56.8	21.9	5,557	Lomé	1,400
Tonga	0.65	0.25	110	Nuku'alofa	2,200
Trinidad & Tobago	5.1	2.0	1,097	Port of Spain	10,000
Tunisia	164	63.2	9,975	Tunis	6,800
Turkey	775	299	68,894	Ankara	7,300
Turkmenistan	488	188	4,863	Ashkhabad	6,700
Turks & Caicos Is. (UK)	0.43	0.17	20	Cockburn Town	9,600
Tuvalu	0.03	0.01	11	Fongafale	1,100
Uganda	241	93.1	26,405	Kampala	1,200
Ukraine	604	233	47,732	Kiev	4,500
United Arab Emirates	83.6	32.3	2,524	Abu Dhabi	22,100
United Kingdom	242	93.4	60,271	London	25,500
United States of America	9,629	3,718	293,028	Washington, DC	36,300
Uruguay	175	67.6	3,399	Montevideo	7,900
Uzbekistan	447	173	26,410	Tashkent	2,600
Vanuatu	12.2	4.7	203	Port-Vila	2,900
Vatican City	0.0004	0.0002	1	Vatican City	N/A
Venezuela	912	352	25,017	Caracas	5,400
Vietnam	332	128	82,690	Hanoi	2,300
Virgin Is. (UK)	0.15	0.06	22	Road Town	16,000
Virgin Is. (US)	0.35	0.13	109	Charlotte Amalie	19,000
Wallis & Futuna Is. (France)	0.20	0.08	16	Mata-Utu	2,000
West Bank (OPT)*	5.9	2.3	2,311	–	800
Western Sahara	266	103	267	El Aaiún	N/A
Yemen	528	204	20,025	Sana'	800
Zambia	753	291	10,462	Lusaka	800
Zimbabwe	391	151	12,672	Harare	2,100

† Gross Domestic Product per capita has been measured using the purchasing power parity method. This enables comparisons to be made between countries through their purchasing power (in US dollars), showing real price levels of goods and services rather than using currency exchange rates.

World Statistics: Cities

This list shows the principal cities with more than 750,000 inhabitants. The figures are taken from the most recent census or estimate available, usually 2000, and as far as possible are the population of the metropolitan area or urban agglomeration (for example, greater New York, Mexico or Paris). All the figures are in thousands. Local name forms have been used for the smaller cities (for example, Thessaloniki).

AFGHANISTAN
Kabul 2,602
ALGERIA
Algiers 1,722
ANGOLA
Luanda 2,697
ARGENTINA
Buenos Aires 12,024
Córdoba 1,368
Rosario 1,279
Mendoza 934
San Miguel de
  Tucumán 792
ARMENIA
Yerevan 1,407
AUSTRALIA
Sydney 4,086
Melbourne 3,466
Brisbane 1,627
Perth 1,381
Adelaide 1,096
AUSTRIA
Vienna 1,807
AZERBAIJAN
Baku 1,792
BANGLADESH
Dhaka 12,519
Chittagong 3,651
Khulna 1,442
Rajshahi 1,035
BELARUS
Minsk 1,717
BELGIUM
Brussels 964
BOLIVIA
La Paz 1,487
Santa Cruz 1,035
Cochabamba 797
BRAZIL
São Paulo 17,962
Rio de Janeiro 10,652
Belo Horizonte 4,224
Pôrto Alegre 3,757
Recife 3,346
Salvador 3,238
Fortaleza 3,066
Curitiba 2,562
Brasília 2,051
Belém 1,658
Manaus 1,467
Campinas 1,434
Santos 1,270
Goiânia 1,117
São José dos
  Campos 972
São Luís 968
Maceió 886
Teresina 848
Campo Grande 821
Natal 806
BULGARIA
Sofia 1,187
BURKINA FASO
Ouagadougou 831
BURMA (MYANMAR)
Rangoon 4,393
Mandalay 770
CAMBODIA
Phnom Penh 1,070
CAMEROON
Douala 1,642
Yaoundé 1,420
CANADA
Toronto 4,881
Montréal 3,511
Vancouver 2,079
Ottawa 1,107
Calgary 972
Edmonton 957
CHILE
Santiago 5,467
CHINA
Shanghai 12,887
Beijing 10,839
Tianjin 9,156
Hong Kong 6,860
Wuhan 5,169
Chongqing 4,900
Shenyang 4,828
Guangzhou 3,893
Chengdu 3,294
Xi'an 3,123
Changchun 3,093
Harbin 2,928
Nanjing 2,740
Zibo 2,675
Dalian 2,628
Jinan 2,568
Guiyang 2,533
Linyi 2,498
Taiyuan 2,415
Qingdao 2,316
Zhengzhou 2,070
Zaozhuang 2,048
Liupanshui 2,023
Handan 1,996
Jinxi 1,821
Lu'an 1,818
Hangzhou 1,780
Tianmen 1,779
Changsha 1,775

Wanxian 1,759
Lanzhou 1,730
Nanchang 1,722
Kunming 1,701
Yantai 1,681
Tangshan 1,671
Xuzhou 1,636
Xiantao 1,614
Shijiazhuang 1,603
Heze 1,600
Yancheng 1,562
Yulin 1,558
Xinghua 1,556
Tai'an 1,503
Pingxiang 1,502
Anshan 1,453
Luoyang 1,451
Jilin 1,435
Qiqihar 1,435
Suining, Sichuan 1,428
Ürümqi 1,415
Fushun 1,413
Fuzhou 1,397
Neijiang 1,393
Changde 1,374
Zhanjiang 1,368
Huainan 1,354
Yiyang 1,343
Xintai 1,325
Baotou 1,319
Dongguan 1,319
Nanning 1,311
Weifang 1,287
Wenzhou 1,269
Hefei 1,242
Huaian 1,232
Yueyang 1,213
Suqian 1,189
Tianshui 1,187
Suzhou 1,183
Shantou 1,176
Ningbo 1,173
Yuzhou 1,173
Datong 1,165
Jingmen 1,153
Leshan 1,137
Shenzhen 1,131
Wuxi 1,127
Xiaoshan 1,124
Zaoyang 1,121
Yixing 1,108
Yongzhou 1,097
Chifeng 1,087
Huzhou 1,077
Daqing 1,076
Zigong 1,072
Mianyang 1,065
Nanchong 1,055
Fuyu 1,025
Jining, Shandong 1,019
Hohhot 978
Xinyi, Guangdong 973
Benxi 957
Jixi 949
Liuzhou 928
Xiangxiang 908
Yichun, Heilongjiang 904
Xianyang 896
Linqing 891
Changzhou 886
Zhangjiagang 886
Zhangjiakou 880
Jiamusi 874
Yichun, Jiangxi 871
Zhaotong 851
Yuyao 848
Jinzhou 834
Xuanzhou 823
Huaibei 814
Xinyu 808
Mudanjiang 801
Hengyang 799
Jiaxing 791
Anshun 789
Fuxin 785
Tongliao 785
Hunjiang 772
Kaifeng 769
COLOMBIA
Bogotá 6,771
Medellín 2,866
Cali 2,233
Barranquilla 1,683
Bucaramanga 937
Cartagena 845
Cúcuta 772
CONGO
Brazzaville 1,306
CONGO (DEMOCRATIC
  REPUBLIC OF THE)
Kinshasa 5,054
Lubumbashi 965
Mbuji-Mayi 806
COSTA RICA
San José 961
CROATIA
Zagreb 1,067
CUBA
Havana 2,256
CZECH REPUBLIC
Prague 1,203

DENMARK
Copenhagen 1,332
DOMINICAN REPUBLIC
Santo Domingo 2,563
Santiago de los
  Caballeros 804
ECUADOR
Guayaquil 2,118
Quito 1,616
EGYPT
Cairo 9,462
Alexandria 3,506
Shubrâ el Kheima 937
EL SALVADOR
San Salvador 1,341
ETHIOPIA
Addis Ababa 2,645
FINLAND
Helsinki 937
FRANCE
Paris 9,630
Lyons 1,353
Marseilles 1,290
Lille 991
Nice 889
Toulouse 761
Bordeaux 754
GEORGIA
Tbilisi 1,406
GERMANY
Berlin 3,387
Hamburg 1,705
Munich 1,195
Cologne 963
GHANA
Accra 1,868
GREECE
Athens 3,116
Thessaloniki 789
GUATEMALA
Guatemala City 3,242
GUINEA
Conakry 1,232
HAITI
Port-au-Prince 1,769
HONDURAS
Tegucigalpa 949
HUNGARY
Budapest 1,819
INDIA
Mumbai 16,086
Kolkata 13,058
Delhi 12,441
Chennai 6,353
Bangalore 5,567
Hyderabad 5,445
Ahmedabad 4,427
Pune 3,655
Surat 2,699
Kanpur 2,641
Jaipur 2,259
Lucknow 2,221
Nagpur 2,089
Patna 1,658
Indore 1,597
Vadodara 1,465
Bhopal 1,425
Coimbatore 1,420
Ludhiana 1,368
Cochin 1,340
Visakhapatnam 1,309
Agra 1,293
Varanasi 1,199
Madurai 1,187
Meerut 1,143
Nashik 1,117
Jabalpur 1,100
Jamshedpur 1,081
Asansol 1,065
Bhilainagar-Durg 1,049
Dhanbad 1,046
Allahabad 1,035
Faridabad 1,018
Vijayawada 999
Rajkot 974
Amritsar 955
Srinagar 954
Ghaziabad 928
Trivandrum 885
Calicut 875
Aurangabad 868
Gwalior 855
Solapur 853
Ranchi 844
Tiruchchirapalli 837
Jodhpur 833
Guwahati 797
Chandigarh 791
Hubli-Dharwad 776
Mysore 776
INDONESIA
Jakarta 11,018
Bandung 3,409
Surabaya 2,461
Medan 1,879
Palembang 1,422
Ujung Pandang 1,051
Bandar Lampung 915
Malang 787
Semarang 787
Tegal 762

Bogor 761
IRAN
Tehran 6,979
Mashhad 1,990
Esfahan 1,381
Tabriz 1,274
Karaj 1,200
Shiraz 1,124
Qom 888
Ahvaz 871
Bakhtaran 771
IRAQ
Baghdad 4,865
Basra 1,338
Mosul 1,131
Irbil 840
IRELAND
Dublin 985
ISRAEL
Tel Aviv-Yafo 2,001
ITALY
Rome 2,649
Milan 1,183
Naples 993
Turin 857
IVORY COAST
  (CÔTE D'IVOIRE)
Abidjan 3,790
JAPAN
Tokyo 12,064
Yokohama 6,427
Osaka 2,599
Nagoya 2,172
Sapporo 1,922
Kobe 1,493
Kyoto 1,468
Fukuoka 1,341
Kawasaki 1,250
Hiroshima 1,126
Kitakyushu 1,011
Sendai 1,008
Chiba 887
Sakai 792
JORDAN
Amman 1,148
KAZAKHSTAN
Almaty 1,130
KENYA
Nairobi 2,233
KOREA, NORTH
Pyŏngyang 3,124
Hamhung 821
KOREA, SOUTH
Seoul 9,888
Pusan 3,830
Inch'on 2,884
Taegu 2,675
Taejŏn 1,522
Kwangju 1,379
Sŏngnam 1,353
Ulsan 1,340
Ansan 984
Puch'on 900
Suwŏn 876
P'ohang 790
KUWAIT
Kuwait City 879
LATVIA
Riga 811
LEBANON
Beirut 2,070
LIBYA
Tripoli 1,733
Benghazi 829
MADAGASCAR
Antananarivo 1,603
MALAYSIA
Kuala Lumpur 1,379
MALI
Bamako 1,114
MEXICO
Mexico City 18,066
Guadalajara 3,697
Monterrey 3,267
Puebla 1,888
Toluca 1,455
Tijuana 1,297
León 1,293
Ciudad Juárez 1,239
Torreón 1,012
San Luis Potosí 857
Mérida 849
Querétaro 798
Mexicali 771
Culiacán 750
MONGOLIA
Ulan Bator 764
MOROCCO
Casablanca 3,357
Rabat 1,616
Fès 907
Marrakesh 822
MOZAMBIQUE
Maputo 1,094
NEPAL
Katmandu 1,176
NETHERLANDS
Amsterdam 1,105
Rotterdam 1,078
NEW ZEALAND
Auckland 1,102

NICARAGUA
Managua 1,009
NIGER
Niamey 775
NIGERIA
Lagos 8,665
Ibadan 1,549
Ogbomosho 809
NORWAY
Oslo 779
PAKISTAN
Karachi 10,032
Lahore 5,452
Faisalabad 2,142
Rawalpindi 1,521
Gujranwala 1,325
Multan 1,263
Hyderabad 1,221
Peshawar 1,066
Islamabad 791
PANAMA
Panamá 1,173
PARAGUAY
Asunción 1,262
PERU
Lima 7,443
PHILIPPINES
Manila 9,950
Davao 1,146
POLAND
Warsaw 1,626
Lódz 815
PORTUGAL
Lisbon 3,861
Porto 1,940
PUERTO RICO
San Juan 2,217
ROMANIA
Bucharest 2,001
RUSSIA
Moscow 8,367
Saint Petersburg 4,635
Nizhniy Novgorod 1,332
Novosibirsk 1,321
Yekaterinburg 1,218
Omsk 1,174
Samara 1,132
Ufa 1,102
Kazan 1,063
Chelyabinsk 1,045
Perm 1,014
Rostov 1,012
Volgograd 1,000
Voronezh 918
Saratov 881
Simbirsk 864
Krasnoyarsk 840
Togliatti 771
SAUDI ARABIA
Riyadh 3,180
Jedda 1,490
Mecca 770
SENEGAL
Dakar 2,078
SERBIA AND
  MONTENEGRO
Belgrade 1,673
SIERRA LEONE
Freetown 822
SINGAPORE
Singapore City 4,131
SOMALIA
Mogadishu 1,162
SOUTH AFRICA
Johannesburg 2,950
Cape Town 2,930
Durban / eThekwini 2,391
Pretoria / Tshwane 1,590
Port Elizabeth 1,006
SPAIN
Madrid 3,017
Barcelona 1,527
SUDAN
Khartoum 2,742
SWEDEN
Stockholm 1,612
Gothenburg 778
SWITZERLAND
Zürich 939
SYRIA
Aleppo 2,229
Damascus 2,144
Homs 811
TAIWAN
Taipei 2,550
Kaohsiung 1,463
T'aichung 950
TANZANIA
Dar es Salaam 2,115
THAILAND
Bangkok 7,372
TUNISIA
Tunis 1,892
TURKEY
Istanbul 8,953
Ankara 3,203
Izmir 2,250
Bursa 1,184
Adana 1,133
Gaziantep 862
Konya 761

UGANDA
Kampala 1,213
UKRAINE
Kiev 2,621
Kharkov 1,521
Dnepropetrovsk 1,122
Donetsk 1,065
Odessa 1,027
Zaporozhye 863
Lvov 794
UNITED ARAB
  EMIRATES
Abu Dhabi 928
Dubai 886
UNITED KINGDOM
London 8,089
Birmingham 2,373
Manchester 2,353
Liverpool 852
Glasgow 832
UNITED STATES OF
  AMERICA
New York 17,800
Los Angeles 11,789
Chicago 8,308
Philadelphia 5,149
Miami 4,919
Dallas–Fort Worth 4,146
Boston 4,032
Washington 3,934
Detroit 3,903
Houston 3,823
Atlanta 3,500
San Francisco 3,229
Phoenix 2,907
Seattle 2,712
San Diego 2,674
Minneapolis–
  St Paul 2,389
St Louis 2,078
Baltimore 2,076
Tampa–
  St Petersburg 2,062
Denver 1,985
Cleveland 1,787
Pittsburgh 1,753
Portland 1,583
San Jose 1,538
San Bernardino 1,507
Cincinnati 1,503
Norfolk–
  Virginia Beach 1,394
Sacramento 1,393
Kansas City 1,362
San Antonio 1,328
Las Vegas 1,314
Milwaukee 1,309
Indianapolis 1,219
Providence 1,175
Orlando 1,157
Columbus 1,133
New Orleans 1,009
Buffalo 977
Memphis 972
Austin 902
Stamford 889
Salt Lake City 888
Jacksonville 882
Louisville 864
Hartford 852
Richmond 819
Charlotte 759
URUGUAY
Montevideo 1,324
UZBEKISTAN
Tashkent 2,148
VENEZUELA
Caracas 3,153
Maracaibo 1,901
Valencia 1,893
Maracay 1,100
Ciudad Guayana 966
Barquisimeto 923
VIETNAM
Ho Chi Minh City 4,619
Hanoi 3,751
Haiphong 1,676
YEMEN
Sana' 1,327
ZAMBIA
Lusaka 1,653
ZIMBABWE
Harare 1,791
Bulawayo 824

World Statistics: Distances

The table shows air distances in miles and kilometres between 30 major cities. Known as 'Great Circle' distances, these measure the shortest routes between the cities, which aircraft use wherever possible. The maps show the world centred on six cities, and illustrate, for example, why direct flights from Japan to northern America and Europe are across the Arctic regions. The maps have been constructed on an Azimuthal Equidistant projection, on which all distances measured through the centre point are true to scale. The red lines are drawn at 5,000, 10,000 and 15,000 km from the central city.

In the table below, distances above the diagonal are in miles; distances below the diagonal are in kilometres (km).

	Beijing	Bombay (Mumbai)	Buenos Aires	Cairo	Calcutta (Kolkata)	Caracas	Chicago	Hong Kong	Honolulu	Johannesburg	Lagos	London	Los Angeles	Mexico City	Moscow	Nairobi	New York	Paris	Rio de Janeiro	Rome	Singapore	Sydney	Tokyo	Wellington
Beijing		2956	11972	4688	2031	8947	6588	1220	5070	7276	7119	5057	6251	7742	3600	5727	6828	5106	10773	5049	2783	5561	1304	6700
Bombay (Mumbai)	4757		9275	2706	1034	9024	8048	2683	8024	4334	4730	4467	8700	9728	3126	2816	7793	4356	8332	3837	2432	6313	4189	7686
Buenos Aires	19268	14925		7341	10268	3167	5599	11481	7558	5025	4919	6917	6122	4591	8374	6463	5298	6867	1214	6929	9867	7332	11410	6202
Cairo	7544	4355	11814		3541	6340	6127	5064	8838	3894	2432	2180	7580	7687	1803	2197	5605	1994	6149	1325	5137	8959	5947	10268
Calcutta (Kolkata)	3269	1664	16524	5699		9609	7978	1653	7048	5256	5727	4946	8152	9494	3438	3839	7921	4883	9366	4486	1800	5678	3195	7055
Caracas	14399	14522	5096	10203	15464		2502	10166	6009	6847	4810	4664	3612	2228	6175	7173	2131	4738	2825	5196	11407	9534	8801	8154
Chicago	10603	12953	9011	3206	12839	4027		7783	4247	8689	5973	3949	1742	1694	4971	8005	711	4132	5311	4809	9369	9243	6299	8358
Hong Kong	1963	4317	18478	8150	2659	16360	12526		5543	6669	7360	5980	7232	8775	4439	5453	8047	5984	11001	5769	1615	4582	1786	5857
Honolulu	8160	12914	12164	14223	11343	9670	6836	8921		11934	10133	7228	2558	3781	7036	10739	4958	7437	8290	8026	6721	5075	3854	4669
Johannesburg	11710	6974	8088	6267	8459	11019	13984	10732	19206		2799	5637	10362	9063	5692	1818	7979	5426	4420	4811	5381	6860	8418	7308
Lagos	11457	7612	7916	3915	9216	7741	9612	11845	16308	4505		3118	7713	6879	3886	2366	5268	2929	3750	2510	6925	9643	8376	9973
London	8138	7190	11131	3508	7961	7507	6356	9623	11632	9071	5017		5442	5552	1552	4237	3463	212	5778	889	6743	10558	5942	11691
Los Angeles	10060	14000	9852	12200	13120	5812	2804	11639	4117	16676	12414	8758		1549	6070	9659	2446	5645	6310	6331	8776	7502	5475	6719
Mexico City	12460	15656	7389	12372	15280	3586	2726	14122	6085	14585	11071	8936	2493		6664	9207	2090	5717	4780	6365	10321	8058	7024	6897
Moscow	5794	5031	13477	2902	5534	9938	8000	7144	11323	9161	6254	2498	9769	10724		3942	4666	1545	7184	1477	5237	9008	4651	10283
Nairobi	9216	4532	10402	3536	6179	11544	12883	8776	17282	2927	3807	6819	15544	14818	6344		7358	4029	5548	3350	4635	7552	6996	8490
New York	10988	12541	8526	9020	12747	3430	1145	12950	7980	12841	8477	5572	3936	3264	7510	11842		3626	4832	4280	9531	9935	6741	8951
Paris	8217	7010	11051	3210	7858	7625	6650	9630	11968	8732	4714	342	9085	9200	2486	6485	5836		5708	687	6671	10539	6038	11798
Rio de Janeiro	17338	13409	1953	9896	15073	4546	8547	17704	13342	7113	6035	9299	10155	7693	11562	8928	7777	9187		5725	9763	8389	11551	7367
Rome	8126	6175	11151	2133	7219	8363	7739	9284	12916	7743	4039	1431	10188	10243	2376	5391	6888	1105	9214		6229	10143	6127	11523
Singapore	4478	3914	15879	8267	2897	18359	15078	2599	10816	8660	11145	10852	14123	16610	8428	7460	15339	10737	15712	10025		3915	3306	5298
Sydney	8949	10160	11800	14418	9138	15343	14875	7374	8168	11040	15519	16992	12073	12969	14497	12153	15989	16962	13501	16324	6300		4861	1383
Tokyo	2099	6742	18362	9571	5141	14164	10137	2874	6202	13547	13480	9562	8811	11304	7485	11260	10849	9718	18589	9861	5321	7823		5762
Wellington	10782	12370	9981	16524	11354	13122	13451	9427	7513	11761	16050	18814	10814	11100	16549	13664	14405	18987	11855	18545	8526	2226	9273	

Northern Hemisphere

MEXICO CITY
19 26°N 99 4°W

LONDON
51 28°N 0 27°W

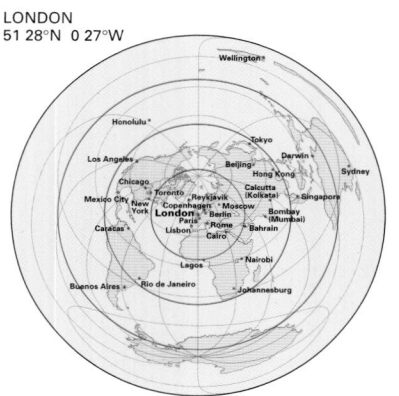

TOKYO
35 33°N 139 46°E

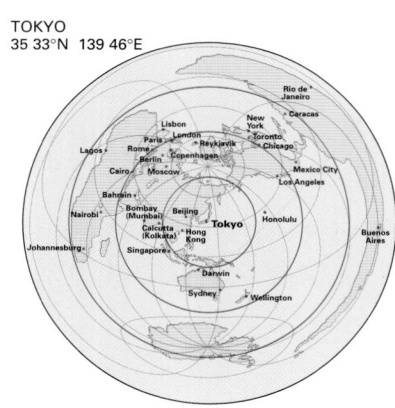

Southern Hemisphere

RIO DE JANEIRO
22 50°S 43 15°W

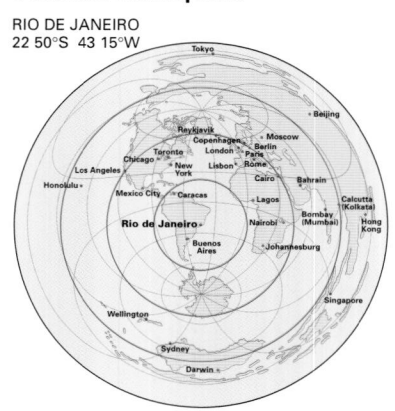

SINGAPORE
1 21°N 103 54°E

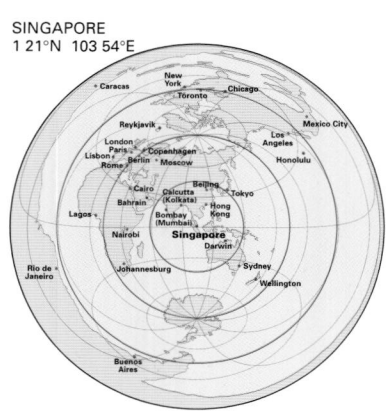

SYDNEY
33 56°S 151 10°E

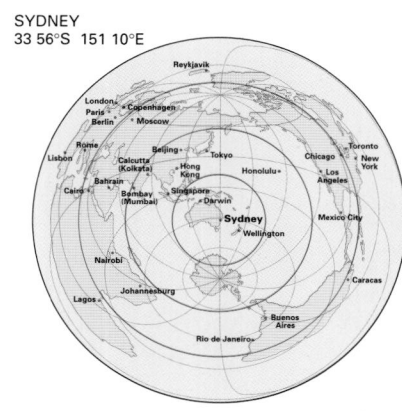

World Statistics: Climate

Rainfall and temperature figures are provided for more than 70 cities around the world. As climate is affected by altitude, the height of each city is shown in metres beneath its name. For each location, the top row of figures shows the total rainfall or snow in millimetres, and the bottom row the average temperature in degrees Celsius; the total annual rainfall and average annual temperature are at the end of the rows.

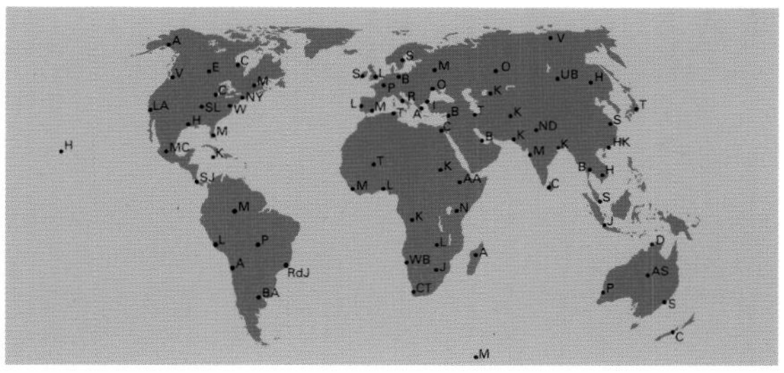

EUROPE	Jan.	Feb.	Mar.	Apr.	May	June	July	Aug.	Sept.	Oct.	Nov.	Dec.	Year
Athens, Greece	62	37	37	23	23	14	6	7	15	51	56	71	402
107 m	10	10	12	16	20	25	28	28	24	20	15	11	18
Berlin, Germany	46	40	33	42	49	65	73	69	48	49	46	43	603
55 m	–1	0	4	9	14	17	19	18	15	9	5	1	9
Istanbul, Turkey	109	92	72	46	38	34	34	30	58	81	103	119	816
14 m	5	6	7	11	16	20	23	23	20	16	12	8	14
Lisbon, Portugal	111	76	109	54	44	16	3	4	33	62	93	103	708
77 m	11	12	14	16	17	20	22	23	21	18	14	12	17
London, UK	54	40	37	37	46	45	57	59	49	57	64	48	593
5 m	4	5	7	9	12	16	18	17	15	11	8	5	11
Málaga, Spain	61	51	62	46	26	5	1	3	29	64	64	62	474
33 m	12	13	16	17	19	29	25	26	23	20	16	13	18
Moscow, Russia	39	38	36	37	53	58	88	71	58	45	47	54	624
156 m	–13	–10	–4	6	13	16	18	17	12	6	–1	–7	4
Odesa, Ukraine	57	62	30	21	34	34	42	37	37	13	35	71	473
64 m	–3	–1	2	9	15	20	22	22	18	12	9	1	10
Paris, France	56	46	35	42	57	54	59	64	55	50	51	50	619
75 m	3	4	8	11	15	18	20	19	17	12	7	4	12
Rome, Italy	71	62	57	51	46	37	15	21	63	99	129	93	744
17 m	8	9	11	14	18	22	25	25	22	17	13	10	16
Shannon, Irish Republic	94	67	56	53	61	57	77	79	86	86	96	117	929
2 m	5	5	7	9	12	14	16	16	14	11	8	6	10
Stockholm, Sweden	43	30	25	31	34	45	61	76	60	48	53	48	554
44 m	–3	–3	–1	5	10	15	18	17	12	7	3	0	7

ASIA	Jan.	Feb.	Mar.	Apr.	May	June	July	Aug.	Sept.	Oct.	Nov.	Dec.	Year
Bahrain	8	18	13	8	<3	0	0	0	0	0	18	18	81
5 m	17	18	21	25	29	32	33	34	31	28	24	19	26
Bangkok, Thailand	8	20	36	58	198	160	160	175	305	206	66	5	1,397
2 m	26	28	29	30	29	29	28	28	28	28	26	25	28
Beirut, Lebanon	191	158	94	53	18	3	<3	<3	5	51	132	185	892
34 m	14	14	16	18	22	24	27	28	26	24	19	16	21
Colombo, Sri Lanka	89	69	147	231	371	224	135	109	160	348	315	147	2,365
7 m	26	26	27	28	28	27	27	27	27	27	26	26	27
Harbin, China	6	5	10	23	43	94	112	104	46	33	8	5	488
160 m	–18	–15	–5	6	13	19	22	21	14	4	–6	–16	3
Ho Chi Minh, Vietnam	15	3	13	43	221	330	315	269	335	269	114	56	1,984
9 m	26	27	29	30	29	28	28	28	27	27	27	26	28
Hong Kong, China	33	46	74	137	292	394	381	361	257	114	43	31	2,162
33 m	16	15	18	22	26	28	28	28	27	25	21	18	23
Jakarta, Indonesia	300	300	211	147	114	97	64	43	66	112	142	203	1,798
8 m	26	26	27	27	27	27	27	27	27	27	27	26	27
Kabul, Afghanistan	31	36	94	102	20	5	3	3	<3	15	20	10	338
1,815 m	–3	–1	6	13	18	22	25	24	20	14	7	3	12
Karachi, Pakistan	13	10	8	3	3	18	81	41	13	<3	3	5	196
4 m	19	20	24	28	30	31	30	29	28	28	24	20	26
Kazalinsk, Kazakhstan	10	10	13	13	15	5	5	8	8	10	13	15	125
63 m	–12	–11	–3	6	18	23	25	23	16	8	–1	–7	7
Kolkata (Calcutta), India	10	31	36	43	140	297	325	328	252	114	20	5	1,600
6 m	20	22	27	30	30	30	29	29	29	28	23	19	26
Mumbai (Bombay), India	3	3	3	<3	18	485	617	340	264	64	13	3	1,809
11 m	24	24	26	28	30	29	27	27	27	28	27	26	27
New Delhi, India	23	18	13	8	13	74	180	172	117	10	3	10	640
218 m	14	17	23	28	33	34	31	30	29	26	20	15	25
Omsk, Russia	15	8	8	13	31	51	51	51	28	25	18	20	318
85 m	–22	–19	–12	–1	10	16	18	16	10	1	–11	–18	–1
Shanghai, China	48	58	84	94	94	180	147	142	130	71	51	36	1,135
7 m	4	5	9	14	20	24	28	28	23	19	12	7	16
Singapore	252	173	193	188	173	173	170	196	178	208	254	257	2,413
10 m	26	27	28	28	28	28	28	27	27	27	27	27	27
Tehran, Iran	46	38	46	36	13	3	3	3	3	8	20	31	246
1,220 m	2	5	9	16	21	26	30	29	25	18	12	6	17
Tokyo, Japan	48	74	107	135	147	165	142	152	234	208	97	56	1,565
6 m	3	4	7	13	17	21	25	26	23	17	11	6	14
Ulan Bator, Mongolia	<3	<3	3	5	10	28	76	51	23	5	5	3	208
1,325 m	–26	–21	–13	–1	6	14	16	14	8	–1	–13	–22	–3
Verkhoyansk, Russia	5	5	3	5	8	23	28	25	13	8	8	5	134
100 m	–50	–45	–32	–15	0	12	14	9	2	–15	–38	–48	–17

AFRICA	Jan.	Feb.	Mar.	Apr.	May	June	July	Aug.	Sept.	Oct.	Nov.	Dec.	Year
Addis Ababa, Ethiopia	<3	3	25	135	213	201	206	239	102	28	<3	0	1,151
2,450 m	19	20	20	20	19	18	18	19	21	22	21	20	20
Antananarivo, Madagas.	300	279	178	53	18	8	8	10	18	61	135	287	1,356
1,372 m	21	21	21	19	18	15	14	15	17	19	21	21	19
Cairo, Egypt	5	5	5	3	3	<3	0	0	<3	<3	3	5	28
116 m	13	15	18	21	25	28	28	28	26	24	20	15	22
Cape Town, S. Africa	15	8	18	48	79	84	89	66	43	31	18	10	508
17 m	21	21	20	17	14	13	12	13	14	16	18	19	17
Johannesburg, S. Africa	114	109	89	38	25	8	8	8	23	56	107	125	709
1,665 m	20	20	18	16	13	10	11	13	16	18	19	20	16
Khartoum, Sudan	<3	<3	<3	<3	3	8	53	71	18	5	<3	0	158
390 m	24	25	28	31	33	34	32	31	32	32	28	25	29
Kinshasa, Congo (D.R.)	135	145	196	196	158	8	3	3	31	119	221	142	1,354
325 m	26	26	27	27	26	24	23	24	25	26	26	26	25
Lagos, Nigeria	28	46	102	150	269	460	279	64	140	206	69	25	1,836
3 m	27	28	29	28	28	26	26	25	26	26	28	28	27
Lusaka, Zambia	231	191	142	18	3	<3	<3	0	<3	10	91	150	836
1,277 m	21	22	21	21	19	16	16	18	22	24	23	22	21
Monrovia, Liberia	31	56	97	216	516	973	996	373	744	772	236	130	5,138
23 m	26	26	27	27	26	25	24	25	25	25	26	26	26
Nairobi, Kenya	38	64	125	211	158	46	15	23	31	53	109	86	958
1,820 m	19	19	19	19	18	16	16	16	18	19	18	18	18
Timbuktu, Mali	<3	<3	3	<3	5	23	79	81	38	3	<3	<3	231
301 m	22	24	28	32	34	35	32	30	32	31	28	23	29
Tunis, Tunisia	64	51	41	36	18	8	3	8	33	51	48	61	419
66 m	10	11	13	16	19	23	26	27	25	20	16	11	18
Walvis Bay, Namibia	<3	5	8	3	3	<3	<3	3	<3	<3	<3	<3	23
7 m	19	19	19	18	17	16	15	14	14	15	17	18	18

AUSTRALIA, NEW ZEALAND AND ANTARCTICA	Jan.	Feb.	Mar.	Apr.	May	June	July	Aug.	Sept.	Oct.	Nov.	Dec.	Year
Alice Springs, Australia	43	33	28	10	15	13	8	8	8	18	31	38	252
579 m	29	28	25	20	15	12	12	14	18	23	26	28	21
Christchurch, N. Zealand	56	43	48	48	66	66	69	48	46	43	48	56	638
10 m	16	16	14	12	9	6	6	7	9	12	14	16	11
Darwin, Australia	386	312	254	97	15	3	<3	3	13	51	119	239	1,491
30 m	29	29	29	29	28	26	25	26	28	29	30	29	28
Mawson, Antarctica	11	30	20	10	44	180	4	40	3	20	0	0	362
14 m	0	–5	–10	–14	–15	–16	–18	–18	–19	–13	–5	–1	–11
Perth, Australia	8	10	20	43	130	180	170	149	86	56	20	13	881
60 m	23	23	22	19	16	14	13	13	15	16	19	22	18
Sydney, Australia	89	102	127	135	127	117	117	76	73	71	73	73	1,181
42 m	22	22	21	18	15	13	12	13	15	18	19	21	17

NORTH AMERICA	Jan.	Feb.	Mar.	Apr.	May	June	July	Aug.	Sept.	Oct.	Nov.	Dec.	Year
Anchorage, Alaska, USA	20	18	15	10	13	18	41	66	66	56	25	23	371
40 m	–11	–8	–5	2	7	12	14	13	9	2	–5	–11	2
Chicago, Illinois, USA	51	51	66	71	86	89	84	81	79	66	61	51	836
251 m	–4	–3	2	9	14	20	23	22	19	12	5	–1	10
Churchill, Man., Canada	15	13	18	23	32	44	46	58	51	43	39	21	402
13 m	–28	–26	–20	–10	–2	6	12	11	5	–2	–12	–22	–7
Edmonton, Alta., Canada	25	19	19	22	43	77	89	78	39	17	16	25	466
676 m	–15	–10	–5	4	11	15	17	16	11	6	–4	–10	3
Honolulu, Hawaii, USA	104	66	79	48	25	18	23	28	36	48	64	104	643
12 m	23	18	19	20	22	24	25	26	26	24	22	19	22
Houston, Texas, USA	89	76	84	91	119	117	99	99	104	94	89	109	1,171
12 m	12	13	17	21	24	27	28	29	26	22	16	12	21
Kingston, Jamaica	23	15	23	31	102	89	38	91	99	180	74	36	800
34 m	25	25	25	26	26	28	28	28	27	27	26	26	26
Los Angeles, Calif., USA	79	76	71	25	10	3	<3	<3	5	15	31	66	381
95 m	13	14	14	16	17	19	21	22	21	18	16	14	17
Mexico City, Mexico	13	5	10	20	53	119	170	152	130	51	18	8	747
2,309 m	12	13	16	18	19	19	17	18	18	16	14	13	16
Miami, Florida, USA	71	53	64	81	173	178	155	160	203	234	71	51	1,516
8 m	20	20	22	23	25	27	28	28	27	25	22	21	24
Montréal, Que., Canada	72	65	74	74	66	82	90	92	88	76	81	87	946
57 m	–10	–9	–3	–6	13	18	21	20	15	9	2	–7	6
New York City, NY, USA	94	97	91	81	81	84	107	109	86	89	76	91	1,092
96 m	–1	–1	3	10	16	20	23	23	21	15	7	2	11
St Louis, Mo., USA	58	64	89	97	114	114	89	86	81	74	71	64	1,001
173 m	0	1	7	13	19	24	26	26	22	15	8	2	14
San José, Costa Rica	15	5	20	46	229	241	211	241	305	300	145	41	1,798
1,146 m	19	19	21	21	22	21	21	21	21	20	20	19	20
Vancouver, BC, Canada	154	115	101	60	52	45	32	41	67	114	150	182	1,113
14 m	3	5	6	9	12	15	17	17	14	10	6	4	10
Washington, DC, USA	86	76	91	84	94	99	112	109	94	74	66	79	1,064
22 m	1	2	7	12	18	23	25	24	20	14	8	3	13

SOUTH AMERICA	Jan.	Feb.	Mar.	Apr.	May	June	July	Aug.	Sept.	Oct.	Nov.	Dec.	Year
Antofagasta, Chile	0	0	0	<3	<3	3	5	3	<3	3	<3	0	13
94 m	21	21	20	18	16	15	14	14	15	16	18	19	17
Buenos Aires, Argentina	79	71	109	89	76	61	56	61	79	86	84	99	950
27 m	23	23	21	17	13	9	10	11	13	15	19	22	16
Lima, Peru	3	<3	<3	<3	5	5	8	8	8	3	3	<3	41
120 m	23	24	24	22	19	17	17	16	17	18	19	21	20
Manaus, Brazil	249	231	262	221	170	84	58	38	46	107	142	203	1,811
44 m	28	28	28	27	28	28	28	28	29	29	29	28	28
Paraná, Brazil	287	236	239	102	13	<3	3	5	28	127	231	310	1,582
260 m	23	23	23	23	23	21	21	22	24	24	24	23	23
Rio de Janeiro, Brazil	125	122	130	107	79	53	41	43	66	79	104	137	1,082
61 m	26	26	25	24	22	21	21	21	21	22	23	25	23

World Statistics: Physical Dimensions

Each topic list is divided into continents and within a continent the items are listed in order of size. The bottom part of many of the lists is selective in order to give examples from as many different countries as possible. The order of the continents is as in the atlas, Europe through to South America. The world top ten are shown in square brackets; in the case of mountains this has not been done because the world top 30 are all in Asia. The figures are rounded as appropriate.

WORLD, CONTINENTS, OCEANS

THE WORLD

	km²	miles²	%
The World	509,450,000	196,672,000	–
Land	149,450,000	57,688,000	29.3
Water	360,000,000	138,984,000	70.7
Asia	44,500,000	17,177,000	29.8
Africa	30,302,000	11,697,000	20.3
North America	24,241,000	9,357,000	16.2
South America	17,793,000	6,868,000	11.9
Antarctica	14,100,000	5,443,000	9.4
Europe	9,957,000	3,843,000	6.7
Australia & Oceania	8,557,000	3,303,000	5.7
Pacific Ocean	155,557,000	60,061,000	46.4
Atlantic Ocean	76,762,000	29,638,000	22.9
Indian Ocean	68,556,000	26,470,000	20.4
Southern Ocean	20,327,000	7,848,000	6.1
Arctic Ocean	14,056,000	5,427,000	4.2

SEAS

PACIFIC

	km²	miles²
South China Sea	2,974,600	1,148,500
Bering Sea	2,268,000	875,000
Sea of Okhotsk	1,528,000	590,000
East China & Yellow	1,249,000	482,000
Sea of Japan	1,008,000	389,000
Gulf of California	162,000	62,500
Bass Strait	75,000	29,000

ATLANTIC

	km²	miles²
Caribbean Sea	2,766,000	1,068,000
Mediterranean Sea	2,516,000	971,000
Gulf of Mexico	1,543,000	596,000
Hudson Bay	1,232,000	476,000
North Sea	575,000	223,000
Black Sea	462,000	178,000
Baltic Sea	422,170	163,000
Gulf of St Lawrence	238,000	92,000

INDIAN

	km²	miles²
Red Sea	438,000	169,000
Persian Gulf	239,000	92,000

MOUNTAINS

EUROPE

		m	ft
Elbrus	Russia	5,642	18,510
Mont Blanc	France/Italy	4,807	15,771
Monte Rosa	Italy/Switzerland	4,634	15,203
Dom	Switzerland	4,545	14,911
Liskamm	Switzerland	4,527	14,852
Weisshorn	Switzerland	4,505	14,780
Taschorn	Switzerland	4,490	14,730
Matterhorn/Cervino	Italy/Switzerland	4,478	14,691
Mont Maudit	France/Italy	4,465	14,649
Dent Blanche	Switzerland	4,356	14,291
Nadelhorn	Switzerland	4,327	14,196
Grandes Jorasses	France/Italy	4,208	13,806
Jungfrau	Switzerland	4,158	13,642
Barre des Ecrins	France	4,103	13,461
Gran Paradiso	Italy	4,061	13,323
Piz Bernina	Italy/Switzerland	4,049	13,284
Eiger	Switzerland	3,970	13,025
Monte Viso	Italy	3,841	12,602
Grossglockner	Austria	3,797	12,457
Wildspitze	Austria	3,772	12,382
Monte Disgrazia	Italy	3,678	12,066
Mulhacén	Spain	3,478	11,411
Pico de Aneto	Spain	3,404	11,168
Etna	Italy	3,340	10,958
Zugspitze	Germany	2,962	9,718
Musala	Bulgaria	2,925	9,596
Olympus	Greece	2,917	9,570
Triglav	Slovenia	2,863	9,393
Monte Cinto	France (Corsica)	2,710	8,891
Galdhøpiggen	Norway	2,469	8,100
Ben Nevis	UK	1,342	4,403

ASIA

		m	ft
Everest	China/Nepal	8,850	29,035
K2 (Godwin Austen)	China/Kashmir	8,611	28,251
Kanchenjunga	India/Nepal	8,598	28,208
Lhotse	China/Nepal	8,516	27,939
Makalu	China/Nepal	8,481	27,824
Cho Oyu	China/Nepal	8,201	26,906
Dhaulagiri	Nepal	8,172	26,811
Manaslu	Nepal	8,156	26,758
Nanga Parbat	Kashmir	8,126	26,660
Annapurna	Nepal	8,078	26,502
Gasherbrum	China/Kashmir	8,068	26,469
Broad Peak	China/Kashmir	8,051	26,414
Xixabangma	China	8,012	26,286
Kangbachen	India/Nepal	7,902	25,925
Jannu	India/Nepal	7,902	25,925
Gayachung Kang	Nepal	7,897	25,909
Himalchuli	Nepal	7,893	25,896
Disteghil Sar	Kashmir	7,885	25,869
Nuptse	Nepal	7,879	25,849
Khunyang Chhish	Kashmir	7,852	25,761
Masherbrum	Kashmir	7,821	25,659
Nanda Devi	India	7,817	25,646
Rakaposhi	Kashmir	7,788	25,551
Batura	Kashmir	7,785	25,541
Namche Barwa	China	7,756	25,446
Kamet	India	7,756	25,446
Soltoro Kangri	Kashmir	7,742	25,400
Gurla Mandhata	China	7,728	25,354
Trivor	Pakistan	7,720	25,328
Kongur Shan	China	7,719	25,324
Tirich Mir	Pakistan	7,690	25,229
K'ula Shan	Bhutan/China	7,543	24,747
Pik Kommunizma	Tajikistan	7,495	24,590
Demavend	Iran	5,604	18,386
Ararat	Turkey	5,165	16,945
Gunong Kinabalu	Malaysia (Borneo)	4,101	13,455
Yu Shan	Taiwan	3,997	13,113
Fuji-San	Japan	3,776	12,388

AFRICA

		m	ft
Kilimanjaro	Tanzania	5,895	19,340
Mt Kenya	Kenya	5,199	17,057
Ruwenzori (Margherita)	Uganda/Congo (D.R.)	5,109	16,762
Ras Dashen	Ethiopia	4,620	15,157
Meru	Tanzania	4,565	14,977
Karisimbi	Rwanda/Congo (D.R.)	4,507	14,787
Mt Elgon	Kenya/Uganda	4,321	14,176
Batu	Ethiopia	4,307	14,130
Guna	Ethiopia	4,231	13,882
Toubkal	Morocco	4,165	13,665
Irhil Mgoun	Morocco	4,071	13,356
Mt Cameroun	Cameroon	4,070	13,353
Amba Ferit	Ethiopia	3,875	13,042
Pico del Teide	Spain (Tenerife)	3,718	12,198
Thabana Ntlenyana	Lesotho	3,482	11,424
Emi Koussi	Chad	3,415	11,204
Mt aux Sources	Lesotho/South Africa	3,282	10,768
Mt Piton	Réunion	3,069	10,069

OCEANIA

		m	ft
Puncak Jaya	Indonesia	5,029	16,499
Puncak Trikora	Indonesia	4,730	15,518
Puncak Mandala	Indonesia	4,702	15,427
Mt Wilhelm	Papua New Guinea	4,508	14,790
Mauna Kea	USA (Hawai'i)	4,205	13,796
Mauna Loa	USA (Hawai'i)	4,169	13,681
Aoraki Mt Cook	New Zealand	3,753	12,313
Mt Balbi	Solomon Is.	2,439	8,002
Orohena	Tahiti	2,241	7,352
Mt Kosciuszko	Australia	2,230	7,316

NORTH AMERICA

		m	ft
Mt McKinley (Denali)	USA (Alaska)	6,194	20,321
Mt Logan	Canada	5,959	19,551
Pico de Orizaba	Mexico	5,610	18,405
Mt St Elias	USA/Canada	5,489	18,008
Popocatépetl	Mexico	5,452	17,887

NORTH AMERICA (continued)

		m	ft
Mt Foraker	USA (Alaska)	5,304	17,401
Iztaccihuatl	Mexico	5,286	17,342
Lucania	Canada	5,226	17,146
Mt Steele	Canada	5,073	16,644
Mt Bona	USA (Alaska)	5,005	16,420
Mt Blackburn	USA (Alaska)	4,996	16,391
Mt Sanford	USA (Alaska)	4,940	16,207
Mt Wood	Canada	4,848	15,905
Nevado de Toluca	Mexico	4,670	15,321
Mt Fairweather	USA (Alaska)	4,663	15,298
Mt Hunter	USA (Alaska)	4,442	14,573
Mt Whitney	USA	4,418	14,495
Mt Elbert	USA	4,399	14,432
Mt Harvard	USA	4,395	14,419
Mt Rainier	USA	4,392	14,409
Blanca Peak	USA	4,372	14,344
Longs Peak	USA	4,345	14,255
Tajumulco	Guatemala	4,220	13,845
Grand Teton	USA	4,197	13,770
Mt Waddington	Canada	3,994	13,104
Mt Robson	Canada	3,954	12,972
Chirripó Grande	Costa Rica	3,837	12,589
Pico Duarte	Dominican Rep.	3,175	10,417

SOUTH AMERICA

		m	ft
Aconcagua	Argentina	6,962	22,841
Bonete	Argentina	6,872	22,546
Ojos del Salado	Argentina/Chile	6,863	22,516
Pissis	Argentina	6,779	22,241
Mercedario	Argentina/Chile	6,770	22,211
Huascarán	Peru	6,768	22,204
Llullaillaco	Argentina/Chile	6,723	22,057
Nudo de Cachi	Argentina	6,720	22,047
Yerupaja	Peru	6,632	21,758
N. de Tres Cruces	Argentina/Chile	6,620	21,719
Incahuasi	Argentina/Chile	6,601	21,654
Cerro Galan	Argentina	6,600	21,654
Tupungato	Argentina/Chile	6,570	21,555
Sajama	Bolivia	6,520	21,391
Illimani	Bolivia	6,485	21,276
Coropuna	Peru	6,425	21,079
Ausangate	Peru	6,384	20,945
Cerro del Toro	Argentina	6,380	20,932
Siula Grande	Peru	6,356	20,853
Chimborazo	Ecuador	6,267	20,561
Alpamayo	Peru	5,947	19,511
Cotapaxi	Ecuador	5,896	19,344
Pico Cristóbal Colón	Colombia	5,800	19,029
Pico Bolivar	Venezuela	5,007	16,427

ANTARCTICA

		m	ft
Vinson Massif		4,897	16,066
Mt Kirkpatrick		4,528	14,855
Mt Markham		4,349	14,268

OCEAN DEPTHS

ATLANTIC OCEAN

	m	ft	
Puerto Rico (Milwaukee) Deep	9,220	30,249	[7]
Cayman Trench	7,680	25,197	[10]
Gulf of Mexico	5,203	17,070	
Mediterranean Sea	5,121	16,801	
Black Sea	2,211	7,254	
North Sea	660	2,165	
Baltic Sea	463	1,519	
Hudson Bay	258	846	

INDIAN OCEAN

	m	ft
Java Trench	7,450	24,442
Red Sea	2,635	8,454
Persian Gulf	73	239

PACIFIC OCEAN

	m	ft	
Mariana Trench	11,022	36,161	[1]
Tonga Trench	10,882	35,702	[2]
Japan Trench	10,554	34,626	[3]
Kuril Trench	10,542	34,587	[4]
Mindanao Trench	10,497	34,439	[5]
Kermadec Trench	10,047	32,962	[6]

PACIFIC OCEAN (continued)		m	ft	
Peru–Chile Trench		8,050	26,410	[8]
Aleutian Trench		7,822	25,662	[9]

ARCTIC OCEAN		m	ft
Molloy Deep		5,608	18,399

LAND LOWS

		m	ft
Caspian Sea	Europe	−28	−92
Dead Sea	Asia	−411	−1,348
Lake Assal	Africa	−156	−512
Lake Eyre North	Oceania	−16	−52
Death Valley	North America	−86	−282
Valdés Peninsula	South America	−40	−131

RIVERS

EUROPE		km	miles	
Volga	Caspian Sea	3,700	2,300	
Danube	Black Sea	2,850	1,770	
Ural	Caspian Sea	2,535	1,575	
Dnepr (Dnipro)	Black Sea	2,285	1,420	
Kama	Volga	2,030	1,260	
Don	Black Sea	1,990	1,240	
Petchora	Arctic Ocean	1,790	1,110	
Oka	Volga	1,480	920	
Belaya	Kama	1,420	880	
Dnister (Dniester)	Black Sea	1,400	870	
Vyatka	Kama	1,370	850	
Rhine	North Sea	1,320	820	
N. Dvina	Arctic Ocean	1,290	800	
Desna	Dnepr (Dnipro)	1,190	740	
Elbe	North Sea	1,145	710	
Wisla	Baltic Sea	1,090	675	
Loire	Atlantic Ocean	1,020	635	

ASIA		km	miles	
Yangtze	Pacific Ocean	6,380	3,960	[3]
Yenisey–Angara	Arctic Ocean	5,550	3,445	[5]
Huang He	Pacific Ocean	5,464	3,395	[6]
Ob–Irtysh	Arctic Ocean	5,410	3,360	[7]
Mekong	Pacific Ocean	4,500	2,795	[9]
Amur	Pacific Ocean	4,442	2,760	[10]
Lena	Arctic Ocean	4,402	2,735	
Irtysh	Ob	4,250	2,640	
Yenisey	Arctic Ocean	4,090	2,540	
Ob	Arctic Ocean	3,680	2,285	
Indus	Indian Ocean	3,100	1,925	
Brahmaputra	Indian Ocean	2,900	1,800	
Syrdarya	Aral Sea	2,860	1,775	
Salween	Indian Ocean	2,800	1,740	
Euphrates	Indian Ocean	2,700	1,675	
Vilyuy	Lena	2,650	1,645	
Kolyma	Arctic Ocean	2,600	1,615	
Amudarya	Aral Sea	2,540	1,575	
Ural	Caspian Sea	2,535	1,575	
Ganges	Indian Ocean	2,510	1,560	
Si Kiang	Pacific Ocean	2,100	1,305	
Irrawaddy	Indian Ocean	2,010	1,250	
Tarim–Yarkand	Lop Nor	2,000	1,240	
Tigris	Indian Ocean	1,900	1,180	

AFRICA		km	miles	
Nile	Mediterranean	6,670	4,140	[1]
Congo	Atlantic Ocean	4,670	2,900	[8]
Niger	Atlantic Ocean	4,180	2,595	
Zambezi	Indian Ocean	3,540	2,200	
Oubangi/Uele	Congo (D.R.)	2,250	1,400	
Kasai	Congo (D.R.)	1,950	1,210	
Shaballe	Indian Ocean	1,930	1,200	
Orange	Atlantic Ocean	1,860	1,155	
Cubango	Okavango Delta	1,800	1,120	
Limpopo	Indian Ocean	1,770	1,100	
Senegal	Atlantic Ocean	1,640	1,020	
Volta	Atlantic Ocean	1,500	930	

AUSTRALIA		km	miles
Murray–Darling	Southern Ocean	3,750	2,330
Darling	Murray	3,070	1,905
Murray	Southern Ocean	2,575	1,600
Murrumbidgee	Murray	1,690	1,050

NORTH AMERICA		km	miles	
Mississippi–Missouri	Gulf of Mexico	6,020	3,740	[4]
Mackenzie	Arctic Ocean	4,240	2,630	
Mississippi	Gulf of Mexico	4,120	2,560	
Missouri	Mississippi	3,780	2,350	
Yukon	Pacific Ocean	3,185	1,980	
Rio Grande	Gulf of Mexico	3,030	1,880	

NORTH AMERICA (continued)		km	miles
Arkansas	Mississippi	2,340	1,450
Colorado	Pacific Ocean	2,330	1,445
Red	Mississippi	2,040	1,270
Columbia	Pacific Ocean	1,950	1,210
Saskatchewan	Lake Winnipeg	1,940	1,205
Snake	Columbia	1,670	1,040
Churchill	Hudson Bay	1,600	990
Ohio	Mississippi	1,580	980
Brazos	Gulf of Mexico	1,400	870
St Lawrence	Atlantic Ocean	1,170	730

SOUTH AMERICA		km	miles	
Amazon	Atlantic Ocean	6,450	4,010	[2]
Paraná–Plate	Atlantic Ocean	4,500	2,800	
Purus	Amazon	3,350	2,080	
Madeira	Amazon	3,200	1,990	
São Francisco	Atlantic Ocean	2,900	1,800	
Paraná	Plate	2,800	1,740	
Tocantins	Atlantic Ocean	2,750	1,710	
Orinoco	Atlantic Ocean	2,740	1,700	
Paraguay	Paraná	2,550	1,580	
Pilcomayo	Paraná	2,500	1,550	
Araguaia	Tocantins	2,250	1,400	
Juruá	Amazon	2,000	1,240	
Xingu	Amazon	1,980	1,230	
Ucayali	Amazon	1,900	1,180	
Marañón	Amazon	1,600	990	
Uruguay	Plate	1,600	990	

LAKES

EUROPE		km²	miles²
Lake Ladoga	Russia	17,700	6,800
Lake Onega	Russia	9,700	3,700
Saimaa system	Finland	8,000	3,100
Vänern	Sweden	5,500	2,100
Rybinskoye Res.	Russia	4,700	1,800

ASIA		km²	miles²	
Caspian Sea	Asia	371,000	143,000	[1]
Lake Baikal	Russia	30,500	11,780	[8]
Aral Sea	Kazakhstan/Uzbekistan	28,687	11,086	[10]
Tonlé Sap	Cambodia	20,000	7,700	
Lake Balqash	Kazakhstan	18,500	7,100	
Lake Dongting	China	12,000	4,600	
Lake Ysyk	Kyrgyzstan	6,200	2,400	
Lake Orumiyeh	Iran	5,900	2,300	
Lake Koko	China	5,700	2,200	
Lake Poyang	China	5,000	1,900	
Lake Khanka	China/Russia	4,400	1,700	
Lake Van	Turkey	3,500	1,400	

AFRICA		km²	miles²	
Lake Victoria	East Africa	68,000	26,000	[3]
Lake Tanganyika	Central Africa	33,000	13,000	[6]
Lake Malawi/Nyasa	East Africa	29,600	11,430	[9]
Lake Chad	Central Africa	25,000	9,700	
Lake Turkana	Ethiopia/Kenya	8,500	3,290	
Lake Volta	Ghana	8,480	3,270	
Lake Bangweulu	Zambia	8,000	3,100	
Lake Rukwa	Tanzania	7,000	2,700	
Lake Mai-Ndombe	Congo (D.R.)	6,500	2,500	
Lake Kariba	Zambia/Zimbabwe	5,300	2,000	
Lake Albert	Uganda/Congo (D.R.)	5,300	2,000	
Lake Nasser	Egypt/Sudan	5,200	2,000	
Lake Mweru	Zambia/Congo (D.R.)	4,900	1,900	
Lake Cabora Bassa	Mozambique	4,500	1,700	
Lake Kyoga	Uganda	4,400	1,700	
Lake Tana	Ethiopia	3,630	1,400	

AUSTRALIA		km²	miles²
Lake Eyre	Australia	8,900	3,400
Lake Torrens	Australia	5,800	2,200
Lake Gairdner	Australia	4,800	1,900

NORTH AMERICA		km²	miles²	
Lake Superior	Canada/USA	82,350	31,800	[2]
Lake Huron	Canada/USA	59,600	23,010	[4]
Lake Michigan	USA	58,000	22,400	[5]
Great Bear Lake	Canada	31,800	12,280	[7]
Great Slave Lake	Canada	28,500	11,000	
Lake Erie	Canada/USA	25,700	9,900	
Lake Winnipeg	Canada	24,400	9,400	
Lake Ontario	Canada/USA	19,500	7,500	
Lake Nicaragua	Nicaragua	8,200	3,200	
Lake Athabasca	Canada	8,100	3,100	
Smallwood Reservoir	Canada	6,530	2,520	
Reindeer Lake	Canada	6,400	2,500	
Nettilling Lake	Canada	5,500	2,100	
Lake Winnipegosis	Canada	5,400	2,100	

SOUTH AMERICA		km²	miles²
Lake Titicaca	Bolivia/Peru	8,300	3,200
Lake Poopo	Bolivia	2,800	1,100

ISLANDS

EUROPE		km²	miles²	
Great Britain	UK	229,880	88,700	[8]
Iceland	Atlantic Ocean	103,000	39,800	
Ireland	Ireland/UK	84,400	32,600	
Novaya Zemlya (N.)	Russia	48,200	18,600	
W. Spitzbergen	Norway	39,000	15,100	
Novaya Zemlya (S.)	Russia	33,200	12,800	
Sicily	Italy	25,500	9,800	
Sardinia	Italy	24,000	9,300	
N.E. Spitzbergen	Norway	15,000	5,600	
Corsica	France	8,700	3,400	
Crete	Greece	8,350	3,200	
Zealand	Denmark	6,850	2,600	

ASIA		km²	miles²	
Borneo	South-east Asia	744,360	287,400	[3]
Sumatra	Indonesia	473,600	182,860	[6]
Honshu	Japan	230,500	88,980	[7]
Sulawesi (Celebes)	Indonesia	189,000	73,000	
Java	Indonesia	126,700	48,900	
Luzon	Philippines	104,700	40,400	
Mindanao	Philippines	101,500	39,200	
Hokkaido	Japan	78,400	30,300	
Sakhalin	Russia	74,060	28,600	
Sri Lanka	Indian Ocean	65,600	25,300	
Taiwan	Pacific Ocean	36,000	13,900	
Kyushu	Japan	35,700	13,800	
Hainan	China	34,000	13,100	
Timor	Indonesia	33,600	13,000	
Shikoku	Japan	18,800	7,300	
Halmahera	Indonesia	18,000	6,900	
Ceram	Indonesia	17,150	6,600	
Sumbawa	Indonesia	15,450	6,000	
Flores	Indonesia	15,200	5,900	
Samar	Philippines	13,100	5,100	
Negros	Philippines	12,700	4,900	
Bangka	Indonesia	12,000	4,600	
Palawan	Philippines	12,000	4,600	
Panay	Philippines	11,500	4,400	
Sumba	Indonesia	11,100	4,300	
Mindoro	Philippines	9,750	3,800	

AFRICA		km²	miles²	
Madagascar	Indian Ocean	587,040	226,660	[4]
Socotra	Indian Ocean	3,600	1,400	
Réunion	Indian Ocean	2,500	965	
Tenerife	Atlantic Ocean	2,350	900	
Mauritius	Indian Ocean	1,865	720	

OCEANIA		km²	miles²	
New Guinea	Indonesia/Papua NG	821,030	317,000	[2]
New Zealand (S.)	Pacific Ocean	150,500	58,100	
New Zealand (N.)	Pacific Ocean	114,700	44,300	
Tasmania	Australia	67,800	26,200	
New Britain	Papua New Guinea	37,800	14,600	
New Caledonia	Pacific Ocean	19,100	7,400	
Viti Levu	Fiji	10,500	4,100	
Hawai'i	Pacific Ocean	10,450	4,000	
Bougainville	Papua New Guinea	9,600	3,700	
Guadalcanal	Solomon Is.	6,500	2,500	
Vanua Levu	Fiji	5,550	2,100	
New Ireland	Papua New Guinea	3,200	1,200	

NORTH AMERICA		km²	miles²	
Greenland	Atlantic Ocean	2,175,600	839,800	[1]
Baffin Is.	Canada	508,000	196,100	[5]
Victoria Is.	Canada	212,200	81,900	[9]
Ellesmere Is.	Canada	212,000	81,800	[10]
Cuba	Caribbean Sea	110,860	42,800	
Newfoundland	Canada	110,680	42,700	
Hispaniola	Dominican Rep./Haiti	76,200	29,400	
Banks Is.	Canada	67,000	25,900	
Devon Is.	Canada	54,500	21,000	
Melville Is.	Canada	42,400	16,400	
Vancouver Is.	Canada	32,150	12,400	
Somerset Is.	Canada	24,300	9,400	
Jamaica	Caribbean Sea	11,400	4,400	
Puerto Rico	Atlantic Ocean	8,900	3,400	
Cape Breton Is.	Canada	4,000	1,500	

SOUTH AMERICA		km²	miles²	
Tierra del Fuego	Argentina/Chile	47,000	18,100	
Falkland Is. (East)	Atlantic Ocean	6,800	2,600	
South Georgia	Atlantic Ocean	4,200	1,600	
Galapagos (Isabela)	Pacific Ocean	2,250	870	

World: Regions in the News

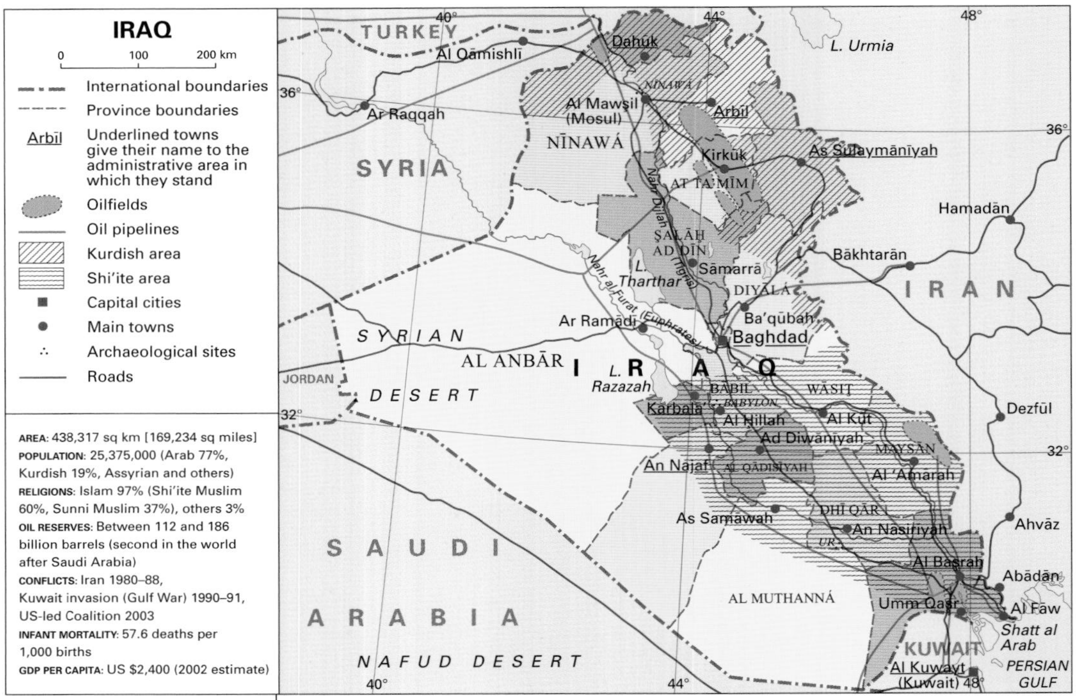

IRAQ

0 100 200 km

- –·–·– International boundaries
- – – – Province boundaries
- Arbil Underlined towns give their name to the administrative area in which they stand
- Oilfields
- Oil pipelines
- Kurdish area
- Shi'ite area
- ■ Capital cities
- ● Main towns
- ∴ Archaeological sites
- —— Roads

AREA: 438,317 sq km [169,234 sq miles]
POPULATION: 25,375,000 (Arab 77%, Kurdish 19%, Assyrian and others)
RELIGIONS: Islam 97% (Shi'ite Muslim 60%, Sunni Muslim 37%), others 3%
OIL RESERVES: Between 112 and 186 billion barrels (second in the world after Saudi Arabia)
CONFLICTS: Iran 1980–88, Kuwait invasion (Gulf War) 1990–91, US-led Coalition 2003
INFANT MORTALITY: 57.6 deaths per 1,000 births
GDP PER CAPITA: US $2,400 (2002 estimate)

Iraq map labels
TURKEY · Al Qamishli · Dahuk · L. Urmia · Ar Raqqah · Al Mawsil (Mosul) · Arbil · NINAWA · Kirkūk · As Sulaymānīyah · SYRIA · AT TA'MIM · Hamadān · Bākhtarān · ŞALĀH AD DĪN · Sāmarrā · DIYĀLĀ · IRAN · L. Tharthar · Nahr al-Furāt · Ar Ramādī · Ba'qūbah · Baghdad · JORDAN · SYRIAN DESERT · AL ANBĀR · BABIL · Razazah · BABYLON · WĀSIT · Karbalā · Al Hillah · Al Kūt · An Najaf · Ad Dīwānīyah · AL QĀDISĪYAH · MAYSĀN · Al 'Amārah · SAUDI ARABIA · As Samāwah · DHĪ QĀR · An Nāsirīyah · Ahvāz · Abādān · AL MUTHANNĀ · Al Başrah · NAFUD DESERT · Umm Qaşr · KUWAIT · Al Faw · Al Kuwayt (Kuwait) · Shatt al Arab · PERSIAN GULF · Dezfūl

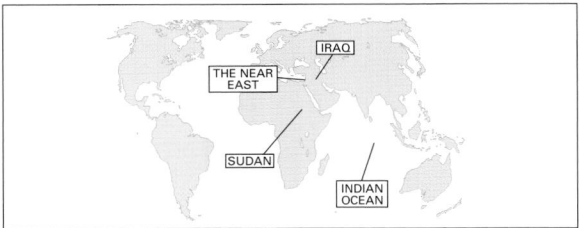

INDIAN OCEAN TSUNAMI

0 500 1000 km

- ▲ Destructive boundary (plates colliding)
- ↙ Direction of movement along plate boundaries
- ◎ Epicentre of earthquake on 26 December 2004
- ○ Affected towns
- —— Constructive boundary (plates moving apart)
- —— Conservative boundary (plates sliding past each other)
- —— Affected coastline
- ◉ Epicentre of earthquake on 28 March 2005
- ■ Capital cities
- ● Main towns

Tsunami map labels and tolls
New Delhi · ARABIAN PLATE · AFRICAN PLATE · Muqdisho · SOMALIA 150 dead · KENYA 1 dead · TANZANIA 10 dead · Mahé · SEYCHELLES 3 dead · Equator · Arabian Sea · Mumbai (Bombay) · Bangalore · Chennai (Madras) · Madurai · Colombo · Malé · MALDIVES 82 dead, 26 missing · INDIA 10,776 dead, 5,640 missing · Kolkata (Calcutta) · Dhaka · BANGLADESH 2 dead · BURMA (MYANMAR) 59 dead · Rangoon (Yangon) · Bay of Bengal · Andaman Is. (India) · Bangkok · THAILAND 5,395 dead, 2,993 missing · Nicobar Is. (India) · Phuket · Banda Aceh · Pinang · Medan · EURASIAN PLATE · SRI LANKA 30,974 dead, 4,698 missing, 100,000 homeless (est.) · MALAYSIA 68 dead · Kuala Lumpur · Singapore · Sumatra · INDIAN AUSTRALIAN PLATE · INDONESIA 122,232 dead, 113,937 missing, 500,000 homeless (est.) · Jakarta · INDIAN OCEAN · Kunming · Hanoi

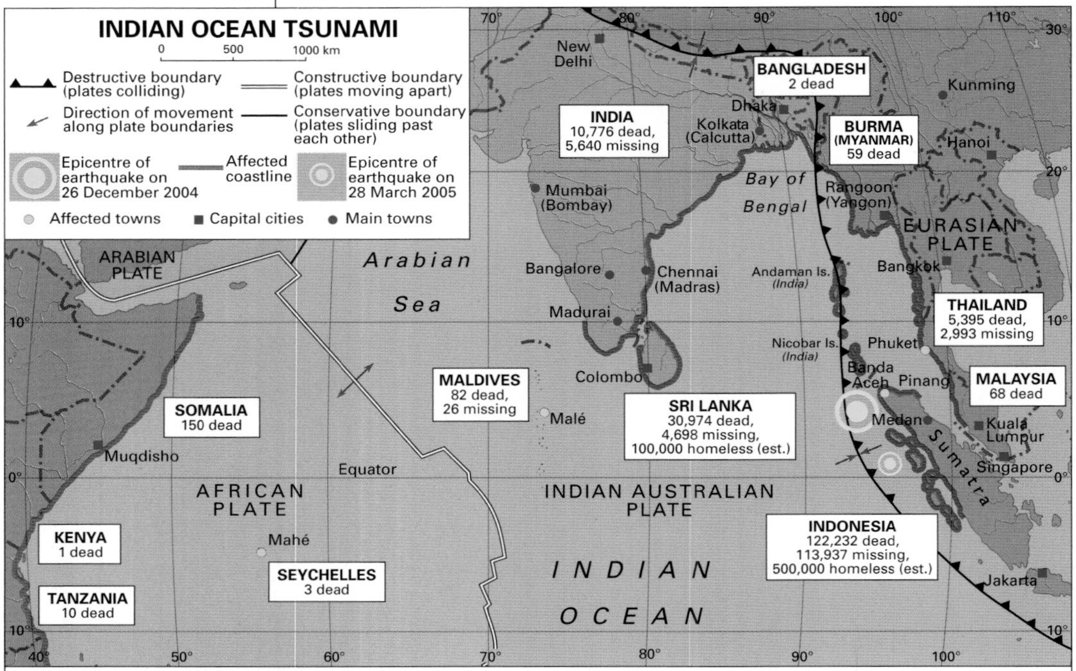

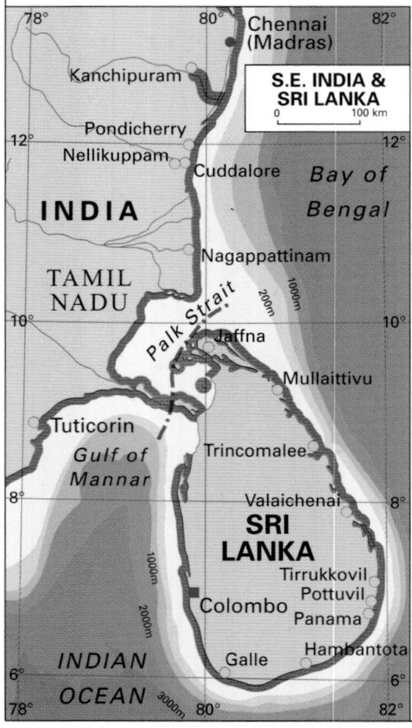

Total death toll: 169,752 dead, 127,294 missing

The 26 December 2004 earthquake measured 9.3 on the Richter Scale, whereas the earthquake on 28 March 2005 measured 8.7. The Richter Scale is a logarithmic scale, so in terms of energy released, the earthquake on 26 December was five times larger than the one on 28 March and was the second largest in recorded history. The December earthquake generated waves that, once they reached the land, were up to 20 m [65 ft] in height.

Timeline:
26 December 2004
0100 GMT	Earthquake occurs
0130 GMT	Tsunami hits Sumatra
0230 GMT	Thailand hit
0300 GMT	Sri Lanka and India hit
0430 GMT	Maldives hit
0700 GMT	East Africa hit

Aid Recipients:
Recipient	Pledges	Donations received (at 22 March 2005)
Indonesia	US $929 million	US $220.8 million
Sri Lanka	US $413.5 million	US $249 million
India	US $57.9 million	US $56.7 million
Thailand	US $13.3 million	US $7.5 million
Somalia	US $9.4 million	US $3 million

S.E. INDIA & SRI LANKA
0 100 km
Chennai (Madras) · Kanchipuram · Pondicherry · Nellikuppam · Cuddalore · Nagapattinam · INDIA · TAMIL NADU · Bay of Bengal · Palk Strait · Jaffna · Mullaittivu · Tuticorin · Gulf of Mannar · Trincomalee · Valaichenai · Tirrukkovil · Pottuvil · SRI LANKA · Colombo · Panama · Hambantota · Galle · INDIAN OCEAN

S. THAILAND
0 100 km
BURMA · Ranong · Isthmus of Kra · Ko Ra · Ko Phra Thong · Khao Lak · THAILAND · Phuket · Krabi · Ko Phi Phi · Gulf of Thailand · INDIAN OCEAN · Ko Talibong · Ko Batong · Hat Yai · Langkawi · MALAYSIA

W. INDONESIA
0 100 km
We · Sabang · Breueh · Banda Aceh · Bireuen · Calang · Lhokseumawe · ACEH · Meulaboh · INDONESIA · Medan · Bakungan · SUMATERA UTARA · Sibigo · Sinabang · Simeulue · Tuangku · Nias · INDIAN OCEAN

THE NEAR EAST

35°E

- –·–·– 1949 Armistice Line
- –··–··– 1950 Armistice Line
- – – – 1974 Cease-fire Line
- Palestinian control
- Joint Israeli/Palestinian control
- ● Efrata Main Jewish settlements
- □ Halhul Main Palestinian Arab towns
- —— Israeli security fence completed
- —— Israeli security fence under construction or planned

Near East map labels
LEBANON · Saydā · Bekaa Valley · Litani · Şūr (Tyre) · Qiryat Shemona · SYRIA · Nahariyya · Golan Heights (under Israeli occupation) · Akko · Zefat · Yam Kinneret · Hefa · Terverya · Nazerat · ISRAEL · Irbid · Baka al Sharqiya · Jenin · Tūbās · Hadera · Shavei Shomron · Elon More · Netanya · Tūlkarm · Nablus · Imanuel · Qalqilya · Kedumim · Kfar Tapuah · Karne Shomron · Ariel · Shiloh · Elkana · Tel Aviv-Yafo · West Bank · Rehovot · Rām Allāh · Beit El · El Bīrah · As Salt · Al Arīhā (Jericho) · Ammān · Ashdod · Jerusalem · Maale Adumim · Ashqelon · Bayt Lahm · Bethlehem · Efrata · Alei Sinai · Nisanit · Gaza · Halhul · Tkoa · Dead Sea · Netzarin · Al Khalīl (Hebron) · Qiryat Arba · Gaza Strip · Kfar Darom · Gadid · Khān Yūnis · Be'er Sheva · MEDITERRANEAN SEA · JORDAN · EGYPT

ISRAEL
POPULATION: 6,199,000 (inc. Israeli settlers in West Bank, Gaza Strip and Golan Heights)
INFANT MORTALITY: 6.2 deaths per 1,000 births
GDP PER CAPITA: US $19,500 (2002 estimate)

West Bank
POPULATION: 2,311,000 (Muslim 75%, Jewish 17%)
INFANT MORTALITY: 21.2 deaths per 1,000 births
GDP PER CAPITA: US $800 (2002 estimate)

Gaza Strip
POPULATION: 1,325,000 (Muslim 98.7%, Christian 0.7%, Jewish 0.6%)
INFANT MORTALITY: 24.8 deaths per 1,000 births
GDP PER CAPITA: US $600 (2002 estimate)

JORDAN
POPULATION: 5,611,000 (Palestinian Arab 50%)

LEBANON
POPULATION: 3,777,000 (Palestinian Arab 11%)

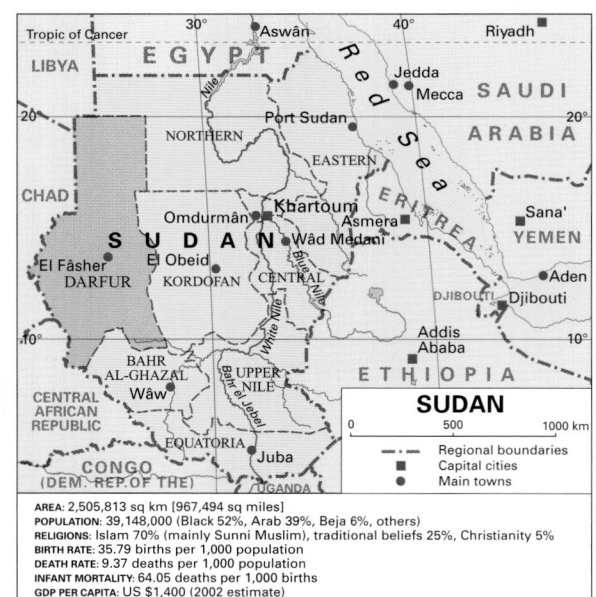

SUDAN

0 500 1000 km

- – – – Regional boundaries
- ■ Capital cities
- ● Main towns

Sudan map labels
Tropic of Cancer · Aswân · Riyadh · LIBYA · EGYPT · Jedda · Mecca · SAUDI ARABIA · NORTHERN · Port Sudan · CHAD · Omdurmân · Khartoum · Asmara · Sana' · YEMEN · El Fâsher · DARFUR · El Obeid · KORDOFAN · Wâd Medani · EASTERN · CENTRAL · ERITREA · Aden · DJIBOUTI · Djibouti · SUDAN · BAHR AL-GHAZAL · Wâw · UPPER NILE · Addis Ababa · CENTRAL AFRICAN REPUBLIC · White Nile · Bahr el Arab · Blue Nile · EQUATORIA · Juba · ETHIOPIA · CONGO (DEM. REP. OF THE) · UGANDA · Red Sea

AREA: 2,505,813 sq km [967,494 sq miles]
POPULATION: 39,148,000 (Black 52%, Arab 39%, Beja 6%, others)
RELIGIONS: Islam 70% (mainly Sunni Muslim), traditional beliefs 25%, Christianity 5%
BIRTH RATE: 35.79 births per 1,000 population
DEATH RATE: 9.37 deaths per 1,000 population
INFANT MORTALITY: 64.05 deaths per 1,000 births
GDP PER CAPITA: US $1,400 (2002 estimate)

Sudan has more internally displaced people than any other country (4.4 million in 2004). Up to 1.6 million people have left their homes and 70,000 are estimated to have been killed since conflict began in the Darfur region in early 2003.

The largest country in Africa, Sudan is about one quarter the size of the USA, or 10 times the size of the UK. The country's inhabitants are divided into three main groups: those in the north, consisting of Muslim Arab and Nubian peoples; those in the south, consisting of traditional Nilotic and Bantu peoples; and those in the west, most of whom immigrated from western Africa in the 20th century.

WORLD EXPLORER

CONTENTS

Mountains and volcanoes	2–3	Sea and ocean cruises	18–19
Deserts and canyons	4–5	Winter sports	20–21
Lakes and waterfalls	6–7	Great beaches	22–23
Wildlife in the Americas and Europe	8–9	Festivals	24–25
Wildlife in Africa, Asia and Australasia	10–11	Historic sites in the Americas	26–27
Marine wildlife	12–13	Historic sites in Europe	28–29
Great railway journeys	14–15	Historic sites in Africa, Asia and Australasia	30–31
River and canal journeys	16–17	Theme parks	32

Mountains and volcanoes

The world's mountains provide a huge variety of magnificent scenery, ranging from the tree-covered Blue Mountains of Australia, little more than 1,070 m (3,500 ft) high, to the towering snow-covered Himalayan peaks of Nepal and China, several of which are over 8,000 m (26,000 ft) high. Many are accessible by road, or sometimes by train or cable car, but walking, even if only a short distance, is usually the best way to experience the breathtaking views that they offer.

◄ **Rocky Mountains, Banff National Park, Canada**
Pointed peaks and sheer cliffs contribute to a magnificent landscape. Over 1,600 km (1,000 miles) of trails pass by glaciers, turquoise lakes and forests of pine, fir and spruce. In the town of Banff a cable car rises to the top of Sulfur Mountain, 2,263 m (7,440 ft) high.
Best time to visit: June–September

THE AMERICAS

Mount McKinley, Denali National Park, Alaska, USA
The USA's highest mountain at 6,194 m (20,321 ft) is in a spectacular wilderness of snow-covered peaks and glaciers with wildlife that includes brown bears, caribou, moose and marmots. Activities include river rafting and sightseeing by plane.
Best time to visit: June–August

Popocatepetl Volcano ('Smoking Mountain'), Sierra Nevada, Mexico
A cloud of smoke often hovers above the massive crater of Popocatepetl, which is

▲ **Sierra Nevada, Yosemite National Park, USA**
The Californian Yosemite National Park is famous for its sheer-sided granite domes, such as the Half Dome and the 1,066 m (3,500 ft) high El Capitan, which rise above forests and emerald lakes. Among the many species of flowers and trees to be found in the park are ancient giant sequoias over 60 m (200 ft) high, one of which is estimated to be 2,700 years old. An added attraction are the Yosemite Falls which, with a drop of 739 m (2,425 ft), are the highest in North America. Walkers can escape the summer crowds by using the 1,280 km (800 miles) of trails.
Best time to visit: May–September

5,452 m (17,887 ft) high. It is possible to climb and descend the mountain in one very long day with the aid of a guide.
Best time to climb: November–March

Cotopaxi and Chimborazo Volcanoes, Ecuador
The two highest active volcanoes in the world are in a country where the main road is known as the 'Avenue of the Volcanoes'. Non-mountaineers can climb Cotopaxi (5,896 m/19,344 ft) and get near to the top of Chimborazo (6,267 m/20,561 ft).
Best time to climb: January–April

Cordillera Blanca, Huascaran National Park, Peru
With 663 glaciers, the peaks of the Cordillera Blanca, more than 50 of which rise to heights of between 5,000 and 6,000 m (16,500 and 19,700 ft), are a great attraction for ice climbers. Huarez is the main climbing centre. An alternative for those who prefer to trek is the richly glaciated Huayhuash range.
Best time to visit: July–September

EUROPE

Landmannalaugar, Iceland
A combination of volcanic and geothermal activity has produced a unique landscape in Landmannalaugar, where mountain peaks (little more than 1,070 m/3,500 ft high) rise above a landscape of convoluted lava fields and blue mountain lakes, and hot springs provide open-air baths.
Best time to visit: July–early September

Mount Vesuvius, Italy
The volcano of Vesuvius dominates the landscape around Naples. Although it lost its plume of smoke after erupting in 1944, it is still active. A bus from Pompeii goes to within 1.5 km (1 mile) of the summit (1,277 m/4,189 ft).
Time to visit: All seasons

AFRICA

Atlas Mountains, Morocco
Canyons with dramatic rock formations are to be found in these rugged mountains that rise to a height of over 3,900 m (13,000 ft). Organized treks pass by numerous isolated Berber villages, far from the road from Marrakech, which winds up to a mountain pass 2,275 m (7,467 ft) high.
Best time to visit: June–October

Mount Kilimanjaro, Tanzania
Africa's highest mountain rises majestically to 5,895 m (19,340 ft) above the plains of Amboseli National Park. It is possible to trek to the top for stunning views over Kenya and Tanzania, along

• Town/city with major airport

▲ Mont Blanc, Alps, France
Europe's highest mountain rises to a height of 4,807 m (15,760 ft). A splendid view of it can be had from the peak of the Aiguille de Midi, a granite spear 3,840 m (12,600 ft) high, that is reached by a steep 3 km (2-mile) ascent in a cable car from Chamonix. Below Mont Blanc is the start of a long-distance ski and walking route, which passes ten of the 12 highest peaks in the Alps on its way to the Matterhorn in Switzerland and Italy.
Best time for walking:
May–September

▼ Mt Bromo, Java
A crater within a vast outer crater, Bromo emits white smoke, as does Mount Semeru, seen here in the distance. Visitors usually stay overnight in a village at the rim of the outer crater, from where it is possible to walk to Bromo at dawn to watch the sun rise up over the outer crater.
Best time to visit:
April–October

routes that pass through farmland and lush forest before reaching alpine-like vegetation and snow-covered rock.
Best time to climb: mid January–late February and late August–September

Drakensberg Mountains, South Africa
Vast pinnacles and blocks of basalt rise to a height of over 3,475 m (11,400 ft) in this range of mountains that also runs through Lesotho. Snowcapped in winter, many of the peaks are an enormous challenge for mountaineers. The Royal Natal National Park has numerous hiking trails.
Best time to visit: April–October

ASIA

Himalayas, Nepal
Within the Himalayas in Nepal are ten of the world's 14 peaks with a height of over 8,000 m (26,000 ft), including Everest (8,850 m/29,035 ft). Far below the snow-capped peaks are terraced hillsides dotted with villages, while above a height of about 2,700 m (9,000 ft) are forests in which rhododendrons bloom between February and April. The most popular base for exploring the mountains is Pokhara. The famous ten-day trek to the mountain town of Jomsom begins here, as does the three-to four-day Annapurna Skyline Trek which provides superb views while being easy enough to be undertaken with children.
Best time to visit: October–April

Karakorams, Pakistan
The jagged peaks of the Karakorams include K2, the world's second highest mountain (8,611 m/28,400 ft). A journey along the Karakoram Highway follows the route of the old Silk Road along the Indus Valley from Rawalpindi to Kashgar in China, sometimes clinging to cliff faces as it winds its way through the mountains up to the Khunjerab Pass at 4,934 m (16,280 ft).
Best time to visit: May–August

Great mountain treks
The following is a selection of great mountain treks that take four or more days. The months given are those in which it is best to undertake each trek.

Long Trail, Vermont, USA (424 km/265 miles; 16–21 days; May–Sept) Easily reached by road, the trail through Vermont's Green Mountains can be walked in sections. It is part of the 3,456 km (2,160-mile) long Appalachian Trail, whose most demanding section is through New Hampshire's White Mountains.

Inca Trail, Peru (4–5 days; April–Sept) By far the best way to approach the spectacular Inca site of Machu Picchu (see *Historic Sites of the Americas*), the Inca Trail begins some distance from Cuzco.

Mont Blanc Circuit, France and Switzerland (10 days; July–Sept) Possibly the finest walk in Europe, it usually starts from Chamonix. With an average altitude of 1,525 m (5,000 ft), it links the seven valleys surrounding Mont Blanc.

Annapurna Circuit, Nepal (17 days; Oct–Nov and March–April) Regarded as Nepal's classic trek, it goes through many types of landscape *(see picture below)*, and reaches a height of 5,416 m (17,765 ft), as well as providing superb views of Annapurna and Dhaulagiri.

Everest Trek, Nepal (14–16 days; Oct–Nov and March–April) A trek from Jiri to the Everest Base Camp on the Khumbu Glacier provides wonderful views of Everest. It is possible to fly back to Katmandu from Lukla, three days' walk away.

Milford Track, New Zealand (54 km/34 miles; 4 days; Oct–April) A walk that is regarded as a must by most New Zealanders ends at the breathtaking Milford Sound (see *Sea and ocean cruises*). The number of walkers is limited and booking well ahead is necessary.

Mayon Volcano, Philippines
Often described as the world's most perfect volcano cone, Mayon (2,462 m/8,075 ft) is still very active. An eruption in 1993 killed 70 people. It can be climbed in two days but it is essential to do so with a guide.
Best time to climb: December–May

Mt Kinabalu, Borneo, Malaysia
It is possible to walk rather than climb to the top of the highest mountain in South-east Asia (4,010 m/13,455 ft). It does, however, take two days and hiring a guide is compulsory. The view from the top sometimes stretches to the Philippines.
Best time to climb: April–September

Huangshan, China
The Chinese regard the 72-peak Huang-shan range as one of the great natural attractions of their country. Some 30 peaks rise to over 1,500 m (4,900 ft). There are two main walking routes up the side of the range, and an eight-minute cable-car ride from Yungusi to the top.
Best time to visit: spring and autumn

Mt Fuji, Japan
The perfectly symmetrical cone of Japan's highest mountain (3,776 m/12,388 ft), which last erupted in 1707, is climbed by people of all ages in the summer. A road goes to the fourth and fifth 'stations', from where it takes four or five hours to climb to the crater. This is best reached at dawn, before the clouds gather.
Best time to climb: July–August

AUSTRALASIA

Blue Mountains, New South Wales, Australia
Reaching a height of just over 1,070 m (3,500 ft), the Blue Mountains – with their densely forested slopes, sandstone chasms, dramatic rock formations and waterfalls – provide a beautiful environment in which to drive and walk. As well as a network of trails there are a number of interesting villages and towns, of which the largest, Katoomba, is served by a railway from Sydney just 80 km (50 miles) away.
Time to visit: All seasons

Cradle Mountain/Lake St Clair National Park, Tasmania, Australia
Australia's best mountain trails and rugged alpine scenery are to be found around Cradle Mountain. Jagged peaks, the highest of which is Mt Ossa (1,617 m/5,300 ft), rise above tarns and lakes in deep valleys.
Best time to visit: November–March

Deserts and canyons

For the adventurous traveller, the stunning landscapes of rock and sand which make up some of the world's most inhospitable environments offer a challenge not to be missed. From the vast sand seas of the Sahara Desert to the deep canyons and distinctive rock formations of the south-western United States, there is an extraordinary range of landforms to explore.

NORTH AMERICA

Bryce Canyon, Utah, USA

On a more human scale than the Grand Canyon, Bryce Canyon is not really a canyon at all but a natural amphitheatre filled with dazzling orange, red and pink rock pinnacles – known as 'hoodoos' – overlooking spectacularly colourful ravines. This surreal landscape can be explored on foot along a network of marked trails, or simply enjoyed from one of the viewpoints along the rim of the amphitheatre.

Monument Valley, Arizona, USA

With its majestic rock pillars towering over a barren, desert landscape, Monument Valley is an awe-inspiring sight. It has been made famous as a backdrop to numerous Hollywood westerns and is now part of the Navajo Reservation. A 27 km (17-mile) road tour of the valley takes two to three hours and offers stunning views of this unforgettable place.

Zion Canyon, Utah, USA

The road through the steep-sided Zion Canyon can become crowded in summer,

and it is worth leaving the car to follow one of the short trails to the Emerald Pools or the hanging gardens at Weeping Rock. Longer trails lead from the canyon to the desert plateau above and offer spectacular views of the contrasting landscapes.

SOUTH AMERICA

Colca Canyon, Peru

High in the Andes the River Colca runs through a gorge which is twice the depth of the Grand Canyon, past ancient Inca granaries cut into the rock and green slopes covered by pre-Inca terracing. This astonishingly beautiful landscape, complete with smoking volcano in the background, is home to the Collagua and Cabana people, whose traditional way of life is punctuated with lively festivals.

Atacama Desert, Chile

Overlooked by a ruined pre-Inca fortress, the picturesque oasis village of San Pedro de Atacama, with its adobe buildings and excellent archeological museum, makes a good base for exploring the canyons, saltpans and stark landscapes of the surrounding desert. One of the most beautiful places to visit is the Valle de la Luna, where the multi-coloured desert formations are a magnet for photographers and filmmakers.

EUROPE

Almerían Desert, Spain

The setting for the film *Lawrence of Arabia* as well as many 'spaghetti westerns', the Almerían Desert is an extraordinary, almost lunar landscape of sand dunes dissected by dried-up river beds and littered with sandstone cones. Film sets are open to the public at Mini-Hollywood.

Timanfaya National Park, Lanzarote, Canary Islands

On an island where it rarely rains, a series of volcanic eruptions in the 1730s created an extraordinary apocalyptic landscape. Guided tours go to an area of solidified lava and volcanic cones, aptly called the Mountains of Fire, where a dry bush dropped into a crevice will burst into flames and meals at a solitary restaurant are barbecued on a volcano.

AFRICA

Draa Valley, the Sahara, Morocco

From the town of Ouarzazate, with its dramatic kasbah, the Draa river runs south-east through a rich landscape of dramatic gorges, agricultural land and kasbahs towards the Sahara. After around 160 km (100 miles), the river reaches the former frontier fort of Zagora, which makes a good base for exploring the desert.

▲ **Grand Canyon, Arizona, USA**
Carved by the Colorado River out of the multi-coloured rock of the Arizona Desert, the Grand Canyon is one of North America's most awe-inspiring natural features. Drives and trails around its rim – 443 km (277 miles) in length – provide stunning views. Visitors can walk or ride mules down one of the vertiginous trails to the valley floor, 1.7 km (1 mile) below, or try rafting on the river.

▲ **Sonoran Desert, USA/Mexico**
Almost encircling the Gulf of California and covering 310,000 sq km (120,00 sq miles), the Sonoran Desert is the hottest of North America's deserts. Tucson, Arizona, serves as a base for tours into the desert, including archaeological tours. Nearby are the excellent Arizona-Sonora Desert Museum and the protected desert habitat of Organ Pipe Cactus National Monument where visitors can see the giant saguaro and organ pipe cacti which have come to symbolize the area. There are good trails and scenic drives around the park, and plenty of desert wildlife to watch.

• Town/city with major airport

Saharan oases, Tunisia

The shifting sand dunes around the town of Douz are an excellent example of the landscape popularly associated with the Sahara Desert. In fact the desert, which covers an area of 8,600,000 sq km (3,320,000 sq miles), has extensive stony plains, rock-strewn plateaux, mountains and large oasis depressions as well as seas of sand. Douz is a good base for camel safaris and for exploring the more isolated southern oases. To the north-west the town of Tozeur, with its beautiful 12th-century mosque, is set beside a vast oasis fed by over 200 springs. It serves as an excellent starting point for four-wheel-drive tours into the desert and to the nearby beautiful mountain oases, such as Tamerza, Mides and Chebika.

Guided expeditions of up to a week can include camel riding and stargazing under the immense Saharan sky.

Ténéré Desert, Niger

For desert purists the seemingly endless sea of sand that is the Ténéré Desert is perhaps the most beautiful part of the Sahara. A two-week round trip from the desert city of Agadez might pass through a massive dinosaur cemetery on the way to the classic oasis town of Bilma and the prehistoric cave paintings of the Djado Plateau. Crossing the Ténéré is notoriously challenging and often dangerous, but the experience is unforgettable.

Sinai Desert, Egypt

Inland from the coastal resorts of the Sinai Peninsula is a hot, desolate wilderness sprinkled with oases and ancient settlements. They include the 6th-century monastery of St Catherine, which stands at the foot of Mount Sinai, where Moses is said to have received the Ten Commandments from God. Camel treks and jeep safaris take visitors into the aptly-named Wilderness of Wanderings, in the centre of the peninsula.

North Kenyan Desert

In sharp contrast to the developed south of Kenya, the North Kenyan Desert is a vast tract of scrubland inhabited by ancient nomadic tribes whose way of life has changed little over the centuries. A rich diversity of desert landscapes here includes scrub desert – which bursts into colour after rainfall – and lunar, volcanic areas. There are lush oases and river-cut canyons too, but the reason most people come here is to see the 'Jade Sea', Lake Turkana, with its profusion of birdlife, hippos and Nile crocodiles.

Namib Desert, Namibia

Stretching for 1,930 km (1,200 miles) down the length of the Namibian coastline to the mouth of the Orange River in South Africa, the Namib is a strip of desert with an average width of 110 km (70 miles). The highest sand dunes in the world – sometimes exceeding 244 m (800 ft) – are to be found at Sossus Vlei, in the Namib-Naukluft National Park. The northern section is known as Skeleton Coast because of the many shipwrecks that lie on the ocean bed nearby.

Blyde River Canyon, South Africa

The view over the canyon from the spot known as God's Window is one of the highlights of any visit to the beautiful Blyde River Nature Reserve, in the Drakensberg. There are two trails down into the canyon – which in some places is over 700 m (2,300 ft) deep – from Bourke's Luck Portholes, where strange natural rock formations can be seen.

ASIA AND AUSTRALASIA

Thar Desert, Rajasthan, India

Within the Rajasthan Desert National Park two areas of interest to tourists can be reached easily from the attractive city of Jaisalmer with its 12th-century fort. One is the Akal Fossil Park where the petrified trunks of 25 trees once covered by the sea lie on a bare hillside. The second is the 3 km (2-mile) long Sam Dunes, just 40 km (25 miles) from Jaisalmer. The dunes are usually crowded with tourists taking camel rides, but it is possible to escape the crowds and go on safaris of several days, by either jeep or camel.

Gobi Desert, Mongolia

For 70 years part of the Soviet Union, the Gobi Desert has only recently become accessible to western travellers. Its greatest attraction is the red sandstone Flaming Cliffs, 80 km (50 miles) north-west of Dalandzadgad, which became famous in the 1920s when the explorer and scientist Roy Chapman Andrews (on whom the character of Indiana Jones was based) discovered fossilized dinosaur remains there. Still rich in dinosaur fossils, the cliffs are just north of the vast Three Beauties National Park with a landscape of mountains, canyons, gravel and sand.

▼ **Wadi Rum, Jordan**
Soaring vertically from the desert floor of Wadi Rum are the massive rock formations known as jebels for which the area is famous. Vehicles and camels can be hired in the Bedouin settlement of Rum, but it is hard to beat the experience of walking through this extraordinary, silent landscape and sleeping out in the desert under the stars.

◄ **Uluru National Park, Northern Territory, Australia**
The largest sandstone monolith in the world, Uluru (Ayers Rock) is a magnificent sight, particularly at sunset when it appears to burn from within. Some 40 km (25 miles) to the west are the Olgas – 36 enormous granite domes – which, like Uluru, are an important Aboriginal site. Access is restricted, but visitors can experience their haunting beauty by following the trail through the Valley of the Winds.

Lakes and waterfalls

From the azure tranquillity of Lake Garda in Italy to the thundering roar of Zimbabwe's Victoria Falls, the great lakes and waterfalls of the world are set amidst dramatically beautiful scenery. Many resorts offer watersports as well as long-distance trails for ramblers and horse-riders.

▶ **Lake Maligne, Jasper National Park, Canada**
The glacier-fed Lake Maligne – shown here at dawn – is set among the snow-covered peaks of Jasper National Park, the biggest and wildest of Canada's four Rocky Mountain national parks at 10,400 sq km (4,000 sq miles). Boat and hiking tours, fishing, rafting and riding are available, while the independent explorer can hire a boat or walk along the excellent network of trails.

▼ **Angel Falls, Venezuela**
The world's highest waterfall with an uninterrupted drop of 2,650 ft (807 m), Angel Falls are 16 times the height of Niagara Falls. Although often shrouded in mist, the Falls are at their most spectacular during the rainy season (June–November) when the volume of water is greatest and when visitors can travel by motorized canoe along the river to Devil's Canyon at the foot of the Falls.

▼ **Lake Argentino, Argentina**
The south-western arm of Lake Argentino is periodically dammed by the Moreno Glacier, from which icebergs regularly break off and crash into the channel below. Visitors can see, hear and photograph the glacier in safety from a series of platforms and viewing points. The massive Upsala Glacier on the northern arm of the lake can be reached by boat from Puerto Bandera.

NORTH AMERICA

Niagara Falls, Canada/USA
The most-visited waterfall in the world, Niagara Falls has been developed as a tourist attraction offering every possible viewing experience, including cable cars, helicopter rides, viewing towers, boats and even tunnels in the rockface. Despite the commercialization, this massive, perpetual curtain of falling water lives up to its reputation as one of the wonders of the natural world.

Waterton-Glacier Park, Montana and Alberta, Canada/USA
Silver lakes are a major feature of the landscape of mountain peaks, waterfalls and hanging valleys, carved by glaciers 10,000 years ago, in the Waterton-Glacier Park. There are spectacular trails for walkers of all levels, and the Going-to-the-Sun Road through the park is considered to be one of the USA's driving highlights.

Lake Tahoe, California, USA
High in the Sierra Nevada mountains on the border between California and Nevada, Lake Tahoe is a popular year-round holiday destination. In winter the area is packed with skiers (see *Winter sports*) while summer brings people seeking the cooler temperatures of the mountains and the crystal waters and sandy beaches of the lake. On the California side, there is swimming, boating, fishing and walking, while the Nevada side offers a glittering nightlife of restaurants and casinos.

SOUTH AMERICA

Iguaçu Falls, Brazil
The torrential waters of the Iguaçu River plunge more than 75 m (250 ft) over a huge, crescent-shaped cliff into the gorge below in a series of some 275 separate waterfalls. Surrounded by lush rainforest, the 4 km (2.5-mile) wide cascades can be viewed from platforms and paths on both sides of the Falls.

Lake Titicaca, Bolivia
High in the Altiplano the clear blue waters of Lake Titicaca bring an oasis of life and colour to the parched landscape. At 8,340 sq km (3,220 sq miles), it is the largest lake in South America, with many lakeside settlements. Boat trips can be made to the floating reed islands inhabited by the Uros, and to ancient Inca ruins on the sacred islands of the Sun and Moon.

Lake Llanquihue, Chile
A reflection of the perfect cone of Volcano Orsono can be seen in this immense lake which lies amid gently rolling pastureland. Towns on the shore include Frutillar Bajo, a popular summer resort with black-sand beaches, and Puerto Varas, a centre for 'adventure' activities such as rafting, riding, hiking and climbing.

EUROPE

Lake Siljan, Sweden
In a land of around 96,000 lakes, Siljan is noted as a centre of Swedish folk tradition and art. Locals and visitors arrive in boats reminiscent of Viking longships during midsummer celebrations at the lakeside church of Rättvik, and traditional mystery plays are performed annually in the open-air theatre at Leksand. Visitors can watch traditional painted wooden horses being made at Nusnäs, and visit the studio of the painter Anders Zorn, who lived in the lakeside town of Mora.

Lake District, England
Famous as the haunt of the Romantic Poets, the Lake District is a beautiful and varied landscape of hills, mountains, lakes and rivers, encompassing a wide range of scenery within a relatively small area. The southern lakes – including Windermere, Coniston and Grasmere – are surrounded by gentle green slopes and attract enormous numbers of visitors in summer.

The wilder north, with its sheer, forbidding crags is more spectacular and much less crowded. Boating is popular on the larger lakes, and a network of paths makes the area a haven for walkers and climbers.

Lake Lucerne, Switzerland

The picturesque medieval town of Lucerne with its famous Kapellbrücke bridge makes an excellent base for exploring this beautiful lake and its mountain surroundings. Visitors can go on a lake cruise and stop off at some of the peaceful villages along the shore, or take the oldest mountain railway in Europe to Mount Rigi for wonderful views of the Alpine scenery.

Lake Garda, Italy

The largest of Italy's lakes, Lake Garda is certainly one of its most beautiful. Sheltered from the north-east by the Dolomites, its climate is particularly gentle, with orange and lemon groves flourishing on its banks. Dotted around the lake are many attractive and historic resort towns – some dating back to Roman times – and romantic hillside villas.

AFRICA

Lake Bosumtwi, Ghana

Sacred to the Asante people, the crater lake of Bosumtwi is the deepest natural lake in Ghana, and its waters are still rising. Its beautiful setting among thickly wooded crater walls makes it a relaxing place to go fishing, boating and swimming. Motorboat trips across the lake are available, and walks around the shore can include visits to lakeside villages.

Murchison Falls, Uganda

The sheer force of the Nile as it shoots through a narrow cleft in the rocks and crashes over a 30 m (100 ft) precipice is what makes Murchison Falls so spectacular. A journey up the river from Paraa Camp to the base of the falls is also an excellent way to see some of the wildlife of the Murchison Falls National Park, including crocodiles, elephants, hippos, giraffes, buffalo, waterbucks and many bird species.

Lake Baringo, Kenya

Encircled by mountains and rich in bird and animal life, Lake Baringo is a fascinating and beautiful place to visit. The shoreline is home to crocodiles and herds of hippos and the area is famous for its hundreds of bird species, attracting birdwatchers from all over the world. A resident ornithologist offers guided walks, and there are also horse rides, camel rides and boat trips to the lake's islands.

ASIA

Lake Toba, Sumatra

Encircled by steep crags – once the rim of an enormous ancient volcano – Lake Toba is the largest crater lake in the world. The area is home to the Toba Batak people, whose brightly painted houses with distinctive crescent-shaped roofs can be seen around the lake. The beautiful island of Samosir is a popular tourist destination

with excellent trekking and rafting as well as interesting megalithic tombs to visit.

Lake Batur, Bali

The largest lake in Bali, Lake Batur is a crater lake and is sacred to the Balinese as the home of the goddess Dewi Danu. The hot springs at Toya Bungkah are said to have healing properties, and the lakeside temple of Pura Jati presides over a holy bathing place. From Toyah Bungkah there are trekking routes up to the summit of Gunung Batur, the soaring 1,717 m (5,630 ft) high volcano which dominates the lake.

Lake Karakul, Tajikistan

At a height of 3,600 m (11,800 ft) in the foothills of the Pamir mountains, Lake Karakul's setting is remote and beautiful. Flanked by the massive Mount Kongur to the north and the magnificent Mount Muztaghata to the south, Karakul is the home of the Kirgiz people and their herds of sheep, goats, horses and camels. It takes a day to walk around the lake, after which walkers can stay overnight in a traditional felt-covered *yurt* at the visitors' camp.

Lake Chuzenji-ko and Kegon Waterfall, Japan

Visitors to Lake Chuzenji-ko and the dramatic Kegon Waterfall are well provided for with cable cars and platforms from which to gaze at the spectacular view, especially popular in autumn when the

leaves are changing colour. Beside the lake is a colourful shrine after which both the town and lake are named.

AUSTRALASIA

Lake Rotorua, New Zealand

Bubbling hot springs, vertical jets of steam and scalding geysers make Rotorua an exciting place to visit. There are lakeside bath houses where visitors can sample the waters, as well as cruises and facilities for a wide range of watersports on the lake and nearby rivers. Maoris have lived beside the lake for around 700 years, and there are many cultural attractions on offer, some more authentic than others.

▲ Keli Mutu, Flores, Indonesia

An extinct volcano, Keli Mutu has three extraordinary crater lakes. Not only is each lake a different colour, but the colours change over decades from vivid green through to deep red and intense turquoise as mineral layers dissolve.

◄ Victoria Falls, Zimbabwe

The 1.7 km (1-mile) wide Victoria Falls are made up of five separate waterfalls which plummet more than 100 m (320 ft) into the gorge below. The Falls are a popular base for adrenaline-boosting activities, such as bungee jumping, white-water rafting and riverboarding, and tours of every description can be taken from operators based in Victoria Falls town.

7

Wildlife in the Americas and Europe

From the bears and moose of the Alaskan wilderness, to the jaguars and toucans of the Central American forests, to the condors and rheas of Patagonia, the Americas have an amazing variety of wildlife. Europe by contrast is famed for its seabirds, and the vast flocks of migrant wildfowl that gather in its wetlands.

▶ Torres del Paine National Park, Chile
An awe-inspiring landscape of forests, glaciers, shimmering lakes, thundering cascades and soaring granite pillars, Torres del Paine National Park in Patagonia is a haven for wildlife, including guanacos, rheas, flamingos, condors and the shy huemul (Chilean deer). There is an excellent network of short- and long-distance trails through the park.

▼ Wrangell-St Elias National Park, Alaska, USA
Of all the Alaskan national parks, Wrangell-St Elias is the best for wildlife watching. This vast landscape of mountains and glaciers is home to moose, wolves, wolverines, bears, beavers and herds of caribou. There are several campsites but few other facilities for visitors in this true wilderness park.

NORTH AMERICA

Wood Buffalo National Park, Alberta/NW Territories, Canada
Canada's largest national park, Wood Buffalo is famous for its free-roaming buffalo herd. Among other inhabitants are lynx, bears and hundreds of bird species, including a river rookery of rare white pelicans and the few remaining whooping cranes in the world. Fort Smith has some accommodation, but canoeing along the rivers and camping are perhaps the best ways to explore this wilderness of forest, marsh and grassland.

Yellowstone National Park, Wyoming, USA
Famous for its many geothermal geysers and hot springs, Yellowstone Park is also home to one of the largest and most diverse populations of mammals in North America. Inhabitants include bison, moose, elks, Bighorn sheep, beavers and marmots as well as lynx, bobcats, wolves and coyotes. Millions of visitors flock to Yellowstone every year, but despite the inevitable tourist development, most of the park is still a true wilderness.

Everglades National Park, Florida, USA
The largest sub-tropical wilderness on the North American mainland, Everglades National Park is a vast area of swamps, mangrove forests and grasslands. It is the only place in the world where alligators and crocodiles live side by side, and there are still a few panthers and black bears. Canoe trails and boat tours are the best way to view the abundant wildlife, which includes a huge variety of bird species.

CENTRAL AMERICA

Braulio Carrillo Park, Costa Rica
Many different habitats exist in Braulio Carrillo, a large area of rainforest covering a range of altitudes from just above sea level to 3,000 m (9,850 ft). Each has its own distinct flora and fauna, although the astonishingly lush vegetation can make spotting animals such as tapirs, sloths, ocelots, jaguars and pumas difficult. The park's abundant birdlife includes toucans, quetzels, umbrella birds, guans and eagles.

Corcovado National Park, Costa Rica
Set on the remote Osa peninsula, Corcovado National Park encompasses coastal mangrove swamps, pristine cloud forests and rocky canyons. Many of Costa Rica's endangered species live here, including tapirs, caymans and jaguars, while crocodiles swim in its waters and turtles lay their eggs on the park's deserted beaches. Ranger stations provide simple accommodation and advice.

Darién National Park, Panama
More than 500 bird species have been seen in the pristine rainforest of Darién National Park, among them many endangered species such as the harpy eagle. Indeed, Cerro Pirre mountain is considered by many birdwatchers to be one of the best sites in the world. Boat trips and forest walks are ideal ways to view the abundant wildlife, although visitors should seek advice on when it is safe to travel because of possible paramilitary activity.

Cockscomb Basin Wildlife Sanctuary, Belize
Beneath the peaks of the Cockscomb mountain range, the dense rainforest of the Cockscomb Basin is home to around 600 jaguars as well as tapirs, anteaters, armadillos and otters. Nearly 300 bird species have been reported in this lush jungle, and a wide variety of reptiles and amphibians are readily visible. Excellent forest trails make this a very rewarding place for wildlife watchers.

SOUTH AMERICA

Podocarpus National Park, Ecuador
Encompassing a wide range of habitats at different altitudes, Podocarpus (near Loja) has many rare plant and animal species, such as the Andean fox, the Andean speckled bear and the mountain tapir. Birdlife is abundant, and it is easy to see many fascinating species. This is, however, a park in peril, with the authorities struggling to protect the environment from poachers, loggers and others. For visitors prepared to rough it, there is much to enjoy in this landscape of lakes, mountains and rainforest.

Manu Biosphere Reserve, Peru
Altitudes range from 200 m (650 ft) to over 4,000 m (13,000 ft) in this area of rainforest near Cuzco. An astonishing 850 bird species are found here, and mammals include jaguars, ocelots, otters and many primate species. The reserve is divided into zones, with restricted visitor access in some areas. A stay in the Reserved Zone, which is set aside for ecotourism and research, must be arranged in advance, but offers the best jungle experience.

▲ Monteverde Cloud Forest Reserve, Costa Rica
Festooned with bromeliads and orchids, the towering rainforest trees of Monteverde Cloud Forest provide shelter for an enormous variety of wildlife including tapirs, monkeys, coatimundis and armadillos, as well as more than 400 bird species. The reserve was established in 1950 by a group of Quakers, who have developed a range of unobtrusive facilities for visitors, including simple accommodation and excellent guided walks.

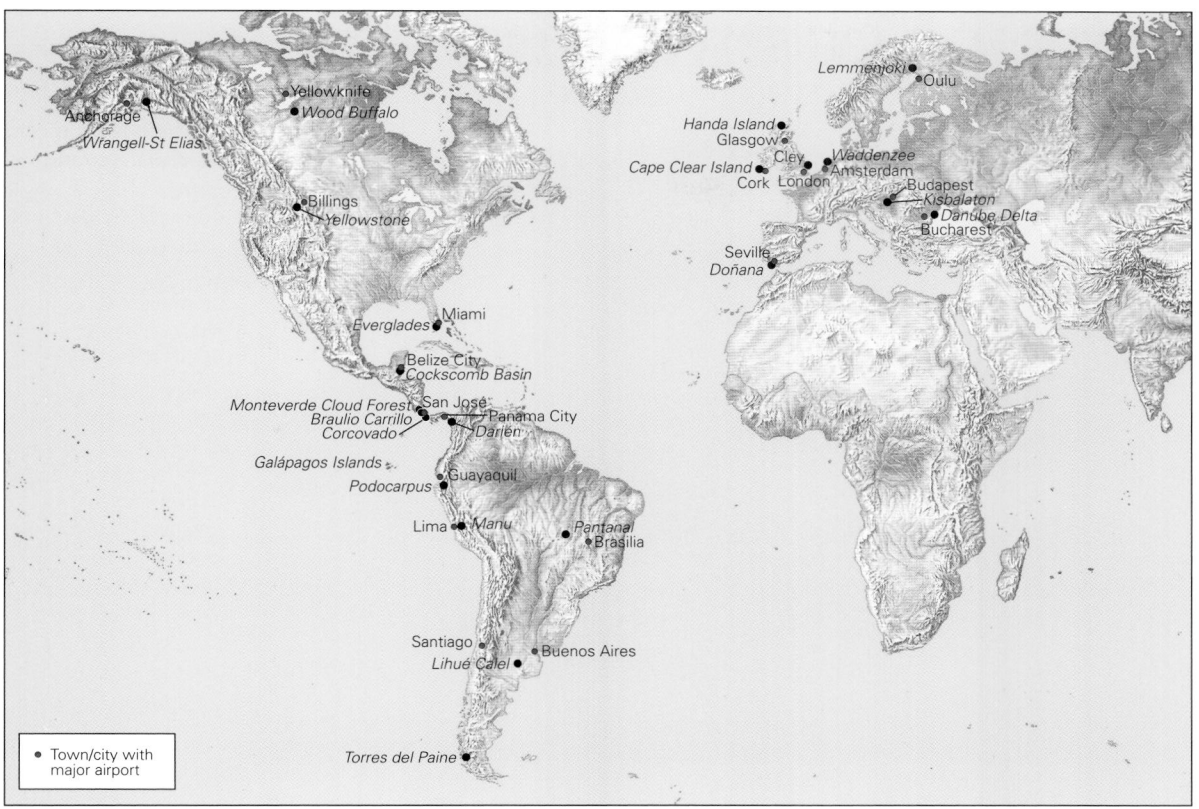

Town/city with major airport

▶ Handa Island, Scotland

The sea cliffs of Handa Island are one of north-west Europe's largest seabird nesting sites, with the high cliff ledges attracting guillemots, razorbills and kittiwakes in enormous numbers. Fulmars, puffins and shags also nest here, while the island's moorland is home to great and Arctic skuas, red-throated divers, shelducks, ringed plovers, wheatears, meadow pipits and skylarks. The island can be visited for the day by boat from the mainland village of Tarbet, near Loch Laxford.

Pantanal, Brazil

A vast swamp covering an area the size of Great Britain, the Pantanal is perhaps the best place to see wildlife in the Americas. Animals wander freely around the wide open spaces, making it relatively easy for visitors to spot such creatures as alligators, jaguars and anacondas, and birds such as the giant red-necked stork. There are organized tours by boat or jeep and on horseback, with overnight accommodation at converted ranch houses.

Lihué Calel National Park, Argentina

An arid landscape of low, pink granite mountains and scrub forest, Lihué Calel (south-west of Santa Rosa) is home to several wild cat species and other mammals such as guanacos, Patagonian foxes, Patagonian hares and chinchillas. Birdlife is plentiful, too, and includes many species of birds of prey. The park has an excellent campsite and visitor centre.

EUROPE

Lemmenjoki National Park, Lappland, Finland

Lemmenjoki (near Inarijärvi) is one of the most extensive areas of uninhabited, forested wilderness in Europe (2,855 sq km/1,102 sq miles). Wide rivers flow through a landscape of peatland and spruce- and birch-forested hills, home to brown bears, golden eagles, foxes, lynx, wolverines and moose. There are also plenty of semi-domesticated reindeer.

Cape Clear Island, Ireland

Ireland's southernmost inhabited island, tiny Cape Clear is famous for its birds. It has breeding populations of chough, black guillemot and rock dove and is visited by many migrant species in August–October, including the rare bee-eater, little bittern, night and purple herons, and great reed warbler, as well as many seabirds. The Bird Observatory has a full-time bird-warden and offers simple accommodation.

Cley Marshes, Norfolk, England

One of Britain's leading birdwatching reserves, Cley Marshes (near Sheringham) has many thatched hides offering excellent views of thousands of water birds. Migrating waders stop in the area on their way to and from their Arctic breeding grounds, and in summer bitterns and avocets breed here. Wildfowl such as teals, widgeons and shovelers are plentiful in winter.

Waddenzee, The Netherlands

Regarded by birdwatchers as the most important intertidal area in Europe, Waddenzee has huge populations of waders and wildfowl. One of the best areas to see the birds is around Schiermonnikoog, particularly at high tide. Among the birds present in summer are avocets, godwits and ruffs, while in winter they include Bewick's swans, barnacle geese, marsh and hen harriers and white-tailed eagles.

Kisbalaton Reserve, Lake Balaton, Hungary

With its reed beds, the Kisbalaton Reserve provides the perfect environment for marsh birds to breed. Night, purple and squacco herons are all to be found here along with little and great white egrets, spoonbills, marsh harriers and several warblers. From October huge flocks of migrating ducks and geese stop in the reserve on their journey south.

Danube Delta, Romania

One of Europe's last unspoiled ecosystems, consisting of forest, lakes, reed beds and marshland, the Danube Delta is home to huge numbers of birds. Due to the lack of tourist facilities, it is probably best-visited in an organized group, ideally from late May–June. Species include bitterns, pygmy cormorants, white pelicans, night, purple and squacco herons, spoonbills, ruddy shelducks, honey buzzards, bee-eaters and white-tailed eagles.

Doñana National Park, Spain

Huge sand dunes and the seasonally flooded plains (*marismas*) behind them provide ideal conditions for a great variety of birdlife in one of Europe's most important wildlife habitats. Peregrines, stone-curlews and short-toed eagles are to be seen in the dunes, while the marismas are feeding grounds for white storks, spoonbills, night and purple herons and colonies of little and cattle egrets.

Galápagos Islands and ecotourism

Lying 960 km (600 miles) off the coast of Ecuador, the fragile wilderness of the Galápagos Islands provides a habitat for a surprising combination of penguins and corals as well as giant tortoises, land and marine iguanas, sperm whales, sea lions, fur seals, orca whales, sharks and a variety of tropical fish. Many of the species living here are found nowhere else in the world, making the Galápagos a vital laboratory for the study of animal and plant life. Access to the islands is strictly controlled and limited to 50 designated visitor sites. The development of ecotourism in the Galápagos Islands aims to ensure the preservation of the habitats and wildlife while enabling tourists to visit and learn about this unique environment.

Wildlife in Africa, Asia and Australasia

An African safari is one of the world's great wildlife-watching experiences. Vast stretches of open savanna are home to the 'big five' – lion, leopard, elephant, rhinoceros and buffalo – as well as herds of zebra and gazelle. The endangered Indian tiger and exotic komodo dragon are just two of the animals that attract visitors to Asia, while Australia has its own unique fauna, including kangaroo, koala and duck-billed platypus.

◄ **Masai Mara National Reserve, Kenya**
Kenya's greatest concentration of wildlife can be seen in Masai Mara, where cheetahs, hyenas, zebras, hartebeest, hippos and crocodiles share the territory with the 'big five'. During the summer enormous herds of wildebeest, zebras and gazelles arrive from the Serengeti on the first stage of their dramatic annual migration.

AFRICA

Abuko Nature Reserve, Gambia
In this small reserve, mangroves, gallery forest and savanna combine to attract over 270 bird species – including the world's largest and smallest kingfishers – making it one of the best birdwatching sites in West Africa. Abuko is also known for its troops of colobus, patas and vervet monkeys.

Niokolo-Koba National Park, Senegal
Some 80 mammal species, including lions, leopards, elephants, waterbucks, bush-bucks, baboons and chimpanzees live in Niokolo-Koba, along with around 350 bird species. The best time to see the animals is when they gather at waterholes during the hot season in April and May.

Tsavo (East and West), Kenya
Tsavo East and Tsavo West combine to make one of the world's biggest national parks, covering an area of 21,000 sq km (8,000 sq miles). As well as the 'big five', the animals include cheetahs, giraffes, zebras, crocodiles, hippos, porcupines and mongooses. Tsavo East is a popular safari destination while at Tsavo West the excellent facilities include underwater hides for hippo watching.

Ngorongoro Crater, Tanzania
Protected within a circle of thickly-forested crater walls, Ngorongoro Crater is an expanse of grassland and forest measuring 14 km (9 miles) across and teeming with wildlife. Elephants, leopards, hyenas, bushbucks, buffalo, wildebeest, elands, warthogs, gazelles and ostriches live alongside the rare black rhinoceros and the handsome black-maned lion, while Lake Makat is home to flocks of flamingos and other water birds.

Jozani Reserve, Zanzibar, Tanzania
The largest remaining area of indigenous forest on Zanzibar, Jozani Reserve is home to a variety of birds and butterflies, as well as a number of rare mammals, including the red colobus monkey, which can only be found here.

Bwindi National Park, Uganda
Half of all the world's endangered mountain gorillas live in Bwindi National Park, an area of hilly rainforest. The park supports a rich variety of animal life including chimpanzees, golden cats, civets, leopards, bushpigs and giant forest hogs. Small groups of visitors who have booked several months in advance can go on guided gorilla-tracking expeditions.

Chobe National Park, Botswana
Encompassing habitats that range from marshland to forest, Chobe is home to a great variety of wildlife, including the rare puku and red lechwe antelope. Other inhabitants include lions, cheetahs, buffalo, giraffes, elephants, zebras, jackals, warthogs, hippos, crocodiles, hyenas, antelopes and wildebeest, as well as an abundance of birdlife. The animals can be viewed from boats on the Chobe River.

Kruger National Park, South Africa
A vast game reserve covering almost 20,000 sq km (7,400 sq miles), Kruger Park is home to around 137 mammal species, including lions, elephants, rhinoceros, leopards, buffalo, zebras, giraffes, impalas, wildebeest, hippos and crocodiles, as well as the rare roan and sable antelopes and oribi. The northern part is especially noted for its birdlife, including the highest density of birds of prey anywhere in the world.

Bird Island, Seychelles
Huge colonies of seabirds nest on the tiny, coral Bird Island. The sooty tern, fairy tern and common noddy are everywhere, while passing migrants add to the interest for birdwatchers. The island is also home to large numbers of giant turtles.

▼ **Serengeti National Park, Tanzania**
Covering 14,763 sq km (5,700 sq miles) and including woodland and mountains, as well as huge tracts of open grassland, the Serengeti is home to the 'big five' plus cheetahs, hyenas, zebras, giraffes, gazelles and many others. It also has around 500 bird species. It is most famous for the spectacular summer migration of gazelles, wildebeest and zebras, when around 2 million animals set off on a 800 km (500-mile) trek to fresh feeding grounds.

▲ **Etosha National Park, Namibia**
One of the most important wildlife reserves in Africa, Etosha covers a vast 20,000 sq km (7,720 sq miles) of woodland and grassland surrounding the Etosha Pan – an immense saline desert. Animals living here include springboks, impalas, kudu, wildebeest, hartebeest, roan antelopes, elands, zebras, elephants and the rare white rhinoceros, as well as predators such as lions, leopards, cheetahs, caracals, jackals and hyenas. There are around 340 bird species, including eagles, ostriches and secretary birds. Accommodation to suit all budgets is available.

ASIA

Kaziranga National Park, Assam, India

Famous as the home of the rare one-horned Great Indian Rhinoceros – most of the surviving 1,500 are here – Kaziranga (east of Gauhati) also has tigers, bears, elephants, bison and many bird species. A good way to travel around the tall-grass and swampy terrain is on an elephant. The park is only open from November to April.

Keoladeo Ghana National Park, Rajasthan, India

Formerly known as the Bharatpur Bird Sanctuary, Keoladeo is famous for its breeding populations of native water birds as well as its thousands of migrating birds which arrive every year from China and Siberia, including herons, storks, snake birds and the rare Siberian crane. The best time to visit is from October to February, when the migratory birds are in residence.

Sundarbans Wildlife Sanctuary, India/Bangladesh

Home to one of the largest remaining tiger populations in India, the Sundarbans Wildlife Sanctuary covers 6,695 sq km (2,585 sq miles) of mangrove swamp in the vast Ganges delta. Tigers are not often spotted by visitors, but a boat excursion through the peaceful mangroves will reveal many other animals – monkeys, wild pigs, spotted deer, crocodiles and fishing cats, as well as a profusion of birdlife.

Kanha National Park, Madhya Pradesh, India

Kipling set his *Jungle Book* in this beautiful landscape of forests, rivers and grasslands (near Mandla). Kanha is the only home of the barasingha (swamp deer) and it also plays an important role in the preservation of the tiger, leopard, chital, sambar and gaur (Indian bison). The park is open November–May, with sightings increasing from March onwards as the hot weather brings out the animals in search of water. Excursions are available.

Khao Yai National Park, Thailand

Encompassing a variety of habitats, from mountains clad in evergreen forest to lowland scrub and grassland, Khao Yai (north-east of Bangkok) has an abundance of wildlife, including elephants, gibbons, porcupines, tigers, leopards, Indian munjaks, Malaysian sun bears and several species of deer and monkey. There are over 250 bird species here, too, including the great hornbill and many colourful parrots and parakeets. Visitors can venture deep into the forest on several excellent trails, some of which require guides.

Taman Negara, Malaysia

Covering 4,340 sq km (1,676 sq miles) of ancient tropical rainforest, Taman Negara is a haven for hundreds of species of birds and animals, while its vegetation includes some of the world's rarest orchids. Inhabitants include tapirs, bears, elephants and gibbons. The park, which is the most visited in Pahang, has an elevated canopy walkway, and jungle hides in the trees, where visitors can spend the night.

Komodo National Park, Indonesia

The world's largest lizard, the astonishing 3 m (10 ft) long Komodo dragon, is found only on Komodo and a few neighbouring small islands. Guided treks usually include visits to dragon feeding places, and allow visitors to see some of the other wildlife of the park, such as wild pigs, deer, monkeys, water buffalo and eagles.

Ujung Kulon National Park, Indonesia

The last remaining low-relief forest on Java, in the far west, Ujung Kulon National Park is the only home of the one-horned Javan rhinoceros. Other inhabitants include the Javan gibbon, Javan tiger, muntjac (barking deer), chevrotain (mouse deer), green sea turtle and crocodile.

AUSTRALASIA

Eungella National Park, Queensland, Australia

With its tall, ancient rainforest trees, rocky creeks and spectacular waterfalls, Eungella is an extraordinarily beautiful place to watch wildlife. Among its inhabitants are kangaroos, possums, feathertail gliders, pythons and the native Eungella honey-eater, but the star attraction is the shy duck-billed platypus, which can be seen around the riverbanks at dawn and dusk.

Otago Peninsula, New Zealand

A remarkable variety of wildlife is concentrated on the Otago Peninsula. Seals and other marine life can be seen along the rocky coastline, while the inlets and beaches shelter numerous waders and waterfowl. A protected albatross nesting-site at Taiaroa Head is open to the public once the eggs are laid, and yellow-eyed penguins can be seen at close quarters from an excellent conservation reserve.

Catlins Forest Park, New Zealand

Ancient rainforest runs down to the rocky inlets and estuaries of the coast, offering a variety of habitats for some of New Zealand's rarest plants and animals. There are colonies of Hooker's sea lion and yellow-eyed penguin, and much birdlife. Two- and four-day ecotours are available.

◄ **Royal Chitwan National Park, Nepal**
With its lush sub-tropical jungle and floodplain swamp, Chitwan National Park is a natural habitat for animals such as the tiger, Indian rhinoceros and leopard. Tours on foot, by jeep or on the back of an elephant are best undertaken between October and March.

▼ **Kakadu National Park, Northern Territory, Australia**
Australia's largest national park, Kakadu encompasses a spectacular collection of rainforest, ravines and wetlands along the South Alligator River. These varied habitats shelter a vast array of wildlife, including 1,500 species of butterflies and moths, 75 reptile species, including crocodiles, 25 species of frog and one third of all Australia's bird species. Mammals include kangaroos, wallabies, walleroos, dingoes and many species of bat.

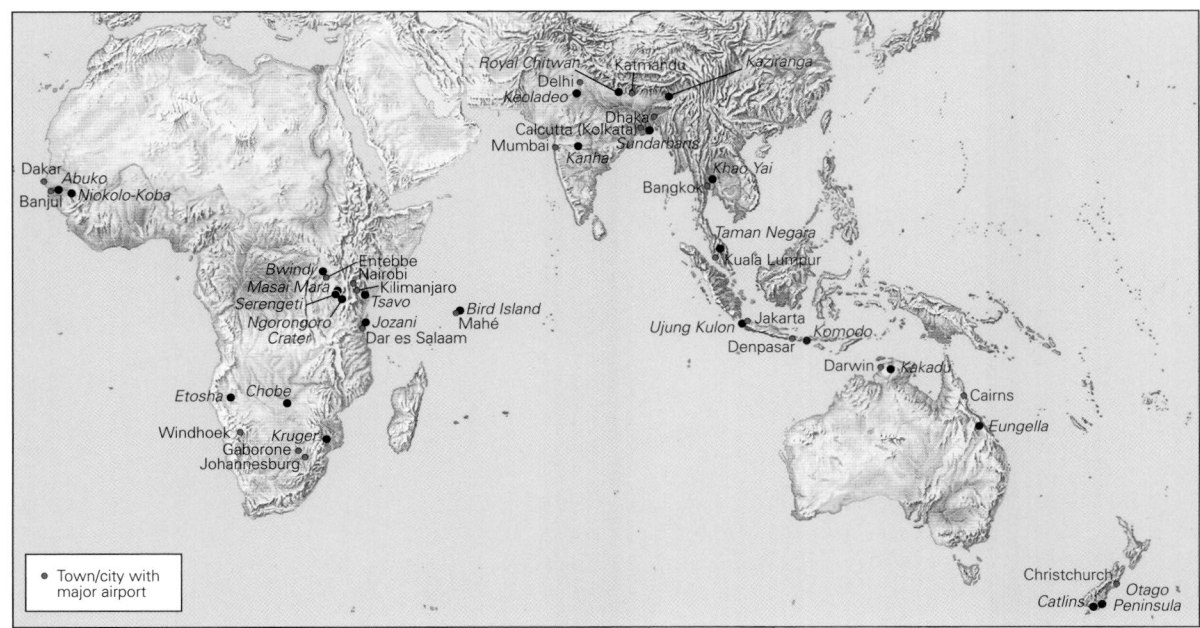

- Town/city with major airport

Marine wildlife

With whale numbers recovering strongly following the world ban on hunting, many seaports in North America, South Africa and Australasia offer boat trips to watch whales and other large fish and mammals. In the warm waters of the tropics, coral reefs teeming with vividly coloured sealife can be explored by scuba divers and snorkellers or viewed from the comfort of a glass-bottomed boat.

◀ **Florida Keys, USA**
Among many places in the Caribbean that serve as a base for viewing or swimming with dolphins is Florida Keys. Consisting of 45 islands surrounded by spectacular corals, Florida Keys also provides a perfect environment for scuba diving.

THE AMERICAS

Johnstone Strait, Canada
The sea between Vancouver Island and the mainland is one of the best places in the world to see orcas (killer whales), the largest and most powerful predators on earth, and minke whales.

Hudson Bay, Canada
Beluga whales can be seen in June, July and August in the bay's Arctic waters. Particularly large numbers spend these months in the Churchill River estuary, an area famous for its polar bears.

Cape Breton and Grand Manan Islands, Canada
Whale-watching boat trips take place around both islands. Off Grand Manan, in the Bay of Fundy, up to 20 whale species, including the rare northern right whale and the finback, can be seen.

Massachusetts Bay, USA
Stellwagen Bank in Massachusetts Bay is a feeding ground for humpback, finback and minke whales from April to October. It is a world-renowned whale-watching area, attracting around 1.5 million whale watchers a year. The coastal towns of New England offer a range of boat trips.

Caribbean Sea, Cayman Islands
The islands are famous among scuba divers for their exceptionally clear waters and deep diving with spectacular sponge colonies and a wide range of reef fish. Those interested in larger species can see dolphins, barracudas and sharks – including silky sharks – here.

Caribbean Sea, Belize
The barrier reef of Belize is the largest in the western hemisphere, and second only to Australia's in the world. Between the reef and the mainland lie more than 175 cays and atolls (coral islands and rings) offering some of the best diving opportunities in the world. The extraordinary Blue Hole at the centre of Lighthouse Reef is a circular shaft over 120 m (395 ft) deep which was once a cavern underneath the sea bed. Half Moon Caye offers one of Belize's most spectacular wall dives, with an almost sheer drop overhung with wonderful coral spurs, rich in marine life.

Caribbean Sea, Venezuela
There is good diving to be had around the offshore islands of Venezuela, especially in the archipelago of Los Roques with its white sand beaches and beautiful coral reefs. The Parque Nacional Morrocoy on the north-west coast of Venezuela is very popular for snorkelling.

Paracas National Park, Peru
A boat trip around the offshore islands within this national park provides an opportunity to see dolphins, seals and sea lions, as well as pelicans and the great Andean condors that inhabit the cliffs.

AFRICA AND THE INDIAN OCEAN

Canary Islands
The waters around the islands provide sheltered feeding grounds for pilot whales, not usually seen so close to shore, and there are many boat trips available from Tenerife. Unfortunately, whale watching is not properly regulated here and whales have been injured by the boats.

Red Sea, Egypt
Hurghada is a good base for snorkelling and diving around the coral reefs of the Red Sea. Jolanda Reef, at the tip of the Sinai Peninsula in the Ras Muhammad National Park, is a spectacular column of coral 800 m (2,625 ft) high. The park is best approached from the Sharm el Sheikh resort.

▲ **Point Reyes, California, USA**
Grey whales can be seen from Point Reyes, north of San Francisco, between October and January as they migrate down the coast of Canada and the USA to the Gulf of California. Between December and March they can be found at Guerrero Negro in Mexico, where they gather to calve.

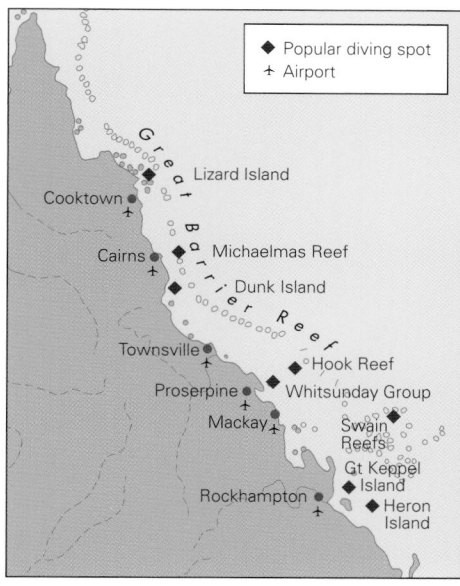

Popular diving spot
+ Airport

Pemba, Zanzibar and Mafia, Tanzania

The three main islands off the Tanzanian coast are surrounded by spectacular coral reefs which are home to a wide variety of marine species including bat fish, lion fish, turtles and rays. They offer some of the best diving opportunities in the world from August to December. Mafia Island is also a favourite breeding ground for giant turtles.

Cape of Good Hope, South Africa

In a country which has the strictest whale protection laws in the world, most whale watching takes place from the shore. The 'Whale Route' is a spectacularly scenic road along the coast from Cape Town, around the Cape of Good Hope, to the Indian Ocean, with many official whale-viewing sites. The town of Hermanus (the self-proclaimed 'whale capital' of South Africa) makes a good base. From June to October southern right whales, once hunted to near-extinction, can be seen swimming in these waters.

Seychelles

The outlying islands in particular offer world-class diving. The reef-ringed shores are a paradise for snorkellers, with over 150 species of tropical reef fish and 30 species of coral. Dolphins, porpoises, sharks and barracudas can also be seen. There are four marine national parks and diving schools with good facilities.

Maldives

Without doubt the Maldives are the best place in the Indian Ocean for diving. There are hundreds of diving sites, with something for everyone from beginners to experts. The more adventurous can explore shipwrecks as well as spectacular caves and terraces of coral. There is also plenty of scope for snorkellers.

► Tortuguero Park, Costa Rica

In the company of a guide, limited numbers of visitors can watch green turtles at their largest nesting site in the western hemisphere. The turtles lay their eggs on the beach between July and October, the peak time being late August.

Australia's Great Barrier Reef

The Great Barrier Reef is the largest structure on earth made by living organisms. It is a chain of coral reefs 2,000 km (1,200 miles) long, encompassing more than 600 islands and cays. About 20 of these islands have resort facilities, with Heron Island and Lizard Island both especially popular with divers. There are around 2,000 species of fish living on the reef and the area is home to many marine mammals, including the rare dugong and several species of whale. The best time to visit the reef is between April and December. Cairns is the mainland base for most reef activities and offers all kinds of tours.

ASIA

Ang Thong National Marine Park, Thailand

Boat trips around 42 limestone islands, many eroded into fantastic shapes, provide opportunities for seeing a variety of wildlife – including dolphins, turtles and sea otters – and for snorkelling and diving.

Similan Islands, Thailand

The gently sloping coral reefs and deep gorges around the Similan Islands feature a huge variety of marine life, including turtles, manta rays and whale sharks.

Sipadan Island, Sabah, Malaysia

An amazing undersea 'wall', teeming with marine life that includes whale sharks, manta rays, turtles and tuna, makes Sipadan one of the world's great diving destinations. The island is the tip of an underwater mountain, making it possible to dive from the beach.

Bunaken Island, Sulawesi, Indonesia

Perhaps the most famous marine destination in Indonesia, Bunaken Island near Manado serves as the main base for exploring the stunning coral reefs known as the 'sea gardens of Sulawesi'.

AUSTRALASIA AND THE PACIFIC

Kaikoura, New Zealand

A world-famous whale-watching centre, Kaikoura caters for 30,000 whale watchers

a year. The deepwater canyons near the shore are home to sperm whales.

Hawaii, USA

The extraordinary song of the humpback whale can be heard in the waters around Hawaii from November to May, after which these rare animals return to their summer feeding grounds in the near-polar waters of the north Pacific. Whale watching is strictly regulated, but there are plenty of boat trips on offer. Hawaii also has coral reefs, though with fewer species than on other Indo-Pacific reefs. Diving is popular, with lessons being provided in the crater lake of the extinct Molokini volcano. Excursions in submarines down to a depth of 50 m (160 ft) offer superb views of the underwater world through portholes.

Rangiroa, Tuamotu Islands

Among many excellent diving sites in French Polynesia, this is possibly the best, with outstanding coral, sharks, dolphins, barracudas and rays.

Marquesas Islands

The oxygen-rich water around the islands, which is thick with plankton, supports a variety of marine creatures, including hammerhead and white-tipped sharks, leopard and manta rays, tuna and barracudas. There are around 20 dive sites, including some impressive caves.

▲ Malindi and Wasini Island, Kenya

One of a number of good diving and snorkelling spots in Kenya, Malindi also offers excursions in glass-bottomed boats to the nearby coral reef. The Kisite Marine National Park on Wasini Island, in the far south, provides spectacular diving safaris.

Great railway journeys

From the luxury of the Orient-Express to the spartan rigours of the Trans-Siberian Railway, the world's great train journeys exert an irresistible lure for many travellers, passing through spectacular landscapes. Journeys vary in length from a few hours to a fortnight, and the more sought-after trains must be booked well in advance.

NORTH AMERICA

Green Mountain Flyer, Vermont, USA
Distance: 21 km (13 miles)
A vintage train takes passengers through the beautiful Vermont countryside, running alongside the Connecticut River for part of the way. Largely a tourist service, the peak period is during October when the autumn colours are at their best.

Coast Starlight, USA
Distance: 2,235 km (1,389 miles)
A journey from Seattle to Los Angeles, through the magnificent landscapes of the west coast of the USA, includes amongst its highlights the mountains of the Oregon Cascades and the Californian Coast Range. South of Oakland the track runs along the edge of the Pacific Ocean, passing several of California's most popular beaches.

Los Mochis to Chihuahua, Mexico
Distance: 655 km (407 miles)
This 14-hour journey is one of contrasting landscapes, from the tropical Pacific coastlands to the high northern plateau by way of the magnificent Copper Canyon (Barranca del Cobre). Longer and deeper than Arizona's Grand Canyon, this is an area of steeply wooded gorges and spectacular mountain peaks.

SOUTH AMERICA

Guayaquil to Quito, Ecuador
Distance: 463 km (288 miles)
For those who relish danger as well as breathtaking scenery, this line – which has been called 'the world's greatest roller-coaster' – is a must. It climbs high into the Andes, zigzagging perilously to an altitude of 3,609 m (11,840 ft) and passing directly under a waterfall. Trains are erratic and often break down.

Central Railway, Peru
Distance: 335 km (208 miles)
The highest railway in the world, this takes passengers on an eight- to nine-hour journey across the Andes, from Lima to Huancayo. Dizzy heights, sheer drops, zigzags, loops and tunnels abound.

EUROPE

Flåm Railway, Norway
Distance: 20 km (12 miles)
Dropping 865 m (2,838 ft) in just 20 km (12 miles), this is one of the steepest non-rack railways in the world. Beginning with a view over the Kjosfossen lake and waterfall, the train weaves its way from Myrdal towards Aurlands Fjord and Flåm through a series of tunnels, with spectacular views between tunnels and snow shelters.

► Palace on Wheels
India's most luxurious train, originally hauled by the *Desert Queen*, takes passengers on an eight-day tour that begins and ends in Delhi. It includes Jaipur and the other major cities of Rajasthan, and Agra.

◄ Glacier Express, Switzerland
Distance: 290 km (180 miles)
An exhilarating seven-and-a-half hour journey in the Swiss Alps, between the ski resorts of St Moritz and Zermatt, is provided by this train. Extraordinary feats of engineering are displayed as it weaves its way through the mountains, travelling through 91 tunnels, crossing 291 bridges and negotiating hairpin bends and steep ascents.

West Highland Line, Scotland
Distance: 264 km (164 miles)
Running between Glasgow and Mallaig, this line provides one of the most spectacular railway journeys in Britain. The route is particularly dramatic between Fort William and Mallaig, with a series of viaducts and tunnels through the mountains high above the Atlantic coast.

Venice Simplon-Orient-Express, Europe
Distance: 1,714 km (1,065 miles)
Passengers travel in style on a train that re-creates the romance of the golden age of rail as it crosses Europe from London to Venice, via Paris, Zürich, Innsbruck and Verona, in 32 hours. Orient-Express trains also run to Rome and Istanbul on a variety of routes that go through Venice, Florence, Lucerne, Budapest and Bucharest.

Andalusian Express, Spain
Distance: 740 km (460 miles)
The luxurious *Al Andalus* follows a circular route from Seville through the beautiful Andalusian countryside, with its citrus and olive groves, vineyards and hilltop villages. There are opportunties to stop off and see the sites at Córdoba, Granada, Antequera and Ronda.

▲ Canadian, Canada
Distance: 2,776 miles (4,4467 km)
On a 69-hour journey that begins in Toronto, this train passes through some of the most beautiful scenery on earth. The prairie lands of Manitoba and Saskatchewan give way to the cattle ranches of Alberta, from where the train climbs into the Rockies. Here it passes lakes, glaciers and the dramatic Fraser Canyon before reaching Vancouver.

Useful web addresses
all preceded by www.

Canadian trains:
viarail.ca

US trains:
amtrak.com

European trains:
raileurope.com

Orient-Express:
orient-expresstrains.com

Pride of Africa:
rovos.co.za

Palace on Wheels:
palaceonwheels.net

Eastern and Oriental Express:
orient-expresstrains.com/eando/train

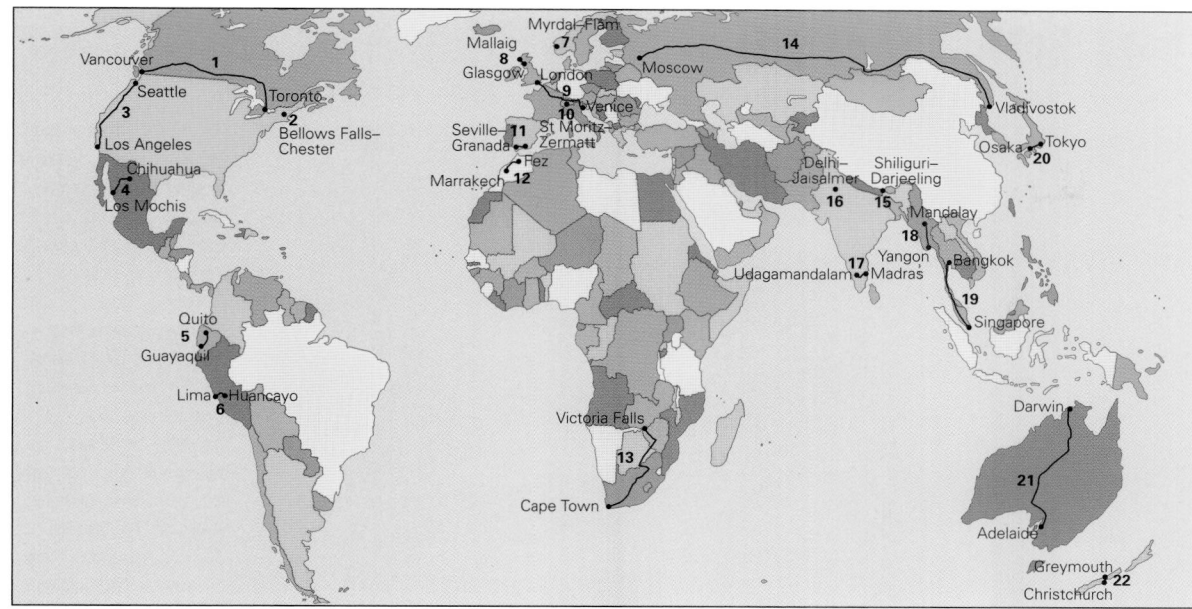

1	Canadian, Canada
2	Green Mountain Flyer, USA
3	Coast Starlight, USA
4	Los Mochis to Chihuahua, Mexico
5	Guayaquil to Quito, Ecuador
6	Central Railway, Peru
7	Flåm Railway, Norway
8	West Highland Line, Scotland
9	Venice Simplon-Orient-Express, Europe
10	Glacier Express, Switzerland
11	Andalusian Express, Spain
12	Marrakech Express, Morocco
13	Pride of Africa, Southern Africa
14	Trans-Siberian Railway, Russia
15	Darjeeling Himalayan Railway, India
16	Palace on Wheels, India
17	Madras to Udagamandalam, India
18	Mandalay Express, Burma (Myanmar)
19	Eastern and Oriental Express, Thailand and Malaysia
20	Tokyo to Osaka, Japan
21	The Ghan, Australia
22	TranzAlpine Express, New Zealand

AFRICA

Marrakech Express, Morocco
Distance: 583 km (362 miles)
Passing through Morocco's four imperial cities, this nine-hour journey begins in Marrakech, near the foot of the High Atlas Mountains, and travels north through the desert to Casablanca. From here the line follows the Atlantic coast to Rabat then gradually heads back inland through orchards and olive groves to Meknès and on to Fès.

Pride of Africa, Southern Africa
Distance: 3,2000 km (2,000 miles)
The journey from Cape Town in this luxurious train is full of romance and drama. In the early stages the train travels through a landscape of vineyards and farmland and across the Karoo Desert to Pretoria. Passengers can enjoy watching wildlife as the journey continues through the African bush across Botswana and Zimbabwe to the spectacular Victoria Falls on the Zambian border.

ASIA

Madras to Udagamandalam, India
Distance: 640 km (400 miles)
This 16-hour journey takes travellers from the plains of Madras through a colourful rural landscape and up into the beautiful Nilgiri hills to the famous hill station of Udagamandalam, formerly known as Ootacamund, or Ooty. The train passes through some of the most dramatic scenery India has to offer, climbing steeply on India's only rack railway to the gentler landscapes of the Deccan Plateau.

Darjeeling Himalayan Railway, India
Distance: 88 km (55 miles)
The tiny engine used on this railway, which is a UNESCO heritage site, takes passengers from Shiliguri on the hot Bengal plains to the mountain climate of Darjeeling in the Himalayas. The journey involves steep ascents and precipitous curves, climbing 2,164 m (7,100 ft). On the way the train passes through Ghoom, which is the second highest station in the world at 2,258 m (7,408 ft) above sea level.

Mandalay Express, Burma (Myanmar)
Distance: 616 km (385 miles)
By no means a tourist train, the Express offers the traveller a truly local experience as it makes its way slowly north from Yangon (formerly Rangoon) through a landscape of rice fields and golden-spired pagodas. The crowded train makes numerous – often unscheduled – stops along the way, making it an unpredictable and colourful journey. Best undertaken between November and February, the journey takes around 16 hours.

Eastern and Oriental Express, Thailand and Malaysia
Distance: 1,943 km (1,207 miles)
Starting in Bangkok, this train takes 52 hours to travel south through the terraced farmlands of Thailand and the rubber plantations and jungles of Malaysia to Singapore. It represents the height of luxury in train travel, while International Express trains that follow the same route provide a more down-to-earth experience.

AUSTRALASIA

The Ghan, Australia
Distance: 2,962 km (1,851 miles)
Named after the Afghan camel-drivers who once transported provisions along its route, the Ghan passenger train made its first journey from Adelaide to Darwin in February 2004. In 47 hours the train passes through vine-covered hills to the craggy mountains of the MacDonnell Ranges, the multi-coloured desert of central Australia and the woodland of the north, much to the delight of train enthusiasts who long campaigned for the line north of Alice Springs to be completed.

◄ **Tokyo to Osaka, Japan**
Distance: 518 km (322 miles)
The Nozomi Express – the fastest scheduled train service in the world – travels at speeds of up to 300 km/h (186 mph) along this line. Not quite as fast, the Hikari Express completes the journey in just over three hours. However, the scenery, which includes Mount Fuji, can best be appreciated from the slower 'bullet' trains.

TranzAlpine Express, New Zealand
Distance: 233 km (154 miles)
Travelling from Christchurch on the South Island's east coast to Greymouth on the west coast, the Express takes passengers on a four-and-a-half hour journey through a variety of landscapes. After crossing the farmlands of the Canterbury Plains it follows the Waimakariri River gorge into the mountainous Arthur's Pass National Park, where it enters the long Otira tunnel. From here the line descends through lush rainforest, passing lakes Poerua and Brunner, to Greymouth.

Trans-Siberian Railway, Russia
Distance: 9,297 km (5,776 miles)
The southern shore of Lake Baikal is on the route of the Trans-Siberian Railway, the world's longest, and possibly most famous, railway. The eight-day journey takes passengers from Moscow to Vladivostok via the Urals, the forested wilderness of Siberia, and the Transbaikalian Mountains.

In the early days of the railway, built between 1891 and 1916, a ferry was used in summer to carry the train across Lake Baikal, while in winter, when the lake froze, temporary rails were laid over the ice. The Siberian landscape is particularly beautiful in winter when it is covered with snow. In the spring there are carpets of wild flowers while in autumn there are the golden colours of the birch forests.

River and canal journeys

The world's great boat journeys give travellers a unique perspective on the countries through which they pass: rivers and canals were the highways of the past, and there are often opportunities to visit historic sites or natural habitats. Whether you are steaming down the Mississippi in a paddleboat, gliding through the French countryside past castles and vineyards or exploring the tributaries of the Amazon, the pace of the journey gives ample time to enjoy the beauty of the surroundings.

NORTH AMERICA

St Lawrence, Canada

From Kingston, where Lake Ontario flows into the majestic St Lawrence River, a six-night journey can be made on a replica steamboat to Montréal (see *World Cities*) and Québec (see *Historic sites in the Americas*). Just east of Kingston the river is dotted with literally a Thousand Islands, many of which have summer houses and opulent mansions set amid forests of yellow birch, silver maple and red and white trillium. In the spring the trillium trees are covered by white blossom.

Upper Mississippi, USA

In the summer months, seven-day cruises by paddleboat run between Minneapolis/St Paul and St Louis. There are also three-day cruises between St Louis and Memphis. The upper river, flowing through relatively flat countryside, is wide, slow moving and dotted with islands, but the stretch immediately below St Louis flows between rocky bluffs. Days spent cruising are alternated with sightseeing tours of such places as the boyhood home of Mark Twain, in Hannibal, Memphis, and a historic Native American site in Burlington, Iowa.

▶ **St Petersburg to Moscow, Russia**
This seven-day cruise passes through a network of rivers, lakes and canals in the richly wooded region of Southern Karelia, and down the upper reaches of the Volga River. Ports of call include the ancient town of Yaroslavl, the attractive Karelian capital of Petrozavodsk, and the Church of the Transfiguration on the island of Kizhi in Lake Onega, with its 22 wooden domes, constructed without a single nail.

CENTRAL AND SOUTH AMERICA

Amazon, Peru and Brazil

Cruises of between three and ten days along the Amazon River, starting from the remote but elegant Peruvian town of Iquitos, or from the brash and bustling Manaus in Brazil, are a relatively comfortable way to see the abundant wildlife of the rainforest. Many companies adopt an educational approach and include lectures on the local flora and fauna. Some include an opportunity to explore smaller tributaries by canoe. For the adventurous independent traveller who is prepared to rough it, a six-day journey by local riverboat from the Atlantic port of Belém to Manaus offers an unforgettable experience of local life and culture.

Orinoco Delta, Venezuela

The vast Orinoco Delta – a maze of channels running between countless forested islands – is one of Venezuela's wildest regions. The area is home to the indigenous Warao people, known for their skilled carving and basketwork, whose houses on stilts can be seen on the riverbanks. Boat tours into the delta can be arranged from the town of Tucupita, and usually last for between two and four days.

EUROPE

Shropshire Union Canal, UK

From Autherley, a 100 km (60-mile) journey can be taken on a slow-moving barge along the Shropshire Union Canal. Deep wooded cuttings, peaceful rural landscapes, medieval market towns and quiet villages are all passed at little more than walking pace. The ancient city of Chester, with its Roman ruins and medieval city walls, is a highlight of the journey. The canal ends at Ellesmere Port on the River Mersey, where there is an excellent boating museum.

Rhine, Switzerland, Germany and the Netherlands

A ten-day journey down the Rhine from Basel to Arnhem combines stunning scenery with a chance to visit the historic towns and cities along its banks. After flowing through the German Black Forest, the river passes romantic clifftop castles, sloping vineyards and picturesque villages on its way to the cities of the north: Bonn, Cologne and Düsseldorf. A detour up the River Neckar to the historic town of Heidelberg is often included.

◀ **Lower Mississippi, USA**
A seven-day cruise by paddleboat can be taken from Memphis to New Orleans. The Mississippi twists and turns on its way to the marshlands bordering the coast. There are opportunities to visit some of the historic sites of the Deep South, including the Civil War battlefields of Vicksburg, and the elegant mansion at Oak Alley Plantation, and to sample some of the local Creole and Cajun cuisine.

▲ **The Burgundy Canal, France**
Passing through a landscape of wooded valleys and sleepy villages, the six-day journey on a barge from Tonnere to Dijon along the Burgundy Canal provides an opportunity to see the beautiful 16th-century chateaux of Tanlay and Ancy le Franc and the 12th-century Cistercian Abbey of Fontenay. The region is famous for its *grand cru* vineyards and its robust cuisine, and there are plenty of opportunities to enjoy both along the way.

Douro, Portugal

Most cruises on the Douro are round trips of seven to nine days, beginning and ending in Porto. Once the boat leaves the coastal plain, it passes between spectacularly terraced vineyards, in an area unspoilt by major roads. Ports of call include the picturesque towns of Lamego and Vila Real. The region is the centre of Portugal's port wine production, and all cruises include a visit to a vineyard to sample the local produce.

Danube, Hungary, Slovak Republic, Austria and Germany

A Danube cruise of around eight days combines sightseeing tours of some of Central Europe's most historic towns and cities with an opportunity to relax on board, watching rich farmland and terraced slopes slip past. A cruise up-river from Budapest to Regensburg includes frequent stops, enabling passengers to explore Bratislava, Vienna, Linz and Passau, and to visit the sumptuous Baroque palace of Schönbrunn and the Benedictine Abbey in Melk. Since the boat berths overnight, passengers can also enjoy some nightlife ashore, and attend specially organized classical concerts.

AFRICA

River Gambia National Park, Gambia

A day trip on the river from Janjanbureh (Georgetown) or Kuntaur provides an opportunity to view crocodiles and hippos at close range. As the rice fields and coconut trees on the banks give way to dense forest, it may also be possible to glimpse monkeys, baboons and many species of birds.

Niger, Mali

A journey along the River Niger as it curves through the semi-desert of the Sahel is the classic way to see and experience the life of this area. Local passenger boats are scheduled to take seven days, but can take as long as 14 to travel between Gao and Koulikoro. The most popular section is the two days or so between Mopti and Korioumé, the stopping point for visits to the ancient desert city of Timbuktu. Also highly recommended is a detour up the River Bani to the beautiful old town of Djenné, where the mosque is a stunning example of construction using mud bricks and render.

ASIA AND AUSTRALASIA

Backwaters of Kerala, India

The eight-hour journey through the backwaters of Kerala, from Kollam (Quilon) to Alappuzha, is popular with tourists. Passengers are transported along a network of rivers, canals and lagoons, overhung with dense tropical foliage that every so often gives way to open paddy fields. Brightly coloured birds and ancient buildings can be glimpsed on the banks, and the Keralan people can be seen going about their daily lives.

Gorges of the Yangtze, China

Time is running out for those who want to experience the full splendour of a cruise along the Yangtze River as it passes between the rocky pinnacles of the Three Gorges. The controversial Three Gorges Dam project is due to be completed in 2009, and the flooding that will eventually create a 560 km (350-mile) long reservoir is well under way. The dam itself has become a tourist attraction. In the meantime, three- to four-day cruises from Chongqing to Wuhan, through the magnificent Qutang, Wuhang and Xiling gorges, continue to provide stunning views of a dramatic natural landscape. It is also possible to take a longer cruise from Shanghai to Chongqing.

Sepik, Papua New Guinea

The Sepik River twists and turns its way from the central mountains of Papua New Guinea through jungles, swamps and grasslands to the sea. Most cruises start from a remote inland location, to which passengers are transferred from Port Moresby by small plane. There is then a leisurely journey through the rainforest, with stops at riverside villages, some of which are on stilts. The people of the region are renowned for their woodcarving and traditional art, each village having its own distinctive style.

Murray, South Australia

A six-day cruise on a paddelboat, beginning and ending at Mannum, passes through colourful scenery, including verdant wetlands, brick-red plains, sandstone cliffs and deep blue lagoons. The cruise may also include a visit to the old river port of Morgan and an opportunity to hear about Aboriginal customs from elders at the Ngaut Ngaut Conservation Park.

◄ Nile, Egypt

A week-long cruise up the Nile from Luxor to Aswan and back combines visits to magnificent historic sites – such as the huge temple of Karnak and the tombs in the Valley of the Kings at Luxor – with periods of relaxation on board an air-conditioned riverboat. There are also opportunities to take camel rides into the desert that lies beyond the narrow fertile strip on either side of the river. From Aswan, where it is possible to sail on the river in a *felucca* (pictured here), a short flight takes passengers to the splendid temple of Abu Simbel, above the shores of Lake Nasser. Abu Simbel can also be reached by taking a luxury three-day cruise on the lake. Created by the building of the Aswan Dam, the lake itself is an impressive sight.

Useful web addresses
all preceded by www.
rivercruises.com
smallshipcruises.com
burgundy-canal.com
travelchinaguide.com/cruise
americanweststeamboat.com

▼ Li, China

The 80 km (50-mile) journey down the Li River from Guilin to the beautiful town of Yangshuo passes through a landscape of precipitous peaks, with names such as Paint Brush Hill and Five Tigers Catch a Goat Hill. Gliding past bamboo-lined riverbanks and picturesque villages, the trip and a bus-ride back to Guilin takes one day.

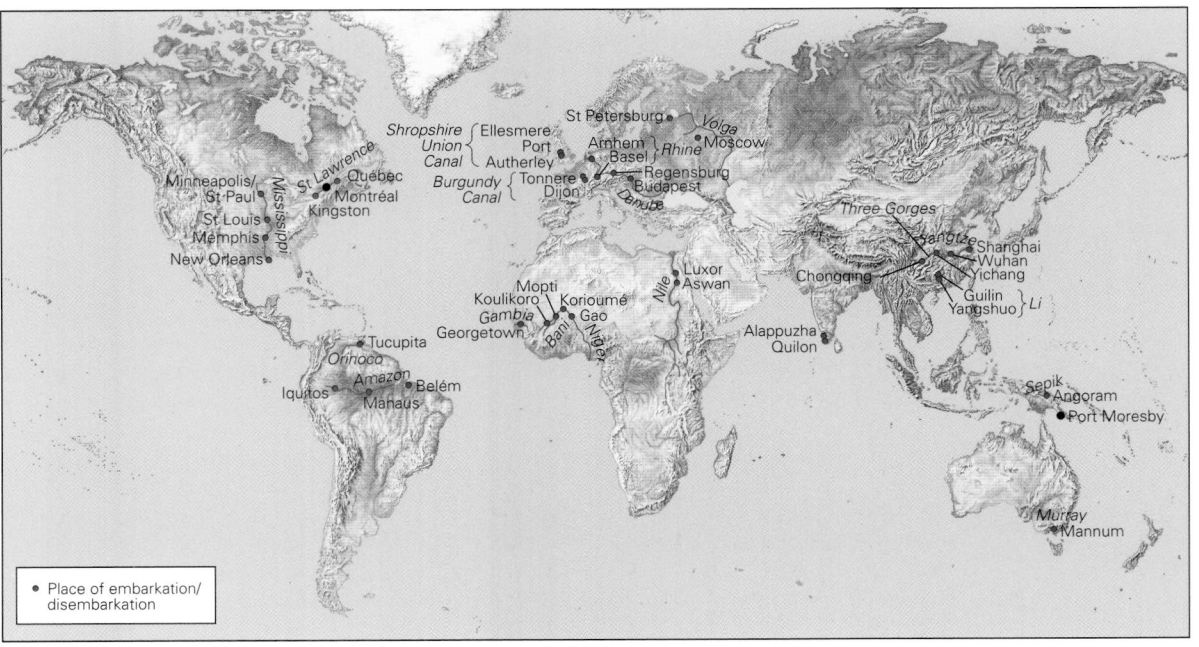

• Place of embarkation/disembarkation

Sea and ocean cruises

Cruises attract all kinds of travellers and cater for an increasingly wide range of tastes. The steep-sided inlets of Alaska, Chile, Norway and New Zealand allow cruise liners to hug the coast, providing matchless views of these dramatic landscapes. Caribbean cruises allow almost daily shore visits, for shopping and exploring. Transatlantic cruises provide lavish on-board entertainment during the long sea passages. Cruise companies also vary in their appeal: some include lectures on the places they visit; others take a far less serious approach!

◄ **The Caribbean**
There are numerous variations on the Caribbean cruise, but virtually all have relatively short sea passages and a visit to a different island almost every day. There are organized trips to the rain-forests of Puerto Rico and sites of European colonial history. Some passengers, however, prefer to spend their time simply enjoying the islands' magnificent beaches.

NORTH AMERICA AND THE ATLANTIC

Alaska/British Columbia
The main attractions of a cruise in this area are the spectacular mountain scenery and the opportunity to see whales and seals, bears and birds of prey at close hand. Ships hug the coastline, entering steep-sided fjords and sailing close to the mouths of glaciers. Ports of call include Juneau, Alaska's capital, the 'gold rush' town of Skagway, and the Russian settlement of Sitka, with its onion domes.

Mexican Riviera
Mexico's west coast is becoming an increasingly popular area for relatively short cruises to catch the late-summer sunshine. For some tourists, the attractions are miles of unspoilt beaches fringed by jungle, such as those at Manzanillo and Zihuatanejo, and being able to go marlin fishing. For others they are the opportunities to experience Mexican culture and to visit the chic resort of Puerto Vallarta.

Atlantic Isles (Canaries, Madeira)
The Atlantic Isles are a popular cruise destination, particularly in winter and spring, when the lower mountain slopes are brilliant with flowers. Shore visits in Madeira usually include the novelty of a ride in a bullock cart or wicker sled on the mountain roads, while a trip to the summit of Tenerife's Mount Teide (3,718 m/12,000 ft) provides spectacular views of the surrounding islands.

Transatlantic cruises
Cruises link Europe with New York or Boston, with ports further south, such as Miami, and also with various Caribbean islands. The most direct, more northerly, route is for those wishing to enjoy the elaborate onboard entertainment, high standard of cuisine, and formal social life that are typical of the transatlantic liner. On ships plying more southerly waters, passengers can combine a luxury lifestyle with sunbathing, swimming and various other deck activities.

SOUTH AMERICA

Chilean fjords
Cruises along the most southern 1,000 km (625 miles) of Chile's coastline provide magnificent views of mountains and glaciers. The further south, the colder and less predictable the weather becomes, but for many the thrill of travelling the route of Darwin's *Beagle* and visiting Tierra del Fuego outweighs the risk of storms.

EUROPE

Norwegian fjords
Those cruising the fjords of Norway do so primarily to enjoy the majestic mountain scenery. Waterfalls, glaciers and wildlife can all be viewed from the comfort of the ship, while shore visits include a ride on a spectacular mountain railway from Flåm (see *Great railway journeys*). Some cruises extend as far as Europe's most northern point, where passengers can experience the midnight sun.

Western Mediterranean
One of the joys of a cruise in the Western Mediterranean is the opportunity to sample the local cuisine and wines. Most cruises include a day in the vibrant Spanish city of Barcelona. In Italy, there are brief organized trips to view the art treasures of Pisa and Florence, and the Roman remains of Pompeii (see *Historic sites in Europe*). There are also opportunities to enjoy the high-life in some of the fashionable resorts of the French Riviera, such as St Tropez, to visit the casinos of Monte Carlo, and to watch the Spanish flamenco dancers in Cartagena. Some cruises extend as far as the Adriatic, call in at the fortress town of Dubrovnik and include a day's sightseeing in Venice.

Eastern Mediterranean
A region rich in the remains of earlier civilizations, the Eastern Mediterranean provides much of historic interest, and many cruises have on-board experts to give background lectures. Some of the main sites visited include the Roman town of Ephesus in Turkey, the Ancient Greek ruins of Delos, the Crusader castle of Krak des Chevaliers in Syria, and the pyramids in Egypt (see *Historic sites in Africa*). Most cruises also include opportunities for swimming, snorkelling and sunbathing.

◄ **Antarctica**
Many of the 'expedition cruises' to the Antarctic use converted research ships or ice breakers, which offer less luxurious accommodation than other cruise ships. Passengers are taken ashore in small inflatable craft, and are thus able to get close to the teeming wildlife. There is always the chance of encountering whales in the surrounding seas, as well as sighting beautifully sculpted icebergs.

▲ **North-east America**
The north-eastern seaboard of America offers areas of great natural beauty such as Acadia National Park in Maine, whose fall colours are the focus of October cruises. There is also an opportunity to see the whales that frequent the waters of Stellwagen Bank off the coast of Massachusetts. Included in a wide variety of shore visits are the Canadian fishing town of Lunenburg, the popular US resort of Martha's Vineyard, and the cities of Boston and New York.

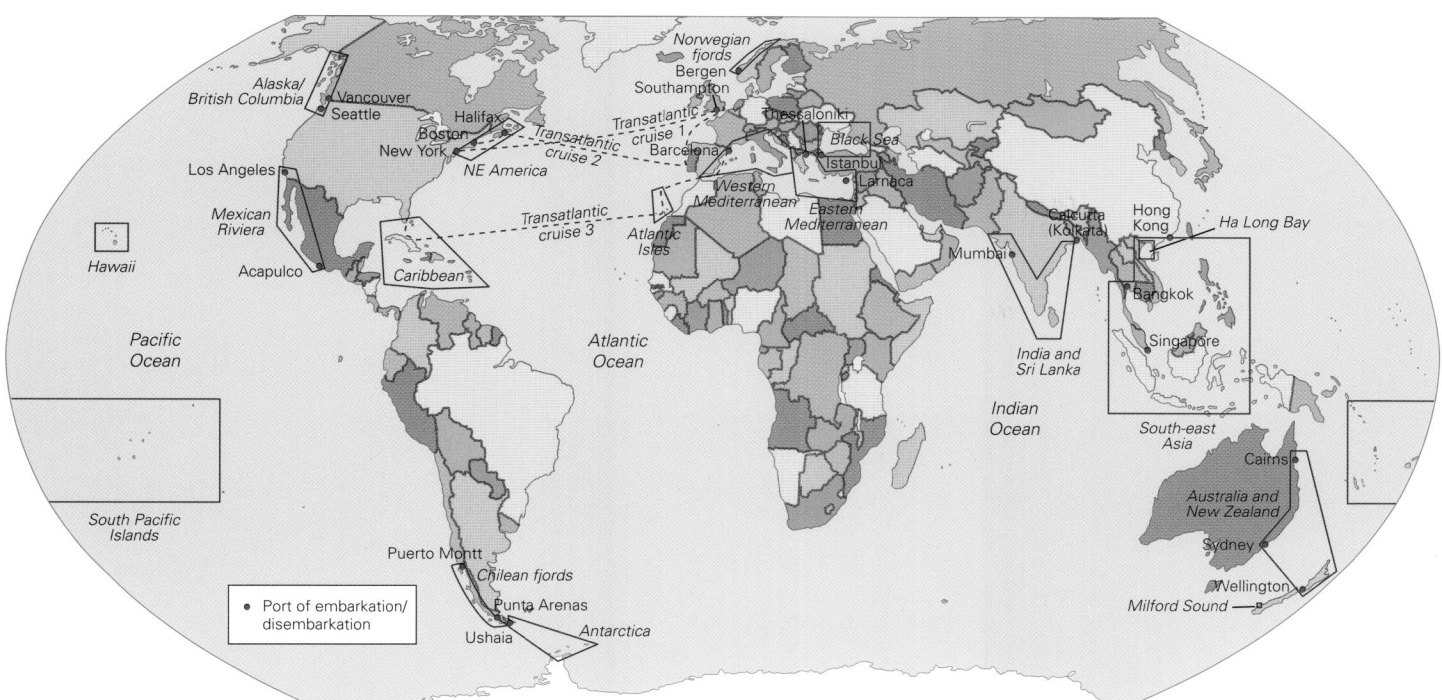

● Port of embarkation/
disembarkation

▼ **Black Sea**
A day in Istanbul (see *World Cities*) is included in most cruises of the Black Sea. The countries bordering the Black Sea provide a rich variety of historic sites, from the medieval churches of Nesebúr in Bulgaria, to the 19th-century opera house in Ukrainian Odessa, the 18th-century palace of Tsar Alexander II on the Crimean peninsula, and the abandoned Byzantine monastery of Sumela, high above the Turkish port of Trabzon.

AFRICA, ASIA AND THE INDIAN OCEAN

India and Sri Lanka
Cruises around the Indian subcontinent provide an opportunity to visit a number of historic sites without the strain of overland travel. A day's sightseeing is followed by a day's relaxation in the relatively cool sea breezes. Many of the sites visited are from India's colonial past – the Dutch fort at Cochin, the former Portuguese colony of Goa, remnants of the British Raj in Madras – but there are also trips to some indigenous sites, such as the Hindu cave temples of Mumbai (Bombay).

South-east Asia
With such a wealth of possible sights and exciting ports of call, there are many varieties of the South-east Asian cruise, which is a popular option for the Christmas break. Most shore visits consist of whistle-stop tours of the port of call, but there are also more adventurous expeditions, such as a visit to an orang-utan

sanctuary in Sarawak, or a trek to catch a glimpse of the famous 'Komodo dragon' (see *Wildlife in Asia*). Many of the cruises visit Bali, with its sandy beaches, terraced rice fields and ornate Hindu temples.

AUSTRALASIA AND THE PACIFIC

Australia and New Zealand
Most cruises of Australia's east coast provide more than one opportunity to stop on the 2,000 km (1,250-mile) long Great Barrier Reef (see *Marine wildlife*). By way of contrast, the natural wonders of New Zealand include the spouting geysers and boiling mud of Rotorua (see *Lakes and waterfalls*), and the dolphins, whales and penguins of the verdant Bay of Islands.

Milford Sound, New Zealand
Milford Sound is perfect for a cruise of just a few hours. It is possible to enjoy lunch while gazing out at towering granite peaks and glaciers, and, on the lower slopes, thick beech forests and waterfalls. There is always the chance of sighting the dolphins, seals, penguins and other sea birds that inhabit the sheltered inlet.

Hawaii, USA
The mountainous Hawaiian island chain was formed by a series of volcanoes, many

of which are still active. Trips to Volcanoes National Park and the world's most active volcano usually include the memorable experience of getting as close as is safe to the actual lava flow. The lower slopes of the mountains are covered in rainforest, home to 20,000 species of orchid and echoing to the sound of waterfalls. Hawaii is a port of call for most Pacific cruises, but it is also possible to take a cruise exclusively of the islands, and so be able to enjoy some of the dramatic beaches and the local culture.

Useful web addresses
all preceded by www.

cruise.com
cruises.about.com
discover-cruises.co.uk
goway.com/cruises
cruiseweb.com
cruisein.co.uk
cruiseinformationservice.co.uk

◄ **Ha Long Bay, Gulf of Tonkin, Vietnam**
'Ha Long' means 'where the dragon plunged into the sea', and the bay contains around 3,000 islands, famous for their sheer, limestone cliffs with honeycombs of caves. A day trip from Haiphong (by motorboat or slower junk) is included in the itineraries of long-distance cruises as well as being available to the independent traveller.

Where, when and for how long?

	Main season	Duration of cruise (in days)
Alaska	May–Sept	7–14
NE America	Aug–Oct	7–14
Mexican Riviera	Sept–Oct	7–10
Atlantic Islands	Apr–Dec	9–14
Transatlantic	April and Sep–Nov	14
Caribbean	Oct–Dec	3–23
Chilean fjords	Oct–May	3–7
Antarctica	mid-Oct–early March	9–12
Norwegian fjords	May–July	7–14
Western Mediterranean	Apr–Nov	12–14
Eastern Mediterranean	Aug–Dec	10–14
Black Sea	Aug–Oct	14
India/Sri Lanka	Dec–Feb	14
South-east Asia	Dec–Feb	8–17
Ha Long, Vietnam	All year	1
Australia/New Zealand	Nov–Apr	14
Milford Sound	Nov–Apr	half day
Hawaii	Sept–Oct	7–14

19

Winter sports

Mountain resorts all over the world are upgrading their facilities: constructing 'ski parks' for snowboarders, installing faster ski-lifts to cut queuing times, and using snow cannons to guarantee good conditions. Now that many of the top resorts can be reached by long-haul flights from either hemisphere, it is possible to enjoy 'winter sports' at any time of year.

THE AMERICAS

Whistler, British Columbia, Canada

Considered one of the top ski resorts in the world, the resort provides access to two mountains with vertical drops of around 1,500 m (5,000 ft). As well as a wide variety of runs, Whistler's crowning glory is its five bowls, which provide plenty of scope for expert skiers and boarders, the latter being well catered for. The base village, which is pedestrian-only, has over 100 restaurants.

Banff, Alberta, Canada

The city of Banff is the gateway to three resorts that are linked by a shuttle bus and share a lift pass. **Lake Louise**, a particularly beautiful resort, is a good choice for families of mixed ability, with a beginners' run from the top of every chair lift. **Sunshine Village** includes 'Delirium Dive', one of the most challenging runs in North America. **Mt Norquay/Mystic Ridge** has a number of runs for the very best skiers and also offers night skiing.

Killington, Vermont, USA

The largest ski area in the eastern USA, Killington spreads over seven mountains. It caters for every level of skier, but is especially suitable for beginners, who have their own network of pistes, and for snowboarders who are provided with their own trail map. Snow cannons ensure good coverage throughout an extended season.

▼ Jackson Hole, Wyoming, USA

One of the most spectacular mountain resorts in the United States, Jackson Hole is most suited to the experienced skier or snowboarder. A 60-person cable car transports skiers from Teton Village to Mount Rendezvous, from where the skilled and intrepid can experience some of the most difficult piste skiing in the world. Other attractions include trips into Yellowstone Park, a swim at 2,460 m (8,000 ft) in the Granite Hot Springs, and sleigh rides to view a huge elk herd.

Lake Tahoe (Squaw Valley, Heavenly) California/Nevada, USA

Lake Tahoe is surrounded by ski resorts. **Squaw Valley** comprises six inter-linked mountain areas, some of which are still open in June. It has excellent facilities for children, including a family fun snow park. **Heavenly** has a spectacular setting, with something to suit skiers and snowboarders of all abilities. Snowboarders are further catered for by specially constructed mountainside features and by a dedicated fun park. A single ski pass is available for all resorts in the area.

Aspen, Colorado, USA

Long considered the smartest ski resort in the United States, Aspen provides an enormous range of facilities and entertainment, including opera. A linked ticket gives access to four mountains. Aspen Mountain and Aspen Highlands are most suitable for intermediates and experts, Buttermilk for beginners, and Snowmass for all levels. Snowboarding is allowed on all but Aspen Mountain.

Valle Nevado, Chile

A purpose-built resort in the Andes, at an altitude of 2,900 m (9,500 ft), Valle Nevado has wide, open pistes and spectacular views. It is also possible to heli-ski.

Gran Catedral (Bariloche), Argentina

Perched on Catedral Mountain, overlooking Lake Nahuel Huapi, Gran Catedral (formerly Bariloche) is Argentina's best-known and most extensive resort. Many visitors are attracted to the area in August for the National Snow Party.

EUROPE

Geilo, Norway

On the edge of the Hardanger plateau, Geilo provides uncomplicated downhill skiing as well as extensive cross-country trails. It is an excellent family resort, with ski schools giving tuition (in English) in snowboarding and cross-country skiing, as well as alpine skiing.

Soldeu/El Tarter, Andorra

For those on a budget, Andorra is a good option, and Soldeu/El Tarter the best of its resorts. Its reputable ski school and gentle slopes make it ideal for the beginner. A drag lift linking it with the neighbouring resorts of Pas de la Casa/Grau Roig has expanded the quality and quantity of runs available for the more experienced skier.

◄ Vail, Colorado, United States

Vail has runs for all abilities and a special family skiing area. Snowboarders are provided with dedicated pistes, a half-pipe and two fun parks. Numerous winter sports are possible, including dog sledding and snowmobiling.

Three Valleys, France

The vast inter-linked ski area of the Three Valleys can be accessed from several resorts. **Courchevel** provides varied skiing, including wooded slopes, but intrepid skiers can also make their way across the whole Three Valleys system. **Méribel** is conveniently placed in the centre of the system. **Val Thorens**, which at 2,320 m (7,544 ft) is Europe's highest ski resort, has three lifts still open in summer.

Chamonix, France

Chamonix is an attractive town set in a steep-sided valley and dominated by Mont Blanc (see *Mountains and volcanoes*). There is extensive, varied skiing on both sides of the valley, linked by bus services. The most famous run, the Vallée Blanche, involves a cable-car ride up to the Aiguille du Midi, followed by a tough walk to the top of the glacier, and a 20 km (13-mile) run down to the valley. The Mont Blanc Ski Pass includes other resorts, giving access to 1,000 km (625 miles) of piste.

▲ Val d'Isère/Tignes, France

Snowboarders and off-piste skiers are among those well catered for by the huge inter-linked system of L'Espace Killy. The system is served by a number of modern resorts. The largest is **Val d'Isère**, which is better suited to more advanced skiers than to beginners, since its easiest skiing is inconveniently located on the upper slopes. **Tignes**, a collection of villages clustered around a mountain lake, offers skiing for much of the year. The lift pass provides access to the whole Espace Killy, as well as a day's skiing at nearby Les Arcs or La Plagne.

Skiing and snowboarding resorts

Level: B = Beginner   I = Intermediate   A = Advanced   Sb = Snowboarding

Resort	Main season	Skiable area or distance	Best-suited level(s)
THE AMERICAS			
Whistler	Nov–Apr	2,863 ha (7,071 acres)	I/A/Sb
Banff	Dec–Apr	3,059 ha (7,558 acres)	I
Killington	Oct–Apr	489 ha (1,209 acres)	B/Sb
Squaw Valley	Nov–May	1,600 ha (4,000 acres)	I/A/Sb
Heavenly	Nov–May	1,942 ha (4,800 acres)	I/A
Jackson Hole	Dec–Apr	1,011 ha (2,500 acres)	A
Aspen	late Nov–Apr	1,936 ha (4,785 acres)	all
Vail	early Nov–late May	2,140 ha (5,289 acres)	all
Valle Nevado	mid-June–mid-Oct	64 km (40 miles)	I/A
Gran Catedral	mid-June–end Sept	640 ha (1,600 acres)	I
EUROPE			
Geilo	Nov–May	25 km (16 miles) 250 km (156 miles) cross-country	B/I
Soldeu/El Tarter	Dec–Mar	74 km (46 miles)	B/I
Three Valleys	Dec–Apr	600 km (374 miles)	all/Sb
Val d'Isère/Tignes	Dec–Apr	300 km (187 miles)	I/A/Sb
Chamonix	Dec–Apr	140 km (87 miles)	A/Sb
Zermatt	Dec–Apr	150 km (93 miles)	I/A
Cervinia	Dec–Mar	80 km (50 miles)	B/I
Wengen/Grindelwald	Dec–Mar	195 km (121 miles)	B/I
St Moritz	Dec–Mar	80 km (50 miles)	I
St Anton	Dec–Apr	170 km (106 miles)	I/A
Söll, Ski-Welt	Dec–Mar	250 km (156 miles)	B/I
Cortina	Dec–Mar	140 km (87 miles)	all
ASIA AND AUSTRALASIA			
Hakuba	Dec–Apr	c. 500 ha (1,250 acres)	all
Perisher Blue	June–Oct	1,250 ha (3,100 acres)	I
The Remarkables	June–Oct	220 ha (550 acres)	I
Coronet Peak	June–Oct	280 ha (700 acres)	I

◀ **Matterhorn (Zermatt, Cervinia), Switzerland/Italy**
The visitor to the Matterhorn area has the choice of staying in the expensive, car-free, Swiss resort of **Zermatt**, or the cheaper, more lively, Italian resort of **Cervinia**. The lift systems of the two resorts are linked. Zermatt provides a huge variety of skiing, from the wooded slopes immediately above the town to the steep runs below the Kleine Matterhorn. The sunny, south-facing slopes of Cervinia provide plenty of runs of intermediate standard. Summer skiing is possible on the highest slopes.

Jungfrau (Wengen, Grindelwald), Switzerland
The slopes of this famous mountain are served by two of Switzerland's best-known resorts. **Wengen**, which considers itself the 'birthplace of Alpine skiing', is an attractive town whose charm is enhanced by a lack of cars (a mountain railway providing the only access). **Grindelwald** is a larger, livelier town. The two are linked by a lift system that provides access to wonderfully varied skiing.

St Moritz, Switzerland
Famous in particular for its glamorous nightlife, St Moritz serves as a gateway to two major lift systems. Corvatsch/Furtshellas provides an opportunity for glacier skiing in both winter and summer. Corviglia provides varied skiing, interspersed by numerous restaurants in spectacular locations.

St Anton, Austria
St Anton attracts skiers from all over the world to its challenging ski runs, with cannon ensuring a good snow coverage. Dramatic off-piste skiing adds to its attraction for the experienced skier and boarder, but there is little for the beginner.

Söll, Ski-Welt, Austria
Söll provides good family skiing. It is ideal for the beginner and intermediate skier, but is not for the adventurous. Its low altitude results in a short season, although snow cannons have been installed.

Cortina, Italy
Surrounded by the distinctive rocky outcrops of the Dolomites, Cortina provides skiing in five main areas. There are runs for a range of skills, including a difficult descent from the Tofana bowl, and the gentle runs of the Socrepes–Pocol area. Cortina is the smartest of the Italian resorts, with a lively nightlife. Activities off the slopes include ice-skating.

ASIA AND AUSTRALASIA

Hakuba, Japan
The village of Hakuba (near Nagano) is the gateway to seven ski areas, providing runs for different standards of skiers, with beginners and intermediates best served by **Hakuba Goryu-Toomi**, and more advanced skiers by **Happo'one** (where night skiing is possible) and **Hakuba 47**.

Perisher Blue, Australia
This winter sports area comprises four resorts, spread over seven mountain peaks, accessed by an underground alpine railway and covered by one ski pass. There is a Nordic Ski Centre at Guthega, and 90 km (55 miles) of cross-country skiing. The main resort town is Jindabyne.

Queenstown (Coronet Peak, The Remarkables), New Zealand
Queenstown provides a residential base for two winter sports areas, The Remarkables and Coronet Peak, with shuttles operating between them. As well as good skiing, both areas offer facilities for snowboarders, including pipes and a terrain park. Families are well catered for, with good ski schools. Heli-skiing is also available.

● Town/city with major airport

21

Great beaches

▶ **Negril, Jamaica**
Negril beach is 11 km (7 miles) long and fringed by trees that hide low-rise hotels and restaurants. While definitely a tourist resort, it still retains a laid-back Jamaican character. Growing environmentalism has led to planning restrictions and active preservation of the surrounding area, including the creation of the Negril Marine Park. This encompasses the Great Morass swamp behind the beach, and the coral reef, cliffs and grottoes that make Negril so popular with scuba divers and snorkellers.

From California to the Caribbean to Australia, the lure of the beach still has a part in most holiday plans. The range is endless – chic and cosmopolitan in the Mediterranean, wild and rugged along the Atlantic shores or palm-fringed coral in the South Pacific. This small selection highlights some of the great beaches that can be linked into a round-the-world trip – whether for the exhilaration of surfing or sailing, or just to do absolutely nothing.

NORTH AMERICA

Venice Beach, Los Angeles, USA
Venice Beach is famous not so much for its wide stretch of sand as for its curving 'boardwalk'. Here, some of LA's more flamboyant citizens display themselves – on foot, skateboard, rollerblade and cycle. The area was originally developed to imitate its European namesake and, although there is no comparison, it is pleasant to stroll along its canals.

Assateague Island, Maryland/Virginia, USA
Assateague Island National Seashore on the Atlantic coast of the Chesapeake Peninsula consists of 60 km (37 miles) of pristine sandy beach, fringed by pine forest and salt marsh. Only a small area of it is accessible by car and the rest of the beach is deserted, except for the more intrepid campers, many of whom come for the fishing and birdwatching. Herds of wild ponies roam the island.

Sanibel Island, Florida, USA
Sanibel's 19 km (12 miles) of beaches are famous for their seashells. Visitors can be seen scouring the seashore or taking boat trips to more remote locations to find the best shells. Around 40% of the island, which can be toured on rented bicycles, is a wildlife preserve and it is also within striking distance of the Florida Everglades (see *Wildlife in the Americas*).

Puerto Escondido, Mexico
The resort of Puerto Escondido has a beach to suit every taste. 'Playa Zicatela' is considered one of the best surfing beaches in North America, but is suitable only for the strongest swimmers. 'Playa Principal' is a more urban beach, with pleasure craft and waterfront restaurants, while the small coves just out of town provide perfect swimming conditions.

THE CARIBBEAN AND SOUTH AMERICA

Magens Bay, St Thomas, US Virgin Islands
The heart-shaped Magens Bay contains a gently sloping sandy beach, surrounded by overhanging trees that provide welcome shade. Protected from the winds and currents, the bay is safe for bathing. Although nude bathing is not allowed on the main beach, it is permitted on the nearby Little Magens Beach. Interesting rock formations on the fringes of the bay are good for snorkelling. The beach is well served by restaurants and bars, carefully hidden among the trees.

Copacabana Beach, Rio de Janeiro, Brazil
Copacabana's 4 km (2.5 miles) of sand is fringed by a wavy black and white mosaic walkway. The beach is provided with modern amenities, such as public showers, kiosks and restaurants, and the shopping centre is only a short walk away. As well as attracting tourists, the beach is a meeting place for the citizens of Rio, and is the focus of the New Year celebrations. It is framed on one side by a huge granite headland and on the other by an imposing World War I fort, below which is an area from which local fishermen still operate.

Viña del Mar, Chile
Known as 'the Garden City' because of the luscious, tropical foliage that lines its boulevards, Viña del Mar also has a beautiful beach. Visitors who tire of the soft white sand and rolling surf can enjoy a tour of the town by horse-drawn carriage, visit the art museum and the extensive botanical gardens. Evening entertainment comes in the form of gourmet restaurants, casinos, discos and concerts.

▲ **Oahu, Hawaiian Islands, USA**
Most visitors to the island of Oahu flock to the string of connected beaches in the resort of Waikiki, just to the east of Honolulu, where the curving sand, studded with palm trees, is backed by a towering wall of high-rise hotels. Those looking for a more peaceful holiday, however, head further around the coast and seek out Waimanalo Beach (above), with its gently shelving, near-white sand and mountain backdrop. On the north coast the calm waters of Waimea Bay in summer also provide excellent swimming, but in winter months it is the centre of the surfing scene, as 10 m (30 ft) waves roll in across the Pacific.

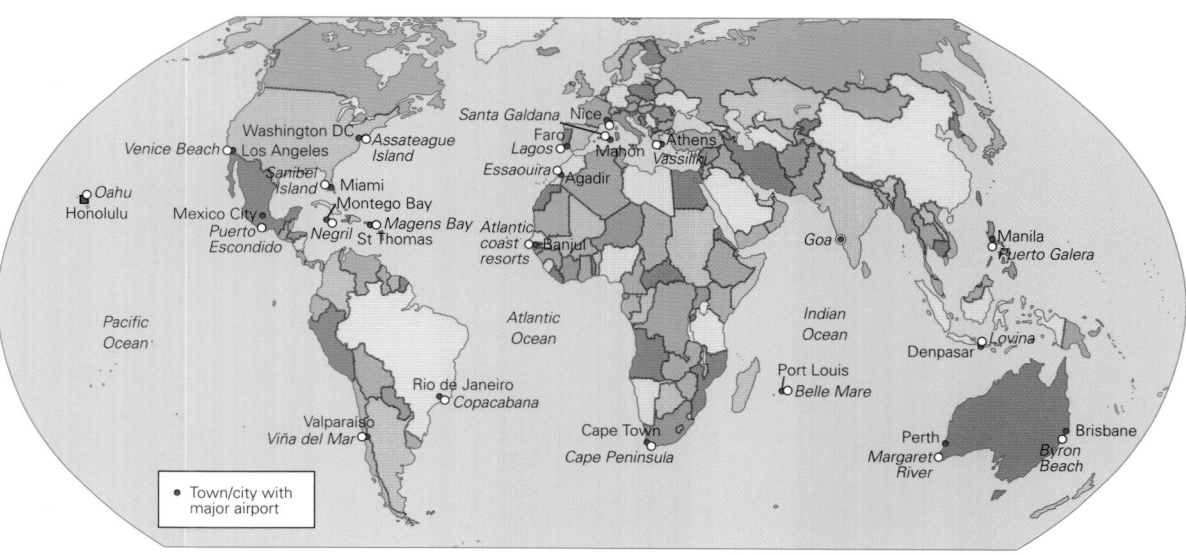

Town/city with major airport

Venice Beach ◦ Los Angeles
Washington DC ◦ Assateague Island
Santa Galdana ◦ Nice
Faro ◦ Lagos ◦ Mahon ◦ Athens
Vassiliki
Essaouira ◦ Agadir
Oahu Honolulu
Sanibel Island ◦ Miami
Montego Bay
Mexico City
Puerto Escondido ◦ Negril ◦ Magens Bay ◦ St Thomas
Atlantic coast resorts ◦ Banjul
Goa
Manila ◦ Puerto Galera
Pacific Ocean
Atlantic Ocean
Indian Ocean
Denpasar
Lovina
Rio de Janeiro ◦ Copacabana
Valparaiso ◦ Viña del Mar
Cape Town
Cape Peninsula
Port Louis ◦ Belle Mare
Perth
Margaret River
Brisbane
Byron Beach

EUROPE

Nice, France
Nice is the largest town on the Côte d'Azur, renowned for the clarity of its light and the colour of its sea. Many famous artists have been inspired by the region, and some are represented in the town's art gallery. The long curved beach is rather pebbly, but its surroundings are attractive, with a wide esplanade on which 'to see and be seen'.

Santa Galdana, Menorca
The Balearic Island least affected by tourism, Menorca is famous for its beaches. The main beach at Santa Galdana can be very crowded in summer, but it is still possible to find relatively unspoilt coves nearby. Just a 1 km (0.5-mile) walk east is the wood-lined sandy beach of Cala Mirjana, where the favourite sport is to jump from rocks into crystal-clear water.

Vassiliki, Levkás, Greece
The small resort of Vassiliki is one of the foremost windsurfing and dinghy sailing centres in the eastern Mediterranean. Set in a bay that provides some shelter for the beginner, it is blessed with reliable winds. The lighter breezes of the morning are followed, after a brief lunchtime lull, by winds strong enough to delight the expert.

AFRICA AND THE INDIAN OCEAN

Essaouira, Morocco
The ancient town of Essaouira provides a fascinating backdrop to 3 km (2 miles) of

▲ Cape Peninsula, South Africa
Among the many beaches on the narrow peninsula south of Cape Town is Boulders Beach, so named because of the huge rocks that provide shelter from the wind. Here, visitors share the sands with a colony of jack-ass penguins. Other resorts on the peninsula, where the ocean water to the west is considerably colder than that of False Bay to the east, include some, such as Fish Hoek, which cater specifically for families, and some, such as the fashionable Clifton area, which attract the young and wealthy. Surfers head for the remote Long Beach at Kommetjie.

sandy shoreline. The commercial life of the town tends to spill over on to the beach, with fishermen offering to cook their catch and camel drivers selling rides, although it is possible to find more secluded areas. The town is the centre of the craft of wood inlay, the local Thuya trees providing the raw material.

Atlantic coast resorts, Gambia
The resorts of Kololi, Kotu, Fajara and Bakau, strung out along a 10 km (6-mile) coastal strip, provide a full range of amenities, including golf courses, equipment for water sports, and swimming pools. Although the sea is relatively safe, there are times when the conditions are unsuitable for all but the strongest swimmer. For those seeking a more authentic African experience, the market town of Serekunda is nearby.

Belle Mare, Mauritius
The coral reef that surrounds much of the island of Mauritius provides a natural breakwater, ensuring calm inshore waters. The beaches are all beautiful, although some have been over-developed or have areas cordoned off by hotels. However, Belle Mare, on the less-developed east coast, still has plenty of public areas. There are also the attractions of a mixed French, Indian and Chinese culture, evident in the island's architecture and cuisine.

ASIA

Goa, India
The dozens of beaches on Goa's 100 km (62-mile) coastline provide plenty of choice. Calangute and Colva, to which young people flocked in the 1970s, are now tourist resorts. However, at both the northern and southern ends of the Goan coast are many relatively unspoilt beaches, including Arambol and Palolem, where beach huts and tree houses provide the main accommodation. At Palolem visitors can take dolphin-watching boat trips.

Puerto Galera, Mindoro, Philippines
A resort area comprising 12 separate coastal districts, Puerto Galera is renowned for its pristine sandy coves, sheltered by a rugged, jungle-covered coastline. Accommodation ranges from

bamboo beach huts to air-conditioned bungalows and family-run hotels. The rich marine life of the area attracts scuba-divers, and equipment for underwater and other marine activities is available for hire.

Lovina, Bali
Although second in size only to Kuta, famous for its surf, Lovina manages to retain the relaxed atmosphere its larger rival has long since lost. Situated on Bali's rugged northern coast, the resort comprises six villages, dotted along 8 km (5 miles) of black-sand beach. Those who enjoy some lively nightlife make for the village of Kalibukbuk. Beach-centred activities include snorkelling and dolphin watching. Excursions can be made inland to nearby hot springs and a Buddhist temple, or further afield to the volcanic regions of Bedugul and Batur.

AUSTRALASIA

Byron Beach, New South Wales, Australia
Byron Beach offers a wide range of beaches. Main Beach is ideal for families, with a life-guard patrol and play equipment shaded by trees, while those wishing for more seclusion head for the smaller coves out on Cape Byron. The area also provides some good surfing and the opportunity to watch passing whales and dolphins. The town itself is less commercial, and better suited to those seeking an alternative lifestyle, than the popular resort of Gold Coast, 50 km (30 miles) to the north.

◄ Lagos, Portugal
Lagos is a busy fishing port and one of the Algarve's oldest settlements, with a long maritime tradition. To the east lie miles of sand dunes and the gently sloping Meia beach. West of the town, the dramatically eroded sandstone cliffs typical of the region form numerous small coves, some of which are only accessible from the sea. Lagos is an excellent base for surfers, who can travel the short distance to Portugal's west-facing beaches if local surf fails. The town provides plenty of interest, from seafood restaurants and bars to the curiosities of the local museum.

▼ Margaret River, Western Australia
Margaret River is among the best surfing areas in Australia, providing conditions to suit both beginners and experts. It also has much for the non-surfer to enjoy, including swimming beaches, river canoeing trips, and visits to local vineyards to taste some of Australia's best wines.

23

Festivals

Whether sacred or profane, festivals throughout the world bring thousands of participants and spectators out on to the streets with grand processions often featuring magnificent costumes and dazzling displays of music and dance, drama and sporting prowess.

THE AMERICAS

▼ Chinese New Year, San Francisco, California, USA

For Chinese communities everywhere, the New Year is a week-long festival. Many celebrations are family-based, but they lead up to a very public grand finale. Chinatown in San Francisco is taken over by the Golden Dragon Parade when hundreds of people, including drummers and other musicians, accompany a 23 m (75 ft) dragon through the streets. The Chinese follow a lunar calendar, which means that their New Year occurs in late January or early February.

Corn Dance Festival, Santa Domingo, New Mexico, USA

At Santa Domingo (near Albuquerque) the Pueblo people honour the harvest goddess, Iyatiko, in the Corn Dance Festival. Celebrants, known as the *koshare*, dress in cornhusks and animal skins to enact the history of their people on a day that is filled with drumming, dancing and feasting. The festival which, unlike many Pueblo ceremonies, is a public event, is always held on 4 August.

Heritage and Jazz Festival, New Orleans, Louisiana, USA

Jazz evolved in New Orleans during the late 19th and early 20th centuries, but the first jazz festival was not until 1968. A major event in the musical calendar and organized by the Heritage and Jazz Festival, it runs over two weekends in April or May. Musicians from all over the world perform in large tents at the Fair Grounds and in smaller venues – clubs, theatres and halls – throughout the city.

Fisherman's Festival, Jamaica

29 June is Saint Peter's day. He is the patron saint of fishermen, and in the fishing ports of Jamaica boats are drawn up to the beach where the owners decorate them with shells and flowers. Long processions follow priests to the edge of the sea where they bless the boats, and the beaches become crowded with steel bands, dancers and family picnics.

Urkupina, Calvario Hill, Bolivia

Early in the 20th century a girl tending her sheep on Calvario Hill had a vision of the Virgin Mary. Now, on 15 August, thousands of pilgrims carrying candles and flowers, and accompanied by musicians, performers and vendors, climb the hill to pay homage to the Virgin. The festivities that follow last for three days.

National Rodeo Festival, Rancagua, Chile

Rodeos take place all over the country and, in late March, the best competitors go to the National Rodeo in Rancagua. This event celebrates the Chilean *huaso* or cowboy. Thousands come to watch as huasos, wearing traditional costume and the heavy spurs unique to Chile, provide exhibitions of horsemanship. The town is given over to feasts of cowboy food and *la cueca*, the erotic folk dance of Chile.

◄ Palio, Siena, Italy

Celebrated every year on 2 July and 16 August, the Palio is a bare-back horserace that dates from the 16th century. Ten horses, each representing one of Siena's *contrade*, or districts, race three times around the crowded central piazza, sometimes barging into each other and unseating their riders. Before the race there is a procession in which men dressed in medieval clothes whirl and twist the *palio*, or flag, of their *contrada*, to the accompaniment of drummers.

EUROPE

Puck Fair, Killorglin, Ireland

A billygoat, King Puck – adorned with ribbons and a crown – opens the three-day Puck Fair every year on 2 August. Musicians from all over Europe perform, and Romanies are among those who entertain the crowds with Irish jigs and stories. The billy is honoured because in the 17th century a herd of goats warned the village of an impending English attack.

Oktober Bierfest, Munich, Germany

The Oktober Bierfest has been an annual event since 1835. It is an important festival for most young visitors to the city and is a huge celebration in honour of beer. It lasts for 16 days from 17 October, and vast beer tents that each house 5,000 drinkers are erected. Food stalls and funfairs add to the festive atmosphere.

Lajkonic, Kraków, Poland

Every year, usually in June, a man dressed as a Tartar rides a mock horse through the streets, accompanied by trumpeters and citizens dressed in medieval costume. He does so in memory of Lajkonic, who in the 13th century killed a Tartar and put on the dead man's clothing before riding into the city to warn that the Tartars were about to attack. The resulting defeat of the Tartars is now celebrated with much pageantry.

San Fermin, Pamplona, Spain

Starting on 6 July and running for eight days, the festival is held in honour of Fermin, patron saint of bullfighters. Each day starts with the playing of drums and pipes, and an effigy of the saint is followed by a procession of matadors and horses, dressed and decorated for the occasion. A rocket signals the release of the bulls from their pen to race through the streets to the bullring. Men run and leap ahead of them, a practice that more than once has resulted in someone being killed. Bull fights and parties fill the evenings.

Mardi Gras Carnaval, Rio de Janeiro, Brazil

All over the Catholic Christian world, there are festivals at Mardi Gras, the last day before the 40 days of Lenten fasting. The Mardi Gras Carnaval in Rio de Janeiro is the most famous. Over the course of two nights the city's 14 main samba schools compete with each other by dancing and parading down the 1 km (0.5-mile) long Sambadrome, watched by thousands of spectators. Each school's parade consists of around 4,000 people in lavish, often extravagant, costumes, accompanied by enormous and elaborate floats, and a band of over 500 drummers. The judging takes place a few days later. Broadcast live on television, it is followed by great celebrations.

Aksu Black Sea Festival, Turkey

The origins of this July festival are very old, dating back to pre-Christian fertility rites. Cybele, the fertility goddess, wore a pebble in her crown and women still throw pebbles into the Black Sea in the hope that this will help them conceive. The highlight of the festival is a performance by male dancers dressed in black and silver, and other artists – musicians, potters, painters and weavers – flock to the site where they perform or sell their work.

AFRICA

Odwira, Ghana

The Asante calendar is filled with religious days and ceremonies, of which the Odwira, usually in August or September, is one of the most important. The high chiefs and priests are involved for some days in secret and sacred rituals, and then the roll of drums announces the start of feasting. It all ends with a grand procession, in which the chiefs are carried in splendid palanquins.

Abu El-Haggag, Luxor, Egypt

Among the ancient ruins of Luxor is a small mosque dedicated to a 12th-century Muslim saint, El-Haggag. Each year, in October or November, thousands of people crowd into Luxor for the saint's *mulid*, or festival, during which Sufis and floats parade the streets. Three model boats are carried about by groups of men, though whether this is in memory of the Ancient Egyptian journey into the Underworld, or of the time when the pilgrimage to Mecca involved a sea crossing, is uncertain.

Timket, Ethiopia

Ethiopian Christians celebrate the baptism of Christ for three days starting on 19 January. The priests, after all-night prayers, emerge from churches carrying holy *tabots* – caskets holding sacred texts – followed by singing children. Multi-coloured umbrellas, signifying high office and authority, are held above the priests. After this religious ceremony, a party mood takes over and there are huge communal meals, music, and excited horse races which sometimes lurch into the spectators.

▶ Ganesh Festival, Mumbai, India

Chowpatty Beach is crowded for ten days in August through to September. Families exchange gifts and women decorate shrines to Shiva, mother of the Hindu elephant-headed god Ganesh. On the tenth day a huge effigy of Ganesh is carried through the streets to be cast into the sea. Drummers and pipers announce its passage, which is followed by a large procession of people dancing and singing.

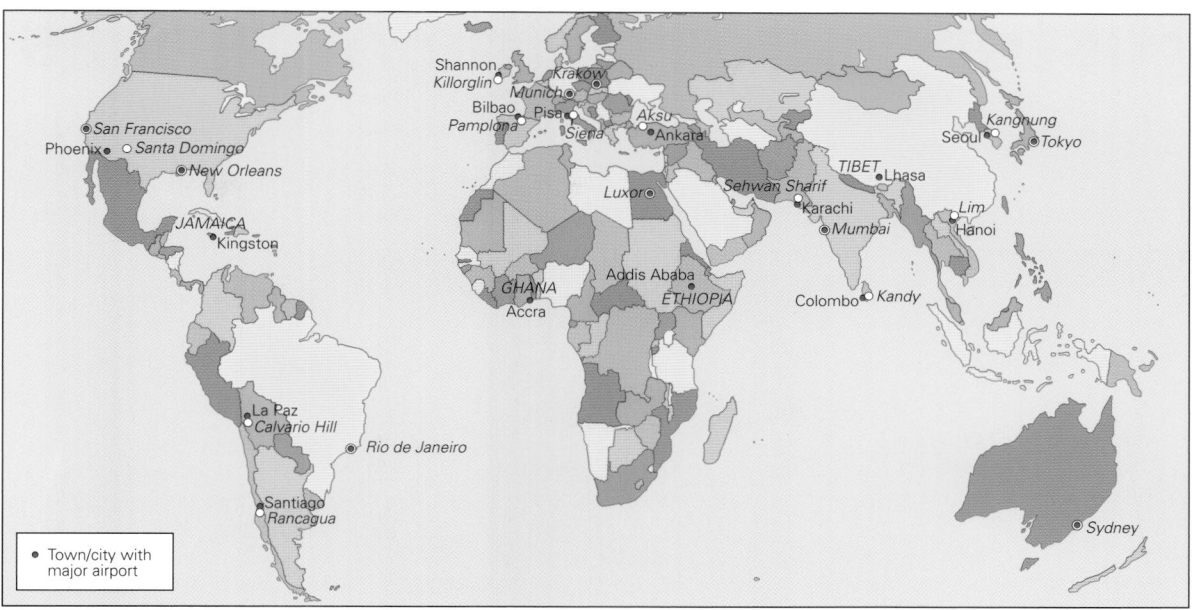

ASIA AND AUSTRALIA

Urs to Lal Shahbaz Qalandar, Sehwan Sharif, Pakistan

All over Pakistan, Muslims celebrate holy men with *urs*, or saints' days. One of the most popular, attracting many thousands of pilgrims, is held in Sehwan Sharif, around the tomb of the 12th-century Iranian scholar-poet Lal Shahbaz Qalandar. For three days, in October or November, Sufis perform their holy, trance-like dances, while drums and gongs beat hour after hour. The entire crowd dances and chants, and many offer votive offerings to the tomb.

Festival of the Tooth, Kandy, Sri Lanka

In the Esala Perhera temple in Kandy is the Tooth Relic of the Buddha. Usually in July, but occasionally in August, there is a spectacular festival in which there are festive meals and dances to celebrate the relic and Buddha. At the festival's climax a great procession of dancers, drummers, temple chieftains, and over 50 elephants in ceremonial attire, goes to the temple, followed by huge crowds of pilgrims.

Ho Lim, Lim, Vietnam

Singers from all over Vietnam pour into the village of Lim (near Bac Ninh) seven days after Tet, the Chinese New Year, in January or February. They participate in a folk-singing contest, and competition is fierce. The crowds who come to listen are also entertained by a circus, street performers, wrestling competitions, and chess games in which people play the parts of the pieces.

Losar, Tibet

The calendar in Tibet follows the lunar cycle. There are two 'New Year' days, but the significant one is Gyalpo Losar, the King's New Year, which is usually in April. People wear new, decorative clothing; the priests fill the temples with chanting, the beating of gongs and the ringing of bells, and new prayer flags are lifted above the temple roofs. Throughout the city, street theatres and musicians perform while people party and play dice in the parks.

Tano, Kangnung, South Korea

This spring festival, usually in April or May, traditionally involved displays of the Korean form of wrestling, *ssirum*, even in the most remote villages. Now, many Koreans spend the holiday watching *ssirum* on television, except in the village of Kangnung. Here they celebrate for five days, not only with wrestling matches but also with performances of the traditional dance called *nong-ak*. The huge crowds also enjoy a spring drink, *chehotang*.

Gay and Lesbian Mardi Gras, Sydney, Australia

Participants pride themselves on outrageous displays and flamboyant costumes during the annual Mardi Gras parade. The street procession comes at the end of a three- to four-week cultural festival in February–March, and ends in a huge party which is restricted to ticket holders. However, revellers throughout the city regard this as an opportunity to party until dawn and beyond.

▲ Sanja Matsuri, Tokyo, Japan

Matsuri – festivals where shrines, or *mikoshi*, believed to contain a god-spirit, are carried through towns and villages – take place all over Japan. However, the biggest event is in Tokyo in April or May. Here the *mikoshi* weigh about 1 tonne each, and 50 men are needed to hoist one through the streets to the Asakusa Temple. Groups of costumed figures, and musicians playing flutes and beating drums, accompany the *mikoshi* on its journey.

Historic sites in the Americas

Amid the rocky canyons of New Mexico, Arizona and Colorado, the dense jungle of Central America and the towering peaks of the Andes lie the spectacular ruins of civilizations that flourished long before 1500 and the arrival of the Europeans. Scattered throughout the continent are the mansions, churches, cathedrals and forts built by European settlers and their descendants since the 16th century.

Mesa Verde and the Anasazi
Mesa Verde National Park in Colorado, USA, contains the ruins of spectacular Anasazi complexes of multi-storey apartments constructed on natural or artificial platforms on the face of canyon cliffs. They are among the remains of hundreds of villages that were built by the Anasazi from the 8th century onwards in south-western USA. Called pueblos by the Spanish, they took various forms. In Chaco Canyon, for example, elaborate complexes of adjoining rooms surrounded circular subterranean ceremonial structures known as *kivas*. The Anasazi began to abandon their pueblos in the 15th century, eventually settling along the Rio Grande. There are many impressive sites worth visiting, but they are usually in remote locations.
Peak season: May–October
Nearest airports: Albuquerque, Santa Fe

▲ **Savannah, Georgia, USA**
The Cotton Exchange is just one of over 1,000 splendid 18th- and 19th-century buildings that have been restored in the historic downtown district of Savannah. Others include the US Customs House and the gold-domed City Hall. Near the city are the Civil War forts of Old Fort Jackson and Fort Pulaski.

NORTH AMERICA

Québec, Canada
Founded by the French in 1608 and now the only walled city in the Americas north of Mexico, Québec has several 17th- and 18th-century buildings. The area by the St Lawrence River has the general appearance of 1759, when the city was captured by the British. On the cliff-top above is the citadel of Cap Diamant, dating from 1820.

Plymouth Plantation, Massachusetts, USA
Costumed actors re-create the life and times of the first permanent colony and a Native American encampment in New England at Plymouth Plantation, a historical theme park. Visitors can go aboard the *Mayflower II*, a reconstruction of the ship that brought the original settlers from England in 1620.

Historic Triangle, Virginia, USA
The colonial towns of Williamsburg, Jamestown and Yorktown comprise the Historic Triangle. **Williamsburg**, Virginia's capital 1699–1780, has a large restored historic district of 17th- and 18th-century buildings with tours led by costumed guides. **Jamestown**, founded in 1607, has some 17th-century ruins, a reconstruction of the 1607 James Fort and full-scale replicas of 17th-century ships. **Yorktown**, the site of the last major battle (1781) in the American Revolution, and besieged during the Civil War, contains fortifications dating from both wars. Other historic sites in Virginia include Thomas Jefferson's house, **Monticello**, George Washington's house, **Mount Vernon**, the plantation house, **Shirley Plantation**, built in the 1660s, and Civil War sites in **Richmond**.

Pueblo de Taos, New Mexico, USA
The largest, multi-storied, adobe (sun-dried brick) structure in the USA, Pueblo de Taos dates from around 1450 and is still inhabited by 1,500 Native Americans. In the town of Taos is the home of Kit Carson, the famous 19th-century mountain man.

Chaco Culture National Historic Park, New Mexico, USA
Impressive Anasazi ruins are to be found in this remote park. Among them is the site of Pueblo Bonito, with remains of a massive plaza surrounded by a semi-circular, five-storey tiered complex of some 200 rooms which once housed up to 1,200 people.

Charleston, USA
A historic centre of Southern culture, Charleston has many colonial buildings. The military relics of the Battery overlook the harbour, while 5 km (3 miles) away is Fort Sumter where the first shot of the Civil War was fired.

San Miguel de Allende, Mexico
An almost totally colonial town, San Miguel de Allende has many attractive houses and churches dating from the 18th century. It is also an important artistic centre, where painting, pottery, sculpture, drama, music and literature all flourish.

Guanajuato, Mexico
A former silver-mining town, founded in the 16th century, Guanajuato has colonial buildings dating from the 17th and 18th centuries among its narrow streets with houses painted in bright colours.

Teotíhuacán, Mexico
Impressive ruins are all that remain of a city which in AD 500 was the sixth largest in the world, with a population of around

Chichén-Itzá and the Maya
Chichén-Itzá in Mexico is a particularly impressive Mayan site that is unique because it displays many features of the Toltecs who occupied the city in the 10th century. Among them is the reclining sculpture of the Toltec rain god. The magnificent remains of the literate Mayan civilization are scattered throughout southern Mexico, Guatemala, Belize and Honduras. Mayan cities expanded rapidly in the 7th and 8th centuries but were then abandoned between the 9th and 13th centuries. Their ruins often include stone-built pyramids crowned by temples and palaces, and courts used in a ritual ball game that involved the sacrifice of the losing team.

There are numerous Mayan sites worth visiting, and it is possible to spend two to three weeks following a route that links the most important in Mexico, Guatemala and Belize.
Peak season: November–April
Nearest airports: See map of 'Mayan Route'

Machu Picchu and the Incas
Machu Picchu in Peru is the most spectacular of many Inca sites in the Andes. Tier upon tier of houses, palaces, temples and defensive walls rise up the side of a high mountain ridge overlooked by the granite pinnacle of Huayana Picchu. The Spaniards failed to find the site in the 16th century, and it was mysteriously abandoned and forgotten until the early 20th century. The Incas developed an enormous empire between the 14th and 15th centuries that extended from modern Ecuador, through Peru to southern Chile. It was conquered by the Spaniards in the 1530s.
Peak season: April–October
Nearest airport: Lima

200,000. Once a centre of pilgrimage, Teotíhuacán includes the remains of hundreds of temples, among them the 70 m (230 ft) high Pyramid of the Sun, built in the 1st century AD and one of the largest buildings in the New World before 1500.

Oaxaca and Monte Albán, Mexico
Oaxaca is a well-preserved colonial town with a cathedral and many other buildings dating from the 16th century onwards. Just 10 km (6 miles) away are the impressive ruins of Monte Albán, which from the 7th century BC served as a centre of worship for many different peoples, including the Maya. Surrounding a huge man-made plateau are the remains of pyramids, a ball court, burial chambers with beautiful murals, and carvings of dancers.

Palenque, Mexico
A Mayan site in a clearing in the jungle, Palenque has numerous buildings with particularly beautiful decoration. They include the Temple of Inscriptions, a stepped pyramid with a 25 m (80 ft) tunnel that leads to a crypt containing the sarcophagus of a 7th-century Mayan king.

Uxmal, Mexico
One of the most beautiful pre-1500 sites in Mexico, Uxmal has Classical Maya architecture. The chief building is the smooth-sided El Adivino, or Pyramid of the Soothsayer, up which there is an almost vertical climb to the 35 m (115 ft) high summit that is crowned by a temple. Nearby is the Governor's Palace, which features a frieze with 103 masks.

CENTRAL AMERICA AND THE CARIBBEAN

Caracol, Belize
An amazing Mayan site deep in the rainforest, Caracol is still being excavated. The ruins, whose full extent has only recently become apparent, include a pyramid 42 m (140 ft) high.

Tikal, Guatemala
Possibly the greatest Mayan site, Tikal is surrounded on all sides by jungle. The remains of 3,000 buildings can be seen, some with painted carvings. The pyramid-like Temple of the Great Jaguar, built in AD 700, is considered the world's best example of Mayan temple construction.

Trinidad, Cuba
Cuba's best-preserved colonial town, Trinidad has many buildings that reflect the town's prosperity as a centre of the sugar trade in the 18th and 19th centuries.

SOUTH AMERICA

Cuzco and the Urubumba Valley, Peru
Former capital of the Incas high in the Andes, Cuzco contains extensive Inca ruins mixed with colonial churches, palaces, houses and a 17th-century cathedral. An attractive and lively town, it is the main starting point for people visiting Machu Picchu (by train or a four-day trek) and other Inca ruins in the Urubumba Valley.

Nazca Lines, Peru
People of the Nazca culture (375 BC–AD 650) created gigantic lines by removing stones to expose the desert soil beneath. The lines, which depict geometrical shapes, birds – one with a wing-span of over 100 m (328 ft) – and animals, are best seen from the air, in a local plane.

Potosí, Bolivia
Founded in 1545 as a silver-mining town, Potosí was the largest city in the Americas in the early 17th century. Today it has over 2,000 colonial buildings, including several 18th-century Baroque churches.

Olinda, Brazil
One of the best-preserved colonial cities in Brazil, on a hill overlooking the Atlantic, Olinda has many 16th- to 18th-century buildings. It is a major cultural centre, with art galleries, music and festivals.

Ouro Prêto, Brazil
A beautiful colonial town founded in 1711, Ouro Prêto has cobblestone roads, statues, fountains, churches, a palace and a theatre. It also serves as a base for exploring other colonial towns in Minas Gerais province, such as Diamantina.

San Ignacio Mini, Argentina
The most impressive of the ruins of Jesuit mission villages in the Misiones region, San Ignacio Mini had 4,356 Guarani inhabitants before the Jesuits were expelled from Spanish territory in 1767. The ruins of only three other missions indicate their former splendour: Sao Miguel in Brazil, and Jesús and Trinidad in Paraguay.

Major cities with historic sites
(see *World Cities*)
- Boston
- Buenos Aires
- Cartagena
- Chicago
- Havana
- Lima
- Los Angeles
- Miami
- Mexico City
- Montréal
- New Orleans
- New York
- Panama
- Quito
- Rio de Janeiro
- San Francisco
- Sucre
- Washington

Historic sites in Europe

There is a huge variety of historic sites in Europe, ranging from prehistoric monuments over 5,000 years old to 19th-century castles. Ruins of the architectural achievements of the Classical Greek and Roman civilizations contrast with what are often perfectly preserved cathedrals, churches, monasteries, castles, palaces and civic buildings dating from the 11th century onwards.

◄ Neuschwanstein Castle, Germany

The ultimate fairytale castle, Neuschwanstein (near Fussen) was built in 1869–86 and is the most famous of Ludwig II's castles inspired by Wagner's vision of medieval Germany. It has a wide range of architectural styles, and its tall white marble towers topped by cone-shaped pinnacles, which have been copied by Disneyworld, are instantly recognizable.

Rock of Cashel, Ireland

Poised dramatically above the town of Cashel in County Tipparary stands a limestone outcrop, 109 m (358 ft) high, known as the Rock of Cashel. It is topped by a group of medieval ecclesiastical ruins, which include a bishop's palace, the 13th-century St Patrick's Cathedral, and the adjoining 12th-century Romanesque St Cormac's chapel.

Caernarfon Castle, Wales

Considered to be the finest of the castles built by Edward I of England after his conquest of Wales in 1283, Caernarfon Castle is exceptionally well preserved. Constructed as a royal palace as well as a military stronghold, it dominates the surrounding walled town, which was also founded by Edward.

Stonehenge, England

The most famous prehistoric monument in Europe, Stonehenge is a circular arrangement of massive standing stones, surrounded by earthworks, whose function is a subject of controversy. Built in stages between c. 3100 BC and c. 1000 BC, it may have been an astronomical observatory, a temple or a secular ceremonial centre. Its distinctive stone trilithons – pairs of uprights topped with horizontal lintels – are an impressive landmark on the Salisbury Plain.

▼ Meteora, Greece

Perched on top of natural rock pinnacles which rise hundreds of metres from the flat plain of Thessaly, near Tríkkala, is a group of Greek orthodox monasteries, some of which are still inhabited today. The highest of these – at 533 m (1,749 ft) is Great Meteoron, which was built from 1356 with a domed church added in the 16th century.

Bruges, Belgium

Once one of Europe's greatest trading centres, Bruges is a well-preserved medieval city with narrow streets and canals spanned by picturesque bridges. Within its 13th-century walls are many historic buildings, including the magnificent Gothic Town Hall and the medieval Cloth Hall. The Groeninge Museum contains paintings by the 15th-century Flemish masters.

Mont-St-Michel, France

Rising dramatically out of the Bay of St-Michel is a steep, rocky island with a medieval abbey on its summit. Buildings and fortifications have been added since the 11th century, resulting in a mixture of styles and shapes which culminate in the 19th-century spire of the church.

Versailles, France

Built for Louis XIV, the 'Sun King', the vast Baroque palace of Versailles was the envy of all Europe in the 17th century. Today, visitors flock to see the Hall of Mirrors – where the Treaty of Versailles was signed at the end of World War I – and to wander between the elaborate fountains in the magnificent formal gardens.

Heidelberg, Germany

Majestically set on the banks of the River Neckar and dominated by the romantic ruins of the castle, Heidelberg is one of Germany's most beautiful and best preserved historic towns, with many fascinating buildings. Its 600-year-old university provides a youthful atmosphere on the streets, especially in the evenings.

Petrodvorets, Russia

An imperial palace in the Baroque style, Petrodvorets was built by Peter the Great after he had visited Versailles. It is set in beautiful parkland interwoven by a system of fountains, cascades and waterways connected to the sea.

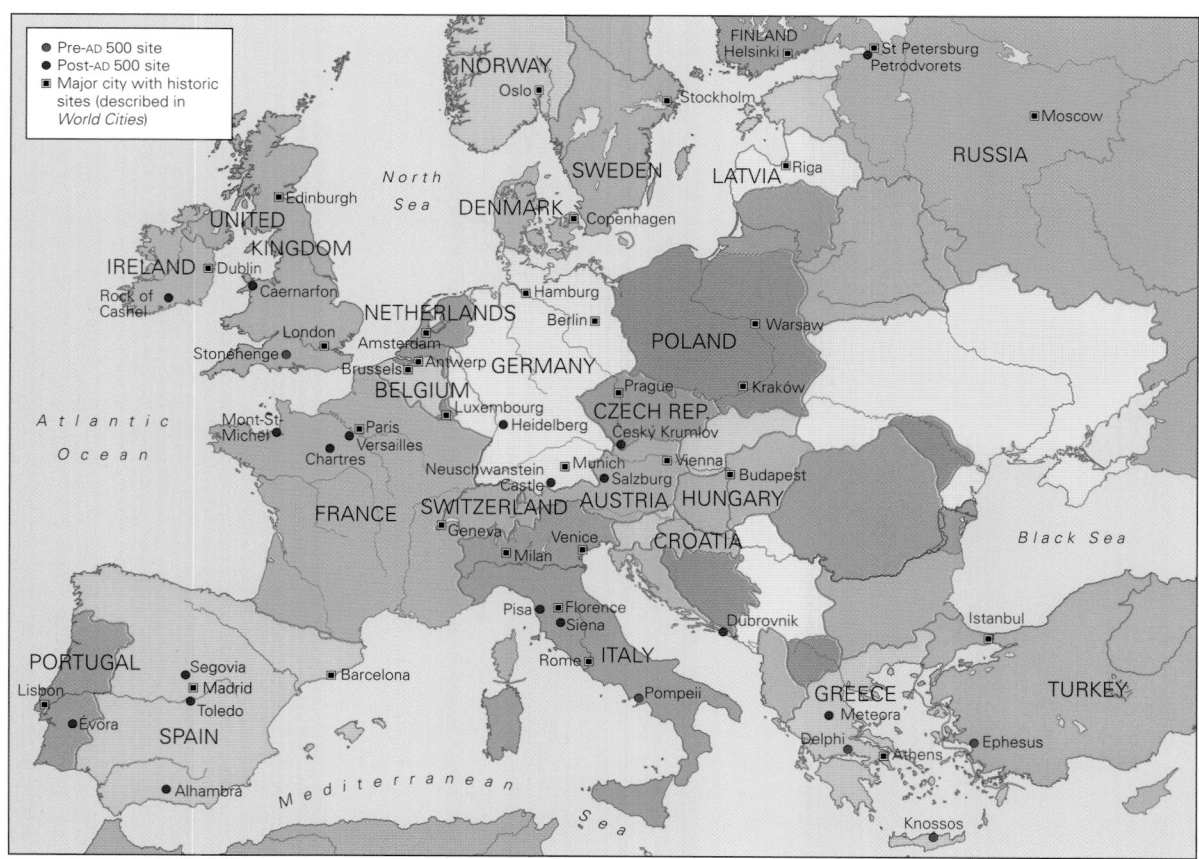

- ● Pre-AD 500 site
- ● Post-AD 500 site
- ■ Major city with historic sites (described in *World Cities*)

Salzburg, Austria

Set in a magnificent subalpine landscape, Salzburg is a picturesque city with many fine Baroque churches and a grand Italianate cathedral, the first of its kind to be built north of the Alps. The simple apartment where Mozart was born is a place of pilgrimage for music lovers.

Český Krumlov, Czech Republic

One of Europe's most picturesque towns, Český Krumlov has hardly changed since the 18th century. Its beautiful medieval and Renaissance buildings are almost encircled by the Vltava River and overlooked by a magnificent castle. Originally a Gothic fortress, Krumlov Castle was rebuilt in the 16th century as a fortified palace.

Évora, Portugal

An attractive city with a history dating back to Roman times, Évora has a walled medieval centre with a distinctly Moorish atmosphere, and many fine Renaissance buildings from its time as a royal residence. The church of São Francisco is a good example of the Portuguese Manueline style of architecture, combining Gothic and Moorish influences.

Toledo, Spain

An ancient city of steep, winding streets lined with elegant if sombre buildings, Toledo is a splendid monument to the many cultures that have flourished here in the past. Moorish, Jewish and Christian traditions are all represented, and parts of the city walls date from the 6th century, when the Visigoths made Toledo their capital. The cathedral is a particularly fine example of the Spanish Gothic.

Segovia, Spain

Set on a rock, Segovia is a delightful old town with a fairytale castle and a 1st-century Roman aqueduct. Other notable buildings include the palace of La Granja, the 16th-century Gothic cathedral and the 12-sided, 13th-century Templar church of Vera Cruz.

Pisa, Italy

The famous Leaning Tower of Pisa is just one of a quartet of ecclesiastical buildings which make up the beautiful Campo dei Miracoli (Field of Miracles) in this medieval walled city. The black and white marble facades of the Duomo and Baptistery, decorated by a succession of distinguished sculptors, are perfect examples of the Pisan Romanesque style, while the cloistered cemetery of Camposanto contains 14th-century frescoes.

Siena, Italy

Surrounded by city walls, Siena's medieval centre, with its narrow, winding streets, fine buildings and palaces, is wonderfully preserved. It is dominated by the Piazza del Campo, a large, shell-shaped square where the spectacular horserace known as the Corsa del Palio is held (see *Festivals*).

Delphi, Greece

In a stunning location, at the foot of Mount Parnassós, lie the impressive ruins of a sanctuary dedicated to Apollo, whose oracle was the most important in Classical Greece. The ruins include the 4th-century BC Temple of Apollo, the Doric Treasury of Athens, a theatre restored by the Romans, and a well-preserved stadium where the Pythian games were held.

Knossós, Crete

The ruined palace of Knossós is one of the few remains of the Minoan civilization, which flourished c. 3000–1100 BC. The first palace at Knossós was built around 2000 BC, and was rebuilt after an earthquake in c. 1720 BC. Excavations have revealed workshops, storerooms, dwellings and ceremonial rooms, one of which contains a gypsum throne.

Dubrovnik, Croatia

The fortifications of the ancient port of Dubrovnik rise straight from the Adriatic, and the double line of city walls encompass two palaces, two monasteries and many churches and other historic buildings, mostly dating from the 15th and 16th centuries. The narrow, winding streets of the old city are free from motor vehicles.

Ephesus, Turkey

The extensive and well-preserved ruins of the ancient city of Ephesus are one of Turkey's most popular historic sites, containing buildings from ancient Greek, Roman and Byzantine times. Among those dating from the Roman period are several temples, a theatre, a library, terraced houses, public baths and latrines, as well as some fine mosaics and wall paintings.

▲ **The Alhambra, Granada, Spain**
The most splendid example of Moorish architecture in Spain is the hilltop Alhambra palace, which was built in the 13th–14th centuries. The unassuming fortress walls contain a richly decorated interior made up of many halls and courtyards, with fountains and pools throughout.

▲ **Chartres Cathedral, France**
Built in the middle of the 13th century, and almost unaltered since, the great cathedral of Notre Dame at Chartres is an exceptionally fine example of high Gothic architecture, with its flying buttresses, vaulted ceilings, intricate stonework and beautifully detailed stained glass. A rare 13th-century labyrinth design on the floor, a Renaissance choir screen and the glowing stained glass of the rose window all add to the beauty and impact of the building.

Pompeii and the Romans

Pompeii is an exceptional historic site because, when the eruption of Vesuvius in AD 79 engulfed the city in volcanic debris, the life of the people, their homes and streets, public spaces and palaces were preserved as if frozen in time. Excavations have revealed a wealth of detailed information about the everyday life of citizens of the Roman Empire, including their public notices, graffiti, brothels, latrines, furnishings and food. At its greatest extent, in the 1st–4th centuries AD, the Roman Empire encircled the Mediterranean Sea, reaching north as far as Britain and south into Egypt. Remains of Roman theatres, temples, baths, arenas, villas and other buildings can be found at sites throughout Europe and north Africa.

Major cities with historic sites
(see *World Cities*)
• Amsterdam
• Antwerp
• Athens
• Barcelona
• Berlin
• Brussels
• Budapest
• Copenhagen
• Dublin
• Edinburgh
• Florence
• Geneva
• Hamburg
• Helsinki
• Istanbul
• Kraków
• Lisbon
• London
• Luxembourg
• Madrid
• Milan
• Moscow
• Munich
• Oslo
• Paris
• Prague
• Reykjavik
• Riga
• Rome
• St Petersburg
• Stockholm
• Vienna
• Warsaw
• Venice

Historic sites in Africa, Asia and Australasia

Africa is the home of the imposing ruins of ancient Egypt – one of the world's first civilizations. With the Middle East, it also has historic sites that reflect the competing influences of Christianity and Islam. In Asia, vast temple complexes, often adorned with wonderful sculptures, are among the remains of great empires, while in Australia, Aboriginal rock paintings are evidence of a culture that flourished long before the Europeans arrived.

◄ **Angkor, Cambodia**
The magnificent ruins at Angkor, capital of the Khmer empire, merit more than one day of sight-seeing. The best-preserved of the buildings is the 12th-century sandstone temple of Angkor Wat, which symbolizes the Hindu universe. Surrounded by pools, it is lavishly decorated with statues and bas-reliefs that are the longest in the world. Around 1.5 km (1 mile) away is the temple complex of Angkor Thom, within which is the Buddhist temple of Bayon with reliefs depicting everyday life.

AFRICA AND THE MIDDLE EAST

Dogon cliffside villages, Mali

Built among the rocks at the foot of the Bandiagara escarpment are the picturesque traditional houses, temples, granaries and meeting places of the Dogon people, whose culture has survived since the 14th century. The area can be reached only on foot and conditions can be gruelling. The best time to visit is December, for the harvest celebrations.

Rock churches of Lalibela, Ethiopia

Carved out of the red volcanic rock of the central highlands are 11 extraordinary medieval churches containing rare and beautiful frescoes, elaborate carvings and bas-reliefs. A complex network of tunnels and passageways connects the churches, some of which are hidden in deep trenches while others have been cut into the cliff face. The best time to visit is the Ethiopian Christmas (7 January) and Easter.

Kilwa Kisiwani, Tanzania

Once an Islamic city-state, the island of Kilwa Kisiwani has extensive ruins, which include a 12th-century mosque, several palaces and grand houses, and a 15th-century Portuguese fort. The impressive 14th-century cliff-top palace of Husuni Kubwa has a 30 m (98 ft) high dome and over 100 rooms.

Zanzibar, Tanzania

The buildings of Zanzibar Town's 'old quarter', Stone Town, reflect its colourful history as an important trading centre, particularly in the 19th century. A maze of narrow streets contain a sultan's palace, an ochre-coloured Arab fort, and the home of the notorious slave trader Tippu Tip, as well as numerous bazaars.

Great Zimbabwe, Zimbabwe

The extensive ruins of a major medieval city dating from the 10th century onwards, Great Zimbabwe is made up of curved stone walls and enclosures which incorporate features of the landscape into their design. The Elliptical Building, with an unusual conical tower and a diameter of almost 100 m (328 ft), is the largest ancient structure in sub-Saharan Africa.

Akko, Israel

The ancient walled port of Akko contains many relics of its long and distinguished history, including the underground 12th-century Crusader vaults and halls, the Ottoman Turkish citadel, and the beautiful 18th-century El Jazzar mosque. A remarkable 18th-century Turkish bath-house has been sensitively restored.

Petra, Jordan

Carved out of red sandstone mountains, the majestic remains of the desert city of Petra include two theatres, the High Place of Sacrifice, a temple and many elaborate tombs. The majority date from the period c. 100 BC –AD 150, when Petra was at the height of its prosperity as an important centre of trade. It had strong links with the Greek Hellenistic world, which are reflected in the Classical facades of its tombs.

ASIA

Mohenjodaro, Pakistan

The excavated remains of a city, Mohenjodaro is the most impressive of all the sites relating to the civilization that flourished in the Indus Valley c. 2600–1800 BC. The site consists of a raised citadel, with public buildings that include an assembly hall and a Great Bath, and a lower town containing residential and industrial areas.

▼ **Ajanta and Ellora Caves, near Aurangabad, India**
Cut into a spectacular horseshoe-shaped cliff, the Buddhist temples and monasteries of Ajanta are decorated with wall-paintings which are among the greatest examples of early Indian art. The series of rock-cut temples at Ellora includes the 8th-century Hindu Kailasa temple which is renowned for its exceptional sculptures of gods and mythological figures.

The Pyramids and Ancient Egypt

Khafre's Sphinx, 73 m (240 ft) in length and carved from a limestone outcrop, stands near the three pyramids at Giza. The most famous of the Egyptian pyramids, they were built as spectacular royal tombs over 4,500 years ago, during the period of the Old Kingdom. The largest at Giza is nearly 150 m (500 ft) high. The last of the Old Kingdom dynasties collapsed c. 2180 BC, but central government was restored by the dynasties of the Middle Kingdom (c. 2055–1650 BC) and New Kingdom (c. 1550–1070 BC). In the era of the New Kingdom, vast temples and lavishly painted royal tombs were constructed, most notably those either side of the River Nile at Luxor and overlooking Lake Nasser at Abu Simbel (see *River and canal journeys*).

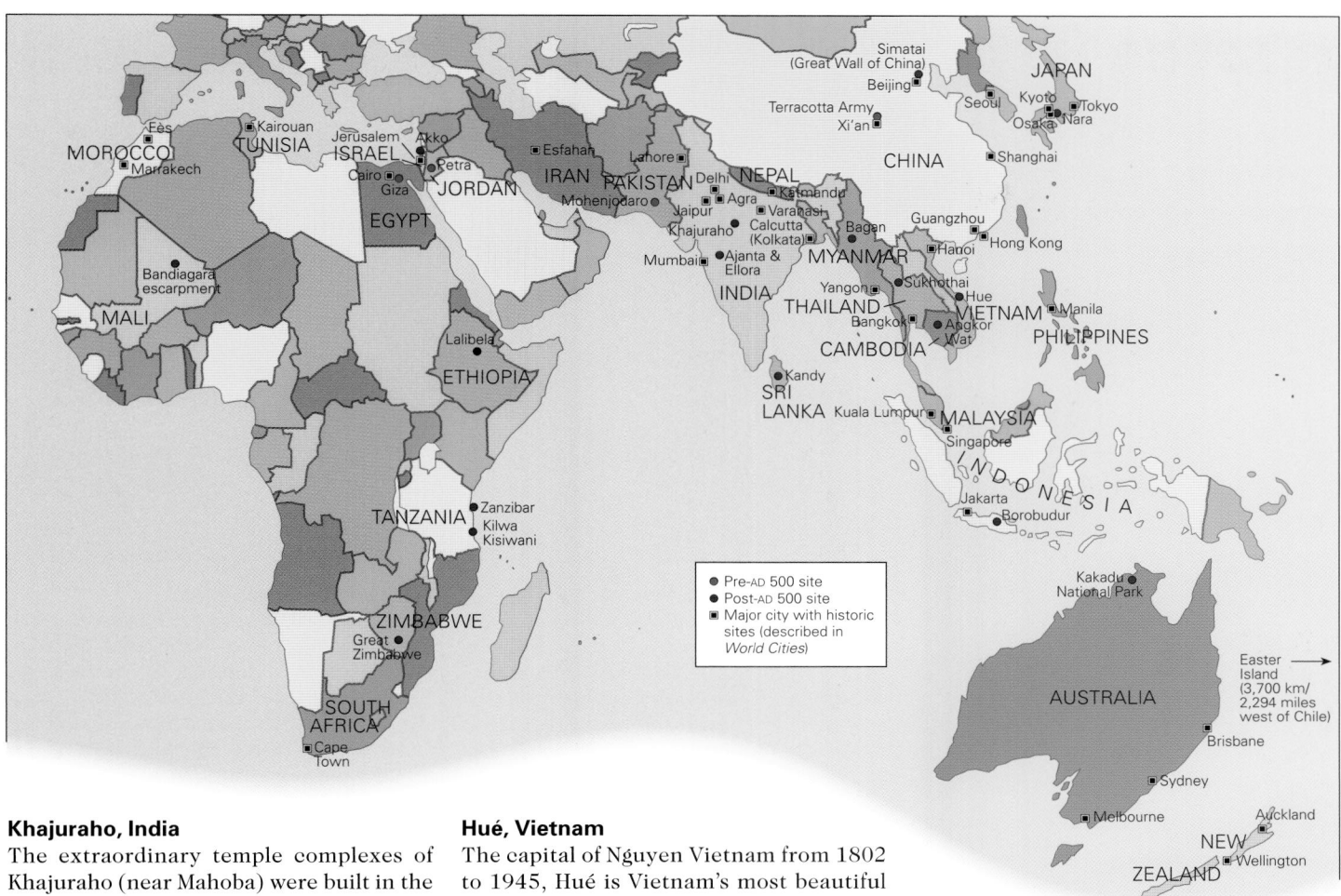

Major cities with historic sites
(see *World Cities*)
AFRICA
• Cairo
• Cape Town
• Fès
• Kairouan
• Marrakech
ASIA
• Agra
• Bangkok
• Beijing
• Calcutta
  (Kolkata)
• Delhi
• Esfahan
• Guangzhou
  (Canton)
• Hanoi
• Hong Kong
• Jaipur
• Jakarta
• Jerusalem
• Katmandu
• Kuala Lumpur
• Kyoto
• Lahore
• Manila
• Mumbai
• Osaka
• Seoul
• Singapore
• Tokyo
• Varanasi
• Xi'an
• Yangon
AUSTRALASIA
• Auckland
• Brisbane
• Melbourne
• Sydney
• Wellington

Khajuraho, India

The extraordinary temple complexes of Khajuraho (near Mahoba) were built in the 10th and 11th centuries by the Hindu Chandela dynasty, but were abandoned in the 14th century. Rediscovered in the jungle in 1838, they were carefully restored and are now famous for their sensual and erotic sculptures depicting human, divine, animal and mythological subjects.

Kandy and the Cultural Triangle, Sri Lanka

Famous for its temple and Festival of the Tooth (see *Festivals*), Kandy is one of three former Sinhalese capitals that together form a 'Cultural Triangle'. The other two are Anuradhapura, a huge site with the remains of palaces and temples dating back to the 3rd century BC, and the more compact and better-preserved Polonnaruwa, around 1,000 years old. Within the triangle is the 1st-century BC cave-temple of Dambulla, with 150 Buddha images, and the impressive 6th-century palace-fortress of Sigiriya. Built on top of 'Lion Rock', this is decorated with frescoes and includes a water garden.

Bagan, Burma (Myanmar)

Built between the 11th and the 13th centuries, Bagan (Pagan, near Pakkoku) became known as 'the city of 4 million pagodas', and was the capital of a vast realm. Today it is an important archeological site covering about 40 sq km (15 sq miles) with over 2,000 structures still standing. Among the most impressive are the Temple of Ananda and the Shwezigon Pagoda, with glazed plaques showing scenes from the life of Buddha.

Old Sukhothai, Thailand

The ruins of the 13th-century capital of the Sukhothai empire have been preserved as a 70 sq km (27 sq mile) historical park. They contain numerous temples set in a landscape of lakes, trees and lawns. The most impressive is Wat Mahathat, with fine stucco work and carved Buddhas.

Hué, Vietnam

The capital of Nguyen Vietnam from 1802 to 1945, Hué is Vietnam's most beautiful city. The magnificent moated citadel with its ten fortified gates contains a palace, a mandarin hall and a museum. In the hills to the south of the city there are seven elaborate royal tombs.

Borobudur, Java, Indonesia

Rising like a squat pyramid from the Kedu Plain, Borobudur (near Yogyakarta) is a colossal 9th-century Buddhist stupa (temple) built by the Sailendra dynasty. The largest monument in the southern hemisphere, it covers 200 sq m (2,153 sq ft) and includes over 500 shrines with seated Buddhas. The walls of the stupa, which has five square and four circular terraces, are decorated with bas-reliefs.

Great Wall of China, Simatai, China

Stretching from the Central Asian desert to the Yellow Sea, the Great Wall is over 2,240 km (1,400 miles) long, averages over 6 m (20 ft) in height, and has a central walkway nearly 4 m (13 ft) wide. Much of what exists today dates from the 14th–16th centuries. The Wall can be visited at Badaling, just 70 km (45 miles) from Beijing. However, a less crowded section is at Simatai, 110 km (68 miles) from Beijing, where there are wonderful views to the distant mountains.

Nara, Japan

The ancient city of Nara has many beautiful pagodas, shrines, gardens and temples, the most famous of which is the 8th-century Eastern Great Temple, the Tadai-Ji. Its Great Buddha Hall houses Japan's largest bronze statue of Buddha; the hall itself is the largest wooden building in the world.

AUSTRALASIA AND THE PACIFIC

Kakadu National Park, Australia

Thousands of Aboriginal rock paintings cover the walls of the caves and cliffs of the ancient Aboriginal lands in Kakadu National Park (see also *Wildlife in Australasia*). The paintings, some of which are estimated to be over 20,000 years old, provide a continuous link with the past for the several hundred Aboriginal people who still live there today.

Easter Island statues, Polynesia

The extraordinary stone statues of Easter Island are the legacy of a lost culture which flourished on the island between around AD 400 and 1600. More than 800 colossal stone heads were erected all around the island's coast. The volcanic crater from which the stone was quarried still contains hundreds of unfinished statues, including the 20 m (65 ft) high El Gigante.

◄ **Army of Terracotta Warriors, near Xi'an, China**
The massive underground mausoleum of China's first emperor, Shi Huang Di, who died in 210 BC, contains an army of around 7,500 life-size terracotta soldiers. Standing in military formation, they are a unique sight.

Theme parks

Inspired by the phenomenon of Disneyland, Los Angeles, the top theme parks around the world are irresistible to children both young and old, as well as adults. The combination of charm and fantasy with white-knuckle rides and superb service guarantees a successful family visit, and since most are located near major cities it is easy to incorporate them into a longer itinerary.

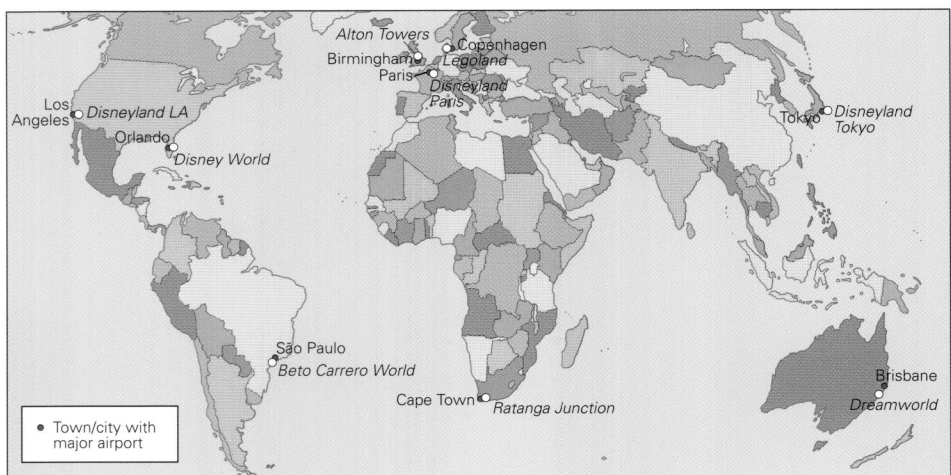

Town/city with major airport

▲ Alton Towers, England

The combination of a ruined stately home, wooded parkland and over 100 rides means that Alton Towers (in Staffordshire) provides entertainment for all tastes. For the benefit of its younger visitors it puts on shows featuring characters from storybooks and songs, such as 'Peter Rabbit and Friends on Ice'. Its more challenging rides have a much darker theme, with names such as Nemesis and Oblivion.

Useful web addresses
preceded by www.

themeparks.about.com

funguide.com/country

disney.go.com

Disneyland, Los Angeles, USA

Disneyland, founded in 1955, is the original Disney theme park, and Mainstreet, Frontierland and Fantasyland – representations of American life and its dreams – have been duplicated in Disney theme parks around the world. Visitors are attracted not only by rides like the runaway train of Big Thunder Mountain, the parade of Disney characters and the famous nightly firework show, but also out of nostalgia and a desire to experience what is itself now a historic site.

Beto Carrero World, Santa Catarina, Brazil

The most extensive theme park in Brazil, Beto Carrero World (near Itajai) combines thrilling rides, shows and a zoo. Its themed areas cover a range of cultures, including a German House complete with beer cellar, a Viking longboat and a Wild West area. Its shows are similarly wide-ranging and feature the legend of Excalibur. Its white-knuckle rides include the free-falling Tower of Terror, and Star World Mountain, with two 360-degree loops. The animal park includes African wildlife and a large collection of cobras.

Disneyland Paris, France

Although based on the same formula as the Los Angeles theme park, the marketing for Disneyland Paris emphasizes the educational element. There are 'Discovery rides', such as the 'Mississippi Steamboat' which provides information about life in frontier towns, while the Swiss Family Robinson tree-house demonstrates practical survival tips. Most visitors, however, go for the glamour of the shows and parades, and the thrill of the rides. These include being catapulted 'From the Earth to the Moon' on a Jules Verne style rocket.

Legoland, Billund, Denmark

Legoland, in which everything is built out of lego, is divided into themed areas, such as Pirateland and Castleland, where children recognize, and are able to interact with, their favourite lego characters. Although the park is aimed primarily at children, providing them with opportunities to play creatively, adults are also charmed by the intricate scale models of real, if somewhat idealized, scenes.

Ratanga Junction, Cape Town, South Africa

Africa's first theme park opened in the late 1990s. It takes as its theme the wildlife of Africa, with rides such as The Cobra, Monkey Falls, and Crocodile Gorge, in which visitors can experience white-water rafting in controlled conditions. A diamond mine is featured, with an underground runaway mine train providing the thrills. There are also less alarming rides for all the family, and 'interactive play areas' for young children.

Disneyland Tokyo, Japan

With many of the same attractions as other Disney theme parks, Disneyland Tokyo is unashamedly American in its culture. Rides range from the gentle Mark Twain Riverboat to the exciting Space Mountain. Around 200 Disney characters, from the earliest cartoons through to the present day, take part in the regular 'Disney's Dreams' parade.

Dreamworld, Queensland, Australia

Thrilling rides and shows are combined with a wildlife park and conservation zone in Dreamworld (near Gold Coast). The Tower of Terror roller coaster reaches speeds of 160 km (100 miles) per hour as it descends from a height of 115 m (375 ft). The Giant Drop uses the same structure to release passengers vertically so that they experience momentary weightlessness. In an 'interactive tiger exhibition' tigers swim with their trainers, while in the Koala Park visitors can handle koalas and watch other native Australian animals.

Walt Disney World, Orlando, Florida, USA

The massive Walt Disney World in Florida encompasses four separate theme parks. At Magic Kingdom there are rides graded for every taste, from those in Fantasyland aimed specifically at younger children, to the Space Mountain rocket trip, which is not for the faint-hearted. The Epcot Centre aims to re-create the atmosphere and architecture of different countries, including Norway, China and Italy. Visitors can eat food typical of the region, and enjoy themed rides, shows and videos. Disney MGM re-creates urban areas, such as New York Street and Hollywood Boulevard, and uses computer technology to enable visitors to come face to face with characters from recent films. The newest of the parks, Animal Kingdom, combines a safari park with typical Disney features, including thrilling rides, exhibitions and shows.

WORLD CITIES

CITY MAPS

Amsterdam	2	Canton	8	Lagos	14	Munich	20	Singapore	27
Athens	2	Cape Town	8	Lisbon	14	New York	21	Stockholm	28
Atlanta	3	Chicago	9	London	15	Osaka	22	Sydney	28
Baghdad	3	Copenhagen	10	Lima	16	Oslo	22	Tokyo	29
Bangkok	3	Delhi	10	Los Angeles	16	Paris	23	Tehran	30
Barcelona	4	Dublin	11	Madrid	17	Prague	24	Tianjin	30
Beijing	4	Edinburgh	11	Manila	17	Rio de Janeiro	24	Toronto	30
Berlin	5	Helsinki	12	Melbourne	17	Rome	25	Vienna	31
Boston	6	Hong Kong	12	Mexico City	18	San Francisco	25	Warsaw	31
Brussels	6	Istanbul	12	Miami	18	St Petersburg	26	Washington	32
Budapest	7	Jakarta	13	Milan	18	Santiago	26	Wellington	32
Buenos Aires	7	Jerusalem	13	Montréal	19	São Paulo	26		
Cairo	7	Johannesburg	13	Moscow	19	Seoul	26		
Calcutta	8	Karachi	14	Mumbai	20	Shanghai	27	INDEX	33–39

CITY GAZETTEER 40–48

CITY MAPS

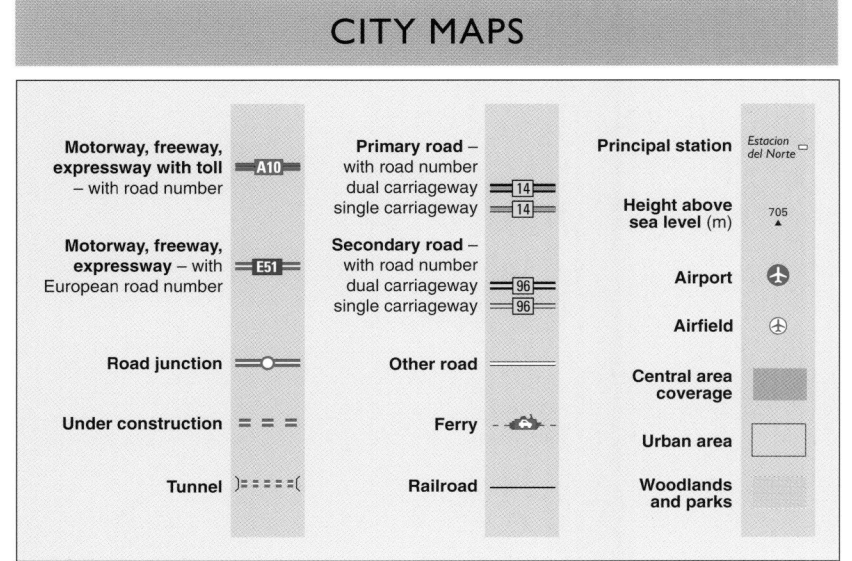

CENTRAL AREA MAPS

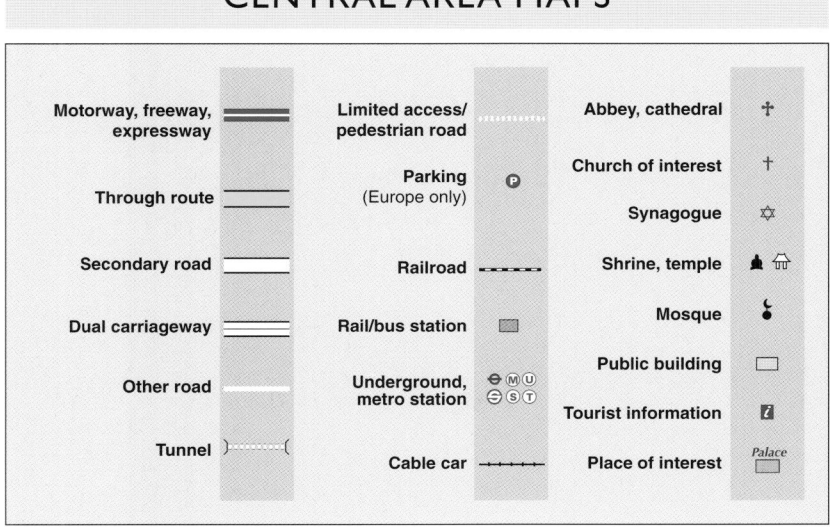

AMSTERDAM

km 0 — 5
miles 0 — 3

N8 Assendelft
Westzaan
Zaandam
Zaanstad
Oostzaan
Zaandijk
A8 E22 A7
Het Twiske
Wijde Wormer
4° 50′
Ilpendam
Monnickendam
N247
N235
Gouw zee
Waterland
Den Ilp
Landsmeer
Broek in Waterland
Zuiderwoude
N247
Noordzeekanaal
N203
N202
Tuindorp Oostzaan
Buiksloot
Nieuwendam
S101
S116
A10
AMSTERDAM
Zunderdorp
Holysloot
Ransdorp
E35
A
Zwanenburg
N5
Centraal Sta.
Anne Frankhuis
Rijksmus.
Zoo
Het IJ
IJ-meer
Sloter-park
Rembrandt-park
Vondel-park
Stedelijk Mus.
S100
S112
Water-graafsmeer
Diemen
Muiden
A9
Osdorp
A10
Sloten
A4
Badhoevedorp
Het Nieuwe Meer
52° 20′
A2
A4
N232
E35
Amsterdamse Bos
Buitenveldert
Amsterdam Zuidoost
A1 E231
52° 20′
Weesp
E19
LUCHTHAVEN SCHIPHOL
A9
Amstelveen
A9
A9
N236
Bovenkerk
Ouderkerk
B
Aalsmeer
Bovenkerker Polder
Abcoude
Ankeveense Plassen
N201
Uithoorn
Westeinder Plassen
Vinkeveense Plassen
Baambrugge
Nederhorst
E35 A2
4° 50′
East from Greenwich
5° 00′

1   2   3

CENTRAL AMSTERDAM

km 0 — 1
miles 0 — 0.5

Westerpark
HAARLEMMERWEG
HAARLEMMER STR
Noorder Kerk
Centraal Station
DE RUIJTERKADE
NOORD
HET IJ
IJ Haven
PIET HEINKADE
a
Markt Centraal
Anne Frankhuis
Wester Kerk
Spaar-potten-Mus.
Dam Rak
St. Nicolaas Kerk
PRINS HENDRIK KADE
Scheepvaart-museum
KATTEN-BURGERGR.
Koninklijk Paleis
Nationaal Monument
Oude Kerk
De Waag
Oosterdok
KATTEN. B. OOSTEN.
Czaar Peterstraat
ROZENGRACHT
Beurs
Nieuw markt en Schans
B. GRACHT B. GRACHT
Cruquiuskade
b
Historisch Mus.
Universiteit
Rembrandt-huis
Plantage Doklaan
Planetarium
Artis Zoo
Kinkerstraat
NASSAUKADE
Univ. Bibl.
Allard Pierson Museum
Musiek theater
AMSTEL
Plantage Middenlaan
Aquarium
MAURITSKADE
Hoogte Kadijk
Singel
Rembrandts plein
Heren gracht
Waterlooplein
Amstelhof
OOST
Tropenmuseum
OVERTOOM
Keizers gracht
Theater Carré
MIDDEN
Filmmuseum
Prinsen gracht
Weesperplein
Sarphatistraat
Oosterpark
Linnaeuskade
Vondelpark
Rijksmuseum
Van Goghmus.
Weteringschans
MAURITSKADE
Wertheim-bachstr.
Muiderpoort Station
OUD ZUID
Stedelijk Mus.
Frederiks plein
Sarphatipark
Onze Lieve Vrouwe Gasthuis
Oosterpark
Willemsparkweg
Concert-gebouw
STADHOUDERS KADE
Albert Cuypstr
WIBAUT STRAAT
Wijtenbachstr.
De Lairessestraat
Van Baerlestr.
HOBBEMAKADE
1 Jan v. Goijenstr.
Ceuntuurbaan
Van Woustraat
Rinddik
WATERGRAAFSMEER
c
Apollolaan
Reijnier Vinkeleskade
Steenstraat
FERDINAND BOLSTRAAT
AMSTELDIJK
Hogeweg
Middenweg
NIEUW ZUID
Olympiaplein
2 van der Helst
Lutmastraat
Transvaalkade
Prins Bernhard plein
VRIES LAAN
Gerrit v. d. Veen straat
Van Hilgaertstr.
Amstel Kanaal
Amstel
Nobelweg
 Commer straat
GOOISEWEG
STADIONWEG
Churchillaan
CHURCHILLAAN
Amstel Station
Juliana plein
Kruislaan
HUGO
Stadionkade

1   2   3

ATHENS

km 0 — 5
miles 0 — 3

23° 40′
Néa Liósia
Petroúpolis
Verdi
Néa Ionía
23° 50′
Diflistiria
Aγ. Aváleos
8
Khaidhárion
Filadhélfia
Patisia
E75
1
Filotheï
83
Khalándrion
A
Skaramangás
E94
Dháfni
Sepolia
Psikhikón
54
Óros
Peristérion
Galátsion
Attiki
Aγ. Paraskeví
468
Lioumi
Kolokinthóu
Kolonos
Kipséli
Kholargós
Glika Nera
Kóridhallós
Aiyáleo
Larisa
Neapolis
Ampelokípi
Zográfos
Néapolis
ATHÍNAI
Tavros
Akrópoli
Stadhion
Koupónia
Aγ. Gheorghios
Dhamarakia
Aγ. I. Rendis
Gargáreta
Kaisariani
Pangrati
Víron
B
Níkaia
Moskhaton
Kallithéa
Dháfni
Imittós
Óros Imittós
Dhrapetsón
N. Smírni
Aγ. Dhimítrios
Ilioúpolis
Piraiévs
N. Fáliron
P. Fáliron
Kalamákion
N. Alexandhria
1026 Évzonos
Peania
Órmos Fáliros
Alimos
Aryiróupolis
Saronikós
Ellinikó
765
Kólpos
Glifádha
37° 50′
37° 50′
Iráklion, Khania, Kithnos, Kos, Míkonos, Mílos, Náxos, Paros, Ródhos, Sámos
Voula
Kitsi
C
Idrousa
Vari
Barako 230
91
C. Kavouri
Vouliagméni
Varkiza
Ayía Marina
23° 40′
23° 50′

1   2   3

CENTRAL ATHENS

km 0 — 1
miles 0 — 0.5

KODRICTONOS
EVELPIDON
Vergovitsis
Pedion Areos
PATISSION
ALEXANDRAS
a
LEOFOROS
Larisa
Pl. Victorias
Peloponnisos
Neof. Metaxá Ipirou
IPPOKRATOUS
28 OKTOVRIOU
Lofos Strefi
Ethniko Arheologiko Mousseio
ACHARNON
Metsovou
Likavitos
Ayios Nikolaos
Théatro
Ayios Georgios
CHALKOKONDILI
Ethniko Mousseio
Evangelismos
AG. KONSTANTINOU
PATISSION
Omonia
Opera
Ethniki Vivliothiki
Panepistimio
Ayios Dionysios
SOFIAS
b
ELEFTHERIOU VENIZELOU
Akadimia
Kolonaki
STADIOU
Benaki
PIREOS
Pl. Omonia
EOLOU
VASILISSIS
KONSTANTINOU
Klafthmonos
Vizandinó Mousseio
Alexander Soutsos Mousseio
Keramikós
Kanari
ERMOU
Pl. Syntagma
Vouli
Lýkiou
Anaktora
ERMOU
Mitropolis
Ethnikos Kipos
VASILEOS
PLAKA
Záppeio
Monastiraki
Adrianou
Arhéa Agora
Thissio
Kendriki Agora
Kendrikó Lysiou
Parthenon
Ários Págos
Áyios Marína
LEOFOROS OLGAS
Akrópoli
Náos Olimpíou Diós
ARDITOU
c
AREOPAGITOU
DIONYSIOU
Lófos Nimfón
Pnika
SINGROU
APOSTOLOU PAVLOU
KALLIROIS
Filopáppou
Dora Stratou Théatro

1   2   3

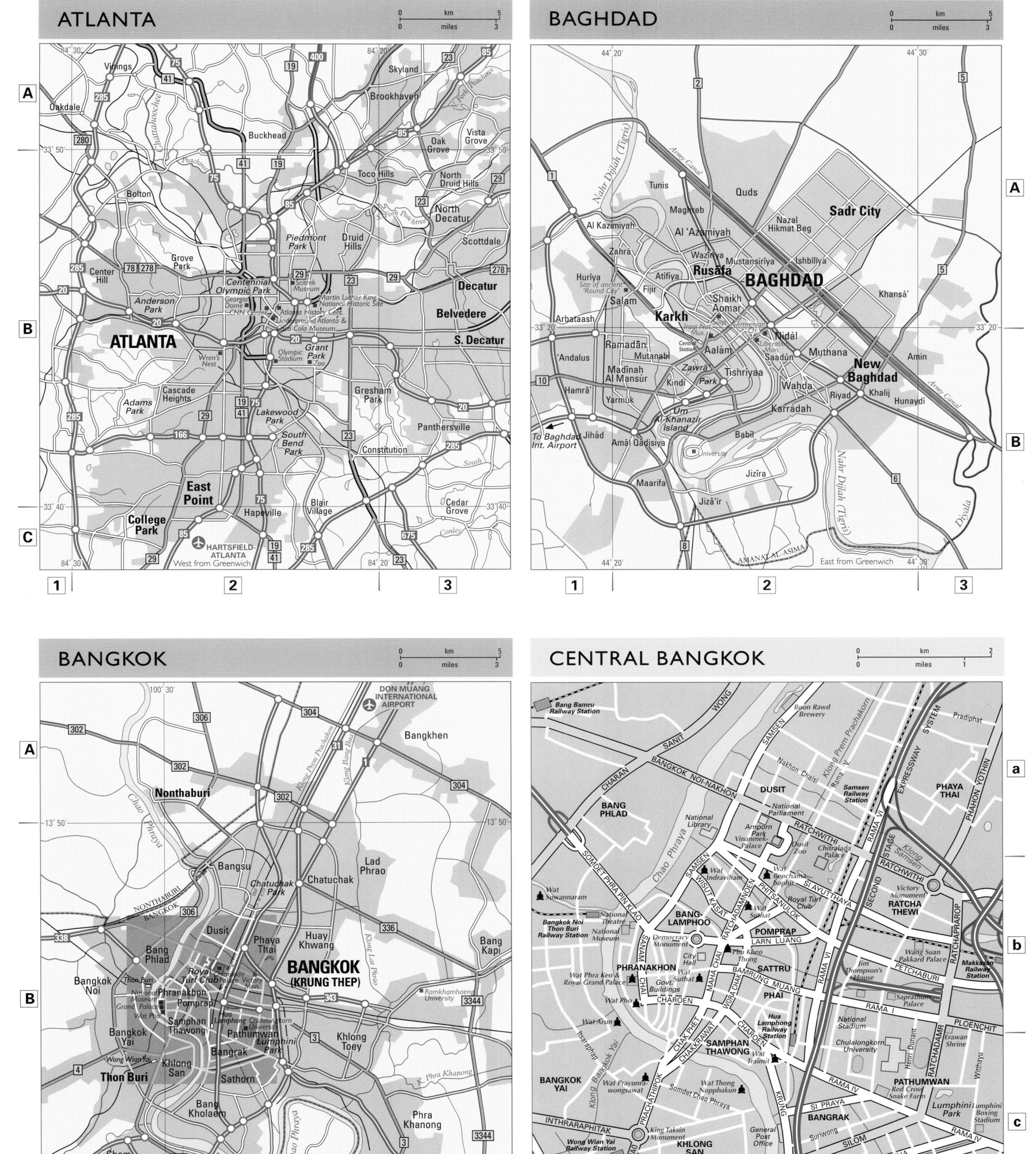

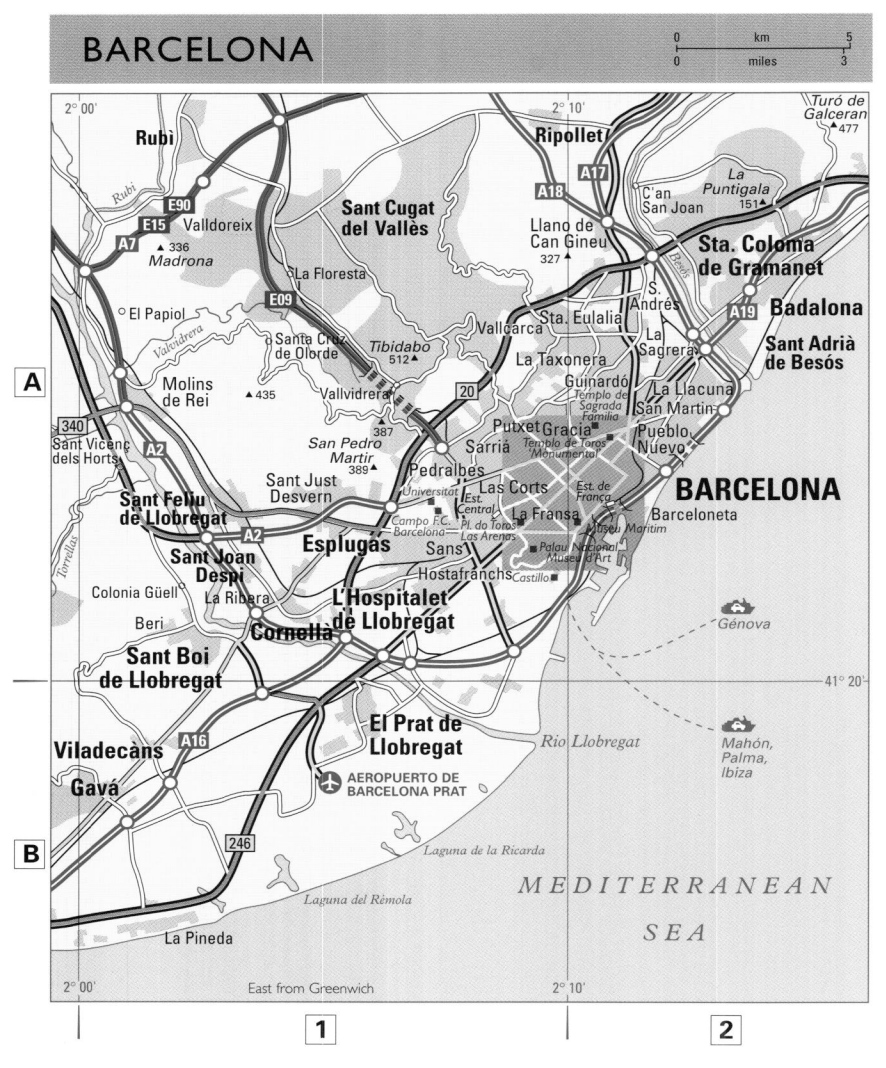

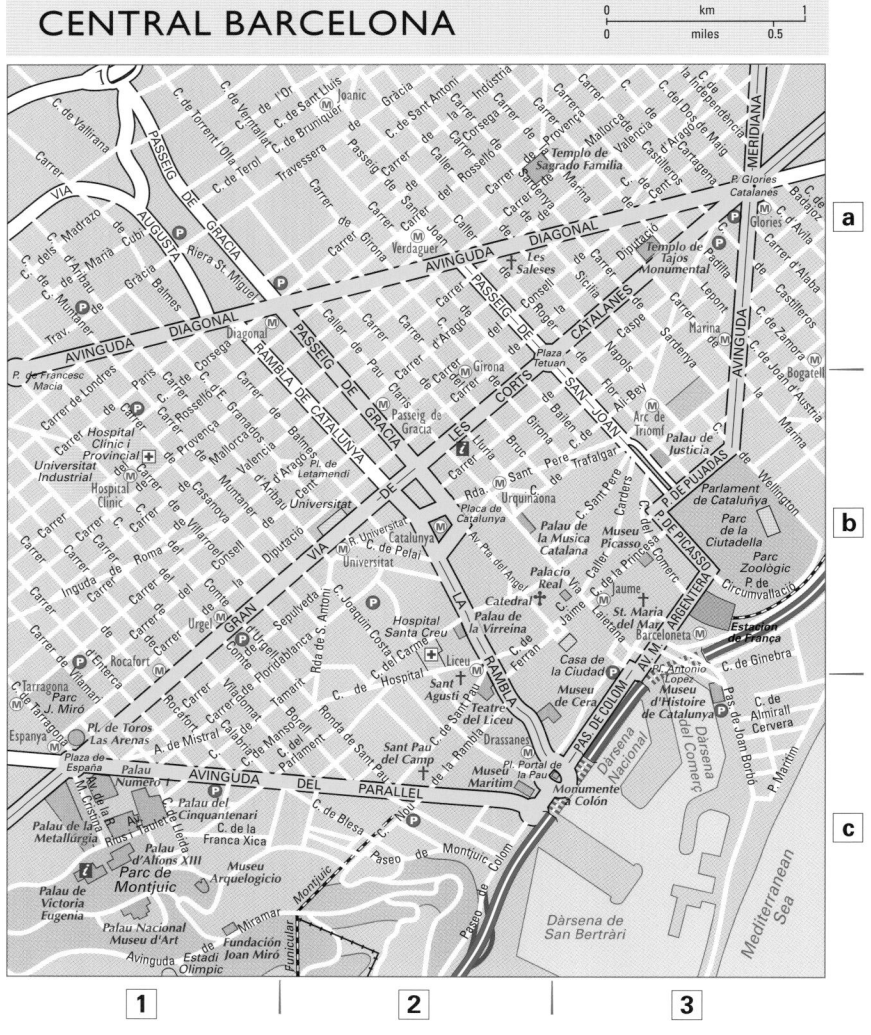

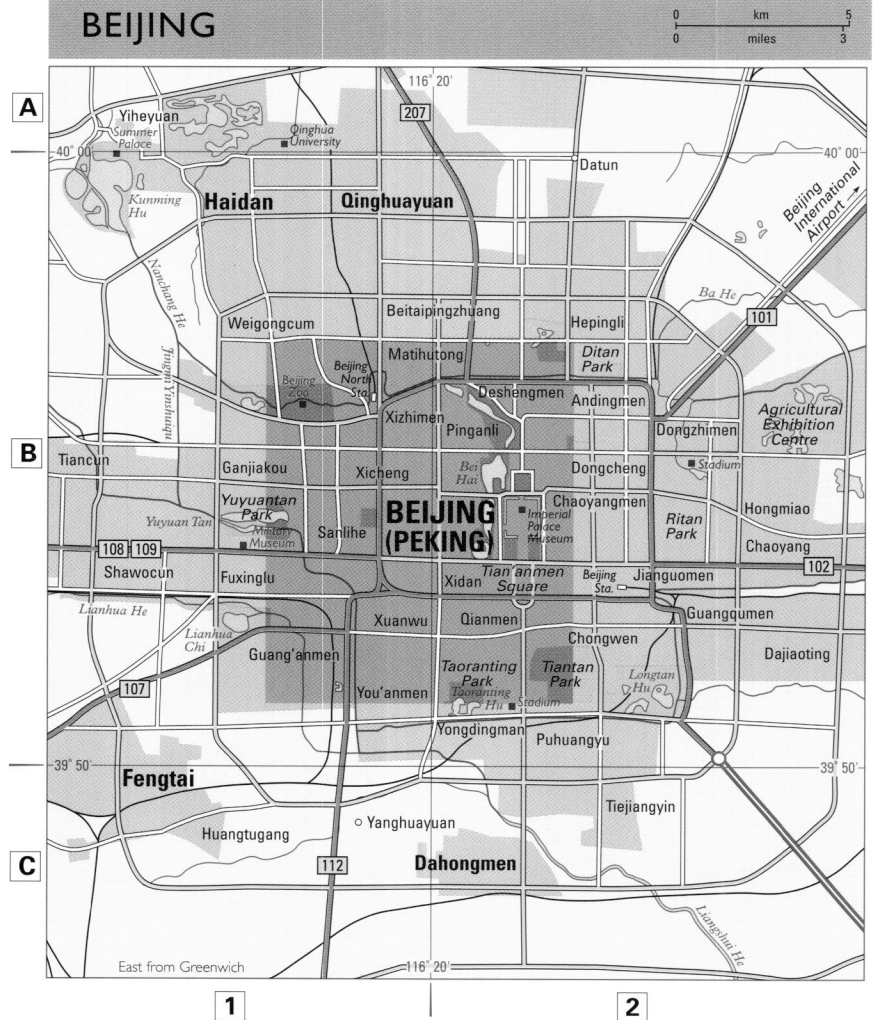

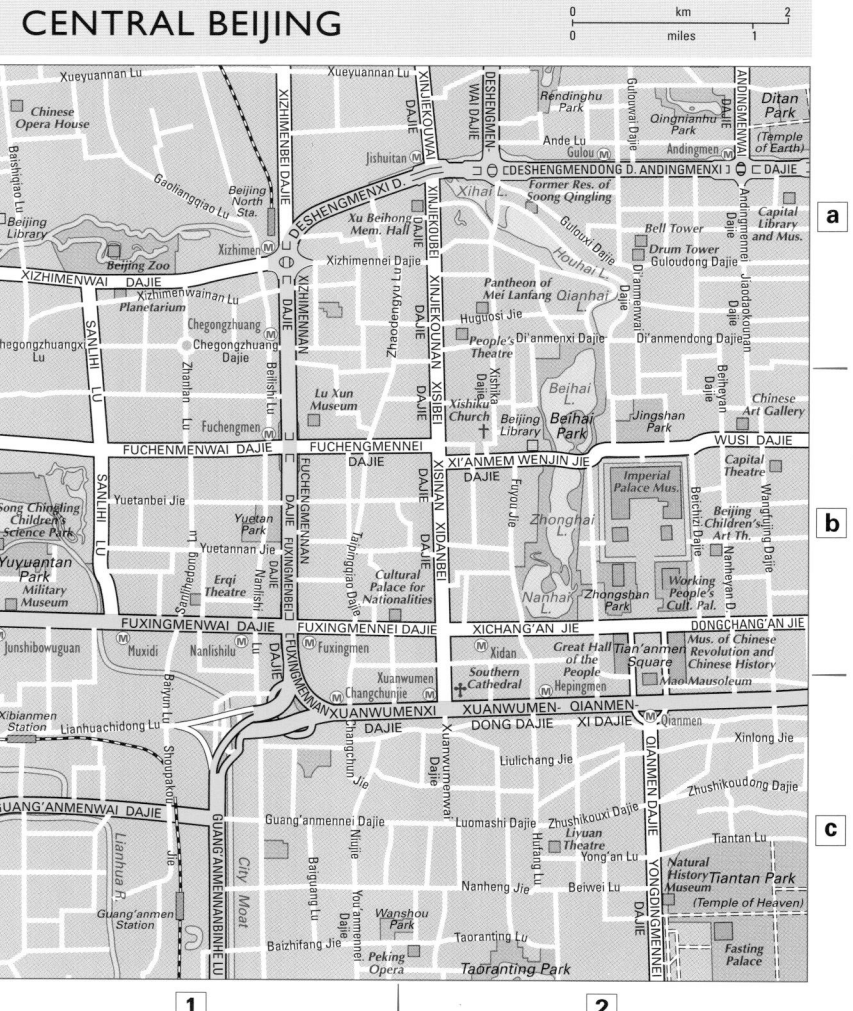

BERLIN

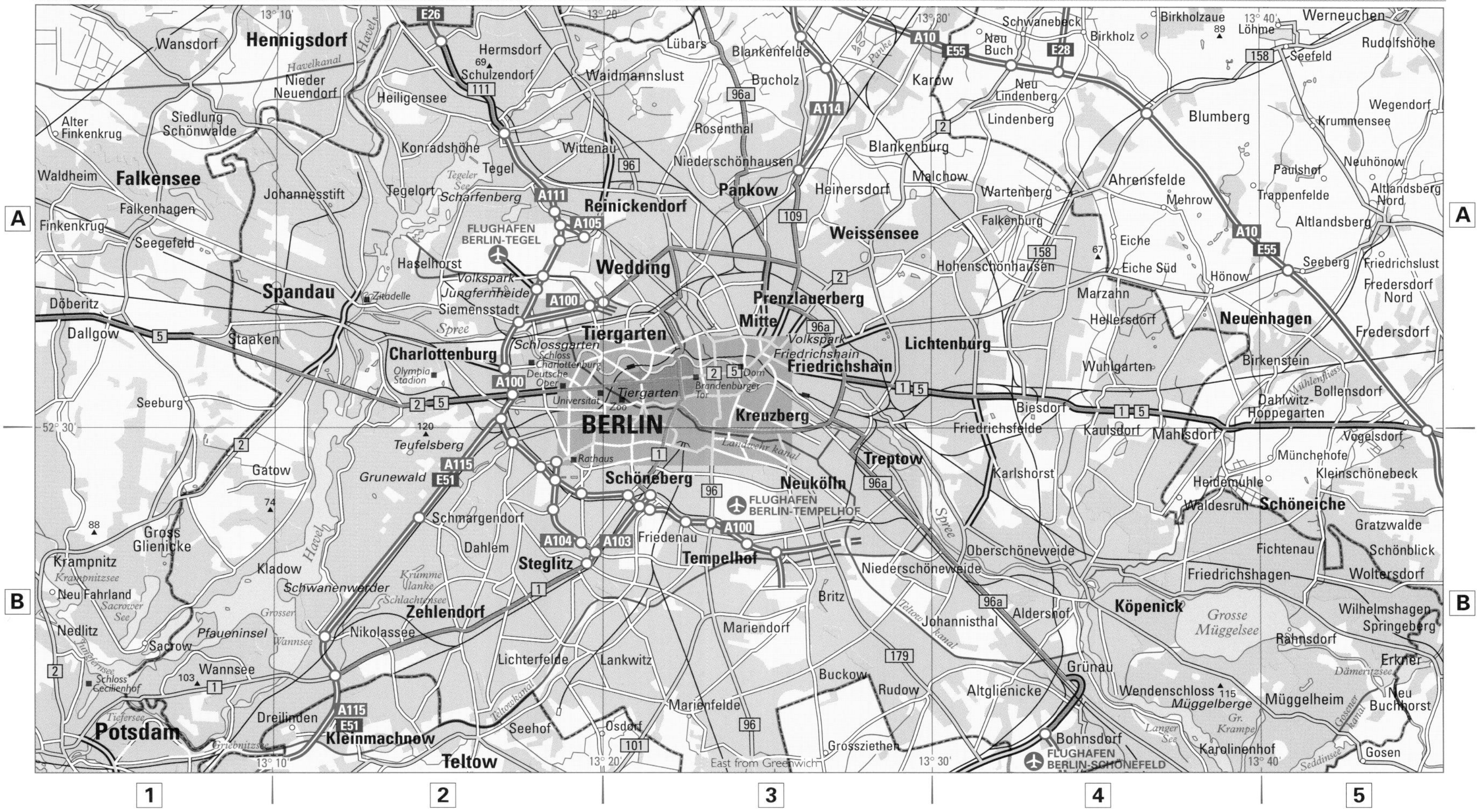

km 0 — 5
miles 0 — 3

A

Wansdorf · Hennigsdorf · Hermsdorf · Schulzendorf · Waidmannslust · Lübars · Blankenfelde · Buchholz · Schwanebeck · Birkholzaue · Löhme · Werneuchen · Rudolfshöhe
Alter Finkenkrug · Siedlung Schönwalde · Nieder Neuendorf · Heiligensee · Tegelort · Scharfenberg · Tegel · Rosenthal · Niederschönhausen · Karow · Neu Lindenberg · Lindenberg · Blumberg · Krummensee · Neuhönow · Wegendorf
Waldheim · Falkensee · Johannesstift · Konradshöhe · Wittenau · Blankenburg · Malchow · Wartenberg · Ahrensfelde · Mehrow · Trappenfelde · Altlandsberg Nord
Finkenkrug · Falkenhagen · **Reinickendorf** · **Pankow** · Heinersdorf · Falkenburg · Hohenschönhausen · Hellersdorf · Eiche · Eiche Süd · Hönow · Seeberg · Friedrichslust · Altlandsberg
Seegefeld · **Spandau** · Haselhorst · FLUGHAFEN BERLIN-TEGEL · Volkspark Jungfernheide · Siemensstadt · **Wedding** · **Weissensee** · Marzahn · **Neuenhagen** · Fredersdorf Nord · Fredersdorf
Döberitz · Dallgow · Staaken · Spree · **Charlottenburg** · Schlossgarten · **Tiergarten** · **Prenzlauerberg** · **Mitte** · **Lichtenburg** · Wuhlgarten · Birkenstein · Bollensdorf
Olympia Stadion · Deutsche Oper · **BERLIN** · **Friedrichshain** · Volkspark Friedrichshain · Biesdorf · Dahlwitz-Hoppegarten
Seeburg · Teufelsberg · Universität · Tiergarten · Brandenburger Tor · **Kreuzberg** · Kaulsdorf · Mahlsdorf · Vogelsdorf

BERLIN

Grunewald · Rathaus · **Schöneberg** · **Neukölln** · **Treptow** · Karlshorst · Münchehofe · Kleinschönebeck
Gatow · Schmargendorf · Dahlem · Friedenau · FLUGHAFEN BERLIN-TEMPELHOF · Oberschöneweide · Heidemühle · Waldesruh · **Schöneiche** · Gratzwalde

B

Krampnitz · Gross Glienicke · Kladow · Schwanenwerder · **Steglitz** · **Tempelhof** · Niederschöneweide · Schönblick · Woltersdorf
Neu Fahrland · Sacrow · Pfaueninsel · **Zehlendorf** · Lichterfelde · Lankwitz · Britz · Johannisthal · Adlershof · **Köpenick** · Grosse Müggelsee · Wilhelmshagen · Springeberg · Erkner
Nedlitz · Pfaueninsel · Nikolassee · Mariendorf · Buckow · Rudow · Grünau · Wendenschloss · Müggelberge · Rahnsdorf · Müggelheim
Wannsee · Schloss Cecilienhof · Mariendorf · Altglienicke · Müggelheim · Neu Buchhorst
Potsdam · Dreilinden · **Kleinmachnow** · Seehof · Osdorf · Grossziethen · Bohnsdorf · FLUGHAFEN BERLIN-SCHÖNEFELD · Karolinenhof · Gosen
Teltow · Marienfelde · East from Greenwich

CENTRAL BERLIN

km 0 — 1
miles 0 — 0.5

CHARLOTTENBURG · **TIERGARTEN** · **MITTE** · **KREUZBERG** · **WILMERSDORF**

a

Schwarzer Weg · Hutten Str. · Turmstrasse · Krankenhaus Moabit · Friedhof · Hannoversche · Rosa-Luxemburg-Pl. · Volksbühne
Kaiserin Augusta Allee · Hansatheater · Alt-Moabit · St. Johannis-Kirche · Lehrter stadtbf. · Charité Krankenhaus · Deutsche Th. und Kammerspiele · Friedrichstadtpalast · Oranienburger Tor
Quedlinburger Str. · Spree · Invalidenstr. · Bode Mus. · Pergamonmus. · Alexanderplatz
Otto-Suhr-Allee · Deutsche Oper · Bellevue · Schloss Bellevue · Haus der Kulturen der Welt · John Foster Dulles Allee · Reichstag · Unter den Linden · Palast d. Rep. · Jannowitzbrücke
Bismarckstrasse · Technische Universität · Tiergarten · Strasse des 17 Juni · Brandenburger Tor · Komische Oper · Staats Oper · Gendarmenmarkt

b

Kantstrasse · Savignypl. · Zoologischer Garten · TIERGARTEN · Grosser Weg · Philharmonie · Kulturforum · National Galerie · Potsdamer Pl. · Bundesministerien · Leipziger Str. · Spittelmarkt · Köpenicker Str.
Budapester Str. · Kurfürstendamm · Europa Center · Wittenbergpl. · Lützow Ufer · Schöneberger Ufer · Anhalter Bf. · Jacobikirche · St. Michael-Kirch

c

WILMERSDORF · Hohenzollerndamm · Bundeshaus · Nollendorfpl. · Bülowstr. · Mus. für Verkehr und Technik · Krankenhaus am Urban · **KREUZBERG** · Kottbusser Tor
Pariser Str. · Preussen park · Kleistpark · Yorckstrasse · Mehringdamm · Friedhof Mehringdamm · Böckler Park · Skalitzer Str.
Konstanzerstrasse · Fehrbelliner Pl. · Grune Wald Strasse · Gneisenaustrasse · Bergmann Str. · Hasen Heide

BOSTON

km 5
miles 3

Great Meadows 71°20'
Nat. Wildlife Refuge
Bedford
Burlington
Woburn
Wakefield
Marblehead
East Acton
West Bedford
Stoneham
North Saugus
Breakheart
Reservation
Greenwood
Clifton
Lynn
Swampscott
Concord
North
Lexington
LAURENCE G.
HANSCOM FIELD
Saugus
Cliftondale
West Lynn
Winchester
Melrose
Mt. Hood
Mem. Park
Nahant Bay
West Concord
Minute Man
Natural History
Park
Lexington
East
Lexington
Arlington
Heights
West
Medford
Malden
Revere
Nahant
ATLANTIC
OCEAN
Fairhaven Hill
Lincoln
Medford
East Point
South Lincoln
Arlington
East
Arlington
Everett
Beachmont
Nahant
Harbor
North Sudbury
Cambridge
Reservoir
Belmont
Wellington
Chelsea
Orient
Heights
Winthrop
Broad
Sound
ESSEX
SUFFOLK
Sudbury
Silver Hill
Waltham
Waverley
Somerville
Charlestown
East
Boston
Goodman Hill
Kendall
Green
Cambridge
Watertown
BOSTON
Logan
INTERNATIONAL
AIRPORT
Massachusetts Bay
Wayland
Weston
Allston
Brighton
Boston
Harbor
Deer
Island
South
Sudbury
Auburndale
Newton
Newtonville
South
Boston
Spectacle
Island
42°20'
Saxonville
Chestnut
Hill
Roxbury
Old Harbor
Thompson
Island
Long
Island
Georges
Island
Point Allerton
Framingham
Brookline
Jamaica
Plain
Franklin
Park
Grove
Hall
Fields
Corner
Dorchester Bay
Hull
Peddocks Island
Wellesley
Needham
Heights
Oak Hill
Roslindale
Dorchester
North
Quincy
Quincy Bay
Grape
Island
Hingham Bay
Nantasket
Beach
Natick
Needham
W. Roxbury
Mattapan
Adams
Shore
Houghs
Neck
North
Cohasset
Brush Hill
Hyde Park
Stony Brook
Res.
Milton
Quincy
Wollaston
Hingham
Dedham

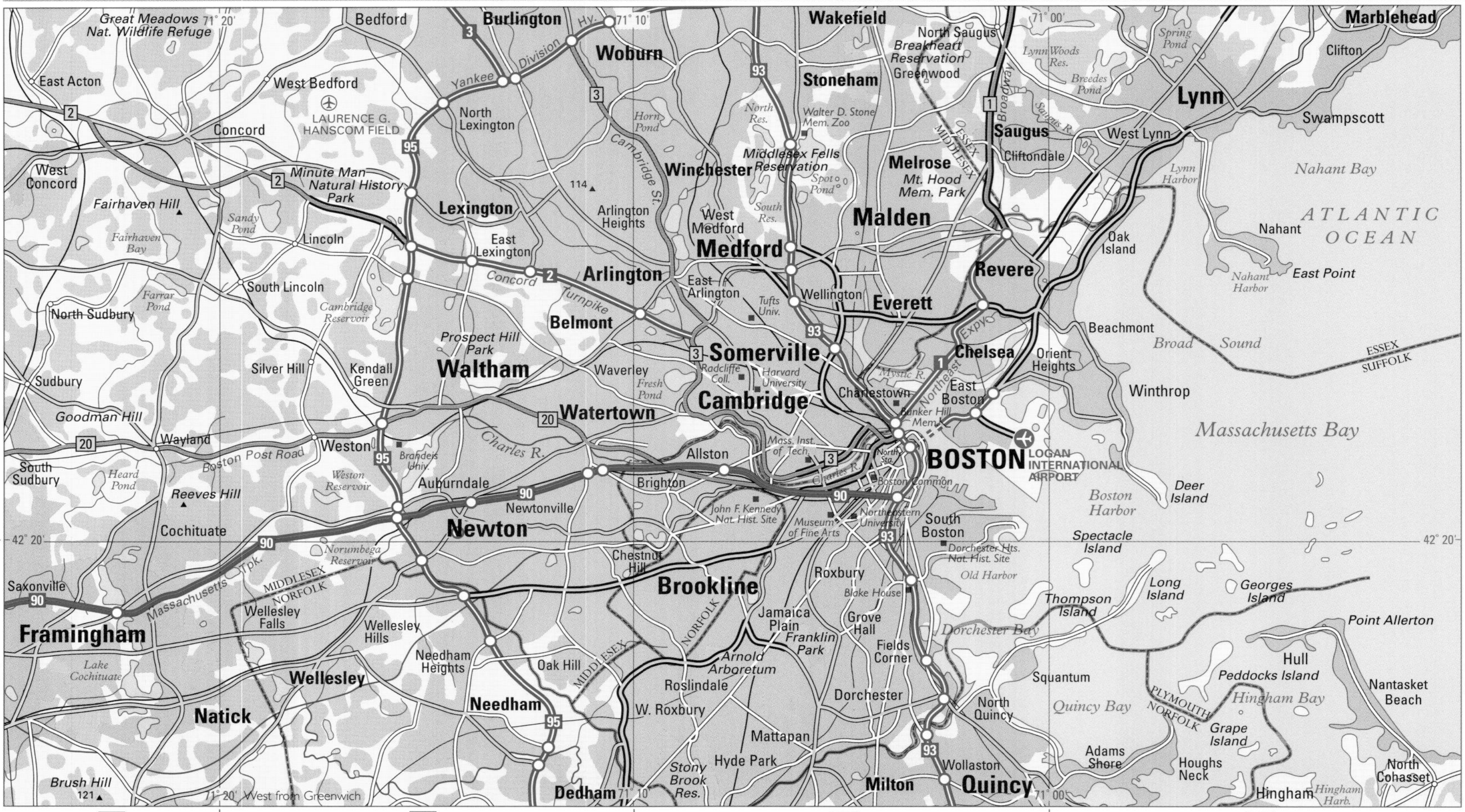

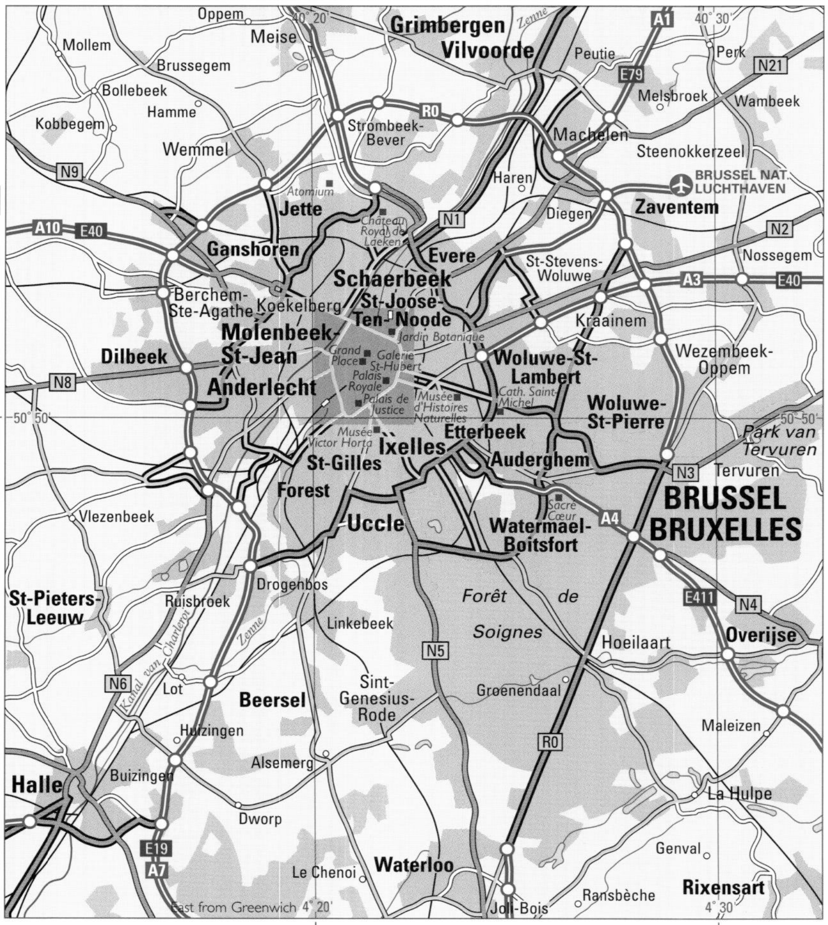

BRUSSELS

km 5
miles 3

Oppem
Grimbergen
Vilvoorde
A1
Mollem
Meise
Peutie
Brussegem
Strombeek-
Bever
Machelen
BRUSSEL NAT.
LUCHTHAVEN
Bollebeek
Hamme
Wemmel
Haren
Zaventem
N9
Atomium
Jette
Evere
St-Stevens-
Woluwe
Ganshoren
Schaerbeek
St-Joost-
Ten-Noode
Kraainem
Wezembeek-
Oppem
Berchem-
Ste-Agathe
Koekelberg
Molenbeek-
St-Jean
Woluwe-St-
Lambert
Dilbeek
Anderlecht
Woluwe-
St-Pierre
Park van
Tervuren
Ixelles
Etterbeek
Auderghem
St-Gilles
Forest
BRUSSEL
BRUXELLES
Uccle
Watermael-
Boitsfort
St-Pieters-
Leeuw
Ruisbroek
Forêt de
Soignes
Overijse
Vlezenbeek
Drogenbos
Linkebeek
Beersel
Sint-
Genesius-
Rode
Groenendaal
Hoeilaart
Halle
Buizingen
Huizingen
Alsemberg
Dworp
Waterloo
Le Chenoi
Genval
Rixensart

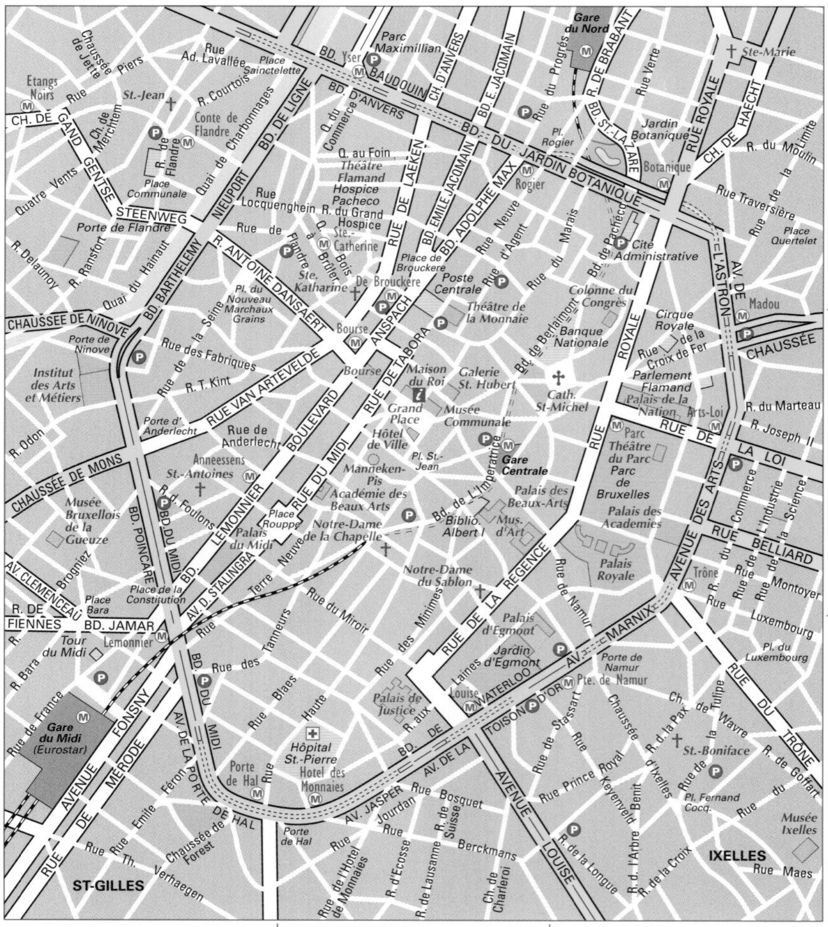

CENTRAL BRUSSELS

km 0.5
miles

ST-GILLES
IXELLES

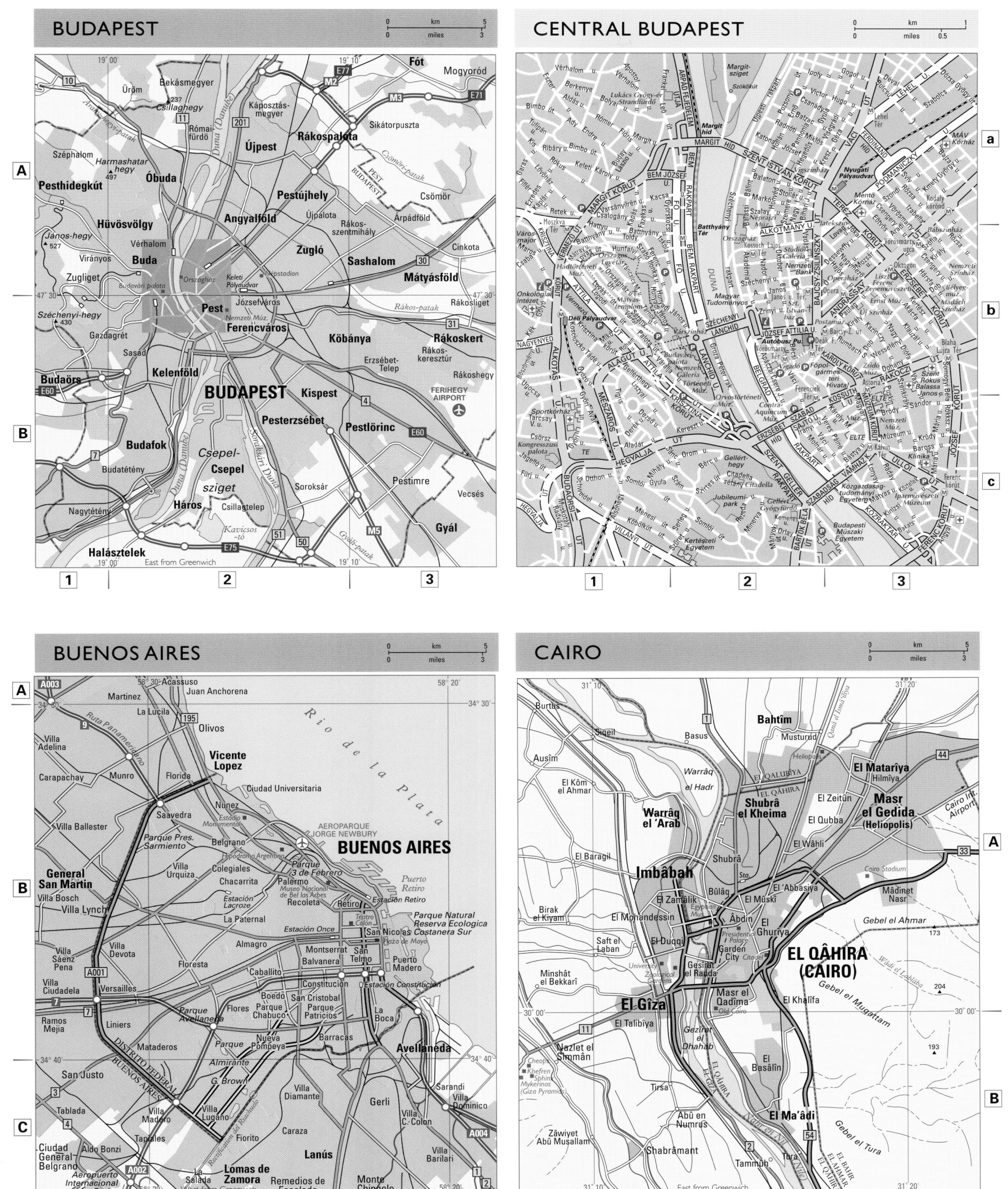

CALCUTTA (KOLKATA)

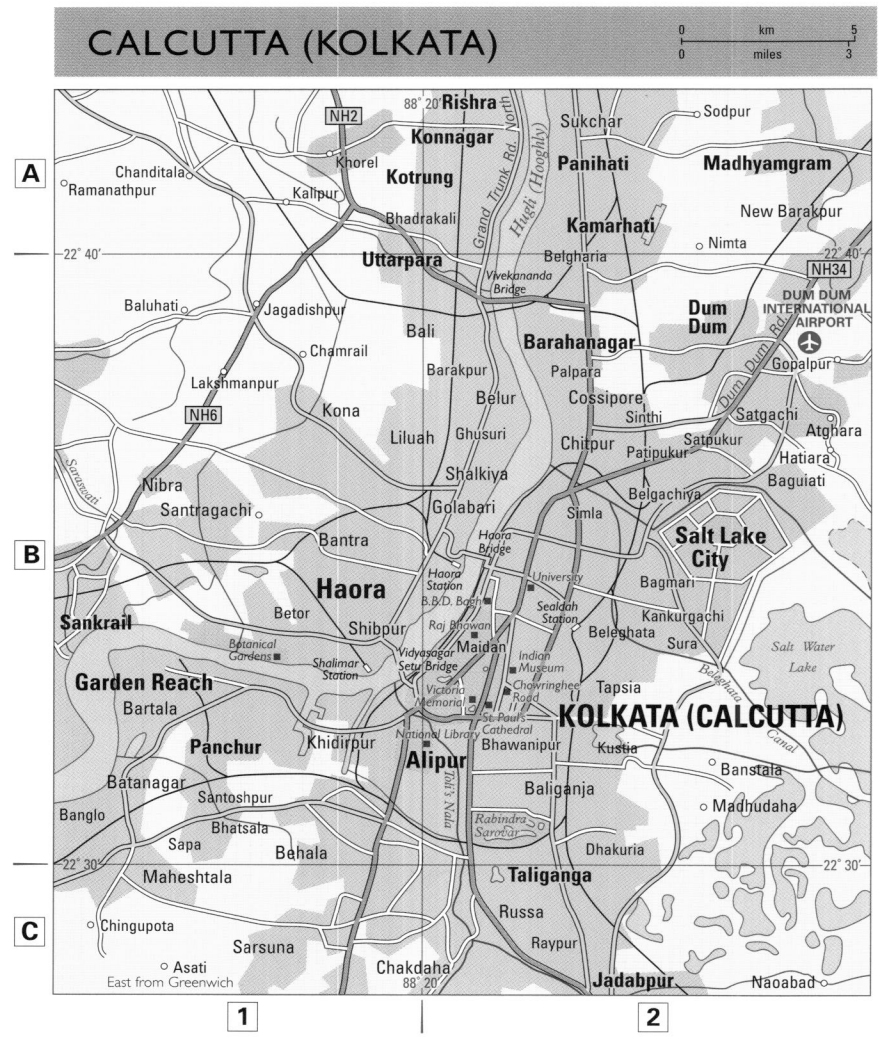

CANTON

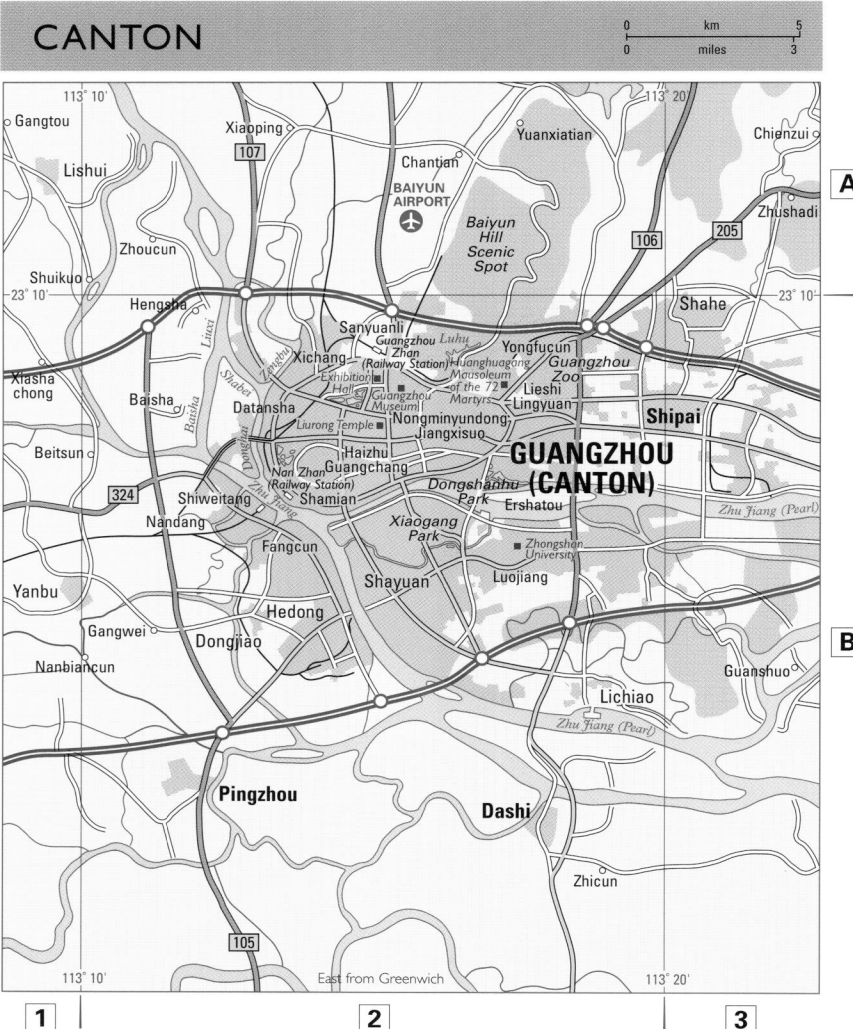

CAPE TOWN

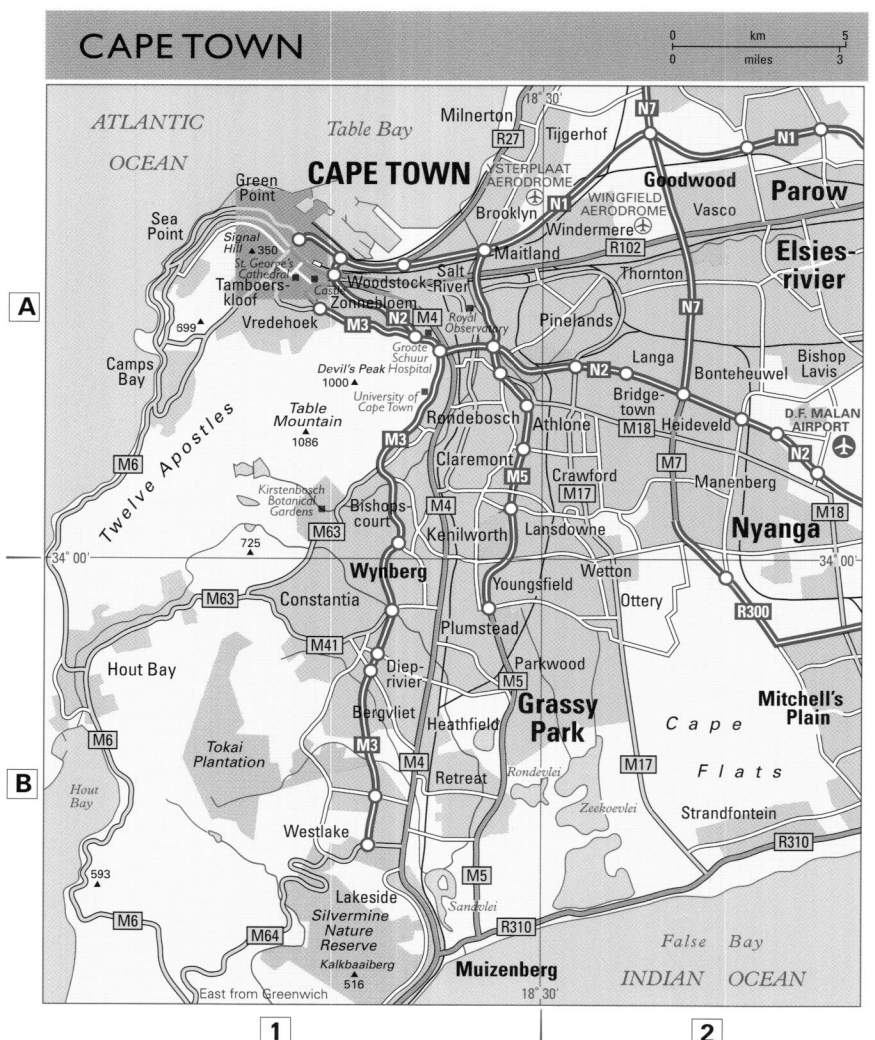

CENTRAL CAPE TOWN

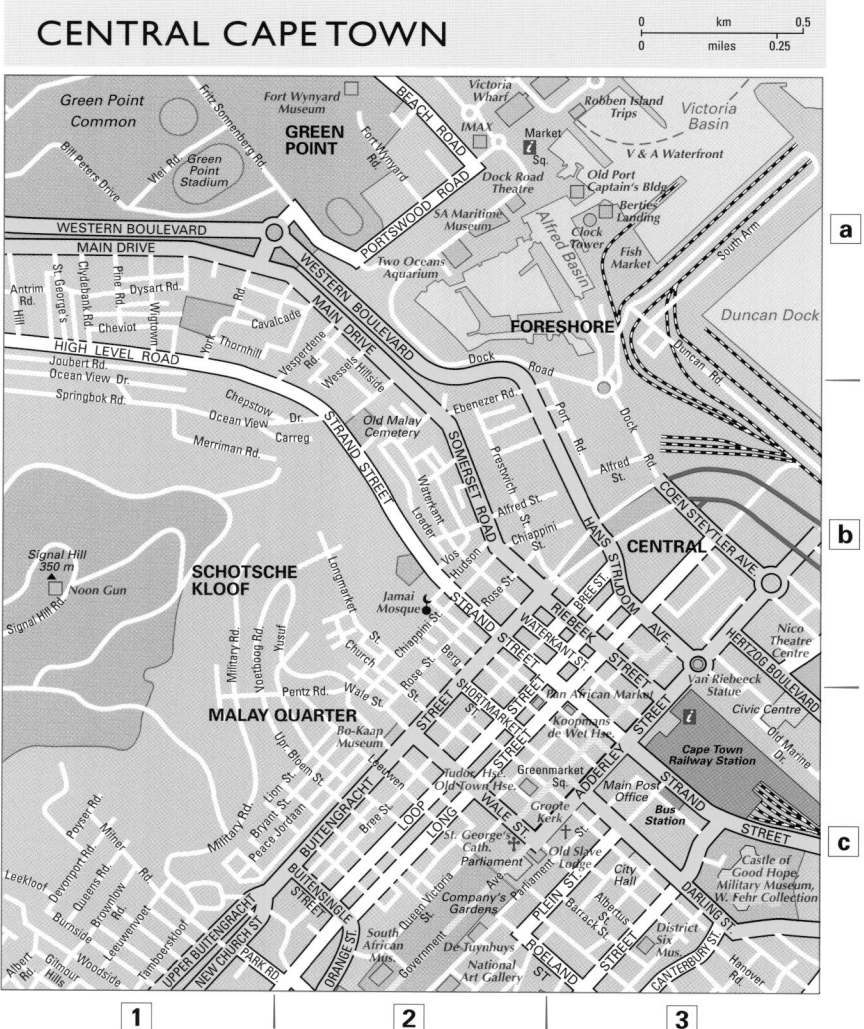

CHICAGO

km 5
miles 3

LAKE MICHIGAN

Evanston
Northwestern University
Baha'i Temple
Wilmette
Skokie
Morton Grove
Glenview
Glenview Countryside
Niles
Park Ridge
Des Plaines
CHICAGO O'HARE INTERNATIONAL AIRPORT
Rosemont
Schiller Park
Franklin Park
Northlake
Stone Park
Melrose Park
Bellwood
Maywood
Westchester
La Grange Park
La Grange
Brookfield
North Riverside
Riverside
Lyons
Broadview
Miller Meadow
Forest Park
Oak Park
Elmwood Park
River Forest
River Grove
Harwood Heights
Norridge
Norwood Park
Edison Park
Dunning
Portage Park
Belmont Cragin
Austin
Cicero
Berwyn
Stickney
Summit
McCook
Hodgkins
Countryside
Indian Head Park
Willow Springs
Argonne Forest
Palos Hills Forest
Palos Park
Palos Heights
Worth
Palos Hills
Hickory Hills
Justice
Bridgeview
Bedford Park
Burbank
Chicago Ridge
Oak Lawn
Hometown
Ashburn
Chicago Lawn
Marquette Park
Hayford
Gage Park
Brighton Park
McKinley Park
Bridgeport
Douglas Park
Garfield Park
Humboldt Park
West Town
Logan Square
Avondale
Irving Park
Lakeview
Wrigley Field
Uptown
Rogers Park
Loyola University
Lincoln Park
Old Town
Near North
Gold Coast
John Hancock Center
Navy Pier
The Loop
CHICAGO
Chinatown
Univ. of Illinois at Chicago
United Center
Comiskey Park
Sherman Park
Ogden Park
Englewood
Washington Park
Univ. of Chicago
Hyde Park
Mus. of Science & Industry
South Shore
Chatham
Roseland
Morgan Park
Beverly
Mount Greenwood
Merrionette Park
Evergreen Park
Blue Island
Robbins
Alsip
Calumet Park
South Deering
Lake Calumet
Dan Ryan Expwy.
Kennedy Expwy.
Eisenhower Expwy.
Stevenson Expwy.
Edens Expwy.
Tri-State Tollway
Bishop Ford Mem. Expwy.
Chicago Skyway
CHICAGO MIDWAY AIRPORT
Frank Lloyd Wright Home
Field Museum
Grant Park
Burnham Park
Soldier Field
Adler Planetarium
Lincoln Park Zoo
Belmont Harbor
North Shore Channel
Des Plaines River
Chicago Sanitary and Ship Canal

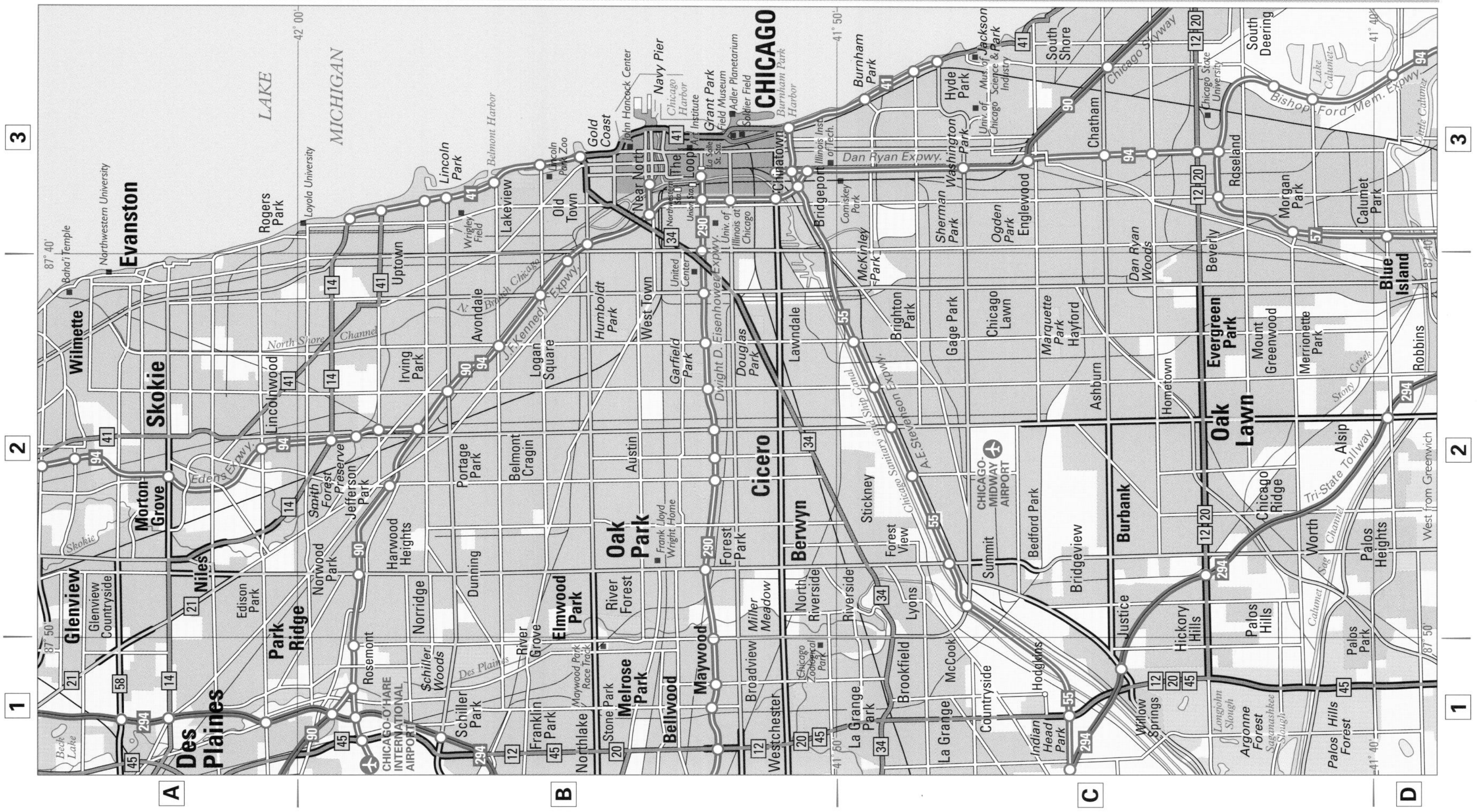

3 | 2 | 1
A | B | C | D

CENTRAL CHICAGO

km 1
miles 0.5

Outer Harbor
Navy Pier
Olive Park
Ohio St. Beach
Lake Point Tower
Streeter Dr.
LAKE MICHIGAN
Chicago Harbor
Adler Planetarium
Shedd Aquarium
E. Solidarity Dr.
Merrill C. Meigs Field
Burnham Park Harbor
McCormack Place East
McCormack Place West
Soldier Field
Field Museum of Nat. History
Burnham Park
SOUTH LAKE SHORE DRIVE EAST
SOUTH LAKE SHORE DRIVE WEST
LAKE SHORE DR.
Grant Park
Buckingham Fountain
Art Institute of Chicago
Chicago Yacht Club
Ogden Slip
NORTH LAKE SHORE DRIVE
Oak St. Beach
GOLD COAST
John Hancock Center
Water Tower Place
Northwestern Memorial Hosp.
E CHICAGO AVE
E Chestnut St
E Delaware Pl
E Oak St
E Division St
E Superior St
E Huron St
E Erie St
E Ontario St
E Grand Ave
E Illinois St
MICHIGAN AVENUE
N State Street
N Rush St
N Wabash Ave
Wrigley Bldg.
Tribune Tower
Marshall Field's
Prudential Building
Randolph St. Sta.
Van Buren St. Sta.
Roosevelt Road Sta.
COLUMBUS DRIVE
Monroe Drive
Jackson Dr.
Balbo Dr.
E Randolph
E Lake St
E Wacker Dr
E South Water St
E Monroe
E Madison
E Washington
E Adams St
E Jackson Dr
E Congress
E Harrison St
E Balbo Ave
E 8th St
E 11th St
E 13th St
E 14th St
E 16th St
E 18th St
E 21st St
E Cermak Rd
SOUTH MICHIGAN AVENUE
SOUTH STATE STREET
S Calumet Ave
S Prairie Ave
S Indiana Ave
S Wabash Ave
W Cermak Rd
ROOSEVELT ROAD
S Clark Street
S State St
S Wentworth Ave
CHINATOWN
SOUTH LOOP
PRINTER'S ROW
THE LOOP
NEAR NORTH
RIVER NORTH
NEW ORLEANS ST
W DIVISION ST
W CHICAGO AVENUE
W Oak St
W Huron St
W Erie St
W Ontario St
W Ohio St
W Grand Ave
W Illinois St
W Kinzie St
W Lake St
W Randolph St
W Washington
W Madison
W Monroe
W Adams St
W Jackson Blvd
W Van Buren St
W Congress Pkwy
W Harrison St
W Polk St
N Larrabee Street
N Hudson Avenue
N Kingsbury St
N Franklin St
N Wells St
N LASALLE
N Clark St
N Dearborn St
N Clinton St
N Canal St
S Canal St
S Clinton St
Merchandise Mart
Sears Tower
La Salle St. Sta.
Union Sta.
Northwestern Sta.
Main Post Office
Opera Ho.
City Hall-County Bldg.
N WACKER DR
S WACKER DR
Chicago River
North Branch
South Branch
CHICAGO RIVER
W 18th St
COPYRIGHT PHILIP'S

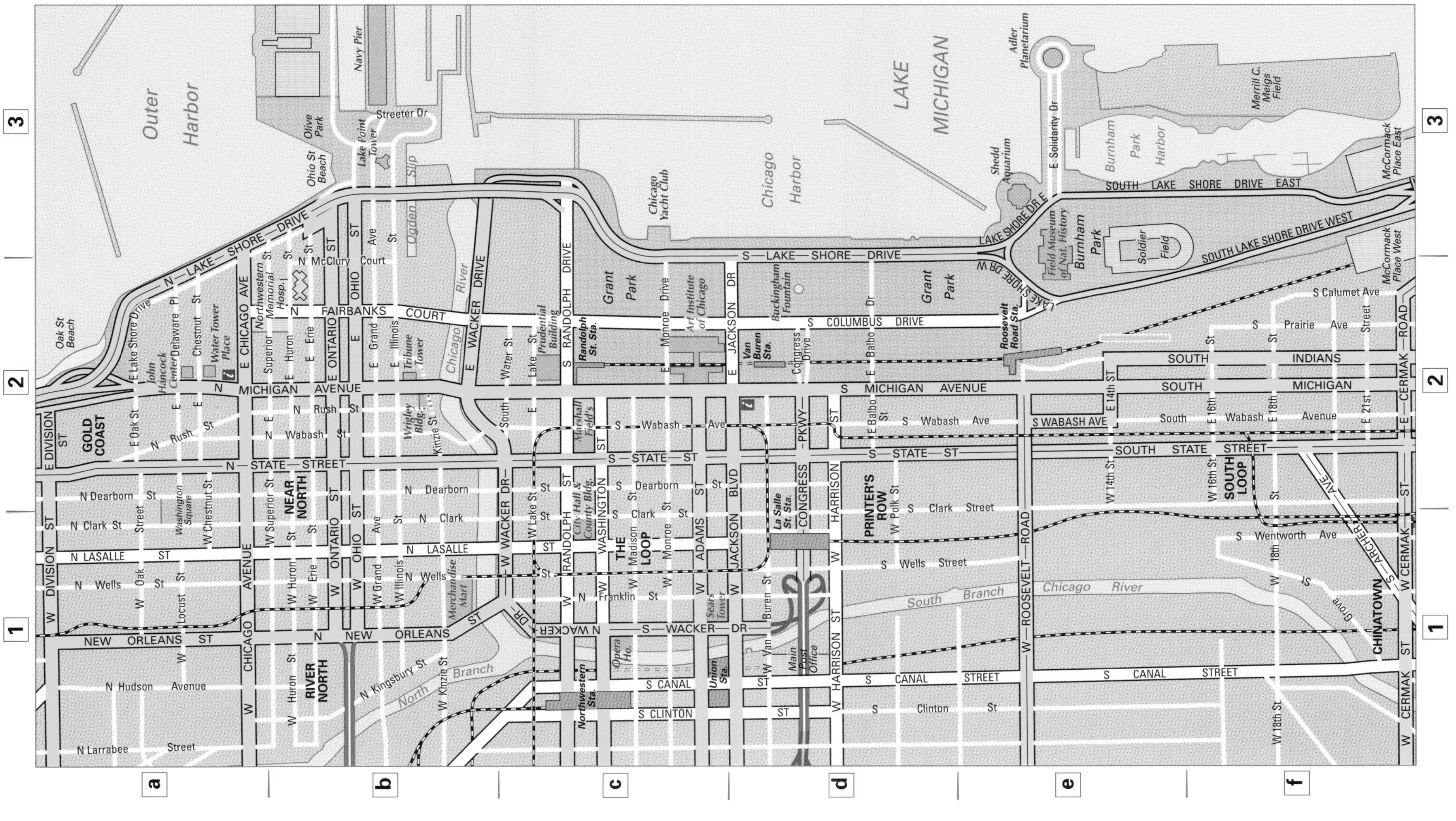

3 | 2 | 1
a | b | c | d | e | f

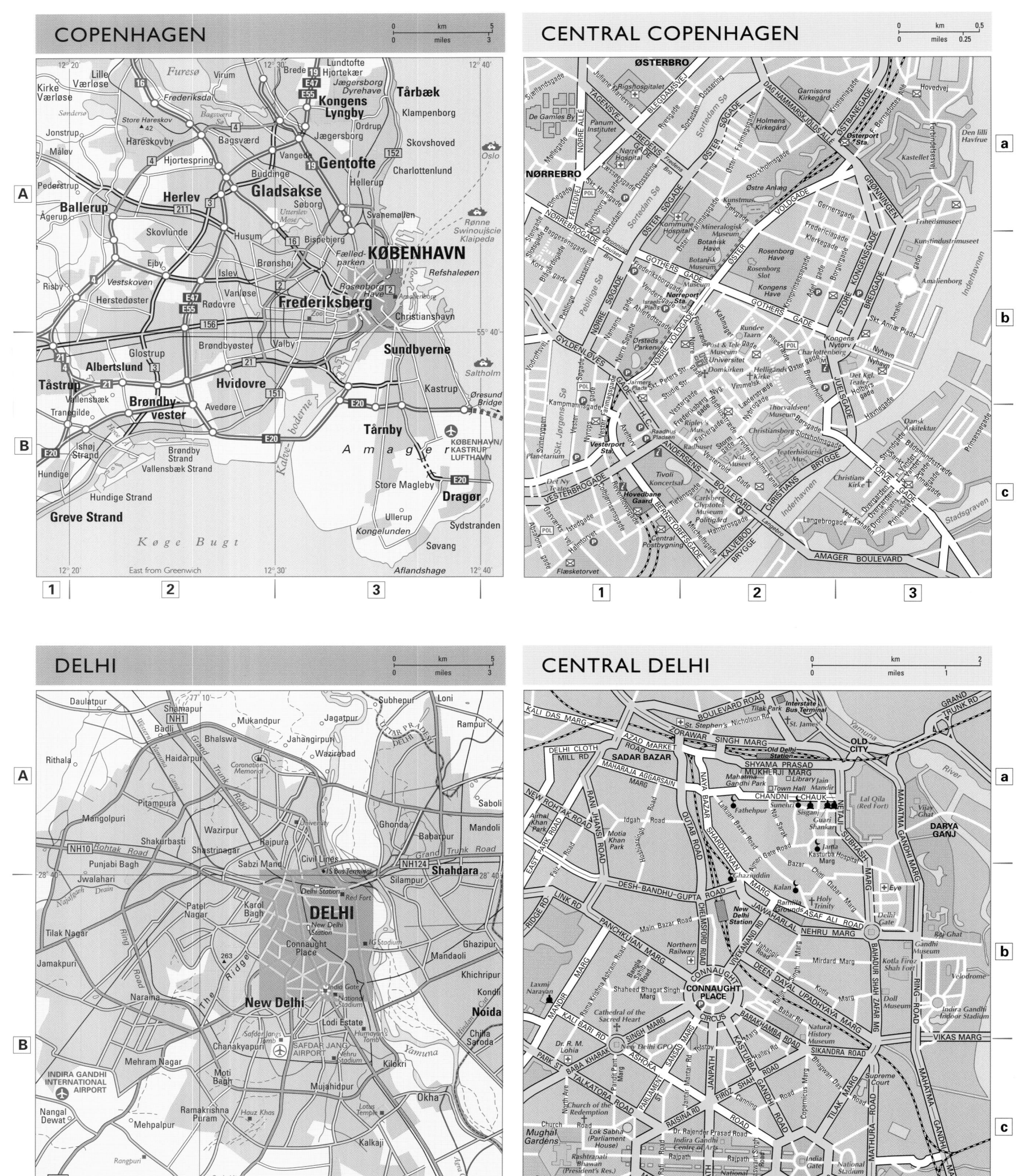

COPENHAGEN

km 5
miles 3

12° 20' Lille Værløse Virum Lundtofte Hjortekær 12° 40'
Kirke Værløse 16 Frederiksdal Brede Jægersborg Tårbæk
Værløse E47 Dyrehave Klampenborg
Søndersø E55 Kongens Lyngby
Jonstrup Store Hareskov 42 Bagsværd Sø Ordrup Skovshoved
Måløv Hareskovby Bagsværd Jægersborg 152 Oslo
Pederstrup 4 Hjortespring Buddinge Vangede 19 Gentofte Charlottenlund
A Herlev Gladsakse Søborg Hellerup
Ballerup 211 Svanemøllen
Agerup Skovlunde Husum 16 Bispebjerg Utterslev Mose Fælled- parken Refshaleøen
Risby 4 Vestskoven Ejby Brønshøj Islev **KØBENHAVN**
Hørstedøster Vanløse Rosenborg Have Amalienborg
E47 Rødovre Zoo **Frederiksberg** Christianshavn
E55 156 Brøndbyøster Valby 55° 40'
21 Glostrup Sundbyerne
4 Albertslund 3 21
Tåstrup 21 Hvidovre 151 Kastrup
Vallensbæk Avedøre Øresund Bridge
Brøndby vester Brøndby Strand Saltholm
Tranegilde E20 E20 Tårnby KØBENHAVN/ KASTRUP LUFTHAVN
B E20 Ishøj Strand Vallensbæk Strand Amager E20
Hundige Store Magleby **Dragør**
Hundige Strand Ullerup Sydstranden
Greve Strand Kongelunden Søvang

Køge Bugt

12° 20' East from Greenwich 12° 30' Aflandshage 12° 40'

1 **2** **3**

CENTRAL COPENHAGEN

km 0,5
miles 0,25

ØSTERBRO
Rigshospitalet Garnisons Kirkegård Hovedvej
De Gamles By Panum Institutet Holmens Kirkegård Østerport Sta. Den lille Havfrue
NØRREBRO Nørre Hospital Kastellet Frihedsmuseet
Kommune Hospital Kunstmus. Østre Anlæg Kunstindustrimuseet
Botanisk Have Rosenborg Have Amalienborg
Botanisk Museum Rosenborg Slot Kongens Have
Nørreport Sta. Nyhavn
a
Rundee Taarn Kongens Nytorv Det Kgl. Teater
Ørsteds Parken Universitet Helligånds Kirke Dansk Arkitektur
Domkirken Vimmelsk.
b
Rådhus Pladsen Thorvaldsen Museum Christiansborg Slotsholmen Christians Kirke
Vesterport Sta. Ripley's Mus. Nat. Museet Teaterhistorisk Mus.
Planetarium BOULEVARD
Det Ny Teater Tivoli Koncertsal CHRISTIANS Stadsgraven
Hovedbane Gaard Ny Carlsberg Glyptotek Politigård Langebrogade
VESTERBROGADE Central Postbygning AMAGER BOULEVARD
c
Flæsketorvet

1 **2** **3**

DELHI

km 5
miles 3

Daulatpur Shamapur NH1 Subhepur Loni
Badli Bhalswa Mukandpur Jagatpur Rampur
Rithala Haidarpur Jahangirpuri Wazirabad UTTAR PRADESH DELHI
Mangolpuri Pitampura Coronation Memorial Saboli
A Shakurbasti Wazirpur University Ghonda Babarpur Mandoli
Punjabi Bagh Shastrinagar Rajpura Grand Trunk Road
NH10 Rohtak Road Sabzi Mand Civil Lines IS Bus Terminal NH124 **Shahdara**
Jwalahari Nangloi Drain Silampur 28° 40'
Tilak Nagar Patel Nagar Karol Bagh Delhi Station Red Fort
Jamakpuri **DELHI** New Delhi Station Ghazipur
263 Connaught Place Mandaoli
Ring Road The Ridge IG Stadium Khichripur
Naraina India Gate **New Delhi** Kondli **Noida**
Chanakyapuri National Stadium Lodi Estate Chila Saroda
B Mehram Nagar Safdar Jangs Tomb Humayun's Tomb Yamuna
INDIRA GANDHI INTERNATIONAL AIRPORT Moti Bagh SAFDAR JANG AIRPORT Nehru Stadium Kilokri
Ramakrishna Puram Mujahidpur Okha
Nangal Dewat Hauz Khas Lotus Temple
NH8 Mehpalpur Kalkaji
Rangpuri Qutb Minar
Mahrauli NH2
East from Greenwich 77° 10' Tughlakabad

1 **2**

CENTRAL DELHI

km 2
miles 1

BOULEVARD ROAD Tilak Park Interstate Bus Terminal GRAND TRUNK RD.
KALI DAS MARG St. Stephen's Nicholson Road St. James Yamuna River
ZORAWAR SINGH MARG Old Delhi Station **OLD CITY**
DELHI CLOTH MILL RD. **SADAR BAZAR** SHYAMA PRASAD MUKHERJI MARG Mahatma Gandhi Park Library Jain
MAHARAJA AGGARSAIN MARG Town Hall Mandir Lal Qila (Red Fort) Vijay Ghat
NEW ROHTAK ROAD Ajmal Khan Park CHANDNI CHAUK Fathepur Sunehri Sisgani NETAJI **DARYA GANJ**
RAN JHANS ROAD Motia Khan Park Idgah QUTAB ROAD Gauri Shankar Jama Masjid MAHATMA GANDHI MARG
EAST PARK ROAD Fair Gate Kasturba Hospital Marg
NEW ROHTAK ROAD Ghaziuddin Bazar Chitli Tabar Eye
DESH-BANDHU-GUPTA ROAD Kalan SUBHASH Delhi Gate Raj Ghat
LINK RD. New Delhi Station Bamila Holy Trinity BAHADUR SHAH ZAFAR MARG Gandhi Museum
RIDGE RD. Northern Railway ASAF ALI ROAD Kotla Firoz Shah Fort Velodrome
Laxmi Narayan Main Bazar Road JAWAHARLAL NEHRU MARG Doll Museum Indira Gandhi Indoor Stadium
Shaheed Bhagat Singh Marg Jahangir House **CONNAUGHT PLACE** Mirdard Marg Kotla RING ROAD **VIKAS MARG**
PANCHKUAN MARG Rama Krishna Ashram Marg DEEN DAYAL UPADHYAYA MARG
MANDIR Cathedral of the Sacred Heart Kali Bari Marg CONNAUGHT CIRCUS Baba Kharak BARAKHAMBA ROAD Natural History Museum
Dr. R. M. Lohia New Delhi GPO KASTURBA GANDHI MARG SIKANDRA ROAD Supreme Court
PARK ST. ASHOKA SANSAD JANPATH Firoz Shah Rd. Bhagwan Das TILAK MARG **MATHURA GANDHI MARG**
TALKATORA ROAD BABA KHARAK PARLIAMENT Church of the Redemption Pandit Pant Marg Mantar Rd. Copernicus National Stadium
Church Road RAISINA RD. Lok Sabha (Parliament House) Dr. Rajender Prasad Road India Gate Purana Qila (Old Fort)
Mughal Gardens Indira Gandhi Centre of Arts SHERSHAH RD.
Rashtrapati Bhawan (President's Res.) Rajpath South Ave Thyagraj Maulana Azad Rd. MOTILAL NEHRU MG National Museum AKBAR ROAD SHAHJAHAN KAMRAJ MG **NEW DELHI**

1 **2** **3**

DUBLIN

CENTRAL DUBLIN

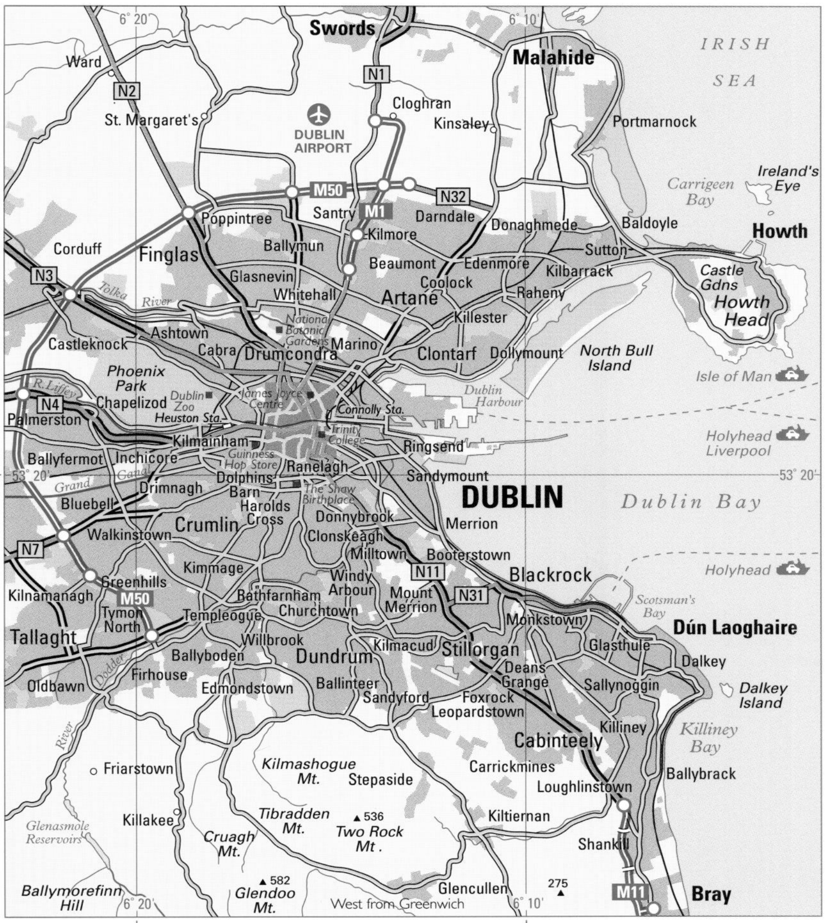

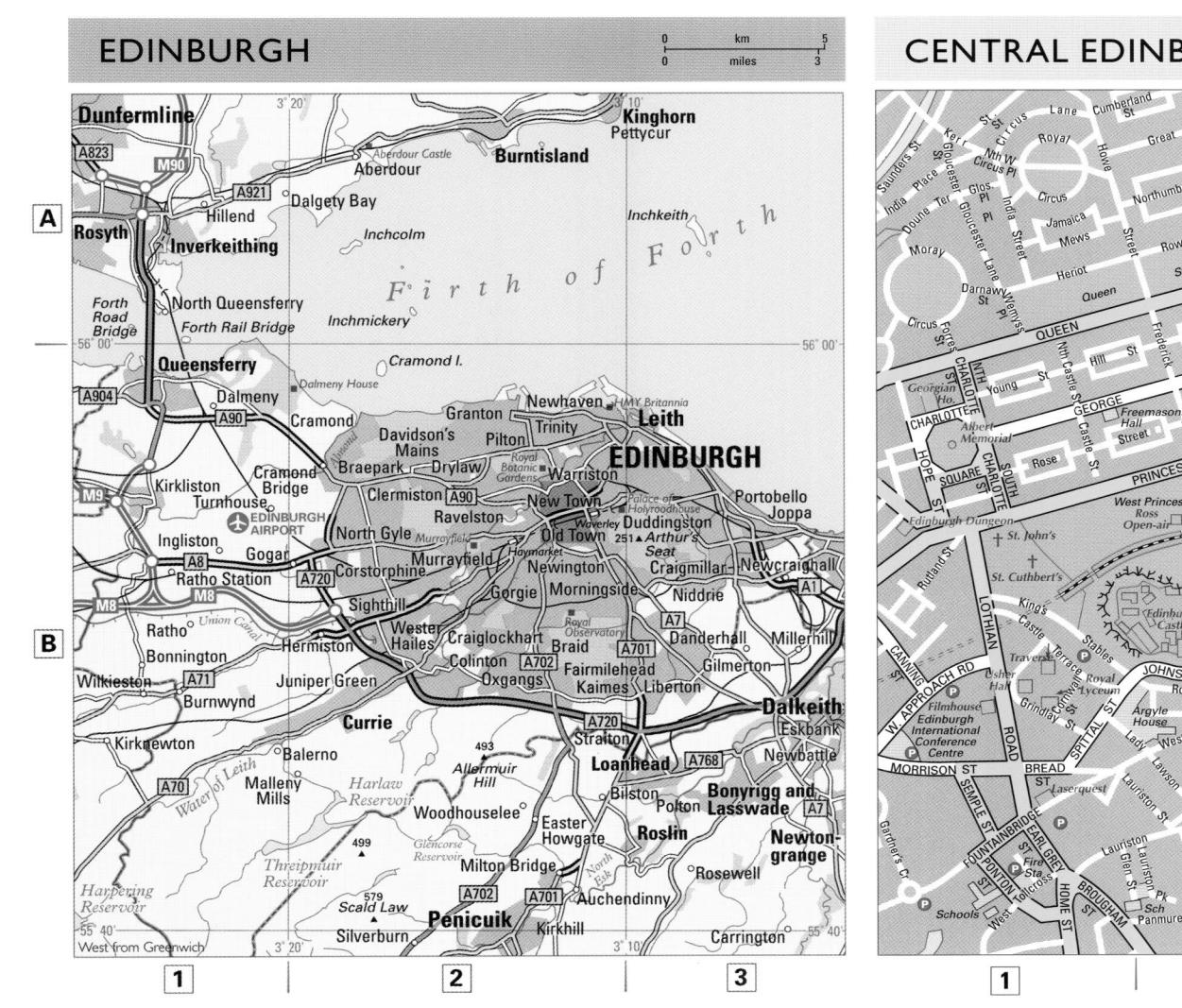

EDINBURGH

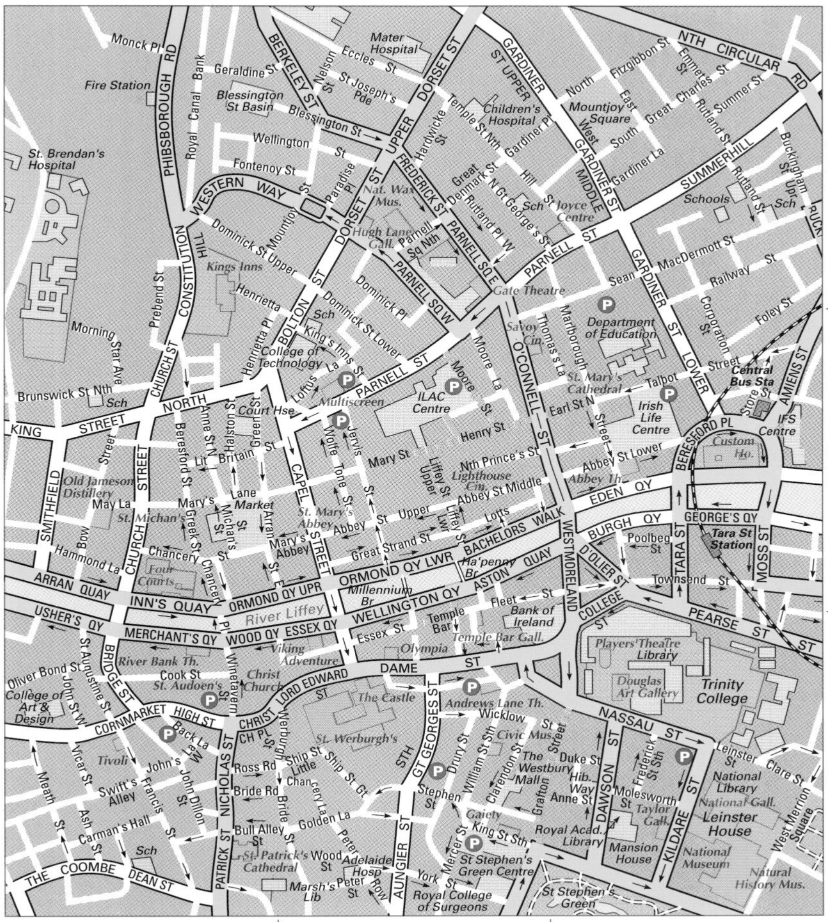

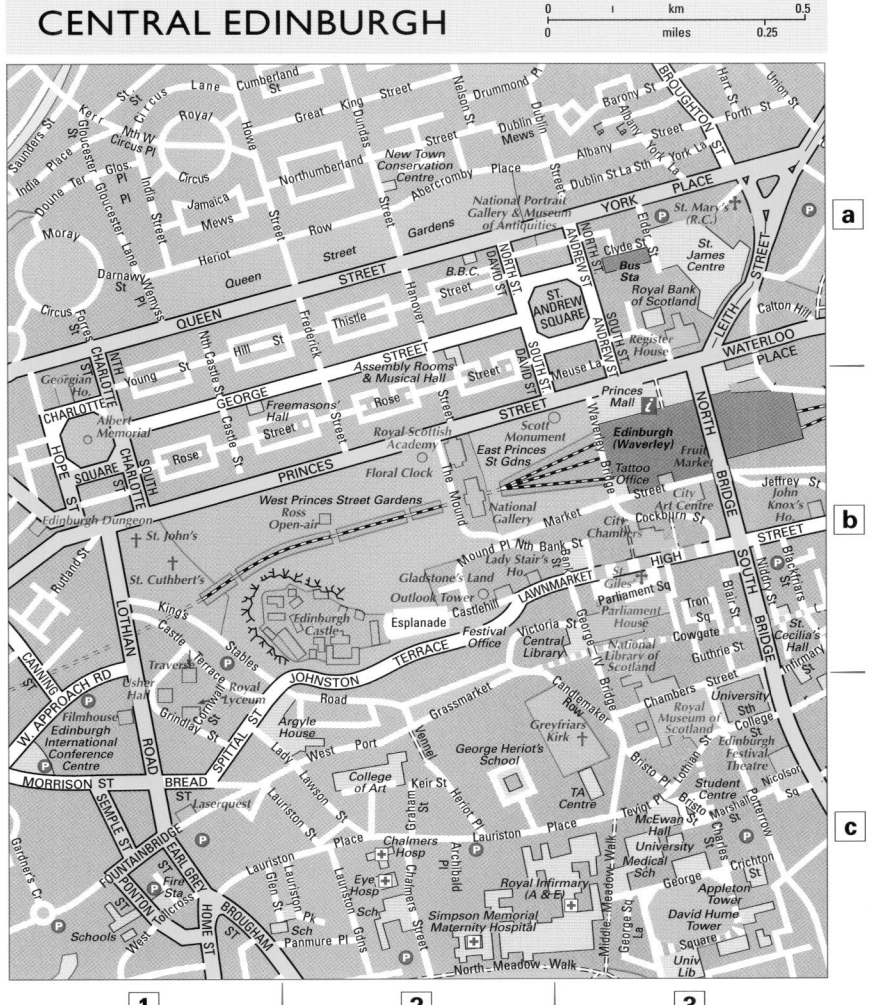

CENTRAL EDINBURGH

COPYRIGHT PHILIP'S

HELSINKI

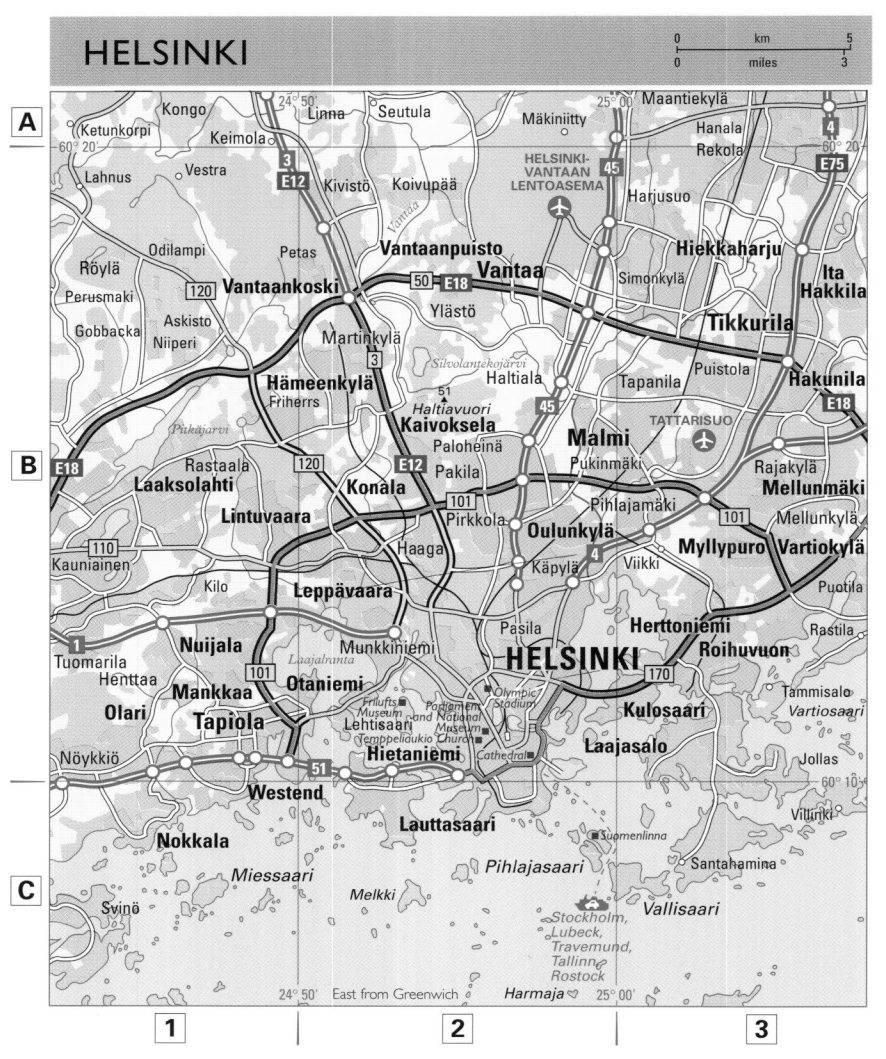

ISTANBUL

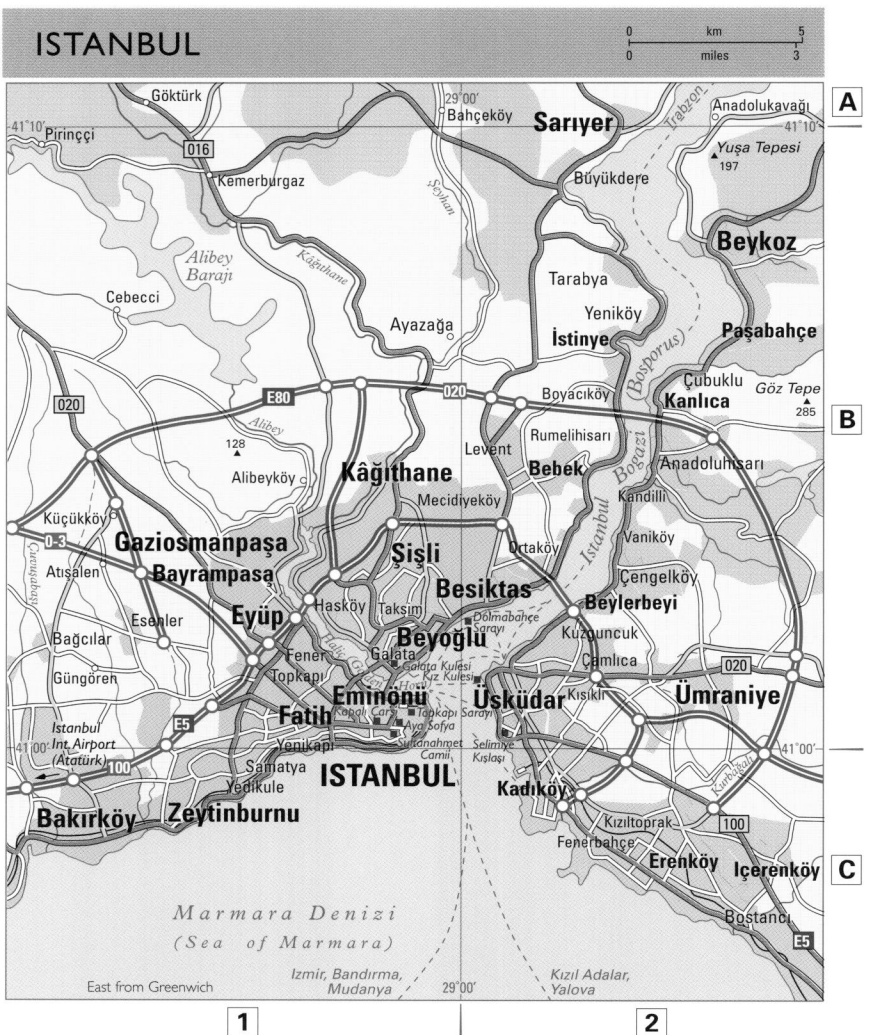

HONG KONG

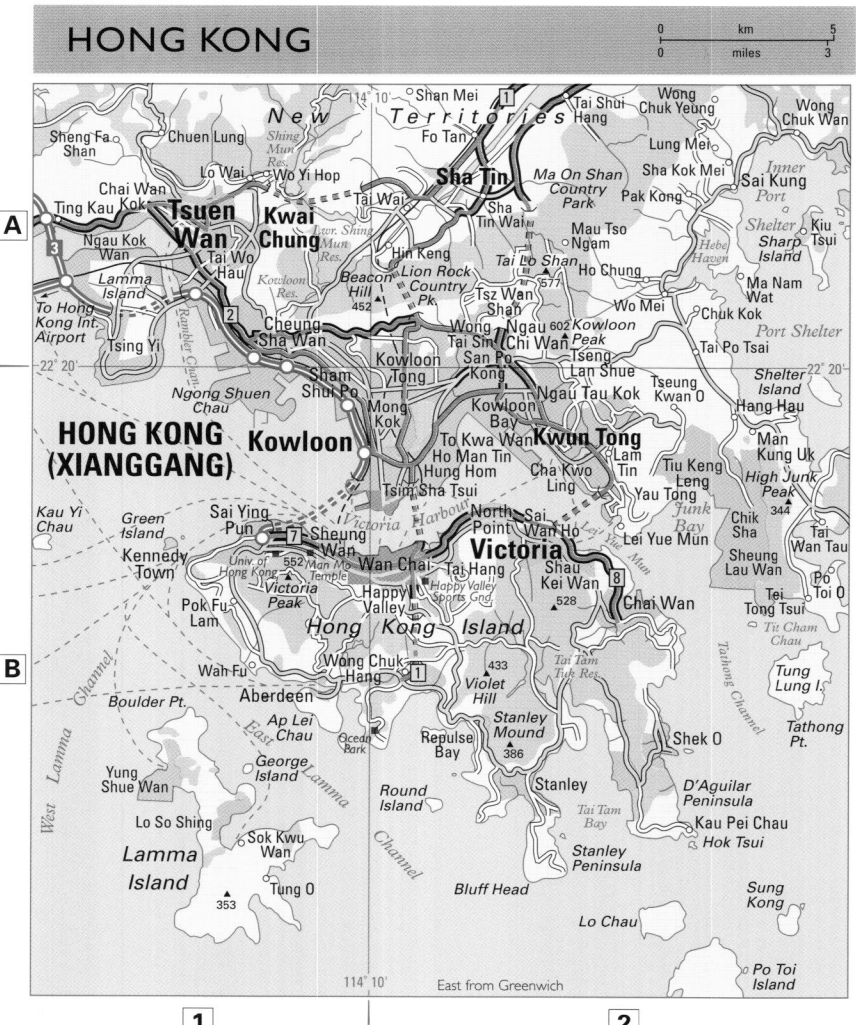

CENTRAL HONG KONG

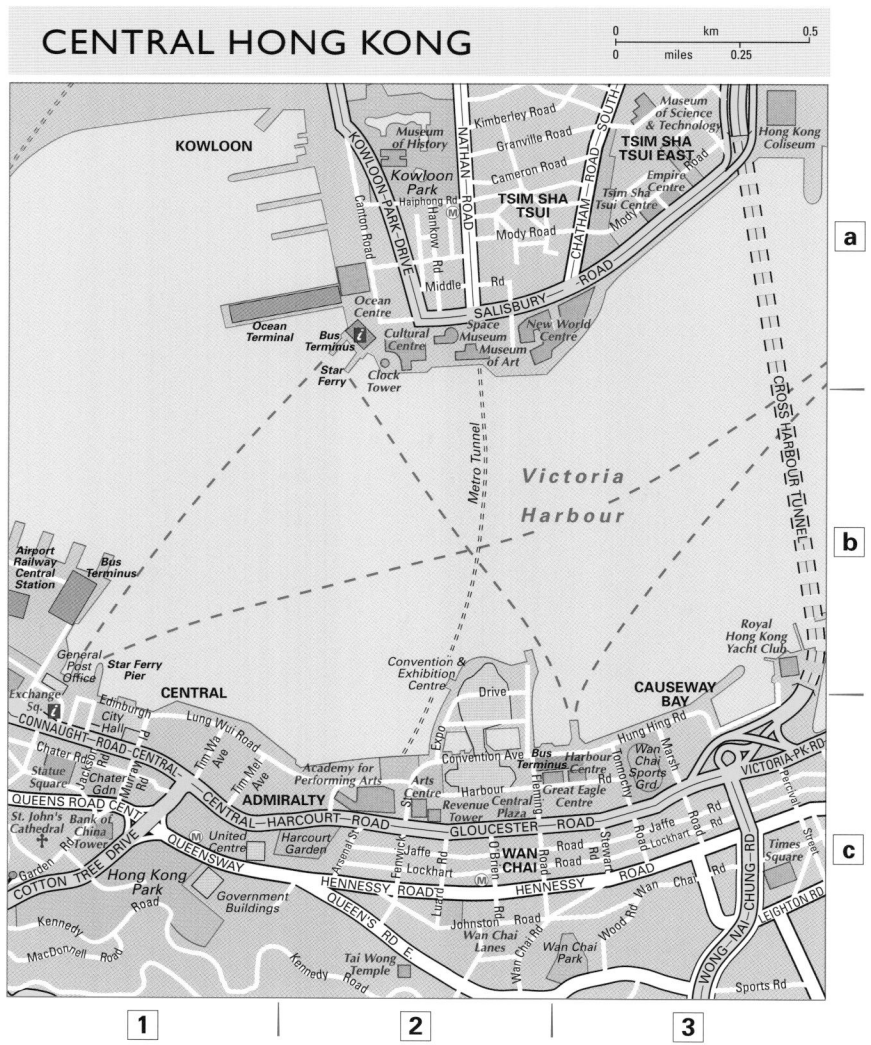

JERUSALEM

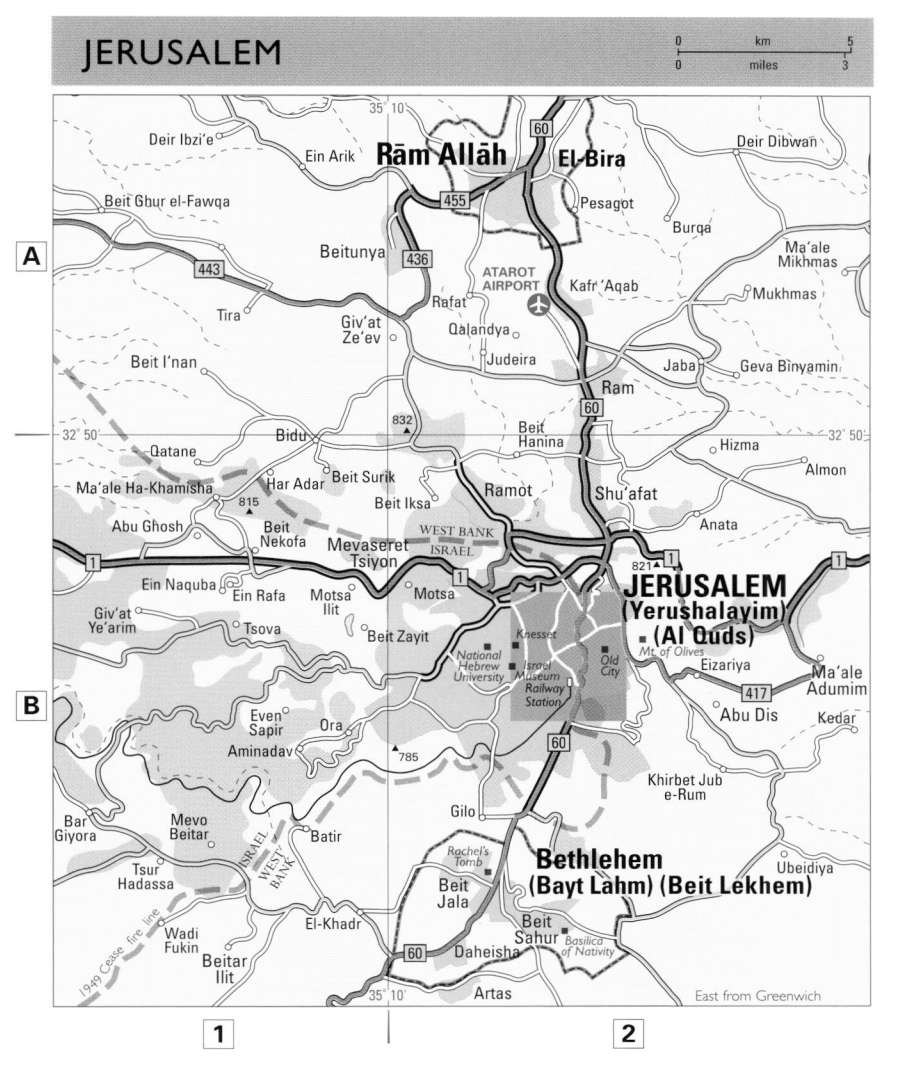

CENTRAL JERUSALEM

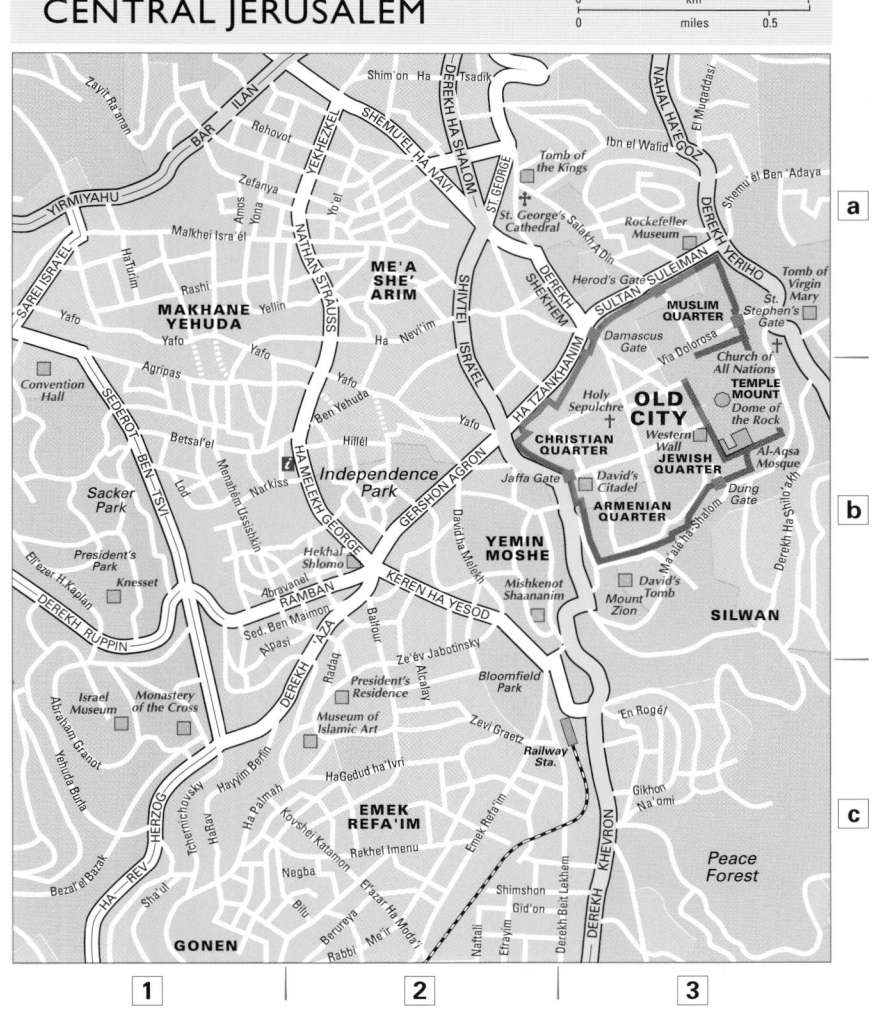

JAKARTA

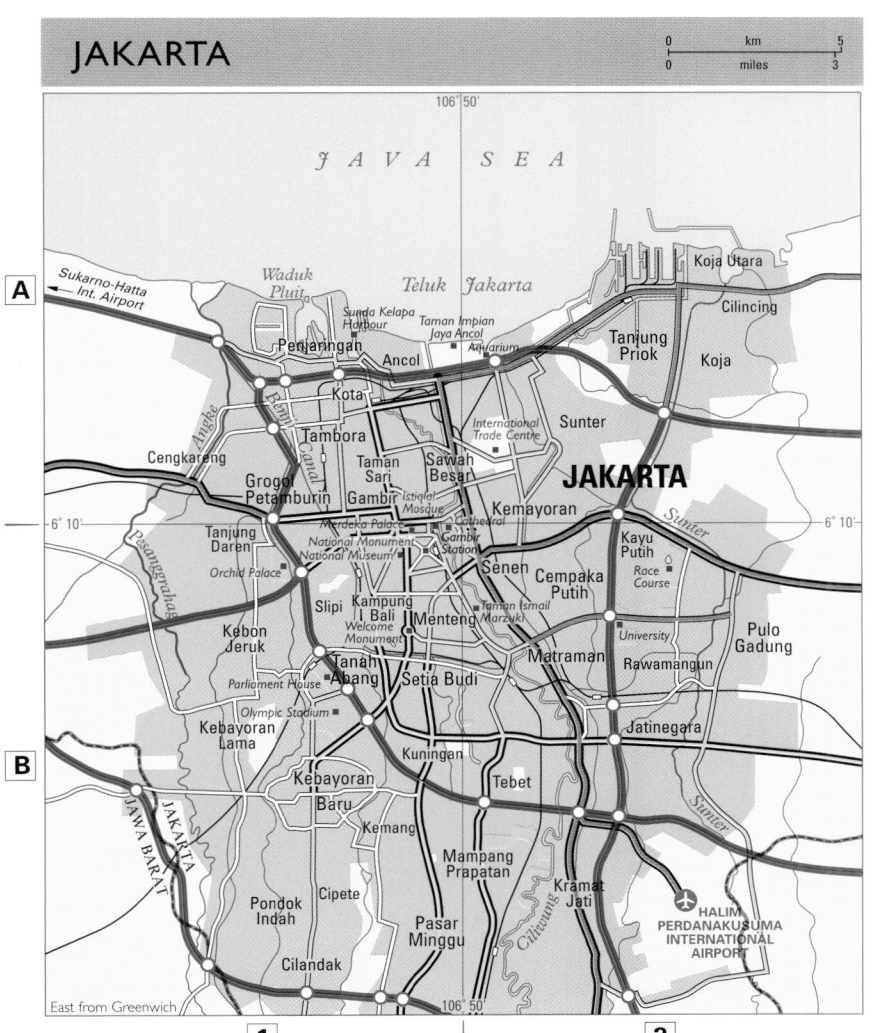

JOHANNESBURG

COPYRIGHT PHILIP'S

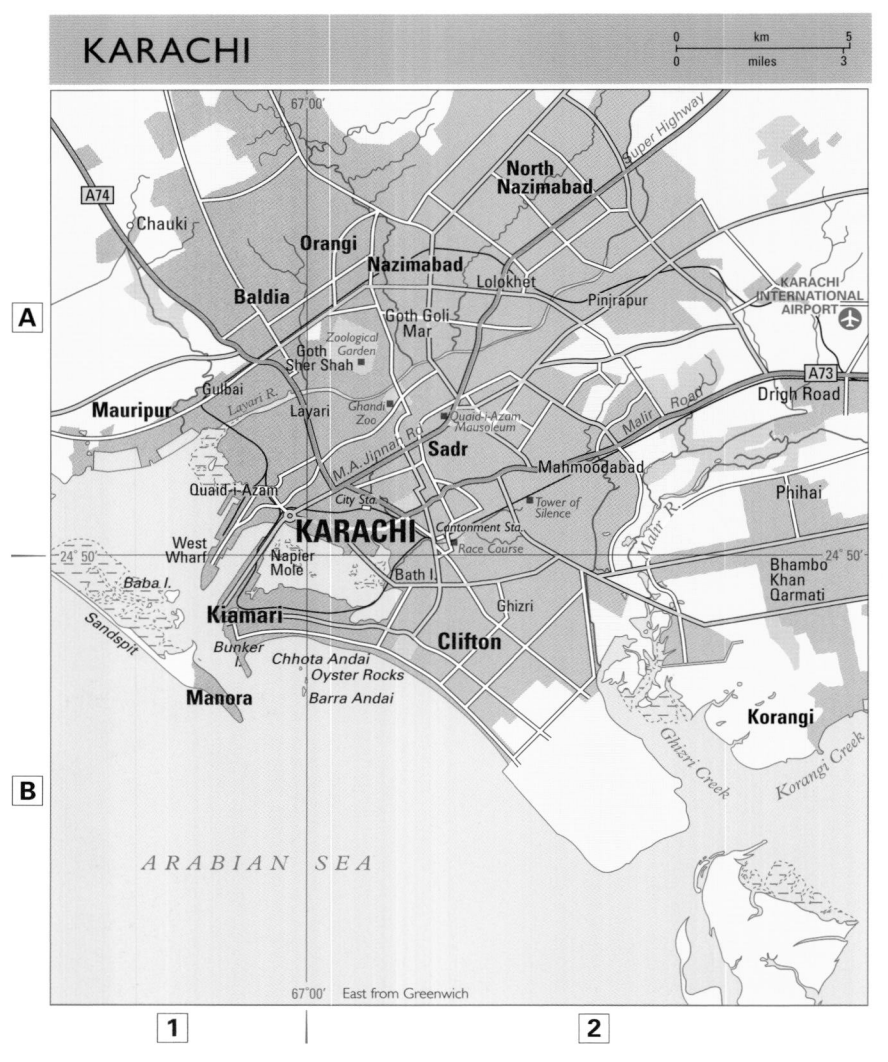

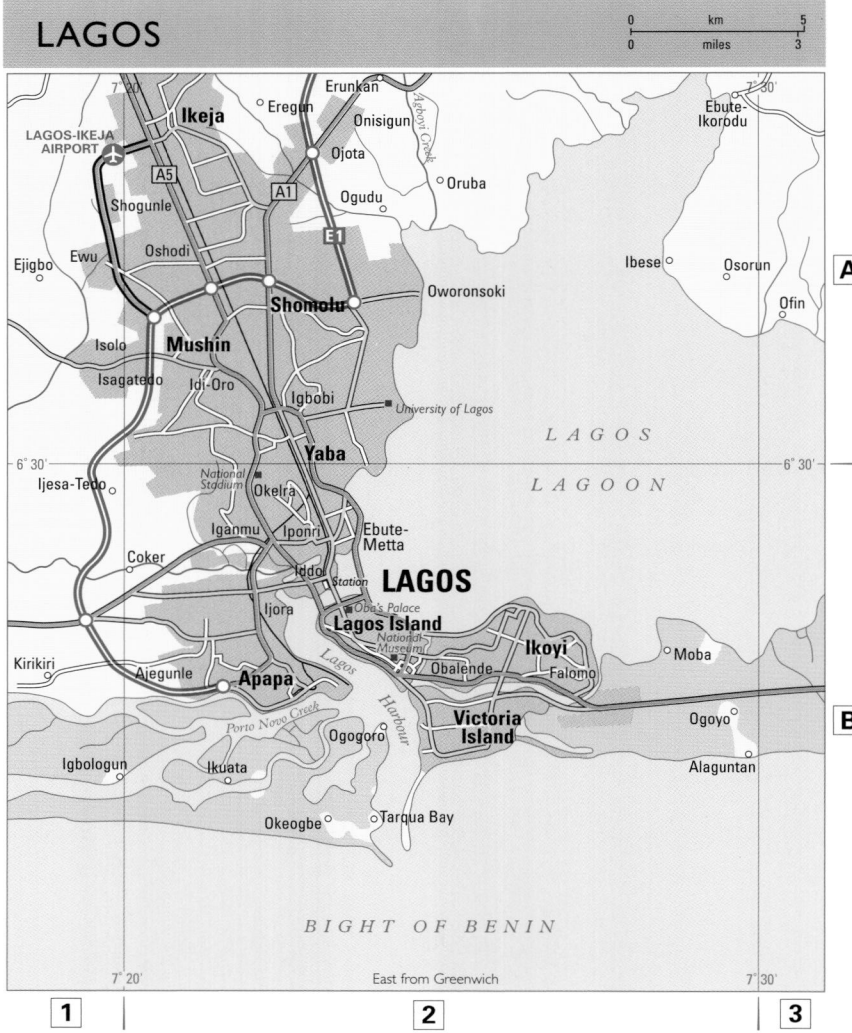

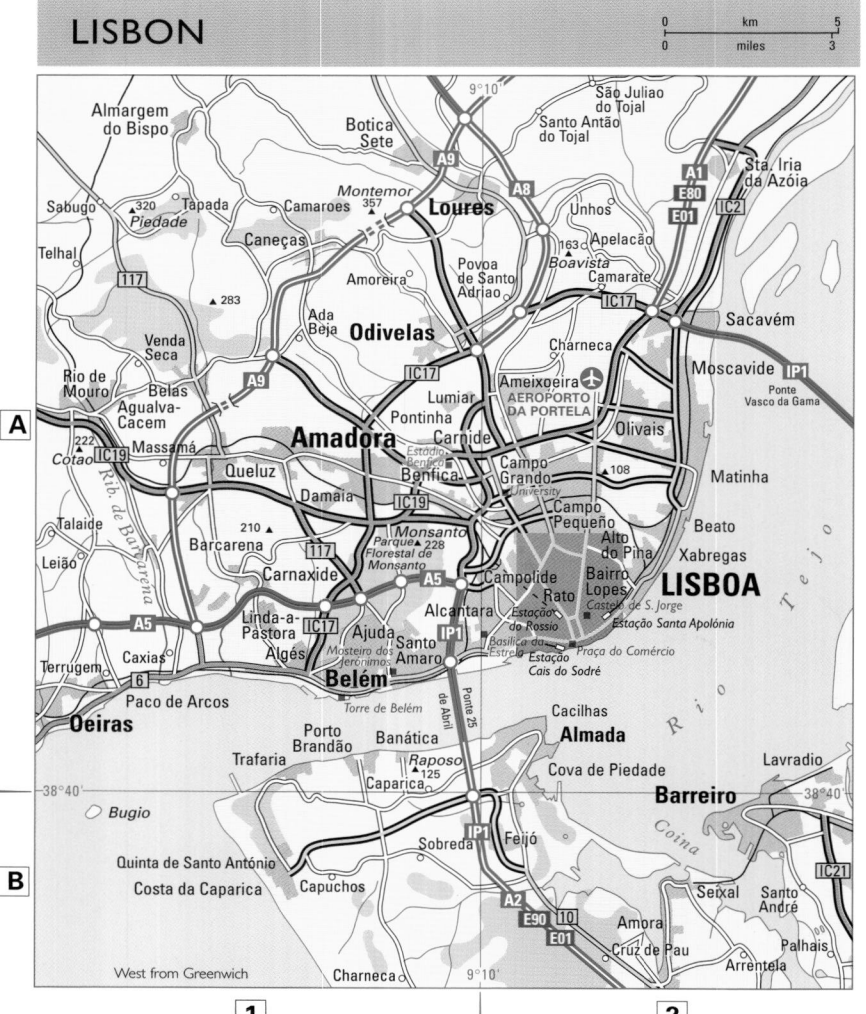

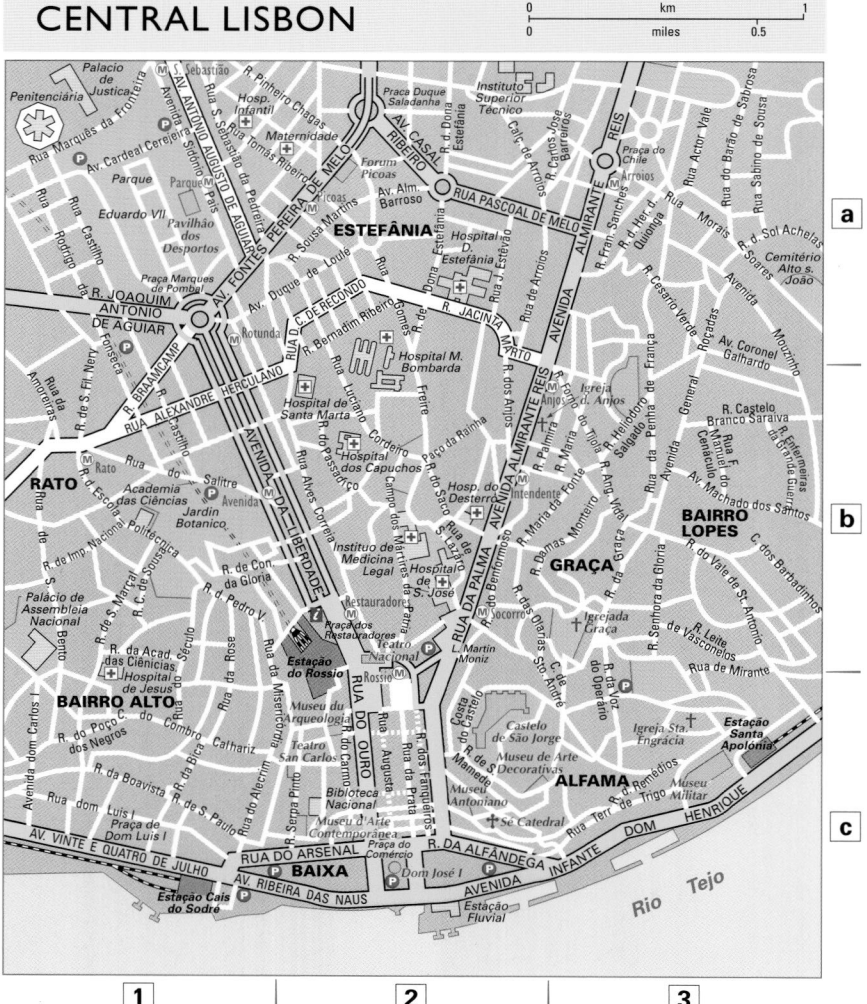

LONDON

km 0 — 5
miles 0 — 3

Northwood · Hatch End · Stanmore · Mill Hill · Barnet · Finchley · Burnt Oak · Colindale · Hendon · M1 · Church End · Wood Green · Noel Park · Woodford Green · To Stansted Airport · Woodford · GREATER LONDON · Hainault · Havering-atte-Bower · Harold Hill

Pinner Green · Harrow Weald · Belmont · Queensbury · Kingsbury · East Finchley · Muswell Hill · Hornsey · Tottenham · A406 · Clayhall · Barkingside · Collier Row · Gidea Park · Gallows Corner · Romford

Ruislip Common · Eastcote · Pinner · Wealdstone · HARROW · Greenhill · Kenton · A1 · Finsbury Park · Highgate · Crouch End · HARINGEY · Walthamstow · A10 · Clapton · Leyton · Leytonstone · WALTHAM FOREST · A12 · Chadwell Heath · Goodmayes · Seven Kings · Newbury Park · REDBRIDGE · Havering · Hornchurch

Ruislip · Rayners Lane · West Harrow · South Harrow · Harrow School · Harrow on the Hill · Wembley · BRENT · Hampstead Garden Suburb · Golders Green · Child's Hill · Hampstead Heath · Kenwood House · Highbury · Stoke Newington · HACKNEY · Bethnal Green · Bow · West Ham · East Ham · A13 · BARKING · DAGENHAM · Becontree · Elm Park

HILLINGDON · Cowley · South Ruislip · Northolt · Perivale · A40 · Greenford · Willesden Green · CAMDEN · Regent's Park · London Zoo · Maida Vale · HOLBORN · Finsbury · SHOREDITCH · TOWER HAMLETS · POPLAR · Canning Town · LONDON CITY · North Woolwich · Beckton · Creekmouth · Rainham

Hayes End · Hayes · Southall · Hanwell · EALING · ACTON · Shepherd's Bush · Notting Hill · Paddington · HYDE PARK · WESTMINSTER · CITY · Wapping · Limehouse · Millennium Dome · Thamesmead · River Thames · Wennington

West Drayton · Sipson · Harlington · Cranford · HEATHROW · Heston · Osterley Park · Brentford · Gunnersbury · Turnham Green · Chiswick · HAMMERSMITH · KENSINGTON · CHELSEA · Vauxhall · SOUTHWARK · BERMONDSEY · Rotherhithe · Isle of Dogs · A102 · Woolwich · Plumstead · Abbey Wood · West Heath · Belvedere · Erith

Isleworth · Syon Park · Kew · Barnes · FULHAM · BATTERSEA · LAMBETH · LONDON · Camberwell · Peckham · New Cross · Deptford · GREENWICH · Charlton · Greenwich Observatory · Kidbrooke · Shooters Hill · East Wickham · Welling · Bexleyheath · Barnehurst · Crayford · DARTFORD

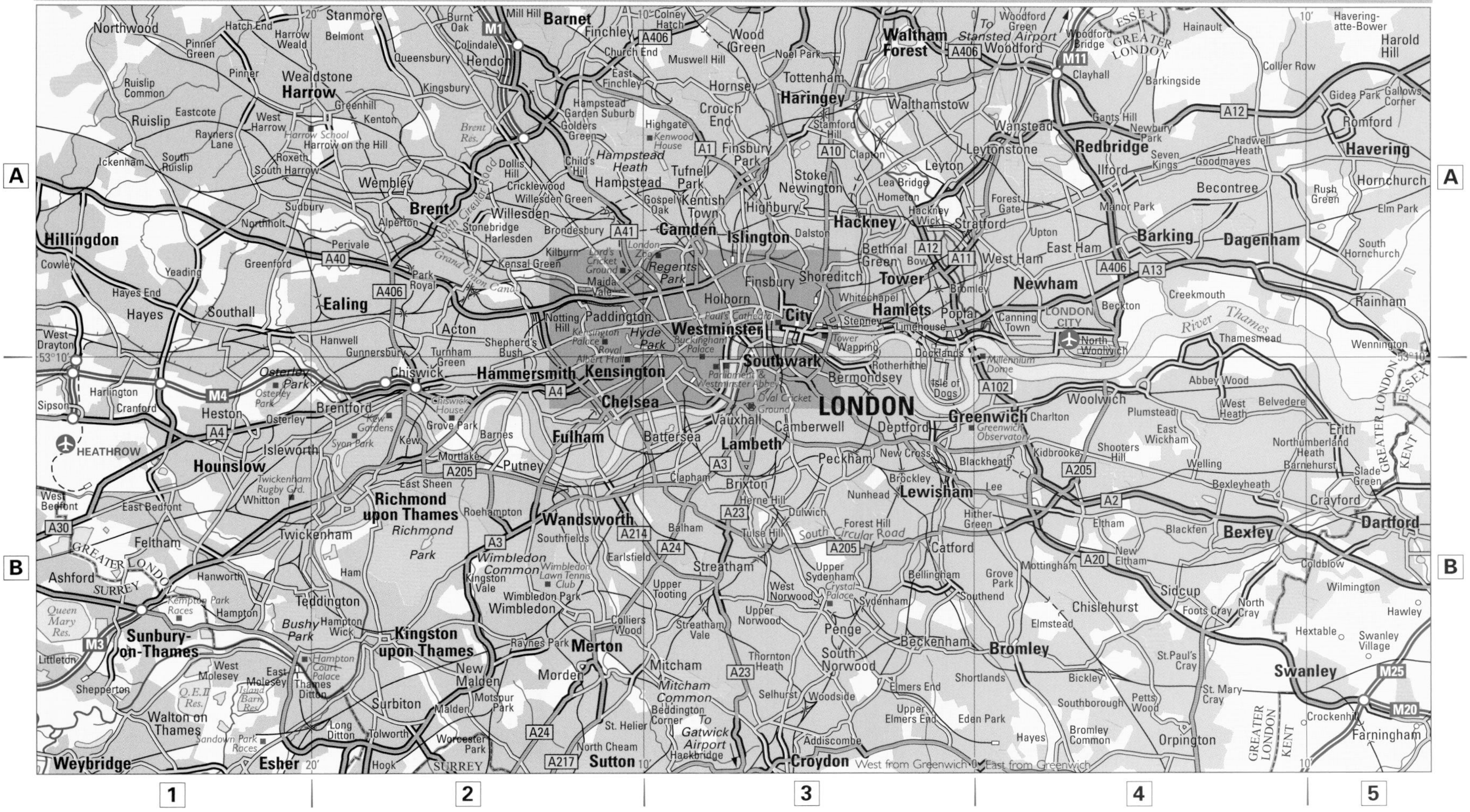

HOUNSLOW · Twickenham Rugby Gd. · Whitton · East Sheen · Roehampton · PUTNEY · Clapham · Brixton · Herne Hill · Dulwich · Nunhead · Brockley · LEWISHAM · Lee · Hither Green · Eltham · Blackfen · New Eltham · A20 · Sidcup · BEXLEY · Coldblow · Wilmington · Hawley

West Bedfont · East Bedfont · Feltham · RICHMOND UPON THAMES · Richmond Park · Southfields · Earlsfield · WANDSWORTH · Balham · Streatham · West Norwood · Upper Sydenham · Sydenham · Grove Park · Mottingham · Chislehurst · Foots Cray · St. Paul's Cray · North Cray · Hextable · Swanley Village

GREATER LONDON · SURREY · Ashford · Hanworth · Teddington · Ham · Wimbledon Common · Kingston Vale · Wimbledon Park · Upper Tooting · A214 · A24 · Colliers Wood · Upper Norwood · Crystal Palace · Bellingham · Catford · A205 · Eltham · A2 · Bexley · Sidcup · M25 · SWANLEY

Kempton Park Races · Hampton · Bushy Park · Kingston upon Thames · WIMBLEDON · Kingston upon Thames · Streatham Vale · Thornton Heath · Penge · South Norwood · Beckenham · Bromley · Elmstead · Bickley · Southborough · Petts Wood · St. Mary Cray · Orpington · GREATER LONDON · KENT · Crockenhill

Queen Mary Res. · M3 · Sunbury-on-Thames · West Molesey · Thames Ditton · New Malden · Morden · Mitcham Common · Beddington Corner · Upper Norwood · South Norwood · Woodside · Shortlands · Bromley Common · Hayes · Eden Park · Elmers End · Upper Elmers End · Crockenhill · Farningham

Littleton · Shepperton · Walton on Thames · Q.E.II Res. · East Molesey · Hampton Court Palace · Long Ditton · Surbiton · Tolworth · Motspur Park · MERTON · Mitcham · Carshalton · Wallington · St. Helier · North Cheam · Worcester Park · A217 · SUTTON · Hackbridge · To Gatwick Airport · M20

Weybridge · Esher · Hook · Malden · Chessington · A24 · St. Helier · CROYDON · Addiscombe · West from Greenwich · East from Greenwich · GREATER LONDON · KENT · Farningham

1 · 2 · 3 · 4 · 5

A · B

CENTRAL LONDON

km 0 — 2
miles 0 — 1

KENSAL RISE · ST. JOHN'S WOOD · Hospital of St. John & Elizabeth · King's Cross · HOXTON · St. Pancras · King's Cross Thameslink · Old Street · SHOREDITCH

WEST KILBURN · Queen's Park · Kilburn · Maida Vale · REGENT'S PARK · London Zoo · Euston · New British Lib. · City Rd. · CLERKENWELL · Wesley's Chapel

MAIDA VALE · WESTBOURNE GREEN · Lord's Cricket Gd. · London Mosque · Open Air Theatre · Queen Mary's Gardens · B.T. Tower · BLOOMSBURY · Russell Sq. · British Museum · FARRINGDON · Barbican · Mus. of London · Moorgate · Liverpool St. · Whitechapel Art Gall.

PADDINGTON · Royal Oak · Madame Tussaud's · Planetarium · MARYLEBONE · Wallace Collection · Oxford Circus · SOHO · Covent Gdn · HOLBORN · CITY · St. Paul's Cath. · Bank · Leadenhall · Aldgate · Tower Hill

BAYSWATER · NOTTING HILL · Notting Hill Gate · KENSINGTON GARDENS · HYDE PARK · Marble Arch · MAYFAIR · Piccadilly Circus · Leicester Sq. · National Gall. · Charing Cross · STRAND · Temple Ch. · Somerset Ho. · Fenchurch St. · The Monument · Tower of London · River Thames

Holland Park Ave. · Holland Park · Kensington Palace · Serpentine Gallery · Apsley House & Wellington Mus. · ST. JAMES'S · Trafalgar Sq. · Banqueting Hall · WHITEHALL · Downing Street · Cabinet War Rooms · BFI London IMAX · National · Waterloo East · SOUTHWARK · London Bridge · London Dungeon · HMS Belfast · Tower Gateway (DLR) · The Design Museum

KENSINGTON · Commonwealth Institute · Olympia · Olympia Exhibition Halls · High St Kensington · Imperial Coll. Science · Nat. History & Geological Mus. · KNIGHTSBRIDGE · BELGRAVIA · Buckingham Palace · Queen's Gall. · New Scot. Yd. · Westminster · Houses of Parliament · Westminster Abbey · St. Thomas' Hosp. · London Eye · County Hall · Hayward Gall. · Royal Festival Halls · Waterloo International · BOROUGH · Guy's Hosp. · NEWINGTON · Elephant & Castle · The Carriage · BERMONDSEY

HAMMERSMITH · WEST KENSINGTON · Earl's Court Exhibition Hall · SOUTH KENSINGTON · Brompton Oratory · Victoria & Albert Mus. · Brompton Hosp. · Royal Marsden Hosp. · Sloane Sq. · PIMLICO · VICTORIA · Victoria Coach Sta. · Tate Britain · Imperial War Mus. · Cuming Mus. · LAMBETH · WALWORTH

WEST KENSINGTON · Baron's Ct · Hammersmith Cemetery · West Brompton · CHELSEA · Chelsea & Westminster Hosp. · Royal Hosp. · Chelsea Royal Hosp. · PIMLICO · Vauxhall · Vauxhall Bridge · KENNINGTON · The Oval Cricket Gd. · Burgess Park

CHELSEA · CHELSEA EMBANKMENT · Chelsea Bridge · River Thames · The Oval

1 · 2 · 3 · 4 · 5

a · b · c

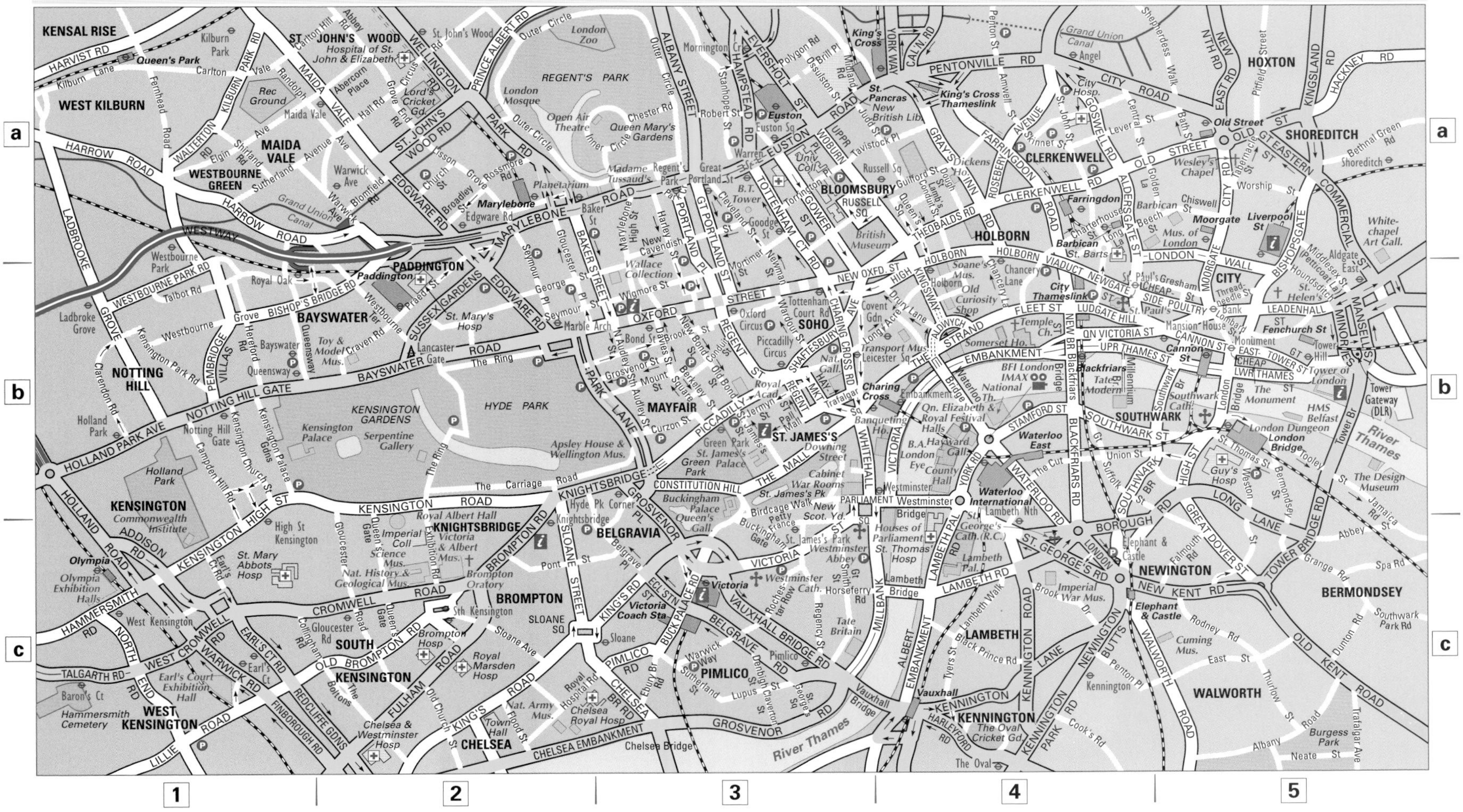

COPYRIGHT PHILIP'S

LOS ANGELES

km 5
miles 3

Tarzana · 101 · Sepulveda Flood Control Basin · Van Nuys · 170 · Burbank · Verdugo Mts. · 2 · San Rafael Hills · Flint Peak 555 · Rose Bowl · Altadena · 210 · San Gabriel Mts.

Encino · 101 · San Fernando Valley · North Hollywood · Disney Studios · 5 · 134 · Glendale · Pasadena · Sierra Madre · Colorado Fwy. · Monrovia

216 · Sherman Oaks · 405 · Studio City · 101 · C.B.S. Studios · Universal Studios · Warner Bros. Studios · Cahuenga Peak 555 · Griffith Park · Zoo · Golden State Fwy. · Glendale Galleria · Eagle Rock · 134 · California Inst. of Tech. · Arcadia

Encino Reservoir · Stone Canyon Reservoir · Santa Monica Mts. · 459 · Beverly Glen · Franklin Reservoir · Hollywood Bowl · Hollywood · Mann's Chinese Theatre · Sunset Blvd. · Highland Park · Garvanza · Southwest Museum · El Sereno · 110 · South Pasadena · San Marino · 19 · Temple City

Bel Air · University of California Los Angeles · Beverly Hills · West Hollywood · Santa Monica Blvd. · Paramount Studios · 2 · Hollywood Fwy. · Dodger Stadium · Lincoln Heights · California State Univ. · Alhambra · San Gabriel · Rosemead · 10

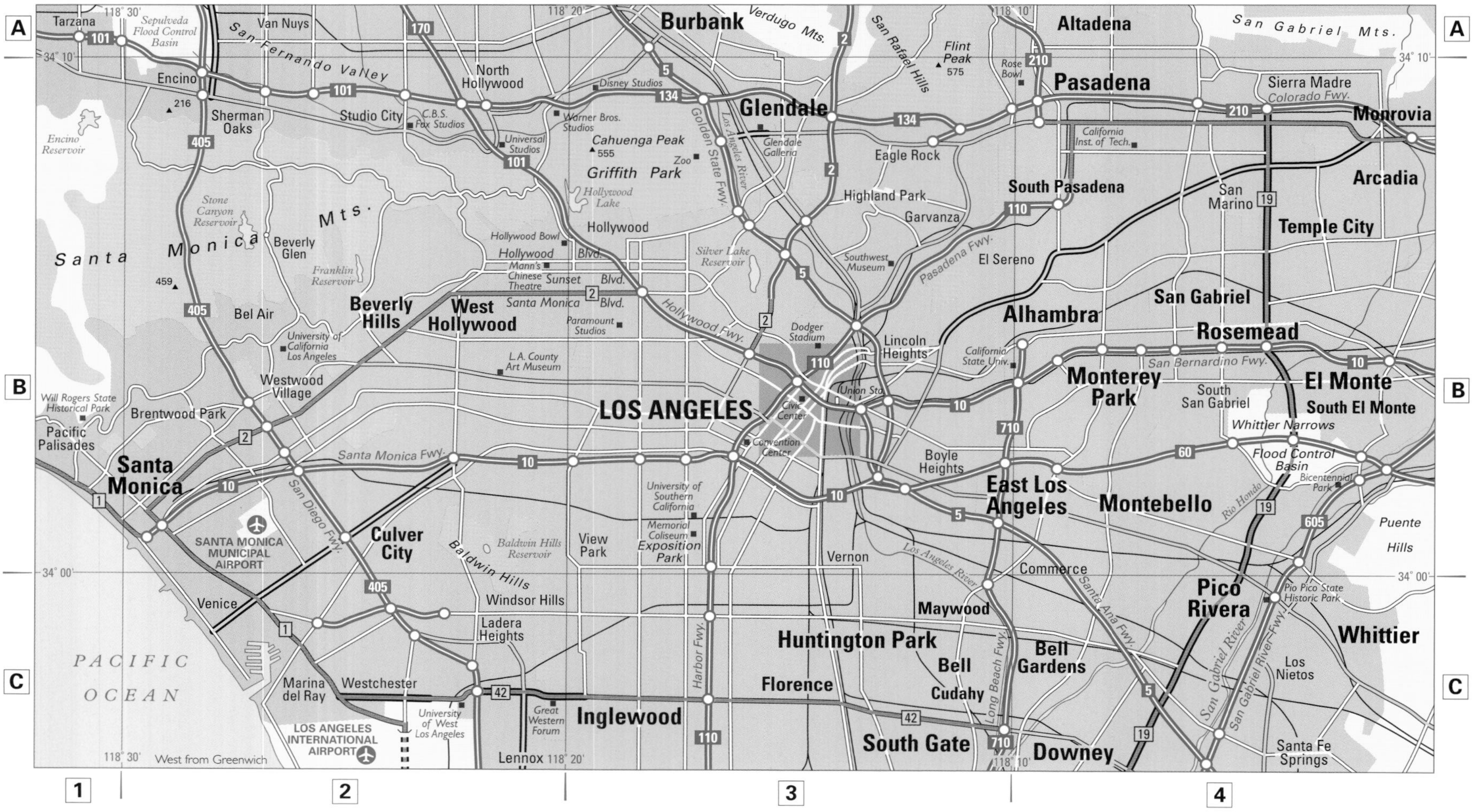

Will Rogers State Historical Park · Westwood Village · Brentwood Park · 2 · L.A. County Art Museum · LOS ANGELES · Civic Center · Union Sta. · 110 · Monterey Park · South San Gabriel · San Bernardino Fwy. · El Monte · South El Monte · Whittier Narrows

Pacific Palisades · Santa Monica · 10 · 1 · Santa Monica Fwy. · Convention Center · Boyle Heights · East Los Angeles · 710 · 60 · Flood Control Basin · Bicentennial Park

Culver City · San Diego Fwy. · Baldwin Hills · View Park · University of Southern California · Memorial Coliseum · Exposition Park · Vernon · Montebello · Rio Hondo · 19 · 605 · Puente Hills

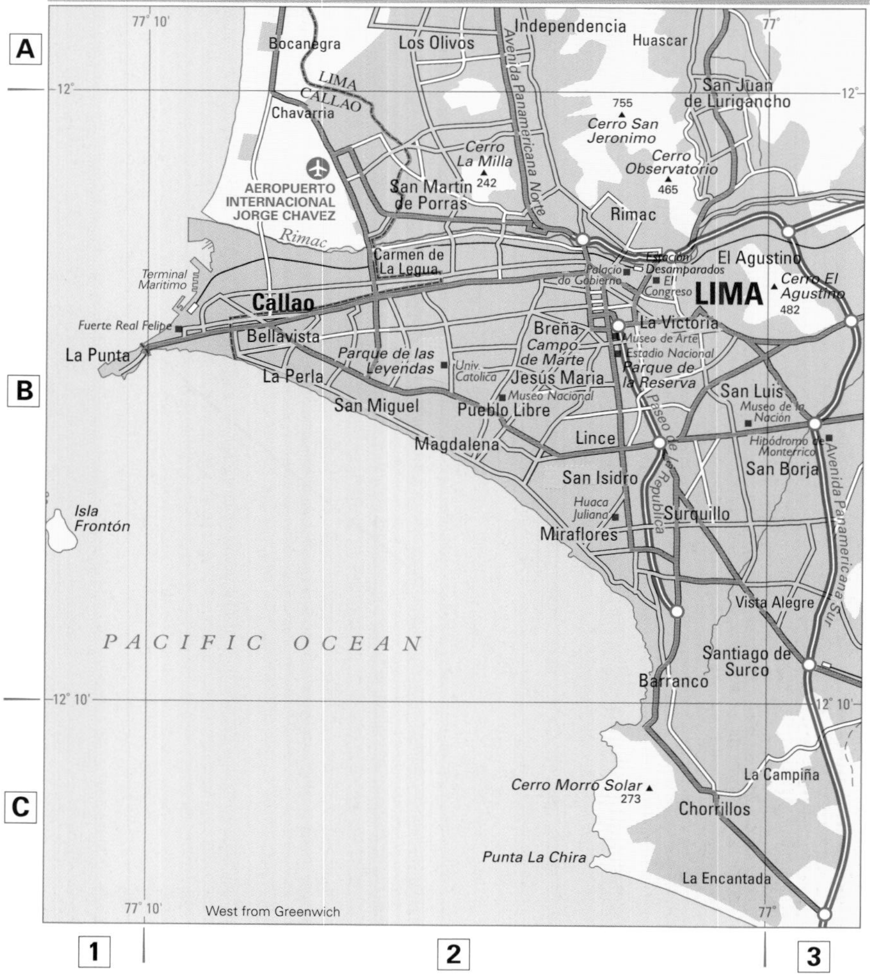

Santa Monica Municipal Airport · Venice · 405 · Baldwin Hills Reservoir · Windsor Hills · Commerce · Santa Ana Fwy. · Pico Rivera · Pio Pico State Historic Park · Whittier

Pacific Ocean · Marina del Ray · Westchester · 1 · University of West Los Angeles · Great Western Forum · Inglewood · Maywood · Bell · Cudahy · Huntington Park · Florence · Bell Gardens · San Gabriel River · Los Nietos · Santa Fe Springs

Los Angeles International Airport · Lennox · 42 · 110 · South Gate · 710 · Downey · 19

West from Greenwich

LIMA

km 5
miles 3

Bocanegra · Los Olivos · Independencia · Huascar · LIMA CALLAO · Chavarria · Cerro San Jeronimo 755 · San Juan de Lurigancho · Cerro La Milla · San Martin de Porras · 242 · Cerro Observatorio 465 · Rimac

Terminal Maritimo · Carmen de la Legua · Rimac · Estación Desamparados · Palacio de Gobierno · Congreso · El Agustino · Cerro El Agustino 482 · LIMA

Callao · Fuerte Real Felipe · Bellavista · Breña · Campo de Marte · Museo de Arte · La Victoria

La Punta · La Perla · Parque de las Leyendas · Univ. Catolica · Jesús Maria · Estadio Nacional · Parque de Reserva · San Luis · Museo de la Nación

San Miguel · Pueblo Libre · Lince · San Borja

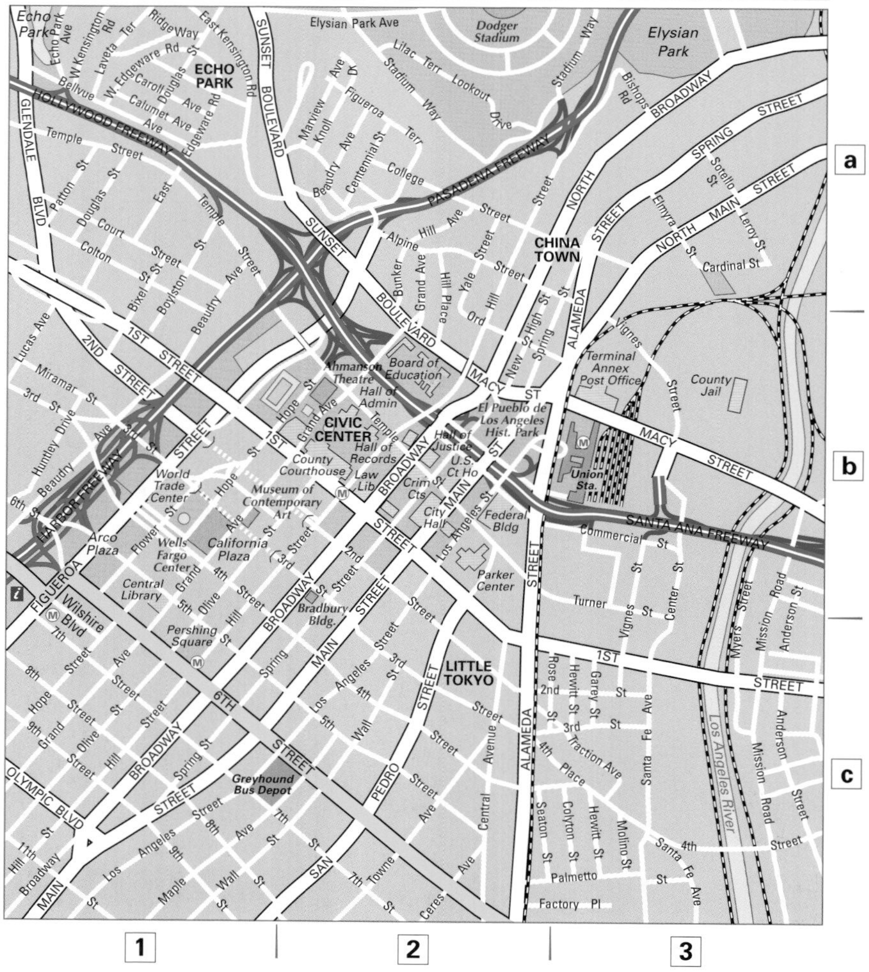

Magdalena · San Isidro · Huaca Juliana · Surquillo · Hipódromo Monterrico · Avenida Panamericana Sur

Miraflores · Vista Alegre

PACIFIC OCEAN · Isla Frontón · Santiago de Surco · Barranco · La Campiña · Cerro Morro Solar 273 · Chorrillos · Punta La Chira · La Encantada

West from Greenwich

CENTRAL LOS ANGELES

km
miles 0.5

Echo Park · Elysian Park Ave · Dodger Stadium · Elysian Park · Sunset Boulevard · China Town · Civic Center · Terminal Annex Post Office · County Jail · El Pueblo de Los Angeles Hist. Park · Union Sta. · Little Tokyo · Greyhound Bus Depot · Olympic Blvd. · Los Angeles River

Figueroa Blvd · Central Library · Pershing Square · Broadway · Main Street · Alameda

MADRID

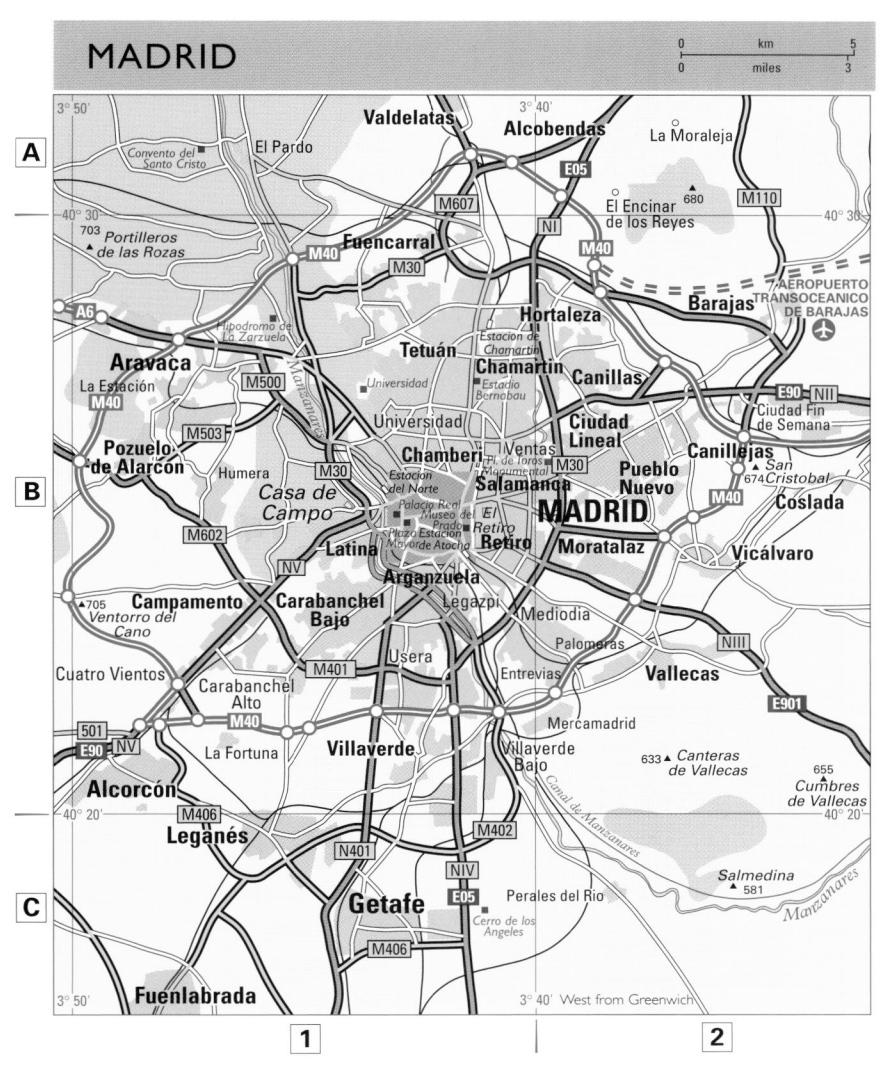

CENTRAL MADRID

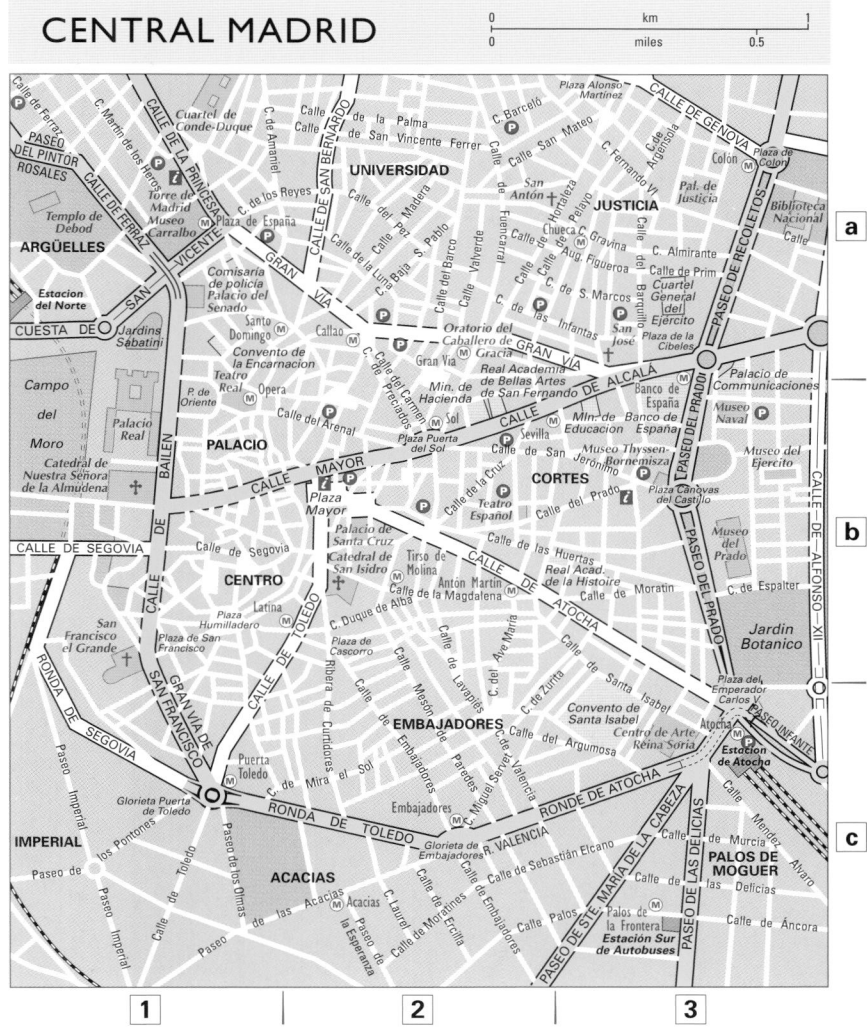

MANILA

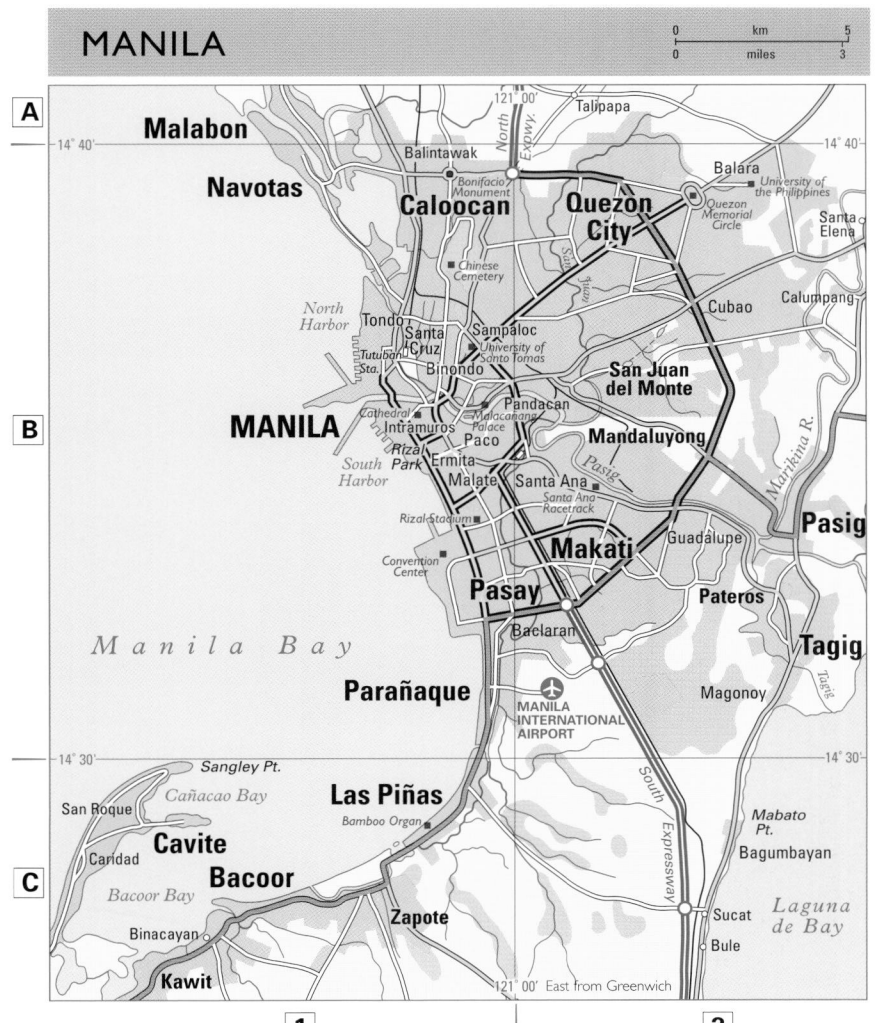

MELBOURNE

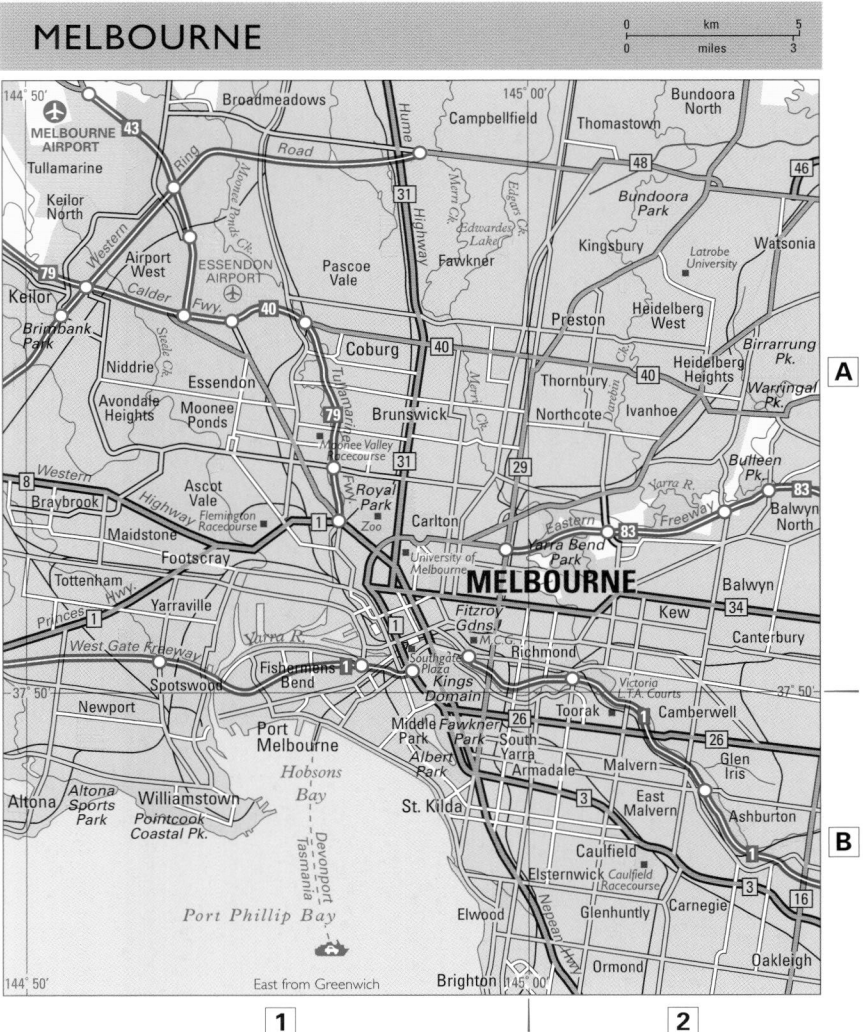

MEXICO CITY

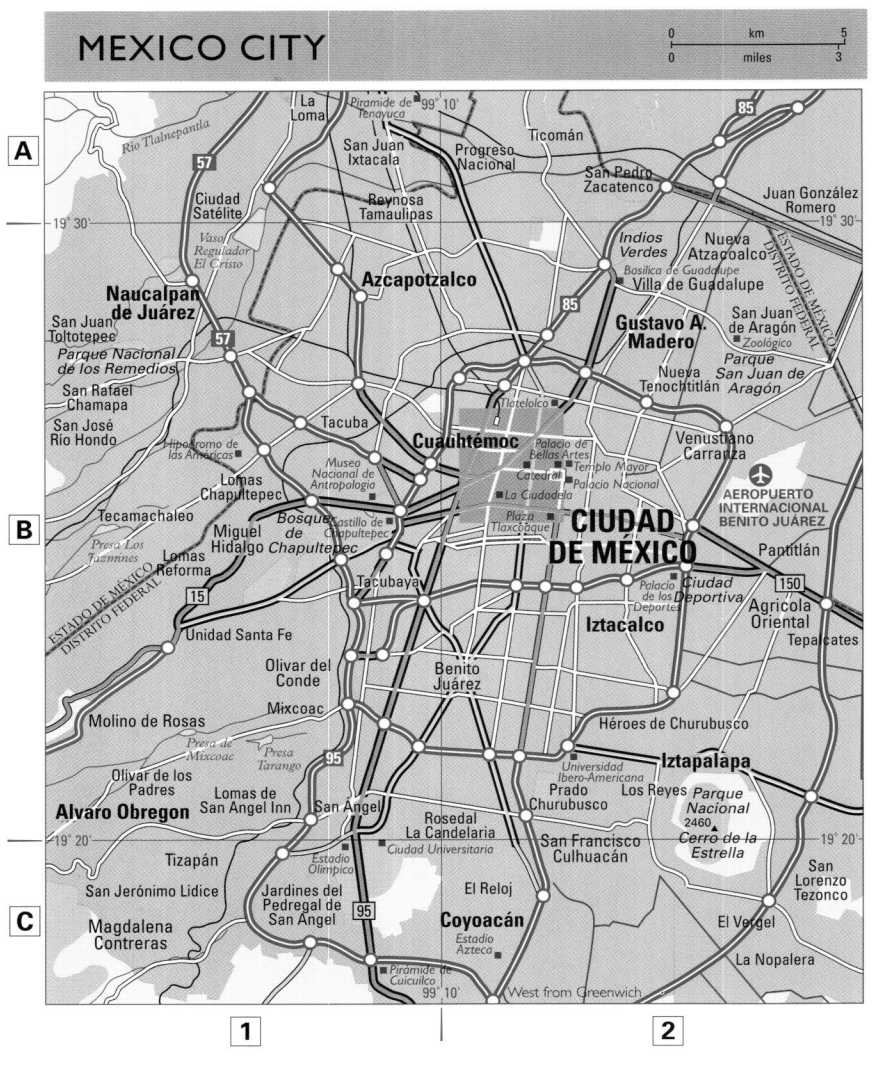

CENTRAL MEXICO CITY

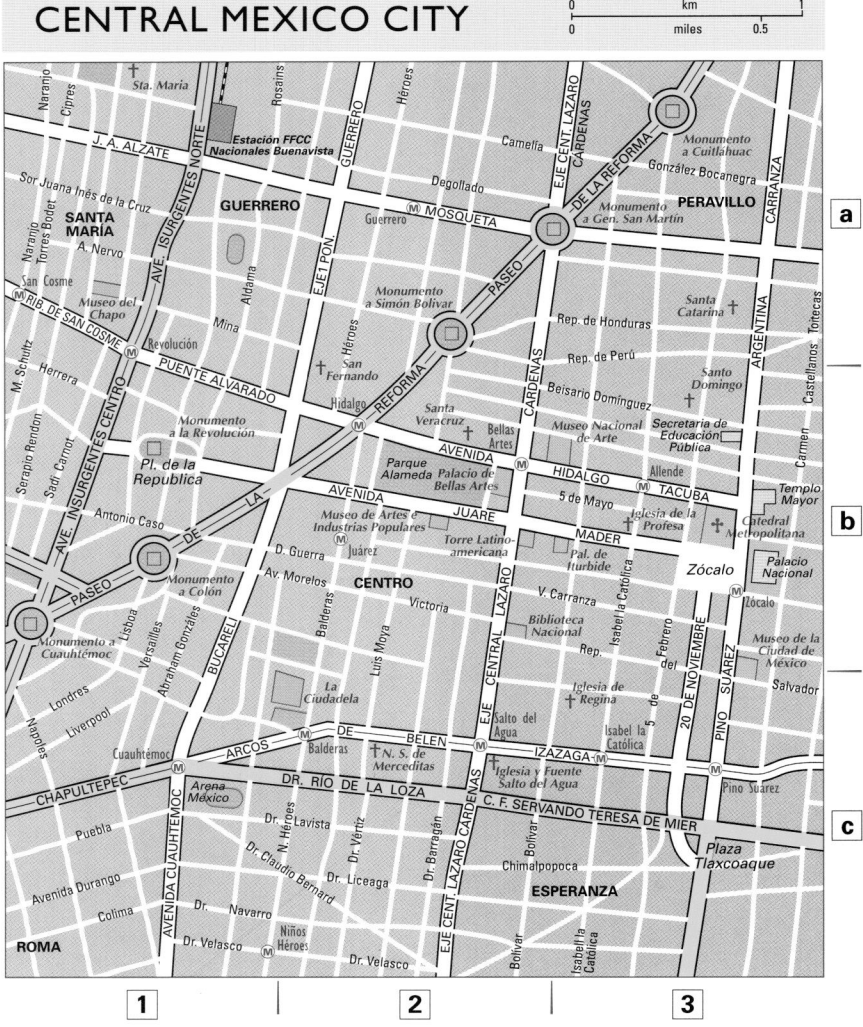

MIAMI

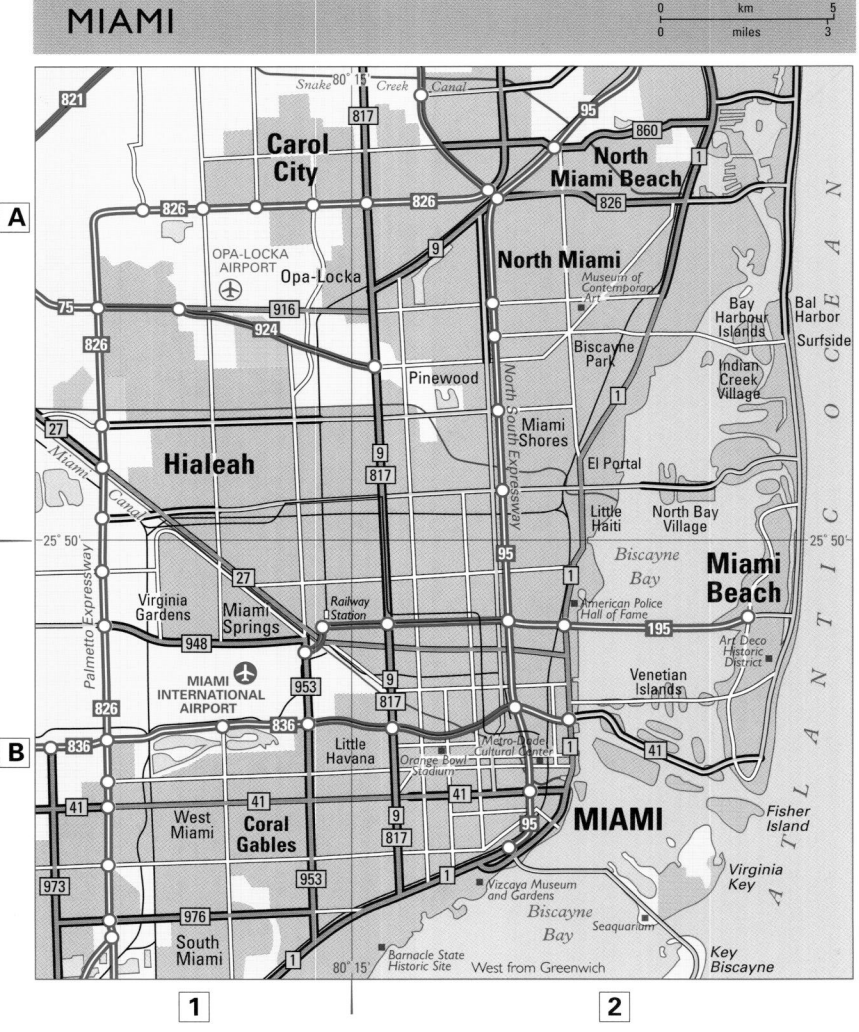

MILAN

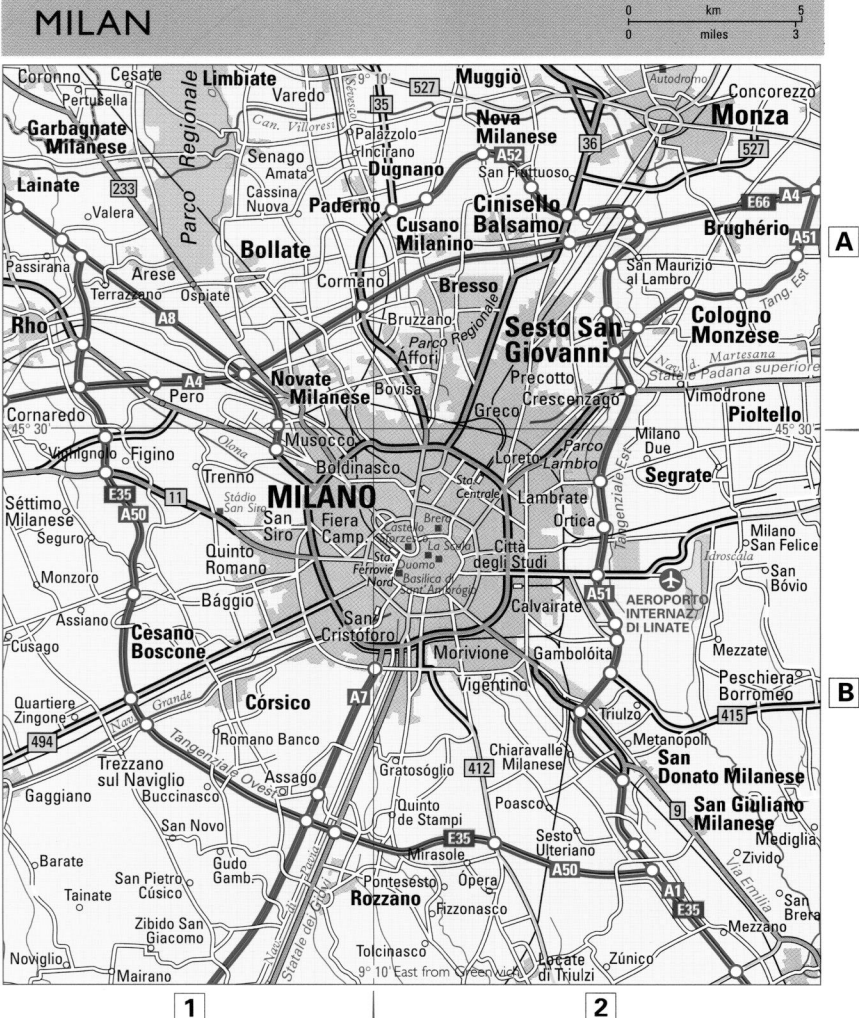

MOSCOW

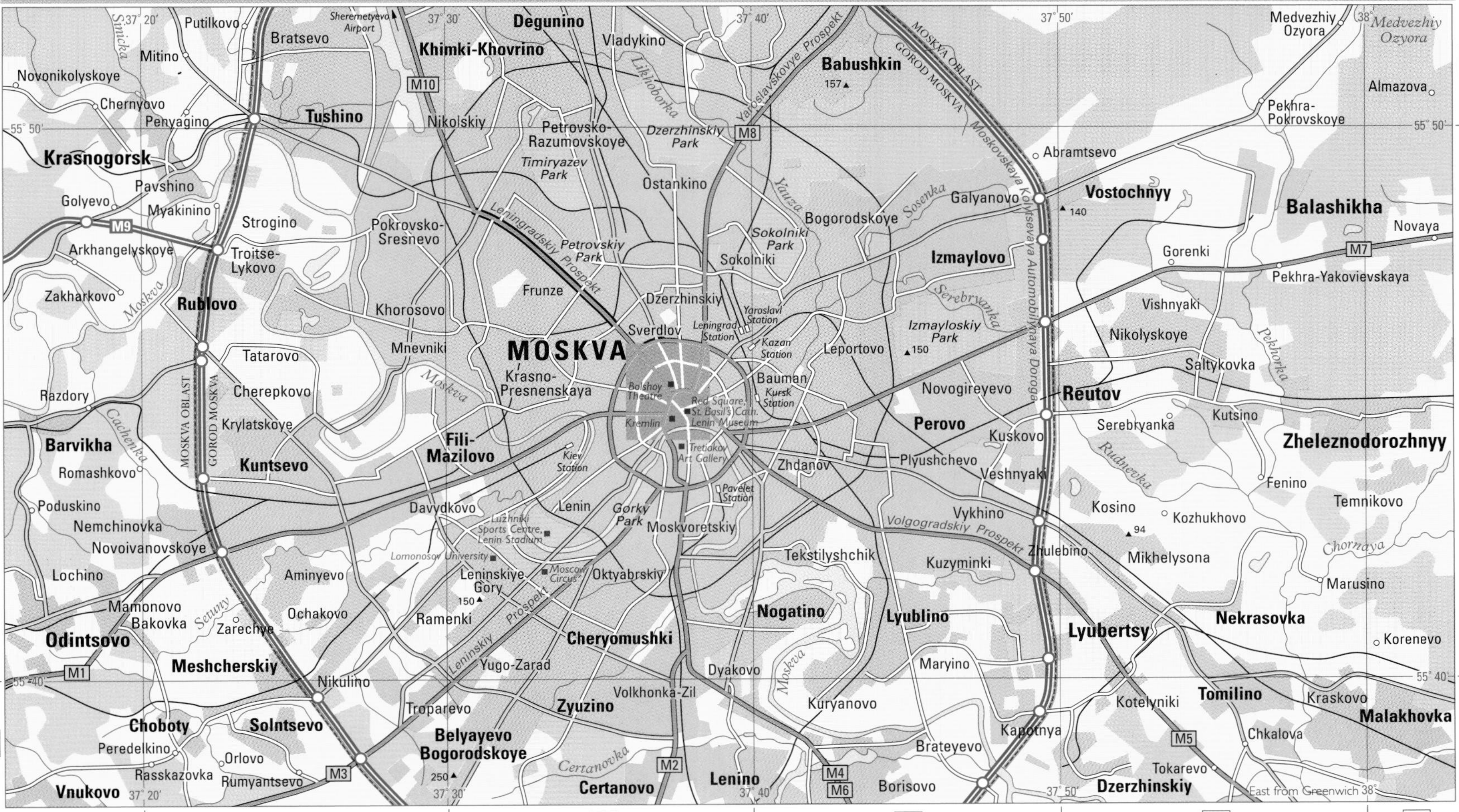

km
miles

A

Novonikolyskoye
Mitino
Putilkovo
Bratsevo
Sheremetyevo Airport
Degunino
Khimki-Khovrino
Vladykino
Babushkin
157 ▲
Medvezhiy Ozyora
Medvezhiy Ozyora
Almazova
Pekhra-Pokrovskoye

Krasnogorsk
Chernyovo
Penyagino
Tushino
Nikolskiy
Petrovsko-Razumovskoye
Dzerzhinskiy Park
Timiryazev Park
Ostankino
Bogorodskoye
Galyanovo
Vostochnyy
140 ▲
Balashikha
Novaya

Pavshino
Golyevo
Myakinino
Strogino
Pokrovsko-Sresnevo
Petrovskiy Park
Sokolniki Park
Sokolniki
Izmaylovo
Gorenki
Pekhra-Yakovievskaya

B

Arkhangelyskoye
Troitse-Lykovo
Khorosovo
Frunze
Dzerzhinskiy
Leningrad Station
Yaroslavl Station
Kazan Station
Izmayloskiy Park
150 ▲
Vishnyaki
Nikolyskoye
Saltykovka

Zakharkovo
Rublovo
Tatarovo
Mnevniki
Krasno-Presnenskaya
MOSKVA
Bolshoy Theatre
Bauman
Kursk Station
Novogireyevo
Reutov
Serebryanka
Kutsino

Razdory
Cherepkovo
Krylatskoye
Fili-Mazilovo
Red Square
St. Basil's Cath
Lenin Museum
Kremlin
Kiev Station
Perovo
Kuskovo
Zheleznodorozhnyy

Barvikha
Romashkovo
Kuntsevo
Tretiakov Art Gallery
Zhdanov
Plyushchevo
Veshnyaki
Fenino
Temnikovo

Poduskino
Nemchinovka
Novoivanovskoye
Davydkovo
Lenin
Gorky Park
Moskvoretskiy
Tekstilyshchik
Vykhino
Kosino
Kozhukhovo
Mikhelysona
Marusino

Lochino
Aminyevo
Luzhniki Sports Centre, Lenin Stadium
Leninskiye-Gory
Oktyabrskiy
Kuzyminki
Zhulebino
94 ▲
Chornaya

Mampnovo
Bakovka
Ochakovo
Zarechya
Ramenki
Yugo-Zarad
Nogatino
Lyublino
Nekrasovka

Odintsovo
Meshcherskiy
Nikulino
Cheryomushki
Dyakovo
Maryino
Kuryanovo
Lyubertsy
Korenevo

Choboty
Peredelkino
Solntsevo
Orlovo
Troparevo
Belyayevo Bogorodskoye
Zyuzino
Volkhonka-Zil
Tomilino
Kraskovo

Rasskazovka
Rumyantsevo
Certanovka
Lenino
Brateyevo
Kotelyniki
Chkalova
Malakhovka

Vnukovo
Certanovo
Borisovo
Tokarevo
Dzerzhinskiy

East from Greenwich 38°

1 2 3 4 5 6

MONTRÉAL

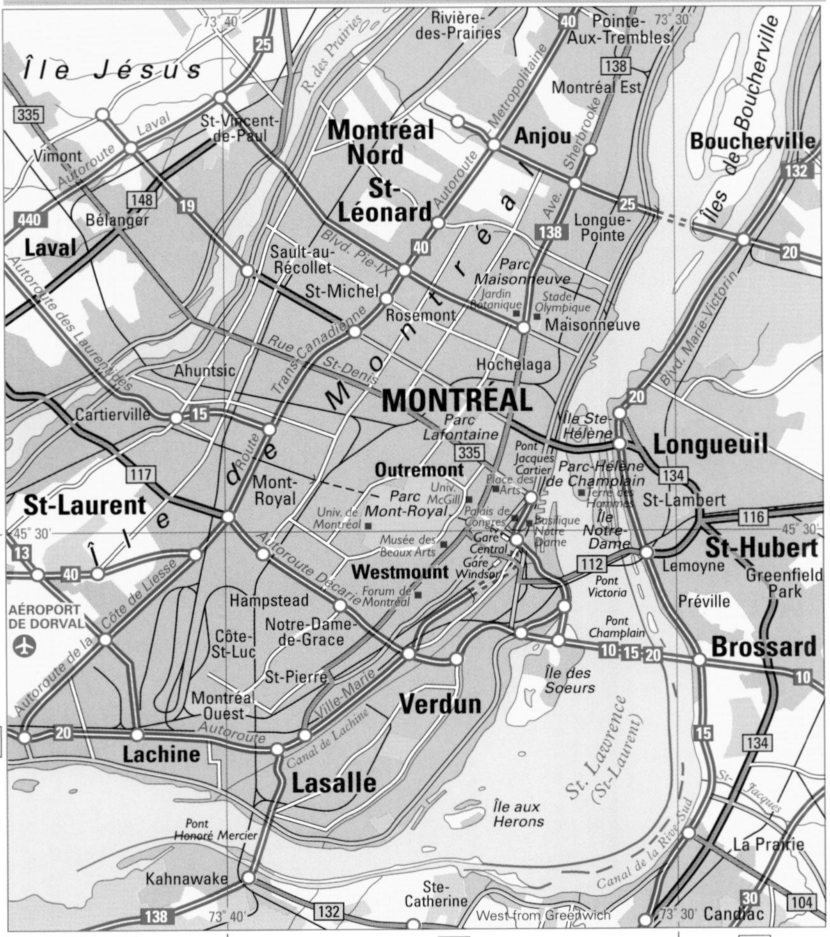

km
miles

Île Jésus

Rivière-des-Prairies
Pointe-Aux-Trembles
Montréal Est
Boucherville

St-Vincent-de-Paul
Montréal Nord
St-Léonard
Anjou

A

Laval
Bélanger
Sault-au-Récollet
St-Michel
Longue-Pointe
Boucherville

Ahuntsic
Rosemont
Parc Maisonneuve
Maisonneuve
Hochelaga

Cartierville
MONTRÉAL
Parc Lafontaine
Villa Ste-Hélène

St-Laurent
Mont-Royal
Outremont
Parc Mont-Royal
Univ. McGill
Parc Hélène / Île Champlain
Longueuil
St-Lambert

Westmount
Musée des Beaux Arts
Palais des Congrès
Basilique Notre-Dame
Gare Central
Gare Windsor
St-Hubert
Lemoyne
Préville
Greenfield Park

AÉROPORT DE DORVAL
Hampstead
Notre-Dame-de-Grace
Côte-St-Luc
Forum de Montréal
Pont Victoria
Pont Champlain
Brossard

St-Pierre
Montréal Ouest
Île des Sœurs

B

Lachine
Verdun
Ville de Lachine
Canal de Lachine
St-Laurent (St-Lawrent)
La Prairie

Lasalle
Pont Honoré Mercier
Île aux Herons
Canal de la Rive Sud

Kahnawake
Ste-Catherine
Candiac

West from Greenwich 73° 30'

1 2 3

CENTRAL MOSCOW

km
miles

Svetnoy Boulevard
SAD-SAMOTECHNAYA
SAD-SUHAREVSKAYA
SAD-SPASSKAYA
Suharevskaya
Sergievskiy Per.

Mayakovskiy Ploshchad
Tchaikovsky Concert Hall
Old Moscow Circus
Trubnaya Pl.
PETROVSKIY BOULEVARD
ROZHDE-STYENSKIY BOULEVARD
U. SRETENKA

Youth Theatre
Russian Cinema
Pushkinskaya
Convent of the Nativity of the Virgin

a

Sadovich
Museum of the Revolution
Pushkin Ploshchad
PETROVKA
Petrovskiy Passage
Varsonofevsky Per.
Turgenevskaya Turgenevskaya Pl.
Chisty Prudy

Gorky Theatre
Stoleshnikov
Bolshoy Ulitsa
Kuznetskiy Most
Detskiy Theatre
Lubyanka

MAL BRONNAYA ULITSA
Chekhov Theatre
Central Post Office
Okhotny Ryad
TEATRALNIY PROJ.
Ploshchad Lubyanskaya
NOVAYA PL.
Polytechnic Museum

Gorky House Museum
Revolution Theatre
Theatre Square
Slavansky Bazar
Bolshoy Per. Deyatbinskaya

NIKITSKY BLD
University
Revolution Square
Manezhnaya Ploshchad
Lenin Museum
Historical Museum
Gum Shopping Arcade
Kitai Gorod

b

Moscow Conservatoire
Central Exhibition Hall
Red Square
Vladimirskaya Peredolak

Arbatskaya Ploshchad
VOZDVIZHENKA U.
Museum of Russian Architecture
Arsenal
Lenin Mausoleum
St. Basil's Cathedral
ULITSA VARVARKA

ULITSA ARBAT
U. ZNAMENKA
Aleksandrov Sad
Council of Ministers
Presidium of the Supreme Soviet
Central Concert Hall

Palace of Congress
Lenin State Library
Ivan Square
Kremlin
Terem Palace
Cathedral Square
Armoury Palace
Archangel Cathedral
Kremlin Palace

c

Pushkin Fine Arts Museum
MOSKVORETS NAB.
RAUSHSKAYA NAB.

Ryleyev Ulitsa
Kropotkinskaya
Moscow Swimming Pool
KREMLEVSKAYA NABEREZHNAYA
BOLOTNAYA NAB.
Vodootvodny Kanal
OVCHINNIKOVSKAYA
KADASHEVSKAYA NAB.
SADOVNICHESKAYA

1 2 3

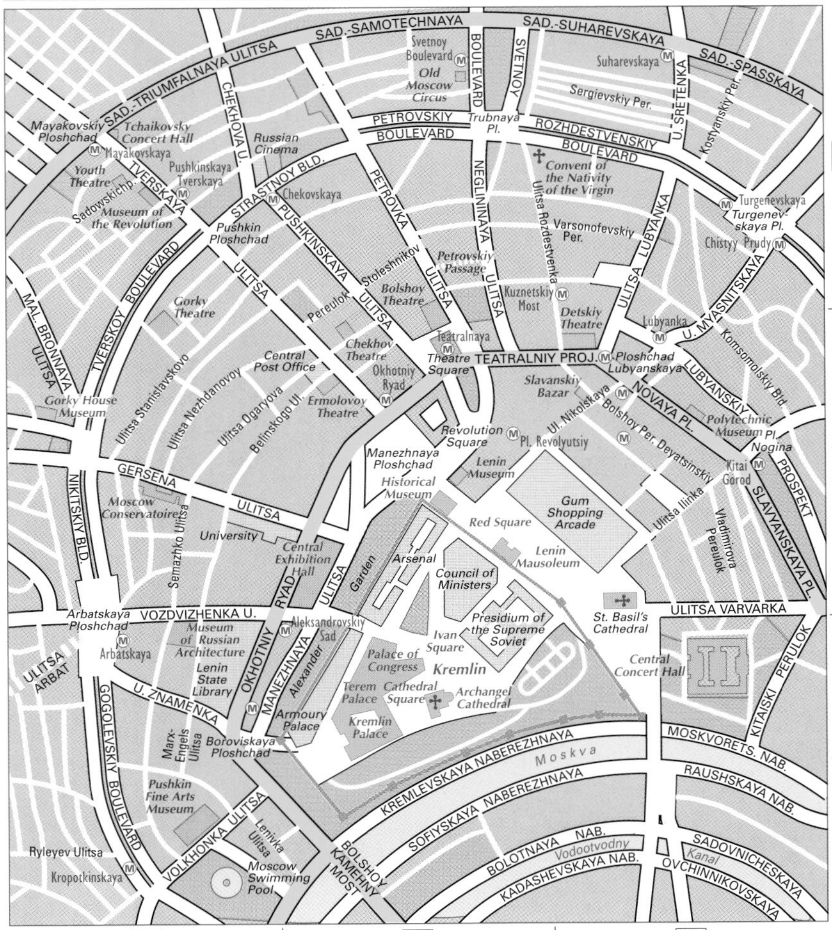

COPYRIGHT PHILIP'S

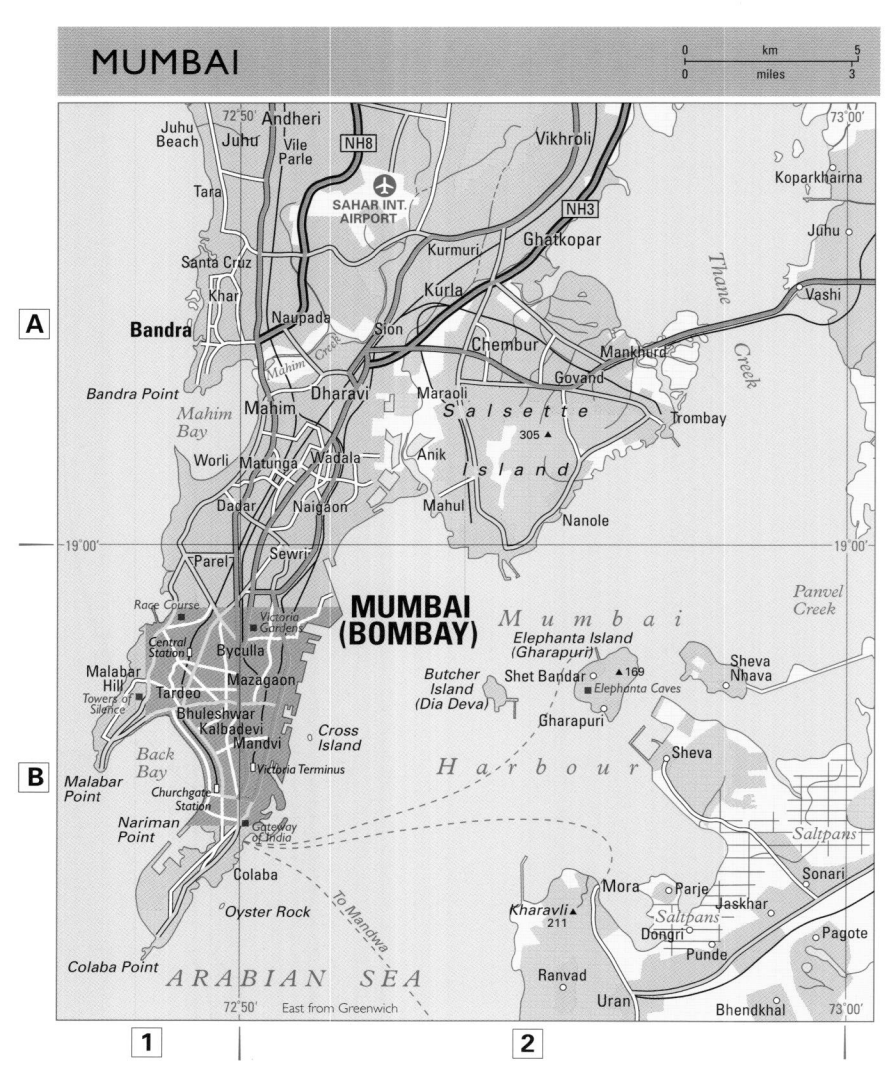

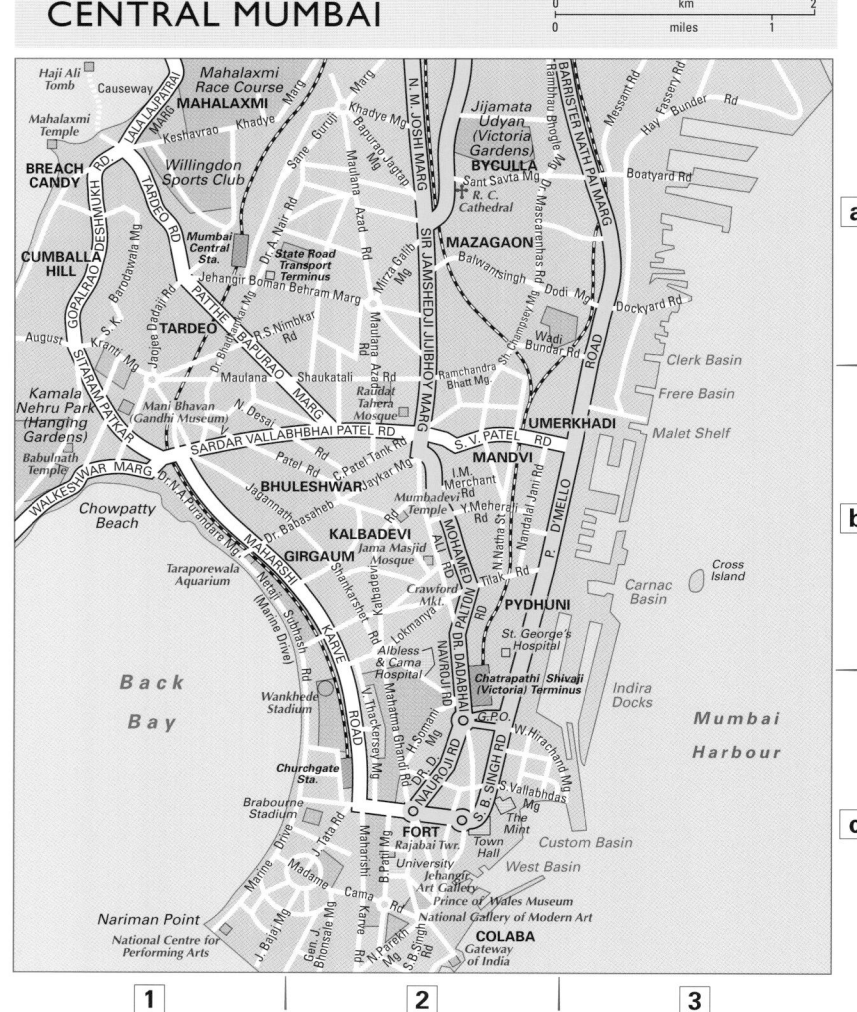

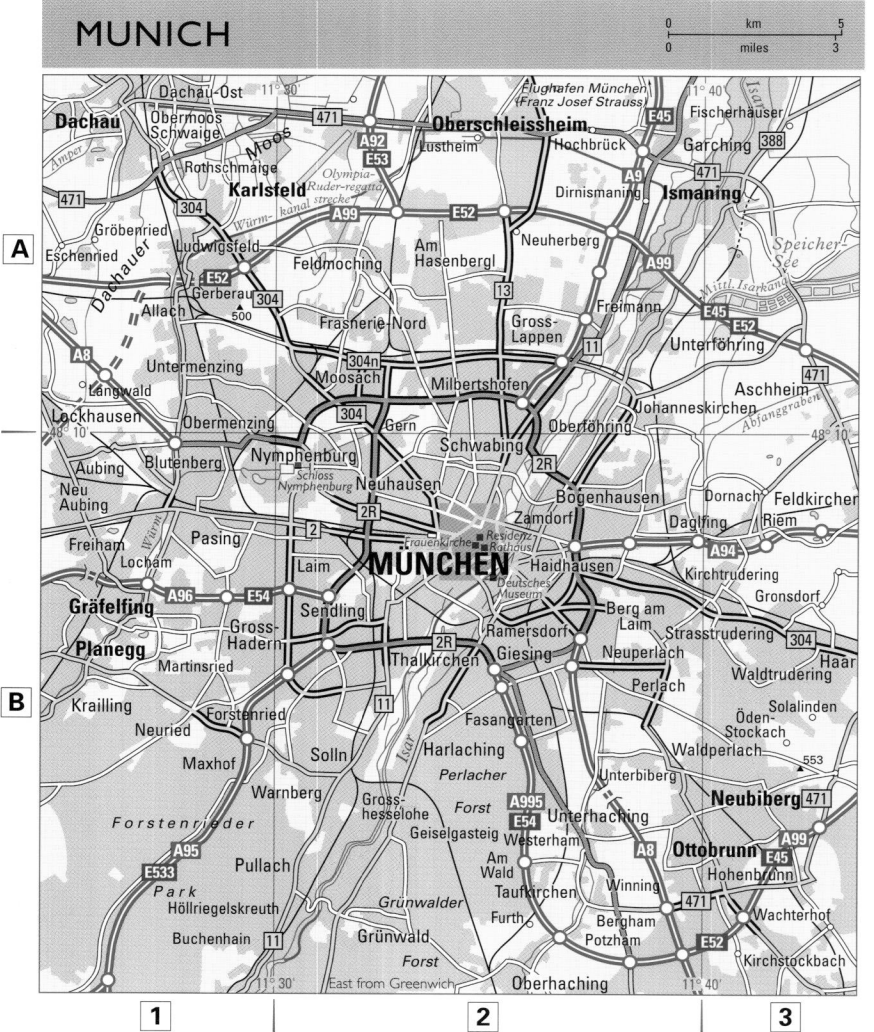

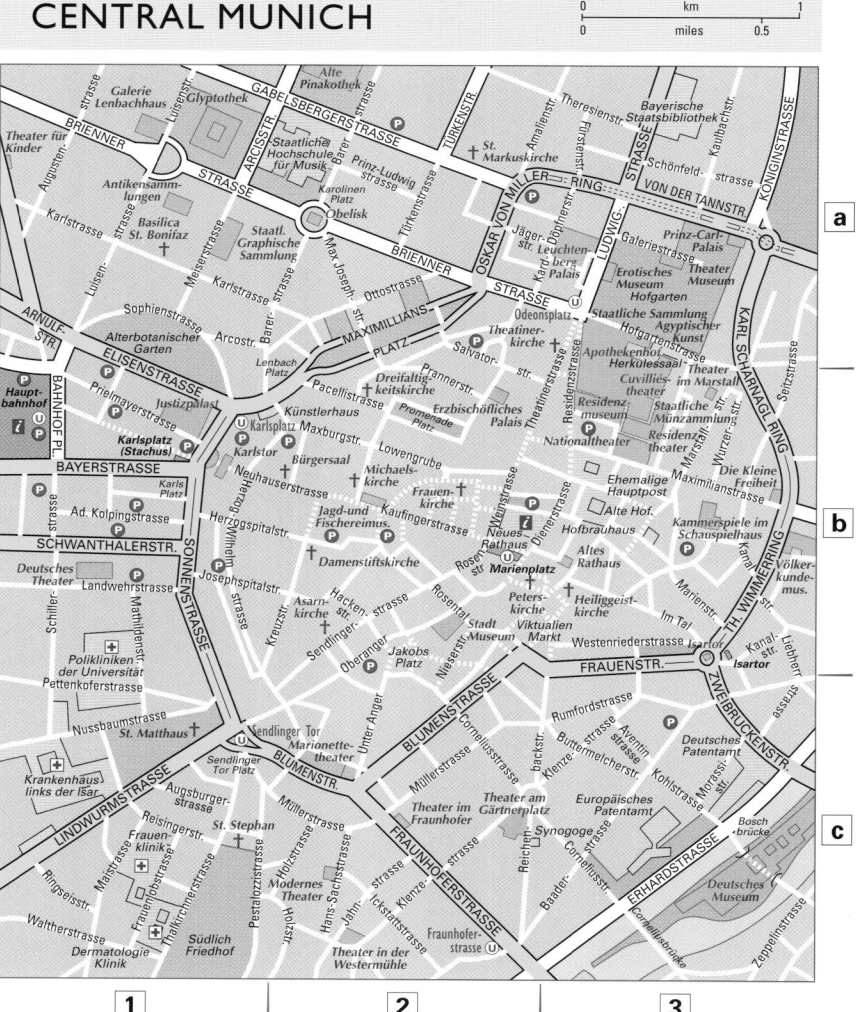

COPYRIGHT PHILIP'S

NEW YORK

0 km 5
0 miles 3

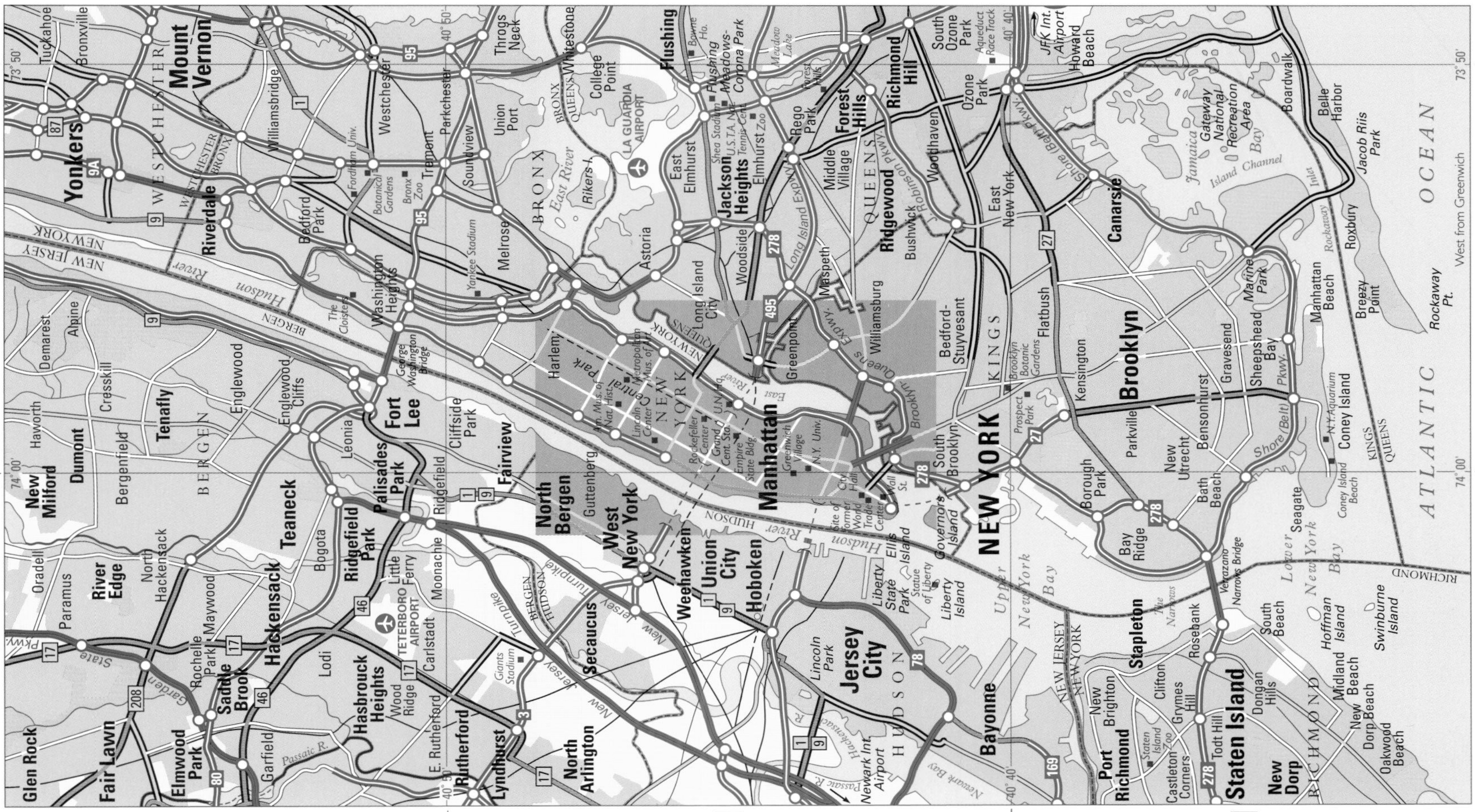
Yonkers
Mount Vernon
Riverdale
Fort Lee
Palisades Park
Teaneck
Hackensack
North Bergen
West New York
Union City
Hoboken
Jersey City
Bayonne
Manhattan
NEW YORK
Brooklyn
Flushing
Jackson Heights
Forest Hills
Richmond Hill
Ridgewood
Canarsie
Staten Island
Stapleton
Port Richmond
New Dorp
Secaucus
Rutherford
Lyndhurst
North Arlington
Fair Lawn
Glen Rock
Hudson
ATLANTIC OCEAN
Upper New York Bay
Lower New York Bay
LA GUARDIA AIRPORT
TETERBORO AIRPORT
BRONX
QUEENS
KINGS
RICHMOND
BERGEN
HUDSON
NEW JERSEY
NEW YORK

CENTRAL NEW YORK

0 km 2
0 miles 1

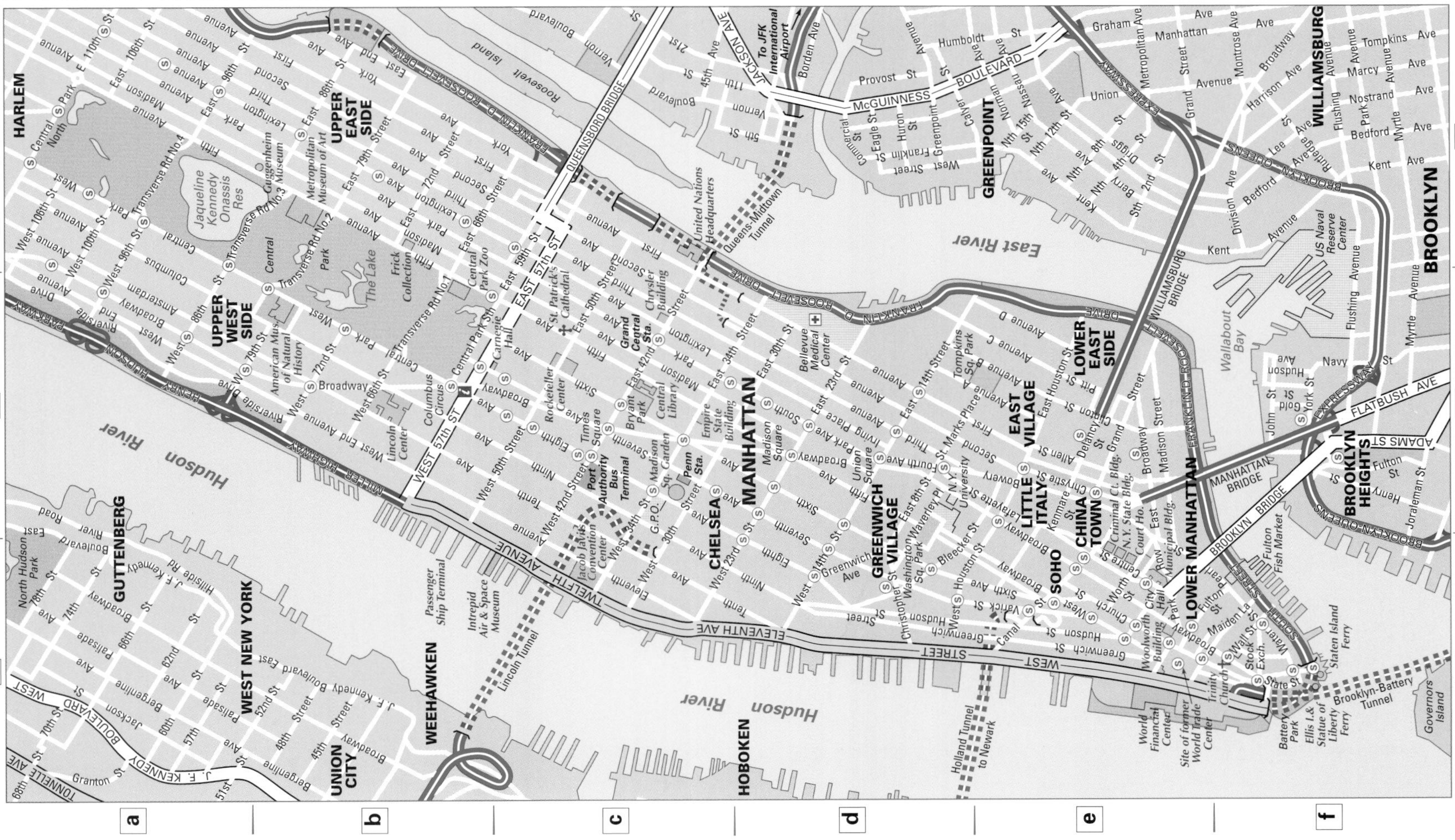
HARLEM
UPPER EAST SIDE
UPPER WEST SIDE
MANHATTAN
CHELSEA
GREENWICH VILLAGE
EAST VILLAGE
LOWER EAST SIDE
LITTLE ITALY
CHINA TOWN
SOHO
LOWER MANHATTAN
GREENPOINT
WILLIAMSBURG
BROOKLYN
BROOKLYN HEIGHTS
GUTTENBERG
WEST NEW YORK
WEEHAWKEN
UNION CITY
HOBOKEN
Hudson River
East River
Roosevelt Island
Central Park
Jacqueline Kennedy Onassis Res
Lincoln Tunnel
Holland Tunnel to Newark
Brooklyn-Battery Tunnel
Queens-Midtown Tunnel
QUEENSBORO BRIDGE
WILLIAMSBURG BRIDGE
MANHATTAN BRIDGE
BROOKLYN BRIDGE
Governors Island
Ellis I. & Statue of Liberty Ferry
Staten Island Ferry
United Nations Headquarters
Empire State Building
Penn Sta.
Grand Central Sta.
Port Authority Bus Terminal
Site of former World Trade Center
Wallabout Bay

OSAKA

km 0 — 5
miles 0 — 3

135° 10' 135° 20' 135° 30'

▲509 Funasaka Takarazuka Hirakata
Karato Arima ▲462 1 Kori
▲598 ▲722 Yamada Senriyama Yamada
Rokkō-Zan 932 Kwansei Gakuin University 171 Settsu Kadoma
Tanigami Yamada Itami OSAKA INTERNATIONAL AIRPORT Toyonaka Neyagawa
428 Iwazono Hirota 173 Suita
Obu-tōge Maya-Zan ▲699 Rokkō Tunnel Kadoma
▲365 Nishinomiya Higashiyodogawa Shijonawate
Ōbu Okamoto Asahi 1 Moriguchi 170
Nada Ashiaya 43 Naruo Jūsō Daitō
Fukiai Higashinada Amagasaki Oyodo Miyakojima Jōtō Kōnoike
▲403 Umeda Kita Osaka Castle Higashinari Ishikiri
Ikuta Nishiyodogawa Fukushima Higashi 308
KŌBE Rokkō Island Konohana Aji Minami Ikuno
Port Island Nishi Nanwa ŌSAKA Higashiōsaka
34° 40' Nagata Kōbe Harbour Minato Tennōji Stadium Shitennoji Temple 34° 40'
Suma Osaka Aquarium Taishō Zoo Abeno Kizuri Yamamoto
Suntory Museum Liberty Osaka Museum Kyūhōji
Osaka Harbour Nishinari Yao
Higashisumiyoshi Tainaka 25
Sumiyoshi Shrine Sumiyoshi 26
Sakai Harbour Ikeuchi YAO AIRPORT Onchi

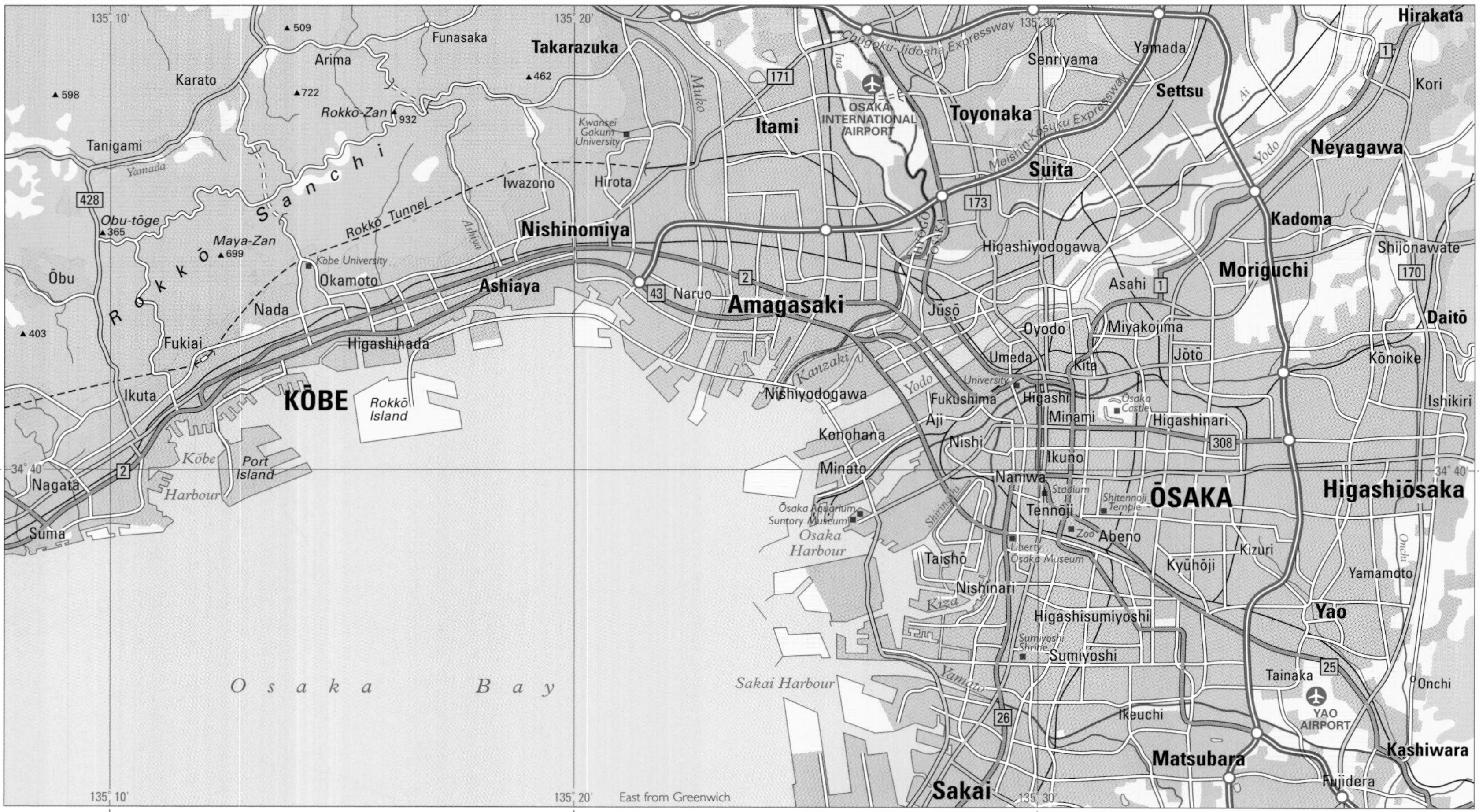

O s a k a   B a y

Matsubara Kashiwara
Sakai 135° 30' Fujidera

East from Greenwich

1 2 3 4

OSLO

km 0 — 5
miles 0 — 3

60° 00' 10° 30' 10° 40' 10° 50' 60° 00'

By OSLO AKERSHUS Tryvannshøgda ▲531 Maridalen
Bogstadvatn Sognsvatn ▲418 Maridalsvatnet Alnsjøen
Burudvatn Holmenkollen Kjelsås
Ila Røa Ris RING 3 Ullevål Gorud
Bærums Verk Lijordet Rødtvet 163
Bryn Haslum Ullern Skøyen OSLO RING 2 Sinsen Alna
▲379 Lysaker Universitet Vestbane sto. 4 Tøyen E6
Kolsås 160 Stabekk Norsk Folke Museum Rådhuset Sentralsta. Bryn
Tanum 164 Bærum 166 E18 Bygdøy Akershus Slott Ryen Oppsal
Høvik Hovedøya Bøler
Sandvika Snarøya Lindøya Bekkelaget E18 E6
Slependen Forshebu Ormøya Lambertseter Østmarkkapellet
Nesøya Frederikshavn Helsingborg København Hirtshals, Kiel Nordstrand
Hvalstad Nesbru Østøya Nesoddtangen Ljabru
Brønnøya Oksval Malmøya 155 Hauketo
Asker 165 Flaskebekk Skoklefall
E18 Konglungen Holmenkollen Bunnefjorden Klemetsrud
59° 50'
167 Vollen Oslofjorden 157 ▲215 Ingierstrand E6
Blakstad Torvvik Kolbotn
Nesodden 156 Myrvoll E6
Slemmestad Fjellstrand Hasle 152
Svestad Oppegård
10° 30' Nærsnes Garder 10° 40' East from Greenwich Blylaget ▲134 E18 Oppegård 10° 50'

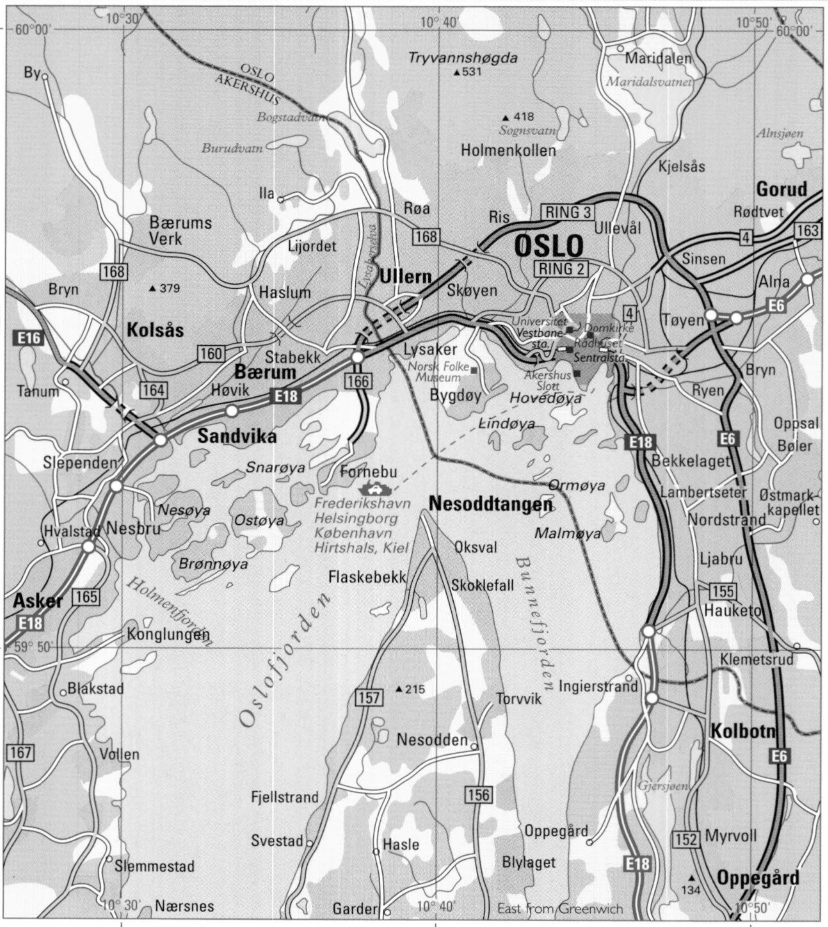

1 2 3 4

CENTRAL OSLO

km 0 — 0.5
miles 0 — 0.25

Parkveien Welhavens gate Stensberg gt. Riksshospitalet Vår Frelsers Gravlund Westye Egebergs gate Nordre gate Korsgata
Hegdehaugsveien Vor Frue hospitalet Damstredet Rostedsgate Brennsveien Gønald Meyers gata
Hoffsvn. Bruns gate Akersveien Dops gate a
Nordahl Kunstindustri mus. St. Olavs-kirke Deichmanske bibliotek Akerselva
Slotts parken ST. OLAVS GATE Thor Olsens gate Maribes gate Øster gate Hausmans gate
Det Kongelige Slottet Historisk museum Fredens Youngs Torget Bernt Ankers gate Christian Krohgs gate
Dronningparken Nasjonal galleriet HAMMERSBORG TUNNELEN Henrik Ibsens gate Brugata
DRAMMENSVEIEN Universitet Det Norske Teater Operaen STENERSGATA Oslo Spektrum
Ibsen-museet National theatret GRENSEN Stortorget Jernbane-torget b
Ruseløkk Johans T Grønland Buss-terminalen
Stenersen-museet Konserthuset Stortingsgata Karl Johans gate Domkirke T Sentralstasjon NYLANDSVEIEN
Vestbane stasjonen Kronpr. Fridtjof Nansens plass Stortinget Biskop Gunnerus gate Havnegata
Dokkveien Rådhuset Hovedpost kontor P BISPEGATA
Teater-museet Christiania torv Tolbugata Børsen
Museet for samtidskunst Arkitekt museet Radhusgata Astrup Fearnley-museet
Piperviken Hjembruogt-museet P Myntgata
Akershus Slott og festning Forsvars-museet Bjørvika Bispevika
Festningskaia Frederikshavn, Helsingborg, København

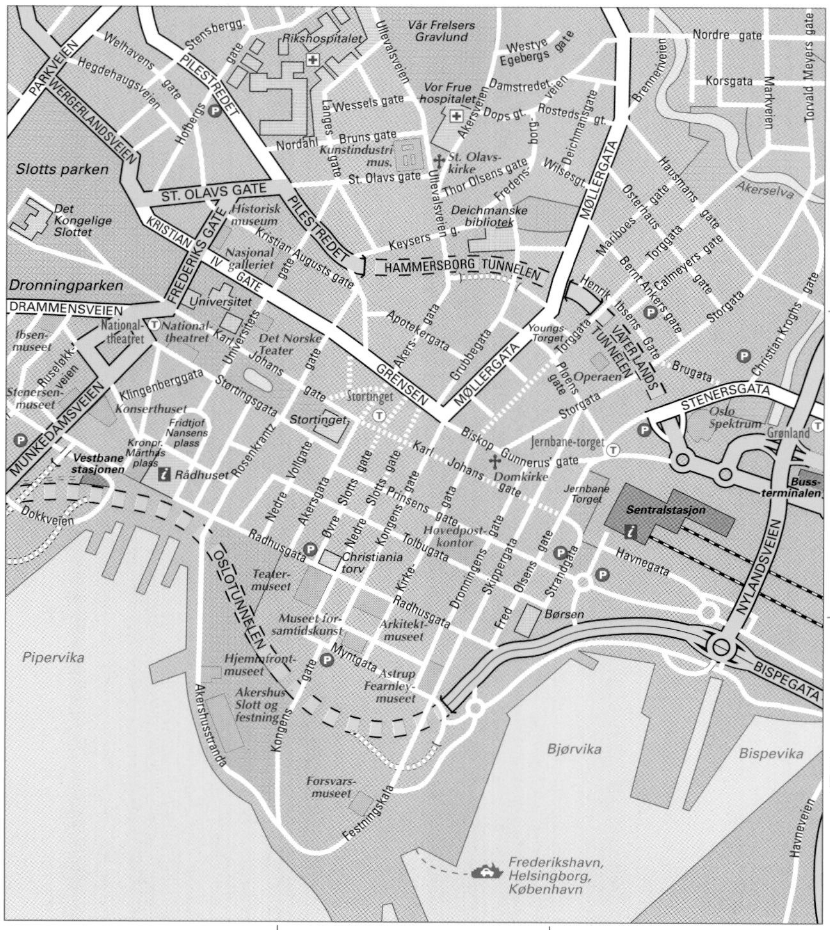

a b c

1 2 3

PARIS

km
miles

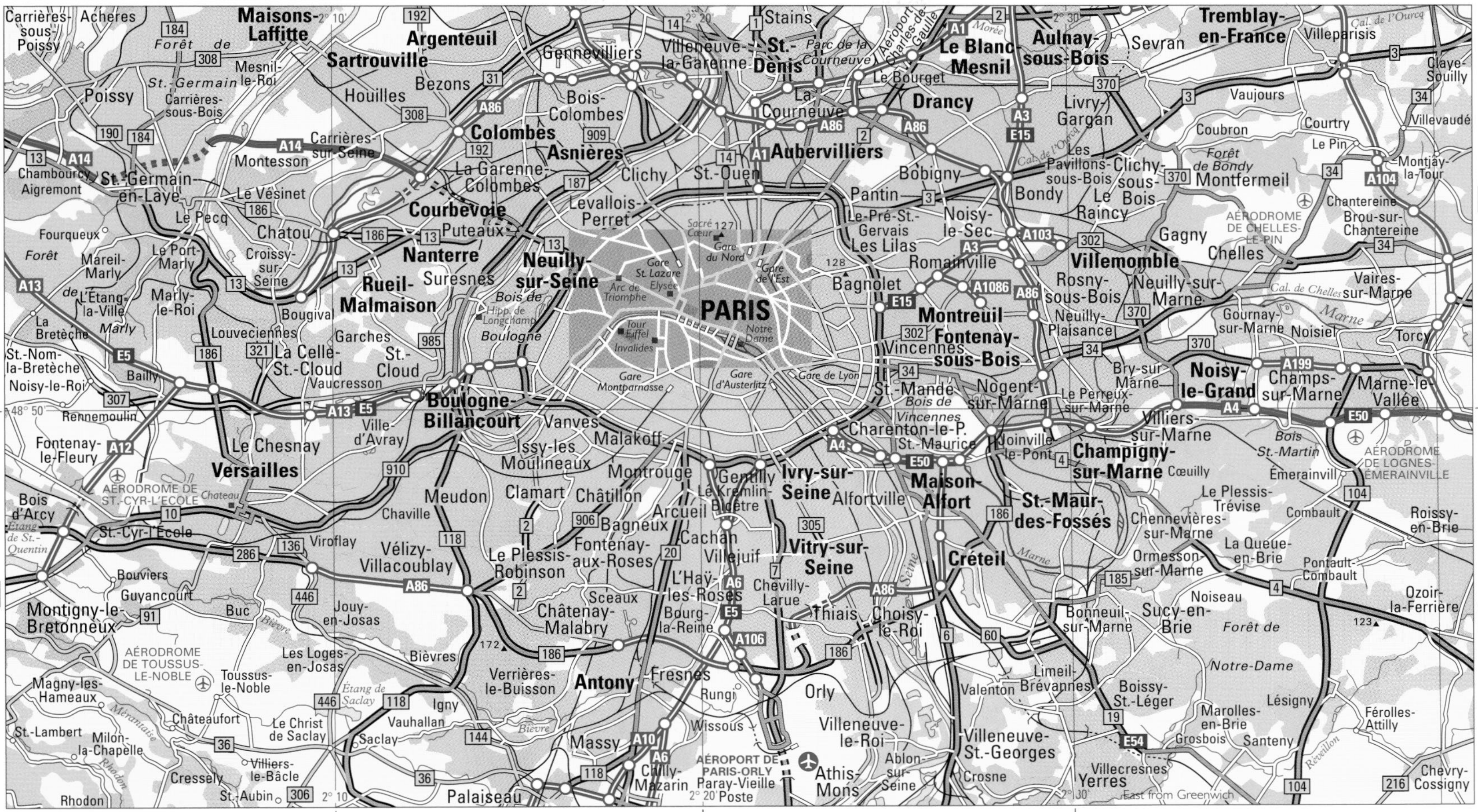

CENTRAL PARIS

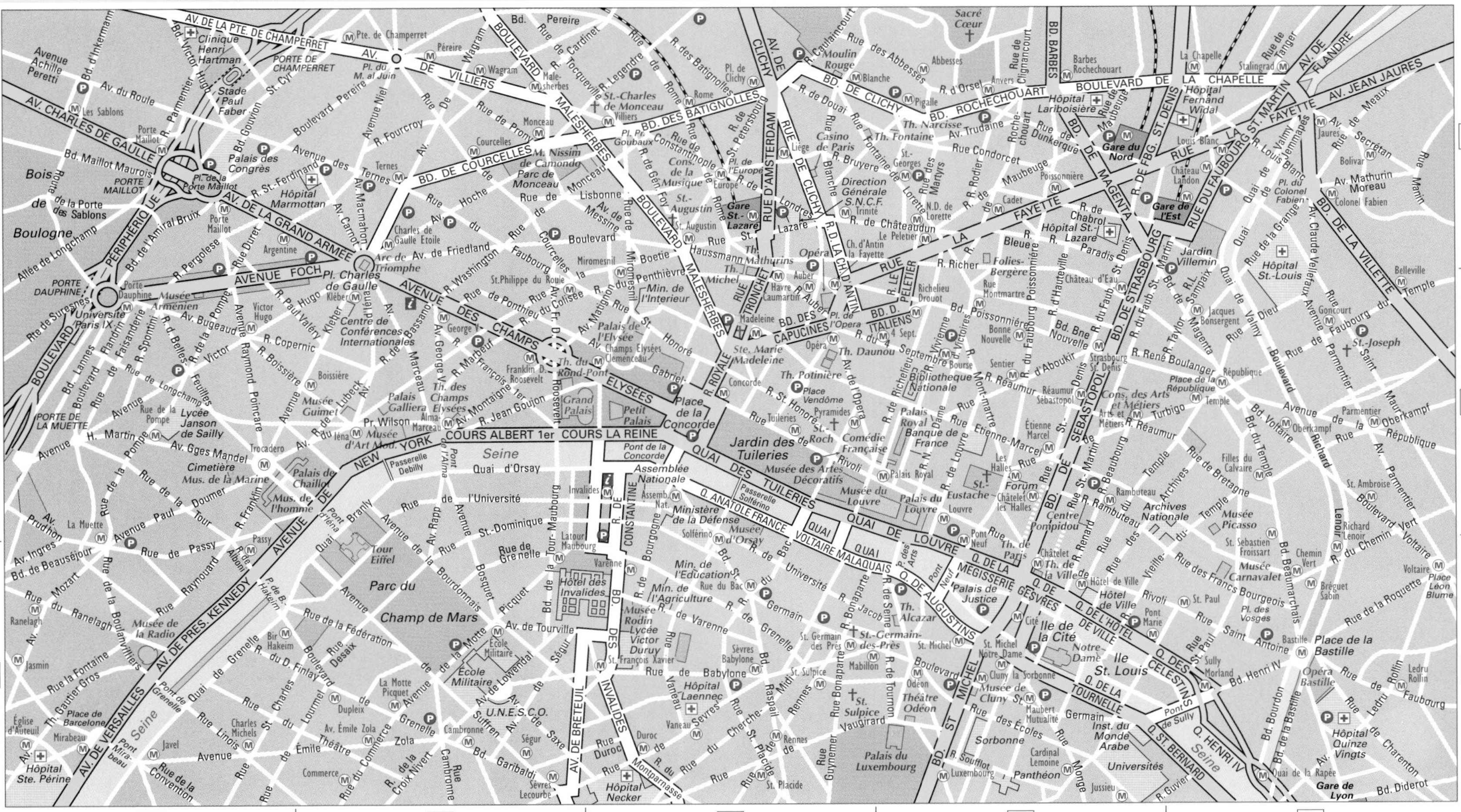

km
miles

PRAGUE

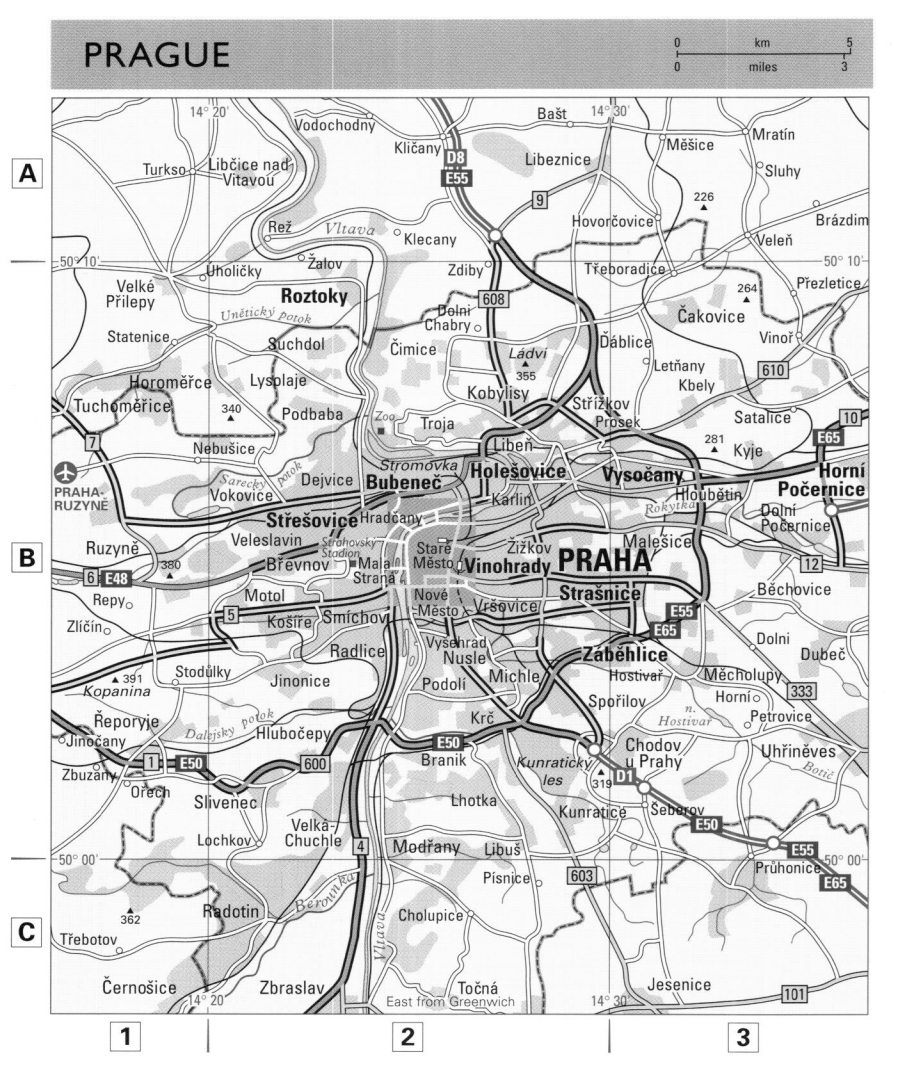

CENTRAL PRAGUE

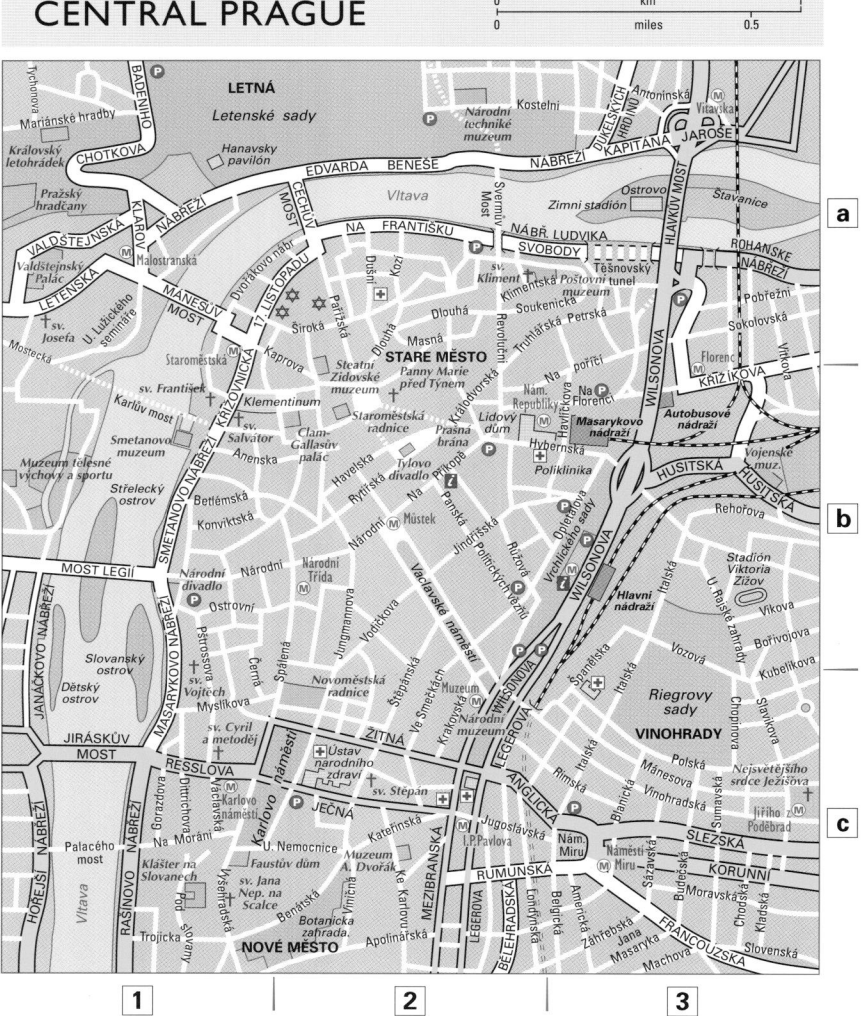

RIO DE JANEIRO

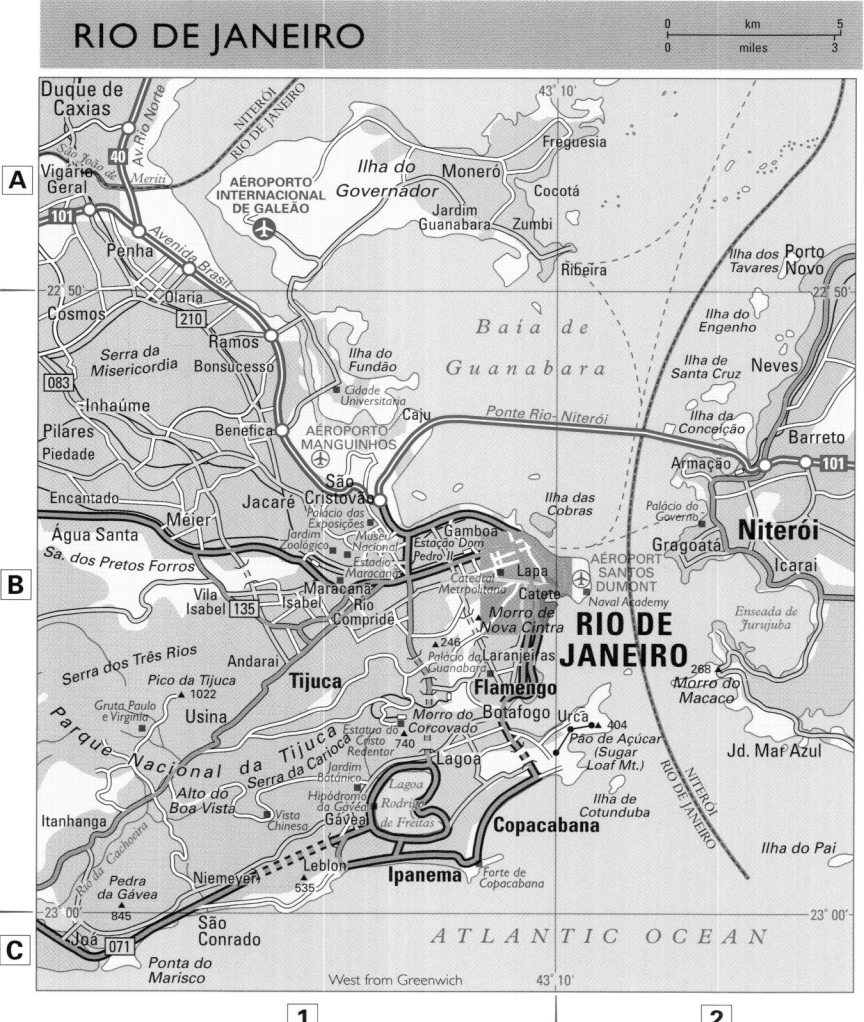

CENTRAL RIO DE JANEIRO

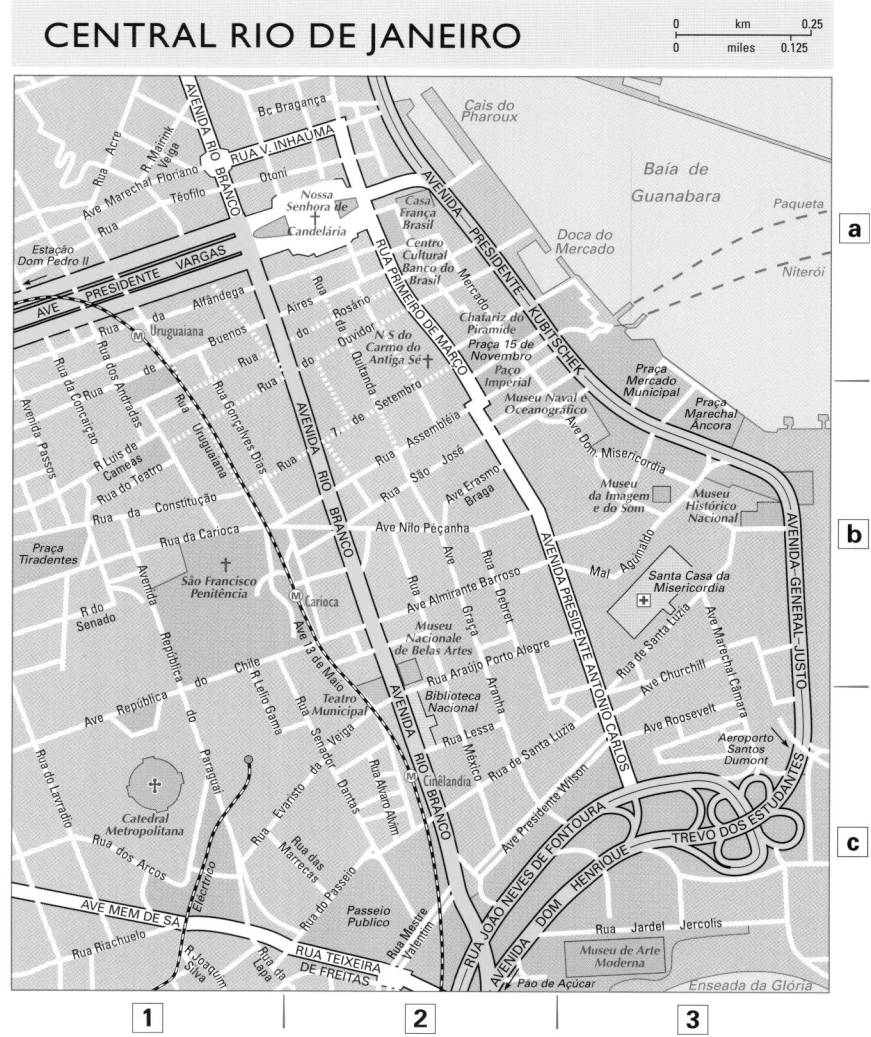

COPYRIGHT PHILIP'S

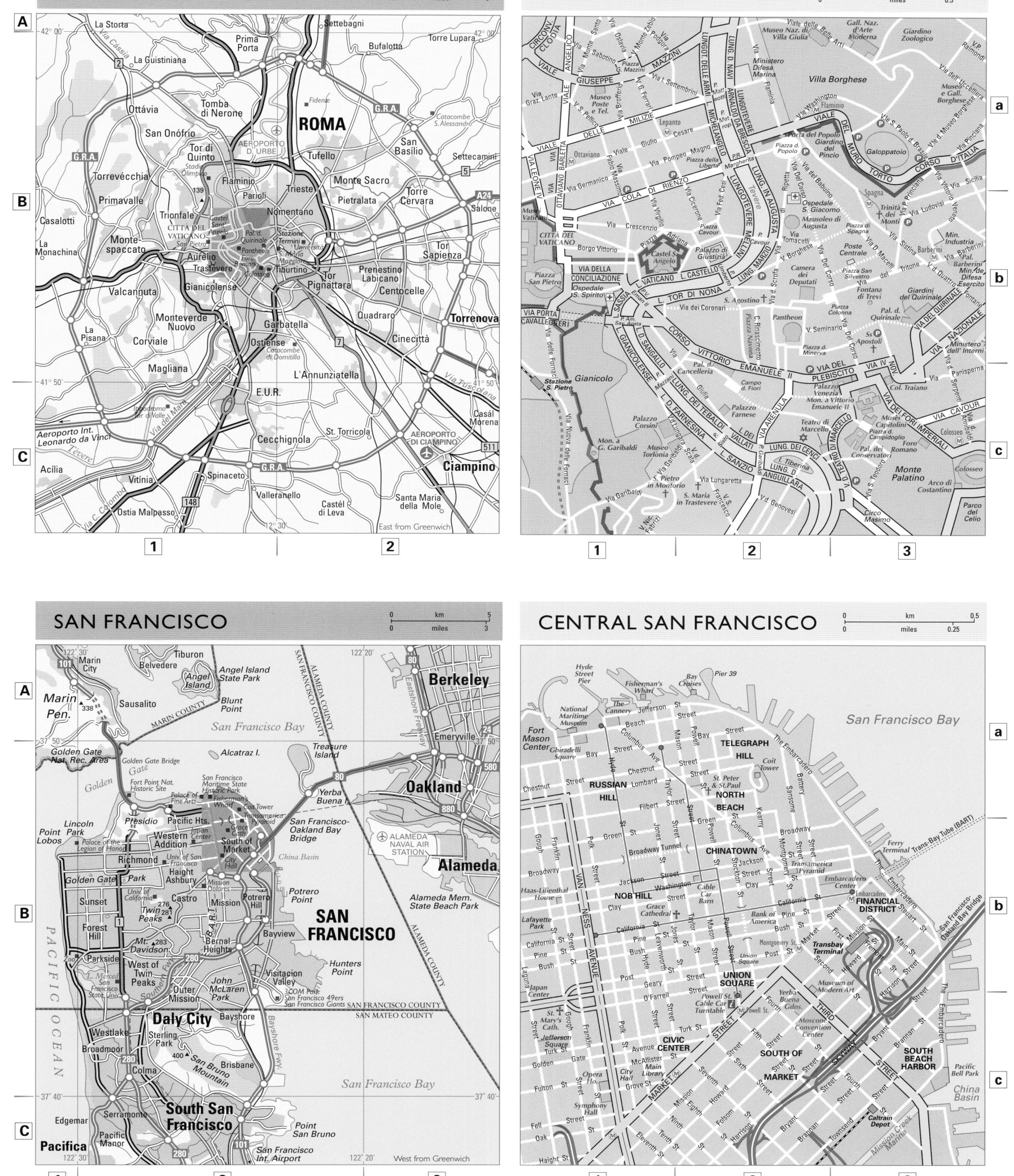

ROME

	1	2
A		
B		
C		

La Storta · Settebagni · Prima Porta · La Guistiniana · Torre Lupara · Bufalotta · Ottávia · Tomba di Nerone · Fidene · ROMA · San Basílio · San Onófrio · Tufello · Settecamini · Tor di Quinto · Torrevécchia · Flaminio · Monte Sacro · Trieste · Parioli · Nomentano · Pietralata · Torre Cervara · Salone · Primavalle · Trionfale · CITTÀ DEL VATICANO · San Pietro · Pal. d. Quirinale · Stazione Termini · Università · Tiburtino · Tor Sapienza · Casalotti · La Monachina · Aurelio Trastévere · Tor Pignattara · Prenestino Labicano · Centocelle · Valcannuta · Gianicolense · Garbatella · Quadraro · Torrenova · Monteverde Nuovo · Cinecittà · La Pisana · Corviale · Ostiense · Catacombe di Domitilla · L'Annunziatella · Magliana · E.U.R. · Cecchignola · Casál Morena · Acília · Ippodromo · St. Torricola · AEROPORTO DI CIAMPINO · Vitínia · Spinaceto · Ciampino · Ostia Malpasso · Valleranello · Castél di Leva · Santa Maria della Mole

Aeroporto Int. Leonardo da Vinci · East from Greenwich

CENTRAL ROME

	1	2	3
a			
b			
c			

Villa Borghese · Gall. Naz. d'Arte Moderna · Giardino Zoologico · Museo Naz. di Villa Giulia · Museo e Gall. Borghese · Porta del Popolo · Piazza d. Popolo · Giardino del Pincio · Galoppatoio · Spagna · Trinità dei Monti · CITTÀ DEL VATICANO · Castel S. Angelo · Piazza San Pietro · Piazza di Spagna · Pantheon · Piazza Navona · Campo d. Fiori · Palazzo Venezia · Mon. a Vittorio Emanuele II · Monte Palatino · Colosseo · Arco di Costantino · Gianicolo · Stazione S. Pietro · Mon. a G. Garibaldi · Museo Torlónia · S. Maria in Trastevere · Parco del Celio

SAN FRANCISCO

	1	2	3
A			
B			
C			

Marin City · Tiburon · Angel Island State Park · Berkeley · Marin Pen. · Belvedere · Angel Island · Blunt Point · Sausalito · MARIN COUNTY · ALAMEDA COUNTY · San Francisco Bay · Emeryville · Golden Gate Nat. Rec. Area · Alcatraz I. · Treasure Island · Oakland · Golden Gate Bridge · Fort Point Nat. Historic Site · San Francisco Maritime State Historic Park · Yerba Buena I. · San Francisco-Oakland Bay Bridge · ALAMEDA NAVAL AIR STATION · Lincoln Park · Palace of Fine Arts · Presidio · Pacific Hts. · Fisherman's Wharf · Coit Tower · Transamerica Pyramid · China Basin · Alameda · Point Lobos · Palace of the Legion of Honor · Western Addition · Japan Center · South of Market · City Hall · Alameda Mem. State Beach Park · Richmond · Univ. of San Francisco · Golden Gate Park · Haight Ashbury · Mission Dolores · Potrero Point · SAN FRANCISCO · Sunset · Univ. of California · Castro · Mission · Potrero Hill · PACIFIC OCEAN · Forest Hill · Twin Peaks · Bayview · Mt. Davidson · Bernal Heights · Parkside · West of Twin Peaks · Hunters Point · Outer Mission · John McLaren Park · Visitacion Valley · San Francisco 49ers · San Francisco Giants · SAN FRANCISCO COUNTY · SAN MATEO COUNTY · Daly City · Bayshore · Westlake · Sterling Park · San Bruno Mountain · Brisbane · Broadmoor · Colma · San Francisco Bay · Edgemar · Serramonte · South San Francisco · Point San Bruno · Pacifica · Pacific Manor · San Francisco Int. Airport

West from Greenwich

CENTRAL SAN FRANCISCO

	1	2	3
a			
b			
c			

Hyde Street Pier · Fisherman's Wharf · Bay Cruises · Pier 39 · National Maritime Museum · The Cannery · Jefferson Street · San Francisco Bay · Fort Mason Center · Ghirardelli Square · TELEGRAPH HILL · Coit Tower · RUSSIAN HILL · St. Peter & St. Paul · NORTH BEACH · The Embarcadero · Trans-Bay Tube (BART) · Broadway Tunnel · CHINATOWN · Transamerica Pyramid · Ferry Terminal · Embarcadero Center · Haas-Lilienthal House · NOB HILL · Cable Car Barn · FINANCIAL DISTRICT · San Francisco-Oakland Bay Bridge · Lafayette Park · Grace Cathedral · Bank of America · Union Square · Transbay Terminal · Japan Center · UNION SQUARE · Yerba Buena Gdns. · Museum of Modern Art · St. Mary's Cath. · Powell St. Cable Car Turntable · CIVIC CENTER · Moscone Convention Center · SOUTH OF MARKET · SOUTH BEACH HARBOR · Jefferson Square · Opera Ho. · City Hall · MARKET · Pacific Bell Park · Symphony Hall · China Basin · Caltrain Depot · Mission Creek Marina

COPYRIGHT PHILIP'S

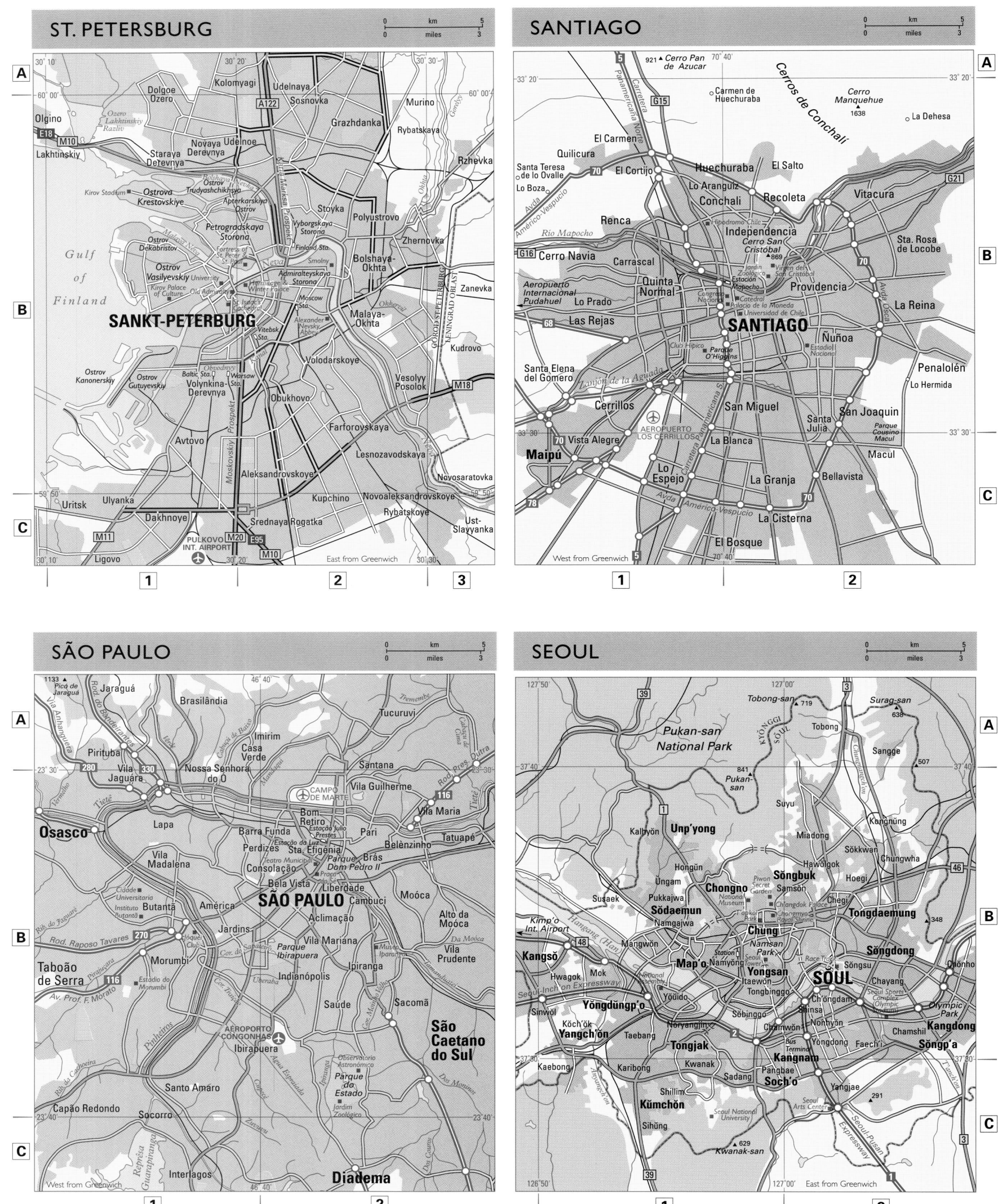

ST. PETERSBURG

km 0 — 5
miles 0 — 3

Olgino
Dolgoe Ozero
Kolomyagi
Udelnaya
Sosnovka
Murino
A122
Ozero Lakhtinskiy Razliv
Grazhdanka
Rybatskaya
E18 M10
Lakhtinskiy
Novaya Derevnya
Udelnoe
Staraya Derevnya
Rzhevka
Kirov Stadium
Ostrova Trudyashchikhsya
Ostrova Krestovskiye
Apterkarskiya Ostrov
Stoyka
Polyustrovo
Petrogradskaya Storona
Vyborgskaya Storona
Zhernovka
Ostrova Dekabristov
Fortress of St. Peter
Finland Sta.
Bolshaya-Okhta
Ostrov Vasilyevskiy
University
Hermitage Winter Palace
Admiralteyskaya Storona
Smolny
St. Isaac's Cathedral
Moscow Sta.
Zanevka
Kirov Palace of Culture
Old Admiralty
Alexander Nevsky Abbey
SANKT-PETERBURG
Vitebsk Sta.
Malaya-Okhta
Okkervil
Kudrovo
LENINGRAD OBLAST
Gulf
of
Finland
Ostrov Kanonerskiy
Baltic Sta.
Obvodnyy Canal
Volodarskoye
Ostrov Gutuyevskiy
Warsaw Sta.
Volynkina-Derevnya
Vesolyy Posolok
M18
Obukhovo
Farforovskaya
Avtovo
Lesnozavodskaya
Novosaratovka
Aleksandrovskoye
Uritsk
Ulyanka
Kupchino
Novoaleksandrovskoye
Dakhnoye
Srednaya Rogatka
Rybatskoye
M11
Ust-Slavyanka
PULKOVO INT. AIRPORT
M20
E95
Ligovo
M10

SANTIAGO

km 0 — 5
miles 0 — 3

921 Cerro Pan de Azucar
5
70° 40'
Cerros de Conchalí
Carmen de Huechuraba
Cerro Manquehue 1638
La Dehesa
Carretera Panamericana Norte
G15
El Carmen
Quilicura
Huechuraba
El Salto
70
El Cortijo
Lo Aranguiz
Vitacura
G21
Santa Teresa de lo Ovalle
Lo Boza
Conchali
Recoleta
Avda Vespucio
Renca
Independencia
Sta. Rosa de Locobe
Río Mapocho
Hipódromo Chile
Cerro San Cristóbal 869
70
G16 Cerro Navia
Carrascal
Jardin Zoológico
Virgen del San Cristóbal
Providencia
Quinta Normal
Estación Mapocho
Congreso Nacional
Palacio de la Moneda
La Reina
Aeropuerto Internacional Pudahuel
Lo Prado
Catedral
Universidad de Chile
Avda Oscar
68
Las Rejas
SANTIAGO
Ñuñoa
Santa Elena del Gomero
Club Hípico
Parque O'Higgins
Estadio Nacional
Penalolén
Cañon de la Aguada
Lo Hermida
Cerrillos
San Miguel
Santa Julia
San Joaquin
Parque Cousiño Macul
AEROPUERTO LOS CERRILLOS
70
Vista Alegre
La Blanca
Macul
Maipú
Lo Espejo
La Granja
Bellavista
78
Avda Américo Vespucio
70
La Cisterna
El Bosque
5
West from Greenwich
70° 40'

SÃO PAULO

km 0 — 5
miles 0 — 3

1133 Pico de Jaraguá
Jaraguá
Brasilândia
Tucuruvi
Tremembé
Via Anhanguera
Rod. dos Bandeirantes
Piritúba
Imirim
Casa Verde
Cabuçu de Cima
280
Vila Jaguára
330
Nossa Senhora do Ó
Santana
Rod. Pres. Dutra
Tietê
CAMPO DE MARTE
Vila Guilherme
116
Osasco
Lapa
Bom Retiro
Estação Júlio Prestes
Pari
Vila Maria
Tatuapé
Vila Madalena
Barra Funda
Estação da Luz
Perdizes
Sta. Efigênia
Belènzinho
Teatro Municipal
Parque Dom Pedro II
Brás
Cidade Universitária
Consolação
SÃO PAULO
Cambuci
Moóca
Instituto Butantã
Butantã
Bela Vista
Liberdade
270
América
Jardins
Aclimação
Alto da Moóca
Rod. Raposo Tavares
Jóquei Club
Parque Ibirapuera
Vila Mariana
Vila Prudente
Taboão de Serra
Morumbi
Indianópolis
Ipiranga
Da Moóca
116
Estádio do Morumbi
Saúde
Sacomã
Av. Prof. F. Morato
AEROPORTO CONGONHAS
São Caetano do Sul
Ibirapuera
Observatório Astronômico
Santo Amaro
Parque do Estado
Capão Redondo
Socorro
Jardim Zoológico
Interlagos
Represa Guarapiranga
West from Greenwich
46° 40'
Diadema

SEOUL

km 0 — 5
miles 0 — 3

127° 50'
127° 00'
3
39
Tobong-san 719
Surag-san 638
Pukan-san National Park
Tobong
Sangge
507
KYŎNGGI
1
Suyu
Kongnŭng
841 Pukan-san
Miadong
Sŏkkwan
Chungwha
Kalbyŏn
Unp'yong
46
Hongŭn
Susaek
Ûngam
Pukkajwa
Chongno
Samsŏn
Hoegi
Chegi
Piwon Secret Garden
Songbuk
Kimp'o Int. Airport
Namgajwa
Changdok Palace
Tongdaemung
348
Hangang (Han)
Sŏdaemun
Ch'ung
Namsan Park
Songsu
48
Mangwŏn
Map'o
Station
Namyŏng
Songdong
Kangsŏ
Hwagok
Mok
National Cemetery
Yongsan
Chongam
Chŏnho
Seoul Tower
Itaewŏn
SŎUL
Chayang
Hwagok
Yŏŭido
Tongbinggo
Shinsa
Seoul Sports Complex (Olympic Stadium)
Seoul-Inch'on Expressway
Sinwŏl
Köch'ök
Sŏbinggo
Olympic Park
Yŏngdŭngp'o
Taebang
Noryangjin
Chamwŏn
Nonhyŏn
Yongdong
Kangdong
Yangch'ŏn
Kaebong
Tongjak
Bus Terminal
Faech'i
Songp'a
Kangnam
Pangbae
Shillim
Karibong
Kwanak
Sadang
P'ongbae
Soch'o
Yangjae
Sŏul Arts Center
Kümch'ŏn
Seoul National University
291
Sihŭng
Seoul-Pusan Expressway
3
629 Kwanak-san
126° 50'
127° 00'
East from Greenwich
39

SHANGHAI

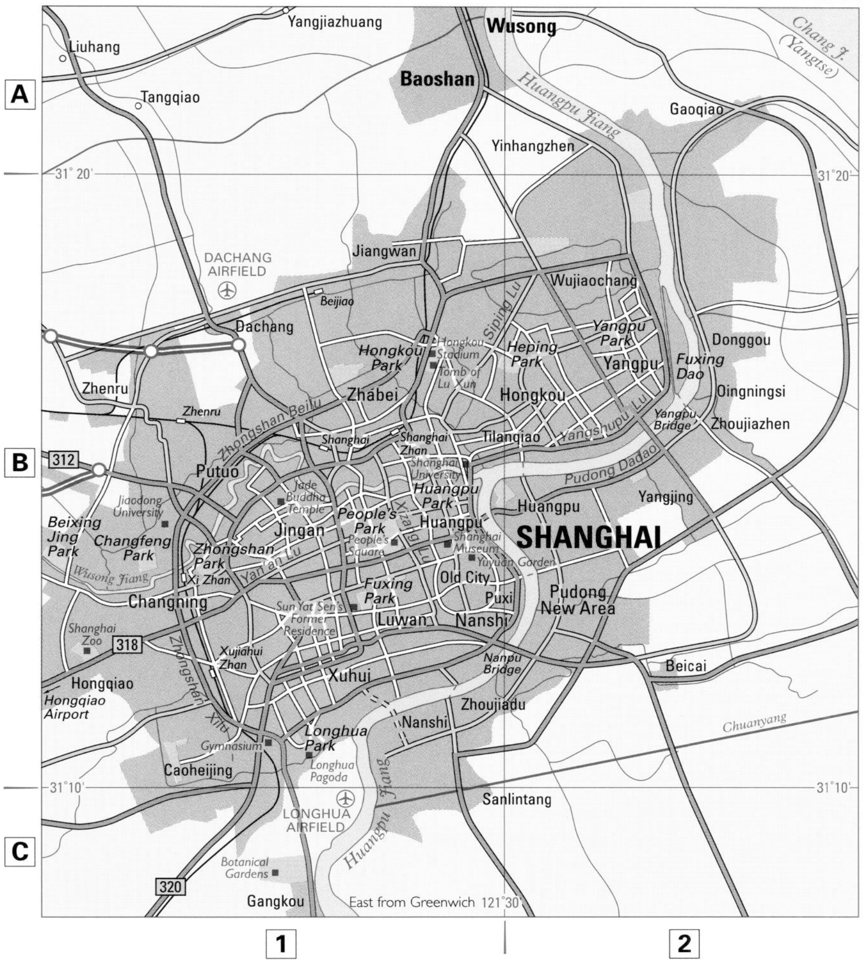

km 0 5
miles 0 3

A

Liuhang
Yangjiazhuang
Wusong
Tangqiao
Baoshan
Yinhangzhen
Gaoqiao
Huangpu Jiang
Chang J. (Yangtse)
31° 20'
31°20'
DACHANG AIRFIELD
Jiangwan
Dachang
Wujiaochang
Donggou
Beijiao
Zhenru
Hongkou Stadium
Heping Park
Yangpu Park
Yangpu
Fuxing Dao
Zhenru
Tomb of Lu Xun
Hongkou
Yangpu Bridge
Zhoujiazhen
312
Putuo
Zhabei
Shanghai Zhan
Tilangiao
Qingningsi
Jiaodong University
Jade Buddha Temple
People's Park
Huangpu Park
Huangpu
Yangjing
B
Beixing Jing Park
Changfeng Park
Jingan
Peoples Sq
Shanghai Museum
SHANGHAI
Pudong Dadao
Zhongshan Park
Xi Zhan
Yan'an Lu
Fuxing Park
Old City
Pudong New Area
Changning
Sun Yat Sen's Former Residence
Luwan
Puxi
318
Shanghai Zoo
Xujiahui
Xu Zhan
Nanshi
Beicai
Gymnasium
Nanpu Bridge
Zhoujiadu
Caoheijing
Longhua Park
Nanshi
Longhua Pagoda
Sanlintang
Chuanyang
31° 10'
31°10'
C
Botanical Gardens
LONGHUA AIRFIELD
320
Gangkou
East from Greenwich 121°30'

1   2

CENTRAL SINGAPORE

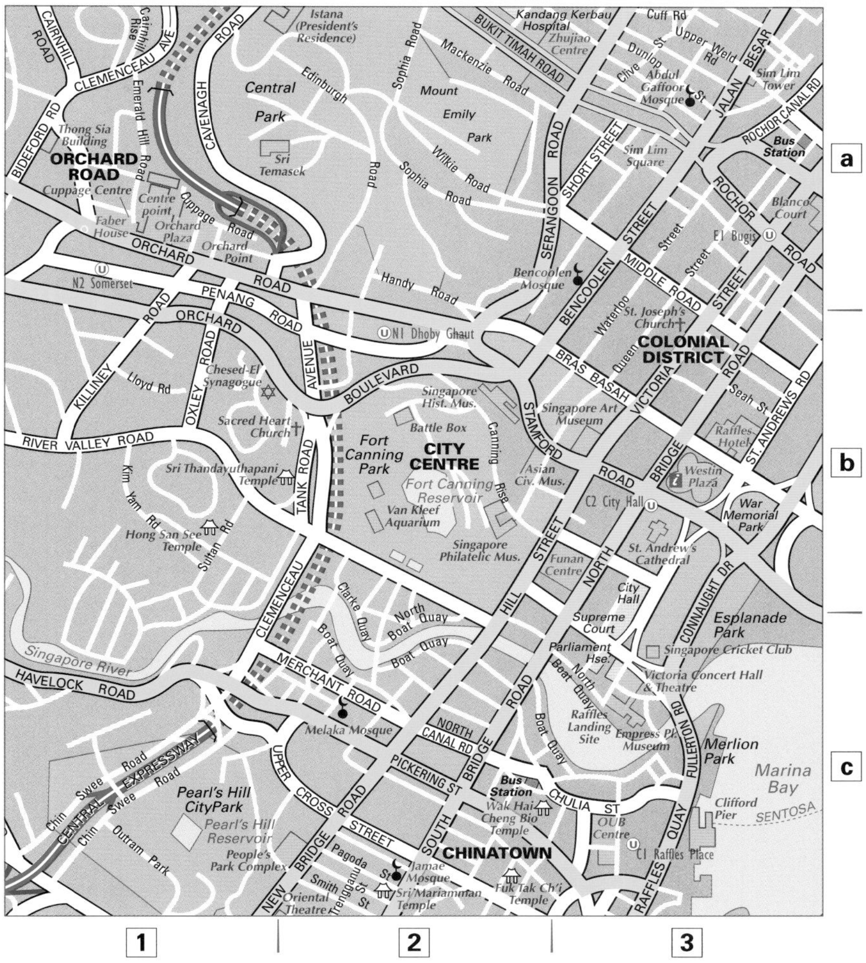

km 0 1
miles 0 0.5

Kandang Kerbau Hospital
CAIRNHILL ROAD
Cairnhill Rise
Istana (President's Residence)
BUKIT TIMAH ROAD
Zhujiao Centre
Cuff Rd
Upper Weld Rd
CLEMENCEAU AVE
Central Park
Edinburgh
Emerald Hill
Mount Sophia
Mackenzie Road
Dunlop
Abdul Gafoor Mosque
Sun Lim Tower
a
BIDEFORD RD
Thong Sia Building
Sri Temasck
Wilkie Road
SERANGOON ROAD
SHORT STREET
Sin Lim Square
ROCHOR CANAL RD
Bus Station
ORCHARD ROAD
Cuppage Centre
Faber House
Centre point
Orchard Plaza
Orchard Point
Sophia Road
Handy Road
Bencoolen Mosque
BENCOOLEN
MIDDLE ROAD
Blanco Court
ROCHOR ROAD
El Bugis Street
N2 Somerset
ORCHARD
PENANG ROAD
Dhoby Ghaut
Waterloo
St. Joseph's Church
COLONIAL DISTRICT
b
KILLINEY ROAD
Lloyd Rd
Chesed-El Synagogue
ORCHARD
AVENUE
BOULEVARD
BRAS BASAH
Singapore Art Museum
VICTORIA STREET
Seah St
Raffles Hotel
Westin Plaza
OXLEY RD
Sacred Heart Church
Singapore Hist. Mus.
Battle Box
Asian Civ. Mus.
ST ANDREWS RD
War Memorial Park
RIVER VALLEY ROAD
Sri Thandayuthapani Temple
Fort Canning Park
CITY CENTRE
Fort Canning Reservoir
Asian Civ. Mus.
C2 City Hall
St. Andrew's Cathedral
b
Hong San See Temple
TANK ROAD
Van Kleef Aquarium
Singapore Philatelic Mus.
STAMFORD
Funan Centre
NORTH BRIDGE
Supreme Court
City Hall
Esplanade Park
CLEMENCEAU
Sultan Mosque
Clarke Quay
North Boat Quay
Parliament Hse
Raffles Landing Site
Victoria Concert Hall & Theatre
Singapore Cricket Club
MERCHANT ROAD
Boat Quay
South Boat Quay
HILL STREET
Empress Pl
Fullerton Rd
Empress Pl. Museum
Merlion Park
c
HAVELOCK ROAD
Singapore River
Melaka Mosque
NORTH CANAL RD
Melaka Mosque
PICKERING ST
Bus Station
Wak Hai Cheng Bio Temple
CHULA ST
Marina Bay
Clifford Pier
SENTOSA
Chin Swee Road
Pearl's Hill CityPark
UPPER CROSS ROAD
CANAL RD
Melaka Mosque
NEW BRIDGE
SOUTH BRIDGE
Pagoda St
OLB Centre
Raffles Quay
c
CENTRAL EXPRESSWAY
Outram Park
Pearl's Hill Reservoir
People's Park Complex
New Oriental Theatre
Smith St
CHINATOWN
Jamae Mosque
Sri Mariamman Temple
Tak Chi Temple

1   2   3

SINGAPORE

km 0 10
miles 0 6

Johor Baharu
103°40'
Malaya
Sembawang
Selat Johor
103°50'
Pulau Seletar
104°00'
MALAYSIA SINGAPORE
Kranji Ind. Est.
Woodlands New Town
Chong Pang
Yishun New Town
Punggol Point
Pulau Ubin
Pulau Tekong Kechil
Pulau Tekong
A
Lim Chu Kang
Sarimbun Res.
Seletar Expy.
Nee Soon
SELETAR AIRPORT
Pulau Serangoon
Tg. Ladang
A
Sarimbun ▲85
Murai Res.
Ama Keng
Zoological Gardens Seletar Reservoir
Jalan Kayu
Punggol
Loyang Ind. Est.
Changi
Choa Chu Kang
Poyan Res.
Kranji Expy.
St Tongh
Sg. Kranji
Bukit Panjang Nature Reserve
Upper Peirce Reservoir
Seletar Hills
Serangoon Harbour
Pasir Ris
Bulim
Bukit Panjang
132
Ang Mo Kio
Chia Keng
PAYA LEBAR AIRPORT
Yan Kit
CHANGI INTERNATIONAL AIRPORT
(Choa Chu Kang 88▲)
Bt. Panjang
Bukit Timah Nature Reserve
▲162
MacRitchie Reservoir
Serangoon
Tampines
Nanyang University
106
Bukit Batok Nature Parks
Air View Park
Raffles Park
Pan Island Expy.
Paya Lebar
Tai Seng
Bedok Reservoir
Kg Landang
Simei
Tanah Merah Golf Course
1° 20'N
Jurong
Bt. Peropok ▲
Jurong Industrial Estate
Clementi
Maryland
Victoria Park
University of Singapore Botanic Gardens
Toa Payoh
Dunearn
Geylang Serai
Geylang
Chai Chee
Bedok
1° 20'N
Tuas
62▲
Chinese & Japanese Gardens
Jurong Town
Pandan Res.
Holland Village
Queenstown
Katong
Frankel
East Coast Park
B
Pulau Pesek
Selat Jurong
Pulau Merlimau
Pasir Panjang
Kg Tanjong Penjuru
Telok Blangah
Buona Vista Park
Mt. 105 Fabour
Kallang Park
National Stadium
East Coast Pkwy.
B
Pulau Ayer Chawan
Pulau Seraya
105
World Trade Centre
SINGAPORE
Pulau Ayer Merbau
Cable Car
P. Brani
Thian Hock Keng
City Hall
St Andrew's Cath
Pulau Sakra
Selat Pandan
P. Bukum
Sentosa
Straits of Singapore
Selat Sinki
103°40'
103°50'
East from Greenwich
104°00'

1   2   3   4

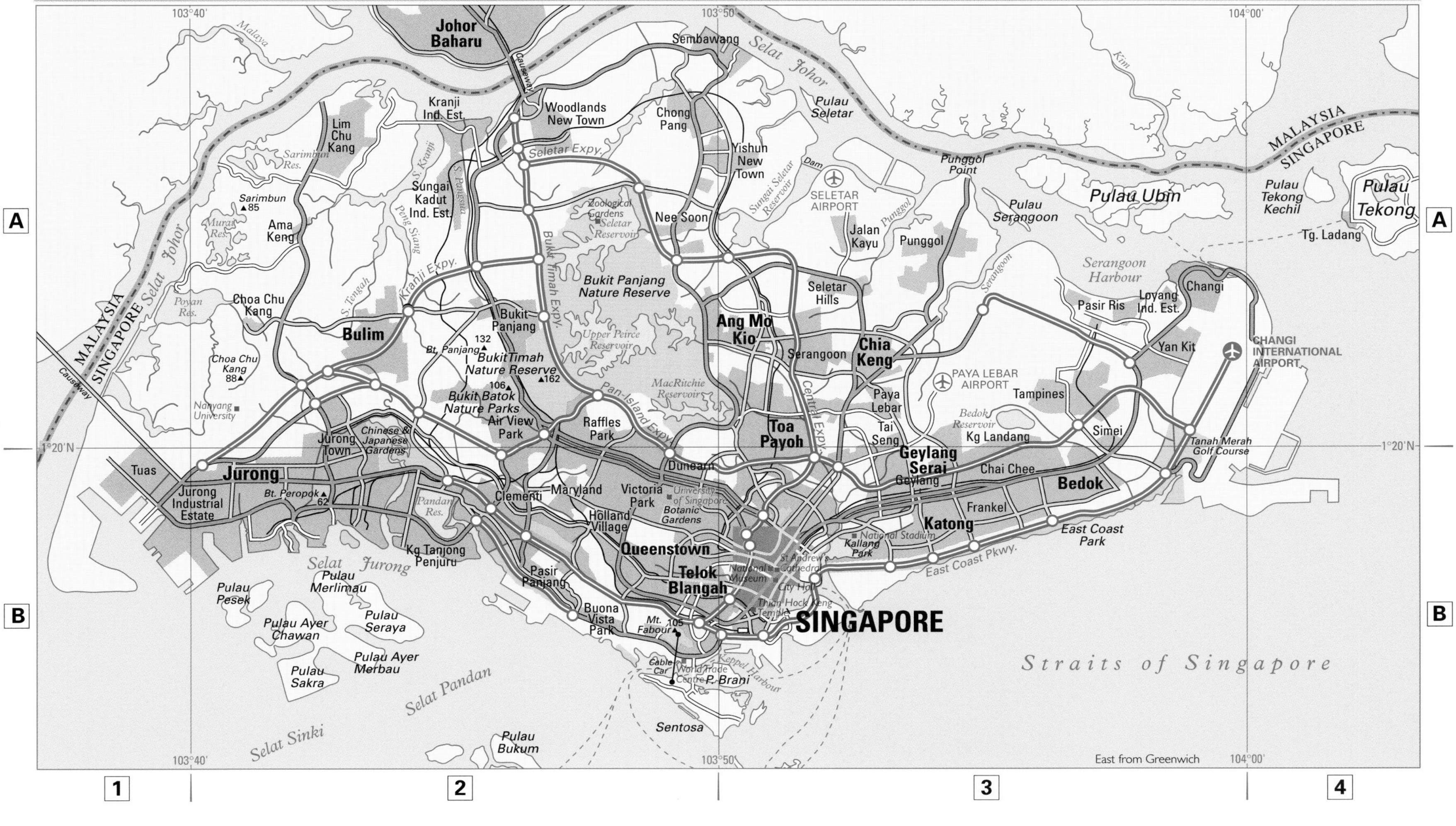

COPYRIGHT PHILIP'S

STOCKHOLM

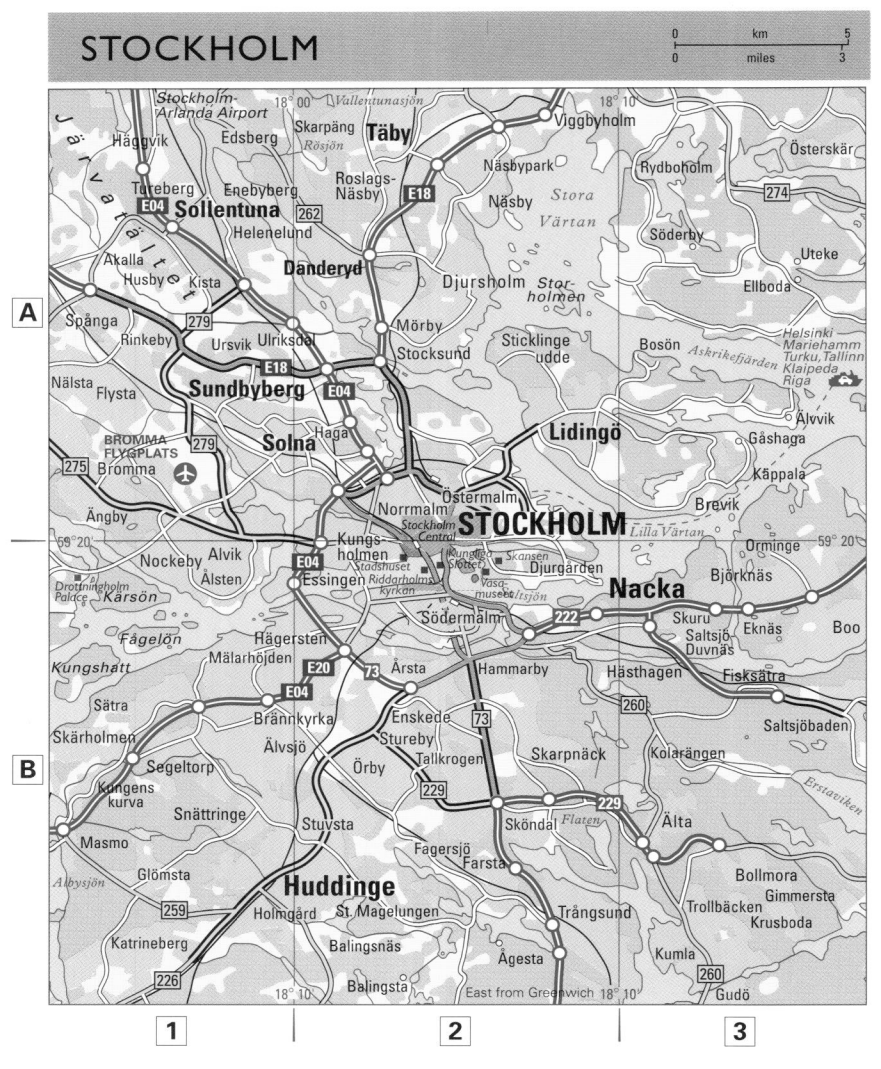

CENTRAL STOCKHOLM

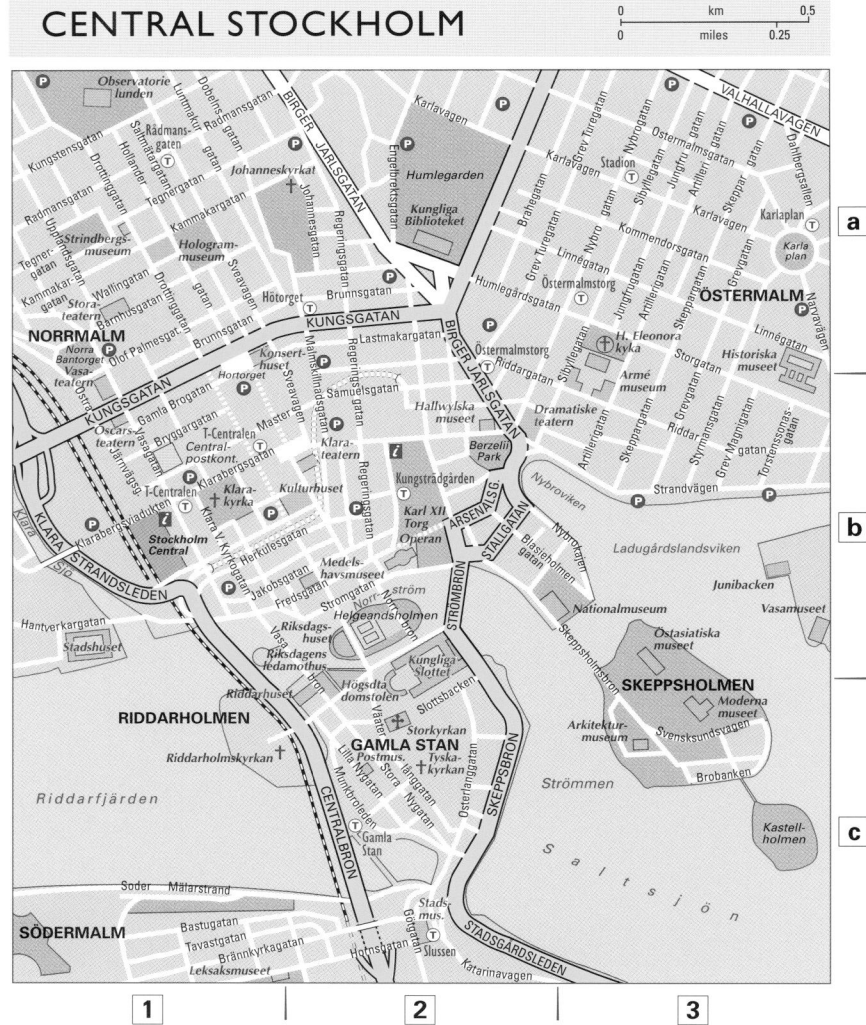

SYDNEY

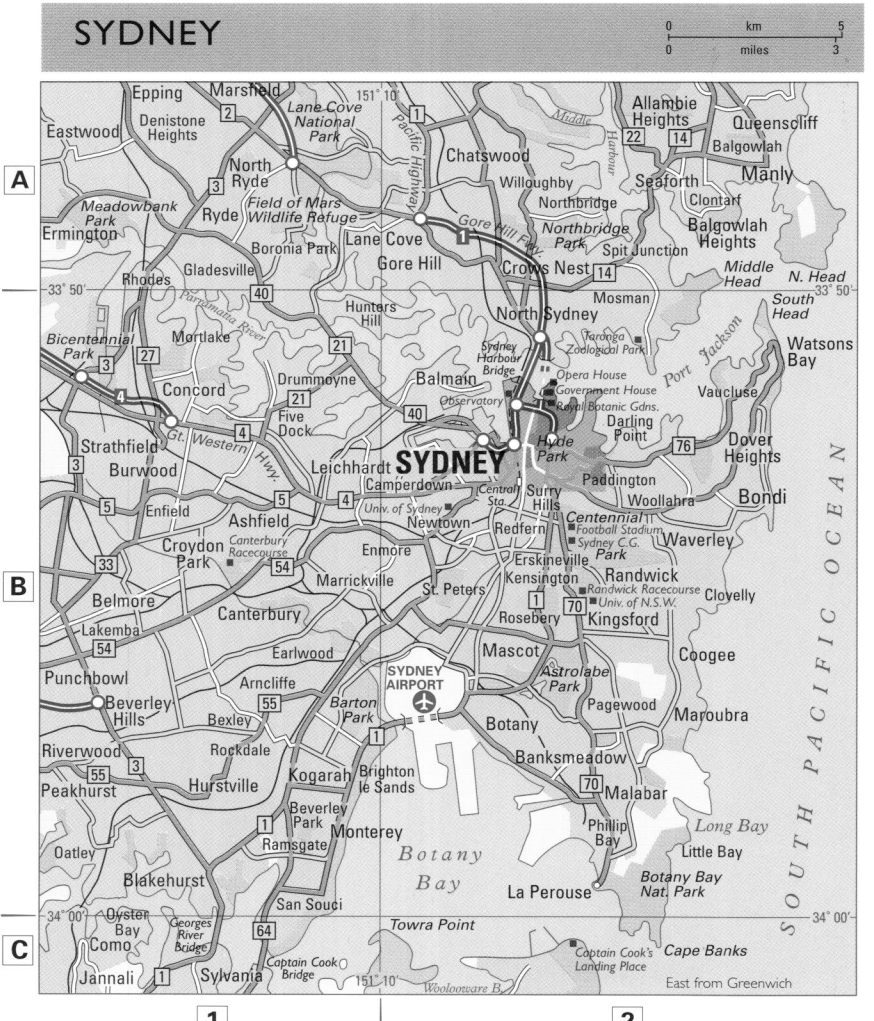

CENTRAL SYDNEY

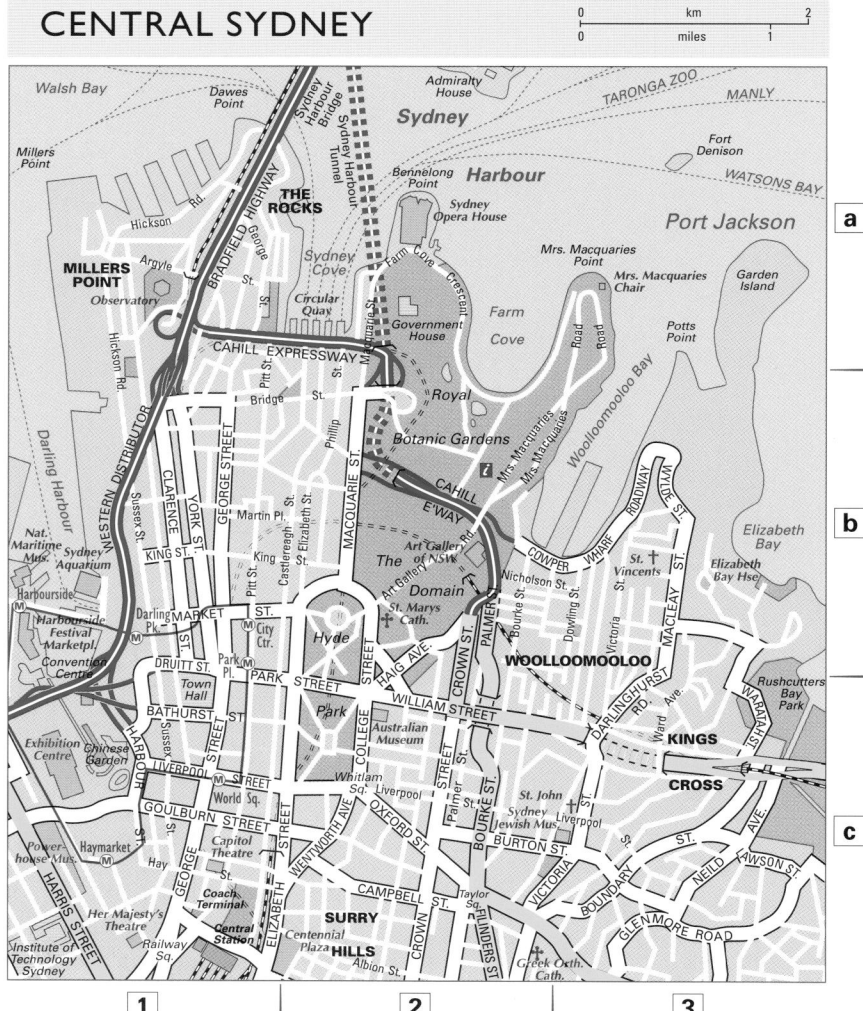

TOKYO

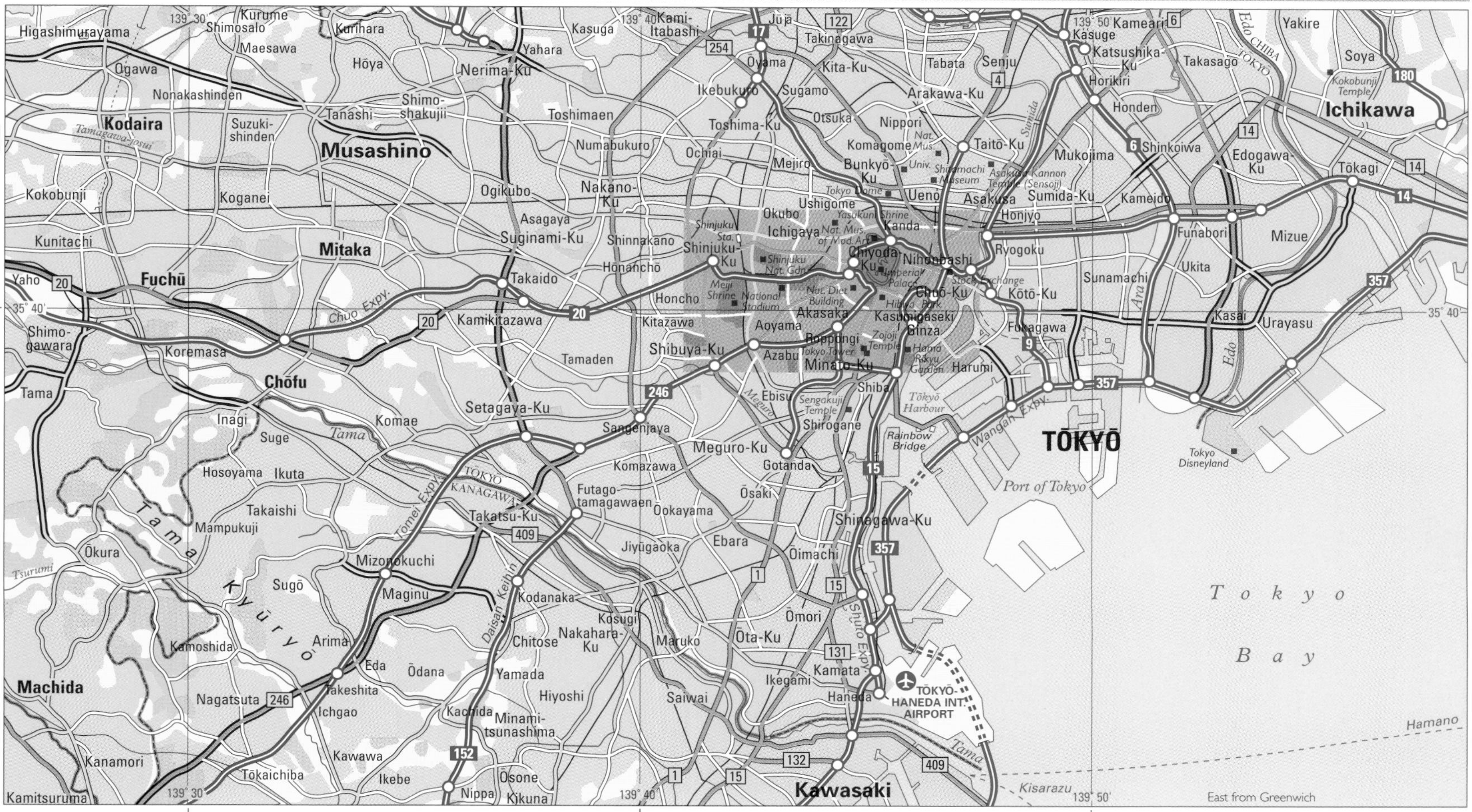

0 km 5
0 miles 3

139° 30'
Higashimurayama Kurume Shimosato Kurihara Kasuga Jūjo Takinagawa Kami-Itabashi
Ogawa Shimo-shakujii Oyama Kita-Ku Tabata Senju Katsushika-Ku Takasago Soya
Kodaira Hōya Maesawa Yahara Ikebukuro Sugamo Otsuka Arakawa-Ku Horikiri Honden Kokubunji Temple
Nonakashinden Toshimaen Toshima-Ku Nippori Komagome Shinkoiwa Edogawa-Ku Ichikawa
Musashino Suzuki-shinden Tanashi Numabukuro Nakano-Ku Ochiai Mejiro Bunkyō-Ku Univ. Ushigome Asakusa Sumida-Ku Kameido Tōkagi
Kodaira Koganei Ogikubo Asagaya Suginami-Ku Okubo Shinjuku-Ku Ichigaya Kanda Nihonbashi Mukojima Honjyō Funabori Mizue 14
Kunitachi **Mitaka** Honancho Shinnakano Shinjuku Sta. Chiyoda-Ku Chūō-Ku Ryogoku Kōtō-Ku Sunamachi 357
Yaho 20 **Fuchū** Takaido Kamikitazawa Honcho Akasaka Kasumigaseki Ginza Fukagawa Kasai Urayasu 35° 40'
Shimo-gawara Koremasa Kitazawa Shibuya-Ku Aoyama Roppongi Minato-Ku Harumi 357
Chōfu Inagi Tamaden Setagaya-Ku Azabu Ebisu Shiba Tōkyō Harbour 9
Tama Suge Komae Sangenjaya Meguro-Ku Shirogane Sengakuji Temple **TŌKYŌ**
Hosoyama Ikuta Futago-tamagawaen Komazawa Gotanda Shirogane Rainbow Bridge Tokyo Disneyland Port of Tokyo
Takaishi Takatsu-Ku Ookayama Ōsaki 15
Mampukuji Mizonokuchi Jiyūgaoka Ebara Shinagawa-Ku
Machida Ōkura Maginu Kodanaka Oimachi 357 *T o k y o*
Kamoshida Arima Chitose Nakahara-Ku Ōmori Ōta-Ku *B a y*
Nagatsuta 246 Eda Ōdana Yamada Maruko Kamata Ikegami
Kanamori Takeshita Ichigao Kawawa Hiyoshi Saiwai Haneda **TŌKYŌ-HANEDA INT. AIRPORT**
Kamitsuruma Tōkaichiba Ikebe Minami-tsunashima 152 Ōsone Nippa Kikuna 132 **Kawasaki** Kisarazu 409 Hamano
139° 30' 139° 40' 139° 50' East from Greenwich

CENTRAL TOKYO

0 km 1
0 miles 0.5

OTAKIBASHI-DORI SHOKUAN-DORI OKUBO-DORI OKUBO-DORI OKUBO-DORI MEJIRO-DORI HAKUSAN-DORI Ochanomizu AKIHABARA ASAKUSABASHI
OME KAIDO **ŌKUBO** Nicolai-do Church Akihabara Station
SHINJUKU-KU Hanazono-jinja Shrine YASUKUNI-DORI Yasukuni-jinja Shrine Kudankita Jimbocho Shin-ochanomizu Transport Mus. **KANDA** Akihabara KODENMACHO
Sumitomo Bldg Shinjuku **ICHIGAYA** Kudanshita Science Technology Museum **JIMBOCHŌ** Ogawamachi Awajicho Iwamotocho YASUKUNI-DORI
Shinjuku Central Park Tokyo City Hall Shinjuku Sta. Shinjuku-gyoemmae **YOTSUYA** Budokan Kitano-maru Park Kandaheisei Edogawabashi Kodenmacho KANDA
YAMATE-DORI KŌEN-DORI Minami-shinjuku Station Shinjuku-gyoen-mae YASUKUNI-DORI Yotsuyasanchōme Ichigaya **SANBANCHŌ** Nat. Mus. of Modern Art Takebashi Otemachi **MARUNŌUCHI** Mitsukoshimae Ningyocho
KOSHU-DORI Shinjuku-National Garden Yotsuya Yotsuya Sta. Kōjimachi Hanzomon **CHIYODA-KU** Fukiage Imperial Garden East Garden Tokyo Otemachi Stock Exchange
Yoyogi Sta. Sendagaya Sta. Shinanomachi Sta. SHINJUKU-DORI St. Ignatius National Theatre Imperial Palace Tokyo Sta. Nihonbashi Kite Mus. NIHONBASHI
Sword Museum MEIJI-DORI GAIEN-NISHI-DORI Nagatacho SOTOBORI-DORI Sakuradamon Outer Garden Niyubashi-mae **CHŪŌ-KU** Kayabacho
Sangūbashi Sta. Meiji Shrine Treasurehouse National Stadium Jingū Outer Garden Akasaka Palace Suntory Art Museum Jingū Inner Garden Government Buildings National Diet Building Government Buildings Hibiya Bridgestone Mus. of Art Tokyo International Forum
Meiji Shrine Inner Garden Jingū Baseball Stadium AOYAMA-DORI Kokkaigijidomae **KASUMIGASEKI** Nissei Theatre Ginza-itchome Hatchobori
Meiji-jingū Shrine Togu Memorial Hall Aoyama-itch ōme Akasaka Kasumigaseki Park Sony Centre Ginza Kabuki-za Theatre Shintomicho
Yoyogi Park Harajuku Sta. Gaienmae **AKASAKA** Nogi-jinja Shrine Uchisaiwaicho Kasumigaseki **GINZA** Higashi-ginza St. Luke's Int. Hospital
Yoyogi-hachiman Sta. Meiji-jingū-mae Aoyama Cemetery Nogizaka SAKURADA-DORI **SHIMBASHI** Shimbashi Tsukiji Tsukiji Hongan-ji Temple **TSUKIJI**
INOKASHIRA-DORI Kanze No Play Theatre OMOTESANDO-DORI Oriental Bazaar Omotesandō **TORANOMON** Reinansaka Church Kamiyacho Atago-yama Central Wholesale Market
SHIBUYA-KU Shibuya Sta. MEIJI-DORI AOYAMA-DORI **AOYAMA** Nezu Art Museum Roppongi HIGASHI-DORI Toranomon DAIICHI KEIHIN-DORI Hama Rikyū Garden Sumida-Gawa
YAMATE-DORI DOGEN-ZAKA KOMAZAWA-DORI **ROPPONGI** Tokyo Tower **MINATO-KU** Shiba Park Zojoji Temple **SHIBA** Hamamatsucho Station Daimon HARUMI KYOSUMI-DORI
AZABU Haneda Airport Shibakoen MITSUME-DORI

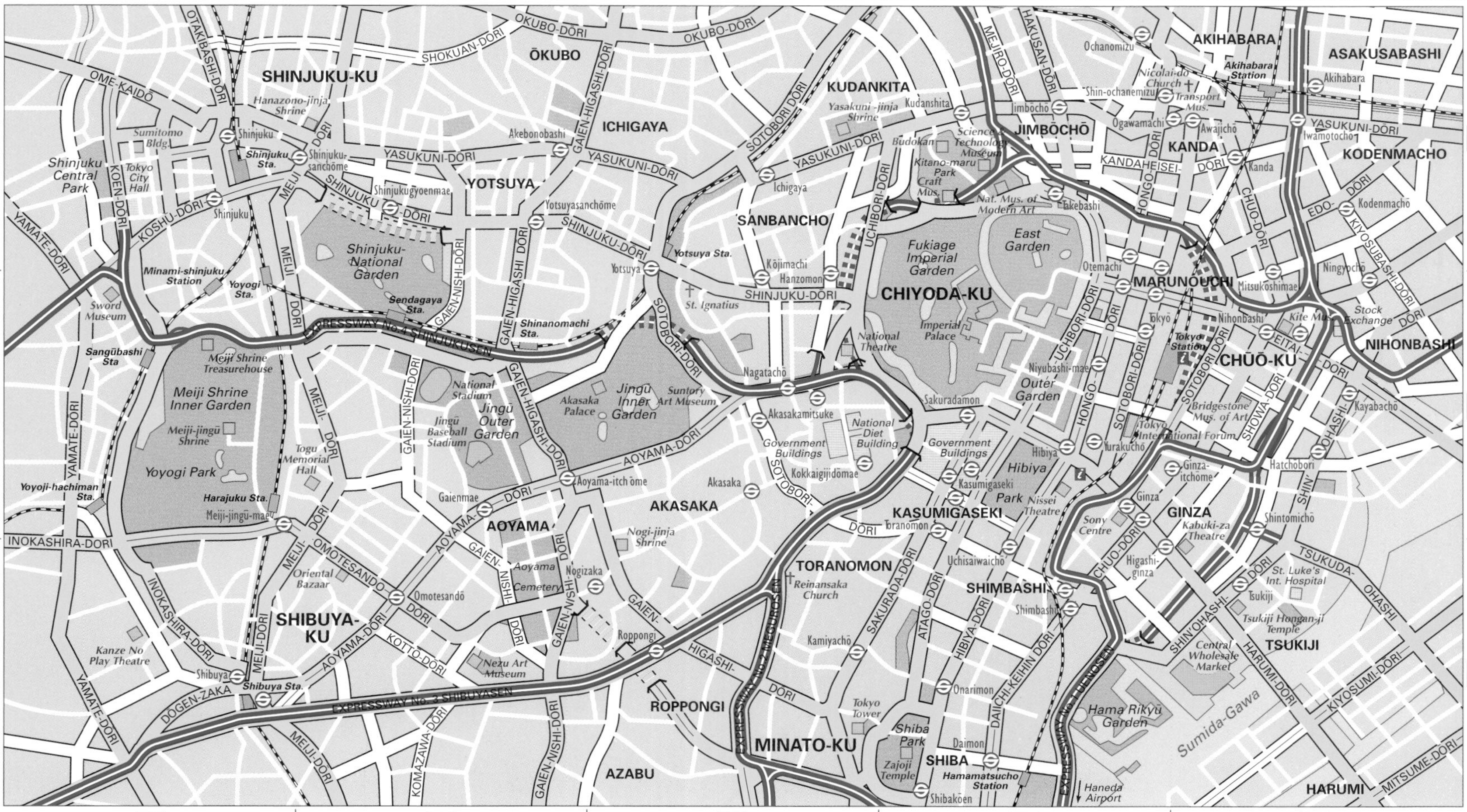

COPYRIGHT PHILIP'S

TEHRAN

km 5
miles 3

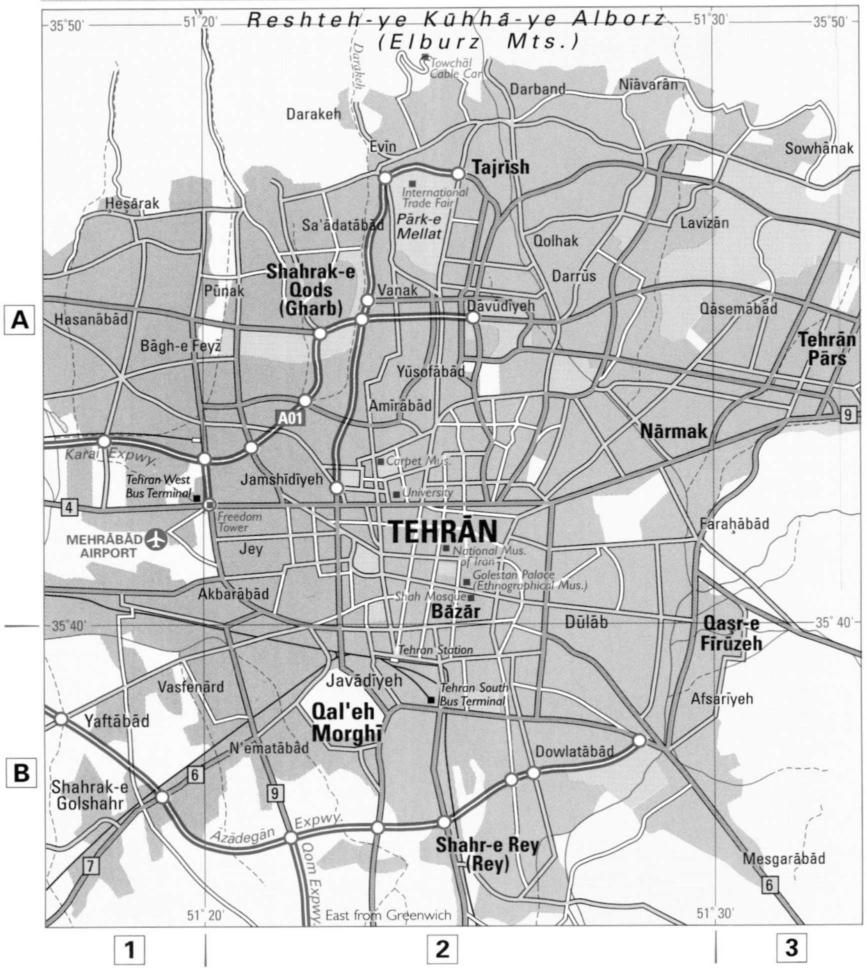

Reshteh-ye Kūhhā-ye Alborz
(Elburz Mts.)

Towchāl Cable Car
Darakeh
Darband
Niāvarān
Darakeh
Evin
Sowhānak
Tajrīsh
International Trade Fair
Pārk-e Mellat
Sa'ādatābād
Qolhak
Lavīzān
Hesārak
Vanak
Qo lhak
Darrūs
Shahrak-e Qods (Gharb)
Pūnak
Dāvūdīyeh
Qāsemābād
Hasanābād
Yūsofābād
Bāgh-e Feyz
Tehrān Pārs
A01
Amīrābād
Nārmak
Karaj Expwy
Jamshīdīyeh
Tehran West Bus Terminal
University
Farahābād
MEHRĀBĀD AIRPORT
Freedom Tower
Jey
Carpet Mus.
National Mus. of Iran
Golestan Palace (Ethnographical Mus.)
Akbarābād
Shah Mosque
Bāzār
Dūlāb
Qasr-e Fīrūzeh
Tehran Station
Javādīyeh
Vasfenārd
Tehran South Bus Terminal
Afsarīyeh
Yaftābād
Qal'eh Morghī
N'ematābād
Dowlatābād
Shahrak-e Golshahr
Āzādegān
Dom Expwy
Shahr-e Rey (Rey)
Mesgarābād

East from Greenwich

TIANJIN

km 5
miles 3

205
Xiaodian
Beicang
Da Yunhe
Yixingbu
Dabizhuang
Hanjiashu
Zhangguizhuang
Ziya He
Xinkai He
Nandian
Dingzigu
Xigu Park
Stadium
Tianjin Xi Zhan (Railway Station)
Xigu
Hebei
Qingde Qiao
104
Hongqiao
The Grand Mosque
Dabei (Grand Mercy) Temple
Ximenwai
Old Chinese District I
Dongmenwai
Tianjin Zhan (Railway Station)
Dongjuzi
Da Yinhe (Grand Canal)
Nanmenwai
Hedong
Zhangguizhuang
TIANJIN (TIENTSIN)
Tianjin University
Antiques Market
Dazhigu
Nankai University
Nānkai
Heping
Renmin Park
Tiaoyuan Pavilion
Shuishang Park
Xinanlou
Aquatic Park
Balitai
Natural History Museum
Jianshan Park
Hexi
Liqizhuang
Húidui
105
205
Hai He

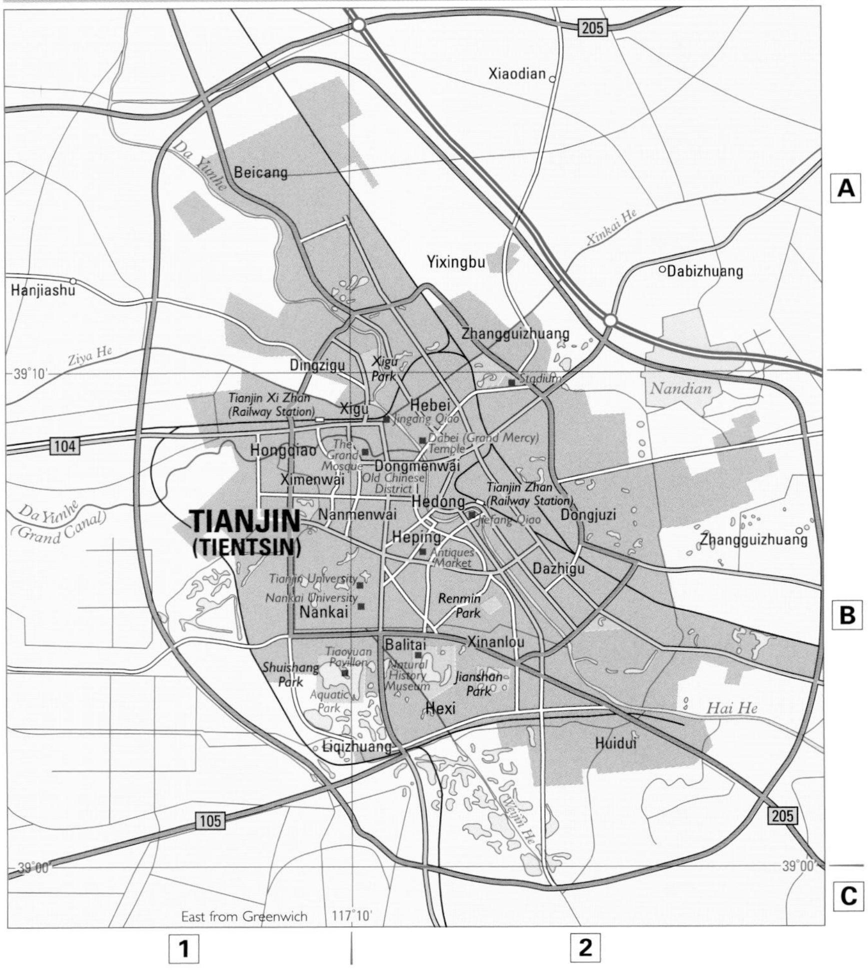

East from Greenwich

TORONTO

km 5
miles 3

27
407
Thornhill
Concord
Edgeley
York Toronto
Newtonbrook
Markham
Metro Toronto Zoo
Fairport
Brown
Rouge
Little Rouge
401
Rouge Hill
West Rouge
Port Union
Pine Grove
Woodbridge
Fisherville
York University
Willowdale
48
Agincourt
Malvern
Highland Creek
2A
North York
Northmount
Lansing
404
Humber Summit
Black Creek Pioneer Village
401
Woburn
West Hill
Beaumonte Heights
Armour Heights
York Mills
Bendale
Thistletown
400
DOWNSVIEW AIRPORT
Wexford
Scarborough
Kipling Heights
Downsview
Lawrence Heights
York Mills
Don Mills
Cliffside
427
Rexdale
Humberlea
401
Ontario Science Centre
Danforth
Malton
Weston
11
Thorncliffe
2
Woodbine Race Track
27
11
Wilket Creek Park
Dentonia Park
TORONTO INTERNATIONAL AIRPORT (LESTER B. PEARSON)
409
401
Forest Hill
Leaside
Birch Cliff
Humber Valley Village
York
East York
5
Kew Gardens
Hanlon
Mount Dennis
Casa Loma
Riverdale Park
Lambton Mills
University of Toronto
Parliament Buildings
Etobicoke
Swansea
5
City Hall
CN Tower & SkyDome
TORONTO
Islington
High Park
Old Fort York
Union Sta.
Gardiner Expwy
Kingsway
Parkdale
TORONTO CITY CENTRE AIRPORT
Markland Wood
427
Humber Bay
Exhibition Place
Toronto Harbour
Burnhamthorpe
Summerville
Ontario Place
Toronto Islands
Gibraltar Point
LAKE ONTARIO
Cooksville
Mississauga
Long Branch
New Toronto
Mimico
2

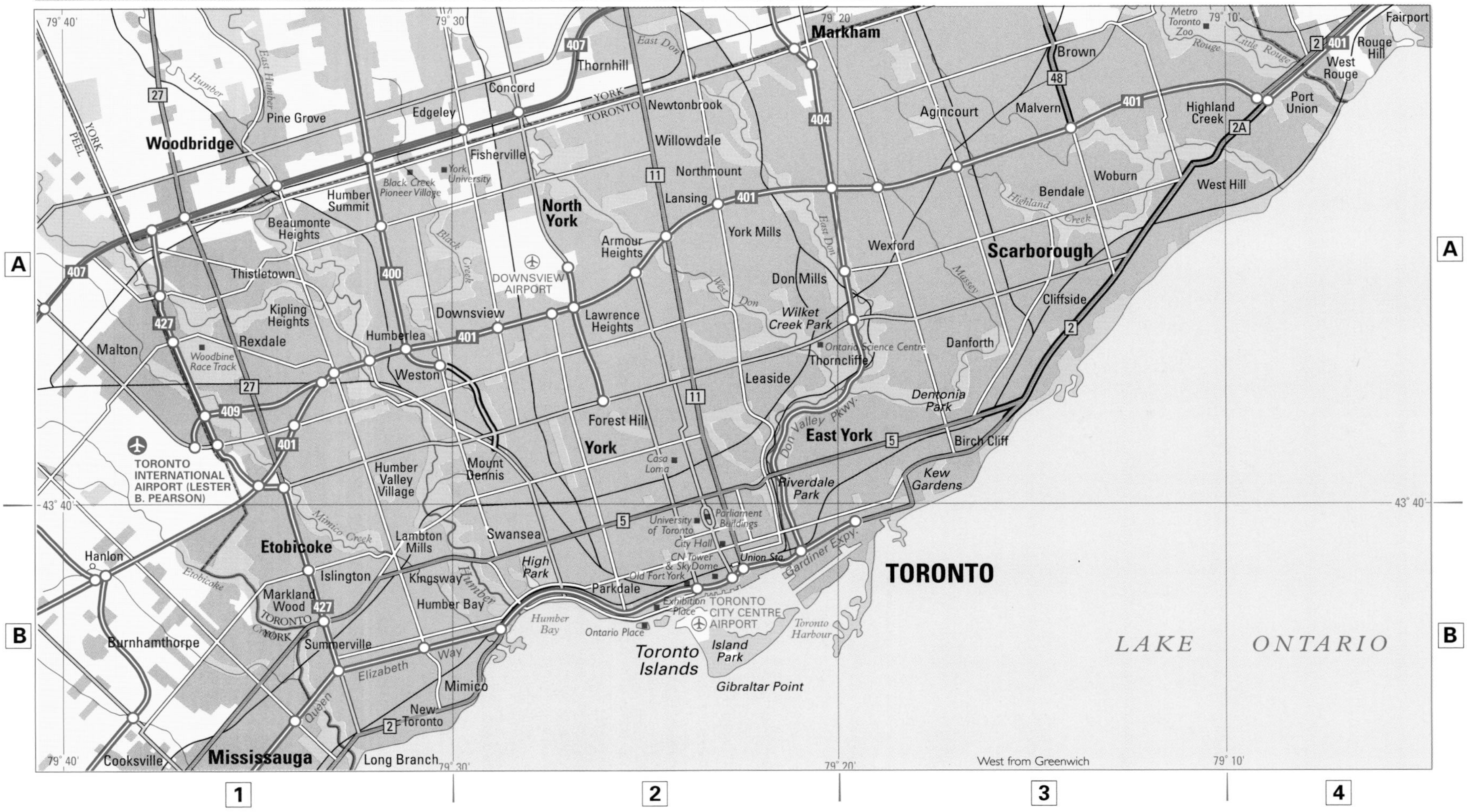

West from Greenwich

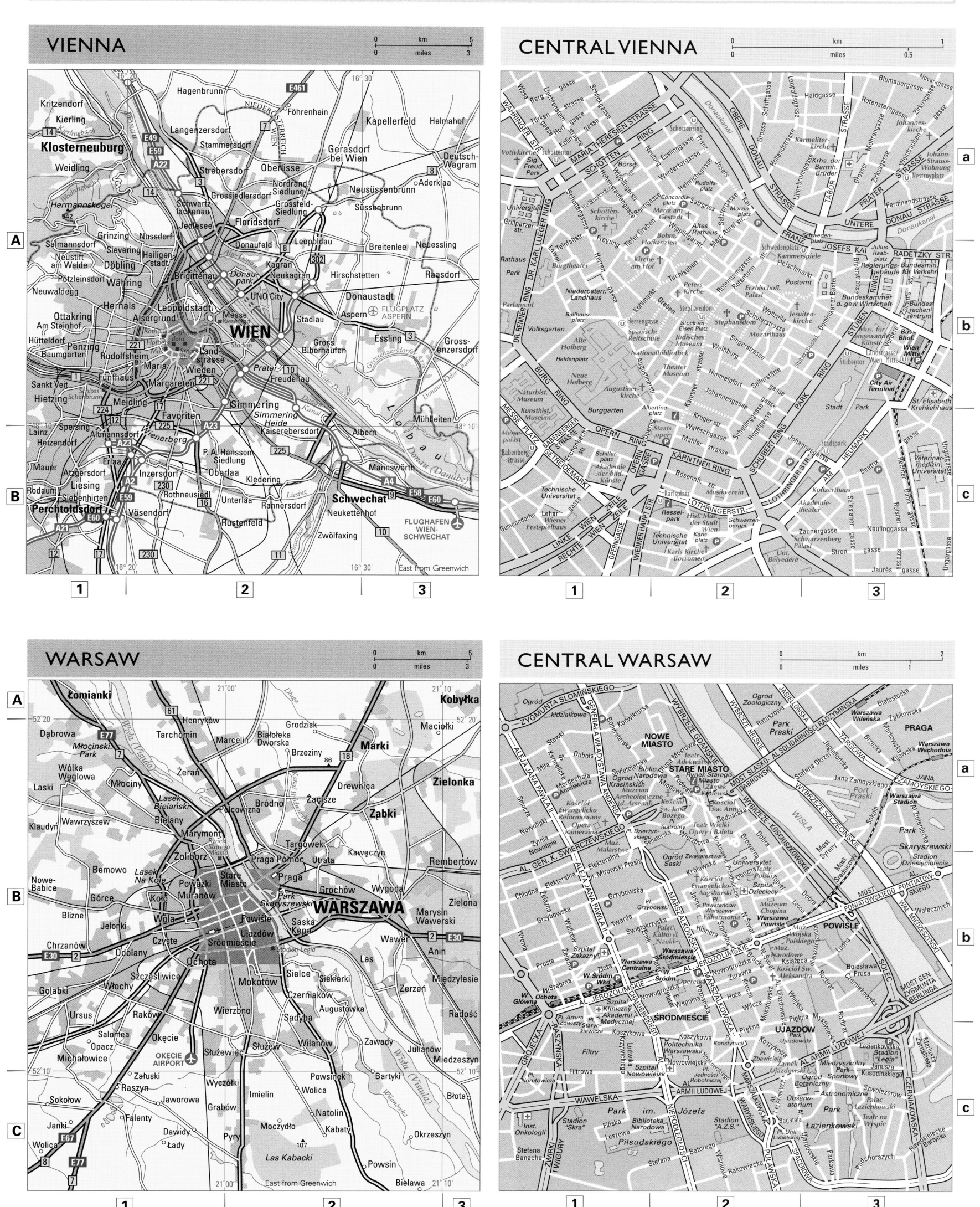

WASHINGTON

km 0 — 5
miles 0 — 3

77°20' 77°10' 77°00' 76°50'

A 39°00'

Dranesville
Great Falls
Potomac
Cabin John Regional Park
Chevy Chase View
Oak View
Silver Spring
Adelphi
Greenbelt
Woodmont
Avenel
Langley Park
College Park
Lewisdale
Berwyn Heights
Lanham
Great Falls Park
99
Cabin John
Glen Echo
Chevy Chase
Rock Creek Park
Takoma Park
Univ. of Maryland
University Park
Greenbelt Park
East Pines
New Carrollton
Seabrook
Bethesda
Glen Mar Park
Somerset
Westgate
Brookmont
Brightwood
Chillum
Hyattsville
Riverdale
Edmonston
Landover Hills
Glenarden
John Hanson Hwy
50

B 39°00'

Reston
MARYLAND
VIRGINIA
Langley
Univ. of the Dist. of Col.
The Catholic University of America
Mount Rainier
Bladensburg
Kent Village
95/495
McLean
Belle View
American University
Washington Cath.
Washington Nat. Zoological Park
WASHINGTON
Trinity College
National Arboretum
Kenilworth Aquatic Gardens
Cheverly
Fairmount Heights
Palmer Park
Tysons Corner
Pimmit Hills
Franklin Park
Northern Va. Reg. Park
Marymount University
Georgetown
The White House
Vietnam Veterans Mem.
Union Station
DISTRICT OF COLUMBIA
Seat Pleasant
Hunters Valley
Dunn Loring
Rosslyn
Lincoln Memorial
U.S. Capitol
Library of Congress
Vienna
Vale
Oakton
Lee Hwy.
Falls Church
Seven Corners
Arlington
29
Arlington Nat. Cemetery
Jefferson Memorial
Fort Dupont Park
Capitol Heights
Kettering
Hillwood
66
Pentagon
50
Mason Mem. Br.
East Potomac Park
Anacostia
Oakland
Millwood
Ritchie
Arlington Blvd.
ARLINGTON FAIRFAX
Broyhill Park
East Arlington
395
Coral Hills
District Heights
50
66
Annalee Heights
495
Holmes Run Acres
Culmore
Baileys Crossroads
Parklawn
WASHINGTON NATIONAL AIRPORT
Anacostia R.
PRINCE GEORGES
Forestville
29
Fairfax
George Mason University
Accotink Creek
Little River Tpk.
Lake Barcroft
Holmes Run
Potomac River
295
Forest Heights
Glassmanor
Silver Hill
Suitland
Hillcrest Heights
Morningside
38°50'

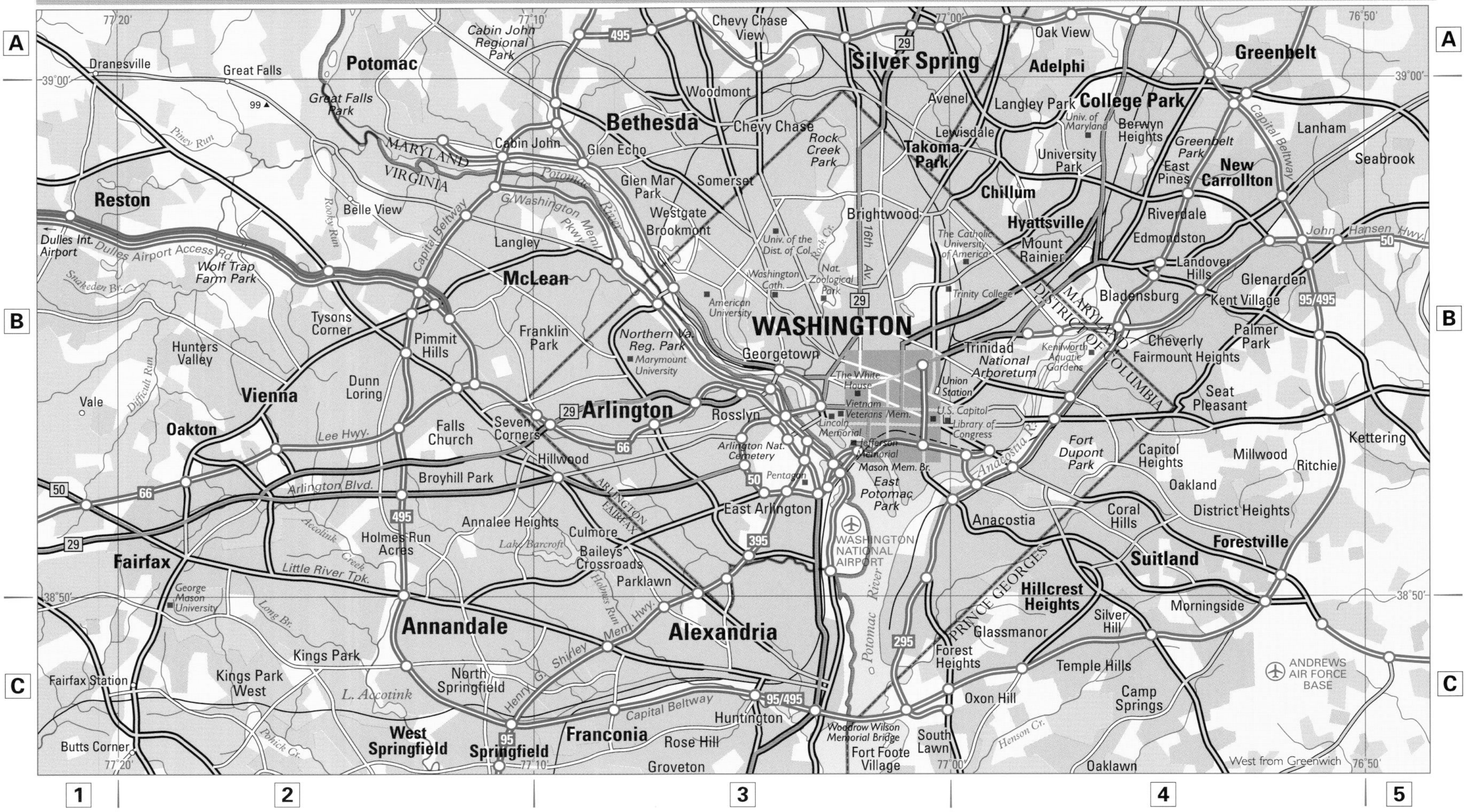

C 38°50'

Fairfax Station
Kings Park West
Kings Park
L. Accotink
North Springfield
Henry G. Shirley Mem. Hwy.
Annandale
Alexandria
Temple Hills
Camp Springs
ANDREWS AIR FORCE BASE
Butts Corner
95
West Springfield
Springfield
Franconia
Rose Hill
Huntington
Woodrow Wilson Memorial Bridge
Capital Beltway
95/495
Oxon Hill
Honson Cr.
Groveton
Fort Foote Village
South Lawn
Oaklawn
West from Greenwich

77°20' 77°10' 77°00' 76°50'

1 2 3 4 5

CENTRAL WASHINGTON

km 0 — 0.5
miles 0 — 0.5

a
P St.
16th St.
Logan Circle
Island Ave.
13th St.
12th St.
11th St.
10th St.
9th St.
7th St.
New Jersey Ave.
P St.
North Capitol St.
NORTH WEST
Scott Circle
Rhode Island Ave.
N St.
Connecticut Ave.
M St.
Thomas Circle
Massachusetts Ave.
Mt. Vernon Sq.-UDC
6th St.
New York Ave.
L St.
Vermont Ave.
L St.
1st St.
Farragut North
Farragut West
McPherson Sq.
Franklin Square
Mt. Vernon Square
K St.
New York Ave.
Massachusetts Ave.
K St.
b
Pennsylvania Ave.
Lafayette Square
H St.
Convention Center
Metro Center
Gallery Place
Nat. Mus. of American Art
Union Station
World Bank
G St.
F St.
National Place
F St.
Judiciary Sq.
F St.
D St.
Louisiana Ave.
Union Station Plaza
Columbus Circle
The White House
Pennsylvania Ave.
Fords Theater
Archives
Navy Memorial
CONSTITUTION
Supreme Court
E St.
Dept. of the Interior
Zero Milestone
Federal Triangle
Nat. Museum of Natural History
CONSTITUTION AVE.
U.S. Capitol
Library of Congress
C St.
The Ellipse
Madison Dr.
National Gallery of Art
National Air & Space Museum
Botanic Gardens
CONSTITUTION AVE.
Nat. Museum of American History
The Mall
Smithsonian Institute
Grant Statue
Reflecting Pool
D. C. War Memorial
Washington Monument
Jefferson Dr.
Hirshhorn Museum
INDEPENDENCE AVE.
INDEPENDENCE AVE.
c
Tidal Basin
US Holocaust Memorial Museum
L'Enfant Plaza
Federal Center SW
M
Capitol South
M
Jefferson Memorial
Outlet Bridge
14th St.
7th St.
SOUTHWEST FREEWAY
New Jersey Ave.
Potomac R.
Francis Case Mem. Bridge
Maine Ave.
SOUTH WEST
G St.
E St.
South Capitol St.
East Potomac Park
Washington Channel
Waterfront
M
M St.

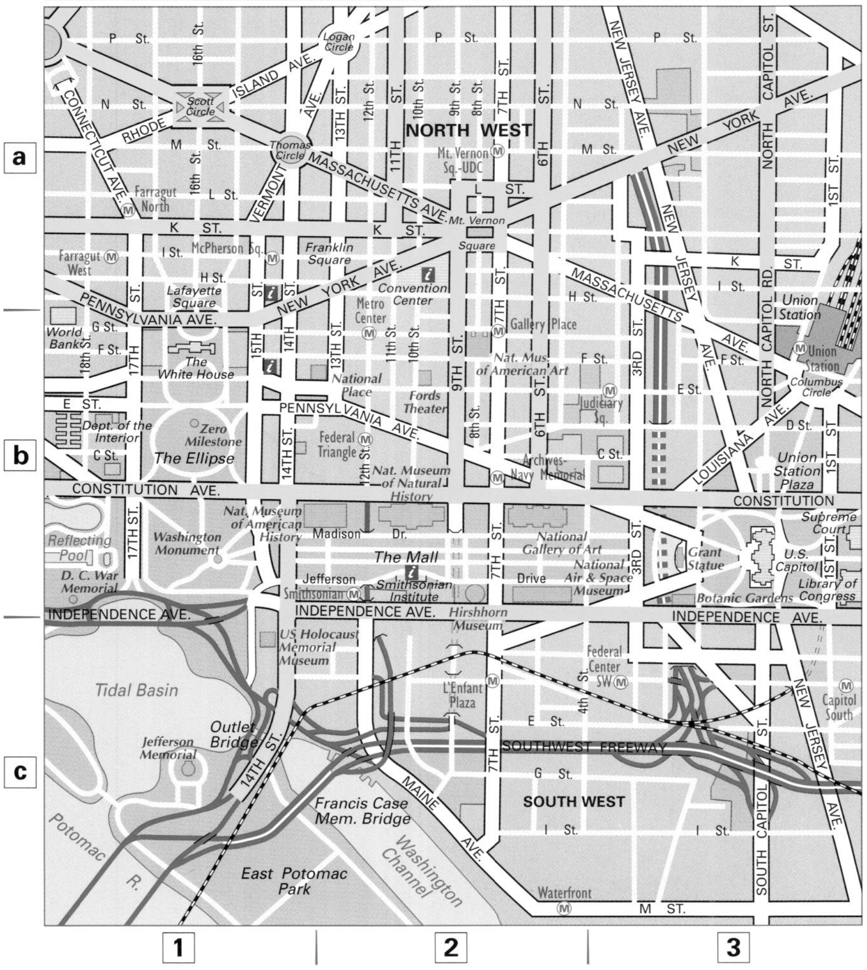

1 2 3

WELLINGTON

km 0 — 5
miles 0 — 3

175°50'

A 41°10'

Cook Strait
Rock Pt.
Elsdon
Porirua
Porirua East
58
459 Colonial Knob
Linden
Haywards
Pipinui Pt.
Tawa
408
Western Hutt Road
Manor Park
Stokes Valley
Redwood
457 Belmont
Taita
Avalon

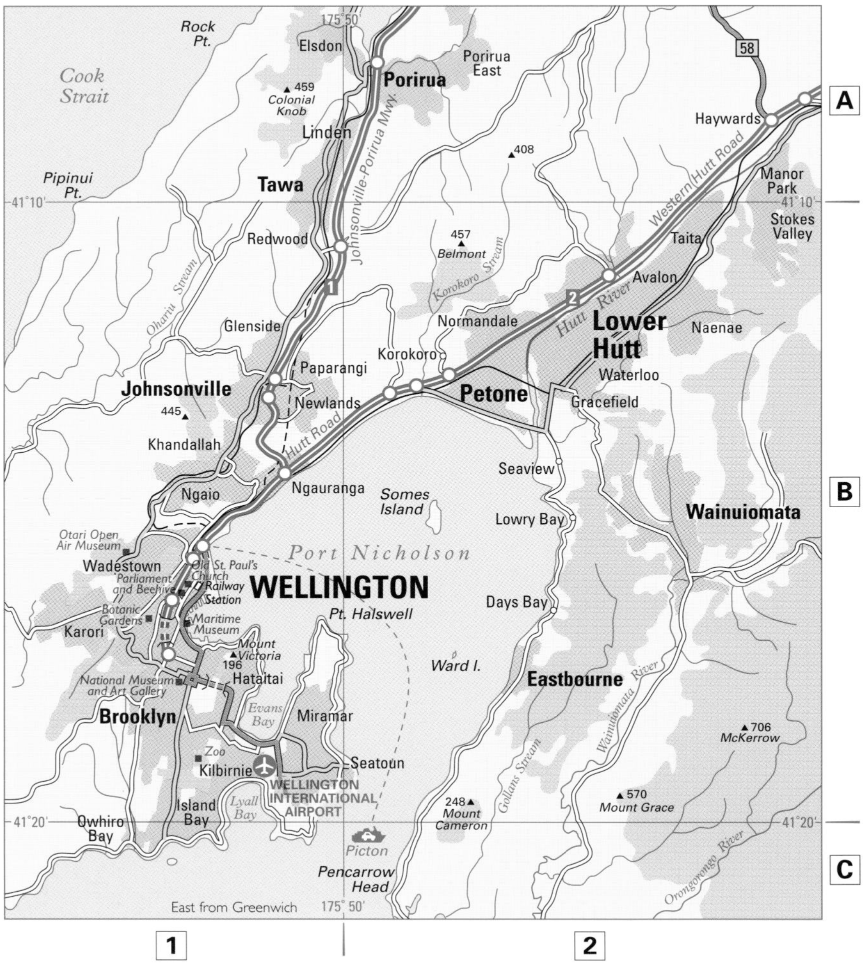

B 41°10'

Glenside
Johnsonville Porirua Mwy.
Korokoro Stream
Normandale
Naenae
Lower Hutt
Korokoro
Waterloo
Johnsonville
445
Paparangi
Newlands
Petone
Gracefield
Hutt Road
Khandallah
Seaview
Ngaio
Ngauranga
Somes Island
Lowry Bay
Wainuiomata
Otari Open Air Museum
Wadestown
Port Nicholson
Days Bay
Parliament and Beehive
Old St. Paul's Church
Railway Station
Ward I.
WELLINGTON
Maritime Museum
Pt. Halswell
Eastbourne
Karori
Botanic Gardens
Mount Victoria 196
National Museum and Art Gallery
Hataitai
Miramar
Evans Bay
Brooklyn
Seatoun
Wellington International Airport
248 Mount Cameron
570 Mount Grace
706 McKerrow
Zoo
Kilbirnie
Lyall Bay
Island Bay
Owhiro Bay
Picton
Pencarrow Head
Orongorongo River
Wainuiomata River
Gollans Stream

C 41°20'

East from Greenwich 175°50'

1 2

INDEX TO CITY MAPS

The index contains the names of all the principal places and features shown on the City Maps. Each name is followed by an additional entry in italics giving the name of the City Map within which it is located.

The number in bold type which follows each name refers to the number of the City Map page where that feature or place will be found.

The letter and figure which are immediately after the page number give the grid square on the map within which the feature or place is situated. The letter represents the latitude and the figure the longitude. Upper case letters refer to the City Maps, lower case letters to the Central Area Maps. The full geographic reference is provided in the border of the City Maps.

The location given is the centre of the city, suburb or feature and is not necessarily the name. Rivers, canals and roads are indexed to their name. Rivers carry the symbol → after their name.

An explanation of the alphabetical order rules and a list of the abbreviations used are to be found at the beginning of the World Map Index.

A

Aalām, *Baghdad* **3** B2
Aalsmeer, *Amsterdam* **2** B1
Abbey Wood, *London* **15** B4
Abcoude, *Amsterdam* **2** B2
Âbdin, *Cairo* **7** A2
Abeno, *Osaka* **22** B4
Aberdeen, *Hong Kong* **12** B2
Aberdour, *Edinburgh* **11** A2
Aberdour Castle, *Edinburgh* **11** A2
Abfanggraben →, *Munich* **20** A3
Ablon-sur-Seine, *Paris* **23** B3
Abramtsevo, *Moscow* **19** B4
Abu Dis, *Jerusalem* **13** B2
Abû en Numrus, *Cairo* **7** B2
Abu Ghosh, *Jerusalem* **13** B1
Acacias, *Madrid* **17** c2
Acassuso, *Buenos Aires* **7** A1
Accotink Cr. →, *Washington* **32** B2
Acheres, *Paris* **23** A1
Acília, *Rome* **25** C1
Aclimação, *São Paulo* **26** B2
Acton, *London* **15** A2
Açúcar, Pão de, *Rio de Janeiro* **24** B2
Ada Beja, *Lisbon* **14** A1
Adams Park, *Atlanta* **3** B2
Adams Shore, *Boston* **6** B4
Addiscombe, *London* **15** B3
Adelphi, *Washington* **32** A4
Aderklaa, *Vienna* **31** A3
Admiralteyskaya Storona, *St. Petersburg* **26** B2
Áffori, *Milan* **18** A2
Aflandshage, *Copenhagen* **10** B3
Afsarīyeh, *Tehran* **30** B2
Agboyi Cr. →, *Lagos* **14** A2
Ågerup, *Copenhagen* **10** A1
Ågesta, *Stockholm* **28** B2
Agincourt, *Toronto* **30** A3
Agora, Arhéa, *Athens* **2** c1
Agra Canal, *Delhi* **10** B2
Agricola Oriental, *Mexico City* **18** B2
Agua Espraiada →, *São Paulo* **26** B2
Agualva-Cacem, *Lisbon* **14** A1
Agustino, Cerro El, *Lima* **16** B2
Ahrensfelde, *Berlin* **5** A4
Ahuntsic, *Montreal* **19** A1
Ai →, *Osaka* **22** A4
Aigremont, *Paris* **23** A1
Air View Park, *Singapore* **27** A2
Airport West, *Melbourne* **17** A1
Aiyaleo, *Athens* **2** B2
Aiyáleos, Óros, *Athens* **2** B1
Ajegunle, *Lagos* **14** B2
Aji, *Osaka* **22** A3
Ajuda, *Lisbon* **14** A1
Akalla, *Stockholm* **28** A1
Akasaka, *Tokyo* **29** b3
Akbarābād, *Tehran* **30** A2
Akershus Slott, *Oslo* **22** A3
Akihabara, *Tokyo* **29** a5
Akrópolis, *Athens* **2** c2
Al 'Azamiyah, *Baghdad* **3** A2
Al Quds = Jerusalem, *Jerusalem* **13** B2
Alaguntan, *Lagos* **14** B2
Alameda, *San Francisco* **25** B3
Alameda, Parque, *Mexico City* **18** b2
Alameda Memorial State Beach Park, *San Francisco* **25** B3
Albern, *Vienna* **31** B2
Albert Park, *Melbourne* **17** B1
Alberton, *Johannesburg* **13** B2
Albertslund, *Copenhagen* **10** B2
Albysjön, *Stockholm* **28** B1
Alcantara, *Lisbon* **14** A1
Alcatraz I., *San Francisco* **25** B2
Alcobendas, *Madrid* **17** A2
Alcorcón, *Madrid* **17** B1
Aldershof, *Berlin* **5** B4
Aldo Bonzi, *Buenos Aires* **7** C1
Aleksandrovskoye, *St. Petersburg* **26** B2
Alexander Nevsky Abbey, *St. Petersburg* **26** B2
Alexander Soutzos Moussío, *Athens* **2** b3
Alexandra, *Johannesburg* **13** A2
Alexandra, *Singapore* **27** B2
Alexandria, *Washington* **32** C3
Alfama, *Lisbon* **14** c3
Alfortville, *Paris* **23** B3
Algés, *Lisbon* **14** A1
Alhambra, *Los Angeles* **16** B4
Alibey →, *Istanbul* **12** B1
Alibey Barajı, *Istanbul* **12** B1
Alibeyköy, *Istanbul* **12** B1
Alimos, *Athens* **2** B2
Alipur, *Calcutta* **8** B1
Allach, *Munich* **20** A1
Allambie Heights, *Sydney* **28** A2
Allard Pierson Museum, *Amsterdam* **2** b2
Allermuir Hill, *Edinburgh* **11** B2
Allerton, Pt., *Boston* **6** B4
Allston, *Boston* **6** A3
Almada, *Lisbon* **14** A2
Almagro, *Buenos Aires* **7** B2
Almargem do Bispo, *Lisbon* **14** A1
Almazovo, *Moscow* **19** A6
Almirante G. Brown, Parque, *Buenos Aires* **7** C2
Almon, *Jerusalem* **13** B2
Almond →, *Edinburgh* **11** B2
Alnabru, *Oslo* **22** A4
Alnsjøen, *Oslo* **22** A4
Alperton, *London* **15** A2
Alpine, *New York* **21** A2
Alrode, *Johannesburg* **13** B2
Alsemerg, *Brussels* **6** B1
Alsergrund, *Vienna* **31** A2
Alsip, *Chicago* **9** C2
Ålsten, *Stockholm* **28** B1
Älta, *Stockholm* **28** B3
Altadena, *Los Angeles* **16** A4
Alte-Donau →, *Vienna* **31** A2
Alte Hofburg, *Vienna* **31** b1
Alter Finkenkrug, *Berlin* **5** A1
Altes Rathaus, *Munich* **20** b3
Altglienicke, *Berlin* **5** B4
Altlandsberg, *Berlin* **5** A5
Altlandsberg Nord, *Berlin* **5** A5
Altmannsdorf, *Vienna* **31** B1
Alto da Moóca, *São Paulo* **26** B2
Alto do Pina, *Lisbon* **14** A2
Altona, *Melbourne* **17** B1
Alvaro Obregon, *Mexico City* **18** B1
Alvik, *Stockholm* **28** B1
Älvsjo, *Stockholm* **28** B2
Älvvik, *Stockholm* **28** A3
Am Hasenbergl, *Munich* **20** A2
Am Steinhof, *Vienna* **31** A1
Am Wald, *Munich* **20** B2
Ama Keng, *Singapore* **27** A2
Amadora, *Lisbon* **14** A1
Amagasaki, *Osaka* **22** A3
Amager, *Copenhagen* **10** B3
Amāl Qādisiya, *Baghdad* **3** B2
Amalienborg, *Copenhagen* **10** b3
Amata, *Milan* **18** A1
Ameixoeira, *Lisbon* **14** A2
América, *São Paulo* **26** B1
Amin, *Baghdad* **3** B2
Aminadov, *Jerusalem* **13** B1
Aminyevo, *Moscow* **19** B2
Amīrābād, *Tehran* **30** A2
Amora, *Lisbon* **14** B2
Amoreira, *Lisbon* **14** A1
Ampelokipi, *Athens* **2** B2
Amper →, *Munich* **20** A1
Amstel, *Amsterdam* **2** b2
Amstel →, *Amsterdam* **2** c2
Amstel-Drecht-Kanaal, *Amsterdam* **2** B2
Amstel Station, *Amsterdam* **2** c3
Amstelhof, *Amsterdam* **2** b2
Amstelveen, *Amsterdam* **2** B2
Amsterdam, *Amsterdam* **2** A2
Amsterdam-Rijnkanaal, *Amsterdam* **2** B3
Amsterdam Zoo, *Amsterdam* **2** b3
Amsterdam Zuidoost, *Amsterdam* **2** B2
Amsterdamse Bos, *Amsterdam* **2** B1
Anacostia, *Washington* **32** B4
Anadoluhisarı, *Istanbul* **12** B2
Anadolukavağı, *Istanbul* **12** A2
Anata, *Jerusalem* **13** B2
Ancol, *Jakarta* **13** A1
'Andalus, *Baghdad* **3** B1
Andarai, *Rio de Janeiro* **24** B1
Anderlecht, *Brussels* **6** A1
Anderson Park, *Atlanta* **3** B2
Andingmen, *Beijing* **4** B2
Andrews Air Force Base, *Washington* **32** C4
Ang Mo Kio, *Singapore* **27** A3
Ängby, *Stockholm* **28** A1
Angel I., *San Francisco* **25** A2
Angel Island State Park, *San Francisco* **25** A2
Angke, Kali →, *Jakarta* **13** A1
Angyalföld, *Budapest* **7** A2
Anik, *Mumbai* **20** A2
Anin, *Warsaw* **31** B2
Anjou, *Montreal* **19** A2
Annalee Heights, *Washington* **32** B2
Annandale, *Washington* **32** C2
Anne Frankhuis, *Amsterdam* **2** a1
Antony, *Paris* **23** B2
Anyangch'on, *Seoul* **26** C1
Aoyama, *Tokyo* **29** b2
Ap Lei Chau, *Hong Kong* **12** B1
Apapa, *Lagos* **14** B2
Apelacão, *Lisbon* **14** A2
Apterkarskiy Ostrov, *St. Petersburg* **26** B2
Ar Kazimiyah, *Baghdad* **3** B1
Ara →, *Tokyo* **29** A4
Arakawa-Ku, *Tokyo* **29** A3
Arany-hegyi-patak →, *Budapest* **7** A2
Aravaca, *Madrid* **17** B1
Arbataash, *Baghdad* **3** A1
Arc de Triomphe, *Paris* **23** a2
Arcadia, *Los Angeles* **16** B4
Arceuil, *Paris* **23** B2
Arco Plaza, *Los Angeles* **16** b1
Arese, *Milan* **18** A1
Arganzuela, *Madrid* **17** B1
Argenteuil, *Paris* **23** A2
Argonne Forest, *Chicago* **9** C1
Argüelles, *Madrid* **17** a1
Arima, *Osaka* **22** A2
Arima, *Tokyo* **29** B2
Ários Págos, *Athens* **2** c1
Arkhangelyskoye, *Moscow* **19** B1
Arlington, *Boston* **6** A2
Arlington, *Washington* **32** B3
Arlington Heights, *Boston* **6** A2
Arlington Nat. Cemetery, *Washington* **32** B3
Armação, *Rio de Janeiro* **24** B2
Armadale, *Melbourne* **17** B2
Armenian Quarter, *Jerusalem* **13** b3
Armour Heights, *Toronto* **30** A2
Arncliffe, *Sydney* **28** B1
Arnold Arboretum, *Boston* **6** B3
Árpádföld, *Budapest* **7** A3
Arrentela, *Lisbon* **14** B2
Årsta, *Stockholm* **28** B2
Art Institute, *Chicago* **9** c2
Artane, *Dublin* **11** A2
Artas, *Jerusalem* **13** B2
Arthur's Seat, *Edinburgh* **11** B3
Aryiróupolis, *Athens* **2** B2
Asagaya, *Tokyo* **29** A2
Asahi, *Osaka* **22** A4
Asakusa, *Tokyo* **29** A3
Asakusabashi, *Tokyo* **29** a5
Asati, *Calcutta* **8** C1
Aschheim, *Munich* **20** A3
Ascot Vale, *Melbourne* **17** A1
Ashburn, *Chicago* **9** C2
Ashburton, *Melbourne* **17** B2
Ashfield, *Sydney* **28** B1
Ashford, *London* **15** B1
Ashiya, *Osaka* **22** A2
Ashiya →, *Osaka* **22** A2
Ashtown, *Dublin* **11** A2
Askisto, *Helsinki* **12** B1
Askrikefjärden, *Stockholm* **28** A3
Asnières, *Paris* **23** A2
Aspern, *Vienna* **31** A2
Aspern, Flugplatz, *Vienna* **31** A3
Assago, *Milan* **18** B1
Assemblée Nationale, *Paris* **23** b3
Assendelft, *Amsterdam* **2** A1
Assiano, *Milan* **18** B1
Astoria, *New York* **21** B2
Astrolabe Park, *Sydney* **28** B2
Atarot Airport, *Jerusalem* **13** A2
Atghara, *Calcutta* **8** B2
Athens = Athínai, *Athens* **2** B2
Athínai, *Athens* **2** B2
Athis-Mons, *Paris* **23** B3
Athlone, *Cape Town* **8** A2
Atholl, *Johannesburg* **13** A2
Atīfīya, *Baghdad* **3** A2
Atişalen, *Istanbul* **12** B1
Atlanta, *Atlanta* **3** B2
Atlanta History Center, *Atlanta* **3** B2
Atomium, *Brussels* **6** A2
Attiki, *Athens* **2** A2
Atzgersdorf, *Vienna* **31** B1
Aubervilliers, *Paris* **23** A3
Aubing, *Munich* **20** B1
Auburndale, *Boston* **6** A2
Aucherdinny, *Edinburgh* **11** B2
Auckland Park, *Johannesburg* **13** B2
Auderghem, *Brussels* **6** B2
Augusta, Mausoleo di, *Rome* **25** b2
Augustówka, *Warsaw* **31** B2
Aulnay-sous-Bois, *Paris* **23** A3
Aurelio, *Rome* **25** B1
Ausîm, *Cairo* **7** A1
Austerlitz, Gare d', *Paris* **23** A3
Austin, *Chicago* **9** B2
Avalon, *Wellington* **32** B2
Avedøre, *Copenhagen* **10** B2
Avellaneda, *Buenos Aires* **7** C2
Avenel, *Washington* **32** B4
Avondale, *Chicago* **9** B2
Avondale Heights, *Melbourne* **17** A1
Avtovo, *St. Petersburg* **26** B1
Ayazağa, *Istanbul* **12** B1
Ayer Chawan, P., *Singapore* **27** B2
Ayer Merbau, P., *Singapore* **27** B2
Ayía Marina, *Athens* **2** C3
Ayía Paraskevi, *Athens* **2** A2
Áyios Dhimitrios, *Athens* **2** B2
Áyios Ioánnis Rendis, *Athens* **2** B1
Azabu, *Tokyo* **29** c3
Azcapotzalco, *Mexico City* **18** B1
Azteca, Estadia, *Mexico City* **18** C2
Azucar, Cerro Pan de, *Santiago* **26** A1

B

Baambrugge, *Amsterdam* **2** B2
Baba I., *Karachi* **14** B1
Babarpur, *Delhi* **10** A2
Babushkin, *Moscow* **19** A4
Back B., *Mumbai* **20** B1
Baclaran, *Manila* **17** B2
Bacoor, *Manila* **17** C1
Bacoor B., *Manila* **17** C1
Badalona, *Barcelona* **4** A2
Badhoevedorp, *Amsterdam* **2** A1
Badli, *Delhi* **10** A1
Bærum, *Oslo* **22** A2
Bağcılar, *Istanbul* **12** B1
Bàggio, *Milan* **18** B1
Bāgh-e-Feyz, *Tehran* **30** A1
Baghdād, *Baghdad* **3** A2
Bagmari, *Calcutta* **8** B2
Bagneux, *Paris* **23** B2
Bagnolet, *Paris* **23** A3
Bagsværd, *Copenhagen* **10** A2
Bagsværd Sø, *Copenhagen* **10** A2
Baguiati, *Calcutta* **8** B2
Bagumbayan, *Manila* **17** C2
Bahçeköy, *Istanbul* **12** A1
Bahtîm, *Cairo* **7** A2
Baileys Crossroads, *Washington* **32** B3
Bailly, *Paris* **23** A1
Bairro Alto, *Lisbon* **14** c1
Bairro Lopes, *Lisbon* **14** b3
Baisha, *Canton* **8** B2
Baisha →, *Canton* **8** B2
Baixa, *Lisbon* **14** c2
Baiyun Airport, *Canton* **8** A2
Baiyun Hill Scenic Spot, *Canton* **8** B2
Bakırköy, *Istanbul* **12** C1
Bakovka, *Moscow* **19** B2
Bal Harbor, *Miami* **18** A2
Balara, *Manila* **17** B2
Balashikha, *Moscow* **19** B5
Baldia, *Karachi* **14** A1
Baldoyle, *Dublin* **11** A3
Baldwin Hills, *Los Angeles* **16** B2
Baldwin Hills Res., *Los Angeles* **16** B2
Balgowlah, *Sydney* **28** A2
Balgowlah Heights, *Sydney* **28** A2
Balham, *London* **15** B3
Bali, *Calcutta* **8** B1
Baliganja, *Calcutta* **8** B2
Balingsnäs, *Stockholm* **28** B2
Balingsta, *Stockholm* **28** B2
Balintawak, *Manila* **17** B1
Balitai, *Tianjin* **30** B2
Ballerup, *Copenhagen* **10** A2
Ballinteer, *Dublin* **11** B2
Ballyboden, *Dublin* **11** B2
Ballybrack, *Dublin* **11** B3
Ballyfermot, *Dublin* **11** A1
Ballymorefinn Hill, *Dublin* **11** B1
Ballymun, *Dublin* **11** A2
Balmain, *Sydney* **28** B2
Baluhati, *Calcutta* **8** B1
Balvanera, *Buenos Aires* **7** B2
Balwyn, *Melbourne* **17** A2
Balwyn North, *Melbourne* **17** A2
Banática, *Lisbon* **14** A1
Banco do Brasil, Centro Cultural, *Rio de Janeiro* **24** a2
Bandra, *Mumbai* **20** A1
Bandra Pt., *Mumbai* **20** A1
Bang Kapi, *Bangkok* **3** B2
Bang Kholaem, *Bangkok* **3** A2
Bang Na, *Bangkok* **3** B2
Bang Phlad, *Bangkok* **3** a1
Bangkhen, *Bangkok* **3** A2
Bangkok = Krung Thep, *Bangkok* **3** B2
Bangkok Noi, *Bangkok* **3** B1
Bangkok Yai, *Bangkok* **3** B1
Banglamphoo, *Bangkok* **3** b2
Banglo, *Calcutta* **8** B1
Bangrak, *Bangkok* **3** B2
Bangsu, *Bangkok* **3** B2
Bank, *London* **15** b5
Bank of America, *San Francisco* **25** b2
Bank of China Tower, *Hong Kong* **12** c1
Banks, C., *Sydney* **28** C2
Banksmeadow, *Sydney* **28** B2
Banstala, *Calcutta* **8** B2
Bantra, *Calcutta* **8** B1
Baoshan, *Shanghai* **27** A1
Bar Giyora, *Jerusalem* **13** B1
Barahanagar, *Calcutta* **8** B2
Barajas, *Madrid* **17** B2
Barajas, Aeropuerto Transoceanico de, *Madrid* **17** B2
Barakpur, *Calcutta* **8** A2
Barberini, Palazzo, *Rome* **25** b3
Barbican, *London* **15** a4
Barcarena, *Lisbon* **14** A1
Barcarena, Rib. de →, *Lisbon* **14** A1
Barcelona, *Barcelona* **4** A2
Barcelona-Prat, Aeropuerta de, *Barcelona* **4** B1
Barceloneta, *Barcelona* **4** A2
Barking, *London* **15** A4
Barkingside, *London* **15** A4
Barnes, *London* **15** B2
Barnet, *London* **15** A2
Barra Andai, *Karachi* **14** B2
Barra Funda, *São Paulo* **26** B2
Barracas, *Buenos Aires* **7** B2
Barranco, *Lima* **16** B2
Barreiro, *Lisbon* **14** B2
Barreto, *Rio de Janeiro* **24** B2
Bartala, *Calcutta* **8** B1
Barton Park, *Sydney* **28** B1
Bartyki, *Warsaw* **31** C2
Barvikha, *Moscow* **19** B1
Bastille, Place de la, *Paris* **23** c5
Basus, *Cairo* **7** A2
Batanagar, *Calcutta* **8** B1
Bath Beach, *New York* **21** C1
Bath I., *Karachi* **14** B2
Batir, *Jerusalem* **13** B1
Batok, Bukit, *Singapore* **27** A2
Battersea, *London* **15** B3
Battery Park, *New York* **21** f1
Bauman, *Moscow* **19** B4
Baumgarten, *Vienna* **31** A1
Bay Harbour Islands, *Miami* **18** A2
Bay Ridge, *New York* **21** C1
Bayonne, *New York* **21** B1
Bayshore, *San Francisco* **25** B3
Bayswater, *London* **15** b2
Bayt Lahm = Bethlehem, *Jerusalem* **13** B2
Bayview, *San Francisco* **25** B2
Bāzār, *Tehran* **30** A2
Beachmont, *Boston* **6** A4
Beacon Hill, *Hong Kong* **12** A2
Beato, *Lisbon* **14** A2
Beaumont, *Dublin* **11** A2
Beaumonte Heights, *Toronto* **30** A1
Bebek, *Istanbul* **12** B2
Běchovice, *Prague* **24** B3
Beck L., *Chicago* **9** A1
Beckenham, *London* **15** B3
Beckton, *London* **15** A4
Becontree, *London* **15** A4
Beddington Corner, *London* **15** B3
Bedford, *Boston* **6** A2
Bedford Park, *Chicago* **9** C2
Bedford Park, *New York* **21** A2
Bedford Stuyvesant, *New York* **21** B2
Bedford View, *Johannesburg* **13** B2
Bedok, *Singapore* **27** B3
Bedok, Res., *Singapore* **27** A3
Beersel, *Brussels* **6** B1
Behala, *Calcutta* **8** B1
Bei Hai, *Beijing* **4** B2
Beicai, *Shanghai* **27** B2
Beicang, *Tianjin* **30** A1
Beihai Park, *Beijing* **4** b2
Beijing, *Beijing* **4** B1
Beit Ghur el-Fawqa, *Jerusalem* **13** A1
Beit Hanina, *Jerusalem* **13** B2
Beit Iksa, *Jerusalem* **13** B2
Beit I'nan, *Jerusalem* **13** A1
Beit Jala, *Jerusalem* **13** B2
Beit Lekhem = Bethlehem, *Jerusalem* **13** B2
Beit Nekofa, *Jerusalem* **13** B1
Beit Sahur, *Jerusalem* **13** B2
Beit Surik, *Jerusalem* **13** B1
Beit Zayit, *Jerusalem* **13** B1
Beitaipingzhuan, *Beijing* **4** B1
Beitar Ilit, *Jerusalem* **13** B1
Beitsun, *Canton* **8** B2
Beitunya, *Jerusalem* **13** A2
Beixing Jing Park, *Shanghai* **27** B1
Békásmegyer, *Budapest* **7** A2
Bekkelaget, *Oslo* **22** A3
Bel Air, *Los Angeles* **16** B2
Bela Vista, *São Paulo* **26** B2
Bélanger, *Montreal* **19** A1
Belas, *Lisbon* **14** A1
Belas Artes, Museu Nacionale de, *Rio de Janeiro* **24** b2
Beleghata, *Calcutta* **8** B2
Belém, *Lisbon* **14** A1
Belém, Torre de, *Lisbon* **14** A1
Belènzinho, *São Paulo* **26** B2
Belgachiya, *Calcutta* **8** B2
Belgharia, *Calcutta* **8** B2
Belgrano, *Buenos Aires* **7** B2
Belgravia, *London* **15** c3
Bell, *Los Angeles* **16** C3
Bell Gardens, *Los Angeles* **16** C4
Bell Tower, *Beijing* **4** a2
Bellavista, *Lima* **16** B2
Bellavista, *Santiago* **26** C2
Belle Harbor, *New York* **21** C2
Belle View, *Washington* **32** B2
Bellevue, Schloss, *Berlin* **5** a2
Bellingham, *London* **15** B3
Bellwood, *Chicago* **9** B1
Belmont, *Boston* **6** A2
Belmont, *London* **15** A2
Belmont, *Wellington* **32** B2
Belmont Harbor, *Chicago* **9** B3
Belmore, *Sydney* **28** B1
Belur, *Calcutta* **8** B2
Belvedere, *Atlanta* **3** B3
Belvedere, *London* **15** B4
Belvedere, *San Francisco* **25** A2
Belyayevo Bogorodskoye, *Moscow* **19** C3
Bemowo, *Warsaw* **31** B1
Benaki, Moussío, *Athens* **2** b3
Bendale, *Toronto* **30** A3
Bendkhal, *Mumbai* **20** B2
Benefica, *Rio de Janeiro* **24** B1
Benfica, *Lisbon* **14** A1
Benito Juárez, *Mexico City* **18** B2
Benito Juárez, Aeropuerto Int., *Mexico City* **18** B2
Bensonhurst, *New York* **21** C2
Berchem-Sainte-Agathe, *Brussels* **6** A1
Berg am Laim, *Munich* **20** B2
Bergenfield, *New York* **21** A2
Bergham, *Munich* **20** B2
Bergvliet, *Cape Town* **8** B1
Beri, *Barcelona* **4** A1
Berkeley, *San Francisco* **25** A3
Berlin, *Berlin* **5** A3
Bermondsey, *London* **15** B3
Bernabeu, Estadio, *Madrid* **17** B1
Bernal Heights, *San Francisco* **25** B2
Berwyn, *Chicago* **9** B2
Berwyn Heights, *Washington* **32** B4
Besiktas, *Istanbul* **12** B2
Besós →, *Barcelona* **4** A2
Bethesda, *Washington* **32** B3
Bethlehem, *Jerusalem* **13** B2
Bethnal Green, *London* **15** A3
Betor, *Calcutta* **8** B1
Beurs, *Amsterdam* **2** b2
Beverley Hills, *Sydney* **28** B1
Beverley Park, *Sydney* **28** B1
Beverly, *Chicago* **9** C3
Beverly Glen, *Los Angeles* **16** B2
Beverly Hills, *Los Angeles* **16** B2
Bexley, *London* **15** B4
Bexley, *Sydney* **28** B1
Bexleyheath, *London* **15** B4
Beykoz, *Istanbul* **12** B2
Beylerbeyi, *Istanbul* **12** B2
Beyoğlu, *Istanbul* **12** B1
Bezons, *Paris* **23** A2
Bezuidenhout Park, *Johannesburg* **13** B2
Bhadrakali, *Calcutta* **8** A2
Bhalswa, *Delhi* **10** A2
Bhambo Khan Qarmati, *Karachi* **14** B2
Bhatsala, *Calcutta* **8** B1
Bhawanipur, *Calcutta* **8** B2
Bhuleshwar, *Mumbai* **20** b2
Białołeka Dworska, *Warsaw* **31** B2
Biblioteca Nacional, *Rio de Janeiro* **24** c2
Bicentennial Park, *Sydney* **28** B1
Bickley, *London* **15** B4
Bidu, *Jerusalem* **13** B1
Bielany, *Warsaw* **31** B1
Bielawa, *Warsaw* **31** C2
Biesdorf, *Berlin* **5** A4
Bièvre →, *Paris* **23** B1
Bièvres, *Paris* **23** B2
Bilston, *Edinburgh* **11** B2
Binacayan, *Manila* **17** C1
Binondo, *Manila* **17** B1
Birak el Kiyam, *Cairo* **7** A1
Birch Cliff, *Toronto* **30** A3
Birkenstein, *Berlin* **5** A5
Birkholz, *Berlin* **5** A4
Birkholzaue, *Berlin* **5** A4
Birrarrung Park, *Melbourne* **17** A2
Biscayne Bay, *Miami* **18** B2
Biscayne Park, *Miami* **18** A2
Bishop Lavis, *Cape Town* **8** A2
Bishopscourt, *Cape Town* **8** A1
Bispebjerg, *Copenhagen* **10** A3
Biwon Secret Garden, *Seoul* **26** B1
Björknas, *Stockholm* **28** B3
Black Cr. →, *Toronto* **30** A2
Blackfen, *London* **15** B4
Blackheath, *London* **15** B4
Blackrock, *Dublin* **11** B2
Bladensburg, *Washington* **32** B4
Blair Village, *Atlanta* **3** C2
Blairgowrie, *Johannesburg* **13** A2
Blakehurst, *Sydney* **28** B1
Blakstad, *Oslo* **22** B1
Blankenburg, *Berlin* **5** A3
Blankenfelde, *Berlin* **5** A3
Blizne, *Warsaw* **31** B1
Bloomsbury, *London* **15** a3
Błota, *Warsaw* **31** C3
Blue Island, *Chicago* **9** C2
Bluebell, *Dublin* **11** B1
Bluff Hd., *Hong Kong* **12** B2
Blumberg, *Berlin* **5** A4
Blunt Pt., *San Francisco* **25** A2
Blutenberg, *Munich* **20** B1
Blylaget, *Oslo* **22** B3
Bo-Kaap Museum, *Cape Town* **8** c2
Boa Vista, Alto do, *Rio de Janeiro* **24** B1
Boardwalk, *New York* **21** C3
Boavista, *Lisbon* **14** A2
Bobigny, *Paris* **23** A3
Bocanegra, *Lima* **16** A2
Boedo, *Buenos Aires* **7** B2
Bogenhausen, *Munich* **20** B2
Bogorodskoye, *Moscow* **19** B4
Bogota, *New York* **21** A1
Bogstadvatnet, *Oslo* **22** A2
Bohnsdorf, *Berlin* **5** B4
Bois-Colombes, *Paris* **23** A2
Bois-d'Arcy, *Paris* **23** B1
Boissy-St.-Léger, *Paris* **23** B4
Boldinasco, *Milan* **18** B1
Bøler, *Oslo* **22** A4
Bollate, *Milan* **18** A1
Bollebeek, *Brussels* **6** A1
Bollensdorf, *Berlin* **5** A5
Bollmora, *Stockholm* **28** B3
Bolshaya-Okhta, *St. Petersburg* **26** B2
Bolton, *Atlanta* **3** B2
Bom Retiro, *São Paulo* **26** B2
Bombay = Mumbai, *Mumbai* **20** B2
Bondi, *Sydney* **28** B2
Bondy, *Paris* **23** A3
Bondy, Forêt de, *Paris* **23** A4
Bonifacio Monument, *Manila* **17** B1
Bonneuil-sur-Marne, *Paris* **23** B4
Bonnington, *Edinburgh* **11** B1
Bonnyrig and Lasswade, *Edinburgh* **11** B3
Bonsucesso, *Rio de Janeiro* **24** B1
Bonteheuwel, *Cape Town* **8** A2
Boo, *Stockholm* **28** A3
Booterstown, *Dublin* **11** B2
Borisovo, *Moscow* **19** C4
Borle, *Mumbai* **20** A2
Boronia Park, *Sydney* **28** A1
Borough Park, *New York* **21** C2
Bosmont, *Johannesburg* **13** B1
Bosön, *Stockholm* **28** A3
Bosporus = Istanbul Boğazi, *Istanbul* **12** B2
Bostancı, *Istanbul* **12** C2
Boston Harbor, *Boston* **6** A4
Botafogo, *Rio de Janeiro* **24** B1
Botanisk Have, *Copenhagen* **10** b2
Botany, *Sydney* **28** B2
Botany B., *Sydney* **28** B2
Botany Bay Nat. Park, *Sydney* **28** B2
Botič →, *Prague* **24** B3
Botica Sete, *Lisbon* **14** A1
Boucherville, *Montreal* **19** A3
Boucherville, Îs. de, *Montreal* **19** A3
Bougival, *Paris* **23** A1
Boulder Pt., *Hong Kong* **12** B1
Boulogne, Bois de, *Paris* **23** A2
Boulogne-Billancourt, *Paris* **23** A2
Bourg-la-Reine, *Paris* **23** B2
Bouviers, *Paris* **23** B1
Bovenkerk, *Amsterdam* **2** B2
Bovenkerker Polder, *Amsterdam* **2** B2
Bovisa, *Milan* **18** A2
Bow, *London* **15** A3
Bowery, *New York* **21** e2
Boyacıköy, *Istanbul* **12** B2
Boyle Heights, *Los Angeles* **16** B3
Bradbury Building, *Los Angeles* **16** b2
Braepark, *Edinburgh* **11** B2
Braid, *Edinburgh* **11** B2
Bramley, *Johannesburg* **13** A2
Brandenburger Tor, *Berlin* **5** A3
Brani, P., *Singapore* **27** B3
Branik, *Prague* **24** B2
Brännkyrka, *Stockholm* **28** B2
Brás, *São Paulo* **26** B2
Brasilândia, *São Paulo* **26** A1
Brateyevo, *Moscow* **19** C4
Bratsevo, *Moscow* **19** A2
Bray, *Dublin* **11** B3
Braybrook, *Melbourne* **17** A1
Brázdim, *Prague* **24** A3
Breach Candy, *Mumbai* **20** a1
Breakheart Reservation, *Boston* **6** A3
Brede, *Copenhagen* **10** A3
Breeds Pond, *Boston* **6** A4
Breezy Point, *New York* **21** C2
Breitenlee, *Vienna* **31** A3
Breña, *Lima* **16** B2
Brent, *London* **15** A2
Brent Res., *London* **15** A2
Brentford, *London* **15** B2
Brentwood Park, *Los Angeles* **16** B2
Brera, *Milan* **18** B2
Bresso, *Milan* **18** A2
Brevik, *Stockholm* **28** A3
Břevnov, *Prague* **24** B2
Bridgeport, *Chicago* **9** B3
Bridgetown, *Cape Town* **8** A2
Bridgeview, *Chicago* **9** C2
Brighton, *Boston* **6** A3
Brighton, *Melbourne* **17** B1
Brighton le Sands, *Sydney* **28** B1
Brighton Park, *Chicago* **9** C2
Brightwood, *Washington* **32** B3
Brigittenau, *Vienna* **31** A2
Brimbank Park, *Melbourne* **17** A1
Brisbane, *San Francisco* **25** B2
British Museum, *London* **15** a3
Britz, *Berlin* **5** B3
Brixton, *London* **15** B3
Broad Sd., *Boston* **6** A4
Broadmeadows, *Melbourne* **17** A1
Broadmoor, *San Francisco* **25** B2
Broadview, *Chicago* **9** B1
Broadway, *New York* **21** e1
Brockley, *London* **15** B3
Bródno, *Warsaw* **31** B2
Bródnowski, Kanal, *Warsaw* **31** B2
Broek in Waterland, *Amsterdam* **2** A2
Bromley, *London* **15** B4
Bromley Common, *London* **15** B4
Bromma, *Stockholm* **28** A1
Bromma flygplats, *Stockholm* **28** A1
Brompton, *London* **15** c2
Brøndby Strand, *Copenhagen* **10** B2
Brøndbyøster, *Copenhagen* **10** B2
Brøndbyvester, *Copenhagen* **10** B2
Brondesbury, *London* **15** A2
Brønnøya, *Oslo* **22** A2
Brønshøj, *Copenhagen* **10** A2
Bronxville, *New York* **21** A3
Brookfield, *Chicago* **9** C1

34 Brookhaven

Brookhaven, *Atlanta* 3 A2
Brookline, *Boston* 6 B3
Brooklyn, *Cape Town* 8 A1
Brooklyn, *New York* 21 C2
Brooklyn, *Wellington* 32 B1
Brooklyn Bridge, *New York* 21 f2
Brookmont, *Washington* 32 B3
Brossard, *Montreal* 19 B3
Brou-sur-Chantereine, *Paris* 23 A4
Brown, *Toronto* 30 A3
Broyhill Park, *Washington* 32 B2
Brughério, *Milan* 18 A2
Brunswick, *Melbourne* 17 A1
Brush Hill, *Boston* 6 B1
Brussegem, *Brussels* 6 A1
Brussel Nat. Luchthaven, *Brussels* 6 A2
Brussels = Bruxelles, *Brussels* 6 A2
Bruxelles, *Brussels* 6 A2
Bruzzano, *Milan* 18 A2
Bry-sur-Marne, *Paris* 23 A4
Bryanston, *Johannesburg* 13 A1
Bryn, *Oslo* 22 A1
Brzeziny, *Warsaw* 31 B2
Bubeneč, *Prague* 24 B2
Buc, *Paris* 23 B1
Buchenhain, *Munich* 20 B1
Buchholz, *Berlin* 5 A3
Buckhead, *Atlanta* 3 A2
Buckingham Palace, *London* 15 b3
Buckow, *Berlin* 5 B3
Buda, *Budapest* 7 A2
Budafok, *Budapest* 7 B2
Budaörs, *Budapest* 7 B1
Budapest, *Budapest* 7 B2
Budatétény, *Budapest* 7 B2
Budavaripalota, *Budapest* 7 b2
Buddinge, *Copenhagen* 10 A3
Budokan, *Tokyo* 29 a4
Buena Vista, *San Francisco* 25 B2
Buenos Aires, *Buenos Aires* 7 B2
Bufalotta, *Rome* 25 B2
Bugio, *Lisbon* 14 B1
Buiksloot, *Amsterdam* 2 A2
Buitenveldert, *Amsterdam* 2 B2
Buizingen, *Brussels* 6 B1
Bukit Panjang Nature Reserve, *Singapore* 27 A2
Bukit Timah Nature Reserve, *Singapore* 27 A2
Bukum, P., *Singapore* 27 B2
Bûlâq, *Cairo* 7 A2
Bule, *Manila* 17 C2
Bulim, *Singapore* 27 A2
Bullen Park, *Melbourne* 17 A2
Bundoora North, *Melbourne* 17 A2
Bundoora Park, *Melbourne* 17 A2
Bunker I., *Karachi* 14 B1
Bunkyo-Ku, *Tokyo* 29 A3
Bunnefjorden, *Oslo* 22 A3
Buona Vista Park, *Singapore* 27 B2
Burbank, *Chicago* 9 C2
Burbank, *Los Angeles* 16 A3
Burlington, *Boston* 6 A2
Burnham Park, *Chicago* 9 c2
Burnham Park Harbor, *Chicago* 9 B3
Burnhamthorpe, *Toronto* 30 B1
Burnt Oak, *London* 15 A2
Burntisland, *Edinburgh* 11 A2
Burnwynd, *Edinburgh* 11 B1
Burqa, *Jerusalem* 13 A2
Burtus, *Cairo* 7 A1
Burudvatn, *Oslo* 22 A2
Burwood, *Sydney* 28 B1
Bushwick, *New York* 21 B2
Bushy Park, *London* 15 B1
Butantã, *São Paulo* 26 B1
Butcher I., *Mumbai* 20 B2
Butts Corner, *Washington* 32 C2
Büyükdere, *Istanbul* 12 B2
Byculla, *Mumbai* 20 B2
Bygdøy, *Oslo* 22 A3

C

C.N. Tower, *Toronto* 30 B2
Cabaçu de Cima →, *São Paulo* 26 A2
Caballito, *Buenos Aires* 7 B2
Cabin John, *Washington* 32 B2
Cabin John Regional Park, *Washington* 32 A2
Cabinteely, *Dublin* 11 B3
Cabra, *Dublin* 11 A2
Cabuçú de Baixo →, *São Paulo* 26 A1
Cachan, *Paris* 23 B2
Cachenka →, *Moscow* 19 B1
Cachoeira, Rib. da →, *São Paulo* 26 B1
Cacilhas, *Lisbon* 14 A2
Cahuenga Pk., *Los Angeles* 16 B3
Cairo = El Qâhira, *Cairo* 7 A2
Caju, *Rio de Janeiro* 24 B1
Čakovice, *Prague* 24 B3
Calcutta = Kolkata, *Calcutta* 8 B2
California Inst. of Tech., *Los Angeles* 16 B4
California Plaza, *Los Angeles* 16 b1
California State Univ., *Los Angeles* 16 B3
Callao, *Lima* 16 B2
Caloocan, *Manila* 17 B1
Calumet Park, *Chicago* 9 C3
Calumet Sag Channel →, *Chicago* 9 C2
Calumpang, *Manila* 17 B2
Calvairate, *Milan* 18 B2
Camarate, *Lisbon* 14 A2
Camaroes, *Lisbon* 14 A1
Camberwell, *London* 15 B3
Camberwell, *Melbourne* 17 B2
Cambridge, *Boston* 6 A3
Cambridge Res., *Boston* 6 A2
Cambuci, *São Paulo* 26 B2
Camden, *London* 15 A3
Cameron, Mt., *Wellington* 32 B2
Çamlıca, *Istanbul* 12 B2
Camp Springs, *Washington* 32 C4
Campamento, *Madrid* 17 B1
Campbellfield, *Melbourne* 17 A1
Camperdown, *Sydney* 28 B2
Campidoglio, *Rome* 25 c3
Campo, Casa de, *Madrid* 17 B1
Campo F.C. Barcelona, *Barcelona* 4 A1
Campo Grando, *Lisbon* 14 A2
Campo Pequeño, *Lisbon* 14 A2
Campolide, *Lisbon* 14 A2
Camps Bay, *Cape Town* 8 A1
C'an San Joan, *Barcelona* 4 A2
Cañacao B., *Manila* 17 C1
Canarsie, *New York* 21 C2
Cancelleria, Palazzo dei, *Rome* 25 c2
Candiac, *Montreal* 19 B3
Caneças, *Lisbon* 14 A1
Canillas, *Madrid* 17 B2
Canillejas, *Madrid* 17 B2
Canning Town, *London* 15 A4
Canteras de Vallecas, *Madrid* 17 B2
Canterbury, *Melbourne* 17 A2
Canterbury, *Sydney* 28 B1
Canton = Guangzhou, *Canton* 8 B2
Caoheijing, *Shanghai* 27 B1
Capão Redondo, *São Paulo* 26 B1
Caparica, *Lisbon* 14 A2
Caparica, Costa da, *Lisbon* 14 B1
Cape Flats, *Cape Town* 8 B2
Cape Town, *Cape Town* 8 A1
Capitol Heights, *Washington* 32 B4
Capitol Hill, *Washington* 32 B4
Capitolini, Musei, *Rome* 25 c3
Captain Cook Bridge, *Sydney* 28 C1
Captain Cook Landing Place Park, *Sydney* 28 C2
Capuchos, *Lisbon* 14 B1
Carabanchel Alto, *Madrid* 17 B1
Carabanchel Bajo, *Madrid* 17 B1
Carapachay, *Buenos Aires* 7 B1
Caraza, *Buenos Aires* 7 C2
Caridad, *Manila* 17 C1
Carioca, Sa. da, *Rio de Janeiro* 24 B1
Carlstadt, *New York* 21 A1
Carlton, *Melbourne* 17 A1
Carmen de Huechuraba, *Santiago* 26 B1
Carmen de la Legua, *Lima* 16 B2
Carnaxide, *Lisbon* 14 A1
Carnegie, *Melbourne* 17 B2
Carnegie Hall, *New York* 21 c2
Carnide, *Lisbon* 14 A1
Carol City, *Miami* 18 A1
Carrascal, *Santiago* 26 B1
Carrickmines, *Dublin* 11 B3
Carrières-sous-Bois, *Paris* 23 A1
Carrières-sous-Poissy, *Paris* 23 A1
Carrières-sur-Seine, *Paris* 23 A2
Carrigeen Bay, *Dublin* 11 A3
Cartierville, *Montreal* 19 A1
Casa Verde, *São Paulo* 26 A1
Casál Morena, *Rome* 25 C2
Casalotti, *Rome* 25 B1
Cascade Heights, *Atlanta* 3 B2
Castél di Leva, *Rome* 25 C2
Castel Sant'Angelo, *Rome* 25 B1
Castle, *Dublin* 11 c2
Castle, *Edinburgh* 11 b2
Castle of Good Hope, *Cape Town* 8 c3
Castleknock, *Dublin* 11 A1
Castleton Corners, *New York* 21 C1
Catedral Metropolitana, *Mexico City* 18 b3
Catedral Metropolitana, *Rio de Janeiro* 24 c1
Catete, *Rio de Janeiro* 24 B1
Catford, *London* 15 B3
Caulfield, *Melbourne* 17 B2
Causeway Bay, *Hong Kong* 12 c3
Cavite, *Manila* 17 C1
Caxias, *Lisbon* 14 A1
Cebecci, *Istanbul* 12 B1
Cecchignola, *Rome* 25 C2
Cecilienhof, Schloss, *Berlin* 5 B1
Cedar Grove, *Atlanta* 3 C3
Cempaka Putih, *Jakarta* 13 B2
Çengelköy, *Istanbul* 12 B2
Cengkareng, *Jakarta* 13 A1
Centennial Park, *Sydney* 28 B2
Center Hill, *Atlanta* 3 B2
Centocelle, *Rome* 25 B2
Centraal Station, *Amsterdam* 2 a2
Central Park, *New York* 21 B2
Cerillos, *Santiago* 26 B1
Cerro de la Estrella, *Mexico City* 18 B2
Cerro de los Angeles, *Madrid* 17 C1
Cerro Navia, *Santiago* 26 B1
Certanovka →, *Moscow* 19 C3
Certanovo, *Moscow* 19 C3
Cesano Boscone, *Milan* 18 B1
Cesate, *Milan* 18 A1
Cha Kwo Ling, *Hong Kong* 12 B2
Chacarrita, *Buenos Aires* 7 B2
Chadwell Heath, *London* 15 A4
Chai Chee, *Singapore* 27 B3
Chai Wan, *Hong Kong* 12 B2
Chai Wan Kok, *Hong Kong* 12 A1
Chaillot, Palais de, *Paris* 23 b2
Chakdaha, *Calcutta* 8 C1
Chamartin, *Madrid* 17 B1
Chamberi, *Madrid* 17 B1
Chambourcy, *Paris* 23 A1
Champ de Mars, Parc du, *Paris* 23 c2
Champigny-sur-Marne, *Paris* 23 B4
Champlain, Pont, *Montreal* 19 B2
Champs Elysées, Avenue des, *Paris* 23 b2
Champs-sur-Marne, *Paris* 23 A4
Chamrail, *Calcutta* 8 B1
Chamshil, *Seoul* 26 B2
Chamwŏn, *Seoul* 26 B2
Chanakyapuri, *Delhi* 10 B2
Chanditala, *Calcutta* 8 A1
Changfeng Park, *Shanghai* 27 B1
Changi, *Singapore* 27 A3
Changi Int. Airport, *Singapore* 27 A3
Changning, *Shanghai* 27 B1
Chantereine, *Paris* 23 A4
Chantian, *Canton* 8 A2
Chao Phraya →, *Bangkok* 3 B2
Chaoyang, *Beijing* 4 B2
Chaoyangmen, *Beijing* 4 B2
Chapelizod, *Dublin* 11 A1
Chapultepec, Bosque de, *Mexico City* 18 B1
Chapultepec, Castillo de, *Mexico City* 18 B1
Charenton-le-Pont, *Paris* 23 B3
Charing Cross, *London* 15 b4
Charleroi, Kanal de →, *Brussels* 6 B1
Charles Bridge, *Prague* 24 b1
Charles Square, *Prague* 24 c1
Charlestown, *Boston* 6 A3
Charlottenburg, *Berlin* 5 A2
Charlottenburg, Schloss, *Berlin* 5 A2
Charlottenlund, *Copenhagen* 10 A3
Charlton, *London* 15 B4
Charneca, *Lisbon* 14 A2
Charneca, *Lisbon* 14 B1
Châteaufort, *Paris* 23 B1
Châtenay-Malabry, *Paris* 23 B2
Chatham, *Chicago* 9 C3
Châtillon, *Paris* 23 B2
Chatou, *Paris* 23 A1
Chatpur, *Calcutta* 8 B2
Chatswood, *Sydney* 28 A2
Chatuchak, *Bangkok* 3 B2
Chatuchak Park, *Bangkok* 3 B2
Chauki, *Karachi* 14 A1
Chavarria, *Lima* 16 B2
Chaville, *Paris* 23 B2
Chayang, *Seoul* 26 B2
Chegi, *Seoul* 26 B2
Chelles, *Paris* 23 A4
Chelles, Canal de, *Paris* 23 A4
Chells-le-Pin, Aérodrome, *Paris* 23 A4
Chelsea, *Boston* 6 A3
Chelsea, *London* 15 B2
Chelsea, *New York* 21 c1
Chembur, *Mumbai* 20 A2
Chennevières-sur-Marne, *Paris* 23 B4
Cheops, *Cairo* 7 B1
Cherepkovo, *Moscow* 19 B2
Chernyovo, *Moscow* 19 A1
Cheryomushki, *Moscow* 19 B3
Chestnut Hill, *Boston* 6 B2
Cheung Sha Wan, *Hong Kong* 12 A1
Cheverly, *Washington* 32 B4
Chevilly-Larue, *Paris* 23 B3
Chevry-Cossigny, *Paris* 23 B4
Chevy Chase, *Washington* 32 B3
Chevy Chase View, *Washington* 32 A3
Chia Keng, *Singapore* 27 A3
Chiaravalle Milanese, *Milan* 18 B2
Chicago, *Chicago* 9 B3
Chicago Harbor, *Chicago* 9 B3
Chicago Lawn, *Chicago* 9 C2
Chicago-Midway Airport, *Chicago* 9 C2
Chicago-O'Hare Int. Airport, *Chicago* 9 B1
Chicago Ridge, *Chicago* 9 C2
Chicago Sanitary and Ship Canal, *Chicago* 9 C2
Chienzui, *Canton* 8 A3
Chik Sha, *Hong Kong* 12 B2
Child's Hill, *London* 15 A2
Chilla Saroda, *Delhi* 10 B2
Chillum, *Washington* 32 B4
Chilly-Mazarin, *Paris* 23 B2
Chinatown, *Los Angeles* 16 a3
Chinatown, *New York* 21 e2
Chinatown, *San Francisco* 25 b2
Chinatown, *Singapore* 27 c2
Chingupota, *Calcutta* 8 C1
Chislehurst, *London* 15 B4
Chiswick, *London* 15 B2
Chiswick House, *London* 15 B2
Chitose, *Tokyo* 29 B2
Chitralada Palace, *Bangkok* 3 B2
Chiyoda-Ku, *Tokyo* 29 b4
Chkalova, *Moscow* 19 C5
Choa Chu Kang, *Singapore* 27 A2
Choboty, *Moscow* 19 C2
Chodov u Prahy, *Prague* 24 B3
Chōfu, *Tokyo* 29 B2
Choisy-le-Roi, *Paris* 23 B3
Cholupice, *Prague* 24 C2
Chom Thong, *Bangkok* 3 B1
Chong Pang, *Singapore* 27 A2
Ch'ŏngdam, *Seoul* 26 B2
Chongmyo Royal Shrine, *Seoul* 26 B1
Chongno, *Seoul* 26 B1
Chongwen, *Beijing* 4 B2
Chŏnho, *Seoul* 26 B2
Chopin, Muzeum, *Warsaw* 31 b2
Chornaya →, *Moscow* 19 B6
Chorrillos, *Lima* 16 C2
Chowpatty Beach, *Mumbai* 20 b1
Christian Quarter, *Jerusalem* 13 b3
Christiansborg, *Copenhagen* 10 c2
Christianshavn, *Copenhagen* 10 A3
Chrysler Building, *New York* 21 c2
Chrzanów, *Warsaw* 31 B1
Chuen Lung, *Hong Kong* 12 A1
Chuk Kok, *Hong Kong* 12 A2
Chulalongkom Univ., *Bangkok* 3 B2
Chung, *Seoul* 26 B1
Chunghwa, *Seoul* 26 B2
Chungnangch'on →, *Seoul* 26 B1
Chūō-Ku, *Tokyo* 29 b5
Church End, *London* 15 A2
Churchtown, *Dublin* 11 B2
Ciampino, *Rome* 25 C2
Ciampino, Aeroporto di, *Rome* 25 C2
Cicero, *Chicago* 9 B2
Cilandak, *Jakarta* 13 B1
Cilincing, *Jakarta* 13 A2
Ciliwung →, *Jakarta* 13 B2
Čimice, *Prague* 24 B2
Cinecittà, *Rome* 25 B2
Cinisello Bálsamo, *Milan* 18 A2
Cinkota, *Budapest* 7 A3
Cipete, *Jakarta* 13 B1
Citadella, *Budapest* 7 c2
Citta degli Studi, *Milan* 18 B2
Città del Vaticano, *Rome* 25 B1
City, *London* 15 A3
City Hall, *New York* 21 e1
Ciudad Deportiva, *Mexico City* 18 B2
Ciudad Fin de Semana, *Madrid* 17 B2
Ciudad General Belgrano, *Buenos Aires* 7 C1
Ciudad Lineál, *Madrid* 17 B2
Ciudad Satélite, *Mexico City* 18 A1
Ciudad Universitaria, *Buenos Aires* 7 B2
Ciudad Universitaria, *Mexico City* 18 C1
Ciutadella, Parc de la, *Barcelona* 4 b3
Civic Center, *Los Angeles* 16 b2
Clamart, *Paris* 23 B2
Clapham, *London* 15 B3
Clapton, *London* 15 A3
Claremont, *Cape Town* 8 A1
Clayhall, *London* 15 A4
Clerkenwell, *London* 15 a4
Clermiston, *Edinburgh* 11 B2
Clichy, *Paris* 23 A2
Clichy-sous-Bois, *Paris* 23 A4
Cliffside, *Toronto* 30 A3
Cliffside Park, *New York* 21 B2
Clifton, *Boston* 6 A4
Clifton, *Karachi* 14 B2
Clifton, *New York* 21 C1
Cliftondale, *Boston* 6 A3
Cloghran, *Dublin* 11 A2
Clonskeagh, *Dublin* 11 B2
Clontarf, *Dublin* 11 A2
Clontarf, *Sydney* 28 A2
Clovelly, *Sydney* 28 B2
Cobras, I. das, *Rio de Janeiro* 24 B2
Coburg, *Melbourne* 17 A1
Cochituate, *Boston* 6 A1
Cochituate, L., *Boston* 6 B1
Cocotá, *Rio de Janeiro* 24 A1
Cœuilly, *Paris* 23 B4
Coina, *Lisbon* 14 B2
Coit Tower, *San Francisco* 25 a2
Coker, *Lagos* 14 B2
Colaba, *Mumbai* 20 B1
Colaba Pt., *Mumbai* 20 B1
Colegiales, *Buenos Aires* 7 B2
Colindale, *London* 15 A2
Colinton, *Edinburgh* 11 B2
College Park, *Atlanta* 3 C2
College Park, *Washington* 32 B4
College Point, *New York* 21 B2
Collégien, *Paris* 23 A4
Collier Row, *London* 15 A4
Colliers Wood, *London* 15 B2
Colma, *San Francisco* 25 B2
Colney Hatch, *London* 15 A3
Cologno Monzese, *Milan* 18 A2
Colombes, *Paris* 23 A2
Colón, Monumente, *Barcelona* 4 c3
Colon, Plaza de, *Madrid* 17 a3
Colonia Güell, *Barcelona* 4 A1
Colonial Knob, *Wellington* 32 A1
Colosseo, *Rome* 25 c3
Columbus Circus, *New York* 21 b2
Combault, *Paris* 23 B4
Comércio, Praça do, *Lisbon* 14 A2
Commerce, *Los Angeles* 16 B4
Como, *Sydney* 28 C1
Company's Gardens, *Cape Town* 8 c2
Conceição, I. da, *Rio de Janeiro* 24 B2
Concertgebouw, *Amsterdam* 2 c1
Conchali, *Santiago* 26 B2
Concord, *Boston* 6 A1
Concord, *Sydney* 28 B1
Concord, *Toronto* 30 A2
Concorde, Place de la, *Paris* 23 b3
Concorezzo, *Milan* 18 A2
Coney Island, *New York* 21 C2
Congonhas, Aéroporto, *São Paulo* 26 B2
Connaught Place, *Delhi* 10 B2
Conservatori, Palazzo dei, *Rome* 25 c3
Consolação, *São Paulo* 26 B2
Constantia, *Cape Town* 8 B1
Constitución, *Buenos Aires* 7 B2
Constitution, *Atlanta* 3 B2
Convention and Exhibition Centre, *Hong Kong* 12 b2
Coogee, *Sydney* 28 B2
Cook Str., *Wellington* 32 A1
Cooksville, *Toronto* 30 B1
Coolock, *Dublin* 11 A2
Copacabana, *Rio de Janeiro* 24 B1
Copenhagen = København, *Copenhagen* 10 A2
Coral Gables, *Miami* 18 B2
Coral Hills, *Washington* 32 B4
Corcovado, Morro do, *Rio de Janeiro* 24 B1
Corduff, *Dublin* 11 A1
Cormano, *Milan* 18 A2
Cornaredo, *Milan* 18 A1
Córsico, *Milan* 18 B1
Corsini, Palazzo, *Rome* 25 c1
Corviale, *Rome* 25 B1
Coslada, *Madrid* 17 B2
Cossigny, *Paris* 23 B4
Cossipore, *Calcutta* 8 B2
Costantino, Arco di, *Rome* 25 c3
Costorphine, *Edinburgh* 11 B2
Cotao, *Lisbon* 14 A1
Côte St.-Luc, *Montreal* 19 B2
Cotunduba, I. de, *Rio de Janeiro* 24 B2
Coubron, *Paris* 23 A4
Countryside, *Chicago* 9 C1
Courbevoie, *Paris* 23 A2
Courtry, *Paris* 23 A4
Covent Garden, *London* 15 b4
Cowgate, *Edinburgh* 11 b3
Cowley, *London* 15 A1
Coyoacán, *Mexico City* 18 B2
Cragin, *Chicago* 9 B2
Craighall Park, *Johannesburg* 13 A2
Craiglockhart, *Edinburgh* 11 B2
Craigmillar, *Edinburgh* 11 B3
Cramond, *Edinburgh* 11 B2
Cramond Bridge, *Edinburgh* 11 B1
Cramond I., *Edinburgh* 11 B2
Cranford, *London* 15 B1
Crawford, *Cape Town* 8 A2
Crayford, *London* 15 B5
Creekmouth, *London* 15 A4
Crescenzago, *Milan* 18 A2
Cressely, *Paris* 23 B1
Cresskill, *New York* 21 A2
Creteil, *Paris* 23 B3
Cricklewood, *London* 15 A2
Cristo Redentor, Estatua do, *Rio de Janeiro* 24 B1
Crockenhill, *London* 15 B4
Croissy-Beaubourg, *Paris* 23 B4
Croissy-sur-Seine, *Paris* 23 A1
Crosby, *Johannesburg* 13 B1
Crosne, *Paris* 23 B3
Cross I., *Mumbai* 20 B2
Crouch End, *London* 15 A3
Crown Mine, *Johannesburg* 13 B1
Crows Nest, *Sydney* 28 A2
Croydon, *London* 15 B3
Croydon Park, *Sydney* 28 B1
Cruagh Mt., *Dublin* 11 B2
Crumlin, *Dublin* 11 B2
Cruz de Pau, *Lisbon* 14 B2
Crystal Palace, *London* 15 B3
Csepel, *Budapest* 7 B2
Csepelsziget, *Budapest* 7 B2
Csillaghegy, *Budapest* 7 A2
Csillagtelep, *Budapest* 7 B2
Csömör, *Budapest* 7 A3
Csömöri-patak →, *Budapest* 7 A3
Cuatro Vientos, *Madrid* 17 B1
Cuauhtémoc, *Mexico City* 18 B2
Cubao, *Manila* 17 B2
Çubuklu, *Istanbul* 12 B2
Cudahy, *Los Angeles* 16 C3
Cuicuilco, Pirámido de, *Mexico City* 18 C1
Culver City, *Los Angeles* 16 B2
Cumballa Hill, *Mumbai* 20 a1
Cumbres de Vallecas, *Madrid* 17 B2
Cupecé, *São Paulo* 26 B1
Currie, *Edinburgh* 11 B2
Cusago, *Milan* 18 B1
Cusano Milanino, *Milan* 18 A2
Custom House, *Dublin* 11 b3
Çuvuşabaşi →, *Istanbul* 12 B1
Czernriaków, *Warsaw* 31 B2
Czyste, *Warsaw* 31 B1

D

D.F. Malan Airport, *Cape Town* 8 A2
Da Moóca →, *São Paulo* 26 B2
Da Yunhe →, *Tianjin* 30 A1
Dabizhuang, *Tianjin* 30 A2
Ďablice, *Prague* 24 B2
Dąbrowa, *Warsaw* 31 B1
Dachang, *Shanghai* 27 B1
Dachang Airfield, *Shanghai* 27 B1
Dachau-Ost, *Munich* 20 A1
Dachauer Moos, *Munich* 20 A1
Dadar, *Mumbai* 20 A1
Dagenham, *London* 15 A4
Daglfing, *Munich* 20 B2
Daheisha, *Jerusalem* 13 B2
Dahlem, *Berlin* 5 B2
Dahlwitz-Hoppegarten, *Berlin* 5 A5
Dahongmen, *Beijing* 4 C2
Daitō, *Osaka* 22 A4
Dajiaoting, *Beijing* 4 B2
Dakhnoye, *St. Petersburg* 26 C1
Dalejský potok →, *Prague* 24 B2
Dalgety Bay, *Edinburgh* 11 A1
Dalkeith, *Edinburgh* 11 B3
Dalkey, *Dublin* 11 B3
Dalkey Island, *Dublin* 11 B3
Dallgow, *Berlin* 5 A1
Dalmeny, *Edinburgh* 11 B1
Dalston, *London* 15 A3
Daly City, *San Francisco* 25 B2
Dam, *Amsterdam* 2 b2
Dam Rak, *Amsterdam* 2 a2
Damaia, *Lisbon* 14 A1
Dämeritzsee, *Berlin* 5 B5
Dan Ryan Woods, *Chicago* 9 C2
Danderhall, *Edinburgh* 11 B3
Danderyd, *Stockholm* 28 A2
Danforth, *Toronto* 30 A3
Darakeh, *Tehran* 30 A2
Darband, *Tehran* 30 A2
Darling Harbour, *Sydney* 28 b1
Darling Point, *Sydney* 28 B2
Darndale, *Dublin* 11 A2
Darrūs, *Tehran* 30 A2
Dartford, *London* 15 B5
Darya Ganj, *Delhi* 1 a3
Dashi, *Canton* 8 B2
Datansha, *Canton* 8 B2
Datun, *Beijing* 4 B2
Daulatpur, *Delhi* 10 A1
David's Citadel, *Jerusalem* 13 b3
David's Tomb, *Jerusalem* 13 b3
Davidson, Mt., *San Francisco* 25 B2
Davidson's Mains, *Edinburgh* 11 B2
Dāvūdiyeh, *Tehran* 30 A2
Davydkovo, *Moscow* 19 B2
Dawidy, *Warsaw* 31 C1
Days Bay, *Wellington* 32 B2
Dazhigu, *Tianjin* 30 B2
De Waag, *Amsterdam* 2 b2
Decatur, *Atlanta* 3 B3
Dedham, *Boston* 6 B2
Deer I., *Boston* 6 A4
Degunino, *Moscow* 19 A3
Deir Dibwan, *Jerusalem* 13 A2
Deir Ibzi'e, *Jerusalem* 13 A1
Dejvice, *Prague* 24 B2
Dekabristov, Ostrov, *St. Petersburg* 26 B1
Delhi, *Delhi* 10 B2
Delhi Gate, *Delhi* 1 b3
Demarest, *New York* 21 A2
Den Ilp, *Amsterdam* 2 A2
Denistone Heights, *Sydney* 28 A1
Dentonia Park, *Toronto* 30 A3
Deptford, *London* 15 B3
Deputati, Camera dei, *Rome* 25 b2
Des Plaines, *Chicago* 9 A1
Des Plaines →, *Chicago* 9 B1
Deshengmen, *Beijing* 4 B2
Deutsch-Wagram, *Vienna* 31 A3
Deutsche Oper, *Berlin* 5 A2
Deutscher Museum, *Munich* 20 B2
Devil's Peak, *Cape Town* 8 A1
Dháfni, *Athens* 2 B2
Dhakuria, *Calcutta* 8 B2
Dhamarakia, *Athens* 2 B1
Dharavi, *Mumbai* 20 A2
Dhrapersón, *Athens* 2 B1
Diadema, *São Paulo* 26 C2
Diegen, *Brussels* 6 A2
Diemen, *Amsterdam* 2 A2
Diepkloof, *Johannesburg* 13 B1
Dieprivier, *Cape Town* 8 B1
Difficult Run →, *Washington* 32 B2
Dilbeek, *Brussels* 6 A1
Dinzigu, *Tianjin* 30 A1
Dirnismaning, *Munich* 20 A2
District Heights, *Washington* 32 B4
Ditan Park, *Beijing* 4 a2
Diyāla →, *Baghdad* 3 B3
Djursholm, *Stockholm* 28 A2
Döberitz, *Berlin* 5 A1
Döbling, *Vienna* 31 A2
Docklands, *London* 15 A3
Dodder, R. →, *Dublin* 11 B1
Dodger Stadium, *Los Angeles* 16 B3
Dolgoe Ozero, *St. Petersburg* 26 A1
Doll Museum, *Delhi* 1 b3
Dollis Hill, *London* 15 A2
Dollymount, *Dublin* 11 A2
Dolni, *Prague* 24 B3
Dolni Chabry, *Prague* 24 B2
Dolni Počernice, *Prague* 24 B3
Dolphins Barn, *Dublin* 11 B2
Dom Pedro II, Parque, *São Paulo* 26 B2
Domain, The, *Sydney* 28 b2
Dome of the Rock, *Jerusalem* 13 b3
Don Mills, *Toronto* 30 A2
Don Muang Int. Airport, *Bangkok* 3 A2
Donaghmede, *Dublin* 11 A3
Donau-Oder Kanal, *Vienna* 31 A3
Donaufeld, *Vienna* 31 A2
Donaupark, *Vienna* 31 A2
Donaustadt, *Vienna* 31 A2
Dongan Hills, *New York* 21 C1
Dongcheng, *Beijing* 4 B2
Donggou, *Shanghai* 27 B2
Dongjiao, *Canton* 8 B2
Dongjuzi, *Tianjin* 30 B2
Dongmenwai, *Tianjin* 30 B2
Dongri, *Mumbai* 20 B2
Dongshanhu Park, *Canton* 8 B2
Dongzhimen, *Beijing* 4 B2
Donnybrook, *Dublin* 11 B2
Doornfontein, *Johannesburg* 13 B2
Dorchester, *Boston* 6 B3
Dorchester B., *Boston* 6 B3
Dornach, *Munich* 20 B3
Dorval, Aéroport de, *Montreal* 19 B1
Dos Couros →, *São Paulo* 26 C2
Dos Moninos →, *São Paulo* 26 C2
Douglas Park, *Chicago* 9 B2
Dover Heights, *Sydney* 28 B2
Dowlatābād, *Tehran* 30 B2
Downey, *Los Angeles* 16 C4
Downsview, *Toronto* 30 A1
Dragør, *Copenhagen* 10 B3
Drancy, *Paris* 23 A3
Dranesville, *Washington* 32 A1
Dreilinden, *Berlin* 5 B2
Drewnica, *Warsaw* 31 B2
Drigh Road, *Karachi* 14 A2
Drimnagh, *Dublin* 11 B2
Drogenbos, *Brussels* 6 B1
Druid Hills, *Atlanta* 3 B2
Drum Towwer, *Beijing* 4 a2
Drumcondra, *Dublin* 11 A2
Drummoyne, *Sydney* 28 B1
Drylaw, *Edinburgh* 11 B2
Dubeč, *Prague* 24 B3
Dublin, *Dublin* 11 A2
Dublin Airport, *Dublin* 11 A2
Dublin Bay, *Dublin* 11 B3
Dublin Harbour, *Dublin* 11 A2
Duddingston, *Edinburgh* 11 B3
Dugnano, *Milan* 18 A2
Dūlāb, *Tehran* 30 B2
Dulwich, *London* 15 B3
Dum Dum, *Calcutta* 8 B2
Dum Dum Int. Airport, *Calcutta* 8 B2
Dumont, *New York* 21 A2
Dún Laoghaire, *Dublin* 11 B3
Duna →, *Budapest* 7 A2
Duncan Dock, *Cape Town* 8 a3
Dundrum, *Dublin* 11 B2
Dunearn, *Singapore* 27 B2
Dunfermline, *Edinburgh* 11 A1
Dunn Loring, *Washington* 32 B2
Dunning, *Chicago* 9 B2
Dunvegan, *Johannesburg* 13 A2
Duomo, *Milan* 18 B2
Duque de Caxias, *Rio de Janeiro* 24 A1
Dusit, *Bangkok* 3 B2
Dusit Zoo, *Bangkok* 3 a2
Dworp, *Brussels* 6 B1
Dyakovo, *Moscow* 19 B3
Dzerzhinskiy, *Moscow* 19 C5
Dzerzhinskiy, *Moscow* 19 B3
Dzerzhinskiy Park, *Moscow* 19 B3

E

Eagle Rock, *Los Angeles* 16 B3
Ealing, *London* 15 A2
Earl's Court, *London* 15 c1
Earlsfield, *London* 15 B2
Earlwood, *Sydney* 28 B1
East Acton, *Boston* 6 A1
East Arlington, *Boston* 6 A3
East Arlington, *Washington* 32 B3
East Bedfont, *London* 15 B1
East Boston, *Boston* 6 A3
East Don →, *Toronto* 30 A2
East Elmhurst, *New York* 21 B2
East Finchley, *London* 15 A2
East Ham, *London* 15 A4
East Humber →, *Toronto* 30 A1
East Lamma Channel, *Hong Kong* 12 B1
East Lexington, *Boston* 6 A2
East Los Angeles, *Los Angeles* 16 B3
East Molesey, *London* 15 B1
East New York, *New York* 21 B2
East Pines, *Washington* 32 B4
East Point, *Atlanta* 3 B2
East Potomac Park, *Washington* 32 B3
East Pt., *Boston* 6 A4
East River →, *New York* 21 B2
East Rutherford, *New York* 21 A1
East Sheen, *London* 15 B2
East Village, *New York* 21 e2
East Wickham, *London* 15 B4
East York, *Toronto* 30 A2
Eastbourne, *Wellington* 32 B2
Eastcote, *London* 15 A1
Easter Howgate, *Edinburgh* 11 B2
Eastwood, *Sydney* 28 A1
Ebara, *Tokyo* 29 B3
Ebisu, *Tokyo* 29 B3
Ebute-Ikorodu, *Lagos* 14 A2
Ebute-Metta, *Lagos* 14 B2
Echo Park, *Los Angeles* 16 a1
Eda, *Tokyo* 29 B2
Edendale, *Johannesburg* 13 A2
Edenmore, *Dublin* 11 A2
Edgars Cr. →, *Melbourne* 17 A1
Edgeley, *Toronto* 30 A1
Edgemar, *San Francisco* 25 C2
Edinburgh, *Edinburgh* 11 B2
Edison Park, *Chicago* 9 A2
Edmondston, *Washington* 32 B4
Edmondstown, *Dublin* 11 B2
Edo →, *Tokyo* 29 B4
Edogawa-Ku, *Tokyo* 29 A4
Edsberg, *Stockholm* 28 A1
Edwards L., *Melbourne* 17 A1
Eiche, *Berlin* 5 A4
Eiche Sud, *Berlin* 5 A4
Eiffel, Tour, *Paris* 23 A2
Ein Arik, *Jerusalem* 13 A1
Ein Naquba, *Jerusalem* 13 B1
Ein Rafa, *Jerusalem* 13 B1
Eizariya, *Jerusalem* 13 B2
Ejby, *Copenhagen* 10 A2
Ejigbo, *Lagos* 14 A1
Ekeberg, *Oslo* 22 A3
Eknäs, *Stockholm* 28 B3
El 'Abbasiya, *Cairo* 7 A2
El Agustino, *Lima* 16 B2
El Baragil, *Cairo* 7 A1
El Basâlîn, *Cairo* 7 B2
El-Bira, *Jerusalem* 13 A2
El Bosque, *Santiago* 26 C2
El Carmen, *Santiago* 26 B1
El Cortijo, *Santiago* 26 B1
El Duqqi, *Cairo* 7 A2
El Encinar de los Reyes, *Madrid* 17 A2
El Ghurîya, *Cairo* 7 A2
El Gîza, *Cairo* 7 A2
El-Khadr, *Jerusalem* 13 B1
El Khalîfa, *Cairo* 7 A2
El Kôm el Ahmar, *Cairo* 7 A2
El Ma'âdi, *Cairo* 7 B2
El Matarîya, *Cairo* 7 A2
El Mohandessin, *Cairo* 7 A2
El Monte, *Los Angeles* 16 B4
El Mûskî, *Cairo* 7 A2
El Pardo, *Madrid* 17 A1
El Portal, *Miami* 18 A2
El Prat de Llobregat, *Barcelona* 4 B1
El Pueblo de L.A. Historic Park, *Los Angeles* 16 b2
El Qâhira, *Cairo* 7 A2
El Qubba, *Cairo* 7 A2
El Reloj, *Mexico City* 18 C2
El Retiro, *Madrid* 17 B1
El Salto, *Santiago* 26 B2
El Sereno, *Los Angeles* 16 B3
El Talibîya, *Cairo* 7 B2
El Vergel, *Mexico City* 18 C2
El Wâhli, *Cairo* 7 A2
El Zamâlik, *Cairo* 7 A2
El Zeitûn, *Cairo* 7 A2
Elephanta Caves, *Mumbai* 20 B2
Elephanta I., *Mumbai* 20 B2
Ellboda, *Stockholm* 28 A3
Ellinikón, *Athens* 2 B2
Ellis I., *New York* 21 B1
Elm Park, *London* 15 A5
Elmers End, *London* 15 B3
Elmhurst, *New York* 21 B2
Elmstead, *London* 15 B4
Elmwood Park, *Chicago* 9 B2
Elmwood Park, *New York* 21 A1
Elsdon, *Wellington* 32 A1
Elsiesrivier, *Cape Town* 8 A2
Elsternwick, *Melbourne* 17 B2
Eltham, *London* 15 B4
Elwood, *Melbourne* 17 B1
Élysée, *Paris* 23 A2
Elysian Park, *Los Angeles* 16 a3
Embajadores, *Madrid* 17 c2
Embarcadero Center, *San Francisco* 25 b3
Emek Refa'im, *Jerusalem* 13 c2
Émerainville, *Paris* 23 B4
Emeryville, *San Francisco* 25 A3
Eminönü, *Istanbul* 12 B1
Emmarentia, *Johannesburg* 13 A2
Empire State Building, *New York* 21 c2
Encantado, *Rio de Janeiro* 24 B1
Encino, *Los Angeles* 16 B2
Encino Res., *Los Angeles* 16 B1
Enebyberg, *Stockholm* 28 A1
Enfield, *Sydney* 28 B1
Engenho, I. do, *Rio de Janeiro* 24 B2
Englewood, *Chicago* 9 C3
Englewood, *New York* 21 A2
Englewood Cliffs, *New York* 21 A2
Enmore, *Sydney* 28 B2
Enskede, *Stockholm* 28 B2
Entrevias, *Madrid* 17 B1
Epping, *Sydney* 28 A1
Erawan Shrine, *Bangkok* 3 c3
Eregun, *Lagos* 14 A2
Erenköy, *Istanbul* 12 C2
Erith, *London* 15 B5
Erlaa, *Vienna* 31 B1
Ermington, *Sydney* 28 A1
Ermita, *Manila* 17 B1
Ershatou, *Canton* 8 B2
Erskineville, *Sydney* 28 B2
Erunkan, *Lagos* 14 A2
Erzsébet-Telep, *Budapest* 7 B3
Eschenried, *Munich* 20 A1
Esenler, *Istanbul* 12 B1
Esher, *London* 15 B1
Eskbank, *Edinburgh* 11 B3
Esperanza, *Mexico City* 18 c3
Esplanade Park, *Singapore* 27 c3
Esplugas, *Barcelona* 4 A1
Esposizione Univ. di Roma (E.U.R.), *Rome* 25 C1
Essendon, *Melbourne* 17 A1
Essendon Airport, *Melbourne* 17 A1
Essingen, *Stockholm* 28 B1
Essling, *Vienna* 31 A3
Est, Gare de l', *Paris* 23 a5
Estadio Maracanã, *Rio de Janeiro* 24 B1
Estado, Parque do, *São Paulo* 26 B2
Estefânia, *Lisbon* 14 a2
Estrela, Basilica da, *Lisbon* 14 A2
Ethnikó Arheologiko Moussío, *Athens* 2 a2
Etobicoke, *Toronto* 30 B1
Etobicoke Cr. →, *Toronto* 30 B1
Etterbeek, *Brussels* 6 B2
Euston, *London* 15 a3
Evanston, *Chicago* 9 A2
Even Sapir, *Jerusalem* 13 B1
Evere, *Brussels* 6 A2
Everett, *Boston* 6 A3
Evergreen Park, *Chicago* 9 C2
Evīn, *Tehran* 30 A2
Évzonos, *Athens* 2 B2
Ewu, *Lagos* 14 A1
Exchange Square, *Hong Kong* 12 c1
Exposições, Palácio das, *Rio de Janeiro* 24 B1
Eyüp, *Istanbul* 12 B1

F

Fabour, Mt., *Singapore* 27 B2
Faechi, *Seoul* 26 B2
Fælledparken, *Copenhagen* 10 A3
Fågelön, *Stockholm* 28 B1
Fagersjö, *Stockholm* 28 B2
Fair Lawn, *New York* 21 A1
Fairfax, *Washington* 32 B2
Fairfax Station, *Washington* 32 C2
Fairhaven Bay, *Boston* 6 A1
Fairhaven Hill, *Boston* 6 A1
Fairland, *Johannesburg* 13 A1
Fairmilehead, *Edinburgh* 11 B2
Fairmount Heights, *Washington* 32 B4
Fairport, *Toronto* 30 A4
Fairview, *New York* 21 B2
Falenty, *Warsaw* 31 C1
Fálirou, Órmos, *Athens* 2 B2
Falkenburg, *Berlin* 5 A4
Falkenhagen, *Berlin* 5 A1
Falkensee, *Berlin* 5 A1
Falls Church, *Washington* 32 B2
Falomo, *Lagos* 14 B2
False Bay, *Cape Town* 8 B2
Fangcun, *Canton* 8 B2
Faraḩābād, *Tehran* 30 A2
Farforovskaya, *St. Petersburg* 26 B2
Farningham, *London* 15 B5
Farrar Pond, *Boston* 6 A1
Farsta, *Stockholm* 28 B2
Fasanerie-Nord, *Munich* 20 A2
Fasangarten, *Munich* 20 B2
Fasting Palace, *Beijing* 4 c2
Fatih, *Istanbul* 12 B1
Favoriten, *Vienna* 31 B2
Fawkner, *Melbourne* 17 A1

Fawkner Park, Melbourne .. 17 B1
Feijó, Lisbon 14 B2
Feldkirchen, Munich 20 B3
Feldmoching, Munich 20 A2
Feltham, London 15 B1
Fener, Istanbul 12 B1
Fenerbahçe, Istanbul 12 C2
Fengtai, Beijing 4 C1
Fenino, Moscow 19 B5
Ferencváros, Budapest ... 7 B2
Ferihegyi Airport, Budapest . 7 B3
Ferndale, Johannesburg ... 13 A2
Férolles-Attilly, Paris 23 B4
Fichtenau, Berlin 5 B5
Fields Corner, Boston 6 B3
Fiera Camp, Milan 18 B1
Fifth Avenue, New York ... 21 b3
Figino, Milan 18 B1
Fijir, Baghdad 3 A2
Filadhélfia, Athens 2 A2
Fili-Mazilovo, Moscow ... 19 B2
Filothei, Athens 2 A2
Finchley, London 15 A2
Finglas, Dublin 11 A2
Finsbury, London 15 A3
Finsbury Park, London ... 15 A3
Fiorito, Buenos Aires 7 C2
Firhouse, Dublin 11 B2
Fischerhäuser, Munich ... 20 A3
Fisher Island, Miami 18 B2
Fishermans Bend, Melbourne 17 A1
Fisherman's Wharf,
    San Francisco 25 a1
Fisherville, Toronto 30 A2
Fiskästra, Stockholm ... 28 B3
Fitzroy Gardens, Melbourne 17 A1
Five Dock, Sydney 28 B1
Fjellstrand, Oslo 22 B2
Flamengo, Rio de Janeiro .. 24 B1
Flaminio, Rome 25 B1
Flaskebekk, Oslo 22 A2
Flatbush, New York 21 C2
Flaten, Stockholm 28 B2
Flemington Racecourse,
    Melbourne 17 A1
Flint Pk., Los Angeles ... 16 B3
Florence, Los Angeles ... 16 C3
Florence Bloom Bird
    Sanctuary, Johannesburg . 13 A2
Florentia, Johannesburg .. 13 A2
Flores, Buenos Aires 7 B2
Floresta, Buenos Aires ... 7 B2
Florida, Buenos Aires ... 7 B2
Florida, Johannesburg ... 13 B1
Floridsdorf, Vienna 31 A2
Flushing, New York 21 B2
Flushing Meadows Corona
    Park, New York 21 B2
Flysta, Stockholm 28 A1
Fo Tan, Hong Kong 12 A2
Föhrenhain, Vienna 31 A2
Fontainebleau, Johannesburg 13 A1
Fontenay-aux-Roses, Paris . 23 B2
Fontenay-le-Fleury, Paris .. 23 B1
Fontenay-sous-Bois, Paris . 23 A3
Foots Cray, London 15 B4
Footscray, Melbourne ... 17 A1
Foreshore, Cape Town ... 8 a3
Forest, Brussels 6 B1
Forest Gate, London 15 A4
Forest Heights, Washington . 32 C3
Forest Hill, London 15 B3
Forest Hill, Toronto 30 A2
Forest Hills, New York ... 21 B2
Forest Park, Chicago 9 B2
Forest View, Chicago ... 9 C2
Forestville, Washington .. 32 B4
Fornebu, Oslo 22 A2
Fornebu Airport, Oslo ... 22 A2
Foro Romano, Rome 25 c3
Forstenried, Munich 20 B1
Forstenrieder Park, Munich . 20 B1
Fort, Mumbai 20 c2
Fort Canning Park, Singapore 27 B2
Fort Dupont Park,
    Washington 32 B4
Fort Foote Village,
    Washington 32 C3
Fort Lee, New York 21 A2
Fort Mason Center,
    San Francisco 25 a1
Forth, Firth of, Edinburgh . 11 A2
Forth Rail Bridge, Edinburgh 11 A1
Forth Road Bridge,
    Edinburgh 11 A1
Fót, Budapest 7 A3
Fourqueux, Paris 23 A1
Foxrock, Dublin 11 B2
Framingham, Boston 6 B1
Franconia, Washington ... 32 C3
Frankel, Singapore 27 B3
Franklin Park, Boston ... 6 B3
Franklin Park, Chicago ... 9 B1
Franklin Park, Washington . 32 B3
Franklin Res., Los Angeles . 16 B2
Frauenkirche, Munich ... 20 B2
Frederiksberg, Copenhagen . 10 A3
Frederiksdal, Copenhagen . 10 A2
Fredersdorf, Berlin 5 A5
Freguesia, Rio de Janeiro .. 24 A1
Freidrichshain, Volkspark,
    Berlin 5 A4
Freiham, Munich 20 A1
Freimann, Munich 20 A2
Fresh Pond, Boston 6 A2
Fresnes, Paris 23 B2
Freudenau, Vienna 31 B1
Friarstown, Dublin 11 B1
Frick Collection, New York . 21 b3
Friedenau, Berlin 5 b3
Friedrichsfelde, Berlin ... 5 B4
Friedrichshagen, Berlin .. 5 B4
Friedrichshain, Berlin ... 5 A3
Friedrichslust, Berlin ... 5 A3
Friherrs, Helsinki 12 B1
Frontón, I., Lima 16 B1
Frunze, Moscow 19 B3
Fuchū, Tokyo 29 A1
Fuencarral, Madrid 17 B1
Fuenlabrada, Madrid ... 17 C1
Fujidera, Osaka 22 B4
Fukagawa, Tokyo 29 B3
Fukiage Imperial Garden,
    Tokyo 29 a4
Fukiai, Osaka 22 A3
Fukushima, Osaka 22 A3
Fulham, London 15 B2
Funabori, Tokyo 29 B4
Funasaka, Osaka 22 A2
Fundão, I. do, Rio de Janeiro 24 A1
Fünfhaus, Vienna 31 A2
Furesø, Copenhagen ... 10 A2
Furth, Munich 20 B3
Futago-tamagawacn, Tokyo . 29 B2
Fuxing Dam, Shanghai ... 27 B1
Fuxing Park, Shanghai ... 27 B1
Fuxinglu, Beijing 4 B1

G

Gage Park, Chicago 9 C2
Gagny, Paris 23 A4
Galata, Istanbul 12 B1
Galátsion, Athens 2 A2
Galeão, Aéroporto Int. de,
    Rio de Janeiro 24 A1
Galyanovo, Moscow 19 B4
Gambir, Jakarta 13 A1
Gamboa, Rio de Janeiro .. 24 B1
Gambólota, Milan 18 B2
Gamla Stan, Stockholm .. 28 c2
Gamlebyen, Oslo 22 A3
Gangtou, Canton 8 A1
Gangwei, Canton 8 B2
Ganjiakou, Beijing 4 B1
Ganshoren, Brussels ... 6 A1
Gants Hill, London 15 A4
Gaoqiao, Shanghai 27 A2
Garbagnate Milanese, Milan 18 A1
Garbatella, Rome 25 B2
Garches, Paris 23 A2
Garching, Munich 20 A3
Garden City, Cairo 7 A2
Garden Reach, Calcutta .. 8 B2
Garder, Oslo 22 B2
Garfield, New York 21 A1
Garfield Park, Chicago .. 9 B2
Gargareta, Athens 2 B2
Garland, Los Angeles ... 16 B3
Gåshaga, Stockholm ... 28 A3
Gateway National Recreation
    Area, New York 21 C2
Gateway of India, Mumbai . 20 B2
Gatow, Berlin 5 B1
Gávea, Rio de Janeiro ... 24 B1
Gávea, Pedra da,
    Rio de Janeiro 24 B1
Gazdagrét, Budapest ... 7 B1
Gebel el Ahmar, Cairo ... 7 A2
Gebel el Muqattam, Cairo . 7 A2
Gebel el Tura, Cairo ... 7 B2
Geiselgasteig, Munich ... 20 B2
General San Martin,
    Buenos Aires 7 B1
Gennevilliers, Paris 23 A2
Gentilly, Paris 23 B3
Gentofte, Copenhagen .. 10 A3
Genval, Brussels 6 B2
George I., Hong Kong ... 12 B2
Georges I., Boston 6 B4
Georges River Bridge, Sydney 28 C1
Georgetown, Washington . 32 B3
Georgia Dome, Atlanta .. 3 b2
Gerasdorf bei Wien, Vienna 31 A2
Gerberau, Munich 20 A1
Gerli, Buenos Aires 7 C2
Germiston, Johannesburg . 13 B2
Gern, Munich 20 B2
Gesîrat el Rauda, Cairo .. 7 A2
Getafe, Madrid 17 C1
Geva Binyamin, Jerusalem . 13 A2
Geylang Serai, Singapore . 27 B3
Gezîrat el Dhahab, Cairo .. 7 A2
Gharapuri, Mumbai 20 B2
Ghatkopar, Mumbai ... 20 A2
Ghazipur, Delhi 10 B2
Ghizri, Karachi 14 B2
Ghizri Cr. →, Karachi ... 14 B2
Ghonda, Delhi 10 A2
Ghusuri, Calcutta 8 B2
Gianicolense, Rome 25 B1
Gianicolo, Rome 25 c1
Gibraltar Pt., Toronto ... 30 B2
Gidea Park, London 15 A5
Giesing, Munich 20 B2
Gilmerton, Edinburgh .. 11 B3
Gilo, Jerusalem 13 B2
Gimmersta, Stockholm .. 28 B3
Ginza, Tokyo 29 b5
Girgaum, Mumbai 20 B2
Giv'at Ye'arim, Jerusalem . 13 B1
Giv'at Ze'ev, Jerusalem .. 13 A2
Giza Pyramids = Pyramids,
    Cairo 7 B1
Gjersjøen, Oslo 22 B3
Gladesville, Sydney 28 B1
Gladsakse, Copenhagen .. 10 A2
Glasnevin, Dublin 11 A2
Glassmanor, Washington . 32 C3
Glasthule, Dublin 11 B3
Glen Iris, Melbourne ... 17 B2
Glen Mar Park, Washington 32 B3
Glen Rock, New York ... 21 A1
Glenanden, Washington . 32 B4
Glenasmole Reservoirs,
    Dublin 11 B1
Glencorse Res., Edinburgh 11 B2
Glencullen, Dublin 11 B2
Glendale, Los Angeles .. 16 B3
Glendoo Mt., Dublin ... 11 B2
Glenhuntly, Melbourne .. 17 B2
Glenside, Wellington ... 32 B1
Glenview, Chicago 9 A2
Glenview Countryside,
    Chicago 9 A2
Glenvista, Johannesburg . 13 B2
Glifádha, Athens 2 B2
Glómsta, Stockholm ... 28 B1
Glostrup, Copenhagen .. 10 B2
Gogar, Edinburgh 11 B2
Golābāk, Tehran 12 A1
Golabari, Calcutta 8 B2
Golabki, Warsaw 31 B1
Gold Coast, Chicago ... 9 a2
Golden Gate, San Francisco 25 B2
Golden Gate Bridge,
    San Francisco 25 B2
Golden Gate Park,
    San Francisco 25 B2
Golden Horn, Istanbul .. 12 B1
Golders Green, London .. 15 A2
Gollans Stream →,
    Wellington 32 B2
Golyevo, Moscow 19 B1
Goodman Hill, Boston .. 6 A1
Goodmayes, London ... 15 A4
Goodwood, Cape Town .. 8 A2
Gopalpur, Calcutta 8 B2
Górce, Warsaw 31 B1
Gore Hill, Sydney 28 A2
Gorely →, St. Petersburg . 26 B3
Gorenki, Moscow 19 B5
Gorgie, Edinburgh 11 B2
Gorky Park, Moscow ... 19 B3
Gosen, Berlin 5 B5
Gosener kanal, Berlin ... 5 B5
Gotanda, Tokyo 29 B3
Goth Goli Mar, Karachi .. 14 A2
Goth Sher Shah, Karachi . 14 A1
Gournay-sur-Marne, Paris . 23 A4
Governador, I. do,
    Rio de Janeiro 24 A1
Governor's I., New York . 21 B1

Graben, Vienna 31 b2
Grabów, Warsaw 31 C1
Graça, Lisbon 14 A3
Grace, Mt., Wellington .. 32 B2
Grace Cathedral,
    San Francisco 25 b1
Gracefield, Wellington .. 32 B2
Gracia, Barcelona 4 A2
Gräfelfing, Munich 20 B1
Gragoatá, Rio de Janeiro . 24 B2
Grand Central Station,
    New York 21 c2
Grand Union Canal, London 15 A2
Grande Place, Brussels .. 6 b2
Grant Park, Atlanta ... 3 B2
Grant Park, Chicago ... 9 c2
Granton, Edinburgh ... 11 B2
Grape I., Boston 6 B4
Grassy Park, Cape Town . 8 B2
Gratosóglio, Milan 18 B2
Gratzwalde, Berlin 5 B5
Gravesend, New York ... 21 C2
Grazhdanka, St. Petersburg . 26 B2
Great Falls, Washington .. 32 B2
Great Falls Park, Washington 32 B2
Great Hall of the People,
    Beijing 4 b2
Great Meadows National
    Wildlife Refuge, Boston . 6 A1
Greco, Milan 18 A2
Green I., Hong Kong ... 12 B1
Green Point, Cape Town . 8 A1
Greenbelt, Washington .. 32 A4
Greenbelt Park, Washington 32 B4
Greenfield Park, Montreal . 19 B3
Greenford, London 15 A1
Greenhill, London 15 A2
Greenhills, Dublin 11 B1
Greenmarket Square,
    Cape Town 8 c2
Greenpoint, New York .. 21 B2
Greenwich, London ... 15 B3
Greenwich Observatory,
    London 15 B3
Greenwich Village, New York 21 B2
Greenwood, Boston 6 A3
Grefsen, Oslo 22 A3
Gresham Park, Atlanta .. 3 B2
Greve Strand, Copenhagen 10 B1
Greyfriars Kirk, Edinburgh 11 c2
Griebnitzsee, Berlin ... 5 B1
Griffen Park, Los Angeles . 16 B3
Grimbergen, Brussels .. 6 A2
Grinzing, Vienna 31 A2
Gröbenried, Munich ... 20 A1
Gröchow, Warsaw 31 B2
Grodzisk, Warsaw 31 A1
Groenendaal, Brussels .. 6 B2
Grogol Petamburin, Jakarta . 13 A1
Gronsdorf, Munich 20 B3
Grorud, Oslo 22 A4
Gross Glienicke, Berlin .. 5 B1
Gross-Hadern, Munich .. 20 B1
Gross-Lappen, Munich .. 20 A2
Grosse Krampe, Berlin .. 5 B5
Grosse Müggelsee, Berlin . 5 B4
Grossenzersdorf, Vienna . 31 A2
Grossenzersdorfer Arm →,
    Vienna 31 A3
Grosser Biberhaufen, Vienna 31 A2
Grosser Wannsee, Berlin . 5 B2
Grossfeld-Siedlung, Vienna 31 A2
Grosshesselohe, Munich .. 20 B2
Grossjedlersdorf, Vienna . 31 A2
Grosszieten, Berlin 5 B3
Grove Hall, Boston 6 B3
Grove Park, Atlanta ... 3 B2
Grove Park, London 15 B4
Grove Park, London 15 A2
Groveton, Washington .. 32 C3
Grünau, Berlin 5 B4
Grünewald, Berlin 5 B2
Grünwald, Munich 20 B2
Grünwalder Forst, Munich . 20 B2
Grymes Hill, New York .. 21 C1
Guadalupe, Manila 17 B2
Guadalupe, Basilica de,
    Mexico City 18 B2
Guanabara, B. de,
    Rio de Janeiro 24 B1
Guanabara, Jardim,
    Rio de Janeiro 24 A1
Guanabara, Palácio da,
    Rio de Janeiro 24 B1
Guang'anmen, Beijing .. 4 B1
Guanguang, Beijing 4 B1
Guangzhou, Canton ... 8 B2
Guanshuo, Canton 8 B3
Gudö, Stockholm 28 B3
Güell, Parque de, Barcelona 4 A2
Guerrero, Mexico City .. 18 a1
Guggenheim Museum,
    New York 21 b3
Guinardó, Barcelona ... 4 A2
Gulbai, Karachi 14 A1
Güngören, Istanbul 12 B1
Gunnersbury, London .. 15 B2
Gustavo A. Madero,
    Mexico City 18 B2
Guttenberg, New York .. 21 B1
Gutyevskiy, Ostrov,
    St. Petersburg 26 B1
Guyancourt, Paris 23 B1
Gyál, Budapest 7 B3
Gyáli-patak →, Budapest . 7 B2

H

Haaga, Helsinki 12 B2
Haar, Munich 20 B3
Hackbridge, London ... 15 B3
Hackensack, New York .. 21 A1
Hackensack →, New York . 21 B1
Hackney, London 15 A3
Hackney Wick, London .. 15 A3
Haga, Stockholm 28 A2
Hagenbrum, Vienna ... 31 A2
Hägersten, Stockholm .. 28 B1
Haght, Stockholm 28 A2
Hai He →, Tianjin 30 B2
Haidan, Beijing 4 B1
Haidarpur, Delhi 10 A1
Haidhausen, Munich ... 20 B2
Haight-Ashbury,
    San Francisco 25 B2
Hainault, London 15 A4
Haizhu Guangchang, Canton 8 B2
Hakunila, Helsinki 12 B3
Halasztelek, Budapest .. 7 B1
Haliç = Golden Horn,
    Istanbul 12 B1
Halim Perdanakusuma
    International Airport,
    Jakarta 13 B2

Halle, Brussels 6 B1
Haltiala, Helsinki 12 B2
Haltiavuori, Helsinki ... 12 B2
Ham, London 15 B2
Hämeenkylä, Helsinki ... 12 B1
Hammarby, Stockholm .. 28 B2
Hamme, Brussels 6 A1
Hammersmith, London .. 15 B2
Hampstead, London ... 15 A2
Hampstead, Montreal ... 19 B2
Hampstead Garden Suburb,
    London 15 A2
Hampstead Heath, London . 15 A2
Hampton, London 15 B1
Hampton Court Palace,
    London 15 B1
Hampton Wick, London .. 15 B1
Hamra', Baghdad 3 B1
Hanala, Helsinki 12 A3
Haneda, Tokyo 29 B3
Hang Hau, Hong Kong .. 12 B2
Hanging Gardens, Mumbai 20 b1
Hanjiashu, Tianjin 30 B2
Hanlon, Toronto 30 B2
Hanwell, London 15 A1
Hanworth, London 15 B1
Haora, Calcutta 8 B1
Hapeville, Atlanta 3 C2
Happy Valley, Hong Kong . 12 A2
Har Adar, Jerusalem ... 13 B1
Haren, Brussels 6 A2
Hareskovby, Copenhagen . 10 A2
Haringey, London 15 A3
Harjusuo, Helsinki 12 B3
Harlaching, Munich ... 20 B2
Harlaw Res., Edinburgh .. 11 B2
Harlem, New York 21 B2
Harlesden, London 15 A2
Harlington, London ... 15 B1
Harmaja, Helsinki 12 C2
Harmashatar hegy, Budapest 7 A2
Harolds Cross, Dublin .. 11 B2
Háros, Budapest 7 B2
Harperring Reservoir,
    Edinburgh 11 B1
Harrow, London 15 A1
Harrow on the Hill, London 15 A1
Harrow School, London .. 15 A1
Harrow Weald, London .. 15 A1
Hartsfield-Atlanta
    International Airport,
    Atlanta 3 C2
Harumi, Tokyo 29 c5
Harvard Univ., Boston .. 6 A3
Harwood Heights, Chicago . 9 B2
Hasanäbäd, Tehran 30 A1
Hasbrouck Heights,
    New York 21 A1
Haselhorst, Berlin 5 A2
Hasköy, Istanbul 12 B1
Hasle, Oslo 22 A3
Haslum, Oslo 22 A2
Hästhagen, Stockholm .. 28 B2
Hataitai, Wellington ... 32 B1
Hatch End, London 15 A1
Hatiara, Calcutta 8 B2
Hauketo, Oslo 22 A3
Havel →, Berlin 5 A2
Havelkanal, Berlin 5 A2
Havering, London 15 A5
Havering-atte-Bower,
    London 15 A5
Hawôlgok, Seoul 26 B2
Haworth, New York ... 21 A2
Hayes, London 15 B4
Hayes, London 15 A1
Hayes End, London 15 A1
Hayford, Chicago 9 C2
Hayward, Washington .. 32 A2
Heard Pond, Boston ... 6 A1
Heathfield, Cape Town .. 8 B1
Heathrow Airport, London . 15 B1
Hebe Haven, Hong Kong . 12 A2
Hebei, Tianjin 30 B2
Hedong, Canton 8 B2
Hedong, Tianjin 30 B2
Heidelberg Heights,
    Melbourne 17 A2
Heidelberg West, Melbourne 17 A2
Heidemühle, Berlin 5 B5
Heideveld, Cape Town .. 8 A2
Heiligensee, Berlin 5 A2
Heiligenstadt, Vienna ... 31 A2
Heinersdorf, Berlin 5 A3
Heldenplatz, Vienna ... 31 b1
Hélène Champlain, Parc,
    Montreal 19 A2
Helenelund, Stockholm .. 28 A1
Heliopolis = Masr el Gedida,
    Cairo 7 A2
Hellersdorf, Berlin 5 A4
Hellinikon, Copenhagen . 10 A3
Helmahof, Vienna 31 A1
Helsingfors = Helsinki,
    Helsinki 12 B2
Helsinki, Helsinki 12 B2
Helsinki Airport, Helsinki . 12 B2
Hendon, London 15 A2
Hengsha, Canton 8 B2
Hennigsdorf, Berlin 5 A2
Henrykôw, Warsaw 31 B2
Henson Cr. →, Washington . 32 C4
Henttaa, Helsinki 12 B1
Heping, Tianjin 30 B2
Heping Park, Shanghai .. 27 B2
Hepingli, Beijing 4 B2
Herley, Copenhagen ... 10 A2
Herman Eckstein Park,
    Johannesburg 13 A2
Hermannskogel, Vienna . 31 A1
Hermiston, Edinburgh .. 11 B2
Hermitage and Winter Palace,
    St. Petersburg 26 B1
Hermsdorf, Berlin 5 A3
Hernals, Vienna 31 A2
Herne Hill, London 15 B3
Héroes de Churubusco,
    Mexico City 18 B2
Herons, I. aux, Montreal . 19 B2
Herstedøster, Copenhagen . 10 A2
Herttoniemi, Helsinki ... 12 B3
Heşärak, Tehran 30 A1
Heston, London 15 B1
Hetzendorf, Vienna 31 A2
Hexi, Tianjin 30 B2
Hextable, London 15 B5
Hialeah, Miami 18 A1
Hickory Hills, Chicago .. 9 C2
Hiekkaharju, Helsinki ... 12 B3
Hietaniemi, Helsinki ... 12 B2
Hietzing, Vienna 31 A2
Higashi, Osaka 22 A4
Higashimurayama, Tokyo . 29 A1
Higashinada, Osaka ... 22 A3
Higashinari, Osaka 22 A4
Higashiōsaka, Osaka ... 22 A4
Higashisumiyoshi, Osaka . 22 B4
Higashiyodogawa, Osaka . 22 A3

High Park, Toronto 30 B2
Highbury, London 15 A3
Highgate, London 15 A3
Highland Cr. →, Toronto . 30 A3
Highland Creek, Toronto . 30 A3
Highland Park, Los Angeles 16 B3
Highlands North,
    Johannesburg 13 A2
Hillcrest Heights, Washington 32 C4
Hillend, Edinburgh 11 A1
Hillingdon, London 15 A1
Hillwood, Washington .. 32 B3
Hilmîya, Cairo 7 A2
Hin Keng, Hong Kong .. 12 A2
Hingham, Boston 6 B4
Hingham B., Boston 6 B4
Hingham Harbor, Boston . 6 B4
Hirakata, Osaka 22 A4
Hirota, Osaka 22 A3
Hirschstetten, Vienna ... 31 A2
Histórico Nacional, Museu,
    Rio de Janeiro 24 b3
Hither Green, London .. 15 B3
Hiyoshi, Tokyo 29 B2
Hizma, Jerusalem 13 B2
Hjortekær, Copenhagen . 10 A2
Hjortespring, Copenhagen . 10 A2
Hlubočepy, Prague 24 B2
Ho Chung, Hong Kong .. 12 A2
Ho Man Tin, Hong Kong . 12 B2
Hoboken, New York ... 21 B1
Hobsons B., Melbourne .. 17 B1
Hochbrück, Munich ... 20 A2
Hochelaga, Montreal ... 19 A2
Hodgkins, Chicago 9 C1
Hoegi, Seoul 26 B2
Hoeilaart, Brussels 6 B2
Hofberg, Vienna 31 A2
Hoffman I., New York .. 21 C1
Hofgarten, Munich 20 a3
Högsdtadomstolen,
    Stockholm 28 c2
Hohenbrunn, Munich .. 20 B3
Hohenschönhausen, Berlin 5 A4
Holborn, London 15 a4
Holešovice, Prague 24 B2
Holland Village, Singapore 27 B2
Höllriegelskreuth, Munich . 20 B1
Hollywood, Los Angeles . 16 B3
Holmenkollen, Oslo ... 22 A2
Holmes Run Acres,
    Washington 32 B2
Holmgård, Stockholm .. 28 B2
Holstein, Amsterdam ... 2 A3
Holysloot, Amsterdam .. 2 A3
Hometown, Chicago ... 9 C2
Hōnanchō, Tokyo 29 A3
Honcho, Tokyo 29 A3
Honden, Tokyo 29 A3
Hondo, Rio →, Los Angeles 16 B4
Hong Kong, Hong Kong . 12 B2
Hong Kong I., Hong Kong . 12 B2
Hong Kong Park, Hong Kong 12 c1
Hongkou, Shanghai ... 27 B1
Hongkou Park, Shanghai . 27 B1
Hongmiao, Beijing 4 B2
Hongqiao, Shanghai ... 27 B1
Hongqiao, Tianjin 30 B2
Hongqiao Airport, Shanghai 27 B1
Hongün, Seoul 26 B1
Honjyo, Tokyo 29 A3
Honoré Mercier, Pont,
    Montreal 19 B1
Hönow, Berlin 5 A4
Hooghly = Hugli →, Calcutta 8 B2
Hook, London 15 B2
Horikiri, Tokyo 29 A4
Horn Pond, Boston 6 A2
Hornchurch, London ... 15 A5
Horni, Prague 24 B3
Horni Počernice, Prague . 24 A3
Hornsey, London 15 A3
Horomĕřice, Prague 24 A1
Hortaleza, Madrid 17 B2
Hosoyama, Tokyo 29 B2
Hostafranchs, Barcelona . 4 A1
Hostivař, Prague 24 B3
Hôtel des Invalides, Paris . 23 c2
Houbětin, Prague 24 B3
Houghs Neck, Boston ... 6 B4
Houghton, Johannesburg . 13 B2
Houilles, Paris 23 A2
Hounslow, London 15 B1
Houses of Parliament,
    London 15 c3
Hout Bay, Cape Town ... 8 B1
Hove Å →, Copenhagen . 10 A1
Hovedøya, Oslo 22 A3
Høvik, Oslo 22 A2
Hovorčovice, Prague ... 24 A3
Howard Beach, New York . 21 C2
Howth, Dublin 11 A3
Howth Head, Dublin ... 11 A3
Hoxton, London 15 a5
Hōya, Tokyo 29 A2
Hradčany, Prague 24 B2
Huanghuagang Mausoleum of
    the 72 Martyrs, Canton . 8 B2
Huangpu, Shanghai ... 27 B1
Huangpu Jiang →, Shanghai 27 B1
Huangpu Park, Shanghai . 27 B1
Huangtugang, Beijing .. 4 C1
Huascar, Lima 16 A2
Huay Khwang, Bangkok . 3 B2
Huddinge, Stockholm .. 28 B2
Hudson →, New York ... 21 A2
Huechuraba, Santiago .. 26 B1
Huertas de San Beltran,
    Barcelona 4 A1
Hugli →, Calcutta 8 B2
Huidui, Tianjin 30 B2
Huizingen, Brussels ... 6 B1
Hull, Boston 6 B4
Humber →, Toronto ... 30 A1
Humber B., Toronto ... 30 A1
Humber Summit, Toronto . 30 A1
Humber Valley Village,
    Toronto 30 A1
Humberlea, Toronto ... 30 A1
Humboldt Park, Chicago . 9 B2
Humera, Madrid 17 B1
Hunaydî, Baghdad 3 B2
Hundige, Copenhagen .. 10 B1
Hundige Strand, Copenhagen 10 B2
Hung Hom, Hong Kong . 12 B2
Hunters Hill, Sydney ... 28 B1
Hunters Pt., San Francisco . 25 B2
Hunters Valley, Washington 32 B2
Huntington, Washington . 32 C3
Huntington Park, Los Angeles 16 C3
Hurîya, Baghdad 3 A1
Hurstville, Sydney 28 B1
Husby, Stockholm 28 A1
Husum, Copenhagen ... 10 A2
Hutt R. →, Wellington .. 32 B2

Hütteldorf, Vienna 31 A1
Hüvösvölgy, Budapest .. 7 A2
Hvalstad, Oslo 22 A1
Hvalstrand, Oslo 22 A2
Hvidovre, Copenhagen .. 10 B2
Hyattsville, Washington . 32 B4
Hyde Park, Boston 6 B3
Hyde Park, Chicago 9 C3
Hyde Park, Johannesburg . 13 A2
Hyde Park, London 15 A2
Hyde Park, Sydney 28 B2

I

Ibese, Lagos 14 A2
Ibirapuera, São Paulo ... 26 B2
Ibirapuera, Parque, São Paulo 26 B2
Icarai, Rio de Janeiro ... 24 B2
Içerenkôy, Istanbul 12 C2
Ichgao, Tokyo 29 B2
Ichigaya, Tokyo 29 a3
Ichikawa, Tokyo 29 A4
Ickenham, London 15 A1
Iddo, Lagos 14 B2
Idi-Oro, Lagos 14 A2
Iganmu, Lagos 14 B2
Igbobi, Lagos 14 A2
Igbologun, Lagos 14 B1
Igny, Paris 23 B2
IJ, Het →, Amsterdam .. 2 A2
IJ-meer, Amsterdam ... 2 A3
IJtunnel, Amsterdam ... 2 a3
Ikebe, Tokyo 29 B2
Ikebukuro, Tokyo 29 A3
Ikegami, Tokyo 29 B3
Ikeja, Lagos 14 A2
Ikeuchi, Osaka 22 B4
Ikoyi, Lagos 14 B2
Ikuata, Lagos 14 A2
Ikuno, Osaka 22 A4
Ikuta, Osaka 22 A2
Ikuta, Tokyo 29 B2
Ila, Oslo 22 A2
Ilford, London 15 A4
Ilioúpolis, Athens 2 B2
Ilpendam, Amsterdam .. 2 A2
Ilsos →, Athens 2 B2
Imagem e do Som, Museu da,
    Rio de Janeiro 24 b3
Imbābah, Cairo 7 A2
Imielin, Warsaw 31 C2
Imirim, São Paulo 26 A2
Imittós, Athens 2 B2
Imittós, Óros, Athens ... 2 B2
Imperial Palace Museum,
    Beijing 4 b2
Inagi, Tokyo 29 B1
Incheom, Edinburgh ... 11 A2
Inchicore, Dublin 11 A1
Inchkeith, Edinburgh .. 11 A3
Inchmickery, Edinburgh . 11 A2
Inciramo, Milan 18 A1
Independencia, Lima ... 16 A2
Independencia, Santiago . 26 B2
India Gate, Delhi 1 c2
Indian Creek Village, Miami 18 A2
Indian Head Park, Chicago 9 C1
Indianópolis, São Paulo . 26 B2
Indios Verdes, Mexico City 18 B2
Indira Gandhi International
    Airport, Delhi 10 B1
Industria, Johannesburg . 13 B1
Ingierstrand, Oslo 22 B3
Inglewood, Los Angeles . 16 C3
Ingliston, Edinburgh ... 11 B1
Inhaúme, Rio de Janeiro . 24 B1
Inner Port Shelter,
    Hong Kong 12 A2
Interlagos, São Paulo ... 26 C2
Intramuros, Manila ... 17 B1
Invalides, Paris 23 A2
Inverkeithing, Edinburgh . 11 A1
Inzersdorf, Vienna 31 B2
Ipanema, Rio de Janeiro . 24 B1
Ipiranga, São Paulo ... 26 B2
Iponri, Lagos 14 B2
Ireland's Eye, Dublin ... 11 A3
Irving Park, Chicago ... 9 B2
Isabel, Rio de Janeiro ... 24 B1
Isagatedo, Lagos 14 A1
Ischia, Chicago 9 C2
Ishbîliya, Baghdad 3 A2
Ishikiri, Osaka 22 A4
Ishøj Strand, Copenhagen 10 B2
Island Bay, Wellington .. 32 B1
Island Park, Toronto ... 30 B2
Isle of Dogs, London ... 15 B3
Islev, Copenhagen 10 A2
Isleworth, London 15 B2
Islington, London 15 A3
Islington, Toronto 30 B1
Ismaning, Munich 20 A3
Ismayloskiy Park, Moscow 19 B4
Issy-les-Moulineaux, Paris . 23 A2
Istanbul, Istanbul 12 C1
Istanbul Boğazi, Istanbul . 12 B2
Istinye, Istanbul 12 B2
Itä Hakkila, Helsinki ... 12 B3
Itaewôn, Seoul 26 B1
Itahanga, Rio de Janeiro . 24 B1
Itami, Osaka 22 A3
Ivanhoe, Melbourne ... 17 A2
Iwazono, Osaka 22 A3
Ixelles, Brussels 6 B2
Izmaylovo, Moscow ... 19 B4
Iztacalco, Mexico City .. 18 B2
Iztapalapa, Mexico City . 18 B2

Jaguaré, Rib. do →,
    São Paulo 26 B1
Jahangirpur, Delhi 10 A2
Jakarta, Jakarta 13 A2
Jakarta, Teluk, Jakarta .. 13 A1
Jalan Kayu, Singapore .. 27 A3
Jamaica B., New York ... 21 C3
Jamaica Plain, Boston .. 6 B3
Jamakpuri, Delhi 10 B1
Jamshîdîyeh, Tehran ... 30 A2
Janki, Warsaw 31 C1
Jannali, Sydney 28 C1
Japan Center, San Francisco 25 b1
Jaraguá, São Paulo 26 A1
Jaraguá, Pico de, São Paulo 26 A1
Jardim Paulista, São Paulo . 26 B1
Jardin Botanique, Brussels . 6 a3
Järvatältet, Stockholm .. 28 A1
Jaskhar, Mumbai 20 B2
Jatinegara, Jakarta 13 B2
Javâdîyeh, Tehran 30 B2
Jaworowa, Warsaw 31 C1
Jedlesee, Vienna 31 A2
Jefferson Memorial,
    Washington 32 c1
Jefferson Park, Chicago . 9 B2
Jelonki, Warsaw 31 B1
Jerónimos, Mosteiro dos,
    Lisbon 14 A1
Jersey City, New York .. 21 B1
Jerusalem, Jerusalem ... 13 B2
Jésus, I., Montreal 19 A1
Jesús Maria, Lima 16 B2
Jette, Brussels 6 A1
Jewish Quarter, Jerusalem . 13 b3
Jey, Tehran 30 B2
Jianguomen, Beijing ... 4 B2
Jiangwan, Shanghai ... 27 B1
Jianshan Park, Tianjin .. 30 B2
Jihād, Baghdad 3 B1
Jim Thompson's House,
    Bangkok 3 b3
Jimbōchō, Tokyo 29 a4
Jingan, Shanghai 27 B1
Jingu Outer Garden, Tokyo 29 b2
Jinočany, Prague 24 B1
Jinonice, Prague 24 B2
Jiyūgaoka, Tokyo 29 B3
Jizā'ir, Baghdad 3 B2
Jìzîra, Baghdad 3 B2
Johannesburg, Johannesburg 13 B2
Johanneskirchen, Munich . 20 A2
Johannesstift, Berlin ... 5 A2
Johannisthal, Berlin ... 5 B4
John Hancock Center,
    Chicago 9 a2
John McLaren Park,
    San Francisco 25 B2
Johnsonville, Wellington . 32 B1
Joinville-le-Pont, Paris .. 23 B3
Joli-Bois, Brussels 6 B2
Jollas, Helsinki 12 B3
Jonstrup, Copenhagen .. 10 A2
Joppa, Edinburgh 11 B3
Jorge Chavez, Aeropuerto
    Int., Lima 16 B2
Jôsefa Piłsudskiego Park,
    Warsaw 31 B1
Jôtô, Osaka 22 A4
Jouy-en-Josas, Paris ... 23 B2
Juan Anchorena,
    Buenos Aires 7 A2
Juan González Romero,
    Mexico City 18 A2
Judeira, Jerusalem 13 A2
Juhu, Mumbai 20 A2
Jūjā, Tokyo 29 A3
Jukskeirivier →,
    Johannesburg 13 A2
Julianów, Warsaw 31 B2
Jungfernheide, Volkspark,
    Berlin 5 A2
Jungfernsee, Berlin 5 B1
Juniper Green, Edinburgh . 11 B2
Junk B., Hong Kong 12 B2
Jurong, Singapore 27 B2
Jurong, Selat, Singapore . 27 B2
Jurong Industrial Estate,
    Singapore 27 B1
Jurujuba, Enseada de,
    Rio de Janeiro 24 B2
Jūsō, Osaka 22 A3
Justice, Chicago 9 C2
Justicia, Madrid 17 a3
Jwalahari, Delhi 10 B1

K

Kabaty, Warsaw 31 C2
Kadikôy, Istanbul 12 C2
Kadoma, Osaka 22 A4
Kaebong, Seoul 26 C1
Kafr 'Aqab, Jerusalem .. 13 A2
Kâğıthane, Istanbul ... 12 B1
Kâğıthane →, Istanbul .. 12 B1
Kagran, Vienna 31 A2
Kahnawake, Montreal .. 19 B1
Kaimes, Edinburgh 11 B2
Kaisariani, Athens 2 B2
Kaiser Wilhelm Kirche, Berlin 5 b2
Kaisersberdorf, Vienna .. 31 A3
Kaivoksela, Helsinki ... 12 B2
Kalamákion, Athens ... 2 B2
Kalbadevi, Mumbai ... 20 b2
Kalhyôn, Seoul 26 B1
Kalipur, Calcutta 8 A1
Kalkaji, Delhi 10 B2
Kallithéa, Athens 2 B2
Kalveboderne, Copenhagen 10 B3
Kamarhati, Calcutta ... 8 A2
Kameari, Tokyo 29 A4
Kameido, Tokyo 29 A4
Kami-Itabashi, Tokyo ... 29 A3
Kamikitazawa, Tokyo ... 29 B2
Kamitsuruma, Tokyo ... 29 B1
Kamoshida, Tokyo 29 B2
Kampong Landang, Singapore 27 A3
Kampong Tanjong Penjuru,
    Singapore 27 B1
Kampung Bali, Jakarta .. 13 B1
Kanda, Tokyo 29 a5
Kandilli, Istanbul 12 B2
Kangnam, Seoul 26 B2
Kangsŏ, Seoul 26 B1
Kankurgachi, Calcutta .. 8 B2
Kanlıca, Istanbul 12 B2
Kanonerskiy, Ostrov,
    St. Petersburg 26 B1
Kanzaki →, Osaka 22 A3
Kapellerfeld, Vienna ... 31 A2

36 Káposztásmegyer

Káposztásmegyer, *Budapest* 7 A2
Kapotnya, *Moscow* 19 C4
Käppala, *Stockholm* 28 A3
Käpylä, *Helsinki* 12 B2
Karachi, *Karachi* 14 A2
Karachi Int. Airport, *Karachi* 14 A2
Karato, *Osaka* 22 A2
Karibong, *Seoul* 26 C1
Karkh, *Baghdad* 3 A2
Karlin, *Prague* 24 B2
Karlsfeld, *Munich* 20 A1
Karlshorst, *Berlin* 5 B4
Karlsplatz, *Munich* 20 b1
Karntner Strasse, *Vienna* 31 b2
Karol Bagh, *Delhi* 10 B2
Karolinenhof, *Berlin* 5 B4
Karori, *Wellington* 32 B1
Karow, *Berlin* 5 A3
Karrādah, *Baghdad* 3 B2
Kärsön, *Stockholm* 28 B1
Kasai, *Tokyo* 29 B4
Kashiwara, *Osaka* 22 B4
Kastellet, *Copenhagen* 10 a3
Kastrup, *Copenhagen* 10 B3
Kastrup Lufthavn, *Copenhagen* 10 B3
Kasuga, *Tokyo* 29 A2
Kasuge, *Tokyo* 29 A3
Kasumigaseki, *Tokyo* 29 b4
Katong, *Singapore* 27 B3
Katrineberg, *Stockholm* 28 B1
Katsushika-Ku, *Tokyo* 29 A4
Kau Pei Chau, *Hong Kong* 12 B2
Kau Yi Chau, *Hong Kong* 12 B1
Kaulsdorf, *Berlin* 5 B4
Kauniainen, *Helsinki* 12 B1
Kawasaki, *Tokyo* 29 B3
Kawawa, *Tokyo* 29 B2
Kawęczyn, *Warsaw* 31 B2
Kayu Putih, *Jakarta* 13 B2
Kbely, *Prague* 24 B3
Kebayoran Baru, *Jakarta* 13 B1
Kebayoran Lama, *Jakarta* 13 B1
Kebon Jeruk, *Jakarta* 13 B1
Kedar, *Jerusalem* 13 B2
Keilor, *Melbourne* 17 A1
Keilor North, *Melbourne* 17 A1
Keimola, *Helsinki* 12 A1
Kelenföld, *Budapest* 7 B2
Kelvin, *Johannesburg* 13 A2
Kemang, *Jakarta* 13 B1
Kemayoran, *Jakarta* 13 B2
Kemerburgaz, *Istanbul* 12 B1
Kempton Park Races, *London* 15 B1
Kendall Green, *Boston* 6 A2
Kenilworth, *Cape Town* 8 A1
Kennedy Town, *Hong Kong* 12 B1
Kennington, *London* 15 c4
Kensal Green, *London* 15 A2
Kensal Rise, *London* 15 a1
Kensington, *Johannesburg* 13 B2
Kensington, *London* 15 B2
Kensington, *New York* 21 C2
Kensington, *Sydney* 28 B2
Kensington Palace, *London* 15 A2
Kent Village, *Washington* 32 B4
Kentish Town, *London* 15 A3
Kenton, *London* 15 A2
Kenwood House, *London* 15 A3
Kepa, *Warsaw* 31 B2
Keppel Harbour, *Singapore* 27 B2
Keramíkos, *Athens* 2 b1
Kettering, *Washington* 32 B5
Kew, *London* 15 B2
Kew, *Melbourne* 17 A2
Kew Gardens, *London* 15 B2
Kew Gardens, *Toronto* 30 B3
Key Biscayne, *Miami* 18 B2
Khaidhárion, *Athens* 2 A1
Khalándrion, *Athens* 2 A2
Khalīj, *Baghdad* 3 B2
Khandallah, *Wellington* 32 B1
Khansā', *Baghdad* 3 A2
Kharavli, *Mumbai* 20 B2
Khefren, *Cairo* 7 B1
Khichripur, *Delhi* 10 B2
Khidirpur, *Calcutta* 8 B1
Khimki-Khovrino, *Moscow* 19 A3
Khirbet Jub e-Rum, *Jerusalem* 13 B2
Khlong San, *Bangkok* 3 B2
Khlong Toey, *Bangkok* 3 B2
Kholargós, *Athens* 2 B2
Khorel, *Calcutta* 8 A1
Khorosovo, *Moscow* 19 B2
Kiamari, *Karachi* 14 B1
Kierling, *Vienna* 31 A1
Kierlingbach →, *Vienna* 31 A1
Kifisós →, *Athens* 2 B2
Kikuna, *Tokyo* 29 B2
Kilbarrack, *Dublin* 11 A3
Kilbirnie, *Wellington* 32 B1
Kilburn, *London* 15 A2
Killakee, *Dublin* 11 B2
Killester, *Dublin* 11 A2
Killiney, *Dublin* 11 B3
Killiney Bay, *Dublin* 11 B3
Kilmacud, *Dublin* 11 B2
Kilmainham, *Dublin* 11 A2
Kilmashogue Mt., *Dublin* 11 B2
Kilmore, *Dublin* 11 A2
Kilnamanagh, *Dublin* 11 B1
Kilo, *Helsinki* 12 B1
Kilokri, *Delhi* 10 B2
Kiltiernan, *Dublin* 11 B2
Kimmage, *Dublin* 11 B2
Kindi, *Baghdad* 3 B2
Kinghorn, *Edinburgh* 11 A2
King's Cross, *London* 15 a4
Kings Cross, *Sydney* 28 c3
Kings Domain, *Melbourne* 17 A1
Kings Park, *Washington* 32 C2
Kings Park West, *Washington* 32 C2
Kingsbury, *London* 15 A2
Kingsbury, *Melbourne* 17 A2
Kingsford, *Sydney* 28 B2
Kingston upon Thames, *London* 15 B2
Kingston Vale, *London* 15 B2
Kingsway, *Toronto* 30 B1
Kinsaley, *Dublin* 11 A2
Kipling Heights, *Toronto* 30 A1
Kipséli, *Athens* 2 B2
Kirchstockbach, *Munich* 20 B3
Kirchtrudering, *Munich* 20 B3
Kirikiri, *Lagos* 14 B1
Kirke Værløse, *Copenhagen* 10 A1
Kirkhill, *Edinburgh* 11 B2
Kirkliston, *Edinburgh* 11 B1
Kirknewton, *Edinburgh* 11 B1
Kirov Palace of Culture, *St. Petersburg* 26 B1
Kısıklı, *Istanbul* 12 B2
Kispest, *Budapest* 7 B2
Kista, *Stockholm* 28 A1
Kita, *Osaka* 22 A4
Kita-Ku, *Tokyo* 29 A3
Kitazawa, *Tokyo* 29 B3
Kiu Tsiu, *Hong Kong* 12 A2
Kivistö, *Helsinki* 12 B2
Kızıltoprak, *Istanbul* 12 C2
Kizu →, *Osaka* 22 B3
Kizuri, *Osaka* 22 B4
Kjelsås, *Oslo* 22 A3
Kladow, *Berlin* 5 B1
Klampenborg, *Copenhagen* 10 A3
Klaudyń, *Warsaw* 31 B1
Klecany, *Prague* 24 A2
Kledering, *Vienna* 31 B2
Klein Jukskei →, *Johannesburg* 13 A1
Kleinmachnow, *Berlin* 5 B2
Kleinschönebeck, *Berlin* 5 B5
Klemetsrud, *Oslo* 22 A4
Kličany, *Prague* 24 A2
Klipriviersberg Nature Reserve, *Johannesburg* 13 B2
Klosterneuburg, *Vienna* 31 A1
Knesset, *Jerusalem* 13 b1
Knightsbridge, *London* 15 c2
Kőbánya, *Budapest* 7 B2
Kobbegem, *Brussels* 6 A1
Kōbe, *Osaka* 22 A2
Kōbe Harbour, *Osaka* 22 B2
København, *Copenhagen* 10 A2
Kobylisy, *Prague* 24 B2
Kobyłka, *Warsaw* 31 A3
Kŏch'ŏk, *Seoul* 26 B1
Kodaira, *Tokyo* 29 A1
Kodanaka, *Tokyo* 29 B2
Kodenmacho, *Tokyo* 29 a5
Koekelberg, *Brussels* 6 A1
Koganei, *Tokyo* 29 A2
Kogarah, *Sydney* 28 B1
Køge Bugt, *Copenhagen* 10 B2
Koivupää, *Helsinki* 12 B2
Koja, *Jakarta* 13 A2
Koja Utara, *Jakarta* 13 A2
Kokobunji, *Tokyo* 29 A1
Kokobunji-Temple, *Tokyo* 29 A4
Kolarängen, *Stockholm* 28 B3
Kolbotn, *Oslo* 22 B3
Kolkata, *Calcutta* 8 B2
Koło, *Warsaw* 31 B1
Kolokinthóu, *Athens* 2 B2
Kolomyagi, *St. Petersburg* 26 A1
Kolónos, *Athens* 2 B2
Kolsås, *Oslo* 22 A2
Komae, *Tokyo* 29 B2
Komagome, *Tokyo* 29 A3
Komazawa, *Tokyo* 29 B3
Kona, *Calcutta* 8 B1
Konala, *Helsinki* 12 B2
Kondli, *Delhi* 10 B2
Kongelige Slottet, *Oslo* 22 a1
Kongelunden, *Copenhagen* 10 B3
Kongens Lyngby, *Copenhagen* 10 A3
Kongnŭng, *Seoul* 26 B2
Kongo, *Helsinki* 12 A1
Koninklijk Paleis, *Amsterdam* 2 b2
Konnagar, *Calcutta* 8 A2
Konohana, *Osaka* 22 A3
Kōnoike, *Osaka* 22 A4
Konradshöhe, *Berlin* 5 A2
Kopanina, *Prague* 24 B1
Koparkhairna, *Mumbai* 20 A2
Köpenick, *Berlin* 5 B4
Korangi, *Karachi* 14 B2
Koremasa, *Tokyo* 29 B1
Korenevo, *Moscow* 19 B6
Kori, *Osaka* 22 A4
Koridhallós, *Athens* 2 B1
Korokoro, *Wellington* 32 B2
Korokoro Stream →, *Wellington* 32 B2
Kosino, *Moscow* 19 B5
Kosugi, *Tokyo* 29 B2
Kota, *Jakarta* 13 A1
Kotelyniki, *Moscow* 19 C5
Kōtō-Ku, *Tokyo* 29 A3
Kotrung, *Calcutta* 8 A2
Kouponia, *Athens* 2 B2
Kowloon, *Hong Kong* 12 B1
Kowloon Park, *Hong Kong* 12 a2
Kowloon Peak, *Hong Kong* 12 A2
Kowloon Res., *Hong Kong* 12 A1
Kowloon Tong, *Hong Kong* 12 A2
Kozhukhovo, *Moscow* 19 B5
Kraainem, *Brussels* 6 A2
Krailling, *Munich* 20 B1
Krampnitz, *Berlin* 5 B1
Krampnitzsee, *Berlin* 5 B1
Kranji, Sungei →, *Singapore* 27 A2
Kranji Industrial Estate, *Singapore* 27 A2
Kraskovo, *Moscow* 19 C5
Krasno-Presnenskaya, *Moscow* 19 B3
Krasnogorsk, *Moscow* 19 B1
Krč, *Prague* 24 B2
Krestovskiye, Ostrov, *St. Petersburg* 26 B1
Kreuzberg, *Berlin* 5 A3
Kritzendorf, *Vienna* 31 A1
Krumme Lanke, *Berlin* 5 B2
Krummensee, *Berlin* 5 A5
Krung Thep, *Bangkok* 3 B2
Krusboda, *Stockholm* 28 B3
Krylatskoye, *Moscow* 19 B2
Küçükköy, *Istanbul* 12 B1
Kudankita, *Tokyo* 29 a3
Kudrovo, *St. Petersburg* 26 B3
Kulosaari, *Helsinki* 12 B3
Kulturforum, *Berlin* 5 b3
Kultury i Nauki, Palac, *Warsaw* 31 b2
Kŭmch'ŏn, *Seoul* 26 C1
Kumla, *Stockholm* 28 B3
Kungens kurva, *Stockholm* 28 B1
Kungliga Slottet, *Stockholm* 28 b2
Kungshatt, *Stockholm* 28 B1
Kungsholmen, *Stockholm* 28 A2
Kuningan, *Jakarta* 13 B1
Kunitachi, *Tokyo* 29 A1
Kunming Hu, *Beijing* 4 B1
Kunratice, *Prague* 24 B2
Kunsthistorischesmuseum, *Vienna* 31 b1
Kuntsevo, *Moscow* 19 B2
Kupchino, *St. Petersburg* 26 B2
Kurbağalı →, *Istanbul* 12 C2
Kurihara, *Tokyo* 29 A2
Kurla, *Mumbai* 20 A2
Kurmuri, *Mumbai* 20 A2
Kurume, *Tokyo* 29 A2
Kuryanovo, *Moscow* 19 C4
Kuskovo, *Moscow* 19 B4
Kustia, *Calcutta* 8 B2
Kutsino, *Moscow* 19 B5
Kuzguncuk, *Istanbul* 12 B2
Kuzyminki, *Moscow* 19 B4
Kwai Chung, *Hong Kong* 12 A1
Kwanak, *Seoul* 26 C1
Kwanak-san, *Seoul* 26 C1
Kyje, *Prague* 24 B3
Kyūhōji, *Osaka* 22 B4

L

La Blanca, *Santiago* 26 C2
La Boca, *Buenos Aires* 7 B2
La Bretèche, *Paris* 23 A1
La Campiña, *Lima* 16 C2
La Celle-St.-Cloud, *Paris* 23 A1
La Ciudadela, *Mexico City* 18 c2
La Courneuve, *Paris* 23 A3
La Dehesa, *Santiago* 26 B2
La Encantada, *Lima* 16 C2
La Estación, *Madrid* 17 B1
La Floresta, *Barcelona* 4 A1
La Fortuna, *Madrid* 17 B1
La Fransa, *Barcelona* 4 A1
La Garenne-Colombes, *Paris* 23 A2
La Giustiniana, *Rome* 25 B1
La Grange, *Chicago* 9 C1
La Grange Park, *Chicago* 9 C1
La Granja, *Santiago* 26 C2
La Guardia Airport, *New York* 21 B2
La Hulpe, *Brussels* 6 B2
La Llacuna, *Barcelona* 4 A2
La Loma, *Mexico City* 18 A1
La Lucila, *Buenos Aires* 7 B2
La Maladrerie, *Paris* 23 A1
La Milla, Cerro, *Lima* 16 B2
La Monachina, *Rome* 25 B1
La Moraleja, *Madrid* 17 A2
La Nopalera, *Mexico City* 18 C2
La Paternal, *Buenos Aires* 7 B2
La Perla, *Lima* 16 B2
La Perouse, *Sydney* 28 B2
La Pineda, *Barcelona* 4 B1
La Pisana, *Rome* 25 B1
La Prairie, *Montreal* 19 B3
La Punta, *Lima* 16 B1
La Puntigala, *Barcelona* 4 A2
La Queue-en-Brie, *Paris* 23 B4
La Reina, *Santiago* 26 B2
La Ribera, *Barcelona* 4 A1
La Sagrera, *Barcelona* 4 A2
La Salada, *Buenos Aires* 7 C2
La Scala, *Milan* 18 B2
La Storta, *Rome* 25 A1
La Taxonera, *Barcelona* 4 A2
La Victoria, *Lima* 16 B2
Laajalahti, *Helsinki* 12 B1
Laajasalo, *Helsinki* 12 B3
Laaksolahti, *Helsinki* 12 B1
Lablâba, W. el →, *Cairo* 7 A2
Lac Cisterna, *Santiago* 26 C2
Lachine, *Montreal* 19 B1
Lad Phrao, *Bangkok* 3 B2
Ladera Heights, *Los Angeles* 16 C2
Ládví, *Prague* 24 B2
Łady, *Warsaw* 31 C1
Lafontaine, Parc, *Montreal* 19 A2
Lagoa, *Rio de Janeiro* 24 B1
Lagos, *Lagos* 14 B2
Lagos Harbour, *Lagos* 14 B2
Lagos-Ikeja Airport, *Lagos* 14 A1
Lagos Island, *Lagos* 14 B2
Lagos Lagoon, *Lagos* 14 B2
Laguna de B., *Manila* 17 C2
Laim, *Munich* 20 B2
Lainate, *Milan* 18 A1
Lainz, *Vienna* 31 B1
Lakemba, *Sydney* 28 B1
Lakeside, *Cape Town* 8 B1
Lakeside, *Johannesburg* 13 A2
Lakeview, *Chicago* 9 B3
Lakewood Park, *Atlanta* 3 B2
Lakhtinskiy, *St. Petersburg* 26 B1
Lakhtinskiy Razliv, Oz., *St. Petersburg* 26 B1
Lakshmanpur, *Calcutta* 8 B1
Lal Qila, *Delhi* 1 a3
Lam Tin, *Hong Kong* 12 B2
Lambert, *Oslo* 22 A3
Lambeth, *London* 15 B3
Lambrate, *Milan* 18 B2
Lambro, Parco, *Milan* 18 B2
Lambton Mills, *Toronto* 30 B1
Lamma I., *Hong Kong* 12 B1
Landover Hills, *Washington* 32 B4
Landsmeer, *Amsterdam* 2 A2
Landstrasse, *Vienna* 31 A2
Landwehr kanal, *Berlin* 5 B3
Lane Cove, *Sydney* 28 A1
Lane Cove National Park, *Sydney* 28 A1
Langa, *Cape Town* 8 A2
Langenzersdorf, *Vienna* 31 A2
Langer See, *Berlin* 5 B4
Langley, *Washington* 32 B2
Langley Park, *Washington* 32 B4
Langwald, *Munich* 20 A1
Lanham, *Washington* 32 B4
Lankwitz, *Berlin* 5 B3
L'Annunziatella, *Rome* 25 C2
Lansdowne, *Cape Town* 8 A2
Lansing, *Toronto* 30 A2
Lanús, *Buenos Aires* 7 C2
Lapa, *Rio de Janeiro* 24 B1
Laranjeiras, *Rio de Janeiro* 24 B1
Larísa Sta., *Athens* 2 a1
Las, *Warsaw* 31 B2
Las Corts, *Barcelona* 4 A1
Las Kabacki, *Warsaw* 31 C2
Las Pinas, *Manila* 17 C1
Las Rejas, *Santiago* 26 B1
Lasalle, *Montreal* 19 B2
Lasek Bielański, *Warsaw* 31 B1
Lasek Na Kole, *Warsaw* 31 B1
Laski, *Warsaw* 31 B1
Latina, *Madrid* 17 B1
Laurence G. Hanscom Field, *Boston* 6 A2
Lauttasaari, *Helsinki* 12 C2
Laval, *Montreal* 19 A1
Lavīzān, *Tehran* 30 A2
Lavradio, *Lisbon* 14 A2
Lawndale, *Chicago* 9 B2
Lawrence Heights, *Toronto* 30 A2
Layari, *Karachi* 14 A2
Layari →, *Karachi* 14 A1
Lazare, Gare St., *Paris* 23 a3
Łazienkowski, Palac, *Warsaw* 31 c3
Łazienkowski Park, *Warsaw* 31 B2
Le Blanc-Mesnil, *Paris* 23 A3
Le Bourget, *Paris* 23 A3
Le Chenoi, *Brussels* 6 B2
Le Chesnay, *Paris* 23 B1
Le Christ de Saclay, *Paris* 23 B2
Le Kremlin-Bicêtre, *Paris* 23 B3
Le Mesnil-le-Roi, *Paris* 23 A1
Le Pecq, *Paris* 23 A1
Le Perreux, *Paris* 23 A3
Le Pin, *Paris* 23 A4
Le Plessis-Robinson, *Paris* 23 B2
Le Plessis-Trévise, *Paris* 23 B4
Le Port-Marly, *Paris* 23 A1
Le Pré-St.-Gervais, *Paris* 23 A3
Le Raincy, *Paris* 23 A4
Le Vésinet, *Paris* 23 A1
Lea Bridge, *London* 15 A3
Leaside, *Toronto* 30 A2
Leblon, *Rio de Janeiro* 24 B1
Lee, *London* 15 B4
Leganés, *Madrid* 17 C1
Legazpi, *Madrid* 17 B1
Lehtisaari, *Helsinki* 12 B2
Lei Yue Mun, *Hong Kong* 12 B2
Leião, *Lisbon* 14 A1
Leicester Square, *London* 15 b3
Leichhardt, *Sydney* 28 B1
Leith, *Edinburgh* 11 B3
Lemoyne, *Montreal* 19 B3
Lenin, *Moscow* 19 B3
Lenino, *Moscow* 19 C3
Leninskiye Gory, *Moscow* 19 B3
Lennox, *Los Angeles* 16 C2
Leonia, *New York* 21 A2
Leopardstown, *Dublin* 11 B2
Leopoldau, *Vienna* 31 A2
Leopoldstadt, *Vienna* 31 A2
Leportovo, *Moscow* 19 B4
Leppävaara, *Helsinki* 12 B1
Les Lilas, *Paris* 23 A3
Les Loges-en-Josas, *Paris* 23 B1
Les Pavillons-sous-Bois, *Paris* 23 A4
Lésigny, *Paris* 23 B4
Lesnozavodskaya, *St. Petersburg* 26 B2
L'Étang-la-Ville, *Paris* 23 A1
Letná, *Prague* 24 a1
Letňany, *Prague* 24 B3
Levallois-Perret, *Paris* 23 A2
Levent, *Istanbul* 12 B2
Lewisdale, *Washington* 32 B4
Lewisham, *London* 15 B3
Lexington, *Boston* 6 A2
Leyton, *London* 15 A3
Leytonstone, *London* 15 A4
L'Hay-les-Roses, *Paris* 23 B3
L'Hospitalet de Llobregat, *Barcelona* 4 A1
Lhotka, *Prague* 24 B2
Liangshui He →, *Beijing* 4 C2
Lianhua Chi, *Beijing* 4 B1
Lianhua He →, *Beijing* 4 B1
Libčice nad Vitavou, *Prague* 24 A2
Libeň, *Prague* 24 B2
Liberdade, *São Paulo* 26 B2
Liberdade, Ave da, *Lisbon* 14 b1
Liberton, *Edinburgh* 11 B3
Liberty I., *New York* 21 B1
Liberty State Park, *New York* 21 B1
Libeznice, *Prague* 24 A2
Library of Congress, *Washington* 32 c3
Libuš, *Prague* 24 B2
Lichiao, *Canton* 8 B2
Lichtenburg, *Berlin* 5 A4
Lichterfelde, *Berlin* 5 B2
Lidingö, *Stockholm* 28 A2
Lieshi Lingyuan, *Canton* 8 B2
Liesing, *Vienna* 31 B1
Liesing →, *Vienna* 31 B2
Liffey, R. →, *Dublin* 11 A1
Ligovo, *St. Petersburg* 26 C1
Lijordet, *Oslo* 22 A2
Likavitos, *Athens* 2 b3
Likhoborka →, *Moscow* 19 A3
Lilla Värtan, *Stockholm* 28 A3
Lille Værløse, *Copenhagen* 10 A2
Liluah, *Calcutta* 8 B1
Lim Chu Kang, *Singapore* 27 A2
Lima, *Lima* 16 B2
Limbiate, *Milan* 18 A1
Limehouse, *London* 15 A3
Limeil-Brévannes, *Paris* 23 B3
Linate, Aeroporto Internazionale di, *Milan* 18 B2
Linbropark, *Johannesburg* 13 A2
Lincoln, *Boston* 6 A2
Lincoln Center, *New York* 21 b2
Lincoln Heights, *Los Angeles* 16 B3
Lincoln Park, *Chicago* 9 B3
Lincoln Park, *New York* 21 B1
Lincoln Park, *San Francisco* 25 B1
Lincolnwood, *Chicago* 9 A2
Linda-a-Pastora, *Lisbon* 14 A1
Linden, *Johannesburg* 13 A2
Linden, *Wellington* 32 A1
Lindenberg, *Berlin* 5 A4
Lindøya, *Oslo* 22 A3
Liniers, *Buenos Aires* 7 B1
Linkebeek, *Brussels* 6 B2
Linksfield, *Johannesburg* 13 A2
Linmeyer, *Johannesburg* 13 B2
Linna, *Helsinki* 12 A2
Lintuvaara, *Helsinki* 12 B1
Lion Rock Country Park, *Hong Kong* 12 A2
Lioúmi, *Athens* 2 B2
Liqizhuang, *Tianjin* 30 B2
Lisboa, *Lisbon* 14 A2
Lisbon = Lisboa, *Lisbon* 14 A2
Lishui, *Canton* 8 A1
Little B., *Sydney* 28 B2
Little Calumet →, *Chicago* 9 D3
Little Ferry, *New York* 21 A1
Little Italy, *New York* 21 e2
Little Mermaid, *Copenhagen* 10 a3
Little Rouge →, *Toronto* 30 A4
Little Tokyo, *Los Angeles* 16 c2
Liuhang, *Shanghai* 27 A1
Liurong Temple, *Canton* 8 B2
Liuxi →, *Canton* 8 B2
Liverpool Street, *London* 15 a5
Livry-Gargan, *Paris* 23 A4
Ljan, *Oslo* 22 A3
Llano de Can Gineu, *Barcelona* 4 A2
Llobregat →, *Barcelona* 4 A1
Lo Aranguiz, *Santiago* 26 B2
Lo Boza, *Santiago* 26 B1
Lo Chau, *Hong Kong* 12 B2
Lo Espejo, *Santiago* 26 C1
Lo Hermida, *Santiago* 26 B2
Lo Prado, *Santiago* 26 B1
Lo So Shing, *Hong Kong* 12 B1
Lo Wai, *Hong Kong* 12 A1
Loanhead, *Edinburgh* 11 B3
Lobau, *Vienna* 31 A3
Lobos, Pt., *San Francisco* 25 B1
Locham, *Munich* 20 B1
Lochino, *Moscow* 19 B1
Lochkov, *Prague* 24 B2
Lockhausen, *Munich* 20 A1
Lodi, *New York* 21 A1
Lodi Estate, *Delhi* 10 B2
Logan Int. Airport, *Boston* 6 A4
Logan Square, *Chicago* 9 B2
Lognes-Émerainville, Aérodrome de, *Paris* 23 B4
Löhme, *Berlin* 5 A5
Lolokhet, *Karachi* 14 A2
Lomas Chapultepec, *Mexico City* 18 B1
Lomas de San Angel Inn, *Mexico City* 18 B1
Lomas de Zamora, *Buenos Aires* 7 C2
Lombardy East, *Johannesburg* 13 A2
Łomianki, *Warsaw* 31 A1
Lomus Reforma, *Mexico City* 18 B1
London, *London* 15 A3
London Bridge, *London* 15 b5
London City Airport, *London* 15 A4
London Zoo, *London* 15 A3
Long B., *Sydney* 28 B2
Long Branch, *Toronto* 30 B1
Long Brook →, *Washington* 32 C2
Long Ditton, *London* 15 B2
Long I., *Boston* 6 B4
Long Island City, *New York* 21 B2
Long Street, *Cape Town* 8 c2
Longchamp, Hippodrôme de, *Paris* 23 A2
Longhua Pagoda, *Shanghai* 27 B1
Longhua Park, *Shanghai* 27 B1
Longjohn Slough, *Chicago* 9 C1
Longtan Hu →, *Beijing* 4 B2
Longue-Pointe, *Montreal* 19 A2
Longueuil, *Montreal* 19 A3
Loni, *Delhi* 10 A2
Loop, The, *Chicago* 9 c1
Lord's Cricket Ground, *London* 15 A2
Loreto, *Milan* 18 B2
Los Angeles Int. Airport, *Los Angeles* 16 C2
Los Cerrillos, Aeropuerto, *Santiago* 26 B1
Los Nietos, *Los Angeles* 16 C4
Los Olivos, *Lima* 16 A2
Los Reyes, *Mexico City* 18 B2
Lot, *Brussels* 6 B1
Loughlinstown, *Dublin* 11 B3
Loures, *Lisbon* 14 A1
Louveciennes, *Paris* 23 A1
Louvre, Musée du, *Paris* 23 b4
Louvre, Palais du, *Paris* 23 b4
Lower East Side, *New York* 21 e2
Lower Hutt, *Wellington* 32 B2
Lower Manhattan, *New York* 21 e1
Lower New York B., *New York* 21 C1
Lower Shing Mun Res., *Hong Kong* 12 A1
Lowry Bay, *Wellington* 32 B2
Lu Xun Museum, *Beijing* 4 b1
Lübars, *Berlin* 5 A3
Ludwigsfeld, *Munich* 20 A1
Luhu, *Canton* 8 B2
Lumiar, *Lisbon* 14 A2
Lumphini Park, *Bangkok* 3 B2
Lundtofte, *Copenhagen* 10 A3
Lung Mei, *Hong Kong* 12 A2
Luojiang, *Canton* 8 B2
Lustheim, *Munich* 20 A2
Luwan, *Shanghai* 27 B1
Luxembourg, Palais du, *Paris* 23 c4
Luzhniki Sports Centre, *Moscow* 19 B3
Lyndhurst, *New York* 21 B1
Lynn, *Boston* 6 A4
Lynn Harbor, *Boston* 6 A4
Lynn Woods Res., *Boston* 6 A3
Lyon, Gare de, *Paris* 23 c5
Lyons, *Chicago* 9 C2
Lysaker, *Oslo* 22 A2
Lysakerselva →, *Oslo* 22 A2
Lysolaje, *Prague* 24 B2
Lyubertsy, *Moscow* 19 B5
Lyublino, *Moscow* 19 B4

M

Ma Nam Wat, *Hong Kong* 12 A2
Ma On Shan Country Park, *Hong Kong* 12 A2
Ma'ale Adumim, *Jerusalem* 13 B2
Ma'ale Ha Khamisha, *Jerusalem* 13 B1
Ma'ale Mikhmas, *Jerusalem* 13 A2
Maantiekylä, *Helsinki* 12 A3
Maarifa, *Baghdad* 3 B2
Mabato Pt., *Manila* 17 C2
Macaco, Morro do, *Rio de Janeiro* 24 B2
McCook, *Chicago* 9 C2
Machelen, *Brussels* 6 A2
Machida, *Tokyo* 29 B1
Maciołki, *Warsaw* 31 B2
McKerrow, *Wellington* 32 B2
McKinley Park, *Chicago* 9 C2
Mclean, *Washington* 32 B2
Macopocho, R. →, *Santiago* 26 B1
MacRitchie Res., *Singapore* 27 A2
Macul, *Santiago* 26 C2
Madame Tussaud's, *London* 15 a3
Madhudaha, *Calcutta* 8 B2
Madhyamgram, *Calcutta* 8 A2
Madīnah Al Mansūr, *Baghdad* 3 B2
Mâdinet Nasr, *Cairo* 7 A2
Madison Avenue, *New York* 21 c2
Madison Square, *New York* 21 d2
Madrid, *Madrid* 17 B1
Madrona, *Barcelona* 4 A1
Maesawa, *Tokyo* 29 A2
Magdalena, *Lima* 16 B2
Magdalena Contreras, *Mexico City* 18 C1
Maghreb, *Baghdad* 3 A2
Maginu, *Tokyo* 29 B2
Magliana, *Rome* 25 B1
Magny-les-Hameaux, *Paris* 23 B1
Magonoy, *Manila* 17 B2
Mahalaxmi, *Mumbai* 20 a1
Maheshtala, *Calcutta* 8 C1
Mahim, *Mumbai* 20 A2
Mahim B., *Mumbai* 20 A1
Mahlsdorf, *Berlin* 5 A4
Mahmoodabad, *Karachi* 14 A2
Mahrauli, *Delhi* 10 B1
Mahul, *Mumbai* 20 A2
Maida Vale, *London* 15 a1
Maidstone, *Melbourne* 17 A1
Maipú, *Santiago* 26 C1
Maisonneuve, Parc, *Montreal* 19 A2
Maisons-Alfort, *Paris* 23 B3
Maisons-Laffitte, *Paris* 23 A1
Maissoneuve, *Montreal* 19 A2
Maitland, *Cape Town* 8 A1
Makati, *Manila* 17 B2
Mäkiniitty, *Helsinki* 12 A2
Mala Straná, *Prague* 24 B2
Malabar, *Mumbai* 20 B1
Malabar, *Sydney* 28 B2
Malabar Hill, *Mumbai* 20 B1
Malabar Pt., *Mumbai* 20 B1
Malabon, *Manila* 17 B1
Malacañang Palace, *Manila* 17 B1
Malahide, *Dublin* 11 A3
Malakhovka, *Moscow* 19 C6
Malakoff, *Paris* 23 B2
Mälarhöjaen, *Stockholm* 28 B1
Malate, *Manila* 17 B1
Malay Quarter, *Cape Town* 8 c2
Malaya Neva, *St. Petersburg* 26 B1
Malaya-Okhta, *St. Petersburg* 26 B2
Malchow, *Berlin* 5 A3
Malden, *Boston* 6 A3
Malden, *London* 15 B2
Maleizen, *Brussels* 6 B3
Malešice, *Prague* 24 B3
Malir →, *Karachi* 14 B2
Mall, The, *Washington* 32 b2
Malleny Mills, *Edinburgh* 11 B2
Malmi, *Helsinki* 12 B2
Malmøya, *Oslo* 22 A3
Måløv, *Copenhagen* 10 A2
Malpasso, Ost., *Rome* 25 C1
Malton, *Toronto* 30 A1
Malvern, *Johannesburg* 13 B2
Malvern, *Melbourne* 17 B2
Malvern, *Toronto* 30 A3
Mamonovo, *Moscow* 19 B2
Mampang Prapatan, *Jakarta* 13 B1
Mampukuji, *Tokyo* 29 B2
Man Budrukh, *Mumbai* 20 A2
Man Khurd, *Mumbai* 20 A2
Mandaluyong, *Manila* 17 B2
Mandaoli, *Delhi* 10 B2
Mandaqui →, *São Paulo* 26 A2
Mandoli, *Delhi* 10 A2
Mandvi, *Mumbai* 20 B2
Manenberg, *Cape Town* 8 A2
Mang Kung Uk, *Hong Kong* 12 B2
Mangolpuri, *Delhi* 10 A1
Manguinhos, Aéroporto, *Rio de Janeiro* 24 B1
Mangwŏn, *Seoul* 26 B1
Manhattan, *New York* 21 B2
Manhattan Beach, *New York* 21 C2
Manila, *Manila* 17 B1
Manila B., *Manila* 17 B1
Manila Int. Airport, *Manila* 17 B2
Mankkaa, *Helsinki* 12 B1
Manly, *Sydney* 28 A2
Mannswörth, *Vienna* 31 B3
Manor Park, *London* 15 A4
Manor Park, *Wellington* 32 A2
Manora, *Karachi* 14 B1
Manquehue, Cerro, *Santiago* 26 B2
Manzanares, Canal de, *Madrid* 17 C2
Mao Mausoleum, *Beijing* 4 c2
Map'o, *Seoul* 26 B1
Maracanã, *Rio de Janeiro* 24 B1
Maraoli, *Mumbai* 20 A2
Marblehead, *Boston* 6 A4
Marcelin, *Warsaw* 31 B1
Mareil-Marly, *Paris* 23 A1
Margareten, *Vienna* 31 A2
Maria, *Vienna* 31 A2
Maridalen, *Oslo* 22 A3
Maridalsvatnet, *Oslo* 22 A3
Mariendorf, *Berlin* 5 B3
Marienfelde, *Berlin* 5 B3
Marienplatz, *Munich* 20 b2
Marikina →, *Manila* 17 B2
Marin City, *San Francisco* 25 A1
Marin Headlands State Park, *San Francisco* 25 A2
Marin Pen., *San Francisco* 25 A1
Marina del Rey, *Los Angeles* 16 C2
Marine Drive, *Mumbai* 20 b1
Marino, *Dublin* 11 A2
Maritim, Museu, *Barcelona* 4 c2
Markham, *Toronto* 30 A2
Marki, *Warsaw* 31 B2
Markland Wood, *Toronto* 30 B1
Marly, Forêt de, *Paris* 23 A1
Marly-le-Roi, *Paris* 23 A1
Marne →, *Paris* 23 B3
Marne-la-Vallée, *Paris* 23 A4
Marolles-en-Brie, *Paris* 23 B4
Maroubra, *Sydney* 28 B2
Marquette Park, *Chicago* 9 C2
Marrickville, *Sydney* 28 B1
Marsfield, *Sydney* 28 A1
Marshall Field's, *Chicago* 9 c2
Marte, Campo de, *São Paulo* 26 B2
Martesana, Navíglio della, *Milan* 18 A2
Martin Luther King National Historic Site, *Atlanta* 3 B2
Martinez, *Buenos Aires* 7 A1
Martinkylä, *Helsinki* 12 B2
Martinsried, *Munich* 20 B1
Maruko, *Tokyo* 29 B3
Marunouchi, *Tokyo* 29 b4
Marusino, *Moscow* 19 B5
Maryino, *Moscow* 19 B4
Maryland, *Singapore* 27 B2
Marylebone, *London* 15 A2
Marymont, *Warsaw* 31 B1
Marysin Wawerski, *Warsaw* 31 B2
Marzahn, *Berlin* 5 A4
Mascot, *Sydney* 28 B2
Masmo, *Stockholm* 28 B1
Maspeth, *New York* 21 B2
Masr el Gedida, *Cairo* 7 A2
Masr el Qadîma, *Cairo* 7 A2
Massachusetts B., *Boston* 6 A4
Massachusett's Inst. of Tech., *Boston* 6 A3
Massamá, *Lisbon* 14 A1
Massey →, *Toronto* 30 A3
Massy, *Paris* 23 B2
Matihutong, *Beijing* 4 B1
Matinha, *Lisbon* 14 A2
Matramam, *Jakarta* 13 B2
Matsubara, *Osaka* 22 B4
Mattapan, *Boston* 6 B3
Mátyásföld, *Budapest* 7 A3
Mátyástemplom, *Budapest* 7 b1
Mau Tso Ngam, *Hong Kong* 12 A2
Mauer, *Vienna* 31 B1
Mauripur, *Karachi* 14 A1
Maxhof, *Munich* 20 B1
Maya-Zan, *Osaka* 22 A2
Mayfair, *Johannesburg* 13 B2
Mayfair, *London* 15 b3
Mayor, Plaza, *Madrid* 17 b2
Maywood, *Chicago* 9 B1
Maywood, *Los Angeles* 16 C3
Maywood, *New York* 21 A1
Mazagaon, *Mumbai* 20 a2
Me'a She' Arim, *Jerusalem* 13 a2
Meadowbank Park, *Sydney* 28 A1
Měcholupy, *Prague* 24 B3
Měčice, *Prague* 24 A3
Mecidiyeköy, *Istanbul* 12 B2
Medford, *Boston* 6 A3
Mediodia, *Madrid* 17 B2
Medvezhiy Ozyora, *Moscow* 19 A5
Meguro →, *Tokyo* 29 B3
Meguro-Ku, *Tokyo* 29 B3
Mehpalpur, *Delhi* 10 B1
Mehrābād Airport, *Tehran* 30 A1
Mehram Nagar, *Delhi* 10 B1
Mehrow, *Berlin* 5 A4
Mei Lanfang, *Beijing* 4 a2
Meidling, *Vienna* 31 A2
Méier, *Rio de Janeiro* 24 B1
Meiji Shrine, *Tokyo* 29 b1
Meise, *Brussels* 6 A1
Mejiro, *Tokyo* 29 A3
Melbourne, *Melbourne* 17 A1
Melbourne Airport, *Melbourne* 17 A1
Melkki, *Helsinki* 12 C2
Mellunkylä, *Helsinki* 12 B3
Mellunmäki, *Helsinki* 12 B3
Melrose, *Boston* 6 A3
Melrose, *New York* 21 B2
Melrose Park, *Chicago* 9 B1
Melsbroek, *Brussels* 6 A2
Menteng, *Jakarta* 13 B1
Mérantaise →, *Paris* 23 B1
Mercamadrid, *Madrid* 17 B2
Merced, L., *San Francisco* 25 B2
Meredale, *Johannesburg* 13 B1
Merlimau, P., *Singapore* 27 B2
Merri Cr. →, *Melbourne* 17 A1
Merrion, *Dublin* 11 B2
Merrionette Park, *Chicago* 9 C2
Merton, *London* 15 B2
Mesgarābād, *Tehran* 30 B3
Meshcherskiy, *Moscow* 19 B2
Messe, *Vienna* 31 A2
Messe-palast, *Vienna* 31 c1
Metanópoli, *Milan* 18 B2
Metropolitan Museum of Art, *New York* 21 b3
Meudon, *Paris* 23 B2
Mevaseret Tsiyon, *Jerusalem* 13 B1
Mevo Beitar, *Jerusalem* 13 B1
México, Ciudad de, *Mexico City* 18 B1
Meyersdal, *Johannesburg* 13 B2
Mezzano, *Milan* 18 B2
Mezzate, *Milan* 18 B2
Miadong, *Seoul* 26 B2
Miami, *Miami* 18 B2
Miami Beach, *Miami* 18 B2
Miami Canal →, *Miami* 18 A1
Miami Int. Airport, *Miami* 18 B1
Miami Shores, *Miami* 18 A2
Miami Springs, *Miami* 18 B1
Miasto, *Warsaw* 31 B2
Michałowice, *Warsaw* 31 B1
Michigan Avenue, *Chicago* 9 b2
Michle, *Prague* 24 B2
Middle Harbour, *Sydney* 28 A2
Middle Hd., *Sydney* 28 A2
Middle Park, *Melbourne* 17 B1
Middle Village, *New York* 21 B2
Middlesex Fells Reservation, *Boston* 6 A3
Midi, Gare du, *Brussels* 6 c1
Midland Beach, *New York* 21 C1
Miedzeszyn, *Warsaw* 31 B3
Międzylesie, *Warsaw* 31 B3
Miessaari, *Helsinki* 12 C1
Miguel Hidalgo, *Mexico City* 18 B1
Mikhelysona, *Moscow* 19 B5
Milano, *Milan* 18 B1
Milano Due, *Milan* 18 B2
Milano San Felice, *Milan* 18 B2
Milbertshofen, *Munich* 20 A2
Mill Hill, *London* 15 A2
Millennium Dome, *London* 15 A4
Miller Meadow, *Chicago* 9 B2
Millerhill, *Edinburgh* 11 B3
Millers Point, *Sydney* 28 a1
Milltown, *Dublin* 11 B2
Millwood, *Washington* 32 B4
Milnerton, *Cape Town* 8 A1
Milon-la-Chapelle, *Paris* 23 B1
Milton, *Boston* 6 B3
Milton Bridge, *Edinburgh* 11 B2
Mimico, *Toronto* 30 B2
Minami, *Osaka* 22 A4
Minamitsunashima, *Tokyo* 29 B2
Minato, *Osaka* 22 B3
Minato-Ku, *Tokyo* 29 c3
Minshât el Bekkarî, *Cairo* 7 A1
Minute Man Nat. Hist. Park, *Boston* 6 A2
Miraflores, *Lima* 16 B2
Miramar, *Wellington* 32 B1
Misericordia, Sa. da, *Rio de Janeiro* 24 B1
Mission, *San Francisco* 25 B2
Mississauga, *Toronto* 30 B1
Mitaka, *Tokyo* 29 A2
Mitcham, *London* 15 B2
Mitcham Common, *London* 15 B3
Mitchell's Plain, *Cape Town* 8 B2
Mitino, *Moscow* 19 A2
Mitte, *Berlin* 5 A3
Mittel Isarkanal →, *Munich* 20 A3
Mixcoac, *Mexico City* 18 B1
Mixcoac, Presa de, *Mexico City* 18 B1
Miyakojima, *Osaka* 22 A4
Mizonokuchi, *Tokyo* 29 B2
Mizue, *Tokyo* 29 A4
Młocinski Park, *Warsaw* 31 B1
Młociny, *Warsaw* 31 B1
Mnevniki, *Moscow* 19 B2
Moba, *Lagos* 14 B2
Moczydło, *Warsaw* 31 C2
Modderfontein, *Johannesburg* 13 A2
Modřany, *Prague* 24 B2
Mogyoród, *Budapest* 7 A3
Moinho Velho, Cor. →, *São Paulo* 26 B2
Mok, *Seoul* 26 B1
Mokotów, *Warsaw* 31 B2
Molenbeek-Saint-Jean, *Brussels* 6 A1
Molino de Rosas, *Mexico City* 18 B1
Mollem, *Brussels* 6 A1
Mollins de Rey, *Barcelona* 4 A1
Mondeor, *Johannesburg* 13 B2
Moneda, Palacio de la, *Santiago* 26 B2
Moneró, *Rio de Janeiro* 24 A1
Mong Kok, *Hong Kong* 12 B2
Monkstown, *Dublin* 11 B3
Monnickendam, *Amsterdam* 2 A3
Monrovia, *Los Angeles* 16 B4
Monsanto, *Lisbon* 14 A1
Monsanto, Parque Florestal de, *Lisbon* 14 A1
Mont Royal, *Montreal* 19 A2
Mont-Royal, Parc, *Montreal* 19 A2
Montana de Montjuich, *Barcelona* 4 A1
Monte Chingolo, *Buenos Aires* 7 C2
Monte Palatino, *Rome* 25 c3

Rainham 37

Montebello, *Los Angeles* 16 B4
Montemor, *Lisbon* 14 A1
Monterey Park, *Los Angeles* 16 B4
Montespaccato, *Rome* 25 B1
Montesson, *Paris* 23 A1
Monteverde Nuovo, *Rome* 25 B1
Montfermeil, *Paris* 23 A4
Montigny-le-Bretonneux, *Paris* 23 B1
Montjay-la-Tour, *Paris* 23 A4
Montjuic, Parc de, *Barcelona* 4 c1
Montparnasse, Gare, *Paris* 23 A2
Montréal, *Montreal* 19 A2
Montréal, Î. de, *Montreal* 19 A2
Montréal, Univ. de, *Montreal* 19 B2
Montréal Est, *Montreal* 19 A2
Montréal Nord, *Montreal* 19 A2
Montréal Ouest, *Montreal* 19 B1
Montreuil, *Paris* 23 A3
Montrouge, *Paris* 23 B2
Montserrat, *Buenos Aires* 7 B2
Monza, *Milan* 18 A2
Monzoro, *Milan* 18 B1
Moóca, *São Paulo* 26 B2
Moonachie, *New York* 21 B1
Moonee Ponds, *Melbourne* 17 A1
Moonee Valley Racecourse, *Melbourne* 17 A1
Moosach, *Munich* 20 A2
Mora, *Mumbai* 20 B2
Moratalaz, *Madrid* 17 B2
Mörby, *Stockholm* 28 A2
Morden, *London* 15 B2
Morée →, *Paris* 23 A3
Morgan Park, *Chicago* 9 C3
Moriguchi, *Osaka* 22 A4
Morivione, *Milan* 18 B2
Morningside, *Edinburgh* 11 B2
Morningside, *Johannesburg* 13 A2
Morningside, *Washington* 32 C4
Morro Solar, Cerro, *Lima* 16 C2
Mortlake, *London* 15 B2
Mortlake, *Sydney* 28 B1
Morton Grove, *Chicago* 9 A2
Morumbi, *São Paulo* 26 B1
Moscavide, *Lisbon* 14 A2
Moscow = Moskva, *Moscow* 19 B3
Moskhaton, *Athens* 2 B2
Moskva, *Moscow* 19 B3
Moskva →, *Moscow* 19 B2
Moskvoretskiy, *Moscow* 19 B3
Mosman, *Sydney* 28 A2
Móstoles, *Madrid* 17 C1
Moti Bagh, *Delhi* 10 B2
Motol, *Prague* 24 B1
Motsa, *Jerusalem* 13 B2
Motsa Ilit, *Jerusalem* 13 B1
Motspur Park, *London* 15 B2
Mottingham, *London* 15 B4
Moulin Rouge, *Paris* 23 a3
Mount Dennis, *Toronto* 30 A2
Mount Greenwood, *Chicago* 9 C2
Mount Hood Memorial Park, *Boston* 6 A3
Mount Merrion, *Dublin* 11 B2
Mount Rainier, *Washington* 32 B4
Mount Vernon, *New York* 21 A3
Mount Vernon Square, *Washington* 32 a2
Mount Zion, *Jerusalem* 13 b3
Mozarthaus, *Vienna* 31 b2
Müggelberge, *Berlin* 5 B4
Müggelheim, *Berlin* 5 B5
Muggiò, *Milan* 18 A2
Mughal Gardens, *Delhi* 1 c1
Mühleiten, *Vienna* 31 A3
Mühlenfliess →, *Berlin* 5 A5
Muiden, *Amsterdam* 2 A3
Muiderpoort Station, *Amsterdam* 2 b3
Muizenberg, *Cape Town* 8 B1
Mujahidpur, *Delhi* 10 B2
Mukandpur, *Delhi* 10 A2
Mukhmas, *Jerusalem* 13 A2
Muko →, *Osaka* 22 A3
Mukojima, *Tokyo* 29 A3
Mulbarton, *Johannesburg* 13 B2
Mumbai, *Mumbai* 20 B2
Mumbai Harbour, *Mumbai* 20 B2
Münchehofe, *Berlin* 5 B5
München, *Munich* 20 B2
Munich = München, *Munich* 20 B2
Munkkiniemi, *Helsinki* 12 B2
Munro, *Buenos Aires* 7 B1
Murai Res., *Singapore* 27 A2
Muranów, *Warsaw* 31 B1
Murino, *St. Petersburg* 26 B2
Murrayfield, *Edinburgh* 11 B2
Musashino, *Tokyo* 29 A2
Museu Nacional, *Rio de Janeiro* 24 B1
Mushin, *Lagos* 14 A2
Musiektheater, *Amsterdam* 2 b2
Muslim Quarter, *Jerusalem* 13 a3
Musocco, *Milan* 18 B1
Mustansirīya, *Baghdad* 3 A2
Musturud, *Cairo* 7 A2
Muswell Hill, *London* 15 A3
Mutanabi, *Baghdad* 3 B2
Muthana, *Baghdad* 3 B2
Myakinino, *Moscow* 19 B2
Mykerinos, *Cairo* 7 B1
Myllypuro, *Helsinki* 12 B3

N

Nacka, *Stockholm* 28 B3
Nada, *Osaka* 22 A2
Naenae, *Wellington* 32 B2
Nærsnes, *Oslo* 22 B1
Nagata, *Osaka* 22 B1
Nagatsuta, *Tokyo* 29 B2
Nagytétény, *Budapest* 7 B1
Nahant, *Boston* 6 A4
Nahant B., *Boston* 6 A4
Nahant Harbor, *Boston* 6 A4
Nahr Dijlah →, *Baghdad* 3 B2
Najafgarh Drain →, *Delhi* 10 B1
Nakahara-Ku, *Tokyo* 29 B2
Nakano-Ku, *Tokyo* 29 A2
Namgajwa, *Seoul* 26 B1
Namsan Park, *Seoul* 26 B1
Namyŏng, *Seoul* 26 B1
Nanbiancun, *Canton* 8 B1
Nanchang He →, *Beijing* 4 B1
Nandang, *Canton* 8 B2
Nandian, *Tianjin* 30 A2
Nangal Dewat, *Delhi* 10 B1
Naniwa, *Osaka* 22 B3
Nankai, *Tianjin* 30 B1
Nanmenwai, *Tianjin* 30 B2
Nanole, *Mumbai* 20 A2
Nanpu Bridge, *Shanghai* 27 B2
Nanshi, *Shanghai* 27 B1
Nantasket Beach, *Boston* 6 B4
Nanterre, *Paris* 23 A2
Naoabad, *Calcutta* 8 C2
Napier Mole, *Karachi* 14 B1
Naraina, *Delhi* 10 B1
Nariman Point, *Mumbai* 20 c1
Nariman Pt., *Mumbai* 20 B1
Nārmak, *Tehran* 30 A2
Naruo, *Osaka* 22 A3
Näsby, *Stockholm* 28 A2
Näsbypark, *Stockholm* 28 A2
Nathan Road, *Hong Kong* 12 a2
Natick, *Boston* 6 B2
National Maritime Museum, *San Francisco* 25 a1
National Museum, *Bangkok* 3 b1
Nationalmuseum, *Stockholm* 28 b2
Natolin, *Warsaw* 31 C2
Naturhistorischesmuseum, *Vienna* 31 b1
Naucalpan de Juárez, *Mexico City* 18 B1
Naupada, *Mumbai* 20 A2
Navíglio di Pavia, *Milan* 18 B1
Navíglio Grande, *Milan* 18 B1
Navona, Piazza, *Rome* 25 b2
Navotas, *Manila* 17 B1
Navy Pier, *Chicago* 9 b3
Nazal Hikmat Beg, *Baghdad* 3 A2
Nazimabad, *Karachi* 14 A2
Nazlet el Simmân, *Cairo* 7 B1
Néa Alexandhria, *Athens* 2 B2
Néa Faliron, *Athens* 2 B1
Néa Ionía, *Athens* 2 A2
Néa Liósia, *Athens* 2 A2
Néa Smírni, *Athens* 2 B2
Neapolis, *Athens* 2 B2
Near North, *Chicago* 9 b2
Nebušice, *Prague* 24 B1
Nederhorst, *Amsterdam* 2 B3
Nedlitz, *Berlin* 5 B1
Nee Soon, *Singapore* 27 A2
Needham Heights, *Boston* 6 B2
Nekrasovka, *Moscow* 19 B5
N'ematābād, *Tehran* 30 B2
Nemchinovka, *Moscow* 19 B1
Nemzeti Muz, *Budapest* 7 c3
Neponsit, *New York* 21 C2
Nerima-Ku, *Tokyo* 29 A3
Nesodden, *Oslo* 22 B3
Nesoddtangen, *Oslo* 22 A3
Nesøya, *Oslo* 22 A2
Neu Aubing, *Munich* 20 B1
Neu Buch, *Berlin* 5 A4
Neu Buchhorst, *Berlin* 5 B5
Neu Fahrland, *Berlin* 5 B1
Neu Lindenberg, *Berlin* 5 A4
Neubiberg, *Munich* 20 B3
Neue Hofburg, *Vienna* 31 b1
Neuenhagen, *Berlin* 5 A4
Neuessling, *Vienna* 31 A3
Neuhausen, *Munich* 20 B2
Neuherberg, *Munich* 20 A2
Neuhönow, *Berlin* 5 A5
Neuilly-Plaisance, *Paris* 23 A4
Neuilly-sur-Marne, *Paris* 23 A4
Neuilly-sur-Seine, *Paris* 23 A2
Neukagran, *Vienna* 31 A2
Neukettenhof, *Vienna* 31 B2
Neukölln, *Berlin* 5 B3
Neuperlach, *Munich* 20 B2
Neuried, *Munich* 20 B1
Neustift am Walde, *Vienna* 31 A1
Neusüssenbrunn, *Vienna* 31 A2
Neuwaldegg, *Vienna* 31 A1
Neva →, *St. Petersburg* 26 B2
Neves, *Rio de Janeiro* 24 B2
New Baghdād, *Baghdad* 3 B2
New Barakpur, *Calcutta* 8 A2
New Brighton, *New York* 21 C1
New Canada, *Johannesburg* 13 B1
New Canada Dam, *Johannesburg* 13 B1
New Carrollton, *Washington* 32 B4
New Cross, *London* 15 B3
New Delhi, *Delhi* 10 B2
New Dorp, *New York* 21 C1
New Dorp Beach, *New York* 21 C1
New Malden, *London* 15 B2
New Milford, *New York* 21 A1
New Territories, *Hong Kong* 12 A1
New Toronto, *Toronto* 30 B1
New Town, *Edinburgh* 11 B2
New Utrecht, *New York* 21 C2
Newark B., *New York* 21 B1
Newbattle, *Edinburgh* 11 B3
Newbury Park, *London* 15 A4
Newcraighall, *Edinburgh* 11 B3
Newham, *London* 15 A4
Newhaven, *Edinburgh* 11 B2
Newington, *Edinburgh* 11 B2
Newington, *London* 15 c5
Newlands, *Johannesburg* 13 B1
Newlands, *Wellington* 32 B1
Newport, *Melbourne* 17 B1
Newton, *Boston* 6 B2
Newtonbrook, *Toronto* 30 A2
Newtongrange, *Edinburgh* 11 B3
Newtonville, *Boston* 6 A2
Newtown, *Sydney* 28 B2
Neyagawa, *Osaka* 22 A4
Ngaio, *Wellington* 32 B1
Ngau Chi Wan, *Hong Kong* 12 A2
Ngau Tau Kok, *Hong Kong* 12 B2
Ngauranga, *Wellington* 32 B1
Ngong Shuen Chau, *Hong Kong* 12 B1
Ngua Kok Wan, *Hong Kong* 12 A1
Nīāvarān, *Tehran* 30 A2
Nibra, *Calcutta* 8 B1
Nidāl, *Baghdad* 3 B2
Niddrie, *Edinburgh* 11 B3
Niddrie, *Melbourne* 17 A1
Nieder Neuendorf, *Berlin* 5 A2
Niederschöneweide, *Berlin* 5 B3
Niederschönhausen, *Berlin* 5 A3
Niemeyer, *Rio de Janeiro* 24 B1
Nieuw Zuid, *Amsterdam* 2 c2
Nieuwe Kerk, *Amsterdam* 2 b2
Nieuwendam, *Amsterdam* 2 A2
Nihonbashi, *Tokyo* 29 b5
Niipperi, *Helsinki* 12 B1
Níkaia, *Athens* 2 B1
Nikolassee, *Berlin* 5 B2
Nikolskiy, *Moscow* 19 B2
Nikolyskoye, *Moscow* 19 B5
Nikulino, *Moscow* 19 B2
Nil, Nahr en →, *Cairo* 7 B2
Nile = Nil, Nahr en →, *Cairo* 7 B2
Niles, *Chicago* 9 A2
Nimta, *Calcutta* 8 A2
Ningyuan, *Tianjin* 30 B2
Nippa, *Tokyo* 29 B2
Nippori, *Tokyo* 29 A3
Nishi, *Osaka* 22 A3
Nishinari, *Osaka* 22 B3
Nishiyodogawa, *Osaka* 22 A3
Niterói, *Rio de Janeiro* 24 B2
Nob Hill, *San Francisco* 25 b1
Nockeby, *Stockholm* 28 B1
Noel Park, *London* 15 A3
Nogatino, *Moscow* 19 B4
Nogent-sur-Marne, *Paris* 23 A3
Noida, *Delhi* 10 B2
Noiseau, *Paris* 23 B4
Noisiel, *Paris* 23 A4
Noisy-le-Grand, *Paris* 23 A4
Noisy-le-Roi, *Paris* 23 A1
Noisy-le-Sec, *Paris* 23 A3
Nokkala, *Helsinki* 12 C1
Nomentano, *Rome* 25 B2
Nonakashinden, *Tokyo* 29 A2
Nongminyundong Jiangxisuo, *Canton* 8 B2
Nonhyŏn, *Seoul* 26 B2
Nonthaburi, *Bangkok* 3 A1
Noon Gun, *Cape Town* 8 b1
Noorder Kerk, *Amsterdam* 2 a1
Noordgesig, *Johannesburg* 13 B1
Noordzeekanaal, *Amsterdam* 2 A1
Nord, Gare du, *Paris* 23 a4
Nordrand-Siedlung, *Vienna* 31 A2
Nordstrand, *Oslo* 22 A3
Normandale, *Wellington* 32 B2
Nørrebro, *Copenhagen* 10 a1
Norridge, *Chicago* 9 B2
Norrmalm, *Stockholm* 28 a1
North Arlington, *New York* 21 B1
North Bay Village, *Miami* 18 A2
North Bergen, *New York* 21 B1
North Branch Chicago River →, *Chicago* 9 B2
North Bull Island, *Dublin* 11 A3
North Cambridge, *Boston* 6 A3
North Cheam, *London* 15 B2
North Cohasset, *Boston* 6 B4
North Cray, *London* 15 B4
North Decatur, *Atlanta* 3 B3
North Druid Hills, *Atlanta* 3 B3
North Esk →, *Edinburgh* 11 B2
North Gyle, *Edinburgh* 11 B2
North Hackensack, *New York* 21 A1
North Harbor, *Manila* 17 B1
North Hd., *Sydney* 28 A2
North Hollywood, *Los Angeles* 16 B2
North Lexington, *Boston* 6 A2
North Miami, *Miami* 18 A2
North Miami Beach, *Miami* 18 A2
North Nazimabad, *Karachi* 14 A2
North Pt., *Hong Kong* 12 B2
North Queensferry, *Edinburgh* 11 A1
North Quincy, *Boston* 6 B3
North Res., *Boston* 6 A3
North Riverside, *Chicago* 9 B2
North Saugus, *Boston* 6 A3
North Shore Channel →, *Chicago* 9 B2
North Springfield, *Washington* 32 C2
North Sudbury, *Boston* 6 A1
North Sydney, *Sydney* 28 B2
North Woolwich, *London* 15 A4
North York, *Toronto* 30 A2
Northbridge, *Sydney* 28 A2
Northbridge Park, *Sydney* 28 A2
Northcliff, *Johannesburg* 13 A1
Northcote, *Melbourne* 17 A2
Northlake, *Chicago* 9 B1
Northmount, *Toronto* 30 A2
Northolt, *London* 15 A1
Northumberland Heath, *London* 15 B5
Northwood, *London* 15 A1
Norumbega Res., *Boston* 6 B2
Norwood, *Johannesburg* 13 A2
Norwood Park, *Chicago* 9 B2
Noryangjin, *Seoul* 26 B1
Nossa Senhora de Candelária, *Rio de Janeiro* 24 a2
Nossa Senhora do Ó, *São Paulo* 26 B1
Nossegem, *Brussels* 6 A3
Notre-Dame, *Paris* 23 c4
Notre-Dame, Bois, *Paris* 23 B4
Notre-Dame-de-Grace, *Montreal* 19 B2
Notting Hill, *London* 15 b1
Nova Milanese, *Milan* 18 A2
Novate Milanese, *Milan* 18 A1
Novaya Derevnya, *St. Petersburg* 26 A1
Nové Město, *Prague* 24 B2
Novoaleksandrovskoye, *St. Petersburg* 26 B2
Novogireyevo, *Moscow* 19 B4
Novoivanovskoye, *Moscow* 19 B1
Novonikolyskoye, *Moscow* 19 A1
Novosaratovka, *St. Petersburg* 26 B3
Nowe-Babice, *Warsaw* 31 B1
Nöykkiö, *Helsinki* 12 B1
Nueva Atzacoalco, *Mexico City* 18 B2
Nueva Pompeya, *Buenos Aires* 7 C2
Nueva Tenochtitlán, *Mexico City* 18 B2
Nuijala, *Helsinki* 12 B1
Numabukuro, *Tokyo* 29 A2
Nunez, *Buenos Aires* 7 B2
Nunhead, *London* 15 B3
Ñuñoa, *Santiago* 26 B2
Nusle, *Prague* 24 B2
Nussdorf, *Vienna* 31 A2
Nyanga, *Cape Town* 8 A2
Nymphenburg, *Munich* 20 B2
Nymphenburg, Schloss, *Munich* 20 B2

O

Oak Grove, *Atlanta* 3 A3
Oak Island, *Boston* 6 A4
Oak Lawn, *Chicago* 9 C2
Oak Park, *Chicago* 9 B2
Oak View, *Washington* 32 A4
Oakdale, *Atlanta* 3 A2
Oakland, *San Francisco* 25 B3
Oakland, *Washington* 32 B4
Oaklawn, *Washington* 32 C4
Oakleigh, *Melbourne* 17 B2
Oakton, *Washington* 32 B2
Oakwood Beach, *New York* 21 C1
Oatley, *Sydney* 28 B1
Obalende, *Lagos* 14 B2
Oba's Palace, *Lagos* 14 B2
Oberföhring, *Munich* 20 B2
Oberhaching, *Munich* 20 B2
Oberlaa, *Vienna* 31 B2
Oberlisse, *Vienna* 31 A2
Obermenzing, *Munich* 20 A1
Obermoos Schwaige, *Munich* 20 A1
Oberschleissheim, *Munich* 20 A2
Oberschöneweide, *Berlin* 5 B4
Observatory, *Johannesburg* 13 B2
Observatory, *Sydney* 28 a1
Ōbu, *Osaka* 22 A1
Obu-tōge, *Osaka* 22 A1
Óbuda, *Budapest* 7 A2
Obukhovo, *St. Petersburg* 26 B2
Obvodnyy Kanal, *St. Petersburg* 26 B1
Ocean Park, *Hong Kong* 12 B2
Ochakovo, *Moscow* 19 B2
Ochota, *Warsaw* 31 B1
O'Connell Street, *Dublin* 11 b2
Ōdana, *Tokyo* 29 B2
Öden-Stockach, *Munich* 20 B3
Odilampi, *Helsinki* 12 B1
Odintsovo, *Moscow* 19 B1
Odivelas, *Lisbon* 14 A1
Odolany, *Warsaw* 31 B1
Oeiras, *Lisbon* 14 A1
Ofin, *Lagos* 14 A3
Ogawa, *Tokyo* 29 A1
Ogden Park, *Chicago* 9 C2
Ogikubo, *Tokyo* 29 A2
Ogogoro, *Lagos* 14 B2
Ogoyo, *Lagos* 14 B2
Ogudu, *Lagos* 14 A2
Ohariu Stream →, *Wellington* 32 B1
O'Higgins, Parque, *Santiago* 26 B2
Ōimachi, *Tokyo* 29 B3
Ojota, *Lagos* 14 A2
Okamoto, *Osaka* 22 A2
Okęcie, *Warsaw* 31 B1
Okęcie Airport, *Warsaw* 31 B1
Okelra, *Lagos* 14 B2
Okeogbe, *Lagos* 14 B2
Okha, *Delhi* 10 B2
Okhta →, *St. Petersburg* 26 B2
Okkervil →, *St. Petersburg* 26 B2
Okrzeszyn, *Warsaw* 31 C2
Oksval, *Oslo* 22 A3
Oktyabrskiy, *Moscow* 19 B3
Ōkubo, *Tokyo* 29 a2
Ōkura, *Tokyo* 29 B1
Olari, *Helsinki* 12 B1
Olaria, *Rio de Janeiro* 24 B1
Old Admiralty, *St. Petersburg* 26 B1
Old City, *Delhi* 1 a3
Old City, *Jerusalem* 13 b3
Old City, *Shanghai* 27 B1
Old Fort = Purana Qila, *Delhi* 1 c3
Old Harbor, *Boston* 6 B3
Old Town, *Chicago* 9 B3
Old Town, *Edinburgh* 11 B2
Oldbawn, *Dublin* 11 B1
Olgino, *St. Petersburg* 26 A1
Olimpico, Estadio, *Mexico City* 18 C1
Olivais, *Lisbon* 14 A2
Olivar de los Padres, *Mexico City* 18 B1
Olivar del Conde, *Mexico City* 18 B1
Olivos, *Buenos Aires* 7 B2
Olona →, *Milan* 18 B1
Olympia, *London* 15 c1
Olympic Stadium, *Helsinki* 12 B2
Olympique, Stade, *Montreal* 19 A2
Omonias, Pl., *Athens* 2 b1
Ōmori, *Tokyo* 29 B3
Onchi, *Osaka* 22 B4
Onchi →, *Osaka* 22 B4
Onisigun, *Lagos* 14 A2
Ōokayama, *Tokyo* 29 B3
Oosterpark, *Amsterdam* 2 b3
Oostzaan, *Amsterdam* 2 A2
Opa-Locka, *Miami* 18 A1
Opa-Locka Airport, *Miami* 18 A1
Opacz, *Warsaw* 31 B1
Opera House, *Sydney* 28 a2
Ophirton, *Johannesburg* 13 B2
Oppegård, *Oslo* 22 B3
Oppem, *Brussels* 6 A1
Oppsal, *Oslo* 22 A4
Ora, *Jerusalem* 13 B1
Oradell, *New York* 21 A1
Orange Bowl Stadium, *Miami* 18 B2
Orangi, *Karachi* 14 A2
Orchard Road, *Singapore* 27 a1
Ordrup, *Copenhagen* 10 A3
Orech, *Prague* 24 B1
Øresund, *Copenhagen* 10 A3
Orient Heights, *Boston* 6 A4
Orlando Dam, *Johannesburg* 13 B1
Orlando East, *Johannesburg* 13 B1
Orlovo, *Moscow* 19 C2
Orly, *Paris* 23 B3
Ormesson-sur-Marne, *Paris* 23 B4
Ormond, *Melbourne* 17 B2
Ormøya, *Oslo* 22 A3
Orpington, *London* 15 B4
Orsay, Musée d', *Paris* 23 b3
Országház, *Budapest* 7 b2
Országos Levétár, *Budapest* 7 b1
Ortaköy, *Istanbul* 12 B2
Ortica, *Milan* 18 B2
Oruba, *Lagos* 14 A2
Orvostörteneti Múz., *Budapest* 7 c2
Ōsaka, *Osaka* 22 B4
Osaka B., *Osaka* 22 B2
Osaka Castle, *Osaka* 22 A4
Osaka Harbour, *Osaka* 22 B3
Osaka International Airport, *Osaka* 22 A3
Ōsaki, *Tokyo* 29 B3
Osasco, *São Paulo* 26 B1
Osdorf, *Berlin* 5 B3
Osdorp, *Amsterdam* 2 A1
Oshodi, *Lagos* 14 A2
Oslo, *Oslo* 22 A3
Oslofjorden, *Oslo* 22 B2
Ōsone, *Tokyo* 29 B2
Osorun, *Lagos* 14 A2
Ospiate, *Milan* 18 A1
Ostankino, *Moscow* 19 B3
Östasiatiskamuséet, *Stockholm* 28 b3
Österalm, *Stockholm* 28 a3
Østerbro, *Copenhagen* 10 a1
Osterley, *London* 15 B1
Osterley Park, *London* 15 B1
Östermalm, *Stockholm* 28 A2
Österskär, *Stockholm* 28 A3
Ostiense, *Rome* 25 B1
Østmarkkapellet, *Oslo* 22 A4
Østøya, *Oslo* 22 A2
Østre Aker, *Oslo* 22 A3
Ōta-Ku, *Tokyo* 29 B3
Otaniemi, *Helsinki* 12 B1
Otari Open Air Museum, *Wellington* 32 B1
Otsuka, *Tokyo* 29 A3
Ottakring, *Vienna* 31 A1
Ottávia, *Rome* 25 B1
Ottery, *Cape Town* 8 B2
Ottobrunn, *Munich* 20 B3
Oud Zuid, *Amsterdam* 2 b1
Oude Kerk, *Amsterdam* 2 b2
Ouderkerk, *Amsterdam* 2 B2
Oulunkylä, *Helsinki* 12 B2
Ourcq, Canal de l', *Paris* 23 A3
Outer Mission, *San Francisco* 25 B2
Outremont, *Montreal* 19 A2
Overijse, *Brussels* 6 B3
Owhiro Bay, *Wellington* 32 C1
Oworonsoki, *Lagos* 14 A2
Oxford Street, *London* 15 b3
Oxgangs, *Edinburgh* 11 B2
Oxon Hill, *Washington* 32 C4
Oyodo, *Osaka* 22 A3
Oyster B., *Sydney* 28 C1
Oyster Rock, *Mumbai* 20 B1
Oyster Rocks, *Karachi* 14 B2
Ozoir-la-Ferrière, *Paris* 23 B4
Ozone Park, *New York* 21 B2

P

Pacific Heights, *San Francisco* 25 B2
Pacific Manor, *San Francisco* 25 C2
Pacific Palisades, *Los Angeles* 16 B1
Pacifica, *San Francisco* 25 C2
Paco, *Manila* 17 B1
Paco de Arcos, *Lisbon* 14 A1
Paco Imperial, *Rio de Janeiro* 24 a2
Paddington, *London* 15 b2
Paddington, *Sydney* 28 B2
Paderno, *Milan* 18 A1
Pagewood, *Sydney* 28 B2
Pagote, *Mumbai* 20 B2
Pai, I. do, *Rio de Janeiro* 24 B2
Pak Kong, *Hong Kong* 12 A2
Pakila, *Helsinki* 12 B2
Palacio de Bellas Artes, *Mexico City* 18 b2
Palacio de Communicaciones, *Madrid* 17 a3
Palacio Nacional, *Mexico City* 18 b3
Palacio Real, *Barcelona* 4 b3
Palacio Real, *Madrid* 17 b1
Palaión Fáliron, *Athens* 2 B2
Palais de Justice, *Brussels* 6 c2
Palais Royal, *Paris* 23 b4
Palais Royale, *Brussels* 6 b3
Palaiseau, *Paris* 23 B2
Palau Nacional Museu d'Art, *Barcelona* 4 c1
Palazzolo, *Milan* 18 A1
Palermo, *Buenos Aires* 7 B2
Palhais, *Lisbon* 14 B2
Palisades Park, *New York* 21 A1
Palmer Park, *Washington* 32 B4
Palmerston, *Dublin* 11 A1
Paloheinä, *Helsinki* 12 B2
Palomeras, *Madrid* 17 B2
Palos Heights, *Chicago* 9 D2
Palos Hills, *Chicago* 9 C2
Palos Hills Forest, *Chicago* 9 C1
Palos Park, *Chicago* 9 C1
Palpara, *Calcutta* 8 B2
Panchur, *Calcutta* 8 B1
Pandacan, *Manila* 17 B2
Pandan, Selat, *Singapore* 27 B2
Pandan Res., *Singapore* 27 B2
Panepistimio, *Athens* 2 b2
Pangbae, *Seoul* 26 C1
Pangrati, *Athens* 2 B2
Pangsua, Sungei →, *Singapore* 27 A2
Panihati, *Calcutta* 8 A2
Panjang, Bukit, *Singapore* 27 A2
Panje, *Mumbai* 20 B2
Panke →, *Berlin* 5 A3
Pankow, *Berlin* 5 A3
Panthéon, *Paris* 23 c4
Pantheon, *Rome* 25 b2
Pantin, *Paris* 23 A3
Pantitlán, *Mexico City* 18 B2
Panvel Cr. →, *Mumbai* 20 B2
Paparangi, *Wellington* 32 B1
Papiol, *Barcelona* 4 A1
Paramus, *New York* 21 A1
Paranaque, *Manila* 17 B1
Paray-Vieille-Poste, *Paris* 23 B3
Parco Regionale, *Milan* 18 A1
Parel, *Mumbai* 20 B1
Pari, *São Paulo* 26 B2
Parioli, *Rome* 25 B1
Paris, *Paris* 23 A3
Paris-Orly, Aéroport de, *Paris* 23 B3
Pārk-e Mellat, *Tehran* 30 A2
Park Ridge, *Chicago* 9 A1
Park Royal, *London* 15 A2
Parkchester, *New York* 21 B2
Parkdale, *Toronto* 30 B2
Parkhurst, *Johannesburg* 13 A2
Parklawn, *Washington* 32 B3
Parkmore, *Johannesburg* 13 A2
Parkside, *San Francisco* 25 B2
Parktown, *Johannesburg* 13 B2
Parktown North, *Johannesburg* 13 A2
Parkview, *Johannesburg* 13 A2
Parkville, *New York* 21 C2
Parkwood, *Cape Town* 8 B1
Parkwood, *Johannesburg* 13 A2
Parow, *Cape Town* 8 A2
Parque Chabuco, *Buenos Aires* 7 B2
Parque Patricios, *Buenos Aires* 7 B2
Parramatta →, *Sydney* 28 A1
Parthenon, *Athens* 2 c2
Paşabahçe, *Istanbul* 12 B2
Pasadena, *Los Angeles* 16 B4
Pasar Minggu, *Jakarta* 13 B1
Pasay, *Manila* 17 B1
Pascoe Vale, *Melbourne* 17 A1
Paseo de la Reforma, *Mexico City* 18 b2
Pasig, *Manila* 17 B2
Pasig →, *Manila* 17 B2
Pasila, *Helsinki* 12 B2
Pasing, *Munich* 20 B1
Pasir Panjang, *Singapore* 27 B2
Pasir Ris, *Singapore* 27 A3
Passaic →, *New York* 21 B1
Passirana, *Milan* 18 A1
Patel Nagar, *Delhi* 10 B1
Pateros, *Manila* 17 B2
Pathersville, *Atlanta* 3 B3
Pathumwan, *Bangkok* 3 B2
Patipukur, *Calcutta* 8 B2
Patisia, *Athens* 2 A2
Paulo E. Virginia, Gruta, *Rio de Janeiro* 24 B1
Paulshof, *Berlin* 5 A5
Pavshino, *Moscow* 19 B1
Paya Lebar, *Singapore* 27 A3
Peachtree →, *Atlanta* 3 B2
Peakhurst, *Sydney* 28 B1
Peania, *Athens* 2 B3
Peckham, *London* 15 B3
Peddocks I., *Boston* 6 B4
Pederstrup, *Copenhagen* 10 A2
Pedralbes, *Barcelona* 4 A1
Pedregal de San Angel, Jardines del, *Mexico City* 18 C1
Pekhorka →, *Moscow* 19 C6
Pekhra-Pokrovskoye, *Moscow* 19 A5
Pekhra-Yakovievskaya, *Moscow* 19 B5
Peking = Beijing, *Beijing* 4 B1
Pelcowizna, *Warsaw* 31 B2
Pelopónnisos Sta., *Athens* 2 a1
Penalolén, *Santiago* 26 B2
Pencarrow Hd., *Wellington* 32 C2
Peng Siang →, *Singapore* 27 A2
Penge, *London* 15 B3
Penha, *Rio de Janeiro* 24 A1
Penicuik, *Edinburgh* 11 B2
Penjaringan, *Jakarta* 13 A1
Penn Station, *New York* 21 c2
Pennsylvania Avenue, *Washington* 32 b1
Pentland Hills, *Edinburgh* 11 B1
Penyagino, *Moscow* 19 A2
Penzing, *Vienna* 31 A1
People's Park, *Shanghai* 27 B1
People's Square, *Shanghai* 27 B1
Perales del Rio, *Madrid* 17 C2
Peravillo, *Mexico City* 18 a3
Perchtoldsdorf, *Vienna* 31 B1
Perdizes, *São Paulo* 26 B2
Peredelkino, *Moscow* 19 C2
Pergamon Museum, *Berlin* 5 a4
Peristérion, *Athens* 2 A2
Perivale, *London* 15 A2
Perk, *Brussels* 6 A2
Perlach, *Munich* 20 B2
Perlacher Forst, *Munich* 20 B2
Pero, *Milan* 18 A1
Peropok, Bukit, *Singapore* 27 B2
Perovo, *Moscow* 19 B4
Pershing Square, *Los Angeles* 16 c1
Pertusella, *Milan* 18 A1
Pesagot, *Jerusalem* 13 A2
Pesanggrahag, Kali →, *Jakarta* 13 B1
Peschiera Borromeo, *Milan* 18 B2
Pesek, P., *Singapore* 27 B2
Pest, *Budapest* 7 B2
Pesterzsébet, *Budapest* 7 B2
Pesthidegkút, *Budapest* 7 A1
Pestimre, *Budapest* 7 B3
Pestlörinc, *Budapest* 7 B3
Pestújhely, *Budapest* 7 A2
Petas, *Helsinki* 12 B2
Petone, *Wellington* 32 B2
Petrogradskaya Storona, *St. Petersburg* 26 B2
Petroúpolis, *Athens* 2 A2
Petrovice, *Prague* 24 B3
Petrovskiy Park, *Moscow* 19 B3
Petrovsko-Razumovskoye, *Moscow* 19 B3
Pettycur, *Edinburgh* 11 A2
Peutie, *Brussels* 6 A2
Pfaueninsel, *Berlin* 5 B1
Phaya Thai, *Bangkok* 3 B2
Phihai, *Karachi* 14 A2
Phillip B., *Sydney* 28 B2
Phoenix Park, *Dublin* 11 A2
Phra Khanong, *Bangkok* 3 B2
Phra Pradaeng, *Bangkok* 3 C2
Phranakhon, *Bangkok* 3 B1
Picasso, Museu, *Barcelona* 4 c2
Piccadilly, *London* 15 b3
Pico Rivera, *Los Angeles* 16 C4
Piedade, *Lisbon* 14 A1
Piedade, *Rio de Janeiro* 24 B1
Piedade, Cova da, *Lisbon* 14 A2
Piedmont Park, *Atlanta* 3 B2
Pietralata, *Rome* 25 B2
Pihlajamäki, *Helsinki* 12 B2
Pihlajasaari, *Helsinki* 12 C2
Pilares, *Rio de Janeiro* 24 B1
Pilton, *Edinburgh* 11 B2
Pimlico, *London* 15 c3
Pimmit Hills, *Washington* 32 B2
Pine Grove, *Toronto* 30 A1
Pinewood, *Miami* 18 A2
Piney Run →, *Washington* 32 B2
Pinganli, *Beijing* 4 B2
Pingzhou, *Canton* 8 B2
Pinheiros →, *São Paulo* 26 B1
Pinjrapur, *Karachi* 14 A2
Pinner, *London* 15 A1
Pinner Green, *London* 15 A1
Pioltello, *Milan* 18 A2
Pipinui Pt., *Wellington* 32 A1
Piraévs, *Athens* 2 B1
Pirajuçara →, *São Paulo* 26 B1
Pirinççi, *Istanbul* 12 B1
Pirituba, *São Paulo* 26 A1
Pirkkola, *Helsinki* 12 B2
Písnice, *Prague* 24 C2
Pitampura, *Delhi* 10 A1
Pitkäjärvi, *Helsinki* 12 B1
Planegg, *Munich* 20 B1
Plumstead, *Cape Town* 8 B1
Plumstead, *London* 15 B4
Plyushchevo, *Moscow* 19 B4
Pníka, *Athens* 2 c1
Po Toi I., *Hong Kong* 12 B2
Po Toi O, *Hong Kong* 12 B2
Poasco, *Milan* 18 B2
Podbaba, *Prague* 24 B2
Podoli, *Prague* 24 B2
Poduskino, *Moscow* 19 B1
Pointe-Aux-Trembles, *Montreal* 19 A2
Poissy, *Paris* 23 A1
Pok Fu Lam, *Hong Kong* 12 B1
Pokrovsko-Sresnevo, *Moscow* 19 B2
Polton, *Edinburgh* 11 B3
Polyustrovo, *St. Petersburg* 26 B2
Pompidou, Centre, *Paris* 23 b4
Pomprap, *Bangkok* 3 B2
Pondok Indah, *Jakarta* 13 B1
Ponta do Marisco, *Rio de Janeiro* 24 C1
Pontault-Combault, *Paris* 23 B4
Pontinha, *Lisbon* 14 A1
Poplar, *London* 15 A3
Popolo, Porta del, *Rome* 25 a2
Poppintree, *Dublin* 11 A2
Porirua, *Wellington* 32 A2
Porirua East, *Wellington* 32 A2
Port I., *Osaka* 22 A2
Port Melbourne, *Melbourne* 17 B1
Port Nicholson, *Wellington* 32 B2
Port Philip Bay, *Melbourne* 17 B1
Port Richmond, *New York* 21 C1
Port Shelter, *Hong Kong* 12 A2
Port Union, *Toronto* 30 A4
Portage Park, *Chicago* 9 B2
Portal de la Pau, Pl., *Barcelona* 4 c2
Portela, Aeroporto da, *Lisbon* 14 A2
Portmarnock, *Dublin* 11 A3
Porto Brandão, *Lisbon* 14 A1
Porto Novo, *Rio de Janeiro* 24 A2
Porto Novo Cr. →, *Lagos* 14 B2
Portobello, *Edinburgh* 11 B3
Portrero, *San Francisco* 25 B3
Potomac, *Washington* 32 A2
Potomac →, *Washington* 32 B3
Potrero Pt., *San Francisco* 25 B2
Potsdam, *Berlin* 5 B1
Potsdamer Platz, *Berlin* 5 b3
Potzham, *Munich* 20 B2
Pötzleinsdorf, *Vienna* 31 A1
Povoa de Santo Adriao, *Lisbon* 14 A2
Powązki, *Warsaw* 31 B1
Powiśle, *Warsaw* 31 B2
Powsin, *Warsaw* 31 C2
Powsinek, *Warsaw* 31 C2
Poyan Res., *Singapore* 27 A2
Pozuelo de Alarcon, *Madrid* 17 B1
Prado, Museo del, *Madrid* 17 b3
Prado Churubusco, *Mexico City* 18 B2
Praga, *Warsaw* 31 B2
Prague = Praha, *Prague* 24 B2
Praha, *Prague* 24 B2
Praha-Ruzyně Airport, *Prague* 24 B1
Praires, R. des →, *Montreal* 19 A2
Prater, *Vienna* 31 A2
Precotto, *Milan* 18 A2
Prenestino Labicano, *Rome* 25 B2
Prenzlauerberg, *Berlin* 5 A3
Preston, *Melbourne* 17 A1
Pretos Forros, Sa. dos, *Rio de Janeiro* 24 B1
Préville, *Montreal* 19 B3
Přezletice, *Prague* 24 B3
Prima Porta, *Rome* 25 B1
Primavalle, *Rome* 25 B1
Primrose, *Johannesburg* 13 B2
Princes Street, *Edinburgh* 11 b2
Printer's Row, *Chicago* 9 d2
Progreso Nacional, *Mexico City* 18 A2
Prosek, *Prague* 24 B3
Prospect Hill Park, *Boston* 6 A2
Providencia, *Santiago* 26 B2
Prudential Building, *Chicago* 9 c2
Průhonice, *Prague* 24 C3
Psikhikón, *Athens* 2 A2
Pudong New Area, *Shanghai* 27 B2
Pueblo Libre, *Lima* 16 B2
Pueblo Nuevo, *Barcelona* 4 A2
Pueblo Nuevo, *Madrid* 17 B2
Puerta del Sol, Plaza, *Madrid* 17 b2
Puerto Madero, *Buenos Aires* 7 B2
Puerto Retiro, *Buenos Aires* 7 B2
Puhuangyu, *Beijing* 4 B2
Puistola, *Helsinki* 12 B3
Pukan-san, *Seoul* 26 B1
Pukinmäki, *Helsinki* 12 B2
Pukkajwa, *Seoul* 26 B1
Pulkovo Int. Airport, *St. Petersburg* 26 C1
Pullach, *Munich* 20 B1
Pulo Gadung, *Jakarta* 13 B2
Pūnak, *Tehran* 30 A2
Punchbowl, *Sydney* 28 B1
Punde, *Mumbai* 20 B2
Punggol, *Singapore* 27 A3
Punggol, Sungei →, *Singapore* 27 A3
Punggol Pt., *Singapore* 27 A3
Punjabi Bagh, *Delhi* 10 A1
Puotila, *Helsinki* 12 B3
Purana Qila, *Delhi* 1 c3
Puteaux, *Paris* 23 A2
Putilkovo, *Moscow* 19 A2
Putney, *London* 15 B2
Putuo, *Shanghai* 27 B1
Putxet, *Barcelona* 4 A1
Puxi, *Shanghai* 27 B1
Pydhuni, *Mumbai* 20 b2
Pyramids, *Cairo* 7 B1
Pyry, *Warsaw* 31 C1

Q

Qalandya, *Jerusalem* 13 A2
Qal'eh Morghī, *Tehran* 30 B2
Qanâ el Ismâ'ilîya, *Cairo* 7 A2
Qāsemābād, *Tehran* 30 A3
Qasr-e Firūzeh, *Tehran* 30 B3
Qatane, *Jerusalem* 13 B1
Qianmen, *Beijing* 4 B2
Qinghuayuan, *Beijing* 4 B1
Qingningsi, *Shanghai* 27 B2
Qolhak, *Tehran* 30 A2
Quadraro, *Rome* 25 B2
Quaid-i-Azam, *Karachi* 14 A1
Quartiere Zingone, *Milan* 18 B1
Quds, *Baghdad* 3 A2
Queen Mary Res., *London* 15 B1
Queen Street, *Edinburgh* 11 a1
Queensbury, *London* 15 A2
Queenscliffe, *Sydney* 28 A2
Queensferry, *Edinburgh* 11 B1
Queenstown, *Singapore* 27 B2
Quellerina, *Johannesburg* 13 A1
Queluz, *Lisbon* 14 A1
Quezon City, *Manila* 17 B2
Quezon Memorial Circle, *Manila* 17 B2
Quilicura, *Santiago* 26 B1
Quincy, *Boston* 6 B3
Quincy B., *Boston* 6 B4
Quinta Normal, *Santiago* 26 B1
Quinto de Stampi, *Milan* 18 B2
Quinto Romano, *Milan* 18 B1
Quirinale, *Rome* 25 B1
Quirinale, Palazzo dei, *Rome* 25 b3

R

Raasdorf, *Vienna* 31 A3
Rådhuset, *Oslo* 22 A3
Radlice, *Prague* 24 B2
Radość, *Warsaw* 31 B3
Radotin, *Prague* 24 C2
Rafat, *Jerusalem* 13 A2
Raffles Hotel, *Singapore* 27 b3
Raffles Park, *Singapore* 27 B2
Raheny, *Dublin* 11 A3
Rahnsdorf, *Berlin* 5 B5
Rainham, *London* 15 A5

38 Raj Ghat

Raj Ghat, Delhi 1 b3
Rajakylä, Helsinki 12 B3
Rajpath, Delhi 1 c2
Rajpura, Delhi 10 A2
Rákos-patak →, Budapest 7 B3
Rákoshegy, Budapest 7 B3
Rákoskeresztúr, Budapest 7 B3
Rákoskert, Budapest 7 B3
Rákosliget, Budapest 7 B3
Rákospalota, Budapest 7 A2
Rákosszentmihály, Budapest 7 A2
Raków, Warsaw 31 B1
Ram, Jerusalem 13 A2
Rām Allāh, Jerusalem 13 A2
Ramadān, Baghdad 3 B2
Ramakrishna Puram, Delhi 10 B1
Ramanathpur, Calcutta 8 A1
Rambla, La, Barcelona 4 b2
Rambler Channel, Hong Kong 12 A1
Ramenki, Moscow 19 B2
Ramersdorf, Munich 20 B2
Ramos, Rio de Janeiro 24 B1
Ramos Mejia, Buenos Aires 7 B1
Ramot, Jerusalem 13 B2
Rampur, Delhi 10 A2
Ramsgate, Sydney 28 B1
Rand Afrikaans Univ., Johannesburg 13 B2
Rand Airport, Johannesburg 13 B2
Randburg, Johannesburg 13 A1
Randhart, Johannesburg 13 B2
Randpark Ridge, Johannesburg 13 A1
Randwick, Sydney 28 B2
Ranelagh, Dublin 11 A2
Rannersdorf, Vienna 31 B2
Ransbèche, Brussels 6 B2
Ransdorp, Amsterdam 2 A2
Ranvad, Mumbai 20 B2
Raposo, Lisbon 14 A1
Rashtrapati Bhawan, Delhi 1 c1
Rasskazovka, Moscow 19 C2
Rastaala, Helsinki 12 B1
Rastila, Helsinki 12 B3
Raszyn, Warsaw 31 C1
Ratcha Thewi, Bangkok 3 b3
Rathfarnham, Dublin 11 B2
Ratho, Edinburgh 11 B1
Ratho Station, Edinburgh 11 B1
Rato, Lisbon 14 A2
Ravelston, Edinburgh 11 B2
Rawamangun, Jakarta 13 B2
Rayners Lane, London 15 A1
Raynes Park, London 15 B2
Raypur, Calcutta 8 C2
Razdory, Moscow 19 B1
Real Felipe, Fuerte, Lima 16 B2
Recoleta, Buenos Aires 7 B2
Recoleta, Santiago 26 B2
Red Fort = Lal Qila, Delhi 1 a3
Redbridge, London 15 A4
Redfern, Sydney 28 B2
Redwood, Wellington 32 B1
Reeves Hill, Boston 6 A1
Refshaleøen, Copenhagen 10 A3
Regents Park, Johannesburg 13 B2
Regent's Park, London 15 a2
Rego Park, New York 21 B2
Reichstag, Berlin 5 a3
Reina Sofia, Centro de Arte, Madrid 17 c3
Reinickendorf, Berlin 5 A3
Rekola, Helsinki 12 B3
Rembertów, Warsaw 31 B2
Rembrandthuis, Amsterdam 2 b2
Rembrandtpark, Amsterdam 2 A2
Rembrandtsplein, Amsterdam 2 b2
Remedios, Parque Nacional de los, Mexico City 18 B1
Remedios de Escalada, Buenos Aires 7 C2
Rémola, Laguna del, Barcelona 4 B1
Renca, Santiago 26 B1
Renmin Park, Tianjin 30 B2
Rennemoulin, Paris 23 A1
Řeporyje, Prague 24 B1
Republica, Plaza de la, Mexico City 18 b1
République, Place de la, Paris 23 b5
Repulse Bay, Hong Kong 12 B2
Repy, Prague 24 B1
Residenz, Munich 20 B2
Residenzmuseum, Munich 20 b3
Reston, Washington 32 B2
Retiro, Buenos Aires 7 B2
Retiro, Madrid 17 B1
Retreat, Cape Town 8 B1
Reutov, Moscow 19 B5
Réveillon →, Paris 23 B4
Revere, Boston 6 A3
Rexdale, Toronto 30 A1
Reynosa Tamaulipas, Mexico City 18 A1
Rho, Milan 18 A1
Rhodes, Sydney 28 A1
Rhodon, Paris 23 B1
Rhodon →, Paris 23 B1
Ribeira, Rio de Janeiro 24 A1
Ricarda, Laguna de la, Barcelona 4 B1
Richmond, Melbourne 17 A2
Richmond, San Francisco 25 B2
Richmond Hill, New York 21 B2
Richmond Park, London 15 B2
Richmond upon Thames, London 15 B2
Riddarholmen, Stockholm 28 c1
Riddarhuset, Stockholm 28 c2
Ridgefield, New York 21 B1
Ridgefield Park, New York 21 A1
Ridgewood, New York 21 B2
Riem, Munich 20 B3
Rijksmuseum, Amsterdam 2 b1
Rikers I., New York 21 B2
Riksdagensledamothus, Stockholm 28 b2
Riksdagshuset, Stockholm 28 b2
Rimac, Lima 16 B2
Ringsend, Dublin 11 A2
Rinkeby, Stockholm 28 A1
Rio Compride, Rio de Janeiro 24 B1
Rio de Janeiro, Rio de Janeiro 24 B1
Rio de la Plata, Buenos Aires 7 B2
Rio de Mouro, Lisbon 14 A1
Ripollet, Barcelona 4 A1
Ris, Oslo 22 A3
Risby, Copenhagen 10 A1
Rishra, Calcutta 8 A2
Ritchie, Washington 32 B4
Rithala, Delhi 10 A1
Rive Sud, Canal de la, Montreal 19 B2
River Edge, New York 21 A1
River Forest, Chicago 9 B2
River Grove, Chicago 9 B1
Riverdale, New York 21 A2
Riverdale, Washington 32 B4
Riverdale Park, Toronto 30 A2
Riverlea, Johannesburg 13 B1
Riverside, Chicago 9 C2
Riverwood, Sydney 28 B1
Rivière-des-Praires, Montreal 19 A2
Rixensart, Brussels 6 B3
Riyad, Baghdad 3 B2
Rizal Park, Manila 17 B1
Rizal Stadium, Manila 17 B1
Røa, Oslo 22 A2
Robbins, Chicago 9 D2
Robertsham, Johannesburg 13 B2
Rochelle Park, New York 21 A1
Rock Cr. →, Washington 32 B3
Rock Creek Park, Washington 32 B3
Rock Pt., Wellington 32 A1
Rockaway Pt., New York 21 C2
Rockdale, Sydney 28 B1
Rockefeller Center, New York 21 c2
Rodaon, Vienna 31 B1
Rødovre, Copenhagen 10 A2
Rodrigo de Freitas, L., Rio de Janeiro 24 B1
Roehampton, London 15 B2
Rogers Park, Chicago 9 A2
Roihuvuori, Helsinki 12 B3
Roissy-en-Brie, Paris 23 B4
Rokin, Amsterdam 2 b2
Rokkō I., Osaka 22 A2
Rokkō Sanchi, Osaka 22 A2
Rokkō-Zan, Osaka 22 A2
Rokytka →, Prague 24 B3
Roma, Rome 25 B1
Római-Fürdö, Budapest 7 A2
Romainville, Paris 23 A3
Romano Banco, Milan 18 B1
Romashkovo, Moscow 19 B1
Rome = Roma, Rome 25 B1
Romford, London 15 A5
Rondebosch, Cape Town 8 A1
Roppongi, Tokyo 29 c3
Rose Hill, Washington 32 C3
Rosebank, New York 21 C1
Rosebery, Sydney 28 B2
Rosedal La Candelaria, Mexico City 18 B2
Roseland, Chicago 9 C3
Rosemead, Los Angeles 16 B4
Rosemont, Montreal 19 A2
Rosenborg Have, Copenhagen 10 A3
Rosenthal, Berlin 5 A3
Rosettenville, Johannesburg 13 B2
Rosewell, Edinburgh 11 B3
Rosherville Dam, Johannesburg 13 B2
Rösjön, Stockholm 28 A2
Roslags-Näsby, Stockholm 28 A2
Roslin, Edinburgh 11 B3
Roslindale, Boston 6 B3
Rosny-sous-Bois, Paris 23 A4
Rosslyn, Washington 32 B3
Rosyth, Edinburgh 11 A1
Rotherhithe, London 15 B3
Rothneusiedl, Vienna 31 B2
Rothschmaige, Munich 20 A1
Rouge Hill, Toronto 30 A4
Round I., Hong Kong 12 B2
Roxbury, Boston 6 B3
Roxeth, London 15 A1
Royal Botanic Garden, Edinburgh 11 B2
Royal Botanic Gardens, Sydney 28 b2
Royal Grand Palace, Bangkok 3 b1
Royal Observatory, Edinburgh 11 B2
Royal Park, Melbourne 17 A1
Royal Turf Club, Bangkok 3 b2
Röylä, Helsinki 12 B1
Rozas, Portilleros de las, Madrid 17 B1
Roztoky, Prague 24 B2
Rozzano, Milan 18 B1
Rubi →, Barcelona 4 A1
Rublovo, Moscow 19 B2
Rudnevka →, Moscow 19 B5
Rudolfsheim, Vienna 31 A2
Rudolfshöhe, Berlin 5 A5
Rudow, Berlin 5 B3
Rueil-Malmaison, Paris 23 A2
Ruisbroek, Brussels 6 B1
Ruislip, London 15 A1
Rumelihisarı, Istanbul 12 B2
Rumyantsevo, Moscow 19 C2
Rungis, Paris 23 B3
Rusāfa, Baghdad 3 A2
Rush Green, London 15 A5
Russa, Calcutta 8 C2
Russian Hill, San Francisco 25 a1
Rustenfeld, Vienna 31 B2
Rutherford, New York 21 B1
Ruzyně, Prague 24 B1
Rybatskaya, St. Petersburg 26 B2
Rydboholm, Stockholm 28 A3
Ryde, Sydney 28 A1
Rynek, Warsaw 31 a2
Ryogoku, Tokyo 29 A3
Rzhevka, St. Petersburg 26 B3

S

Sa'ādatābād, Tehran 30 A2
Saadūn, Baghdad 3 B2
Saavedra, Buenos Aires 7 B2
Saboli, Delhi 10 A2
Sabugo, Lisbon 14 A1
Sabzi Mand, Delhi 10 A2
Sacavém, Lisbon 14 A2
Saclay, Paris 23 B2
Saclay, Étang de, Paris 23 B1
Sacomã, São Paulo 26 B2
Sacré Cœur, Paris 23 a4
Sacrow, Berlin 5 B1
Sacrower See, Berlin 5 B1
Sadang, Seoul 26 C1
Sadar Bazar, Delhi 1 a1
Saddle Brook, New York 21 A1
Sadr, Karachi 14 A2
Sadr City, Baghdad 3 A2
Sadyba, Warsaw 31 B2
Saft el Laban, Cairo 7 A2
Saganashkee Slough, Chicago 9 C1
Sagene, Oslo 22 A3
Sagrada Familia, Templo de, Barcelona 4 A2
Sagrado Familia, Templo de, Barcelona 4 a2
Sahar Int. Airport, Mumbai 20 A2
Sai Kung, Hong Kong 12 A2
Sai Wan Ho, Hong Kong 12 B2
Sai Ying Pun, Hong Kong 12 B1
St.-Aubin, Paris 23 B1
St.-Cloud, Paris 23 A2
St.-Cyr-l'École, Paris 23 B1
St.-Cyr-l'École, Aérodrome de, Paris 23 B1
St.-Denis, Paris 23 A3
St.-Germain, Forêt de, Paris 23 A1
St.-Germain-en-Laye, Paris 23 A1
St. Giles Cathedral, Edinburgh 11 b2
St-Gilles, Brussels 6 B2
St. Helier, London 15 B2
St.-Hubert, Montreal 19 B3
St. Hubert, Galerie, Brussels 6 b2
St. Isaac's Cathedral, St. Petersburg 26 B1
St. Jacques →, Montreal 19 B3
St. James's, London 15 b3
St. John's Cathedral, Hong Kong 12 c1
St-Joose-Ten-Noode, Brussels 6 A2
St. Kilda, Melbourne 17 B1
St. Lambert, Montreal 19 A3
St.-Lambert, Paris 23 B1
St.-Laurent, Montreal 19 A1
St. Lawrence →, Montreal 19 B2
St.-Lazare, Gare, Paris 23 A2
St.-Léonard, Montreal 19 A2
St. Magelungen, Stockholm 28 B2
St.-Mandé, Paris 23 A3
St. Margaret's, Dublin 11 A2
St.-Martin, Bois, Paris 23 B4
St. Mary Cray, London 15 B4
St.-Maur-des-Fossés, Paris 23 B3
St.-Maurice, Paris 23 B3
St.-Michel, Montreal 19 A2
St. Nikolaus-Kirken, Prague 24 B2
St.-Ouen, Paris 23 A3
St. Patrick's Cathedral, Dublin 11 c1
St. Patrick's Cathedral, New York 21 c2
St. Paul's Cathedral, London 15 b4
St. Paul's Cray, London 15 B4
St. Peters, Sydney 28 B2
St. Petersburg = Sankt Peterburg, St. Petersburg 26 B1
St.-Pierre, Montreal 19 B2
St-Pieters-Leeuw, Brussels 6 B1
St.-Quentin, Étang de, Paris 23 B1
St. Stephen's Green, Dublin 11 c3
St-Stevens-Woluwe, Brussels 6 A2
St.-Vincent-de-Paul, Montreal 19 A2
Ste.-Catherine, Montreal 19 B2
Ste.-Hélène, Î., Montreal 19 A2
Saiwai, Tokyo 29 B3
Sakai, Osaka 22 B3
Sakai Harbour, Osaka 22 B3
Sakra, P., Singapore 27 B2
Salam, Baghdad 3 A2
Salamanca, Madrid 17 B1
Sâllynoggin, Dublin 11 B3
Salmannsdorf, Vienna 31 A1
Salmedina, Madrid 17 C2
Salomea, Warsaw 31 B1
Salsette I., Mumbai 20 A2
Salt Lake City, Calcutta 8 B2
Salt River, Cape Town 8 A1
Salt Water L., Calcutta 8 B2
Saltsjö-Duvnäs, Stockholm 28 B3
Saltykovka, Moscow 19 B5
Samatya, Istanbul 12 C1
Sampaloc, Manila 17 B1
Samphan Thawong, Bangkok 3 B2
Samsŏn, Seoul 26 B2
San Andrés, Barcelona 4 A2
San Angel, Mexico City 18 B1
San Angelo, Castel, Rome 25 b1
San Basilio, Rome 25 B2
San Borja, Lima 16 B3
San Bóvio, Milan 18 B2
San Bruno, Pt., San Francisco 25 C2
San Bruno Mt., San Francisco 25 B2
San Cristobal, Buenos Aires 7 B2
San Cristobal, Madrid 17 B2
San Cristóbal, Cerro, Santiago 26 B2
San Cristoforo, Milan 18 B1
San Donato Milanese, Milan 18 B2
San Francisco, San Francisco 25 B2
San Francisco B., San Francisco 25 B3
San Francisco Culhuacán, Mexico City 18 C2
San Fruttuoso, Milan 18 A2
San Gabriel, Los Angeles 16 B4
San Giuliano Milanese, Milan 18 B2
San Isidro, Lima 16 B2
San Jerónimo Lidice, Mexico City 18 C1
San Joaquin, Santiago 26 B2
San José Rio Hondo, Mexico City 18 B1
San Juan →, Manila 17 B2
San Juan de Aragón, Mexico City 18 B2
San Juan de Aragón, Parque, Mexico City 18 B2
San Juan de Lurigancho, Lima 16 A2
San Juan del Monte, Manila 17 B2
San Juan Ixtacala, Mexico City 18 A1
San Juan Toltotepec, Mexico City 18 B1
San Just Desvern, Barcelona 4 A1
San Justo, Buenos Aires 7 C1
San Lorenzo Tezonco, Mexico City 18 C2
San Luis, Lima 16 B2
San Marino, Los Angeles 16 B4
San Martin, Barcelona 4 A2
San Martin de Porras, Lima 16 B2
San Miguel, Lima 16 B2
San Miguel, Santiago 26 B2
San Nicolas, Buenos Aires 7 B2
San Onófrio, Rome 25 B1
San Pedro Martir, Barcelona 4 A1
San Pedro Zacatenco, Mexico City 18 A2
San Pietro, Piazza, Rome 25 b1
San Po Kong, Hong Kong 12 A2
San Rafael Chamapa, Mexico City 18 B1
San Rafael Hills, Los Angeles 16 A3
San Roque, Manila 17 B2
San Siro, Milan 18 B1
San Souci, Sydney 28 B1
San Telmo, Buenos Aires 7 B2
San Vicenc dels Horts, Barcelona 4 A1
Sanbancho, Tokyo 29 a3
Sandown, Johannesburg 13 A2
Sandown Park Races, London 15 B1
Sandton, Johannesburg 13 A2
Sandvika, Oslo 22 A2
Sandy Pond, Boston 6 A2
Sandyford, Dublin 11 B2
Sandymount, Dublin 11 B2
Sangenjaya, Tokyo 29 B2
Sangge, Seoul 26 B2
Sangley Pt., Manila 17 C1
Sankrail, Calcutta 8 B1
Sankt Peterburg, St. Petersburg 26 B1
Sankt Veit, Vienna 31 A1
Sanlihe, Beijing 4 B1
Sanlintang, Shanghai 27 C1
Sans, Barcelona 4 A1
Sant Agusti, Barcelona 4 c2
Sant Ambrogio, Basilica di, Milan 18 B2
Sant Boi de Llobregat, Barcelona 4 A1
Sant Cugat, Barcelona 4 A1
Sant Feliu de Llobregat, Barcelona 4 A1
Sant Joan Despi, Barcelona 4 A1
Sant Maria del Mar, Barcelona 4 b3
Sant Pau del Camp, Barcelona 4 c2
Santa Ana, Manila 17 B2
Santa Coloma de Gramanet, Barcelona 4 A2
Santa Cruz, Manila 17 B1
Santa Cruz, Mumbai 20 A1
Santa Cruz, I. de, Rio de Janeiro 24 B2
Santa Cruz de Olorde, Barcelona 4 A1
Santa Efigénia, São Paulo 26 B2
Santa Elena, Manila 17 B2
Santa Elena del Gomero, Santiago 26 B1
Santa Eulalia, Barcelona 4 A2
Santa Fe Springs, Los Angeles 16 C4
Santa Iria da Azóia, Lisbon 14 A2
Santa Julia, Santiago 26 C2
Santa Maria, Mexico City 18 a1
Santa Monica, Los Angeles 16 B2
Santa Monica Mts., Los Angeles 16 B2
Santa Rosa De Locobe, Santiago 26 B2
Santa Teresa de la Ovalle, Santiago 26 B1
Santahamina, Helsinki 12 C3
Santana, São Paulo 26 A2
Santeny, Paris 23 B4
Santiago, Santiago 26 B2
Santiago de Surco, Lima 16 B2
Santo Amaro, Lisbon 14 A1
Santo Amaro, São Paulo 26 B1
Santo Andre, Lisbon 14 B2
Santo Antão do Tojal, Lisbon 14 A2
Santo António, Qta. de, Lisbon 14 B1
Santo Tomas, Univ. of, Manila 17 B1
Santos Dumont, Aéroport, Rio de Janeiro 24 B2
Santoshpur, Calcutta 8 B1
Santragachi, Calcutta 8 B1
Santry, Dublin 11 A2
Sanyuanli, Canton 8 B2
São Caetano do Sul, São Paulo 26 B2
São Conrado, Rio de Janeiro 24 C1
São Cristovão, Rio de Janeiro 24 B1
São Francisco Penitência, Rio de Janeiro 24 b1
São Jorge, Castelo de, Lisbon 14 A2
São Juliao do Tojal, Lisbon 14 A2
São Paulo, São Paulo 26 B2
Sapa, Calcutta 8 B1
Sapateiro, Cor. do →, São Paulo 26 B1
Sarandi, Buenos Aires 7 C2
Saraswati →, Calcutta 8 A1
Sarecky potok →, Prague 24 B2
Sarimbun, Singapore 27 A2
Sarimbun Res., Singapore 27 A2
Sarıyer, Istanbul 12 A2
Saronikós Kólpos, Athens 2 B1
Sarriá, Barcelona 4 A1
Sarsuna, Calcutta 8 C1
Sartrouville, Paris 23 A2
Sasad, Budapest 7 B2
Sashalom, Budapest 7 A3
Saska, Warsaw 31 B2
Satalice, Prague 24 B3
Satgachi, Calcutta 8 B2
Sathorn, Bangkok 3 B2
Satpukur, Calcutta 8 B2
Sätra, Stockholm 28 B1
Sattru Pha, Bangkok 3 b2
Saúde, São Paulo 26 B2
Saugus, Boston 6 A3
Saugus →, Boston 6 A3
Sault-au-Récollet, Montreal 19 A2
Sausalito, San Francisco 25 A2
Sawah Besar, Jakarta 13 A1
Saxonville, Boston 6 B1
Scald Law, Edinburgh 11 B2
Scarborough, Toronto 30 A3
Sceaux, Paris 23 B2
Schaerbeek, Brussels 6 A2
Scharfenberg, Berlin 5 A2
Scheepvartmuseum, Amsterdam 2 b3
Schiller Park, Chicago 9 B1
Schiller Woods, Chicago 9 B1
Schiphol, Luchthaven, Amsterdam 2 B1
Schlachtensee, Berlin 5 B2
Schlossgarten, Berlin 5 A2
Schmargendorf, Berlin 5 B2
Schönblick, Berlin 5 B5
Schönbrunn, Schloss, Vienna 31 A1
Schöneberg, Berlin 5 B3
Schöneiche, Berlin 5 B5
Schönwalde, Berlin 5 A1
Schotschekloof, Cape Town 8 b1
Schulzendorf, Berlin 5 A2
Schwabing, Munich 20 B2
Schwanebeck, Berlin 5 A4
Schwanenwerder, Berlin 5 B2
Schwarzlackenau, Vienna 31 A2
Schwechat, Vienna 31 B2
Scitrek Museum, Atlanta 3 B2
Scott Monument, Edinburgh 11 b2
Scottdale, Atlanta 3 B3
Sea Point, Cape Town 8 A1
Seabrook, Washington 32 B5
Seacliff, San Francisco 25 B2
Seaforth, Sydney 28 A2
Seagate, New York 21 C1
Sears Tower, Chicago 9 c1
Seat Pleasant, Washington 32 B4
Seaview, Wellington 32 B2
Šeberov, Prague 24 B3
Secaucus, New York 21 B1
Seddinsee, Berlin 5 B5
Seeberg, Berlin 5 A5
Seeburg, Berlin 5 A1
Seefeld, Berlin 5 A5
Seegefeld, Berlin 5 A1
Seehof, Berlin 5 B2
Segeltorp, Stockholm 28 B1
Segrate, Milan 18 B2
Seguro, Milan 18 B1
Seine →, Paris 23 B3
Seixal, Lisbon 14 B2
Selby, Johannesburg 13 B2
Seletar, P., Singapore 27 A3
Seletar Hills, Singapore 27 A3
Seletar Res., Singapore 27 A2
Selhurst, London 15 B3
Sembawang, Singapore 27 A2
Senago, Milan 18 A1
Sendinger Tor Platz, Munich 20 c1
Sendling, Munich 20 B2
Senju, Tokyo 29 A3
Senriyama, Osaka 22 A4
Sentosa, P., Singapore 27 B2
Seoul = Sŏul, Seoul 26 B2
Seoul National Univ., Seoul 26 C1
Seoul Tower, Seoul 26 B1
Sepolia, Athens 2 A2
Sepulveda Flood Control Basin, Los Angeles 16 A2
Serangoon, Singapore 27 A3
Serangoon, P., Singapore 27 A3
Serangoon, Sungei →, Singapore 27 A3
Serangoon Harbour, Singapore 27 A3
Seraya, P., Singapore 27 B2
Serebryanka, Moscow 19 B5
Serebryanka →, Moscow 19 B4
Serramonte, San Francisco 25 C2
Sesto San Giovanni, Milan 18 A2
Sesto Ulteriano, Milan 18 B2
Setagaya-Ku, Tokyo 29 B2
Seter, Oslo 22 A3
Setia Budi, Jakarta 13 B1
Settebagni, Rome 25 A2
Settecamini, Rome 25 B2
Séttimo Milanese, Milan 18 B1
Settsu, Osaka 22 A4
Setuny →, Moscow 19 B2
Seutula, Helsinki 12 A2
Seven Corners, Washington 32 B3
Seven Kings, London 15 A4
Sévesco →, Milan 18 A1
Sevran, Paris 23 A4
Sewri, Mumbai 20 B2
Sforzesso, Castello, Milan 18 B2
Sha Kok Mei, Hong Kong 12 A2
Sha Tin, Hong Kong 12 A2
Sha Tin Wai, Hong Kong 12 A2
Shabrâmant, Cairo 7 B2
Shahdara, Delhi 10 A2
Shahe, Canton 8 B2
Shahr-e Rey, Tehran 30 B2
Shahrak-e Golshahr, Tehran 30 B1
Shahrak-e Qods, Tehran 30 A2
Shaikh Aomar, Baghdad 3 A2
Shakurbasti, Delhi 10 A1
Shalkiya, Calcutta 8 B2
Sham Shui Po, Hong Kong 12 B1
Shamapur, Delhi 10 A1
Shamian, Canton 8 B2
Shan Mei, Hong Kong 12 A2
Shanghai, Shanghai 27 B2
Shankill, Dublin 11 B3
Sharp I., Hong Kong 12 A2
Shastrinagar, Delhi 10 A2
Shau Kei Wan, Hong Kong 12 B2
Shawocun, Beijing 4 B1
Shayuan, Canton 8 B2
Sheepshead Bay, New York 21 C2
Shek O, Hong Kong 12 B2
Shelter I., Hong Kong 12 B2
Sheng Fa Shan, Hong Kong 12 A1
Shepherds Bush, London 15 A2
Shepperton, London 15 B1
Sherman Oaks, Los Angeles 16 B2
Sherman Park, Chicago 9 C2
Shet Bandar, Mumbai 20 B2
Sheung Lau Wan, Hong Kong 12 B2
Sheung Wan, Hong Kong 12 B1
Sheva, Mumbai 20 B2
Sheva Nhava, Mumbai 20 B2
Shiba, Tokyo 29 c4
Shibpur, Calcutta 8 B1
Shibuya-Ku, Tokyo 29 c1
Shijōnawate, Osaka 22 A4
Shillim, Seoul 26 C1
Shimogawara, Tokyo 29 B1
Shimosalo, Tokyo 29 A2
Shimoshakujii, Tokyo 29 A2
Shinagawa-Ku, Tokyo 29 B3
Shing Mun Res., Hong Kong 12 A1
Shinjuku-Ku, Tokyo 29 a1
Shinjuku National Garden, Tokyo 29 a2
Shinkoiwa, Tokyo 29 A4
Shinnakano, Tokyo 29 A3
Shinsa, Seoul 26 B2
Shipai, Canton 8 B3
Shirinashi →, Osaka 22 B3
Shirogane, Tokyo 29 B3
Shiweitang, Canton 8 B2
Shogunle, Lagos 14 A2
Shomolu, Lagos 14 A2
Shooters Hill, London 15 B4
Shoreditch, London 15 a5
Shortlands, London 15 B4
Shu' afat, Jerusalem 13 B2
Shubrâ, Cairo 7 A2
Shubrâ el Kheima, Cairo 7 A2
Shuikuo, Canton 8 A2
Shuishang Park, Tianjin 30 B1
Sidcup, London 15 B4
Siebenhirten, Vienna 31 B1
Siedlung, Berlin 5 A1
Siekierki, Warsaw 31 B2
Sielce, Warsaw 31 B2
Siemensstadt, Berlin 5 A2
Sierra Madre, Los Angeles 16 B4
Sievering, Vienna 31 A2
Sighthill, Edinburgh 11 B2
Signal Hill, Cape Town 8 A1
Sihŭng, Seoul 26 C1
Sikátorpuszta, Budapest 7 A3
Silampur, Delhi 10 B2
Silver Hill, Boston 6 A2
Silver Hill, Washington 32 C4
Silver Spring, Washington 32 A3
Silvermine Nature Reserve, Cape Town 8 B1
Silvolantekojärvi, Helsinki 12 B2
Simei, Singapore 27 A3
Simla, Calcutta 8 B2
Simmering, Vienna 31 A2
Simmering Heide, Vienna 31 A2
Simonkylä, Helsinki 12 B3
Singapore, Singapore 27 B3
Singapore, Univ. of, Singapore 27 B2
Sinicka →, Moscow 19 A1
Sinki, Selat, Singapore 27 B2
Sint-Genesius-Rode, Brussels 6 B2
Sinwŏl, Seoul 26 B1
Sion, Mumbai 20 A2
Sipson, London 15 B1
Siqeil, Cairo 7 A1
Şişli, Istanbul 12 B1
Skansen, Stockholm 28 B2
Skärholmen, Stockholm 28 B1
Skarpäng, Stockholm 28 A2
Skarpnäck, Stockholm 28 B2
Skaryszewski Park, Warsaw 31 B2
Skeppsholmen, Stockholm 28 c3
Skokie, Chicago 9 A2
Skokie →, Chicago 9 A2
Skoklefall, Oslo 22 A3
Sköndal, Stockholm 28 B2
Skovlunde, Copenhagen 10 A2
Skovshoved, Copenhagen 10 A3
Skuru, Stockholm 28 B3
Skyland, Atlanta 3 A3
Slade Green, London 15 B5
Slemmestad, Oslo 22 B1
Slependen, Oslo 22 A2
Slipi, Jakarta 13 B1
Slivenec, Prague 24 B2
Sloten, Amsterdam 2 A1
Sloterpark, Amsterdam 2 A1
Sluhy, Prague 24 A3
Służew, Warsaw 31 B2
Służewiec, Warsaw 31 B2
Smíchov, Prague 24 B2
Smith Forest Preserve, Chicago 9 B2
Smithsonian Institute, Washington 32 b2
Smolny, St. Petersburg 26 B2
Snake Creek Canal →, Miami 18 A2
Snarøya, Oslo 22 A2
Snättringe, Stockholm 28 B1
Sŏbinggo, Seoul 26 B1
Søborg, Copenhagen 10 A2
Sobreda, Lisbon 14 B1
Soch'o, Seoul 26 C1
Sŏdaemun, Seoul 26 B1
Söderby, Stockholm 28 A3
Södermalm, Stockholm 28 B2
Sodpur, Calcutta 8 A2
Soeurs, Î. des, Montreal 19 B2
Sognsvatn, Oslo 22 A3
Soho, London 15 b3
Soho, New York 21 e1
Soignes, Forêt de, Brussels 6 B2
Sok Kwu Wan, Hong Kong 12 B1
Sŏkkwan, Seoul 26 B2
Sokolniki, Moscow 19 B4
Sokolniki Park, Moscow 19 B4
Sokołów, Warsaw 31 C1
Solalinden, Munich 20 B3
Soldier Field, Chicago 9 e3
Sollentuna, Stockholm 28 A1
Solln, Munich 20 B2
Solna, Stockholm 28 A1
Solntsevo, Moscow 19 C2
Somerset, Washington 32 B3
Somerville, Boston 6 A3
Somes Is., Wellington 32 B2
Sonari, Mumbai 20 B2
Søndersø, Copenhagen 10 A2
Sŏngbuk, Seoul 26 B2
Sŏngdong, Seoul 26 B2
Sŏngp'a, Seoul 26 B2
Sŏngsu, Seoul 26 B2
Soong Qingling, Former Res. of, Beijing 4 a2
Soroksár, Budapest 7 B2
Soroksari Duna →, Budapest 7 B2
Sosenka →, Moscow 19 B4
Sosnovka, St. Petersburg 26 B2
Sŏul, Seoul 26 B2
Soundview, New York 21 B2
South Beach, New York 21 C1
South Beach Harbor, San Francisco 25 c3
South Bend Park, Atlanta 3 B2
South Boston, Boston 6 A3
South Brooklyn, New York 21 B2
South Decatur, Atlanta 3 B3
South Deering, Chicago 9 C3
South El Monte, Los Angeles 16 B4
South Gate, Los Angeles 16 C3
South Harbor, Manila 17 B1
South Harrow, London 15 A1
South Hd., Sydney 28 B2
South Hills, Johannesburg 13 B2
South Hornchurch, London 15 A5
South Kensington, London 15 c2
South Lawn, Washington 32 C3
South Lincoln, Boston 6 A2
South Miami, Miami 18 B1
South Norwood, London 15 B3
South of Market, San Francisco 25 B2
South Ozone Park, New York 21 B3
South Pasadena, Los Angeles 16 B4
South Res., Boston 6 A3
South Ruislip, London 15 A1
South San Francisco, San Francisco 25 C2
South San Gabriel, Los Angeles 16 B4
South Shore, Chicago 9 C3
South Sudbury, Boston 6 A1
Southall, London 15 A1
Southborough, London 15 B4
Southend, London 15 B3
Southfields, London 15 B2
Southwark, London 15 B3
Søvang, Copenhagen 10 B3
Soweto, Johannesburg 13 B1
Sowhānak, Tehran 30 A3
Soya, Tokyo 29 A4
Spandau, Berlin 5 A1
Spånga, Stockholm 28 A1
Spanische Reitschule, Vienna 31 b1
Spectacle I., Boston 6 A4
Speicher-See, Munich 20 A3
Speising, Vienna 31 B1
Sphinx, Cairo 7 B1
Spinaceto, Rome 25 C1
Spit Junction, Sydney 28 A2
Spořilov, Prague 24 B3
Spot Pond, Boston 6 A3
Spotswood, Melbourne 17 B1
Spree →, Berlin 5 A2
Spring Pond, Boston 6 A4
Springeberg, Berlin 5 B5
Springfield, Washington 32 C2
Squantum, Boston 6 B3
Srednaya Rogatka, St. Petersburg 26 C2
Śródmieście, Warsaw 31 B2
Staaken, Berlin 5 A1
Stabekk, Oslo 22 A2
Stadhion, Athens 2 c3
Stadhuis, Amsterdam 2 b2
Stadlau, Vienna 31 A2
Stadshuset, Stockholm 28 b1
Stains, Paris 23 A3
Stamford Hill, London 15 A3
Stammersdorf, Vienna 31 A2
Stanley, Hong Kong 12 B2
Stanley Mound, Hong Kong 12 B2
Stanley Pen., Hong Kong 12 B2
Stanmore, London 15 A2
Stapleton, New York 21 C1
Star Ferry, Hong Kong 12 a2
Staraya Derevnya, St. Petersburg 26 B1
Stare, Warsaw 31 B2
Staré Město, Prague 24 B2
Starego Miasto, Warsaw 31 a2
Staten Island Zoo, New York 21 C1
Statenice, Prague 24 B1
Statue Square, Hong Kong 12 c1
Stedelijk Museum, Amsterdam 2 c1
Steele Creek, Melbourne 17 A1
Steenokkerzeel, Brussels 6 A2
Steglitz, Berlin 5 B2
Stepaside, Dublin 11 B2
Stephansdom, Vienna 31 b2
Stepney, London 15 A3
Sterling Park, San Francisco 25 B2
Sticklinge udde, Stockholm 28 A2
Stickney, Chicago 9 C2
Stillorgan, Dublin 11 B2
Stockholm, Stockholm 28 B2
Stocksund, Stockholm 28 A2
Stodůlky, Prague 24 B1
Stoke Newington, London 15 A3
Stokes Valley, Wellington 32 B2
Stone Canyon Res., Los Angeles 16 B2
Stone Park, Chicago 9 B1
Stonebridge, London 15 A2
Stoneham, Boston 6 A3
Stony Brook Res., Boston 6 B3
Stora Värtan, Stockholm 28 A2
Store Hareskov, Copenhagen 10 A2
Store Magleby, Copenhagen 10 B3
Storholmen, Stockholm 28 A2
Stoyka, St. Petersburg 26 B2
Straiton, Edinburgh 11 B3
Strand, London 15 b4
Strandfontein, Cape Town 8 B2
Strašnice, Prague 24 B2
Strasstrudering, Munich 20 B3
Stratford, London 15 A4
Strathfield, Sydney 28 B1
Streatham, London 15 B3
Streatham Vale, London 15 B3
Strebersdorf, Vienna 31 A2
Střešovice, Prague 24 B2
Střížkov, Prague 24 B2
Strogino, Moscow 19 B2
Strombeek-Bever, Brussels 6 A2
Stromovka, Prague 24 B2
Studio City, Los Angeles 16 B2
Stureby, Stockholm 28 B2
Stuvsta, Stockholm 28 B2
Subhepur, Delhi 10 A2
Sucat, Manila 17 C2
Suchdol, Prague 24 B2
Sucy-en-Brie, Paris 23 B4
Sudbury, Boston 6 A1
Sugamo, Tokyo 29 A3
Sugar Loaf Mt. = Açúcar, Pão de, Rio de Janeiro 24 B2
Suge, Tokyo 29 B2
Suginami-Ku, Tokyo 29 A2
Sugō, Tokyo 29 B2
Suita, Osaka 22 A4
Suitland, Washington 32 B4
Sukchar, Calcutta 8 A2
Suma, Osaka 22 B1
Sumida →, Tokyo 29 A3
Sumida-Ku, Tokyo 29 A3
Sumiyoshi, Osaka 22 B4
Summerville, Toronto 30 B1
Summit, Chicago 9 C2
Sunamachi, Tokyo 29 A4
Sunbury-on-Thames, London 15 B1
Sundbyberg, Stockholm 28 A1
Sundbyerne, Copenhagen 10 B3
Sung Kong, Hong Kong 12 B2
Sungei Kadut Industrial Estate, Singapore 27 A2
Sungei Selatar Res., Singapore 27 A3
Sunter, Jakarta 13 A2
Sunter, Kali →, Jakarta 13 B2
Suomenlinna, Helsinki 12 C2
Supreme Court, Washington 32 b3
Sura, Calcutta 8 B2
Surag-san, Seoul 26 A2
Surbiton, London 15 B2
Suresnes, Paris 23 A2
Surfside, Miami 18 A2
Surquillo, Lima 16 B2
Surrey Hills, Sydney 28 B2
Susaek, Seoul 26 B1
Süssenbrunn, Vienna 31 A2
Sutton, Dublin 11 A3
Sutton, London 15 B2
Suyu, Seoul 26 B2
Suzukishinden, Tokyo 29 A2
Svanemøllen, Copenhagen 10 A3
Sverdlov, Moscow 19 B3
Svestad, Oslo 22 B2
Svinö, Helsinki 12 C1
Swampscott, Boston 6 A4
Swanley, London 15 B4
Swansea, Toronto 30 B2
Swinburne I., New York 21 C1
Swords, Dublin 11 A2
Sydenham, Johannesburg 13 A2
Sydney, Sydney 28 B2
Sydney, Univ. of, Sydney 28 B2
Sydney Airport, Sydney 28 B2
Sydney Harbour Bridge, Sydney 28 B2
Sydstranden, Copenhagen 10 B3
Sylvania, Sydney 28 C1
Syntagma, Pl., Athens 2 b3
Syon Park, London 15 B2
Szczęsliwice, Warsaw 31 B1
Széchnenyi-hegy, Budapest 7 B1
Szent Istvánbaz, Budapest 7 b2
Széphalom, Budapest 7 A1

T

Tabata, Tokyo 29 A3
Tablada, Buenos Aires 7 C1
Table Bay, Cape Town 8 A1
Table Mountain, Cape Town 8 A1
Taboão da Serra, São Paulo 26 B1
Täby, Stockholm 28 A2
Tacuba, Mexico City 18 B1
Tacubaya, Mexico City 18 B1
Taebang, Seoul 26 B1

Zyuzino 39

Tagig, *Manila* 17 B2
Tagig →, *Manila* 17 B2
Tai Hang, *Hong Kong* 12 B2
Tai Lo Shan, *Hong Kong* 12 A2
Tai Po Tsai, *Hong Kong* 12 A2
Tai Seng, *Singapore* 27 A3
Tai Shui Hang, *Hong Kong* 12 A2
Tai Tam B., *Hong Kong* 12 B2
Tai Tam Tuk Res., *Hong Kong* 12 B2
Tai Wai, *Hong Kong* 12 A1
Tai Wan Tau, *Hong Kong* 12 B2
Tai Wo Hau, *Hong Kong* 12 A1
Tainaka, *Osaka* 22 B4
Taishō, *Osaka* 22 B3
Taita, *Wellington* 32 B2
Tajrīsh, *Tehran* 30 A2
Takaido, *Tokyo* 29 A2
Takaishi, *Tokyo* 29 B2
Takarazuka, *Osaka* 22 A2
Takasago, *Tokyo* 29 A4
Takatsu-Ku, *Tokyo* 29 B2
Takeshita, *Tokyo* 29 B2
Takinegawa, *Tokyo* 29 A3
Takoma Park, *Washington* 32 B3
Taksim, *Istanbul* 12 B1
Talaide, *Lisbon* 14 A1
Taliganga, *Calcutta* 8 B2
Talipapa, *Manila* 17 A2
Tallaght, *Dublin* 11 B1
Tallkrogen, *Stockholm* 28 B2
Tama, *Tokyo* 29 B1
Tama →, *Tokyo* 29 B2
Tama Kyūryō, *Tokyo* 29 B2
Tamaden, *Tokyo* 29 B2
Tamagawa-josui →, *Tokyo* 29 A1
Taman Sari, *Jakarta* 13 A1
Tamanduateí →, *São Paulo* 26 B2
Tamboerskloof, *Cape Town* 8 A1
Tambora, *Jakarta* 13 A1
Tammisalo, *Helsinki* 12 B3
Tammûh, *Cairo* 7 B2
Tampines, *Singapore* 27 A3
Tanah Abang, *Jakarta* 13 B1
Tanigami, *Osaka* 22 A2
Tanjung Duren, *Jakarta* 13 B1
Tanjung Priok, *Jakarta* 13 A2
Tanum, *Oslo* 22 A1
Taoranting Park, *Beijing* 4 c2
Tapada, *Lisbon* 14 A1
Tapanila, *Helsinki* 12 B3
Tapiales, *Buenos Aires* 7 C1
Tapiola, *Helsinki* 12 B1
Tapsia, *Calcutta* 8 B2
Tara, *Mumbai* 20 A1
Tarabya, *Istanbul* 12 B2
Tarango, Presa, *Mexico City* 18 B1
Tårbæk, *Copenhagen* 10 A3
Tarchomin, *Warsaw* 31 B1
Tardeo, *Mumbai* 20 B1
Targówek, *Warsaw* 31 B2
Tårnby, *Copenhagen* 10 B3
Tarqua Bay, *Lagos* 14 B2
Tåstrup, *Copenhagen* 10 B1
Tatarovo, *Moscow* 19 B2
Tathong Channel, *Hong Kong* 12 B2
Tathong Pt., *Hong Kong* 12 B2
Tatuapé, *São Paulo* 26 B2
Taufkirchen, *Munich* 20 B2
Tavares, I. dos, *Rio de Janeiro* 24 A2
Távros, *Athens* 2 B2
Tawa, *Wellington* 32 A1
Teaneck, *New York* 21 A1
Teatro Municipal, *Rio de Janeiro* 24 c2
Tebet, *Jakarta* 13 B2
Tecamachaleo, *Mexico City* 18 B1
Teddington, *London* 15 B1
Tegel, *Berlin* 5 A2
Tegel, Flughafen, *Berlin* 5 A2
Tegeler See, *Berlin* 5 A2
Tegelort, *Berlin* 5 A2
Tehrān, *Tehran* 30 A2
Tehrān Pārs, *Tehran* 30 A3
Tei Tong Tsui, *Hong Kong* 12 B2
Tejo, Rio →, *Lisbon* 14 A2
Tekstilyshchik, *Moscow* 19 B4
Telegraph hill, *San Francisco* 25 a2
Telhal, *Lisbon* 14 A1
Telok Blangah, *Singapore* 27 B2
Teltow, *Berlin* 5 B2
Teltow kanal, *Berlin* 5 B3
Temnikovo, *Moscow* 19 B6
Tempelhof, *Berlin* 5 B3
Tempelhof, Flughafen, *Berlin* 5 B3
Temple City, *Los Angeles* 16 B4
Temple Hills Park, *Washington* 32 C4
Temple Mount, *Jerusalem* 13 b3
Templeogue, *Dublin* 11 B2
Templo Mayor, *Mexico City* 18 b3
Tenafly, *New York* 21 A2
Tenayuca, Piramide de, *Mexico City* 18 A1
Tengah →, *Singapore* 27 A2
Tennoji, *Osaka* 22 B4
Tepalcates, *Mexico City* 18 B2
Terrazzano, *Milan* 18 A1
Terrugem, *Lisbon* 14 A1
Tervuren, *Brussels* 6 B3
Tervuren, Park van, *Brussels* 6 B3
Tetuán, *Madrid* 17 B1
Teufelsberg, *Berlin* 5 B2
Tévere →, *Rome* 25 B1
Thalkirchen, *Munich* 20 B2
Thames →, *London* 15 A4
Thames Ditton, *London* 15 B1
Thamesmead, *London* 15 A4
Thana Cr. →, *Mumbai* 20 A2
The Loop, *Chicago* 9 B3
The Ridge, *Delhi* 10 B2
The Wilds, *Johannesburg* 13 B2
Theater Carré, *Amsterdam* 2 b2
Théatro Dionissou, *Athens* 2 c2
Thiais, *Paris* 23 B3
Thissío, *Athens* 2 c1
Thistletown, *Toronto* 30 A1
Thomastown, *Melbourne* 17 A2
Thompson I., *Boston* 6 B4
Thon Buri, *Bangkok* 3 B1
Thornbury, *Melbourne* 17 A2
Thorncliffe, *Toronto* 30 A2
Thornhill, *Toronto* 30 A2
Thornton, *Cape Town* 8 A2
Thornton Heath, *London* 15 B3
Threipmuir Res., *Edinburgh* 11 B2
Throgs Neck, *New York* 21 B3
Thyssen Bornemisza, Museo, *Madrid* 17 b3
Tian'anmen Square, *Beijing* 4 B2
Tiancun, *Beijing* 4 B1
Tianjin, *Tianjin* 30 B1
Tiantan Park, *Beijing* 4 c2
Tibidabo, *Barcelona* 4 A1
Tibradden Mt., *Dublin* 11 B2
Tiburon, *San Francisco* 25 A2
Tiburtino, *Rome* 25 B2
Ticomán, *Mexico City* 18 A2
Tiefersee, *Berlin* 5 B1
Tiejiangyin, *Beijing* 4 C2
Tientsin = Tianjin, *Tianjin* 30 B1
Tiergarten, *Berlin* 5 A3
Tietê →, *São Paulo* 26 B2
Tigerhof, *Cape Town* 8 A2
Tigris = Nahr Dijlah →, *Baghdad* 3 B2
Tijuca, *Rio de Janeiro* 24 B1
Tijuca, Parque Nacional da, *Rio de Janeiro* 24 B1
Tijuca, Pico da, *Rio de Janeiro* 24 B1
Tikkurila, *Helsinki* 12 B3
Tilak Nagar, *Delhi* 10 B1
Tilanqiao, *Shanghai* 27 B1
Timah, Bukit, *Singapore* 27 A2
Times Square, *New York* 21 c2
Timiryazev Park, *Moscow* 19 B3
Ting Kau, *Hong Kong* 12 A1
Tira, *Jerusalem* 13 A1
Tirsa, *Cairo* 7 B2
Tishrīyaa, *Baghdad* 3 B2
Tiu Keng Leng, *Hong Kong* 12 B2
Tivoli, *Copenhagen* 10 a3
Tizapán, *Mexico City* 18 C1
Tlalnepantla →, *Mexico City* 18 A1
To Kwai Wan, *Hong Kong* 12 B2
Toa Payoh, *Singapore* 27 A3
Tobong, *Seoul* 26 B2
Tobong-san, *Seoul* 26 A2
Točná, *Prague* 24 C2
Toco Hills, *Atlanta* 3 B2
Todt Hill, *New York* 21 C1
Tōkagi, *Tokyo* 29 A4
Tokai Plantation, *Cape Town* 8 B1
Tōkaichiba, *Tokyo* 29 B2
Tokarevo, *Moscow* 19 C5
Tōkyō, *Tokyo* 29 B3
Tokyo B., *Tokyo* 29 B4
Tokyo-Haneda Int. Airport, *Tokyo* 29 B3
Tokyo Harbour, *Tokyo* 29 B3
Tolka R. →, *Dublin* 11 A1
Tolworth, *London* 15 B2
Tomb of Lu Xun, *Shanghai* 27 B1
Tomb of the Kings, *Jerusalem* 13 a2
Tomba di Nerone, *Rome* 25 B1
Tomilino, *Moscow* 19 C5
Tondo, *Manila* 17 B1
Tongbinggo, *Seoul* 26 B1
Tongjak, *Seoul* 26 B1
Tongmaemung, *Seoul* 26 B2
Tongqiao, *Shanghai* 27 A1
Toorak, *Melbourne* 17 B2
Topkapı, *Istanbul* 12 B1
Tor di Quinto, *Rome* 25 B1
Tor Pignattara, *Rome* 25 B2
Tor Sapienza, *Rome* 25 B2
Toranomon, *Tokyo* 29 c3
Torcy, *Paris* 23 A4
Toronto, *Toronto* 30 B3
Toronto, Univ. of, *Toronto* 30 B2
Toronto Harbour, *Toronto* 30 B2
Toronto I., *Toronto* 30 B2
Toronto Int. Airport, *Toronto* 30 A1
Toros Las Arenas, Pl. de, *Barcelona* 4 c1
Toros Monumental, Templo de, *Barcelona* 4 a3
Torre Latino-americana, *Mexico City* 18 b2
Torre Lupara, *Rome* 25 B2
Torre Nova, *Rome* 25 B2
Torrellas →, *Barcelona* 4 A1
Torrevécchia, *Rome* 25 B1
Toshima-Ku, *Tokyo* 29 A3
Toshimaen, *Tokyo* 29 A2
Tottenham, *London* 15 A3
Tottenham, *Melbourne* 17 A1
Tour Eiffel, *Paris* 23 c2
Toussus-le-Noble, *Paris* 23 B1
Toussus-le-Noble, Aérodrome de, *Paris* 23 B1
Tower Bridge, *London* 15 b5
Tower Hamlets, *London* 15 A3
Tower of London, *London* 15 A3
Towra Pt., *Sydney* 28 C2
Tøyen, *Oslo* 22 A3
Toyonaka, *Osaka* 22 A3
Trafalgar Square, *London* 15 b3
Trafaria, *Lisbon* 14 A1
Traição, Cor. →, *São Paulo* 26 B2
Tranegilde, *Copenhagen* 10 B2
Trångsund, *Stockholm* 28 B2
Transamerica Pyramid, *San Francisco* 25 b2
Transbay Terminal, *San Francisco* 25 b3
Trappenfelde, *Berlin* 5 A4
Trastévere, *Rome* 25 B1
Treasure I., *San Francisco* 25 B2
Třeboradice, *Prague* 24 B3
Třebotov, *Prague* 24 C1
Tremblay-en-France, *Paris* 23 A4
Tremembe →, *São Paulo* 26 A2
Tremont, *New York* 21 A2
Trenno, *Milan* 18 B1
Treptow, *Berlin* 5 B3
Trés Rios, Sa. dos, *Rio de Janeiro* 24 B1
Trevi, Fontana di, *Rome* 25 b3
Trezzano sul Navíglio, *Milan* 18 B1
Tribune Tower, *Chicago* 9 b2
Trieste, *Rome* 25 B2
Trinidad, *Washington* 32 B4
Trinity, *Edinburgh* 11 B2
Trinity College, *Dublin* 11 c3
Trionfale, *Rome* 25 B1
Triulzo, *Milan* 18 B2
Trocadero, *Paris* 23 b1
Troitse-Lykovo, *Moscow* 19 B2
Troja, *Prague* 24 B2
Trollbäcken, *Stockholm* 28 B3
Trombay, *Mumbai* 20 A2
Troparevo, *Moscow* 19 C2
Tropenmuseum, *Amsterdam* 2 b3
Trudyashchikhsya, Ostrov, *St. Petersburg* 26 B1
Tryvasshøgda, *Oslo* 22 A3
Tseng Lan Shue, *Hong Kong* 12 A2
Tsim Sha Tsui, *Hong Kong* 12 a2
Tsing Yi, *Hong Kong* 12 A1
Tsova, *Jerusalem* 13 B1
Tsuen Wan, *Hong Kong* 12 A1
Tsukiji, *Tokyo* 29 c5
Tsur Hadassa, *Jerusalem* 13 B1
Tsurumi →, *Tokyo* 29 B3
Tsz Wan Shan, *Hong Kong* 12 A2
Tuas, *Singapore* 27 B1
Tuchoměřice, *Prague* 24 B1
Tuckahoe, *New York* 21 A3
Tucuruvi, *São Paulo* 26 A2
Tufello, *Rome* 25 B2
Tufnell Park, *London* 15 A3
Tughlakabad, *Delhi* 10 B2
Tuileries, Jardin des, *Paris* 23 b3
Tuindorp Oostzaan, *Amsterdam* 2 A2
Tullamarine, *Melbourne* 17 A1
Tulse Hill, *London* 15 B3
Tung Lung I., *Hong Kong* 12 B2
Tung O, *Hong Kong* 12 B1
Tunis, *Baghdad* 3 A2
Tuomarila, *Helsinki* 12 B1
Tureberg, *Stockholm* 28 A1
Turffontein, *Johannesburg* 13 B2
Turkso, *Prague* 24 A1
Turnham Green, *London* 15 B2
Turnhouse, *Edinburgh* 11 B1
Tuscolana, Via, *Rome* 25 B2
Tushino, *Moscow* 19 A2
Twelve Apostles, *Cape Town* 8 A1
Twickenham, *London* 15 B1
Twickenham Rugby Ground, *London* 15 B1
Twin Peaks, *San Francisco* 25 B2
Two Rock Mt., *Dublin* 11 B2
Tymon North, *Dublin* 11 B1
Tysons Corner, *Washington* 32 B2

U

U.S. Capitol, *Washington* 32 b3
Ubeidiya, *Jerusalem* 13 B2
Uberaba →, *São Paulo* 26 B2
Ubin, P., *Singapore* 27 A3
Uccle, *Brussels* 6 B2
Udelnaya, *St. Petersburg* 26 A2
Udelnoe, *St. Petersburg* 26 B1
Udlding, *Munich* 20 A1
Ueno, *Tokyo* 29 A3
Üholičky, *Prague* 24 B1
Uhříněves, *Prague* 24 B3
Uithoorn, *Amsterdam* 2 B1
Újpalota, *Budapest* 7 A2
Újpest, *Budapest* 7 A2
Ukita, *Tokyo* 29 A4
Ullerup, *Copenhagen* 10 B3
Ullevål, *Oslo* 22 A3
Ulriksdal, *Stockholm* 28 A1
Ulyanka, *St. Petersburg* 26 B1
Um Al-Khanazir Island, *Baghdad* 3 B2
Umeda, *Osaka* 22 A3
Umerkhadi, *Mumbai* 20 b2
Ümraniye, *Istanbul* 12 B2
Underground Atlanta, *Atlanta* 3 B2
Unětický potok →, *Prague* 24 B2
Ŭngam, *Seoul* 26 B1
Unhos, *Lisbon* 14 A2
Unidad Santa Fe, *Mexico City* 18 B1
Union City, *New York* 21 B1
Union Port, *New York* 21 B2
Union Square, *New York* 21 d2
Union Square, *San Francisco* 25 b2
Union Station, *Washington* 32 b3
United Nations H.Q., *New York* 21 c3
Universidad, *Madrid* 17 B1
Universidad de Chile, *Santiago* 26 B2
University Park, *Washington* 32 B4
Unp'yong, *Seoul* 26 B1
Unter den Linden, *Berlin* 5 a4
Unterbiberg, *Munich* 20 B2
Unterföhring, *Munich* 20 A3
Unterhaching, *Munich* 20 B2
Unterlaa, *Vienna* 31 B2
Untermenzing, *Munich* 20 A1
Upper East Side, *New York* 21 b3
Upper Elmers End, *London* 15 B3
Upper New York B., *New York* 21 C1
Upper Norwood, *London* 15 B3
Upper Peirce Res., *Singapore* 27 A2
Upper Sydenham, *London* 15 B3
Upper Tooting, *London* 15 B3
Upper West Side, *New York* 21 a2
Upton, *London* 15 A4
Uptown, *Chicago* 9 B2
Uran, *Mumbai* 20 B2
Urayasu, *Tokyo* 29 B4
Urbe, Aeroporto d', *Rome* 25 B2
Urca, *Rio de Janeiro* 24 B2
Uritsk, *St. Petersburg* 26 C1
Üröm, *Budapest* 7 A2
Ursus, *Warsaw* 31 B1
Ursvik, *Stockholm* 28 A1
Usera, *Madrid* 17 B1
Ushigome, *Tokyo* 29 A3
Usina, *Rio de Janeiro* 24 B1
Üsküdar, *Istanbul* 12 B2
Ust-Slavyanka, *St. Petersburg* 26 C3
Uteke, *Stockholm* 28 A3
Utrata, *Warsaw* 31 B2
Uttarpara, *Calcutta* 8 B1
Utterslev Mose, *Copenhagen* 10 A2

V

Vadaul, *Mumbai* 20 A2
Vaires-sur-Marne, *Paris* 23 A4
Valby, *Copenhagen* 10 B2
Valcannuta, *Rome* 25 B1
Valdelatas, *Madrid* 17 A1
Vale, *Washington* 32 B1
Valenton, *Paris* 23 B3
Valera, *Milan* 18 A1
Vallcarca, *Barcelona* 4 A1
Valldoreix, *Barcelona* 4 A1
Vallecas, *Madrid* 17 B2
Vallensbæk, *Copenhagen* 10 B2
Vallensbæk Strand, *Copenhagen* 10 B2
Vallentunasjön, *Stockholm* 28 A2
Valleranello, *Rome* 25 C1
Vallisaari, *Helsinki* 12 C3
Vallvidrera, *Barcelona* 4 A1
Valvidrera →, *Barcelona* 4 A1
Van Goghmuseum, *Amsterdam* 2 c1
Vanak, *Tehran* 30 A2
Vangede, *Copenhagen* 10 A3
Vaniköy, *Istanbul* 12 B2
Vanløse, *Copenhagen* 10 A2
Vantaa, *Helsinki* 12 B2
Vantaa →, *Helsinki* 12 B2
Vantaankoski, *Helsinki* 12 B2
Vantaanpuisto, *Helsinki* 12 B2
Vanves, *Paris* 23 B2
Varedo, *Milan* 18 A1
Varkiza, *Athens* 2 C2
Varszínház, *Budapest* 7 b2
Vartiokylä, *Helsinki* 12 B3
Vartiosaari, *Helsinki* 12 B3
Vasamuseet, *Stockholm* 28 b3
Vasco, *Cape Town* 8 A2
Vasfanārd, *Tehran* 30 B2
Vashi, *Mumbai* 20 A2
Vasilyevskiy, Ostrov, *St. Petersburg* 26 B1
Vaso Regulador El Cristo, *Mexico City* 18 B1
Vaucluse, *Sydney* 28 B2
Vaucresson, *Paris* 23 A1
Vauhallan, *Paris* 23 B2
Vaujours, *Paris* 23 A4
Vauxhall, *London* 15 c4
Vecsés, *Budapest* 7 B3
Veleň, *Prague* 24 A3
Veleslavin, *Prague* 24 B2
Vélizy-Villacoublay, *Paris* 23 B2
Velka-Chuchle, *Prague* 24 B2
Velké Přilepy, *Prague* 24 B1
Venda Seca, *Lisbon* 14 A1
Venetian Islands, *Miami* 18 B2
Venezia, Palazzo, *Rome* 25 c2
Venice, *Los Angeles* 16 C2
Ventas, *Madrid* 17 B1
Ventorro del Cano, *Madrid* 17 B1
Venustiano Carranza, *Mexico City* 18 B2
Verde →, *São Paulo* 26 A1
Verdi, *Athens* 2 A2
Verdun, *Montreal* 19 B2
Vérhalom, *Budapest* 7 A2
Vermelho →, *São Paulo* 26 B1
Vernon, *Los Angeles* 16 B3
Verrières-le-Buisson, *Paris* 23 B2
Versailles, *Buenos Aires* 7 B1
Versailles, *Paris* 23 B1
Veshnyaki, *Moscow* 19 B4
Vesolyy Posolok, *St. Petersburg* 26 B2
Vestra, *Helsinki* 12 B1
Vestskoven, *Copenhagen* 10 A2
Vicálvaro, *Madrid* 17 B2
Vicente Lopez, *Buenos Aires* 7 B2
Victoria, *Hong Kong* 12 B2
Victoria, *London* 15 c3
Victoria, Mt., *Wellington* 32 B1
Victoria, Pont, *Montreal* 19 B2
Victoria and Albert Waterfront, *Cape Town* 8 a1
Victoria Gardens, *Mumbai* 20 B2
Victoria Harbour, *Hong Kong* 12 B1
Victoria Island, *Lagos* 14 B2
Victoria L., *Johannesburg* 13 B2
Victoria Lawn Tennis Courts, *Melbourne* 17 B2
Victoria Park, *Singapore* 27 B2
Victoria Peak, *Hong Kong* 12 B1
Victoria Wharf, *Cape Town* 8 a2
Vienna = Wien, *Vienna* 31 A2
Vienna, *Washington* 32 B2
View Park, *Los Angeles* 16 B3
Vigário Geral, *Rio de Janeiro* 24 A1
Vigentino, *Milan* 18 B2
Viggbyholm, *Stockholm* 28 A2
Vighignolo, *Milan* 18 B1
Viikki, *Helsinki* 12 B3
Vikhroli, *Mumbai* 20 A2
Vila Guilherme, *São Paulo* 26 B2
Vila Isabel, *Rio de Janeiro* 24 B1
Vila Jaguára, *São Paulo* 26 B1
Vila Madalena, *São Paulo* 26 B1
Vila Maria, *São Paulo* 26 B2
Vila Mariana, *São Paulo* 26 B2
Vila Prudente, *São Paulo* 26 B2
Viladecans, *Barcelona* 4 B1
Vile Parle, *Mumbai* 20 A2
Villa Adelina, *Buenos Aires* 7 B1
Villa Ballester, *Buenos Aires* 7 B1
Villa Barilari, *Buenos Aires* 7 C2
Villa Borghese, *Rome* 25 a3
Villa Bosch, *Buenos Aires* 7 B1
Villa C. Colon, *Buenos Aires* 7 C2
Villa Ciudadela, *Buenos Aires* 7 B1
Villa de Guadalupe, *Mexico City* 18 B2
Villa Devoto, *Buenos Aires* 7 B1
Villa Diamante, *Buenos Aires* 7 C2
Villa Dominico, *Buenos Aires* 7 C3
Villa Lugano, *Buenos Aires* 7 C2
Villa Lynch, *Buenos Aires* 7 B1
Villa Madero, *Buenos Aires* 7 C1
Villa Sáenz Pena, *Buenos Aires* 7 B1
Villa Urquiza, *Buenos Aires* 7 B2
Villaverde, *Madrid* 17 B1
Villaverde Bajo, *Madrid* 17 B1
Ville-d'Avray, *Paris* 23 B2
Villecresnes, *Paris* 23 B4
Villejuif, *Paris* 23 B3
Villemomble, *Paris* 23 A4
Villeneuve-la-Garenne, *Paris* 23 A2
Villeneuve-le-Roi, *Paris* 23 B3
Villeneuve-St.-Georges, *Paris* 23 B3
Villeparisis, *Paris* 23 A4
Villevaudé, *Paris* 23 A4
Villiers-le-Bâcle, *Paris* 23 B1
Villiers-sur-Marne, *Paris* 23 B4
Villinki, *Helsinki* 12 C3
Villoresi, Canale, *Milan* 18 A1
Vilvoorde, *Brussels* 6 A2
Vimodrone, *Milan* 18 A2
Vimont, *Montreal* 19 A1
Vinanmek Palace, *Bangkok* 3 a2
Vincennes, *Paris* 23 A3
Vincennes, Bois de, *Paris* 23 B3
Vinings, *Atlanta* 3 A2
Vinohrady, *Prague* 24 c3
Vinoř, *Prague* 24 B3
Violet Hill, *Hong Kong* 12 B2
Virányos, *Budapest* 7 A1
Virgen del San Cristóbal, *Santiago* 26 B2
Virginia Gardens, *Miami* 18 B1
Virginia Key, *Miami* 18 B2
Viroflay, *Paris* 23 B2
Víron, *Athens* 2 B2
Virum, *Copenhagen* 10 A2
Vishnyaki, *Moscow* 19 B5
Visitacion Valley, *San Francisco* 25 B2
Vista Alegre, *Lima* 16 B3
Vista Alegre, *Santiago* 26 C1
Vista Grove, *Atlanta* 3 A3
Vitacura, *Santiago* 26 B2
Vitinia, *Rome* 25 C1
Vitry-sur-Seine, *Paris* 23 B3
Vizandinó, Moussío, *Athens* 2 b3
Vladykino, *Moscow* 19 A3
Vlezenbeek, *Brussels* 6 B1
Vltava →, *Prague* 24 A2
Vnukovo, *Moscow* 19 C1
Vokovice, *Prague* 24 B2
Volgelsdorf, *Berlin* 5 B5
Volkhonka-Zil, *Moscow* 19 C3
Vollen, *Oslo* 22 B1
Volodarskoye, *St. Petersburg* 26 B2
Volynkina-Derevnya, *St. Petersburg* 26 B1
Vondelpark, *Amsterdam* 2 A2
Vösendorf, *Vienna* 31 B2
Vostochnyy, *Moscow* 19 B5
Voula, *Athens* 2 C2
Vouliagmeni, *Athens* 2 C2
Vredehoek, *Cape Town* 8 A1
Vršovice, *Prague* 24 B2
Vyborgskaya Storona, *St. Petersburg* 26 B2
Vykhino, *Moscow* 19 B4
Vyšehrad, *Prague* 24 B2

W

Wachterhof, *Munich* 20 B3
Wadala, *Mumbai* 20 A2
Wadestown, *Wellington* 32 B1
Wadi Fukin, *Jerusalem* 13 B1
Wah Fu, *Hong Kong* 12 B1
Wahda, *Baghdad* 3 B2
Währing, *Vienna* 31 A2
Waidmannslust, *Berlin* 5 A3
Wainuiomata, *Wellington* 32 B2
Wainuiomata R. →, *Wellington* 32 B2
Wakefield, *Boston* 6 A3
Waldesruh, *Berlin* 5 B4
Waldperlach, *Munich* 20 B3
Waldtrudering, *Munich* 20 B3
Walkinstown, *Dublin* 11 B1
Wall Street, *New York* 21 f1
Waltham, *Boston* 6 A2
Waltham Forest, *London* 15 A3
Walthamstow, *London* 15 A3
Walton on Thames, *London* 15 B1
Wambeek, *Brussels* 6 A3
Wan Chai, *Hong Kong* 12 B2
Wan Chai Lanes, *Hong Kong* 12 c2
Wandsworth, *London* 15 B2
Wankhede Stadium, *Mumbai* 20 c2
Wannsee, *Berlin* 5 B1
Wansdorf, *Berlin* 5 A1
Wanstead, *London* 15 A4
Wapping, *London* 15 A3
Ward, *Dublin* 11 A1
Ward I., *Wellington* 32 B2
Warnberg, *Munich* 20 B2
Warrâq el 'Arab, *Cairo* 7 A2
Warrâq el Hadr, *Cairo* 7 A2
Warringen Park, *Melbourne* 17 A2
Warriston, *Edinburgh* 11 B2
Warsaw = Warszawa, *Warsaw* 31 B2
Warszawa, *Warsaw* 31 B2
Wartenberg, *Berlin* 5 A4
Washington, *Washington* 32 B3
Washington Heights, *New York* 21 A2
Washington Monument, *Washington* 32 b1
Washington Nat. Airport, *Washington* 32 B3
Washington Park, *Chicago* 9 C3
Wat Arun, *Bangkok* 3 b1
Wat Pho, *Bangkok* 3 b1
Wat Phra Keo, *Bangkok* 3 b1
Wat Traimit, *Bangkok* 3 c2
Water of Leith, *Edinburgh* 11 B1
Water Tower Place, *Chicago* 9 a2
Watergraafsmeer, *Amsterdam* 2 A2
Waterland, *Amsterdam* 2 A2
Waterloo, *Brussels* 6 B2
Waterloo, *Wellington* 32 B2
Waterloo International, *London* 15 b4
Watermael-Boitsfort, *Brussels* 6 B2
Watertown, *Boston* 6 A2
Watsonia, *Melbourne* 17 A2
Waverley, *Boston* 6 A2
Waverley, *Johannesburg* 13 A2
Waverley, *Sydney* 28 B2
Waverley Station, *Edinburgh* 11 b3
Wawer, *Warsaw* 31 B2
Wawrzyszew, *Warsaw* 31 B1
Wayland, *Boston* 6 A1
Wazirabad, *Delhi* 10 A2
Wazīrīya, *Baghdad* 3 A2
Wazirpur, *Delhi* 10 A2
Wealdstone, *London* 15 A1
Wedding, *Berlin* 5 A3
Weehawken, *New York* 21 B1
Weesp, *Amsterdam* 2 B3
Weidling, *Vienna* 31 A1
Weidlingbach, *Vienna* 31 A1
Weigongcum, *Beijing* 4 B1
Weijin He →, *Tianjin* 30 B2
Weissensee, *Berlin* 5 A3
Wellesley, *Boston* 6 B2
Wellesley Falls, *Boston* 6 B2
Wellesley Hills, *Boston* 6 B2
Welling, *London* 15 B4
Wellington, *Boston* 6 A3
Wellington, *Wellington* 32 B1
Wells Fargo Center, *Los Angeles* 16 b1
Weltevreden Park, *Johannesburg* 13 A1
Wembley, *London* 15 A2
Wemmel, *Brussels* 6 A1
Wemmer Pan, *Johannesburg* 13 B2
Wenceslas Square, *Prague* 24 b2
Wendenschloss, *Berlin* 5 B4
Wenhuagong, *Tianjin* 30 B2
Wennington, *London* 15 A5
Werneuchen, *Berlin* 5 A5
West Bedford, *Boston* 6 A2
West Concord, *Boston* 6 A1
West Don →, *Toronto* 30 A2
West Drayton, *London* 15 A1
West Ham, *London* 15 A4
West Harrow, *London* 15 A1
West Heath, *London* 15 B4
West Hill, *Toronto* 30 A3
West Hollywood, *Los Angeles* 16 B2
West Kensington, *London* 15 c1
West Kilburn, *London* 15 a1
West Lamma Channel, *Hong Kong* 12 B1
West Lynn, *Boston* 6 A4
West Medford, *Boston* 6 A3
West Miami, *Miami* 18 B1
West Molesey, *London* 15 B1
West New York, *New York* 21 B1
West of Twin Peaks, *San Francisco* 25 B2
West Park, *Johannesburg* 13 A1
West Rouge, *Toronto* 30 A4
West Roxbury, *Boston* 6 B3
West Springfield, *Washington* 32 C2
West Town, *Chicago* 9 B2
West Wharf, *Karachi* 14 B1
Westbourne Green, *London* 15 a1
Westchester, *Chicago* 9 B1
Westchester, *Los Angeles* 16 C2
Westchester, *New York* 21 A2
Westcliff, *Johannesburg* 13 B2
Westdene, *Johannesburg* 13 B1
Westend, *Helsinki* 12 C1
Wester Hailes, *Edinburgh* 11 B2
Westerham, *Munich* 20 B2
Western Addition, *San Francisco* 25 B2
Western Wall, *Jerusalem* 13 b3
Westgate, *Washington* 32 B3
Westlake, *Cape Town* 8 B1
Westlake, *San Francisco* 25 B2
Westminster, *London* 15 A3
Westmount, *Montreal* 19 B2
Weston, *Boston* 6 A2
Weston, *Toronto* 30 A1
Weston Res., *Boston* 6 A2
Westwood Village, *Los Angeles* 16 B2
Westzaan, *Amsterdam* 2 A1
Wetton, *Cape Town* 8 B2
Wexford, *Toronto* 30 A3
Weybridge, *London* 15 B1
Wezembeek-Oppem, *Brussels* 6 A2
White House, The, *Washington* 32 b1
Whitechapel, *London* 15 A3
Whitehall, *Dublin* 11 A2
Whitehall, *London* 15 b3
Whittier, *Los Angeles* 16 C4
Whitton, *London* 15 B1
Wieden, *Vienna* 31 A2
Wien, *Vienna* 31 A2
Wien-Schwechat, Flughafen, *Vienna* 31 B3
Wienerberg, *Vienna* 31 B2
Wierzbno, *Warsaw* 31 B2
Wijde Wormer, *Amsterdam* 2 A2
Wilanów, *Warsaw* 31 B2
Wilanówka →, *Warsaw* 31 C2
Wilhelmshagen, *Berlin* 5 B5
Wilket Creek Park, *Toronto* 30 A2
Wilkieston, *Edinburgh* 11 B1
Willbrook, *Dublin* 11 B2
Willesden, *London* 15 A2
Willesden Green, *London* 15 A2
Williamsbridge, *New York* 21 A2
Williamsburg, *New York* 21 B2
Williamstown, *Melbourne* 17 B1
Willoughby, *Sydney* 28 A2
Willow Springs, *Chicago* 9 C1
Willowdale, *Toronto* 30 A2
Wilmersdorf, *Berlin* 5 c1
Wilmette, *Chicago* 9 A2
Wilmington, *London* 15 B5
Wilshire Boulevard, *Los Angeles* 16 c1
Wimbledon, *London* 15 B2
Wimbledon Common, *London* 15 B2
Wimbledon Park, *London* 15 B2
Wimbledon Tennis Ground, *London* 15 B2
Winchester, *Boston* 6 A3
Windermere, *Cape Town* 8 A2
Windsor, *Johannesburg* 13 A1
Windsor Hills, *Los Angeles* 16 C2
Windy Arbour, *Dublin* 11 B2
Winning, *Munich* 20 B2
Winthrop, *Boston* 6 A4
Wissous, *Paris* 23 B2
Wittenau, *Berlin* 5 A2
Witwatersrand, Univ. of, *Johannesburg* 13 B2
Włochy, *Warsaw* 31 B1
Wo Mei, *Hong Kong* 12 A2
Wo Yi Hop, *Hong Kong* 12 A1
Woburn, *Boston* 6 A3
Woburn, *Toronto* 30 A3
Woduk Pluit, *Jakarta* 13 A1
Wola, *Warsaw* 31 B1
Wolf Trap Farm Park, *Washington* 32 B2
Wolica, *Warsaw* 31 C2
Wolica, *Warsaw* 31 C1
Wólka Węglowa, *Warsaw* 31 B1
Wollaston, *Boston* 6 B3
Woltersdorf, *Berlin* 5 B5
Woluwe-Saint-Lambert, *Brussels* 6 A2
Woluwe-Saint-Pierre, *Brussels* 6 A2
Wong Chuk Hang, *Hong Kong* 12 B2
Wong Chuk Wan, *Hong Kong* 12 A2
Wong Chuk Yeung, *Hong Kong* 12 A2
Wong Tai Sin, *Hong Kong* 12 A2
Wood Green, *London* 15 A3
Wood Ridge, *New York* 21 A1
Woodbridge, *Toronto* 30 A1
Woodford, *London* 15 A4
Woodford Bridge, *London* 15 A4
Woodford Green, *London* 15 A4
Woodhaven, *New York* 21 B2
Woodhouselee, *Edinburgh* 11 B2
Woodlands New Town, *Singapore* 27 A2
Woodmont, *Washington* 32 B3
Woodside, *London* 15 B3
Woodside, *New York* 21 B2
Woodstock, *Cape Town* 8 A1
Woollahra, *Sydney* 28 B2
Woolloomooloo, *Sydney* 28 b2
Woolooware B., *Sydney* 28 C1
Woolwich, *London* 15 B4
Woolworth Building, *New York* 21 e1
World Trade Center, site of former, *New York* 21 B1
Worli, *Mumbai* 20 A1
Worth, *Chicago* 9 C2
Wren's Nest, *Atlanta* 3 B2
Wrigley Building, *Chicago* 9 b2
Wuhlgarten, *Berlin* 5 A4
Wujiaochang, *Shanghai* 27 B2
Würm →, *Munich* 20 B1
Würm-kanal, *Munich* 20 A1
Wusong, *Shanghai* 27 A1
Wyczółki, *Warsaw* 31 C1
Wygoda, *Warsaw* 31 B2
Wynberg, *Cape Town* 8 B1

X

Xabregas, *Lisbon* 14 A2
Xianggang = Hong Kong, *Hong Kong* 12 B1
Xiaodian, *Tianjin* 30 A2
Xiaogang Park, *Canton* 8 B2
Xiaoping, *Canton* 8 A2
Xiasha chong, *Canton* 8 B1
Xichang, *Canton* 8 B2
Xicheng, *Beijing* 4 B1
Xidan, *Beijing* 4 B2
Xigu Park, *Tianjin* 30 A2
Xigucun, *Tianjin* 30 A1
Ximenwai, *Tianjin* 30 B1
Xinanlou, *Tianjin* 30 B2
Xinkai He →, *Tianjin* 30 A2
Xizhimen, *Beijing* 4 B1
Xu Beihong Mem. Hall, *Beijing* 4 a1
Xuanwu, *Beijing* 4 B1
Xuhui, *Shanghai* 27 B1

Y

Yaba, *Lagos* 14 A2
Yaftābād, *Tehran* 30 B1
Yahara, *Tokyo* 29 A2
Yaho, *Tokyo* 29 A1
Yakire, *Tokyo* 29 A4
Yamada, *Osaka* 22 A4
Yamada, *Tokyo* 29 B2
Yamamoto, *Osaka* 22 B4
Yamato →, *Osaka* 22 B3
Yamuna →, *Delhi* 10 B2
Yan Kit, *Singapore* 27 A3
Yanbu, *Canton* 8 B1
Yangch'ŏn, *Seoul* 26 B1
Yanghuayuan, *Beijing* 4 C1
Yangjae, *Seoul* 26 C2
Yangjiazhuang, *Shanghai* 27 A1
Yangpu, *Shanghai* 27 B2
Yangpu Park, *Shanghai* 27 B2
Yao, *Osaka* 22 B4
Yao Airport, *Osaka* 22 B4
Yarmūk, *Baghdad* 3 B1
Yarra →, *Melbourne* 17 A1
Yarra Bend Park, *Melbourne* 17 A2
Yarraville, *Melbourne* 17 A1
Yau Tong, *Hong Kong* 12 B2
Yauza →, *Moscow* 19 A4
Yeading, *London* 15 A1
Yedikule, *Istanbul* 12 C1
Yemin Moshe, *Jerusalem* 13 b2
Yenikapı, *Istanbul* 12 B1
Yeniköy, *Istanbul* 12 B2
Yerba Buena Gardens, *San Francisco* 25 c2
Yerba Buena I., *San Francisco* 25 B2
Yerres, *Paris* 23 B4
Yerushalayim = Jerusalem, *Jerusalem* 13 B2
Yiheyuan, *Beijing* 4 A1
Yinhangzhen, *Shanghai* 27 A2
Yishun New Town, *Singapore* 27 A3
Yixingbu, *Tianjin* 30 A2
Ylästö, *Helsinki* 12 B2
Yodo →, *Osaka* 22 A4
Yongdingman, *Beijing* 4 B2
Yŏngdong, *Seoul* 26 B2
Yŏngdŭngp'o, *Seoul* 26 B1
Yongfucun, *Canton* 8 B2
Yongjing, *Shanghai* 27 B2
Yongsan, *Seoul* 26 B1
Yonkers, *New York* 21 A2
York, *Toronto* 30 A2
York Mills, *Toronto* 30 A2
Yotsuya, *Tokyo* 29 a2
You'anmen, *Beijing* 4 B1
Yŏŭido, *Seoul* 26 B1
Youndsfield, *Cape Town* 8 B1
Yuanxiatian, *Canton* 8 A2
Yugo-Zarad, *Moscow* 19 B3
Yung Shue Wan, *Hong Kong* 12 B1
Yūsofābād, *Tehran* 30 A2
Yuyuantan Park, *Beijing* 4 b2

Z

Zaandam, *Amsterdam* 2 A1
Zaandijk, *Amsterdam* 2 A1
Zaanstad, *Amsterdam* 2 A1
Záběhlice, *Prague* 24 B2
Ząbki, *Warsaw* 31 B2
Żacisze, *Warsaw* 31 B2
Zahrā, *Baghdad* 3 A1
Zakharkovo, *Moscow* 19 B1
Žalov, *Prague* 24 A2
Załuski, *Warsaw* 31 C1
Zamdorf, *Munich* 20 B2
Zamek Królewski, *Warsaw* 31 a2
Zamek Ujazdowski, *Warsaw* 31 c3
Zanevka, *St. Petersburg* 26 B3
Zapote, *Manila* 17 C1
Záppeio, *Athens* 2 c2
Zarechye, *Moscow* 19 B2
Zaventem, *Brussels* 6 A2
Zawady, *Warsaw* 31 B2
Zâwiyet Abû Musallam, *Cairo* 7 B1
Zawrā' Park, *Baghdad* 3 B2
Zbraslav, *Prague* 24 C2
Zbuzany, *Prague* 24 B1
Zdiby, *Prague* 24 B2
Zeekoevlei, *Cape Town* 8 B2
Zehlendorf, *Berlin* 5 B2
Zenne →, *Brussels* 6 B1
Żerań, *Warsaw* 31 B1
Zerzeń, *Warsaw* 31 B2
Zeytinburnu, *Istanbul* 12 C1
Zhabei, *Shanghai* 27 B1
Zhangguizhuang, *Tianjin* 30 B2
Zhdanov, *Moscow* 19 B4
Zheleznodorozhnyy, *Moscow* 19 B6
Zhenru, *Shanghai* 27 B1
Zhernovka, *St. Petersburg* 26 B2
Zhicun, *Canton* 8 B2
Zhongshan Park, *Beijing* 4 b2
Zhongshan Park, *Shanghai* 27 B1
Zhoucun, *Canton* 8 A2
Zhoujiadu, *Shanghai* 27 B1
Zhoujiazhen, *Shanghai* 27 B2
Zhu Jiang →, *Canton* 8 B3
Zhulebino, *Moscow* 19 B5
Zhushadi, *Canton* 8 A3
Zielona, *Warsaw* 31 B3
Zielonka, *Warsaw* 31 B2
Ziya He →, *Tianjin* 30 A1
Žižkov, *Prague* 24 B2
Zličín, *Prague* 24 B1
Zócalo, *Mexico City* 18 b3
Zografos, *Athens* 2 B2
Żoliborz, *Warsaw* 31 B1
Zonnenbloem, *Cape Town* 8 A1
Zoo, *Beijing* 4 a1
Zugliget, *Budapest* 7 B1
Zugló, *Budapest* 7 A2
Zuiderwoude, *Amsterdam* 2 A3
Zumbi, *Rio de Janeiro* 24 A1
Zunderdorp, *Amsterdam* 2 A2
Zuvuvu →, *São Paulo* 26 C1
Zwanenburg, *Amsterdam* 2 A1
Zwölfaxing, *Vienna* 31 B2
Zyuzino, *Moscow* 19 C3

CITY GAZETTEER

The entries below provide information on places of interest in cities throughout the world that have particularly large numbers of visitors, whether in a business or tourist capacity. The map page reference at the start of an entry indicates that one or more relevant maps are included in the City Maps section.

Accra, Ghana

Accra is not the most beautiful city in West Africa, but its people are considered to be among the friendliest and best educated. It has several lively markets and a National Museum with displays of West African art and artefacts. Near the city are some beautiful sandy beaches, although visitors should be alert to the powerful undertow. Further along the coast are forts and castles that once served as slave-trading centres, including St George's Castle at Elmina, the oldest European structure in sub-Saharan Africa.

Agra, India

Agra is visited primarily for its architectural wonders, especially the 17th-century Taj Mahal. This magical building, a symbol of Mughal emperor Shah Jahan's love for his favourite wife, Mumtaz Mahal, captures the imagination even when crowded with tourists in the heat of the day. Agra's 16th-century Red Fort contains elaborately decorated royal apartments and gardens that give a vivid impression of life at the Mughal court. Just 40 km (25 miles) away is the Mughal 'ghost city' of Fatehpur Sikri which was abandoned almost immediately after it had been built in the 1570s.

Taj Mahal, Agra

Amsterdam, The Netherlands   *Map page 2*

In the centre of Amsterdam is a network of canals, crossed by around a thousand bridges and edged with tree-lined streets of 17th- and 18th-century gabled houses. Canal cruises are an excellent way to get to know the city, and visitors can also hire bicycles – a major form of transport in Amsterdam. Among the museums are the Rijksmuseum, with its famous art collection, the Van Gogh Museum, and the Stedelijk Museum, housing modern art. The heart of the city is Dam Square, with the royal palace and Anne Frank's house (now a museum) close by. Rembrandt's house can also be visited in an area full of bars, nightclubs and restaurants.

Antwerp, Belgium

A vibrant city with much to see, Antwerp – on the River Scheldt and Europe's second largest port – deserves to be a highly rated tourist destination. At the heart of its beautiful old town is the Great Market, with a 16th-century town hall. Nearby, among cobbled streets lined with bars, restaurants and shops, is the impressive Gothic cathedral with paintings by Rubens, the city's most famous artist. There is also much to attract those who want a really enjoyable night on the town.

Athens, Greece   *Map page 2*

Athens is a curious mixture of ancient and modern, where ugly concrete tower blocks rub shoulders with Classical monuments. Dominating the centre of the city are the ruins on the Acropolis, dating from the 5th century BC and crowned by the magnificent Parthenon. Other interesting ruins include the Temple of Olympian Zeus, the largest temple in Greece. The National Archaeological Museum houses gold artefacts from Mycenae and spectacular Minoan frescoes. Nestling beneath the Acropolis is the engaging Pláka quarter, with its small Byzantine churches and bustling tavernas. For most visitors the centre of Athens is Sindagma Square, with its large hotels, banks and open-air cafés. Ferries to the islands depart from the port of Piraeus, 10 km (6 miles) from the square.

Atlanta, Georgia, USA   *Map page 3*

Beneath the glittering high-rise buildings of Atlanta's modern financial centre lies 'Underground Atlanta' – the revitalized old centre, complete with cobbled, gas-lit streets and packed with shops and restaurants. The piazza above it is filled with street entertainers and flanked by the Coca-Cola Museum. Atlanta is most famously associated with Martin Luther King, and an area of the city is devoted to his memory and to the history of the civil rights movement. The Centennial Olympic Park, with its Fountain of Rings, is an entertaining outdoor venue, and the adjacent CNN Center provides an interesting studio tour.

Auckland, New Zealand

The heart of Auckland is the magnificent Waitemata Harbour, where sailing is a popular pastime. The city is not renowned for its nightlife, but it is pleasant to walk its streets, perhaps following the 13 km (8-mile) Coast-to-Coast Walkway from the Ferry Building to Manukau Harbour. On the route, in an area of parkland known as The Domain, is the Auckland Museum, with a unique collection of Maori and Pacific Island artefacts. Beyond is the inner suburb of Parnell, with its colonial buildings, east of which is Underwater World, a particularly impressive aquarium. There are several city beaches, and surfing beaches beyond the Waitakere Ranges.

Bangkok, Thailand   *Map page 3*

With its choking traffic, Bangkok can be both a daunting and an exhilarating city for short-stay visitors. Something of the old Siam can be uncovered by using the river-bus service to visit the Royal Grand Palace and the ornate Temple of the Emerald Buddha (Wat Phra Keo). Other Buddhist temples include the Temple of the Dawn (Wat Arun), whose 82 m (266 ft) high gilded stupa is best seen from the Chao Phraya River. At Jim Thompson's House there is an extraordinary private museum of Thai domestic architecture. The network of canals, with their floating markets, is well worth exploring, as are the shops for silk and other textiles, clothes, jewellery and handicrafts. Night-time entertainment includes traditional dancing and Thai boxing.

Floating market, Bangkok

Barcelona, Spain   *Map page 4*

The capital of Catalonia and Spain's second city, Barcelona is a major port with a fashionable, cosmopolitan cultural life. Particularly enjoyable is strolling along the Ramblas, a broad avenue which bisects central Barcelona, and has a vibrant street life. At the southern end is the renovated harbour area, with shops, restaurants and tapas bars. The district of greatest historic interest is the Barri Gòtic, where medieval houses cluster around the great Gothic cathedral, La Seu. Barcelona has over 50 museums and galleries, including world-class museums dedicated to the works of Picasso and Miró, but it is the buildings of Antonio Gaudí that are most often associated with the city. His incomplete Sagrada Família Cathedral has become a symbol for Barcelona, and is perhaps the most fantastic of all his eccentric creations.

Beijing, China   *Map page 4*

Despite Beijing's daunting scale, extreme climate and heavy traffic, its sights are well worth visiting. They include the massive Tiananmen Square, the Mao Mausoleum, the Great Hall of the People, the Imperial Palace (Forbidden City), the buildings of the Summer Palace along the shore of Kunming Lake, and the 15th-century Temple of Heaven. Beijing has many interesting parks, including Beihai Park with its historic buildings and exquisite Jade Island. However, perhaps the most famous attraction of all is the Great Wall, which can be visited at Badaling, just 70 km (40 miles) north-west of the city, on a trip that also takes in the Ming tombs in the Shisan Ling Valley.

Berlin, Germany   *Map page 5*

After decades of being divided into West and East Berlin, the city is once again the capital of a united Germany. From the modern dome on the renovated Reichstag building there are fine views of the new buildings rising in the former no-man's-land between the two sectors, whose distinct character can still be felt. The city's youthful 'alternative' scene also continues to thrive, as does its famous nightlife in and around, for example, Savignyplatz in the west and the Scheunenviertel in the east. To the east of the Brandenburg Gate is an area of grand old squares and streets containing Berlin's main museums, including the Pergamon, with its collection of Ancient, Oriental and Islamic art. To the west is the landscaped Tiergarten, the famous zoo, with its exotic pastiche architecture, and the wealthy, modern heart of former West Berlin.

Boston, Massachusetts, USA   *Map page 6*

The oldest areas of Boston have a European feel, their street plan based on meandering farm tracks. The Beacon Hill district contains splendid 19th-century brick houses and narrow alleyways, and the Massachusetts State House. A 'Freedom Trail', marked by a line of red bricks, takes the visitor past 17th- and 18th-century buildings, some of which are associated with the American Revolution. There are also guided tours of the USA's oldest surviving battleship – the USS *Constitution*, built in 1797 – moored in Boston Harbour. Across the Charles River lies Cambridge, with Harvard University and Square. Boston is a relatively unthreatening city for visitors, with a lively intellectual and artistic life, and a 'necklace' of city parks and tree-lined streets within a compact central area.

Brisbane, Queensland, Australia

The relaxed atmosphere and compactness of its centre make Brisbane a pleasant place to stroll around. Its historic precinct, next to the Botanic Gardens, contains some fine 19th-century buildings, among them the Treasury. South of the River Brisbane is the State Art Gallery and the Cultural Centre, which includes two theatres and a superb concert hall. Day trips are possible to the beaches of the Gold and Sunshine Coasts.

Brussels, Belgium   *Map page 6*

The centre of government for the European Union, Brussels is renowned for its excellent restaurants and shops, with everything from flea markets to the designer boutiques in the Galéries St Hubert. The imposing Hôtel de Ville, the gilded 17th-century houses and the Maison du Roi make the Grand-Place one of the world's most beautiful central squares. To the east lies the Gothic cathedral, the Palais Royale and the Royal Art Museums, containing both ancient and modern art. The city is full of fine examples of Art Nouveau architecture, including the museum dedicated to the founder of the movement, Victor Horta. A popular tourist site is the irreverent 17th-century statue, Manneken Pis.

Budapest, Hungary   *Map page 7*

The Danube and Parliament building, Budapest

Formerly two cities, Buda and Pest, on opposite sides of the Danube, the capital of Hungary is a fascinating destination. The Castle Hill district of Buda includes the cobbled streets and medieval houses of the Old Town, and the Royal Palace (Budavári palota), containing the national art gallery and museum. The Fishermen's Bastion gives sweeping views over the city. A network of grand 19th-century boulevards forms the centre of the larger, more cosmopolitan Pest, with its imposing Parliament building (Orzágház).

There are many elegant spa baths (gyógyfürdo) dotted around the city, and extensive Roman remains, including an amphitheatre, at Óbuda and Rómaifürdo. Famous for its cafés, Budapest has excellent restaurants and offers a huge range of entertainment, including opera, jazz and discos.

Buenos Aires, Argentina   *Map page 7*

The centre of Buenos Aires is laid out on a grand scale, with wide boulevards, imposing 19th-century buildings, modern tower blocks, and spacious plazas. Around this area, however, are the more intimate districts (*barrios*), each with its distinctive character. San Telmo is the artists' quarter, while La Boca, with its brightly painted houses, is the city's port district. The most fashionable district, Recoleta, houses the National Museum of Art, but is best known for the ornate tombs of its cemetery.

La Boca, Buenos Aires

Cairo, Egypt   *Map page 7*

The largest city in Africa, Cairo is full of hooting taxis and bustling crowds. Modern buildings have risen next to the minarets of the old mosques, while a maze of markets provide potential bargains. The Pyramids of Giza are visible from the upper storeys of buildings all over the city. Famous worldwide for its unrivalled collection of antiquities, the Egyptian Museum houses the treasures of the Pharaoh Tutankhamun, and more than 100,000 other relics and antiquities from all periods of ancient Egyptian history. Experiences not to be missed include the *Son et Lumière* that takes place daily by the Sphinx at Giza, and drifting on the Nile in a *felucca* while watching the sun sink below the Cairo skyline.

Calcutta (Kolkata), India   *Map page 8*

The capital of West Bengal, Calcutta (Kolkata) is regarded by many as the cultural and intellectual centre of India. It also has a reputation for extreme poverty and squalor. One of the great colonial cities of Asia, its main historic sites date from the days of the British Raj and include the white marble Victoria Memorial, the neo-Gothic St Paul's Cathedral, and the Indian Museum, with sculptures from all over India. These buildings are all in the vicinity of the Maidan, one of the largest city parks in the world, where hundreds of different interests – among them yoga, cricket and riding – are regularly pursued, and live entertainment is provided.

Canton (Guangzhou), China   *Map page 8*

An economic success but a planning disaster, Guangzhou holds more attraction for the business traveller than for those seeking historic sites.

There are, however, numerous decaying French and British colonial buildings on Shamian Island, which provides a haven of peace from the bustle of Guangzhou's streets. A climb to the top of the 11th-century Temple of Six Banyan Trees provides a fine view. Another way of seeing the city is to take a cruise on the Pearl River.

Cape Town, South Africa   *Map page 8*

South Africa's oldest city, Cape Town has several buildings of historic interest, including the Castle of Good Hope, the Old Town House, the Tuynhuis and the Parliament building. Artefacts from all over Africa are sold at the Saturday market in Greenmarket Square. The city lies below the spectacular Table Mountain, accessible by cable car. There are numerous good beaches, such as those at Clifton and Camps Bay on the cold Atlantic Ocean, and at Muizenberg and Fishoek on the warmer Indian Ocean. The old docks have been developed as the Victoria and Albert Waterfront, which boasts a range of restaurants. Boat trips run from here to the infamous Robben Island, where Nelson Mandela was imprisoned.

Cartagena, Colombia

Several impressive 16th-century forts overlook the channel leading to the bay of Cartagena, evidence of the city's origins as an imperial Spanish stronghold. Huge 17th- and 18th-century walls surround narrow streets, palaces, churches, monasteries and plazas. The Palace of the Inquisition is a fine example of colonial architecture, with its magnificent Baroque gateway.

Chicago, Illinois, USA   *Map page 9*

Built on the shore of Lake Michigan, Chicago played a key role in the economic development of the USA, serving as a railhead for the cattle trade of the Midwest. Its skyline includes skyscrapers dating from the 1890s, buildings in the International Style of the 1950s, and particularly fine examples of more recent architecture. The Sears Tower provides fantastic views of four states from its Space Deck. A closer view can be had on a boat trip up the Chicago River or from 'The Loop', an elevated railway that lends its name to the area it encircles. There are several important museums, including the vast Museum of Science and Industry and the Art Institute of Chicago. For outdoor pursuits, there is the extensive Grant Park, bordering the lake. The city is renowned for its rich musical life and, as well as a world-class symphony orchestra, there is a multitude of clubs offering blues, jazz, rock and folk music.

Skyline with Sears Tower, Chicago

Cologne, Germany

Despite the almost total destruction of central Cologne during World War II, many historic buildings have been restored to their former glory, including the massive and beautiful twin-towered Gothic cathedral (Dom). Among the museums and art galleries are the Roman-Germanic Museum and the Imhoff-Stollwek Museum of Chocolate. The city's unique beer, *kslsch*, can be sampled in the numerous beer halls. Short boat trips on the Rhine provide views of the impressive riverfront, while longer boat excursions go to, for example, Königswinter and Linz.

Copenhagen, Denmark   *Map page 10*

Scandinavia's largest and liveliest city, Copenhagen has excellent art collections, royal palaces, churches and other historic buildings as well as entertainment late into the night. Punctuated by parks, lakes, fountains and squares, the city is easily explored on foot or bicycle. The old harbour of Nyhavn, with its tall, brightly painted buildings, is packed with pavement cafés and bars, while the Latin Quarter is good for restaurants. From the top of the Round Tower (Rundee Taarn), Europe's oldest functioning observatory, there are magnificent views over the city. The famous Tivoli Gardens is a delightfully varied amusement park dating from 1843. A bridge now links Copenhagen to the attractive Swedish city of Malmö.

Delhi, India   *Map page 10*

Red Fort, Delhi

The capital of India, Delhi is a city with two centres: New Delhi, which was established by the British in 1911, and Old Delhi, whose present layout dates from the 17th century. The streets of the old town, and in particular Chandni Chauk, are famously frenetic. The massive walls of the Red Fort and the Lahore Gate enclose a host of palace buildings, although many have been stripped of their fine decoration. India's largest mosque, the Jama Masjid, is also in the old town. The new city, with its broad avenues and imposing marble buildings, contains some older sites, including the 16th-century tomb of Humayun and the 12th-century Qutb Minar tower.

Dublin, Ireland   *Map page 11*

Built on the River Liffey, Ireland's capital contains elegant 18th-century buildings, two Norman cathedrals, a castle, and some fine museums, three of them in Leinster House. One of the oldest books in the world, the 9th-century illuminated Book of Kells, is housed in Trinity College library, while the Writers' Museum pays homage to local literary figures such as W. B. Yeats, James Joyce and Oscar Wilde. Dublin has a relaxed, friendly atmosphere, and plenty of pubs and restaurants. In summer, outdoor events are often held in Phoenix Park. The famous Easter Uprising of 1916 is commemorated at Kilmainham Jail, where many heroes of Irish independence were once incarcerated.

Edinburgh, Scotland   *Map page 11*

Set on a dramatic rock that soars 76 m (250 ft) from the valley floor, the Old Town of Edinburgh is a collection of historic buildings, towering tenements and narrow passages huddling beneath a romantic castle. The Royal Mile, lined with 16th- and 17th-century buildings, leads from the castle to the royal residence of Holyrood. The Royal Museum lies to its south, as does the lively Grassmarket district with its bars and restaurants. The small but elegant National Gallery sits in Princes Street Gardens to the north. Beyond lie graceful Georgian squares, terraces and crescents of the New Town. Scotland's capital has a rich cultural life, including the world-famous International and Fringe festivals.

Esfahan, Iran

On the four sides of the vast central square of Esfahan, with its formal lawns and pool, are the delicately tiled façades of public buildings. These include the opulent Royal Mosque and the magnificent entrance to the bazaar, whose crowded streets twist and turn towards the steps of the Great Mosque, a complex of buildings spanning a 700-year period. Among other historic sites are the shrine of Imamzadeh Ahmad and several royal palaces. Esfahan's high altitude keeps it relatively cool, making it pleasant to stroll through the streets and parks, and sample the many teahouses.

Fès, Morocco

The old part of Fès – Fès el-Bali – is one of the largest living medieval cities in the world. A fascinating labyrinth of some 94,000 streets and lanes, its covered bazaars are crammed with every conceivable sort of craft workshop, restaurants and market stalls, as well as extensive dye pits and tanneries. On the edge of the old town, the Museum of Moroccan Arts houses a splendid collection of artefacts, including colourful tribal carpets and the city's famous blue pottery.

Florence, Italy

The pedestrianized streets in the beautiful centre of Florence enable visitors to wander about freely, visiting such well-known Renaissance sites as the cathedral, with its red-roofed dome, and the spacious Piazza della Signoria, dominated by the crenellated Palazzo Vecchio. Between the piazza and the River Arno is the Uffizi Gallery, containing famous works by Botticelli and Titian among many others. The 14th-century Ponte Vecchio bridge, lined on both sides with jewellery and gift shops, provides a route to the imposing Pitti Palace. The city's churches range in style from the exquisite San Miniato, through the austere Santo Croce to the classically inspired San Lorenzo. Of the many religious frescoes, those by Fra Angelico in the monastery of San Marco, and by Masaccio in the church of Santa Maria del Carmine, stand out. The Bargello has a fine collection of sculpture, while the Accademia houses Michelangelo's *David*.

Cathedral with Brunelleshci's dome, Florence

Geneva, Switzerland

Geneva enjoys one of the world's most dramatic locations, straddling the Rhône where it leaves Lake Geneva, and overlooked by the Alps on one side and the Jura mountains on the other. A cosmopolitan, French-speaking city, it is a world centre for banking and commerce as well as for international organizations, such as the Red Cross. South of the river, the oldest part has excellent museums, galleries and historic buildings, including St Peter's Cathedral, where John Calvin preached. Geneva lives up to its reputation for efficiency, cleanliness and safety, but all this comes at a price: restaurants, clubs and other entertainments are smart and expensive.

Hamburg, Germany

Germany's largest port (there are daily harbour tours from March to November), Hamburg combines its busy commercial life with a graceful, old-world charm. Situated on the River Elbe and criss-crossed by a network of canals, at its heart is the Alster lake, where boating is a popular pastime in the summer. The city has many extensive parks, stylish shopping arcades, elegant boulevards, museums and art galleries, among them the Kunsthalle with a fine collection of art spanning several centuries. There are numerous inviting café-bars and all-night entertainment, most notably in the St Pauli Quarter, where The Beatles famously performed in the 1960s.

Hanoi, Vietnam

Built on the Red River, around several large lakes, Hanoi has both peaceful tree-lined avenues and parks, and a bustling old city where almost anything can be purchased, including silk, lacquerware, puppets and jewellery. Bikes are the main form of transport. The city's many religious buildings include the One-Pillar Pagoda and the 11th-century Temple of Literature. Ho Chi Minh's mausoleum provides a memorable experience, with visitors being escorted to view the embalmed body. A day trip can be made to the Perfume Pagoda – actually a complex of pagodas and Buddhist shrines carved out of limestone cliffs. A cruise from Haiphong around the limestone islands of Halong Bay is also recommended.

Havana, Cuba

Ironically for a country that is proud of its independence from imperialism, one of the main attractions of Cuba's capital is its colonial past. The vast open space of Plaza de la Revolución and the post-colonial buildings of the Vedado district are worth seeing, but it is the boulevards and squares of Old Havana that are most fascinating.

The palaces surrounding the Plaza de Armas, the Baroque cathedral and the elegant thoroughfare 'The Paseo' are all fine examples of colonial architecture. There are few cars on the streets, but many bicycles. There are also many nightclubs, where salsa is the predominant dance style.

Capitol building and Grand Theatre, Havana

Helsinki, Finland   *Map page 12*

Helsinki is almost surrounded by water and is full of the sounds and scents of the sea. Among its architectural gems are the 19th-century Neo-classical buildings of Senate Square – which also contains the blue-domed Lutheran Cathedral – and the rock-hewn church of Temppeliauko (1969) where many concerts are held. Although its combination of attractive buildings, good restaurants and excellent art galleries and museums make it a year-round tourist destination, Helsinki really comes to life in summer, with open-air cafés, concerts, and boat trips to the ruined fortress on nearby Suomenlinna Island.

Hong Kong, China   *Map page 12*

Most visitors to Hong Kong take the short ferry ride from Kowloon across the harbour, with its spectacular view of the high-rise buildings on the waterfront of Hong Kong Island. A visit to the Man Mo temple, with its ornate interior, provides a complete contrast. A funicular goes to the top of Victoria Peak where there are shady paths through lush vegetation. The Tsim Sha Tsui area of Kowloon contains a group of modern exhibition buildings, including the Space Museum and the Hong Kong Museum of History, as well as air-conditioned shopping malls. A ferry goes to the islands of Lamma, where there are relatively uncrowded beaches, country walks and seafood restaurants. A hydrofoil goes to Macau.

Istanbul, Turkey   *Map page 12*

Formerly known as Constantinople, Istanbul has an imperial history dating back to the time of the Roman Empire. Its strategic position straddling the Bosporus Strait makes it both a European and an Asian city. Among the churches built in the 6th century by Emperor Constantine is the domed Hagia Sophia (Aya Sofya), which was converted into a mosque in 1453 and is now a museum. The 17th-century Blue Mosque (Sultanahmet Camii) is a masterpiece of Ottoman architecture, while the Topkapi Palace, with its imperial treasury stuffed with gold and jewels, is on every itinerary. In old Istanbul is the labyrinthine Kapali Carsi (the world's largest covered bazaar) where more than 4,000 shops and stalls sell carpets, jewellery, ceramics, brass and leatherware. A fascinating mixture of both the ancient and modern, Istanbul also has a renowned cuisine.

Jaipur, India

Known as the 'Pink City' because of the salmon-coloured wash applied to many of its buildings, Jaipur is the capital of the colourful state of Rajasthan. It is divided into areas dedicated to specialist activities, such as elephant-handling or the sale of textiles, silver or gems. Within the walled town are the Palace of Winds (Hawa Mahal), with its delicately screened windows, the City Palace – now a museum – and Jai Singh's extraordinary Observatory, with its huge angular stone instruments. Nearby is the hill town and Rajput palace complex of Amber.

Jakarta, Indonesia   *Map page 13*

Jakarta's glinting high-rise office blocks contrast sharply with the cobbled square at the heart of what was 18th-century Batavia (now known as Kota). Much can be discovered of this colonial period at the dock of Sunda Kelapa, where many magnificent schooners are moored and a maritime museum has been created in an old warehouse. The National Museum has excellent displays on Indonesia's ethnic groups. There is a theme park at Taman Impian Jaya Ancol, and Balinese dancing and traditional music at Taman Ismail Marzuki. Jakarta also offers a fine range of restaurants.

Jerusalem, Israel   *Map page 13*

The focus of most visits to Jerusalem is the Old City with its different quarters. The heart of the Christian quarter is the Church of the Holy Sepulchre, the site of Christ's crucifixion. This is reached along the Via Dolorosa, much of which passes through the Muslim quarter, with its impressive Mamluk architecture. The Western (Wailing) Wall is in the Jewish quarter, which also contains the multi-layered Temple Mount Excavations. The Armenian quarter, the centre of the Armenian Church, contains the impressive Citadel. Towering over all these is the golden Dome of the Rock, a sacred Muslim site in the Temple Mount compound.

Dome of the Rock, Jerusalem

Johannesburg, South Africa   *Map page 13*

The richest city in Africa, Johannesburg is also a lively centre of South African culture. Museum-Africa has collections relating to the history and art of all sections of the community, while the nearby Market Theatre Complex, which contains four theatres, is an attractive place in which to eat and drink, and listen to music. Visitors, however, should be aware of the high crime rate in the downtown area, and enjoy instead the restaurants and gardens of northern suburbs such as Rosebank and Melville. Outside the city is Soweto, the vast black township which has a lively music and theatre scene but is best visited on a guided tour.

Kairouan, Tunisia

An important centre for the Muslim faith, Tunisia's holy city has over 130 mosques, including the 9th-century Great Mosque, which once doubled as a fortress. A special permit is required to visit the holy sites. Kairouan's maze of buildings and narrow, winding streets is enclosed by ancient city walls, and it is a fascinating place in which to stroll. Artisans carry out the traditional trades of weaving and carpentry, and carpet sellers try to attract visitors to their stalls in the souk (bazaar).

Karachi, Pakistan   *Map page 14*

Developed as a city by the British from the 1840s, Karachi is a business rather than a tourist centre. It does, however, have many colourful bazaars in Saddar, the central district, which specialize in such products as jewellery, cloth, dried fruit and bottles. It also has a fascinating coastline which can be viewed on a traditional lateen-sailed boat trip from the harbour. Clifton Beach, with its camel rides and fairground, is well equipped for families, while other, rather less commercialized beaches are a short drive away.

Katmandu, Nepal

Street scene, Katmandu

Katmandu is a popular holiday destination – an intriguing mixture of modern buildings and narrow, traffic-clogged streets with intricately carved temples and shrines. Many of these ancient buildings are grouped around Durbar Square, including the Jaganath Temple, with its erotic carvings. The Old Royal Palace houses an interesting museum. Jochne, better known as 'Freak Street', is a focal point for many visitors, with its fascinating shops, cheap hotels and restaurants. Outside the city are three huge temples: the Hindu Pashupatinath complex, with its riverside ghats, and the Buddhist stupas of Boudhanath and Swayambunath.

Kraków, Poland

Having come through World War II virtually unscathed, and with not a high-rise building in sight, Kraków's densely packed old centre is full of historic churches and picturesque streets and squares. The central market square, which is reputed to be the largest medieval town square in Europe, contains a number of interesting buildings, among them the largely 16th-century Cloth Hall. The square is also the focus of the city's vigorous cultural life. There are several jazz and cabaret clubs in the Old Town, as well as numerous attractive cafés, bars and restaurants. To the south are the castle and cathedral of Wawel, behind which lies Kazimierz, the gradually reviving Jewish district.

Kuala Lumpur, Malaysia

A city that has sprung up since the 1860s, Kuala Lumpur is short on historic sites but has plenty to offer the visitor. Its colonial, 19th-century heart is Merdeka Square. Nearby is the most spectacular of the city's mosques, Masjid Jamek. Chinatown and Little India provide much of interest, and Malaysian craftwork and antiques can be bought at the Art Deco Central Market. The 'Golden Triangle' business area includes the Petronas Twin Towers, one of the world's tallest buildings. The Lake Gardens contain a Bird Park, Orchid Garden and Butterfly Park. A half-hour drive outside the city are the Batu Caves, used as Hindu temples. Day trips can be made to the historic city of Malacca and the Genting Highlands Casino Complex.

Kyoto, Japan

Japan's capital for over 1,000 years, Kyoto has numerous Buddhist temples, Shinto shrines, palaces and gardens. Despite extensive modern development, there are still traditional wooden houses and craft shops in the back streets. A city that is particularly spectacular when clad in either cherry blossom or autumnal colours, its main sights include the 1,001 gilded statues of Buddha lined up in the Hall of the Thirty-Three Bays, the view from the temple of Kiyomizu-dera, and the intriguing gardens of Ginkaku-ji. Other famous gardens include the lake-garden of Kinkaku-ji, and the 500-year-old garden of Ryoan-ji. The city of Nara, 35 km (22 miles) south, contains the huge bronze Buddha of Todai-ji, and other fine examples of early Japanese art and architecture.

Temple of Kiyomizu-dera, Kyoto

Lagos, Nigeria　　　　　　　　　　*Map page 14*

Although no longer the capital of Nigeria, Lagos is by far the largest city in West Africa. At its heart lies Lagos Island, a business centre whose skyline is spiked by skyscrapers. The National Museum provides a fascinating insight into the country's cultural heritage and includes works of art dating back 2,800 years, including beautiful Benin bronzes. The city's main attraction, however, is modern African music, and many of the country's best-known singers have nightclubs here.

Lahore, Pakistan

Lahore is renowned for its Mughal architecture. The most attractive of its many mosques is that of Wazir Kahn, covered in intricate glazed mosaic tiles, but the largest is the Badshahi Mosque. The massive walls of Lahore Fort surround a compound of elegant buildings. Away from the centre is Jahangir's tomb and the Shalimar Garden, with its geometrically arranged terraces, ponds, fountains and, in February and March, its spectacular flowers.

Las Vegas, Nevada, USA

A city whose population grew from 30 to half a million in just 90 years, Las Vegas is continually reinventing itself, with the casinos on The Strip providing ever bigger and better spectacles. The most famous is Caesar's Palace, with staff dressed as centurions and Cleopatra lookalikes. New York, New York entices with its replica skyscrapers and a Statue of Liberty. Treasure Island has a mock sea battle, Mirage an erupting volcano and Circus Circus live fire-eaters. Food and lodging are cheap, particularly midweek, with the real profits being made on the gambling tables and slot machines. Las Vegas is popular for outrageous weddings, with services being conducted in the most unlikely places – in a 'drive-through' chapel, the nearby Grand Canyon, or even in mid-air.

The Strip, Las Vegas

Lima, Peru　　　　　　　　　　*Map page 16*

A once-beautiful city, Lima has suffered badly at the hands of modern developers. It is worth visiting primarily for its fine museums, which provide background information about Peru's Inca sites. It is also a useful base from which to explore the surrounding countryside, including the beautiful beaches to the south, over which towers the temple complex of Pachacamac.

Lisbon, Portugal　　　　　　　　　　*Map page 14*

There are many hills to climb and much to see in Portugal's capital. Stretching north from the Rio Tejo, the Baixa district – rebuilt after the devastating earthquake of 1755 – contains many of the city's museums and theatres. The old Moorish area, the Alfama, survived the earthquake and its warren of narrow streets, stairways and squares leads up to the hilltop Castle of St George, with magnificent views. On the edge of the city the Belém area contains fine examples of 16th-century architecture, including the marvellous Jerônimos Monastery and the famous white Belém Tower. At night the haunting traditional *fado* music is played in bars in, for example, the Bairro Alto district. Day trips can be made to the hill town of Sintra or to the beaches on the Estoril coast.

London, England　　　　　　　　　　*Map page 15*

Europe's largest city, London is a lively, cosmopolitan metropolis, offering a huge range of attractions to the visitor. From the grand squares of Knightsbridge and Belgravia to the business district of the City, central London is made up of a mosaic of areas, each with its own distinctive atmosphere and architectural style. Historic buildings include the Tower of London (containing the Crown Jewels), St Paul's Cathedral, Westminster Abbey, the Houses of Parliament and Buckingham Palace. Among the many art galleries are the Tate Modern, housed in a converted power station on the South Bank of the River Thames, and The National Gallery, overlooking Trafalgar Square. The British Museum contains a monumental collection of Egyptian, Greek and Roman artefacts. Soho, Piccadilly and Covent Garden form the heart of the theatre district, with numerous restaurants, clubs and bars. Day excursions can be made to Hampton Court Palace, Windsor Castle, Canterbury Cathedral, the Royal Pavilion in Brighton, and the historic university towns of Oxford and Cambridge.

Los Angeles, California, USA　　　　*Map page 16*

Among the skyscrapers in Los Angeles' downtown area are some notable public buildings, including the Museum of Contemporary Art. To the southwest is Exposition Park, home to three museums, including the interactive California Space Center. Most visitors, however, flock to Hollywood in search of film stars, although the big names have long since left for more salubrious neighbourhoods, such as Beverly Hills and elegant Bel Air. Other attractions include the Warner Bros. Studio Tour, and the thrilling rides at Universal Studios. On the coast, the long sandy beach linking Santa Monica and Venice is a magnet for Los Angeles' more colourful characters.

Luxembourg City, Luxembourg

The picturesque old walled city of Luxembourg perches above the Pétrusse and Alzette valleys, overlooked by the ruins of its ancient fortress with a labyrinth of defensive tunnels and underground chambers (the casemates), which is a UNESCO World Heritage Site. Running between the Citadelle du St Esprit, which provides spectacular views, and the Grand Ducal Palace is the elegant Chemin de la Corniche, one of Europe's most beautiful pedestrian promenades.

Madrid, Spain　　　　　　　　　　*Map page 17*

Spain's capital is a huge metropolis with a remarkable collection of museums and art galleries, beautiful parks and a famously vibrant nightlife centred on Plaza de Santa Ana. The city is made up of a number of districts (*barrios*), each with its own distinct character. The area of most interest to visitors is around the 17th-century Plaza Mayor, with the elaborately decorated Royal Palace, the Opera House (Teatro Real) and the famous Prado Museum all within easy reach. The city has a vivacious character and a buzzing street life. Tapas bars are everywhere, and shoppers can explore the busy Gran Via or the atmospheric Rastro flea market centred on Plaza de Cascorro. Excursions can be made to the austere monastery of El Escorial and to the historic towns of Toledo, Segovia, Avila and Aranjuez.

Plaza Mayor, Madrid

Manila, Philippines
Map page 17

Many people visit Manila purely for its bars and nightlife, and the city provides plenty to choose from in the business district of Makati and the streets behind Roxes Boulevard. The walled area known as Intramuros contains the most significant historic sites, including Fort Santiago and the imposing Romanesque cathedral. Rizal Park, projecting out into Manila Bay, contains a lagoon, a spectacular fountain, a replica of Beijing's Summer Palace, a Japanese Garden and planetarium. Manila's Chinatown (on the border of Santa Cruz and Binondo) is the place to go for silk, porcelain and Chinese dumplings.

Marrakech, Morocco

Famous for its lively street life, Marrakech is also known for the pink colour that dominates the city from the earth walls around the old town centre to the flat-roofed houses. Every evening in Djemaa El Fna, the old town's central square, acrobats, snake charmers and storytellers perform. Nearby is the labyrinthine souk (bazaar), with its hundreds of small shops selling jewellery, carpets, metalware and leather. There are several beautiful gardens, and the Museum of Arts contains a magnificent display of carpets. Just an hour's drive away are the spectacular High Atlas mountains.

The souk, Marrakech

Melbourne, Victoria, Australia
Map page 17

Central Melbourne, on the north bank of the River Yarra, is a striking blend of past and present. Ornate 19th-century buildings sit alongside towering skyscrapers, as in Collins Street where the 1980s Rialto Towers provide splendid views from an Observation Deck. Elsewhere, the Old Melbourne Gaol is a major historic attraction and there are many fine parks and gardens, including the outstanding Botanic Gardens. The city's multi-ethnic nature is apparent in the popular Queen Victoria Market and in the huge variety of restaurants. Outside the centre several inner suburbs, each with a distinct character, can be explored by tram. Places of interest nearby include the Yarra Valley with its wineries and wildlife sanctuaries, and Phillip Island with its penguins.

Mexico City, Mexico
Map page 18

It is worth braving the traffic and pollution of Mexico City to see the impressive architecture of the buildings surrounding the main square (Zócalo), including the National Palace, with its murals by Diego Rivera. Nearby are the fascinating excavations of an Aztec temple (Templo Mayor). Bosque de Chapultepec, with its boating lakes, gardens and zoo, provides some relief from the hectic street life. It is also home to the outstanding

Museo de Antropologia, whose indoor and outdoor exhibition spaces house the world's greatest collection of Mexican art and artefacts. Just 48 km (30 miles) away from the centre are the splendid ruins of the ancient city of Teotihuacán.

Miami, Florida, USA
Map page 18

Miami is spread out along the fragmented coastline of Biscayne Bay. The Spanish language predominates and the downtown area, with its modern tower blocks, is greatly enlivened by the Latin American street life. Little Havana and Little Haiti are two areas worth visiting for their strong culture. The city's most elegant neighbourhood is Coral Gables, built as a 'model suburb' in the 1920s. Miami Beach, on an island linked to the mainland by causeways, has many fine examples of Art Deco buildings and miles of sandy beaches, hotels and bars.

Milan, Italy
Map page 18

Famous as a world centre for design and fashion, and for its grand opera house, La Scala, Milan has many historic buildings alongside its modern skyscrapers. The enormous Gothic cathedral dominates the main square, Piazza del Duomo, and the nearby convent of Santa Maria delle Grazie houses Leonardo da Vinci's fresco *The Last Supper*. Italy's most beautiful shopping arcade, the Galleria Vittorio Emanuele II, runs between the cathedral and La Scala. The Castello Sforzesco, a striking red-brick castle which was once the seat of the Dukes of Milan, houses the excellent municipal art collections. Excursions can be made to the old university town of Pavia and to the lake resorts such as Varenna and Bellagio on Lake Como, and Stresa on Lake Maggiore.

Montréal, Québec, Canada
Map page 19

Situated on the St Lawrence River, Montréal is Canada's second-largest city. The multi-ethnic nature of its population, of whom around 60% are French-speaking, is evident in the diversity of its cuisine and cultural festivals. The Parisian-style old city has numerous 17th-, 18th- and 19th-century buildings, among them the Neo-gothic Basilique Notre-Dame. By the river a public space has been created out of the old shipyards, complete with exhibitions and amusements. Boat trips can be taken up and down the St Lawrence, including one through the Lachine Rapids. The collection in the Art Museum is wide-ranging and includes a display of Inuit art. There are also particularly interesting Botanic Gardens.

Moscow, Russia
Map page 19

Moscow radiates outwards from the Kremlin in a series of rings, of which the innermost is of greatest interest to visitors and is small enough to be explored on foot. Among the buildings enclosed by the thick red-brick walls of the Kremlin are three imposing palaces and the Archangel Cathedral. Outside is Red Square, with the exotic, multi-coloured domes of St Basil's Cathedral, the Lenin Mausoleum, the Historical Museum and the magnificent 19th-century state department store, GUM, facing each other across the famous cobbled parade ground. There are also numerous literary museums and art galleries. The palatial metro system with its glittering chandeliers and fabulous marble architecture should not be missed.

St Basil's Cathedral, Moscow

Mumbai (Bombay), India
Map page 20

Home to India's thriving film industry, Mumbai also has the largest slum area of any city in Asia. The influence of the British colonial heritage is apparent in the Victorian Gothic buildings of the Fort district, the triumphal Gateway of India arch, and the red double-decker buses. The frenetic streets and bazaars are, however, pure India. Malabar Hill, with its Hanging Gardens, provides some relief from the crowds, as do the Mahatma Gandhi Museum and an impressive new National Gallery of Modern Art. Most visitors take a boat trip across the large harbour to Elephanta Island, to see the Hindu temples hewn out of the rock.

Munich, Germany
Map page 20

Munich is a cosmopolitan city, close to the Bavarian Alps, with many beautiful buildings and a wide variety of theatres, museums, galleries and restaurants. In the centre of the old town is the Marienplatz with its famous old town hall (Rathaus), and several historic churches. Many visitors shop in the glamorous Maximilianstrasse and spend an evening at the opera or drink in one of the city's many historic beer cellars, such as the famous Hofbräuhaus. Another attraction is the beer festival in October. Just outside the city is the Baroque palace of Nymphenburg.

Nairobi, Kenya

East Africa's most modern city has broad streets lined with jacaranda trees. The compact city centre can be walked in 20 minutes, but visitors should be aware that street robberies are a growing problem. The National Museum details the history of Kenyan tribal groups. Close to the city is the Bomas of Kenya, where traditional dances and songs are performed, and the Nairobi National Park where zebras, giraffes, lions, leopards and rhinos are among the animals that can be seen, particularly from July to September.

New Orleans, Louisiana, USA

Its fantastic mix of cultures – French, Spanish, Native American, African and Caribbean – makes New Orleans one of America's most stimulating cities. It is famous as the 'cradle of jazz', and trad jazz is still played in Preservation Hall. The best way to see the elegant architecture of the French Quarter is on foot, starting in Jackson Square – a park that is surrounded by some of the city's most important public buildings, including the Louisiana State Museum. Many visitors go to New Orleans simply to enjoy its restaurants, including the Creole and Cajun cuisines, both variations on the French. Popular times to visit are during the Mardi Gras carnival in February or March, and the annual Jazz Festival in April or May.

New York, NY, USA
Map page 21

Manhattan and the Statue of Liberty, New York

New York is the ultimate destination for those who love cities, with most of its main attractions on Manhattan Island. However, its famous skyline was changed forever following the destruction of the twin towers of the World Trade Center on 11 September 2001; the 1930s Empire State Building is now the city's tallest building. The dozens of art galleries include the Metropolitan Museum of Art and the Guggenheim Museum of predominantly 20th-century art. The ferry to Staten Island provides panoramic views of Manhattan, while the Circle Line runs ferries across the harbour to the Statue of Liberty and Ellis Island. Districts to be toured on foot include Greenwich Village, with its cafés, SoHo, renowned for its art galleries and boutiques, and Little Italy. Some visitors are drawn to the city by stores such as Bloomingdales, others by its nightlife. Providing a haven from the big-city traffic is Central Park, where there is often live entertainment.

Osaka, Japan
Map page 22

The Japanese city most welcoming to foreign visitors, Osaka is enjoyed mainly for its lively nightlife and varied cuisine. It has some fine historic sites, such as the castle and the red-painted Sumiyoshi Shinto shrine to the gods of the sea. Its museums include the Liberty Osaka Museum of Human Rights and the Suntory Museum of 20th-century graphic art. The spectacular Osaka Aquarium is another attraction.

Oslo, Norway
Map page 22

The oldest of Scandinavia's capitals, Oslo is an attractive city situated at the head of Oslofjord. The impressive medieval Akershus castle contains grand staterooms, dungeons and the Norwegian Resistance Museum. The Munch Museum has over 5,000 drawings and paintings by Edvard Munch, while in the beautiful Vigeland Park, sculptures by Gustav Vigeland are on permanent display. Across the harbour is the Bygdøy peninsula with good beaches, an open-air folk museum and maritime museums containing Viking ships as well as Thor Heyerdahl's raft, *Kon-Tiki*.

Panama City, Panama

Bristling with skyscrapers and fronted by palm-fringed beaches, Panama is a thriving modern city. In the Casco Viejo district, grand Spanish colonial buildings overlook the Bay of Panama from the tip of a fortified peninsula. The old sea wall provides excellent views across the bay and there are restaurants in its restored colonial dungeons. Other attractions include the 17th-century Presidential Palace, the cathedral and the Panama Canal. The 16th-century ruins of Old Panama (Panamá Viejo) lie 6.5 km (4 miles) to the east.

Paris, France
Map page 23

Famously beautiful in springtime, Paris is fascinating at any time of year. Packed with historic buildings, world-famous art collections, fine restaurants and street cafés, it is one of the world's most elegant cities. Compact enough to explore on foot, the centre is made up of a number of distinct areas or *quartiers*, each with its own character. On a hill crowned by the basilica of Sacré-Coeur is Montmartre, with its village-like atmosphere, street artists, nearby flea markets and a splendid view over the city. The Notre Dame Cathedral and Sainte Chapelle are on the peaceful Île de la Cité, an island in the River Seine. The Picasso Museum is set among the beautiful old houses and courtyards of the Marais. The colourful Pompidou Centre looms above the galleries and cafés of the Beaubourg. The Louvre occupies a vast stretch of the Right Bank of the Seine, and there is a magnificent unbroken view through the Tuileries gardens and along the Champs Elysées to the Arc de Triomphe. Attractions on the Left Bank include the Musée d'Orsay – containing a huge collection of Impressionist art – and the Eiffel Tower. Excursions can be made to the royal palaces of Versailles and Fontainebleu, Monet's house at Giverney, and the beautiful cathedral at Chartres.

The Seine and Notre Dame, Paris

Perth, Western Australia, Australia

Situated on a sweep of the Swan River, Perth has lots of sunshine and an easy-going atmosphere. Its centre is relatively compact and dominated by skyscrapers, among which are scattered some Victorian buildings, such as the ornate Government House and the Old Flour Mill. A few miles to the west lie excellent sandy beaches and opportunities for surfing, while cruise companies offer dolphin- and whale-watching trips. The port of Fremantle, just 20 km (12 miles) away, is worth visiting, as is Rottnest Island.

Prague, Czech Republic
Map page 24

With a centre full of beautiful buildings covering 900 years of architecture it is easy to see why Prague, on the River Vitava, is one of Europe's top tourist attractions. Prague Castle (Prazsky Hrad), encompassing the 10th-century Church of St George and the Gothic St Vitus' Cathedral, is the focus of most visits to the city. Other architectural treasures include Baroque and Rococo palaces and the Neoclassical National Theatre (Náordní divadlo). The Old Jewish Quarter (Josefov) contains the Jewish Cemetery and several synagogues, including the Old-New Synagogue (Staranová). Prague's rich cultural life centres especially on its music – it is home to two fine orchestras. It is also arguably the beer-drinking capital of the world, and has several famous beer halls as well as numerous pubs and bars.

Quito, Ecuador

At a height of 2,850 m (9,350 ft), Quito escapes the oppressive temperature and pollution of many Latin American cities. The historic centre, with its whitewashed buildings and red roofs, is a UNESCO heritage site and includes a 16th-century monastery and cathedral, as well as a number of museums. There is also a fascinating vivarium, with displays of many of Ecuador's reptiles, both living and dead.

Reykjavik, Iceland

The world's northernmost capital, Reykjavik is a small modern city with colourful buildings, fashionable shops and a lively nightlife. The Arni Magnússon Institute houses a famous collection of Icelandic saga manuscripts, while the National Museum in the Old Town displays relics from the earliest days of settlement. The modern church of Hallgrímskirkja is built in the shape of a lava mountain and offers excellent views over the city from its 75 m (246 ft) high tower.

Riga, Latvia

A bustling industrial city, Riga also has a waterfront castle, a medieval centre and a lively cultural life. Places to visit include the cavernous Dome Cathedral, the Riga Motor Museum, an open-air ethnographical museum and St Peter's Church – with a view over Old Riga from the spire, which is reached by a lift. To the west, a string of resort towns known collectively as Jurmala stretches for 20 km (12 miles) along the coast, with peaceful beaches and good restaurants.

Rio de Janeiro, Brazil
Map page 24

With a spectacular location at the entrance to a bay, Rio has two famous landmarks that provide breathtaking views: Corcovado Mountain, topped by a huge statue of Christ, and Sugar Loaf Mountain. There are many museums, including the National Historical and the wide-ranging National. The city is best known, however, for its lively beaches, including Copacabana, and the more upmarket Ipanema. At night, the bars, clubs and discos of Rio resound to jazz and rock. There are samba shows primarily for tourists as well as more authentic dancehalls. A particularly popular time to visit is during the spectacular Mardi Gras Carnaval, in February or March.

View from Sugar Loaf Mountain, Rio de Janeiro

Rome, Italy
Map page 25

The historic capital of the Roman Empire, of Latin Christendom and now of Italy, Rome is exceptionally rich in treasures from many eras. Ancient buildings include the Colosseum, the Arch of Constantine, Trajan's Column, the Roman Forum

and the Pantheon. Among the early Christian sites are the famous catacombs and the basilicas of Santa Maria Maggiore and San Giovanni in Laterano (near the Colosseum). Michelangelo's Piazza del Campidoglio – bordered by three palaces – is a fine example of Renaissance town planning, but Rome is known more for its Baroque buildings and squares, and landmarks such as the Trevi Fountain and the Spanish Steps. In the centre of Rome, the Vatican City is the world's smallest independent state, containing St Peter's Square, St Peter's Basilica, the Sistine Chapel and ten museums. Increased pedestrianization of the centre has made it easier to enjoy the exuberant street life for which the city is famous.

St Petersburg, Russia   *Map page 26*

Situated in the Neva River delta, St Petersburg is a city of canals, bridges and elegant architecture. Founded in 1703 by Peter the Great, its oldest landmark is the massive Peter-Paul Fortress, with the slender spire of the Cathedral of St Peter and St Paul rising above it. At the heart of the city is Palace Square, dominated by the pastel-coloured façade of the Winter Palace. The palace is part of the Hermitage Museum, which contains one of the world's greatest collections of European art. Along the Nevsky Prospekt are the former homes of many famous Russians as well as several palaces, department stores, theatres, restaurants, churches and the richly decorated Kazan Cathedral. Day trips can be taken to several summer palaces, among them Pushkin and Petrodvorets.

San Francisco, California, USA   *Map page 25*

One of the USA's most spectacular cities, San Francisco's trademarks are its elegant suspension bridges (Golden Gate and Oakland Bay Bridge) and the street cars that service the steep streets. It is also famous as America's gay capital, the main focus of the gay community being the Castro district. The city has a thriving Chinatown, and its North Beach area (between Russian and Telegraph hills) has long been associated with alternative culture. The northern waterfront includes the famous and crowded Fisherman's Wharf development, with its numerous restaurants. The Golden Gate Park is home to several specialist gardens, art galleries and museums. A boat takes visitors to Alcatraz, the notorious island prison.

Santiago, Chile   *Map page 26*

Santiago is a sprawling city set on a wide plain at the foot of the Andes. However, its central area is relatively compact, and its tree-lined streets and landscaped parks are pleasant to explore on foot, with diversions to the Museum of Pre-Colombian Art in the Real Casa de Aduana and the Santiago Museum, close to the cathedral. A funicular goes to the peak of San Cristóbal and the Pablo Neruda Museum. Day trips can be made to the beaches of Valparaiso and the ski resort of Valle Nevado.

São Paulo, Brazil   *Map page 26*

Although much of São Paulo is modern, the area around the central square (Praça da Sé) contains several interesting old buildings, such as the whitewashed Palácio do Colégio, (a 19th-century replica of Baroque buildings), the Igreja de Santo Antônio and the Solar da Marquesa de Santos. The city has plenty of nightlife and a varied cuisine,

some of its best bars and restaurants being in the suburb known as the Jardins. The nearby Parque do Ibirapuera is a centre for sporting activities and home to several of the city's museums, as well as providing a haven of peace in its 'reading woods'.

Seattle, Washington, USA

The sparkling skyscrapers of downtown Seattle, including the trademark 'flying saucer' of the Space Needle, rise from the shores of Elliott Bay against the spectacular backdrop of the snowy peak of Mount Rainier. A recent surge in the city's prosperity (Seattle is home to the Microsoft Corporation) has led to much new building and the restoration of the historic centre. The city is a centre for contemporary arts and music, the embodiment of which is the high-tech Experience Music Project building. It also contains the headquarters of the Boeing Corporation, whose out-of-town Museum of Flight is a popular attraction.

Seoul, South Korea   *Map page 26*

Secret Garden of palace of Ch'angdok, Seoul

Selected as the site of the ruling dynasty's capital in 1394, Seoul today consists of a series of linked districts, each with its own centre. The National Assembly and financial institutions are on the small island of Youido. Spread around the old centre is a series of royal palaces, the best preserved of which is Ch'angdok, with its Secret Garden of wooded hills and ponds. T'apkol Park is a good place to meet the locals, while Namsan Park is home to the Botanic Gardens, and also to Seoul Tower, which provides a fine view of the city.

Shanghai, China   *Map page 27*

Rapidly regaining its status as a major trading and commercial centre, Shanghai's colonial past is clearly visible in the massive 1920s Neoclassical buildings of its waterfront trading area, famous as 'The Bund'. The maze of narrow streets in the Old City and the crowded bazaar of Yuyuan Park provide a complete contrast. Chinese culture is celebrated in the impressive collection of paintings, ceramics, calligraphy, and sculpture in the new Shanghai Museum. Just 80 km (50 miles) away are the famous city gardens of Suzhou, some of which are over 1,000 years old.

Singapore City, Singapore   *Map page 27*

Singapore is a popular 'stopover' city because it is relatively compact, has an efficient infrastructure and its shopping malls are a source of bargains. Amid the high-rise developments are colonial, Chinese, Malay and Indian enclaves that have retained their character, and some fine historic buildings, such as Coleman's Parliament building, the Buddhist Temple of Heavenly Happiness (Thian Hock Keng Temple) and the colourful Sri

Mariamman Hindu Temple. On the riverside are the restored old shops of Boat and Clarke Quays, both of which are relatively lively nightspots. To the south a cable car and causeway go to the island of Sentosa, which has beaches and attractions such as the impressive Underwater World, while to the north is the well-designed zoo, which features a night safari park. To the west attractions include the Jurong Bird Park and Tang Dynasty City.

Stockholm, Sweden   *Map page 28*

Built on 14 islands, between Lake Mälaren and the Baltic Sea, Stockholm is a beautiful city with numerous parks. It has an essentially modern feel, with many fine 20th-century buildings, although there is still a medieval Old Town (Gamla Stan), with narrow streets and a 15th-century cathedral (Storkyrkan). A ferry goes to Drottningholm – the royal family's island castle, complete with lakeside gardens and an 18th-century theatre. The island of Djurgarden is home to an open-air museum of Swedish vernacular architecture (Skansen) and the cathedral-like building that covers the *Vasa* – a beautifully restored 17th-century warship.

Sydney, NSW, Australia   *Map page 28*

Australia's oldest and largest city is built around a beautiful harbour that is both a major port and recreational area. Best known for its sail-shaped opera house and striking steel-arched harbour bridge, Sydney also has excellent beaches such as Manly, which can be reached by ferry, and the famous Bondi. In the centre, ferries and harbour cruises set out from Circular Quay, near which is The Rocks, with a restored historic quarter. Another area of waterside redevelopment is Darling Harbour, not far from which is the bustling Sydney Fish Market. Away from the harbour, inner suburbs worth visiting include Glebe, Newtown and Paddington, each with a distinct character and attractive 19th-century terraced houses. With an exciting mix of Asian and European cultures, the city offers a cosmopolitan choice of restaurants, theatres and music. The many museums and art galleries include the Australian Museum, which has a gallery devoted to Aboriginal history. A day trip can be made by train to the spectacular Blue Mountains only 80 km (50 miles) away.

Opera House, Sydney

Tehran, Iran   *Map page 30*

Most visitors to Tehran concentrate on its excellent museums. The National Museum and the Golestan Palace Museum house many ancient objects, including those taken from famous sites such as Persepolis. The Museum of Glass and Ceramics is well designed and organized, and the Reza Abbasis Museum displays Islamic art. For those willing to brave the heat and noise, Iran has an extensive bazaar.

Tianjin, China
Map page 30

The centre of Tianjin, for decades an important trading port, is a mixture of international architectural styles – British, French, German and Japanese – from the late 19th century. The Ancient Culture Street, a major draw for visitors, is an attempt to re-create the feel of ancient China. For a more authentic experience of Chinese culture, it is worth going to the Antiques Market and taking a walk through the Hai River Park.

Tokyo, Japan
Map page 29

Visitors to Tokyo, faced with a vast urban sprawl, normally work outwards from the Imperial Palace and the surrounding gardens, which contain the remains of Edo Castle. Immediately to the east is the downtown area, with a wide choice of restaurants and shops and some fine examples of modern architecture, including the Tokyo International Forum, with a 60 m (200 ft) high glass atrium. To the west is the Meijii Shrine, set in attractive gardens. The city centre has many art galleries, exhibiting both Japanese and European art. However, many of the largest museums, including the Tokyo National Museum, are further north, in Ueno. The adjacent Asakusa district reveals a more tranquil world of wooden houses, temples and shrines, including the magnificent temple of Senso-ji.

Toronto, Ontario, Canada
Map page 30

Standing on the shore of Lake Ontario, Toronto is Canada's leading commercial city. In its centre is the tallest free-standing structure in the world: the CN Tower. Glass-fronted lifts transport visitors to the Space Deck, 442 m (1,400 ft high), from where it is possible to see as far as Niagara Falls. The city's museums include the Royal Ontario Museum and the Gallery of Inuit Art. Along the waterfront an area of old warehouses has been developed as the Harbourfront Park, with hotels, theatres, shops and restaurants. Toronto's large immigrant population has helped create a vibrant city culture, with a thriving music scene.

Vancouver, British Columbia, Canada

Built around a natural harbour, Vancouver is a major port and city of inlets and green spaces, set against a mountain backdrop. The downtown area contains a cluster of sparkling, glass-fronted skyscrapers. Vancouver has a thriving Chinatown and a dynamic artistic and musical scene that encompasses classical, jazz and rock music. Of the many museums, the Museum of Anthropology is the finest. Stanley Park – a peninsula containing a large area of semi-wilderness – has three of Vancouver's many city beaches and the Vancouver Aquarium. Nearby is Vancouver Island, with its rainforest and glacial mountain peaks.

Varanasi, India

Built on the banks of the sacred River Ganges, Varanasi is famous for the flights of stone steps (ghats), lining 5 km (3 miles) of the river banks, where Hindu pilgrims bathe in the waters and cremate their dead. The old town consists of a maze of narrow alleyways at the heart of which is the Golden Temple, dedicated to the god Shiva. The city is also sacred for Buddhists, and at nearby Sarnath there is a collection of restored temples.

Venice, Italy

Distant view of Church of Santa Maria delle Salute, Venice

Built on a collection of islands and criss-crossed by 177 canals, Venice is a city like no other, where boats are the only means of transport. A journey by gondola or vaporetto along the Grand Canal passes many grand palaces, including the Gothic Ca' d'Oro and Ca' Foscari, the Renaissance Palazzo Grimani and the Baroque Rezzonico. The familiar landmark of the Rialto Bridge presides over the busiest shopping area in Venice. Around St Mark's Square is the stunning 11th-century Byzantine Basilica, the Pala d'Oro, and the Doge's Palace. A lift to the top of the towering Campanile provides exceptional views over the city and the lagoon, across which lies the Lido, with beaches and hotels. The Accademia contains the world's most comprehensive collection of Venetian art, including paintings by Titian, while the Peggy Guggenheim collection is one of the most important of 20th-century art outside the USA.

Vienna, Austria
Map page 31

Formerly the capital of the Habsburg and Austro-Hungarian empires, today's Vienna preserves an atmosphere of historic grandeur. A city of cafés, beer cellars, parks and elegant boulevards, it has a centre, the Innere Stadt, that is sufficiently compact to be explored on foot. It contains numerous Baroque churches and palaces, the magnificent Gothic St Stephen's Cathedral, and the Hofburg – the Habsburgs' imperial palace, which is now home to the famous Spanish Riding School. Among the city's many museums are the Kunsthistorisches (Art History Museum), with an unrivalled collection of paintings by Peter Breugel the Elder, and the fine 18th-century Belvedere palace complex which features paintings by Klimt and Schiele among others. Outside the centre is Schönbrunn, the Habsburgs' impressive summer palace, and the Prater (in Leopoldstadt), a vast park featuring Vienna's giant ferris wheel. To the north the hills of Kahlenberg and Leopoldsberg provide magnificent views over the city.

Warsaw, Poland
Map page 31

The old centre of Warsaw, on the left bank of the River Vistula, was reduced to rubble during World War II, but it has been meticulously rebuilt and is now a UNESCO World Heritage site. All the buildings appear to date from the 18th century or earlier. They include St John's Cathedral and the Renaissance and Baroque merchants' houses surrounding the Old Market Square (Rynek Starego Miasta). There is also the excellent Historical Museum of Warsaw, many lively cafés and some fine restaurants. Outside the Old Town is the beautiful Lazienki park and palace complex and, 6 km (4 miles) further south, the restored Baroque Wilanów park and palace.

Washington DC, USA
Map page 32

The main public buildings of Washington DC are grouped on and around the National Mall – a broad swathe of parkland containing the Washington Monument, the Lincoln and Jefferson memorials, and the V-shaped polished black stone wall incised with thousands of names, which commemorates the Americans who fell in Vietnam. On the north side of the Mall is the White House, and overlooking all from the eastern end is the Capitol building, with its 55 m (180 ft) high rotunda. Home to the House of Representatives and the Senate, it is open to visitors. The National Gallery of Art and the National Air and Space Museum are two of the many museums. Central Washington DC can be dangerous at night. Georgetown is more relaxed, with its restaurants, bars and handsome streets. Within easy reach of the city are Chesapeake Bay and several Civil War battle sites.

Wellington, New Zealand
Map page 32

Overlooked by Mount Victoria, Wellington is the political and commercial capital of New Zealand. Wooden Victorian houses climb the steep hills surrounding the magnificent harbour of Port Nicholson, and a cable car provides a spectacular view of the city. Among the historic buildings in the centre are the Old Government Buildings, while the city's museums include the recently opened Museum of New Zealand (Te Papa). A lively, cosmopolitan city, Wellington has an exciting cultural scene, as evidenced in February and March by the annual Fringe Festival and the biennial International Festival of the Arts.

View over the harbour, Wellington

Xi'an, China

As well as being a base from which to visit the famous Army of Terracotta Warriors, Xi'an possesses its own historic sites. These include the impressive city walls that all but surround the old town, and the 64 m (200 ft) high Big Goose Pagoda. Xi'an also has a strong Islamic culture and its Great Mosque is the largest in China. The Shaanxi Provincial Museum presents a fascinating history of the Silk Road.

Yangon (Rangoon), Burma (Myanmar)

The main focus of any visit to Yangon will be the magnificent Shwedagon stupa. The stupa is 90 m (290 ft) high and shaped like a bell. Completely covered in gold, it is surrounded by a host of smaller gilded stupas, statues, temples and pavilions. Of the many other Buddhist sites around the city, the huge reclining Buddha at Chaukhtatgyi Paya is the most impressive. Two large lakes provide areas of recreation, and the many tree-lined streets and areas of near-jungle give some parts an almost rural feel.

WORLD MAPS

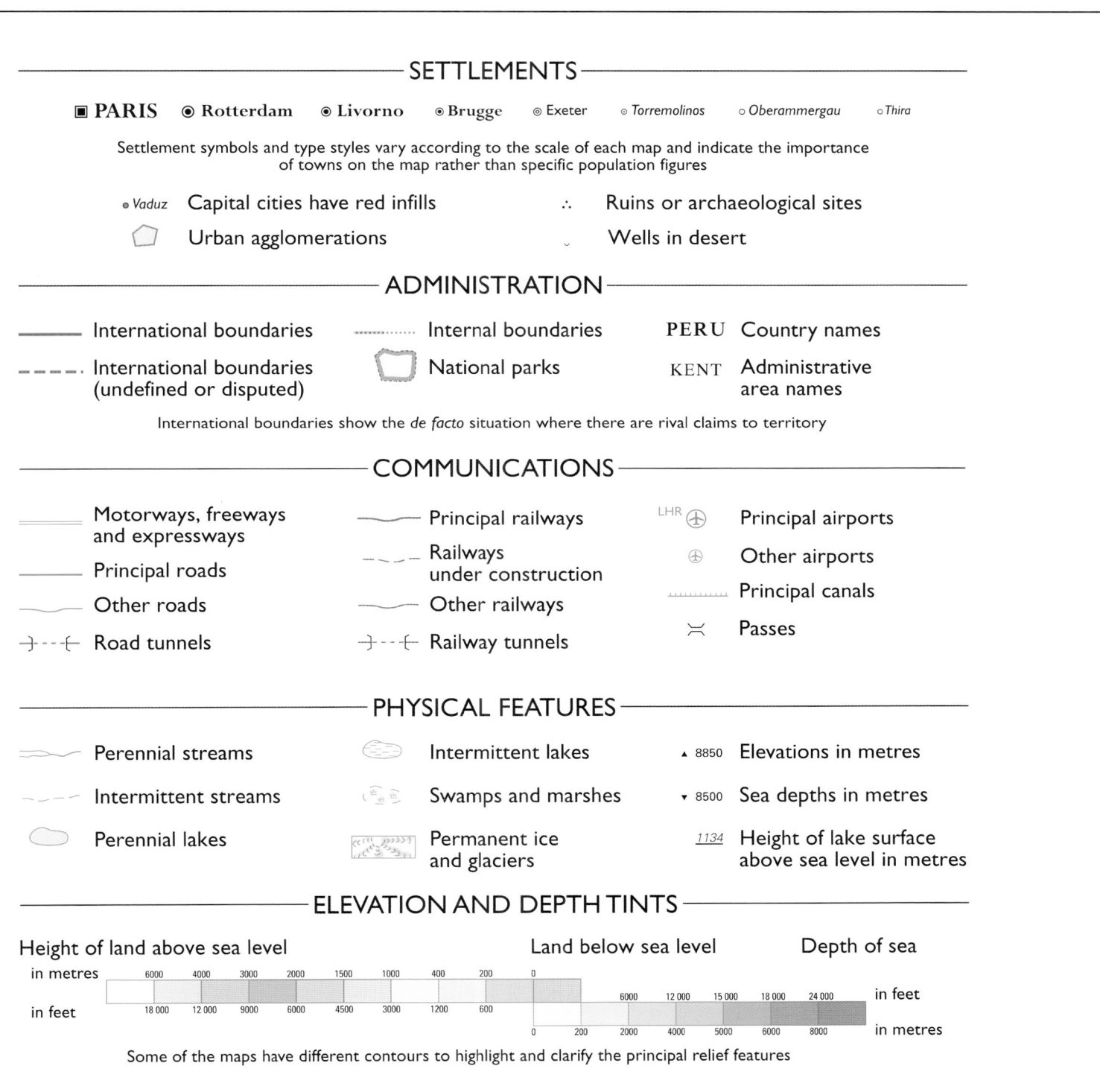

SETTLEMENTS

■ PARIS ◉ Rotterdam ◉ Livorno ◉ Brugge ◉ Exeter ○ Torremolinos ○ Oberammergau ○ Thira

Settlement symbols and type styles vary according to the scale of each map and indicate the importance of towns on the map rather than specific population figures

● Vaduz Capital cities have red infills ∴ Ruins or archaeological sites

Urban agglomerations Wells in desert

ADMINISTRATION

International boundaries Internal boundaries PERU Country names

International boundaries (undefined or disputed) National parks KENT Administrative area names

International boundaries show the *de facto* situation where there are rival claims to territory

COMMUNICATIONS

Motorways, freeways and expressways Principal railways LHR Principal airports

Principal roads Railways under construction Other airports

Other roads Other railways Principal canals

Road tunnels Railway tunnels Passes

PHYSICAL FEATURES

Perennial streams Intermittent lakes ▲ 8850 Elevations in metres

Intermittent streams Swamps and marshes ▼ 8500 Sea depths in metres

Perennial lakes Permanent ice and glaciers 1134 Height of lake surface above sea level in metres

ELEVATION AND DEPTH TINTS

Height of land above sea level   Land below sea level   Depth of sea

in metres   6000 4000 3000 2000 1500 1000 400 200 0

6000 12 000 15 000 18 000 24 000   in feet

in feet   18 000 12 000 9000 6000 4500 3000 1200 600

0 200 2000 4000 5000 6000 8000   in metres

Some of the maps have different contours to highlight and clarify the principal relief features

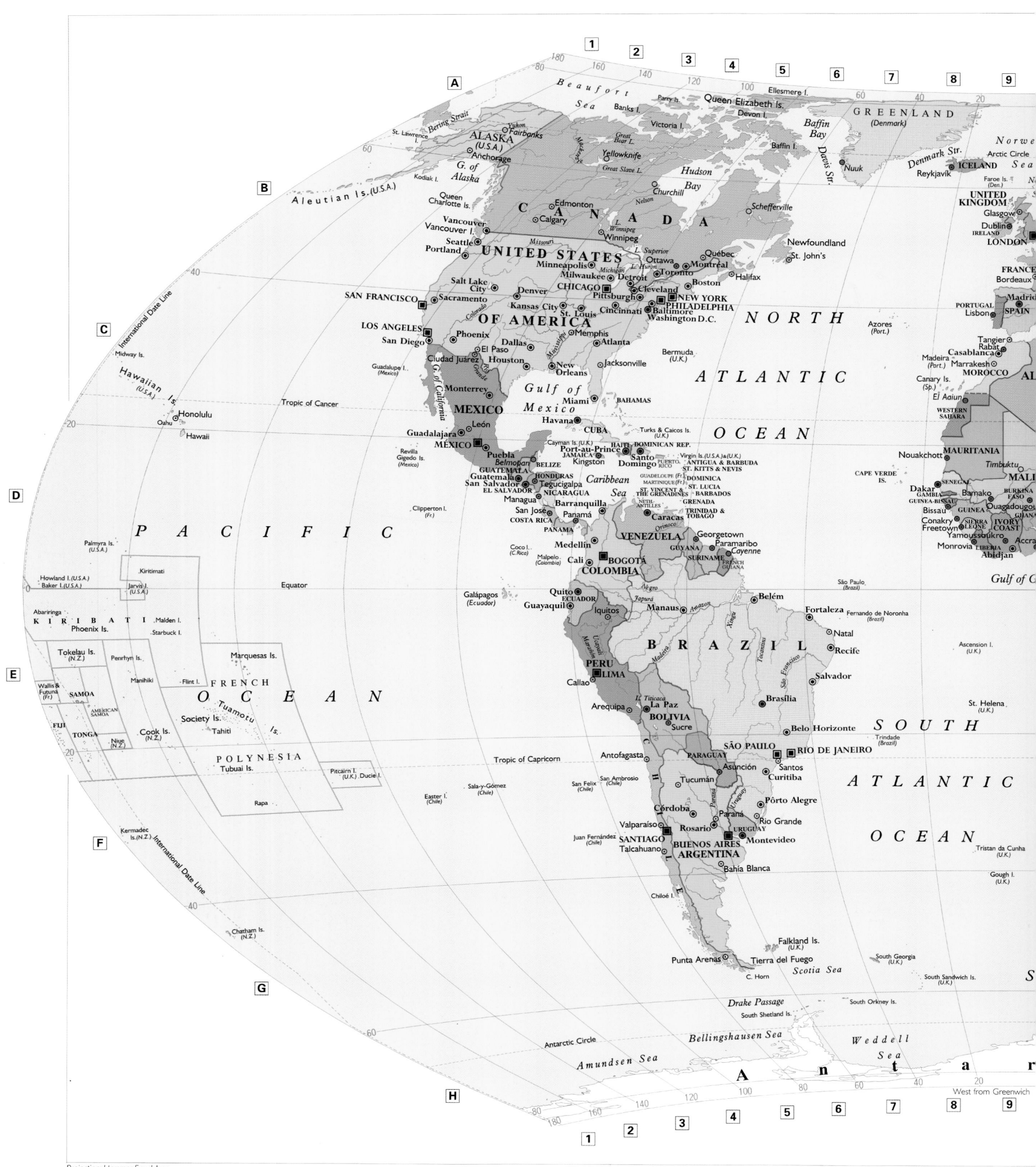

Projection: Hammer Equal Area

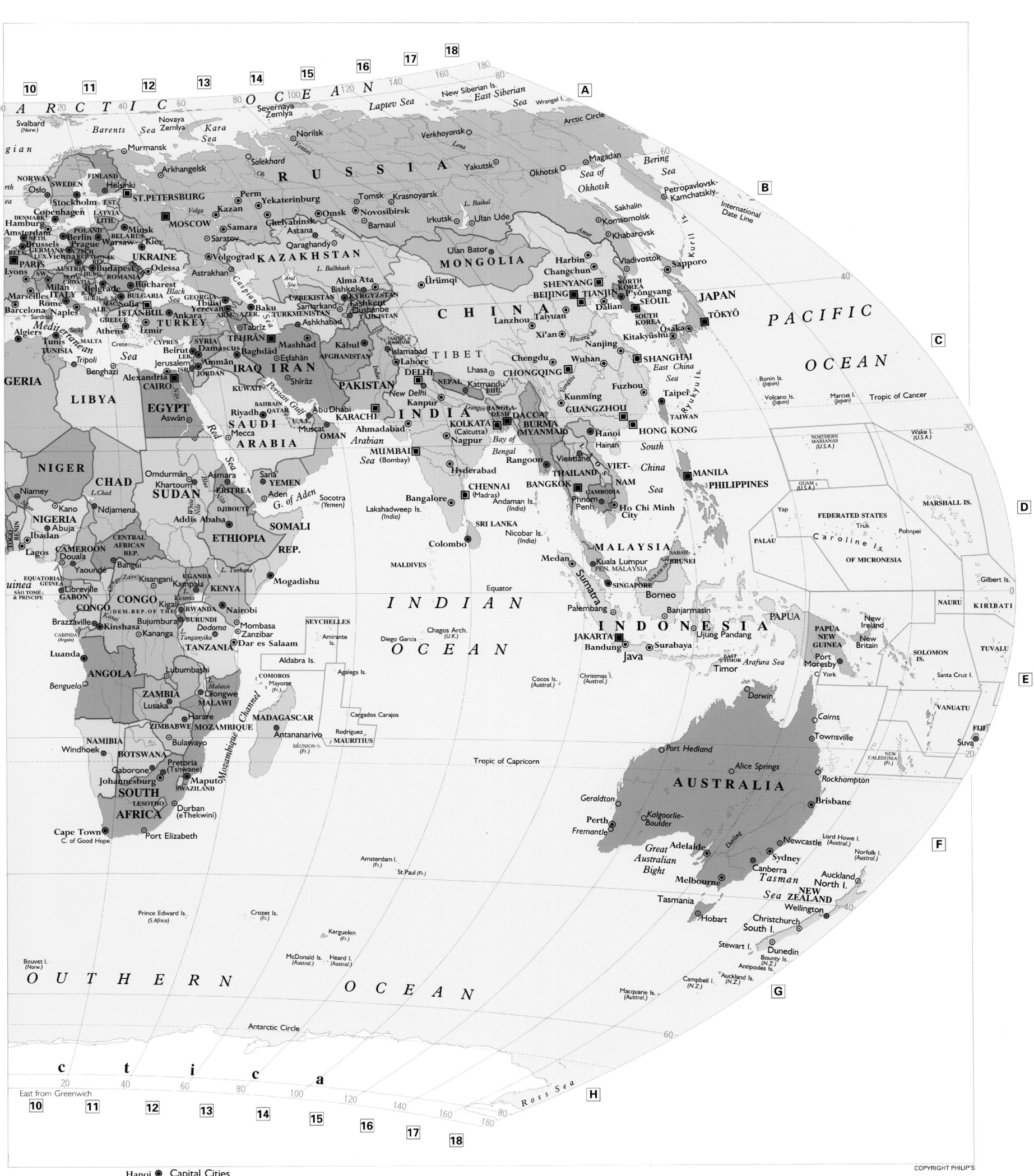

Hanoi ● Capital Cities

1:31 100 000

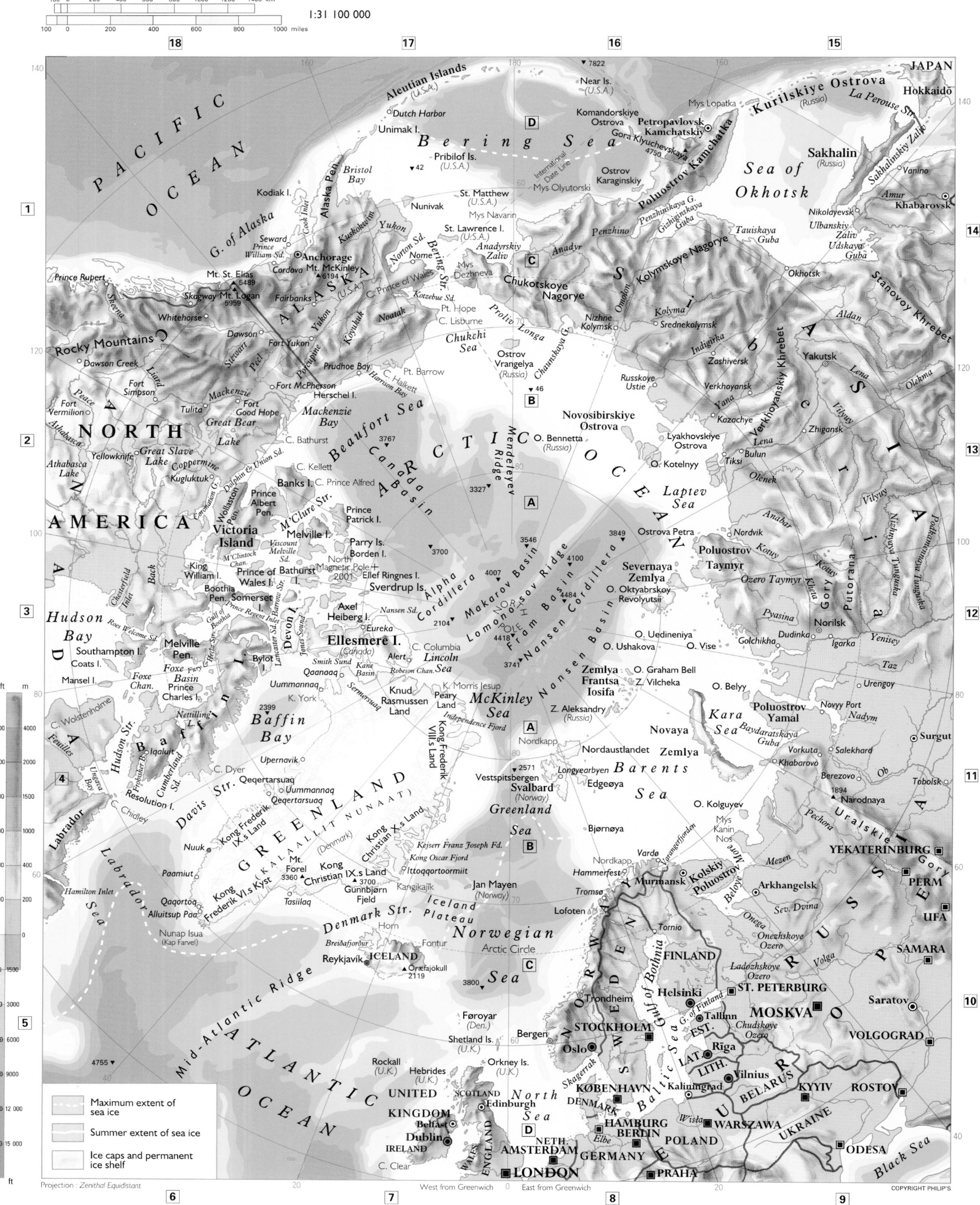

Legend:
- Maximum extent of sea ice
- Summer extent of sea ice
- Ice caps and permanent ice shelf

Projection : Zenithal Equidistant

West from Greenwich   East from Greenwich

COPYRIGHT PHILIP'S

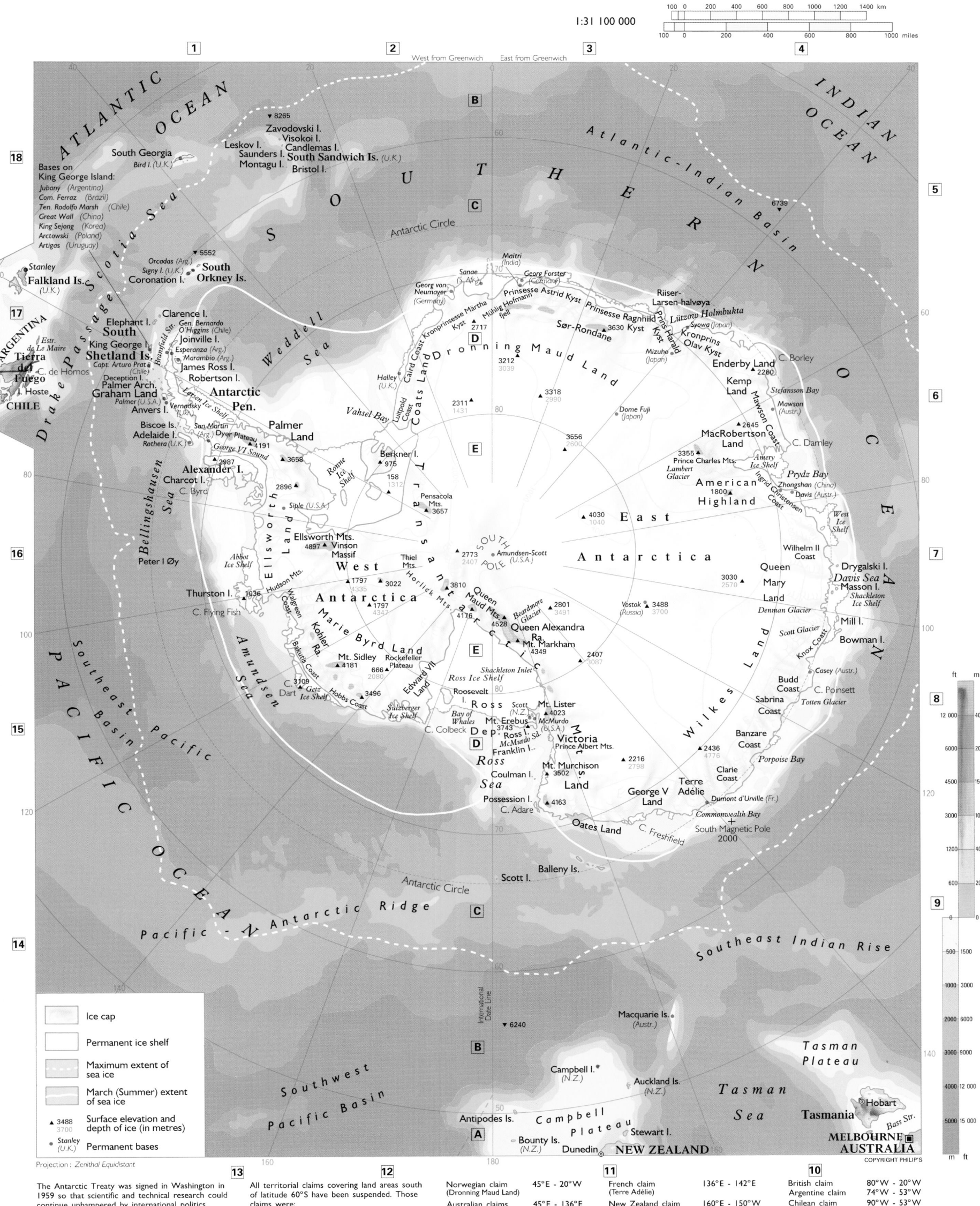

ANTARCTICA 5

1:31 100 000

West from Greenwich | East from Greenwich

ATLANTIC OCEAN

INDIAN OCEAN

SOUTHERN

Atlantic-Indian Basin

▼ 8265

Zavodovski I.
Visokoi I.
Leskov I. Candlemas I.
Saunders I. South Sandwich Is. (U.K.)
Montagu I. Bristol I.

South Georgia
Bird I. (U.K.)

Bases on King George Island:
Jubany (Argentina)
Com. Ferraz (Brazil)
Ten. Rodolfo Marsh (Chile)
Great Wall (China)
King Sejong (Korea)
Arctowski (Poland)
Artigas (Uruguay)

Antarctic Circle

6739 ▲

▼ 5552

Orcadas (Arg.)
Signy I. (U.K.) South Orkney Is.
Coronation I.

Stanley
Falkland Is.
(U.K.)

ARGENTINA

Clarence I.
Elephant I.
South Gen. Bernardo O'Higgins (Chile)
King George I. Joinville I.
Shetland Is. Esperanza (Arg.)
Capt. Arturo Prat (Chile) Marambio (Arg.)
Deception I. James Ross I.
Robertson I.

Tierra del Fuego
C. de Hornos
I. Hoste
CHILE

Drake Passage

Scotia Sea

Weddell Sea

Maitri (India)
Sanae (S. Afr.)
Georg von Neumayer (Germany)
Georg Forster (Germany)

Prinsesse Astrid Kyst
Prinsesse Ragnhild Kyst
Mühlig Hofmann fjell
Kronprinsesse Martha Kyst
2717

Riiser-Larsen-halvøya
Prins Harald Kyst
Lützow Holmbukta
Syowa (Japan)
Kronprins Olav Kyst

Palmer Arch.
Anvers I.
Palmer (U.S.A.)
Vernadsky (U.K.)

Graham Land
Antarctic Pen.

Dronning Maud Land
Coats Land
Caird Coast
Kronprinsesse Martha

3630 Kyst
3212
3039

3318
2990

Enderby Land
Kemp Land
Mawson (Austr.)
2280
C. Borley
Stefansson Bay

Biscoe Is.
Adelaide I.
Rothera (U.K.)
San Martín (Arg.)
Dyer Plateau

Palmer Land
Halley (U.K.)
Vahsel Bay

3656
2600

Mizuho (Japan)
Dome Fuji (Japan)
2311
1431

MacRobertson Land
2645
Prince Charles Mts.
3355
3491
C. Darnley

2987
C. Byrd
Alexander I.
Charcot I.

Bellingshausen Sea

George VI Sound
3191

3658
Ronne Ice Shelf
Berkner I.
975
158
1312

Lambert Glacier
Amery Ice Shelf

American Highland
1800
Zhongshan (China)
Davis (Austr.)
Prydz Bay
Ingrid Christensen Coast
Zhongshan

Peter I Øy

2896

Siple (U.S.A.)
Pensacola Mts.
3657

4030
1040

East Antarctica

Wilhelm II Coast
West Ice Shelf

Ellsworth Mts.
4897
Vinson Massif

Thiel Mts.
2773
3810
4335

SOUTH POLE
Amundsen-Scott (U.S.A.)
2407

3030
2570

Queen Mary Land

Drygalski I.
Davis Sea
Masson I.
Shackleton Ice Shelf

Thurston I.
1036
C. Flying Fish

Hudson Mts.
1797
3022
Horlick Mts.

Queen Maud Mts.
4176
4528
Beardmore Glacier
2801
3491

Vostok (Russia)
3488
3700

Denman Glacier
Scott Glacier
Knox Coast
Totten Glacier

Mill I.
Bowman I.

West Antarctica

Marie Byrd Land

Kohler Ra.

1797
4341

Queen Alexandra Ra.
Mt. Markham
4349

2407
3087

Budd Coast
Sabrina Coast
Casey (Austr.)
C. Poinsett

Mt. Sidley
4181
Rockefeller Plateau
666
2080

Edward VII Land

Shackleton Inlet
Ross Ice Shelf

Banzare Coast

Bakutis Coast
C. 3109
Dart
Getz Ice Shelf
Hobbs Coast
3496

Salzberger Ice Shelf

Roosevelt I.
Ross Sea
Bay of Whales
C. Colbeck

Scott (N.Z.)
Mt. Lister
4023
Mt. Erebus
3743
Ross I.
McMurdo (U.S.A.)
McMurdo Sd.
Franklin I.

Mt. Murchison
3502

Victoria Land
Prince Albert Mts.

2436
4776

Clarie Coast
Porpoise Bay

2216
2798

Terre Adélie
Dumont d'Urville (Fr.)
Commonwealth Bay
South Magnetic Pole
2000

Coulman I.
Possession I.
C. Adare
4163

George V Land
Oates Land
C. Freshfield

Balleny Is.

Scott I.

Antarctic Circle

Pacific-Antarctic Ridge

Southeast Pacific Basin

PACIFIC OCEAN

Amundsen Sea

Southeast Indian Rise

▼ 6240

International Date Line

Macquarie Is. (Austr.)

Tasman Plateau

Southwest Pacific Basin

Campbell I. (N.Z.)

Auckland Is. (N.Z.)

Tasman Sea

Hobart
Tasmania
Bass Str.

Antipodes Is.
Campbell Plateau
Bounty Is. (N.Z.)
Stewart I.
Dunedin
NEW ZEALAND

MELBOURNE
AUSTRALIA
COPYRIGHT PHILIP'S

Legend

- Ice cap
- Permanent ice shelf
- Maximum extent of sea ice
- March (Summer) extent of sea ice
- ▲ 3488 / 3700 Surface elevation and depth of ice (in metres)
- ● Stanley (U.K.) Permanent bases

Projection : Zenithal Equidistant

The Antarctic Treaty was signed in Washington in 1959 so that scientific and technical research could continue unhampered by international politics.

All territorial claims covering land areas south of latitude 60°S have been suspended. Those claims were:

Norwegian claim (Dronning Maud Land)	45°E - 20°W
Australian claims	45°E - 136°E 142°E - 160°E
French claim (Terre Adélie)	136°E - 142°E
New Zealand claim (Ross Dependency)	160°E - 150°W
British claim	80°W - 20°W
Argentine claim	74°W - 53°W
Chilean claim	90°W - 53°W

ft m
12 000 / 4000
9000 / 3000
6000 / 2000
4500 / 1500
3000 / 1000
1800 / 600
600 / 200
0 / 0

m / ft
1500
3000
6000
9000
12 000
15 000

1:17 800 000

100 0 100 200 300 400 500 600 700 800 km
100 0 100 200 300 400 500 miles

Projection: Bonne

COPYRIGHT PHILIP'S

Ural Mountains

Obshchi Syrt

Caspian Depression

Caspian Sea

Volga

Ural

Caucasus

Elbruz 5642

Pontine Mts.

Kurdistan

L. Urmia
L. Van
Ararat 5165

Mesopotamia

Tigris
Euphrates

Volga Hts.

Kama
Iz
Iz
Pechora
Narodnaya 1894

U r a l s

Pechora
Mezen
N. Dvina
Oka
Volga

Central Russian Uplands

Don
Donets
Basin
Donets

Tsimlyansk Res.

Manych

Kerch
Kuban
Terek

Sea of Azov
Str. of Kerch
Crimea

Black Sea

Bosporus

Anatolia (Asia Minor)

Taurus Mts.
Erciyas Dağ 3916

L. Tuz

Kızıl Irmak

Rybinsk Res.

L. Onega
Str. of
Chudskoye
L. Ladoga

W. Dvina

Pripet

Bug

Dnieper

Ukraine

Dniester

Prut

Danube

Balkans

Rhodope

Sea of Marmara
Dardanelles
Mt. Ida 1766

Ægean Sea

Rhodes
Cyprus
Crete

White Sea

Kola Pen.

Kanin Pen.

Finland
Karelia

L. Onega

G. of Finland
Åland

European Plain

North European Plain

Niemen

Odra

Elbe

Carpathians
Tatra 2655
Moravian Hts.
Sudeten
Bohemian Forest

Transylvanian Alps
Plain of Hungary
Tisza
Drava
Sava
Danube
Wallachia

Dinaric Alps

Adriatic Sea

Pindus

Morea

Olympus 2917

Str. of Otranto

Ionian Is.

Ionian Sea

C. Matapan

Lapland
Njordknold

Inari
Torne

Scandinavia

Vesterålen
Lofoten
Kebnekaise 2111

G. of Bothnia

Indals
Ume
Mälaren

Gotland
Öland
Bornholm

Baltic Sea

Jutland

Vänern
Vättern

Kattegat
Skagerrak

Fyn
Sjælland
Møns Klint

Glittertind 2469
Galdhøpiggen 2469

Norwegian Sea

North Cape
Bjørnøy
Arctic Circle

Iceland
Hofsjökull
Öræfajökull 2119
Hekla 1491

SOUTH EAST ICELAND

Faroe Is.

Shetland Is.
Orkney Is.
Fair Isle
Hebrides

Great Britain
Ben Nevis 1343
British Isles
Snowdon 1085

Ireland

North Sea
Dogger
Fisher
German Bight
Helgoland

Forties
Humber
Thames
Tyne
Forth
Cromarty

English Channel
Channel Is.
Brittany

Celtic Sea
Land's End
Plymouth
Lundy

FASTNET
SOLE
SHANNON
ROCKALL
BAILEY
FAEROES

Rockall

ATLANTIC OCEAN

Bay of Biscay

Gironde
Garonne
Loire
Seine

Massif Central
Cévennes
Puy de Sancy 1886

Pyrenees
Pic de Néthou 3404
G. of Lions

Jura
Vosges
Black Forest
Ardennes
Rhine
Rhône
Saône

Alps
Mont Blanc 4807

Apennines
Gran Sasso d'Italia 2914
Po
Tiber
Vesuvius 1277

Ligurian Sea
Corsica
Sardinia

Tyrrhenian Sea

Str. of Bonifacio
C. Bon
Pantelleria
Sicily
Etna 3340
Str. of Messina
Calabria 4070
Malta

Balearic Is.
Minorca
Majorca
Ibiza

Cantabrian Mts.
Old Castile
New Castile

Iberian Peninsula
Duero
Ebro
Tagus

Sierra Morena
Andalusia
Sierra Nevada 3478
Guadalquivir
Guadiana

Str. of Gibraltar

C. de São Vicente
C. da Roca
C. Finisterre

Africa
Plateau of the Shotts

Mediterranean Sea

East from Greenwich
West from Greenwich

ROCKALL Sea areas named in weather forecasts

m ft
15 000 5000
12 000 4000
3000
2000
6000 1000
3000 600
1200 400
600 200
0
200 600
1000 3000
2000 6000
4000 12 000
ft m

1:17 800 000

100 0 100 200 300 400 500 600 700 800 km
100 0 100 200 300 400 500 miles

COPYRIGHT PHILIP'S

C D E F G H J

ICELAND
Reykjavik

NORWEGIAN Sea

ATLANTIC OCEAN

Tromsø
Narvik
Kiruna
Hammerfest

SWEDEN
NORWAY
FINLAND
Gulf of Bothnia
Luleå
Vaasa
Tampere
Turku
Helsinki

Trondheim
Bergen
Stavanger
Oslo
Gävle
Uppsala
Stockholm
Örebro
Jönköping
Göteborg
Gothenburg
Malmö

DENMARK
Ålborg
Århus
Copenhagen
Kiel
Kattegat
Skagerrak

North Sea
Shetland Is.
Orkney Is.
Faroe Is. (Den.)
Hebrides
SCOTLAND
Aberdeen
Dundee
Edinburgh
Glasgow
N. IRELAND
Belfast
IRELAND
Dublin
Cork
UNITED KINGDOM
WALES
ENGLAND
Newcastle-upon-Tyne
Leeds
Manchester
Liverpool
Sheffield
Birmingham
Cardiff
Bristol
LONDON
Southampton
Plymouth
English Channel
Channel Is.

White Sea
Murmansk
Arkhangelsk
N. Dvina
L. Onega
L. Ladoga

St. Petersburg
Vyborg
Lake Chudskoye
ESTONIA
Tallinn
LATVIA
Riga
LITHUANIA
Kaunas
Vilnius
Kaliningrad (Russia)

R U S S I A
MOSCOW
Nizhniy Tagil
Yekaterinburg
Chelyabinsk
Magnitogorsk
Perm
Ufa
Kotlas
Kirov
Kazan
Simbirsk
Samara
Saratov
Penza
Uralsk
Orenburg
Tambov
Voronezh
Tula
Orel
Kursk
Ryazan
Yaroslavl
Vologda
Kostroma
Ivanovo
Nizhniy Novgorod
Rybinsk Res.
Smolensk
Vitebsk
W. Dvina
Mahilyow
Minsk
BELARUS
Homel
Pripet
Brest
Volga

KAZAKHSTAN
Ural

Caspian Sea
Astrakhan
Volgograd
Makhachkala
Baku
AZERBAIJAN
ARMENIA
Yerevan
GEORGIA
Tbilisi

IRAN
Tabriz
Araks

IRAQ
Baghdad
Tigris
Euphrates
SYRIA
Aleppo
T U R K E Y
Erzurum
Diyarbakir
Kayseri
Adana
Konya
Ankara
Izmir
Bursa
ISTANBUL
Bosporus
CYPRUS
Nicosia

Black Sea
Constanta
Varna
Odessa
Nikolayev
Kherson
Krivoy Rog
Zaporozhye
Dnepropetrovsk
Donetsk
Kharkov
Rostov
Taganrog
Krasnodar
Stavropol
Crimea
Sevastopol
Samsun
Antalya
Rhodes

U K R A I N E
Kiev
Zhytomyr
Chernihiv
Lvov
Dniester
Bug
Dnieper
Galati
MOLDOVA
Kishinev

POLAND
Warsaw
Gdansk
Szczecin
Bydgoszcz
Białystok
Poznań
Łódź
Lublin
Wrocław
Kraków
Katowice
Vistula
Oder

ROMANIA
Bucharest
Cluj-Napoca
Timişoara
Braşov
Ploieşti
Danube
BULGARIA
Sofia
Plovdiv
SERBIA & MONTENEGRO
Belgrade
Niš
MACEDONIA
Skopje
ALBANIA
Tiranë
BOSNIA-HERZ.
Sarajevo
CROATIA
Zagreb
Split
HUNGARY
Budapest
Debrecen
Miskolc
SLOVAK REP.
Bratislava
CZECH REP.
Prague
Ostrava
AUSTRIA
Vienna
Linz
Graz
Salzburg
Innsbruck
SLOVENIA
Ljubljana
Trieste

GERMANY
Berlin
Hamburg
Bremen
Hannover
Magdeburg
Leipzig
Dresden
Chemnitz
Halle
Dortmund
Essen
Cologne
Düsseldorf
Frankfurt am Main
Stuttgart
Nuremberg
Munich
Elbe
Rhine
NETHER-LANDS
Amsterdam
The Hague
Rotterdam
BELGIUM
Brussels
Antwerp
LUX.
Luxembourg
Meuse

FRANCE
PARIS
Lille
Le Havre
Rouen
Strasbourg
Dijon
Nantes
Loire
Limoges
Lyons
St-Étienne
Grenoble
Bordeaux
Garonne
Toulouse
Rhône
Nice
Marseilles
Toulon
Brest
Seine
Bay of Biscay
Gironde
ANDORRA
Andorra-la-Vella

SWITZERLAND
Zürich
Geneva
Bern
Basle

ITALY
Rome
Milan
Turin
Genoa
Venice
Bologna
Florence
Naples
Bari
Táranto
Palermo
Messina
Catánia
Sicily
Sardinia
Cágliari
Corsica
Ajaccio
Tiber
SAN MARINO
MONACO

Adriatic Sea
Tyrrhenian Sea
Ionian Sea
Ægean Sea
GREECE
Athens
Patras
Thessaloniki
Corfu
Crete

MALTA
Valletta
Pantelleria (Italy)

SPAIN
Madrid
Barcelona
Valencia
Zaragoza
Bilbao
Valladolid
Málaga
Córdoba
Granada
Seville
Alicante
Murcia
Cádiz
La Coruña
Vigo
Ebro
Balearic Is.
Minorca
Majorca
Ibiza
Palma
Gibraltar (U.K.)
Str. of Gibraltar

PORTUGAL
Lisbon
Porto
Douro
Tagus
Guadiana

Mediterranean Sea

MOROCCO
Tangier
Ceuta (Sp.)
Melilla

ALGERIA
Algiers
Annaba
Constantine
A f r i c a

TUNISIA
Tunis

West from Greenwich
East from Greenwich
Arctic Circle

Projection: Bonne

■ LONDON Capital Cities

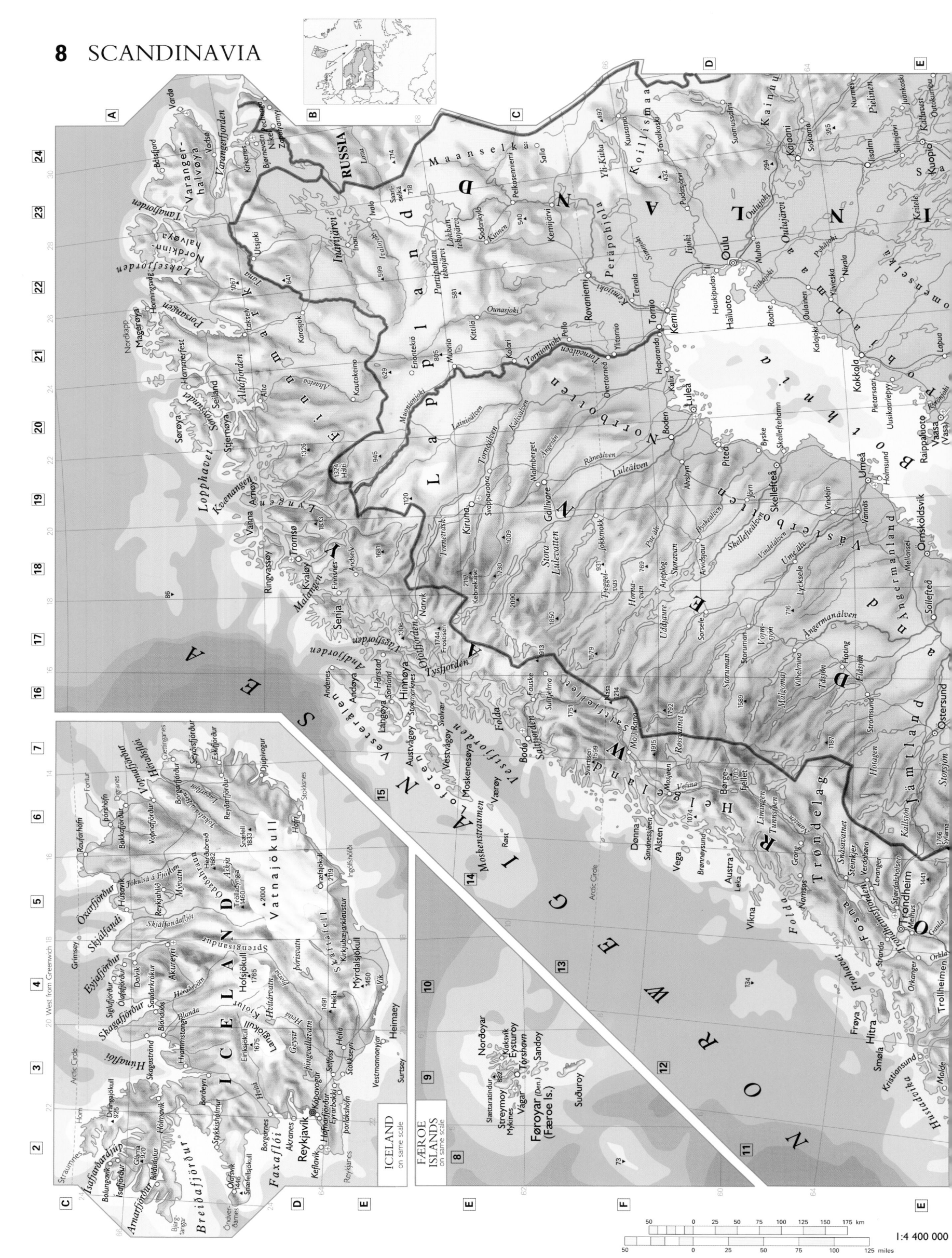

ICELAND
on same scale

FÆROE
ISLANDS
on same scale

1:4 400 000

East from Greenwich

Projection: Conical with two standard parallels

1:1 800 000

10 0 10 20 30 40 50 60 70 80 km
10 0 10 20 30 40 50 miles

13

SCOTLAND

Kintyre
Mull of Oa
Brodick
Arran
Campbeltown
Firth of Clyde

Inishtrahull
Malin Hd.
Lough Swilly
Fanad Hd.
Mulroy B.
Malin
Carndonagh
Moville
Giants Causeway
Rathlin I.
Ballycastle
Fair Hd.
Mull of Kintyre
Ailsa Craig
Tory I.
Sheep Haven
Horn Hd.
Inishowen Pen.
Portstewart
Portrush
Mts. of Antrim
L. Ryan
Bloody Foreland
Gweedore
Errigal 752
Rathmelton
Buncrana
L. Foyle
Coleraine
Limavady
Ballymoney 554
Garron Pt.
GLENARIFF
Carnryan
Stranraer
Aran I.
The Rosses
683
Letterkenny
GLENVEAGH
Londonderry
Bann
Ballymena
Larne
Portpatrick
Inishfree B.
Derryveagh Mts.
LONDONDERRY
Sawel Mt. Roe
Magherafelt
Randalstown Ballyclare
Mts. 269
Crohy Hd.
Gweebarra B.
DONEGAL
Glenties
Lifford
Strabane
683 Sperrin Mts.
NORTHERN
Antrim
Newtownabbey
Belfast L.
Carrickfergus
Dawros Hd.
Lavagh More 676
Finn
Sion Mills
Newtownstewart
Moneymore
Cookstown
Lough Neagh
Belfast
Bangor
Donaghadee
Newtownards
Loughros More B.
601 Killybegs
Donegal
Castlederg
TYRONE
Omagh
Coalisland
Dungannon
IRELAND
Lisburn
Comber
Ards Pen.
Rossan Pt.
Slieve League
St. John's Pt.
Ballyshannon
Erne
Irvinestown
Enniskillen
Dromore
Aughnacloy
Armagh
DOWN
Strangford L.
Portaferry
Donegal Bay
Bundoran
Lower L. Erne
FERMANAGH
Monaghan
Middletown
Craigavon
Lurgan
Lagan
Banbridge
Ballynahinch
Ballyquintin Pt.
Bundoran
Upper Erne
Clones
MONAGHAN
Castleblaney
Keady
Portadown
Dundrum
Downpatrick
St. John's Pt.
Sligo Bay
Sligo
Manorhamilton
L. Allen
Belturbet
Annalee
Cootehill
Newry
Mourne Mts.
852 Slieve Donard
Newcastle
Dundrum B.
Killala B.
Killala
LEITRIM
Leitrim
Cavan
Carrickmacross
577 Slieve Gullion
Warrenpoint
Kilkeel
Broad Haven
Erris Hd.
Ballina
Sligo
CAVAN
L. Gowna
Kingscourt
Dundalk
Greenore
Carlingford L.
Mullet Pen.
Belmullet
380
Charlestown
Boyle
Carrick-on-Shannon
L. Sheelin
Oldcastle
Louth
Ardee
Dunleer
Dundalk Bay
Inishkea North
Inishkea South
Blacksod Bay
Swinford
Ballaghaderreen
Granard
Ceanannus Mor (Kells)
LOUTH
Clogher Hd.
Achill Hd.
672
Corraun Pen.
806
Nephin
MAYO
Newport
Castlebar
Knock
ROSCOMMON
Castlerea
Longford
Castlepollard
Blackwater
Drogheda
Balbriggan
Achill I.
Clare I.
Clew Bay
Westport
Ballyhaunis
Claremorris
Roscommon
LONGFORD
An Uaimh (Navan)
Rush
Inishturk
Killary Harbour
765 Croagh Patrick
819 Mweelrea
Ballinrobe
Glennamaddy
IRELAND
Trim
Royal Canal
Swords
Lambay I.
Inishbofin
Inishshark
Connemara
Lough Mask
Tuam
Inny
MEATH
Athboy
Boyne
Malahide
CONNEMARA
Clifden
Oughterard
Lough Corrib
WESTMEATH
Leinster
DUB
Howth Hd.
Slyne Hd.
GALWAY
Athenry
Lough Ree
Moate
Mullingar
Edenderry
Maynooth
DUBLIN
Dublin
Dun Laoghaire
Galway
Athlone
Ballinasloe
Clara
Daingean
Bog of Allen
KILDARE
Clondalkin
Bertraghboy B.
Kilkieran B.
Galway Bay
Black Hd.
Loughrea
Suck
Tullamore
OFFALY
Portarlington
Droichead Nua
Naas
Bray
Greystones
Aran Is.
Inishmore
Inishmaan
Inisheer
368 Slieve Aughty
Gort
Portumna
Shannon
Birr
Mountmellick
Port Laoise
Monasterevin
Athy
Kilcock
754
Wicklow Mts.
Cliffs of Moher
Hags Hd.
BURREN
Lough Derg
Slieve Bloom 528 Arden
Roscrea
Mountrath
LAOIS
Carlow
Tullow
Arklow
Liscannor Bay
Ennistimon
Tulla
Nenagh
Templemore
Durrow
Wicklow
Wicklow Hd.
Mal Bay
Mutton I.
Ennis
Killaloe
Thurles
Kilkenny
Callan
CARLOW
Muine Bheag
Shillelagh
Lugnaquilla 926
Avoca
Rathdrum
Kilkee
Sixmilebridge
CLARE
694 Keeper Hill
TIPPERARY
KILKENNY
796 Mt. Leinster
Bunclody
Gorey
Loop Hd.
Kilrush
Limerick
Golden Vale
Cashel
Nore
Barrow
Slaney
WEXFORD
Cahore Pt.
Mouth of the Shannon
Foynes
Rathkeale
Tipperary
Slievenamon 722
Enniscorthy
Ballybunion
LIMERICK
Newcastle West
Caher
Carrick-on-Suir
New Ross
Wexford
Kerry Hd.
Munster
Kilfinnane
Galtymore 920
Galty Mts.
Clonmel
Wexford Harbour
Rosslare
Rosslare Harbour
Brandon B.
Tralee B.
Listowel
Feale
Rath Luirc
Mitchelstown
Knockmealdown Mts. 795
Comeragh Mts. 792
Waterford
Tramore
Greenore Pt.
Smerwick Harbour
Tralee
Maine
Newmarket
Buttevant
Fermoy
WATERFORD
Tramore B.
Waterford Harbour
Brandon Mt. 953
Slieve Mish 853
Killarney
Kanturk
Mallow
Blackwater
Lismore
Dungarvan
Dungarvan Harbour
Hook Hd.
Saltee Is.
Carnsore Pt.
Dingle
Laune
Boggeragh Mts.
Youghal
Youghal B.
Great Blasket I.
Dunmore Hd.
Dingle Bay
Killorglin
L. Leane
646
CORK
Blarney
Midleton
St. David's Hd.
St. David's
Inishvickillane
Carrauntoohill 1041
KILLARNEY
Macgillycuddy's Reeks
Cork
WALES
St. Brides Bay
Valencia I.
Cahersiveen
Kenmare
Lee
Passage West
Cobh
Crosshaven
Cork Harbour
Puffin I.
707
Macroom
Bandon
Kinsale
Great Skellig
Caha Mts.
Glengarriff
Dunmanway
Clonakilty
Old Head of Kinsale
115
Ballinskelligs B.
Scariff I.
Kenmare River
686
Bantry
Skibbereen
Clonakilty B.
Dursey I.
Castletown Bearhaven
Bear I.
Bantry Bay
Dunmanus B.
Long I.
Sherkin I.
Galley Hd.
Crow Hd.
Skull
Baltimore
Clear I.
123
Mizen Hd.
C. Clear
CELTIC SEA
Fastnet Rock

ATLANTIC OCEAN

NORTH CHANNEL

IRISH SEA

St. George's Channel

Projection: Lambert's Conformal Conic
West from Greenwich
COPYRIGHT PHILIP'S

ft m
1500 500
600 200
300 100
0 0
50 150
100 300
200 600
500 1500
1000 3000
2000 6000
m ft

National Parks

1:1 800 000

10 0 10 20 30 40 50 60 70 80 km
10 0 10 20 30 40 50 miles

Key to Scottish unitary authorities on map
1 CITY OF ABERDEEN
2 DUNDEE CITY
3 WEST DUNBARTONSHIRE
4 EAST DUNBARTONSHIRE
5 CITY OF GLASGOW
6 INVERCLYDE
7 RENFREWSHIRE
8 EAST RENFREWSHIRE
9 NORTH LANARKSHIRE
10 FALKIRK
11 CLACKMANNANSHIRE
12 WEST LOTHIAN
13 CITY OF EDINBURGH
14 MIDLOTHIAN

ORKNEY IS. on same scale

ORKNEY

North Ronaldsay
Papa Westray
Westray
Eday
Sanday
Rousay
Stronsay
Shapinsay
Stromness
Mainland
Kirkwall
St. Mary's
Hoy
Scapa Flow
Burray
Burwick
South Ronaldsay
Dunnet Hd.
Stroma
Duncansby Head
John o' Groats
Thurso
Sinclair's Bay
Pentland Firth

SHETLAND IS. on same scale

Muckle Flugga
Unst
Haroldswick
Yell
Ulsta
Fetlar
Out Skerries
Esha Ness
St. Magnus Bay
Sullom Voe
Whalsay
Papa Stour
Voe
Bressay
Walls
Scalloway
Lerwick
Foula
West Burra
Boddam
Sumburgh Hd.
Yell Sound
North Channel

Flannan Is.
Butt of Lewis
C. Wrath
Durness
Pt. of Stoer
Strathy Pt.
Dounreay
Dunnet Hd.
Thurso
Hoy
Scapa Flow
Burwick
Stroma
John o' Groats
Pentland Firth

Gallan Hd.
Broad Bay
Eye Peninsula
Stornoway
Lewis
Toe Hd.
Scarp
Clisham
Harris
Tarbert
Pabbay
Berneray
North Uist
Lochmaddy
Baleshare
Grimsay
Benbecula
Ardivachar Pt.
South Uist
Lochboisdale
Eriskay
Barra
Castlebay
Vatersay
Sandray
Barra Hd.

WESTERN ISLES

Reay Forest
Ben Hope 927
Ben More Assynt 998
Lochinver
Rubha Coigeach
Enard B.
L. Assynt
Ullapool
L. Broom
Gruinard B.
Greenstone Pt.
L. Ewe
Gairloch
L. Maree
L. Torridon
Rubha Hunish
Uig
Raasay
Portree
Dunvegan
Skye
Cuillin Hills 992
Kyle of Lochalsh
Kyleakin
Glenelg
Armadale
S. of Sleat
Mallaig
Arisaig
L. Morar
Rhum (Rùm)
Eigg
Muck
Canna
Coll
Tiree
Tobermory
Mull
Ben More 966
Iona
Staffa
Ulva
Kerrera
Oban
Lismore
Seil
Luing
Scarba
Colonsay
Oronsay
Jura
Islay
Bowmore
Port Ellen
Rhinns Pt.
Mull of Oa
Gigha
Campbeltown
Mull of Kintyre

Sutherland
Caithness
961
Tongue
Naver
Halkirk
Thurso
Wick
Lybster
Ord of Caithness
Helmsdale
Brora
Golspie
Lairg
Oykel
Bonar Bridge
Tain
Dornoch Firth
Tarbat Ness
Cromarty
Invergordon
Alness
Dingwall
Strathpeffer
Muir of Ord
Beauly
Inverness
Nairn
Forres
Elgin
Lossiemouth
Portknockie
Portsoy
Rosehearty
Kinnairds Hd.
Fraserburgh
Peterhead
Buchan Ness
Cruden Bay
Ellon
Oldmeldrum
Inverurie
Kintore
Dyce
Westhill
Aberdeen 1
Girdle Ness
Peterculter
Banchory
Stonehaven
Inverbervie
Laurencekirk
Brechin
Montrose
Arbroath
Carnoustie
Monifieth
Forfar
Kirriemuir
Blairgowrie
Alyth
Coupar Angus
Scone
Perth
Dundee
St. Andrews
Fife Ness
Leuchars
Cupar
Falkland
Leven
Anstruther
Buckhaven
Kirkcaldy
Glenrothes
Cowdenbeath
Dunfermline
Kinross
Alloa
Stirling
Callander
Dunblane
Crieff
Auchterarder
Aberfeldy
Pitlochry
Blair Atholl
Kingussie
Aviemore
Grantown-on-Spey
Tomintoul
Ballater
Aboyne
Braemar
Dufftown
Keith
Huntly
Turriff
Macduff
Banff
Cullen
Buckie
Fochabers
Rothes
Charlestown of Aberlour
Alford

HIGHLAND
MORAY
ABERDEENSHIRE
BUCHAN
ANGUS
PERTH AND KINROSS
FIFE

Ben Nevis 1342
Fort William
Kinlochleven
Ballachulish
Glencoe
L. Linnhe
Morvern
L. Sunart
L. Shiel
L. Moidart
Pt. of Ardnamurchan
Loch Ness
Glen Moriston
Fort Augustus
L. Arkaig
Loch Lochy
L. Laggan
Loch Rannoch
Rannoch Moor
Ben Lawers 1214
Crianlarich
Ben More 1174
Ben Lomond 973
Loch Lomond
LOCH LOMOND AND THE TROSSACHS
Inveraray
Lochgilphead
Tarbert
ARGYLL AND BUTE
Helensburgh
Dunoon
Gourock
Greenock
Port Glasgow
Rothesay
Bute
Largs
Ardrossan
Saltcoats
Kilwinning
Irvine
Troon
Prestwick
Ayr
Maybole
Girvan
Ailsa Craig
NORTH AYRSHIRE
EAST AYRSHIRE
SOUTH AYRSHIRE
Arran
Goat Fell 874
Brodick
Kilbrannan Sd.
Firth of Clyde

Dumbarton
Clydebank
Glasgow
Paisley
Hamilton
Motherwell
East Kilbride
Wishaw
Carluke
Lanark
Biggar
Strathaven
Kilmarnock
Cumnock
Sanquhar
Dalmellington
Moffat
SOUTH LANARKSHIRE
Peebles
Galashiels
Melrose
Selkirk
Hawick
Jedburgh
Kelso
Coldstream
Duns
Berwick-upon-Tweed
Eyemouth
St. Abb's Head
SCOTTISH BORDERS
The Cheviot 816
Broad Law 840
Moorfoot Hills
Lammermuir Hills
Pentland Hills
Edinburgh
Leith
Musselburgh
Haddington
Dalkeith
Bonnyrigg
Penicuik
Livingston
Bo'ness
Grangemouth
Falkirk
Cumbernauld
Airdrie
Coatbridge
Kirkintilloch
Denny
Bannockburn
EAST LOTHIAN
North Berwick
Dunbar

DUMFRIES & GALLOWAY
Dumfries
Annan
Gretna
Lockerbie
Langholm
Locharbriggs
Moffat
New Galloway
Castle Douglas
Dalbeattie
Kirkcudbright
Gatehouse of Fleet
Newton Stewart
Wigtown
Stranraer
Cairnryan
Portpatrick
Whithorn
Luce Bay
Mull of Galloway
Burrow Hd.
L. Ryan
Solway Firth

ENGLAND
NORTHUMBERLAND
CUMBRIA
DURHAM
Newcastle-upon-Tyne
Gateshead
Blaydon
Carlisle
Hexham
Haltwhistle
Alston
Appleby-in-Westmorland
Penrith
Keswick
Cockermouth
Workington
Maryport
Whitehaven
St. Bees Hd.
Silloth
Wigton
Brampton
Alnwick
Amble
Morpeth
Stanley
Consett
Crook
Bishop Auckland
Barnard Castle
Brough
Kielder Water
Ullswater
Derwent Water
Cross Fell 893
Skiddaw
Helvellyn 950
Hadrian's Wall
Holy I.
Farne Is.
Bamburgh
Wooler
Flodden

NORTHERN IRELAND
Belfast
Larne
Carrickfergus
Bangor
Newtownards
Donaghadee
Belfast L.

ATLANTIC OCEAN
NORTH SEA
NORTH CHANNEL
North Minch
Little Minch
Sea of the Hebrides
Inner Hebrides
Outer Hebrides
Moray Firth
Firth of Tay
Firth of Forth
Sound of Jura
Passage of Tiree
Firth of Lorn

SCOTLAND
Grampian Mountains
Cairngorm Mts. 1309
CAIRNGORMS
Northwest Highlands
Southern Uplands
Ben Macdhui 1309
Lochnagar 1154

Projection: Lambert's Conformal Conic
West from Greenwich
COPYRIGHT PHILIP'S

ft m
3000 1000
1500 500
600 200
300 150
0 100
150 300
600 1500
1000 3000
m ft

☐ Forest Parks in Scotland

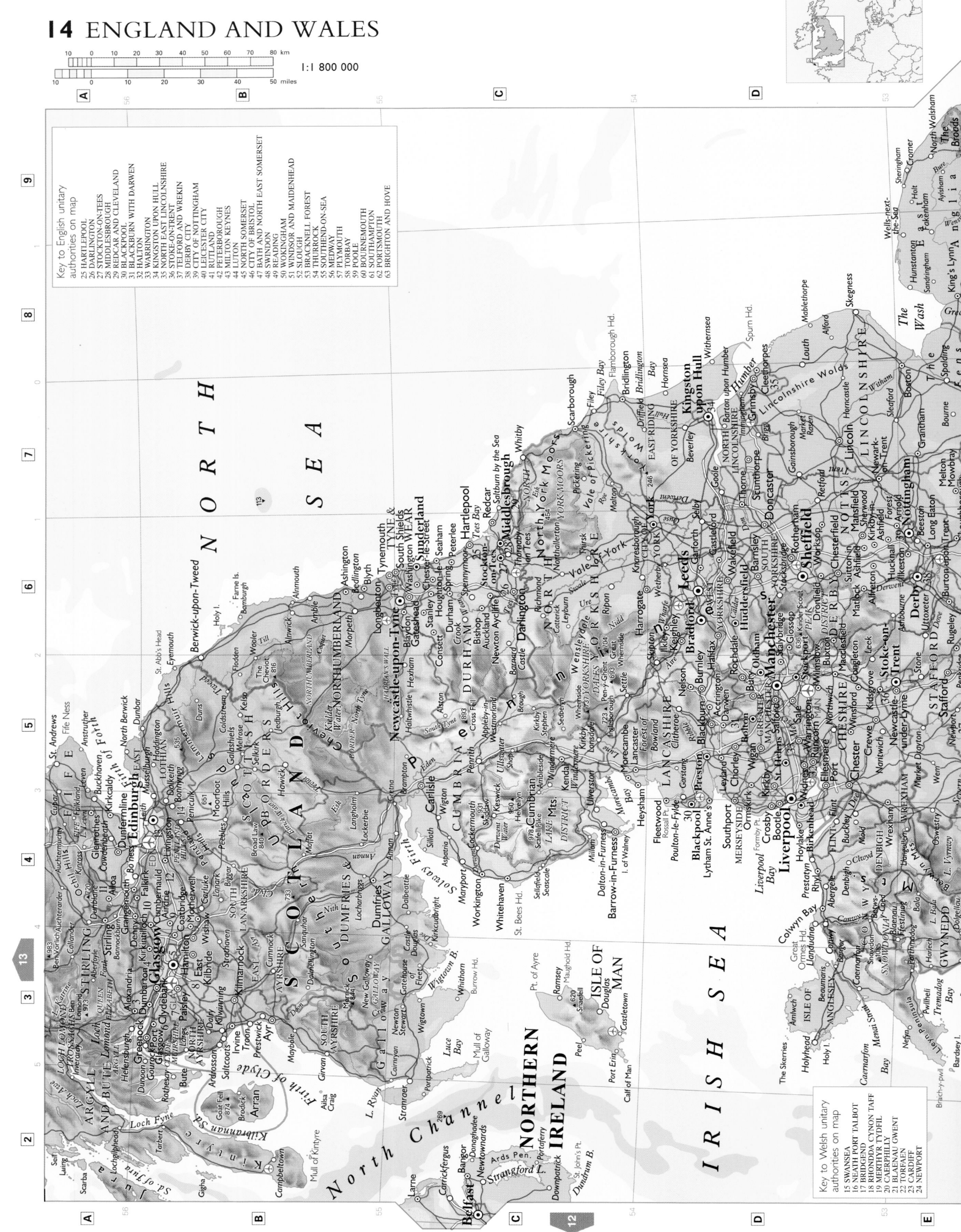

1:1 800 000

Key to English unitary authorities on map
25 HARTLEPOOL
26 DARLINGTON
27 STOCKTON-ON-TEES
28 MIDDLESBROUGH
29 REDCAR AND CLEVELAND
30 BLACKPOOL
31 BLACKBURN WITH DARWEN
32 HALTON
33 WARRINGTON
34 KINGSTON UPON HULL
35 NORTH EAST LINCOLNSHIRE
36 NORTH LINCOLNSHIRE
37 STOKE-ON-TRENT
37 TELFORD AND WREKIN
38 DERBY CITY
39 CITY OF NOTTINGHAM
40 LEICESTER CITY
41 RUTLAND
42 PETERBOROUGH
43 MILTON KEYNES
44 LUTON
45 NORTH SOMERSET
46 CITY OF BRISTOL
47 BATH AND NORTH EAST SOMERSET
48 SWINDON
49 READING
50 WOKINGHAM
51 WINDSOR AND MAIDENHEAD
52 SLOUGH
53 BRACKNELL FOREST
54 THURROCK
55 MEDWAY
56 SOUTHEND-ON-SEA
57 PLYMOUTH
58 TORBAY
59 POOLE
60 BOURNEMOUTH
61 SOUTHAMPTON
62 PORTSMOUTH
63 BRIGHTON AND HOVE

Key to Welsh unitary authorities on map
15 SWANSEA
16 NEATH PORT TALBOT
17 BRIDGEND
18 RHONDDA CYNON TAFF
19 MERTHYR TYDFIL
20 CAERPHILLY
21 BLAENAU GWENT
22 TORFAEN
23 CARDIFF
24 NEWPORT

50   0   25   50   75   100   125   150   175 km
50   0   25   50   75   100   125 miles

1:4 400 000

1   **2**   **3**   **4**   **5**   **6**   **7**   **8**   **9**

A   T   L   A   N   T   I   C   O   C   E   A   N

NORWAY
Bergen
Askøy
Osøyro
Stord
Bømlo
Leirvik
Haugesund
Kopervik
Åkrahamn
Stavanger
Sandnes
Bryne
Nærbø

Shetland Is.
Yell
Unst
Fetlar
Foula
Mainland
Lerwick
Fair Isle

Orkney Is.
Westray
Sanday
Stronsay
Mainland
Kirkwall
Hoy
South Ronaldsay

C. Wrath
Pentland Firth
Thurso
Wick
Helmsdale

Lewis
Stornoway
St. Kilda
Harris
789
North Uist
Benbecula
South Uist
Barra
Outer Hebrides
North Minch
Sea of the Hebrides
Inner Hebrides
Skye
Portree
Rhum
Eigg
Coll
Tiree
Tobermory
Mull
Colonsay
Jura
Islay

North West Highlands
Ullapool
Lairg
Golspie
Tain
Dingwall
Nairn
Inverness
Glen More
L. Ness
Aviemore
1182
Ben Nevis
1342
Fort William
Mallaig
Oban
L. Awe
L. Lomond
Grampian Mts.
1214
Forfar
Montrose
Arbroath

Moray Firth
Buckie
Banff
Elgin
Fraserburgh
Huntly
Peterhead
Inverurie
Aberdeen
1311
Ballater
Stonehaven

SCOTLAND
973
Stirling
Perth
St. Andrews
Dundee
Glenrothes
Kirkcaldy
Dunfermline
Dunbar
Dumbarton
Greenock
Glasgow
Paisley
Motherwell
Edinburgh
East Kilbride
Hamilton
Irvine
Berwick-upon-Tweed
Kilmarnock
Galashiels
Ayr
Southern Uplands
840
Jedburgh
816
Hawick
Cheviot Hills
Campbeltown
Arran
Girvan
Dumfries
Alnwick

N   O   R   T   H   S   E   A

Malin Hd.
Buncrana
Aran I.
Letterkenny
Coleraine
Ballymena
Larne
Lifford
Londonderry
Donegal
Omagh
NORTHERN IRELAND
Antrim
Bangor
U
Lough Neagh
Belfast
Bundoran
Lower L. Erne
Enniskillen
Clones
Portadown
Lisburn
Lurgan
Armagh
Newry
Mull of Galloway
Whitehaven
Kirkcudbright
Annan
Carlisle
Workington
Hexham
Gateshead
Durham
Newcastle-upon-Tyne
South Shields
Sunderland
Hartlepool
Redcar
Middlesbrough
Stockton-on-Tees
Darlington
Pennines
893
Cumbrian Mts.
978
Scarborough

Sligo
L. Conn
Ballina
Castlebar
Westport
Lough Mask
Connemara
Lough Corrib
Galway B.
Galway
Aran Is.
Ennis
Kilrush
Shannon
953
Dingle
Carrauntoohill 1041
Macgillycuddy's Reeks
Valencia I.
Tralee
Killarney
Kilkenny
Listowel
Mallow
Bantry
Bandon
Kinsale
Cork
Cóbh
Youghal
Dungarvan
C. Clear

Leitrim
Cavan
Castleblaney
Dundalk
Drogheda
Boyne
Roscommon
Longford
Athlone
Lough Ree
Mullingar
Ceanannus Mor
IRELAND
Ballinasloe
Tullamore
Birr
Liffey
Nenagh
Tipperary
Thurles
Limerick
Lough Derg
Clonmel
Carrick-on-Suir
Waterford
99
Fishguard

Douglas
I. of Man
Barrow-in-Furness
Lancaster
Harrogate
York
Beverley
Bridlington
UNITED KINGDOM
Blackpool
Keighley
Leeds
Kingston upon Hull
Preston
Burnley
Bradford
Blackburn
Halifax
Huddersfield
Barnsley
Scunthorpe
Grimsby
Bolton
Doncaster
Rotherham
Louth
Manchester
Oldham
Sheffield
Stockport
636
Liverpool
Warrington
Chester
Crewe
Chesterfield
Mansfield
Lincoln
Skegness
Boston
The Wash

Holyhead
Anglesey
Colwyn Bay
Bangor
Wrexham
Stoke on Trent
Derby
Nottingham
Cromer
Snowdon 1085
Stafford
Telford
Grantham
King's Lynn
ENGLAND
Shrewsbury
Leicester
Norwich
Great Yarmouth
Lowestoft
Cambrian Mts.
Welshpool
Nuneaton
Peterborough
Thetford
Wolverhampton
Coventry
Corby
BIRMINGHAM
Rugby
Northampton
Ely
Bury St. Edmunds
Ipswich
Cardigan Bay
Aberystwyth
Redditch
Royal Leamington Spa
Bedford
Felixstowe
Worcester
Milton Keynes
Harwich
Hereford
Stevenage
Colchester
WALES
886
Cheltenham
Luton
Harlow
Chelmsford
Carmarthen
Brecon
Cwmbran
Gloucester
Oxford
Hemel Hempstead
Basildon
Merthyr Tydfil
Cotswold Hills
High Wycombe
Watford
Southend-on-Sea
Neath
Rhondda
Newport
Swindon
Slough
Llanelli
Cardiff
Bristol
Newbury
Reading
LONDON
Chatham
Margate
Port Talbot
Barry
Bath
Thames
Canterbury
Swansea
Weston-super-Mare
Maidstone
Dover
Bristol Channel
Reigate
Str. of Dover
Barnstaple
Exmoor
Salisbury
Winchester
Guildford
Crawley
Ashford
Folkestone
Taunton
Yeovil
Basingstoke
Bude
618
Southampton
Fareham
Havant
Hastings
Eastbourne
Dartmoor
Exeter
Bournemouth
Poole
Portsmouth
Brighton
Worthing
Newquay
Exmouth
Weymouth
Newport
Isle of Wight
Truro
Torbay
Plymouth
St. Austell
Land's End
Penzance
Falmouth
Isles of Scilly

IRISH SEA
North Channel
Firth of Clyde
Dublin
Dun Laoghaire
Bray
Port Laoise
Athy
Carlow
Wicklow Mts.
926
Wexford
Arklow
Rosslare
St. George's Channel

Haverfordwest
Milford Haven
Pembroke

C E L T I C   S E A

E N G L I S H   C H A N N E L

C. de la Hague
Pte. de Barfleur
Alderney
Cherbourg
St. Peter Port
Guernsey
Sark
Valognes
Cotentin
Le Havre
Bolbec
Rouen
Channel Is. (U.K.)
St. Helier
Jersey
Bayeux
Trouville-sur-Mer
Caen
Lisieux
Elbeuf
Seine
West from Greenwich

FRANCE
Fécamp
Pays de Caux
Dieppe
Abbeville
St-Quentin
Le Tréport
Amiens
Laon
Picardie
Le Touquet-Paris-Plage
33
Boulogne-sur-Mer
Gris-Nez
St-Omer
Béthune
Lille
Villeneuve-d'Ascq
Calais
Dunkerque
Bruay-la-Buissière
Lens
Valenciennes
Cambrai
Flandre
Artois
Tourcoing
Roubaix
Tournai
Mechelen

BELGIUM
Brussel (Bruxelles)
Gent
Brugge
Oostende
Zeebrugge
Antwerpen

NETHERLANDS
Texel
Den Helder
Alkmaar
Haarlem
's-Gravenhage (Den Haag)
Hoek van Holland
ROTTERDAM
Dordrecht
Vlissingen

1224
316
238
1182
16
36

Projection: Conical with two standard parallels

18   **19**

COPYRIGHT PHILIP'S

ft   m
3000   1000
1500   500
600   200
0   0
150
300
600
1500
3000
6000
m   ft

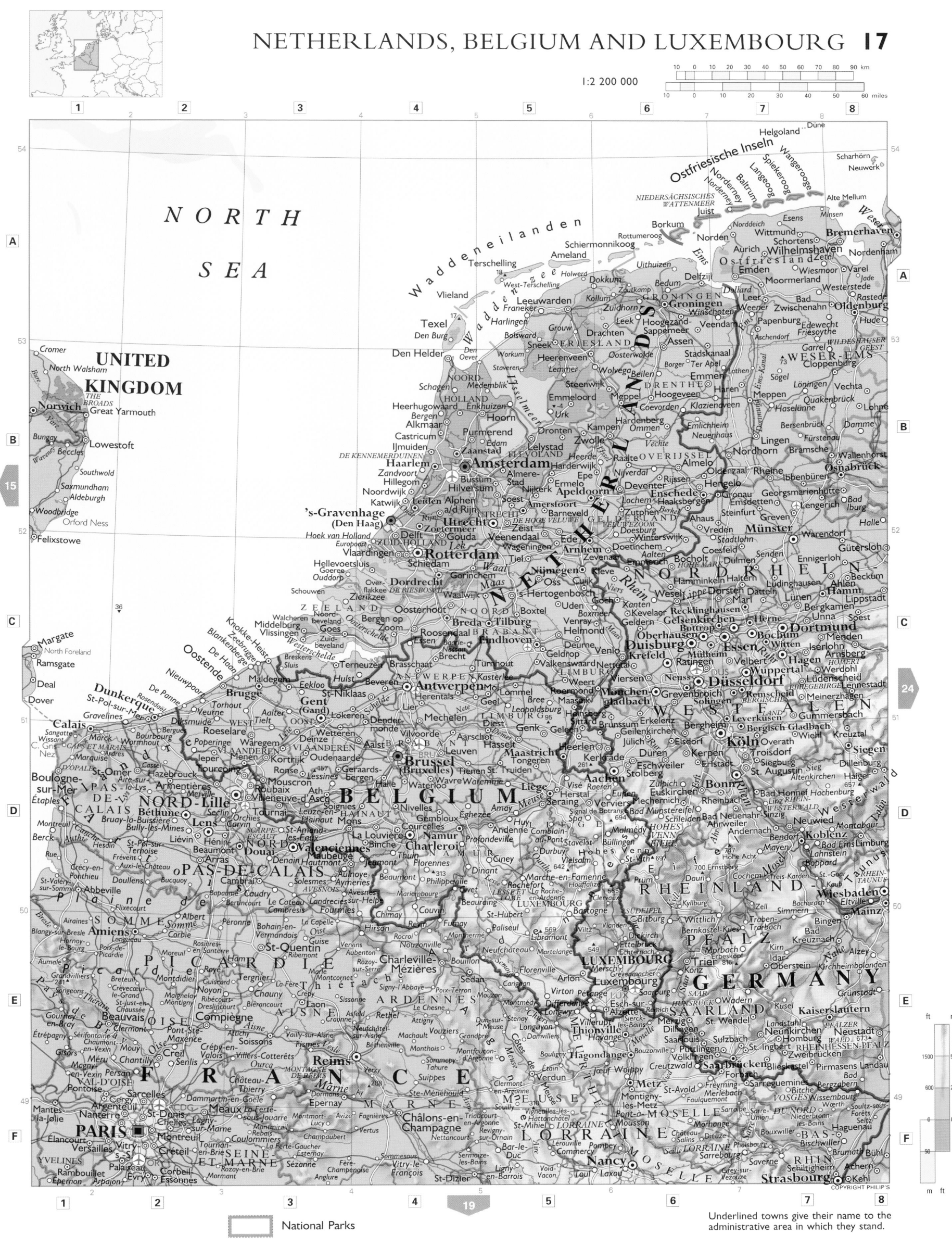

1:2 200 000

National Parks

Underlined towns give their name to the administrative area in which they stand.

COPYRIGHT PHILIP'S

10 0 10 20 30 40 50 60 70 80 90 km

1:2 200 000

10 0 10 20 30 40 50 60 miles

DÉPARTEMENTS IN THE PARIS AREA
1 Ville de Paris   3 Val-de-Marne
2 Seine-St-Denis   4 Hauts-de-Seine

Projection : Lambert's Conformal Conic

West from Greenwich

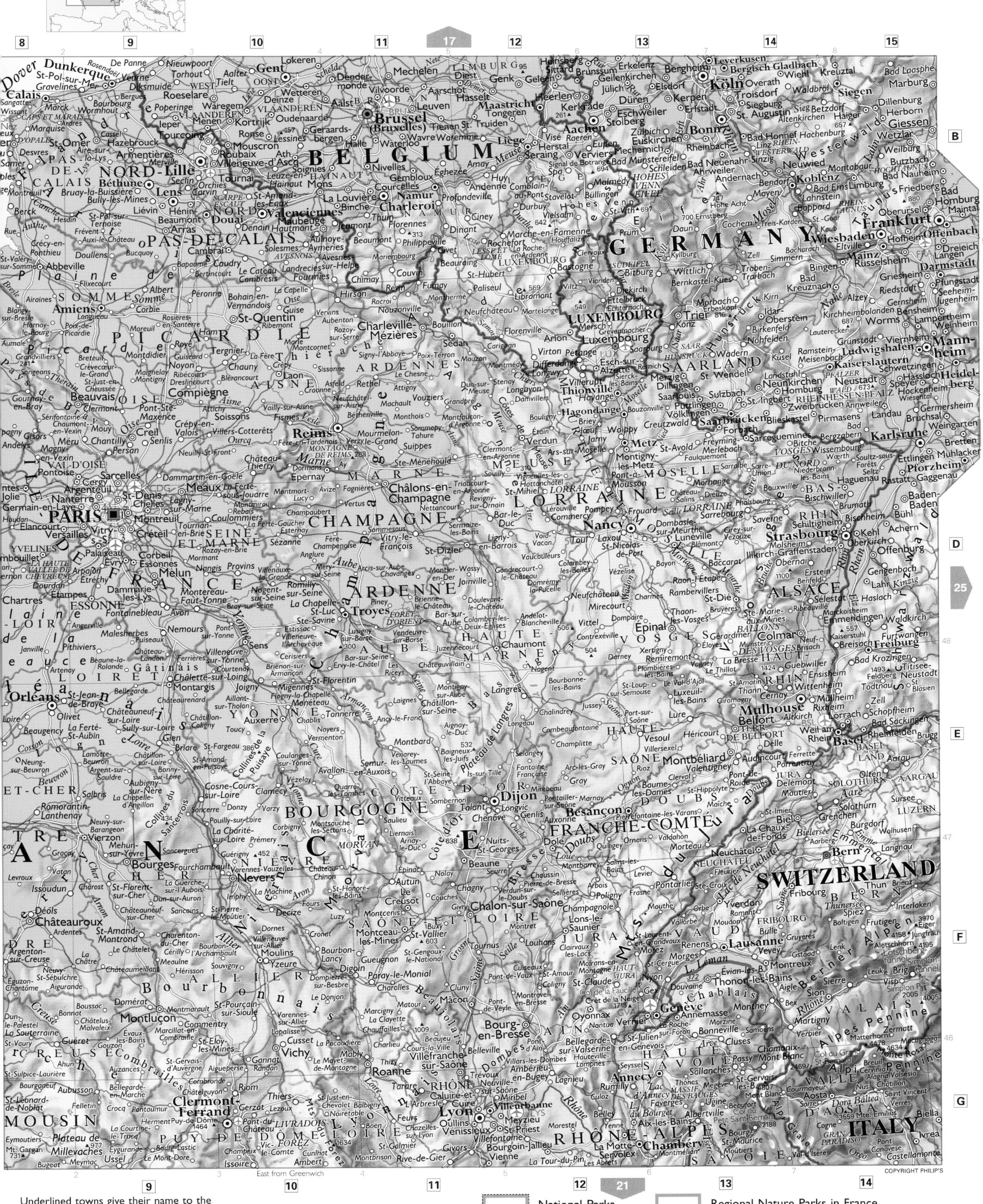

Underlined towns give their name to the administrative area in which they stand.

National Parks   Regional Nature Parks in France

East from Greenwich

COPYRIGHT PHILIP'S

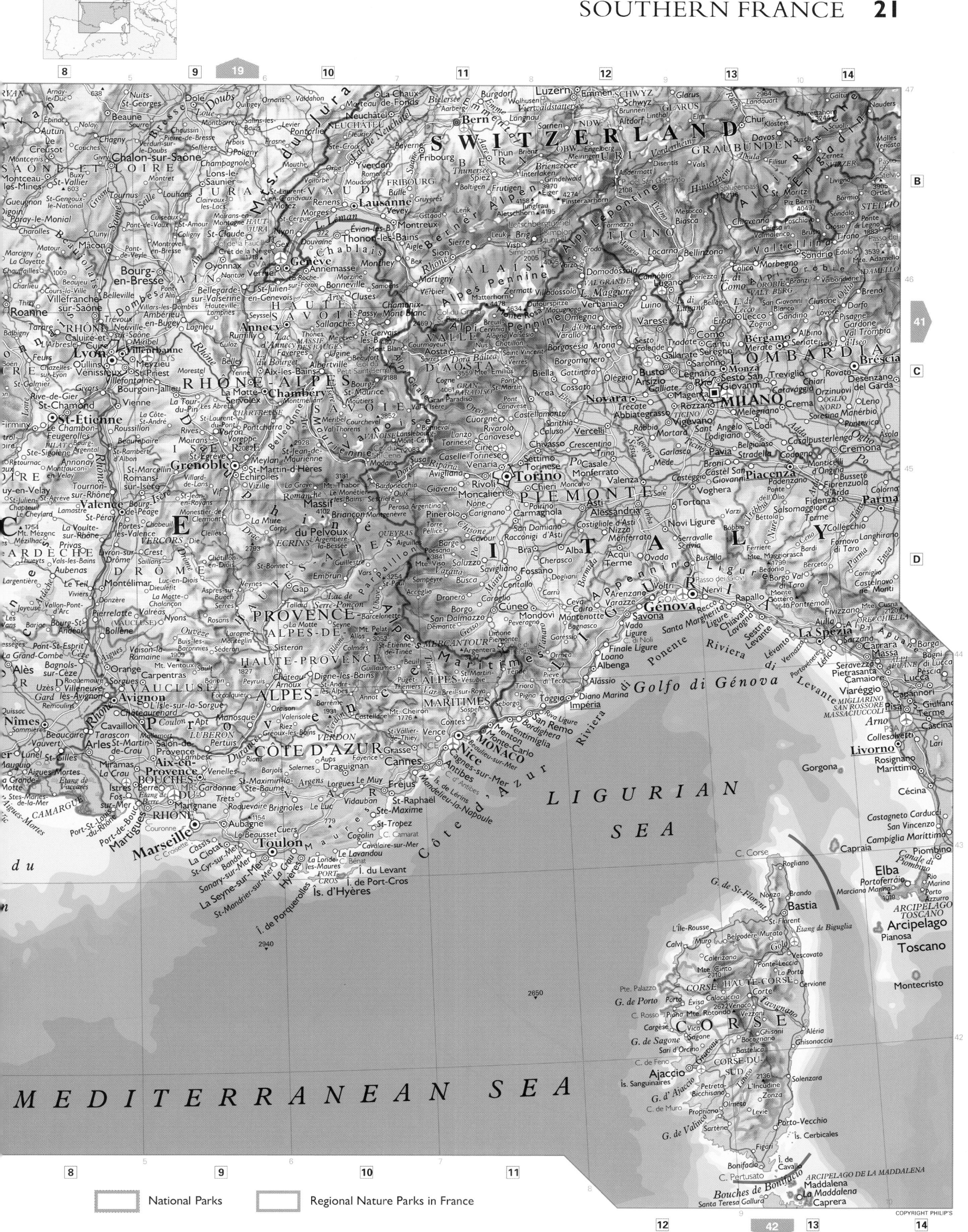

National Parks   Regional Nature Parks in France

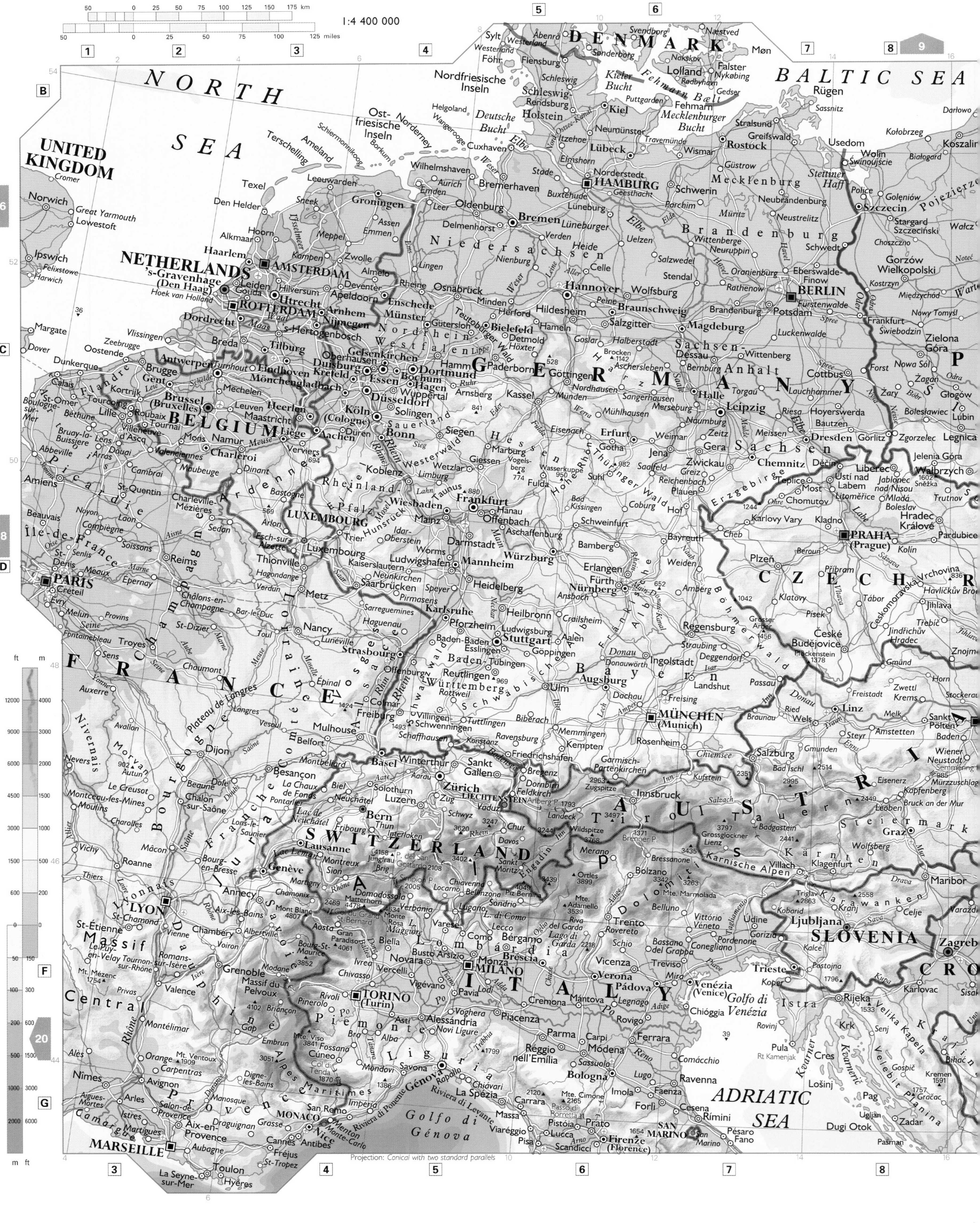

1:4 400 000

50 0 25 50 75 100 125 150 175 km
50 0 25 50 75 100 125 miles

NORTH SEA

BALTIC SEA

DENMARK

UNITED KINGDOM

NETHERLANDS

BELGIUM

LUXEMBOURG

GERMANY

FRANCE

SWITZERLAND

CZECH

AUSTRIA

SLOVENIA

ITALY

ADRIATIC SEA

Projection: Conical with two standard parallels

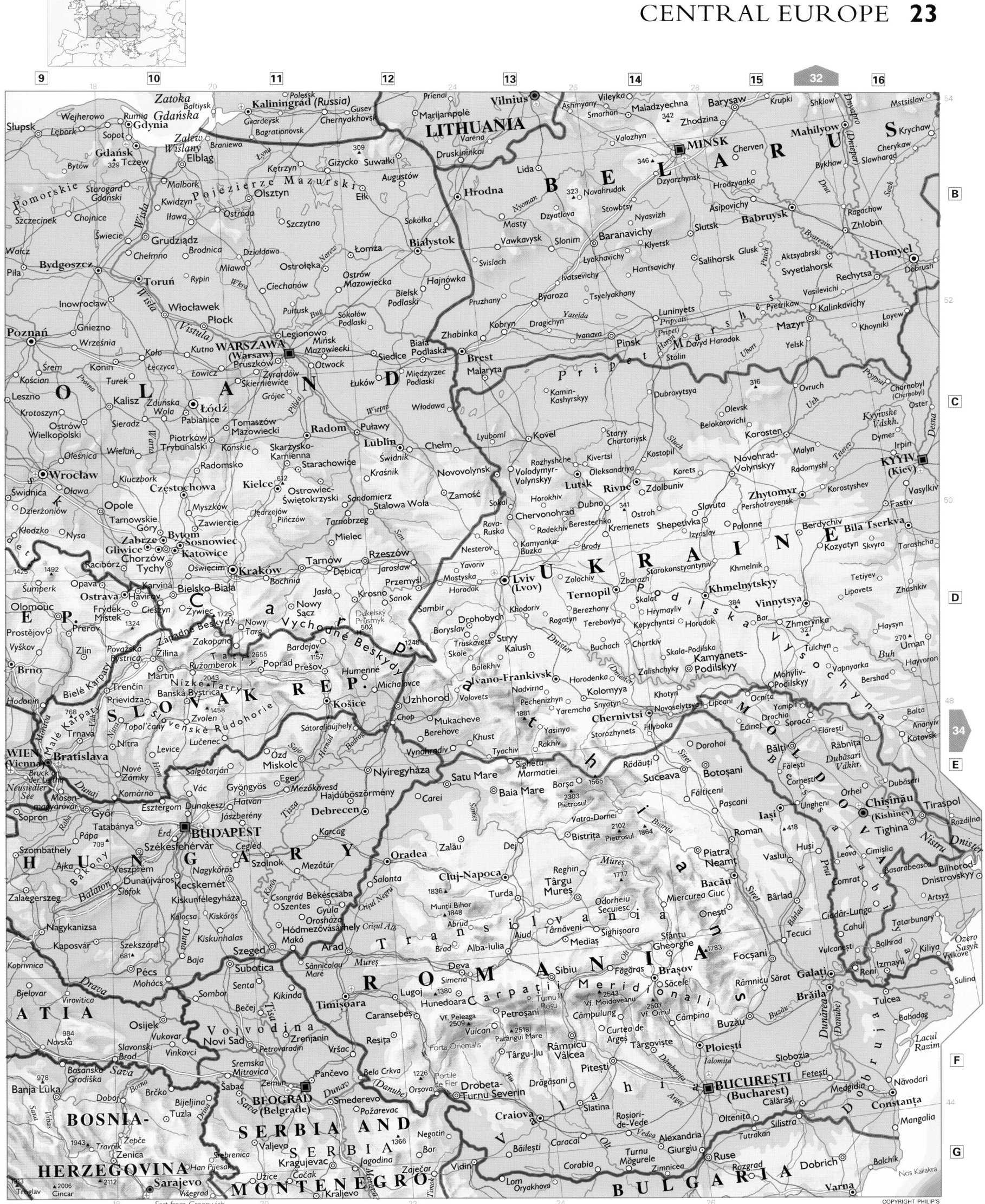

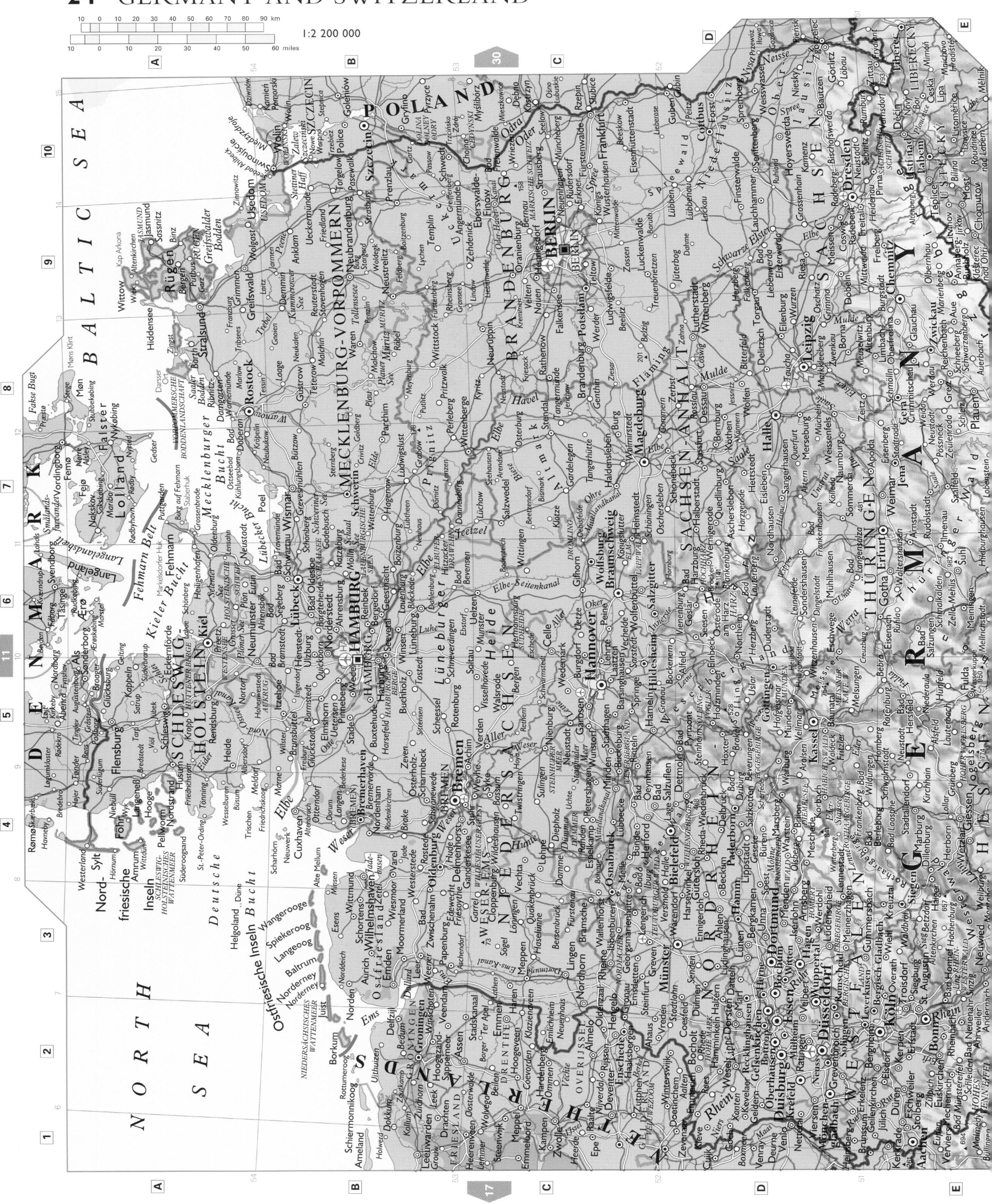

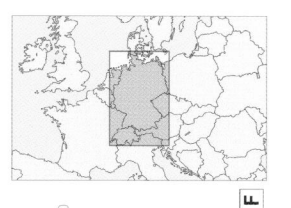

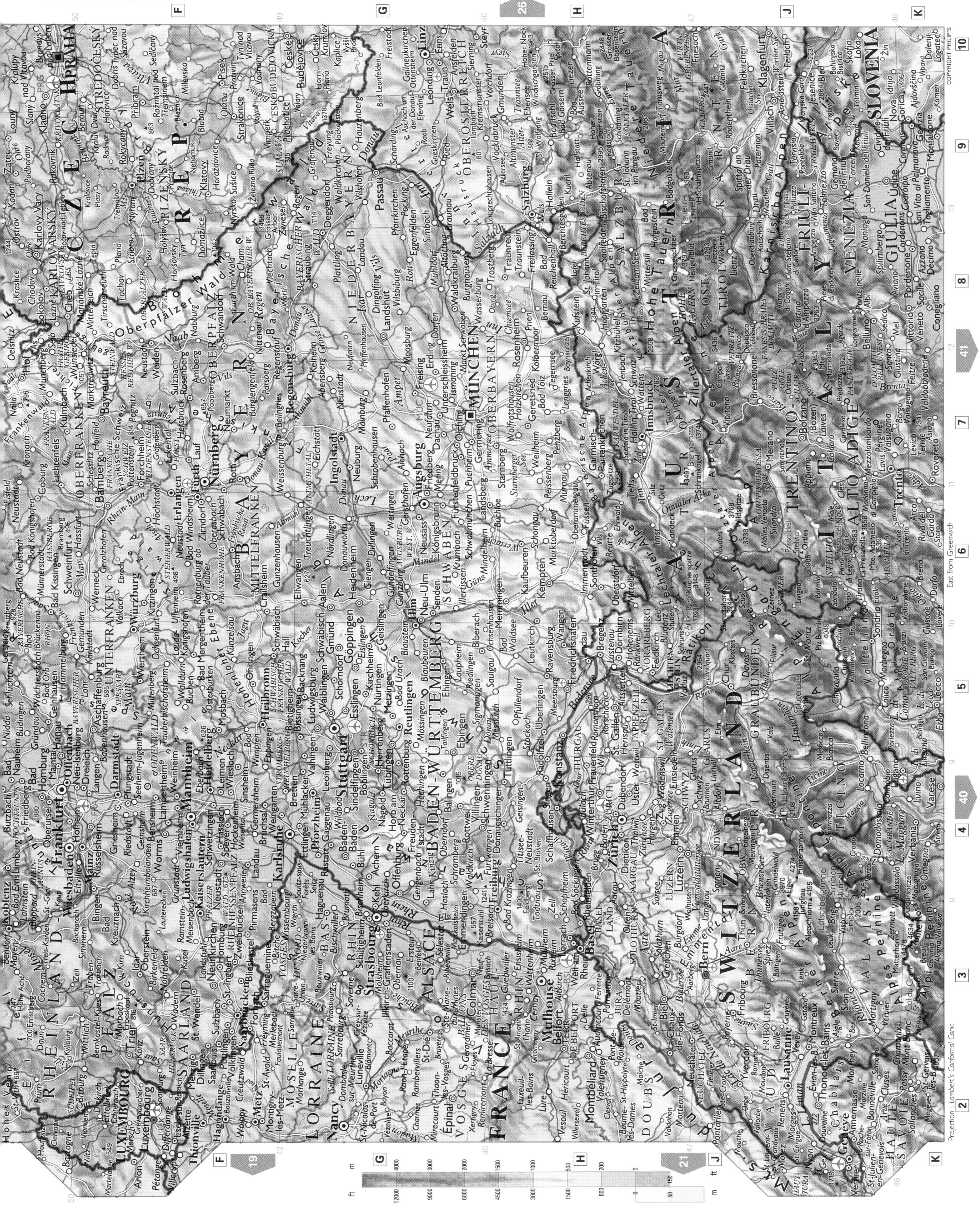

41

Nature Parks in Germany

National Parks

Underlined towns give their name to the administrative area in which they stand.

COPYRIGHT PHILIP'S

Projection: Lambert's Conformal Conic

East from Greenwich

1:2 200 000

National Parks

COPYRIGHT PHILIP'S

Underlined towns give their name to the
administrative area in which they stand.

1:2 200 000

Administrative divisions in Croatia:
1 Brodsko-Posavska
2 Koprivničko-Križevačka
4 Medimurska
5 Osječko-Baranjska
6 Požeško-Slavonska
8 Virovitičko-Podravska
9 Vukovarsko-Srijemska

Inter-entity boundaries as agreed
- - - - at the 1995 Dayton Peace Agreement

East from Greenwich

National Parks

Underlined towns give their name to the
administrative area in which they stand.

COPYRIGHT PHILIP'S

1:2 200 000

Gulf of Riga

BALTIC SEA

SWEDEN

LATVIA

LITHUANIA

KALININGRAD (Russia)

POMORSKIE

WARMIŃSKO-MAZURSKIE

ZACHODNIO-POMORSKIE

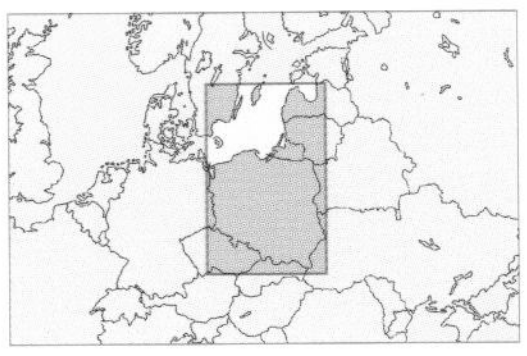

Riga · Jūrmala · Jelgava · Šiauliai · Kaunas · Marijampolė · Hrodna

Ventspils · Liepāja · Klaipėda · Kaliningrad · Elbląg

Gdynia · Gdańsk · Sopot · Słupsk · Koszalin

Gotland (Sweden) · Öland (Sweden) · Visby · Kalmar

Bornholm (Denmark)

Underlined towns give their name to the
administrative area in which they stand.

National Parks

COPYRIGHT PHILIP'S

Projection: Lambert's Conformal Conic

East from Greenwich

POLAND

MAZOWIECKIE

WARSZAWA

PODLASKIE

LUBELSKIE

PODKARPACKIE

MAŁOPOLSKIE

ŚWIĘTOKRZYSKIE

ŁÓDZKIE

ŚLĄSKIE

OPOLSKIE

DOLNOŚLĄSKIE

WIELKOPOLSKIE

LUBUSKIE

POMORSKIE

KUJAWSKO-POMORSKIE

BELARUS

UKRAINE

SLOVAK REP.

CZECH REP.

AUSTRIA

GERMANY

Kraków
Wrocław
Poznań
Łódź
Lublin
Kielce
Radom
Częstochowa
Katowice
Bydgoszcz
Toruń
Białystok
Brno

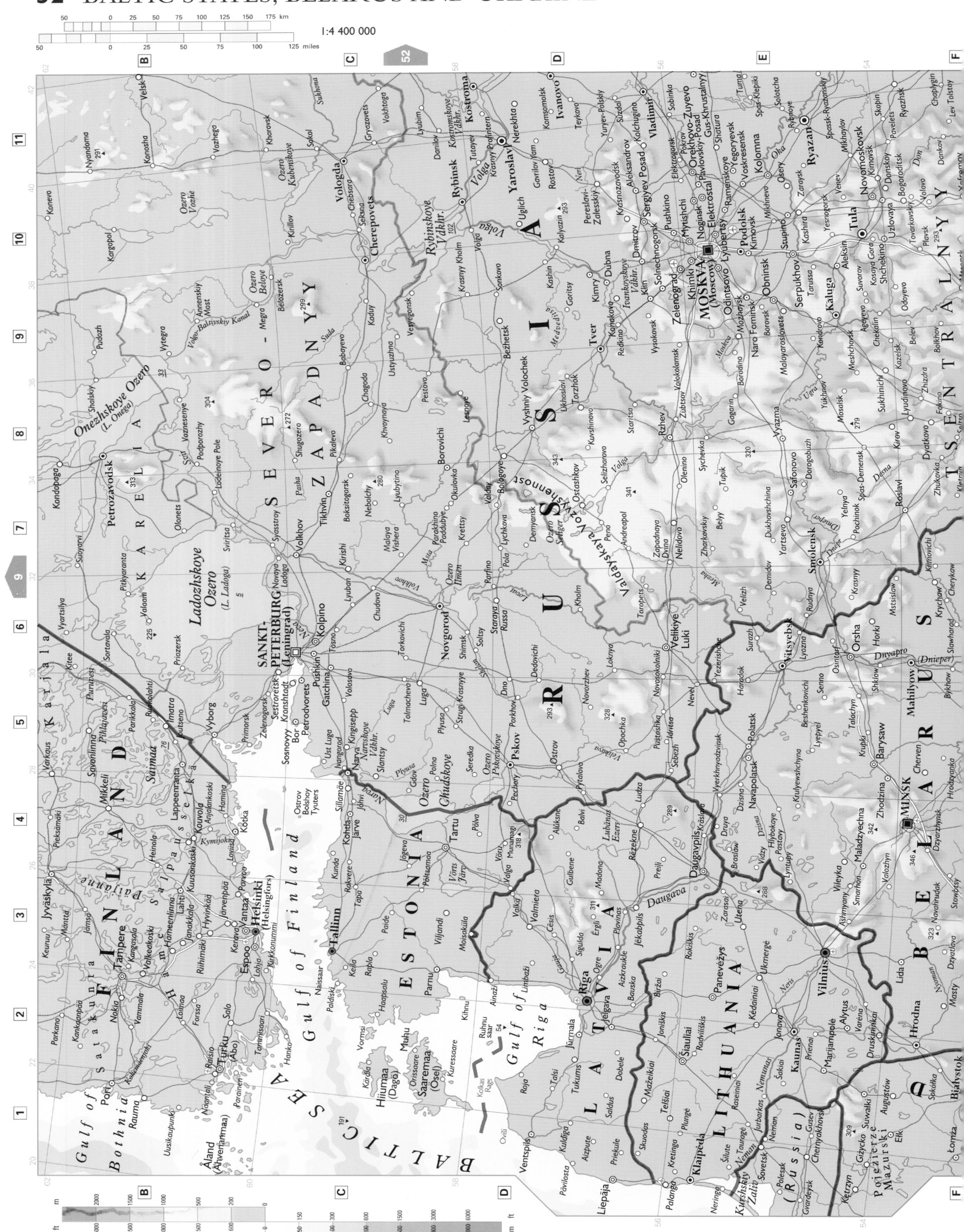

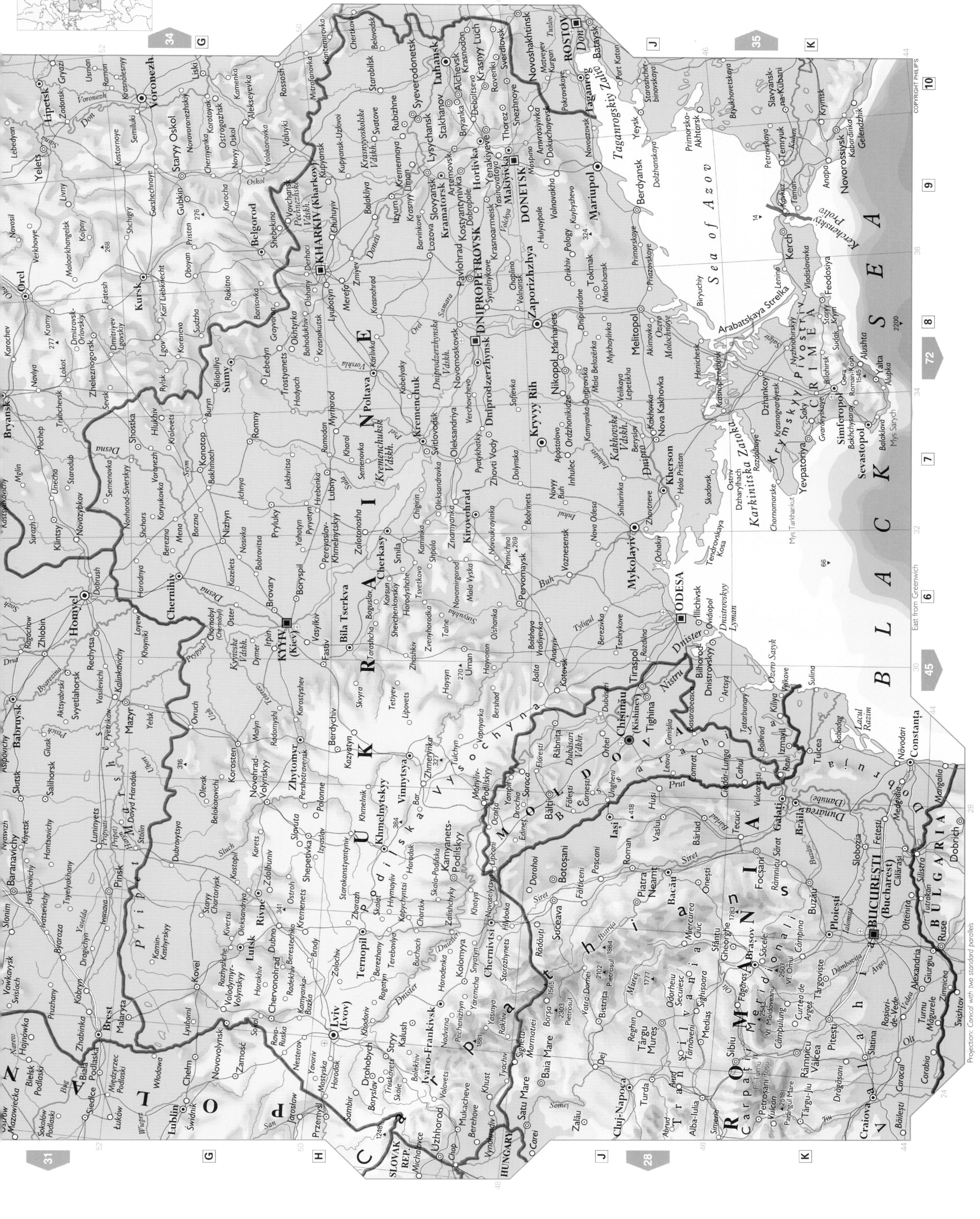

UKRAINE

KHARKIV (Kharkov)

DNIPROPETROVSK

DONETSK

Luhansk

Zaporizhzhya

Kryvyy Rih

Mykolayiv

ODESA

KYYIV (Kiev)

Poltava

Sumy

Chernihiv

Homyel

Babruysk

Brest

Pinsk

Lviv (Lvov)

Ivano-Frankivsk

Ternopil

Rivne

Lutsk

Khmelnytskyy

Vinnytsya

Chernivtsi

MOLDOVA

Chişinău (Kishinev)

Tiraspol

ROMANIA

BUCUREŞTI (Bucharest)

Iaşi

Braşov

Galaţi

Constanţa

BULGARIA

Ruse

Voronezh

Orel

Bryansk

Kursk

Belgorod

Rostov

Taganrog

Mariupol

Novorossiysk

CRIMEA

Simferopol

Sevastopol

Yalta

Kerch

Sea of Azov

BLACK SEA

SLOVAK REP.

HUNGARY

Uzhhorod

Mukacheve

Satu Mare

Cluj-Napoca

Sibiu

Craiova

Ploieşti

Danube

Dniester

Don

East from Greenwich

Projection: Conical with two standard parallels

COPYRIGHT PHILIP'S

1:4 400 000

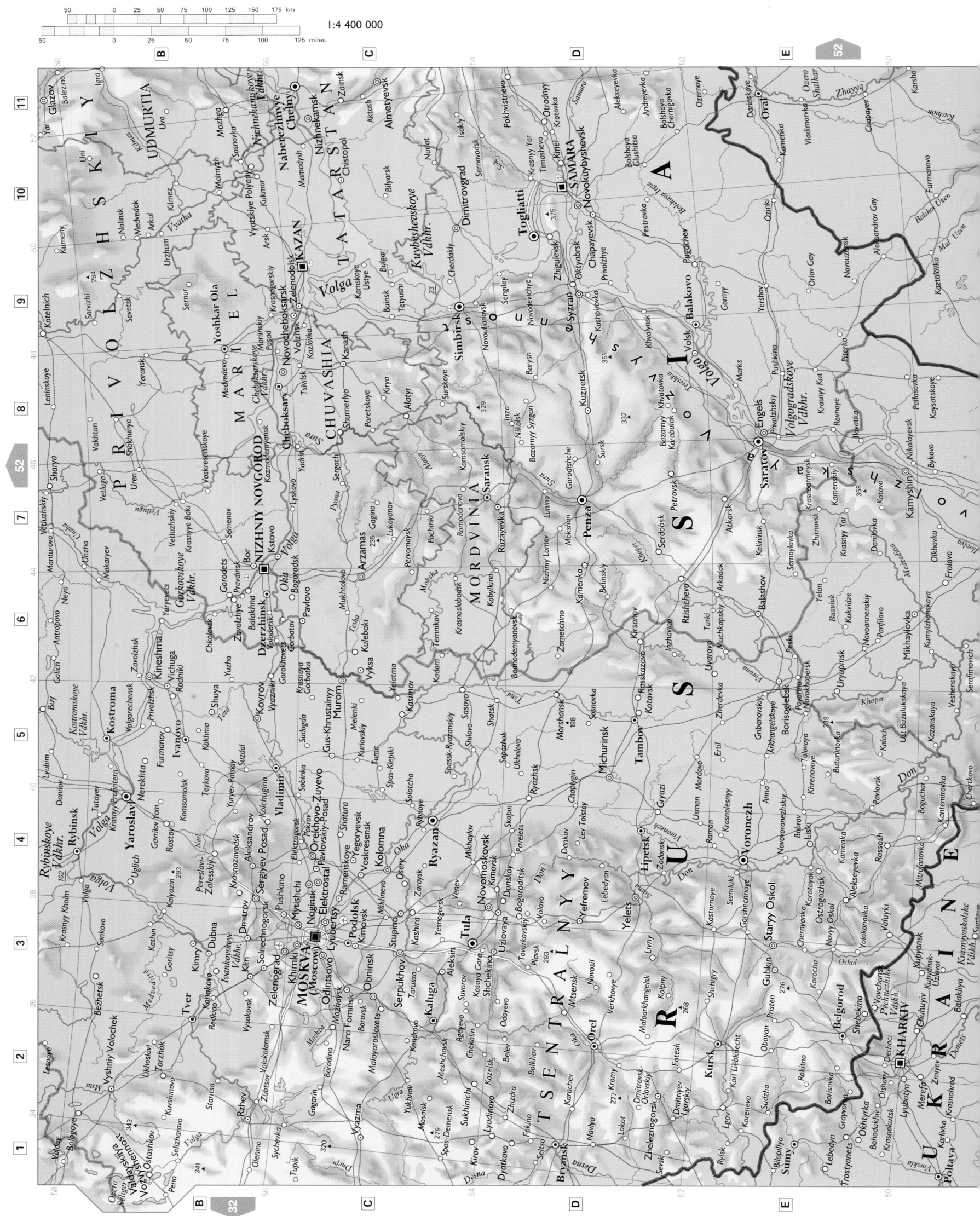

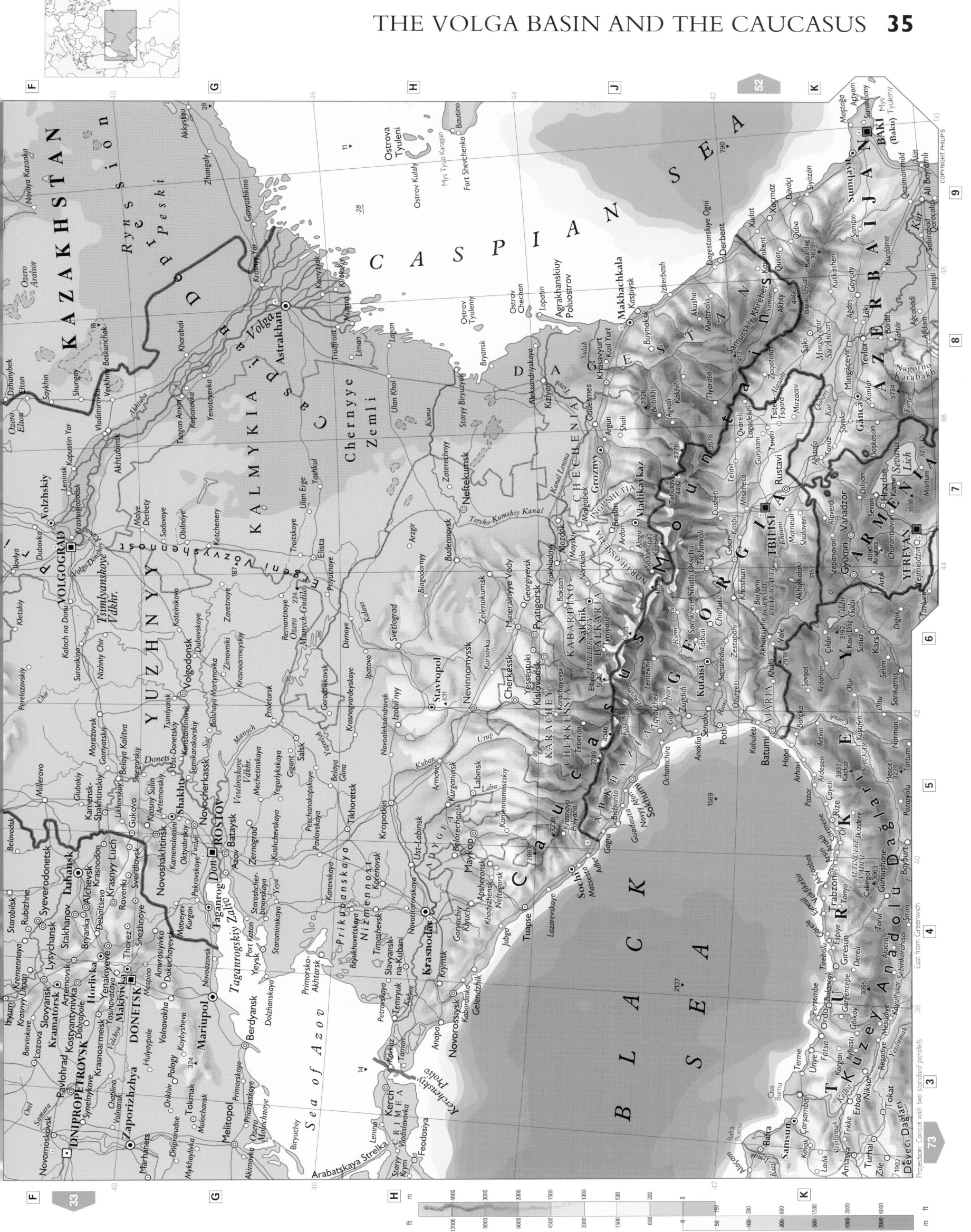

CASPIAN SEA

BLACK SEA

KAZAKHSTAN

AZERBAIJAN

ARMENIA

GEORGIA

TURKEY

Sea of Azov

Projection: Conic with two standard parallels
East from Greenwich

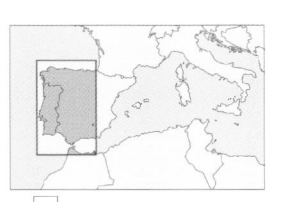

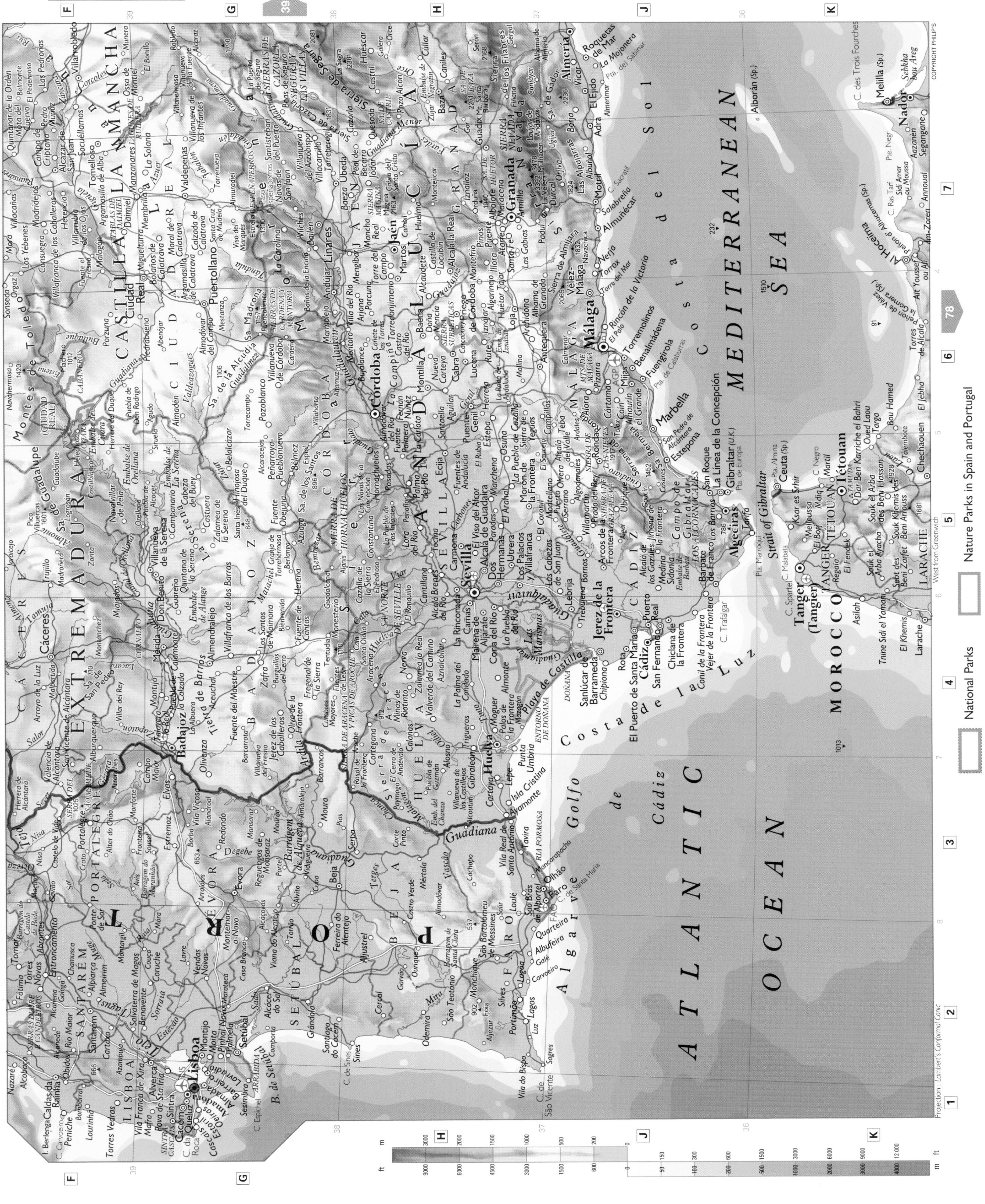

ATLANTIC OCEAN
MEDITERRANEAN SEA
Golfo de Cádiz
Costa de la Luz
Costa del Sol
Strait of Gibraltar
EXTREMADURA
CASTILLA-LA MANCHA
ANDALUCÍA
PORTUGAL
MOROCCO
Lisboa
Sevilla
Córdoba
Granada
Málaga
Cádiz
Huelva
Badajoz
Cáceres
Jaén
Almería
Gibraltar (U.K.)
Tanger (Tangier)
Tétouan
Ceuta (Sp.)
Melilla (Sp.)
National Parks
Nature Parks in Spain and Portugal
Projection: Lambert's Conformal Conic
West from Greenwich
COPYRIGHT PHILIP'S

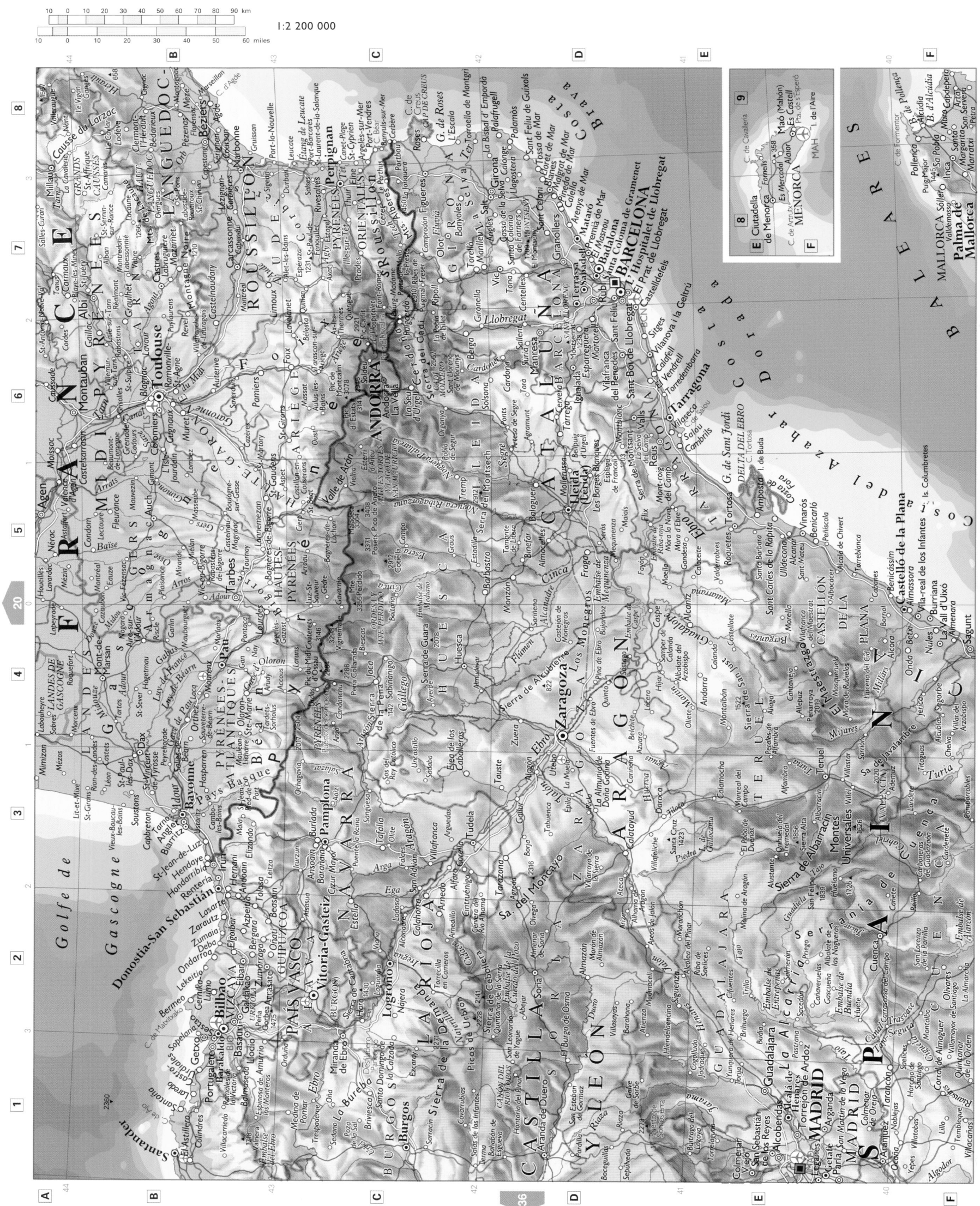

1:2 200 000

ALGER (ALGIERS)

MEDITERRANEAN SEA

BALEARIC ISLANDS

ISLAS BALEARES

Golfo de Valencia

Valencia

Costa Blanca

Costa del Sol

Formentera

Eivissa (Ibiza)

CASTILLA-LA MANCHA

CIUDAD REAL

MURCIA

ALMERÍA

GRANADA

Valencia

Alicante

Elche

Cartagena

Murcia

Lorca

Almería

Granada

Albacete

MÉDEA

TIARET

RELIZANE

MASCARA

ORAN (OUAHRAN)

TÉMOUCHENT

Sidi-bel-Abbès

Mostaganem

Blida

Médéa

West from Greenwich

East from Greenwich

Nature Parks in Spain

National Parks

Projection: Lambert's Conformal Conic

1:2 200 000

National Parks

Underlined towns give their name to the
administrative area in which they stand.

East from Greenwich

Administrative divisions in Croatia:
1 Brodsko-Posavska
2 Koprivničko-Križevačka
3 Krapinsko-Zagorska
4 Medimurska
5 Požeško-Slavonska
7 Varaždinska
8 Virovitičko-Podravska
10 Zagreba čka

Nature Parks in Italy

Inter-entity boundaries as agreed
at the 1995 Dayton Peace Agreement

COPYRIGHT PHILIP'S

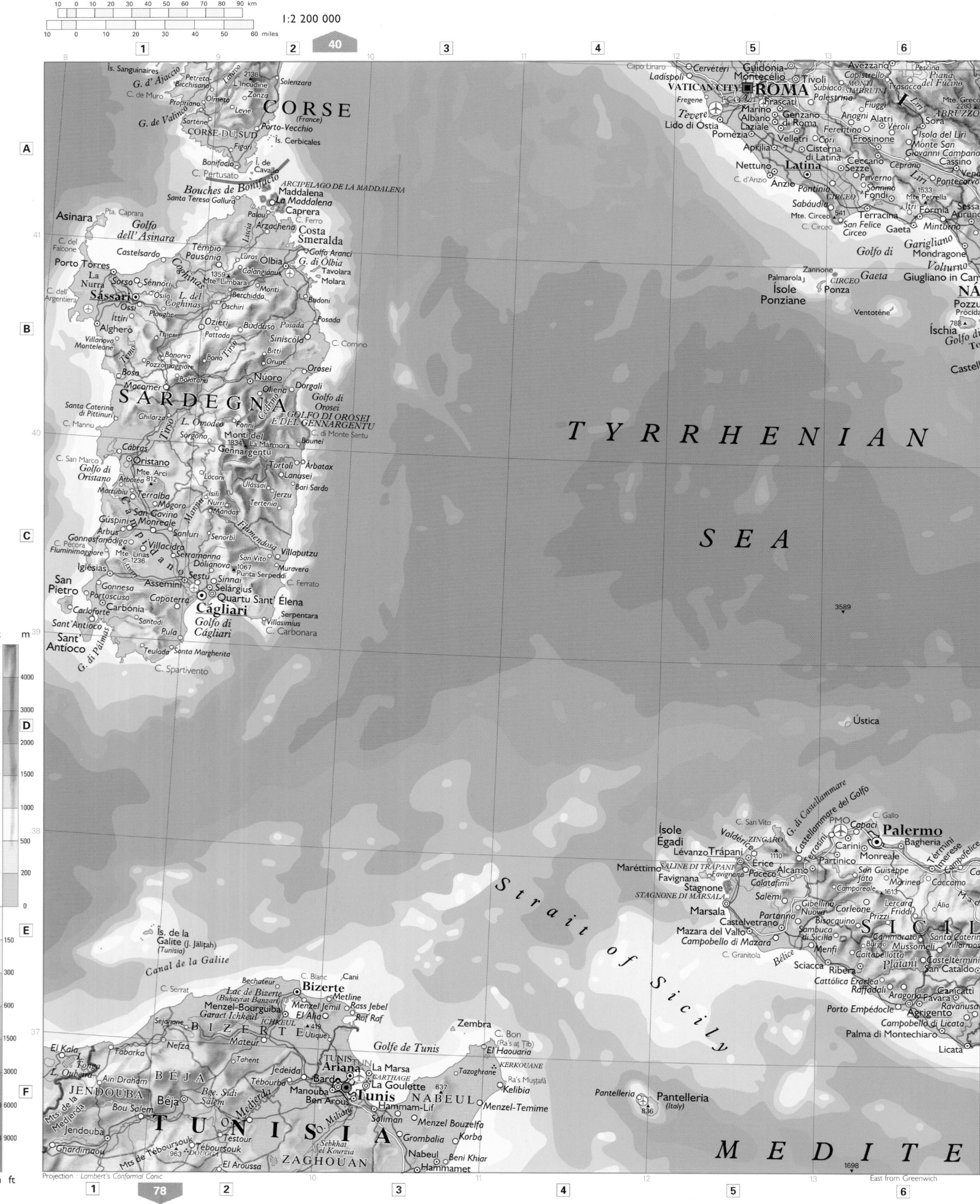

1:2 200 000

Projection : Lambert's Conformal Conic

East from Greenwich

Nature Parks in Italy   National Parks

Underlined towns give their name to the administrative area in which they stand.

1:2 200 000

Inter-entity boundaries as agreed
at the 1995 Dayton Peace Agreement

National Parks

Underlined towns give their name to the administrative area in which they stand.

COPYRIGHT PHILIP'S

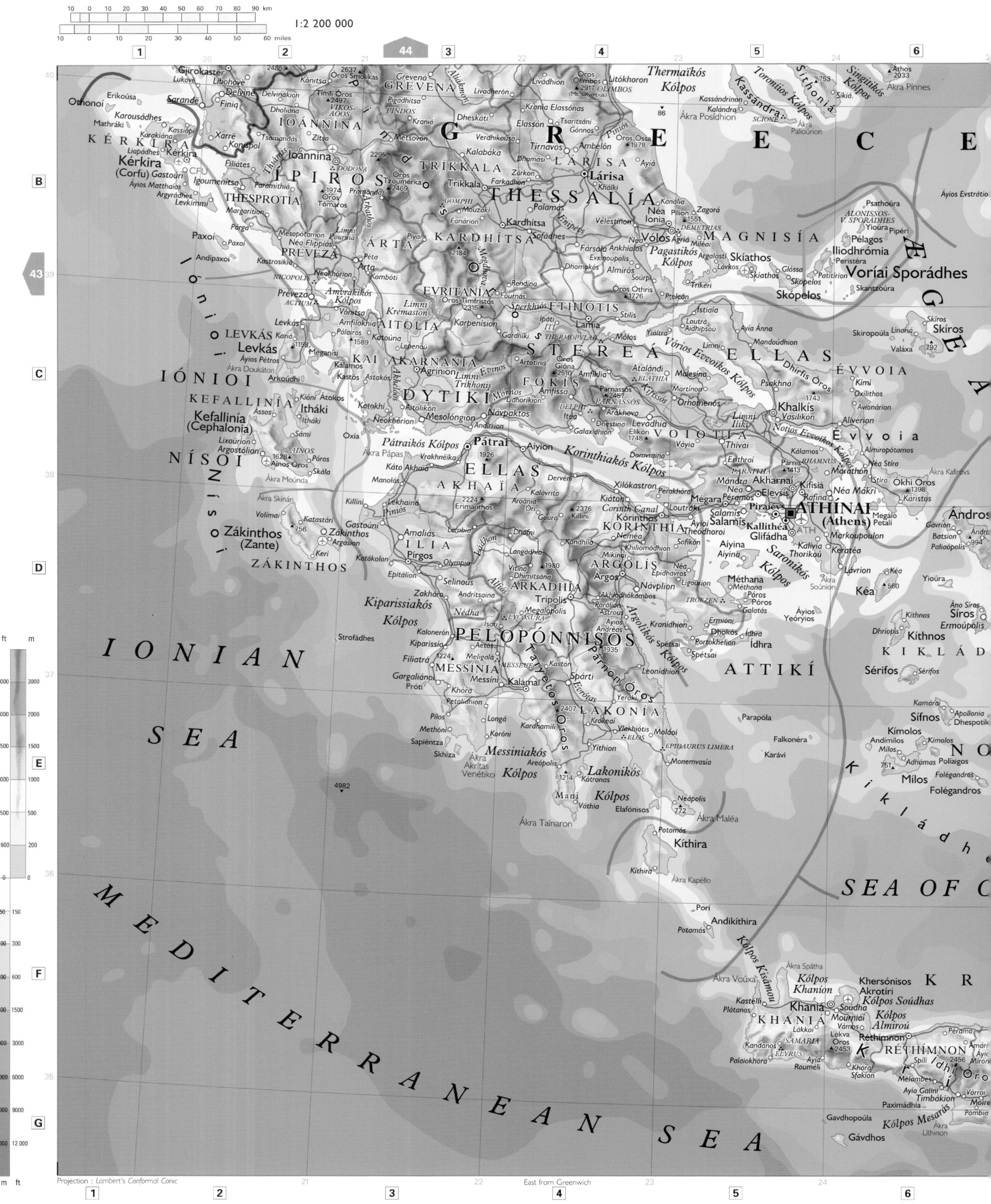

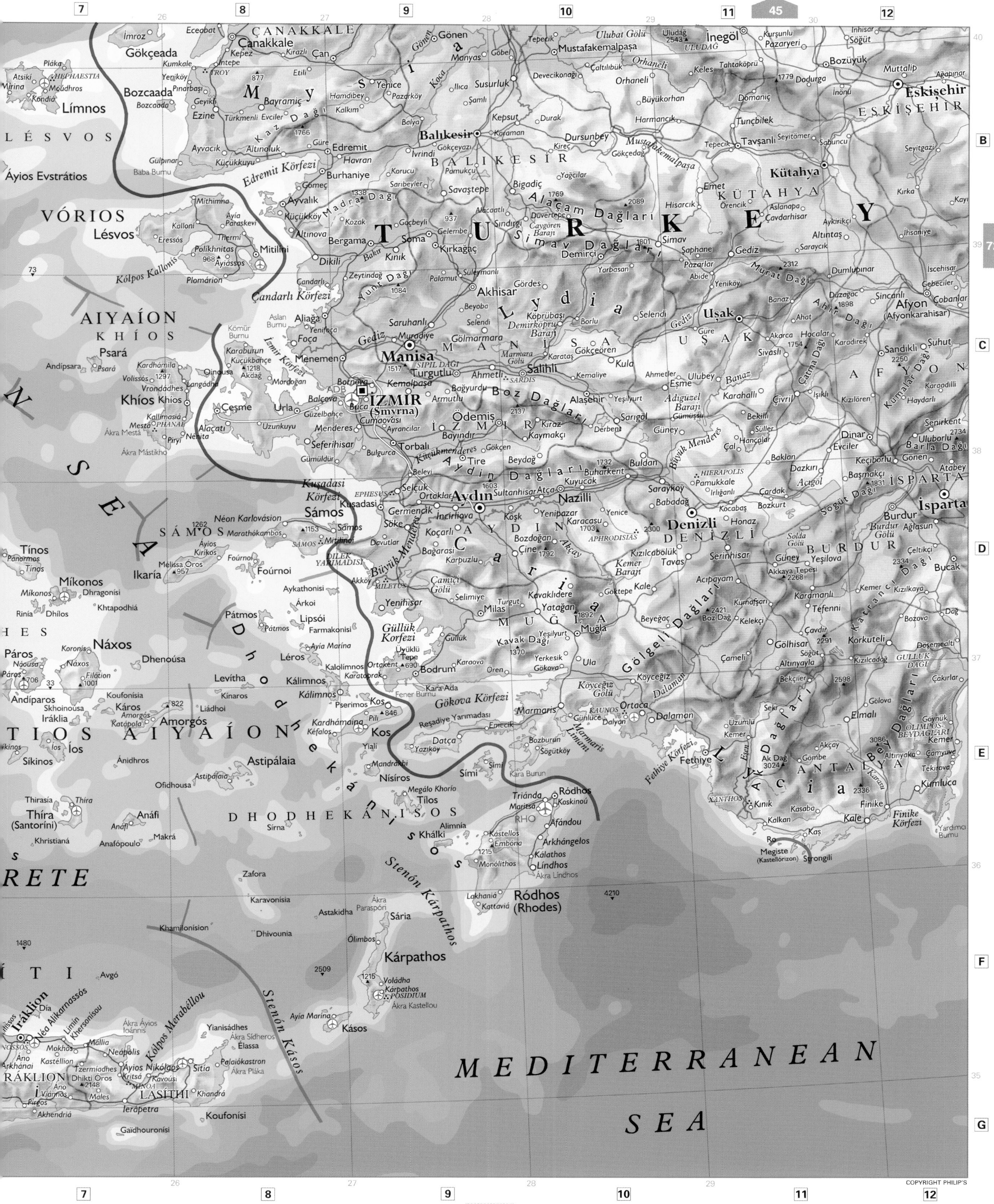

Grid references (top)
7 8 9 10 11 **45** 12

MY S I a

Plák
Atsiki
Mírina
Kondiá
HEPHAESTIA
Moúdhros
Límnos

Eceabat
Kumkale
TROY
Kilitbahir
ÇANAKKALE
Kepez
Çanakkale
İntepe
Pınarbaşı
İmroz
Gökçeada

Gönen
Gönel
Tepecik
Mustafakemalpaşa
Manyas
Göbel
Ulubat Gölü
İnegöl
Kurşunlu
Pazaryeri
İnhisar
Söğüt
Bozüyük
Müttalip
Ağapınar
Eskişehir

L É S V O S
VÓRIOS

Bayramiç
Çan
Yenice
Ezine
Türkmenli
Eviler
Geyikli
Hamdibey
Pazarköy
Kalkım
Balya
Gönen

Susurluk
İlıca
Devecikonağı
Orhaneli
Büyükorhan
Harmancık
Dursunbey
Tepecik
Tavşanlı
Seyitömer
Sabuncu
Domaniç
Tunçbilek

Balıkesir
B A L I K E S İ R
Karaman
Gökçeyazı
Gökçedağ
Mustafakemalpaşa
Kireç
Emet
Orencik
Aslanapa
Çavdarhisar
Kütahya
K Ü T A H Y A
Kırka

Áyios Evstrátios

Edremit Körfezi
Edremit
Havran
Burhaniye
Gömeç
Ayvalık
Küçükkuyu
Altınoluk
Ayvacık
Gülpınar
Baba Burnu

İvrindi
Korucu
Pamukçu
Savaştepe
Bigadiç
Yağcılar
Alaçam Dağları
Hisarcık
Orencik
Çavdarhisar
Aykırıkçı
Altıntaş
İhsaniye

Lésvos

Mithimna
Ayía Paraskeví
Kalloní
Eressós
Políkhnitas
Ayíassos
Thermí
Mitilíni

Madra Dağı
Kozak
Bergama
Soma
Kırkağaç
Akhisar
Beyoba
Selendi
Selendi
Demirci
Simav
Şaphane
Gediz
Pazarlar
Abide
Yeniköy
Dumlupınar
İscehisar

A İ Y A İ O N
K H Í O S
Psará
Andípsara
Psará

Küçükköy
Dikili
Çandarlı Körfezi
Çandarlı
Zeytindağ
Palamut
Yund Dağı
Süleymanlı
Gördes
Borlu
Selendi
Köprübaşı
Demirköprü Barajı
Uşak
U Ş A K
Güre
Banaz
Ahat
Düzağaç
Sincanlı
Afyon
(Afyonkarahisar)
Cobanlar

T U R K E Y

Khíos Khios
Kallimasiá
Mestá
PHANAÍ
Ákra Mestá
Piryí
Nénita
Ákra Mástikho

Kömür Burnu
Aslan Burnu
Karaburun
Küçükbahçe
Akdağ
Foça
Yenifoça
Menemen
Muradiye
Gediz
Manisa
M A N İ S A
SIPIL DAĞI
Saruhanlı
Gölmarmara
Marmara Gölü
Turgutlu
Salihli
SARDIS
Kemaliye
Kula
Ahmetler
Eşme
Ulubey
Banaz
Karahallı
Civril
Sivaslı
Karacadağ
Karadirek
Sandıklı
Suhut
Kızılören
Haydarlı

Çeşme
Urla
Balçova
İZMİR
(Smyrna)
Buca
Güzelbahçe
Uzunkuyu
Alaçatı
Menderes
Seferihisar
Gümüldür

Kemalpaşa
Armutlu
Boz Dağları
Alaşehir
Yeşilyurt
Sarıgöl
Adıgüzel Barajı
Gümüşsu
Güney
Bekilli
Süller
Dinar
Keçiborlu
Uluborlu
Barla Dağı
Gönen
Atabey

İ Z M İ R
Ödemiş
Bayındır
Torbalı
Tire
Gökçen
Kiraz
Kaymakçı
Derbent
Güney
Hançalar
Çal
Büyük Menderes
Baklan
Dazkırı
Acıgöl
Başmakçı
Isparta
İ S P A R T A

Kuşadası Körfezi
EPHESUS
Selçuk
Kuşadası
Germencik
İncirliova
Küçükmenderes
Belevi
Aydın Dağları
Buharkent
Buldan
Sarayköy
HIERAPOLIS
Pamukkale
İrlıganlı
Kocabaş
Çardak
Burdur
Ağlasun
Burdur
B U R D U R

Sámos
Néon Karlovásion
Marathókambos
Sámos
SÁMOS
Mitilíni
Söke
Koçarlı
Köşk
Yenipazar
Karacasu
APHRODISIAS
Nazilli
Babadağ
Denizli
D E N İ Z L İ
Honaz
Solda Gölü
Güney
Yeşilova
Çeltikçi
Bucak

Tínos
Pánormos
Tínos
Ákra Papás

DİLEK YARIMADASI
Davutlar
Bağarası
A Y D I N
Aydın
Sultanhisar
Atça
Kuyucak
Bozdoğan
Kızılcabölük
Serinhisar
Tavas
Kemer Barajı
Akkaya Tepesi
Kemer
Karamanlı
Tefenni
Bozova
Dağ

Mikonos
Míkonos
Dhragonísi

İkaría
Mélissa Óros
Áyios Kírikos
Foúrnoi
Foúrnoi

Büyük Menderes
Ákköy
MILETUS
Yenihisar
Çamiçi Gölü
Selimiye
Turgut
Kavaklıdere
Göktepe
Kale
Acıpayam
Akkaya Tepesi
Gölhisar
Söğüt
Altınyayla
Kızılcadağ

Páros
Náoussa
Páros
Náxos
Koronis
Dhilos
Rinía

Árkoi
Lipsói
Farmakonísi
Güllük Körfezi
Uyuklu Tepe
Ortakent
Milas
Yatağan
Muğla
M U Ğ L A
Muğla
Beyağaç
Gölgeli Dağları
Çavdır
Çameli
Korkuteli

Náxos
Koufonísia
Iráklia

Pátmos
Pátmos
Léros
Ayía Marína
Kálimnos
Güllük
Karaova
Ören
Yeşilyurt
Boz Dağ
Kelekçi
Kemer
Kızılcaağ
G U L L U K D A Ğ I

Andíparos
Koufonísia
Káros
Amorgós
Katápola
Liádhoi
Levítha
Kínaros
Kálimnos
Kalolimnos
Ortakent
Karatoprak
Bodrum
Kara Ada
Kavak Dağı
Yerkesik
Gökova
Ula
Köyceğiz Gölü
Dalaman
Antalya
A N T A L Y A

T I O S   A İ Y A İ O N
Síkinos
Íos
Íos
Anídhros
Astipálaia
Ofidhousa
Astipálaia

Pserimos
Kos
Kos
Kardhámaina
Kéfalos
Yalı
Gökova Körfezi
Reşadiye Yarımadası
Marmaris
Günlüce
Dalyan
Ortaca
Dalaman
Köyceğiz
D H O D H E K Á N I S O S

Thirasía
Thíra
Thíra
(Santoríni)
Khristianá
Anáfi
Anáfi
Anafópoulo
Makrá
Sírna

Nísiros
Megálo Khorió
Tílos
Datça
Yazıköy
Bozburun
Söğütköy
Sími
Epének
Marmaris Limanı
Kaunos
Uzunlu
Dalaman
Kemer
Fethiye
Akçay
Gömbe
L Y C İ A
A K D A Ğ L A R I
Elmalı
Kumluca

Nísiros
Khálki
Kastellós
Embóna
Arkhángelos
Kalathos
Líndhos
Monólithos
Ákra Líndhos
RHODES
Triánda
Maritsa
Ródhos
Koskinoú
Afándou

XANTHOS
Kınık
Kasaba
Kalkan
Kaş
Ro
Megísti
(Kastellórizon)
Strongili
Finike
Kale
Finike Körfezi
Yardımcı Burnu

Zafora
Stenón Kárpathos
Astakídha
Ákra Parasporí
Sária
Lakhaniá
Kattaviá
Ródhos
(Rhodes)

C R E T E

Karavonísia
Khamilonísion
Dhivounía
Ákra Pláka
Ólimbos
Karavonísia

Voládha
Kárpathos
POSIDIUM
Ákra Kastéllou

Iráklion
Día
Néa Alikarnassós
Límin Khersonísou
Mália
Neápolis
Áyios Nikólaos
Sitía
Kásos

Mokhós
Kastéllion
Dhíkti Óros
MINOA
Kritsá
Gourniá
Ierápetra
Koufonísi
Gaïdhouronísi

M E D I T E R R A N E A N

S E A

National Parks

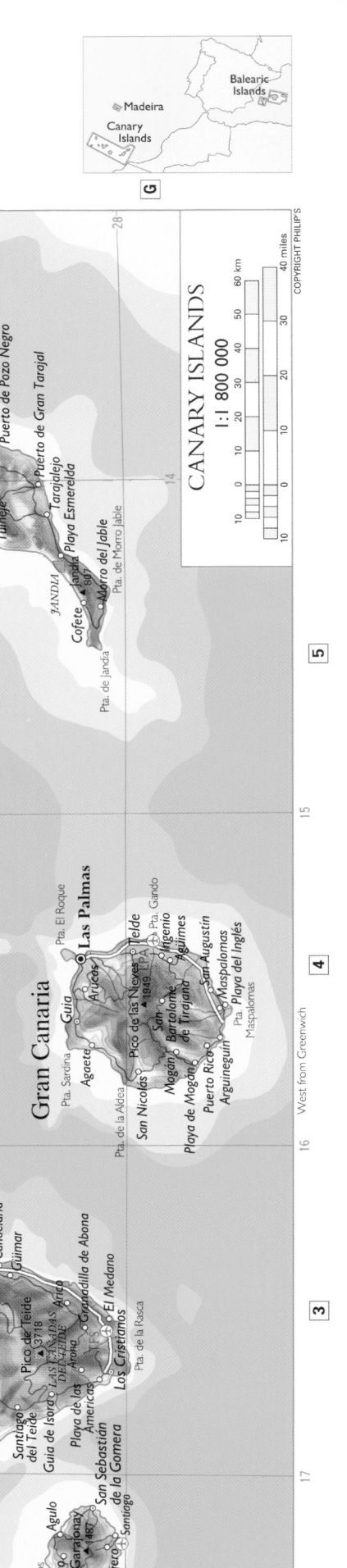

Madeira
Canary Islands
Balearic Islands

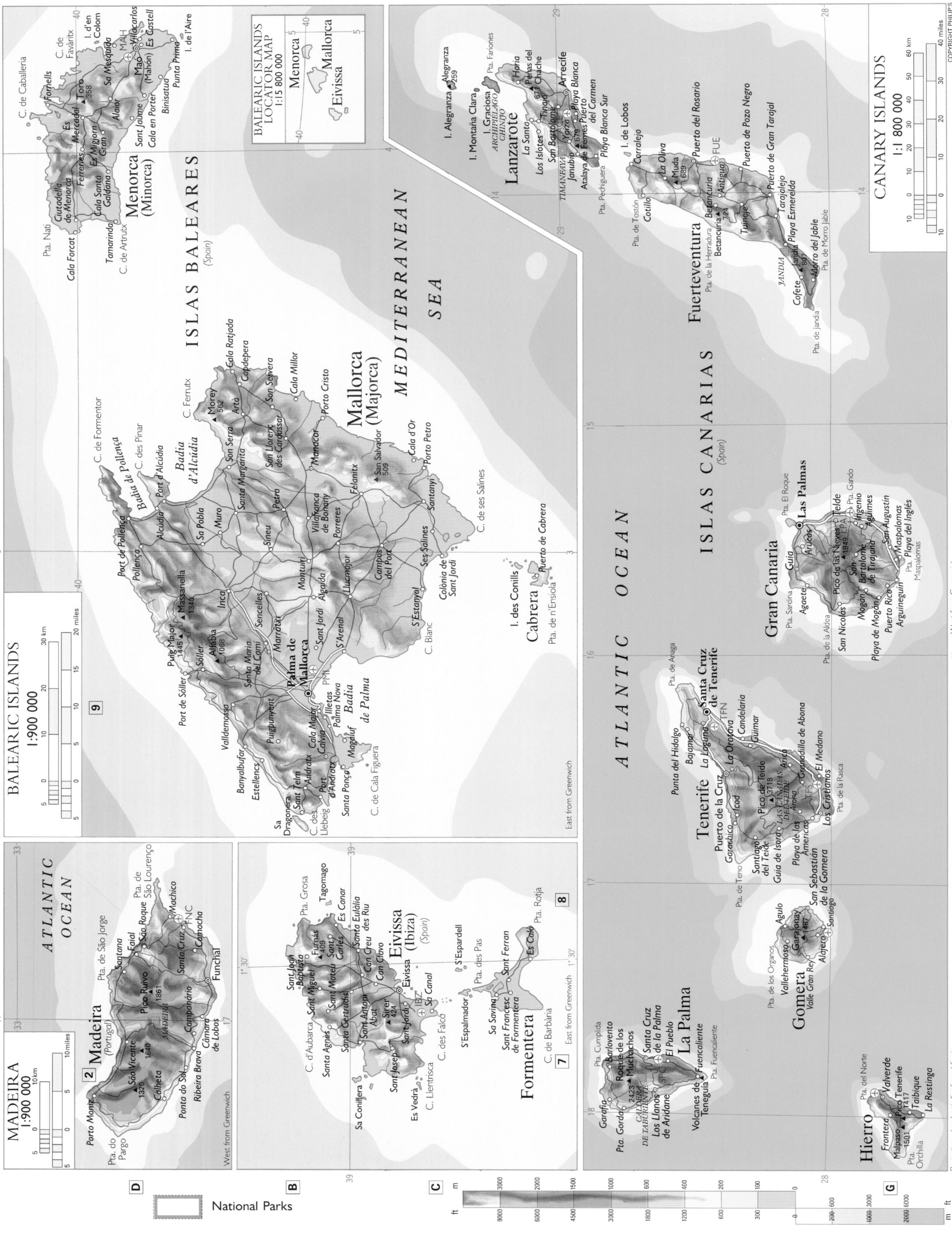

BALEARIC ISLANDS
LOCATOR MAP
1:15 800 000

Menorca
Mallorca
Eivissa

Menorca (Minorca)

C. de Caballeria
Pta. Nati
Fornells
C. de Favàritx
I. d'en Colom
Villacarlos
Es Castell
I. de l'Aire
Punta Prima
Ciutadella de Menorca
Cala Santa Galdana
Tamarinda
C. d'Artrux
Ferreres
Es Mercadal
Alaior
Toro 358
Maó (Mahón)
MAH
Sant Jaume
Cala en Porter
Binisatud
Mercadal

ISLAS BALEARES (Spain)

Mallorca (Majorca)

C. de Formentor
C. de Pollença
Port de Pollença
Pollença
Badia de Pollença
C. del Pinar
C. des Pinar
Port d'Alcúdia
Alcúdia
Badia d'Alcúdia
Muro
Sa Pobla
Inca
Santa Margarita
Petra
Son Serra
San Llorenç des Cardassar
Artà
Capdepera
Cala Ratjada
Son Servera
Cala Millor
Porto Cristo
Manacor
Vilafranca de Bonany
Felanitx
San Salvador 509
Cala d'Or
Porto Petro
Santanyí
C. de ses Salines
Ses Salines
Campos del Port
Llucmajor
Montuïri
Porreres
Algaida
Sineu
Sencelles
Santa Maria del Camí
Marratxí
Santa Eugènia
Puigpunyent
Palma de Mallorca
PM
Badia de Palma
S'Arenal
Palma Nova
Illetas
Cala Major
Calvià
Magaluf
C. de Cala Figuera
Andratx
Port d'Andratx
Sant Telm
Sa Dragonera
C. des Llebeig
Estellencs
Banyalbufar
Valldemossa
Puig Major 1445
Port de Sóller
Sóller
Massanella 1348
Alaró 1068
Norey 562
C. Ferrutx
Sant Jordi
Marratxí
Santa Ponça
Colònia de Sant Jordi
S'Estanyol
C. Blanc
Pta. de n'Ensiola
Puerto de Cabrera

Cabrera
I. des Conills

MEDITERRANEAN SEA

East from Greenwich

BALEARIC ISLANDS
1:900 000

Madeira (Portugal)

ATLANTIC OCEAN
Porto Moniz
Pta. do Pargo
Pta. de São Lourenço
Pta. de São Jorge
Santana
Faial
São Roque
Santa Cruz
Machico
Camacha
Funchal
Pico Ruivo 1861
Curral das Freiras
Campanário
Ponta do Sol
Ribeira Brava
Câmara de Lobos
Calheta
São Vicente 1320
FNC
West from Greenwich

MADEIRA
1:900 000

Eivissa (Ibiza) (Spain)

Pta. Grossa
Tagomago
Es Canar
Santa Eulalia del Riu
Sant Carles
Sant Joan Baptista
Sant Miquel
Sant Mateu
Santa Gertrudis
Can Clavo
Santa Agnès
Sant Antoni Abat
Sant Josep
Sant Jordi
Eivissa 424
IBZ
C. des Falcó
Sa Conillera
Es Vedrà
C. Llentrisca
Funás 409

Formentera
S'Espalmador
Sa Savina
Sant Francesc de Formentera
Es Caló
Pta. des Pas
Pta. Rotja
C. de Barbària
S'Espardell

East from Greenwich

National Parks

ISLAS CANARIAS (Spain)

Lanzarote
I. Alegranza 289
I. Montaña Clara
I. Graciosa
ARCHIPIÉLAGO CHINIJO
La Santa
Los Islotes
Haria
Peñas del Chache 671
Arrecife
Guatiza
Playa Blanca
Puerto del Carmen
San Bartolomé
TIMANFAYA
Pta. Pechiguera
Playa Blanca Sur
I. de Lobos
Corralejo
Pta. Fanones

Fuerteventura
La Oliva
Muda 689
Betancuria
Antigua
FUE
Puerto del Rosario
Tuineje
Tarajalejo
Pta. de Tostón
Cotillo
Pta. de la Herradura
Gran Tarajal
Puerto de Pozo Negro
Puerto de Gran Tarajal
Atalaya de Femés
Morro del Jable
Cofete
Jandía
JANDIA
Pta. de Jandía
Playa de Morro del Jable

Gran Canaria
Las Palmas
Pta. El Roque
Telde
Gando
Pta. Gando
Ingenio
Agüimes
San Agustín
Maspalomas
Pico de las Nieves 1949
Tejeda
San Bartolomé de Tirajana
Mogán
Guía
Arucas
Agaete
San Nicolás
Pta. Sardina
Pta. de la Aldea
Playa de Mogán
Puerto Rico
Arguineguín
Pta. Playa del Inglés

Tenerife
Pico del Teide 3718
Santa Cruz de Tenerife
TFN
La Laguna
La Orotava
Puerto de la Cruz
Candelaria
Güimar
Garachico
Icod
La Guancha
Adeje
Arona
Granadilla de Abona
El Médano
Los Cristianos
Playa de las Américas
Punta del Hidalgo
Pta. de Anaga
Bajamar
Pta. de Teno
LAS CAÑADAS
DEL TEIDE

Gomera
San Sebastián de la Gomera
Garajonay 1487
Hermigua
Agulo
Vallehermoso
Valle Gran Rey
Alojera
Santiago
Pta. de los Órganos

La Palma
Santa Cruz de la Palma
Los Llanos de Aridane
El Paso
Barlovento
Puntallana
Fuencaliente
Tenegula
Volcanes de Teneguía
Garafía
Puntagorda
Roque de los Muchachos 2423
CALDERA DE TABURIENTE
Pta. Cumplida
El Pueblo
Pta. Fuencaliente

Hierro
Valverde
Frontera
Pico de Tenerife 1501
Malpaso
Taibique
La Restinga
Pta. del Norte
Pta. Orchilla

ATLANTIC OCEAN

West from Greenwich

CANARY ISLANDS
1:1 800 000

COPYRIGHT PHILIP'S

Projection: Lambert's Conformal Conic

m   ft
9000
6000
4500
3000
1800
1200
600
300
150
0

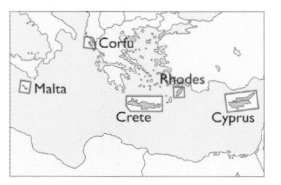

CRETE
1:1 200 000

CYPRUS
1:1 200 000

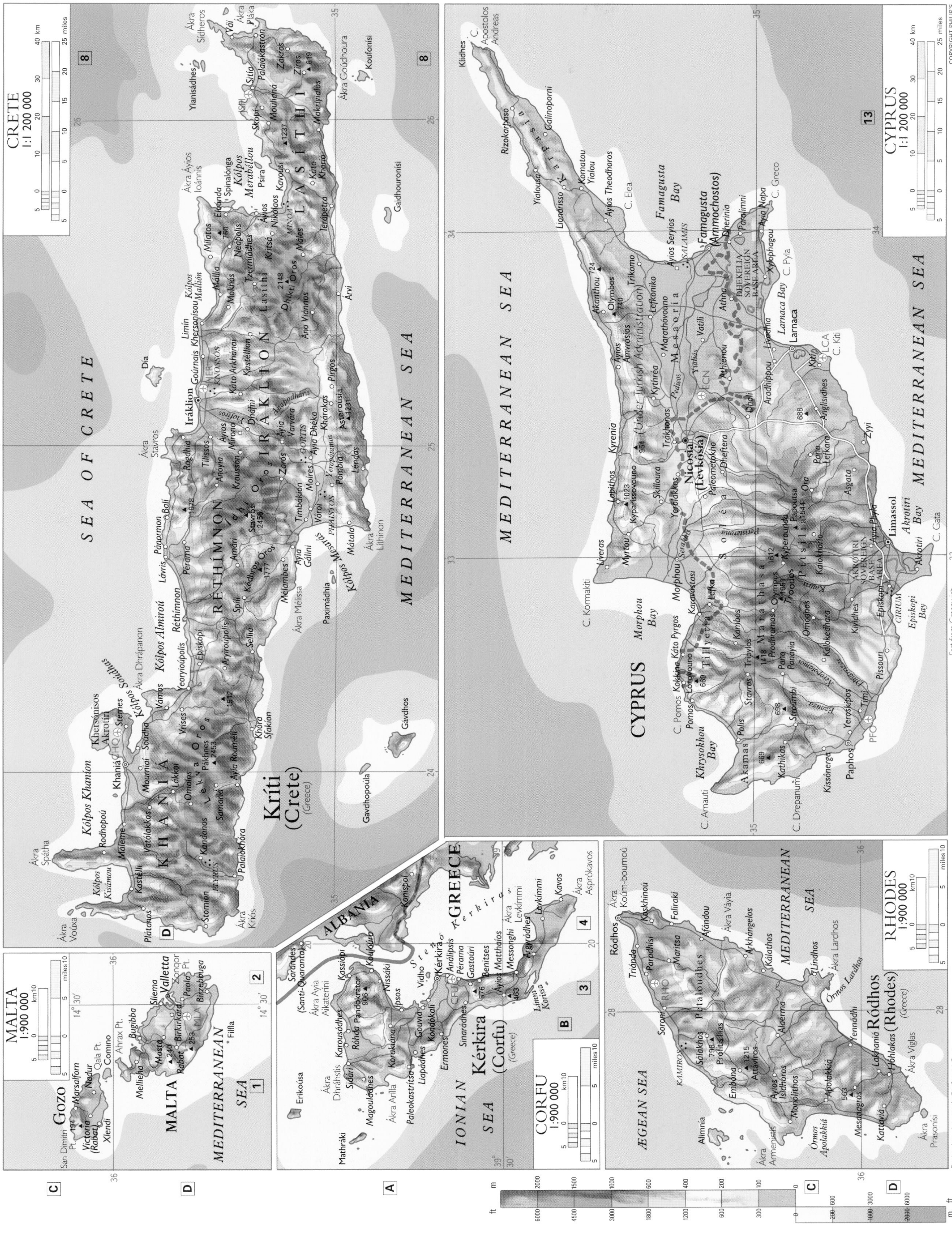

MALTA
1:900 000

CORFU
1:900 000

RHODES
1:900 000

Projection: Lambert's Conformal Conic

COPYRIGHT PHILIP'S

East from Greenwich

SEA OF CRETE

MEDITERRANEAN SEA

IONIAN SEA

AEGEAN SEA

Kríti (Crete) (Greece)

Kérkira (Corfu) (Greece)

Ródhos (Rhodes) (Greece)

CYPRUS

GREECE

ALBANIA

Nicosia (Levkosía)

Famagusta (Ammóchostos)

Limassol

Larnaca

Iráklion

Khaniá

Valletta

GOZO

1:44 400 000

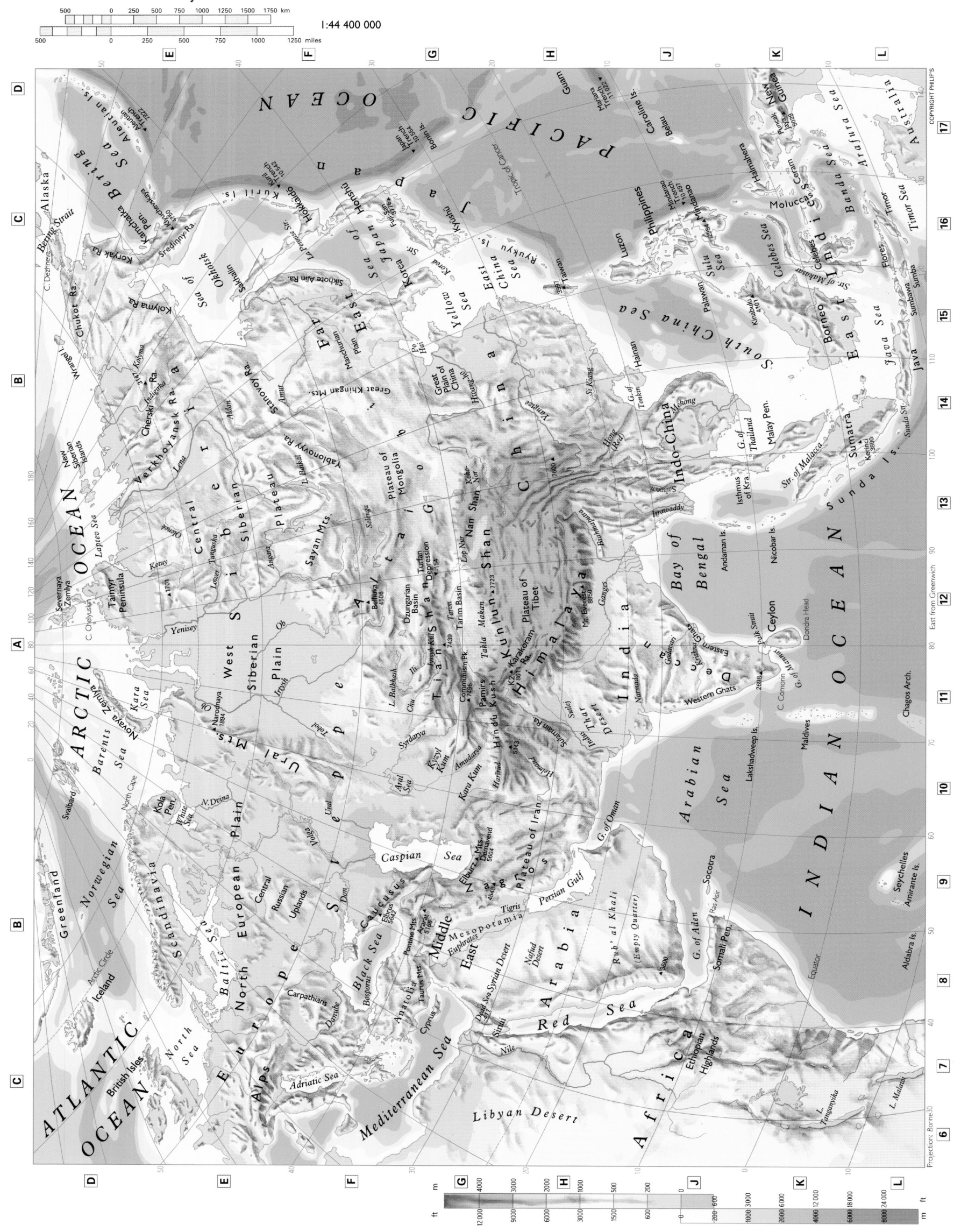

Projection: Bonne.
East from Greenwich

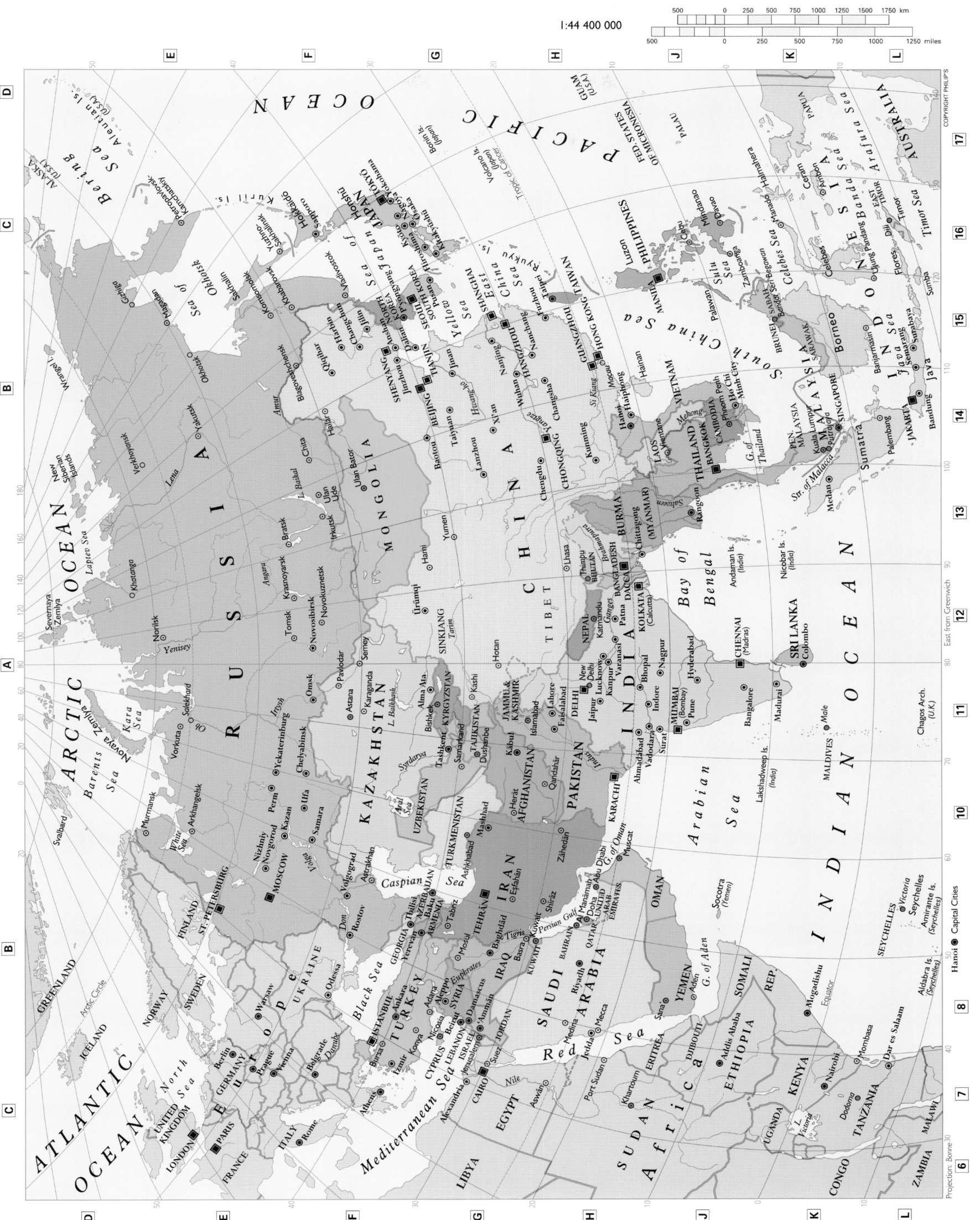

1:44 400 000

500   0   250   500   750   1000   1250   1500   1750 km

500   0   250   500   750   1000   1250 miles

COPYRIGHT PHILIP'S

Projection: Bonne

East from Greenwich

Hanoi ● Capital Cities

1:17 800 000

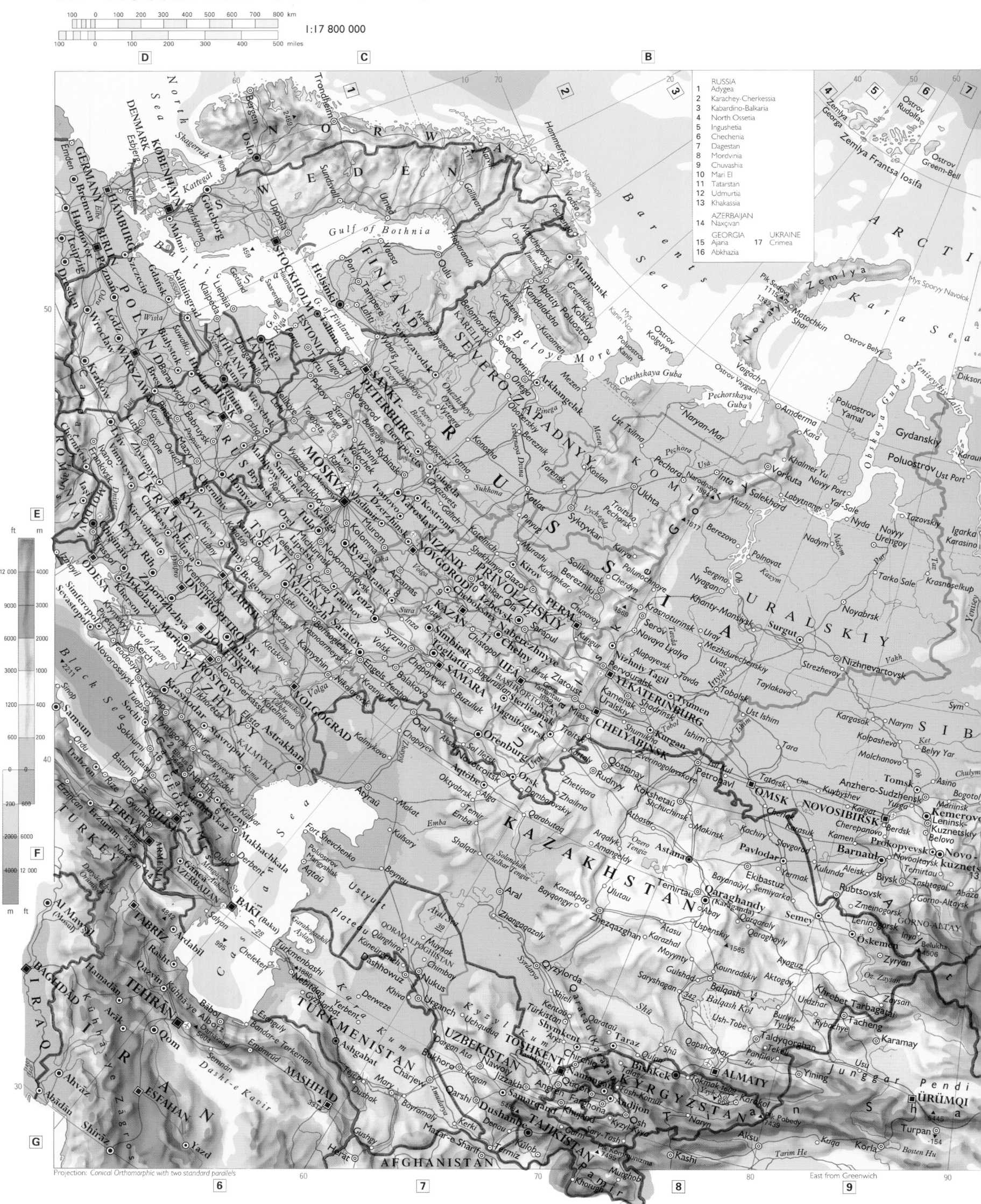

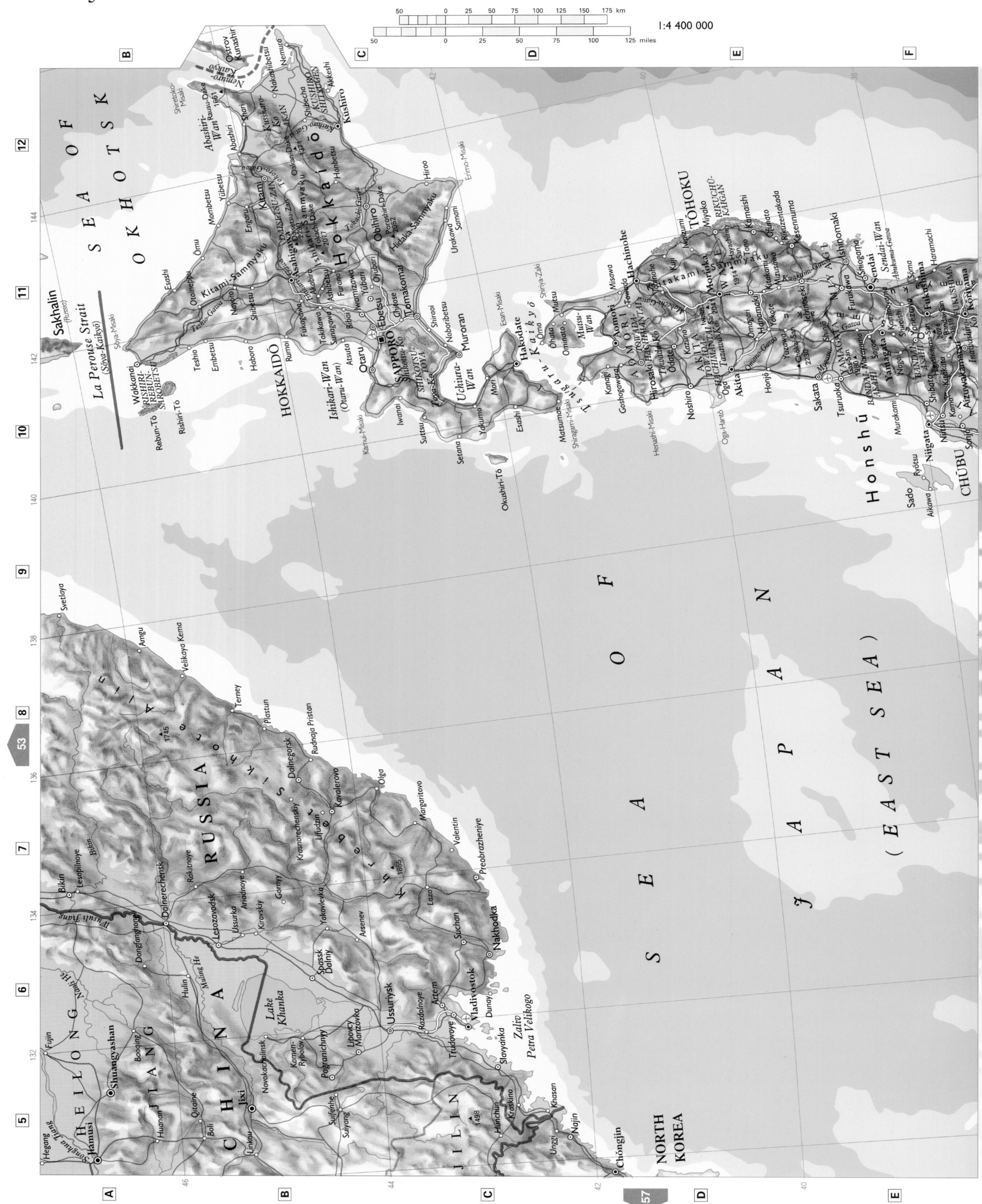

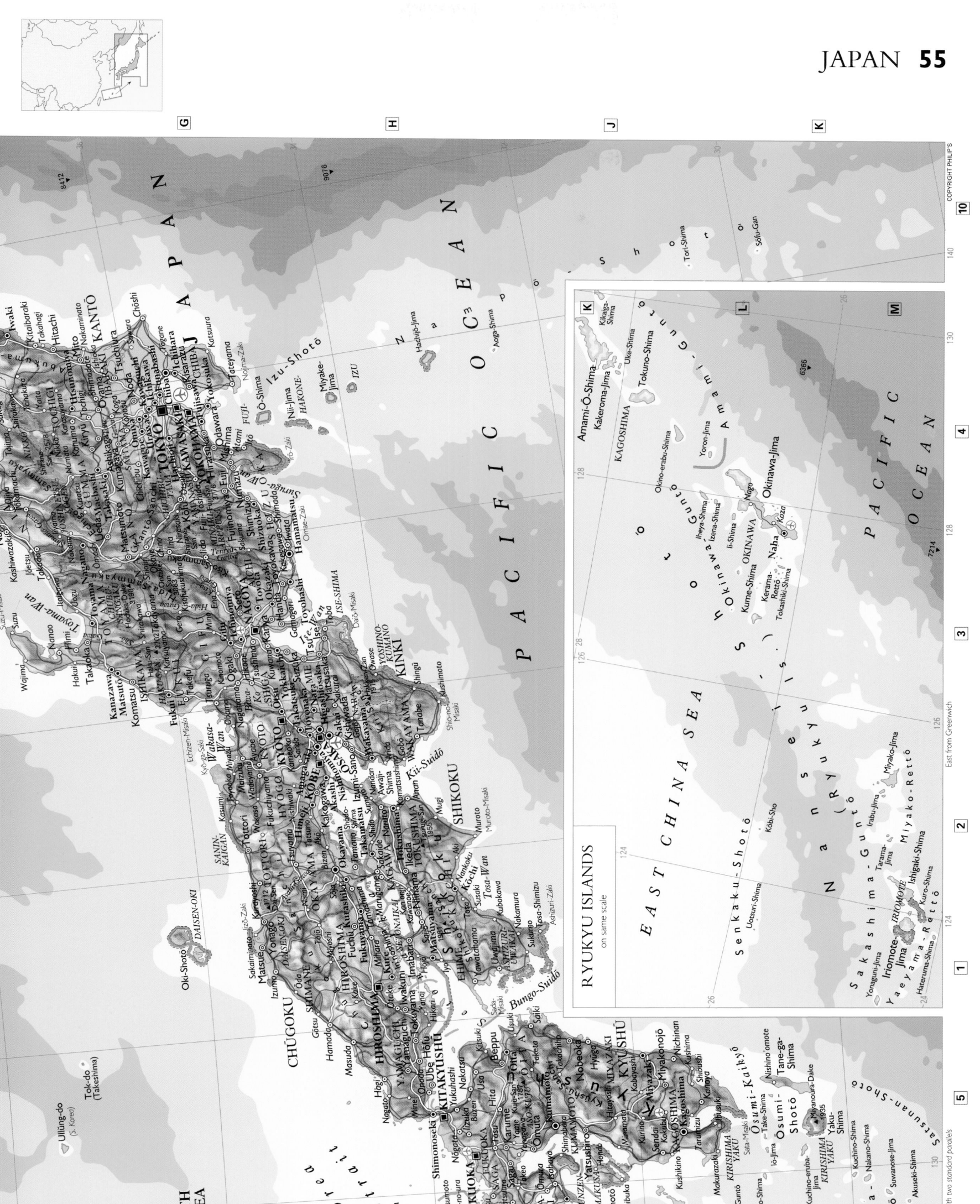

G H J K

10

COPYRIGHT PHILIP'S

140

P A C I F I C   O C E A N

K

Amami-Ō-Shima

Kikaiga-Shima

Uke-Shima

Tokuno-Shima

L

130

6365

M

KAGOSHIMA

Okino-erabu-Shima

Yoron-Jima

Iheya-Shima
Izena-Shima

Ii-Shima

OKINAWA

Nago

Okinawa-Jima

Naha

Koza

7214

P A C I F I C   O C E A N

Kume-Shima

Kerama-Rettō

Tokashiki-Shima

128

128

4

O k i n a w a   -   G u n t ō

3

28

26

130

RYUKYU ISLANDS
on same scale

E A S T   C H I N A   S E A

124

124

126

126

East from Greenwich

Senkaku-Shotō

Uotsuri-Shima

Kōbi-Sho

N a n s e i - (R y u k y u) -   S h o t ō

Iriomote-
IRIOMOTE

Yonaguni-Shima

Sakishima - Guntō

Tarama-
Jima

Inabu-Jima

Miyako-Jima

Miyako-Rettō

Ishigaki-Jima

Kuro-Shima

Y a e y a m a - S h i m a - R e t t ō

Hateruma-Shima

26

24

2

1

SOUTH
KOREA

Pohang

Ulsan

Yŏngdŏk

Ullŭng-do
(S. Korea)

Tok-do
(Takeshima)

38

36

34

F

K o r e a   S t r a i t

Tsushima
(Japan)

Iki

Go-noura

Katsumoto

Nagata

Nagoya

Hirado

Sasebo

Goto-
Rettō

Fukue-
Shima

SAIKAI

Nakadori-
Shima

Nomo-
Zaki

Fukue

SHIMANE

CHŪGOKU

DAISEN-OKI

Oki-Shotō

Sakaiminato

Masuda

Hagi

Matsue

Yonago

Tottori

SANIN-
KAIGAN

Hamada

Ōda

Izumo

Iwami

Mine

Onoda

Ube

Hōfu

Yamaguchi

Iwakuni

YAMAGUCHI

KITAKYUSHU

Shimonoseki

FUKUOKA

Nagata

Nōgata

Buzen

Iizuka

Yukuhashi

Nakatsu

Usa

Beppu

OITA

Hita

Kitsuki

Usuki

Saeki

Takeda

Nobeoka

MIYAZAKI

Hyūga

Takanabe

K y ū s h ū

KUMAMOTO

Yatsushiro

Hondo

AMAKUSA-
SHOTŌ

Koshiki-
Rettō

Kuchino-eraku-Jima

Uji-Guntō

Kuro-Shima

Satsunan-Shotō

Akuseki-Shima

Suwanose-Jima

Nakano-Shima

Kuchino-Shima

T o k a r a - R e t t ō

KIRISHIMA
YAKU

Sendai

Kushikino

Ijūin

KAGOSHIMA

Makurazaki

Ibusuki

Kanoya

Sata-Misaki

Ōsumi-
Shotō

Ōsumi-Kaikyō

Tane-ga-
Shima

Nishino'omote

Yaku-
Shima

Miyakonojō

Nichinan

Kushima

Shibushi

Tarumizu

Ō S U M I

S A T S U M A

NAGASAKI

SAGA

Ōmura

Isahaya

UNZEN-
AMAKUSA

Shimabara

FUKUOKA

Karatsu

Imari

Tōsu

Kurume

Ōmuta

Yame

Yanagawa

Ōkawa

Hitoyoshi

Shimanto

E A S T   C H I N A   S E A

5

4

J

K

30

32

Projection: Conical with two standard parallels

Scale bar:
9000 6000 4500 3000 2000 1500 1000 400 200 0
m ft 3000 6000 12 000 18 000 24 000
ft 600 1200 2000 4000 6000 8000
G H

KINKI

CHIBA

KANTŌ

TOKYO

J A P A N

9076

8412

IBARAKI

Mito

Hitachi

Iwaki

Kitaibaraki

Takahagi

Chōshi

Katsuura

Nojima-Zaki

Tateyama

Yokosuka

Yokohama

KANAGAWA

KAWASAKI

Odawara

Atami

Ō-Shima

HAKONE

Nii-Jima

Miyake-
Jima

IZU

Izu-Shotō

Hachijō-Jima

Aoga-Shima

Tori-Shima

Sōfu-Gan

Niijimazaki

Shimoda

Numazu

Shizuoka

Hamamatsu

Tsu

ISE-SHIMA

MIE

NAGOYA

GIFU

AICHI

SHIGA

KYOTO

KINKI

KOBE

OSAKA

HYOGO

Wakayama

WAKAYAMA

YOSHINO-
KUMANO

Shingū

Kushimoto

Shio-no-Misaki

Tanabe

Kainan

Gobō

Awaji-
Shima

Kii-Suidō

SHIKOKU

Tokushima

TOKUSHIMA

KAGAWA

Takamatsu

Naruto

Muroto

Muroto-Misaki

Kōchi

KŌCHI

Tosa-Wan

Nankoku

Susaki

Kubokawa

Nakamura

Sukumo

Tosa-Shimizu

Ashizuri-Zaki

EHIME

Matsuyama

Uwajima

UWAKAI

Bungo-Suidō

HIROSHIMA

Kure

Okayama

OKAYAMA

Fukuyama

Onomichi

Kurashiki

Mihara

Tamano

Marugame

Imabari

Saijō

Niihama

Iyo

Hikari

Tokuyama

Daisen

Izuhara

PACIFIC OCEAN

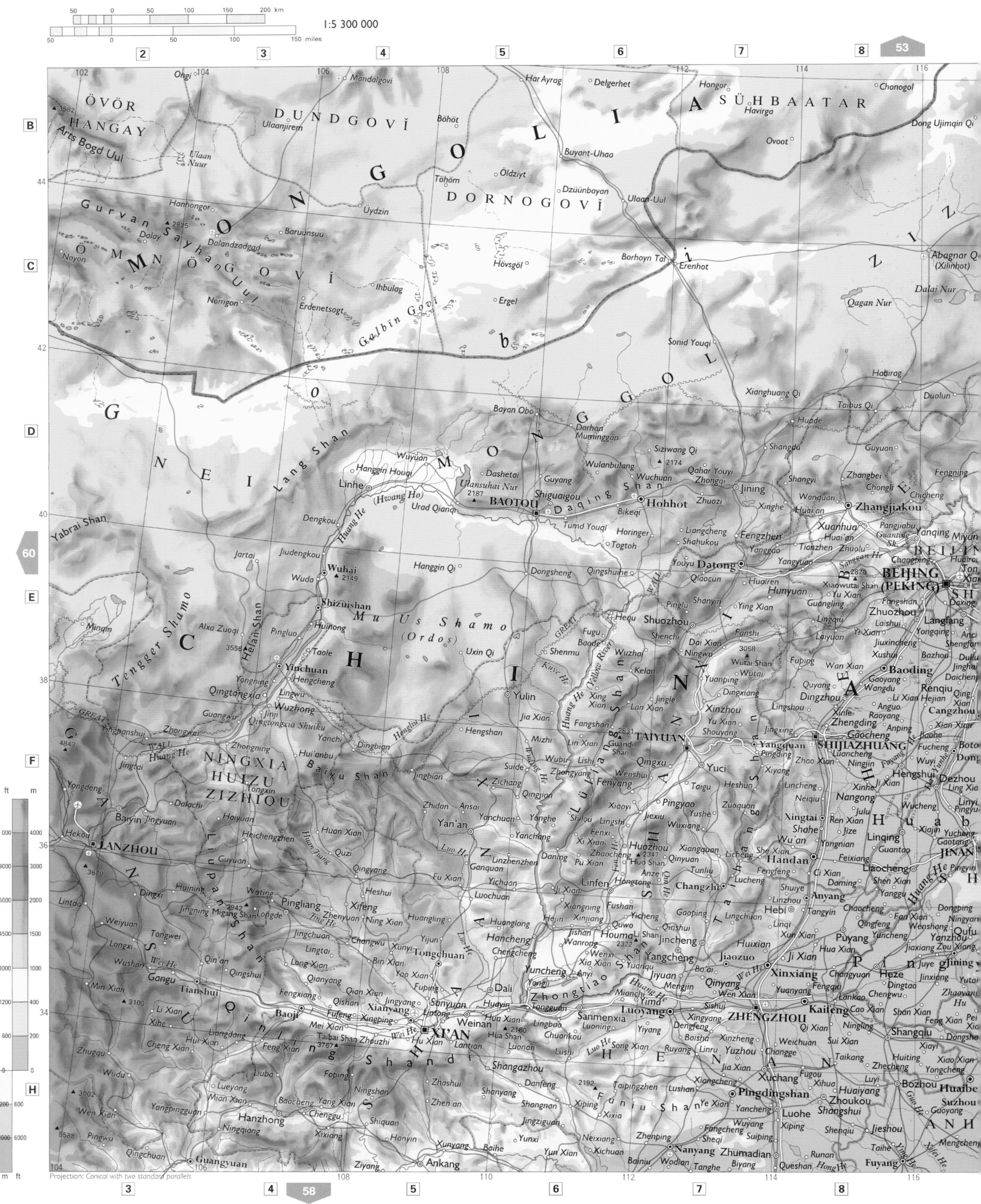

1:5 300 000

Projection: Conical with two standard parallels

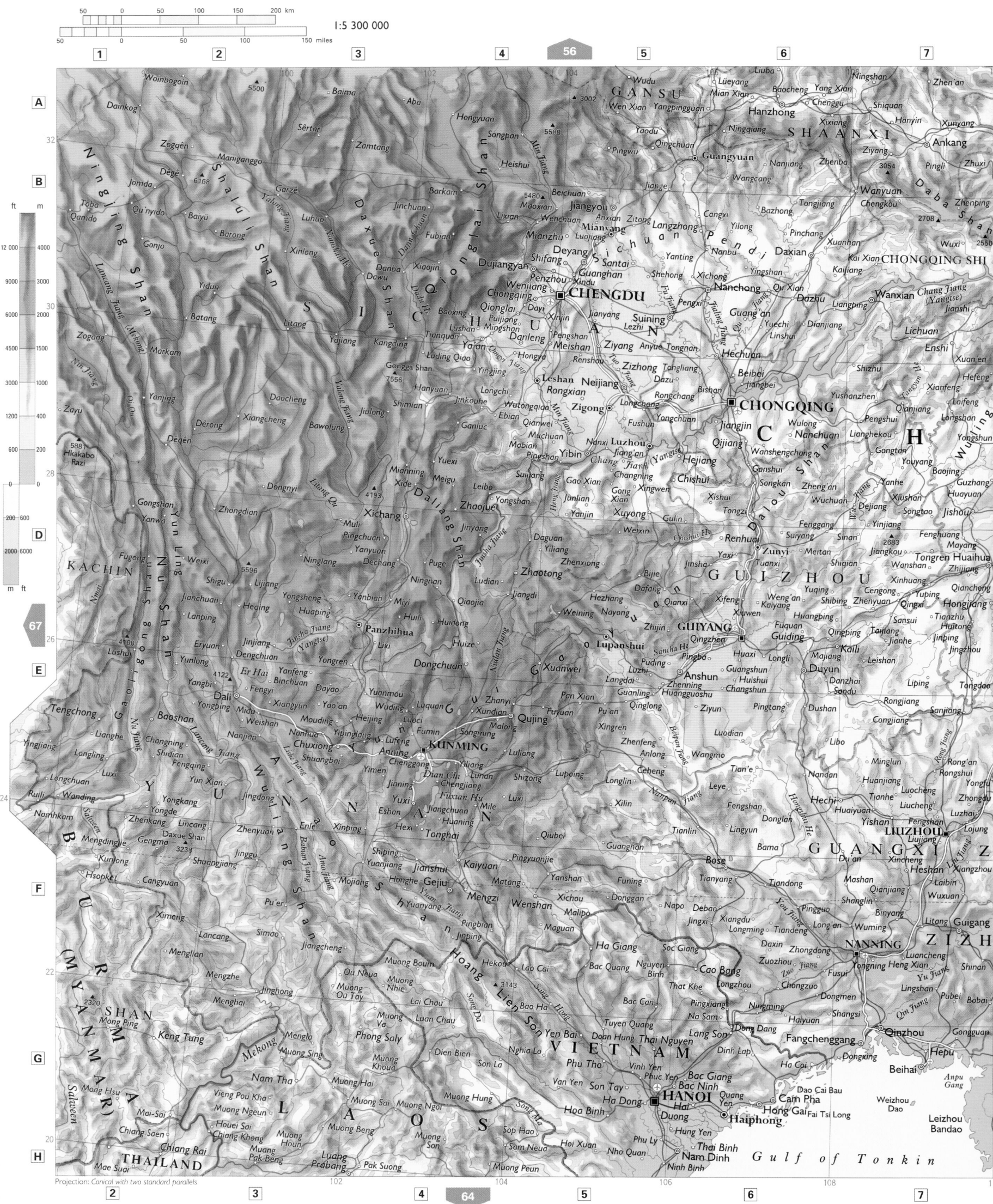

1:5 300 000

Projection: Conical with two standard parallels

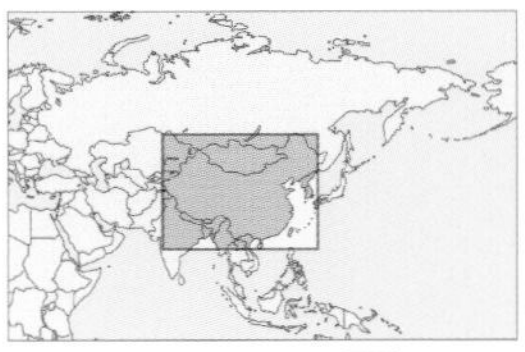

1:17 800 000

100 0 100 200 300 400 500 600 700 800 km
100 0 100 200 300 400 500 miles

COPYRIGHT PHILIP'S

East from Greenwich

Projection: Bonne

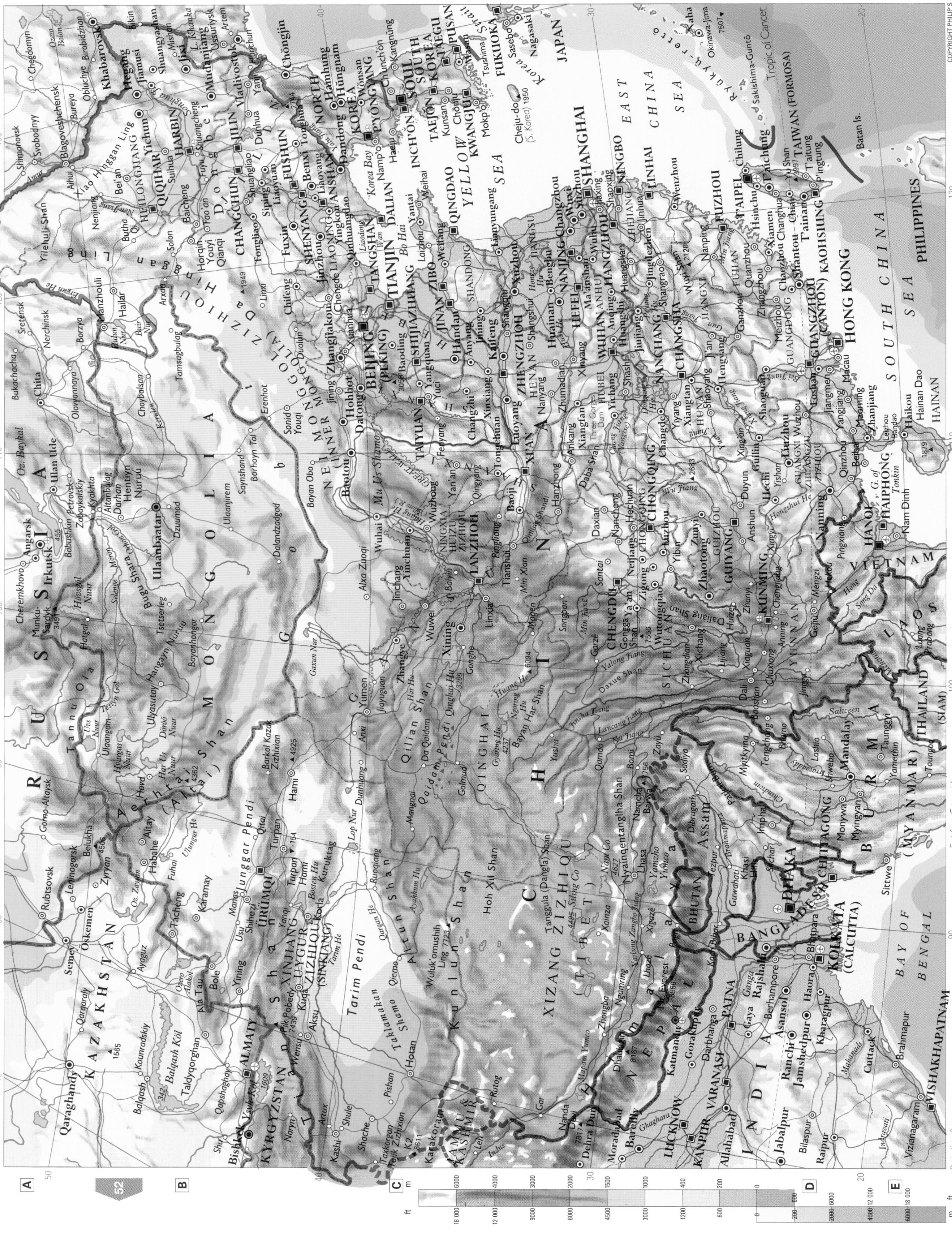

1:6 700 000

50   0   100   150   200   250   300 km
50   0   50   100   150   200 miles

59

A

*Dongsha Dao
(China)*

Itbayat I.
Batan Is.
Batan I.

PACIFIC

20

Balintang Channel

B

Calayan I.
Dalupiri I.   Babuyan
Babuyan   Islands
Fuga I.   Camiguin I.

Babuyan Channel

OCEAN

Mayraira Pt.

Claveria
Bacarra   Bangui
San Nicolas   Laoag   Aparri   Santa Ana
Batac   Kabugao   Gonzaga
Cabugao   Tuao   Gattaran
Bongued   Tuguegarao
Vigan   Cagayan
Santa   Mt. Cresta
Candon   Maria   Libuagan   Iga   1685
Tagudin   Roxas   Ilagan   Palanan Pt.
Bontoc   San Mateo   Palanan
Balaoan   MT.   Santiago   **Luzon**
San Fernando   DATA   Solano   C. San Ildefonso
Bolinao   2928   Cordon   Cosiguran
Lingayen   HUNDRED   Baguio   Bayombong
Alaminos   ISLANDS   Rosario   Mt. Anacaun
Lingayen   Gulf   Dagupan   1852
San Carlos   San Monuel
Santa Cruz   Bayambang   San Jose   Baler Bay
Moncada   Cuyapo   Baler
Masinloc   Camiling   Victoria   AURORA MEMORIAL
Iba   2037   La   Cabanatuan
Tarlac   Paz   Gapan   Polillo I.
Concepcion   Dingalan   Patnanongan I.
Mt. Pinatubo   Angeles   San Fernando   Jomalig I.
1780   San Antonio   Malabon   Polillo I.
Olongapo   Caloocan
Oroni   Quezon City   Lamon Bay
Bataan   Manila   **MANILA**   Paracale
Mariveles   Bay   Pasay   Santa Cruz   Labo   Pandan
Cavite   Dasmariñas   Santa Cruz   Daet   Viga   Catanduanes
Nasugbu   Laguna de Bay   Lucban   Atimonan   Calabanga   San Andres
Tagaytay   San   Lucena   Calauag   BICOL   Virac
Balayan   Pablo   Calabanga   Mt. Isarog   Legazpi
Lubang   Lemery   Lipa   Lopez   Catanauan   1976   Naga   Tabaco   Rapu Rapu I.
Is.   Batangas   Lobo   Tayabas Bay   Nabua   2421   Mayon Vol.
Verde I. Pass   Iriga   Sorsogon
C. Calavite   Baac   Marin-   Donsol   Gubat
Calapan   duque   Magallanes   San Bernardino Str.
LAKE   Victoria   Bulan   Irosin
Mamburao   NAUJAN   Romblon   Sibuyan I.
Mindoro   Mt. Baco   Pinamalayan   SIBUYAN   Laoang
Sablayan   2487   Ticao I.   Mondragon
Bongabong   Aroroy   Masbate   Catarman   Gamay
APO REEF   Roxas   Tablas I.   Odiongan   Mandaon   Mibagos   Arteche
San Jose   Ilin I.   Masbate   Oras
Busuanga I.   Semirara Is.   SEA   Calbayog   Taft

SOUTH
CHINA
SEA

PHILIPPINE
SEA

PHILIPPINES

Culion I.   Calamian   Placer   Catbalogan   Paranas
Group   Pandan   Kalibo   VISAYAN   Bilinan I.   Catbiran   Santa   Borongan
Linapacan Str.   Roxas   SEA   Calubian   Rita   Basey
Linapacan I.   Dao   Ajuy   Bantayan I.   Carigara   General MacArthur
Cuyo Is.   Tibiao   2117   Passi   Cadiz   Palompon   Leyte   Tacloban   Guiuan
Taytay   Bugasong   Panay   Sara   Bogo   Ormoc   Dulag   Homonhon I.
Cuyo West Pass   Cuyo   San Jose   Iloilo   Silay   Victorias   Tuburan   Camotes Is.   Leyte Gulf
Cayo East Pass   Guimaras   Jordan   San Carlos   Danao   Baybay   Abuyog
Bacolod   La   2450   CENTRAL CEBU   Camotes
Palawan   Hinigaran   Carlota   Mandaue   Sea   Sogod   San Juan   Dinagat I.
ST PAUL   Binalbagan   Cebu   Bato   Surigao Str.
1593   Himamaylan   Guihulngan   Carcar   Panaon I.   Dinagat
Irahuan   Kabankalan   Maasin   Siargao I.
Honda Bay   Sipalay   Bais   Argao   Bohol I.   Surigao   Placer
Puerto Princesa   Hinoba-an   Tanjay   Oslob   RAJAH   Bucas Grande I.
Cagayan Is.   Negros   Dumaguete   Tagbilaran   SIKATUNA   Carrascal
Bayawan   Bohol   Camiguin I.   Cabadbaran   Lanuza
Siaton   Siquijor I.   Talisayan   Tandag
Zamboanguita   Nasipit   Tago

SULU
SEA

*TUBBATAHA
REEFS*

Mt. Mantalingajan   Dipolog   Butuan   Marihatag
2085   Dapitan   Esperanza   Lianga
SEA   Balingasag   Talacogon   Hinatuan
C. Buliluyan   Manukan   Iligan   Opol   Cagayan de Oro   Bislig
Bugsuk I.   Oroquieta   Bay   MT. OZAMIZ   Malaybalay
Sindangan   MALINDANG   Iligan   2938   Malaybalay
Labason   2815   Marawi City   Bunawan
Siocon   Tubod   L. Lanao   Cateel
Balabac I.   Kabasalan   Pagadian   Mindanao   Baganga
Balambangan   Sibuca   Malabang   Panabo
Bangi   Sibuguey   Parang   Midsayap   Pantukan   Manay
Kudat   Jembongan   Suba Talan   Bay   Illana   Tagum
Senaja   Olutanga   Cotabato   Pikit   Mt. Apo   Davao
Langkon   Pangutaran   Bay   Datu Piang   2954   Digos   San Isidro
Tenghilan   Group   Moro Gulf   Talayan   Davao
Kota Belud   G. Kinabalu   Basilan Str.   Kalamansig   Koronadal   Gulf
Kota   4101   Zamboanga   Lebak   Malita
Kinabalu   Basilan I.   Isabela   Lamitan   Palimbang   2083   General
Papar   Telok   Pilas   Siasi   Santos
Labuk   Sandakan   Group   Jolo   Samales   Kiamba
Keningau   Turtle Is.   Parang   Group   Sarangani Is.
Melalap   Talipao   Tinaca Pt.
SABAH   Siasi   Jolo
MALAYSIA   Tapul   Group
Silam   Tapul I. Pata I.
Borneo   Tawi-tawi   Sibutu   *CELEBES*
Group   Group   *SEA*

INDONESIA   Kep. Talaud

10 497

Mindanao Trench

Projection: Lambert's Conformal Conic   East from Greenwich   COPYRIGHT PHILIP'S

National Parks

ft   m
9000   3000
6000   2000
4500   1500
3000   1000
1200   400
600   200
0   0
200   600
4000   12 000
8000   24 000
m   ft

Projection: Mercator

East from Greenwich

JAVA AND MADURA
1:6 700 000

50   0   50   100   150   200   250   300 km
50   0   50   100   150   200 miles

BALI
1:1 800 000

10   0   10   20   30 km
10   0   10   20 miles

PHILIPPINES

Clayeria, Babuyan Chan., C. Engaño, Bacarra, Laoag, Aparri, Batac, Tuao, Bangued, Vigan, Bontoc, Tuguegarao, Ilagan, Palanan Pt., Palanan, Casiguran, San Fernando, Baler, Solano, Bayombong, Baguio, Bolinao, Lingayen G., San Jose, Cabanatuan, Dagupan, Tarlac, Angeles, San Fernando, Polillo Is., Olongapo, Mt. Pinatubo, Bataan, Malolos, Quezon City, MANILA, Cavite, Santa Cruz, Daet, Manila B., Calamba, Batangas, Lucena, Calauag, Naga, Virac, Lubang Is., Calapan, Marinduque, Catanduanes, Mindoro, Tabaco, Mayon Volcano, Legazpi, Lagonoy Gulf, Halcon, Sablayan, Romblon, Burias, Bulan, Sorsogon, Masbate, Catarman, Samar, San Jose, Tablas, Sea, Masbate, Taft, Semirara Is., Panay, Roxas, Calbayog, Borongan, General MacArthur, Cuyo, Pototan, Iloilo, Visayan Sea, Leyte, Tacloban, Cadiz, Cuyo Is., San Carlos, Mandaue, Baybay, Guiuan, Cebu, Maasin, Dinagat, Taytay, San Jose de Buenavista, Bacolod, Bohol Sea, Talibon, Siargao, Puerto Princesa, Dumaguete, Negros, Tanjay, Siquijor, Camiguin, Tandag, Dipolog, Butuan, Lianga, Sindangan, Oroquieta, Cagayan de Oro, Liloy, Ozami, Iligan, Malaybalay, Cateel, Boganga, Zamboanga, Pagadian, Parang, Cotabato, Tagum, Davao, Isabela, Lebak, Kidapawan, Mt. Apo, Mati, Basilan, Jolo, Talayan, Kiamba, Digos, General Santos, Sarangani B., Tinaca Pt., Siasi, Tapul Group, Sarangani, Tawitawi

LUZON, MINDANAO, PALAWAN

SULU SEA, **CELEBES SEA**, **Mindanao Trench**

Lahad Datu, Semporna, Sebuku, Sandakan, Cagayan Is., Pangutaran Group, Sibutu Passage

JAVA / JAWA

BANTEN, JAKARTA, Merak, Serang, Tangerang, Bogor, Bandung, Rangkasbitung, Sukabumi, Cianjur, Purwakarta, Subang, Karawang, Indramayu, Cirebon, Kuningan, Tegal, Pekalongan, SEMARANG, Pati, Rembang, Tuban, Madura, Sumenep, Pamekasan, Sampang, SURABAYA, Gresik, Sidoarjo, Pasuruan, Probolinggo, Situbondo, Bondowoso, Banyuwangi, Jember, Malang, Kediri, Madiun, Surakarta, Yogyakarta, Magelang, Salatiga, Garut, Tasikmalaya, Ciamis, Purwokerto, Banyumas, Kebumen, Wonosobo, Boyolali

BALI

Singaraja, Gilimanuk, Ketapang, Lovina, Tejakula, Kubutambahan, Seririt, Negara, Gunung Agung 3142, Bangli, Klungkung, Candi Dasa, Karangasem (Amlapura), Denpasar, Kuta, Sanur, Nusa Dua, Ubud, Gianyar, Sukawati, Tabanan, Jimbaran, Uluwatu, Nusa Penida, Selat Lombok, **Lombok**, Mataram, Ampenan, Lembar, Gerung

INDIAN OCEAN

SULAWESI (Celebes)

Manado, Kema, Tondano, Gorontalo, Kotamobagu, Tomini, Toli-Toli, Buol, Palu, Donggala, Poso, Luwuk, Kolonodale, Kendari, Kolaka, Watampone, Ujung Pandang, Bulukumba, Bantaeng, Sinjai, Majene, Mamuju, Masamba, Palopo, Pare-pare, Pinrang

CELEBES SEA, **MOLUCCA SEA**, **Teluk Tomini**, **Teluk Bone**

Halmahera, Ternate, Tidore, Tobelo, Morotai, Bacan, Obi, Buru, Seram (Ceram), Ambon, Buton, Wangiwangi

MALUKU, **BANDA SEA**, **FLORES SEA**

Gunungapi, Kepulauan Kai, Tual, Kai Besar, Dobo, Kepulauan Aru, Kepulauan Tanimbar, Saumlaki, Yamdena, Larat

PAPUA / IRIAN JAYA

Sorong, Manokwari, Biak, Jazirah Doberai, Fakfak, Kaimana, Nabire, Teluk Cenderawasih, Jayapura, Sentani, Pegunungan Van Rees, **Pegunungan Maoke**, Pegunungan Sudirman, Puncak Jaya 4702, Jayawijaya, Mandala, Oksibil, Timika, Tembagapura, Agats, Merauke, Muting, Okaba, Kimaam, Pulau Dolak

PAPUA NEW GUINEA

PACIFIC OCEAN, **ARAFURA SEA**, Equator

NUSA TENGGARA TIMUR

Sumbawa, Sunda Is., Flores, Sumba, Ende, Ruteng, Aimere, Maumere, Larantuka, Adonara, Lomblen, Pantar, Alor, Kalabahi, Atauro, Dili, Baucau, Viqueque, **EAST TIMOR**, Kupang, Roti, Sawu Sea

COPYRIGHT PHILIP'S

94

COPYRIGHT PHILIP'S

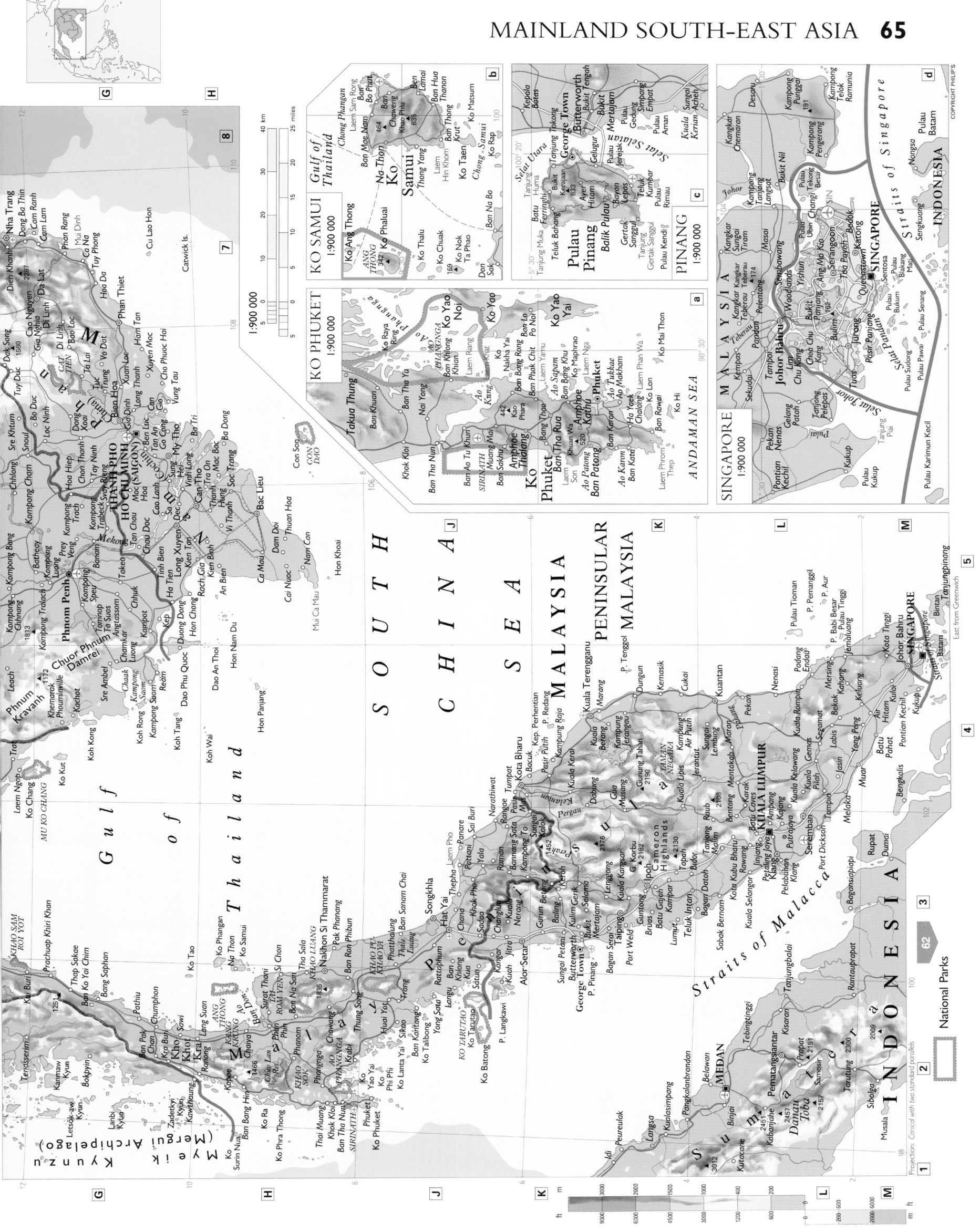

KO SAMUI 1:900 000

Gulf of Thailand

Ko Samui

PINANG 1:900 000

Pulau Pinang

George Town
Butterworth

KO PHUKET 1:900 000

ANDAMAN SEA

Ko Phuket

SINGAPORE 1:900 000

PENINSULAR MALAYSIA

MALAYSIA

SINGAPORE

Straits of Singapore

INDONESIA

S O U T H   C H I N A   S E A

Gulf
of
Thailand

Straits of Malacca

I N D O N E S I A

Kyunzu
(Mergui Archipelago)
Myeik

National Parks

Projection: Conical with two standard parallels   East from Greenwich

1:8 900 000

Projection: Conical with two standard parallels

Continuation Southwards on same scale

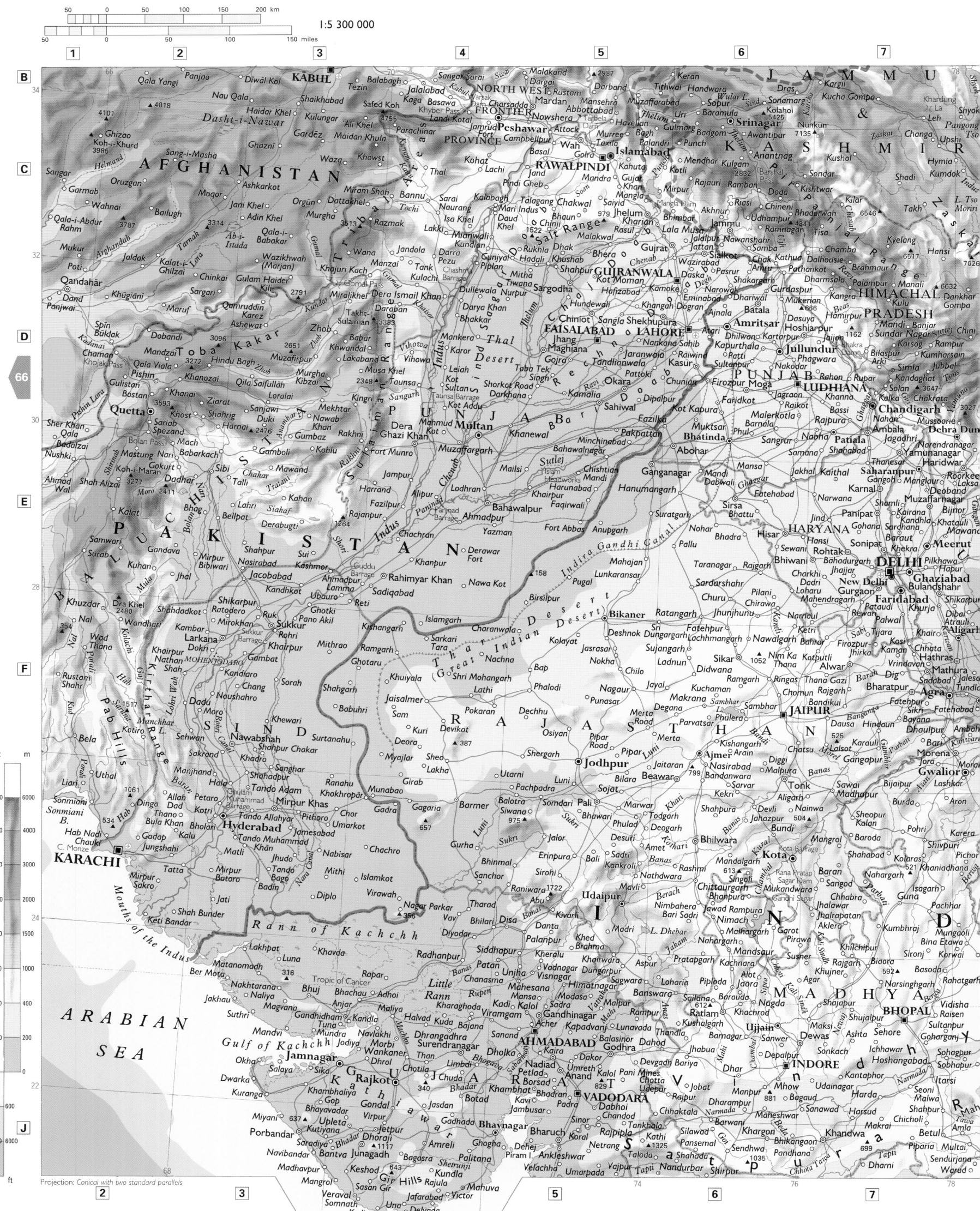

50   0   50   100   150   200 km
1:5 300 000
50   0   50   100   150 miles

Projection: Conical with two standard parallels

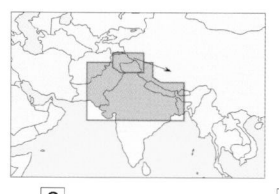

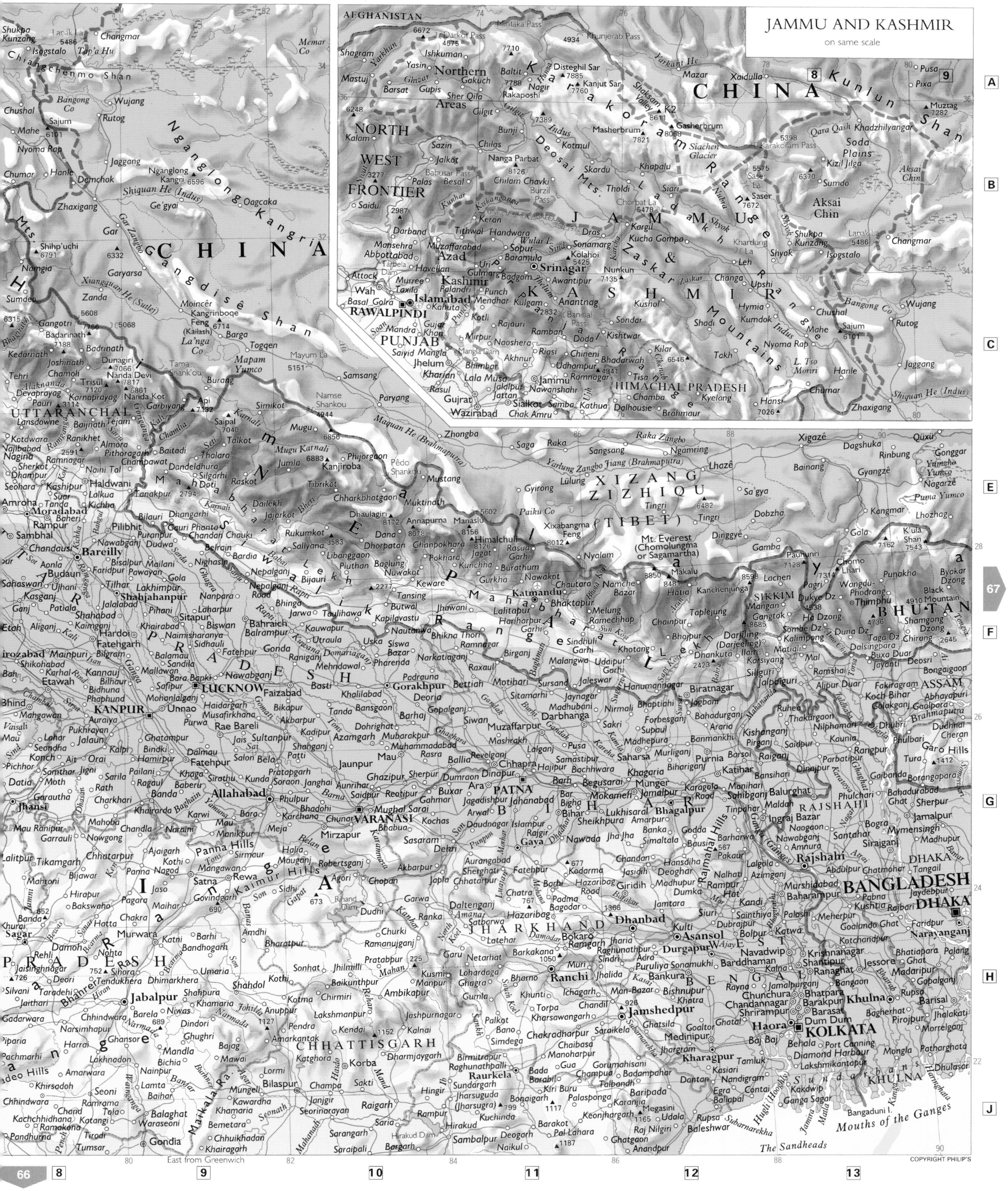

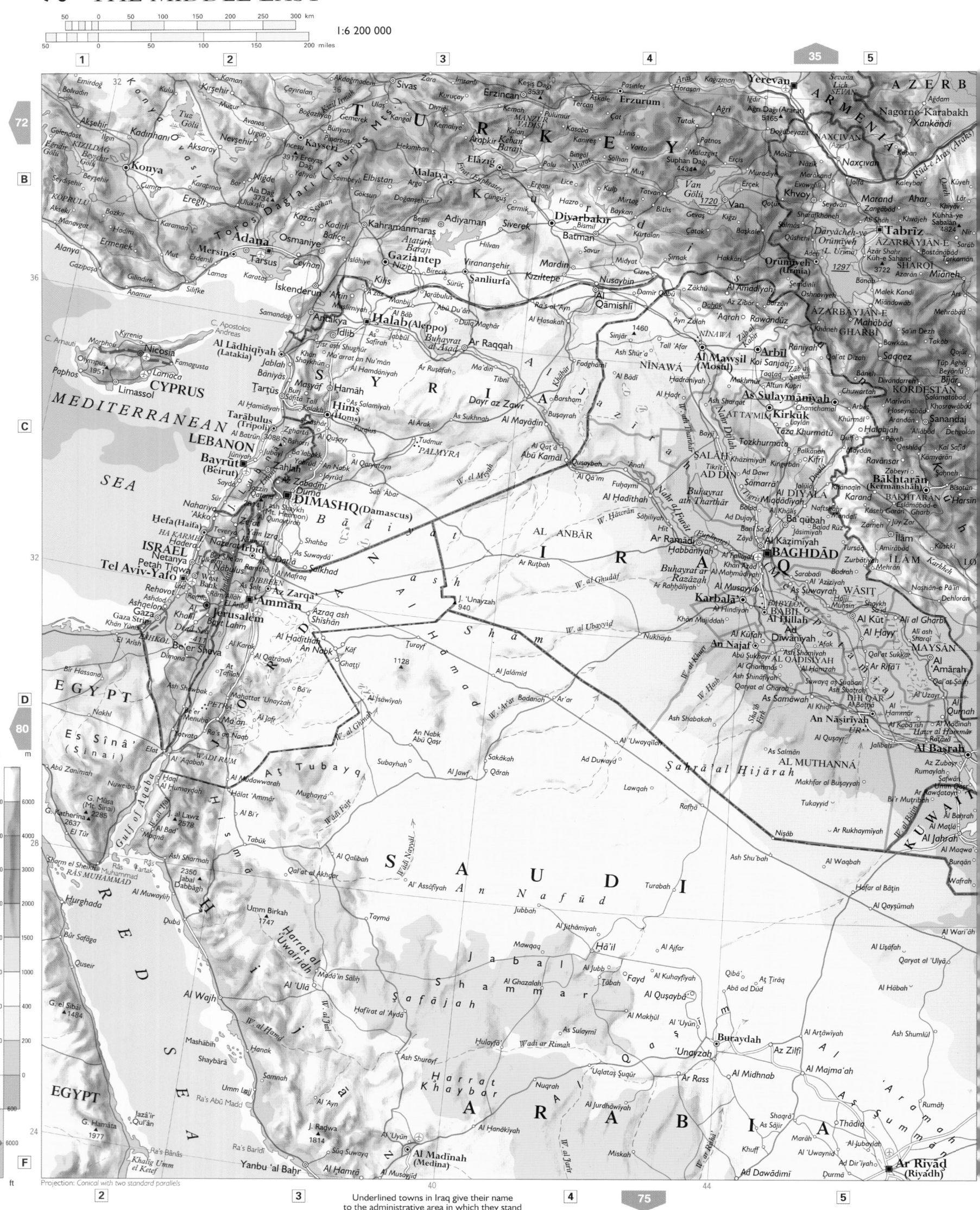

1:6 200 000

Projection: Conical with two standard parallels

Underlined towns in Iraq give their name
to the administrative area in which they stand

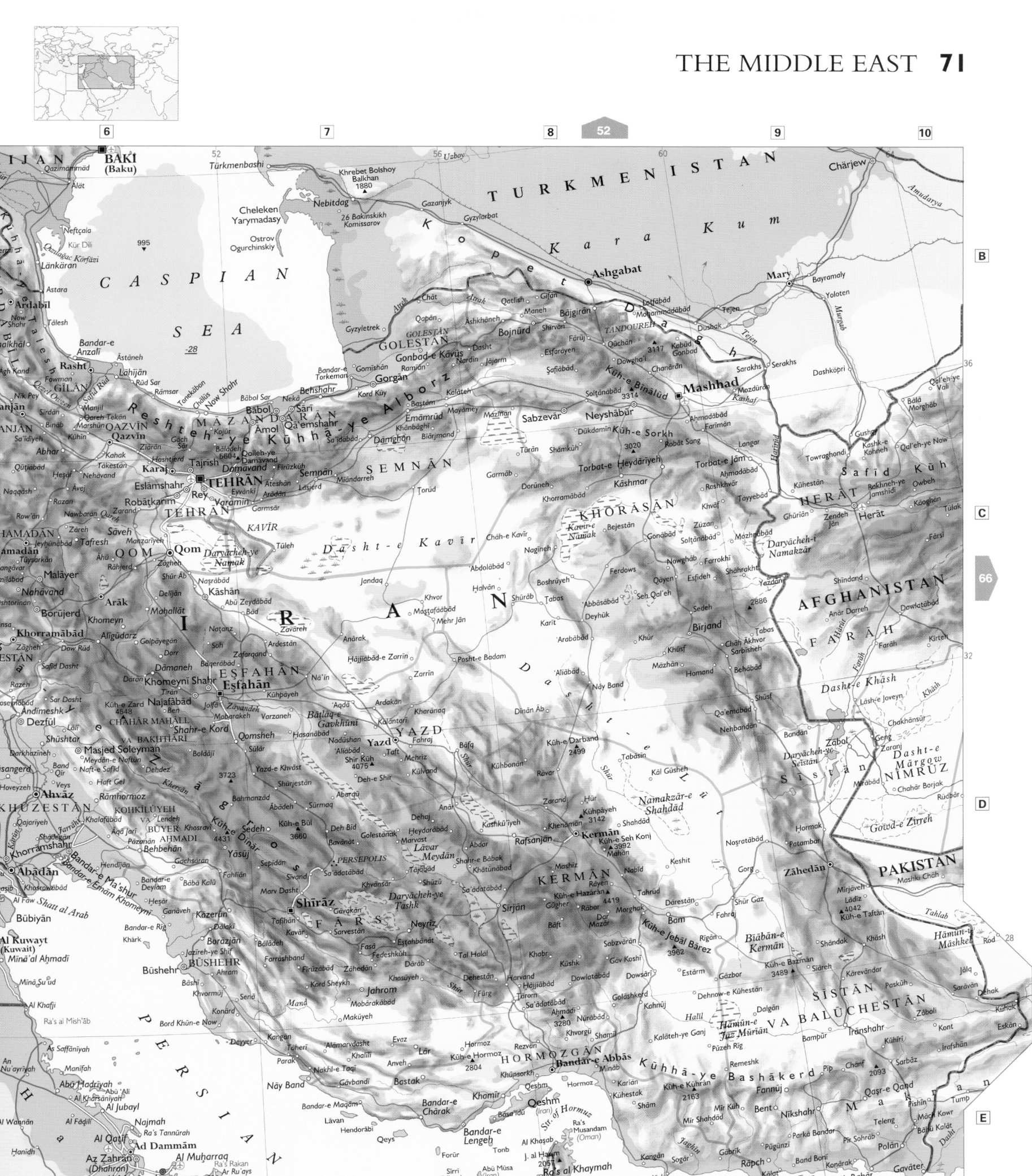

1 : 4 400 000

50 0 25 50 75 100 125 150 175 km
50 0 25 50 75 100 125 miles

BULGARIA

B L A C K   S E A

Stara Zagora
Yambol
Aytos
Burgas
Nos Emine
Michurin
Elkhovo

Kırklareli
Edirne
Pınarhisar
Demirköy
İğneada Burnu
Orestiás
Arda
Babaeski
Vize
Saray
Üzünköprü
Hayrabolu
Muratlı
Çorlu
Çatalca
Silivri
İstanbul Boğazı (Bosporus)
İpsala
Keşan
Malkara
Tekirdağ
Büyükçekmece
İSTANBUL
Kartal
Kocaeli (İzmit)
Gebze
Darıca
Şile
Kandıra
Sakarya (Adapazarı)
Hendek
Düzce

Kerempe Burnu
İnce Burun
Sinop
Kurucaşile
Cide
İnebolu
Abana
Çatalzeytin
Ayancık
Gerze
Amasra
Zonguldak
Kilimli
Devrekâni
Küre Dağları
Bafra Burnu
Bafra
Samsun
Terme
Ünye
Fatsa
Ordu

Gökçeada
Samothráki
Gökçeada
Eceabat
Gelibolu
Lapseki
Çanakkale
TROY
Biga
Çan
Gönen
Bandırma
Erdek
Marmara
Mudanya
Gemlik
Yalova
Orhangazi
İznik
İznik Gölü
Sapanca
Geyve
Akyazı
Mudurnu
Göynük
Bolu
Gerede
Çerkeş
Kızılcahamam
Çankırı
Kastamonu
Taşköprü
Durağan
Boyabat

Marmara Denizi (Sea of Marmara)

Bozcaada
Ezine
Bayramiç
Edremit
Balya
Susurluk
Bursa
Uludağ
İnegöl
Bilecik
Söğüt
Bozüyük
Eskişehir
Alpu
Mihalıççık
Sivrihisar
Polatlı
ANKARA
Elmadağ
Kırıkkale
Keskin
Bâlâ

Balıkesir
Burhaniye
Ayvalık
Bergama
Soma
Kınık
Akhisar
Demirci
Simav
Gediz
Kütahya
Tavşanlı
Emet
Uşak
Afyon (Afyonkarahisar)
Banaz
Kırka
Seyitgazi
Çifteler
Yunak
Haymana
Yenice
Kulu
Şereflikoçhisar
Tuz Gölü

İzmir (Smyrna)
Manisa
Menemen
Turgutlu
Salihli
Alaşehir
Eşme
Ödemiş
Sarıgöl
Çivril
Sandıklı
Suhut
Bolvadin
Eber Gölü
Akşehir Gölü
Akşehir
Şarkışla

Çeşme
Urla
Seferihisar
Torbalı
Selçuk
EPHESUS
Tire
Nazilli
Aydın
Büyük Menderes
Denizli
Çardak
Dinar
Burdur
Eğridir Gölü
Eğridir
Isparta
Konya
Obruk
Karapınar

Kuşadası
Söke
Milas
Yatağan
Muğla
Bodrum
Marmaris
Köyceğiz
Dalaman
Fethiye
Kaş
Finike
Kumluca
Kemer
Antalya
Manavgat
Serik
Side
ASPENDOS
Alanya
Gazipaşa
Anamur
Anamur Burnu

MEDITERRANEAN SEA

GREECE

Lésvos
Khíos
Sámos
Ikaría
Pátmos
Kálimnos
Kos
Astipálaia
Tílos
Sími
Ródhos (Rhodes)
Kárpathos
Kásos
Dhodhekánisos

CYPRUS
Morphou
Kyrenia
Nicosia
Famagusta
Rizokarpaso
C. Apostolos Andreas
Polis
Troodos
Olympus 1951
Paphos
Episkopi
Limassol
Larnaca

Mersin (İçel)
Tarsus
Adana
Ceyhan
Seyhan Barajı
Osmaniye
İslâhiye
Gaziantep
Nizip
Kilis
İskenderun
İskenderun Körfezi
Antakya
Reyhanlı
HALAB (Aleppo)
İdlib

S Y
Al Lādhiqīyah (Latakia)
Jablah
Bāniyās
Hamāh
Tartūs
Al Hamidiyah
Himş (Homs)
Tarābulus (Tripoli)
Zgharta
Al Batrūn
Bsharri

LEBANON
Jubayl
Junīyah
BAYRŪT (Beirut)
Zahlah
Saydā
Ba'labakk

DIMASHQ (Damascus)
Qaţana
Jaramānah

ISRAEL
Hefa (Haifa)
Nazerat
Netanya
Tel Aviv-Yafo
West Bank
Jerusalem
Ashdod
Ashqelon
Rehovot
Ramla

AMMĀN
Az Zarqā
Irbid
JORDA

Division between Greeks and Turks in Cyprus; Turks to the North.

Projection: Conical with two standard parallels

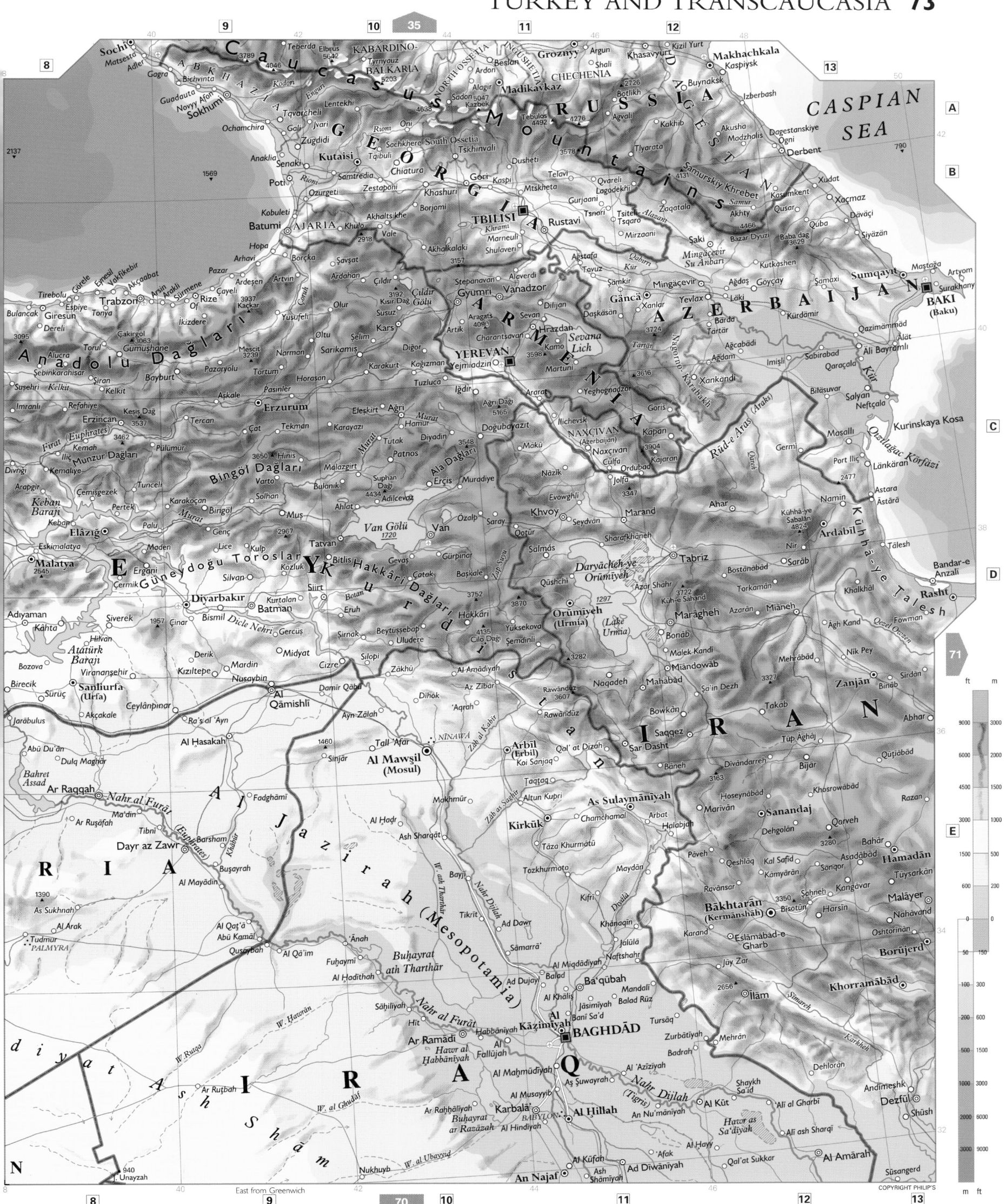

CASPIAN
SEA

Sochi
Matsesta
Adler
Gagra
Guadauta
Novvy Afon
Sokhum
Ochamchira
Gali
Anaklia
Zugdidi
Senaki
Poti
Kobuleti
Batumi AJARIA
Hopa
Arhavi
Pazar
Ardeşen
Çayeli
Rize
Of
Trabzon
Arsin
Sürmene
Akçaabat
Vakfıkebir
Görele
Espiye
Tirebolu
Giresun
Bulancak
Dereli

Teberda
Elbrus 5642
Tyrnyauz
BALKARIA
5203
Kodori
Engur
Lentekhi
Rioni
Oni
Sachkhere
Tqvarcheli
Ochamchira
Sukhum

KABARDINO-
5047 Kazbek
Alagir
Ardon
Beslan
Sadon
4638
Kutaisi
Samtredia
Ozurgeti
Zestaponi
Khulo
Vale
Akhaltsikhe
Khashuri
Borjomi
Akhalkalaki
3157
Savşat
Ardahan
Çıldır
3192 Çıldır
Kısır Dağ
Susuz
Kars
Sarikamiş

North Ossetia
Vladikavkaz
Dusheti
Mtskheta
Gori
Kaspi
TBILISI
Khrami
Rustavi
Marneuli
Shulaveri
Stepanavan
Alaverdi
Gyumri
Vanadzor
Dilijan
ARMENIA
Aragats 4090
Artik
Charantsavan
YEREVAN
Yejmiadzin

INGUSHETIA
Nazran
Groznyy
Argun
Shali
CHECHENIA
Botlikh
2726
Agvali
4492
4276
Kakhib
Tlyarata
3578
Telavi
Qvareli
Lagodekhi
Tsiteli-Alazani
Zaqatala
Şaki
Bazar Dyuzi
4466
Ağstafa
Tovuz
Şəmkir
Gəncə
Xanlar
Daşkəsən
Sevan
Hrazdan
Sevana Lich
3598
Martuni

Khasavyurt
Kizil Yurt
Makhachkala
Kaspiysk
Izberbash
Buynaksk
Dagestanskiye Ogni
Derbent
790
Akusha
Madzhalis
2137

Samurskiy Khrebet
Samur
Kusary
Xudat
Xaçmaz
Qusar
Dəvəçi
Siyəzän
Mingəçevir
Su Anbarı
Ağdaş
Göyçay
Şamaxı
Sumqayit
Maştağa
Artyom
Surakhany
BAKI
(Baku)

AZERBAIJAN
3724
Bərdə
Tərtər
Ağcabədi
Ağdam
Imişli
Sabirabad
Qazımämmäd
Äli Bayramlı
Älät
Salyan
Neftçala
Kürdämir
Qaraçala
Kür
Bitäsuvar
3616

Anadolu Dağları
3095
Torul
Gümüşhane
3063
Çakırgöl
Bayburt
Mescit 3239
Tortum
Oltu
Şelim
Olur
Yusufeli
Artvin
Ardanuç
Norman
Sarikamiş
Kağızman
Dığor
Karakurt
Iğdır
Tuzluca
Ararat
Agri Dağı 5165
Doğubayazıt
Nахçıvan
(Azerbaijan)
Naxçıvan
Culfa
Ordubad
Jolfa
3904
3347
Kajaran
Kapan
Goris
Xankändi
Nagorno-Karabakh
Qubadlı

Şebinkarahisar
Suşehri
Kelkit
Refahiye
İmranlı
Erzincan
Kesiş Dağ 3537
Çat
Aşkale
Erzurum
Pasinler
Horasan
Eleşkirt
Ağrı
Tutak
Patnos
3548
Murat
Karayazı
Tekman
Hınıs
Diyadin
Ala Dağları
Ilıchevsk
Mākū
Qotur
Khvoy
Seydvan
Marand
Ahar
Germi
Port İliç
2477
Länkäran
Astara

Münzur Dağları
3462
Kemah
İliç
Kemaliye
Divriği
Arapgir
Çemişgezek
Keban Baraji
Keban
Pertek
Elâzığ
Maden
Ergani
Çermik
Çınar
Diyarbakır
Bingöl Dağları
3650
Varto
Bingöl
Karliova
Genç
Palu
Solhan
Malazgirt
Bulanık
Muş
Ahlat
Suphan Dağı 4434
Adilcevaz
Erçiş
Muradiye
Özalp
Saray
Nāzik
Evowghli
Qūshchi
Sharafkhāneh
Daryācheh-ye
Orūmiyeh
(Lake Urmia)
Azar Shahr
Kühe-ye Sahand 3722
Tabriz
Bostānābād
Torkamān
Azarān
Miāneh
Sarāb
Bonāb
Nir
Ardabil
Tälesh
Khalkhāl
Āgh Kand
Nik Pey
Zanjān
Bināb
3277
Abhar

Malatya 2545
Eskimalatya
Adıyaman
Kâhta
Hilvan
Siverek
Atatürk Baraji
Bozova
Birecik
Süruç
Şanlıurfa
(Urfa)
Akçakale

Silvan
Güneydoğu Toroslar
Lice
Kulp
Tatvan
Bitlis
Kozluk
Hakkâri Dağları
Siirt
Eruh
Şırnak
Beytüşşebap
Uludere
Çatak
Başkale
Şemdinli
Yüksekova
Cilo Dağı 4135
3752
3870
Orūmiyeh
(Urmia)
1297
Marāgheh

Kuntalan
Batman
Bismil
Dicle Nehri
Gercüş
Midyat
Cizre
Silopi
Zākhū
Al-'Amādiyah
Az Zibār
Dihōk
'Aqrah
Rawāndūz
3607
Rawānduz
Naqadeh
Mahābād
Miāndowāb
3282
Şa'in Dezh
Bowkān
Saqqez
Takāb
Tūp Āghāj
3277
Sirdān

Kızıltepe
Mardin
Derik
Nusaybin
Al Qāmishlī
Damir Qābū
Ra's al 'Ayn
Ceylânpınar
'Ayn Zālah
Tall 'Afar
NĪNAWĀ
Sinjār
1460
Al Ḥasakah
Al Ḥadr

Bahret Assad
Ar Raqqah
Ma'din
Ar Ruşāfah
Fadghāmī
Ash Sharqāt
Makhmūr
Arbīl
(Erbil)
Koi Sanjaq
Qol' at Dizah
Dīvāndarreh
Bijār
Qūţīābād
Khosrowābād
Razan

Al Jazirah
(Mesopotamia)
Tibnī
Barsham
Khābūr
Busayrah
Dayr az Zawr
Al Mayādīn
Altun Kupri
Taqtaq
Kirkūk
Tāza Khurmātū
As Sulaymānīyah
Chamchamal
Arbat
Halabjah
Pāveh
Marivān
Qeshlāq
Kāmyārān
Dehgolān
3163
Sanandaj
Qorveh
3280
Bahār
Asadābād
Sonqor
Kangāvar
Hamadān
Tūysarkān

SYRIA
1390
As Sukhnah
Al Arak
Al Qaṭ'a
Abū Kamāl
Qusaybah
Al Qā'im
'Ānah
Al Hadīthah
Fuḥaymī
Ḥīt

W. ath Tharthār
Buḥayrat ath Tharthār
Bayjī
Tikrīt
Ad Dawr
Sāmarrā'
Balad
Ad Dujayl
Al Khāliṣ
Ba'qūbah
Balad Rūz
Mandalī
2656
Īlām
Badrah
Mehrān
Tursāq
Zurbāţīyah

Nahr al Furāt
(Euphrates)
Nahr Dijlah
Tozkhurmāto
Kifrī
Dyālā
Jalūlā'
Khānaqīn
Karand
Jäy Zar
Naftshahr
3350
Bīsotūn
Bākhtarān
(Kermānshāh)
Hārsīn
Eslāmābād-e Gharb
Malāyer
Nāhāvand
Oshtorīnān
Borūjerd
Khorramābād

R I A
Tudmur
PALMYRA
940
'Unayzah
W. Hawran
W. Ruqq
W. al Ghudaf
Ar Ruṭbah
Nukhayb
W. al Ubayyid
Ash Shām
diyat

I R A Q
Nahr al Furāt
Ar Ramādī
Habbānīyah
Hawr al Ḥabbānīyah
Al Fallūjah
Al Maḥmūdīyah
Al Musayyib
Aş Şuwayrah
Kāẓimīyah
Al Hindīyah
BAGHDĀD
BABYLON
Al Hillah
Karbalā'
An Nu'mānīyah
Al Kūt
Shaykh Sa'd
'Alī al Gharbī
Badrah
Andimeshk
Dezfūl
Shūsh
Süsangerd

Al Kūfah
An Najaf
Ash Shāmīyah
Ad Dīwānīyah
Afak
Al Ḥayy
Qal'at Sukkar
Buḥayrat ar Razāzah
Al Miqdādīyah
Banī Sa'd
'Alī al 'Azīzīyah
Hawr as Sa'dīyah
'Alī ash Sharqī
Al 'Amārah

GEORGIA
ABKHAZIA
Caucasus
Mountains
3789
4046
RUSSIA
DAGESTAN
3629
Baba dag
Kutkäshen
Qəbələ
Qax
Balakən

East from Greenwich
COPYRIGHT PHILIP'S

10 0 10 20 30 40 50 60 70 80 100 km

1:2 200 000

10 0 10 20 30 40 50 60 miles

1 2 3 4 72 5 6

CYPRUS

Paphos
Episkopi
Limassol
Akrotiri
Bay
Episkopi
Bay
C. Gata

M E D I T E R R A N E A N

S E A

Al Ḩamīdīyah
Hims (Homs)
Tall
Kalakh
Shinshār
Furqlus
ASH
SHAMĀL
Al Mīnā'
Tarābulus (Tripoli)
Zgharta
Halbā
Al Qusayr
HIMȘ
Al Batrūn
Qurnat as Sawdā' 3088
Bsharri
Al Labwah
2464
Al Qaryatayn
Jubayl
Qartabā
2616
Ba'labakk
Bi'r Ghadir
Ibrāhīm
An Nabk

LEBANON
BAYRŪT (Beirut)
Bikfayyā
J. Sannīn 2628
Alayh
Zaḩlah
Sirghāyā
Khān Abū Shāmat
Ash Shuwayfāt
JABAL
Ad Dāmūr
LUBNĀN
Hawsh
Mūssá
Az Zabadānī
Dūmā
Sayda (Sidon)
1942
Jazzīn
J. al Bārak
Qatanā
DIMASHQ
DIMASHQ (Damascus)
(DAM.)
An Nabaṭīyah at Taḩta
Kash Shaykh (Mt Hermon)
2814
Al khīyām
Marj 'Uyūn
Al Kiswah
Al Ḩājānah
Sūr (Tyre)
AL
JANŪB
Qiryat
Shemona
Mas'ada
Burāq
Shemona
1197
Al Qunayṭirah
As Sanamayn

SYRIA

Naḩariyya
Me'ona
Ar Rafid
W. Al Ḩarīr
Shahbā
'Akko (Acre)
Zefat
AS SUWAYDĀ
Hagalil
Karmi'el
Yam
Izra
Mifraz
Hefa
Qiryat
HAZAFON
Fiq
Shaykh Miskīn
As Suwaydā 1800
J. al Druz
Hefa (Haifa)
Teverya (Tiberias)
Saḩam al
Șalāh
HEFA
Qiryat Ata
Kinneret
Jawlān
Dar'ā
Malaḩ
Dāliyat el Karmel
Nazerat (Nazareth)
Yarmūk
IRBID
Ar Ramthā
Bușrā ash Shām
Salkhad
KARMEL
Afula
Ţayiba
TEL MEGIDDO
CAESAREA
Umm el Fahm
IRBID
Al Mafraq
Umm al Qittayn
Jenin
'AJLŪN
AL MAFRAQ
Pardes
Hadera
Hanna-Karkur
Bet She'an
J. Umm ad Daraj
Al Mafraq
ISRAEL
Shōmrōn
Tulkarm
SAMARIA 1247
Jarash
Netanya
Tūbās
JIBBEEN
JARASH
HAMERKAZ
Nābulus
N. az Zarqā
Herzliyya
Kafar Sava
SHILO
AL BALQA
Az Zarqā
Benē Beraq
Petaḩ Tiqwa
As Salt
Tel Aviv-Yafo
Ramat Gan
289
Wādi es Sīr
AMMĀN
Bat Yam
West Bank
Karama
Rishon le Ziyyon
Lod
Rām Allāh
Yavne
Ramla
El Arīḩā (Jericho)
Na'ūr
'AMMĀN
Ashdod
Rehovot
AMM
Azraq ash Shīshān
Qiryat Mal'akhi
Bet Shemesh
Jerusalem (Yerushalayim)
ĀZ ZARQĀ
Ashqelon
Qiryat
Gat
Bayt Lahm (Bethlehem)
(Al Quds)
MA'DABĀ
Qiryat
TEL
MA'DĀBĀ
Gaza
LAKHISH
Al Khalīl (Hebron)
W. Al Ḩaydān
Gaza
N. Shiqma
Dhībān
Al Hadītha
Strip
Sederot
Az Ẕāhirīyah
Al Qaṭrānah
Khān Yūnis
Be'er Sheva (Beersheba)
Rafaḩ
Arad
Al Karak
El Daheir
Sedom
AL KARAK
El 'Arīsh
Bor Mashash
Al Mazār
Bûr Sa'îd (Port Said)
Dimona
Bûr Fu'ad
Khalīg el Tīna
Rās Burūn
Sabkhet el
Bardawil
El 'Arîsh
HADAROM
W. al Hasā
W. Bā'ir
Qantara Suweis
Romāni
Bîr el 'Abd
Bîr Lahfan
El 'Arîsh
Qezi'ot
JORDAN
Bîr Garârât
At Tafīlah
Bîr el Duweidar
Bîr Qaṭia
Bîr Kaseiba
Birein
AT TAFĪLAH
Bā'ir
El Qantara
Bîr el Jafir
SHAMÂL
Sedé Bogér
Wāḩid
Bîr Modkûr
SÎNÎ
Muweilḩ
Nijil
J. ash Shawmari
892
El Quseima
Mizpe Ramon
1738
Mahattat 'Unayzah
Ismâ'ilîya
Bîr el Mâlḩi
Bîr Ḩasana
1072
Talâta
ISMÂ'ILÎYA
Hanegev
Wādi
Mūsa
Khamsa
G.Yi 'Allaq
PETRA
El Buheirat
1094
Ma'ān
el Murrat
G. el Kabrit
W. Quraiya
El Agrûd
Wādī
el Kubra
Bîr el Thamâda
W. el Brûk
N. Paran
Mūsa
(Biter Lakes)
MA'ĀN
Gineifa
Bîr Gebeil Ḩisn
Bîr el 'Agaba
El Jafr
Qa'el Jafr
E G Y P T
Bîr Beida
N. Ḩiyyon
El Kuntilla
El Thamad
Bî'r el Mārī
Mahattat ash Shīdīyah
El Suweis (Suez)
Mamarr
Bûr Taufîq
Mitla
Ra's an Naqb
Adabiya
ES SÎNÂ'
1435
'Uyûn Mûsa
(Sinai)
Al Aqaba
Nakhl
AL 'AQABAH
Khalîg
Ain Sudr
W. Ruaḩ
Ghubbet
948
W. el Sḩeira
Bîr Abu Muḩammad
Bîr al Buṭayyḩāt
Bîr al Qaṭṭar
el Bûs
G. el Kabrit
En 'Avrona
SAUDI
Gebel el Tîh
WADI RUM
Bîr
1272
1592 1754
Abu Sandûq
El Wabeira
Batn el Ghûl
Bîr el Biarât
ARABIA
JANÛB
Elat
Rum
At Tubayq
EL
W. Abu Ga'da
Bîr el Heisi
SUWEIS
SÎNÎ
1165
Al 'Aqaba
Bîr Wuseit
Bîr el Taba
Al Mudawwarah
Haql
Gulf of Aqaba

Projection: Polyconic
East from Greenwich
COPYRIGHT PHILIP'S

1 2 80 3 1974 Cease Fire Lines 4 5 National Parks 6

ft m
9000 3000
6000 2000
4500 1500
3000 1000
1200 400
600 200
0
200 600
2000 6000
m ft

1:13 300 000

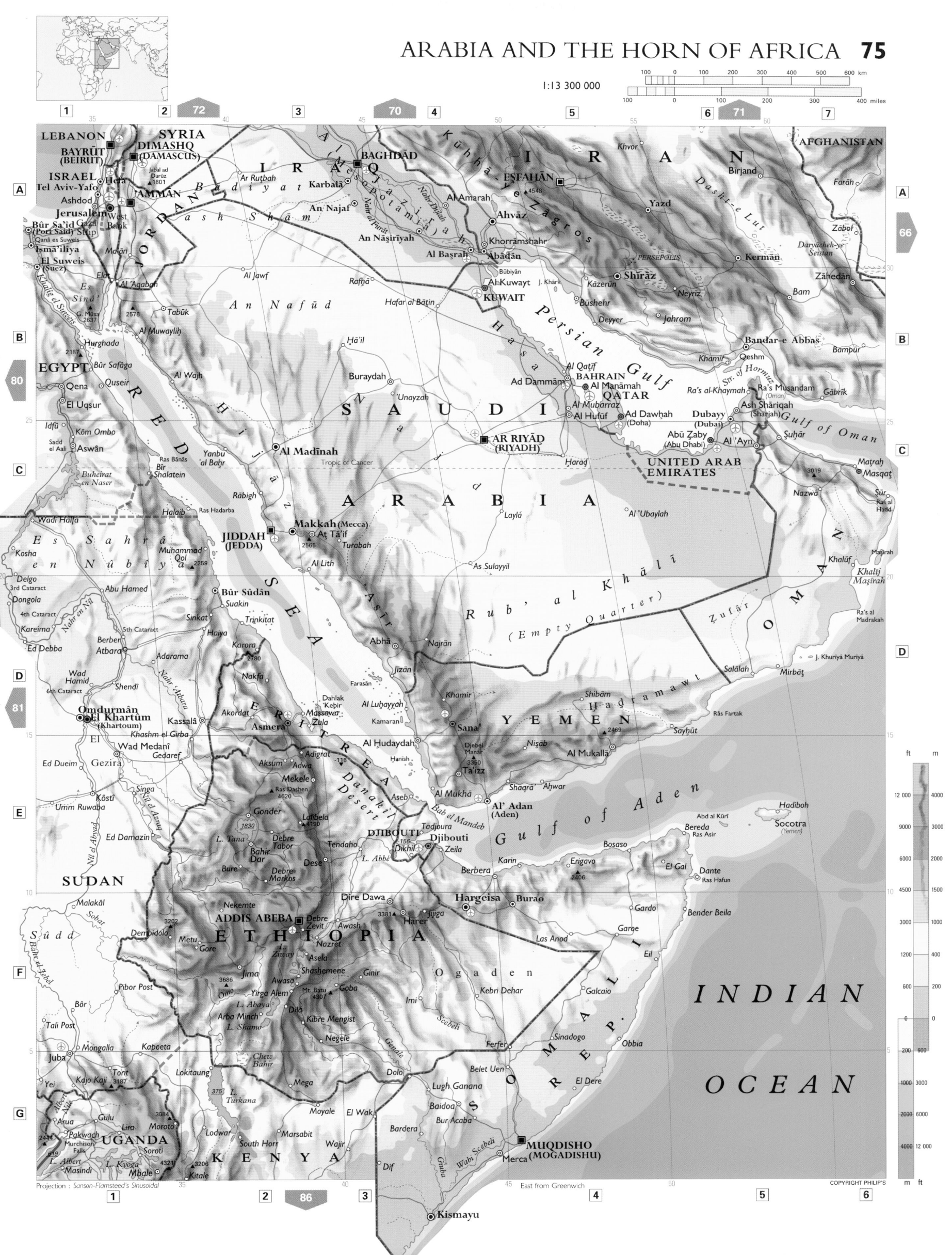

COPYRIGHT PHILIP'S

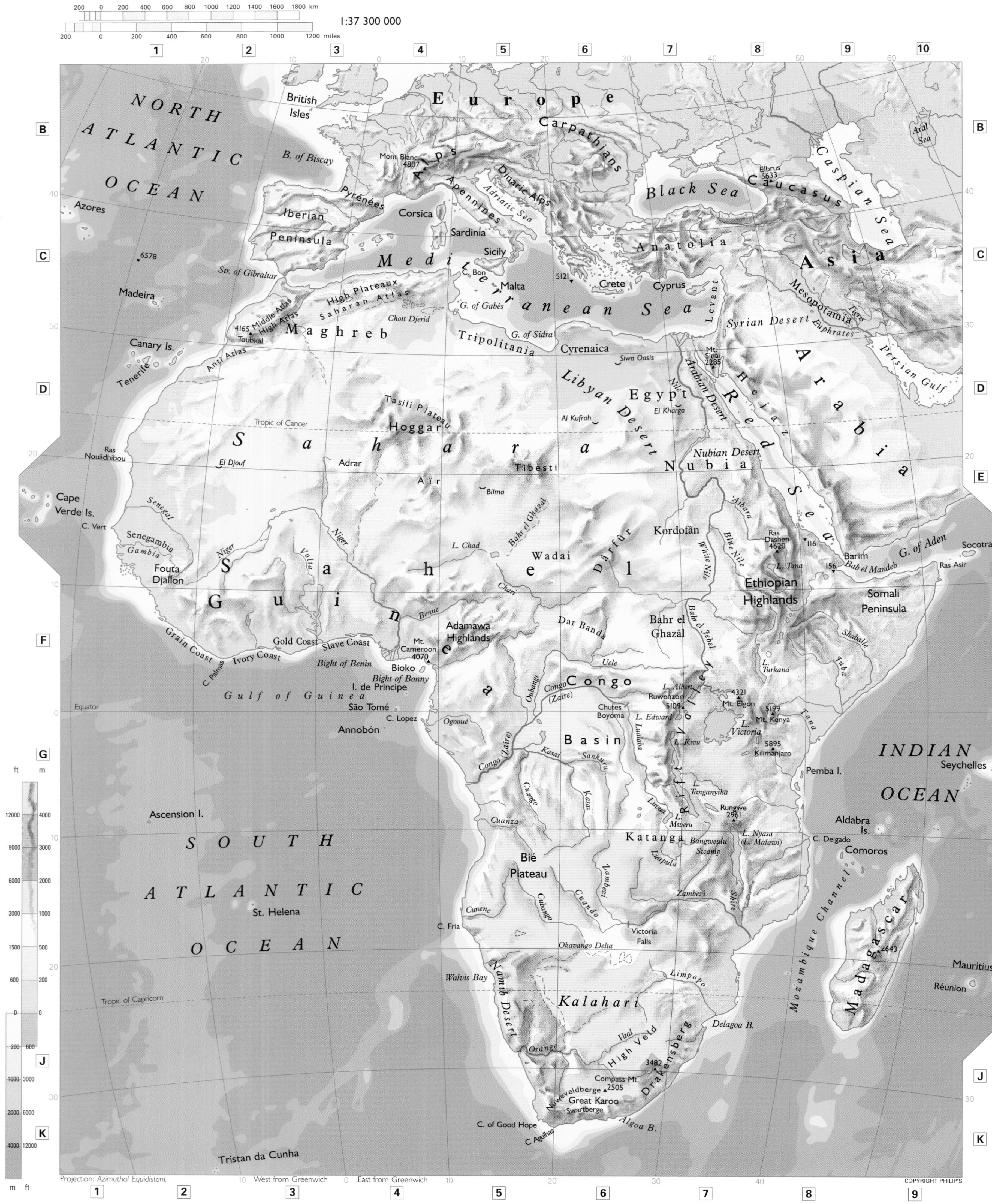

200 0 200 400 600 800 1000 1200 1400 1600 1800 km

1:37 300 000

200 0 200 400 600 800 1000 1200 miles

NORTH ATLANTIC OCEAN

EUROPE

British Isles

B. of Biscay

Carpathians

Alps

Mont Blanc 4807

Pyrénées

Apennines

Dinaric Alps

Adriatic Sea

Elbrus 5633

Black Sea

Caucasus

Caspian Sea

Aral Sea

Azores

Iberian Peninsula

Corsica

Sardinia

Sicily

C. Bon

Malta

Crete

Cyprus

Anatolia

Asia

6578

Madeira

Str. of Gibraltar

High Plateaux

Saharan Atlas

Middle Atlas

High Atlas

4165

Toubkal

Anti Atlas

Maghreb

Chott Djerid

Mediterranean Sea

G. of Gabès

Tripolitania

G. of Sidra

Cyrenaica

Siwa Oasis

Levant

Mesopotamia

Tigris

Euphrates

Syrian Desert

Persian Gulf

Mt. Sinai 2285

Arabian Desert

Hejaz

Red Sea

Arabia

Canary Is.

Tenerife

Tasili Plateau

Tropic of Cancer

Hoggar

Libyan Desert

Egypt

Al Kufrah

El Khārga

Nubia

Nubian Desert

Ras Nouâdhibou

El Djouf

Adrar

Aïr

Bilma

Tibesti

Sahara

Cape Verde Is.

C. Vert

Senegal

Senegambia

Gambia

Fouta Djallon

Niger

Niger

Volta

Sahel

Guinea

L. Chad

Bahr el Ghazal

Wadai

Darfûr

Kordofân

White Nile

Blue Nile

Atbara

Ras Dashen 4620

116

L. Tana

156

Barim

Bab el Mandeb

Ras Asir

G. of Aden

Socotra

Chari

Benue

Adamawa Highlands

Dar Banda

Bahr el Ghazâl

Somali Peninsula

Ethiopian Highlands

Shabelle

Grain Coast

Gold Coast

Slave Coast

Ivory Coast

C. Palmas

Bight of Benin

Mt. Cameroon 4070

Bioko

Bight of Bonny

I. de Principe

Gulf of Guinea

São Tomé

C. Lopez

Ogooué

Ubangi

Uele

Congo (Zaïre)

Congo Basin

Juba

L. Albert

Ruwenzori 5094

Mt. Elgon 4321

Mt. Kenya 5199

L. Turkana

Equator

Annobón

Congo (Zaïre)

Kasai

Sankuru

Chutes Boyoma

L. Edward

L. Kivu

L. Victoria

Kilimanjaro 5895

Tana

Great Rift Valley

Pemba I.

INDIAN OCEAN

Seychelles

Ascension I.

Kasai

Cuango

Cuanza

L. Luitaba

L. Tanganyika

L. Mweru

Rungwe 2961

Katanga

Luapula

Bangweulu Swamp

L. Nyasa (L. Malawi)

Aldabra Is.

Comoros

SOUTH ATLANTIC OCEAN

St. Helena

Bié Plateau

Zambezi

Cubango

Cuando

Zambezi

Shire

C. Delgado

Mozambique Channel

Madagascar

2643

Mauritius

Réunion

C. Fria

Cunene

Okavango Delta

Victoria Falls

Tropic of Capricorn

Walvis Bay

Namib Desert

Kalahari

Vaal

Orange

Limpopo

Delagoa B.

High Veld

Drakensberg

3482

Compass Mt. 2505

Nuweveldberge

Great Karoo

Swartberge

Algoa B.

C. of Good Hope

C. Agulhas

Tristan da Cunha

ft m

12000 4000

9000 3000

6000 2000

3000 1000

1500 500

600 200

0 0

200 600

1000 3000

2000 6000

4000 12000

m ft

Projection: Azimuthal Equidistant

West from Greenwich

East from Greenwich

COPYRIGHT PHILIP'S

1:37 300 000

● Dakar   Capital Cities

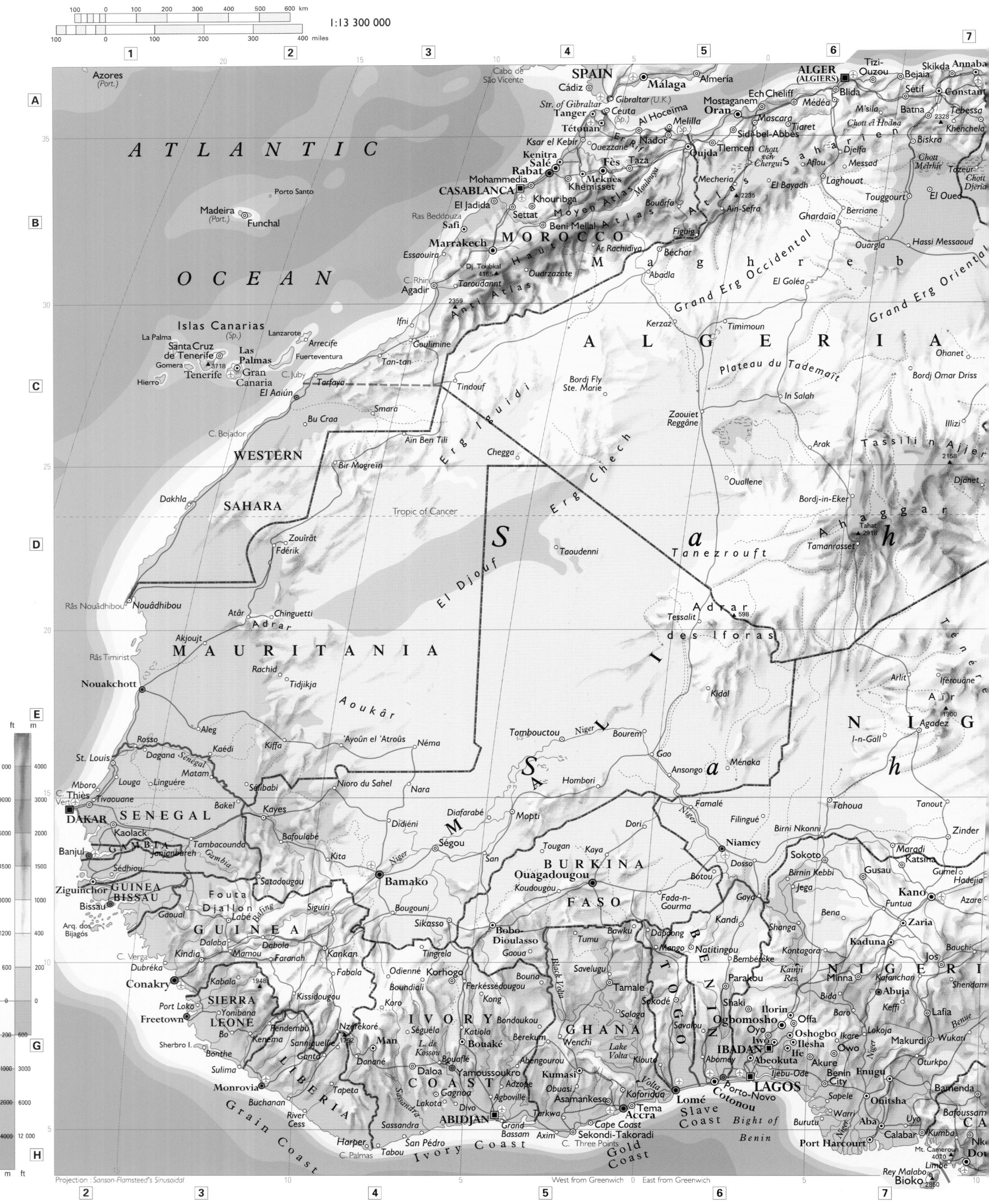

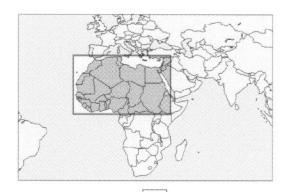

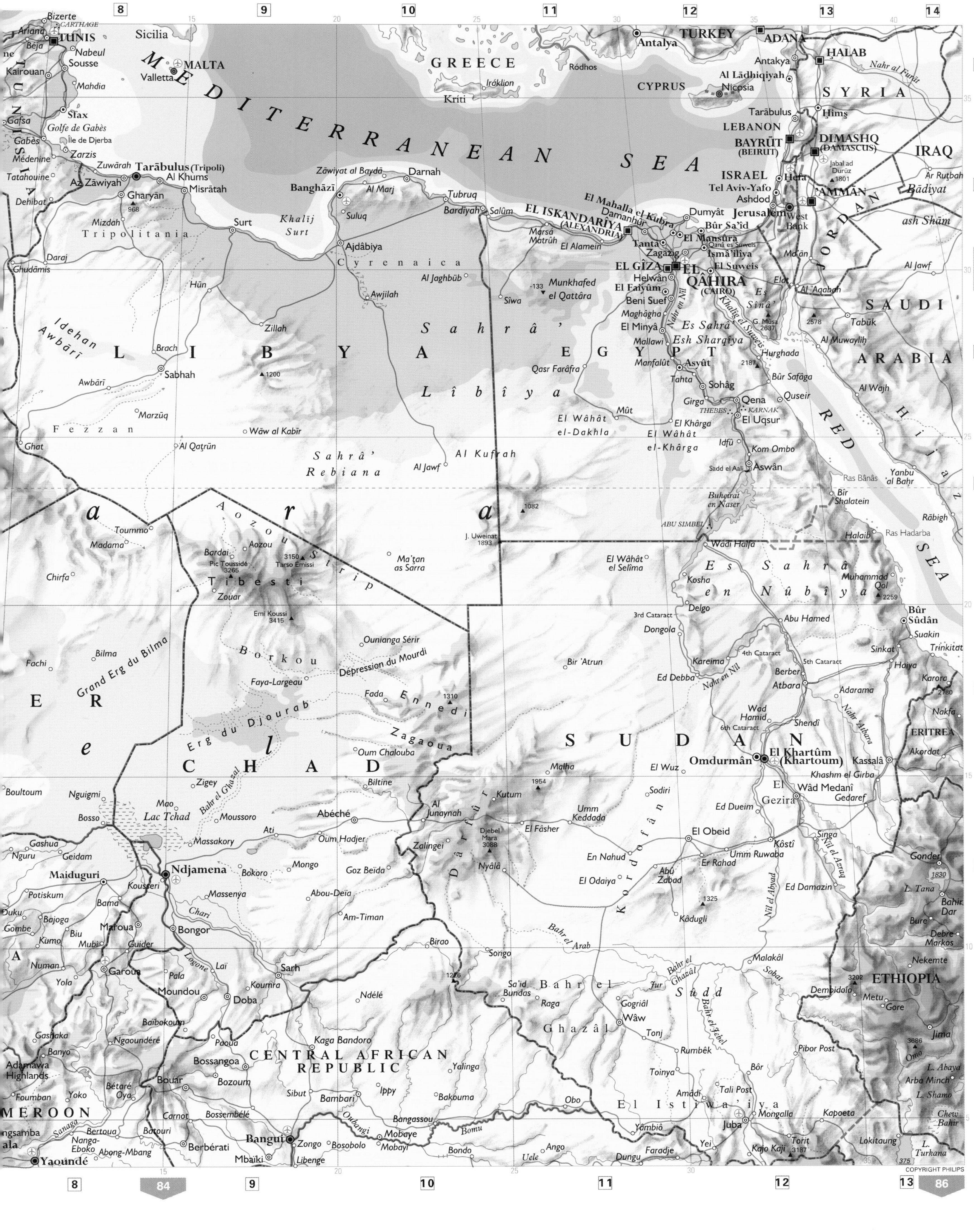

Bizerte
Ariana
Béja
TUNIS
Nabeul
Sousse
CARTHAGE
Sicilia
MALTA
Valletta
GREECE
TURKEY
Antalya
ADANA
Antakya
HALAB
Nahr al Furat
Ródhos
Al Lādhiqiyah
Nicosia
SYRIA
IRAQ
Kairouan
Mahdia
Iráklion
CYPRUS
Kríti
Tarābulus
Hims
Ar Rutbah
Sfax
Gafsa
Golfe de Gabès
LEBANON
BAYRŪT
(BEIRUT)
DIMASHQ
(DAMASCUS)
Gabès
Ile de Djerba
ISRAEL
Jabal ad
Druze
1801
Médenine
Zarzis
MEDITERRANEAN SEA
El Mahalla el Kubra
Tel Aviv-Yafo
Haifa
AMMĀN
Bādiyat
Tataouine
Zuwārah
Tarābulus (Tripoli)
EL ISKANDARĪYA
(ALEXANDRIA)
Damanhûr
Dumyât
Bûr Sa'îd
Jerusalem
West Bank
JORDAN
ash Shām
Dehibat
Az Zāwiyah
Al Khums
Misrātah
Banghāzī
Al Marj
Zāwiyat al Baydâ
Darnah
Tubruq
Bardīyah
Salûm
El Mansūra
Qanâ es Suweis
Ma'ān
Gharyān
968
Surt
Khalīj
Surt
Suluq
Ajdâbiya
Marsa
Matrûh
El Alamein
Zagazig
Tanta
Ismā'îliya
El Suweis
Al Jawf
Mizdah
Tripolitania
Cyrenaica
EL GÎZA
EL QÂHIRA
(CAIRO)
Helwân
El Faiyûm
Beni Suef
Elat
Al 'Aqabah
SAUDI
Daraj
Ghudāmis
Hūn
Al Jaghbūb
Siwa
Munkhafed
el Qattâra
-133
Es
Sinâ
Mûsá
2637
2578
Tabûk
ARABIA
Idehan
Awbārī
LIBYA
Awjilah
Sahrâ'
Lîbîya
El Minyâ
Maghâgha
Es Sahrâ
Esh Sharqîya
Khalig el Suweis
Hurghada
Al Muwaylih
Brach
Zillah
Manfalût
Asyût
Tahta
Sohâg
Bûr Safâga
Al Wajh
Sabhah
1200
Qasr Farâfra
2187
Marzûq
Fezzan
Awbārī
Waw al Kabīr
El Wâhât
el-Dakhla
El Khârga
Girga
Qena
KARNAK
El Khârga
THEBES
El Uqsur
Quseir
Ghat
Al Qatrūn
Sahrâ'
Rebiana
Al Kufrah
Al Jawf
Idfû
Kom Ombo
RED
Ras Bânâs
Yanbu
al Bahr
S a h a r a
Sadd el Aali
Aswân
Hilaz
Toummo
Madama
Aozou
Strip
Ma'tan
as Sarra
1082
J. Uweinat
1893
ABU SIMBEL
Buhetrai
en Naser
Wâdi Halfa
Halaib
Bîr
Shalatein
Ras Hadarba
Rābigh
SEA
Chirfa
Bardai
Pic Toussidé
3265
Aozou
3150
Tarso Emissi
Tibesti
Zouar
Emi Koussi
3415
Es
Sahrâ
en
Nûbîya
El Wâhât
el Selîma
Kosha
Delgo
Muhammad
Qol
2259
Fachi
Bilma
Grand Erg du Bilma
Borkou
Ounianga Sérir
Dépression du Mourdi
Bir 'Atrun
3rd Cataract
Dongola
Abu Hamed
Bûr
Sûdân
Suakin
ERe
Faya-Largeau
Erg du Djourab
Fada
Ennedi
1310
Ed Debba
Nahr en Nîl
Kareima
4th Cataract
Berber
5th Cataract
Atbara
Adarama
Haiya
Karora
780
Nakfa
Akordat
ERITREA
e
CHAD
Zagaoua
Oum Chalouba
SUDAN
Wad
Hamid
6th Cataract
Shendî
Nahr el Atbara
Kassalâ
Zigey
Biltine
Matha
El Khartûm
(Khartoum)
Boultoum
Nguigmi
Bosso
Mao
Lac Tchad
Moussoro
Ati
Abéché
Al Junaynah
Kutum
1954
Umm
Keddada
Sodiri
El Wuz
Omdurmân
El Obeid
Khashm el Girba
Wâd Medanî
El
Gezira
Gedaref
Gashua
Nguru
Geidam
Bahr el Ghazal
Massakory
Oûm Hadjer
Mongo
Goz Beïda
Zalingei
Nyâlâ
Djebel Mara
3088
El Fâsher
En Nahud
Er Rahad
Umm Ruwaba
Kôstî
Singa
Nil el Azraq
Gonder
1830
L. Tana
Maiduguri
Kousseri
Ndjamena
Bokoro
Massenya
Abou-Deïa
Am-Timan
Darfûr
Kordofân
El Odaiya
Abū
Zabad
Ed Dueim
Kâdugli
1325
Ed Damazin
Nil el Abiad
Bahir
Dar
Bure
Debre
Markos
Potiskum
Bama
Maroua
Guider
Bongor
Birao
Songo
Bahr el Arab
Sa'id
Bundas
Bahr el
Ghazâl
Malakâl
Sobat
3202
Nekemte
ETHIOPIA
Duku
Bajoga
Biu
Mubi
Garoua
Pala
Laï
Koumra
Ndélé
Raga
Wâw
Gogrial
Sûdd
Tonj
Rumbêk
Pibor Post
Metu
Gore
Jima
Numan
Yola
Moundou
Doba
1226
Ghazâl
Bôr
Toinya
3686
Omo
Arba Minch
L. Abaya
Gashaka
Banyo
Baibokoum
Ngaoundéré
Kaga Bandoro
Yalinga
Tali Post
L. Shamo
Foumban
Yoko
Bétaré
Oya
Bossangoa
Bozoum
CENTRAL AFRICAN
REPUBLIC
Sibut
Bambari
Ippy
Bakouma
Obo
El Istiwa'iya
Amadi
Mongalla
Kapoeta
Chew
Bahr
375
MEROON
Bétaré
Oya
Bertoua
Nanga-Eboko
Bouar
Bangui
Zongo
Berbérati
Mbaïki
Bosobolo
Mobayi
Bossembélé
Bangassou
Uele
Yâmbiô
Yei
Dungu
Faradje
Kajo Kaji
Torit
Juba
Lokitaung
L.
Turkana
ala
ngsamba-
Yaoundé
Abong-Mbang
Mobaye
Libenge
Bomu
Bondo
Ango
COPYRIGHT PHILIPS

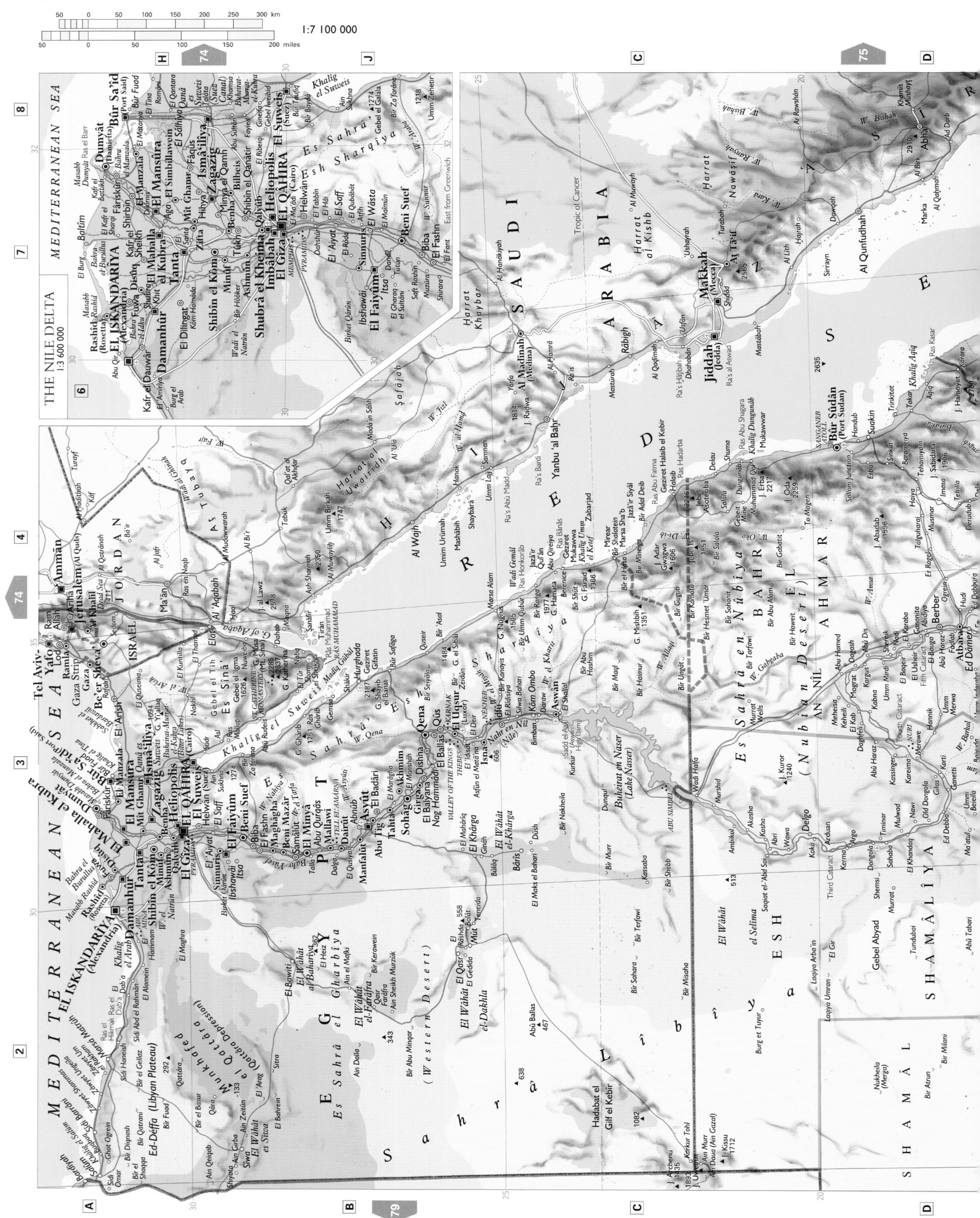

1:7 100 000

THE NILE DELTA
1:3 600 000

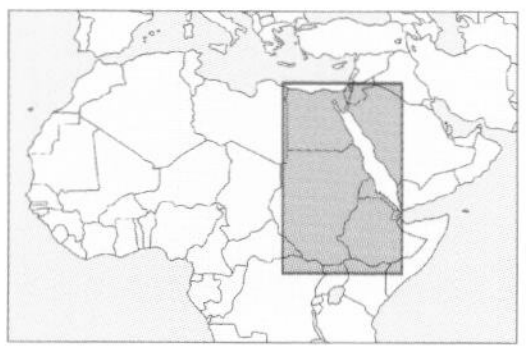

Legend:

∴ UNESCO World Heritage Sites

National Parks

Nature Reserves and Game Reserves

COPYRIGHT PHILIP'S

Projection: Lambert's Equivalent Azimuthal

East from Greenwich

Projection : Lambert's Equivalent Azimuthal

West from Greenwich

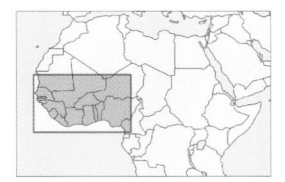

National Parks

Nature Reserves and Game Reserves

∴ UNESCO World Heritage Sites

N. E. NIGERIA
on same scale

East from Greenwich

COPYRIGHT PHILIP'S

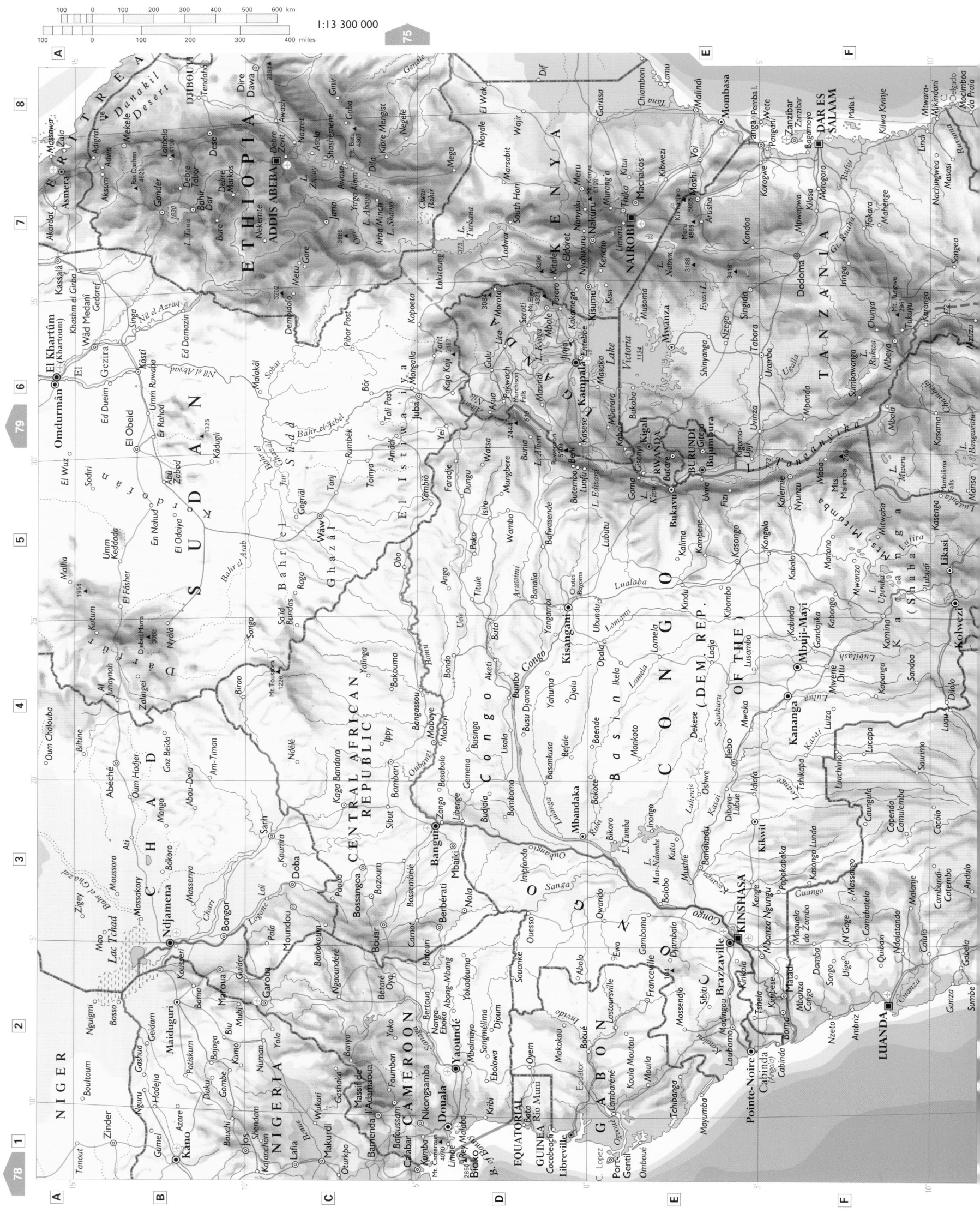

MADAGASCAR
on same scale

INDIAN OCEAN

INDIAN OCEAN

ATLANTIC OCEAN

Projection: Sanson-Flamsteed's Sinusoidal

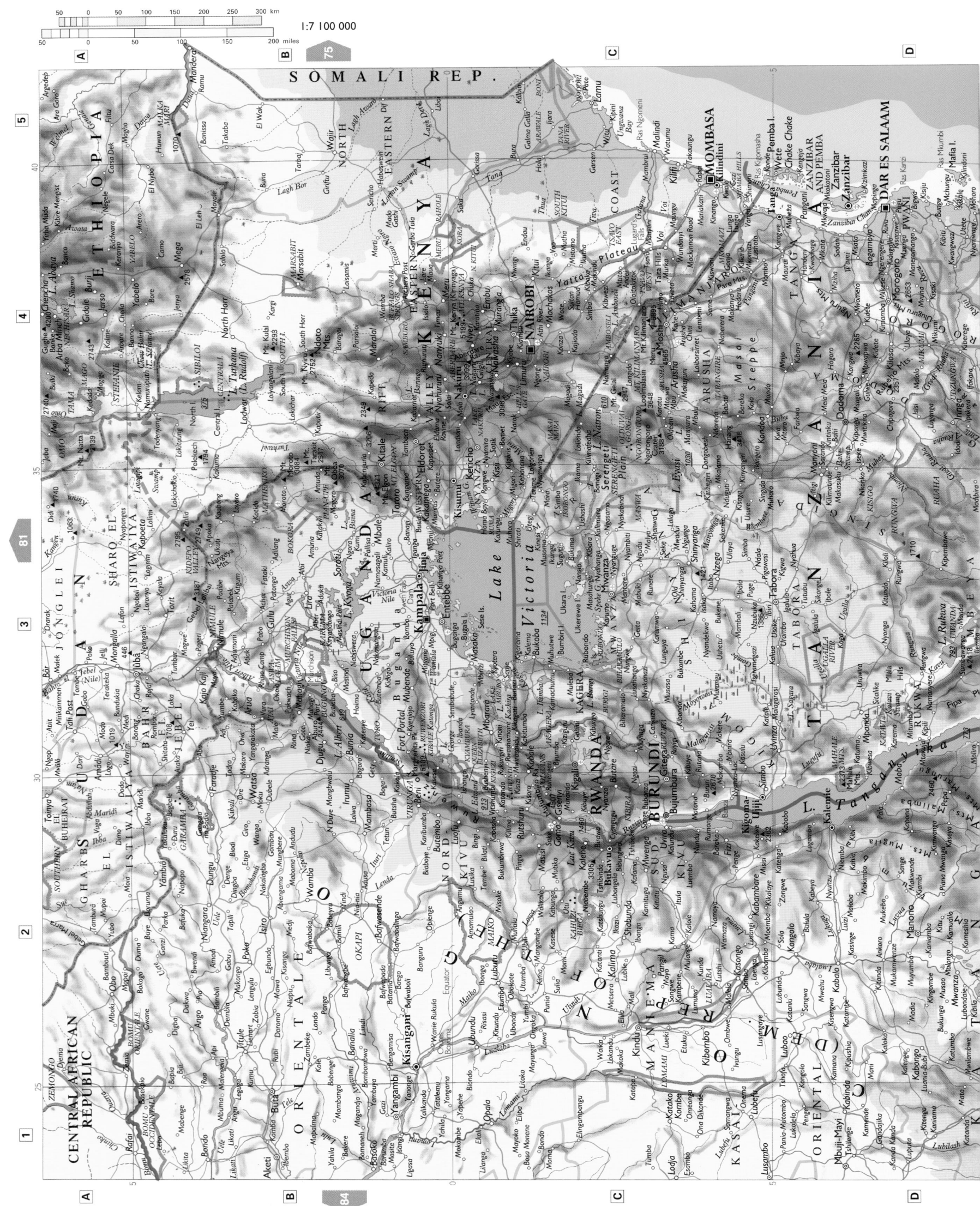

1:7 100 000

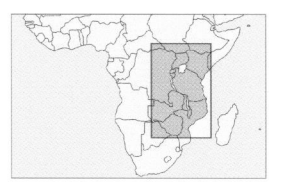

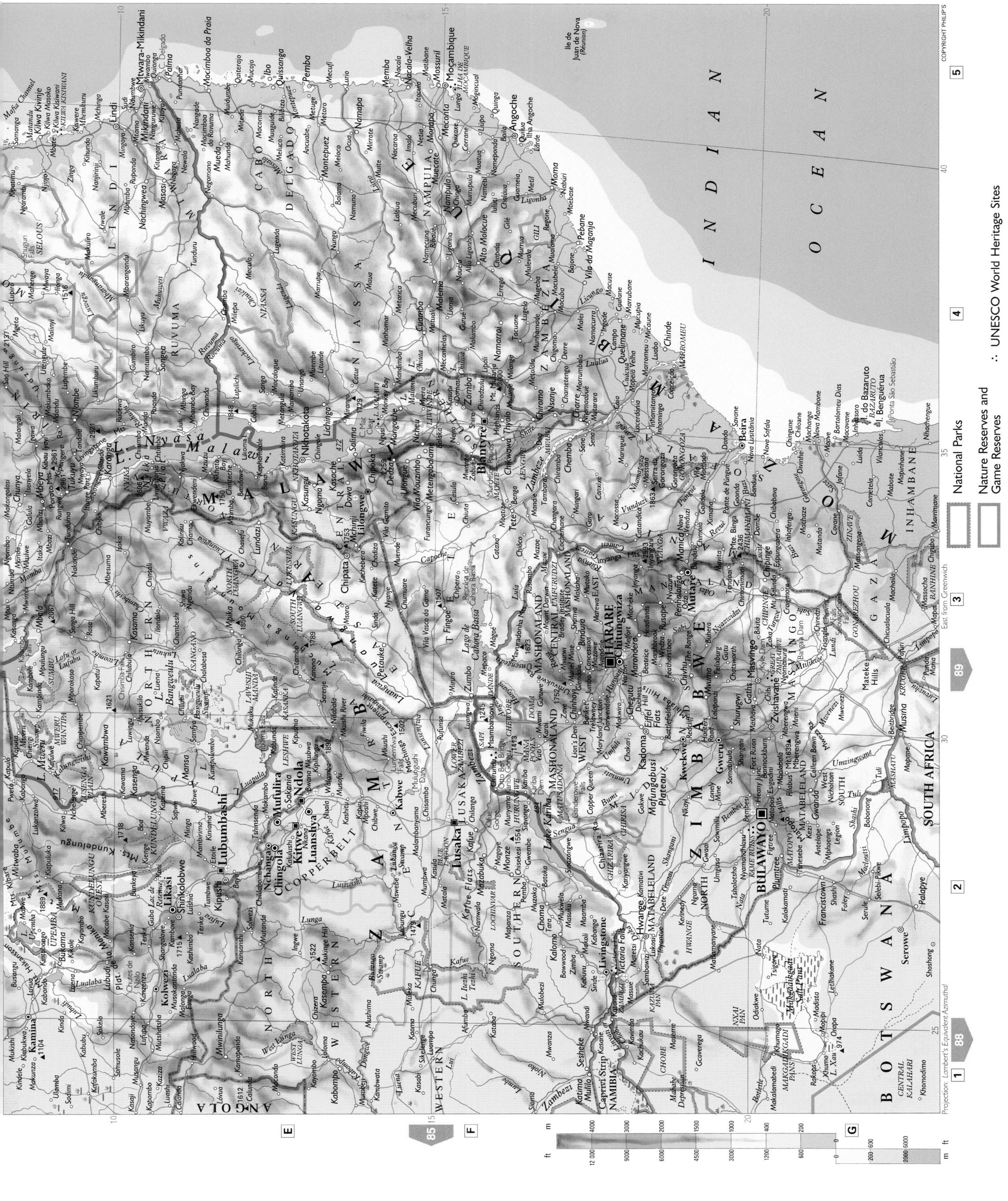

National Parks

Nature Reserves and Game Reserves

∴ UNESCO World Heritage Sites

50 0 50 100 150 200 250 300 km
1:7 100 000
50 0 50 100 150 200 miles

Projection: Lambert's Equivalent Azimuthal

MOZAMBIQUE CHANNEL

ZIMBABWE

MOZAMBIQUE

ZAMBEZIA

MALAWI

MADAGASCAR

INDIAN OCEAN

LIMPOPO

MPUMALANGA

SWAZILAND

LESOTHO

KWAZULU NATAL

EASTERN CAPE

BULAWAYO

HARARE

PRETORIA (Tshwane)

JOHANNESBURG

DURBAN (eThekwini)

ANTANANARIVO

Tropic of Capricorn

MADAGASCAR

on same scale

National Parks

Nature Reserves and
Game Reserves

⋄∴ UNESCO World Heritage Sites

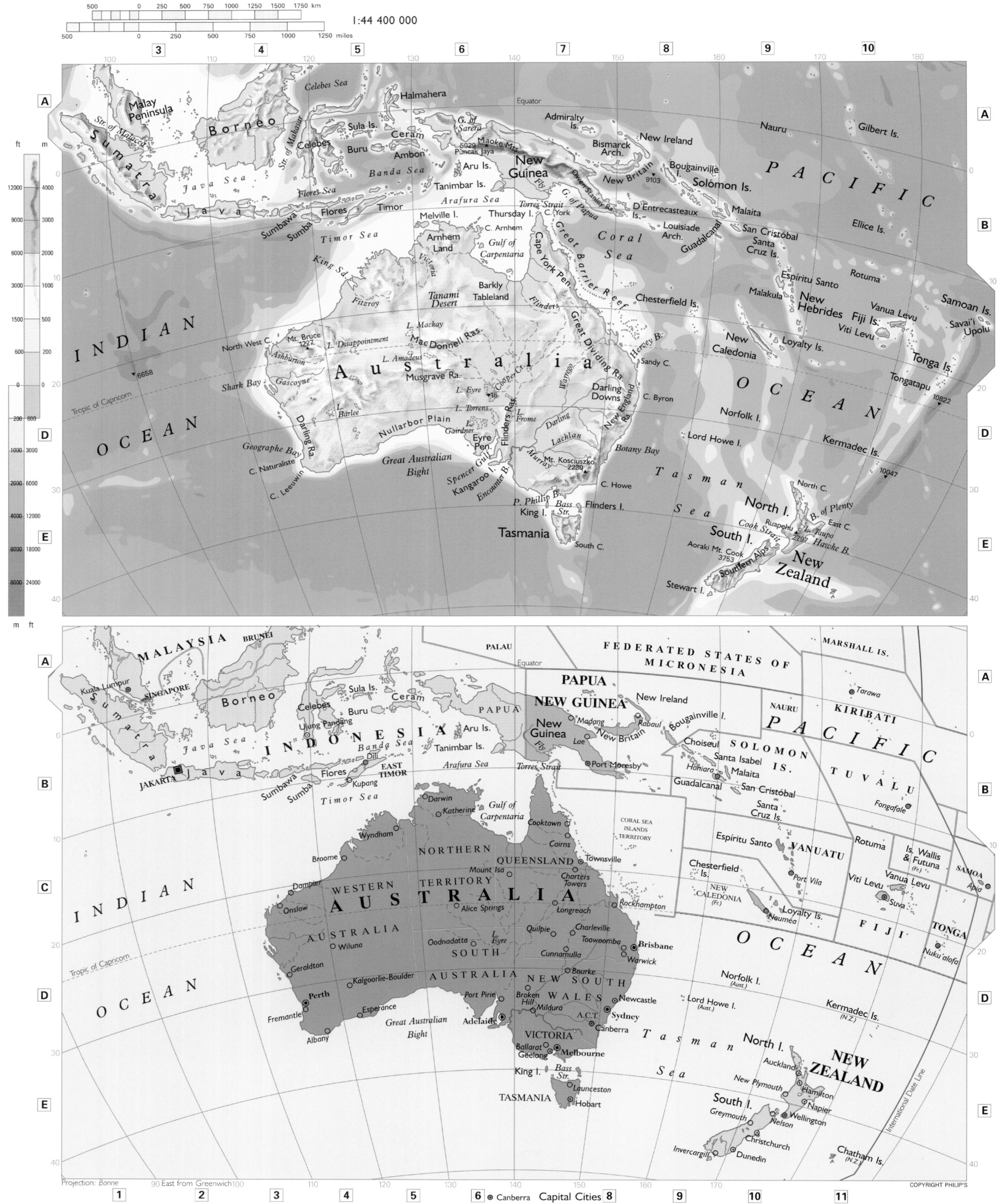

1:44 400 000

500   0   250   500   750   1000   1250   1500   1750 km
500   0   250   500   750   1000   1250 miles

Physical map (top):

Malay Peninsula, Sumatra, Borneo, Celebes Sea, Halmahera, Equator, Admiralty Is., Nauru, Gilbert Is., PACIFIC, Str. of Malacca, Str. of Makasar, Sula Is., Ceram, G. of Sarera, Maoke Mts., 5029 Puncak Jaya, New Ireland, Bismarck Arch., New Britain, Bougainville, 9103, Solomon Is., Celebes, Buru, Ambon, Aru Is., New Guinea, Owen Stanley Ra., D'Entrecasteaux Is., Malaita, Ellice Is., Java Sea, Banda Sea, Tanimbar Is., Fly, G. of Papua, San Cristóbal, Santa Cruz Is., Java, Flores Sea, Flores, Timor, Sumbawa, Sumba, Timor Sea, Arafura Sea, Thursday I., Torres Strait, C. York, Cape York Pen., Coral Sea, Guadalcanal, Espíritu Santo, Rotuma, Samoan Is., Melville I., C. Arnhem, Gulf of Carpentaria, Great Barrier Reef, Chesterfield Is., Malakula, New Hebrides, Fiji Is., Vanua Levu, Savai'i, Upolu, INDIAN, Arnhem Land, Victoria, Barkly Tableland, Flinders, Great Dividing Ra., Hervey B., New Caledonia, Loyalty Is., Viti Levu, Tonga Is., King Sd., Fitzroy, Tanami Desert, Sandy C., Tongatapu, North West C., Mt. Bruce 1227, L. Disappointment, MacDonnell Ras., L. Mackay, Darling Downs, C. Byron, Norfolk I., OCEAN, 6658, Ashburton, L. Amadeus, Australia, Musgrave Ra., Copper Cr., Warrego, Darling, New England Ra., Shark Bay, Gascoyne, L. Eyre, L. Torrens, Lachlan, Lord Howe I., Kermadec Is., Tropic of Capricorn, L. Barlee, Darling Ra., Nullarbor Plain, Gairdner, L. Frome, Murray, Botany Bay, 10047, Geographe Bay, Eyre Pen., Flinders Ra., Mt. Kosciuszko 2230, C. Howe, Tasman Sea, North C., C. Naturaliste, Great Australian Bight, Spencer Gulf, Kangaroo I., Encounter B., P. Phillip B., Bass Str., Flinders I., South C., North I., B. of Plenty, East C., C. Leeuwin, King I., Tasmania, Ruapehu 2797, L. Taupo, Hawke B., South I., Aoraki Mt. Cook 3753, Southern Alps, New Zealand, Stewart I., 10822

Political map (bottom):

MALAYSIA, BRUNEI, PALAU, FEDERATED STATES OF MICRONESIA, MARSHALL IS., Kuala Lumpur, SINGAPORE, Sumatra, Borneo, Sula Is., Ceram, PAPUA, PAPUA NEW GUINEA, New Ireland, NAURU, Tarawa, KIRIBATI, New Guinea, Madang, Rabaul, Bougainville I., PACIFIC, Celebes, Buru, INDONESIA, Ujung Pandang, Aru Is., New Britain, Choiseul, SOLOMON IS., Santa Isabel, Java Sea, Banda Sea, Dili, Tanimbar Is., Lae, Fly, Honiara, Malaita, TUVALU, JAKARTA, Java, EAST TIMOR, Arafura Sea, Torres Strait, Port Moresby, Guadalcanal, San Cristóbal, Sumbawa, Sumba, Kupang, Santa Cruz Is., Fongafale, Timor Sea, Darwin, Katherine, Gulf of Carpentaria, CORAL SEA ISLANDS TERRITORY, Espíritu Santo, VANUATU, Rotuma, Is. Wallis & Futuna (Fr.), SAMOA, Cooktown, Chesterfield Is., Port Vila, Viti Levu, Vanua Levu, Wyndham, NORTHERN, Cairns, Apia, Broome, TERRITORY, Mount Isa, Townsville, NEW CALEDONIA (Fr.), Loyalty Is., Suva, Dampier, WESTERN, QUEENSLAND, Charters Towers, Nouméa, FIJI, Onslow, AUSTRALIA, Alice Springs, Longreach, Rockhampton, TONGA, INDIAN, AUSTRALIA, Quilpie, Charleville, OCEAN, Nuku'alofa, Wiluna, Oodnadatta, L. Eyre, Toowoomba, Brisbane, Cunnamulla, Warwick, Tropic of Capricorn, SOUTH, Norfolk I. (Aust.), Geraldton, Kalgoorlie-Boulder, AUSTRALIA, NEW SOUTH, Bourke, Perth, Port Pirie, Broken Hill, WALES, Newcastle, Lord Howe I. (Aust.), Kermadec Is. (N.Z.), Fremantle, Esperance, Mildura, A.C.T., Sydney, Albany, Great Australian Bight, Adelaide, VICTORIA, Canberra, Tasman, North I., NEW ZEALAND, Ballarat, Melbourne, Sea, Auckland, Geelong, King I., Bass Str., New Plymouth, Hamilton, TASMANIA, Launceston, South I., Napier, Hobart, Greymouth, Nelson, Wellington, International Date Line, Invercargill, Christchurch, Chatham Is. (N.Z.), Dunedin

Projection: Bonne   90 East from Greenwich 100

COPYRIGHT PHILIP'S

● Canberra   Capital Cities

1:5 300 000

50   0   50   100   150   200 km
50   0   50   100   150 miles

North
Island

South
Island

TASMAN
SEA

PACIFIC
OCEAN

AUCKLAND
Takapuna
Manukau
Papakura
Pukekohe
Mercer
Waiuku
Waikato
Huntly
Morrinsville
Te Aroha
Raglan
Kawhia
Te Awamutu
Hamilton
Cambridge
Tauranga
Whakatane
Kawerau
Rotorua
Te Puke
Opotiki
Taneatua
Putaruru
Tokoroa
Mokai
Wairakei
Kinleith
Taupo
Ongarue
Taumarunui
Turangi
Mokau

Houhora Heads
C. Reinga
C. Maria
van Diemen
North C.
Rangaunu B.
Doubtless B.
Mangonui
Whangaroa Harb.
Ahipara B.
Kaitaia
Tauroa Pt.
Okaihau
Waitangi
Opua
Rawene
Kaikohe
Hokianga Harbour
B. of Islands
C. Brett
Hikurangi
Whangarei
Whangarei Harb.
Bream Hd.
Bream B.
Waipoua
Forest
Dargaville
Waipu
Little
Barrier I.
Warkworth
C. Rodney
Great Barrier I.
Helensville
Kaipara Harbour
C. Colville
Cuvier I.
Coromandel
Whitianga
Thames
Whangamata
Mayor I.
Waihi
Tauranga Harb.
Mount
Maunganui

Bay of
Plenty

Whakaari
(White I.)
Runaway
East C.

Raukumara Ra.
Hikurangi
1753
Motu
Waipiro
Tolaga Bay
UREWERA
Ormond
Gisborne
Poverty Bay
Waikaremoana
Nuhaka
Wairoa
Waikokopu
Mahia Pen.

New Plymouth
Mt. Taranaki or Mt. Egmont
2518
Inglewood
C. Egmont
Opunake
Kapuni
Stratford
EGMONT
Eltham
Hawera
Patea
Waverley
WHANGANUI
Whangamomona
Ohakune
Raetihi
Ruapehu 2797
TONGARIRO
Taihape
Mangaweka
Hunterville
Marton
Bulls
Halcombe
Feilding

Waiouru
Ruahine Ra.
Bay
View
C. Kidnappers
Napier
Hastings
Waipawa
Waipukurau
Dannevirke
Woodville
Pahiatua
Eketahuna
C. Turnagain

**Palmerston
North**
Foxton
Shannon
Levin
Otaki
Masterton
Carterton
Greytown
Martinborough
Paraparaumu
Kapiti I.
Featherston
Upper Hutt
Petone
Lower Hutt
Wellington
L. Wairarapa
Cook Strait

C. Farewell
Collingwood
Golden
B.
Takaka
ABEL
TASMAN
D'Urville I.
Tasman
B.
KAHURANGI
Karamea
Karamea
Bight
Tasman
Mts.
Motueka
Pelorus
Tadmor
Nelson
Havelock
Richmond
Wakefield
Picton
Seddonville
Granity
Lyell
Matiri Ra.
Murchison
Wairau
Blenheim
Seddon
Ward
Westport
Inangahua
NELSON
LAKES
Tapuae-o-Uenuku 2885
Punakaiki
Mt. Travers 2338
PAPAROA
Reefton
Clarence
Blackball
Lewis
Pass
Spenser
Mts.
Hanmer
Springs
Kaikoura
Runanga
Greymouth
Stillwater
Waiau
Kumara
L. Brunner
Jacksons
Culverden
Hurunui
Hokitika
ARTHUR'S
PASS
Waikari
Ross
Arthur's P.
Amberley
Oxford
Waipara
Abut Hd.
Rangiora
Kaiapoi
Pegasus Bay
New Brighton
Christchurch
Coleridge
Springfield
Lyttelton
Whitecliffs
Riccarton
Methven
Lincoln
Banks Pen.
Staveley
Akaroa
Little River
WESTLAND
Mt. Cook
3753
Aoraki
Mount Cook
MT. COOK
Southbridge
Ellesmere
Rakaia
Tekapo
Rangitata
Ashburton
Canterbury
Bight
Jackson B.
Okuru
Haast
MOUNT
ASPIRING
L. Pukaki
Fairlie
L. Tekapo
Canterbury
Plains
Mt.
Aspiring
3027
Earnslaw
2818
L. Hawea
L. Wanaka
Ohau
Pukaki
Temuka
Timaru
Milford Sd.
Sutherland Falls
Milford
Sound
Bligh Sound
George Sound
Wanaka
Arrowtown
Cromwell
Dunstan
Mts.
St.
Andrews
Waimate
Tokarahi
Ngapara
Kurow
Secretary I.
Doubtful Sd.
L. Te Anau
Kingston
L. Wakatipu
Queenstown
Clyde
Alexandra
Naseby
Ida
Kakanui
Mts.
Oamaru
Maheno
Hampden
Palmerston
FIORDLAND
L. Manapouri
Eyre
Mts.
Mossburn
Lumsden
Garvie
Mts.
Umbrella
Mts.
Roxburgh
Manuherikia
Dunback
Port Chalmers
Otago Harbour
C. Saunders
Breaksea Sd.
Resolution I.
Dusky Sd.
Manapouri
Te Anau
Southland
Nightcaps
Ohai
Edievale
Kelso
Tapanui
Lawrence
Milton
Mosgiel
Dunedin
Clinton
Balclutha
Kaitangata
Chalky
Inlet
Preservation
Inlet
Te Waewae B.
Orepuki
Riverton
Tuatapere
Clifden
Winton
Otautau
Gore
Mataura
Wyndham
Owaka
Nugget Pt.
Solander I.
Invercargill
South Invercargill
Bluff
Ruapuke I.
Takanui
Tahakopa
Foveaux Str.
Halfmoon Bay
Stewart I.
(Rakiura)
RAKIURA
Port Pegasus
South West C.

Southern Alps
Tiritiri o te Moana

Otago
Taieri
Clutha

Southland

National Parks

Projection : Conical with two standard parallels
East from Greenwich
COPYRIGHT PHILIP'S

SAMOAN ISLANDS
1:10 700 000

SAMOA
Savai'i
Apia
Upolu
AMERICAN
SAMOA
Pago Pago
Tutuila
West from
Greenwich

FIJI AND TONGA
1:10 700 000

50   0   50   100   150   200 km
50   0   50   100   150 miles

Futuna
Wallis & Futuna (Fr.)
Niuafo'ou
(Tonga)
Thikombia
Labasa
Vanua Levu
Yasawa Group
Taveuni
Koro
Vanua Balavu
FIJI
Lautoka
1323
Viti Levu
Nandi
Levuka
Ovalau
Gau
Koro Sea
Lakeba
Lau
Group
Suva
Moala
Vava'u
PACIFIC
OCEAN
Kandavu
Vatoa
Tofua
TONGA
(Friendly Is.)
Tongatapu
Nuku'alofa
East from Greenwich
West from Greenwich

ft   m
9000   3000
6000   2000
3000   1000
1200   400
600   200
0
200   600
2000   6000
4000   12 000
6000   18 000
m   ft

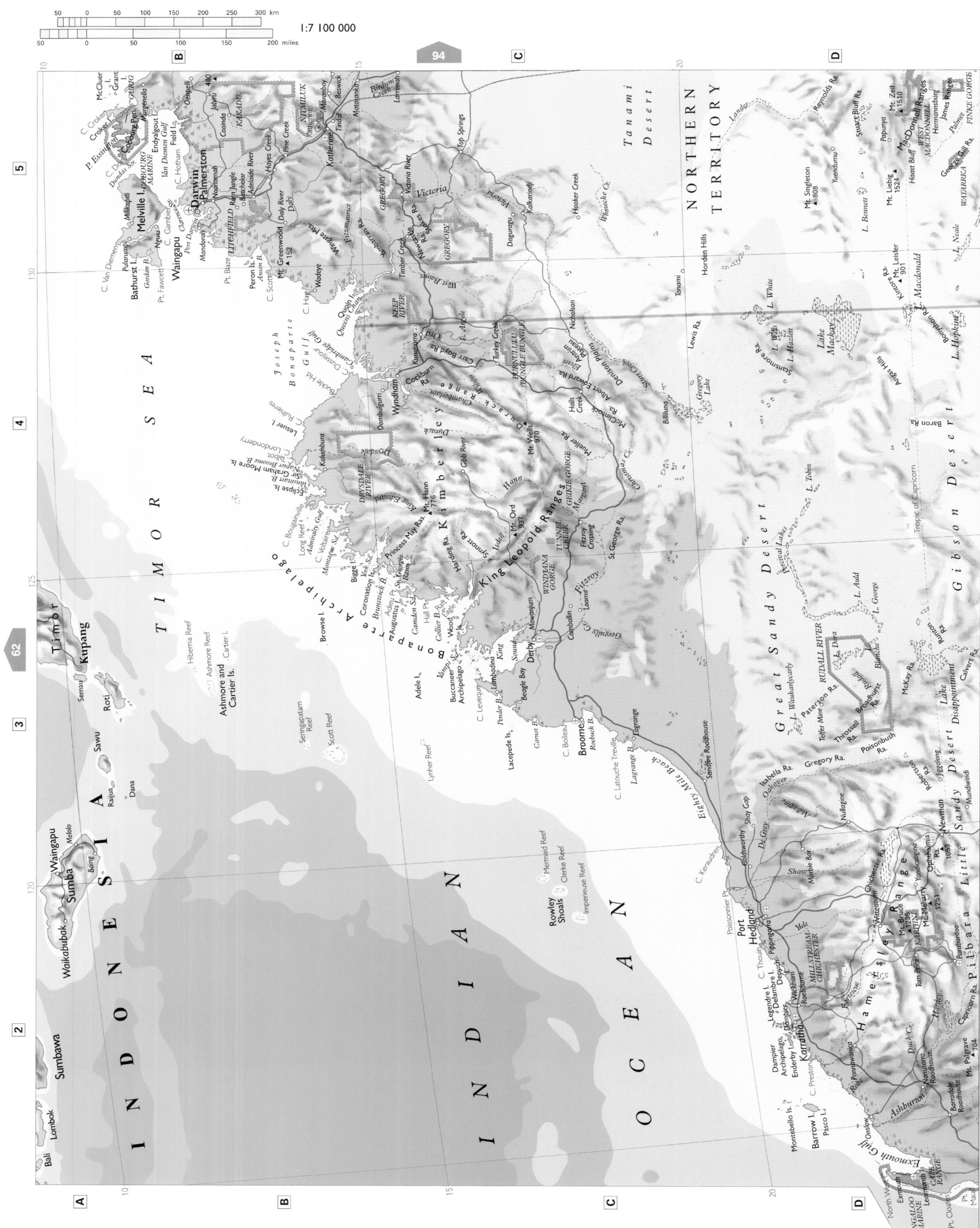

1:7 100 000

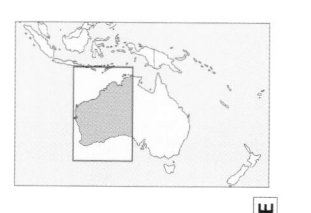

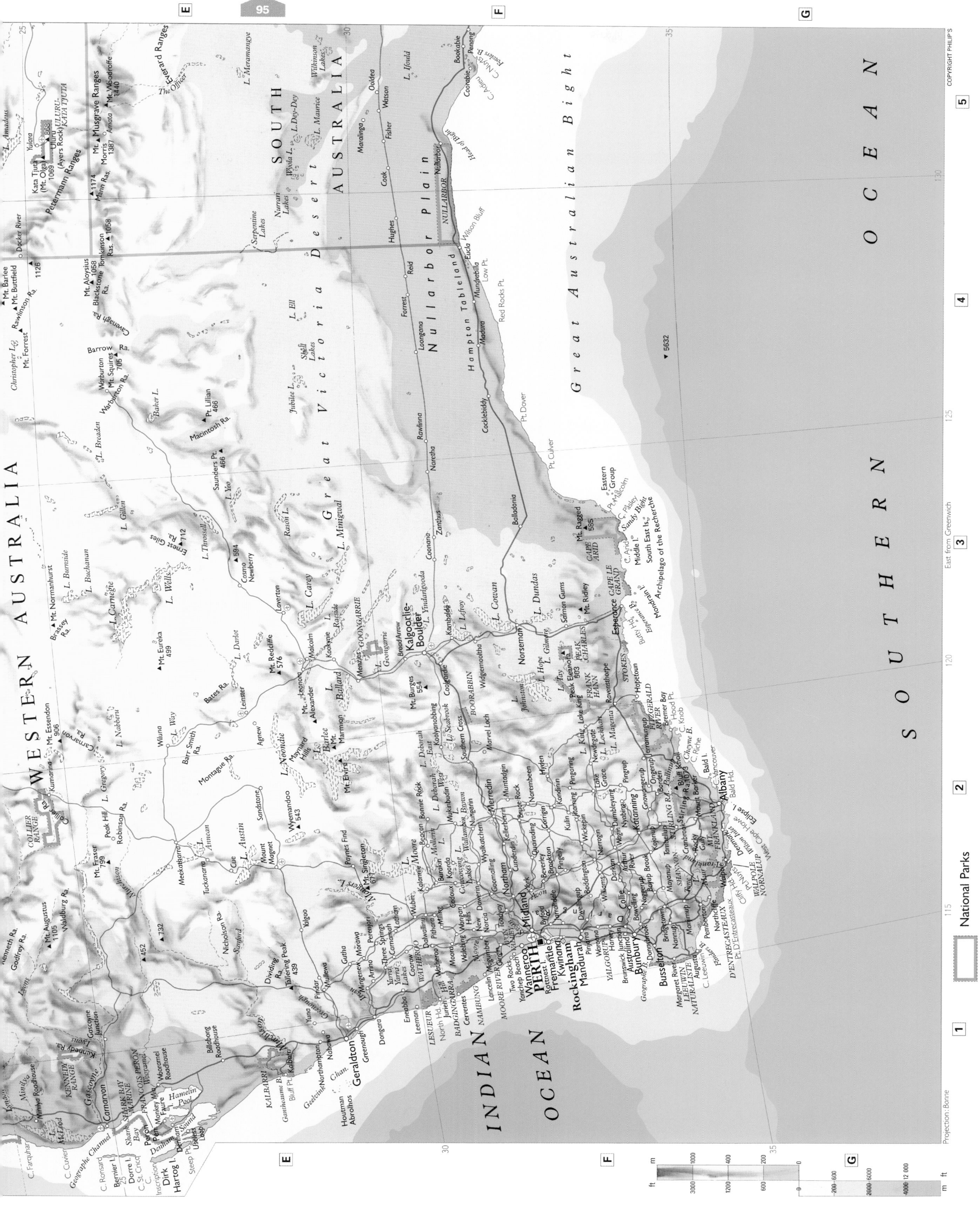

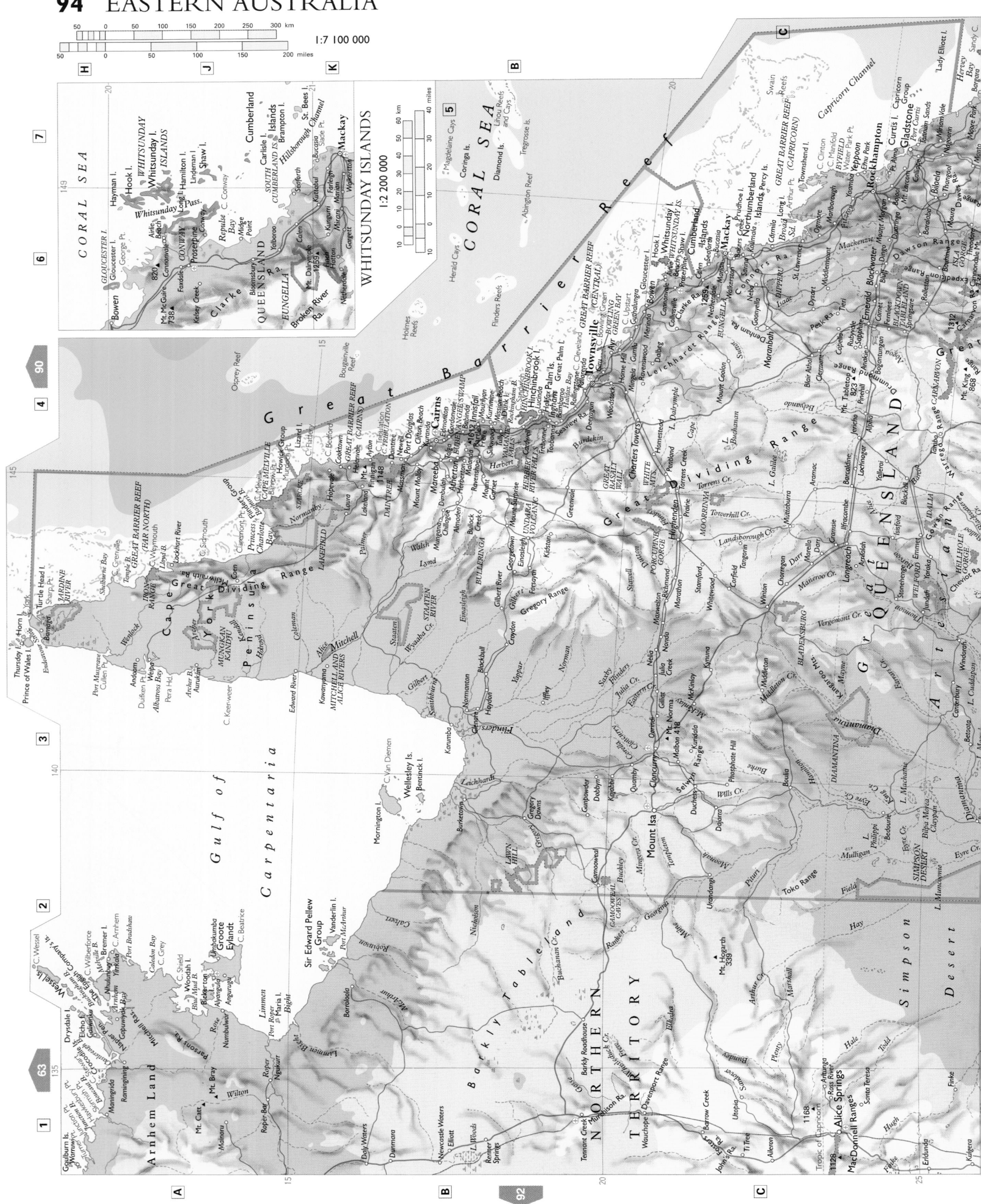

WHITSUNDAY ISLANDS
1:2 200 000

1:7 100 000

COPYRIGHT PHILIP'S

TASMAN SEA

BRISBANE
Gold Coast
Sunshine Coast
Hervey Bay
Maryborough
Bundaberg

Coffs Harbour
Port Macquarie
Taree
Tuncurry-Forster

Newcastle
Gosford
SYDNEY
Windsor
Maitland
Cessnock
Wollongong
Nowra-Bomaderry
Kiama

Campbelltown

Armidale
Tamworth
Toowoomba
Warwick

QUEENSLAND

NEW SOUTH WALES

Dubbo
Orange
Bathurst
Parkes
Lithgow
Katoomba
Penrith

Canberra
Queanbeyan
Goulburn

Broken Hill

Dividing Range
Great Dividing Range
Darling Downs

Cobar
Bourke

Wagga Wagga
Albury-Wodonga
Wangaratta
Shepparton
Bendigo
Echuca

Mildura

SOUTH AUSTRALIA

Lake Eyre
Lake Eyre (North)
Lake Torrens
Lake Gairdner
Lake Frome

Sturt Stony Desert

Flinders Ranges

Port Augusta
Whyalla
Port Pirie
ADELAIDE
Elizabeth
Gawler
Murray Bridge
Kangaroo I.

Mount Gambier

VICTORIA

MELBOURNE
Geelong
Ballarat
Werribee
Sunbury
Dandenong
Frankston
Mornington
Warrnambool
Horsham

Gippsland
Sale
Traralgon
Morwell
Bairnsdale

Bass Strait
King Island
Flinders Island
Furneaux Group
Cape Barren I.

TASMANIA
Launceston
Devonport
Burnie
Hobart

National Parks

East from Greenwich

on same scale

km
m   ft
1500 4500
1000 3000
600   1800
400   1200
200   600
0   0
200   600
2000 6000
4000 12 000
m

Projection: Bonne

93

7   8   9   10

6

1   2   3   4   5

Okhotsk   Poluostrov Kamchatka   *Bering Sea*

B   **MOSKVA**   Yekaterinburg   Tomsk   *Lena*   Sea of Okhotsk   Petropavlovsk -Kamchatskiy   Komandorskiye Ostrova (*Russia*)   Near Is. (*U.S.A.*)   Andreanof Is.
Volga   *Ob*   Novosibirsk   Irkutsk   Chita   Blagoveshchensk   *Amur*   Sakhalin   7822   *Aleutian*
Astana (Aqmola)   Semey   50   *Oz. Baykal*   Khabarovsk   *La Perouse Str.*   Kurilskiye Ostrova (*Russia*)   Kuril Trench   *Aleutian Trench*

KAZAKHSTAN   *Aral Sea*   *Balqash Köl*   Ulaanbaatar   **MONGOLIA**   Harbin   Changchun   Vladivostok   Hakodate   ▼10,542   *Emperor Seamount Chain*   *Hawai*

C   Almaty   Ürümqi   **SHENYANG**   Sapporo   Sea of Japan
Toshkent   *Altai*   **BEIJING**   **TIANJIN**   Dalian   NORTH KOREA   **SŎUL**   Sendai
KYRGYZSTAN   Taiyuan   SOUTH KOREA   Nagoya   Fuji-San 3776   **TOKYO**   Midway Is. (*U.S.A.*)
TAJIKISTAN   **C H I N A**   *Huang He*   Qingdao   Kyōto   Yokohama

D   **AFGHANISTAN**   Kabul   Srinagar   *Kunlun Shan*   Lanzhou   Xi'an   Kitakyūshū   Osaka **JAPAN**   Lisianski I. (*U.S.A.*)
PAKISTAN   Lahore   *Himalaya*   XIZANG   Nanjing   *Yellow Sea*   Shikoku   10,554   *Japan Trench*
DELHI   Lhasa   **CHONGQING**   Wuhan   *Kyūshū*
Kanpur   Mt. Everest 8850   **HANGZHOU**   *Cheng Jiang*   Changsha   **SHANGHAI**

E   *Ganga*   NEPAL   *Brahmaputra*   Kunming   Fuzhou   *East China Sea*   Ogasawara Guntō (*Japan*)
KOLKATA (Calcutta)   **DHAKA**   **GUANGZHOU**   Taipei   *Ryūkyū-retto* (*Japan*)   Kazan-Rettō (*Japan*)   Minami-Tori-Shima (*Japan*)
I N D I A   BANGLADESH   Mandalay   **HONG KONG**   Macau   **TAIWAN**   *South Honshu Ridge*
BURMA   Hanoi   *Marcus*   Wake I. (*U.S.A.*)   *Necker Ridge*

F   Hyderabad   *Bay of Bengal*   Rangoon   *Salween*   LAOS   Hainan   C. Engano   **NORTHERN MARIANAS** (*U.S.A.*)   **MARSHALL IS.**
CHENNAI (Madras)   **THAILAND**   Luzon   Saipan   Bikini Atoll   *International Dateline*   **P A**
BANGKOK   *Mekong*   Paracel Is.   **MANILA**   GUAM (*U.S.A.*)   Enewetak Atoll
Andaman Is. (*India*)   CAMBODIA   Mindoro   **PHILIPPINES**   11,022   *Mariana Trench*

G   SRI LANKA   Nicobar Is. (*India*)   Phnom Penh   *G. of Thailand*   Palawan   Samar 10,497   Yap   *Caroline Is.*   Truk   *M i c r o n e s i a*   Dalap-Uliga-Darrit
Colombo   Thanh Pho Ho Chi Minh   *South China Sea*   **MALAYSIA**   4101   Mindanao   Koror   Jaluit I.
Kuala Lumpur   PEN. MALAYSIA   BRUNEI   SABAH   *Sulu Sea*   *Mindanao Trench*   **PALAU**   **FEDERATED STATES OF MICRONESIA**   Pohnpei ● Palikir   Butaritari

SINGAPORE   *Sumatera*   SARAWAK   *Celebes Sea*   *M e l*   Tarawa   Gilbert Is.   Howland I. (*U.S.A.*)
Palembang   Borneo   Halmahera   **PAPUA NEW GUINEA**   **NAURU**   Banaba   Baker I. (*U.S.A.*)
Sunda   **I N D O N E S I A**   Ujung Pandang   Sulawesi   Buru   Seram   Puncak Jaya 5029 ▲ PAPUA   Admiralty Is.   New Ireland   *a*   **KIR**   *O*
Java Sea   **JAKARTA**   *Flores Sea*   *Banda Sea*   *Maluku*   New Guinea   Bismarck Arch.   Rabaul   Phoenix Is.   Abariringa Enderbury I.
Selat Sunda   Surabaya   Jawa   Bali   Sumbawa   Flores   7440   Lae   Bougainville   New Britain   **SOLOMON IS.**   Fongafale
Sunda Islands   *Java Trench*   Sumba   EAST TIMOR   Timor   Port Moresby   Honiara   **TUVALU**   Tokelau Is. (*N.Z.*)

INDIAN   Christmas I. (*Austral.*)   Cocos Is. (*Austral.*)   *Arafura Sea*   *Torres Strait*   C. York   Guadalcanal   Santa Cruz I. 9165   Rotuma   Is. Wallis & Futuna (*Fr.*)   **SAMOA**   Apia
C. Arnhem   *Gulf of Carpentaria*   *Coral Sea*   Louisiade Arch.   Espiritu Santo   Vanua Levu   Viti Levu   **FIJI**   Suva   Nuku'alofa
Darwin   Broome   Cairns   **VANUATU**   Is. Chesterfield   Port Vila   7570   Is. Loyauté   **TONGA**

OCEAN   North West C.   *Great Barrier Reef*   Townsville   NEW CALEDONIA (*Fr.*)   Nouméa   10,822   *Tonga Trench*
AUSTRALIA   Mount Isa ●   Rockhampton   *Great Dividing Ra.*   Norfolk I. (*Austral.*)
Geraldton   Alice Springs   **Brisbane**   Lord Howe I. (*Austral.*)   Kermadec Is. (*N.Z.*)

L   Nouvelle Amsterdam (*Fr.*)   I. St. Paul (*Fr.*)   *L. Eyre*   *Murray*   *Darling*   Kermadec Trench ▼10,047
Perth   Sydney   Canberra   *Tasman Sea*   **NEW ZEALAND**
Great Australian Bight   Albany   Adelaide   Mt. Kosciuszko 2230   Auckland

M   *Mid-Indian Ridge*   **Melbourne**   *Bass Str.*   Aoraki Mt. Cook 3753   Christchurch   Chatham Is. (*N.Z.*)
Tasmania   Hobart   Dunedin   Bounty Is. (*N.Z.*)
Is. Crozet (*Fr.*)   Invercargill   Antipodes Is. (*N.Z.*)

N   Kerguelen (*Fr.*)   Heard I. (*Austral.*)   Auckland Is. (*N.Z.*)   Campbell I. (*N.Z.*)   Macquarie Is. (*Austral.*)

Elevation scale

ft	m
12 000	4000
9000	3000
6000	2000
3000	1000
1500	500
600	200
0	0
600	200
3000	1000
6000	2000
12 000	4000
18 000	6000
24 000	8000
m ft	

Arctic Circle

ALASKA
(U.S.A.)
Anchorage
5959
Juneau

Bristol Bay
Gulf of Alaska

Is. (U.S.A.)

Prince of Wales I.
(U.S.A.) Prince Rupert
Queen Charlotte Is.
(Canada)

C A N A D A

R O C K Y

Edmonton

L. Winnipeg

Calgary

Regina

Winnipeg

N O R T H

Newfoundland

Vancouver
Vancouver I.
Victoria
Seattle
Portland

Boise

Snake

Minneapolis

Missouri

L. Superior

L. Michigan

Québec

St. Lawrence

St. John's

Montréal

L. Huron
Ontario
Toronto
Detroit
L. Erie
Buffalo
Pittsburgh

Ottawa
Boston

NEW YORK CITY
PHILADELPHIA
Baltimore
Washington D.C.

C. Mendocino

Salt Lake
City

Denver

Colorado

CHICAGO

Kansas City

St. Louis
Cincinnati

Sacramento

SAN FRANCISCO

6741

4418

Mts.

UNITED STATES

Oklahoma City
Memphis

A T L A N T I C

6741

LOS ANGELES
San Diego

Phoenix

Dallas

Mississippi

Atlanta

Appalachian Mts.

C. Hatteras

Bermuda
(U.K.)

Ciudad
Juárez

Houston

San Antonio

New
Orleans

Jacksonville

Guadalupe
(Mex.)

Baja California

M E X

Gulf of Mexico

Miami

Sargasso Sea

Golfo de California

Monterrey

BAHAMAS

Florida Str.

O C E A N

Tropic of Cancer

Honolulu

Oahu
4205
Hawaii

HAWAIIAN IS.
(U.S.A.)

C. San Lucas

La Habana

West Indies

Johnston I.
(U.S.A.)

C I F I C

Guadalajara

MEXICO
5610
Puebla

I. Clipperton
(Fr.)

Mérida

Canal de Yucatán

7680

9200

HAITI

DOMINICAN REP.

JAMAICA

Kingston

PUERTO
RICO
(U.S.A.)

Leeward
Is.

Acapulco

Is. Revilla Gigedo
(Mex.)

Caribbean Sea

BARBADOS

Palmyra Is.
(U.S.A.)

Teraina

North West Christmas I. Ridge

Tabuaeran

Kiritimati

GUATEMALA
Guatemala
San Salvador
EL SALVADOR

BELIZE

HONDURAS

NICARAGUA

Managua

Windward Is.

COSTA
RICA

San José

Barranquilla

Maracaibo

Medellín

Colón
Panama
PANAMA

CARACAS

VENEZUELA

O C E A N

Jarvis I.
(U.S.A.)

Line Is.

Equator

Galápagos
(Ecuador)

I. del Coco
(Costa Rica)

I. de Malpelo
(Colombia)

Orinoco

Cali
COLOMBIA

Bogotá

I B A T I

Malden I.

Starbuck I.

Quito
ECUADOR

Amazonas

AMER.
SAMOA
(U.S.A.)

Tongareva
Pukapuka
Manihiki

Vostok I.

Caroline I.
(Millennium I.)

Is. Marquises

Guayaquil

C. Palinas

Iquitos

BRAZIL

Flint I.

Trujillo

Suwarrow Is.

Is. de la
Société

Papeete
Tahiti

Is. Tuamotu

6369

PERU

LIMA

Cuzco

Nevada Ancohuma
6550

Niue
(N.Z.)

Cook Is.
(N.Z.)

Rarotonga

Austral Seamount Chain

Is. Tubuai

Tuamotu

FRENCH POLYNESIA

Mururoa

Ridge

Arequipa
6866
Peru-
Arica

L. Titicaca

La Paz
BOLIVIA

Iquique
Chile

Tropic of Capricorn

Antofagasta

PARAGUAY

Asunción

San Felix
(Chile)

San Ambrosio
(Chile)

Ducie I.

Pitcairn I.
(U.K.)

Sala-y-Gómez
(Chile)

Peru-Chile Trench

8050
Trench

San Miguel
de Tucumán

Rapa

I. de Pascua
(Chile)

Pôrto
Alegre

Arch. de
Juan Fernández
(Chile)

Córdoba

Valparaíso

Aconcagua
6960
Rosario

URUGUAY

Montevideo

SANTIAGO
Concepción

BUENOS
AIRES

Río de la Plata

Patagonia
Cordillera de los Andes

ARGENTINA

Chile Rise

S O U T H

A T L A N T I C

6212

O C E A N

Pacific-Antarctic Ridge

East Pacific Ridge

Punta Arenas

Est. de Magallanes
Tierra del Fuego

C. de Hornos

Falkland Is.
(U.K.)

South Georgia
(U.K.)

West from Greenwich

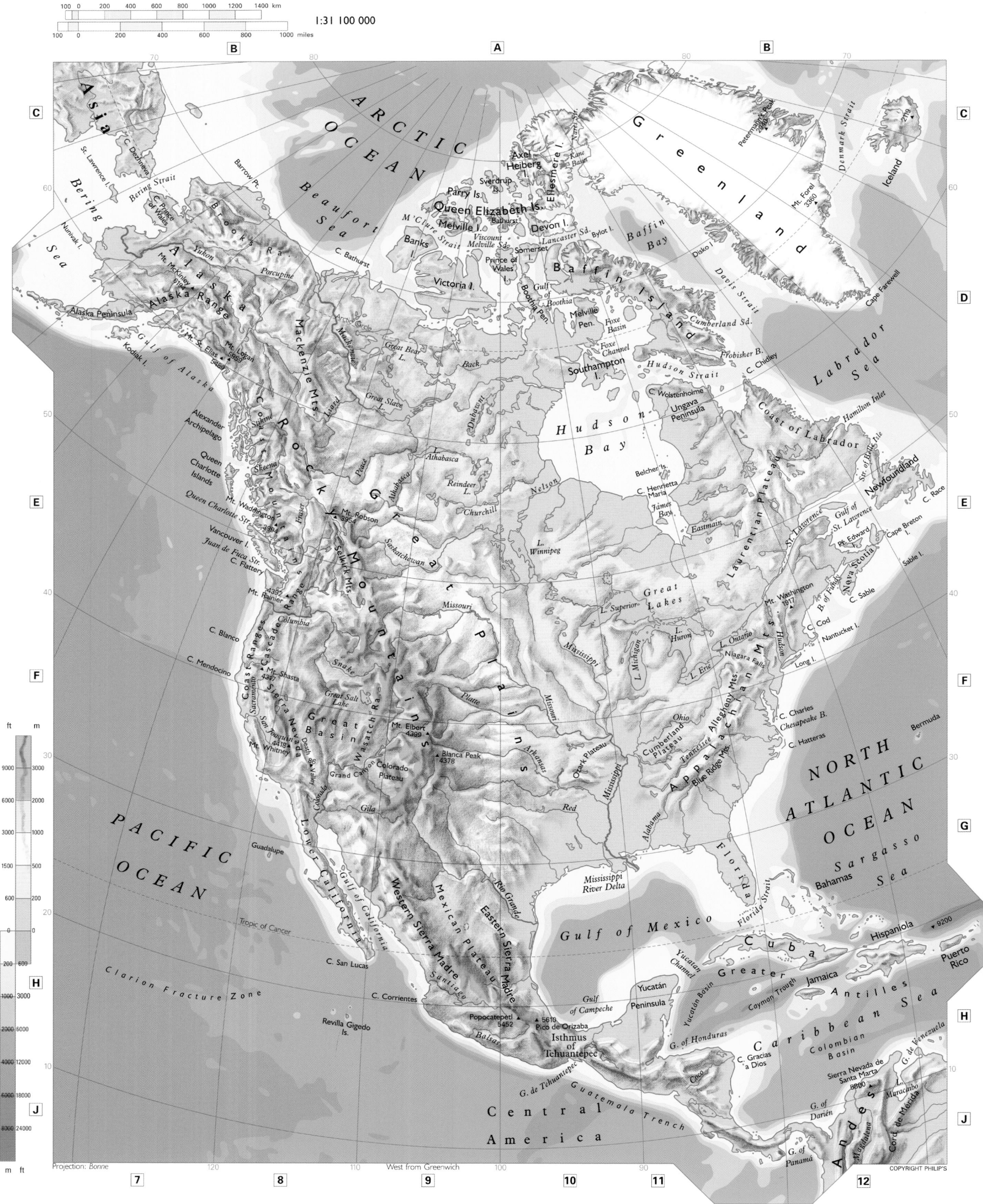

100 0 200 400 600 800 1000 1200 1400 km

1:31 100 000

100 0 200 400 600 800 1000 miles

Projection: Bonne

West from Greenwich

COPYRIGHT PHILIP'S

Asia

ARCTIC OCEAN

Greenland

Iceland

Denmark Strait

Petermann Peak 2940

Mt. Forel 3360

Cape Farewell

Kane Basin

Axel Heiberg

Ellesmere I.

Sverdrup Is.

Parry Is.

Queen Elizabeth Is.

Melville I.

Bathurst

Devon I.

Lancaster Sd.

Bylot I.

Disko I.

Davis Strait

M'Clure Strait

Viscount Melville Sd.

Somerset

Banks

Prince of Wales

Gulf of Boothia

Boothia Pen.

Baffin Bay

Baffin Island

Cumberland Sd.

Victoria I.

St. Lawrence I.

C. Dezhneva

Bering Strait

Nunivak I.

C. Prince of Wales

Bering Sea

Barrow Pt.

Beaufort Sea

C. Bathurst

Melville Pen.

Foxe Basin

Foxe Channel

Frobisher B.

C. Chidley

Labrador Sea

Brooks Ra.

Mt. McKinley 6194

Yukon

Alaska Range

Porcupine

Arctic Circle

Great Bear L.

Back

Southampton I.

Hudson Strait

Ungava Peninsula

C. Wolstenholme

Hamilton Inlet

Coast of Labrador

Alaska Peninsula

Kodiak I.

Gulf of Alaska

Mt. S. Elias 5489

Mt. Logan 5950

Mackenzie Mts.

Liard

Mackenzie

Great Slave L.

Dubawnt

Hudson Bay

Belcher Is.

C. Henrietta Maria

James Bay

Eastmain

Newfoundland

Alexander Archipelago

Queen Charlotte Islands

Queen Charlotte Str.

Stikine

Skeena

Rocky Mountains

Peace

Athabasca

Athabasca

Reindeer L.

Churchill

Nelson

L. Winnipeg

Saskatchewan

Laurentian Plateau

St. Lawrence

Gulf of St. Lawrence

C. Race

Vancouver I.

Juan de Fuca Str.

C. Flattery

Mt. Robson 3954

Mt. Waddington 3994

Selkirk Mts.

Columbia

Great Plains

Missouri

Great Lakes

L. Superior

L. Michigan

L. Huron

L. Ontario

L. Erie

Niagara Falls

Mt. Washington 1917

B. of Fundy

Pte. Edward

Cape Breton I.

Nova Scotia

C. Sable

Str. of Belle Isle

C. Blanco

C. Mendocino

Mt. 4352

Cascade Ranges

Mt. Rainier 4392

Coast Ranges

Mt. Shasta 4347

Snake

Platte

Missouri

Mississippi

Ohio

Cumberland Plateau

Tennessee

Allegheny Mts.

Appalachian Mts.

Hudson

C. Cod

Nantucket I.

Long I.

C. Charles

Chesapeake B.

C. Hatteras

Sacramento

Sierra Nevada

San Joaquin

Great Basin

Great Salt Lake

Wasatch Ra.

Mt. Elbert 4399

Blanca Peak 4378

Colorado Plateau

Ozark Plateau

Blue Ridge Mts.

Bermuda

Mt. Whitney 4419

Death Valley 86

Grand Canyon

Colorado

Gila

Arkansas

Red

Mississippi

Alabama

NORTH ATLANTIC OCEAN

PACIFIC OCEAN

Guadalupe

Lower California

Gulf of California

Tropic of Cancer

C. San Lucas

Western Sierra Madre

Mexican Plateau

Eastern Sierra Madre

Rio Grande

Mississippi River Delta

Gulf of Mexico

Florida

Florida Strait

Bahamas

Sargasso Sea

Cuba

Hispaniola

9200

Puerto Rico

Clarion Fracture Zone

Revilla Gigedo Is.

C. Corrientes

Santiago

Balsas

Popocatepetl 5452

Pico de Orizaba 5610

Isthmus of Tehuantepec

Gulf of Campeche

Yucatán

Yucatán Peninsula

Yucatán Channel

Yucatan Basin

Cayman Trough

Jamaica

G. of Honduras

Greater Antilles

Caribbean Sea

Colombian Basin

Sierra Nevada de Santa Marta 5800

G. de Venezuela

Maracaibo

C. Gracias a Dios

Coco

G. de Tehuantepec

Guatemala Trench

CENTRAL AMERICA

G. of Darién

G. of Panamá

Andes

Cord. de Mérida

Magdalena

ft m

9000 3000

6000 2000

3000 1000

1500 500

600 200

0 0

200 600

1000 3000

2000 6000

4000 12000

6000 18000

8000 24000

m ft

1:31 100 000

100 0 200 400 600 800 1000 1200 1400 km
100 0 200 400 600 800 1000 miles

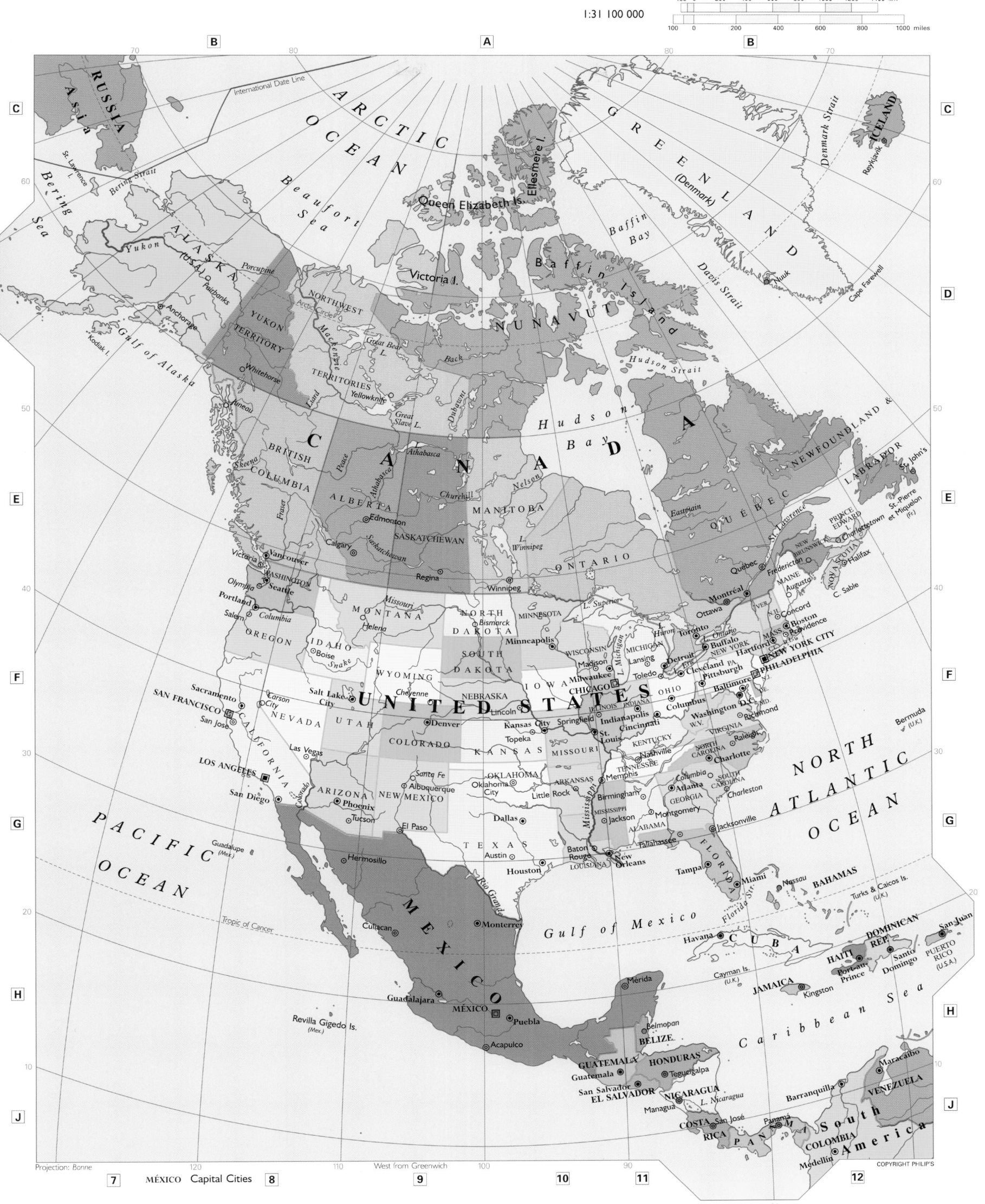

RUSSIA

Asia

St. Lawrence I.

Bering
Strait

Bering
Sea

ARCTIC OCEAN

International Date Line

GREENLAND

ICELAND

Reykjavik

Denmark Strait

Beaufort
Sea

Queen Elizabeth Is.

Ellesmere I.

Baffin
Bay

Davis Strait

Cape Farewell

(Denmark)

Kodiak I.

Gulf of Alaska

Yukon

ALASKA
(U.S.A.)

Porcupine

Fairbanks

Anchorage

Arctic Circle

NORTHWEST

YUKON
TERRITORY

Whitehorse

Juneau

Mackenzie

Great Bear
L.

Back

TERRITORIES

Yellowknife

Great
Slave L.

NUNAVUT

Baffin Island

Nuuk

Hudson Strait

C A N A D A

Hudson

Bay

NEWFOUNDLAND &
LABRADOR

St. John's

BRITISH
COLUMBIA

Skeena

Fraser

Peace

Athabasca

Athabasca

ALBERTA

Edmonton

Calgary

Saskatchewan

SASKATCHEWAN

Churchill

Nelson

MANITOBA

L.
Winnipeg

Regina

Eastmain

QUÉBEC

St. Lawrence

Québec

Fredericton

NEW
BRUNSWICK

PRINCE
EDWARD

St-Pierre
et Miquelon
(Fr)

Charlottetown

NOVA
SCOTIA

Halifax

C. Sable

Victoria

Vancouver

Olympia

WASHINGTON

Seattle

Portland

Salem

OREGON

Columbia

MONTANA

Missouri

Helena

IDAHO

Boise

Snake

Winnipeg

L. Superior

ONTARIO

NORTH
DAKOTA

Bismarck

MINNESOTA

Ottawa

Montréal

VER.

N.H.

Concord

MAINE

Augusta

MASS.

Boston

Providence

Toronto

Ontario

L. Huron

WISCONSIN

MICHIGAN

Madison

Minneapolis

Milwaukee

Lansing

Detroit

Buffalo

NEW YORK

Hartford

CONN.

NEW YORK CITY

SOUTH
DAKOTA

WYOMING

Cheyenne

IOWA

NEBRASKA

ILLINOIS

INDIANA

CHICAGO

Toledo

L. Erie

Cleveland

PA.

Pittsburgh

OHIO

Columbus

PHILADELPHIA

Baltimore

DEL.

MD.

Washington D.C.

Richmond

Sacramento

SAN FRANCISCO

San Jose

Carson
City

NEVADA

Salt Lake
City

UTAH

U N I T E D   S T A T E S

Denver

COLORADO

Lincoln

Kansas City

Topeka

KANSAS

St.
Louis

Springfield

Indianapolis

MISSOURI

Cincinnati

KENTUCKY

Nashville

TENNESSEE

W.V.

VIRGINIA

NORTH
CAROLINA

Raleigh

Charlotte

SOUTH
CAROLINA

Columbia

Bermuda
(U.K.)

LOS ANGELES

CALIFORNIA

San Diego

Las Vegas

Colorado

ARIZONA

Phoenix

Tucson

Santa Fe

Albuquerque

NEW MEXICO

El Paso

OKLAHOMA

Oklahoma
City

ARKANSAS

Little Rock

Memphis

Dallas

T E X A S

Austin

Houston

Mississippi

MISSISSIPPI

Jackson

Birmingham

ALABAMA

Montgomery

Atlanta

GEORGIA

Charleston

Jacksonville

Tallahassee

LOUISIANA

Baton
Rouge

New
Orleans

FLORIDA

Tampa

Miami

NORTH

ATLANTIC

OCEAN

PACIFIC

OCEAN

Guadalupe
(Mex.)

Tropic of Cancer

Hermosillo

Culiacan

M E X I C O

Monterrey

Rio Grande

Gulf of Mexico

Havana

CUBA

Nassau

BAHAMAS

Florida Str.

Turks & Caicos Is.
(U.K.)

DOMINICAN
REP.

San Juan

PUERTO
RICO
(U.S.A.)

Revilla Gigedo Is.
(Mex.)

Guadalajara

MÉXICO

Puebla

Mérida

Belmopan

BELIZE

Acapulco

GUATEMALA

Guatemala

HONDURAS

Tegucigalpa

San Salvador

EL SALVADOR

NICARAGUA

Managua

L. Nicaragua

COSTA
RICA

San José

Cayman Is.
(U.K.)

JAMAICA

Kingston

HAITI

Port-au-
Prince

Santo
Domingo

Caribbean
Sea

Maracaibo

Barranquilla

VENEZUELA

PANAMA

Panamá

COLOMBIA

Medellín

South America

Projection: Bonne

MÉXICO Capital Cities

West from Greenwich

1:13 300 000

Projection : Bonne

ALASKA
1:26 700 000

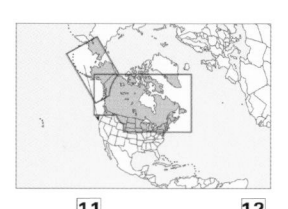

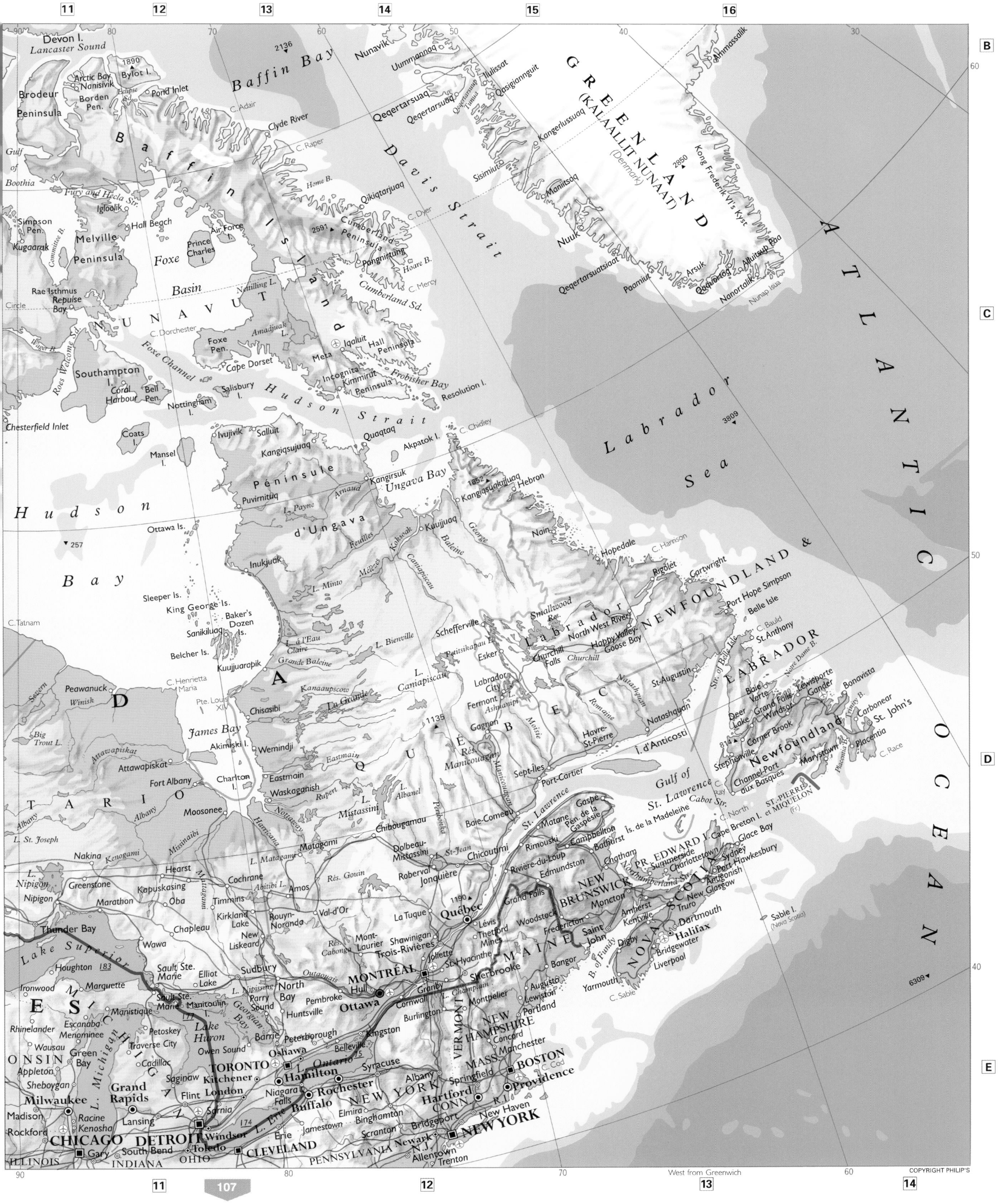

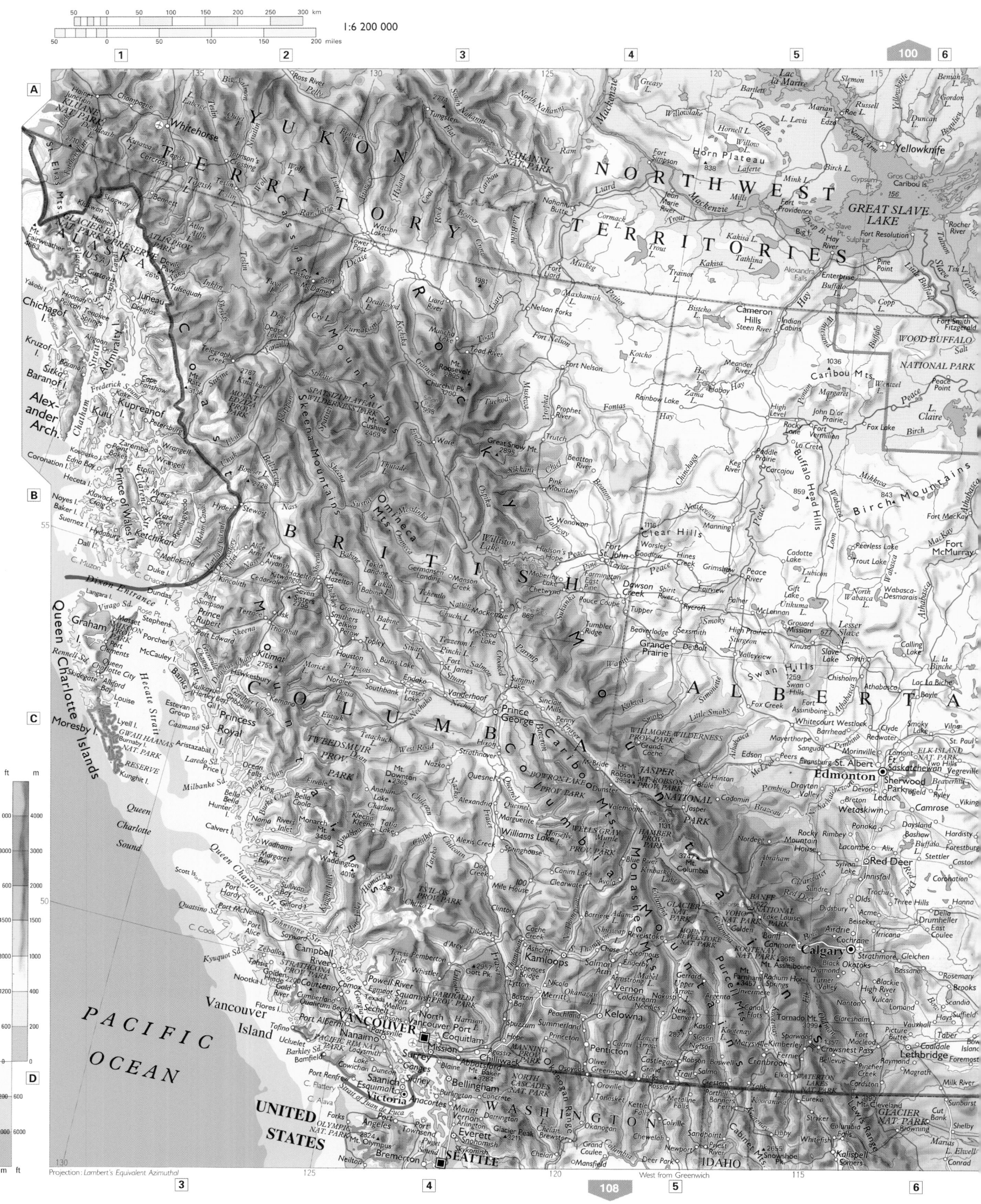

National Parks

1:6 200 000

Projection: Lambert's Equivalent Azimuthal

National Parks

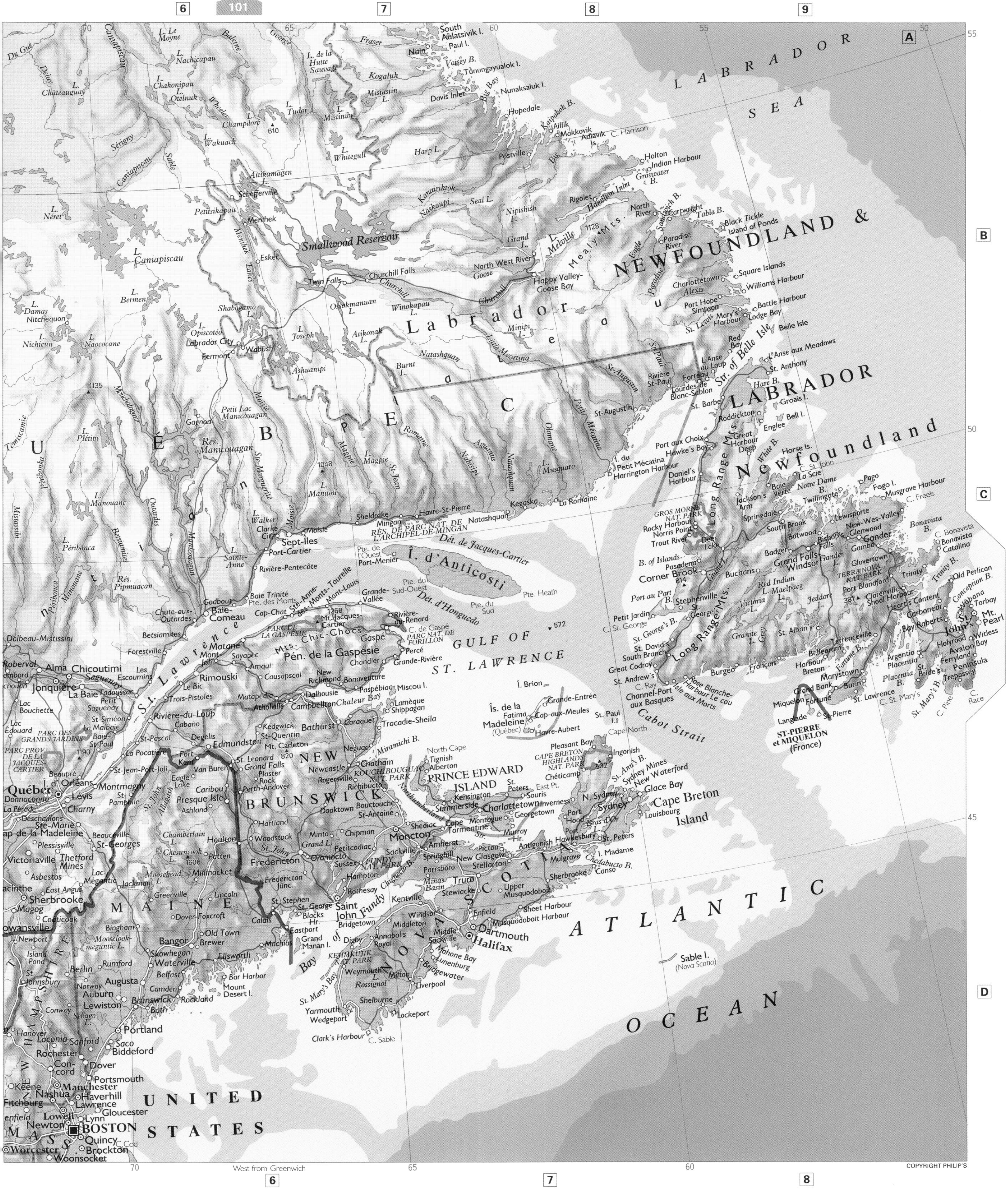

LABRADOR SEA

NEWFOUNDLAND & LABRADOR

Labrador

QUÉBEC

Newfoundland

GULF OF ST. LAWRENCE

Î. d'Anticosti

Cabot Strait

ST-PIERRE et MIQUELON (France)

PRINCE EDWARD ISLAND

NEW BRUNSWICK

NOVA SCOTIA

Cape Breton Island

MAINE

NEW HAMPSHIRE

UNITED STATES

MASS.

ATLANTIC OCEAN

Sable I. (Nova Scotia)

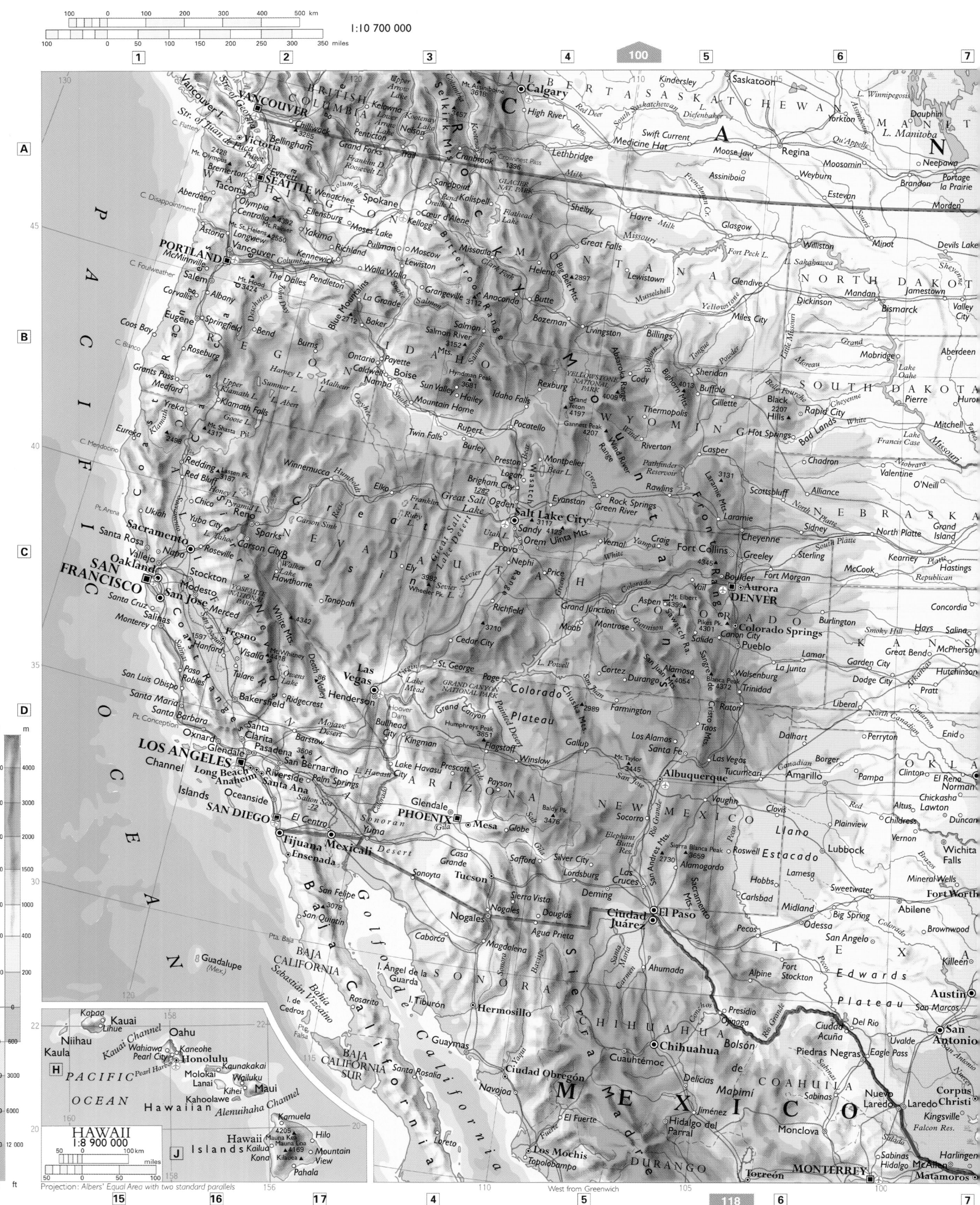

1:10 700 000

Projection: Albers' Equal Area with two standard parallels

West from Greenwich

HAWAII
1:8 900 000

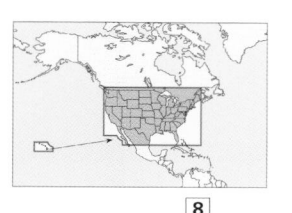

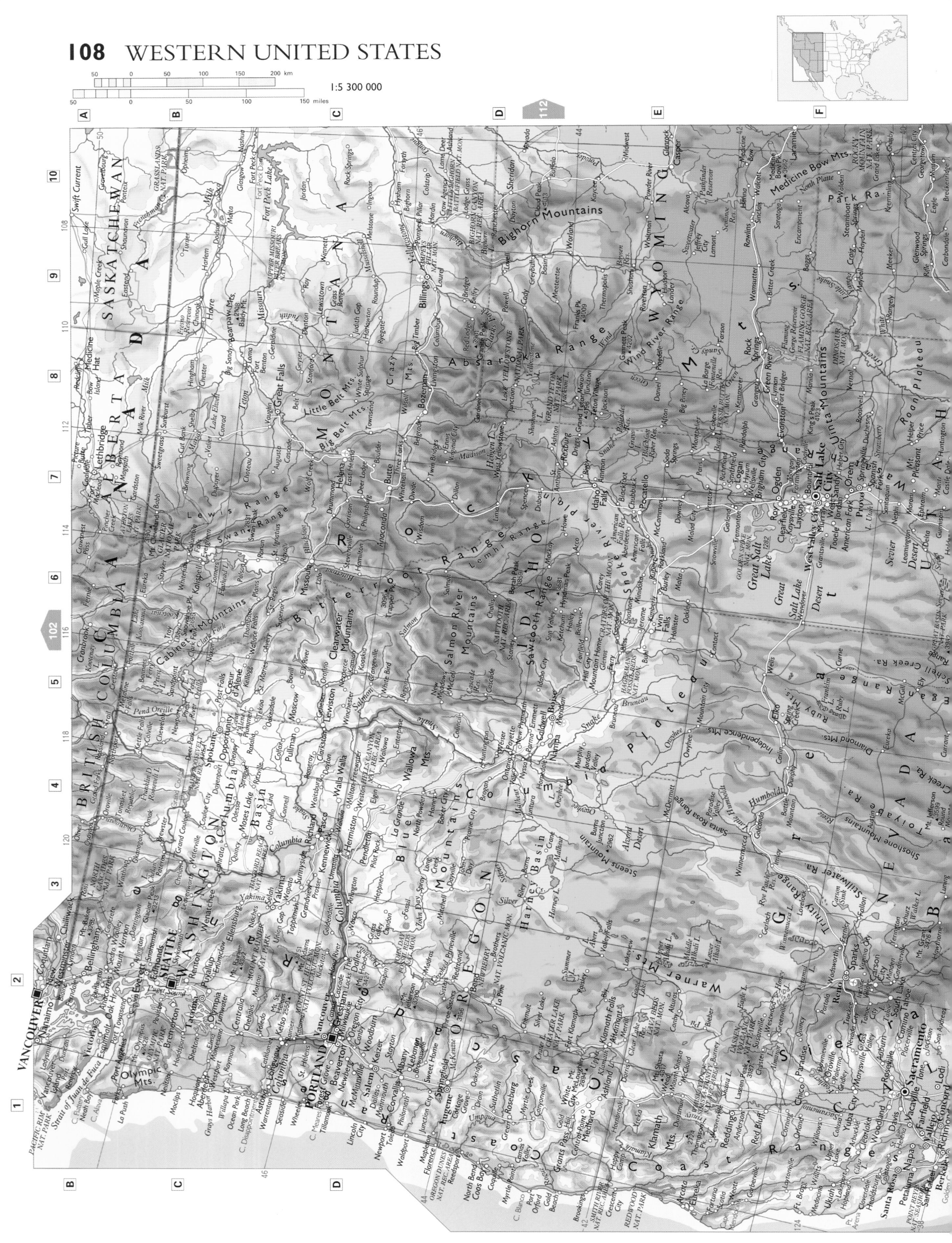

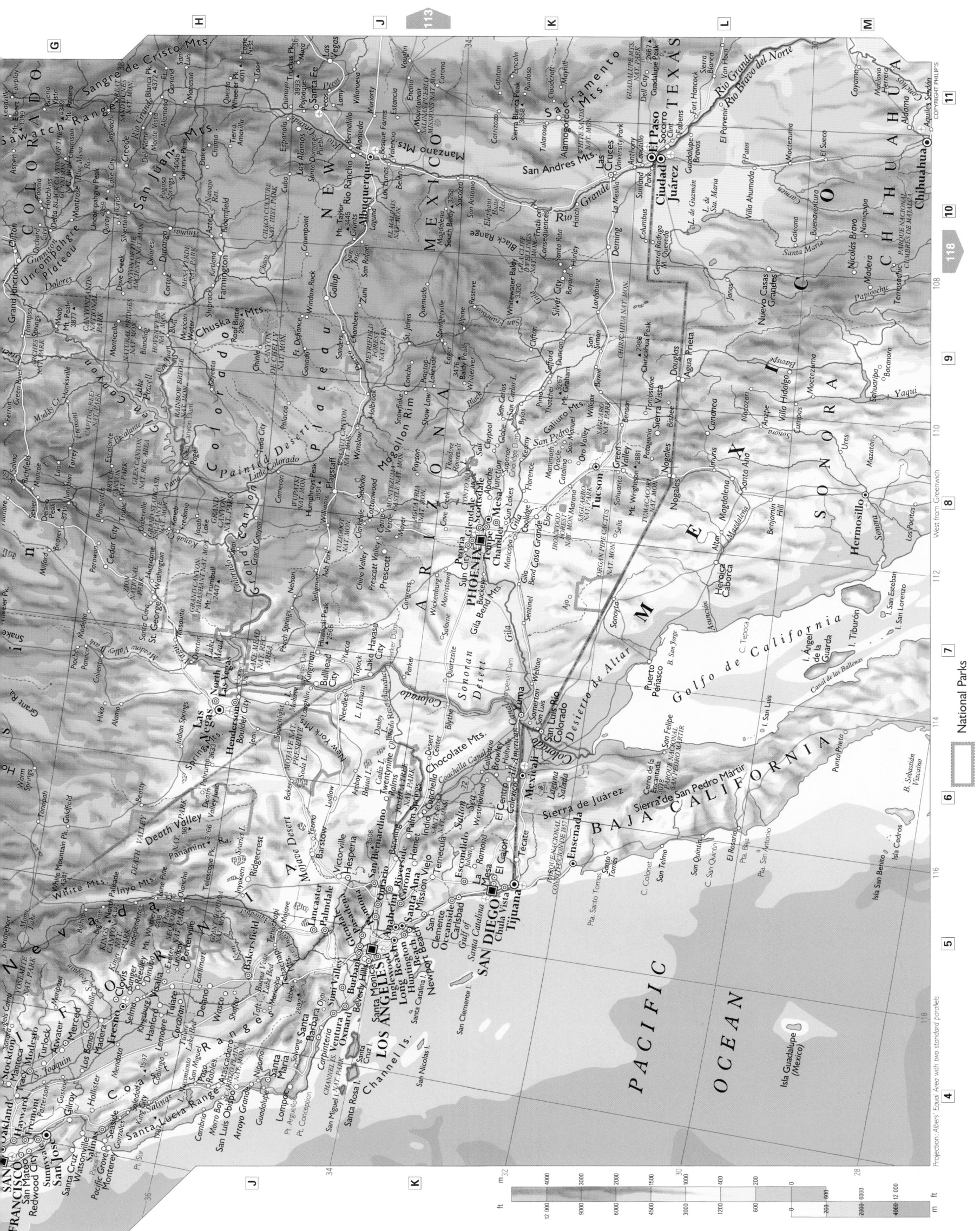

National Parks

COPYRIGHT PHILIP'S

Projection: Albers' Equal Area with two standard parallels

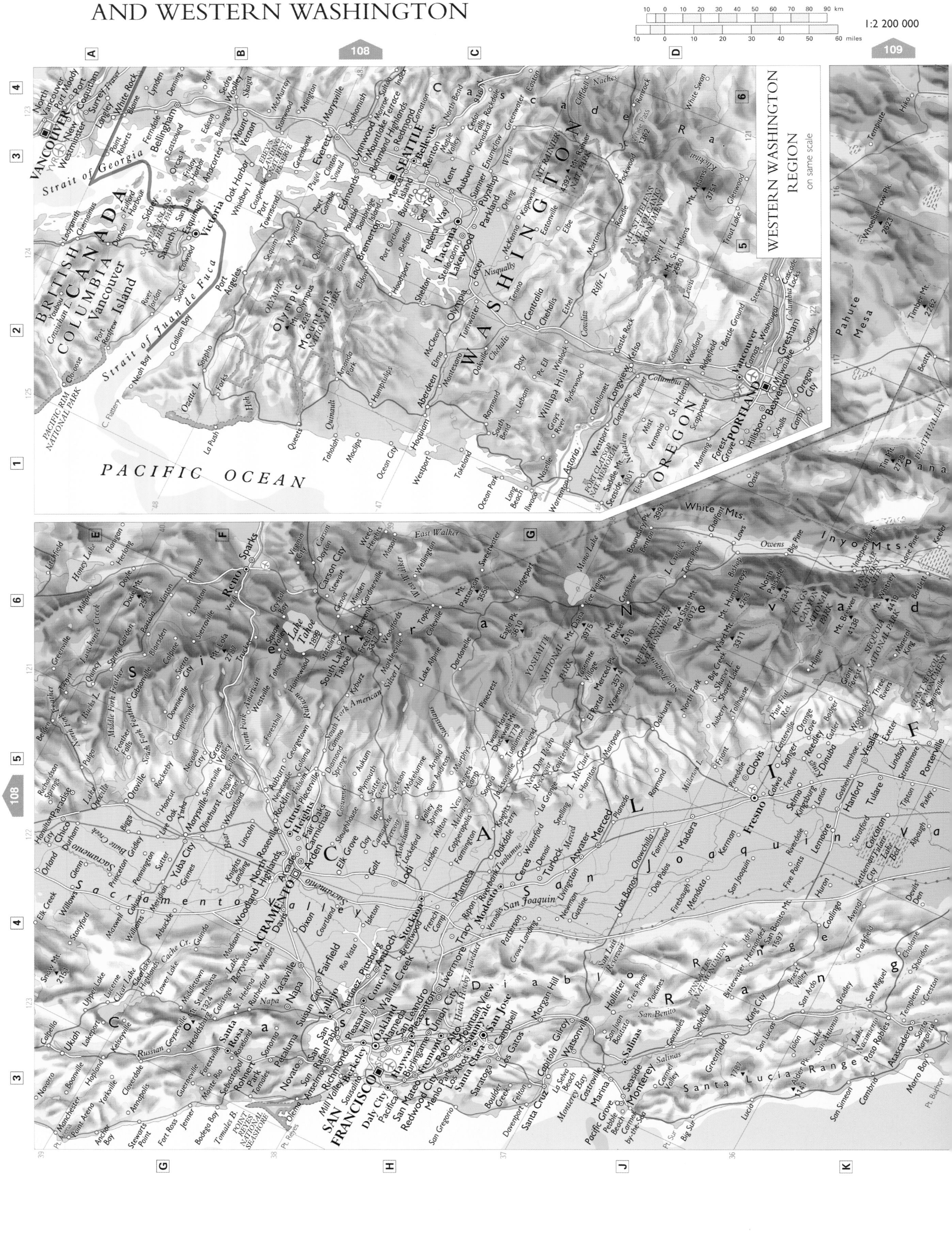

10 0 10 20 30 40 50 60 70 80 90 km
10 0 10 20 30 40 50 60 miles

1:2 200 000

WESTERN WASHINGTON
REGION
on same scale

PACIFIC OCEAN

BRITISH COLUMBIA

Vancouver Island

Strait of Georgia

Strait of Juan de Fuca

OLYMPIC Mountains NATIONAL PARK
Mt Olympus 2428

WASHINGTON

VANCOUVER
New Westminster
Victoria
Bellingham
Everett
SEATTLE
Bellevue
Bremerton
Tacoma
Lakewood
Olympia
Centralia
Chehalis
Aberdeen
Hoquiam

MT. RAINIER NAT. PARK
4392 Mt Rainier

MT ST. HELENS NAT. VOLCANIC MONUMENT
Mt St. Helens 2550

OREGON
PORTLAND
Beaverton
Hillsboro
Oregon City
Vancouver
Gresham
Milwaukie

Columbia
Longview
Kelso
Astoria

White Mts.

Inyo Mts.
Owens
Big Pine
Bishop

N e v a d a

Pahute Mesa

DEATH VALLEY
Panamint

SIERRA NEVADA

Reno
Sparks
Carson City
Lake Tahoe 1899
South Lake Tahoe

Mono Lake

YOSEMITE NATIONAL PARK

KINGS CANYON NATIONAL PARK
Mt Whitney 4418

SEQUOIA NATIONAL PARK

C A L I F O R N I A

Sacramento Valley

SACRAMENTO
Citrus Heights
Carmichael
Arden-Arcade
Roseville
North Highlands
Woodland
Davis
Chico
Oroville
Yuba City
Marysville
Lodi
Stockton
Elk Grove
Galt

Modesto
Turlock
Merced
San Joaquin

Fresno
Clovis
Madera
Chowchilla
Visalia
Tulare
Hanford
Porterville
Lindsay
Exeter
Reedley
Dinuba
Selma
Sanger

San Joaquin Valley

SAN FRANCISCO
Oakland
Berkeley
San Jose
Santa Clara
Sunnyvale
Mountain View
Palo Alto
Redwood City
San Mateo
Daly City
Fremont
Hayward
San Leandro
Alameda
Pleasanton
Livermore
Walnut Creek
Concord
Antioch
Pittsburg
Martinez
Vallejo
Fairfield
Vacaville
Napa
Santa Rosa
Petaluma
San Rafael
Novato

Diablo Range

Santa Cruz
Watsonville
Salinas
Monterey
Pacific Grove
Carmel-by-the-Sea
Marina
Seaside
Hollister
Gilroy
Morgan Hill
Los Gatos
Saratoga
Campbell
Capitola

Santa Lucia Range
Paso Robles
Atascadero
San Luis Reservoir
Big Sur
Point Sur

1:5 300 000

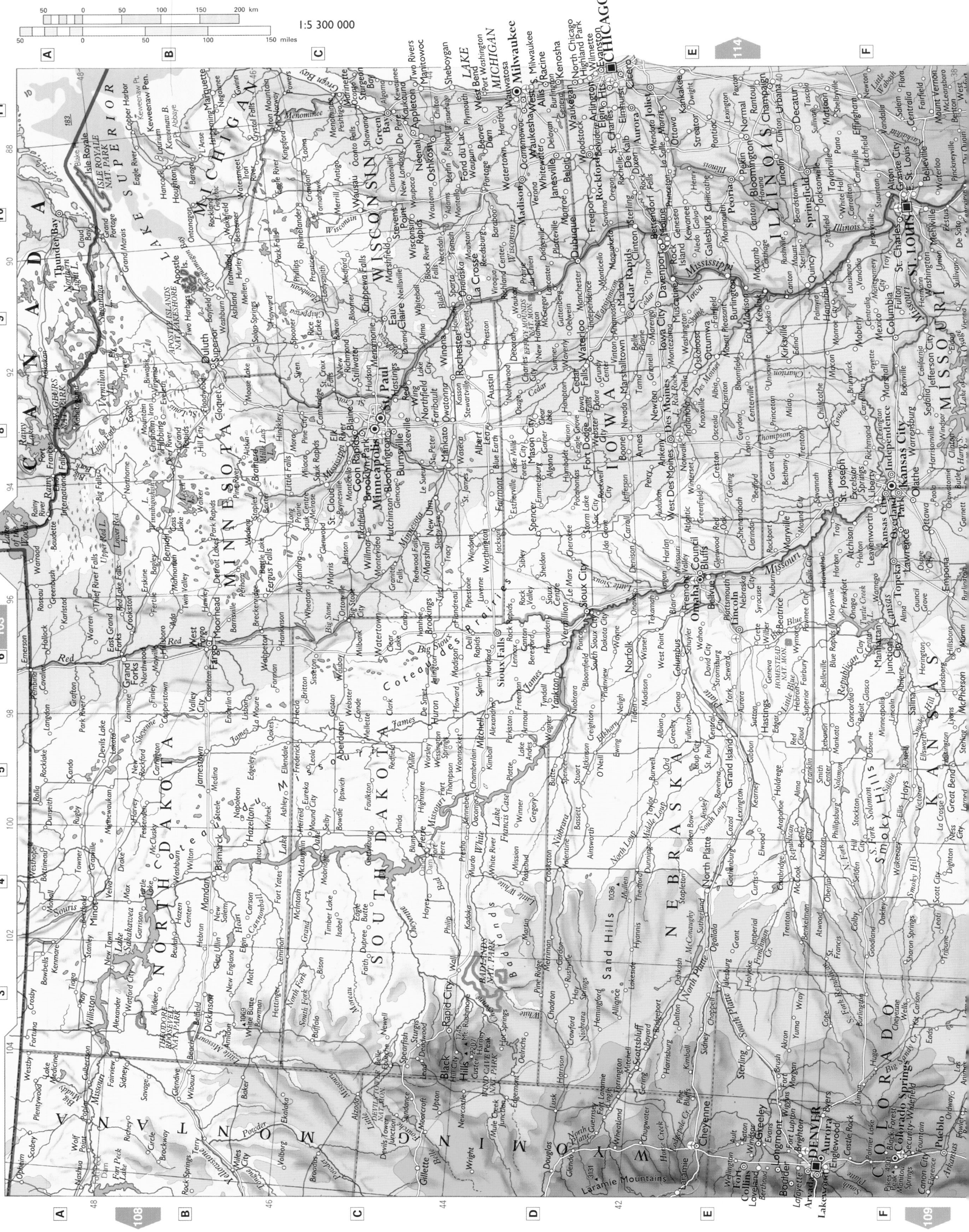

50 0 50 100 150 200 km
50 0 50 100 150 miles

CANADA

LAKE SUPERIOR

MICHIGAN

WISCONSIN

MINNESOTA

NORTH DAKOTA

SOUTH DAKOTA

NEBRASKA

IOWA

ILLINOIS

MISSOURI

KANSAS

COLORADO

WYOMING

MONTANA

LAKE MICHIGAN

CHICAGO

Milwaukee

Minneapolis

St. Paul

Duluth

Bismarck

Pierre

Des Moines

Omaha

Lincoln

Topeka

Kansas City

St. Louis

Denver

Colorado Springs

Pueblo

Sioux Falls

Fargo

Grand Forks

Rapid City

ISLE ROYALE NAT. PARK

APOSTLE ISLANDS NAT LAKESHORE

THEODORE ROOSEVELT NAT. PARK

BADLANDS NAT. PARK

WIND CAVE NAT PARK

VOYAGEURS NAT PARK

LAKE OF THE WOODS

Coteau des Prairies

Sand Hills

Black Hills

Smoky Hills

Missouri

Mississippi

Platte

James

Red

Souris

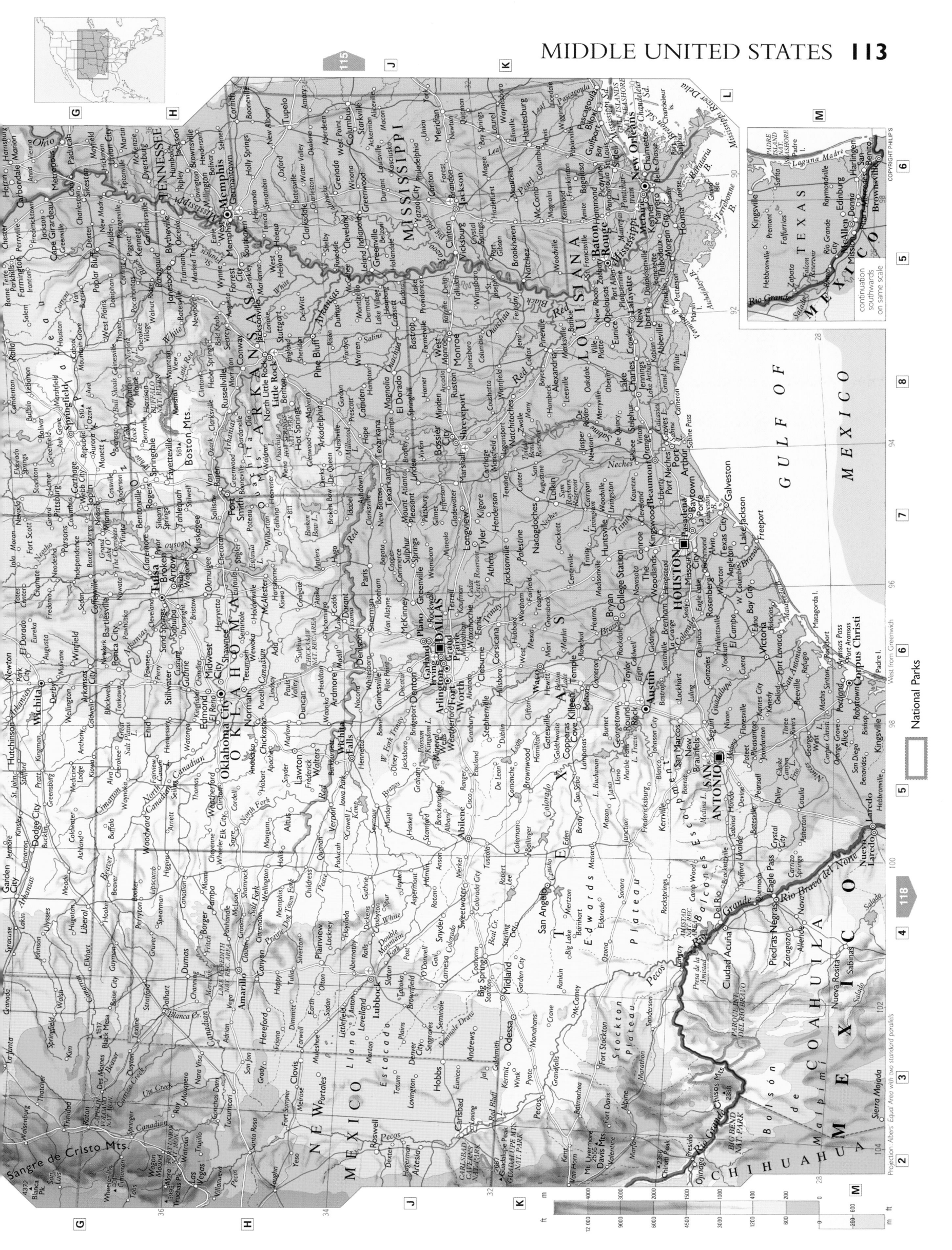

National Parks

Projection: Albers' Equal Area with two standard parallels

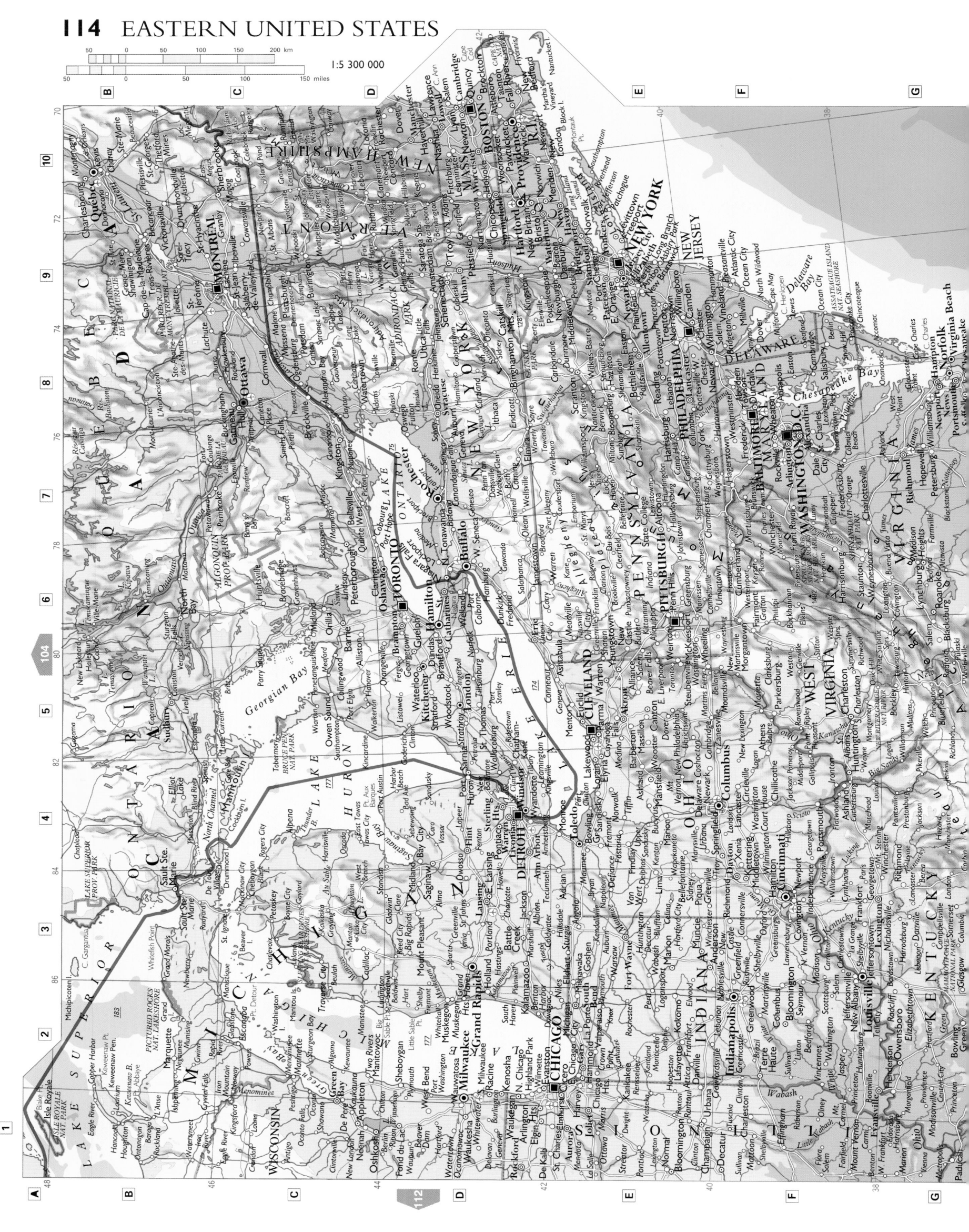

1:5 300 000

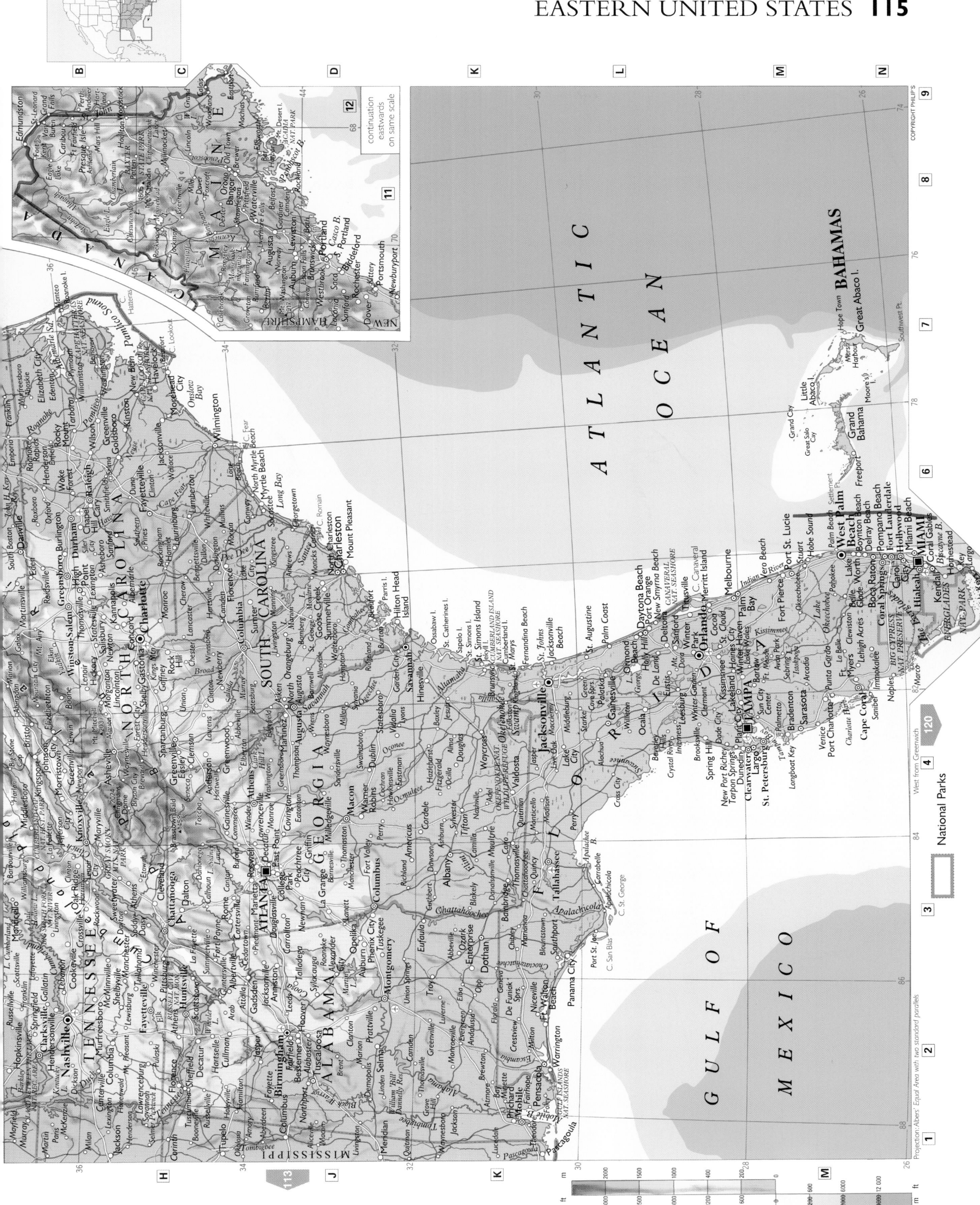

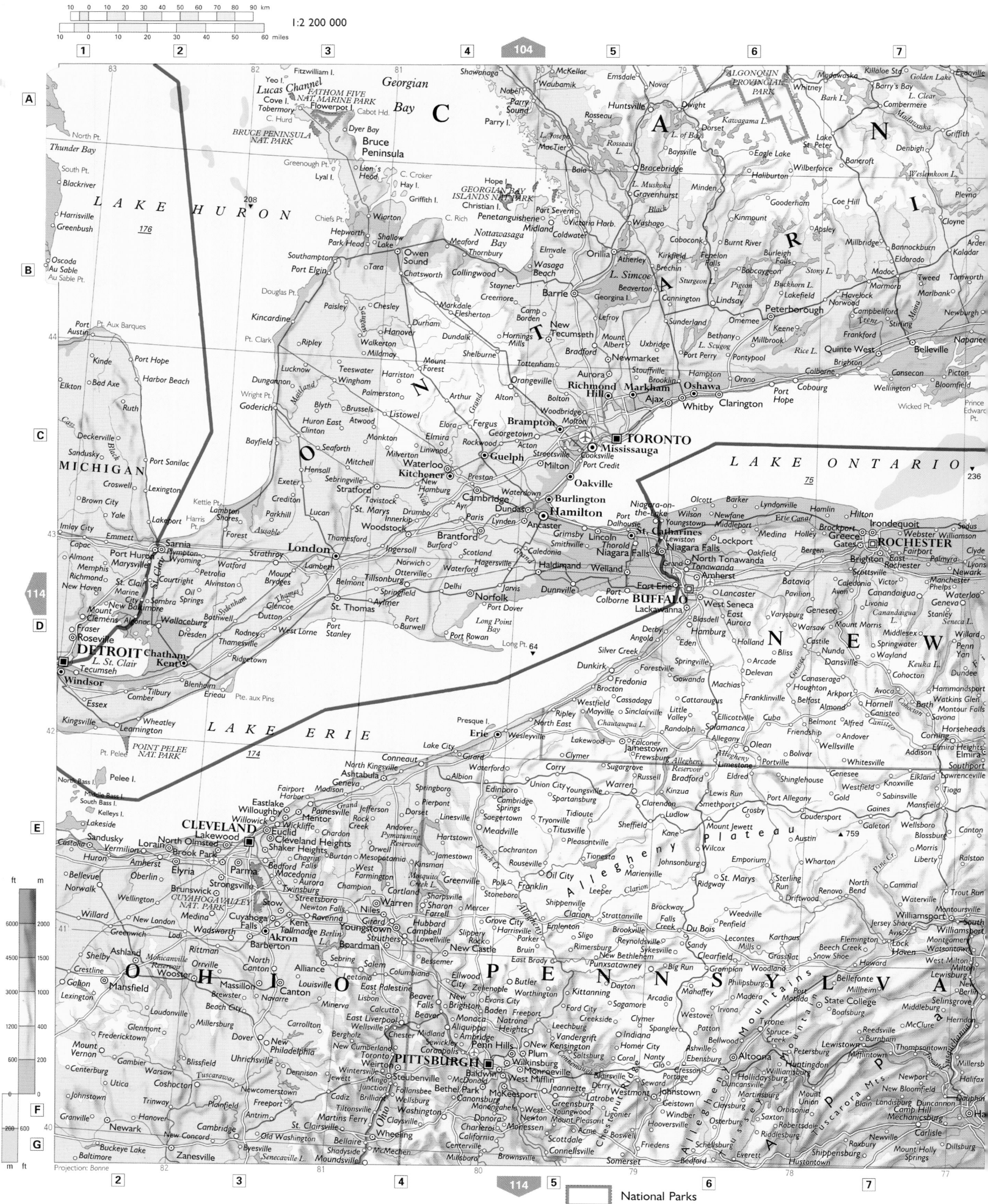

1:2 200 000

National Parks

Projection: Bonne

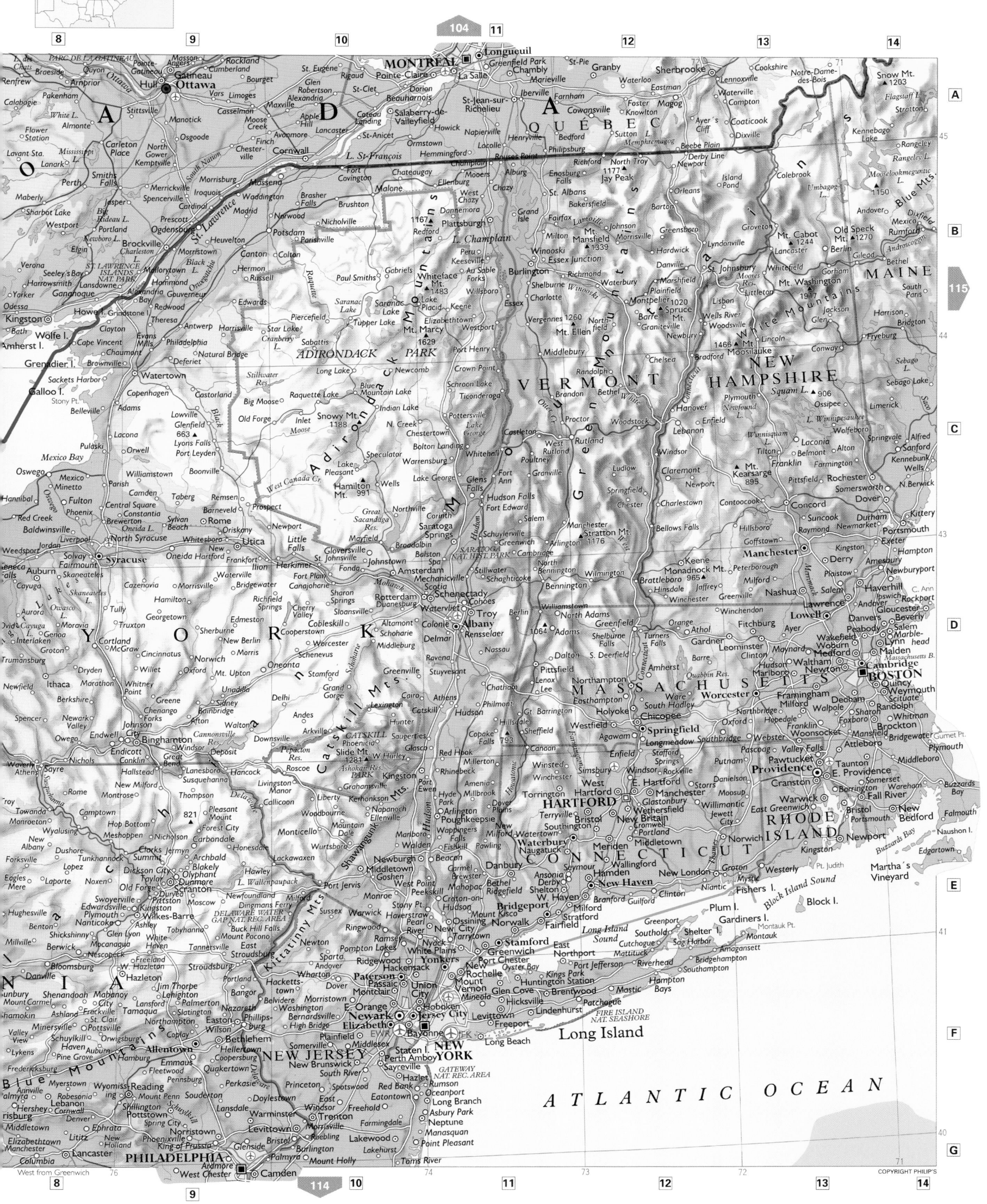

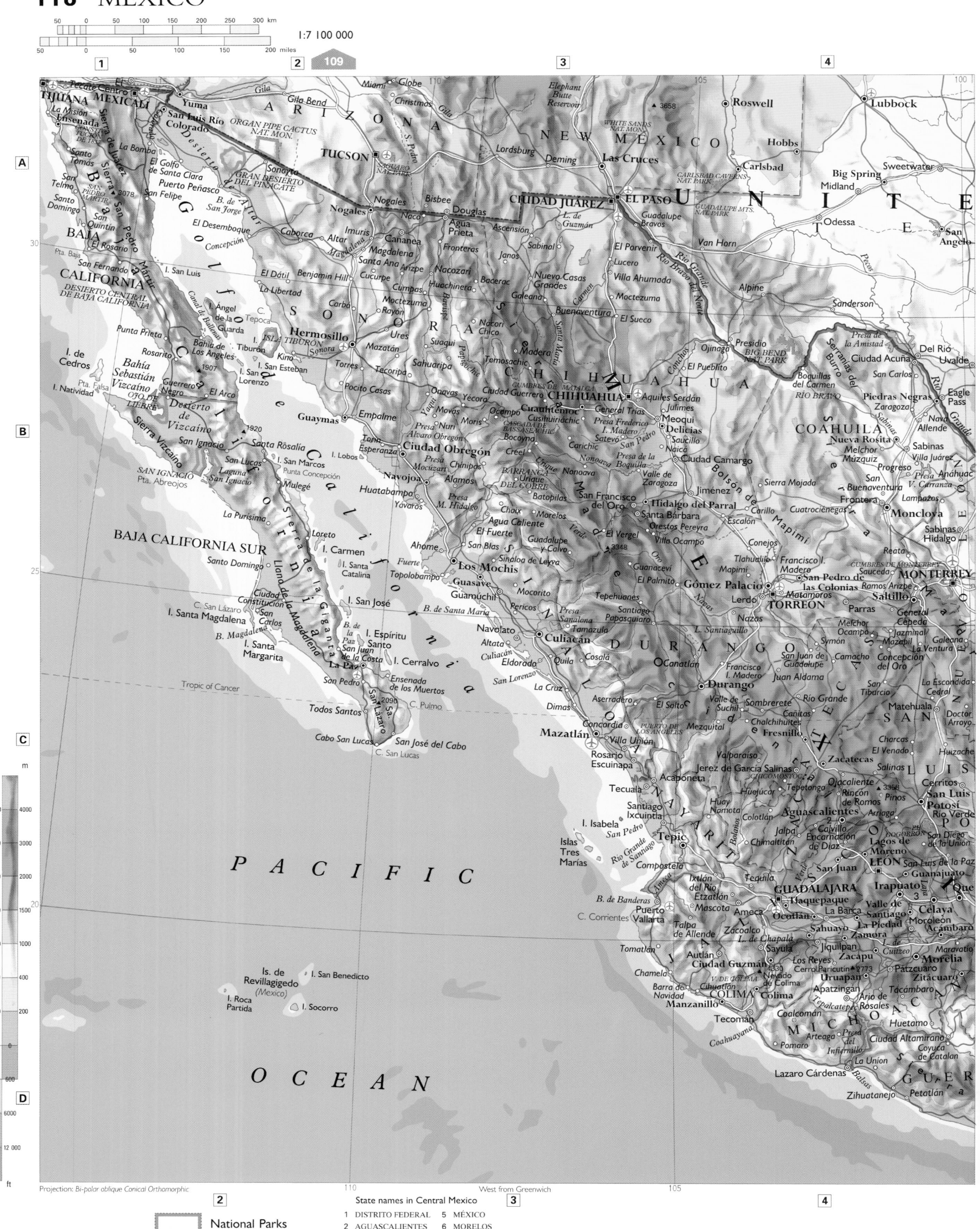

50   0   50   100   150   200   250   300 km
1:7 100 000

50   0   50   100   150
200 miles

109

1   2   3   4

Scale bar (elevation)

ft	m
12 000	4000
9000	3000
6000	2000
4500	1500
3000	1000
1200	400
600	200
	0
200	600
2000	6000
4000	12 000
m	ft

Projection: Bi-polar oblique Conical Orthomorphic

West from Greenwich

National Parks

State names in Central Mexico

1 DISTRITO FEDERAL   5 MÉXICO
2 AGUASCALIENTES   6 MORELOS
3 GUANAJUATO   7 QUERÉTARO
4 HIDALGO   8 TLAXCALA

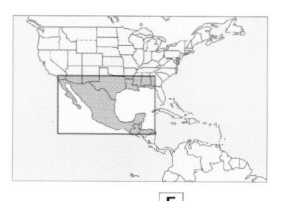

1:7 100 000

50 0 50 100 150 200 250 300 km
50 0 50 100 150 200 miles

JAMAICA
1:2 700 000

10 0 10 20 30 40 50 km
10 0 10 20 30 miles

a

CARIBBEAN SEA

Montego Bay • Falmouth • Runaway Bay • St. Ann's Bay
Lucea • Wakefield • Ocho Rios • Galina Point • Port Maria
Negril • Cambridge • The Cockpit Country • Mount Denham 985▲ • Dry Harbour Mountains • Moneague • Annotto Bay
South Negril Pt. • Maggotty • Don Figuero Mts. • Linstead • The Blue Mountains • John Crow • Port Antonio
Savanna-la-Mar • Black River • Santa Cruz Mts. • Mandeville • Spanish Town • Blue Mountain Peak 2256▲ • Mts.
Great Pedro Bluff • May Pen • Portmore • KINGSTON • Morant Point
Alligator Pond • Portland Bight • Port Morant
Portland Point • Morant Bay

GULF OF MEXICO

Canal de Yucatán

A

I. Desterrada
I. Pérez (Mexico)
C. Catoche
Punta Yalkubul
I. San Antonio
Dzilam de Bravo • Rio Lagartos • El Cuyo
Progreso • Motul • Temax • Tizimín • Cancún
Mérida • Izamal • Valladolid • Puerto Morelos
Maxcanú • Sotuta • CHICHEN ITZA • Isla Cozumel
Calkiní • Ticul • Peto • Cozumel
Campeche • Tekax • Bolonchentical • Vigia Chico
Champotón • Hopelchen • Felipe Carrillo Puerto • B. de la Ascensión
Chenkán • San José Carpizo • SIAN KA'AN
Ciudad del Carmen • Pedro Antonio Santos • B. del Espíritu Santo
MEXICO • QUINTANA ROO • Bacalar
PANTANOS DE CENTLA • CAMPECHE • Chetumal • B. de Chetumal
Palizada • CALAKMUL • Corozal • Banco Chinchorro
Balcanán • MIRADOR-RIO AZUL • Orange Walk
Tenosique • LAGUNA DEL TIGRE • Ambergris Cay
Ocosingo • Uaxactún • San Pedro
La Independencia • L. Petén Itzá • TIKAL • Belize City • Turneffe Is.
Comitán • SIERRA DE LACANDON • Flores • Belmopan • Middlesex
MONTES AZULES • La Libertad • Benque Viejo • BELIZE
Sebol • GHIQUIBUL • Dangriga
LAGUNAS DE MONTEBELLO • Maya Mts.
San Luis • Golfo de Honduras
GUATEMALA • Coban • San Antonio • Monkey River
Cuilco 3993▲ • SIERRA DE LOS CUCHUMATANES • L. de Izabal • Livingston • Is. de la Bahía
San Marcos • Huehuetenango • Sierra de las Minas • Puerto Barrios • Roatán
Totonicapán • Sololá • Zacapa • San Pedro Sula • La Ceiba • Trujillo • Camarón
Ayutla • ATITLAN • ANTIGUA • Chiquimula • Santa Rosa de Copán • El Progreso • Olanchito • Brus Laguna
Retalhuleu • Mazatenango • GUATEMALA • Esquipulas • Comayagua • Juticalpa • RIO PLATANO • Laguna Caratasca
Coatepeque • Amatitlán • HONDURAS • Yoro • Catacamas • C. Falso
Escuintla • La Esperanza • La Paz • Tegucigalpa • Mosquitia
Santa Ana • San José • La Paz • Danlí • C. Gracias a Dios
Ahuachapán • Sonsonate • Cojutepeque • Zacatecoluca • Nacaome • Choluteca • Puerto Cabo Gracias á Dios
Acajutla • Nueva San Salvador • San Miguel • La Unión • Jinotega • Kisalaya
SAN SALVADOR • Usulután • G. de Fonseca • Estelí • Cord. Isabelia • Cayos Miskitos (Nicaragua)
EL SALVADOR • Chinandega • Matagalpa • Siuna • Puerto Cabezas
G. de Morazán • Corinto • León • Muy Muy • SASLAYA
NICARAGUA • Boaco • Rio Grande
MANAGUA • Masaya • Juigalpa • Prinzapolca
Diriamba • Granada • Santo Domingo • I. de Providencia (Colombia)
Jinotepe • Rivas • Lago de Nicaragua • Bluefields • Cayos Roncador (Colombia)
San Juan del Sur • I. de Ometepe • El Bluff • I. de San Andrés (Colombia)
B. de Salinas • San Carlos • Is. del Maiz • Cayos de Albuquerque (Colombia)
Santa Elena • Los Chiles • San Juan del Norte
Liberia • Cord. de Guanacaste • San Juan • Pta. Mico
Santa Cruz • Cord. Central • Guápiles • Siquirres
Carmona • Alajuela • SAN JOSÉ • Limón
Puntarenas • Cartago • Bribri • Bocas del Toro
COSTA RICA • Pandora • Panama Canal • Portobelo
Puerto Quepos • Chirripó • Buenos Aires • AMISTAD • Colón • Serrania de San Blas
B. de Coronado • Puerto Cortés • Chiriquí • G. de los Mosquitos • PANAMÁ • Golfo del Darién
Corcovado • San Vito • Volcán Baru • Boquete • Pen. de Azuero • Arch. de las Perlas
Pen. de Osa • Golfito • Concepción • David • Santiago • Chitré • DARIÉN
Puerto Armuelles • Remedios • Aguadulce • Las Tablas • El Real
Pta. Burica • Sona • Pocri • Yaviza
G. de Chiriquí • Pen. de Azuero • Garachine
I. de Coiba • I. de Cebaco • GOIBA • Punta Mariato • La Palma
I. Jicarón • Tonosí • CERRO HOYA

USA
West Palm Beach • West End
Fort Myers • Naples • Boca Raton • Freeport • Grand Bahama • Hope Town
The Everglades • Fort Lauderdale • Northwest Providence Channel • Great Abaco I.
C. Romano • Hialeah • Bimini Is. • Berry Is. • Little Abaco I.
MIAMI • Nicolls Town • Nassau • Eleuthera • Dunmore Town
EVERGLADES NAT. PARK • New Providence • Governor's Harbour
Florida Bay • C. Sable • Andros Town • Portsmouth (Rock Sound)
Dry Tortugas (U.S.A.) • Great Guana Cay • Great Exuma I.
Key West • Adelaide • George Town
LA HABANA (Havana) • Guanabacoa • Cay Sal Bank • Andros Island
Mariano • Santa Cruz del Norte • Canal Nicholas • Straits of Florida
Guanajay • Matanzas • Great Bahama Bank • BAH
Bahía Honda • Cárdenas • Jumentos Cays
La Esperanza • San Antonio Batabanó • Jovellanos • Colón • Sagua la Grande • Caibarién • Duncan Town
Pinar del Río • de los Baños • Jaguey Grande • Santa Clara • Morón • Cayo Romano
Guane • San Luis • Cienfuegos • Placetas • Ciego de Ávila • Nuevitas
Corrientes • La Fé • I. de la Juventud • Trinidad • Júcaro • Sancti Spíritus • Arch. de Camagüey • Puerto Manotí
Arch. de los Canarreos • Tunas de Zaza • Camagüey • Puerto Padre
Santa Cruz del Sur • Victoria de las Tunas • Gibara • HOLGUÍN
Arch. de Jardines de la Reina • Golfo de Guacanayabo • Bayamo • Palma Soriano
CUBA • Manzanillo • Sierra Maestra 1974▲
Cayman Islands (U.K.) • Cayman Brac • Little Cayman • C. Cruz • SANTIAGO DE CUBA
George Town • Grand Cayman • 7680▼
Is. Santanilla (Swan Islands) (Honduras) • GREATER
Bajo Nuevo (Colombia) • CARIB
Montego Bay • St. Ann's Bay
Lucea • Falmouth • Port Maria • Annotto Bay
Negril • Cambridge • JAMAICA • Port Antonio
South Negril Pt. • Savanna-la-Mar • Black River • Mandeville • Spanish Town • KINGSTON • Port Morant
May Pen • Morant Pt.
Pedro Cays (Jamaica)
CARTAGE

Inset b — GUADELOUPE
Pte. de la Grande Vigie
Port-Louis • Grande-Terre
Petit-Canal
Ste-Rose • Moule
Pointe-Noire • Pointe-à-Pitre • La Désirade
Basse-Terre • Gosier • Ste-Anne • Pointe des Châteaux
Bouillante • GUADELOUPE (Fr.) • Îles de la Petite Terre
Capesterre-Belle-Eau • Marie-Galante
SOUFRIÈRE 1467▲ • St-Louis • 204▲
Basse-Terre • Trois-Rivières • Grand-Bourg • Capesterre
Îles des Saintes • Pte. des Bases

b

Inset c — MARTINIQUE
Cap St-Martin • Basse-Pointe
Le Prêcheur • Ste-Marie • Presqu'île de la Caravelle
Montagne Pelée 1463▲ • La Trinité
St-Pierre • Le Robert
Schoelcher • St-Joseph • Le François
Fort-de-France • Le Lamentin
MARTINIQUE (Fr.) • Rivière-Salée • Le St-Esprit
Rivière-Pilote • Le Marin
Pte. d'Enfer

c

GUADELOUPE AND MARTINIQUE
1:1 800 000

10 0 10 20 30 40 50 60 km
10 0 10 20 30 40 miles

PACIFIC OCEAN

PUERTO RICO d
1:2 700 000
10   0   10   20   30 miles
10   0   10   20   30   40   50 km

ATLANTIC OCEAN

PUERTO RICO (U.S.A.)

Pta. Aguijereada
Isabela
Aguadilla
Arecibo
Barceloneta
Manati
Vega Baja
SAN JUAN
Mayagüez
San Sebastian
Utuado
Adjuntas
Cordillera Central
Cerro de Punta 1338
Uroyan Mts.
Yauco
San German
Guanica
Ponce
Guayama
Pta. Aguila
Caguas
Cayey
Coamp
Humacoa
Yabucoa
Naguabo
Fajardo
Pta. Puerca
Culebra
Dewey
Vieques
Esperanza
Rio Grande
Carolina
Sierra de Liquillo
I. Caja de Muertos

VIRGIN ISLANDS e
1:1 800 000
10   0   10   20   30 km
10   0   10   20 miles

Rufling Pt.
The Settlement
Anegada
East Pt.
Virgin Islands (U.K.)
Jost Van Dyke I.
Great Camanoe
Guana I.
Tortola
Road Town
Beef I.
Spanish Town
Virgin Gorda
Virgin Is. (U.S.A.)
Hans Lollik I.
Cruz Bay
Peter I.
VIRGIN IS.
Charlotte Amalie
St. Thomas I.
St. John I.

ST. LUCIA f
1:890 000
5   0   10 km
5   0   10 miles

Cap Point
Pte. Hardy
Gros Islet
Esperance Bay
Castries
Marquis
Babonneau
L'Anse la Raye
Canaries
Millet
Dennery
Soufrière
Soufrière Bay
Mt. Gimie 750 1950
Petit Piton 796
Trou Gras Pt.
Micoud
Vierge Pt.
Gros Piton Pt.
Gros Piton
Choiseul
ST. LUCIA
Laborie
Vieux Fort
C. Moule à Chique

BARBADOS g
1:890 000
5   0   10 km
5   0   10 miles

North Point
Crabhill
Spring Hall
Fustic
Boscobelle
Portland
245 Belleplaine
Speightstown
Westmoreland
Bathsheba
BARBADOS
Alleynes Bay
340 Mt. Hillaby
Hillcrest
Holetown
Martin's Bay
Massiah Street
Black Rock
Jackson
Bridgefield
Ellerton
Six Cross Roads
Ragged Pt.
Edey
Bridgetown
Ivy
Oistins
The Crane
Carlisle Bay
Worthing
Oistins Bay
St. Martins
BGI Chancery Lane
South Point

ATLANTIC OCEAN

AMAS

ATLANTIC OCEAN

Arthur's Town
The Bight
Cat I.
San Salvador I.
Conception I.
Rum Cay
Long I.
Tropic of Cancer
Clarence Town
Samana Cay
Sandy Cay
Cay Verde
Crooked I.
Albert Town
Snug Corner
Acklins I.
Plana Cays
Mira por vos Cay
Mayaguana I.
Cay Santo Domingo
Hogsty Reef
Little Inagua I.
Turks & Caicos (U.K.)
Caicos Is.
Cockburn Town
Turks Is.
Banes
Antilla
Lake Rose
Inagua
Matthew Town
Great Inagua I.
Mayari
Moa
Baracoa
Guantanamo
GUANTANAMO BAY (U.S.A.)
Pta. de Maisi
Maisi
Î. de la Tortue
Monte Cristi
LA ISABELA
Santiago de los Cabelleros
Paso de los Vientos (Windward Passage)
Cap-Haïtien
Puerto Plata
San Francisco de Macorís
Milwaukee Deep 9200
Puerto Rico Trench
Jean Rabel
Port-de-Paix
Fort Liberté
La Vega
Nagua
Samana
Cap-à-Foux
G. de la Gonâve
Gonaïves
Hinche
Central
Cord
3175
Pico Duarte
FUITISES
Sanchez
Sabana de la Mar
C. Engaño
Bayamón
SAN JUAN
Anegada
Sombrero (U.K.)
Jérémie
Î. de la Gonâve
St-Marc
ARMANDO BERMUDEZ
Hato Mayor
Arecibo
Carolina
Virgin Gorda
Tortola
Road Town
Anguilla (U.K.)
HAITI
PORT-AU-PRINCE
DOMINICAN REP.
San Pedro de Macorís
Higuey
La Romana
Aguadilla
1338
Fajardo
Virgin Is. (U.K.)
Charlotte Amalie
St.-Martin (Fr.)
Navassa I. (U.S.A.)
Dame Marie
Massif de la Hotte
Petit Goâve
2280
SANTO DOMINGO
ESTE
B. de Yuma
Mayagüez
Ponce
Caguas
Guayama
Virgin Is. (U.S.A.)
St. Thomas
Anegada Passage
St. Maarten (Neth.)
St.-Barthélemy (Fr.)
Les Cayes
Aquin
Jacmel
SIERRA DE BAHORUCO
Aroa Ban
San Cristóbal
I. Saona
Isla Mona
Christiansted
Saba (Neth.)
Barbuda
Pointe-à-Gravois
à Vache
Barahona
Compostela
L. Enriquillo
I. Beata
C. Beata
Mona Passage
PUERTO RICO (U.S.A.)
Frederiksted
St. Croix (U.S.A.)
St. Eustatius (Neth.)
ST. KITTS & NEVIS
Basseterre
Nevis
ANTIGUA & BARBUDA
St. John's
Antigua
Redonda
Montserrat (U.K.)
Hispaniola
Antilles
Pedernales

Antilles

BEAN SEA

I. de Aves (Venezuela)

Ste-Rose
Moule
La Désirade
GUADELOUPE (Fr.)
1467
Pointe-à-Pitre
Basse-Terre
Marie-Galante (Fr.)
Grand-Bourg
I. des Saintes (Fr.)
Dominica Passage
Portsmouth
144?
DOMINICA
Roseau
MORNE TROIS PITONS
Martinique Passage
Mt. Pelée 1397
Ste-Marie
Fort-de-France
Le François
Rivière-Pilote
MARTINIQUE (Fr.)
St. Lucia Channel
Castries
Soufrière
ST. LUCIA
St. Vincent Passage
Soufrière 1234
St. Vincent
Speightstown
Kingstown
Bridgetown
BARBADOS
Hillsborough
ST. VINCENT & THE GRENADINES
St. George's
GRENADA

Leeward Islands
Lesser Antilles
Windward Islands

Lesser Antilles

Aruba (Neth.)
Oranjestad
Curaçao
Bonaire
I. Blanquilla (Ven.)
Tobago
MACURIA
C. San Román
Willemstad
NETH. ANTILLES
Is. Las Aves (Ven.)
ARC. LOS ROQUES
I. Orchila (Ven.)
Is. Los Hermanos (Ven.)
Scarborough
Port of Spain
Galera
Pta. Gallinas
Pen. de la Guajira
Pta. Espada
Punto Fijo
Is. Los Roques (Ven.)
I. La Tortuga (Ven.)
NUEVA ESPARTA
I. de Margarita
Is. Los Testigos (Ven.)
Trinidad
Arima
Rio Claro
COLOMBIA
Santa Marta
TAYRONA
Ríohacha
Uribia
Golfo de Venezuela
Punta Cardón
MEDANOS DE CORO
La Vela de Coro
CUEVA DEL GUACHARO
CERRO EL COPEY
La Asunción
Porlamar
LAGUNA LA RESTINGA
Pen. de Paria
Carupano
Río Caribe
Güira
San Fernando
TRINIDAD & TOBAGO
BARRANQUILLA
Ciénaga
SIERRA NEVADA DE STA. MARTA
5800
San Rafael
Altagracia
FALCÓN
Tucacas
Puerto Cabello
HENRI PITTIER
Maiquetia
La Guaira
VARGAS
CARACAS
C. Codera
Higuerote
Puerto La Cruz
Cumana
MOCHIMA
G. de Paria
TURIMIQUIRE
SUCRE
Caripito
Maturín
Soledad
Baranoa
Sabanalarga
Maracaibo
Cabimas
Ciudad Ojeda
LARA
Mene Grande
San Felipe
YARACUY
Valencia
CARABOBO
ARAGUA
Villa de Cura
MIRANDA
Los Teques
Ocumare del Tuy
Río Chico
Barcelona
Caicara
DELTA
MONAGAS
Tucupita
NA
Arjona
Calamar
MAGDALENA
Plato
Zambrano
César
Valledupar
Agustin Codazzi
Villa del Rosario
La Concepción
Machiques
Lago de Maracaibo
BARQUISIMETO
Yaritagua
Yaracuy de los Morros
San Carlos
COJEDES
San Juan de los Morros
El Sombrero
GUÁRICO
Valle de la Pascua
Pariaguan
Anaco
Cantaura
El Tigre
AMACURO
Sincelejo
Mompós
Magangué
Sincé
San Planeta
NDOBA
Ayapel
libano
Simiti
BOLÍVAR
ZULIA
PERIJA
CIÉNAGAS DEL CATATUMBO
Betijoque
TRUJILLO
Valera
PORTUGUESA
Acarigua
Guanare
El Baúl
Calabozo
Santa María de Ipire
Ciudad Guayana
Sierra Imataca
El Pao
El Carmen
San Marta
leju
Corozal
El Banco
CATATUMBO-BARI
San Carlos del Zulia
Encontrados
MÉRIDA
Cord. de Mérida
Ciudad Bolivia
BARINAS
Libertad
Barinas
Portuguesa
AGUARO-GUARIQUITO
ANZOÁTEGUI
Ciudad Bolívar
Upata
Guri
Arona
Majagual
El Barco
CESAR NORTE
DE
Ocaña
SIERRA NEVADA
San Carlos
Puerto de Nutrias
San Fernando de Apure
Apure
Los Barrancos
Guasipati
Tumeremo
San Planeta
Rica
DOBA
Caucasia
SANTANDER
Cúcuta
TÁCHIRA
San Cristóbal
Barbara
PARAMOS DE EL COJAL
Ciudad Bolivar
Bruzual
Achaguas
Arauca
Caicara
Mapire
Orinoco
Tigre
Embalse de Guri
C. Callao
VENEZUELA

West from Greenwich
COPYRIGHT PHILIP'S

ft
600   6000   12 000   18 000   24 000
m
200   2000   4000   6000   8000

☐ National Parks

4000   3000   2000   1500   1000   400   200   0
12 000   9000   6000   4500   3000   2000   1200   600

1:31 100 000

Projection: Lambert's Azimuthal Equal Area

COPYRIGHT PHILIP'S

1:31 100 000

COPYRIGHT PHILIP'S

■ LIMA Capital Cities

1:14 200 000

Projection: Sanson-Flamsteed's Sinusoidal

ATLANTIC OCEAN

TRINIDAD AND TOBAGO
1:2 200 000
10 0 10 20 30 40 50 km
10 0 10 20 30 miles

Tobago
Charlotteville   North Pt.
Castara   565▲ Ridge   Little Tobago
Plymouth   Roxborough
Buccoo Reef   Scarborough
Crown Pt.   Rocky Bay

VENEZUELA
Pen. de Paria
Macuro
Monos I.   Corozal Pt.
Güiria   Maraval
Dragon's Mouth
Golfo de Paria
Port of Spain   San Juan   Arima   Gugico
Chaguanas   Caroni   Talparo   Sangre Grande   Upper Manzanilla
Couva   Narva Swamp   Cocos Bay
Point Lisas
Otaheite Bay   Gasparillo   Rio Claro   Guataro Pt.
San Fernando   Pierreville
Brighton   La Brea   Princes Town   Mayaro Bay
Point Fortin   Penal   Basse Terre   Guayaguayare
Cedros Bay   Palo Seco   Siparia   Galeota Pt.
Bonasse   Pitch Lake   La Lune   Trinity Hills   304
Icacos Pt.   Erin Pt.   Moruga
Serpent's Mouth
VENEZUELA   Pta. Bombedor
West from Greenwich

La Vache Pt.   Chupara Pt.   Blanchisseuse   Sans Souci
Maracas Bay Village   Northern Range   Matelot   Toco
936   940▲Mt. Aripo   Salibea   Galera Pt.
Tunapuna Valencia   Redhead
Matura Bay

Trinidad
ATLANTIC OCEAN

Charlotteville

SURINAME   FRENCH GUIANA

town
Amsterdam
Nieuw Nickerie
Totness   Nieuw Amsterdam
Kwakoegron   Moengo
Albina   St-Laurent   Iracoubo   Sinnamary
Prof. Van Blommestein-meer   Kourou   Cayenne
Julianatop ▲1230   Kaw   C. Orange   Approuague
Tafelberg   St Georges
Oiapoque
Camopi

Serra Tumucumaque
Amapá
Amapá
Merirumá   Serra do Navio   Araguari
Macapá
Mazagão   I. Caviana
Afuá   I. Mexiana   C. Maguarinho   Equator
Chaves   Curuçá Salinópolis
Breves   Marajó   Salvaterra   Vigia   Bragança
I. Grande de Gurupá   Soure   Curuçá
Almeirim   Gurupá   BELÉM   Viseu
Pôrto de Moz   Castanhal   Viseu
Cametá   Abaetetuba   Turiaçu

Óbidos   Prainha   Breves   Curralinho   Gururupu
Faro   Monte Alegre   Baião   B. de São Marcos
Alenquer   Santarém   Altamira   São Luís   Barreirinhas
Belterra   Aveiro   Tucuruí   Rosário   Tutóia   Luís Correia
Itaituba   Brasília Legal   Pinheiro   Itapecuru-Mirim   Parnaíba   Camocim
Marabá   Bacabal   Caxias   Piripiri   Granja   Itapipoca   Caucaia   FORTALEZA
MARANHÃO   Codó   Campo Maior   Ipu   Quixadá   Sobral   Maranguape   Cascavel
Imperatriz   Teresina   CEARÁ   Baturité   Aracati
São João do Araguaia   Barra do Corda   Senador Pompeu   Russas   Mossoró
Carajás   Grajaú   Pôrto Franco   Amarante   Valença do Piauí   Iguatu   Caicó   RIO GRANDE DO NORTE   Areia Branca
Estreito   Colinas   Picos   Cajazeiras   Sousa   Patos   Currais Novos   Natal
Carolina   Loreto   Nova Iorque   Oeiras   Crato   Juazeiro do Norte   PARAÍBA   Canguaretama
Conceição do Araguaia   Araguaína   PIAUÍ   Paulistana   Salgueiro   Campina Grande   João Pessoa
Araguacema   Riachão   Uruçuí   Chapada do Araripe   Pesqueira   Caruaru   PERNAMBUCO   Olinda   RECIFE
Palmas   São João do Piauí   Jaboatão
TOCANTINS   Pedro Afonso   Serra Dois Irmãos   Petrolina   Garanhuns   Palmares   Vitória de Santo Antão
Santa Filomena   Caracol   Nova Casa Nova   Juàzeiro   Palmeira dos Índios   Cabo de Santo Agostinho

BRAZIL

TO GROSSO
Diamantino
Cuiabá   Mato Grosso
MATO GROSSO DO SUL

Planalto do Mato Grosso

Santo Antônio
Rondonópolis

Campo Grande

GOIÁS

Goiânia
Anápolis

BRASÍLIA
DIST. FED.

Formosa
Luziânia

BAHIA

Barreiras
Ibotirama   Itaberaba
Bom Jesus da Lapa   Serra do Sincorá
Feira de Santana
Cachoeira   Santo Amaro
Valença   SALVADOR
B. de Todos os Santos

Jequié
Itabuna   Ilhéus
Vitória da Conquista   Canavieiras
Ubaitaba
Belmonte
Pôrto Seguro

MINAS GERAIS

Uberlândia
BELO HORIZONTE

ESPÍRITO SANTO

Vitória
Vila Velha

São Paulo (Braz.)

Fernando de Noronha (Braz.)

Rocas

Maceió   ALAGOAS   SERGIPE   Aracaju
São Cristóvão   Estância

6059▾

Trindade (Braz.)

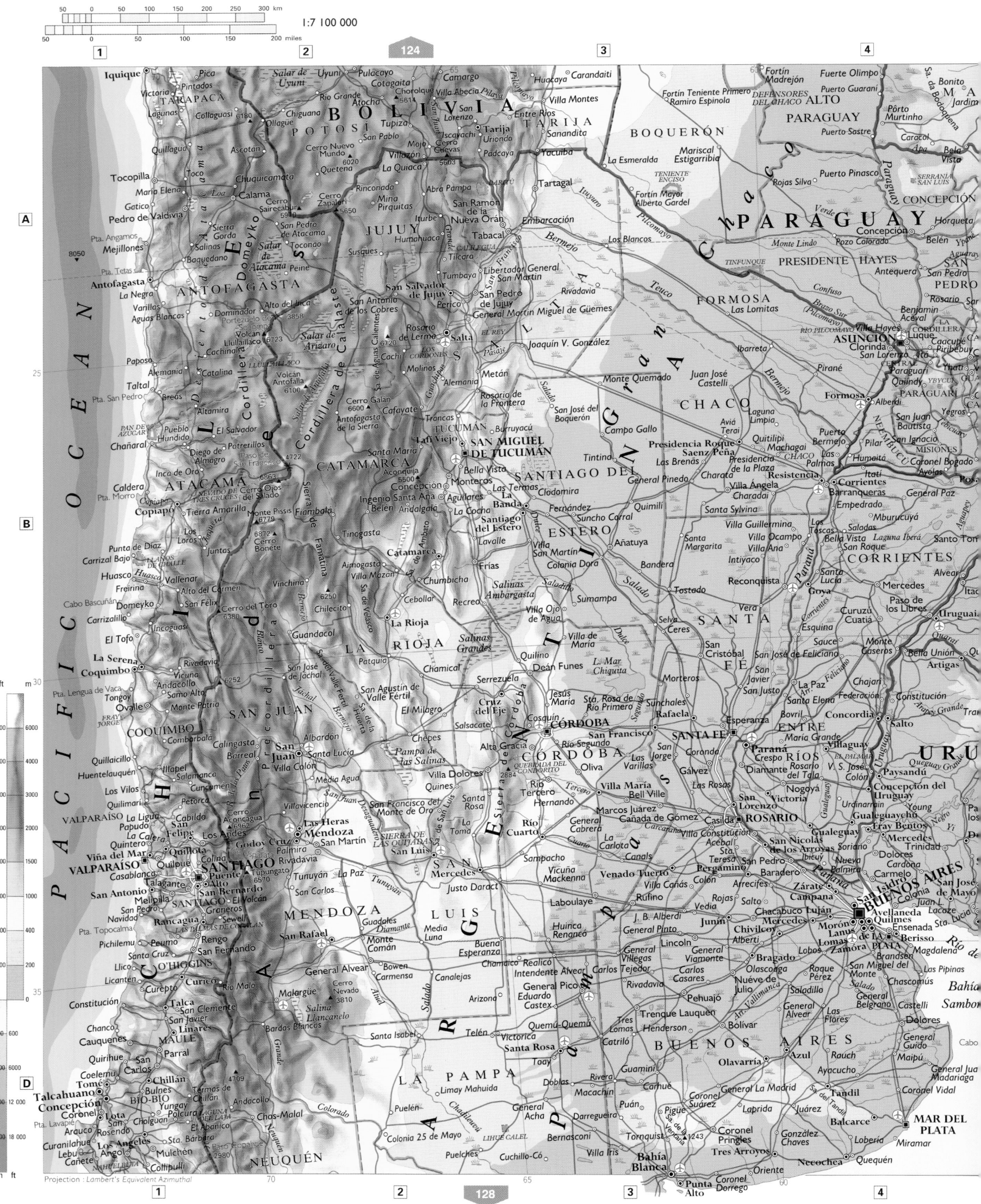

1:7 100 000

Projection : Lambert's Equivalent Azimuthal

National Parks

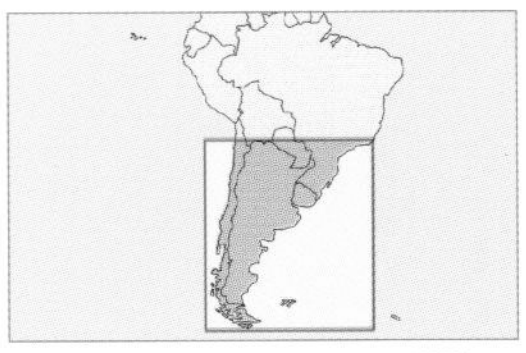

1:14 200 000

Projection: Sanson-Flamsteed's Sinusoidal

West from Greenwich

COPYRIGHT PHILIP'S

PARAGUAY

BRASIL

URUGUAY

ARGENTINA

CHILE

PACIFIC OCEAN

SOUTH ATLANTIC OCEAN

FALKLAND ISLANDS (ISLAS MALVINAS) (U.K.)
West Falkland, East Falkland, Stanley, Port Darwin

South Georgia (U.K.)

Tierra del Fuego

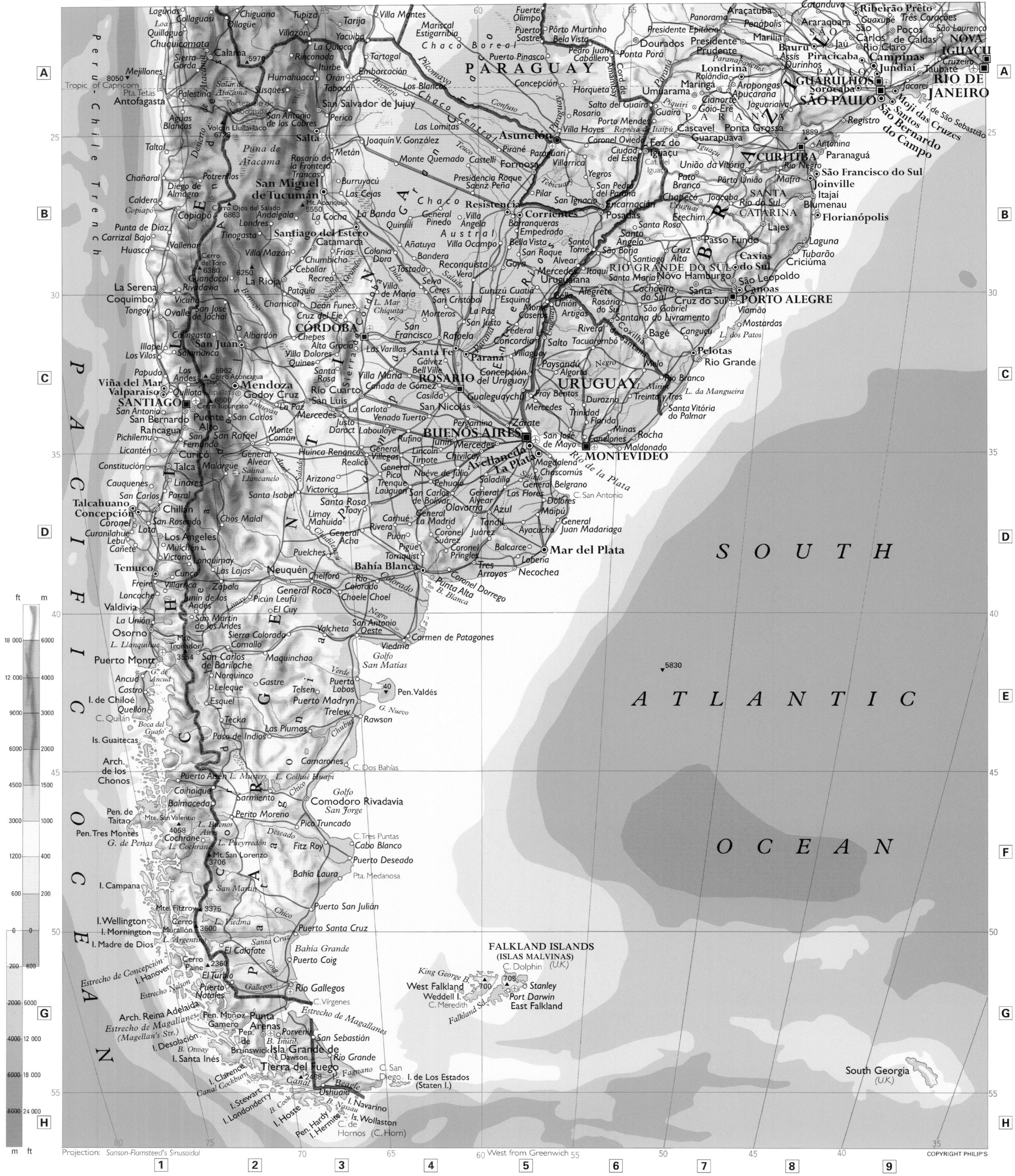

INDEX TO WORLD MAPS

How to use the index

The index contains the names of all the principal places and features shown on the World Maps. Each name is followed by an additional entry in italics giving the country or region within which it is located. The alphabetical order of names composed of two or more words is governed primarily by the first word and then by the second. This is an example of the rule:

Mīr Kūh, *Iran*	....	**71 E8**
Mīr Shahdād, *Iran*	....	**71 E8**
Mira, *Italy*	....	**41 C9**
Mira por vos Cay, *Bahamas*	..	**121 B5**
Miraj, *India*	....	**66 F2**

Physical features composed of a proper name (Erie) and a description (Lake) are positioned alphabetically by the proper name. The description is positioned after the proper name and is usually abbreviated:

Erie, L., *N. Amer.* **116 D4**

Where a description forms part of a settlement or administrative name however, it is always written in full and put in its true alphabetic position:

Mount Morris, *U.S.A.* **116 D7**

Names beginning with M' and Mc are indexed as if they were spelled Mac. Names beginning St. are alphabetised under Saint, but Sankt, Sint, Sant', Santa and San are all spelt in full and are alphabetised accordingly. If the same place name occurs two or more times in the index and all are in the same country, each is followed by the name of the administrative subdivision in which it is located. For example:

Jackson, Ky., *U.S.A.*	....	**114 G4**
Jackson, Mich., *U.S.A.*	....	**114 D3**
Jackson, Minn., *U.S.A.*	......	**112 D7**

The number in bold type which follows each name in the index refers to the number of the map page where that feature or place will be found. This is usually the largest scale at which the place or feature appears.

The letter and figure which are in bold type immediately after the page number give the grid square on the map page, within which the feature is situated. The letter represents the latitude and the figure the longitude. A lower case letter immediately after the page number refers to an inset map on that page.

In some cases the feature itself may fall within the specified square, while the name is outside. This is usually the case only with features which are larger than a grid square.

Rivers are indexed to their mouths or confluences, and carry the symbol → after their names. The following symbols are also used in the index: ■ country, ☑ overseas territory or dependency, □ first order administrative area, △ national park, ◠ other park (provincial park, nature reserve or game reserve), ✈ (LHR) principal airport (and location identifier).

How to pronounce place names

English-speaking people usually have no difficulty in reading and pronouncing correctly English place names. However, foreign place name pronunciations may present many problems. Such problems can be minimised by following some simple rules. However, these rules cannot be applied to all situations, and there will be many exceptions.

1. In general, stress each syllable equally, unless your experience suggests otherwise.
2. Pronounce the letter 'a' as a broad 'a' as in 'arm'.
3. Pronounce the letter 'e' as a short 'e' as in 'elm'.
4. Pronounce the letter 'i' as a cross between a short 'i' and long 'e', as the two 'i's in 'California'.
5. Pronounce the letter 'o' as an intermediate 'o' as in 'soft'.
6. Pronounce the letter 'u' as an intermediate 'u' as in 'sure'.
7. Pronounce consonants hard, except in the Romance-language areas where 'g's are likely to be pronounced softly like 'j' in 'jam'; 'j' itself may be pronounced as 'y'; and 'x's may be pronounced as 'h'.
8. For names in mainland China, pronounce 'q' like the 'ch' in 'chin', 'x' like the 'sh' in 'she', 'zh' like the 'j' in 'jam', and 'z' as if it were spelled 'dz'. In general pronounce 'a' as in 'father', 'e' as in 'but', 'i' as in 'keep', 'o' as in 'or', and 'u' as in 'rule'.

Moreover, English has no diacritical marks (accent and pronunciation signs), although some languages do. The following is a brief and general guide to the pronunciation of those most frequently used in the principal Western European languages.

		Pronunciation as in
French	é	day and shows that the e is to be pronounced; e.g. Orléans.
	è	mare
	î	used over any vowel and does not affect pronunciation; shows contraction of the name, usually omission of 's' following a vowel.
	ç	's' before 'a', 'o' and 'u'.
	ë, ï, ü	over 'e', 'i' and 'u' when they are used with another vowel and shows that each is to be pronounced.
German	ä	fate
	ö	fur
	ü	no English equivalent; like French 'tu'
Italian	à, é	over vowels and indicates stress.
Portuguese	ã, õ	vowels pronounced nasally.
	ç	boss
	á	shows stress
	ô	shows that a vowel has an 'i' or 'u' sound combined with it.
Spanish	ñ	canyon
	ü	pronounced as w and separately from adjoining vowels.
	á	usually indicates that this is a stressed vowel.

Abbreviations

A.C.T. – Australian Capital Territory
A.R. – Autonomous Region
Afghan. – Afghanistan
Afr. – Africa
Ala. – Alabama
Alta. – Alberta
Amer. – America(n)
Arch. – Archipelago
Ariz. – Arizona
Ark. – Arkansas
Atl. Oc. – Atlantic Ocean
B. – Baie, Bahía, Bay, Bucht, Bugt
B.C. – British Columbia
Bangla. – Bangladesh
Barr. – Barrage
Bos.-H. – Bosnia-Herzegovina
C. – Cabo, Cap, Cape, Coast
C.A.R. – Central African Republic
C. Prov. – Cape Province
Calif. – California
Cat. – Catarata
Cent. – Central
Chan. – Channel
Colo. – Colorado
Conn. – Connecticut
Cord. – Cordillera
Cr. – Creek
Czech. – Czech Republic
D.C. – District of Columbia
Del. – Delaware
Dem. – Democratic
Dep. – Dependency
Des. – Desert
Dét. – Détroit
Dist. – District
Dj. – Djebel
Domin. – Dominica
Dom. Rep. – Dominican Republic
E. – East

E. Salv. – El Salvador
Eq. Guin. – Equatorial Guinea
Est. – Estrecho
Falk. Is. – Falkland Is.
Fd. – Fjord
Fla. – Florida
Fr. – French
G. – Golfe, Golfo, Gulf, Guba, Gebel
Ga. – Georgia
Gt. – Great, Greater
Guinea-Biss. – Guinea-Bissau
H.K. – Hong Kong
H.P. – Himachal Pradesh
Hants. – Hampshire
Harb. – Harbor, Harbour
Hd. – Head
Hts. – Heights
I.(s). – Île, Ilha, Insel, Isla, Island, Isle
Ill. – Illinois
Ind. – Indiana
Ind. Oc. – Indian Ocean
Ivory C. – Ivory Coast
J. – Jabal, Jebel
Jaz. – Jazīrah
Junc. – Junction
K. – Kap, Kapp
Kans. – Kansas
Kep. – Kepulauan
Ky. – Kentucky
L. – Lac, Lacul, Lago, Lagoa, Lake, Limni, Loch, Lough
La. – Louisiana
Ld. – Land
Liech. – Liechtenstein
Lux. – Luxembourg
Mad. P. – Madhya Pradesh
Madag. – Madagascar
Man. – Manitoba

Mass. – Massachusetts
Md. – Maryland
Me. – Maine
Medit. S. – Mediterranean Sea
Mich. – Michigan
Minn. – Minnesota
Miss. – Mississippi
Mo. – Missouri
Mont. – Montana
Mozam. – Mozambique
Mt.(s) – Mont, Montaña, Mountain
Mte. – Monte
Mti. – Monti
N. – Nord, Norte, North, Northern, Nouveau
N.B. – New Brunswick
N.C. – North Carolina
N. Cal. – New Caledonia
N. Dak. – North Dakota
N.H. – New Hampshire
N.I. – North Island
N.J. – New Jersey
N. Mex. – New Mexico
N.S. – Nova Scotia
N.S.W. – New South Wales
N.W.T. – North West Territory
N.Y. – New York
N.Z. – New Zealand
Nac. – Nacional
Nat. – National
Nebr. – Nebraska
Neths. – Netherlands
Nev. – Nevada
Nfld. & L. – Newfoundland and Labrador
Nic. – Nicaragua
O. – Oued, Ouadi
Occ. – Occidentale
Okla. – Oklahoma

Ont. – Ontario
Or. – Orientale
Oreg. – Oregon
Os. – Ostrov
Oz. – Ozero
P. – Pass, Passo, Pasul, Pulau
P.E.I. – Prince Edward Island
Pa. – Pennsylvania
Pac. Oc. – Pacific Ocean
Papua N.G. – Papua New Guinea
Pass. – Passage
Peg. – Pegunungan
Pen. – Peninsula, Péninsule
Phil. – Philippines
Pk. – Peak
Plat. – Plateau
Prov. – Province, Provincial
Pt. – Point
Pta. – Ponta, Punta
Pte. – Pointe
Qué. – Québec
Queens. – Queensland
R. – Rio, River
R.I. – Rhode Island
Ra. – Range
Raj. – Rajasthan
Recr. – Recreational, Récréatif
Reg. – Region
Rep. – Republic
Res. – Reserve, Reservoir
Rhld-Pfz. – Rheinland-Pfalz
S. – South, Southern, Sur
Si. Arabia – Saudi Arabia
S.C. – South Carolina
S. Dak. – South Dakota
S.I. – South Island
S. Leone – Sierra Leone
Sa. – Serra, Sierra
Sask. – Saskatchewan

Scot. – Scotland
Sd. – Sound
Serbia & M.. – Serbia & Montenegro
Sev. – Severnaya
Sib. – Siberia
Sprs. – Springs
St. – Saint
Sta. – Santa
Ste. – Sainte
Sto. – Santo
Str. – Strait, Stretto
Switz. – Switzerland
Tas. – Tasmania
Tenn. – Tennessee
Terr. – Territory, Territoire
Tex. – Texas
Tg. – Tanjung
Trin. & Tob. – Trinidad & Tobago
U.A.E. – United Arab Emirates
U.K. – United Kingdom
U.S.A. – United States of America
Ut. P. – Uttar Pradesh
Va. – Virginia
Vdkhr. – Vodokhranilishche
Vdskh. – Vodoskhovyshche
Vf. – Vírful
Vic. – Victoria
Vol. – Volcano
Vt. – Vermont
W. – Wadi, West
W. Va. – West Virginia
Wall. & F. Is. – Wallis and Futuna Is.
Wash. – Washington
Wis. – Wisconsin
Wlkp. – Wielkopolski
Wyo. – Wyoming
Yorks. – Yorkshire

A

A 'Âli an Nîl □, *Sudan* 81 F3
A Baña, *Spain* 36 C2
A Cañiza, *Spain* 36 C2
A Coruña, *Spain* 36 B2
A Estrada, *Spain* 36 C2
A Fonsagrada, *Spain* 36 B3
A Guarda, *Spain* 36 D2
A Gudiña, *Spain* 36 C3
A Rúa, *Spain* 36 C3
Aachen, *Germany* 24 E2
Aalborg = Ålborg, *Denmark* .. 11 G3
Aalen, *Germany* 25 G6
Aalst, *Belgium* 17 D4
Aalten, *Neths.* 17 C6
Aalter, *Belgium* 17 C3
Äänekoski, *Finland* 9 E21
Aarau, *Switz.* 25 H4
Aarberg, *Switz.* 25 H3
Aare →, *Switz.* 25 H4
Aargau □, *Switz.* 25 H4
Aarhus = Århus, *Denmark* 11 H4
Aarschot, *Belgium* 17 D4
Aba, *China* 58 A3
Aba, *Dem. Rep. of the Congo* .. 86 B3
Aba, *Nigeria* 83 D6
Âbâ, Jazîrat, *Sudan* 81 E3
Abaco I., *Bahamas* 120 A4
Abadab, J., *Sudan* 80 D4
Ābādān, *Iran* 71 D6
Abade, *Ethiopia* 81 F4
Ābādeh, *Iran* 71 D7
Abadin, *Spain* 36 B3
Abadla, *Algeria* 78 B5
Abaetetuba, *Brazil* 125 D9
Abagnar Qi, *China* 56 C9
Abah, Tanjung, *Indonesia* .. 63 K18
Abai, *Paraguay* 127 B4
Abak, *Nigeria* 83 E6
Abakaliki, *Nigeria* 83 D6
Abakan, *Russia* 53 D10
Abala, *Niger* 83 C5
Abalak, *Niger* 83 B6
Abalemma, *Niger* 83 B6
Abana, *Turkey* 72 B6
Abancay, *Peru* 124 F4
Abano Terme, *Italy* 41 C8
Abarán, *Spain* 39 G3
Abariringa, *Kiribati* 96 H10
Abarqū, *Iran* 71 D7
Abashiri, *Japan* 54 B12
Abashiri-Wan, *Japan* 54 C12
Abaújszántó, *Hungary* 28 B6
Abava →, *Latvia* 30 A8
Ābay = Nîl el Azraq →, *Sudan* 81 D3
Abay, *Kazakhstan* 52 E8
Abaya, L., *Ethiopia* 81 F4
Abayita-Shala Lakes △, *Ethiopia* 81 F4
Abaza, *Russia* 52 D9
Abbadia di Fiastra △, *Italy* . 41 E10
Abbadia San Salvatore, *Italy* . 41 F8
'Abbāsābād, *Iran* 71 C8
Abbay = Nîl el Azraq →, *Sudan* 81 D3
Abbaye, Pt., *U.S.A.* 114 B1
Abbé, L., *Ethiopia* 81 E5
Abbeville, *France* 19 B8
Abbeville, Ala., *U.S.A.* 115 K3
Abbeville, La., *U.S.A.* 113 L8
Abbeville, S.C., *U.S.A.* 115 H4
Abbiategrasso, *Italy* 40 C5
Abbot Ice Shelf, *Antarctica* . 5 D16
Abbottabad, *Pakistan* 68 B5
Abd al Kūrī, *Yemen* 75 E5
Abdar, *Iran* 71 D7
'Abdolābād, *Iran* 71 C8
Abdulpur, *Bangla.* 69 G13
Abéché, *Chad* 79 F10
Abejar, *Spain* 38 D2
Abekr, *Sudan* 81 E2
Abel Tasman △, *N.Z.* 91 J4
Abengourou, *Ivory C.* 82 D4
Åbenójar, *Spain* 37 G6
Åbenrå, *Denmark* 11 J3
Abensberg, *Germany* 25 G7
Abeokuta, *Nigeria* 83 D5
Aber, *Uganda* 86 B3
Aberaeron, *U.K.* 15 E3
Aberayron = Aberaeron, *U.K.* . 15 E3
Aberchirder, *U.K.* 13 D6
Abercorn, *Australia* 95 D5
Aberdare, *U.K.* 15 F4
Aberdare △, *Kenya* 86 C4
Aberdare Ra., *Kenya* 86 C4
Aberdeen, *Australia* 95 E5
Aberdeen, *Canada* 103 C7
Aberdeen, *S. Africa* 88 E3
Aberdeen, *U.K.* 13 D6
Aberdeen, Ala., *U.S.A.* 115 J1
Aberdeen, Idaho, *U.S.A.* 108 E7
Aberdeen, Md., *U.S.A.* 114 F7
Aberdeen, S. Dak., *U.S.A.* .. 112 C5
Aberdeen, Wash., *U.S.A.* 110 D3
Aberdeen, City of □, *U.K.* .. 13 D6
Aberdeenshire □, *U.K.* 13 D6
Aberdovey = Aberdyfi, *U.K.* .. 15 E3
Aberdyfi, *U.K.* 15 E3
Aberfeldy, *U.K.* 13 E5
Aberfoyle, *U.K.* 13 E4
Abergavenny, *U.K.* 15 F4
Abergele, *U.K.* 14 D4
Abernathy, *U.S.A.* 113 J4
Abert, L., *U.S.A.* 108 E3
Aberystwyth, *U.K.* 15 E3
Abhā, *Si. Arabia* 75 D3
Abhar, *Iran* 71 B6
Abhayapuri, *India* 69 F14
Abia □, *Nigeria* 83 D6
Abide, *Turkey* 47 C11
Abidiya, *Sudan* 80 D3

Abidjan, *Ivory C.* 82 D4
Abilene, Kans., *U.S.A.* 112 F6
Abilene, Tex., *U.S.A.* 113 J5
Abingdon, *U.K.* 15 F6
Abingdon, *U.S.A.* 115 G5
Abington Reef, *Australia* ... 94 B4
Abitau →, *Canada* 103 B7
Abitibi →, *Canada* 104 B3
Abitibi, L., *Canada* 104 C4
Abiy Adi, *Ethiopia* 81 E4
Abkhaz Republic = Abkhazia □, *Georgia* 35 J5
Abkhazia □, *Georgia* 35 J5
Abminga, *Australia* 95 D1
Abnûb, *Egypt* 80 B3
Åbo = Turku, *Finland* 9 F20
Abocho, *Nigeria* 83 D6
Abohar, *India* 68 D6
Aboisso, *Ivory C.* 82 D4
Abomey, *Benin* 83 D5
Abong-Mbang, *Cameroon* 84 D2
Abonnema, *Nigeria* 83 E6
Abony, *Hungary* 28 C5
Aboso, *Ghana* 82 D4
Abou-Deïa, *Chad* 79 F9
Aboyne, *U.K.* 13 D6
Abra Pampa, *Argentina* 126 A2
Abraham L., *Canada* 102 C5
Abrantes, *Portugal* 37 F2
Abreojos, Pta., *Mexico* 118 B2
Abri, Esh Shamâliya, *Sudan* . 80 C3
Abri, Janub Kordofân, *Sudan* . 81 E3
Abrolhos, Banka, *Brazil* 122 E7
Abrud, *Romania* 28 D8
Abruzzo □, *Italy* 41 F10
Absaroka Range, *U.S.A.* 108 D9
Abtenau, *Austria* 26 D6
Abu, *India* 68 G5
Abū al Abyad, *U.A.E.* 71 E7
Abū al Khaṣīb, *Iraq* 71 D6
Abū 'Alī, *Si. Arabia* 71 E6
Abū 'Alī →, *Lebanon* 74 A4
Abu Ballas, *Egypt* 80 C2
Abu Deleiq, *Sudan* 81 D3
Abu Dhabi = Abū Ẕāby, *U.A.E.* . 71 E7
Abu Dis, *Sudan* 80 D3
Abu Dom, *Sudan* 81 D3
Abū Du'ān, *Syria* 70 B3
Abu el Gairi, W. →, *Egypt* .. 74 F2
Abu Fatma, Ras, *Sudan* 80 C4
Abu Gabra, *Sudan* 81 E2
Abu Ga'da, W. →, *Egypt* 74 F1
Abu Gelba, *Sudan* 81 E3
Abu Gubeiha, *Sudan* 81 E3
Abu Habl, Khawr →, *Sudan* ... 81 E3
Abū Ḥadrīyah, *Si. Arabia* ... 71 E6
Abu Hamed, *Sudan* 80 D3
Abu Haraz, An Nîl al Azraq, *Sudan* 80 D3
Abu Haraz, El Gezira, *Sudan* . 81 E3
Abu Haraz, Esh Shamâliya, *Sudan* 80 D3
Abu Higar, *Sudan* 81 E3
Abū Kamāl, *Syria* 70 C4
Abu Kuleiwat, *Sudan* 81 E2
Abū Madd, Ra's, *Si. Arabia* . 70 E3
Abū Mariariq, *Sudan* 81 E2
Abū Mendi, *Ethiopia* 81 E4
Abū Mūsā, *U.A.E.* 71 E7
Abū Qaşr, *Si. Arabia* 70 D3
Abu Qir, *Egypt* 80 H7
Abu Qireiya, *Egypt* 80 C4
Abu Qurqās, *Egypt* 80 B3
Abu Shagara, Ras, *Sudan* 80 C4
Abu Shanab, *Sudan* 81 E2
Abū Şukhayr, *Iraq* 70 D5
Abū Sultân, *Egypt* 80 H8
Abu Tabari, *Sudan* 80 D2
Abu Tig, *Egypt* 80 B3
Abu Tiga, *Sudan* 81 E3
Abu Tineitin, *Sudan* 81 D3
Abu Uruq, *Sudan* 81 D3
Abu Zabad, *Sudan* 81 E2
Abū Ẕāby, *U.A.E.* 71 E7
Abū Zeydābād, *Iran* 71 C6
Abuja, *Nigeria* 83 D6
Abukuma-Gawa →, *Japan* 54 E10
Abukuma-Sammyaku, *Japan* ... 54 F10
Abunã, *Brazil* 124 E5
Abunã →, *Brazil* 124 E5
Abune Yosef, *Ethiopia* 81 E4
Abut Hd., *N.Z.* 91 K3
Abuye Meda, *Ethiopia* 81 E4
Abwong, *Sudan* 81 F3
Åby, *Sweden* 11 F10
Aby, Lagune, *Ivory C.* 82 D4
Abyad, *Sudan* 81 E2
Åbybro, *Denmark* 11 G3
Acadia □, *U.S.A.* 115 C11
Açailândia, *Brazil* 125 D9
Acajutla, El Salv. 120 D2
Acámbaro, *Mexico* 118 D4
Acanthus, *Greece* 44 F7
Acaponeta, *Mexico* 118 C3
Acapulco, *Mexico* 119 D5
Acaraí, Serra, *Brazil* 124 C7
Acarigua, *Venezuela* 124 B5
Acatlán, *Mexico* 119 D5
Acayucan, *Mexico* 119 D6
Accéglio, *Italy* 40 D4
Accomac, *U.S.A.* 114 G8
Accous, *France* 20 E3
Accra, *Ghana* 83 D4
Accrington, *U.K.* 14 D5
Acebal, *Argentina* 126 C3
Acebo □, *Indonesia* 62 D1
Acerra, *Italy* 43 B7
Aceuchal, *Spain* 37 G4
Achalpur, *India* 66 J10
Acheng, *China* 57 B14

Achenkirch, *Austria* 26 D4
Achensee, *Austria* 26 D4
Acher, *India* 68 H5
Achern, *Germany* 25 G4
Achill Hd., *Ireland* 12 C1
Achill I., *Ireland* 12 C1
Achim, *Germany* 24 B5
Achinsk, *Russia* 53 D10
Acıgöl, *Turkey* 47 D11
Acıpayam, *Turkey* 47 D11
Acireale, *Italy* 43 E8
Ackerman, *U.S.A.* 113 J10
Acklins I., *Bahamas* 121 B5
Acme, *Canada* 102 C6
Acme, *U.S.A.* 116 F5
Aconcagua, Cerro, *Argentina* . 126 C2
Aconquija, Mt., *Argentina* .. 126 B2
Açores, Is. dos, Atl. Oc. ... 78 A1
Acornhoek, S. Africa 89 C5
Acquapendente, *Italy* 41 F8
Acquasanta Terme, *Italy* 41 F10
Acquasparta, *Italy* 41 F9
Acquaviva delle Fonti, *Italy* . 43 B9
Acqui Terme, *Italy* 40 D5
Acraman, L., *Australia* 95 E2
Acre = 'Akko, *Israel* 74 C4
Acre □, *Brazil* 124 E4
Acre →, *Brazil* 124 E5
Acri, *Italy* 43 C9
Acs, *Hungary* 28 C3
Actium, *Greece* 46 C2
Acton, *Canada* 116 C4
Acuña, *Mexico* 118 B4
Ad Dammām, *Si. Arabia* 71 E6
Ad Dāmūr, *Lebanon* 74 B4
Ad Dawādimī, *Si. Arabia* 70 E5
Ad Dawḥah, *Qatar* 71 E6
Ad Dawr, *Iraq* 70 C4
Ad Dir'iyah, *Si. Arabia* 70 E5
Ad Dīwānīyah, *Iraq* 70 D5
Ad Dujayl, *Iraq* 70 C5
Ad Duwayd, *Si. Arabia* 70 D4
Ada, *Ghana* 83 D5
Ada, Serbia & M. 28 E5
Ada, Minn., *U.S.A.* 112 B6
Ada, Okla., *U.S.A.* 113 H6
Adabiya, *Egypt* 74 F1
Adair, C., *Canada* 101 A12
Adaja →, *Spain* 36 D6
Adak I., *U.S.A.* 100 C2
Adamaoua, Massif de l', *Cameroon* 83 D7
Adamawa □, *Nigeria* 83 D7
Adamawa Highlands = Adamaoua, Massif de l', *Cameroon* 83 D7
Adamello △, *Italy* 40 B7
Adamello, Mte., *Italy* 40 B7
Adami Tulu, *Ethiopia* 81 F4
Adaminaby, *Australia* 95 F4
Adams, Mass., *U.S.A.* 117 D11
Adams, N.Y., *U.S.A.* 117 C8
Adams, Wis., *U.S.A.* 112 D10
Adams, Mt., *U.S.A.* 110 D5
Adam's Bridge, Sri Lanka 66 Q11
Adams L., *Canada* 102 C5
Adam's Peak, Sri Lanka 66 R12
Adamuz, *Spain* 37 G6
Adana, *Turkey* 70 B2
Adanero, *Spain* 36 E6
Adapazarı = Sakarya, *Turkey* . 72 B4
Adar Gwagwa, J., *Sudan* 80 C4
Adarama, *Sudan* 81 D3
Adare, C., *Antarctica* 5 D11
Adarte, *Eritrea* 81 E5
Adaut, *Indonesia* 63 F8
Adavale, *Australia* 95 D3
Adda →, *Italy* 40 C6
Addis Ababa = Addis Abeba, *Ethiopia* 81 F4
Addis Abeba, *Ethiopia* 81 F4
Addis Alem, *Ethiopia* 81 F4
Addis Zemen, *Ethiopia* 81 E4
Addison, *U.S.A.* 116 D7
Addo, S. Africa 88 E4
Addo △, S. Africa 88 E4
Adebour, *Niger* 83 C7
Ādeh, *Iran* 70 B5
Adel, *U.S.A.* 115 K4
Adelaide, *Australia* 95 E2
Adelaide, S. Africa 88 E4
Adelaide, *Bahamas* 120 A4
Adelaide I., *Antarctica* ... 5 C17
Adelaide Pen., *Canada* 100 B10
Adelaide River, *Australia* .. 92 B5
Adelaide Village, *Bahamas* .. 120 A4
Adelanto, *U.S.A.* 111 L9
Adele I., *Australia* 92 C3
Adélie, Terre, *Antarctica* .. 5 C10
Adelie Land = Adélie, Terre, *Antarctica* 5 C10
Adelsk, *Belarus* 30 E10
Ademuz, *Spain* 38 E3
Aden = Al 'Adan, *Yemen* 75 E4
Aden, G. of, *Asia* 75 E4
Adendorp, S. Africa 88 E3
Aderbissinat, *Niger* 83 B6
Adh Dhayd, *U.A.E.* 71 E7
Adhoi, *India* 68 H4
Adi, *Indonesia* 63 E8
Adi Arkai, *Ethiopia* 81 E4
Adi Daro, *Ethiopia* 81 E4
Adi Keyih, *Eritrea* 81 E4
Adi Kwala, *Eritrea* 81 E4
Adi Ugri, *Eritrea* 81 E4
Adieu, C., *Australia* 93 F5
Adieu Pt., *Australia* 92 C3
Adigala, *Ethiopia* 81 E5
Adilabad, *India* 66 K11
Adilcevaz, *Turkey* 73 C10

Adirondack △, *U.S.A.* 117 C10
Adirondack Mts., *U.S.A.* 117 C10
Adis Abeba = Addis Abeba, *Ethiopia* 81 F4
Adıyaman, *Turkey* 73 D8
Adjohon, *Benin* 83 D5
Adjud, *Romania* 29 D12
Adjumani, *Uganda* 86 B3
Adjuntas, *Puerto Rico* ..... 121 d
Adlavik Is., *Canada* 105 B8
Adler, *Russia* 35 J4
Admer, *Algeria* 83 A6
Admiralty G., *Australia* 92 B4
Admiralty I., *U.S.A.* 102 B2
Admiralty Is., *Papua N. G.* . 96 H6
Adnan Menderes, Izmir ✈ (ADB), *Turkey* 47 C9
Ado, *Nigeria* 83 D5
Ado-Ekiti, *Nigeria* 83 D6
Adok, *Sudan* 81 F3
Adola, *Ethiopia* 81 E5
Adonara, *Indonesia* 63 F6
Adoni, *India* 66 M10
Adony, *Hungary* 28 C3
Adour →, *France* 20 E2
Adra, *India* 69 H12
Adra, *Spain* 37 J7
Adrano, *Italy* 43 E7
Adrar, *Mauritania* 78 D3
Adrar des Iforas, *Algeria* .. 78 C5
Adria, *Italy* 41 C9
Adrian, Mich., *U.S.A.* 114 E3
Adrian, Tex., *U.S.A.* 113 H3
Adriatic Sea, Medit. S. 6 G3
Adua, *Indonesia* 63 E7
Adwa, *Ethiopia* 81 E4
Adygea □, *Russia* 35 H5
Adzhar Republic = Ajaria □, *Georgia* 35 K6
Adzopé, *Ivory C.* 82 D4
Ægean Sea, Medit. S. 47 C7
Aerhtai Shan, *Mongolia* 60 B4
Ærø, *Denmark* 11 K4
Ærøskøbing, *Denmark* 11 K4
Aëtós, *Greece* 46 D3
'Afak, *Iraq* 70 C5
Afándou, *Greece* 49 C10
Afar □, *Ethiopia* 81 E5
Afghanistan ■, *Asia* 66 C4
Afikpo, *Nigeria* 83 D6
Aflou, *Algeria* 78 B6
Afogados da Brígada, *Brazil* ... [not present]
Afragóla, *Italy* 43 B7
Afram →, *Ghana* 83 D4
Afrera, *Ethiopia* 81 E5
Africa 76 E6
'Afrīn, *Syria* 70 B3
Afşin, *Turkey* 72 C7
Afton, N.Y., *U.S.A.* 117 D9
Afton, Wyo., *U.S.A.* 108 E8
Afuá, *Brazil* 125 D8
'Afula, *Israel* 74 C4
Afyon, *Turkey* 47 C12
Afyon □, *Turkey* 47 C12
Afyonkarahisar = Afyon, *Turkey* 47 C12
Aga, *Egypt* 80 H7
Agadès = Agadez, *Niger* 83 B6
Agadez, *Niger* 83 B6
Agadir, *Morocco* 78 B4
Agaete, Canary Is. 48 G4
Agapi, Ethiopia .... [not present]
Agaie, *Nigeria* 83 D6
Again, *Sudan* 81 F2
Agalega Is., *Mauritius* 3 E12
Ağapınar, *Turkey* 47 B12
Agar, *India* 68 H7
Agaro, *Ethiopia* 81 F4
Agartala, *India* 67 H17
Agāş, *Romania* 29 D11
Agassiz, *Canada* 102 D4
Agats, *Indonesia* 63 F9
Agawam, *U.S.A.* 117 D12
Agbélouvé, *Togo* 83 D5
Agboville, *Ivory C.* 82 D4
Ağcabādi, *Azerbaijan* 35 K8
Ağdam, *Azerbaijan* 35 L8
Ağdaş, *Azerbaijan* 35 K8
Agde, *France* 20 E7
Agde, C. d', *France* 20 E7
Agdzhabedi = Ağcabādi, *Azerbaijan* 35 K8
Agen, *France* 20 D4
Agerbæk, *Denmark* 11 J2
Agersø, *Denmark* 11 J5
Ageyevo, *Russia* 32 E9
Āgh Kand, *Iran* 71 B6
Aghireşu, *Romania* 29 D8
Aginskoye, *Russia* 53 D12
Ağlasun, *Turkey* 47 D12
Agly →, *France* 20 F7
Agnew, *Australia* 93 E3
Agnibilékrou, *Ivory C.* 82 D4
Agnita, *Romania* 29 E9
Agnone, *Italy* 41 G11
Agofie, *Ghana* 83 D5
Agogna →, *Italy* 40 C5
Agogo, *Sudan* 81 F2
Agôn, *Sweden* 10 C11
Agon Coutainville, *France* .. 18 C5
Ágordo, *Italy* 41 B9
Agori, *India* 69 G10
Agouna, *Benin* 83 D5
Agout →, *France* 20 E5
Agra, *India* 68 F7
Agrakhanskiy Poluostrov, *Russia* 35 J8
Agramunt, *Spain* 38 D6
Agreda, *Spain* 38 D3
Ağri →, *Italy* 43 B9
Agri →, *Italy* 43 B9
Ağrı Dağı, *Turkey* 70 B5
Ağrı Karakose = Ağrı, *Turkey* . 73 C10
Agriá, *Greece* 46 B5

Agrigento, *Italy* 42 E6
Agrínion, *Greece* 46 C3
Agrópoli, *Italy* 43 B7
Ağstafa, *Azerbaijan* 35 K7
Agua Caliente, Baja Calif., *Mexico* 111 N10
Agua Caliente, Sinaloa, *Mexico* 118 B3
Agua Caliente Springs, *U.S.A.* 111 N10
Água Clara, *Brazil* 125 H8
Agua Fria △, *U.S.A.* 109 J8
Agua Hechicero, *Mexico* 111 N10
Agua Prieta, *Mexico* 118 A3
Aguadilla, *Puerto Rico* .... 121 d
Aguadulce, *Panama* 120 E3
Aguanga, *U.S.A.* 111 M10
Aguanish, *Canada* 105 B7
Aguanus →, *Canada* 105 B7
Aguapey →, *Argentina* 126 B4
Aguaray Guazú →, *Paraguay* . 126 A4
Aguarico →, *Ecuador* 124 D3
Aguas →, *Spain* 38 D4
Aguaro-Guariquito △, *Venezuela* 121 E6
Aguas Blancas, *Chile* 126 A2
Aguas Calientes, Sierra de, *Argentina* 126 B2
Aguascalientes, *Mexico* 118 C4
Aguascalientes □, *Mexico* ... 118 C4
Agudo, *Spain* 37 G6
Águeda, *Portugal* 36 E2
Águeda →, *Spain* 36 D4
Aguelhok, *Mali* 83 B5
Aguié, *Niger* 83 C6
Aguila, Punta, *Puerto Rico* . 121 d
Aguilafuente, *Spain* 36 D6
Aguilar, *Spain* 37 H6
Aguilar de Campóo, *Spain* ... 36 C6
Aguilares, *Argentina* 126 B2
Águilas, *Spain* 39 H3
Agüimes, Canary Is. 48 G4
Aguja, C. de la, *Colombia* .. 122 B3
Agujereada, Pta., *Puerto Rico* 121 d
Agulaa, *Ethiopia* 81 E4
Agulhas, C., S. Africa 88 E3
Agulo, Canary Is. 48 F2
Agung, Gunung, *Indonesia* ... 63 J18
Agur, *Uganda* 86 B3
Agusan →, *Phil.* 61 G6
Ağva, *Turkey* 45 E13
Agvali, *Russia* 35 J8
Aha Mts., *Botswana* 88 B3
Ahaggar, *Algeria* 78 D7
Ahamansu, *Ghana* 83 D5
Ahar, *Iran* 70 B5
Ahat, *Turkey* 47 C11
Ahaus, *Germany* 24 C2
Ahipara B., *N.Z.* 91 F4
Ahir Dağı, *Turkey* 47 C12
Ahiri, *India* 66 K12
Ahlat, *Turkey* 73 C10
Ahlen, *Germany* 24 D3
Ahmad Wal, *Pakistan* 68 E1
Ahmadabad, *India* 68 H5
Aḥmadābād, Khorāsān, *Iran* .. 71 C9
Aḥmadābād, Khorāsān, *Iran* .. 71 C8
Aḥmadī, *Iran* 71 E8
Ahmadnagar, *India* 66 K9
Ahmadpur, *Pakistan* 68 E4
Ahmadpur Lamma, *Pakistan* .. 68 E4
Ahmar, *Ethiopia* 81 F5
Ahmedabad = Ahmadabad, *India* 68 H5
Ahmednagar = Ahmadnagar, *India* 66 K9
Ahmetbey, *Turkey* 45 E11
Ahmetler, *Turkey* 47 C11
Ahmetli, *Turkey* 47 C9
Ahoada, *Nigeria* 83 D6
Ahome, *Mexico* 118 B3
Ahoskie, *U.S.A.* 115 G7
Ahr →, *Germany* 24 E3
Ahram, *Iran* 71 D6
Ahrax Pt., *Malta* 49 D1
Ahrensbök, *Germany* 24 A6
Ahrensburg, *Germany* 24 B6
Āhū, *Iran* 71 C6
Ahuachapán, El Salv. 120 D2
Ahun, *France* 19 F9
Åhus, *Sweden* 11 J8
Ahvāz, *Iran* 71 D6
Ahvenanmaa, *Finland* 9 F19
Aḥwar, *Yemen* 75 E4
Ahzar →, *Mali* 83 B5
Ai →, *India* 69 F14
Ai-Ais, *Namibia* 88 D2
Ai-Ais and Fish River Canyon △, *Namibia* 88 C2
Aichach, *Germany* 25 G7
Aichi □, *Japan* 55 G8
Aigle, *Switz.* 25 J2
Aignay-le-Duc, *France* 19 E11
Aigoual, Mt., *France* 20 D7
Aigre, *France* 20 C4
Aigua, *Uruguay* 127 C5
Aigueperse, *France* 19 F10
Aigues →, *France* 21 D8
Aigues-Mortes, *France* 21 E8
Aigues-Mortes, G. d', *France* . 21 E8
Aigües Tortes y Lago San Mauricio △, *Spain* 38 C4
Aiguilles, *France* 21 D10
Aiguillon, *France* 20 D4
Aigurande, *France* 19 F8
Aihui, *China* 60 A7
Aija, *Peru* 124 E3
Aikawa, *Japan* 54 E9
Aiken, *U.S.A.* 115 J5
Ailao Shan, *China* 58 F3
Aileron, *Australia* 94 C1
Aillant-sur-Tholon, *France* . 19 E10
Aillik, *Canada* 105 A8
Ailsa Craig, *U.K.* 13 F3
Aim, *Russia* 53 D14
Aimere, *Indonesia* 63 F6

Aimogasta, Argentina ... 126 B2
Ain □, France ... 19 F12
Ain ➤, France ... 21 C9
Aïn Ben Tili, Mauritania ... 78 C4
Ain Dalla, Egypt ... 80 B2
Ain el Mafki, Egypt ... 80 B2
Ain Girba, Egypt ... 80 B2
Ain Murr, Sudan ... 80 C2
Aïn Sefra, Algeria ... 78 B5
Ain Sheikh Murzûk, Egypt ... 80 B2
Ain Sudr, Egypt ... 74 F2
Ain Sukhna, Egypt ... 80 J8
Ain Zeitûn, Egypt ... 80 B2
Ainaži, Latvia ... 9 H21
Aínos Óros, Greece ... 46 C2
Ainsworth, U.S.A. ... 112 D5
Aiquile, Bolivia ... 124 G5
Aïr, Niger ... 83 B6
Air Force I., Canada ... 101 B12
Air Hitam, Malaysia ... 65 M4
Airaines, France ... 19 C8
Airdrie, Canada ... 102 C6
Airdrie, U.K. ... 13 F5
Aire ➤, France ... 19 C11
Aire ➤, U.K. ... 14 D7
Aire, I. de l', Spain ... 48 B11
Aire-sur-la-Lys, France ... 19 B9
Aire-sur-l'Adour, France ... 20 E3
Airlie Beach, Australia ... 94 J6
Airvault, France ... 18 F6
Aisch ➤, Germany ... 25 F6
Aisne □, France ... 19 C10
Aisne ➤, France ... 19 C9
Ait, India ... 69 G8
Aitana, Sierra de, Spain ... 39 G4
Aitkin, U.S.A. ... 112 B8
Aitolía kai Akarnanía □, Greece ... 46 C3
Aitolikón, Greece ... 46 C3
Aiud, Romania ... 29 D8
Aix-en-Provence, France ... 21 E9
Aix-la-Chapelle = Aachen, Germany ... 24 E2
Aix-les-Bains, France ... 21 C9
Aixe-sur-Vienne, France ... 20 C5
Áyina, Greece ... 46 D5
Aiyínion, Greece ... 44 F6
Aíyion, Greece ... 46 C4
Aizawl, India ... 67 H18
Aizenay, France ... 18 F5
Aizkraukle, Latvia ... 9 H21
Aizpute, Latvia ... 9 H19
Aizuwakamatsu, Japan ... 54 F9
Ajaccio, France ... 21 G12
Ajaccio, G. d', France ... 21 G12
Ajai ➤, Uganda ... 86 B3
Ajaigarh, India ... 69 G9
Ajalpan, Mexico ... 119 D5
Ajanta Ra., India ... 66 J9
Ajari Rep. = Ajaria □, Georgia ... 35 K6
Ajaria □, Georgia ... 35 K6
Ajax, Canada ... 116 C5
Ajdābiyā, Libya ... 79 B10
Ajdovščina, Slovenia ... 41 C10
Ajibar, Ethiopia ... 81 E4
Ajka, Hungary ... 28 C2
'Ajlūn, Jordan ... 74 C4
'Ajlūn □, Jordan ... 74 C4
'Ajmān, U.A.E. ... 71 E7
Ajmer, India ... 68 F6
Ajnala, India ... 68 D6
Ajo, U.S.A. ... 109 K7
Ajo, C. de, Spain ... 36 B7
Ajok, Sudan ... 81 F2
Ajuy, Phil. ... 61 F5
Ak Dağ, Turkey ... 47 E11
Ak Dağları, Muğla, Turkey ... 47 E11
Ak Dağları, Sivas, Turkey ... 72 C7
Akaba, Togo ... 83 D5
Akabira, Japan ... 54 C11
Akagera △, Rwanda ... 86 C3
Akaki Beseka, Ethiopia ... 81 F4
Akala, Sudan ... 81 D4
Akamas, Cyprus ... 49 D11
Akan △, Japan ... 54 C12
Akanthou, Cyprus ... 49 D12
Akarca, Turkey ... 47 C11
Akaroa, N.Z. ... 91 K4
Akasha, Sudan ... 80 C3
Akashi, Japan ... 55 G7
Akbarpur, Bihar, India ... 69 G10
Akbarpur, Ut. P., India ... 69 F10
Akçaabat, Turkey ... 73 B8
Akçadağ, Turkey ... 72 C7
Akçakale, Turkey ... 73 D8
Akçaova, Turkey ... 72 B4
Akçaova, Turkey ... 45 E13
Akçay, Turkey ... 47 E11
Akçay ➤, Turkey ... 47 D10
Akdağ, Turkey ... 47 C8
Akdağmadeni, Turkey ... 72 C6
Akelamo, Indonesia ... 63 D7
Åkers styckebruk, Sweden ... 10 E11
Åkersberga, Sweden ... 10 E12
Aketi, Dem. Rep. of the Congo ... 84 D4
Akhaïa □, Greece ... 46 C3
Akhalkalaki, Georgia ... 35 K6
Akhaltsikhe, Georgia ... 35 K6
Akharnaí, Greece ... 46 C5
Akhelóös ➤, Greece ... 46 C3
Akhendriá, Greece ... 47 G7
Akhisar, Turkey ... 47 C9
Akhladhókambos, Greece ... 46 D4
Akhmîm, Egypt ... 80 B3
Akhnur, India ... 69 C6
Akhtopol, Bulgaria ... 45 D11
Akhtuba ➤, Russia ... 35 F8
Akhtubinsk, Russia ... 35 F8
Akhty, Russia ... 35 K8
Akhtyrka = Okhtyrka, Ukraine ... 33 G8
Aki, Japan ... 55 H6
Akimiski I., Canada ... 104 B3

Akimovka, Ukraine ... 33 J8
Åkirkeby, Denmark ... 11 J8
Akita, Japan ... 54 E10
Akita □, Japan ... 54 E10
Akjoujt, Mauritania ... 82 B2
Akka, Mali ... 82 B4
Akkaya Tepesi, Turkey ... 47 D11
Akkeshi, Japan ... 54 C12
'Akko, Israel ... 74 C4
Akköy, Turkey ... 47 D9
Aklampa, Benin ... 83 D5
Aklavik, Canada ... 100 B6
Aklera, India ... 68 G7
Akmené, Lithuania ... 30 B9
Akmenrags, Latvia ... 30 B8
Akō, Japan ... 55 G7
Ako, Nigeria ... 83 C7
Akōbō, Sudan ... 81 F3
Akobo ➤, Ethiopia ... 81 F3
Akola, India ... 66 J10
Akonolinga, Cameroon ... 83 E7
Akor, Mali ... 82 C3
Akordat, Eritrea ... 81 D4
Akosombo Dam, Ghana ... 83 D5
Akot, Sudan ... 81 F3
Akoupé, Ivory C. ... 82 D4
Akpatok I., Canada ... 101 B13
Åkrahamn, Norway ... 9 G11
Åkranes, Iceland ... 8 D2
Akreïjit, Mauritania ... 82 B3
Akrítas Venétiko, Ákra, Greece ... 46 E3
Akron, Colo., U.S.A. ... 112 E3
Akron, Ohio, U.S.A. ... 116 E3
Akrotiri, Cyprus ... 49 E11
Akrotíri, Ákra, Greece ... 45 F9
Akrotiri Bay, Cyprus ... 49 E12
Aksai Chin, China ... 69 B8
Aksaray, Turkey ... 70 B2
Aksay, Kazakhstan ... 52 D6
Akşehir, Turkey ... 70 B1
Akşehir Gölü, Turkey ... 72 C4
Akstafa = Ağstafa, Azerbaijan ... 35 K7
Aksu, China ... 60 B3
Aksu ➤, Turkey ... 72 D4
Aksum, Ethiopia ... 81 E4
Aktash, Russia ... 34 C11
Aktogay, Kazakhstan ... 52 E8
Aktsyabrski, Belarus ... 33 F5
Aktyubinsk = Aqtöbe, Kazakhstan ... 52 D6
Aku, Nigeria ... 83 D6
Akure, Nigeria ... 83 D6
Akureyri, Iceland ... 8 D4
Akuseki-Shima, Japan ... 55 K4
Akusha, Russia ... 35 J8
Akwa-Ibom □, Nigeria ... 83 E6
Akyab = Sittwe, Burma ... 67 J18
Akyazı, Turkey ... 72 B4
Al 'Adan, Yemen ... 75 E4
Al Aḩsā = Hasa □, Si. Arabia ... 71 E6
Al Ajfar, Si. Arabia ... 70 E4
Al Amādīyah, Iraq ... 70 B4
Al 'Amārah, Iraq ... 70 D5
Al 'Aqabah, Jordan ... 74 F4
Al 'Aqabah □, Jordan ... 74 F4
Al Arak, Syria ... 70 C3
Al 'Aramah, Si. Arabia ... 70 E5
Al 'Arṭāwīyah, Si. Arabia ... 70 E5
Al 'Āṣimah = 'Ammān □, Jordan ... 74 D5
Al 'Assāfīyah, Si. Arabia ... 70 D3
Al 'Ayn, Si. Arabia ... 70 E3
Al 'Ayn, U.A.E. ... 71 E7
Al 'Azīzīyah, Iraq ... 70 C5
Al Bāb, Syria ... 70 B3
Al Bad', Si. Arabia ... 70 D2
Al Bādī, Iraq ... 70 C4
Al Baḩrah, Kuwait ... 70 D5
Al Baḩral Mayyit = Dead Sea, Asia ... 74 D4
Al Balqā □, Jordan ... 74 C4
Al Bārūk, J., Lebanon ... 74 B4
Al Baṣrah, Iraq ... 70 D5
Al Baṭḩā, Iraq ... 70 D5
Al Batrūn, Lebanon ... 74 A4
Al Baydā, Libya ... 79 B10
Al Biqā □, Lebanon ... 74 A5
Al Bi'r, Si. Arabia ... 70 D3
Al Burayj, Syria ... 74 A5
Al Faḑilī, Si. Arabia ... 71 E6
Al Fallūjah, Iraq ... 70 C4
Al Fāw, Iraq ... 71 D6
Al Fujayrah, U.A.E. ... 71 E8
Al Ghadaf, W. ➤, Jordan ... 74 D5
Al Ghammās, Iraq ... 70 D5
Al Ghazālah, Si. Arabia ... 70 E4
Al Ḩadīthah, Iraq ... 70 C4
Al Ḩadīthah, Si. Arabia ... 74 D6
Al Ḩadr, Iraq ... 70 C4
Al Ḩājānah, Syria ... 74 B5
Al Hajar al Gharbī, Oman ... 71 E8
Al Ḩāmad, Si. Arabia ... 70 D3
Al Ḩamdānīyah, Syria ... 70 C3
Al Ḩamīdīyah, Syria ... 74 A4
Al Ḩammār, Iraq ... 70 D5
Al Ḩamrā', Si. Arabia ... 70 E3
Al Ḩamzah, Iraq ... 70 D5
Al Ḩanākīyah, Si. Arabia ... 70 E4
Al Ḩarīr, W. ➤, Syria ... 74 C4
Al Ḩasā, W. ➤, Jordan ... 74 D4
Al Ḩasakah, Syria ... 70 B4
Al Ḩayy, Iraq ... 70 C5
Al Ḩayz, Iraq ... 70 C4
Al Ḩijānah, Syria ... 74 B5
Al Ḩillah, Iraq ... 70 C5
Al Ḩillah, Si. Arabia ... 75 B4
Al Ḩindīyah, Iraq ... 70 C5
Al Ḩirmil, Lebanon ... 74 A5
Al Ḩudaydah, Yemen ... 75 E3
Al Ḩufūf, Si. Arabia ... 71 E6
Al Ḩumaydah, Si. Arabia ... 70 D2

Al Ḩunayy, Si. Arabia ... 71 E6
Al Isāwīyah, Si. Arabia ... 70 D3
Al Jafr, Jordan ... 74 E5
Al Jāfūrah, Si. Arabia ... 71 E7
Al Jaghbūb, Libya ... 79 C10
Al Jahrah, Kuwait ... 70 D5
Al Jalāmīd, Si. Arabia ... 70 D3
Al Jamalīyah, Qatar ... 71 E6
Al Janūb □, Lebanon ... 74 B4
Al Jawf, Libya ... 79 D10
Al Jawf, Si. Arabia ... 70 D3
Al Jazirah, Iraq ... 70 C5
Al Jithāmīyah, Si. Arabia ... 70 E4
Al Jubayl, Si. Arabia ... 71 E6
Al Jubaylah, Si. Arabia ... 70 E5
Al Jubb, Si. Arabia ... 70 E4
Al Junaynah, Sudan ... 79 F10
Al Kabā'ish, Iraq ... 70 D5
Al Karak, Jordan ... 74 D4
Al Karak □, Jordan ... 74 E5
Al Kāzimīyah, Iraq ... 70 C5
Al Khābūra, Oman ... 71 F8
Al Khafji, Si. Arabia ... 71 E6
Al Khalīl, West Bank ... 74 D4
Al Khāliṣ, Iraq ... 70 C5
Al Kharsānīyah, Si. Arabia ... 71 E6
Al Khaṣab, Oman ... 71 E8
Al Khawr, Qatar ... 71 E6
Al Khiḑr, Iraq ... 70 D5
Al Khiyām, Lebanon ... 74 B4
Al Khums, Libya ... 79 B8
Al Kiswah, Syria ... 74 B5
Al Kūfah, Iraq ... 70 C5
Al Kufrah, Libya ... 79 D10
Al Kuhayfiyah, Si. Arabia ... 70 E4
Al Kūt, Iraq ... 70 C5
Al Kuwayt, Kuwait ... 70 D5
Al Labwah, Lebanon ... 74 A5
Al Lādhiqīyah, Syria ... 70 C2
Al Līth, Si. Arabia ... 75 C3
Al Liwā', Oman ... 71 E8
Al Luḩayyah, Yemen ... 75 D3
Al Madīnah, Iraq ... 70 D5
Al Madīnah, Si. Arabia ... 70 E3
Al Mafraq, Jordan ... 74 C5
Al Mafraq □, Jordan ... 74 C5
Al Maḩmūdīyah, Iraq ... 70 C5
Al Majma'ah, Si. Arabia ... 70 E5
Al Makhruq, W. ➤, Jordan ... 74 D6
Al Makhūl, Si. Arabia ... 70 E4
Al Manāmah, Bahrain ... 71 E6
Al Maqwa', Kuwait ... 70 D5
Al Marj, Libya ... 79 B10
Al Maṭlā, Kuwait ... 70 D5
Al Mawjib, W. ➤, Jordan ... 74 D4
Al Mawṣil, Iraq ... 70 B4
Al Mayādin, Syria ... 70 C4
Al Mazār, Jordan ... 74 D4
Al Midhnab, Si. Arabia ... 70 E5
Al Mīnā', Lebanon ... 74 A4
Al Miqdādīyah, Iraq ... 70 C5
Al Mubarraz, Si. Arabia ... 71 E6
Al Mudawwarah, Jordan ... 74 F5
Al Mughayrā', U.A.E. ... 71 E7
Al Muḩarraq, Bahrain ... 71 E6
Al Mukallā, Yemen ... 75 E4
Al Mukhā, Yemen ... 75 E3
Al Musayjīd, Si. Arabia ... 70 E3
Al Musayyib, Iraq ... 70 C5
Al Muthanná □, Iraq ... 70 D5
Al Muwayh, Si. Arabia ... 80 C5
Al Muwaylih, Si. Arabia ... 70 E2
Al Owuho = Otukpa, Nigeria ... 83 D6
Al Qādisīyah □, Iraq ... 70 D5
Al Qā'im, Iraq ... 70 C4
Al Qalībah, Si. Arabia ... 70 D3
Al Qāmishlī, Syria ... 70 B4
Al Qaryatayn, Syria ... 74 A6
Al Qaṣīm, Si. Arabia ... 70 E4
Al Qaṭ'ā, Syria ... 70 C4
Al Qaṭīf, Si. Arabia ... 71 E6
Al Qaṭrānah, Jordan ... 74 D5
Al Qaṭrūn, Libya ... 79 D9
Al Qayṣūmah, Si. Arabia ... 70 D5
Al Quds = Jerusalem, Israel ... 74 D4
Al Qunayṭirah, Syria ... 74 C4
Al Qunfudhah, Si. Arabia ... 80 D5
Al Qurnah, Iraq ... 70 D5
Al Quṣayr, Iraq ... 70 D5
Al Quṣayr, Syria ... 74 A5
Al Quṭayfah, Syria ... 74 B5
Al 'Ubaylah, Si. Arabia ... 75 C5
Al 'Udaylīyah, Si. Arabia ... 71 E6
Al 'Ulā, Si. Arabia ... 70 E3
Al 'Uqayr, Si. Arabia ... 71 E6
Al 'Uwaynid, Si. Arabia ... 70 E5
Al 'Uwayqīlah, Si. Arabia ... 70 D4
Al 'Uyūn, Ḩijāz, Si. Arabia ... 70 E3
Al 'Uyūn, Najd, Si. Arabia ... 70 E4
Al 'Uzayr, Iraq ... 70 D5
Al Wajh, Si. Arabia ... 70 E3
Al Wakrah, Qatar ... 71 E6
Al Waqbah, Si. Arabia ... 70 D5
Al Wari'āh, Si. Arabia ... 70 E5
Ala, Italy ... 40 C8
Ala Dağ, Turkey ... 70 B2
Alabama □, U.S.A. ... 115 J2
Alabama ➤, U.S.A. ... 115 K2
Alaca, Turkey ... 72 B6
Alaçam, Turkey ... 72 B6
Alaçam Dağları, Turkey ... 47 B10
Alacant = Alicante, Spain ... 39 G4
Alaçatı, Turkey ... 47 C8
Alachua, U.S.A. ... 115 L4
Alaejos, Spain ... 36 D5
Alaérma, Greece ... 49 C9
Alagir, Russia ... 35 J7
Alagna Valsésia, Italy ... 40 C4
Alagoa Grande, Brazil ... 125 E11

Alagoas □, Brazil ... 125 E11
Alagoinhas, Brazil ... 125 F11
Alagón, Spain ... 38 D3
Alagón ➤, Spain ... 36 F4
Alaior, Spain ... 48 B11
Alajero, Canary Is. ... 48 F2
Alajuela, Costa Rica ... 120 D3
Alakamisy, Madag. ... 89 C8
Alaknanda ➤, India ... 69 D8
Alakol, Ozero, Kazakhstan ... 60 B3
Alamarvdasht, Iran ... 71 E7
Alamata, Ethiopia ... 81 E4
Alameda, Calif., U.S.A. ... 110 H4
Alameda, N. Mex., U.S.A. ... 109 J10
Alaminos, Phil. ... 61 C3
Alamo, U.S.A. ... 111 J11
Alamo Crossing, U.S.A. ... 111 L13
Alamogordo, U.S.A. ... 109 K11
Alamos, Mexico ... 118 B3
Alamosa, U.S.A. ... 109 H11
Åland = Ahvenanmaa, Finland ... 9 F19
Alandroal, Portugal ... 37 G3
Ålands hav, Europe ... 9 F18
Alange, Embalse d', Spain ... 37 G4
Alania = North Ossetia □, Russia ... 35 J7
Alanís, Spain ... 37 G5
Alanya, Turkey ... 70 B1
Alaotra, Farihin', Madag. ... 89 B8
Alapayevsk, Russia ... 52 D7
Alappuzha = Alleppey, India ... 66 Q10
Alar del Rey, Spain ... 36 C6
Alaraz, Spain ... 36 E5
Alarcón, Embalse de, Spain ... 38 F2
Alarobia-Vohiposa, Madag. ... 89 C8
Alaşehir, Turkey ... 47 C10
Alaska □, U.S.A. ... 100 B5
Alaska, G. of, Pac. Oc. ... 100 C5
Alaska Peninsula, U.S.A. ... 100 C4
Alaska Range, U.S.A. ... 100 B4
Alássio, Italy ... 40 E5
Älät, Azerbaijan ... 35 L9
Alatri, Italy ... 41 G10
Alatyr, Russia ... 34 C8
Alatyr ➤, Russia ... 34 C8
Alausí, Ecuador ... 124 D3
Álava □, Spain ... 38 C2
Alava, C., U.S.A. ... 108 B1
Alaverdi, Armenia ... 35 K7
Alavo = Alavus, Finland ... 9 E20
Alavus, Finland ... 9 E20
Alawoona, Australia ... 95 E3
'Alayh, Lebanon ... 74 B4
Alazani ➤, Azerbaijan ... 35 K8
Alba, Italy ... 40 D5
Alba □, Romania ... 29 D8
Alba Adriática, Italy ... 41 F10
Alba de Tormes, Spain ... 36 E5
Alba-Iulia, Romania ... 29 D8
Albac, Romania ... 28 D7
Albacete, Spain ... 39 F3
Albacete □, Spain ... 39 G3
Albacutya, L., Australia ... 95 F3
Ålbæk, Denmark ... 11 G4
Ålbæk Bugt, Denmark ... 11 G4
Albaida, Spain ... 39 G4
Albalate de las Nogueras, Spain ... 38 E2
Albalate del Arzobispo, Spain ... 38 D4
Alban, France ... 20 E6
Albanel, L., Canada ... 104 B5
Albania ■, Europe ... 44 E4
Albano Laziale, Italy ... 41 G9
Albany, Australia ... 93 G2
Albany, Ga., U.S.A. ... 115 K3
Albany, N.Y., U.S.A. ... 117 D11
Albany, Oreg., U.S.A. ... 108 D2
Albany, Tex., U.S.A. ... 113 J5
Albany ➤, Canada ... 104 B3
Albardón, Argentina ... 126 C2
Albarracín, Spain ... 38 E3
Albarracín, Sierra de, Spain ... 38 E3
Albatera, Spain ... 39 G4
Albatross B., Australia ... 94 A3
Albegna ➤, Italy ... 41 F8
Albemarle, U.S.A. ... 115 H5
Albemarle Sd., U.S.A. ... 115 H7
Albenga, Italy ... 40 D5
Alberche ➤, Spain ... 36 F6
Alberdi, Paraguay ... 126 B4
Albères, Mts., France ... 20 F6
Alberga ➤, Sweden ... 11 F10
Alberga, The ➤, Australia ... 95 D2
Albersdorf, Germany ... 24 A5
Albert, France ... 19 C9
Albert, L., Africa ... 86 B3
Albert, L., Australia ... 95 F2
Albert Edward Ra., Australia ... 92 C4
Albert Lea, U.S.A. ... 112 D8
Albert Nile ➤, Uganda ... 86 B3
Albert Town, Bahamas ... 121 B5
Alberta □, Canada ... 102 C6
Alberti, Argentina ... 126 D3
Albertinia, S. Africa ... 88 E3
Albertirsa, Hungary ... 28 C4
Alberton, Canada ... 105 C7
Albertville, France ... 21 C10
Albertville, U.S.A. ... 115 H2
Albi, France ... 20 E6
Albia, U.S.A. ... 112 E8
Albina, Suriname ... 125 B8
Albina, Ponta, Angola ... 88 B1
Albino, Italy ... 40 C6
Albion, Mich., U.S.A. ... 114 D3
Albion, Nebr., U.S.A. ... 112 E6
Albion, Pa., U.S.A. ... 116 E4
Albocácer, Spain ... 38 E5
Alborán, Medit. S. ... 37 K7
Albolote, Spain ... 37 H7
Alborea, Spain ... 39 F3
Ålborg, Denmark ... 11 G3
Ålborg Bugt, Denmark ... 11 H4
Alborz, Reshteh-ye Kūhhā-ye, Iran ... 71 C7

Albox, Spain ... 39 H2
Albufeira, Portugal ... 37 H2
Albula ➤, Switz. ... 25 J5
Albuñol, Spain ... 37 J7
Albuquerque, U.S.A. ... 109 J10
Albuquerque, Cayos de, Caribbean ... 120 D3
Alburg, U.S.A. ... 117 B11
Alburno, Mte., Italy ... 43 B8
Alburquerque, Spain ... 37 F4
Albury = Albury-Wodonga, Australia ... 95 F4
Albury-Wodonga, Australia ... 95 F4
Alcácer do Sal, Portugal ... 37 G2
Alcáçovas, Portugal ... 37 G2
Alcalá de Chivert, Spain ... 38 E5
Alcalá de Guadaira, Spain ... 37 H5
Alcalá de Henares, Spain ... 36 E7
Alcalá de los Gazules, Spain ... 37 J5
Alcalá del Júcar, Spain ... 39 F3
Alcalá del Río, Spain ... 37 H5
Alcalá del Valle, Spain ... 37 J5
Alcalá la Real, Spain ... 37 H7
Álcamo, Italy ... 42 E5
Alcanadre, Spain ... 38 C2
Alcanadre ➤, Spain ... 38 D4
Alcanar, Spain ... 38 E5
Alcanede, Portugal ... 37 F2
Alcanena, Portugal ... 37 F2
Alcañices, Spain ... 36 D4
Alcañiz, Spain ... 38 D4
Alcântara, Brazil ... 125 D10
Alcántara, Spain ... 36 F4
Alcántara, Embalse de, Spain ... 36 F4
Alcantarilla, Spain ... 39 H3
Alcaracejos, Spain ... 37 G6
Alcaraz, Spain ... 39 G2
Alcaraz, Sierra de, Spain ... 39 G2
Alcaudete, Spain ... 37 H6
Alcázar de San Juan, Spain ... 37 F7
Alchevsk, Ukraine ... 33 H10
Alcira = Alzira, Spain ... 39 F4
Alcobaça, Portugal ... 37 F2
Alcobendas, Spain ... 36 E7
Alcolea del Pinar, Spain ... 38 D2
Alcora, Spain ... 38 E4
Alcorcón, Spain ... 36 E7
Alcoutim, Portugal ... 37 H3
Alcova, U.S.A. ... 108 E10
Alcoy, Spain ... 39 G4
Alcubierre, Sierra de, Spain ... 38 D4
Alcublas, Spain ... 38 F4
Alcúdia, Spain ... 48 B10
Alcúdia, B. d', Spain ... 48 B10
Alcudia, Sierra de la, Spain ... 37 G6
Aldabra Is., Seychelles ... 77 G8
Aldama, Mexico ... 119 C5
Aldan, Russia ... 53 D13
Aldan ➤, Russia ... 53 C13
Aldea, Pta. de la, Canary Is. ... 48 G4
Aldeburgh, U.K. ... 15 E9
Alder Pk., U.S.A. ... 110 K5
Alderney, U.K. ... 15 H5
Aldershot, U.K. ... 15 F7
Åled, Sweden ... 11 H6
Aledo, U.S.A. ... 112 E9
Alefa, Ethiopia ... 81 E4
Aleg, Mauritania ... 82 B2
Alegranza, Canary Is. ... 48 E6
Alegranza, I., Canary Is. ... 48 E6
Alegre, Brazil ... 127 A7
Alegrete, Brazil ... 127 B4
Aleisk, Russia ... 52 D9
Aleksandriya = Oleksandriya, Kirovohrad, Ukraine ... 33 H7
Aleksandriya = Oleksandriya, Rivne, Ukraine ... 33 G4
Aleksandriyskaya, Russia ... 35 J8
Aleksandrov, Russia ... 32 D10
Aleksandrov Gay, Russia ... 34 E9
Aleksandrovac, Serbia & M. ... 44 C5
Aleksandrovac, Serbia & M. ... 44 B5
Aleksandrovka = Oleksandrovka, Ukraine ... 33 H7
Aleksandrovo, Bulgaria ... 45 C8
Aleksandrovsk-Sakhalinskiy, Russia ... 53 D15
Aleksandrów Kujawski, Poland ... 31 F5
Aleksandrów Łódzki, Poland ... 31 G6
Aleksandry, Z., Russia ... 4 A10
Alekseyevka, Samara, Russia ... 34 D10
Alekseyevka, Voronezh, Russia ... 33 G10
Aleksin, Russia ... 32 E9
Aleksinac, Serbia & M. ... 44 C5
Além Paraíba, Brazil ... 127 A7
Alemania, Argentina ... 126 B2
Alemania, Chile ... 126 B2
Alençon, France ... 18 D7
Alenquer, Brazil ... 125 D8
Alenuihaha Channel, U.S.A. ... 106 H17
Alépé, Ivory C. ... 82 D4
Aleppo = Ḩalab, Syria ... 70 B3
Aléria, France ... 21 F13
Alert, Canada ... 4 A4
Alès, France ... 21 D8
Aleşd, Romania ... 28 C7
Alessándria, Italy ... 40 D5
Ålestrup, Denmark ... 11 H3
Ålesund, Norway ... 9 E12
Alet-les-Bains, France ... 20 F6
Aletschhorn, Switz. ... 25 J4
Aleutian Is., Pac. Oc. ... 100 C2
Aleutian Trench, Pac. Oc. ... 96 C10
Alexander, U.S.A. ... 112 B3
Alexander, Mt., Australia ... 93 E3
Alexander Arch., U.S.A. ... 100 C6
Alexander Bay, S. Africa ... 88 D2
Alexander City, U.S.A. ... 115 J3
Alexander I., Antarctica ... 5 C17
Alexandra, Australia ... 95 F4
Alexandra, N.Z. ... 91 L2
Alexandra Falls, Canada ... 102 A5

Alexandria = El Iskandarîya,
  Egypt 80 H7
Alexandria, *B.C., Canada* ... 102 C4
Alexandria, *Ont., Canada* ... 117 A10
Alexandria, *Romania* 29 G10
Alexandria, *S. Africa* 88 E4
Alexandria, *U.K.* 13 F4
Alexandria, *La., U.S.A.* 113 K8
Alexandria, *Minn., U.S.A.* ... 112 C7
Alexandria, *S. Dak., U.S.A.* . 112 D6
Alexandria, *Va., U.S.A.* 114 G7
Alexandria Bay, *U.S.A.* 117 B9
Alexandrina, L., *Australia* ... 95 F2
Alexandroúpolis, *Greece* 45 F9
Alexis →, *Canada* 105 B8
Alexis Creek, *Canada* 102 C4
Alfabia, *Spain* 48 B9
Alfambra, *Spain* 38 E3
Alfândega da Fé, *Portugal* ... 36 D4
Alfaro, *Spain* 38 C3
Alfatar, *Bulgaria* 45 C11
Alfaz del Pi, *Spain* 39 G4
Alfeld, *Germany* 24 D5
Alfenas, *Brazil* 127 A6
Alfiós →, *Greece* 46 D3
Alföld, *Hungary* 28 D5
Alfonsine, *Italy* 41 D9
Alford, *Aberds., U.K.* 13 D6
Alford, *Lincs., U.K.* 14 D8
Alfred, *Maine, U.S.A.* 117 C14
Alfred, *N.Y., U.S.A.* 116 D7
Alfreton, *U.K.* 14 D6
Alfta, *Sweden* 10 C10
Alga, *Kazakhstan* 52 E6
Algaida, *Spain* 48 B9
Algar, *Spain* 37 J5
Ålgård, *Norway* 9 G11
Algarinejo, *Spain* 37 H6
Algarve, *Portugal* 37 J2
Algeciras, *Spain* 37 J5
Algemesí, *Spain* 39 F4
Alger, *Algeria* 78 A6
Alger ✈ (ALG), *Algeria* 39 J8
Algeria ■, *Africa* 78 C6
Alghero, *Italy* 42 B1
Älghult, *Sweden* 11 G9
Algiers = Alger, *Algeria* ... 78 A6
Algoa B., *S. Africa* 88 E4
Algodonales, *Spain* 37 J5
Algodor →, *Spain* 36 F7
Algoma, *U.S.A.* 114 C2
Algona, *U.S.A.* 112 D7
Algonac, *U.S.A.* 116 D2
Algonquin △, *Canada* 104 C4
Algorta, *Uruguay* 128 C5
Alhama de Almería, *Spain* .. 37 J8
Alhama de Aragón, *Spain* ... 38 D3
Alhama de Granada, *Spain* .. 37 H7
Alhama de Murcia, *Spain* ... 39 H3
Alhambra, *U.S.A.* 111 L8
Alhaurín el Grande, *Spain* .. 37 J6
Alhucemas = Al Hoceïma,
  Morocco 78 A5
'Alī al Gharbī, *Iraq* 70 C5
'Alī ash Sharqī, *Iraq* 70 C5
Äli Bayramlı, *Azerbaijan* ... 35 L9
'Alī Khēl, *Afghan.* 68 C3
Ali Sahîh, *Djibouti* 81 E5
Ali Shāh, *Iran* 70 B5
Ália, *Italy* 42 E6
'Alīābād, *Khorāsān, Iran* ... 71 C8
'Alīābād, *Kordestān, Iran* .. 70 C5
'Alīābād, *Yazd, Iran* 71 D7
Aliaga, *Spain* 38 E4
Aliağa, *Turkey* 47 C8
Aliákmon →, *Greece* 44 F6
Alibo, *Ethiopia* 81 F4
Alibori →, *Benin* 83 C5
Alibunar, *Serbia & M.* 28 E5
Alicante, *Spain* 39 G4
Alicante □, *Spain* 39 G4
Alicante ✈ (ALC), *Spain* ... 39 G4
Alice, *S. Africa* 88 E4
Alice, *U.S.A.* 113 M5
Alice →, *Queens., Australia* . 94 C3
Alice →, *Queens., Australia* . 94 B3
Alice, Punta, *Italy* 43 C10
Alice Arm, *Canada* 102 B3
Alice Springs, *Australia* 94 C1
Alicedale, *S. Africa* 88 E4
Aliceville, *U.S.A.* 115 J1
Alicudi, *Italy* 43 D7
Aliganj, *India* 69 F8
Aligarh, *Raj., India* 68 G7
Aligarh, *Ut. P., India* 68 F8
Alīgūdarz, *Iran* 71 C6
Alijó, *Portugal* 36 D3
Alimía, *Greece* 49 C9
Alingsås, *Sweden* 11 G6
Alipur, *Pakistan* 68 E4
Alipur Duar, *India* 67 F16
Aliquippa, *U.S.A.* 116 F4
Alishan, *Taiwan* 59 F13
Aliste →, *Spain* 36 D5
Alitus = Alytus, *Lithuania* .. 9 J21
Alivérion, *Greece* 46 C6
Aliwal North, *S. Africa* 88 E4
Alix, *Canada* 102 C6
Aljezur, *Portugal* 37 H2
Aljustrel, *Portugal* 37 H2
Alkamari, *Niger* 83 C7
Alkmaar, *Neths.* 17 B4
All American Canal, *U.S.A.* . 109 K6
Allada, *Benin* 83 D5
Allagash →, *U.S.A.* 115 B11
Allah Dad, *Pakistan* 68 G2
Allahabad, *India* 69 G9
Allan, *Canada* 103 C7
Allanche, *France* 20 C6
Allanridge, *S. Africa* 88 D4
Allaqi, Wadi →, *Egypt* 80 C3
Allariz, *Spain* 36 C3

Allassac, *France* 20 C5
Ålleberg, *Sweden* 11 F7
Allegany, *U.S.A.* 116 D6
Allegheny →, *U.S.A.* 116 F5
Allegheny Mts., *U.S.A.* 114 G6
Allegheny Reservoir, *U.S.A.* . 116 E6
Allègre, *France* 20 C7
Allègre, Pte., *Guadeloupe* ... 120 b
Allen, Bog of, *Ireland* 12 C5
Allen, L., *Ireland* 12 B3
Allendale, *U.S.A.* 115 J5
Allende, *Mexico* 118 B4
Allentown, *U.S.A.* 117 F9
Allentsteig, *Austria* 26 C8
Alleppey, *India* 66 Q10
Allepuz, *Spain* 38 E4
Aller →, *Germany* 24 C5
Alleynes B., *Barbados* ..... 121 g
Alliance, *Nebr., U.S.A.* 112 D3
Alliance, *Ohio, U.S.A.* 116 F3
Allier □, *France* 19 F9
Allier →, *France* 19 F10
Alliford Bay, *Canada* 102 C2
Alligator Pond, *Jamaica* .... 120 a
Allinge, *Denmark* 11 J8
Alliston = New Tecumseth,
  Canada 116 B5
Alloa, *U.K.* 13 E5
Allones, *France* 18 D8
Allora, *Australia* 95 D5
Allos, *France* 21 D10
Alluitsup Paa, *Greenland* ... 101 B15
Alma, *Canada* 105 C5
Alma, *Ga., U.S.A.* 115 K4
Alma, *Kans., U.S.A.* 112 F6
Alma, *Mich., U.S.A.* 114 D3
Alma, *Nebr., U.S.A.* 112 E5
Alma Ata = Almaty, *Kazakhstan* 52 E8
Almacelles, *Spain* 38 D5
Almada, *Portugal* 37 G1
Almadén, *Australia* 94 B3
Almadén, *Spain* 37 G6
Almanor, L., *U.S.A.* 108 F3
Almansa, *Spain* 39 G3
Almanza, *Spain* 36 C5
Almanzor, Pico, *Spain* 36 E5
Almanzora →, *Spain* 39 H3
Almaş, Munţii, *Romania* ... 28 F7
Almassora, *Spain* 38 F4
Almaty, *Kazakhstan* 52 E8
Almazán, *Spain* 38 D2
Almeirim, *Brazil* 125 D8
Almeirim, *Portugal* 37 F2
Almelo, *Neths.* 17 B6
Almenar de Soria, *Spain* ... 38 D2
Almenara, *Spain* 38 F4
Almendra, Embalse de, *Spain* 36 D4
Almendralejo, *Spain* 37 G4
Almere-Stad, *Neths.* 17 B5
Almería, *Spain* 37 J8
Almería □, *Spain* 39 H2
Almería, G. de, *Spain* 39 J2
Almetyevsk, *Russia* 34 C11
Älmhult, *Sweden* 11 H8
Almirante, *Panama* 120 E3
Almiropótamos, *Greece* 46 C6
Almirós, *Greece* 46 B4
Almiroú, Kólpos, *Greece* ... 49 D6
Almodôvar, *Portugal* 37 H2
Almodóvar del Campo, *Spain* 37 G6
Almodóvar del Río, *Spain* .. 37 H5
Almond, *U.S.A.* 116 D7
Almont, *U.S.A.* 116 D1
Almonte, *Canada* 117 A8
Almonte, *Spain* 37 H4
Almora, *India* 69 E8
Almoradí, *Spain* 39 G4
Almorox, *Spain* 36 E6
Almoustarat, *Mali* 83 B5
Älmsta, *Sweden* 10 E12
Almudévar, *Spain* 38 C4
Almuñécar, *Spain* 37 J7
Almunge, *Sweden* 10 E12
Almuradiel, *Spain* 37 G7
Alness, *U.K.* 13 D4
Alnmouth, *U.K.* 14 B6
Alnwick, *U.K.* 14 B6
Aloi, *Uganda* 86 B3
Alon, *Burma* 67 H19
Alonissos-Voríai Sporades △,
  Greece 46 B6
Alor, *Indonesia* 63 F6
Alor Setar, *Malaysia* 65 J3
Álora, *Spain* 37 J6
Alosno, *Spain* 37 H3
Alot, *India* 68 H6
Aloysius, Mt., *Australia* 93 E4
Alpaugh, *U.S.A.* 110 K7
Alpe Apuane △, *Italy* 40 D7
Alpedrinha, *Portugal* 36 E3
Alpena, *U.S.A.* 114 C4
Alpes-de-Haute-Provence □,
  France 21 D10
Alpes-Maritimes □, *France* .. 21 E11
Alpha, *Australia* 94 C4
Alpha Cordillera, *Arctic* 4 A2
Alphen aan den Rijn, *Neths.* . 17 B4
Alpiarça, *Portugal* 37 F2
Alpine, *Ariz., U.S.A.* 109 K9
Alpine, *Calif., U.S.A.* 111 N10
Alpine, *Tex., U.S.A.* 113 K3
Alps, *Europe* 6 F7
Alpu, *Turkey* 72 C4
Alqueta, Barragem do, *Portugal* 37 G3
Alrø, *Denmark* 11 J4
Als, *Denmark* 11 K3
Alsace □, *France* 19 D14
Alsask, *Canada* 103 C7
Alsasua, *Spain* 38 C2
Alsek →, *U.S.A.* 102 B1
Alsfeld, *Germany* 24 E5

Alsten, *Norway* 8 D15
Alstermo, *Sweden* 11 H9
Alston, *U.K.* 14 C5
Alta, *Norway* 8 B20
Alta, Sierra, *Spain* 38 E3
Alta Gracia, *Argentina* 126 C3
Alta Sierra, *U.S.A.* 111 K8
Altaelva →, *Norway* 8 B20
Altafjorden, *Norway* 8 A20
Altai = Aerhtai Shan, *Mongolia* 60 B4
Altamaha →, *U.S.A.* 115 K5
Altamira, *Brazil* 125 D8
Altamira, *Chile* 126 B2
Altamira, *Mexico* 119 C5
Altamira, Cuevas de, *Spain* . 36 B6
Altamont, *U.S.A.* 117 D10
Altamura, *Italy* 43 B9
Altanbulag, *Mongolia* 60 A5
Altar, *Mexico* 118 A2
Altar, Desierto de, *Mexico* .. 118 B2
Altata, *Mexico* 118 C3
Altavista, *U.S.A.* 114 G6
Altay, *China* 60 B3
Altdorf, *Switz.* 25 J4
Alte Mellum, *Germany* 24 B4
Altea, *Spain* 39 G4
Altenberg, *Germany* 24 E9
Altenbruch, *Germany* 24 B4
Altenburg, *Germany* 24 E8
Altenkirchen,
  Mecklenburg-Vorpommern,
  Germany 24 A9
Altenkirchen, *Rhld.-Pfz.,*
  Germany 24 E3
Altenmarkt, *Austria* 26 D7
Alter do Chão, *Portugal* 37 F3
Altınoluk, *Turkey* 47 B8
Altınova, *Turkey* 47 B8
Altıntaş, *Turkey* 47 B12
Altınyaka, *Turkey* 47 E12
Altınyayla, *Turkey* 47 D11
Altiplano, *Bolivia* 122 E4
Altkirch, *France* 19 E14
Altmark, *Germany* 24 C7
Altmühl →, *Germany* 25 G7
Altmühltal △, *Germany* 25 G7
Altmunster, *Austria* 26 D6
Alto Adige = Trentino-Alto
  Adige □, *Italy* 41 B8
Alto Araguaia, *Brazil* 125 G8
Alto Cuchumatanes =
  Cuchumatanes, Sierra de los,
  Guatemala 120 C1
Alto del Carmen, *Chile* 126 B1
Alto del Inca, *Chile* 126 A2
Alto Garda Bresciano △, *Italy* 40 C7
Alto Ligonha, *Mozam.* 87 F4
Alto Molocue, *Mozam.* 87 F4
Alto Paraguay □, *Paraguay* .. 126 A4
Alto Paraná □, *Paraguay* ... 127 B5
Alton, *Canada* 116 C4
Alton, *U.K.* 15 F7
Alton, *Ill., U.S.A.* 112 F9
Alton, *N.H., U.S.A.* 117 C13
Altona, *Canada* 103 D9
Altoona, *U.S.A.* 116 F6
Altötting, *Germany* 25 G8
Altstätten, *Switz.* 25 H5
Altun Kupri, *Iraq* 70 C5
Altun Shan, *China* 60 C3
Alturas, *U.S.A.* 108 F3
Altus, *U.S.A.* 113 H5
Alubijid, *Phil.* 61 G6
Alucra, *Turkey* 73 B8
Aluk, *Sudan* 81 F2
Alūksne, *Latvia* 9 H22
Alunda, *Sweden* 10 E12
Alunite, *U.S.A.* 111 K12
Aluoro →, *Ethiopia* 81 F3
Alupka, *Ukraine* 33 K8
Alushta, *Ukraine* 33 K8
Alusi, *Indonesia* 63 F8
Alustante, *Spain* 38 E3
Alva, *U.S.A.* 113 G5
Alvaiázere, *Portugal* 36 F2
Älvängen, *Sweden* 11 G6
Alvão □, *Portugal* 36 D3
Alvarado, *Mexico* 119 D5
Alvarado, *U.S.A.* 113 J6
Alvaro Obregón, Presa, *Mexico* 118 B3
Älvdalen, *Sweden* 10 C8
Alvear, *Argentina* 126 B4
Alverca, *Portugal* 37 G1
Alvesta, *Sweden* 11 H8
Alvin, *U.S.A.* 113 L7
Alvinston, *Canada* 116 D3
Alvito, *Portugal* 37 G3
Älvkarleby, *Sweden* 10 D11
Alvord Desert, *U.S.A.* 108 E4
Älvros, *Sweden* 10 B8
Älvsbyn, *Sweden* 8 D19
Alwar, *India* 68 F7
Alxa Zuoqi, *China* 56 E3
Alyangula, *Australia* 94 A2
Alyata = Älät, *Azerbaijan* ... 35 L9
Alyth, *U.K.* 13 E5
Alytus, *Lithuania* 9 J21
Alzada, *U.S.A.* 112 C2
Alzey, *Germany* 25 F4
Alzira, *Spain* 39 F4
Am Timan, *Chad* 79 F10
Amadeus, L., *Australia* 93 D5
Amadi, *Dem. Rep. of the Congo* 86 B2
Amâdi, *Sudan* 81 F3
Amadjuak L., *Canada* 101 B12
Amadora, *Portugal* 37 G1
Amagansett, *U.S.A.* 117 F12
Amager, *Denmark* 11 J6
Amagunze, *Nigeria* 83 D6
Amahai, *Indonesia* 63 E7
Amakusa-Shotō, *Japan* 55 H5

Åmål, *Sweden* 10 E6
Amalfi, *Italy* 43 B7
Amaliás, *Greece* 46 D3
Amalner, *India* 66 J9
Amamapare, *Indonesia* 63 E9
Amambaí, *Brazil* 127 A4
Amambaí →, *Brazil* 127 A5
Amambay □, *Paraguay* 127 A4
Amambay, Cordillera de,
  S. Amer. 127 A4
Amami-Guntō, *Japan* 55 L4
Amami-Ō-Shima, *Japan* 55 L4
Aman, Pulau, *Malaysia* ..... 65 c
Amaná, L., *Brazil* 124 D6
Amanat →, *India* 69 G11
Amanda Park, *U.S.A.* 110 C3
Amangeldy, *Kazakhstan* 52 D7
Amantea, *Italy* 43 C9
Amapá, *Brazil* 125 C8
Amapá □, *Brazil* 125 C8
Amara, *Sudan* 81 E3
Amara □, *Ethiopia* 81 E4
Amarante, *Brazil* 125 E10
Amarante, *Portugal* 36 D2
Amaranth, *Canada* 103 C9
Amareleja, *Portugal* 37 G3
Amargosa →, *U.S.A.* 111 J10
Amargosa Range, *U.S.A.* ... 111 J10
Amári, *Greece* 49 D6
Amarillo, *U.S.A.* 113 H4
Amarkantak, *India* 69 H9
Amârna, Tell el', *Sudan* 80 B3
Amaro, Mte., *Italy* 41 F11
Amarpur, *India* 69 G12
Amarti, *Eritrea* 81 E5
Amarwara, *India* 69 H8
Amasra, *Turkey* 72 B5
Amassama, *Nigeria* 83 D6
Amasya, *Turkey* 72 B6
Amata, *Australia* 93 E5
Amatikulu, *S. Africa* 89 D5
Amatitlán, *Guatemala* 120 D1
Amatrice, *Italy* 41 F10
Amay, *Belgium* 17 D5
Amazon = Amazonas →,
  S. Amer. 125 D9
Amazonas □, *Brazil* 124 E6
Amazonas □, *S. Amer.* 125 D9
Amba Ferit, *Ethiopia* 81 E4
Ambah, *India* 68 F8
Ambahakily, *Madag.* 89 C7
Ambahita, *Madag.* 89 C8
Ambala, *India* 68 D7
Ambalavao, *Madag.* 89 C8
Ambalindum, *Australia* 94 C2
Ambanja, *Madag.* 89 A8
Ambararata, *Madag.* 89 B8
Ambarchik, *Russia* 53 C17
Ambarijeby, *Madag.* 89 A8
Ambaro, Helodranon', *Madag.* 89 A8
Ambato, *Ecuador* 124 D3
Ambato, Sierra de, *Argentina* 126 B2
Ambato Boeny, *Madag.* 89 B8
Ambatofinandrahana, *Madag.* 89 C8
Ambatolampy, *Madag.* 89 B8
Ambatomainty, *Madag.* 89 B8
Ambatomanoina, *Madag.* ... 89 B8
Ambatondrazaka, *Madag.* ... 89 B8
Ambatosoratra, *Madag.* 89 B8
Ambelón, *Greece* 46 B4
Amberg, *Germany* 25 F7
Ambergris Cay, *Belize* 119 D7
Ambérieu-en-Bugey, *France* . 21 C9
Amberley, *N.Z.* 91 K4
Ambert, *France* 20 C7
Ambidédi, *Mali* 82 C2
Ambikapur, *India* 69 H10
Ambikol, *Sudan* 80 C3
Ambilobé, *Madag.* 89 A8
Ambinanindrano, *Madag.* ... 89 C8
Ambinanitelo, *Madag.* 89 B8
Ambinda, *Madag.* 89 B8
Amble, *U.K.* 14 B6
Ambleside, *U.K.* 14 C5
Ambo, *Peru* 124 F3
Amboahangy, *Madag.* 89 C8
Ambodifototra, *Madag.* 89 B8
Ambodilazana, *Madag.* 89 B8
Ambodiriana, *Madag.* 89 B8
Ambohidratrimo, *Madag.* ... 89 B8
Ambohidray, *Madag.* 89 B8
Ambohimahamasina, *Madag.* . 89 C8
Ambohimahasoa, *Madag.* ... 89 C8
Ambohimanga, *Madag.* 89 C8
Ambohimitombo, *Madag.* ... 89 C8
Ambohitra, *Madag.* 89 A8
Amboise, *France* 18 E8
Ambon, *Indonesia* 63 E7
Ambondro, *Madag.* 89 D8
Amborompotsy, *Madag.* 89 C8
Ambositra, *Madag.* 89 C8
Ambovombe, *Madag.* 89 D8
Amboy, *U.S.A.* 111 L11
Amboyna Cay, *S. China Sea* . 62 C4
Ambridge, *U.S.A.* 116 F4
Ambriz, *Angola* 84 F2
Amchitka I., *U.S.A.* 100 C1
Amderma, *Russia* 52 C7
Amdhi, *India* 69 H9
Ameca, *Mexico* 118 C4
Ameca →, *Mexico* 118 C3
Amecameca, *Mexico* 119 D5
Ameland, *Neths.* 17 A5
Amélia, *Italy* 41 F9
Amendolara, *Italy* 43 C9
Amenia, *U.S.A.* 117 E11
American Falls, *U.S.A.* 108 E7
American Falls Reservoir, *U.S.A.* 108 E7
American Fork, *U.S.A.* 108 F8
American Highland, *Antarctica* 5 D6

American Samoa ☑, *Pac. Oc.* . 91 B13
Americana, *Brazil* 127 A6
Americus, *U.S.A.* 115 K3
Amerigo Vespucci, Firenze ✈
  (FLR), *Italy* 40 E8
Amersfoort, *Neths.* 17 B5
Amersfoort, *S. Africa* 89 D4
Amery Ice Shelf, *Antarctica* . 5 C6
Ames, *Spain* 36 C2
Ames, *U.S.A.* 112 E8
Amesbury, *U.S.A.* 117 D14
Amet, *India* 68 G5
Amfíklia, *Greece* 46 C4
Amfilokhía, *Greece* 46 C3
Amfípolis, *Greece* 44 F7
Ámfissa, *Greece* 46 C4
Amga, *Russia* 53 C14
Amga →, *Russia* 53 C14
Amgu, *Russia* 53 E14
Amgun →, *Russia* 53 D14
Amherst, *Canada* 105 C7
Amherst, *Mass., U.S.A.* 117 D12
Amherst, *N.Y., U.S.A.* 116 D6
Amherst, *Ohio, U.S.A.* 116 E2
Amherst I., *Canada* 117 B8
Amherstburg, *Canada* 104 D3
Amiata, Mte., *Italy* 41 F8
Amidon, *U.S.A.* 112 B3
Amiens, *France* 19 C9
Amindaion, *Greece* 44 F5
Åminne, *Sweden* 11 G7
Amino, *Ethiopia* 81 G5
Amīrābād, *Iran* 70 C5
Amirante Is., *Seychelles* 50 K9
Amisk △, *Canada* 103 B9
Amisk L., *Canada* 103 C8
Amistad △, *U.S.A.* 113 L4
Amistad, Presa de la, *Mexico* 118 B4
Amite, *U.S.A.* 113 K9
Amla, *India* 68 J8
Amlapura = Karangasem,
  Indonesia 63 J18
Amlia I., *U.S.A.* 100 C2
Amlwch, *U.K.* 14 D3
Amm Adam, *Sudan* 81 D4
'Ammān, *Jordan* 74 D4
'Ammān □, *Jordan* 74 D5
'Ammān ✈ (AMM), *Jordan* . 74 D5
Ammanford, *U.K.* 15 F4
Ammassalik = Tasiilaq,
  Greenland 4 C6
Ammerån →, *Sweden* 10 A10
Ammersee, *Germany* 25 G7
Ammochostos = Famagusta,
  Cyprus 49 D12
Ammon, *U.S.A.* 108 E8
Amnat Charoen, *Thailand* ... 64 E5
Amnura, *Bangla.* 69 G13
Amo Jiang →, *China* 58 F3
Åmol, *Iran* 71 B7
Amorgós, *Greece* 47 E7
Amory, *U.S.A.* 115 J1
Amos, *Canada* 104 C4
Åmot, *Norway* 9 G13
Åmotfors, *Sweden* 10 E6
Amoy = Xiamen, *China* 59 E12
Ampanavoana, *Madag.* 89 B9
Ampang, *Malaysia* 65 L3
Ampangalana, Lakandranon',
  Madag. 89 C8
Ampanihy, *Madag.* 89 C7
Amparafaravola, *Madag.* 89 B8
Amparihy, *Madag.* 89 C8
Ampasinambo, *Madag.* 89 C8
Ampasindava, Helodranon',
  Madag. 89 A8
Ampasindava, Saikanosy, *Madag.* 89 A8
Ampenan, *Indonesia* 63 K18
Amper, *Nigeria* 83 D6
Amper →, *Germany* 25 G7
Ampezzo, *Italy* 41 B9
Amphoe Kathu, *Thailand* ... 65 a
Amphoe Thalang, *Thailand* .. 65 a
Ampitsikinana, *Réunion* 89 A8
Ampombiantambo, *Madag.* .. 89 A8
Amposta, *Spain* 38 E5
Ampotaka, *Madag.* 89 D7
Ampoza, *Madag.* 89 C7
Amqui, *Canada* 105 C6
Amravati, *India* 66 J10
Amreli, *India* 68 J4
Amritsar, *India* 68 D6
Amroha, *India* 69 E8
Amrum, *Germany* 24 A4
Amsterdam, *Neths.* 17 B4
Amsterdam, *U.S.A.* 117 D10
Amsterdam ✈ (AMS), *Neths.* 17 B4
Amsterdam, I. = Nouvelle-
  Amsterdam, Î., *Ind. Oc.* .. 3 F13
Amstetten, *Austria* 26 C7
Amudarya →, *Uzbekistan* .. 52 E6
Amundsen Gulf, *Canada* 100 A7
Amundsen-Scott, *Antarctica* . 5 E
Amundsen Sea, *Antarctica* .. 5 D15
Amungen, *Sweden* 10 C9
Amuntai, *Indonesia* 62 E5
Amur →, *Russia* 53 D15
Amur, W. →, *Sudan* 80 D3
Amurang, *Indonesia* 63 D6
Amursio, *Spain* 38 B1
Amursk, *Russia* 53 D14
Amusco, *Spain* 36 C6
Amvrakikós Kólpos, *Greece* . 46 C2
Amvrosiyivka, *Ukraine* 33 J10
Amyderya = Amudarya →,
  Uzbekistan 52 E6
An Anbâr □, *Iraq* 70 C4
An Bien, *Vietnam* 65 H5
An Hoa, *Vietnam* 64 E7
An Nabatîyah at Tahta, *Lebanon* 74 B4
An Nabk, *Si. Arabia* 70 D3
An Nabk, *Syria* 74 A5

An Nafūd, *Si. Arabia* ... 70 D4
An Najaf, *Iraq* ... 70 C5
An Nāşirīyah, *Iraq* ... 70 D5
An Nhon, *Vietnam* ... 64 F7
An Nîl □, *Sudan* ... 80 D3
An Nîl el Abyad □, *Sudan* ... 81 E3
An Nîl el Azraq □, *Sudan* ... 81 E3
An Nu'ayrīyah, *Si. Arabia* ... 71 E6
An Nu'mānīyah, *Iraq* ... 73 F11
An Nuwayb'ī, W. →, *Si. Arabia* ... 74 F3
An Uaimh, *Ireland* ... 12 C5
Anabar →, *Russia* ... 53 B12
'Anabtā, *West Bank* ... 74 C4
Anaconda, *U.S.A.* ... 108 C7
Anacortes, *U.S.A.* ... 110 B4
Anacuao, Mt., *Phil.* ... 61 C4
Anadarko, *U.S.A.* ... 113 H5
Anadia, *Portugal* ... 36 E2
Anadolu, *Turkey* ... 72 C5
Anadyr, *Russia* ... 53 C18
Anadyr →, *Russia* ... 53 C18
Anadyrskiy Zaliv, *Russia* ... 53 C19
Anáfi, *Greece* ... 47 E7
Anafópoulo, *Greece* ... 47 E7
Anaga, Pta. de, *Canary Is.* ... 48 F3
Anagni, *Italy* ... 41 G10
'Ānah, *Iraq* ... 70 C4
Anaheim, *U.S.A.* ... 111 M9
Anahim Lake, *Canada* ... 102 C3
Anáhuac, *Mexico* ... 118 B4
Anakapalle, *India* ... 67 L13
Anakie, *Australia* ... 94 C4
Anaklia, *Georgia* ... 35 J5
Analalava, *Madag.* ... 89 A8
Analavoka, *Madag.* ... 89 C8
Análipsis, *Greece* ... 49 A3
Anambar →, *Pakistan* ... 68 D3
Anambas, Kepulauan, *Indonesia* ... 62 D3
Anambas Is. = Anambas, Kepulauan, *Indonesia* ... 62 D3
Anambra □, *Nigeria* ... 83 D6
Anamosa, *U.S.A.* ... 112 D9
Anamur, *Turkey* ... 70 B2
Anamur Burnu, *Turkey* ... 72 D5
Anan, *Japan* ... 55 H7
Anand, *India* ... 68 H5
Anánes, *Greece* ... 46 E6
Anantapur, *India* ... 66 M10
Anantnag, *India* ... 69 C6
Ananyiv, *Ukraine* ... 29 C14
Anapa, *Russia* ... 33 K9
Anapodháris →, *Greece* ... 49 E7
Anápolis, *Brazil* ... 125 G9
Anapu →, *Brazil* ... 125 D8
Anār, *Iran* ... 71 D7
Anārak, *Iran* ... 71 C7
Anarisfjällen, *Sweden* ... 10 A7
Anas →, *India* ... 68 H5
Anatolia = Anadolu, *Turkey* ... 72 C5
Anatsogno, *Madag.* ... 89 C7
Añatuya, *Argentina* ... 126 B3
Anaunethad L., *Canada* ... 103 A8
Anbyŏn, *N. Korea* ... 57 E14
Ancares □, *Spain* ... 36 C4
Ancares, Sierra de, *Spain* ... 36 C4
Ancaster, *Canada* ... 116 C5
Ancenis, *France* ... 18 E5
Anchor Bay, *U.S.A.* ... 110 G3
Anchorage, *U.S.A.* ... 100 B5
Anci, *China* ... 56 E9
Ancohuma, Nevado, *Bolivia* ... 124 G5
Ancón, *Peru* ... 124 F3
Ancona, *Italy* ... 41 E10
Ancud, *Chile* ... 128 E2
Ancud, G. de, *Chile* ... 128 E2
Ancy-le-Franc, *France* ... 19 E11
Andacollo, *Argentina* ... 126 D1
Andacollo, *Chile* ... 126 C1
Andaingo, *Madag.* ... 89 B8
Andalgalá, *Argentina* ... 126 B2
Åndalsnes, *Norway* ... 9 E12
Andalucía □, *Spain* ... 37 H6
Andalusia = Andalucía □, *Spain* ... 37 H6
Andalusia, *U.S.A.* ... 115 K2
Andaman Is., *Ind. Oc.* ... 50 H13
Andaman Sea, *Ind. Oc.* ... 62 B1
Andamooka Opal Fields, *Australia* ... 95 E2
Andapa, *Madag.* ... 89 A8
Andara, *Namibia* ... 88 B3
Andelot-Blancheville, *France* ... 19 D12
Andenes, *Norway* ... 8 B17
Andenne, *Belgium* ... 17 D5
Andéranboukane, *Mali* ... 83 B5
Andermatt, *Switz.* ... 25 J4
Andernach, *Germany* ... 24 E4
Andernos-les-Bains, *France* ... 20 D2
Anderslöv, *Sweden* ... 11 J7
Anderson, *Alaska, U.S.A.* ... 100 B5
Anderson, *Calif., U.S.A.* ... 108 F2
Anderson, *Ind., U.S.A.* ... 114 E3
Anderson, *Mo., U.S.A.* ... 113 G7
Anderson, *S.C., U.S.A.* ... 115 H4
Anderson →, *Canada* ... 100 B7
Anderstorp, *Sweden* ... 11 G7
Andes, *U.S.A.* ... 117 D10
Andes, Cord. de los, *S. Amer.* ... 124 H5
Andfjorden, *Norway* ... 8 B17
Andhra Pradesh □, *India* ... 66 L11
Andijon, *Uzbekistan* ... 52 E8
Andikíthira, *Greece* ... 46 F5
Andilamena, *Madag.* ... 89 B8
Andīmeshk, *Iran* ... 71 C6
Andímilos, *Greece* ... 46 E6
Andíparos, *Greece* ... 47 D7
Andípaxoi, *Greece* ... 46 B2
Andípsara, *Greece* ... 47 C7
Andírrion, *Greece* ... 46 C3
Andizhan = Andijon, *Uzbekistan* ... 52 E8
Andoain, *Spain* ... 38 B2
Andoany, *Madag.* ... 89 A8

Andohahela △, *Madag.* ... 89 C8
Andong, *S. Korea* ... 57 F15
Andongwei, *China* ... 57 G10
Andoom, *Australia* ... 94 A3
Andorra, *Spain* ... 38 E4
Andorra ■, *Europe* ... 20 F5
Andorra La Vella, *Andorra* ... 20 F5
Andover, *Maine, U.S.A.* ... 117 B14
Andover, *Mass., U.S.A.* ... 117 D13
Andover, *N.J., U.S.A.* ... 117 F10
Andover, *N.Y., U.S.A.* ... 116 D7
Andover, *Ohio, U.S.A.* ... 116 E4
Andøya, *Norway* ... 8 B16
Andradina, *Brazil* ... 125 H8
Andrahary, Mt., *Madag.* ... 89 A8
Andramasina, *Madag.* ... 89 B8
Andranopasy, *Madag.* ... 89 C7
Andranovory, *Madag.* ... 89 C7
Andratx, *Spain* ... 48 B9
Andreanof Is., *U.S.A.* ... 100 C2
Andreapol, *Russia* ... 32 D7
Andrews, *S.C., U.S.A.* ... 115 J6
Andrews, *Tex., U.S.A.* ... 113 J3
Andreyevka, *Russia* ... 34 D10
Ándria, *Italy* ... 43 A9
Andriamena, *Madag.* ... 89 B8
Andriandampy, *Madag.* ... 89 C8
Andriba, *Madag.* ... 89 B8
Andrijevica, *Serbia & M.* ... 44 D3
Andringitra △, *Madag.* ... 89 C8
Andritsaina, *Greece* ... 46 D3
Androka, *Madag.* ... 89 C7
Ándros, *Greece* ... 46 D6
Andros I., *Bahamas* ... 120 B4
Andros Town, *Bahamas* ... 120 B4
Androscoggin →, *U.S.A.* ... 117 C14
Andrychów, *Poland* ... 31 J6
Andújar, *Spain* ... 37 G6
Andulo, *Angola* ... 84 G3
Aneby, *Sweden* ... 11 G8
Anegada, *Br. Virgin Is.* ... 121 e
Anegada Passage, *W. Indies* ... 121 C7
Aného, *Togo* ... 83 D5
Anenni-Noi, *Moldova* ... 29 D14
Aneto, Pico de, *Spain* ... 38 C5
Anfu, *China* ... 59 D10
Ang Mo Kio, *Singapore* ... 65 d
Ang Thong, *Thailand* ... 64 E3
Ang Thong △, *Thailand* ... 65 H2
Ang Thong, Ko, *Thailand* ... 65 b
Angamos, Punta, *Chile* ... 126 A1
Angara →, *Russia* ... 53 D10
Angara-Débou, *Benin* ... 83 C5
Angarab, *Ethiopia* ... 81 E4
Angarbaka, *Sudan* ... 81 F1
Angarsk, *Russia* ... 53 D11
Angas Hills, *Australia* ... 92 D4
Angaston, *Australia* ... 95 E2
Ånge, *Sweden* ... 10 B9
Ángel, Salto = Angel Falls, *Venezuela* ... 124 B6
Ángel de la Guarda, I., *Mexico* ... 118 B2
Angel Falls, *Venezuela* ... 124 B6
Angeles, *Phil.* ... 61 D4
Ängelholm, *Sweden* ... 11 H6
Angels Camp, *U.S.A.* ... 110 G6
Ängelsberg, *Sweden* ... 10 E10
Anger →, *Ethiopia* ... 81 F4
Angereb →, *Ethiopia* ... 81 E4
Ångermanälven →, *Sweden* ... 10 B11
Ångermanland, *Sweden* ... 8 E18
Angermünde, *Germany* ... 24 B9
Angers, *Canada* ... 117 A9
Angers, *France* ... 18 E6
Angerville, *France* ... 19 D9
Ängesån →, *Sweden* ... 8 C20
Angikuni L., *Canada* ... 103 A9
Angkor, *Cambodia* ... 64 F4
Anglès, *Spain* ... 38 D7
Anglesey, Isle of □, *U.K.* ... 14 D3
Anglet, *France* ... 20 E2
Angleton, *U.S.A.* ... 113 L7
Anglin →, *France* ... 20 B4
Anglure, *France* ... 19 D10
Angmagssalik = Tasiilaq, *Greenland* ... 4 C6
Ango, *Dem. Rep. of the Congo* ... 86 B2
Angoche, *Mozam.* ... 87 F4
Angoche, I., *Mozam.* ... 87 F4
Angol, *Chile* ... 126 D1
Angola, *Ind., U.S.A.* ... 114 E3
Angola, *N.Y., U.S.A.* ... 116 D5
Angola ■, *Africa* ... 85 G3
Angoulême, *France* ... 20 C4
Angoumois, *France* ... 20 C4
Angra dos Reis, *Brazil* ... 127 A7
Angrapa →, *Russia* ... 30 D8
Angren, *Uzbekistan* ... 52 E8
Angtassom, *Cambodia* ... 65 G5
Angu, *Dem. Rep. of the Congo* ... 86 B1
Anguang, *China* ... 57 B12
Anguilla ☒, *W. Indies* ... 121 C7
Anguo, *China* ... 56 E8
Angurugu, *Australia* ... 94 A2
Angus □, *U.K.* ... 13 E6
Angwa →, *Zimbabwe* ... 89 B5
Anhanduí →, *Brazil* ... 127 A5
Anholt, *Denmark* ... 11 H5
Anhua, *China* ... 59 C8
Anhui □, *China* ... 59 B11
Anhwei = Anhui □, *China* ... 59 B11
Anichab, *Namibia* ... 88 C1
Ánidhros, *Greece* ... 47 E7
Anié, *Togo* ... 83 D5
Anina, *Romania* ... 28 E6
Aninoasa, *Romania* ... 29 F9
Anivorano, *Madag.* ... 89 B8
Anjalankoski, *Finland* ... 9 F22

Anjar, *India* ... 68 H4
Anji, *China* ... 59 B12
Anjou, *France* ... 18 E6
Anjozorobe, *Madag.* ... 89 B8
Anju, *N. Korea* ... 57 E13
Anka, *Nigeria* ... 83 C6
Ankaboa, Tanjona, *Madag.* ... 89 C7
Ankang, *China* ... 56 H5
Ankara, *Turkey* ... 72 C5
Ankaramena, *Madag.* ... 89 C8
Ankaratra, *Madag.* ... 85 H9
Ankarsrum, *Sweden* ... 11 G10
Ankasakasa, *Madag.* ... 89 B7
Ankavandra, *Madag.* ... 89 B8
Ankazoabo, *Madag.* ... 89 C7
Ankazobe, *Madag.* ... 89 B8
Ankeny, *U.S.A.* ... 112 E8
Ankilimalinika, *Madag.* ... 89 C7
Ankilizato, *Madag.* ... 89 C8
Ankisabe, *Madag.* ... 89 B8
Anklam, *Germany* ... 24 B9
Ankober, *Ethiopia* ... 81 F4
Ankoro, *Dem. Rep. of the Congo* ... 86 D2
Ankororoka, *Madag.* ... 89 D8
Anlong, *China* ... 58 E5
Anlu, *China* ... 59 B9
Anmyŏn-do, *S. Korea* ... 57 F14
Ånn, *Sweden* ... 10 A6
Ann, C., *U.S.A.* ... 117 D14
Ann Arbor, *U.S.A.* ... 114 D4
Anna, *Russia* ... 34 E5
Anna, *U.S.A.* ... 113 G10
Annaba, *Algeria* ... 78 A7
Annaberg-Buchholz, *Germany* ... 24 E9
Annalee →, *Ireland* ... 12 B4
Annam, *Vietnam* ... 64 E7
Annamitique, Chaîne, *Asia* ... 64 D6
Annan, *U.K.* ... 13 G5
Annan →, *U.K.* ... 13 G5
Annapolis, *U.S.A.* ... 114 F7
Annapolis Royal, *Canada* ... 105 D6
Annapurna, *Nepal* ... 69 E10
Annean, L., *Australia* ... 93 E2
Anneberg, *Sweden* ... 11 G8
Annecy, *France* ... 21 C10
Annecy, Lac d', *France* ... 21 C10
Annemasse, *France* ... 19 F13
Annenskiy Most, *Russia* ... 32 B9
Anning, *China* ... 58 E4
Anniston, *U.S.A.* ... 115 J3
Annobón, *Atl. Oc.* ... 77 G4
Annonay, *France* ... 21 C8
Annot, *France* ... 21 E10
Annotto B., *Jamaica* ... 120 a
Annville, *U.S.A.* ... 117 F8
Annweiler, *Germany* ... 25 F3
Áno Arkhánai, *Greece* ... 47 F7
Áno Porróia, *Greece* ... 44 E7
Áno Síros, *Greece* ... 46 D6
Áno Viánnos, *Greece* ... 49 D7
Anorotsangana, *Madag.* ... 89 A8
Anosibe, *Madag.* ... 89 B8
Anou Mellene, *Mali* ... 83 B5
Anoumaba, *Ivory C.* ... 82 D4
Anóyia, *Greece* ... 49 D6
Anping, *Hebei, China* ... 56 E8
Anping, *Liaoning, China* ... 57 D12
Anpu Gang, *China* ... 58 G7
Anqing, *China* ... 59 B11
Anqiu, *China* ... 57 F10
Anren, *China* ... 59 D9
Ansager, *Denmark* ... 11 J2
Ansai, *China* ... 56 F5
Ansbach, *Germany* ... 25 F6
Anse la Raye, *St. Lucia* ... 121 f
Anseba →, *Eritrea* ... 81 D4
Ansfelden, *Austria* ... 26 C7
Anshan, *China* ... 57 D12
Anshun, *China* ... 58 D5
Ansião, *Portugal* ... 36 F2
Ansley, *U.S.A.* ... 112 E5
Ansó, *Spain* ... 38 C4
Ansoain, *Spain* ... 38 C3
Anson, *U.S.A.* ... 113 J5
Anson B., *Australia* ... 92 B5
Ansongo, *Mali* ... 83 B5
Ansonia, *U.S.A.* ... 117 E11
Anstruther, *U.K.* ... 13 E6
Ansudu, *Indonesia* ... 63 E9
Antabamba, *Peru* ... 124 F4
Antakya, *Turkey* ... 70 B3
Antalaha, *Madag.* ... 89 A9
Antalya, *Turkey* ... 72 D4
Antalya □, *Turkey* ... 47 E12
Antalya Körfezi, *Turkey* ... 72 D4
Antambohobe, *Madag.* ... 89 C8
Antanambao-Manampotsy, *Madag.* ... 89 B8
Antanambe, *Madag.* ... 89 B8
Antananarivo, *Madag.* ... 89 B8
Antananarivo □, *Madag.* ... 89 B8
Antanifotsy, *Madag.* ... 89 B8
Antanimbaribe, *Madag.* ... 89 C7
Antanimora, *Madag.* ... 89 C8
Antarctic Pen., *Antarctica* ... 5 C18
Antarctica ... 5 E3
Antelope, *Zimbabwe* ... 87 G2
Antequera, *Paraguay* ... 126 A4
Antequera, *Spain* ... 37 H6
Antero, Mt., *U.S.A.* ... 109 G10
Antevamena, *Madag.* ... 89 C7
Anthemoús, *Greece* ... 44 F7
Anthony, *Kans., U.S.A.* ... 113 G5
Anthony, *N. Mex., U.S.A.* ... 109 K10
Anti Atlas, *Morocco* ... 78 C4
Anti-Lebanon = Ash Sharqi, Al Jabal, *Lebanon* ... 74 B5
Antibes, *France* ... 21 E11
Antibes, C. d', *France* ... 21 E11

Anticosti, Î. d', *Canada* ... 105 C7
Antifer, C. d', *France* ... 18 C7
Antigo, *U.S.A.* ... 112 C10
Antigonish, *Canada* ... 105 C7
Antigua, *Canary Is.* ... 48 F5
Antigua, *Guatemala* ... 120 D1
Antigua, *W. Indies* ... 121 C7
Antigua & Barbuda ■, *W. Indies* ... 121 C7
Antilla, *Cuba* ... 120 B4
Antilles = West Indies, *Cent. Amer.* ... 121 D7
Antioch, *U.S.A.* ... 110 G5
Antioche, Pertuis d', *France* ... 20 B2
Antioquia, *Colombia* ... 124 B3
Antipodes Is., *Pac. Oc.* ... 96 M9
Antlers, *U.S.A.* ... 113 H7
Antoetra, *Madag.* ... 89 C8
Antofagasta, *Chile* ... 126 A1
Antofagasta □, *Chile* ... 126 A2
Antofagasta de la Sierra, *Argentina* ... 126 B2
Antofalla, *Argentina* ... 126 B2
Antofalla, Salar de, *Argentina* ... 126 B2
Anton, *U.S.A.* ... 113 J3
Antongila, Helodrano, *Madag.* ... 89 B8
Antonibé, *Madag.* ... 89 B8
Antonibé, Presqu'île d', *Madag.* ... 89 A8
Antonina, *Brazil* ... 127 B6
Antrain, *France* ... 18 D5
Antrim, *U.K.* ... 12 B5
Antrim, *U.S.A.* ... 116 F3
Antrim □, *U.K.* ... 12 B5
Antrim, Mts. of, *U.K.* ... 12 A5
Antrim Plateau, *Australia* ... 92 C4
Antrodoco, *Italy* ... 41 F10
Antropovo, *Russia* ... 34 A6
Antsakabary, *Madag.* ... 89 B8
Antsalova, *Madag.* ... 89 B7
Antsenavolo, *Madag.* ... 89 C8
Antsiafabositra, *Madag.* ... 89 B8
Antsirabe, *Antananarivo, Madag.* ... 89 B8
Antsirabe, *Antsiranana, Madag.* ... 89 A8
Antsirabe, *Mahajanga, Madag.* ... 89 B8
Antsiranana, *Madag.* ... 89 A8
Antsiranana □, *Madag.* ... 89 A8
Antsohihy, *Madag.* ... 89 A8
Antsohimbondrona Seranana, *Madag.* ... 89 A8
Antu, *China* ... 57 C15
Antwerp = Antwerpen, *Belgium* ... 17 C4
Antwerp, *U.S.A.* ... 117 B9
Antwerpen, *Belgium* ... 17 C4
Antwerpen □, *Belgium* ... 17 C4
Anupgarh, *India* ... 68 E5
Anuppur, *India* ... 69 H9
Anuradhapura, *Sri Lanka* ... 66 Q12
Anveh, *Iran* ... 71 E7
Anvers = Antwerpen, *Belgium* ... 17 C4
Anvers I., *Antarctica* ... 5 C17
Anwen, *China* ... 59 C13
Anxi, *Fujian, China* ... 59 E12
Anxi, *Gansu, China* ... 60 B4
Anxian, *China* ... 58 B5
Anxiang, *China* ... 59 C9
Anxious B., *Australia* ... 95 E1
Anyama, *Ivory C.* ... 82 D4
Anyang, *China* ... 56 F8
Anyer-Kidul, *Indonesia* ... 63 G11
Anyi, *Jiangxi, China* ... 59 C10
Anyi, *Shanxi, China* ... 56 G6
Anyuan, *China* ... 59 E10
Anyue, *China* ... 58 B5
Anza, *U.S.A.* ... 111 M10
Anze, *China* ... 56 F7
Anzhero-Sudzhensk, *Russia* ... 52 D9
Ánzio, *Italy* ... 42 A5
Ao Makham, *Thailand* ... 65 a
Ao Phangnga △, *Thailand* ... 65 a
Aoga-Shima, *Japan* ... 55 H9
Aoiz, *Spain* ... 38 C3
Aomen = Macau, *China* ... 59 F9
Aomori, *Japan* ... 54 D10
Aomori □, *Japan* ... 54 D10
Aonla, *India* ... 69 E8
Aoraki Mount Cook, *N.Z.* ... 91 K3
Aosta, *Italy* ... 40 C4
Aotearoa = New Zealand ■, *Oceania* ... 91 J6
Aoudéras, *Niger* ... 83 B6
Aoukâr, *Mauritania* ... 82 B3
Aozou, Couloir d', *Chad* ... 79 D9
Apa →, *S. Amer.* ... 126 A4
Apache, *U.S.A.* ... 113 H5
Apache Junction, *U.S.A.* ... 109 K8
Apalachee B., *U.S.A.* ... 115 L4
Apalachicola, *U.S.A.* ... 115 L3
Apalachicola →, *U.S.A.* ... 115 L3
Apam, *Ghana* ... 83 D4
Apapa, *Nigeria* ... 83 D5
Apaporis →, *Colombia* ... 124 D5
Aparados da Serra △, *Brazil* ... 127 B5
Aparri, *Phil.* ... 61 B4
Apateu, *Romania* ... 28 D6
Apatin, *Serbia & M.* ... 28 E4
Apatity, *Russia* ... 52 C4
Apatzingán, *Mexico* ... 118 D4
Apeldoorn, *Neths.* ... 17 B5
Apen, *Germany* ... 24 B3
Apennines = Appennini, *Italy* ... 40 D7
Aphrodisias, *Turkey* ... 47 D10
Apia, *Samoa* ... 91 A13
Apiacás, Serra dos, *Brazil* ... 124 E7
Apies →, *S. Africa* ... 89 D4
Apizaco, *Mexico* ... 119 D5
Aplao, *Peru* ... 124 G4
Apo, Mt., *Phil.* ... 63 C7
Apolakkiá, *Greece* ... 49 C9
Apolakkiá, Órmos, *Greece* ... 49 C9
Apolda, *Germany* ... 24 D7
Apollonia, *Greece* ... 46 E6
Apolo, *Bolivia* ... 124 F5
Aporé →, *Brazil* ... 125 G8

Apostle Is., *U.S.A.* ... 112 B9
Apostle Islands △, *U.S.A.* ... 112 B9
Apóstoles, *Argentina* ... 127 B4
Apostolos Andreas, C., *Cyprus* ... 49 D13
Apostolovo, *Ukraine* ... 33 J7
Apoteri, *Guyana* ... 124 C7
Appalachian Mts., *U.S.A.* ... 114 G6
Äppelbo, *Sweden* ... 10 D8
Appennini, *Italy* ... 40 D7
Appennino Ligure, *Italy* ... 40 D6
Appenzell-Ausser Rhoden □, *Switz.* ... 25 H5
Appenzell-Inner Rhoden □, *Switz.* ... 25 H5
Appiano, *Italy* ... 41 B8
Apple Hill, *Canada* ... 117 A10
Apple Valley, *U.S.A.* ... 111 L9
Appleby-in-Westmorland, *U.K.* ... 14 C5
Appledore, *U.K.* ... 15 F3
Appleton, *U.S.A.* ... 114 C1
Approuague →, *Fr. Guiana* ... 125 C8
Apricena, *Italy* ... 41 G12
Aprília, *Italy* ... 42 A5
Apsheronsk, *Russia* ... 35 H4
Apsley, *Canada* ... 116 B6
Apt, *France* ... 21 E9
Apuane, Alpi, *Italy* ... 40 D7
Apucarana, *Brazil* ... 127 A5
Apulia = Púglia □, *Italy* ... 43 A9
Apure →, *Venezuela* ... 124 B5
Apurímac →, *Peru* ... 124 F4
Apuseni, Munții, *Romania* ... 28 D7
Āqā Jarī, *Iran* ... 71 D6
Aqaba = Al 'Aqabah, *Jordan* ... 74 F4
Aqaba, G. of, *Red Sea* ... 70 D2
'Aqabah, Khalīj al = Aqaba, G. of, *Red Sea* ... 70 D2
'Aqdā, *Iran* ... 71 C7
Aqīq, *Sudan* ... 80 D4
Aqīq, Khalīg, *Sudan* ... 80 D4
'Aqrah, *Iraq* ... 70 B4
Aqtaū, *Kazakhstan* ... 52 E6
Aqtöbe, *Kazakhstan* ... 52 D6
Aquidauana, *Brazil* ... 125 H7
Aquiles Serdán, *Mexico* ... 118 B3
Aquin, *Haiti* ... 121 C5
Aquitaine □, *France* ... 20 D3
Ar Rachidiya = Er Rachidia, *Morocco* ... 78 B5
Ar Rafid, *Syria* ... 74 C4
Ar Raḩḩālīyah, *Iraq* ... 70 C4
Ar Ramādī, *Iraq* ... 70 C4
Ar Ramthā, *Jordan* ... 74 C5
Ar Raqqah, *Syria* ... 70 C3
Ar Rass, *Si. Arabia* ... 70 E4
Ar Rawshān, *Si. Arabia* ... 80 C5
Ar Rifā'ī, *Iraq* ... 70 D5
Ar Riyāḑ, *Si. Arabia* ... 70 E5
Ar Ru'ays, *Qatar* ... 71 E6
Ar Rukhaymīyah, *Iraq* ... 70 D5
Ar Ruşāfah, *Syria* ... 70 C3
Ar Ruţbah, *Iraq* ... 70 C4
Ara, *India* ... 69 G11
Ara Goro, *Ethiopia* ... 81 F5
Ara Tera, *Ethiopia* ... 81 F5
Arab, *U.S.A.* ... 115 H2
'Arab, Bahr el →, *Sudan* ... 81 F2
Arab, Khalīg el, *Egypt* ... 80 A2
Arab, Shatt al →, *Asia* ... 71 D6
'Araba, W. →, *Egypt* ... 80 J8
'Arabābād, *Iran* ... 71 C8
Araban, *Turkey* ... 72 D7
Arabatskaya Strelka, *Ukraine* ... 33 K8
Arabba, *Italy* ... 41 B8
Arabia, *Asia* ... 50 G8
Arabian Desert = Es Sahrâ' Esh Sharqīya, *Egypt* ... 80 B3
Arabian Gulf = Persian Gulf, *Asia* ... 71 E6
Arabian Sea, *Ind. Oc.* ... 50 H10
Araç, *Turkey* ... 72 B5
Aracaju, *Brazil* ... 125 F11
Aracati, *Brazil* ... 125 D11
Araçatuba, *Brazil* ... 127 A5
Aracena, *Spain* ... 37 H4
Aracena, Sierra de, *Spain* ... 37 H4
Aračinovo, *Macedonia* ... 44 D5
Araçuaí, *Brazil* ... 125 G10
'Arad, *Israel* ... 74 D4
Arad, *Romania* ... 28 D6
Arad □, *Romania* ... 28 D6
Arădān, *Iran* ... 71 C7
Aradhippou, *Cyprus* ... 49 E12
Arafura Sea, *E. Indies* ... 96 H5
Aragats, *Armenia* ... 35 K7
Aragón □, *Spain* ... 38 D4
Aragón →, *Spain* ... 38 C3
Aragona, *Italy* ... 42 E6
Araguacema, *Brazil* ... 125 E9
Araguaia →, *Brazil* ... 125 E9
Araguaína, *Brazil* ... 125 E9
Araguari, *Brazil* ... 125 G9
Araguari →, *Brazil* ... 125 C9
Arain, *India* ... 68 F6
Arak, *Algeria* ... 78 C6
Arāk, *Iran* ... 71 C6
Araka, *Sudan* ... 81 G3
Arakan Coast, *Burma* ... 67 K19
Arakan Yoma, *Burma* ... 67 K19
Arákhova, *Greece* ... 46 C4
Arakli, *Turkey* ... 73 B8
Araks = Aras, Rūd-e →, *Asia* ... 35 K9
Aral, *Kazakhstan* ... 52 E7
Aral Sea, *Asia* ... 52 E7
Aral Tengizi = Aral Sea, *Asia* ... 52 E7
Aralsk = Aral, *Kazakhstan* ... 52 E7
Aralskoye More = Aral Sea, *Asia* ... 52 E7
Aralsor, Ozero, *Kazakhstan* ... 35 F9
Aramac, *Australia* ... 94 C4
Aran I., *Ireland* ... 12 B3
Aran Is., *Ireland* ... 12 C2
Aranda de Duero, *Spain* ... 36 D7
Arandān, *Iran* ... 70 C5

Arandelovac, Serbia & M. 44 B4
Aranjuez, Spain 36 E7
Aranos, Namibia 88 C2
Aransas Pass, U.S.A. 113 M6
Aranyaprathet, Thailand 64 F4
Araouane, Mali 82 B4
Arapahoe, U.S.A. 112 E5
Arapey Grande →, Uruguay 126 C4
Arapgir, Turkey 70 B3
Arapiraca, Brazil 125 E11
Arapongas, Brazil 127 A5
Ar'ar, Si. Arabia 70 D4
Araranguá, Brazil 127 B6
Araraquara, Brazil 125 H9
Araras, Serra das, Brazil 127 B5
Ararat, Armenia 73 C11
Ararat, Australia 95 F3
Ararat, Mt. = Ağrı Dağı, Turkey 70 B5
Araria, India 69 F12
Araripe, Chapada do, Brazil 125 E11
Araruama, L. de, Brazil 127 A7
Aras, Rūd-e →, Asia 35 K9
Aratäne, Mauritania 82 B3
Arauca, Colombia 124 B4
Arauca →, Venezuela 124 B5
Arauco, Chile 126 D1
Arawa, Ethiopia 81 F5
Arawale △, Kenya 86 C5
Araxá, Brazil 125 G9
Araya, Pen. de, Venezuela 124 A6
Arba Gugu, Ethiopia 81 F5
Arba Minch, Ethiopia 81 F4
Arbat, Iraq 70 C5
Árbatax, Italy 42 C2
Arbi, Ethiopia 81 F4
Arbīl, Iraq 70 C5
Arboga, Sweden 10 E9
Arbois, France 19 F12
Arbore, Ethiopia 81 F4
Arboréa, Italy 42 C1
Arborfield, Canada 103 C8
Arborg, Canada 103 C9
Arbre du Ténéré, Niger 83 B7
Arbroath, U.K. 13 E6
Arbuckle, U.S.A. 110 F4
Arbus, Italy 42 C1
Arc →, France 21 C10
Arc-lès-Gray, France 19 E12
Arcachon, France 20 D2
Arcachon, Bassin d', France 20 D2
Arcade, Calif., U.S.A. 111 L8
Arcade, N.Y., U.S.A. 116 D6
Arcadia, Fla., U.S.A. 115 M5
Arcadia, La., U.S.A. 113 J8
Arcadia, Pa., U.S.A. 116 F6
Arcata, U.S.A. 108 F1
Arcévia, Italy 41 E9
Archangel = Arkhangelsk, Russia 52 C5
Archar, Bulgaria 44 C6
Archbald, U.S.A. 117 E9
Archena, Spain 39 G3
Archer →, Australia 94 A3
Archer B., Australia 94 A3
Archer Bend = Mungkan
  Kandju △, Australia 94 A3
Archers Post, Kenya 86 B4
Arches △, U.S.A. 109 G9
Archidona, Spain 37 H6
Archipel-de-Mingan △, Canada . 105 B7
Archipiélago Chinijo △,
  Canary Is. 48 E6
Archipiélago Los Roques △,
  Venezuela 121 D6
Arci, Mte., Italy 42 C1
Arcidosso, Italy 41 F8
Arcipelago de la Maddalena △,
  Italy 42 A2
Arcipelago Toscano △, Italy 40 F7
Arcis-sur-Aube, France 19 D11
Arckaringa Cr. →, Australia 95 D2
Arco, Italy 40 C7
Arco, U.S.A. 108 E7
Arcos de Jalón, Spain 38 D2
Arcos de la Frontera, Spain 37 J5
Arcos de Valdevez, Portugal 36 D2
Arcot, India 66 N11
Arcozelo, Portugal 36 E3
Arctic Bay, Canada 101 A11
Arctic Ocean, Arctic 4 B18
Arctic Red River = Tsiigehtchic,
  Canada 100 B6
Arctowski, Antarctica 5 C18
Arda →, Bulgaria 45 E10
Arda →, Italy 40 C7
Ardabīl, Iran 71 B6
Ardabīl □, Iran 71 B6
Ardahan, Turkey 73 B10
Ardakān = Sepīdān, Iran 71 D7
Ardakān, Iran 71 C7
Ardala, Sweden 11 F7
Ardales, Spain 37 J6
Ardèche □, France 21 D8
Ardèche →, France 21 D8
Ardee, Ireland 12 C5
Arden, Canada 116 B8
Arden, Denmark 11 H3
Arden, Calif., U.S.A. 110 G5
Arden, Nev., U.S.A. 111 J11
Ardenne, Belgium 17 E5
Ardennes = Ardenne, Belgium .. 17 E5
Ardennes □, France 19 C11
Ardentes, France 19 F8
Arderin, Ireland 12 C4
Ardeşen, Turkey 73 B9
Ardestān, Iran 71 C7
Árdhas →, Greece 45 E10
Ardhéa, Greece 44 F6
Ardila →, Portugal 37 G3
Ardino, Bulgaria 45 E9
Ardivachar Pt., U.K. 13 D1
Ardlethan, Australia 95 E4
Ardmore, Okla., U.S.A. 113 H6

Ardmore, Pa., U.S.A. 117 G9
Ardnamurchan, Pt. of, U.K. 13 E2
Ardnave Pt., U.K. 13 F2
Ardon, Russia 35 J7
Ardore, Italy 43 D9
Ardres, France 19 B8
Ardrossan, Australia 95 E2
Ardrossan, U.K. 13 F4
Ards Pen., U.K. 12 B6
Arduan, Sudan 80 D3
Ardud, Romania 28 C7
Arecibo, Puerto Rico ...... 121 d
Areia Branca, Brazil 125 E11
Arena, Pt., U.S.A. 110 G3
Arenal, Honduras 120 C2
Arenal, Sweden 11 F10
Arenas = Las Arenas, Spain 36 B6
Arenas de San Pedro, Spain 36 E5
Arendal, Norway 9 G13
Arendsee, Germany 24 C7
Arenys de Mar, Spain 38 D7
Arenzano, Italy 40 D5
Areópolis, Greece 46 E4
Arequipa, Peru 124 G4
Arero, Ethiopia 81 G4
Arès, France 20 D2
Arévalo, Spain 36 D6
Arezzo, Italy 41 E8
Arga →, Spain 38 C3
Arga, Turkey 70 B3
Argalastí, Greece 46 B5
Argamasilla de Alba, Spain 37 F7
Argamasilla de Calatrava, Spain 37 G6
Arganda, Spain 36 E7
Arganil, Portugal 36 E2
Argedeb, Ethiopia 81 F5
Argelès-Gazost, France 20 E3
Argelès-sur-Mer, France 20 F7
Argens →, France 21 E10
Argent-sur-Sauldre, France 19 E9
Argenta, Canada 102 C5
Argenta, Italy 41 D8
Argentan, France 18 D6
Argentário, Mte., Italy 41 F8
Argentat, France 20 C5
Argentera, Italy 40 D4
Argenteuil, France 19 D9
Argentia, Canada 105 C9
Argentiera, C. dell', Italy 42 B1
Argentina ■, S. Amer. 128 D3
Argentina, Colombia 124 C3
Argentine Basin, S. Amer. 122 H5
Argentino, L., Argentina 128 G2
Argenton-Château, France 18 F6
Argenton-sur-Creuse, France .. 19 F8
Argeş □, Romania 29 F9
Argeş →, Romania 29 F11
Arghandab →, Afghan. 68 D1
Argheile, Ethiopia 81 F5
Argo, Sudan 80 D3
Argolikós Kólpos, Greece 46 D4
Argolís □, Greece 46 D4
Argonne, France 19 C12
Árgos, Greece 46 D4
Árgos Orestikón, Greece 44 F5
Argostólion, Greece 46 C2
Arguedas, Spain 38 C3
Arguello, Pt., U.S.A. 111 L6
Arguineguín, Canary Is. 48 G4
Argun →, Russia 35 J7
Argun, Russia 53 D13
Argungu, Nigeria 83 C5
Argus Pk., U.S.A. 111 K9
Argyle, L., Australia 92 C4
Argyll, U.K. 13 E4
Argyll & Bute □, U.K. 13 E3
Arhavi, Turkey 73 B9
Århus, Denmark 11 H4
Århus Amtskommune □,
  Denmark 11 H4
Ariadnoye, Russia 54 B7
Ariamsvlei, Namibia 88 D2
Ariano Irpino, Italy 43 A8
Aribinda, Burkina Faso 83 C4
Arica, Chile 124 G4
Arica, Colombia 124 D4
Arico, Canary Is. 48 F3
Arid, C., Australia 93 F3
Arida, Japan 55 G7
Ariège □, France 20 F5
Ariège →, France 20 E5
Arieş →, Romania 29 D8
Arihā, Israel 80 A4
Arilje, Serbia & M. 44 C4
Arílla, Ákra, Greece 49 A3
Arima, Trin. & Tob. 121 D7
Arinos →, Brazil 124 F7
Ario de Rosales, Mexico 118 D4
Ariogala, Lithuania 30 C10
Aripo, Mt., Trin. & Tob. 125 K15
Aripuanã, Brazil 124 E6
Aripuanã →, Brazil 124 E6
Ariquemes, Brazil 124 E6
Arisaig, U.K. 13 E3
Arīsh, W. el →, Egypt 80 A3
Arissa, Ethiopia 81 E5
Aristazabal I., Canada 102 C3
Arivonimamo, Madag. 89 B8
Ariza, Spain 38 D2
Arizaro, Salar de, Argentina .. 126 A2
Arizona, Argentina 126 D2
Arizona □, U.S.A. 109 J8
Arizpe, Mexico 118 A2
Årjäng, Sweden 10 E6
Arjeplog, Sweden 8 D18
Arjepluovre = Arjeplog, Sweden 8 D18
Arjona, Colombia 124 A3
Arjona, Spain 37 H6
Arjuna, Indonesia 63 G15
Arka, Russia 53 C15
Arkadak, Russia 34 E6
Arkadelphia, U.S.A. 113 H8
Arkadhía □, Greece 46 D4

Arkaig, L., U.K. 13 E3
Arkalyk = Arqalyk, Kazakhstan . 52 D7
Arkansas □, U.S.A. 113 H8
Arkansas →, U.S.A. 113 J9
Arkansas City, U.S.A. 113 G6
Arkaroola, Australia 95 E2
Árkathos →, Greece 46 B3
Arkhángelos, Greece 49 C10
Arkhangelsk, Russia 52 C5
Arkhangelskoye, Russia 34 E5
Arki, India 68 D7
Arkiko, Eritrea 81 D4
Arklow, Ireland 12 D5
Árkoi, Greece 47 D8
Arkona, Kap, Germany 24 A9
Arkösund, Sweden 11 F10
Arkport, U.S.A. 116 D7
Arkticheskiy, Mys, Russia 53 A10
Arkul, Russia 34 B10
Arkville, U.S.A. 117 D10
Árla, Sweden 10 E10
Arlanda, Stockholm ✈ (ARN),
  Sweden 10 E11
Arlanza →, Spain 36 C6
Arlanzón →, Spain 36 C6
Arlbergpass, Austria 26 D3
Arles, France 21 E8
Arli, Burkina Faso 83 C5
Arli △, Burkina Faso 83 C5
Arlington, S. Africa 89 D4
Arlington, N.Y., U.S.A. 117 E11
Arlington, Oreg., U.S.A. 108 D3
Arlington, S. Dak., U.S.A. 112 C6
Arlington, Tex., U.S.A. 113 J6
Arlington, Va., U.S.A. 114 F7
Arlington, Vt., U.S.A. 117 C11
Arlington, Wash., U.S.A. 110 B4
Arlington Heights, U.S.A. 114 D2
Arlit, Niger 78 E7
Arlon, Belgium 17 E5
Arltunga, Australia 94 C1
Armagh, U.K. 12 B5
Armagh □, U.K. 12 B5
Armagnac, France 20 E4
Armançon →, France 19 E10
Armando Bermudez △,
  Dom. Rep. 121 C5
Armavir, Russia 35 H5
Armenia, Colombia 124 C3
Armenia ■, Asia 35 K7
Armeniş, Romania 28 E7
Armenistís, Ákra, Greece 49 C9
Armentières, France 19 B9
Armidale, Australia 95 E5
Armilla, Spain 37 H7
Armorique △, France 18 D3
Armour, U.S.A. 112 D5
Armstrong, B.C., Canada 102 C5
Armstrong, Ont., Canada 104 B2
Armutlu, Bursa, Turkey 45 F12
Armutlu, İzmir, Turkey 47 C9
Arnaía, Greece 44 F7
Arnarfjörður, Iceland 8 D2
Arnaud →, Canada 101 B12
Arnauti, C., Cyprus 49 D11
Arnay-le-Duc, France 19 E11
Arnedillo, Spain 38 C2
Arnedo, Spain 38 C2
Arnett, U.S.A. 113 G5
Arnhem, Neths. 17 C5
Arnhem, C., Australia 94 A2
Arnhem B., Australia 94 A2
Arnhem Land, Australia 94 A1
Árnissa, Greece 44 F5
Arno →, Italy 40 E7
Arno Bay, Australia 95 E2
Arnold, U.K. 14 D6
Arnold, U.S.A. 110 G6
Arnoldstein, Austria 26 E6
Arnon →, France 19 E9
Arnot, Canada 103 B9
Arnøy, Norway 8 A19
Arnprior, Canada 117 A8
Arnsberg, Germany 24 D4
Arnsberger Wald △, Germany . 24 D4
Arnstadt, Germany 24 E6
Aroab, Namibia 88 D2
Aroánia Óri, Greece 46 D4
Aroche, Spain 37 H4
Arochuku, Nigeria 83 D6
Arolsen, Germany 24 D5
Aron, India 68 G6
Aron →, France 19 F10
Arona, Canary Is. 48 F3
Arona, Italy 40 C5
Aroona, Ría de, Spain 36 C2
Aroroy, Phil. 61 E5
Arpajon, France 19 D9
Arpajon-sur-Cère, France 20 D6
Arpaşu de Jos, Romania 29 E9
Arqalyk, Kazakhstan 52 D7
Arrah = Ara, India 69 G11
Arraiolos, Portugal 37 G3
Arran, U.K. 13 F3
Arras, France 19 B9
Arrasate, Spain 38 B2
Arrats →, France 20 D4
Arreau, France 20 F4
Arrecife, Canary Is. 48 F6
Arrecifes, Argentina 126 C3
Arrée, Mts. d', France 18 D3
Arriaga, Chiapas, Mexico 119 D6
Arriaga, San Luis Potosí, Mexico 118 C4
Arribes del Duero △, Spain 36 D4
Arrilalah, Australia 94 C3
Arrino, Australia 93 E2
Arriondas, Spain 36 B5
Arromanches-les-Bains, France . 18 C6
Arronches, Portugal 37 F3

Arros →, France 20 E3
Arrow, L., Ireland 12 B3
Arrowhead, L., U.S.A. 111 L9
Arrowtown, N.Z. 91 L2
Arroyo de la Luz, Spain 37 F4
Arroyo Grande, U.S.A. 111 K6
Års, Denmark 11 H3
Ars, Iran 70 B5
Ars-sur-Moselle, France 19 C13
Arsenault L., Canada 103 B7
Arsenev, Russia 54 B6
Arsi □, Ethiopia 81 F4
Arsiero, Italy 41 C8
Arsin, Turkey 73 B8
Arsk, Russia 34 B9
Ársunda, Sweden 10 D10
Árta, Greece 46 B3
Artà, Spain 48 B10
Arteaga, Mexico 118 D4
Arteche, Phil. 61 E6
Arteijo = Arteixo, Spain 36 B2
Arteixo, Spain 36 B2
Artem = Artyom, Azerbaijan .. 35 K10
Artem, Russia 54 C6
Artemovsk, Russia 53 D10
Artemovsk, Ukraine 33 H9
Artemovskiy, Russia 35 G5
Artenay, France 19 D8
Artern, Germany 24 D7
Artesa de Segre, Spain 38 D6
Artesia = Mosomane, Botswana 88 C4
Artesia, U.S.A. 113 J2
Arthington, Liberia 82 D2
Arthur, Canada 116 C4
Arthur →, Australia 95 G3
Arthur Cr. →, Australia 94 C2
Arthur Pt., Australia 94 C5
Arthur River, Australia 93 F2
Arthur's Pass, N.Z. 91 K3
Arthur's Pass △, N.Z. 91 K3
Arthur's Town, Bahamas 121 B4
Artigas, Antarctica 5 C18
Artigas, Uruguay 126 C4
Artik, Armenia 35 K6
Artillery L., Canada 103 A7
Artois, France 19 B9
Artotína, Greece 46 C4
Artrutx, C. de, Spain 48 B10
Artsyz, Ukraine 29 D14
Artvin, Turkey 73 B9
Artyom, Azerbaijan 35 K10
Aru, Kepulauan, Indonesia 63 F8
Aru Is. = Aru, Kepulauan,
  Indonesia 63 F8
Arua, Uganda 86 B3
Aruanã, Brazil 125 F8
Aruba ☑, W. Indies 121 D6
Arucas, Canary Is. 48 F4
Arudy, France 20 E3
Arun →, Nepal 69 F12
Arun →, U.K. 15 G7
Arunachal Pradesh □, India .. 67 F19
Arusha, Tanzania 86 C4
Arusha □, Tanzania 86 C4
Arusha △, Tanzania 86 C4
Arusha Chini, Tanzania 86 C4
Aruwimi →, Dem. Rep. of
  the Congo 86 B1
Arvada, Colo., U.S.A. 112 F2
Arvada, Wyo., U.S.A. 108 D10
Arve →, France 19 F13
Árvi, Greece 49 E7
Arviat, Canada 103 A10
Arvidsjaur, Sweden 8 D18
Arvika, Sweden 10 E6
Arvin, U.S.A. 111 K8
Arwal, India 69 G11
Arxan, China 60 B6
Aryd, Sweden 11 H8
Aryiádhes, Greece 49 B3
Aryiroúpolis, Greece 49 D6
Arys, Kazakhstan 52 E7
Arzachena, Italy 42 A2
Arzamas, Russia 34 C6
Arzgir, Russia 35 H7
Arzignano, Italy 41 C8
Arzúa, Spain 36 C2
Aš, Czech Rep. 26 A5
Ås, Sweden 10 A8
As Pontes de García Rodríguez,
  Spain 36 B3
Aş Şafā, Syria 74 B6
As Saffānīyah, Si. Arabia 71 E6
As Safīrah, Syria 70 B3
Aş Şahm, Oman 71 E8
As Sājir, Si. Arabia 70 E5
As Salamīyah, Syria 70 C3
As Salmān, Iraq 70 D5
As Salţ, Jordan 74 C4
As Sal'w'a, Qatar 71 E6
As Samāwah, Iraq 70 D5
As Sanamayn, Syria 74 B5
As Sohar = Şuḩār, Oman 71 E8
As Sukhnah, Syria 70 C3
As Sulaymānīyah, Iraq 70 C5
As Sulaymī, Si. Arabia 70 E4
As Sulayyil, Si. Arabia 75 C4
As Summān, Si. Arabia 70 E5
As Suwaydā, Syria 74 C5
As Suwaydā □, Syria 74 C5
As Suwayq, Oman 71 F8
Aş Şuwayrah, Iraq 70 C5
Åsa, Sweden 11 G6
Asab, Namibia 88 D2
Asaba, Nigeria 83 D6
Asad, Buhayrat al, Syria 70 C3
Asadābād, Iran 73 E13
Asafo, Ghana 82 D4
Asahi-Gawa →, Japan 55 G6
Asahigawa, Japan 54 C11
Asale, L., Ethiopia 81 E5

Asamankese, Ghana 83 D4
Asan →, India 69 F8
Asansol, India 69 H12
Åsarna, Sweden 10 B8
Asayita, Ethiopia 81 E5
Asbe Teferi, Ethiopia 81 F5
Asbesberge, S. Africa 88 D3
Asbestos, Canada 105 C5
Asbury Park, U.S.A. 117 F10
Ascea, Italy 43 B8
Ascensión, Mexico 118 A3
Ascensión, B. de la, Mexico .. 119 D7
Ascension I., Atl. Oc. 77 G2
Aschach an der Donau, Austria . 26 C7
Aschaffenburg, Germany 25 F5
Aschendorf, Germany 24 B3
Aschersleben, Germany 24 D7
Asciano, Italy 41 E8
Áscoli Piceno, Italy 41 F10
Áscoli Satriano, Italy 43 A8
Ascope, Peru 124 E3
Ascotán, Chile 126 A2
Aseb, Eritrea 81 E5
Åseda, Sweden 11 G9
Asela, Ethiopia 81 F4
Åsen, Sweden 10 C7
Asenovgrad, Bulgaria 45 D8
Aserradero, Mexico 118 C3
Asfeld, France 19 C11
Asfûn el Matâ'na, Egypt 80 B3
Asgata, Cyprus 49 E12
Ash Fork, U.S.A. 109 J7
Ash Grove, U.S.A. 113 G8
Ash Shabakah, Iraq 70 D4
Ash Shamāl □, Lebanon 74 A5
Ash Shāmīyah, Iraq 70 D5
Ash Shāriqah, U.A.E. 71 E7
Ash Sharmah, Si. Arabia 70 D2
Ash Sharqāt, Iraq 70 C4
Ash Sharqi, Al Jabal, Lebanon . 74 B5
Ash Shaţrah, Iraq 70 D5
Ash Shawbak, Jordan 70 D2
Ash Shawmari, J., Jordan 74 E5
Ash Shināfīyah, Iraq 70 D5
Ash Shu'bah, Si. Arabia 70 D5
Ash Shumlūl, Si. Arabia 70 E5
Ash Shūr'a, Iraq 70 C4
Ash Shurayf, Si. Arabia 70 E3
Ash Shuwayfāt, Lebanon 74 B4
Ashanti □, Ghana 83 D4
Ashau, Vietnam 64 D6
Ashbourne, U.K. 14 D6
Ashburn, U.S.A. 115 K4
Ashburton, N.Z. 91 K3
Ashburton →, Australia 92 D1
Ashcroft, Canada 102 C4
Ashdod, Israel 74 D3
Ashdown, U.S.A. 113 J7
Asheboro, U.S.A. 115 H6
Ashern, Canada 103 C9
Asherton, U.S.A. 113 L5
Asheville, U.S.A. 115 H4
Ashewat, Pakistan 68 D3
Asheweig →, Canada 104 B2
Ashford, Australia 95 D5
Ashford, U.K. 15 F8
Ashgabat, Turkmenistan 52 F6
Ashibetsu, Japan 54 C11
Ashikaga, Japan 55 F9
Ashington, U.K. 14 B6
Ashizuri-Uwakai △, Japan 55 H6
Ashizuri-Zaki, Japan 55 H6
Ashkarkot, Afghan. 68 C2
Ashkhabad = Ashgabat,
  Turkmenistan 52 F6
Āshkhāneh, Iran 71 B8
Ashland, Kans., U.S.A. 113 G5
Ashland, Ky., U.S.A. 114 F4
Ashland, Mont., U.S.A. 108 D10
Ashland, Ohio, U.S.A. 116 F2
Ashland, Oreg., U.S.A. 108 E2
Ashland, Pa., U.S.A. 117 F8
Ashland, Va., U.S.A. 114 G7
Ashland, Wis., U.S.A. 112 B9
Ashley, N. Dak., U.S.A. 112 B5
Ashley, Pa., U.S.A. 117 E9
Ashmore and Cartier Is., Ind. Oc. 92 B3
Ashmore Reef, Australia 92 B3
Ashmûn, Egypt 80 H7
Ashmyany, Belarus 9 J21
Ashokan Reservoir, U.S.A. 117 E10
Ashqelon, Israel 74 D3
Ashta, India 68 H7
Ashtabula, U.S.A. 116 E4
Ashton, S. Africa 88 E3
Ashton, U.S.A. 108 D8
Ashuanipi, L., Canada 105 B6
Ashuapmushuan →, Canada .. 104 C5
Ashville, U.S.A. 116 F6
'Āşī →, Asia 72 D6
Asia 50 E12
Asia, Kepulauan, Indonesia .. 63 D8
Asiago, Italy 41 C8
Asifabad, India 66 K11
Asinara, Italy 42 A1
Asinara, G. dell', Italy 42 A1
Asino, Russia 52 D9
Asipovichy, Belarus 32 F5
'Asīr □, Si. Arabia 75 D3
Asir, Ras, Somali Rep. 75 E5
Aşkale, Turkey 73 C9
Askersund, Sweden 11 F8
Askham, S. Africa 88 D3
Askim, Norway 9 G14
Askja, Iceland 8 D5
Asköy, Norway 9 F11
Asl, Egypt 80 B3
Aslan Burnu, Turkey 47 C8
Aslanapa, Turkey 47 B11
Asmara = Asmera, Eritrea 81 D4
Asmera, Eritrea 81 D4
Asnæs, Denmark 11 J4

Åsnen, *Sweden* 11 H8
Aso Kuju △, *Japan* 55 H5
Åsola, *Italy* 40 C7
Asosa, *Ethiopia* 81 E3
Asoteriba, Jebel, *Sudan* 80 C4
Aspatria, *U.K.* 14 C4
Aspe, *Spain* 39 G4
Aspen, *U.S.A.* 109 G10
Aspendos, *Turkey* 72 D4
Aspermont, *U.S.A.* 113 J4
Aspet, *France* 20 E4
Aspiring, Mt., *N.Z.* 91 L2
Aspres-sur-Buëch, *France* ... 21 D9
Asprókavos, Ákra, *Greece* ... 49 B4
Aspromonte △, *Italy* 43 D8
Aspur, *India* 68 H6
Asquith, *Canada* 103 C7
Assab = Aseb, *Eritrea* 81 E5
Assâba, Massif de l', *Mauritania* . 82 B2
Assagny △, *Ivory C.* 82 D4
Assaikio, *Nigeria* 83 D6
Assam □, *India* 67 G18
Assamakka, *Niger* 83 B6
Assateague Island △, *U.S.A.* . 114 F8
Asse, *Belgium* 17 D4
Assémini, *Italy* 42 C1
Assen, *Neths.* 17 A6
Assens, *Denmark* 11 J3
Assini, *Ivory C.* 82 D4
Assiniboia, *Canada* 103 D7
Assiniboine ➤, *Canada* 103 D9
Assiniboine, Mt., *Canada* ... 102 C5
Assis, *Brazil* 127 A5
Assisi, *Italy* 41 E9
Ássos, *Greece* 46 C2
Assynt, L., *U.K.* 13 C3
Astaffort, *France* 20 D4
Astakídha, *Greece* 47 F8
Astakós, *Greece* 46 C3
Astana, *Kazakhstan* 52 D8
Åstäneh, *Iran* 71 B6
Astara, *Azerbaijan* 71 B6
Åstärā, *Iran* 73 C13
Asteroúsia, *Greece* 49 E7
Asti, *Italy* 40 D5
Astipálaia, *Greece* 47 E8
Astorga, *Spain* 36 C4
Astoria, *U.S.A.* 110 D3
Åstorp, *Sweden* 11 H6
Astrakhan, *Russia* 35 G9
Astudillo, *Spain* 36 C6
Asturias □, *Spain* 36 B5
Asturias ✈ (OVD), *Spain* ... 36 B4
Asunción, *Paraguay* 126 B4
Asunción Nochixtlán, *Mexico* . 119 D5
Åsunden, *Sweden* 11 F9
Asutri, *Sudan* 81 D4
Aswa ➤, *Uganda* 86 B3
Aswa-Lolim △, *Uganda* 86 B3
Aswad, Ra's al, *Si. Arabia* .. 80 C4
Aswân, *Egypt* 80 C3
Aswân Dam = Sadd el Aali, *Egypt* 80 C3
Asyût, *Egypt* 80 B3
Asyûti, Wadi ➤, *Egypt* 80 B3
Aszód, *Hungary* 28 C4
At Tafilah, *Jordan* 74 E4
At Tafilah □, *Jordan* 74 E4
Aţ Ta'if, *Si. Arabia* 75 C3
At Ta'mīm □, *Iraq* 70 C5
Aţ Ţirāq, *Si. Arabia* 70 E5
Aţ Ţubayq, *Si. Arabia* 70 D3
Atabey, *Turkey* 47 D12
Atacama □, *Chile* 126 B2
Atacama, Desierto de, *Chile* . 126 A2
Atacama, Salar de, *Chile* 126 A2
Atakpamé, *Togo* 83 D5
Ataländi, *Greece* 46 C4
Atalaya, *Peru* 124 F4
Atalaya de Femes, *Canary Is.* . 48 F6
Atami, *Japan* 55 G9
Atapupu, *E. Timor* 63 F6
Atâr, *Mauritania* 78 D3
Atarfe, *Spain* 37 H7
Atari, *Pakistan* 68 D6
Atascadero, *U.S.A.* 110 K6
Atasu, *Kazakhstan* 52 E8
Ataturk, Istanbul ✈ (IST), *Turkey* 45 F12
Atatürk Baraji, *Turkey* 73 D8
Atauro, *E. Timor* 63 F7
'Atbara, *Sudan* 80 D3
'Atbara, Nahr ➤, *Sudan* 80 D3
Atbasar, *Kazakhstan* 52 D7
Atça, *Turkey* 47 D10
Atchafalaya B., *U.S.A.* 113 L9
Atchison, *U.S.A.* 112 F7
Atebubu, *Ghana* 83 D4
Ateca, *Spain* 38 D3
Aterno ➤, *Italy* 41 F10
Åteshān, *Iran* 71 C7
Atesine, Alpi, *Italy* 41 B8
Atessa, *Italy* 41 F11
Atfih, *Egypt* 80 J7
Ath, *Belgium* 17 D3
Athabasca, *Canada* 102 C6
Athabasca ➤, *Canada* 103 B6
Athabasca, L., *Canada* 103 B7
Athabasca Sand Dunes △,
  Canada 103 B7
Athboy, *Ireland* 12 C5
Athenry, *Ireland* 12 C3
Athens = Athínai, *Greece* 46 D5
Athens, Ala., *U.S.A.* 115 H2
Athens, Ga., *U.S.A.* 115 J4
Athens, N.Y., *U.S.A.* 117 D11
Athens, Ohio, *U.S.A.* 114 F4
Athens, Pa., *U.S.A.* 117 E8
Athens, Tenn., *U.S.A.* 115 H3
Athens, Tex., *U.S.A.* 113 J7
Atherley, *Canada* 116 B5
Atherton, *Australia* 94 B4
Athiéme, *Benin* 83 D5

Athienou, *Cyprus* 49 D12
Athínai, *Greece* 46 D5
Athínai ✈ (ATH), *Greece* 46 D5
Athlone, *Ireland* 12 C4
Athna, *Cyprus* 49 D12
Athol, *U.S.A.* 117 D12
Atholl, Forest of, *U.K.* 13 E5
Atholville, *Canada* 105 C6
Áthos, *Greece* 45 F8
Athy, *Ireland* 12 C5
Ati, *Chad* 79 F9
Ati, *Sudan* 81 E2
Atiak, *Uganda* 86 B3
Atienza, *Spain* 38 D2
Atiit, *Sudan* 81 F3
Atik L., *Canada* 103 B9
Atikameg ➤, *Canada* 104 B3
Atikokan, *Canada* 104 C1
Atikonak L., *Canada* 105 B7
Atimonan, *Phil.* 61 E4
Atitlán △, *Cent. Amer.* 119 E6
Atka, *Russia* 53 C16
Atka I., *U.S.A.* 100 C2
Atkarsk, *Russia* 34 E7
Atkinson, *U.S.A.* 112 D5
Atlanta, Ga., *U.S.A.* 115 J3
Atlanta, Tex., *U.S.A.* 113 J7
Atlantic, *U.S.A.* 112 E7
Atlantic City, *U.S.A.* 114 F8
Atlantic-Indian Basin, *Antarctica* 5 B4
Atlantic-Indian Ridge, *Atl. Oc.* . 5 B3
Atlantic Ocean 2 E9
Atlas Mts. = Haut Atlas, *Morocco* 78 B4
Atlin, *Canada* 102 B2
Atlin △, *Canada* 102 B2
Atlin, L., *Canada* 102 B2
Atmore, *U.S.A.* 115 K2
Atoka, *U.S.A.* 113 H6
Atokos Nisís, *Greece* 46 C2
Átokos Nisís, *Greece* 46 C2
Atoyac, *U.S.A.* 111 K9
Atrai ➤, *Bangla.* 69 G13
Atrak = Atrek ➤, *Turkmenistan* 71 B8
Åtran, *Sweden* 11 G6
Åtran ➤, *Sweden* 11 H6
Atrauli, *India* 68 E8
Atrek ➤, *Turkmenistan* 71 B8
Atri, *Italy* 41 F10
Atsiki, *Greece* 47 B7
Atsoum Mts., *Cameroon* 83 D7
Atsuta, *Japan* 54 C10
Attalla, *U.S.A.* 115 H2
Attapu, *Laos* 64 E6
Attáviros, *Greece* 49 C9
Attawapiskat, *Canada* 104 B3
Attawapiskat ➤, *Canada* 104 B3
Attawapiskat L., *Canada* 104 B2
Attersee, *Austria* 26 D6
Attica, Ind., *U.S.A.* 114 E2
Attica, Ohio, *U.S.A.* 116 E2
Attichy, *France* 19 C10
Attigny, *France* 19 C11
Attika = Attikí □, *Greece* 46 D5
Attikamegen L., *Canada* 105 B6
Attikí □, *Greece* 46 D5
Attleboro, *U.S.A.* 117 E13
Attock, *Pakistan* 68 C5
Attopeu = Attapu, *Laos* 64 E6
Attu I., *U.S.A.* 100 C1
Attur, *India* 66 P11
Atuel ➤, *Argentina* 126 D2
Åtvidaberg, *Sweden* 11 F10
Atwater, *U.S.A.* 110 H6
Atwood, *Canada* 116 C3
Atwood, *U.S.A.* 112 F4
Atyraū, *Kazakhstan* 52 E6
Au Sable, *U.S.A.* 116 B1
Au Sable ➤, *U.S.A.* 114 C4
Au Sable Forks, *U.S.A.* 117 B11
Au Sable Pt., *U.S.A.* 116 B1
Aubagne, *France* 21 E9
Aubarca, C. d', *Spain* 48 B7
Aube □, *France* 19 D11
Aube ➤, *France* 19 D10
Aubenas, *France* 21 D8
Aubenton, *France* 19 C11
Auberry, *U.S.A.* 110 H7
Aubigny-sur-Nère, *France* ... 19 E9
Aubin, *France* 20 D6
Aubrac, Mts. d', *France* 20 D7
Auburn, Ala., *U.S.A.* 115 J3
Auburn, Calif., *U.S.A.* 110 G5
Auburn, Ind., *U.S.A.* 114 E3
Auburn, Maine, *U.S.A.* 115 C10
Auburn, N.Y., *U.S.A.* 117 D8
Auburn, Nebr., *U.S.A.* 112 E7
Auburn, Pa., *U.S.A.* 117 F8
Auburn, Wash., *U.S.A.* 110 C4
Auburn Ra., *Australia* 95 D5
Auburndale, *U.S.A.* 115 L5
Aubusson, *France* 20 C6
Auce, *Latvia* 30 B9
Auch, *France* 20 E4
Auchi, *Nigeria* 83 D6
Auchterarder, *U.K.* 13 E5
Auchtermuchty, *U.K.* 13 E5
Auckland, *N.Z.* 91 G5
Auckland Is., *Pac. Oc.* 96 N8
Aude □, *France* 20 E6
Aude ➤, *France* 20 E7
Auden, *Canada* 104 B2
Auderville, *France* 18 C5
Audierne, *France* 18 D2
Audincourt, *France* 19 E13
Audo Ra., *Ethiopia* 81 F5
Audubon, *U.S.A.* 112 E7
Aue, *Germany* 24 E8
Auerbach, *Germany* 24 E8
Augathella, *Australia* 95 D4
Aughnacloy, *U.K.* 12 B5
Augrabies Falls, *S. Africa* 88 D3
Augrabies Falls △, *S. Africa* . 88 D3

Augsburg, *Germany* 25 G6
Augsburg-Westliche Wälder △,
  Germany 25 G6
Augusta, *Australia* 93 F2
Augusta, *Italy* 43 E8
Augusta, Ark., *U.S.A.* 113 H9
Augusta, Ga., *U.S.A.* 115 J5
Augusta, Kans., *U.S.A.* 113 G6
Augusta, Maine, *U.S.A.* 101 D13
Augusta, Mont., *U.S.A.* 108 C7
Augustenborg, *Denmark* 11 K3
Augustów, *Poland* 30 E9
Augustus, Mt., *Australia* 93 D2
Augustus I., *Australia* 92 C3
Aukan, *Eritrea* 81 D5
Aukrug △, *Germany* 24 A5
Aukum, *U.S.A.* 110 G6
Auld, L., *Australia* 92 D3
Aulla, *Italy* 40 D6
Aulnay, *France* 20 B3
Aulne ➤, *France* 18 D2
Aulnoye-Aymeries, *France* ... 19 B10
Ault, *France* 18 B8
Ault, *U.S.A.* 112 E2
Aulus-les-Bains, *France* 20 F5
Aumale, *France* 19 C8
Aumont-Aubrac, *France* 20 D7
Auna, *Nigeria* 83 C5
Auning, *Denmark* 11 H4
Aunis, *France* 20 B3
Auponhia, *Indonesia* 63 E7
Aups, *France* 21 E10
Aur, Pulau, *Malaysia* 65 L5
Auraiya, *India* 69 F8
Aurangabad, Bihar, India 69 G11
Aurangabad, Maharashtra, India 66 K9
Auray, *France* 18 E4
Aurich, *Germany* 24 B3
Aurillac, *France* 20 D6
Auronzo di Cadore, *Italy* 41 B9
Aurora, *S. Africa* 88 E2
Aurora, Colo., *U.S.A.* 112 F2
Aurora, Ill., *U.S.A.* 114 E1
Aurora, Mo., *U.S.A.* 113 G8
Aurora, N.Y., *U.S.A.* 117 D8
Aurora, Nebr., *U.S.A.* 112 E6
Aurora, Ohio, *U.S.A.* 116 E3
Aurukun, *Australia* 94 A3
Aus, *Namibia* 88 D2
Ausable ➤, *Canada* 116 C3
Auschwitz = Oświęcim, *Poland* 31 H6
Austerlitz = Slavkov u Brna,
  Czech Rep. 27 B9
Austin, Minn., *U.S.A.* 112 D8
Austin, Nev., *U.S.A.* 108 G5
Austin, Pa., *U.S.A.* 116 E6
Austin, Tex., *U.S.A.* 113 K6
Austin, L., *Australia* 93 E2
Austin I., *Canada* 103 A10
Austra, *Norway* 8 D14
Austral Is. = Tubuai Is.,
  French Polynesia 97 K13
Austral Seamount Chain, *Pac. Oc.* 97 K13
Australia ■, *Oceania* 96 K5
Australian Capital Territory □,
  Australia 95 F4
Australind, *Australia* 93 F2
Austria ■, *Europe* 26 E7
Austvågøy, *Norway* 8 B16
Auterive, *France* 20 E5
Authie ➤, *France* 19 B8
Authon-du-Perche, *France* ... 18 D7
Autlán, *Mexico* 118 D4
Autun, *France* 19 F11
Auvergne □, *France* 20 C7
Auvergne, Mts. d', *France* ... 20 C6
Auvézère ➤, *France* 20 C4
Auxerre, *France* 19 E10
Auxi-le-Château, *France* 19 B9
Auxonne, *France* 19 E12
Auzances, *France* 19 F9
Ava, *U.S.A.* 113 G8
Avallon, *France* 19 E10
Avalon, *U.S.A.* 111 M8
Avalon Pen., *Canada* 105 C9
Avanos, *Turkey* 70 B2
Avaré, *Brazil* 127 A6
Ávas, *Greece* 45 F9
Avawatz Mts., *U.S.A.* 111 K10
Avdan Dağı, *Turkey* 45 F13
Avdira, *Brazil* 125 D7
Aveiro, *Portugal* 36 E2
Aveiro □, *Portugal* 36 E2
Åvej, *Iran* 71 C6
Avellaneda, *Argentina* 126 C4
Avellino, *Italy* 43 B7
Avenal, *U.S.A.* 110 K6
Aversa, *Italy* 43 B7
Avery, *U.S.A.* 108 C6
Aves, I. de, *W. Indies* 121 C7
Aves, Is. las, *Venezuela* 121 D6
Avesnes-sur-Helpe, *France* ... 19 B10
Avesnois ➤, *France* 19 B10
Avesta, *Sweden* 10 D10
Aveyron □, *France* 20 D6
Aveyron ➤, *France* 20 D5
Avezzano, *Italy* 41 F10
Avgó, *Greece* 47 F7
Aviá Terai, *Argentina* 126 B3
Aviano, *Italy* 41 B9
Aviemore, *U.K.* 13 D5
Avigliana, *Italy* 40 C4
Avigliano, *Italy* 43 B8
Avignon, *France* 21 E8
Ávila, *Spain* 36 E6
Ávila □, *Spain* 36 E6
Ávila, Sierra de, *Spain* 36 E6
Avila Beach, *U.S.A.* 111 K6
Avilés, *Spain* 36 B5
Avintes, *Portugal* 36 D2
Avionárion, *Greece* 46 C6

Avis, *Portugal* 37 F3
Avis, *U.S.A.* 116 E7
Avísio ➤, *Italy* 40 B8
Aviz = Avis, *Portugal* 37 F3
Avize, *France* 19 D11
Avlum, *Denmark* 11 H2
Avoca ➤, *Australia* 95 F3
Avoca, *U.S.A.* 116 D7
Avoca ➤, *Australia* 95 F3
Avoca ➤, *Ireland* 12 D5
Avola, *Canada* 102 C5
Avola, *Italy* 43 F8
Avon ➤, *Australia* 116 D7
Avon ➤, *Australia* 93 F2
Avon ➤, *Bristol, U.K.* 15 F5
Avon ➤, *Dorset, U.K.* 15 G6
Avon ➤, *Warks., U.K.* 15 E5
Avon Park, *U.S.A.* 115 M5
Avondale, *Zimbabwe* 87 F3
Avonlea, *Canada* 103 D8
Avonmore, *Canada* 117 A10
Avonmouth, *U.K.* 15 F5
Avramov, *Bulgaria* 45 D10
Avranches, *France* 18 D5
Avre ➤, *France* 18 D8
Avrig, *Romania* 29 E9
Avrillé, *France* 18 E6
Avtovac, *Bos.-H.* 44 C2
Awag el Baqar, *Sudan* 81 E3
A'waj ➤, *Syria* 74 B5
Awaji-Shima, *Japan* 55 G7
'Awālī, *Bahrain* 71 E6
Awantipur, *India* 69 C6
Awasa, *Ethiopia* 81 F4
Awash, *Ethiopia* 81 F4
Awash, *Ethiopia* 81 F5
Awash ➤, *Ethiopia* 81 E5
Awaso, *Ghana* 82 D4
Awatere ➤, *N.Z.* 91 J5
Awbārī, *Libya* 79 C8
Awbārī □, *Libya* 79 C8
Awe, L., *U.K.* 13 E3
Aweil, *Sudan* 81 F2
Awgu, *Nigeria* 83 D6
Awjilah, *Libya* 79 C10
Awka, *Nigeria* 83 D6
Ax-les-Thermes, *France* 20 F5
Axat, *France* 20 F6
Axe ➤, *U.K.* 15 F5
Axel Heiberg I., *Canada* 98 A10
Axim, *Ghana* 82 E4
Axintele, *Romania* 29 F11
Axiós ➤, *Greece* 44 F6
Axminster, *U.K.* 15 G4
Ay, *France* 19 C11
Ayabaca, *Peru* 124 D3
Ayabe, *Japan* 55 G7
Ayacucho, *Argentina* 126 D4
Ayacucho, *Peru* 124 F4
Ayaguz, *Kazakhstan* 52 E9
Ayamé, *Ivory C.* 82 D4
Ayamonte, *Spain* 37 H3
Ayan, *Russia* 53 D14
Ayancık, *Turkey* 72 B6
Ayas, *Turkey* 72 B5
Ayaviri, *Peru* 124 F4
Aybastı, *Turkey* 72 B7
Aydın, *Turkey* 72 D2
Aydın □, *Turkey* 47 D9
Aydın Dağları, *Turkey* 47 D10
Ayelu, *Ethiopia* 81 E5
Ayenngré, *Togo* 83 D5
Ayer, *U.S.A.* 117 D13
Ayer Hitam, *Malaysia* .... 65 c
Ayerbe, *Spain* 38 C4
Ayer's Cliff, *Canada* 117 A12
Ayers Rock, *Australia* 93 E5
Ayiá, *Greece* 46 B4
Ayia Aikateríni, Ákra, *Greece* . 49 A3
Ayía Ánna, *Greece* 46 C5
Ayia Dhéka, *Greece* 49 D6
Ayía Gálini, *Greece* 49 D6
Ayía Marína, *Kásos, Greece* . 47 F8
Ayía Marína, *Léros, Greece* .. 47 D8
Ayia Napa, *Cyprus* 49 E13
Ayía Paraskeví, *Greece* 47 B8
Ayia Phyla, *Cyprus* 49 E12
Ayía Rouméli, *Greece* 49 D5
Ayía Varvára, *Greece* 49 D7
Ayiássos, *Greece* 47 B8
Áyioi Theódhoroi, *Greece* ... 46 D5
Áyion Óros □, *Greece* 45 F8
Áyios Amvrósios, *Cyprus* 49 D12
Áyios Andréas, *Greece* 46 D4
Áyios Evstrátios, *Greece* 45 E8
Áyios Ioánnis, Ákra, *Greece* . 49 D7
Áyios Isídhoros, *Greece* 49 C9
Áyios Kiríkos, *Greece* 47 D8
Áyios Matthaíos, *Greece* 49 B3
Áyios Mírono, *Greece* 47 F7
Áyios Nikólaos, *Greece* 49 D7
Áyios Pétros, *Greece* 46 C2
Áyios Seryios, *Cyprus* 49 D12
Áyios Theódhoros, *Cyprus* ... 49 D13
Áyios Yeóryios, *Greece* 46 D5
Aykathonísi, *Greece* 47 D8
Aykırıkçi, *Turkey* 47 B12
Aylesbury, *U.K.* 15 F7
Aylmer, *Canada* 116 D4
Aylmer, L., *Canada* 100 B8
'Ayn, Wādī al, *Oman* 71 F7
Ayn Dār, *Si. Arabia* 71 E7
Ayn Zālah, *Iraq* 70 B4
Ayna, *Spain* 39 G2
Ayod, *Sudan* 81 F3
Ayolas, *Paraguay* 126 B4
Ayon, Ostrov, *Russia* 53 C17
Ayora, *Spain* 39 F3
Ayorou, *Niger* 83 C5
'Ayoûn el 'Atroûs, *Mauritania* . 82 B3

Ayr, *Australia* 94 B4
Ayr, *Canada* 116 C4
Ayr, *U.K.* 13 F4
Ayr ➤, *U.K.* 13 F4
Ayrancı, *Turkey* 72 D5
Ayrancılar, *Turkey* 47 C9
Ayre, Pt. of, *I. of Man* 14 C3
Aysha, *Ethiopia* 81 E5
Ayton, *Australia* 94 B4
Aytos, *Bulgaria* 45 D11
Aytoska Planina, *Bulgaria* ... 45 D11
Ayu, Kepulauan, *Indonesia* .. 63 D8
Ayutla, *Guatemala* 120 D1
Ayutla, *Mexico* 119 D5
Ayvacık, *Turkey* 72 C2
Ayvalık, *Turkey* 47 B8
Az Zabadānī, *Syria* 74 B5
Az Ẓāhirīyah, *West Bank* 74 D3
Aẕ Ẕahrān, *Si. Arabia* 71 E6
Az Zarqā', *Jordan* 74 C5
Az Zarqā', *U.A.E.* 71 E7
Az Zarqā' □, *Jordan* 74 C5
Az Zāwiyah, *Libya* 79 B8
Az Zibār, *Iraq* 70 B5
Az Zilfī, *Si. Arabia* 70 E5
Az Zubayr, *Iraq* 70 D5
Az Zuqur, *Yemen* 81 E5
Azad Kashmir □, *Pakistan* ... 69 C5
Azambuja, *Portugal* 37 F2
Azamgarh, *India* 69 F10
Azángaro, *Peru* 124 F4
Azaoua, *Niger* 83 B5
Azaouad, *Mali* 82 B4
Azaouak, Vallée de l', *Mali* ... 83 B5
Āẕar Shahr, *Iran* 70 B5
Azara, *Nigeria* 83 D6
Azarán, *Iran* 70 B5
Azärbaijan = Azerbaijan ■, *Asia* 35 K9
Āẕarbāyjān-e Gharbī □, *Iran* .. 70 B5
Āẕarbāyjān-e Sharqī □, *Iran* .. 70 B5
Azare, *Nigeria* 83 C7
Azay-le-Rideau, *France* 18 E7
A'zāz, *Syria* 70 B3
Azbine = Aïr, *Niger* 83 B6
Azerbaijan ■, *Asia* 35 K9
Azerbaijchan = Azerbaijan ■,
  Asia 35 K9
Azezo, *Ethiopia* 81 E4
Azimganj, *India* 69 G13
Aznalcóllar, *Spain* 37 H4
Azogues, *Ecuador* 124 D3
Azores = Açores, Is. dos, *Atl. Oc.* 78 A1
Azov, *Russia* 35 G4
Azov, Sea of, *Europe* 33 J9
Azovskoye More = Azov, Sea of,
  Europe 33 J9
Azpeitia, *Spain* 38 B2
Azraq ash Shīshān, *Jordan* ... 74 D5
Aztec, *U.S.A.* 109 H10
Azúa de Compostela, *Dom. Rep.* 121 C5
Azuaga, *Spain* 37 G5
Azuara, *Spain* 38 D4
Azuer ➤, *Spain* 37 F7
Azuero, Pen. de, *Panama* 120 E3
Azul, *Romania* 29 E10
Azul, *Argentina* 126 D4
Azusa, *U.S.A.* 111 L9
Azzano Décimo, *Italy* 41 C9

B

Ba Be △, *Vietnam* 64 A5
Ba Don, *Vietnam* 64 D6
Ba Dong, *Vietnam* 65 H6
Ba Ngoi = Cam Lam, *Vietnam* . 65 G7
Ba Tri, *Vietnam* 65 G6
Ba Vi △, *Vietnam* 64 B5
Ba Xian = Bazhou, *China* 56 E9
Baa, *Indonesia* 63 F6
Baamonde, *Spain* 36 B3
Baardeere = Bardera, *Somali Rep.* 75 G3
Baarle-Nassau, *Belgium* 17 C4
Bab el Mandeb, *Red Sea* 75 E3
Baba, *Bulgaria* 44 D7
Bābā, Koh-i-, *Afghan.* 66 B5
Baba Burnu, *Turkey* 47 B8
Baba dag, *Azerbaijan* 35 K9
Bābā Kalū, *Iran* 71 D6
Babadag, *Romania* 29 F13
Babadağ, *Turkey* 47 D10
Babaeski, *Turkey* 45 E11
Babahoyo, *Ecuador* 124 D3
Babai = Sarju ➤, *India* 69 F9
Babana, *Nigeria* 83 C5
Babanusa, *Sudan* 81 E2
Babar, *Indonesia* 63 F7
Babar, *Pakistan* 68 D3
Babarkach, *Pakistan* 68 E3
Babayevo, *Russia* 32 C8
Babb, *U.S.A.* 108 B7
Babenhausen, *Germany* 25 F4
Băbeni, *Romania* 29 F9
Baberu, *India* 69 G9
Babi Besar, Pulau, *Malaysia* .. 65 L4
Babia Gora, *Europe* 31 J6
Babian Jiang ➤, *China* 58 F3
Bābil □, *Iraq* 70 C5
Babile, *Ethiopia* 81 F5
Babimost, *Poland* 31 F2
Babinda, *Australia* 94 B4
Babine, *Canada* 102 B3
Babine ➤, *Canada* 102 B3
Babine L., *Canada* 102 C3
Babiogórski △, *Poland* 31 J6
Babo, *Indonesia* 63 E8
Babócsa, *Hungary* 28 D2
Bābol, *Iran* 71 B7
Bābol Sar, *Iran* 71 B7

Baborów, Poland — 31 H5
Babruysk, Belarus — 33 F5
Babuhri, India — 68 F3
Babuna, Macedonia — 44 E5
Babura, Nigeria — 83 C6
Babusar Pass, Pakistan — 69 B5
Babushkin, Russia — 60 A5
Babušnica, Serbia & M. — 44 C6
Babuyan Chan., Phil. — 61 B4
Babylon, Iraq — 70 C5
Bač, Serbia & M. — 28 E4
Bâc →, Moldova — 29 D14
Bac Can, Vietnam — 58 F5
Bac Giang, Vietnam — 58 G6
Bac Lieu, Vietnam — 65 H5
Bac Ninh, Vietnam — 58 G6
Bac Phan, Vietnam — 64 B5
Bac Quang, Vietnam — 58 F5
Bacabal, Brazil — 125 D10
Bacalar, Mexico — 119 D7
Bacan, Kepulauan, Indonesia — 63 E7
Bacarra, Phil. — 61 B4
Bacău, Romania — 29 D11
Bacău □, Romania — 29 D11
Baccarat, France — 19 D13
Bacerac, Mexico — 118 A3
Bāceşti, Romania — 29 D12
Bach Long Vi, Dao, Vietnam — 64 B6
Bach Ma →, Vietnam — 64 D6
Bacharach, Germany — 25 E3
Bachhwara, India — 69 G11
Bachuma, Ethiopia — 81 F4
Bačina, Serbia & M. — 44 C5
Back →, Canada — 100 B9
Bačka Palanka, Serbia & M. — 28 E4
Bačka Topola, Serbia & M. — 28 E4
Bäckebo, Sweden — 11 H10
Bäckefors, Sweden — 11 F6
Bäckhammar, Sweden — 10 E8
Bački Petrovac, Serbia & M. — 28 E4
Backnang, Germany — 25 G5
Baco, Mt., Phil. — 61 E4
Bacolod, Phil. — 61 F5
Bacqueville-en-Caux, France — 18 C8
Bács-Kiskun □, Hungary — 28 D4
Bácsalmás, Hungary — 28 D4
Bacuag = Placer, Phil. — 61 G6
Bacuk, Malaysia — 65 J4
Bād, Iran — 71 C7
Bad →, U.S.A. — 112 C4
Bad Aussee, Austria — 26 D6
Bad Axe, U.S.A. — 116 C2
Bad Bergzabern, Germany — 25 F3
Bad Berleburg, Germany — 24 D4
Bad Bevensen, Germany — 24 B6
Bad Bramstedt, Germany — 24 B5
Bad Brückenau, Germany — 25 E5
Bad Doberan, Germany — 24 A7
Bad Driburg, Germany — 24 D5
Bad Ems, Germany — 25 E3
Bad Frankenhausen, Germany — 24 D7
Bad Freienwalde, Germany — 24 C10
Bad Goisern, Austria — 26 D6
Bad Harzburg, Germany — 24 D6
Bad Hersfeld, Germany — 24 E5
Bad Hofgastein, Austria — 26 D6
Bad Homburg, Germany — 25 E4
Bad Honnef, Germany — 24 E3
Bad Iburg, Germany — 24 C4
Bad Ischl, Austria — 26 D6
Bad Kissingen, Germany — 25 E6
Bad Königshofen, Germany — 25 E6
Bad Kreuznach, Germany — 25 F3
Bad Krozingen, Germany — 25 H3
Bad Laasphe, Germany — 24 E4
Bad Lands, U.S.A. — 112 D3
Bad Langensalza, Germany — 24 D6
Bad Lauterberg, Germany — 24 D6
Bad Leonfelden, Austria — 26 C7
Bad Liebenwerda, Germany — 24 D9
Bad Mergentheim, Germany — 25 F5
Bad Münstereifel, Germany — 24 E2
Bad Nauheim, Germany — 25 E4
Bad Neuenahr-Ahrweiler, Germany — 24 E3
Bad Neustadt, Germany — 25 E6
Bad Oeynhausen, Germany — 24 C4
Bad Oldesloe, Germany — 24 B6
Bad Orb, Germany — 25 E5
Bad Pyrmont, Germany — 24 D5
Bad Reichenhall, Germany — 25 H8
Bad Säckingen, Germany — 25 H3
Bad Salzuflen, Germany — 24 C4
Bad Salzungen, Germany — 24 E6
Bad Schwartau, Germany — 24 B6
Bad Segeberg, Germany — 24 B6
Bad St. Leonhard, Austria — 26 E7
Bad Tölz, Germany — 25 H7
Bad Urach, Germany — 25 G5
Bad Vöslau, Austria — 27 D9
Bad Waldsee, Germany — 25 H5
Bad Wildungen, Germany — 24 D5
Bad Wimpfen, Germany — 25 F5
Bad Windsheim, Germany — 25 F6
Bad Zwischenahn, Germany — 24 B4
Bada Barabil, India — 69 H11
Badagara, India — 66 P9
Badagri, Nigeria — 83 D5
Badajós, L., Brazil — 124 D6
Badajoz, Spain — 37 G4
Badajoz □, Spain — 37 G4
Badakhshān □, Afghan. — 66 A7
Badalona, Spain — 38 D7
Badalzai, Afghan. — 68 E1
Badampahar, India — 67 H15
Badanah, Si. Arabia — 70 D4
Badarinath, India — 69 D8
Badas, Kepulauan, Indonesia — 62 D3
Baddo →, Pakistan — 66 F4
Bade, Indonesia — 63 F9
Badeggi, Nigeria — 83 D6
Badéguichéri, Niger — 83 C6

Baden, Austria — 27 C9
Baden, Switz. — 25 H4
Baden, U.S.A. — 116 F4
Baden-Baden, Germany — 25 G4
Baden-Württemberg □, Germany — 25 G4
Badgastein, Austria — 26 D6
Badger, Canada — 105 C8
Badger, U.S.A. — 110 J7
Bādghīs □, Afghan. — 66 B3
Badgingarra △, Australia — 93 F2
Badgom, India — 69 B6
Badia Polésine, Italy — 41 C8
Badiar △, Guinea — 82 C2
Badin, Pakistan — 68 G3
Badinka △, Mali — 82 C3
Badlands △, U.S.A. — 112 D3
Badogo, Mali — 82 C3
Badoumbé, Mali — 82 C2
Badrah, Iraq — 70 C5
Badrinath, India — 69 D8
Badulla, Sri Lanka — 66 R12
Badung, Selat, Indonesia — 63 K18
Baena, Spain — 37 H6
Baeza, Spain — 37 H7
Bafang, Cameroon — 83 D7
Bafatá, Guinea-Biss. — 82 C2
Baffin B., Canada — 101 A13
Baffin I., Canada — 101 B12
Bafia, Cameroon — 83 E7
Bafilo, Togo — 83 D5
Bafing △, Mali — 82 C2
Bafing →, Mali — 82 C2
Bafliyūn, Syria — 70 B3
Bafoulabé, Mali — 82 C2
Bafoussam, Cameroon — 83 D7
Bāfq, Iran — 71 D7
Bafra, Turkey — 72 B6
Bafra Burnu, Turkey — 72 B7
Bāft, Iran — 71 D8
Bafut, Cameroon — 83 D7
Bafwasende, Dem. Rep. of the Congo — 86 B2
Bagam, Niger — 83 B6
Bagamoyo, Tanzania — 86 D4
Bagan Datoh, Malaysia — 65 L3
Bagan Serai, Malaysia — 65 K3
Baganga, Phil. — 61 H7
Bagani, Namibia — 88 B3
Bagansiapiapi, Indonesia — 62 D2
Bagasra, India — 68 J4
Bagaud, India — 68 H6
Bagawi, Sudan — 81 E3
Bagbag, Sudan — 81 D3
Bagdad, U.S.A. — 111 L11
Bagdarin, Russia — 53 D12
Bagé, Brazil — 127 C5
Bagenalstown = Muine Bheag, Ireland — 12 D5
Baggs, U.S.A. — 108 F10
Bagh, Pakistan — 69 C5
Baghain →, India — 69 G9
Baghdād, Iraq — 70 C5
Bagheria, Italy — 42 D6
Baghlān, Afghan. — 66 A6
Baghlān □, Afghan. — 66 B6
Bagley, U.S.A. — 112 B7
Bagnara Cálabra, Italy — 43 D8
Bagnasco, Italy — 40 D5
Bagnères-de-Bigorre, France — 20 E4
Bagnères-de-Luchon, France — 20 F4
Bagni di Lucca, Italy — 40 D7
Bagno di Romagna, Italy — 41 E8
Bagnoles-de-l'Orne, France — 18 D6
Bagnols-sur-Cèze, France — 21 D8
Bagnorégio, Italy — 41 F9
Bago = Pegu, Burma — 67 L20
Bagodar, India — 69 G11
Bagrationovsk, Russia — 9 J19
Bagrdan, Serbia & M. — 44 B5
Baguio, Phil. — 61 C4
Bağyurdu, Turkey — 47 C9
Bagzane, Monts, Niger — 83 B6
Bah, India — 69 F8
Bahabón de Esgueva, Spain — 36 D7
Bahadurganj, India — 69 F12
Bahadurgarh, India — 68 E7
Bahama, Canal Viejo de, W. Indies — 120 B4
Bahamas ■, N. Amer. — 121 B5
Bahār, Iran — 73 E13
Baharampur, India — 69 G13
Baharîya, El Wâhât al, Egypt — 80 B2
Baharu Pandan = Pandan, Malaysia — 65 d
Bahawalnagar, Pakistan — 68 E5
Bahawalpur, Pakistan — 68 E4
Bahçe, Turkey — 72 D7
Bahçecik, Turkey — 45 F13
Baheri, India — 69 E8
Bahgul →, India — 69 F8
Bahi, Tanzania — 86 D4
Bahi Swamp, Tanzania — 86 D4
Bahía = Salvador, Brazil — 125 F11
Bahía □, Brazil — 125 F10
Bahía, Is. de la, Honduras — 120 C2
Bahía Blanca, Argentina — 126 D3
Bahía de Caráquez, Ecuador — 124 D2
Bahía Honda, Cuba — 120 B3
Bahía Laura, Argentina — 128 F3
Bahía Negra, Paraguay — 124 H7
Bahir Dar, Ethiopia — 81 E4
Bahmanzād, Iran — 71 D6
Bahr el Ahmar □, Sudan — 80 D4
Bahr el Ghazâl □, Sudan — 81 F2
Bahr el Jabal □, Sudan — 81 G3
Bahraich, India — 69 F9
Bahrain ■, Asia — 71 E6
Bahror, India — 68 F7
Bāhū Kalāt, Iran — 71 E9
Bai, Mali — 82 C4
Bai Bung, Mui = Ca Mau, Mui, Vietnam — 65 H5

Bai Duc, Vietnam — 64 C5
Bai Thuong, Vietnam — 64 C5
Baia de Aramă, Romania — 28 E7
Baia Mare, Romania — 29 C8
Baia-Sprie, Romania — 29 C8
Baião, Brazil — 125 D9
Baïbokoum, Chad — 79 G9
Baicheng, China — 57 B12
Băicoi, Romania — 29 E10
Baidoa, Somali Rep. — 75 G3
Baie-Comeau, Canada — 105 C6
Baie-St-Paul, Canada — 105 C5
Baie-Trinité, Canada — 105 C6
Baie Verte, Canada — 105 C8
Baignes-Ste-Radegonde, France — 20 C3
Baigneux-les-Juifs, France — 19 E11
Baihar, India — 69 H9
Baihe, China — 56 H6
Baijnath, India — 69 E8
Baikal, L. = Baykal, Oz., Russia — 53 D11
Baikunthpur, India — 69 H10
Baile Atha Cliath = Dublin, Ireland — 12 C5
Băile Govora, Romania — 29 E9
Băile Herculane, Romania — 28 F7
Băile Olăneşti, Romania — 29 E9
Băile Tuşnad, Romania — 29 D10
Bailén, Spain — 37 G7
Băileşti, Romania — 29 F8
Baima, China — 58 A3
Bain-de-Bretagne, France — 18 E5
Bainbridge, Ga., U.S.A. — 115 K3
Bainbridge, N.Y., U.S.A. — 117 D9
Baing, Indonesia — 63 F6
Bainiu, China — 56 H7
Baiona, Spain — 36 C2
Bā'ir, Jordan — 74 E5
Bairiki = Tarawa, Kiribati — 96 G9
Bairin Youqi, China — 57 C10
Bairin Zuoqi, China — 57 C10
Bairnsdale, Australia — 95 F4
Bais, Phil. — 61 G5
Baisha, China — 56 G7
Baissa, Nigeria — 83 D7
Baitadi, Nepal — 69 E9
Baixa Limia-Sierra do Xurés △, Spain — 36 D2
Baiyin, China — 56 F3
Baiyü, China — 58 B2
Baiyu Shan, China — 56 F4
Baiyuda, Sudan — 80 D3
Baj Baj, India — 69 H13
Baja, Hungary — 28 D3
Baja, Pta., Mexico — 118 B1
Baja California, Mexico — 118 A1
Baja California □, Mexico — 118 B2
Baja California Sur □, Mexico — 118 B2
Bajag, India — 69 H9
Bajamar, Canary Is. — 48 F3
Bajana, India — 68 H4
Bajatrejo, Indonesia — 63 J17
Bajera, Indonesia — 63 J18
Bājgīrān, Iran — 71 B8
Bajimba, Mt., Australia — 95 D5
Bajina Bašta, Serbia & M. — 44 C3
Bajmok, Serbia & M. — 28 E4
Bajo Nuevo, Caribbean — 120 C4
Bajoga, Nigeria — 83 C7
Bajool, Australia — 94 C5
Bak, Hungary — 28 D1
Bakar, Croatia — 41 C11
Bakasi Pen., Cameroon — 83 E6
Bakel, Senegal — 82 C2
Baker, Calif., U.S.A. — 111 K10
Baker, Mont., U.S.A. — 112 B2
Baker, L., Canada — 100 B10
Baker, Mt., U.S.A. — 108 B3
Baker City, U.S.A. — 108 D5
Baker I., Pac. Oc. — 96 G10
Baker I., U.S.A. — 102 B2
Baker L., Australia — 93 E4
Baker Lake, Canada — 100 B10
Bakers Creek, Australia — 94 C4
Bakers Dozen Is., Canada — 104 A4
Bakersfield, Calif., U.S.A. — 111 K8
Bakersfield, Vt., U.S.A. — 117 B12
Bakhchysaray, Ukraine — 33 K7
Bakhmach, Ukraine — 33 G7
Bākhtarān, Iran — 70 C5
Bākhtarān □, Iran — 70 C5
Bakı, Azerbaijan — 35 K9
Bakır →, Turkey — 47 C9
Bakırdaği, Turkey — 72 C6
Bakkafjörður, Iceland — 8 C6
Baklan, Turkey — 47 C11
Bako, Ethiopia — 81 F4
Bako, Ivory C. — 82 D3
Bakony, Hungary — 28 C2
Bakony Forest = Bakony, Hungary — 28 C2
Bakori, Nigeria — 83 C6
Bakouma, C.A.R. — 84 C4
Baksan, Russia — 35 J6
Bakswaho, India — 69 G8
Baku = Bakı, Azerbaijan — 35 K9
Bakundi, Nigeria — 83 D7
Bakutis Coast, Antarctica — 5 D15
Baky = Bakı, Azerbaijan — 35 K9
Bala, Canada — 116 A5
Bala, Senegal — 82 C2
Bâlâ, Turkey — 72 C5
Bala, U.K. — 14 E4
Bala, L., U.K. — 14 E4
Balabac I., Phil. — 62 C5
Balabac Str., E. Indies — 62 C5
Balabagh, Afghan. — 68 B4
Ba'labakk, Lebanon — 74 B5
Balabalangan, Kepulauan, Indonesia — 62 E5
Bălăciţa, Romania — 29 F8
Balad, Iraq — 70 C5
Balad Rūz, Iraq — 70 C5

Bālādeh, Fārs, Iran — 71 D6
Bālādeh, Māzandaran, Iran — 71 B6
Balaghat, India — 66 J12
Balaghat Ra., India — 66 K10
Balaguer, Spain — 38 D5
Balakhna, Russia — 34 B6
Balaklava, Ukraine — 33 K7
Balakliya, Ukraine — 33 H9
Balakovo, Russia — 34 D8
Balamau, India — 69 F9
Bălan, Romania — 29 D10
Balancán, Mexico — 119 D6
Balanivka, Ukraine — 29 B14
Balashov, Russia — 34 E6
Balasinor, India — 68 H5
Balasore = Baleshwar, India — 67 J15
Balassagyarmat, Hungary — 28 B4
Balât, Egypt — 80 B2
Balaton, Hungary — 28 D2
Balaton-Felvidéki △, Hungary — 28 D2
Balatonboglár, Hungary — 28 D2
Balatonfüred, Hungary — 28 D2
Balatonszentgyörgy, Hungary — 28 D2
Balayan, Phil. — 61 E4
Balazote, Spain — 39 G2
Balbieriškis, Lithuania — 30 D10
Balbigny, France — 21 C8
Balbina, Reprêsa de, Brazil — 124 D7
Balboa, Panama — 120 E4
Balbriggan, Ireland — 12 C5
Balcarce, Argentina — 126 D4
Balcarres, Canada — 103 C8
Bălcești, Romania — 29 F8
Balchik, Bulgaria — 45 C12
Balclutha, N.Z. — 91 M2
Balcones Escarpment, U.S.A. — 113 L5
Bald Hd., Australia — 93 G2
Bald I., Australia — 93 F2
Bald Knob, U.S.A. — 113 H9
Baldock L., Canada — 103 B9
Baldwin, Mich., U.S.A. — 114 D3
Baldwin, Pa., U.S.A. — 116 F5
Baldwinsville, U.S.A. — 117 C8
Baldy Mt., U.S.A. — 108 B9
Baldy Peak, U.S.A. — 109 K9
Bale, Croatia — 41 C10
Bale, Ethiopia — 81 F5
Bale □, Ethiopia — 81 F5
Bale Mts. △, Ethiopia — 81 F4
Baleares, Is., Spain — 48 B10
Balearic Is. = Baleares, Is., Spain — 48 B10
Baleine = Whale →, Canada — 105 A6
Baleine, Petite R. de la →, Canada — 104 A4
Băleni, Romania — 29 E12
Baler, Phil. — 61 D4
Baler Bay, Phil. — 61 D4
Baleshare, U.K. — 13 D1
Baleshwar, India — 67 J15
Balezino, Russia — 34 B11
Balfate, Honduras — 120 C2
Balfour, S. Africa — 89 D4
Balham →, Iran — 71 B8
Bali, Cameroon — 83 D7
Balí, Greece — 49 D6
Bali, India — 68 G5
Bali, Indonesia — 63 J18
Bali □, Indonesia — 63 J18
Bali, Selat, Indonesia — 63 J17
Bali Sea, Indonesia — 63 J17
Balia, S. Leone — 82 D2
Baliapal, India — 69 J12
Baligród, Poland — 31 J9
Balik Pulau, Malaysia — 65 c
Balıkeşir, Turkey — 47 B9
Balıkeşir □, Turkey — 47 B9
Balıklıçeşme, Turkey — 45 F11
Balikpapan, Indonesia — 62 E5
Balimbing, Phil. — 63 C5
Baling, Malaysia — 65 K3
Balingen, Germany — 25 G4
Balinț, Romania — 28 E6
Balintang Channel, Phil. — 61 B4
Balipara, India — 67 F18
Balkan Mts. = Stara Planina, Bulgaria — 44 C7
Balkhash = Balqash, Kazakhstan — 52 E8
Balkhash, Ozero = Balqash Köl, Kazakhstan — 52 E8
Balla, Bangla. — 67 G17
Ballachulish, U.K. — 13 E3
Balladonia, Australia — 93 F3
Ballaghaderreen, Ireland — 12 C3
Ballarat, Australia — 95 F3
Ballard, L., Australia — 93 E3
Ballater, U.K. — 13 D5
Ballé, Mali — 82 B3
Ballena Gris = Ojo de Liebre △, Mexico — 118 B2
Ballenas, Canal de, Mexico — 118 B2
Balleny Is., Antarctica — 5 C11
Balleroy, France — 18 C6
Ballerup, Denmark — 11 J6
Balli, Turkey — 45 F11
Ballia, India — 69 G11
Ballina, Australia — 95 D5
Ballina, Ireland — 12 B2
Ballinasloe, Ireland — 12 C3
Ballinger, U.S.A. — 113 K5
Ballinrobe, Ireland — 12 C2
Ballinskelligs B., Ireland — 12 E1
Ballon, France — 18 D7
Ballons des Vosges △, France — 19 E14
Ballsh, Albania — 44 F3
Ballston Spa, U.S.A. — 117 D11
Ballybunion, Ireland — 12 D2
Ballycastle, U.K. — 12 A5
Ballyclare, U.K. — 12 B5
Ballyhaunis, Ireland — 12 C3
Ballymena, U.K. — 12 B5
Ballymoney, U.K. — 12 A5
Ballymote, Ireland — 12 B3
Ballynahinch, U.K. — 12 B6

Ballyquintin Pt., U.K. — 12 B6
Ballyshannon, Ireland — 12 B3
Balmaceda, Chile — 128 F2
Balmaseda, Spain — 38 B1
Balmazújváros, Hungary — 28 C6
Balmertown, Canada — 103 C10
Balmoral, Australia — 95 F3
Balmorhea, U.S.A. — 113 K3
Balochistan = Baluchistan □, Pakistan — 66 F4
Balonne →, Australia — 95 D4
Balotra, India — 68 G5
Balqash, Kazakhstan — 52 E8
Balqash Köl, Kazakhstan — 52 E8
Balrampur, India — 69 F10
Balranald, Australia — 95 E3
Balş, Romania — 29 F9
Balsas, Mexico — 119 D5
Balsas →, Brazil — 125 D9
Balsas →, Mexico — 118 D4
Bålsta, Sweden — 10 E11
Balston Spa, U.S.A. — 117 D11
Balta, Romania — 28 F7
Balta, Ukraine — 29 B14
Baltanás, Spain — 36 D6
Bălți, Moldova — 29 C12
Baltic Sea, Europe — 9 H18
Baltîm, Egypt — 80 H7
Baltimore, Ireland — 12 E2
Baltimore, Md., U.S.A. — 114 F7
Baltimore, Ohio, U.S.A. — 116 G2
Baltit, Pakistan — 69 A6
Baltiysk, Russia — 9 J18
Baltrum, Germany — 24 B3
Baluchistan □, Pakistan — 66 F4
Balurghat, India — 69 G13
Balvi, Latvia — 9 H22
Balya, Turkey — 47 B9
Bam, Iran — 71 D8
Bama, China — 58 E6
Bama, Nigeria — 83 C7
Bamaga, Australia — 94 A3
Bamaji L., Canada — 104 B1
Bamako, Mali — 82 C3
Bamba, Mali — 83 B4
Bambari, C.A.R. — 84 C4
Bambaroo, Australia — 94 B4
Bambara Maoundé, Mali — 82 B4
Bamberg, Germany — 25 F6
Bamberg, U.S.A. — 115 J5
Bambesi, Ethiopia — 81 F3
Bambey, Senegal — 82 C1
Bambili, Dem. Rep. of the Congo — 86 B2
Bamboi, Ghana — 82 D4
Bamburgh, U.K. — 14 B6
Bamenda, Cameroon — 83 D7
Bamfield, Canada — 102 D3
Bāmīān □, Afghan. — 66 B5
Bamiancheng, China — 57 C13
Bamkin, Cameroon — 83 D7
Bampūr, Iran — 71 E9
Ban, Burkina Faso — 82 C4
Ban Ao Tu Khun, Thailand — 65 a
Ban Ban, Laos — 64 C4
Ban Bang Hin, Thailand — 65 H2
Ban Bang Khu, Thailand — 65 a
Ban Bang Rong, Thailand — 65 a
Ban Bo Phut, Thailand — 65 b
Ban Chaweng, Thailand — 65 b
Ban Chiang Klang, Thailand — 64 C3
Ban Chik, Laos — 64 D4
Ban Choho, Thailand — 64 E4
Ban Dan Lan Hoi, Thailand — 64 D2
Ban Don = Surat Thani, Thailand — 65 H2
Ban Don, Vietnam — 64 F6
Ban Don, Ao →, Thailand — 65 H2
Ban Dong, Thailand — 64 C3
Ban Hong, Thailand — 64 C2
Ban Hua Thanon, Thailand — 65 b
Ban Kaeng, Thailand — 64 D3
Ban Kantang, Thailand — 65 J2
Ban Karon, Thailand — 65 a
Ban Kata, Thailand — 65 a
Ban Keun, Laos — 64 C4
Ban Khai, Thailand — 64 F3
Ban Kheun, Laos — 64 B3
Ban Khlong Khian, Thailand — 65 a
Ban Khlong Kua, Thailand — 65 J3
Ban Khuan, Thailand — 65 a
Ban Khuan Mao, Thailand — 65 J2
Ban Ko Yai Chim, Thailand — 65 G2
Ban Kok, Thailand — 64 D4
Ban Laem, Thailand — 64 F2
Ban Lamai, Thailand — 65 b
Ban Lao Ngam, Laos — 64 E6
Ban Le Kathe, Thailand — 64 E2
Ban Lo Po Noi, Thailand — 65 a
Ban Mae Chedi, Thailand — 64 C2
Ban Mae Laeng, Thailand — 64 B2
Ban Mae Nam, Thailand — 65 b
Ban Mae Sariang, Thailand — 64 C1
Ban Mê Thuột = Buon Ma Thuot, Vietnam — 64 F7
Ban Mi, Thailand — 64 E3
Ban Muong Mo, Laos — 64 C4
Ban Na Bo, Thailand — 65 b
Ban Na Mo, Laos — 64 D5
Ban Na San, Thailand — 65 H2
Ban Na Tong, Laos — 64 B3
Ban Nam Bac, Laos — 64 B4
Ban Nam Ma, Laos — 64 A3
Ban Ngang, Laos — 64 E6
Ban Nong Bok, Laos — 64 D5
Ban Nong Boua, Laos — 64 E6
Ban Nong Pling, Thailand — 64 E3
Ban Pak Chan, Thailand — 65 G2
Ban Patong, Thailand — 65 a
Ban Phai, Thailand — 64 D4
Ban Phak Chit, Thailand — 65 a
Ban Pong, Thailand — 64 F2
Ban Rawai, Thailand — 65 a

Ban Ron Phibun, *Thailand* 65 H2
Ban Sakhu, *Thailand* .... 65 a
Ban Sanam Chai, *Thailand* 65 J3
Ban Sangka, *Thailand* 64 E3
Ban Tak, *Thailand* 64 D2
Ban Tako, *Thailand* 64 E4
Ban Tha Dua, *Thailand* 64 D2
Ban Tha Li, *Thailand* 64 D3
Ban Tha Nun, *Thailand* .... 65 a
Ban Tha Rua, *Thailand* .... 65 a
Ban Tha Yu, *Thailand* .... 65 a
Ban Thahine, *Laos* 64 E5
Ban Thong Krut, *Thailand* ..... 65 b
Ban Xien Kok, *Laos* 64 B3
Ban Yen Nhan, *Vietnam* 64 B6
Banaba, *Kiribati* 96 H8
Banalia, *Dem. Rep. of the Congo* 86 B2
Banam, *Cambodia* 65 G5
Banamba, *Mali* 82 C3
Banana Is., *S. Leone* 82 D2
Bananal, I. do, *Brazil* 125 F8
Banaras = Varanasi, *India* 69 G10
Banas →, *Gujarat, India* 68 H4
Banas →, *Mad. P., India* 69 G9
Bânâs, Ras, *Egypt* 80 C4
Banaz, *Turkey* 47 C11
Banaz →, *Turkey* 47 C11
Banbridge, *U.K.* 12 B5
Banbury, *U.K.* 15 E6
Banchory, *U.K.* 13 D6
Banco, *Ethiopia* 81 F4
Bancroft, *Canada* 116 A7
Band, *Romania* 29 D9
Band Bonī, *Iran* 71 E8
Band Qīr, *Iran* 71 D6
Banda, *Mad. P., India* 69 G8
Banda, *Ut. P., India* 69 G9
Banda, Kepulauan, *Indonesia* .. 63 E7
Banda Aceh, *Indonesia* 62 C1
Banda Banda, Mt., *Australia* .. 95 E5
Banda Elat, *Indonesia* 63 F8
Banda Is. = Banda, Kepulauan,
  Indonesia 63 E7
Banda Sea, *Indonesia* 63 F7
Bandai-Asahi △, *Japan* 54 F10
Bandai-San, *Japan* 54 F10
Bandama →, *Ivory C.* 82 D3
Bandama Blanc →, *Ivory C.* 82 D3
Bandama Rouge →, *Ivory C.* 82 D4
Bandān, *Iran* 71 D9
Bandanaira, *Indonesia* 63 E7
Bandanwara, *India* 68 F6
Bandar = Machilipatnam, *India* 67 L12
Bandar-e Abbās, *Iran* 71 E8
Bandar-e Anzalī, *Iran* 71 B6
Bandar-e Būshehr = Būshehr,
  Iran 71 D6
Bandar-e Chārak, *Iran* 71 E7
Bandar-e Deylam, *Iran* 71 D6
Bandar-e Emām Khomeynī, *Iran* . 71 D6
Bandar-e Lengeh, *Iran* 71 E7
Bandar-e Maqām, *Iran* 71 E7
Bandar-e Ma'shur, *Iran* 71 D6
Bandar-e Rīg, *Iran* 71 D6
Bandar-e Torkeman, *Iran* 71 B7
Bandar Lampung =
  Tanjungkarang Telukbetung,
  Indonesia 62 F3
Bandar Maharani = Muar,
  Malaysia 65 L4
Bandar Penggaram = Batu Pahat,
  Malaysia 65 M4
Bandar Seri Begawan, *Brunei* .. 62 C4
Bandar Sri Aman, *Malaysia* 62 D4
Bandawe, *Malawi* 87 E3
Bande, *Spain* 36 C3
Bandeira, Pico da, *Brazil* 127 A7
Bandera, *Argentina* 126 B3
Banderas, B. de, *Mexico* 118 C3
Bandhogarh, *India* 69 H9
Bandi →, *India* 68 F6
Bandiagara, *Mali* 82 C4
Bandikui, *India* 68 F7
Bandırma, *Turkey* 45 F11
Bandjarmasin = Banjarmasin,
  Indonesia 62 E4
Bandol, *France* 21 E9
Bandon, *Ireland* 12 E3
Bandon →, *Ireland* 12 E3
Bandula, *Mozam.* 87 F3
Bandundu, *Dem. Rep. of
  the Congo* 84 E3
Bandung, *Indonesia* 63 G12
Bané, *Burkina Faso* 83 C4
Bǎneasa, *Romania* 29 E12
Bāneh, *Iran* 70 C5
Bañeres, *Spain* 39 G4
Banes, *Cuba* 121 B4
Banff, *Canada* 102 C5
Banff, *U.K.* 13 D6
Banff △, *Canada* 102 C5
Banfora, *Burkina Faso* 82 C4
Bang Fai →, *Laos* 64 D5
Bang Hieng →, *Laos* 64 D5
Bang Krathum, *Thailand* 64 D3
Bang Lamung, *Thailand* 64 F3
Bang Mun Nak, *Thailand* 64 D3
Bang Pa In, *Thailand* 64 E3
Bang Rakam, *Thailand* 64 D3
Bang Saphan, *Thailand* 65 G2
Bang Thao, *Thailand* .... 65 a
Bangaduni I., *India* 69 J13
Bangala Dam, *Zimbabwe* 87 G3
Bangalore, *India* 66 N10
Banganga →, *India* 68 F6
Banganté, *Cameroon* 83 D7
Bangaon, *India* 69 H13
Bangassou, *C.A.R.* 84 D4
Banggai, *Indonesia* 63 E6
Banggai, Kepulauan, *Indonesia* 63 E6
Banggai Arch. = Banggai,
  Kepulauan, *Indonesia* 63 E6

Banggi, *Malaysia* 62 C5
Banghāzī, *Libya* 79 B10
Bangjang, *Sudan* 81 E3
Bangka, *Sulawesi, Indonesia* .. 63 D7
Bangka, *Sumatera, Indonesia* .. 62 E3
Bangka, Selat, *Indonesia* 62 E3
Bangka-Belitung □, *Indonesia* . 62 E3
Bangkalan, *Indonesia* 63 G15
Bangkinang, *Indonesia* 62 D2
Bangko, *Indonesia* 62 E2
Bangkok, *Thailand* 64 F3
Bangladesh ■, *Asia* 67 H17
Bangli, *Indonesia* 63 J18
Bangolo, *Ivory C.* 82 D3
Bangong Co, *India* 69 B8
Bangor, *Down, U.K.* 12 B6
Bangor, *Gwynedd, U.K.* 14 D3
Bangor, *Maine, U.S.A.* 101 D13
Bangor, *Pa., U.S.A.* 117 F9
Bangued, *Phil.* 61 C4
Bangui, *C.A.R.* 84 D3
Bangui, *Phil.* 61 B4
Banguru, *Dem. Rep. of the Congo* 86 B2
Bangweulu, L., *Zambia* 87 E3
Bangweulu Swamp, *Zambia* 87 E3
Banhine △, *Mozam.* 89 C5
Baní, *Dom. Rep.* 121 C5
Bani →, *Mali* 82 C4
Bani Bangou, *Niger* 83 B5
Banī Sa'd, *Iraq* 70 C5
Bania, *Ivory C.* 82 D4
Banihal Pass, *India* 69 C6
Banikoara, *Benin* 83 C5
Bāniyās, *Syria* 70 C3
Banja Luka, *Bos.-H.* 28 F2
Banjar, *India* 68 D7
Banjar →, *India* 69 H9
Banjarmasin, *Indonesia* 62 E4
Banjul, *Gambia* 82 C1
Banka, *India* 69 G12
Bankas, *Mali* 82 C4
Bankeryd, *Sweden* 11 G8
Banket, *Zimbabwe* 87 F3
Bankilaré, *Niger* 83 C5
Bankipore, *India* 67 G14
Banks I., *B.C., Canada* 102 C3
Banks I., *N.W.T., Canada* 100 A7
Banks Pen., *N.Z.* 91 K4
Banks Str., *Australia* 95 G4
Bankura, *India* 69 H12
Bankya, *Bulgaria* 44 D7
Banmankhi, *India* 69 G12
Bann →, *Arm., U.K.* 12 B5
Bann →, *L'derry., U.K.* 12 A5
Bannalec, *France* 18 E3
Bannang Sata, *Thailand* 65 J3
Banning, *U.S.A.* 111 M10
Banno, *Ethiopia* 81 G4
Bannockburn, *Canada* 116 B7
Bannockburn, *U.K.* 13 E5
Bannockburn, *Zimbabwe* 87 G2
Bannu, *Pakistan* 66 C7
Bano, *India* 69 H11
Bañolas = Banyoles, *Spain* 38 C7
Banon, *France* 21 D9
Baños de la Encina, *Spain* 37 G7
Baños de Molgas, *Spain* 36 C3
Bánovce nad Bebravou,
  Slovak Rep. 27 C11
Banovići, *Bos.-H.* 28 F3
Bansgaon, *India* 69 F10
Banská Bystrica, *Slovak Rep.* . 27 C12
Banská Štiavnica, *Slovak Rep.* 27 C11
Bansko, *Bulgaria* 44 E7
Banskobystrický □, *Slovak Rep.* 27 C12
Banswara, *India* 68 H6
Bantaeng, *Indonesia* 63 F5
Bantaji, *Nigeria* 83 D7
Bantayan, *Phil.* 61 F5
Banten □, *Indonesia* 63 G11
Bantry, *Ireland* 12 E2
Bantry B., *Ireland* 12 E2
Bantul, *Indonesia* 63 G14
Bantva, *India* 68 J4
Banya, *Bulgaria* 45 D8
Banyak, Kepulauan, *Indonesia* . 62 D1
Banyalbufar, *Spain* 48 B9
Banyo, *Cameroon* 83 D7
Banyoles, *Spain* 38 C7
Banyuls-sur-Mer, *France* 20 F7
Banyumas, *Indonesia* 63 G13
Banyuwangi, *Indonesia* 63 J17
Banzare Coast, *Antarctica* 5 C9
Bao Ha, *Vietnam* 58 F5
Bao Lac, *Vietnam* 64 A5
Bao Loc, *Vietnam* 65 G6
Bao'an = Shenzhen, *China* 59 F10
Baocheng, *China* 56 H4
Baode, *China* 56 E6
Baodi, *China* 57 E9
Baoding, *China* 56 E8
Baoji, *China* 56 G4
Baojing, *China* 58 C7
Baokang, *China* 59 B8
Baoshan, *Shanghai, China* 59 B13
Baoshan, *Yunnan, China* 58 E2
Baotou, *China* 56 D6
Baoxing, *China* 58 B4
Baoying, *China* 57 H10
Bap, *India* 68 F5
Bapatla, *India* 67 M12
Bapaume, *France* 19 B9
Bāqerābād, *Iran* 71 C6
Ba'qūbah, *Iraq* 70 C5
Baquedano, *Chile* 126 A2
Bar, *Serbia & M.* 44 D3
Bar, *Ukraine* 33 H4
Bar Bigha, *India* 69 G11
Bar Harbor, *U.S.A.* 115 C14
Bar-le-Duc, *France* 19 D12
Bar-sur-Aube, *France* 19 D11
Bar-sur-Seine, *France* 19 D11

Bara, *India* 69 G9
Bâra, *Romania* 29 C12
Bara Banki, *India* 69 F9
Barabai, *Indonesia* 62 E5
Baraboo, *U.S.A.* 112 D10
Baracoa, *Cuba* 121 B5
Baradā →, *Syria* 74 B5
Baradero, *Argentina* 126 C4
Baraga, *U.S.A.* 112 B10
Bǎrǎganul, *Romania* 29 F12
Barah →, *India* 68 F6
Barahona, *Dom. Rep.* 121 C5
Barahona, *Spain* 38 D2
Barail Range, *India* 67 G18
Barajas, Madrid ✈ (MAD), *Spain* 36 E7
Baraka, *Sudan* 81 E2
Baraka →, *Sudan* 80 D4
Barakar →, *India* 69 G12
Barakhola, *India* 67 G18
Barakot, *India* 69 J11
Barakpur, *India* 69 H13
Baralaba, *Australia* 94 C4
Baralla, *Spain* 36 C3
Baralzon L., *Canada* 103 B9
Barameiya, *Sudan* 80 D4
Baramula, *India* 69 B6
Baran, *India* 68 G7
Baran →, *Pakistan* 68 G3
Barañain, *Spain* 38 C3
Barna →, *India* 69 G10
Barani, *Burkina Faso* 82 C4
Barankul, *Kazakhstan* .... (see Barrnell)
Baranof, *U.S.A.* 100 C6
Baranów Sandomierski, *Poland* . 31 H8
Baranya □, *Hungary* 28 E3
Baraolt, *Romania* 29 D10
Barapasi, *Indonesia* 63 E9
Barasat, *India* 69 H13
Barat Daya, Kepulauan,
  Indonesia 63 F7
Barataria B., *U.S.A.* 113 L10
Barauda, *India* 68 H6
Baraut, *India* 68 E7
Barbacena, *Brazil* 127 A7
Barban, *Croatia* 41 C11
Barbària, C. de, *Spain* 48 C7
Barbaros, *Turkey* 45 F11
Barbastro, *Spain* 38 C5
Barbate de Franco, *Spain* 37 J5
Barberino di Mugello, *Italy* .. 41 E8
Barberton, *S. Africa* 89 D5
Barberton, *U.S.A.* 116 E3
Barbezieux-St-Hilaire, *France* 20 C3
Barbosa, *Colombia* 124 B4
Barbourville, *U.S.A.* 115 G4
Barbuda, *W. Indies* 121 C7
Bârca, *Romania* 29 G8
Barcaldine, *Australia* 94 C4
Barcarrota, *Spain* 37 G4
Barcellona Pozzo di Gotto, *Italy* 43 D8
Barcelona, *Spain* 38 D7
Barcelona, *Venezuela* 124 A6
Barcelona □, *Spain* 38 D7
Barcelona ✈ (BCN), *Spain* 38 D7
Barceloneta, *Puerto Rico* ..... 121 d
Barcelonette, *France* 21 D10
Barcelos, *Brazil* 124 D6
Barcin, *Poland* 31 F4
Barclayville, *Liberia* 82 E3
Barcoo →, *Australia* 94 D3
Barcs, *Hungary* 28 E2
Barczewo, *Poland* 30 E7
Bārdā, *Azerbaijan* 35 K8
Bardaï, *Chad* 79 D9
Bardas Blancas, *Argentina* 126 D2
Bardawīl, Sabkhet el, *Egypt* .. 74 D2
Barddhaman, *India* 69 H12
Bardejov, *Slovak Rep.* 27 B14
Bardera, *Somali Rep.* 75 G3
Bardi, *Italy* 40 D6
Bardīyah, *Libya* 79 B10
Bardolino, *Italy* 40 C7
Bardonécchia, *Italy* 40 C3
Bardsey I., *U.K.* 14 E3
Bardstown, *U.S.A.* 114 G3
Bareilly, *India* 69 E8
Barela, *India* 69 H9
Barentin, *France* 18 C7
Barenton, *France* 18 D6
Barents Sea, *Arctic* 50 B7
Barentu, *Eritrea* 81 D4
Barfleur, *France* 18 C5
Barfleur, Pte. de, *France* 18 C5
Barga, *Italy* 40 D7
Bargara, *Australia* 94 C5
Bargas, *Spain* 36 F6
Bârgăului Bistrița, *Romania* .. 29 C9
Barge, *Italy* 40 D4
Bargnop, *Sudan* 81 F2
Bargteheide, *Germany* 24 B6
Barguzin, *Russia* 53 D11
Barh, *India* 69 G11
Barhaj, *India* 69 F10
Barharwa, *India* 69 G12
Barhi, *India* 69 G11
Bari, *India* 68 F7
Bari, *Italy* 43 A9
Bari Doab, *Pakistan* 68 D5
Bari Sadri, *India* 68 G6
Bari Sardo, *Italy* 42 C2
Barīdī, Ra's, *Si. Arabia* 70 E3
Barīm, *Yemen* 76 E8
Barinas, *Venezuela* 124 B4
Baring, C., *Canada* 100 B8
Baringo, L., *Kenya* 86 B4
Bârîs, *Egypt* 80 C3
Barisal, *Bangla.* 67 H17
Barisal □, *Bangla.* 67 H17
Barisan, Bukit, *Indonesia* 62 E2
Barito →, *Indonesia* 62 E4

Baritú △, *Argentina* 126 A3
Barjac, *France* 21 D8
Barjols, *France* 21 E10
Bark L., *Canada* 116 A7
Barka = Baraka →, *Sudan* 80 D4
Barkakana, *India* 69 H11
Barkam, *China* 58 B4
Barker, *U.S.A.* 116 C6
Barkley, L., *U.S.A.* 115 G2
Barkley Sound, *Canada* 102 D3
Barkly East, *S. Africa* 88 E4
Barkly Roadhouse, *Australia* .. 94 B2
Barkly Tableland, *Australia* .. 94 B2
Barkly West, *S. Africa* 88 D3
Barkol, Wadi →, *Sudan* 80 D3
Barla Dağı, *Turkey* 47 C12
Bârlad, *Romania* 29 D12
Bârlad →, *Romania* 29 E12
Barlee, L., *Australia* 93 E2
Barlee, Mt., *Australia* 93 D4
Barletta, *Italy* 43 A9
Barlinek, *Poland* 31 F2
Barlovento, *Canary Is.* 48 F2
Barlow L., *Canada* 103 A8
Barmedman, *Australia* 95 E4
Barmer, *India* 68 G4
Barmera, *Australia* 95 E3
Barmouth, *U.K.* 14 E3
Barmstedt, *Germany* 24 B5
Barna →, *India* 69 G10
Barnagar, *India* 68 H6
Barnala, *India* 68 D6
Barnard Castle, *U.K.* 14 C6
Barnaul, *Russia* 52 D9
Barnesville, *U.S.A.* 115 J3
Barnet □, *U.K.* 15 F7
Barneveld, *Neths.* 17 B5
Barneveld, *U.S.A.* 117 C9
Barneville-Cartevert, *France* . 18 C5
Barnhart, *U.S.A.* 113 K4
Barnsley, *U.K.* 14 D6
Barnstable Bay = Bideford Bay,
  U.K. 15 F3
Barnsville, *U.S.A.* 112 B6
Barnwell, *U.S.A.* 115 J5
Baro, *Nigeria* 83 D6
Baro →, *Ethiopia* 81 F3
Baroda = Vadodara, *India* 68 H5
Baroda, *India* 68 G7
Baroe, *S. Africa* 88 E3
Baron Ra., *Australia* 92 D4
Barong, *China* 58 B2
Barotseland, *Zambia* 85 H4
Barouéli, *Mali* 82 C3
Barpeta, *India* 67 F17
Barques, Pt. Aux, *U.S.A.* 116 B2
Barquísimeto, *Venezuela* 124 A5
Barr, Ras el, *Egypt* 80 H7
Barr Smith Range, *Australia* .. 93 E3
Barra, *Brazil* 125 F10
Barra, *U.K.* 13 E1
Barra, Sd. of, *U.K.* 13 D1
Barra de Navidad, *Mexico* 118 D4
Barra do Corda, *Brazil* 125 E9
Barra do Piraí, *Brazil* 127 A7
Barra Falsa, Pta. da, *Mozam.* . 89 C6
Barra Mansa, *Brazil* 127 A7
Barraba, *Australia* 95 E5
Barrackpur = Barakpur, *India* . 69 H13
Barradale Roadhouse, *Australia* 92 D1
Barrafranca, *Italy* 43 E7
Barraigh = Barra, *U.K.* 13 E1
Barranca, *Lima, Peru* 124 F3
Barranca, *Loreto, Peru* 124 D3
Barranca del Cobre △, *Mexico* . 118 B3
Barrancabermeja, *Colombia* 124 B4
Barrancas, *Venezuela* 124 B6
Barrancos, *Portugal* 37 G4
Barranqueras, *Argentina* 126 B4
Barranquilla, *Colombia* 124 A4
Barraute, *Canada* 104 C4
Barre, *Mass., U.S.A.* 117 D12
Barre, *Vt., U.S.A.* 117 B12
Barreal, *Argentina* 126 C2
Barreiras, *Brazil* 125 F10
Barreirinhas, *Brazil* 125 D10
Barreiro, *Portugal* 37 G1
Barrême, *France* 21 E10
Barretos, *Brazil* 125 H9
Barrhead, *Canada* 102 C6
Barrie, *Canada* 116 B5
Barrier Ra., *Australia* 95 E3
Barrière, *Canada* 102 C4
Barrington, *U.S.A.* 117 E13
Barrington L., *Canada* 103 B8
Barrington Tops, *Australia* ... 95 E5
Barringun, *Australia* 95 D4
Barro do Garças, *Brazil* 125 G8
Barron, *U.S.A.* 112 C9
Barrow, *U.S.A.* 100 A4
Barrow →, *Ireland* 12 D5
Barrow Creek, *Australia* 94 C1
Barrow I., *Australia* 92 D2
Barrow-in-Furness, *U.K.* 14 C4
Barrow Pt., *Australia* 94 A3
Barrow Pt., *U.S.A.* 98 B4
Barrow Ra., *Australia* 93 E4
Barrow Str., *Canada* 4 B3
Barruecopardo, *Spain* 36 D4
Barruelo de Santullán, *Spain* . 36 C6
Barry, *U.K.* 15 F4
Barry's Bay, *Canada* 116 A7
Barsalogho, *Burkina Faso* 83 C4
Barsat, *Pakistan* 69 A5
Barsham, *Syria* 70 C4
Barsi, *India* 66 K9
Barsinghausen, *Germany* 24 C5
Barsoi, *India* 67 G15
Barstow, *U.S.A.* 111 L9

Barth, *Germany* 24 A8
Barthélemy, Col, *Vietnam* 64 C5
Bartica, *Guyana* 124 B7
Bartin, *Turkey* 72 B5
Bartle Frere, *Australia* 94 B4
Bartlesville, *U.S.A.* 113 G7
Bartlett, *U.S.A.* 110 J8
Bartlett, L., *Canada* 102 A5
Bartolomeu Dias, *Mozam.* 87 G4
Barton, *U.S.A.* 117 B12
Barton upon Humber, *U.K.* 14 D7
Bartoszyce, *Poland* 30 D7
Bartow, *U.S.A.* 115 M5
Barú, Volcan, *Panama* 120 E3
Barumba, *Dem. Rep. of the Congo* 86 B1
Baruth, *Germany* 24 C9
Baruunsuu, *Mongolia* 56 C3
Barwani, *India* 68 H6
Barwice, *Poland* 30 E3
Barycz →, *Poland* 31 G3
Barysaw, *Belarus* 32 E5
Barysh, *Russia* 34 D8
Barzān, *Iraq* 70 B5
Bârzava, *Romania* 28 D6
Bas-Rhin □, *France* 19 D14
Bašaid, *Serbia & M.* 28 E5
Bâsa'idū, *Iran* 71 E7
Basal, *Pakistan* 68 C5
Basankusa, *Dem. Rep. of
  the Congo* 84 D3
Basarabeasca, *Moldova* 29 D13
Basarabi, *Romania* 29 F13
Basarabia = Bessarabiya,
  Moldova 33 J5
Basauri, *Spain* 38 B2
Basawa, *Afghan.* 68 B4
Bascuñán, C., *Chile* 126 B1
Basel, *Switz.* 25 H3
Basel, Euroairport ✈ (BSL),
  Europe 19 E14
Basel-Landschaft □, *Switz.* ... 25 H3
Basento →, *Italy* 43 B9
Bashākerd, Kūhhā-ye, *Iran* 71 E8
Bashaw, *Canada* 102 C6
Bāshī, *Iran* 71 D6
Bashkir Republic =
  Bashkortostan □, *Russia* 52 D6
Bashkortostan □, *Russia* 52 D6
Bashtanivka, *Ukraine* 29 E14
Basibasy, *Madag.* 89 C7
Basilan I., *Phil.* 61 H5
Basilan Str., *Phil.* 61 H5
Basildon, *U.K.* 15 F8
Basile, *Eq. Guin.* 83 E6
Basilicata □, *Italy* 43 B9
Basim = Washim, *India* 66 J10
Basin, *U.S.A.* 108 D9
Basingstoke, *U.K.* 15 F6
Baška, *Croatia* 41 D11
Başkale, *Turkey* 73 C10
Baskatong, Rés., *Canada* 104 C4
Basle = Basel, *Switz.* 25 H3
Basoda, *India* 68 H7
Basoka, *Dem. Rep. of the Congo* 86 B1
Basongo, *Dem. Rep. of the Congo* 86 B1
Basque, Pays, *France* 20 E2
Basque Provinces = País Vasco □,
  Spain 38 C2
Basra = Al Başrah, *Iraq* 70 D5
Bass Str., *Australia* 95 F4
Bassano, *Canada* 102 C6
Bassano del Grappa, *Italy* 41 C8
Bassar, *Togo* 83 D5
Bassas da India, *Ind. Oc.* 85 J7
Basse-Normandie □, *France* 18 D6
Basse-Pointe, *Martinique* ..... 120 c
Basse Santa-Su, *Gambia* 82 C2
Basse-Terre, *Guadeloupe* ...... 120 b
Basse Terre, *Trin. & Tob.* 125 K15
Bassein, *Burma* 67 L19
Basseterre, *St. Kitts & Nevis* 121 C7
Bassett, *U.S.A.* 112 D5
Bassi, *India* 68 D7
Bassigny, *France* 19 E12
Bassikounou, *Mauritania* 82 B3
Bassila, *Benin* 83 D5
Bassum, *Germany* 24 C4
Båstad, *Sweden* 11 H6
Bastak, *Iran* 71 E7
Baştām, *Iran* 71 B7
Bastar, *India* 67 K12
Bastelica, *France* 21 F13
Basti, *India* 69 F10
Bastia, *France* 21 F13
Bastogne, *Belgium* 17 D5
Bastrop, *La., U.S.A.* 113 J9
Bastrop, *Tex., U.S.A.* 113 K6
Bat Yam, *Israel* 74 C3
Bata, *Eq. Guin.* 84 D1
Bata, *Romania* 28 D7
Bataan □, *Phil.* 61 D4
Batabanó, *Cuba* 120 B3
Batabanó, G. de, *Cuba* 120 B3
Batac, *Phil.* 61 B4
Batagai, *Russia* 53 C14
Batajnica, *Serbia & M.* 44 B4
Batak, *Bulgaria* 45 E8
Batala, *India* 68 D6
Batalha, *Portugal* 36 F2
Batama, *Dem. Rep. of the Congo* 86 B2
Batamay, *Russia* 53 C13
Batang, *Indonesia* 63 G13
Batang, *Phil.* 61 E4
Batangas, *Phil.* 61 E4
Batanta, *Indonesia* 63 E8
Batatais, *Brazil* 127 A6
Batavia, *U.S.A.* 116 D6
Bataysk, *Russia* 33 J10
Batchelor, *Australia* 92 B5
Batdambang, *Cambodia* 64 F4

Batemans B., *Australia* 95 F5
Batemans Bay, *Australia* 95 F5
Bates Ra., *Australia* 93 E3
Batesburg-Leesville, *U.S.A.* ... 115 J5
Batesville, *Ark., U.S.A.* 113 H9
Batesville, *Miss., U.S.A.* 113 H10
Batesville, *Tex., U.S.A.* 113 L5
Bath, *Canada* 117 B8
Bath, *U.K.* 15 F5
Bath, *Maine, U.S.A.* 115 D11
Bath, *N.Y., U.S.A.* 116 D7
Bath & North East Somerset □,
  U.K. 15 F5
Batheay, *Cambodia* 65 G5
Bathsheba, *Barbados* .... 121 g
Bathurst, *Australia* 95 E4
Bathurst, *Canada* 105 C6
Bathurst, *S. Africa* 88 E4
Bathurst, C., *Canada* 100 A7
Bathurst B., *Australia* 94 A3
Bathurst Harb., *Australia* 95 G4
Bathurst I., *Australia* 92 B5
Bathurst I., *Canada* 98 B3
Bathurst Inlet, *Canada* 100 B9
Bati, *Ethiopia* 81 E5
Batie, *Burkina Faso* 82 D4
Batman, *Turkey* 70 B4
Baṭn al Ghūl, *Jordan* 74 F4
Batna, *Algeria* 78 A7
Batobato = San Isidro, *Phil.* .. 61 H7
Batočina, *Serbia & M.* 44 B5
Batoka, *Zambia* 87 F2
Baton Rouge, *U.S.A.* 113 K9
Batong, Ko, *Thailand* 65 J2
Bátonyterenye, *Hungary* 28 C4
Batopilas, *Mexico* 118 B3
Batouri, *Cameroon* 84 D2
Båtsfjord, *Norway* 8 A23
Battambang = Batdambang,
  Cambodia 64 F4
Batticaloa, *Sri Lanka* 66 R12
Battipáglia, *Italy* 43 B7
Battle, *U.K.* 15 G8
Battle →, *Canada* 103 C7
Battle Creek, *U.S.A.* 114 D3
Battle Ground, *U.S.A.* 110 E4
Battle Harbour, *Canada* 105 B8
Battle Lake, *U.S.A.* 112 B7
Battle Mountain, *U.S.A.* 108 F5
Battlefields, *Zimbabwe* 87 F2
Battleford, *Canada* 103 C7
Battonya, *Hungary* 28 D6
Batu, *Ethiopia* 81 F4
Batu, Kepulauan, *Indonesia* ... 62 E1
Batu Caves, *Malaysia* 65 L3
Batu Ferringhi, *Malaysia* ..... 65 c
Batu Gajah, *Malaysia* 65 K3
Batu Is. = Batu, Kepulauan,
  Indonesia 62 E1
Batu Pahat, *Malaysia* 65 M4
Batuata, *Indonesia* 63 F6
Batugondang, Tanjung, *Indonesia* 63 J17
Batukau, Gunung, *Indonesia* .. 63 J18
Batur, *Indonesia* 63 J18
Batur, Gunung, *Indonesia* 63 J18
Baturaja, *Indonesia* 62 E2
Baturité, *Brazil* 125 D11
Baturiti, *Indonesia* 63 J18
Bau, *Malaysia* 62 D4
Baubau, *Indonesia* 63 F6
Baucau, *E. Timor* 63 F7
Bauchi, *Nigeria* 83 C6
Bauchi □, *Nigeria* 83 C7
Baud, *France* 18 E3
Baudette, *U.S.A.* 112 A7
Bauer, C., *Australia* 95 E1
Bauhinia, *Australia* 94 C4
Baukau = Baucau, *E. Timor* ... 63 F7
Bauld, C., *Canada* 101 C14
Baume-les-Dames, *France* 19 E13
Baunatal, *Germany* 24 D5
Baunei, *Italy* 42 B2
Baure, *Nigeria* 83 C6
Bauru, *Brazil* 127 A6
Bausi, *India* 69 G12
Bauska, *Latvia* 9 H21
Bautino, *Kazakhstan* 35 H10
Bautzen, *Germany* 24 D10
Bauya, *S. Leone* 82 D2
Bavănāt, *Iran* 71 D7
Bavanište, *Serbia & M.* 28 F5
Bavaria = Bayern □, *Germany* . 25 G7
Båven, *Sweden* 10 E10
Bavispe →, *Mexico* 118 B3
Bawdwin, *Burma* 67 H20
Bawean, *Indonesia* 62 F4
Bawku, *Ghana* 83 C4
Bawlake, *Burma* 67 K20
Bawolung, *China* 58 C3
Baxley, *U.S.A.* 115 K4
Baxoi, *China* 58 B1
Baxter, *U.S.A.* 112 B7
Baxter Springs, *U.S.A.* 113 G7
Baxter State △, *U.S.A.* 115 B11
Bay, L. de, *Phil.* 61 D4
Bay City, *Mich., U.S.A.* 114 D4
Bay City, *Tex., U.S.A.* 113 L7
Bay Minette, *U.S.A.* 115 K2
Bay Roberts, *Canada* 105 C9
Bay St. Louis, *U.S.A.* 113 K10
Bay Springs, *U.S.A.* 113 K10
Bay View, *N.Z.* 91 H6
Baya, *Dem. Rep. of the Congo* . 87 E2
Bayamo, *Cuba* 120 B4
Bayamón, *Puerto Rico* .... 121 d
Bayan Har Shan, *China* 60 C4
Bayan Hot = Alxa Zuoqi, *China* 56 E3
Bayan Lepas, *Malaysia* .... 65 c
Bayan Obo, *China* 56 D5

Bayan-Ovoo = Erdenetsogt,
  Mongolia 56 C4
Bayana, *India* 68 F7
Bayanaúyl, *Kazakhstan* 52 D8
Bayandalay, *Mongolia* 56 C2
Bayanhongor, *Mongolia* 60 B5
Bayard, *N. Mex., U.S.A.* 109 K9
Bayard, *Nebr., U.S.A.* 112 E3
Bayawan, *Phil.* 61 G5
Baybay, *Phil.* 61 F6
Bayburt, *Turkey* 73 B9
Baydhabo = Baidoa, *Somali Rep.* 75 G3
Bayelsa □, *Nigeria* 83 E6
Bayerische Alpen, *Germany* ... 25 H7
Bayerische Rhön △, *Germany* .. 25 E6
Bayerischer Spessart △, *Germany* 25 F6
Bayerischer Wald, *Germany* ... 25 G8
Bayern □, *Germany* 25 G7
Bayeux, *France* 18 C6
Bayfield, *Canada* 116 C3
Bayfield, *U.S.A.* 112 B9
Bayındır, *Turkey* 47 C9
Bayjī, *Iraq* 70 C4
Baykal, Oz., *Russia* 53 D11
Baykan, *Turkey* 70 B4
Baykonur = Bayqongyr,
  Kazakhstan 52 E7
Baynes Mts., *Namibia* 88 B1
Bayombong, *Phil.* 61 C4
Bayon, *France* 19 D13
Bayona = Baiona, *Spain* 36 C2
Bayonne, *France* 20 E2
Bayonne, *U.S.A.* 117 F10
Bayovar, *Peru* 124 E2
Bayqongyr, *Kazakhstan* 52 E7
Bayram-Ali = Bayramaly,
  Turkmenistan 52 F7
Bayramaly, *Turkmenistan* 52 F7
Bayramiç, *Turkey* 47 B8
Bayreuth, *Germany* 25 F7
Bayrischzell, *Germany* 25 H8
Bayrūt, *Lebanon* 74 B4
Bays, L. of, *Canada* 116 A5
Baysville, *Canada* 116 A5
Bayt Lahm, *West Bank* 74 D4
Baytown, *U.S.A.* 113 L7
Bayun, *Indonesia* 63 J18
Bayzo, *Niger* 83 C5
Baza, *Spain* 37 H8
Bazar Dyuzi, *Russia* 35 K8
Bazardüzü = Bazar Dyuzi, *Russia* 35 K8
Bazarny Karabulak, *Russia* ... 34 D8
Bazarnyy Syzgan, *Russia* 34 D8
Bazaruto △, *Mozam.* 89 C6
Bazaruto, I. do, *Mozam.* 89 C6
Bazas, *France* 20 D3
Bazhong, *China* 58 B6
Bazhou, *China* 56 E9
Bazmān, Kūh-e, *Iran* 71 D9
Beach, *U.S.A.* 112 B3
Beach City, *U.S.A.* 116 F3
Beachport, *Australia* 95 F3
Beachy Hd., *U.K.* 15 G8
Beacon, *Australia* 93 F2
Beacon, *U.S.A.* 117 E11
Beaconsfield, *Australia* 95 G4
Beagle, Canal, *S. Amer.* 128 H3
Beagle Bay, *Australia* 92 C3
Bealanana, *Madag.* 89 A8
Beals Cr. →, *U.S.A.* 113 J4
Beamsville, *Canada* 116 C5
Bear →, *Calif., U.S.A.* 110 G5
Bear →, *Utah, U.S.A.* 106 D4
Béar, C., *France* 20 F7
Bear I., *Ireland* 12 E1
Bear L., *Canada* 103 B9
Bear L., *U.S.A.* 108 F8
Beardmore, *Canada* 104 C2
Beardmore Glacier, *Antarctica* . 5 E11
Beardstown, *U.S.A.* 112 F9
Bearma →, *India* 69 G8
Béarn, *France* 20 E3
Bearpaw Mts., *U.S.A.* 108 B9
Bearskin Lake, *Canada* 104 B1
Beas →, *India* 68 D6
Beas de Segura, *Spain* 37 G8
Beasain, *Spain* 38 B2
Beata, C., *Dom. Rep.* 121 C5
Beata, I., *Dom. Rep.* 121 C5
Beatrice, *U.S.A.* 112 E6
Beatrice, *Zimbabwe* 87 F3
Beatrice, C., *Australia* 94 A2
Beatton →, *Canada* 102 B4
Beatton River, *Canada* 102 B4
Beatty, *U.S.A.* 110 J10
Beaucaire, *France* 21 E8
Beauce, Plaine de la, *France* .. 19 D8
Beauceville, *Canada* 105 C5
Beaudesert, *Australia* 95 D5
Beaufort, *France* 21 C10
Beaufort, *Malaysia* 62 C5
Beaufort, *N.C., U.S.A.* 115 H7
Beaufort, *S.C., U.S.A.* 115 J5
Beaufort Sea, *Arctic* 98 B5
Beaufort West, *S. Africa* 88 E3
Beaugency, *France* 19 E8
Beauharnois, *Canada* 117 A11
Beaujeu, *France* 19 F11
Beaujolais, *France* 19 F11
Beaulieu →, *Canada* 102 A6
Beaulieu-sur-Dordogne, *France* 20 D5
Beaulieu-sur-Mer, *France* 21 E11
Beauly, *U.K.* 13 D4
Beauly →, *U.K.* 13 D4
Beaumaris, *U.K.* 14 D3
Beaumont, *Belgium* 17 D4
Beaumont, *France* 20 D4
Beaumont, *U.S.A.* 113 K7
Beaumont-de-Lomagne, *France* 20 E5
Beaumont-le-Roger, *France* ... 18 C7
Beaumont-sur-Sarthe, *France* . 18 D7
Beaune, *France* 19 E11

Beaune-la-Rolande, *France* 19 D9
Beaupré, *Canada* 105 C5
Beaupréau, *France* 18 E6
Beauraing, *Belgium* 17 D4
Beaurepaire, *France* 21 C9
Beausejour, *Canada* 103 C9
Beauval, *Canada* 103 B7
Beauvais, *France* 19 C9
Beauvoir-sur-Mer, *France* 18 F4
Beauvoir-sur-Niort, *France* ... 20 B3
Beaver, *Okla., U.S.A.* 113 G4
Beaver, *Pa., U.S.A.* 116 F4
Beaver, *Utah, U.S.A.* 109 G7
Beaver →, *B.C., Canada* 102 B4
Beaver →, *Ont., Canada* 104 A2
Beaver →, *Sask., Canada* 103 B7
Beaver →, *U.S.A.* 113 G5
Beaver City, *U.S.A.* 112 E5
Beaver Creek, *Canada* 100 B5
Beaver Dam, *U.S.A.* 112 D10
Beaver Falls, *U.S.A.* 116 F4
Beaver Hill L., *Canada* 103 C10
Beaver I., *U.S.A.* 114 C3
Beaverhill L., *Canada* 102 C6
Beaverlodge, *Canada* 102 B5
Beaverstone →, *Canada* 104 B2
Beaverton, *Canada* 116 B5
Beaverton, *U.S.A.* 110 E4
Beawar, *India* 68 F6
Bebedouro, *Brazil* 127 A6
Bebera, Tanjung, *Indonesia* ... 63 K18
Beboa, *Madag.* 89 B7
Bebra, *Germany* 24 E5
Becan, *Mexico* 119 D7
Beccles, *U.K.* 15 E9
Bečej, *Serbia & M.* 28 E5
Beceni, *Romania* 29 E11
Becerreá, *Spain* 36 C3
Béchar, *Algeria* 78 B5
Bechyně, *Czech Rep.* 26 B7
Beckley, *U.S.A.* 114 G5
Beckum, *Germany* 24 D4
Beclean, *Romania* 29 C9
Bečov nad Teplou, *Czech Rep.* 26 A5
Bečva →, *Czech Rep.* 27 B10
Bédar, *Spain* 39 H3
Bédarieux, *France* 20 E7
Beddouza, Ras, *Morocco* 78 B4
Bedele, *Ethiopia* 81 F4
Bederkesa, *Germany* 24 B4
Bedeso, *Ethiopia* 81 F5
Bedford, *Canada* 117 A12
Bedford, *S. Africa* 88 E4
Bedford, *U.K.* 15 E7
Bedford, *Ind., U.S.A.* 114 F2
Bedford, *Iowa, U.S.A.* 112 E7
Bedford, *Ohio, U.S.A.* 116 E3
Bedford, *Pa., U.S.A.* 116 F6
Bedford, *Va., U.S.A.* 114 G6
Bedford, C., *Australia* 94 B4
Bedfordshire □, *U.K.* 15 E7
Będków, *Poland* 31 G6
Bednja →, *Croatia* 41 B13
Bednodemyanovsk, *Russia* 34 D6
Bedok, *Singapore* .... 65 d
Bedónia, *Italy* 40 D7
Bedourie, *Australia* 94 C2
Bedum, *Neths.* 17 A6
Będzin, *Poland* 31 H6
Beebe Plain, *Canada* 117 A12
Beech Creek, *U.S.A.* 116 E7
Beef I., *Br. Virgin Is.* .... 121 e
Beelitz, *Germany* 24 C8
Beenleigh, *Australia* 95 D5
Be'er Menuḥa, *Israel* 70 D2
Be'er Sheva, *Israel* 74 D3
Beersheba = Be'er Sheva, *Israel* 74 D3
Beeskow, *Germany* 24 C10
Beestekraal, *S. Africa* 89 D4
Beeston, *U.K.* 14 E6
Beetzendorf, *Germany* 24 C7
Beeville, *U.S.A.* 113 L6
Befale, *Dem. Rep. of the Congo* 84 D4
Befandriana, Mahajanga, *Madag.* 89 B8
Befandriana, Toliara, *Madag.* . 89 C7
Befasy, *Madag.* 89 C7
Befotaka, *Antsiranana, Madag.* 89 A8
Befotaka, Fianarantsoa, *Madag.* 89 C8
Bega, *Australia* 95 F4
Bega, Canalul, *Romania* 28 E5
Bégard, *France* 18 D3
Beğendik, *Turkey* 45 F10
Begoro, *Ghana* 83 D4
Begusarai, *India* 69 G12
Behābād, *Iran* 71 C8
Behala, *India* 69 H13
Behara, *Madag.* 89 C8
Behbehān, *Iran* 71 D6
Behm Canal, *U.S.A.* 102 B2
Behshahr, *Iran* 71 B7
Bei Jiang →, *China* 59 F9
Bei'an, *China* 60 B7
Beibei, *China* 58 C6
Beichuan, *China* 58 B5
Beihai, *China* 58 G7
Beijing, *China* 56 E9
Beijing □, *China* 56 E9
Beilen, *Neths.* 17 B6
Beiliu, *China* 59 F8
Beipan Jiang →, *China* 58 E5
Beipiao, *China* 57 D11
Beira, *Mozam.* 87 F3
Beirut = Bayrūt, *Lebanon* 74 B4
Beiseker, *Canada* 102 C6
Beitaolaizhao, *China* 57 B13
Beitbridge, *Zimbabwe* 87 G3
Beiuș, *Romania* 28 D7

Beizhen = Binzhou, *China* 57 F10
Beizhen, *China* 57 D11
Beizhengzhen, *China* 57 B12
Béja, *Portugal* 37 G3
Béja, *Tunisia* 79 A7
Beja □, *Portugal* 37 H3
Bejaïa, *Algeria* 78 A7
Béjar, *Spain* 36 E5
Bejestān, *Iran* 71 C8
Bekaa Valley = Al Biqâ, *Lebanon* 74 A5
Bekçiler, *Turkey* 47 E11
Békés, *Hungary* 28 D6
Békés □, *Hungary* 28 D6
Békéscsaba, *Hungary* 28 D6
Bekilli, *Turkey* 47 C11
Bekily, *Madag.* 89 C8
Bekisopa, *Madag.* 89 C8
Bekitro, *Madag.* 89 C8
Bekodoka, *Madag.* 89 B8
Bekoji, *Ethiopia* 81 F4
Bekok, *Malaysia* 65 L4
Bekopaka, *Madag.* 89 B7
Bekuli, *Indonesia* 63 J17
Bekwai, *Ghana* 83 D4
Bela, *India* 69 G10
Bela, *Pakistan* 68 F2
Bela Bela, *S. Africa* 89 C4
Bela Crkva, *Serbia & M.* 28 F6
Bela Palanka, *Serbia & M.* ... 44 C6
Bela Vista, *Brazil* 126 A4
Bela Vista, *Mozam.* 89 D5
Bélábre, *France* 20 B5
Belalcázar, *Spain* 37 G5
Belan →, *India* 69 G9
Belanovica, *Serbia & M.* 44 B4
Belarus ■, *Europe* 32 F4
Belau = Palau ■, *Pac. Oc.* ... 96 G5
Belavenona, *Madag.* 89 C8
Belawan, *Indonesia* 62 D1
Belaya, *Ethiopia* 81 E4
Belaya Glina, *Russia* 35 G5
Belaya Kalitva, *Russia* 35 F5
Belaya Tserkov = Bila Tserkva,
  Ukraine 33 H6
Belcești, *Romania* 29 C12
Belchatów, *Poland* 31 G6
Belcher Is., *Canada* 104 A3
Belchite, *Spain* 38 D4
Belden, *U.S.A.* 110 E5
Beled Weyne = Belet Uen,
  Somali Rep. 75 G4
Belém, *Brazil* 125 D9
Belén, *Argentina* 126 B2
Belén, *Paraguay* 126 A4
Belen, *U.S.A.* 109 J10
Belene, *Bulgaria* 45 C9
Beleni, *Turkey* 72 D7
Bélesta, *France* 20 F5
Belet Uen, *Somali Rep.* 75 G4
Belev, *Russia* 32 F9
Belevi, *Turkey* 47 C9
Belfair, *U.S.A.* 110 C4
Belfast, *S. Africa* 89 D5
Belfast, *U.K.* 12 B6
Belfast, *Maine, U.S.A.* 115 C11
Belfast, *N.Y., U.S.A.* 116 D6
Belfast L., *U.K.* 12 B6
Belfield, *U.S.A.* 112 B3
Belfort, *France* 19 E13
Belfort, Territoire de □, *France* 19 E13
Belfry, *U.S.A.* 108 D9
Belgaum, *India* 66 M9
Belgioioso, *Italy* 40 C6
Belgium ■, *Europe* 17 D4
Belgodère, *France* 21 F13
Belgorod, *Russia* 33 G9
Belgorod-Dnestrovskiy =
  Bilhorod-Dnistrovskyy,
  Ukraine 33 J6
Belgrade = Beograd, *Serbia & M.* 44 B4
Belgrade, *U.S.A.* 108 D8
Belhaven, *U.S.A.* 115 H7
Beli Drim →, *Europe* 44 D4
Beli Manastir, *Croatia* 28 E3
Beli Timok →, *Serbia & M.* .. 44 C6
Bélice →, *Italy* 42 E5
Belimbing, *Indonesia* 63 J18
Belinskiy, *Russia* 34 D6
Beliton Is. = Belitung, *Indonesia* 62 E3
Belitung, *Indonesia* 62 E3
Beliu, *Romania* 28 D6
Belize ■, *Cent. Amer.* 119 D7
Belize City, *Belize* 119 D7
Beljakovci, *Macedonia* 44 D5
Beljanica, *Serbia & M.* 44 B5
Belkovskiy, Ostrov, *Russia* ... 53 B14
Bell →, *Canada* 104 C4
Bell I., *Canada* 105 B8
Bell-Irving →, *Canada* 102 B3
Bell Peninsula, *Canada* 101 B11
Bell Ville, *Argentina* 126 C3
Bella, *Italy* 43 B8
Bella Bella, *Canada* 102 C3
Bella Coola, *Canada* 102 C3
Bella Unión, *Uruguay* 126 C4
Bella Vista, *Corrientes, Argentina* 126 B4
Bella Vista, *Tucuman, Argentina* 126 B2
Bellac, *France* 20 B5
Bellágio, *Italy* 40 C6
Bellaire, *U.S.A.* 116 F4
Bellária, *Italy* 41 D9
Bellary, *India* 66 M10
Bellata, *Australia* 95 D4
Belle-Chasse, *U.S.A.* 113 L10
Belle Fourche, *U.S.A.* 112 C3
Belle Fourche →, *U.S.A.* 112 C3
Belle Glade, *U.S.A.* 115 M5
Belle-Île, *France* 18 E3
Belle Isle, *Canada* 105 B8
Belle Isle, Str. of, *Canada* ... 105 B8
Belle Plaine, *U.S.A.* 112 E8

Belle Yella, *Liberia* 82 D3
Belledonne, *France* 21 C10
Bellefontaine, *U.S.A.* 114 E4
Bellefonte, *U.S.A.* 116 F7
Bellegarde, *France* 19 E9
Bellegarde-en-Marche, *France* . 20 C6
Bellegarde-sur-Valserine, *France* 19 F12
Bellême, *France* 18 D7
Belleoram, *Canada* 105 C8
Belleplaine, *Barbados* .... 121 g
Belleville, *Canada* 116 B7
Belleville, *France* 19 F11
Belleville, *Ill., U.S.A.* 112 F10
Belleville, *Kans., U.S.A.* 112 F6
Belleville, *N.Y., U.S.A.* 117 C8
Belleville-sur-Vie, *France* 18 F5
Bellevue, *Canada* 102 D6
Bellevue, *Idaho, U.S.A.* 108 E6
Bellevue, *Nebr., U.S.A.* 112 E7
Bellevue, *Ohio, U.S.A.* 116 E2
Bellevue, *Wash., U.S.A.* 110 C4
Belley, *France* 21 C9
Bellin = Kangirsuk, *Canada* .. 101 B13
Bellinge, *Denmark* 11 J4
Bellingen, *Australia* 95 E5
Bellingham, *U.S.A.* 100 D7
Bellingshausen Sea, *Antarctica* 5 C17
Bellinzona, *Switz.* 25 J5
Bello, *Colombia* 124 B3
Bellows Falls, *U.S.A.* 117 C12
Bellpat, *Pakistan* 68 E3
Bellpuig d'Urgell, *Spain* 38 D6
Belluno, *Italy* 41 B9
Bellwood, *U.S.A.* 116 F6
Bélmez, *Spain* 37 G5
Belmont, *Canada* 116 D3
Belmont, *S. Africa* 88 D3
Belmont, *U.S.A.* 116 D6
Belmonte, *Brazil* 125 G11
Belmonte, *Portugal* 36 E3
Belmopan, *Belize* 119 D7
Belmullet, *Ireland* 12 B2
Belo Horizonte, *Brazil* 125 G10
Belo-sur-Mer, *Madag.* 89 C7
Belo-Tsiribihina, *Madag.* 89 B7
Belogorsk = Bilohirsk, *Ukraine* 33 K8
Belogorsk, *Russia* 53 D13
Belogradchik, *Bulgaria* 44 C6
Belogradets, *Bulgaria* 45 C11
Beloha, *Madag.* 89 D8
Beloit, *Kans., U.S.A.* 112 F5
Beloit, *Wis., U.S.A.* 112 D10
Belokorovichi, *Ukraine* 33 G5
Belomorsk, *Russia* 52 C4
Belonia, *India* 67 H17
Belopolye = Bilopillya, *Ukraine* 33 G8
Belorechensk, *Russia* 35 H4
Belorussia = Belarus ■, *Europe* 32 F4
Beloslav, *Bulgaria* 45 C11
Belovo, *Bulgaria* 45 D8
Belovo, *Russia* 52 D9
Belovodsk, *Ukraine* 33 H10
Beloye, Ozero, *Russia* 32 B9
Beloye More, *Russia* 52 C4
Belozem, *Bulgaria* 45 D9
Belozersk, *Russia* 32 B9
Belpasso, *Italy* 43 E7
Belpre, *U.S.A.* 114 F5
Belrain, *India* 69 E9
Belt, *U.S.A.* 108 C8
Beltana, *Australia* 95 E2
Belterra, *Brazil* 125 D8
Beltinci, *Slovenia* 41 B13
Belton, *S.C., U.S.A.* 115 H4
Belton L., *U.S.A.* 113 K6
Beltsy = Bălți, *Moldova* 29 C12
Belturbet, *Ireland* 12 B4
Belukha, *Russia* 52 E9
Beluran, *Malaysia* 62 C5
Beluša, *Slovak Rep.* 27 B11
Belušić, *Serbia & M.* 44 C5
Belvedere Maríttimo, *Italy* ... 43 C8
Belvès, *France* 20 D5
Belvidere, *Ill., U.S.A.* 112 D10
Belvidere, *N.J., U.S.A.* 117 F9
Belvis de la Jara, *Spain* 36 F6
Belyando →, *Australia* 94 C4
Belyy, *Russia* 32 E7
Belyy, Ostrov, *Russia* 52 B8
Belyy Yar, *Russia* 52 D9
Belz, *Ukraine* 31 H11
Belżec, *Poland* 31 H10
Belzig, *Germany* 24 C8
Belzoni, *U.S.A.* 113 J9
Bełżyce, *Poland* 31 G9
Bemaraha, Lembalemban' i,
  Madag. 89 B7
Bemarivo, *Antsiranana,
  Madag.* 89 A9
Bemarivo →, *Mahajanga, Madag.* 89 B8
Bemavo, *Madag.* 89 C8
Bembéréke, *Benin* 83 C5
Bembesi, *Zimbabwe* 87 F2
Bembesi →, *Zimbabwe* 87 F2
Bembézar →, *Spain* 37 H5
Bembibre, *Spain* 36 C4
Bemetara, *India* 69 J9
Bemidji, *U.S.A.* 112 B7
Bemolanga, *Madag.* 89 B8
Ben, *Iran* 71 C6
Ben Cruachan, *U.K.* 13 E3
Ben Dearg, *U.K.* 13 D4
Ben En △, *Vietnam* 64 C5
Ben Hope, *U.K.* 13 C4
Ben Lawers, *U.K.* 13 E4
Ben Lomond, *N.S.W., Australia* 95 E5
Ben Lomond, *Tas., Australia* .. 95 G4
Ben Lomond, *U.K.* 13 E4
Ben Lomond △, *Australia* 95 G4
Ben Luc, *Vietnam* 65 G6

Ben Macdhui, U.K. — 13 D5
Ben Mhor, U.K. — 13 D1
Ben More, Arg. & Bute, U.K. — 13 E2
Ben More, Stirl., U.K. — 13 E4
Ben More Assynt, U.K. — 13 C4
Ben Nevis, U.K. — 13 E3
Ben Quang, Vietnam — 64 D6
Ben Vorlich, U.K. — 13 E4
Ben Wyvis, U.K. — 13 D4
Bena, Nigeria — 83 C6
Benalla, Australia — 95 F4
Benalmádena, Spain — 37 J6
Bénat, C., France — 21 E10
Benavente, Portugal — 37 G2
Benavente, Spain — 36 C5
Benavides, U.S.A. — 113 M5
Benavides de Órbigo, Spain — 36 C5
Benbecula, U.K. — 13 D1
Benbonyathe, Australia — 95 E2
Bend, U.S.A. — 108 D3
Bender Beila, Somali Rep. — 75 F5
Bendery = Tighina, Moldova — 29 D14
Bendigo, Australia — 95 F3
Bendorf, Germany — 24 E3
Benē Beraq, Israel — 74 C3
Bénéna, Mali — 82 C4
Benenitra, Madag. — 89 C8
Benešov, Czech Rep. — 26 B7
Benevento, Italy — 43 A7
Benfeld, France — 19 D14
Benga, Mozam. — 87 F3
Bengal, Bay of, Ind. Oc. — 67 M17
Bengalūru = Bangalore, India — 66 N10
Bengbis, Cameroon — 83 E7
Bengbu, China — 57 H9
Benghazi = Banghāzī, Libya — 79 B10
Bengkalis, Indonesia — 62 D2
Bengkulu, Indonesia — 62 E2
Bengkulu □, Indonesia — 62 E2
Bengough, Canada — 103 D7
Bengtsfors, Sweden — 10 E6
Benguela, Angola — 85 G2
Benguérua, I., Mozam. — 89 C6
Benha, Egypt — 80 H7
Beni, Dem. Rep. of the Congo — 86 B2
Beni →, Bolivia — 124 F5
Beni Mazâr, Egypt — 80 B3
Beni Mellal, Morocco — 78 B4
Beni Suef, Egypt — 80 J7
Beniah L., Canada — 102 A6
Benicarló, Spain — 38 E5
Benicàssim, Spain — 38 E5
Benicia, U.S.A. — 110 G4
Benidorm, Spain — 39 G4
Benin ■, Africa — 83 D5
Benin →, Nigeria — 83 D6
Benin, Bight of, W. Afr. — 83 E5
Benin City, Nigeria — 83 D6
Benisa, Spain — 39 G5
Benitses, Greece — 49 A3
Benjamin Aceval, Paraguay — 126 A4
Benjamin Constant, Brazil — 124 D4
Benjamin Hill, Mexico — 118 A2
Benkelman, U.S.A. — 112 E4
Benkovac, Croatia — 41 D12
Bennett, Canada — 102 B2
Bennett, L., Australia — 92 D5
Bennetta, Ostrov, Russia — 53 B15
Bennettsville, U.S.A. — 115 H6
Bennichchāb, Mauritania — 82 B1
Bennington, N.H., U.S.A. — 117 D11
Bennington, Vt., U.S.A. — 117 D11
Bénodet, France — 18 E2
Benoni, S. Africa — 89 D4
Benque Viejo del Carmen, Belize — 119 D7
Bensheim, Germany — 25 F4
Benson, Ariz., U.S.A. — 109 L8
Benson, Minn., U.S.A. — 112 C7
Bent, Iran — 71 E8
Benteng, Indonesia — 63 F6
Bentinck I., Australia — 94 B2
Bentiu, Sudan — 81 F2
Bento Gonçalves, Brazil — 127 B5
Benton, Ark., U.S.A. — 113 H8
Benton, Calif., U.S.A. — 110 H8
Benton, Ill., U.S.A. — 112 G10
Benton, Pa., U.S.A. — 117 E8
Benton Harbor, U.S.A. — 114 D2
Bentong, Malaysia — 65 L3
Bentonville, U.S.A. — 113 G7
Bentu Liben, Ethiopia — 81 F4
Benue □, Nigeria — 83 D6
Benue →, Nigeria — 83 D6
Benxi, China — 57 D12
Beo, Indonesia — 63 D7
Beograd, Serbia & M. — 44 B4
Beograd ✈ (BEG), Serbia & M. — 44 C4
Beoumi, Ivory C. — 82 D3
Bepan Jiang →, China — 58 E6
Beppu, Japan — 55 H5
Beqaa Valley = Al Biqâ, Lebanon — 74 A5
Ber Mota, India — 68 H3
Berach →, India — 68 G6
Beraketa, Madag. — 89 C7
Berane, Serbia & M. — 44 D3
Berat, Albania — 44 F3
Berau, Teluk, Indonesia — 63 E8
Beravina, Madag. — 89 B8
Berber, Sudan — 80 D3
Berbera, Somali Rep. — 75 E4
Berbérati, C.A.R. — 84 D3
Berbice →, Guyana — 124 B7
Berceto, Italy — 40 D6
Berchidda, Italy — 42 B2
Berchtesgaden, Germany — 25 H8
Berchtesgaden △, Germany — 25 H8
Berck, France — 19 B8
Berdichev = Berdychiv, Ukraine — 33 H5
Berdsk, Russia — 52 D9
Berdyansk, Ukraine — 33 J9
Berdychiv, Ukraine — 33 H5

Berea, U.S.A. — 114 G3
Berebere, Indonesia — 63 D7
Bereda, Somali Rep. — 75 E5
Berehomet, Ukraine — 29 B10
Berehove, Ukraine — 28 B7
Berekum, Ghana — 82 D4
Berenice, Egypt — 80 C4
Berens →, Canada — 103 C9
Berens I., Canada — 103 C9
Berens River, Canada — 103 C9
Beresford, U.S.A. — 112 D6
Berestechko, Ukraine — 33 G3
Bereşti, Romania — 29 D12
Beretău →, Romania — 28 C6
Berettyó →, Hungary — 28 D6
Berettyóújfalu, Hungary — 28 C6
Berevo, Mahajanga, Madag. — 89 B7
Berevo, Toliara, Madag. — 89 B7
Bereza = Byaroza, Belarus — 33 F3
Berezhany, Ukraine — 33 H3
Berezina = Byarezina →, Belarus — 33 F6
Berezivka, Ukraine — 33 J6
Berezna, Ukraine — 33 G6
Bereznik, Russia — 52 C5
Berezniki, Russia — 52 D6
Berezovo, Russia — 52 C7
Berezyne, Ukraine — 29 D14
Berga, Spain — 38 C6
Berga, Sweden — 11 G10
Bérgamo, Italy — 40 C6
Bergantes →, Spain — 38 B2
Bergby, Sweden — 10 D11
Bergedorf, Germany — 24 B6
Bergeforsen, Sweden — 10 B11
Bergen, Mecklenburg-Vorpommern, Germany — 24 A9
Bergen, Niedersachsen, Germany — 24 C5
Bergen, Neths. — 17 B4
Bergen, Norway — 9 F11
Bergen op Zoom, Neths. — 17 C4
Bergerac, France — 20 D4
Bergheim, Germany — 24 E2
Bergholz, U.S.A. — 116 F4
Bergisch Gladbach, Germany — 17 D7
Bergisches Land □, Germany — 24 E3
Bergkamen, Germany — 24 D3
Bergkvara, Sweden — 11 H10
Bergshamra, Sweden — 10 E12
Bergsjö, Sweden — 10 C11
Bergstrasse-Odenwald △, Germany — 25 F1
Bergues, France — 19 B9
Bergviken, Sweden — 10 C10
Bergville, S. Africa — 89 D4
Berhala, Selat, Indonesia — 62 E2
Berhampore = Baharampur, India — 69 G13
Berhampur = Brahmapur, India — 67 K14
Berheci →, Romania — 29 E12
Bering Sea, Pac. Oc. — 100 C1
Bering Strait, Pac. Oc. — 100 B3
Beringovskiy, Russia — 53 C18
Berisso, Argentina — 126 C4
Berja, Spain — 37 J8
Berkeley, U.S.A. — 110 H4
Berkner I., Antarctica — 5 D18
Berkovitsa, Bulgaria — 44 C7
Berkshire □, U.K. — 117 D08
Berkshire Downs, U.K. — 15 F6
Berlanga, Spain — 37 G5
Berlenga, I., Portugal — 37 F1
Berlin, Germany — 24 C9
Berlin, Md., U.S.A. — 114 F8
Berlin, N.H., U.S.A. — 117 B13
Berlin, N.Y., U.S.A. — 117 D11
Berlin, Wis., U.S.A. — 114 D1
Berlin □, Germany — 24 C9
Berlin L., U.S.A. — 116 E4
Berlin Tegel ✈ (TXL), Germany — 24 C9
Bermeja, Sierra, Spain — 37 J5
Bermejo →, Formosa, Argentina — 126 B4
Bermejo →, San Juan, Argentina — 126 C2
Bermen, L., Canada — 105 B6
Bermeo, Spain — 38 B2
Bermillo de Sayago, Spain — 36 D4
Bermuda ☑, Atl. Oc. — 98 F13
Bern, Switz. — 25 J3
Bern □, Switz. — 25 J3
Bernalda, Italy — 43 B9
Bernalillo, U.S.A. — 109 J10
Bernardo de Irigoyen, Argentina — 127 B5
Bernardo O'Higgins □, Chile — 126 C1
Bernardsville, U.S.A. — 117 F10
Bernasconi, Argentina — 126 D3
Bernau, Bayern, Germany — 25 H8
Bernau, Brandenburg, Germany — 24 C9
Bernay, France — 18 C7
Bernburg, Germany — 24 D7
Berndorf, Austria — 26 D9
Berne = Bern, Switz. — 25 J3
Berne □ = Bern □, Switz. — 25 J3
Berner Alpen, Switz. — 25 J3
Berneray, U.K. — 13 D1
Bernier I., Australia — 93 D1
Bernina, Piz, Switz. — 25 J5
Bernkastel-Kues, Germany — 25 F3
Beroroha, Madag. — 89 C8
Béroubouay, Benin — 83 C5
Beroun, Czech Rep. — 26 B7
Berounka →, Czech Rep. — 26 B7
Berovo, Macedonia — 44 E6
Berre, Étang de, France — 21 E9
Berre-l'Étang, France — 21 E9
Berri, Australia — 95 E3
Berriane, Algeria — 78 B6
Berry, Australia — 95 E5
Berry, France — 19 F8
Berry Is., Bahamas — 120 A4
Berryessa L., U.S.A. — 110 G4
Berryville, U.S.A. — 113 G8

Berseba, Namibia — 88 D2
Bersenbrück, Germany — 24 C3
Bershad, Ukraine — 29 B14
Berthold, U.S.A. — 112 A4
Berthoud, U.S.A. — 112 E2
Bertincourt, France — 19 B9
Bertoua, Cameroon — 84 D2
Bertraghboy B., Ireland — 12 C2
Berwick, U.S.A. — 117 E8
Berwick-upon-Tweed, U.K. — 14 B6
Berwyn Mts., U.K. — 14 E4
Beryslav, Ukraine — 33 J7
Berzasca, Romania — 28 F6
Berzence, Hungary — 28 D2
Besal, Pakistan — 69 B5
Besalampy, Madag. — 89 B7
Besançon, France — 19 E13
Besar, Indonesia — 62 E5
Beshenkovichi, Belarus — 32 E5
Beška, Serbia & M. — 28 E5
Beslan, Russia — 35 J7
Besna Kobila, Serbia & M. — 44 D6
Besnard L., Canada — 103 B7
Besni, Turkey — 70 B3
Besor, N. →, Egypt — 74 D3
Bessarabiya, Moldova — 33 J5
Bessarabka = Basarabeasca, Moldova — 29 D13
Bessèges, France — 21 D8
Bessemer, Ala., U.S.A. — 115 J2
Bessemer, Mich., U.S.A. — 112 B9
Bessemer, Pa., U.S.A. — 116 F4
Bessin, France — 18 C6
Bessines-sur-Gartempe, France — 20 B5
Beswick, Australia — 92 B5
Bet She'an, Israel — 74 C4
Bet Shemesh, Israel — 74 D4
Betafo, Madag. — 89 B8
Betancuria, Canary Is. — 48 F5
Betanzos, Spain — 36 B2
Bétaré Oya, Cameroon — 84 C2
Betatao, Madag. — 89 B8
Bétera, Spain — 39 F4
Bétérou, Benin — 83 D5
Bethal, S. Africa — 89 D4
Bethanien, Namibia — 88 D2
Bethany, Canada — 116 B6
Bethany, U.S.A. — 112 E7
Bethel, Alaska, U.S.A. — 100 B3
Bethel, Conn., U.S.A. — 117 E11
Bethel, Maine, U.S.A. — 117 B14
Bethel, Vt., U.S.A. — 117 C12
Bethel Park, U.S.A. — 116 F4
Bethenville, France — 19 C11
Bethlehem = Bayt Lahm, West Bank — 74 D4
Bethlehem, S. Africa — 89 D4
Bethlehem, U.S.A. — 117 F9
Bethulie, S. Africa — 88 E4
Béthune, France — 19 B9
Béthune →, France — 18 C8
Betioky, Madag. — 89 C7
Betong, Thailand — 65 K3
Betoota, Australia — 94 D3
Betor, Ethiopia — 81 E4
Betroka, Madag. — 89 C8
Betsiamites, Canada — 105 C6
Betsiamites →, Canada — 105 C6
Betsiboka →, Madag. — 89 B8
Bettendorf, U.S.A. — 112 E9
Bettiah, India — 69 F11
Bettna, Sweden — 11 F10
Béttola, Italy — 40 D6
Betul, India — 66 J10
Betung, Malaysia — 62 D4
Betws-y-Coed, U.K. — 14 D4
Betxi, Spain — 38 F4
Betzdorf, Germany — 24 E3
Beuil, France — 21 D10
Beulah, Mich., U.S.A. — 114 C2
Beulah, N. Dak., U.S.A. — 112 B4
Beuvron →, France — 18 E8
Beveren, Belgium — 17 C4
Beverley, Australia — 93 F2
Beverley, U.K. — 14 D7
Beverley Hills, U.S.A. — 115 L4
Beverly, U.S.A. — 117 D14
Beverly Hills, U.S.A. — 111 L8
Beverungen, Germany — 24 D5
Bevoalavo, Madag. — 89 D7
Bewas →, India — 69 H8
Bex, Switz. — 25 J3
Bexhill, U.K. — 15 G8
Bey Dağları, Turkey — 47 E12
Beyānlū, Iran — 70 C5
Beyazköy, Turkey — 45 E11
Beyçayırı, Turkey — 45 F10
Beydağ, Turkey — 47 C10
Beyeğaç, Turkey — 47 D10
Beyin, Ghana — 82 D4
Beykoz, Turkey — 45 E13
Beyla, Guinea — 82 D3
Beynat, France — 20 C5
Beyneu, Kazakhstan — 52 E6
Beyoba, Turkey — 47 C9
Beyoğlu, Turkey — 45 E12
Beypazarı, Turkey — 72 B4
Beyşehir, Turkey — 72 D4
Beyşehir Gölü, Turkey — 70 B1
Beytüşşebap, Turkey — 73 D10
Bezdan, Serbia & M. — 28 E3
Béziers, France — 20 E7
Bezwada = Vijayawada, India — 67 L12
Bhabua, India — 69 G10
Bhachau, India — 66 H7
Bhadar →, Gujarat, India — 68 H5
Bhadar →, Gujarat, India — 68 J3
Bhadgaon = Bhaktapur, Nepal — 69 F11
Bhadohi, India — 69 G10
Bhadra, India — 68 E6

Bhadrakh, India — 67 J15
Bhadran, India — 68 H5
Bhadravati, India — 66 N9
Bhag, Pakistan — 68 E2
Bhagalpur, India — 69 G12
Bhagirathi →, Uttaranchal, India — 69 D8
Bhagirathi →, W. Bengal, India — 69 H13
Bhakkar, Pakistan — 68 D4
Bhakra Dam, India — 68 D7
Bhaktapur, Nepal — 69 F11
Bhamo, Burma — 67 G20
Bhandara, India — 66 J11
Bhanpura, India — 68 G6
Bhanrer Ra., India — 69 H8
Bhaptiahi, India — 69 F12
Bharat = India ■, Asia — 66 K11
Bharatpur, Chhattisgarh, India — 69 H9
Bharatpur, Raj., India — 68 F7
Bharno, India — 69 H11
Bharuch, India — 66 J8
Bhatinda, India — 68 D6
Bhatpara, India — 69 H13
Bhattu, India — 68 E6
Bhaun, Pakistan — 68 C5
Bhaunagar = Bhavnagar, India — 66 J8
Bhavnagar, India — 66 J8
Bhawari, India — 68 G5
Bhayavadar, India — 68 J4
Bhera, Pakistan — 68 C5
Bhikangaon, India — 68 J6
Bhilsa = Vidisha, India — 68 H7
Bhilwara, India — 68 G6
Bhima →, India — 66 L10
Bhimbar, Pakistan — 69 C6
Bhind, India — 69 F8
Bhinga, India — 69 F9
Bhinmal, India — 68 G5
Bhiwandi, India — 66 K8
Bhiwani, India — 68 E7
Bhogava →, India — 68 H5
Bhola, Bangla. — 67 H17
Bholari, Pakistan — 68 G3
Bhopal, India — 68 H7
Bhubaneshwar, India — 67 J14
Bhuj, India — 68 H3
Bhumiphol Res., Thailand — 64 D2
Bhusawal, India — 66 J9
Bhutan ■, Asia — 67 F17
Biafra, B. of = Bonny, Bight of, Africa — 83 E6
Biak, Indonesia — 63 E9
Biała, Poland — 31 H4
Biała →, Poland — 31 H7
Biała Piska, Poland — 30 E9
Biała Podlaska, Poland — 31 F10
Biała Rawska, Poland — 31 G7
Białobrzegi, Poland — 31 G7
Białogard, Poland — 30 D2
Białowieski △, Poland — 31 F10
Białowieża, Poland — 31 F10
Biały Bór, Poland — 30 E3
Białystok, Poland — 31 E10
Biancavilla, Italy — 43 E7
Bianco, Italy — 43 D9
Biankouma, Ivory C. — 82 D3
Biaora, India — 68 H7
Biārjmand, Iran — 71 B7
Biaro, Indonesia — 63 D7
Biarritz, France — 20 E2
Bias, Indonesia — 63 J18
Biasca, Switz. — 25 J4
Biba, Egypt — 80 J7
Bibai, Japan — 54 C10
Bibbiena, Italy — 41 E8
Bibby I., Canada — 103 A10
Bibel →, Spain — 36 C3
Biberach, Germany — 25 G5
Bibiani, Ghana — 82 D4
Bibungwa, Dem. Rep. of the Congo — 86 C2
Bicaj, Albania — 44 E4
Bicaz, Romania — 29 D11
Bicazu Ardelean, Romania — 29 D10
Bíccari, Italy — 43 A8
Bicester, U.K. — 15 F6
Bichena, Ethiopia — 81 E4
Bicheno, Australia — 95 G4
Bichia, India — 69 H9
Bichvinta, Georgia — 35 J5
Bickerton I., Australia — 94 A2
Bicske, Hungary — 28 C3
Bida, Nigeria — 83 D6
Bidar, India — 66 L10
Biddeford, U.S.A. — 115 D10
Biddwara, Ethiopia — 81 F4
Bideford, U.K. — 15 F3
Bideford Bay, U.K. — 15 F3
Bidhuna, India — 69 F8
Bidor, Malaysia — 65 K3
Bie, Sweden — 10 E10
Bié, Planalto de, Angola — 85 G3
Bieber, U.S.A. — 108 F3
Biebrza →, Poland — 31 E9
Biebrzański △, Poland — 30 E9
Biecz, Poland — 31 J8
Biel, Switz. — 25 H3
Bielawa, Poland — 31 H3
Bielefeld, Germany — 24 C4
Bielersee, Switz. — 25 H3
Biella, Italy — 40 C5
Bielsk Podlaski, Poland — 31 F10
Bielsko-Biała, Poland — 31 J6
Bien Hoa, Vietnam — 65 G6
Bienne = Biel, Switz. — 25 H3
Bienvenida, Spain — 37 G4
Bienville, L., Canada — 104 A5
Bierné, France — 18 E6
Bierun, Poland — 31 H6
Bierutów, Poland — 31 G4
Biescas, Spain — 38 C4
Biese →, Germany — 24 C7
Biesiesfontein, S. Africa — 88 E2

Bieszczadzki △, Poland — 31 J9
Bietigheim-Bissingen, Germany — 25 G5
Bieżuń, Poland — 31 F6
Biferno →, Italy — 41 G12
Big →, Canada — 105 B8
Big B., Canada — 105 A7
Big Bear City, U.S.A. — 111 L10
Big Bear Lake, U.S.A. — 111 L10
Big Belt Mts., U.S.A. — 108 C8
Big Bend, Swaziland — 89 D5
Big Bend △, U.S.A. — 113 L3
Big Black →, U.S.A. — 113 K9
Big Blue →, U.S.A. — 112 F6
Big Creek, U.S.A. — 110 H7
Big Cypress △, U.S.A. — 115 M5
Big Cypress Swamp, U.S.A. — 115 M5
Big Falls, U.S.A. — 112 A8
Big Fork →, U.S.A. — 112 A8
Big Horn Mts. = Bighorn Mts., U.S.A. — 108 D10
Big I., Canada — 102 A5
Big Lake, U.S.A. — 113 K4
Big Moose, U.S.A. — 117 C10
Big Muddy Cr. →, U.S.A. — 112 A2
Big Pine, U.S.A. — 110 H8
Big Piney, U.S.A. — 108 E8
Big Rapids, U.S.A. — 114 D3
Big Rideau L., Canada — 117 B8
Big River, Canada — 103 C7
Big Run, U.S.A. — 116 F6
Big Sable Pt., U.S.A. — 114 C2
Big Salmon →, Canada — 102 A2
Big Sand L., Canada — 103 B9
Big Sandy, U.S.A. — 108 B8
Big Sandy →, U.S.A. — 114 F4
Big Sandy Cr. →, U.S.A. — 112 F3
Big Sioux →, U.S.A. — 112 D6
Big South Fork △, U.S.A. — 115 G3
Big Spring, U.S.A. — 113 J4
Big Stone City, U.S.A. — 112 C6
Big Stone Gap, U.S.A. — 115 G4
Big Stone L., U.S.A. — 112 C6
Big Sur, U.S.A. — 110 J5
Big Timber, U.S.A. — 108 D9
Big Trout L., Canada — 104 B2
Big Trout Lake, Canada — 104 B2
Biğa, Turkey — 45 F11
Biga →, Turkey — 45 F11
Bigadiç, Turkey — 47 B10
Biganos, France — 20 D3
Biggar, Canada — 103 C7
Biggar, U.K. — 13 F5
Bigge I., Australia — 92 B4
Biggenden, Australia — 95 D5
Biggleswade, U.K. — 15 E7
Biggs, U.S.A. — 110 F5
Bighorn, U.S.A. — 108 C10
Bighorn →, U.S.A. — 108 C10
Bighorn Canyon △, U.S.A. — 108 D9
Bighorn Mts., U.S.A. — 108 D10
Bignona, Senegal — 82 C1
Bigorre, France — 20 E4
Bigstone L., Canada — 103 C9
Biguglia, Étang de, France — 21 F13
Bigwa, Tanzania — 86 D4
Bihać, Bos.-H. — 41 D12
Bihar, India — 69 G11
Bihar □, India — 69 G12
Biharamulo, Tanzania — 86 C3
Biharamulo △, Tanzania — 86 C3
Bihariganj, India — 69 G12
Biharkeresztes, Hungary — 28 C6
Bihor □, Romania — 28 D7
Bihor, Munții, Romania — 28 D7
Bijagós, Arquipélago dos, Guinea-Biss. — 82 C1
Bijaipur, India — 68 F7
Bijapur, Chhattisgarh, India — 67 K12
Bijapur, Karnataka, India — 66 L9
Bījār, Iran — 70 C5
Bijawar, India — 69 G8
Bijeljina, Bos.-H. — 28 F4
Bijelo Polje, Serbia & M. — 44 C3
Bijie, China — 58 D5
Bijnor, India — 68 E8
Bikaner, India — 68 E5
Bikapur, India — 69 F10
Bikeqi, China — 56 D6
Bikfayyā, Lebanon — 74 B4
Bikin, Russia — 53 E14
Bikin →, Russia — 54 A7
Bikini Atoll, Marshall Is. — 96 F8
Bikita, Zimbabwe — 89 C5
Bikoué, Cameroon — 83 E7
Bila Tserkva, Ukraine — 33 H6
Bilanga, Burkina Faso — 83 C4
Bilara, India — 68 F5
Bilaspur, Chhattisgarh, India — 69 H10
Bilaspur, Punjab, India — 68 D7
Bilāsuvar, Azerbaijan — 73 C13
Bilauk Taungdan, Thailand — 64 F2
Bilbao, Spain — 38 B2
Bilbao ✈ (BIO), Spain — 36 B8
Bilbeis, Egypt — 80 H7
Bilbo = Bilbao, Spain — 38 B2
Bilbor, Romania — 29 C10
Bilce-Zolote, Ukraine — 29 B11
Bilciureşti, Romania — 29 F10
Bíldudalur, Iceland — 8 D2
Bílé Karpaty, Europe — 27 B11
Bileća, Bos.-H. — 44 D2
Bilecik, Turkey — 72 B4
Bilgoraj, Poland — 31 H9
Bilgram, India — 69 F9
Bilhaur, India — 69 F9
Bilhorod-Dnistrovskyy, Ukraine — 33 J6
Bilibino, Russia — 53 C17
Bilibiza, Mozam. — 87 E5
Bilisht, Albania — 44 F5
Billabong Roadhouse, Australia — 93 E2
Billdal, Sweden — 11 G5

Billiluna, *Australia*	92	C4
Billings, *U.S.A.*	108	D9
Billiton Is. = Belitung, *Indonesia*	62	E3
Billsta, *Sweden*	10	A12
Billund, *Denmark*	11	J3
Bilma, *Niger*	79	E8
Bilo Gora, *Croatia*	28	E2
Biloela, *Australia*	94	C5
Bilohirsk, *Ukraine*	33	K8
Bilopillya, *Ukraine*	33	G8
Biloxi, *U.S.A.*	113	K10
Bilpa Morea Claypan, *Australia*	94	D3
Biltine, *Chad*	79	F10
Bilyarsk, *Russia*	34	C10
Bima, *Indonesia*	63	F5
Bimban, *Egypt*	80	C3
Bimbila, *Ghana*	83	D5
Bimini Is., *Bahamas*	120	A4
Bin Xian, *Heilongjiang, China*	57	B14
Bin Xian, *Shaanxi, China*	56	G5
Bin Yauri, *Nigeria*	83	C5
Bina-Etawah, *India*	68	G8
Bināb, *Iran*	71	B6
Binalbagan, *Phil.*	61	F5
Binalong, *Australia*	95	E4
Bīnālūd, Kūh-e, *Iran*	71	B8
Binatang = Bintangor, *Malaysia*	62	D4
Binche, *Belgium*	17	D4
Binchuan, *China*	58	E3
Binder, *Chad*	83	D7
Bindki, *India*	69	F9
Bindslev, *Denmark*	11	G4
Bindura, *Zimbabwe*	87	F3
Binefar, *Spain*	38	D5
Bingara, *Australia*	95	D5
Bingen, *Germany*	25	F3
Bingerville, *Ivory C.*	82	D4
Bingham, *U.S.A.*	115	C11
Binghamton, *U.S.A.*	117	D9
Bingöl, *Turkey*	70	B4
Bingöl Dağları, *Turkey*	73	C9
Bingsjö, *Sweden*	10	C9
Binh Dinh = An Nhon, *Vietnam*	64	F7
Binh Khe, *Vietnam*	64	F7
Binh Son, *Vietnam*	64	E7
Binhai, *China*	57	G10
Binic, *France*	18	D4
Binisatua, *Spain*	48	B11
Binjai, *Indonesia*	62	D3
Binji, *Nigeria*	83	C5
Binnaway, *Australia*	95	E4
Binongko, *Indonesia*	63	F6
Binscarth, *Canada*	103	C8
Binshangul Gumuz □, *Ethiopia*	81	E3
Bint Goda, *Sudan*	81	E3
Bintan, *Indonesia*	62	D2
Bintangor, *Malaysia*	62	D4
Bintulu, *Malaysia*	62	D4
Bintuni, *Indonesia*	63	E8
Binyang, *China*	58	F7
Binz, *Germany*	24	A9
Binzert = Bizerte, *Tunisia*	79	A7
Binzhou, *China*	57	F10
Bío Bío □, *Chile*	126	D1
Biograd na Moru, *Croatia*	41	E12
Biogradska Gora △, *Serbia & M.*	44	D3
Bioko, *Eq. Guin.*	83	E6
Biokovo, *Croatia*	41	E14
Bipindi, *Cameroon*	83	E7
Bir, *India*	66	K9
Bir, Ras, *Djibouti*	81	E5
Bîr Abu Hashim, *Egypt*	80	C3
Bîr Abu Minqar, *Egypt*	80	B2
Bîr Abu Muḥammad, *Egypt*	74	F3
Bi'r ad Dabbāghāt, *Jordan*	74	E4
Bîr Adal Deib, *Sudan*	80	C4
Bi'r al Butayyiḥāt, *Jordan*	74	F4
Bi'r al Mārī, *Jordan*	74	E4
Bi'r al Qattār, *Jordan*	74	F4
Bîr 'Asal, *Egypt*	80	B3
Bîr Atrun, *Sudan*	80	D2
Bîr Beiḍa, *Egypt*	74	E3
Bîr Diqnash, *Egypt*	80	A2
Bîr el 'Abd, *Egypt*	74	D2
Bîr el Basur, *Egypt*	80	B2
Bîr el Biarât, *Egypt*	74	F3
Bîr el Duweidar, *Egypt*	74	E1
Bîr el Garârât, *Egypt*	74	D2
Bîr el Gellaz, *Egypt*	80	A2
Bîr el Heisi, *Egypt*	74	F3
Bîr el Jafir, *Egypt*	74	E1
Bîr el Mâlḥi, *Egypt*	74	E2
Bîr el Shaqqa, *Egypt*	80	A2
Bîr el Thamâda, *Egypt*	74	E2
Bîr Fuad, *Egypt*	80	A2
Bîr Gebeil Ḥisn, *Egypt*	74	E2
Bi'r Ghadir, *Syria*	74	A6
Bîr Haimur, *Egypt*	80	C3
Bîr Ḥasana, *Egypt*	74	E2
Bîr Hōoker, *Egypt*	80	H7
Bîr Kanayis, *Egypt*	80	C3
Bîr Kaseiba, *Egypt*	74	E2
Bîr Kerawein, *Egypt*	80	B2
Bîr Lahfân, *Egypt*	74	E2
Bîr Madkûr, *Egypt*	74	E1
Bîr Maql, *Egypt*	80	C3
Bîr Mîneiga, *Egypt*	80	C2
Bîr Misaha, *Egypt*	80	C2
Bîr Mogreïn, *Mauritania*	78	C3
Bîr Murr, *Egypt*	80	C3
Bi'r Muṭribah, *Kuwait*	70	D5
Bîr Nakheila, *Egypt*	80	C3
Bîr Qaṭia, *Egypt*	74	E1
Bîr Qatrani, *Egypt*	80	A2
Bîr Ranga, *Egypt*	80	C3
Bîr Sahara, *Egypt*	80	C2
Bîr Seiyâla, *Egypt*	80	B3
Bîr Shalatein, *Egypt*	80	C3
Bîr Shebb, *Egypt*	80	C2
Bîr Shût, *Egypt*	80	C4
Bîr Terfawi, *Egypt*	80	C2
Bîr Umm Qubûr, *Egypt*	80	C3
Bîr Ungât, *Egypt*	80	C3
Bîr Za'farâna, *Egypt*	80	J8
Bîr Zeidûn, *Egypt*	80	B3
Biramféro, *Guinea*	82	C3
Biratnagar, *Nepal*	69	F12
Birawa, *Dem. Rep. of the Congo*	86	C2
Birch →, *Canada*	102	B6
Birch Hills, *Canada*	103	C7
Birch I., *Canada*	103	C9
Birch L., *N.W.T., Canada*	102	A5
Birch L., *Ont., Canada*	104	B1
Birch Mts., *Canada*	102	B6
Birch River, *Canada*	103	C8
Birchip, *Australia*	95	F3
Birchiș, *Romania*	28	E7
Bird, *Canada*	103	B10
Bird I. = Aves, I. de, *W. Indies*	121	C7
Bird I., *Antarctica*	5	B1
Birdsville, *Australia*	94	D2
Birdum Cr. →, *Australia*	92	C5
Birecik, *Turkey*	70	B3
Birein, *Israel*	74	E3
Bireuen, *Indonesia*	62	C1
Biri →, *Sudan*	81	F2
Birifo, *Gambia*	82	C2
Birigui, *Brazil*	127	A5
Birjand, *Iran*	71	C8
Birkenfeld, *Germany*	25	F3
Birkenhead, *U.K.*	14	D4
Birkerød, *Denmark*	11	J6
Birket Qârûn, *Egypt*	80	J7
Birkfeld, *Austria*	26	D8
Bîrlad = Bârlad, *Romania*	29	D12
Birmingham, *U.K.*	15	E6
Birmingham, *U.S.A.*	115	J2
Birmingham International ✈ (BHX), *U.K.*	15	E6
Birmitrapur, *India*	67	H14
Birni Ngaouré, *Niger*	83	C5
Birni Nkonni, *Niger*	83	C6
Birnin Gwari, *Nigeria*	83	C6
Birnin Kebbi, *Nigeria*	83	C5
Birnin Kudu, *Nigeria*	83	C6
Birobidzhan, *Russia*	53	E14
Birr, *Ireland*	12	C4
Birrie →, *Australia*	95	D4
Birsilpur, *India*	68	E5
Birsk, *Russia*	52	D6
Birštonas, *Lithuania*	30	D11
Birtle, *Canada*	103	C8
Birur, *India*	66	N9
Biryuchiy, *Ukraine*	33	J8
Biržai, *Lithuania*	9	H21
Birzebbugga, *Malta*	49	D2
Bisa, *Indonesia*	63	E7
Bisáccia, *Italy*	43	A8
Bisacquino, *Italy*	42	E6
Bisalpur, *India*	69	E8
Bisbee, *U.S.A.*	109	L9
Biscarrosse, *France*	20	D2
Biscarrosse et de Parentis, Étang de, *France*	20	D2
Biscéglie, *Italy*	43	A9
Bischheim, *France*	19	D14
Bischofshofen, *Austria*	26	D6
Bischofswerda, *Germany*	24	D10
Bischwiller, *France*	19	D14
Biscoe Is., *Antarctica*	5	C17
Biscotasing, *Canada*	104	C3
Biševo, *Croatia*	41	F13
Bisha, *Eritrea*	81	D4
Bishah, W. →, *Si. Arabia*	80	C5
Bishan, *China*	58	C6
Bishkek, *Kyrgyzstan*	52	E8
Bishnupur, *India*	69	H12
Bisho, *S. Africa*	89	E4
Bishop, *Calif., U.S.A.*	110	H8
Bishop, *Tex., U.S.A.*	113	M6
Bishop Auckland, *U.K.*	14	C6
Bishop's Falls, *Canada*	105	C8
Bishop's Stortford, *U.K.*	15	F8
Bisignano, *Italy*	43	C9
Bisina, L., *Uganda*	86	B3
Biskra, *Algeria*	78	B7
Biskupiec, *Poland*	30	E7
Bismarck, *U.S.A.*	112	B4
Bismarck Arch., *Papua N. G.*	96	H7
Bismark, *Germany*	24	C7
Bismil, *Turkey*	73	D9
Biso, *Uganda*	86	B3
Bison, *U.S.A.*	112	C3
Bîsotûn, *Iran*	70	C5
Bispgården, *Sweden*	10	A10
Bissagos = Bijagós, Arquipélago dos, *Guinea-Biss.*	82	C1
Bissau, *Guinea-Biss.*	82	C1
Bissaula, *Nigeria*	83	D7
Bissikrima, *Guinea*	82	C2
Bissorã, *Guinea-Biss.*	82	C1
Bistcho L., *Canada*	102	B5
Bistreț, *Romania*	29	G8
Bistrica = Ilirska-Bistrica, *Slovenia*	41	C11
Bistrița, *Romania*	29	C9
Bistrița →, *Romania*	29	D11
Bistrița Năsăud □, *Romania*	29	C9
Bistriței, Munții, *Romania*	29	C10
Biswan, *India*	69	F9
Bisztynek, *Poland*	30	D7
Bitburg, *Germany*	25	F2
Bitche, *France*	19	C14
Bithynia, *Turkey*	72	B4
Bitlis, *Turkey*	70	B4
Bitola, *Macedonia*	44	E5
Bitolj = Bitola, *Macedonia*	44	E5
Bitonto, *Italy*	43	A9
Bitter Creek, *U.S.A.*	108	F9
Bitter L. = Buheirat-Murrat-el-Kubra, *Egypt*	80	H8
Bitterfeld, *Germany*	24	D8
Bitterfontein, *S. Africa*	88	E2
Bitterroot →, *U.S.A.*	108	C6
Bitterroot Range, *U.S.A.*	108	D6
Bitterwater, *U.S.A.*	110	J6
Bitti, *Italy*	42	B2
Bittou, *Burkina Faso*	83	C4
Biu, *Nigeria*	83	C7
Bivolari, *Romania*	29	C12
Bivolu, Vf., *Romania*	29	C10
Biwa-Ko, *Japan*	55	G8
Biwabik, *U.S.A.*	112	B8
Bixad, *Romania*	29	C8
Bixby, *U.S.A.*	113	H7
Biyang, *China*	56	H7
Biysk, *Russia*	52	D9
Bizana, *S. Africa*	89	E4
Bizen, *Japan*	55	G7
Bizerte, *Tunisia*	79	A7
Bjargtangar, *Iceland*	8	D1
Bjärnum, *Sweden*	11	H7
Bjästa, *Sweden*	10	A12
Bjelasica, *Serbia & M.*	44	D3
Bjelašnica, *Bos.-H.*	28	G3
Bjelovar, *Croatia*	41	C13
Bjerringbro, *Denmark*	11	H3
Björbo, *Sweden*	10	D8
Björklinge, *Sweden*	10	D11
Björneborg = Pori, *Finland*	9	F19
Björneborg, *Sweden*	10	E8
Bjørnevatn, *Norway*	8	B23
Bjørnøya, *Arctic*	4	B8
Bjursås, *Sweden*	10	D9
Bjuv, *Sweden*	11	H6
Bla, *Mali*	82	C3
Blace, *Serbia & M.*	44	C5
Blachownia, *Poland*	31	H5
Black = Da →, *Vietnam*	58	G5
Black →, *Canada*	116	B5
Black →, *Ariz., U.S.A.*	109	K8
Black →, *Ark., U.S.A.*	113	H9
Black →, *Mich., U.S.A.*	116	D2
Black →, *N.Y., U.S.A.*	117	C8
Black →, *Wis., U.S.A.*	112	D9
Black Bay Pen., *Canada*	104	C2
Black Birch L., *Canada*	103	B7
Black Canyon of the Gunnison △, *U.S.A.*	109	G10
Black Diamond, *Canada*	102	C6
Black Duck →, *Canada*	104	A2
Black Forest = Schwarzwald, *Germany*	25	G4
Black Forest, *U.S.A.*	112	F2
Black Hd., *Ireland*	12	C2
Black Hills, *U.S.A.*	112	D3
Black I., *Canada*	103	C9
Black L., *Canada*	103	B7
Black L., *Mich., U.S.A.*	114	C3
Black L., *N.Y., U.S.A.*	117	B9
Black Lake, *Canada*	103	B7
Black Mesa, *U.S.A.*	113	G3
Black Mt. = Mynydd Du, *U.K.*	15	F4
Black Mts., *U.K.*	15	F4
Black Range, *U.S.A.*	109	K10
Black River, *Jamaica*	120	a
Black River Falls, *U.S.A.*	112	C9
Black Rock, *Barbados*	121	g
Black Sea, *Eurasia*	6	G12
Black Tickle, *Canada*	105	B8
Black Volta →, *Africa*	82	D4
Black Warrior →, *U.S.A.*	115	J2
Blackall, *Australia*	94	C4
Blackball, *N.Z.*	91	K3
Blackbull, *Australia*	94	B3
Blackburn, *U.K.*	14	D5
Blackburn with Darwen □, *U.K.*	14	D5
Blackdown Tableland △, *Australia*	94	C4
Blackfoot, *U.S.A.*	108	E7
Blackfoot →, *U.S.A.*	108	C7
Blackfoot River Reservoir, *U.S.A.*	108	E8
Blackpool, *U.K.*	14	D4
Blackpool □, *U.K.*	14	D4
Blackriver, *U.S.A.*	116	B1
Blacksburg, *U.S.A.*	114	G5
Blacksod B., *Ireland*	12	B1
Blackstone, *U.S.A.*	114	G7
Blackstone Ra., *Australia*	93	E4
Blackwater = West Road →, *Canada*	102	C4
Blackwater, *Australia*	94	C4
Blackwater →, *Meath, Ireland*	12	C4
Blackwater →, *Waterford, Ireland*	12	D4
Blackwater →, *U.K.*	12	B5
Blackwell, *U.S.A.*	113	G6
Blackwells Corner, *U.S.A.*	111	K7
Bladensburg △, *Australia*	94	C3
Blaenau Ffestiniog, *U.K.*	14	E4
Blaenau Gwent □, *U.K.*	15	F4
Blagaj, *Bos.-H.*	44	C1
Blagnac, *France*	20	E5
Blagnac, Toulouse ✈ (TLS), *France*	20	E5
Blagodarnoye = Blagodarnyy, *Russia*	35	H6
Blagodarnyy, *Russia*	35	H6
Blagoevgrad, *Bulgaria*	44	D7
Blagoveshchensk, *Russia*	53	D13
Blahkiuh, *Indonesia*	63	J18
Blain, *France*	18	E5
Blain, *U.S.A.*	116	F7
Blaine, *Minn., U.S.A.*	112	C8
Blaine, *Wash., U.S.A.*	110	B4
Blaine Lake, *Canada*	103	C7
Blair, *U.S.A.*	112	E6
Blair Athol, *Australia*	94	C4
Blair Atholl, *U.K.*	13	E5
Blairgowrie, *U.K.*	13	E5
Blairsden, *U.S.A.*	110	F6
Blairsville, *U.S.A.*	116	F5
Blaj, *Romania*	29	D8
Blakang Mati, Pulau, *Singapore*	65	d
Blake Pt., *U.S.A.*	112	A10
Blakely, *Ga., U.S.A.*	115	K3
Blakely, *Pa., U.S.A.*	117	E9
Blâmont, *France*	19	D13
Blanc, C., *Italy*	48	B9
Blanc, Mont, *Europe*	21	C10
Blanc-Sablon, *Canada*	105	B8
Blanca, B., *Argentina*	128	D4
Blanca Peak, *U.S.A.*	109	H11
Blanche, C., *Australia*	95	E1
Blanche, L., *S. Austral., Australia*	95	D2
Blanche, L., *W. Austral., Australia*	92	D3
Blanchisseuse, *Trin. & Tob.*	125	K15
Blanco, *S. Africa*	88	E3
Blanco, *U.S.A.*	113	K5
Blanco →, *Argentina*	126	C2
Blanco, C., *Costa Rica*	120	E2
Blanco, C., *U.S.A.*	108	E1
Blanda →, *Iceland*	8	D3
Blandford Forum, *U.K.*	15	G5
Blanding, *U.S.A.*	109	H9
Blanes, *Spain*	38	D7
Blangy-sur-Bresle, *France*	19	C8
Blanice →, *Czech Rep.*	26	B7
Blankaholm, *Sweden*	11	G10
Blankenberge, *Belgium*	17	C3
Blankenburg, *Germany*	24	D6
Blanquefort, *France*	20	D3
Blanquillo, *Uruguay*	127	C4
Blansko, *Czech Rep.*	27	B9
Blantyre, *Malawi*	87	F4
Blarney, *Ireland*	12	E3
Blasdell, *U.S.A.*	116	D6
Błaszki, *Poland*	31	G5
Blatná, *Czech Rep.*	26	B6
Blato, *Croatia*	41	F13
Blaubeuren, *Germany*	25	G5
Blaustein, *Germany*	25	G5
Blåvands Huk, *Denmark*	11	J2
Blaydon, *U.K.*	14	C6
Blaye, *France*	20	C3
Blaye-les-Mines, *France*	20	D6
Blayney, *Australia*	95	E4
Blaze, Pt., *Australia*	92	B5
Błażowa, *Poland*	31	J9
Bleckede, *Germany*	24	B6
Bled, *Slovenia*	41	B11
Bleiburg, *Austria*	26	E7
Blejești, *Romania*	29	F10
Blekinge, *Sweden*	9	H16
Blekinge län □, *Sweden*	11	H9
Blenheim, *Canada*	116	D3
Blenheim, *N.Z.*	91	J4
Bléone →, *France*	21	D10
Blérancourt, *France*	19	C10
Bletchley, *U.K.*	15	F7
Blida, *Algeria*	78	A6
Blidö, *Sweden*	10	E12
Blidsberg, *Sweden*	11	G7
Blieskastel, *Germany*	25	F3
Bligh Sound, *N.Z.*	91	L1
Blind River, *Canada*	104	C3
Blinisht, *Albania*	44	E3
Bliss, *Idaho, U.S.A.*	108	E6
Bliss, *N.Y., U.S.A.*	116	D6
Blissfield, *U.S.A.*	116	F3
Blitar, *Indonesia*	63	H15
Blitta, *Togo*	83	D5
Block I., *U.S.A.*	117	E13
Block Island Sd., *U.S.A.*	117	E13
Bloemfontein, *S. Africa*	88	D4
Bloemhof, *S. Africa*	88	D4
Blois, *France*	18	E8
Blomskog, *Sweden*	10	E6
Blomstermåla, *Sweden*	11	H10
Blönduós, *Iceland*	8	D3
Blongas, *Indonesia*	63	K19
Błonie, *Poland*	31	F7
Bloodvein →, *Canada*	103	C9
Bloody Foreland, *Ireland*	12	A3
Bloomer, *U.S.A.*	112	C9
Bloomfield, *Canada*	116	C7
Bloomfield, *Iowa, U.S.A.*	112	E8
Bloomfield, *N. Mex., U.S.A.*	109	H10
Bloomfield, *Nebr., U.S.A.*	112	D6
Bloomington, *Ill., U.S.A.*	112	E10
Bloomington, *Ind., U.S.A.*	114	F2
Bloomington, *Minn., U.S.A.*	112	C8
Bloomsburg, *U.S.A.*	117	F8
Bloomsbury, *Australia*	94	J6
Blora, *Indonesia*	63	G14
Blossburg, *U.S.A.*	116	E7
Blouberg, *S. Africa*	89	C4
Blountstown, *U.S.A.*	115	K3
Bludenz, *Austria*	26	D2
Blue Earth, *U.S.A.*	112	D7
Blue Hole △, *Belize*	120	C2
Blue Lagoon △, *Zambia*	87	F2
Blue Mesa Reservoir, *U.S.A.*	109	G10
Blue Mountain Lake, *U.S.A.*	117	C10
Blue Mountain Pk., *Jamaica*	120	a
Blue Mts., *Jamaica*	120	a
Blue Mts., *Maine, U.S.A.*	117	B14
Blue Mts., *Oreg., U.S.A.*	108	D4
Blue Mts., *Pa., U.S.A.*	117	F8
Blue Mud B., *Australia*	94	A2
Blue Nile = Nîl el Azraq →, *Sudan*	81	D3
Blue Rapids, *U.S.A.*	112	F6
Blue Ridge Mts., *U.S.A.*	115	G5
Blue River, *Canada*	102	C5
Bluefield, *U.S.A.*	114	G5
Bluefields, *Nic.*	120	D3
Bluff, *N.Z.*	91	M2
Bluff, *U.S.A.*	109	H9
Bluff Knoll, *Australia*	93	F2
Bluff Pt., *Australia*	93	E1
Bluffton, *U.S.A.*	114	E3
Blumenau, *Brazil*	127	B6
Blunt, *U.S.A.*	112	C5
Bly, *U.S.A.*	108	E3
Blyde River Canyon △, *S. Africa*	89	C5
Blyth, *Canada*	116	C3
Blyth, *U.K.*	14	B6
Blythe, *U.S.A.*	111	M12
Blytheville, *U.S.A.*	113	H10
Bo, *S. Leone*	82	D2
Bo Duc, *Vietnam*	65	G6
Bo Hai, *China*	57	E10
Bo Xian = Bozhou, *China*	56	H8
Boa Vista, *Brazil*	124	C6
Boac, *Phil.*	61	E4
Boaco, *Nic.*	120	D2
Bo'ai, *China*	56	G7
Boal, *Spain*	36	B4
Boalsburg, *U.S.A.*	116	F7
Boane, *Mozam.*	89	D5
Boardman, *U.S.A.*	116	E4
Bobadah, *Australia*	95	E4
Bobai, *China*	58	F7
Bobbili, *India*	67	K13
Bóbbio, *Italy*	40	D6
Bobcaygeon, *Canada*	116	B6
Böblingen, *Germany*	25	G5
Bobo-Dioulasso, *Burkina Faso*	82	C4
Bobolice, *Poland*	30	E3
Boboshevo, *Bulgaria*	44	D7
Bobov Dol, *Bulgaria*	44	D6
Bóbr →, *Poland*	31	F2
Bobraomby, Tanjon' i, *Madag.*	89	A8
Bobrinets, *Ukraine*	33	H7
Bobrov, *Russia*	34	E5
Bobrovitsa, *Ukraine*	33	G6
Bobruysk = Babruysk, *Belarus*	33	F5
Boby, Pic, *Madag.*	85	J9
Boca de Drago, *Venezuela*	125	K15
Bôca do Acre, *Brazil*	124	E5
Boca Raton, *U.S.A.*	115	M5
Bocanda, *Ivory C.*	82	D4
Bocas del Toro, *Panama*	120	E3
Boceguillas, *Spain*	36	D7
Bochnia, *Poland*	31	J7
Bocholt, *Germany*	24	D2
Bochum, *Germany*	24	D3
Bockenem, *Germany*	24	C6
Boćki, *Poland*	31	F10
Bocognano, *France*	21	F13
Bocoyna, *Mexico*	118	B3
Bocșa, *Romania*	28	E6
Boda, *Dalarna, Sweden*	10	C9
Böda, *Kalmar, Sweden*	11	G11
Boda, *Västernorrland, Sweden*	10	B10
Bodafors, *Sweden*	11	G8
Bodaybo, *Russia*	53	D12
Boddam, *U.K.*	13	B7
Boddington, *Australia*	93	F2
Bode Sadu, *Nigeria*	83	D5
Bodega Bay, *U.S.A.*	110	G3
Boden, *Sweden*	8	D19
Bodensee, *Europe*	25	H5
Bodenteich, *Germany*	24	C6
Bodhan, *India*	66	K10
Bodinga, *Nigeria*	83	C6
Bodmin, *U.K.*	15	G3
Bodmin Moor, *U.K.*	15	G3
Bodø, *Norway*	8	C16
Bodrog →, *Hungary*	28	B6
Bodrum, *Turkey*	47	D9
Bódva →, *Hungary*	28	B5
Boën, *France*	21	C8
Boende, *Dem. Rep. of the Congo*	84	E4
Boerne, *U.S.A.*	113	L5
Boesmans →, *S. Africa*	88	E4
Boffa, *Guinea*	82	C2
Bogalusa, *U.S.A.*	113	K10
Bogan →, *Australia*	95	D4
Bogan Gate, *Australia*	95	E4
Bogandé, *Burkina Faso*	83	C4
Bogantungan, *Australia*	94	C4
Bogata, *U.S.A.*	113	J7
Bogatić, *Serbia & M.*	44	B3
Boğazkale, *Turkey*	72	B6
Boğazlıyan, *Turkey*	72	C6
Bogen, *Sweden*	10	D6
Bogense, *Denmark*	11	J4
Bogetići, *Serbia & M.*	44	D2
Boggabilla, *Australia*	95	D5
Boggabri, *Australia*	95	E5
Boggeragh Mts., *Ireland*	12	D3
Boglan = Solhan, *Turkey*	70	B4
Bognor Regis, *U.K.*	15	G7
Bogo, *Phil.*	61	F6
Bogodukhov = Bohodukhiv, *Ukraine*	33	G8
Bogol Manya, *Ethiopia*	81	G5
Bogong, Mt., *Australia*	95	F4
Bogor, *Indonesia*	63	G12
Bogoroditsk, *Russia*	32	F10
Bogorodsk, *Russia*	34	B6
Bogoso, *Ghana*	82	D4
Bogotá, *Colombia*	124	C4
Bogotol, *Russia*	52	D9
Bogou, *Togo*	83	C5
Bogra, *Bangla.*	67	G16
Boguchany, *Russia*	53	D10
Boguchar, *Russia*	34	F5
Bogué, *Mauritania*	82	B2
Boguslav, *Ukraine*	33	H6
Boguszów-Gorce, *Poland*	31	H3
Bohain-en-Vermandois, *France*	19	C10
Bohdan, *Ukraine*	29	B9
Bohemian Forest = Böhmerwald, *Germany*	25	F9
Bohinjska Bistrica, *Slovenia*	41	B11
Böhmerwald, *Germany*	25	F9
Bohmte, *Germany*	24	C4
Bohodukhiv, *Ukraine*	33	G8
Bohol □, *Phil.*	61	G6
Bohol Sea, *Phil.*	63	C6
Bohongou, *Burkina Faso*	83	C5
Böhönye, *Hungary*	28	D2
Bohorodchany, *Ukraine*	29	B9

Bohuslän, Sweden ... 11 F5
Boi, Nigeria ... 83 D6
Boi, Pta. de, Brazil ... 127 A6
Boiaçu, Brazil ... 124 D6
Boileau, C., Australia ... 92 C3
Boing'o, Sudan ... 81 F3
Boiro, Spain ... 36 C2
Boise, U.S.A. ... 108 E5
Boise City, U.S.A. ... 113 G3
Boissevain, Canada ... 103 D8
Bóite →, Italy ... 41 B9
Boitzenburg, Germany ... 24 B9
Boizenburg, Germany ... 24 B6
Bojador, C., W. Sahara ... 78 C3
Bojana →, Albania ... 44 E3
Bojano, Italy ... 43 A7
Bojanowo, Poland ... 31 G3
Bøjden, Denmark ... 11 J4
Bojnūrd, Iran ... 71 B8
Bojonegoro, Indonesia ... 63 G14
Boju, Nigeria ... 83 D6
Boka, Serbia & M. ... 28 E5
Boka Kotorska, Serbia & M. ... 44 D2
Bokala, Ivory C. ... 82 D4
Bokani, Nigeria ... 83 D6
Bokaro, India ... 69 H11
Boké, Guinea ... 82 C2
Bokhara →, Australia ... 95 D4
Bokkos, Nigeria ... 83 D6
Boknafjorden, Norway ... 9 G11
Bokora △, Uganda ... 86 B3
Bokoro, Chad ... 79 F9
Bokpyin, Burma ... 65 G2
Boksitogorsk, Russia ... 32 C7
Bol, Croatia ... 41 E13
Bolama, Guinea-Biss. ... 82 C1
Bolan →, Pakistan ... 68 E2
Bolan Pass, Pakistan ... 66 E5
Bolaños →, Mexico ... 118 C4
Bolaños de Calatrava, Spain ... 37 G7
Bolayır, Turkey ... 45 F10
Bolbec, France ... 18 C7
Boldājī, Iran ... 71 D6
Boldeşti-Scăeni, Romania ... 29 E11
Bole, China ... 60 B3
Bole, Ethiopia ... 81 F4
Bole, Ghana ... 82 D4
Bolekhiv, Ukraine ... 33 H2
Bolesławiec, Poland ... 31 G2
Bolgatanga, Ghana ... 83 C4
Bolgrad = Bolhrad, Ukraine ... 29 E13
Bolhrad, Ukraine ... 29 E13
Bolinao, Phil. ... 61 C3
Bolintin-Vale, Romania ... 29 F10
Bolívar, Argentina ... 126 D3
Bolivar, Mo., U.S.A. ... 113 G8
Bolivar, N.Y., U.S.A. ... 116 D6
Bolivar, Tenn., U.S.A. ... 113 H10
Bolivia ■, S. Amer. ... 124 G6
Bolivian Plateau = Altiplano, Bolivia ... 122 G4
Boljevac, Serbia & M. ... 44 C5
Bolkhov, Russia ... 32 F9
Bolków, Poland ... 31 H3
Bollebygd, Sweden ... 11 G6
Bollène, France ... 21 D8
Bollnäs, Sweden ... 10 C10
Bollon, Australia ... 95 D4
Bollstabruk, Sweden ... 10 B11
Bolmen, Sweden ... 11 H7
Bolobo, Dem. Rep. of the Congo ... 84 E3
Bologna, Italy ... 41 D8
Bologna ✈ (BLQ), Italy ... 41 D8
Bologoye, Russia ... 32 D8
Bolon, Ozero, Russia ... 60 B8
Bolonchenticul, Mexico ... 119 D7
Bolótana, Italy ... 42 B1
Boloven, Cao Nguyen, Laos ... 64 E6
Bolpur, India ... 69 H12
Bolsena, Italy ... 41 F8
Bolsena, L. di, Italy ... 41 F8
Bolshakovo, Russia ... 30 D8
Bolshaya Chernigovka, Russia ... 34 D10
Bolshaya Glushitsa, Russia ... 34 D10
Bolshaya Martynovka, Russia ... 35 G5
Bolshaya Vradiyevka, Ukraine ... 33 J6
Bolshevik, Ostrov, Russia ... 53 B11
Bolshoy Anyuy →, Russia ... 53 C17
Bolshoy Begichev, Ostrov, Russia ... 53 B12
Bolshoy Kavkas = Caucasus Mountains, Eurasia ... 35 J7
Bolshoy Lyakhovskiy, Ostrov, Russia ... 53 B15
Bolshoy Tyuters, Ostrov, Russia ... 9 G22
Bolsward, Neths. ... 17 A5
Bolt Head, U.K. ... 15 G4
Boltaña, Spain ... 38 C5
Boltigen, Switz. ... 25 J3
Bolton, Canada ... 116 C5
Bolton, U.K. ... 14 D5
Bolton Landing, U.S.A. ... 117 C11
Bolu, Turkey ... 72 B4
Bolungavík, Iceland ... 8 C2
Boluo, China ... 59 F10
Bolvadin, Turkey ... 70 B1
Bolzano, Italy ... 41 B8
Bom Jesus da Lapa, Brazil ... 125 F10
Boma, Dem. Rep. of the Congo ... 84 F2
Bombala, Australia ... 95 F4
Bombarral, Portugal ... 37 F1
Bombay = Mumbai, India ... 66 K8
Bombedor, Pta., Venezuela ... 125 L15
Bomboma, Dem. Rep. of the Congo ... 84 D3
Bombombwa, Dem. Rep. of the Congo ... 86 B2
Bomi Hills, Liberia ... 82 D2
Bomili, Dem. Rep. of the Congo ... 86 B2
Bømlo, Norway ... 9 G11
Bomokandi →, Dem. Rep. of the Congo ... 86 B2
Bomu →, C.A.R. ... 84 D4

Bon, C., Tunisia ... 76 C5
Bon Sar Pa, Vietnam ... 64 F6
Bonāb, Iran ... 73 D12
Bonaigarh, India ... 69 J11
Bonaire, Neth. Ant. ... 121 D6
Bonampak, Mexico ... 119 D6
Bonang, Australia ... 95 F4
Bonanza, Nic. ... 120 D3
Bonaparte Arch., Australia ... 92 B3
Bonar Bridge, U.K. ... 13 D4
Bonasse, Trin. & Tob. ... 125 K15
Bonaventure, Canada ... 105 C6
Bonavista, Canada ... 105 C9
Bonavista, C., Canada ... 105 C9
Bonavista B., Canada ... 105 C9
Bondeno, Italy ... 41 D8
Bondo, Dem. Rep. of the Congo ... 86 B1
Bondoukou, Ivory C. ... 82 D4
Bondowoso, Indonesia ... 63 G15
Bone, Teluk, Indonesia ... 63 E6
Bonerate, Indonesia ... 63 F6
Bonerate, Kepulauan, Indonesia ... 63 F6
Bo'ness, U.K. ... 13 E5
Bonete, Cerro, Argentina ... 126 B2
Bong Son = Hoai Nhon, Vietnam ... 64 E7
Bonga, Ethiopia ... 81 F4
Bongabong, Phil. ... 61 E4
Bongor, Chad ... 79 F9
Bongouanou, Ivory C. ... 82 D4
Bonham, U.S.A. ... 113 J6
Boni, Mali ... 82 B4
Boni △, Kenya ... 86 C5
Bonifacio, France ... 21 G13
Bonifacio, Bouches de, Medit. S. ... 42 A2
Bonin Is. = Ogasawara Gunto, Pac. Oc. ... 96 K6
Bonke, Ethiopia ... 81 F4
Bonkoukou, Niger ... 83 C5
Bonn, Germany ... 24 E3
Bonnat, France ... 19 F8
Bonne Terre, U.S.A. ... 113 G9
Bonnétable, France ... 18 D7
Bonneval, France ... 21 C11
Bonneval-sur-Arc, France ... 18 D8
Bonneville, France ... 19 F13
Bonney, L., Australia ... 95 F3
Bonnie Rock, Australia ... 93 F2
Bonny, Nigeria ... 83 E6
Bonny →, Nigeria ... 83 E6
Bonny, Bight of, Africa ... 83 E6
Bonny-sur-Loire, France ... 19 E9
Bonnyrigg, U.K. ... 13 F5
Bonnyville, Canada ... 103 C6
Bono, Italy ... 42 B2
Bonoi, Indonesia ... 63 E9
Bonorva, Italy ... 42 B1
Bonsall, U.S.A. ... 111 M9
Bontang, Indonesia ... 62 D5
Bontebok △, S. Africa ... 88 E3
Bonthe, S. Leone ... 82 D2
Bontoc, Phil. ... 61 C4
Bonyeri, Ghana ... 82 D4
Bonyhád, Hungary ... 28 D3
Bonython Ra., Australia ... 92 D4
Bookabie, Australia ... 93 F5
Booker, U.S.A. ... 113 G4
Boola, Guinea ... 82 D3
Booligal, Australia ... 95 E3
Boonah, Australia ... 95 D5
Boone, Iowa, U.S.A. ... 112 D8
Boone, N.C., U.S.A. ... 115 G5
Booneville, Ark., U.S.A. ... 113 H8
Booneville, Miss., U.S.A. ... 115 H1
Boonville, Calif., U.S.A. ... 110 F3
Boonville, Ind., U.S.A. ... 114 F2
Boonville, Mo., U.S.A. ... 112 F8
Boonville, N.Y., U.S.A. ... 117 C9
Boorabbin △, Australia ... 93 F3
Boorindal, Australia ... 95 E4
Boorowa, Australia ... 95 E4
Boosaaso = Bosaso, Somali Rep. ... 75 E4
Boothia, Gulf of, Canada ... 101 A11
Boothia Pen., Canada ... 100 A10
Bootle, U.K. ... 14 D4
Booué, Gabon ... 84 E2
Boppard, Germany ... 25 E3
Boquete, Panama ... 120 E3
Boquilla, Presa de la, Mexico ... 118 B3
Boquillas del Carmen, Mexico ... 118 B4
Bor, Czech Rep. ... 26 B5
Bor, Russia ... 34 B7
Bor, Serbia & M. ... 44 B6
Bôr, Sudan ... 81 F3
Bor, Sweden ... 11 G8
Bor, Turkey ... 72 D6
Bor Mashash, Israel ... 74 D3
Borah Peak, U.S.A. ... 108 D7
Borang, Sudan ... 81 G3
Borås, Sweden ... 11 G6
Borāzjān, Iran ... 71 D6
Borba, Brazil ... 124 D7
Borba, Portugal ... 37 G3
Borborema, Planalto da, Brazil ... 122 D7
Borcea, Romania ... 29 F12
Borçka, Turkey ... 73 B9
Bord Khūn-e Now, Iran ... 71 D6
Borda, C., Australia ... 95 F2
Bordeaux, France ... 20 D3
Bordeaux ✈ (BOD), France ... 20 D3
Borden, Australia ... 93 F2
Borden-Carleton, Canada ... 105 C7
Borden I., Canada ... 4 B2
Borden Pen., Canada ... 101 A11
Border Ranges △, Australia ... 95 D5
Borders = Scottish Borders □, U.K. ... 13 F6
Bordertown, Australia ... 95 F3
Borðeyri, Iceland ... 8 D3
Bordighera, Italy ... 40 E4
Bordj Fly Ste. Marie, Algeria ... 78 C5

Bordj-in-Eker, Algeria ... 78 D7
Bordj Omar Driss, Algeria ... 78 C7
Bore, Ethiopia ... 81 G4
Borehamwood, U.K. ... 15 F7
Borek Wielkopolski, Poland ... 31 G4
Borensberg, Sweden ... 11 F9
Borgå = Porvoo, Finland ... 9 F21
Borgarfjörður, Iceland ... 8 D7
Borgarnes, Iceland ... 8 D3
Børgefjellet, Norway ... 8 D15
Borger, Neths. ... 17 B6
Borger, U.S.A. ... 113 H4
Borgholm, Sweden ... 11 H10
Bórgia, Italy ... 43 D9
Borgo San Dalmazzo, Italy ... 40 D4
Borgo San Lorenzo, Italy ... 41 E8
Borgo Val di Taro, Italy ... 40 D6
Borgo Valsugana, Italy ... 41 B8
Borgomanero, Italy ... 40 C5
Borgorose, Italy ... 41 F10
Borgosésia, Italy ... 40 C5
Borhoyn Tal, Mongolia ... 56 C6
Bori, Nigeria ... 83 E6
Borikhane, Laos ... 64 C4
Borisoglebsk, Russia ... 34 E6
Borisov = Barysaw, Belarus ... 32 E5
Borisovka, Russia ... 33 G9
Borja, Peru ... 124 D3
Borja, Spain ... 38 D3
Borjas Blancas = Les Borges Blanques, Spain ... 38 D5
Borjomi, Georgia ... 35 K6
Børkop, Denmark ... 11 J3
Borkou, Chad ... 79 E9
Borkum, Germany ... 24 B2
Borlänge, Sweden ... 10 D9
Borley, C., Antarctica ... 5 C5
Bórmio, Italy ... 40 B7
Borna, Germany ... 24 D8
Borne Sulinowo, Poland ... 30 E3
Borneo, E. Indies ... 62 D5
Bornholm, Denmark ... 11 J8
Bornholms Amtskommune □, Denmark ... 11 J8
Bornholmsgattet, Europe ... 11 J8
Borno □, Nigeria ... 83 C7
Bornos, Spain ... 37 J5
Bornova, Turkey ... 47 C9
Bornu Yassa, Nigeria ... 83 C7
Boro →, Sudan ... 81 F2
Borodino, Russia ... 32 E8
Borodino, Ukraine ... 29 D14
Borogontsy, Russia ... 53 C14
Boromo, Burkina Faso ... 82 C4
Boron, U.S.A. ... 111 L9
Borongan, Phil. ... 61 F6
Borotangba Mts., C.A.R. ... 81 F2
Borotou, Ivory C. ... 82 D3
Borovan, Bulgaria ... 44 C7
Borovichi, Russia ... 32 C7
Borovsk, Russia ... 32 E9
Borrby, Sweden ... 11 J8
Borrego Springs, U.S.A. ... 111 M10
Borriol, Spain ... 38 E4
Borroloola, Australia ... 94 B2
Borşa, Cluj, Romania ... 29 D8
Borşa, Maramureş, Romania ... 29 C9
Borsad, India ... 68 H5
Borsec, Romania ... 29 D10
Borshchiv, Ukraine ... 29 B11
Borsod-Abaúj-Zemplén □, Hungary ... 28 B6
Bort-les-Orgues, France ... 20 C6
Borth, U.K. ... 15 E3
Börtnan, Sweden ... 10 B7
Borūjerd, Iran ... 71 C6
Borynya, Ukraine ... 31 J10
Boryslav, Ukraine ... 31 J10
Boryspil, Ukraine ... 33 G6
Borzhomi = Borjomi, Georgia ... 35 K6
Borzna, Ukraine ... 33 G7
Borzya, Russia ... 53 D12
Bosa, Italy ... 42 B1
Bosanska Dubica, Bos.-H. ... 41 C13
Bosanska Gradiška, Bos.-H. ... 28 E2
Bosanska Kostajnica, Bos.-H. ... 41 C13
Bosanska Krupa, Bos.-H. ... 41 D13
Bosanski Brod, Bos.-H. ... 28 E2
Bosanski Novi, Bos.-H. ... 41 C13
Bosanski Petrovac, Bos.-H. ... 41 D13
Bosanski Šamac, Bos.-H. ... 28 E3
Bosansko Grahovo, Bos.-H. ... 41 D13
Bosaso, Somali Rep. ... 75 E4
Boscastle, U.K. ... 15 G3
Boscobelle, Barbados ... 121 g
Bose, China ... 58 F7
Boshan, China ... 57 F9
Boshof, S. Africa ... 88 D4
Boshrūyeh, Iran ... 71 C8
Bosilegrad, Serbia & M. ... 44 D6
Boskovice, Czech Rep. ... 27 B9
Bosna →, Bos.-H. ... 28 E3
Bosna i Hercegovina = Bosnia-Herzegovina ■, Europe ... 28 G2
Bosnia-Herzegovina ■, Europe ... 28 G2
Bosnik, Indonesia ... 63 E9
Bosobolo, Dem. Rep. of the Congo ... 84 D3
Bosporus = İstanbul Boğazı, Turkey ... 45 E13
Bosque Farms, U.S.A. ... 109 J10
Bossangoa, C.A.R. ... 84 C3
Bossé Bangou, Niger ... 83 C5
Bossier City, U.S.A. ... 113 J8
Bosso, Niger ... 83 C7
Bosso, Dallol →, Niger ... 83 C5
Bostan, Pakistan ... 68 D2
Bostānābād, Iran ... 70 B5
Bosten Hu, China ... 60 B3
Boston, U.K. ... 14 E7

Boston, U.S.A. ... 117 D13
Boston Bar, Canada ... 102 D4
Boston Mts., U.S.A. ... 113 H8
Bosumtwi, L., Ghana ... 83 D4
Boswell, Canada ... 102 D5
Boswell, U.S.A. ... 116 F5
Botad, India ... 68 H4
Botan →, Turkey ... 73 D10
Botene, Laos ... 64 D3
Botev, Bulgaria ... 45 D8
Botevgrad, Bulgaria ... 44 D7
Bothaville, S. Africa ... 88 D4
Bothnia, G. of, Europe ... 8 E19
Bothwell, Australia ... 95 G4
Bothwell, Canada ... 116 D3
Boticas, Portugal ... 36 D3
Botletle →, Botswana ... 88 C3
Botlikh, Russia ... 35 J8
Botna →, Moldova ... 29 D14
Botoroaga, Romania ... 29 F10
Botoşani, Romania ... 29 C11
Botoşani □, Romania ... 29 C11
Botou, Burkina Faso ... 83 C5
Botricello, Italy ... 43 D9
Botro →, Ivory C. ... 82 D3
Botswana ■, Africa ... 88 C3
Bottineau, U.S.A. ... 112 A4
Bottnaryd, Sweden ... 11 G7
Bottrop, Germany ... 17 C6
Botucatu, Brazil ... 127 A6
Botwood, Canada ... 105 C8
Bou Djébéha, Mali ... 82 B4
Boû Rjeïmât, Mauritania ... 82 B1
Bouaflé, Ivory C. ... 82 D3
Bouaké, Ivory C. ... 82 D3
Bouar, C.A.R. ... 84 C3
Bouârfa, Morocco ... 78 B5
Boucaut B., Australia ... 94 A1
Bouches-du-Rhône □, France ... 21 E9
Boucle de Baoulé △, Mali ... 82 C3
Boucles de la Seine Normande △, France ... 18 C7
Bouctouche, Canada ... 105 C7
Bougainville, C., Australia ... 92 B4
Bougainville I., Papua N. G. ... 96 H7
Bougainville Reef, Australia ... 94 B4
Bougie = Bejaïa, Algeria ... 78 A7
Bougouni, Mali ... 82 C3
Bouillon, Belgium ... 17 E5
Boukombé, Benin ... 83 C5
Boulal, Mali ... 82 B3
Boulazac, France ... 20 C4
Boulder, Colo., U.S.A. ... 112 E2
Boulder, Mont., U.S.A. ... 108 C7
Boulder City, U.S.A. ... 111 K12
Boulder Creek, U.S.A. ... 110 H4
Boulder Dam = Hoover Dam, U.S.A. ... 111 K12
Bouli, Mauritania ... 82 B2
Boulia, Australia ... 94 C2
Bouligny, France ... 19 C12
Boulogne →, France ... 18 E5
Boulogne-sur-Gesse, France ... 20 E4
Boulogne-sur-Mer, France ... 19 B8
Bouloire, France ... 18 E7
Boulouli, Mali ... 82 B3
Boultoum, Niger ... 83 C7
Boûmdeïd, Mauritania ... 82 B2
Boun Neua, Laos ... 64 B3
Boun Tai, Laos ... 64 B3
Bouna, Ivory C. ... 82 D4
Boundary Peak, U.S.A. ... 110 H8
Boundiali, Ivory C. ... 82 D3
Bountiful, U.S.A. ... 108 F8
Bounty Is., Pac. Oc. ... 96 M9
Boura, Mali ... 82 C4
Bourbon-Lancy, France ... 19 F10
Bourbon-l'Archambault, France ... 19 F10
Bourbonnais, France ... 19 F10
Bourbonne-les-Bains, France ... 19 E12
Bourbourg, France ... 19 B9
Bourdel L., Canada ... 104 A5
Bourem, Mali ... 83 B4
Bourg, France ... 20 C3
Bourg-Argental, France ... 21 C8
Bourg-de-Péage, France ... 21 C9
Bourg-en-Bresse, France ... 19 F12
Bourg-Lastic, France ... 20 C6
Bourg-Madame, France ... 20 F5
Bourg-St-Andéol, France ... 21 D8
Bourg-St-Maurice, France ... 21 C10
Bourganeuf, France ... 20 C5
Bourges, France ... 19 E9
Bourget, Canada ... 117 A9
Bourget, Lac du, France ... 21 C9
Bourgneuf, B. de, France ... 18 E4
Bourgneuf-en-Retz, France ... 18 E5
Bourgogne, France ... 19 F11
Bourgoin-Jallieu, France ... 21 C9
Bourgueil, France ... 18 E7
Bourke, Australia ... 95 E4
Bourne →, U.K. ... 14 E7
Bournemouth, U.K. ... 15 G6
Bournemouth □, U.K. ... 15 G6
Bouroum, Burkina Faso ... 83 C4
Bouse, U.S.A. ... 111 M13
Boussac, France ... 19 F9
Boussé, Burkina Faso ... 83 C4
Boussouma, Burkina Faso ... 83 C4
Boutilimit, Mauritania ... 82 B2
Boutonne →, France ... 20 C3
Bouvet I. = Bouvetøya, Antarctica ... 3 G10
Bouvetøya, Antarctica ... 3 G10
Bouxwiller, France ... 19 D14
Bouza, Niger ... 83 C6
Bouzonville, France ... 19 C13
Bova Marina, Italy ... 43 E8
Bovalino Marina, Italy ... 43 D9

Bovino, Italy ... 43 A8
Bovril, Argentina ... 126 C4
Bow →, Canada ... 102 C6
Bow Island, Canada ... 102 D6
Bowbells, U.S.A. ... 112 A3
Bowdle, U.S.A. ... 112 C5
Bowelling, Australia ... 93 F2
Bowen, Argentina ... 126 D2
Bowen, Australia ... 94 J6
Bowen Mts., Australia ... 95 F4
Bowie, Ariz., U.S.A. ... 109 K9
Bowie, Tex., U.S.A. ... 113 J6
Bowkān, Iran ... 70 B5
Bowland, Forest of, U.K. ... 14 D5
Bowling Green, Ky., U.S.A. ... 114 G2
Bowling Green, Ohio, U.S.A. ... 114 E4
Bowling Green, C., Australia ... 94 B4
Bowling Green Bay △, Australia ... 94 B4
Bowman, U.S.A. ... 112 B3
Bowman I., Antarctica ... 5 C8
Bowmanville = Clarington, Canada ... 116 C6
Bowmore, U.K. ... 13 F2
Bowral, Australia ... 95 E5
Bowraville, Australia ... 95 E5
Bowron →, Canada ... 102 C4
Bowron Lake △, Canada ... 102 C4
Bowser L., Canada ... 102 B3
Bowsman, Canada ... 103 C8
Bowwood, Zambia ... 87 F2
Box Cr. →, Australia ... 95 E3
Boxholm, Sweden ... 11 F9
Boxmeer, Neths. ... 17 C5
Boxtel, Neths. ... 17 C5
Boyabat, Turkey ... 72 B6
Boyalıca, Turkey ... 45 F13
Boyang, China ... 59 C11
Boyce, U.S.A. ... 113 K8
Boyd L., Canada ... 104 B4
Boyle, Canada ... 102 C6
Boyle, Ireland ... 12 C3
Boyne →, Ireland ... 12 C5
Boyne City, U.S.A. ... 114 C3
Boynitsa, Bulgaria ... 44 C6
Boynton Beach, U.S.A. ... 115 M5
Boyolali, Indonesia ... 63 G14
Boyoma, Chutes, Dem. Rep. of the Congo ... 86 B2
Boysen Reservoir, U.S.A. ... 108 E9
Boyuibe, Bolivia ... 124 G6
Boyup Brook, Australia ... 93 F2
Boz Burun, Turkey ... 45 F12
Boz Dağ, Turkey ... 47 D11
Boz Dağları, Turkey ... 47 C10
Bozan, Turkey ... 47 E10
Bozburun, Turkey ... 47 E10
Bozcaada, Turkey ... 72 C2
Bozdoğan, Turkey ... 47 D10
Bozeman, U.S.A. ... 108 D8
Bozen = Bolzano, Italy ... 41 B8
Boževac, Serbia & M. ... 44 B5
Bozhou, China ... 56 H8
Bozkır, Turkey ... 72 D5
Bozkurt, Turkey ... 47 D11
Bozouls, France ... 20 D6
Bozoum, C.A.R. ... 84 C3
Bozova, Antalya, Turkey ... 47 D12
Bozova, Sanliurfa, Turkey ... 73 D8
Bozovici, Romania ... 28 F7
Bozüyük, Turkey ... 47 B12
Bra, Italy ... 40 D4
Braås, Sweden ... 11 G9
Brabant □, Belgium ... 17 D4
Brabant L., Canada ... 103 B8
Brabrand, Denmark ... 11 H4
Brač, Croatia ... 41 E13
Bracadale, L., U.K. ... 13 D2
Bracciano, Italy ... 41 F9
Bracciano, L. di, Italy ... 41 F9
Bracebridge, Canada ... 116 A5
Brach, Libya ... 79 C8
Bracieux, France ... 18 E8
Bräcke, Sweden ... 10 B9
Brackettville, U.S.A. ... 113 L4
Bracknell, U.K. ... 15 F7
Bracknell Forest □, U.K. ... 15 F7
Brad, Romania ... 28 D7
Brádano →, Italy ... 43 B9
Bradenton, U.S.A. ... 115 M4
Bradford, Canada ... 116 B5
Bradford, U.K. ... 14 D6
Bradford, Pa., U.S.A. ... 116 E6
Bradford, Vt., U.S.A. ... 117 C12
Bradley, Ark., U.S.A. ... 113 J8
Bradley, Calif., U.S.A. ... 110 K6
Bradley Institute, Zimbabwe ... 87 F3
Brady, U.S.A. ... 113 K5
Brædstrup, Denmark ... 11 J3
Braeside, Canada ... 117 A8
Braga, Portugal ... 36 D2
Braga □, Portugal ... 36 D2
Bragadiru, Romania ... 29 G10
Bragado, Argentina ... 126 D3
Bragança, Brazil ... 125 D9
Bragança, Portugal ... 36 D4
Bragança □, Portugal ... 36 D4
Bragança Paulista, Brazil ... 127 A6
Brahestad = Raahe, Finland ... 8 D21
Brahmanbaria, Bangla. ... 67 H17
Brahmani →, India ... 67 J15
Brahmapur, India ... 67 K14
Brahmaputra →, Asia ... 67 H13
Braich-y-pwll, U.K. ... 14 E3
Braidwood, Australia ... 95 F4
Brăila, Romania ... 29 E12
Brăila □, Romania ... 29 E12
Brainerd, U.S.A. ... 112 B7
Braintree, U.K. ... 15 F8
Braintree, U.S.A. ... 117 D14
Brak →, S. Africa ... 88 D3
Brake, Germany ... 24 B4

Brakel, Germany 24 D5
Bräkne-Hoby, Sweden 11 H9
Brakwater, Namibia 88 C2
Brålanda, Sweden 11 F6
Bramberg, Germany 25 E6
Bramdrupdam, Denmark 11 J3
Bramming, Denmark 11 J2
Brämön, Sweden 10 B11
Brampton, Canada 116 C5
Brampton, U.K. 14 C5
Bramsche, Germany 24 C3
Bramton I., Australia 94 J7
Branco →, Brazil 124 D6
Brandberg, Namibia 88 C1
Brandberg △, Namibia 88 C1
Brande, Denmark 11 J3
Brandenburg = Neubrandenburg,
    Germany 24 B9
Brandenburg, Germany 24 C8
Brandenburg □, Germany 24 C9
Brandfort, S. Africa 88 D4
Brandø, France 21 F13
Brandon, Canada 103 D9
Brandon, U.S.A. 117 C11
Brandon B., Ireland 12 D1
Brandon Mt., Ireland 12 D1
Brandsen, Argentina 126 D4
Brandvlei, S. Africa 88 E3
Brandýs nad Labem, Czech Rep. 26 A7
Brăneşti, Romania 29 F11
Branford, U.S.A. 117 E12
Braniewo, Poland 30 D6
Bransfield Str., Antarctica ... 5 C18
Brańsk, Poland 31 F9
Branson, U.S.A. 113 G8
Brantford, Canada 116 C4
Brantôme, France 20 C4
Branzi, Italy 40 B6
Bras d'Or L., Canada 105 C7
Brasher Falls, U.S.A. 117 B10
Brasil, Planalto, Brazil 122 E6
Brasiléia, Brazil 124 F5
Brasília, Brazil 125 G9
Brasília Legal, Brazil 125 D7
Braslaw, Belarus 9 J22
Braslovče, Slovenia 41 B12
Braşov, Romania 29 E10
Braşov □, Romania 29 E10
Brass, Nigeria 83 E6
Brass →, Nigeria 83 E6
Brassac-les-Mines, France 20 C7
Brasschaat, Belgium 17 C4
Brassey, Banjaran, Malaysia ... 62 D5
Brassey Ra., Australia 93 E3
Brasstown Bald, U.S.A. 115 H4
Brastad, Sweden 11 F5
Brastavăţu, Romania 29 G9
Bratan = Morozov, Bulgaria ... 45 D9
Brateş, Romania 29 E11
Bratislava, Slovak Rep. 27 C10
Bratislava M.R. Štefánik ✈
    (BTS), Slovak Rep. 27 C10
Bratislavský □, Slovak Rep. ... 27 C10
Bratsigovo, Bulgaria 45 D8
Bratsk, Russia 53 D11
Brattleboro, U.S.A. 117 D12
Bratunac, Bos.-H. 28 F4
Braunau, Austria 26 C6
Braunschweig, Germany 24 C6
Braunton, U.K. 15 F3
Bravicea, Moldova 29 C13
Bråviken, Sweden 11 F10
Bravo del Norte, Rio = Grande,
    Rio →, U.S.A. 113 N6
Brawley, U.S.A. 111 N11
Bray, Ireland 12 C5
Bray, Mt., Australia 94 A1
Bray-sur-Seine, France 19 D10
Brazeau →, Canada 102 C5
Brazil, U.S.A. 114 F2
Brazil ■, S. Amer. 125 F9
Brazilian Highlands = Brasil,
    Planalto, Brazil 122 E6
Brazo Sur →, S. Amer. 126 B4
Brazos →, U.S.A. 113 L7
Brazzaville, Congo 84 E3
Brčko, Bos.-H. 28 F3
Brda →, Poland 31 E5
Brdy, Czech Rep. 26 B6
Breaden, L., Australia 93 E4
Breaksea Sd., N.Z. 91 L1
Bream B., N.Z. 91 F5
Bream Hd., N.Z. 91 F5
Breas, Chile 126 B1
Breaza, Romania 29 E10
Brebes, Indonesia 63 G13
Brechin, Canada 116 B5
Brechin, U.K. 13 E6
Brecht, Belgium 17 C4
Breckenridge, Colo., U.S.A. .. 108 G10
Breckenridge, Minn., U.S.A. .. 112 B6
Breckenridge, Tex., U.S.A. ... 113 J5
Breckland, U.K. 15 E8
Břeclav, Czech Rep. 27 C9
Brecon, U.K. 15 F4
Brecon Beacons, U.K. 15 F4
Brecon Beacons △, U.K. 15 F4
Breda, Neths. 17 C4
Bredaryd, Sweden 11 G7
Bredasdorp, S. Africa 88 E3
Bredebro, Denmark 11 J2
Bredstedt, Germany 24 A4
Bree, Belgium 17 C5
Bregalnica →, Macedonia 44 E6
Bregenz, Austria 26 D2
Bregovo, Bulgaria 44 B6
Bréhal, France 18 D5
Bréhat, Î. de, France 18 D4
Breiðafjörður, Iceland 8 D2
Breil-sur-Roya, France 21 E11
Breisach, Germany 25 G3
Brejo, Brazil 125 D10

Bremen, Germany 24 B4
Bremen □, Germany 24 B4
Bremer Bay, Australia 93 F2
Bremer I., Australia 94 A2
Bremerhaven, Germany 24 B4
Bremerton, U.S.A. 110 C4
Bremervörde, Germany 24 B5
Brenes, Spain 37 H5
Brenham, U.S.A. 113 K6
Brenne, France 20 B5
Brenne △, France 20 B5
Brennerpass, Austria 26 D4
Breno, Italy 40 C7
Brent, U.S.A. 115 J2
Brentwood, U.K. 15 F8
Brentwood, Calif., U.S.A. 110 H5
Brentwood, N.Y., U.S.A. 117 F11
Bréscia, Italy 40 C7
Breskens, Neths. 17 C3
Breslau = Wrocław, Poland ... 31 G4
Bresle →, France 18 B8
Bressanone, Italy 41 B8
Bressay, U.K. 13 A7
Bresse, France 19 F12
Bressuire, France 18 F6
Brest, Belarus 33 F2
Brest, France 18 D2
Brest-Litovsk = Brest, Belarus .. 33 F2
Bretagne □, France 18 D3
Breţcu, Romania 29 D11
Bretenoux, France 20 D5
Breteuil, Eure, France 18 D7
Breteuil, Oise, France 19 C9
Breton, Canada 102 C6
Breton, Pertuis, France 20 B2
Breton Sd., U.S.A. 113 L10
Brett, C., N.Z. 91 F5
Bretten, Germany 25 F4
Breuil-Cervínia, Italy 40 C4
Brevard, U.S.A. 115 H4
Breves, Brazil 125 D8
Brewarrina, Australia 95 E4
Brewer, U.S.A. 115 C11
Brewer, Mt., U.S.A. 110 J8
Brewerville, Liberia 82 D2
Brewster, N.Y., U.S.A. 117 E11
Brewster, Ohio, U.S.A. 116 F3
Brewster, Wash., U.S.A. 108 B4
Brewster, Kap = Kangikajik,
    Greenland 4 B6
Brewton, U.S.A. 115 K2
Breyten, S. Africa 89 D5
Breza, Bos.-H. 28 F3
Brežice, Slovenia 41 C12
Březnice, Czech Rep. 26 B6
Breznik, Bulgaria 44 D6
Brezno, Slovak Rep. 27 C12
Brezoi, Romania 29 E9
Brezovica, Serbia & M. 44 D5
Brezovo, Bulgaria 45 D9
Briançon, France 21 D10
Briare, France 19 E9
Bribie I., Australia 95 D5
Bribri, Costa Rica 120 E3
Briceni, Moldova 29 B12
Bricquebec, France 18 C5
Bridgefield, Barbados ...... 121 g
Bridgehampton, U.S.A. 117 F12
Bridgend, U.K. 15 F4
Bridgend □, U.K. 15 F4
Bridgeport, Calif., U.S.A. ... 110 G7
Bridgeport, Conn., U.S.A. ... 117 E11
Bridgeport, Nebr., U.S.A. ... 112 E3
Bridgeport, Tex., U.S.A. 113 J6
Bridger, U.S.A. 108 D9
Bridgeton, U.S.A. 114 F8
Bridgetown, Australia 93 F2
Bridgetown, Barbados ...... 121 g
Bridgetown, Canada 105 D6
Bridgewater, Canada 105 D7
Bridgewater, Mass., U.S.A. .. 117 E14
Bridgewater, N.Y., U.S.A. ... 117 D9
Bridgewater, C., Australia ... 95 F3
Bridgewater-Gagebrook,
    Australia 95 G4
Bridgnorth, U.K. 15 E5
Bridgton, U.S.A. 117 B14
Bridgwater, U.K. 15 F5
Bridgwater B., U.K. 15 F4
Bridlington, U.K. 14 C7
Bridlington B., U.K. 14 C7
Bridport, Australia 95 G4
Bridport, U.K. 15 G5
Briec, France 18 D2
Brienne-le-Château, France .. 19 D11
Brienon-sur-Armançon, France 19 E10
Brienz, Switz. 25 J4
Brienzersee, Switz. 25 J3
Brière △, France 18 E4
Brig, Switz. 25 J3
Brigg, U.K. 14 D7
Brigham City, U.S.A. 108 F7
Bright, Australia 95 F4
Brighton, Australia 95 F2
Brighton, Canada 116 B7
Brighton, Trin. & Tob. 125 K15
Brighton, U.K. 15 G7
Brighton, Colo., U.S.A. 108 G2
Brighton, N.Y., U.S.A. 116 C7
Brignogan-Plage, France 18 D2
Brignoles, France 21 E10
Brihuega, Spain 38 E2
Brikama, Gambia 82 C1
Brilliant, U.S.A. 116 F4
Brilon, Germany 24 D4
Bríndisi, Italy 43 B10
Brinje, Croatia 41 D12
Brinkley, U.S.A. 113 H9
Brinnon, U.S.A. 110 C4
Brion, Î., Canada 105 C7

Brionne, France 18 C7
Brionski, Croatia 41 D10
Brioude, France 20 C7
Briouze, France 18 D6
Brisbane, Australia 95 D5
Brisbane →, Australia 95 D5
Brisighella, Italy 41 D8
Bristol, U.K. 15 F5
Bristol, Conn., U.S.A. 117 E12
Bristol, Pa., U.S.A. 117 F10
Bristol, R.I., U.S.A. 117 E13
Bristol, Tenn., U.S.A. 115 G4
Bristol, City of □, U.K. 15 F5
Bristol B., U.S.A. 100 C4
Bristol Channel, U.K. 15 F3
Bristol I., Antarctica 5 B1
Bristol L., U.S.A. 109 J5
Bristow, U.S.A. 113 H6
Britain = Great Britain, Europe . 6 E5
British Columbia □, Canada .. 102 C3
British Indian Ocean Terr. =
    Chagos Arch. ☒, Ind. Oc. . 50 K11
British Isles, Europe 6 D4
British Virgin Is. ☒, W. Indies . 121 e
Brits, S. Africa 89 D4
Britstown, S. Africa 88 E3
Britt, Canada 104 C3
Britton, U.S.A. 112 C6
Brittany = Bretagne □, France . 18 D3
Britton, U.S.A. 20 C5
Brive-la-Gaillarde, France ... 20 C5
Briviesca, Spain 36 C7
Brixen = Bressanone, Italy ... 41 B8
Brixham, U.K. 15 G4
Brnaze, Croatia 41 E13
Brněnský □, Czech Rep. 27 B9
Brno, Czech Rep. 27 B9
Broach = Bharuch, India 66 J8
Broad →, U.S.A. 115 J5
Broad Arrow, Australia 93 F3
Broad B., U.K. 13 C2
Broad Haven, Ireland 12 B2
Broad Law, U.K. 13 F5
Broad Sd., Australia 94 C4
Broadalbin, U.S.A. 117 C10
Broadback →, Canada 104 B4
Broadhurst Ra., Australia ... 92 D3
Broads △, U.K. 15 E9
Broads, The, U.K. 14 E9
Broadus, U.S.A. 112 C2
Broager, Denmark 11 K3
Broaroad, Sweden 11 H8
Brocēni, Latvia 30 B9
Brochet, Canada 103 B8
Brochet, L., Canada 103 B8
Brocken, Germany 24 D6
Brockport, U.S.A. 116 C7
Brockton, U.S.A. 117 D13
Brockville, Canada 117 B9
Brockway, Mont., U.S.A. ... 112 B2
Brockway, Pa., U.S.A. 116 E6
Brocton, U.S.A. 116 D5
Brod, Macedonia 44 E5
Brodarevo, Serbia & M. 44 C3
Brodeur Pen., Canada 101 A11
Brodhead, Mt., U.S.A. 116 E7
Brodick, U.K. 13 F3
Brodnica, Poland 31 E6
Brody, Ukraine 33 G3
Brogan, U.S.A. 108 D5
Broglie, France 18 C7
Brok, Poland 31 F8
Broken Arrow, U.S.A. 113 G7
Broken Bow, Nebr., U.S.A. .. 112 E5
Broken Bow, Okla., U.S.A. .. 113 H7
Broken Bow Lake, U.S.A. ... 113 H7
Broken Hill, Australia 95 E3
Broken River Ra., Australia .. 94 K6
Brokind, Sweden 11 F9
Bromley □, U.K. 15 F8
Bromo, Indonesia 63 G15
Bromölla, Sweden 11 H8
Bromsgrove, U.K. 15 E5
Brønderslev, Denmark 11 G3
Brong-Ahafo □, Ghana 82 D4
Broni, Italy 40 C6
Bronkhorstspruit, S. Africa .. 89 D4
Brønnøysund, Norway 8 D15
Bronte, Italy 43 E7
Brook Park, U.S.A. 116 E4
Brookhaven, U.S.A. 113 K9
Brookings, Oreg., U.S.A. 108 E1
Brookings, S. Dak., U.S.A. ... 112 C6
Brooklin, Canada 116 C6
Brooklyn Park, U.S.A. 112 C8
Brooks, Canada 102 C6
Brooks Range, U.S.A. 100 B5
Brooksville, U.S.A. 115 L4
Brookton, Australia 93 F2
Brookville, U.S.A. 116 E5
Broom, L., U.K. 13 D3
Broome, Australia 92 C3
Broons, France 18 D4
Brora, U.K. 13 C5
Brora →, U.K. 13 C5
Brørup, Denmark 11 J2
Brösarp, Sweden 11 J8
Brosna →, Ireland 12 C4
Broşteni, Mehedinţi, Romania . 28 F7
Broşteni, Suceava, Romania .. 29 C10
Brothers, U.S.A. 108 E3
Brou, France 18 D8
Brouage, France 20 C2
Brough, U.K. 14 C5
Brough Hd., U.K. 13 B5
Broughton Island = Qikiqtarjuaq,
    Canada 101 B13
Broumov, Czech Rep. 27 A9
Brovary, Ukraine 33 G6
Brovst, Denmark 11 G3
Brown, L., Australia 93 F2
Brown, Pt., Australia 95 E1
Brown City, U.S.A. 116 C2

Brown Willy, U.K. 15 G3
Brownfield, U.S.A. 113 J3
Browning, U.S.A. 108 B7
Brownsville, Oreg., U.S.A. ... 108 D2
Brownsville, Pa., U.S.A. 116 F5
Brownsville, Tenn., U.S.A. ... 113 H10
Brownsville, Tex., U.S.A. 113 N6
Brownville, U.S.A. 117 C9
Brownwood, U.S.A. 113 K5
Browse I., Australia 92 B3
Bruas, Malaysia 65 K3
Bruay-la-Buissière, France ... 19 B9
Bruce, Mt., Australia 92 D2
Bruce Pen., Canada 116 B3
Bruce Peninsula □, Canada .. 116 A3
Bruce Rock, Australia 93 F2
Bruche →, France 19 D14
Bruchsal, Germany 25 F4
Bruck an der Leitha, Austria .. 27 C9
Bruck an der Mur, Austria ... 26 D8
Brue →, U.K. 15 F5
Bruges = Brugge, Belgium ... 17 C3
Brugg, Switz. 25 H4
Brugge, Belgium 17 C3
Bruin, U.S.A. 116 E5
Brûlé, Canada 102 C5
Brûlon, France 18 E6
Brumado, Brazil 125 F10
Brumath, France 19 D14
Brumunddal, Norway 9 F14
Bruneau, U.S.A. 108 E6
Bruneau →, U.S.A. 108 E6
Bruneck = Brunico, Italy 41 B8
Brunei = Bandar Seri Begawan,
    Brunei 62 C4
Brunei ■, Asia 62 D4
Brunflo, Sweden 10 A8
Brunico, Italy 41 B8
Brunna, Sweden 10 E11
Brunnen, Switz. 25 J4
Brunner, L., N.Z. 91 K3
Brunsbüttel, Germany 24 B5
Brunssum, Neths. 17 D5
Brunswick = Braunschweig,
    Germany 24 C6
Brunswick, Ga., U.S.A. 115 K5
Brunswick, Maine, U.S.A. ... 115 D11
Brunswick, Md., U.S.A. 114 F7
Brunswick, Mo., U.S.A. 112 F8
Brunswick, Ohio, U.S.A. 116 E3
Brunswick, Pen. de, Chile ... 128 G2
Brunswick B., Australia 92 C3
Brunswick Junction, Australia . 93 F2
Bruntál, Czech Rep. 27 B10
Bruny I., Australia 95 G4
Brus Laguna, Honduras 120 C3
Brusartsi, Bulgaria 44 C7
Brush, U.S.A. 112 E3
Brushton, U.S.A. 117 B10
Brusio, Switz. 25 J6
Brusque, Brazil 127 B6
Brussel, Belgium 17 D4
Brussel ✈ (BRU), Belgium ... 17 D5
Brussels = Brussel, Belgium .. 17 D4
Brussels, Canada 116 C3
Brusy, Poland 30 E4
Bruthen, Australia 95 F4
Bruxelles = Brussel, Belgium .. 17 D4
Bruyères, France 19 D13
Bruz, France 18 D5
Brwinów, Poland 31 F7
Bryagovo, Bulgaria 45 E9
Bryan, Ohio, U.S.A. 114 E3
Bryan, Tex., U.S.A. 113 K6
Bryan, Mt., Australia 95 E2
Bryanka, Ukraine 33 H10
Bryansk, Bryansk, Russia ... 33 F8
Bryansk, Dagestan, Russia ... 35 H8
Bryanskoye = Bryansk, Russia . 35 H8
Bryce Canyon △, U.S.A. 109 H7
Bryne, Norway 9 G11
Bryson City, U.S.A. 115 H4
Bryukhovetskaya, Russia 33 K10
Brza Palanka, Serbia & M. ... 44 B6
Brzeg, Poland 31 H4
Brzeg Dolny, Poland 31 G3
Brześć Kujawski, Poland 31 F5
Brzesko, Poland 31 J7
Brzeziny, Poland 31 G6
Brzozów, Poland 31 J9
Bsharri, Lebanon 74 A5
Bū Baqarah, U.A.E. 71 E8
Bu Craa, W. Sahara 78 C3
Bū Ḥasā, U.A.E. 71 F7
Bua, Sweden 11 G6
Bua Yai, Thailand 64 E4
Buapinang, Indonesia 63 E6
Buba, Guinea-Biss. 82 C2
Bubanza, Burundi 86 C2
Bubaque, Guinea-Biss. 82 C1
Bube, Ethiopia 81 F4
Bübiyän, Kuwait 71 D6
Buca, Turkey 47 C9
Bucak, Turkey 47 D12
Bucaramanga, Colombia 124 B4
Bucas Grande I., Phil. 61 G6
Bucasia, Australia 94 K7
Buccaneer Arch., Australia ... 92 C3
Buccino, Italy 43 B8
Buccoo Reef, Trin. & Tob. ... 125 J16
Bucecea, Romania 29 C11
Bucegi △, Romania 29 E10
Buchach, Ukraine 33 H3
Buchan, U.K. 13 D6
Buchan Ness, U.K. 13 D7
Buchanan, Canada 103 C8
Buchanan, Liberia 82 D2
Buchanan, L., Queens., Australia 94 C4
Buchanan, L., W. Austral.,
    Australia 93 E3
Buchanan, L., U.S.A. 113 K5
Buchanan Cr. →, Australia ... 94 B2

Buchans, Canada 105 C8
Bucharest = Bucureşti, Romania 29 F11
Buchen, Germany 25 F5
Buchholz, Germany 24 B5
Buchloe, Germany 25 G6
Buchon, Pt., U.S.A. 110 K6
Buciumi, Romania 28 C8
Buck Hill Falls, U.S.A. 117 E9
Bückeburg, Germany 24 C5
Buckeye, U.S.A. 109 K7
Buckeye Lake, U.S.A. 116 G2
Buckhannon, U.S.A. 114 F5
Buckhaven, U.K. 13 E5
Buckhorn L., Canada 116 B6
Buckie, U.K. 13 D6
Buckingham, Canada 104 C4
Buckingham, U.K. 15 F7
Buckingham B., Australia ... 94 A2
Buckinghamshire □, U.K. ... 15 F7
Buckle Hd., Australia 92 B4
Buckleboo, Australia 95 E2
Buckley, U.K. 14 D4
Buckley →, Australia 94 C2
Bucklin, U.S.A. 113 G5
Bucks L., U.S.A. 110 F5
Bucquoy, France 19 B9
Bucureşti, Romania 29 F11
Bucureşti Otopeni ✈ (OTP),
    Romania 45 B10
Bucyrus, U.S.A. 114 E4
Budacu, Vf., Romania 29 C10
Budalin, Burma 67 H19
Budaörs, Hungary 28 C3
Budapest, Hungary 28 C3
Budapest □, Hungary 28 C3
Budapest ✈ (BUD), Hungary ... 28 C3
Budaun, India 69 E8
Budd Coast, Antarctica 5 C8
Buddusò, Italy 42 B2
Bude, U.K. 15 G3
Budennovsk, Russia 35 H7
Budeşti, Romania 29 F11
Budeyi, Ukraine 29 B14
Budge Budge = Baj Baj, India . 69 H13
Budgewoi, Australia 95 E5
Budia, Spain 38 E2
Büdingen, Germany 25 E5
Budjala, Dem. Rep. of the Congo 84 D3
Budoni, Italy 42 B2
Búdrio, Italy 41 D8
Budva, Serbia & M. 44 D2
Budzyń, Poland 31 F3
Buea, Cameroon 83 E6
Buellton, U.S.A. 111 L6
Buena Esperanza, Argentina . 126 C2
Buena Park, U.S.A. 111 M9
Buena Vista, Colo., U.S.A. ... 109 G10
Buena Vista, Va., U.S.A. 114 G6
Buena Vista Lake Bed, U.S.A. . 111 K7
Buenaventura, Colombia 124 C3
Buenaventura, Mexico 118 B3
Buendía, Embalse de, Spain .. 38 E2
Buenos Aires, Argentina 126 C4
Buenos Aires, Costa Rica 120 E3
Buenos Aires □, Argentina ... 126 D4
Buenos Aires, L., Chile 128 F2
Buffalo, Mo., U.S.A. 113 G8
Buffalo, N.Y., U.S.A. 116 D6
Buffalo, Okla., U.S.A. 113 G5
Buffalo, S. Dak., U.S.A. 112 C3
Buffalo, Wyo., U.S.A. 108 D10
Buffalo →, Canada 102 A5
Buffalo →, S. Africa 89 D5
Buffalo Head Hills, Canada .. 102 B5
Buffalo L., Alta., Canada 102 C6
Buffalo L., N.W.T., Canada .. 102 A5
Buffalo Narrows, Canada ... 103 B7
Buffalo Springs, Kenya 86 B4
Buffels →, S. Africa 88 D2
Buford, U.S.A. 115 H4
Bug = Buh →, Ukraine 33 J6
Bug →, Poland 31 F8
Buga, Colombia 124 C3
Bugala I., Uganda 86 C3
Buganda, Uganda 86 C3
Buganga, Uganda 86 C3
Bugasong, Phil. 61 F5
Bugeat, France 20 C5
Bugel, Tanjung, Indonesia ... 63 G14
Bugibba, Malta 49 D1
Bugojno, Bos.-H. 28 F2
Bugsuk, Phil. 62 C5
Buguma, Nigeria 83 E6
Bugun Shara, Mongolia 60 B5
Bugungu △, Uganda 86 B3
Buguruslan, Russia 52 D6
Buh →, Ukraine 33 J6
Buharkent, Turkey 47 D10
Buheirat-Murrat-el-Kubra, Egypt 80 H8
Buhera, Zimbabwe 89 B5
Bühl, Germany 25 G4
Buhl, U.S.A. 108 E6
Buhuşi, Romania 29 D11
Bui △, Ghana 82 D4
Builth Wells, U.K. 15 E4
Buinsk, Russia 34 C9
Buir Nur, Mongolia 60 B6
Buis-les-Baronnies, France ... 21 D9
Buitrago del Lozoya, Spain ... 36 E7
Bujalance, Spain 37 H6
Bujanovac, Serbia & M. 44 D5
Bujaraloz, Spain 38 D4
Buje, Croatia 41 C10
Bujumbura, Burundi 86 C2
Bük, Hungary 28 C1
Buk, Poland 31 F3
Bukachacha, Russia 53 D12
Bukama, Dem. Rep. of the Congo 87 D2
Bukavu, Dem. Rep. of the Congo 86 C2
Bukene, Tanzania 86 C3
Bukhara = Bukhoro, Uzbekistan 52 F7

Bukhoro, Uzbekistan 52 F7
Bukima, Tanzania 86 C3
Bukit Badung, Indonesia 63 K18
Bukit Kerajaan, Malaysia 65 c
Bukit Mertajam, Malaysia 65 c
Bukit Ni, Malaysia 65 d
Bukit Panjang, Singapore 65 d
Bukit Tengah, Malaysia 65 c
Bukittinggi, Indonesia 62 E2
Bükk, Hungary 28 B5
Bükki △, Hungary 28 B5
Bukoba, Tanzania 86 C3
Bukum, Pulau, Singapore 65 d
Bukuru, Nigeria 83 D6
Bukuya, Uganda 86 B3
Būl, Kuh-e, Iran 71 D7
Bula, Guinea-Biss. 82 C1
Bula, Indonesia 63 E8
Bülach, Switz. 25 H4
Bulahdelah, Australia 95 E5
Bulan, Phil. 61 E5
Bulancak, Turkey 73 B8
Bulandshahr, India 68 E7
Bulanık, Turkey 73 C10
Bûlâq, Egypt 80 B3
Bulawayo, Zimbabwe 87 G2
Buldan, Turkey 47 C10
Bulgar, Russia 34 C9
Bulgaria ■, Europe 45 D9
Bulgheria, Monte, Italy 43 B8
Bulgurca, Turkey 47 C9
Buli, Teluk, Indonesia 63 D7
Buliluyan, C., Phil. 61 G2
Bulim, Singapore 65 d
Bulki, Ethiopia 81 F4
Bulkley →, Canada 102 B3
Bull Shoals L., U.S.A. 113 G8
Bullaque →, Spain 37 G6
Bullas, Spain 39 G3
Bulle, Switz. 25 J3
Bulleringa △, Australia 94 B3
Bullhead City, U.S.A. 111 K12
Büllingen, Belgium 17 D6
Bullock Creek, Australia 94 B3
Bulloo →, Australia 95 D3
Bulloo L., Australia 95 D3
Bulls, N.Z. 91 J5
Bully-les-Mines, France 19 B9
Bulnes, Chile 126 D1
Bulqizë, Albania 44 E4
Bulsar = Valsad, India 66 J8
Bultfontein, S. Africa 88 D4
Bulukumba, Indonesia 63 F6
Bulun, Russia 53 B13
Bumba, Dem. Rep. of the Congo 84 D4
Bumbeşti-Jiu, Romania 29 E8
Bumbiri I., Tanzania 86 C3
Bumbuna, S. Leone 82 D2
Bumhpa Bum, Burma 67 F20
Bumi →, Zimbabwe 87 F2
Buna, Kenya 86 B4
Bunawan, Phil. 61 G6
Bunazi, Tanzania 86 C3
Bunbury, Australia 93 F2
Bunclody, Ireland 12 D5
Buncrana, Ireland 12 A4
Bundaberg, Australia 95 C5
Bünde, Germany 24 C4
Bundey →, Australia 94 C2
Bundi, India 68 G6
Bundjalung △, Australia 95 D5
Bundoran, Ireland 12 B3
Bundukia, Sudan 81 F3
Bung Kan, Thailand 64 C4
Bunga →, Nigeria 83 C6
Bungay, U.K. 15 E9
Bungil Cr. →, Australia 95 D4
Bungle Bungle = Purnululu △, Australia 92 C4
Bungo-Suidō, Japan 55 H6
Bungoma, Kenya 86 B3
Bungotakada, Japan 55 H5
Bungu, Tanzania 86 D4
Bunia, Dem. Rep. of the Congo 86 B3
Bunji, Pakistan 69 B6
Bunkie, U.S.A. 113 K8
Bunnell, U.S.A. 115 L5
Buñol, Spain 39 F4
Bunsuru, Nigeria 83 C5
Buntok, Indonesia 62 E4
Bununu Dass, Nigeria 83 C6
Bununu Kasa, Nigeria 83 D6
Bunya Mts. △, Australia 95 D5
Bünyan, Turkey 72 C6
Bunyu, Indonesia 62 D5
Bunza, Nigeria 83 C5
Buol, Indonesia 63 D6
Buon Brieng, Vietnam 64 F7
Buon Ma Thuot, Vietnam 64 F7
Buong Long, Cambodia 64 F6
Buorkhaya, Mys, Russia 53 B14
Buqayq, Si. Arabia 71 E6
Buqbuq, Egypt 80 A2
Bur Acaba, Somali Rep. 75 G3
Bûr Fuad, Egypt 80 H8
Bûr Safâga, Egypt 70 E2
Bûr Sa'îd, Egypt 80 H8
Bûr Sûdân, Sudan 80 D4
Bûr Taufiq, Egypt 80 J8
Bura, Kenya 86 C4
Burakin, Australia 93 F2
Buram, Sudan 81 E2
Burao, Somali Rep. 75 F4
Burāq, Syria 74 B5
Buraydah, Si. Arabia 70 E4
Burbank, U.S.A. 111 L8
Burda, India 68 G6
Burdekin →, Australia 94 B4
Burdur, Turkey 47 D12
Burdur □, Turkey 47 D12
Burdur Gölü, Turkey 47 D12
Burdwan = Barddhaman, India 69 H12
Bure, Gojam, Ethiopia 81 E4
Bure, Ilubabor, Ethiopia 81 F4
Bure →, U.K. 14 E9
Büren, Germany 24 D4
Bureya →, Russia 53 E13
Burford, Canada 116 C4
Burg, Germany 24 C7
Burg auf Fehmarn, Germany 24 A7
Burg el Arab, Egypt 80 H6
Burg et Tuyur, Sudan 80 C2
Burg Stargard, Germany 24 B9
Burgas, Bulgaria 45 D11
Burgas □, Bulgaria 45 D10
Burgaski Zaliv, Bulgaria 45 D11
Burgdorf, Germany 24 C6
Burgdorf, Switz. 25 H3
Burgenland □, Austria 27 D9
Burgeo, Canada 105 C8
Burgersdorp, S. Africa 88 E4
Burges, Mt., Australia 93 F3
Burghausen, Germany 25 G8
Burghead, U.K. 13 D5
Búrgio, Italy 42 E6
Burglengenfeld, Germany 25 F8
Burgohondo, Spain 36 E6
Burgos, Spain 36 C7
Burgos □, Spain 36 C7
Burgstädt, Germany 24 E8
Burgsvik, Sweden 11 G12
Burguillos del Cerro, Spain 37 G4
Burgundy = Bourgogne □, France 19 F11
Burhaniye, Turkey 47 B8
Burhanpur, India 66 J10
Burhi Gandak →, India 69 G12
Burhner →, India 69 H9
Buri Pen., Eritrea 81 D4
Burias I., Phil. 61 E5
Burica, Pta., Costa Rica 120 E3
Burien, U.S.A. 110 C4
Burigi ⌂, Tanzania 86 C3
Burigi, L., Tanzania 86 C3
Burin, Canada 105 C8
Buriram, Thailand 64 E4
Burj Sāfitā, Syria 70 C3
Burji, Ethiopia 81 F4
Burkburnett, U.S.A. 113 H5
Burke →, Australia 94 C2
Burke Chan., Canada 102 C3
Burketown, Australia 94 B2
Burkina Faso ■, Africa 82 C4
Burk's Falls, Canada 104 C4
Burlada, Spain 38 C3
Burleigh Falls, Canada 116 B6
Burley, U.S.A. 108 E7
Burlingame, U.S.A. 110 H4
Burlington, Canada 116 C5
Burlington, Colo., U.S.A. 112 F3
Burlington, Iowa, U.S.A. 112 E9
Burlington, Kans., U.S.A. 112 F7
Burlington, N.C., U.S.A. 115 G6
Burlington, N.J., U.S.A. 117 F10
Burlington, Vt., U.S.A. 117 B11
Burlington, Wash., U.S.A. 110 B4
Burlington, Wis., U.S.A. 114 D1
Burlyu-Tyube, Kazakhstan 52 E8
Burma ■, Asia 67 J20
Burnaby I., Canada 102 C2
Burnet, U.S.A. 113 K5
Burney, U.S.A. 108 F3
Burnham, U.S.A. 116 F7
Burnham-on-Sea, U.K. 15 F5
Burnie, Australia 95 G4
Burnley, U.K. 14 D5
Burns, U.S.A. 108 E4
Burns Lake, Canada 102 C3
Burnside →, Canada 100 B9
Burnside, L., Australia 93 E3
Burnsville, U.S.A. 112 C8
Burnt, L., Canada 105 B7
Burnt River, Canada 116 B6
Burntwood →, Canada 103 B9
Burntwood L., Canada 103 B8
Burqān, Kuwait 70 D5
Burra, Australia 95 E2
Burra, Nigeria 83 C6
Burray, U.K. 13 C6
Burrel, Albania 44 E4
Burren △, Ireland 12 C3
Burren Junction, Australia 95 E4
Burriana, Spain 38 F4
Burrinjuck Res., Australia 95 F4
Burro, Serranías del, Mexico 118 B4
Burrow Hd., U.K. 13 G4
Burrum Coast △, Australia 95 D5
Burruyacú, Argentina 126 B3
Burry Port, U.K. 15 F3
Bursa, Turkey 45 F13
Burseryd, Sweden 11 G7
Burstall, Canada 103 C7
Burton, Ohio, U.S.A. 116 E3
Burton, S.C., U.S.A. 115 J5
Burton, L., Canada 104 B4
Burton upon Trent, U.K. 14 E6
Buru, Indonesia 63 E7
Burullus, Bahra el, Egypt 80 H7
Burûn, Râs, Egypt 74 D2
Burundi ■, Africa 86 C3
Bururi, Burundi 86 C2
Burutu, Nigeria 83 D6
Burwell, U.S.A. 112 E5
Burwick, U.K. 13 C5
Bury, U.K. 14 D5
Bury St. Edmunds, U.K. 15 E8
Buryatia □, Russia 53 D11
Buryn, Ukraine 33 G7
Burzenin, Poland 31 G5
Busalla, Italy 40 D5
Busan = Pusan, S. Korea 57 G15
Busango Swamp, Zambia 87 E2
Buşayrah, Syria 70 C4
Busca, Italy 40 D4
Bushat, Albania 44 E3
Būshehr, Iran 71 D6
Būshehr □, Iran 71 D6
Bushell, Canada 103 B7
Bushenyi, Uganda 86 C3
Bushire = Būshehr, Iran 71 D6
Bushtyna, Ukraine 29 B8
Busie, Ghana 82 C4
Businga, Dem. Rep. of the Congo 84 D4
Busko-Zdrój, Poland 31 H7
Busovača, Bos.-H. 28 F2
Buşra ash Shām, Syria 74 C5
Busselton, Australia 93 F2
Busseri →, Sudan 81 F2
Busseto, Italy 40 D7
Bussière-Badil, France 20 C4
Bussolengo, Italy 40 C7
Bussum, Neths. 17 B5
Buşteni, Romania 29 E10
Busto, C., Spain 36 B4
Busto Arsízio, Italy 40 C5
Busu Djanoa, Dem. Rep. of the Congo 84 D4
Busuanga I., Phil. 61 E3
Büsum, Germany 24 A4
Busungbiu, Indonesia 63 J17
Buta, Dem. Rep. of the Congo 86 B1
Butare, Rwanda 86 C2
Butaritari, Kiribati 96 G9
Bute, U.K. 13 F3
Bute Inlet, Canada 102 C4
Butemba, Uganda 86 B3
Butembo, Dem. Rep. of the Congo 86 B2
Buteni, Romania 28 D7
Butera, Italy 43 E7
Butha Qi, China 60 B7
Butiaba, Uganda 86 B3
Butler, Mo., U.S.A. 112 F7
Butler, Pa., U.S.A. 116 F5
Buton, Indonesia 63 E6
Butte, Mont., U.S.A. 108 C7
Butte, Nebr., U.S.A. 112 D5
Butte Creek →, U.S.A. 110 F5
Butterworth = Gcuwa, S. Africa 89 E4
Butterworth, Malaysia 65 c
Buttevant, Ireland 12 D3
Buttfield, Mt., Australia 93 D4
Button B., Canada 103 B10
Buttonwillow, U.S.A. 111 K7
Butty Hd., Australia 93 F3
Butuan, Phil. 61 G6
Butuku-Luba, Eq. Guin. 83 E6
Butung = Buton, Indonesia 63 E6
Buturlinovka, Russia 34 E5
Butzbach, Germany 25 E4
Bützow, Germany 24 B7
Buur Hakaba = Bur Acaba, Somali Rep. 75 G3
Buxa Duar, India 69 F13
Buxar, India 69 G10
Buxtehude, Germany 24 B5
Buxton, U.K. 14 D6
Buxy, France 19 F11
Buy, Russia 34 A5
Buynaksk, Russia 35 J8
Buyo, Ivory C. 82 D3
Buyo, L. de, Ivory C. 82 D3
Büyük Menderes →, Turkey 47 D9
Büyükçekmece, Turkey 45 E12
Büyükkarıştiran, Turkey 45 E11
Büyükkemikli Burnu, Turkey 45 F10
Büyükorhan, Turkey 47 B10
Büyükyoncalı, Turkey 45 E11
Buzançais, France 18 F8
Buzău, Romania 29 E11
Buzău □, Romania 29 E11
Buzău →, Romania 29 E12
Buzău, Pasul, Romania 29 E11
Buzen, Japan 55 H5
Buzet, Croatia 41 C10
Buzi →, Mozam. 87 F3
Buziaş, Romania 28 E6
Buzuluk, Russia 52 D6
Buzuluk →, Russia 34 E6
Buzzards B., U.S.A. 117 E14
Buzzards Bay, U.S.A. 117 E14
Bwana Mkubwe, Dem. Rep. of the Congo 87 E2
Bwindi △, Uganda 86 C2
Byala, Ruse, Bulgaria 45 C9
Byala, Varna, Bulgaria 45 D11
Byala Slatina, Bulgaria 44 C7
Byarezina →, Belarus 33 F6
Byaroza, Belarus 33 F3
Bychawa, Poland 31 G9
Byczyna, Poland 31 G5
Bydgoszcz, Poland 31 E5
Byelarus = Belarus ■, Europe 32 F4
Byelorussia = Belarus ■, Europe 32 F4
Byers, U.S.A. 112 F2
Byesville, U.S.A. 116 G3
Byfield △, Australia 94 C5
Byford, Australia 93 F2
Bykhaw, Belarus 32 F6
Bykhov = Bykhaw, Belarus 32 F6
Bykovo, Russia 34 F7
Bylas, U.S.A. 109 K8
Bylot, Canada 103 B10
Bylot I., Canada 101 A12
Byrd, C., Antarctica 5 C17
Byrock, Australia 95 E4
Byron, C., Australia 95 D5
Byron Bay, Australia 95 D5
Byrranga, Gory, Russia 53 B11
Byrranga Mts. = Byrranga, Gory, Russia 53 B11
Byrum, Denmark 11 G5
Byske, Sweden 8 D19
Byskeälven →, Sweden 8 D19
Bystrytsya, Ukraine 29 B9
Bystrzyca →, Dolnośląskie, Poland 31 G3
Bystrzyca →, Lubelskie, Poland 31 G9
Bystrzyca Kłodzka, Poland 31 H3
Bytča, Slovak Rep. 27 B11
Bytkiv, Ukraine 29 B9
Bytom, Poland 31 H5
Bytom Odrzański, Poland 31 G2
Bytów, Poland 30 D4
Byumba, Rwanda 86 C3
Bzenec, Czech Rep. 27 C10
Bzura →, Poland 31 F7

C

Ca →, Vietnam 64 C5
Ca Mau, Vietnam 65 H5
Ca Mau, Mui, Vietnam 65 H5
Ca Na, Vietnam 65 G7
Caacupé, Paraguay 126 B4
Caaguazú △, Paraguay 127 B4
Caála, Angola 85 G3
Caamaño Sd., Canada 102 C3
Caazapá, Paraguay 126 B4
Caazapá □, Paraguay 127 B4
Cabadbaran, Phil. 61 G6
Cabalian = San Juan, Phil. 61 F6
Caballeria, C. de, Spain 48 A11
Cabana, Spain 36 B2
Cabañaquinta, Spain 36 B5
Cabanatuan, Phil. 61 D4
Cabañeros ⌂, Spain 37 F6
Cabanes, Spain 38 E5
Cabano, Canada 105 C6
Čabar, Croatia 41 C11
Cabazon, U.S.A. 111 M10
Cabedelo, Brazil 125 E12
Cabeza del Buey, Spain 37 G5
Cabezón de la Sal, Spain 36 B6
Cabildo, Chile 126 C1
Cabimas, Venezuela 124 A4
Cabinda, Angola 84 F2
Cabinda □, Angola 84 F2
Cabinet Mts., U.S.A. 108 C6
Cabo Blanco, Argentina 128 F3
Cabo de Gata-Níjar ⌂, Spain 39 J2
Cabo Frio, Brazil 127 A7
Cabo Pantoja, Peru 124 D3
Cabonga, Réservoir, Canada 104 C4
Cabool, U.S.A. 113 G8
Caboolture, Australia 95 D5
Cabora Bassa Dam = Cahora Bassa, Represa de, Mozam. 87 F3
Caborca, Mexico 118 A2
Cabot, Mt., U.S.A. 117 B13
Cabot Hd., Canada 116 A3
Cabot Str., Canada 105 C8
Cabra, Spain 37 H6
Cabra del Santo Cristo, Spain 37 H7
Cábras, Italy 42 C1
Cabrera, Spain 48 B9
Cabrera △, Spain 39 F7
Cabrera, Sierra, Spain 36 C4
Cabri, Canada 103 C7
Cabriel →, Spain 39 F3
Cabugao, Phil. 61 C4
Cacabelos, Spain 36 C4
Caçador, Brazil 127 B5
Čačak, Serbia & M. 44 C4
Caçapava do Sul, Brazil 127 C5
Cáccamo, Italy 42 E6
Cacém, Portugal 37 G1
Cáceres, Brazil 124 G7
Cáceres, Spain 37 F4
Cáceres □, Spain 36 F5
Cache Bay, Canada 104 C4
Cache Cr. →, U.S.A. 110 G5
Cache Creek, Canada 102 C4
Cacheu, Guinea-Biss. 82 C1
Cachi, Argentina 126 B2
Cachimbo, Serra do, Brazil 125 E7
Cachinal de la Sierra, Chile 126 A2
Cachoeira, Brazil 125 F11
Cachoeira do Sul, Brazil 127 C5
Cachoeiro de Itapemirim, Brazil 127 A7
Cachopo, Portugal 37 H3
Cacine, Guinea-Biss. 82 C1
Cacoal, Brazil 124 F6
Cacólo, Angola 84 G3
Caconda, Angola 85 G3
Čadca, Slovak Rep. 27 B11
Caddo, U.S.A. 113 H6
Cader Idris, U.K. 15 E4
Cadereyta, Mexico 118 B5
Cadí, Sierra del, Spain 38 C6
Cadí-Moixeró ⌂, Spain 38 C3
Cadibarrawirracanna, L., Australia 95 D2
Cadillac, France 20 D3
Cadillac, U.S.A. 114 C3
Cadiz, Phil. 61 F5
Cádiz, Spain 37 J4
Cadiz, Calif., U.S.A. 111 L11
Cadiz, Ohio, U.S.A. 116 F4
Cádiz □, Spain 37 J5
Cádiz, G. de, Spain 37 J3
Cadiz L., U.S.A. 109 J6
Cadney Park, Australia 95 D1
Cadomin, Canada 102 C5
Cadotte Lake, Canada 102 B5
Cadours, France 20 E5
Cadoux, Australia 93 F2
Caen, France 18 C6
Caernarfon, U.K. 14 D3
Caernarfon B., U.K. 14 D3
Caernarvon = Caernarfon, U.K. 14 D3
Caerphilly, U.K. 15 F4
Caerphilly □, U.K. 15 F4
Caesarea, Israel 74 C3
Caetité, Brazil 125 F10
Cafayate, Argentina 126 B2
Cafu, Angola 88 B2
Cagayan →, Phil. 61 B4
Cagayan de Oro, Phil. 61 G6
Cagayan Is., Phil. 61 G4
Cagayan Sulu I., Phil. 61 H3
Cagli, Italy 41 E9
Cágliari, Italy 42 C2
Cágliari, G. di, Italy 42 C2
Cagnano Varano, Italy 41 G12
Cagnes-sur-Mer, France 21 E11
Caguán →, Colombia 124 D4
Caguas, Puerto Rico 121 d
Caha Mts., Ireland 12 E2
Cahama, Angola 88 B1
Caher, Ireland 12 D4
Caherciveen, Ireland 12 E1
Cahora Bassa, L. de, Mozam. 87 F3
Cahora Bassa, Represa de, Mozam. 87 F3
Cahore Pt., Ireland 12 D5
Cahors, France 20 D5
Cahul, Moldova 29 E13
Cai Bau, Dao, Vietnam 58 G6
Cai Nuoc, Vietnam 65 H5
Caia, Mozam. 87 F4
Caianda, Angola 87 E1
Caibarién, Cuba 120 B4
Caibiran, Phil. 61 F6
Caicara, Venezuela 124 B5
Caicó, Brazil 125 E11
Caicos Is., Turks & Caicos 121 B5
Caicos Passage, W. Indies 121 B5
Caidian, China 59 B10
Căinari, Moldova 29 D14
Caird Coast, Antarctica 5 D1
Cairn Gorm, U.K. 13 D5
Cairngorm Mts., U.K. 13 D5
Cairngorms △, U.K. 13 D5
Cairnryan, U.K. 13 G3
Cairns, Australia 94 B4
Cairns L., Canada 103 C10
Cairo = El Qâhira, Egypt 80 H7
Cairo, Ga., U.S.A. 115 K3
Cairo, Ill., U.S.A. 113 G10
Cairo, N.Y., U.S.A. 117 D11
Cairo Montenotte, Italy 40 D5
Caithness, U.K. 13 C5
Caithness, Ord of, U.K. 13 C5
Caja de Muertos, I., Puerto Rico 121 d
Cajamarca, Peru 124 E3
Cajarc, France 20 D5
Cajàzeiras, Brazil 125 E11
Čajetina, Serbia & M. 44 C3
Çakirgol, Turkey 73 B8
Çakırlar, Turkey 47 E12
Čakovec, Croatia 41 B13
Çal, Turkey 47 C11
Cala, Spain 37 H4
Cala →, Spain 37 H4
Cala Cadolar, Punta de = Rotja, Pta., Spain 39 G6
Cala d'Or, Spain 48 B10
Cala en Porter, Spain 48 B11
Cala Figuera, C. de, Spain 48 B9
Cala Forcat, Spain 48 B10
Cala Major, Spain 48 B9
Cala Mezquida = Sa Mesquida, Spain 48 B11
Cala Millor, Spain 48 B10
Cala Ratjada, Spain 48 B10
Cala Santa Galdana, Spain 48 B10
Calabanga, Phil. 61 E5
Calabar, Nigeria 83 E6
Calabogie, Canada 117 A8
Calabozo, Venezuela 124 B5
Calábria □, Italy 43 C9
Calábria △, Italy 43 C9
Calaburras, Pta. de, Spain 37 J6
Calaceite, Spain 38 D5
Calacuccia, France 21 F13
Calafat, Romania 28 G7
Calafate, Argentina 128 G2
Calafell, Spain 38 D6
Calahorra, Spain 38 C3
Calais, France 19 B8
Calais, U.S.A. 115 C12
Calakmul ⌂, Mexico 119 D7
Calalaste, Cord. de, Argentina 126 B2
Calama, Brazil 124 E6
Calama, Chile 126 A2
Calamar, Colombia 124 A4
Calamian Group, Phil. 61 F3
Calamocha, Spain 38 E3
Calamonte, Spain 37 G4
Călan, Romania 28 E7
Calañas, Spain 37 H4
Calanda, Spain 38 E4
Calang, Indonesia 62 D1
Calangiánus, Italy 42 B2
Calapan, Phil. 61 E4
Călărasi, Moldova 29 C13
Călăraşi, Romania 29 F12
Călăraşi □, Romania 29 F12
Calasparra, Spain 39 G3
Calatafimi, Italy 42 E5
Calatayud, Spain 38 D3
Călăţele, Romania 28 D8
Calato = Kálathos, Greece 47 E10
Calauag, Phil. 61 E5
Calavà, C., Italy 43 D7
Calavite, C., Phil. 61 E4
Calayan, Phil. 61 B4
Calbayog, Phil. 61 E6
Calca, Peru 124 F4
Calcasieu L., U.S.A. 113 L8
Calcutta = Kolkata, India 69 H13
Caldaro, Italy 41 B8
Caldas da Rainha, Portugal 37 F1
Caldas de Reis, Spain 36 C2
Calder →, U.K. 14 D6
Caldera, Chile 126 B1

Caldera de Taburiente △, Canary Is. ... 48 F2
Caldwell, Idaho, U.S.A. ... 108 E5
Caldwell, Kans., U.S.A. ... 113 G6
Caldwell, Tex., U.S.A. ... 113 K6
Caledon, S. Africa ... 88 E2
Caledon →, S. Africa ... 88 E4
Caledon B., Australia ... 94 A2
Caledonia, Canada ... 116 C5
Caledonia, U.S.A. ... 116 D7
Calella, Spain ... 38 D7
Calemba, Angola ... 88 B2
Calen, Australia ... 94 J6
Calenzana, France ... 21 F12
Caletones, Chile ... 126 C1
Calexico, U.S.A. ... 111 N11
Calf of Man, I. of Man ... 14 C3
Calgary, Canada ... 102 C6
Calheta, Madeira ... 48 D2
Calhoun, U.S.A. ... 115 H3
Cali, Colombia ... 124 C3
Calicut, India ... 66 P9
Caliente, U.S.A. ... 109 H6
California, Mo., U.S.A. ... 112 F8
California, Pa., U.S.A. ... 116 F5
California □, U.S.A. ... 110 H7
California, Baja, Mexico ... 118 A1
California, Baja, T.N. = Baja California □, Mexico ... 118 B2
California, Baja, T.S. = Baja California Sur □, Mexico ... 118 B2
California, G. de, Mexico ... 118 B2
California City, U.S.A. ... 111 K9
California Hot Springs, U.S.A. ... 111 K8
Calilegua △, Argentina ... 126 B3
Călimănești, Romania ... 29 E9
Călimani, Munții, Romania ... 29 C10
Calingasta, Argentina ... 126 C2
Calipatria, U.S.A. ... 111 M11
Calistoga, U.S.A. ... 110 G4
Calitri, Italy ... 43 B8
Calitzdorp, S. Africa ... 88 E3
Callabonna, L., Australia ... 95 D3
Callac, France ... 18 D3
Callan, Ireland ... 12 D4
Callander, U.K. ... 13 E4
Callao, Peru ... 124 F3
Calles, Mexico ... 119 C5
Callicoon, U.S.A. ... 117 E9
Calling Lake, Canada ... 102 B6
Calliope, Australia ... 94 C5
Callosa de Ensarriá, Spain ... 39 G4
Callosa de Segura, Spain ... 39 G4
Calne, U.K. ... 15 F6
Calola, Angola ... 88 B2
Calolbon = San Andres, Phil. ... 61 E6
Calonge, Spain ... 38 D8
Caloocan, Phil. ... 61 D4
Calore →, Italy ... 43 A7
Caloundra, Australia ... 95 D5
Calpe, Spain ... 39 G5
Calpella, U.S.A. ... 110 F3
Calpine, U.S.A. ... 110 F6
Calstock, Canada ... 104 C3
Caltabellotta, Italy ... 42 E6
Caltagirone, Italy ... 43 E7
Caltanissetta, Italy ... 43 E7
Çaltılıbük, Turkey ... 45 G12
Caluire-et-Cuire, France ... 19 G11
Calulo, Angola ... 84 G2
Caluso, Italy ... 40 C4
Calvados □, France ... 18 C6
Calvert →, Australia ... 94 B2
Calvert I., Canada ... 102 C3
Calvert Ra., Australia ... 92 D3
Calvi, France ... 21 F12
Calviá, Spain ... 39 F7
Calvillo, Mexico ... 118 C4
Calvinia, S. Africa ... 88 E2
Calvo, Mte., Italy ... 41 G12
Calwa, U.S.A. ... 110 J7
Calzada Almuradiel = Almuradiel, Spain ... 37 G7
Calzada de Calatrava, Spain ... 37 G7
Cam →, U.K. ... 15 E8
Cam Lam, Vietnam ... 65 G7
Cam Pha, Vietnam ... 58 G6
Cam Ranh, Vietnam ... 65 G7
Cam Xuyen, Vietnam ... 64 C6
Camabatela, Angola ... 84 F3
Camacha, Madeira ... 48 D3
Camacho, Mexico ... 118 C4
Camacupa, Angola ... 85 G3
Camagüey, Cuba ... 120 B4
Camaiore, Italy ... 40 E7
Camaná, Peru ... 124 G4
Camanche Reservoir, U.S.A. ... 110 G6
Camaquã, Brazil ... 127 C5
Camaquã →, Brazil ... 127 C5
Câmara de Lobos, Madeira ... 48 D3
Camarat, C., France ... 21 E10
Camaret-sur-Mer, France ... 18 D2
Camargo, Mexico ... 119 B5
Camargue, France ... 21 E8
Camargue △, France ... 21 E8
Camarillo, U.S.A. ... 111 L7
Camariñas, Spain ... 36 B1
Camarón, C., Honduras ... 120 C2
Camarones, Argentina ... 128 E3
Camas, Spain ... 37 H4
Camas, U.S.A. ... 110 E4
Camas Valley, U.S.A. ... 108 E2
Camballin, Australia ... 92 C3
Cambará, Brazil ... 127 A5
Cambay = Khambhat, India ... 68 H5
Cambay, G. of = Khambhat, G. of, India ... 66 J8
Cambil, Spain ... 37 H7
Cambo-les-Bains, France ... 20 E2
Cambodia ■, Asia ... 64 F5
Camborne, U.K. ... 15 G2

Cambrai, France ... 19 B10
Cambre, Spain ... 36 B2
Cambria, U.S.A. ... 110 K5
Cambrian Mts., U.K. ... 15 E4
Cambridge, Canada ... 116 C4
Cambridge, Jamaica ... 120 a
Cambridge, N.Z. ... 91 G5
Cambridge, U.K. ... 15 E8
Cambridge, Mass., U.S.A. ... 117 D13
Cambridge, Minn., U.S.A. ... 112 C8
Cambridge, N.Y., U.S.A. ... 117 C11
Cambridge, Nebr., U.S.A. ... 112 E4
Cambridge, Ohio, U.S.A. ... 116 F3
Cambridge Bay = Ikaluktutiak, Canada ... 100 B9
Cambridge G., Australia ... 92 B4
Cambridge Springs, U.S.A. ... 116 E4
Cambridgeshire □, U.K. ... 15 E7
Cambrils, Spain ... 38 D6
Cambuci, Brazil ... 127 A7
Cambundi-Catembo, Angola ... 84 G3
Camden, Ala., U.S.A. ... 115 K2
Camden, Ark., U.S.A. ... 113 J8
Camden, Maine, U.S.A. ... 115 C11
Camden, N.J., U.S.A. ... 117 G9
Camden, N.Y., U.S.A. ... 117 C9
Camden, S.C., U.S.A. ... 115 H5
Camden Sd., Australia ... 92 C3
Camdenton, U.S.A. ... 113 F8
Camelford, U.K. ... 15 G3
Çameli, Turkey ... 47 D11
Camenca, Moldova ... 29 D13
Camerino, Italy ... 41 E10
Cameron, Ariz., U.S.A. ... 109 J8
Cameron, La., U.S.A. ... 113 L8
Cameron, Mo., U.S.A. ... 112 F7
Cameron, Tex., U.S.A. ... 113 K6
Cameron Highlands, Malaysia ... 65 K3
Cameron Hills, Canada ... 102 B5
Cameroon ■, Africa ... 79 G7
Camerota, Italy ... 43 B8
Cameroun →, Cameroon ... 83 E6
Cameroun, Mt., Cameroon ... 83 E6
Cametá, Brazil ... 125 D9
Çamiçi Gölü, Turkey ... 47 D9
Camiguin □, Phil. ... 61 G6
Camiguin I., Phil. ... 61 B4
Camiling, Phil. ... 61 D4
Camilla, U.S.A. ... 115 K3
Caminha, Portugal ... 36 D2
Camino, U.S.A. ... 110 G6
Camira Creek, Australia ... 95 D5
Cammal, U.S.A. ... 116 E7
Camocim, Brazil ... 125 D10
Camooweal, Australia ... 94 B2
Camooweal Caves △, Australia ... 94 C2
Camopi, Fr. Guiana ... 125 C8
Camotes Is., Phil. ... 61 F6
Camotes Sea, Phil. ... 61 F6
Camp Borden, Canada ... 116 B5
Camp Hill, U.S.A. ... 116 F8
Camp Nelson, U.S.A. ... 111 J8
Camp Pendleton, U.S.A. ... 111 M9
Camp Verde, U.S.A. ... 109 J8
Camp Wood, U.S.A. ... 113 L5
Campagna, Italy ... 43 B8
Campana, Argentina ... 126 C4
Campana, Madeira ... 48 D2
Campana, I., Chile ... 128 F1
Campanário, Madeira ... 48 D2
Campanario, Spain ... 37 G5
Campánia □, Italy ... 43 B7
Campbell, S. Africa ... 88 D3
Campbell, Calif., U.S.A. ... 110 H5
Campbell, Ohio, U.S.A. ... 116 E4
Campbell I., Pac. Oc. ... 96 N8
Campbell L., Canada ... 103 A7
Campbell River, Canada ... 102 C3
Campbell Town, Australia ... 95 G4
Campbellford, Canada ... 116 B7
Campbellpur, Pakistan ... 68 C5
Campbellsville, U.S.A. ... 114 G3
Campbellton, Canada ... 105 C6
Campbelltown, Australia ... 95 E5
Campbeltown, U.K. ... 13 F3
Campeche, Mexico ... 119 D6
Campeche □, Mexico ... 119 D6
Campeche, Golfo de, Mexico ... 119 D6
Campello, Spain ... 39 G4
Camperdown, Australia ... 95 F3
Camperville, Canada ... 103 C8
Campi Salentina, Italy ... 43 B11
Câmpia Turzii, Romania ... 29 D8
Campidano, Italy ... 42 C1
Campíglia Maríttima, Italy ... 40 E7
Campillo de Altobuey, Spain ... 39 F3
Campillos, Spain ... 37 H6
Câmpina, Romania ... 29 E10
Campina Grande, Brazil ... 125 E11
Campinas, Brazil ... 127 A6
Campli, Italy ... 41 F10
Campo, Spain ... 38 C5
Campo de Criptana, Spain ... 37 F7
Campo de Gibraltar, Spain ... 37 J5
Campo Grande, Brazil ... 125 H8
Campo Maior, Brazil ... 125 D10
Campo Maior, Portugal ... 37 F3
Campo Mourão, Brazil ... 127 A5
Campo Túres, Italy ... 41 B8
Campobasso, Italy ... 43 A7
Campobello di Licata, Italy ... 42 E6
Campobello di Mazara, Italy ... 42 E5
Campofelice di Roccella, Italy ... 42 E6
Campomarino, Italy ... 41 G12
Camporeale, Italy ... 42 E6
Camporrobles, Spain ... 38 F3
Campos, Brazil ... 127 A7
Campos Belos, Brazil ... 125 F9
Campos del Port, Spain ... 48 B10
Campos Novos, Brazil ... 127 B5
Camprodón, Spain ... 38 C7

Camptonville, U.S.A. ... 110 F5
Camptown, U.S.A. ... 117 E8
Câmpulung, Argeş, Romania ... 29 E10
Câmpulung, Suceava, Romania ... 29 C10
Câmpuri, Romania ... 29 D11
Camrose, Canada ... 102 C6
Camsell Portage, Canada ... 103 B7
Çamyuva, Turkey ... 47 E12
Can, Turkey ... 45 F11
Can Clavo, Spain ... 48 C7
Can Creu, Spain ... 48 C7
Can Gio, Vietnam ... 65 G6
Can Tho, Vietnam ... 65 G5
Canaan, U.S.A. ... 117 D11
Canada ■, N. Amer. ... 100 C10
Canada Basin, Arctic ... 4 B18
Cañada de Gómez, Argentina ... 126 C3
Canadian, U.S.A. ... 113 H4
Canadian →, U.S.A. ... 113 H7
Canajoharie, U.S.A. ... 117 D10
Çanakkale, Turkey ... 45 F10
Çanakkale □, Turkey ... 45 F10
Çanakkale Boğazı, Turkey ... 45 F10
Canal Flats, Canada ... 102 C5
Canalejas, Argentina ... 126 D2
Canals, Argentina ... 126 C3
Canals, Spain ... 39 G4
Canandaigua, U.S.A. ... 116 D7
Canandaigua L., U.S.A. ... 116 D7
Cananea, Mexico ... 118 A2
Canarias, Is., Atl. Oc. ... 48 F4
Canaries, St. Lucia ... 121 f
Canarreos, Arch. de los, Cuba ... 120 B3
Canary Is. = Canarias, Is., Atl. Oc. ... 48 F4
Canaseraga, U.S.A. ... 116 D7
Canatlán, Mexico ... 118 C4
Canaveral, U.S.A. ... 115 L5
Canaveral, C., U.S.A. ... 115 L5
Cañaveruelas, Spain ... 38 E2
Canavieiras, Brazil ... 125 G11
Canberra, Australia ... 95 F4
Canby, Calif., U.S.A. ... 108 F3
Canby, Minn., U.S.A. ... 112 C6
Canby, Oreg., U.S.A. ... 110 E4
Cancale, France ... 18 D5
Canche →, France ... 19 B8
Cancún, Mexico ... 119 C7
Candanchu, Spain ... 38 C4
Çandarlı, Turkey ... 47 C8
Çandarlı Körfezi, Turkey ... 47 C8
Candas, Spain ... 36 B5
Candé, France ... 18 E5
Candela, Italy ... 43 A8
Candelaria, Argentina ... 127 B4
Candelaria, Canary Is. ... 48 F3
Candelario △, Spain ... 36 E5
Candeleda, Spain ... 36 E5
Candelo, Australia ... 95 F4
Candi Dasa, Indonesia ... 63 J18
Candia = Iráklion, Greece ... 49 D7
Candia, Sea of = Crete, Sea of, Greece ... 47 E7
Candle L., Canada ... 103 C7
Candlemas I., Antarctica ... 5 B1
Cando, U.S.A. ... 112 A5
Canea = Khaniá, Greece ... 49 D6
Canelli, Italy ... 40 D5
Canelones, Uruguay ... 127 C4
Canet-Plage, France ... 20 F7
Cañete, Chile ... 126 D1
Cañete, Peru ... 124 F3
Cañete, Spain ... 38 E3
Cañete de las Torres, Spain ... 37 H6
Cangas, Spain ... 36 C2
Cangas de Narcea, Spain ... 36 B4
Cangas de Onís, Spain ... 36 B5
Cangnan, China ... 59 D13
Canguaretama, Brazil ... 125 E11
Canguçu, Brazil ... 127 C5
Canguçu, Serra do, Brazil ... 127 C5
Cangwu, China ... 59 F8
Cangxi, China ... 58 B5
Cangyuan, China ... 58 F2
Cangzhou, China ... 56 E9
Caniapiscau →, Canada ... 105 A6
Caniapiscau, L. de, Canada ... 105 B6
Canicattì, Italy ... 42 E6
Canicattini Bagni, Italy ... 43 E8
Caniles, Spain ... 37 H8
Canim Lake, Canada ... 102 C4
Canindeyu □, Paraguay ... 127 A5
Canino, Italy ... 41 F8
Canisteo, U.S.A. ... 116 D7
Canisteo →, U.S.A. ... 116 D7
Canmore, Canada ... 102 C5
Cann River, Australia ... 95 F4
Canna, U.K. ... 13 D2
Cannanore, India ... 66 P9
Cannes, France ... 21 E11
Canning Town = Port Canning, India ... 69 H13
Cannington, Canada ... 116 B5
Cannóbio, Italy ... 40 B5
Cannock, U.K. ... 15 E5
Cannon Ball →, U.S.A. ... 112 B4
Cannondale Mt., Australia ... 94 D4
Cannonsville Reservoir, U.S.A. ... 117 D9
Cannonvale, Australia ... 94 J6
Canoas, Brazil ... 127 B5
Canoe L., Canada ... 103 B7
Canon City, U.S.A. ... 108 G2
Cañón de Rio Blanco △, Mexico ... 119 D5
Cañón del Río Lobos △, Spain ... 36 D7
Cañón del Sumidero △, Mexico ... 119 D5
Canora, Canada ... 103 C8
Canosa di Púglia, Italy ... 43 A9

Canowindra, Australia ... 95 E4
Canso, Canada ... 105 C7
Cantabria □, Spain ... 36 B7
Cantabria, Sierra de, Spain ... 38 C2
Cantabrian Mts. = Cantábrica, Cordillera, Spain ... 36 C5
Cantábrica, Cordillera, Spain ... 36 C5
Cantal, Plomb du, France ... 20 C6
Cantanhede, Portugal ... 36 E2
Cantavieja, Spain ... 38 E4
Cantavir, Serbia & M. ... 28 E4
Cantemir, Moldova ... 29 D13
Canterbury, Australia ... 94 D3
Canterbury □, N.Z. ... 91 K3
Canterbury, U.K. ... 15 F9
Canterbury Bight, N.Z. ... 91 L3
Canterbury Plains, N.Z. ... 91 K3
Cantil, U.S.A. ... 111 K9
Cantillana, Spain ... 37 H5
Canton = Guangzhou, China ... 59 F9
Canton, Ga., U.S.A. ... 115 H3
Canton, Ill., U.S.A. ... 112 E9
Canton, Miss., U.S.A. ... 113 J9
Canton, Mo., U.S.A. ... 112 E9
Canton, N.Y., U.S.A. ... 117 B9
Canton, Ohio, U.S.A. ... 116 F3
Canton, Pa., U.S.A. ... 116 E8
Canton, S. Dak., U.S.A. ... 112 D6
Canton L., U.S.A. ... 113 G5
Cantù, Italy ... 40 C6
Canudos, Brazil ... 124 E7
Canumã →, Brazil ... 124 D7
Canutama, Brazil ... 124 E6
Canutillo, U.S.A. ... 109 L10
Canvey, U.K. ... 15 F8
Canyon, U.S.A. ... 113 H4
Canyon De Chelly △, U.S.A. ... 109 H9
Canyon of the Ancients △, U.S.A. ... 109 H9
Canyonlands △, U.S.A. ... 109 G9
Canyonville, U.S.A. ... 108 E2
Cao Bang, Vietnam ... 58 F6
Cao He →, China ... 57 D13
Cao Lanh, Vietnam ... 65 G5
Cao Xian, China ... 56 G8
Cáorle, Italy ... 41 C9
Cap-aux-Meules, Canada ... 105 C7
Cap-Chat, Canada ... 105 C6
Cap-de-la-Madeleine, Canada ... 104 C5
Cap-Haïtien, Haiti ... 121 C5
Cap Pt., St. Lucia ... 121 f
Capac, U.S.A. ... 116 C2
Capáccio, Italy ... 43 B8
Capaci, Italy ... 42 D6
Capanaparo →, Venezuela ... 124 B5
Capánnori, Italy ... 40 E7
Capbreton, France ... 20 E2
Capdenac, France ... 20 D6
Capdepera, Spain ... 38 F8
Cape →, Australia ... 94 C4
Cape Arid △, Australia ... 93 F3
Cape Barren I., Australia ... 95 G4
Cape Breton Highlands △, Canada ... 105 C7
Cape Breton I., Canada ... 105 C7
Cape Charles, U.S.A. ... 114 G8
Cape Coast, Ghana ... 83 D4
Cape Cod △, U.S.A. ... 114 E10
Cape Coral, U.S.A. ... 115 M5
Cape Dorset, Canada ... 101 B12
Cape Fear →, U.S.A. ... 115 H6
Cape Girardeau, U.S.A. ... 113 G10
Cape Hatteras △, U.S.A. ... 115 H8
Cape Lee △, Australia ... 93 F3
Cape Lookout △, U.S.A. ... 115 H7
Cape May, U.S.A. ... 114 F8
Cape May Point, U.S.A. ... 114 F8
Cape Melville △, Australia ... 94 A3
Cape Mount △, Liberia ... 82 D2
Cape Peninsula △, S. Africa ... 88 E2
Cape Range △, Australia ... 92 D1
Cape Tormentine, Canada ... 105 C7
Cape Town, S. Africa ... 88 E2
Cape Tribulation △, Australia ... 94 B4
Cape Verde Is. ■, Atl. Oc. ... 77 E1
Cape Vincent, U.S.A. ... 117 B8
Cape York Peninsula, Australia ... 94 A3
Capela, Brazil ... 125 F11
Capella, Australia ... 94 C4
Capendu, France ... 20 E6
Capestang, France ... 20 E7
Capesterre-Belle-Eau, Guadeloupe ... 120 b
Capesterre-de-Marie-Galante, Guadeloupe ... 120 b
Capim →, Brazil ... 125 D9
Capistrello, Italy ... 41 G10
Capitan, U.S.A. ... 109 K11
Capitol Reef △, U.S.A. ... 109 G8
Capitola, U.S.A. ... 110 J5
Capizzi, Italy ... 43 E7
Capoche →, Mozam. ... 87 F3
Capodichino, Nápoli ✈ (NAP), Italy ... 43 B7
Capoterra, Italy ... 42 C1
Cappadocia, Turkey ... 72 C6
Capraia, Italy ... 40 E6
Caprara, Pta., Italy ... 42 A1
Caprarola, Italy ... 41 F9
Capreol, Canada ... 104 C3
Caprera, Italy ... 42 A2
Capri, Italy ... 43 B7
Capricorn Group, Australia ... 94 C5
Capricorn Ra., Australia ... 92 D2
Caprino Veronese, Italy ... 40 C7
Caprivi Game △, Namibia ... 88 B3
Caprivi Strip, Namibia ... 88 B3
Caps et Marais d'Opale △, France ... 19 B9
Captain's Flat, Australia ... 95 F4
Captieux, France ... 20 D3
Capulin Volcano △, U.S.A. ... 113 G3

Caracal, Romania ... 29 F9
Caracas, Venezuela ... 124 A5
Caracol, Mato Grosso do Sul, Brazil ... 126 A4
Caracol, Piauí, Brazil ... 125 E10
Caráglio, Italy ... 40 D4
Carajás, Brazil ... 125 E8
Carajás, Serra dos, Brazil ... 125 E8
Carangola, Brazil ... 127 A7
Caransebeş, Romania ... 28 E7
Carantec, France ... 18 D3
Caraquet, Canada ... 105 C6
Caraş Severin □, Romania ... 28 E7
Caraşova, Romania ... 28 E6
Caratasca, L., Honduras ... 120 C3
Caratinga, Brazil ... 125 G10
Caraúbas, Brazil ... 125 E11
Caravaca de la Cruz, Spain ... 39 G3
Caravággio, Italy ... 40 C6
Caravela, Guinea-Biss. ... 82 C1
Caravelas, Brazil ... 125 G11
Caraveli, Peru ... 124 G4
Caravelle, Presqu'île de la, Martinique ... 120 c
Caràzinho, Brazil ... 127 B5
Carballino = O Carballiño, Spain ... 36 C2
Carballo, Spain ... 36 B2
Carberry, Canada ... 103 D9
Carbó, Mexico ... 118 B2
Carbonara, C., Italy ... 42 C2
Carbondale, Colo., U.S.A. ... 108 G10
Carbondale, Ill., U.S.A. ... 113 G10
Carbondale, Pa., U.S.A. ... 117 E9
Carbonear, Canada ... 105 C9
Carboneras, Spain ... 39 J3
Carboneras de Guadazón, Spain ... 38 F3
Carbónia, Italy ... 42 C1
Carcabuey, Spain ... 37 H6
Carcagente = Carcaixent, Spain ... 39 F4
Carcaixent, Spain ... 39 F4
Carcajou, Canada ... 102 B5
Carcar, Phil. ... 61 F5
Carcarana →, Argentina ... 126 C3
Carcasse, C., Haiti ... 121 C5
Carcassonne, France ... 20 E6
Carcross, Canada ... 102 A2
Çardak, Çanakkale, Turkey ... 45 F10
Çardak, Denizli, Turkey ... 47 D11
Cardamon Hills, India ... 66 Q10
Cardeña, Spain ... 37 G6
Cárdenas, Cuba ... 120 B3
Cárdenas, San Luis Potosí, Mexico ... 119 C5
Cárdenas, Tabasco, Mexico ... 119 D6
Cardenete, Spain ... 38 F3
Cardiff, U.K. ... 15 F4
Cardiff □, U.K. ... 15 F4
Cardiff-by-the-Sea, U.S.A. ... 111 M9
Cardigan, U.K. ... 15 E3
Cardigan B., U.K. ... 15 E3
Cardinal, Canada ... 117 B9
Cardona, Spain ... 38 D6
Cardona, Uruguay ... 126 C4
Cardoner →, Spain ... 38 D6
Cardoso, Ilha do, Brazil ... 127 B5
Cardston, Canada ... 102 D6
Cardwell, Australia ... 94 B4
Careen L., Canada ... 103 B7
Carei, Romania ... 28 C7
Careme = Ciremay, Indonesia ... 63 G13
Carentan, France ... 18 C5
Carey, U.S.A. ... 108 E7
Carey, L., Australia ... 93 E3
Carey L., Canada ... 103 A8
Careysburg, Liberia ... 82 D2
Cargèse, France ... 21 F12
Carhaix-Plouguer, France ... 18 D3
Carhué, Argentina ... 126 D3
Caria, Turkey ... 47 D10
Cariacica, Brazil ... 125 H10
Cariati, Italy ... 43 C9
Caribbean Sea, W. Indies ... 121 D5
Cariboo Mts., Canada ... 102 C4
Caribou, U.S.A. ... 115 B12
Caribou →, Man., Canada ... 103 B10
Caribou →, N.W.T., Canada ... 102 A3
Caribou I., Canada ... 104 C2
Caribou Is., Canada ... 102 A6
Caribou L., Man., Canada ... 103 B9
Caribou L., Ont., Canada ... 104 B2
Caribou Mts., Canada ... 102 B5
Caribou River △, Canada ... 103 B9
Caribrod = Dimitrovgrad, Serbia & M. ... 44 C6
Carichic, Mexico ... 118 B3
Carigara, Phil. ... 61 F6
Carignan, France ... 19 C12
Carignano, Italy ... 40 D4
Carillo, Mexico ... 118 B4
Carinda, Australia ... 95 E4
Cariñena, Spain ... 38 D3
Carinhanha, Brazil ... 125 F10
Carinhanha →, Brazil ... 125 F10
Carini, Italy ... 42 D6
Cariño, Spain ... 36 B3
Carínola, Italy ... 42 A6
Carinthia = Kärnten □, Austria ... 26 E7
Caripito, Venezuela ... 124 A6
Carlet, Spain ... 39 F4
Carleton, Mt., Canada ... 105 C6
Carleton Place, Canada ... 117 A8
Carletonville, S. Africa ... 88 D4
Cârlibaba, Romania ... 29 C10
Carlin, U.S.A. ... 108 F5
Carlingford L., U.K. ... 12 B5
Carlinville, U.S.A. ... 112 F10
Carlisle, U.K. ... 14 C5
Carlisle, U.S.A. ... 116 F7
Carlisle B., Barbados ... 121 g
Carlisle I., Australia ... 94 J7
Carlit, Pic, France ... 20 F5

Carloforte, *Italy* 42 C1
Carlos Casares, *Argentina* 126 D3
Carlos Tejedor, *Argentina* 126 D3
Carlow, *Ireland* 12 D5
Carlow □, *Ireland* 12 D5
Carlsbad, *Calif., U.S.A.* 111 M9
Carlsbad, *N. Mex., U.S.A.* 113 J2
Carlsbad Caverns △, *U.S.A.* ... 113 J2
Carluke, *U.K.* 13 F5
Carlyle, *Canada* 103 D8
Carmacks, *Canada* 100 B6
Carmagnola, *Italy* 40 D4
Carman, *Canada* 103 D9
Carmarthen, *U.K.* 15 F3
Carmarthen B., *U.K.* 15 F3
Carmarthenshire □, *U.K.* 15 F3
Carmaux, *France* 20 D6
Carmel, *U.S.A.* 117 E10
Carmel-by-the-Sea, *U.S.A.* 110 J5
Carmel Valley, *U.S.A.* 110 J5
Carmelo, *Uruguay* 126 C4
Carmen, *Colombia* 124 B3
Carmen, *Paraguay* 127 B4
Carmen →, *Mexico* 118 A3
Carmen, I., *Mexico* 118 B2
Carmen de Patagones, *Argentina* 128 A4
Cármenes, *Spain* 36 C5
Carmensa, *Argentina* 126 D2
Carmi, *Canada* 102 D5
Carmi, *U.S.A.* 114 F1
Carmichael, *U.S.A.* 110 G5
Carmila, *Australia* 94 C4
Carmona, *Costa Rica* 120 E2
Carmona, *Spain* 37 H5
Carn Ban, *U.K.* 13 D4
Carn Eige, *U.K.* 13 D3
Carnamah, *Australia* 93 E2
Carnarvon, *Australia* 93 D1
Carnarvon, *S. Africa* 88 E3
Carnarvon △, *Australia* 94 C4
Carnarvon Ra., *Queens., Australia* 94 D4
Carnarvon Ra., *W. Austral.,
    Australia* 93 E3
Carnation, *U.S.A.* 110 C5
Carndonagh, *Ireland* 12 A4
Carnduff, *Canada* 103 D8
Carnegie, *U.S.A.* 116 F4
Carnegie, *Australia* 93 E3
Carnic Alps = Karnische Alpen,
    Europe 26 E6
Carniche Alpi = Karnische Alpen,
    Europe 26 E6
Carnot, *C.A.R.* 84 D3
Carnot, *Australia* 95 E2
Carnot B., *Australia* 92 C3
Carnoustie, *U.K.* 13 E6
Carnsore Pt., *Ireland* 12 D5
Caro, *U.S.A.* 114 D4
Carol City, *U.S.A.* 115 N5
Carolina, *Brazil* 125 E9
Carolina, *Puerto Rico* ..... 121 d
Carolina, *S. Africa* 89 D5
Caroline I., *Kiribati* 97 H12
Caroline Is., *Micronesia* ... 96 G7
Caroni →, *Trin. & Tob.* 125 K15
Caroni →, *Venezuela* 124 B6
Caronie = Nébrodi, Monti, *Italy* . 43 E7
Caroona, *Australia* 95 E5
Carpathians, *Europe* 6 F10
Carpaţii Meridionali, *Romania* .. 29 E9
Carpentaria, G. of, *Australia* . 94 A2
Carpentras, *France* 21 D9
Carpi, *Italy* 40 D7
Cărpineni, *Moldova* 29 D13
Carpinteria, *U.S.A.* 111 L7
Carpio, *Spain* 36 D5
Carr Boyd Ra., *Australia* ... 92 C4
Carrabelle, *U.S.A.* 115 L3
Carral, *Spain* 36 B2
Carranza, Presa V., *Mexico* .. 118 B4
Carrara, *Italy* 40 D7
Carrascal, *Phil.* 61 G6
Carrascosa del Campo, *Spain* .. 38 E2
Carrauntoohill, *Ireland* ... 12 D2
Carrick-on-Shannon, *Ireland* . 12 C3
Carrick-on-Suir, *Ireland* ... 12 D4
Carrickfergus, *U.K.* 12 B6
Carrickmacross, *Ireland* ... 12 C5
Carrieton, *Australia* 95 E2
Carrington, *U.S.A.* 112 B5
Carrión →, *Spain* 36 D6
Carrión de los Condes, *Spain* . 36 C6
Carrizal Bajo, *Chile* 126 B1
Carrizalillo, *Chile* 126 B1
Carrizo Cr. →, *U.S.A.* 113 G3
Carrizo Plain ◠, *U.S.A.* 110 K7
Carrizo Springs, *U.S.A.* ... 113 L5
Carrizozo, *U.S.A.* 109 K11
Carroll, *U.S.A.* 112 D7
Carrollton, *Ga., U.S.A.* ... 115 J3
Carrollton, *Ill., U.S.A.* ... 112 F9
Carrollton, *Ky., U.S.A.* ... 114 F3
Carrollton, *Mo., U.S.A.* ... 112 F8
Carrollton, *Ohio, U.S.A.* ... 116 F3
Carron →, *U.K.* 13 D4
Carron, L., *U.K.* 13 D3
Carrot →, *Canada* 103 C8
Carrot River, *Canada* 103 C8
Carrouges, *France* 18 D6
Carrù, *Italy* 40 D4
Carruthers, *Canada* 103 C7
Carsa Dek, *Ethiopia* 81 F4
Çarşamba, *Turkey* 72 B7
Carsóli, *Italy* 41 F10
Carson, *Calif., U.S.A.* 111 M8
Carson, *N. Dak., U.S.A.* ... 112 B4
Carson →, *U.S.A.* 110 F8
Carson City, *U.S.A.* 110 F7
Carson Sink, *U.S.A.* 108 G4
Cartagena, *Colombia* 124 A3
Cartagena, *Spain* 39 H4
Cartago, *Colombia* 124 C3

Cartago, *Costa Rica* 120 E3
Cártama, *Spain* 37 J6
Cartaxo, *Portugal* 37 F2
Cartaya, *Spain* 37 H3
Cartersville, *U.S.A.* 115 H3
Carterton, *N.Z.* 91 J5
Carthage, *Tunisia* 42 F3
Carthage, *Ill., U.S.A.* 112 E9
Carthage, *Mo., U.S.A.* 113 G7
Carthage, *N.Y., U.S.A.* 114 D8
Carthage, *Tex., U.S.A.* 113 J7
Cartier I., *Australia* 92 B3
Cartwright, *Canada* 105 B8
Caruaru, *Brazil* 125 E11
Carúpano, *Venezuela* 124 A6
Caruthersville, *U.S.A.* 113 G10
Carvin, *France* 19 B9
Carvoeiro, *Brazil* 124 D6
Carvoeiro, C., *Portugal* 37 F1
Cary, *U.S.A.* 115 H6
Casa, Pas de la = Envalira, Port
    d', *Europe* 38 C6
Casa Branca, *Portugal* 37 G2
Casa Grande, *U.S.A.* 109 K8
Casablanca, *Chile* 126 C1
Casablanca, *Morocco* 78 B4
Casacalenda, *Italy* 41 G11
Casalbordino, *Italy* 41 F11
Casale Monferrato, *Italy* ... 40 C5
Casalmaggiore, *Italy* 40 D7
Casalpusterlengo, *Italy* 40 C6
Casamance →, *Senegal* 82 C1
Casarano, *Italy* 43 B11
Casares, *Spain* 37 J5
Casas Ibáñez, *Spain* 39 F3
Casasimarro, *Spain* 39 F2
Casatejada, *Spain* 36 F5
Casavieja, *Spain* 36 E6
Cascada de Basaseachic △,
    Mexico 118 B3
Cascade, *Idaho, U.S.A.* 108 D5
Cascade, *Mont., U.S.A.* 108 C8
Cascade Locks, *U.S.A.* 110 E5
Cascade Ra., *U.S.A.* 110 D5
Cascade Reservoir, *U.S.A.* .. 108 D5
Cascais, *Portugal* 37 G1
Cascavel, *Brazil* 127 A5
Cáscina, *Italy* 40 E7
Casco B., *U.S.A.* 115 D10
Caselle Torinese, *Italy* 40 C4
Caserta, *Italy* 43 A7
Casey, *Antarctica* 5 C8
Caseyr, Raas = Asir, Ras,
    Somali Rep. 75 E5
Cashel, *Ireland* 12 D4
Casiguran, *Phil.* 61 C5
Casilda, *Argentina* 126 C3
Casimcea, *Romania* 29 F13
Casino, *Australia* 95 D5
Casiquiare →, *Venezuela* ... 124 C5
Čáslav, *Czech Rep.* 26 B8
Casma, *Peru* 124 E3
Casmalia, *U.S.A.* 111 L6
Cásola Valsénio, *Italy* 41 D8
Cásoli, *Italy* 41 F11
Caspe, *Spain* 38 D4
Casper, *U.S.A.* 108 E10
Caspian Depression, *Eurasia* . 35 G9
Caspian Sea, *Eurasia* 52 E6
Cass Lake, *U.S.A.* 112 B7
Cassà de la Selva, *Spain* ... 38 D7
Cassadaga, *U.S.A.* 116 D5
Cassano allo Iónio, *Italy* .. 43 C9
Cassel, *France* 19 B9
Casselman, *Canada* 117 A9
Casselton, *U.S.A.* 112 B6
Cassiar, *Canada* 102 B3
Cassiar Mts., *Canada* 102 B2
Cassino, *Italy* 42 A6
Cassis, *France* 21 E9
Cassville, *U.S.A.* 113 G8
Castagneto Carducci, *Italy* .. 40 E7
Castaic, *U.S.A.* 111 L8
Castalia, *U.S.A.* 116 E2
Castanhal, *Brazil* 125 D9
Castara, *Trin. & Tob.* 125 J16
Castéggio, *Italy* 40 C6
Castejón de Monegros, *Spain* . 38 D4
Castèl di Sangro, *Italy* 41 G11
Castèl San Giovanni, *Italy* .. 40 C6
Castèl San Pietro Terme, *Italy* . 41 D8
Castelbuono, *Italy* 43 E7
Castelfidardo, *Italy* 41 E10
Castelfiorentino, *Italy* 40 E7
Castelfranco Emília, *Italy* .. 40 D8
Castelfranco Véneto, *Italy* .. 41 C8
Casteljaloux, *France* 20 D4
Castellabate, *Italy* 43 B7
Castellammare, G. di, *Italy* . 42 D5
Castellammare del Golfo, *Italy* . 42 D5
Castellammare di Stábia, *Italy* . 43 B7
Castellamonte, *Italy* 40 C4
Castellane, *France* 21 E10
Castellaneta, *Italy* 43 B9
Castelli, *Argentina* 126 D4
Castelló de la Plana, *Spain* . 38 F4
Castellón de la Plana □, *Spain* . 38 E4
Castellote, *Spain* 38 E4
Castelmáuro, *Italy* 41 G11
Castelnau-de-Médoc, *France* .. 20 C3
Castelnau-Magnoac, *France* ... 20 E4
Castelnaudary, *France* 20 E5
Castelnovo ne' Monti, *Italy* . 40 D7
Castelnuovo di Val di Cécina,
    Italy 40 E7
Castelo, *Brazil* 127 A7
Castelo Branco, *Portugal* ... 36 F3
Castelo Branco □, *Portugal* . 36 F3
Castelo de Paiva, *Portugal* .. 36 D2
Castelo de Vide, *Portugal* ... 37 F3
Castelsardo, *Italy* 42 B1
Castelsarrasin, *France* 20 D5

Casteltérmini, *Italy* 42 E6
Castelvetrano, *Italy* 42 E5
Casterton, *Australia* 95 F3
Castets, *France* 20 E2
Castiglion Fiorentino, *Italy* . 41 E8
Castiglione del Lago, *Italy* .. 41 E9
Castiglione della Pescáia, *Italy* . 40 F7
Castiglione delle Stiviere, *Italy* . 40 C7
Castilblanco, *Spain* 37 F5
Castile, *U.S.A.* 116 D6
Castilla, Playa de, *Spain* ... 37 J4
Castilla-La Mancha □, *Spain* . 6 H5
Castilla y Leon □, *Spain* ... 36 D6
Castillo de Locubín, *Spain* .. 37 H7
Castillon-en-Couserans, *France* . 20 F4
Castillonès, *France* 20 D4
Castillos, *Uruguay* 127 C5
Castle Dale, *U.S.A.* 108 G8
Castle Douglas, *U.K.* 13 G5
Castle Rock, *Colo., U.S.A.* . 112 F2
Castle Rock, *Wash., U.S.A.* . 110 D4
Castlebar, *Ireland* 12 C2
Castlebay, *U.K.* 13 E1
Castleblaney, *Ireland* 12 B5
Castlederg, *U.K.* 12 B4
Castleford, *U.K.* 14 D6
Castlegar, *Canada* 102 D5
Castlemaine, *Australia* 95 F3
Castlepollard, *Ireland* 12 C4
Castlerea, *Ireland* 12 C3
Castlereagh →, *Australia* ... 95 E4
Castlereagh B., *Australia* ... 94 A2
Castleton, *U.S.A.* 117 C11
Castletown, *I. of Man* 14 C3
Castletown Bearhaven, *Ireland* . 12 E2
Castor, *Canada* 102 C6
Castor →, *Canada* 104 B4
Castorland, *U.S.A.* 117 C9
Castres, *France* 20 E6
Castricum, *Neths.* 17 B4
Castries, *St. Lucia* .... 121 f
Castril, *Spain* 37 H8
Castro, *Brazil* 127 A6
Castro, *Chile* 128 E2
Castro Alves, *Brazil* 125 F11
Castro del Río, *Spain* 37 H6
Castro Verde, *Portugal* 37 H2
Castro-Urdiales, *Spain* 36 B7
Castrojeriz, *Spain* 36 C6
Castropol, *Spain* 36 B4
Castroreale, *Italy* 43 D8
Castrovillari, *Italy* 43 C9
Castroville, *U.S.A.* 110 J5
Castuera, *Spain* 37 G5
Çat, *Turkey* 73 C9
Cat Ba △, *Vietnam* 64 B6
Cat Ba, Dao, *Vietnam* 64 B6
Cat I., *Bahamas* 121 B4
Cat L., *Canada* 104 B1
Cat Lake, *Canada* 104 B1
Cat Tien △, *Vietnam* 65 G6
Čata, *Slovak Rep.* 27 D11
Catacamas, *Honduras* 120 D2
Cataguases, *Brazil* 127 A7
Catalão, *Brazil* 125 G9
Çatalca, *Turkey* 45 E12
Catalina, *Canada* 105 C9
Catalina, *Chile* 126 B2
Catalina, *U.S.A.* 109 K8
Catalonia = Cataluña □, *Spain* . 38 D6
Cataluña □, *Spain* 38 D6
Çatalzeytin, *Turkey* 72 B6
Catamarca, *Argentina* 126 B2
Catamarca □, *Argentina* 126 B2
Catanauan, *Phil.* 61 E5
Catanduanes □, *Phil.* 61 E6
Catanduva, *Brazil* 127 A6
Catánia, *Italy* 43 E8
Catánia, G. di, *Italy* 43 E8
Catanzaro, *Italy* 43 D9
Catarman, *Phil.* 61 E6
Catatumbo-Barí △, *Colombia* . 121 E5
Catbalogan, *Phil.* 61 F6
Cateel, *Phil.* 61 H7
Catembe, *Mozam.* 89 D5
Caterham, *U.K.* 15 F7
Cathcart, *S. Africa* 88 E4
Cathlamet, *U.S.A.* 110 D3
Catio, *Guinea-Biss.* 82 C1
Catlettsburg, *U.S.A.* 114 F4
Çatma Dağı, *Turkey* 47 C11
Catoche, C., *Mexico* 119 C7
Cátria, Mte., *Italy* 41 E9
Catriló, *Argentina* 126 D3
Catrimani, *Brazil* 124 C6
Catrimani →, *Brazil* 124 C6
Catskill, *U.S.A.* 117 D11
Catskill △, *U.S.A.* 117 D10
Catskill Mts., *U.S.A.* 117 D10
Catt, Mt., *Australia* 94 A1
Cattaraugus, *U.S.A.* 116 D6
Catterick, *U.K.* 14 C6
Cáttólica, *Italy* 41 E9
Cáttólica Eraclea, *Italy* ... 42 E6
Catuala, *Angola* 88 B2
Catuane, *Mozam.* 89 D5
Catur, *Mozam.* 87 E4
Catwick Is., *Vietnam* 65 G7
Cauca →, *Colombia* 124 B4
Caucaia, *Brazil* 125 D11
Caucasus Mountains, *Eurasia* . 35 J7
Caudry, *France* 19 B10
Caulnes, *France* 18 D4
Caulónia, *Italy* 43 D9
Caungula, *Angola* 84 F3
Cauquenes, *Chile* 126 D1
Caura →, *Venezuela* 124 B6
Căuşani, *Moldova* 29 D14
Causapscal, *Canada* 105 C6

Caussade, *France* 20 D5
Causse-Méjean, *France* 20 D7
Causses du Quercy ◠, *France* . 20 D5
Cauterets, *France* 20 F3
Cauvery →, *India* 66 P11
Caux, Pays de, *France* 18 C7
Cava de' Tirreni, *Italy* 43 B7
Cávado →, *Portugal* 36 D2
Cavagrande del Cassibile ◠, *Italy* . 43 F8
Cavaillon, *France* 21 E9
Cavalaire-sur-Mer, *France* ... 21 E10
Cavalese, *Italy* 41 B8
Cavalier, *U.S.A.* 112 A6
Cavalla = Cavally →, *Africa* . 82 E3
Cavallo, Î. de, *France* 21 G13
Cavally →, *Africa* 82 E3
Cavan, *Ireland* 12 B4
Cavan □, *Ireland* 12 C4
Cavárzere, *Italy* 41 C9
Çavdarhisar, *Turkey* 47 B11
Çavdır, *Turkey* 47 D11
Cave Creek, *U.S.A.* 109 K7
Cavenagh Ra., *Australia* ... 93 E4
Cavendish, *Australia* 95 F3
Caviana, I., *Brazil* 125 C8
Cavite, *Phil.* 61 D4
Cavnic, *Romania* 29 C8
Cavour, *Italy* 40 D4
Cavtat, *Croatia* 44 D2
Cawndilla L., *Australia* 95 E3
Cawnpore = Kanpur, *India* ... 69 F9
Caxias, *Brazil* 125 D10
Caxias do Sul, *Brazil* 127 B5
Çay, *Turkey* 72 C4
Cay Sal Bank, *Bahamas* 120 B4
Cayambe, *Ecuador* 124 C3
Çaycuma, *Turkey* 72 B5
Çayeli, *Turkey* 73 B9
Cayenne, *Fr. Guiana* 125 B8
Cayey, *Puerto Rico* .... 121 d
Caygören Baraji, *Turkey* ... 47 B10
Cayiralan, *Turkey* 72 C6
Caylus, *France* 20 D5
Cayman Brac, *Cayman Is.* ... 120 C4
Cayman Is. ☑, *W. Indies* ... 120 C3
Cayman Trough, *Caribbean* ... 98 H11
Cayres, *France* 20 D7
Cayuga, *Canada* 116 D5
Cayuga, *U.S.A.* 117 D8
Cayuga L., *U.S.A.* 117 D8
Cazalla de la Sierra, *Spain* . 37 H5
Cazaux et de Sanguinet, Étang de,
    France 20 D2
Cazenovia, *U.S.A.* 117 D9
Cazères, *France* 20 E5
Cazin, *Bos.-H.* 41 D12
Cazombo, *Angola* 85 G4
Cazorla, *Spain* 37 H7
Cazorla, Sierra de, *Spain* .. 37 G8
Cea →, *Spain* 36 C5
Ceamurlia de Jos, *Romania* .. 29 F13
Ceará = Fortaleza, *Brazil* .. 125 D11
Ceará □, *Brazil* 125 E11
Ceará Mirim, *Brazil* 125 E11
Ceauru, L., *Romania* 29 F8
Cebaco, I. de, *Panama* 120 E3
Ceballos, *Argentina* 126 B2
Cebollar, *Argentina* 126 B2
Cebollera, Sierra de, *Spain* . 38 D2
Cebreros, *Spain* 36 E6
Cebu, *Phil.* 61 F5
Čečava, *Bos.-H.* 28 F2
Ceccano, *Italy* 42 A6
Cece, *Hungary* 28 D3
Cechi, *Ivory C.* 82 D4
Cecil Plains, *Australia* 95 D5
Cécina, *Italy* 40 E7
Cécina →, *Italy* 40 E7
Ceclavín, *Spain* 36 F4
Cedar →, *U.S.A.* 112 E9
Cedar City, *U.S.A.* 109 H7
Cedar Creek Reservoir, *U.S.A.* . 113 J6
Cedar Falls, *Iowa, U.S.A.* .. 112 D8
Cedar Falls, *Wash., U.S.A.* . 110 C5
Cedar Key, *U.S.A.* 115 L4
Cedar L., *Canada* 103 C8
Cedar Rapids, *U.S.A.* 112 E9
Cedartown, *U.S.A.* 115 H3
Cedarvale, *Canada* 102 B3
Cedarville, *S. Africa* 89 E4
Cedeira, *Spain* 36 B2
Cedral, *Mexico* 118 C4
Cedrino →, *Italy* 42 B2
Cedro, *Brazil* 125 E11
Cedros, I. de, *Mexico* 118 B1
Cedros B., *Trin. & Tob.* ... 125 K15
Ceduna, *Australia* 95 E1
Cedynia, *Poland* 31 F1
Cée, *Spain* 36 C1
Ceerigaabo = Erigavo,
    Somali Rep. 75 E4
Cefalù, *Italy* 43 D7
Cega →, *Spain* 36 D6
Cegléd, *Hungary* 28 C4
Cehegín, *Spain* 39 G3
Ceheng, *China* 58 E5
Cehu-Silvaniei, *Romania* ... 29 C8
Ceica, *Romania* 28 D7
Ceira →, *Portugal* 36 E2
Cekik, *Indonesia* 63 J17
Čelákovice, *Czech Rep.* 26 A7
Celano, *Italy* 41 F10
Celanova, *Spain* 36 C3
Celaque △, *Honduras* 120 D1
Celaya, *Mexico* 118 C4
Celebes = Sulawesi, *Indonesia* . 63 E6
Celebes Sea, *Indonesia* 63 D6
Čelić, *Bos.-H.* 28 F3
Celina, *U.S.A.* 114 E3

Celinac, *Bos.-H.* 28 F2
Celje, *Slovenia* 41 B12
Celldömölk, *Hungary* 28 C2
Celle, *Germany* 24 C6
Celorico da Beira, *Portugal* . 36 E3
Celtic Sea, *Atl. Oc.* 6 E4
Çeltikçi, *Turkey* 47 D12
Çemişgezek, *Turkey* 73 C8
Cenderwasih, Teluk, *Indonesia* . 63 E9
Cengong, *China* 58 D7
Ceno →, *Italy* 40 D7
Centallo, *Italy* 40 D4
Centelles, *Spain* 38 D7
Center, *N. Dak., U.S.A.* ... 112 B4
Center, *Tex., U.S.A.* 113 K7
Centerburg, *U.S.A.* 116 F2
Centerville, *Calif., U.S.A.* . 110 J7
Centerville, *Iowa, U.S.A.* .. 112 E8
Centerville, *Pa., U.S.A.* ... 116 F5
Centerville, *Tenn., U.S.A.* . 115 H2
Centerville, *Tex., U.S.A.* .. 113 K7
Cento, *Italy* 41 D8
Central = Tsentralnyy □, *Russia* . 34 D3
Central □, *Ghana* 83 D4
Central □, *Kenya* 86 C4
Central □, *Malawi* 87 E3
Central □, *Zambia* 87 E2
Central, Cordillera, *Colombia* . 124 C4
Central, Cordillera, *Costa Rica* . 120 D3
Central, Cordillera, *Dom. Rep.* . 121 C5
Central, Cordillera, *Phil.* .. 61 C4
Central, Cordillera, *Puerto Rico* . 121 d
Central African Rep. ■, *Africa* . 79 G9
Central America, *America* 98 H11
Central Butte, *Canada* 103 C7
Central City, *Colo., U.S.A.* . 108 G11
Central City, *Ky., U.S.A.* .. 114 G2
Central City, *Nebr., U.S.A.* . 112 E6
Central I., *Kenya* 86 B4
Central Island △, *Kenya* ... 86 B4
Central Kalahari ◠, *Botswana* . 88 C3
Central Makran Range, *Pakistan* . 66 F4
Central Patricia, *Canada* ... 104 B1
Central Point, *U.S.A.* 108 E2
Central Russian Uplands, *Europe* . 6 E13
Central Siberian Plateau, *Russia* . 50 C14
Central Square, *U.S.A.* 117 C8
Centralia, *U.S.A.* 112 F10
Centralia, *Mo., U.S.A.* 112 F8
Centralia, *Wash., U.S.A.* ... 110 D4
Cenxi, *China* 59 F8
Ceotina □, *Bos.-H.* 44 C2
Cephalonia = Kefallinía, *Greece* . 46 C2
Čepin, *Croatia* 28 E3
Ceprano, *Italy* 42 A6
Ceptura, *Romania* 29 E11
Cepu, *Indonesia* 63 G14
Ceram = Seram, *Indonesia* ... 63 E7
Ceram Sea = Seram Sea,
    Indonesia 63 E7
Cerbère, *France* 20 F7
Cercal, *Portugal* 37 H2
Cercedilla, *Spain* 38 C6
Cère →, *France* 20 D5
Cerea, *Italy* 41 C8
Ceredigion □, *U.K.* 15 E3
Ceres, *Argentina* 126 B3
Ceres, *S. Africa* 88 E2
Ceres, *U.S.A.* 110 H6
Céret, *France* 20 F6
Cergy, *France* 19 C9
Cerignola, *Italy* 43 A8
Cerigo = Kíthira, *Greece* ... 46 E5
Cérilly, *France* 19 F9
Cerisiers, *France* 19 D10
Cerizay, *France* 18 F6
Çerkeş, *Turkey* 72 B5
Çerkezköy, *Turkey* 45 E12
Cerknica, *Slovenia* 41 C11
Cerkovica, *Bulgaria* 45 C8
Cermerno, *Serbia & M.* 44 C4
Çermik, *Turkey* 73 C8
Cerna, *Romania* 29 E13
Cerna →, *Romania* 29 F8
Cernavodă, *Romania* 29 F13
Cernay, *France* 19 E14
Černik, *Croatia* 28 E2
Cerralvo, I., *Mexico* 118 C3
Çerrik, *Albania* 44 E3
Cerritos, *Mexico* 118 C4
Cerro Chato, *Uruguay* 127 C4
Cerro Corá △, *Paraguay* 127 A4
Cerro el Copey △, *Venezuela* . 121 D7
Cerro Hoya △, *Panama* 120 E3
Cerro Saroche △, *Venezuela* . 121 D6
Certaldo, *Italy* 40 E8
Cervaro →, *Italy* 43 A8
Cervati, Monte, *Italy* 43 B8
Cerventes, *Australia* 93 F2
Cervera, *Spain* 38 D6
Cervera de Pisuerga, *Spain* .. 36 C6
Cervera del Río Alhama, *Spain* . 38 C3
Cervéteri, *Italy* 41 F9
Cérvia, *Italy* 41 D9
Cervignano del Friuli, *Italy* . 41 C10
Cervione, *France* 21 F13
Cervo, *Spain* 36 B3
Cesarò, *Italy* 43 E7
Cesenático, *Italy* 41 D9
Cēsis, *Latvia* 9 H21
Česká Lípa, *Czech Rep.* 26 A7
Česká Třebová, *Czech Rep.* .. 27 B9
České Budějovice, *Czech Rep.* . 26 C7
Českobudějovický □, *Czech Rep.* . 26 B7
Českomoravská Vrchovina,
    Czech Rep. 26 B8
Český Brod, *Czech Rep.* 26 A7
Český Krumlov, *Czech Rep.* .. 26 C7

Český Těšín, *Czech Rep.*   27 B11
Česma →, *Croatia*   41 C13
Çeşme, *Turkey*   47 C8
Cessnock, *Australia*   95 E5
Cesson-Sévigné, *France*   18 D5
Cestas, *France*   20 D3
Cestos →, *Liberia*   82 D3
Cestos Sehnkwehn △, *Liberia*   82 D3
Cetate, *Romania*   28 F8
Cetin Grad, *Croatia*   41 C12
Cetina →, *Croatia*   41 E13
Cetinje, *Serbia & M.*   44 D2
Cetraro, *Italy*   43 C8
Ceuta, *N. Afr.*   78 A4
Ceva, *Italy*   40 D3
Cévennes, *France*   20 D7
Cévennes △, *France*   20 D7
Ceyhan, *Turkey*   70 B2
Ceyhan →, *Turkey*   72 D6
Ceylânpınar, *Turkey*   73 D9
Ceylon = Sri Lanka ■, *Asia*   66 R12
Cèze →, *France*   21 D8
Cha-am, *Thailand*   64 F2
Cha Pa, *Vietnam*   64 A4
Chabanais, *France*   20 C4
Chabeuil, *France*   21 D9
Chablais, *France*   19 F13
Chablis, *France*   19 E10
Chacabuco, *Argentina*   126 C3
Chachapoyas, *Peru*   124 E3
Chachoengsao, *Thailand*   64 F3
Chachran, *Pakistan*   66 E7
Chachro, *Pakistan*   68 G4
Chaco △, *Argentina*   126 B4
Chaco □, *Argentina*   126 B3
Chaco □, *Paraguay*   126 B4
Chaco →, *U.S.A.*   109 H9
Chaco Austral, *S. Amer.*   128 C4
Chaco Boreal, *S. Amer.*   124 H6
Chaco Central, *S. Amer.*   128 A4
Chaco Culture △, *U.S.A.*   109 H10
Chacon, C., *U.S.A.*   102 C2
Chad ■, *Africa*   79 F8
Chad, L. = Tchad, L., *Chad*   79 F8
Chadan, *Russia*   53 D10
Chadileuvú →, *Argentina*   126 D2
Chadiza, *Zambia*   87 E3
Chadron, *U.S.A.*   112 D3
Chadyr-Lunga = Ciadâr-Lunga, *Moldova*   29 D13
Chae Hom, *Thailand*   64 C2
Chae Son △, *Thailand*   64 C2
Chaem →, *Thailand*   64 C2
Chaeryŏng, *N. Korea*   57 E13
Chagai Hills = Chāh Gay Hills, *Afghan.*   66 E3
Chagda, *Russia*   53 D14
Chaghcharān, *Afghan.*   66 B4
Chagny, *France*   19 F11
Chagoda, *Russia*   32 C8
Chagos Arch. ☒, *Ind. Oc.*   50 K11
Chagres △, *Panama*   120 E4
Chagrin Falls, *U.S.A.*   116 E3
Chaguanas, *Trin. & Tob.*   125 K15
Chāh Ākhvor, *Iran*   71 C8
Chāh Bahar, *Iran*   71 E9
Chāh-e Kavīr, *Iran*   71 C8
Chāh Gay Hills, *Afghan.*   66 E3
Chahar Burjak, *Afghan.*   66 D3
Chahār Maḥāll va Bakhtīarī □, *Iran*   71 C6
Chaibasa, *India*   67 H14
Chaillé-les-Marais, *France*   20 B2
Chainat, *Thailand*   64 E3
Chaiya, *Thailand*   65 H2
Chaiyaphum, *Thailand*   64 E4
Chaj Doab, *Pakistan*   68 C5
Chajari, *Argentina*   126 C4
Chak Amru, *Pakistan*   68 C6
Chaka, *Sudan*   81 G3
Chakar →, *Pakistan*   68 E3
Chakari, *Zimbabwe*   89 B4
Chake Chake, *Tanzania*   86 D4
Chakhānsūr, *Afghan.*   66 D3
Chakonipau, L., *Canada*   105 A6
Chakradharpur, *India*   69 H11
Chakrata, *India*   68 D7
Chakwal, *Pakistan*   68 C5
Chala, *Peru*   124 G4
Chalais, *France*   20 C4
Chalchihuites, *Mexico*   118 C4
Chalcis = Khalkís, *Greece*   46 C5
Châlette-sur-Loing, *France*   19 D9
Chaleur B., *Canada*   105 C6
Chalfant, *U.S.A.*   110 H8
Chalhuanca, *Peru*   124 F4
Chalindrey, *France*   19 E12
Chaling, *China*   59 D9
Chalisgaon, *India*   66 J9
Chalk River, *Canada*   104 C4
Chalky Inlet, *N.Z.*   91 M1
Challans, *France*   18 F5
Challapata, *Bolivia*   124 G5
Challis, *U.S.A.*   108 D6
Chalmette, *U.S.A.*   113 L10
Chalon-sur-Saône, *France*   19 F11
Chalonnes-sur-Loire, *France*   18 E6
Châlons-en-Champagne, *France*   19 D11
Châlus, *France*   20 C4
Chālūs, *Iran*   71 B6
Cham, *Germany*   25 F8
Cham, Cu Lao, *Vietnam*   64 E7
Chama, *U.S.A.*   109 H10
Chamaicó, *Argentina*   126 D3
Chaman, *Pakistan*   66 D5
Chamba, *India*   68 C7
Chamba, *Tanzania*   87 E4
Chambal →, *India*   69 F8
Chamberlain, *U.S.A.*   112 D5
Chamberlain →, *Australia*   92 C4
Chamberlain L., *U.S.A.*   115 B11
Chambers, *U.S.A.*   109 J9

Chambersburg, *U.S.A.*   114 F7
Chambéry, *France*   21 C9
Chambeshi →, *Zambia*   84 G6
Chambly, *Canada*   117 A11
Chambord, *Canada*   105 C5
Chamboulive, *France*   20 C5
Chamchamal, *Iraq*   70 C5
Chamela, *Mexico*   118 D3
Chamical, *Argentina*   126 C2
Chamkar Luong, *Cambodia*   65 G4
Chamoli, *India*   69 D8
Chamonix-Mont Blanc, *France*   21 C10
Champa, *India*   69 H10
Champagne, *Canada*   102 A1
Champagne, *France*   19 D11
Champagnole, *France*   19 F12
Champaign, *U.S.A.*   114 E1
Champassak, *Laos*   64 E5
Champaubert, *France*   19 D10
Champawat, *India*   69 E9
Champdeniers-St-Denis, *France*   20 B3
Champdoré, L., *Canada*   105 A6
Champeix, *France*   20 C7
Champion, *U.S.A.*   116 E4
Champlain, *U.S.A.*   117 B11
Champlain, L., *U.S.A.*   117 B11
Champlitte, *France*   19 E12
Champotón, *Mexico*   119 D6
Champua, *India*   69 H11
Chamusca, *Portugal*   37 F2
Chana, *Thailand*   65 J3
Chañaral, *Chile*   126 B1
Chanārān, *Iran*   71 B8
Chanasma, *India*   68 H5
Chancery Lane, *Barbados*   121 g
Chanco, *Chile*   126 D1
Chand, *India*   69 J8
Chandan, *India*   69 G12
Chandan Chauki, *India*   69 E9
Chandannagar, *India*   69 H13
Chandausi, *India*   69 E8
Chandeleur Is., *U.S.A.*   113 L10
Chandeleur Sd., *U.S.A.*   113 L10
Chandigarh, *India*   68 D7
Chandil, *India*   69 H12
Chandler, *Australia*   95 D1
Chandler, *Canada*   105 C7
Chandler, *Ariz., U.S.A.*   109 K8
Chandler, *Okla., U.S.A.*   113 H6
Chandod, *India*   68 J5
Chandpur, *Bangla.*   67 H17
Chandrapur, *India*   66 K11
Chānf, *Iran*   71 E9
Chang, *Pakistan*   68 F3
Chang, Ko, *Thailand*   65 F4
Ch'ang Chiang = Chang Jiang →, *China*   59 B13
Chang Jiang →, *China*   59 B13
Changa, *India*   69 C7
Changanacheri, *India*   66 Q10
Changane →, *Mozam.*   89 C5
Changbai, *China*   57 D15
Changbai Shan, *China*   57 C15
Changchiak'ou = Zhangjiakou, *China*   56 D8
Ch'angchou = Changzhou, *China*   59 B12
Changchun, *China*   57 C13
Changchunling, *China*   57 B13
Changde, *China*   59 C8
Changdo-ri, *N. Korea*   57 E14
Changfeng, *China*   59 A11
Changhai = Shanghai, *China*   59 B13
Changhua, *China*   59 B12
Changhua, *Taiwan*   59 E13
Changhŭng, *S. Korea*   57 G14
Changhŭngni, *N. Korea*   57 D15
Changi, *Singapore*   65 d
Changi, Singapore ✈ (SIN), *Singapore*   65 M4
Changjiang, *China*   64 C7
Changjin, *N. Korea*   57 D14
Changjin-chŏsuji, *N. Korea*   57 D14
Changle, *China*   59 E12
Changli, *China*   57 E10
Changling, *China*   57 B12
Changlun, *Malaysia*   65 J3
Changning, *Hunan, China*   59 D9
Changning, *Sichuan, China*   58 C5
Changning, *Yunnan, China*   58 E2
Changping, *China*   56 D9
Changsha, *China*   59 C9
Changshan, *China*   59 C12
Changshu, *China*   59 B13
Changshun, *China*   58 D6
Changtai, *China*   59 E11
Changting, *China*   59 E11
Changwu, *China*   56 G4
Changxing, *China*   59 B12
Changyang, *China*   59 B8
Changyi, *China*   57 F10
Changyŏn, *N. Korea*   57 E13
Changyuan, *China*   56 G8
Changzhi, *China*   56 F7
Changzhou, *China*   59 B12
Chanhanga, *Angola*   88 B1
Chania = Khaniá, *Greece*   49 D6
Chanlar = Xanlar, *Azerbaijan*   35 K8
Channapatna, *India*   66 N10
Channel Is., *U.K.*   15 H5
Channel Is., *U.S.A.*   111 M7
Channel Islands △, *U.S.A.*   111 L7
Channel-Port aux Basques, *Canada*   105 C8
Channel Tunnel, *Europe*   15 F9
Channing, *U.S.A.*   113 H3
Chantada, *Spain*   36 C3
Chanthaburi, *Thailand*   64 F4
Chantilly, *France*   19 C9
Chantonnay, *France*   18 F5
Chantrey Inlet, *Canada*   100 B10
Chanute, *U.S.A.*   113 G7
Chanza →, *Spain*   37 H3

Chao Hu, *China*   59 B11
Chao Phraya →, *Thailand*   64 F3
Chao Phraya Lowlands, *Thailand*   56 F8
Chaocheng, *China*   56 F8
Chaohu, *China*   59 B11
Chaoyang, *Guangdong, China*   59 F11
Chaoyang, *Liaoning, China*   57 D11
Chaozhou, *China*   59 F11
Chapais, *Canada*   104 C5
Chapala, *Mozam.*   87 F4
Chapala, L. de, *Mexico*   118 C4
Chapayev, *Kazakhstan*   34 E10
Chapayevsk, *Russia*   34 D9
Chapecó, *Brazil*   127 B5
Chapel Hill, *U.S.A.*   115 H6
Chapleau, *Canada*   104 C3
Chaplin, *Canada*   103 C7
Chaplin L., *Canada*   103 C7
Chaplino, *Ukraine*   33 H9
Chaplygin, *Russia*   32 F11
Chappell, *U.S.A.*   112 E3
Chapra = Chhapra, *India*   69 G11
Chara, *Russia*   53 D12
Charadai, *Argentina*   126 B4
Charagua, *Bolivia*   124 G6
Charambirá, Punta, *Colombia*   124 C3
Charaña, *Bolivia*   124 G5
Charantsavan, *Armenia*   35 K7
Charanwala, *India*   68 F5
Charata, *Argentina*   126 B3
Charcas, *Mexico*   118 C4
Charcot I., *Antarctica*   5 C17
Chard, *U.K.*   15 G5
Chardon, *U.S.A.*   116 E3
Chardzhou = Chärjew, *Turkmenistan*   52 F7
Charente □, *France*   20 C4
Charente →, *France*   20 C2
Charente-Maritime □, *France*   20 C3
Chari →, *Chad*   79 F8
Chārīkār, *Afghan.*   66 B6
Chariton →, *U.S.A.*   112 F8
Chau Doc, *Vietnam*   65 G5
Charkhari, *India*   69 G8
Charkhi Dadri, *India*   68 E7
Charleroi, *Belgium*   17 D4
Charleroi, *U.S.A.*   116 F5
Charles, C., *U.S.A.*   114 G8
Charles City, *U.S.A.*   112 D8
Charles de Gaulle, Paris ✈ (CDG), *France*   19 D9
Charles L., *Canada*   103 B6
Charles Town, *U.S.A.*   114 F7
Charleston, *Ill., U.S.A.*   114 F1
Charleston, *Miss., U.S.A.*   113 H9
Charleston, *Mo., U.S.A.*   113 G10
Charleston, *S.C., U.S.A.*   115 J6
Charleston, *W. Va., U.S.A.*   114 F5
Charleston L., *Canada*   117 B9
Charleston Peak, *U.S.A.*   111 J11
Charlestown, *Ireland*   12 C3
Charlestown, *S. Africa*   89 D4
Charlestown, *Ind., U.S.A.*   114 F3
Charlestown, *N.H., U.S.A.*   117 C12
Charlestown of Aberlour, *U.K.*   13 D5
Charleville = Rath Luirc, *Ireland*   12 D3
Charleville, *Australia*   95 D4
Charleville-Mézières, *France*   19 C11
Charlevoix, *U.S.A.*   114 C3
Charlieu, *France*   19 F11
Charlotte, *Mich., U.S.A.*   114 D3
Charlotte, *N.C., U.S.A.*   115 H5
Charlotte, *Vt., U.S.A.*   117 B11
Charlotte Amalie, *U.S. Virgin Is.*   121 e
Charlotte Harbor, *U.S.A.*   115 M4
Charlotte L., *Canada*   102 C3
Charlottenberg, *Sweden*   10 E6
Charlottesville, *U.S.A.*   114 F6
Charlottetown, *Nfld. & L., Canada*   105 B8
Charlottetown, *P.E.I., Canada*   105 C7
Charlotteville, *Trin. & Tob.*   125 J16
Charlton, *Australia*   95 F3
Charlton, *U.S.A.*   112 E8
Charlton I., *Canada*   104 B4
Charmes, *France*   19 D13
Charny, *Canada*   105 C5
Charnyany, *Belarus*   31 G11
Charolles, *France*   19 F11
Chârost, *France*   19 F9
Charre, *Mozam.*   87 F4
Charroux, *France*   20 B4
Charsadda, *Pakistan*   68 B4
Charters Towers, *Australia*   94 C4
Chartres, *France*   18 D8
Chartreuse △, *France*   21 C9
Chascomús, *Argentina*   126 D4
Chasefu, *Zambia*   87 E3
Chashma Barrage, *Pakistan*   68 C4
Chasseneuil-sur-Bonnieure, *France*   20 C4
Chāt, *Iran*   71 B7
Chatal Balkan = Udvoy Balkan, *Bulgaria*   45 D10
Château-Arnoux-St-Auban, *France*   21 D10
Château-Chinon, *France*   19 E10
Château-d'Oëx, *Switz.*   25 J3
Château-d'Olonne, *France*   20 B2
Château-du-Loir, *France*   18 E7
Château-Gontier, *France*   18 E6
Château-la-Vallière, *France*   18 E7
Château-Landon, *France*   19 D9
Château-Renard, *France*   19 E9
Château-Renault, *France*   18 E7
Château-Salins, *France*   19 D13
Château-Thierry, *France*   19 C10
Châteaubourg, *France*   18 D5
Châteaubriant, *France*   18 E5
Châteaudun, *France*   18 D8
Châteaugay, *U.S.A.*   117 B10
Châteaugiron, *France*   18 D5

Châteauguay, L., *Canada*   105 A5
Châteaulin, *France*   18 D2
Châteaumeillant, *France*   19 F9
Châteauneuf-du-Faou, *France*   18 D3
Châteauneuf-sur-Charente, *France*   20 C3
Châteauneuf-sur-Cher, *France*   19 F9
Châteauneuf-sur-Loire, *France*   19 E9
Châteaurenard, *France*   21 E8
Châteauroux, *France*   19 F8
Châteauvillain, *France*   19 D11
Châteaux, Pte. des, *Guadeloupe*   120 b
Châtelaillon-Plage, *France*   20 B2
Châtelguyon, *France*   20 C7
Châtellerault, *France*   18 F7
Châtelus-Malvaleix, *France*   19 F9
Chatham = Chatham-Kent, *Canada*   116 D2
Chatham = Miramichi, *Canada*   105 C6
Chatham, *U.K.*   15 F8
Chatham, *U.S.A.*   117 D11
Chatham Is., *Pac. Oc.*   96 M10
Chatham-Kent, *Canada*   116 D2
Châtillon, *Italy*   40 C4
Châtillon-Coligny, *France*   19 E9
Châtillon-en-Diois, *France*   21 D9
Châtillon-sur-Indre, *France*   18 F8
Châtillon-sur-Loire, *France*   19 E9
Châtillon-sur-Seine, *France*   19 E11
Chatmohar, *Bangla.*   69 G13
Chatra, *India*   69 G11
Chatrapur, *India*   67 K14
Chats, L. des, *Canada*   117 A8
Chatsu, *India*   68 F6
Chatsworth, *Canada*   116 B4
Chatsworth, *Zimbabwe*   87 F3
Chättagām = Chittagong, *Bangla.*   67 H17
Chattahoochee, *U.S.A.*   115 K3
Chattahoochee →, *U.S.A.*   115 K3
Chattanooga, *U.S.A.*   115 H3
Chatteris, *U.K.*   15 E8
Chaturat, *Thailand*   64 E3
Chaudes-Aigues, *France*   20 D7
Chauffailles, *France*   19 F11
Chaukan Pass, *Burma*   67 F20
Chaumont, *France*   19 D12
Chaumont, *U.S.A.*   117 B8
Chaumont-en-Vexin, *France*   19 C8
Chaumont-sur-Loire, *France*   18 E8
Chaunay, *France*   20 B4
Chaunskaya G., *Russia*   4 C18
Chauny, *France*   19 C10
Chausey, Îs., *France*   18 D5
Chaussin, *France*   19 F12
Chautauqua L., *U.S.A.*   116 D5
Chauvigny, *France*   18 F7
Chauvin, *Canada*   103 C6
Chavanges, *France*   19 D11
Chaves, *Brazil*   125 D9
Chaves, *Portugal*   36 D3
Chawang, *Thailand*   65 H2
Chazelles-sur-Lyon, *France*   21 C8
Chazy, *U.S.A.*   117 B11
Cheb, *Czech Rep.*   26 A5
Cheboksarskoye Vdkhr., *Russia*   34 B8
Cheboksary, *Russia*   34 B8
Cheboygan, *U.S.A.*   114 C3
Chebsara, *Russia*   32 C10
Chech, Erg, *Africa*   78 D5
Chechelnyk, *Ukraine*   29 B14
Chechen, Ostrov, *Russia*   35 H8
Chechenia □, *Russia*   35 J7
Checheno-Ingush Republic = Chechenia □, *Russia*   35 J7
Chechnya = Chechenia □, *Russia*   35 J7
Chech'ŏn, *S. Korea*   57 F15
Chęciny, *Poland*   31 H7
Checotah, *U.S.A.*   113 H7
Chedabucto B., *Canada*   105 C7
Cheduba I., *Burma*   67 K18
Cheepie, *Australia*   95 D4
Chef-Boutonne, *France*   20 B3
Chegdomyn, *Russia*   53 D14
Chegga, *Mauritania*   78 C4
Chegutu, *Zimbabwe*   87 F3
Chehalis, *U.S.A.*   110 D4
Chehalis →, *U.S.A.*   110 D3
Cheile Nerei-Beusnița △, *Romania*   28 F6
Cheiron, Mt., *France*   21 E10
Cheju do, *S. Korea*   57 H14
Chekalin, *Russia*   32 E9
Chekhovo, *Russia*   30 D7
Chekiang = Zhejiang □, *China*   59 C13
Chel = Kuru, Bahr el →, *Sudan*   81 F2
Chela, Sa. da, *Angola*   88 B1
Chelan, *U.S.A.*   108 C4
Chelan, L., *U.S.A.*   108 B3
Cheleken, *Turkmenistan*   52 F6
Cheleken Yarymadasy, *Turkmenistan*   71 B7
Chelforó, *Argentina*   128 D3
Chelkar = Shalqar, *Kazakhstan*   52 E6
Chelkar Tengiz, Solonchak, *Kazakhstan*   52 E7
Chella, *Ethiopia*   81 F4
Chelles, *France*   19 D9
Chełm, *Poland*   31 G10
Chełmno, *Poland*   31 E5
Chelmsford, *U.K.*   15 F8
Chełmża, *Poland*   31 E5
Chelsea, *U.S.A.*   117 C12
Cheltenham, *U.K.*   15 F5
Chelva, *Spain*   38 F4
Chelyabinsk, *Russia*   52 D7
Chelyuskin, C. = Chelyuskin, Mys, *Russia*   53 B11
Chelyuskin, Mys, *Russia*   53 B11
Chemainus, *Canada*   110 B3
Chemba, *Mozam.*   85 H6
Chembar = Belinskiy, *Russia*   34 D6

Chemillé, *France*   18 E6
Chemnitz, *Germany*   24 E8
Chemult, *U.S.A.*   108 E3
Chen, Gora, *Russia*   53 C15
Chenab →, *Pakistan*   68 D4
Chenango Forks, *U.S.A.*   117 D9
Chencha, *Ethiopia*   81 F4
Chenchiang = Zhenjiang, *China*   59 A12
Cheney, *U.S.A.*   108 C5
Cheng Xian, *China*   56 H3
Chengbu, *China*   59 D8
Chengcheng, *China*   56 G5
Chengchou = Zhengzhou, *China*   56 G7
Chengde, *China*   57 D9
Chengdong Hu, *China*   59 A11
Chengdu, *China*   58 B5
Chenggong, *China*   58 E4
Chenggu, *China*   56 H4
Chenghai, *China*   59 F11
Chengjiang, *China*   58 E4
Chengkou, *China*   58 B7
Ch'engmai, *China*   64 C7
Ch'engtu = Chengdu, *China*   58 B5
Chengwu, *China*   56 G8
Chengxi Hu, *China*   59 A11
Chengyang, *China*   57 F11
Chenjiagang, *China*   57 G10
Chenkán, *Mexico*   119 D6
Chennai, *India*   66 N12
Chenôve, *France*   19 E12
Chenxi, *China*   59 C8
Chenzhou, *China*   59 E9
Cheo Reo, *Vietnam*   62 B3
Chepelare, *Bulgaria*   45 E8
Chepén, *Peru*   124 E3
Chepes, *Argentina*   126 C2
Chepo, *Panama*   120 E4
Chepstow, *U.K.*   15 F5
Chequamegon B., *U.S.A.*   112 B9
Cher □, *France*   19 E9
Cher →, *France*   18 E7
Chéradi, *Italy*   43 B10
Cherasco, *Italy*   40 D4
Cheraw, *U.S.A.*   115 H6
Cherbourg, *France*   18 C5
Cherdakly, *Russia*   34 C9
Cherdyn, *Russia*   52 C6
Cheremkhovo, *Russia*   53 D11
Cherepanovo, *Russia*   52 D9
Cherepovets, *Russia*   32 C9
Chergui, Chott ech., *Algeria*   78 B6
Cherikov = Cherykaw, *Belarus*   32 F6
Cherkasy, *Ukraine*   33 H7
Cherkessk, *Russia*   35 H6
Cherlak, *Russia*   52 D8
Chernaya, *Russia*   53 B9
Chernelytsya, *Ukraine*   29 B10
Chernigov = Chernihiv, *Ukraine*   33 G6
Chernihiv, *Ukraine*   33 G6
Chernivetska □, *Ukraine*   29 B10
Chernivtsi, *Ukraine*   29 B10
Chernivtsi, *Ukraine*   29 B10
Chernobyl = Chornobyl, *Ukraine*   33 G6
Chernogorsk, *Russia*   53 D10
Chernomorskoye = Chornomorske, *Ukraine*   33 K7
Chernovtsy = Chernivtsi, *Ukraine*   29 B10
Chernyakhovsk, *Russia*   9 J19
Chernyanka, *Russia*   33 G9
Chernysheyskiy, *Russia*   53 C12
Chernyye Zemli, *Russia*   35 H8
Cherokee, *Iowa, U.S.A.*   112 D7
Cherokee, *Okla., U.S.A.*   113 G5
Cherokee Village, *U.S.A.*   113 G9
Cherokees, Grand Lake O' The, *U.S.A.*   113 G7
Cherrapunji, *India*   67 G17
Cherry Valley, *Calif., U.S.A.*   111 M10
Cherry Valley, *N.Y., U.S.A.*   117 D10
Cherskiy, *Russia*   53 C17
Cherskogo Khrebet, *Russia*   53 C15
Chertkovo, *Russia*   33 H11
Cherven, *Belarus*   32 F5
Cherven-Bryag, *Bulgaria*   45 C8
Chervonoarmiyske, *Ukraine*   29 E13
Chervonohrad, *Ukraine*   33 G3
Cherwell →, *U.K.*   15 F6
Cherykaw, *Belarus*   32 F6
Chesapeake, *U.S.A.*   114 G7
Chesapeake B., *U.S.A.*   114 G7
Cheshire □, *U.K.*   14 D5
Cheshskaya Guba, *Russia*   52 C5
Cheshunt, *U.K.*   15 F7
Chesil Beach, *U.K.*   15 G5
Chesley, *Canada*   116 B3
Cheste, *Spain*   39 F4
Chester, *U.K.*   14 D5
Chester, *Calif., U.S.A.*   108 F3
Chester, *Ill., U.S.A.*   113 G10
Chester, *Mont., U.S.A.*   108 B8
Chester, *Pa., U.S.A.*   114 F8
Chester, *S.C., U.S.A.*   115 H5
Chester, *Vt., U.S.A.*   117 C12
Chester, *W. Va., U.S.A.*   116 F4
Chester-le-Street, *U.K.*   14 C6
Chesterfield, *U.K.*   14 D6
Chesterfield, Is., *N. Cal.*   96 J7
Chesterfield Inlet, *Canada*   100 B10
Chesterton Ra., *Australia*   95 D4
Chesterton Range △, *Australia*   95 D4
Chestertown, *U.S.A.*   117 C11
Chesterville, *Canada*   117 A9
Chestnut Ridge, *U.S.A.*   116 F5
Chesuncook L., *U.S.A.*   115 C11
Chéticamp, *Canada*   105 C7
Chetrosu, *Moldova*   29 B12
Chetumal, *Mexico*   119 D7
Chetumal, B. de, *Mexico*   119 D7
Chetwynd, *Canada*   102 B4
Chevanceaux, *France*   20 C3

Cheviot, The, *U.K.* 14 B5
Cheviot Hills, *U.K.* 14 B5
Cheviot Ra., *Australia* 94 D3
Chew Bahir, *Ethiopia* 81 G4
Chewelah, *U.S.A.* 108 B5
Chewore △, *Zimbabwe* 87 F2
Cheyenne, *Okla., U.S.A.* 113 H5
Cheyenne, *Wyo., U.S.A.* 112 E2
Cheyenne ➜, *U.S.A.* 112 C4
Cheyenne Wells, *U.S.A.* 112 F3
Cheyne B., *Australia* 93 F2
Chhabra, *India* 68 G7
Chhaktala, *India* 68 H6
Chhapra, *India* 69 G11
Chhata, *India* 68 F7
Chhatarpur, *Jharkhand, India* .. 69 G11
Chhatarpur, *Mad. P., India* 69 G8
Chhattisgarh □, *India* 69 J10
Chhep, *Cambodia* 64 F5
Chhindwara, *Mad. P., India* 69 H8
Chhindwara, *Mad. P., India* 69 H8
Chhlong, *Cambodia* 65 F5
Chhota Tawa ➜, *India* 68 H7
Chhoti Kali Sindh ➜, *India* 68 G6
Chhuikhadan, *India* 69 J9
Chhuk, *Cambodia* 65 G5
Chi ➜, *Thailand* 64 E5
Chiai, *Taiwan* 59 F13
Chiali, *Taiwan* 59 F13
Chiamboni, *Somali Rep.* 84 E8
Chianciano Terme, *Italy* 41 E8
Chiang Dao, *Thailand* 64 C2
Chiang Kham, *Thailand* 64 C3
Chiang Khan, *Thailand* 64 D3
Chiang Khong, *Thailand* 58 G3
Chiang Mai, *Thailand* 64 C2
Chiang Rai, *Thailand* 58 H2
Chiang Saen, *Thailand* 58 G3
Chianti, *Italy* 41 E8
Chiapa ➜, *Mexico* 119 D6
Chiapa de Corzo, *Mexico* 119 D6
Chiapas □, *Mexico* 119 D6
Chiaramonte Gulfi, *Italy* 43 E7
Chiaravalle, *Italy* 41 E10
Chiaravalle Centrale, *Italy* 43 D9
Chiari, *Italy* 40 C6
Chiatura, *Georgia* 35 J6
Chiautla, *Mexico* 119 D5
Chiávari, *Italy* 40 D6
Chiavenna, *Italy* 40 B6
Chiba, *Japan* 55 G10
Chiba □, *Japan* 55 G10
Chibabava, *Mozam.* 89 C5
Chibemba, *Cunene, Angola* 85 H2
Chibemba, *Huila, Angola* 88 B2
Chibi, *Zimbabwe* 89 C5
Chibia, *Angola* 85 H2
Chibougamau, *Canada* 104 C5
Chibougamau, L., *Canada* 104 C5
Chibuk, *Nigeria* 83 C7
Chibuto, *Mozam.* 89 C5
Chic-Chocs, Mts., *Canada* 105 C6
Chicacole = Srikakulam, *India* .. 67 K13
Chicago, *U.S.A.* 114 E2
Chicago Heights, *U.S.A.* 114 E2
Chichagof I., *U.S.A.* 100 C6
Chichén-Itzá, *Mexico* 119 C7
Chicheng, *China* 56 D8
Chichester, *U.K.* 15 G7
Chichester Ra., *Australia* 92 D2
Chichibu, *Japan* 55 F9
Chichibu-Tama △, *Japan* 55 G9
Chichóli, *India* 68 H8
Chickasaw ➜, *U.S.A.* 113 H6
Chickasha, *U.S.A.* 113 H6
Chiclana de la Frontera, *Spain* .. 37 J4
Chico, *U.S.A.* 110 F5
Chico ➜, *Chubut, Argentina* .. 128 E3
Chico ➜, *Santa Cruz, Argentina* 128 G3
Chicomo, *Mozam.* 89 C5
Chicomostoc, *Mexico* 118 C4
Chicontepec, *Mexico* 119 C5
Chicopee, *U.S.A.* 117 D12
Chicoutimi, *Canada* 105 C5
Chicualacuala, *Mozam.* 89 C5
Chidambaram, *India* 66 P11
Chidenguele, *Mozam.* 89 C5
Chidley, C., *Canada* 101 B13
Chiducuane, *Mozam.* 89 C5
Chiede, *Angola* 88 B2
Chiefs Pt., *Canada* 116 B3
Chiem Hoa, *Vietnam* 64 A5
Chiemsee, *Germany* 25 H8
Chiengi, *Zambia* 87 D2
Chiengmai = Chiang Mai,
  Thailand 64 C2
Chienti ➜, *Italy* 41 E10
Chieri, *Italy* 40 C4
Chiers ➜, *France* 19 C11
Chiesa in Valmalenco, *Italy* 40 B6
Chiese ➜, *Italy* 40 C7
Chieti, *Italy* 41 F11
Chifeng, *China* 57 C10
Chigirin, *Ukraine* 33 H7
Chignecto B., *Canada* 105 C7
Chiguana, *Bolivia* 126 A2
Chigwell, *U.K.* 15 F8
Chiha-ri, *N. Korea* 57 E14
Chihli, G. of = Bo Hai, *China* .. 57 E10
Chihuahua, *Mexico* 118 B3
Chihuahua □, *Mexico* 118 B3
Chiili = Shīeli, *Kazakhstan* 52 E7
Chik Bollapur, *India* 66 N10
Chikmagalur, *India* 66 N9
Chikwawa, *Malawi* 87 F3
Chilac, *Mexico* 119 D5
Chilam Chavki, *Pakistan* 69 B6
Chilanga, *Zambia* 87 F2
Chilapa, *Mexico* 119 D5
Chilas, *Pakistan* 69 B6

Chilaw, *Sri Lanka* 66 R11
Chilcotin ➜, *Canada* 102 C4
Childers, *Australia* 95 D5
Childress, *U.S.A.* 113 H4
Chile ■, *S. Amer.* 128 D2
Chile Rise, *Pac. Oc.* 97 L18
Chilecito, *Argentina* 126 B2
Chilete, *Peru* 124 E3
Chilia, Brațul ➜, *Romania* 29 E14
Chililabombwe, *Zambia* 87 E2
Chilin = Jilin, *China* 57 C14
Chilka L., *India* 67 K14
Chilko ➜, *Canada* 102 C4
Chilko L., *Canada* 102 C4
Chillagoe, *Australia* 94 B3
Chillán, *Chile* 126 D1
Chillicothe, *Ill., U.S.A.* 112 E10
Chillicothe, *Mo., U.S.A.* 112 F8
Chillicothe, *Ohio, U.S.A.* 114 F4
Chilliwack, *Canada* 102 D4
Chilo, *India* 68 F5
Chiloane, I., *Mozam.* 89 C5
Chiloé, I. de, *Chile* 128 E2
Chilpancingo, *Mexico* 119 D5
Chiltern Hills, *U.K.* 15 F7
Chilton, *U.S.A.* 114 C1
Chilubi, *Zambia* 87 E2
Chilubula, *Zambia* 87 E3
Chilumba, *Malawi* 87 E3
Chilung, *Taiwan* 59 E13
Chilwa, L., *Malawi* 87 F4
Chimaltitán, *Mexico* 118 C4
Chimán, *Panama* 120 E4
Chimanimani, *Zimbabwe* 89 B5
Chimanimani △, *Zimbabwe* .. 87 F3
Chimay, *Belgium* 17 D4
Chimayo, *U.S.A.* 109 H11
Chimbay, *Uzbekistan* 52 E6
Chimborazo, *Ecuador* 124 D3
Chimbote, *Peru* 124 E3
Chimkent = Shymkent,
  Kazakhstan 52 E7
Chimoio, *Mozam.* 87 F3
Chimpembe, *Zambia* 87 D2
Chin □, *Burma* 67 J18
Chin Ling Shan = Qinling Shandi,
  China 56 H5
China, *Mexico* 119 B5
China ■, *Asia* 60 D6
China, Great Plain of, *Asia* 50 F15
China Lake, *U.S.A.* 111 K9
Chinan = Jinan, *China* 56 F9
Chinandega, *Nic.* 120 D2
Chinati Peak, *U.S.A.* 113 L2
Chincha Alta, *Peru* 124 F3
Chinchaga ➜, *Canada* 102 B5
Chinchilla, *Australia* 95 D5
Chinchilla de Monte Aragón,
  Spain 39 G3
Chinchorro, Banco, *Mexico* 119 D7
Chinchou = Jinzhou, *China* 57 D11
Chincoteague, *U.S.A.* 114 G8
Chinde, *Mozam.* 87 F4
Chindo, *S. Korea* 57 G14
Chindwin ➜, *Burma* 67 J19
Chineni, *India* 69 C6
Chinga, *Mozam.* 87 F4
Chingola, *Zambia* 87 E2
Chingole, *Malawi* 87 E3
Ch'ingtao = Qingdao, *China* .. 57 F11
Chingune, *Mozam.* 89 C5
Chinhae, *S. Korea* 57 G15
Chinhanguanine, *Mozam.* 89 D5
Chinhoyi, *Zimbabwe* 87 F3
Chini, *India* 68 D8
Chiniot, *Pakistan* 68 D5
Chínipas, *Mexico* 118 B3
Chinji, *Pakistan* 68 C5
Chinju, *S. Korea* 57 G15
Chinle, *U.S.A.* 109 H9
Chinmen, *Taiwan* 59 E13
Chinmen Tao, *Taiwan* 59 E12
Chinnampo = Namp'o, *N. Korea* 57 E13
Chino, *Japan* 55 G9
Chino, *U.S.A.* 111 L9
Chino Valley, *U.S.A.* 109 J7
Chinon, *France* 18 E7
Chinook, *U.S.A.* 108 B9
Chinsali, *Zambia* 87 E3
Chióggia, *Italy* 41 C9
Chíos = Khíos, *Greece* 47 C8
Chipata, *Zambia* 87 E3
Chiperceni, *Moldova* 29 C13
Chipinge, *Zimbabwe* 87 G3
Chipinge △, *Zimbabwe* 87 G3
Chipiona, *Spain* 37 J4
Chipley, *U.S.A.* 115 K3
Chipman, *Canada* 105 C6
Chipoka, *Malawi* 87 E3
Chippenham, *U.K.* 15 F5
Chippewa ➜, *U.S.A.* 112 C8
Chippewa Falls, *U.S.A.* 112 C9
Chipping Norton, *U.K.* 15 F6
Chiprovtsi, *Bulgaria* 44 C6
Chiputneticook Lakes, *U.S.A.* .. 115 C11
Chiquián, *Peru* 124 F3
Chiquibul △, *Belize* 120 C2
Chiquimula, *Guatemala* 120 D2
Chiquinquira, *Colombia* 124 B4
Chir ➜, *Russia* 35 F6
Chirala, *India* 66 M12
Chiramba, *Mozam.* 87 F3
Chirawa, *India* 68 E6
Chirchiq, *Uzbekistan* 52 E7
Chiredzi, *Zimbabwe* 89 C5
Chiricahua △, *U.S.A.* 109 K9
Chiricahua Peak, *U.S.A.* 109 L9
Chiriquí, G. de, *Panama* 120 E3
Chiriquí, L. de, *Panama* 120 E3
Chirisa △, *Zimbabwe* 87 F2
Chirivira Falls, *Zimbabwe* 87 G3

Chirmiri, *India* 67 H13
Chirnogi, *Romania* 29 F11
Chirpan, *Bulgaria* 45 D9
Chirripó Grande, Cerro,
  Costa Rica 120 E3
Chirundu, *Zimbabwe* 89 B4
Chisamba, *Zambia* 87 E2
Chisapani Garhi, *Nepal* 67 F14
Chisasibi, *Canada* 104 B4
Ch'ishan, *Taiwan* 59 F13
Chisholm, *Canada* 102 C6
Chisholm, *U.S.A.* 112 B8
Chishtian Mandi, *Pakistan* 68 E5
Chishui, *China* 58 C5
Chishui He ➜, *China* 58 C5
Chisimaio, *Somali Rep.* 77 G8
Chisimba Falls, *Zambia* 87 E3
Chişinău, *Moldova* 29 C13
Chişinău ✈ (KIV), *Moldova* .. 29 C13
Chişineu Criş, *Romania* 28 D6
Chisone ➜, *Italy* 40 D4
Chisos Mts., *U.S.A.* 113 L3
Chistopol, *Russia* 34 C10
Chita, *Russia* 53 D12
Chitipa, *Malawi* 87 D3
Chitose, *Japan* 54 C10
Chitral, *Pakistan* 66 B7
Chitré, *Panama* 120 E3
Chittagong, *Bangla.* 67 H17
Chittagong □, *Bangla.* 67 G17
Chittaurgarh, *India* 68 G6
Chittoor, *India* 66 N11
Chitungwiza, *Zimbabwe* 87 F3
Chiusi, *Italy* 41 E8
Chiva, *Spain* 39 F4
Chivasso, *Italy* 40 C4
Chivhu, *Zimbabwe* 87 F3
Chivilcoy, *Argentina* 126 C4
Chiwanda, *Tanzania* 87 E3
Chixi, *China* 59 G9
Chizarira, *Zimbabwe* 87 F2
Chizarira △, *Zimbabwe* 87 F2
Chizera, *Zambia* 87 E2
Chkalov = Orenburg, *Russia* .. 52 D6
Chkolovsk, *Russia* 34 B6
Chloride, *U.S.A.* 111 K12
Chlumec nad Cidlinou,
  Czech Rep. 26 A8
Chmielnik, *Poland* 31 H7
Cho, *Vietnam* 58 G5
Cho-do, *N. Korea* 57 E13
Cho Phuoc Hai, *Vietnam* 65 G6
Choa Chu Kang, *Singapore* .. 65 d
Choba, *Kenya* 86 B4
Chobe △, *Botswana* 88 B4
Choch'iwŏn, *S. Korea* 57 F14
Chociwel, *Poland* 30 E2
Chocolate Mts., *U.S.A.* 111 M11
Choctawhatchee ➜, *U.S.A.* .. 115 K3
Chodecz, *Poland* 31 F6
Chodov, *Czech Rep.* 26 A5
Chodziez, *Poland* 31 F3
Choele Choel, *Argentina* 128 D3
Choiseul, *St. Lucia* .... 121 f
Choix, *Mexico* 118 B3
Chojna, *Poland* 31 F1
Chojnice, *Poland* 30 E4
Chojnów, *Poland* 31 G2
Chōkai-San, *Japan* 54 E10
Choke Canyon L., *U.S.A.* 113 L5
Choke Mts., *Ethiopia* 81 E4
Chokurdakh, *Russia* 53 B15
Cholame, *U.S.A.* 110 K6
Cholet, *France* 18 E6
Cholguan, *Chile* 126 D1
Choluteca, *Honduras* 120 D2
Choluteca ➜, *Honduras* 120 D2
Chom Bung, *Thailand* 64 F2
Chom Thong, *Thailand* 64 C2
Choma, *Zambia* 87 F2
Chomolungma = Everest, Mt.,
  Nepal 69 E12
Chomun, *India* 68 F6
Chomutov, *Czech Rep.* 26 A6
Chon Buri, *Thailand* 64 F3
Chon Thanh, *Vietnam* 65 G6
Ch'onan, *S. Korea* 57 F14
Chone, *Ecuador* 124 D3
Chong Kai, *Cambodia* 64 F4
Chong Mek, *Thailand* 64 E5
Chong Phangan, *Thailand* .... 65 b
Chong Samui, *Thailand* ...... 65 b
Chongde, *China* 59 B13
Chŏngdo, *S. Korea* 57 G15
Chŏngha, *S. Korea* 57 F15
Chŏngju, *S. Korea* 57 F14
Chŏngju, *N. Korea* 57 E13
Chongli, *China* 56 D8
Chongming, *China* 59 B13
Chongming Dao, *China* 59 B13
Chongqing, *Chongqing, China* .. 58 C6
Chongqing, *Sichuan, China* 58 B4
Chongqing Shi □, *China* 58 C6
Chongren, *China* 59 D11
Chonguene, *Mozam.* 89 C5
Chŏngŭp, *S. Korea* 57 G14
Chongyi, *China* 59 E10
Chongzuo, *China* 58 F6
Chŏnju, *S. Korea* 57 G14
Chonos, Arch. de los, *Chile* .. 128 F2
Chop, *Ukraine* 28 B7
Chopim ➜, *Brazil* 127 B5
Chor, *Pakistan* 68 G3
Chorbat La, *India* 69 B7
Chorley, *U.K.* 14 D5
Chorna, *Ukraine* 29 C14
Chornobyl, *Ukraine* 33 G6
Chornomorske, *Ukraine* 33 K7
Chorolque, Cerro, *Bolivia* 126 A2
Choroszcz, *Poland* 31 E9

Chorregon, *Australia* 94 C3
Chorro el Indio △, *Venezuela* .. 121 E5
Chortkiv, *Ukraine* 33 H3
Ch'ŏrwon, *S. Korea* 57 E14
Chorzele, *Poland* 31 E7
Chorzów, *Poland* 31 H5
Chos-Malal, *Argentina* 126 D1
Chosan, *N. Korea* 57 D13
Choszczno, *Poland* 31 E2
Choteau, *U.S.A.* 108 C7
Chotěboř, *Czech Rep.* 26 B8
Chotila, *India* 68 H4
Chotta Udepur, *India* 68 H6
Chowchilla, *U.S.A.* 110 H6
Choybalsan, *Mongolia* 60 B6
Christchurch, *N.Z.* 91 K4
Christchurch, *U.K.* 15 G6
Christian I., *Canada* 116 B4
Christiana, *S. Africa* 88 D4
Christiansfeld, *Denmark* 11 J3
Christiansted, *U.S. Virgin Is.* .. 121 C7
Christie ➜, *Canada* 103 A6
Christina ➜, *Canada* 103 B6
Christmas Cr. ➜, *Australia* .. 92 C4
Christmas I. = Kiritimati, *Kiribati* 97 G12
Christmas I., *Ind. Oc.* 96 J2
Christopher L., *Australia* 93 D4
Chrudim, *Czech Rep.* 26 B8
Chrzanów, *Poland* 31 H6
Chtimba, *Malawi* 87 E3
Chū = Shū, *Kazakhstan* 52 E8
Chū = Shū ➜, *Kazakhstan* .. 50 E10
Chu ➜, *Vietnam* 64 C5
Chu Lai, *Vietnam* 64 E7
Chuak, Ko, *Thailand* .... 65 b
Ch'uanchou = Quanzhou, *China* 59 E12
Chuankou, *China* 56 G6
Chubbuck, *U.S.A.* 108 E7
Chūbu □, *Japan* 55 F8
Chubu-Sangaku △, *Japan* 55 F8
Chubut ➜, *Argentina* 128 E3
Chuchi L., *Canada* 102 B4
Chuda, *India* 68 H4
Chudovo, *Russia* 32 C6
Chudskoye, Ozero, *Russia* 9 G22
Chūgoku □, *Japan* 55 G6
Chūgoku-Sanchi, *Japan* 55 G6
Chuguyev = Chuhuyiv, *Ukraine* 33 H9
Chugwater, *U.S.A.* 112 E2
Chuhuyiv, *Ukraine* 33 H9
Chukchi Sea, *Russia* 53 C19
Chukotskoye Nagorye, *Russia* .. 53 C18
Chula Vista, *U.S.A.* 111 N9
Chulman, *Russia* 53 D13
Chulucanas, *Peru* 124 E2
Chulym ➜, *Russia* 52 D9
Chum Phae, *Thailand* 64 D4
Chum Saeng, *Thailand* 64 E3
Chumar, *India* 69 C8
Chumbicha, *Argentina* 126 B2
Chumerna, *Bulgaria* 45 D9
Chumikan, *Russia* 53 D14
Chumphon, *Thailand* 65 G2
Chumuare, *Mozam.* 87 E3
Chumunjin, *S. Korea* 57 F15
Chuna ➜, *Russia* 53 D10
Chun'an, *China* 59 C12
Ch'unch'ŏn, *S. Korea* 57 F14
Chunchura, *India* 69 H13
Chunga, *Zambia* 87 F2
Chŭnggang-ŭp, *N. Korea* 57 D14
Chunghwa, *N. Korea* 57 E13
Ch'ungju, *S. Korea* 57 F14
Chungking = Chongqing, *China* .. 58 C6
Chungli, *Taiwan* 59 E13
Ch'ungmu, *S. Korea* 57 G15
Chungt'iaoshan = Zhongtiao
  Shan, *China* 56 G6
Chungyang Shanmo, *Taiwan* .. 59 F13
Chunian, *Pakistan* 68 D6
Chunya, *Tanzania* 87 D3
Chunyang, *China* 57 C15
Chupara Pt., *Trin. & Tob.* 125 K15
Chuquibamba, *Peru* 124 G4
Chuquicamata, *Chile* 126 A2
Chur, *Switz.* 25 J5
Churachandpur, *India* 67 G18
Church Stretton, *U.K.* 15 E5
Churchill, *Canada* 103 B10
Churchill ➜, *Man., Canada* .. 103 B10
Churchill ➜, *Nfld. & L., Canada* 105 B7
Churchill, C., *Canada* 103 B10
Churchill Falls, *Canada* 105 B7
Churchill L., *Canada* 103 B7
Churchill Pk., *Canada* 102 B3
Churki, *India* 69 H10
Churu, *India* 68 E6
Churún Merú = Angel Falls,
  Venezuela 124 B6
Chushal, *India* 69 C8
Chuska Mts., *U.S.A.* 109 H9
Chusovoy, *Russia* 52 D6
Chute-aux-Outardes, *Canada* .. 105 C6
Chuuronjang, *N. Korea* 57 D15
Chuvash Republic = Chuvashia □,
  Russia 34 C8
Chuvashia □, *Russia* 34 C8
Chuwārtah, *Iraq* 70 C5
Chuxiong, *China* 58 E3
Chuy, *Uruguay* 127 C5
Chuzhou, *China* 59 A12
Chynadiyeve, *Ukraine* 28 B7
Ci Xian, *China* 56 F8
Ciacova, *Romania* 28 E6
Ciadâr-Lunga, *Moldova* 29 D13
Ciamis, *Indonesia* 63 G13
Cianjur, *Indonesia* 63 G13
Cianorte, *Brazil* 127 A5
Cibola, *U.S.A.* 111 M12
Cicero, *U.S.A.* 114 E2
Cidacos ➜, *Spain* 38 C3
Cide, *Turkey* 72 B5

Ciénagas del Catatumbo △,
  Venezuela 121 E5
Ciechanów, *Poland* 31 F7
Ciechanowiec, *Poland* 31 F9
Ciechocinek, *Poland* 31 F5
Ciego de Ávila, *Cuba* 120 B4
Ciénaga, *Colombia* 124 A4
Cienfuegos, *Cuba* 120 B3
Cierp-Gaud, *France* 20 F4
Cíes, Is., *Spain* 36 C2
Cieszanów, *Poland* 31 H10
Cieszyn, *Poland* 31 J5
Cieza, *Spain* 39 G3
Cifteler, *Turkey* 72 C4
Cifuentes, *Spain* 38 E2
Cihanbeyli, *Turkey* 72 C5
Cihuatlán, *Mexico* 118 D4
Cijara △, *Spain* 37 F6
Cijara, Embalse de, *Spain* 37 F6
Cijulang, *Indonesia* 63 G13
Cilacap, *Indonesia* 63 G13
Çıldır, *Turkey* 73 B10
Çıldır Gölü, *Turkey* 73 B10
Cilento e Vallo di Diano △, *Italy* 43 B8
Cili, *China* 59 C8
Cilibia, *Romania* 29 E12
Cilicia, *Turkey* 72 D5
Cill Chainnigh = Kilkenny,
  Ireland 12 D4
Cilo Dağı, *Turkey* 73 D10
Cima, *U.S.A.* 111 K11
Cimarron, *Kans., U.S.A.* 113 G4
Cimarron, *N. Mex., U.S.A.* .. 113 G2
Cimarron ➜, *U.S.A.* 113 G6
Cimişlia, *Moldova* 29 D13
Cimone, Mte., *Italy* 40 D7
Çınar, *Turkey* 73 D9
Çınarcık, *Turkey* 45 F13
Cinca ➜, *Spain* 38 D5
Cincar, *Bos.-H.* 28 G2
Cincinnati, *U.S.A.* 114 F3
Cincinnatus, *U.S.A.* 117 D9
Çine, *Turkey* 47 D10
Ciney, *Belgium* 17 D5
Cíngoli, *Italy* 41 E10
Cinigiano, *Italy* 41 F8
Cinto, Mte., *France* 21 F12
Cintruénigo, *Spain* 38 C3
Ciocile, *Romania* 29 F12
Ciolănești din Deal, *Romania* .. 29 F10
Ciorani, *Romania* 29 F11
Ciovo, *Croatia* 41 E13
Circeo, Mte., *Italy* 42 A6
Çırçır, *Turkey* 72 C7
Circle, *Alaska, U.S.A.* 100 B5
Circle, *Mont., U.S.A.* 112 B2
Circleville, *U.S.A.* 114 F4
Cirebon, *Indonesia* 63 G13
Ciremay, *Indonesia* 63 G13
Cirencester, *U.K.* 15 F6
Cireşu, *Romania* 28 F7
Cirey-sur-Vezouze, *France* .. 19 D13
Ciriè, *Italy* 40 C4
Cirium, *Cyprus* 49 E11
Cirò, *Italy* 43 C10
Cirò Marina, *Italy* 43 C10
Ciron ➜, *France* 20 D3
Cisco, *U.S.A.* 113 J5
Cislău, *Romania* 29 E11
Cisna, *Poland* 31 J9
Cisnădie, *Romania* 29 E9
Cisterna di Latina, *Italy* 42 A5
Cisternino, *Italy* 43 B10
Cistierna, *Spain* 36 C5
Citeli-Ckaro = Tsiteli-Tsqaro,
  Georgia 35 K8
Citlaltépetl = Orizaba, Pico de,
  Mexico 119 D5
Citrus Heights, *U.S.A.* 110 G5
Citrusdal, *S. Africa* 88 E2
Città di Castello, *Italy* 41 E9
Città Sant' Angelo, *Italy* 41 F11
Cittadella, *Italy* 41 C8
Cittaducale, *Italy* 41 F9
Cittanova, *Italy* 43 D9
Ciuc, Munții, *Romania* 29 D11
Ciucaş, Vf., *Romania* 29 E10
Ciucea, *Romania* 28 D7
Ciuciulea, *Moldova* 29 C12
Ciuciuleni, *Moldova* 29 C13
Ciudad Altamirano, *Mexico* .. 118 D4
Ciudad Bolívar, *Venezuela* .. 124 B6
Ciudad Camargo, *Mexico* 118 B3
Ciudad de Valles, *Mexico* 119 C5
Ciudad del Carmen, *Mexico* .. 119 D6
Ciudad del Este, *Paraguay* .. 127 B5
Ciudad Delicias = Delicias,
  Mexico 118 B3
Ciudad Guayana, *Venezuela* .. 124 B6
Ciudad Guerrero, *Mexico* 118 B3
Ciudad Guzmán, *Mexico* 118 D4
Ciudad Juárez, *Mexico* 118 A3
Ciudad Madero, *Mexico* 119 C5
Ciudad Mante, *Mexico* 119 C5
Ciudad Obregón, *Mexico* 118 B3
Ciudad Real, *Spain* 37 G7
Ciudad Real □, *Spain* 37 G7
Ciudad Rodrigo, *Spain* 36 E4
Ciudad Victoria, *Mexico* 119 C5
Ciudadela, *Spain* 48 B10
Ciulnița, *Romania* 29 F12
Ciumeghiu, *Romania* 28 D6
Ciuperceni, *Romania* 28 F8
Civa Burnu, *Turkey* 72 B7
Cividale del Friuli, *Italy* 41 B10
Civita Castellana, *Italy* 41 F9
Civitanova Marche, *Italy* 41 E10
Civitavécchia, *Italy* 41 F8
Civray, *France* 20 B4
Çivril, *Turkey* 47 C11
Cixerri ➜, *Italy* 42 C1

Cixi, *China* 59 B13
Cizre, *Turkey* 70 B4
Cizur Mayor, *Spain* 38 C3
Clackmannanshire □, *U.K.* ... 13 E5
Clacton-on-Sea, *U.K.* 15 F9
Clain →, *France* 18 F7
Claire, L., *Canada* 102 B6
Clairton, *U.S.A.* 116 F5
Clairvaux-les-Lacs, *France* . 19 F12
Claise →, *France* 20 B5
Clallam Bay, *U.S.A.* 110 B2
Clamecy, *France* 19 E10
Clanton, *U.S.A.* 115 J2
Clanwilliam, *S. Africa* 88 E2
Clara, *Ireland* 12 C4
Claraville, *U.S.A.* 111 K8
Clare, *Australia* 95 E2
Clare, *U.S.A.* 114 D3
Clare □, *Ireland* 12 D3
Clare →, *Ireland* 12 C2
Clare I., *Ireland* 12 C1
Claremont, *Calif., U.S.A.* .. 111 L9
Claremont, *N.H., U.S.A.* 117 C12
Claremont Pt., *Australia* ... 94 A3
Claremore, *U.S.A.* 113 G7
Claremorris, *Ireland* 12 C3
Clarence →, *Australia* 95 D5
Clarence →, *N.Z.* 91 K4
Clarence, I., *Chile* 128 G2
Clarence I., *Antarctica* 5 C18
Clarence Str., *Australia* ... 92 B5
Clarence Town, *Bahamas* 121 B5
Clarendon, *Pa., U.S.A.* 116 E5
Clarendon, *Tex., U.S.A.* 113 H4
Clarenville-Shoal Harbour,
   Canada 105 C9
Claresholm, *Canada* 102 D6
Clarie Coast, *Antarctica* ... 5 C9
Clarinda, *U.S.A.* 112 E7
Clarington, *Canada* 116 C6
Clarion, *Iowa, U.S.A.* 112 D8
Clarion, *Pa., U.S.A.* 116 E5
Clarion →, *U.S.A.* 116 E5
Clarion Fracture Zone, *Pac. Oc.* . 98 H7
Clark, *U.S.A.* 112 C6
Clark, Pt., *Canada* 116 B3
Clark Fork, *U.S.A.* 108 B5
Clark Fork →, *U.S.A.* 108 B5
Clarkdale, *U.S.A.* 109 J7
Clarke City, *Canada* 105 B6
Clarke I., *Australia* 95 G4
Clarke Ra., *Australia* 94 J6
Clark's Fork →, *U.S.A.* 108 D9
Clark's Harbour, *Canada* 105 D6
Clarks Hill L., *U.S.A.* 115 J4
Clarks Summit, *U.S.A.* 117 E9
Clarksburg, *U.S.A.* 114 F5
Clarksdale, *U.S.A.* 113 H9
Clarksville, *Ark., U.S.A.* .. 113 H8
Clarksville, *Tenn., U.S.A.* . 115 G2
Clarksville, *Tex., U.S.A.* .. 113 J7
Clatskanie, *U.S.A.* 110 D3
Claude, *U.S.A.* 113 H4
Claveria, *Phil.* 61 B4
Clay, *U.S.A.* 110 G5
Clay Center, *U.S.A.* 112 F6
Claypool, *U.S.A.* 109 K8
Claysburg, *U.S.A.* 116 F6
Claysville, *U.S.A.* 116 F4
Clayton, *N. Mex., U.S.A.* ... 113 G3
Clayton, *N.Y., U.S.A.* 117 B8
Clear, C., *Ireland* 12 E2
Clear, L., *Canada* 116 A7
Clear Hills, *Canada* 102 B5
Clear I., *Ireland* 12 E2
Clear L., *U.S.A.* 110 F4
Clear Lake, *Iowa, U.S.A.* ... 112 D8
Clear Lake, *S. Dak., U.S.A.* 112 C6
Clear Lake Reservoir, *U.S.A.* 108 F3
Clearfield, *Pa., U.S.A.* 116 E6
Clearfield, *Utah, U.S.A.* ... 108 F8
Clearlake, *U.S.A.* 108 G2
Clearlake Highlands, *U.S.A.* 110 G4
Clearwater, *Canada* 102 C4
Clearwater, *U.S.A.* 115 M4
Clearwater →, *Alta., Canada* 102 C6
Clearwater →, *Alta., Canada* 103 B6
Clearwater L., *Canada* 103 C9
Clearwater Lake △, *Canada* .. 103 C8
Clearwater Mts., *U.S.A.* 108 C6
Clearwater River △, *Canada* . 103 B7
Cleburne, *U.S.A.* 113 J6
Clee Hills, *U.K.* 15 E5
Cleethorpes, *U.K.* 14 D7
Cleeve Cloud, *U.K.* 15 F6
Clelles, *France* 21 D9
Clemson, *U.S.A.* 115 H4
Clerke Reef, *Australia* 92 C2
Clermont, *Australia* 94 C4
Clermont, *France* 19 C9
Clermont, *U.S.A.* 115 L5
Clermont-en-Argonne, *France* 19 C12
Clermont-Ferrand, *France* ... 20 C7
Clermont-l'Hérault, *France* . 20 E7
Clerval, *France* 19 E13
Clervaux, *Lux.* 17 D6
Cles, *Italy* 40 B8
Clevedon, *U.K.* 15 F5
Cleveland, *Miss., U.S.A.* ... 113 J9
Cleveland, *Ohio, U.S.A.* 116 E3
Cleveland, *Okla., U.S.A.* ... 113 G6
Cleveland, *Tenn., U.S.A.* ... 115 H3
Cleveland, *Tex., U.S.A.* 113 K7
Cleveland, C., *Australia* ... 94 B4
Cleveland, Mt., *U.S.A.* 108 B7
Cleveland Heights, *U.S.A.* .. 116 E3
Clevelândia, *Brazil* 127 B5
Clew B., *Ireland* 12 C2
Clewiston, *U.S.A.* 115 M5
Clifden, *Ireland* 12 C1
Clifden, *N.Z.* 91 M1
Cliffdell, *U.S.A.* 110 D5

Cliffy Hd., *Australia* 93 G2
Clifton, *Australia* 95 D5
Clifton, *Ariz., U.S.A.* 109 K9
Clifton, *Colo., U.S.A.* 109 G9
Clifton, *Tex., U.S.A.* 113 K6
Clifton Beach, *Australia* ... 94 B4
Climax, *Canada* 103 D7
Clinch →, *U.S.A.* 115 H3
Clingmans Dome, *U.S.A.* 115 H4
Clint, *U.S.A.* 109 L10
Clinton, *B.C., Canada* 102 C4
Clinton, *Ont., Canada* 116 C3
Clinton, *N.Z.* 91 M2
Clinton, *Ark., U.S.A.* 113 H8
Clinton, *Conn., U.S.A.* 117 E12
Clinton, *Ill., U.S.A.* 112 E10
Clinton, *Ind., U.S.A.* 114 F2
Clinton, *Iowa, U.S.A.* 112 E9
Clinton, *Mass., U.S.A.* 117 D13
Clinton, *Miss., U.S.A.* 113 J9
Clinton, *Mo., U.S.A.* 112 F8
Clinton, *N.C., U.S.A.* 115 H6
Clinton, *Okla., U.S.A.* 113 H5
Clinton, *S.C., U.S.A.* 115 H5
Clinton, *Tenn., U.S.A.* 115 G3
Clinton, *Wash., U.S.A.* 110 C4
Clinton C., *Australia* 94 C5
Clinton Colden L., *Canada* .. 100 B9
Clintonville, *U.S.A.* 112 C10
Clipperton, I., *Pac. Oc.* ... 97 F17
Clisham, *U.K.* 13 D2
Clisson, *France* 18 E5
Clitheroe, *U.K.* 14 D5
Clo-oose, *Canada* 110 B2
Cloates, Pt., *Australia* 92 D1
Clocolan, *S. Africa* 89 D4
Clodomira, *Argentina* 126 B3
Clogher Hd., *Ireland* 12 C5
Clonakilty, *Ireland* 12 E3
Clonakilty B., *Ireland* 12 E3
Cloncurry, *Australia* 94 C3
Cloncurry →, *Australia* 94 B3
Clondalkin, *Ireland* 12 C5
Clones, *Ireland* 12 B4
Clonmel, *Ireland* 12 D4
Cloppenburg, *Germany* 24 C4
Cloquet, *U.S.A.* 112 B8
Clorinda, *Argentina* 126 B4
Cloud Bay, *Canada* 104 C2
Cloud Peak, *U.S.A.* 108 D10
Cloudcroft, *U.S.A.* 109 K11
Cloverdale, *U.S.A.* 110 G4
Clovis, *Calif., U.S.A.* 110 J7
Clovis, *N. Mex., U.S.A.* 113 H3
Cloyes-sur-le-Loir, *France* . 18 E8
Cloyne, *Canada* 116 B7
Cluj □, *Romania* 29 D8
Cluj-Napoca, *Romania* 29 D8
Clunes, *Australia* 95 F3
Cluny, *France* 19 F11
Cluses, *France* 19 F13
Clusone, *Italy* 40 C6
Clutha →, *N.Z.* 91 M2
Clwyd □, *U.K.* 14 D4
Clwyd →, *U.K.* 14 D4
Clyde, *Canada* 102 C6
Clyde, *N.Z.* 91 L2
Clyde, *U.S.A.* 116 C8
Clyde →, *U.K.* 13 F4
Clyde, Firth of, *U.K.* 13 F3
Clyde Muirshiel △, *U.K.* 13 F4
Clyde River, *Canada* 101 A13
Clydebank, *U.K.* 13 F4
Clymer, *N.Y., U.S.A.* 116 D5
Clymer, *Pa., U.S.A.* 116 D5
Ćmielów, *Poland* 31 H8
Côa →, *Portugal* 36 D3
Coachella, *U.S.A.* 111 M10
Coachella Canal, *U.S.A.* 111 N12
Coahoma, *U.S.A.* 113 J4
Coahuayana →, *Mexico* 118 D4
Coahuila □, *Mexico* 118 B4
Coal →, *Canada* 102 B3
Coalane, *Mozam.* 87 F4
Coalcomán, *Mexico* 118 D4
Coaldale, *Canada* 102 D6
Coalgate, *U.S.A.* 113 H6
Coalinga, *U.S.A.* 110 J6
Coalisland, *U.K.* 12 B5
Coalville, *U.K.* 14 E6
Coalville, *U.S.A.* 108 F8
Coamo, *Puerto Rico* .... 121 d
Coari, *Brazil* 124 D6
Coast □, *Kenya* 86 C4
Coast Mts., *Canada* 102 C3
Coast Ranges, *U.S.A.* 110 G4
Coatbridge, *U.K.* 13 F4
Coatepec, *Mexico* 119 D5
Coatepeque, *Guatemala* 120 D1
Coatesville, *U.S.A.* 114 F8
Coaticook, *Canada* 117 A13
Coats I., *Canada* 101 B11
Coats Land, *Antarctica* 5 D1
Coatzacoalcos, *Mexico* 119 D6
Coba, *Mexico* 119 C7
Cobadin, *Romania* 29 F13
Cobalt, *Canada* 104 C4
Cobán, *Guatemala* 120 C1
Çobanlar, *Turkey* 47 C12
Cobar, *Australia* 95 E4
Cóbh, *Ireland* 12 E3
Cobija, *Bolivia* 124 F5
Cobleskill, *U.S.A.* 117 D10
Coboconk, *Canada* 116 B6
Cobourg, *Canada* 116 C6
Cobourg △, *Australia* 92 B5
Cobourg Pen., *Australia* 92 B5
Cobram, *Australia* 95 F4
Cóbué, *Mozam.* 87 E3
Coburg, *Germany* 25 E6
Coca, *Spain* 36 D6
Cocanada = Kakinada, *India* . 67 L13
Cocentaina, *Spain* 39 G4

Cochabamba, *Bolivia* 124 G5
Cochem, *Germany* 25 E3
Cochemane, *Mozam.* 87 F3
Cochin, *India* 66 Q10
Cochin China = Nam-Phan,
   Vietnam 65 G6
Cochran, *U.S.A.* 115 J4
Cochrane, *Alta., Canada* 102 C6
Cochrane, *Ont., Canada* 104 C3
Cochrane, *Chile* 128 F2
Cochrane →, *Canada* 103 B8
Cochrane, L., *Chile* 128 F2
Cochranton, *U.S.A.* 116 E4
Cockburn, *Australia* 95 E3
Cockburn, Canal, *Chile* 128 G2
Cockburn I., *Canada* 104 C3
Cockburn Ra., *Australia* 92 C4
Cockermouth, *U.K.* 14 C4
Cocklebiddy, *Australia* 93 F4
Cockpit Country, The, *Jamaica* 120 a
Coco →, *Cent. Amer.* 120 D3
Coco, I. del, *Pac. Oc.* 97 G19
Cocoa, *U.S.A.* 115 L5
Cocobeach, *Gabon* 84 D1
Cocora, *Romania* 29 F12
Cocos B., *Trin. & Tob.* 125 K15
Cocos Is., *Ind. Oc.* 96 J1
Cod, C., *U.S.A.* 114 D10
Codajás, *Brazil* 124 D6
Codigoro, *Italy* 41 D9
Codlea, *Romania* 29 E10
Codó, *Brazil* 125 D10
Codogno, *Italy* 40 C6
Codróipo, *Italy* 41 C10
Codru, Munţii, *Romania* 28 D7
Cody, *U.S.A.* 108 D9
Coe Hill, *Canada* 116 B7
Coelemu, *Chile* 126 D1
Coen, *Australia* 94 A3
Coesfeld, *Germany* 24 D3
Cœur d'Alene, *U.S.A.* 108 C5
Cœur d'Alene L., *U.S.A.* 108 C5
Coevorden, *Neths.* 17 B6
Cofete, *Canary Is.* 48 F5
Coffeyville, *U.S.A.* 113 G7
Coffin B., *Australia* 95 E2
Coffin Bay, *Australia* 95 E2
Coffin Bay Peninsula, *Australia* 95 E2
Coffs Harbour, *Australia* ... 95 E5
Cofre de Perote △, *Mexico* .. 119 D5
Cofrentes, *Spain* 39 F3
Cogalnic →, *Moldova* 29 E14
Cogealac, *Romania* 29 F13
Coghinas →, *Italy* 42 B1
Coghinas, L. del, *Italy* 42 B2
Cognac, *France* 20 C3
Cogne, *Italy* 40 C4
Cogolin, *France* 21 E10
Cogolludo, *Spain* 38 E1
Cohocton, *U.S.A.* 116 D7
Cohocton →, *U.S.A.* 116 D7
Cohoes, *U.S.A.* 117 D11
Cohuna, *Australia* 95 F3
Coiba, I., *Panama* 120 E3
Coig →, *Argentina* 128 G3
Coigeach, Rubha, *U.K.* 13 C3
Coihaique, *Chile* 128 F2
Coimbatore, *India* 66 P10
Coimbra, *Brazil* 124 G7
Coimbra, *Portugal* 36 E2
Coimbra □, *Portugal* 36 E2
Coín, *Spain* 37 J6
Coipasa, Salar de, *Bolivia* . 124 G5
Cojimies, *Ecuador* 124 C3
Cojocna, *Romania* 29 D8
Cojutepequé, *El Salv.* 120 D2
Çoka, *Serbia & M.* 28 E5
Cokeville, *U.S.A.* 108 E8
Colac, *Australia* 95 F3
Colatina, *Brazil* 125 G10
Colbeck, C., *Antarctica* 5 D13
Colborne, *Canada* 116 C7
Colby, *U.S.A.* 112 F4
Colchester, *U.K.* 15 F8
Cold L., *Canada* 103 C7
Coldstream, *Canada* 102 C5
Coldstream, *U.K.* 13 F6
Coldwater, *Canada* 116 B5
Coldwater, *Kans., U.S.A.* ... 113 G5
Coldwater, *Mich., U.S.A.* ... 114 E3
Colebrook, *U.S.A.* 117 B13
Coleman, *U.S.A.* 113 K5
Coleman →, *Australia* 94 B3
Colenso, *S. Africa* 89 D4
Coleraine, *Australia* 95 F3
Coleraine, *U.K.* 12 A5
Coleridge, L., *N.Z.* 91 K3
Colesberg, *S. Africa* 88 E4
Coleville, *U.S.A.* 110 G7
Colfax, *Calif., U.S.A.* 110 F6
Colfax, *La., U.S.A.* 113 K8
Colfax, *Wash., U.S.A.* 108 C5
Colhué Huapi, L., *Argentina* 128 F3
Colibaşi, *Moldova* 29 E13
Colibaşi, *Romania* 29 F9
Cólico, *Italy* 40 B6
Coligny, *France* 19 F12
Coligny, *S. Africa* 89 D4
Colima, *Mexico* 118 D4
Colima □, *Mexico* 118 D4
Colima, Nevado de, *Mexico* .. 118 D4
Colina, *Chile* 126 C1
Colina do Norte, *Guinea-Biss.* 82 C2
Colinas, *Brazil* 125 E10
Colindres, *Spain* 36 B7
Coll, *U.K.* 13 E2
Collaguasi, *Chile* 126 A2
Collarada, Peña, *Spain* 38 C4
Collarenebri, *Australia* 95 D4
Colle di Val d'Elsa, *Italy* . 40 E8
Collécchio, *Italy* 40 D7

Colleen Bawn, *Zimbabwe* 87 G2
College Park, *U.S.A.* 115 J3
College Station, *U.S.A.* 113 K6
Collesalvetti, *Italy* 40 E7
Colli Euganei △, *Italy* 41 C8
Collie, *Australia* 93 F2
Collier B., *Australia* 92 C3
Collier Ra., *Australia* 93 D2
Collier Range △, *Australia* . 93 D2
Collina, Passo di, *Italy* ... 40 D7
Collingwood, *Canada* 116 B4
Collingwood, *N.Z.* 91 J4
Collins, *Canada* 104 B2
Collinsville, *Australia* 94 C4
Collipulli, *Chile* 126 D1
Collooney, *Ireland* 12 B3
Colmar, *France* 19 D14
Colmars, *France* 21 D10
Colmenar, *Spain* 37 J6
Colmenar de Oreja, *Spain* ... 36 E7
Colmenar Viejo, *Spain* 36 E7
Colo →, *Australia* 95 E5
Cologne = Köln, *Germany* 24 E2
Colom, I. d'en, *Spain* 48 B11
Coloma, *U.S.A.* 110 G6
Colomb-Béchar = Béchar, *Algeria* 78 B5
Colombey-les-Belles, *France* 19 D12
Colombey-les-Deux-Églises,
   France 19 D11
Colombia ■, *S. Amer.* 124 C4
Colombian Basin, *S. Amer.* .. 98 H12
Colombo, *Sri Lanka* 66 R11
Colomiers, *France* 20 E5
Colón, *Buenos Aires, Argentina* 126 C3
Colón, *Entre Ríos, Argentina* 126 C4
Colón, *Cuba* 120 B3
Colón, *Panama* 120 E4
Colón, Arch. de, *Ecuador* ... 97 H18
Colonia del Sacramento, *Uruguay* 126 C4
Colonia Dora, *Argentina* 126 B3
Colonial Beach, *U.S.A.* 114 F7
Colonie, *U.S.A.* 117 D11
Colonna, C., *Italy* 43 C10
Colonsay, *Canada* 103 C7
Colonsay, *U.K.* 13 E2
Colorado □, *U.S.A.* 109 G10
Colorado →, *Argentina* 128 D4
Colorado →, *N. Amer.* 109 L6
Colorado →, *U.S.A.* 113 L7
Colorado City, *U.S.A.* 113 J4
Colorado Plateau, *U.S.A.* ... 109 H8
Colorado River Aqueduct, *U.S.A.* 111 L12
Colorado Springs, *U.S.A.* ... 112 F2
Colorno, *Italy* 40 D7
Colstrip, *U.S.A.* 108 D10
Colton, *U.S.A.* 117 B10
Columbia, *Ky., U.S.A.* 114 G3
Columbia, *La., U.S.A.* 113 J8
Columbia, *Miss., U.S.A.* 113 K10
Columbia, *Mo., U.S.A.* 112 F8
Columbia, *Pa., U.S.A.* 117 F8
Columbia, *S.C., U.S.A.* 115 J5
Columbia, *Tenn., U.S.A.* 115 H2
Columbia →, *N. Amer.* 110 D2
Columbia, C., *Canada* 4 A4
Columbia, District of □, *U.S.A.* 114 F7
Columbia, Mt., *Canada* 102 C5
Columbia Basin, *U.S.A.* 108 C4
Columbia Falls, *U.S.A.* 108 B6
Columbia Mts., *Canada* 102 C5
Columbia Plateau, *U.S.A.* ... 108 D5
Columbiana, *U.S.A.* 116 F4
Columbretes, Is., *Spain* 38 F5
Columbus, *Ga., U.S.A.* 115 J3
Columbus, *Ind., U.S.A.* 114 F3
Columbus, *Kans., U.S.A.* 113 G7
Columbus, *Miss., U.S.A.* 115 J1
Columbus, *Mont., U.S.A.* 108 D9
Columbus, *N. Mex., U.S.A.* .. 109 L10
Columbus, *Nebr., U.S.A.* 112 E6
Columbus, *Ohio, U.S.A.* 114 F4
Columbus, *Tex., U.S.A.* 113 L6
Colunga, *Spain* 36 B5
Colusa, *U.S.A.* 110 F4
Colville, *U.S.A.* 108 B5
Colville →, *U.S.A.* 100 A4
Colville, C., *N.Z.* 91 G5
Colwood, *Canada* 110 B3
Colwyn Bay, *U.K.* 14 D4
Coma, *Ethiopia* 81 F4
Comácchio, *Italy* 41 D9
Comalcalco, *Mexico* 119 D6
Comallo, *Argentina* 128 E2
Comana, *Romania* 29 F11
Comanche, *U.S.A.* 113 K5
Comandante Ferraz, *Antarctica* 5 C18
Comănești, *Romania* 29 D11
Comarnic, *Romania* 29 E10
Comayagua, *Honduras* 120 D2
Combahee →, *U.S.A.* 115 J5
Combarbalá, *Chile* 126 C1
Combe Martin, *U.K.* 15 F3
Combeaufontaine, *France* 19 E12
Comber, *Canada* 116 D2
Comber, *U.K.* 12 B6
Combermere, *Canada* 116 A7
Comblain-au-Pont, *Belgium* .. 17 D5
Combourg, *France* 18 D5
Combrailles, *France* 19 F9
Combronde, *France* 20 C7
Comeragh Mts., *Ireland* 12 D4
Comet, *Australia* 94 C4
Comilla, *Bangla.* 67 H17
Comino, *Malta* 49 C1
Cómino, C., *Italy* 42 B2
Cómiso, *Italy* 43 F7
Comitán, *Mexico* 119 D6
Commentry, *France* 19 F9
Commerce, *Ga., U.S.A.* 115 H4
Commerce, *Tex., U.S.A.* 113 J7

Commercy, *France* 19 D12
Committee B., *Canada* 101 B11
Commonwealth B., *Antarctica* 5 C10
Commoron Cr. →, *Australia* .. 95 D5
Communism Pk. = Kommunizma,
   Pik, *Tajikistan* 52 F8
Como, *Italy* 40 C6
Como, Lago di, *Italy* 40 B6
Comodoro Rivadavia, *Argentina* 128 F3
Comoé →, *Ivory C.* 82 D4
Comorâşte, *Romania* 28 E6
Comorin, C., *India* 66 Q10
Comoro Is. = Comoros ■,
   Ind. Oc. 77 H8
Comoros ■, *Ind. Oc.* 77 H8
Comox, *Canada* 102 D4
Compiègne, *France* 19 C9
Comporta, *Portugal* 37 G2
Compostela, *Mexico* 118 C4
Comprida, I., *Brazil* 127 A6
Compton, *Canada* 117 A13
Compton, *U.S.A.* 111 M8
Comrat, *Moldova* 29 D13
Con Cuong, *Vietnam* 64 C5
Con Dao △, *Vietnam* 65 H6
Con Son, *Vietnam* 65 H6
Conakry, *Guinea* 82 D2
Conara, *Australia* 95 G4
Concarneau, *France* 18 E3
Conceição, *Mozam.* 87 F4
Conceição da Barra, *Brazil* . 125 G11
Conceição do Araguaia, *Brazil* 125 E9
Concepción, *Argentina* 126 B2
Concepción, *Bolivia* 124 G6
Concepción, *Chile* 126 D1
Concepción, *Mexico* 119 D6
Concepción, *Paraguay* 126 A4
Concepción □, *Chile* 126 D1
Concepción, Est. de, *Chile* . 128 G2
Concepción, L., *Bolivia* 124 G6
Concepción, Punta, *Mexico* .. 118 B2
Concepción del Oro, *Mexico* . 118 C4
Concepción del Uruguay,
   Argentina 126 C4
Conception, Pt., *U.S.A.* 111 L6
Conception B., *Canada* 105 C9
Conception B., *Namibia* 88 C1
Conception I., *Bahamas* 121 B4
Concession, *Zimbabwe* 87 F3
Conchas Dam, *U.S.A.* 113 H2
Conches-en-Ouche, *France* ... 18 D7
Concho, *U.S.A.* 109 J9
Concho →, *U.S.A.* 113 K5
Conchos →, *Chihuahua, Mexico* 118 B4
Conchos →, *Tamaulipas, Mexico* 119 B5
Concord, *Calif., U.S.A.* 110 H4
Concord, *N.C., U.S.A.* 115 H5
Concord, *N.H., U.S.A.* 117 C13
Concordia, *Argentina* 126 C4
Concórdia, *Brazil* 124 D5
Concordia, *Mexico* 118 C3
Concordia, *U.S.A.* 112 F6
Concrete, *U.S.A.* 108 B3
Condamine, *Australia* 95 D5
Condat, *France* 20 C6
Conde, *U.S.A.* 112 C5
Condé-sur-Noireau, *France* .. 18 D6
Condeúba, *Brazil* 125 F10
Condobolin, *Australia* 95 E4
Condom, *France* 20 E4
Condon, *U.S.A.* 108 D3
Conegliano, *Italy* 41 C9
Conejera, I. = Conills, I. des,
   Spain 48 B9
Conejos, *Mexico* 118 B4
Conemaugh →, *U.S.A.* 116 F5
Conero △, *Italy* 41 E10
Confolens, *France* 20 B4
Confuso →, *Paraguay* 126 B4
Congaz, *Moldova* 29 D13
Conghua, *China* 59 F9
Congjiang, *China* 58 E7
Congleton, *U.K.* 14 D5
Congo (Kinshasa) = Congo, Dem.
   Rep. of the ■, *Africa* ... 84 E4
Congo ■, *Africa* 84 E3
Congo →, *Africa* 84 F2
Congo, Dem. Rep. of the ■,
   Africa 84 E4
Congo Basin, *Africa* 84 E4
Congonhas, *Brazil* 127 A7
Congress, *U.S.A.* 109 J7
Conil de la Frontera, *Spain* 37 J4
Conills, I. des, *Spain* 48 B9
Coniston, *Canada* 104 C3
Conjeeveram = Kanchipuram,
   India 66 N11
Conklin, *Canada* 103 B6
Conklin, *U.S.A.* 117 D9
Conn, L., *Ireland* 12 B2
Connacht □, *Ireland* 12 C2
Conneaut, *U.S.A.* 116 E4
Connecticut □, *U.S.A.* 117 E12
Connecticut →, *U.S.A.* 117 E12
Connell, *U.S.A.* 108 C4
Connellsville, *U.S.A.* 116 F5
Connemara □, *Ireland* 12 C2
Connemara △, *Ireland* 12 C2
Connerré, *France* 18 D7
Connersville, *U.S.A.* 114 F3
Connors Ra., *Australia* 94 C4
Conques, *France* 20 D6
Conquest, *Canada* 103 C7
Conrad, *U.S.A.* 108 B8
Conran, C., *Australia* 95 F4
Conroe, *U.S.A.* 113 K7
Consecon, *Canada* 116 C7
Conselheiro Lafaiete, *Brazil* 127 A7
Conselve, *Italy* 41 C8
Consett, *U.K.* 14 C6
Consort, *Canada* 103 C6

Constance = Konstanz, Germany 25 H5
Constance, L. = Bodensee, Europe 25 H5
Constanţa, Romania 29 F13
Constanţa □, Romania 29 F13
Constantia, U.S.A. 117 C8
Constantina, Spain 37 H5
Constantine, Algeria 78 A7
Constitución, Chile 126 D1
Constitución, Uruguay 126 C4
Constitucion de 1857 △, Mexico 118 A1
Consuegra, Spain 37 F7
Consul, Canada 103 D7
Contact, U.S.A. 108 F6
Contai, India 69 J12
Contamana, Peru 124 E4
Contamine, Italy 41 C9
Contas →, Brazil 125 F11
Contes, France 21 E11
Contoocook, U.S.A. 117 C13
Contra Costa, Mozam. 89 D5
Contres, France 18 E8
Contrexéville, France 19 D12
Contwoyto L., Canada 100 B8
Conversano, Italy 43 B10
Conway = Conwy, U.K. 14 D4
Conway = Conwy →, U.K. 14 D4
Conway, Australia 94 J6
Conway, Ark., U.S.A. 113 H8
Conway, N.H., U.S.A. 117 C13
Conway, S.C., U.S.A. 115 J6
Conway, C., Australia 94 J6
Conway, L., Australia 95 D2
Conwy, U.K. 14 D4
Conwy □, U.K. 14 D4
Conwy →, U.K. 14 D4
Coober Pedy, Australia 95 D1
Cooch Behar = Koch Bihar, India 67 F16
Cooinda, Australia 92 B5
Cook, Australia 93 F5
Cook, U.S.A. 112 B8
Cook, B., Chile 128 H3
Cook, C., Canada 102 C3
Cook, Mt. = Aoraki Mount Cook, N.Z. 91 K3
Cook Inlet, U.S.A. 100 C4
Cook Is., Pac. Oc. 97 J12
Cook Strait, N.Z. 91 J5
Cookeville, U.S.A. 115 G3
Cookhouse, S. Africa 88 E4
Cookshire, Canada 117 A13
Cookstown, U.K. 12 B5
Cooksville, Canada 116 C5
Cooktown, Australia 94 B4
Coolabah, Australia 95 E4
Cooladdi, Australia 95 D4
Coolah, Australia 95 E4
Coolamon, Australia 95 E4
Coolgardie, Australia 93 F3
Coolidge, U.S.A. 109 K8
Coolidge Dam, U.S.A. 109 K8
Cooloola △, Australia 95 D5
Cooma, Australia 95 F4
Coon Rapids, U.S.A. 112 C8
Coonabarabran, Australia 95 E4
Coonamble, Australia 95 E4
Coonana, Australia 93 F3
Coondapoor, India 66 N9
Coongie, Australia 95 D2
Coongoola, Australia 95 D4
Cooninie, L., Australia 95 D2
Cooper, U.S.A. 113 J7
Cooper Cr. →, Australia 95 D2
Cooperstown, N. Dak., U.S.A. 112 B5
Cooperstown, N.Y., U.S.A. 117 D10
Coorabie, Australia 93 F5
Coorong, The, Australia 95 F2
Coorow, Australia 93 E2
Cooroy, Australia 95 D5
Coos Bay, U.S.A. 108 E1
Coosa →, U.S.A. 115 J2
Cootamundra, Australia 95 E4
Cootehill, Ireland 12 B4
Copahue Paso, Argentina 126 D1
Copainalá, Mexico 119 D6
Copake Falls, U.S.A. 117 D11
Copalnic Mănăştur, Romania 29 C8
Copán, Honduras 120 D2
Cope, U.S.A. 112 F3
Cope, C., Spain 39 H3
Copenhagen = København, Denmark 11 J6
Copenhagen, U.S.A. 117 C9
Copertino, Italy 43 B11
Copiapó, Chile 126 B1
Copiapó →, Chile 126 B1
Coplay, U.S.A. 117 F9
Copp L., Canada 102 A6
Copparo, Italy 41 D8
Coppename →, Suriname 125 B7
Copper Harbor, U.S.A. 114 B2
Copper Queen, Zimbabwe 87 F2
Copperas Cove, U.S.A. 113 K6
Copperbelt □, Zambia 87 E2
Coppermine = Kugluktuk, Canada 100 B8
Coppermine →, Canada 100 B8
Copperopolis, U.S.A. 110 H6
Copşa Mică, Romania 29 D9
Coquet →, U.K. 14 B6
Coquille, U.S.A. 108 E1
Coquimbo, Chile 126 C1
Coquimbo □, Chile 126 C1
Corabia, Romania 29 G9
Coracora, Peru 124 G4
Coraki, Australia 95 D5
Coral, U.S.A. 116 F5
Coral Gables, U.S.A. 115 N5
Coral Harbour, Canada 101 B11
Coral Sea, Pac. Oc. 96 J7
Coral Springs, U.S.A. 115 M5
Coraopolis, U.S.A. 116 F4
Corato, Italy 43 A9
Corbeil-Essonnes, France 19 D9

Corbie, France 19 C9
Corbières, France 20 F6
Corbigny, France 19 E10
Corbin, U.S.A. 114 G3
Corbones →, Spain 37 H5
Corbu, Romania 29 F13
Corby, U.K. 15 E7
Corcaigh = Cork, Ireland 12 E3
Corcoran, U.S.A. 110 J7
Corcovado △, Costa Rica 120 E3
Cordele, U.S.A. 115 K4
Cordell, U.S.A. 113 H5
Cordenòns, Italy 41 C9
Cordes-sur-Ciel, France 20 D5
Córdoba, Argentina 126 C3
Córdoba, Mexico 119 D5
Córdoba, Spain 37 H6
Córdoba □, Argentina 126 C3
Córdoba □, Spain 37 G6
Córdoba, Sierra de, Argentina 126 C3
Cordon, Phil. 61 C4
Cordova, U.S.A. 100 B5
Corella, Spain 38 C3
Corella →, Australia 94 B3
Corfield, Australia 94 C3
Corfu = Kérkira, Greece 49 A3
Corfu ✈ (CFU), Greece 46 B1
Corfu, Str. of, Greece 49 A4
Corgo = O Corgo, Spain 36 C3
Cori, Italy 42 A5
Coria, Spain 36 F4
Coria del Río, Spain 37 H4
Coringa Is., Australia 94 B4
Corigliano Cálabro, Italy 43 C9
Corinth = Kórinthos, Greece 46 D4
Corinth, Miss., U.S.A. 115 H1
Corinth, N.Y., U.S.A. 117 C11
Corinth, G. of = Korinthiakós Kólpos, Greece 46 C4
Corinth Canal, Greece 46 D4
Corinto, Brazil 125 G10
Corinto, Nic. 120 D2
Cork, Ireland 12 E3
Cork □, Ireland 12 E3
Cork Harbour, Ireland 12 E3
Corlay, France 18 D3
Corleone, Italy 42 E6
Corleto Perticara, Italy 43 B9
Çorlu, Turkey 45 E11
Cormack L., Canada 102 A4
Cormòns, Italy 41 C10
Cormorant, Canada 103 C8
Cormorant L., Canada 103 C8
Corn Is. = Maíz, Is. del, Nic. 120 D3
Cornalvo △, Spain 37 F4
Cornélio Procópio, Brazil 127 A5
Corner Brook, Canada 105 C8
Corneşti, Moldova 29 C13
Corníglio, Italy 40 D7
Corning, Ark., U.S.A. 113 G9
Corning, Calif., U.S.A. 108 G2
Corning, Iowa, U.S.A. 112 E7
Corning, N.Y., U.S.A. 116 D7
Corno Grande, Italy 41 F10
Cornwall, Canada 117 A10
Cornwall, U.S.A. 117 F8
Cornwall □, U.K. 15 G3
Corny Pt., Australia 95 E2
Coro, Venezuela 124 A5
Coroatá, Brazil 125 D10
Corocoro, Bolivia 124 G5
Coroico, Bolivia 124 G5
Coromandel, N.Z. 91 G5
Coromandel Coast, India 66 N12
Corona, Calif., U.S.A. 111 M9
Corona, N. Mex., U.S.A. 109 J11
Coronach, Canada 103 D7
Coronado, U.S.A. 111 N9
Coronado, B. de, Costa Rica 120 E3
Coronados, Is. los, U.S.A. 111 N9
Coronation, Canada 102 C6
Coronation Gulf, Canada 100 B8
Coronation I., Antarctica 5 C18
Coronation Is., Australia 92 B3
Coronda, Argentina 126 C3
Coronel, Chile 126 D1
Coronel Bogado, Paraguay 126 B4
Coronel Dorrego, Argentina 126 D3
Coronel Oviedo, Paraguay 126 B4
Coronel Pringles, Argentina 126 D3
Coronel Suárez, Argentina 126 D3
Coronel Vidal, Argentina 126 D4
Coropuna, Nevado, Peru 124 G4
Çorovodë, Albania 44 F4
Corowa, Australia 95 F4
Corozal, Belize 119 D7
Corozal □, Belize 119 D7
Corozal Pt., Trin. & Tob. 125 K15
Corps, France 21 D9
Corpus, Argentina 127 B4
Corpus Christi, U.S.A. 113 M6
Corpus Christi, L., U.S.A. 113 L6
Corral de Almaguer, Spain 36 F7
Corralejo, Canary Is. 48 F6
Corraun Pen., Ireland 12 C2
Corréggio, Italy 40 D7
Corrente, C. das, Mozam. 89 C6
Corrèze □, France 20 C5
Corrèze →, France 20 C5
Corrib, L., Ireland 12 C2
Corridónia, Italy 41 E10
Corrientes, Argentina 126 B4
Corrientes □, Argentina 126 B4
Corrientes →, Argentina 126 C4
Corrientes →, Peru 124 D4
Corrientes, C., Colombia 124 B3
Corrientes, C., Cuba 120 B3
Corrientes, C., Mexico 118 C3
Corrigan, U.S.A. 113 K7
Corrigin, Australia 93 F2
Corse △, France 21 F13
Corse □, France 21 G13

Corse, C., France 21 E13
Corse-du-Sud □, France 21 G13
Corsica = Corse □, France 21 G13
Corsicana, U.S.A. 113 J6
Corte, France 21 F13
Corte Pinto, Portugal 37 H3
Cortegana, Spain 37 H4
Cortés, Mar de = California, G. de, Mexico 118 B2
Cortez, U.S.A. 109 H9
Cortina d'Ampezzo, Italy 41 B9
Cortland, N.Y., U.S.A. 117 D8
Cortland, Ohio, U.S.A. 116 E4
Cortona, Italy 41 E8
Corubal →, Guinea-Biss. 82 C2
Coruche, Portugal 37 G2
Çoruh →, Turkey 35 K5
Çorum, Turkey 72 B6
Corumbá, Brazil 124 G7
Corund, Romania 29 D10
Corunna = A Coruña, Spain 36 B2
Corvallis, U.S.A. 108 D2
Corvette, L. de la, Canada 104 B5
Corydon, U.S.A. 112 E8
Cosalá, Mexico 118 C3
Cosamaloapan, Mexico 119 D5
Cosenza, Italy 43 C9
Coşereni, Romania 29 F11
Coshocton, U.S.A. 116 F3
Cosmo Newberry, Australia 93 E3
Cosne-Cours-sur-Loire, France 19 E9
Coso Junction, U.S.A. 111 J9
Coso Pk., U.S.A. 111 J9
Cospeito, Spain 36 B3
Cosquín, Argentina 126 C3
Cossato, Italy 40 C5
Cossé-le-Vivien, France 18 E6
Cosson →, France 18 E8
Costa Blanca, Spain 39 G4
Costa Brava, Spain 38 D8
Costa del Sol, Spain 37 J6
Costa Dorada, Spain 38 D6
Costa Mesa, U.S.A. 111 M9
Costa Rica ■, Cent. Amer. 120 E3
Costa Smeralda, Italy 42 A2
Costeşti, Romania 29 F9
Costigliole d'Asti, Italy 40 D5
Cosumnes →, U.S.A. 110 G5
Coswig, Sachsen, Germany 24 D9
Coswig, Sachsen-Anhalt, Germany 24 D8
Cotabato, Phil. 61 H6
Cotagaita, Bolivia 126 A2
Côte d'Azur, France 21 E11
Côte-d'Ivoire = Ivory Coast ■, Africa 82 D4
Côte d'Or, France 19 E11
Côte-d'Or □, France 19 E11
Coteau des Prairies, U.S.A. 112 C6
Coteau du Missouri, U.S.A. 112 B4
Cotentin, France 18 C5
Côtes-d'Armor □, France 18 D4
Côtes de Meuse, France 19 C12
Côtes-du-Nord = Côtes-d'Armor □, France 18 D4
Cotiella, Spain 38 C5
Cotillo, Canary Is. 48 F5
Cotiujeni, Moldova 29 C13
Cotonou, Benin 83 D5
Cotopaxi, Ecuador 124 D3
Cotronei, Italy 43 C9
Cotswold Hills, U.K. 15 F5
Cottage Grove, U.S.A. 108 E2
Cottbus, Germany 24 D10
Cottonwood, U.S.A. 109 J7
Cotulla, U.S.A. 113 L5
Coubre, Pte. de la, France 20 C2
Couches, France 19 F11
Couço, Portugal 37 G2
Coudersport, U.S.A. 116 E6
Couedic, C. du, Australia 95 F2
Couëron, France 18 E5
Couesnon →, France 18 D5
Couhé, France 20 B4
Coulanges-sur-Yonne, France 19 E10
Coulee City, U.S.A. 108 C4
Coulman I., Antarctica 5 D11
Coulommiers, France 19 D10
Coulon →, France 21 E9
Coulonge →, Canada 104 C4
Coulonges-sur-l'Autize, France 20 B3
Coulounieix-Chamiers, France 20 C4
Coulterville, U.S.A. 110 H6
Council, U.S.A. 108 D5
Council Bluffs, U.S.A. 112 E7
Council Grove, U.S.A. 112 F6
Coupeville, U.S.A. 110 B4
Courantyne →, S. Amer. 124 B7
Courcelles, Belgium 17 D4
Courchevel, France 21 C10
Courçon, France 20 B3
Courmayeur, Italy 40 C3
Couronne, C., France 21 E9
Cours-la-Ville, France 19 F11
Coursan, France 20 E7
Courseulles-sur-Mer, France 18 C6
Courtenay, Canada 102 D4
Courtenay, France 19 D10
Courtland, U.S.A. 110 G5
Courtrai = Kortrijk, Belgium 17 D3
Courtright, Canada 116 D2
Coushatta, U.S.A. 113 J8
Couva, Trin. & Tob. 125 K15
Couvin, Belgium 17 D4
Covarrubias, Spain 36 C7
Covasna, Romania 29 E11
Covasna □, Romania 29 E10
Cove I., Canada 116 A3
Coventry, U.K. 15 E6
Covilhã, Portugal 36 E3

Covington, Ga., U.S.A. 115 J4
Covington, Ky., U.S.A. 114 F3
Covington, Okla., U.S.A. 113 G6
Covington, Tenn., U.S.A. 113 H10
Covington, Va., U.S.A. 114 G5
Cowal, L., Australia 95 E4
Cowan, L., Australia 93 F3
Cowan, L., Canada 103 C7
Cowangie, Australia 95 F3
Cowansville, Canada 117 A12
Coward Springs, Australia 95 D2
Cowcowing Lakes, Australia 93 F2
Cowdenbeath, U.K. 13 E5
Cowell, Australia 95 E2
Cowes, U.K. 15 G6
Cowichan L., Canada 110 B2
Cowlitz →, U.S.A. 110 D4
Cowra, Australia 95 E4
Cox, Spain 39 G4
Coxilha Grande, Brazil 127 B5
Coxim, Brazil 125 G8
Cox's Bazar, Bangla. 67 J17
Coyote Wells, U.S.A. 111 N11
Coyuca de Benítez, Mexico 119 D4
Coyuca de Catalan, Mexico 118 D4
Cozad, U.S.A. 112 E5
Cozes, France 20 C3
Cozumel, Mexico 119 C7
Cozumel, Isla, Mexico 119 C7
Crab Hill, Barbados 121 g
Cracow = Kraków, Poland 31 H6
Cracow, Australia 95 D5
Cradle Mt.-Lake St. Clair △, Australia 95 G4
Cradock, Australia 95 E2
Cradock, S. Africa 88 E4
Craig, U.S.A. 108 F10
Craigavon, U.K. 12 B5
Craigmore, Zimbabwe 87 G3
Craik, Canada 103 C7
Crailsheim, Germany 25 F6
Craiova, Romania 29 F8
Cramsie, Australia 94 C3
Cranberry L., U.S.A. 117 B10
Cranberry Portage, Canada 103 C8
Cranbrook, Australia 93 F2
Cranbrook, Canada 102 D5
Crandon, U.S.A. 112 C10
Crane, Oreg., U.S.A. 108 E4
Crane, Tex., U.S.A. 113 K3
Cranston, U.S.A. 117 E13
Craon, France 18 E6
Craonne, France 19 C10
Crapone-sur-Arzon, France 20 C7
Crasna, Romania 29 D12
Crasna →, Romania 28 C7
Crasnei, Munţii, Romania 29 C8
Crateús, Brazil 125 E10
Crater L., U.S.A. 108 E2
Crater Lake △, U.S.A. 108 E2
Craters of the Moon △, U.S.A. 108 E7
Crati →, Italy 43 C9
Crato, Brazil 125 E11
Crato, Portugal 37 F3
Craven, L., Canada 104 B4
Crawford, U.S.A. 112 D3
Crawfordsville, U.S.A. 114 E2
Crawley, U.K. 15 F7
Crazy Mts., U.S.A. 108 C8
Crean L., Canada 103 C7
Crécy-en-Ponthieu, France 19 B8
Crediton, Canada 116 C3
Crediton, U.K. 15 G4
Cree →, Canada 103 B7
Cree →, U.K. 13 G4
Cree L., Canada 103 B7
Creede, U.S.A. 109 H10
Creekside, U.S.A. 116 F5
Creel, Mexico 118 B3
Creemore, Canada 116 B4
Creighton, Canada 103 C8
Creighton, U.S.A. 112 D6
Creil, France 19 C9
Crema, Italy 40 C6
Cremona, Italy 40 C7
Crepaja, Serbia & M. 28 E5
Crépy, France 19 C10
Crépy-en-Valois, France 19 C9
Cres, Croatia 41 D11
Crescent City, U.S.A. 108 F1
Crescentino, Italy 40 C5
Crespino, Argentina 126 C3
Crespo, Argentina 126 C3
Cresson, U.S.A. 116 F6
Crest, France 21 D9
Cresta, Mt., Phil. 61 C5
Crestline, Calif., U.S.A. 111 L9
Crestline, Ohio, U.S.A. 116 F2
Creston, Canada 102 D5
Creston, Calif., U.S.A. 110 K6
Creston, Iowa, U.S.A. 112 E7
Crestview, Calif., U.S.A. 110 H8
Crestview, Fla., U.S.A. 115 K2
Crêt de la Neige, France 19 F12
Crete = Kríti, Greece 49 D7
Crete, U.S.A. 112 E6
Crete, Sea of, Greece 47 E7
Créteil, France 19 D9
Creus, C. de, Spain 38 C8
Creuse □, France 19 F9
Creuse →, France 20 B4
Creutzwald, France 19 C13
Creuzburg, Germany 24 D6
Crèvecœur-le-Grand, France 19 C9
Crevillente, Spain 39 G4
Crewe, U.K. 14 D5
Crewkerne, U.K. 15 G5
Crianlarich, U.K. 13 E4
Criciúma, Brazil 127 B6
Cricova, Moldova 29 C13
Crieff, U.K. 13 E5
Crikvenica, Croatia 41 C11
Crimea □, Ukraine 33 K8

Crimean Pen. = Krymskyy Pivostriv, Ukraine 33 K8
Crimmitschau, Germany 24 E8
Cristuru Secuiesc, Romania 29 D10
Crişul Alb →, Romania 28 D6
Crişul Negru →, Romania 28 D6
Crişul Repede →, Romania 28 D5
Criuleni, Moldova 29 C14
Crivitz, Germany 24 B7
Crna →, Macedonia 44 E5
Crna Gora = Montenegro □, Serbia & M. 44 D3
Crna Gora, Macedonia 44 D5
Crna Reka = Crna →, Macedonia 44 E5
Crna Trava, Serbia & M. 44 D6
Crni Drim →, Macedonia 44 E4
Crni Timok →, Serbia & M. 44 C6
Crnoljeva Planina, Serbia & M. 44 D5
Črnomelj, Slovenia 41 C12
Croagh Patrick, Ireland 12 C2
Croatia ■, Europe 41 C13
Crocker, Banjaran, Malaysia 62 C5
Crockett, U.S.A. 113 K7
Crocodile = Krokodil →, Mozam. 89 D5
Crocodile Is., Australia 94 A1
Crocq, France 20 C6
Crodo, Italy 40 B5
Crohy Hd., Ireland 12 B3
Croisette, C., France 21 E9
Croisic, Pte. du, France 18 E4
Croix, L. La, Canada 104 C1
Croker, C., Australia 92 B5
Croker, C., Canada 116 B4
Croker I., Australia 92 B5
Cromarty, U.K. 13 D4
Cromer, U.K. 14 E9
Cromwell, N.Z. 91 L2
Cromwell, U.S.A. 117 E12
Cronat, France 19 F10
Crook, U.K. 14 C6
Crooked →, Canada 102 C4
Crooked →, U.S.A. 108 D3
Crooked I., Bahamas 121 B5
Crooked Island Passage, Bahamas 121 B5
Crookston, Minn., U.S.A. 112 B6
Crookston, Nebr., U.S.A. 112 D4
Crookwell, Australia 95 E4
Cropane-Micone △, Italy 43 D9
Crosby, U.K. 14 D4
Crosby, N. Dak., U.S.A. 112 A3
Crosby, Pa., U.S.A. 116 E6
Crosbyton, U.S.A. 113 J4
Crosía, Italy 43 C9
Cross →, Nigeria 83 E6
Cross City, U.S.A. 115 L4
Cross Fell, U.K. 14 C5
Cross L., Canada 103 C9
Cross Lake, Canada 103 C9
Cross River □, Nigeria 83 D6
Cross River △, Nigeria 83 D6
Cross Sound, U.S.A. 100 C6
Crossett, U.S.A. 113 J9
Crosshaven, Ireland 12 E3
Crossville, U.S.A. 115 G3
Croswell, U.S.A. 116 C2
Croton-on-Hudson, U.S.A. 117 E11
Crotone, Italy 43 C10
Crow →, Canada 102 B4
Crow Agency, U.S.A. 108 D10
Crow Hd., Ireland 12 E1
Crowell, U.S.A. 113 J5
Crowley, U.S.A. 113 K8
Crowley, L., U.S.A. 110 H8
Crown Point, Ind., U.S.A. 114 E2
Crown Point, N.Y., U.S.A. 117 C11
Crown Pt., Trin. & Tob. 125 J16
Crownpoint, U.S.A. 109 J9
Crows Landing, U.S.A. 110 H5
Crows Nest, Australia 95 D5
Crowsnest Pass, Canada 102 D6
Croydon, Australia 94 B3
Croydon □, U.K. 15 F7
Crozet, Is., Ind. Oc. 3 G12
Crozon, France 18 D2
Cruz, C., Cuba 120 C4
Cruz Alta, Brazil 127 B5
Cruz Bay, U.S. Virgin Is. 121 e
Cruz de Incio, Spain 36 C3
Cruz del Eje, Argentina 126 C3
Cruzeiro, Brazil 127 A7
Cruzeiro do Oeste, Brazil 127 A5
Cruzeiro do Sul, Brazil 124 E4
Cry L., Canada 102 B3
Crystal Bay, U.S.A. 110 F7
Crystal Brook, Australia 95 E2
Crystal City, U.S.A. 113 L5
Crystal Falls, U.S.A. 114 B1
Crystal River, U.S.A. 115 L4
Crystal Springs, U.S.A. 113 K9
Csenger, Hungary 28 D5
Csongrád, Hungary 28 D5
Csongrád □, Hungary 28 D5
Csorna, Hungary 28 C2
Csurgo, Hungary 28 D2
Cu Lao Hon, Vietnam 65 G7
Cua Rao, Vietnam 64 C5
Cuácua →, Mozam. 87 F4
Cuamato, Angola 88 B2
Cuamba, Mozam. 87 E4
Cuando →, Angola 85 H4
Cuando Cubango □, Angola 88 B3
Cuangar, Angola 88 B2
Cuango = Kwango →, Dem. Rep. of the Congo 84 E3
Cuanza →, Angola 84 F2
Cuarto →, Argentina 126 C3
Cuatrociénegas, Mexico 118 B4
Cuauhtémoc, Mexico 118 B3
Cuba, Portugal 37 G3
Cuba, N. Mex., U.S.A. 109 J10
Cuba, N.Y., U.S.A. 116 D6
Cuba ■, W. Indies 120 B4

Cubango →, Africa 88 B3
Çubuk, Turkey 72 B5
Cuc Phuong △, Vietnam 64 B5
Cuchumatanes, Sierra de los,
  Guatemala 120 C1
Cuckfield, U.K. 15 F7
Cucuí, Brazil 124 C5
Cucurpe, Mexico 118 A2
Cúcuta, Colombia 124 B4
Cudalbi, Romania 29 E12
Cuddalore, India 66 P11
Cuddapah, India 66 M11
Cuddapan, L., Australia 94 D3
Cudillero, Spain 36 B4
Cue, Australia 93 E2
Cuéllar, Spain 36 D6
Cuenca, Ecuador 124 D3
Cuenca, Spain 38 E2
Cuenca □, Spain 38 F3
Cuenca, Serranía de, Spain .. 38 F3
Cuenca Alta del Manzanares △,
  Spain 36 E7
Cuerdo del Pozo, Embalse de la,
  Spain 38 D2
Cuernavaca, Mexico 119 D5
Cuero, U.S.A. 113 L6
Cuers, France 21 E10
Cueva de la Quebrada del
  Toro △, Venezuela 121 D6
Cuevas del Almanzora, Spain . 39 H4
Cuevo, Bolivia 124 H6
Cugir, Romania 29 E8
Cugnaux, France 20 E5
Cuhai-Bakony →, Hungary ... 28 C2
Cuiabá, Brazil 125 G7
Cuiabá →, Brazil 125 G7
Cuijk, Neths. 17 C5
Cuilco, Guatemala 120 C1
Cuillin Hills, U.K. 13 D2
Cuillin Sd., U.K. 13 D2
Cuiseaux, France 19 F12
Cuito →, Angola 88 B3
Cuitzeo, L. de, Mexico 118 D4
Cujmir, Romania 28 F7
Cukai, Malaysia 65 K4
Culbertson, U.S.A. 112 A2
Culcairn, Australia 95 F4
Culebra, Isla de, Puerto Rico 121 d
Culebra, Sierra de la, Spain .. 36 D4
Culfa, Azerbaijan 73 C11
Culgoa →, Australia 95 D4
Culgoa Flood Plain △, Australia . 95 D4
Culiacán, Mexico 118 C3
Culiacán →, Mexico 118 C3
Culik, Indonesia 63 J18
Culion, Phil. 61 F4
Cúllar, Spain 37 H8
Cullarin Ra., Australia 95 E4
Cullen, U.K. 13 D6
Cullen Pt., Australia 94 A3
Cullera, Spain 39 F4
Cullman, U.S.A. 115 H2
Cullompton, U.K. 15 G4
Culoz, France 21 C9
Culpeper, U.S.A. 114 F7
Culuene →, Brazil 125 F8
Culver, Pt., Australia 93 F3
Culverden, N.Z. 91 K4
Cumaná, Venezuela 124 A6
Cumaovası, Turkey 47 C9
Cumberland, B.C., Canada ... 102 D4
Cumberland, Ont., Canada ... 117 A9
Cumberland, U.S.A. 114 F6
Cumberland →, U.S.A. 115 G2
Cumberland, L., U.S.A. 115 G3
Cumberland Gap △, U.S.A. .. 115 G4
Cumberland I., U.S.A. 115 K5
Cumberland Is., Australia .. 94 J7
Cumberland Island △, U.S.A. 115 K5
Cumberland L., Canada 103 C8
Cumberland Pen., Canada 101 B13
Cumberland Plateau, U.S.A. .. 115 H3
Cumberland Sd., Canada 101 B13
Cumbernauld, U.K. 13 F5
Cumborah, Australia 95 D4
Cumbres de Majalca △, Mexico 118 B3
Cumbres de Monterrey △, Mexico 118 B4
Cumbres Mayores, Spain 37 G4
Cumbria □, U.K. 14 C5
Cumbrian Mts., U.K. 14 C5
Cumbum, India 66 M11
Cuminá →, Brazil 125 D7
Cummings Mt., U.S.A. 111 K8
Cummins, Australia 95 E2
Cumnock, Australia 95 E4
Cumnock, U.K. 13 F4
Cumpas, Mexico 118 B3
Cumplida, Pta., Canary Is. .. 48 F2
Çumra, Turkey 72 D5
Cunco, Chile 128 D2
Cuncumén, Chile 126 C1
Cunderdin, Australia 93 F2
Cunene →, Angola 88 B1
Cúneo, Italy 40 D4
Çüngüş, Turkey 73 C8
Cunillera, I. = Sa Conillera, Spain 48 C7
Cunlhat, France 20 C7
Cunnamulla, Australia 95 D4
Cuorgnè, Italy 40 C4
Cupar, Canada 103 C8
Cupar, U.K. 13 E5
Cupcini, Moldova 29 B12
Cupica, G. de, Colombia 124 B3
Ćuprija, Serbia & M. 44 C5
Curaçao, Neth. Ant. 121 D6
Curanilahue, Chile 126 D1
Curaray →, Peru 124 D4
Cure →, France 19 E10
Curepto, Chile 126 D1
Curiapo, Venezuela 124 B6
Curicó, Chile 126 C1
Curinga, Italy 43 D9

Curitiba, Brazil 127 B6
Curitibanos, Brazil 127 B5
Currabubula, Australia 95 E5
Currais Novos, Brazil 125 E11
Curralinho, Brazil 125 D9
Current →, U.S.A. 113 G9
Currane, Australia 95 F3
Curtis, U.S.A. 108 F6
Curtea de Argeş, Romania ... 29 E9
Curtici, Romania 28 D6
Curtis, U.S.A. 112 E4
Curtis Group, Australia 95 F4
Curtis I., Australia 94 C5
Curuápanema →, Brazil 125 D7
Curuçá, Brazil 125 D9
Curuguaty, Paraguay 127 A4
Curuzú Cuatiá, Argentina ... 126 B4
Curvelo, Brazil 125 G10
Cushing, U.S.A. 113 H6
Cushing, Mt., Canada 102 B3
Cusihuiriáchic, Mexico 118 B3
Cusna, Mte., Italy 40 D7
Cusset, France 19 F10
Custer, U.S.A. 112 D3
Cut Bank, U.S.A. 108 B7
Cutchogue, U.S.A. 117 E12
Cuthbert, U.S.A. 115 K3
Cutler, U.S.A. 110 J7
Cutro, Italy 43 C9
Cuttaburra →, Australia 95 D3
Cuttack, India 67 J14
Cuvier, C., Australia 93 D1
Cuvier I., N.Z. 91 G5
Cuxhaven, Germany 24 B4
Cuyahoga Falls, U.S.A. 116 E3
Cuyahoga Valley △, U.S.A. .. 116 E3
Cuyapo, Phil. 61 D4
Cuyo, Phil. 61 F4
Cuyo East Pass, Phil. 61 F4
Cuyo West Pass, Phil. 61 F4
Cuyuni →, Guyana 124 B7
Cuzco, Bolivia 124 H5
Cuzco, Peru 124 F4
Čvrsnica, Bos.-H. 28 G2
Cwmbran, U.K. 15 F4
Cyangugu, Rwanda 86 C2
Cybinka, Poland 31 F1
Cyclades = Kikládhes, Greece . 46 E6
Cygnet, Australia 95 G4
Cynthiana, U.S.A. 114 F3
Cypress Hills, Canada 103 D7
Cypress Hills △, Canada 103 D7
Cyprus ■, Asia 49 E12
Cyrenaica, Libya 79 C10
Czaplinek, Poland 30 E3
Czar, Canada 103 C6
Czarna →, Łódzkie, Poland .. 31 G6
Czarna →, Świętokrzyskie,
  Poland 31 H8
Czarna Białostocka, Poland . 31 E10
Czarna Woda, Poland 30 E5
Czarne, Poland 30 E3
Czarnków, Poland 31 F3
Czech Rep. ■, Europe 26 B8
Czechowice-Dziedzice, Poland 31 J5
Czempiń, Poland 31 F3
Czeremcha, Poland 31 F10
Czerniejewo, Poland 31 F4
Czersk, Poland 30 E4
Czerwieńsk, Poland 31 F2
Czerwionka-Leszczyny, Poland 31 H5
Częstochowa, Poland 31 H6
Człopa, Poland 31 E3
Człuchów, Poland 30 E4
Czyżew-Osada, Poland 31 F9

D

Da →, Vietnam 58 G5
Da Hinggan Ling, China 60 B7
Da Lat, Vietnam 65 G7
Da Nang, Vietnam 64 D7
Da Qaidam, China 60 C4
Da Yunhe →, China 57 G11
Da'an, China 57 B13
Daan Viljoen △, Namibia 88 C2
Dab'a, Ras el, Egypt 80 H6
Daba Shan, China 58 B7
Dabai, Nigeria 83 C6
Dabakala, Ivory C. 82 D4
Dabas, Hungary 28 C4
Dabat, Ethiopia 81 E4
Dabbagh, Jabal, Si. Arabia .. 70 E2
Dabhoi, India 68 H5
Dąbie, Poland 31 F5
Dabnou, Niger 83 C6
Dabo = Pasirkuning, Indonesia 62 E2
Dabola, Guinea 82 C2
Dabou, Ivory C. 82 D4
Daboya, Ghana 83 D4
Dąbrovolya, Belarus 31 F10
Dąbrowa Białostocka, Poland 30 E10
Dąbrowa Górnicza, Poland ... 31 H6
Dąbrowa Tarnowska, Poland .. 31 H7
Dabu, China 59 E11
Dabung, Malaysia 65 K4
Dabus →, Ethiopia 81 E4
Dacato →, Ethiopia 81 F5
Dacca = Dhaka, Bangla. 69 H14
Dacca = Dhaka □, Bangla. ... 69 G14
Dachau, Germany 25 G7
Dachstein, Hoher, Austria .. 26 D6

Dačice, Czech Rep. 26 B8
Dadanawa, Guyana 124 C7
Daday, Turkey 72 B5
Dade City, U.S.A. 115 L4
Dadhar, Pakistan 68 E2
Dadiya, Nigeria 83 D7
Dadra & Nagar Haveli □, India 66 J8
Dadri = Charkhi Dadri, India 68 E7
Dadu, Pakistan 68 F2
Dadu He →, China 58 C4
Daet, Phil. 61 D5
Dafang, China 58 D5
Dagana, Senegal 82 B1
Dagash, Sudan 80 D3
Dagestan □, Russia 35 J8
Dagestanskiye Ogni, Russia . 35 J9
Daggett, U.S.A. 111 L10
Daghestan Republic =
  Dagestan □, Russia 35 J8
Daghfeli, Sudan 80 D3
Dağlıq Qarabağ = Nagorno-
  Karabakh □, Azerbaijan ... 70 D5
Dagö = Hiiumaa, Estonia 9 G20
Dagu, China 57 E9
Daguan, China 58 D4
Dagupan, Phil. 61 C4
Daguragu, Australia 92 C5
Dahab, Egypt 80 B3
Dahlak □, Eritrea 81 D5
Dahlak Kebir, Eritrea 81 D5
Dahlenburg, Germany 24 B6
Dahlonega, U.S.A. 115 H4
Dahme, Germany 24 D9
Dahod, India 68 H6
Dahong Shan, China 59 B9
Dahra, Senegal 82 B1
Dahshûr, Egypt 80 J7
Dahûk, Iraq 70 B3
Dai Hao, Vietnam 64 C6
Dai-Sen, Japan 55 G6
Dai Shan, China 59 B14
Dai Xian, China 56 E7
Daicheng, China 56 E9
Daimiel, Spain 37 F7
Daingean, Ireland 12 C4
Dainkog, China 58 A1
Daintree, Australia 94 B4
Daintree △, Australia 94 B4
Daiō-Misaki, Japan 55 G8
Dair, J. ed, Sudan 81 E3
Dairût, Egypt 80 B3
Daisen-Oki △, Japan 55 G6
Daisetsu-Zan, Japan 54 C11
Daisetsu-Zan △, Japan 54 C11
Dajarra, Australia 94 C2
Dajin Chuan →, China 58 B3
Dak Dam, Cambodia 64 F6
Dak Nhe, Vietnam 64 E6
Dak Pek, Vietnam 64 E6
Dak Song, Vietnam 65 F6
Dak Sui, Vietnam 64 E6
Dakar, Senegal 82 C1
Dakhla, W. Sahara 78 D2
Dakhla, El Wâhât el-, Egypt . 80 B2
Dakingari, Nigeria 83 C5
Dakor, India 68 H5
Dakoro, Niger 83 C6
Dakota City, U.S.A. 112 D6
Đakovica, Serbia & M. 44 D4
Đakovo, Croatia 28 E3
Dalaba, Guinea 82 C2
Dalachi, China 56 F3
Dalai Nur, China 56 C9
Dālakī, Iran 71 D6
Dalälven →, Sweden 10 D10
Dalaman, Turkey 47 E10
Dalaman →, Turkey 47 E10
Dalandzadgad, Mongolia 56 C3
Dalap-Uliga-Darrit, Marshall Is. 96 G9
Dalarna, Sweden 10 D8
Dalarnas län □, Sweden 10 C8
Dālbandīn, Pakistan 66 E4
Dalbeattie, U.K. 13 G5
Dalbeg, Australia 94 C4
Dalbosjön, Sweden 11 F6
Dalby, Australia 95 D5
Dalby, Sweden 11 J7
Dalby Söderskog △, Sweden .. 11 J7
Dale City, U.S.A. 114 F7
Dale Hollow L., U.S.A. 115 G3
Dalga, Egypt 80 B3
Dalgán, Iran 71 E8
Dalhart, U.S.A. 113 G3
Dalhousie, Canada 105 C6
Dalhousie, India 68 C6
Dali, Shaanxi, China 56 G5
Dali, Yunnan, China 58 E3
Dalian, China 57 E11
Daliang Shan, China 58 D4
Daling He →, China 57 D11
Dāliyat el Karmel, Israel .. 74 C4
Dalj, Croatia 28 E3
Dalkeith, U.K. 13 F5
Dallas, Oreg., U.S.A. 108 D2
Dallas, Tex., U.S.A. 113 J6
Dalli, Ethiopia 81 E5
Dalmā, U.A.E. 71 E7
Dalmacija, Croatia 41 E13
Dalmas, L., Canada 105 B5
Dalmatia = Dalmacija, Croatia 41 E13
Dalmau, India 69 F9
Dalmellington, U.K. 13 F4
Dalnegorsk, Russia 53 E14
Dalnerechensk, Russia 53 E14
Dalnevostochnyy □, Russia .. 53 C14
Daloa, Ivory C. 82 D3
Dalong Shan, China 58 C6
Dalry, U.K. 13 F4
Dalrymple, L., Australia ... 94 C4
Dalrymple, Mt., Australia .. 94 K8
Dals Långed, Sweden 11 F6

Dalsjöfors, Sweden 11 G7
Dalsland, Sweden 11 F6
Daltenganj, India 69 H11
Dalton, Ga., U.S.A. 115 H3
Dalton, Mass., U.S.A. 117 D11
Dalton, Nebr., U.S.A. 112 E3
Dalton-in-Furness, U.K. 14 C4
Dalupiri I., Phil. 61 B4
Dalvík, Iceland 8 D4
Dálvvadis = Jokkmokk, Sweden 8 C18
Dalwallinu, Australia 93 F2
Daly →, Australia 92 B5
Daly City, U.S.A. 110 H4
Daly L., Canada 103 B7
Daly River, Australia 92 B5
Daly Waters, Australia 94 B1
Dalyan, Turkey 47 E10
Dam Doi, Vietnam 65 H5
Dam Ha, Vietnam 64 B6
Daman, India 66 J8
Dāmaneh, Iran 71 C6
Damanhûr, Egypt 80 H7
Damant L., Canada 103 A7
Damanzhuang, China 56 E9
Damar, Indonesia 63 F7
Damaraland, Namibia 88 C2
Damascus = Dimashq, Syria .. 74 B5
Damaturu, Nigeria 83 C7
Damāvand, Iran 71 C7
Damāvand, Qolleh-ye, Iran .. 71 C7
Damba, Angola 84 F3
Dâmbovița □, Romania 29 F10
Dâmbovița →, Romania 29 F11
Dâmbovnic →, Romania 29 F10
Dame Marie, Haiti 121 C5
Dāmghān, Iran 71 B7
Dāmienesti, Romania 29 D11
Damietta = Dumyât, Egypt ... 80 H7
Daming, China 56 F8
Damīr Qābū, Syria 70 B4
Dammam = Ad Dammām,
  Si. Arabia 71 E6
Dammarie-les-Lys, France ... 19 D9
Dammartin-en-Goële, France . 19 C9
Damme, Germany 24 C4
Damoder →, India 69 H12
Damoh, India 69 H8
Dampier, Australia 92 D2
Dampier, Selat, Indonesia .. 63 E8
Dampier Arch., Australia ... 92 D2
Damrei, Chuor Phnum,
  Cambodia 65 G4
Damvillers, France 19 C12
Dan-Gulbi, Nigeria 83 C6
Dan Xian, China 64 C7
Dana, Indonesia 63 F6
Dana, L., Canada 104 B4
Dana, Mt., U.S.A. 110 H7
Danakil Desert, Ethiopia ... 81 E5
Danané, Ivory C. 82 D3
Danao, Phil. 61 F6
Danau Poso, Indonesia 63 E6
Danba, China 58 B3
Danbury, U.S.A. 117 E11
Danby L., U.S.A. 109 J6
Dand, Afghan. 68 D1
Dande △, Zimbabwe 87 F3
Dandeldhura, Nepal 69 E9
Dandeli, India 66 M9
Dandenong, Australia 95 F4
Dandil, Egypt 80 J7
Dandong, China 57 D13
Danfeng, China 56 H6
Dangan Liedao, China 59 F10
Dangé-St-Romain, France 20 B4
Dângeni, Romania 29 C11
Dangla, Ethiopia 81 E4
Dangla Shan = Tanggula Shan,
  China 60 C4
Dangora, Nigeria 83 C6
Dangouadougou, Burkina Faso 82 C4
Dangrek, Phnom, Thailand ... 64 E5
Dangriga, Belize 119 D7
Dangshan, China 56 G9
Dangtu, China 59 B12
Dangyang, China 59 B8
Dani, Burkina Faso 83 C4
Daniel, U.S.A. 108 E8
Daniel's Harbour, Canada ... 105 B8
Danielskuil, S. Africa 88 D3
Danielson, U.S.A. 117 E13
Danilov, Russia 32 C11
Danilovgrad, Serbia & M. ... 44 D3
Danilovka, Russia 34 E7
Daning, China 56 F6
Danja, Nigeria 83 C6
Danjiangkou, China 59 A8
Danjiangkou Shuiku, China .. 59 A8
Dank, Oman 71 F8
Dankalwa, Nigeria 83 C7
Dankama, Nigeria 83 C6
Dankhar Gompa, India 66 C11
Dankov, Russia 32 F10
Danleng, China 58 B4
Danlí, Honduras 120 D2
Dannemora, U.S.A. 117 B11
Dannenberg, Germany 24 B7
Dannevirke, N.Z. 91 J6
Dannhauser, S. Africa 89 D5
Dansville, U.S.A. 116 D7
Danta, India 68 G5
Dantan, India 69 H12
Danube = Dunărea →, Europe . 29 E14
Danvers, U.S.A. 117 D14
Danville, Ill., U.S.A. 114 E2
Danville, Ky., U.S.A. 114 G3
Danville, Pa., U.S.A. 117 F8
Danville, Va., U.S.A. 115 G6

Danville, Vt., U.S.A. 117 B12
Danyang, China 59 B12
Danzhai, China 58 D6
Danzig = Gdańsk, Poland 30 D5
Dão →, Portugal 36 E2
Dao Xian, China 59 E8
Daocheng, China 58 C3
Daoukro, Ivory C. 82 D4
Dapaong, Togo 83 C5
Dapchi, Nigeria 83 C7
Dapitan, Phil. 61 G5
Daqing Shan, China 56 D6
Daqu Shan, China 59 B14
Dar Banda, Africa 76 F4
Dar el Beida = Casablanca,
  Morocco 78 B4
Dar es Salaam, Tanzania 86 D4
Dar Mazār, Iran 71 D8
Dar'ā, Syria 74 C5
Dar'ā □, Syria 74 C5
Dārāb, Iran 71 D7
Daraban, Pakistan 68 D4
Darabani, Romania 29 B11
Daraina, Madag. 89 A8
Daraj, Libya 79 B8
Dārān, Iran 71 C6
Daravica, Serbia & M. 44 D4
Daraw, Egypt 80 C3
Dārayyā, Syria 74 B5
Darazo, Nigeria 83 C7
Darband, Pakistan 68 B5
Darband, Kūh-e, Iran 71 D8
Darbhanga, India 69 F11
D'Arcy, Canada 102 C4
Darda, Croatia 28 E3
Dardanelle, Ark., U.S.A. ... 113 H8
Dardanelle, Calif., U.S.A. . 110 G7
Dardanelles = Çanakkale Boğazı,
  Turkey 45 F10
Dare →, Ethiopia 81 F5
Darende, Turkey 72 C7
Dārestān, Iran 71 D8
Darfo, Italy 40 C7
Dârfûr, Sudan 79 F10
Dargai, Pakistan 68 B4
Dargan Ata, Turkmenistan ... 52 E7
Dargaville, N.Z. 91 F4
Dargol, Niger 83 C5
Darhan, Mongolia 60 B5
Darhan Muminggan Lianheqi,
  China 56 D6
Dari, Sudan 81 F3
Darıca, Turkey 72 B3
Darién, G. del, Colombia ... 124 B3
Darién □, Panama 120 E4
Dariganga = Ovoot, Mongolia . 56 B7
Darinskoye, Kazakhstan 34 E10
Darjeeling = Darjiling, India 69 F13
Darjiling, India 69 F13
Darkan, Australia 93 F2
Darkhana, Pakistan 68 D5
Darkhazīneh, Iran 71 D6
Darkot Pass, Pakistan 69 A5
Darling →, Australia 95 E3
Darling Downs, Australia ... 95 D5
Darling Ra., Australia 93 F2
Darlington, U.K. 14 C6
Darlington, U.S.A. 115 H6
Darlington □, U.K. 14 C6
Darlington, L., S. Africa .. 88 E4
Darlot, L., Australia 93 E3
Darłowo, Poland 30 D3
Dărmănești, Bacău, Romania . 29 D11
Dărmănești, Suceava, Romania 29 C11
Darmstadt, Germany 25 F4
Darnah, Libya 79 B10
Darnall, S. Africa 89 D5
Darney, France 19 D13
Darnley, C., Antarctica 5 C6
Darnley B., Canada 100 B7
Daroca, Spain 38 D3
Darou-Mousti, Senegal 82 B1
Darr →, Australia 94 C3
Darra Pezu, Pakistan 68 C4
Darrequeira, Argentina 126 D3
Darrington, U.S.A. 108 B3
Darsser Ort, Germany 24 A8
Dart →, U.K. 15 G4
Dart, C., Antarctica 5 D14
Dartford, U.K. 15 F8
Dartmoor, U.K. 15 G4
Dartmoor △, U.K. 15 G4
Dartmouth, Canada 105 D7
Dartmouth, U.K. 15 G4
Dartmouth Res., Australia .. 95 D4
Dartuch, C. = Artrutx, C. de,
  Spain 48 B10
Daruvar, Croatia 28 E2
Darvaza, Turkmenistan 52 E6
Darvel, Teluk = Lahad Datu,
  Teluk, Malaysia 63 D5
Darwen, U.K. 14 D5
Darwendale, Zimbabwe 89 B5
Darwha, India 66 J10
Darwin, Australia 92 B5
Darwin, U.S.A. 111 J9
Darya Khan, Pakistan 68 D4
Daryoi Amu = Amudarya →,
  Uzbekistan 52 E6
Dās, U.A.E. 71 E7
Dashen, Ras, Ethiopia 81 E4
Dashetai, China 56 D5
Dashhowuz, Turkmenistan 52 E6
Dashkesan = Daşkäsän,
  Azerbaijan 35 K7
Dashköpri, Turkmenistan 71 B9
Dasht, Iran 71 B8
Dasht →, Pakistan 66 G2
Daska, Pakistan 68 C6
Daşkäsän, Azerbaijan 35 K7
Dassa, Benin 83 D5
Dasuya, India 68 D6

Datça, Turkey 47 E9
Datia, India 69 G8
Datian, China 59 E11
Datong, Anhui, China 59 B11
Datong, Shanxi, China 56 D7
Dattakhel, Pakistan 68 C3
Datteln, Germany 24 D3
Datu, Tanjung, Indonesia 62 D3
Datu Piang, Phil. 61 H6
Datuk, Tanjong = Datu, Tanjung, Indonesia 62 D3
Daua = Dawa →, Africa 81 G5
Daud Khel, Pakistan 68 C4
Daudnagar, India 69 G11
Daugava →, Latvia 9 H21
Daugavpils, Latvia 9 J22
Daulpur, India 68 F7
Daun, Germany 25 E2
Dauphin, Canada 103 C8
Dauphin, U.S.A. 116 F8
Dauphin L., Canada 103 C9
Dauphiné, France 21 C9
Daura, Borno, Nigeria 83 C7
Daura, Katsina, Nigeria 83 C6
Dausa, India 68 F7
Dāvāçi, Azerbaijan 35 K9
Davangere, India 66 M9
Davao, Phil. 61 H6
Davao G., Phil. 61 H6
Dāvar Panāh = Sarāvān, Iran 71 E9
Davenport, Calif., U.S.A. 110 H4
Davenport, Iowa, U.S.A. 112 E9
Davenport, Wash., U.S.A. 108 C4
Davenport Ra., Australia 94 C1
Daventry, U.K. 15 E6
David, Panama 120 E3
David City, U.S.A. 112 E6
David Gorodok = Davyd Haradok, Belarus 33 F4
Davidson, Canada 103 C7
Davis, Antarctica 5 C6
Davis, U.S.A. 110 G5
Davis Dam, U.S.A. 111 K12
Davis Inlet, Canada 105 A7
Davis Mts., U.S.A. 113 K2
Davis Sea, Antarctica 5 C7
Davis Str., N. Amer. 101 B14
Davo →, Ivory C. 82 D3
Davos, Switz. 25 J5
Davutlar, Turkey 47 D9
Davy L., Canada 103 B7
Davyd Haradok, Belarus 33 F4
Dawa →, Africa 81 G5
Dawaki, Bauchi, Nigeria 83 D6
Dawaki, Kano, Nigeria 83 C6
Dawei = Tavoy, Burma 64 E2
Dawes Ra., Australia 94 C5
Dawlish, U.K. 15 G4
Dawna Ra., Burma 64 D2
Dawros Hd., Ireland 12 B3
Dawson, Canada 100 B6
Dawson, U.S.A. 115 K3
Dawson, I., Chile 128 G2
Dawson B., Canada 103 C8
Dawson Creek, Canada 102 B4
Dawson Inlet, Canada 103 A10
Dawson Ra., Australia 94 C4
Dawu, Hubei, China 59 B9
Dawu, Sichuan, China 58 B3
Dax, France 20 E2
Daxian, China 58 B6
Daxin, China 58 F6
Daxindian, China 57 F11
Daxinggou, China 57 C15
Daxue Shan, Sichuan, China 58 B3
Daxue Shan, Yunnan, China 58 F2
Dayao, China 58 E3
Daye, China 59 B10
Dayet en Naharat, Mali 82 B4
Dayi, China 58 B4
Daylesford, Australia 95 F3
Dayong, China 59 C8
Dayr az Zawr, Syria 70 C4
Daysland, Canada 102 C6
Dayton, Nev., U.S.A. 110 F7
Dayton, Ohio, U.S.A. 114 F3
Dayton, Pa., U.S.A. 116 F5
Dayton, Tenn., U.S.A. 115 H3
Dayton, Wash., U.S.A. 108 C4
Dayton, Wyo., U.S.A. 108 D10
Daytona Beach, U.S.A. 115 L5
Dayu, China 59 E10
Dayville, U.S.A. 108 D4
Dazhu, China 58 B6
Dazkırı, Turkey 47 D11
Dazu, China 58 C5
De Aar, S. Africa 88 E3
De Biesbosch, Neths. 17 C4
De Funiak Springs, U.S.A. 115 K2
De Grey →, Australia 92 D2
De Haan, Belgium 17 C3
De Hoge Veluwe △, Neths. 17 B5
De Hoop △, S. Africa 88 E3
De Kalb, U.S.A. 112 E10
De Kennemerduinen △, Neths. 17 B4
De Land, U.S.A. 115 L5
De Leon, U.S.A. 113 J5
De Panne, Belgium 17 C2
De Pere, U.S.A. 114 C1
De Queen, U.S.A. 113 H7
De Quincy, U.S.A. 113 K8
De Ridder, U.S.A. 113 K8
De Smet, U.S.A. 112 C6
De Soto, U.S.A. 112 F9
De Tour Village, U.S.A. 114 C4
De Witt, U.S.A. 113 H9
Dead Sea, Asia 74 D3
Deadwood, U.S.A. 112 C3
Deadwood L., Canada 102 B3
Deal, U.K. 15 F9
Deal I., Australia 95 F4
Dealesville, S. Africa 88 D4

De'an, China 59 C10
Dean →, Canada 102 C3
Dean, Forest of, U.K. 15 F5
Dean Chan., Canada 102 C3
Deán Funes, Argentina 126 C3
Dease →, Canada 102 B3
Dease L., Canada 102 B2
Dease Lake, Canada 102 B2
Death Valley, U.S.A. 111 J10
Death Valley △, U.S.A. 111 J10
Death Valley Junction, U.S.A. 111 J10
Deauville, France 18 C7
Deba, Spain 38 B2
Deba Habe, Nigeria 83 C7
Debaltsevo, Ukraine 33 H10
Debao, China 58 F6
Debar, Macedonia 44 E4
Debark, Ethiopia 81 E4
Debden, Canada 103 C7
Dębica, Poland 31 H8
Dęblin, Poland 31 G8
Dębno, Poland 31 F1
Débo, L., Mali 82 B4
DeBolt, Canada 102 B5
Deborah East, L., Australia 93 F2
Deborah West, L., Australia 93 F2
Debrc, Serbia & M. 44 B3
Debre Birhan, Ethiopia 81 F4
Debre Markos, Ethiopia 81 E4
Debre May, Ethiopia 81 E4
Debre Sina, Ethiopia 81 F4
Debre Tabor, Ethiopia 81 E4
Debre Zebit, Ethiopia 81 E4
Debre Zeyit, Ethiopia 81 F4
Debrecen, Hungary 28 C6
Debrzno, Poland 30 E4
Dečani, Serbia & M. 44 D4
Decatur, Ala., U.S.A. 115 H2
Decatur, Ga., U.S.A. 115 J3
Decatur, Ill., U.S.A. 112 F10
Decatur, Ind., U.S.A. 114 E3
Decatur, Tex., U.S.A. 113 J6
Decazeville, France 20 D6
Deccan, India 66 L11
Deception Bay, Australia 95 D5
Deception I., Antarctica 5 C17
Deception L., Canada 103 B8
Dechang, China 58 D4
Dechhu, India 68 F5
Děčín, Czech Rep. 26 A7
Decize, France 19 F10
Deckerville, U.S.A. 116 C2
Decollatura, Italy 43 C9
Decorah, U.S.A. 112 D9
Deda, Romania 29 D9
Dédéagach = Alexandroúpolis, Greece 45 F9
Deder, Ethiopia 81 F5
Dedham, U.S.A. 117 D13
Dédougou, Burkina Faso 82 C4
Dedovichi, Russia 32 D5
Dedza, Malawi 87 E3
Dee →, Aberds., U.K. 13 D6
Dee →, Dumf. & Gall., U.K. 13 G4
Dee →, Wales, U.K. 14 D4
Deep B., Canada 102 A5
Deepwater, Australia 95 D5
Deer →, Canada 103 B10
Deer L., Canada 103 C10
Deer Lake, Nfld. & L., Canada 105 C8
Deer Lake, Ont., Canada 103 C10
Deer Lodge, U.S.A. 108 C7
Deer Park, U.S.A. 108 C5
Deer River, U.S.A. 112 B8
Deeragun, Australia 94 B4
Deerdepoort, S. Africa 88 C4
Deferiet, U.S.A. 117 B9
Defiance, U.S.A. 114 E3
Degana, India 68 F6
Dêgê, China 58 B2
Degebe →, Portugal 37 G3
Degeberga, Sweden 11 J8
Dégelis, Canada 105 C6
Degema, Nigeria 83 E6
Degerfors, Sweden 10 E8
Degerhamn, Sweden 11 H10
Deggendorf, Germany 25 G8
Degh →, Pakistan 68 D5
Değirmendere, Turkey 45 F13
Deh Bīd, Iran 71 D7
Deh-e Shīr, Iran 71 D7
Dehaj, Iran 71 D7
Dehak, Iran 71 E9
Dehdez, Iran 71 D6
Dehej, India 68 J5
Dehestān, Iran 71 D7
Dehgolān, Iran 70 C5
Dehibat, Tunisia 79 B8
Dehlorān, Iran 70 C5
Dehnow-e Kūhestān, Iran 71 E8
Dehra Dun, India 68 D8
Dehri, India 69 G11
Dehua, China 59 E12
Dehui, China 57 B13
Deim Zubeir, Sudan 81 F2
Deinze, Belgium 17 D3
Dej, Romania 29 C8
Deka →, Zimbabwe 88 B4
Dekemhare, Eritrea 81 D4
Dekese, Dem. Rep. of the Congo 84 E4
Del Mar, U.S.A. 111 N9
Del Norte, U.S.A. 109 H10
Del Rio, U.S.A. 113 L4
Delai, Sudan 80 D4
Delambre I., Australia 92 D2
Delami, Sudan 81 E3
Delano, U.S.A. 111 K7
Delano Peak, U.S.A. 109 G7
Delareyville, S. Africa 88 D4
Delaronde L., Canada 103 C7

Delavan, U.S.A. 112 D10
Delaware, U.S.A. 114 E4
Delaware □, U.S.A. 114 F8
Delaware →, U.S.A. 114 F8
Delaware B., U.S.A. 114 F8
Delaware Water Gap △, U.S.A. 117 E10
Delay →, Canada 105 A5
Delbrück, Germany 24 D4
Delčevo, Macedonia 44 E6
Delegate, Australia 95 F4
Delémont, Switz. 25 H3
Delevan, U.S.A. 116 D6
Delft, Neths. 17 B4
Delfzijl, Neths. 17 A6
Delgado, C., Mozam. 87 E5
Delgerhet, Mongolia 56 B6
Delgo, Sudan 80 C3
Delhi, Canada 116 D4
Delhi, India 68 E7
Delhi, La., U.S.A. 113 J9
Delhi, N.Y., U.S.A. 117 D10
Deli Jovan, Serbia & M. 44 B6
Delia, Canada 102 C6
Delice, Turkey 72 C6
Delicias, Mexico 118 B3
Delījān, Iran 71 C6
Déline, Canada 100 B7
Delisle, Canada 103 C7
Delitzsch, Germany 24 D8
Dell City, U.S.A. 109 L11
Dell Rapids, U.S.A. 112 D6
Delle, France 19 E14
Delmar, U.S.A. 117 D11
Delmenhorst, Germany 24 B4
Delnice, Croatia 41 C11
Delonga, Ostrova, Russia 53 B15
Deloraine, Australia 95 G4
Deloraine, Canada 103 D8
Delphi, Greece 46 C4
Delphi, U.S.A. 114 E2
Delphos, U.S.A. 114 E3
Delportshoop, S. Africa 88 D3
Delray Beach, U.S.A. 115 M5
Delsbo, Sweden 10 C10
Delta, Colo., U.S.A. 109 G9
Delta, Utah, U.S.A. 108 G7
Delta □, Nigeria 83 D6
Delta del Ebro △, Spain 38 E5
Delta del Po △, Italy 41 D9
Delta du Saloum △, Senegal 82 C1
Delta Dunărea △, Romania 29 E14
Delta Junction, U.S.A. 100 B5
Deltona, U.S.A. 115 L5
Delungra, Australia 95 D5
Delvada, India 68 J4
Delvinákion, Greece 46 B2
Delvinë, Albania 44 G4
Delyatyn, Ukraine 29 B9
Demak, Indonesia 63 G14
Demanda, Sierra de la, Spain 38 C2
Demavend = Damāvand, Qolleh-ye, Iran 71 C7
Dembecha, Ethiopia 81 E4
Dembi, Ethiopia 81 F4
Dembia, Dem. Rep. of the Congo 86 B2
Dembidolo, Ethiopia 81 F3
Demchok, India 69 C8
Demer →, Belgium 17 D4
Demetrias, Greece 46 B5
Demidov, Russia 32 E6
Deming, N. Mex., U.S.A. 109 K10
Deming, Wash., U.S.A. 110 B4
Demini →, Brazil 124 D6
Demirci, Turkey 47 B10
Demirköprü Baraji, Turkey 47 C10
Demirköy, Turkey 45 E11
Demmin, Germany 24 B9
Demonte, Italy 40 D4
Demopolis, U.S.A. 115 J2
Dempo, Indonesia 62 E2
Demyansk, Russia 32 D7
Den Burg, Neths. 17 A4
Den Chai, Thailand 64 D3
Den Haag = 's-Gravenhage, Neths. 17 B4
Den Helder, Neths. 17 B4
Den Oever, Neths. 17 B5
Denain, France 19 B10
Denair, U.S.A. 110 H6
Denau, Uzbekistan 52 F7
Denbigh, Canada 116 A7
Denbigh, U.K. 14 D4
Denbighshire □, U.K. 14 D4
Dendang, Indonesia 62 E3
Dendermonde, Belgium 17 C4
Deneba, Ethiopia 81 F4
Dengchuan, China 58 E3
Denge, Nigeria 83 C6
Dengfeng, China 56 G7
Dengi, Nigeria 83 D6
Dengkou, China 56 D4
Dengzhou, China 59 A9
Denham, Australia 93 E1
Denham, Mt., Jamaica 120 a
Denham Ra., Australia 94 C4
Denham Sd., Australia 93 E1
Denholm, Canada 103 C7
Denia, Spain 39 G5
Denial B., Australia 95 E1
Deniliquin, Australia 95 F3
Denison, Iowa, U.S.A. 112 E7
Denison, Tex., U.S.A. 113 J6
Denison Plains, Australia 92 C4
Denizli, Turkey 47 D11
Denizli □, Turkey 47 D11
Denman Glacier, Antarctica 5 C7
Denmark, Australia 93 F2
Denmark ■, Europe 11 J3
Denmark Str., Atl. Oc. 4 C6
Dennery, St. Lucia 121 f
Dennison, U.S.A. 116 F3
Denny, U.K. 13 E5

Denpasar, Indonesia 63 K18
Denpasar ✈ (DPS), Indonesia 63 K18
Denton, Mont., U.S.A. 108 C9
Denton, Tex., U.S.A. 113 J6
D'Entrecasteaux △, Australia 93 F2
D'Entrecasteaux, Pt., Australia 93 F2
Denu, Ghana 83 D5
Denver, Colo., U.S.A. 112 F2
Denver, Pa., U.S.A. 117 F8
Denver City, U.S.A. 113 J3
Deoband, India 68 E7
Deogarh, India 68 G5
Deoghar, India 69 G12
Deolali, India 66 K8
Deoli = Devli, India 68 G6
Déols, France 19 F8
Deora, India 68 F4
Deori, India 69 H8
Deoria, India 69 F10
Deosai Mts., Pakistan 69 B6
Deosri, India 69 F14
Depalpur, India 68 H6
Deping, China 57 F9
Deposit, U.S.A. 117 D9
Depuch I., Australia 92 D2
Deputatskiy, Russia 53 C14
Dêqên, China 58 C2
Deqing, China 59 F8
Dera Ghazi Khan, Pakistan 68 D4
Dera Ismail Khan, Pakistan 68 D4
Derabugti, Pakistan 68 E3
Derawar Fort, Pakistan 68 E4
Derbent, Russia 35 J9
Derbent, Turkey 47 C10
Derby, Australia 92 C3
Derby, U.K. 14 E6
Derby, Conn., U.S.A. 117 E11
Derby, Kans., U.S.A. 113 G6
Derby, N.Y., U.S.A. 116 D6
Derby City □, U.K. 14 E6
Derby Line, U.S.A. 117 B12
Derbyshire □, U.K. 14 D6
Đerdap, Serbia & M. 44 B6
Derdepoort, S. Africa 88 C4
Dereham, U.K. 15 E8
Derecske, Hungary 28 C6
Dereköy, Turkey 45 E11
Dereli, Turkey 73 B8
Derg →, U.K. 12 B4
Derg, L., Ireland 12 D3
Dergachi = Derhaci, Ukraine 33 G9
Dergaon, India 67 F19
Derhaci, Ukraine 33 G9
Derik, Turkey 73 D9
Derinkuyu, Turkey 72 C6
Dermantsi, Bulgaria 45 C8
Dermott, U.S.A. 113 J9
Derry = Londonderry, U.K. 12 B4
Derry = Londonderry □, U.K. 12 B4
Derry, N.H., U.S.A. 117 D13
Derry, Pa., U.S.A. 116 F5
Derryveagh Mts., Ireland 12 B3
Derudub, Sudan 80 D4
Derval, France 18 E5
Dervéni, Greece 46 C4
Derventa, Bos.-H. 28 F2
Derwent →, Cumb., U.K. 14 C4
Derwent →, Derby, U.K. 14 E6
Derwent →, N. Yorks., U.K. 14 D7
Derwent Water, U.K. 14 C4
Des Moines, Iowa, U.S.A. 112 E8
Des Moines, N. Mex., U.S.A. 113 G3
Des Moines →, U.S.A. 112 E9
Desa, Romania 28 G8
Desaguadero →, Argentina 126 C2
Desaguadero →, Bolivia 124 G5
Desantne, Ukraine 29 E14
Desar, Malaysia 65 d
Descanso, Pta., Mexico 111 N9
Descartes, France 20 B4
Deschaillons-sur-St-Laurent, Canada 105 C5
Deschambault L., Canada 103 C8
Deschutes →, U.S.A. 108 D3
Dese, Ethiopia 81 E4
Deseado →, Argentina 128 F3
Desenzano del Garda, Italy 40 C7
Desert Center, U.S.A. 111 M11
Desert Hot Springs, U.S.A. 111 M10
Deshnok, India 68 F5
Desierto Central de Baja California △, Mexico 118 B2
Desna →, Ukraine 33 G6
Desnățui →, Romania 29 G8
Desolación, I., Chile 128 G2
Despeñaperros, △, Spain 37 G7
Despeñaperros, Paso, Spain 37 G7
Despotovac, Serbia & M. 44 B5
Dessau, Germany 24 D8
Dessye = Dese, Ethiopia 81 E4
D'Estrees B., Australia 95 F2
Desuri, India 68 G5
Desvres, France 19 B8
Det Udom, Thailand 64 E5
Deta, Romania 28 E6
Dete, Zimbabwe 88 B4
Đetinja →, Serbia & M. 44 C4
Detmold, Germany 24 D4
Detour, Pt., U.S.A. 114 C2
Detroit, U.S.A. 116 D1
Detroit Lakes, U.S.A. 112 B7
Detva, Slovak Rep. 27 C12
Deurne, Neths. 17 C5
Deutsch-Luxemburgischer △, Germany 25 E13
Deutsche Bucht, Germany 24 A4
Deutschlandsberg, Austria 26 E8
Deux-Sèvres □, France 18 F6
Deva, Romania 28 E7
Devakottai, India 66 Q11
Devaprayag, India 69 D8

Dévaványa, Hungary 28 C5
Deveci Dağları, Turkey 72 B7
Devecikonağı, Turkey 45 G12
Devecser, Hungary 28 C2
Develi, Turkey 72 C6
Deventer, Neths. 17 B6
Deveron →, U.K. 13 D6
Devesel, Romania 28 F7
Devgadh Bariya, India 68 H5
Devikot, India 68 F4
Devils Den, U.S.A. 110 K7
Devils Lake, U.S.A. 112 A5
Devils Paw, Canada 102 B2
Devils Postpile △, U.S.A. 110 H7
Devils Tower △, U.S.A. 112 C2
Devils Tower Junction, U.S.A. 112 C2
Devin, Bulgaria 45 E8
Devine, U.S.A. 113 L5
Devizes, U.K. 15 F6
Devli, India 68 G6
Devnya, Bulgaria 45 C11
Devon, Canada 102 C6
Devon □, U.K. 15 G4
Devon I., Canada 98 B11
Devonport, Australia 95 G4
Devonport, N.Z. 91 G5
Devrek, Turkey 72 B4
Devrekâni, Turkey 72 B5
Devrez →, Turkey 72 B6
Dewas, India 68 H7
Dewetsdorp, S. Africa 88 D4
Dewey, Puerto Rico 121 d
Dexing, China 59 C11
Dexter, Maine, U.S.A. 115 C11
Dexter, Mo., U.S.A. 113 G10
Dexter, N. Mex., U.S.A. 113 J2
Deyang, China 58 B5
Deyhūk, Iran 71 C8
Deyyer, Iran 71 E6
Dezadeash L., Canada 102 A1
Dezfūl, Iran 71 C6
Dezhneva, Mys, Russia 53 C19
Dezhou, China 56 F9
Dhadhar →, India 69 G11
Dháfni, Kríti, Greece 49 D7
Dháfni, Pelóponnisos, Greece 46 D4
Dhahaban, Si. Arabia 80 C4
Dhahiriya = Az Zāhirīyah, West Bank 74 D3
Dhahran = Az Zahrān, Si. Arabia 71 E6
Dhak, Pakistan 68 C5
Dhaka, Bangla. 69 H14
Dhaka □, Bangla. 69 G14
Dhali, Cyprus 49 D12
Dhamási, Greece 46 B4
Dhampur, India 69 E8
Dhamtari, India 67 J12
Dhanbad, India 69 H12
Dhangarhi, Nepal 67 E12
Dhankuta, Nepal 69 F12
Dhar, India 68 H6
Dharampur, India 68 H6
Dharamsala = Dharmsala, India 68 C7
Dhariwal, India 68 D6
Dharla →, Bangla. 69 G13
Dharmapuri, India 66 N11
Dharmjaygarh, India 69 H10
Dharmsala, India 68 C7
Dharni, India 68 J7
Dharwad, India 66 M9
Dhasan →, India 69 G8
Dhaulagiri, Nepal 69 E10
Dhebar, L., India 68 G6
Dheftera, Cyprus 49 D12
Dhenkanal, India 67 J14
Dhenoúsa, Greece 47 D7
Dherinia, Cyprus 49 D12
Dheskáti, Greece 44 G5
Dhespotikó, Greece 46 E6
Dhestina, Greece 46 C4
Dhī Qār □, Iraq 70 D5
Dhiarrizos →, Cyprus 49 E11
Dhībān, Jordan 74 D4
Dhidhimótikhon, Greece 45 E10
Dhíkti Óros, Greece 49 D7
Dhilianáta, Greece 46 C2
Dhílos, Greece 47 D7
Dhilwan, India 68 D6
Dhimarkhera, India 69 H9
Dhimitsána, Greece 46 D4
Dhírfis Óros, Greece 46 C5
Dhodhekánisos, Greece 47 E8
Dhodhekánisos □, Greece 47 E8
Dhokós, Greece 46 D5
Dholiana, Greece 46 B2
Dholka, India 68 H5
Dhomokós, Greece 46 B4
Dhoraji, India 68 J4
Dhoxáton, Greece 45 E8
Dhragonísi, Greece 47 D7
Dhráhstis, Ákra, Greece 49 A3
Dhrangadhra, India 68 H4
Dhrápanon, Ákra, Greece 49 D6
Dhriópis, Greece 46 D6
Dhrol, India 68 H4
Dhuburi, India 67 F16
Dhule, India 66 J9
Di-ib, W. →, Sudan 80 C4
Di Linh, Vietnam 65 G7
Di Linh, Cao Nguyen, Vietnam 65 G7
Día, Greece 49 D7
Diabakania, Guinea 82 C2
Diablo, Mt., U.S.A. 110 H5
Diablo Range, U.S.A. 110 H5
Diafarabé, Mali 82 C4
Diala, Mali 82 C3
Dialakoro, Mali 82 C3
Dialakoto, Senegal 82 C2
Diallassagou, Mali 82 C4
Diamante, Argentina 126 C3

Diamante, Italy 43 C8
Diamante →, Argentina 126 C2
Diamantina, Brazil 125 G10
Diamantina △, Australia 94 C3
Diamantina →, Australia 95 D2
Diamantino, Brazil 125 F7
Diamond Bar, U.S.A. 111 L9
Diamond Harbour, India 69 H13
Diamond Is., Australia 94 B5
Diamond Mts., U.S.A. 108 G6
Diamond Springs, U.S.A. 110 G6
Dian Chi, China 58 E4
Dianalund, Denmark 11 J5
Dianbai, China 59 G8
Diancheng, China 59 G8
Dianjiang, China 58 B6
Diano Marina, Italy 40 E5
Dianra, Ivory C. 82 D3
Diapaga, Burkina Faso 83 C5
Diapangou, Burkina Faso 83 C5
Diariguila, Guinea 82 C2
Dībā, U.A.E. 71 E8
Dibai, India 68 E8
Dibaya-Lubue, Dem. Rep. of
  the Congo 84 E3
Dibbeen △, Jordan 74 C4
Dibete, Botswana 88 C4
Dibrugarh, India 67 F19
Dickens, U.S.A. 113 J4
Dickinson, U.S.A. 112 B3
Dickson, U.S.A. 115 G2
Dickson City, U.S.A. 117 E9
Dicle Nehri →, Turkey 73 D9
Dicomano, Italy 41 E8
Didesa, W. →, Ethiopia 81 E4
Didi, Sudan 81 F3
Didiéni, Mali 82 C3
Didsbury, Canada 102 C6
Didwana, India 68 F6
Die, France 21 D9
Diébougou, Burkina Faso 82 C4
Diecke, Guinea 82 D3
Diefenbaker, L., Canada 103 C7
Diego de Almagro, Chile 126 B1
Diego Garcia, Ind. Oc. 3 E13
Diekirch, Lux. 17 E6
Diéma, Mali 82 C3
Diembéring, Senegal 82 C1
Diemelsee △, Germany 24 D4
Dien Ban, Vietnam 64 E7
Dien Bien, Vietnam 58 G4
Dien Khanh, Vietnam 65 F7
Diepholz, Germany 24 C4
Dieppe, France 18 C8
Dierks, U.S.A. 113 H8
Diest, Belgium 17 D5
Dietikon, Switz. 25 H4
Dieulefit, France 21 D9
Dieuze, France 19 D13
Dif, Somali Rep. 75 G3
Differdange, Lux. 17 E5
Dig, India 68 F7
Digba, Dem. Rep. of the Congo 86 B2
Digby, Canada 105 D6
Diggi, India 68 F6
Dighinala, Bangla. 67 H18
Dighton, U.S.A. 112 F4
Digna, Mali 82 C3
Digne-les-Bains, France 21 D10
Digoin, France 19 F11
Digor, Turkey 73 B10
Digos, Phil. 61 H6
Digranes, Iceland 8 C6
Digul →, Indonesia 63 F9
Digya △, Ghana 83 D5
Dihang = Brahmaputra →, Asia 69 H13
Dijlah, Nahr →, Asia 70 D5
Dijon, France 19 E12
Dikhil, Djibouti 81 E5
Dikili, Turkey 47 B8
Dikirnis, Egypt 80 H7
Dikkil = Dikhil, Djibouti 81 E5
Dikson, Russia 52 B9
Dikwa, Nigeria 83 C7
Dila, Ethiopia 81 F4
Dilek Yarimadisi △, Turkey .. 47 D9
Dili, E. Timor 63 F7
Dilijan, Armenia 35 K7
Dilizhan = Dilijan, Armenia .. 35 K7
Dilj, Croatia 28 E3
Dillenburg, Germany 24 E4
Dilley, U.S.A. 113 L5
Dilli = Delhi, India 68 E7
Dilling, Sudan 81 E2
Dillingen, Bayern, Germany .. 25 G6
Dillingen, Saarland, Germany . 25 F2
Dillingham, U.S.A. 100 C4
Dillon, Canada 103 B7
Dillon, Mont., U.S.A. 108 D7
Dillon, S.C., U.S.A. 115 H6
Dillon →, Canada 103 B7
Dillsburg, U.S.A. 116 F7
Dilly, Mali 82 C3
Dilolo, Dem. Rep. of the Congo 84 G4
Dilove, Ukraine 29 C9
Dimas, Mexico 118 C3
Dimashq, Syria 74 B5
Dimashq □, Syria 74 B5
Dimbaza, S. Africa 89 E4
Dimbokro, Ivory C. 82 D4
Dimboola, Australia 95 F3
Dîmbovița = Dâmbovița →,
  Romania 29 F11
Dimbulah, Australia 94 B4
Dimitrovgrad, Bulgaria 45 D9
Dimitrovgrad, Russia 34 C9
Dimitrovgrad, Serbia & M. ... 44 C6
Dimitrovo = Pernik, Bulgaria . 44 D7
Dimmitt, U.S.A. 113 H3
Dimo, Sudan 81 F2

Dimona, Israel 74 D4
Dimovo, Bulgaria 44 C6
Dinagat, Phil. 61 F6
Dinajpur, Bangla. 67 G16
Dinan, France 18 D4
Dīnān Āb, Iran 71 C8
Dinant, Belgium 17 D4
Dinapur, India 69 G11
Dinar, Turkey 47 C12
Dīnār, Kūh-e, Iran 71 D6
Dinara Planina, Croatia 41 D13
Dinard, France 18 D4
Dinaric Alps = Dinara Planina,
  Croatia 41 D13
Dindanko, Mali 82 C3
Dinder △, Sudan 81 E4
Dinder, Nahr ed →, Sudan .. 81 E3
Dindigul, India 66 P11
Dindori, India 69 H9
Ding Xian = Dingzhou, China . 56 E8
Dinga, Pakistan 68 G2
Dingalan, Phil. 61 D4
Dingbian, China 56 F4
Dingelstädt, Germany 24 D6
Dingle, Ireland 12 D1
Dingle, Sweden 11 F5
Dingle B., Ireland 12 D1
Dingmans Ferry, U.S.A. 117 E10
Dingnan, China 59 E10
Dingo, Australia 94 C4
Dingolfing, Germany 25 G8
Dingtao, China 56 G8
Dinguira, Mali 82 C2
Dinguiraye, Guinea 82 C2
Dingwall, U.K. 13 D4
Dingxi, China 56 G3
Dingxiang, China 56 E7
Dingyuan, China 59 A11
Dingzhou, China 56 E8
Dinh, Mui, Vietnam 65 G7
Dinh Lap, Vietnam 58 G6
Dinira △, Venezuela 121 E6
Dinokwe, Botswana 88 C4
Dinorwic, Canada 103 D10
Dinosaur △, Canada 102 C6
Dinosaur ○, U.S.A. 108 F9
Dinuba, U.S.A. 110 J7
Diö, Sweden 11 H8
Dioila, Mali 82 C3
Dioka, Mali 82 C2
Diongoï, Mali 82 C3
Diósgyőr, Hungary 28 B5
Diosig, Romania 28 C7
Diougani, Mali 82 C4
Diouloulou, Senegal 82 C1
Dioura, Mali 82 C3
Diourbel, Senegal 82 C1
Dipalpur, Pakistan 68 D5
Diplo, Pakistan 68 G3
Dipolog, Phil. 61 G5
Dippern △, Australia 94 C4
Dir, Pakistan 66 B7
Diré, Mali 82 B4
Dire Dawa, Ethiopia 81 F5
Diriamba, Nic. 120 D2
Dirk Hartog I., Australia 93 E1
Dirranbandi, Australia 95 D4
Disa, India 68 G5
Disa, Sudan 81 E3
Disappointment, C., U.S.A. .. 108 C2
Disappointment, L., Australia . 92 D3
Disaster B., Australia 95 F4
Discovery B., Australia 95 F3
Disentis Muster, Switz. 25 J4
Dishna, Egypt 80 B3
Disina, Nigeria 83 C6
Disko = Qeqertarsuaq, Greenland 101 B5
Disna = Dzisna →, Belarus .. 32 K5
Diss, U.K. 15 E9
Disteghil Sar, Pakistan 69 A6
Distrito Federal □, Brazil ... 125 G9
Distrito Federal □, Mexico .. 119 D5
Disûq, Egypt 80 H7
Diu, India 68 J4
Dīvāndarreh, Iran 70 C5
Dives →, France 18 C6
Dives-sur-Mer, France 18 C6
Divichi = Dăvăçi, Azerbaijan . 35 K9
Divide, U.S.A. 108 D7
Dividing Ra., Australia 93 E2
Divinópolis, Brazil 125 H10
Divjake, Albania 44 F3
Divnoye, Russia 35 H6
Divo, Ivory C. 82 D3
Divriği, Turkey 73 C8
Dīwāl Kol, Afghan. 68 B2
Dixie Mt., U.S.A. 110 F6
Dixon, Calif., U.S.A. 110 G5
Dixon, Ill., U.S.A. 112 E10
Dixon Entrance, U.S.A. 100 C6
Dixville, Canada 117 A13
Diyadin, Turkey 73 C10
Diyālā □, Iraq 70 C5
Diyālā →, Iraq 70 C5
Diyarbakır, Turkey 70 B4
Diyodar, India 68 G4
Djakarta = Jakarta, Indonesia 63 G12
Djamba, Angola 88 B1
Djambala, Congo 84 E2
Djanet, Algeria 78 D7
Djawa = Jawa, Indonesia 62 F3
Djelfa, Algeria 78 B6
Djema, C.A.R. 86 A2
Djenné, Mali 82 C4
Djerba, I. de, Tunisia 79 B8
Djerid, Chott, Tunisia 78 B7
Djibo, Burkina Faso 83 C4
Djibouti, Djibouti 81 E5
Djibouti ■, Africa 81 E5
Djolu, Dem. Rep. of the Congo 84 D4
Djougou, Benin 83 D5
Djoum, Cameroon 84 D2

Djourab, Erg du, Chad 79 E9
Djugu, Dem. Rep. of the Congo 86 B3
Djúpivogur, Iceland 8 D6
Djurås, Sweden 10 D9
Djurö, Sweden 11 F7
Djursland, Denmark 11 H4
Dmitriya Lapteva, Proliv, Russia 53 B15
Dmitriyev Lgovskiy, Russia .. 33 F8
Dmitrov, Russia 32 D9
Dmitrovsk-Orlovskiy, Russia . 33 F8
Dnepr = Dnipro →, Ukraine . 33 J7
Dneprodzerzhinsk =
  Dniprodzerzhynsk, Ukraine . 33 H8
Dneprodzerzhinskoye Vdkhr. =
  Dniprodzerzhynske Vdskh.,
  Ukraine 33 H8
Dnepropetrovsk =
  Dnipropetrovsk, Ukraine 33 H8
Dneprorudnoye = Dniprorudne,
  Ukraine 33 J8
Dnestr = Dnister →, Ukraine . 33 J6
Dnieper = Dnipro →, Ukraine 33 J7
Dniester = Dnister →, Europe . 33 J6
Dnipro →, Ukraine 33 J7
Dniprodzerzhynsk, Ukraine .. 33 H8
Dniprodzerzhynske Vdskh.,
  Ukraine 33 H8
Dnipropetrovsk, Ukraine 33 H8
Dniprorudne, Ukraine 33 J8
Dnister →, Europe 33 J6
Dnistrovskyy Lyman, Ukraine 33 J6
Dno, Russia 32 D5
Dnyapro = Dnipro →, Ukraine 33 J7
Doaktown, Canada 105 C6
Doan Hung, Vietnam 58 G5
Doany, Madag. 89 A8
Doba, Chad 79 G9
Dobandi, Pakistan 68 D2
Dobbiaco, Italy 41 B9
Dobbyn, Australia 94 B3
Dobele, Latvia 9 H20
Döbeln, Germany 24 D9
Doberai, Jazirah, Indonesia .. 63 E8
Dobiegniew, Poland 31 F2
Doblas, Argentina 126 D3
Dobo, Indonesia 63 F8
Doboj, Bos.-H. 28 F3
Dobra, Wielkopolskie, Poland 31 G5
Dobra, Zachodnio-Pomorskie,
  Poland 30 E2
Dobra, Dâmbovița, Romania . 29 F10
Dobra, Hunedoara, Romania . 28 E7
Dobre Miasto, Poland 30 E7
Dobreşti, Romania 28 D7
Dobrich, Bulgaria 45 C11
Dobrinishta, Bulgaria 44 E7
Dobříš, Czech Rep. 26 B7
Dobrodzień, Poland 31 H5
Dobromyl, Ukraine 31 J9
Dobron, Ukraine 28 B7
Dobropole, Ukraine 33 H9
Dobrovolsk, Russia 30 D9
Dobruja, Europe 29 F13
Dobrush, Belarus 33 F6
Dobrzany, Poland 30 E2
Dobrzyń nad Wisłą, Poland .. 31 F6
Doc, Mui, Vietnam 64 D6
Docker River, Australia 93 D4
Docksta, Sweden 10 A12
Doctor Arroyo, Mexico 118 C4
Doda, India 69 C6
Doda, L., Canada 104 C4
Dodecanese = Dhodhekánisos,
  Greece 47 E8
Dodge City, U.S.A. 113 G5
Dodge L., Canada 103 B7
Dodgeville, U.S.A. 112 D9
Dodo, Cameroon 83 D7
Dodo, Sudan 81 F2
Dodola, Ethiopia 81 F4
Dodoma, Tanzania 86 D4
Dodoma □, Tanzania 86 D4
Dodona, Greece 46 B2
Dodori △, Kenya 86 C5
Dodsland, Canada 103 C7
Dodson, U.S.A. 108 B9
Dodurga, Turkey 47 B11
Doesburg, Neths. 17 B6
Doetinchem, Neths. 17 C6
Dog Creek, Canada 102 C4
Dog L., Man., Canada 103 C9
Dog L., Ont., Canada 104 C2
Doğanşehir, Turkey 72 C7
Dogliani, Italy 40 D4
Dogondoutchi, Niger 83 C5
Dogran, Pakistan 68 D5
Doğubayazıt, Turkey 70 B5
Doguéraoua, Niger 83 C6
Doha = Ad Dawḥah, Qatar .. 71 E6
Dohazari, Bangla. 67 H18
Dohrighat, India 69 F10
Doi, Indonesia 63 D7
Doi Inthanon △, Thailand ... 64 C2
Doi Khuntan △, Thailand 64 C2
Doi Luang, Thailand 64 C2
Doi Luang △, Thailand 64 C2
Doi Saket, Thailand 64 C2
Doi Suthep △, Thailand 64 C2
Dois Irmãos, Sa., Brazil 125 E10
Dojransko Jezero, Macedonia . 44 E6
Dokkum, Neths. 17 A5
Dokri, Pakistan 68 F3
Dokuchayevsk, Ukraine 33 J9
Dolac, Serbia & M. 44 D4
Dolak, Pulau, Indonesia 63 F9
Dolbeau-Mistassini, Canada . 105 C5
Dole, France 19 E12
Doleib, Wadi →, Sudan 81 E3
Dolenji Logatec, Slovenia ... 41 C11

Dolgellau, U.K. 14 E4
Dolgelley = Dolgellau, U.K. .. 14 E4
Dolhasca, Romania 29 C11
Dolianova, Italy 42 C2
Dolinskaya = Dolynska, Ukraine 33 H7
Dolj □, Romania 29 F8
Dollard, Neths. 17 A7
Dolna Banya, Bulgaria 44 D7
Dolni Chiflik, Bulgaria 45 D11
Dolni Dŭbnik, Bulgaria 45 C8
Dolnośląskie □, Poland 31 G3
Dolný Kubín, Slovak Rep. ... 27 B12
Dolo, Ethiopia 81 G5
Dolo, Italy 41 C9
Dolomites = Dolomiti, Italy .. 41 B8
Dolomiti, Italy 41 B8
Dolomiti Bellunesi △, Italy .. 41 B9
Dolores, Argentina 126 D4
Dolores, Uruguay 126 C4
Dolores, U.S.A. 109 H9
Dolores →, U.S.A. 109 G9
Dolovo, Serbia & M. 28 F5
Dolphin, C., Falk. Is. 128 G5
Dolphin and Union Str., Canada 100 B8
Dolsk, Poland 31 G4
Dolyna, Ukraine 29 B9
Dolynska, Ukraine 33 H7
Dolynske, Ukraine 29 C14
Dolzhanskaya, Russia 33 J9
Dom Pedrito, Brazil 127 C5
Doma, Nigeria 83 D6
Doma △, Zimbabwe 87 F3
Domaniç, Turkey 47 B11
Domariaganj →, India 69 F10
Domasi, Malawi 87 F4
Domažlice, Czech Rep. 26 B5
Dombarovskiy, Russia 52 D6
Dombås, Norway 9 E13
Dombasle-sur-Meurthe, France 19 D13
Dombes, France 21 C9
Dombóvár, Hungary 28 D3
Dombrád, Hungary 28 B6
Domel I. = Letsôk-aw Kyun,
  Burma 65 G2
Domérat, France 19 F9
Domeyko, Chile 126 B1
Domeyko, Cordillera, Chile .. 126 A2
Domfront, France 18 D6
Dominador, Chile 126 A2
Dominica ■, W. Indies 121 C7
Dominica Passage, W. Indies . 121 C7
Dominican Rep. ■, W. Indies 121 C5
Dömitz, Germany 24 B7
Domme, France 20 D5
Domneşti, Romania 29 E9
Domodóssola, Italy 40 B5
Domogled-Valea Cernei △,
  Romania 28 F7
Dompaire, France 19 D13
Dompierre-sur-Besbre, France 19 F10
Dompim, Ghana 82 D4
Domrémy-la-Pucelle, France . 19 D12
Domville, Mt., Australia 95 D5
Domvraína, Greece 46 C4
Domžale, Slovenia 41 B11
Don →, Russia 33 J10
Don →, Aberds., U.K. 13 D6
Don →, S. Yorks., U.K. 14 D7
Don, C., Australia 92 B5
Don Benito, Spain 37 G5
Don Figuereo Mts., Jamaica . 120 a
Don Sak, Thailand .... 65 b
Dona Ana = Nhamaabué,
  Mozam. 87 F4
Doña Mencía, Spain 37 H6
Donaghadee, U.K. 12 B6
Donald, Australia 95 F3
Donaldsonville, U.S.A. 113 K9
Donalsonville, U.S.A. 115 K3
Doñana △, Spain 37 J4
Donau = Dunărea →, Europe 29 E14
Donau →, Austria 27 C10
Donau Auen △, Austria 27 C9
Donaueschingen, Germany .. 25 H4
Donauwörth, Germany 25 G6
Doncaster, U.K. 14 D6
Dondo, Mozam. 87 F3
Dondo, Teluk, Indonesia 63 D6
Dondra Head, Sri Lanka 66 S12
Dondușeni, Moldova 29 B12
Donegal, Ireland 12 B3
Donegal □, Ireland 12 B4
Donegal B., Ireland 12 B3
Donets →, Russia 35 G5
Donets Basin, Ukraine 6 F13
Donetsk, Ukraine 33 J9
Dong Ba Thin, Vietnam 65 F7
Dong Dang, Vietnam 58 G6
Dong Giam, Vietnam 64 C5
Dong Ha, Vietnam 64 D6
Dong Hene, Laos 64 D5
Dong Hoi, Vietnam 64 D6
Dong Jiang →, China 59 F10
Dong Khe, Vietnam 58 A6
Dong Ujimqin Qi, China 56 B9
Dong Van, Vietnam 64 A5
Dong Xoai, Vietnam 65 G6
Donga, Nigeria 83 D7
Donga →, Nigeria 83 D7
Dong'an, China 59 D8
Dongara, Australia 93 E1
Dongbei, China 53 E13
Dongchuan, China 58 D5
Dongfang, China 59 D7
Dongfeng, China 57 C13
Donggala, Indonesia 63 E5
Donggan, China 58 F5
Dongguan, China 59 F9
Dongguang, China 56 F9

Donghai Dao, China 59 G8
Dongjingcheng, China 57 B15
Dongkou, China 59 D8
Donglan, China 58 E6
Dongliu, China 59 B11
Dongmen, China 58 F6
Dongning, China 57 B16
Dongnyi, China 58 C3
Dongola, Sudan 80 D3
Dongping, China 56 G9
Dongsha Dao, China 59 G11
Dongshan, China 59 F11
Dongsheng, China 56 E6
Dongtai, China 57 H11
Dongting Hu, China 59 C9
Dongtou, China 59 D13
Dongxiang, China 59 C11
Dongxing, China 58 G7
Dongyang, China 59 C13
Dongzhi, China 59 B11
Donington, C., Australia 95 E2
Doniphan, U.S.A. 113 G9
Donja Stubica, Croatia 41 C12
Donji Dušnik, Serbia & M. .. 44 C6
Donji Miholjac, Croatia 28 E3
Donji Milanovac, Serbia & M. 44 B6
Donji Vakuf, Bos.-H. 28 F2
Dønna, Norway 8 C15
Donna, U.S.A. 113 M5
Donnaconna, Canada 105 C5
Donnelly's Crossing, N.Z. ... 91 F4
Donnybrook, Australia 93 F2
Donnybrook, S. Africa 89 D4
Donora, U.S.A. 116 F5
Donostia = Donostia-San
  Sebastián, Spain 38 B3
Donostia-San Sebastián, Spain 38 B3
Donskoy, Russia 32 F10
Donsol, Phil. 61 E5
Donzère, France 21 D8
Donzy, France 19 E10
Doon →, U.K. 13 F4
Dora, L., Australia 92 D3
Dora Báltea →, Italy 40 C5
Dora Ripária →, Italy 40 C4
Doran L., Canada 103 A7
Dorchester, U.K. 15 G5
Dorchester, C., Canada 101 B12
Dordabis, Namibia 88 C2
Dordogne □, France 20 C4
Dordogne →, France 20 C3
Dordrecht, Neths. 17 C4
Dordrecht, S. Africa 88 E4
Dore →, France 20 C7
Dore, Mts., France 20 C6
Doré L., Canada 103 C7
Doré Lake, Canada 103 C7
Dorfen, Germany 25 G8
Dorgali, Italy 42 B2
Dori, Burkina Faso 83 C4
Doring →, S. Africa 88 E2
Doringbos, S. Africa 88 E2
Dorking, U.K. 15 F7
Dormaa-Ahenkro, Ghana ... 82 D4
Dormans, France 19 C10
Dormo, Ras, Eritrea 81 E5
Dornbirn, Austria 26 D2
Dornes, France 19 F10
Dorneşti, Romania 29 C11
Dornie, U.K. 13 D3
Dornoch, U.K. 13 D4
Dornoch Firth, U.K. 13 D4
Dornogovĭ □, Mongolia 56 C6
Doro, Mali 83 B4
Dorog, Hungary 28 C3
Dorogobuzh, Russia 32 E7
Dorohoi, Romania 29 C11
Döröö Nuur, Mongolia 60 B4
Dorr, Iran 71 C6
Dorre I., Australia 93 E1
Dorrigo, Australia 95 E5
Dorris, U.S.A. 108 F3
Dorset, Canada 116 A6
Dorset, U.S.A. 116 E4
Dorset □, U.K. 15 G5
Dorsten, Germany 24 D2
Dortmund, Germany 24 D3
Dortmund-Ems-Kanal →,
  Germany 24 D3
Dörtyol, Turkey 72 D7
Dorum, Germany 24 B4
Doruma, Dem. Rep. of the Congo 86 B2
Dorûneh, Iran 71 C8
Dos Bahías, C., Argentina ... 128 E3
Dos Hermanas, Spain 37 H5
Dos Palos, U.S.A. 110 J6
Dösemealtı, Turkey 47 D12
Dosso, Niger 83 C5
Dosso ○, Niger 83 C5
Dothan, U.S.A. 115 K3
Doty, U.S.A. 110 D3
Douai, France 19 B10
Douako, Guinea 82 D2
Douala, Cameroon 83 E6
Douarnenez, France 18 D2
Doubabougou, Mali 82 C3
Double Island Pt., Australia . 95 D5
Double Mountain Fork →,
  U.S.A. 113 J4
Doubrava, Czech Rep. 26 A8
Doubs □, France 19 E13
Doubs →, France 19 F12
Doubtful Sd., N.Z. 91 L1
Doubtless B., N.Z. 91 F4
Doudeville, France 18 C7
Doué-la-Fontaine, France ... 18 E6
Douentza, Mali 82 C4
Douglas, I. of Man 14 C3
Douglas, S. Africa 88 D3
Douglas, Ariz., U.S.A. 109 L9
Douglas, Ga., U.S.A. 115 K4

Douglas, *Wyo., U.S.A.* 112 D2
Douglas Apsley △, *Australia* 95 G4
Douglas Chan., *Canada* 102 C3
Douglas Pt., *Canada* 116 B3
Douglasville, *U.S.A.* 115 J3
Doukáton, Ákra, *Greece* 46 C2
Douna, *Mali* 82 C3
Dounreay, *U.K.* 13 C5
Dourada, Serra, *Brazil* 125 F9
Dourados, *Brazil* 127 A5
Dourados ~, *Brazil* 127 A5
Dourados, Serra dos, *Brazil* 127 A5
Dourdan, *France* 19 D9
Douro ~, *Europe* 36 D2
Douvaine, *France* 19 F13
Douvres-la-Délivrande, *France* 18 C6
Douze ~, *France* 20 E3
Dove ~, *U.K.* 14 E6
Dove Creek, *U.S.A.* 109 H9
Dover, *Australia* 95 G4
Dover, *U.K.* 15 F9
Dover, *Del., U.S.A.* 114 F8
Dover, *N.H., U.S.A.* 117 C14
Dover, *N.J., U.S.A.* 117 F10
Dover, *Ohio, U.S.A.* 116 F3
Dover, Pt., *Australia* 93 F4
Dover, Str. of, *Europe* 15 G9
Dover-Foxcroft, *U.S.A.* 115 C11
Dover Plains, *U.S.A.* 117 E11
Dovey = Dyfi ~, *U.K.* 15 E3
Dovhe, *Ukraine* 29 B8
Dovrefjell, *Norway* 9 E13
Dow Rūd, *Iran* 71 C6
Dowa, *Malawi* 87 E3
Dowagiac, *U.S.A.* 114 E2
Dowerin, *Australia* 93 F2
Dowgha'i, *Iran* 71 B8
Dowlatābād, *Iran* 71 D8
Down □, *U.K.* 12 B5
Downey, *Calif., U.S.A.* 111 M8
Downey, *Idaho, U.S.A.* 108 E7
Downham Market, *U.K.* 15 E8
Downieville, *U.S.A.* 110 F6
Downpatrick, *U.K.* 12 B6
Downpatrick Hd., *Ireland* 12 B2
Downsville, *U.S.A.* 117 D10
Downton, Mt., *Canada* 102 C4
Dowsārī, *Iran* 71 D8
Doyle, *U.S.A.* 110 E6
Doylestown, *U.S.A.* 117 F9
Dozois, Rés., *Canada* 104 C4
Dra Khel, *Pakistan* 68 F2
Drac ~, *France* 21 C9
Dračevo, *Macedonia* 44 E5
Drachten, *Neths.* 17 A6
Drăgănești, *Moldova* 29 C13
Drăgănești-Olt, *Romania* 29 F9
Drăgănești-Vlașca, *Romania* 29 F10
Dragaš, *Serbia & M.* 44 D4
Drăgășani, *Romania* 29 F9
Dragichyn, *Belarus* 33 F3
Dragocvet, *Serbia & M.* 44 C5
Dragon's Mouth = Boca de Drago, *Venezuela* 125 K15
Dragovishtitsa, *Bulgaria* 44 D6
Draguignan, *France* 21 E10
Drahove, *Ukraine* 29 B8
Drain, *U.S.A.* 108 E2
Drake, *U.S.A.* 112 B4
Drake Passage, *S. Ocean* 5 B17
Drakensberg, *S. Africa* 89 D4
Dráma, *Greece* 45 E8
Dráma □, *Greece* 45 E8
Drammen, *Norway* 9 G14
Drangajökull, *Iceland* 8 C2
Dranov, Ostrov, *Romania* 29 F14
Dras, *India* 69 B6
Drau = Drava ~, *Croatia* 28 E3
Drava ~, *Croatia* 28 E3
Dravograd, *Slovenia* 41 B12
Drawa ~, *Poland* 31 F2
Drawieński △, *Poland* 31 F2
Drawno, *Poland* 31 E2
Drawsko Pomorskie, *Poland* 30 E2
Drayton Valley, *Canada* 102 C6
Dreieich, *Germany* 25 E4
Dren, *Serbia & M.* 44 C4
Drenthe □, *Neths.* 17 B6
Drepanum, C., *Cyprus* 49 E11
Dresden, *Canada* 116 D2
Dresden, *Germany* 24 D9
Dreux, *France* 18 D8
Drezdenko, *Poland* 31 F2
Driffield, *U.K.* 14 C7
Driftwood, *U.S.A.* 116 E6
Driggs, *U.S.A.* 108 E8
Drin ~, *Albania* 44 D3
Drin i Zi ~, *Albania* 44 E4
Drina ~, *Bos.-H.* 44 B3
Drincea ~, *Romania* 28 F7
Drinjača ~, *Bos.-H.* 28 F4
Drissa = Vyerkhnyadzvinsk, *Belarus* 32 E4
Drniš, *Croatia* 41 E13
Drøbak, *Norway* 9 G14
Drobeta-Turnu Severin, *Romania* 28 F7
Drobin, *Poland* 31 F6
Drochia, *Moldova* 29 B12
Drogheda, *Ireland* 12 C5
Drogichin = Dragichyn, *Belarus* 33 F3
Drogobych = Drohobych, *Ukraine* 31 J10
Drohiczyn, *Poland* 31 F9
Drohobych, *Ukraine* 31 J10
Droichead Atha = Drogheda, *Ireland* 12 C5
Droichead Nua, *Ireland* 12 C5
Droitwich, *U.K.* 15 E5
Drôme □, *France* 21 D9
Drôme ~, *France* 21 D8

Dromedary, C., *Australia* 95 F5
Drömling △, *Germany* 24 C7
Dromore, *U.K.* 12 B4
Dromore West, *Ireland* 12 B3
Dronero, *Italy* 40 D4
Dronfield, *U.K.* 14 D6
Dronne ~, *France* 20 C3
Dronten, *Neths.* 17 B5
Dropt ~, *France* 20 D3
Drosendorf, *Austria* 26 C8
Droué, *France* 18 D8
Drumbo, *Canada* 116 C4
Drumheller, *Canada* 102 C6
Drummond, *U.S.A.* 108 C7
Drummond I., *U.S.A.* 114 C4
Drummond Pt., *Australia* 95 E2
Drummond Ra., *Australia* 94 C4
Drummondville, *Canada* 104 C5
Drumright, *U.S.A.* 113 H6
Druskininkai, *Lithuania* 9 J20
Drut ~, *Belarus* 33 F6
Druya, *Belarus* 32 E4
Druzhba, *Bulgaria* 45 C12
Druzhina, *Russia* 53 C15
Drvar, *Bos.-H.* 41 D13
Drvenik, *Croatia* 41 E13
Drwęca ~, *Poland* 31 E5
Dry Harbour Mts., *Jamaica* 120 a
Dry Tortugas, *U.S.A.* 120 B3
Dryanovo, *Bulgaria* 45 D9
Dryden, *Canada* 103 D10
Dryden, *U.S.A.* 117 D8
Drygalski I., *Antarctica* 5 C7
Drysdale ~, *Australia* 92 B4
Drysdale I., *Australia* 94 A2
Drysdale River △, *Australia* 92 B4
Drzewica, *Poland* 31 G7
Drzewiczka ~, *Poland* 31 G7
Dschang, *Cameroon* 83 D7
Du Bois, *U.S.A.* 116 E6
Du Gué ~, *Canada* 104 A5
Du He, *China* 59 A8
Du Quoin, *U.S.A.* 112 G10
Du'an, *China* 58 F7
Duanesburg, *U.S.A.* 117 D10
Duaringa, *Australia* 94 C4
Duarte, Pico, *Dom. Rep.* 121 D5
Dubā, *Si. Arabia* 70 E2
Dubai = Dubayy, *U.A.E.* 71 E7
Dubăsari, *Moldova* 29 C14
Dubăsari Vdkhr., *Moldova* 29 C13
Dubawnt ~, *Canada* 103 A8
Dubawnt L., *Canada* 103 A8
Dubayy, *U.A.E.* 71 E7
Dubbo, *Australia* 95 E4
Dubele, *Dem. Rep. of the Congo* 86 B2
Dübendorf, *Switz.* 25 H4
Dubica, *Croatia* 41 C13
Dublin, *Ireland* 12 C5
Dublin, *Ga., U.S.A.* 115 J4
Dublin, *Tex., U.S.A.* 113 J5
Dublin □, *Ireland* 12 C5
Dublin ✈ (DUB), *Ireland* 12 C5
Dubna, *Russia* 32 D9
Dubnica nad Váhom, *Slovak Rep.* 27 C11
Dubno, *Ukraine* 33 G3
Dubois, *U.S.A.* 108 D7
Dubossary = Dubăsari, *Moldova* 29 C14
Dubossary Vdkhr. = Dubăsari Vdkhr., *Moldova* 29 C13
Dubove, *Ukraine* 29 B8
Dubovka, *Russia* 35 F7
Dubovskoye, *Russia* 35 G6
Dubrajpur, *India* 69 H12
Dubréka, *Guinea* 82 D2
Dubrovitsa = Dubrovytsya, *Ukraine* 33 G4
Dubrovnik, *Croatia* 44 D2
Dubrovytsya, *Ukraine* 33 G4
Dubuque, *U.S.A.* 112 D9
Dubysa ~, *Lithuania* 30 C10
Duchang, *China* 59 C11
Duchesne, *U.S.A.* 108 F8
Duchess, *Australia* 94 C2
Ducie I., *Pac. Oc.* 97 K15
Duck ~, *U.S.A.* 115 G2
Duck Cr. ~, *Australia* 92 D2
Duck Lake, *Canada* 103 C7
Duck Mountain △, *Canada* 103 C8
Duckwall, Mt., *U.S.A.* 110 H6
Dudhi, *India* 67 G13
Dudinka, *Russia* 53 C9
Dudley, *U.K.* 15 E5
Dudwa, *India* 69 E9
Duékoué, *Ivory C.* 82 D3
Dueñas, *Spain* 36 D6
Duero = Douro ~, *Europe* 36 D2
Dufftown, *U.K.* 13 D5
Dufourspitz, *Switz.* 25 K3
Dūghī Kalā, *Afghan.* 66 C3
Dugi Otok, *Croatia* 41 D11
Dugo Selo, *Croatia* 41 C13
Duifken Pt., *Australia* 94 A3
Duisburg, *Germany* 24 D2
Duiwelskloof, *S. Africa* 89 C5
Dujiangyan, *China* 58 B4
Duk Fadiat, *Sudan* 81 F3
Duk Faiwil, *Sudan* 81 F3
Dukat, *Albania* 44 F3
Dūkdamīn, *Iran* 71 C8
Dukelský Průsmyk, *Slovak Rep.* 27 B14
Dukhān, *Qatar* 71 E6
Dukhovshchina, *Russia* 32 E7
Duki, *Pakistan* 66 D6
Dukla, *Poland* 31 J8
Duku, *Bauchi, Nigeria* 83 C7
Duku, *Sokoto, Nigeria* 83 C5
Dulag, *Phil.* 61 F6
Dulce, *U.S.A.* 109 H10

Dulce ~, *Argentina* 126 C3
Dulce, G., *Costa Rica* 120 E3
Dulf, *Iraq* 70 C5
Dŭlgopol, *Bulgaria* 45 C11
Dulit, Banjaran, *Malaysia* 62 D4
Duliu, *China* 56 E9
Dullewala, *Pakistan* 68 D4
Dullstroom, *S. Africa* 89 D5
Dülmen, *Germany* 24 D3
Dulovo, *Bulgaria* 45 C11
Duluth, *U.S.A.* 112 B8
Dum Dum, *India* 69 H13
Dum Duma, *India* 67 F19
Dūmā, *Syria* 74 B5
Dumaguete, *Phil.* 61 G5
Dumai, *Indonesia* 62 D2
Dumaran, *Phil.* 61 F3
Dumas, *Ark., U.S.A.* 113 J9
Dumas, *Tex., U.S.A.* 113 H4
Dumayr, *Syria* 74 B5
Dumbarton, *U.K.* 13 F4
Dumbier, *Slovak Rep.* 27 C12
Dumbleyung, *Australia* 93 F2
Dumboa, *Nigeria* 83 C7
Dumbrăveni, *Romania* 29 D9
Dumfries, *U.K.* 13 F5
Dumfries & Galloway □, *U.K.* 13 F5
Dumitrești, *Romania* 29 E11
Dumka, *India* 69 G12
Dumlupınar, *Turkey* 47 C12
Dümmer, *Germany* 24 C4
Dümmer ○, *Germany* 24 C4
Dumoine ~, *Canada* 104 C4
Dumoine, L., *Canada* 104 C4
Dumraon, *India* 69 G11
Dumyât, *Egypt* 80 H7
Dumyât, Masabb, *Egypt* 80 H7
Dún Dealgan = Dundalk, *Ireland* 12 B5
Dún Laoghaire, *Ireland* 12 C5
Dun-le-Palestel, *France* 19 F8
Dun-sur-Auron, *France* 19 F9
Dun-sur-Meuse, *France* 19 C12
Duna = Dunărea ~, *Europe* 29 E14
Duna ~, *Hungary* 28 E3
Duna-Drava △, *Hungary* 28 D3
Duna-völgyi-föcsatorna, *Hungary* 28 D3
Dunaföldvár, *Hungary* 28 D3
Dunagiri, *India* 69 D8
Dunaj = Dunărea ~, *Europe* 29 E14
Dunaj ~, *Slovak Rep.* 27 D11
Dunajec ~, *Poland* 31 H7
Dunajská Streda, *Slovak Rep.* 27 C10
Dunakeszi, *Hungary* 28 C4
Dunapataj, *Hungary* 28 D4
Dunărea ~, *Europe* 29 E14
Dunaszekcső, *Hungary* 28 D3
Dunaújváros, *Hungary* 28 D3
Dunav = Dunărea ~, *Europe* 29 E14
Dunavăţu de Jos, *Romania* 29 F14
Dunavtsi, *Bulgaria* 44 C6
Dunay, *Russia* 54 C6
Dunayivtsi, *Ukraine* 29 B11
Dunback, *N.Z.* 91 L3
Dunblane, *U.K.* 13 E5
Duncan, *Canada* 102 D4
Duncan, *Ariz., U.S.A.* 109 K9
Duncan, *Okla., U.S.A.* 113 H6
Duncan, L., *Canada* 104 B4
Duncan, L., *Canada* 102 A6
Duncan Town, *Bahamas* 120 B4
Duncansby Head, *U.K.* 13 C5
Duncansville, *U.S.A.* 116 F6
Dundalk, *Canada* 116 B4
Dundalk, *Ireland* 12 B5
Dundalk, *U.S.A.* 114 F7
Dundalk Bay, *Ireland* 12 C5
Dundaga, *Latvia* 30 A9
Dundas = Uummannaq, *Greenland* 4 B4
Dundas = Uummannaq, *Greenland* 4 B5
Dundas, *Canada* 116 C5
Dundas, L., *Australia* 93 F3
Dundas I., *Canada* 102 C2
Dundas Str., *Australia* 92 B5
Dundee, *S. Africa* 89 D5
Dundee, *U.K.* 13 E6
Dundee, *U.S.A.* 116 D8
Dundee City □, *U.K.* 13 E6
Dundgovĭ □, *Mongolia* 56 B4
Dundrum, *U.K.* 12 B6
Dundrum B., *U.K.* 12 B6
Dunedin, *N.Z.* 91 L3
Dunedin, *U.S.A.* 115 L4
Dunfermline, *U.K.* 13 E5
Dungannon, *Canada* 116 C3
Dungannon, *U.K.* 12 B5
Dungarpur, *India* 68 H5
Dungarvan, *Ireland* 12 D4
Dungarvan Harbour, *Ireland* 12 D4
Dungeness, *U.K.* 15 G8
Dungo, L. do, *Angola* 88 B2
Dungog, *Australia* 95 E5
Dungu, *Dem. Rep. of the Congo* 86 B2
Dungun, *Malaysia* 65 K4
Dungunâb, *Sudan* 80 C4
Dungunâb, Khalîg, *Sudan* 80 C4
Dunhua, *China* 57 C15
Dunhuang, *China* 60 B4
Dunk I., *Australia* 94 B4
Dunkassa, *Benin* 83 C5
Dunkeld, *Australia* 95 K4
Dunkeld, *U.K.* 13 E5
Dunkerque, *France* 19 A9
Dunkery Beacon, *U.K.* 15 F4
Dunkirk = Dunkerque, *France* 19 A9
Dunkirk, *U.S.A.* 116 D5
Dunkuj, *Sudan* 81 E3

Dunkwa, *Central, Ghana* 82 D4
Dunkwa, *Central, Ghana* 83 D4
Dúnleary = Dún Laoghaire, *Ireland* 12 C5
Dunleer, *Ireland* 12 C5
Dunmanus B., *Ireland* 12 E2
Dunmanway, *Ireland* 12 E2
Dunmara, *Australia* 94 B1
Dunmore, *U.S.A.* 117 E9
Dunmore Hd., *Ireland* 12 D1
Dunmore Town, *Bahamas* 120 A4
Dunn, *U.S.A.* 115 H6
Dunnellon, *U.S.A.* 115 L4
Dunnet Hd., *U.K.* 13 C5
Dunning, *U.S.A.* 112 E4
Dunnville, *Canada* 116 D5
Dunolly, *Australia* 95 F3
Dunoon, *U.K.* 13 F4
Dunphy, *U.S.A.* 108 F5
Dunqul, *Egypt* 80 C3
Duns, *U.K.* 13 F6
Dunseith, *U.S.A.* 112 A4
Dunsmuir, *U.S.A.* 108 F2
Dunstable, *U.K.* 15 F7
Dunstan Mts., *N.Z.* 91 L2
Dunster, *Canada* 102 C5
Dunvegan, *U.K.* 13 D2
Dunvegan L., *Canada* 103 A7
Duolun, *China* 56 C9
Duong Dong, *Vietnam* 65 G4
Dupree, *U.S.A.* 112 C4
Dupuyer, *U.S.A.* 108 B7
Duque de Caxias, *Brazil* 127 A7
Durack ~, *Australia* 92 C4
Durack Ra., *Australia* 92 C4
Durağan, *Turkey* 72 B6
Durak, *Turkey* 47 B10
Durance ~, *France* 21 E8
Durand, *U.S.A.* 112 C9
Durango, *Mexico* 118 C4
Durango, *U.S.A.* 109 H10
Durango □, *Mexico* 118 C4
Durankulak, *Bulgaria* 45 C12
Durant, *Miss., U.S.A.* 113 J10
Durant, *Okla., U.S.A.* 113 J6
Duratón ~, *Spain* 36 D6
Durazno, *Uruguay* 126 C4
Durazzo = Durrës, *Albania* 44 E3
Durban, *France* 20 F6
Durban, *S. Africa* 89 D5
Durbuy, *Belgium* 17 D5
Dúrcal, *Spain* 37 J7
Ðurđevac, *Croatia* 28 D2
Düren, *Germany* 24 E2
Durg, *India* 67 J12
Durgapur, *India* 69 H12
Durham, *Canada* 116 B4
Durham, *U.K.* 14 C6
Durham, *Calif., U.S.A.* 110 F5
Durham, *N.C., U.S.A.* 115 H6
Durham, *N.H., U.S.A.* 117 C14
Durham □, *U.K.* 14 C6
Durlești, *Moldova* 29 C13
Durmā, *Si. Arabia* 70 E5
Durmitor, *Serbia & M.* 44 C3
Durmitor △, *Serbia & M.* 44 C3
Durness, *U.K.* 13 C4
Durrës, *Albania* 44 E3
Durrow, *Ireland* 12 D4
Dursey I., *Ireland* 12 E1
Dursley, *U.K.* 15 F5
Dursunbey, *Turkey* 47 B10
Durtal, *France* 18 E6
Duru, *Dem. Rep. of the Congo* 86 B2
Duru Gölü, *Turkey* 45 E12
Durusu, *Turkey* 45 E12
Durūz, Jabal ad, *Jordan* 74 C5
D'Urville, Tanjung, *Indonesia* 63 E9
D'Urville I., *N.Z.* 91 J4
Duryea, *U.S.A.* 117 E9
Dūsh, *Egypt* 80 C3
Dushak, *Turkmenistan* 52 F7
Dushan, *China* 58 E6
Dushanbe, *Tajikistan* 52 F7
Dushore, *U.S.A.* 117 E8
Dusky Sd., *N.Z.* 91 L1
Dussejour, C., *Australia* 92 B4
Düsseldorf, *Germany* 24 D2
Düsseldorf Rhein-Ruhr ✈ (DUS), *Germany* 24 D2
Duszniki-Zdrój, *Poland* 31 H3
Dutch Harbor, *U.S.A.* 100 C3
Dutlwe, *Botswana* 88 C3
Dutsan Wai, *Nigeria* 83 C6
Dutton, *Canada* 116 D3
Dutton ~, *Australia* 94 C3
Duved, *Sweden* 10 A6
Düvertepe, *Turkey* 47 B10
Duwayhin, Khawr, *U.A.E.* 71 E6
Duyun, *China* 58 D6
Düzağac, *Turkey* 47 C12
Düzce, *Turkey* 72 B4
Dve Mogili, *Bulgaria* 45 C9
Dvina, Severnaya ~, *Russia* 52 C5
Dvinsk = Daugavpils, *Latvia* 9 J22
Dvor, *Croatia* 41 C13
Dvůr Králové nad Labem, *Czech Rep.* 26 A8
Dwarka, *India* 68 H3
Dwellingup, *Australia* 93 F2
Dwight, *Canada* 116 A5
Dwight, *U.S.A.* 114 E1
Dyakove, *Ukraine* 28 B7
Dyatkovo, *Russia* 33 F8
Dyatlovo = Dzyatlava, *Belarus* 32 F3
Dyce, *U.K.* 13 D6
Dyer, C., *Canada* 101 B13
Dyer Bay, *Canada* 116 A3
Dyer Plateau, *Antarctica* 5 D17
Dyersburg, *U.S.A.* 113 G10

Dyfi ~, *U.K.* 15 E3
Dyje ~, *Czech Rep.* 27 C9
Dymer, *Ukraine* 33 G6
Dynów, *Poland* 31 J9
Dysart, *Australia* 94 C4
Dyviziya 29 E14
Dzerzhinsk, *Russia* 34 B6
Dzhalinda, *Russia* 53 D13
Dzhambul = Taraz, *Kazakhstan* 52 E8
Dzhankoy, *Ukraine* 33 K8
Dzhanybek, *Kazakhstan* 34 F8
Dzharylhach, Ostriv, *Ukraine* 33 J7
Dzhezkazgan = Zhezqazghan, *Kazakhstan* 52 E7
Dzhizak = Jizzakh, *Uzbekistan* 52 E7
Dzhugdzur, Khrebet, *Russia* 53 D14
Dzhulynk, *Ukraine* 29 B14
Dzhuryn, *Ukraine* 29 B13
Dzhvari = Jvari, *Georgia* 35 J6
Dzialdowo, *Poland* 31 E7
Dzialoszyce, *Poland* 31 H7
Dzialoszyn, *Poland* 31 G5
Dzibilcháltún, *Mexico* 119 C7
Dzibilchaltun, *Yucatán, Mexico* 119 C7
Dzierzgoń, *Poland* 30 E6
Dzierzoniów, *Poland* 31 H3
Dzilam de Bravo, *Mexico* 119 C7
Dzisna, *Belarus* 32 E5
Dzisna ~, *Belarus* 32 E5
Dziwnów, *Poland* 30 D1
Dzungaria = Junggar Pendi, *China* 60 B3
Dzungarian Basin = Junggar Pendi, *China* 60 B3
Dzuumod, *Mongolia* 60 B5
Dzyarzhynsk, *Belarus* 32 F4
Dzyatlava, *Belarus* 32 F3

E

E.C. Manning △, *Canada* 102 D4
Eabamet L., *Canada* 104 B2
Eads, *U.S.A.* 112 F3
Eagar, *U.S.A.* 109 J9
Eagle, *Alaska, U.S.A.* 100 B5
Eagle, *Colo., U.S.A.* 108 G10
Eagle ~, *Canada* 105 B8
Eagle Butte, *U.S.A.* 112 C4
Eagle Grove, *U.S.A.* 112 D8
Eagle L., *Canada* 103 D10
Eagle L., *Calif., U.S.A.* 108 F3
Eagle L., *Maine, U.S.A.* 115 B11
Eagle Lake, *Canada* 116 A6
Eagle Lake, *Maine, U.S.A.* 115 B11
Eagle Lake, *Tex., U.S.A.* 113 L6
Eagle Mountain, *U.S.A.* 111 M11
Eagle Nest, *U.S.A.* 109 H11
Eagle Pass, *U.S.A.* 113 L4
Eagle Pk., *U.S.A.* 110 G7
Eagle Pt., *Australia* 92 C3
Eagle River, *Mich., U.S.A.* 114 B1
Eagle River, *Wis., U.S.A.* 112 C10
Eaglehawk, *Australia* 95 F3
Eagles Mere, *U.S.A.* 117 E8
Ealing □, *U.K.* 15 F7
Ear Falls, *Canada* 103 C10
Earle, *U.S.A.* 113 H9
Earlimart, *U.S.A.* 111 K7
Earn ~, *U.K.* 13 E5
Earn, L., *U.K.* 13 E4
Earnslaw, Mt., *N.Z.* 91 L2
Earth, *U.S.A.* 113 H3
Easley, *U.S.A.* 115 H4
East Anglia, *U.K.* 14 E9
East Angus, *Canada* 105 C5
East Antarctica, *Antarctica* 5 D7
East Aurora, *U.S.A.* 116 D6
East Ayrshire □, *U.K.* 13 F4
East Bengal, *Bangla.* 67 H17
East Beskids = Vychodné Beskydy, *Europe* 27 B15
East Brady, *U.S.A.* 116 F5
East C., *N.Z.* 91 G7
East Chicago, *U.S.A.* 114 E2
East China Sea, *Asia* 60 C7
East Coulee, *Canada* 102 C6
East Dereham = Dereham, *U.K.* 15 E8
East Dunbartonshire □, *U.K.* 13 F4
East Falkland, *Falk. Is.* 128 G5
East Grand Forks, *U.S.A.* 112 B6
East Greenwich, *U.S.A.* 117 E13
East Grinstead, *U.K.* 15 F8
East Hartford, *U.S.A.* 117 E12
East Helena, *U.S.A.* 108 C8
East Indies, *Asia* 50 K15
East Kilbride, *U.K.* 13 F4
East Lansing, *U.S.A.* 114 D3
East Liverpool, *U.S.A.* 116 F4
East London, *S. Africa* 89 E4
East Lothian □, *U.K.* 13 F6
East Main = Eastmain, *Canada* 104 B4
East Northport, *U.S.A.* 117 F11
East Orange, *U.S.A.* 117 F10
East Pacific Ridge, *Pac. Oc.* 97 J17
East Palestine, *U.S.A.* 116 F4
East Pine, *Canada* 102 B4
East Point, *U.S.A.* 115 J3
East Providence, *U.S.A.* 117 E13
East Pt., *Br. Virgin Is.* 121 e
East Pt., *Canada* 105 C7
East Renfrewshire □, *U.K.* 13 F4
East Retford = Retford, *U.K.* 14 D7
East Riding of Yorkshire □, *U.K.* 14 D7
East Rochester, *U.S.A.* 116 C7
East St. Louis, *U.S.A.* 112 F9
East Schelde = Oosterschelde ~, *Neths.* 17 C4
East Sea = Japan, Sea of, *Asia* 54 E7
East Siberian Sea, *Russia* 53 B17

East Stroudsburg, *U.S.A.* 117 E9
East Sussex □, *U.K.* 15 G8
East Tawas, *U.S.A.* 114 C4
East Timor ■, *Asia* 63 F7
East Toorale, *Australia* 95 E4
East Walker ➤, *U.S.A.* 110 G7
East Windsor, *U.S.A.* 117 F10
Eastbourne, *N.Z.* 91 J5
Eastbourne, *U.K.* 15 G8
Eastend, *Canada* 103 D7
Easter I. = Pascua, I. de, *Chile* .. 97 K17
Eastern □, *Ghana* 83 D4
Eastern □, *Kenya* 86 C4
Eastern □, *S. Leone* 82 D2
Eastern Cape □, *S. Africa* 88 E4
Eastern Cr. ➤, *Australia* 94 C3
Eastern Ghats, *India* 66 N11
Eastern Group = Lau Group, *Fiji* . 91 C9
Eastern Group, *Australia* 93 F3
Eastern Transvaal =
  Mpumalanga □, *S. Africa* 89 D5
Easterville, *Canada* 103 C9
Easthampton, *U.S.A.* 117 D12
Eastlake, *U.S.A.* 116 E3
Eastland, *U.S.A.* 113 J5
Eastleigh, *U.K.* 15 G6
Eastmain, *Canada* 104 B4
Eastmain ➤, *Canada* 104 B4
Eastman, *Canada* 117 A12
Eastman, *U.S.A.* 115 J4
Easton, *Md., U.S.A.* 114 F7
Easton, *Pa., U.S.A.* 117 F9
Easton, *Wash., U.S.A.* 110 C5
Eastpointe, *U.S.A.* 116 D2
Eastport, *U.S.A.* 115 C12
Eastsound, *U.S.A.* 110 B4
Eaton, *U.S.A.* 112 E2
Eatonia, *Canada* 103 C7
Eatonton, *U.S.A.* 115 J4
Eatontown, *U.S.A.* 117 F10
Eatonville, *U.S.A.* 110 C4
Eau Claire, *U.S.A.* 112 C9
Eau Claire, L. à l', *Canada* ... 104 A5
Eauze, *France* 20 E4
Eban, *Nigeria* 83 D5
Ebbegebirge △, *Germany* 24 D3
Ebbw Vale, *U.K.* 15 F4
Ebeltoft, *Denmark* 11 H4
Ebeltoft Vig, *Denmark* 11 H4
Ebensburg, *U.S.A.* 116 F6
Ebensee, *Austria* 26 D6
Eber Gölü, *Turkey* 72 C4
Eberbach, *Germany* 25 F4
Eberswalde-Finow, *Germany* 24 C9
Ebetsu, *Japan* 54 C10
Ebey's Landing △, *U.S.A.* 110 B4
Ebian, *China* 58 C4
Ebingen, *Germany* 25 G5
Éboli, *Italy* 43 B8
Ebolowa, *Cameroon* 83 E7
Ebonyi □, *Nigeria* 83 D6
Ebrach, *Germany* 25 F6
Ébrié, Lagune, *Ivory C.* 82 D4
Ebro ➤, *Spain* 38 E5
Ebro, Embalse del, *Spain* 36 C7
Ebstorf, *Germany* 24 B6
Eceabat, *Turkey* 45 F10
Ech Chéliff, *Algeria* 78 A6
Echigo-Sammyaku, *Japan* 55 F9
Échirolles, *France* 21 C9
Echizen-Misaki, *Japan* 55 G7
Echmiadzin = Yejmiadzin,
  Armenia 35 K7
Echo Bay, *N.W.T., Canada* 100 B8
Echo Bay, *Ont., Canada* 104 C3
Echoing ➤, *Canada* 104 B1
Echterdingen, Stuttgart ✈ (STR),
  Germany 25 G5
Echternach, *Lux.* 17 E6
Echuca, *Australia* 95 F3
Ecija, *Spain* 37 H5
Eckental, *Germany* 25 F7
Eckernförde, *Germany* 24 A5
Eclipse I., *Australia* 93 G2
Eclipse Is., *Australia* 92 B4
Eclipse Sd., *Canada* 101 A11
Écommoy, *France* 18 E7
Écouché, *France* 18 D6
Ecrins ➤, *France* 21 D10
Ecuador ■, *S. Amer.* 124 D3
Écueillé, *France* 18 E8
Ed, *Sweden* 11 F5
Ed Dabbura, *Sudan* 80 D3
Ed Da'ein, *Sudan* 81 E2
Ed Damazin, *Sudan* 79 F12
Ed Dâmer, *Sudan* 80 D3
Ed Dar el Beida = Casablanca,
  Morocco 78 B4
Ed Debba, *Sudan* 80 D3
Ed-Déffa, *Egypt* 80 A2
Ed Deim, *Sudan* 81 E2
Ed Dueim, *Sudan* 81 E3
Edam, *Canada* 103 C7
Edam, *Neths.* 17 B5
Edane, *Sweden* 10 E6
Eday, *U.K.* 13 B6
Edd, *Eritrea* 81 E5
Eddrachillis B., *U.K.* 13 C3
Eddystone, *U.K.* 15 G3
Eddystone Pt., *Australia* 95 G4
Ede, *Neths.* 17 B5
Ede, *Nigeria* 83 D5
Édéa, *Cameroon* 83 E7
Edebäck, *Sweden* 10 E7
Edehon L., *Canada* 103 A9
Edelény, *Hungary* 28 B5
Eden, *Australia* 95 F4
Eden, *N.C., U.S.A.* 115 G6
Eden, *N.Y., U.S.A.* 116 D6
Eden, *Tex., U.S.A.* 113 K5
Eden ➤, *U.K.* 14 C4
Edenburg, *S. Africa* 88 D4

Edendale, *S. Africa* 89 D5
Edenderry, *Ireland* 12 C4
Edenton, *U.S.A.* 115 G7
Edenville, *S. Africa* 89 D4
Eder ➤, *Germany* 24 D5
Eder-Stausee, *Germany* 24 D4
Edewecht, *Germany* 24 B3
Edgar, *U.S.A.* 112 E6
Edgartown, *U.S.A.* 117 E14
Edge Hill, *U.K.* 15 E6
Edgefield, *U.S.A.* 115 J5
Edgeley, *U.S.A.* 112 B5
Edgemont, *U.S.A.* 112 D3
Edgeøya, *Svalbard* 4 B9
Edievale, *N.Z.* 91 L2
Edina, *Liberia* 82 D2
Edina, *U.S.A.* 112 E8
Edinboro, *U.S.A.* 116 E4
Edinburg, *U.S.A.* 113 M5
Edinburgh, *U.K.* 13 F5
Edinburgh ✈ (EDI), *U.K.* 13 F5
Edinburgh, City of □, *U.K.* 13 F5
Edineț, *Moldova* 29 B12
Edirne, *Turkey* 45 E10
Edirne □, *Turkey* 45 E10
Edison, *U.S.A.* 110 B4
Edithburgh, *Australia* 95 F2
Edmeston, *U.S.A.* 117 D9
Edmond, *U.S.A.* 113 H6
Edmonds, *U.S.A.* 110 C4
Edmonton, *Australia* 94 B4
Edmonton, *Canada* 102 C6
Edmund L., *Canada* 104 B1
Edmundston, *Canada* 105 C6
Edna, *U.S.A.* 113 L6
Edo □, *Nigeria* 83 D6
Edolo, *Italy* 40 B7
Edremit, *Turkey* 47 B9
Edremit Körfezi, *Turkey* 47 B8
Edsbro, *Sweden* 10 E12
Edsbyn, *Sweden* 10 C9
Edson, *Canada* 102 C5
Eduardo Castex, *Argentina* 126 D3
Edward ➤, *Australia* 95 F3
Edward, L., *Africa* 86 C2
Edward River, *Australia* 94 A3
Edward VII Land, *Antarctica* ... 5 E13
Edwards, *Calif., U.S.A.* 111 L9
Edwards, *N.Y., U.S.A.* 117 B9
Edwards Air Force Base, *U.S.A.* . 111 L9
Edwards Plateau, *U.S.A.* 113 K4
Edwardsville, *U.S.A.* 117 E9
Edxná, *Mexico* 119 D6
Edzo, *Canada* 102 A5
Eeklo, *Belgium* 17 C3
Eferding, *Austria* 26 C7
Effigy Mounds △, *U.S.A.* 112 D9
Effingham, *U.S.A.* 114 F1
Eforie, *Romania* 29 F13
Ega ➤, *Spain* 38 C3
Egadi, Ísole, *Italy* 42 E5
Egan Range, *U.S.A.* 108 G6
Eganville, *Canada* 116 A7
Eger = Cheb, *Czech Rep.* 26 A5
Eger, *Hungary* 28 C5
Eger ➤, *Hungary* 28 C5
Egersund, *Norway* 9 G12
Egg L., *Canada* 103 B7
Eggegebirge Südlicher
  Teutoburger Wald △, *Germany* . 24 D4
Eggenburg, *Austria* 26 C8
Eggenfelden, *Germany* 25 G8
Éghezée, *Belgium* 17 D4
Égletons, *France* 20 C6
Egmont, *Canada* 102 D4
Egmont △, *N.Z.* 91 H5
Egmont, C., *N.Z.* 91 H4
Egmont, Mt. = Taranaki, Mt.,
  N.Z. 91 H5
Egra, *India* 69 J12
Eğridir, *Turkey* 72 D4
Eğridir Gölü, *Turkey* 70 B1
Egtved, *Denmark* 11 J3
Egume, *Nigeria* 83 D6
Éguzon-Chantôme, *France* 19 F8
Egvekinot, *Russia* 53 C19
Egyek, *Hungary* 28 C5
Egypt ■, *Africa* 80 B3
Eha Amufu, *Nigeria* 83 D6
Ehime □, *Japan* 55 H6
Ehingen, *Germany* 25 G5
Ehrenberg, *U.S.A.* 111 M12
Ehrwald, *Austria* 26 D3
Eibar, *Spain* 38 B2
Eichstätt, *Germany* 25 G7
Eider ➤, *Germany* 24 A4
Eidsvold, *Australia* 95 D5
Eidsvoll, *Norway* 9 F14
Eifel, *Germany* 25 E2
Eiffel Flats, *Zimbabwe* 87 F3
Eiger, *Switz.* 40 B5
Eigg, *U.K.* 13 E2
Eighty Mile Beach, *Australia* .. 92 C3
Eil, *Somali Rep.* 75 F4
Eil, L., *U.K.* 13 E3
Eildon, *Australia* 95 F4
Eildon, L., *Australia* 95 F4
Eilenburg, *Germany* 24 D8
Ein el Luweiqa, *Sudan* 81 E3
Einasleigh, *Australia* 94 B3
Einasleigh ➤, *Australia* 94 B3
Einbeck, *Germany* 24 D5
Eindhoven, *Neths.* 17 C5
Einsiedeln, *Switz.* 25 H4
Eire = Ireland ■, *Europe* 12 C4
Eiríksjökull, *Iceland* 8 D3
Eirunepé, *Brazil* 124 E5
Eiseb ➤, *Namibia* 88 C2
Eisenach, *Germany* 24 E6
Eisenberg, *Germany* 24 E7
Eisenerz, *Austria* 26 D7
Eisenhüttenstadt, *Germany* 24 C10

Eisenkappel, *Austria* 26 E7
Eisenstadt, *Austria* 27 D9
Eisfeld, *Germany* 25 E6
Eisleben, *Germany* 24 D7
Eislingen, *Germany* 25 G5
Eivissa, *Spain* 48 C7
Eixe, Serra do, *Spain* 36 C4
Ejea de los Caballeros, *Spain* . 38 C3
Ejeda, *Madag.* 89 C7
Ejura, *Ghana* 83 D4
Ejutla, *Mexico* 119 D5
Ekalaka, *U.S.A.* 112 C2
Ekenäs = Tammisaari, *Finland* .. 9 F20
Ekenässjön, *Sweden* 11 G9
Ekerö, *Sweden* 10 E11
Eket, *Nigeria* 83 E6
Eketahuna, *N.Z.* 91 J5
Ekhínos, *Greece* 45 E9
Ekibastuz, *Kazakhstan* 52 D8
Ekiti □, *Nigeria* 83 D6
Ekoli, *Dem. Rep. of the Congo* . 86 C1
Ekoln, *Sweden* 10 E11
Ekshärad, *Sweden* 10 D7
Eksjö, *Sweden* 11 G8
Ekuma ➤, *Namibia* 88 B2
Ekwan ➤, *Canada* 104 B3
Ekwan Pt., *Canada* 104 B3
El Aaiún, *W. Sahara* 78 C3
El Abanico, *Chile* 126 D1
El Abbasiya, *Sudan* 81 E3
El 'Agrûd, *Egypt* 74 E3
El Ait, *Sudan* 81 E2
El 'Aiyat, *Egypt* 80 J7
El Alamein, *Egypt* 80 A2
El 'Aqaba, W. ➤, *Egypt* 74 E2
El 'Arag, *Egypt* 80 B2
El Arahal, *Spain* 37 H5
El Arīḥā, *West Bank* 74 D4
El 'Arîsh, *Egypt* 74 D2
El 'Arîsh, W. ➤, *Egypt* 74 D2
El Asnam = Ech Chéliff, *Algeria* . 78 A6
El Astillero, *Spain* 36 B7
El Badâri, *Egypt* 80 B3
El Bahrein, *Egypt* 80 B2
El Ballâs, *Egypt* 80 B3
El Balyana, *Egypt* 80 B3
El Baqeir, *Sudan* 80 D3
El Barco de Ávila, *Spain* 36 E5
El Barco de Valdeorras = O
  Barco, *Spain* 36 C4
El Bauga, *Sudan* 80 D3
El Bawiti, *Egypt* 80 B2
El Bayadh, *Algeria* 78 B6
El Bierzo, *Spain* 36 C4
El Bluff, *Nic.* 120 D3
El Bonillo, *Spain* 39 G2
El Brûk, W. ➤, *Egypt* 74 E2
El Buheirat □, *Sudan* 81 F3
El Burgo de Osma, *Spain* 38 D1
El Cajon, *U.S.A.* 111 N10
El Campo, *U.S.A.* 113 L6
El Centro, *U.S.A.* 111 N11
El Cerro, *Bolivia* 124 G6
El Cerro de Andévalo, *Spain* ... 37 H4
El Compadre, *Mexico* 111 N10
El Coronil, *Spain* 37 H5
El Cuy, *Argentina* 128 D3
El Cuyo, *Mexico* 119 C7
El Dab'a, *Egypt* 80 H6
El Daheir, *Egypt* 74 D3
El Dátil, *Mexico* 118 B2
El Deir, *Egypt* 80 B3
El Dere, *Somali Rep.* 75 G4
El Descanso, *Mexico* 111 N10
El Desemboque, *Mexico* 118 A2
El Dilingat, *Egypt* 80 H7
El Diviso, *Colombia* 124 C3
El Djouf, *Mauritania* 78 D4
El Dorado, *Ark., U.S.A.* 113 J8
El Dorado, *Kans., U.S.A.* 113 G6
El Dorado, *Venezuela* 124 B6
El 'Ein, *Sudan* 81 D2
El Ejido, *Spain* 37 J8
El Escorial, *Spain* 36 E6
El Espinar, *Spain* 36 D6
El Faiyûm, *Egypt* 80 J7
El Fâsher, *Sudan* 81 E2
El Fashn, *Egypt* 80 J7
El Ferrol = Ferrol, *Spain* 36 B2
El Fifi, *Sudan* 81 E2
El Fuerte, *Mexico* 118 B3
El Ga'a, *Sudan* 81 E2
El Gal, *Somali Rep.* 75 E5
El Garef, *Sudan* 81 E3
El Gebir, *Sudan* 81 E2
El Gedida, *Egypt* 80 B2
El Geneina = Al Junaynah, *Sudan* . 79 F10
El Geteina, *Sudan* 81 E3
El Gezira □, *Sudan* 81 E3
El Gir, *Sudan* 80 D2
El Gîza, *Egypt* 80 J7
El Gogorron △, *Mexico* 118 C4
El Goléa, *Algeria* 78 B6
El Grau, *Spain* 39 G4
El Guácharo △, *Venezuela* 121 D7
El Guache △, *Venezuela* 121 E6
El Hagiz, *Sudan* 81 D4
El Hâi, *Egypt* 80 J7
El Hammam, *Egypt* 80 A2
El Hawata, *Sudan* 81 E3
El Heiz, *Egypt* 80 B2
El Hideib, *Sudan* 81 E2
El Hilla, *Sudan* 81 E2
El 'Idisât, *Egypt* 80 B3
El Iskandarîya, *Egypt* 80 H7
El Istiwa'iya, *Sudan* 79 G11
El Jadida, *Morocco* 78 B4
El Jardal, *Honduras* 120 D2
El Jebelein, *Sudan* 81 E3
El Kab, *Sudan* 80 D3
El Kabrît, G., *Egypt* 74 F2
El Kafr el Sharqi, *Egypt* 80 H7

El Kamlin, *Sudan* 81 D3
El Karaba, *Sudan* 80 D3
El Kere, *Ethiopia* 81 F5
El Khandaq, *Sudan* 80 D3
El Khârga, *Egypt* 80 B3
El Khartûm, *Sudan* 81 D3
El Khartûm □, *Sudan* 81 D3
El Khartûm Bahrî, *Sudan* 81 D3
El Kuntilla, *Egypt* 74 E3
El Laqâwa, *Sudan* 81 E2
El Leh, *Ethiopia* 81 G4
El Leiya, *Sudan* 81 D4
El Maestrazgo, *Spain* 38 E4
El Mafâza, *Sudan* 81 E3
El Maghra, *Egypt* 80 A2
El Mahalla el Kubra, *Egypt* 80 H7
El Mahârîq, *Egypt* 80 B3
El Maîmûn, *Egypt* 80 J7
El Maks el Bahari, *Egypt* 80 C3
El Masid, *Sudan* 81 D3
El Masnou, *Spain* 38 D7
El Matariya, *Egypt* 80 H8
El Meda, *Ethiopia* 81 F5
El Medano, *Canary Is.* 48 F3
El Metemma, *Sudan* 81 D3
El Milagro, *Argentina* 126 C2
El Minyâ, *Egypt* 80 B3
El Monte, *U.S.A.* 111 L8
El Montseny, *Spain* 38 D7
El Mreyye, *Mauritania* 82 B3
El Niybo, *Ethiopia* 81 G4
El Obeid, *Sudan* 81 E3
El Odaiya, *Sudan* 81 E2
El Oro, *Mexico* 119 D4
El Oued, *Algeria* 78 B7
El Palmar △, *Argentina* 126 C4
El Palmito, Presa, *Mexico* 118 B3
El Paso, *U.S.A.* 109 L10
El Paso Robles, *U.S.A.* 110 K6
El Pedernoso, *Spain* 39 F2
El Pedroso, *Spain* 37 H5
El Pinacate y Gran Desierto de
  Altar = Gran Desierto del
  Pinacate △, *Mexico* 118 A2
El Pobo de Dueñas, *Spain* 38 E3
El Portal, *U.S.A.* 110 H7
El Porvenir, *Mexico* 118 A3
El Prat de Llobregat, *Spain* ... 38 D7
El Progreso, *Honduras* 120 C2
El Pueblito, *Mexico* 118 B3
El Pueblo, *Canary Is.* 48 F2
El Puente del Arzobispo, *Spain* . 36 F5
El Puerto de Santa María, *Spain* . 37 J4
El Qâhira, *Egypt* 80 H7
El Qantara, *Egypt* 74 E1
El Qasr, *Egypt* 80 B2
El Qubbât, *Egypt* 80 J7
El Queseima, *Egypt* 74 E3
El Qusîya, *Egypt* 80 B3
El Râshda, *Egypt* 80 B2
El Real, *Panama* 124 B3
El Reno, *U.S.A.* 113 H6
El Rey △, *Argentina* 126 A3
El Ridisiya, *Egypt* 80 C3
El Rio, *U.S.A.* 111 L7
El Ronquillo, *Spain* 37 H4
El Roque, Pta., *Canary Is.* 48 F4
El Rosarito, *Mexico* 118 B2
El Rubio, *Spain* 37 H5
El Saff, *Egypt* 80 J7
El Saheira, W. ➤, *Egypt* 74 E2
El Salto, *Mexico* 118 C3
El Salvador ■, *Cent. Amer.* 120 D2
El Sauce, *Nic.* 120 D2
El Saucejo, *Spain* 37 H5
El Shallal, *Egypt* 80 C3
El Simbillawein, *Egypt* 80 H7
El Sueco, *Mexico* 118 B3
El Suweis, *Egypt* 80 J8
El Tabbîn, *Egypt* 80 J7
El Tamarâni, W. ➤, *Egypt* 74 E3
El Thamad, *Egypt* 74 F3
El Tigre, *Venezuela* 124 B6
El Tîh, Gebal, *Egypt* 74 F2
El Tîna, *Egypt* 80 H8
El Tîna, Khalîg, *Egypt* 74 D1
El Tofo, *Chile* 126 B1
El Tránsito, *Chile* 126 B1
El Tûr, *Egypt* 70 D2
El Turbio, *Argentina* 128 G2
El Uqsur, *Egypt* 80 B3
El Valle △, *Spain* 39 H3
El Venado, *Mexico* 118 C4
El Vendrell, *Spain* 38 D6
El Vergel, *Mexico* 118 B3
El Vigía, *Venezuela* 124 B4
El Viso del Alcor, *Spain* 37 H5
El Wabeira, *Egypt* 74 F2
El Wak, *Kenya* 86 B5
El Waqf, *Egypt* 80 B3
El Weguet, *Ethiopia* 81 F5
El Wuz, *Sudan* 81 D3
Elafónisos, *Greece* 46 E4
Élancourt, *France* 19 D8
Élassa, *Greece* 47 F8
Elassón, *Greece* 46 B4
Elat, *Israel* 74 F3
Eláthia, *Greece* 46 C4
Elâzığ, *Turkey* 70 B3
Elba, *Italy* 40 F7
Elba, *U.S.A.* 115 K2
Elbasan, *Albania* 44 E4
Elbe, *U.S.A.* 110 D4
Elbe ➤, *Europe* 24 B4
Elbe-Seitenkanal, *Germany* 24 B6
Elbert, Mt., *U.S.A.* 109 G10
Elberton, *U.S.A.* 115 H4

Elbeuf, *France* 18 C8
Elbidtan, *Turkey* 70 B3
Elbing = Elbląg, *Poland* 30 D6
Elbistan, *Turkey* 72 C7
Elbląg, *Poland* 30 D6
Elbow, *Canada* 103 C7
Elbrus, *Asia* 35 J6
Elbufer-Drawehn △, *Germany* ... 24 B6
Elburz Mts. = Alborz, Reshteh-ye
  Kūhhā-ye, *Iran* 71 C7
Elche, *Spain* 39 G4
Elche de la Sierra, *Spain* 39 G2
Elcho I., *Australia* 94 A2
Elda, *Spain* 39 G4
Elde ➤, *Germany* 24 B7
Eldon, *Mo., U.S.A.* 112 F8
Eldon, *Wash., U.S.A.* 110 C3
Eldora, *U.S.A.* 112 D8
Eldorado, *Argentina* 127 B5
Eldorado, *Canada* 116 B7
Eldorado, *Mexico* 118 C3
Eldorado, *Ill., U.S.A.* 114 G1
Eldorado, *Tex., U.S.A.* 113 K4
Eldorado Springs, *U.S.A.* 113 G8
Eldoret, *Kenya* 86 B4
Eldred, *U.S.A.* 116 E6
Elea, C., *Cyprus* 49 D13
Eleanora, Pk., *Australia* 93 F3
Elefantes ➤, *Africa* 89 C5
Elektrogorsk, *Russia* 32 E10
Elektrostal, *Russia* 32 E10
Elele, *Nigeria* 83 D6
Elena, *Bulgaria* 45 D9
Elephant Butte Reservoir, *U.S.A.* . 109 K10
Elephant I., *Antarctica* 5 C18
Eleshnitsa, *Bulgaria* 44 E7
Eleşkirt, *Turkey* 73 C10
Eleuthera, *Bahamas* 120 B4
Elevsís, *Greece* 46 C5
Elevtheroúpolis, *Greece* 45 F8
Elgin, *Canada* 117 B8
Elgin, *U.K.* 13 D5
Elgin, *Ill., U.S.A.* 114 D1
Elgin, *N. Dak., U.S.A.* 112 B4
Elgin, *Oreg., U.S.A.* 108 D5
Elgin, *Tex., U.S.A.* 113 K6
Elgoibar, *Spain* 38 B2
Elgon, Mt., *Africa* 86 B3
Eliase, *Indonesia* 63 F8
Elikón, *Greece* 46 C4
Elim, *Namibia* 88 B2
Elim, *S. Africa* 88 E2
Elin Pelin, *Bulgaria* 44 D7
Elista, *Russia* 35 G7
Elizabeth, *Australia* 95 E2
Elizabeth, *U.S.A.* 117 F10
Elizabeth City, *U.S.A.* 115 G7
Elizabethton, *U.S.A.* 115 G4
Elizabethtown, *Ky., U.S.A.* 114 G3
Elizabethtown, *N.Y., U.S.A.* ... 117 B11
Elizabethtown, *Pa., U.S.A.* 117 F8
Elizondo, *Spain* 38 B3
Ełk, *Poland* 30 E9
Elk ➤, *Canada* 102 C5
Elk ➤, *Poland* 30 E9
Elk ➤, *U.S.A.* 115 H2
Elk City, *U.S.A.* 113 H5
Elk Creek, *U.S.A.* 110 F4
Elk Grove, *U.S.A.* 110 G5
Elk Island △, *Canada* 102 C6
Elk Lake, *Canada* 104 C3
Elk Point, *Canada* 103 C6
Elk River, *Idaho, U.S.A.* 108 C5
Elk River, *Minn., U.S.A.* 112 C8
Elkedra ➤, *Australia* 94 C2
Elkhart, *Ind., U.S.A.* 114 E3
Elkhart, *Kans., U.S.A.* 113 G4
Elkhorn, *Canada* 103 D8
Elkhorn ➤, *U.S.A.* 112 E6
Elkhovo, *Bulgaria* 45 D10
Elkin, *U.S.A.* 115 G5
Elkins, *U.S.A.* 114 F6
Elkland, *U.S.A.* 116 E7
Elko, *Canada* 102 D5
Elko, *U.S.A.* 108 F6
Elkton, *U.S.A.* 116 C1
Ell, L., *Australia* 93 E4
Ellef Ringnes I., *Canada* 4 B2
Ellen, Mt., *U.S.A.* 117 B12
Ellenburg, *U.S.A.* 117 B11
Ellendale, *U.S.A.* 112 B5
Ellensburg, *U.S.A.* 108 C3
Ellenville, *U.S.A.* 117 E10
Ellerton, *Barbados* .... 121 g
Ellery, Mt., *Australia* 95 F4
Ellesmere, L., *N.Z.* 91 M4
Ellesmere I., *Canada* 98 B11
Ellesmere Port, *U.K.* 14 D5
Ellice Is. = Tuvalu ■, *Pac. Oc.* . 96 H9
Ellicottville, *U.S.A.* 116 D6
Elliot, *Australia* 94 B1
Elliot, *S. Africa* 89 E4
Elliot Lake, *Canada* 104 C3
Elliotdale = Xhora, *S. Africa* . 89 E4
Ellis, *Australia* 112 F5
Elliston, *Australia* 95 E1
Ellisville, *U.S.A.* 113 K10
Ellon, *U.K.* 13 D6
Ellore = Eluru, *India* 67 L12
Ellsworth, *Kans., U.S.A.* 112 F5
Ellsworth, *Maine, U.S.A.* 115 C11
Ellsworth Land, *Antarctica* 5 D16
Ellsworth Mts., *Antarctica* 5 D16
Ellwangen, *Germany* 25 G6
Ellwood City, *U.S.A.* 116 F4
Elm, *Switz.* 25 J5
Elm-Lappwald △, *Germany* 24 C6
Elma, *Canada* 103 D9
Elma, *U.S.A.* 110 D3
Elmadağ, *Turkey* 72 C5
Elmalı, *Turkey* 47 E11

Elmhurst, *U.S.A.* 114 E2
Elmina, *Ghana* 83 D4
Elmira, *Canada* 116 C4
Elmira, *U.S.A.* 116 D8
Elmira Heights, *U.S.A.* 116 D8
Elmore, *Australia* 95 F3
Elmore, *U.S.A.* 111 M11
Elmshorn, *Germany* 24 B5
Elmvale, *Canada* 116 B5
Elne, *France* 20 F6
Elora, *Canada* 116 C4
Elos, *Greece* 46 E4
Eloúnda, *Greece* 49 D7
Eloy, *U.S.A.* 109 K8
Éloyes, *France* 19 D13
Elrose, *Canada* 103 C7
Elsdorf, *Germany* 24 E2
Elsie, *U.S.A.* 110 E3
Elsinore = Helsingør, *Denmark* 11 H6
Elster →, *Germany* 24 D7
Elsterwerda, *Germany* 24 D9
Eltham, *N.Z.* 91 H5
Elton, *Russia* 35 F8
Elton, Ozero, *Russia* 35 F8
Eltville, *Germany* 25 E4
Eluru, *India* 67 L12
Elvas, *Portugal* 37 G3
Elven, *France* 18 E4
Elverum, *Norway* 9 F14
Elvire →, *Australia* 92 C4
Elvire, Mt., *Australia* 93 E2
Elvo →, *Italy* 40 C5
Elwell, L., *U.S.A.* 108 B8
Elwood, Ind., *U.S.A.* 114 E3
Elwood, Nebr., *U.S.A.* 112 E5
Elx = Elche, *Spain* 39 G4
Ely, *U.K.* 15 E8
Ely, Minn., *U.S.A.* 112 B9
Ely, Nev., *U.S.A.* 108 G6
Elyria, *U.S.A.* 116 E2
Elyrus, *Greece* 46 F5
Elz →, *Germany* 25 G3
Emådalen, *Sweden* 10 C8
Emāmrūd, *Iran* 71 B7
Emån →, *Sweden* 11 G10
Emba, *Kazakhstan* 52 E6
Emba →, *Kazakhstan* 52 E6
Embarcación, *Argentina* 126 A3
Embarras Portage, *Canada* 103 B6
Embetsu, *Japan* 54 B10
Embi = Emba, *Kazakhstan* 52 E6
Embi = Emba →, *Kazakhstan* 52 E6
Embóna, *Greece* 49 C9
Embrun, *France* 21 D10
Embu, *Kenya* 86 C4
Emden, *Germany* 24 B3
Emecik, *Turkey* 47 E9
Emerald, *Australia* 94 C4
Emerson, *Canada* 103 D9
Emet, *Turkey* 47 B11
Emi Koussi, *Chad* 79 E9
Emília-Romagna □, *Italy* 40 D8
Emilius, Mte., *Italy* 40 C4
Eminabad, *Pakistan* 68 C6
Emine, Nos, *Bulgaria* 45 D11
Emirdağ, *Turkey* 72 C4
Emissi, Tarso, *Chad* 79 D9
Emlenton, *U.S.A.* 116 E5
Emlichheim, *Germany* 24 C2
Emmaboda, *Sweden* 11 H9
Emmaus, *S. Africa* 88 D4
Emmaus, *U.S.A.* 117 F9
Emme →, *Switz.* 25 H3
Emmeloord, *Neths.* 17 B5
Emmen, *Neths.* 17 B6
Emmen, *Switz.* 25 H4
Emmendingen, *Germany* 25 G3
Emmental, *Switz.* 25 J3
Emmerich, *Germany* 24 D2
Emmet, *Australia* 94 C3
Emmetsburg, *U.S.A.* 112 D7
Emmett, Idaho, *U.S.A.* 108 E5
Emmett, Mich., *U.S.A.* 116 D2
Emmonak, *U.S.A.* 100 B3
Emo, *Canada* 103 D10
Emőd, *Hungary* 28 C5
Emona, *Bulgaria* 45 D11
Empalme, *Mexico* 118 B2
Empangeni, *S. Africa* 89 D5
Empedrado, *Argentina* 126 B4
Emperor Seamount Chain, *Pac. Oc.* 96 D9
Empoli, *Italy* 40 E7
Emporia, Kans., *U.S.A.* 112 F6
Emporia, Va., *U.S.A.* 115 G7
Emporium, *U.S.A.* 116 E6
Empress, *Canada* 103 C7
Empty Quarter = Rub' al Khālī, *Si. Arabia* 75 D4
Ems →, *Germany* 24 B3
Emsdale, *Canada* 116 A5
Emsdetten, *Germany* 24 C3
Emu, *China* 57 C15
Emu Park, *Australia* 94 C5
'En 'Avrona, *Israel* 74 F4
En Nahud, *Sudan* 81 E2
En Nofalab, *Sudan* 81 D3
Ena, *Japan* 55 G8
Enana, *Namibia* 88 B2
Enånger, *Sweden* 10 C11
Enard B., *U.K.* 13 C3
Enare = Inarijärvi, *Finland* 8 B22
Enarotali, *Indonesia* 63 E9
Encampment, *U.S.A.* 108 F10
Encantadas, Serra, *Brazil* 127 C5
Encarnación, *Paraguay* 127 B4
Encarnación de Diaz, *Mexico* 118 C4
Enchi, *Ghana* 82 D4
Encinitas, *U.S.A.* 111 M9
Encino, *U.S.A.* 109 J11
Encounter B., *Australia* 95 F2
Encs, *Hungary* 28 B6
Endako, *Canada* 102 C3
Ende, *Indonesia* 63 F6
Endeavour Str., *Australia* 94 A3
Endelave, *Denmark* 11 J4
Enderby, *Canada* 102 C5
Enderby I., *Australia* 92 D2
Enderby Land, *Antarctica* 5 C5
Enderlin, *U.S.A.* 112 B6
Endicott, *U.S.A.* 117 D8
Endwell, *U.S.A.* 117 D8
Endyalgout I., *Australia* 92 B5
Eneabba, *Australia* 93 E2
Enewetak Atoll, *Marshall Is.* 96 F8
Enez, *Turkey* 45 F10
Enfer, Pte. d', *Martinique* 120 c
Enfield, *Canada* 105 D7
Enfield, Conn., *U.S.A.* 117 E12
Enfield, N.H., *U.S.A.* 117 C12
Engadin, *Switz.* 25 J6
Engaño, C., *Dom. Rep.* 121 C6
Engaño, C., *Phil.* 63 A6
Engaru, *Japan* 54 B11
Engcobo, *S. Africa* 89 E4
Engelberg, *Switz.* 25 J4
Engels, *Russia* 34 E8
Engemann L., *Canada* 103 B7
Engershatu, *Eritrea* 81 D4
Enggano, *Indonesia* 62 F2
England →, *Australia* 113 H9
England □, *U.K.* 15 E5
Englee, *Canada* 105 B8
Englehart, *Canada* 104 C4
Englewood, *Canada* 112 F2
English →, *Canada* 103 C10
English Bazar = Ingraj Bazar, *India* 69 G13
English Channel, *Europe* 15 G6
English Company's Is., The, *Australia* 94 A2
English River, *Canada* 104 C1
Engures ezers, *Latvia* 30 A10
Enguri →, *Georgia* 35 J5
Enid, *U.S.A.* 113 G6
Enipévs →, *Greece* 46 B4
Enkhuizen, *Neths.* 17 B5
Enköping, *Sweden* 10 E11
Enle, *China* 58 F3
Enna, *Italy* 43 E7
Ennadai, *Canada* 103 A8
Ennadai L., *Canada* 103 A8
Ennedi, *Chad* 79 E10
Enngonia, *Australia* 95 D4
Ennigerloh, *Germany* 24 D4
Ennis, *Ireland* 12 D3
Ennis, Mont., *U.S.A.* 108 D8
Ennis, Tex., *U.S.A.* 113 J6
Enniscorthy, *Ireland* 12 D5
Enniskillen, *Ireland* 12 B4
Ennistimon, *Ireland* 12 D2
Enns, *Austria* 26 C7
Enns →, *Austria* 26 C7
Enontekiö, *Finland* 8 B20
Enosburg Falls, *U.S.A.* 117 B12
Enping, *China* 59 F9
Enriquillo, L., *Dom. Rep.* 121 C5
Enschede, *Neths.* 17 B6
Ensenada, *Argentina* 126 C4
Ensenada, *Mexico* 118 A1
Ensenada de los Muertos, *Mexico* 118 C2
Enshi, *China* 58 B7
Ensiola, Pta. de n', *Spain* 48 B9
Ensisheim, *France* 19 E14
Entebbe, *Uganda* 86 B3
Enterprise, *Canada* 102 A5
Enterprise, Ala., *U.S.A.* 115 K3
Enterprise, Oreg., *U.S.A.* 108 D5
Entorno de Doñana, *Spain* 37 J4
Entraygues-sur-Truyère, *France* 20 D6
Entre Ríos, *Bolivia* 126 A3
Entre Ríos □, *Argentina* 126 C4
Entrepeñas, Embalse de, *Spain* 38 E2
Entroncamento, *Portugal* 37 F2
Enugu, *Nigeria* 83 D6
Enugu □, *Nigeria* 83 D6
Enugu Ezike, *Nigeria* 83 D6
Enumclaw, *U.S.A.* 110 C5
Envalira, Port d', *Europe* 38 C6
Envermeu, *France* 18 C8
Enviken, *Sweden* 10 D9
Enying, *Hungary* 28 D3
Enza →, *Italy* 40 D7
Eólie, Ís., *Italy* 43 D7
Epanomí, *Greece* 44 F6
Epe, *Neths.* 17 B5
Epe, *Nigeria* 83 D5
Épernay, *France* 19 C10
Épernon, *France* 19 D8
Ephesus, *Turkey* 47 D9
Ephraim, *U.S.A.* 108 G8
Ephrata, Pa., *U.S.A.* 117 F8
Ephrata, Wash., *U.S.A.* 108 C4
Epidaurus Limera, *Greece* 46 E5
Épila, *Spain* 38 D3
Épinac, *France* 19 F11
Épinal, *France* 19 D13
Episkopi, *Cyprus* 49 E11
Episkopí, *Greece* 49 D7
Episkopi Bay, *Cyprus* 49 E11
Epitálion, *Greece* 46 D3
Eppan = Appiano, *Italy* 41 B8
Eppingen, *Germany* 25 F4
Epsom, *U.K.* 15 F7
Epukiro, *Namibia* 88 C2
Equatoria = El Istiwa'iya, *Sudan* 79 G11
Equatorial Guinea ■, *Africa* 84 D1
Er Hai, *China* 58 E3
Er Rachidia, *Morocco* 78 B5
Er Rahad, *Sudan* 81 E3
Er Rif, *Morocco* 78 A5
Er Rogel, *Sudan* 80 D4
Er Roseires, *Sudan* 81 E3
Er Rua'at, *Sudan* 81 E3
Eraclea, *Italy* 41 C9
Erāwadī Myit = Irrawaddy →, *Burma* 67 M19
Erāwadī Myitwanya = Irrawaddy, Mouths of the, *Burma* 67 M19
Erba, *Italy* 40 C6
Erba, *Sudan* 80 D4
Erba, J., *Sudan* 80 C4
Erbaa, *Turkey* 72 B7
Erbeskopf, *Germany* 25 F3
Erbil = Arbīl, *Iraq* 70 B5
Erbu, *Ethiopia* 81 E3
Erçek, *Turkey* 70 B4
Erçiş, *Turkey* 73 C10
Erciyaş Dağı, *Turkey* 70 B2
Érd, *Hungary* 28 C3
Erdao Jiang →, *China* 57 C14
Erdek, *Turkey* 45 F11
Erdemli, *Turkey* 72 D6
Erdene = Ulaan-Uul, *Mongolia* 56 B6
Erdenetsogt, *Mongolia* 56 C4
Erding, *Germany* 25 G7
Erdre →, *France* 18 E5
Erebus, Mt., *Antarctica* 5 D11
Erechim, *Brazil* 127 B5
Ereğli, Konya, *Turkey* 70 B2
Ereğli, Zonguldak, *Turkey* 72 B4
Erei, Monti, *Italy* 43 E7
Erenhot, *China* 56 C7
Eresma →, *Spain* 36 D6
Eressós, *Greece* 47 B7
Erfenisdam, *S. Africa* 88 D4
Erfstadt, *Germany* 24 E2
Erft →, *Germany* 24 D2
Erfurt, *Germany* 24 E7
Ergani, *Turkey* 70 B3
Ergel, *Mongolia* 56 C5
Ergene →, *Turkey* 45 E10
Ergeni Vozvyshennost, *Russia* 35 G7
Érgli, *Latvia* 9 H21
Erhlin, *Taiwan* 59 F13
Eria →, *Spain* 36 C5
Eriba, *Sudan* 81 D4
Eriboll, L., *U.K.* 13 C4
Érice, *Italy* 42 D5
Erie, *U.S.A.* 116 D4
Erie, L., *N. Amer.* 116 D4
Erie Canal, *U.S.A.* 116 C7
Erieau, *Canada* 116 D3
Erigavo, *Somali Rep.* 75 E4
Erikoúsa, *Greece* 49 A3
Eriksdale, *Canada* 103 C9
Erímanthos, *Greece* 46 D3
Erimo-misaki, *Japan* 54 D11
Erin Pt., *Trin. & Tob.* 125 K15
Erinpura, *India* 68 G5
Eriskay, *U.K.* 13 D1
Erithraí, *Greece* 46 C5
Eritrea ■, *Africa* 81 E4
Erjas →, *Portugal* 36 F3
Erkelenz, *Germany* 24 D2
Erkner, *Germany* 24 C9
Erlangen, *Germany* 25 F6
Erldunda, *Australia* 94 D1
Ermelo, *Neths.* 17 B5
Ermelo, *S. Africa* 89 D4
Ermenak, *Turkey* 70 B2
Ermil, *Sudan* 81 E2
Ermióni, *Greece* 46 D5
Ermones, *Greece* 49 A3
Ernakulam, *India* 66 Q10
Erne →, *Ireland* 12 B4
Erne, Lower L., *U.K.* 12 B4
Erne, Upper L., *U.K.* 12 B4
Ernest Giles Ra., *Australia* 93 E3
Ernstberg, *Germany* 25 E2
Erode, *India* 66 P10
Eromanga, *Australia* 95 D3
Erongo, *Namibia* 88 C2
Erquy, *France* 18 D4
Erramala Hills, *India* 66 M11
Errer →, *Ethiopia* 81 F5
Errigal, *Ireland* 12 A3
Erris Hd., *Ireland* 12 B1
Erskë, *Albania* 44 F4
Erskine, *U.S.A.* 112 B7
Erstein, *France* 19 D14
Ertholmene, *Denmark* 11 J9
Ertil, *Russia* 34 E5
Ertis = Irtysh →, *Russia* 52 C7
Eruh, *Turkey* 73 D10
Eruwa, *Nigeria* 83 D5
Ervy-le-Châtel, *France* 19 D10
Erwin, *U.S.A.* 115 G4
Eryuan, *China* 58 D2
Erzgebirge, *Germany* 24 E8
Erzin, *Russia* 53 D10
Erzincan, *Turkey* 70 B3
Erzurum, *Turkey* 70 B4
Es Caló, *Spain* 48 C8
Es Canar, *Spain* 48 B8
Es Mercadal, *Spain* 48 B11
Es Migjorn Gran, *Spain* 48 B11
Es Safiya, *Sudan* 81 D3
Es Sahrâ' Esh Sharqîya, *Egypt* 80 B3
Es Sînâ', *Egypt* 74 F3
Es Sûkî, *Sudan* 81 E3
Esambo, *Dem. Rep. of the Congo* 86 C1
Esan-Misaki, *Japan* 54 D10
Esashi, Hokkaidō, *Japan* 54 B11
Esashi, Hokkaidō, *Japan* 54 D10
Esbjerg, *Denmark* 11 J2
Esbo = Espoo, *Finland* 9 F21
Escalante, *U.S.A.* 109 H8
Escalante →, *U.S.A.* 109 H8
Escalón, *Mexico* 118 B4
Escambia →, *U.S.A.* 115 K2
Escanaba, *U.S.A.* 114 C2
Esch-sur-Alzette, *Lux.* 17 E6
Eschede, *Germany* 24 C6
Eschwege, *Germany* 24 D6
Eschweiler, *Germany* 24 E2
Escondido, *U.S.A.* 111 M9
Escravos →, *Nigeria* 83 D6
Escuinapa, *Mexico* 118 C3
Escuintla, *Guatemala* 120 D1
Eséka, *Cameroon* 83 E7
Eşen →, *Turkey* 47 E11
Esenguly, *Turkmenistan* 52 F6
Esens, *Germany* 24 B3
Esenyurt, *Turkey* 45 E12
Esera →, *Spain* 38 C5
Eşfahān, *Iran* 71 C6
Eşfahān □, *Iran* 71 C6
Esfarāyen, *Iran* 71 B8
Esfīdeh, *Iran* 71 C8
Esgueva →, *Spain* 36 D6
Esh Sham = Dimashq, *Syria* 74 B5
Esh Shamâlîya □, *Sudan* 80 D2
Esha Ness, *U.K.* 13 A7
Eshan, *China* 58 E4
Esher, *U.K.* 15 F7
Eshkol △, *Israel* 74 D3
Eshowe, *S. Africa* 89 D5
Esiama, *Ghana* 82 E4
Esigodini, *Zimbabwe* 89 C4
Esil = Ishim →, *Russia* 52 D8
Esino →, *Italy* 41 E10
Esira, *Madag.* 89 C8
Esk →, Cumb., *U.K.* 13 G5
Esk →, N. Yorks., *U.K.* 14 C7
Eskān, *Iran* 71 E9
Esker, *Canada* 105 B6
Eskifjörður, *Iceland* 8 D7
Eskilsäter, *Sweden* 11 F7
Eskilstuna, *Sweden* 10 E10
Eskimalatya, *Turkey* 73 C8
Eskimo Point = Arviat, *Canada* 103 A10
Eskişehir, *Turkey* 47 B12
Eskişehir □, *Turkey* 47 B12
Esla →, *Spain* 36 D4
Eslāmābād-e Gharb, *Iran* 70 C5
Eslāmshahr, *Iran* 71 C6
Eslöv, *Sweden* 11 J7
Eşme, *Turkey* 47 C10
Esmeraldas, *Ecuador* 124 C3
Esnagi L., *Canada* 104 C3
Espalion, *France* 20 D6
Espanola, *Canada* 104 C3
Espanola, *U.S.A.* 109 H10
Esparreguera, *Spain* 38 D6
Esparta, *Costa Rica* 120 E3
Espelkamp, *Germany* 24 C4
Esperance, *Australia* 93 F3
Esperance B., *Australia* 93 F3
Esperance Harbour, *St. Lucia* 121 f
Esperanza, *Antarctica* 5 C18
Esperanza, *Argentina* 126 C3
Esperanza, *Phil.* 61 G6
Esperanza, *Puerto Rico* 121 d
Espéraza, *France* 20 F6
Espichel, C., *Portugal* 37 G1
Espiel, *Spain* 37 G5
Espigão, Serra do, *Brazil* 127 B5
Espinazo, Sierra del = Espinhaço, Serra do, *Brazil* 125 G10
Espinhaço, Serra do, *Brazil* 125 G10
Espinho, *Portugal* 36 D2
Espinilho, Serra do, *Brazil* 127 B5
Espinosa de los Monteros, *Spain* 36 B7
Espírito Santo □, *Brazil* 125 H10
Espírito Santo, *Vanuatu* 96 J8
Espíritu Santo, B. del, *Mexico* 119 D7
Espíritu Santo, I., *Mexico* 118 C2
Espita, *Mexico* 119 C7
Espiye, *Turkey* 73 B8
Espluga de Francolí, *Spain* 38 D6
Espoo, *Finland* 9 F21
Espuña, Sierra de, *Spain* 39 H3
Espungabera, *Mozam.* 89 C5
Esquel, *Argentina* 128 E2
Esquimalt, *Canada* 102 D4
Esquina, *Argentina* 126 C4
Essaouira, *Morocco* 78 B4
Essebie, *Dem. Rep. of the Congo* 86 B3
Essen, *Belgium* 17 C4
Essen, *Germany* 24 D3
Essendon, Mt., *Australia* 93 E3
Essequibo →, *Guyana* 124 B7
Essex, *Canada* 116 D2
Essex, Calif., *U.S.A.* 111 L11
Essex, N.Y., *U.S.A.* 117 B11
Essex □, *U.K.* 15 F8
Essex Junction, *U.S.A.* 117 B11
Esslingen, *Germany* 25 G5
Essonne □, *France* 19 D9
Estaca de Bares, C. de, *Spain* 36 B3
Estadilla, *Spain* 38 C5
Estados, I. de Los, *Argentina* 128 G4
Estagel, *France* 20 F6
Eştahbānāt, *Iran* 71 D7
Estância, *Brazil* 125 F11
Estancia, *U.S.A.* 109 J10
Estārm, *Iran* 71 D8
Estarreja, *Portugal* 36 E2
Estats, Pic d', *Spain* 38 C6
Estcourt, *S. Africa* 89 D4
Este, *Italy* 41 C8
Esteli △, *Dom. Rep.* 121 C6
Esteli, *Nic.* 120 D2
Estella, *Spain* 38 C2
Estellencs, *Spain* 48 B9
Estena →, *Spain* 37 F6
Estepa, *Spain* 37 H6
Estepona, *Spain* 37 J5
Esterhazy, *Canada* 103 C8
Esternay, *France* 19 D10
Esterri d'Aneu, *Spain* 38 C6
Estevan, *Canada* 103 D8
Estevan Group, *Canada* 102 C3
Estherville, *U.S.A.* 112 D7
Estissac, *France* 19 D10
Eston, *Canada* 103 C7
Estonia ■, *Europe* 9 G21
Estoril, *Portugal* 37 G1
Estouk, *Mali* 83 B5
Estreito, *Brazil* 125 E9
Estrela, Serra da, *Portugal* 36 E3
Estrella, *Portugal* 37 G7
Estremoz, *Portugal* 37 G3
Estrondo, Serra do, *Brazil* 125 E9
Esztergom, *Hungary* 28 C3
Et Tidra, *Mauritania* 82 B1
Etah, *India* 69 F8
Étain, *France* 19 C12
Étampes, *France* 19 D9
Etanga, *Namibia* 88 B1
Étaples, *France* 19 B8
Etawah, *India* 69 F8
Etawney L., *Canada* 103 B9
Ete, *Nigeria* 83 D6
eThekwini = Durban, *S. Africa* 89 D5
Ethel, *U.S.A.* 110 D4
Ethelbert, *Canada* 103 C8
Ethiopia ■, *Africa* 75 F3
Ethiopian Highlands, *Ethiopia* 50 J7
Etili, *Turkey* 45 G10
Etive, L., *U.K.* 13 E3
Etna, *Italy* 43 E7
Etoile, *Dem. Rep. of the Congo* 87 E2
Etosha, S. *Namibia* 88 B2
Etosha Pan, *Namibia* 88 B2
Etowah, *U.S.A.* 115 H3
Étréchy, *France* 19 D9
Étrépagny, *France* 19 C8
Étretat, *France* 18 C7
Etropole, *Bulgaria* 45 D8
Ettelbruck, *Lux.* 17 E6
Ettrick Water →, *U.K.* 13 F6
Etuku, *Dem. Rep. of the Congo* 86 C2
Etulia, *Moldova* 29 E13
Etzatlán, *Mexico* 118 C4
Etzná, *Mexico* 119 D6
Etzná-Tixmucuy = Edzná, *Mexico* 119 D6
Eu, *France* 18 B8
Eubenangee Swamp △, *Australia* 94 B4
Euboea = Évvoia, *Greece* 46 C6
Eucla, *Australia* 93 F4
Euclid, *U.S.A.* 116 E3
Eucumbene, L., *Australia* 95 F4
Eudora, *U.S.A.* 113 J9
Eufaula, Ala., *U.S.A.* 115 K3
Eufaula, Okla., *U.S.A.* 113 H7
Eufaula L., *U.S.A.* 113 H7
Eugene, *U.S.A.* 108 E2
Eugowra, *Australia* 95 E4
Eulo, *Australia* 95 D4
Eungella △, *Australia* 94 C4
Eunice, La., *U.S.A.* 113 K8
Eunice, N. Mex., *U.S.A.* 113 J3
Eupen, *Belgium* 17 D6
Euphrates = Furāt, Nahr al →, *Asia* 70 D5
Eure □, *France* 18 C8
Eure →, *France* 18 C8
Eure-et-Loir □, *France* 18 D8
Eureka, *Canada* 4 B3
Eureka, Calif., *U.S.A.* 108 F1
Eureka, Kans., *U.S.A.* 113 G6
Eureka, Mont., *U.S.A.* 108 B6
Eureka, Nev., *U.S.A.* 108 G5
Eureka, S. Dak., *U.S.A.* 112 C5
Eureka, Mt., *Australia* 93 E3
Euroa, *Australia* 95 F4
Europa, Île, *Ind. Oc.* 85 J8
Europa, Picos de, *Spain* 36 B6
Europa, Pta. de, *Gib.* 37 J5
Europe 6 E10
Europoort, *Neths.* 17 C4
Euskirchen, *Germany* 24 E2
Eustis, *U.S.A.* 115 L5
Eutin, *Germany* 24 A6
Eutsuk L., *Canada* 102 C3
Evale, *Angola* 88 B2
Evans, *U.S.A.* 112 E2
Evans, L., *Canada* 104 B4
Evans City, *U.S.A.* 116 F4
Evans Head, *Australia* 95 D5
Evans Mills, *U.S.A.* 117 B9
Evansburg, *Canada* 102 C5
Evanston, Ill., *U.S.A.* 114 E2
Evanston, Wyo., *U.S.A.* 108 F8
Evansville, *U.S.A.* 114 G2
Évaux-les-Bains, *France* 19 F9
Evaz, *Iran* 71 E7
Evciler, Afyon, *Turkey* 47 C11
Evciler, Çanakkale, *Turkey* 47 B8
Eveleth, *U.S.A.* 112 B8
Evensk, *Russia* 53 C16
Everard, L., *Australia* 95 E1
Everard Ranges, *Australia* 93 E5
Everest, Mt., *Nepal* 69 E12
Everett, Pa., *U.S.A.* 116 F6
Everett, Wash., *U.S.A.* 110 C4
Everglades △, *U.S.A.* 115 N5
Everglades, The, *U.S.A.* 115 N5
Everglades City, *U.S.A.* 115 N5
Evergreen, Ala., *U.S.A.* 115 K2
Evergreen, Mont., *U.S.A.* 108 B6
Everöd, *Sweden* 11 J8
Evertsberg, *Sweden* 10 C7
Evesham, *U.K.* 15 E6
Évian-les-Bains, *France* 19 F13
Évinos →, *Greece* 46 C3
Évisa, *France* 21 F12
Evje, *Norway* 9 G12
Évora, *Portugal* 37 G3
Évora □, *Portugal* 37 G3
Evowghlī, *Iran* 70 B5
Évreux, *France* 18 C8
Evritanía □, *Greece* 46 B3
Évron, *France* 18 D6

Évros □, *Greece* 45 E10
Évros ➤, *Greece* 72 B2
Evrótas ➤, *Greece* 46 E4
Évry, *France* 19 D9
Évvoia, *Greece* 46 C6
Évvoia □, *Greece* 46 C5
Evxinoúpolis, *Greece* 46 B4
Ewe, L., *U.K.* 13 D3
Ewing, *U.S.A.* 112 D5
Ewo, *Congo* 84 E2
Exaltación, *Bolivia* 124 F5
Excelsior Springs, *U.S.A.* ... 112 F7
Excideuil, *France* 20 C5
Exe ➤, *U.K.* 15 G4
Exeter, *Canada* 116 C3
Exeter, *U.K.* 15 G4
Exeter, *Calif., U.S.A.* 110 J7
Exeter, *N.H., U.S.A.* 117 D14
Exmoor, *U.K.* 15 F4
Exmoor △, *U.K.* 15 F4
Exmouth, *Australia* 92 D1
Exmouth, *U.K.* 15 G4
Exmouth G., *Australia* 92 D1
Expedition △, *Australia* 95 D4
Expedition Ra., *Australia* ... 94 C4
Extremadura □, *Spain* 37 F4
Exuma Sound, *Bahamas* 120 B4
Eyasi, L., *Tanzania* 86 C4
Eye Pen., *U.K.* 13 C2
Eyemouth, *U.K.* 13 F6
Eygues = Aigues ➤, *France* ... 21 D8
Eygurande, *France* 19 C9
Eyjafjörður, *Iceland* 8 C4
Eymet, *France* 20 D4
Eymoutiers, *France* 20 C5
Eynesil, *Turkey* 73 B8
Eyre (North), L., *Australia* . 95 D2
Eyre (South), L., *Australia* . 95 D2
Eyre Mts., *N.Z.* 91 L2
Eyre Pen., *Australia* 95 E2
Eysturoy, *Færoe Is.* 8 E9
Eyvānkī, *Iran* 71 C6
Ez Zeidab, *Sudan* 80 D3
Ezcaray, *Spain* 38 C1
Ežerelis, *Lithuania* 30 D10
Ezhou, *China* 59 B10
Ezine, *Turkey* 47 B8
Ezouza ➤, *Cyprus* 49 E11

F

F.Y.R.O.M. = Macedonia ■,
 Europe 44 E5
Fabala, *Guinea* 82 D3
Fabens, *U.S.A.* 109 L10
Fabero, *Spain* 36 C4
Fåborg, *Denmark* 11 J4
Fabriano, *Italy* 41 E9
Făcăeni, *Romania* 29 F12
Fachi, *Niger* 79 E8
Fada, *Chad* 79 E10
Fada-n-Gourma, *Burkina Faso* . 83 C5
Fadd, *Hungary* 28 D3
Faddor, *Sudan* 81 F3
Faddeyevskiy, Ostrov, *Russia* 53 B15
Fadghāmī, *Syria* 70 C4
Fadlab, *Sudan* 80 D3
Faenza, *Italy* 41 D8
Færoe Is. = Føroyar, *Atl. Oc.* 8 F9
Fafa, *Mali* 83 B5
Fafe, *Portugal* 36 D2
Fagam, *Nigeria* 83 C7
Făgăras, *Romania* 29 E9
Făgăras, Munţii, *Romania* 29 E9
Fågelmara, *Sweden* 11 H9
Fagerhult, *Sweden* 11 G9
Fagersta, *Sweden* 10 D9
Făget, *Romania* 28 E7
Făget, Munţii, *Romania* 29 C8
Fagnano, L., *Argentina* 128 G3
Fagnières, *France* 19 D11
Faguibine, L., *Mali* 82 B4
Fahlīān, *Iran* 71 D6
Fahraj, *Kermān, Iran* 71 D8
Fahraj, *Yazd, Iran* 71 D7
Fai Tsi Long, *Vietnam* 58 G6
Faial, *Madeira* 48 D3
Fair Haven, *U.S.A.* 114 D9
Fair Hd., *U.K.* 12 A5
Fair Oaks, *U.S.A.* 110 G5
Fairbanks, *U.S.A.* 100 B5
Fairbury, *U.S.A.* 112 E6
Fairfax, *U.S.A.* 117 B11
Fairfield, *Ala., U.S.A.* 115 J2
Fairfield, *Calif., U.S.A.* ... 110 G4
Fairfield, *Conn., U.S.A.* 117 E11
Fairfield, *Idaho, U.S.A.* 108 E6
Fairfield, *Ill., U.S.A.* 114 F1
Fairfield, *Iowa, U.S.A.* 112 E9
Fairfield, *Tex., U.S.A.* 113 K7
Fairford, *Canada* 103 C9
Fairhope, *U.S.A.* 115 K2
Fairlie, *N.Z.* 91 L3
Fairmead, *U.S.A.* 110 H6
Fairmont, *Minn., U.S.A.* 112 D7
Fairmont, *W. Va., U.S.A.* 114 F5
Fairmount, *Calif., U.S.A.* ... 111 L8
Fairmount, *N.Y., U.S.A.* 91 J4
Fairplay, *U.S.A.* 109 G11
Fairport, *U.S.A.* 116 C7
Fairport Harbor, *U.S.A.* 116 E3
Fairview, *Canada* 102 B5
Fairview, *Mont., U.S.A.* 112 B2
Fairview, *Okla., U.S.A.* 113 G5
Fairweather, Mt., *U.S.A.* 102 B1
Faisalabad, *Pakistan* 68 D5
Faith, *U.S.A.* 112 C3
Faizabad, *India* 69 F10

Fajardo, *Puerto Rico* .... 121 d
Fajr, W. ➤, *Si. Arabia* 70 D3
Fakenham, *U.K.* 14 E8
Fåker, *Sweden* 10 A8
Fakfak, *Indonesia* 63 E8
Fakiya, *Bulgaria* 45 D11
Fakobli, *Ivory C.* 82 D3
Fakse, *Denmark* 11 J6
Fakse Bugt, *Denmark* 11 J6
Fakse Ladeplads, *Denmark* 11 J6
Faku, *China* 57 C12
Falaba, *S. Leone* 82 D2
Falaise, *France* 18 D6
Falaise, Mui, *Vietnam* 64 C5
Falakrón Óros, *Greece* 44 E7
Falam, *Burma* 67 H18
Falces, *Spain* 38 C3
Fălciu, *Romania* 29 D13
Falcó, C. des, *Spain* 48 C7
Falcón, Presa, *Mexico* 119 B5
Falcon Lake, *Canada* 103 D9
Falcon Reservoir, *U.S.A.* 113 M5
Falconara Maríttima, *Italy* .. 41 E10
Falcone, C. del, *Italy* 42 B1
Falconer, *U.S.A.* 116 D5
Faléa, *Mali* 82 C2
Falémé ➤, *Senegal* 82 C2
Falerum, *Sweden* 11 F10
Faleshty = Fălești, *Moldova* . 29 C12
Fălești, *Moldova* 29 C12
Falfurrias, *U.S.A.* 113 M5
Falher, *Canada* 102 B5
Falirakí, *Greece* 49 C10
Falkenberg, *Germany* 24 D9
Falkenberg, *Sweden* 11 H6
Falkensee, *Germany* 24 C9
Falkirk, *U.K.* 13 F5
Falkirk □, *U.K.* 13 F5
Falkland, *U.K.* 13 E5
Falkland Is. ☑, *Atl. Oc.* 128 G5
Falkland Sd., *Falk. Is.* 128 G5
Falkonéra, *Greece* 46 E5
Falköping, *Sweden* 11 F7
Fall River, *U.S.A.* 117 E13
Fallbrook, *U.S.A.* 111 M9
Fallon, *U.S.A.* 108 G4
Falls City, *U.S.A.* 112 E7
Falls Creek, *U.S.A.* 116 E6
Falmouth, *Jamaica* .... 120 a
Falmouth, *U.K.* 15 G2
Falmouth, *U.S.A.* 117 E14
Falsa, Pta., *Mexico* 118 B1
False B., *S. Africa* 88 E2
Falso, C., *Honduras* 120 C3
Falster, *Denmark* 11 K5
Fălticeni, *Romania* 29 C11
Falun, *Sweden* 10 D9
Famagusta, *Cyprus* 49 D12
Famagusta Bay, *Cyprus* 49 D13
Famalé, *Niger* 78 F6
Famatina, Sierra de, *Argentina* 126 B2
Family L., *Canada* 103 C9
Famoso, *U.S.A.* 111 K7
Fan Xian, *China* 56 G8
Fana, *Mali* 82 C3
Fanad Hd., *Ireland* 12 A4
Fanárion, *Greece* 46 B3
Fandriana, *Madag.* 89 C8
Fánes-Sénnes e Braies △, *Italy* 41 B9
Fang, *Thailand* 58 H2
Fang Xian, *China* 59 A8
Fangaga, *Sudan* 80 D4
Fangak, *Sudan* 81 F3
Fangchang, *China* 59 B12
Fangcheng, *China* 56 H7
Fangchenggang, *China* 58 G7
Fangliao, *Taiwan* 59 F13
Fangshan, *China* 56 E6
Fangzi, *China* 57 F10
Fani i Madh ➤, *Albania* 44 E4
Fanjakana, *Madag.* 89 C8
Fanjiatun, *China* 57 C13
Fannich, L., *U.K.* 13 D4
Fannūj, *Iran* 71 E8
Fanø, *Denmark* 11 J2
Fano, *Italy* 41 E10
Fanshi, *China* 56 E7
Fao = Al Fāw, *Iraq* 71 D6
Faqirwali, *Pakistan* 68 E5
Fâqûs, *Egypt* 80 H7
Far East = Dalnevostochnyy □,
 Russia 53 C14
Far East, *Asia* 50 E16
Fara in Sabina, *Italy* 41 F9
Faradje, *Dem. Rep. of the Congo* 86 B2
Farafangana, *Madag.* 89 C8
Faráfra, El Wâhât el-, *Egypt* . 80 B2
Farāh, *Afghan.* 66 C3
Farāh □, *Afghan.* 66 C3
Farahalana, *Madag.* 89 A9
Faraid, Gebel, *Egypt* 80 C4
Farako, *Ivory C.* 82 D4
Faramana, *Burkina Faso* 82 C4
Faranah, *Guinea* 82 C2
Farasān, Jazā'ir, *Si. Arabia* 75 D3
Farasan Is. = Farasān, Jazā'ir,
 Si. Arabia 75 D3
Faratsiho, *Madag.* 89 B8
Fardes ➤, *Spain* 37 H7
Fareham, *U.K.* 15 G6
Farewell C. = Nunap Isua,
 Greenland 101 C15
Färgelanda, *Sweden* 11 F5
Farghona, *Uzbekistan* 52 E8
Fargo, *U.S.A.* 112 B6
Fär'iah, W. al ➤, *West Bank* . 74 C4
Faribault, *U.S.A.* 112 C8
Faridabad, *India* 68 E6
Faridkot, *India* 68 D6
Faridpur, *Bangla.* 69 H13

Faridpur, *India* 69 E8
Färila, *Sweden* 10 C9
Farim, *Guinea-Biss.* 82 C1
Farīmān, *Iran* 71 C8
Farina, *Australia* 95 E2
Fariones, Pta., *Canary Is.* .. 48 E6
Fâriskûr, *Egypt* 80 H7
Färjestaden, *Sweden* 11 H10
Farkadhón, *Greece* 46 B4
Farleigh, *Australia* 94 K7
Farmakonisi, *Greece* 47 D9
Farmerville, *U.S.A.* 113 J8
Farmingdale, *U.S.A.* 117 F10
Farmington, *Canada* 102 B4
Farmington, *Calif., U.S.A.* .. 110 H6
Farmington, *Maine, U.S.A.* ... 115 C10
Farmington, *Mo., U.S.A.* 113 G9
Farmington, *N.H., U.S.A.* 117 C13
Farmington, *N. Mex., U.S.A.* . 109 H9
Farmington, *Utah, U.S.A.* 108 F8
Farmington ➤, *U.S.A.* 117 E12
Farmville, *U.S.A.* 114 G6
Färnäs, *Sweden* 10 D8
Farne Is., *U.K.* 14 B6
Färnebofjärden △, *Sweden* 10 D10
Farnham, *Canada* 117 A12
Farnham, Mt., *Canada* 102 C5
Faro, *Brazil* 125 D7
Faro, *Canada* 100 B6
Faro, *Portugal* 37 H3
Fårö, *Sweden* 9 H18
Faro □, *Portugal* 37 H2
Faro ✈ (FAO), *Portugal* 37 H3
Fårösund, *Sweden* 11 G13
Farquhar, C., *Australia* 93 D1
Farrars Cr. ➤, *Australia* 94 D3
Farrāshband, *Iran* 71 D7
Farrell, *U.S.A.* 116 E4
Farrokhī, *Iran* 71 C8
Farruch, C. = Ferrutx, C., *Spain* 48 B10
Fārs □, *Iran* 71 D7
Fársala, *Greece* 46 B4
Farsø, *Denmark* 11 H3
Farson, *U.S.A.* 108 E9
Farsund, *Norway* 9 G12
Fartak, Râs, *Si. Arabia* 70 D2
Fartak, Ra's, *Yemen* 75 D5
Fârţāneşti, *Romania* 29 E12
Fartura, Serra da, *Brazil* ... 127 B5
Faru, *Nigeria* 83 C6
Fārūj, *Iran* 71 B8
Fårup, *Denmark* 11 H3
Farvel, Kap = Nunap Isua,
 Greenland 101 C15
Farwell, *U.S.A.* 113 H3
Fāryāb □, *Afghan.* 66 B4
Fasā, *Iran* 71 D7
Fasano, *Italy* 43 B10
Fashoda, *Sudan* 81 F3
Fassa, *Mali* 82 C3
Fastiv, *Ukraine* 33 G5
Fastnet Rock, *Ireland* 12 E2
Fastov = Fastiv, *Ukraine* 33 G5
Fatagar, Tanjung, *Indonesia* . 63 E8
Fatehabad, *Haryana, India* .. 68 E6
Fatehabad, *Ut. P., India* 68 F8
Fatehgarh, *India* 69 F8
Fatehpur, *Bihar, India* 69 G11
Fatehpur, *Raj., India* 68 F6
Fatehpur, *Ut. P., India* 69 G9
Fatehpur, *Ut. P., India* 69 F9
Fatehpur Sikri, *India* 68 F6
Fatesh, *Russia* 33 F8
Fathai, *Sudan* 81 F3
Fathom Five △, *Canada* 116 A3
Fatick, *Senegal* 82 C1
Fatima, *Canada* 105 C7
Fátima, *Portugal* 37 F2
Fatoya, *Guinea* 82 C3
Fatsa, *Turkey* 72 B7
Faucille, Col de la, *France* . 19 F13
Faulkton, *U.S.A.* 112 C5
Faulquemont, *France* 19 C13
Faure I., *Australia* 93 E1
Făurei, *Romania* 29 E12
Fauresmith, *S. Africa* 88 D4
Fauske, *Norway* 8 C16
Favara, *Italy* 42 E6
Favàritx, C. de, *Spain* 48 B11
Faverges, *France* 21 C10
Favignana, *Italy* 42 E5
Favignana, I., *Italy* 42 E5
Fawcett, Pt., *Australia* 92 B5
Fawn ➤, *Canada* 104 A2
Fawnskin, *U.S.A.* 111 L10
Faxaflói, *Iceland* 8 D2
Faxälven ➤, *Sweden* 10 A10
Faya-Largeau, *Chad* 79 E9
Fayd, *Si. Arabia* 70 E4
Faydiyah, *Egypt* 80 H8
Fayence, *France* 21 E10
Fayette, *Ala., U.S.A.* 115 J2
Fayette, *Mo., U.S.A.* 112 F8
Fayetteville, *Ark., U.S.A.* .. 113 G7
Fayetteville, *N.C., U.S.A.* .. 115 H6
Fayetteville, *Tenn., U.S.A.* . 115 H2
Fayón, *Spain* 38 D5
Fazao-Malfakassa △, *Togo* 83 D5
Fazilka, *India* 68 D6
Fazilpur, *Pakistan* 68 E4
Feale ➤, *Ireland* 12 D2
Feather ➤, *U.S.A.* 108 G3
Feather Falls, *U.S.A.* 110 F5
Featherston, *N.Z.* 91 J5
Featherstone, *Zimbabwe* 87 F3
Fécamp, *France* 18 C7
Fedala = Mohammedia, *Morocco* 78 B4
Federación, *Argentina* 126 C4
Federal, *Argentina* 128 C5

Federal Capital Terr. □, *Nigeria* 83 D6
Federal Way, *U.S.A.* 110 C4
Fedeshkūh, *Iran* 71 D7
Fehérgyarmat, *Hungary* 28 C7
Fehmarn, *Germany* 24 A7
Fehmarn Bælt, *Europe* 11 K5
Fehmarn Belt = Fehmarn Bælt,
 Europe 11 K5
Fei Xian, *China* 57 G9
Feijó, *Brazil* 124 E4
Feilding, *N.Z.* 91 J5
Feira de Santana, *Brazil* 125 F11
Feixi, *China* 59 B11
Feixiang, *China* 56 F8
Fejér □, *Hungary* 28 C3
Fejø, *Denmark* 11 K5
Feke, *Turkey* 72 D6
Fekete ➤, *Hungary* 28 E3
Felanitx, *Spain* 48 B10
Feldbach, *Austria* 26 E8
Feldberg, *Baden-W., Germany* . 25 H3
Feldberg,
 Mecklenburg-Vorpommern,
 Germany 24 B9
Feldkirch, *Austria* 26 D2
Feldkirchen, *Austria* 26 E7
Felipe Carrillo Puerto, *Mexico* 119 D7
Felixburg, *Zimbabwe* 89 B5
Felixstowe, *U.K.* 15 F9
Felletin, *France* 20 C6
Fellingsbro, *Sweden* 10 E9
Felton, *U.S.A.* 110 H4
Feltre, *Italy* 41 B8
Femer Bælt = Fehmarn Bælt,
 Europe 11 K5
Femø, *Denmark* 11 K5
Femunden, *Norway* 9 E14
Fen He ➤, *China* 56 G6
Fene, *Spain* 36 B2
Fenelon Falls, *Canada* 116 B6
Fener Burnu, *Turkey* 47 E9
Feneroa, *Ethiopia* 81 E4
Feng Xian, *Jiangsu, China* ... 56 G9
Feng Xian, *Shaanxi, China* ... 56 H4
Fengári, *Greece* 45 F9
Fengcheng, *Jiangxi, China* ... 59 C10
Fengcheng, *Liaoning, China* .. 57 D13
Fengfeng, *China* 56 F8
Fenggang, *China* 58 D6
Fenghua, *China* 59 C13
Fenghuang, *China* 58 D7
Fengkai, *China* 59 F8
Fengle, *China* 59 B9
Fengning, *China* 56 D9
Fengqing, *China* 58 E2
Fengqiu, *China* 56 G8
Fengrun, *China* 57 E10
Fengshan, *Guangxi Zhuangzu,*
 China 58 E7
Fengshan, *Guangxi Zhuangzu,*
 China 58 E6
Fengshan, *Taiwan* 59 F13
Fengshun, *China* 59 F11
Fengtai, *Anhui, China* 59 A11
Fengtai, *Beijing, China* 56 E9
Fengxian, *China* 59 B13
Fengxiang, *China* 56 G4
Fengxin, *China* 59 C10
Fengyang, *China* 57 H9
Fengyi, *China* 58 E3
Fengyüan, *Taiwan* 59 E13
Fengzhen, *China* 56 D7
Feno, C. de, *France* 21 G12
Fenoarivo, *Fianarantsoa, Madag.* 89 C8
Fenoarivo, *Madag.* 89 C8
Fenoarivo Afovoany, *Madag.* .. 89 B8
Fenoarivo Atsinanana, *Madag.* 89 B8
Fens, The, *U.K.* 14 E7
Fensmark, *Denmark* 11 J5
Fenton, *U.S.A.* 114 D4
Fenxi, *China* 56 F6
Fenyang, *China* 56 F6
Fenyi, *China* 59 D10
Feodosiya, *Ukraine* 33 K8
Fère-Champenoise, *France* 19 D10
Fère-en-Tardenois, *France* ... 19 C10
Ferentino, *Italy* 41 G10
Ferfer, *Somali Rep.* 75 F4
Fergana = Farghona, *Uzbekistan* 52 E8
Fergus, *Canada* 116 C4
Fergus Falls, *U.S.A.* 112 B6
Feričanci, *Croatia* 28 E2
Ferihegy, Budapest ✈ (BUD),
 Hungary 28 C4
Ferkéssédougou, *Ivory C.* 82 D3
Ferlach, *Austria* 26 E7
Ferland, *Canada* 104 B2
Ferlo, Vallée du, *Senegal* ... 82 B2
Ferlo-Nord △, *Senegal* 82 B2
Ferlo-Sud △, *Senegal* 82 B2
Fermanagh □, *U.K.* 12 B4
Fermo, *Italy* 41 E10
Fermont, *Canada* 105 B6
Fermoselle, *Spain* 36 D4
Fermoy, *Ireland* 12 D3
Fernán Núñez, *Spain* 37 H6
Fernández, *Argentina* 126 B3
Fernandina Beach, *U.S.A.* 115 K5
Fernando de Noronha, *Brazil* . 125 D12
Fernando Póo = Bioko, *Eq. Guin.* 83 E6
Ferndale, *U.S.A.* 110 B4
Fernie, *Canada* 102 D5
Fernlees, *Australia* 94 C4
Fernley, *U.S.A.* 108 G4
Ferozepore = Firozpur, *India* 68 D6
Férrai, *Greece* 45 F10
Ferrandina, *Italy* 43 B9
Ferrara, *Italy* 41 D8

Ferrato, C., *Italy* 42 C2
Ferreira do Alentejo, *Portugal* 37 G2
Ferreñafe, *Peru* 124 E3
Ferrerías, *Spain* 48 B11
Ferret, C., *France* 20 D2
Ferrette, *France* 19 E14
Ferriday, *U.S.A.* 113 K9
Ferriere, *Italy* 40 D6
Ferrières, *France* 19 D9
Ferro, Capo, *Italy* 42 A2
Ferrol, *Spain* 36 B2
Ferron, *U.S.A.* 109 G8
Ferrutx, C., *Spain* 48 B10
Ferryland, *Canada* 105 C9
Fertile, *U.S.A.* 112 B6
Fertőszentmiklós, *Hungary* ... 28 C1
Fertotavi △, *Hungary* 28 C1
Fès, *Morocco* 78 B5
Fessenden, *U.S.A.* 112 B5
Festus, *U.S.A.* 112 F9
Feté Bowé, *Senegal* 82 C2
Feteşti, *Romania* 29 F12
Fethiye, *Turkey* 47 E11
Fethiye Körfezi, *Turkey* 47 E10
Fetlar, *U.K.* 13 A8
Feuilles ➤, *Canada* 101 C12
Feurs, *France* 21 C8
Fez = Fès, *Morocco* 78 B5
Fezzan, *Libya* 79 C8
Fiambalá, *Argentina* 126 B2
Fianarantsoa, *Madag.* 89 C8
Fianarantsoa □, *Madag.* 89 B8
Fiche, *Ethiopia* 81 F4
Fichtelgebirge, *Germany* 25 E7
Fichtelgebirge △, *Germany* ... 25 E8
Ficksburg, *S. Africa* 89 D4
Fidenza, *Italy* 40 D7
Fiditi, *Nigeria* 83 D5
Field ➤, *Australia* 94 C2
Field I., *Australia* 92 B5
Fieni, *Romania* 29 E10
Fier, *Albania* 44 F3
Fierzë, *Albania* 44 D4
Fife □, *U.K.* 13 E5
Fife □, *U.K.* 13 E5
Fife Ness, *U.K.* 13 E6
Fifth Cataract, *Sudan* 80 D3
Figari, *France* 21 G13
Figeac, *France* 20 D6
Figeholm, *Sweden* 11 G10
Figline Valdarno, *Italy* 41 E8
Figtree, *Zimbabwe* 87 G2
Figueira Castelo Rodrigo,
 Portugal 36 E4
Figueira da Foz, *Portugal* ... 36 E2
Figueiró dos Vinhos, *Portugal* 36 F2
Figueres, *Spain* 38 C7
Figuig, *Morocco* 78 B5
Fihaonana, *Madag.* 89 B8
Fiherenana, *Madag.* 89 C8
Fiherenana ➤, *Madag.* 89 C7
Fiji ■, *Pac. Oc.* 91 C8
Fik, *Ethiopia* 81 F5
Fika, *Nigeria* 83 C7
Filabres, Sierra de los, *Spain* 37 H8
Filabusi, *Zimbabwe* 89 C4
Filadélfia, *Italy* 43 D9
Fil'akovo, *Slovak Rep.* 27 C12
Filey, *U.K.* 14 C7
Filey B., *U.K.* 14 C7
Filfla, *Malta* 49 D1
Filiaşi, *Romania* 29 F8
Filiátes, *Greece* 46 B2
Filiatrá, *Greece* 46 D3
Filicudi, *Italy* 43 D7
Filingué, *Niger* 83 C5
Filiouri ➤, *Greece* 45 E9
Filipstad, *Sweden* 10 E8
Filisur, *Switz.* 25 J5
Fillmore, *Calif., U.S.A.* 111 L8
Fillmore, *Utah, U.S.A.* 109 G7
Filótion, *Greece* 47 D7
Filottrano, *Italy* 41 E10
Filtu, *Ethiopia* 81 F5
Fina △, *Mali* 82 C3
Finale Emília, *Italy* 41 D8
Finale Lígure, *Italy* 40 D5
Fiñana, *Spain* 37 H8
Finch, *Canada* 117 A9
Finch Hatton, *Australia* 94 K6
Findhorn ➤, *U.K.* 13 D5
Findlay, *U.S.A.* 114 E4
Finger L., *Canada* 104 B1
Finger Lakes, *U.S.A.* 117 D8
Fíngoè, *Mozam.* 87 E3
Finike, *Turkey* 47 E12
Finike Körfezi, *Turkey* 47 E12
Finiq, *Albania* 44 G4
Finistère □, *France* 18 D3
Finisterre = Fisterra, *Spain* 36 C1
Finisterre, C. = Fisterra, C., *Spain* 36 C1
Finke, *Australia* 94 D1
Finke Gorge △, *Australia* 92 D5
Finland ■, *Europe* 8 E22
Finland, G. of, *Europe* 9 G21
Finlay ➤, *Canada* 102 B3
Finley, *Australia* 95 F4
Finley, *U.S.A.* 112 B6
Finn ➤, *Ireland* 12 B4
Finnerödja, *Sweden* 11 F8
Finnigan, Mt., *Australia* 94 B4
Finniss, C., *Australia* 95 E1
Finnmark, *Norway* 8 B20
Finnsnes, *Norway* 8 B18
Finspång, *Sweden* 11 F9
Finsteraarhorn, *Switz.* 25 J4
Finsterwalde, *Germany* 24 D9
Fiora ➤, *Italy* 41 F8
Fiordland △, *N.Z.* 91 L1
Fiorenzuola d'Arda, *Italy* ... 40 D6
Fīq, *Syria* 74 C4

Firat = Furāt, Nahr al →, Asia .. 70 D5
Fire Island ○, U.S.A. 117 F11
Firebag →, Canada 103 B6
Firebaugh, U.S.A. 110 J6
Firedrake L., Canada 103 A8
Firenze, Italy 41 E8
Firenze Amerigo Vespucci ✈ (FLR), Italy 40 E8
Firenze Pisa ✈ (PSA), Italy ... 40 E7
Firenzuola, Italy 41 D8
Firk, Sha'ib →, Iraq 70 D5
Firmi, France 20 D6
Firminy, France 21 C8
Firozabad, India 69 F8
Firozpur, India 68 D6
Firozpur-Jhirka, India 68 F7
Fīrūzābād, Iran 71 D7
Fīrūzkūh, Iran 71 C7
Firvale, Canada 102 C3
Fish →, Namibia 88 D2
Fish →, S. Africa 88 E3
Fish River Canyon, Namibia ... 88 D2
Fisher, Australia 93 F5
Fisher B., Canada 103 C9
Fishers I., U.S.A. 117 E13
Fishguard, U.K. 15 E3
Fishing L., Canada 103 C9
Fishkill, U.S.A. 117 E11
Fismes, France 19 C10
Fisterra, Spain 36 C1
Fisterra, C., Spain 36 C1
Fitchburg, U.S.A. 117 D13
Fitz Roy, Argentina 128 F3
Fitzgerald, Canada 102 B6
Fitzgerald, U.S.A. 115 K4
Fitzgerald River △, Australia .. 93 F3
Fitzmaurice →, Australia 92 B5
Fitzroy →, Queens., Australia .. 94 C5
Fitzroy →, W. Austral., Australia 92 C3
Fitzroy, Mte., Argentina 128 F2
Fitzroy Crossing, Australia 92 C4
Fitzwilliam I., Canada 116 A3
Fiuggi, Italy 41 G10
Fiume = Rijeka, Croatia 41 C11
Fiumicino, Roma ✈ (FCO), Italy 41 G9
Five Points, U.S.A. 110 J6
Fivizzano, Italy 40 D7
Fizi, Dem. Rep. of the Congo ... 86 C2
Fjällbacka, Sweden 11 F5
Fjärdhundra, Sweden 10 E10
Fjellerup, Denmark 11 H4
Fjerritslev, Denmark 11 G3
Fjugesta, Sweden 10 E8
Flagstaff, U.S.A. 109 J8
Flagstaff L., U.S.A. 115 C10
Flaherty I., Canada 104 A4
Flåm, Norway 9 F12
Flambeau →, U.S.A. 112 C9
Flamborough Hd., U.K. 14 C7
Fläming, Germany 24 C8
Flaming Gorge ○, U.S.A. 108 F9
Flaming Gorge Reservoir, U.S.A. 108 F9
Flamingo, Teluk, Indonesia 63 F9
Flanders = Flandre, Europe ... 19 B9
Flandre, Europe 19 B9
Flandre-Occidentale = West-Vlaanderen □, Belgium ... 17 D2
Flandre-Orientale = Oost-Vlaanderen □, Belgium ... 17 C3
Flandreau, U.S.A. 112 C6
Flanigan, U.S.A. 110 E7
Flannan Is., U.K. 13 C1
Flåsjön, Sweden 8 D16
Flat →, Canada 102 A3
Flathead L., U.S.A. 108 C7
Flattery, C., Australia 94 A4
Flattery, C., U.S.A. 110 B2
Flatwoods, U.S.A. 114 F4
Fleetwood, U.K. 14 D4
Fleetwood, U.S.A. 117 F9
Flekkefjord, Norway 9 G12
Flemington, U.S.A. 116 E2
Flen, Sweden 10 E10
Flensburg, Germany 24 A5
Flers, France 18 D6
Flesherton, Canada 116 B4
Flesko, Tanjung, Indonesia 63 D6
Fleurance, France 20 E4
Fleurier, Switz. 25 J2
Fleurieu Pen., Australia 95 F2
Flevoland □, Neths. 17 B5
Flin Flon, Canada 103 C8
Flinders →, Australia 94 B3
Flinders B., Australia 93 F2
Flinders Group, Australia 94 A3
Flinders I., S. Austral., Australia . 95 E1
Flinders I., Tas., Australia 95 G4
Flinders Ranges, Australia 95 E2
Flinders Reefs, Australia 94 B4
Flint, U.K. 14 D4
Flint, U.S.A. 114 D4
Flint →, U.S.A. 115 K3
Flint I., Kiribati 97 J12
Flintshire □, U.K. 14 D4
Fliseryd, Sweden 11 G10
Flix, Spain 38 D5
Flixecourt, France 19 B9
Floby, Sweden 11 F7
Floda, Sweden 11 G6
Flodden, U.K. 14 B5
Flogny-la-Chapelle, France ... 19 E10
Floodwood, U.S.A. 112 B8
Flora, U.S.A. 114 F1
Florac, France 20 D7
Florala, U.S.A. 115 K2
Florence = Firenze, Italy 41 E8
Florence, Ala., U.S.A. 115 H2
Florence, Ariz., U.S.A. 109 K8
Florence, Colo., U.S.A. 112 F2
Florence, Oreg., U.S.A. 108 E1
Florence, S.C., U.S.A. 115 H6

Florence, L., Australia 95 D2
Florencia, Colombia 124 C3
Florennes, Belgium 17 D4
Florensac, France 20 E7
Florenville, Belgium 17 E5
Flores, Guatemala 120 C2
Flores, Indonesia 63 F6
Flores I., Canada 102 D3
Flores Sea, Indonesia 63 F6
Floresti, Moldova 29 C13
Floresville, U.S.A. 113 L5
Floriano, Brazil 125 E10
Florianópolis, Brazil 127 B6
Florida, Cuba 120 B4
Florida, Uruguay 127 C4
Florida □, U.S.A. 115 L5
Florida, Straits of, U.S.A. 120 B4
Florida B., U.S.A. 120 B3
Florida Keys, U.S.A. 115 N5
Florídia, Italy 43 E8
Flórina, Greece 44 F5
Flórina □, Greece 44 F5
Florø, Norway 9 F11
Flower Station, Canada 117 A8
Flowerpot I., Canada 116 A3
Floydada, U.S.A. 113 J4
Fluk, Indonesia 63 E7
Flúmen →, Spain 38 D4
Flumendosa →, Italy 42 C2
Fluminimaggiore, Italy 42 C1
Flushing = Vlissingen, Neths. .. 17 C3
Fluviá →, Spain 38 C8
Flying Fish, C., Antarctica 5 D15
Foam Lake, Canada 103 C8
Foča, Bos.-H. 44 C2
Foça, Turkey 47 C8
Fochabers, U.K. 13 D5
Focșani, Romania 29 E12
Fódécontéa, Guinea 82 C2
Fogang, China 59 F9
Fóggia, Italy 43 A8
Foggo, Nigeria 83 C6
Foglia →, Italy 41 E9
Fogo, Canada 105 C9
Fogo I., Canada 105 C9
Fohnsdorf, Austria 26 D7
Föhr, Germany 24 A4
Foia, Portugal 37 H2
Foix, France 20 F5
Fojnica, Bos.-H. 28 G2
Fokino, Russia 32 F8
Fokís □, Greece 46 C4
Fokku, Nigeria 83 C5
Folda, Nord-Trøndelag, Norway 8 D14
Folda, Nordland, Norway 8 C16
Földeák, Hungary 28 D5
Folégandros, Greece 46 E6
Foley, Botswana 88 C4
Foley, U.S.A. 115 K2
Foleyet, Canada 104 C3
Folgefonni, Norway 9 F12
Foligno, Italy 41 F9
Folkestone, U.K. 15 F9
Folkston, U.S.A. 115 K5
Follansbee, U.S.A. 116 F4
Follónica, Italy 40 F7
Follónica, G. di, Italy 40 F7
Folsom L., U.S.A. 110 G5
Foltești, Romania 29 E13
Fond-du-Lac, Canada 103 B7
Fond du Lac, U.S.A. 112 D10
Fond-du-Lac →, Canada 103 B7
Fonda, U.S.A. 117 D10
Fondi, Italy 42 A6
Fonfría, Spain 36 D4
Fongafale, Tuvalu 96 H9
Fonni, Italy 42 B2
Fonsagrada = A Fonsagrada, Spain 36 B3
Fonseca, G. de, Cent. Amer. ... 120 D2
Font-Romeu-Odeillo-Via, France 20 F5
Fontaine-Française, France 19 E12
Fontainebleau, France 19 D9
Fontana, U.S.A. 111 L9
Fontas →, Canada 102 B4
Fonte Boa, Brazil 124 D5
Fontem, Cameroon 83 D6
Fontenay-le-Comte, France 20 B3
Fontenelle Reservoir, U.S.A. .. 108 E8
Fontur, Iceland 8 C6
Fonyód, Hungary 28 D2
Foochow = Fuzhou, China 59 D12
Foping, China 56 H5
Forbach, France 19 C13
Forbes, Australia 95 E4
Forbesganj, India 69 F12
Forcados, Nigeria 83 D6
Forcados →, Nigeria 83 D6
Forcalquier, France 21 E9
Forchheim, Germany 25 F7
Ford City, Calif., U.S.A. 111 K7
Ford City, Pa., U.S.A. 116 F5
Førde, Norway 9 F11
Ford's Bridge, Australia 95 D4
Fordyce, U.S.A. 113 J8
Forécariah, Guinea 82 D2
Forel, Mt., Greenland 98 C16
Foremost, Canada 102 D6
Forest, Canada 116 C3
Forest, U.S.A. 113 J10
Forest City, Iowa, U.S.A. 112 D8
Forest City, N.C., U.S.A. 115 H5
Forest City, Pa., U.S.A. 117 E9
Forestburg, Canada 102 C6
Foreste Casentinesi-Monte Falterona-Campigna △, Italy . 41 E8
Foresthill, U.S.A. 110 F6
Forestier Pen., Australia 95 G4
Forestville, Canada 105 C6
Forestville, Calif., U.S.A. 110 G4

Forestville, N.Y., U.S.A. 116 D5
Forêt d'Orient ○, France 19 D11
Forez, Mts. du, France 20 C7
Forfar, U.K. 13 E6
Forillon △, Canada 105 C7
Forks, U.S.A. 110 C2
Forksville, U.S.A. 117 E8
Forlì, Italy 41 D9
Forman, U.S.A. 112 B6
Formazza, Italy 40 B5
Formby Pt., U.K. 14 D4
Formentera, Spain 48 C7
Formentor, C. de, Spain 48 B10
Former Yugoslav Republic of Macedonia = Macedonia ■, Europe 44 E5
Fórmia, Italy 42 A6
Formígine, Italy 40 D7
Formosa = Taiwan ■, Asia ... 59 F13
Formosa, Argentina 126 B4
Formosa, Brazil 125 G9
Formosa □, Argentina 126 B4
Formosa, Serra, Brazil 125 F8
Formosa B. = Ungwana B., Kenya 86 C5
Fornells, Spain 48 A11
Fornos de Algodres, Portugal .. 36 E3
Fornovo di Taro, Italy 40 D7
Føroyar, Atl. Oc. 8 F9
Forres, U.K. 13 D5
Forrest, Australia 93 F4
Forrest, Mt., Australia 93 D4
Forrest City, U.S.A. 113 H9
Fors, Sweden 10 D10
Forsayth, Australia 94 B3
Forshaga, Sweden 10 E7
Förslöv, Sweden 11 H6
Forsmo, Sweden 10 A11
Forssa, Finland 9 F20
Forst, Germany 24 D10
Forsvik, Sweden 11 F8
Forsyth, U.S.A. 108 C10
Fort Abbas, Pakistan 68 E5
Fort Albany, Canada 104 B3
Fort Ann, U.S.A. 117 C11
Fort Assiniboine, Canada 102 C6
Fort Augustus, U.K. 13 D4
Fort Beaufort, S. Africa 88 E4
Fort Benton, U.S.A. 108 C8
Fort Bragg, U.S.A. 108 G2
Fort Bridger, U.S.A. 108 F8
Fort Chipewyan, Canada 103 B6
Fort Clatsop ○, U.S.A. 110 D3
Fort Collins, U.S.A. 112 E2
Fort-Coulonge, Canada 104 C4
Fort Covington, U.S.A. 117 B10
Fort Davis, U.S.A. 113 K3
Fort Defiance, U.S.A. 109 J9
Fort-de-France, Martinique .... 120 c
Fort Dodge, U.S.A. 112 D7
Fort Edward, U.S.A. 117 C11
Fort Erie, Canada 116 D6
Fort Fairfield, U.S.A. 115 B12
Fort Frances, Canada 103 D10
Fort Franklin = Déline, Canada . 100 B7
Fort Garland, U.S.A. 109 H11
Fort George = Chisasibi, Canada 104 B4
Fort Good Hope, Canada 100 B7
Fort Hancock, U.S.A. 109 L11
Fort Hope, Canada 104 B2
Fort Irwin, U.S.A. 111 K10
Fort Kent, U.S.A. 115 B11
Fort Klamath, U.S.A. 108 E3
Fort Laramie, U.S.A. 112 D2
Fort Lauderdale, U.S.A. 115 M5
Fort Liard, Canada 102 A4
Fort Liberté, Haiti 121 C5
Fort Lupton, U.S.A. 112 E2
Fort MacKay, Canada 102 B6
Fort Macleod, Canada 102 D6
Fort McMurray, Canada 102 B6
Fort McPherson, Canada 100 B6
Fort Madison, U.S.A. 112 E9
Fort Meade, U.S.A. 115 M5
Fort Morgan, U.S.A. 112 E3
Fort Myers, U.S.A. 115 M5
Fort Nelson, Canada 102 B4
Fort Nelson →, Canada 102 B4
Fort Norman = Tulita, Canada .. 100 B7
Fort Payne, U.S.A. 115 H3
Fort Peck, U.S.A. 108 B10
Fort Peck Dam, U.S.A. 108 C10
Fort Peck L., U.S.A. 108 C10
Fort Pierce, U.S.A. 115 M5
Fort Pierre, U.S.A. 112 C4
Fort Plain, U.S.A. 117 D10
Fort Portal, Uganda 86 B3
Fort Providence, Canada 102 A5
Fort Qu'Appelle, Canada 103 C8
Fort Resolution, Canada 102 A6
Fort Rixon, Zimbabwe 87 G2
Fort Ross, U.S.A. 110 G3
Fort Rupert = Waskaganish, Canada 104 B4
Fort St. James, Canada 102 C4
Fort St. John, Canada 102 B4
Fort Saskatchewan, Canada ... 102 C6
Fort Scott, U.S.A. 113 G7
Fort Severn, Canada 104 A2
Fort Shevchenko, Kazakhstan .. 35 H10
Fort Simpson, Canada 102 A4
Fort Smith, Canada 102 B6
Fort Smith, U.S.A. 113 H7
Fort Stockton, U.S.A. 113 K3
Fort Sumner, U.S.A. 113 H2
Fort Thompson, U.S.A. 112 C5
Fort Valley, U.S.A. 115 J4
Fort Vermilion, Canada 102 B5
Fort Walton Beach, U.S.A. 115 K2
Fort Wayne, U.S.A. 114 E3
Fort William, U.K. 13 E3

Fort Worth, U.S.A. 113 J6
Fort Yates, U.S.A. 112 B4
Fort Yukon, U.S.A. 100 B5
Fortaleza, Brazil 125 D11
Forteau, Canada 105 B8
Fortescue →, Australia 92 D2
Forth →, U.K. 13 E5
Forth, Firth of, U.K. 13 E6
Fortore →, Italy 41 G12
Fortrose, U.K. 13 D4
Fortuna, Spain 39 G3
Fortuna, Calif., U.S.A. 108 F1
Fortuna, N. Dak., U.S.A. 112 A3
Fortune, Canada 105 C8
Fortune B., Canada 105 C8
Forūr, Iran 71 E7
Fos-sur-Mer, France 21 E8
Foshan, China 59 F9
Fosna, Norway 8 E14
Fosnavåg, Norway 9 E11
Foso, Ghana 83 D4
Fossano, Italy 40 D4
Fossil, U.S.A. 108 D3
Fossil Butte ○, U.S.A. 108 F8
Fossombrone, Italy 41 E9
Foster →, Canada 103 B7
Fosters Ra., Australia 94 C1
Fostoria, U.S.A. 114 E4
Fotadrevo, Madag. 89 C8
Fouesnant, France 18 E2
Fougères, France 18 D5
Foul Pt., Sri Lanka 66 Q12
Foula, U.K. 13 A6
Foulalaba, Mali 82 C3
Foulness I., U.K. 15 F8
Foulpointe, Madag. 89 B8
Foulweather, C., U.S.A. 106 B2
Foumban, Cameroon 83 D7
Foumbot, Cameroon 83 D7
Foundiougne, Senegal 82 C1
Fountain, U.S.A. 112 F2
Fountain Springs, U.S.A. 111 K8
Fourchambault, France 19 E10
Fouriesburg, S. Africa 88 D4
Fourmies, France 19 B11
Fournás, Greece 46 B3
Foúrnoi, Greece 47 D8
Fours, France 19 F10
Fourth Cataract, Sudan 80 D3
Fouta Djalon, Guinea 82 C2
Foux, Cap-à-, Haiti 121 C5
Foveaux Str., N.Z. 91 M2
Fowey, U.K. 15 G3
Fowler, Calif., U.S.A. 110 J7
Fowler, Colo., U.S.A. 112 F3
Fowlers B., Australia 93 F5
Fowman, Iran 71 B6
Fox →, Canada 103 B10
Fox Creek, Canada 102 C5
Fox Lake, Canada 102 B6
Fox Valley, Canada 103 C7
Foxboro, U.S.A. 117 D13
Foxdale, Australia 94 J6
Foxe Basin, Canada 101 B12
Foxe Chan., Canada 101 B11
Foxe Pen., Canada 101 B12
Foxen, Sweden 10 E5
Foxton, N.Z. 91 J5
Foyle, Lough, U.K. 12 A4
Foynes, Ireland 12 D2
Foz, Spain 36 B3
Foz do Cunene, Angola 88 B1
Foz do Iguaçu, Brazil 127 B5
Frackville, U.S.A. 117 F8
Fraga, Spain 38 D5
Fraile Muerto, Uruguay 127 C5
Fram Basin, Arctic ...... 4 A
Framingham, U.S.A. 117 D13
Frampol, Poland 31 H9
Franca, Brazil 125 H9
Francavilla al Mare, Italy 41 F11
Francavilla Fontana, Italy 43 B10
France ■, Europe 7 F6
Frances, Australia 95 F3
Frances →, Canada 102 A3
Frances L., Canada 102 A3
Franceville, Gabon 84 E2
Franche-Comté □, France 19 F12
Francis Case, L., U.S.A. 112 D5
Francisco Beltrão, Brazil 127 B5
Francisco I. Madero, Coahuila, Mexico 118 B4
Francisco I. Madero, Durango, Mexico 118 C4
Francistown, Botswana 89 C4
Francofonte, Italy 43 E7
François, Canada 105 C8
François L., Canada 102 C3
François Peron △, Australia ... 93 E1
Franeker, Neths. 17 A5
Frank Hann △, Australia 93 F3
Frankado, Djibouti 81 E5
Frankenberg, Germany 24 D4
Frankenhöhe ○, Germany 25 F6
Frankenthal, Germany 25 F5
Frankenwald, Germany 25 E7
Frankford, S. Africa 89 D4
Frankford, Canada 116 B7
Frankfort, Ind., U.S.A. 114 E2
Frankfort, Kans., U.S.A. 112 F6
Frankfort, Ky., U.S.A. 114 F3
Frankfort, N.Y., U.S.A. 117 C9
Frankfurt, Brandenburg, Germany 24 C10
Frankfurt, Hessen, Germany ... 25 E4
Frankfurt ✈ (FRA), Germany . 25 E4
Fränkische Alb, Germany 25 F7
Fränkische Rezat →, Germany . 25 F7
Fränkische Saale →, Germany . 25 E5
Fränkische Schweiz, Germany . 25 F7

Frankische Schweiz-Veldensteiner Forst ○, Germany 25 F7
Frankland →, Australia 93 G2
Franklin, Ky., U.S.A. 115 G2
Franklin, La., U.S.A. 113 L9
Franklin, Mass., U.S.A. 117 D13
Franklin, N.H., U.S.A. 117 C13
Franklin, Nebr., U.S.A. 112 E5
Franklin, Pa., U.S.A. 116 E5
Franklin, Va., U.S.A. 115 G7
Franklin, W. Va., U.S.A. 114 F6
Franklin B., Canada 100 B7
Franklin D. Roosevelt L., U.S.A. 108 B4
Franklin-Gordon Wild Rivers △, Australia 95 G4
Franklin I., Antarctica 5 D11
Franklin L., U.S.A. 108 F6
Franklin Mts., Canada 100 B7
Franklin Str., Canada 100 A10
Franklinton, U.S.A. 113 K9
Franklinville, U.S.A. 116 D6
Franks Pk., U.S.A. 108 E9
Frankston, Australia 95 F4
Frånö, Sweden 10 B11
Fransfontein, Namibia 88 C2
Fränsta, Sweden 10 B10
Frantsa Iosifa, Zemlya, Russia .. 52 A6
Franz, Canada 104 C3
Franz Josef Land = Frantsa Iosifa, Zemlya, Russia 52 A6
Franz Josef Strauss, München ✈ (MUC), Germany 25 G7
Franzburg, Germany 24 A8
Frascati, Italy 41 G9
Fraser, U.S.A. 116 D2
Fraser →, B.C., Canada 102 D4
Fraser →, Nfld. & L., Canada .. 105 A7
Fraser, Mt., Australia 93 E2
Fraser I., Australia 95 D5
Fraser Lake, Canada 102 C4
Fraserburg, S. Africa 88 E3
Fraserburgh, U.K. 13 D6
Fraserdale, Canada 104 C3
Frashër, Albania 44 F4
Frătești, Romania 29 G10
Frauenfeld, Switz. 25 H4
Fray Bentos, Uruguay 126 C4
Fray Jorge △, Chile 126 C1
Frechilla, Spain 36 C6
Fredericia, Denmark 11 J3
Frederick, Md., U.S.A. 114 F7
Frederick, Okla., U.S.A. 113 H5
Frederick, S. Dak., U.S.A. 112 C5
Fredericksburg, Pa., U.S.A. ... 117 F8
Fredericksburg, Tex., U.S.A. .. 113 K5
Fredericksburg, Va., U.S.A. ... 114 F7
Fredericktown, Mo., U.S.A. ... 113 G9
Fredericktown, Ohio, U.S.A. .. 116 F2
Frederico I. Madero, Presa, Mexico 118 B3
Frederico Westphalen, Brazil .. 127 B5
Fredericton, Canada 105 C6
Fredericton Junction, Canada .. 105 C6
Frederiksborg Amtskommune □, Denmark 11 J6
Frederikshåb = Paamiut, Greenland 101 B15
Frederikshamn = Hamina, Finland 9 F22
Frederikshavn, Denmark 11 G4
Frederikssund, Denmark 11 J6
Frederiksted, U.S. Virgin Is. ... 121 C7
Frederiksværk, Denmark 11 J6
Fredonia, Ariz., U.S.A. 109 H7
Fredonia, Kans., U.S.A. 113 G7
Fredonia, N.Y., U.S.A. 116 D5
Fredriksberg, Sweden 10 D8
Fredrikstad, Norway 9 G14
Free State □, S. Africa 88 D4
Freehold, U.S.A. 117 F10
Freel Peak, U.S.A. 110 G7
Freeland, U.S.A. 117 E9
Freels, C., Canada 105 C9
Freeman, Calif., U.S.A. 111 K9
Freeman, S. Dak., U.S.A. 112 D6
Freeport, Bahamas 120 A4
Freeport, Ill., U.S.A. 112 D10
Freeport, N.Y., U.S.A. 117 F11
Freeport, Ohio, U.S.A. 116 F3
Freeport, Pa., U.S.A. 116 F5
Freeport, Tex., U.S.A. 113 L7
Freetown, S. Leone 82 D2
Frégate, L. de la, Canada 104 B5
Fregenal de la Sierra, Spain ... 37 G4
Fregene, Italy 41 G9
Fréhel, C., France 18 D4
Freiberg, Germany 24 E9
Freibourg = Fribourg, Switz. .. 25 J3
Freiburg, Baden-W., Germany . 25 H3
Freiburg, Niedersachsen, Germany 24 B5
Freilassing, Germany 25 H8
Freire, Chile 128 D2
Freirina, Chile 126 B1
Freising, Germany 25 G7
Freistadt, Austria 26 C7
Freital, Germany 24 D9
Fréjus, France 21 E10
Fremantle, Australia 93 F2
Fremont, Calif., U.S.A. 110 H4
Fremont, Mich., U.S.A. 114 D3
Fremont, Nebr., U.S.A. 112 E6
Fremont, Ohio, U.S.A. 114 E4
Fremont →, U.S.A. 109 G8
French Camp, U.S.A. 110 H5
French Cays = Plana Cays, Bahamas 121 B5
French Creek →, U.S.A. 116 E5
French Guiana ☑, S. Amer. 125 C8

French Polynesia ⊘, *Pac. Oc.* ... 97 K13
Frenchman Cr. ➤, *N. Amer.* 108 B10
Frenchman Cr. ➤, *U.S.A.* 112 E4
Frenštát pod Radhoštěm,
  Czech Rep. 27 B11
Fresco, *Ivory C.* 82 D3
Fresco ➤, *Brazil* 125 E8
Freshfield, C., *Antarctica* 5 C10
Fresnay-sur-Sarthe, *France* 18 D7
Fresnillo, *Mexico* 118 C4
Fresno, *U.S.A.* 110 J7
Fresno Alhandiga, *Spain* 36 E5
Fresno Reservoir, *U.S.A.* 108 B9
Freudenstadt, *Germany* 25 G4
Frévent, *France* 19 B9
Frew ➤, *Australia* 94 C2
Frewsburg, *U.S.A.* 116 D5
Freycinet △, *Australia* 95 A4
Freycinet Pen., *Australia* 95 G4
Freyming-Merlebach, *France* ... 19 C13
Freyung, *Germany* 25 G9
Fria, *Guinea* 82 C2
Fria, C., *Namibia* 88 B1
Friant, *U.S.A.* 110 J7
Frías, *Argentina* 126 B2
Fribourg, *Switz.* 25 J3
Fribourg □, *Switz.* 25 J3
Fridafors, *Sweden* 11 H8
Friday Harbor, *U.S.A.* 110 B3
Friedberg, *Bayern, Germany* ... 25 G6
Friedberg, *Hessen, Germany* ... 25 E4
Friedens, *U.S.A.* 116 F6
Friedland, *Germany* 24 B9
Friedrichshafen, *Germany* 25 H5
Friedrichskoog, *Germany* 24 A4
Friedrichstadt, *Germany* 24 A5
Friendship, *U.S.A.* 116 D6
Friesach, *Austria* 26 E7
Friesack, *Germany* 24 C8
Friesland □, *Neths.* 17 A5
Friesoythe, *Germany* 24 B3
Friggesund, *Sweden* 10 C10
Frillesås, *Sweden* 11 G6
Frinnaryd, *Sweden* 11 G8
Frio ➤, *U.S.A.* 113 L5
Frio, C., *Brazil* 122 F6
Friol, *Spain* 36 B3
Friona, *U.S.A.* 113 H3
Fristad, *Sweden* 11 G6
Fritch, *U.S.A.* 113 H4
Fritsla, *Sweden* 11 G6
Fritzlar, *Germany* 24 D5
Friuli-Venézia Giulia □, *Italy* ... 41 B9
Frobisher B., *Canada* 101 B13
Frobisher Bay = Iqaluit, *Canada* 101 B13
Frobisher L., *Canada* 103 B7
Frohavet, *Norway* 8 E13
Frohnleiten, *Austria* 26 D8
Frolovo, *Russia* 34 F6
Frombork, *Poland* 30 D6
Frome, *U.K.* 15 F5
Frome ➤, *U.K.* 15 G5
Frome, L., *Australia* 95 E2
Frome, The ➤, *Australia* 95 D2
Frómista, *Spain* 36 C6
Front Range, *U.S.A.* 106 C5
Front Royal, *U.S.A.* 114 F6
Fronteira, *Portugal* 37 F3
Frontera, *Canary Is.* 48 G2
Frontera, *Mexico* 119 D6
Fronteras, *Mexico* 118 A3
Frontignan, *France* 20 E7
Frosinone, *Italy* 42 A6
Frostburg, *U.S.A.* 114 F6
Frostisen, *Norway* 8 B17
Frouard, *France* 19 D13
Frövi, *Sweden* 10 E9
Frøya, *Norway* 8 E13
Frumoasa, *Romania* 29 D10
Frunze = Bishkek, *Kyrgyzstan* . 52 E8
Frunzivka, *Ukraine* 29 C14
Fruška Gora, *Serbia & M.* ... 28 E4
Fruška Gora △, *Serbia & M.* ... 44 A3
Frutal, *Brazil* 125 H9
Frutigen, *Switz.* 25 J3
Frýdek-Místek, *Czech Rep.* ... 27 B11
Frýdlant, *Czech Rep.* 26 A8
Fryeburg, *U.S.A.* 117 B14
Fryvaldov = Jeseník, *Czech Rep.* 27 A10
Fthiótis □, *Greece* 46 C4
Fu Jiang ➤, *China* 58 C6
Fu Xian = Wafangdian, *China* . 57 E11
Fu Xian, *China* 56 G5
Fu'an, *China* 59 D12
Fubian, *China* 58 B4
Fucécchio, *Italy* 40 E7
Fucheng, *China* 56 F9
Fuchou = Fuzhou, *China* 59 D12
Fuchū, *Japan* 55 G6
Fuchuan, *China* 59 E8
Fuchun Jiang ➤, *China* 59 B13
Fúcino, Piana del, *Italy* 41 F10
Fuding, *China* 59 D13
Fuencaliente, *Canary Is.* 48 F2
Fuencaliente, *Spain* 37 G6
Fuencaliente, Pta., *Canary Is.* . 48 F2
Fuengirola, *Spain* 37 J6
Fuenlabrada, *Spain* 36 E7
Fuensalida, *Spain* 36 E6
Fuente-Álamo, *Spain* 39 G3
Fuente-Álamo de Murcia, *Spain* 39 H3
Fuente de Cantos, *Spain* 37 G4
Fuente del Maestre, *Spain* 37 G4
Fuente el Fresno, *Spain* 37 F7
Fuente Obejuna, *Spain* 37 G5
Fuente Palmera, *Spain* 37 H5
Fuentes de Andalucía, *Spain* ... 37 H5
Fuentes de Ebro, *Spain* 38 D4
Fuentes de León, *Spain* 37 G4
Fuentes de Oñoro, *Spain* 36 E4
Fuentesaúco, *Spain* 36 D5

Fuerte ➤, *Mexico* 118 B3
Fuerte Olimpo, *Paraguay* 126 A4
Fuerteventura, *Canary Is.* 48 F6
Fuerteventura ✈ (FUE),
  Canary Is. 48 F6
Fufeng, *China* 56 G5
Fuga I., *Phil.* 61 B4
Fugou, *China* 58 D2
Fugong, *China* 58 D2
Fugou, *China* 56 G8
Fugu, *China* 56 E6
Fuhai, *China* 60 B3
Fuḥaymī, *Iraq* 70 C4
Fuhlsbüttel, Hamburg ✈ (HAM),
  Germany 24 B5
Fuji, *Japan* 55 G9
Fuji-Hakone-Izu △, *Japan* ... 55 G9
Fuji-San, *Japan* 55 G9
Fuji-Yoshida, *Japan* 55 G9
Fujian □, *China* 59 E12
Fujinomiya, *Japan* 55 G9
Fujisawa, *Japan* 55 G9
Fujiyama, Mt. = Fuji-San, *Japan* . 55 G9
Fukagawa, *Japan* 54 C11
Fukien = Fujian □, *China* ... 59 E12
Fukuchiyama, *Japan* 55 G7
Fukue-Shima, *Japan* 55 H4
Fukui, *Japan* 55 F8
Fukui □, *Japan* 55 G8
Fukuoka, *Japan* 55 H5
Fukuoka □, *Japan* 55 H5
Fukushima, *Japan* 54 F10
Fukushima □, *Japan* 54 F10
Fukuyama, *Japan* 55 G6
Fulacunda, *Guinea-Biss.* 82 C1
Fulda, *Germany* 24 E5
Fulda ➤, *Germany* 24 D5
Fulford Harbour, *Canada* 110 B3
Fuliang, *China* 59 C11
Fullerton, *Calif., U.S.A.* 111 M9
Fullerton, *Nebr., U.S.A.* 112 E6
Fulongquan, *China* 57 B13
Fülöpszállás, *Hungary* 28 D4
Fulton, *Mo., U.S.A.* 112 F9
Fulton, *N.Y., U.S.A.* 117 C8
Fuluälven ➤, *Sweden* 10 C7
Fulufjället, *Sweden* 10 C6
Fumay, *France* 19 C11
Fumel, *France* 20 D4
Fumin, *China* 58 E4
Funabashi, *Japan* 55 G10
Funafuti = Fongafale, *Tuvalu* . 96 H9
Funäsdalen, *Sweden* 10 B6
Funchal, *Madeira* 48 D3
Funchal ✈ (FNC), *Madeira* ... 48 D3
Fundación, *Colombia* 124 A4
Fundão, *Portugal* 36 E3
Fundu Moldovei, *Romania* ... 29 C10
Fundulea, *Romania* 29 F11
Fundy, *Canada* 105 C6
Fundy, B. of, *Canada* 105 D6
Funhalouro, *Mozam.* 89 C5
Funing, *Hebei, China* 57 E10
Funing, *Jiangsu, China* 57 H10
Funing, *Yunnan, China* 58 F5
Funiu Shan, *China* 56 H7
Funsi, *Ghana* 82 C4
Funtua, *Nigeria* 83 C6
Fuping, *Hebei, China* 56 E8
Fuping, *Shaanxi, China* 56 G5
Fuqing, *China* 59 E12
Fuquan, *China* 58 D6
Furano, *Japan* 54 C11
Furāt, Nahr al ➤, *Asia* 70 D5
Fürg, *Iran* 71 D7
Furmanov, *Russia* 34 B5
Furmanovo, *Kazakhstan* 34 F9
Furnás, *Spain* 48 B8
Furnas, Reprêsa de, *Brazil* ... 127 A6
Furneaux Group, *Australia* ... 95 G4
Furqlus, *Syria* 74 A6
Fürstenau, *Germany* 24 C3
Fürstenberg, *Germany* 24 B9
Fürstenfeld, *Austria* 26 D9
Fürstenfeldbruck, *Germany* ... 25 G7
Fürstenwalde, *Germany* 24 C10
Fürth, *Germany* 25 F6
Furth im Wald, *Germany* 25 F8
Furtwangen, *Germany* 25 G4
Furudal, *Sweden* 10 C9
Furukawa, *Japan* 54 E10
Furulund, *Sweden* 11 J7
Fury and Hecla Str., *Canada* . 101 B11
Fusagasuga, *Colombia* 124 C4
Fuscaldo, *Italy* 43 C9
Fushan, *Shandong, China* 57 F11
Fushan, *Shanxi, China* 56 G6
Fushë Arrëz, *Albania* 44 D4
Fushë Krujë, *Albania* 44 E3
Fushun, *Liaoning, China* 57 D12
Fushun, *Sichuan, China* 58 C5
Fusong, *China* 57 C14
Füssen, *Germany* 25 H6
Fustic, *Barbados* .... 121 g
Fusui, *China* 58 F6
Futog, *Serbia & M.* 28 E4
Futuna, *Wall. & F. Is.* 91 B8
Fuwa, *Egypt* 80 H7
Fuxian Hu, *China* 58 E4
Fuxin, *China* 57 C11
Fuyang, *Anhui, China* 56 H8
Fuyang, *Zhejiang, China* 59 B12
Fuyang He ➤, *China* 56 E9
Fuying Dao, *China* 59 D13
Fuyu, *China* 57 B13
Fuyuan, *China* 58 E5
Füzesgyarmat, *Hungary* 28 C6
Fuzhou, *China* 59 D12
Fylde, *U.K.* 14 D5
Fyn, *Denmark* 11 J4
Fyne, L., *U.K.* 13 F3
Fyns Amtskommune □, *Denmark* 11 J4
Fynshav, *Denmark* 11 K3

G

Ga, *Ghana* 82 D4
Gaanda, *Nigeria* 83 C7
Gabarin, *Nigeria* 83 C7
Gabas ➤, *France* 20 E3
Gabela, *Angola* 84 G2
Gabès, *Tunisia* 79 B8
Gabès, G. de, *Tunisia* 79 B8
Gabgaba, W. ➤, *Egypt* 80 C3
Gabin, *Poland* 31 F6
Gabon ■, *Africa* 84 E2
Gaborone, *Botswana* 88 C4
Gabriels, *U.S.A.* 117 B10
Gabrovo, *Bulgaria* 45 D9
Gacé, *France* 18 D7
Gäch Sār, *Iran* 71 B6
Gachsārān, *Iran* 71 D6
Gacko, *Bos.-H.* 44 C2
Gadag, *India* 66 M9
Gadamai, *Sudan* 81 D4
Gadap, *Pakistan* 68 G2
Gadarwara, *India* 69 H8
Gadebusch, *Germany* 24 B7
Gadein, *Sudan* 81 F2
Gadhada, *India* 68 J4
Gádor, Sierra de, *Spain* 37 J8
Gadra, *Pakistan* 68 G4
Gadsden, *U.S.A.* 115 H3
Gadwal, *India* 66 L10
Gadyach = Hadyach, *Ukraine* . 33 G8
Găeşti, *Romania* 29 F10
Gaeta, *Italy* 42 A6
Gaeta, G. di, *Italy* 42 A6
Gaffney, *U.S.A.* 115 H5
Gafsa, *Tunisia* 78 B7
Gagarawa, *Nigeria* 83 C6
Gagaria, *India* 68 G4
Gagarin, *Russia* 32 E8
Gağğauzia □, *Moldova* 29 D13
Gaggenau, *Germany* 25 G4
Gaghamni, *Sudan* 81 E2
Gagino, *Russia* 34 C7
Gagliano del Capo, *Italy* 43 C11
Gagnef, *Sweden* 10 D9
Gagnoa, *Ivory C.* 82 D3
Gagnon, *Canada* 105 B6
Gagnon, L., *Canada* 103 A6
Gagra, *Georgia* 35 J5
Gahini, *Rwanda* 86 C3
Gahmar, *India* 69 G10
Gai Xian = Gaizhou, *China* ... 57 D12
Gaïdhouronísi, *Greece* 49 E7
Gail, *U.S.A.* 113 J4
Gail ➤, *Austria* 26 E6
Gaillac, *France* 20 E5
Gaillimh = Galway, *Ireland* ... 12 C2
Gaillon, *France* 18 C8
Gaines, *U.S.A.* 116 E7
Gainesville, *Fla., U.S.A.* 115 L4
Gainesville, *Ga., U.S.A.* 115 H4
Gainesville, *Mo., U.S.A.* 113 G8
Gainesville, *Tex., U.S.A.* 113 J6
Gainsborough, *U.K.* 14 D7
Gairdner, L., *Australia* 95 E2
Gairloch, *U.K.* 13 D3
Gairloch, L., *U.K.* 13 D3
Gaizhou, *China* 57 D12
Gaj, *Croatia* 28 E2
Gaj ➤, *Pakistan* 68 F2
Gakuch, *Pakistan* 69 A5
Galala, Gebel el, *Egypt* 80 J8
Galán, Cerro, *Argentina* 126 B2
Galana ➤, *Kenya* 86 C5
Galanta, *Slovak Rep.* 27 C10
Galapagar, *Spain* 36 E7
Galápagos = Colón, Arch. de,
  Ecuador 97 H18
Galashiels, *U.K.* 13 F6
Galatás, *Greece* 46 D5
Galați, *Romania* 29 E13
Galați □, *Romania* 29 E12
Galatia, *Turkey* 72 C5
Galatina, *Italy* 43 B11
Galátone, *Italy* 43 B11
Galax, *U.S.A.* 115 G5
Galaxídhion, *Greece* 46 C4
Galcaio, *Somali Rep.* 75 F4
Galdhøpiggen, *Norway* 9 F12
Galeana, *Chihuahua, Mexico* . 118 A3
Galeana, *Nuevo León, Mexico* . 118 A3
Galegu, *Sudan* 81 E4
Galela, *Indonesia* 63 D7
Galena, *U.S.A.* 100 B4
Galera ➤, *Spain* 39 H2
Galera Pt., *Trin. & Tob.* 121 D7
Galeota Pt., Trin. & Tob. 125 K16
Galera, *Spain* 39 H2
Galesburg, *U.S.A.* 112 E9
Galeton, *U.S.A.* 116 E7
Galga, *Ethiopia* 81 F4
Gali, *Georgia* 35 J5
Galicea Mare, *Romania* 29 F8
Galich, *Russia* 34 A6
Galiche, *Bulgaria* 44 C7
Galicia □, *Spain* 36 C3
Galičica △, *Macedonia* 44 E4
Galilee = Hagalil, *Israel* 74 C4
Galilee, L., *Australia* 94 C4
Galilee, Sea of = Yam Kinneret,
  Israel 74 C4
Galim, *Cameroon* 83 D7
Galina Pt., *Jamaica* .... 120 a
Galinoporni, *Cyprus* 49 D13
Galion, *U.S.A.* 116 F2
Galiuro Mts., *U.S.A.* 109 K8
Galiwinku, *Australia* 94 A2
Gallan Hd., *U.K.* 13 C1
Gallarate, *Italy* 40 C5

Gallatin, *U.S.A.* 115 G2
Galle, *Sri Lanka* 66 R12
Gállego ➤, *Spain* 38 D4
Gallegos ➤, *Argentina* 128 G3
Galletti ➤, *Ethiopia* 81 F5
Galley Hd., *Ireland* 12 E3
Galliate, *Italy* 40 C5
Gallinas, Pta., *Colombia* 124 A4
Gallipoli = Gelibolu, *Turkey* . 45 F10
Gallípoli, *Italy* 43 B10
Gallipolis, *U.S.A.* 114 F4
Gällivare, *Sweden* 8 C19
Gallneukirchen, *Austria* 26 C7
Gällö, *Sweden* 10 B9
Gallo, C., *Italy* 42 D6
Gallocanta, L. de, *Spain* 38 E3
Galloo I., *U.S.A.* 117 C8
Galloway, *U.K.* 13 F4
Galloway ⌒, *U.K.* 13 F4
Galloway, Mull of, *U.K.* 13 G4
Gallup, *U.S.A.* 109 J9
Gallur, *Spain* 38 D3
Galoya, *Sri Lanka* 66 Q12
Galt, *U.S.A.* 110 G5
Galten, *Denmark* 11 H3
Galtür, *Austria* 26 E3
Galty Mts., *Ireland* 12 D3
Galtymore, *Ireland* 12 D3
Galva, *U.S.A.* 112 E9
Galve de Sorbe, *Spain* 38 D1
Galveston, *U.S.A.* 113 L7
Galveston B., *U.S.A.* 113 L7
Gálvez, *Argentina* 126 C3
Galway, *Ireland* 12 C2
Galway □, *Ireland* 12 C2
Galway B., *Ireland* 12 C2
Gam ➤, *Vietnam* 64 B5
Gamagōri, *Japan* 55 G8
Gamari, L., *Ethiopia* 81 E5
Gamawa, *Nigeria* 83 C7
Gamay, *Phil.* 61 E6
Gamba, *China* 83 C4
Gambat, *Pakistan* 68 F3
Gambela, *Ethiopia* 81 F3
Gambela □, *Ethiopia* 81 F3
Gambela △, *Ethiopia* 81 F3
Gambela-Hizboch □, *Ethiopia* . 81 F3
Gambhir ➤, *India* 68 F6
Gambia ■, *W. Afr.* 82 C1
Gambia ➤, *W. Afr.* 82 C1
Gambier, *U.S.A.* 116 F2
Gambier, C., *Australia* 92 B5
Gambier Is., *Australia* 95 C9
Gambo, *Canada* 105 C9
Gamboli, *Pakistan* 68 E3
Gamboma, *Congo* 84 E3
Gamka ➤, *S. Africa* 88 E3
Gamkab ➤, *Namibia* 88 D2
Gamla Uppsala, *Sweden* 10 E11
Gamlakarleby = Kokkola, *Finland* . 8 E20
Gamleby, *Sweden* 11 G10
Gammon ➤, *Canada* 103 C9
Gammon Ranges △, *Australia* . 95 E2
Gamo-Gofa, *Ethiopia* 81 F4
Gamou, *Niger* 83 C6
Gamtoos ➤, *S. Africa* 88 E4
Gan, *France* 20 E3
Gan Goriama, Mts., *Cameroon* . 83 D7
Gan Jiang ➤, *China* 59 C11
Ganado, *U.S.A.* 109 J9
Gananita, *Sudan* 80 D3
Gananoque, *Canada* 117 B8
Ganāveh, *Iran* 71 D6
Gäncä, *Azerbaijan* 35 K8
Gancheng, *China* 64 C7
Gand = Gent, *Belgium* 17 C3
Ganda, *Angola* 85 G2
Gandajika, *Dem. Rep. of
  the Congo* 84 F4
Gandak ➤, *India* 69 G11
Gandava, *Pakistan* 68 E2
Gander, *Canada* 105 C9
Gander L., *Canada* 105 C9
Ganderkesee, *Germany* 24 B4
Ganderowe Falls, *Zimbabwe* . 87 F2
Gandesa, *Spain* 38 D5
Gandhi Sagar, *India* 68 G6
Gandhinagar, *India* 68 H5
Gandi, *Nigeria* 83 C6
Gandía, *Spain* 39 G4
Gandino, *Italy* 40 C6
Gando, Pta., *Canary Is.* 48 G4
Gandole, *Nigeria* 83 D7
Gâneb, *Mauritania* 82 B2
Ganedidalem = Gani, *Indonesia* . 63 E7
Ganetti, *Sudan* 80 D3
Ganga ➤, *India* 69 H14
Ganga Sagar, *India* 69 J13
Gangan ➤, *India* 69 E8
Ganganagar, *India* 68 E5
Gangapur, *India* 68 F7
Gangara, *Niger* 83 C6
Gangaw, *Burma* 67 H19
Gangdisê Shan, *China* 67 D12
Ganges = Ganga ➤, *India* ... 69 H14
Ganges, *Canada* 102 D4
Ganges, *France* 20 E7
Ganges, Mouths of the, *India* . 69 J14
Gânghester, *Sweden* 11 G7
Gangi, *Italy* 43 E7
Gangoh, *India* 68 E7
Gangotri, *India* 69 D8
Gangtok, *India* 67 F16
Gangu, *China* 56 G3
Gangyao, *China* 57 B14
Gani, *Indonesia* 63 E7
Ganj, *India* 69 F8
Ganluc, *China* 58 C4
Gannat, *France* 19 F10
Gannett Peak, *U.S.A.* 108 E9
Ganquan, *China* 56 F5

Gänserndorf, *Austria* 27 C9
Ganshui, *China* 58 C6
Gansu □, *China* 56 G3
Ganta, *Liberia* 82 D3
Gantheaume, C., *Australia* 95 F2
Gantheaume B., *Australia* 93 E1
Gantsevichi = Hantsavichy,
  Belarus 33 F4
Ganye, *Nigeria* 83 D7
Ganyem = Genyem, *Indonesia* . 63 E10
Ganyu, *China* 57 G10
Ganzhou, *China* 59 E10
Gao, *Mali* 83 B4
Gao Xian, *China* 58 C5
Gao'an, *China* 59 C10
Gaochun, *China* 59 B12
Gaohe, *China* 59 F9
Gaohebu, *China* 59 B11
Gaokeng, *China* 59 D9
Gaolan Dao, *China* 59 G9
Gaoligong Shan, *China* 58 E2
Gaomi, *China* 57 F10
Gaoming, *China* 59 F9
Gaoping, *China* 56 G7
Gaotang, *China* 56 F9
Gaoua, *Burkina Faso* 82 C4
Gaoual, *Guinea* 82 C2
Gaoxiong = Kaohsiung, *Taiwan* . 59 F13
Gaoyang, *China* 56 E8
Gaoyao, *China* 59 F9
Gaoyou, *China* 59 A12
Gaoyou Hu, *China* 57 H10
Gaoyuan, *China* 57 F9
Gaozhou, *China* 59 G8
Gap, *France* 21 D10
Gapan, *Phil.* 61 D4
Gapat ➤, *India* 69 G10
Gapuwiyak, *Australia* 94 A2
Gar, *China* 60 C2
Garabogazköl Aylagy,
  Turkmenistan 52 E6
Garachico, *Canary Is.* 48 F3
Garachiné, *Panama* 120 E4
Garafia, *Canary Is.* 48 F2
Garah, *Australia* 95 D4
Garajonay, *Canary Is.* 48 F2
Garamba ➤, *Dem. Rep. of
  the Congo* 86 B2
Garango, *Burkina Faso* 83 C4
Garanhuns, *Brazil* 125 E11
Garautha, *India* 69 G8
Garawe, *Liberia* 82 E3
Garba Tula, *Kenya* 86 B4
Garberville, *U.S.A.* 108 F2
Garbiyang, *India* 69 D9
Garbsen, *Germany* 24 C5
Gard □, *France* 21 D8
Gard ➤, *France* 21 E8
Garda, L. di, *Italy* 40 C7
Gardanne, *France* 21 E9
Gårdby, *Sweden* 11 H10
Garde L., *Canada* 103 A7
Gardelegen, *Germany* 24 C7
Garden City, *Ga., U.S.A.* ... 115 J5
Garden City, *Kans., U.S.A.* . 113 G4
Garden City, *Tex., U.S.A.* . 113 K4
Garden Grove, *U.S.A.* 111 M9
Gardez, *Afghan.* 68 C3
Gardhíki, *Greece* 46 C3
Gardiner, *Maine, U.S.A.* ... 115 C11
Gardiner, *Mont., U.S.A.* ... 108 D8
Gardiners I., *U.S.A.* 117 E12
Gardner, *U.S.A.* 117 D13
Gardner Canal, *Canada* 102 C3
Gardnerville, *U.S.A.* 110 G7
Gardno, Jezioro, *Poland* 30 D4
Gardo, *Somali Rep.* 75 F4
Gardone Val Trómpia, *Italy* ... 40 C7
Gárdony, *Hungary* 28 C3
Garešnica, *Croatia* 41 C13
Garéssio, *Italy* 40 D5
Garey, *U.S.A.* 111 L6
Garfield, *U.S.A.* 108 C5
Garforth, *U.K.* 14 D6
Gargaliánoi, *Greece* 46 D3
Gargan, Mt., *France* 20 C5
Gargano, △, *Italy* 41 G12
Gargett, *Australia* 94 K6
Gargouna, *Mali* 83 B5
Gargždai, *Lithuania* 30 C8
Garibaldi △, *Canada* 102 D4
Gariep, L., *S. Africa* 88 E4
Garies, *S. Africa* 88 E2
Garigliano ➤, *Italy* 42 A6
Garissa, *Kenya* 86 C4
Garkida, *Nigeria* 83 C7
Garko, *Nigeria* 83 C6
Garland, *Tex., U.S.A.* 113 J6
Garland, *Utah, U.S.A.* 108 F7
Garlasco, *Italy* 40 C5
Garliava, *Lithuania* 30 D10
Garlin, *France* 20 E3
Garm, *Tajikistan* 52 F8
Garmāb, *Iran* 71 C8
Garmisch-Partenkirchen,
  Germany 25 H7
Garmo, Qullai = Kommunizma,
  Pik, *Tajikistan* 52 F8
Garmsār, *Iran* 71 C7
Garner, *U.S.A.* 112 D8
Garnett, *U.S.A.* 112 F7
Garo Hills, *India* 69 G14
Garoe, *Somali Rep.* 75 F4
Garonne ➤, *France* 20 B3
Garonne, Canal Latéral à la,
  France 20 D4
Garoowe = Garoe, *Somali Rep.* . 75 F4
Garot, *India* 68 G6
Garoua, *Cameroon* 83 D7
Garpenberg, *Sweden* 10 D10
Garphyttan, *Sweden* 10 E8

Garrauli, *India* 69 G8
Garrel, *Germany* 24 C4
Garrigues, *France* 20 E7
Garrison, Mont., U.S.A. 108 C7
Garrison, N. Dak., U.S.A. 112 B4
Garrison Res. = Sakakawea, L.,
   U.S.A. 112 B4
Garron Pt., *U.K.* 12 A6
Garrovillas, *Spain* 37 F4
Garrucha, *Spain* 39 H3
Garry →, *U.K.* 13 E5
Garry, L., *Canada* 100 B9
Garsen, *Kenya* 86 C5
Gärsnäs, *Sweden* 11 J8
Garson L., *Canada* 103 B6
Garstang, *U.K.* 14 D5
Gartempe →, *France* 20 B4
Gartz, *Germany* 24 B10
Garu, *Ghana* 83 C4
Garu, *India* 69 H11
Garub, *Namibia* 88 D2
Garut, *Indonesia* 63 G12
Garvão, *Portugal* 37 H2
Garvie Mts., *N.Z.* 91 L2
Garwa = Garoua, *Cameroon* 83 D7
Garwa, *India* 69 G10
Garwolin, *Poland* 31 G8
Gary, *U.S.A.* 114 E2
Garz, *Germany* 24 A9
Garzê, *China* 58 B3
Garzón, *Colombia* 124 C3
Gas-San, *Japan* 54 E10
Gasan Kuli = Esenguly,
   Turkmenistan 52 F6
Gascogne, *France* 20 E4
Gascogne, G. de, *Europe* 20 E2
Gascony = Gascogne, *France* .. 20 E4
Gascoyne →, *Australia* 93 D1
Gascoyne Junction, *Australia* . 93 E2
Gascueña, *Spain* 38 E2
Gash, Wadi →, *Ethiopia* 81 D4
Gash-Setit →, *Eritrea* 81 D4
Gashagar, *Nigeria* 83 C7
Gashaka, *Nigeria* 83 D7
Gashaka-Gumti △, *Nigeria* 83 D7
Gasherbrum, *Pakistan* 69 B7
Gashua, *Nigeria* 83 C7
Gasparillo, *Trin. & Tob.* ... 125 K15
Gaspé, *Canada* 105 C7
Gaspé, C., *Canada* 105 C7
Gaspé Pen. = Gaspésie, Pén. de
   la, *Canada* 105 C6
Gaspésie △, *Canada* 105 C6
Gaspésie, Pén. de la, *Canada* . 105 C6
Gassan, *Burkina Faso* 82 C4
Gassol, *Nigeria* 83 D7
Gasteiz = Vitoria-Gasteiz, *Spain* 38 C2
Gastonia, *U.S.A.* 115 H5
Gastoúni, *Greece* 46 D3
Gastoúri, *Greece* 46 B1
Gastre, *Argentina* 128 E3
Gästrikland, *Sweden* 10 D10
Gata, C., *Cyprus* 49 E12
Gata, C. de, *Spain* 39 J2
Gata, Sierra de, *Spain* 36 E4
Gataga →, *Canada* 102 B3
Gătaia, *Romania* 28 E6
Gatchina, *Russia* 32 C6
Gatehouse of Fleet, *U.K.* 13 G4
Gates, *U.S.A.* 116 C7
Gatesville, *U.S.A.* 113 K6
Gateway △, *U.S.A.* 117 F11
Gaths, *Zimbabwe* 87 G3
Gatico, *Chile* 126 A1
Gâtinais, *France* 19 D9
Gâtine, Hauteurs de, *France* . 20 B3
Gatineau, *Canada* 117 A9
Gatineau □, *Canada* 104 C4
Gatineau →, *Canada* 104 C4
Gattaran, *Phil.* 61 B4
Gattinara, *Italy* 40 C5
Gatton, *Australia* 95 D5
Gatun, L., *Panama* 120 E4
Gatwick, London ✈ (LGW), *U.K.* . 15 F7
Gatyana, *S. Africa* 89 E4
Gau, *Fiji* .... 91 a
Gaucín, *Spain* 37 J5
Gauer L., *Canada* 103 B9
Gauhati = Guwahati, *India* ... 67 F17
Gauja →, *Latvia* 9 H21
Gaula →, *Norway* 8 E14
Gauri Phanta, *India* 69 E9
Gausta, *Norway* 9 G13
Gauteng □, *S. Africa* 89 D4
Gāv Koshī, *Iran* 71 D8
Gāvakān, *Iran* 71 D7
Gavallai △, *Liberia* 82 D3
Gavarnie, *France* 20 F3
Gāvāter, *Iran* 71 E9
Gāvbandī, *Iran* 71 E7
Gavdhopoúla, *Greece* 49 E6
Gávdhos, *Greece* 49 E6
Gavi, *Italy* 40 D5
Gavião, *Portugal* 37 F3
Gaviota, *U.S.A.* 111 L6
Gävkhūnī, Bāţlāq-e, *Iran* 71 C7
Gävle, *Sweden* 10 D11
Gävleborgs län □, *Sweden* ... 10 C10
Gävlebukten, *Sweden* 10 D11
Gavorrano, *Italy* 40 F7
Gavray, *France* 18 D5
Gavrilov Yam, *Russia* 32 D10
Gávrion, *Greece* 46 D6
Gawachab, *Namibia* 88 D2
Gawilgarh Hills, *India* 66 J10
Gawler, *Australia* 95 E2
Gawu, *Nigeria* 83 D6
Gaxun Nur, *China* 60 B5
Gaya, *India* 69 G11
Gaya, *Niger* 83 C5
Gaya, *Nigeria* 83 C6

Gayéri, *Burkina Faso* 83 C5
Gaylord, *U.S.A.* 114 C3
Gayndah, *Australia* 95 D5
Gaysin = Haysyn, *Ukraine* 29 B14
Gayvoron = Hayvoron, *Ukraine* . 29 B14
Gaza, *Gaza Strip* 74 D3
Gaza □, *Mozam.* 89 C5
Gaza Strip ☑, *Asia* 74 D3
Gazanjyk, *Turkmenistan* 71 B7
Gazaoua, *Niger* 83 C6
Gāzbor, *Iran* 71 D8
Gazi, Dem. Rep. of the Congo .. 86 B1
Gaziantep, *Turkey* 70 B3
Gazimağosa = Famagusta, *Cyprus* 49 D12
Gazipaşa, *Turkey* 72 D5
Gbarnga, *Liberia* 82 D3
Gbekebo, *Nigeria* 83 D5
Gboko, *Nigeria* 83 D6
Gbongan, *Nigeria* 83 D5
Gcoverega, *Botswana* 88 B3
Gcuwa, *S. Africa* 89 E4
Gdańsk, *Poland* 30 D5
Gdansk ✈ (GDN), *Poland* 30 D5
Gdańska, Zatoka, *Poland* 30 D6
Gdov, *Russia* 9 G22
Gdynia, *Poland* 30 D5
Geba →, *Guinea-Biss.* 82 C1
Gebe, *Indonesia* 63 D7
Gebeciler, *Turkey* 47 C12
Gebeit Mine, *Sudan* 80 C4
Gebel Abyad, *Sudan* 80 D2
Gebel Iweibid, *Egypt* 80 H8
Gebze, *Turkey* 45 F13
Gecha, *Ethiopia* 81 F4
Gedaref, *Sudan* 81 E4
Gedaref □, *Sudan* 81 E4
Gediz, *Turkey* 47 B11
Gediz →, *Turkey* 47 C8
Gedo, *Ethiopia* 81 F4
Gèdre, *France* 20 F4
Gedser, *Denmark* 11 K5
Gedung, Pulau, *Malaysia* ..... 65 c
Geegully Cr. →, *Australia* ... 92 C3
Geel, *Belgium* 17 C4
Geelong, *Australia* 95 F3
Geelvink B. = Cenderwasih,
   Teluk, *Indonesia* 63 E9
Geelvink Chan., *Australia* ... 93 E1
Geesthacht, *Germany* 24 B6
Geidam, *Nigeria* 83 C7
Geikie →, *Canada* 103 B8
Geikie Gorge △, *Australia* ... 92 C4
Geilenkirchen, *Germany* 24 E2
Geili, *Sudan* 81 D3
Geisingen, *Germany* 25 H4
Geislingen, *Germany* 25 G5
Geistown, *U.S.A.* 116 F6
Geita, *Tanzania* 86 C3
Gejiu, *China* 58 F4
Gel →, *Sudan* 81 F2
Gel, Meydān-e, *Iran* 71 D7
Gel River, *Sudan* 81 F2
Gela, *Italy* 43 E7
Gela, G. di, *Italy* 43 F7
Gelahun, *Liberia* 82 D2
Gelang Patah, *Malaysia* ...... 65 d
Gelderland □, *Neths.* 17 B6
Geldern, *Germany* 24 D2
Geldrop, *Neths.* 17 C5
Geleen, *Neths.* 17 D5
Gelehun, *S. Leone* 82 D2
Gelembe, *Turkey* 47 B9
Gelemso, *Ethiopia* 81 F5
Gelendost, *Turkey* 72 C4
Gelendzhik, *Russia* 33 K10
Gelibolu, *Turkey* 45 F10
Gelibolu Yarımadası, *Turkey* . 45 F10
Gelidonya Burnu, *Turkey* 72 D4
Gelnhausen, *Germany* 25 E5
Gelnica, *Slovak Rep.* 27 C13
Gelsenkirchen, *Germany* 24 D3
Gelting, *Germany* 24 A5
Gelugur, *Malaysia* .... 65 c
Gemas, *Malaysia* 65 L4
Gembloux, *Belgium* 17 D4
Gembu, *Nigeria* 83 D7
Gemena, Dem. Rep. of the Congo . 84 D3
Gemerek, *Turkey* 70 B3
Gemla, *Sweden* 11 H8
Gemlik, *Turkey* 45 F13
Gemlik Körfezi, *Turkey* 45 F12
Gemona del Friuli, *Italy* ... 41 B10
Gemsa, *Egypt* 80 B3
Gemsbok △, *Botswana* 88 D3
Gemünden, *Germany* 25 E5
Genale →, *Ethiopia* 81 F4
Genç, *Turkey* 73 C9
Gençay, *France* 20 B4
Geneina, Gebel, *Egypt* 80 B3
General Acha, *Argentina* 126 D3
General Alvear, Buenos Aires,
   Argentina 126 D4
General Alvear, Mendoza,
   Argentina 126 D2
General Artigas, *Paraguay* .. 126 B4
General Belgrano, *Argentina* . 126 D4
General Bernardo O'Higgins,
   Antarctica 5 C18
General Cabrera, *Argentina* . 126 C3
General Cepeda, *Mexico* 118 B4
General Guido, *Argentina* ... 126 D4
General Juan Madariaga,
   Argentina 126 D4
General La Madrid, *Argentina* 126 D3
General MacArthur, *Phil.* 61 F6
General Martín Miguel de
   Güemes, Argentina 126 A3
General Paz, *Argentina* 126 B4
General Pico, *Argentina* 126 D3
General Pinedo, *Argentina* .. 126 B3
General Pinto, *Argentina* ... 126 C3
General Roca, *Argentina* 128 D3

General Santos, *Phil.* 61 H6
General Toshevo, *Bulgaria* .. 45 C12
General Trevino, *Mexico* 119 B5
General Trías, *Mexico* 118 B3
General Viamonte, *Argentina* 126 D3
General Villegas, *Argentina* 126 D3
Genesee, Idaho, U.S.A. 108 C5
Genesee, Pa., U.S.A. 116 E7
Genesee →, *U.S.A.* 116 C7
Geneseo, Ill., U.S.A. 112 E9
Geneseo, N.Y., U.S.A. 116 D7
Geneva = Genève, *Switz.* 25 J2
Geneva, Ala., U.S.A. 115 K3
Geneva, N.Y., U.S.A. 116 D8
Geneva, Nebr., U.S.A. 112 E6
Geneva, Ohio, U.S.A. 116 E4
Geneva, L. = Léman, L., *Europe* 19 F13
Geneva, L., *U.S.A.* 114 D1
Genève, *Switz.* 25 J2
Gengenbach, *Germany* 25 G4
Gengma, *China* 58 F2
Genichesk = Henichesk, *Ukraine* 33 J8
Genil →, *Spain* 37 H5
Genk, *Belgium* 17 D5
Genlis, *France* 19 E12
Gennargentu, Mti. del, *Italy* . 42 B2
Gennes, *France* 18 E6
Genoa = Génova, *Italy* 40 D5
Genoa, Australia 95 F4
Genoa, N.Y., U.S.A. 117 D8
Genoa, Nebr., U.S.A. 112 E6
Genoa, Nev., U.S.A. 110 F7
Génova, *Italy* 40 D5
Génova ✈ (GOA), *Italy* 40 D5
Génova, G. di, *Italy* 40 E6
Genriyetty, Ostrov, *Russia* .. 53 B16
Gent, *Belgium* 17 C3
Genteng, Bali, Indonesia 63 J17
Genteng, Jawa, Indonesia 63 G12
Genthin, *Germany* 24 C8
Genyem, *Indonesia* 63 E10
Genzano di Lucánia, *Italy* ... 43 B9
Genzano di Roma, *Italy* 41 G9
Geoagiu, *Romania* 29 E8
Geographe B., *Australia* 93 F2
Geographe Chan., *Australia* .. 93 D1
Geokchay = Göyçay, *Azerbaijan* 35 K8
Georg Forster, *Antarctica* 5 D3
Georg von Neumayer, *Antarctica* 5 D17
Georga, Zemlya, *Russia* 52 A5
George, S. Africa 105 A6
George →, *Canada* 105 A6
George, L., N.S.W., Australia . 95 F4
George, L., S. Austral., Australia 95 F3
George, L., W. Austral., Australia 92 D3
George, L., Uganda 86 B3
George, L., Fla., U.S.A. 115 L5
George, L., N.Y., U.S.A. 117 C11
George Gill Ra., *Australia* .. 92 D5
George Pt., *Australia* 94 J6
George River = Kangiqsualujjuaq,
   Canada 101 C13
George Sound, *N.Z.* 91 L1
George Town, Australia 95 G4
George Town, Bahamas 120 B4
George Town, Cayman Is. 120 C3
George Town, Malaysia .... 65 c
George V Land, *Antarctica* 5 C10
George VI Sound, *Antarctica* .. 5 D17
Georgetown, *U.S.A.* 113 L5
Georgetown = Janjanbureh,
   Gambia 82 C2
Georgetown, Australia 94 B3
Georgetown, Ont., Canada 116 C5
Georgetown, P.E.I., Canada .. 105 C7
Georgetown, Guyana 124 B7
Georgetown, Calif., U.S.A. .. 110 G6
Georgetown, Colo., U.S.A. .. 108 G11
Georgetown, Ky., U.S.A. 114 F3
Georgetown, N.Y., U.S.A. 117 D9
Georgetown, Ohio, U.S.A. 114 F4
Georgetown, S.C., U.S.A. 115 J6
Georgetown, Tex., U.S.A. 113 K6
Georgia □, *U.S.A.* 115 K5
Georgia ■, *Asia* 35 K6
Georgia, Str. of, *Canada* ... 102 D4
Georgian B., *Canada* 116 A4
Georgian Bay Islands △, *Canada* 116 B5
Georgina →, *Australia* 94 C2
Georgina I., *Canada* 116 B5
Georgiyevsk, *Russia* 35 H6
Georgsmarienhütte, *Germany* .. 24 C4
Gera, *Germany* 24 E8
Geraardsbergen, *Belgium* 17 D3
Geral, Serra, *Brazil* 127 B6
Geral de Goiás, Serra, *Brazil* 125 F9
Geraldine, *U.S.A.* 108 C8
Geraldton, Australia 93 E1
Geraldton, Canada 104 C2
Gérardmer, *France* 19 D13
Gerçüş, *Turkey* 73 D9
Gerede, *Turkey* 72 B5
Gerês, Sierra do, *Portugal* .. 36 D3
Gereshk, *Afghan.* 66 D4
Geretsried, *Germany* 25 H7
Gérgal, *Spain* 39 H2
Gerik, *Malaysia* 65 K3
Gering, *U.S.A.* 112 E3
Gerlach, *U.S.A.* 108 F4
Gerlachovský štít, Slovak Rep. . 27 B13
German Planina, *Macedonia* ... 44 D6
Germansen Landing, *Canada* .. 102 B4
Germantown, *U.S.A.* 113 M10
Germany ■, *Europe* 24 E6
Germencik, *Turkey* 47 D9
Germering, *Germany* 25 G7
Germersheim, *Germany* 25 F4
Germī, *Iran* 71 B6
Germiston, S. Africa 89 D4
Gernika-Lumo, *Spain* 38 B2
Gernsheim, *Germany* 25 F4
Gero, *Japan* 55 G8

Gerokgak, *Indonesia* 63 J17
Gerolzhofen, *Germany* 25 F6
Gerona = Girona, *Spain* 38 D7
Gerrard, *Canada* 102 C5
Gers □, *France* 20 E4
Gers →, *France* 20 D4
Gersfeld, *Germany* 24 E5
Gersthofen, *Germany* 25 G6
Gertak Sanggul, *Malaysia* .... 65 c
Gertak Sanggul, Tanjung,
   Malaysia .... 65 c
Gerung, *Indonesia* 63 K19
Gerzat, *France* 20 C7
Gerze, *Turkey* 72 B6
Geseke, *Germany* 24 D4
Geser, *Indonesia* 63 E8
Gesso →, *Italy* 40 D4
Getafe, *Spain* 36 E7
Getinge, *Sweden* 11 H6
Gettysburg, Pa., U.S.A. 114 F7
Gettysburg, S. Dak., U.S.A. . 112 C5
Getxo, *Spain* 38 B2
Getz Ice Shelf, *Antarctica* ... 5 D14
Gevaş, *Turkey* 73 C10
Gévaudan, *France* 20 D7
Gevgelija, *Macedonia* 44 E6
Gévora →, *Spain* 37 G4
Gewani, *Ethiopia* 81 E5
Gex, *France* 19 F13
Geyikli, *Turkey* 47 B8
Geyser, *U.S.A.* 108 C8
Geyserville, *U.S.A.* 110 G4
Geyve, *Turkey* 72 B4
Ghâbat el Arab = Wang Kai,
   Sudan 81 F2
Ghabeish, *Sudan* 81 E2
Ghaggar →, *India* 68 E6
Ghaghara →, *India* 69 G11
Ghaghara, *India* 69 G13
Ghagra →, *India* 69 H11
Ghagra, *India* 69 F9
Ghalla, Wadi el →, *Sudan* 81 E2
Ghana ■, *W. Afr.* 83 D4
Ghansor, *India* 69 H9
Ghanzi, *Botswana* 88 C3
Gharb el Istiwa'iya □, *Sudan* . 81 G3
Gharb Kordofân □, *Sudan* 81 E2
Ghardaïa, *Algeria* 78 B6
Ghârib, G., *Egypt* 80 B3
Gharig, *Sudan* 81 E2
Gharyān, *Libya* 79 B8
Ghat, *Libya* 79 D8
Ghatal, *India* 69 H12
Ghatampur, *India* 69 F9
Ghats, Eastern, *India* 66 N11
Ghats, Western, *India* 66 N9
Ghatsila, *India* 69 H12
Ghaţţī, Si. Arabia 70 D3
Ghawdex = Gozo, *Malta* 49 C1
Ghazal, Bahr el →, *Chad* 79 F9
Ghazâl, Bahr el →, *Sudan* 81 F3
Ghaziabad, *India* 68 E7
Ghazipur, *India* 69 G10
Ghazni, *Afghan.* 68 C3
Ghaznī □, *Afghan.* 66 C6
Ghedi, *Italy* 40 C7
Ghelari, *Romania* 28 E7
Ghent = Gent, *Belgium* 17 C3
Gheorghe Gheorghiu-Dej =
   Onești, Romania 29 D11
Gheorgheni, *Romania* 29 D10
Gherla, *Romania* 29 C8
Ghidigeni, *Romania* 29 D12
Ghilarza, *Italy* 42 B1
Ghimeș-Făget, *Romania* 29 D11
Ghīnah, Wādī al →, Si. Arabia . 70 D3
Ghisonaccia, *France* 21 F13
Ghisoni, *France* 21 F13
Ghizao, *Afghan.* 66 C1
Ghizar →, *Pakistan* 69 A5
Ghot Ogrein, *Egypt* 80 A2
Ghotaru, *India* 68 F4
Ghotki, *Pakistan* 68 E3
Ghowr □, *Afghan.* 66 C4
Ghudāf, W. al →, *Iraq* 70 C4
Ghudāmis, *Libya* 77 C7
Ghudāmis □, *Libya* 79 B8
Ghughri, *India* 69 H9
Ghugus, *India* 66 K11
Ghulam Mohammad Barrage,
   Pakistan 68 G3
Ghūrīān, *Afghan.* 66 B2
Gia Dinh, *Vietnam* 65 G6
Gia Lai = Plei Ku, *Vietnam* .. 64 F7
Gia Nghia, *Vietnam* 65 G6
Gia Ngoc, *Vietnam* 64 E7
Gia Vuc, *Vietnam* 64 E7
Giannutri, *Italy* 40 F8
Giant Forest, *U.S.A.* 110 J8
Giant Mts. = Krkonoše,
   Czech Rep. 26 A8
Giant Sequoia △, *U.S.A.* 110 K8
Giants Causeway, *U.K.* 12 A5
Gianyar, *Indonesia* 63 K18
Giarabub = Al Jaghbūb, *Libya* 79 C10
Giarre, *Italy* 43 E8
Giaveno, *Italy* 40 C4
Gibara, *Cuba* 120 B4
Gibb River, *Australia* 92 C4
Gibbon, *U.S.A.* 112 E5
Gibe →, *Ethiopia* 81 F4
Gibellina Nuova, *Italy* 42 E5
Gibeon, *Namibia* 88 D2
Gibraleón, *Spain* 37 H4
Gibraltar ☑, *Europe* 37 J5
Gibraltar, Str. of, *Medit. S.* 37 K5
Gibraltar Range △, *Australia* . 95 D5
Gibsons, *Canada* 102 D4
Gibsonville, *U.S.A.* 110 F6

Giddings, *U.S.A.* 113 K6
Gidole, *Ethiopia* 81 F4
Giebnegáisi = Kebnekaise,
   Sweden 8 C18
Gien, *France* 19 E9
Giengen, *Germany* 25 G6
Giessen, *Germany* 24 E4
Gīfān, *Iran* 71 B8
Gifatin, Geziret, *Egypt* 80 B3
Gifhorn, *Germany* 24 C6
Gift Lake, *Canada* 102 B5
Gifu, *Japan* 55 G8
Gifu □, *Japan* 55 G8
Gigant, *Russia* 35 G5
Giganta, Sa. de la, *Mexico* . 118 B2
Gigen, *Bulgaria* 45 C8
Gigha, *U.K.* 13 F3
Gíglio, *Italy* 40 F7
Gignac, *France* 20 E7
Gigüela →, *Spain* 37 F7
Gijón, *Spain* 36 B5
Gil I., *Canada* 102 C3
Gila →, *U.S.A.* 109 K6
Gila Bend, *U.S.A.* 109 K7
Gila Bend Mts., *U.S.A.* 109 K7
Gila Cliff Dwellings △, *U.S.A.* 109 K9
Gīlān □, *Iran* 71 B6
Gilău, *Romania* 29 D8
Gilbert →, *Australia* 94 B3
Gilbert Is., *Kiribati* 96 G9
Gilbert River, *Australia* 94 B3
Gilead, *U.S.A.* 117 B14
Gilf el Kebîr, Hadabat el, *Egypt* 80 C2
Gilford I., *Canada* 102 C3
Gilgandra, *Australia* 95 E4
Gilgil, *Kenya* 86 C4
Gilgit, *India* 69 B6
Gilgit →, *Pakistan* 69 B6
Gili →, *Mozam.* 87 F4
Gilimanuk, *Indonesia* 63 J17
Giljeva Planina, Serbia & M. . 103 B10
Gillam, *Canada* 103 B10
Gilleleje, *Denmark* 11 H6
Gillen, L., *Australia* 93 E3
Gilles, L., *Australia* 95 E2
Gillette, *U.S.A.* 112 C2
Gilliat, *Australia* 94 C3
Gillingham, *U.K.* 15 F8
Gilmer, *U.S.A.* 113 J7
Gilmore, L., *Australia* 93 F3
Gilo →, *Ethiopia* 81 F3
Gilort →, *Romania* 29 F8
Gilroy, *U.S.A.* 110 H5
Gimbi, *Ethiopia* 81 F4
Gimie, Mt, St. Lucia .... 121 f
Gimli, *Canada* 103 C9
Gimo, *Sweden* 10 D12
Gimone →, *France* 20 E5
Gimont, *France* 20 E4
Gin Gin, *Australia* 95 D5
Ginâh, *Egypt* 80 B3
Gineifa, *Egypt* 80 H8
Gingin, *Australia* 93 F2
Gingindlovu, S. Africa 89 D5
Ginir, *Ethiopia* 81 F5
Ginosa, *Italy* 43 B9
Ginzo de Limia = Xinzo de Limia,
   Spain 36 C3
Gióia, G. di, *Italy* 43 D8
Gióia del Colle, *Italy* 43 B9
Gióia Táuro, *Italy* 43 D8
Gioiosa Iónica, *Italy* 43 D9
Gioiosa Marea, *Italy* 43 D7
Gióna, Óros, *Greece* 46 C4
Giovi, Passo dei, *Italy* 40 D5
Giovinazzo, *Italy* 43 A9
Gir Hills, *India* 68 J4
Girab, *India* 68 F4
Girâfi, W. →, *Egypt* 74 F3
Giraltovce, Slovak Rep. 27 B14
Girard, Kans., U.S.A. 113 G7
Girard, Ohio, U.S.A. 116 E4
Girard, Pa., U.S.A. 116 E4
Girdle Ness, *U.K.* 13 D6
Giresun, *Turkey* 73 B8
Girga, *Egypt* 80 B3
Giri →, *India* 68 D7
Giridih, *India* 69 G12
Girifalco, *Italy* 43 D9
Girne = Kyrenia, *Cyprus* 49 D12
Giro, *Nigeria* 83 C5
Giromagny, *France* 19 E13
Giron = Kiruna, *Sweden* 8 C19
Girona, *Spain* 38 D7
Girona □, *Spain* 38 C7
Gironde □, *France* 20 D3
Gironde →, *France* 20 C2
Gironella, *Spain* 38 C6
Girraween △, *Australia* 95 D5
Giru, *Australia* 94 B4
Girvan, *U.K.* 13 F4
Gisborne, *N.Z.* 91 H7
Gisenyi, *Rwanda* 86 C2
Gislaved, *Sweden* 11 G7
Gisors, *France* 19 C8
Gitega, *Burundi* 86 C2
Giuba →, Somali Rep. 75 G3
Giugliano in Campania, *Italy* 43 B7
Giuliano, *Italy* 41 F10
Giurgeni, *Romania* 29 F12
Giurgiu, *Romania* 29 G10
Giurgiu □, *Romania* 29 F10
Giurgiuleşti, *Moldova* 29 E13
Give, *Denmark* 11 J3
Givet, *France* 19 B11
Givors, *France* 21 C8
Givry, *France* 19 F11
Giyon, *Ethiopia* 81 F4
Giza = El Gîza, *Egypt* 80 J7
Gizhiga, *Russia* 53 C17
Gizhiginskaya Guba, *Russia* . 53 C16
Giżycko, *Poland* 30 D8

Gizzeria, *Italy* 43 D9
Gjalicë e Lumës, Mal., *Albania* . 44 D4
Gjegjan, *Albania* 44 E4
Gjirokastër, *Albania* 44 F4
Gjøvik, *Norway* 9 F14
Gjuhës, Kep i, *Albania* 44 F3
Glace Bay, *Canada* 105 C8
Glacier △, *Canada* 102 C5
Glacier △, *U.S.A.* 108 B7
Glacier Bay △, *U.S.A.* 102 B1
Glacier Peak, *U.S.A.* 108 B3
Gladewater, *U.S.A.* 113 J7
Gladstone, *Queens., Australia* . 94 C5
Gladstone, *S. Austral., Australia* . 95 E2
Gladstone, *Canada* 103 C9
Gladstone, *U.S.A.* 114 C2
Gladwin, *U.S.A.* 114 D3
Glafsfjorden, *Sweden* 10 E6
Glagah, *Indonesia* 63 J17
Głogów Małopolski, *Poland* ... 31 H8
Gláma = Glomma →, *Norway* . 9 G14
Gláma, *Iceland* 8 D2
Glamis, *U.S.A.* 111 N11
Glamoč, *Bos.-H.* 41 D13
Glamorgan, Vale of □, *U.K.* ... 15 F4
Glamsbjerg, *Denmark* 11 J4
Glarus, *Switz.* 25 H5
Glarus □, *Switz.* 25 J5
Glasco, *Kans., U.S.A.* 112 F6
Glasco, *N.Y., U.S.A.* 117 D11
Glasgow, *U.K.* 13 F4
Glasgow, *Ky., U.S.A.* 114 G3
Glasgow, *Mont., U.S.A.* 108 B10
Glasgow, City of □, *U.K.* 13 F4
Glasgow International ✈ (GLA),
   U.K. 13 F4
Glaslyn, *Canada* 103 C7
Glastonbury, *U.K.* 15 F5
Glastonbury, *U.S.A.* 117 E12
Glauchau, *Germany* 24 E8
Glava, *Sweden* 10 E6
Glavice, *Croatia* 41 E13
Glazov, *Russia* 34 A11
Gleichen, *Canada* 102 C6
Gleisdorf, *Austria* 26 D8
Gleiwitz = Gliwice, *Poland* ... 31 H5
Glen, *U.S.A.* 117 B13
Glen Affric, *U.K.* 13 D3
Glen Canyon, *U.S.A.* 109 H8
Glen Canyon △, *U.S.A.* 109 H8
Glen Canyon Dam, *U.S.A.* 109 H8
Glen Coe, *U.K.* 13 E3
Glen Cove, *U.S.A.* 117 F11
Glen Garry, *U.K.* 13 D3
Glen Innes, *Australia* 95 D5
Glen Lyon, *U.S.A.* 117 E8
Glen Mor, *U.K.* 13 D4
Glen More, *U.K.* 13 D5
Glen Moriston, *U.K.* 13 D4
Glen Robertson, *Canada* 117 A10
Glen Spean, *U.K.* 13 E4
Glen Ullin, *U.S.A.* 112 B4
Glénan, Îs. de, *France* 18 E3
Glenariff △, *Ireland* 12 A5
Glencoe, *Canada* 116 D3
Glencoe, *S. Africa* 89 D5
Glencoe, *U.S.A.* 112 C7
Glendale, *Ariz., U.S.A.* 109 K7
Glendale, *Calif., U.S.A.* 111 L8
Glendale, *Zimbabwe* 87 F3
Glendive, *U.S.A.* 112 B2
Glendo, *U.S.A.* 112 D2
Glenelg →, *Australia* 95 F3
Glenfield, *U.S.A.* 117 C9
Glengarriff, *Ireland* 12 E2
Glenmorgan, *Australia* 95 D4
Glenn, *U.S.A.* 110 F4
Glennallen, *U.S.A.* 100 B5
Glennamaddy, *Ireland* 12 C3
Glenns Ferry, *U.S.A.* 108 E6
Glenore, *Australia* 94 B3
Glenreagh, *Australia* 95 E5
Glenrock, *U.S.A.* 108 E11
Glenrothes, *U.K.* 13 E5
Glens Falls, *U.S.A.* 117 C11
Glenside, *U.S.A.* 117 F9
Glenties, *Ireland* 12 B3
Glenveagh △, *Ireland* 12 A3
Glenville, *U.S.A.* 114 F5
Glenwood, *Canada* 105 C9
Glenwood, *Ark., U.S.A.* 113 H8
Glenwood, *Iowa, U.S.A.* 112 E7
Glenwood, *Minn., U.S.A.* 112 C7
Glenwood, *Wash., U.S.A.* 110 D5
Glenwood Springs, *U.S.A.* ... 108 G10
Glettinganes, *Iceland* 8 D7
Glifádha, *Greece* 46 D5
Glimåkra, *Sweden* 11 H8
Glina, *Croatia* 41 C13
Glinojeck, *Poland* 31 F7
Gliwice, *Poland* 31 H5
Globe, *U.S.A.* 109 K8
Glodeanu Siliștea, *Romania* . 29 F11
Glodeni, *Moldova* 29 C12
Glödnitz, *Austria* 26 E7
Gloggnitz, *Austria* 26 D8
Głogów, *Poland* 31 G3
Głogówek, *Poland* 31 H4
Glomma →, *Norway* 9 G14
Glorieuses, Is., *Ind. Oc.* ... 89 A8
Glóssa, *Greece* 46 B5
Glossop, *U.K.* 14 D6
Gloucester, *Australia* 95 E5
Gloucester, *U.K.* 15 F5
Gloucester, *U.S.A.* 117 D14
Gloucester I., *Australia* 94 J6
Gloucester Island △, *Australia* . 94 J6
Gloucester Point, *U.S.A.* ... 114 G7
Gloucestershire □, *U.K.* 15 F5
Gloversville, *U.S.A.* 117 C10

Glovertown, *Canada* 105 C9
Główno, *Poland* 31 G6
Głubczyce, *Poland* 31 H4
Glubokiy, *Russia* 35 F5
Glubokoye = Hlybokaye, *Belarus* . 32 E4
Głuchołazy, *Poland* 31 H4
Glücksburg, *Germany* 24 A5
Glückstadt, *Germany* 24 B5
Glukhov = Hlukhiv, *Ukraine* . 33 G7
Glusk, *Belarus* 33 F5
Głuszyca, *Poland* 31 H3
Glyngøre, *Denmark* 11 H2
Gmünd, *Kärnten, Austria* 26 E6
Gmünd, *Niederösterreich, Austria* . 26 C8
Gmunden, *Austria* 26 D6
Gnarp, *Sweden* 10 B11
Gnesta, *Sweden* 10 E11
Gniew, *Poland* 30 E5
Gniewkowo, *Poland* 31 F5
Gniezno, *Poland* 31 F4
Gnjilane, *Serbia & M.* 44 D5
Gnoien, *Germany* 24 B8
Gnosjö, *Sweden* 11 G7
Gnowangerup, *Australia* 93 F2
Goa, *India* 66 M8
Goa □, *India* 66 M8
Goalen Hd., *Australia* 95 F5
Goalpara, *India* 67 F17
Goaltor, *India* 69 H12
Goalundo Ghat, *Bangla.* 69 H13
Goaso, *Ghana* 82 D4
Goat Fell, *U.K.* 13 F3
Goba, *Ethiopia* 81 F4
Goba, *Mozam.* 89 D5
Gobabis, *Namibia* 88 C2
Göbel, *Turkey* 45 F12
Gobi, *Asia* 56 C6
Gobō, *Japan* 55 H7
Gobo, *Sudan* 81 F3
Göçbeyli, *Turkey* 47 B9
Goch, *Germany* 24 D2
Gochas, *Namibia* 88 C2
Godalming, *U.K.* 15 F7
Godavari →, *India* 67 L13
Godavari Pt., *India* 67 L13
Godbout, *Canada* 105 C6
Godda, *India* 69 G12
Godech, *Bulgaria* 44 C7
Goderich, *Canada* 116 C3
Goderville, *France* 18 C7
Godfrey Ra., *Australia* 93 D2
Godhavn = Qeqertarsuaq,
   Greenland 101 B14
Godhra, *India* 68 H5
Gödöllő, *Hungary* 28 C4
Godoy Cruz, *Argentina* 126 C2
Gods →, *Canada* 104 A1
Gods L., *Canada* 104 B1
Gods River, *Canada* 103 C10
Godthåb = Nuuk, *Greenland* .. 101 B14
Goeie Hoop, Kaap die = Good
   Hope, C. of, *S. Africa* 88 E2
Goéland, L. au, *Canada* 104 C4
Goélands, L. aux, *Canada* ... 105 A7
Goeree, *Neths.* 17 C3
Goes, *Neths.* 17 C3
Goffstown, *U.S.A.* 117 C13
Gogama, *Canada* 104 C3
Gogebic, L., *U.S.A.* 112 B10
Goggetti, *Ethiopia* 81 F4
Gogolin, *Poland* 31 H5
Gogonou, *Benin* 83 C5
Gogra = Ghaghara →, *India* . 69 G11
Gogrial, *Sudan* 81 F2
Gogti, *Ethiopia* 81 E5
Gohana, *India* 68 E7
Goharganj, *India* 68 H7
Goi →, *India* 68 H6
Goiânia, *Brazil* 125 G9
Goiás, *Brazil* 125 G8
Goiás □, *Brazil* 125 F9
Goio-Erê, *Brazil* 127 A5
Góis, *Portugal* 36 E2
Gojam, *Ethiopia* 81 E4
Gojeb, Wabi →, *Ethiopia* 81 F4
Gojō, *Japan* 55 G7
Gojra, *Pakistan* 68 D5
Gökçeada, *Turkey* 45 F9
Gökçedağ, *Turkey* 47 B10
Gökçeören, *Turkey* 47 C10
Gökçeyazı, *Turkey* 47 B9
Gökırmak →, *Turkey* 72 B6
Gökova, *Turkey* 47 D10
Gökova Körfezi, *Turkey* 47 E9
Göksu →, *Turkey* 72 D6
Göksun, *Turkey* 72 C7
Gökteik, *Burma* 67 H20
Göktepe, *Turkey* 47 D10
Gokurt, *Pakistan* 68 E2
Gokwe, *Zimbabwe* 89 B4
Gola, *India* 69 E9
Golakganj, *India* 69 F13
Golan Heights = Hagolan, *Syria* . 74 C4
Gołańcz, *Poland* 31 F4
Goläshkerd, *Iran* 71 E8
Golaya Pristen = Hola Pristan,
   Ukraine 33 J7
Gölbaşı, *Adıyaman, Turkey* .. 72 D7
Gölbaşı, *Ankara, Turkey* 72 C5
Golchikha, *Russia* 4 B12
Golconda, *U.S.A.* 108 F5
Gölcük, *Kocaeli, Turkey* 45 F13
Gölcük, *Niğde, Turkey* 72 C6
Gold, *U.S.A.* 116 E7
Gold Beach, *U.S.A.* 108 E1
Gold Coast, *W. Afr.* 83 E4
Gold Hill, *U.S.A.* 108 E2
Gold River, *Canada* 102 D3
Gołdap, *Poland* 30 D9

Goldberg, *Germany* 24 B8
Golden, *Canada* 102 C5
Golden B., *N.Z.* 91 J4
Golden Gate, *U.S.A.* 108 H2
Golden Gate Highlands △,
   S. Africa 89 D4
Golden Hinde, *Canada* 102 D3
Golden Lake, *Canada* 116 A7
Golden Spike △, *U.S.A.* 108 F7
Golden Vale, *Ireland* 12 D3
Goldendale, *U.S.A.* 108 D3
Goldfield, *U.S.A.* 109 H5
Goldsand L., *Canada* 103 B8
Goldsboro, *U.S.A.* 115 H7
Goldsmith, *U.S.A.* 113 K3
Goldsworthy, *Australia* 92 D2
Goldthwaite, *U.S.A.* 113 K5
Golegã, *Portugal* 37 F2
Golestān □, *Iran* 71 B7
Golestānak, *Iran* 71 D7
Goleta, *U.S.A.* 111 L7
Golfito, *Costa Rica* 120 E3
Golfo Aranci, *Italy* 42 B2
Golfo di Orosei e del
   Gennargentu △, *Italy* 42 B2
Gölgeli Dağları, *Turkey* 47 D10
Gölhisar, *Turkey* 47 D11
Goliad, *U.S.A.* 113 L6
Golija, *Serbia & M.* 44 C2
Golija, *Serbia & M.* 44 C4
Golina, *Poland* 31 F5
Gölköy, *Turkey* 72 B7
Göllersdorf, *Austria* 26 C9
Gölmarmara, *Turkey* 47 C9
Golo →, *France* 21 F13
Gólova, *Turkey* 47 E12
Golpāyegān, *Iran* 71 C6
Gölpazarı, *Turkey* 72 B4
Golra, *Pakistan* 68 C5
Golspie, *U.K.* 13 D5
Golub-Dobrzyń, *Poland* 31 E6
Golubac, *Serbia & M.* 44 B5
Golyam Perelik, *Bulgaria* ... 45 E8
Golyama Kamchiya →, *Bulgaria* . 45 C11
Goma, *Dem. Rep. of the Congo* . 86 C2
Gomal Pass, *Pakistan* 68 D3
Gomati →, *India* 69 G10
Gombari, *Dem. Rep. of the Congo* . 86 B2
Gombe, *Nigeria* 83 C7
Gombe →, *Tanzania* 86 C3
Gombe □, *Nigeria* 83 C7
Gombi, *Nigeria* 83 C7
Gomel = Homyel, *Belarus* 33 F6
Gomera, *Canary Is.* 48 F2
Gómez Palacio, *Mexico* 118 B4
Gomīshān, *Iran* 71 B7
Gommern, *Germany* 24 C7
Gomogomo, *Indonesia* 63 F8
Gomoh, *India* 67 H15
Gomotartsi, *Bulgaria* 44 B6
Gompa = Ganta, *Liberia* 82 D3
Gomphi, *Greece* 46 B3
Gonābād, *Iran* 71 C8
Gonaïves, *Haiti* 121 C5
Gonarezhou △, *Zimbabwe* 87 G3
Gonâve, G. de la, *Haiti* 121 C5
Gonâve, Île de la, *Haiti* ... 121 C5
Gonbad-e Kāvūs, *Iran* 71 B7
Gonda, *India* 69 F9
Gondal, *India* 68 J4
Gonder, *Ethiopia* 81 E4
Gondia, *India* 66 J12
Gondola, *Mozam.* 87 F3
Gondomar, *Portugal* 36 D2
Gondrecourt-le-Château, *France* . 19 D12
Gönen, *Balıkesir, Turkey* ... 45 F11
Gönen, *Isparta, Turkey* 47 D12
Gönen →, *Turkey* 45 F11
Gong Xian, *China* 58 C5
Gong'an, *China* 59 B9
Gongcheng, *China* 59 E8
Gongga Shan, *China* 58 C3
Gongguan, *China* 58 G7
Gonghe, *China* 60 C5
Gongola →, *Nigeria* 83 D7
Gongolgon, *Australia* 95 E4
Gongshan, *China* 58 D2
Gongtan, *China* 58 C7
Gongzhuling, *China* 57 C13
Goniadz, *Poland* 30 E9
Goniri, *Nigeria* 83 C7
Gonjo, *China* 58 B2
Gonnesa, *Italy* 42 C1
Gónnos, *Greece* 46 B4
Gonnosfanádiga, *Italy* 42 C1
Gonzaga, *Phil.* 61 B5
Gonzales, *Calif., U.S.A.* ... 110 J5
Gonzales, *Tex., U.S.A.* 113 L6
González Chaves, *Argentina* . 126 D3
Good Hope, C. of, *S. Africa* . 88 E2
Gooderham, *Canada* 116 B6
Goodhouse, *S. Africa* 88 D2
Gooding, *U.S.A.* 108 E6
Goodland, *U.S.A.* 112 F4
Goodlow, *Canada* 102 B4
Goodooga, *Australia* 95 D4
Goodsprings, *U.S.A.* 111 K11
Goole, *U.K.* 14 D7
Goolgowi, *Australia* 95 E4
Goomalling, *Australia* 93 F2
Goomeri, *Australia* 95 D5
Goonda, *Mozam.* 87 F3
Goondiwindi, *Australia* 95 D5
Goongarrie △, *Australia* 93 F3
Goongarrie, L., *Australia* ... 93 F3
Goonyella, *Australia* 94 C4
Goose →, *Canada* 105 B7
Goose Creek, *U.S.A.* 115 J5
Goose L., *U.S.A.* 108 F3

Gop, *India* 66 H6
Gopalganj, *India* 69 F11
Göppingen, *Germany* 25 G5
Gor, *Spain* 37 H8
Góra, *Dolnośląskie, Poland* . 31 G3
Góra, *Mazowieckie, Poland* .. 31 F7
Góra Kalwaria, *Poland* 31 G8
Gorakhpur, *India* 69 F10
Goražde, *Bos.-H.* 28 G3
Gorbatov, *Russia* 34 B6
Gorbea, Peña, *Spain* 38 B2
Gorda, *U.S.A.* 110 K5
Gorda, Pta., *Canary Is.* 48 F2
Gorda, Pta., *Nic.* 120 D3
Gordan B., *Australia* 92 B5
Gördes, *Turkey* 47 C10
Gordon, *U.S.A.* 112 D3
Gordon →, *Australia* 95 G4
Gordon L., *Alta., Canada* ... 103 B6
Gordon L., *N.W.T., Canada* .. 102 A6
Gordonvale, *Australia* 94 B4
Gore, *Ethiopia* 81 F4
Gore, *N.Z.* 91 M2
Gore Bay, *Canada* 104 C3
Görele, *Turkey* 73 B8
Goreme, *Turkey* 72 C6
Gorey, *Ireland* 12 D5
Gorg, *Iran* 71 D8
Gorgān, *Iran* 71 B7
Gorgona, *Italy* 40 E6
Gorgona, I., *Colombia* 124 C3
Gorgora, *Ethiopia* 81 E4
Gorgoram, *Nigeria* 83 C7
Gorham, *U.S.A.* 117 B13
Gori, *Georgia* 35 J7
Goriganga →, *India* 69 E9
Goris, *Armenia* 73 C12
Gorízia, *Italy* 41 C10
Gorj □, *Romania* 29 E8
Gorki = Horki, *Belarus* 32 E6
Gorki = Nizhniy Novgorod,
   Russia 34 B7
Gorkiy = Nizhniy Novgorod,
   Russia 34 B7
Gorkovskoye Vdkhr., *Russia* . 34 B6
Gorleston, *U.K.* 15 E9
Gorlice, *Poland* 31 J8
Görlitz, *Germany* 24 D10
Gorlovka = Horlivka, *Ukraine* . 33 H10
Gorman, *U.S.A.* 111 L8
Gorna Dzhumaya = Blagoevgrad,
   Bulgaria 44 D7
Gorna Oryakhovitsa, *Bulgaria* . 45 C9
Gornja Radgona, *Slovenia* ... 41 B13
Gornja Tuzla, *Bos.-H.* 28 F3
Gornji Grad, *Slovenia* 41 B11
Gornji Milanovac, *Serbia & M.* . 44 B4
Gornji Vakuf, *Bos.-H.* 28 G2
Gorno Ablanovo, *Bulgaria* ... 45 C9
Gorno-Altay □, *Russia* 52 D9
Gorno-Altaysk, *Russia* 52 D9
Gornyatskiy, *Russia* 35 F5
Gornyy, *Saratov, Russia* 34 E9
Gornyy, *Sib., Russia* 54 B6
Gorodenka = Horodenka,
   Ukraine 29 B10
Gorodets, *Russia* 34 B6
Gorodishche = Horodyshche,
   Ukraine 33 H6
Gorodishche, *Russia* 34 D7
Gorodnya = Horodnya, *Ukraine* . 33 G6
Gorodok = Haradok, *Belarus* . 32 E6
Gorodok = Horodok, *Ukraine* . 33 H2
Gorodovikovsk, *Russia* 35 G5
Gorokhov = Horokhiv, *Ukraine* . 33 G3
Gorokhovets, *Russia* 34 B6
Gorom Gorom, *Burkina Faso* .. 83 C4
Goromonzi, *Zimbabwe* 87 F3
Gorong, Kepulauan, *Indonesia* . 63 E8
Gorongose →, *Mozam.* 89 B5
Gorongosa △, *Mozam.* 89 C5
Gorongoza, *Mozam.* 87 F3
Gorongoza, Sa. da, *Mozam.* .. 87 F3
Gorontalo, *Indonesia* 63 D6
Gorontalo □, *Indonesia* 63 D6
Goronyo, *Nigeria* 83 C6
Górowo Iławeckie, *Poland* ... 30 D7
Gorron, *France* 18 D6
Gorshechnoye, *Russia* 33 G10
Gort, *Ireland* 12 C3
Gortis, *Greece* 49 D6
Góry Bystrzyckie, *Poland* ... 31 H3
Goryachiy Klyuch, *Russia* ... 35 H4
Gorzkowice, *Poland* 31 G6
Górzno, *Poland* 31 E6
Gorzów Śląski, *Poland* 31 G5
Gorzów Wielkopolski, *Poland* . 31 F2
Gosford, *Australia* 95 E5
Goshen, *Calif., U.S.A.* 110 J7
Goshen, *N.Y., U.S.A.* 117 E10
Goshogawara, *Japan* 54 D10
Goslar, *Germany* 24 D6
Gospič, *Croatia* 41 D12
Gosport, *U.K.* 15 G6
Gossas, *Senegal* 82 C1
Gosse →, *Australia* 94 B1
Gossi, *Mali* 83 B4
Gossinga, *Sudan* 81 F2
Gostivar, *Macedonia* 44 E4
Gostyń, *Poland* 31 G4
Gostynin, *Poland* 31 F6
Göta älv →, *Sweden* 11 G6
Göta kanal, *Sweden* 11 F9
Götaland, *Sweden* 11 G7
Göteborg, *Sweden* 11 G5
Götene, *Sweden* 11 F7
Gotești, *Moldova* 29 D13
Gotha, *Germany* 24 E6

Gothenburg = Göteborg, *Sweden* . 11 G5
Gothenburg, *U.S.A.* 112 E4
Gothèye, *Niger* 83 C5
Gotland, *Sweden* 11 G12
Gotlands län □, *Sweden* 11 G12
Gotō-Rettō, *Japan* 55 H4
Gotse Delchev, *Bulgaria* 44 E7
Gotska Sandön, *Sweden* 9 G18
Götsu, *Japan* 55 G6
Gott Pk., *Canada* 102 C4
Góttero, Monte, *Italy* 40 D6
Göttingen, *Germany* 24 D5
Gottwald = Zmiyev, *Ukraine* . 33 H9
Gottwaldov = Zlín, *Czech Rep.* . 27 B10
Goubangzi, *China* 57 D11
Gouda, *Neths.* 17 B4
Goúdhoura, Ákra, *Greece* 49 E8
Goudiry, *Senegal* 82 C2
Goudoumaria, *Niger* 83 C7
Gough I., *Atl. Oc.* 2 G9
Gouin, Rés., *Canada* 104 C5
Gouitafla, *Ivory C.* 82 D3
Goulburn, *Australia* 95 E4
Goulburn Is., *Australia* 94 A1
Goulia, *Ivory C.* 82 C3
Goulimine, *Morocco* 78 C3
Goumbou, *Mali* 82 B3
Gouménissa, *Greece* 44 F6
Goundam, *Mali* 82 B4
Goúra, *Greece* 46 D4
Gourbassi, *Mali* 82 C2
Gourdon, *France* 20 D5
Gouré, *Niger* 83 C7
Gourin, *France* 18 D3
Gourits →, *S. Africa* 88 E3
Gourma-Rharous, *Mali* 83 B4
Goúrnais, *Greece* 49 D7
Gournay-en-Bray, *France* 19 C8
Gourock, *U.K.* 13 F4
Goursi, *Burkina Faso* 82 C4
Gouverneur, *U.S.A.* 117 B9
Gouviá, *Greece* 49 A3
Gouzon, *France* 19 F9
Governador Valadares, *Brazil* . 125 G10
Governor's Harbour, *Bahamas* . 120 A4
Govindgarh, *India* 69 G9
Gowan Ra., *Australia* 94 D4
Gowanda, *U.S.A.* 116 D6
Gower, *U.K.* 15 F3
Gowna, L., *Ireland* 12 C4
Goya, *Argentina* 126 B4
Göyçay, *Azerbaijan* 35 K8
Goyder Lagoon, *Australia* ... 95 D2
Goyllarisquisga, *Peru* 124 F3
Göynük, *Antalya, Turkey* 47 E12
Göynük, *Bolu, Turkey* 72 B4
Goz Beïda, *Chad* 79 F10
Goz Regeb, *Sudan* 81 D4
Gozdnica, *Poland* 31 G2
Gozo, *Malta* 49 C1
Graaff-Reinet, *S. Africa* ... 88 E3
Grabo, *Ivory C.* 82 D3
Grabow, *Germany* 24 B7
Grabów nad Prosną, *Poland* .. 31 G5
Gračac, *Croatia* 41 D12
Gračanica, *Bos.-H.* 28 F3
Graçay, *France* 19 E8
Gracias a Dios, C., *Honduras* . 120 D3
Graciosa, I., *Canary Is.* ... 48 E6
Grad Sofiya □, *Bulgaria* 44 D7
Gradac, *Serbia & M.* 44 C3
Gradačac, *Bos.-H.* 28 F3
Gradeška Planina, *Macedonia* . 44 E6
Gradets, *Bulgaria* 45 D10
Gradište, *Slovenia* 41 B12
Grădiștea de Munte, *Romania* . 29 E8
Grado, *Italy* 41 C10
Grado, *Spain* 36 B4
Grady, *U.S.A.* 113 H3
Graeca, Lacul, *Romania* 29 F11
Grafenau, *Germany* 25 G9
Gräfenberg, *Germany* 25 F7
Grafham Water, *U.K.* 15 E7
Grafton, *Australia* 95 D5
Grafton, *N. Dak., U.S.A.* ... 112 A6
Grafton, *W. Va., U.S.A.* 114 F5
Graham, *Canada* 104 C1
Graham, *U.S.A.* 113 J5
Graham, Mt., *U.S.A.* 109 K9
Graham Bell, Ostrov = Greem-
   Bell, Ostrov, *Russia* 52 A7
Graham I., *Canada* 102 C2
Graham Land, *Antarctica* 5 C17
Grahamstown, *S. Africa* 88 E4
Grahamsville, *U.S.A.* 117 E10
Grahovo, *Serbia & M.* 44 D2
Graie, Alpi, *Europe* 21 C11
Grain Coast, *W. Afr.* 82 E3
Grajagan, *Indonesia* 63 K17
Grajagan, Teluk, *Indonesia* . 63 K17
Grajaú, *Brazil* 125 E9
Grajaú →, *Brazil* 125 D10
Grajewo, *Poland* 30 E9
Gramada, *Bulgaria* 44 C6
Gramat, *France* 20 D5
Grammichele, *Italy* 43 E7
Grámmos, Óros, *Greece* 44 F4
Grampian, *U.S.A.* 116 F6
Grampian Highlands = Grampian
   Mts., *U.K.* 13 E5
Grampian Mts., *U.K.* 13 E5
Grampians, The, *Australia* .. 95 F3
Gramsh, *Albania* 44 F4
Gran Canaria, *Canary Is.* ... 48 G4
Gran Chaco, *S. Amer.* 126 B3
Gran Desierto del Pinacate △,
   Mexico 118 A2
Gran Paradiso, *Italy* 40 C4
Gran Sasso d'Itália, *Italy* . 41 F10
Gran Sasso e Monti Della
   Laga △, *Italy* 41 F10

Granada, *Nic.* 120 D2
Granada, *Spain* 37 H7
Granada, *U.S.A.* 113 F3
Granada □, *Spain* 37 H7
Granadilla de Abona, *Canary Is.* 48 F3
Granard, *Ireland* 12 C4
Granbury, *U.S.A.* 113 J6
Granby, *Canada* 117 A12
Granby, *U.S.A.* 108 F11
Grand →, *Canada* 116 D5
Grand →, *Mo., U.S.A.* 112 F8
Grand →, *S. Dak., U.S.A.* 112 C4
Grand Bahama I., *Bahamas* 120 A4
Grand Bank, *Canada* 105 C8
Grand Bassam, *Ivory C.* 82 D4
Grand Béréby, *Ivory C.* 82 E3
Grand-Bourg, *Guadeloupe* 120 b
Grand Canal = Yun Ho →, *China* 57 E9
Grand Canyon, *U.S.A.* 109 H7
Grand Canyon △, *U.S.A.* 109 H7
Grand Canyon-Parashant △, *U.S.A.* 109 H7
Grand Cayman, *Cayman Is.* 120 C3
Grand Centre, *Canada* 103 C6
Grand Cess, *Liberia* 82 E3
Grand Coulee, *U.S.A.* 108 C4
Grand Coulee Dam, *U.S.A.* 108 C4
Grand Falls, *Canada* 105 C6
Grand Falls-Windsor, *Canada* 105 C8
Grand Forks, *Canada* 102 D5
Grand Forks, *U.S.A.* 112 B6
Grand Gorge, *U.S.A.* 117 D10
Grand Haven, *U.S.A.* 114 D2
Grand I., *Mich., U.S.A.* 114 B2
Grand I., *N.Y., U.S.A.* 116 D6
Grand Island, *U.S.A.* 112 E5
Grand Isle, *La., U.S.A.* 113 L9
Grand Isle, *Vt., U.S.A.* 117 B11
Grand Junction, *U.S.A.* 109 G9
Grand L., *N.B., Canada* 105 C6
Grand L., *Nfld. & L., Canada* 105 C8
Grand L., *Nfld. & L., Canada* 105 B7
Grand L., *U.S.A.* 113 L8
Grand Lahou, *Ivory C.* 82 D3
Grand Lake, *U.S.A.* 108 F11
Grand-Lieu, L. de, *France* 18 E5
Grand Manan I., *Canada* 105 D6
Grand Marais, *Canada* 112 B9
Grand Marais, *U.S.A.* 114 B3
Grand-Mère, *Canada* 104 C5
Grand Popo, *Benin* 83 D5
Grand Portage, *U.S.A.* 112 B10
Grand Prairie, *U.S.A.* 113 J6
Grand Rapids, *Canada* 103 C9
Grand Rapids, *Mich., U.S.A.* 114 D2
Grand Rapids, *Minn., U.S.A.* 112 B8
Grand St-Bernard, Col du, *Europe* 25 K3
Grand Staircase-Escalante △, *U.S.A.* 109 H8
Grand Teton, *U.S.A.* 108 E8
Grand Teton △, *U.S.A.* 108 D8
Grand Union Canal, *U.K.* 15 E7
Grand-Vigie, Pte. de la, *Guadeloupe* 120 b
Grandas de Salime, *Spain* 36 B4
Grande →, *Jujuy, Argentina* 126 A2
Grande →, *Mendoza, Argentina* 126 D2
Grande →, *Bolivia* 124 G6
Grande →, *Bahia, Brazil* 125 F10
Grande →, *Minas Gerais, Brazil* 125 H8
Grande, B., *Argentina* 128 G3
Grande, Rio →, *U.S.A.* 113 N6
Grande Baleine, R. de la →, *Canada* 104 A4
Grande Cache, *Canada* 102 C5
Grande Casse, Pte. de la, *France* 21 C10
Grande-Entrée, *Canada* 105 C7
Grande Prairie, *Canada* 102 B5
Grande-Rivière, *Canada* 105 C7
Grande-Terre, *Guadeloupe* 120 b
Grande-Vallée, *Canada* 105 C6
Grandfalls, *U.S.A.* 113 K3
Grândola, *Portugal* 37 G2
Grandpré, *France* 19 C11
Grands Causses △, *France* 20 D6
Grands-Jardins △, *Canada* 105 C5
Grandview, *Canada* 103 C8
Grandview, *U.S.A.* 108 C4
Grandvilliers, *France* 19 C8
Graneros, *Chile* 126 C1
Grangemouth, *U.K.* 13 E5
Granger, *U.S.A.* 108 F9
Grängesberg, *Sweden* 10 D9
Grangeville, *U.S.A.* 108 D5
Granisle, *Canada* 102 C3
Granite City, *U.S.A.* 112 F9
Granite Falls, *U.S.A.* 112 C7
Granite L., *Canada* 105 C8
Granite Mt., *U.S.A.* 111 M10
Granite Pk., *U.S.A.* 108 D9
Graniteville, *U.S.A.* 117 B12
Granitola, C., *Italy* 42 E5
Granity, *N.Z.* 91 J3
Granja, *Brazil* 125 D10
Granja de Moreruela, *Spain* 36 D5
Granja de Torrehermosa, *Spain* 37 G5
Gränna, *Sweden* 11 F8
Granollers, *Spain* 38 D7
Gransee, *Germany* 24 B9
Grant, *U.S.A.* 112 E4
Grant, Mt., *U.S.A.* 108 G4
Grant City, *U.S.A.* 112 E7
Grant I., *Australia* 92 B5
Grant Range, *U.S.A.* 109 G6
Grantham, *U.K.* 14 E7
Grantown-on-Spey, *U.K.* 13 D5
Grants, *U.S.A.* 109 J10
Grants Pass, *U.S.A.* 108 E2
Grantsville, *U.S.A.* 108 F7
Granville, *France* 18 D5
Granville, *N. Dak., U.S.A.* 112 A4

Granville, *N.Y., U.S.A.* 117 C11
Granville, *Ohio, U.S.A.* 116 F2
Granville L., *Canada* 103 B8
Graskop, *S. Africa* 89 C5
Gräsö, *Sweden* 10 D12
Grass →, *Canada* 103 B9
Grass Range, *U.S.A.* 108 C9
Grass River △, *Canada* 103 C8
Grass Valley, *Calif., U.S.A.* 110 F6
Grass Valley, *Oreg., U.S.A.* 108 D3
Grassano, *Italy* 43 B9
Grasse, *France* 21 E10
Grassflat, *U.S.A.* 116 F6
Grasslands △, *Canada* 103 D7
Grassy, *Australia* 95 G3
Gråsten, *Denmark* 11 K3
Gråstorp, *Sweden* 11 F6
Gratkorn, *Austria* 26 D8
Graulhet, *France* 20 E5
Graus, *Spain* 38 C5
Grave, Pte. de, *France* 20 C2
Gravelbourg, *Canada* 103 D7
Gravelines, *France* 19 A9
's-Gravenhage, *Neths.* 17 B4
Gravenhurst, *Canada* 116 B5
Gravesend, *Australia* 95 D5
Gravesend, *U.K.* 15 F8
Gravina in Púglia, *Italy* 43 B9
Gravois, Pointe-à-, *Haiti* 121 C5
Gravone →, *France* 21 G12
Gray, *France* 19 E12
Grayling, *U.S.A.* 114 C3
Grays, *U.K.* 15 F8
Grays Harbor, *U.S.A.* 108 C1
Grays L., *U.S.A.* 108 E8
Grays River, *U.S.A.* 110 D3
Grayvoron, *Russia* 33 G8
Graz, *Austria* 26 D8
Grdelica, *Serbia & M.* 44 D6
Greasy L., *Canada* 102 A4
Great Abaco I. = Abaco I., *Bahamas* 120 A4
Great Artesian Basin, *Australia* 94 C3
Great Australian Bight, *Australia* 93 F5
Great Bahama Bank, *Bahamas* 120 B4
Great Barrier I., *N.Z.* 91 G5
Great Barrier Reef, *Australia* 94 B4
Great Barrier Reef △, *Australia* 94 B4
Great Barrington, *U.S.A.* 117 D11
Great Basalt Wall △, *Australia* 94 B4
Great Basin, *U.S.A.* 108 G5
Great Basin △, *U.S.A.* 108 G6
Great Bear →, *Canada* 100 B7
Great Bear L., *Canada* 100 B7
Great Belt = Store Bælt, *Denmark* 11 J4
Great Bend, *Kans., U.S.A.* 112 F5
Great Bend, *Pa., U.S.A.* 117 E9
Great Blasket I., *Ireland* 12 D1
Great Britain, *Europe* 6 E5
Great Camanoe, *Br. Virgin Is.* 121 e
Great Codroy, *Canada* 105 C8
Great Dividing Ra., *Australia* 94 C4
Great Driffield = Driffield, *U.K.* 14 C7
Great Exuma I., *Bahamas* 120 B4
Great Falls, *U.S.A.* 108 C8
Great Fish = Groot Vis →, *S. Africa* 88 E4
Great Guana Cay, *Bahamas* 120 A4
Great Inagua I., *Bahamas* 121 B5
Great Indian Desert = Thar Desert, *India* 68 F5
Great Karoo, *S. Africa* 88 E3
Great Khingan Mts. = Da Hinggan Ling, *China* 60 B7
Great Lake, *Australia* 95 G4
Great Lakes, *N. Amer.* 98 E11
Great Malvern, *U.K.* 15 E5
Great Miami →, *U.S.A.* 114 F3
Great Ormes Head, *U.K.* 14 D4
Great Ouse →, *U.K.* 14 E8
Great Palm I., *Australia* 94 B4
Great Pedro Bluff, *Jamaica* 120 a
Great Plains, *N. Amer.* 98 E9
Great Ruaha →, *Tanzania* 86 D4
Great Sacandaga L., *U.S.A.* 117 C10
Great Saint Bernard Pass = Grand St-Bernard, Col du, *Europe* 25 K3
Great Salt L., *U.S.A.* 108 F7
Great Salt Lake Desert, *U.S.A.* 108 F7
Great Salt Plains L., *U.S.A.* 113 G5
Great Sand Dunes △, *U.S.A.* 109 H11
Great Sandy △, *Australia* 95 D5
Great Sandy Desert, *Australia* 92 D3
Great Sangi = Sangihe, Pulau, *Indonesia* 63 D7
Great Scarcies →, *S. Leone* 82 D2
Great Skellig, *Ireland* 12 E1
Great Slave L., *Canada* 102 A5
Great Smoky Mts. △, *U.S.A.* 115 H4
Great Snow Mt., *Canada* 102 B4
Great Stour = Stour →, *U.K.* 15 F9
Great Victoria Desert, *Australia* 93 E4
Great Wall, *Antarctica* 5 C18
Great Wall, *China* 56 E5
Great Whernside, *U.K.* 14 C6
Great Yarmouth, *U.K.* 15 E9
Great Zab = Zāb al Kabīr →, *Iraq* 70 C4
Great Zimbabwe, *Zimbabwe* 87 G3
Greater Antilles, *W. Indies* 121 C5
Greater London □, *U.K.* 15 F7
Greater Manchester □, *U.K.* 14 D5
Greater St. Lucia Wetlands △, *S. Africa* 89 D5
Greater Sudbury = Sudbury, *Canada* 104 C3
Greater Sunda Is., *Indonesia* 62 F4
Grebbestad, *Sweden* 11 F5
Grebenka = Hrebinka, *Ukraine* 33 G7
Greco, C., *Cyprus* 49 E13
Greco, Mte., *Italy* 41 G10

Gredos, Sierra de, *Spain* 36 E6
Greece, *U.S.A.* 116 C7
Greece ■, *Europe* 46 B3
Greeley, *Colo., U.S.A.* 112 E2
Greeley, *Nebr., U.S.A.* 112 E5
Green-Bell, Ostrov, *Russia* 52 A7
Green →, *U.S.A.* 108 E2
Green →, *Ky., U.S.A.* 114 G2
Green →, *Utah, U.S.A.* 109 G9
Green B., *U.S.A.* 114 C2
Green Bay, *U.S.A.* 114 C2
Green C., *Australia* 95 F5
Green Cove Springs, *U.S.A.* 115 L5
Green Lake, *Canada* 103 C7
Green Mts., *U.S.A.* 117 C12
Green River, *Utah, U.S.A.* 109 G8
Green River, *Wyo., U.S.A.* 108 F9
Green Valley, *U.S.A.* 109 L8
Greenbank, *U.S.A.* 110 B4
Greenbush, *Mich., U.S.A.* 116 B1
Greenbush, *Minn., U.S.A.* 112 A6
Greencastle, *U.S.A.* 114 F2
Greene, *U.S.A.* 117 D9
Greenfield, *Calif., U.S.A.* 110 J5
Greenfield, *Calif., U.S.A.* 111 K8
Greenfield, *Ind., U.S.A.* 114 F3
Greenfield, *Iowa, U.S.A.* 112 E7
Greenfield, *Mass., U.S.A.* 117 D12
Greenfield, *Mo., U.S.A.* 113 G8
Greenfield Park, *Canada* 117 A11
Greenland ☒, *N. Amer.* 4 C5
Greenland Sea, *Arctic* 4 B7
Greenock, *U.K.* 13 F4
Greenore, *Ireland* 12 B5
Greenore Pt., *Ireland* 12 D5
Greenough, *Australia* 93 E1
Greenough →, *Australia* 93 E1
Greenough Pt., *Canada* 116 B3
Greenport, *U.S.A.* 117 E12
Greensboro, *Ga., U.S.A.* 115 J4
Greensboro, *N.C., U.S.A.* 115 G6
Greensboro, *Vt., U.S.A.* 117 B12
Greensburg, *Ind., U.S.A.* 114 F3
Greensburg, *Kans., U.S.A.* 113 G5
Greensburg, *Pa., U.S.A.* 116 F5
Greenstone Pt., *U.K.* 13 D3
Greenvale, *Australia* 94 B4
Greenville, *Liberia* 82 D3
Greenville, *Ala., U.S.A.* 115 K2
Greenville, *Calif., U.S.A.* 110 E6
Greenville, *Maine, U.S.A.* 115 C11
Greenville, *Mich., U.S.A.* 114 D3
Greenville, *Miss., U.S.A.* 113 J9
Greenville, *Mo., U.S.A.* 113 G9
Greenville, *N.C., U.S.A.* 115 H7
Greenville, *N.H., U.S.A.* 117 D13
Greenville, *N.Y., U.S.A.* 117 D10
Greenville, *Ohio, U.S.A.* 114 E3
Greenville, *Pa., U.S.A.* 116 E4
Greenville, *S.C., U.S.A.* 115 H4
Greenville, *Tenn., U.S.A.* 115 G4
Greenville, *Tex., U.S.A.* 113 J6
Greenwater Lake △, *Canada* 103 C8
Greenwich, *Conn., U.S.A.* 117 E11
Greenwich, *N.Y., U.S.A.* 117 C11
Greenwich, *Ohio, U.S.A.* 116 E2
Greenwich □, *U.K.* 15 F8
Greenwood, *Canada* 102 D5
Greenwood, *Ark., U.S.A.* 113 H7
Greenwood, *Ind., U.S.A.* 114 F2
Greenwood, *Miss., U.S.A.* 113 J9
Greenwood, *S.C., U.S.A.* 115 H4
Greenwood, Mt., *Australia* 92 B5
Gregbe, *Ivory C.* 82 D3
Gregory, *U.S.A.* 112 D5
Gregory △, *Australia* 92 C5
Gregory →, *Australia* 94 B2
Gregory, L., *S. Austral., Australia* 95 D2
Gregory, L., *W. Austral., Australia* 93 D3
Gregory Downs, *Australia* 94 B2
Gregory L., *Australia* 92 D4
Gregory Ra., *Queens., Australia* 94 B3
Gregory Ra., *W. Austral., Australia* 92 D3
Greiffenberg, *Germany* 24 B9
Greifswald, *Germany* 24 A9
Greifswalder Bodden, *Germany* 24 A9
Grein, *Austria* 26 C7
Greiz, *Germany* 24 E8
Gremikha, *Russia* 52 C4
Grenå, *Denmark* 11 H4
Grenada, *U.S.A.* 113 J10
Grenada ■, *W. Indies* 121 D7
Grenade, *France* 20 E5
Grenadier I., *U.S.A.* 117 B8
Grenadines, The, *St. Vincent* 121 D7
Grenchen, *Switz.* 25 H3
Grenen, *Denmark* 11 G4
Grenfell, *Australia* 95 E4
Grenfell, *Canada* 103 C8
Grenoble, *France* 21 C9
Grenville, C., *Australia* 94 A3
Grenville Chan., *Canada* 102 C3
Gréoux-les-Bains, *France* 21 E9
Gresham, *U.S.A.* 110 E4
Gresik, *Indonesia* 63 G15
Gretna, *U.K.* 13 F5
Greven, *Germany* 24 C3
Grevená, *Greece* 44 F5
Grevená □, *Greece* 44 F5
Grevenbroich, *Germany* 24 D2
Grevenmacher, *Lux.* 17 E6
Grevesmühlen, *Germany* 24 B7
Grevestrand, *Denmark* 11 J6
Grey →, *Canada* 105 C8
Grey →, *N.Z.* 91 K3
Grey, C., *Australia* 94 A2
Grey Ra., *Australia* 95 D3
Greybull, *U.S.A.* 108 D9
Greymouth, *N.Z.* 91 K3
Greystones, *Ireland* 12 C5
Greytown, *N.Z.* 91 J5

Greytown, *S. Africa* 89 D5
Gribanovskiy, *Russia* 34 E5
Gribbell I., *Canada* 102 C3
Gribës, Mal i, *Albania* 44 F3
Gridley, *U.S.A.* 110 F5
Griekwastad, *S. Africa* 88 D3
Griesheim, *Germany* 25 F4
Grieskirchen, *Austria* 26 C6
Griffin, *U.S.A.* 115 J3
Griffith, *Australia* 95 E4
Griffith, *Canada* 116 A7
Griffith I., *Canada* 116 B4
Grignols, *France* 20 D3
Grigoriopol, *Moldova* 29 C14
Grimaylov = Hrymayliv, *Ukraine* 33 H4
Grimes, *U.S.A.* 110 F5
Grimma, *Germany* 24 D8
Grimmen, *Germany* 24 A9
Grimsay, *U.K.* 13 D1
Grimsby, *Canada* 116 C5
Grimsby, *U.K.* 14 D7
Grimshaw, *Canada* 102 B5
Grimslöv, *Sweden* 11 H8
Grimstad, *Norway* 9 G13
Grimsey, *Iceland* 8 C5
Grindelwald, *Switz.* 25 J4
Grindsted, *Denmark* 11 J2
Grindstone I., *Canada* 117 B8
Grindu, *Romania* 29 F11
Grinnell, *U.S.A.* 112 E8
Grintavec, *Slovenia* 41 B11
Gris-Nez, C., *France* 19 B8
Grisolles, *France* 20 E5
Grisons = Graubünden □, *Switz.* 25 J5
Grisslehamn, *Sweden* 10 D12
Grmeč Planina, *Bos.-H.* 41 D13
Groais I., *Canada* 105 B8
Grobiņa, *Latvia* 30 B8
Groblersdal, *S. Africa* 89 D4
Grobming, *Austria* 26 D6
Grocka, *Serbia & M.* 44 B4
Gródek, *Poland* 31 E10
Grodków, *Poland* 31 H4
Grodno = Hrodna, *Belarus* 30 E10
Grodzisk Mazowiecki, *Poland* 31 F7
Grodzisk Wielkopolski, *Poland* 31 F3
Grodzyanka = Hrodzyanka, *Belarus* 32 F5
Groesbeck, *U.S.A.* 113 K6
Groix, *France* 18 E3
Groix, Î. de, *France* 18 E3
Grójec, *Poland* 31 G7
Gronau, *Niedersachsen, Germany* 24 C5
Gronau, *Nordrhein-Westfalen, Germany* 24 C3
Grong, *Norway* 8 D15
Grönhögen, *Sweden* 11 H10
Groningen, *Neths.* 17 A6
Groningen □, *Neths.* 17 A6
Groom, *U.S.A.* 113 H4
Groot →, *S. Africa* 88 E3
Groot Berg →, *S. Africa* 88 E2
Groot-Brakrivier, *S. Africa* 88 E3
Groot Karasberge, *Namibia* 88 D2
Groot-Kei →, *S. Africa* 89 E4
Groot Vis →, *S. Africa* 88 E4
Grootdrink, *S. Africa* 88 D3
Groote Eylandt, *Australia* 94 A2
Grootfontein, *Namibia* 88 B2
Grootlaagte →, *Africa* 88 C3
Grootvloer →, *S. Africa* 88 E3
Gros C., *Canada* 102 A6
Gros Islet, *St. Lucia* 121 f
Gros Morne △, *Canada* 105 C8
Gros Piton, *St. Lucia* 121 f
Gros Piton Pt., *St. Lucia* 121 f
Grósio, *Italy* 40 B7
Grosne →, *France* 19 F11
Grossa, Pta., *Spain* 48 B8
Grossenbrode, *Germany* 24 A7
Grossenhain, *Germany* 24 D9
Grosser Arber, *Germany* 25 F9
Grosser Plöner See, *Germany* 24 A6
Grosseto, *Italy* 41 F8
Grossgerungs, *Austria* 26 C7
Grossglockner, *Austria* 26 D5
Groswater B., *Canada* 105 B8
Groton, *Conn., U.S.A.* 117 E12
Groton, *N.Y., U.S.A.* 117 D8
Groton, *S. Dak., U.S.A.* 112 C5
Grottáglie, *Italy* 43 B10
Grottaminarda, *Italy* 43 A8
Grottammare, *Italy* 41 F10
Grouard Mission, *Canada* 102 B5
Grouin, Pte. du, *France* 18 D5
Groundhog →, *Canada* 104 C3
Grouw, *Neths.* 17 A5
Grove City, *U.S.A.* 116 E4
Grove Hill, *U.S.A.* 115 K2
Groveland, *U.S.A.* 110 H6
Grover City, *U.S.A.* 111 K6
Groves, *U.S.A.* 113 L8
Groveton, *U.S.A.* 117 B13
Grožnjan, *Croatia* 41 C10
Groznyy, *Russia* 35 J7
Grubišno Polje, *Croatia* 28 E2
Grudovo = Sredets, *Bulgaria* 45 D11
Grudusk, *Poland* 31 E7
Grudziądz, *Poland* 30 E5
Gruinard B., *U.K.* 13 D3
Gruissan, *France* 20 E7
Grumo Áppula, *Italy* 43 A9
Grums, *Sweden* 10 E7
Grünberg, *Germany* 24 E5
Gründau, *Germany* 25 E5
Grünstadt, *Germany* 25 F4
Gruppo di Tessa △, *Italy* 40 B8
Gruver, *U.S.A.* 113 G4
Gruyères, *Switz.* 25 J3
Gruža, *Serbia & M.* 44 C4

Gryazi, *Russia* 33 F10
Gryazovets, *Russia* 32 C11
Grybów, *Poland* 31 J7
Grycksbo, *Sweden* 10 D9
Gryfice, *Poland* 30 E2
Gryfino, *Poland* 31 E1
Gryfów Śląski, *Poland* 31 G2
Grythyttan, *Sweden* 10 E8
Gua, *India* 67 H14
Gua Musang, *Malaysia* 65 K3
Guacanayabo, G. de, *Cuba* 120 B4
Guachípas →, *Argentina* 126 B2
Guadajoz →, *Spain* 37 H6
Guadalajara, *Mexico* 118 C4
Guadalajara, *Spain* 38 E1
Guadalajara □, *Spain* 38 E2
Guadalcanal, *Solomon Is.* 96 H8
Guadalcanal, *Spain* 37 G5
Guadalén →, *Spain* 37 G7
Guadalmena →, *Argentina* 126 C2
Guadalete →, *Spain* 37 J4
Guadalimar →, *Spain* 37 G7
Guadalmena →, *Spain* 37 G3
Guadalmez →, *Spain* 37 G5
Guadalope →, *Spain* 38 D4
Guadalquivir →, *Spain* 37 J4
Guadalupe = Guadeloupe ☒, *W. Indies* 120 b
Guadalupe, *Mexico* 111 N10
Guadalupe, *Spain* 37 F5
Guadalupe, *U.S.A.* 111 L6
Guadalupe →, *Mexico* 111 N10
Guadalupe →, *U.S.A.* 113 L6
Guadalupe, Sierra de, *Spain* 37 F5
Guadalupe Bravos, *Mexico* 118 A3
Guadalupe I., *Pac. Oc.* 98 G8
Guadalupe Mts. △, *U.S.A.* 113 K2
Guadalupe Peak, *U.S.A.* 113 K2
Guadalupe y Calvo, *Mexico* 118 B3
Guadarrama, Sierra de, *Spain* 36 E7
Guadauta, *Georgia* 35 J5
Guadeloupe ☒, *Guadeloupe* 120 b
Guadeloupe ☒, *W. Indies* 120 b
Guadeloupe Passage, *W. Indies* 121 C7
Guadiamar →, *Spain* 37 J4
Guadiana →, *Portugal* 37 H3
Guadiana Menor →, *Spain* 37 H7
Guadiaro →, *Spain* 37 J5
Guadiato →, *Spain* 37 H5
Guadiela →, *Spain* 38 E2
Guadix, *Spain* 37 H7
Guafo, Boca del, *Chile* 128 E2
Guaico, *Trin. & Tob.* 125 K15
Guainía □, *Colombia* 124 C5
Guaíra, *Brazil* 127 A5
Guaíra □, *Paraguay* 126 B4
Guaitecas, Is., *Chile* 128 E2
Guajará-Mirim, *Brazil* 124 F5
Guajira, Pen. de la, *Colombia* 124 A4
Gualán, *Guatemala* 120 C2
Gualdo Tadino, *Italy* 41 E9
Gualeguay, *Argentina* 126 C4
Gualeguaychú, *Argentina* 126 C4
Gualequay →, *Argentina* 126 C4
Guam ☒, *Pac. Oc.* 96 F6
Guaminí, *Argentina* 126 D3
Guamúchil, *Mexico* 118 B3
Guana I., *Br. Virgin Is.* 121 e
Guanabara, *Brazil* 120 B3
Guanacaste △, *Costa Rica* 120 D2
Guanacaste, Cordillera del, *Costa Rica* 120 D2
Guanaceví, *Mexico* 118 B3
Guanahani = San Salvador I., *Bahamas* 121 B5
Guanajay, *Cuba* 120 B3
Guanajuato, *Mexico* 118 C4
Guanajuato □, *Mexico* 118 C4
Guandacol, *Argentina* 126 B2
Guane, *Cuba* 120 B3
Guang'an, *China* 58 B6
Guangchang, *China* 59 D11
Guangde, *China* 59 B12
Guangdong □, *China* 59 F9
Guangfeng, *China* 59 C12
Guanghan, *China* 58 B5
Guangling, *China* 56 E8
Guangnan, *China* 58 E5
Guangning, *China* 59 F9
Guangrao, *China* 57 F10
Guangshui, *China* 59 B9
Guangshun, *China* 58 D6
Guangwu, *China* 56 F3
Guangxi Zhuangzu Zizhiqu □, *China* 58 F7
Guangyuan, *China* 58 A5
Guangze, *China* 59 D11
Guangzhou, *China* 59 F9
Guánica, *Puerto Rico* 121 d
Guanipa →, *Venezuela* 124 B6
Guanling, *China* 58 E5
Guannan, *China* 57 G10
Guantánamo, *Cuba* 121 B4
Guantánamo B., *Cuba* 121 C4
Guantao, *China* 56 F8
Guanyang, *China* 59 E8
Guanyun, *China* 57 G10
Guápiles, *Costa Rica* 120 D3
Guapo B., *Trin. & Tob.* 125 K15
Guaporé, *Brazil* 127 B5
Guaporé →, *Brazil* 124 F5
Guaqui, *Bolivia* 124 G5
Guara, Sierra de, *Spain* 38 C4
Guaramacal △, *Venezuela* 121 E5
Guarapari, *Brazil* 127 A7
Guarapuava, *Brazil* 127 B5
Guaratinguetá, *Brazil* 127 A6
Guaratuba, *Brazil* 127 B6
Guarda, *Portugal* 36 E3
Guarda □, *Portugal* 36 E3

Guardafui, C. = Asir, Ras, Somali Rep. 75 E5
Guardamar del Segura, Spain 39 G4
Guardavalle, Italy 43 D9
Guárdia Sanframondi, Italy 43 A7
Guardiagrele, Italy 41 F11
Guardo, Spain 36 C6
Guareña, Spain 37 G4
Guareña →, Spain 36 D5
Guárico □, Venezuela 124 B5
Guarujá, Brazil 127 A6
Guarulhos, Brazil 127 A6
Guarus, Brazil 127 A7
Guasave, Mexico 118 B3
Guasdualito, Venezuela 124 B4
Guastalla, Italy 40 D7
Guatemala, Guatemala 120 D1
Guatemala ■, Cent. Amer. 120 C1
Guatemala Trench, Pac. Oc. 98 H10
Guatopo △, Venezuela 121 D6
Guatuaro Pt., Trin. & Tob. 125 K16
Guaviare →, Colombia 124 C5
Guaxupé, Brazil 127 A6
Guayaguayare, Trin. & Tob. 125 K15
Guayama, Puerto Rico 121 d
Guayaquil, Ecuador 124 D3
Guayaquil, G. de, Ecuador 124 D2
Guaymas, Mexico 118 B2
Guba, Dem. Rep. of the Congo 87 E2
Guba, Ethiopia 81 E4
Gûbâl, Madiq, Egypt 80 B3
Gubat, Phil. 61 E6
Gúbbio, Italy 41 E9
Guben, Germany 24 D10
Gubin, Poland 31 G1
Gubio, Nigeria 83 C7
Gubkin, Russia 33 G9
Guča, Serbia & M. 44 C4
Gucheng, China 59 A8
Gudata = Guadauta, Georgia 35 J5
Gudbrandsdalen, Norway 9 F14
Guddu Barrage, Pakistan 66 E6
Gudenå →, Denmark 11 H4
Gudermes, Russia 35 J8
Gudhjem, Denmark 11 J8
Gudur, India 66 M11
Guebwiller, France 19 E14
Guecho = Getxo, Spain 38 B2
Guékédou, Guinea 82 D2
Guele Mendouka, Cameroon 83 E7
Guelmine = Goulimine, Morocco 78 C3
Guelph, Canada 116 C4
Guémené-Penfao, France 18 E5
Guémené-sur-Scorff, France 18 D3
Guéné, Benin 83 C5
Guer, France 18 E4
Guérande, France 18 E4
Guéret, France 19 F8
Guérigny, France 19 E10
Guerneville, U.S.A. 110 G4
Guernica = Gernika-Lumo, Spain 38 B2
Guernsey, U.K. 15 H5
Guernsey, U.S.A. 112 D2
Guerrero □, Mexico 119 D5
Guessou-Sud, Benin 83 C5
Gueugnon, France 19 F11
Guéyo, Ivory C. 82 D3
Gughe, Ethiopia 81 F4
Gügher, Iran 71 D8
Guglionesi, Italy 41 G11
Guhakolak, Tanjung, Indonesia 63 G11
Gui Jiang →, China 59 F8
Guia, Canary Is. 48 F4
Guia de Isora, Canary Is. 48 F3
Guia Lopes da Laguna, Brazil 127 A4
Guiana Highlands, S. Amer. 122 C4
Guibéroua, Ivory C. 82 D3
Guichi, China 59 B11
Guider, Cameroon 83 D7
Guidiguir, Niger 83 C6
Guidimouni, Niger 83 C6
Guiding, China 58 D6
Guidong, China 59 D9
Guidónia-Montecélio, Italy 41 F9
Guiers, L. de, Senegal 82 B1
Guigang, China 58 F7
Guiglo, Ivory C. 82 D3
Guihulñgan, Phil. 61 F5
Guijá, Mozam. 89 C5
Guijuelo, Spain 36 E5
Guildford, U.K. 15 F7
Guilford, U.S.A. 117 E12
Guilin, China 59 E8
Guillaume-Delisle, L., Canada 104 A4
Guillaumes, France 21 D10
Guillestre, France 21 D10
Guilvinec, France 18 E2
Güimar, Canary Is. 48 F3
Guimarães, Portugal 36 D2
Guimaras □, Phil. 61 F5
Guinda, U.S.A. 110 G4
Guinea, Africa 76 F4
Guinea ■, W. Afr. 82 C2
Guinea, Gulf of, Atl. Oc. 83 E5
Guinea-Bissau ■, Africa 82 C2
Güines, Cuba 120 B3
Guingamp, France 18 D3
Guinguinéo, Senegal 82 C1
Guipavas, France 18 D2
Guiping, China 59 F8
Guipúzcoa □, Spain 38 B2
Guir →, Mali 82 B4
Guirel, Mauritania 82 B3
Güiria, Venezuela 124 A6
Guiscard, France 19 C10
Guise, France 19 C10
Guitiriz, Spain 36 B3
Guitri, Ivory C. 82 D3
Guiuan, Phil. 61 F6
Guixi, China 59 C11
Guiyang, Guizhou, China 58 D6
Guiyang, Hunan, China 59 E9

Guizhou □, China 58 D6
Gujan-Mestras, France 20 D2
Gujar Khan, Pakistan 68 C5
Gujarat □, India 68 H4
Gujiang, China 59 D10
Gujranwala, Pakistan 68 C6
Gujrat, Pakistan 68 C6
Gukovo, Russia 35 F5
Gulbarga, India 66 L10
Gulbene, Latvia 9 H22
Gulf, The = Persian Gulf, Asia 71 E6
Gulf Islands △, U.S.A. 115 C12
Gulfport, U.S.A. 113 K10
Gulgong, Australia 95 E4
Gulin, China 58 C5
Gulistan, Pakistan 68 D2
Gull Lake, Canada 103 C7
Gullbrandstorp, Sweden 11 H6
Gullspång, Sweden 11 F8
Güllük, Turkey 47 D9
Güllük Daği △, Turkey 47 E12
Güllük Korfezi, Turkey 47 D9
Gulma, Nigeria 83 C5
Gulmarg, India 69 B6
Gulnar, Turkey 72 D5
Gülpınar, Turkey 47 B8
Gülşehir, Turkey 72 C6
Gulshad, Kazakhstan 52 E8
Gulu, Uganda 86 B3
Gŭlŭbovo, Bulgaria 45 D9
Gulud, J., Sudan 81 E2
Gulwe, Tanzania 86 D4
Gulyaypole = Hulyaypole, Ukraine 33 J9
Gumal →, Pakistan 68 D4
Gumbaz, Pakistan 68 D3
Gumel, Nigeria 83 C6
Gumiel de Hizán, Spain 36 D7
Gumla, India 69 H11
Gumlu, Australia 94 B4
Gummersbach, Germany 24 D3
Gummi, Nigeria 83 C6
Gümüldür, Turkey 47 C9
Gümüşçay, Turkey 45 F11
Gümüşhacıköy, Turkey 72 B6
Gümüşhane, Turkey 73 B8
Gümüşsu, Turkey 47 C11
Gumzai, Indonesia 63 F8
Guna, Ethiopia 81 F4
Guna, India 68 G7
Gundelfingen, Germany 25 G6
Güney, Burdur, Turkey 47 D11
Güney, Denizli, Turkey 47 C11
Güneydoğu Toroslar, Turkey 73 C9
Gunisao →, Canada 103 C9
Gunisao L., Canada 103 C9
Gunjyal, Pakistan 68 C4
Günlüce, Turkey 47 E10
Gunnarskog, Sweden 10 E6
Gunnbjørn Fjeld, Greenland 4 C6
Gunnebo, Sweden 11 G10
Gunnedah, Australia 95 E5
Gunnewin, Australia 95 D4
Gunningbar Cr. →, Australia 95 E4
Gunnison, Colo., U.S.A. 109 G10
Gunnison, Utah, U.S.A. 108 G8
Gunnison →, U.S.A. 109 G9
Guntakal, India 66 M10
Guntersville, U.S.A. 115 H2
Guntong, Malaysia 65 K3
Guntur, India 67 L12
Gunungapi, Indonesia 63 F7
Gunungsitoli, Indonesia 62 D1
Günz →, Germany 25 G6
Gunza, Angola 84 G2
Günzburg, Germany 25 G6
Gunzenhausen, Germany 25 F6
Guo He →, China 57 H9
Guoyang, China 56 H9
Gupis, Pakistan 69 A5
Gura Humorului, Romania 29 C10
Gura-Teghii, Romania 29 E11
Gurag, Ethiopia 81 F4
Gurahonț, Romania 28 D7
Gurdaspur, India 68 C6
Gurdon, U.S.A. 113 J8
Güre, Balıkesir, Turkey 47 B8
Güre, Uşak, Turkey 47 C11
Gurgaon, India 68 E7
Gürgentepe, Turkey 72 B7
Gurghiu, Munții, Romania 29 D10
Gurgueia →, Brazil 125 E10
Gurha, India 68 G4
Guri, Embalse de, Venezuela 124 B6
Gurig △, Australia 92 B5
Gurin, Nigeria 83 D7
Gurjaani, Georgia 35 K7
Gurk →, Austria 26 E7
Gurkha, Nepal 69 E11
Gurley, Australia 95 D4
Gurnet Point, U.S.A. 117 D14
Guro, Mozam. 87 F3
Gürpınar, Ist., Turkey 45 F12
Gürpınar, Van, Turkey 73 C10
Gürsu, Turkey 45 F13
Gurué, Mozam. 87 F4
Gurun, Malaysia 65 K3
Gürün, Turkey 72 C7
Gurupá, Brazil 125 D8
Gurupá, I. Grande de, Brazil 125 D8
Gurupi, Brazil 125 F9
Gurupi →, Brazil 125 D9
Guruwe, Zimbabwe 89 B5
Guryev = Atyraū, Kazakhstan 52 E6
Guryevsk, Russia 30 D7
Gus-Khrustalnyy, Russia 34 C5
Gusau, Nigeria 83 C6
Gusev, Russia 9 J20
Gushan, China 57 E12
Gushgy, Turkmenistan 52 F7

Gushi, China 59 A10
Gushiago, Ghana 83 D4
Gusinje, Serbia & M. 44 D3
Gusinoozersk, Russia 53 D11
Gúspini, Italy 42 C1
Güssing, Austria 27 D9
Gustavsberg, Sweden 10 E12
Gustavus, U.S.A. 102 B1
Gustine, U.S.A. 110 H6
Güstrow, Germany 24 B8
Gusum, Sweden 11 F10
Guta = Kolárovo, Slovak Rep. 27 D10
Gütersloh, Germany 24 D4
Gutha, Australia 93 E2
Guthalungra, Australia 94 B4
Guthrie, Okla., U.S.A. 113 H6
Guthrie, Tex., U.S.A. 113 J4
Gutian, China 59 D12
Guttenberg, U.S.A. 112 D9
Gutu, Zimbabwe 89 B5
Guwahati, India 67 F17
Guy Fawkes River △, Australia 95 D5
Guyana ■, S. Amer. 124 C7
Guyane française = French Guiana ☒, S. Amer. 125 C8
Guyang, China 56 D6
Guyenne, France 20 D4
Guymon, U.S.A. 113 G4
Guyra, Australia 95 E5
Guyuan, Hebei, China 56 D8
Guyuan, Ningxia Huizu, China 56 G4
Güzelbahçe, Turkey 47 C8
Güzelyurt = Morphou, Cyprus 49 D11
Guzhang, China 58 C7
Guzhen, China 57 H9
Guzmán, L. de, Mexico 118 A3
Gvardeysk, Russia 9 J19
Gvardeyskoye, Ukraine 33 K8
Gwa, Burma 67 L19
Gwaai, Zimbabwe 87 F2
Gwaai →, Zimbabwe 87 F2
Gwabegar, Australia 95 E4
Gwadabawa, Nigeria 83 C6
Gwädar, Pakistan 66 G3
Gwagwada, Nigeria 83 C6
Gwaii Haanas △, Canada 102 C2
Gwalior, India 68 F8
Gwanara, Nigeria 83 D5
Gwanda, Zimbabwe 87 G2
Gwandu, Nigeria 83 C5
Gwane, Dem. Rep. of the Congo 86 B2
Gwaram, Nigeria 83 C7
Gwarzo, Nigeria 83 C6
Gwda →, Poland 31 E3
Gweebarra B., Ireland 12 B3
Gweedore, Ireland 12 A3
Gweru, Zimbabwe 87 F2
Gwi, Nigeria 83 D6
Gwinn, U.S.A. 114 B2
Gwio Kura, Nigeria 83 C7
Gwoza, Nigeria 83 C7
Gwydir →, Australia 95 D4
Gwynedd □, U.K. 14 E3
Gyandzha = Gäncä, Azerbaijan 35 K8
Gyaring Hu, China 60 C4
Gydanskiy Poluostrov, Russia 52 C8
Gympie, Australia 95 D5
Gyomaendrőd, Hungary 28 D5
Gyöngyös, Hungary 28 C4
Győr, Hungary 28 C2
Győr-Moson-Sopron □, Hungary 28 C2
Gypsum Pt., Canada 102 A6
Gypsumville, Canada 103 C9
Gyueshevo, Bulgaria 44 D6
Gyula, Hungary 28 D6
Gyumri, Armenia 35 K6
Gyzylarbat, Turkmenistan 52 F6
Gyzyletrek, Turkmenistan 71 B7
Gzhatsk = Gagarin, Russia 32 E8

H

Ha 'Arava →, Israel 74 E4
Ha Coi, Vietnam 58 G6
Ha Dong, Vietnam 58 G5
Ha Giang, Vietnam 58 F5
Ha Karmel △, Israel 74 C4
Ha Tien, Vietnam 65 G5
Ha Tinh, Vietnam 64 C5
Ha Trung, Vietnam 64 C5
Ha Yaek Chalong, Thailand 65 a
Haaksbergen, Neths. 17 B6
Haapsalu, Estonia 9 G20
Haarlem, Neths. 17 B4
Haast →, N.Z. 91 K2
Haast Bluff, Australia 92 D5
Hab →, Pakistan 68 G3
Hab Nadi Chauki, Pakistan 68 G2
Habahe, China 60 B3
Habaswein, Kenya 86 B4
Habay, Canada 102 B5
Habbānīyah, Iraq 70 C4
Habbānīyah, Hawr al, Iraq 73 F10
Habichtswald △, Germany 24 D5
Habo, Sweden 11 G8
Haboro, Japan 54 B10
Habshān, U.A.E. 71 F7
Hachenburg, Germany 24 E3
Hachijō-Jima, Japan 55 H9
Hachinohe, Japan 54 D10
Hachiōji, Japan 55 G9
Hachŏn, N. Korea 57 D15
Hacıbektaş, Turkey 72 C6
Hacılar, Turkey 72 C6
Hachās, Sweden 10 B8
Hackensack, U.S.A. 117 F10
Hackettstown, U.S.A. 117 F10

Hadali, Pakistan 68 C5
Hadarba, Ras, Sudan 80 C4
Hadarom □, Israel 74 E4
Hadd, Ra's al, Oman 75 C6
Haddington, U.K. 13 F6
Hadejia, Nigeria 83 C7
Hadejia →, Nigeria 83 C7
Hadera, Israel 74 C3
Hadera, N. →, Israel 74 C3
Haderslev, Denmark 11 J3
Hadhramaut = Hadramawt, Yemen 75 D4
Hadiboh, Yemen 75 E5
Hadım, Turkey 72 D5
Hadong, S. Korea 57 G14
Hadramawt, Yemen 75 D4
Hadrānīyah, Iraq 70 C4
Hadrian's Wall, U.K. 14 B5
Hadsten, Denmark 11 H4
Hadsund, Denmark 11 H4
Hadyach, Ukraine 33 G8
Haeju, N. Korea 57 E13
Haenam, S. Korea 57 G14
Haenertsburg, S. Africa 89 C4
Haerhpin = Harbin, China 57 B14
Hafar al Bāṭin, Si. Arabia 70 D5
Hafik, Turkey 72 C7
Hafīrat al 'Aydā, Si. Arabia 70 E3
Hafit, Oman 71 F7
Hafizabad, Pakistan 68 C5
Haflong, India 67 G18
Hafnarfjörður, Iceland 8 D3
Haft Gel, Iran 71 D6
Hafun, Ras, Somali Rep. 75 E5
Hagalil, Israel 74 C4
Hagby, Sweden 11 H10
Hagen, Germany 24 D3
Hagenow, Germany 24 B7
Hagerman, U.S.A. 113 J2
Hagerman Fossil Beds △, U.S.A. 108 E6
Hagerstown, U.S.A. 114 F7
Hagersville, Canada 116 D4
Hagetmau, France 20 E3
Hagfors, Sweden 10 D7
Hagi, Japan 55 G5
Hagolan, Syria 74 C4
Hagondange, France 19 C13
Hags Hd., Ireland 12 D2
Hague, C. de la, France 18 C5
Hague, The = 's-Gravenhage, Neths. 17 B4
Haguenau, France 19 D14
Hai Duong, Vietnam 58 G6
Hai'an, Guangdong, China 59 G8
Hai'an, Jiangsu, China 59 A13
Haicheng, Fujian, China 59 E11
Haicheng, Liaoning, China 57 D12
Haidar Khel, Afghan. 68 C3
Haidarābād = Hyderabad, India 66 L11
Haidargarh, India 69 F9
Haifa = Hefa, Israel 74 C4
Haifeng, China 59 F10
Haiger, Germany 24 E4
Haikou, China 60 D6
Hā'il, Si. Arabia 70 E4
Hailar, China 60 B6
Hailey, U.S.A. 108 E6
Haileybury, Canada 104 C4
Hailin, China 57 B15
Hailing Dao, China 59 G8
Hailong, China 57 C13
Hailuoto, Finland 8 D21
Haimen, Guangdong, China 59 F11
Haimen, Jiangsu, China 59 B13
Hainan □, China 60 E5
Hainaut □, Belgium 17 D4
Hainburg, Austria 27 C9
Haines, Alaska, U.S.A. 102 B1
Haines, Oreg., U.S.A. 108 D5
Haines City, U.S.A. 115 L5
Haines Junction, Canada 102 A1
Hainfeld, Austria 26 C8
Haining, China 59 B13
Haiphong, Vietnam 58 G6
Haitan Dao, China 59 E12
Haiti ■, W. Indies 121 C5
Haiya, Sudan 80 D4
Haiyan, China 59 B13
Haiyang, China 57 F11
Haiyuan, Guangxi Zhuangzu, China 58 F6
Haiyuan, Ningxia Huizu, China 56 F3
Haizhou, China 57 G10
Haizhou Wan, China 57 G10
Hajdú-Bihar □, Hungary 28 C6
Hajdúböszörmény, Hungary 28 C6
Hajdúdorog, Hungary 28 C6
Hajdúhadház, Hungary 28 C6
Hajdúnánás, Hungary 28 C6
Hajdúsámson, Hungary 28 C6
Hajdúszoboszló, Hungary 28 C6
Hajipur, India 69 G11
Hājjī Muḥsin, Iraq 70 C5
Hājjīābād, Iran 71 D7
Hājjīābād-e Zarrīn, Iran 71 C7
Hajnówka, Poland 31 F10
Hakansson, Mts., Dem. Rep. of the Congo 87 D2
Hakkâri, Turkey 70 B4
Hakkâri Dağları, Turkey 73 C10
Hakken-Zan, Japan 55 G7
Hakodate, Japan 54 D10
Hakos, Namibia 88 C2
Håksberg, Sweden 10 D9
Haku-San, Japan 55 F8
Haku-San, Japan 55 F8
Hakui, Japan 55 F8

Hālat 'Ammār, Si. Arabia 70 D3
Halbā, Lebanon 74 A5
Halberstadt, Germany 24 D7
Halcombe, N.Z. 91 J5
Halcon, Phil. 63 B6
Halde Fjäll = Haltiatunturi, Finland 8 B19
Halden, Norway 9 G14
Haldensleben, Germany 24 C7
Haldia, India 67 H16
Haldimand, Canada 116 D5
Haldwani, India 69 E8
Hale →, Australia 94 C2
Halesowen, U.K. 15 E5
Halesworth, U.K. 15 E9
Haleyville, U.S.A. 115 H2
Half Assini, Ghana 82 D4
Halfmoon Bay, N.Z. 91 M2
Halfway →, Canada 102 B4
Halia, India 69 G10
Haliburton, Canada 116 A6
Halifax, Australia 94 B4
Halifax, Canada 105 D7
Halifax, U.K. 14 D6
Halifax, U.S.A. 116 F8
Halifax B., Australia 94 B4
Halifax I., Namibia 88 D2
Halīl →, Iran 71 E8
Halkirk, U.K. 13 C5
Hall Beach = Sanirajak, Canada 101 B11
Hall in Tirol, Austria 26 D4
Hall Pen., Canada 101 B13
Hall Pt., Australia 92 C3
Hallabro, Sweden 11 H9
Halland, Sweden 9 H15
Hallands □, Sweden 11 H6
Hallands Väderö, Sweden 11 H6
Hallandsås, Sweden 11 H7
Hällbybrunn, Sweden 10 E10
Halle, Belgium 17 D4
Halle, Nordrhein-Westfalen, Germany 24 C4
Halle, Sachsen-Anhalt, Germany 24 D7
Hällefors, Sweden 10 E8
Hälleforsnäs, Sweden 10 E10
Hallein, Austria 26 D6
Hällekis, Sweden 11 F7
Hallen, Sweden 10 A8
Hallett, Australia 95 E2
Hallettsville, U.S.A. 113 L6
Hallim, S. Korea 57 H14
Hallingdalselvi →, Norway 9 F13
Hallock, U.S.A. 112 A6
Halls Creek, Australia 92 C4
Hallsberg, Sweden 10 E9
Hallstahammar, Sweden 10 E10
Hallstatt, Austria 26 D6
Hallstavik, Sweden 10 D12
Hallstead, U.S.A. 117 E9
Halmahera, Indonesia 63 D7
Halmeu, Romania 28 C8
Halmstad, Sweden 11 H6
Hals, Denmark 11 H4
Hälsingborg = Helsingborg, Sweden 11 H6
Hälsingland, Sweden 10 C10
Halstead, U.K. 15 F8
Haltern, Germany 24 D3
Haltiatunturi, Finland 8 B19
Halton □, U.K. 14 D5
Haltwhistle, U.K. 14 C5
Hālūl, Qatar 71 E7
Halvad, India 68 H4
Halvān, Iran 71 C8
Ham, France 19 C10
Ham Tan, Vietnam 65 G6
Ham Yen, Vietnam 64 A5
Hamab, Namibia 88 D2
Hamad, Sudan 81 D3
Hamada, Japan 55 G6
Hamadān, Iran 71 C6
Hamadān □, Iran 71 C6
Hamāh, Syria 70 C3
Hamamatsu, Japan 55 G8
Hamar, Norway 9 F14
Hamâta, Gebel, Egypt 70 E2
Hambantota, Sri Lanka 66 R12
Hamber △, Canada 102 C5
Hamburg, Germany 24 B5
Hamburg, Ark., U.S.A. 113 J9
Hamburg, N.Y., U.S.A. 116 D6
Hamburg, Pa., U.S.A. 117 F9
Hamburg □, Germany 24 B5
Hamburg Fuhlsbüttel ✈ (HAM), Germany 24 B5
Hamd, W. al →, Si. Arabia 70 E3
Hamden, U.S.A. 117 E12
Hamdibey, Turkey 47 B9
Häme, Finland 9 F20
Hämeenlinna, Finland 9 F21
Hamélé, Ghana 82 C4
Hamelin Pool, Australia 93 E1
Hameln, Germany 24 C5
Hamerkaz □, Israel 74 C3
Hamersley Ra., Australia 92 D2
Hamhung, N. Korea 57 E14
Hami, China 60 B4
Hamilton, Australia 95 F3
Hamilton, Canada 116 C5
Hamilton, N.Z. 91 G5
Hamilton, U.K. 13 F4
Hamilton, Ala., U.S.A. 115 H1
Hamilton, Mont., U.S.A. 108 C6
Hamilton, N.Y., U.S.A. 117 D9
Hamilton, Ohio, U.S.A. 114 F3
Hamilton, Tex., U.S.A. 113 K5
Hamilton →, Australia 94 C2
Hamilton, The →, Australia 95 D2
Hamilton City, U.S.A. 110 F4
Hamilton I., Australia 94 J6
Hamilton Inlet, Canada 105 B8
Hamilton Mt., U.S.A. 117 C10

Hamina, *Finland* 9 F22
Hamirpur, *H.P., India* 68 D7
Hamirpur, *Ut. P., India* 69 G9
Hamitabat, *Turkey* 45 E11
Hamlet, *U.S.A.* 115 H6
Hamley Bridge, *Australia* 95 E2
Hamlin = Hameln, *Germany* ... 24 C5
Hamlin, *N.Y., U.S.A.* 116 C7
Hamlin, *Tex., U.S.A.* 113 J4
Hamm, *Germany* 24 D3
Ḥammār, Hawr al, *Iraq* 70 D5
Hammarstrand, *Sweden* 10 A10
Hammeren, *Denmark* 11 J8
Hammerfest, *Norway* 8 A20
Hammerum, *Denmark* 11 H3
Hamminkeln, *Germany* 24 D2
Hammond, *Ind., U.S.A.* 114 E2
Hammond, *La., U.S.A.* 113 K9
Hammond, *N.Y., U.S.A.* 117 B9
Hammondsport, *U.S.A.* 116 D7
Hammonton, *U.S.A.* 114 F8
Hamneda, *Sweden* 11 H7
Hamoyet, Jebel, *Sudan* 80 D4
Hampden, *N.Z.* 91 L3
Hampshire □, *U.K.* 15 F6
Hampshire Downs, *U.K.* 15 F6
Hampton, *N.B., Canada* 105 C6
Hampton, *Ont., Canada* 116 C6
Hampton, *Ark., U.S.A.* 113 J8
Hampton, *Iowa, U.S.A.* 112 D8
Hampton, *N.H., U.S.A.* 117 D14
Hampton, *S.C., U.S.A.* 115 J5
Hampton, *Va., U.S.A.* 114 G7
Hampton Bays, *U.S.A.* 117 F12
Hampton Tableland, *Australia* .. 93 F4
Hamra, *Sweden* 10 C8
Hamrat esh Sheykh, *Sudan* 81 E2
Hamur, *Turkey* 73 C10
Hamyang, *S. Korea* 57 G14
Han Jiang →, *China* 59 F11
Han Shui, *China* 58 A7
Han Shui →, *China* 59 B10
Hanak, *Si. Arabia* 70 E3
Hanamaki, *Japan* 54 E10
Hanang, *Tanzania* 86 C4
Hanau, *Germany* 25 E4
Hanbogd = Ihbulag, *Mongolia* .. 56 C4
Hançalar, *Turkey* 47 C11
Hâncești, *Moldova* 29 D13
Hancheng, *China* 56 G6
Hanchuan, *China* 59 B9
Hancock, *Mich., U.S.A.* 112 B10
Hancock, *N.Y., U.S.A.* 117 E9
Handa, *Japan* 55 G8
Handan, *China* 56 F8
Handeni, *Tanzania* 86 D4
Handlová, *Slovak Rep.* 27 C11
Handub, *Sudan* 80 D4
Handwara, *India* 69 B6
Hanegev, *Israel* 74 E4
Hanford, *U.S.A.* 110 J7
Hanford Reach △, *U.S.A.* 108 C4
Hang Chat, *Thailand* 64 C2
Hang Dong, *Thailand* 64 C2
Hangang →, *S. Korea* 57 F14
Hangayn Nuruu, *Mongolia* 60 B4
Hangchou = Hangzhou, *China* .. 59 B13
Hanggin Houqi, *China* 56 D4
Hanggin Qi, *China* 56 E5
Hangu, *China* 57 E9
Hangzhou, *China* 59 B13
Hangzhou Wan, *China* 59 B13
Hanhongor, *Mongolia* 56 C3
Hanidh, *Si. Arabia* 71 E6
Ḥanīsh, *Yemen* 75 E3
Haniska, *Slovak Rep.* 27 C14
Hanjiang, *China* 59 E12
Hankinson, *U.S.A.* 112 B6
Hankö, *Finland* 9 G20
Hankou, *China* 59 B10
Hanksville, *U.S.A.* 109 G8
Hanle, *India* 69 C8
Hanmer Springs, *N.Z.* 91 K4
Hann →, *Australia* 92 C4
Hann, Mt., *Australia* 92 C4
Hanna, *Canada* 102 C6
Hanna, *U.S.A.* 108 F10
Hannah B., *Canada* 104 B4
Hannibal, *Mo., U.S.A.* 112 F9
Hannibal, *N.Y., U.S.A.* 117 C8
Hannik, *Sudan* 80 D3
Hannover, *Germany* 24 C5
Hanö, *Sweden* 11 H8
Hanöbukten, *Sweden* 11 J8
Hanoi, *Vietnam* 58 G5
Hanover = Hannover, *Germany* . 24 C5
Hanover, *Canada* 116 B3
Hanover, *S. Africa* 88 E3
Hanover, *N.H., U.S.A.* 117 C12
Hanover, *Ohio, U.S.A.* 116 F2
Hanover, *Pa., U.S.A.* 114 F7
Hanover, I., *Chile* 128 G2
Hans Lollik I., *U.S. Virgin Is.* .. 121 e
Hansdiha, *India* 69 G12
Hanshou, *China* 59 C8
Hansi, *India* 68 E6
Hanson, L., *Australia* 95 E2
Hanstholm, *Denmark* 11 G2
Hantsavichy, *Belarus* 33 F4
Hanumangarh, *India* 68 E6
Hanyin, *China* 58 A7
Hanyuan, *China* 58 C4
Hanzhong, *China* 56 H4
Haora, *India* 69 H13
Haoxue, *China* 59 B9
Haparanda, *Sweden* 8 D21
Happy, *U.S.A.* 113 H4
Happy Camp, *U.S.A.* 108 F2
Happy Valley-Goose Bay,
  Canada 105 B7

Hapsu, *N. Korea* 57 D15
Hapur, *India* 68 E7
Ḥaql, *Si. Arabia* 74 F3
Har, *Indonesia* 63 F8
Har-Ayrag, *Mongolia* 56 B5
Har Hu, *China* 60 C4
Har Us Nuur, *Mongolia* 60 B4
Har Yehuda, *Israel* 74 D3
Ḥaraḍ, *Si. Arabia* 75 C4
Haradok, *Belarus* 32 E6
Häradsbäck, *Sweden* 11 H8
Haranomachi, *Japan* 54 F10
Harare, *Zimbabwe* 87 F3
Harat, *Eritrea* 81 D4
Harbin, *China* 57 B14
Harbiye, *Turkey* 72 D7
Harbo, *Sweden* 10 D11
Harboør, *Denmark* 11 H2
Harbor Beach, *U.S.A.* 116 C2
Harbour Breton, *Canada* 105 C8
Harbour Deep, *Canada* 105 B8
Harburg, *Germany* 24 B5
Harburger Berge △, *Germany* .. 24 B5
Hårby, *Denmark* 11 J4
Harda, *India* 68 H7
Hardangerfjorden, *Norway* ... 9 F12
Hardangervidda, *Norway* 9 F12
Hardap △, *Namibia* 88 C2
Hardap Dam, *Namibia* 88 C2
Hardenberg, *Neths.* 17 B6
Harderwijk, *Neths.* 17 B5
Hardey →, *Australia* 92 D2
Hardin, *U.S.A.* 108 D10
Harding, *S. Africa* 89 E4
Harding Ra., *Australia* 92 C3
Hardisty, *Canada* 102 C6
Hardoi, *India* 69 F9
Hardwar = Haridwar, *India* ... 68 E8
Hardwick, *U.S.A.* 117 B12
Hardy, Pen., *Chile* 128 H3
Hardy, Pte., *St. Lucia* ...... 121 f
Hare B., *Canada* 105 B8
Hareid, *Norway* 9 E12
Haren, *Germany* 24 C3
Harer, *Ethiopia* 81 F5
Harerge, *Ethiopia* 81 F5
Hareto, *Ethiopia* 81 F4
Harfleur, *France* 18 C7
Hargeisa, *Somali Rep.* 75 F3
Harghita □, *Romania* 29 D10
Harghita, Munţii, *Romania* ... 29 D10
Hargshamn, *Sweden* 10 D12
Hari →, *Indonesia* 62 E2
Haria, *Canary Is.* 48 E6
Haridwar, *India* 68 E8
Harim, Jabal al, *Oman* 71 E8
Haringhata →, *Bangla.* 67 J16
Harīrūd →, *Asia* 66 A2
Härjedalen, *Sweden* 10 B7
Harlan, *Iowa, U.S.A.* 112 E7
Harlan, *Ky., U.S.A.* 115 G4
Hârlău, *Romania* 29 C11
Harlech, *U.K.* 14 E3
Harlem, *U.S.A.* 108 B9
Hårlev, *Denmark* 11 J6
Harlingen, *Neths.* 17 A5
Harlingen, *U.S.A.* 113 M6
Harlow, *U.K.* 15 F8
Harlowton, *U.S.A.* 108 C9
Harmancık, *Turkey* 47 B11
Harmånger, *Sweden* 10 C11
Harmil, *Eritrea* 81 D5
Harnai, *Pakistan* 68 D2
Harney Basin, *U.S.A.* 108 E4
Harney L., *U.S.A.* 108 E4
Harney Peak, *U.S.A.* 112 D3
Härnön, *Sweden* 10 B12
Härnösand, *Sweden* 10 B11
Haro, *Spain* 38 C2
Haroldswick, *U.K.* 13 A8
Harp L., *Canada* 105 A7
Harper, *Liberia* 82 E3
Harplinge, *Sweden* 11 H6
Harr, *Mauritania* 82 B2
Harrai, *India* 69 H8
Harrand, *Pakistan* 68 E4
Ḥarrat Khaybar, *Si. Arabia* .. 80 B5
Ḥarrat Nawāṣīf, *Si. Arabia* .. 80 C5
Harricana →, *Canada* 104 B4
Harriman, *U.S.A.* 115 H3
Harrington Harbour, *Canada* . 105 B8
Harris, *U.K.* 13 D2
Harris, L., *Australia* 95 E2
Harris, Sd. of, *U.K.* 13 D1
Harris Pt., *Canada* 116 C2
Harrisburg, *Ill., U.S.A.* 113 G10
Harrisburg, *Nebr., U.S.A.* ... 112 E3
Harrisburg, *Pa., U.S.A.* 116 F8
Harrismith, *S. Africa* 89 D4
Harrison, *Ark., U.S.A.* 113 G8
Harrison, *Maine, U.S.A.* 117 B14
Harrison, *Nebr., U.S.A.* 112 D3
Harrison, C., *Canada* 105 B8
Harrison, Canada 102 D4
Harrisonburg, *U.S.A.* 114 F6
Harrisonville, *U.S.A.* 112 F7
Harriston, *Canada* 116 C4
Harrisville, *Mich., U.S.A.* ... 116 B1
Harrisville, *N.Y., U.S.A.* 117 B9
Harrisville, *Pa., U.S.A.* 116 E5
Harrodsburg, *U.S.A.* 114 G3
Harrogate, *U.K.* 14 C6
Harrow □, *U.K.* 15 F7
Harrowsmith, *Canada* 117 B8
Harry S. Truman Reservoir,
  U.S.A. 112 F7
Harsefeld, *Germany* 24 B5
Harsewinkel, *Germany* 24 D4
Harsin, *Iran* 70 C5
Hârşova, *Romania* 29 F12
Harstad, *Norway* 8 B17
Harsud, *India* 68 H7

Hart, *U.S.A.* 114 D2
Hart, L., *Australia* 95 E2
Hartbees →, *S. Africa* 88 D3
Hartberg, *Austria* 26 D8
Hartford, *Conn., U.S.A.* 117 E12
Hartford, *Ky., U.S.A.* 114 G2
Hartford, *S. Dak., U.S.A.* ... 112 D6
Hartford, *Wis., U.S.A.* 114 D1
Hartford City, *U.S.A.* 114 E3
Hartland, *Canada* 105 C6
Hartland Pt., *U.K.* 15 F3
Hartlepool, *U.K.* 14 C6
Hartlepool □, *U.K.* 14 C6
Hartley Bay, *Canada* 102 C3
Hartmannberge, *Namibia* 88 B1
Hartney, *Canada* 103 D8
Hartselle, *U.S.A.* 115 H2
Hartshorne, *U.S.A.* 113 H7
Hartstown, *U.S.A.* 116 E4
Hartsville, *U.S.A.* 115 H5
Hartswater, *S. Africa* 88 D3
Hartwell, *U.S.A.* 115 H4
Harunabad, *Pakistan* 68 E5
Harvand, *Iran* 71 D7
Harvey, *Australia* 93 F2
Harvey, *Ill., U.S.A.* 114 E2
Harvey, *N. Dak., U.S.A.* 112 B5
Harwich, *U.K.* 15 F9
Haryana □, *India* 68 E7
Haryn →, *Belarus* 33 F4
Harz, *Germany* 24 D6
Harz △, *Germany* 24 D6
Harzgerode, *Germany* 24 D7
Hasa □, *Si. Arabia* 71 E6
Hasaheisa, *Sudan* 81 E3
Ḥasanābād, *Iran* 71 C7
Ḥasb, W. →, *Iraq* 70 D5
Hasdo →, *India* 69 J10
Haselünne, *Germany* 24 C3
Hashimoto, *Japan* 55 G7
Hashtjerd, *Iran* 71 C6
Haskell, *U.S.A.* 113 J5
Hasköy, *Turkey* 45 E10
Haslach, *Germany* 25 G4
Hasle, *Denmark* 11 J8
Haslemere, *U.K.* 15 F7
Haslev, *Denmark* 11 J5
Hasparren, *France* 20 E2
Hassa, *Turkey* 72 D7
Hassberge △, *Germany* 25 E6
Hassela, *Sweden* 10 B10
Hasselt, *Belgium* 17 D5
Hassfurt, *Germany* 25 E6
Hassi Messaoud, *Algeria* 78 B7
Hässleholm, *Sweden* 11 H7
Hassloch, *Germany* 25 F4
Hästholmen, *Sweden* 11 F8
Hastings, *N.Z.* 91 H6
Hastings, *U.K.* 15 G8
Hastings, *Mich., U.S.A.* 114 D3
Hastings, *Minn., U.S.A.* 112 C8
Hastings, *Nebr., U.S.A.* 112 E5
Hastings Ra., *Australia* 95 E5
Hästveda, *Sweden* 11 H7
Hat, *Ukraine* 28 B7
Hat Yai, *Thailand* 65 J3
Hatanbulag = Ergel, *Mongolia* .. 56 C5
Hatay = Antalya, *Turkey* 72 D7
Hatch, *U.S.A.* 109 K10
Hatchet L., *Canada* 103 B8
Ḥaţeg, *Romania* 28 E7
Hateruma-Shima, *Japan* 55 M1
Hatfield P.O., *Australia* 95 E3
Hatgal, *Mongolia* 60 A5
Hathras, *India* 68 F8
Hatia, *Bangla.* 67 H17
Ḥāṭibah, Ra's, *Si. Arabia* ... 80 C4
Hato Mayor, *Dom. Rep.* 121 C6
Hatta, *India* 69 G8
Hattah, *Australia* 95 E3
Hatteras, C., *U.S.A.* 115 H8
Hattiesburg, *U.S.A.* 113 K10
Hatvan, *Hungary* 28 C4
Hau Bon = Cheo Reo, *Vietnam* .. 62 B3
Hau Duc, *Vietnam* 64 E7
Haugesund, *Norway* 9 G11
Haukipudas, *Finland* 8 D21
Haultain →, *Canada* 103 B7
Hauraki G., *N.Z.* 91 G5
Hausruck, *Austria* 26 C6
Haut Atlas, *Morocco* 78 B4
Haut-Jura △, *France* 19 F9
Haut-Languedoc △, *France* ... 20 E6
Haut Niger △, *Guinea* 82 C2
Haut-Rhin □, *France* 19 E14
Haute-Corse □, *France* 21 F13
Haute-Garonne □, *France* 20 E5
Haute-Loire □, *France* 20 C7
Haute-Marne □, *France* 19 D12
Haute-Normandie □, *France* .. 18 C7
Haute-Saône □, *France* 19 E13
Haute-Savoie □, *France* 21 C10
Haute-Vienne □, *France* 20 C5
Hautes-Alpes □, *France* 21 D10
Hautes Fagnes = Hohe Venn,
  Belgium 17 D6
Hautes Fagnes = Hohes Venn-
  Eifel △, *Europe* 24 E2
Hautes-Pyrénées □, *France* .. 20 F4
Hauteville-Lompnès, *France* .. 21 C9
Hautmont, *France* 19 B10
Hauts-de-Seine □, *France* ... 19 D9
Hauts Plateaux, *Algeria* 76 C4
Hauzenberg, *Germany* 25 G9
Havana = La Habana, *Cuba* ... 120 B3
Havana, *U.S.A.* 112 E9
Havant, *U.K.* 15 G7
Havârna, *Romania* 29 B11
Havasor = Kızıl, *Turkey* 70 B4
Havasu, L., *U.S.A.* 111 L12

Havdhem, *Sweden* 11 G12
Havel →, *Germany* 24 C8
Havelian, *Pakistan* 68 B5
Havelock, *Canada* 116 B7
Havelock, *N.Z.* 91 J4
Havelock, *U.S.A.* 115 H7
Haverfordwest, *U.K.* 15 F3
Haverhill, *U.K.* 15 E8
Haverhill, *U.S.A.* 117 D13
Haverstraw, *U.S.A.* 117 E11
Håverud, *Sweden* 11 F6
Havirga, *Mongolia* 56 B7
Havířov, *Czech Rep.* 27 B11
Havlíčkův Brod, *Czech Rep.* .. 26 B8
Havneby, *Denmark* 11 J2
Havran, *Turkey* 47 B9
Havre, *U.S.A.* 108 B9
Havre-Aubert, *Canada* 105 C7
Havre-St.-Pierre, *Canada* 105 B7
Havsa, *Turkey* 45 E10
Havza, *Turkey* 72 B6
Haw →, *U.S.A.* 115 H6
Hawaii □, *U.S.A.* 106 H16
Hawaii I., *Pac. Oc.* 106 J17
Hawaiian Is., *Pac. Oc.* 106 H17
Hawaiian Ridge, *Pac. Oc.* 97 E11
Hawarden, *U.S.A.* 112 D6
Hawea, L., *N.Z.* 91 L2
Hawera, *N.Z.* 91 H5
Hawick, *U.K.* 13 F6
Hawk Junction, *Canada* 104 C3
Hawke B., *N.Z.* 91 H6
Hawker, *Australia* 95 E2
Hawkesbury, *Canada* 104 C5
Hawkesbury I., *Canada* 102 C3
Hawkesbury Pt., *Australia* ... 94 A1
Hawkinsville, *U.S.A.* 115 J4
Hawley, *Minn., U.S.A.* 112 B6
Hawley, *Pa., U.S.A.* 117 E9
Ḥawrān, W. →, *Iraq* 70 C4
Hawsh Mūssá, *Lebanon* 74 B4
Hawthorne, *U.S.A.* 108 G4
Hay, *Australia* 95 E3
Hay →, *Australia* 94 C2
Hay →, *Canada* 102 A5
Hay, C., *Australia* 92 B4
Hay I., *Canada* 116 B4
Hay L., *Canada* 102 B5
Hay-on-Wye, *U.K.* 15 E4
Hay River, *Canada* 102 A5
Hay Springs, *U.S.A.* 112 D3
Haya = Tehoru, *Indonesia* ... 63 E7
Hayachine-San, *Japan* 54 E10
Hayange, *France* 19 C13
Haydarlı, *Turkey* 47 C12
Hayden, *U.S.A.* 108 F10
Haydon, *Australia* 94 B3
Hayes, *U.S.A.* 112 C4
Hayes →, *Canada* 104 A1
Hayes Creek, *Australia* 92 B5
Hayle, *U.K.* 15 G2
Hayling I., *U.K.* 15 G7
Haymana, *Turkey* 72 C5
Haymen I., *Australia* 94 J6
Hayrabolu, *Turkey* 45 E11
Hays, *Canada* 102 C6
Hays, *U.S.A.* 112 F5
Haysyn, *Ukraine* 29 B14
Hayvoron, *Ukraine* 29 B14
Hayward, *Calif., U.S.A.* 110 H4
Hayward, *Wis., U.S.A.* 112 B9
Haywards Heath, *U.K.* 15 G7
Ḥazafon □, *Israel* 74 C4
Hazārān, Kūh-e, *Iran* 71 D8
Hazard, *U.S.A.* 114 G4
Hazaribag, *India* 69 H11
Hazaribag Road, *India* 69 G11
Hazebrouck, *France* 19 B9
Hazelton, *Canada* 102 B3
Hazelton, *U.S.A.* 112 B4
Hazen, *U.S.A.* 112 B4
Hazlehurst, *Ga., U.S.A.* 115 K4
Hazlehurst, *Miss., U.S.A.* ... 113 K9
Hazlet, *U.S.A.* 117 F10
Hazleton, *U.S.A.* 117 F9
Hazlett, L., *Australia* 92 D4
Hazro, *Turkey* 70 B4
He Xian, *Anhui, China* 59 B12
He Xian, *Guangxi Zhuangzu,
  China* 59 E8
Head of Bight, *Australia* 93 F5
Headlands, *Zimbabwe* 87 F3
Healdsburg, *U.S.A.* 110 G4
Healdton, *U.S.A.* 113 H6
Healesville, *Australia* 95 F4
Heany Junction, *Zimbabwe* 89 C4
Heard I., *Ind. Oc.* 3 G13
Hearne, *U.S.A.* 113 K6
Hearst, *Canada* 104 C3
Heart →, *U.S.A.* 112 B4
Heart's Content, *Canada* 105 C9
Heath, Pte., *Canada* 105 C7
Heathrow, London ✈ (LHR),
  U.K. 15 F7
Heavener, *U.S.A.* 113 H7
Hebbronville, *U.S.A.* 113 M5
Hebei □, *China* 56 E9
Hebel, *Australia* 95 D4
Heber, *U.S.A.* 111 N11
Heber City, *U.S.A.* 108 F8
Heber Springs, *U.S.A.* 113 H9
Hebgen L., *U.S.A.* 108 D8
Hebi, *China* 56 G8
Hebrides, Sea of the, *U.K.* .. 13 D2
Hebron = Al Khalīl, *West Bank* .. 74 D4
Hebron, *Canada* 101 C13
Hebron, *N. Dak., U.S.A.* 112 B3
Hebron, *Nebr., U.S.A.* 112 E6
Heby, *Sweden* 10 E10
Hecate Str., *Canada* 102 C2

Heceta I., *U.S.A.* 102 B2
Hechi, *China* 58 E7
Hechingen, *Germany* 25 G4
Hechuan, *China* 58 B6
Hecla, *U.S.A.* 112 C5
Hecla I., *Canada* 103 C9
Hédé, *France* 18 D5
Hede, *Sweden* 10 B7
Hedemora, *Sweden* 10 D9
Hedensted, *Denmark* 11 J3
Hedesunda, *Sweden* 10 D10
Heerde, *Neths.* 17 B6
Heerenveen, *Neths.* 17 B5
Heerhugowaard, *Neths.* 17 B4
Heerlen, *Neths.* 17 D5
Ḥefa, *Israel* 74 C4
Ḥefa □, *Israel* 74 C4
Hefei, *China* 59 B11
Hefeng, *China* 59 C8
Hegalig, *Sudan* 81 E3
Hegang, *China* 60 B8
Heiban, *Sudan* 81 E3
Heichengzhen, *China* 56 F4
Heide, *Germany* 24 A5
Heidelberg, *Germany* 25 F4
Heidelberg, *S. Africa* 88 E3
Heidenau, *Germany* 24 E9
Heidenheim, *Germany* 25 G6
Heijing, *China* 58 E3
Heilbad Heiligenstadt, *Germany* . 24 D6
Heilbron, *S. Africa* 89 D4
Heilbronn, *Germany* 25 F5
Heiligenblut, *Austria* 26 D5
Heiligenhafen, *Germany* 24 A6
Heilongjiang □, *China* 60 B7
Heilunkiang = Heilongjiang □,
  China 60 B7
Heimaey, *Iceland* 8 E3
Heinola, *Finland* 9 F22
Heinsberg, *Germany* 24 D2
Heinze Kyun, *Burma* 64 E11
Heishan, *China* 57 D12
Heishui, *Liaoning, China* 57 C10
Heishui, *Sichuan, China* 58 A4
Hejaz = Ḥijāz □, *Si. Arabia* .. 70 E3
Hejian, *China* 56 E9
Hejiang, *China* 58 C5
Hejin, *China* 56 G6
Hekimhan, *Turkey* 70 B3
Hekla, *Iceland* 8 E4
Hekou, *Guangdong, China* 59 F9
Hekou, *Yunnan, China* 58 F4
Hel, *Poland* 30 D5
Helagsfjället, *Sweden* 10 B6
Helan Shan, *China* 56 E3
Helechosa, *Spain* 37 F6
Helen Atoll, *Pac. Oc.* 63 D8
Helena, *Ark., U.S.A.* 113 H9
Helena, *Mont., U.S.A.* 108 C7
Helendale, *U.S.A.* 111 L9
Helensburgh, *U.K.* 13 E4
Helensville, *N.Z.* 91 G5
Helenvale, *Australia* 94 B4
Helgasjön, *Sweden* 11 H8
Helgeland, *Norway* 8 C15
Helgoland, *Germany* 24 A3
Heligoland = Helgoland,
  Germany 24 A3
Heligoland B. = Deutsche Bucht,
  Germany 24 A4
Heliopolis, *Egypt* 80 H7
Hella, *Iceland* 8 E3
Hellertown, *U.S.A.* 117 F9
Hellespont = Çanakkale Boğazı,
  Turkey 45 F10
Hellevoetsluis, *Neths.* 17 C4
Hellhole Gorge △, *Australia* .. 94 D3
Hellín, *Spain* 39 G3
Hells Canyon △, *U.S.A.* 108 D5
Hell's Gate △, *Kenya* 86 C4
Helmand □, *Afghan.* 66 D4
Helmand →, *Afghan.* 66 D2
Helme →, *Germany* 24 D7
Helmeringhausen, *Namibia* ... 88 D2
Helmond, *Neths.* 17 C5
Helmsdale, *U.K.* 13 C5
Helmsdale →, *U.K.* 13 C5
Helmstedt, *Germany* 24 C7
Helong, *China* 57 C15
Helper, *U.S.A.* 108 G8
Helsingborg, *Sweden* 11 H6
Helsinge, *Denmark* 11 H6
Helsingfors = Helsinki, *Finland* . 9 F21
Helsingør, *Denmark* 11 H6
Helsinki, *Finland* 9 F21
Helska, Mierzeja, *Poland* 30 D5
Helston, *U.K.* 15 G2
Helvellyn, *U.K.* 14 C4
Helwân, *Egypt* 80 J7
Hemel Hempstead, *U.K.* 15 F7
Hemet, *U.S.A.* 111 M10
Hemingford, *U.S.A.* 112 D3
Hemmingford, *Canada* 117 A11
Hempstead, *U.S.A.* 113 K6
Hemse, *Sweden* 11 G12
Hemsön, *Sweden* 10 B12
Hemsö, *Sweden* 11 F5
Henan □, *China* 56 H8
Henares →, *Spain* 36 E7
Henashi-Misaki, *Japan* 54 D9
Hendaye, *France* 20 E2
Hendek, *Turkey* 72 B4
Henderson, *Argentina* 126 D3
Henderson, *Ky., U.S.A.* 114 G2
Henderson, *N.C., U.S.A.* 115 G6
Henderson, *Nev., U.S.A.* 111 J12
Henderson, *Tenn., U.S.A.* ... 115 H1
Henderson, *Tex., U.S.A.* 113 J7
Hendersonville, *N.C., U.S.A.* . 115 H4
Hendersonville, *Tenn., U.S.A.* . 115 G2
Hendījān, *Iran* 71 D6

Hendorābī, Iran ... 71 E7
Heng Jiang, China ... 58 C5
Heng Xian, China ... 58 F7
Hengcheng, China ... 56 E4
Hëngchun, Taiwan ... 59 F13
Hengdaohezi, China ... 57 B15
Hengelo, Neths. ... 17 B6
Hengfeng, China ... 59 C10
Hengshan, Hunan, China ... 59 D9
Hengshan, Shaanxi, China ... 56 F5
Hengshui, China ... 56 F8
Hengyang, China ... 59 D9
Henichesk, Ukraine ... 33 J8
Hénin-Beaumont, France ... 19 B9
Henley-on-Thames, U.K. ... 15 F7
Henlopen, C., U.S.A. ... 114 F8
Hennan, Sweden ... 10 B9
Hennebont, France ... 18 E3
Hennenman, S. Africa ... 88 D4
Hennessey, U.S.A. ... 113 G6
Hennigsdorf, Germany ... 24 C9
Henri Pittier △, Venezuela ... 121 D6
Henrietta, U.S.A. ... 113 J5
Henrietta, Ostrov = Genriyetty, Ostrov, Russia ... 53 B16
Henrietta Maria, C., Canada ... 104 A3
Henry, U.S.A. ... 112 E10
Henryetta, U.S.A. ... 113 H7
Henryville, Canada ... 117 A11
Hensall, Canada ... 116 C3
Henstedt-Ulzburg, Germany ... 24 B5
Hentiesbaai, Namibia ... 88 C1
Hentiyn Nuruu, Mongolia ... 60 B5
Henty, Australia ... 95 F4
Henzada, Burma ... 67 L19
Hephaestia, Greece ... 47 B7
Heping, China ... 59 E10
Heppner, U.S.A. ... 108 D4
Hepu, China ... 58 G7
Hepworth, Canada ... 116 B3
Heqing, China ... 58 D3
Hequ, China ... 56 E6
Héraðsflói, Iceland ... 8 D6
Héraðsvötn →, Iceland ... 8 D4
Heraklion = Iráklion, Greece ... 49 D7
Herald Cays, Australia ... 94 B4
Herāt, Afghan. ... 66 B3
Herāt □, Afghan. ... 66 B3
Hérault □, France ... 20 E7
Hérault →, France ... 20 E7
Herbault, France ... 18 E8
Herbert →, Australia ... 94 B4
Herbert River Falls △, Australia ... 94 B4
Herberton, Australia ... 94 B4
Herbertsdale, S. Africa ... 88 E3
Herbignac, France ... 18 E4
Herborn, Germany ... 24 E4
Herby, Poland ... 31 H5
Herceg-Novi, Serbia & M. ... 44 D2
Herchmer, Canada ... 103 B10
Herðubreið, Iceland ... 8 D5
Hereford, U.K. ... 15 E5
Hereford, U.S.A. ... 113 H3
Herefordshire □, U.K. ... 15 E5
Hereke, Turkey ... 45 F13
Herencia, Spain ... 37 F7
Herentals, Belgium ... 17 C4
Herford, Germany ... 24 C4
Héricourt, France ... 19 E13
Herington, U.S.A. ... 112 F6
Herisau, Switz. ... 25 H5
Hérisson, France ... 19 F9
Herkimer, U.S.A. ... 117 D10
Herlong, U.S.A. ... 110 E6
Herm, U.K. ... 15 H5
Hermakivka, Ukraine ... 29 B11
Hermann, U.S.A. ... 112 F9
Hermannsburg, Australia ... 92 D5
Hermannsburg, Germany ... 24 C6
Hermanus, S. Africa ... 88 E2
Herment, France ... 20 C6
Hermidale, Australia ... 95 E4
Hermiston, U.S.A. ... 108 D4
Hermite, I., Chile ... 128 H3
Hermon, U.S.A. ... 117 B9
Hermon, Mt. = Shaykh, J. ash-, Lebanon ... 74 B4
Hermosillo, Mexico ... 118 B2
Hernád →, Hungary ... 28 C6
Hernandarias, Paraguay ... 127 B5
Hernandez, U.S.A. ... 110 J6
Hernando, Argentina ... 126 C3
Hernando, U.S.A. ... 113 H10
Hernani, Spain ... 38 B3
Herndon, U.S.A. ... 116 F8
Herne, Germany ... 17 C7
Herne Bay, U.K. ... 15 F9
Herning, Denmark ... 11 H2
Heroica = Caborca, Mexico ... 118 A2
Heroica Nogales = Nogales, Mexico ... 118 A2
Heron Bay, Canada ... 104 C2
Herradura, Pta. de la, Canary Is. ... 48 F5
Herreid, U.S.A. ... 112 C4
Herrenberg, Germany ... 25 G4
Herrera, Spain ... 37 H6
Herrera de Alcántara, Spain ... 37 F3
Herrera de Pisuerga, Spain ... 36 C6
Herrera del Duque, Spain ... 37 F5
Herrestad, Sweden ... 11 F5
Herrin, U.S.A. ... 113 G10
Herriot, Canada ... 103 B8
Herrljunga, Sweden ... 11 F7
Hersbruck, Germany ... 25 F7
Herschel I., Canada ... 4 C1
Hershey, U.S.A. ... 117 F8
Hersonissos, Greece ... 49 D7
Herstal, Belgium ... 17 D5
Hertford, U.K. ... 15 F7
Hertfordshire □, U.K. ... 15 F7
's-Hertogenbosch, Neths. ... 17 C5

Hertsa, Ukraine ... 29 B11
Hertzogville, S. Africa ... 88 D4
Hervás, Spain ... 36 E5
Hervey B., Australia ... 94 C5
Herzberg, Brandenburg, Germany ... 24 D9
Herzberg, Niedersachsen, Germany ... 24 D6
Herzliyya, Israel ... 74 C3
Herzogenburg, Austria ... 26 C8
Ḥeşār, Fārs, Iran ... 71 D6
Ḥeşār, Markazī, Iran ... 71 C6
Hesdin, France ... 19 B9
Heshan, China ... 58 F7
Heshui, China ... 56 G5
Heshun, China ... 56 F7
Hesperia, U.S.A. ... 111 L9
Hesse = Hessen □, Germany ... 24 E4
Hessen □, Germany ... 24 E4
Hessenreuther und Manteler Wald △, Germany ... 25 F8
Hestra, Sweden ... 11 G7
Hetch Hetchy Aqueduct, U.S.A. ... 110 H5
Hettinger, U.S.A. ... 112 C3
Hettstedt, Germany ... 24 D7
Heuvelton, U.S.A. ... 117 B9
Heves, Hungary ... 28 C5
Heves □, Hungary ... 28 C5
Hewitt, U.S.A. ... 113 K6
Hexham, U.K. ... 14 C5
Hexi, Yunnan, China ... 58 E4
Hexi, Zhejiang, China ... 59 D12
Hexigten Qi, China ... 57 C9
Ḥeydarābād, Iran ... 71 D7
Heyuan, China ... 59 F10
Heywood, Australia ... 95 F3
Heze, China ... 56 G8
Hezhang, China ... 58 D5
Hi, Ko, Thailand ... 65 a
Hi Vista, U.S.A. ... 111 L9
Hialeah, U.S.A. ... 115 N5
Hiawatha, U.S.A. ... 112 F7
Hibbing, U.S.A. ... 112 B8
Hibbs B., Australia ... 95 G4
Hibernia Reef, Australia ... 92 B3
Hickman, U.S.A. ... 113 G10
Hickory, U.S.A. ... 115 H5
Hicks, Pt., Australia ... 95 F4
Hicks L., Canada ... 103 A9
Hicksville, U.S.A. ... 117 F11
Hida, Romania ... 29 C8
Hida-Gawa →, Japan ... 55 G8
Hida-Sammyaku, Japan ... 55 F8
Hidaka-Sammyaku, Japan ... 54 C11
Hidalgo, Mexico ... 119 C5
Hidalgo □, Mexico ... 119 C5
Hidalgo, Presa M., Mexico ... 118 B3
Hidalgo del Parral, Mexico ... 118 B3
Hiddensee, Germany ... 24 A9
Hieflau, Austria ... 26 D7
Hiendelaencina, Spain ... 38 D2
Hierro, Canary Is. ... 48 G1
Higashiajima-San, Japan ... 54 F10
Higashiōsaka, Japan ... 55 G7
Higgins, U.S.A. ... 113 G4
Higgins Corner, U.S.A. ... 110 F5
High Bridge, U.S.A. ... 117 F10
High Level, Canada ... 102 B5
High Point, U.S.A. ... 115 H6
High Prairie, Canada ... 102 B5
High River, Canada ... 102 C6
High Tatra = Tatry, Slovak Rep. ... 27 B13
High Veld, Africa ... 76 J6
High Wycombe, U.K. ... 15 F7
Highland □, U.K. ... 13 D4
Highland Park, U.S.A. ... 114 D2
Highmore, U.S.A. ... 112 C5
Highrock L., Man., Canada ... 103 B8
Highrock L., Sask., Canada ... 103 B7
Higüey, Dom. Rep. ... 121 C6
Hihya, Egypt ... 80 H7
Hiiumaa, Estonia ... 9 G20
Híjar, Spain ... 38 D4
Ḥijāz □, Si. Arabia ... 70 E3
Hijo = Tagum, Phil. ... 61 H6
Hikari, Japan ... 55 H5
Hikmak, Ras el, Egypt ... 80 A2
Hiko, U.S.A. ... 110 H11
Hikone, Japan ... 55 G8
Hikurangi, Gisborne, N.Z. ... 91 H6
Hikurangi, Northland, N.Z. ... 91 F5
Hildburghausen, Germany ... 24 E6
Hildesheim, Germany ... 24 C5
Hill →, Australia ... 93 F2
Hill City, Idaho, U.S.A. ... 108 E6
Hill City, Kans., U.S.A. ... 112 F5
Hill City, S. Dak., U.S.A. ... 112 D3
Hill Island L., Canada ... 103 A7
Hillaby, Mt., Barbados ... 121 g
Hillared, Sweden ... 11 G7
Hillcrest, Barbados ... 121 g
Hillcrest Center, U.S.A. ... 111 K8
Hillegom, Neths. ... 17 B4
Hillerød, Denmark ... 11 J6
Hillerstorp, Sweden ... 11 G7
Hillsboro, Kans., U.S.A. ... 112 F6
Hillsboro, N. Dak., U.S.A. ... 112 B6
Hillsboro, Ohio, U.S.A. ... 114 F4
Hillsboro, Oreg., U.S.A. ... 110 E4
Hillsboro, Tex., U.S.A. ... 113 J6
Hillsborough, Grenada ... 121 D7
Hillsborough, U.S.A. ... 117 C13
Hillsborough Channel, Australia ... 94 J7
Hillsdale, Mich., U.S.A. ... 114 E3
Hillsdale, N.Y., U.S.A. ... 117 D11
Hillsport, Canada ... 104 C2
Hillston, Australia ... 95 E4
Hilo, U.S.A. ... 106 J17
Hilton, U.S.A. ... 116 C7
Hilton Head Island, U.S.A. ... 115 J5
Hilvan, Turkey ... 73 D8

Hilversum, Neths. ... 17 B5
Himachal Pradesh □, India ... 68 D7
Himalaya, Asia ... 69 E11
Himamaylan, Phil. ... 61 F5
Himarë, Albania ... 44 F3
Himatnagar, India ... 66 H8
Himeji, Japan ... 55 G7
Himi, Japan ... 55 F8
Himmerland, Denmark ... 11 H3
Ḥimṣ, Syria ... 74 A5
Ḥimṣ □, Syria ... 74 A6
Hinche, Haiti ... 121 C5
Hinchinbrook I., Australia ... 94 B4
Hinchinbrook Island △, Australia ... 94 B4
Hinckley, U.K. ... 15 E6
Hinckley, U.S.A. ... 112 B8
Hindaun, India ... 68 F7
Hindmarsh, L., Australia ... 95 F3
Hindsholm, Denmark ... 11 J4
Hindu Bagh, Pakistan ... 68 D2
Hindu Kush, Asia ... 66 B7
Hindupur, India ... 66 N10
Hines Creek, Canada ... 102 B5
Hinesville, U.S.A. ... 115 K5
Hinganghat, India ... 66 J11
Hingham, U.S.A. ... 108 B8
Hingir, India ... 69 J10
Hingoli, India ... 66 K10
Hinigaran, Phil. ... 61 F5
Hinis, Turkey ... 73 C9
Hinna = Imi, Ethiopia ... 81 F5
Hinna, Nigeria ... 83 C7
Hinnerup, Denmark ... 11 H4
Hinnøya, Norway ... 8 B16
Hinojosa del Duque, Spain ... 37 G5
Hinsdale, U.S.A. ... 117 D12
Hinterrhein →, Switz. ... 25 J5
Hinton, Canada ... 102 C5
Hinton, U.S.A. ... 114 G5
Hīrā →, India ... 69 H8
Hirapur, India ... 69 G8
Hiratsuka, Japan ... 55 G9
Hirfanlı Barajı, Turkey ... 72 C5
Hiroo, Japan ... 54 C11
Hirosaki, Japan ... 54 D10
Hiroshima, Japan ... 55 G6
Hiroshima □, Japan ... 55 G6
Hirson, France ... 19 C11
Hirtshals, Denmark ... 11 G3
Hisar, India ... 68 E6
Hisarcık, Turkey ... 47 B11
Hisaria, Bulgaria ... 45 D8
Hisb, Sha'ib = Ḥasb, W. →, Iraq ... 70 D5
Ḥismá, Si. Arabia ... 70 D3
Hispaniola, W. Indies ... 121 C5
Ḥīt, Iraq ... 70 C4
Hita, Japan ... 55 H5
Hitachi, Japan ... 55 F10
Hitchin, U.K. ... 15 F7
Hitoyoshi, Japan ... 55 H5
Hitra, Norway ... 8 E13
Hitzacker, Germany ... 24 B7
Hixon, Canada ... 102 C4
Ḥiyyon, N. →, Israel ... 74 E4
Hjalmar L., Canada ... 103 A7
Hjälmaren, Sweden ... 10 E9
Hjältevad, Sweden ... 11 G9
Hjo, Sweden ... 11 F8
Hjørring, Denmark ... 11 G3
Hjortkvarn, Sweden ... 11 F9
Hkakabo Razi, Burma ... 67 E20
Hlinsko, Czech Rep. ... 26 B8
Hlobane, S. Africa ... 89 D5
Hlohovec, Slovak Rep. ... 27 C10
Hlučín, Czech Rep. ... 27 B11
Hluhluwe, S. Africa ... 89 D5
Hluhluwe →, S. Africa ... 89 C5
Hlukhiv, Ukraine ... 33 G7
Hlyboka, Ukraine ... 29 B10
Hlybokaye, Belarus ... 32 E4
Hnúšťa, Slovak Rep. ... 27 C12
Ho, Ghana ... 83 D5
Ho Chi Minh City = Thanh Pho Ho Chi Minh, Vietnam ... 65 G6
Ho Thuong, Vietnam ... 64 C5
Hoa Binh, Vietnam ... 58 G5
Hoa Da, Vietnam ... 65 G7
Hoa Hiep, Vietnam ... 65 G5
Hoai Nhon, Vietnam ... 64 E7
Hoang Lien Son, Vietnam ... 58 F4
Hoanib →, Namibia ... 88 B2
Hoare B., Canada ... 101 B13
Hoarusib →, Namibia ... 88 B2
Hobart, Australia ... 95 G4
Hobart, U.S.A. ... 113 H5
Hobbs, U.S.A. ... 113 J3
Hobbs Coast, Antarctica ... 5 D14
Hobe Sound, U.S.A. ... 115 M5
Hoboken, U.S.A. ... 117 F10
Hobro, Denmark ... 11 H3
Hoburgen, Sweden ... 11 H12
Hocalar, Turkey ... 47 C11
Hochfeld, Namibia ... 88 C2
Hochharz △, Germany ... 24 D6
Hochschwab, Austria ... 26 D8
Höchstadt, Germany ... 25 F6
Hochtaunus △, Germany ... 25 E4
Hockenheim, Germany ... 25 F4
Hodaka-Dake, Japan ... 55 F8
Hodeida = Al Ḥudaydah, Yemen ... 75 E3
Hodgeville, Canada ... 103 C7
Hodgson, Canada ... 103 C9
Hódmezővásárhely, Hungary ... 28 D5
Hodna, Chott el, Algeria ... 78 A6
Hodonín, Czech Rep. ... 27 C10
Hoeamdong, N. Korea ... 57 C16
Hœdic, Î. de, France ... 18 E4
Hoek van Holland, Neths. ... 17 C4

Hoengsŏng, S. Korea ... 57 F14
Hoeryong, N. Korea ... 57 C15
Hoeyang, N. Korea ... 57 E14
Hof, Germany ... 25 E7
Hofgeismar, Germany ... 24 D5
Hofheim, Germany ... 25 E4
Hofmeyr, S. Africa ... 88 E4
Höfn, Iceland ... 8 D6
Hofors, Sweden ... 10 D10
Hofsjökull, Iceland ... 8 D4
Hōfu, Japan ... 55 G5
Hogan Group, Australia ... 95 F4
Höganäs, Sweden ... 11 H6
Hogarth, Mt., Australia ... 94 C2
Hoggar = Ahaggar, Algeria ... 78 D7
Högsäter, Sweden ... 11 F6
Högsby, Sweden ... 11 G10
Högsjö, Sweden ... 10 E9
Hogsty Reef, Bahamas ... 121 B5
Hoh →, U.S.A. ... 110 C2
Hohe Acht, Germany ... 25 E3
Hohe Tauern, Austria ... 26 D5
Hohe Tauern △, Austria ... 26 D5
Hohe Venn, Belgium ... 17 D6
Hohenau, Austria ... 27 C9
Hohenems, Austria ... 26 D2
Hohenloher Ebene, Germany ... 25 F5
Hohenwald, U.S.A. ... 115 H2
Hohenwestedt, Germany ... 24 A5
Hoher Rhön = Rhön, Germany ... 24 E5
Hoher Vogelsberg △, Germany ... 24 D5
Hohes Venn-Eifel △, Europe ... 24 E2
Hohhot, China ... 56 D6
Hóhlakas, Greece ... 49 D9
Hohoe, Ghana ... 83 D5
Hoi An, Vietnam ... 64 E7
Hoi Xuan, Vietnam ... 58 G5
Hoisington, U.S.A. ... 112 F5
Højer, Denmark ... 11 K2
Hōjō, Japan ... 55 H6
Hok, Sweden ... 11 G8
Hökensås, Sweden ... 11 G8
Hökerum, Sweden ... 11 G7
Hokianga Harbour, N.Z. ... 91 F4
Hokitika, N.Z. ... 91 K3
Hokkaidō □, Japan ... 54 C11
Hol-Hol, Djibouti ... 81 E5
Hola Pristan, Ukraine ... 33 J7
Holbæk, Denmark ... 11 J5
Holbrook, Australia ... 95 F4
Holbrook, U.S.A. ... 109 J8
Holden, U.S.A. ... 108 G7
Holdenville, U.S.A. ... 113 H6
Holdrege, U.S.A. ... 112 E5
Holešov, Czech Rep. ... 27 B10
Holetown, Barbados ... 121 g
Holguín, Cuba ... 120 B4
Holíč, Slovak Rep. ... 27 C10
Holice, Czech Rep. ... 26 A8
Höljes, Sweden ... 10 D6
Hollabrunn, Austria ... 26 C9
Holland, Mich., U.S.A. ... 114 D2
Holland, N.Y., U.S.A. ... 116 D6
Hollandale, U.S.A. ... 113 J9
Holley, U.S.A. ... 116 C6
Hollfeld, Germany ... 25 F7
Hollidaysburg, U.S.A. ... 116 F6
Hollis, U.S.A. ... 113 H5
Hollister, Calif., U.S.A. ... 110 J5
Hollister, Idaho, U.S.A. ... 108 E6
Höllviken = Höllviksnäs, Sweden ... 11 J6
Höllviksnäs, Sweden ... 11 J6
Holly Hill, U.S.A. ... 115 L5
Holly Springs, U.S.A. ... 113 H10
Hollywood, U.S.A. ... 115 N5
Holman, Canada ... 100 A8
Hólmavík, Iceland ... 8 D3
Holmen, U.S.A. ... 112 D9
Holmes Reefs, Australia ... 94 B4
Holmsjö, Sweden ... 11 H9
Holmsjön, Västernorrland, Sweden ... 10 B10
Holmsjön, Västernorrland, Sweden ... 10 B9
Holmsland Klit, Denmark ... 11 J2
Holmsund, Sweden ... 8 E19
Holod, Romania ... 28 D7
Holovne, Ukraine ... 31 G11
Holozubyntsi, Ukraine ... 29 B11
Holroyd →, Australia ... 94 A3
Holstebro, Denmark ... 11 H2
Holsteinische Schweiz △, Germany ... 24 A6
Holsworthy, U.K. ... 15 G3
Holton, Canada ... 105 B8
Holton, U.S.A. ... 112 F7
Holtville, U.S.A. ... 111 N11
Holwerd, Neths. ... 17 A5
Holy I., Angl., U.K. ... 14 D3
Holy I., Northumberland, U.K. ... 14 B6
Holyhead, U.K. ... 14 D3
Holyoke, Colo., U.S.A. ... 112 E3
Holyoke, Mass., U.S.A. ... 117 D12
Holyrood, Canada ... 105 C9
Holzkirchen, Germany ... 25 H7
Holzminden, Germany ... 24 D5
Homa Bay, Kenya ... 86 C3
Homalin, Burma ... 67 G19
Homand, Iran ... 71 C8
Homathko →, Canada ... 102 C4
Homberg, Germany ... 24 D5
Hombori, Mali ... 83 B4
Homburg, Germany ... 25 F3
Home Hill, Australia ... 94 B4
Homedale, U.S.A. ... 108 E5
Homer, Alaska, U.S.A. ... 100 C4
Homer, La., U.S.A. ... 113 J8
Homer City, U.S.A. ... 116 F5
Homert △, Germany ... 24 D4

Homestead, Australia ... 94 C4
Homestead, U.S.A. ... 115 N5
Homestead △, U.S.A. ... 112 E6
Homewood, U.S.A. ... 110 F6
Homoine, Mozam. ... 89 C6
Homoljske Planina, Serbia & M. ... 44 B5
Homorod, Romania ... 29 D10
Homs = Ḥimṣ, Syria ... 74 A5
Homyel, Belarus ... 33 F6
Hon Chong, Vietnam ... 65 G5
Hon Me, Vietnam ... 64 C5
Honan = Henan □, China ... 56 H8
Honaz, Turkey ... 47 D11
Honbetsu, Japan ... 54 C11
Honcut, U.S.A. ... 110 F5
Honda Bay, Phil. ... 61 G3
Hondeklipbaai, S. Africa ... 88 E2
Hondo, Japan ... 55 H5
Hondo, U.S.A. ... 113 L5
Hondo, Rio →, Belize ... 119 D7
Honduras ■, Cent. Amer. ... 120 D2
Honduras, G. de, Caribbean ... 120 C2
Hønefoss, Norway ... 9 F14
Honesdale, U.S.A. ... 117 E9
Honey L., U.S.A. ... 110 E6
Honfleur, France ... 18 C7
Høng, Denmark ... 11 J5
Hong →, Vietnam ... 58 F5
Hong Gai, Vietnam ... 58 G6
Hong He →, China ... 56 H8
Hong Hu →, China ... 59 C9
Hong Kong □, China ... 59 F10
Hong'an, China ... 59 B10
Hongch'ŏn, S. Korea ... 57 F14
Honghai Wan, China ... 59 F10
Honghe, China ... 58 F4
Honghu, China ... 59 C9
Hongjiang, China ... 58 D7
Hongliu He →, China ... 56 F5
Hongor, Mongolia ... 56 B7
Hongsa, Laos ... 64 C3
Hongshui He →, China ... 58 F7
Hongsŏng, S. Korea ... 57 F14
Hongtong, China ... 56 F6
Honguedo, Détroit d', Canada ... 105 C7
Hongwon, N. Korea ... 57 E14
Hongya, China ... 58 C4
Hongyuan, China ... 58 A4
Hongze Hu, China ... 57 H10
Honiara, Solomon Is. ... 96 H7
Honiton, U.K. ... 15 G4
Honjō, Japan ... 54 E10
Honkorâb, Ras, Egypt ... 80 C4
Honningsvåg, Norway ... 8 A21
Hönö, Sweden ... 11 G5
Honolulu, U.S.A. ... 106 H16
Hontoria del Pinar, Spain ... 38 D1
Hood, Mt., U.S.A. ... 108 D3
Hood, Pt., Australia ... 93 F2
Hood River, U.S.A. ... 108 D3
Hoodsport, U.S.A. ... 110 C3
Hooge, Germany ... 24 A4
Hoogeveen, Neths. ... 17 B6
Hoogezand-Sappemeer, Neths. ... 17 A6
Hooghly = Hugli →, India ... 69 J13
Hooghly-Chinsura = Chunchura, India ... 69 H13
Hook Hd., Ireland ... 12 D5
Hook I., Australia ... 94 J6
Hook of Holland = Hoek van Holland, Neths. ... 17 C4
Hooker, U.S.A. ... 113 G4
Hooker Creek, Australia ... 92 C5
Hoonah, U.S.A. ... 102 B1
Hooper Bay, U.S.A. ... 100 B3
Hoopeston, U.S.A. ... 114 E2
Hoopstad, S. Africa ... 88 D4
Höör, Sweden ... 11 J7
Hoorn, Neths. ... 17 B5
Hoover, U.S.A. ... 115 J2
Hoover Dam, U.S.A. ... 111 K12
Hooversville, U.S.A. ... 116 F6
Hop Bottom, U.S.A. ... 117 E9
Hopa, Turkey ... 73 B9
Hope, Canada ... 102 D4
Hope, Ariz., U.S.A. ... 111 M13
Hope, Ark., U.S.A. ... 113 J8
Hope, L., S. Austral., Australia ... 95 D2
Hope, L., W. Austral., Australia ... 93 F3
Hope, Pt., U.S.A. ... 4 C17
Hope I., Canada ... 116 B4
Hope Town, Bahamas ... 120 A4
Hopedale, Canada ... 105 A7
Hopedale, U.S.A. ... 117 D13
Hopefield, S. Africa ... 88 E2
Hopei = Hebei □, China ... 56 E9
Hopelchén, Mexico ... 119 D7
Hopetoun, Vic., Australia ... 95 F3
Hopetoun, W. Austral., Australia ... 93 F3
Hopetown, S. Africa ... 88 D3
Hopevale, Australia ... 94 B4
Hopewell, U.S.A. ... 114 G7
Hopfgarten, Austria ... 26 D5
Hopkins, L., Australia ... 92 D4
Hopkinsville, U.S.A. ... 115 G2
Hopland, U.S.A. ... 110 G3
Hoquiam, U.S.A. ... 110 D3
Hora Hoverla, Ukraine ... 29 B9
Horasan, Turkey ... 73 B10
Horažďovice, Czech Rep. ... 26 B6
Horb, Germany ... 25 G4
Hörby, Sweden ... 11 J7
Horcajo de Santiago, Spain ... 38 F1
Worden Hills, Australia ... 92 D5
Horezu, Romania ... 29 E8
Horgen, Switz. ... 25 H4
Horgoš, Serbia & M. ... 28 D4
Hořice, Czech Rep. ... 26 A8
Horinchove, Ukraine ... 29 B8
Horinger, China ... 56 D6

Horki, *Belarus* 32 E6
Horlick Mts., *Antarctica* 5 E15
Horlivka, *Ukraine* 33 H10
Hormak, *Iran* 71 D9
Hormoz, *Iran* 71 E7
Hormoz, Jaz.-ye, *Iran* 71 E8
Hormozgān □, *Iran* 71 E8
Hormuz, Kūh-e, *Iran* 71 E7
Hormuz, Str. of, *The Gulf* 71 E8
Horn, *Austria* 26 C8
Horn, *Iceland* 8 C2
Horn, *Sweden* 11 G9
Horn →, *Canada* 102 A5
Horn, Cape = Hornos, C. de,
  Chile 128 H3
Horn Head, *Ireland* 12 A3
Horn I., *Australia* 94 A3
Horn Plateau, *Canada* 102 A5
Hornachuelos, *Spain* 37 H5
Hornavan, *Sweden* 8 C17
Hornbeck, *U.S.A.* 113 K8
Hornbrook, *U.S.A.* 108 F2
Hornburg, *Germany* 24 C6
Horncastle, *U.K.* 14 D7
Horndal, *Sweden* 10 D10
Hornell, *U.S.A.* 116 D7
Hornell L., *Canada* 102 A5
Hornepayne, *Canada* 104 C3
Horní Planá, *Czech Rep.* 26 C7
Hornings Mills, *Canada* 116 B4
Hornitos, *U.S.A.* 110 H6
Hornos, C. de, *Chile* 128 H3
Hornoy-le-Bourg, *France* 19 C8
Hornsea, *U.K.* 14 D7
Hornslandet, *Sweden* 10 C11
Hörnum, *Germany* 24 A4
Horobetsu = Noboribetsu, *Japan* . 54 C10
Horodenka, *Ukraine* 29 B10
Horodnya, *Ukraine* 33 G7
Horodok, Khmelnytskyy, *Ukraine* . 33 H4
Horodok, Lviv, *Ukraine* 33 H2
Horodyshche, *Ukraine* 33 H6
Horokhiv, *Ukraine* 33 G3
Horovice, *Czech Rep.* 26 B6
Horqin Youyi Qianqi, *China* 57 A12
Horqueta, *Paraguay* 126 A4
Horred, *Sweden* 11 G6
Horse Creek, *U.S.A.* 112 E3
Horse I., *Canada* 103 C9
Horse Is., *Canada* 105 B8
Horsefly L., *Canada* 102 C4
Horseheads, *U.S.A.* 116 D8
Horsens, *Denmark* 11 J3
Horsham, *Australia* 95 F3
Horsham, *U.K.* 15 F7
Horšovský Týn, *Czech Rep.* ... 26 B5
Horten, *Norway* 9 G14
Hortobágy →, *Hungary* 28 C6
Hortobágyi △, *Hungary* 28 C6
Horton, *U.S.A.* 112 F7
Horton →, *Canada* 100 B7
Horwood L., *Canada* 104 C3
Hosaina, *Ethiopia* 81 F4
Hose, Gunung-Gunung, *Malaysia* . 62 D4
Ḥoseynābād, Khuzestān, *Iran* ... 71 C6
Ḥoseynābād, Kordestān, *Iran* ... 70 C5
Hoshangabad, *India* 68 H7
Hoshiarpur, *India* 68 D6
Hospet, *India* 66 M10
Hoste, I., *Chile* 128 H3
Hostens, *France* 20 D3
Hot, *Thailand* 64 C2
Hot Creek Range, *U.S.A.* 108 G6
Hot Springs, Ark., *U.S.A.* 113 H8
Hot Springs, S. Dak., *U.S.A.* .. 112 D3
Hot Springs △, *U.S.A.* 113 H8
Hotagen, *Sweden* 8 E16
Hotan, *China* 60 C2
Hotazel, *S. Africa* 88 D3
Hotchkiss, *U.S.A.* 109 G10
Hotham, C., *Australia* 92 B5
Hoting, *Sweden* 8 D17
Hotolisht, *Albania* 44 E4
Hotte, Massif de la, *Haiti* 121 C5
Hottentotsbaai, *Namibia* 88 D1
Houat, Î. de, *France* 18 E4
Houdan, *France* 19 D8
Houei Sai, *Laos* 58 G3
Houeillès, *France* 20 D4
Houffalize, *Belgium* 17 D5
Houghton, Mich., *U.S.A.* 112 B10
Houghton, N.Y., *U.S.A.* 116 D6
Houghton L., *U.S.A.* 114 C3
Houghton-le-Spring, *U.K.* 14 C6
Houhora Heads, *N.Z.* 91 F4
Houlton, *U.S.A.* 115 B12
Houma, *U.S.A.* 113 L9
Houndé, *Burkina Faso* 82 C4
Hourtin, *France* 20 C2
Hourtin-Carcans, Étang d',
  France 20 C2
Housatonic →, *U.S.A.* 117 E11
Houston, *Canada* 102 C3
Houston, Mo., *U.S.A.* 113 G9
Houston, Tex., *U.S.A.* 113 L7
Hout →, *S. Africa* 89 C4
Houtkraal, *S. Africa* 88 E3
Houtman Abrolhos, *Australia* ... 93 E1
Hovd, *Mongolia* 60 B4
Hove, *U.K.* 15 G7
Hovenweep △, *U.S.A.* 109 H9
Hoveyzeh, *Iran* 71 D6
Hovmantorp, *Sweden* 11 H9
Hövsgöl, *Mongolia* 56 C5
Hövsgöl Nuur, *Mongolia* 60 A5
Hovsta, *Sweden* 10 E9
Howakil, *Eritrea* 81 D5
Howar, Wadi →, *Sudan* 81 D2
Howard, *Australia* 95 D5
Howard, Pa., *U.S.A.* 116 F7
Howard, S. Dak., *U.S.A.* 112 C6

Howe, *U.S.A.* 108 E7
Howe, C., *Australia* 95 F5
Howe I., *Canada* 117 B8
Howell, *U.S.A.* 114 D4
Howick, *Canada* 117 A11
Howick, *S. Africa* 89 D5
Howick Group, *Australia* 94 A4
Howitt, L., *Australia* 95 D2
Howland I., *Pac. Oc.* 96 G10
Howrah = Haora, *India* 69 H13
Howth Hd., *Ireland* 12 C5
Höxter, *Germany* 24 D5
Hoy, *U.K.* 13 C5
Hoya, *Germany* 24 C5
Høyanger, *Norway* 9 F12
Hoyerswerda, *Germany* 24 D10
Hoylake, *U.K.* 14 D4
Hoyos, *Spain* 36 E4
Hpa-an = Pa-an, *Burma* 67 L20
Hpungan Pass, *Burma* 67 F20
Hradec Králové, *Czech Rep.* ... 26 A8
Hrádek, *Czech Rep.* 27 C9
Hranice, *Czech Rep.* 27 B10
Hrazdan, *Armenia* 35 K7
Hrebenka, *Ukraine* 33 G7
Hrodna, *Belarus* 30 E10
Hrodzyanka, *Belarus* 32 F5
Hron →, *Slovak Rep.* 27 D11
Hrubieszów, *Poland* 31 H10
Hrubý Jeseník, *Czech Rep.* ... 27 A10
Hrvatska = Croatia ■, *Europe* .. 41 C13
Hrymayliv, *Ukraine* 33 H4
Hrynyava, *Ukraine* 29 C9
Hsenwi, *Burma* 67 H20
Hsiamen = Xiamen, *China* 59 E12
Hsian = Xi'an, *China* 56 G5
Hsinchu, *Taiwan* 59 E13
Hsinhailien = Lianyungang, *China* 57 G10
Hsinying, *Taiwan* 59 F13
Hsopket, *Burma* 58 F2
Hsüchou = Xuzhou, *China* 57 G9
Hu Xian, *China* 56 G5
Hua Hin, *Thailand* 64 F2
Hua Xian, Henan, *China* 56 G8
Hua Xian, Shaanxi, *China* 56 G5
Hua'an, *China* 59 E11
Huab →, *Namibia* 88 B2
Huacheng, *China* 59 E10
Huachinera, *Mexico* 118 A3
Huacho, *Peru* 124 F3
Huade, *China* 56 D7
Huadian, *China* 57 C14
Huadu, *China* 59 F9
Huai Had △, *Thailand* 64 D5
Huai He →, *China* 59 A14
Huai Nam Dang △, *Thailand* ... 64 C2
Huai Yot, *Thailand* 65 J2
Huai'an, Hebei, *China* 56 D8
Huai'an, Jiangsu, *China* 57 H10
Huaibei, *China* 56 G9
Huaibin, *China* 59 A10
Huaide = Gongzhuling, *China* .. 57 C13
Huaidezhen, *China* 57 C13
Huaihua, *China* 58 D7
Huaiji, *China* 59 F9
Huainan, *China* 59 A11
Huaining, *China* 59 B11
Huairen, *China* 56 E7
Huairou, *China* 56 D9
Huaiyang, *China* 56 H8
Huaiyin, *China* 57 H10
Huaiyuan, Anhui, *China* 57 H9
Huaiyuan, Guangxi Zhuangzu,
  China 58 E7
Huajianzi, *China* 57 D13
Huajuapan de Leon, *Mexico* ... 119 D5
Hualapai Peak, *U.S.A.* 109 J7
Hualien, *Taiwan* 59 E13
Huallaga →, *Peru* 124 E3
Huambo, *Angola* 85 G3
Huan Jiang →, *China* 56 G5
Huan Xian, *China* 56 F4
Huancabamba, *Peru* 124 E3
Huancane, *Peru* 124 G5
Huancavelica, *Peru* 124 F3
Huancayo, *Peru* 124 F3
Huanchaca, *Bolivia* 124 H5
Huang Hai = Yellow Sea, *China* . 57 G12
Huang He →, *China* 57 F10
Huang Xian, *China* 57 F11
Huangchuan, *China* 59 A10
Huanggang, *China* 59 B10
Huangguoshu, *China* 58 E5
Huangling, *China* 56 G5
Huanglong, *China* 56 G5
Huanglongtan, *China* 59 A8
Huangmei, *China* 59 B10
Huangpi, *China* 59 B10
Huangping, *China* 58 D6
Huangshan, *China* 59 C12
Huangshi, *China* 59 B10
Huangsongdian, *China* 57 C14
Huangyan, *China* 59 C13
Huangyangsi, *China* 59 D8
Huaning, *China* 58 E4
Huanjiang, *China* 58 E7
Huantai, *China* 57 F9
Huánuco, *Peru* 124 E3
Huaping, *China* 58 D3
Huaraz, *Peru* 124 E3
Huarmey, *Peru* 124 F3
Huarong, *China* 59 C9
Huascarán, *Peru* 124 E3
Huasco, *Chile* 126 B1
Huasco →, *Chile* 126 B1
Huasna, *U.S.A.* 111 K6
Huatabampo, *Mexico* 118 B3
Huauchinango, *Mexico* 119 C5
Huautla de Jiménez, *Mexico* ... 119 D5
Huaxi, *China* 58 D6
Huay Namota, *Mexico* 118 C4

Huayin, *China* 56 G6
Huayuan, *China* 58 C7
Huayuan, *China* 58 B6
Huazhou, *China* 59 G8
Hubbard, Ohio, *U.S.A.* 116 E4
Hubbard, Tex., *U.S.A.* 113 K6
Hubbart Pt., *Canada* 103 B10
Hubei □, *China* 59 B9
Hubli, *India* 66 M9
Huch'ang, N. *Korea* 57 D14
Hucknall, *U.K.* 14 D6
Huddersfield, *U.K.* 14 D6
Hude, *Germany* 24 B4
Hudi, *Sudan* 80 D3
Hudiksvall, *Sweden* 10 C11
Hudson, *Canada* 104 B1
Hudson, Mass., *U.S.A.* 117 D13
Hudson, N.Y., *U.S.A.* 117 D11
Hudson, Wis., *U.S.A.* 112 C8
Hudson, Wyo., *U.S.A.* 108 E9
Hudson →, *U.S.A.* 117 F10
Hudson Bay, Nunavut, *Canada* . 101 C11
Hudson Bay, Sask., *Canada* ... 103 C8
Hudson Falls, *U.S.A.* 117 C11
Hudson Mts., *Antarctica* 5 D16
Hudson Str., *Canada* 101 B13
Hudson's Hope, *Canada* 102 B4
Hue, *Vietnam* 64 D6
Huebra →, *Spain* 36 D4
Huedin, *Romania* 28 D8
Huehuetenango, *Guatemala* ... 120 C1
Huejúcar, *Mexico* 118 C4
Huélamo, *Spain* 38 E3
Huelgoat, *France* 18 D3
Huelma, *Spain* 37 H7
Huelva, *Spain* 37 H4
Huelva □, *Spain* 37 H4
Huelva →, *Spain* 37 H5
Huentelauquén, *Chile* 126 C1
Huércal-Overa, *Spain* 39 H3
Huerta, Sa. de la, *Argentina* .. 126 C2
Huertas, C. de las, *Spain* 39 G4
Huerva →, *Spain* 38 D4
Huesca, *Spain* 38 C4
Huesca □, *Spain* 38 C5
Huéscar, *Spain* 39 H2
Huetamo, *Mexico* 118 D4
Huete, *Spain* 38 E2
Hugh →, *Australia* 94 D1
Hughenden, *Australia* 94 C3
Hughes, *Australia* 93 F4
Hughesville, *U.S.A.* 117 E8
Hugli →, *India* 69 J13
Hugo, Colo., *U.S.A.* 112 F3
Hugo, Okla., *U.S.A.* 113 H7
Hugoton, *U.S.A.* 113 G4
Hui Xian = Huixian, *China* 56 G7
Hui Xian, *China* 56 H4
Hui'an, *China* 59 E12
Hui'anbu, *China* 56 F4
Huichang, *China* 59 E10
Huichapán, *Mexico* 119 C5
Huidong, Guangdong, *China* ... 59 F10
Huidong, Sichuan, *China* 58 D4
Huifa He →, *China* 57 C14
Huila, Nevado del, *Colombia* .. 124 C3
Huilai, *China* 59 F11
Huili, *China* 58 D4
Huimin, *China* 57 F9
Huinan, *China* 57 C14
Huinca Renancó, *Argentina* ... 126 C3
Huining, *China* 56 G3
Huinong, *China* 56 E4
Huisache, *Mexico* 118 C4
Huishui, *China* 58 D6
Huisne →, *France* 18 E7
Huiting, *China* 56 G9
Huitong, *China* 58 D7
Huixian, *China* 56 G7
Huixtla, *Mexico* 119 D6
Huize, *China* 58 D4
Huizhou, *China* 59 F10
Hukawng Valley, *Burma* 67 F20
Hukou, *China* 59 C11
Ḥuksan-chedo, S. *Korea* 57 G13
Hukuntsi, *Botswana* 88 C3
Ḥulayfā', *Si. Arabia* 70 E4
Hulin He →, *China* 57 B12
Hull = Kingston upon Hull, *U.K.* 14 D7
Hull, *Canada* 117 A9
Hull →, *U.K.* 14 D7
Hulst, *Neths.* 17 C4
Hultsfred, *Sweden* 11 G9
Hulun Nur, *China* 60 B6
Hulyaypole, *Ukraine* 33 J9
Huma, Tanjung, *Malaysia* .... 65 c
Humacao, *Puerto Rico* ...... 121 d
Humahuaca, *Argentina* 126 A2
Humaitá, *Brazil* 124 E6
Humaitá, *Paraguay* 126 B4
Humansdorp, *S. Africa* 88 E3
Humara, J., *Sudan* 81 D3
Humbe, *Angola* 88 B1
Humber →, *U.K.* 14 D7
Humboldt, *Canada* 103 C7
Humboldt, Iowa, *U.S.A.* 112 D7
Humboldt, Tenn., *U.S.A.* 113 H10
Humboldt →, *U.S.A.* 108 F4
Humboldt Gletscher =
  Sermersuaq, *Greenland* 4 B4
Hume, *U.S.A.* 110 J8
Hume, L., *Australia* 95 F4
Humenné, *Slovak Rep.* 27 C14
Hummelsta, *Sweden* 10 E10
Humphreys, Mt., *U.S.A.* 110 H8
Humphreys Peak, *U.S.A.* 109 J8
Humpolec, *Czech Rep.* 26 B8
Humptulips, *U.S.A.* 110 C3
Hūn, *Libya* 79 C9
Hun Jiang →, *China* 57 D13
Húnaflói, *Iceland* 8 D3
Hunan □, *China* 59 D9

Hunchun, *China* 57 C16
Hundested, *Denmark* 11 J5
Hundewali, *Pakistan* 68 D5
Hundred Mile House, *Canada* .. 102 C4
Hunedoara, *Romania* 28 E7
Hunedoara □, *Romania* 28 E7
Hünfeld, *Germany* 24 E5
Hung Yen, *Vietnam* 58 G6
Hungary ■, *Europe* 27 D12
Hungary, Plain of, *Europe* 6 F10
Hungerford, *Australia* 95 D3
Hŭngnam, N. *Korea* 57 E14
Hungt'ou Hsü, *Taiwan* 59 G13
Huni Valley, *Ghana* 82 D4
Hunneberg, *Sweden* 11 F6
Hunnebostrand, *Sweden* 11 F5
Hunsberge, *Namibia* 88 D2
Hunsrück, *Germany* 25 F3
Hunstanton, *U.K.* 14 E8
Hunte →, *Germany* 24 B4
Hunter, *U.S.A.* 117 D10
Hunter I., *Australia* 95 G3
Hunter I., *Canada* 102 C3
Hunter Ra., *Australia* 95 E5
Hunters Road, *Zimbabwe* 87 F2
Hunterville, *N.Z.* 91 H5
Huntingburg, *U.S.A.* 114 F2
Huntingdon, *Canada* 104 C5
Huntingdon, *U.K.* 15 E7
Huntingdon, *U.S.A.* 116 F6
Huntington, Ind., *U.S.A.* 114 E3
Huntington, N.Y., *U.S.A.* 117 F11
Huntington, Oreg., *U.S.A.* ... 108 D5
Huntington, Utah, *U.S.A.* 108 G8
Huntington, W. Va., *U.S.A.* .. 114 F4
Huntington Beach, *U.S.A.* ... 111 M9
Huntly, *N.Z.* 91 G5
Huntly, *U.K.* 13 D6
Huntsville, *Canada* 116 A5
Huntsville, Ala., *U.S.A.* 115 H2
Huntsville, Tex., *U.S.A.* 113 K7
Hunyani →, *Zimbabwe* 87 F3
Hunyuan, *China* 56 E7
Hunza →, *India* 69 B6
Huo Xian = Huozhou, *China* .. 56 F6
Huong Khe, *Vietnam* 64 C5
Huonville, *Australia* 95 G4
Huoqiu, *China* 59 A11
Huoshan, Anhui, *China* 59 A12
Huoshan, Anhui, *China* 59 B11
Huoshao Dao = Lü-Tao, *Taiwan* 59 F13
Huozhou, *China* 56 F6
Hupeh = Hubei □, *China* 59 B9
Ḥūr, *Iran* 71 D8
Hurbanovo, *Slovak Rep.* 27 D11
Hurd, C., *Canada* 116 A3
Hure Qi, *China* 57 C11
Hurezani, *Romania* 29 F8
Hurghada, *Egypt* 80 B3
Hurley, N. Mex., *U.S.A.* 109 K9
Hurley, Wis., *U.S.A.* 112 B9
Huron, Calif., *U.S.A.* 110 J6
Huron, Ohio, *U.S.A.* 116 E2
Huron, S. Dak., *U.S.A.* 112 C5
Huron, L., *U.S.A.* 116 B2
Huron East, *Canada* 116 C3
Hurricane, *U.S.A.* 109 H7
Hurso, *Ethiopia* 81 F5
Hurungwe △, *Zimbabwe* 87 F2
Hurunui →, *N.Z.* 91 K4
Hurup, *Denmark* 11 H2
Húsavík, *Iceland* 8 C5
Huşi, *Romania* 29 D13
Huskvarna, *Sweden* 11 G8
Hustadvika, *Norway* 8 E12
Hustontown, *U.S.A.* 116 F6
Hustopeče, *Czech Rep.* 27 C9
Husum, *Germany* 24 A5
Husum, *Sweden* 10 A13
Hutchinson, Kans., *U.S.A.* ... 113 F6
Hutchinson, Minn., *U.S.A.* ... 112 C7
Hutte Sauvage, L. de la, *Canada* 105 A7
Hüttenberg, *Austria* 26 E7
Hüttener Berge △, *Germany* .. 24 A5
Hutton, Mt., *Australia* 95 D4
Huwei, *Ethiopia* 81 G5
Huy, *Belgium* 17 D5
Huzhou, *China* 59 B13
Hvalpsund, *Denmark* 11 H3
Hvammstangi, *Iceland* 8 D3
Hvar, *Croatia* 41 E13
Hvarski Kanal, *Croatia* 41 E13
Hvítá →, *Iceland* 8 D3
Hvizdets, *Ukraine* 29 B10
Hwachŏn-chŏsuji, S. *Korea* ... 57 E14
Hwang Ho = Huang He →, *China* 57 F10
Hwange, *Zimbabwe* 87 F2
Hwange △, *Zimbabwe* 88 B4
Hyannis, Mass., *U.S.A.* 114 E10
Hyannis, Nebr., *U.S.A.* 112 E4
Hyargas Nuur, *Mongolia* 60 B4
Hybo, *Sweden* 10 C10
Hydaburg, *U.S.A.* 102 B2
Hyde Park, *U.S.A.* 117 E11
Hyden, *Australia* 93 F2
Hyder, *U.S.A.* 102 B2
Hyderabad, *India* 66 L11
Hyderabad, *Pakistan* 68 G3
Hyères, *France* 21 E10
Hyères, Îs. d', *France* 21 F10
Hyesan, N. *Korea* 57 D15
Hyland →, *Canada* 102 B3
Hyltebruk, *Sweden* 11 H7
Hymia, *India* 69 C8
Hyndman Peak, *U.S.A.* 108 E6
Hyōgo □, *Japan* 55 G7
Hyrum, *U.S.A.* 108 F8
Hysham, *U.S.A.* 108 C10

I-n-Gall, *Niger* 83 B6
I-n-Oudad, *Algeria* 83 A5
I-n-Ouzzal, *Algeria* 83 A5
I-n-Tadreft, *Niger* 83 B6
Iablaniţa, *Romania* 28 F7
Iaco →, *Brazil* 124 E5
Iacobeni, *Romania* 29 C10
Iakora, *Madag.* 89 C8
Ialomiţa □, *Romania* 29 F12
Ialomiţa →, *Romania* 29 F12
Ialoveni, *Moldova* 29 D13
Ialpug →, *Moldova* 29 E13
Ianca, *Romania* 29 E12
Iara, *Romania* 29 D8
Iarda, *Ethiopia* 81 E4
Iargara, *Moldova* 29 D13
Iaşi, *Romania* 29 C12
Iaşi □, *Romania* 29 C12
Íasmos, *Greece* 45 E9
Ib →, *India* 69 J10
Iba, *Phil.* 61 D3
Ibadan, *Nigeria* 83 D5
Ibagué, *Colombia* 124 C3
Iballë, *Albania* 44 D4
Ibăneşti, Botoşani, *Romania* .. 29 B11
Ibăneşti, Mureş, *Romania* 29 D9
Ibar →, *Serbia & M.* 44 C4
Ibaraki □, *Japan* 55 F10
Ibarra, *Ecuador* 124 C3
Ibba, *Sudan* 81 G2
Ibba, Bahr →, *Sudan* 81 F2
Ibbenbüren, *Germany* 24 C3
Ibembo, *Dem. Rep. of the Congo* 86 B1
Ibera, L., *Argentina* 126 B4
Iberian Peninsula, *Europe* ... 6 H5
Iberville, *Canada* 117 A11
Iberville, Lac d', *Canada* 104 A5
Ibi, *Nigeria* 83 D6
Ibi, *Spain* 39 G4
Ibiá, *Brazil* 125 G9
Ibiapaba, Sa. da, *Brazil* 125 D10
Ibicuí →, *Brazil* 127 B4
Ibicuy, *Argentina* 126 C4
Ibiza = Eivissa, *Spain* 48 C7
Ibiza = Eivissa, *Spain* 39 G6
Íblei, Monti, *Italy* 43 E7
Ibo, *Mozam.* 87 E5
Ibonma, *Indonesia* 63 E8
Ibotirama, *Brazil* 125 F10
Ibrāhīm →, *Lebanon* 74 A4
'Ibrī, *Oman* 71 F8
Ibriktepe, *Turkey* 45 E10
Ibshawāi, *Egypt* 80 J7
Ibu, *Indonesia* 63 D7
Ibusuki, *Japan* 55 J5
Ica, *Peru* 124 F3
Içá →, *Brazil* 124 D5
Icacos Pt., *Trin. & Tob.* 125 K15
Içana, *Brazil* 124 C5
Içana →, *Brazil* 124 C5
Içel = Mersin, *Turkey* 70 B2
Iceland ■, *Europe* 8 D4
Iceland Plateau, *Arctic* 4 C7
Ich'ang = Yichang, *China* ... 59 B8
Ichchapuram, *India* 67 K14
Ichhawar, *India* 68 H7
Ichihara, *Japan* 55 G10
Ichikawa, *Japan* 55 G9
Ichilo →, *Bolivia* 124 G6
Ichinohe, *Japan* 54 D10
Ichinomiya, *Japan* 55 G8
Ichinoseki, *Japan* 54 E10
Ichnya, *Ukraine* 33 G7
Icod, *Canary Is.* 48 F3
Ida Grove, *U.S.A.* 112 D7
Idabel, *U.S.A.* 113 J7
Idaga Hamus, *Ethiopia* 81 E4
Idah, *Nigeria* 83 D6
Idaho □, *U.S.A.* 108 D7
Idaho City, *U.S.A.* 108 E6
Idaho Falls, *U.S.A.* 108 E7
Idalia △, *Australia* 94 C3
Idanha-a-Nova, *Portugal* 36 F3
Idar-Oberstein, *Germany* 25 F3
Idensalmi = Iisalmi, *Finland* .. 8 E22
Idfû, *Egypt* 80 C3
Ídhi Óros, *Greece* 49 D6
Ídhra, *Greece* 46 D5
Idi, *Indonesia* 62 C1
Idiofa, *Dem. Rep. of the Congo* 84 E3
Idku, Bahra el, *Egypt* 80 H7
Idlib, *Syria* 70 C3
Idre, *Sweden* 10 C6
Idria, *U.S.A.* 110 J6
Idrija, *Slovenia* 41 C11
Idritsa, *Russia* 32 D5
Idutywa, *S. Africa* 89 E4
Ieper, *Belgium* 17 D2
Ierápetra, *Greece* 49 E7
Ierissós, *Greece* 44 F7
Iernut, *Romania* 29 D9
Iesi, *Italy* 41 E10
Iésolo, *Italy* 41 C9
Ifach, Peñón de, *Spain* 39 G5
Ifakara, *Tanzania* 84 F7
'Ifāl, W. al →, *Si. Arabia* ... 70 D2
Ifanadiana, *Madag.* 89 C8
Ife, *Nigeria* 83 D5
Iférouâne, *Niger* 83 B6
Iffley, *Australia* 94 B3
Ifon, *Nigeria* 83 D6
Iforas, Adrar des, *Africa* 83 B5
Ifould, L., *Australia* 93 F5
Iganga, *Uganda* 86 B3
Igarapava, *Brazil* 125 H9
Igarka, *Russia* 52 C9

Igatimi, *Paraguay* 127 A4
Igbetti, *Nigeria* 83 D5
Igbo-Ora, *Nigeria* 83 D5
Igboho, *Nigeria* 83 D5
Igbor, *Nigeria* 83 D6
Iğdır, *Turkey* 73 C11
Igelfors, *Sweden* 11 F9
Iggesund, *Sweden* 10 C11
Iglésias, *Italy* 42 C1
Igloolik, *Canada* 101 B11
Igluligaarjuk = Chesterfield Inlet,
  Canada 100 B10
Iglulik = Igloolik, *Canada* 101 B11
'Igma, Gebel el, *Egypt* 80 B3
Ignace, *Canada* 104 C1
Iğneada, *Turkey* 45 E11
Iğneada Burnu, *Turkey* 45 E12
Igoumenítsa, *Greece* 46 B2
Igra, *Russia* 34 B11
Iguaçu △, *Brazil* 127 B5
Iguaçu ➤, *Brazil* 127 B5
Iguaçu, Cat. del, *Brazil* 127 B5
Iguaçu Falls = Iguaçu, Cat. del,
  Brazil 127 B5
Iguala, *Mexico* 119 D5
Igualada, *Spain* 38 D6
Iguassu = Iguaçu ➤, *Brazil* 127 B5
Iguatu, *Brazil* 125 E11
Iguazú △, *Argentina* 127 B5
Iguidi, Erg, *Africa* 78 C4
Iguéla, *Gabon* 84 E1
Iharana, *Madag.* 89 A9
Ihbulag, *Mongolia* 56 C4
Iheya-Shima, *Japan* 55 L3
Ihiala, *Nigeria* 83 D6
Ihosy, *Madag.* 89 C8
Ihotry, Farihy, *Madag.* 89 C7
Ihugh, *Nigeria* 83 D6
Ii, *Finland* 8 D21
Ii-Shima, *Japan* 55 L3
Iida, *Japan* 55 G8
Iijoki ➤, *Finland* 8 D21
Iisalmi, *Finland* 8 E22
Iiyama, *Japan* 55 F9
Iizuka, *Japan* 55 H5
Ijebu-Igbo, *Nigeria* 83 D5
Ijebu-Ode, *Nigeria* 83 D5
IJmuiden, *Neths.* 17 B4
Ijo älv = Iijoki ➤, *Finland* 8 D21
IJssel ➤, *Neths.* 17 B5
IJsselmeer, *Neths.* 17 B5
Ijuí, *Brazil* 127 B5
Ijuí ➤, *Brazil* 127 B4
Ikalamavony, *Madag.* 89 C8
Ikale, *Nigeria* 83 D6
Ikaluktutiak, *Canada* 100 B9
Ikang, *Nigeria* 83 E6
Ikara, *Nigeria* 83 C6
Ikare, *Nigeria* 83 D6
Ikaría, *Greece* 47 D8
Ikast, *Denmark* 11 H3
Ikeda, *Japan* 55 G6
Ikeja, *Nigeria* 83 D5
Ikela, *Dem. Rep. of the Congo* .. 84 E4
Ikerre-Ekiti, *Nigeria* 83 D6
Ikhtiman, *Bulgaria* 44 D7
Iki, *Japan* 55 H4
Ikimba L., *Tanzania* 86 C3
Ikire, *Nigeria* 83 D5
Ikizdere, *Turkey* 73 B9
Ikom, *Nigeria* 83 D6
Ikongo, *Madag.* 89 C8
Ikopa ➤, *Madag.* 89 B8
Ikorongo △, *Tanzania* 86 C3
Ikot Ekpene, *Nigeria* 83 D6
Ikparjuk = Arctic Bay, *Canada* 101 A11
Ikungu, *Tanzania* 86 C3
Ikurun, *Nigeria* 83 D5
Ila, *Nigeria* 83 D5
Ilagan, *Phil.* 61 C4
Ilaka, *Madag.* 89 B8
Ilâm, *Iran* 70 C5
Ilam, *Nepal* 69 F12
Ilam □, *Iran* 70 C5
Ilan, *Taiwan* 59 E13
Ilanskiy, *Russia* 53 D10
Ilaro, *Nigeria* 83 D5
Ilatane, *Niger* 83 B5
Iława, *Poland* 30 E6
Ile ➤, *Kazakhstan* 52 E8
Île-à-la-Crosse, *Canada* 103 B7
Île-à-la-Crosse, Lac, *Canada* .. 103 B7
Île-de-France □, *France* 19 D9
Ileanda, *Romania* 29 C8
Ilebo, *Dem. Rep. of the Congo* .. 84 E4
Ilek, *Russia* 52 D6
Ilero, *Nigeria* 83 D5
Ilesha, *Kwara, Nigeria* 83 D5
Ilesha, *Oyo, Nigeria* 83 D5
Ilford, *Canada* 103 B9
Ilfracombe, *Australia* 94 C3
Ilfracombe, *U.K.* 15 F3
Ilgaz, *Turkey* 72 B5
Ilgaz Dağları, *Turkey* 72 B5
Ilgın, *Turkey* 72 C4
Ilha de Moçambique, *Mozam.* .. 87 F5
Ílhavo, *Portugal* 36 E2
Ilhéus, *Brazil* 125 F11
Ili = Ile ➤, *Kazakhstan* 52 E8
Ilia, *Romania* 28 E7
Ilía □, *Greece* 46 D3
Iliamna L., *U.S.A.* 100 C4
Iliç, *Turkey* 73 C8
Ilıca, *Turkey* 47 B9
Ilichevsk, *Azerbaijan* 73 C11
Iligan, *Phil.* 61 G6
Iligan Bay, *Phil.* 61 G6
Ilıkí, L., *Greece* 46 C5
Ilin I., *Phil.* 61 E4
Iliodhrómia, *Greece* 46 B5
Ilion, *U.S.A.* 117 D9
Ilirska-Bistrica, *Slovenia* 41 C11
Ilkeston, *U.K.* 14 E6

Ilkley, *U.K.* 14 D6
Illampu = Ancohuma, Nevado,
  Bolivia 124 G5
Illana B., *Phil.* 61 H5
Illapel, *Chile* 126 C1
Ille-et-Vilaine □, *France* 18 D5
Ille-sur-Têt, *France* 20 F6
Illéla, *Niger* 83 C6
Iller ➤, *Germany* 25 G5
Illertissen, *Germany* 25 G6
Illescas, *Spain* 36 E7
Illetas, *Spain* 48 B9
Illichivsk, *Ukraine* 33 J6
Illiers-Combray, *France* 18 D8
Illimani, Nevado, *Bolivia* 124 G5
Illinois □, *U.S.A.* 112 E10
Illinois ➤, *U.S.A.* 112 F9
Ilizi, *Algeria* 78 C7
Illkirch-Graffenstaden, *France* .. 19 D14
Íllora, *Spain* 37 H7
Ilm ➤, *Germany* 24 D7
Ilmajoki, *Finland* 9 E20
Ilmen, Ozero, *Russia* 32 C6
Ilmenau, *Germany* 24 E6
Ilnytsya, *Ukraine* 28 B7
Ilo, *Peru* 124 G4
Ilobu, *Nigeria* 83 D5
Iloilo, *Phil.* 61 F5
Ilora, *Nigeria* 83 D5
Ilorin, *Nigeria* 83 D5
Ilovatka, *Russia* 34 E7
Ilovlya, *Russia* 35 F7
Ilovlya ➤, *Russia* 35 F7
Iłowa, *Poland* 31 G2
Ilubabor, *Ethiopia* 81 F4
Ilva Mică, *Romania* 29 C9
Ilwaco, *U.S.A.* 110 D2
Ilwaki, *Indonesia* 63 F7
Ilyichevsk = Illichivsk, *Ukraine* .. 33 J6
Iłża, *Poland* 31 G8
Itzanka ➤, *Poland* 31 G8
Imabari, *Japan* 55 G6
Imaloto ➤, *Madag.* 89 C8
Imamoğlu, *Turkey* 72 D6
Imandra, Ozero, *Russia* 52 C5
Imanombo, *Madag.* 89 C8
Imari, *Japan* 55 H4
Imasa, *Sudan* 80 D4
Imathía □, *Greece* 44 F6
Imatra, *Finland* 32 B5
Iménas, *Mali* 83 B5
imeni 26 Bakinskikh
  Komissarov = Neftçala,
  Azerbaijan 71 B6
imeni 26 Bakinskikh Komissarov,
  Turkmenistan 71 B7
Imeri, Serra, *Brazil* 124 C5
Imerimandroso, *Madag.* 89 B8
Imi, *Ethiopia* 81 F5
Imishly = Imişli, *Azerbaijan* 35 L9
Imişli, *Azerbaijan* 35 L9
Imlay, *U.S.A.* 108 F4
Imlay City, *U.S.A.* 116 D1
Immaseri, *Sudan* 81 D2
Immenstadt, *Germany* 25 H6
Immingham, *U.K.* 14 D7
Immokalee, *U.S.A.* 115 M5
Imo □, *Nigeria* 83 D6
Imo ➤, *Nigeria* 83 E6
Ímola, *Italy* 41 D8
Imotski, *Croatia* 41 E14
Imperatriz, *Brazil* 125 E9
Impéria, *Italy* 40 E5
Imperial, *Canada* 103 C7
Imperial, *Calif., U.S.A.* 111 N11
Imperial, *Nebr., U.S.A.* 112 E4
Imperial Beach, *U.S.A.* 111 N9
Imperial Dam, *U.S.A.* 111 N12
Imperial Reservoir, *U.S.A.* 111 N12
Imperial Valley, *U.S.A.* 111 N11
Imperieuse Reef, *Australia* 92 C2
Impfondo, *Congo* 84 D3
Imphal, *India* 67 G18
Imphy, *France* 19 F10
Imranlı, *Turkey* 73 C8
Imroz = Gökçeada, *Turkey* .. 45 F9
Imroz, *Turkey* 45 F9
Imst, *Austria* 26 D3
Imuris, *Mexico* 118 A2
Imuruan B., *Phil.* 63 B5
In Akhmed, *Mali* 83 B4
In Aleï, *Mali* 82 B4
In Delimane, *Mali* 83 B5
In Guezzam, *Algeria* 83 B6
In Koufi, *Mali* 83 B5
In Salah, *Algeria* 78 C6
In Tallak, *Mali* 83 B5
In Tebezas, *Mali* 83 B5
Ina, *Japan* 55 G8
Inagua △, *Bahamas* 121 B5
Inangahua, *N.Z.* 91 J3
Inanwatan, *Indonesia* 63 E8
Iñapari, *Peru* 124 F5
Inari, *Finland* 8 B22
Inarijärvi, *Finland* 8 B22
Inawashiro-Ko, *Japan* 54 F10
Inca, *Spain* 48 B9
Inca de Oro, *Chile* 126 B2
Incaguasi, *Chile* 126 B1
Ince Burun, *Turkey* 72 A6
Incekum Burnu, *Turkey* 72 D5
Incesu, *Turkey* 70 B2
Inch'ŏn, *S. Korea* 57 F14
Incio = Cruz de Incio, *Spain* .. 36 C3
Incirliova, *Turkey* 47 D9
Incline Village, *U.S.A.* 108 G4
Incomáti ➤, *Mozam.* 89 D5
Incudine, Mte., *France* 21 G13
Inda Silase, *Ethiopia* 81 E4
Indal, *Sweden* 10 B11
Indalsälven ➤, *Sweden* 10 B11
Indaw, *Burma* 67 G20

Indbir, *Ethiopia* 81 F4
Independence, *Calif., U.S.A.* 110 J8
Independence, *Iowa, U.S.A.* 112 D9
Independence, *Kans., U.S.A.* 113 G7
Independence, *Ky., U.S.A.* 114 F3
Independence, *Mo., U.S.A.* 112 F7
Independence Fjord, *Greenland* .. 4 A6
Independence Mts., *U.S.A.* 108 F5
Independenţa, *Romania* 29 E12
Index, *U.S.A.* 110 C5
India ■, *Asia* 66 K11
Indian ➤, *U.S.A.* 115 M5
Indian Cabins, *Canada* 102 B5
Indian Harbour, *Canada* 105 B8
Indian Head, *Canada* 103 C8
Indian Lake, *U.S.A.* 117 C10
Indian Ocean 50 K11
Indian Springs, *U.S.A.* 111 J11
Indiana, *U.S.A.* 116 F5
Indiana □, *U.S.A.* 114 F3
Indianapolis, *U.S.A.* 114 F2
Indianola, *Iowa, U.S.A.* 112 E8
Indianola, *Miss., U.S.A.* 113 J9
Indigirka ➤, *Russia* 53 B15
Indija, *Serbia & M.* 28 E5
Indio, *U.S.A.* 111 M10
Indira Gandhi Canal, *India* 68 F5
Indo-China, *Asia* 50 H14
Indonesia ■, *Asia* 62 F5
Indore, *India* 68 H6
Indramayu, *Indonesia* 63 G13
Indravati ➤, *India* 67 K12
Indre □, *France* 19 F8
Indre ➤, *France* 18 E7
Indre-et-Loire □, *France* 18 E7
Indulkana, *Australia* 95 D1
Indura, *Belarus* 30 E10
Indus ➤, *Pakistan* 68 G2
Indus, Mouths of the, *Pakistan* .. 68 H3
Inebolu, *Turkey* 72 B5
Inecik, *Turkey* 45 F11
İnegöl, *Turkey* 45 F13
Ineu, *Romania* 28 D6
Infantes = Villanueva de los
  Infantes, *Spain* 37 G7
Infiernillo, Presa del, *Mexico* .. 118 D4
Infiesto, *Spain* 36 B5
Ingelstad, *Sweden* 11 H8
Ingenio, *Canary Is.* 48 G4
Ingenio Santa Ana, *Argentina* .. 126 B2
Ingersoll, *Canada* 116 C4
Ingham, *Australia* 94 B4
Ingleborough, *U.K.* 14 C5
Inglewood, *Queens., Australia* .. 95 D5
Inglewood, *Vic., Australia* 95 F3
Inglewood, *N.Z.* 91 H5
Inglewood, *U.S.A.* 111 M8
Ingólfshöfði, *Iceland* 8 E5
Ingolstadt, *Germany* 25 G7
Ingomar, *U.S.A.* 108 C10
Ingonish, *Canada* 105 C7
Ingore, *Guinea-Biss.* 82 C1
Ingraj Bazar, *India* 69 G13
Ingrid Christensen Coast,
  Antarctica 5 C6
Ingul = Inhul ➤, *Ukraine* 33 J7
Ingulec = Inhulec ➤, *Ukraine* .. 33 J7
Ingulets = Inhulets ➤, *Ukraine* .. 33 J7
Inguri = Enguri ➤, *Georgia* .. 35 J5
Ingushetia □, *Russia* 35 J7
Ingwavuma, *S. Africa* 89 D5
Inhaca, *Mozam.* 89 D5
Inhafenga, *Mozam.* 89 C5
Inhambane, *Mozam.* 89 C6
Inhambane □, *Mozam.* 89 C5
Inhaminga, *Mozam.* 87 F4
Inharrime, *Mozam.* 89 C6
Inharrime ➤, *Mozam.* 89 C6
Inhisar, *Turkey* 47 A12
Inhul ➤, *Ukraine* 33 J7
Inhulec, *Ukraine* 33 J7
Inhulets ➤, *Ukraine* 33 J7
Iniesta, *Spain* 39 F3
Ining = Yining, *China* 52 E9
Inírida ➤, *Colombia* 124 C5
Inishbofin, *Ireland* 12 C1
Inisheer, *Ireland* 12 C2
Inishfree B., *Ireland* 12 A3
Inishkea North, *Ireland* 12 B1
Inishkea South, *Ireland* 12 B1
Inishmaan, *Ireland* 12 C2
Inishmore, *Ireland* 12 C2
Inishowen Pen., *Ireland* 12 A4
Inishshark, *Ireland* 12 C1
Inishturk, *Ireland* 12 C1
Inishvickillane, *Ireland* 12 D1
Injibara, *Ethiopia* 81 E4
Injune, *Australia* 95 D4
Inklin ➤, *Canada* 102 B2
Inland Kaikoura Ra., *N.Z.* 91 J4
Inland Sea = Setonaikai, *Japan* .. 55 G6
Inle L., *Burma* 67 J20
Inlet, *U.S.A.* 117 C10
Inn ➤, *Austria* 26 C6
Innamincka, *Australia* 95 D3
Inner Hebrides, *U.K.* 13 E2
Inner Mongolia = Nei Monggol
  Zizhiqu □, *China* 56 D7
Inner Sound, *U.K.* 13 D3
Innerkip, *Canada* 116 C4
Innetalling I., *Canada* 104 A4
Innisfail, *Australia* 94 B4
Innisfail, *Canada* 102 C6
In'noshima, *Japan* 55 G6
Innsbruck, *Austria* 26 D4
Innviertel, *Austria* 26 C7
Inny ➤, *Ireland* 12 C4
Inongo, *Dem. Rep. of the Congo* .. 84 E3
Inönü, *Turkey* 47 B12
Inoucdjouac = Inukjuak, *Canada* 101 C12
Inowrocław, *Poland* 31 F5
Inpundong, *N. Korea* 57 D14

Inscription, C., *Australia* 93 E1
Insein, *Burma* 67 L20
Insjön, *Sweden* 10 D9
Ińsko, *Poland* 30 E2
Însurăţei, *Romania* 29 F12
Inta, *Russia* 52 C6
Intendente Alvear, *Argentina* .. 126 D3
Intepe, *Turkey* 47 A8
Interlaken, *Switz.* 25 J3
Interlaken, *U.S.A.* 117 D8
International Falls, *U.S.A.* 112 A8
Intiyaco, *Argentina* 126 B3
Întorsura Buzăului, *Romania* .. 29 E11
Inukjuak, *Canada* 101 C12
Inútil, B., *Chile* 128 G2
Inuvik, *Canada* 100 B6
Inveraray, *U.K.* 13 E3
Inverbervie, *U.K.* 13 E6
Invercargill, *N.Z.* 91 M2
Inverclyde □, *U.K.* 13 F4
Inverell, *Australia* 95 D5
Invergordon, *U.K.* 13 D4
Inverloch, *Australia* 95 F4
Invermere, *Canada* 102 C5
Inverness, *Canada* 105 C7
Inverness, *U.K.* 13 D4
Inverness, *U.S.A.* 115 L4
Inverurie, *U.K.* 13 D6
Investigator Group, *Australia* .. 95 E1
Investigator Str., *Australia* 95 F2
Inya, *Russia* 52 D9
Inyanga, *Zimbabwe* 87 F3
Inyangani, *Zimbabwe* 87 F3
Inyantue, *Zimbabwe* 88 B4
Inyo Mts., *U.S.A.* 110 J9
Inyokern, *U.S.A.* 111 K9
Inza, *Russia* 34 D8
Inzhavino, *Russia* 34 D6
Iō-Jima, *Japan* 55 J5
Ioánnina, *Greece* 46 B2
Ioánnina □, *Greece* 46 B2
Iola, *U.S.A.* 113 G7
Ion Corvin, *Romania* 29 F12
Iona, *U.K.* 13 E2
Ionia, *U.S.A.* 114 D3
Ionian Is. = Iónioi Nísoi, *Greece* . 46 C2
Ionian Sea, *Medit. S.* 6 H9
Iónioi Nísoi, *Greece* 46 C2
Iónioi Nísoi □, *Greece* 46 C2
Íos, *Greece* 47 E7
Iowa □, *U.S.A.* 112 D8
Iowa ➤, *U.S.A.* 112 E9
Iowa City, *U.S.A.* 112 E9
Iowa Falls, *U.S.A.* 112 D8
Iowa Park, *U.S.A.* 113 J5
Ipala, *Tanzania* 86 C3
Ipameri, *Brazil* 125 G9
Ipáti, *Greece* 46 C4
Ipatinga, *Brazil* 125 G10
Ipatovo, *Russia* 35 H6
Ipel' ➤, *Europe* 27 D11
Ipiales, *Colombia* 124 C3
Ipin = Yibin, *China* 58 C5
Ipiros □, *Greece* 46 B2
Ipixuna, *Brazil* 124 E4
Ipoh, *Malaysia* 65 K3
Ippy, *C.A.R.* 84 C4
Ipsala, *Turkey* 45 F10
Ipsárion, Óros, *Greece* 45 F8
Ipswich, *Australia* 95 D5
Ipswich, *U.K.* 15 E9
Ipswich, *Mass., U.S.A.* 117 D14
Ipswich, *S. Dak., U.S.A.* 112 C5
Ipu, *Brazil* 125 D10
Iqaluit, *Canada* 101 B13
Iquique, *Chile* 124 H4
Iquitos, *Peru* 124 D4
Irabu-Jima, *Japan* 55 M2
Iracoubo, *Fr. Guiana* 125 B8
Irafshān, *Iran* 71 E9
Irahuan, *Phil.* 61 G3
Iráklia, Kikládhes, *Greece* 47 E7
Iráklia, Sérrai, *Greece* 44 E7
Iráklion, *Greece* 49 D7
Iráklion □, *Greece* 49 D7
Irala, *Paraguay* 127 B5
Iran ■, *Asia* 71 C7
Iran, Gunung-Gunung, *Malaysia* 62 D4
Iran, Plateau of, *Asia* 50 F9
Iran Ra. = Iran, Gunung-Gunung,
  Malaysia 62 D4
Irānshahr, *Iran* 71 E9
Irapuato, *Mexico* 118 C4
Iraq ■, *Asia* 70 C5
Irati, *Brazil* 127 B5
Irbes saurums, *Latvia* 30 A9
Irbid, *Jordan* 74 C4
Irbid □, *Jordan* 74 C5
Iregua ➤, *Spain* 38 C7
Ireland ■, *Europe* 12 C4
Irele, *Nigeria* 83 D6
Irgiz, Bolshaya ➤, *Russia* 34 D9
Irhyangdong, *N. Korea* 57 D15
Iri, *S. Korea* 57 G14
Irian Jaya = Papua □, *Indonesia* .. 63 E9
Irié, *Guinea* 82 D3
Iriga, *Phil.* 61 E5
Iringa, *Tanzania* 86 D4
Iringa □, *Tanzania* 86 D4
Iriomote △, *Japan* 55 M1
Iriomote-Jima, *Japan* 55 M1
Iriona, *Honduras* 120 C2
Iriri ➤, *Brazil* 125 D8
Irish Republic ■, *Europe* 12 C4
Irish Sea, *Europe* 14 D3
Irkutsk, *Russia* 53 D11
Irlığanlı, *Turkey* 47 D11
Irma, *Canada* 103 C6
Irō-Zaki, *Japan* 55 G9
Iroise, Mer d', *France* 18 D2
Iron Baron, *Australia* 95 E2

Iron Gate = Portile de Fier,
  Europe 28 F7
Iron Knob, *Australia* 95 E2
Iron Mountain, *U.S.A.* 114 C1
Iron Range △, *Australia* 94 A3
Iron River, *U.S.A.* 112 B10
Irondequoit, *U.S.A.* 116 C7
Ironton, *Mo., U.S.A.* 113 G9
Ironton, *Ohio, U.S.A.* 114 F4
Ironwood, *U.S.A.* 112 B9
Ironwood Forest △, *U.S.A.* 109 K8
Iroquois, *Canada* 117 B9
Iroquois Falls, *Canada* 104 C3
Irosin, *Phil.* 61 E6
Irpin, *Ukraine* 33 G6
Irrara Cr. ➤, *Australia* 95 D4
Irrawaddy □, *Burma* 67 L19
Irrawaddy ➤, *Burma* 67 M19
Irrawaddy, Mouths of the, *Burma* 67 M19
Irricana, *Canada* 102 C6
Irshava, *Ukraine* 28 B8
Irsina, *Italy* 43 B9
Irtysh ➤, *Russia* 52 C7
Irumu, *Dem. Rep. of the Congo* .. 86 B2
Irún, *Spain* 38 B3
Irunea = Pamplona, *Spain* 38 C3
Irurzun, *Spain* 38 C3
Irvine, *U.K.* 13 F4
Irvine, *Calif., U.S.A.* 111 M9
Irvine, *Ky., U.S.A.* 114 G4
Irvinestown, *U.K.* 12 B4
Irving, *U.S.A.* 113 J6
Irvona, *U.S.A.* 116 F6
Irwin ➤, *Australia* 93 E1
Irymple, *Australia* 95 E3
Is, Jebel, *Sudan* 80 C4
Is-sur-Tille, *France* 19 E12
Isa, *Nigeria* 83 C6
Isa Khel, *Pakistan* 68 C4
Isaac ➤, *Australia* 94 C4
Isabel, *U.S.A.* 112 C4
Isabela, *Phil.* 61 H5
Isabela, *Puerto Rico* .... 121 d
Isabela, I., *Mexico* 118 C3
Isabelia, Cord., *Nic.* 120 D2
Isabella Ra., *Australia* 92 D3
Isaccea, *Romania* 29 E13
Ísafjarðardjúp, *Iceland* 8 C2
Ísafjörður, *Iceland* 8 C2
Isagarh, *India* 68 G7
Isahaya, *Japan* 55 H5
Isaka, *Tanzania* 86 C3
Işalniţa, *Romania* 29 F8
Isalo △, *Madag.* 89 C8
Isan ➤, *India* 69 F9
Isana = Içana ➤, *Brazil* 124 C5
Isangano △, *Zambia* 87 E3
Isanlu Makutu, *Nigeria* 83 D6
Isar ➤, *Germany* 25 G8
Isarco ➤, *Italy* 41 B8
Ísari, *Greece* 46 D3
Iscehisar, *Turkey* 47 C12
Íscar, *Spain* 36 D6
Íschia, *Italy* 42 B6
Isdell ➤, *Australia* 92 C3
Ise, *Japan* 55 G8
Ise-Shima △, *Japan* 55 G8
Ise-Wan, *Japan* 55 G8
Isefjord, *Denmark* 11 J5
Isel ➤, *Austria* 26 E5
Iseo, *Italy* 40 C7
Iseo, L. d', *Italy* 40 C7
Iseramagazi, *Tanzania* 86 C3
Isère □, *France* 21 C9
Isère ➤, *France* 21 D8
Iserlohn, *Germany* 24 D3
Isérnia, *Italy* 43 A7
Iseyin, *Nigeria* 83 D5
Isfahan = Eşfahān, *Iran* 71 C6
Ishëm, *Albania* 44 E3
Ishigaki-Shima, *Japan* 55 M2
Ishikari-Gawa ➤, *Japan* 54 C10
Ishikari-Sammyaku, *Japan* 54 C11
Ishikari-Wan, *Japan* 54 C10
Ishikawa □, *Japan* 55 F8
Ishim, *Russia* 52 D7
Ishim ➤, *Russia* 52 D8
Ishinomaki, *Japan* 54 E10
Ishioka, *Japan* 55 F10
Ishkuman, *Pakistan* 69 A5
Ishpeming, *U.S.A.* 114 B2
Isigny-sur-Mer, *France* 18 C5
Isıklar Dağı, *Turkey* 45 F11
Işıklı, *Turkey* 47 C11
Isil Kul, *Russia* 52 D8
Ísili, *Italy* 42 C2
Isiolo, *Kenya* 86 B4
Isiro, *Dem. Rep. of the Congo* ... 86 B2
Isisford, *Australia* 94 C3
Iskenderun, *Turkey* 70 B3
Iskenderun Körfezi, *Turkey* .. 72 D6
Iskilip, *Turkey* 72 B6
Iskŭr ➤, *Bulgaria* 45 C8
Iskŭr, Yazovir, *Bulgaria* 44 D7
Iskut ➤, *Canada* 102 B2
Isla ➤, *U.K.* 13 E5
Isla Coiba △, *Panama* 120 E3
Isla Cristina, *Spain* 37 H3
Isla de Salamanca △, *Colombia* 121 D5
Isla Gorge △, *Australia* 94 D4
Isla Tiburón y San Esteban △,
  Mexico 118 B2
Isla Vista, *U.S.A.* 111 L7
Islâhiye, *Turkey* 72 D7
Islam Headworks, *Pakistan* 68 E5
Islamabad, *Pakistan* 68 C5
Islamgarh, *Pakistan* 68 F4
Islamkot, *Pakistan* 68 G4
Islampur, *India* 69 G11
Island L., *Canada* 103 C10
Island Lagoon, *Australia* 95 E2
Island Pond, *U.S.A.* 117 B13

Islands, B. of, *Canada* 105 C8
Islands, B. of, *N.Z.* 91 F5
Islay, *U.K.* 13 F2
Isle →, *France* 20 D3
Isle aux Morts, *Canada* 105 C8
Isle of Wight □, *U.K.* 15 G6
Isle Royale △, *U.S.A.* 114 B1
Isleton, *U.S.A.* 110 G5
Ismail = Izmayil, *Ukraine* .. 29 E13
Ismâ'ilîya, *Egypt* 80 H8
Ismaning, *Germany* 25 G7
Isna, *Egypt* 80 B3
Isoanala, *Madag.* 89 C8
Isogstalo, *India* 69 B8
Ísola del Liri, *Italy* 41 G10
Ísola della Scala, *Italy* 40 C7
Ísola di Capo Rizzuto, *Italy* . 43 D10
Isparta, *Turkey* 47 D12
Isperikh, *Bulgaria* 45 C10
Íspica, *Italy* 43 F7
Israel ■, *Asia* 74 D3
Isratu, *Eritrea* 81 D4
Issakly, *Russia* 34 C10
Issia, *Ivory C.* 82 D3
Issoire, *France* 20 C7
Issoudun, *France* 19 F8
Issyk-Kul, Ozero = Ysyk-Köl, *Kyrgyzstan* 52 E8
Ist, *Croatia* 41 D11
Istállós-kő, *Hungary* 28 B5
Istanbul, *Turkey* 45 E12
Istanbul □, *Turkey* 45 E12
Istanbul ✗ (IST), *Turkey* .. 45 F12
Istanbul Boğazı, *Turkey* ... 45 E13
Istiaía, *Greece* 46 C5
Istok, *Serbia & M.* 44 D4
Istokpoga, L., *U.S.A.* 115 M5
Istra, *Croatia* 41 C10
Istres, *France* 21 E8
Istria = Istra, *Croatia* ... 41 C10
Itá, *Paraguay* 126 B4
Itaberaba, *Brazil* 125 F10
Itabira, *Brazil* 125 G10
Itabirito, *Brazil* 127 A7
Itabuna, *Brazil* 125 F11
Itacaúnas →, *Brazil* 125 E9
Itacoatiara, *Brazil* 124 D7
Itaipú, Reprêsa de, *Brazil* . 127 B5
Itaituba, *Brazil* 125 D7
Itajaí, *Brazil* 127 B6
Itajubá, *Brazil* 127 A6
Itaka, *Tanzania* 87 D3
Itala △, *S. Africa* 89 D5
Italy ■, *Europe* 7 G8
Itamaraju, *Brazil* 125 G11
Itampolo, *Madag.* 89 C7
Itandrano, *Madag.* 89 C8
Itapecuru-Mirim, *Brazil* .. 125 D10
Itaperuna, *Brazil* 127 A7
Itapetininga, *Brazil* 127 A6
Itapeva, *Brazil* 127 A6
Itapicuru →, *Bahia, Brazil* . 125 F11
Itapicuru →, *Maranhão, Brazil* . 125 D10
Itapipoca, *Brazil* 125 D11
Itapuá □, *Paraguay* 127 B4
Itaquari, *Brazil* 127 A7
Itaquí, *Brazil* 126 B4
Itararé, *Brazil* 127 A6
Itarsi, *India* 68 H7
Itatí, *Argentina* 126 B4
Itatiaia △, *Brazil* 127 A7
Itbayat, *Phil.* 61 A4
Itchen →, *U.K.* 15 G6
Itéa, *Greece* 46 C4
Itezhi Tezhi, L., *Zambia* .. 87 F2
Ithaca = Itháki, *Greece* ... 46 C2
Ithaca, *U.S.A.* 117 D8
Itháki, *Greece* 46 C2
Iti △, *Greece* 46 C4
Itiquira →, *Brazil* 125 G7
Itō, *Japan* 55 G9
Itoigawa, *Japan* 55 F8
Iton →, *France* 18 C8
Itonamas →, *Bolivia* 124 F6
Itri, *Italy* 42 A6
Itsa, *Egypt* 80 J7
Íttiri, *Italy* 42 B1
Ittoqqortoormiit, *Greenland* . 4 B6
Itu, *Brazil* 127 A6
Itu, *Nigeria* 83 D6
Itu Aba I., *S. China Sea* .. 62 B4
Ituiutaba, *Brazil* 125 G9
Itumbiara, *Brazil* 125 G9
Ituna, *Canada* 103 C8
Itunge Port, *Tanzania* ... 87 D3
Iturbe, *Argentina* 126 A2
Ituri →, *Dem. Rep. of the Congo* . 86 B2
Iturup, Ostrov, *Russia* ... 53 E15
Ituxi →, *Brazil* 124 E6
Ituyuro →, *Argentina* ... 126 A3
Itzehoe, *Germany* 24 B5
Ivaí →, *Brazil* 127 A5
Ivalo, *Finland* 8 B22
Ivalojoki →, *Finland* ... 8 B22
Ivanava, *Belarus* 33 F3
Ivančice, *Czech Rep.* ... 27 B9
Ivane-Puste, *Ukraine* ... 29 B11
Ivăneşti, *Romania* 29 D12
Ivangorod, *Russia* 32 C5
Ivanhoe, *Australia* 95 E3
Ivanhoe, *Calif., U.S.A.* .. 110 J7
Ivanhoe, *Minn., U.S.A.* .. 112 C6
Ivanhorod, *Ukraine* 29 B14
Ivanić Grad, *Croatia* ... 41 C13
Ivanjica, *Serbia & M.* ... 44 C4
Ivanjska, *Bos.-H.* 28 F2
Ivankoyskoye Vdkhr., *Russia* .. 32 D9
Ivano-Frankivsk, *Ukraine* . 29 B9
Ivano-Frankivska □, *Ukraine* . 29 B9
Ivanovo = Ivanava, *Belarus* . 33 F3
Ivanovo, *Russia* 32 D11

Ivanšćica, *Croatia* 41 B13
Ivato, *Madag.* 89 C8
Ivatsevichy, *Belarus* ... 33 F3
Ivaylovgrad, *Bulgaria* ... 45 E10
Ivinheima, *Brazil* 127 A5
Ivinhema, *Brazil* 127 A5
Ivohibe, *Madag.* 89 C8
Ivory Coast, *W. Afr.* ... 82 E4
Ivory Coast ■, *Africa* ... 82 D4
Ivösjön, *Sweden* 11 H8
Ivrea, *Italy* 40 C4
Ivrindi, *Turkey* 47 B9
Ivujivik, *Canada* 101 B12
Ivybridge, *U.K.* 15 G4
Iwaizumi, *Japan* 54 E10
Iwaki, *Japan* 55 F10
Iwakuni, *Japan* 55 G6
Iwamizawa, *Japan* 54 C10
Iwanai, *Japan* 54 C10
Iwata, *Japan* 55 G8
Iwate □, *Japan* 54 E10
Iwate-San, *Japan* 54 E10
Iwo, *Nigeria* 83 D5
Iwonicz-Zdrój, *Poland* .. 31 J8
Ixiamas, *Bolivia* 124 F5
Ixopo, *S. Africa* 89 E5
Ixtepec, *Mexico* 119 D5
Ixtlán del Río, *Mexico* .. 118 C4
Iyal Bakhit, *Sudan* 81 E2
Iyo, *Japan* 55 H6
Izabal, L. de, *Guatemala* . 120 C2
Izamal, *Mexico* 119 C7
Izberbash, *Russia* 35 J8
Izbica, *Poland* 31 H10
Izbica Kujawska, *Poland* . 31 F5
Izbiceni, *Romania* 29 G9
Izena-Shima, *Japan* ... 55 L3
Izgrev, *Bulgaria* 45 C10
Izhevsk, *Russia* 52 D6
Izmayil, *Ukraine* 29 E13
Izmir, *Turkey* 47 C9
Izmir □, *Turkey* 47 C9
Izmir Adnan Menderes ✗ (ADB), *Turkey* 47 C9
Izmir Körfezi, *Turkey* ... 47 C8
Izmit = Kocaeli, *Turkey* .. 45 F13
Iznájar, *Spain* 37 H6
Iznalloz, *Spain* 37 H7
Iznik, *Turkey* 72 B3
Iznik Gölü, *Turkey* 45 F13
Izobil'nyy, *Russia* 35 H5
Izola, *Slovenia* 41 C10
Izra, *Syria* 74 C5
Iztochni Rodopi, *Bulgaria* . 45 E9
Izúcar de Matamoros, *Mexico* .. 119 D5
Izumi-Sano, *Japan* 55 G7
Izumo, *Japan* 55 G6
Izyaslav, *Ukraine* 33 G4
Izyum, *Ukraine* 33 H9

J

Jaba, *Ethiopia* 81 F4
Jabal at Ta'ir, *Red Sea* .. 81 D5
Jabalón →, *Spain* 37 G6
Jabalpur, *India* 69 H8
Jabbūl, *Syria* 70 B3
Jabiru, *Australia* 92 B5
Jablah, *Syria* 70 C3
Jablanac, *Croatia* 41 D11
Jablanica, *Bos.-H.* 28 G2
Jablonec nad Nisou, *Czech Rep.* . 26 A8
Jablonica, *Slovak Rep.* .. 27 C10
Jablonowo Pomorskie, *Poland* . 30 E6
Jablunkov, *Czech Rep.* .. 27 B11
Jaboatão, *Brazil* 125 E11
Jaboticabal, *Brazil* ... 127 A6
Jabukovac, *Serbia & M.* . 44 B6
Jaca, *Spain* 38 C4
Jacareí, *Brazil* 127 A6
Jacarèzinho, *Brazil* ... 127 A6
Jackman, *U.S.A.* 115 C10
Jacksboro, *U.S.A.* 113 J5
Jackson, *Barbados* .... 121 g
Jackson, *Ala., U.S.A.* .. 115 K2
Jackson, *Calif., U.S.A.* .. 110 G6
Jackson, *Ky., U.S.A.* ... 114 G4
Jackson, *Mich., U.S.A.* .. 114 D3
Jackson, *Minn., U.S.A.* .. 112 D7
Jackson, *Miss., U.S.A.* .. 113 J9
Jackson, *Mo., U.S.A.* ... 113 G10
Jackson, *N.H., U.S.A.* .. 117 B13
Jackson, *Ohio, U.S.A.* .. 114 F4
Jackson, *Tenn., U.S.A.* .. 115 H1
Jackson, *Wyo., U.S.A.* .. 108 E8
Jackson B., *N.Z.* 91 K2
Jackson L., *U.S.A.* 108 E8
Jacksons, *N.Z.* 91 K3
Jackson's Arm, *Canada* .. 105 C8
Jacksonville, *Ala., U.S.A.* . 115 J3
Jacksonville, *Ark., U.S.A.* . 113 H8
Jacksonville, *Calif., U.S.A.* . 110 H6
Jacksonville, *Fla., U.S.A.* . 115 K5
Jacksonville, *Ill., U.S.A.* . 112 F9
Jacksonville, *N.C., U.S.A.* . 115 H7
Jacksonville, *Tex., U.S.A.* . 113 K7
Jacksonville Beach, *U.S.A.* . 115 K5
Jacmel, *Haiti* 121 C5
Jacob Lake, *U.S.A.* 109 H7
Jacobabad, *Pakistan* ... 68 E3
Jacobina, *Brazil* 125 F10
Jacques-Cartier ⌒, *Canada* . 105 C7
Jacques-Cartier, Dét. de, *Canada* . 105 C7
Jacques-Cartier, Mt., *Canada* . 105 C6
Jacqueville, *Ivory C.* ... 82 D4
Jacuí →, *Brazil* 127 C5
Jacumba, *U.S.A.* 111 N10

Jacundá →, *Brazil* 125 D8
Jade, *Germany* 24 B4
Jadebusen, *Germany* ... 24 B4
Jadovnik, *Serbia & M.* .. 44 C3
Jadraque, *Spain* 38 E2
Jaén, *Peru* 124 E3
Jaén, *Spain* 37 H7
Jaén □, *Spain* 37 H7
Jafarabad, *India* 68 J4
Jaffa = Tel Aviv-Yafo, *Israel* . 74 C3
Jaffa, C., *Australia* ... 95 F2
Jaffna, *Sri Lanka* 66 Q12
Jaffray, *Canada* 103 D10
Jaffrey, *U.S.A.* 117 D12
Jagadhri, *India* 68 D7
Jagadishpur, *India* 69 G11
Jagdalpur, *India* 67 K13
Jagersfontein, *S. Africa* . 88 D4
Jaghīn →, *Iran* 71 E8
Jagodina, *Serbia & M.* .. 44 B5
Jagraon, *India* 66 D9
Jagst →, *Germany* ... 25 F5
Jagtial, *India* 66 K11
Jaguariaíva, *Brazil* ... 127 A6
Jaguaribe →, *Brazil* ... 125 D11
Jagüey Grande, *Cuba* ... 120 B3
Jahanabad, *India* 69 G11
Jahazpur, *India* 68 G6
Jahrom, *Iran* 71 D7
Jaijon, *India* 68 D7
Jailolo, *Indonesia* 63 D7
Jailolo, Selat, *Indonesia* . 63 D7
Jaipur, *India* 68 F6
Jais, *India* 69 F9
Jaisalmer, *India* 68 F4
Jaisinghnagar, *India* ... 69 H8
Jaitaran, *India* 68 F5
Jaithari, *India* 69 H8
Jajarm, *Iran* 71 B8
Jajce, *Bos.-H.* 28 F2
Jakam →, *India* 68 H6
Jakarta, *Indonesia* ... 63 G12
Jakhal, *India* 68 E6
Jakhau, *India* 68 H3
Jakobstad = Pietarsaari, *Finland* . 8 E20
Jakupica, *Macedonia* ... 44 E5
Jal, *U.S.A.* 113 J3
Jalālābād, *Afghan.* ... 68 B4
Jalalabad, *India* 69 F8
Jalalpur Jattan, *Pakistan* . 68 C6
Jalama, *U.S.A.* 111 L6
Jalapa, *Guatemala* 120 D2
Jalapa Enríquez = Xalapa, *Mexico* . 119 D5
Jalasjärvi, *Finland* ... 9 E20
Jalaun, *India* 69 F8
Jaldhaka →, *Bangla.* ... 69 F13
Jalesar, *India* 68 F8
Jaleswar, *Nepal* 69 F11
Jalgaon, *India* 66 J9
Jalībah, *Iraq* 70 D5
Jalingo, *Nigeria* 83 D7
Jalisco □, *Mexico* 118 D4
Jalkot, *Pakistan* 69 B5
Jallas →, *Spain* 36 C1
Jalna, *India* 66 K9
Jalón →, *Spain* 38 D3
Jalor, *India* 68 G5
Jalpa, *Mexico* 118 C4
Jalpaiguri, *India* 67 F16
Jaluit I., *Marshall Is.* .. 96 G8
Jalūlā, *Iraq* 70 C5
Jamaari, *Nigeria* 83 C6
Jamaica ■, *W. Indies* .. 120 a
Jamalpur, *Bangla.* 67 G16
Jamalpur, *India* 69 G12
Jamalpurganj, *India* ... 69 H13
Jamanxim →, *Brazil* .. 125 D7
Jambewangi, *Indonesia* . 63 J17
Jambi, *Indonesia* 62 E2
Jambi □, *Indonesia* ... 62 E2
Jambusar, *India* 68 H5
James →, *S. Dak., U.S.A.* . 112 D6
James →, *Va., U.S.A.* .. 114 G7
James B., *Canada* 104 B3
James Ranges, *Australia* . 92 D5
James Ross I., *Antarctica* . 5 C18
Jamestown, *Australia* .. 95 E2
Jamestown, *S. Africa* .. 88 E4
Jamestown, *N. Dak., U.S.A.* . 112 B5
Jamestown, *N.Y., U.S.A.* . 116 D5
Jamestown, *Pa., U.S.A.* . 116 E4
Jamīlābād, *Iran* 71 C6
Jamiltepec, *Mexico* ... 119 D5
Jamira →, *India* 69 J13
Jämjö, *Sweden* 11 H9
Jamkhandi, *India* 66 L9
Jammerbugt, *Denmark* .. 11 G3
Jammu, *India* 68 C6
Jammu & Kashmir □, *India* . 69 B7
Jamnagar, *India* 68 H4
Jamni →, *India* 69 G8
Jampur, *Pakistan* 68 E4
Jamrud, *Pakistan* 68 C4
Jämsä, *Finland* 9 F21
Jamshedpur, *India* ... 69 H12
Jamtara, *India* 69 H12
Jämtland, *Sweden* ... 8 E15
Jämtlands län □, *Sweden* . 10 B7
Jan L., *Canada* 103 C8
Jan Mayen, *Arctic* ... 4 B7
Janakkala, *Finland* ... 9 F21
Janaúba, *Brazil* 125 G10
Jand, *Pakistan* 68 C5
Jandaq, *Iran* 71 C7
Jandía, *Canary Is.* 48 F5
Jandía △, *Canary Is.* ... 48 F5
Jandía, Pta. de, *Canary Is.* . 48 F5
Jandola, *Pakistan* 68 C4
Jandowae, *Australia* .. 95 D5
Jándula →, *Spain* 37 G6
Janesville, *U.S.A.* 112 D10

Janga, *Ghana* 83 C4
Jangamo, *Mozam.* 89 C6
Janghai, *India* 69 G10
Janikowo, *Poland* 31 F5
Janin = Ioánnina □, *Greece* . 46 B2
Janja, *Bos.-H.* 28 F4
Janjanbureh, *Gambia* ... 82 C2
Janjevo, *Serbia & M.* ... 44 D5
Janjgir, *India* 69 J10
Janjina, *Croatia* 41 F14
Janjina, *Madag.* 89 C8
Janos, *Mexico* 118 A3
Jánoshalma, *Hungary* .. 28 D4
Jánosháza, *Hungary* ... 28 C2
Jánossomorja, *Hungary* . 28 C2
Janów, *Poland* 31 H6
Janów Lubelski, *Poland* . 31 H9
Janów Podlaski, *Poland* . 31 F10
Janowiec Wielkopolski, *Poland* . 31 F4
Januária, *Brazil* 125 G10
Janub □, *Sudan* 81 F2
Janub Dârfûr □, *Sudan* . 81 E2
Janub Kordofân □, *Sudan* . 81 E3
Janûb Sînî □, *Egypt* ... 74 F2
Janubio, *Canary Is.* ... 48 F6
Janville, *France* 19 D8
Janzé, *France* 18 E5
Jaora, *India* 68 H6
Japan ■, *Asia* 55 G8
Japan, Sea of, *Asia* ... 54 E7
Japan Trench, *Pac. Oc.* .. 96 D6
Japen = Yapen, *Indonesia* . 63 E9
Japla, *India* 69 G11
Japurá →, *Brazil* 124 D5
Jaquarão, *Brazil* 127 C5
Jaqué, *Panama* 120 E4
Jarābulus, *Syria* 70 B3
Jaraicejo, *Spain* 37 F5
Jaraíz de la Vera, *Spain* . 36 E5
Jarama →, *Spain* 36 E7
Jaramānah, *Syria* 72 F7
Jarandilla, *Spain* 36 E5
Jaranwala, *Pakistan* ... 68 D5
Jarash, *Jordan* 74 C4
Jarash □, *Jordan* 74 C4
Järbo, *Sweden* 10 D10
Jardim, *Brazil* 126 A4
Jardín □, *Spain* 39 G2
Jardine River △, *Australia* . 94 A3
Jardines de la Reina, Arch. de los, *Cuba* . 120 B4
Jargalang, *China* 57 C12
Jari →, *Brazil* 125 D8
Jarīr, W. al →, *Si. Arabia* . 70 E4
Jarmen, *Germany* 24 B9
Järna, *Dalarna, Sweden* . 10 D8
Järna, *Stockholm, Sweden* . 10 E11
Jarnac, *France* 20 C3
Jarny, *France* 19 C12
Jarocin, *Poland* 31 G4
Jaromĕř, *Czech Rep.* ... 26 A8
Jarosław, *Poland* 31 H9
Järpås, *Sweden* 11 F6
Järpen, *Sweden* 10 A7
Jarrahdale, *Australia* .. 93 F2
Jarrahi →, *Iran* 71 D6
Jarres, Plaine des, *Laos* . 64 C4
Jarso, *Ethiopia* 81 F4
Jartai, *China* 56 E3
Jarud Qi, *China* 57 B11
Järvenpää, *Finland* ... 9 F21
Jarvis, *Canada* 116 D4
Jarvis I., *Pac. Oc.* 97 H12
Jarvorník, *Czech Rep.* .. 27 A10
Järvsö, *Sweden* 10 C10
Jarwa, *India* 69 F10
Jaša Tomić, *Serbia & M.* . 28 E5
Jasdan, *India* 68 H4
Jashpurnagar, *India* ... 69 H11
Jasidih, *India* 69 G12
Jasień, *Poland* 31 G2
Jāsimīyah, *Iraq* 70 C5
Jasin, *Malaysia* 65 L4
Jāsk, *Iran* 71 E8
Jasło, *Poland* 31 J8
Jasmund, *Germany* ... 24 A9
Jasmund △, *Germany* .. 24 A9
Jaso, *India* 69 G9
Jasper, *Alta., Canada* .. 102 C5
Jasper, *Ont., Canada* .. 117 B9
Jasper, *Ala., U.S.A.* ... 115 J2
Jasper, *Fla., U.S.A.* ... 115 K4
Jasper, *Ind., U.S.A.* ... 114 F2
Jasper, *Tex., U.S.A.* ... 113 K8
Jasper △, *Canada* 102 C5
Jasrasar, *India* 68 F5
Jastarnia, *Poland* 30 D5
Jastrebarsko, *Croatia* .. 41 C12
Jastrowie, *Poland* 30 E3
Jastrzębie Zdrój, *Poland* . 31 J5
Jász-Nagykun-Szolnok □, *Hungary* . 28 C5
Jászapáti, *Hungary* ... 28 C5
Jászárokszállás, *Hungary* . 28 C4
Jászberény, *Hungary* .. 28 C4
Jászkisér, *Hungary* ... 28 C5
Jászladány, *Hungary* .. 28 C5
Jataí, *Brazil* 125 G8
Jati, *Pakistan* 68 G3
Jatibarang, *Indonesia* .. 63 G13
Jatiluwih, *Indonesia* ... 63 J18
Jatinegara, *Indonesia* .. 63 G12
Játiva = Xàtiva, *Spain* .. 39 G4
Jättendal, *Sweden* ... 10 C11
Jaú, *Brazil* 127 A6
Jauja, *Peru* 124 F3
Jaunpur, *India* 69 G10
Java = Jawa, *Indonesia* .. 62 F3
Java Sea, *Indonesia* ... 62 F3
Java Trench, *Ind. Oc.* ... 62 F3
Javalambre, Sa. de, *Spain* . 38 E4

Jávea, *Spain* 39 G5
Jawa, *Indonesia* 62 F3
Jawa Barat □, *Indonesia* . 63 G12
Jawa Tengah □, *Indonesia* . 63 G14
Jawa Timur □, *Indonesia* . 63 G15
Jawad, *India* 68 G6
Jawor, *Poland* 31 G3
Jaworzno, *Poland* 31 H6
Jaworzyna Śląska, *Poland* . 31 H3
Jay Peak, *U.S.A.* 117 B12
Jaya, Puncak, *Indonesia* . 63 E9
Jayanti, *India* 67 F16
Jayapura, *Indonesia* ... 63 E10
Jayawijaya, Pegunungan, *Indonesia* . 63 E9
Jaynagar, *India* 67 F15
Jayrūd, *Syria* 70 C3
Jayton, *U.S.A.* 113 J4
Jāz Mūrīān, Hāmūn-e, *Iran* . 71 E8
Jazīreh-ye Shīf, *Iran* ... 71 D6
Jazminal, *Mexico* 118 C4
Jazzīn, *Lebanon* 74 B4
Jean, *U.S.A.* 111 K11
Jean Marie River, *Canada* . 102 A4
Jean-Rabel, *Haiti* 121 C5
Jeanerette, *U.S.A.* ... 113 L9
Jeannette, Ostrov = Zhannetty, Ostrov, *Russia* . 53 B16
Jeannette, *U.S.A.* 116 F5
Jebāl Bārez, Kūh-e, *Iran* . 71 D8
Jebba, *Nigeria* 83 D5
Jebel, Bahr el →, *Sudan* . 81 F3
Jebel Dud, *Sudan* 81 E3
Jebel Qerri, *Sudan* ... 81 D3
Jedburgh, *U.K.* 13 F6
Jedda = Jiddah, *Si. Arabia* . 75 C2
Jeddore L., *Canada* ... 105 C8
Jedlicze, *Poland* 31 J8
Jędrzejów, *Poland* ... 31 H7
Jedwabne, *Poland* 31 E9
Jeetzel →, *Germany* .. 24 B7
Jefferson, *Iowa, U.S.A.* . 112 D7
Jefferson, *Ohio, U.S.A.* . 116 E4
Jefferson, *Tex., U.S.A.* . 113 J7
Jefferson, Mt., *Nev., U.S.A.* . 108 G5
Jefferson, Mt., *Oreg., U.S.A.* . 108 D3
Jefferson City, *Mo., U.S.A.* . 112 F8
Jefferson City, *Tenn., U.S.A.* . 115 G4
Jeffersontown, *U.S.A.* .. 114 F3
Jeffersonville, *U.S.A.* .. 114 F3
Jeffrey City, *U.S.A.* ... 108 E10
Jega, *Nigeria* 83 C5
Jeju = Cheju do, *S. Korea* . 57 H14
Jēkabpils, *Latvia* 9 H21
Jekyll I., *U.S.A.* 115 K5
Jelcz-Laskowice, *Poland* . 31 G4
Jelenia Góra, *Poland* .. 31 H2
Jelgava, *Latvia* 9 H20
Jelgava □, *Latvia* 30 B10
Jelica, *Serbia & M.* ... 44 C4
Jelli, *Sudan* 81 F3
Jelšava, *Slovak Rep.* ... 27 C13
Jemaja, *Indonesia* 65 L5
Jemaluang, *Malaysia* .. 65 L4
Jember, *Indonesia* 63 H15
Jembongan, *Malaysia* .. 62 C5
Jena, *Germany* 24 E7
Jena, *U.S.A.* 113 K8
Jenbach, *Austria* 26 D4
Jenīn, *West Bank* 74 C4
Jenkins, *U.S.A.* 114 G4
Jenner, *U.S.A.* 110 G3
Jennings, *U.S.A.* 113 K8
Jepara, *Indonesia* 63 G14
Jeparit, *Australia* 95 F3
Jequié, *Brazil* 125 F10
Jequitinhonha, *Brazil* .. 125 G10
Jequitinhonha →, *Brazil* . 125 G11
Jerantut, *Malaysia* ... 65 L4
Jerejak, Pulau, *Malaysia* . 65 c
Jérémie, *Haiti* 121 C5
Jerez, Punta, *Mexico* .. 119 C5
Jerez de García Salinas, *Mexico* . 118 C4
Jerez de la Frontera, *Spain* . 37 J4
Jerez de los Caballeros, *Spain* . 37 G4
Jericho = El Arīḥā, *West Bank* . 74 D4
Jericho, *Australia* 94 C4
Jerichow, *Germany* ... 24 C8
Jerid, Chott el = Djerid, Chott, *Tunisia* . 78 B7
Jerilderie, *Australia* ... 95 F4
Jermyn, *U.S.A.* 117 E9
Jerome, *U.S.A.* 108 E6
Jerramungup, *Australia* . 93 F2
Jersey, *U.K.* 15 H5
Jersey City, *U.S.A.* ... 117 F10
Jersey Shore, *U.S.A.* .. 116 E7
Jerseyville, *U.S.A.* ... 112 F9
Jerusalem, *Israel* 74 D4
Jervis B., *Australia* ... 95 F5
Jervis Inlet, *Canada* .. 102 C4
Jerzu, *Italy* 42 C2
Jesenice, *Slovenia* ... 41 B11
Jeseník, *Czech Rep.* ... 27 A10
Jesenké, *Slovak Rep.* .. 27 C13
Jesi = Iesi, *Italy* 41 E10
Jessnitz, *Germany* ... 24 D8
Jessore, *Bangla.* 67 H16
Jesup, *U.S.A.* 115 K5
Jesús Carranza, *Mexico* . 119 D5
Jesús María, *Argentina* . 126 C3
Jetmore, *U.S.A.* 113 F5
Jetpur, *India* 68 J4
Jeumont, *France* 19 B11
Jevnaker, *Norway* ... 9 F14
Jewett, *U.S.A.* 116 F3
Jewett City, *U.S.A.* ... 117 E13
Jeyḩūnābād, *Iran* 71 C6
Jeypore, *India* 67 K13

Jha Jha, *India* 69 G12
Jhaarkand = Jharkhand □, *India* 69 H11
Jhabua, *India* 68 H6
Jhajjar, *India* 68 E7
Jhal, *Pakistan* 68 E2
Jhal Jhao, *Pakistan* 66 F4
Jhalawar, *India* 68 G7
Jhalida, *India* 69 H11
Jhalrapatan, *India* 68 G7
Jhang Maghiana, *Pakistan* 68 D5
Jhansi, *India* 69 G8
Jhargram, *India* 69 H12
Jharia, *India* 69 H12
Jharkhand □, *India* 69 H11
Jharsuguda, *India* 67 J14
Jhelum, *Pakistan* 68 C5
Jhelum ➤, *Pakistan* 68 D5
Jhilmilli, *India* 69 H10
Jhudo, *Pakistan* 68 G3
Jhunjhunu, *India* 68 E6
Ji-Paraná, *Brazil* 124 F6
Ji Xian, *Hebei, China* 56 F8
Ji Xian, *Henan, China* 56 G8
Ji Xian, *Shanxi, China* 56 F6
Jia Xian, *Henan, China* 56 H7
Jia Xian, *Shaanxi, China* ... 56 E6
Jiading, *China* 59 B13
Jiahe, *China* 59 E9
Jialing Jiang ➤, *China* 58 C6
Jiamusi, *China* 60 B8
Ji'an, *Jiangxi, China* 59 D10
Ji'an, *Jilin, China* 57 D14
Jianchang, *China* 57 D11
Jianchangying, *China* 57 D10
Jianchuan, *China* 58 D2
Jiande, *China* 59 C12
Jiang'an, *China* 58 C5
Jiangbei, *China* 58 C6
Jiangcheng, *China* 58 F3
Jiangchuan, *China* 58 E4
Jiangdi, *China* 58 D4
Jiangdu, *China* 59 A12
Jiange, *China* 58 A5
Jianghua, *China* 59 E8
Jiangjin, *China* 58 C6
Jiangkou, *China* 58 D7
Jiangle, *China* 59 D11
Jiangling, *China* 59 B9
Jiangmen, *China* 59 F9
Jiangning, *China* 59 B12
Jiangshan, *China* 59 C12
Jiangsu □, *China* 57 H11
Jiangxi □, *China* 59 D11
Jiangyan, *China* 59 A13
Jiangyin, *China* 59 B13
Jiangyong, *China* 59 E8
Jiangyou, *China* 58 B5
Jianhe, *China* 58 D7
Jianli, *China* 59 C9
Jianning, *China* 59 D11
Jian'ou, *China* 59 D12
Jianshi, *China* 58 B7
Jianshui, *China* 58 F4
Jianyang, *Fujian, China* 59 D12
Jianyang, *Sichuan, China* ... 58 B5
Jiao Xian = Jiaozhou, *China* . 57 F11
Jiaohe, *China* 56 E9
Jiaohe, *Jilin, China* 57 C14
Jiaojiang, *China* 59 C13
Jiaoling, *China* 59 E11
Jiaozhou, *China* 57 F11
Jiaozhou Wan, *China* 57 F11
Jiaozuo, *China* 56 G7
Jiashan, *China* 59 B13
Jiawang, *China* 57 G9
Jiaxiang, *China* 56 G9
Jiaxing, *China* 59 B13
Jiayi = Chiai, *Taiwan* 59 F13
Jiayu, *China* 59 C9
Jibiya, *Nigeria* 83 C6
Jibou, *Romania* 29 C8
Jibuti = Djibouti ■, *Africa* 81 E5
Jicarón, I., *Panama* 120 E3
Jičín, *Czech Rep.* 26 A8
Jiddah, *Si. Arabia* 75 C2
Jido, *India* 67 E19
Jieshou, *China* 56 H8
Jiexiu, *China* 56 F6
Jieyang, *China* 59 F11
Jigawa □, *Nigeria* 83 C6
Jiggalong, *Australia* 92 D3
Jigni, *India* 69 G8
Jihlava, *Czech Rep.* 26 B8
Jihlava ➤, *Czech Rep.* 27 C9
Jihlavský □, *Czech Rep.* 26 B8
Jihočeský □, *Czech Rep.* 26 B7
Jihomoravský □, *Czech Rep.* . 27 B9
Jijiga, *Ethiopia* 75 F3
Jikamshi, *Nigeria* 83 C6
Jikau, *Sudan* 81 F3
Jilin, *China* 57 C14
Jilin □, *China* 57 C14
Jiloca ➤, *Spain* 38 D3
Jilong = Chilung, *Taiwan* ... 59 E13
Jim Thorpe, *U.S.A.* 117 F9
Jima, *Ethiopia* 81 F4
Jimbaran, Teluk, *Indonesia* . 63 K18
Jimbolia, *Romania* 28 E5
Jimena de la Frontera, *Spain* 37 J5
Jiménez, *Mexico* 118 B4
Jimo, *China* 57 F11
Jin Jiang ➤, *China* 59 C10
Jin Xian = Jinzhou, *China* .. 56 E8
Jin Xian, *China* 57 E11
Jinan, *China* 56 F9
Jinchang, *China* 60 C5
Jincheng, *China* 56 G7
Jinchuan, *China* 58 B4
Jind, *India* 68 E7
Jindabyne, *Australia* 95 F4
Jindřichův Hradec, *Czech Rep.* 26 B8
Jing He ➤, *China* 56 G5

Jing Shan, *China* 59 B8
Jing Xian, *China* 59 B12
Jing'an, *China* 59 C10
Jingbian, *China* 56 F5
Jingchuan, *China* 56 G4
Jingde, *China* 59 B12
Jingdezhen, *China* 59 C11
Jingdong, *China* 58 E3
Jinggangshan, *China* 59 D10
Jinggu, *China* 58 F3
Jinghai, *China* 56 E9
Jinghong, *China* 58 G3
Jingjiang, *China* 59 A13
Jingle, *China* 56 E6
Jingmen, *China* 59 B9
Jingning, *China* 56 G3
Jingpo Hu, *China* 57 C15
Jingshan, *China* 59 B9
Jingtai, *China* 56 F3
Jingxi, *China* 58 F6
Jingxing, *China* 56 E8
Jingyang, *China* 56 G5
Jingyu, *China* 57 C14
Jingyuan, *China* 56 F3
Jingzhou, *China* 58 D7
Jingziguan, *China* 56 H6
Jinhua, *China* 59 C12
Jining, *Nei Monggol Zizhiqu, China* 56 D7
Jining, *Shandong, China* 56 G9
Jinja, *Uganda* 86 B3
Jinjang, *Malaysia* 65 L3
Jinji, *China* 56 F4
Jinjiang, *Fujian, China* 59 E12
Jinjiang, *Yunnan, China* 58 D3
Jinjini, *Ghana* 82 D4
Jinkou, *China* 59 B10
Jinkouhe, *China* 58 C4
Jinmen Dao, *China* 59 E12
Jinnah Barrage, *Pakistan* ... 66 C7
Jinning, *China* 58 E4
Jinotega, *Nic.* 120 D2
Jinotepe, *Nic.* 120 D2
Jinping, *Guizhou, China* 58 D7
Jinping, *Yunnan, China* 58 F4
Jinsha, *China* 58 D6
Jinsha Jiang ➤, *China* 58 C5
Jinshan, *China* 59 B13
Jinshi, *China* 59 C8
Jintan, *China* 59 B12
Jinxi, *Jiangxi, China* 59 D11
Jinxi, *Liaoning, China* 57 D11
Jinxian, *China* 59 C11
Jinxiang, *China* 56 G9
Jinyang, *China* 58 D4
Jinyun, *China* 59 C13
Jinzhai, *China* 59 B10
Jinzhou, *Hebei, China* 56 E8
Jinzhou, *Liaoning, China* ... 57 D11
Jiparaná ➤, *Brazil* 124 E6
Jipijapa, *Ecuador* 124 D2
Jiquilpan, *Mexico* 118 D4
Jishan, *China* 56 G6
Jishou, *China* 58 C7
Jishui, *China* 59 D10
Jisr ash Shughūr, *Syria* 70 C3
Jitarning, *Australia* 93 F2
Jitra, *Malaysia* 65 J3
Jiu ➤, *Romania* 29 G8
Jiudengkou, *China* 56 E4
Jiujiang, *Guangdong, China* . 59 F9
Jiujiang, *Jiangxi, China* ... 59 C10
Jiuling Shan, *China* 59 C10
Jiulong = Kowloon, *China* ... 59 F10
Jiulong ➤, *China* 58 C3
Jiutai, *China* 57 B13
Jiuxincheng, *China* 56 E8
Jiuyuhang, *China* 59 B12
Jixi, *Anhui, China* 59 B12
Jixi, *Heilongjiang, China* .. 57 B16
Jiyang, *China* 57 F9
Jiyuan, *China* 56 G7
Jīzān, *Si. Arabia* 75 D3
Jize, *China* 56 F8
Jizera ➤, *Czech Rep.* 26 A7
Jizl, Wādī al ➤, *Si. Arabia* . 70 E3
Jizō-Zaki, *Japan* 55 G6
Jizzakh, *Uzbekistan* 52 E7
Joaçaba, *Brazil* 127 B5
Joal Fadiout, *Senegal* 82 C1
João Pessoa, *Brazil* 125 E12
Joaquín V. González, *Argentina* 126 B3
Jobat, *India* 68 H6
Jobourg, Nez de, *France* 18 C5
Jódar, *Spain* 37 H7
Jodhpur, *India* 68 F5
Jodiya, *India* 68 H4
Jōetsu, *Japan* 55 F9
Jœuf, *France* 19 C12
Jofane, *Mozam.* 89 C5
Jogbani, *India* 69 F12
Jõgeva, *Estonia* 9 G22
Jogjakarta = Yogyakarta, *Indonesia* 63 G14
Johannesburg, *S. Africa* 89 D4
Johannesburg, *U.S.A.* 111 K9
Johansfors, *Sweden* 11 H9
Johilla ➤, *India* 69 H9
John Crow Mts., *Jamaica* ... 120 a
John Day, *U.S.A.* 108 D4
John Day ➤, *U.S.A.* 108 D3
John Day Fossil Beds △, *U.S.A.* 108 D4
John D'Or Prairie, *Canada* . 102 B5
John F. Kennedy International, New York ✈ (JFK), *U.S.A.* 117 F11
John H. Kerr Reservoir, *U.S.A.* 115 G6
John o' Groats, *U.K.* 13 C5
Johnnie, *U.S.A.* 111 J10
Johnson, *Kans., U.S.A.* 113 G4
Johnson, *Vt., U.S.A.* 117 B12
Johnson City, *N.Y., U.S.A.* . 117 D9

Johnson City, *Tenn., U.S.A.* 115 G4
Johnson City, *Tex., U.S.A.* 113 K5
Johnsonburg, *U.S.A.* 116 E6
Johnsondale, *U.S.A.* 111 K8
Johnsons Crossing, *Canada* . 102 A2
Johnston, L., *Australia* 93 F3
Johnston Falls = Mambilima Falls, *Zambia* 87 E2
Johnston I., *Pac. Oc.* 97 F11
Johnstone Str., *Canada* 102 C3
Johnstown, *N.Y., U.S.A.* ... 117 C10
Johnstown, *Ohio, U.S.A.* ... 116 F2
Johnstown, *Pa., U.S.A.* 116 F6
Johor, Selat, *Asia* .... 65 d
Johor Bahru, *Malaysia* ...... 65 d
Jõhvi, *Estonia* 9 G22
Joigny, *France* 19 E10
Joinville, *Brazil* 127 B6
Joinville, *France* 19 D12
Joinville I., *Antarctica* ... 5 C18
Jojutla, *Mexico* 119 D5
Jokkmokk, *Sweden* 8 C18
Jökulsá á Bru ➤, *Iceland* .. 8 D6
Jökulsá á Fjöllum ➤, *Iceland* 8 C5
Jolfā, *Āzarbājān-e Sharqī, Iran* 70 B5
Jolfā, *Esfahan, Iran* 71 C6
Joliet, *U.S.A.* 114 E1
Joliette, *Canada* 104 C5
Jolo, *Phil.* 61 J4
Jolon, *U.S.A.* 110 K5
Jomalig I., *Phil.* 61 D5
Jombang, *Indonesia* 63 G15
Jomda, *China* 58 B2
Jonava, *Lithuania* 9 J21
Jones Sound, *Canada* 4 B3
Jonesboro, *Ark., U.S.A.* ... 113 H9
Jonesboro, *La., U.S.A.* 113 J8
Jong ➤, *S. Leone* 82 D2
Jonglei, *Sudan* 81 F3
Jonglei □, *Sudan* 81 F3
Joniškis, *Lithuania* 9 H20
Jönköping, *Sweden* 11 G8
Jönköpings län □, *Sweden* ... 11 G8
Jonquière, *Canada* 105 C5
Jonsered, *Sweden* 11 G6
Jonzac, *France* 20 C3
Joplin, *U.S.A.* 113 G7
Jora, *India* 68 F6
Jordan, *Mont., U.S.A.* 108 C10
Jordan, *N.Y., U.S.A.* 117 C8
Jordan ■, *Asia* 74 E5
Jordan ➤, *Asia* 74 D4
Jordan Valley, *U.S.A.* 108 E5
Jordanów, *Poland* 31 J6
Jorhat, *India* 67 F19
Jörn, *Sweden* 8 D19
Jorong, *Indonesia* 62 E4
Jørpeland, *Norway* 9 G11
Jorquera ➤, *Chile* 126 B2
Jos, *Nigeria* 83 D6
Jos Plateau, *Nigeria* 83 D6
Jošanička Banja, *Serbia & M.* 44 C4
José Batlle y Ordóñez, *Uruguay* 127 C4
Joseni, *Romania* 29 D10
Joseph, *Nfld. & L., Canada* 105 B6
Joseph, L., *Ont., Canada* .. 116 A5
Joseph Bonaparte G., *Australia* 92 B4
Joshinath, *India* 69 D8
Joshinetsu-Kōgen △, *Japan* . 55 F9
Joshua Tree, *U.S.A.* 111 L10
Joshua Tree △, *U.S.A.* 111 M10
Josselin, *France* 18 E4
Jost Van Dyke, *Br. Virgin Is.* 121 e
Jostedalsbreen, *Norway* 9 F12
Jotunheimen, *Norway* 9 F13
Joubertberg, *Namibia* 88 B1
Joué-lès-Tours, *France* 18 E7
Jourdanton, *U.S.A.* 113 L5
Joutseno, *Finland* 32 B5
Jovellanos, *Cuba* 120 B3
Joyeuse, *France* 21 D8
Józefów, *Lubelskie, Poland* . 31 H10
Józefów, *Mazowieckie, Poland* 31 F8
Ju Xian, *China* 57 F10
Juan Aldama, *Mexico* 118 C4
Juan Bautista Alberdi, *Argentina* 126 C3
Juan de Fuca Str., *Canada* . 110 B3
Juan de Nova, *Ind. Oc.* 89 B7
Juan Fernández, Arch. de, *Pac. Oc.* 97 L20
Juan José Castelli, *Argentina* 126 B3
Juan L. Lacaze, *Uruguay* ... 126 C4
Juárez, *Argentina* 126 D4
Juárez, *Mexico* 111 N11
Juárez, Sierra de, *Mexico* . 118 A1
Juàzeiro, *Brazil* 125 E10
Juàzeiro do Norte, *Brazil* . 125 E11
Juba = Giuba ➤, *Somali Rep.* 75 G3
Juba, *Sudan* 81 G3
Jubany, *Antarctica* 5 C18
Jubayl, *Lebanon* 74 A4
Jubbah, *Si. Arabia* 70 D4
Jubbal, *India* 68 D7
Jubbulpore = Jabalpur, *India* 69 H8
Jūbek, *Germany* 24 A5
Jubga, *Russia* 35 H4
Jubilee L., *Australia* 93 E4
Juby, C., *Morocco* 78 C3
Júcar = Xúquer ➤, *Spain* ... 39 F4
Júcaro, *Cuba* 120 B4
Juchitán, *Mexico* 119 D5
Judaea = Har Yehuda, *Israel* 74 D3
Judenburg, *Austria* 26 D7
Judith ➤, *U.S.A.* 108 C9
Judith, Pt., *U.S.A.* 117 E13
Judith Gap, *U.S.A.* 108 C9
Juelsminde, *Denmark* 11 J4
Jugoslavia = Serbia & Montenegro ■, *Europe* 44 C4
Juigalpa, *Nic.* 120 D2
Juillac, *France* 20 C5

Juist, *Germany* 24 B2
Juiz de Fora, *Brazil* 127 A7
Jujuy □, *Argentina* 126 A2
Julesburg, *U.S.A.* 112 E3
Juli, *Peru* 124 G5
Julia Cr. ➤, *Australia* 94 C3
Julia Creek, *Australia* 94 C3
Juliaca, *Peru* 124 G4
Julian, *U.S.A.* 111 M10
Julian, L., *Canada* 104 B4
Julian Alps = Julijske Alpe, *Slovenia* 41 B11
Julianatop, *Suriname* 125 C7
Julianehåb = Qaqortoq, *Greenland* 101 B6
Jülich, *Germany* 24 E2
Julijske Alpe, *Slovenia* ... 41 B11
Julimes, *Mexico* 118 B3
Jullundur, *India* 68 D6
Julu, *China* 56 F8
Jumbo, *Zimbabwe* 87 F3
Jumbo Pk., *U.S.A.* 111 J12
Jumentos Cays, *Bahamas* ... 120 B4
Jumilla, *Spain* 39 G3
Jumla, *Nepal* 69 E10
Jumna = Yamuna ➤, *India* .. 69 G9
Junagadh, *India* 68 J4
Junction, *Tex., U.S.A.* 113 K5
Junction, *Utah, U.S.A.* 109 G7
Junction B., *Australia* 94 A1
Junction City, *Kans., U.S.A.* 112 F6
Junction City, *Oreg., U.S.A.* 108 D2
Junction Pt., *Australia* ... 94 A1
Jundah, *Australia* 94 C3
Jundiaí, *Brazil* 127 A6
Juneau, *U.S.A.* 102 B2
Junee, *Australia* 95 E4
Jungfrau, *Switz.* 25 J3
Junggar Pendi, *China* 60 B3
Jungshahi, *Pakistan* 68 G2
Jūniyah, *Lebanon* 74 B4
Junian, *China* 58 C5
Junín, *Argentina* 126 C3
Junín de los Andes, *Argentina* 128 D2
Juniata ➤, *U.S.A.* 116 F7
Junín, *Argentina* 126 C3
Juntas, *Chile* 126 B2
Juntura, *U.S.A.* 108 E4
Jur, Nahr el ➤, *Sudan* 81 F2
Jura = Jura, Mts. du, *Europe* 19 F13
Jura = Schwäbische Alb, *Germany* 25 G5
Jura, *U.K.* 13 F3
Jura □, *France* 19 F12
Jura □, *Switz.* 25 H3
Jūra ➤, *Lithuania* 30 C9
Jura, Mts. du, *Europe* 19 F13
Jura, Sd. of, *U.K.* 13 F3
Jurbarkas, *Lithuania* 9 J20
Jurien, *Australia* 93 F2
Jurilovca, *Romania* 29 F13
Jūrmala, *Latvia* 9 H20
Jurong, *China* 59 B12
Jurong, *Singapore* .... 65 d
Juruá ➤, *Brazil* 124 D5
Juruena, *Brazil* 124 F7
Juruena ➤, *Brazil* 124 E7
Juruti, *Brazil* 125 D7
Jussey, *France* 19 E12
Justo Daract, *Argentina* ... 126 C2
Jutaí ➤, *Brazil* 124 D5
Jüterbog, *Germany* 24 D9
Juticalpa, *Honduras* 120 D2
Jutland = Jylland, *Denmark* 11 H3
Juventud, I. de la, *Cuba* .. 120 B3
Juvigny-sous-Andaine, *France* 18 D6
Jūy Zar, *Iran* 70 C5
Juye, *China* 56 G9
Juzennecourt, *France* 19 D11
Jvari, *Georgia* 35 J6
Jwaneng, *Botswana* 88 C3
Jyderup, *Denmark* 11 J5
Jylland, *Denmark* 11 H3
Jyväskylä, *Finland* 9 E21

K

K2, *Pakistan* 69 B7
Ka ➤, *Nigeria* 83 C5
Kaap Plateau, *S. Africa* ... 88 D3
Kaapkruis, *Namibia* 88 C1
Kaapstad = Cape Town, *S. Africa* 88 E2
Kaba, *Guinea* 82 C2
Kabaena, *Indonesia* 63 F6
Kabala, *S. Leone* 82 D2
Kabale, *Uganda* 86 C3
Kabalo, *Dem. Rep. of the Congo* 86 D2
Kabambare, *Dem. Rep. of the Congo* 86 C2
Kabango, *Dem. Rep. of the Congo* 87 D2
Kabanjahe, *Indonesia* 62 D1
Kabankalan, *Phil.* 61 G5
Kabara, *Mali* 82 B4
Kabardinka, *Russia* 33 K10
Kabardino-Balkar Republic = Kabardino-Balkaria □, *Russia* 35 J6
Kabardino-Balkaria □, *Russia* 35 J6
Kabarega Falls = Murchison Falls, *Uganda* 86 B3
Kabasalan, *Phil.* 61 H5
Kabat, *Indonesia* 63 J17
Kabba, *Nigeria* 83 D6
Kabetogama, *U.S.A.* 112 A8
Kabi, *Nigeria* 83 C7
Kabin Buri, *Thailand* 64 F3
Kabinakagami L., *Canada* ... 104 C3
Kabinda, *Dem. Rep. of the Congo* 84 F4
Kabna, *Sudan* 80 D3
Kabompo, *Zambia* 87 E1
Kabompo ➤, *Zambia* 85 G4

Kabondo, *Dem. Rep. of the Congo* 87 D2
Kabongo, *Dem. Rep. of the Congo* 86 D2
Kabou, *Togo* 83 D5
Kabr, *Sudan* 81 E2
Kabrousse, *Senegal* 82 C1
Kabūd Gonbad, *Iran* 71 B8
Kabugao, *Phil.* 61 B4
Kābul, *Afghan.* 68 B3
Kābul □, *Afghan.* 66 B6
Kābul ➤, *Pakistan* 68 C5
Kabunga, *Dem. Rep. of the Congo* 86 C2
Kaburuang, *Indonesia* 63 D7
Kabushiya, *Sudan* 81 D3
Kabwe, *Zambia* 87 E2
Kačanik, *Serbia & M.* 44 D5
Kačergine, *Lithuania* 30 D10
Kachchh, Gulf of, *India* ... 68 H3
Kachchh, Rann of, *India* ... 68 H4
Kachchhidhana, *India* 69 J8
Kachebera, *Zambia* 87 E3
Kachia, *Nigeria* 83 D6
Kachikau, *Botswana* 88 B3
Kachin □, *Burma* 58 D1
Kachira, L., *Uganda* 86 C3
Kachiry, *Kazakhstan* 52 D8
Kachisi, *Ethiopia* 81 F4
Kachnara, *India* 68 H6
Kachot, *Cambodia* 65 G4
Kaçkar, *Turkey* 73 B9
Kadan, *Czech Rep.* 26 A6
Kadan Kyun, *Burma* 64 F2
Kadanai ➤, *Afghan.* 68 D1
Kadarkút, *Hungary* 28 D2
Kadavu, *Fiji* 91 D8
Kade, *Ghana* 83 D4
Kadhimain = Al Kāzimīyah, *Iraq* 70 C5
Kadi, *India* 68 H5
Kadina, *Australia* 95 E2
Kadınhanı, *Turkey* 72 C5
Kadiolo, *Mali* 82 C3
Kadipur, *India* 69 F10
Kadirli, *Turkey* 70 B3
Kadiyevka = Stakhanov, *Ukraine* 33 H10
Kadododo, *Sudan* 81 E2
Kadoka, *U.S.A.* 112 D4
Kadom, *Russia* 34 C5
Kadoma, *Zimbabwe* 87 F2
Kādugli, *Sudan* 81 E2
Kaduna, *Nigeria* 83 C6
Kaduna □, *Nigeria* 83 C6
Kaduy, *Russia* 32 C9
Kaédi, *Mauritania* 82 B2
Kaélé, *Cameroon* 83 C7
Kaeng Khoï, *Thailand* 64 E3
Kaeng Kra Chan △, *Thailand* 64 F2
Kaeng Tana △, *Thailand* 64 E5
Kaesŏng, *N. Korea* 57 F14
Kāf, *Si. Arabia* 70 D3
Kafan = Kapan, *Armenia* 70 B5
Kafanchan, *Nigeria* 83 D6
Kafareti, *Nigeria* 83 C7
Kaffrine, *Senegal* 82 C1
Kafin, *Nigeria* 83 D6
Kafin Madaki, *Nigeria* 83 C6
Kafinda, *Zambia* 87 E3
Kafirévs, Ákra, *Greece* 46 C6
Kafr el Battikh, *Egypt* 80 H7
Kafr el Dauwâr, *Egypt* 80 H7
Kafr el Sheikh, *Egypt* 80 H7
Kafue, *Zambia* 87 F2
Kafue ➤, *Zambia* 85 H5
Kafue Flats, *Zambia* 87 F2
Kafulwe, *Zambia* 87 D2
Kaga, *Afghan.* 68 B4
Kaga Bandoro, *C.A.R.* 84 C3
Kagan, *Uzbekistan* 52 F7
Kagarko, *Nigeria* 83 D6
Kagawa □, *Japan* 55 G7
Kagera □, *Tanzania* 86 C3
Kagera ➤, *Uganda* 86 C3
Kağızman, *Turkey* 70 B4
Kagmar, *Sudan* 81 E3
Kagoshima, *Japan* 55 J5
Kagoshima □, *Japan* 55 J5
Kagul = Cahul, *Moldova* 29 E13
Kahak, *Iran* 71 B6
Kahama, *Tanzania* 86 C3
Kahan, *Pakistan* 68 E3
Kahang, *Malaysia* 65 L4
Kahayan ➤, *Indonesia* 62 E4
Kahe, *Tanzania* 86 C4
Kahnūj, *Iran* 71 E8
Kahoka, *U.S.A.* 112 E9
Kahoolawe, *U.S.A.* 106 H16
Kahramanmaraş, *Turkey* 70 B3
Kâhta, *Turkey* 73 D8
Kahul, Ozero, *Ukraine* 29 E13
Kahurangi △, *N.Z.* 91 J4
Kahuta, *Pakistan* 68 C5
Kahuzi-Biega △, *Dem. Rep. of the Congo* 86 C2
Kai, Kepulauan, *Indonesia* . 63 F8
Kai Besar, *Indonesia* 63 F8
Kai Is. = Kai, Kepulauan, *Indonesia* 63 F8
Kai Kecil, *Indonesia* 63 F8
Kai Xian, *China* 58 B7
Kaiama, *Nigeria* 83 D5
Kaiapoi, *N.Z.* 91 K4
Kaieteur Falls, *Guyana* ... 124 B7
Kaifeng, *China* 56 G8
Kaihua, *China* 59 C12
Kaijiang, *China* 58 B6
Kaikohe, *N.Z.* 91 F4
Kaikoura, *N.Z.* 91 K4
Kailahun, *S. Leone* 82 D2
Kailash = Kangrinboqê Feng, *China* 69 D9
Kaili, *China* 58 D6
Kailu, *China* 57 C11

Kailua Kona, *U.S.A.* 106 J17
Kaimana, *Indonesia* 63 E8
Kaimanawa Mts., *N.Z.* 91 H5
Kaimganj, *India* 69 F8
Kaimur Hills, *India* 69 G10
Kainab ➤, *Namibia* 88 D2
Kainji Dam, *Nigeria* 83 D5
Kainji Lake △, *Nigeria* 83 C5
Kainji Res., *Nigeria* 83 C5
Kainuu, *Finland* 8 D23
Kaipara Harbour, *N.Z.* 91 G5
Kaiping, *China* 59 F9
Kaipokok B., *Canada* 105 B8
Kaira, *India* 68 H5
Kairana, *India* 68 E7
Kaironi, *Indonesia* 63 E8
Kairouan, *Tunisia* 79 A8
Kaiserslautern, *Germany* 25 F3
Kaiserstuhl, *Germany* 25 G3
Kaitaia, *N.Z.* 91 F4
Kaitangata, *N.Z.* 91 M2
Kaithal, *India* 68 E7
Kaitu ➤, *Pakistan* 68 C4
Kaiyang, *China* 58 D6
Kaiyuan, *Liaoning, China* 57 C13
Kaiyuan, *Yunnan, China* 58 F4
Kajaani, *Finland* 8 D22
Kajabbi, *Australia* 94 C3
Kajana = Kajaani, *Finland* ... 8 D22
Kajang, *Malaysia* 65 L3
Kajaran, *Armenia* 73 C12
Kajiado, *Kenya* 86 C4
Kajo Kaji, *Sudan* 81 G3
Kajuru, *Nigeria* 83 C6
Kaka, *Sudan* 81 E3
Kakabeka Falls, *Canada* 104 C2
Kakamas, *S. Africa* 88 D3
Kakamega, *Kenya* 86 B3
Kakanj, *Bos.-H.* 28 F3
Kakanui Mts., *N.Z.* 91 L3
Kakata, *Liberia* 82 D2
Kakdwip, *India* 69 J13
Kake, *Japan* 55 G6
Kake, *U.S.A.* 102 B2
Kakegawa, *Japan* 55 G9
Kakeroma-Jima, *Japan* 55 K4
Kakhib, *Russia* 35 J8
Kakhovka, *Ukraine* 33 J7
Kakhovske Vdskh., *Ukraine* ... 33 J7
Kakinada, *India* 67 L13
Kakisa ➤, *Canada* 102 A5
Kakisa L., *Canada* 102 A5
Kakogawa, *Japan* 55 G7
Kakum △, *Ghana* 83 D4
Kakwa ➤, *Canada* 102 C5
Kāl Gūsheh, *Iran* 71 D8
Kal Safīd, *Iran* 70 C5
Kala, *Nigeria* 83 C7
Kalaallit Nunaat = Greenland Ø,
  N. Amer. 4 C5
Kalabagh, *Pakistan* 68 C4
Kalabahi, *Indonesia* 63 F6
Kalabáka, *Greece* 46 B3
Kalabana, *Mali* 82 C3
Kalach, *Russia* 34 E5
Kalach na Donu, *Russia* 35 F6
Kaladan ➤, *Burma* 67 J18
Kaladar, *Canada* 116 B7
Kalahari, *Africa* 88 C3
Kalahari Gemsbok △, *S. Africa* 88 D3
Kalajoki, *Finland* 8 D20
Kalakamati, *Botswana* 89 C4
Kalakan, *Russia* 53 D12
K'alak'unlun Shank'ou =
  Karakoram Pass, *Asia* 69 B7
Kalam, *Pakistan* 69 B5
Kalama, *Dem. Rep. of the Congo* 86 C2
Kalama, *U.S.A.* 110 E4
Kalámai, *Greece* 46 D4
Kalamariá, *Greece* 44 F6
Kalamazoo, *U.S.A.* 114 D3
Kalamazoo ➤, *U.S.A.* 114 D2
Kalambo Falls, *Tanzania* 87 D3
Kálamos, *Greece* 46 C5
Kálamos Nisís, *Greece* 46 C2
Kalan, *Turkey* 70 B3
Kalankalan, *Guinea* 82 C3
Kalannie, *Australia* 93 F2
Kalāntarī, *Iran* 71 C7
Kalao, *Indonesia* 63 F6
Kalaotoa, *Indonesia* 63 F6
Kälarne, *Sweden* 10 B10
Kalasin, *Thailand* 64 D4
Kālat, *Iran* 71 E8
Kalat, *Pakistan* 66 E5
Kalāteh, *Iran* 71 B7
Kalāteh-ye Ganj, *Iran* 71 E8
Kálathos, *Greece* 47 E10
Kalaus ➤, *Russia* 35 H7
Kalávrita, *Greece* 46 C4
Kalbarri, *Australia* 93 E1
Kalbarri △, *Australia* 93 E11
Kale, *Antalya, Turkey* 47 E12
Kale, *Denizli, Turkey* 47 D10
Kalecik, *Turkey* 72 B5
Kalegauk Kyun, *Burma* 67 M20
Kalehe, *Dem. Rep. of the Congo* 86 C2
Kalema, *Tanzania* 86 C3
Kalemie, *Dem. Rep. of the Congo* 86 D2
Kalety, *Poland* 31 H5
Kalewa, *Burma* 67 H19
Kaleybar, *Iran* 70 B5
Kalgoorlie-Boulder, *Australia* . 93 F3
Kali ➤, *India* 69 F8
Kali Sindh ➤, *India* 68 G6
Kaliakra, Nos, *Bulgaria* 45 C12
Kalianda, *Indonesia* 62 F3
Kalibo, *Phil.* 61 F5
Kalima, *Dem. Rep. of the Congo* 86 C2
Kalimantan, *Indonesia* 62 E4
Kalimantan Barat □, *Indonesia* 62 E4

Kalimantan Selatan □, *Indonesia* 62 E5
Kalimantan Tengah □, *Indonesia* 62 E4
Kalimantan Timur □, *Indonesia* 62 D5
Kálimnos, *Greece* 47 D8
Kalimpong, *India* 69 F13
Kaliningrad, *Russia* 9 J19
Kaliningrad ✈ (KGD), *Russia* . 30 D7
Kalininsk, *Russia* 34 E7
Kalinkavichy, *Belarus* 33 F5
Kalinkovichi = Kalinkavichy,
  Belarus 33 F5
Kalinovik, *Bos.-H.* 44 C2
Kalipetrovo, *Bulgaria* 45 B11
Kaliro, *Uganda* 86 B3
Kalirrákhi, *Greece* 45 F8
Kalispell, *U.S.A.* 108 B6
Kalisz, *Poland* 31 G5
Kalisz Pomorski, *Poland* 31 E2
Kaliua, *Tanzania* 86 D3
Kalívia Thorikoú, *Greece* 46 D5
Kalix = Kalixälven ➤, *Sweden* . 8 D20
Kalix, *Sweden* 8 D20
Kalixälven ➤, *Sweden* 8 D20
Kalka, *India* 68 D7
Kalkan, *Turkey* 47 E11
Kalkarindji, *Australia* 92 C5
Kalkaska, *U.S.A.* 114 C3
Kalkfeld, *Namibia* 88 C2
Kalkfontein, *Botswana* 88 C3
Kalkım, *Turkey* 47 B9
Kalkrand, *Namibia* 88 C2
Kållandsö, *Sweden* 11 F7
Kallavesi, *Finland* 8 E22
Källby, *Sweden* 11 F7
Kallimasiá, *Greece* 47 C8
Kallinge, *Sweden* 11 H9
Kallithéa, *Greece* 46 D5
Kallmet, *Albania* 44 E3
Kalloní, *Greece* 47 B8
Kallonís, Kólpos, *Greece* 47 B8
Kallsjön, *Sweden* 8 E15
Kalmalo, *Nigeria* 83 C6
Kalmar, *Sweden* 11 H10
Kalmar län □, *Sweden* 11 G10
Kalmar sund, *Sweden* 11 H10
Kalmyk Republic = Kalmykia □,
  Russia 35 G8
Kalmykia □, *Russia* 35 G8
Kalmykovo, *Kazakhstan* 52 E6
Kalna, *India* 69 H13
Kalnai, *India* 69 H10
Kalocsa, *Hungary* 28 D4
Kalofer, *Bulgaria* 45 D8
Kalokhorio, *Cyprus* 49 E12
Kaloko, *Dem. Rep. of the Congo* 86 D2
Kalol, *Gujarat, India* 68 H5
Kalol, *Gujarat, India* 68 H5
Kalolímnos, *Greece* 47 D9
Kalomo, *Zambia* 87 F2
Kalonerón, *Greece* 46 D3
Kalpi, *India* 69 F8
Kaltern = Caldaro, *Italy* 41 B8
Kaltungo, *Nigeria* 83 D7
Kalu, *Pakistan* 68 G2
Kaluga, *Russia* 32 E9
Kalulushi, *Zambia* 87 E2
Kalundborg, *Denmark* 11 J5
Kalush, *Ukraine* 33 H3
Kałuszyn, *Poland* 31 F8
Kalutara, *Sri Lanka* 66 R12
Kalvarija, *Lithuania* 30 D10
Kalyan, *India* 66 K8
Kalyazin, *Russia* 32 D9
Kam, *Albania* 44 D4
Kam ➤, *Nigeria* 83 D7
Kama, *Dem. Rep. of the Congo* . 86 C2
Kama ➤, *Russia* 6 D16
Kamachumu, *Tanzania* 86 C3
Kamaishi, *Japan* 54 E10
Kamalia, *Pakistan* 68 D5
Kaman, *India* 68 F6
Kaman, *Turkey* 72 C5
Kamanjab, *Namibia* 88 B2
Kamapanda, *Zambia* 87 E1
Kamarān, *Yemen* 75 D3
Kamativi, *Zimbabwe* 88 B4
Kamba, *Nigeria* 83 C5
Kambalda, *Australia* 93 F3
Kambar, *Pakistan* 68 F3
Kambia, *S. Leone* 82 D2
Kambolé, *Togo* 83 D5
Kambolé, *Zambia* 87 D3
Kambos, *Cyprus* 49 D11
Kambove, *Dem. Rep. of
  the Congo* 87 E2
Kamchatka, Poluostrov, *Russia* 53 D16
Kamchatka Pen. = Kamchatka,
  Poluostrov, *Russia* 53 D16
Kamchiya ➤, *Bulgaria* 45 C11
Kame Ruins, *Zimbabwe* 87 G2
Kamen, *Russia* 52 D9
Kamen-Rybolov, *Russia* 54 B6
Kamenica, *Serbia & M.* 44 C4
Kamenica, *Serbia & M.* 44 B3
Kamenice nad Lipou, *Czech Rep.* 26 B8
Kamenjak, Rt, *Croatia* 41 D10
Kamenka = Kaminka, *Ukraine* . 33 H7
Kamenka, *Kazakhstan* 34 E10
Kamenka, *Penza, Russia* 34 D6
Kamenka, *Voronezh, Russia* .. 33 G10
Kamenka Bugskaya = Kamyanka-
  Buzka, *Ukraine* 33 G3
Kamennomostskiy, *Russia* 35 H5
Kameno, *Bulgaria* 45 D11
Kamenolomni, *Russia* 35 G5
Kamensk-Shakhtinskiy, *Russia* 35 F5
Kamensk Uralskiy, *Russia* 52 D7
Kamenskiy, *Russia* 34 E7

Kamenskoye, *Russia* 53 C17
Kamenyak, *Bulgaria* 45 C10
Kamenz, *Germany* 24 D10
Kameoka, *Japan* 55 G7
Kamiah, *U.S.A.* 108 C5
Kamień Krajeński, *Poland* 30 E4
Kamień Pomorski, *Poland* 30 E1
Kamienna ➤, *Poland* 31 G8
Kamienna Góra, *Poland* 31 H3
Kamieńsk, *Poland* 31 G6
Kamieskroon, *S. Africa* 88 E2
Kamilukuak L., *Canada* 103 A8
Kamin-Kashyrskyy, *Ukraine* .. 33 G3
Kamina, *Dem. Rep. of the Congo* 87 D2
Kaminak L., *Canada* 103 A10
Kaministiquia, *Canada* 104 C1
Kaminka, *Ukraine* 33 H7
Kaminoyama, *Japan* 54 E10
Kamiros, *Greece* 49 C9
Kamituga, *Dem. Rep. of
  the Congo* 86 C2
Kamla ➤, *India* 69 G12
Kamloops, *Canada* 102 C4
Kamnik, *Slovenia* 41 B11
Kamo, *Armenia* 35 K7
Kamo, *Japan* 54 F9
Kamoke, *Pakistan* 68 C6
Kamp ➤, *Austria* 26 C8
Kampala, *Uganda* 86 B3
Kampar, *Malaysia* 65 K3
Kampar ➤, *Indonesia* 62 D2
Kampen, *Neths.* 17 B5
Kampene, *Dem. Rep. of
  the Congo* 84 C5
Kamphaeng Phet, *Thailand* ... 64 D2
Kampinoski △, *Poland* 31 F7
Kampolombo, L., *Zambia* 87 E2
Kampong Chhnang, *Cambodia* . 65 F5
Kampong Pengerang, *Malaysia* 65 d
Kampong Punggai, *Malaysia* .. 65 d
Kampong Saom, *Cambodia* 65 G4
Kampong Saom, Chaak,
  Cambodia 65 G4
Kampong Tanjong Langsat,
  Malaysia .... 65 d
Kampong Telok Ramunia,
  Malaysia .... 65 d
Kampong To, *Thailand* 65 J3
Kampot, *Cambodia* 65 G5
Kampti, *Burkina Faso* 82 C4
Kampuchea = Cambodia ■, *Asia* 64 F5
Kampung Air Putih, *Malaysia* . 65 K4
Kampung Jerangau, *Malaysia* . 65 K4
Kampung Raja, *Malaysia* 65 K4
Kampungbaru = Tolitoli,
  Indonesia 63 D6
Kamrau, Teluk, *Indonesia* 63 E8
Kamsack, *Canada* 103 C8
Kamsai, *Guinea* 82 C2
Kamskoye Ustye, *Russia* 34 C9
Kamuchawie L., *Canada* 103 B8
Kamui-Misaki, *Japan* 54 C10
Kamyanets-Podilskyy, *Ukraine* 29 B11
Kamyanka-Buzka, *Ukraine* 33 G3
Kamyanka-Dniprovska, *Ukraine* 33 J8
Kamyanyets, *Belarus* 31 F10
Kamyanyuki, *Belarus* 31 F10
Kamyshin, *Russia* 34 E7
Kamyzyak, *Russia* 35 G9
Kan ➤, *Russia* 53 D10
Kan, *Sudan* 81 F3
Kanaaupscow ➤, *Canada* 101 C12
Kanaaupscow, *Canada* 104 B4
Kanab, *U.S.A.* 109 H7
Kanab ➤, *U.S.A.* 109 H7
Kanagi, *Japan* 54 D10
Kanairiktok ➤, *Canada* 105 A7
Kanália, *Greece* 46 B4
Kananga, *Dem. Rep. of the Congo* 84 F4
Kanash, *Russia* 34 C8
Kanaskat, *U.S.A.* 110 C5
Kanastraíon, Ákra = Palioúrion,
  Ákra, *Greece* 44 G7
Kanawha ➤, *U.S.A.* 114 F4
Kanazawa, *Japan* 55 F8
Kanchanaburi, *Thailand* 64 E2
Kanchenjunga, *Nepal* 69 F13
Kanchipuram, *India* 66 N11
Kańczuga, *Poland* 31 J9
Kandaghat, *India* 68 D7
Kandahar = Qandahār, *Afghan.* 66 D4
Kandalaksha, *Russia* 52 C4
Kandangan, *Indonesia* 62 E5
Kandanghaur, *Indonesia* 63 G13
Kandanos, *Greece* 49 D5
Kandava, *Latvia* 30 A9
Kandavu = Kadavu, *Fiji* 91 D8
Kandhíla, *Greece* 46 D4
Kandhkot, *Pakistan* 68 E3
Kandhla, *India* 68 E7
Kandi, *Benin* 83 C5
Kandi, *India* 69 H13
Kandiaro, *Pakistan* 68 F3
Kandıra, *Turkey* 72 B4
Kandla, *India* 68 H4
Kandos, *Australia* 95 E4
Kandreho, *Madag.* 89 B8
Kandy, *Sri Lanka* 66 R12
Kane, *U.S.A.* 116 E6
Kane Basin, *Greenland* 98 B12
Kanel, *Senegal* 82 B2
Kanevskaya, *Russia* 35 G4
Kanfanar, *Croatia* 41 C10
Kang, *Botswana* 88 C3
Kang Krung △, *Thailand* 65 H2
Kangal, *Turkey* 72 C7
Kangān, *Fārs, Iran* 71 E7
Kangān, *Hormozgān, Iran* 71 E8
Kangar, *Malaysia* 65 J3
Kangaré, *Mali* 82 C3

Kangaroo I., *Australia* 95 F2
Kangaroo Mts., *Australia* 94 C3
Kangasala, *Finland* 9 F21
Kangāvar, *Iran* 71 C6
Kangding, *China* 58 B3
Kangdong, *N. Korea* 57 E14
Kangean, Kepulauan, *Indonesia* 62 F5
Kangean Is. = Kangean,
  Kepulauan, *Indonesia* 62 F5
Kangen ➤, *Sudan* 81 F3
Kanggye, *N. Korea* 57 D14
Kanggyŏng, *S. Korea* 57 F14
Kanghwa, *S. Korea* 57 F14
Kangikajik, *Greenland* 4 B6
Kangiqcliniq = Rankin Inlet,
  Canada 100 B10
Kangiqsualujjuaq, *Canada* 101 C13
Kangiqsujuaq, *Canada* 101 B12
Kangiqtugaapik = Clyde River,
  Canada 101 A13
Kangirsuk, *Canada* 101 B13
Kangkar Chemaran, *Malaysia* . 65 d
Kangkar Sungai Tiram, *Malaysia* 65 d
Kangkar Teberau, *Malaysia* ... 65 d
Kangnŭng, *S. Korea* 57 F15
Kangping, *China* 57 C12
Kangra, *India* 68 C7
Kangrinboqe Feng, *China* 69 D9
Kangto, *China* 67 F18
Kanhar ➤, *India* 69 G10
Kani, *Ivory C.* 82 D3
Kaniama, *Dem. Rep. of the Congo* 86 D1
Kaniapiskau = Caniapiscau ➤,
  Canada 105 A6
Kaniapiskau, L. = Caniapiscau, L.
  de, *Canada* 105 B6
Kanin, Poluostrov, *Russia* 52 C5
Kanin Nos, Mys, *Russia* 52 C5
Kanin Pen. = Kanin, Poluostrov,
  Russia 52 C5
Kaninė, *Albania* 44 F3
Kaniva, *Australia* 95 F3
Kanjiža, *Serbia & M.* 28 D5
Kanjut Sar, *Pakistan* 69 A6
Kankaanpää, *Finland* 9 F20
Kankakee, *U.S.A.* 114 E2
Kankakee ➤, *U.S.A.* 114 E1
Kankan, *Guinea* 82 C3
Kankendy = Xankändi,
  Azerbaijan 70 B5
Kanker, *India* 67 J12
Kankossa, *Mauritania* 82 B2
Kankroli, *India* 68 G5
Kannapolis, *U.S.A.* 115 H5
Kannauj, *India* 69 F8
Kannod, *India* 66 H10
Kano, *Nigeria* 83 C6
Kano □, *Nigeria* 83 C6
Kan'onji, *Japan* 55 G6
Kanoroba, *Ivory C.* 82 D3
Kanowit, *Malaysia* 62 D4
Kanoya, *Japan* 55 J5
Kanpetlet, *Burma* 67 J18
Kanpur, *India* 69 F9
Kansas □, *U.S.A.* 112 F6
Kansas ➤, *U.S.A.* 112 F7
Kansas City, *Kans., U.S.A.* 112 F7
Kansas City, *Mo., U.S.A.* 112 F7
Kansenia, *Dem. Rep. of the Congo* 87 E2
Kansk, *Russia* 53 D10
Kansŏng, *S. Korea* 57 E15
Kansu = Gansu □, *China* 56 G3
Kantaphor, *India* 68 H7
Kantchari, *Burkina Faso* 83 C5
Kantché, *Niger* 83 C6
Kanté, *Togo* 83 D5
Kantemirovka, *Russia* 33 H10
Kantharalak, *Thailand* 64 E5
Kantli ➤, *India* 68 E6
Kantō □, *Japan* 55 F9
Kantō-Sanchi, *Japan* 55 G9
Kanturk, *Ireland* 12 D3
Kanuma, *Japan* 55 F9
Kanus, *Namibia* 88 D2
Kanye, *Botswana* 88 C4
Kanzenze, *Dem. Rep. of
  the Congo* 87 E2
Kanzi, Ras, *Tanzania* 86 D4
Kao Phara, *Thailand* .... 65 a
Kaohsiung, *Taiwan* 59 F13
Kaokoveld, *Namibia* 88 B1
Kaolack, *Senegal* 82 C1
Kaoshan, *China* 57 B13
Kapaa, *U.S.A.* 106 G15
Kapadvanj, *India* 68 H5
Kapaklı, *Turkey* 45 E11
Kapan, *Armenia* 70 B5
Kapanga, *Dem. Rep. of the Congo* 84 F4
Kapchagai = Qapshaghay,
  Kazakhstan 52 E8
Kapela = Velika Kapela, *Croatia* 41 C12
Kapéllo, Ákra, *Greece* 46 E5
Kapema, *Dem. Rep. of the Congo* 87 E2
Kapfenberg, *Austria* 26 D8
Kapı Dağı, *Turkey* 45 F11
Kapiri Mposhi, *Zambia* 87 E2
Kāpīsā □, *Afghan.* 66 B6
Kapiskau ➤, *Canada* 104 B3
Kapit, *Malaysia* 62 D4
Kapiti I., *N.Z.* 91 J5
Kaplan, *U.S.A.* 113 K8
Kaplice, *Czech Rep.* 26 C7
Kapoe, *Thailand* 65 H2
Kapoeta, *Sudan* 81 G3
Kápolnásnyék, *Hungary* 28 C3
Kapos ➤, *Hungary* 28 D3
Kaposvár, *Hungary* 28 D2
Kapowsin, *U.S.A.* 110 D4
Kappeln, *Germany* 24 A5
Kappelshamn, *Sweden* 11 G12
Kapps, *Namibia* 88 C2
Kaprije, *Croatia* 41 E12

Kapsan, *N. Korea* 57 D15
Kapsukas = Marijampolė,
  Lithuania 9 J20
Kaptai L., *Bangla.* 67 H18
Kapuas ➤, *Indonesia* 62 E3
Kapuas Hulu, Pegunungan,
  Malaysia 62 D4
Kapuas Hulu Ra. = Kapuas Hulu,
  Pegunungan, *Malaysia* 62 D4
Kapulo, *Dem. Rep. of the Congo* 87 D2
Kapunda, *Australia* 95 E2
Kapuni, *N.Z.* 91 H5
Kapurthala, *India* 68 D6
Kapuskasing, *Canada* 104 C3
Kapuskasing ➤, *Canada* 104 C3
Kapustin Yar, *Russia* 35 F7
Kaputar, *Australia* 95 E5
Kaputir, *Kenya* 86 B4
Kapuvár, *Hungary* 28 C2
Kara, *Russia* 52 C7
Karā, W. ➤, *Si. Arabia* 80 C5
Kara Ada, *Turkey* 47 E9
Kara Bogaz Gol, Zaliv =
  Garabogazköl Aylagy,
  Turkmenistan 52 E6
Kara Burun, *Turkey* 47 E9
Kara Kalpak Republic =
  Qoraqalpoghistan □,
  Uzbekistan 52 E6
Kara Kum, *Turkmenistan* 52 F6
Kara Sea, *Russia* 52 B7
Karaadilli, *Turkey* 47 C12
Karabiğa, *Turkey* 45 F11
Karabük, *Turkey* 72 B5
Karaburun, *Albania* 44 F3
Karaburun, *Turkey* 47 C8
Karabutak = Qarabutaq,
  Kazakhstan 52 E7
Karacabey, *Turkey* 45 F12
Karacakılavuz, *Turkey* 45 E11
Karacaköy, *Turkey* 45 E12
Karacasu, *Turkey* 47 D10
Karachala = Qaraçala, *Azerbaijan* 35 L9
Karachayevsk, *Russia* 35 J5
Karachev, *Russia* 33 F8
Karachey-Cherkessia □, *Russia* 35 J5
Karachi, *Pakistan* 68 G2
Karad, *India* 66 L9
Karadirek, *Turkey* 47 C12
Karaga, *Ghana* 83 D4
Karaganda = Qaraghandy,
  Kazakhstan 52 E8
Karagayly = Qaraghayly,
  Kazakhstan 52 E8
Karaginskiy, Ostrov, *Russia* ... 53 D17
Karagola Road, *India* 69 G12
Karagüney Dağları, *Turkey* ... 72 B6
Karahallı, *Turkey* 47 C11
Karaikal, *India* 66 P11
Karaikkudi, *India* 66 P11
Karaisali, *Turkey* 72 D6
Karaj, *Iran* 71 C6
Karak, *Malaysia* 65 L4
Karakalpakstan =
  Qoraqalpoghistan □,
  Uzbekistan 52 E6
Karakelong, *Indonesia* 63 D7
Karakitang, *Indonesia* 63 D7
Karakoçan, *Turkey* 73 C9
Karakol, *Kyrgyzstan* 52 E8
Karakoram Pass, *Asia* 69 B7
Karakoram Ra., *Pakistan* 69 B7
Karakurt, *Turkey* 73 B10
Karakuwisa, *Namibia* 88 B2
Karalon, *Russia* 53 D12
Karama, *Jordan* 74 D4
Karaman, *Balıkesir, Turkey* ... 47 B9
Karaman, *Konya, Turkey* 70 B2
Karamanlı, *Turkey* 47 D11
Karamay, *China* 60 B3
Karambu, *Indonesia* 62 E5
Karamea Bight, *N.Z.* 91 J3
Karamnasa ➤, *India* 69 G10
Karamürsel, *Turkey* 45 F13
Karand, *Iran* 70 C5
Karangana, *Mali* 82 C3
Karanganyar, *Indonesia* 63 G13
Karangasem, *Indonesia* 63 J18
Karanjia, *India* 69 J11
Karankasso, *Burkina Faso* 82 C4
Karaova, *Turkey* 47 D9
Karapınar, *Turkey* 72 D5
Karasburg, *Namibia* 88 D2
Karasino, *Russia* 52 C9
Karasjok, *Norway* 8 B21
Karasu ➤, *Turkey* 72 B4
Karasu ➤, *Turkey* 47 E12
Karasuk, *Russia* 52 D8
Karasuyama, *Japan* 55 F10
Karataş, *Adana, Turkey* 72 D6
Karataş, *Manisa, Turkey* 47 C10
Karataş Burnu, *Turkey* 72 D6
Karatau, Khrebet = Qarataū,
  Kazakhstan 52 E7
Karatoprak, *Turkey* 47 D9
Karatsu, *Japan* 55 H5
Karaul, *Russia* 52 B9
Karauli, *India* 68 F7
Karavastasë, L. e, *Albania* 44 F3
Karávi, *Greece* 46 E5
Karavostasi, *Cyprus* 49 D11
Karawang, *Indonesia* 63 G12
Karawanken, *Europe* 26 E7
Karayazı, *Turkey* 73 C10
Karazhal, *Kazakhstan* 52 E8
Karbalā', *Iraq* 70 C5
Kårböle, *Sweden* 10 C9
Karcag, *Hungary* 28 C5
Karcha ➤, *Pakistan* 69 B7
Karchana, *India* 69 G9
Karczew, *Poland* 31 F8
Kardam, *Bulgaria* 45 C12

Kardeljovo = Ploče, *Croatia* 41 E14
Kardhámila, *Greece* 47 C8
Kardhamíli, *Greece* 46 E4
Kardhítsa, *Greece* 46 B3
Kardhítsa □, *Greece* 46 B3
Kärdla, *Estonia* 9 G20
Kareeberge, *S. Africa* 88 E3
Kareha ➜, *India* 69 G12
Kareima, *Sudan* 80 D3
Karelia □, *Russia* 52 C4
Karelian Republic = Karelia □,
  Russia 52 C4
Karera, *India* 68 G8
Kārevāndar, *Iran* 71 E9
Kargasok, *Russia* 52 D9
Kargat, *Russia* 52 D9
Kargı, *Turkey* 72 B6
Kargil, *India* 69 B7
Kargopol, *Russia* 32 B10
Kargowa, *Poland* 31 F2
Karguéri, *Niger* 83 C7
Karhal, *India* 69 F8
Kariá, *Greece* 46 C2
Kariaí, *Greece* 45 F8
Karīān, *Iran* 71 E8
Karianga, *Madag.* 89 C8
Kariba, *Zimbabwe* 87 F2
Kariba, L., *Zimbabwe* 87 F2
Kariba Dam, *Zimbabwe* 87 F2
Kariba Gorge, *Zambia* 87 F2
Karibib, *Namibia* 88 C2
Karijini △, *Australia* 92 D2
Karimata, Kepulauan, *Indonesia* .. 62 E3
Karimata, Selat, *Indonesia* 62 E3
Karimata Is. = Karimata,
  Kepulauan, *Indonesia* 62 E3
Karimnagar, *India* 66 K11
Karimun Kecil, Pulau, *Indonesia* . 65 d
Karimunjawa, Kepulauan,
  Indonesia 62 F4
Karin, *Somali Rep.* 75 E4
Káristos, *Greece* 46 C6
Karīt, *Iran* 71 C8
Kariya, *Japan* 55 G8
Kariyangwe, *Zimbabwe* 89 B4
Karjala, *Finland* 32 A5
Karkaralinsk = Qarqaraly,
  Kazakhstan 52 E8
Karkheh ➜, *Iran* 70 D5
Karkinitska Zatoka, *Ukraine* 33 K7
Karkinitskiy Zaliv = Karkinitska
  Zatoka, *Ukraine* 33 K7
Karkuk = Kirkūk, *Iraq* 70 C5
Karkur Tohl, *Egypt* 80 C2
Karl Liebknecht, *Russia* 33 G8
Karleby = Kokkola, *Finland* 8 E20
Karlholmsbruk, *Sweden* 10 D11
Karlino, *Poland* 30 D2
Karlivka, *Ukraine* 33 H8
Karlobag, *Croatia* 41 D12
Karlovac, *Croatia* 41 C12
Karlovarský □, *Czech Rep.* 26 A5
Karlovka = Karlivka, *Ukraine* 33 H8
Karlovo, *Bulgaria* 45 D8
Karlovy Vary, *Czech Rep.* 26 A5
Karlsbad = Karlovy Vary,
  Czech Rep. 26 A5
Karlsborg, *Sweden* 11 F8
Karlshamn, *Sweden* 11 H8
Karlskoga, *Sweden* 10 E8
Karlskrona, *Sweden* 11 H9
Karlsruhe, *Germany* 25 F4
Karlstad, *Sweden* 10 E7
Karlstad, *U.S.A.* 112 A6
Karlstadt, *Germany* 25 F5
Karma, *Niger* 83 C5
Karmēlava, *Lithuania* 30 D11
Karmi'el, *Israel* 74 C4
Karnak, *Egypt* 80 B3
Karnal, *India* 68 E7
Karnali ➜, *Nepal* 69 E9
Karnaphuli Res. = Kaptai L.,
  Bangla. 67 H18
Karnaprayag, *India* 69 D8
Karnataka □, *India* 66 N10
Karnes City, *U.S.A.* 113 L6
Karnische Alpen, *Europe* 26 E6
Karnobat, *Bulgaria* 45 D10
Kärnten □, *Austria* 26 E6
Karo, *Mali* 82 C4
Karoi, *Zimbabwe* 87 F2
Karon, Ao, *Thailand* .... 65 a
Karonga, *Malawi* 87 D3
Karoo △, *S. Africa* 88 E3
Karoonda, *Australia* 95 F2
Karor, *Pakistan* 68 D4
Karora, *Sudan* 80 D4
Káros, *Greece* 47 E7
Karounga, *Mali* 82 B3
Karousádhes, *Greece* 46 B1
Karpacz, *Poland* 31 H2
Karpasia, *Cyprus* 49 D13
Kárpathos, *Greece* 47 F9
Kárpathos, Stenón, *Greece* 47 F9
Karpatskiy △, *Ukraine* 29 B9
Karpenísion, *Greece* 46 C3
Karpuz Burnu = Apostolos
  Andreas, C., *Cyprus* 49 D13
Karpuzlu, *Turkey* 47 D9
Karratha, *Australia* 92 D2
Kars, *Turkey* 73 B10
Karsakpay, *Kazakhstan* 52 E7
Karsha, *Kazakhstan* 34 F10
Karshi = Qarshi, *Uzbekistan* 52 F7
Karsiyang, *India* 69 F13
Karsog, *India* 68 D7
Karst = Kras, *Croatia* 41 C10
Kartal, *Turkey* 45 F13
Kartál Óros, *Greece* 45 E9
Kartaly, *Russia* 52 D7
Kartapur, *India* 68 D6
Karthaus, *U.S.A.* 116 E6

Kartuzy, *Poland* 30 D5
Karufa, *Indonesia* 63 E8
Karuma △, *Uganda* 86 B3
Karumba, *Australia* 94 B3
Karumo, *Tanzania* 86 C3
Karumwa, *Tanzania* 86 C3
Kārūn ➜, *Iran* 71 D6
Karungu, *Kenya* 86 C3
Karup, *Denmark* 11 H3
Karur, *India* 66 M9
Karwan ➜, *India* 68 F8
Karwar, *India* 66 M9
Karwendel △, *Austria* 26 D4
Karwi, *India* 69 G9
Kaş, *Turkey* 47 E11
Kasaba, *Turkey* 47 E11
Kasache, *Malawi* 87 E3
Kasai ➜, *Dem. Rep. of the Congo* 84 E3
Kasai-Oriental □, *Dem. Rep. of*
  the Congo 86 D1
Kasaji, *Dem. Rep. of the Congo* .. 87 E1
Kasama, *Zambia* 87 E3
Kasan-dong, *N. Korea* 57 D14
Kasane, *Namibia* 88 B3
Kasanga, *Tanzania* 87 D3
Kasanka △, *Zambia* 87 E3
Kasar, Ras, *Sudan* 80 D4
Kasaragod, *India* 66 N9
Kasba L., *Canada* 103 A8
Kāseh Garān, *Iran* 70 C5
Kasempa, *Zambia* 87 E2
Kasenga, *Dem. Rep. of the Congo* 87 E2
Kasese, *Uganda* 86 B3
Kasewa, *Zambia* 87 E2
Kasganj, *India* 69 F8
Kashabowie, *Canada* 104 C1
Kashaf, *Iran* 71 C9
Kāshān, *Iran* 71 C6
Kashechewan, *Canada* 104 B3
Kashgar = Kashi, *China* 60 C2
Kashi, *China* 60 C2
Kashimbo, *Dem. Rep. of*
  the Congo 87 E2
Kashin, *Russia* 32 D9
Kashipur, *India* 69 E8
Kashira, *Russia* 32 E10
Kashiwazaki, *Japan* 55 F9
Kashk-e Kohneh, *Afghan.* 66 B3
Kashkū'īyeh, *Iran* 71 D7
Kashmar, *Iran* 71 C8
Kashmir, *Asia* 69 C7
Kashmor, *Pakistan* 68 E3
Kashpirovka, *Russia* 34 D9
Kashun Noerh = Gaxun Nur,
  China 60 B5
Kasiari, *India* 69 H12
Kasimov, *Russia* 34 C5
Kasinge, *Dem. Rep. of the Congo* 86 D2
Kasiruta, *Indonesia* 63 E7
Kaskaskia ➜, *U.S.A.* 112 G10
Kaskattama ➜, *Canada* 103 B10
Kaskinen, *Finland* 9 E19
Kaskö = Kaskinen, *Finland* 9 E19
Kaslo, *Canada* 102 D5
Kasmere L., *Canada* 103 B8
Kasongo, *Dem. Rep. of the Congo* 86 C2
Kasongo Lunda, *Dem. Rep. of*
  the Congo 84 F3
Kásos, *Greece* 47 F8
Kásos, Stenón, *Greece* 47 F8
Kaspi, *Georgia* 35 K7
Kaspichan, *Bulgaria* 45 C11
Kaspiysk, *Russia* 35 J8
Kaspiyskiy, *Russia* 35 H8
Kassab ed Doleib, *Sudan* 81 E3
Kassaba, *Egypt* 80 C2
Kassalā, *Sudan* 81 D4
Kassalā □, *Sudan* 81 D4
Kassándra, *Greece* 44 F7
Kassándrinon, *Greece* 44 F7
Kassel, *Germany* 24 D5
Kassinger, *Sudan* 80 D3
Kassiópi, *Greece* 49 A3
Kasson, *U.S.A.* 112 C8
Kastamonu, *Turkey* 72 B5
Kastav, *Croatia* 41 C11
Kastélli, *Greece* 49 D5
Kastéllion, *Greece* 49 D7
Kastellórizon = Megiste, *Greece* . 47 E11
Kástellos, *Greece* 47 E9
Kastellou, Ákra, *Greece* 47 F9
Kasterlee, *Belgium* 17 C4
Kastlösa, *Sweden* 11 H10
Kastóri, *Greece* 46 D4
Kastoría, *Greece* 44 F5
Kastoría □, *Greece* 44 F5
Kastorías, Límni, *Greece* 44 F5
Kastornoye, *Russia* 33 G10
Kastós Nisís, *Greece* 46 C2
Kastrosikiá, *Greece* 46 B2
Kastrup, København ✈ (CPH),
  Denmark 11 J6
Kastsyukovichy, *Belarus* 32 F7
Kasulu, *Tanzania* 86 C3
Kasumi, *Japan* 55 G7
Kasumkent, *Russia* 35 K9
Kasungu, *Malawi* 87 E3
Kasungu △, *Malawi* 87 E3
Kasur, *Pakistan* 68 D6
Kata Tjuta = Olga, Mt., *Australia* 93 E5
Kataba, *Zambia* 87 F2
Katagum, *Nigeria* 83 C7
Katahdin, Mt., *U.S.A.* 115 C11
Katako Kombe, *Dem. Rep. of*
  the Congo 86 C1
Katákolon, *Greece* 46 D3
Katale, *Tanzania* 86 C3
Katanda, *Katanga, Dem. Rep. of*
  the Congo 86 D1
Katanda, *Nord-Kivu, Dem. Rep.*
  of the Congo 86 C2

Katanga □, *Dem. Rep. of*
  the Congo 86 D2
Katangi, *India* 66 J11
Katanning, *Australia* 93 F2
Katastári, *Greece* 46 D2
Katavi △, *Tanzania* 86 D3
Katavi Swamp, *Tanzania* 86 D3
Kateríni, *Greece* 44 F6
Katghora, *India* 69 H10
Katha, *Burma* 67 G20
Katherina, Gebel, *Egypt* 70 D2
Katherine, *Australia* 92 B5
Katherine Gorge, *Australia* 92 B5
Kathi, *India* 68 J6
Kathiawar, *India* 68 H4
Kathikas, *Cyprus* 49 E11
Kathmandu = Katmandu, *Nepal* . 69 F11
Kathua, *India* 68 C6
Kati, *Mali* 82 C3
Katihar, *India* 69 G12
Katima Mulilo, *Zambia* 88 B3
Katimbira, *Malawi* 87 E3
Katingan = Mendawai ➜,
  Indonesia 62 E4
Katiola, *Ivory C.* 82 D3
Katlabukh, Ozero, *Ukraine* 29 E14
Katlanovo, *Macedonia* 44 E5
Katmandu, *Nepal* 69 F11
Katni, *India* 69 H9
Káto Akhaïa, *Greece* 46 C3
Káto Arkhánai, *Greece* 49 D7
Káto Khorió, *Greece* 49 D7
Káto Pyrgos, *Cyprus* 49 D11
Káto Stavros, *Greece* 44 F7
Katokhí, *Greece* 46 C3
Katompe, *Dem. Rep. of the Congo* 86 D2
Katong, *Singapore* .... 65 d
Katonga ➜, *Uganda* 86 B3
Katoomba, *Australia* 95 E5
Katoúna, *Greece* 46 C3
Katowice, *Poland* 31 H6
Katranci Dağı, *Turkey* 47 D12
Katrine, L., *U.K.* 13 E4
Katrineholm, *Sweden* 10 E10
Katsepe, *Madag.* 89 B8
Katsina, *Nigeria* 83 C6
Katsina □, *Nigeria* 83 C6
Katsina Ala, *Nigeria* 83 D6
Katsina Ala ➜, *Nigeria* 83 D6
Katsumoto, *Japan* 55 H4
Katsuura, *Japan* 55 G10
Katsuyama, *Japan* 55 F8
Kattaviá, *Greece* 49 D9
Kattegat, *Denmark* 11 H5
Katthammarsvik, *Sweden* 11 G12
Katul, J., *Sudan* 81 E2
Katumba, *Dem. Rep. of the Congo* 86 D2
Katwa, *India* 69 H13
Katwijk, *Neths.* 17 B4
Kāty Wrocławskie, *Poland* 31 G3
Kauai, *U.S.A.* 106 H15
Kauai Channel, *U.S.A.* 106 H15
Kaub, *Germany* 25 E3
Kaudom △, *Namibia* 88 B3
Kaufbeuren, *Germany* 25 H6
Kaufman, *U.S.A.* 113 J6
Kauhajoki, *Finland* 9 E20
Kaukauna, *U.S.A.* 114 C1
Kaukauveld, *Namibia* 88 C3
Kaunakakai, *U.S.A.* 106 H16
Kaunas, *Lithuania* 9 J20
Kaunas ✈ (KUN), *Lithuania* 30 D11
Kaunia, *Bangla.* 69 G13
Kaunos, *Turkey* 47 E10
Kaura Namoda, *Nigeria* 83 C6
Kauru, *Nigeria* 83 C6
Kautokeino, *Norway* 8 B20
Kauwapur, *India* 69 F10
Kavacha, *Russia* 53 C17
Kavadarci, *Macedonia* 44 E6
Kavajë, *Albania* 44 E3
Kavak, *Turkey* 72 B7
Kavak Dağı, *Turkey* 47 D10
Kavaklı, *Turkey* 45 E11
Kavaklıdere, *Turkey* 47 D10
Kavalerovo, *Russia* 54 B7
Kavali, *India* 66 M12
Kavála, *Greece* 45 F8
Kavála □, *Greece* 45 E8
Kavála Kólpos, *Greece* 45 F8
Kavār, *Iran* 71 D7
Kavarna, *Bulgaria* 45 C12
Kavi, *India* 68 H5
Kavimba, *Botswana* 88 B3
Kavīr, Dasht-e, *Iran* 71 C7
Kavkaz, *Russia* 33 K9
Kävlinge, *Sweden* 11 J7
Kavos, *Greece* 49 B4
Kavoúsi, *Greece* 47 F7
Kaw, *Fr. Guiana* 125 C8
Kawa, *Sudan* 81 E3
Kawagama L., *Canada* 116 A6
Kawagoe, *Japan* 55 G9
Kawaguchi, *Japan* 55 G9
Kawambwa, *Zambia* 87 D2
Kawanoe, *Japan* 55 G6
Kawardha, *India* 69 J9
Kawasaki, *Japan* 55 G9
Kawasi, *Indonesia* 63 E7
Kawerau, *N.Z.* 91 H6
Kawhia, *N.Z.* 91 H5
Kawhia Harbour, *N.Z.* 91 H5
Kawio, Kepulauan, *Indonesia* 63 D7
Kawnro, *Burma* 67 H21
Kawthaung, *Burma* 65 H2
Kawthoolei = Kayin □, *Burma* ... 67 L20
Kawthule = Kayin □, *Burma* 67 L20
Kaxholmen, *Sweden* 11 G8
Kaya, *Burkina Faso* 83 C4
Kayah □, *Burma* 67 K20
Kayalıköy Baraji, *Turkey* 45 E11
Kayan ➜, *Indonesia* 62 D5

Kaycee, *U.S.A.* 108 E10
Kayeli, *Indonesia* 63 E7
Kayenta, *U.S.A.* 109 H8
Kayes, *Mali* 82 C2
Kayı, *Turkey* 47 B12
Kayima, *S. Leone* 82 D2
Kayin □, *Burma* 67 L20
Kaymakçı, *Turkey* 47 C10
Kayoa, *Indonesia* 63 D7
Kayomba, *Zambia* 87 E1
Kaysatskoye, *Russia* 34 F8
Kayseri, *Turkey* 70 B2
Kaysville, *U.S.A.* 108 F8
Kaz Dağı, *Turkey* 47 B8
Kazachye, *Russia* 53 B14
Kazakhstan ■, *Asia* 52 E7
Kazan, *Russia* 34 C9
Kazan ➜, *Canada* 103 A9
Kazan-Rettō, *Pac. Oc.* 96 F6
Kazanlŭk, *Bulgaria* 45 D9
Kazanskaya, *Russia* 34 F5
Kazatin = Kozyatyn, *Ukraine* 33 H5
Kazaure, *Nigeria* 83 C6
Kazbek, *Russia* 35 J7
Kāzerūn, *Iran* 71 D6
Kazi Magomed = Qazimämmäd,
  Azerbaijan 35 K9
Kazimierz Dolny, *Poland* 31 G8
Kazimierza Wielka, *Poland* 31 H7
Kazincbarcika, *Hungary* 28 B5
Kazlų Rūda, *Lithuania* 30 D10
Kaztalovka, *Kazakhstan* 34 F9
Kazuma Pan △, *Zimbabwe* 87 F2
Kazuno, *Japan* 54 D10
Kazym ➜, *Russia* 52 C7
Kcynia, *Poland* 31 F4
Ké-Macina, *Mali* 82 C3
Kéa, *Greece* 46 D6
Keady, *U.K.* 12 B5
Kearney, *U.S.A.* 112 E5
Kearny, *U.S.A.* 109 K8
Kearsarge, Mt., *U.S.A.* 117 C13
Keban, *Turkey* 73 C8
Keban Baraji, *Turkey* 70 B3
Kebbi □, *Nigeria* 83 C5
Kébi, *Ivory C.* 82 D3
Kebnekaise, *Sweden* 8 C18
Kebri Dehar, *Ethiopia* 75 F3
Kebumen, *Indonesia* 63 G13
Kecel, *Hungary* 28 D4
Kechika ➜, *Canada* 102 B3
Keçiborlu, *Turkey* 47 D12
Kecskemét, *Hungary* 28 D4
Kedada, *Ethiopia* 81 F4
Kedarnath, *India* 69 D8
Kedgwick, *Canada* 105 C6
Kediri, *Indonesia* 63 G15
Kedjebi, *Ghana* 83 D5
Kédougou, *Senegal* 82 C2
Kędzierzyn-Koźle, *Poland* 31 H5
Keeler, *U.S.A.* 110 J9
Keeley L., *Canada* 103 C7
Keeling Is. = Cocos Is., *Ind. Oc.* . 96 J1
Keelung = Chilung, *Taiwan* 59 E13
Keene, *Canada* 116 B6
Keene, Calif., *U.S.A.* 111 K8
Keene, N.H., *U.S.A.* 117 D12
Keene, N.Y., *U.S.A.* 117 B11
Keep River △, *Australia* 92 C4
Keeper Hill, *Ireland* 12 D3
Keer-Weer, C., *Australia* 94 A3
Keeseville, *U.S.A.* 117 B11
Keetmanshoop, *Namibia* 88 D2
Keewatin, *Canada* 103 D10
Keewatin ➜, *Canada* 103 B8
Kefa, *Ethiopia* 81 F4
Kefallinía, *Greece* 46 C2
Kefallinía □, *Greece* 46 C2
Kéfalos, *Greece* 47 E8
Kefamenanu, *Indonesia* 63 F6
Kefar Sava, *Israel* 74 C3
Keffi, *Nigeria* 83 D6
Keffin Hausa, *Nigeria* 83 C6
Keflavík, *Iceland* 8 D2
Keftya, *Ethiopia* 81 E4
Keg River, *Canada* 102 B5
Kegaska, *Canada* 105 B7
Keheili, *Sudan* 80 D3
Kehl, *Germany* 25 G3
Keighley, *U.K.* 14 D6
Keila, *Estonia* 9 G21
Keimoes, *S. Africa* 88 D3
Keita, *Niger* 83 C6
Keitele, *Finland* 8 E22
Keith, *Australia* 95 F3
Keith, *U.K.* 13 D6
Keizer, *U.S.A.* 108 D2
Kejimkujik △, *Canada* 105 D6
Kejserr Franz Joseph Fd.,
  Greenland 4 B6
Kekri, *India* 68 G6
Kelam, *Ethiopia* 81 G4
Kelamet, *Eritrea* 81 D4
Kelan, *China* 56 E6
Kelang = Klang, *Malaysia* 65 L3
Kelantan □, *Malaysia* 65 J4
Kelan ➜, *Malaysia* 65 J4
Kelan, *India* .... 66 65 c
Kelheim, *Germany* 25 G7
Kelibia, *Tunisia* 53 A1
Kelkit, *Turkey* 73 B8
Kelkit ➜, *Turkey* 72 B7
Kellerberrin, *Australia* 93 F2
Kellett, C., *Canada* 4 B1
Kelleys I., *U.S.A.* 116 E2
Kellogg, *U.S.A.* 108 C5
Kells = Ceanannus Mor, *Ireland* . 12 C5
Kelmė, *Lithuania* 30 C9
Kelmentsi, *Ukraine* 29 B11

Kelokedhara, *Cyprus* 49 E11
Kelowna, *Canada* 102 D5
Kelsey Creek, *Australia* 94 K3
Kelseyville, *U.S.A.* 110 G4
Kelso, *N.Z.* 91 L2
Kelso, *U.K.* 13 F6
Kelso, *U.S.A.* 110 D4
Keluang, *Malaysia* 65 L4
Kelvington, *Canada* 103 C8
Kem, *Russia* 52 C4
Kem ➜, *Russia* 52 C4
Kema, *Indonesia* 63 D7
Kemah, *Turkey* 70 B3
Kemaliye, Erzincan, *Turkey* 73 C8
Kemaliye, Manisa, *Turkey* 47 C10
Kemalpaşa, *Turkey* 47 C9
Kemaman, *Malaysia* 62 D2
Kemano, *Canada* 102 C3
Kemasik, *Malaysia* 65 K4
Kembolcha, *Ethiopia* 81 E4
Kemer, Antalya, *Turkey* 47 E12
Kemer, Burdur, *Turkey* 47 D12
Kemer, Muğla, *Turkey* 47 E11
Kemer Baraji, *Turkey* 47 D10
Kemerovo, *Russia* 52 D9
Kemeru △, *Latvia* 30 B10
Kemi, *Finland* 8 D21
Kemi älv = Kemijoki ➜, *Finland* . 8 D21
Kemi träsk = Kemijärvi, *Finland* . 8 C22
Kemijärvi, *Finland* 8 C22
Kemijoki ➜, *Finland* 8 D21
Kemmerer, *U.S.A.* 108 F8
Kemmuna = Comino, *Malta* 49 C1
Kemp, L., *U.S.A.* 113 J5
Kemp Land, *Antarctica* 5 C5
Kempas, *Malaysia* .... 65 d
Kempsey, *Australia* 95 E5
Kempt, L., *Canada* 104 C5
Kempten, *Germany* 25 H6
Kempton, *Australia* 95 G4
Kemptville, *Canada* 117 B9
Ken ➜, *India* 69 G9
Kenai, *U.S.A.* 100 B4
Kenamuke Swamp, *Sudan* 69 H10
Kendal, *Indonesia* 63 G14
Kendal, *U.K.* 14 C5
Kendall, *Australia* 95 E5
Kendall, *U.S.A.* 115 N5
Kendall ➜, *Australia* 94 A3
Kendallville, *U.S.A.* 114 E3
Kendari, *Indonesia* 63 E6
Kendawangan, *Indonesia* 62 E4
Kende, *Nigeria* 83 C5
Kendi, Pulau, *Malaysia* .... 65 c
Kendrapara, *India* 67 J15
Kendrew, *S. Africa* 88 E3
Kene Thao, *Laos* 64 C3
Kenedy, *U.S.A.* 113 L6
Kenema, *S. Leone* 82 D2
Keng Kok, *Laos* 64 D5
Keng Tawng, *Burma* 67 J21
Keng Tung, *Burma* 58 G2
Kengeja, *Tanzania* 86 D4
Kenhardt, *S. Africa* 88 D3
Kéniéba, *Mali* 82 C2
Kenitra, *Morocco* 78 B4
Kenli, *China* 57 F10
Kenmare, *Ireland* 12 E2
Kenmare, *U.S.A.* 112 A3
Kenmare River, *Ireland* 12 E2
Kennebago Lake, *U.S.A.* 117 A14
Kennebec, *U.S.A.* 112 D5
Kennebec ➜, *U.S.A.* 115 D11
Kennebunk, *U.S.A.* 117 C14
Kennedy, *Zimbabwe* 88 B4
Kennedy Ra., *Australia* 93 D2
Kennedy Range △, *Australia* 93 D2
Kenner, *U.S.A.* 113 L9
Kennet ➜, *U.K.* 15 F7
Kenneth Ra., *Australia* 93 D2
Kennett, *U.S.A.* 113 G9
Kennewick, *U.S.A.* 108 C4
Kenogami ➜, *Canada* 104 B3
Kenora, *Canada* 103 D10
Kenosha, *U.S.A.* 114 D2
Kensington, *Canada* 105 C7
Kent, Ohio, *U.S.A.* 116 E3
Kent, Tex., *U.S.A.* 113 K2
Kent, Wash., *U.S.A.* 110 C4
Kent □, *U.K.* 15 F8
Kent Group, *Australia* 95 F4
Kent Pen., *Canada* 100 B9
Kentau, *Kazakhstan* 52 E7
Kentland, *U.S.A.* 114 E2
Kenton, *U.S.A.* 114 E4
Kentucky □, *U.S.A.* 114 G3
Kentucky ➜, *U.S.A.* 114 F3
Kentucky L., *U.S.A.* 115 G2
Kentville, *Canada* 105 C7
Kentwood, *U.S.A.* 113 K9
Kenya ■, *Africa* 86 B4
Kenya, Mt., *Kenya* 86 C4
Keo Neua, Deo, *Vietnam* 64 C5
Keokuk, *U.S.A.* 112 E9
Keonjhargarh, *India* 69 J11
Kep, *Cambodia* 64 B6
Kep, *Vietnam* 64 B6
Kepala Batas, *Malaysia* .... 65 c
Kepez, *Turkey* 45 F10
Kepi, *Indonesia* 63 F9
Kępice, *Poland* 30 D3
Kępno, *Poland* 31 G4
Kepsut, *Turkey* 47 B10
Kerala □, *India* 66 P10
Kerama-Rettō, *Japan* 55 L3
Keran, *Pakistan* 69 B5
Keran △, *Togo* 83 C5
Kerang, *Australia* 95 F3
Keranyo, *Ethiopia* 81 F4
Kerao ➜, *Sudan* 81 E3
Keratéa, *Greece* 46 D5
Keraudren, C., *Australia* 92 C2

Kerava, Finland 9 F21
Kerch, Ukraine 33 K9
Kerchenskiy Proliv, Black Sea 33 K9
Kerchoual, Mali 83 B5
Kerempe Burnu, Turkey 72 A5
Keren, Eritrea 81 D4
Kerewan, Gambia 82 C1
Kerguelen, Ind. Oc. 3 G13
Keri, Greece 46 D2
Keri Kera, Sudan 81 E3
Kericho, Kenya 86 C4
Kerinci, Indonesia 62 E2
Kerki, Turkmenistan 52 F7
Kerkínitis, Límni, Greece 44 E7
Kérkira, Greece 49 A3
Kérkira □, Greece 46 B1
Kérkira ✈ (CFU), Greece 46 B1
Kerkouane, Tunisia 42 F4
Kerkrade, Neths. 17 D6
Kerma, Sudan 80 D3
Kermadec Is., Pac. Oc. 96 L10
Kermadec Trench, Pac. Oc. 96 L10
Kermān, Iran 71 D8
Kerman, U.S.A. 110 J6
Kermān □, Iran 71 D8
Kermān □, Iran 71 D8
Kermān, Bīābān-e, Iran 71 D8
Kermānshāh = Bākhtarān, Iran 70 C5
Kermen, Bulgaria 45 D10
Kermit, U.S.A. 113 K3
Kern ➤, U.S.A. 111 K7
Kernhof, Austria 26 D8
Kernow = Cornwall □, U.K. 15 G3
Kernville, U.S.A. 111 K8
Keroh, Malaysia 65 K3
Kérou, Benin 83 C5
Kérouane, Guinea 82 D3
Kerpen, Germany 24 E2
Kerrera, U.K. 13 E3
Kerrobert, Canada 103 C7
Kerrville, U.S.A. 113 K5
Kerry □, Ireland 12 D2
Kerry Hd., Ireland 12 D2
Kersa, Ethiopia 81 F5
Kerulen ➤, Asia 60 B6
Kervo = Kerava, Finland 9 F21
Kerzaz, Algeria 78 C5
Kesagami ➤, Canada 104 B4
Kesagami L., Canada 104 B3
Keşan, Turkey 45 F10
Kesennuma, Japan 54 E10
Keshit, Iran 71 D8
Keşiş Dağ, Turkey 73 C8
Keskin, Turkey 72 C5
Kestell, S. Africa 89 D4
Kestenga, Russia 52 C4
Keswick, U.K. 14 C4
Keszthely, Hungary 28 D2
Ket ➤, Russia 52 D9
Keta, Ghana 83 D5
Keta Lagoon, Ghana 83 D5
Ketapang, Bali, Indonesia 63 J17
Ketapang, Kalimantan, Indonesia 62 E4
Ketchenery, Russia 35 G7
Ketchikan, U.S.A. 102 B2
Ketchum, U.S.A. 108 E6
Kete Krachi, Ghana 83 D4
Ketef, Khalîg Umm el, Egypt 70 F2
Kétou, Benin 83 D5
Ketri, India 68 E6
Kętrzyn, Poland 30 D8
Kettering, U.K. 15 E7
Kettering, U.S.A. 114 F3
Kettle ➤, Canada 103 B11
Kettle Falls, U.S.A. 108 B4
Kettle Pt., Canada 116 C2
Kettleman City, U.S.A. 110 J7
Kęty, Poland 31 J6
Keuka L., U.S.A. 116 D7
Keuruu, Finland 9 E21
Kevelaer, Germany 24 D2
Kewanee, U.S.A. 112 E10
Kewaunee, U.S.A. 114 C2
Keweenaw B., U.S.A. 114 B1
Keweenaw Pen., U.S.A. 114 B2
Keweenaw Pt., U.S.A. 114 B2
Key Largo, U.S.A. 115 N5
Key West, U.S.A. 107 F10
Keyala, Sudan 81 G3
Keynsham, U.K. 15 F5
Keyser, U.S.A. 114 F6
Kezhma, Russia 53 D11
Kezi, Zimbabwe 89 C4
Kežmarok, Slovak Rep. 27 B13
Kgalagadi Transfrontier △, Africa 88 D3
Khabarovsk, Russia 53 E14
Khabr, Iran 71 D8
Khābūr ➤, Syria 70 C4
Khachmas = Xaçmaz, Azerbaijan 35 K9
Khachrod, India 68 H6
Khadari, W. el ➤, Sudan 81 E2
Khadro, Pakistan 68 F3
Khadyzhensk, Russia 35 H4
Khadzhilyangar, China 69 B8
Khaga, India 69 G9
Khagaria, India 69 G12
Khaipur, Pakistan 68 E5
Khair, India 68 F7
Khairabad, India 69 F9
Khairagarh, India 69 J9
Khairpur, Pakistan 68 F3
Khairpur Nathan Shah, Pakistan 68 F2
Khairwara, India 68 H5
Khaisor ➤, Pakistan 68 D3
Khajuri Kach, Pakistan 68 C3
Khakassia □, Russia 52 D9
Khakhea, Botswana 88 C3
Khalafābād, Iran 71 D6
Khalilabad, India 69 F10
Khalīlī, Iran 71 E7
Khalkhāl, Iran 71 B6
Khálki, Dhodhekánisos, Greece 47 E9

Khálki, Thessalía, Greece 46 B4
Khalkidhikí □, Greece 44 F7
Khalkís, Greece 46 C5
Khalmer Yu, Russia 52 C7
Khalūf, Oman 75 C6
Kham Keut, Laos 64 C5
Khamaria, India 69 H9
Khambhaliya, India 68 H3
Khambhat, India 68 H5
Khambhat, G. of, India 66 J8
Khamilonísion, Greece 47 F8
Khamīr, Iran 71 E7
Khamir, Yemen 75 D3
Khamsa, Egypt 74 E1
Khan ➤, Namibia 88 C2
Khān Abū Shāmat, Syria 74 B5
Khān Azād, Iraq 70 C5
Khān Mujiddah, Iraq 70 C4
Khān Shaykhūn, Syria 70 C3
Khān Yūnis, Gaza Strip 74 D3
Khanai, Pakistan 68 D2
Khānaqīn, Iraq 70 C5
Khānbāghī, Iran 71 B7
Khandrá, Greece 47 F8
Khandwa, India 66 J10
Khandyga, Russia 53 C14
Khāneh, Iran 70 B5
Khanewal, Pakistan 68 D4
Khangah Dogran, Pakistan 68 D5
Khanh Duong, Vietnam 64 F7
Khaniá, Greece 49 D6
Khaniá □, Greece 49 D6
Khaniadhana, India 68 G8
Khanion, Kólpos, Greece 49 D5
Khanka, L., Asia 53 E14
Khankendy = Xankändi, Azerbaijan 70 B5
Khanna, India 68 D7
Khanozai, Pakistan 68 D2
Khanpur, Pakistan 68 E4
Khanty-Mansiysk, Russia 52 C7
Khao Laem △, Thailand 64 E2
Khao Laem Res., Thailand 64 E2
Khao Luang △, Thailand 65 H2
Khao Phlu, Thailand 65 b
Khao Pu-Khao Ya △, Thailand 65 J2
Khao Sam Roi Yot △, Thailand 65 F2
Khao Sok △, Thailand 65 H2
Khao Yai △, Thailand 64 E3
Khaoen Si Nakarin △, Thailand 64 E2
Khapalu, Pakistan 69 B7
Khapcheranga, Russia 53 E12
Kharabali, Russia 35 G8
Kharaghoda, India 68 H4
Kharagpur, India 69 H12
Khárakas, Greece 49 D7
Kharan Kalat, Pakistan 66 E4
Kharānaq, Iran 71 C7
Kharda, India 66 K9
Khardung La, India 69 B7
Kharg = Khārk, Jazīreh-ye, Iran 71 D6
Khârga, El Wâhât-el, Egypt 80 B3
Khargon, India 66 J9
Khari ➤, India 68 G6
Kharian, Pakistan 68 C5
Kharit, Wadi el ➤, Egypt 80 C3
Khārk, Jazīreh-ye, Iran 71 D6
Kharkiv, Ukraine 33 H9
Kharkov = Kharkiv, Ukraine 33 H9
Kharmanli, Bulgaria 45 E9
Kharovsk, Russia 32 C11
Kharsawangarh, India 69 H11
Kharta, Turkey 72 B3
Khartoum = El Khartûm, Sudan 81 D3
Khasan, Russia 54 C5
Khasavyurt, Russia 35 J8
Khāsh, Iran 66 E2
Khashm el Girba, Sudan 81 E4
Khashum, Sudan 81 E2
Khashuri, Georgia 35 J6
Khaskovo, Bulgaria 45 E9
Khaskovo □, Bulgaria 45 E9
Khatanga, Russia 53 B11
Khatanga ➤, Russia 53 B11
Khatauli, India 68 E7
Khatra, India 69 H12
Khātūnābād, Iran 71 D7
Khatyrka, Russia 53 C18
Khavda, India 68 H3
Khaybar, Ḥarrat, Si. Arabia 70 E4
Khayelitsha, S. Africa 85 L3
Khāzimiyah, Iraq 70 C4
Khazzân Jabal al Awliyâ, Sudan 81 D3
Khe Bo, Vietnam 64 C5
Khe Long, Vietnam 64 B5
Khe Sanh, Vietnam 64 D6
Khed Brahma, India 66 G8
Khekra, India 68 E7
Khemarak Phouminville, Cambodia 65 G4
Khemisset, Morocco 78 B4
Khemmarat, Thailand 64 D5
Khenāmān, Iran 71 D8
Khenchela, Algeria 78 A7
Khersān ➤, Iran 71 D6
Khérson, Greece 44 E6
Kherson, Ukraine 33 J7
Khersónisos Akrotíri, Greece 49 D6
Kheta ➤, Russia 53 B11
Khewari, Pakistan 68 F3
Khilchipur, India 68 G7
Khiliomódhion, Greece 46 D4
Khilok, Russia 53 D12
Khimki, Russia 32 E9
Khíos, Greece 47 C8
Khíos □, Greece 47 C8
Khirsadoh, India 69 H8
Khiuma = Hiiumaa, Estonia 9 G20
Khiva, Uzbekistan 52 E7
Khīyāv, Iran 70 B5
Khlebarovo, Bulgaria 45 C10
Khlong Khlung, Thailand 64 D2

Khmelnik, Ukraine 33 H4
Khmelnitskiy = Khmelnytskyy, Ukraine 33 H4
Khmelnytskyy, Ukraine 33 H4
Khmer Rep. = Cambodia ■, Asia 64 F5
Khoai, Hon, Vietnam 65 H5
Khodoriv, Ukraine 33 H3
Khodzent = Khūjand, Tajikistan 52 E7
Khojak Pass, Afghan. 68 D2
Khok Kloi, Thailand 65 a
Khok Pho, Thailand 65 J3
Kholm, Russia 32 D6
Kholmsk, Russia 53 E15
Khomas Hochland, Namibia 88 C2
Khombole, Senegal 82 C1
Khomeyn, Iran 71 C6
Khomeynī Shahr, Iran 71 C6
Khomodino, Botswana 88 C3
Khon Kaen, Thailand 64 D4
Khong ➤, Cambodia 64 F5
Khong Sedone, Laos 64 E5
Khonuu, Russia 53 C15
Khoper ➤, Russia 34 F6
Khor el 'Atash, Sudan 81 E3
Khóra, Greece 46 D3
Khóra Sfakíon, Greece 49 D6
Khorāsān □, Iran 71 C8
Khorat = Nakhon Ratchasima, Thailand 64 E4
Khorat, Cao Nguyen, Thailand 64 E4
Khorixas, Namibia 88 C1
Khorol, Ukraine 33 H7
Khorramābād, Khorāsān, Iran 71 C8
Khorramābād, Lorestān, Iran 71 C6
Khorrāmshahr, Iran 71 D6
Khorugh, Tajikistan 52 F8
Khosravī, Iran 71 D6
Khosrowābād, Khuzestān, Iran 71 D6
Khosrowābād, Kordestān, Iran 70 C5
Khost, Pakistan 68 D2
Khosūyeh, Iran 71 D7
Khotyn, Ukraine 29 B11
Khouribga, Morocco 78 B4
Khowst, Afghan. 68 C3
Khowst □, Afghan. 66 C3
Khoyniki, Belarus 33 G5
Khrami ➤, Georgia 35 K7
Khrenovoye, Russia 34 E5
Khrisoúpolis, Greece 45 F8
Khristianá, Greece 47 E7
Khrysokhou B., Cyprus 49 D11
Khtapodhiá, Greece 47 D7
Khu Khan, Thailand 64 E5
Khuan Wa, Thailand 65 a
Khudzhand = Khūjand, Tajikistan 52 E7
Khuff, Si. Arabia 70 E5
Khūgīānī, Afghan. 68 D2
Khuis, Botswana 88 D3
Khuiyala, India 68 F4
Khūjand, Tajikistan 52 E7
Khujner, India 68 H7
Khulna, Bangla. 67 H16
Khulna □, Bangla. 67 H16
Khulo, Georgia 35 K6
Khumago, Botswana 88 C3
Khūnsorkh, Iran 71 E8
Khunti, India 69 H11
Khūr, Iran 71 C8
Khurai, India 68 G8
Khurayṣ, Si. Arabia 71 E6
Khureit, Sudan 81 E2
Khurīyā Murīyā, Jazā'ir, Oman 75 D6
Khurja, India 68 E7
Khūrmāl, Iraq 70 C5
Khurr, Wādī al, Iraq 70 C4
Khūsf, Iran 71 C8
Khush, Afghan. 66 C3
Khushab, Pakistan 68 C5
Khust, Ukraine 29 B8
Khutse △, Botswana 88 C3
Khuzdar, Pakistan 68 F2
Khūzestān □, Iran 71 D6
Khvāf, Iran 71 C9
Khvājeh, Iran 70 B5
Khvalynsk, Russia 34 D9
Khvānsār, Iran 71 D7
Khvatovka, Russia 34 D8
Khvor, Iran 71 C7
Khvorgū, Iran 71 E8
Khvormūj, Iran 71 D6
Khvoy, Iran 70 B5
Khvoynaya, Russia 32 C8
Khyriv, Ukraine 28
Kiabukwa, Dem. Rep. of the Congo 87 D1
Kiama, Australia 95 E5
Kiamba, Phil. 61 H6
Kiambi, Dem. Rep. of the Congo 86 D2
Kiambu, Kenya 86 C4
Kiang West △, Gambia 82 C1
Kiangara, Madag. 89 B8
Kiangsi = Jiangxi □, China 59 D11
Kiangsu = Jiangsu □, China 57 H11
Kiáton, Greece 46 C4
Kibæk, Denmark 11 H2
Kibale △, Uganda 86 B3
Kibanga Port, Uganda 86 B3
Kibara, Tanzania 86 C3
Kibare, Mts., Dem. Rep. of the Congo 86 D2
Kibira △, Burundi 86 C2
Kibombo, Dem. Rep. of the Congo 86 C2
Kibondo, Tanzania 86 C3
Kibre Mengist, Ethiopia 81 F4
Kibumbu, Burundi 86 C2
Kibungo, Rwanda 86 C3
Kibuye, Burundi 86 C2
Kibuye, Rwanda 86 C2
Kibwesa, Tanzania 86 D2
Kibwezi, Kenya 86 C4

Kicasalih, Turkey 45 E10
Kičevo, Macedonia 44 E4
Kichha, India 69 E8
Kichha ➤, India 69 E8
Kicking Horse Pass, Canada 102 C5
Kidal, Mali 83 B5
Kidderminster, U.K. 15 E5
Kidepo Valley △, Uganda 86 B3
Kidete, Tanzania 86 D4
Kidira, Senegal 82 C2
Kidnappers, C., N.Z. 91 H6
Kidsgrove, U.K. 14 D5
Kidston, Australia 94 B3
Kidugallo, Tanzania 86 D4
Kiel, Germany 24 A6
Kiel Canal = Nord-Ostsee-Kanal, Germany 24 A5
Kielce, Poland 31 H7
Kielder Water, U.K. 14 B5
Kieler Bucht, Germany 24 A6
Kiembara, Burkina Faso 82 C4
Kien Binh, Vietnam 65 H5
Kien Tan, Vietnam 65 G5
Kienge, Dem. Rep. of the Congo 87 E2
Kiessé, Niger 83 C5
Kiev = Kyyiv, Ukraine 33 G6
Kifaya, Guinea 82 C2
Kiffa, Mauritania 82 B2
Kifisiá, Greece 46 C5
Kifissós ➤, Greece 46 C5
Kifrī, Iraq 70 C5
Kigali, Rwanda 86 C3
Kigarama, Tanzania 86 C3
Kigelle, Sudan 81 F3
Kigezi △, Uganda 86 C2
Kigoma □, Tanzania 86 D3
Kigoma-Ujiji, Tanzania 86 C2
Kigomasha, Ras, Tanzania 86 C4
Kığızı, Turkey 70 B4
Kihei, U.S.A. 106 H16
Kihnu, Estonia 9 G21
Kii-Sanchi, Japan 55 G8
Kii-Suidō, Japan 55 H7
Kikaiga-Shima, Japan 55 K4
Kikinda, Serbia & M. 28 E5
Kikládhes □, Greece 46 E6
Kikládhes □, Greece 46 D6
Kikwit, Dem. Rep. of the Congo 84 E3
Kil, Sweden 10 E7
Kilafors, Sweden 10 C10
Kilar, India 68 C7
Kilauea Crater, U.S.A. 106 J17
Kilbrannan Sd., U.K. 13 F3
Kilchu, N. Korea 57 D15
Kilcoy, Australia 95 D5
Kildare, Ireland 12 C5
Kildare □, Ireland 12 C5
Kileikli, Sudan 81 E2
Kilfinnane, Ireland 12 D3
Kilgore, U.S.A. 113 J7
Kilibo, Benin 83 D5
Kilifi, Kenya 86 C4
Kilimanjaro, Tanzania 86 C4
Kilimanjaro □, Tanzania 86 C4
Kilimli, Turkey 72 B4
Kilindini, Kenya 86 C4
Kilis, Turkey 70 B3
Kiliya, Ukraine 29 E14
Kilkee, Ireland 12 D2
Kilkeel, U.K. 12 B5
Kilkenny, Ireland 12 D4
Kilkenny □, Ireland 12 D4
Kilkieran B., Ireland 12 C2
Kilkís, Greece 44 F6
Kilkís □, Greece 44 E6
Killala, Ireland 12 B2
Killala B., Ireland 12 B2
Killaloe, Canada 116 A7
Killaloe, Ireland 12 D3
Killarney, Australia 95 D5
Killarney, Canada 103 D9
Killarney, Ireland 12 D2
Killarney △, Ireland 12 D2
Killary Harbour, Ireland 12 C2
Killdeer, U.S.A. 112 B3
Killeberg, Sweden 11 H8
Killeen, U.S.A. 113 K6
Killin, U.K. 13 E4
Killíni, Ilía, Greece 46 D3
Killíni, Korinthía, Greece 46 D4
Killorglin, Ireland 12 D2
Killybegs, Ireland 12 B3
Kilmarnock, U.K. 13 F4
Kilmez, Russia 34 B10
Kilmez ➤, Russia 34 B10
Kilmore, Australia 95 F3
Kilondo, Tanzania 87 D3
Kilosa, Tanzania 86 D4
Kilrush, Ireland 12 D2
Kilwa Kisiwani, Tanzania 87 D4
Kilwa Kivinje, Tanzania 87 D4
Kilwa Masoko, Tanzania 87 D4
Kilwinning, U.K. 13 F4
Kim, U.S.A. 113 G3
Kim ➤, Cameroon 83 D7
Kimaam, Indonesia 63 F9
Kimamba, Tanzania 86 D4
Kimba, Australia 95 E2
Kimball, Nebr., U.S.A. 112 E3
Kimball, S. Dak., U.S.A. 112 D5
Kimberley, Australia 92 C4
Kimberley, Canada 102 D5
Kimberley, S. Africa 88 D3

Kimparana, Mali 82 C4
Kimpese, Dem. Rep. of the Congo 84 F2
Kimry, Russia 32 D9
Kimstad, Sweden 11 F9
Kinabalu, Gunung, Malaysia 62 C5
Kínaros, Greece 47 E8
Kinaskan L., Canada 102 B2
Kinbasket L., Canada 102 C5
Kincardine, Canada 116 B3
Kincolith, Canada 102 C3
Kinda, Dem. Rep. of the Congo 87 D2
Kindberg, Austria 26 D8
Kinde, U.S.A. 116 C2
Kinder Scout, U.K. 14 D6
Kindersley, Canada 103 C7
Kindia, Guinea 82 D2
Kindu, Dem. Rep. of the Congo 86 C2
Kinel, Russia 34 D10
Kineshma, Russia 34 B6
Kinesi, Tanzania 86 C3
King, L., Australia 93 F2
King, Mt., Australia 94 D4
King City, U.S.A. 110 J5
King Cr. ➤, Australia 94 C2
King Edward ➤, Australia 92 B4
King Frederick VI Land = Kong Frederik VI Kyst, Greenland 101 B15
King George B., Falk. Is. 128 G4
King George I., Antarctica 5 C18
King George Is., Canada 101 C11
King I. = Kadan Kyun, Burma 64 F2
King I., Australia 95 F3
King I., Canada 102 C3
King Leopold Ranges, Australia 92 C4
King of Prussia, U.S.A. 117 F9
King Sd., Australia 92 C3
King Sejong, Antarctica 5 C18
King William I., Canada 100 B10
King William's Town, S. Africa 88 E4
Kingait = Cape Dorset, Canada 101 B12
Kingaok = Bathurst Inlet, Canada 100 B9
Kingaroy, Australia 95 D5
Kingfisher, U.S.A. 113 H6
Kingirbān, Iraq 70 C5
Kingisepp = Kuressaare, Estonia 9 G20
Kingisepp, Russia 32 C5
Kingman, Ariz., U.S.A. 111 K12
Kingman, Kans., U.S.A. 113 G5
Kingoonya, Australia 95 E2
Kingri, Pakistan 68 D3
Kings ➤, U.S.A. 110 J7
Kings Canyon △, U.S.A. 110 J8
King's Lynn, U.K. 14 E8
Kings Mountain, U.S.A. 115 H5
Kings Park, U.S.A. 117 F11
King's Peak, U.S.A. 108 F8
Kingsbridge, U.K. 15 G4
Kingsburg, U.S.A. 110 J7
Kingscote, Australia 95 F2
Kingscourt, Ireland 12 C5
Kingsford, U.S.A. 114 C1
Kingsland, U.S.A. 115 K5
Kingsley, U.S.A. 112 D7
Kingsport, U.S.A. 115 G4
Kingston, Canada 117 B8
Kingston, Jamaica 120 a
Kingston, N.Z. 91 L2
Kingston, N.H., U.S.A. 117 D13
Kingston, N.Y., U.S.A. 117 E11
Kingston, Pa., U.S.A. 117 E9
Kingston, R.I., U.S.A. 117 E13
Kingston South East, Australia 95 F2
Kingston upon Hull, U.K. 14 D7
Kingston upon Hull □, U.K. 14 D7
Kingston-upon-Thames □, U.K. 15 F7
Kingstown, St. Vincent 121 D7
Kingstree, U.S.A. 115 J6
Kingsville, Canada 116 D2
Kingsville, U.S.A. 113 M6
Kingussie, U.K. 13 D4
Kingwood, U.S.A. 113 K7
Kınık, Antalya, Turkey 47 E11
Kınık, Izmir, Turkey 47 B9
Kinistino, Canada 103 C7
Kinkala, Congo 84 E2
Kinki □, Japan 55 H8
Kinleith, N.Z. 91 H5
Kinlochleven, U.K. 13 E4
Kinmount, Canada 116 B6
Kinna, Sweden 11 G6
Kinnairds Hd., U.K. 13 D6
Kinnared, Sweden 11 G7
Kinnarp, Sweden 11 F7
Kinneviken, Sweden 11 F7
Kino, Mexico 118 B2
Kinoje ➤, Canada 104 B3
Kinomoto, Japan 55 G8
Kinoni, Uganda 86 C3
Kinoosao, Canada 103 B8
Kinross, U.K. 13 E5
Kinsale, Ireland 12 E3
Kinsale, Old Hd. of, Ireland 12 E3
Kinsha = Chang Jiang ➤, China 59 B13
Kinshasa, Dem. Rep. of the Congo 84 E3
Kinsley, U.S.A. 113 G5
Kinsman, U.S.A. 116 E4
Kinston, U.S.A. 115 H7
Kintampo, Ghana 83 D4
Kintamani, Indonesia 63 J18
Kintore, U.K. 13 D6
Kintore Ra., Australia 92 D4
Kintyre, U.K. 13 F3
Kintyre, Mull of, U.K. 13 F3
Kinushseo ➤, Canada 104 A3
Kinuso, Canada 102 B5
Kinyangiri, Tanzania 86 C3
Kinyeti, Sudan 81 G3
Kinzig ➤, Germany 25 G3
Kinzua, U.S.A. 116 E6
Kinzua Dam, U.S.A. 116 E6
Kióni, Greece 46 C2

Kiosk, Canada 104 C4
Kiowa, Kans., U.S.A. 113 G5
Kiowa, Okla., U.S.A. 113 H7
Kipahigan L., Canada 103 B8
Kipanga, Tanzania 86 D4
Kiparissía, Greece 46 D3
Kiparissiakós Kólpos, Greece ... 46 D3
Kipawa, L., Canada 104 C4
Kipembawe, Tanzania 86 D3
Kipengere Ra., Tanzania 87 D3
Kipili, Tanzania 86 D3
Kipini, Kenya 86 C5
Kipling, Canada 103 C8
Kippure, Ireland 12 C5
Kipushi, Dem. Rep. of the Congo 87 E2
Kirane, Mali 82 B2
Kiranomena, Madag. 89 B8
Kiraz, Turkey 47 C10
Kirazlı, Turkey 45 F10
Kirchhain, Germany 24 E4
Kirchheim, Germany 25 G5
Kirchheimbolanden, Germany . 25 F3
Kirchschlag, Austria 27 D9
Kireç, Turkey 47 B10
Kirensk, Russia 53 D11
Kirghizia = Kyrgyzstan ■, Asia 52 E8
Kirghizstan = Kyrgyzstan ■, Asia 52 E8
Kiribati ■, Pac. Oc. 96 H10
Kırıkhan, Turkey 72 D7
Kırıkkale, Turkey 72 C5
Kirillov, Russia 32 C10
Kirin = Jilin, China 57 C14
Kirinyaga = Kenya, Mt., Kenya 86 C4
Kirishi, Russia 32 C7
Kirishima Yaku △, Japan ... 55 J5
Kiritimati, Kiribati 97 G12
Kırka, Turkey 47 B12
Kirkağaç, Turkey 47 B9
Kirkby, U.K. 14 D5
Kirkby-in-Ashfield, U.K. ... 14 D6
Kirkby Lonsdale, U.K. 14 C5
Kirkby Stephen, U.K. 14 C5
Kirkcaldy, U.K. 13 E5
Kirkcudbright, U.K. 13 G4
Kirkee, India 66 K8
Kirkenes, Norway 8 B23
Kirkfield, Canada 116 B6
Kirkintilloch, U.K. 13 F4
Kirkjubæjarklaustur, Iceland ... 8 E4
Kirkkonummi, Finland 9 F21
Kirkland Lake, Canada 104 C3
Kırklareli, Turkey 45 E11
Kırklareli □, Turkey 45 E11
Kirksville, U.S.A. 112 E8
Kirkük, Iraq 70 C5
Kirkwall, U.K. 13 C6
Kirkwood, S. Africa 88 E4
Kirn, Germany 25 F3
Kirov, Kaluga, Russia 32 E8
Kirov, Kirov, Russia 52 D5
Kirovabad = Gäncä, Azerbaijan 35 K8
Kirovograd = Kirovohrad, Ukraine ... 33 H7
Kirovohrad, Ukraine 33 H7
Kirovskiy, Astrakhan, Russia . 35 H9
Kirovskiy, Kamchatka, Russia . 53 D16
Kirovskiy, Primorsk, Russia . 54 B6
Kirriemuir, U.K. 13 E5
Kirsanov, Russia 34 D6
Kırşehir, Turkey 70 B2
Kirtachi, Niger 83 C5
Kirthar Range, Pakistan ... 68 F2
Kirtland, U.S.A. 109 H9
Kiruna, Sweden 8 C18
Kirundu, Dem. Rep. of the Congo 86 C2
Kirya, Russia 34 C8
Kiryū, Japan 55 F9
Kisa, Sweden 11 G9
Kisaga, Tanzania 86 C3
Kisalaya, Nic. 120 D3
Kisalföld, Hungary 28 C2
Kisámou, Kólpos, Greece ... 49 D5
Kisanga, Dem. Rep. of the Congo 86 B2
Kisangani, Dem. Rep. of the Congo ... 86 B2
Kisar, Indonesia 63 F7
Kisarawe, Tanzania 86 D4
Kisarazu, Japan 55 G9
Kisbér, Hungary 28 C3
Kishanganga →, Pakistan ... 69 B5
Kishanganj, India 69 F13
Kishangarh, Raj., India ... 68 F6
Kishangarh, Raj., India ... 68 F4
Kishi, Nigeria 83 D5
Kishinev = Chişinău, Moldova 29 C13
Kishiwada, Japan 55 G7
Kishtwar, India 69 C6
Kisielice, Poland 30 E6
Kisigo →, Tanzania 86 D3
Kisii, Kenya 86 C3
Kisiju, Tanzania 86 D4
Kisir, Turkey 73 B10
Kisizi, Uganda 86 C2
Kiskomárom = Zalakomár, Hungary ... 28 D2
Kiskőrei-víztároló, Hungary . 28 C5
Kiskőrös, Hungary 28 D4
Kiskundorozsma, Hungary .. 28 D5
Kiskunfélegyháza, Hungary . 28 D4
Kiskunhalas, Hungary 28 D4
Kiskunmajsa, Hungary 28 D4
Kiskunsági △, Hungary 28 D4
Kislovodsk, Russia 35 J6
Kismayu = Chisimaio, Somali Rep. ... 77 G8
Kiso-Gawa →, Japan 55 G8
Kiso-Sammyaku, Japan 55 G8
Kisofukushima, Japan 55 G8
Kisoro, Uganda 86 C2
Kissidougou, Guinea 82 D2
Kissimmee, U.S.A. 115 L5
Kissimmee →, U.S.A. 115 M5

Kississing L., Canada 103 B8
Kissónerga, Cyprus 49 E11
Kissu, J., Sudan 80 C2
Kistanje, Croatia 41 E12
Kisújszállás, Hungary 28 C5
Kisumu, Kenya 86 C3
Kisvárda, Hungary 28 B7
Kiswani, Tanzania 86 C4
Kiswere, Tanzania 87 D4
Kit Carson, U.S.A. 112 F3
Kita, Mali 82 C3
Kitaibaraki, Japan 55 F10
Kitakami, Japan 54 E10
Kitakami-Gawa →, Japan .. 54 E10
Kitakami-Sammyaku, Japan . 54 E10
Kitakata, Japan 54 F9
Kitakyūshū, Japan 55 H5
Kitale, Kenya 86 B4
Kitami, Japan 54 C11
Kitami-Sammyaku, Japan ... 54 B11
Kitangiri, L., Tanzania 86 C3
Kitaya, Tanzania 87 E5
Kitchener, Canada 116 C4
Kitee, Finland 32 A6
Kitega = Gitega, Burundi .. 86 C2
Kitengo, Dem. Rep. of the Congo 86 D1
Kitgum, Uganda 86 B3
Kíthira, Greece 46 E5
Kíthnos, Greece 46 D6
Kiti, Cyprus 49 E12
Kiti, C., Cyprus 49 E12
Kitimat, Canada 102 C3
Kitinen →, Finland 8 C22
Kitiyab, Sudan 81 D3
Kítros, Greece 44 F6
Kitsman, Ukraine 29 B10
Kitsuki, Japan 55 H5
Kittakittaooloo, L., Australia . 95 D2
Kittanning, U.S.A. 116 F5
Kittatinny Mts., U.S.A. ... 117 F10
Kittery, U.S.A. 115 D10
Kittilä, Finland 8 C21
Kitui, Kenya 86 C4
Kitwanga, Canada 102 B3
Kitwe, Zambia 87 E2
Kitzbühel, Austria 26 D5
Kitzbühler Alpen, Austria .. 26 D5
Kitzingen, Germany 25 F6
Kivarli, India 68 G5
Kivertsi, Ukraine 33 G3
Kividhes, Cyprus 49 E11
Kivik, Sweden 11 J8
Kivotós, Greece 44 F5
Kivu, L., Dem. Rep. of the Congo 86 C2
Kiyev = Kyyiv, Ukraine 33 G6
Kiyevskoye Vdkhr. = Kyyivske Vdskh., Ukraine ... 33 G6
Kıyıköy, Turkey 45 E12
Kızıl Adalar, Turkey 45 F13
Kızıl Irmak →, Turkey 72 B6
Kizil Jilga, China 69 B8
Kizil Yurt, Russia 35 J8
Kızılcabölük, Turkey 47 D11
Kızılcadağ, Turkey 47 D11
Kızılcahamam, Turkey 72 B5
Kızılhisar, Turkey 72 D3
Kızılırmak, Turkey 72 B5
Kızılkaya, Turkey 47 D12
Kızılören, Turkey 47 C12
Kızıltepe, Turkey 70 B4
Kizimkazi, Tanzania 86 D4
Kizlyar, Russia 35 J8
Kizyl-Arvat = Gyzylarbat, Turkmenistan ... 52 F6
Kjellerup, Denmark 11 H3
Kjölur, Iceland 8 D4
Kladanj, Bos.-H. 28 F3
Kladnica, Serbia & M. 44 C4
Kladno, Czech Rep. 26 A7
Kladovo, Serbia & M. 44 B6
Klaeng, Thailand 64 F3
Klagenfurt, Austria 26 E7
Klagshamn, Sweden 11 J6
Klaipėda, Lithuania 9 J19
Klaipėda □, Lithuania 30 C8
Klaksvík, Faeroe Is. 8 E9
Klamath →, U.S.A. 108 F1
Klamath Falls, U.S.A. 108 E3
Klamath Mts., U.S.A. 108 F2
Klamono, Indonesia 63 E8
Klang, Malaysia 65 L3
Klanjec, Croatia 41 B12
Klappan →, Canada 102 B3
Klarälven →, Sweden 10 E7
Klässbol, Sweden 10 E6
Klatovy, Czech Rep. 26 B6
Klawer, S. Africa 88 E2
Klazienaveen, Neths. 17 B6
Klé, Mali 82 C3
Klecko, Poland 31 F4
Kleczew, Poland 31 F5
Kleena Kleene, Canada ... 102 C4
Klein-Karas, Namibia 88 D2
Klekovača, Bos.-H. 41 D13
Klembivka, Ukraine 29 B13
Klenoec, Macedonia 44 E4
Klenovec, Slovak Rep. 27 C12
Klerksdorp, S. Africa 88 D4
Kletnya, Russia 32 F7
Kletsk = Klyetsk, Belarus . 33 F4
Kletskiy, Russia 35 F6
Kleve, Germany 24 D2
Klickitat, U.S.A. 108 D3
Klickitat →, U.S.A. 110 E5
Klidhes, Cyprus 49 D13
Klimovichi, Belarus 32 F6
Klin, Russia 32 D9
Klina, Serbia & M. 44 D4
Klinaklini →, Canada 102 C3
Klintehamn, Sweden 11 G12
Klintsy, Russia 33 F7

Klip →, S. Africa 89 D4
Klipdale, S. Africa 88 E2
Klippan, Sweden 11 H7
Klipplaat, S. Africa 88 E3
Klisura, Bulgaria 45 D8
Kljajićevo, Serbia & M. ... 28 E4
Ključ, Bos.-H. 41 D13
Kłobuck, Poland 31 H5
Klockestrand, Sweden 10 B11
Kłodawa, Poland 31 F5
Kłodzko, Poland 31 H3
Klong Wang Chao △, Thailand 64 D2
Klos, Albania 44 E4
Klosterneuburg, Austria ... 27 C9
Klosters, Switz. 25 J5
Klötze, Germany 24 C7
Klouto, Togo 83 D5
Kluane △, Canada 102 A1
Kluane L., Canada 100 B6
Kluczbork, Poland 31 H5
Klukwan, U.S.A. 102 B1
Klungkung, Indonesia 63 K18
Klyetsk, Belarus 33 F4
Klyuchevskaya, Gora, Russia 53 D17
Knäred, Sweden 11 H7
Knaresborough, U.K. 14 C6
Knee L., Man., Canada ... 104 A1
Knee L., Sask., Canada ... 103 B7
Knezha, Bulgaria 45 C8
Knight Inlet, Canada 102 C3
Knighton, U.K. 15 E4
Knights Ferry, U.S.A. 110 H6
Knights Landing, U.S.A. .. 110 G5
Knin, Croatia 41 D13
Knislinge, Sweden 11 H8
Knittelfeld, Austria 26 D7
Knivsta, Sweden 10 E11
Knjaževac, Serbia & M. .. 44 C6
Knob, C., Australia 93 F2
Knock, Ireland 12 C3
Knockmealdown Mts., Ireland 12 D4
Knokke-Heist, Belgium ... 17 C3
Knossós, Greece 49 D7
Knowlton, Canada 117 A12
Knox, U.S.A. 114 E2
Knox Coast, Antarctica ... 5 C8
Knoxville, Iowa, U.S.A. ... 112 E8
Knoxville, Pa., U.S.A. 116 E7
Knoxville, Tenn., U.S.A. .. 115 H4
Knud Rasmussen Land, Greenland ... 4 A5
Knysna, S. Africa 88 E3
Knyszyn, Poland 30 E9
Ko Kha, Thailand 64 C2
Ko Tarutao △, Thailand .. 65 J2
Ko Yao, Thailand .... 65 a
Koartac = Quaqtaq, Canada 101 B13
Koba, Indonesia 63 F8
Kobarid, Slovenia 41 B10
Kobayashi, Japan 55 J5
Kōbe, Japan 55 G7
Kobelyaky, Ukraine 33 H8
København, Denmark 11 J6
København ✈ (CPH), Denmark . 11 J6
Københavns Amtskommune □, Denmark ... 11 J6
Kobenni, Mauritania 82 B3
Kōbi-Sho, Japan 55 M1
Koblenz, Germany 25 E3
Kobo, Ethiopia 81 E4
Kobryn, Belarus 33 F3
Kobuleti, Georgia 35 K5
Kobylin, Poland 31 G4
Kobyłka, Poland 31 F8
Kobylkino, Russia 34 C6
Koca →, Turkey 45 F11
Kocabaş, Turkey 47 D11
Kocaeli, Turkey 45 F13
Kocaeli □, Turkey 45 F13
Kočane, Serbia & M. 44 C5
Kočani, Macedonia 44 E6
Koçarlı, Turkey 47 D9
Koceljevo, Serbia & M. .. 44 B3
Kočevje, Slovenia 41 C11
Koch Bihar, India 67 F16
Kochang, S. Korea 57 G14
Kochas, India 69 G10
Kocher →, Germany 25 F5
Kochi = Cochin, India ... 66 Q10
Kōchi, Japan 55 H6
Kōchi □, Japan 55 H6
Kochiu = Gejiu, China ... 58 F4
Kock, Poland 31 G9
Kodarma, India 69 G11
Kode, Sweden 11 G5
Kodiak, U.S.A. 100 C4
Kodiak I., U.S.A. 100 C4
Kodinar, India 68 J4
Kodok, Sudan 81 F3
Kodori →, Georgia 35 J5
Kodyma, Ukraine 29 B14
Koedoesberge, S. Africa .. 88 E3
Koes, Namibia 88 D2
Kofçaz, Turkey 45 E11
Koffiefontein, S. Africa .. 88 D4
Kofiau, Indonesia 63 E7
Köflach, Austria 26 D8
Koforidua, Ghana 83 D4
Kōfu, Japan 55 G9
Koga, Japan 55 F9
Kogaluc →, Canada 105 A7
Køge, Denmark 11 J6
Køge Bugt, Denmark 11 J6
Kogi □, Nigeria 83 D6
Kogin Baba, Nigeria 83 D7
Koh-i-Khurd, Afghan. ... 68 C1
Koh-i-Maran, Pakistan .. 68 E2
Kohat, Pakistan 68 C4
Kohima, India 67 G19

Kohkīlūyeh va Būyer Aḥmadī □, Iran ... 71 D6
Kohler Ra., Antarctica ... 5 D15
Kohlu, Pakistan 68 E3
Kohtla-Järve, Estonia 9 G22
Kohylnyk →, Ukraine 29 E14
Koi Sanjaq, Iraq 70 B5
Koin-dong, N. Korea 57 D14
Koinare, Bulgaria 45 C8
Koindu, S. Leone 82 D2
Kojetín, Czech Rep. 27 B10
Kojŏ, N. Korea 57 E14
Kojonup, Australia 93 F2
Kojūr, Iran 71 B6
Koka, Sudan 80 C3
Kokand = Qŭqon, Uzbekistan 52 E8
Kokas, Indonesia 63 E8
Kokava, Slovak Rep. 27 C12
Kokchetav = Kökshetaū, Kazakhstan ... 52 D7
Kokemäenjoki →, Finland . 9 F19
Kokhma, Russia 34 B5
Koki, Senegal 82 B1
Kokkola, Finland 8 E20
Koko, Nigeria 83 C5
Koko Kyunzu, Burma 67 M18
Kokolopozo, Ivory C. 82 D3
Kokomo, U.S.A. 114 E2
Kokoro, Niger 83 C5
Koksan, N. Korea 57 E14
Kökshetaū, Kazakhstan .. 52 D7
Koksoak →, Canada 101 C13
Kokstad, S. Africa 89 E4
Kokubu, Japan 55 J5
Kola, Indonesia 63 F8
Kola Pen. = Kolskiy Poluostrov, Russia ... 52 C4
Kolachi →, Pakistan 68 F2
Kolahoi, India 69 B6
Kolahun, Liberia 82 D2
Kolaka, Indonesia 63 E6
Kolar, India 66 N11
Kolar Gold Fields, India . 66 N11
Kolaras, India 68 G6
Kolari, Finland 8 C20
Kolárovo, Slovak Rep. ... 27 D10
Kolašin, Serbia & M. ... 44 D3
Kolayat, India 68 F8
Kolback, Sweden 10 E10
Kolbäckån →, Sweden .. 10 E10
Kolbermoor, Germany ... 25 H8
Kolbuszowa, Poland 31 H8
Kolchugino, Russia 32 D10
Kolda, Senegal 82 C2
Koldegi, Sudan 81 E3
Kolding, Denmark 11 J3
Kolepom = Dolak, Pulau, Indonesia ... 63 F9
Kolguyev, Ostrov, Russia . 52 C5
Kolhapur, India 66 L9
Kolia, Ivory C. 82 D3
Kolín, Czech Rep. 26 A8
Kolind, Denmark 11 H4
Kolkas rags, Latvia 9 H20
Kolkata, India 69 H13
Kollam = Quilon, India .. 66 Q10
Kölleda, Germany 24 D7
Kollum, Neths. 17 A6
Kolmanskop, Namibia ... 88 D2
Köln, Germany 24 E2
Kolno, Poland 30 E8
Koło, Poland 31 F5
Kołobrzeg, Poland 30 D2
Kolochava, Ukraine 29 B8
Kolokani, Mali 82 C3
Koloko, Burkina Faso ... 82 C3
Kololo, Ethiopia 81 F5
Kolomna, Russia 32 E10
Kolomyya, Ukraine 29 B10
Kolondiéba, Mali 82 C3
Kolonodale, Indonesia .. 63 E6
Kolonowskie, Poland ... 31 H5
Kolosib, India 67 G18
Kolpashevo, Russia 52 D9
Kolpino, Russia 32 C6
Kolpny, Russia 33 F9
Kolskiy Poluostrov, Russia 52 C4
Kolsva, Sweden 10 E9
Kolubara →, Serbia & M. . 44 B4
Koluszki, Poland 31 G6
Kolwezi, Dem. Rep. of the Congo 87 E2
Kolyma →, Russia 53 C17
Kolymskoye Nagorye, Russia 53 C16
Kôm Hamâda, Egypt 80 H7
Kôm Ombo, Egypt 80 C3
Komadugu Gana →, Nigeria 83 C7
Komandorskiye Is. = Komandorskiye Ostrova, Russia ... 53 D17
Komandorskiye Ostrova, Russia 53 D17
Komárno, Slovak Rep. ... 27 D11
Komárom, Hungary 28 C3
Komárom-Esztergom □, Hungary 28 C3
Komatipoort, S. Africa ... 89 D5
Komatou Yialou, Cyprus .. 49 D13
Komatsu, Japan 55 F8
Komatsushima, Japan ... 55 H7
Kombissiri, Burkina Faso . 83 C4
Kombori, Burkina Faso .. 82 C4
Kombóti, Greece 46 B3
Komen, Slovenia 41 C10
Komenda, Ghana 83 D4
Komi □, Russia 52 C6
Komiža, Croatia 41 E13
Komló, Hungary 28 D3
Kommunars = Alchevsk, Ukraine ... 33 H10
Kommunizma, Pik, Tajikistan 52 F8
Komodo, Indonesia 63 F5
Komoé →, Ivory C. 82 D4

Komoran, Pulau, Indonesia . 63 F9
Komoro, Japan 55 F9
Komotini, Greece 45 E9
Komovi, Serbia & M. 44 D3
Kompasberg, S. Africa ... 88 E3
Kompong Bang, Cambodia . 65 F5
Kompong Cham, Cambodia . 65 F5
Kompong Chhnang = Kampong Chhnang, Cambodia ... 65 F5
Kompong Chikreng, Cambodia 64 F5
Kompong Kleang, Cambodia 64 F5
Kompong Luong, Cambodia 65 G5
Kompong Pranak, Cambodia 64 F5
Kompong Som = Kampong Saom, Cambodia ... 65 G4
Kompong Som, Chhung = Kampong Saom, Chaak, Cambodia ... 65 G4
Kompong Speu, Cambodia .. 65 G5
Kompong Sralau, Cambodia 64 E5
Kompong Thom, Cambodia . 64 F5
Kompong Trabeck, Cambodia 64 F5
Kompong Trabeck, Cambodia 65 G5
Kompong Trach, Cambodia . 65 G5
Kompong Tralach, Cambodia 65 G5
Komrat = Comrat, Moldova 29 D13
Komsberg, S. Africa 88 E3
Komsomolets, Ostrov, Russia 53 A10
Komsomolsk, Amur, Russia 53 D14
Komsomolsk, Ivanovo, Russia 32 D11
Komsomolskiy, Russia ... 34 C7
Kömür Burnu, Turkey 47 C8
Kon Tum, Vietnam 64 E7
Kon Tum, Plateau du, Vietnam 64 E7
Kona, Mali 82 C4
Konakovo, Russia 32 D9
Konarhā □, Afghan. 66 B7
Konārī, Iran 71 D6
Konch, India 69 G8
Konde, Tanzania 86 C4
Kondiá, Greece 47 B7
Kondinin, Australia 93 F2
Kondoa, Tanzania 86 C4
Kondópaga, Russia 32 A8
Kondratyevo, Russia 53 D10
Kondrovo, Russia 32 E8
Konduga, Nigeria 83 C7
Köneürgench, Turkmenistan 52 E6
Konevo, Russia 32 A10
Kong = Khong →, Cambodia 64 E5
Kong, Ivory C. 82 D4
Kong, Koh, Cambodia ... 65 G4
Kong Christian IX Land, Greenland ... 4 C6
Kong Christian X Land, Greenland ... 4 B6
Kong Frederik IX Land, Greenland ... 4 C5
Kong Frederik VI Kyst, Greenland ... 101 B15
Kong Frederik VIII Land, Greenland ... 4 B6
Kong Oscar Fjord, Greenland 4 B6
Kongeå →, Denmark 11 J2
Kongerslev, Denmark 11 H4
Kongju, S. Korea 57 F14
Konglu, Burma 67 F20
Kongola, Namibia 88 B3
Kongolo, Kasai-Or., Dem. Rep. of the Congo ... 86 D1
Kongolo, Katanga, Dem. Rep. of the Congo ... 86 D2
Kongor, Sudan 81 F3
Kongoussi, Burkina Faso .. 83 C4
Kongsberg, Norway 9 G13
Kongsvinger, Norway 9 F15
Kongwa, Tanzania 86 D4
Koni, Dem. Rep. of the Congo 87 E2
Koni, Mts., Dem. Rep. of the Congo ... 87 E2
Koniakari, Mali 82 C2
Koniecpol, Poland 31 H6
Königs Wusterhausen, Germany 24 C9
Königsbrunn, Germany ... 25 G6
Königslutter, Germany ... 24 C6
Konin, Poland 31 F5
Konispol, Albania 44 G4
Kónitsa, Greece 46 A2
Konjic, Bos.-H. 28 G2
Konkiep, Namibia 88 D2
Konkouré →, Guinea ... 82 D2
Könnern, Germany 24 D7
Kono, S. Leone 82 D2
Konongo, Ghana 83 D4
Konosha, Russia 32 B11
Kōnosu, Japan 55 F9
Konotop, Ukraine 33 G7
Konsankoro, Guinea 82 D3
Końskie, Poland 31 G7
Konstancin-Jeziorna, Poland 31 F8
Konstantinovka = Kostyantynivka, Ukraine .. 33 H9
Konstantinovsk, Russia .. 35 G5
Konstantynów Łódźki, Poland 31 G6
Konstanz, Germany 25 H5
Kont, Iran 71 E9
Kontagora, Nigeria 83 C6
Kontcha, Cameroon 83 D7
Konya, Turkey 70 B2
Konya Ovası, Turkey 72 C5
Konz, Germany 25 F2
Konza, Kenya 86 C4
Koocanusa, L., Canada .. 108 B6
Wookynie, Australia 93 E3
Woolyanobbing, Australia 93 F2
Wooniba, Australia 95 E1
Woorawatha, Australia .. 95 E4
Woorda, Australia 93 F2
Wooskia, U.S.A. 108 C6
Kootenay △, Canada ... 102 C5
Kootenay →, U.S.A. ... 102 D5

Kootenay L., *Canada* 102 D5
Kootjieskolk, *S. Africa* 88 E3
Kopanovka, *Russia* 35 G8
Kopaonik, *Serbia & M.* 44 C4
Kopaonik △, *Serbia & M.* 44 C4
Kópavogur, *Iceland* 8 D3
Kopayhorod, *Ukraine* 29 B12
Koper, *Slovenia* 41 C10
Kopervik, *Norway* 9 G11
Kopet Dagh, *Asia* 71 B8
Kopi, *Australia* 95 E2
Köping, *Sweden* 10 E10
Köpingsvik, *Sweden* 11 H10
Kopište, *Croatia* 41 F13
Koplik, *Albania* 44 D3
Köpmanholmen, *Sweden* 10 A12
Kopparberg, *Sweden* 10 E9
Koppeh Dāgh = Kopet Dagh,
  Asia 71 B8
Koppies, *S. Africa* 89 D4
Koppom, *Sweden* 10 E6
Koprivlen, *Bulgaria* 44 E7
Koprivnica, *Croatia* 41 B13
Kopřivnice, *Czech Rep.* 27 B11
Koprivshtitsa, *Bulgaria* 45 D8
Köprübaşı, *Turkey* 47 C10
Kopychyntsi, *Ukraine* 33 H3
Kora △, *Kenya* 86 C4
Korab, *Macedonia* 44 E4
Korakiána, *Greece* 49 A3
Koral, *India* 68 J5
Korarou, L., *Mali* 82 B4
Korba, *India* 69 H10
Korbach, *Germany* 24 D4
Korbu, △, *Malaysia* 65 K3
Korçë, *Albania* 44 F4
Korčula, *Croatia* 41 F13
Korčulanski Kanal, *Croatia* .. 41 E13
Kord Kūy, *Iran* 71 B7
Kord Sheykh, *Iran* 71 D7
Kordestan = Kurdistan, *Asia* .. 73 D10
Kordestān □, *Iran* 70 C5
Kordofân, *Sudan* 79 F11
Koré Mayroua, *Niger* 83 C5
Korea, North ■, *Asia* 57 E14
Korea, South ■, *Asia* 57 G15
Korea Bay, *Korea* 57 E13
Korea Strait, *Asia* 57 H15
Korem, *Ethiopia* 81 E4
Korenevo, *Russia* 33 G8
Korenovsk, *Russia* 35 H4
Korets, *Ukraine* 33 G4
Korfantów, *Poland* 31 H4
Korgan, *Turkey* 72 B7
Korgus, *Sudan* 80 D3
Korhogo, *Ivory C.* 82 D3
Koribundu, *S. Leone* 82 D2
Korienzé, *Mali* 82 B4
Korinthía, *Greece* 46 D4
Korinthiakós Kólpos, *Greece* .. 46 C4
Kórinthos, *Greece* 46 D4
Korioumé, *Mali* 82 B4
Koríssa, Límni, *Greece* 49 B3
Kōriyama, *Japan* 54 F10
Korkuteli, *Turkey* 47 D12
Körmend, *Hungary* 28 C1
Kornat, *Croatia* 41 E12
Kornat △, *Croatia* 41 E12
Korneshty = Corneşti, *Moldova* .. 29 C13
Korneuburg, *Austria* 27 C9
Kórnik, *Poland* 31 F4
Koro, *Fiji* 91 C8
Koro, *Ivory C.* 82 D3
Koro, *Mali* 82 C4
Koro Sea, *Fiji* 91 C9
Korocha, *Russia* 33 G9
Köroğlu Dağları, *Turkey* 72 B5
Korogwe, *Tanzania* 86 D4
Koroleve, *Ukraine* 29 B8
Koronadal, *Phil.* 61 H6
Koróni, *Greece* 46 E3
Korónia, Limni, *Greece* 44 F7
Koronís, *Greece* 47 D7
Koronowo, *Poland* 31 E4
Koropets, *Ukraine* 29 B10
Koror, *Palau* 96 G5
Körös →, *Hungary* 28 D5
Körös Maros △, *Hungary* 28 D5
Köröstarcsa, *Hungary* 28 D6
Korosten, *Ukraine* 33 G5
Korostyshev, *Ukraine* 33 G5
Korotoyak, *Russia* 33 G10
Korraraika, Helodranon' i,
  Madag. 89 B7
Korsakov, *Russia* 53 E15
Korsberga, *Sweden* 11 G9
Korshiv, *Ukraine* 29 B10
Korshunovo, *Russia* 53 D12
Korsør, *Denmark* 11 J5
Korsun Shevchenkovskiy,
  Ukraine 33 H6
Korsze, *Poland* 30 D8
Korti, *Sudan* 80 D3
Kortrijk, *Belgium* 17 D3
Korucu, *Turkey* 47 B9
Korwai, *India* 68 G8
Koryakskoye Nagorye, *Russia* .. 53 C18
Koryŏng, *S. Korea* 57 G15
Koryukovka, *Ukraine* 33 G7
Kos, *Greece* 47 E9
Kosa, *Ethiopia* 81 F4
Kosaya Gora, *Russia* 32 E9
Kościan, *Poland* 31 F3
Kościerzyna, *Poland* 30 D4
Kosciusko, *U.S.A.* 113 J10
Kosciuszko, Mt., *Australia* .. 95 F4
Kösély →, *Hungary* 28 C6
Kosha, *Sudan* 80 C3
Koshava, *Bulgaria* 44 B7
K'oshih = Kashi, *China* 60 C2
Koshiki-Rettō, *Japan* 55 J4

Kosi, *India* 68 F7
Kosi →, *India* 69 E8
Košice, *Slovak Rep.* 27 C14
Košický □, *Slovak Rep.* 27 C14
Kosiv, *Ukraine* 29 B10
Kosjerić, *Serbia & M.* 44 B3
Köşk, *Turkey* 47 D10
Koskinoú, *Greece* 49 C10
Koslan, *Russia* 52 C5
Kosmach, *Ukraine* 29 B9
Kosŏng, *N. Korea* 57 E15
Kosovo □, *Serbia & M.* 44 D4
Kosovo Polje, *Serbia & M.* .. 44 D5
Kosovska Kamenica, *Serbia & M.* .. 44 D5
Kosovska Mitrovica, *Serbia & M.* .. 44 D4
Kossou, L. de, *Ivory C.* 82 D3
Kosta, *Sweden* 11 H9
Kostajnica, *Croatia* 41 C13
Kostanjevica, *Slovenia* 41 C12
Kostenets, *Bulgaria* 44 D7
Koster, *S. Africa* 88 D4
Kôstî, *Sudan* 81 E3
Kostinbrod, *Bulgaria* 44 D7
Kostolac, *Serbia & M.* 44 B5
Kostopil, *Ukraine* 33 G4
Kostroma, *Russia* 32 D11
Kostromskoye Vdkhr., *Russia* .. 32 D11
Kostrzhivka, *Ukraine* 29 B10
Kostrzyn, *Lubuskie, Poland* .. 31 F1
Kostrzyn, *Wielkopolskie, Poland* .. 31 F4
Kostyantynivka, *Ukraine* 33 H9
Kostyukovichi = Kastsyukovichy,
  Belarus 32 F7
Koszalin, *Poland* 30 D3
Kőszeg, *Hungary* 28 C1
Kot Addu, *Pakistan* 68 D4
Kot Kapura, *India* 68 D6
Kot Moman, *Pakistan* 68 C5
Kot Sultan, *Pakistan* 68 D4
Kota, *India* 68 G6
Kota Barrage, *India* 68 G6
Kota Belud, *Malaysia* 62 C5
Kota Bharu, *Malaysia* 65 J4
Kota Kinabalu, *Malaysia* 62 C5
Kota Kubu Bharu, *Malaysia* .. 65 L3
Kota Tinggi, *Malaysia* 65 M4
Kotaagung, *Indonesia* 62 F2
Kotabaru, *Indonesia* 62 E5
Kotabumi, *Indonesia* 62 E2
Kotamobagu, *Indonesia* 63 D6
Kotcho L., *Canada* 102 B4
Kotdwara, *India* 69 E8
Kotel, *Bulgaria* 45 D10
Kotelnich, *Russia* 34 A9
Kotelnikovo, *Russia* 35 G6
Kotelnyy, Ostrov, *Russia* .. 53 B14
Kothari →, *India* 68 G6
Köthen, *Germany* 24 D7
Kothi, *Chhattisgarh, India* .. 69 H10
Kothi, *Mad. P., India* 69 G9
Kotiro, *Pakistan* 68 F2
Kotka, *Finland* 9 F22
Kotlas, *Russia* 52 C5
Kotlenska Planina, *Bulgaria* .. 45 D10
Kotli, *Pakistan* 68 C5
Kotma, *India* 69 H9
Kotmul, *Pakistan* 69 B6
Koton-Karifi, *Nigeria* 83 D6
Kotonkoro, *Nigeria* 83 C6
Kotor, *Serbia & M.* 44 D2
Kotor Varoš, *Bos.-H.* 28 F2
Kotoriba, *Croatia* 41 B13
Kotovo, *Russia* 34 E7
Kotovsk, *Russia* 34 D5
Kotovsk, *Ukraine* 33 J5
Kotputli, *India* 68 F7
Kotri, *Pakistan* 68 G3
Kótronas, *Greece* 46 E4
Kötschach-Mauthen, *Austria* .. 26 E6
Kotturu, *India* 66 M10
Kotuy →, *Russia* 53 B11
Kotyuzhany, *Ukraine* 29 B12
Kotzebue, *U.S.A.* 100 B3
Kouchibouguac △, *Canada* 105 C6
Koudougou, *Burkina Faso* 82 C4
Koufonísi, *Greece* 49 E8
Koufonísia, *Greece* 47 E7
Kougaberge, *S. Africa* 88 E3
Kouibli, *Ivory C.* 82 D3
Kouilou →, *Congo* 84 E2
Koula Moutou, *Gabon* 84 E2
Koulen = Kulen, *Cambodia* 64 F5
Koulikoro, *Mali* 82 C3
Kouloúra, *Greece* 49 A3
Koúm-bournoú, Ákra, *Greece* .. 49 C10
Koumala, *Australia* 94 C4
Koumankou, *Mali* 82 C3
Koumbia, *Burkina Faso* 82 C4
Koumbia, *Guinea* 82 C2
Koumboum, *Guinea* 82 C2
Koumpenntoum, *Senegal* 82 C2
Koumra, *Chad* 79 G9
Koun-Fao, *Ivory C.* 82 D4
Koundara, *Guinea* 82 C2
Koundian, *Guinea* 82 C3
Koungheul, *Senegal* 82 C2
Kounradskiy, *Kazakhstan* 52 E8
Kountze, *U.S.A.* 113 K7
Koupéla, *Burkina Faso* 83 C4
Kourémalé, *Mali* 82 C3
Kouris →, *Cyprus* 49 E11
Kourou, *Fr. Guiana* 125 B8
Kourouba, *Mali* 82 C3
Kouroukoto, *Mali* 82 C3
Kouroussa, *Guinea* 82 C3
Kourouninkoto, *Mali* 82 C3
Koussane, *Senegal* 82 C2
Koussanar, *Senegal* 82 C2
Kousséri, *Cameroon* 79 F8
Koutiala, *Mali* 82 C3

Kouto, *Ivory C.* 82 D3
Kouvé, *Togo* 83 D5
Kouvola, *Finland* 9 F22
Kovačica, *Serbia & M.* 28 E5
Kovel, *Ukraine* 33 G3
Kovin, *Serbia & M.* 28 F5
Kovrov, *Russia* 34 B5
Kowal, *Poland* 31 F6
Kowalewo Pomorskie, *Poland* .. 31 E5
Kowanyama, *Australia* 94 B3
Kowloon, *China* 59 F10
Kowŏn, *N. Korea* 57 E14
Koyampattur = Coimbatore, *India* .. 66 P10
Koyulhisar, *Turkey* 72 B7
Koyunyeri, *Turkey* 45 F10
Koza, *Japan* 55 L3
Kozak, *Turkey* 47 B9
Kozan, *Turkey* 70 B2
Kozáni, *Greece* 44 F5
Kozáni □, *Greece* 44 F5
Kozara, *Bos.-H.* 41 D14
Kozara △, *Bos.-H.* 28 F2
Kozarac, *Bos.-H.* 41 D13
Kozelets, *Ukraine* 33 G6
Kozhikode = Calicut, *India* .. 66 P9
Koziegłowy, *Poland* 31 H6
Kozienice, *Poland* 31 G8
Kozje, *Slovenia* 41 B12
Kozloduy, *Bulgaria* 44 C7
Kozlovets, *Bulgaria* 45 C9
Kozlovka, *Russia* 34 C9
Kozludzha = Suvorovo,
  Bulgaria 45 C11
Kozluk, *Turkey* 73 C9
Koźmin, *Poland* 31 G4
Kozuchów, *Poland* 31 G2
Kozyatyn, *Ukraine* 33 H5
Kpabia, *Ghana* 83 D4
Kpalimé, *Togo* 83 D5
Kpandae, *Ghana* 83 D4
Kpessi, *Togo* 83 D5
Kra, Isthmus of = Kra, Kho Khot,
  Thailand 65 G2
Kra, Kho Khot, *Thailand* 65 G2
Kra Buri, *Thailand* 65 G2
Kraai →, *S. Africa* 88 E4
Krabi, *Thailand* 65 H2
Krachen, *Cambodia* 64 F6
Kragan, *Indonesia* 63 G14
Kragerø, *Norway* 9 G13
Kragujevac, *Serbia & M.* 44 B4
Krajenka, *Poland* 31 E3
Krakatau = Rakata, Pulau,
  Indonesia 62 F3
Krakatoa = Rakata, Pulau,
  Indonesia 62 F3
Krakor, *Cambodia* 64 F5
Kraków, *Poland* 31 H6
Kraków ✈ (KRK), *Poland* 31 H6
Kralanh, *Cambodia* 64 F4
Králíky, *Czech Rep.* 27 A9
Kraljevo, *Serbia & M.* 44 C4
Královéhradecký □, *Czech Rep.* .. 26 A8
Královský Chlmec, *Slovak Rep.* .. 27 C14
Kralupy nad Vltavou, *Czech Rep.* .. 26 A7
Kramatorsk, *Ukraine* 33 H9
Kramfors, *Sweden* 10 B11
Kraniá, *Greece* 44 G5
Kranía Elassónas, *Greece* 46 B4
Kranídhion, *Greece* 46 D5
Kranj, *Slovenia* 41 B11
Kranjska Gora, *Slovenia* 41 B10
Krankskop, *S. Africa* 89 D5
Krapina, *Croatia* 41 B12
Krapina →, *Croatia* 41 C12
Krapkowice, *Poland* 31 H4
Kras, *Croatia* 41 C10
Kraskino, *Russia* 53 E14
Kraslava, *Latvia* 32 E4
Kraslice, *Czech Rep.* 26 A5
Krasnaya Gorbatka, *Russia* .. 34 C5
Krasnaya Polyana, *Russia* 35 J5
Krasne, *Ukraine* 29 D14
Krasni Okny, *Ukraine* 29 C14
Kraśnik, *Poland* 31 H9
Krasnoarmeisk, *Ukraine* 33 H9
Krasnoarmeysk, *Russia* 34 E7
Krasnoarmeyskiy, *Russia* 35 G6
Krasnobród, *Poland* 31 H10
Krasnodar, *Russia* 35 H4
Krasnodon, *Ukraine* 33 H10
Krasnogorskiy, *Russia* 34 B9
Krasnograd = Krasnohrad,
  Ukraine 33 H8
Krasnogvardeysk, *Ukraine* 33 K8
Krasnogvardeyskoye, *Russia* .. 35 H5
Krasnohrad, *Ukraine* 33 H8
Krasnokutsk, *Ukraine* 33 G8
Krasnolesnyy, *Russia* 33 G10
Krasnoperekopsk, *Ukraine* .. 33 J7
Krasnorechenskiy, *Russia* .. 54 B7
Krasnoselkup, *Russia* 52 C9
Krasnoslobodsk, *Mordvinia*,
  Russia 34 C6
Krasnoslobodsk, *Volgograd*,
  Russia 35 F7
Krasnoturinsk, *Russia* 52 D7
Krasnoyarsk, *Russia* 53 D10
Krasnoyarskoye, *Russia* 30 D8
Krasnoye = Krasnyy, *Russia* .. 32 E6
Krasnoyilsk, *Ukraine* 29 C10
Krasnozavodsk, *Russia* 32 D10
Krasnoznamensk, *Russia* 30 D9
Krasny Sulin, *Russia* 33 H11
Krasnystaw, *Poland* 31 H10
Krasnyy, *Russia* 32 E6
Krasnyy Kholm, *Russia* 32 C9
Krasnyy Kut, *Russia* 34 E8
Krasnyy Liman, *Ukraine* 33 H9

Krasnyy Luch, *Ukraine* 33 H10
Krasnyy Profintern, *Russia* .. 32 D11
Krasnyy Yar, *Astrakhan, Russia* .. 35 G9
Krasnyy Yar, *Samara, Russia* .. 34 D10
Krasnyy Yar, *Volgograd, Russia* .. 34 E7
Krasnyye Baki, *Russia* 34 B7
Krasnyyoskolske Vdskh., *Ukraine* .. 33 H9
Kraszna →, *Hungary* 28 B7
Kratie = Kracheh, *Cambodia* .. 64 F6
Kratovo, *Macedonia* 44 D6
Krau, *Indonesia* 63 E10
Kravanh, Chuor Phnum,
  Cambodia 65 G4
Krefeld, *Germany* 24 D2
Krémaston, Límni, *Greece* 46 C3
Kremen, *Croatia* 41 D12
Kremenchuk, *Ukraine* 33 H7
Kremenchuksk Vdskh., *Ukraine* .. 33 H7
Kremenets, *Ukraine* 33 G3
Kremennaya, *Ukraine* 33 H10
Kremges = Svitlovodsk, *Ukraine* .. 33 H7
Kremmen, *Germany* 24 C9
Kremmling, *U.S.A.* 108 F10
Kremnica, *Slovak Rep.* 27 C11
Krems, *Austria* 26 C8
Kremsmünster, *Austria* 26 C7
Kretinga, *Lithuania* 9 J19
Krettsy, *Russia* 32 C7
Kreuzberg, *Germany* 25 E5
Kreuztal, *Germany* 24 E4
Kría Vrísi, *Greece* 44 F6
Kribi, *Cameroon* 83 E6
Krichem, *Bulgaria* 45 D8
Krichev = Krychaw, *Belarus* .. 32 F6
Krim, *Slovenia* 41 C11
Kriós, Ákra, *Greece* 49 D5
Krishna →, *India* 67 M12
Krishnanagar, *India* 69 H13
Kristdala, *Sweden* 11 G10
Kristiansand, *Norway* 9 G13
Kristianstad, *Sweden* 11 H8
Kristiansund, *Norway* 8 E12
Kristiinankaupunki, *Finland* .. 9 E19
Kristinehamn, *Sweden* 10 E8
Kristinestad =
  Kristiinankaupunki, *Finland* .. 9 E19
Kríti, *Greece* 49 D7
Kritsá, *Greece* 49 D7
Kriva →, *Macedonia* 44 D5
Kriva Palanka, *Macedonia* 44 D6
Krivaja →, *Bos.-H.* 28 F3
Krivelj, *Serbia & M.* 44 B6
Křivoklátsko △, *Czech Rep.* .. 26 A6
Krivoy Rog = Kryvyy Rih,
  Ukraine 33 J7
Križevci, *Croatia* 41 B13
Krk, *Croatia* 41 C11
Krka △, *Croatia* 41 E12
Krka →, *Slovenia* 41 C12
Krkonoše, *Czech Rep.* 26 A8
Krkonoše △, *Czech Rep.* 26 A8
Krnov, *Czech Rep.* 27 A10
Krobia, *Poland* 31 G3
Krokeaí, *Greece* 46 E4
Krokek, *Sweden* 11 F10
Krokodil →, *Mozam.* 89 D5
Krokom, *Sweden* 10 A8
Krokowa, *Poland* 30 D5
Krolevets, *Ukraine* 33 G7
Kroměříž, *Czech Rep.* 27 B10
Krompachy, *Slovak Rep.* 27 C13
Kromy, *Russia* 33 F8
Kronach, *Germany* 25 E7
Krong Kaoh Kong, *Cambodia* .. 62 B2
Kronobergs län □, *Sweden* .. 11 H8
Kronprins Olav Kyst, *Antarctica* .. 5 C5
Kronprinsesse Märtha Kyst,
  Antarctica 5 D2
Kronshtadt, *Russia* 32 C5
Kroonstad, *S. Africa* 88 D4
Kröpelin, *Germany* 24 A7
Kropotkin, *Russia* 35 H5
Kropp, *Germany* 24 A5
Krosna, *Lithuania* 30 D10
Krośniewice, *Poland* 31 F6
Krosno, *Poland* 31 J8
Krosno Odrzańskie, *Poland* .. 31 F2
Krotoszyn, *Poland* 31 G4
Krotovka, *Russia* 34 D10
Kroussón, *Greece* 49 D6
Krrabë, *Albania* 44 E3
Krško, *Slovenia* 41 C12
Krstača, *Serbia & M.* 44 D4
Kruger △, *S. Africa* 89 C5
Krugersdorp, *S. Africa* 89 D4
Kruisfontein, *S. Africa* 88 E3
Krujë, *Albania* 44 E3
Krulevshchina = Krulyewshchyna,
  Belarus 32 E4
Krulyewshchyna, *Belarus* 32 E4
Krumbach, *Germany* 25 G6
Krumë, *Albania* 44 D4
Krumovgrad, *Bulgaria* 45 E9
Krung Thep = Bangkok, *Thailand* .. 64 F3
Krupanj, *Serbia & M.* 44 B3
Krupina, *Slovak Rep.* 27 C12
Krupinica →, *Slovak Rep.* .. 27 C11
Krupki, *Belarus* 32 E5
Kruševac, *Serbia & M.* 44 C5
Kruševo, *Macedonia* 44 E5
Krushelnyksya, *Ukraine* 31 J10
Kruszwica, *Poland* 31 F5
Krychaw, *Belarus* 32 F6
Krymsk, *Russia* 33 K10
Krymskyy Poluostrov = Krymskyy
  Pivostriv, *Ukraine* 33 K8
Krymskyy Pivostriv, *Ukraine* .. 33 K8
Krynica, *Poland* 31 J7
Krynica Morska, *Poland* 30 D6
Krynki, *Poland* 31 E10
Krynychne, *Ukraine* 29 E13
Kryvyy Rih, *Ukraine* 33 J7

Kryzhopil, *Ukraine* 29 B13
Krzepice, *Poland* 31 H5
Krzeszów, *Poland* 31 H9
Krzna →, *Poland* 31 F10
Krzywiń, *Poland* 31 G3
Krzyż Wielkopolski, *Poland* .. 31 F2
Ksar el Kebir, *Morocco* 78 B4
Ksar es Souk = Er Rachidia,
  Morocco 78 B5
Książ Wielkopolski, *Poland* .. 31 F4
Kstovo, *Russia* 34 B7
Ku, W. el →, *Sudan* 81 E2
Kuah, *Malaysia* 65 J2
Kuala Belait, *Malaysia* 62 D4
Kuala Berang, *Malaysia* 65 K4
Kuala Dungun = Dungun,
  Malaysia 65 K4
Kuala Kangsar, *Malaysia* 65 K3
Kuala Kelawang, *Malaysia* .. 65 L4
Kuala Kerai, *Malaysia* 65 K4
Kuala Kerian, *Malaysia* ...... 65 c
Kuala Lipis, *Malaysia* 65 K4
Kuala Lumpur, *Malaysia* 65 L3
Kuala Nerang, *Malaysia* 65 J3
Kuala Pilah, *Malaysia* 65 L4
Kuala Rompin, *Malaysia* 65 L4
Kuala Selangor, *Malaysia* .. 65 L3
Kuala Sepetang, *Malaysia* .. 65 K3
Kuala Terengganu, *Malaysia* .. 65 K4
Kualajelai, *Indonesia* 62 E4
Kualakapuas, *Indonesia* 62 E4
Kualakurun, *Indonesia* 62 E4
Kualapembuang, *Indonesia* .. 62 E4
Kualasimpang, *Indonesia* 62 D1
Kuancheng, *China* 57 D10
Kuandang, *Indonesia* 63 D6
Kuandian, *China* 57 D13
Kuangchou = Guangzhou, *China* .. 59 F9
Kuanshan, *Taiwan* 59 F13
Kuantan, *Malaysia* 65 L4
Kuba = Quba, *Azerbaijan* 35 K9
Kuban →, *Russia* 33 K9
Kuban Depression =
  Prikubanskaya Nizmennost,
  Russia 35 H4
Kubenskoye, Ozero, *Russia* .. 32 C10
Kubokawa, *Japan* 55 H6
Kubrat, *Bulgaria* 45 C10
Kubu, *Indonesia* 63 J18
Kubutambahan, *Indonesia* 63 J18
Kucar, Tanjung, *Indonesia* .. 63 K18
Kučevo, *Serbia & M.* 44 B5
Kucha Gompa, *India* 69 B7
Kuchaman, *India* 68 F6
Kuchenspitze, *Austria* 26 D3
Kuchinda, *India* 69 J11
Kuching, *Malaysia* 62 D4
Kuchino-eruba-Jima, *Japan* .. 55 J5
Kuchino-Shima, *Japan* 55 K4
Kuchinotsu, *Japan* 55 H5
Kuchl, *Austria* 26 D6
Kuchurhan →, *Ukraine* 29 D14
Kucing = Kuching, *Malaysia* .. 62 D4
Kuçovë, *Albania* 44 F3
Küçükbahçe, *Turkey* 47 C8
Küçükköy, *Turkey* 47 B8
Küçükkuyu, *Turkey* 47 B8
Küçükmenderes →, *Turkey* 47 D9
Kud →, *Pakistan* 68 F2
Kuda, *India* 66 H7
Kudat, *Malaysia* 62 C5
Kudirkos Naumiestis, *Lithuania* .. 30 D9
Kudowa-Zdrój, *Poland* 31 H3
Kudus, *Indonesia* 63 G14
Kudymkar, *Russia* 52 D6
Kueiyang = Guiyang, *China* .. 58 D6
Kufra Oasis = Al Kufrah, *Libya* .. 79 D10
Kufstein, *Austria* 26 D5
Kugaaruk = Pelly Bay, *Canada* .. 101 B11
Kugong I., *Canada* 104 A4
Kūhak, *Iran* 66 F3
Kuhan, *Pakistan* 68 E2
Kühbonān, *Iran* 71 D8
Kühestak, *Iran* 71 E8
Kuhin, *Iran* 71 B6
Kühīrī, *Iran* 71 E9
Kuhnsdorf, *Austria* 26 E7
Kūhpāyeh, *Esfahan, Iran* 71 C7
Kūhpāyeh, *Kermān, Iran* 71 D8
Kührān, Kūh-e, *Iran* 71 E8
Kui Buri, *Thailand* 65 F2
Kuiseb →, *Namibia* 88 C1
Kuito, *Angola* 85 G3
Kuiu I., *U.S.A.* 102 B2
Kujang, *N. Korea* 57 E14
Kujawsko-Pomorskie □, *Poland* .. 30 E5
Kuji, *Japan* 54 D10
Kujū-San, *Japan* 55 H5
Kukava, *Ukraine* 29 B12
Kukavica, *Serbia & M.* 44 D5
Kukawa, *Nigeria* 83 C7
Kukës, *Albania* 44 D4
Kukmor, *Russia* 34 B10
Kukup, *Malaysia* .... 65 d
Kukup, Pulau, *Malaysia* .... 65 d
Kukvidze, *Russia* 34 E6
Kula, *Bulgaria* 44 C6
Kula, *Serbia & M.* 28 E4
Kula, *Turkey* 47 C10
Kulachi, *Pakistan* 68 D4
Kulai, *Malaysia* 65 M4
Kulaly, Ostrov, *Kazakhstan* .. 35 H10
Kulasekarappattinam, *India* .. 66 Q11
Kulautuva, *Lithuania* 30 D10
Kuldīga, *Latvia* 9 H19
Kuldīga □, *Latvia* 30 B8
Kuldu, *Sudan* 81 E2
Kulebaki, *Russia* 34 C6
Kulen, *Cambodia* 64 F5
Kulen Vakuf, *Bos.-H.* 41 D13
Kulgam, *India* 69 C6

Kulgera, *Australia* 94 D1
Kulim, *Malaysia* 65 K3
Kulin, *Australia* 93 F2
Kulkayu = Hartley Bay, *Canada* . 102 C3
Kullen, *Sweden* 11 H6
Kulmbach, *Germany* 25 E7
Kŭlob, *Tajikistan* 52 F7
Kulp, *Turkey* 73 C9
Kulpawn ➤, *Ghana* 83 D4
Kulsary, *Kazakhstan* 52 E6
Kulti, *India* 69 H12
Kulu, *India* 68 D7
Kulu, *Turkey* 72 C5
Kulumbura, *Australia* 92 B4
Kulunda, *Russia* 52 D8
Kulungar, *Afghan.* 68 C3
Kŭlvand, *Iran* 71 D7
Kulwin, *Australia* 95 F3
Kulyab = Kŭlob, *Tajikistan* 52 F7
Kuma ➤, *Russia* 35 H8
Kumafşarı, *Turkey* 47 D11
Kumaganum, *Nigeria* 83 C7
Kumagaya, *Japan* 55 F9
Kumai, *Indonesia* 62 E4
Kumalar Dağı, *Turkey* 47 C12
Kumamba, Kepulauan, *Indonesia* 63 E9
Kumamoto, *Japan* 55 H5
Kumamoto □, *Japan* 55 H5
Kumanovo, *Macedonia* 44 D5
Kumara, *N.Z.* 91 K3
Kumarina, *Australia* 93 D2
Kumasi, *Ghana* 82 D4
Kumba, *Cameroon* 83 E6
Kumbağ, *Turkey* 45 F11
Kumbakonam, *India* 66 P11
Kumbarilla, *Australia* 95 D5
Kumbhraj, *India* 68 G7
Kumbia, *Australia* 95 D5
Kumbo, *Cameroon* 83 D7
Kŭmch'ŏn, *N. Korea* 57 E14
Kumdok, *India* 69 C8
Kume-Shima, *Japan* 55 L3
Kumeny, *Russia* 34 A9
Kumharsain, *India* 68 D7
Kŭmhwa, *S. Korea* 57 E14
Kumi, *Uganda* 86 B3
Kumkale, *Turkey* 45 G10
Kumla, *Sweden* 10 E9
Kumluca, *Turkey* 47 E12
Kummerower See, *Germany* 24 B8
Kumo, *Nigeria* 83 C7
Kumo älv = Kokemäenjoki ➤,
   Finland 9 F19
Kumon Bum, *Burma* 67 F20
Kumylzhenskaya, *Russia* 34 F6
Kunágota, *Hungary* 28 D6
Kunashir, Ostrov, *Russia* 53 E15
Kunda, *Estonia* 9 G22
Kunda, *India* 69 G9
Kundar ➤, *Pakistan* 68 D3
Kundelungu △, *Dem. Rep. of*
   the Congo 87 E2
Kundelungu Ouest △, *Dem. Rep.*
   of the Congo 87 D2
Kundian, *Pakistan* 68 C4
Kundla, *India* 68 J4
Kung, Ao, *Thailand* .... 65 a
Kunga ➤, *Bangla.* 69 J13
Kungälv, *Sweden* 11 G5
Kunghit I., *Canada* 102 C2
Kungrad = Qŭnghirot, *Uzbekistan* 52 E6
Kungsängen, *Sweden* 10 E11
Kungsbacka, *Sweden* 11 G6
Kungsgården, *Sweden* 10 D10
Kungshamn, *Sweden* 11 F5
Kungsör, *Sweden* 10 E10
Kungur, *Russia* 52 D6
Kungurri, *Australia* 94 K6
Kunhar ➤, *Pakistan* 69 B5
Kunhegyes, *Hungary* 28 C5
Kuningan, *Indonesia* 63 G13
Kunlong, *Burma* 58 F2
Kunlun Shan, *Asia* 60 C3
Kunming, *China* 58 E4
Kunmadaras, *Hungary* 28 C5
Kunów, *Poland* 31 H8
Kunsan, *S. Korea* 57 G14
Kunshan, *China* 59 B13
Kunszentmárton, *Hungary* 28 D5
Kunszentmiklós, *Hungary* 28 C4
Kuntaur, *Senegal* 82 C2
Kununurra, *Australia* 92 C4
Kunwari ➤, *India* 69 F8
Kunya-Urgench = Köneürgench,
   Turkmenistan 52 E6
Künzelsau, *Germany* 25 F5
Kuopio, *Finland* 8 E22
Kupa ➤, *Croatia* 41 C13
Kupang, *Indonesia* 63 F6
Kupreanof I., *U.S.A.* 102 B2
Kupres, *Bos.-H.* 28 G2
Kupyansk, *Ukraine* 33 H9
Kupyansk-Uzlovoi, *Ukraine* ... 33 H9
Kuqa, *China* 60 B3
Kür ➤, *Azerbaijan* 73 C13
Kür Dili, *Azerbaijan* 71 B6
Kura = Kür ➤, *Azerbaijan* ... 73 C13
Kuranda, *Australia* 94 B4
Kuranga, *India* 68 H3
Kurashiki, *Japan* 55 G6
Kurayoshi, *Japan* 55 G6
Kürdämir, *Azerbaijan* 35 K9
Kurdistan, *Asia* 73 D10
Kŭrdzhali, *Bulgaria* 45 E9
Kure, *Japan* 55 G6
Küre, *Turkey* 72 B5
Küre Dağları, *Turkey* 72 B6
Kuressaare, *Estonia* 9 G20
Kurgan, *Russia* 52 D7
Kurganinsk, *Russia* 35 H5
Kurgannaya = Kurganinsk, *Russia* 35 H5
Kuri, *India* 68 F4

Kuria Maria Is. = Khurīyā Murīyā,
   Jazā'ir, *Oman* 75 D6
Kuridala, *Australia* 94 C3
Kurigram, *Bangla.* 67 G16
Kurikka, *Finland* 9 E20
Kuril Is. = Kurilskiye Ostrova,
   Russia 53 E15
Kuril Trench, *Pac. Oc.* 96 C7
Kurilsk, *Russia* 53 E15
Kurilskiye Ostrova, *Russia* ... 53 E15
Kurino, *Japan* 55 J5
Kurinskaya Kosa = Kür Dili,
   Azerbaijan 71 B6
Kurkur, *Egypt* 80 C3
Kurlovskiy, *Russia* 34 C5
Kurmuk, *Sudan* 81 E3
Kurnool, *India* 66 M11
Kuro-Shima, *Kagoshima, Japan* . 55 J4
Kuro-Shima, *Okinawa, Japan* .. 55 M2
Kuror, J., *Sudan* 80 C3
Kurow, *N.Z.* 91 L3
Kurów, *Poland* 31 G9
Kurram ➤, *Pakistan* 68 C4
Kurri Kurri, *Australia* 95 E5
Kurrimine, *Australia* 94 B4
Kursavka, *Russia* 35 H6
Kurshskaya Kosa △, *Russia* ... 30 C7
Kurshskiy Zaliv, *Russia* 9 J19
Kuršių Nerijos △, *Lithuania* .. 30 C8
Kursk, *Russia* 33 G9
Kuršumlija, *Serbia & M.* 44 C5
Kuršumlijska Banja, *Serbia & M.* 44 C5
Kurşunlu, *Bursa, Turkey* 45 F13
Kurşunlu, *Çankırı, Turkey* ... 72 B5
Kurtalan, *Turkey* 73 D9
Kurtbey, *Turkey* 45 E10
Kuru, *Sudan* 81 F2
Kuru, Bahr el ➤, *Sudan* 81 F2
Kuruçaşile, *Turkey* 72 B5
Kuruçay, *Turkey* 70 B3
Kuruktag, *China* 60 B3
Kuruman, *S. Africa* 88 D3
Kuruman ➤, *S. Africa* 88 D3
Kurume, *Japan* 55 H5
Kurunegala, *Sri Lanka* 66 R12
Kurya, *Russia* 52 C6
Kus Gölü, *Turkey* 45 F11
Kuşadası, *Turkey* 72 D2
Kuşadası Körfezi, *Turkey* 47 D8
Kusamba, *Indonesia* 63 K18
Kusatsu, *Japan* 55 F9
Kusawa L., *Canada* 102 A1
Kusel, *Germany* 25 F3
Kushaka, *Nigeria* 83 C6
Kushalgarh, *India* 68 H6
Kushchevskaya, *Russia* 35 G4
Kusheriki, *Nigeria* 83 C6
Kushikino, *Japan* 55 J5
Kushima, *Japan* 55 J5
Kushimoto, *Japan* 55 H7
Kushiro, *Japan* 54 C12
Kushiro-Gawa ➤, *Japan* 54 C12
Kushiro Shitsugen △, *Japan* .. 54 C12
Kūshk, *Iran* 71 D8
Kushka = Gushgy, *Turkmenistan* 52 F7
Kūshkī, *Iran* 70 C5
Kushnytsya, *Ukraine* 29 B8
Kushol, *India* 69 C7
Kushtia, *Bangla.* 67 H16
Kushum ➤, *Kazakhstan* 34 F10
Kuskokwim B., *U.S.A.* 100 C3
Kusmi, *India* 69 H10
Kussharo-Ko, *Japan* 54 C12
Kustanay = Qostanay,
   Kazakhstan 52 D7
Kut, Ko, *Thailand* 65 G4
Kuta, *Indonesia* 63 K18
Kütahya, *Turkey* 47 B12
Kütahya □, *Turkey* 47 B11
Kutaisi, *Georgia* 35 J6
Kutaraja = Banda Aceh,
   Indonesia 62 C1
Kutch, Gulf of = Kachchh, Gulf
   of, *India* 68 H3
Kutch, Rann of = Kachchh, Rann
   of, *India* 68 H4
Kutina, *Croatia* 41 C13
Kutiyana, *India* 68 J4
Kutjevo, *Croatia* 28 E2
Kutkashen, *Azerbaijan* 35 K8
Kutná Hora, *Czech Rep.* 26 B8
Kutno, *Poland* 31 F6
Kutse, *Botswana* 88 C3
Kuttabul, *Australia* 94 K6
Kutu, *Dem. Rep. of the Congo* 84 E3
Kutum, *Sudan* 81 E1
Kúty, *Slovak Rep.* 27 C10
Kuty, *Ukraine* 29 B10
Kuujjuaq, *Canada* 101 C13
Kuujjuarapik, *Canada* 104 A4
Kuup-tong, *N. Korea* 57 D14
Kuusamo, *Finland* 8 D23
Kuusankoski, *Finland* 9 F22
Kuvshinovo, *Russia* 32 D8
Kuwait = Al Kuwayt, *Kuwait* .. 70 D5
Kuwait ■, *Asia* 70 D5
Kuwana, *Japan* 55 G8
Kuwana ➤, *India* 69 F10
Kuybyshev = Samara, *Russia* .. 34 D10
Kuybyshev, *Russia* 52 D8
Kuybyshevo, *Ukraine* 33 J9
Kuybyshevskoye Vdkhr., *Russia* 34 C9
Kuye He ➤, *China* 56 E6
Küyeh, *Iran* 70 B5
Kuyucak, *Turkey* 47 D10
Kuyumba, *Russia* 53 C10
Kuzey Anadolu Dağları, *Turkey* 72 B7
Kuzmin, *Serbia & M.* 28 E4
Kuznetsk, *Russia* 34 D8
Kuzomen, *Russia* 52 C4
Kvænangen, *Norway* 8 A19

Kværndrup, *Denmark* 11 J4
Kvaløy, *Norway* 8 B18
Kvänum, *Sweden* 11 F7
Kvareli = Qvareli, *Georgia* ... 35 K7
Kvarner, *Croatia* 41 D11
Kvarnerič, *Croatia* 41 D11
Kvicksund, *Sweden* 10 E10
Kvillsfors, *Sweden* 11 G9
Kvismare kanal, *Sweden* 10 E9
Kvissleby, *Sweden* 10 B11
Kwa-Nobuhle, *S. Africa* 85 L5
Kwabhaca, *S. Africa* 89 E4
Kwakhanai, *Botswana* 88 C3
Kwakoegron, *Suriname* 125 B7
Kwale, *Kenya* 86 C4
Kwale, *Nigeria* 83 D6
KwaMashu, *S. Africa* 89 D5
Kwando ➤, *Africa* 88 B3
Kwangchow = Guangzhou, *China* 59 F9
Kwangdaeri, *N. Korea* 57 D14
Kwangju, *S. Korea* 57 G14
Kwango ➤, *Dem. Rep. of*
   the Congo 84 E3
Kwangsi-Chuang = Guangxi
   Zhuangzu Zizhiqu □, *China* . 58 F7
Kwangtung = Guangdong □,
   China 59 F9
Kwara □, *Nigeria* 83 D6
Kwataboahegan ➤, *Canada* .. 104 B3
Kwatisore, *Indonesia* 63 E8
KwaZulu Natal □, *S. Africa* .. 89 D5
Kweichow = Guizhou □, *China* 58 D6
Kwekwe, *Zimbabwe* 87 F2
Kwidzyn, *Poland* 30 E5
Kwiha, *Ethiopia* 81 E4
Kwinana New Town, *Australia* . 93 F2
Kwisa ➤, *Poland* 31 G2
Kwoka, *Indonesia* 63 E8
Kwolla, *Nigeria* 83 D6
Kyabra Cr. ➤, *Australia* 95 D3
Kyabram, *Australia* 95 F4
Kyaikto, *Burma* 64 D1
Kyakhta, *Russia* 53 D11
Kyambura □, *Uganda* 86 C3
Kyancutta, *Australia* 95 E2
Kyaukpadaung, *Burma* 67 J19
Kyaukpyu, *Burma* 67 K18
Kyaukse, *Burma* 67 J20
Kybartai, *Lithuania* 30 D9
Kyburz, *U.S.A.* 110 G6
Kyelang, *India* 68 C7
Kyenjojo, *Uganda* 86 B3
Kyjov, *Czech Rep.* 27 B10
Kyle, *Canada* 103 C7
Kyle Dam, *Zimbabwe* 87 G3
Kyle of Lochalsh, *U.K.* 13 D3
Kyll ➤, *Germany* 25 F2
Kyllburg, *Germany* 25 E2
Kymijoki ➤, *Finland* 9 F22
Kymmene älv = Kymijoki ➤,
   Finland 9 F22
Kyneton, *Australia* 95 F3
Kynuna, *Australia* 94 C3
Kyō-ga-Saki, *Japan* 55 G7
Kyoga, L., *Uganda* 86 B3
Kyogle, *Australia* 95 D5
Kyom ➤, *Sudan* 81 F2
Kyongju, *S. Korea* 57 G15
Kyongpyaw, *Burma* 67 L19
Kyŏngsŏng, *N. Korea* 57 D15
Kyŏto, *Japan* 55 G7
Kyōto □, *Japan* 55 G7
Kyparissovouno, *Cyprus* 49 D12
Kyperounda, *Cyprus* 49 E11
Kyrenia, *Cyprus* 49 D12
Kyrgyzstan ■, *Asia* 52 E8
Kyritz, *Germany* 24 C8
Kyrkhult, *Sweden* 11 H8
Kyrnasivka, *Ukraine* 29 B13
Kyro älv = Kyrönjoki ➤, *Finland* 8 E19
Kyrönjoki ➤, *Finland* 8 E19
Kystatyam, *Russia* 53 C13
Kysucké Nové Mesto, *Slovak Rep.* 27 B11
Kytay, Ozero, *Ukraine* 29 E14
Kythréa, *Cyprus* 49 D12
Kyunhla, *Burma* 67 H19
Kyuquot Sound, *Canada* 102 D3
Kyurdamir = Kürdämir,
   Azerbaijan 35 K9
Kyūshū, *Japan* 55 H5
Kyūshū □, *Japan* 55 H5
Kyūshū-Sanchi, *Japan* 55 H5
Kyustendil, *Bulgaria* 44 D6
Kyusyur, *Russia* 53 B13
Kyyiv, *Ukraine* 33 G6
Kyyivske Vdskh., *Ukraine* 33 G6
Kyzyl, *Russia* 53 D10
Kyzyl Kum, *Uzbekistan* 52 E7
Kyzyl-Kyya, *Kyrgyzstan* 52 E8
Kyzyl-Orda = Qyzylorda,
   Kazakhstan 52 E7

L

La Albuera, *Spain* 37 G4
La Alcarria, *Spain* 38 E2
La Almarcha, *Spain* 38 F2
La Almunia de Doña Godina,
   Spain 38 D3
La Amistad △, *Cent. Amer.* .. 120 E3
La Asunción, *Venezuela* 124 A6
La Baie, *Canada* 105 C5
La Banda, *Argentina* 126 B3
La Barca, *Mexico* 118 C4
La Barge, *U.S.A.* 108 E8
La Bastide-Puylaurent, *France* . 20 D7

La Baule, *France* 18 E4
La Belle, *U.S.A.* 115 M5
La Biche ➤, *Canada* 102 B4
La Biche, L., *Canada* 102 C6
La Bisbal d'Empordà, *Spain* .. 38 D8
La Blanquilla, *Venezuela* 121 D7
La Bomba, *Mexico* 118 A1
La Brea, *Trin. & Tob.* 125 K15
La Brède, *France* 20 D3
La Bresse, *France* 19 D13
La Bureba, *Spain* 36 C7
La Calera, *Chile* 126 C1
La Campana △, *Chile* 126 C1
La Campiña, *Spain* 37 H6
La Canal = Sa Canal, *Spain* .. 48 C7
La Canourgue, *France* 20 D7
La Capelle, *France* 19 C10
La Carlota, *Argentina* 126 C3
La Carlota, *Phil.* 61 F5
La Carlota, *Spain* 37 H6
La Carolina, *Spain* 37 G7
La Cavalerie, *France* 20 D7
La Ceiba, *Honduras* 120 C2
La Chaise-Dieu, *France* 20 C7
La Chapelle d'Angillon, *France* . 19 E9
La Chapelle-St-Luc, *France* ... 19 D11
La Chapelle-sur-Erdre, *France* . 18 E5
La Charité-sur-Loire, *France* .. 19 E10
La Chartre-sur-le-Loir, *France* . 18 E7
La Châtaigneraie, *France* 20 B3
La Châtre, *France* 19 F9
La Chaux-de-Fonds, *Switz.* ... 25 H2
La Chorrera, *Panama* 120 E4
La Ciotat, *France* 21 E9
La Clayette, *France* 19 F11
La Cocha, *Argentina* 126 B2
La Concepción, *Panama* 120 E3
La Concordia, *Mexico* 119 D6
La Coruña = A Coruña, *Spain* . 36 B2
La Coruña □, *Spain* 36 B2
La Côte-St-André, *France* 21 C9
La Courtine, *France* 20 C6
La Crau, *Bouches-du-Rhône,*
   France 21 E8
La Crau, *Var, France* 21 E10
La Crescent, *U.S.A.* 112 D9
La Crete, *Canada* 102 B5
La Crosse, *Kans., U.S.A.* 112 F5
La Crosse, *Wis., U.S.A.* 112 D9
La Cruz, *Costa Rica* 120 D2
La Cruz, *Mexico* 118 C3
La Désirade, *Guadeloupe* ... 120 b
La Escondida, *Mexico* 118 C5
La Esmeralda, *Paraguay* 126 A3
La Esperanza, *Cuba* 120 B3
La Esperanza, *Honduras* 120 D2
La Estrada = A Estrada, *Spain* . 36 C2
La Faouët, *France* 18 D3
La Fayette, *U.S.A.* 115 H3
La Fé, *Cuba* 120 B3
La Fère, *France* 19 C10
La Ferté-Bernard, *France* 18 D7
La Ferté-Gaucher, *France* 19 D10
La Ferté-Macé, *France* 18 D6
La Ferté-St-Aubin, *France* ... 19 E8
La Ferté-sous-Jouarre, *France* . 19 D10
La Ferté-Vidame, *France* 18 D7
La Flèche, *France* 18 E6
La Follette, *U.S.A.* 115 G3
La Fregeneda, *Spain* 36 E4
La Fuente de San Esteban, *Spain* 36 E4
La Gacilly, *France* 18 E4
La Gineta, *Spain* 39 F2
La Grand'Combe, *France* 21 D8
La Grande, *U.S.A.* 108 D4
La Grande ➤, *Canada* 104 B5
La Grande Deux, Rés., *Canada* 104 B4
La Grande-Motte, *France* 21 E8
La Grande Quatre, Rés., *Canada* 104 B5
La Grande Trois, Rés., *Canada* . 104 B4
La Grange, *Calif., U.S.A.* 110 H6
La Grange, *Ga., U.S.A.* 115 J3
La Grange, *Ky., U.S.A.* 114 F3
La Grange, *Tex., U.S.A.* 113 L6
La Grave, *France* 21 C10
La Guaira, *Venezuela* 124 A5
La Guardia = A Guarda, *Spain* . 36 D2
La Gudiña = A Gudiña, *Spain* . 36 C3
La Guerche-de-Bretagne, *France* 18 E5
La Guerche-sur-l'Aubois, *France* 19 F9
La Habana, *Cuba* 120 B3
La Haute Vallée de Chevreuse △,
   France 19 D8
La Haye-du-Puits, *France* 18 C5
La Horra, *Spain* 36 D7
La Independencia, *Mexico* 119 D6
La Isabela, *Dom. Rep.* 121 C5
La Jonquera, *Spain* 38 C7
La Junta, *U.S.A.* 113 F3
La Laguna, *Canary Is.* 48 F3
La Libertad, *Guatemala* 120 C1
La Libertad, *Mexico* 118 B2
La Ligua, *Chile* 126 C1
La Línea de la Concepción, *Spain* 37 J5
La Loche, *Canada* 103 B7
La Londe-les-Maures, *France* .. 21 E10
La Lora, *Spain* 36 C7
La Loupe, *France* 18 D8
La Louvière, *Belgium* 17 D4
La Lune, *Trin. & Tob.* 125 K15
La Machine, *France* 19 F10
La Maddalena, *Italy* 42 A2
La Malbaie, *Canada* 105 C5
La Malinche △, *Mexico* 119 D5
La Mancha, *Spain* 39 F2
La Mariña, *Spain* 36 B3
La Martre, L., *Canada* 102 A5
La Mesa, *U.S.A.* 111 N9
La Misión, *Mexico* 118 A1
La Mothe-Achard, *France* 18 F5
La Motte-Chalançon, *France* .. 21 D9

La Motte-du-Caire, *France* 21 D10
La Motte-Servolex, *France* 21 C9
La Moure, *U.S.A.* 112 B5
La Muela, *Spain* 38 D3
La Mure, *France* 21 D9
La Negra, *Chile* 126 A1
La Oliva, *Canary Is.* 48 F6
La Orotava, *Canary Is.* 48 F3
La Oroya, *Peru* 124 F3
La Pacaudière, *France* 19 F10
La Palma, *Canary Is.* 48 F2
La Palma, *Panama* 120 E4
La Palma del Condado, *Spain* . 37 H4
La Paloma, *Chile* 126 C1
La Pampa □, *Argentina* 126 D2
La Paragua, *Venezuela* 124 B6
La Paz, *Entre Ríos, Argentina* . 126 C4
La Paz, *San Luis, Argentina* .. 126 C2
La Paz, *Bolivia* 124 G5
La Paz, *Honduras* 120 D2
La Paz, *Mexico* 118 C2
La Paz, *Phil.* 61 D4
La Paz Centro, *Nic.* 120 D2
La Pedrera, *Colombia* 124 D5
La Pérade, *Canada* 105 C5
La Perouse Str., *Asia* 54 B11
La Pesca, *Mexico* 119 C5
La Piedad, *Mexico* 118 C4
La Pine, *U.S.A.* 108 E3
La Plata, *Argentina* 126 D4
La Pobla de Lillet, *Spain* 38 C6
La Pocatière, *Canada* 105 C5
La Pola de Gordón, *Spain* ... 36 C5
La Porta, *France* 21 F13
La Porte, *Ind., U.S.A.* 114 E2
La Porte, *Tex., U.S.A.* 113 L7
La Presanella, *Italy* 40 B7
La Puebla = Sa Pobla, *Spain* .. 38 F8
La Puebla de Cazalla, *Spain* .. 37 H5
La Puebla de los Infantes, *Spain* . 37 H5
La Puebla de Montalbán, *Spain* 37 F6
La Puebla del Río, *Spain* 37 H4
La Puerta de Segura, *Spain* .. 37 G8
La Purísima, *Mexico* 118 B2
La Push, *U.S.A.* 110 C2
La Quiaca, *Argentina* 126 A2
La Réole, *France* 20 D3
La Restinga, *Canary Is.* 48 G2
La Rioja, *Argentina* 126 B2
La Rioja □, *Argentina* 126 B2
La Rioja □, *Spain* 38 C2
La Robla, *Spain* 36 C5
La Roche-Bernard, *France* 18 E4
La Roche-Canillac, *France* ... 20 C5
La Roche-en-Ardenne, *Belgium* 17 D5
La Roche-sur-Foron, *France* .. 19 F13
La Roche-sur-Yon, *France* 18 F5
La Rochefoucauld, *France* 20 C4
La Rochelle, *France* 20 B2
La Roda, *Spain* 39 F2
La Roda de Andalucía, *Spain* . 37 H6
La Romana, *Dom. Rep.* 121 C6
La Ronge, *Canada* 103 B7
La Rumorosa, *Mexico* 111 N10
La Sabina = Sa Savina, *Spain* . 48 C7
La Sagra, *Spain* 39 H2
La Salle, *U.S.A.* 112 E10
La Sanabria, *Spain* 36 C4
La Santa, *Canary Is.* 48 E6
La Sarre, *Canada* 104 C4
La Scie, *Canada* 105 C8
La Selva, *Spain* 38 C7
La Selva Beach, *U.S.A.* 110 J5
La Selva del Camp, *Spain* 38 D6
La Serena, *Chile* 126 B1
La Serena, *Spain* 37 G5
La Seu d'Urgell, *Spain* 38 C6
La Seyne-sur-Mer, *France* 21 E9
La Sila, *Italy* 43 C9
La Solana, *Spain* 37 G7
La Soufrière, *St. Vincent* 121 D7
La Souterraine, *France* 19 F8
La Spézia, *Italy* 40 D6
La Suze-sur-Sarthe, *France* ... 18 E7
La Tagua, *Colombia* 124 C3
La Teste-de-Buch, *France* 20 D2
La Tortuga, *Venezuela* 121 D6
La Tour-du-Pin, *France* 21 C9
La Tranche-sur-Mer, *France* .. 18 F5
La Tremblade, *France* 20 C2
La Trinité, *Martinique* .... 120 c
La Tuque, *Canada* 104 C5
La Unión, *Chile* 128 E2
La Unión, *El Salv.* 120 D2
La Unión, *Mexico* 118 D4
La Unión, *Spain* 39 H4
La Urbana, *Venezuela* 124 B5
La Vache Pt., *Trin. & Tob.* ... 125 K15
La Vall d'Uixó, *Spain* 38 F4
La Vecilla de Curveño, *Spain* . 36 C5
La Vega, *Dom. Rep.* 121 C5
La Vela de Coro, *Venezuela* .. 124 A5
La Veleta, *Spain* 37 H7
La Venta, *Mexico* 119 D6
La Ventura, *Mexico* 118 C4
La Voulte-sur-Rhône, *France* .. 21 D8
Laa an der Thaya, *Austria* ... 27 C9
Laaber, Grosse ➤, *Germany* .. 25 G8
Laage, *Germany* 24 B8
Laas Caanood = Las Anod,
   Somali Rep. 75 F4
Laatzen, *Germany* 24 C5
Laba ➤, *Russia* 35 H4
Labason, *Phil.* 61 G5
Labastide-Murat, *France* 20 D5
Labastide-Rouairoux, *France* .. 20 E6
Labbézenga, *Mali* 83 B5
Labe = Elbe ➤, *Europe* 24 B4
Labé, *Guinea* 82 C2
Laberge, L., *Canada* 102 A1
Labin, *Croatia* 41 C11

Labinsk, Russia ... 35 H5
Labis, Malaysia ... 65 L4
Łabiszyn, Poland ... 31 F4
Labo, Phil. ... 61 D5
Laboe, Germany ... 24 A6
Laborec →, Slovak Rep. ... 27 C14
Laborie, St. Lucia ... 121 f
Labouheyre, France ... 20 D3
Laboulaye, Argentina ... 126 C3
Labrador, Canada ... 105 B7
Labrador City, Canada ... 105 B6
Labrador Sea, Atl. Oc. ... 101 C14
Lábrea, Brazil ... 124 E6
Labruguière, France ... 20 E6
Labuan, Malaysia ... 62 C5
Labuan, Pulau, Malaysia ... 62 C5
Labuha, Indonesia ... 63 E7
Labuhan, Indonesia ... 63 G11
Labuhanbajo, Indonesia ... 63 F6
Labuk, Telok, Malaysia ... 62 C5
Labyrinth, L., Australia ... 95 E2
Labytnangi, Russia ... 52 C7
Laç, Albania ... 44 E3
Lac-Bouchette, Canada ... 105 C5
Lac Édouard, Canada ... 104 C5
Lac La Biche, Canada ... 102 C6
Lac la Martre = Wha Ti, Canada ... 100 B8
Lac La Ronge △, Canada ... 103 B7
Lac-Mégantic, Canada ... 105 C5
Lac Thien, Vietnam ... 64 F7
Lacanau, France ... 20 D2
Lacanau, Étang de, France ... 20 D2
Lacantún →, Mexico ... 119 D6
Lacara →, Spain ... 37 G4
Lacaune, France ... 20 E6
Lacaune, Mts. de, France ... 20 E6
Laccadive Is. = Lakshadweep Is., India ... 50 H11
Lacepede B., Australia ... 95 F2
Lacepede Is., Australia ... 92 C3
Lacerdónia, Mozam. ... 87 F4
Lacey, U.S.A. ... 110 C4
Lachhmangarh, India ... 68 F6
Lachi, Pakistan ... 68 C4
Lachine, Canada ... 104 C5
Lachlan →, Australia ... 95 E3
Lachute, Canada ... 104 C5
Lackawanna, U.S.A. ... 116 D6
Lackawaxen, U.S.A. ... 117 E10
Lacolle, Canada ... 117 A11
Lacombe, Canada ... 102 C6
Lacona, U.S.A. ... 117 C8
Láconi, Italy ... 42 C2
Laconia, U.S.A. ... 117 C13
Lacq, France ... 20 E3
Ladakh Ra., India ... 69 C8
Lądek-Zdrój, Poland ... 31 H3
Ládhon →, Greece ... 46 D3
Ladik, Turkey ... 72 B6
Ladismith, S. Africa ... 88 E3
Ladíspoli, Italy ... 41 G9
Lādīz, Iran ... 71 D9
Ladnun, India ... 68 F6
Ladoga, L. = Ladozhskoye Ozero, Russia ... 32 B6
Ladozhskoye Ozero, Russia ... 32 B6
Ladushkin, Russia ... 30 D7
Lady Elliott I., Australia ... 94 C5
Lady Grey, S. Africa ... 88 E4
Ladybrand, S. Africa ... 88 D4
Ladysmith, Canada ... 102 D4
Ladysmith, S. Africa ... 89 D4
Ladysmith, U.S.A. ... 112 C9
Ladyzhnyn, Ukraine ... 29 B14
Lae, Papua N. G. ... 96 H6
Laem Hin Khom, Thailand ... 65 b
Laem Khat, Thailand ... 65 a
Laem Nga, Thailand ... 65 a
Laem Ngop, Thailand ... 65 F4
Laem Pho, Thailand ... 65 J3
Laem Phan Wa, Thailand ... 65 a
Laem Phrom Thep, Thailand ... 65 a
Laem Riang, Thailand ... 65 a
Laem Sam Rong, Thailand ... 65 b
Laem Son, Thailand ... 65 a
Laem Yamu, Thailand ... 65 a
Læsø, Denmark ... 11 G5
Læsø Rende, Denmark ... 11 G4
Lafayette, Colo., U.S.A. ... 112 F2
Lafayette, Ind., U.S.A. ... 114 E2
Lafayette, La., U.S.A. ... 113 K9
Lafayette, Tenn., U.S.A. ... 115 G3
Laferte →, Canada ... 102 A5
Lafia, Nigeria ... 83 D6
Lafiagi, Nigeria ... 83 D6
Lafleche, Canada ... 103 D7
Lafon, Sudan ... 81 F3
Lagan, Sweden ... 11 H7
Lagan →, Sweden ... 11 H6
Lagan →, U.K. ... 12 B6
Lagarfljót →, Iceland ... 8 D6
Lage, Germany ... 24 D4
Lågen →, Oppland, Norway ... 9 F14
Lågen →, Vestfold, Norway ... 9 G14
Lägerdorf, Germany ... 24 B5
Laghouat, Algeria ... 78 B6
Lagnieu, France ... 21 C9
Lagny-sur-Marne, France ... 19 D9
Lago, Italy ... 43 C9
Lago de Sanabria y Entorno △, Spain ... 36 C4
Lagôa, Portugal ... 37 H2
Lagoa do Peixe △, Brazil ... 127 C5
Lagoa Vermelha, Brazil ... 127 B5
Lagoaça, Portugal ... 36 D4
Lagodekhi, Georgia ... 35 K8
Lagonegro, Italy ... 43 B8
Lagonoy G., Phil. ... 61 E5
Lagos, Nigeria ... 83 D5
Lagos, Portugal ... 37 H2
Lagos □, Nigeria ... 83 D5
Lagos de Moreno, Mexico ... 118 C4

Lagrange, Australia ... 92 C3
Lagrange B., Australia ... 92 C3
Laguardia, Spain ... 38 C2
Laguépie, France ... 20 D5
Laguna, Brazil ... 127 B6
Laguna, U.S.A. ... 109 J10
Laguna Beach, U.S.A. ... 111 M9
Laguna de Duera, Spain ... 36 D6
Laguna de la Restinga △, Venezuela ... 121 D6
Laguna del Laja △, Chile ... 126 D1
Laguna del Tigre △, Guatemala ... 120 C1
Laguna Limpia, Argentina ... 126 B4
Lagunas, Chile ... 126 A2
Lagunas, Peru ... 124 E3
Lagunas de Chacahua △, Mexico ... 119 D5
Lagunas de Montebello △, Mexico ... 119 D6
Lagunas de Ruidera △, Spain ... 39 G2
Lahad Datu, Malaysia ... 63 C5
Lahad Datu, Teluk, Malaysia ... 63 D5
Lahan Sai, Thailand ... 64 E4
Lahanam, Laos ... 64 D5
Lahar, India ... 69 F8
Laharpur, India ... 69 F9
Lahat, Indonesia ... 62 E2
Lahewa, Indonesia ... 62 D1
Lāhījān, Iran ... 71 B6
Lahn →, Germany ... 25 E3
Lahnstein, Germany ... 25 E3
Laholm, Sweden ... 11 H7
Laholmsbukten, Sweden ... 11 H6
Lahore, Pakistan ... 68 D6
Lahr, Germany ... 25 G3
Lahri, Pakistan ... 68 E3
Lahti, Finland ... 9 F21
Lahtis = Lahti, Finland ... 9 F21
Laï, Chad ... 79 G9
Lai Chau, Vietnam ... 58 F4
Lai'an, China ... 59 A12
Laibin, China ... 58 F7
Laifeng, China ... 58 C7
L'Aigle, France ... 18 D7
Laignes, France ... 19 E11
L'Aiguillon-sur-Mer, France ... 20 B2
Laila = Layla, Si. Arabia ... 75 C4
Laingsburg, S. Africa ... 88 E3
Lainioälven →, Sweden ... 8 C20
Lairg, U.K. ... 13 C4
Laishui, China ... 56 E8
Laissac, France ... 20 D6
Láives, Italy ... 41 B8
Laiwu, China ... 57 F9
Laixi, China ... 57 F11
Laiyang, China ... 57 F11
Laiyuan, China ... 56 E8
Laizhou, China ... 57 F10
Laizhou Wan, China ... 57 F10
Laja →, Mexico ... 118 C4
Lajere, Nigeria ... 83 C7
Lajes, Brazil ... 127 B5
Lajkovac, Serbia & M. ... 44 B4
Lajosmizse, Hungary ... 28 C4
Lak Sao, Laos ... 64 C5
Lakaband, Pakistan ... 68 D3
Lakamané, Mali ... 82 C3
Lake Alpine, U.S.A. ... 110 G7
Lake Andes, U.S.A. ... 112 D5
Lake Arthur, U.S.A. ... 113 K8
Lake Bindegolly △, Australia ... 95 D3
Lake Cargelligo, Australia ... 95 E4
Lake Charles, U.S.A. ... 113 K8
Lake City, Colo., U.S.A. ... 109 G10
Lake City, Fla., U.S.A. ... 115 K4
Lake City, Mich., U.S.A. ... 114 C3
Lake City, Minn., U.S.A. ... 112 C8
Lake City, Pa., U.S.A. ... 116 D4
Lake City, S.C., U.S.A. ... 115 J6
Lake Cowichan, Canada ... 102 D4
Lake District △, U.K. ... 14 C4
Lake Elsinore, U.S.A. ... 111 M9
Lake Eyre △, Australia ... 95 D2
Lake Gairdner △, Australia ... 95 E2
Lake George, U.S.A. ... 117 C11
Lake Grace, Australia ... 93 F2
Lake Harbour = Kimmirut, Canada ... 101 B13
Lake Havasu City, U.S.A. ... 111 L12
Lake Hughes, U.S.A. ... 111 L8
Lake Isabella, U.S.A. ... 111 K8
Lake Jackson, U.S.A. ... 113 L7
Lake Junction, U.S.A. ... 108 D8
Lake King, Australia ... 93 F2
Lake Lenore, Canada ... 103 C8
Lake Louise, Canada ... 102 C5
Lake Malawi △, Malawi ... 87 E3
Lake Mburo △, Uganda ... 86 C3
Lake Mead △, U.S.A. ... 111 K12
Lake Meredith △, U.S.A. ... 113 H4
Lake Mills, U.S.A. ... 112 D8
Lake Nakuru △, Kenya ... 86 C4
Lake Placid, U.S.A. ... 117 B11
Lake Pleasant, U.S.A. ... 117 C10
Lake Providence, U.S.A. ... 113 J9
Lake Roosevelt △, U.S.A. ... 108 C4
Lake St. Peter, Canada ... 116 A6
Lake Superior △, Canada ... 104 C3
Lake Torrens △, Australia ... 95 E2
Lake Village, U.S.A. ... 113 J9
Lake Wales, U.S.A. ... 115 M5
Lake Worth, U.S.A. ... 115 M5
Lakeba, Fiji ... 91 D9
Lakefield, Canada ... 116 B6
Lakefield △, Australia ... 94 B3
Lakehurst, U.S.A. ... 117 F10
Lakeland, Australia ... 94 B3
Lakeland, U.S.A. ... 115 M5
Lakemba = Lakeba, Fiji ... 91 D9
Lakeport, Calif., U.S.A. ... 110 F4
Lakeport, Mich., U.S.A. ... 116 C2
Lakes Entrance, Australia ... 95 F4
Lakeside, Ariz., U.S.A. ... 109 J9

Lakeside, Calif., U.S.A. ... 111 N10
Lakeside, Nebr., U.S.A. ... 112 D3
Lakeside, Ohio, U.S.A. ... 116 E2
Lakeview, U.S.A. ... 108 E3
Lakewood, Colo., U.S.A. ... 112 G2
Lakewood, N.J., U.S.A. ... 117 F10
Lakewood, N.Y., U.S.A. ... 116 D5
Lakewood, Ohio, U.S.A. ... 116 E3
Lakewood, Wash., U.S.A. ... 110 C4
Lakha, India ... 68 F4
Lakhaniá, Greece ... 49 D9
Lakhimpur, India ... 69 F9
Lakhnadon, India ... 69 H8
Lakhnau = Lucknow, India ... 69 F9
Lakhonpheng, Laos ... 64 E5
Lakhpat, India ... 68 H3
Läki, Azerbaijan ... 35 K8
Lakin, U.S.A. ... 113 G4
Lakitusaki →, Canada ... 104 B3
Lakki, Pakistan ... 68 C4
Lákkoi, Greece ... 49 D5
Lakonía □, Greece ... 46 E4
Lakonikós Kólpos, Greece ... 46 E4
Lakor, Indonesia ... 63 F7
Lakota, Ivory C. ... 82 D3
Lakota, U.S.A. ... 112 A5
Laksar, India ... 68 E8
Laksefjorden, Norway ... 8 A22
Lakselv, Norway ... 8 A21
Lakshadweep Is., India ... 50 H11
Lakshmanpur, India ... 69 H10
Lakshmikantapur, India ... 69 H13
Lala Musa, Pakistan ... 68 C5
Lalaghat, India ... 67 G18
Lalago, Tanzania ... 86 C3
Lalapanzi, Zimbabwe ... 87 F3
Lalapaşa, Turkey ... 45 E10
Lalbenque, France ... 20 D5
L'Albufera, Spain ... 39 F4
Lalganj, India ... 69 G11
Lalgola, India ... 69 G13
Lālī, Iran ... 71 C6
Lalibela, Ethiopia ... 81 E4
Lalin, China ... 57 B14
Lalín, Spain ... 36 C2
Lalin He →, China ... 57 B13
Lalinde, France ... 20 D4
Lalitapur, Nepal ... 69 F11
Lalitpur, India ... 69 G8
Lalkua, India ... 69 E8
Lalsot, India ... 68 F7
Lam, Vietnam ... 64 B6
Lam Pao Res., Thailand ... 64 D4
Lama Kara, Togo ... 83 D5
Lamaing, Burma ... 67 M20
Lamar, Colo., U.S.A. ... 112 F3
Lamar, Mo., U.S.A. ... 113 G7
Lamas, Peru ... 124 E3
Lamastre, France ... 21 D8
Lambach, Austria ... 26 C6
Lamballe, France ... 18 D4
Lambaréné, Gabon ... 84 E2
Lambasa = Labasa, Fiji ... 91 C8
Lambay I., Ireland ... 12 C5
Lambert Glacier, Antarctica ... 5 D6
Lambert's Bay, S. Africa ... 88 E2
Lambesc, France ... 21 E9
Lambeth, Canada ... 116 D3
Lámbia, Greece ... 46 D3
Lambomakondro, Madag. ... 89 C7
Lambro →, Italy ... 40 C6
Lambton Shores, Canada ... 116 C3
Lame, Nigeria ... 83 C6
Lame Deer, U.S.A. ... 108 D10
Lamego, Portugal ... 36 D3
Lamèque, Canada ... 105 C7
Lameroo, Australia ... 95 F3
Lamesa, U.S.A. ... 113 J4
Lamía, Greece ... 46 C4
Lamington △, Australia ... 95 D5
Lamitan, Phil. ... 61 H5
Lammermuir Hills, U.K. ... 13 F6
Lammhult, Sweden ... 11 G8
Lamoille →, U.S.A. ... 117 B11
Lamon B., Phil. ... 61 D5
Lamont, Canada ... 102 C6
Lamont, Calif., U.S.A. ... 111 K8
Lamont, Wyo., U.S.A. ... 108 E10
Lamotte-Beuvron, France ... 19 E9
Lampa, Peru ... 124 G4
Lampang, Thailand ... 64 C2
Lampasas, U.S.A. ... 113 K5
Lampazos de Naranjo, Mexico ... 118 B4
Lampedusa, Italy ... 43 H6
Lampeter, U.K. ... 15 E3
Lampman, Canada ... 103 D8
Lamprechtshausen, Austria ... 26 D5
Lampung □, Indonesia ... 62 F2
Lamta, India ... 69 H9
Lamu, Kenya ... 86 C5
Lamy, U.S.A. ... 109 J11
Lan Xian, China ... 56 E6
Lan Yu = Hungt'ou Hsü, Taiwan ... 59 G13
Lanak La, China ... 69 B8
Lanak'o Shank'ou = Lanak La, China ... 69 B8
Lanao, L., Phil. ... 61 H6
Lanark, Canada ... 117 A8
Lanark, U.K. ... 13 F5
Lanbi Kyun, Burma ... 65 G2
Lancang, China ... 58 F2
Lancang Jiang →, China ... 58 G3
Lancashire □, U.K. ... 14 D5
Lancaster, Canada ... 117 A10
Lancaster, U.K. ... 14 C5
Lancaster, Calif., U.S.A. ... 111 L8
Lancaster, Ky., U.S.A. ... 114 G3
Lancaster, N.H., U.S.A. ... 117 B13
Lancaster, N.Y., U.S.A. ... 116 D6
Lancaster, Ohio, U.S.A. ... 114 F4
Lancaster, Pa., U.S.A. ... 117 F8

Lancaster, S.C., U.S.A. ... 115 H5
Lancaster, Wis., U.S.A. ... 112 D9
Lancaster Sd., Canada ... 101 A11
Lancelin, Australia ... 93 F2
Lanchow = Lanzhou, China ... 56 F2
Lanchyn, Ukraine ... 29 B9
Lanciano, Italy ... 41 F11
Lancun, China ... 57 F11
Łańcut, Poland ... 31 H9
Land Between the Lakes △, U.S.A. ... 115 G1
Landau, Bayern, Germany ... 25 G8
Landau, Rhld-Pfz., Germany ... 25 F4
Landeck, Austria ... 26 D3
Lander, U.S.A. ... 108 E9
Lander →, Australia ... 92 D5
Landerneau, France ... 18 D2
Landes, France ... 20 D2
Landes □, France ... 20 E3
Landes de Gascogne △, France ... 20 D3
Landete, Spain ... 38 F3
Landi Kotal, Pakistan ... 68 B4
Landisburg, U.S.A. ... 116 F7
Landivisiau, France ... 18 D2
Landquart, Switz. ... 25 J5
Landrecies, France ... 19 B10
Land's End, U.K. ... 15 G2
Landsberg, Germany ... 25 G6
Landsborough Cr. →, Australia ... 94 C3
Landsbro, Sweden ... 11 G8
Landshut, Germany ... 25 G8
Landskrona, Sweden ... 11 J6
Landstuhl, Germany ... 25 F3
Landvetter, Sweden ... 11 G6
Lanesboro, U.S.A. ... 117 E9
Lanester, France ... 18 E3
Lanett, U.S.A. ... 115 J3
Lång Jan = Ölands södra udde, Sweden ... 11 H10
Langeac, France ... 20 C7
Langeais, France ... 18 E7
Langeb Baraka →, Sudan ... 80 D4
Langeberg, S. Africa ... 88 E3
Langeberge, S. Africa ... 88 D3
Langeland, Denmark ... 11 K4
Langelands Bælt, Denmark ... 11 K4
Langen, Hessen, Germany ... 25 F4
Langen, Niedersachsen, Germany ... 24 B4
Langenburg, Canada ... 103 C8
Langeneß, Germany ... 24 A4
Langenlois, Austria ... 26 C8
Langeoog, Germany ... 24 B3
Langeskov, Denmark ... 11 J4
Länghem, Sweden ... 11 G7
Langhirano, Italy ... 40 D7
Langholm, U.K. ... 13 F5
Langjökull, Iceland ... 8 D3
Langkawi, Pulau, Malaysia ... 65 J2
Langklip, S. Africa ... 88 D3
Langkon, Malaysia ... 62 C5
Langlade, St-P. & M. ... 105 C8
Langley, Canada ... 110 A4
Langnau, Switz. ... 25 J3
Langogne, France ... 20 D7
Langon, France ... 20 D3
Langøya, Norway ... 8 B16
Langreo, Spain ... 36 B5
Langres, France ... 19 E12
Langres, Plateau de, France ... 19 E12
Langsa, Indonesia ... 62 D1
Långsele, Sweden ... 10 A11
Långshyttan, Sweden ... 10 D10
Langtry, U.S.A. ... 113 L4
Langu, Thailand ... 65 J2
Langue de Barbarie △, Senegal ... 82 C1
Languedoc, France ... 20 E7
Languedoc-Roussillon □, France ... 20 E6
Langxi, China ... 59 B12
Langxiangzhen, China ... 56 E9
Langzhong, China ... 58 B5
Lanigan, Canada ... 103 C7
Lankao, China ... 56 G8
Länkäran, Azerbaijan ... 71 B6
Lanmeur, France ... 18 D3
Lannemezan, France ... 20 E4
Lannilis, France ... 18 D2
Lannion, France ... 18 D3
L'Annonciation, Canada ... 104 C5
Lanouaille, France ... 20 C5
Lanping, China ... 58 D2
Lansdale, U.S.A. ... 117 F9
Lansdowne, Australia ... 95 E5
Lansdowne, Canada ... 117 B8
Lansdowne House, Canada ... 104 B2
L'Anse, U.S.A. ... 114 B1
L'Anse au Loup, Canada ... 105 B8
L'Anse aux Meadows, Canada ... 105 B8
Lansford, U.S.A. ... 117 F9
Lanshan, China ... 59 E9
Lansing, U.S.A. ... 114 D3
Lanslebourg-Mont-Cenis, France ... 21 C10
Lanta Yai, Ko, Thailand ... 65 J2
Lantewa, Nigeria ... 83 C7
Lantian, China ... 56 G5
Lanus, Argentina ... 126 C4

Lanusei, Italy ... 42 C2
Lanuza, Phil. ... 61 G7
Lanxi, China ... 59 C12
Lanzarote, Canary Is. ... 48 F6
Lanzarote ✈ (ACE), Canary Is. ... 48 F6
Lanzhou, China ... 56 F2
Lanzo Torinese, Italy ... 40 C4
Lao →, Italy ... 43 C8
Lao Bao, Laos ... 64 D6
Lao Cai, Vietnam ... 58 F4
Laoag, Phil. ... 61 B4
Laoang, Phil. ... 61 E6
Laoha He →, China ... 57 C11
Laohekou, China ... 59 A8
Laois □, Ireland ... 12 D4
Laon, France ... 19 C10
Laona, U.S.A. ... 114 C1
Laos ■, Asia ... 64 D5
Lapa, Brazil ... 127 B6
Lapai, Nigeria ... 83 D6
Lapalisse, France ... 19 F10
Lapeer, U.S.A. ... 114 D4
Lapeyrade, France ... 20 D3
Lapithos, Cyprus ... 49 D12
Lapland = Lappland, Europe ... 8 B21
Laporte, U.S.A. ... 117 E8
Lapovo, Serbia & M. ... 44 B5
Lappeenranta, Finland ... 9 F23
Lappland, Europe ... 8 B21
Lappo = Lapua, Finland ... 8 E20
Laprida, Argentina ... 126 D3
Lapseki, Turkey ... 45 F10
Laptev Sea, Russia ... 53 B13
Lapua, Finland ... 8 E20
Lăpuş →, Romania ... 29 C8
Lăpuş, Munţii, Romania ... 29 C8
Lăpuşna, Moldova ... 29 D13
Łapy, Poland ... 31 F9
Laqiya Arba'in, Sudan ... 80 C2
Laqiya Umran, Sudan ... 80 D2
L'Áquila, Italy ... 41 F10
Lār, Āzarbāyjān-e Sharqī, Iran ... 70 B5
Lār, Fārs, Iran ... 71 E7
Larabanga, Ghana ... 82 D4
Laragne-Montéglin, France ... 21 D9
Laramie, U.S.A. ... 112 E2
Laramie →, U.S.A. ... 108 F11
Laramie Mts., U.S.A. ... 112 E2
Laranjeiras do Sul, Brazil ... 127 B5
Larantuka, Indonesia ... 63 F6
Larat, Indonesia ... 63 F8
L'Arbresle, France ... 21 C8
Lärbro, Sweden ... 11 G12
Larde, Mozam. ... 87 F4
Larder Lake, Canada ... 104 C4
Lardhos, Ákra = Líndhos, Ákra, Greece ... 49 C10
Lardhos, Órmos, Greece ... 49 C10
Laredo, Spain ... 36 B7
Laredo, U.S.A. ... 113 M5
Laredo Sd., Canada ... 102 C3
Largentière, France ... 21 D8
L'Argentière-la-Bessée, France ... 21 D10
Largo, U.S.A. ... 115 M4
Largs, U.K. ... 13 F4
Lari, Italy ... 40 E7
Lariang, Indonesia ... 63 E5
Larimore, U.S.A. ... 112 B6
Larino, Italy ... 41 G11
Lárisa, Greece ... 46 B4
Lárisa □, Greece ... 46 B4
Larkana, Pakistan ... 68 F3
Larnaca, Cyprus ... 49 E12
Larnaca Bay, Cyprus ... 49 E12
Larne, U.K. ... 12 B6
Larned, U.S.A. ... 112 F5
Laroquebrou, France ... 20 D6
Larose, U.S.A. ... 113 L9
Larrimah, Australia ... 92 C5
Larsen Ice Shelf, Antarctica ... 5 C17
Laruns, France ... 20 F3
Larvik, Norway ... 9 G14
Larzac, Causse du, France ... 20 E7
Las Alpujarras, Spain ... 39 J1
Las Animas, U.S.A. ... 112 F3
Las Anod, Somali Rep. ... 75 F4
Las Arenas, Spain ... 36 B6
Las Batuecas △, Spain ... 36 E4
Las Breñas, Argentina ... 126 B3
Las Cabezas de San Juan, Spain ... 37 J5
Las Cañadas del Teide △, Canary Is. ... 48 F3
Las Cejas, Argentina ... 128 B4
Las Chimeneas, Mexico ... 111 N10
Las Cruces, U.S.A. ... 109 K10
Las Flores, Argentina ... 126 D4
Las Heras, Argentina ... 126 C2
Las Lajas, Argentina ... 128 D2
Las Lomitas, Argentina ... 126 A3
Las Marismas, Spain ... 37 H4
Las Minas, Spain ... 39 G3
Las Navas de la Concepción, Spain ... 37 H5
Las Navas del Marqués, Spain ... 36 E6
Las Palmas, Argentina ... 126 B4
Las Palmas, Canary Is. ... 48 F4
Las Palmas →, Mexico ... 111 N10
Las Palmas ✈ (LPA), Canary Is. ... 48 G4
Las Palmas de Cocalán △, Chile ... 126 C1
Las Pedroñas, Spain ... 39 F2
Las Piedras, Uruguay ... 127 C4
Las Pipinas, Argentina ... 126 D4
Las Plumas, Argentina ... 128 E3
Las Rosas, Argentina ... 126 C3
Las Rozas, Spain ... 36 E7
Las Tablas, Panama ... 120 E3
Las Termas, Argentina ... 126 B3
Las Toscas, Argentina ... 126 B4
Las Truchas, Mexico ... 118 D4
Las Varillas, Argentina ... 126 C3
Las Vegas, N. Mex., U.S.A. ... 109 J11
Las Vegas, Nev., U.S.A. ... 111 J11

Las Vegas McCarran
  International ✈ (LAS), U.S.A.   111   J11
Lasarte, Spain   38   B2
Lascano, Uruguay   127   C5
Lash-e Joveyn, Afghan.   66   D2
Lashburn, Canada   103   C7
Lashio, Burma   67   H20
Lashkar, India   68   F8
Łasin, Poland   30   E6
Lasíthi, Greece   49   D7
Lasíthi □, Greece   49   D7
Lāsjerd, Iran   71   C7
Lask, Poland   31   G6
Łaskarzew, Poland   31   G8
Laško, Slovenia   41   B12
Lassay-les-Châteaux, France   18   D6
Lassen Pk., U.S.A.   108   F3
Lassen Volcanic △, U.S.A.   108   F3
Last Mountain L., Canada   103   C7
Lastchance Cr. ➤, U.S.A.   110   E5
Lastoursville, Gabon   84   E2
Lastovo, Croatia   41   F13
Lastovski Kanal, Croatia   41   F14
Lat Yao, Thailand   64   E2
Latacunga, Ecuador   124   D3
Latakia = Al Lādhiqīyah, Syria   70   C2
Latchford, Canada   104   C4
Latehar, India   69   H11
Laterza, Italy   43   B9
Latham, Australia   93   E2
Lathen, Germany   24   C3
Lathi, India   68   F4
Lathrop Wells, U.S.A.   111   J10
Latiano, Italy   43   B10
Latina, Italy   42   A5
Latisana, Italy   41   C10
Latium = Lazio □, Italy   41   F9
Laton, U.S.A.   110   J7
Latorytsya ➤, Slovak Rep.   27   C14
Latouche Treville, C., Australia   92   C3
Latrobe, Australia   95   G4
Latrobe, U.S.A.   116   F5
Latrónico, Italy   43   B9
Latvia ■, Europe   9   H20
Lau, Nigeria   83   D7
Lau Group, Fiji   91   C9
Lauchhammer, Germany   24   D9
Lauda-Königshofen, Germany   25   F5
Lauenburg, Germany   24   B6
Lauenburgische Seen △, Germany   24   B6
Lauf, Germany   25   F7
Laughlin, U.S.A.   109   J6
Laujar de Andarax, Spain   39   H2
Laukaa, Finland   9   E21
Launceston, Australia   95   G4
Launceston, U.K.   15   G3
Laune ➤, Ireland   12   D2
Launglon Bok, Burma   64   F1
Laupheim, Germany   25   G5
Laura, Australia   94   B3
Laureana di Borrello, Italy   43   D9
Laurel, Miss., U.S.A.   113   K10
Laurel, Mont., U.S.A.   108   D9
Laurencekirk, U.K.   13   E6
Laurens, U.S.A.   115   H4
Laurentian Plateau, Canada   105   B6
Lauria, Italy   43   B8
Laurie L., Canada   103   B8
Laurinburg, U.S.A.   115   H6
Laurium, U.S.A.   114   B1
Lausanne, Switz.   25   J2
Laut, Indonesia   62   D3
Laut, Pulau, Indonesia   62   E5
Laut Kecil, Kepulauan, Indonesia   62   E5
Lauterbach, Germany   24   E5
Lauterecken, Germany   25   F3
Lautoka, Fiji   91   C7
Lauzès, France   20   D5
Lava ➤, Russia   30   D8
Lava Beds △, U.S.A.   108   F3
Lavagh More, Ireland   12   B3
Lavagna, Italy   40   D6
Laval, France   18   D6
Lavalle, Argentina   126   B2
Lavant Station, Canada   117   A8
Lāvar Meydān, Iran   71   D7
Lávara, Greece   45   E10
Lavardac, France   20   D4
Lavaur, France   20   E5
Lavelanet, France   20   F5
Lavello, Italy   43   A8
Laverton, Australia   93   E3
Lavis, Italy   40   B8
Lávkos, Greece   46   B5
Lavos, Portugal   36   E2
Lavradio, Portugal   37   G1
Lavras, Brazil   127   A7
Lavre, Portugal   37   G2
Lávrion, Greece   46   D6
Lávris, Greece   49   D6
Lavumisa, Swaziland   89   D5
Lavushi Manda △, Zambia   87   E3
Lawas, Malaysia   62   D5
Lawele, Indonesia   63   F6
Lawn Hill, Australia   94   B2
Lawng Pit, Burma   67   G20
Lawqah, Si. Arabia   70   D4
Lawra, Ghana   82   C4
Lawrence, N.Z.   91   L2
Lawrence, Kans., U.S.A.   112   F7
Lawrence, Mass., U.S.A.   117   D13
Lawrenceburg, Ind., U.S.A.   114   F3
Lawrenceburg, Tenn., U.S.A.   115   H2
Lawrenceville, Ga., U.S.A.   115   J4
Lawrenceville, Pa., U.S.A.   116   E7
Laws, U.S.A.   110   H8
Lawton, U.S.A.   113   H5
Lawu, Indonesia   63   G14
Lawz, J. al, Si. Arabia   80   B4
Laxå, Sweden   11   F8
Laxford, L., U.K.   13   C3
Laxou, France   19   D13

Lay ➤, France   20   B2
Layla, Si. Arabia   75   C4
Laylān, Iraq   70   C5
Layon ➤, France   18   E6
Layton, U.S.A.   108   F7
Laytonville, U.S.A.   108   G2
Lazarevac, Serbia & M.   44   B4
Lazarevskoye, Russia   35   J4
Lazarivo, Madag.   89   C8
Lazdijai, Lithuania   30   D10
Lazio □, Italy   41   F9
Lazo, Moldova   29   C13
Lazo, Russia   54   C6
Le Beausset, France   21   E9
Le Bic, Canada   105   C6
Le Blanc, France   20   B5
Le Bleymard, France   20   D7
Le Bourgneuf-la-Fôret, France   18   D6
Le Bugue, France   20   D4
Le Cateau Cambrésis, France   19   B10
Le Caylar, France   20   E7
Le Chambon-Feugerolles, France   21   C8
Le Châtelet, France   19   F9
Le Chesne, France   19   C11
Le Cheylard, France   21   D8
Le Conquet, France   18   D2
Le Creusot, France   19   F11
Le Croisic, France   18   E4
Le Donjon, France   19   F10
Le Dorat, France   20   B5
Le François, Martinique   120   c
Le Gosier, Guadeloupe   120   b
Le Grand-Lucé, France   18   E7
Le Grand-Pressigny, France   18   F7
Le Grand-Quevilly, France   18   C8
Le Havre, France   18   C7
Le Lamentin, Martinique   120   c
Le Lion-d'Angers, France   18   E6
Le Louroux-Béconnais, France   18   E6
Le Luc, France   21   E10
Le Lude, France   18   E7
Le Mans, France   18   E7
Le Marin, Martinique   120   c
Le Mars, U.S.A.   112   D6
Le Mayet-de-Montagne, France   19   F10
Le Mêle-sur-Sarthe, France   18   D7
Le Monastier-sur-Gazeille, France   20   D7
Le Monêtier-les-Bains, France   21   D10
Le Mont-Dore, France   20   C6
Le Mont-St-Michel, France   18   D5
Le Moule, Guadeloupe   120   b
Le Muy, France   21   E10
Le Palais, France   18   E3
Le Perthus, France   20   F6
Le Prêcheur, Martinique   120   c
Le Puy-en-Velay, France   20   C7
Le Robert, Martinique   120   c
Le St-Esprit, Martinique   120   c
Le Sueur, U.S.A.   112   C8
Le Teil, France   21   D8
Le Teilleul, France   18   D6
Le Theil, France   18   D7
Le Thillot, France   19   E13
Le Thuy, Vietnam   64   D6
Le Touquet-Paris-Plage, France   19   B8
Le Tréport, France   18   B8
Le Val-d'Ajol, France   19   E13
Le Verdon-sur-Mer, France   20   C2
Le Vigan, France   20   E7
Lea ➤, U.K.   15   F8
Leach, Cambodia   65   F4
Lead, U.S.A.   112   C3
Leader, Canada   103   C7
Leadville, U.S.A.   109   G10
Leaf ➤, U.S.A.   113   K10
Leaf Rapids, Canada   103   B9
Leamington, Canada   116   D2
Leamington, U.S.A.   108   G7
Leamington Spa = Royal
  Leamington Spa, U.K.   15   E6
Le'an, China   59   D10
Leandro Norte Alem, Argentina   127   B4
Leane, L., Ireland   12   D2
Learmonth, Australia   92   D1
Leask, Canada   103   C7
Leatherhead, U.K.   15   F7
Leavenworth, Kans., U.S.A.   112   F7
Leavenworth, Wash., U.S.A.   108   C3
Łeba, Poland   30   D4
Łeba ➤, Poland   30   D4
Lebach, Germany   25   F2
Lebak, Phil.   61   H6
Lebam, U.S.A.   110   D3
Lebane, Serbia & M.   44   D5
Lebanon, Ind., U.S.A.   114   E2
Lebanon, Kans., U.S.A.   112   F5
Lebanon, Ky., U.S.A.   114   G3
Lebanon, Mo., U.S.A.   113   G8
Lebanon, N.H., U.S.A.   117   C12
Lebanon, Oreg., U.S.A.   108   D2
Lebanon, Pa., U.S.A.   117   F8
Lebanon, Tenn., U.S.A.   115   G2
Lebanon ■, Asia   74   B5
Lebec, U.S.A.   111   L8
Lebedyan, Russia   33   F10
Lebedyn, Ukraine   33   G8
Lebel-sur-Quévillon, Canada   104   C4
Lebomboberge, S. Africa   89   C5
Lębork, Poland   30   D4
Lebrija, Spain   37   J4
Łebsko, Jezioro, Poland   30   D4
Lebu, Chile   126   D1
Leca da Palmeira, Portugal   36   D2
Lecce, Italy   43   B11
Lecco, Italy   40   C6
Lecco, L. di, Italy   40   C6
Lécera, Spain   38   D4
Lech, Austria   26   D3
Lech ➤, Germany   25   G6
Lechang, China   59   E9
Lechtaler Alpen, Austria   26   D3

Lecontes Mills, U.S.A.   116   E6
Lectoure, France   20   E4
Łęczna, Poland   31   G9
Łęczyca, Poland   31   F6
Ledesma, Spain   36   D5
Ledong, China   64   C7
Leduc, Canada   102   C6
Lee, U.S.A.   117   D11
Lee ➤, Ireland   12   E3
Lee Vining, U.S.A.   110   H7
Leech L., U.S.A.   112   B7
Leeds, U.K.   14   D6
Leeds, U.S.A.   115   J2
Leek, Neths.   17   A6
Leek, U.K.   14   D5
Leeman, Australia   93   E1
Leeper, U.S.A.   116   E5
Leer, Germany   24   B3
Leesburg, U.S.A.   115   L5
Leesville, U.S.A.   113   K8
Leeton, Australia   95   E4
Leetonia, U.S.A.   116   F4
Leeu Gamka, S. Africa   88   E3
Leeuwarden, Neths.   17   A5
Leeuwin, C., Australia   93   F2
Leeuwin Naturaliste △, Australia   93   F2
Leeward Is., Atl. Oc.   121   C7
Lefka, Cyprus   49   D11
Lefkoniko, Cyprus   49   D12
Lefroy, Canada   116   B5
Lefroy, L., Australia   93   F3
Łeg ➤, Poland   31   H8
Leganés, Spain   36   E7
Legazpi, Phil.   61   E5
Lège-Cap-Ferret, France   20   D2
Lege Hida, Ethiopia   81   F5
Leghorn = Livorno, Italy   40   E7
Legionowo, Poland   31   F8
Legnago, Italy   41   C8
Legnano, Italy   40   C5
Legnica, Poland   31   G3
Legrad, Croatia   41   B13
Leh, India   69   B7
Lehigh Acres, U.S.A.   115   M5
Lehighton, U.S.A.   117   F9
Lehliu, Romania   29   F11
Leho, Sudan   81   F3
Lehrte, Germany   24   C5
Lehututu, Botswana   88   C3
Lei Shui ➤, China   59   D9
Leiah, Pakistan   68   D4
Leibnitz, Austria   26   E8
Leibo, China   58   C4
Leicester, U.K.   15   E6
Leicester City □, U.K.   15   E6
Leicestershire □, U.K.   15   E6
Leichhardt ➤, Australia   94   B2
Leichhardt Ra., Australia   94   C4
Leiden, Neths.   17   B4
Leie ➤, Belgium   17   C3
Leifers = Láives, Italy   41   B8
Leimen, Germany   25   F4
Leine ➤, Germany   24   C5
Leinefelde, Germany   24   D6
Leinster, Australia   93   E3
Leinster □, Ireland   12   C4
Leinster, Mt., Ireland   12   D5
Leipalingis, Lithuania   30   D10
Leipzig, Germany   24   D8
Leiria, Portugal   36   F2
Leiria □, Portugal   36   F2
Leirvik, Norway   9   G11
Leishan, China   58   D7
Leisler, Mt., Australia   92   D4
Leith, U.K.   13   F5
Leith Hill, U.K.   15   F7
Leitha ➤, Europe   27   D10
Leitrim, Ireland   12   B3
Leitrim □, Ireland   12   B4
Leitza, Spain   38   B3
Leiyang, China   59   D9
Leizhou, China   59   G8
Leizhou Bandao, China   58   G7
Leizhou Wan, China   59   G8
Lek ➤, Neths.   17   C4
Leka, Norway   8   D14
Lekáni, Greece   45   E8
Lekbibaj, Albania   44   D3
Lekeitio, Spain   38   B2
Lekhainá, Greece   46   D3
Lekoui, Burkina Faso   82   C4
Leksand, Sweden   10   D9
Lékva Óros, Greece   49   D6
Leland, Mich., U.S.A.   114   C3
Leland, Miss., U.S.A.   113   J9
Lelâng, Sweden   10   E6
Leleque, Argentina   128   E2
Lelystad, Neths.   17   B5
Lem, Denmark   11   H2
Lema, Nigeria   83   C5
Lema Shilindi, Ethiopia   81   G5
Léman, L., Europe   19   F13
Lembar, Indonesia   63   K19
Lembuak, Indonesia   63   K19
Lemera, Dem. Rep. of the Congo   86   C2
Lemery, Phil.   61   E4
Lemhi Ra., U.S.A.   108   D7
Lemmer, Neths.   17   B5
Lemmon, U.S.A.   112   C3
Lemon Grove, U.S.A.   111   N9
Lemoore, U.S.A.   110   J7
Lempdes, France   20   C7
Lemvig, Denmark   11   H2
Lena ➤, Russia   53   B13
Lenart, Slovenia   41   B12
Lenartovce, Slovak Rep.   27   C13
Lencloître, France   18   F7
Léndas, Greece   49   E6
Lendava, Slovenia   41   B13
Lendeh, Iran   71   D6

Lendinara, Italy   41   C8
Lengerich, Germany   24   C3
Lenggong, Malaysia   65   K3
Lenggries, Germany   25   H7
Lengshuijiang, China   59   D8
Lengshuitan, China   59   D8
Lengua de Vaca, Pta., Chile   126   C1
Lenina, Kanal ➤, Russia   35   J7
Lenino, Ukraine   33   K8
Leninogorsk, Kazakhstan   52   D9
Leninsk, Russia   35   F7
Leninsk-Kuznetskiy, Russia   52   D9
Leninskoye, Russia   34   A8
Lenk, Switz.   25   J3
Lenkoran = Länkäran, Azerbaijan   71   B6
Lenmalu, Indonesia   63   E8
Lenne ➤, Germany   24   D3
Lennestadt, Germany   24   D4
Lennox, U.S.A.   112   D6
Lennoxville, Canada   117   A13
Leno, Italy   40   C7
Lenoir, U.S.A.   115   H5
Lenoir City, U.S.A.   115   H3
Lenore L., Canada   103   C8
Lenox, U.S.A.   117   D11
Lens, France   19   B9
Lensahn, Germany   24   A6
Lensk, Russia   53   C12
Lentekhi, Georgia   35   J6
Lenti, Hungary   28   D1
Lentini, Italy   43   E8
Lenwood, U.S.A.   111   L9
Lenya, Burma   62   B1
Lenzen, Germany   24   B7
Léo, Burkina Faso   82   C4
Leoben, Austria   26   D8
Leodhas = Lewis, U.K.   13   C2
Leola, U.S.A.   112   C5
Leominster, U.K.   15   E5
Leominster, U.S.A.   117   D13
León, France   20   E2
León, Mexico   118   C4
León, Nic.   120   D2
León, Spain   36   C5
León, U.S.A.   112   E8
León □, Spain   36   C5
Leon ➤, U.S.A.   113   K6
León, Montes de, Spain   36   C4
Leonardo da Vinci, Roma ✈
  (FCO), Italy   41   G9
Leonardtown, U.S.A.   114   F7
Leonardville, Namibia   88   C2
Leonberg, Germany   25   G5
Leonding, Austria   26   C7
Leonessa, Italy   41   F9
Leonforte, Italy   43   E7
Leongatha, Australia   95   F4
Leonídhion, Greece   46   D4
Leonora, Australia   93   E3
Leopoldina, Brazil   127   A7
Leopoldsburg, Belgium   17   C5
Leoti, U.S.A.   112   F4
Leova, Moldova   29   D13
Leoville, Canada   103   C7
Lepe, Spain   37   H3
Lepel = Lyepyel, Belarus   32   E5
Lepenoú, Greece   46   C3
Leping, China   59   C11
Lépo, L. do, Angola   88   B2
Lepontine, Alpi, Italy   40   B5
Leppävirta, Finland   9   E22
Lepsény, Hungary   28   D3
Lequeitio = Lekeitio, Spain   38   B2
Lercara Friddi, Italy   42   E6
Lerdo, Mexico   118   B4
Léré, Chad   83   D7
Léré, Mali   82   B4
Lere, Bauchi, Nigeria   83   D6
Lere, Kaduna, Nigeria   83   C6
Leribe, Lesotho   89   D4
Lérici, Italy   40   D6
Lérida = Lleida, Spain   38   D5
Lérins, Îs. de, France   21   E11
Lerma, Spain   36   C7
Léros, Greece   47   D8
Lérouville, France   19   D12
Lerum, Sweden   11   G6
Lerwick, U.K.   13   A7
Leş, Romania   28   D6
Les Abrets, France   21   C9
Les Andelys, France   18   C8
Les Borges Blanques, Spain   38   D5
Les Cayes, Haiti   121   C5
Les Coteaux, Canada   117   A10
Les Essarts, France   18   F5
Les Herbiers, France   18   F5
Les Minquiers, Plateau des,
  Chan. Is.   18   D4
Les Pieux, France   18   C5
Les Ponts-de-Cé, France   18   E6
Les Riceys, France   19   E11
Les Sables-d'Olonne, France   20   B2
Les Vans, France   21   D8
Lesbos = Lésvos, Greece   47   B8
L'Escala, Spain   38   C8
Leshan, China   58   C4
Leshwe △, Dem. Rep. of
  the Congo   87   E2
Lésina, Italy   41   G12
Lésina, L. di, Italy   41   G12
Lesjöfors, Sweden   10   E8
Lesko, Poland   31   J9
Leskov I., Antarctica   5   B1
Leskovac, Serbia & M.   44   C5
Leskovik, Albania   44   F4
Leśna, Poland   31   G2
Lesneven, France   18   D2
Leśnica, Poland   31   H5
Lešnica, Serbia & M.   44   B3

Lesnoye, Russia   32   C8
Lesopilnoye, Russia   54   A7
Lesotho ■, Africa   89   D4
Lesozavodsk, Russia   53   E14
Lesparre-Médoc, France   20   C3
Lessay, France   18   C5
Lesse ➤, Belgium   17   D4
Lesse et Lomme △, Belgium   17   D5
Lessebo, Sweden   11   H9
Lesser Antilles, W. Indies   121   D7
Lesser Slave L., Canada   102   B5
Lesser Sunda Is., Indonesia   63   F6
Lessines, Belgium   17   D3
Lester, U.S.A.   110   C5
Lester B. Pearson International,
  Toronto ✈ (YYZ), Canada   116   C5
Lestock, Canada   103   C8
Lesuer I., Australia   92   B4
Lesueur △, Australia   93   F2
Lésvos, Greece   47   B8
Leszno, Poland   31   G3
Letaba, S. Africa   89   C5
Letälven, Sweden   10   E8
Letchworth, U.K.   15   F7
Letea, Ostrov, Romania   29   E15
Lethbridge, Canada   102   D6
Lethem, Guyana   124   C7
Leti, Kepulauan, Indonesia   63   F7
Leti Is. = Leti, Kepulauan,
  Indonesia   63   F7
Letiahau ➤, Botswana   88   C3
Leticia, Colombia   124   D5
Leting, China   57   E10
Letjiesbos, S. Africa   88   E3
Letlhakane, Botswana   88   C4
Letlhakeng, Botswana   88   C3
Letong, Indonesia   62   D3
Letpadan, Burma   67   L19
Letpan, Burma   67   K19
Letsôk-aw Kyun, Burma   65   G2
Letterkenny, Ireland   12   B4
Leu, Romania   29   F9
Leucadia, U.S.A.   111   M9
Leucate, France   20   F7
Leucate, Étang de, France   20   F7
Leuchars, U.K.   13   E6
Leuk, Switz.   25   J3
Leuşeni, Moldova   29   D13
Leuser, G., Indonesia   62   D1
Leutkirch, Germany   25   H6
Leuven, Belgium   17   D4
Leuze-en-Hainaut, Belgium   17   D3
Lev Tolstoy, Russia   32   F10
Levádhia, Greece   46   C4
Levan, Albania   44   F3
Levanger, Norway   8   E14
Levant, Î. du, France   21   E10
Lévanto, Italy   40   D6
Lévanzo, Italy   42   D5
Levelland, U.S.A.   113   J3
Leven, U.K.   13   E6
Leven, L., U.K.   13   E5
Leven, Toraka, Madag.   89   A8
Leveque C., Australia   92   C3
Leverano, Italy   43   B10
Leverkusen, Germany   24   D3
Levice, Slovak Rep.   27   C11
Lévico Terme, Italy   41   C8
Levie, France   21   G13
Levier, France   19   F13
Levin, N.Z.   91   J5
Lévis, Canada   105   C5
Levis, L., Canada   102   A5
Levítha, Greece   47   D8
Levittown, N.Y., U.S.A.   117   F11
Levittown, Pa., U.S.A.   117   F10
Levka, Bulgaria   45   E10
Levkás, Greece   46   C2
Levkás □, Greece   46   C2
Levkímmi, Greece   49   B4
Levkímmi, Ákra, Greece   49   B4
Levkôsia = Nicosia, Cyprus   49   D12
Levoča, Slovak Rep.   27   B13
Levroux, France   19   F8
Levski, Bulgaria   45   C9
Levskigrad = Karlovo, Bulgaria   45   D8
Lewes, U.K.   15   G8
Lewes, U.S.A.   114   F8
Lewin Brzeski, Poland   31   H4
Lewis, U.K.   13   C2
Lewis ➤, U.S.A.   110   E4
Lewis, Butt of, U.K.   13   C2
Lewis Ra., Australia   92   D4
Lewis Range, U.S.A.   108   C7
Lewis Run, U.S.A.   116   E6
Lewisburg, Pa., U.S.A.   116   F8
Lewisburg, Tenn., U.S.A.   115   H2
Lewisburg, W. Va., U.S.A.   114   G5
Lewisporte, Canada   105   C8
Lewiston, Idaho, U.S.A.   108   C5
Lewiston, Maine, U.S.A.   115   C11
Lewiston, N.Y., U.S.A.   116   C5
Lewistown, Mont., U.S.A.   108   C9
Lewistown, Pa., U.S.A.   116   F7
Lexington, Ill., U.S.A.   112   E10
Lexington, Ky., U.S.A.   114   F3
Lexington, Mich., U.S.A.   116   C2
Lexington, Mo., U.S.A.   112   F8
Lexington, N.C., U.S.A.   115   H5
Lexington, N.Y., U.S.A.   117   D10
Lexington, Nebr., U.S.A.   112   E5
Lexington, Ohio, U.S.A.   116   F2
Lexington, Tenn., U.S.A.   115   H1
Lexington, Va., U.S.A.   114   G6
Lexington Park, U.S.A.   114   F7
Leyburn, U.K.   14   C6
Leye, China   58   E6
Leyland, U.K.   14   D5
Leyre ➤, France   20   D2
Leyte □, Phil.   61   F6
Leyte Gulf, Phil.   61   F6

Leżajsk, *Poland* 31 H9
Lezay, *France* 20 B3
Lezhë, *Albania* 44 E3
Lezhi, *China* 58 B5
Lézignan-Corbières, *France* .. 20 E6
Lezoux, *France* 20 C7
Lgov, *Russia* 33 G8
Lhasa, *China* 60 D4
Lhazê, *China* 60 D3
Lhokkruet, *Indonesia* 62 D1
Lhokseumawe, *Indonesia* 62 C1
L'Hospitalet de Llobregat, *Spain* 38 D7
Li, *Thailand* 64 D2
Li Shui →, *China* 59 C9
Li Xian, *Gansu, China* 56 G3
Li Xian, *Hebei, China* 56 E8
Li Xian, *Hunan, China* 59 C8
Liádhoi, *Greece* 47 E8
Liancheng, *China* 59 E11
Liancourt Rocks = Tok-do, *Asia* 55 F5
Lianga, *Phil.* 61 G7
Liangcheng,
　Nei Monggol Zizhiqu, China .. 56 D7
Liangcheng, *Shandong, China* 57 G10
Liangdang, *China* 56 H4
Lianghe, *China* 58 E2
Lianghekou, *China* 58 C7
Liangping, *China* 58 B6
Liangpran, *Indonesia* 62 D4
Lianhua, *China* 59 D9
Lianjiang, *Fujian, China* 59 D12
Lianjiang, *Guangdong, China* 59 G8
Lianping, *China* 59 E10
Lianshan, *China* 59 E9
Lianshanguan, *China* 57 D12
Lianshui, *China* 57 H10
Lianyuan, *China* 59 D8
Lianyungang, *China* 57 G10
Lianzhou, *China* 59 E9
Liao He →, *China* 57 D11
Liaocheng, *China* 56 F8
Liaodong Bandao, *China* 57 E12
Liaodong Wan, *China* 57 D11
Liaoning □, *China* 57 D12
Liaotung, G. of = Liaodong Wan,
　China 57 D11
Liaoyang, *China* 57 D12
Liaoyuan, *China* 57 C13
Liaozhong, *China* 57 D12
Liapádhes, *Greece* 46 B1
Liard →, *Canada* 102 A4
Liard River, *Canada* 102 B3
Liari, *Pakistan* 68 G2
Libau = Liepāja, *Latvia* 9 H19
Libby, *U.S.A.* 108 B6
Libenge, *Dem. Rep. of the Congo* 84 D3
Liberal, *U.S.A.* 113 G4
Liberec, *Czech Rep.* 26 A8
Liberecký □, *Czech Rep.* 26 A8
Liberia, *Costa Rica* 120 D2
Liberia ■, *W. Afr.* 82 D3
Liberty, *Mo., U.S.A.* 112 F7
Liberty, *N.Y., U.S.A.* 117 E10
Liberty, *Pa., U.S.A.* 116 E7
Liberty, *Tex., U.S.A.* 113 K7
Libiąż, *Poland* 31 H6
Lībīya, Sahrâ', *Africa* 79 C10
Libo, *China* 58 E6
Libobo, Tanjung, *Indonesia* .. 63 E7
Libode, *S. Africa* 89 E4
Libohovë, *Albania* 44 F4
Libourne, *France* 20 D3
Libramont, *Belgium* 17 E5
Librazhd, *Albania* 44 E4
Libreville, *Gabon* 84 D1
Libya ■, *N. Afr.* 79 C9
Libyan Desert = Lībīya, Sahrâ',
　Africa 79 C10
Libyan Plateau = Ed-Déffa, *Egypt* 80 A2
Licantén, *Chile* 126 D1
Licata, *Italy* 42 E6
Lice, *Turkey* 73 C9
Licheng, *China* 56 F7
Lichfield, *U.K.* 15 E6
Lichinga, *Mozam.* 87 E4
Lichtenburg, *S. Africa* 88 D4
Lichtenfels, *Germany* 25 E7
Lichuan, *Hubei, China* 58 B7
Lichuan, *Jiangxi, China* 59 D11
Licking →, *U.S.A.* 114 F3
Licosa, Punta, *Italy* 43 B7
Licungo →, *Mozam.* 87 F4
Lida, *Belarus* 9 K21
Liden, *Sweden* 10 B10
Lidhoríkion, *Greece* 46 C4
Lidhult, *Sweden* 11 H7
Lidköping, *Sweden* 11 F7
Lido, *Italy* 41 C9
Lido, *Niger* 83 C5
Lido di Roma = Óstia, Lido di,
　Italy 41 G9
Lidzbark, *Poland* 31 E6
Lidzbark Warmiński, *Poland* .. 30 D7
Liebenwalde, *Germany* 24 C9
Lieberose, *Germany* 24 D10
Liebig, Mt., *Australia* 92 D5
Liebling, *Romania* 28 E6
Liechtenstein ■, *Europe* 25 H5
Liège, *Belgium* 17 D5
Liège □, *Belgium* 17 D5
Liegnitz = Legnica, *Poland* .. 31 G3
Lienart, *Dem. Rep. of the Congo* 86 B2
Lienyünchiangshih =
　Lianyungang, *China* 57 G10
Lienz, *Austria* 26 E5
Liepāja, *Latvia* 9 H19
Liepāja □, *Latvia* 30 B8
Liepājas ezers, *Latvia* 30 B8
Lier, *Belgium* 17 C4
Liernais, *France* 19 E11
Liești, *Romania* 29 E12
Liévin, *France* 19 B9

Lièvre →, *Canada* 104 C4
Liezen, *Austria* 26 D7
Liffey →, *Ireland* 12 C5
Lifford, *Ireland* 12 B4
Liffré, *France* 18 D5
Lifudzin, *Russia* 54 B7
Ligao, *Phil.* 61 E5
Lightning Ridge, *Australia* .. 95 D4
Lignano Sabbiadoro, *Italy* .. 41 C10
Ligny-en-Barrois, *France* 19 D12
Ligonha →, *Mozam.* 87 F4
Ligonier, *U.S.A.* 116 F5
Ligoúrion, *Greece* 46 D5
Ligueil, *France* 18 E7
Liguria □, *Italy* 40 D5
Ligurian Sea, *Medit. S.* 6 G7
Lihou Reefs and Cays, *Australia* 94 B5
Lihue, *U.S.A.* 106 H15
Lihué Calel △, *Argentina* 126 D2
Lijiang, *China* 58 D3
Likasi, *Dem. Rep. of the Congo* 87 E2
Likenäs, *Sweden* 10 D7
Likhoslavl, *Russia* 32 D9
Likhovskoy, *Russia* 33 H11
Likoma I., *Malawi* 87 E3
Likumburu, *Tanzania* 87 D4
L'Île-Bouchard, *France* 18 E7
L'Île-Rousse, *France* 21 F12
Liling, *China* 59 D9
Lilla Edet, *Sweden* 11 F6
Lille, *France* 19 B10
Lille Bælt, *Denmark* 11 J3
Lillebonne, *France* 18 C7
Lillehammer, *Norway* 9 F14
Lillesand, *Norway* 9 G13
Lillhärdal, *Sweden* 10 C8
Lillian Pt., *Australia* 93 E4
Lillo, *Spain* 36 F7
Lillooet, *Canada* 102 C4
Lillooet →, *Canada* 102 D4
Lilongwe, *Malawi* 87 E3
Liloy, *Phil.* 63 C6
Lim →, *Bos.-H.* 44 C3
Lim Chu Kang, *Singapore* .... 65 d
Lima, *Indonesia* 63 E7
Lima, *Peru* 124 F3
Lima, *Mont., U.S.A.* 108 D7
Lima, *Ohio, U.S.A.* 114 E3
Lima →, *Portugal* 36 D2
Liman, *Indonesia* 63 G14
Liman, *Russia* 35 H8
Limanowa, *Poland* 31 J7
Limassol, *Cyprus* 49 E12
Limay →, *Argentina* 128 D3
Limay Mahuida, *Argentina* .. 126 D2
Limbach-Oberfrohna, *Germany* 24 E8
Limbang, *Brunei* 62 D5
Limbara, Mte., *Italy* 42 B2
Limbaži, *Latvia* 9 H21
Limbdi, *India* 68 H4
Limbe, *Cameroon* 83 E6
Limburg, *Germany* 25 E4
Limburg □, *Belgium* 17 C5
Limburg □, *Neths.* 17 C5
Limedsforsen, *Sweden* 10 D7
Limeira, *Brazil* 127 A6
Limenária, *Greece* 45 F8
Limerick, *Ireland* 12 D3
Limerick, *U.S.A.* 117 C14
Limerick □, *Ireland* 12 D3
Limestone, *U.S.A.* 116 D6
Limestone →, *Canada* 103 B10
Limfjorden, *Denmark* 11 H3
Limia = Lima →, *Portugal* .. 36 D2
Limín Khersonísou, *Greece* .. 47 F7
Limingen, *Norway* 8 D15
Limmared, *Sweden* 11 G7
Limmen Bight, *Australia* 94 A2
Limmen Bight →, *Australia* .. 94 B2
Límni, *Greece* 46 C5
Límnos, *Greece* 47 B7
Limoges, *Canada* 117 A9
Limoges, *France* 20 C5
Limón, *Costa Rica* 120 E3
Limon, *U.S.A.* 112 F3
Limone Piemonte, *Italy* 40 D4
Limousin □, *France* 20 C5
Limousin, Plateaux du, *France* 20 C5
Limoux, *France* 20 E6
Limpopo □, *S. Africa* 89 C4
Limpopo →, *Africa* 89 D5
Limuru, *Kenya* 86 C4
Lin Xian, *China* 56 F6
Lin'an, *China* 59 B12
Linapacan I., *Phil.* 61 F3
Linapacan Str., *Phil.* 61 F3
Linares, *Chile* 126 D1
Linares, *Mexico* 119 C5
Linares, *Spain* 37 G7
Linaro, Capo, *Italy* 41 F8
Línas Mte., *Italy* 42 C1
Linate, Milano ✈ (LIN), *Italy* .. 40 C6
Lincang, *China* 58 F3
Lincheng, *China* 56 F8
Linchuan, *China* 59 D11
Lincoln = Beamsville, *Canada* 116 C5
Lincoln, *Argentina* 126 C3
Lincoln, *N.Z.* 91 K4
Lincoln, *U.K.* 14 D7
Lincoln, *Calif., U.S.A.* 110 G5
Lincoln, *Ill., U.S.A.* 112 E10
Lincoln, *Kans., U.S.A.* 112 F5
Lincoln, *Maine, U.S.A.* 115 C11
Lincoln, *N.H., U.S.A.* 117 B13
Lincoln, *N. Mex., U.S.A.* .. 109 K11
Lincoln, *Nebr., U.S.A.* 112 E6
Lincoln City, *U.S.A.* 108 D1
Lincoln Hav = Lincoln Sea, *Arctic* 4 A5
Lincoln Sea, *Arctic* 4 A5
Lincolnshire □, *U.K.* 14 D7
Lincolnshire Wolds, *U.K.* 14 D7

Lincolnton, *U.S.A.* 115 H5
Lind, *U.S.A.* 108 C4
Linda, *U.S.A.* 110 F5
Lindau, *Germany* 25 H5
Lindeman I., *Australia* 94 J7
Linden, *Guyana* 124 B7
Linden, *Ala., U.S.A.* 115 J2
Linden, *Calif., U.S.A.* 110 G5
Linden, *Tex., U.S.A.* 113 J7
Lindenhurst, *U.S.A.* 117 F11
Lindesberg, *Sweden* 10 E9
Lindesnes, *Norway* 9 H12
Líndhos, *Greece* 49 C10
Líndhos, Ákra, *Greece* 49 C10
Lindi, *Tanzania* 87 D4
Lindi □, *Tanzania* 87 D4
Lindi →, *Dem. Rep. of the Congo* 86 B2
Lindö, *Sweden* 11 F10
Lindome, *Sweden* 11 G6
Lindoso, *Portugal* 36 D2
Lindow, *Germany* 24 C8
Lindsay, *Canada* 116 B6
Lindsay, *Calif., U.S.A.* 110 J7
Lindsay, *Okla., U.S.A.* 113 H6
Lindsborg, *U.S.A.* 112 F6
Lindsdal, *Sweden* 11 H10
Line Islands, *Pac. Oc.* 97 H12
Linesville, *U.S.A.* 116 E4
Linfen, *China* 56 F6
Ling Xian, *Hunan, China* 59 D9
Ling Xian, *Shandong, China* 56 F9
Lingao, *China* 64 C7
Lingayen, *Phil.* 63 A6
Lingayen G., *Phil.* 61 C4
Lingbi, *China* 57 H9
Lingbo, *Sweden* 10 C10
Lingchuan, *Guangxi Zhuangzu,
　China* 59 E8
Lingchuan, *Shanxi, China* .. 56 G7
Lingen, *Germany* 24 C3
Lingga, *Indonesia* 62 E2
Lingga, Kepulauan, *Indonesia* 62 E2
Lingga Arch. = Lingga,
　Kepulauan, *Indonesia* 62 E2
Linghem, *Sweden* 11 F9
Lingle, *U.S.A.* 112 D2
Lingqiu, *China* 56 E8
Lingshan, *China* 58 F7
Lingshi, *China* 56 F6
Lingshou, *China* 56 E8
Lingshui, *China* 64 C8
Lingtai, *China* 56 G4
Linguère, *Senegal* 82 B1
Lingui, *China* 59 E8
Lingwu, *China* 56 E4
Lingyuan, *China* 57 D10
Lingyun, *China* 58 E6
Linhai, *China* 59 C13
Linhares, *Brazil* 125 G10
Linhe, *China* 56 D4
Linjiang, *China* 57 D14
Linköping, *Sweden* 11 F9
Linkou, *China* 57 B16
Linli, *China* 59 C8
Linnhe, L., *U.K.* 13 E3
Linqi, *China* 56 G7
Linqing, *China* 56 F8
Linru, *China* 57 F10
Linru, *China* 56 G7
Lins, *Brazil* 127 A6
Linshui, *China* 58 B6
Linstead, *Jamaica* .... 120 a
Linta →, *Madag.* 89 D7
Linth →, *Switz.* 25 H5
Linthal, *Switz.* 25 J5
Linton, *Ind., U.S.A.* 114 F2
Linton, *N. Dak., U.S.A.* 112 B4
Lintong, *China* 56 G5
Linwood, *Canada* 116 C4
Linwu, *China* 59 E9
Linxi, *China* 57 C10
Linxia, *China* 60 C5
Linxiang, *China* 59 C9
Linyanti →, *Africa* 88 B4
Linyi, *China* 57 G10
Linz, *Austria* 26 C7
Linz, *Germany* 24 E3
Linzhenzhen, *China* 56 F5
Linzi, *China* 57 F10
Lion, G. du, *France* 20 E7
Lionárisso, *Cyprus* 49 D13
Lioni, *Italy* 43 B8
Lions, G. of = Lion, G. du, *France* 20 E7
Lion's Den, *Zimbabwe* 87 F3
Lion's Head, *Canada* 116 B3
Liozno = Lyozna, *Belarus* .. 32 E6
Lipa, *Phil.* 61 E4
Lipali, *Mozam.* 87 F4
Lipany, *Slovak Rep.* 27 B13
Lípari, *Italy* 43 D7
Lípari, Is. = Éolie, Ís., *Italy* .. 43 D7
Lipcani, *Moldova* 29 B11
Lipetsk, *Russia* 33 F10
Lipiany, *Poland* 31 E1
Liping, *China* 58 D7
Lipkany = Lipcani, *Moldova* 29 B11
Lipljan, *Serbia & M.* 44 D5
Lipník nad Bečvou, *Czech Rep.* 27 B10
Lipno, *Poland* 31 F6
Lipova, *Romania* 28 D6
Lipovcy Manzovka, *Russia* .. 54 B5
Lipovets, *Ukraine* 33 H5
Lippe →, *Germany* 24 D2
Lippstadt, *Germany* 24 D4
Lipscomb, *U.S.A.* 113 G4
Lipsk, *Poland* 30 E10
Lipsko, *Poland* 31 G8
Lipsói, *Greece* 47 D8
Liptovský Hrádok, *Slovak Rep.* 27 B12
Liptovský Milkuláš, *Slovak Rep.* 27 B12
Liptrap, C., *Australia* 95 F4

Lipu, *China* 59 E8
Liquillo, Sierra de, *Puerto Rico* . 121 d
Lira, *Uganda* 86 B3
Liri →, *Italy* 42 A6
Liria = Llíria, *Spain* 39 F4
Lisala, *Dem. Rep. of the Congo* . 84 D4
Lisboa, *Portugal* 37 G1
Lisboa □, *Portugal* 37 F1
Lisboa ✈ (LIS), *Portugal* .. 37 G1
Lisbon = Lisboa, *Portugal* .. 37 G1
Lisbon, *N. Dak., U.S.A.* 112 B6
Lisbon, *N.H., U.S.A.* 117 B13
Lisbon, *Ohio, U.S.A.* 116 F4
Lisbon Falls, *U.S.A.* 115 D10
Lisburn, *U.K.* 12 B5
Lisburne, C., *U.S.A.* 4 C17
Liscannor B., *Ireland* 12 D2
Liscia →, *Italy* 42 A2
Lishe Jiang →, *China* 58 E3
Lishi, *China* 56 F6
Lishu, *China* 57 C13
Lishui, *Jiangsu, China* 59 B12
Lishui, *Zhejiang, China* 59 C12
Lisianski I., *Pac. Oc.* 96 E10
Lisichansk = Lysychansk, *Ukraine* 33 H10
Lisieux, *France* 18 C7
Liski, *Russia* 33 G10
L'Isle-Jourdain, *Gers, France* .. 20 E5
L'Isle-Jourdain, *Vienne, France* .. 20 B4
L'Isle-sur-la-Sorgue, *France* .. 21 E9
Lisle-sur-Tarn, *France* 20 E5
Lismore, *Australia* 95 D5
Lismore, *Ireland* 12 D4
Lista, *Norway* 9 G12
Lister, Mt., *Antarctica* 5 D11
Liston, *Australia* 95 D5
Listowel, *Canada* 116 C4
Listowel, *Ireland* 12 D2
Lit, *Sweden* 10 A8
Lit-et-Mixe, *France* 20 D2
Litang, *Guangxi Zhuangzu, China* 58 F7
Litang, *Sichuan, China* 58 B3
Litang Qu →, *China* 58 C3
Litani →, *Lebanon* 74 B4
Litchfield, *Calif., U.S.A.* .. 110 E6
Litchfield, *Conn., U.S.A.* .. 117 E11
Litchfield, *Ill., U.S.A.* 112 F10
Litchfield, *Minn., U.S.A.* .. 112 C7
Litchfield △, *Australia* 92 B5
Liteni, *Romania* 29 C11
Lithgow, *Australia* 95 E5
Líthinon, Ákra, *Greece* 49 E6
Lithuania ■, *Europe* 9 J20
Litija, *Slovenia* 41 B11
Lititz, *U.S.A.* 117 F8
Litókhoron, *Greece* 44 F6
Litoměřice, *Czech Rep.* 26 A7
Litomyšl, *Czech Rep.* 27 B9
Litschau, *Austria* 26 C8
Little Abaco, *Bahamas* 120 A4
Little Barrier I., *N.Z.* 91 G5
Little Belt Mts., *U.S.A.* .. 108 C8
Little Bighorn Battlefield △,
　U.S.A. 108 D10
Little Blue →, *U.S.A.* 112 F6
Little Buffalo →, *Canada* .. 102 A6
Little Cayman, *Cayman Is.* .. 120 C3
Little Churchill →, *Canada* .. 103 B9
Little Colorado →, *U.S.A.* .. 109 H8
Little Current, *Canada* 104 C3
Little Current →, *Canada* .. 104 B3
Little Falls, *Minn., U.S.A.* .. 112 C7
Little Falls, *N.Y., U.S.A.* .. 117 C10
Little Fork →, *U.S.A.* 112 A8
Little Grand Rapids, *Canada* .. 103 C9
Little Humboldt →, *U.S.A.* .. 108 F5
Little Inagua I., *Bahamas* .. 121 B5
Little Karoo, *S. Africa* 88 E3
Little Khingan Mts. = Xiao
　Hinggan Ling, *China* 60 B7
Little Lake, *U.S.A.* 111 K9
Little Laut Is. = Laut Kecil,
　Kepulauan, *Indonesia* 62 E5
Little Mecatina = Petit-
　Mécatina →, *Canada* 105 B8
Little Minch, *U.K.* 13 D2
Little Missouri →, *U.S.A.* .. 112 B3
Little Ouse →, *U.K.* 15 E9
Little Rann, *India* 68 H4
Little Red →, *U.S.A.* 113 H9
Little River, *N.Z.* 91 K4
Little Rock, *U.S.A.* 113 H8
Little Ruaha →, *Tanzania* .. 86 D4
Little Sable Pt., *U.S.A.* 114 D2
Little Scarcies →, *S. Leone* 82 D2
Little Sioux →, *U.S.A.* 112 E6
Little Smoky →, *Canada* 102 C5
Little Snake →, *U.S.A.* 108 F9
Little Tobago, *Trin. & Tob.* .. 125 J16
Little Valley, *U.S.A.* 116 D6
Little Wabash →, *U.S.A.* .. 114 G1
Little White →, *U.S.A.* 112 D4
Little Zab = Zāb aş Şaghīr →,
　Iraq 70 C4
Littlefield, *U.S.A.* 113 J3
Littlehampton, *U.K.* 15 G7
Littleton, *U.S.A.* 117 B13
Litvinov, *Czech Rep.* 26 A6
Liu He →, *China* 57 D11
Liu Jiang →, *China* 58 F7
Liuba, *China* 56 H4
Liucheng, *China* 58 E7
Liugou, *China* 57 D10
Liuhe, *China* 57 C13
Liuheng Dao, *China* 59 C14
Liujiang, *China* 58 E7
Liulin, *China* 56 F6
Liuwa Plain, *Zambia* 85 G4
Liuyang, *China* 59 C9
Liuzhou, *China* 58 E7

Liuzhuang, *China* 57 H11
Livada, *Romania* 28 C8
Livadherón, *Greece* 44 F5
Livadhia, *Cyprus* 49 E12
Livádhion, *Greece* 46 A4
Livarot, *France* 18 D7
Live Oak, *Calif., U.S.A.* .. 110 F5
Live Oak, *Fla., U.S.A.* 115 K4
Liveras, *Cyprus* 49 D11
Livermore, *U.S.A.* 110 H5
Livermore, Mt., *U.S.A.* 113 K2
Livermore Falls, *U.S.A.* .. 115 C11
Liverpool, *Canada* 105 D7
Liverpool, *U.K.* 14 D4
Liverpool, *U.S.A.* 117 C8
Liverpool Bay, *U.K.* 14 D4
Liverpool Ra., *Australia* .. 95 E5
Livingston, *Guatemala* 120 C2
Livingston, *U.K.* 13 F5
Livingston, *Ala., U.S.A.* .. 115 J1
Livingston, *Calif., U.S.A.* .. 110 H6
Livingston, *Mont., U.S.A.* .. 108 D8
Livingston, *S.C., U.S.A.* .. 115 J5
Livingston, *Tenn., U.S.A.* .. 115 G3
Livingston, *Tex., U.S.A.* .. 113 K7
Livingston, L., *U.S.A.* 113 K7
Livingston Manor, *U.S.A.* .. 117 E10
Livingstone, *Zambia* 87 F2
Livingstone Mts., *Tanzania* .. 87 D3
Livingstonia, *Malawi* 87 E3
Livno, *Bos.-H.* 28 G2
Livny, *Russia* 33 F9
Livonia, *Mich., U.S.A.* 114 D4
Livonia, *N.Y., U.S.A.* 116 D7
Livorno, *Italy* 40 E7
Livradois-Forez △, *France* .. 20 E7
Livramento, *Brazil* 127 C4
Livron-sur-Drôme, *France* .. 21 D8
Livyntsi, *Ukraine* 29 B11
Liwale, *Tanzania* 87 D4
Liwiec →, *Poland* 31 F8
Liwonde △, *Malawi* 87 E4
Lixi, *China* 58 D3
Lixian, *China* 58 B4
Lixoúrion, *Greece* 46 C2
Liyang, *China* 59 B12
Lizard I., *Australia* 94 A4
Lizard Pt., *U.K.* 15 H2
Lizzano, *Italy* 43 B10
Ljig, *Serbia & M.* 44 B4
Ljubija, *Bos.-H.* 41 D13
Ljubinje, *Bos.-H.* 44 D2
Ljubljana, *Slovenia* 41 B11
Ljubljana ✈ (LJU), *Slovenia* .. 41 B11
Ljubno, *Slovenia* 41 B11
Ljubovija, *Serbia & M.* 44 B3
Ljugarn, *Sweden* 11 G12
Ljung, *Sweden* 11 G7
Ljungan →, *Sweden* 10 B11
Ljungaverk, *Sweden* 10 B10
Ljungby, *Sweden* 11 H7
Ljungbyholm, *Sweden* 11 H10
Ljungdalen, *Sweden* 10 B6
Ljungsbro, *Sweden* 11 F9
Ljungskile, *Sweden* 11 F5
Ljusdal, *Sweden* 10 C10
Ljusfallshammar, *Sweden* .. 11 F9
Ljusnan →, *Sweden* 10 C11
Ljusne, *Sweden* 10 C11
Ljutomer, *Slovenia* 41 B13
Llagostera, *Spain* 38 D7
Llancanelo, Salina, *Argentina* .. 126 D2
Llandeilo, U.K. 15 F4
Llandovery, *U.K.* 15 F4
Llandrindod Wells, *U.K.* .. 15 E4
Llandudno, *U.K.* 14 D4
Llanelli, *U.K.* 15 F3
Llanes, *Spain* 36 B6
Llangollen, *U.K.* 14 E4
Llanidloes, *U.K.* 15 E4
Llano, *U.S.A.* 113 K5
Llano →, *U.S.A.* 113 K5
Llano Estacado, *U.S.A.* .. 113 J3
Llanos, *S. Amer.* 124 C4
Llanos de Challe △, *Chile* .. 126 B1
Llanquihue, L., *Chile* 128 E1
Llanwrtyd Wells, *U.K.* 15 E4
Llebeig, C. des, *Spain* 48 B9
Lleida, *Spain* 38 D5
Lleida □, *Spain* 38 C6
Llentrisca, C., *Spain* 48 C7
Llera, *Mexico* 119 C5
Llerena, *Spain* 37 G5
Lleyn Peninsula, *U.K.* 14 E3
Llico, *Chile* 126 C1
Llíria, *Spain* 39 F4
Llobregat →, *Spain* 38 D7
Llodio, *Spain* 38 B2
Lloret de Mar, *Spain* 38 D7
Lloyd B., *Australia* 94 A3
Lloyd L., *Canada* 103 B7
Lloydminster, *Canada* 103 C7
Llucena del Cid, *Spain* 38 E4
Llucmajor, *Spain* 48 B9
Llullaillaco △, *Chile* 126 A2
Llullaillaco, Volcán, *S. Amer.* .. 126 A2
Lo →, *Vietnam* 64 B5
Loa, *U.S.A.* 109 G8
Loa →, *Chile* 126 A1
Loaita I., *S. China Sea* 62 B4
Loange →, *Dem. Rep. of
　the Congo* 84 E4
Loano, *Italy* 40 D5
Lobatse, *Botswana* 88 D4
Löbau, *Germany* 24 D10
Lobenstein, *Germany* 24 E7
Lobería, *Argentina* 126 D4
Łobez, *Poland* 30 E2
Łobożeok, *Sweden* 11 J7
Łobżek, *Poland* 30 E2
Lobito, *Angola* 85 G2
Lobo →, *Ivory C.* 82 D3

Lobos, *Argentina* 126 D4
Lobos, I., *Mexico* 118 B2
Lobos, I. de, *Canary Is.* 48 F6
Łobżenica, *Poland* 31 E4
Loc Binh, *Vietnam* 64 B6
Loc Ninh, *Vietnam* 65 G6
Locarno, *Switz.* 25 J4
Loch Baghasdail = Lochboisdale,
  U.K. 13 D1
Loch Garman = Wexford, *Ireland* 12 D5
Loch Lomond and the
  Trossachs △, *U.K.* 13 E4
Loch Nam Madadh = Lochmaddy,
  U.K. 13 D1
Lochaber, *U.K.* 13 E3
Locharbriggs, *U.K.* 13 F5
Lochboisdale, *U.K.* 13 D1
Loche, L. La, *Canada* 103 B7
Lochem, *Neths.* 17 B6
Loches, *France* 18 E7
Lochgilphead, *U.K.* 13 E3
Lochinvar △, *Zambia* 87 F2
Lochinver, *U.K.* 13 C3
Lochmaddy, *U.K.* 13 D1
Lochnagar, *Australia* 94 C4
Lochnagar, *U.K.* 13 E5
Łochów, *Poland* 31 F8
Lochy, L., *U.K.* 13 E4
Lock, *Australia* 95 E2
Lock Haven, *U.S.A.* 116 E7
Lockeford, *U.S.A.* 110 G5
Lockeport, *Canada* 105 D6
Lockerbie, *U.K.* 13 F5
Lockhart, *U.S.A.* 113 L6
Lockhart, L., *Australia* 93 F2
Lockhart River, *Australia* ... 94 A3
Lockney, *U.S.A.* 113 H4
Lockport, *U.S.A.* 116 C6
Locminé, *France* 18 E4
Locri, *Italy* 43 D9
Locronan, *France* 18 D2
Lod, *Israel* 74 D3
Lodeinoye Pole, *Russia* 32 B7
Lodève, *France* 20 E7
Lodge Bay, *Canada* 105 B8
Lodge Grass, *U.S.A.* 108 D10
Lodgepole Cr. ➤, *U.S.A.* 112 E2
Lodhran, *Pakistan* 68 E4
Lodi, *Italy* 40 C6
Lodi, *Calif., U.S.A.* 110 G5
Lodi, *Ohio, U.S.A.* 116 E3
Lodja, *Dem. Rep. of the Congo* 86 C1
Lodosa, *Spain* 38 C2
Lödöse, *Sweden* 11 F6
Lodwar, *Kenya* 86 B4
Łódź, *Poland* 31 G6
Łódzkie □, *Poland* 31 G6
Loei, *Thailand* 64 D3
Loengo, *Dem. Rep. of the Congo* 86 C2
Loeriesfontein, *S. Africa* ... 88 E2
Lofa ➤, *Liberia* 83 D2
Lofa Mano △, *Liberia* 82 D2
Lofer, *Austria* 26 D5
Lofoten, *Norway* 8 B15
Lofsdalen, *Sweden* 10 B7
Lofsen ➤, *Sweden* 10 B7
Loftahammar, *Sweden* 11 G10
Loga, *Niger* 83 C5
Logan, *Iowa, U.S.A.* 112 E7
Logan, *Ohio, U.S.A.* 114 F4
Logan, *Utah, U.S.A.* 108 F8
Logan, *W. Va., U.S.A.* 114 G5
Logan, Mt., *Canada* 100 B5
Logandale, *U.S.A.* 111 J12
Logansport, *Ind., U.S.A.* 114 E2
Logansport, *La., U.S.A.* 113 K8
Logirim, *Sudan* 81 G3
Logo, *Sudan* 81 F3
Logone ➤, *Chad* 79 F9
Logroño, *Spain* 38 C2
Logrosán, *Spain* 37 F5
Løgstør, *Denmark* 11 H3
Løgumkloster, *Denmark* 11 J2
Lohals, *Denmark* 11 J4
Lohardaga, *India* 69 H11
Loharia, *India* 68 H6
Loharu, *India* 68 E6
Lohja, *Finland* 9 F21
Löhne, *Germany* 24 C4
Lohr, *Germany* 25 F5
Lohri Wah ➤, *Pakistan* 68 F2
Loi-kaw, *Burma* 67 K20
Loimaa, *Finland* 9 F20
Loir ➤, *France* 18 E6
Loir-et-Cher □, *France* 18 E8
Loire □, *France* 21 C8
Loire ➤, *France* 18 E4
Loire Anjou Touraine △, *France* 18 E6
Loire-Atlantique □, *France* .. 18 E5
Loiret □, *France* 19 E9
Loitz, *Germany* 24 B9
Loja, *Ecuador* 124 D3
Loja, *Spain* 37 H6
Loji = Kawasi, *Indonesia* 63 E7
Lojo = Lohja, *Finland* 9 F21
Løjt Kirkeby, *Denmark* 11 J3
Lojung, *China* 58 E7
Loka, *Sudan* 81 G3
Lokandu, *Dem. Rep. of the Congo* 86 C2
Lokeren, *Belgium* 17 C3
Lokgwabe, *Botswana* 88 C3
Lokhvitsa, *Ukraine* 33 G7
Lokichokio, *Kenya* 86 B3
Lokitaung, *Kenya* 86 B4
Lökkan tekojärvi, *Finland* ... 8 C22
Løkken, *Denmark* 11 G3
Loknya, *Russia* 32 D6
Loko, *Nigeria* 83 D6
Lokoja, *Nigeria* 83 D6
Lokot, *Russia* 33 F8
Lol ➤, *Sudan* 81 F2
Lola, *Guinea* 82 D3

Lola, Mt., *U.S.A.* 110 F6
Lolibai, Gebel, *Sudan* 81 G3
Lolimi, *Sudan* 81 G3
Loliondo, *Tanzania* 86 C4
Lolland, *Denmark* 11 K5
Lollar, *Germany* 24 E4
Lolo, *U.S.A.* 108 C6
Lolodorf, *Cameroon* 83 E7
Lom, *Bulgaria* 44 C7
Lom ➤, *Bulgaria* 44 C7
Lom Kao, *Thailand* 64 D3
Lom Sak, *Thailand* 64 D3
Loma, *U.S.A.* 108 C8
Loma Linda, *U.S.A.* 111 L9
Lomami ➤, *Dem. Rep. of
  the Congo* 86 B1
Lomas de Zamóra, *Argentina* .. 126 C4
Lombadina, *Australia* 92 C3
Lombárdia □, *Italy* 40 C6
Lombardy = Lombárdia □, *Italy* 40 C6
Lombez, *France* 20 E4
Lomblen, *Indonesia* 63 F6
Lombok, *Indonesia* 62 F5
Lombok, Selat, *Indonesia* 63 K18
Lomé, *Togo* 83 D5
Lomela, *Dem. Rep. of the Congo* 84 E4
Lomela ➤, *Dem. Rep. of
  the Congo* 84 E4
Lomgana, *Australia* 93 F4
Lomianki, *Poland* 31 F7
Lomma, *Sweden* 11 J7
Lommel, *Belgium* 17 C5
Lomond, *Canada* 102 C6
Lomond, L., *U.K.* 13 E4
Lomonosov Ridge, *Arctic* ..... 4 A
Lomphat, *Cambodia* 64 F6
Lompobatang, *Indonesia* 63 F5
Lompoc, *U.S.A.* 111 L6
Łomża, *Poland* 31 E9
Lon, Ko, *Thailand* .... 65 a
Loncoche, *Chile* 128 D2
Londa, *India* 66 M9
Londiani, *Kenya* 86 C4
Londinières, *France* 18 C8
London, *Canada* 116 D3
London, *U.K.* 15 F7
London, *Ky., U.S.A.* 114 G3
London, *Ohio, U.S.A.* 114 F4
London, Greater □, *U.K.* 15 F7
London Gatwick ✈ (LGW), *U.K.* 15 F7
London Heathrow ✈ (LHR),
  U.K. 15 F7
London Stansted ✈ (STN), *U.K.* 15 F8
Londonderry, *U.K.* 12 B4
Londonderry □, *U.K.* 12 B4
Londonderry, C., *Australia* .. 92 B4
Londonderry, I., *Chile* 128 H2
Londres, *Argentina* 128 B3
Londrina, *Brazil* 127 A5
Lone Pine, *U.S.A.* 110 J8
Lonely Mine, *Zimbabwe* 89 B4
Long B., *U.S.A.* 115 J6
Long Beach, *Calif., U.S.A.* .. 111 M8
Long Beach, *N.Y., U.S.A.* 117 F11
Long Beach, *Wash., U.S.A.* ... 110 D2
Long Branch, *U.S.A.* 117 F11
Long Creek, *U.S.A.* 108 D4
Long Eaton, *U.K.* 14 E6
Long I., *Australia* 94 J6
Long I., *Bahamas* 121 B4
Long I., *Canada* 104 B4
Long I., *Ireland* 12 E2
Long I., *U.S.A.* 117 F11
Long Island Sd., *U.S.A.* 117 E12
Long L., *Canada* 104 C2
Long Lake, *U.S.A.* 117 C10
Long Point B., *Canada* 116 D4
Long Prairie ➤, *U.S.A.* 112 C7
Long Pt., *Canada* 116 D4
Long Range Mts., *Canada* 105 C8
Long Reef, *Australia* 92 B4
Long Spruce, *Canada* 103 B10
Long Str. = Longa, Proliv, *Russia* 4 C16
Long Thanh, *Vietnam* 65 G6
Long Xian, *China* 56 G4
Long Xuyen, *Vietnam* 65 G5
Longá, *Greece* 46 E3
Longa, Proliv, *Russia* 4 C16
Long'an, *China* 58 F6
Longarone, *Italy* 41 B9
Longbenton, *U.K.* 14 B6
Longboat Key, *U.S.A.* 115 M4
Longchang, *China* 58 C5
Longchi, *China* 58 C4
Longchuan, *Guangdong, China* . 59 E10
Longchuan, *Yunnan, China* 58 E1
Longde, *China* 56 G4
Longeau, *France* 19 E12
Longford, *Australia* 95 G4
Longford, *Ireland* 12 C4
Longford □, *Ireland* 12 C4
Longhai, *China* 59 E11
Longhua, *China* 57 D9
Longido, *Tanzania* 86 C4
Longiram, *Indonesia* 62 E5
Longkou, *Jiangxi, China* 59 D10
Longkou, *Shandong, China* 57 F11
Longlac, *Canada* 104 C2
Longli, *China* 58 D6
Longlin, *China* 58 E5
Longling, *China* 58 E2
Longmeadow, *U.S.A.* 117 D12
Longmen, *China* 59 F10
Longming, *China* 58 F5
Longmont, *U.S.A.* 112 E2
Longnan, *China* 59 E10
Longnawan, *Indonesia* 62 D4
Longobucco, *Italy* 43 C9
Longquan, *China* 59 C12
Longreach, *Australia* 94 C3
Longshan, *China* 58 C7
Longsheng, *China* 59 E8

Longué-Jumelles, *France* 18 E6
Longueau, *France* 19 C9
Longueuil, *Canada* 117 A11
Longuyon, *France* 19 C12
Longvic, *France* 19 E12
Longview, *Tex., U.S.A.* 113 J7
Longview, *Wash., U.S.A.* 110 D4
Longwy, *France* 19 C12
Longxi, *China* 56 G3
Longyan, *China* 59 E11
Longyearbyen, *Svalbard* 4 B8
Longyou, *China* 59 C12
Longzhou, *China* 58 F6
Lonigo, *Italy* 41 C8
Lonja ➤, *Croatia* 41 C13
Lonoke, *U.S.A.* 113 H9
Lonquimay, *Chile* 128 D2
Lons-le-Saunier, *France* 19 F12
Lönsboda, *Sweden* 11 H8
Looe, *U.K.* 15 G3
Lookout, C., *Canada* 104 A3
Lookout, C., *U.S.A.* 115 H7
Loolmalasin, *Tanzania* 86 C4
Loon ➤, *Alta., Canada* 102 B5
Loon ➤, *Man., Canada* 103 B8
Loon Lake, *Canada* 103 C7
Loongana, *Australia* 93 F4
Loop Hd., *Ireland* 12 D2
Lop Buri, *Thailand* 64 E3
Lop Nor = Lop Nur, *China* 60 B4
Lop Nur, *China* 60 B4
Lopare, *Bos.-H.* 28 F3
Lopatin, *Russia* 35 J8
Lopatina, Gora, *Russia* 53 D15
Lopaye, *Sudan* 81 F3
Lopez, *Phil.* 61 E5
Lopez, *U.S.A.* 117 E8
Lopez, C., *Gabon* 84 E1
Lopphavet, *Norway* 8 A19
Lora ➤, *Afghan.* 66 D4
Lora, Hāmūn-i-, *Pakistan* 66 E4
Lora Cr. ➤, *Australia* 95 D2
Lora del Río, *Spain* 37 H5
Lorain, *U.S.A.* 116 E2
Loralai, *Pakistan* 68 D3
Lorca, *Spain* 39 H3
Lord Howe I., *Pac. Oc.* 96 L7
Lord Howe Ridge, *Pac. Oc.* ... 96 L8
Lordsburg, *U.S.A.* 109 K9
Lorestan □, *Iran* 71 C6
Loreto, *Brazil* 125 E9
Loreto, *Italy* 41 E10
Loreto, *Mexico* 118 B2
Lorgues, *France* 21 E10
Lorhosso, *Burkina Faso* 82 C4
Lorient, *France* 18 E3
Lőrinci, *Hungary* 28 C4
Lormi, *India* 69 H9
Lorn, *U.K.* 13 E3
Lorn, Firth of, *U.K.* 13 E3
Lorne, *Australia* 95 F3
Loronyo, *Sudan* 81 G3
Lorovouno, *Cyprus* 49 D11
Lörrach, *Germany* 25 H3
Lorraine △, *France* 19 D12
Lorraine □, *France* 19 D13
Los, *Sweden* 10 C9
Los, Îles de, *Guinea* 82 D2
Los Alamos, *Calif., U.S.A.* .. 111 L6
Los Alamos, *N. Mex., U.S.A.* . 109 J10
Los Alcornocales △, *Spain* ... 37 J5
Los Altos, *U.S.A.* 110 H4
Los Andes, *Chile* 126 C1
Los Angeles, *Chile* 126 D1
Los Angeles, *U.S.A.* 111 M8
Los Angeles, Bahia de, *Mexico* 118 B2
Los Angeles Aqueduct, *U.S.A.* 111 K9
Los Angeles International ✈
  (LAX), *U.S.A.* 111 M8
Los Banos, *U.S.A.* 110 H6
Los Barrios, *Spain* 37 J5
Los Blancos, *Argentina* 126 A3
Los Cardones △, *Argentina* ... 126 B2
Los Chiles, *Costa Rica* 120 D3
Los Corrales de Buelna, *Spain* 36 B6
Los Cristianos, *Canary Is.* .. 48 F3
Los Gallardos, *Spain* 39 H3
Los Gatos, *U.S.A.* 110 H5
Los Haïtises □, *Dom. Rep.* ... 121 C6
Los Hermanos Is., *Venezuela* . 121 D7
Los Islotes, *Canary Is.* 48 E6
Los Llanos de Aridane, *Canary Is.* 48 F2
Los Loros, *Chile* 126 B1
Los Lunas, *U.S.A.* 109 J10
Los Mochis, *Mexico* 118 B3
Los Monegros, *Spain* 38 D4
Los Nietos, *Spain* 39 H4
Los Olivos, *U.S.A.* 111 L6
Los Palacios, *Cuba* 120 B3
Los Palacios y Villafranca, *Spain* 37 H5
Los Reyes, *Mexico* 118 D4
Los Roques Is., *Venezuela* ... 121 D6
Los Santos de Maimona, *Spain* 37 G4
Los Teques, *Venezuela* 124 A5
Los Testigos, Is., *Venezuela* 124 A6
Los Vilos, *Chile* 126 C1
Los Yébenes, *Spain* 37 F7
Łosice, *Poland* 31 F9
Loskop Dam, *S. Africa* 89 D4
Løsning, *Denmark* 11 J3
Lossiemouth, *U.K.* 13 D5
Lossen △, *Sweden* 10 B6
Lostwithiel, *U.K.* 15 G3
Lot □, *France* 20 D5
Lot ➤, *France* 20 D4
Lot-et-Garonne □, *France* 20 D4
Lota, *Chile* 126 D1
Lotagipi Swamp, *Sudan* 81 G3
Loṭfābād, *Iran* 71 B8
Lothair, *S. Africa* 89 D5
Lotorp, *Sweden* 11 F9

Lötschbergtunnel, *Switz.* 25 J3
Löttorp, *Sweden* 11 G11
Lotung, *Taiwan* 59 E13
Loubomo, *Congo* 84 E2
Loudéac, *France* 18 D4
Loudi, *China* 59 D8
Loudonville, *U.S.A.* 116 F2
Loudun, *France* 18 E7
Loue ➤, *France* 19 E12
Louga, *Senegal* 82 B1
Loughborough, *U.K.* 14 E6
Loughrea, *Ireland* 12 C3
Loughros More B., *Ireland* ... 12 B3
Louhans, *France* 19 F12
Louis Trichardt, *S. Africa* .. 89 C4
Louis XIV, Pte., *Canada* 104 B4
Louisa, *U.S.A.* 114 F4
Louisbourg, *Canada* 105 C8
Louise I., *Canada* 102 C2
Louiseville, *Canada* 104 C5
Louisiade Arch., *Papua N. G.* 96 J7
Louisiana, *U.S.A.* 112 F9
Louisiana □, *U.S.A.* 113 K9
Louisville, *Ky., U.S.A.* 114 F3
Louisville, *Miss., U.S.A.* ... 113 J10
Louisville, *Ohio, U.S.A.* 116 F3
Loulay, *France* 20 B3
Loulé, *Portugal* 37 H3
Louny, *Czech Rep.* 26 A6
Loup City, *U.S.A.* 112 E5
Loups Marins, Lacs des, *Canada* 104 A5
Lourdes, *France* 20 E3
Lourinhã, *Portugal* 37 F1
Lousã, *Portugal* 36 E2
Louta, *Burkina Faso* 82 C4
Louth, *Australia* 95 E4
Louth, *Ireland* 12 C5
Louth □, *Ireland* 12 C5
Louth, *U.K.* 14 D7
Loutrá Aidhipsoú, *Greece* 46 C5
Loutráki, *Greece* 46 D4
Louvain = Leuven, *Belgium* ... 17 D4
Louviers, *France* 18 C8
Louwsburg, *S. Africa* 89 D5
Lovat ➤, *Russia* 32 C6
Lovćen, *Serbia & M.* 44 D2
Lovech, *Bulgaria* 45 C8
Lovech □, *Bulgaria* 45 C8
Loveland, *U.S.A.* 112 E2
Lovell, *U.S.A.* 108 D9
Lovelock, *U.S.A.* 108 F4
Lóvere, *Italy* 40 C7
Lövestad, *Sweden* 11 J7
Loviisa, *Finland* 9 F22
Lovisa = Loviisa, *Finland* ... 9 F22
Lovosice, *Czech Rep.* 26 A7
Lovran, *Croatia* 41 C11
Lovrin, *Romania* 28 E5
Lövstabruk, *Sweden* 10 D11
Lövstabukten, *Sweden* 10 D11
Low, L., *Canada* 104 B4
Low Pt., *Australia* 93 F4
Low Tatra = Nízké Tatry,
  Slovak Rep. 27 C12
Lowa, *Dem. Rep. of the Congo* 86 C2
Lowa ➤, *Dem. Rep. of the Congo* 86 C2
Lowell, *U.S.A.* 117 D13
Lowellville, *U.S.A.* 116 E4
Löwen ➤, *Namibia* 88 D2
Lower Alkali L., *U.S.A.* 108 F3
Lower Arrow L., *Canada* 102 D5
Lower Austria =
  Niederösterreich □, *Austria* 26 C8
Lower California = Baja
  California, *Mexico* 118 A1
Lower Hutt, *N.Z.* 91 J5
Lower Lake, *U.S.A.* 110 G4
Lower Manitou L., *Canada* 103 D10
Lower Post, *Canada* 102 B3
Lower Red L., *U.S.A.* 112 B7
Lower Saxony =
  Niedersachsen □, *Germany* .. 24 C4
Lower Tunguska = Tunguska,
  Nizhnyaya ➤, *Russia* 53 C9
Lower Zambezi △, *Zambia* 87 F2
Lowestoft, *U.K.* 15 E9
Lowgar □, *Afghan.* 66 B6
Łowicz, *Poland* 31 F6
Lowville, *U.S.A.* 117 C9
Loxton, *Australia* 95 E3
Loxton, *S. Africa* 88 E3
Loyalton, *U.S.A.* 110 F6
Loyalty Is. = Loyauté, Îs., *N. Cal.* 96 K8
Loyang = Luoyang, *China* 56 G7
Loyauté, Îs., *N. Cal.* 96 K8
Loyev = Loyew, *Belarus* 33 G6
Loyew, *Belarus* 33 G6
Loyoro, *Uganda* 86 B3
Lož, *Slovenia* 41 C11
Lozère □, *France* 20 D7
Loznica, *Serbia & M.* 44 B3
Lozova, *Ukraine* 33 H9
Lü Shan, *China* 59 C11
Lü-Tao, *Taiwan* 59 F13
Lü Xian, *China* 58 D4
Luachimo, *Angola* 84 F4
Luajan ➤, *India* 69 G11
Lualaba ➤, *Dem. Rep. of
  the Congo* 86 B2
Luampa, *Zambia* 87 F1
Lu'an, *China* 59 B11
Luan Chau, *Vietnam* 58 G4
Luan He ➤, *China* 57 E10
Luan Xian, *China* 57 E10
Luancheng, *Guangxi Zhuangzu,
  China* 58 F7
Luancheng, *Hebei, China* 56 F8
Luanco, *Spain* 36 B5
Luanda, *Angola* 84 F2
Luang, Thale, *Thailand* 65 J3

Luang Prabang, *Laos* 58 H4
Luangwa, *Zambia* 87 F3
Luangwa ➤, *Zambia* 87 E3
Luangwa Valley, *Zambia* 87 E3
Luanne, *China* 57 D9
Luanping, *China* 57 D9
Luanshya, *Zambia* 87 E2
Luapula □, *Zambia* 87 E2
Luapula ➤, *Africa* 87 D2
Luarca, *Spain* 36 B4
Luashi, *Dem. Rep. of the Congo* 87 E1
Luau, *Angola* 84 G4
Lubaczów, *Poland* 31 H10
Lubań, *Poland* 31 G2
Lubana, Ozero = Lubānas Ezers,
  Latvia 9 H22
Lubānas Ezers, *Latvia* 9 H22
Lubang, *Phil.* 61 E4
Lubang Is., *Phil.* 63 B6
Lubango, *Angola* 85 G2
Lubao, *Dem. Rep. of the Congo* 86 D2
Lubartów, *Poland* 31 G9
Lubawa, *Poland* 30 E6
Lübbecke, *Germany* 24 C4
Lübben, *Germany* 24 D9
Lübbenau, *Germany* 24 D9
Lubbock, *U.S.A.* 113 J4
Lübeck, *Germany* 24 B6
Lübecker Bucht, *Germany* 24 A6
Lubefu ➤, *Dem. Rep. of the Congo* 86 C1
Lubefu, *Dem. Rep. of
  the Congo* 86 C1
Lubelskie □, *Poland* 31 G9
Lubero = Luofu, *Dem. Rep. of
  the Congo* 86 C2
Luberon △, *France* 21 E9
Lubersac, *France* 20 C5
Lubicon L., *Canada* 102 B5
Lubień Kujawski, *Poland* 31 F6
Lubilash ➤, *Dem. Rep. of
  the Congo* 84 F4
Lubin, *Poland* 31 G3
Lublin, *Poland* 31 G9
Lubliniec, *Poland* 31 H5
Lubnān, Jabal, *Lebanon* 74 B4
Lubniewice, *Poland* 31 F2
Lubny, *Ukraine* 33 G7
Lubomierz, *Poland* 31 G2
Luboń, *Poland* 31 F3
Lubondaja, *Dem. Rep. of
  the Congo* 86 C2
L'ubotín, *Slovak Rep.* 27 B13
Lubraniec, *Poland* 31 F5
Lubsko, *Poland* 31 G1
Lübtheen, *Germany* 24 B7
Lubuagan, *Phil.* 61 C4
Lubudi, *Dem. Rep. of the Congo* 84 F5
Lubudi ➤, *Dem. Rep. of
  the Congo* 87 D2
Lubuklinggau, *Indonesia* 62 E2
Lubuksikaping, *Indonesia* 62 D2
Lubumbashi, *Dem. Rep. of
  the Congo* 87 E2
Lubunda, *Dem. Rep. of the Congo* 86 D2
Lubungu, *Zambia* 87 E2
Lubuskie □, *Poland* 31 F2
Lubutu, *Dem. Rep. of the Congo* 86 C2
Luc An Chau, *Vietnam* 64 A5
Luc-en-Diois, *France* 21 D9
Lucan, *Canada* 116 C3
Lucania, Mt., *Canada* 100 B5
Lucas Channel, *Canada* 116 A3
Lucban, *Phil.* 61 D4
Lucca, *Italy* 40 E7
Lucé, *France* 18 D8
Luce Bay, *U.K.* 13 G4
Lucea, *Jamaica* .... 120 a
Lucedale, *U.S.A.* 115 K1
Lucena, *Phil.* 61 E4
Lucena, *Spain* 37 H6
Lučenec, *Slovak Rep.* 27 C12
Lucera, *Italy* 43 A8
Lucerne = Luzern, *Switz.* 25 H4
Lucerne, *U.S.A.* 110 F4
Lucerne Valley, *U.S.A.* 111 L10
Lucero, *Mexico* 118 A3
Luchena ➤, *Spain* 39 H3
Lucheng, *China* 56 F7
Lucheringa ➤, *Mozam.* 87 E4
Lüchow, *Germany* 24 C7
Luchuan, *China* 59 F8
Lucia, *U.S.A.* 110 J5
Lucinda, *Australia* 94 B4
Luckau, *Germany* 24 D9
Luckenwalde, *Germany* 24 C9
Luckhoff, *S. Africa* 88 D3
Lucknow, *Canada* 116 C3
Lucknow, *India* 69 F9
Luçon, *France* 20 B2
Lüda = Dalian, *China* 57 E11
Luda Kamchiya ➤, *Bulgaria* ... 45 C11
Ludbreg, *Croatia* 41 B13
Lüdenscheid, *Germany* 24 D3
Lüderitz, *Namibia* 88 D2
Lüderitzbaai, *Namibia* 88 D2
Ludhiana, *India* 68 D6
Ludian, *China* 58 D4
Luding Qiao, *China* 58 C4
Lüdinghausen, *Germany* 24 D3
Ludington, *U.S.A.* 114 D2
Ludlow, *U.K.* 15 E5
Ludlow, *Calif., U.S.A.* 111 L10
Ludlow, *Pa., U.S.A.* 116 E6
Ludlow, *Vt., U.S.A.* 117 C12
Ludus, *Romania* 29 D9
Ludvika, *Sweden* 10 D9
Ludwigsburg, *Germany* 25 G5
Ludwigsfelde, *Germany* 24 C9
Ludwigshafen, *Germany* 25 F4
Ludwigslust, *Germany* 24 B7
Ludza, *Latvia* 32 D4
Lueki, *Dem. Rep. of the Congo* 86 C2

Luena, *Dem. Rep. of the Congo* . 87 D2
Luena, *Zambia* 87 E3
Luenha = Ruenya →, *Africa* ... 87 F3
Lüeyang, *China* 56 H4
Lufeng, *Guangdong, China* . 59 F10
Lufeng, *Yunnan, China* .. 58 E4
Lufira →, *Dem. Rep. of the Congo* . 87 D2
Lufkin, *U.S.A.* 113 K7
Lufupa, *Dem. Rep. of the Congo* 87 E1
Luga, *Russia* 32 C5
Luga →, *Russia* 32 C5
Lugano, *Switz.* 25 J4
Lugano, L. di, *Switz.* 40 C6
Lugansk = Luhansk, *Ukraine* .. 33 H10
Lugard's Falls, *Kenya* 86 C4
Lugela, *Mozam.* 87 F4
Lugenda →, *Mozam.* 87 E4
Lugh Ganana, *Somali Rep.* .. 75 G3
Lugnaquillia, *Ireland* 12 D5
Lugo, *Italy* 41 D8
Lugo, *Spain* 36 B3
Lugo □, *Spain* 36 C3
Lugoj, *Romania* 28 E6
Lugovoy = Qulan, *Kazakhstan* .. 52 E8
Luhansk, *Ukraine* 33 H10
Luhe, *China* 59 A12
Luhe →, *Germany* 24 B6
Luhuo, *China* 58 B3
Luiana, *Angola* 88 B3
Luichow Pen. = Leizhou Bandao, *China* 58 G7
Luimneach = Limerick, *Ireland* . 12 D3
Luing, *U.K.* 13 E3
Luino, *Italy* 40 C5
Luís Correia, *Brazil* 125 D10
Luitpold Coast, *Antarctica* .. 5 D1
Luiza, *Dem. Rep. of the Congo* . 84 F4
Luizi, *Dem. Rep. of the Congo* . 86 D2
Luján, *Argentina* 126 C4
Lujiang, *China* 59 B11
Lukang, *Taiwan* 59 E13
Lukanga Swamp, *Zambia* ... 87 E2
Lukavac, *Bos.-H.* 28 F3
Lukenie →, *Dem. Rep. of the Congo* 84 E4
Lukhisaral, *India* 69 G12
Lŭki, *Bulgaria* 45 E8
Lukolela, *Dem. Rep. of the Congo* 86 D1
Lukosi, *Zimbabwe* 87 F2
Lukovë, *Albania* 44 G3
Lukovit, *Bulgaria* 45 C8
Łuków, *Poland* 31 G9
Lukoyanov, *Russia* 34 C7
Lukusuzi △, *Zambia* 87 E3
Luleå, *Sweden* 8 D20
Luleälven →, *Sweden* 8 D19
Lüleburgaz, *Turkey* 45 E11
Luliang, *China* 58 E4
Luling, *U.S.A.* 113 L6
Lulong, *China* 57 E10
Lulonga →, *Dem. Rep. of the Congo* 84 D3
Lulua →, *Dem. Rep. of the Congo* 84 E4
Lumajang, *Indonesia* 63 H15
Lumbala N'guimbo, *Angola* .. 85 G4
Lumberton, *U.S.A.* 115 H6
Lumsden, *Canada* 103 C8
Lumsden, *N.Z.* 91 L2
Lumut, *Malaysia* 65 K3
Lumut, Tanjung, *Indonesia* .. 62 E3
Luna, *India* 68 H3
Lunan, *China* 58 E4
Lunavada, *India* 68 H5
Lunca, *Romania* 29 C10
Lunca Corbului, *Romania* ... 29 F9
Lund, *Sweden* 11 J7
Lundazi, *Zambia* 87 E3
Lunderskov, *Denmark* 11 J3
Lundi →, *Zimbabwe* 87 G3
Lundu, *Malaysia* 62 D3
Lundy, *U.K.* 15 F3
Lune →, *U.K.* 14 C5
Lüneburg, *Germany* 24 B6
Lüneburg Heath = Lüneburger Heide, *Germany* 24 B6
Lüneburger Heide, *Germany* .. 24 B6
Lunel, *France* 21 E8
Lünen, *Germany* 24 D3
Lunenburg, *Canada* 105 D7
Lunéville, *France* 19 D13
Lunga →, *Zambia* 87 E2
Lungi Airport, *S. Leone* 82 D2
Lunglei, *India* 67 H18
Luni, *India* 68 G5
Luni →, *India* 68 G4
Luninets = Luninyets, *Belarus* . 33 F4
Luning, *U.S.A.* 108 G4
Lunino, *Russia* 34 D7
Luninyets, *Belarus* 33 F4
Lunkaransar, *India* 68 E5
Lunsemfwa →, *Zambia* 87 E3
Lunsemfwa Falls, *Zambia* ... 87 E2
Luo He →, *China* 56 G6
Luocheng, *China* 58 E7
Luochuan, *China* 56 G5
Luoci, *China* 58 E4
Luodian, *China* 58 E6
Luoding, *China* 59 F8
Luofu, *Dem. Rep. of the Congo* 86 C2
Luohe, *China* 56 H8
Luojiang, *China* 58 B5
Luonan, *China* 56 G6
Luoning, *China* 56 G6
Luotian, *China* 59 A10
Luoxiao Shan, *China* 59 D10
Luoyang, *China* 56 G7
Luoyuan, *China* 59 D12
Luozigou, *China* 57 C16
Lupanshui, *China* 58 D5
Lupeni, *Romania* 29 E8

Lupilichi, *Mozam.* 87 E4
Łupków, *Poland* 31 J9
Lupoing, *China* 58 E5
Luquan, *China* 58 E4
Luque, *Paraguay* 126 B4
Lúras, *Italy* 42 B2
Luray, *U.S.A.* 114 F6
Lure, *France* 19 E13
Lurgan, *U.K.* 12 B5
Lusaka, *Zambia* 87 F2
Lusaka □, *Zambia* 87 F2
Lusambo, *Dem. Rep. of the Congo* 86 C1
Lusangaye, *Dem. Rep. of the Congo* 86 C2
Luseland, *Canada* 103 C7
Lusenga Plain △, *Zambia* ... 87 D2
Lushan, *Henan, China* 56 H7
Lushan, *Sichuan, China* ... 58 B4
Lushi, *China* 56 G6
Lushnjë, *Albania* 44 F3
Lushoto, *Tanzania* 86 C4
Lushui, *China* 58 E2
Lüshun, *China* 57 E11
Lusignan, *France* 20 B4
Lusigny-sur-Barse, *France* .. 19 D11
Lusk, *U.S.A.* 112 D2
Lussac-les-Châteaux, *France* .. 20 B4
Lustenau, *Austria* 26 D2
Lūt, Dasht-e, *Iran* 71 D8
Luta = Dalian, *China* 57 E11
Lutherstadt Wittenberg, *Germany* 24 D8
Luton, *U.K.* 15 F7
Luton □, *U.K.* 15 F7
Łutselk'e, *Canada* 103 A6
Lutsk, *Ukraine* 33 G3
Lützow Holmbukta, *Antarctica* . 5 C4
Lutzputs, *S. Africa* 88 D3
Luuq = Lugh Ganana, *Somali Rep.* 75 G3
Luverne, *Ala., U.S.A.* 115 K2
Luverne, *Minn., U.S.A.* ... 112 D6
Luvua, *Dem. Rep. of the Congo* . 87 D2
Luvua →, *Dem. Rep. of the Congo* 86 D2
Luvuvhu →, *S. Africa* ... 89 C5
Luwegu →, *Tanzania* 87 D4
Luwuk, *Indonesia* 63 E6
Luxembourg, *Lux.* 17 E6
Luxembourg □, *Belgium* ... 17 E5
Luxembourg ■, *Europe* ... 7 F7
Luxembourg ✈ (LUX), *Lux.* .. 17 E6
Luxeuil-les-Bains, *France* ... 19 E13
Luxi, *Hunan, China* 59 C8
Luxi, *Yunnan, China* 58 E4
Luxi, *Yunnan, China* 58 E2
Luxor = El Uqsur, *Egypt* ... 80 B3
Luy-de-Béarn →, *France* ... 20 E3
Luy-de-France →, *France* ... 20 E3
Luyi, *China* 56 H8
Luz-St-Sauveur, *France* 20 F4
Luzern, *Switz.* 25 H4
Luzern □, *Switz.* 25 H3
Luzhai, *China* 58 E7
Luzhany, *Ukraine* 29 B10
Luzhi, *China* 58 D5
Luzhou, *China* 58 C5
Luziânia, *Brazil* 125 G9
Lužnice →, *Czech Rep.* ... 26 B7
Luzon, *Phil.* 61 D4
Luzon Strait, *Asia* 59 G13
Luzy, *France* 19 F10
Luzzi, *Italy* 43 C9
Lviv, *Ukraine* 33 H3
Lvov = Lviv, *Ukraine* 33 H3
Lwówek, *Poland* 31 F3
Lwówek Śląski, *Poland* 31 G2
Lyakhavichy, *Belarus* 33 F4
Lyakhovskiye, Ostrova, *Russia* . 53 B15
Lyaki = Läki, *Azerbaijan* ... 35 K8
Lyal I., *Canada* 116 B3
Lyaskovets, *Bulgaria* 45 C9
Lyasnaya, *Belarus* 31 F10
Lybster, *U.K.* 13 C5
Lycaonia, *Turkey* 72 D5
Lychen, *Germany* 24 B9
Lychkova, *Russia* 32 C7
Lycia, *Turkey* 47 E11
Lyckebyån →, *Sweden* 11 H9
Lycksele, *Sweden* 8 D18
Lycosura, *Greece* 46 D4
Lydda = Lod, *Israel* 74 D3
Lydenburg, *S. Africa* 89 D5
Lydia, *Turkey* 47 C10
Łydynia →, *Poland* 31 F7
Lyell, *N.Z.* 91 J4
Lyell I., *Canada* 102 C2
Lyepyel, *Belarus* 32 E5
Lykens, *U.S.A.* 117 F8
Lyman, *Ukraine* 29 E14
Lyman, *U.S.A.* 108 F8
Lymanske, *Ukraine* 29 D14
Lyme B., *U.K.* 15 G4
Lyme Regis, *U.K.* 15 G4
Lymington, *U.K.* 15 G6
Łyna →, *Poland* 9 J19
Lynchburg, *U.S.A.* 114 G6
Lynd →, *Australia* 94 B3
Lynd Ra., *Australia* 95 D4
Lynden, *Canada* 116 C4
Lynden, *U.S.A.* 110 B4
Lyndhurst, *Australia* 95 E2
Lyndon →, *Australia* 93 D1
Lyndonville, *N.Y., U.S.A.* .. 116 C6
Lyndonville, *Vt., U.S.A.* ... 117 B12
Lyngen, *Norway* 8 B19
Lynher Reef, *Australia* 92 C3
Lynn, *U.S.A.* 117 D14
Lynn Lake, *Canada* 103 B8
Lynton, *U.K.* 15 F4
Lyntupy, *Belarus* 9 J22

Lynx L., *Canada* 103 A7
Lyon, *France* 21 C8
Lyon St-Exupery ✈ (LYS), *France* 21 C9
Lyonnais, *France* 21 C8
Lyons = Lyon, *France* 21 C8
Lyons, *Ga., U.S.A.* 115 J4
Lyons, *Kans., U.S.A.* 112 F5
Lyons, *N.Y., U.S.A.* 116 C8
Lyons →, *Australia* 93 E2
Lyons Falls, *U.S.A.* 117 C9
Lyozna, *Belarus* 32 E6
Lys = Leie →, *Belgium* ... 17 C3
Lysá nad Labem, *Czech Rep.* .. 26 A7
Lysekil, *Sweden* 11 F5
Lyskovo, *Russia* 34 B7
Lystrup, *Denmark* 11 H4
Lysvik, *Sweden* 10 D7
Lysychansk, *Ukraine* 33 H10
Lytham St. Anne's, *U.K.* ... 14 D4
Lyttelton, *N.Z.* 91 K4
Lytton, *Canada* 102 C4
Lyuban, *Russia* 32 C6
Lyubertsy, *Russia* 32 E9
Lyubim, *Russia* 32 C11
Lyubimets, *Bulgaria* 45 E10
Lyuboml, *Ukraine* 31 G11
Lyubotyn, *Ukraine* 33 H8
Lyubytino, *Russia* 32 C7
Lyudinovo, *Russia* 32 F8

M

M.R. Gomez, Presa, *Mexico* 119 B5
M.R. Stefanik, Bratislava ✈ (BTS), *Slovak Rep.* 27 C10
Ma →, *Vietnam* 58 H5
Ma'adaba, *Jordan* 74 E4
Maamba, *Zambia* 88 B4
Ma'ān, *Jordan* 74 E4
Ma'ān □, *Jordan* 74 F5
Maanselkä, *Finland* 8 C23
Ma'anshan, *China* 59 B12
Maarianhamina, *Finland* ... 9 F18
Ma'arrat an Nu'mān, *Syria* .. 70 C3
Maas →, *Neths.* 17 C4
Maaseik, *Belgium* 17 C5
Maasin, *Phil.* 63 B6
Maastricht, *Neths.* 17 D5
Maave, *Mozam.* 89 C5
Mababe Depression, *Botswana* . 88 B3
Mabalane, *Mozam.* 89 C5
Mabel L., *Canada* 102 C5
Mabenge, *Dem. Rep. of the Congo* 86 B1
Maberly, *Canada* 117 B8
Mabian, *China* 58 C4
Mabil, *Ethiopia* 81 E4
Mablethorpe, *U.K.* 14 D8
Mably, *France* 19 F10
Maboma, *Dem. Rep. of the Congo* 86 B2
Mabonto, *S. Leone* 82 D2
Mabrouk, *Mali* 83 B4
Mabuasehube △, *Botswana* .. 88 D3
Mac Bac, *Vietnam* 65 H6
Macachín, *Argentina* 126 D3
Macaé, *Brazil* 127 A7
Macael, *Spain* 39 H2
Macalister →, *Australia* ... 95 F4
McAlester, *U.S.A.* 113 H7
McAllen, *U.S.A.* 113 M5
MacAlpine L., *Canada* 100 B9
Macamic, *Canada* 104 C4
Macao = Macau, *China* ... 59 F9
Macão, *Portugal* 37 F3
Macapá, *Brazil* 125 C8
Macarao △, *Venezuela* 121 D6
McArthur →, *Australia* ... 94 B2
McArthur, Port, *Australia* .. 94 B2
Macau, *Brazil* 125 E11
Macau, *China* 59 F9
McBride, *Canada* 102 C4
McCall, *U.S.A.* 108 D5
McCamey, *U.S.A.* 113 K3
McCammon, *U.S.A.* 108 E7
McCauley I., *Canada* 102 C2
McCleary, *U.S.A.* 110 C3
Macclenny, *U.S.A.* 115 K4
Macclesfield, *U.K.* 14 D5
M'Clintock Chan., *Canada* .. 100 A9
McClintock Ra., *Australia* .. 92 C4
McCloud, *U.S.A.* 108 F2
McCluer I., *Australia* 92 B5
McClure, *U.S.A.* 116 F7
McClure, L., *U.S.A.* 110 H6
M'Clure Str., *Canada* 98 B8
McClusky, *U.S.A.* 112 B4
McComb, *U.S.A.* 113 K9
McConaughy, L., *U.S.A.* ... 112 E4
McCook, *U.S.A.* 112 E4
McCreary, *Canada* 103 C9
McCullough Mt., *U.S.A.* ... 111 K11
McCusker →, *Canada* 103 B7
McDame, *Canada* 102 B3
McDermitt, *U.S.A.* 108 F5
McDonald, *U.S.A.* 116 F4
Macdonald, L., *Australia* ... 92 D4
McDonald Is., *Ind. Oc.* ... 3 G13
MacDonnell Ranges, *Australia* . 92 D5
McDowell L., *Canada* 104 B1
Maceda, *Spain* 36 C3
Macedonia ■, *Europe* 44 E5
Maceió, *Brazil* 125 E11
Maceira, *Portugal* 36 F2
Macenta, *Guinea* 82 D3
Macerata, *Italy* 41 E10
McFarland, *U.S.A.* 111 K7
McFarlane →, *Canada* 103 B7

Macfarlane, L., *Australia* ... 95 E2
McGehee, *U.S.A.* 113 J9
McGill, *U.S.A.* 108 G6
Macgillycuddy's Reeks, *Ireland* . 12 E2
McGraw, *U.S.A.* 117 D8
McGregor, *U.S.A.* 112 D9
McGregor Ra., *Australia* ... 95 D3
McGuire, Mt, *Australia* ... 94 A3
Mach, *Pakistan* 66 E5
Māch Kowr, *Iran* 71 E9
Machado = Jiparaná →, *Brazil* . 124 E6
Machagai, *Argentina* 126 B3
Machakos, *Kenya* 86 C4
Machala, *Ecuador* 124 D3
Machanga, *Mozam.* 89 C6
Machattie, L., *Australia* ... 94 C2
Machault, *France* 19 C11
Machava, *Mozam.* 89 D5
Machece, *Mozam.* 87 F4
Macheke, *Zimbabwe* 89 B5
Macheng, *China* 59 B10
Machero, *Spain* 37 F6
Machhu →, *India* 68 H4
Machias, *Maine, U.S.A.* ... 115 C12
Machias, *N.Y., U.S.A.* ... 116 D6
Machichi →, *Canada* 103 B10
Machico, *Madeira* 48 D3
Machilipatnam, *India* 67 L12
Machiques, *Venezuela* 124 A4
Machupicchu, *Peru* 124 F4
Machynlleth, *U.K.* 15 E4
Macia, *Mozam.* 89 D5
Maciejowice, *Poland* 31 G8
McIlwraith Ra., *Australia* .. 94 A3
Măcin, *Romania* 29 E13
Macina, *Mali* 82 C4
McInnes L., *Canada* 103 C10
McIntosh, *U.S.A.* 112 C4
McIntosh L., *Canada* 103 B8
Macintosh Ra., *Australia* ... 93 E4
Macintyre →, *Australia* ... 95 D5
Macizo Galaico, *Spain* 36 C3
Mackay, *Australia* 94 K7
Mackay, *U.S.A.* 108 E7
MacKay →, *Canada* 102 B6
Mackay, L., *Australia* 92 D4
McKay Ra., *Australia* 92 D3
McKeesport, *U.S.A.* 116 F5
McKellar, *Canada* 116 A5
McKenna, *U.S.A.* 110 D4
Mackenzie, *Canada* 102 B4
Mackenzie →, *Australia* ... 94 C4
Mackenzie →, *Canada* 100 B6
McKenzie →, *U.S.A.* 108 D2
Mackenzie Bay, *Canada* ... 4 B1
Mackenzie City = Linden, *Guyana* 124 B7
Mackenzie Mts., *Canada* ... 100 B6
Mackinaw City, *U.S.A.* ... 114 C3
McKinlay, *Australia* 94 C3
McKinlay →, *Australia* ... 94 C3
McKinley, Mt., *U.S.A.* ... 100 B4
McKinley Sea, *Arctic* 4 A7
McKinney, *U.S.A.* 113 J6
Mackinnon Road, *Kenya* ... 86 C4
McKittrick, *U.S.A.* 111 K7
Macklin, *Canada* 103 C7
Macksville, *Australia* 95 E5
McLaughlin, *U.S.A.* 112 C4
Maclean, *Australia* 95 D5
McLean, *U.S.A.* 113 H4
McLeansboro, *U.S.A.* 112 F10
Maclear, *S. Africa* 89 E4
Maclear, C., *Malawi* 87 E3
Macleay →, *Australia* 95 E5
McLennan, *Canada* 102 B5
McLeod →, *Canada* 102 C5
MacLeod, B., *Canada* 103 A7
McLeod, L., *Australia* 93 D1
MacLeod Lake, *Canada* ... 102 C4
McLoughlin, Mt., *U.S.A.* .. 108 E2
McMechen, *U.S.A.* 116 G4
McMinnville, *Oreg., U.S.A.* . 108 D2
McMinnville, *Tenn., U.S.A.* . 115 H3
McMurdo Sd., *Antarctica* .. 5 D11
McMurray = Fort McMurray, *Canada* 102 B6
McMurray, *U.S.A.* 110 B4
Macodoene, *Mozam.* 89 C6
Macomb, *U.S.A.* 112 E9
Macomer, *Italy* 42 B1
Mâcon, *France* 19 F11
Macon, *Ga., U.S.A.* 115 J4
Macon, *Miss., U.S.A.* 115 J1
Macon, *Mo., U.S.A.* 112 F8
Macossa, *Mozam.* 87 F3
Macoun L., *Canada* 103 B8
Macovane, *Mozam.* 89 C6
McPherson, *U.S.A.* 112 F6
McPherson Pk., *U.S.A.* ... 111 L7
McPherson Ra., *Australia* .. 95 D5
Macquarie →, *Australia* ... 95 E4
Macquarie Harbour, *Australia* . 95 G4
Macquarie Is., *Pac. Oc.* ... 96 N7
MacRobertson Land, *Antarctica* . 5 D6
Macroom, *Ireland* 12 E3
MacTier, *Canada* 116 A5
Macubela, *Mozam.* 87 F4
Macugnaga, *Italy* 40 C4
Macuira △, *Colombia* 121 D5
Macuiza, *Mozam.* 87 F3
Macumba, The →, *Australia* . 95 D2
Macuro, *Venezuela* 125 K15
Macusani, *Peru* 124 F4
Macuse, *Mozam.* 87 F4
Macuspana, *Mexico* 119 D6
Macusse, *Angola* 88 B3
Ma'dabā □, *Jordan* 74 D4
Madadeni, *S. Africa* 89 D5
Madagali, *Nigeria* 83 C7

Madagascar ■, *Africa* 89 C8
Madā'in Sālih, *Si. Arabia* ... 70 E3
Madama, *Niger* 79 D8
Madame, I., *Canada* 105 C7
Madan, *Bulgaria* 45 E8
Madaoua, *Niger* 83 C6
Madara, *Nigeria* 83 C7
Madaripur, *Bangla.* 67 H17
Madauk, *Burma* 67 L20
Madawaska, *Canada* 116 A7
Madawaska →, *Canada* ... 116 A8
Madaya, *Burma* 67 H20
Madbar, *Sudan* 81 F3
Maddalena, *Italy* 42 A2
Maddaloni, *Italy* 43 A7
Madeira, *Atl. Oc.* 48 D3
Madeira →, *Brazil* 124 D7
Madeleine, Îs. de la, *Canada* . 105 C7
Maden, *Turkey* 73 C8
Madera, *Mexico* 118 B3
Madera, *Calif., U.S.A.* ... 110 J6
Madera, *Pa., U.S.A.* 116 F6
Madha, *India* 66 L9
Madhavpur, *India* 68 J3
Madhepura, *India* 69 F12
Madhubani, *India* 69 F12
Madhupur, *India* 69 G12
Madhya Pradesh □, *India* .. 68 J8
Madidi →, *Bolivia* 124 F5
Madikeri, *India* 66 N9
Madikwe ∩, *S. Africa* 89 D5
Madill, *U.S.A.* 113 H6
Madimba, *Dem. Rep. of the Congo* 84 E3
Ma'din, *Syria* 70 C3
Madina, *Mali* 82 C3
Madinani, *Ivory C.* 82 D3
Madingou, *Congo* 84 E2
Madirovalo, *Madag.* 89 B8
Madison, *Calif., U.S.A.* ... 110 G5
Madison, *Fla., U.S.A.* 115 K4
Madison, *Ind., U.S.A.* ... 114 F3
Madison, *Nebr., U.S.A.* ... 112 E6
Madison, *Ohio, U.S.A.* ... 116 E3
Madison, *S. Dak., U.S.A.* .. 112 D6
Madison, *Wis., U.S.A.* ... 112 D10
Madison →, *U.S.A.* 108 D8
Madison Heights, *U.S.A.* ... 114 G6
Madisonville, *Ky., U.S.A.* .. 114 G2
Madisonville, *Tex., U.S.A.* .. 113 K7
Madista, *Botswana* 88 C4
Madiun, *Indonesia* 63 G14
Madoc, *Canada* 116 B7
Madol, *Sudan* 81 F2
Madon →, *France* 19 D13
Madona, *Latvia* 9 H22
Madonie, *Italy* 42 E6
Madonna di Campíglio, *Italy* . 40 B7
Madra Dağı, *Turkey* 47 B9
Madrakah, Ra's al, *Oman* .. 75 D6
Madras = Chennai, *India* ... 66 N12
Madras = Tamil Nadu □, *India* . 66 P10
Madras, *U.S.A.* 108 D3
Madre, Laguna, *U.S.A.* ... 113 M6
Madre, Sierra, *Phil.* 61 C5
Madre de Dios →, *Bolivia* .. 124 F5
Madre de Dios, I., *Chile* ... 128 G1
Madre del Sur, Sierra, *Mexico* . 119 D5
Madre Occidental, Sierra, *Mexico* 118 B3
Madre Oriental, Sierra, *Mexico* . 118 C5
Madri, *India* 68 G5
Madrid, *Spain* 36 E7
Madrid, *U.S.A.* 117 B9
Madrid □, *Spain* 36 E7
Madrid Barajas ✈ (MAD), *Spain* . 36 E7
Madridejos, *Spain* 37 F7
Madrigal de las Altas Torres, *Spain* 36 D6
Madrona, Sierra, *Spain* ... 37 G6
Madroñera, *Spain* 37 F5
Madu, *Sudan* 81 E2
Madura, *Australia* 93 F4
Madura, *Indonesia* 63 G15
Madura, Selat, *Indonesia* .. 63 G15
Madurai, *India* 66 Q11
Madurantakam, *India* 66 N11
Madzhalis, *Russia* 35 J8
Mae Chan, *Thailand* 64 C2
Mae Hong Son, *Thailand* .. 64 C1
Mae Khlong →, *Thailand* .. 64 F3
Mae Phrik, *Thailand* 64 D2
Mae Ping △, *Thailand* ... 64 D2
Mae Ramat, *Thailand* 64 D2
Mae Rim, *Thailand* 64 C2
Mae Sot, *Thailand* 64 D2
Mae Suai, *Thailand* 58 H2
Mae Tha, *Thailand* 64 C2
Mae Wong △, *Thailand* ... 64 E2
Mae Yom △, *Thailand* ... 64 C3
Maebashi, *Japan* 55 F9
Maella, *Spain* 38 D5
Maesteg, *U.K.* 15 F4
Maestra, Sierra, *Cuba* 120 B4
Maevatanana, *Madag.* 89 B8
Mafeking = Mafikeng, *S. Africa* . 88 D4
Mafeking, *Canada* 103 C8
Maféré, *Ivory C.* 82 D4
Mafeteng, *Lesotho* 88 D4
Maffra, *Australia* 95 F4
Mafia I., *Tanzania* 86 D4
Mafikeng, *S. Africa* 88 D4
Mafra, *Brazil* 127 B6
Mafra, *Portugal* 37 G1
Mafungbusi Plateau, *Zimbabwe* 87 F2
Magadan, *Russia* 53 D16
Magadi, *Kenya* 86 C4
Magadi, L., *Kenya* 86 C4
Magaliesburg, *S. Africa* ... 89 D4
Magallanes, Estrecho de, *Chile* . 128 G2
Magaluf, *Spain* 39 F7
Magangué, *Colombia* 124 B4
Magaria, *Niger* 83 C6

Magburaka, *S. Leone* 82 D2
Magdalen Is. = Madeleine, Îs. de
  la, *Canada* 105 C7
Magdalena, *Argentina* 126 D4
Magdalena, *Bolivia* 124 F6
Magdalena, *Mexico* 118 A2
Magdalena, *U.S.A.* 109 J10
Magdalena �']', *Colombia* 124 A4
Magdalena �']', *Mexico* 118 A2
Magdalena, B., *Mexico* 118 C2
Magdalena, Llano de la, *Mexico* . 118 C2
Magdeburg, *Germany* 24 C7
Magdelaine Cays, *Australia* 94 B5
Magdub, *Sudan* 81 E2
Magee, *U.S.A.* 113 K10
Magelang, *Indonesia* 63 G14
Magellan's Str. = Magallanes,
  Estrecho de, *Chile* 128 G2
Magenta, *Italy* 40 C5
Magenta, L., *Australia* 93 F2
Magerøya, *Norway* 8 A21
Maggia ➜, *Switz.* 25 J4
Maggiorasca, Mte., *Italy* 40 D6
Maggiore, Lago, *Italy* 40 B5
Maggotty, *Jamaica* .... 120 a
Maghâgha, *Egypt* 80 B3
Maghama, *Mauritania* 82 B2
Magherafelt, *U.K.* 12 B5
Maghreb, *N. Afr.* 78 B5
Magione, *Italy* 41 E9
Magistralnyy, *Russia* 53 D11
Maglaj, *Bos.-H.* 28 F3
Magliano in Toscana, *Italy* 41 F8
Máglie, *Italy* 43 B11
Magnac-Laval, *France* 20 B5
Magnetic Pole (North), *Canada* . 4 A2
Magnetic Pole (South), *Antarctica* 5 C9
Magnisía □, *Greece* 46 B5
Magnitogorsk, *Russia* 52 D6
Magnolia, *Ark., U.S.A.* 113 J8
Magnolia, *Miss., U.S.A.* 113 K9
Magny-en-Vexin, *France* 19 C8
Mago △, *Ethiopia* 81 F4
Magog, *Canada* 117 A12
Magoro, *Uganda* 86 B3
Magoša = Famagusta, *Cyprus* . 49 D12
Magouládhes, *Greece* 49 A3
Magoye, *Zambia* 87 F2
Magozal, *Mexico* 119 C5
Magpie, L., *Canada* 105 B7
Magrath, *Canada* 102 D6
Magre ➜, *Spain* 39 F4
Magrur, *Sudan* 81 E3
Magrur, Wadi ➜, *Sudan* 81 D2
Magta Lahjar, *Mauritania* 82 B2
Maguan, *China* 58 F5
Maguarinho, C., *Brazil* 125 D9
Magude, *Mozam.* 89 D5
Magurski △, *Poland* 31 J8
Mağusa = Famagusta, *Cyprus* . 49 D12
Maguse ➜, *Canada* 103 A9
Maguse Pt., *Canada* 103 A10
Magvana, *India* 68 H3
Magwe, *Burma* 67 J19
Magwe, *Sudan* 81 G3
Maha Sarakham, *Thailand* 64 D4
Mahābād, *Iran* 70 B5
Mahabharat Lekh, *Nepal* 69 E10
Mahabo, *Madag.* 89 C7
Mahadeo Hills, *India* 69 H8
Mahaffey, *U.S.A.* 116 F6
Mahagi, *Dem. Rep. of the Congo* 86 B3
Mahajamba ➜, *Madag.* 89 B8
Mahajamba, Helodranon' i,
  Madag. 89 B8
Mahajan, *India* 68 E5
Mahajanga, *Madag.* 89 B8
Mahajanga □, *Madag.* 89 B8
Mahajilo ➜, *Madag.* 89 B8
Mahakam ➜, *Indonesia* 62 E5
Mahalapye, *Botswana* 88 C4
Mahale Mts., *Tanzania* 86 D3
Mahale Mts. △, *Tanzania* 86 D2
Maḥallāt, *Iran* 71 C6
Māhān, *Iran* 71 D8
Mahan ➜, *India* 69 H10
Mahanadi ➜, *India* 67 J15
Mahananda ➜, *India* 69 G12
Mahanoro, *Madag.* 89 B8
Mahanoy City, *U.S.A.* 117 F8
Maharashtra □, *India* 66 J9
Mahasham, W. ➜, *Egypt* 74 E3
Mahasoa, *Madag.* 89 C8
Mahasolo, *Madag.* 89 B8
Mahattat ash Shīdīyah, *Jordan* . 74 F4
Mahattat 'Unayzah, *Jordan* 74 E4
Mahavavy ➜, *Madag.* 89 B8
Mahaxay, *Laos* 64 D5
Mahbubnagar, *India* 66 L10
Mahdah, *Oman* 71 E7
Mahdia, *Tunisia* 79 A8
Mahe, *India* 69 C8
Mahendragarh, *India* 68 E7
Mahenge, *Tanzania* 87 D4
Maheno, *N.Z.* 91 L3
Mahesana, *India* 68 H5
Maheshwar, *India* 68 H6
Mahgawan, *India* 69 F8
Mahi ➜, *India* 68 H5
Mahia Pen., *N.Z.* 91 H6
Mahilyow, *Belarus* 32 F6
Mahinerangi, L., *N.Z.* 91 L2
Mahmiya, *Sudan* 81 D3
Mahmud Kot, *Pakistan* 68 D4
Mahmudia, *Romania* 29 E14
Mahmudiye, *Turkey* 47 B12
Mahmutbey, *Turkey* 45 E12
Mahnomen, *U.S.A.* 112 B7
Mahoba, *India* 69 G8
Mahón = Maó, *Spain* 48 B11
Mahon, Menorca ✈ (MAH),
  Spain 38 F9

Mahone Bay, *Canada* 105 D7
Mahopac, *U.S.A.* 117 E11
Mahuta, *Nigeria* 83 C5
Mahuva, *India* 68 J4
Mahya Daği, *Turkey* 45 E11
Mai-Ndombe, L., *Dem. Rep. of
  the Congo* 84 E3
Mai-Sai, *Thailand* 58 G2
Mai Thon, Ko, *Thailand* ...... 65 a
Maia, *Portugal* 36 D2
Maia, *Spain* 38 B3
Maials, *Spain* 38 D5
Maîche, *France* 19 E13
Maicurú ➜, *Brazil* 125 D8
Máida, *Italy* 43 D9
Maidan Khula, *Afghan.* 68 C3
Maidenhead, *U.K.* 15 F7
Maidstone, *Canada* 103 C7
Maidstone, *U.K.* 15 F8
Maiduguri, *Nigeria* 83 C7
Maiella △, *Italy* 41 F11
Maienfeld, *Switz.* 25 H9
Māieruş, *Romania* 29 E10
Maigatari, *Nigeria* 83 C6
Maignelay Montigny, *France* ... 19 C9
Maigo, *Phil.* 61 G5
Maigudo, *Ethiopia* 81 F4
Maihar, *India* 69 G9
Maijdi, *Bangla.* 67 H17
Maikala Ra., *India* 67 J12
Maiko △, *Dem. Rep. of the Congo* 86 C2
Mailani, *India* 69 E9
Maillezais, *France* 20 B3
Mailsi, *Pakistan* 68 E5
Main ➜, *Germany* 25 F4
Main ➜, *U.K.* 12 B5
Main Range △, *Australia* 95 D5
Main Ridge, *Trin. & Tob.* 125 J16
Mainburg, *Germany* 25 G7
Maine, *France* 18 D6
Maine □, *U.S.A.* 115 C11
Maine ➜, *Ireland* 12 D2
Maine-et-Loire □, *France* 18 E6
Maïne-Soroa, *Niger* 83 C7
Maingkwan, *Burma* 67 F20
Mainit, L., *Phil.* 61 G6
Mainland, *Orkney, U.K.* 13 C5
Mainland, *Shet., U.K.* 13 A7
Mainoru, *Australia* 94 A1
Mainpuri, *India* 69 F8
Maintal, *Germany* 25 E4
Maintenon, *France* 19 D8
Maintirano, *Madag.* 89 B7
Mainz, *Germany* 25 E4
Maipú, *Argentina* 126 D4
Maiquetía, *Venezuela* 124 A5
Máira ➜, *Italy* 40 D4
Mairabari, *India* 67 F18
Maisí, *Cuba* 121 B5
Maisí, Pta. de, *Cuba* 121 B5
Maitland, *N.S.W., Australia* 95 E5
Maitland, *S. Austral., Australia* . 95 E2
Maitland ➜, *Canada* 116 C3
Maitri, *Antarctica* 5 D3
Maiyema, *Nigeria* 83 C5
Maiyuan, *China* 59 E11
Maíz, Is. del, *Nic.* 120 D3
Maizuru, *Japan* 55 G7
Majalengka, *Indonesia* 63 G13
Majene, *Indonesia* 63 E5
Majete △, *Malawi* 87 F3
Majevica, *Bos.-H.* 28 F3
Maji, *Ethiopia* 81 F4
Majiang, *China* 58 D6
Majorca = Mallorca, *Spain* 48 B10
Maka, *Senegal* 82 C2
Makaha, *Zimbabwe* 89 B5
Makak, *Cameroon* 83 E7
Makalamabedi, *Botswana* 88 C3
Makale, *Indonesia* 63 E5
Makamba, *Burundi* 86 C2
Makari, *Cameroon* 83 C7
Makarikari = Makgadikgadi Salt
  Pans, *Botswana* 88 C4
Makarov Basin, *Arctic* .... 4 A
Makarovo, *Russia* 53 D11
Makarska, *Croatia* 41 E14
Makaryev, *Russia* 34 B6
Makasar = Ujung Pandang,
  Indonesia 63 F5
Makasar, Selat, *Indonesia* 63 E5
Makasar, Str. of = Makasar, Selat,
  Indonesia 63 E5
Makat, *Kazakhstan* 52 E6
Makedonija = Macedonia ■,
  Europe 44 E5
Makeni, *S. Leone* 82 D2
Makeyevka = Makiyivka, *Ukraine* 33 H9
Makgadikgadi △, *Botswana* 88 C3
Makgadikgadi Salt Pans,
  Botswana 88 C4
Makhachkala, *Russia* 35 J8
Makhado = Louis Trichardt,
  S. Africa 89 C4
Makharadze = Ozurgeti, *Georgia* 35 K5
Makhfar al Buşayyah, *Iraq* 70 D5
Makhmūr, *Iraq* 70 C4
Makian, *Indonesia* 63 D7
Makindu, *Kenya* 86 C4
Makinsk, *Kazakhstan* 52 D8
Makiv, *Ukraine* 29 B11
Makiyivka, *Ukraine* 33 H9
Makkah, *Si. Arabia* 75 C2
Makkovik, *Canada* 105 A8
Makó, *Hungary* 28 D5
Mako, *Senegal* 82 C2
Makokou, *Gabon* 84 D2
Makongo, *Dem. Rep. of the Congo*
  the Congo 86 B2
Makoro, *Dem. Rep. of the Congo* 86 B2
Maków Mazowiecki, *Poland* ... 31 F8
Maków Podhalański, *Poland* ... 31 J6
Makrá, *Greece* 47 E7

Makrai, *India* 66 H10
Makran Coast Range, *Pakistan* . 66 G4
Makrana, *India* 68 F6
Makrany, *Belarus* 31 G11
Mákri, *Greece* 45 F9
Makriyialos, *Greece* 49 D7
Makunda, *Botswana* 88 C5
Makung, *Taiwan* 59 F12
Makurazaki, *Japan* 55 J5
Makurdi, *Nigeria* 83 D6
Makūyeh, *Iran* 71 D7
Makwassie, *S. Africa* 88 D4
Makwiro, *Zimbabwe* 89 B5
Mâl, *Mauritania* 82 B2
Mal B., *Ireland* 12 D2
Mala, Pta., *Panama* 120 E3
Mala Belozёrka, *Ukraine* 33 J8
Malá Fatra △, *Slovak Rep.* 27 B12
Mala Kapela, *Croatia* 41 D12
Mala Panew ➜, *Poland* 31 H4
Mala Vyska, *Ukraine* 33 H6
Malabang, *Phil.* 61 H6
Malabar Coast, *India* 66 P9
Malabon, *Phil.* 61 D4
Malacca, Straits of, *Indonesia* . 65 L3
Malacky, *Slovak Rep.* 27 C10
Malad City, *U.S.A.* 108 E7
Maladeta, *Spain* 38 C5
Maladzyechna, *Belarus* 32 E4
Málaga, *Spain* 37 J6
Málaga □, *Spain* 37 J6
Malagarasi, *Tanzania* 86 D3
Malagarasi ➜, *Tanzania* 86 D2
Malagasy Rep. = Madagascar ■,
  Africa 89 C8
Malagón, *Spain* 37 F7
Malagón ➜, *Spain* 37 H3
Malahide, *Ireland* 12 C5
Malaimbandy, *Madag.* 89 C8
Malakâl, *Sudan* 81 F3
Malakand, *Pakistan* 68 B4
Malakwal, *Pakistan* 68 C5
Malamala, *Indonesia* 63 E6
Malanda, *Australia* 94 B4
Malang, *Indonesia* 63 G15
Malangen, *Norway* 8 B18
Malanje, *Angola* 84 F3
Mälaren, *Sweden* 10 E11
Malargüe, *Argentina* 126 D2
Malartic, *Canada* 104 C4
Malaryta, *Belarus* 31 G11
Malatya, *Turkey* 70 B3
Malawi ■, *Africa* 87 E3
Malawi, L. = Nyasa, L., *Africa* . 87 E3
Malay Pen., *Asia* 65 J3
Malaya Belozёrka = Mala
  Belozёrka, *Ukraine* 33 J8
Malaya Vishera, *Russia* 32 C7
Malaya Viska = Mala Vyska,
  Ukraine 33 H6
Malaybalay, *Phil.* 61 G6
Malāyer, *Iran* 71 C6
Malaysia ■, *Asia* 65 K4
Malazgirt, *Turkey* 70 B4
Malbaza, *Niger* 83 C6
Malbon, *Australia* 94 C3
Malbooma, *Australia* 95 E1
Malbork, *Poland* 30 D6
Malcésine, *Italy* 40 C7
Malchin, *Germany* 24 B8
Malchow, *Germany* 24 B8
Malcolm, *Australia* 93 E3
Malcolm, Pt., *Australia* 93 F3
Malczyce, *Poland* 31 G3
Maldah, *India* 69 G13
Maldegem, *Belgium* 17 C3
Malden, *Mass., U.S.A.* 117 D13
Malden, *Mo., U.S.A.* 113 G10
Malden I., *Kiribati* 97 H12
Maldon, *U.K.* 15 F8
Maldonado, *Uruguay* 127 C5
Maldonado, Punta, *Mexico* 119 D5
Malè, *Italy* 40 B7
Male, *Maldives* 51 J11
Malé Karpaty, *Slovak Rep.* 27 C10
Maléa, Ákra, *Greece* 46 E5
Malegaon, *India* 66 J9
Malei, *Mozam.* 87 F4
Malek, *Sudan* 81 F3
Malek Kandī, *Iran* 70 B5
Malela, *Dem. Rep. of the Congo* 86 C2
Malema, *Mozam.* 87 E4
Máleme, *Greece* 49 D5
Målerås, *Sweden* 11 H9
Malerkotla, *India* 68 D6
Máles, *Greece* 49 D7
Malesherbes, *France* 19 D9
Maleshevska Planina, *Europe* .. 44 E7
Malesína, *Greece* 46 C5
Malestroit, *France* 18 E4
Malfa, *Italy* 43 D7
Malgobek, *Russia* 35 J7
Malgomaj, *Sweden* 8 D17
Malgrat de Mar, *Spain* 38 D7
Malha, *Sudan* 81 D2
Malhargarh, *India* 68 G6
Malheur ➜, *U.S.A.* 108 D5
Malheur L., *U.S.A.* 108 E4
Mali, *Guinea* 82 C2
Mali ■, *Africa* 82 B4
Mali ➜, *Burma* 67 G20
Mali Kanal, *Serbia & M.* 28 E4
Mali Kyun, *Burma* 64 F2
Malibu, *U.S.A.* 111 L8
Maliku, *Indonesia* 63 E6
Malili, *Indonesia* 63 E6
Mälilla, *Sweden* 11 G9
Malimba, Mts., *Dem. Rep. of
  the Congo* 86 D2

Malin Hd., *Ireland* 12 A4
Malin Pen., *Ireland* 12 A4
Malindi, *Kenya* 86 C5
Malines = Mechelen, *Belgium* .. 17 C4
Malino, *Indonesia* 63 D6
Malinyi, *Tanzania* 87 D4
Malipo, *China* 58 F5
Maliq, *Albania* 44 F4
Malita, *Phil.* 63 C7
Maliwun, *Burma* 62 B1
Maljenje, *Serbia & M.* 44 C5
Malka Mari △, *Kenya* 86 B5
Malkara, *Turkey* 45 F10
Malkinia Górna, *Poland* 31 F9
Malko Tŭrnovo, *Bulgaria* 45 E11
Mallacoota Inlet, *Australia* 95 F4
Mallaig, *U.K.* 13 D3
Mallaoua, *Niger* 83 C6
Mallawan, *India* 69 F9
Mallawi, *Egypt* 80 B3
Mallemort, *France* 21 E9
Málles Venosta, *Italy* 40 B7
Mállia, *Greece* 49 D7
Mallión, Kólpos, *Greece* 49 D7
Mallorca, *Spain* 48 B10
Mallorytown, *Canada* 117 B9
Mallow, *Ireland* 12 D3
Malmbäck, *Sweden* 11 G8
Malmberget, *Sweden* 8 C19
Malmédy, *Belgium* 17 D6
Malmesbury, *S. Africa* 88 E2
Malmivaara = Malmberget,
  Sweden 8 C19
Malmköping, *Sweden* 10 E10
Malmö, *Sweden* 11 J7
Malmslätt, *Sweden* 11 F9
Malmyzh, *Russia* 34 B10
Malnaş, *Romania* 29 D10
Malo Konare, *Bulgaria* 45 D8
Maloarkhangelsk, *Russia* 33 F9
Malolos, *Phil.* 63 B6
Malolotja △, *Swaziland* 89 D5
Malombe L., *Malawi* 87 E4
Malomice, *Poland* 31 G2
Malomir, *Bulgaria* 45 D10
Malone, *U.S.A.* 117 B10
Malong, *China* 58 E4
Małopolskie □, *Poland* 31 J7
Malorad, *Bulgaria* 44 C7
Måløy, *Norway* 9 F11
Maloyaroslovets, *Russia* 32 E9
Malpartida, *Spain* 37 F4
Malpaso, *Canary Is.* 48 G1
Malpelo, I. de, *Colombia* 124 C2
Malpica de Bergantiños, *Spain* . 36 B2
Malpur, *India* 68 H5
Malpura, *India* 68 F6
Mals = Málles Venosta, *Italy* .. 40 B7
Malta, *Idaho, U.S.A.* 108 E7
Malta, *Mont., U.S.A.* 108 B10
Malta ■, *Europe* 49 D2
Malthöhe, *Namibia* 88 C2
Maltepe, *Turkey* 45 F13
Malton, *Canada* 116 C5
Malton, *U.K.* 14 C7
Maluku, *Indonesia* 63 E7
Maluku □, *Indonesia* 63 E7
Maluku Sea = Molucca Sea,
  Indonesia 63 E6
Maluku Utara □, *Indonesia* 63 D7
Malumfashi, *Nigeria* 83 C6
Malung, *Sweden* 10 D7
Malungsfors, *Sweden* 10 D7
Maluwe, *Ghana* 82 D4
Malvan, *India* 66 L8
Malvern, *U.S.A.* 113 H8
Malvern Hills, *U.K.* 15 E5
Malvinas, Is. = Falkland Is. ✍,
  Atl. Oc. 128 G5
Malý Dunaj ➜, *Slovak Rep.* ... 27 D11
Malya, *Tanzania* 86 C3
Malye Derbety, *Russia* 35 G7
Malyn, *Ukraine* 33 G5
Malyy Lyakhovskiy, Ostrov,
  Russia 53 B15
Mama, *Russia* 53 D12
Mamadysh, *Russia* 34 C10
Mamanguape, *Brazil* 125 E11
Mamarr Mitlâ, *Egypt* 74 E1
Mamasa, *Indonesia* 63 E5
Mambasa, *Dem. Rep. of
  the Congo* 86 B2
Mamberamo ➜, *Indonesia* 63 E9
Mambilima Falls, *Zambia* 87 E2
Mambirima, *Dem. Rep. of
  the Congo* 87 E2
Mambo, *Tanzania* 86 C4
Mambrui, *Kenya* 86 C5
Mamburao, *Phil.* 61 E4
Mameigwess L., *Canada* 104 B2
Mamers, *France* 18 D7
Mamfé, *Cameroon* 83 D6
Mammoth, *U.S.A.* 109 K8
Mammoth Cave △, *U.S.A.* 114 G3
Mamonovo, *Russia* 30 D6
Mamoré ➜, *Bolivia* 124 F5
Mamou, *Guinea* 82 C2
Mamoudzou, *Mayotte* 77 H8
Mampata, *Guinea-Biss.* 82 C2
Mampikony, *Madag.* 89 B8
Mampong, *Ghana* 83 D4
Mamry, Jezioro, *Poland* 30 D8
Mamuju, *Indonesia* 63 E5
Mamuno, *Botswana* 88 C3
Mamuras, *Albania* 44 E3
Man, *Ivory C.* 82 D3
Man, I. of, *U.K.* 14 C3
Man-Bazar, *India* 69 H12
Man Na, *Burma* 67 H20
Mana ➜, *Fr. Guiana* 125 B8
Mana Pools △, *Zimbabwe* 87 F2

Manaar, G. of = Mannar, G. of,
  Asia 66 Q11
Manacapuru, *Brazil* 124 D6
Manacor, *Spain* 48 B10
Manado, *Indonesia* 63 D6
Managua, *Nic.* 120 D2
Managua, L. de, *Nic.* 120 D2
Manakara, *Madag.* 89 C8
Manali, *India* 68 C7
Manama = Al Manāmah, *Bahrain* 71 E6
Manambao ➜, *Madag.* 89 B7
Manambato, *Madag.* 89 A8
Manambolo ➜, *Madag.* 89 B7
Manambolosy, *Madag.* 89 B8
Mananara △, *Madag.* 89 B8
Mananara ➜, *Madag.* 89 C8
Mananara Avaratra, *Madag.* 89 B8
Mananjary, *Madag.* 89 C8
Manankoro, *Mali* 82 C3
Manantenina, *Madag.* 89 C8
Manaos = Manaus, *Brazil* 124 D7
Manapire ➜, *Venezuela* 124 B5
Manapouri, *N.Z.* 91 L1
Manapouri, L., *N.Z.* 91 L1
Manaqil, *Sudan* 81 E3
Manār, Jabal, *Yemen* 75 E3
Manaravolo, *Madag.* 89 C8
Manas, *China* 60 B3
Manas ➜, *India* 67 F17
Manaslu, *Nepal* 69 E11
Manasquan, *U.S.A.* 117 F10
Manassa, *U.S.A.* 109 H11
Manatí, *Puerto Rico* .... 121 d
Manaung, *Burma* 67 K18
Manaus, *Brazil* 124 D7
Manavgat, *Turkey* 72 D4
Manawan L., *Canada* 103 B8
Manay, *Phil.* 61 H7
Manbij, *Syria* 70 B3
Mancha Real, *Spain* 37 H7
Manche □, *France* 18 C5
Manchegorsk, *Russia* 52 C4
Manchester, *U.K.* 14 D5
Manchester, *Calif., U.S.A.* 110 G3
Manchester, *Conn., U.S.A.* 117 E12
Manchester, *Ga., U.S.A.* 115 J3
Manchester, *Iowa, U.S.A.* 112 D9
Manchester, *Ky., U.S.A.* 114 G4
Manchester, *N.H., U.S.A.* 117 D13
Manchester, *N.Y., U.S.A.* 116 D7
Manchester, *Pa., U.S.A.* 117 F8
Manchester, *Tenn., U.S.A.* 115 H2
Manchester, *Vt., U.S.A.* 117 C11
Manchester International ✈
  (MAN), *U.K.* 14 D5
Manchester L., *Canada* 103 A7
Manchhar L., *Pakistan* 68 F2
Manchuria = Dongbei, *China* .. 53 E13
Manchurian Plain, *China* 50 E16
Manciano, *Italy* 41 F8
Mancifa, *Ethiopia* 81 F5
Mand ➜, *India* 69 J10
Mand ➜, *Iran* 71 D7
Manda, *Ludewe, Tanzania* 87 E3
Manda, *Mbeya, Tanzania* 86 D3
Manda, *Mbeya, Tanzania* 87 D3
Mandabé, *Madag.* 89 C7
Mandaguari, *Brazil* 127 A5
Mandah = Töhöm, *Mongolia* .. 56 B5
Mandal, *Norway* 9 G12
Mandala, Puncak, *Indonesia* ... 63 E10
Mandalay, *Burma* 67 J20
Mandale = Mandalay, *Burma* .. 67 J20
Mandalgarh, *India* 68 G6
Mandalgovi, *Mongolia* 56 B4
Mandalī, *Iraq* 70 C5
Mandan, *U.S.A.* 112 B4
Mandaon, *Phil.* 61 E5
Mandar, Teluk, *Indonesia* 63 E5
Mándas, *Italy* 42 C2
Mandasor = Mandsaur, *India* .. 68 G6
Mandelieu-la-Napoule, *France* . 21 E10
Mandera, *Kenya* 86 B5
Mandeville, *Jamaica* .... 120 a
Mandi, *India* 68 D7
Mandi Dabwali, *India* 68 E6
Mandiana, *Guinea* 82 C3
Mandimba, *Mozam.* 87 E4
Mandioli, *Indonesia* 63 E7
Mandla, *India* 69 H9
Mandø, *Denmark* 11 J2
Mandorah, *Australia* 92 B5
Mandoto, *Madag.* 89 B8
Mandoúdhion, *Greece* 46 C5
'Mándra, *Greece* 46 C5
Mandra, *Pakistan* 68 C5
Mandráki, *Greece* 47 E9
Mandrare ➜, *Madag.* 89 D8
Mandritsara, *Madag.* 89 B8
Mandronarivo, *Madag.* 89 C8
Mandsaur, *India* 68 G6
Mandurah, *Australia* 93 F2
Manduria, *Italy* 43 B10
Mandvi, *India* 68 H3
Mandya, *India* 66 N10
Mandzai, *Pakistan* 68 D2
Mané, *Burkina Faso* 83 C4
Maneh, *Iran* 71 B8
Manengouba, Mts., *Cameroon* .. 83 E6
Manera, *Madag.* 89 C7
Manérbio, *Italy* 40 C7
Maneroo Cr. ➜, *Australia* 94 C3
Manfalût, *Egypt* 80 B3
Manfredónia, *Italy* 41 G12
Manfredónia, G. di, *Italy* 41 G13
Manga, *Burkina Faso* 83 C4
Manga, *Niger* 82 D3
Mangabeiras, Chapada das, *Brazil* 125 F9
Mangalia, *Romania* 29 G13
Mangalore, *India* 66 N9
Mangan, *India* 69 F13
Mangaung, *S. Africa* 85 K5

Mangawan, *India* 69 G9
Mangaweka, *N.Z.* 91 H5
Manggar, *Indonesia* 62 E3
Manggawitu, *Indonesia* 63 E8
Manggis, *Indonesia* 63 J18
Mangindrano, *Madag.* 89 A8
Mangkalihat, Tanjung, *Indonesia* 63 D5
Mangla, *Pakistan* 68 C5
Mangla Dam, *Pakistan* 69 C5
Manglaur, *India* 68 E7
Mango, *Togo* 83 C5
Mangoche, *Malawi* 87 E4
Mangoky ➤, *Madag.* 89 C7
Mangole, *Indonesia* 63 E6
Mangombe, *Dem. Rep. of
  the Congo* 86 C2
Mangonui, *N.Z.* 91 F4
Mangoro ➤, *Madag.* 89 B8
Mangrol, *Mad. P., India* 68 J4
Mangrol, *Raj., India* 68 G6
Mangualde, *Portugal* 36 E3
Mangueira, L. da, *Brazil* 127 C5
Mangum, *U.S.A.* 113 H5
Mangyshlak, Poluostrov,
  Kazakhstan 52 E6
Manhattan, *U.S.A.* 112 F6
Manhiça, *Mozam.* 89 D5
Mania ➤, *Madag.* 89 B8
Maniago, *Italy* 41 B9
Manica, *Mozam.* 89 B5
Manica □, *Mozam.* 89 B5
Manicaland □, *Zimbabwe* 87 F3
Manicoré, *Brazil* 124 E6
Manicouagan ➤, *Canada* 105 C6
Manicouagan, Rés., *Canada* 105 B6
Maniema □, *Dem. Rep. of
  the Congo* 86 C2
Manīfah, *Si. Arabia* 71 E6
Manifold, C., *Australia* 94 C5
Maniganggo, *China* 58 B2
Manigotagan, *Canada* 103 C9
Manigotagan ➤, *Canada* 103 C9
Manihari, *India* 69 G12
Manihiki, *Cook Is.* 97 J11
Manika, Plateau de la, *Dem. Rep.
  of the Congo* 87 E2
Manikpur, *India* 69 G9
Manila, *Phil.* 61 D4
Manila, *U.S.A.* 108 F9
Manila B., *Phil.* 61 D4
Manilla, *Australia* 95 E5
Manimpé, *Mali* 82 C3
Maningrida, *Australia* 94 A1
Maninian, *Ivory C.* 82 C3
Manipur □, *India* 67 G19
Manipur ➤, *Burma* 67 H19
Manisa, *Turkey* 47 C9
Manisa □, *Turkey* 47 C9
Manistee, *U.S.A.* 114 C2
Manistee ➤, *U.S.A.* 114 C2
Manistique, *U.S.A.* 114 C2
Manitoba □, *Canada* 103 B9
Manitoba, L., *Canada* 103 C9
Manitou, *Canada* 103 D9
Manitou, L., *Canada* 105 B6
Manitou Is., *U.S.A.* 114 C3
Manitou L., *Canada* 103 C7
Manitou Springs, *U.S.A.* 112 F2
Manitoulin I., *Canada* 104 C3
Manitouwadge, *Canada* 104 C2
Manitowoc, *U.S.A.* 114 C2
Manizales, *Colombia* 124 B3
Manja, *Madag.* 89 C7
Manjacaze, *Mozam.* 89 C5
Manjakandriana, *Madag.* 89 B8
Manjhand, *Pakistan* 68 G3
Manjil, *Iran* 71 B6
Manjimup, *Australia* 93 F2
Manjra ➤, *India* 66 K10
Mankato, *Kans., U.S.A.* 112 F5
Mankato, *Minn., U.S.A.* 112 C8
Mankayane, *Swaziland* 89 D5
Mankera, *Pakistan* 68 D4
Mankim, *Cameroon* 83 D7
Mankono, *Ivory C.* 82 D3
Mankota, *Canada* 103 D7
Manlay = Üydzin, *Mongolia* 56 B4
Manlleu, *Spain* 38 C7
Manmad, *India* 66 J9
Mann Ranges, *Australia* 93 E5
Manna, *Indonesia* 62 E2
Mannahill, *Australia* 95 E3
Mannar, *Sri Lanka* 66 Q11
Mannar, G. of, *Asia* 66 Q11
Mannar I., *Sri Lanka* 66 Q11
Mannheim, *Germany* 25 F4
Manning, *Canada* 102 B5
Manning, *Oreg., U.S.A.* 110 E3
Manning, *S.C., U.S.A.* 115 J5
Mannu ➤, *Italy* 42 C2
Mannu, C., *Italy* 42 B1
Mannum, *Australia* 95 E2
Mano, *S. Leone* 82 D2
Mano ➤, *Liberia* 82 D2
Mano River, *Liberia* 82 D2
Manoharpur, *India* 69 H11
Manokwari, *Indonesia* 63 E8
Manolás, *Greece* 46 C3
Manombo, *Madag.* 89 C7
Manono, *Dem. Rep. of the Congo* 86 D2
Manoppello, *Italy* 41 F11
Manosque, *France* 21 E9
Manotick, *Canada* 117 A9
Manouane ➤, *Canada* 105 C5
Manouane, L., *Canada* 105 B5
Manp'o, *N. Korea* 57 D14
Manpojin = Manp'o, *N. Korea* 57 D14
Manpur, *Chhattisgarh, India* 69 H10
Manpur, *Mad. P., India* 68 H6
Manresa, *Spain* 38 D6
Mansa, *Gujarat, India* 68 H5

Mansa, *Punjab, India* 68 E6
Mansa, *Zambia* 87 E2
Månsåsen, *Sweden* 10 A8
Mansehra, *Pakistan* 68 B5
Mansel I., *Canada* 101 B11
Mansfield, *Australia* 95 F4
Mansfield, *U.K.* 14 D6
Mansfield, *La., U.S.A.* 113 J8
Mansfield, *Mass., U.S.A.* 117 D13
Mansfield, *Ohio, U.S.A.* 116 F2
Mansfield, *Pa., U.S.A.* 116 E7
Mansfield, *Mt., U.S.A.* 117 B12
Mansilla de las Mulas, *Spain* 36 C5
Mansle, *France* 20 C4
Mansoa, *Guinea-Biss.* 82 C1
Manson Creek, *Canada* 102 B4
Manta, *Ecuador* 124 D2
Mantadia △, *Madag.* 89 B8
Mantalingajan, Mt., *Phil.* 61 G2
Mantare, *Tanzania* 86 C3
Manteca, *U.S.A.* 110 H5
Manteo, *U.S.A.* 115 H8
Mantes-la-Jolie, *France* 19 D8
Manthani, *India* 66 K11
Manti, *U.S.A.* 108 G8
Mantiqueira, Serra da, *Brazil* 127 A7
Manton, *U.S.A.* 114 C3
Mantorp, *Sweden* 11 F9
Mántova, *Italy* 40 C7
Mänttä, *Finland* 9 E21
Mantua = Mántova, *Italy* 40 C7
Manturovo, *Russia* 34 A7
Manu, *Peru* 124 F4
Manu ➤, *Peru* 124 F4
Manu'a Is., *Amer. Samoa* 91 B14
Manui, *Indonesia* 63 E6
Manukau, *N.Z.* 91 G5
Manuripi ➤, *Bolivia* 124 F5
Many, *U.S.A.* 113 K8
Manyara, L., *Tanzania* 86 C4
Manyas, *Turkey* 45 F11
Manyava, *Ukraine* 29 B9
Manych ➤, *Russia* 35 G5
Manych-Gudilo, Ozero, *Russia* 35 G6
Manyonga ➤, *Tanzania* 86 C3
Manyoni, *Tanzania* 86 D3
Manzai, *Pakistan* 68 C4
Manzala, Bahra el, *Egypt* 80 H7
Manzanar △, *U.S.A.* 110 J7
Manzanares, *Spain* 37 F7
Manzaneda, *Spain* 36 C3
Manzanillo, *Cuba* 120 B4
Manzanillo, *Mexico* 118 D4
Manzanillo, Pta., *Panama* 120 E4
Manzano Mts., *U.S.A.* 109 J10
Manzarīyeh, *Iran* 71 C6
Manzhouli, *China* 60 B6
Manzini, *Swaziland* 89 D5
Mao, *Chad* 79 F9
Maó, *Spain* 48 B11
Maoke, Pegunungan, *Indonesia* 63 E9
Maolin, *China* 57 C12
Maoming, *China* 59 G8
Maopi T'ou, *China* 59 G13
Maoxian, *China* 58 B4
Maoxing, *China* 57 B13
Mapam Yumco, *China* 60 C3
Mapastepec, *Mexico* 119 D6
Maphrao, Ko, *Thailand* .... 65 a
Mapia, Kepulauan, *Indonesia* 63 D8
Mapimí, *Mexico* 118 B4
Mapimí, Bolsón de, *Mexico* 118 B4
Maping, *China* 59 B9
Mapinga, *Tanzania* 86 D4
Mapinhane, *Mozam.* 89 C6
Maple Creek, *Canada* 103 D7
Maple Valley, *U.S.A.* 110 C4
Mapleton, *U.S.A.* 108 D2
Mapuera ➤, *Brazil* 124 D7
Mapulanguene, *Mozam.* 89 C5
Maputo, *Mozam.* 89 D5
Maputo □, *Mozam.* 89 D5
Maputo △, *Mozam.* 89 D5
Maputo, B. de, *Mozam.* 89 D5
Maqiaohe, *China* 57 B16
Maqnā, *Si. Arabia* 70 D2
Maquan He = Brahmaputra ➤,
  Asia 69 H13
Maqueda, *Spain* 36 E6
Maquela do Zombo, *Angola* 84 F3
Maquinchao, *Argentina* 128 E3
Maquoketa, *U.S.A.* 112 D9
Mar, Serra do, *Brazil* 127 B6
Mar Chiquita, L., *Argentina* 126 C3
Mar del Plata, *Argentina* 126 D4
Mar Menor, *Spain* 39 H4
Mara, *Tanzania* 86 C3
Mara □, *Tanzania* 86 C3
Maraã, *Brazil* 124 D5
Marabá, *Brazil* 125 E9
Maracá, I. de, *Brazil* 125 C8
Maracaibo, *Venezuela* 124 A4
Maracaibo, L. de, *Venezuela* 124 B4
Maracaju, *Brazil* 127 A4
Maracas Bay Village,
  Trin. & Tob. 125 K15
Maracay, *Venezuela* 124 A5
Maracena, *Spain* 37 H7
Maradi, *Niger* 83 C6
Marägheh, *Iran* 70 B5
Marāh, *Si. Arabia* 70 E5
Marahoue △, *Ivory C.* 82 D3
Marais du Cotentin et du
  Bessin △, *France* 18 C5
Marais Poitevin, Val de Sèvre et
  Vendée △, *France* 20 B3
Marajó, I. de, *Brazil* 125 D9
Marākand, *Iran* 70 B5
Marakele △, *S. Africa* 89 E4
Maralal, *Kenya* 86 B4

Maralinga, *Australia* 93 F5
Maramaraereğlisi, *Turkey* 45 F11
Marambio, *Antarctica* 5 C18
Marampa, *S. Leone* 82 D2
Maramureş □, *Romania* 29 C9
Maran, *Malaysia* 65 L4
Maranboy, *Australia* 92 B5
Maranchón, *Spain* 38 D2
Marand, *Iran* 70 B5
Marang, *Malaysia* 65 K4
Maranguape, *Brazil* 125 D11
Maranhão = São Luís, *Brazil* 125 D10
Maranhão □, *Brazil* 125 E9
Marano, L. di, *Italy* 41 C10
Maranoa ➤, *Australia* 95 D4
Marañón ➤, *Peru* 124 D4
Marão, *Mozam.* 89 C5
Maraş = Kahramanmaraş, *Turkey* 70 B3
Mărăşeşti, *Romania* 29 E12
Maratea, *Italy* 43 C8
Marateca, *Portugal* 37 G2
Marathasa, *Cyprus* 49 E11
Marathókambos, *Greece* 47 D8
Marathon, *Australia* 94 C3
Marathon, *Canada* 104 C2
Marathón, *Greece* 46 C5
Marathon, *N.Y., U.S.A.* 117 D8
Marathon, *Tex., U.S.A.* 113 K3
Marathóvouno, *Cyprus* 49 D12
Maratua, *Indonesia* 63 D5
Maraval, *Trin. & Tob.* 125 K15
Maravatío, *Mexico* 118 D4
Marawi City, *Phil.* 61 G6
Marāwih, *U.A.E.* 71 E7
Marazliyivka, *Ukraine* 29 D15
Marbella, *Spain* 37 J6
Marble Bar, *Australia* 92 D2
Marble Falls, *U.S.A.* 113 K5
Marblehead, *U.S.A.* 117 D14
Marburg, *Germany* 24 E4
Marcal ➤, *Hungary* 28 C2
Marcali, *Hungary* 28 D2
Marcaria, *Italy* 40 C7
Mărcăuţi, *Moldova* 29 B12
March, *U.K.* 15 E8
Marche, *France* 20 B5
Marche □, *Italy* 41 E10
Marche-en-Famenne, *Belgium* 17 D5
Marchena, *Spain* 37 H5
Marches = Marche □, *Italy* 41 E10
Marchesale △, *Italy* 43 D9
Marciana Marina, *Italy* 40 F7
Marcianise, *Italy* 43 A7
Marcigny, *France* 19 F11
Marcillat-en-Combraille, *France* 19 F9
Marck, *France* 19 B8
Marckolsheim, *France* 19 D14
Marco, *U.S.A.* 115 N5
Marcos Juárez, *Argentina* 126 C3
Mărculeşti, *Moldova* 29 C13
Marcus I. = Minami-Tori-Shima,
  Pac. Oc. 96 E7
Marcus Necker Ridge, *Pac. Oc.* 96 F9
Marcy, Mt., *U.S.A.* 117 B11
Mardan, *Pakistan* 68 B5
Mardarivka, *Ukraine* 29 C14
Mardin, *Turkey* 70 B4
Mårdsjö, *Sweden* 10 A9
Marécchia ➤, *Italy* 41 D9
Maree, L., *U.K.* 13 D3
Mareeba, *Australia* 94 B4
Mareetsane, *S. Africa* 88 D4
Maremma, *Italy* 41 F8
Maremma △, *Italy* 40 F8
Maréna, *Kayes, Mali* 82 C2
Maréna, *Koulikouro, Mali* 82 C3
Marengo, *U.S.A.* 112 E8
Marennes, *France* 20 C2
Marerano, *Madag.* 89 C7
Maréttimo, *Italy* 42 E5
Mareuil, *France* 20 C4
Marfa, *U.S.A.* 113 K2
Marfa Pt., *Malta* 49 D1
Marganets = Marhanets, *Ukraine* 33 J8
Margaret ➤, *Australia* 92 C4
Margaret Bay, *Canada* 102 C3
Margaret L., *Canada* 102 B5
Margaret River, *Australia* 93 F2
Margarita, I. de, *Venezuela* 124 A6
Margarítion, *Greece* 46 B2
Margaritovo, *Russia* 54 C7
Margate, *S. Africa* 89 E5
Margate, *U.K.* 15 F9
Margeride, Mts. de la, *France* 20 D7
Margherita di Savóia, *Italy* 43 A9
Margherita Pk., *Uganda* 86 B3
Marghita, *Romania* 28 C7
Margonin, *Poland* 31 F4
Margosatubig, *Phil.* 61 H5
Märgow, Dasht-e, *Afghan.* 66 D3
Marguerite, *Canada* 102 C4
Marhanets, *Ukraine* 33 J8
Mari El □, *Russia* 34 B8
Mari Indus, *Pakistan* 68 C4
Mari Republic = Mari El □,
  Russia 34 B8
María, Sa. de, *Spain* 39 H2
María Elena, *Chile* 126 A2
María Grande, *Argentina* 126 C4
Maria I., *N. Terr., Australia* 94 A2
Maria I., *Tas., Australia* 95 G4
Maria Island △, *Australia* 95 G4
Maria van Diemen, C., *N.Z.* 91 F4
Mariager, *Denmark* 11 H3
Mariager Fjord, *Denmark* 11 H4
Mariakani, *Kenya* 86 C4
Marian, *Australia* .... 94 b
Marian L., *Canada* 102 A5
Mariana Trench, *Pac. Oc.* 96 F6
Marianao, *Cuba* 120 B3

Marianna, *Ark., U.S.A.* 113 H9
Marianna, *Fla., U.S.A.* 115 K3
Mariannelund, *Sweden* 11 G9
Mariánské Lázně, *Czech Rep.* 26 B5
Marias ➤, *U.S.A.* 108 C8
Mariato, Punta, *Panama* 120 E3
Mariazell, *Austria* 26 D8
Maribo, *Denmark* 11 K5
Maribor, *Slovenia* 41 B12
Marico ➤, *Africa* 88 C4
Maricopa, *Ariz., U.S.A.* 109 K7
Maricopa, *Calif., U.S.A.* 111 K7
Marīdī, *Sudan* 81 G2
Marīdī, Wadi ➤, *Sudan* 81 F2
Marié ➤, *Brazil* 124 D5
Marie Byrd Land, *Antarctica* 5 D14
Marie-Galante, *Guadeloupe* .... 120 b
Mariecourt = Kangiqsujuaq,
  Canada 101 B12
Mariefred, *Sweden* 10 E11
Mariehamn = Maarianhamina,
  Finland 9 F18
Marieholm, *Sweden* 11 J7
Mariembourg, *Belgium* 17 D4
Marienbad = Mariánské Lázně,
  Czech Rep. 26 B5
Marienberg, *Germany* 24 E9
Mariental, *Namibia* 88 C2
Marienville, *U.S.A.* 116 E5
Mariestad, *Sweden* 11 F7
Marietta, *Ga., U.S.A.* 115 J3
Marietta, *Ohio, U.S.A.* 114 F5
Marieville, *Canada* 117 A11
Mariga ➤, *Nigeria* 83 C6
Marignane, *France* 21 E9
Marihatag, *Phil.* 61 G7
Mariinsk, *Russia* 52 D9
Mariinskiy Posad, *Russia* 34 B8
Marijampolė, *Lithuania* 9 J20
Marijampolė □, *Lithuania* 30 D10
Marília, *Brazil* 127 A6
Marín, *Spain* 36 C2
Marina, *U.S.A.* 110 J5
Marinduque, *Phil.* 63 B6
Marine City, *U.S.A.* 116 D2
Marineo, *Italy* 42 E6
Marinette, *U.S.A.* 114 C2
Maringá, *Brazil* 127 A5
Marinha Grande, *Portugal* 36 F2
Marino, *Italy* 41 G9
Marion, *Ala., U.S.A.* 115 J2
Marion, *Ill., U.S.A.* 113 G10
Marion, *Ind., U.S.A.* 114 E3
Marion, *Iowa, U.S.A.* 112 D9
Marion, *Kans., U.S.A.* 112 F6
Marion, *N.C., U.S.A.* 115 H5
Marion, *Ohio, U.S.A.* 114 E4
Marion, *S.C., U.S.A.* 115 H6
Marion, *Va., U.S.A.* 115 G5
Marion, L., *U.S.A.* 115 J5
Mariposa, *U.S.A.* 110 H7
Mariscal Estigarribia, *Paraguay* 126 A3
Maritime Alps = Maritimes,
  Alpes, *Europe* 21 D11
Maritimes, Alpes, *Europe* 21 D11
Maritsa = Évros ➤, *Greece* 72 B2
Maritsá, *Greece* 49 C10
Mariupol, *Ukraine* 33 J9
Mariusa △, *Venezuela* 121 E12
Marīvān, *Iran* 70 C5
Marj 'Uyūn, *Lebanon* 74 B4
Marka = Merca, *Somali Rep.* 75 G3
Marka, *Si. Arabia* 80 D5
Markam, *China* 58 C2
Markaryd, *Sweden* 11 H7
Markdale, *Canada* 116 B4
Marked Tree, *U.S.A.* 113 H9
Markelsdorfer Huk, *Germany* 24 A7
Market Drayton, *U.K.* 14 E5
Market Harborough, *U.K.* 15 E7
Market Rasen, *U.K.* 14 D7
Markham, *Canada* 116 C5
Markham, Mt., *Antarctica* 5 E11
Marki, *Poland* 31 F8
Märkische Schweiz △, *Germany* 24 C10
Markkleeberg, *Germany* 24 D8
Markleeville, *U.S.A.* 110 G7
Markoupoulon, *Greece* 46 D5
Markovac, *Serbia & M.* 44 B5
Markovo, *Russia* 53 C17
Markoye, *Burkina Faso* 83 C5
Marks, *Russia* 34 E8
Marksville, *U.S.A.* 113 K8
Markt Schwaben, *Germany* 25 G7
Marktoberdorf, *Germany* 25 H6
Marktredwitz, *Germany* 25 E8
Marl, *Germany* 24 D3
Marla, *Australia* 95 D1
Marlbank, *Canada* 116 B7
Marlboro, *Mass., U.S.A.* 117 D13
Marlboro, *N.Y., U.S.A.* 117 E11
Marlborough, *Australia* 94 C4
Marlborough, *U.K.* 15 F6
Marlborough Downs, *U.K.* 15 F6
Marlin, *U.S.A.* 113 K6
Marlow, *Germany* 24 A8
Marlow, *U.K.* 15 F7
Marlow, *U.S.A.* 113 H6
Marmagao, *India* 66 M8
Marmande, *France* 20 D4
Marmara, *Turkey* 45 F11
Marmara, Sea of = Marmara
  Denizi, *Turkey* 45 F12
Marmara Denizi, *Turkey* 45 F12
Marmara Gölü, *Turkey* 47 C10
Marmaris, *Turkey* 47 E10
Marmaris Limanı, *Turkey* 47 E10
Marmion, Mt., *Australia* 93 E2
Marmion L., *Canada* 104 C1
Marmolada, Mte., *Italy* 41 B8
Marmolejo, *Spain* 37 G6

Marmora, *Canada* 116 B7
Mármora, La, *Italy* 42 C2
Marnay, *France* 19 E12
Marne, *Germany* 24 B5
Marne □, *France* 19 D11
Marne ➤, *France* 19 D9
Marneuli, *Georgia* 35 K7
Maroala, *Madag.* 89 B8
Maroantsetra, *Madag.* 89 B8
Maroelaboom, *Namibia* 88 B2
Marofandilia, *Madag.* 89 C7
Marojejy △, *Madag.* 89 A8
Marolambo, *Madag.* 89 C8
Maromandia, *Madag.* 89 A8
Maromokotro, *Madag.* 89 A8
Marondera, *Zimbabwe* 87 F3
Maroni ➤, *Fr. Guiana* 125 B8
Marónia, *Greece* 45 F9
Maronne ➤, *France* 20 C5
Maroochydore, *Australia* 95 D5
Maroona, *Australia* 95 F3
Maros ➤, *Hungary* 28 D5
Marosakoa, *Madag.* 89 B8
Maroseranana, *Madag.* 89 B8
Maróstica, *Italy* 41 C8
Marotandrano, *Madag.* 89 B8
Marotaolano, *Madag.* 89 A8
Maroua, *Cameroon* 83 C7
Marovato, *Madag.* 89 B8
Marovoay, *Madag.* 89 B8
Marquard, *S. Africa* 88 D4
Marquesas = Marquises, Îs.,
  French Polynesia 97 H14
Marquette, *U.S.A.* 114 B2
Marquis, *St. Lucia* .... 121 f
Marquise, *France* 19 B8
Marquises, Îs., *French Polynesia* 97 H14
Marra, Djebel, *Sudan* 79 F10
Marra, *Si. Arabia* 81 F2
Marracuene, *Mozam.* 89 D5
Marradi, *Italy* 41 D8
Marrakech, *Morocco* 78 B4
Marratxi, *Spain* 38 F7
Marrawah, *Australia* 95 G3
Marree, *Australia* 95 D2
Marrero, *U.S.A.* 113 L9
Marrimane, *Mozam.* 89 C5
Marromeu, *Mozam.* 89 B6
Marromeu △, *Mozam.* 89 B6
Marroquí, Punta, *Spain* 37 K5
Marrowie Cr. ➤, *Australia* 95 E4
Marrubane, *Mozam.* 87 F4
Marrúbiu, *Italy* 42 C1
Marrupa, *Mozam.* 87 E4
Mars Hill, *U.S.A.* 115 B12
Marsá 'Alam, *Egypt* 80 B3
Marsá Matrûh, *Egypt* 80 A2
Marsá Sha'b, *Sudan* 80 C4
Marsabit, *Kenya* 86 B4
Marsabit △, *Kenya* 86 B4
Marsala, *Italy* 42 E5
Marsalforn, *Malta* 49 C1
Mârşani, *Romania* 29 F9
Marsberg, *Germany* 24 D4
Marsciano, *Italy* 41 F9
Marsden, *Australia* 95 E4
Marseillan, *France* 20 E7
Marseille, *France* 21 E9
Marseille ✈ (MRS), *France* 21 E9
Marseilles = Marseille, *France* 21 E9
Marsh I., *U.S.A.* 113 L9
Marshall, *Liberia* 82 D2
Marshall, *Ark., U.S.A.* 113 H8
Marshall, *Mich., U.S.A.* 114 D3
Marshall, *Minn., U.S.A.* 112 C6
Marshall, *Mo., U.S.A.* 112 F8
Marshall, *Tex., U.S.A.* 113 J7
Marshall ➤, *Australia* 94 C2
Marshall Is. ■, *Pac. Oc.* 96 G9
Marshalltown, *U.S.A.* 112 D8
Marshbrook, *Zimbabwe* 89 B5
Marshfield, *Mo., U.S.A.* 113 G8
Marshfield, *Vt., U.S.A.* 117 B12
Marshfield, *Wis., U.S.A.* 112 C9
Marshun, *Iran* 71 B6
Mársico Nuovo, *Italy* 43 B8
Märsta, *Sweden* 10 E11
Marstal, *Denmark* 11 K4
Marstrand, *Sweden* 11 G5
Mart, *U.S.A.* 113 K6
Marta ➤, *Italy* 41 F8
Martaban, *Burma* 67 L20
Martaban, G. of, *Burma* 67 L20
Martano, *Italy* 43 B11
Martapura, *Kalimantan, Indonesia* 62 E4
Martapura, *Sumatera, Indonesia* 62 E2
Marte, *Nigeria* 83 C7
Martel, *France* 20 D5
Martelange, *Belgium* 17 E5
Martellago, *Italy* 41 C9
Martés, Sierra, *Spain* 39 F4
Martfű, *Hungary* 28 C5
Martha's Vineyard, *U.S.A.* 117 E14
Martigné-Ferchaud, *France* 18 E5
Martigny, *Switz.* 25 J3
Martigues, *France* 21 E9
Martin, *Slovak Rep.* 27 B11
Martin, *S. Dak., U.S.A.* 112 D4
Martin, *Tenn., U.S.A.* 113 G10
Martín ➤, *Spain* 38 D4
Martin, L., *U.S.A.* 115 J3
Martina Franca, *Italy* 43 B10
Martinborough, *N.Z.* 91 J5
Martinez, *Calif., U.S.A.* 110 G4
Martinez, *Ga., U.S.A.* 115 J4
Martínez ✈, *W. Indies* .... 120 c
Martinique Passage, *W. Indies* 121 C7
Martínipolis, *Brazil* 127 A5
Martin's Bay, *Barbados* .... 121 g
Martins Ferry, *U.S.A.* 116 F4
Martinsberg, *Austria* 26 C8

Martinsburg, Pa., U.S.A. 116 F6
Martinsburg, W. Va., U.S.A. 114 F7
Martinsicuro, Italy 41 F10
Martinsville, Ind., U.S.A. 114 F2
Martinsville, Va., U.S.A. 115 G6
Marton, N.Z. 91 J5
Martorell, Spain 38 D6
Martos, Spain 37 H7
Martuni, Armenia 35 K7
Maru, Nigeria 83 C6
Maruf, Afghan. 66 D5
Marugame, Japan 55 G6
Marunga, Angola 88 B3
Marungu, Mts., Dem. Rep. of the Congo 86 D3
Marv Dasht, Iran 71 D7
Marvast, Iran 71 D7
Marvejols, France 20 D7
Marvel Loch, Australia 93 F2
Marwar, India 68 G5
Mary, Turkmenistan 52 F7
Maryborough = Port Laoise, Ireland 12 C4
Maryborough, Queens., Australia 95 D5
Maryborough, Vic., Australia 95 F3
Maryfield, Canada 103 D8
Maryland □, U.S.A. 114 F7
Maryland Junction, Zimbabwe 87 F3
Maryport, U.K. 14 C4
Mary's Harbour, Canada 105 B8
Marystown, Canada 105 C8
Marysville, Canada 102 D5
Marysville, Calif., U.S.A. 110 F5
Marysville, Kans., U.S.A. 112 F6
Marysville, Mich., U.S.A. 116 D2
Marysville, Ohio, U.S.A. 114 E4
Marysville, Wash., U.S.A. 110 B4
Maryville, Mo., U.S.A. 112 E7
Maryville, Tenn., U.S.A. 115 H4
Marzūq, Libya 79 C8
Masahunga, Tanzania 86 C3
Masai, Malaysia 65 d
Masai Mara △, Kenya 86 C4
Masai Steppe, Tanzania 86 C4
Masaka, Uganda 86 C3
Masalembo, Kepulauan, Indonesia 62 F4
Masalima, Kepulauan, Indonesia 62 F5
Masallı, Azerbaijan 73 C13
Masamba, Indonesia 63 E6
Masan, S. Korea 57 G15
Masandam, Ra's, Oman 71 E8
Masasi, Tanzania 87 E4
Masaya, Nic. 120 D2
Masba, Nigeria 83 C7
Masbate, Phil. 61 E5
Máscali, Italy 43 E8
Mascara, Algeria 78 A6
Mascota, Mexico 118 C4
Masela, Indonesia 63 F7
Maseru, Lesotho 88 D4
Mashaba, Zimbabwe 87 G3
Mashābih, Si. Arabia 70 E3
Mashan, China 58 F7
Mashar, Sudan 81 F2
Mashatu △, Botswana 89 C4
Mashegu, Nigeria 83 D6
Masherbrum, Pakistan 69 B7
Mashhad, Iran 71 B8
Mashi, Nigeria 83 C6
Mashīz, Iran 71 D8
Māshkel, Hāmūn-i-, Pakistan 66 E3
Mashki Chāh, Pakistan 66 E3
Mashonaland, Zimbabwe 85 H6
Mashonaland Central □, Zimbabwe 89 B5
Mashonaland East □, Zimbabwe 89 B5
Mashonaland West □, Zimbabwe 89 B4
Mashrakh, India 69 F11
Mashtaga = Maştağa, Azerbaijan 35 K10
Masindi, Uganda 86 B3
Masindi Port, Uganda 86 B3
Maşīrah, Oman 75 C6
Maşīrah, Khalīj, Oman 75 C6
Masisi, Dem. Rep. of the Congo 86 C2
Masjed Soleyman, Iran 71 D6
Mask, L., Ireland 12 C2
Maskin, Oman 71 F8
Maslen Nos, Bulgaria 45 D11
Maslinica, Croatia 41 E13
Masnou = El Masnou, Spain 38 D7
Masoala △, Madag. 89 B9
Masoala, Tanjon' i, Madag. 89 B9
Masoarivo, Madag. 89 B7
Masohi = Amahai, Indonesia 63 E7
Masomeloka, Madag. 89 C8
Mason, Nev., U.S.A. 110 G7
Mason, Tex., U.S.A. 113 K5
Mason City, U.S.A. 112 D8
Maspalomas, Canary Is. 48 G4
Maspalomas, Pta., Canary Is. 48 G4
Masqaṭ, Oman 75 C6
Massa, Italy 40 D7
Massa Maríttima, Italy 40 E7
Massachusetts □, U.S.A. 117 D13
Massachusetts B., U.S.A. 117 D14
Massafra, Italy 43 B10
Massakory, Chad 79 F9
Massanella, Spain 48 B9
Massangena, Mozam. 89 C5
Massango, Angola 84 F3
Massat, France 20 F5
Massawa = Mitsiwa, Eritrea 81 D4
Massena, U.S.A. 117 B10
Massénya, Chad 79 F9
Masset, Canada 102 C2
Masseube, France 20 E4
Massiac, France 20 C7
Massiah Street, Barbados 121 g
Massif Central, France 20 D7
Massif des Bauges △, France 19 G13

Massigui, Mali 82 C3
Massillon, U.S.A. 116 F3
Massinga, Mozam. 89 C6
Massingir, Mozam. 89 C5
Masson-Angers, Canada 117 A9
Masson I., Antarctica 5 C7
Mastanli = Momchilgrad, Bulgaria 45 E9
Masterton, N.Z. 91 J5
Mastic, U.S.A. 117 F12
Mástikho, Ákra, Greece 47 C8
Mastuj, Pakistan 69 A5
Mastung, Pakistan 66 E5
Mastūrah, Si. Arabia 80 C4
Masty, Belarus 32 F3
Masuda, Japan 55 G5
Masvingo, Zimbabwe 87 G3
Masvingo □, Zimbabwe 87 G3
Maswa △, Tanzania 86 C3
Maşyāf, Syria 70 C3
Maszewo, Poland 30 E2
Mat →, Albania 44 E3
Matabeleland, Zimbabwe 85 H5
Matabeleland North □, Zimbabwe 87 F2
Matabeleland South □, Zimbabwe 87 G2
Matachel →, Spain 37 G4
Matachewan, Canada 104 C3
Matadi, Dem. Rep. of the Congo 84 F2
Matagalpa, Nic. 120 D2
Matagami, Canada 104 C4
Matagami, L., Canada 104 C4
Matagorda B., U.S.A. 113 L6
Matagorda I., U.S.A. 113 L6
Matak, Indonesia 62 D3
Mátala, Greece 49 E6
Matam, Senegal 82 B2
Matameye, Niger 83 C6
Matamoros, Campeche, Mexico 119 D6
Matamoros, Coahuila, Mexico 118 B4
Matamoros, Tamaulipas, Mexico 119 B5
Ma'ṭan as Sarra, Libya 79 D10
Matandu →, Tanzania 87 D3
Matane, Canada 105 C6
Matang, China 58 F5
Matankari, Niger 83 C5
Matanomadh, India 68 H3
Matanzas, Cuba 120 B3
Matapa, Botswana 88 C3
Matapan, C. = Taínaron, Ákra, Greece 46 E4
Matapédia, Canada 105 C6
Matapo △, Zimbabwe 87 G2
Matara, Sri Lanka 66 S12
Mataram, Indonesia 63 K19
Matarani, Peru 124 G4
Mataranka, Australia 92 B5
Matarma, Râs, Egypt 74 E1
Mataró, Spain 38 D7
Matarraña →, Spain 38 D5
Mataruška Banja, Serbia & M. 44 C4
Matatiele, S. Africa 89 E4
Mataura, N.Z. 91 M2
Matehuala, Mexico 118 C4
Mateke Hills, Zimbabwe 87 G3
Matelot, Trin. & Tob. 125 K15
Matera, Italy 43 B9
Matese △, Italy 43 A7
Matese, Monti del, Italy 43 A7
Mátészalka, Hungary 28 C7
Matetsi, Zimbabwe 87 F2
Matfors, Sweden 10 B11
Matha, France 20 C3
Matheniko △, Uganda 86 B3
Mathis, U.S.A. 113 L6
Mathráki, Greece 49 A3
Mathura, India 68 F7
Mati, Phil. 61 H7
Matiakoali, Burkina Faso 83 C5
Matiali, India 69 F13
Matías Romero, Mexico 119 D5
Matibane, Mozam. 87 E5
Matiri Ra., N.Z. 91 J4
Matjiesfontein, S. Africa 88 E3
Matla →, India 69 J13
Matlamanyane, Botswana 88 B4
Matli, Pakistan 68 G3
Matlock, U.K. 14 D6
Matna, Sudan 81 E4
Mato Grosso □, Brazil 125 F8
Mato Grosso, Planalto do, Brazil 125 G8
Mato Grosso do Sul □, Brazil 125 G8
Matobo = Matapo △, Zimbabwe 87 G2
Matochkin Shar, Russia 52 B6
Matopo Hills, Zimbabwe 87 G2
Matopos, Zimbabwe 87 G2
Matosinhos, Portugal 36 D2
Matour, France 19 F11
Matroosberg, S. Africa 88 E2
Matsena, Nigeria 83 C7
Matsesta, Russia 35 J4
Matsu Tao, Taiwan 59 E13
Matsue, Japan 55 G6
Matsum, Ko, Thailand 65 b
Matsumae, Japan 54 D10
Matsumoto, Japan 55 F9
Matsusaka, Japan 55 G8
Matsuura, Japan 55 H4
Matsuyama, Japan 55 H6
Mattagami →, Canada 104 B3
Mattancheri, India 66 Q10
Mattawa, Canada 104 C4
Matterhorn, Switz. 25 K3
Mattersburg, Austria 27 D9
Matthew Town, Bahamas 121 B5
Matthews Ridge, Guyana 124 B6
Mattice, Canada 104 C3
Mattituck, U.S.A. 117 F12
Mattō, Japan 55 F8
Mattoon, U.S.A. 114 F1

Matuba, Mozam. 89 C5
Matucana, Peru 124 F3
Matūn = Khowst, Afghan. 68 C3
Matura B., Trin. & Tob. 125 K15
Maturín, Venezuela 124 B6
Matusadona △, Zimbabwe 87 F2
Matveyev Kurgan, Russia 33 J10
Matxitxako, C., Spain 38 B2
Mau, Mad. P., India 69 F8
Mau, Ut. P., India 69 G10
Mau, Ut. P., India 69 G9
Mau Escarpment, Kenya 86 C4
Mau Ranipur, India 69 G8
Maubeuge, France 19 B10
Maubourguet, France 20 E4
Maud, Pt., Australia 92 D1
Maude, Australia 95 E3
Maudin Sun, Burma 67 M19
Maués, Brazil 124 D7
Mauganj, India 67 G12
Maughold Hd., I. of Man 14 C3
Mauguio, France 20 E7
Maui, U.S.A. 106 H16
Maulamyaing = Moulmein, Burma 67 L20
Maule □, Chile 126 D1
Mauléon-Licharre, France 20 E3
Maumee, U.S.A. 114 E4
Maumee →, U.S.A. 114 E4
Maumere, Indonesia 63 F6
Maumusson, Pertuis de, France 20 C2
Maun, Botswana 88 C3
Mauna Kea, U.S.A. 106 J17
Mauna Loa, U.S.A. 106 J17
Maungmagan Kyunzu, Burma 64 E1
Maupin, U.S.A. 108 D3
Maure-de-Bretagne, France 18 E5
Maurepas, L., U.S.A. 113 K9
Maures, France 21 E10
Mauriac, France 20 C6
Maurice, L., Australia 93 E5
Maurice △, Canada 104 C5
Maurienne, France 21 C10
Mauritania ■, Africa 78 E3
Mauritius ■, Ind. Oc. 77 J9
Mauron, France 18 D4
Maurs, France 20 D6
Mauston, U.S.A. 112 D9
Mauterndorf, Austria 26 D6
Mauthen, Austria 26 E6
Mauvezin, France 20 E4
Mauzé-sur-le-Mignon, France 20 B3
Mavli, India 68 G5
Mavrovë, Albania 44 F3
Mavrovo △, Macedonia 44 E4
Mavuradonha Mts., Zimbabwe 87 F3
Mawa, Dem. Rep. of the Congo 86 B2
Mawai, India 69 H9
Mawana, India 68 E7
Mawand, Pakistan 68 E3
Mawk Mai, Burma 67 J20
Mawlaik, Burma 67 H19
Mawlamyine = Moulmein, Burma 67 L20
Mawqaq, Si. Arabia 70 E4
Mawson Base, Antarctica 5 C6
Mawson Coast, Antarctica 5 C6
Max, U.S.A. 112 B4
Maxcanú, Mexico 119 C6
Maxesibeni, S. Africa 89 E4
Maxhamish L., Canada 102 B4
Maxixe, Mozam. 89 C6
Maxville, Canada 117 A10
Maxwell, U.S.A. 110 F4
Maxwelton, Australia 94 C3
May, C., U.S.A. 114 F8
May Pen, Jamaica 120 a
Maya →, Russia 53 D14
Maya Mts., Belize 119 D7
Mayaguana, Bahamas 121 B5
Mayagüez, Puerto Rico 121 d
Mayahi, Niger 83 C6
Mayaky, Ukraine 29 C14
Mayals = Maials, Spain 38 D5
Mayāmey, Iran 71 B7
Mayang, China 58 D7
Mayanup, Australia 93 F2
Mayapán, Mexico 119 C7
Mayapan, Yucatán, Mexico 119 C7
Mayarí, Cuba 121 B4
Mayaro B., Trin. & Tob. 125 K16
Maybell, U.S.A. 108 F9
Maybole, U.K. 13 F4
Maychew, Ethiopia 81 E4
Maydān, Iraq 70 C5
Maydan, Ukraine 29 B8
Maydena, Australia 95 G4
Mayen, Germany 25 E3
Mayenne, France 18 D6
Mayenne □, France 18 D6
Mayenne →, France 18 E6
Mayer, U.S.A. 109 J7
Mayerthorpe, Canada 102 C5
Mayfield, Ky., U.S.A. 115 G1
Mayfield, N.Y., U.S.A. 117 C10
Mayhill, U.S.A. 109 K11
Maykop, Russia 35 H5
Maymyo, Burma 64 A1
Maynard, Mass., U.S.A. 117 D13
Maynard, Wash., U.S.A. 110 C4
Maynard Hills, Australia 93 E2
Mayne →, Australia 94 C3
Maynooth, Ireland 12 C5
Mayo, Canada 100 B6
Mayo □, Ireland 12 C2
Mayo Daga, Nigeria 83 D7
Mayo Faran, Nigeria 83 D7
Mayon Volcano, Phil. 61 E5
Mayor I., N.Z. 91 G6
Mayorga, Spain 36 C5
Mayotte ☐, Ind. Oc. 85 G9
Mayraira Pt., Phil. 61 B4
Maysān □, Iraq 70 D5

Mayskiy, Russia 35 J7
Maysville, U.S.A. 114 F4
Mayu, Indonesia 63 D7
Mayville, N. Dak., U.S.A. 112 B6
Mayville, N.Y., U.S.A. 116 D5
Mayya, Russia 53 C14
Mazabuka, Zambia 87 F2
Mazagán = El Jadida, Morocco 78 B4
Mazagão, Brazil 125 D8
Mazamet, France 20 E6
Mazán, Peru 124 D4
Māzandarān □, Iran 71 B7
Mazapil, Mexico 118 C4
Mazara del Vallo, Italy 42 E5
Mazarrón, Spain 39 H3
Mazarrón, G. de, Spain 39 H3
Mazaruni →, Guyana 124 B7
Mazatán, Mexico 118 B2
Mazatenango, Guatemala 120 D1
Mazatlán, Mexico 118 C3
Mažeikiai, Lithuania 9 H20
Māzhān, Iran 71 C8
Mazīnān, Iran 71 B8
Mazoe, Mozam. 87 F3
Mazoe →, Mozam. 87 F3
Mazowe, Zimbabwe 87 F3
Mazowieckie □, Poland 31 F8
Mazrūb, Sudan 81 E2
Mazu Dao, China 59 D12
Mazurian Lakes = Mazurski, Pojezierze, Poland 30 E7
Mazurski, Pojezierze, Poland 30 E7
Mazyr, Belarus 33 F5
Mbaba, Senegal 82 C1
Mbabane, Swaziland 89 D5
Mbagne, Mauritania 82 B2
M'bahiakro, Ivory C. 82 D4
Mbaïki, C.A.R. 84 D3
Mbala, Zambia 87 D3
Mbalabala, Zimbabwe 89 C4
Mbale, Uganda 86 B3
Mbalmayo, Cameroon 83 E7
Mbam →, Cameroon 83 E7
Mbamba Bay, Tanzania 87 E3
Mbandaka, Dem. Rep. of the Congo 84 D3
Mbanga, Cameroon 83 E6
Mbanza Congo, Angola 84 F2
Mbanza Ngungu, Dem. Rep. of the Congo 84 F2
Mbarangandu, Tanzania 87 D4
Mbarara, Uganda 86 C3
Mbashe →, S. Africa 89 E4
Mbatto, Ivory C. 82 D4
Mbenkuru →, Tanzania 87 D4
Mberengwa, Zimbabwe 87 G2
Mberengwa, Mt., Zimbabwe 87 G2
Mbeuru, Nigeria 83 D6
Mbesuma, Zambia 87 E3
Mbeya, Tanzania 87 D3
Mbeya □, Tanzania 86 D3
M'bili, Sudan 81 F2
Mbinga, Tanzania 87 E4
Mbini = Río Muni □, Eq. Guin. 84 D2
Mboki, C.A.R. 81 F2
M'bonge, Cameroon 83 E6
Mboro, Senegal 82 B1
M'boukou, Rés. de, Cameroon 83 D7
Mboune, Senegal 82 C2
Mbour, Senegal 82 C1
Mbout, Mauritania 82 B2
Mbuji-Mayi, Dem. Rep. of the Congo 86 D1
Mbulu, Tanzania 86 C4
Mburucuyá, Argentina 126 B4
McCarran International, Las Vegas ✈ (LAS), U.S.A. 111 J11
Mchinja, Tanzania 87 D4
Mchinji, Malawi 87 E3
McMurdo, Antarctica 5 D11
Mdantsane, S. Africa 85 L5
Mead, L., U.S.A. 111 J12
Meade, U.S.A. 113 G4
Meadow Lake, Canada 103 C7
Meadow Lake △, Canada 103 C7
Meadow Valley Wash →, U.S.A. 111 J12
Meadville, U.S.A. 116 E4
Meaford, Canada 116 B4
Mealhada, Portugal 36 E2
Mealy Mts., Canada 105 B8
Meander River, Canada 102 B5
Meares, C., U.S.A. 108 D2
Mearim →, Brazil 125 D10
Meath □, Ireland 12 C5
Meath Park, Canada 103 C7
Meaulne, France 19 F9
Meaux, France 19 D9
Mebechi-Gawa →, Japan 54 D10
Mebulu, Tanjung, Indonesia 63 K18
Mecanhelas, Mozam. 87 F4
Mecca = Makkah, Si. Arabia 75 C2
Mecca, U.S.A. 111 M10
Mechanicsburg, U.S.A. 116 F8
Mechanicville, U.S.A. 117 D11
Mechara, Ethiopia 81 F5
Mechelen, Belgium 17 C4
Mecheria, Algeria 78 B5
Mechernich, Germany 24 E2
Mechetinskaya, Russia 35 G5
Mecidiye, Turkey 45 F10
Mecitözü, Turkey 72 B6
Mecklenburg-Vorpommern □, Germany 24 B8
Mecklenburger Bucht, Germany 24 A7
Meconta, Mozam. 87 E4
Mecsek, Hungary 28 D3
Meda, Portugal 36 E3
Medan, Indonesia 62 D1
Médanos de Coro △, Venezuela 121 D6
Medanosa, Pta., Argentina 128 F3
Mede, Italy 40 C5
Médéa, Algeria 78 A6

Mededa, Bos.-H. 28 G4
Medellín, Colombia 124 B3
Medelpad, Sweden 10 B10
Medemblik, Neths. 17 B5
Mederdra, Mauritania 82 B1
Medford, Mass., U.S.A. 117 D13
Medford, Oreg., U.S.A. 108 E2
Medford, Wis., U.S.A. 112 C9
Medgidia, Romania 29 F13
Medi, Sudan 81 F3
Media Agua, Argentina 126 C2
Media Luna, Argentina 126 C2
Medianeira, Brazil 127 B5
Mediaş, Romania 29 D9
Medicina, Italy 41 D8
Medicine Bow, U.S.A. 108 F10
Medicine Bow Pk., U.S.A. 108 F10
Medicine Bow Ra., U.S.A. 108 F10
Medicine Hat, Canada 103 D6
Medicine Lake, U.S.A. 112 A2
Medicine Lodge, U.S.A. 113 G5
Medina = Al Madīnah, Si. Arabia 70 E3
Medina, N. Dak., U.S.A. 112 B5
Medina, N.Y., U.S.A. 116 C6
Medina, Ohio, U.S.A. 116 E3
Medina →, U.S.A. 113 L5
Medina de Pomar, Spain 36 C7
Medina de Ríoseco, Spain 36 D5
Medina del Campo, Spain 36 D6
Medina L., U.S.A. 113 L5
Medina Sidonia, Spain 37 J5
Medinaceli, Spain 38 D2
Medinipur, India 69 H12
Mediterranean Sea, Europe 6 H7
Médoc, France 20 C3
Medulin, Croatia 41 D10
Medveđa, Serbia & M. 44 D5
Medvedevo, Russia 34 B8
Medveditsa →, Tver, Russia 32 D9
Medveditsa →, Volgograd, Russia 34 F6
Medvedok, Russia 34 B10
Medvezhi, Ostrava, Russia 53 B17
Medvezhyegorsk, Russia 52 C4
Medway →, U.K. 15 F8
Medway □, U.K. 15 F8
Medzev, Slovak Rep. 27 C13
Medzilaborce, Slovak Rep. 27 B14
Medžitlija, Macedonia 44 F5
Meekatharra, Australia 93 E2
Meeker, U.S.A. 108 F10
Meelpaeg Res., Canada 105 C8
Meersburg, Germany 25 H5
Meerut, India 68 E7
Meeteetse, U.S.A. 108 D9
Mega, Ethiopia 81 G4
Megálo Khorío, Greece 47 E9
Megálo Petalí, Greece 46 D6
Megalópolis, Greece 46 D4
Meganísi Nisís, Greece 46 C2
Mégara, Greece 46 D5
Megasini, India 69 J12
Megdhova →, Greece 46 B3
Megève, France 21 C10
Meghalaya □, India 67 G17
Meghezez, Ethiopia 81 F4
Meghna →, Bangla. 67 H17
Mégiscane, L., Canada 104 C4
Megiste, Greece 47 E11
Megra, Russia 32 B9
Mehadia, Romania 28 F7
Meharry, Mt., Australia 92 D2
Mehedeby, Sweden 10 D11
Mehedinți □, Romania 28 F7
Meheisa, Sudan 80 D3
Mehlville, U.S.A. 112 F9
Mehndawal, India 69 F10
Mehr Jān, Iran 71 C7
Mehrābād, Iran 70 B5
Mehrān, Iran 70 C5
Mehrīz, Iran 71 D7
Mehun-sur-Yèvre, France 19 E9
Mei Jiang →, China 59 E11
Mei Xian, China 56 G4
Meicheng, China 59 C12
Meichengzhen, China 59 C8
Meichuan, China 59 B10
Meigu, China 58 C4
Meiktila, Burma 67 J19
Meinerzhagen, Germany 24 D3
Meiningen, Germany 24 E6
Meira, Serra de, Spain 36 B3
Meiringen, Switz. 25 J4
Meishan, China 58 B4
Meissen, Germany 24 D9
Meissner, Germany 24 D5
Meissner-Kaufinger Wald △, Germany 24 D5
Meitan, China 58 D6
Meizhou, China 59 E11
Meja, India 69 G10
Mejillones, Chile 126 A1
Mekdela, Ethiopia 81 E4
Mekele, Ethiopia 81 E4
Mekhtar, Pakistan 66 D6
Meknès, Morocco 78 B4
Meko, Nigeria 83 D5
Mekong →, Asia 65 H6
Mekongga, Indonesia 63 E6
Mekrou →, Benin 83 C5
Mekvari = Kür →, Azerbaijan 73 C13
Mel, Italy 41 B9
Melagiri Hills, India 66 N10
Melaka, Malaysia 65 L4
Melalap, Malaysia 62 C5
Mélambes, Greece 49 D6
Melanesia, Pac. Oc. 96 H7
Melaya, Indonesia 63 J17
Melbourne, Australia 95 F4
Melbourne, U.S.A. 115 L5
Melchor Múzquiz, Mexico 118 B4
Melchor Ocampo, Mexico 118 C4
Méldola, Italy 41 D9

Meldorf, Germany 24 A5
Melegnano, Italy 40 C6
Melenci, Serbia & M. 28 E5
Melenki, Russia 34 C5
Mélèzes →, Canada 104 A5
Melfi, Italy 43 B8
Melfort, Canada 103 C8
Melfort, Zimbabwe 87 F3
Melgaço, Portugal 36 C2
Melgar de Fernamental, Spain 36 C6
Melhus, Norway 8 E14
Melide, Spain 36 C2
Meligalá, Greece 46 D3
Melilla, N. Afr. 78 A5
Melilli, Italy 43 E8
Melipilla, Chile 126 C1
Mélissa, Ákra, Greece 49 D6
Mélissa Óros, Greece 47 D8
Melita, Canada 103 D8
Mélito di Porto Salvo, Italy 43 E8
Melitopol, Ukraine 33 J8
Melk, Austria 26 C8
Mellan Fryken, Sweden 10 E7
Mellansel, Sweden 8 E18
Mellbystrand, Sweden 11 H6
Mellegue →, France 20 B3
Melle, France 20 B3
Melle, Germany 24 C4
Mellen, U.S.A. 112 B9
Mellerud, Sweden 11 F6
Mellette, U.S.A. 112 C5
Mellid = Melide, Spain 36 C2
Mellieħa, Malta 49 D1
Mellit, Sudan 81 E2
Mellrichstadt, Germany 24 E6
Melnik, Bulgaria 44 E7
Mělník, Czech Rep. 26 A7
Melnytsya Podilska, Ukraine 29 B11
Melo, Uruguay 127 C5
Melolo, Indonesia 63 F6
Melouprey, Cambodia 64 F5
Melrose, Australia 95 E4
Melrose, U.K. 13 F6
Melrose, Minn., U.S.A. 112 C7
Melrose, N. Mex., U.S.A. 113 H3
Melstone, U.S.A. 108 C10
Melsungen, Germany 24 D5
Melton Mowbray, U.K. 14 E7
Melun, France 19 D9
Melut, Sudan 81 E3
Melville, Canada 103 C8
Melville, C., Australia 94 A3
Melville, I., Canada 105 B8
Melville B., Australia 94 A2
Melville I., Australia 92 B5
Melville I., Canada 98 B8
Melville Pen., Canada 101 B11
Mélykút, Hungary 28 D4
Memaliaj, Albania 44 F3
Memba, Mozam. 87 E5
Memboro, Indonesia 63 F5
Membrilla, Spain 37 G7
Memel = Klaipėda, Lithuania 9 J19
Memel, S. Africa 89 D4
Memmingen, Germany 25 H6
Mempawah, Indonesia 62 D3
Memphis, Egypt 80 J7
Memphis, Mich., U.S.A. 116 D2
Memphis, Tenn., U.S.A. 113 H10
Memphis, Tex., U.S.A. 113 H4
Memphremagog, L., U.S.A. 117 B12
Mena, Ukraine 33 G7
Mena, U.S.A. 113 H7
Mena →, Ethiopia 81 F5
Menai Strait, U.K. 14 D3
Ménaka, Mali 83 B5
Menan = Chao Phraya →, Thailand 64 F3
Menarandra →, Madag. 89 D7
Menard, U.S.A. 113 K5
Menawashei, Sudan 81 E1
Mendawai →, Indonesia 62 E4
Mende, France 20 D7
Mendebo Mts., Ethiopia 81 F4
Menden, Germany 24 D3
Menderes, Turkey 47 C9
Mendez, Mexico 119 B5
Mendhar, India 69 C6
Mendi, Ethiopia 81 F4
Mendip Hills, U.K. 15 F5
Mendocino, U.S.A. 108 G2
Mendocino, C., U.S.A. 108 F1
Mendota, Calif., U.S.A. 110 J6
Mendota, Ill., U.S.A. 112 E10
Mendoyo, Indonesia 63 J17
Mendoza, Argentina 126 C2
Mendoza □, Argentina 126 C2
Mene Grande, Venezuela 124 B4
Menemen, Turkey 47 C9
Menen, Belgium 17 D3
Menfi, Italy 42 E5
Mengdingjie, China 58 F2
Mengeš, Slovenia 41 B11
Menggala, Indonesia 62 E3
Menghai, China 58 G3
Mengíbar, Spain 37 H7
Mengjin, China 56 G7
Mengla, China 58 G3
Menglian, China 58 F2
Mengshan, China 59 E8
Mengyin, China 57 G9
Mengzhe, China 58 F3
Mengzi, China 58 F4
Menihek, Canada 105 B6
Menihek L., Canada 105 B6
Menin = Menen, Belgium 17 D3
Menindee, Australia 95 E3
Menindee L., Australia 95 E3
Meningie, Australia 95 F2
Menjangan, Pulau, Indonesia 63 J17
Menlo Park, U.S.A. 110 H4
Menominee, U.S.A. 114 C2

Menominee →, U.S.A. 114 C2
Menomonie, U.S.A. 112 C9
Menongue, Angola 85 G3
Menorca, Spain 48 B11
Menorca ✈ (MAH), Spain 38 F9
Mentakab, Malaysia 65 L4
Mentawai, Kepulauan, Indonesia 62 E1
Menton, France 21 E11
Mentor, U.S.A. 116 E3
Menzies, Australia 93 E3
Meob B., Namibia 88 C1
Me'ona, Israel 74 B4
Meoqui, Mexico 118 B3
Mepaco, Mozam. 87 F3
Meppel, Neths. 17 B6
Meppen, Germany 24 C3
Mequinenza, Spain 38 D5
Mequinenza, Embalse de, Spain 38 D5
Mer, France 18 E8
Merabéllou, Kólpos, Greece 49 D7
Merak, Indonesia 63 F12
Meramangye, L., Australia 93 E5
Meran = Merano, Italy 41 B8
Merano, Italy 41 B8
Merate, Italy 40 C6
Merauke, Indonesia 63 F10
Merbein, Australia 95 E3
Merbuk, Gunung, Indonesia 63 J17
Merca, Somali Rep. 75 G3
Mercantour △, France 21 D10
Mercato Saraceno, Italy 41 E9
Merced, U.S.A. 110 H6
Merced →, U.S.A. 110 H6
Merced Pk., U.S.A. 110 H7
Mercedes, Buenos Aires, Argentina 126 C4
Mercedes, Corrientes, Argentina 126 B4
Mercedes, San Luis, Argentina 126 C2
Mercedes, Uruguay 126 C4
Mercedes, U.S.A. 113 M6
Merceditas, Chile 126 B1
Mercer, U.S.A. 116 E4
Mercer, N.Z. 91 G5
Mercer Island, U.S.A. 110 C4
Mercury, U.S.A. 111 J11
Mercy, C., Canada 101 B13
Merdrignac, France 18 D4
Mere, U.K. 15 F5
Meredith, C., Falk. Is. 128 G4
Meredith, L., U.S.A. 113 H4
Merefa, Ukraine 33 H9
Merei, Romania 29 E11
Merga = Nukheila, Sudan 80 D2
Mergui, Burma 64 F2
Mergui Arch. = Myeik Kyunzu, Burma 65 G2
Méribel-les-Allues, France 21 C10
Meriç, Turkey 45 F10
Meriç →, Turkey 45 F10
Mérida, Mexico 119 C7
Mérida, Spain 37 G4
Mérida, Venezuela 124 B4
Mérida, Cord. de, Venezuela 124 B4
Meriden, U.K. 15 E6
Meriden, U.S.A. 117 E12
Meridian, Calif., U.S.A. 110 F5
Meridian, Idaho, U.S.A. 108 E5
Meridian, Miss., U.S.A. 115 J1
Mérignac, France 20 D3
Mérinaghène, Senegal 82 B1
Merinda, Australia 94 C4
Mering, Germany 25 G6
Meringa, Nigeria 83 C7
Merir, Pac. Oc. 63 D8
Merirumã, Brazil 125 C8
Merkel, U.S.A. 113 J5
Mermaid Reef, Australia 92 C2
Merowe, Sudan 80 D3
Merredin, Australia 93 F2
Merrick, U.K. 13 F4
Merrickville, Canada 117 B9
Merrill, Oreg., U.S.A. 108 E3
Merrill, Wis., U.S.A. 112 C10
Merrimack →, U.S.A. 117 D14
Merriman, U.S.A. 112 D4
Merritt, Canada 102 C4
Merritt Island, U.S.A. 115 L5
Merriwa, Australia 95 E5
Merry I., Canada 104 A4
Merryville, U.S.A. 113 K8
Mersa Fatma, Eritrea 81 E5
Mersch, Lux. 17 E6
Merse →, Italy 41 E8
Mersea I., U.K. 15 F8
Merseburg, Germany 24 D7
Mersey →, U.K. 14 D4
Merseyside □, U.K. 14 D4
Mersin, Turkey 70 B2
Mersing, Malaysia 65 L4
Merta, India 68 F6
Merta Road, India 68 F5
Merthyr Tydfil, U.K. 15 F4
Merthyr Tydfil □, U.K. 15 F4
Mértola, Portugal 37 H3
Mertzon, U.S.A. 113 K4
Méru, France 19 C9
Meru, Kenya 86 B4
Meru, Tanzania 86 C4
Meru △, Kenya 86 B4
Merville, France 19 B9
Méry-sur-Seine, France 19 D10
Merzifon, Turkey 72 B6
Merzig, Germany 25 F2
Mesa, U.S.A. 109 K8
Mesa Verde △, U.S.A. 109 H9
Mesagne, Italy 43 B10
Mesanagrós, Greece 49 C9
Mesaoria, Cyprus 49 D12
Mesarás, Kólpos, Greece 49 D6
Meschede, Germany 24 D4
Mescit, Turkey 73 B9
Mesfinto, Ethiopia 81 E4

Mesgouez, L., Canada 104 B5
Meshchovsk, Russia 32 E8
Meshed = Mashhad, Iran 71 B8
Meshoppen, U.S.A. 117 E8
Meshra er Req, Sudan 81 F2
Mesilinka →, Canada 102 B4
Mesilla, U.S.A. 109 K10
Meslay-du-Maine, France 18 E6
Mesocco, Switz. 25 J5
Mesolóngion, Greece 46 C3
Mesopotamia = Al Jazirah, Iraq 70 C5
Mesopotamia, U.S.A. 116 E4
Mesopótamon, Greece 46 B2
Mesoraca, Italy 43 C9
Mésou Volímais = Volímai, Greece 46 D2
Mesquite, U.S.A. 109 H6
Messaad, Algeria 78 B6
Messalo →, Mozam. 87 E4
Méssaména, Cameroon 83 E7
Messeue, Greece 46 D3
Messina = Musina, S. Africa 89 C5
Messina, Italy 43 D8
Messina, Str. di, Italy 43 D8
Messíni, Greece 46 D4
Messínia □, Greece 46 D3
Messiniakós Kólpos, Greece 46 E4
Messkirch, Germany 25 H5
Messlingen, Sweden 10 B6
Messonghi, Greece 49 B3
Mesta →, Bulgaria 44 E7
Mestá, Ákra, Greece 47 C7
Mestanza, Spain 37 G6
Mestre, Italy 41 C9
Mesudiye, Turkey 72 B7
Meta →, S. Amer. 124 B5
Meta Incognita Pen., Canada 101 B13
Metabetchouan, Canada 105 C5
Metairie, U.S.A. 113 L9
Metalici, Munţii, Romania 28 D7
Metaline Falls, U.S.A. 108 B5
Metallifere, Colline, Italy 40 E8
Metán, Argentina 126 B3
Metangula, Mozam. 87 E3
Metauro →, Italy 41 E10
Metema, Ethiopia 81 E4
Metengobalame, Mozam. 87 E3
Méthana, Greece 46 D5
Methóni, Greece 46 E3
Methven, N.Z. 91 K3
Metil, Mozam. 87 F4
Metkovets, Bulgaria 44 C7
Metković, Croatia 41 E14
Metlakatla, U.S.A. 100 C6
Metlika, Slovenia 41 C12
Metropolis, U.S.A. 113 G10
Métsovon, Greece 46 B3
Metu, Ethiopia 81 F4
Metz, France 19 C13
Metzingen, Germany 25 G5
Meulaboh, Indonesia 62 D1
Meung-sur-Loire, France 19 E8
Meureudu, Indonesia 62 C1
Meurthe →, France 19 D13
Meurthe-et-Moselle □, France 19 C12
Meuse □, France 19 C12
Meuse →, Europe 17 D5
Meuselwitz, Germany 24 D8
Mexia, U.S.A. 113 K6
Mexiana, I., Brazil 125 D9
Mexicali, Mexico 111 N11
Mexican Plateau, Mexico 98 G9
Mexican Water, U.S.A. 109 H9
México, Mexico 119 D5
Mexico, Maine, U.S.A. 117 B14
Mexico, Mo., U.S.A. 112 F9
Mexico, N.Y., U.S.A. 117 C8
México □, Mexico 119 D5
Mexico ■, Cent. Amer. 118 C4
Mexico, G. of, Cent. Amer. 119 C7
Mexico B., U.S.A. 117 C8
Meydân-e Naftûn, Iran 71 D6
Meydani, Ra's-e, Iran 71 E8
Meyenburg, Germany 24 B8
Meymac, France 20 C6
Meymaneh, Afghan. 66 B4
Meyrueis, France 20 D7
Meyssac, France 20 C5
Meyzieu, France 21 C8
Mezdra, Bulgaria 44 C7
Mèze, France 20 E7
Mezen, Russia 52 C5
Mezen →, Russia 52 C5
Mézenc, Mt., France 21 D8
Mezhdurechenskiy, Russia 52 D7
Mézidon-Canon, France 18 C6
Mézières-en-Brenne, France 20 B5
Mézilhac, France 21 D8
Mézin, France 20 D4
Mezőberény, Hungary 28 D6
Mezőfalva, Hungary 28 D3
Mezőhegyes, Hungary 28 D5
Mezőkovácsháza, Hungary 28 D5
Mezőkövesd, Hungary 28 C5
Mézos, France 20 D2
Mezőtúr, Hungary 28 C5
Mezquital, Mexico 118 C4
Mezzolombardo, Italy 40 B8
Mfolozi →, S. Africa 89 D5
Mgeta, Tanzania 87 D4
Mglin, Russia 33 F7
Mhlaba Hills, Zimbabwe 87 F3
Mhow, India 68 H6
Miahuatlán, Mexico 119 D5
Miajadas, Spain 37 F5
Miami, Fla., U.S.A. 115 N5
Miami, Okla., U.S.A. 113 G7
Miami, Tex., U.S.A. 113 H4
Miami Beach, U.S.A. 115 N5

Mian Xian, China 56 H4
Mianchi, China 56 G6
Miandarreh, Iran 71 C7
Miandowāb, Iran 70 B5
Miandrivazo, Madag. 89 B8
Miāneh, Iran 70 B5
Mianning, China 58 C4
Mianwali, Pakistan 68 C4
Mianyang, China 58 B5
Mianzhu, China 58 B5
Miaoli, Taiwan 59 E13
Miarinarivo, Antananarivo, Madag. 89 B8
Miarinarivo, Toamasina, Madag. 89 B8
Miariravaratra, Madag. 89 C8
Miass, Russia 52 D7
Miastko, Poland 30 E3
Miasteczko Krajeńskie, Poland 31 E4
Mica, S. Africa 89 C5
Micăsasa, Romania 29 D9
Michalovce, Slovak Rep. 27 C14
Michigan □, U.S.A. 114 C3
Michigan, L., U.S.A. 114 D2
Michigan City, U.S.A. 114 E2
Michika, Nigeria 83 C7
Michipicoten I., Canada 104 C2
Michoacan □, Mexico 118 D4
Michurin = Tsarevo, Bulgaria 45 D11
Michurinsk, Russia 34 D5
Mico, Pta., Nic. 120 D3
Micronesia, Pac. Oc. 96 G7
Micronesia, Federated States of ■, Pac. Oc. 96 G7
Mid-Oceanic Ridge, Ind. Oc. 96 M1
Midai, Indonesia 62 D3
Midale, Canada 103 D8
Middelburg, Neths. 17 C3
Middelburg, Eastern Cape, S. Africa 88 E4
Middelburg, Mpumalanga, S. Africa 89 D4
Middelfart, Denmark 11 J3
Middelpos, S. Africa 88 E3
Middelwit, S. Africa 88 C4
Middle Alkali L., U.S.A. 108 F3
Middle Bass I., U.S.A. 116 E2
Middle East, Asia 50 F7
Middle Fork Feather →, U.S.A. 110 F5
Middle I., Australia 93 F3
Middle Loup →, U.S.A. 112 E5
Middle Sackville, Canada 105 D7
Middleboro, U.S.A. 117 E14
Middleburg, Fla., U.S.A. 115 K5
Middleburg, Pa., U.S.A. 116 F7
Middleburgh, U.S.A. 117 D10
Middlebury, U.S.A. 117 B11
Middlemount, Australia 94 C4
Middleport, N.Y., U.S.A. 116 C6
Middleport, Ohio, U.S.A. 114 F4
Middlesboro, U.S.A. 115 G4
Middlesbrough, U.K. 14 C6
Middlesbrough □, U.K. 14 C6
Middlesex, Belize 120 C2
Middlesex, N.J., U.S.A. 117 F10
Middlesex, N.Y., U.S.A. 116 D7
Middleton, Australia 94 C3
Middleton, Canada 105 D6
Middleton Cr. →, Australia 94 C3
Middletown, U.K. 12 B5
Middletown, Calif., U.S.A. 110 G4
Middletown, Conn., U.S.A. 117 E12
Middletown, N.Y., U.S.A. 117 E10
Middletown, Ohio, U.S.A. 114 F3
Middletown, Pa., U.S.A. 117 F8
Midge Point, Australia 94 J6
Midhurst, U.K. 15 G7
Mīdī, Yemen 81 D5
Midi, Canal du →, France 20 E5
Midi d'Ossau, Pic du, France 20 F3
Midi-Pyrénées □, France 20 E5
Midland, Australia 93 F2
Midland, Canada 116 B5
Midland, Calif., U.S.A. 111 M12
Midland, Mich., U.S.A. 114 D3
Midland, Pa., U.S.A. 116 F4
Midland, Tex., U.S.A. 113 K3
Midlands □, Zimbabwe 87 F2
Midleton, Ireland 12 E3
Midlothian, U.S.A. 113 J6
Midlothian □, U.K. 13 F5
Midongy, Tangorombohitr'i, Madag. 89 C8
Midongy Atsimo, Madag. 89 C8
Midou →, France 20 E3
Midouze →, France 20 E3
Midsayap, Phil. 61 H6
Midu, China 58 E3
Midway Is., Pac. Oc. 96 E10
Midway Wells, U.S.A. 111 N11
Midwest, U.S.A. 107 B9
Midwest, Wyo., U.S.A. 108 E10
Midwest City, U.S.A. 113 H6
Midyat, Turkey 70 B4
Midzŏr, Bulgaria 44 C6
Mie □, Japan 55 G8
Miechów, Poland 31 H7
Miedwie, Jezioro, Poland 31 E1
Międzybórz, Poland 31 G4
Międzylesie, Poland 31 H3
Międzyrzec Podlaski, Poland 31 F9
Międzyrzecz, Poland 31 F2
Międzyzdroje, Poland 30 E1
Miejska Górka, Poland 31 G3
Miélan, France 20 E4
Mielec, Poland 31 H8
Mienga, Angola 88 B2
Miercurea-Ciuc, Romania 29 D10
Miercurea Sibiului, Romania 29 E8
Mieres, Spain 36 B5
Mieroszów, Poland 31 H3

Mieso, Ethiopia 81 F5
Mieszkowice, Poland 31 F1
Mifflintown, U.S.A. 116 F7
Mifraz Ḥefa, Israel 74 C4
Migennes, France 19 E10
Migliarino, Italy 41 D8
Migliarino-San Rossore-Massaciuccoli △, Italy 40 E7
Miguel Alemán, Presa, Mexico 119 D5
Miguelturra, Spain 37 G7
Mihăileni, Romania 29 C11
Mihăilești, Romania 29 F10
Mihailovca, Moldova 29 D13
Mihalgazi, Turkey 47 A12
Mihaliççik, Turkey 72 C4
Mihara, Japan 55 G6
Miheşu de Cîmpie, Romania 29 D9
Mijas, Spain 37 J6
Mikese, Tanzania 86 D4
Mikha-Tskhakaya = Senaki, Georgia 35 J6
Mikhailovka = Mykhaylivka, Ukraine 33 J8
Mikhaylov, Russia 32 E10
Mikhaylovgrad = Montana, Bulgaria 44 C7
Mikhaylovka, Russia 34 E6
Mikhnevo, Russia 32 E9
Mikínai, Greece 46 D4
Mikkeli, Finland 9 F22
Mikkwa →, Canada 102 B6
Mikniya, Sudan 81 D3
Mikołajki, Poland 30 E8
Míkonos, Greece 47 D7
Mikrí Préspa, Límni, Greece 44 F5
Mikrón Dhérion, Greece 45 E10
Mikstat, Poland 31 G4
Mikulov, Czech Rep. 27 C9
Mikumi, Tanzania 86 D4
Mikumi △, Tanzania 86 D4
Milaca, U.S.A. 112 C8
Milagro, Ecuador 124 D3
Milagros, Phil. 61 E5
Milan = Milano, Italy 40 C6
Milan, Mo., U.S.A. 112 E8
Milan, Tenn., U.S.A. 115 H1
Milange, Mozam. 87 F4
Milano, Italy 40 C6
Milano Linate ✈ (LIN), Italy 40 C6
Milanoa, Madag. 89 A8
Milâs, Turkey 47 D9
Milatos, Greece 49 D7
Milazzo, Italy 43 D8
Milbank, U.S.A. 112 C6
Milbanke Sd., Canada 102 C3
Milden, Canada 103 C7
Mildenhall, U.K. 15 E8
Mildmay, Canada 116 B3
Mildura, Australia 95 E3
Mile, China 58 E4
Miléai, Greece 46 B5
Miles, Australia 95 D5
Miles City, U.S.A. 112 B2
Mileşti, Moldova 29 C13
Milestone, Canada 103 D8
Mileto, Italy 43 D9
Miletto, Mte., Italy 43 A7
Miletus, Turkey 47 D9
Milevsko, Czech Rep. 26 B7
Milford, Calif., U.S.A. 110 E6
Milford, Conn., U.S.A. 117 E11
Milford, Del., U.S.A. 114 F8
Milford, Mass., U.S.A. 117 D13
Milford, N.H., U.S.A. 117 D13
Milford, Pa., U.S.A. 117 E10
Milford, Utah, U.S.A. 109 G7
Milford Haven, U.K. 15 F2
Milford Sd., N.Z. 91 L1
Milford Sound, N.Z. 91 L1
Milḥ, Baḥr al = Razāzah, Buḩayrat ar, Iraq 70 C4
Milicz, Poland 31 G4
Milikapiti, Australia 92 B5
Miling, Australia 93 F2
Militello in Val di Catánia, Italy 43 E7
Milk →, U.S.A. 108 B10
Milk, Wadi el →, Sudan 80 D3
Milk River, Canada 102 D6
Mill I., Antarctica 5 C8
Mill Valley, U.S.A. 110 H4
Millárs →, Spain 38 F4
Millau, France 20 D7
Millbridge, Canada 116 B7
Millbrook, Canada 116 B6
Millbrook, U.S.A. 117 E11
Mille Lacs, L. des, Canada 104 C1
Mille Lacs L., U.S.A. 112 B8
Milledgeville, U.S.A. 115 J4
Millen, U.S.A. 115 J5
Millennium I. = Caroline I., Kiribati 97 H12
Miller, U.S.A. 112 C5
Millerovo, Russia 35 F5
Millersburg, Ohio, U.S.A. 116 F3
Millersburg, Pa., U.S.A. 116 F8
Millerton, U.S.A. 117 E11
Millerton L., U.S.A. 110 J7
Millet, St. Lucia 121 f
Millevaches, Plateau de, France 20 C6
Millheim, U.S.A. 116 F7
Millicent, Australia 95 F3
Millington, U.S.A. 113 H10
Millinocket, U.S.A. 115 C11
Millmerran, Australia 95 D5
Millom, U.K. 14 C4
Mills L., Canada 102 A5
Millsboro, U.S.A. 116 G5
Millstream-Chichester △, Australia 92 D2
Milltown Malbay, Ireland 12 D2
Millville, N.J., U.S.A. 114 F8
Millville, Pa., U.S.A. 117 E8

Millwood L., U.S.A. 113 J8
Milna, Croatia 41 E13
Milne →, Australia 94 C2
Milo, U.S.A. 115 C11
Mílos, Greece 46 E6
Miłosław, Poland 31 F4
Milot, Albania 44 E3
Milparinka, Australia 95 D3
Miltenberg, Germany 25 F5
Milton, N.S., Canada 105 D7
Milton, Ont., Canada 116 C5
Milton, N.Z. 91 M2
Milton, Calif., U.S.A. 110 G6
Milton, Fla., U.S.A. 115 K2
Milton, Pa., U.S.A. 116 F8
Milton, Vt., U.S.A. 117 B11
Milton-Freewater, U.S.A. 108 D4
Milton Keynes, U.K. 15 E7
Milton Keynes □, U.K. 15 E7
Miluo, China 59 C9
Milverton, Canada 116 C4
Milwaukee, U.S.A. 114 D2
Milwaukee Deep, Atl. Oc. 121 C16
Milwaukie, U.S.A. 110 E4
Mim, Ghana 82 D4
Mimizan, France 20 D2
Mimoň, Czech Rep. 26 A7
Min Jiang →, Fujian, China 59 E12
Min Jiang →, Sichuan, China 58 C5
Min Xian, China 56 G3
Mina Pirquitas, Argentina 126 A2
Minā Su'ud, Si. Arabia 71 D6
Minā'al Aḥmadī, Kuwait 71 D6
Minago →, Canada 103 C9
Minaki, Canada 103 D10
Minamata, Japan 55 H5
Minami-Arapusa △, Japan 55 G9
Minami-Tori-Shima, Pac. Oc. 96 F7
Minas, Uruguay 127 C4
Minas, Sierra de las, Guatemala 120 C2
Minas Basin, Canada 105 C7
Minas de Riotinto, Spain 37 H4
Minas Gerais □, Brazil 125 G9
Minatitlán, Mexico 119 D6
Minbu, Burma 67 J19
Minchinabad, Pakistan 68 D5
Mincio →, Italy 40 C7
Minčol, Slovak Rep. 27 B13
Mindanao, Phil. 61 H6
Mindanao Sea = Bohol Sea, Phil. 63 C6
Mindanao Trench, Pac. Oc. 61 F7
Mindel →, Germany 25 G6
Mindelheim, Germany 25 G6
Minden, Canada 116 B6
Minden, Germany 24 C4
Minden, La., U.S.A. 113 J8
Minden, Nev., U.S.A. 110 G7
Mindiptana, Indonesia 63 F10
Mindoro, Phil. 61 E4
Mindoro Str., Phil. 61 E4
Mine, Japan 55 G5
Minehead, U.K. 15 F4
Mineola, N.Y., U.S.A. 117 F11
Mineola, Tex., U.S.A. 113 J7
Mineral King, U.S.A. 110 J8
Mineral Wells, U.S.A. 113 J5
Mineralnyye Vody, Russia 35 H6
Minersville, U.S.A. 117 F8
Minerva, U.S.A. 116 F3
Minervino Murge, Italy 43 A9
Minetto, U.S.A. 117 C8
Mingäçevir, Azerbaijan 35 K8
Mingäçevir Su Anbarı, Azerbaijan 35 K8
Mingan, Canada 105 B7
Mingechaur = Mingäçevir, Azerbaijan 35 K8
Mingechaurskoye Vdkhr. = Mingäçevir Su Anbarı, Azerbaijan 35 K8
Mingela, Australia 94 B4
Mingenew, Australia 93 E2
Mingera Cr. →, Australia 94 C2
Minggang, China 59 A10
Mingguang, China 59 A11
Mingin, Burma 67 H19
Mingir, Moldova 29 D13
Minglanilla, Spain 39 F3
Minglun, China 58 E7
Mingo Junction, U.S.A. 116 F4
Mingorria, Spain 36 E6
Mingshan, China 58 B4
Mingteke Daban = Mintaka Pass, Pakistan 69 A6
Mingxi, China 59 D11
Mingyuegue, China 57 C15
Minho = Miño →, Spain 36 D2
Minhou, China 59 E12
Minićevo, Serbia & M. 28 C7
Minidoka, U.S.A. 108 E7
Minigwal, L., Australia 93 E3
Minilya, Australia 93 D1
Minilya Roadhouse, Australia 93 D1
Minipi L., Canada 105 B7
Mink L., Canada 102 A5
Minkammen, Sudan 81 F3
Minna, Nigeria 83 D6
Minneapolis, Kans., U.S.A. 112 F6
Minneapolis, Minn., U.S.A. 112 C8
Minnedosa, Canada 103 C9
Minnesota □, U.S.A. 112 B8
Minnesota →, U.S.A. 112 C8
Minnewaukan, U.S.A. 112 A5
Minnipa, Australia 95 E2
Minnitaki L., Canada 104 C1
Mino, Japan 55 G8
Miño, Spain 36 B2
Miño →, Spain 36 D2
Minoa, Greece 47 F7
Minorca = Menorca, Spain 48 B11
Minot, U.S.A. 112 A4
Minqin, China 56 E2
Minqing, China 59 D12

Minsen, Germany 24 B3
Minsk, Belarus 32 F4
Mińsk Mazowiecki, Poland 31 F8
Mintabie, Australia 95 D1
Mintaka Pass, Pakistan 69 A6
Minto, Canada 105 C6
Minto, L., Canada 104 A5
Minton, Canada 103 D8
Minturn, U.S.A. 108 G10
Minturno, Italy 42 A6
Minûf, Egypt 80 H7
Minusinsk, Russia 53 D10
Minutang, India 67 E20
Minya el Qamh, Egypt 80 H7
Minya Konka = Gongga Shan, China 58 C3
Mionica, Bos.-H. 28 F3
Mionica, Serbia & M. 44 B4
Miquelon, Canada 104 C4
Miquelon, St-P. & M. 105 C8
Mir, Niger 83 C7
Mīr Kūh, Iran 71 E8
Mīr Shahdād, Iran 71 E8
Mira, Italy 41 C9
Mira, Portugal 36 E2
Mira →, Portugal 37 H2
Mira por vos Cay, Bahamas 121 B5
Mirabella Eclano, Italy 43 A7
Mirador-Río Azul △, Guatemala 120 C2
Miraj, India 66 L9
Miram Shah, Pakistan 68 C4
Miramar, Argentina 126 D4
Miramar, Mozam. 89 C6
Miramas, France 21 E8
Mirambeau, France 20 C3
Miramichi, Canada 105 C6
Miramichi B., Canada 105 C7
Miramont-de-Guyenne, France 20 D4
Miranda, Brazil 125 H7
Miranda →, Brazil 124 G7
Miranda de Ebro, Spain 38 C2
Miranda do Corvo, Portugal 36 E2
Miranda do Douro, Portugal 36 D4
Mirande, France 20 E4
Mirandela, Portugal 36 D3
Mirándola, Italy 40 D8
Mirandópolis, Brazil 127 A5
Mirango, Malawi 87 E3
Mirani, Australia 94 K6
Mirano, Italy 41 C9
Miras, Albania 44 F4
Mirassol, Brazil 127 A6
Mirbāṭ, Oman 75 D5
Mirear, Egypt 80 C4
Mirebeau, France 18 F7
Mirebeau-sur-Bèze, France 19 E12
Mirecourt, France 19 D13
Mirgorod = Myrhorod, Ukraine 33 H7
Miri, Malaysia 62 D4
Miriam Vale, Australia 94 C5
Miribel, France 19 G11
Mirim, L., S. Amer. 127 C5
Mirnyy, Russia 53 C12
Miroč, Serbia & M. 44 B6
Mirokhan, Pakistan 68 F3
Mirond L., Canada 103 B8
Mirosławiec, Poland 30 E3
Mirpur, Pakistan 69 C5
Mirpur Batoro, Pakistan 68 G3
Mirpur Bibiwari, Pakistan 68 E2
Mirpur Khas, Pakistan 68 G3
Mirpur Sakro, Pakistan 68 G2
Mirria, Niger 83 C6
Mirsk, Poland 31 H2
Mirtağ, Turkey 70 B4
Miryang, S. Korea 57 G15
Mirzaani, Georgia 35 K8
Mirzapur, India 69 G10
Mirzapur-cum-Vindhyachal = Mirzapur, India 69 G10
Misantla, Mexico 119 D5
Misawa, Japan 54 D10
Miscou I., Canada 105 C7
Mish'āb, Ra's al, Si. Arabia 71 D6
Mishan, China 60 B8
Mishawaka, U.S.A. 114 E2
Mishbih, Gebel, Egypt 80 C3
Mishima, Japan 55 G9
Misión, Mexico 111 N10
Misiones □, Argentina 127 B5
Misiones □, Paraguay 126 B4
Miskah, Si. Arabia 70 E4
Miskitos, Cayos, Nic. 120 D3
Miskolc, Hungary 28 B5
Misoke, Dem. Rep. of the Congo 86 C2
Misool, Indonesia 63 E8
Miṣrātah, Libya 79 B9
Missanabie, Canada 104 C3
Missinaibi →, Canada 104 B3
Missinaibi L., Canada 104 C3
Mississagi →, Canada 104 C3
Mississauga, Canada 116 C5
Mississippi □, U.S.A. 113 J10
Mississippi →, U.S.A. 113 L10
Mississippi L., Canada 117 A8
Mississippi River Delta, U.S.A. 113 L9
Mississippi Sd., U.S.A. 113 K10
Missoula, U.S.A. 108 C7
Missouri □, U.S.A. 112 F8
Missouri →, U.S.A. 112 F9
Missouri City, U.S.A. 113 L7
Missouri Valley, U.S.A. 112 E7
Mist, U.S.A. 110 E3
Mistassibi →, Canada 105 B5

Mistassini →, Canada 105 C5
Mistassini, L., Canada 104 B5
Mistastin L., Canada 105 A7
Mistelbach, Austria 27 C9
Misterbianco, Italy 43 E8
Mistinibi, L., Canada 105 A7
Mistissini, Canada 105 C5
Mistretta, Italy 43 E7
Misty L., Canada 103 B8
Misurata = Miṣrātah, Libya 79 B9
Mît Ghamr, Egypt 80 H7
Mitatib, Sudan 81 D4
Mitchell, Australia 95 D4
Mitchell, Canada 116 C3
Mitchell, Nebr., U.S.A. 112 E3
Mitchell, Oreg., U.S.A. 108 D3
Mitchell, S. Dak., U.S.A. 112 D6
Mitchell →, Australia 94 B3
Mitchell, Mt., U.S.A. 115 H4
Mitchell and Alice Rivers △, Australia 94 B3
Mitchell Ranges, Australia 94 A2
Mitchelstown, Ireland 12 D3
Mitha Tiwana, Pakistan 68 C5
Mithi, Pakistan 68 G3
Mithrao, Pakistan 68 F3
Mitilíni, Greece 47 B8
Mitilinoí, Greece 47 D8
Mito, Japan 55 F10
Mitrofanovka, Russia 33 H10
Mitrovica = Kosovska Mitrovica, Serbia & M. 44 D4
Mitsinjo, Madag. 89 B8
Mitsiwa, Eritrea 81 D4
Mitsiwa Channel, Eritrea 81 D5
Mitsukaidō, Japan 55 F9
Mittagong, Australia 95 E5
Mittelberg, Austria 26 D3
Mittelfranken □, Germany 25 F6
Mittellandkanal →, Germany 24 C4
Mittenwalde, Germany 24 C9
Mittersill, Austria 26 D5
Mitterteich, Germany 25 F8
Mittimatalik = Pond Inlet, Canada 101 A12
Mittweida, Germany 24 E8
Mitú, Colombia 124 C4
Mitumba, Tanzania 86 D3
Mitumba, Mts., Dem. Rep. of the Congo 86 D2
Mitwaba, Dem. Rep. of the Congo 87 D2
Mityana, Uganda 86 B3
Mixteco →, Mexico 119 D5
Miyagi □, Japan 54 E10
Miyah, W. el →, Egypt 80 C3
Miyah, W. el →, Syria 70 C3
Miyake-Jima, Japan 55 G9
Miyako, Japan 54 E10
Miyako-Jima, Japan 55 M2
Miyako-Rettō, Japan 55 M2
Miyakonojō, Japan 55 J5
Miyani, India 68 J3
Miyanoura-Dake, Japan 55 J5
Miyazaki, Japan 55 J5
Miyazaki □, Japan 55 H5
Miyazu, Japan 55 G7
Miyet, Bahr el = Dead Sea, Asia 74 D4
Miyi, China 58 D4
Miyoshi, Japan 55 G6
Miyun, China 56 D9
Miyun Shuiku, China 57 D9
Mizan Teferi, Ethiopia 81 F4
Mizdah, Libya 79 B8
Mizen Hd., Cork, Ireland 12 E2
Mizen Hd., Wicklow, Ireland 12 D5
Mizhhirya, Ukraine 29 B8
Mizhi, China 56 F6
Mizil, Romania 29 F11
Mizoram □, India 67 H18
Mizpe Ramon, Israel 74 E3
Mizuho, Antarctica 5 D5
Mizusawa, Japan 54 E10
Mjällby, Sweden 11 H8
Mjöbäck, Sweden 11 G6
Mjölby, Sweden 11 F9
Mjörn, Sweden 11 G6
Mjøsa, Norway 9 F14
Mkata, Tanzania 86 D4
Mkhaya □, Swaziland 89 D5
Mkokotoni, Tanzania 86 D4
Mkomazi, Tanzania 86 C4
Mkomazi →, Tanzania 86 C3
Mkomazi ≏, S. Africa 89 E5
Mkulwe, Tanzania 87 D3
Mkumbi, Ras, Tanzania 86 D4
Mkushi, Zambia 87 E2
Mkushi River, Zambia 87 E2
Mkuze, S. Africa 89 D5
Mkuze →, S. Africa 89 D5
Mladá Boleslav, Czech Rep. 26 A7
Mladenovac, Serbia & M. 44 B4
Mlala Hills, Tanzania 86 D3
Mlange = Mulanje, Malawi 87 F4
Mlanje, Pic, Malawi 85 H7
Mlava →, Serbia & M. 44 B5
Mława, Poland 31 E7
Mlawula △, Swaziland 89 D5
Mljet, Croatia 41 F14
Mljet △, Croatia 41 F14
Mljetski Kanal, Croatia 41 F14
Młynary, Poland 30 D6
Mme, Cameroon 83 D7
Mmabatho, S. Africa 88 D4
Mo i Rana, Norway 8 C16
Moa, Cuba 121 B4
Moa, Indonesia 63 F7
Moa →, S. Leone 82 D2
Moab, U.S.A. 109 G9
Moala, Fiji 91 D8
Moama, Australia 95 F3

Moamba, Mozam. 89 D5
Moate, Ireland 12 C4
Moapa, U.S.A. 111 J12
Mobārakābād, Iran 71 D7
Mobaye, C.A.R. 84 D4
Mobayi, Dem. Rep. of the Congo 84 D4
Moberley Lake, Canada 102 B4
Moberly, U.S.A. 112 F8
Mobile, U.S.A. 115 K1
Mobile B., U.S.A. 115 K2
Mobridge, U.S.A. 112 C4
Moc Chau, Vietnam 64 B5
Moc Hoa, Vietnam 65 G5
Mocabe Kasari, Dem. Rep. of the Congo 87 D2
Moçambique, Mozam. 87 F5
Mocanaqua, U.S.A. 117 E8
Mochima △, Venezuela 121 D7
Mochudi, Botswana 88 C4
Mocimboa da Praia, Mozam. 87 E5
Mociu, Romania 29 D9
Möckeln, Sweden 11 H8
Mockfjärd, Sweden 10 D8
Moclips, U.S.A. 110 C2
Mocoa, Colombia 124 C3
Mococa, Brazil 127 A6
Mocorito, Mexico 118 B3
Moctezuma, Mexico 118 B3
Moctezuma →, Mexico 119 C5
Mocuba, Mozam. 87 F4
Mocúzari, Presa, Mexico 118 B3
Modane, France 21 C10
Modasa, India 68 H5
Modder →, S. Africa 88 D3
Modderrivier, S. Africa 88 D3
Módena, Italy 40 D7
Modena, U.S.A. 109 H7
Modesto, U.S.A. 110 H6
Módica, Italy 43 F7
Modimolle, S. Africa 89 C4
Mödling, Austria 27 C9
Modo, Sudan 81 F3
Modra, Slovak Rep. 27 C10
Modriča, Bos.-H. 28 F3
Moe, Australia 95 F4
Moebase, Mozam. 87 F4
Moëlan-sur-Mer, France 18 E3
Moengo, Suriname 125 B8
Moffat, U.K. 13 F5
Moga, India 68 D6
Mogadishu = Muqdisho, Somali Rep. 75 G4
Mogador = Essaouira, Morocco 78 B4
Mogadouro, Portugal 36 D4
Mogalakwena →, S. Africa 89 C4
Mogami-Gawa →, Japan 54 E10
Mogán, Canary Is. 48 G4
Mogaung, Burma 67 G20
Mogi das Cruzes, Brazil 127 A6
Mogi-Guaçu →, Brazil 127 A6
Mogi-Mirim, Brazil 127 A6
Mogielnica, Poland 31 G7
Mogige, Ethiopia 81 F4
Mogilev = Mahilyow, Belarus 32 F6
Mogilev-Podolskiy = Mohyliv-Podilskyy, Ukraine 29 B12
Mogilno, Poland 31 F4
Mogincual, Mozam. 87 F5
Mogliano Véneto, Italy 41 C9
Mogocha, Russia 53 D12
Mogok, Burma 67 H20
Mogollon Rim, U.S.A. 109 J8
Mógoro, Italy 42 C1
Mograt, Sudan 80 D3
Moguer, Spain 37 H4
Mogumber, Australia 93 F2
Mohács, Hungary 28 E3
Mohales Hoek, Lesotho 88 E4
Mohall, U.S.A. 112 A4
Moḥammadābād, Iran 71 B8
Mohammedia, Morocco 78 B4
Mohana →, India 69 G11
Mohanlalganj, India 69 F9
Mohave, L., U.S.A. 111 K12
Mohawk →, U.S.A. 117 D11
Moheda, Sweden 11 G8
Mohenjodaro, Pakistan 68 F3
Moher, Cliffs of, Ireland 12 D2
Mohicanville Reservoir, U.S.A. 116 F3
Möhne →, Germany 24 D3
Mohoro, Tanzania 86 D4
Mohyliv-Podilskyy, Ukraine 29 B12
Moia, Sudan 81 F2
Moidart, L., U.K. 13 E3
Moineşti, Romania 29 D11
Moira →, Canada 116 B7
Moirans, France 21 C9
Moirans-en-Montagne, France 19 F12
Moíres, Greece 49 D6
Moisaküla, Estonia 9 G21
Moisie, Canada 105 B6
Moisie →, Canada 105 B6
Moissac, France 20 D5
Moita, Portugal 37 G2
Moixent, Spain 39 G4
Möja, Sweden 10 E12
Mojácar, Spain 39 H3
Mojados, Spain 36 D6
Mojave, U.S.A. 111 K8
Mojave ≏, U.S.A. 111 K11
Mojave Desert, U.S.A. 111 L10
Mojiang, China 58 F3
Mojo, Bolivia 126 A2
Mojo, Ethiopia 81 F4
Mojokerto, Indonesia 63 G15
Mokai, N.Z. 91 H5

Mokambo, Dem. Rep. of the Congo 87 E2
Mokameh, India 69 G11
Mokau, N.Z. 91 H5
Mokelumne →, U.S.A. 110 G5
Mokelumne Hill, U.S.A. 110 G6
Mokhós, Greece 49 D7
Mokhotlong, Lesotho 89 D4
Möklinta, Sweden 10 D10
Mokokchung, India 67 F19
Mokolo, Cameroon 83 C7
Mokolo →, S. Africa 89 C4
Mokopane, S. Africa 89 C4
Mokp'o, S. Korea 57 G14
Mokra Gora, Serbia & M. 44 D4
Mokronog, Slovenia 41 C12
Moksha →, Russia 34 C6
Mokshan, Russia 34 D7
Mokwa, Nigeria 83 D6
Mol, Belgium 17 C5
Mola di Bari, Italy 43 A10
Molale, Ethiopia 81 E4
Moláoi, Greece 46 E4
Molara, Italy 42 B2
Molat, Croatia 41 D11
Molchanovo, Russia 52 D9
Mold, U.K. 14 D4
Moldava nad Bodvou, Slovak Rep. 27 C14
Moldavia = Moldova ■, Europe 29 C13
Moldavia, Romania 29 D12
Molde, Norway 8 E12
Moldova ■, Europe 29 C13
Moldova Nouă, Romania 28 F6
Moldoveanu, Vf., Romania 29 E9
Moldoviţa, Romania 29 C10
Mole △, Ghana 83 D4
Mole →, U.K. 15 F7
Mole Creek, Australia 95 G4
Molepolole, Botswana 88 C4
Molfetta, Italy 43 A9
Molina de Aragón, Spain 38 E3
Molina de Segura, Spain 39 G3
Moline, U.S.A. 112 E9
Molinella, Italy 41 D8
Molinos, Argentina 126 B2
Moliro, Dem. Rep. of the Congo 86 D3
Moliterno, Italy 43 B8
Molkom, Sweden 10 E7
Mölle, Sweden 11 H6
Molledo, Spain 36 B6
Mollendo, Peru 124 G4
Mollerin, L., Australia 93 F2
Mollerussa, Spain 38 D5
Mollina, Spain 37 H6
Mölln, Germany 24 B6
Mölnlycke, Sweden 11 G6
Molochansk, Ukraine 33 J8
Molochnoye, Ozero, Ukraine 33 J8
Molodechno = Maladzyechna, Belarus 32 E4
Molodove, Ukraine 29 D14
Molokai, U.S.A. 106 H16
Molong, Australia 95 E4
Molopo →, Africa 88 D3
Mólos, Greece 46 C4
Molsheim, France 19 D14
Molson L., Canada 103 C9
Molteno, S. Africa 88 E4
Molu, Indonesia 63 F8
Molucca Sea, Indonesia 63 E6
Moluccas = Maluku, Indonesia 63 E7
Moma, Dem. Rep. of the Congo 86 C1
Moma, Mozam. 87 F4
Mombasa, Kenya 86 C4
Mombetsu, Japan 54 B11
Mombuey, Spain 36 C4
Momchilgrad, Bulgaria 45 E9
Momi, Dem. Rep. of the Congo 86 C2
Mompós, Colombia 124 B4
Møn, Denmark 11 K6
Mon □, Burma 67 L20
Mona, Canal de la = Mona Passage, W. Indies 121 C6
Mona, Isla, Puerto Rico 121 C6
Mona, Pta., Costa Rica 120 E3
Mona Passage, W. Indies 121 C6
Monaca, U.S.A. 116 F4
Monaco ■, Europe 21 E11
Monadhliath Mts., U.K. 13 D4
Monadnock, Mt., U.S.A. 117 D12
Monaghan, Ireland 12 B5
Monaghan □, Ireland 12 B5
Monahans, U.S.A. 113 K3
Monapo, Mozam. 87 E5
Monar, L., U.K. 13 D3
Monarch Mt., Canada 102 C3
Monashee Mts., Canada 102 C5
Monasterevin, Ireland 12 C4
Monastir = Bitola, Macedonia 44 E5
Moncada, Phil. 61 D4
Moncalieri, Italy 40 C4
Moncalvo, Italy 40 C5
Monção, Portugal 36 C2
Moncarapacho, Portugal 37 H3
Moncayo, Sierra del, Spain 38 D3
Mönchengladbach, Germany 24 D2
Monchique, Portugal 37 H2
Moncks Corner, U.S.A. 115 J5
Monclova, Mexico 118 B4
Moncontour, France 18 D4
Moncton, Canada 105 C7
Mondariz, Spain 36 C2
Mondego →, Portugal 36 E2
Mondego, C., Portugal 36 E2
Mondeodo, Indonesia 63 E6
Mondeville, France 18 C6
Mondolfo, Italy 41 E10
Mondoñedo, Spain 36 B3
Mondovì, Italy 40 D4
Mondragon, Phil. 61 E6

Mondragone, *Italy* 42 A6
Mondrain I., *Australia* 93 F3
Moneague, *Jamaica* .... 120 a
Monemvasía, *Greece* 46 E5
Monessen, *U.S.A.* 116 F5
Monesterio, *Spain* 37 G4
Monestier-de-Clermont, *France* . 21 D9
Monett, *U.S.A.* 113 G8
Moneymore, *U.K.* 12 B5
Monfalcone, *Italy* 41 C10
Monflanquin, *France* 20 D4
Monforte, *Portugal* 37 F3
Monforte de Lemos, *Spain* ... 36 C3
Mong Cai, *Vietnam* 64 B6
Mong Hsu, *Burma* 58 G2
Mong Kung, *Burma* 67 J20
Mong Nai, *Burma* 67 J20
Mong Pawk, *Burma* 67 H21
Mong Ping, *Burma* 58 G2
Mong Ton, *Burma* 67 J21
Mong Wa, *Burma* 67 J22
Mong Yai, *Burma* 67 H21
Mongalla, *Sudan* 81 F3
Mongers, L., *Australia* 93 E2
Monghyr = Munger, *India* ... 69 G12
Mongibello = Etna, *Italy* 43 E7
Mongo, *Chad* 79 F9
Mongo ➜, *S. Leone* 82 D2
Mongolia ■, *Asia* 53 E10
Mongolia, Plateau of, *Asia* ... 50 E14
Mongonu, *Nigeria* 83 C7
Mongu, *Zambia* 85 H4
Mõngua, *Angola* 88 B2
Monifieth, *U.K.* 13 E6
Monistrol-sur-Loire, *France* .. 21 C8
Monkey Bay, *Malawi* 87 E4
Monkey Mia, *Australia* 93 E1
Monkey River Town, *Belize* .. 119 D7
Moṅki, *Poland* 30 E9
Monkoto, *Dem. Rep. of the Congo* 84 E4
Monkton, *Canada* 116 C3
Monmouth, *U.K.* 15 F5
Monmouth, *Ill., U.S.A.* 112 E9
Monmouth, *Oreg., U.S.A.* ... 108 D2
Monmouthshire □, *U.K.* 15 F5
Mono L., *U.S.A.* 110 H7
Monolith, *U.S.A.* 111 K8
Monólithos, *Greece* 49 C9
Monongahela, *U.S.A.* 116 F5
Monópoli, *Italy* 43 B10
Monor, *Hungary* 28 C4
Monos I., *Trin. & Tob.* 125 K15
Monóvar, *Spain* 39 G4
Monreal del Campo, *Spain* .. 38 E3
Monreale, *Italy* 42 D6
Monroe, *Ga., U.S.A.* 115 J4
Monroe, *La., U.S.A.* 113 J8
Monroe, *Mich., U.S.A.* 114 E4
Monroe, *N.C., U.S.A.* 115 H5
Monroe, *N.Y., U.S.A.* 117 E10
Monroe, *Utah, U.S.A.* 109 G7
Monroe, *Wash., U.S.A.* 110 C5
Monroe, *Wis., U.S.A.* 112 D10
Monroe City, *U.S.A.* 112 F9
Monroeton, *U.S.A.* 117 E8
Monroeville, *Ala., U.S.A.* ... 115 K2
Monroeville, *Pa., U.S.A.* 116 F5
Monrovia, *Liberia* 82 D2
Mons, *Belgium* 17 D3
Møns Klint, *Denmark* 11 K6
Monsaraz, *Portugal* 37 G3
Monse, *Indonesia* 63 E6
Monségur, *France* 20 D4
Monsélice, *Italy* 41 C8
Mönsterås, *Sweden* 11 G10
Mont Cenis, Col du, *France* . 21 C10
Mont-de-Marsan, *France* ... 20 E3
Mont-Joli, *Canada* 105 C6
Mont-Laurier, *Canada* 104 C4
Mont-Louis, *Canada* 105 C6
Mont Peko △, *Ivory C.* 82 D3
Mont-roig del Camp, *Spain* .. 38 D5
Mont-St-Michel, Le, *France* . 18 D5
Mont Sangbe △, *Ivory C.* ... 82 D3
Mont-Tremblant △, *Canada* . 104 C5
Montabaur, *Germany* 24 E3
Montagnac, *France* 20 E7
Montagnana, *Italy* 41 C8
Montagne d'Ambre △, *Madag.* 89 A8
Montagne de Reims △, *France* 19 C11
Montagu, *S. Africa* 88 E3
Montagu I., *Antarctica* 5 B1
Montague, *Canada* 105 C7
Montague, I., *Mexico* 118 A2
Montague Ra., *Australia* 93 E2
Montague Sd., *Australia* 92 B4
Montaigu, *France* 18 F5
Montalbán, *Spain* 38 E4
Montalbano Iónico, *Italy* ... 43 B9
Montalbo, *Spain* 38 F2
Montalcino, *Italy* 41 E8
Montalegre, *Portugal* 36 D3
Montalto, *Italy* 43 D8
Montalto di Castro, *Italy* ... 41 F8
Montalto Uffugo, *Italy* 43 C9
Montalvo, *U.S.A.* 111 L7
Montamarta, *Spain* 36 D5
Montana, *Bulgaria* 44 C7
Montaña, *Peru* 124 E4
Montana □, *Bulgaria* 44 C7
Montana □, *U.S.A.* 108 C9
Montaña Clara, I., *Canary Is.* 48 E6
Montañas de Malaga △, *Spain* 37 J6
Montánchez, *Spain* 37 F4
Montargil, *Portugal* 37 F2
Montargis, *France* 19 E9
Montauban, *France* 20 D5
Montauk, *U.S.A.* 117 E13
Montauk Pt., *U.S.A.* 117 E13
Montbard, *France* 19 E11
Montbarrey, *France* 19 E12
Montbéliard, *France* 19 E13

Montblanc, *Spain* 38 D6
Montbrison, *France* 21 C8
Montcalm, Pic de, *France* ... 20 F5
Montceau-les-Mines, *France* . 19 F11
Montcenis, *France* 21 B8
Montclair, *U.S.A.* 117 F10
Montcornet, *France* 19 C11
Montcuq, *France* 20 D5
Montdidier, *France* 19 C9
Monte Albán, *Mexico* 119 D5
Monte Alegre, *Brazil* 125 D8
Monte Azul, *Brazil* 125 G10
Monte-Carlo, *Monaco* 21 E11
Monte Caseros, *Argentina* .. 126 C4
Monte Comán, *Argentina* ... 126 C2
Monte Cristi, *Dom. Rep.* 121 C5
Monte Cucco △, *Italy* 41 E9
Monte Lindo ➜, *Paraguay* .. 126 A4
Monte Patria, *Chile* 126 C1
Monte Quemado, *Argentina* . 126 B3
Monte Redondo, *Portugal* .. 36 F2
Monte Rio, *U.S.A.* 110 G4
Monte San Giovanni Campano,
 Italy 42 A6
Monte San Savino, *Italy* 41 E8
Monte Sant' Ángelo, *Italy* ... 41 G12
Monte Santu, C. di, *Italy* ... 42 B2
Monte Sibillini △, *Italy* 41 F10
Monte Subasio △, *Italy* 41 E9
Monte Vista, *U.S.A.* 109 H10
Monteagudo, *Argentina* 127 B5
Montealegre del Castillo, *Spain* . 39 G3
Montebello, *Canada* 104 C5
Montebello Iónico, *Italy* 43 E8
Montebello Is., *Australia* 92 D2
Montebelluna, *Italy* 41 C9
Montebourg, *France* 18 C5
Montecastrilli, *Italy* 41 F9
Montecatini Terme, *Italy* ... 40 E7
Montecito, *U.S.A.* 111 L7
Montecristo, *Italy* 40 F7
Montefalco, *Italy* 41 F9
Montefiascone, *Italy* 41 F9
Montefrío, *Spain* 37 H7
Montegiórgio, *Italy* 41 E10
Montego Bay, *Jamaica* ..... 120 a
Montehermoso, *Spain* 36 E4
Montejicar, *Spain* 37 H7
Montélimar, *France* 21 D8
Montella, *Italy* 43 B8
Montellano, *Spain* 37 J5
Montemor-o-Novo, *Portugal* . 37 G2
Montemor-o-Velho, *Portugal* 36 E2
Montemorelos, *Mexico* 119 B5
Montendre, *France* 20 C3
Montenegro, *Brazil* 127 B5
Montenegro □, *Serbia & M.* .. 44 D3
Montenero di Bisáccia, *Italy* . 41 G11
Montepuez, *Mozam.* 87 E4
Montepuez ➜, *Mozam.* 87 E5
Montepulciano, *Italy* 41 E8
Montereale, *Italy* 41 F10
Montereau-Faut-Yonne, *France* 19 D9
Monterey, *U.S.A.* 110 J5
Monterey B., *U.S.A.* 110 J5
Montería, *Colombia* 124 B3
Monteros, *Argentina* 126 B2
Monterotondo, *Italy* 41 F9
Monterrey, *Mexico* 118 B4
Montes Azules △, *Mexico* ... 119 D6
Montes Claros, *Brazil* 125 G10
Montesano, *U.S.A.* 110 D3
Montesano sulla Marcellana, *Italy* 43 B8
Montesárchio, *Italy* 43 A7
Montescaglioso, *Italy* 43 B9
Montesilvano, *Italy* 41 F11
Montesinho △, *Portugal* 36 D4
Montevarchi, *Italy* 41 E8
Montevideo, *Uruguay* 127 C4
Montevideo, *U.S.A.* 112 C7
Montezuma, *U.S.A.* 112 E8
Montezuma Castle △, *U.S.A.* . 109 J8
Montfaucon, *France* 18 E5
Montfaucon-d'Argonne, *France* 19 C12
Montfaucon-en-Velay, *France* . 21 C8
Montfort-le-Gesnois, *France* . 18 D7
Montfort-sur-Meu, *France* ... 18 D5
Montfragüe △, *Spain* 36 F5
Montgenèvre, *France* 21 D10
Montgomery, *U.K.* 15 E4
Montgomery, *Ala., U.S.A.* ... 115 J2
Montgomery, *Pa., U.S.A.* ... 116 E8
Montgomery, *W. Va., U.S.A.* . 114 F5
Montgomery City, *U.S.A.* ... 112 F9
Montguyon, *France* 20 C3
Monthermé, *France* 19 C11
Monthey, *Switz.* 25 J2
Monthois, *France* 19 C11
Monti, *Italy* 42 B2
Monti Lucrétili △, *Italy* 41 F9
Monti Picentini △, *Italy* 43 B8
Monti Simbruini △, *Italy* ... 41 G10
Monticelli d'Ongina, *Italy* .. 40 C6
Monticello, *Ark., U.S.A.* 113 J9
Monticello, *Fla., U.S.A.* 115 K4
Monticello, *Ind., U.S.A.* 114 E2
Monticello, *Iowa, U.S.A.* ... 112 D9
Monticello, *Ky., U.S.A.* 115 G3
Monticello, *Minn., U.S.A.* ... 112 C8
Monticello, *Miss., U.S.A.* ... 113 K9
Monticello, *N.Y., U.S.A.* 117 E10
Monticello, *Utah, U.S.A.* ... 109 H9
Montichiari, *Italy* 40 C7
Montier-en-Der, *France* 19 D11
Montignac, *France* 20 C5
Montigny-les-Metz, *France* .. 19 C13
Montigny-sur-Aube, *France* . 19 E11
Montijo, *Portugal* 37 G2
Montijo, *Spain* 37 G4
Montilla, *Spain* 37 H6
Montivilliers, *France* 18 C7

Montluçon, *France* 19 F9
Montmagny, *Canada* 105 C5
Montmarault, *France* 19 F9
Montmartre, *Canada* 103 C8
Montmédy, *France* 19 C12
Montmélian, *France* 21 C10
Montmirail, *France* 19 D10
Montmoreau-St-Cybard, *France* 20 C4
Montmorillon, *France* 20 B4
Montmort-Lucy, *France* 19 D10
Monto, *Australia* 94 C5
Montoire-sur-le-Loir, *France* . 18 E7
Montongbuwoh, *Indonesia* .. 63 K19
Montório al Vomano, *Italy* .. 41 F10
Montoro, *Spain* 37 G6
Montour Falls, *U.S.A.* 116 D8
Montoursville, *U.S.A.* 116 E8
Montpelier, *Idaho, U.S.A.* ... 108 E8
Montpelier, *Vt., U.S.A.* 117 B12
Montpellier, *France* 20 E7
Montpezat-de-Quercy, *France* 20 D5
Montpon-Ménestérol, *France* 20 D4
Montréal, *Canada* 117 A11
Montréal, *Aude, France* 20 E6
Montréal, *Gers, France* 20 E4
Montreal ➜, *Canada* 104 C3
Montreal L., *Canada* 103 C7
Montreal Lake, *Canada* 103 C7
Montredon-Labessonnié, *France* 20 E6
Montrésor, *France* 18 E8
Montret, *France* 19 F12
Montreuil, *Pas-de-Calais, France* 19 B8
Montreuil, *Seine-St-Denis, France* 19 D9
Montreuil-Bellay, *France* ... 18 E6
Montreux, *Switz.* 25 J2
Montrevel-en-Bresse, *France* . 19 F12
Montrichard, *France* 18 E8
Montrose, *U.K.* 13 E6
Montrose, *Colo., U.S.A.* 109 G10
Montrose, *Pa., U.S.A.* 117 E9
Monts, Pte. des, *Canada* 105 C6
Montsalvy, *France* 20 D6
Montsant, Serra de, *Spain* .. 38 D6
Montsauche-les-Settons, *France* 19 E11
Montsec, Serra del, *Spain* ... 38 C5
Montseny △, *Spain* 38 D2
Montserrat, *Spain* 38 D6
Montserrat ☑, *W. Indies* ... 121 C7
Montuenga, *Spain* 36 D6
Montuiri, *Spain* 48 B9
Monywa, *Burma* 67 H19
Monza, *Italy* 40 C6
Monze, *Zambia* 87 F2
Monze, C., *Pakistan* 68 G2
Monzón, *Spain* 38 D5
Mooers, *U.S.A.* 117 B11
Mooi ➜, *S. Africa* 89 D5
Mooi River, *S. Africa* 89 D4
Moonah ➜, *Australia* 94 C2
Moonda, L., *Australia* 94 D3
Moonie, *Australia* 95 D5
Moonie ➜, *Australia* 95 D4
Moonta, *Australia* 95 E2
Moora, *Australia* 93 F2
Moorcroft, *U.S.A.* 112 C2
Moore ➜, *Australia* 93 F2
Moore, L., *Australia* 93 E2
Moore Park, *Australia* 94 C5
Moore River △, *Australia* ... 93 F2
Moorefield, *U.S.A.* 114 F6
Moores Res., *U.S.A.* 117 B13
Moorfoot Hills, *U.K.* 13 F5
Moorhead, *U.S.A.* 112 B6
Moormerland, *Germany* 24 B3
Moorpark, *U.S.A.* 111 L8
Moorreesburg, *S. Africa* 88 E2
Moorrinya △, *Australia* 94 C3
Moosburg, *Germany* 25 G7
Moose ➜, *Canada* 104 B3
Moose ➜, *U.S.A.* 117 C9
Moose Creek, *Canada* 117 A10
Moose Factory, *Canada* 104 B3
Moose Jaw, *Canada* 103 C7
Moose Jaw ➜, *Canada* 103 C7
Moose Lake, *Canada* 103 C8
Moose Lake, *U.S.A.* 112 B8
Moose Mountain △, *Canada* . 103 D8
Moosehead L., *U.S.A.* 115 C11
Mooselookmeguntic L., *U.S.A.* 115 C10
Moosilauke, Mt., *U.S.A.* 117 B13
Moosomin, *Canada* 103 C8
Moosonee, *Canada* 104 B3
Moosup, *U.S.A.* 117 E13
Mopane, *S. Africa* 89 C4
Mopeia Velha, *Mozam.* 87 F4
Mopipi, *Botswana* 88 C3
Mopoi, *C.A.R.* 86 A2
Mopti, *Mali* 82 C4
Moqatta, *Sudan* 81 E4
Moqor, *Afghan.* 68 C2
Moquegua, *Peru* 124 G4
Móra, *Hungary* 28 C3
Mór, *Hungary* 28 C3
Mora, *Cameroon* 83 C7
Móra, *Portugal* 37 G2
Mora, *Spain* 37 F7
Mora, *Sweden* 10 C8
Mora, *Minn., U.S.A.* 112 C8
Mora, *N. Mex., U.S.A.* 109 J11
Mora ➜, *U.S.A.* 113 H2
Mora de Rubielos, *Spain* ... 38 E4
Mòra d'Ebre, *Spain* 38 D5
Mòra la Nova, *Spain* 38 D5
Moradabad, *India* 69 E8
Moradfenobe, *Madag.* 89 B7
Morafenobe, *Madag.* 89 B7
Moraĝ, *Poland* 30 E6
Moral de Calatrava, *Spain* .. 37 G7
Moraleja, *Spain* 36 E4
Moramanga, *Madag.* 89 B8
Moran, *Kans., U.S.A.* 113 G7
Moran, *Wyo., U.S.A.* 108 E8
Moranbah, *Australia* 94 C4
Morano Cálabro, *Italy* 43 C9

Morant Bay, *Jamaica* ...... 120 a
Morant Cays, *Jamaica* 120 C4
Morant Pt., *Jamaica* .... 120 a
Morar, *India* 68 F8
Morar, L., *U.K.* 13 E3
Moratalla, *Spain* 39 G3
Moratuwa, *Sri Lanka* 66 R11
Morava ➜, *Slovak Rep.* 27 C9
Moravia, *U.S.A.* 117 D8
Moravian Hts. = Českomoravská
 Vrchovina, *Czech Rep.* ... 26 B8
Moravica ➜, *Serbia & M.* ... 44 C4
Moraviţa, *Romania* 28 E6
Moravská Třebová, *Czech Rep.* 27 B9
Moravské Budějovice, *Czech Rep.* 26 B8
Morawa, *Australia* 93 E2
Morawhanna, *Guyana* 124 B7
Moray □, *U.K.* 13 D5
Moray Firth, *U.K.* 13 D5
Morbach, *Germany* 25 F3
Morbegno, *Italy* 40 B6
Morbi, *India* 68 H4
Morbihan □, *France* 18 E4
Morcenx, *France* 20 D3
Morcone, *Italy* 43 A7
Mordelles, *France* 18 D5
Morden, *Canada* 103 D9
Mordoğan, *Turkey* 47 C8
Mordovian Republic =
 Mordvinia □, *Russia* 34 C7
Mordovo, *Russia* 34 D5
Mordvinia □, *Russia* 34 C7
Mordy, *Poland* 31 F9
Morea, *Greece* 6 H10
Moreau ➜, *U.S.A.* 112 C4
Morecambe, *U.K.* 14 C5
Morecambe B., *U.K.* 14 C5
Moree, *Australia* 95 D4
Morehead, *U.S.A.* 114 F4
Morehead City, *U.S.A.* 115 H7
Morel ➜, *India* 68 F7
Morelia, *Mexico* 118 D4
Morella, *Australia* 94 C3
Morella, *Spain* 38 E4
Morelos, *Mexico* 118 B3
Morelos □, *Mexico* 119 D5
Moremi △, *Botswana* 88 B3
Morena, *India* 68 F8
Morena, Sierra, *Spain* 37 G7
Moreni, *Romania* 29 F10
Moreno Valley, *U.S.A.* 111 M10
Moresby I., *Canada* 102 C2
Morestel, *France* 21 C9
Moreton I., *Australia* 95 D5
Moreton Island △, *Australia* . 95 D5
Moreuil, *France* 19 C9
Morey, *Spain* 48 B10
Morez, *France* 19 F13
Morgan, *U.S.A.* 108 F8
Morgan City, *U.S.A.* 113 L9
Morgan Hill, *U.S.A.* 110 H5
Morganfield, *U.S.A.* 114 G2
Morganton, *U.S.A.* 115 H5
Morgantown, *U.S.A.* 114 F6
Morgenzon, *S. Africa* 89 D4
Morges, *Switz.* 25 J2
Morghak, *Iran* 71 D8
Morgongåva, *Sweden* 10 E10
Morhange, *France* 19 D13
Morhar ➜, *India* 69 G11
Mori, *Italy* 40 C7
Mori, *Japan* 54 C10
Moriarty, *U.S.A.* 109 J10
Moribaya, *Guinea* 82 D3
Morice L., *Canada* 102 C3
Moriki, *Nigeria* 83 C6
Morinville, *Canada* 102 C6
Morioka, *Japan* 54 E10
Moris, *Mexico* 118 B3
Morlaàs, *France* 20 E3
Morlaix, *France* 18 D3
Mörlunda, *Sweden* 11 G9
Mormanno, *Italy* 43 C8
Mormant, *France* 19 D9
Mornington, *Australia* 95 F4
Mornington, I., *Chile* 128 F1
Mornington I., *Australia* ... 94 B2
Mórnos ➜, *Greece* 46 C3
Moro, *Pakistan* 68 F2
Moro, *Sudan* 81 E3
Moro ➜, *Pakistan* 68 E2
Moro G., *Phil.* 61 H5
Morocco ■, *N. Afr.* 78 B4
Morogoro, *Tanzania* 86 D4
Morogoro □, *Tanzania* 86 D4
Moroleón, *Mexico* 118 C4
Morombe, *Madag.* 89 C7
Morón, *Argentina* 126 C4
Morón, *Cuba* 120 B4
Morón de Almazán, *Spain* .. 38 D2
Morón de la Frontera, *Spain* . 37 H5
Morona ➜, *Peru* 124 D3
Morondava, *Madag.* 89 C7
Morondo, *Ivory C.* 82 D3
Morongo Valley, *U.S.A.* 111 L10
Moroni, *Comoros Is.* 77 H8
Moroni, *U.S.A.* 108 G8
Moronou, *Ivory C.* 82 D4
Morotai, *Indonesia* 63 D7
Moroto, *Uganda* 86 B3
Moroto, Mt., *Uganda* 86 B3
Morozov, *Bulgaria* 45 D9
Morozovsk, *Russia* 35 F5
Morpeth, *U.K.* 14 B6
Morphou, *Cyprus* 49 D11
Morphou Bay, *Cyprus* 49 D11
Morrilton, *U.S.A.* 113 H8
Morrinhos, *Brazil* 125 G9
Morrinsville, *N.Z.* 91 G5
Morris, *Canada* 103 D9
Morris, *Ill., U.S.A.* 112 E10

Morris, *Minn., U.S.A.* 112 C7
Morris, *N.Y., U.S.A.* 117 D9
Morris, *Pa., U.S.A.* 116 E7
Morris, Mt., *Australia* 93 E5
Morris Jesup, Kap, *Greenland* 4 A5
Morrisburg, *Canada* 117 B9
Morristown, *Ariz., U.S.A.* .. 109 K7
Morristown, *N.J., U.S.A.* ... 117 F10
Morristown, *N.Y., U.S.A.* .. 117 B9
Morristown, *Tenn., U.S.A.* . 115 G4
Morrisville, *N.Y., U.S.A.* ... 117 D9
Morrisville, *Pa., U.S.A.* 117 F10
Morrisville, *Vt., U.S.A.* 117 B12
Morro, Pta., *Chile* 126 B1
Morro Bay, *U.S.A.* 110 K6
Morro del Jable, *Canary Is.* . 48 F5
Morro Jable, Pta. de, *Canary Is.* 48 F5
Morrocoy △, *Venezuela* 121 D6
Morrosquillo, G. de, *Colombia* 120 E4
Mörrum, *Sweden* 11 H8
Morrumbene, *Mozam.* 89 C6
Mörrumsån ➜, *Sweden* 11 H8
Mors, *Denmark* 11 H2
Morshansk, *Russia* 34 D5
Mörsil, *Sweden* 10 A7
Mortagne ➜, *France* 19 D13
Mortagne-au-Perche, *France* . 18 D7
Mortagne-sur-Gironde, *France* 20 C3
Mortagne-sur-Sèvre, *France* . 18 F6
Mortain, *France* 18 D6
Mortara, *Italy* 40 C5
Morteau, *France* 19 E13
Morteros, *Argentina* 126 C3
Mortlach, *Canada* 103 C7
Mortlake, *Australia* 95 F3
Morton, *Tex., U.S.A.* 113 J3
Morton, *Wash., U.S.A.* 110 D4
Moruga, *Trin. & Tob.* 125 K15
Morundah, *Australia* 95 E4
Moruya, *Australia* 95 F5
Morvan ➜, *France* 19 E11
Morven, *Australia* 95 D4
Morvern, *U.K.* 13 E3
Morwell, *Australia* 95 F4
Moryń, *Poland* 31 F1
Morzine, *France* 19 F13
Mosalsk, *Russia* 32 E8
Mosbach, *Germany* 25 F5
Mošćenice, *Croatia* 41 C11
Mosciano Sant' Ángelo, *Italy* . 41 F10
Moscos Is., *Burma* 64 E1
Moscow = Moskva, *Russia* .. 32 E9
Moscow, *Idaho, U.S.A.* 108 C5
Moscow, *Pa., U.S.A.* 117 E9
Mosel ➜, *Europe* 19 B14
Moselle = Mosel ➜, *Europe* . 19 B14
Moselle □, *France* 19 D13
Moses Lake, *U.S.A.* 108 C4
Mosgiel, *N.Z.* 91 L3
Moshaweng ➜, *S. Africa* ... 88 D3
Moshi, *Tanzania* 86 C4
Moshupa, *Botswana* 88 C4
Mosina, *Poland* 31 F3
Mosjøen, *Norway* 8 D15
Moskenesøya, *Norway* 8 C15
Moskenstraumen, *Norway* .. 8 C15
Moskva, *Russia* 32 E9
Moskva ➜, *Russia* 32 E10
Moslavačka Gora, *Croatia* .. 41 C13
Mosomane, *Botswana* 88 C4
Mosonmagyaróvár, *Hungary* . 28 C2
Mošorin, *Serbia & M.* 28 E5
Mospino, *Ukraine* 33 J9
Mosquera, *Colombia* 124 C3
Mosquero, *U.S.A.* 113 H3
Mosqueruela, *Spain* 38 E4
Mosquitia, *Honduras* 120 C3
Mosquito Coast = Mosquitia,
 Honduras 120 C3
Mosquito Creek L., *U.S.A.* .. 116 E4
Mosquito L., *Canada* 103 A8
Mosquitos, G. de los, *Panama* 120 E3
Moss, *Norway* 9 G14
Moss Vale, *Australia* 95 E5
Mossbank, *Canada* 103 D7
Mossburn, *N.Z.* 91 L2
Mosselbaai, *S. Africa* 88 E3
Mossendjo, *Congo* 84 E2
Mossgiel, *Australia* 95 E3
Mossingen, *Germany* 25 G5
Mossman, *Australia* 94 B4
Mossoró, *Brazil* 125 E11
Mossuril, *Mozam.* 87 E5
Most, *Czech Rep.* 26 A6
Mosta, *Malta* 49 D1
Mostaganem, *Algeria* 78 A6
Mostar, *Bos.-H.* 28 G2
Mostardas, *Brazil* 127 C5
Mostiska = Mostyska, *Ukraine* 31 J10
Móstoles, *Spain* 36 E7
Mosty = Masty, *Belarus* 32 F3
Mostyska, *Ukraine* 31 J10
Mosul = Al Mawşil, *Iraq* ... 70 B4
Mosûlpo, *S. Korea* 57 H14
Mota, *Ethiopia* 81 E4
Mota del Cuervo, *Spain* ... 39 F2
Mota del Marqués, *Spain* .. 36 D5
Motagua ➜, *Guatemala* ... 120 C2
Motala, *Sweden* 11 F9
Motaze, *Mozam.* 89 C5
Moţca, *Romania* 29 C11
Moth, *India* 69 G8
Motherwell, *U.K.* 13 F5
Motihari, *India* 69 F11
Motilla del Palancar, *Spain* . 39 F3
Motnik, *Slovenia* 41 B11
Motovun, *Croatia* 41 C10
Motozintla de Mendoza, *Mexico* 119 D6
Motril, *Spain* 37 J7
Motru, *Romania* 28 F7
Motru ➜, *Romania* 29 F8

Mott, *U.S.A.* 112 B3
Móttola, *Italy* 43 B10
Motueka, *N.Z.* 91 J4
Motueka →, *N.Z.* 91 J4
Motul, *Mexico* 119 C7
Mouchalagane →, *Canada* .. 105 B6
Moúdhros, *Greece* 47 B7
Mouding, *China* 58 E3
Moudjeria, *Mauritania* 82 B2
Moudon, *Switz.* 25 J2
Mouila, *Gabon* 84 E2
Moulamein, *Australia* 95 F3
Moule à Chique, C., *St. Lucia* 121 f
Mouliana, *Greece* 49 D7
Moulins, *France* 19 F10
Moulmein, *Burma* 67 L20
Moulouya, O. →, *Morocco* .. 78 B5
Moultrie, *U.S.A.* 115 K4
Moultrie, L., *U.S.A.* 115 J5
Mound City, *Mo., U.S.A.* .. 112 E7
Mound City, *S. Dak., U.S.A.* 112 C4
Moundou, *Chad* 79 G9
Moundsville, *U.S.A.* 116 G4
Moung, *Cambodia* 64 F4
Mount Airy, *U.S.A.* 115 G5
Mount Albert, *Canada* 116 B5
Mount Aspiring △, *N.Z.* ... 91 L2
Mount Barker, *S. Austral.,*
    Australia 95 F2
Mount Barker, *W. Austral.,*
    Australia 93 F2
Mount Brydges, *Canada* 116 D3
Mount Burr, *Australia* 95 F3
Mount Carmel = Ha Karmel △,
    Israel 74 C4
Mount Carmel, *Ill., U.S.A.* 114 F2
Mount Carmel, *Pa., U.S.A.* 117 F8
Mount Charleston, *U.S.A.* . 111 J11
Mount Clemens, *U.S.A.* 116 D2
Mount Coolon, *Australia* .. 94 C4
Mount Darwin, *Zimbabwe* ... 87 F3
Mount Desert I., *U.S.A.* .. 115 C11
Mount Dora, *U.S.A.* 115 L5
Mount Edziza △, *Canada* ... 102 B2
Mount Elgon △, *E. Afr.* ... 86 B3
Mount Field △, *Australia* . 95 G4
Mount Fletcher, *S. Africa* 89 E4
Mount Forest, *Canada* 116 C4
Mount Gambier, *Australia* . 95 F3
Mount Garnet, *Australia* .. 94 B4
Mount Holly, *U.S.A.* 117 G10
Mount Holly Springs, *U.S.A.* 116 F7
Mount Hope, *N.S.W., Australia* 95 E4
Mount Hope, *S. Austral.,*
    Australia 95 E2
Mount Isa, *Australia* 94 C2
Mount Jewett, *U.S.A.* 116 E6
Mount Kaputar △, *Australia* 95 E5
Mount Kenya △, *Kenya* 86 C4
Mount Kilimanjaro △, *Tanzania* 86 C4
Mount Kisco, *U.S.A.* 117 E11
Mount Laguna, *U.S.A.* 111 N10
Mount Larcom, *Australia* .. 94 C5
Mount Lofty Ra., *Australia* 95 E2
Mount Magnet, *Australia* .. 93 E2
Mount Maunganui, *N.Z.* 91 G6
Mount Molloy, *Australia* .. 94 B4
Mount Morgan, *Australia* .. 94 C5
Mount Morris, *U.S.A.* 116 D7
Mount Pearl, *Canada* 105 C9
Mount Penn, *U.S.A.* 117 F9
Mount Perry, *Australia* ... 95 D5
Mount Pleasant, *Iowa, U.S.A.* 112 E9
Mount Pleasant, *Mich., U.S.A.* 114 D3
Mount Pleasant, *Pa., U.S.A.* 116 F5
Mount Pleasant, *S.C., U.S.A.* 115 J6
Mount Pleasant, *Tenn., U.S.A.* 115 H2
Mount Pleasant, *Tex., U.S.A.* 113 J7
Mount Pleasant, *Utah, U.S.A.* 108 G8
Mount Pocono, *U.S.A.* 117 E9
Mount Rainier △, *U.S.A.* .. 110 D5
Mount Revelstoke △, *Canada* 102 C5
Mount Robson △, *Canada* ... 102 C5
Mount St. Helens △, *U.S.A.* 110 D4
Mount Selinda, *Zimbabwe* .. 89 C5
Mount Shasta, *U.S.A.* 108 F2
Mount Signal, *U.S.A.* 111 N11
Mount Sterling, *Ill., U.S.A.* 112 F9
Mount Sterling, *Ky., U.S.A.* 114 F4
Mount Surprise, *Australia* 94 B3
Mount Union, *U.S.A.* 116 F7
Mount Upton, *U.S.A.* 117 D9
Mount Vernon, *Ill., U.S.A.* 114 F1
Mount Vernon, *Ind., U.S.A.* 112 F10
Mount Vernon, *N.Y., U.S.A.* 117 F11
Mount Vernon, *Ohio, U.S.A.* 116 F2
Mount Vernon, *Wash., U.S.A.* 110 B4
Mount William △, *Australia* 95 G4
Mountain Ash, *U.K.* 15 F4
Mountain Center, *U.S.A.* .. 111 M10
Mountain City, *Nev., U.S.A.* 108 F6
Mountain City, *Tenn., U.S.A.* 115 G5
Mountain Dale, *U.S.A.* 117 E10
Mountain Grove, *U.S.A.* ... 113 G8
Mountain Home, *Ark., U.S.A.* 113 G8
Mountain Home, *Idaho, U.S.A.* 108 E6
Mountain Iron, *U.S.A.* 112 B8
Mountain Pass, *U.S.A.* 111 K11
Mountain View, *Ark., U.S.A.* 113 H8
Mountain View, *Calif., U.S.A.* 110 H4
Mountain View, *Hawaii, U.S.A.* 106 J17
Mountain Zebra △, *S. Africa* 88 E4
Mountainair, *U.S.A.* 109 J10
Mountlake Terrace, *U.S.A.* 110 C4
Mountmellick, *Ireland* 12 C4
Mountrath, *Ireland* 12 D4
Moura, *Australia* 94 C4
Moura, *Brazil* 124 D6
Moura, *Portugal* 37 G3
Mourão, *Portugal* 37 G3
Mourdi, Dépression du, *Chad* 79 E10

Mourdiah, *Mali* 82 C3
Mourenx, *France* 20 E3
Mouri, *Ghana* 83 D4
Mourilyan, *Australia* 94 B4
Mourmelon-le-Grand, *France* 19 C11
Mourne →, *U.K.* 12 B4
Mourne Mts., *U.K.* 12 B5
Mourniaí, *Greece* 49 D6
Mournies = Mourniaí, *Greece* 49 D6
Mouscron, *Belgium* 17 D3
Moussoro, *Chad* 79 F9
Mouthe, *France* 19 F13
Moutier, *Switz.* 25 H3
Moûtiers, *France* 21 C10
Moutong, *Indonesia* 63 D6
Mouy, *France* 19 C9
Mouzáki, *Greece* 46 B3
Mouzon, *France* 19 C12
Movas, *Mexico* 118 B3
Moville, *Ireland* 12 A4
Mowandjum, *Australia* 92 C3
Moy →, *Ireland* 12 B2
Moyale, *Kenya* 81 G4
Moyamba, *S. Leone* 82 D2
Moyen Atlas, *Morocco* 78 B4
Moyne, L. le, *Canada* 105 A6
Moyo, *Indonesia* 62 F5
Moyobamba, *Peru* 124 E3
Moyyero →, *Russia* 53 C11
Moyynty, *Kazakhstan* 52 E8
Mozambique = Moçambique,
    Mozam. 87 F5
Mozambique ■, *Africa* 87 F4
Mozambique Chan., *Africa* . 89 B7
Mozdok, *Russia* 35 J7
Mozdūrān, *Iran* 71 B9
Mozhaysk, *Russia* 32 E9
Mozhga, *Russia* 34 B11
Mozhnābād, *Iran* 71 C9
Mozirje, *Slovenia* 41 B11
Mozyr = Mazyr, *Belarus* ... 33 F5
Mpanda, *Tanzania* 86 D3
Mpésoba, *Mali* 82 C3
Mphoengs, *Zimbabwe* 89 C4
Mpika, *Zambia* 87 E3
Mpulungu, *Zambia* 87 D3
Mpumalanga, *S. Africa* 89 D5
Mpumalanga □, *S. Africa* .. 89 D5
Mpwapwa, *Tanzania* 86 D4
Mqanduli, *S. Africa* 89 E4
Mqinvartsveri = Kazbek, *Russia* 35 J7
Mrągowo, *Poland* 30 E8
Mramor, *Serbia & M.* 44 C5
Mrkonjić Grad, *Bos.-H.* ... 28 F2
Mrkopalj, *Croatia* 41 C11
Mrocza, *Poland* 31 E4
Msambansovu, *Zimbabwe* 87 F3
M'sila →, *Algeria* 78 A6
Msoro, *Zambia* 87 E3
Msta →, *Russia* 32 C6
Mstislavl = Mstsislaw, *Belarus* 32 E6
Mstsislaw, *Belarus* 32 E6
Mszana Dolna, *Poland* 31 J7
Mszczonów, *Poland* 31 G7
Mtama, *Tanzania* 87 E4
Mtamvuna →, *S. Africa* 89 E5
Mtilikwe →, *Zimbabwe* 87 G3
Mtsensk, *Russia* 32 F9
Mtskheta, *Georgia* 35 K7
Mtubatuba, *S. Africa* 89 D5
Mtwalume, *S. Africa* 89 E5
Mtwara-Mikindani, *Tanzania* 87 E5
Mu Gia, Deo, *Vietnam* 64 D5
Mu Ko Chang △, *Thailand* .. 65 G4
Mu Us Shamo, *China* 56 E5
Muang Chiang Rai = Chiang Rai,
    Thailand 58 H2
Muang Khong, *Laos* 64 E5
Muang Lamphun, *Thailand* .. 64 C2
Muang Mai, *Thailand* ...... 65 a
Muang Pak Beng, *Laos* 58 H4
Muar, *Malaysia* 65 L4
Muarabungo, *Indonesia* 62 E2
Muaraenim, *Indonesia* 62 E2
Muarajuloi, *Indonesia* 62 E4
Muarakaman, *Indonesia* 62 E5
Muaratebo, *Indonesia* 62 E2
Muaratembesi, *Indonesia* .. 62 E2
Muaratewe, *Indonesia* 62 E4
Mubarakpur, *India* 69 F10
Mubarraz = Al Mubarraz,
    Si. Arabia 71 E6
Mubende, *Uganda* 86 B3
Mubi, *Nigeria* 83 C7
Mucajaí →, *Brazil* 124 C6
Muchachos, Roque de los,
    Canary Is. 48 F2
Mücheln, *Germany* 24 D7
Muchinga Mts., *Zambia* 87 E3
Muchkapskiy, *Russia* 34 E6
Muchuan, *China* 58 C5
Muck, *U.K.* 13 E2
Muckadilla, *Australia* 95 D4
Muckle Flugga, *U.K.* 13 A8
Mucur, *Turkey* 72 C6
Mucuri, *Brazil* 125 G11
Mucusso, *Angola* 88 B3
Muda, *Canary Is.* 48 F6
Mudanjiang, *China* 57 B15
Mudanya, *Turkey* 45 F12
Muddy Cr. →, *U.S.A.* 109 H8
Mudgee, *Australia* 95 E4
Mudjatik →, *Canada* 103 B7
Mudurnu, *Turkey* 72 B4
Muecate, *Mozam.* 87 E4
Mueda, *Mozam.* 87 E4
Mueller Ra., *Australia* ... 92 C4
Muerto, Mar, *Mexico* 119 D6
Mufu Shan, *China* 59 C10
Mufulira, *Zambia* 87 E2
Mufumbiro Range, *Africa* .. 86 C2

Mugardos, *Spain* 36 B2
Muge →, *Portugal* 37 F2
Múggia, *Italy* 41 C10
Mughal Sarai, *India* 69 G10
Mughayrā', *Si. Arabia* 70 D3
Mugi, *Japan* 55 H7
Mugia = Muxía, *Spain* 36 B1
Mugila, Mts., *Dem. Rep. of*
    the Congo 86 D2
Muğla, *Turkey* 47 D10
Muğla □, *Turkey* 47 D10
Muglad, *Sudan* 81 E2
Muglizh, *Bulgaria* 45 D9
Mugu, *Nepal* 69 E10
Muhammad, Râs, *Egypt* 70 E2
Muhammad Qol, *Sudan* 80 C4
Muhammadabad, *India* 69 F10
Muhesi →, *Tanzania* 86 D4
Mühlacker, *Germany* 25 G4
Mühldorf, *Germany* 25 G8
Mühlhausen, *Germany* 24 D6
Mühlig Hofmann fjell, *Antarctica* 5 D3
Mühlviertel, *Austria* 26 C7
Muhos, *Finland* 8 D22
Muhu, *Estonia* 9 G20
Muhutwe, *Tanzania* 86 C3
Muine Bheag, *Ireland* 12 D5
Muir, L., *Australia* 93 F2
Muir of Ord, *U.K.* 13 D4
Mujnak = Muynak, *Uzbekistan* 52 E6
Muka, *Tanjung, Malaysia* .. 65 c
Mukacheve, *Ukraine* 28 B7
Mukachevo = Mukacheve,
    Ukraine 28 B7
Mukah, *Malaysia* 62 D4
Mukandwara, *India* 68 G6
Mukawwa, Geziret, *Egypt* .. 80 C4
Mukawwar, *Sudan* 80 C4
Mukdahan, *Thailand* 64 D5
Mukden = Shenyang, *China* . 57 D12
Mukerian, *India* 68 D6
Mukhavyets, *Belarus* 31 F10
Mukhtolovo, *Russia* 34 C6
Mukinbudin, *Australia* 93 F2
Mukishi, *Dem. Rep. of the Congo* 87 D1
Mukomuko, *Indonesia* 62 E2
Mukomwenze, *Dem. Rep. of*
    the Congo 86 D2
Muktsar, *India* 68 D6
Mukur = Moqor, *Afghan.* ... 68 C2
Mukutawa →, *Canada* 103 C9
Mukwela, *Zambia* 87 F2
Mula, *Spain* 39 G3
Mula →, *Pakistan* 68 F2
Mulange, *Dem. Rep. of the Congo* 86 C2
Mulanje, *Malawi* 87 F4
Mulanje, Mt., *Malawi* 87 F4
Mulchén, *Chile* 126 D1
Mulde →, *Germany* 24 D8
Mule Creek Junction, *U.S.A.* 112 D2
Muleba, *Tanzania* 86 C3
Mulejé, *Mexico* 118 B2
Muleshoe, *U.S.A.* 113 H3
Muletta, Gara, *Ethiopia* .. 81 F5
Mulgrave, *Canada* 105 C7
Mulhacén, *Spain* 37 H7
Mülheim, *Germany* 24 D2
Mulhouse, *France* 19 E14
Muli, *China* 58 D3
Muling, *China* 57 B16
Mull, *U.K.* 13 E3
Mull, Sound of, *U.K.* 13 E3
Mullaittivu, *Sri Lanka* ... 66 Q12
Mullen, *U.S.A.* 112 D4
Mullens, *U.S.A.* 114 G5
Muller, Pegunungan, *Indonesia* 62 D4
Mullet Pen., *Ireland* 12 B1
Mullewa, *Australia* 93 E2
Müllheim, *Germany* 25 H3
Mulligan →, *Australia* 94 D2
Mullingar, *Ireland* 12 C4
Mullins, *U.S.A.* 115 H6
Mullsjö, *Sweden* 11 G7
Mullumbimby, *Australia* ... 95 D5
Mulobezi, *Zambia* 87 F2
Mulroy B., *Ireland* 12 A4
Multan, *Pakistan* 68 D4
Mulumbe, Mts., *Dem. Rep. of*
    the Congo 87 D2
Mulungushi Dam, *Zambia* ... 87 E2
Mulvane, *U.S.A.* 113 G6
Mulwad, *Sudan* 80 D3
Mumbai, *India* 66 K8
Mumbwa, *Zambia* 87 F2
Mumra, *Russia* 35 H8
Mun →, *Thailand* 64 E5
Muna, *Indonesia* 63 F6
Munabao, *India* 68 G3
Munamagi, *Estonia* 9 H22
Muncan, *Indonesia* 63 K18
Muncar, *Indonesia* 63 J17
Münchberg, *Germany* 25 E7
Müncheberg, *Germany* 24 C10
München, *Germany* 25 G7
Munchen-Gladbach =
    Mönchengladbach, *Germany* 24 D2
München International ✈ (MUC),
    Germany 25 G7
Muncho Lake, *Canada* 102 B3
Munch'ŏn, *N. Korea* 57 E14
Muncie, *U.S.A.* 114 E3
Muncoonie, L., *Australia* . 94 D2
Mundabbera, *Australia* 95 D5
Munday, *U.S.A.* 113 J5
Münden, *Germany* 24 D5
Münden △, *Germany* 24 D5
Mundiwindi, *Australia* 92 D3
Mundo →, *Spain* 39 G2
Mundo Novo, *Brazil* 125 F10
Mundra, *India* 68 H3
Mundrabilla, *Australia* ... 93 F4
Munera, *Spain* 39 F2

Mungallala, *Australia* 95 D4
Mungallala Cr. →, *Australia* 95 D4
Mungana, *Australia* 94 B3
Mungaoli, *India* 68 G8
Mungari, *Mozam.* 87 F3
Mungbere, *Dem. Rep. of*
    the Congo 86 B2
Mungeli, *India* 69 H9
Munger, *India* 69 G12
Mungkan Kandju △, *Australia* 94 A3
Munich = München, *Germany* 25 G7
Munising, *U.S.A.* 114 B2
Munka-Ljungby, *Sweden* 11 H6
Munkebo, *Denmark* 11 J4
Munkedal, *Sweden* 11 F5
Munkfors, *Sweden* 10 E7
Munku-Sardyk, *Russia* 53 D11
Münnerstadt, *Germany* 25 E6
Muñoz Gamero, Pen., *Chile* 128 G2
Munroe L., *Canada* 103 B9
Munsan, *S. Korea* 57 F14
Münster, *France* 19 D14
Munster, *Niedersachsen,* *Germany* 24 C6
Münster, *Nordrhein-Westfalen,*
    Germany 24 D3
Munster □, *Ireland* 12 D3
Muntadgin, *Australia* 93 F2
Muntele Mare, Vf., *Romania* 29 D8
Muntok, *Indonesia* 62 E3
Munyama, *Zambia* 87 F2
Munzur Dağları, *Turkey* ... 73 C8
Muong Beng, *Laos* 58 G3
Muong Boum, *Vietnam* 58 F4
Muong Et, *Laos* 64 B5
Muong Hai, *Laos* 58 G3
Muong Hiem, *Laos* 64 B4
Muong Houn, *Laos* 58 G3
Muong Hung, *Vietnam* 58 G4
Muong Kau, *Laos* 64 E5
Muong Khao, *Laos* 64 C4
Muong Khoua, *Laos* 58 G4
Muong Liep, *Laos* 64 C3
Muong May, *Laos* 64 E6
Muong Ngeun, *Laos* 58 G3
Muong Ngoi, *Laos* 58 G4
Muong Nhie, *Vietnam* 58 F4
Muong Nong, *Laos* 64 D6
Muong Ou Tay, *Laos* 58 F3
Muong Oua, *Laos* 64 C3
Muong Peun, *Laos* 58 G4
Muong Phalane, *Laos* 64 D5
Muong Phieng, *Laos* 64 C3
Muong Phine, *Laos* 64 D6
Muong Sai, *Laos* 58 G3
Muong Saiapoun, *Laos* 64 C3
Muong Sen, *Vietnam* 64 C5
Muong Sing, *Laos* 58 G3
Muong Son, *Laos* 64 B4
Muong Soui, *Laos* 64 C4
Muong Va, *Laos* 58 G4
Muong Xia, *Vietnam* 64 B5
Muonio, *Finland* 8 C20
Muonio älv = Muonionjoki →,
    Finland 8 C20
Muonioälven = Muonionjoki →,
    Finland 8 C20
Muonionjoki →, *Finland* ... 8 C20
Muping, *China* 57 F11
Mupoi, *Sudan* 81 F2
Muqaddam, Wadi →, *Sudan* .. 80 D3
Muqdisho, *Somali Rep.* 75 G4
Mur →, *Austria* 27 E9
Mûr-de-Bretagne, *France* .. 18 D4
Muradiye, *Manisa, Turkey* . 47 C9
Muradiye, *Van, Turkey* 73 C10
Murakami, *Japan* 54 E9
Murallón, Cerro, *Chile* ... 128 F2
Muranda, *Rwanda* 86 C2
Murang'a, *Kenya* 86 C4
Murashi, *Russia* 52 D5
Murat, *France* 20 C6
Murat →, *Turkey* 73 C9
Murat Dağı, *Turkey* 47 C11
Muratlı, *Turkey* 45 E11
Murato, *France* 21 F13
Murau, *Austria* 26 D7
Murava, *Belarus* 31 F11
Muravera, *Italy* 42 C2
Murayama, *Japan* 54 E10
Murça, *Portugal* 36 D3
Murchison →, *Australia* ... 93 E1
Murchison Falls, *Uganda* .. 86 B3
Murchison Falls △, *Uganda* 86 B3
Murchison Ra., *Australia* . 94 C1
Murchison Rapids, *Malawi* . 87 F3
Murcia, *Spain* 39 G3
Murcia □, *Spain* 39 H3
Murdo, *U.S.A.* 112 D4
Murdoch Pt., *Australia* ... 94 A3
Mûrefte, *Turkey* 45 F11
Mureş □, *Romania* 29 D9
Mureş →, *Romania* 28 D5
Mureşul = Mureş →, *Romania* 28 D5
Muret, *France* 20 E5
Murewa, *Zimbabwe* 89 B5
Murfreesboro, *N.C., U.S.A.* 115 G7
Murfreesboro, *Tenn., U.S.A.* 115 H2
Murgab = Murghob, *Tajikistan* 52 F8
Murgab →, *Turkmenistan* ... 71 B9
Murgenella, *Australia* 92 B5
Murgeni, *Romania* 29 D13
Murgha Kibzai, *Pakistan* .. 68 D3
Murghob, *Tajikistan* 52 F8
Murgon, *Australia* 95 D5
Muri, *India* 69 H11
Muria, *Indonesia* 63 G14
Muriaé, *Brazil* 127 A7
Murias de Paredes, *Spain* . 36 C4
Muriel Mine, *Zimbabwe* 87 F3
Müritz, *Germany* 24 B8
Müritz △, *Germany* 24 B8

Murliganj, *India* 69 G12
Murmansk, *Russia* 52 C4
Murnau, *Germany* 25 H7
Muro, *France* 21 F12
Muro, *Spain* 48 B10
Muro, C. de, *France* 21 G12
Muro de Alcoy, *Spain* 39 G4
Muro Lucano, *Italy* 43 B8
Murom, *Russia* 34 C6
Muroran, *Japan* 54 C10
Muros, *Spain* 36 C1
Muros y de Noya, Ría de, *Spain* 36 C1
Muroto, *Japan* 55 H7
Muroto-Misaki, *Japan* 55 H7
Murovani Kurylivtsi, *Ukraine* 29 B12
Murowana Goślina, *Poland* . 31 F3
Murphy, *U.S.A.* 108 E5
Murphys, *U.S.A.* 110 G6
Murrat, *Sudan* 80 D2
Murrat Wells, *Sudan* 80 C3
Murray, *Ky., U.S.A.* 115 G1
Murray, *Utah, U.S.A.* 108 F8
Murray →, *Australia* 95 F2
Murray →, *U.S.A.* 115 H5
Murray Bridge, *Australia* . 95 F2
Murray Harbour, *Canada* ... 105 C7
Murray River △, *Australia* 95 E3
Murraysburg, *S. Africa* ... 88 E3
Murree, *Pakistan* 68 C5
Murrieta, *U.S.A.* 111 M9
Murro di Porco, Capo, *Italy* 43 F8
Murrumbidgee →, *Australia* 95 E3
Murrumburrah, *Australia* .. 95 E4
Murrurundi, *Australia* 95 E5
Murshid, *Sudan* 80 C3
Murshidabad, *India* 69 G13
Murska Sobota, *Slovenia* .. 41 B13
Murtle L., *Canada* 102 C5
Murtoa, *Australia* 95 F3
Murtosa, *Portugal* 36 E2
Murungu, *Tanzania* 86 C3
Mururoa, *French Polynesia* 97 K14
Murwara, *India* 69 H9
Murwillumbah, *Australia* .. 95 D5
Mürz →, *Austria* 26 D8
Mürzzuschlag, *Austria* 26 D8
Muş, *Turkey* 70 B4
Mûsa, Gebel, *Egypt* 70 D2
Musa Khel, *Pakistan* 68 D3
Mûsa Qal'eh, *Afghan.* 66 C4
Musafirkhana, *India* 69 F9
Musala, *Bulgaria* 44 D7
Musala, *Indonesia* 62 D1
Musan, *N. Korea* 57 C15
Musangu, *Dem. Rep. of the Congo* 87 E1
Musasa, *Tanzania* 86 C3
Musay'īd, *Qatar* 71 E6
Muscat = Masqaṭ, *Oman* 75 C6
Muscatine, *U.S.A.* 112 E9
Musengezi = Unsengedsi →,
    Zimbabwe 87 F3
Musgrave Harbour, *Canada* . 105 C9
Musgrave Ranges, *Australia* 93 E5
Mushie, *Dem. Rep. of the Congo* 84 E3
Mushin, *Nigeria* 83 D5
Musi →, *Indonesia* 62 E2
Musina, *S. Africa* 89 C5
Muskeg →, *Canada* 102 A4
Muskegon, *U.S.A.* 114 D2
Muskegon →, *U.S.A.* 114 D2
Muskegon Heights, *U.S.A.* . 114 D2
Muskogee, *U.S.A.* 113 H7
Muskoka, L., *Canada* 116 B5
Muskwa →, *Canada* 102 B4
Muslīmiyah, *Syria* 70 B3
Musmar, *Sudan* 80 D4
Musofu, *Zambia* 87 E2
Musoma, *Tanzania* 86 C3
Musquaro, L., *Canada* 105 B7
Musquodoboit Harbour, *Canada* 105 D7
Musselburgh, *U.K.* 13 F5
Musselshell →, *U.S.A.* 108 C10
Mussidan, *France* 20 C4
Mussomeli, *Italy* 42 E6
Mussoorie, *India* 68 D8
Mussuco, *Angola* 88 B2
Mustafakemalpaşa, *Turkey* . 45 F12
Mustang, *Nepal* 69 E10
Musters, L., *Argentina* ... 128 F3
Musudan, *N. Korea* 57 D15
Muswellbrook, *Australia* .. 95 E5
Muszyna, *Poland* 31 J7
Mût, *Egypt* 80 B2
Mut, *Turkey* 70 B2
Mutanda, *Mozam.* 89 C5
Mutanda, *Zambia* 87 E2
Mutare, *Zimbabwe* 87 F3
Muting, *Indonesia* 63 F10
Mutki = Mirtağ, *Turkey* ... 70 B4
Mutoko, *Zimbabwe* 89 B5
Mutoray, *Russia* 53 C11
Mutshatsha, *Dem. Rep. of*
    the Congo 87 E1
Mutsu, *Japan* 54 D10
Mutsu-Wan, *Japan* 54 D10
Muttaburra, *Australia* 94 C3
Muttalip, *Turkey* 47 B12
Mutton I., *Ireland* 12 D2
Mutuáli, *Mozam.* 87 E4
Mutum Biyu, *Nigeria* 83 D7
Muweilih, *Egypt* 74 E3
Muxía, *Spain* 36 B1
Muy Muy, *Nic.* 120 D2
Muyinga, *Burundi* 86 C3
Muynak, *Uzbekistan* 52 E6
Muzaffarabad, *Pakistan* ... 69 B5
Muzaffargarh, *Pakistan* ... 68 D4
Muzaffarnagar, *India* 68 E7
Muzaffarpur, *India* 69 F11
Muzafirpur, *Pakistan* 68 D3
Muzhi, *Russia* 52 C7
Muzillac, *France* 18 E4

Muzūra, *Egypt* 80 J7
Mvõlõ, *Sudan* 81 F2
Mvuma, *Zimbabwe* 87 F3
Mvurwi, *Zimbabwe* 87 F3
Mwabvi △, *Malawi* 87 F3
Mwadui, *Tanzania* 86 C3
Mwambo, *Tanzania* 87 E5
Mwandi, *Zambia* 87 F1
Mwanza, *Dem. Rep. of the Congo* 86 D2
Mwanza, *Tanzania* 86 C3
Mwanza, *Zambia* 87 F1
Mwanza □, *Tanzania* 86 C3
Mwaya, *Tanzania* 87 D3
Mweelrea, *Ireland* 12 C2
Mweka, *Dem. Rep. of the Congo* 84 E4
Mwenezi, *Zimbabwe* 87 G3
Mwenezi ➤, *Mozam.* 87 G3
Mwenga, *Dem. Rep. of the Congo* 86 C2
Mweru, L., *Zambia* 87 D2
Mweru Wantipa △, *Zambia* . 87 D2
Mweza Range, *Zimbabwe* ... 87 G3
Mwilambwe, *Dem. Rep. of the Congo* 86 D2
Mwimbi, *Tanzania* 87 D3
Mwinilunga, *Zambia* 87 E1
My Tho, *Vietnam* 65 G6
Myajlar, *India* 68 F4
Myanaung, *Burma* 67 K19
Myanmar = Burma ■, *Asia* . 67 J20
Myaungmya, *Burma* 67 L19
Myedna, *Belarus* 31 G10
Myeik Kyunzu, *Burma* 65 G1
Myers Chuck, *U.S.A.* 102 B2
Myerstown, *U.S.A.* 117 F8
Myingyan, *Burma* 67 J19
Myitkyina, *Burma* 67 G20
Myjava, *Slovak Rep.* 27 C10
Mykhaylivka, *Ukraine* 33 J8
Mykines, *Faeroe Is.* 8 E9
Mykolayiv, *Ukraine* 33 J7
Mymensingh, *Bangla.* 67 G17
Mynydd Du, *U.K.* 15 F4
Mýrdalsjökull, *Iceland* 8 E4
Myrhorod, *Ukraine* 33 H7
Myrtle Beach, *U.S.A.* 115 J4
Myrtle Creek, *U.S.A.* 108 E2
Myrtle Point, *U.S.A.* 108 E1
Myrtou, *Cyprus* 49 D12
Mysia, *Turkey* 45 G11
Myślenice, *Poland* 31 J6
Myślibórz, *Poland* 31 F1
Mysłowice, *Poland* 31 H6
Mysore = Karnataka □, *India* 66 N10
Mysore, *India* 66 N10
Mystic, *U.S.A.* 117 E13
Myszków, *Poland* 31 H6
Myszyniec, *Poland* 30 E8
Mytishchi, *Russia* 32 E9
Mývatn, *Iceland* 8 D5
Mže ➤, *Czech Rep.* 26 B6
Mzimba, *Malawi* 87 E3
Mzimkulu ➤, *S. Africa* 89 E5
Mzimvubu ➤, *S. Africa* 89 E4
Mzuzu, *Malawi* 87 E3

N

Na Hearadh = Harris, *U.K.* ... 13 D2
Na Noi, *Thailand* 64 C3
Na Phao, *Laos* 64 D5
Na Sam, *Vietnam* 58 F6
Na San, *Vietnam* 64 B5
Na Thon, *Thailand* .... 65 b
Naab ➤, *Germany* 25 F8
Na'am, *Sudan* 81 F2
Na'am ➤, *Sudan* 81 F2
Naantali, *Finland* 9 F19
Naas, *Ireland* 12 C5
Nababeep, *S. Africa* 88 D2
Nabawa, *Australia* 93 E1
Nabberu, L., *Australia* 93 E3
Nabburg, *Germany* 25 F8
Naberezhnyye Chelny, *Russia* . 34 C11
Nabeul, *Tunisia* 79 A8
Nabha, *India* 68 D7
Nabīd, *Iran* 71 D8
Nabire, *Indonesia* 63 E9
Nabisar, *Pakistan* 68 G3
Nabisipi ➤, *Canada* 105 B7
Nabiswera, *Uganda* 86 B3
Nāblus = Nābulus, *West Bank* 74 C4
Naboomspruit, *S. Africa* 89 C4
Nabou, *Burkina Faso* 82 C4
Nabua, *Phil.* 61 E5
Nābulus, *West Bank* 74 C4
Nacala, *Mozam.* 87 E5
Nacala-Velha, *Mozam.* 87 E5
Nacaome, *Honduras* 120 D2
Nacaroa, *Mozam.* 87 E4
Naches, *U.S.A.* 108 C3
Naches ➤, *U.S.A.* 110 D6
Nachicapau, L., *Canada* 105 A6
Nachingwea, *Tanzania* 87 E4
Nachna, *India* 68 F4
Náchod, *Czech Rep.* 26 A9
Nacimiento L., *U.S.A.* 110 K6
Naco, *Mexico* 118 A3
Nacogdoches, *U.S.A.* 113 K7
Nácori Chico, *Mexico* 118 B3
Nacozari, *Mexico* 118 A3
Nádendal = Naantali, *Finland* . 9 F19
Nadi, *Fiji* 91 C7
Nadi, *Sudan* 80 D3
Nadiad, *India* 68 H5
Nādlac, *Romania* 28 D5
Nador, *Morocco* 78 B5
Nadur, *Malta* 49 C1

Nadūshan, *Iran* 71 C7
Nadvirna, *Ukraine* 29 B9
Nadvornaya = Nadvirna, *Ukraine* 29 B9
Nadym, *Russia* 52 C8
Nadym ➤, *Russia* 52 C8
Nærbø, *Norway* 9 G11
Næstved, *Denmark* 11 J5
Nafada, *Nigeria* 83 C7
Naft-e Safīd, *Iran* 71 D6
Naftshahr, *Iran* 70 C5
Nafud Desert = An Nafūd, *Si. Arabia* 70 D4
Nag Hammādi, *Egypt* 80 B3
Naga, *Phil.* 61 E5
Nagahama, *Japan* 55 G8
Nagai, *Japan* 54 E10
Nagaland □, *India* 67 G19
Nagano, *Japan* 55 F9
Nagano □, *Japan* 55 F9
Nagaoka, *Japan* 55 F9
Nagappattinam, *India* 66 P11
Nagar ➤, *Bangla.* 69 G13
Nagar Parkar, *Pakistan* 68 G4
Nagasaki, *Japan* 55 H4
Nagasaki □, *Japan* 55 H4
Nagato, *Japan* 55 G5
Nagaur, *India* 68 F5
Nagda, *India* 68 H6
Nagercoil, *India* 66 Q10
Nagina, *India* 69 E8
Nagīneh, *Iran* 71 C8
Nagir, *Pakistan* 69 A6
Naglarby, *Sweden* 10 D9
Nagod, *India* 69 G9
Nagold, *Germany* 25 G4
Nagold ➤, *Germany* 25 G4
Nagoorin, *Australia* 94 C5
Nagorno-Karabakh □, *Azerbaijan* 70 B5
Nagornyy, *Russia* 53 D13
Nagoya, *Japan* 55 G8
Nagpur, *India* 66 J11
Nagua, *Dom. Rep.* 121 C6
Naguabo, *Puerto Rico* ...... 121 d
Nagyatád, *Hungary* 28 D2
Nagyecsed, *Hungary* 28 C7
Nagykálló, *Hungary* 28 C6
Nagykanizsa, *Hungary* 28 D2
Nagykáta, *Hungary* 28 C4
Nagykőrös, *Hungary* 28 C4
Naha, *Japan* 55 L3
Nahan, *India* 68 D7
Nahanni △, *Canada* 102 A4
Nahanni Butte, *Canada* 102 A4
Nahargarh, Mad. P., *India* ... 68 G6
Nahargarh, Raj., *India* 68 G7
Nahariyya, *Israel* 70 C2
Nahāvand, *Iran* 71 C6
Nahe ➤, *Germany* 25 F3
Nahirne, *Ukraine* 29 E13
Nahīya, W. ➤, *Egypt* 80 B3
Nahuelbuta △, *Chile* 126 D13
Nai Yong, *Thailand* .... 65 a
Naicá, *Mexico* 118 B3
Naicam, *Canada* 103 C8
Naikoon △, *Canada* 102 C2
Naila, *Germany* 25 E7
Naimisharanya, *India* 69 F9
Nain, *Canada* 105 A7
Nā'īn, *Iran* 71 C7
Naini Tal, *India* 69 E8
Nainpur, *India* 66 H12
Naintré, *France* 18 F7
Nainwa, *India* 68 G6
Naipu, *Romania* 29 F10
Nairn, *U.K.* 13 D5
Nairobi, *Kenya* 86 C4
Nairobi △, *Kenya* 86 C4
Naissaar, *Estonia* 9 G21
Naita, Mt., *Ethiopia* 81 F4
Naivasha, *Kenya* 86 C4
Naivasha, L., *Kenya* 86 C4
Najac, *France* 20 D5
Najaf = An Najaf, *Iraq* 70 C5
Najafābād, *Iran* 71 C6
Najd, *Si. Arabia* 75 B3
Nájera, *Spain* 38 C2
Najerilla ➤, *Spain* 38 C2
Najibabad, *India* 68 E8
Najin, N. *Korea* 57 C16
Najmah, *Si. Arabia* 71 E6
Najrān, *Si. Arabia* 75 D3
Naju, *S. Korea* 57 G14
Nakadōri-Shima, *Japan* 55 H4
Nakalagba, *Dem. Rep. of the Congo* 86 B2
Nakaminato, *Japan* 55 F10
Nakamura, *Japan* 55 H6
Nakano, *Japan* 55 F9
Nakano-Shima, *Japan* 55 K4
Nakashibetsu, *Japan* 54 C12
Nakfa, *Eritrea* 81 D4
Nakfa △, *Eritrea* 81 D4
Nakha Yai, *Thailand* .... 65 a
Nakhichevan = Naxçıvan, *Azerbaijan* 70 B5
Nakhichevan Rep. = Naxçıvan □, *Azerbaijan* 52 F5
Nakhl, *Egypt* 74 F2
Nakhl-e Taqī, *Iran* 71 E7
Nakhodka, *Russia* 53 E14
Nakhon Nayok, *Thailand* 64 E3
Nakhon Pathom, *Thailand* ... 64 F3
Nakhon Phanom, *Thailand* .. 64 D5
Nakhon Ratchasima, *Thailand* 64 E4
Nakhon Sawan, *Thailand* 64 E3
Nakhon Si Thammarat, *Thailand* 65 H3
Nakhon Thai, *Thailand* 64 D3
Nakhtarana, *India* 68 H3
Nakina, *Canada* 104 B2
Nakło nad Notecią, *Poland* .. 31 E4
Nako, *Burkina Faso* 82 C4
Nakodar, *India* 68 D6

Nakskov, *Denmark* 11 K5
Naktong ➤, *S. Korea* 57 G15
Nakuru, *Kenya* 86 C4
Nakuru, L., *Kenya* 86 C4
Nakusp, *Canada* 102 C5
Nal, *Pakistan* 68 F2
Nal ➤, *Pakistan* 68 G1
Nalázi, *Mozam.* 89 C5
Nalchik, *Russia* 35 J6
Nalęczów, *Poland* 31 G9
Nalerigu, *Ghana* 83 C4
Nalgonda, *India* 66 L11
Nalhati, *India* 69 G12
Naliya, *India* 68 H3
Nallamalai Hills, *India* 66 M11
Nallıhan, *Turkey* 72 B4
Nalón ➤, *Spain* 36 B4
Nam Can, *Vietnam* 65 H5
Nam-ch'on, N. *Korea* 57 E14
Nam Co, *China* 60 C4
Nam Dinh, *Vietnam* 58 G6
Nam Du, Hon, *Vietnam* 65 H5
Nam Nao △, *Thailand* 64 D3
Nam Ngum Dam, *Laos* 64 C4
Nam-Phan, *Vietnam* 65 G6
Nam Phong, *Thailand* 64 D4
Nam Tha, *Laos* 58 G3
Nam Tok, *Thailand* 64 E2
Namacunde, *Angola* 88 B2
Namacurra, *Mozam.* 89 B6
Namak, Daryācheh-ye, *Iran* .. 71 C7
Namak, Kavir-e, *Iran* 71 C8
Namakzār, Daryācheh-ye, *Iran* 71 C9
Namaland, *Namibia* 88 C2
Namangan, *Uzbekistan* 52 E8
Namapa, *Mozam.* 87 E4
Namaqualand, *S. Africa* 88 E2
Namasagali, *Uganda* 86 B3
Namber, *Indonesia* 63 E8
Nambour, *Australia* 95 D5
Nambucca Heads, *Australia* .. 95 E5
Nambung △, *Australia* 93 F2
Namche Bazar, *Nepal* 69 F12
Namchonjŏm = Nam-ch'on, N. *Korea* 57 E14
Namecunda, *Mozam.* 87 E4
Nameponda, *Mozam.* 87 F4
Náměšt' nad Oslavou, *Czech Rep.* 27 B9
Námestovo, *Slovak Rep.* 27 B12
Nametil, *Mozam.* 87 F4
Namew L., *Canada* 103 C8
Namgia, *India* 69 D8
Namhkam, *Burma* 58 E1
Namib Desert, *Namibia* 88 C2
Namib-Naukluft △, *Namibia* . 88 C2
Namibe, *Angola* 85 H2
Namibe □, *Angola* 88 B1
Namibia ■, *Africa* 88 C2
Namibwoestyn = Namib Desert, *Namibia* 88 C2
Namīn, *Iran* 73 C13
Namlea, *Indonesia* 63 E7
Namoi ➤, *Australia* 95 E4
Nampa, *U.S.A.* 108 E5
Nampala, *Mali* 82 B3
Nampo, N. *Korea* 57 E13
Nampō-Shotō, *Japan* 55 J10
Nampula, *Mozam.* 87 F4
Namrole, *Indonesia* 63 E7
Namse Shankou, *China* 67 E13
Namsen ➤, *Norway* 8 D14
Namsos, *Norway* 8 D14
Namtok Chat Trakan △, *Thailand* 64 D3
Namtok Mae Surin △, *Thailand* 64 C2
Namtsy, *Russia* 53 C13
Namtu, *Burma* 67 H20
Namtumbo, *Tanzania* 87 E4
Namu, *Canada* 102 C3
Namur, *Belgium* 17 D4
Namur □, *Belgium* 17 D4
Namutoni, *Namibia* 88 B2
Namwala, *Zambia* 87 F2
Namwŏn, S. *Korea* 57 G14
Namysłów, *Poland* 31 G4
Nan, *Thailand* 64 C3
Nan ➤, *Thailand* 64 E3
Nan-ch'ang = Nanchang, *China* 59 C10
Nan Ling, *China* 59 E8
Nan Xian, *China* 59 C9
Nana, *Romania* 29 F11
Nana Kru, *Liberia* 82 E3
Nanaimo, *Canada* 102 D4
Nanam, N. *Korea* 57 D15
Nanan, *China* 59 E12
Nanango, *Australia* 95 D5
Nan'ao, *China* 59 F11
Nanao, *Japan* 55 F8
Nanbu, *China* 58 B6
Nanchang, Jiangxi, *China* 59 C10
Nanchang, Kiangsi, *China* 59 C10
Nancheng, *China* 59 D11
Nanching = Nanjing, *China* ... 59 A12
Nanchong, *China* 58 B6
Nanchuan, *China* 58 C6
Nancy, *France* 19 D13
Nanda Devi, *India* 69 D8
Nanda Kot, *India* 69 D9
Nandan, *China* 58 E6
Nandan, *Japan* 55 G7
Nanded, *India* 66 K10
Nandewar Ra., *Australia* 95 E5
Nandi = Nadi, *Fiji* 91 C7
Nandigram, *India* 69 H12
Nandurbar, *India* 66 J9
Nandyal, *India* 66 M11
Nanfeng, Jiangxi, *China* 59 D11
Nanfeng, Guangdong, *China* . 59 F8
Nang Rong, *Thailand* 64 E4
Nanga-Eboko, *Cameroon* 83 E7
Nanga Parbat, *Pakistan* 69 B6
Nangade, *Mozam.* 87 E4
Nangapinoh, *Indonesia* 62 E4
Nangarhār □, *Afghan.* 66 B7

Nangatayap, *Indonesia* 62 E4
Nangeya Mts., *Uganda* 86 B3
Nangis, *France* 19 D10
Nangong, *China* 56 F8
Nanhua, *China* 58 E3
Nanhuang, *China* 57 F11
Nanhui, *China* 59 B13
Nanjeko, *Zambia* 87 F1
Nanji Shan, *China* 59 D13
Nanjian, *China* 58 E3
Nanjiang, *China* 58 A6
Nanjing, Fujian, *China* 59 E11
Nanjing, Jiangsu, *China* 59 A12
Nanjirinji, *Tanzania* 87 D4
Nankana Sahib, *Pakistan* 68 D5
Nankang, *China* 59 E10
Nanking = Nanjing, *China* ... 59 A12
Nankoku, *Japan* 55 H6
Nanling, *China* 59 B12
Nanning, *China* 58 F7
Nannup, *Australia* 93 F2
Nanpan Jiang ➤, *China* 58 E6
Nanpara, *India* 69 F9
Nanpi, *China* 56 E9
Nanping, Fujian, *China* 59 D12
Nanping, Henan, *China* 59 C9
Nanri Dao, *China* 59 E12
Nanripe, *Mozam.* 87 E4
Nansei-Shotō = Ryūkyū-rettō, *Japan* 55 M3
Nansen Basin, *Arctic* 4 A10
Nansen Cordillera, *Arctic* .... 4 A
Nansen Sd., *Canada* 4 A3
Nanshan I., S. *China Sea* 62 B5
Nansio, *Tanzania* 86 C3
Nant, *France* 20 D7
Nanterre, *France* 19 D9
Nantes, *France* 18 E5
Nantiat, *France* 20 B5
Nanticoke, *U.S.A.* 117 E8
Nanton, *Canada* 102 C6
Nantong, *China* 59 A13
Nantou, *Taiwan* 59 F13
Nantua, *France* 19 F12
Nantucket I., *U.S.A.* 114 E10
Nantwich, *U.K.* 14 D5
Nanty Glo, *U.S.A.* 116 F6
Nanuque, *Brazil* 125 G10
Nanusa, Kepulauan, *Indonesia* 63 D7
Nanutarra Roadhouse, *Australia* 92 D2
Nanxi, *China* 58 C5
Nanxiong, *China* 59 E10
Nanyang, *China* 56 H7
Nanyi Hu, *China* 59 B12
Nanyuki, *Kenya* 86 B4
Nanzhang, *China* 59 B8
Nao, C. de la, *Spain* 39 G5
Naococane, L., *Canada* 105 B5
Náousa, Imathía, *Greece* 44 F6
Náousa, Kikládhes, *Greece* ... 47 D7
Naozhou Dao, *China* 59 G8
Napa, *U.S.A.* 110 G4
Napa ➤, *U.S.A.* 110 G4
Napanee, *Canada* 116 B8
Napanoch, *U.S.A.* 117 E10
Nape, *Laos* 64 C5
Nape Pass = Keo Neua, Deo, *Vietnam* 64 C5
Napier, *N.Z.* 91 H6
Napier Broome B., *Australia* .. 92 B4
Napier Pen., *Australia* 94 A2
Napierville, *Canada* 117 A11
Naples = Nápoli, *Italy* 43 B7
Naples, *U.S.A.* 115 M5
Napo, *China* 58 F5
Napo ➤, *Peru* 124 D4
Napoleon, N. Dak., *U.S.A.* ... 112 B5
Napoleon, Ohio, *U.S.A.* 114 E3
Nápoli, *Italy* 43 B7
Nápoli, G. di, *Italy* 43 B7
Nápoli Capodichino ✈ (NAP), *Italy* 43 B7
Napopo, Dem. Rep. of the Congo 86 B2
Naqâda, *Egypt* 80 B3
Naqadeh, *Iran* 73 D11
Naqb, Ra's an, *Jordan* 74 F4
Naqqāsh, *Iran* 71 C6
Nara, *Japan* 55 G7
Nara, *Mali* 82 B3
Nara □, *Japan* 55 G8
Nara Canal, *Pakistan* 68 G3
Nara Visa, *U.S.A.* 113 H3
Naracoorte, *Australia* 95 F3
Naradhan, *Australia* 95 E4
Naraini, *India* 69 G9
Narasapur, *India* 67 L12
Narathiwat, *Thailand* 65 J3
Narayanganj, *Bangla.* 67 H17
Narayanpet, *India* 66 L10
Narberth, *U.K.* 15 F3
Narbonne, *France* 20 E7
Narcea ➤, *Spain* 36 B4
Nardin, *Iran* 71 B7
Nardò, *Italy* 43 B11
Narembeen, *Australia* 93 F2
Narendranagar, *India* 68 D8
Nares Str., *Arctic* 98 A13
Naretha, *Australia* 93 F3
Narew ➤, *Poland* 31 F7
Nari ➤, *Pakistan* 68 F2
Narin, *Afghan.* 66 A6
Narindra, Helodranon' i, *Madag.* 89 A8
Narita, *Japan* 55 G10
Nariva Swamp, Trin. & Tob. .. 125 K15
Närke, *Sweden* 10 E8
Narmada ➤, *India* 68 J5
Narman, *Turkey* 73 B9
Narmland, *Sweden* 9 F15
Narnaul, *India* 68 E7
Narni, *Italy* 41 F9
Naro, *Ghana* 82 C4
Naro Fominsk, *Russia* 32 E9

Narodnaya, *Russia* 6 B17
Narok, *Kenya* 86 C4
Narón, *Spain* 36 B2
Narooma, *Australia* 95 F5
Narowal, *Pakistan* 68 C6
Narrabri, *Australia* 95 E4
Narran ➤, *Australia* 95 D4
Narrandera, *Australia* 95 E4
Narrogin, *Australia* 93 F2
Narromine, *Australia* 95 E4
Narrow Hills △, *Canada* 103 C8
Narsimhapur, *India* 69 H8
Narsinghgarh, *India* 68 H7
Nartes, L. e, *Albania* 44 F3
Nartkala, *Russia* 35 J6
Naruto, *Japan* 55 G7
Narva, *Estonia* 32 C5
Narva ➤, *Russia* 9 G22
Narva Bay = Narva Laht, *Estonia* 9 G19
Narva Laht, *Estonia* 9 G19
Narvik, *Norway* 8 B17
Narvskoye Vdkhr., *Russia* ... 32 C5
Narwana, *India* 68 E7
Narwiański △, *Poland* 31 F9
Naryan-Mar, *Russia* 52 C6
Narym, *Russia* 52 D9
Naryn, *Kyrgyzstan* 52 E8
Nasa, *Norway* 8 C16
Năsăud, *Romania* 29 C9
Naseby, *N.Z.* 91 L3
Naselle, *U.S.A.* 110 D3
Naser, Buheirat en, *Egypt* ... 80 C3
Nashua, Mont., *U.S.A.* 108 B10
Nashua, N.H., *U.S.A.* 117 D13
Nashville, Ark., *U.S.A.* 113 J8
Nashville, Ga., *U.S.A.* 115 K4
Nashville, Tenn., *U.S.A.* 115 G2
Našice, *Croatia* 28 E3
Nasielsk, *Poland* 31 F7
Nasik, *India* 66 K8
Nasipit, *Phil.* 61 G6
Nasir, *Sudan* 81 F3
Nasirabad, *India* 68 F6
Nasirabad, *Pakistan* 68 E3
Nasīrīyah = An Nāşirīyah, *Iraq* 70 D5
Naskaupi ➤, *Canada* 105 B7
Naso, *Italy* 43 D7
Nasratabad, *Iran* 71 C6
Naşrīān-e Pā'īn, *Iran* 70 C5
Nass ➤, *Canada* 102 C3
Nassarawa, *Nigeria* 83 D6
Nassarawa □, *Nigeria* 83 D6
Nassau, *Bahamas* 120 A4
Nassau, *U.S.A.* 117 D11
Nassau, B., *Chile* 128 H3
Nasser, L. = Naser, Buheirat en, *Egypt* 80 C3
Nassian, Ivory C. 82 D4
Nässjö, *Sweden* 11 G8
Nastapoka ➤, *Canada* 104 A4
Nastapoka, Is., *Canada* 104 A4
Nasugbu, *Phil.* 61 D4
Näsum, *Sweden* 11 H8
Näsviken, *Sweden* 10 C10
Nata, *Botswana* 88 C4
Nata ➤, *Botswana* 88 C4
Natal, *Brazil* 125 E11
Natal, *Indonesia* 62 D1
Natal, S. *Africa* 85 K6
Natal Drakensberg △, S. *Africa* 89 D4
Natalinci, Serbia & M. 28 F5
Natanz, *Iran* 71 C6
Natashquan, *Canada* 105 B7
Natashquan ➤, *Canada* 105 B7
Natchez, *U.S.A.* 113 K9
Natchitoches, *U.S.A.* 113 K8
Nathalia, *Australia* 95 F4
Nathdwara, *India* 68 G5
Nati, Pta., *Spain* 48 A10
Natimuk, *Australia* 95 F3
Nation ➤, *Canada* 102 B4
National City, *U.S.A.* 111 N9
Natitingou, *Benin* 83 C5
Natividad, I., *Mexico* 118 B1
Natkyizin, *Burma* 64 E1
Natron, L., *Tanzania* 86 C4
Natrona Heights, *U.S.A.* 116 F5
Natrûn, W. el ➤, *Egypt* 80 H7
Nättraby, *Sweden* 11 H9
Natukanaoka Pan, *Namibia* .. 88 B2
Natuna Besar, Kepulauan, *Indonesia* 62 D3
Natuna Is. = Natuna Besar, Kepulauan, *Indonesia* 62 D3
Natuna Selatan, Kepulauan, *Indonesia* 62 D3
Natural Bridge, *U.S.A.* 117 B9
Natural Bridges △, *U.S.A.* ... 109 H8
Naturaliste, C., *Australia* 95 G4
Nau Qala, *Afghan.* 68 B3
Naucelle, *France* 20 D6
Nauders, *Austria* 26 E3
Nauen, *Germany* 24 C8
Naugatuck, *U.S.A.* 117 E11
Naujaat = Repulse Bay, *Canada* 101 B11
Naujoji Akmenė, *Lithuania* .. 30 B9
Naumburg, *Germany* 24 D7
Nā'ūr at Tunayb, *Jordan* 74 D4
Nauru ■, Pac. Oc. 96 H8
Naushahra = Nowshera, *Pakistan* 66 C8
Naushahro, *Pakistan* 68 F3
Naushon I., *U.S.A.* 117 E14
Nauta, *Peru* 124 D4
Nautanwa, *India* 67 F13
Nautla, *Mexico* 119 C5
Nava, *Mexico* 118 B4
Nava del Rey, *Spain* 36 D5
Navadwip, *India* 69 H13
Navahermosa, *Spain* 37 F6
Navahrudak, *Belarus* 32 F3

Navajo Reservoir, *U.S.A.* **109 H10**
Navalcarnero, *Spain* **36 E6**
Navalmoral de la Mata, *Spain* .. **36 F5**
Navalvillar de Pela, *Spain* **37 F5**
Navan = An Uaimh, *Ireland* **12 C5**
Navapolatsk, *Belarus* **32 E5**
Navarin, Mys, *Russia* **4 C16**
Navarino, I., *Chile* **128 H3**
Navarra □, *Spain* **38 C3**
Navarre, *U.S.A.* **116 F3**
Navarro ➤, *U.S.A.* **110 F3**
Navas de San Juan, *Spain* **37 G7**
Navasota, *U.S.A.* **113 K6**
Navassa I., *W. Indies* **121 C5**
Nävekvarn, *Sweden* **11 F10**
Naver ➤, *U.K.* **13 C4**
Navia, *Spain* **36 B4**
Navia ➤, *Spain* **36 B4**
Navia de Suarna, *Spain* **36 C3**
Navibandar, *India* **68 J3**
Navidad, *Chile* **126 C1**
Naviraí, *Brazil* **127 A5**
Navlakhi, *India* **68 H4**
Navlya, *Russia* **33 F8**
Năvodari, *Romania* **29 F13**
Navoi = Nawoiy, *Uzbekistan* .. **52 E7**
Navojoa, *Mexico* **118 B3**
Navolato, *Mexico* **118 C3**
Návpaktos, *Greece* **46 C3**
Návplion, *Greece* **46 D4**
Navrongo, *Ghana* **83 C4**
Navsari, *India* **66 J8**
Nawa Kot, *Pakistan* **68 E4**
Nawab Khan, *Pakistan* **68 D3**
Nawabganj, *Ut. P., India* **69 F9**
Nawabganj, *Ut. P., India* **69 E8**
Nawabshah, *Pakistan* **68 F3**
Nawada, *India* **69 G11**
Nawakot, *Nepal* **69 F11**
Nawalgarh, *India* **68 F6**
Nawanshahr, *India* **69 C6**
Nawar, Dasht-i-, *Afghan.* **68 C3**
Nawi, *Sudan* **80 D3**
Nawoiy, *Uzbekistan* **52 E7**
Naxçıvan, *Azerbaijan* **70 B5**
Naxçıvan □, *Azerbaijan* **52 F5**
Náxos, *Greece* **47 D7**
Nay, *France* **20 E3**
Nay, Mui, *Vietnam* **62 B3**
Nāy Band, *Būshehr, Iran* **71 E7**
Nāy Band, *Khorāsān, Iran* **71 C8**
Nayakhan, *Russia* **53 C16**
Nayarit □, *Mexico* **118 C4**
Nayé, *Senegal* **82 C2**
Nayong, *China* **58 D5**
Nayoro, *Japan* **54 B11**
Nayyāl, W. ➤, *Si. Arabia* **70 D3**
Nazaré, *Brazil* **125 F11**
Nazaré, *Portugal* **37 F1**
Nazareth = Nazerat, *Israel* **74 C4**
Nazareth, *U.S.A.* **117 F9**
Nazas, *Mexico* **118 B4**
Nazas ➤, *Mexico* **118 B4**
Nazca, *Peru* **124 F4**
Naze, The, *U.K.* **15 F9**
Nazerat, *Israel* **74 C4**
Nāzik, *Iran* **70 B5**
Nazilli, *Turkey* **47 D10**
Nazko, *Canada* **102 C4**
Nazko ➤, *Canada* **102 C4**
Nazret, *Ethiopia* **81 F4**
Nazwa, *Oman* **75 C6**
Nchanga, *Zambia* **87 E2**
Ncheu, *Malawi* **87 E3**
Ndala, *Tanzania* **86 C3**
Ndalatando, *Angola* **84 F2**
Ndali, *Benin* **83 D5**
Ndareda, *Tanzania* **86 C4**
Ndélé, *C.A.R.* **84 C4**
Ndiael ➤, *Senegal* **82 B1**
Ndikinimeki, *Cameroon* **83 E7**
N'Dioum, *Senegal* **82 B2**
Ndjamena, *Chad* **79 F8**
Ndola, *Zambia* **87 E2**
Ndoto Mts., *Kenya* **86 B4**
Nduguti, *Tanzania* **86 C3**
Ndumo △, *S. Africa* **89 D5**
Néa Alikarnassós, *Greece* **47 F7**
Néa Ankhíalos, *Greece* **46 B4**
Néa Epídhavros, *Greece* **46 D5**
Néa Flippiás, *Greece* **46 B2**
Néa Ionía, *Greece* **46 B4**
Néa Kallikrátia, *Greece* **44 F7**
Néa Mákri, *Greece* **46 C5**
Néa Moudhaniá, *Greece* **44 F7**
Néa Péramos, *Attikí, Greece* .. **46 C5**
Néa Péramos, *Kaválla, Greece* .. **45 F8**
Néa Víssi, *Greece* **45 E10**
Néa Zíkhna, *Greece* **44 E7**
Neagh, Lough, *U.K.* **12 B5**
Neah Bay, *U.S.A.* **110 B2**
Neale, L., *Australia* **92 D5**
Neales, The ➤, *Australia* **95 D2**
Neamţ □, *Romania* **29 C11**
Neápolis, *Kozáni, Greece* **44 F5**
Neápolis,
  Aitolía kai Akarnanía, Greece . **46 C3**
Neápolis, *Kríti, Greece* **49 D7**
Neápolis, *Lakonía, Greece* **46 E5**
Near Is., *U.S.A.* **100 C1**
Neath, *U.K.* **15 F4**
Neath Port Talbot □, *U.K.* **15 F4**
Nebbou, *Burkina Faso* **83 C4**
Nebelat el Hagana, *Sudan* **81 E2**
Nebine Cr. ➤, *Australia* **95 D4**
Nebitdag, *Turkmenistan* **52 F6**
Nebo, *Australia* **94 C4**
Nebolchy, *Russia* **32 C7**
Nebraska □, *U.S.A.* **112 E5**
Nebraska City, *U.S.A.* **112 E7**
Nébrodi, Monti, *Italy* **43 E7**
Necedah, *U.S.A.* **112 C9**
Nechako ➤, *Canada* **102 C4**
Neches ➤, *U.S.A.* **113 L8**

Nechisar △, *Ethiopia* **81 F4**
Neckar ➤, *Germany* **25 F4**
Neckartal-Odenwald △, *Germany* **25 F5**
Necochea, *Argentina* **126 D4**
Neda, *Spain* **36 B2**
Nedelino, *Bulgaria* **45 E9**
Nedelišće, *Croatia* **41 B13**
Nédha ➤, *Greece* **46 D3**
Nedoboyivtsi, *Ukraine* **29 B11**
Needles, *Canada* **102 D5**
Needles, *U.S.A.* **111 L12**
Needles, The, *U.K.* **15 G6**
Ñeembucú □, *Paraguay* **126 B4**
Neemuch = Nimach, *India* **68 G6**
Neenah, *U.S.A.* **114 C1**
Neepawa, *Canada* **103 C9**
Neftçala, *Azerbaijan* **71 B6**
Neftegorsk, *Russia* **35 H4**
Neftekumsk, *Russia* **35 H7**
Nefyn, *U.K.* **14 E3**
Négala, *Mali* **82 C3**
Negapatam = Nagappattinam,
  India **66 P11**
Negara, *Indonesia* **63 J17**
Negaunee, *U.S.A.* **114 B2**
Negele, *Ethiopia* **81 F4**
Negev Desert = Hanegev, *Israel* . **74 E4**
Negoiul, Vf., *Romania* **29 E9**
Negombo, *Sri Lanka* **66 R11**
Negotin, *Serbia & M.* **44 B6**
Negotino, *Macedonia* **44 E6**
Negra, Peña, *Spain* **36 C4**
Negra, Pta., *Peru* **124 E2**
Negrais, C. = Maudin Sun, *Burma* **67 M19**
Negreşti, *Romania* **29 D12**
Negreşti-Oaş, *Romania* **29 C8**
Negril, *Jamaica* .... **120 a**
Negro ➤, *Argentina* **128 E4**
Negro ➤, *Brazil* **124 D7**
Negro ➤, *Uruguay* **127 C4**
Negros, *Phil.* **61 G5**
Negru Vodă, *Romania* **29 G13**
Neguac, *Canada* **105 C6**
Nehalem ➤, *U.S.A.* **110 E3**
Nehāvand, *Iran* **71 C6**
Nehbandān, *Iran* **71 D9**
Nehoiu, *Romania* **29 E11**
Nei Monggol Zizhiqu □, *China* .. **56 D7**
Neijiang, *China* **58 C5**
Neillsville, *U.S.A.* **112 C9**
Neilton, *U.S.A.* **108 C2**
Neiqiu, *China* **56 F8**
Neiva, *Colombia* **124 C3**
Neixiang, *China* **56 H6**
Nejanilini L., *Canada* **103 B9**
Nejd = Najd, *Si. Arabia* **75 B3**
Nejo, *Ethiopia* **81 F4**
Nekā, *Iran* **71 B7**
Nekemte, *Ethiopia* **81 F4**
Nêkheb, *Egypt* **80 B3**
Neksø, *Denmark* **11 J9**
Nelas, *Portugal* **36 E3**
Nelia, *Australia* **94 C3**
Nelidovo, *Russia* **32 D7**
Neligh, *U.S.A.* **112 D5**
Nelkan, *Russia* **53 D14**
Nellore, *India* **66 M11**
Nelson, *Canada* **102 D5**
Nelson, *N.Z.* **91 J4**
Nelson, *U.K.* **14 D5**
Nelson, *Ariz., U.S.A.* **109 J7**
Nelson, *Nev., U.S.A.* **111 K12**
Nelson ➤, *Canada* **103 C9**
Nelson, C., *Australia* **95 F3**
Nelson, Estrecho, *Chile* **128 G2**
Nelson Forks, *Canada* **102 B4**
Nelson House, *Canada* **103 B9**
Nelson L., *Canada* **103 B8**
Nelson Lakes △, *N.Z.* **91 J4**
Nelspoort, *S. Africa* **88 E3**
Nelspruit, *S. Africa* **89 D5**
Néma, *Mauritania* **82 B3**
Neman = Nemunas ➤, *Lithuania* **9 J19**
Neman, *Russia* **9 J20**
Neméa, *Greece* **46 D4**
Nemeiben L., *Canada* **103 B7**
Nemërçkë, Mal, *Albania* **44 F4**
Nemira, Vf., *Romania* **29 D11**
Nemiscau, *Canada* **104 B4**
Nemiscau, L., *Canada* **104 B4**
Nemours, *France* **19 D9**
Nemšová, *Slovak Rep.* **27 C11**
Nemunas ➤, *Lithuania* **9 J19**
Nemuro, *Japan* **54 C12**
Nemuro-Kaikyō, *Japan* **54 C12**
Nemyriv, *Ukraine* **31 H10**
Nenagh, *Ireland* **12 D3**
Nenasi, *Malaysia* **65 L4**
Nene ➤, *U.K.* **15 E8**
Nénita, *Greece* **47 C8**
Nenjiang, *China* **60 B7**
Neno, *Malawi* **87 F3**
Neodesha, *U.S.A.* **113 G7**
Neokhórion,
  Aitolía kai Akarnanía, Greece . **46 C3**
Neokhórion, *Árta, Greece* **46 B2**
Néon Karlovásion, *Greece* **47 D8**
Néon Petrítsi, *Greece* **44 E7**
Neosho, *U.S.A.* **113 G7**
Neosho ➤, *U.S.A.* **113 H7**
Nepal ■, *Asia* **69 F11**
Nepalganj, *Nepal* **69 E9**
Nepalganj Road, *India* **69 E9**
Nephi, *U.S.A.* **108 G8**
Nephin, *Ireland* **12 B2**
Nepi, *Italy* **41 F9**
Nepomuk, *Czech Rep.* **26 B6**
Neptune, *U.S.A.* **117 F10**
Nera ➤, *Italy* **41 F9**
Nera ➤, *Romania* **28 F6**
Nérac, *France* **20 D4**

Nerang, *Australia* **95 D5**
Neratovice, *Czech Rep.* **26 A7**
Nerchinsk, *Russia* **53 D12**
Nereju, *Romania* **29 E11**
Nerekhta, *Russia* **32 D11**
Néret, L., *Canada* **105 B5**
Neretvanski Kanal, *Croatia* .. **41 E14**
Neringa, *Lithuania* **9 J19**
Neris ➤, *Lithuania* **9 J21**
Nerja, *Spain* **37 J7**
Nerl ➤, *Russia* **32 D11**
Nerpio, *Spain* **39 G2**
Nerva, *Spain* **37 H4**
Nervi, *Italy* **40 D6**
Neryungri, *Russia* **53 D13**
Nescopeck, *U.S.A.* **117 E8**
Nesebŭr, *Bulgaria* **45 D11**
Ness, L., *U.K.* **13 D4**
Ness City, *U.S.A.* **112 F5**
Nesterov, *Russia* **30 D9**
Nesterov, *Ukraine* **33 G2**
Nestórion, *Greece* **44 F5**
Néstos ➤, *Greece* **45 E8**
Nesvady, *Slovak Rep.* **27 D11**
Nesvizh = Nyasvizh, *Belarus* .. **33 F4**
Netanya, *Israel* **74 C3**
Netarhat, *India* **69 H11**
Nete ➤, *Belgium* **17 C4**
Netherdale, *Australia* **94 K6**
Netherlands ■, *Europe* **17 C5**
Netherlands Antilles ☑, *W. Indies* **124 A5**
Neto ➤, *Italy* **43 C10**
Netrang, *India* **68 J5**
Nettancourt, *France* **19 D11**
Nettetal, *Germany* **24 C2**
Nettilling L., *Canada* **101 B12**
Nettuno, *Italy* **42 A5**
Netzahualcoyotl, Presa, *Mexico* . **119 D6**
Neu-Isenburg, *Germany* **25 E4**
Neu-Ulm, *Germany* **25 G6**
Neubrandenburg, *Germany* .. **24 B9**
Neubukow, *Germany* **24 A7**
Neuburg, *Germany* **25 G7**
Neuchâtel, *Switz.* **25 J2**
Neuchâtel □, *Switz.* **25 J2**
Neuchâtel, Lac de, *Switz.* **25 J2**
Neudau, *Austria* **26 D9**
Neuenhagen, *Germany* **24 C9**
Neuenhaus, *Germany* **24 C2**
Neuf-Brisach, *France* **19 D14**
Neufahrn, *Bayern, Germany* .. **25 G8**
Neufahrn, *Bayern, Germany* .. **25 G7**
Neufchâteau, *Belgium* **17 E5**
Neufchâteau, *France* **19 D12**
Neufchâtel-en-Bray, *France* **18 C8**
Neufchâtel-sur-Aisne, *France* .. **19 C11**
Neuhaus, *Germany* **24 B6**
Neuillé-Pont-Pierre, *France* **18 E7**
Neuilly-St-Front, *France* **19 C10**
Neukalen, *Germany* **24 B8**
Neumarkt, *Germany* **25 F7**
Neumünster, *Germany* **24 A5**
Neung-sur-Beuvron, *France* .. **19 E8**
Neunkirchen, *Austria* **26 D9**
Neunkirchen, *Germany* **25 F3**
Neuquén, *Argentina* **128 D3**
Neuquén □, *Argentina* **126 D2**
Neuruppin, *Germany* **24 C8**
Neusäss, *Germany* **25 G6**
Neuse ➤, *U.S.A.* **115 H7**
Neusiedl, *Austria* **27 D9**
Neusiedler See, *Austria* **27 D9**
Neusiedler See-Seewinkel △,
  Austria **27 D9**
Neuss, *Germany* **24 D2**
Neussargues-Moissac, *France* .. **20 C7**
Neustadt, *Bayern, Germany* .. **25 F8**
Neustadt, *Bayern, Germany* .. **25 G7**
Neustadt, *Bayern, Germany* .. **25 E7**
Neustadt, *Brandenburg, Germany* **24 C8**
Neustadt, *Hessen, Germany* .. **24 E5**
Neustadt, *Niedersachsen,
  Germany* **24 C5**
Neustadt, *Rhld.-Pfz., Germany* .. **25 F4**
Neustadt, *Sachsen, Germany* .. **24 D10**
Neustadt, *Schleswig-Holstein,
  Germany* **24 A6**
Neustadt, *Thüringen, Germany* .. **24 E7**
Neustrelitz, *Germany* **24 B9**
Neuvic, *France* **20 C6**
Neuville-sur-Saône, *France* .. **21 C8**
Neuvy-le-Roi, *France* **18 E7**
Neuvy-St-Sépulchre, *France* **19 F8**
Neuvy-sur-Barangeon, *France* .. **19 E9**
Neuwerk, *Germany* **24 B4**
Neuwied, *Germany* **24 E3**
Neva ➤, *Russia* **32 C6**
Nevada, *Iowa, U.S.A.* **112 D8**
Nevada, *Mo., U.S.A.* **113 G7**
Nevada □, *U.S.A.* **108 G5**
Nevada City, *U.S.A.* **110 F6**
Nevado, Cerro, *Argentina* **126 D2**
Nevado de Colima = Volcán de
  Colima △, *Mexico* **118 D4**
Nevado de Tres Cruces △, *Chile* **126 B2**
Nevel, *Russia* **32 D5**
Nevertire, *Australia* **95 E4**
Neville, *Canada* **103 D7**
Nevinnomyssk, *Russia* **35 H6**
Nevis, *St. Kitts & Nevis* **121 C7**
Nevrokop = Gotse Delchev,
  Bulgaria **44 E7**
Nevşehir, *Turkey* **70 B2**
Nevskoye, *Russia* **30 D9**
New ➤, *U.S.A.* **114 F5**
New Aiyansh, *Canada* **102 B3**
New Albany, *Ind., U.S.A.* **114 F3**
New Albany, *Miss., U.S.A.* **113 H10**

New Albany, *Pa., U.S.A.* **117 E8**
New Amsterdam, *Guyana* **124 B7**
New Angledool, *Australia* **95 D4**
New Baltimore, *U.S.A.* **116 D2**
New Bedford, *U.S.A.* **117 E14**
New Berlin, *N.Y., U.S.A.* **117 D9**
New Berlin, *Pa., U.S.A.* **116 F8**
New Bern, *U.S.A.* **115 H7**
New Bethlehem, *U.S.A.* **116 F5**
New Bloomfield, *U.S.A.* **116 F7**
New Boston, *U.S.A.* **113 J7**
New Braunfels, *U.S.A.* **113 L5**
New Brighton, *N.Z.* **91 K4**
New Brighton, *U.S.A.* **116 F4**
New Britain, *Papua N. G.* **96 H7**
New Britain, *U.S.A.* **117 E12**
New Brunswick, *U.S.A.* **117 F10**
New Brunswick □, *Canada* **105 C6**
New Bussa, *Nigeria* **83 D5**
New Caledonia ☑, *Pac. Oc.* .. **96 K8**
New Castle = Castilla-La
  Mancha □, *Spain* **6 H5**
New Castle, *Ind., U.S.A.* **114 F3**
New Castle, *Pa., U.S.A.* **116 F4**
New City, *U.S.A.* **117 E11**
New Concord, *U.S.A.* **116 G3**
New Cumberland, *U.S.A.* **116 F4**
New Cuyama, *U.S.A.* **111 L7**
New Delhi, *India* **68 E7**
New Denver, *Canada* **102 D5**
New Don Pedro Reservoir, *U.S.A.* **110 H6**
New England, *U.S.A.* **107 B12**
New England, *N. Dak., U.S.A.* .. **112 B3**
New England Ra. △, *Australia* .. **95 E5**
New Forest △, *U.K.* **15 G6**
New Galloway, *U.K.* **13 F4**
New Glasgow, *Canada* **105 C7**
New Guinea, *Oceania* **96 H5**
New Hamburg, *Canada* **116 C4**
New Hampshire □, *U.S.A.* **117 C13**
New Hanover, *S. Africa* **89 D5**
New Hartford, *U.S.A.* **117 C9**
New Haven, *Conn., U.S.A.* **117 E12**
New Haven, *Mich., U.S.A.* **116 D2**
New Hazelton, *Canada* **102 B3**
New Hebrides = Vanuatu ■,
  Pac. Oc. **96 J8**
New Holland, *U.S.A.* **117 F8**
New Iberia, *U.S.A.* **113 K9**
New Ireland, *Papua N. G.* **96 H7**
New Jersey □, *U.S.A.* **114 E8**
New Kensington, *U.S.A.* **116 F5**
New Lexington, *U.S.A.* **114 F4**
New Liskeard, *Canada* **104 C4**
New London, *Conn., U.S.A.* .. **117 E12**
New London, *Ohio, U.S.A.* .. **116 E2**
New London, *Wis., U.S.A.* .. **112 C10**
New Madrid, *U.S.A.* **113 G10**
New Martinsville, *U.S.A.* **114 F5**
New Meadows, *U.S.A.* **108 D5**
New Melones L., *U.S.A.* **110 H6**
New Mexico □, *U.S.A.* **109 J10**
New Milford, *Conn., U.S.A.* .. **117 E11**
New Milford, *Pa., U.S.A.* **117 E9**
New Norcia, *Australia* **93 F2**
New Norfolk, *Australia* **95 G4**
New Orleans, *U.S.A.* **113 L9**
New Philadelphia, *U.S.A.* **116 F3**
New Plymouth, *N.Z.* **91 H5**
New Plymouth, *U.S.A.* **108 E5**
New Port Richey, *U.S.A.* **115 L4**
New Providence, *Bahamas* **120 A4**
New Quay, *U.K.* **15 E3**
New Radnor, *U.K.* **15 E4**
New Richmond, *Canada* **105 C6**
New Richmond, *U.S.A.* **112 C8**
New River Gorge △, *U.S.A.* .. **114 G5**
New Roads, *U.S.A.* **113 K9**
New Rochelle, *U.S.A.* **117 F11**
New Rockford, *U.S.A.* **112 B5**
New Romney, *U.K.* **15 G8**
New Ross, *Ireland* **12 D5**
New Salem, *U.S.A.* **112 B4**
New Scone = Scone, *U.K.* **13 E5**
New Siberian I. = Novaya Sibir,
  Ostrov, *Russia* **53 B16**
New Siberian Is. = Novosibirskiye
  Ostrova, *Russia* **53 B15**
New Smyrna Beach, *U.S.A.* .. **115 L5**
New South Wales □, *Australia* .. **95 E4**
New Tecumseth, *Canada* **116 B5**
New Town, *U.S.A.* **112 B3**
New Tredegar, *U.K.* **15 F4**
New Ulm, *U.S.A.* **112 C7**
New Waterford, *Canada* **105 C7**
New-Wes-Valley, *Canada* **105 C9**
New Westminster, *Canada* **110 A4**
New York, *U.S.A.* **117 F11**
New York □, *U.S.A.* **117 D9**
New York J.F. Kennedy
  International ✈ (JFK), *U.S.A.* **117 F11**
New York Mts. △, *U.S.A.* **109 J6**
New Zealand ■, *Oceania* **91 J6**
Newaj ➤, *India* **68 G7**
Newala, *Tanzania* **87 E4**
Newark, *Del., U.S.A.* **114 F8**
Newark, *N.J., U.S.A.* **117 F10**
Newark, *N.Y., U.S.A.* **116 C7**
Newark, *Ohio, U.S.A.* **116 F2**
Newark International ✈ (EWR),
  U.S.A. **117 F10**
Newark-on-Trent, *U.K.* **14 D7**
Newark Valley, *U.S.A.* **117 D8**
Newberg, *U.S.A.* **108 D2**
Newberry, *Mich., U.S.A.* **113 B3**
Newberry, *S.C., U.S.A.* **115 H5**
Newberry □, *U.S.A.* **108 L2**
Newberry Springs, *U.S.A.* **111 L10**

Newburgh, *Canada* **116 B8**
Newburgh, *U.S.A.* **117 E10**
Newbury, *U.K.* **15 F6**
Newbury, *N.H., U.S.A.* **117 B12**
Newbury, *Vt., U.S.A.* **117 B12**
Newburyport, *U.S.A.* **115 D10**
Newcastle, *Australia* **95 E5**
Newcastle, *N.B., Canada* **105 C6**
Newcastle, *Ont., Canada* **104 D4**
Newcastle, *S. Africa* **89 D4**
Newcastle, *U.K.* **12 B6**
Newcastle, *Calif., U.S.A.* **110 G5**
Newcastle, *Wyo., U.S.A.* **112 D2**
Newcastle Emlyn, *U.K.* **15 E3**
Newcastle Ra. △, *Australia* **92 C5**
Newcastle-under-Lyme, *U.K.* .. **14 D5**
Newcastle-upon-Tyne, *U.K.* .. **14 C6**
Newcastle Waters, *Australia* .. **94 B1**
Newcastle West, *Ireland* **12 D2**
Newcomb, *U.S.A.* **117 C10**
Newcomerstown, *U.S.A.* **116 F3**
Newdegate, *Australia* **93 F2**
Newell, *Australia* **94 B4**
Newell, *U.S.A.* **112 C3**
Newfane, *U.S.A.* **116 C6**
Newfield, *U.S.A.* **117 D8**
Newfound L., *U.S.A.* **117 C13**
Newfoundland, *Canada* **105 C8**
Newfoundland, *U.S.A.* **117 E9**
Newfoundland & Labrador □,
  Canada **105 B8**
Newhall, *U.S.A.* **111 L8**
Newhaven, *U.K.* **15 G8**
Newkirk, *U.S.A.* **113 G6**
Newlyn, *U.K.* **15 G2**
Newman, *Australia* **92 D2**
Newman, *U.S.A.* **110 H5**
Newmarket, *Canada* **116 B5**
Newmarket, *Ireland* **12 D3**
Newmarket, *U.K.* **15 E8**
Newmarket, *U.S.A.* **117 C14**
Newnan, *U.S.A.* **115 J3**
Newport, *Ireland* **12 C2**
Newport, *I. of W., U.K.* **15 G6**
Newport, *Newp., U.K.* **15 F5**
Newport, *Ark., U.S.A.* **113 H9**
Newport, *Ky., U.S.A.* **114 F3**
Newport, *N.H., U.S.A.* **117 C12**
Newport, *N.Y., U.S.A.* **117 C9**
Newport, *Oreg., U.S.A.* **108 D1**
Newport, *Pa., U.S.A.* **116 F7**
Newport, *R.I., U.S.A.* **117 E13**
Newport, *Tenn., U.S.A.* **115 H4**
Newport, *Vt., U.S.A.* **117 B12**
Newport, *Wash., U.S.A.* **108 B5**
Newport □, *U.K.* **15 F4**
Newport Beach, *U.S.A.* **111 M9**
Newport News, *U.S.A.* **114 G7**
Newport Pagnell, *U.K.* **15 E7**
Newquay, *U.K.* **15 G2**
Newry, *U.K.* **12 B5**
Newton, *Ill., U.S.A.* **112 F10**
Newton, *Iowa, U.S.A.* **112 E8**
Newton, *Kans., U.S.A.* **113 F6**
Newton, *Mass., U.S.A.* **117 D13**
Newton, *Miss., U.S.A.* **113 J10**
Newton, *N.C., U.S.A.* **115 H5**
Newton, *N.J., U.S.A.* **117 E10**
Newton, *Tex., U.S.A.* **113 K8**
Newton Abbot, *U.K.* **15 G4**
Newton Aycliffe, *U.K.* **14 C6**
Newton Falls, *U.S.A.* **116 E4**
Newton Stewart, *U.K.* **13 G4**
Newtonmore, *U.K.* **13 D4**
Newtown, *U.K.* **15 E4**
Newtownabbey, *U.K.* **12 B6**
Newtownards, *U.K.* **12 B6**
Newtownbarry = Bunclody,
  Ireland **12 D5**
Newtownstewart, *U.K.* **12 B4**
Newville, *U.S.A.* **116 F7**
Nexon, *France* **20 C5**
Neya, *Russia* **34 A6**
Neyrīz, *Iran* **71 D7**
Neyshābūr, *Iran* **71 B8**
Nezhin = Nizhyn, *Ukraine* **33 G6**
Nezperce, *U.S.A.* **108 C5**
Nezvysko, *Ukraine* **29 B10**
Ngabang, *Indonesia* **62 D3**
Ngabordamlu, Tanjung, *Indonesia* **63 F8**
N'Gage, *Angola* **84 F3**
Ngala, *Nigeria* **83 C7**
Ngambé, *Centre, Cameroon* .. **83 D7**
Ngambé, *Littoral, Cameroon* .. **83 E7**
Ngami Depression, *Botswana* .. **88 C3**
Ngamo, *Zimbabwe* **87 F2**
Ngangala, *Sudan* **81 G3**
Nganglong Kangri, *China* **67 C12**
Ngao, *Thailand* **64 C2**
Ngaoundéré, *Cameroon* **84 C2**
Ngapara, *N.Z.* **91 L3**
Ngara, *Tanzania* **86 C3**
Ngawi, *Indonesia* **63 G14**
Nghia Lo, *Vietnam* **58 G5**
Ngobili, *Sudan* **81 G3**
Ngoma, *Malawi* **87 E3**
Ngomahura, *Zimbabwe* **87 G3**
Ngomba, *Tanzania* **87 D3**
Ngop, *Sudan* **81 F3**
Ngoring Hu, *China* **60 C4**
Ngorkou, *Mali* **82 B4**
Ngorongoro, *Tanzania* **86 C4**
Ngorongoro △, *Tanzania* **86 C4**
Ngozi, *Burundi* **86 C2**
Ngudu, *Tanzania* **86 C3**
Nguigmi, *Niger* **79 F8**
Nguila, *Cameroon* **83 E7**
Nguiu, *Australia* **92 B5**
Ngukurr, *Australia* **94 A1**
Ngunga, *Tanzania* **86 C3**
Nguru, *Nigeria* **83 C7**
Nguru Mts., *Tanzania* **86 D4**

Ngusi, Malawi ... 87 E3
Nguyen Binh, Vietnam ... 58 F5
Nha Trang, Vietnam ... 65 F7
Nhacoongo, Mozam. ... 89 C6
Nhamaabué, Mozam. ... 87 F4
Nhamundá →, Brazil ... 125 D7
Nhangulaze, L., Mozam. ... 89 C5
Nhill, Australia ... 95 F3
Nho Quan, Vietnam ... 58 G5
Nhulunbuy, Australia ... 94 A2
Nia-nia, Dem. Rep. of the Congo ... 86 B2
Niafounké, Mali ... 82 B4
Niagara Falls, Canada ... 116 C5
Niagara Falls, U.S.A. ... 116 C6
Niagara-on-the-Lake, Canada ... 116 C5
Niah, Malaysia ... 62 D4
Niamey, Niger ... 83 C5
Niandan-Koro, Guinea ... 82 C3
Nianforando, Guinea ... 82 D2
Niangara, Dem. Rep. of the Congo ... 86 B2
Niangbo, Ivory C. ... 82 D3
Niangoloko, Burkina Faso ... 82 C4
Niantic, U.S.A. ... 117 E12
Niaro, Sudan ... 81 E3
Nias, Indonesia ... 62 D1
Niassa □, Mozam. ... 87 E4
Niassa ○, Mozam. ... 87 E4
Nibāk, Si. Arabia ... 71 E7
Nibe, Denmark ... 11 H3
Nicaragua ■, Cent. Amer. ... 120 D2
Nicaragua, L. de, Nic. ... 120 D2
Nicastro, Italy ... 43 D9
Nice, France ... 21 E11
Nice ✈ (NCE), France ... 21 E11
Niceville, U.S.A. ... 115 K2
Nichicun, L., Canada ... 105 B5
Nichinan, Japan ... 55 J5
Nicholas Channel, W. Indies ... 120 B3
Nicholasville, U.S.A. ... 114 G3
Nichols, U.S.A. ... 117 D8
Nicholson, Australia ... 92 C4
Nicholson, U.S.A. ... 117 E9
Nicholson →, Australia ... 94 B2
Nicholson →, Canada ... 103 A8
Nicholson Ra., Australia ... 93 E2
Nicholville, U.S.A. ... 117 B10
Nicobar Is., Ind. Oc. ... 50 J13
Nicola, Canada ... 102 C4
Nicolls Town, Bahamas ... 120 A4
Nicopolis, Greece ... 46 B2
Nicosia, Cyprus ... 49 D12
Nicosia, Italy ... 43 E7
Nicótera, Italy ... 43 D8
Nicoya, Costa Rica ... 120 D2
Nicoya, G. de, Costa Rica ... 120 E3
Nicoya, Pen. de, Costa Rica ... 120 E2
Nida, Lithuania ... 30 C8
Nidd →, U.K. ... 14 D6
Nidda, Germany ... 25 E5
Nidda →, Germany ... 25 E4
Nidwalden □, Switz. ... 25 J4
Nidzica, Poland ... 31 E7
Niebüll, Germany ... 24 A4
Nied →, Germany ... 19 C13
Niederaula, Germany ... 24 E5
Niederbayern □, Germany ... 25 G8
Niederbronn-les-Bains, France ... 19 D14
Niedere Tauern, Austria ... 26 D7
Niederösterreich □, Austria ... 26 C8
Niedersachsen □, Germany ... 24 C4
Niedersächsisches Wattenmeer △, Germany ... 24 B3
Niekerkshoop, S. Africa ... 88 D3
Niellé, Ivory C. ... 82 C3
Niemba, Dem. Rep. of the Congo ... 86 D2
Niemen = Nemunas →, Lithuania ... 9 J19
Niemodlin, Poland ... 31 H4
Nienburg, Germany ... 24 C5
Niepołomice, Poland ... 31 H7
Niers →, Germany ... 24 D1
Niesky, Germany ... 24 D10
Nieszawa, Poland ... 31 F5
Nieu Bethesda, S. Africa ... 88 E3
Nieuw Amsterdam, Suriname ... 125 B7
Nieuw Nickerie, Suriname ... 125 B7
Nieuwoudtville, S. Africa ... 88 E2
Nieuwpoort, Belgium ... 17 C2
Nieves, Pico de las, Canary Is. ... 48 G4
Nièvre □, France ... 19 E10
Niga, Mali ... 82 C3
Niğde, Turkey ... 70 B2
Nigel, S. Africa ... 89 D4
Niger □, Nigeria ... 83 D6
Niger ■, W. Afr. ... 83 B7
Niger →, W. Afr. ... 83 D6
Niger Delta, Africa ... 83 E6
Nigeria ■, W. Afr. ... 83 D6
Nighasin, India ... 69 E9
Nightcaps, N.Z. ... 91 L2
Nigríta, Greece ... 44 F7
Nii-Jima, Japan ... 55 G9
Niigata, Japan ... 54 E9
Niigata □, Japan ... 55 F9
Niihama, Japan ... 55 H6
Niihau, U.S.A. ... 106 H14
Niimi, Japan ... 55 G6
Niitsu, Japan ... 54 F9
Níjar, Spain ... 39 J2
Nijil, Jordan ... 74 E4
Nijkerk, Neths. ... 17 B5
Nijmegen, Neths. ... 17 C5
Nijverdal, Neths. ... 17 B6
Nik Pey, Iran ... 71 B6
Nike, Nigeria ... 83 D6
Nikiniki, Indonesia ... 63 F6
Nikísiani, Greece ... 45 F8
Nikítas, Greece ... 44 F7
Nikki, Benin ... 83 D5
Nikkō, Japan ... 55 F9
Nikkō △, Japan ... 55 F9
Nikolayev = Mykolayiv, Ukraine ... 33 J7

Nikolayevsk, Russia ... 34 E7
Nikolayevsk-na-Amur, Russia ... 53 D15
Nikolsk, Russia ... 34 D8
Nikolskoye, Russia ... 53 D17
Nikopol, Bulgaria ... 45 C8
Nikopol, Ukraine ... 33 J8
Niksar, Turkey ... 72 B7
Nīkshahr, Iran ... 71 E9
Nikšić, Serbia & M. ... 44 D2
Nîl, Nahr en →, Africa ... 80 H7
Nîl el Abyad →, Sudan ... 81 D3
Nîl el Azraq →, Sudan ... 81 D3
Nila, Indonesia ... 63 F7
Niland, U.S.A. ... 111 M11
Nile = Nîl, Nahr en →, Africa ... 80 H7
Nile Delta, Egypt ... 80 H7
Niles, Mich., U.S.A. ... 114 E2
Niles, Ohio, U.S.A. ... 116 E4
Nilüfer →, Turkey ... 45 F12
Nim Ka Thana, India ... 68 F6
Nimach, India ... 68 G6
Nimbahera, India ... 68 G6
Nîmes, France ... 21 E8
Nimfaíon, Ákra = Pínnes, Ákra, Greece ... 45 F8
Nimmitabel, Australia ... 95 F4
Nimule, Sudan ... 81 G3
Nimule △, Sudan ... 81 G3
Nin, Croatia ... 41 D12
Nindigully, Australia ... 95 D4
Nineveh = Nînawá, Iraq ... 70 B4
Ning Xian, China ... 56 G4
Ningaloo ○, Australia ... 92 D1
Ning'an, China ... 57 B15
Ningbo, China ... 59 C13
Ningcheng, China ... 57 D10
Ningde, China ... 59 D12
Ningdu, China ... 59 D10
Ninggang, China ... 59 D9
Ningguo, China ... 59 B12
Ninghai, China ... 59 C13
Ninghua, China ... 59 D11
Ningi, Nigeria ... 83 C6
Ningjin, China ... 56 F8
Ningjing Shan, China ... 58 C2
Ningling, China ... 58 D3
Ningling, China ... 56 G8
Ningming, China ... 58 F6
Ningnan, China ... 58 D4
Ningpo = Ningbo, China ... 59 C13
Ningqiang, China ... 56 H4
Ningshan, China ... 56 H5
Ningsia Hui A.R. = Ningxia Huizu Zizhiqu □, China ... 56 F4
Ningwu, China ... 56 E7
Ningxia Huizu Zizhiqu □, China ... 56 F4
Ningxiang, China ... 59 C9
Ningyang, China ... 56 G9
Ningyuan, China ... 59 E8
Ninh Binh, Vietnam ... 58 G5
Ninh Giang, Vietnam ... 64 B6
Ninh Hoa, Vietnam ... 64 F7
Ninh Ma, Vietnam ... 64 F7
Nini-Suhien ○, Ghana ... 82 D4
Ninove, Belgium ... 17 D4
Nioaque, Brazil ... 127 A4
Niobrara, U.S.A. ... 112 D6
Niobrara →, U.S.A. ... 112 D6
Niokolo-Koba △, Senegal ... 82 C2
Niono, Mali ... 82 C3
Nionsamoridougou, Guinea ... 82 D3
Nioro du Rip, Senegal ... 82 C1
Nioro du Sahel, Mali ... 82 B3
Niort, France ... 20 B3
Nipawin, Canada ... 103 C8
Nipfjället, Sweden ... 10 C6
Nipigon, Canada ... 104 C2
Nipigon, L., Canada ... 104 C2
Nipishish L., Canada ... 105 B7
Nipissing L., Canada ... 104 C4
Nipomo, U.S.A. ... 111 K6
Nipton, U.S.A. ... 111 K11
Niquelândia, Brazil ... 125 F9
Nīr, Iran ... 70 B5
Nirasaki, Japan ... 55 G9
Nirmal, India ... 66 K11
Nirmali, India ... 69 F12
Niš, Serbia & M. ... 44 C5
Nisa, Portugal ... 37 F3
Nişāb, Si. Arabia ... 70 D5
Nişāb, Yemen ... 75 E4
Nišava →, Serbia & M. ... 44 C5
Niscemi, Italy ... 43 E7
Nishinomiya, Japan ... 55 G7
Nishino'omote, Japan ... 55 J5
Nishiwaki, Japan ... 55 G7
Nísíros, Greece ... 47 E9
Niška Banja, Serbia & M. ... 44 C6
Niskibi →, Canada ... 104 A2
Nisko, Poland ... 31 H9
Nisporeni, Moldova ... 29 C13
Nisqually →, U.S.A. ... 110 C4
Nissáki, Greece ... 49 A3
Nissan →, Sweden ... 11 H6
Nissum Bredning, Denmark ... 11 H2
Nissum Fjord, Denmark ... 11 H2
Nistru = Dnister →, Europe ... 33 J6
Nisutlin →, Canada ... 102 A2
Nitchequon, Canada ... 105 B5
Niterói, Brazil ... 127 A7
Nith →, Canada ... 116 C4
Nith →, U.K. ... 13 F5
Nitmiluk △, Australia ... 92 B5
Nitra, Slovak Rep. ... 27 C11
Nitra →, Slovak Rep. ... 27 D11
Nitriansky □, Slovak Rep. ... 27 C11
Nittenau, Germany ... 25 F8
Niuafo'ou, Tonga ... 91 B11
Niue, Cook Is. ... 97 J11
Niulan Jiang →, China ... 58 D4

Niut, Indonesia ... 62 D4
Niutou Shan, China ... 59 C13
Niuzhuang, China ... 57 D12
Nivala, Finland ... 8 E21
Nivelles, Belgium ... 17 D4
Nivernais, France ... 19 E10
Niwas, India ... 69 H9
Nixon, U.S.A. ... 113 L6
Nizamabad, India ... 66 K11
Nizamghat, India ... 67 E19
Nizhne Kolymsk, Russia ... 53 C17
Nizhnegorskiy = Nyzhnohirskyy, Ukraine ... 33 K8
Nizhnekamsk, Russia ... 34 C10
Nizhneudinsk, Russia ... 53 D10
Nizhnevartovsk, Russia ... 52 C8
Nizhniy Chir, Russia ... 35 F6
Nizhniy Lomov, Russia ... 34 D6
Nizhniy Novgorod, Russia ... 34 B7
Nizhniy Tagil, Russia ... 52 D6
Nizhyn, Ukraine ... 33 G6
Nizip, Turkey ... 70 B3
Nízké Tatry, Slovak Rep. ... 27 C12
Nízké Tatry △, Slovak Rep. ... 27 C12
Nízký Jeseník, Czech Rep. ... 27 B10
Nizza Monferrato, Italy ... 40 D5
Njakwa, Malawi ... 87 E3
Njanji, Zambia ... 87 E3
Njegoš, Serbia & M. ... 44 D2
Njinjo, Tanzania ... 87 D4
Njombe, Tanzania ... 87 D3
Njombe →, Tanzania ... 86 D4
Njurundabommen, Sweden ... 10 B11
Nkambe, Cameroon ... 83 D7
Nkana, Zambia ... 87 E2
Nkandla, S. Africa ... 89 D5
Nkawkaw, Ghana ... 83 D4
Nkayi, Zimbabwe ... 87 F2
Nkhotakota, Malawi ... 87 E3
Nkhotakota △, Malawi ... 87 E3
Nkongsamba, Cameroon ... 83 E6
Nkurenkuru, Namibia ... 88 B2
Nkwanta, Ghana ... 82 D4
Nmai →, Burma ... 58 F2
Noakhali = Maijdi, Bangla. ... 67 H17
Nobel, Canada ... 116 A4
Nobeoka, Japan ... 55 H5
Noblejas, Spain ... 36 F7
Noblesville, U.S.A. ... 114 E3
Noboribetsu, Japan ... 54 C10
Noce →, Italy ... 40 B8
Nocera Inferiore, Italy ... 43 B7
Nocera Umbra, Italy ... 41 E9
Noci, Italy ... 43 B10
Nocona, U.S.A. ... 113 J6
Nocrich, Romania ... 29 E9
Noda, Japan ... 55 G9
Nogales, Mexico ... 118 A2
Nogales, U.S.A. ... 109 L8
Nogaro, France ... 20 E3
Nogat →, Poland ... 30 D6
Nōgata, Japan ... 55 H5
Nogent, France ... 19 D12
Nogent-le-Rotrou, France ... 18 D7
Nogent-sur-Seine, France ... 19 D10
Noginsk, Moskva, Russia ... 32 E10
Noginsk, Tunguska, Russia ... 53 C10
Nogoa →, Australia ... 94 C4
Nogoyá, Argentina ... 126 C4
Nógrád □, Hungary ... 28 C4
Noguera Pallaresa →, Spain ... 38 D5
Noguera Ribagorzana →, Spain ... 38 D5
Nohar, India ... 68 E6
Nohfelden, Germany ... 25 F3
Nohta, India ... 69 H8
Noia, Spain ... 36 C2
Noire, Montagne, France ... 20 E6
Noires, Mts., France ... 18 D3
Noirétable, France ... 20 C7
Noirmoutier, Î. de, France ... 18 F4
Noirmoutier-en-l'Île, France ... 18 F4
Nojane, Botswana ... 88 C3
Nojima-Zaki, Japan ... 55 G9
Nok Kundi, Pakistan ... 66 E3
Nok Ta Phao, Ko, Thailand ... 65 b
Nokaneng, Botswana ... 88 B3
Nokia, Finland ... 9 F20
Nokomis, Canada ... 103 C8
Nokomis L., Canada ... 103 B8
Nola, C.A.R. ... 84 D3
Nola, Italy ... 43 B7
Nolay, France ... 19 F11
Noli, C. di, Italy ... 40 D5
Nolinsk, Russia ... 34 B9
Noma Omuramba →, Namibia ... 88 B3
Nombre de Dios, Panama ... 120 E4
Nome, U.S.A. ... 100 B3
Nomo-Zaki, Japan ... 55 H4
Nonacho L., Canada ... 103 A7
Nonancourt, France ... 18 D8
Nonda, Australia ... 94 C3
None, Italy ... 40 D4
Nong Chang, Thailand ... 64 E2
Nong Het, Laos ... 64 C4
Nong Khai, Thailand ... 64 D4
Nong'an, China ... 57 B13
Nongoma, S. Africa ... 89 D5
Nonoava, Mexico ... 118 B3
Nonthaburi, Thailand ... 64 F3
Nontron, France ... 20 C4
Nonza, France ... 21 F13
Noonamah, Australia ... 92 B5
Noondie, L., Australia ... 93 E2
Noord Brabant □, Neths. ... 17 C5
Noord Holland □, Neths. ... 17 B4
Noordbeveland, Neths. ... 17 C3
Noordoostpolder, Neths. ... 17 B5

Noordwijk, Neths. ... 17 B4
Noosa Heads, Australia ... 95 D5
Nootka I., Canada ... 102 D3
Nopiming ○, Canada ... 103 C9
Nora, Eritrea ... 81 D5
Nora, Sweden ... 10 E9
Noralee, Canada ... 102 C3
Noranda = Rouyn-Noranda, Canada ... 104 C4
Norberg, Sweden ... 10 D9
Nórcia, Italy ... 41 F10
Norco, U.S.A. ... 111 M9
Nord □, France ... 19 B10
Nord-Kivu □, Dem. Rep. of the Congo ... 86 C2
Nord-Ostsee-Kanal, Germany ... 24 A5
Nord-Pas-de-Calais □, France ... 19 B9
Nordaustlandet, Svalbard ... 4 B9
Nordborg, Denmark ... 11 J3
Nordby, Denmark ... 11 J2
Norddeich, Germany ... 24 B3
Nordegg, Canada ... 102 C5
Norden, Germany ... 24 B3
Nordenham, Germany ... 24 B4
Norderney, Germany ... 24 B3
Norderstedt, Germany ... 24 B6
Nordfjord, Norway ... 9 F11
Nordfriesische Inseln, Germany ... 24 A4
Nordhausen, Germany ... 24 D6
Nordhorn, Germany ... 24 C3
Nordøyar, Færoe Is. ... 8 E9
Nordingrå, Sweden ... 10 B12
Nordjyllands Amtskommune □, Denmark ... 11 G4
Nordkapp, Norway ... 8 A21
Nordkapp, Svalbard ... 4 A9
Nordkinnhalvøya, Norway ... 8 A22
Nördlicher Teutoburger Wald-Wiehengebirge △, Germany ... 24 C4
Nördlingen, Germany ... 25 G6
Nordrhein-Westfalen □, Germany ... 24 D3
Nordstrand, Germany ... 24 A4
Nordvik, Russia ... 53 B12
Nore →, Ireland ... 12 D4
Norfolk, Canada ... 116 D4
Norfolk, Nebr., U.S.A. ... 112 D6
Norfolk, Va., U.S.A. ... 114 G7
Norfolk □, U.K. ... 15 E8
Norfolk I., Pac. Oc. ... 96 K8
Norfork L., U.S.A. ... 113 G8
Norilsk, Russia ... 53 C9
Norma, Mt., Australia ... 94 C3
Normal, U.S.A. ... 112 E10
Norman, U.S.A. ... 113 H6
Norman →, Australia ... 94 B3
Norman Wells, Canada ... 100 B7
Normanby →, Australia ... 94 A3
Normandie ○, France ... 18 D6
Normandin, Canada ... 104 C5
Normanhurst, Mt., Australia ... 93 E3
Normanton, Australia ... 94 B3
Normétal, Canada ... 104 C4
Norquay, Canada ... 103 C8
Norquinco, Argentina ... 128 E2
Norra Kvill △, Sweden ... 11 G9
Norra Ulvön, Sweden ... 10 A12
Norrahammar, Sweden ... 11 G8
Norrbottens län □, Sweden ... 8 C19
Nørre Åby, Denmark ... 11 J3
Nørre Alslev, Denmark ... 11 K5
Nørre Nebel, Denmark ... 11 J2
Nørresundby, Denmark ... 11 G3
Norrhult-Klavreström, Sweden ... 11 G9
Norris Point, Canada ... 105 C8
Norristown, U.S.A. ... 117 F9
Norrköping, Sweden ... 11 F10
Norrland, Sweden ... 9 E16
Norrsundet, Sweden ... 10 D11
Norrtälje, Sweden ... 10 E12
Norseman, Australia ... 93 F3
Norsk, Russia ... 53 D14
Norte, Pta. del, Canary Is. ... 48 G2
Norte, Serra do, Brazil ... 124 F7
North, C., Canada ... 105 C7
North Adams, U.S.A. ... 117 D11
North America ... 98 F10
North Arm, Canada ... 102 A5
North Atlantic Ocean, Atl. Oc. ... 2 C7
North Augusta, U.S.A. ... 115 J5
North Ayrshire □, U.K. ... 13 F4
North Bass I., U.S.A. ... 116 E2
North Battleford, Canada ... 103 C7
North Bay, Canada ... 104 C4
North Belcher Is., Canada ... 104 A4
North Bend, Oreg., U.S.A. ... 108 E1
North Bend, Pa., U.S.A. ... 116 E7
North Bend, Wash., U.S.A. ... 110 C5
North Bennington, U.S.A. ... 117 D11
North Berwick, U.K. ... 13 E6
North Berwick, U.S.A. ... 117 C14
North C., Canada ... 105 C7
North C., N.Z. ... 91 F4
North Canadian →, U.S.A. ... 113 H7
North Canton, U.S.A. ... 116 F3
North Cape = Nordkapp, Norway ... 8 A21
North Cape = Nordkapp, Svalbard ... 4 A9
North Caribou L., Canada ... 104 B1
North Carolina □, U.S.A. ... 115 H6
North Cascades △, U.S.A. ... 108 B3
North Channel, Canada ... 104 C3
North Channel, U.K. ... 13 F3
North Charleston, U.S.A. ... 115 J6
North Chicago, U.S.A. ... 114 D2
North Creek, U.S.A. ... 117 C11
North Dakota □, U.S.A. ... 112 B5
North Downs, U.K. ... 15 F8
North East, U.S.A. ... 116 D5
North East Frontier Agency = Arunachal Pradesh □, India ... 67 F19
North East Lincolnshire □, U.K. ... 14 D7

North Eastern □, Kenya ... 86 B5
North Esk →, U.K. ... 13 E6
North European Plain, Europe ... 6 E10
North Foreland, U.K. ... 15 F9
North Fork, U.S.A. ... 110 H7
North Fork American →, U.S.A. ... 110 G5
North Fork Feather →, U.S.A. ... 110 F5
North Fork Grand →, U.S.A. ... 112 C3
North Fork Red →, U.S.A. ... 113 H5
North Frisian Is. = Nordfriesische Inseln, Germany ... 24 A4
North Gower, Canada ... 117 A9
North Hd., Australia ... 93 F1
North Henik L., Canada ... 103 A9
North Highlands, U.S.A. ... 110 G5
North Horr, Kenya ... 86 B4
North I., Kenya ... 86 B4
North I., N.Z. ... 91 H5
North Kingsville, U.S.A. ... 116 E4
North Kitui ○, Kenya ... 86 C4
North Knife →, Canada ... 103 B10
North Koel →, India ... 69 G10
North Korea ■, Asia ... 57 E14
North Lakhimpur, India ... 67 F19
North Lanarkshire □, U.K. ... 13 F5
North Las Vegas, U.S.A. ... 111 J11
North Lincolnshire □, U.K. ... 14 D7
North Little Rock, U.S.A. ... 113 H8
North Loup →, U.S.A. ... 112 E5
North Luangwa △, Zambia ... 87 E3
North Magnetic Pole, Canada ... 4 A2
North Minch, U.K. ... 13 C3
North Moose L., Canada ... 103 C8
North Moose L., Man., Canada ... 103 C8
North Myrtle Beach, U.S.A. ... 115 J6
North Nahanni →, Canada ... 102 A4
North Olmsted, U.S.A. ... 116 E3
North Ossetia □, Russia ... 35 J7
North Pagai, I. = Pagai Utara, Pulau, Indonesia ... 62 E2
North Palisade, U.S.A. ... 110 H8
North Platte, U.S.A. ... 112 E4
North Platte →, U.S.A. ... 112 E4
North Pole, Arctic ... 4 A
North Portal, Canada ... 103 D8
North Powder, U.S.A. ... 108 D5
North Pt., Barbados ... 121 g
North Pt., Trin. & Tob. ... 125 J16
North Pt., U.S.A. ... 116 A1
North Rhine Westphalia = Nordrhein-Westfalen □, Germany ... 24 D3
North River, Canada ... 105 B8
North Ronaldsay, U.K. ... 13 B6
North Saskatchewan →, Canada ... 103 C7
North Sea, Europe ... 16
North Seal →, Canada ... 103 B9
North Somerset □, U.K. ... 15 F5
North Sporades = Vóriai Sporádhes, Greece ... 46 B5
North Sydney, Canada ... 105 C7
North Syracuse, U.S.A. ... 117 C8
North Taranaki Bight, N.Z. ... 91 H5
North Thompson →, Canada ... 102 C4
North Tonawanda, U.S.A. ... 116 C6
North Troy, U.S.A. ... 117 B12
North Truchas Pk., U.S.A. ... 109 J11
North Twin I., Canada ... 104 B4
North Tyne →, U.K. ... 14 B5
North Uist, U.K. ... 13 D1
North Vancouver, Canada ... 102 D4
North Vernon, U.S.A. ... 114 F3
North Wabasca L., Canada ... 102 B6
North Walsham, U.K. ... 14 E9
North West = Severo-Zapadnyy □, Russia ... 52 C4
North-West □, S. Africa ... 88 D4
North West C., Australia ... 92 D1
North West Christmas I. Ridge, Pac. Oc. ... 97 G11
North West Frontier □, Pakistan ... 68 C4
North West Highlands, U.K. ... 13 D4
North West River, Canada ... 105 B7
North Western □, Zambia ... 87 E2
North Wildwood, U.S.A. ... 114 F8
North York Moors, U.K. ... 14 C7
North York Moors △, U.K. ... 14 C7
North Yorkshire □, U.K. ... 14 C6
Northallerton, U.K. ... 14 C6
Northam, Australia ... 93 F2
Northam, S. Africa ... 88 C4
Northampton, Australia ... 93 E1
Northampton, U.K. ... 15 E7
Northampton, Mass., U.S.A. ... 117 D12
Northampton, Pa., U.S.A. ... 117 F9
Northamptonshire □, U.K. ... 15 E7
Northbridge, U.S.A. ... 117 D13
Northcliffe, Australia ... 93 F2
Northeast Providence Chan., W. Indies ... 120 A4
Northeim, Germany ... 24 D6
Northern = Limpopo □, S. Africa ... 89 C4
Northern □, Ghana ... 83 D4
Northern □, Malawi ... 87 E3
Northern □, S. Leone ... 82 D2
Northern □, Zambia ... 87 E3
Northern Areas □, Pakistan ... 69 A5
Northern Cape □, S. Africa ... 88 D3
Northern Circars, India ... 67 L13
Northern Indian L., Canada ... 103 B9
Northern Ireland □, U.K. ... 12 B5
Northern Light L., Canada ... 104 C1
Northern Marianas ☑, Pac. Oc. ... 96 F6
Northern Mid-Atlantic Ridge, Atl. Oc. ... 4 D6
Northern Province □, S. Africa ... 89 C4
Northern Range, Trin. & Tob. ... 125 K15
Northern Territory □, Australia ... 92 D5
Northfield, Minn., U.S.A. ... 112 C8
Northfield, Vt., U.S.A. ... 117 B12
Northland □, N.Z. ... 91 F4
Northome, U.S.A. ... 112 B7

Northport, *Ala., U.S.A.* 115 J2
Northport, *Wash., U.S.A.* 108 B5
Northumberland □, *U.K.* 14 B6
Northumberland C., *Australia* .. 95 F3
Northumberland Is., *Australia* .. 94 C4
Northumberland Str., *Canada* .. 105 C7
Northville, *U.S.A.* 117 C10
Northwest Providence Channel,
W. Indies 120 A4
Northwest Territories □, *Canada* 100 B9
Northwich, *U.K.* 14 D5
Northwood, *Iowa, U.S.A.* 112 D8
Northwood, *N. Dak., U.S.A.* 112 B6
Norton, *U.S.A.* 112 F5
Norton, *Zimbabwe* 87 F3
Norton Sd., *U.S.A.* 100 B3
Nortorf, *Germany* 24 A5
Norwalk, *Calif., U.S.A.* 111 M8
Norwalk, *Conn., U.S.A.* 117 E11
Norwalk, *Iowa, U.S.A.* 112 E8
Norwalk, *Ohio, U.S.A.* 116 E2
Norway, *Maine, U.S.A.* 115 C10
Norway, *Mich., U.S.A.* 114 C2
Norway ■, *Europe* 8 E14
Norway House, *Canada* 103 C9
Norwegian Sea, *Atl. Oc.* 7 B6
Norwich, *Canada* 116 D4
Norwich, *U.K.* 15 E9
Norwich, *Conn., U.S.A.* 117 E12
Norwich, *N.Y., U.S.A.* 117 D9
Norwood, *Canada* 116 B7
Norwood, *U.S.A.* 117 B10
Noshiro, *Japan* 54 D10
Nosivka, *Ukraine* 33 G6
Nosovka = Nosivka, *Ukraine* ... 33 G6
Noṣratābād, *Iran* 71 D8
Noss Hd., *U.K.* 13 C5
Nossebro, *Sweden* 11 F6
Nossob →, *S. Africa* 88 D3
Nossombougou, *Mali* 82 C3
Nosy Barren, *Madag.* 85 H8
Nosy Be, *Madag.* 85 G9
Nosy Boraha, *Madag.* 89 B8
Nosy Lava, *Madag.* 89 A8
Nosy Varika, *Madag.* 89 C8
Noteć →, *Poland* 31 F2
Notikewin →, *Canada* 102 B5
Notio Aigaio = Notios Aiyaíon □ 47 E7
Notios Aiyaíon □ 47 E7
Notios Evvoïkos Kólpos, *Greece* 46 C5
Noto, *Italy* 43 F8
Noto, G. di, *Italy* 43 F8
Notodden, *Norway* 9 G13
Notre Dame B., *Canada* 105 C8
Notre-Dame-de-Koartac =
Quaqtaq, *Canada* 101 B13
Notre-Dame-des-Bois, *Canada* .. 117 A13
Notre-Dame-d'Ivugivic = Ivujivik,
Canada 101 B12
Notre-Dame-du-Nord, *Canada* .. 104 C4
Notsé, *Togo* 83 D5
Nottawasaga B., *Canada* 116 B4
Nottaway →, *Canada* 104 B4
Nottingham, *U.K.* 14 E6
Nottingham, City of □, *U.K.* ... 14 E6
Nottingham I., *Canada* 101 B12
Nottinghamshire □, *U.K.* 14 D6
Nottoway →, *U.S.A.* 114 G7
Notwane →, *Botswana* 88 C4
Nouâdhibou, *Mauritania* 78 D2
Nouâdhibou, Ras, *Mauritania* .. 78 D2
Nouakchott, *Mauritania* 82 B1
Nouâmghâr, *Mauritania* 82 B1
Nouméa, *N. Cal.* 96 K8
Nouna, *Burkina Faso* 82 C4
Noupoort, *S. Africa* 88 E3
Nouveau Comptoir = Wemindji,
Canada 104 B4
Nouvelle-Amsterdam, Î., *Ind. Oc.* 3 F13
Nouvelle-Calédonie = New
Caledonia ☑, *Pac. Oc.* 96 K8
Nouzonville, *France* 19 C11
Nová Baňa, *Slovak Rep.* 27 C11
Nová Bystřice, *Czech Rep.* 26 B8
Nova Casa Nova, *Brazil* 125 E10
Nova Esperança, *Brazil* 127 A5
Nova Friburgo, *Brazil* 127 A7
Nova Gorica, *Slovenia* 41 C10
Nova Gradiška, *Croatia* 28 E2
Nova Iguaçu, *Brazil* 127 A7
Nova Iorque, *Brazil* 125 E10
Nova Kakhovka, *Ukraine* 33 J7
Nova Lamego, *Guinea-Biss.* ... 82 C2
Nova Lima, *Brazil* 127 A7
Nova Lusitânia, *Mozam.* 87 F3
Nova Mambone, *Mozam.* 87 F3
Nova Odesa, *Ukraine* 33 J6
Nová Paka, *Czech Rep.* 26 A8
Nova Pavova, *Serbia & M.* 28 F5
Nova Scotia □, *Canada* 105 C7
Nova Siri, *Italy* 43 B9
Nova Sofala, *Mozam.* 89 C5
Nova Ushytsya, *Ukraine* 29 B12
Nova Varoš, *Serbia & M.* 44 C3
Nova Venécia, *Brazil* 125 G10
Nova Zagora, *Bulgaria* 45 D10
Novaci, *Macedonia* 44 E5
Novaci, *Romania* 29 E8
Novafèltria, *Italy* 41 E9
Novannenskiy = Novoannenskiy,
Russia 34 E6
Novar, *Canada* 116 A5
Novara, *Italy* 40 C5
Novato, *U.S.A.* 110 G4
Novaya Kakhovka = Nova
Kakhovka, *Ukraine* 33 J7
Novaya Kazanka, *Kazakhstan* .. 35 F9
Novaya Ladoga, *Russia* 32 B7
Novaya Lyalya, *Russia* 52 D7
Novaya Sibir, Ostrov, *Russia* .. 53 B16
Novaya Zemlya, *Russia* 52 B6
Nové Město, *Slovak Rep.* 27 C10

Nové Město na Moravě,
Czech Rep. 26 B9
Nové Město nad Metují,
Czech Rep. 27 A9
Nové Zámky, *Slovak Rep.* 27 C11
Novelda, *Spain* 39 G4
Novellara, *Italy* 40 D7
Noventa Vicentina, *Italy* 41 C8
Novgorod, *Russia* 32 C6
Novgorod-Severskiy = Novhorod-
Siverskyy, *Ukraine* 33 G7
Novhorod-Siverskyy, *Ukraine* .. 33 G7
Novi Bečej, *Serbia & M.* 28 E5
Novi Iskar, *Bulgaria* 44 D7
Novi Lígure, *Italy* 40 D5
Novi Knežεvac, *Serbia & M.* ... 28 D5
Novi Pazar, *Bulgaria* 45 C11
Novi Pazar, *Serbia & M.* 44 C4
Novi Sad, *Serbia & M.* 28 E4
Novi Slankamen, *Serbia & M.* .. 28 E5
Novi Travnik, *Bos.-H.* 28 F2
Novi Vinodolski, *Croatia* 41 C11
Novigrad, *Istra, Croatia* 41 C10
Novigrad, *Zadar, Croatia* 41 D12
Novigradsko More, *Croatia* ... 41 D12
Novo Hamburgo, *Brazil* 127 B5
Novo Ivanivka, *Ukraine* 29 E14
Novo Mesto, *Slovenia* 41 C12
Novo Miloševo, *Serbia & M.* ... 28 E5
Novo Remanso, *Brazil* 125 E10
Novoaleksandrovsk, *Russia* 35 H5
Novoaleksandrovskaya =
Novoaleksandrovsk, *Russia* .. 35 H5
Novoaltaysk, *Russia* 52 D9
Novoannenskiy, *Russia* 34 E6
Novoazovsk, *Ukraine* 33 J10
Novocheboksarsk, *Russia* 34 B8
Novocherkassk, *Russia* 35 G5
Novodevichye, *Russia* 34 D9
Novograd-Volynskyy, *Ukraine* .. 33 G4
Novogrudok = Navahrudak,
Belarus 32 F3
Novohrad-Volynskyy, *Ukraine* .. 33 G4
Novokachalinsk, *Russia* 54 B6
Novokhopersk, *Russia* 34 E5
Novokuybyshevsk, *Russia* 34 D9
Novokuznetsk, *Russia* 52 D9
Novomirgorod, *Ukraine* 33 H6
Novomoskovsk, *Russia* 32 E10
Novomoskovsk, *Ukraine* 33 H8
Novopolotsk = Navapolatsk,
Belarus 32 E5
Novorossiysk, *Russia* 33 K9
Novorybnoye, *Russia* 53 B11
Novorzhev, *Russia* 32 D5
Novosej, *Albania* 44 E4
Novoselytsya, *Ukraine* 29 B11
Novoshakhtinsk, *Russia* 33 J10
Novosibirsk, *Russia* 52 D9
Novosibirskiye Ostrova, *Russia* 53 B15
Novosil, *Russia* 33 F9
Novosokolniki, *Russia* 32 D6
Novotitarovskaya, *Russia* 35 H4
Novotroitsk, *Russia* 52 D6
Novoukrayinka, *Ukraine* 33 H6
Novouljanovsk, *Russia* 34 C9
Novouzensk, *Russia* 34 E9
Novovolynsk, *Ukraine* 31 H11
Novovoronezhskiy, *Russia* 33 G10
Novoyavoriske, *Ukraine* 31 J10
Novozybkov, *Russia* 33 F6
Novska, *Croatia* 41 C14
Novvy Urengoy, *Russia* 52 C8
Nový Bor, *Czech Rep.* 26 A7
Novy Bug = Novyy Buh, *Ukraine* 33 J7
Nový Bydžov, *Czech Rep.* 26 A8
Novy Dvor, *Belarus* 31 F11
Novy Dwór Mazowiecki, *Poland* 31 F7
Nový Jičín, *Czech Rep.* 27 B11
Novyy Afon, *Georgia* 35 J5
Novyy Buh, *Ukraine* 33 J7
Novyy Oskol, *Russia* 33 G9
Novyy Port, *Russia* 52 C8
Now Shahr, *Iran* 71 B6
Nowa Deba, *Poland* 31 H8
Nowa Ruda, *Poland* 31 H3
Nowa Sarzyna, *Poland* 31 H9
Nowa Sól, *Poland* 31 G2
Nowata, *U.S.A.* 113 G7
Nowbarān, *Iran* 71 C6
Nowe, *Poland* 30 E5
Nowe Miasteczko, *Poland* 31 G2
Nowe Miasto, *Poland* 31 F7
Nowe Miasto Lubawskie, *Poland* 30 E6
Nowe Skalmierzyce, *Poland* .. 31 G4
Nowe Warpno, *Poland* 30 E1
Nowghāb, *Iran* 71 C8
Nowgong, *Assam, India* 67 F18
Nowgong, *Mad. P., India* 69 G8
Nowogard, *Poland* 30 E2
Nowogród, *Poland* 31 E8
Nowogród Bobrzanski, *Poland* .. 31 G2
Nowogrodziec, *Poland* 31 G2
Nowra, *Australia* 95 E5
Nowshera, *Pakistan* 66 C8
Nowy Dwór Gdański, *Poland* .. 30 D6
Nowy Sącz, *Poland* 31 J7
Nowy Staw, *Poland* 30 D6
Nowy Targ, *Poland* 31 J7
Nowy Tomyśl, *Poland* 31 F3
Nowy Wiśnicz, *Poland* 31 J7
Noxen, *U.S.A.* 117 E8
Noxon, *U.S.A.* 108 C6
Noyabr'sk, *Russia* 52 C8
Noyant, *France* 18 E7
Noyers, *France* 19 E10
Noyon, *France* 19 C9
Noyon, *Mongolia* 56 C2
Nozay, *France* 18 E5
Nsanje, *Malawi* 87 F4
Nsawam, *Ghana* 83 D4
Nsomba, *Zambia* 87 E2

Nsukka, *Nigeria* 83 D6
Ntui, *Cameroon* 83 E7
Nu Jiang →, *China* 58 E2
Nu Shan, *China* 58 E2
Nuba Mts. = Nubah, Jibalan,
Sudan 81 E3
Nubah, Jibalan, *Sudan* 81 E3
Nubia, *Africa* 76 D7
Nubian Desert = Nûbîya, Es
Sahrâ en, *Sudan* 80 C3
Nûbîya, Es Sahrâ en, *Sudan* ... 80 C3
Nubledo, *Spain* 36 B5
Nuboai, *Indonesia* 63 E9
Nucet, *Romania* 28 D7
Nueces →, *U.S.A.* 113 M6
Nueltin L., *Canada* 103 A9
Nueva Carteya, *Spain* 37 H6
Nueva Gerona, *Cuba* 120 B3
Nueva Palmira, *Uruguay* 126 C4
Nueva Rosita, *Mexico* 118 B4
Nueva San Salvador, *El Salv.* 120 D2
Nueva Tabarca, *Spain* 39 G4
Nueve de Julio, *Argentina* ... 126 D3
Nuevitas, *Cuba* 120 B4
Nuevo, G., *Argentina* 128 E4
Nuevo Casas Grandes, *Mexico* 118 A3
Nuevo Guerrero, *Mexico* 119 B5
Nuevo Laredo, *Mexico* 119 B5
Nuevo León □, *Mexico* 118 C5
Nuevo Rocafuerte, *Ecuador* .. 124 D3
Nugget Pt., *N.Z.* 91 M2
Nugrus, Gebel, *Egypt* 80 C3
Nuhaka, *N.Z.* 91 H6
Nuits-St-Georges, *France* 19 E11
Nukey Bluff, *Australia* 95 E2
Nukhayb, *Iraq* 70 C4
Nukheila, *Sudan* 80 D2
Nuku'alofa, *Tonga* 91 E12
Nuku'ulaofa, *Uzbekistan* 52 E6
Nules, *Spain* 38 F4
Nullagine, *Australia* 92 D3
Nullagine →, *Australia* 92 D3
Nullarbor, *Australia* 93 F5
Nullarbor △, *Australia* 93 F2
Nullarbor Plain, *Australia* 93 F4
Numalla, L., *Australia* 95 D3
Numan, *Nigeria* 83 D7
Numata, *Japan* 55 F9
Numatinna →, *Sudan* 81 F2
Numazu, *Japan* 55 G9
Numbulwar, *Australia* 94 A2
Numfoor, *Indonesia* 63 E8
Numurkah, *Australia* 95 F4
Nunaksaluk I., *Canada* 105 A7
Nunap Isua, *Greenland* 101 C15
Nunavut □, *Canada* 101 D8
Nunda, *U.S.A.* 116 D7
Nuneaton, *U.K.* 15 E6
Nungarin, *Australia* 93 F2
Nungo, *Mozam.* 87 E4
Nungwe, *Tanzania* 86 C3
Nunivak I., *U.S.A.* 100 B3
Nunkun, *India* 69 C7
Núoro, *Italy* 42 B2
Nūrābād, *Iran* 71 E8
Nure →, *Italy* 40 C6
Nuremberg = Nürnberg, *Germany* 25 F7
Nuri, *Mexico* 118 B3
Nuri, *Sudan* 80 D3
Nurioopta, *Australia* 95 E2
Nuristān □, *Afghan.* 66 B7
Nurlat, *Russia* 34 C10
Nurmes, *Finland* 8 E23
Nürnberg, *Germany* 25 F7
Nurpur, *Pakistan* 68 D4
Nurra, La, *Italy* 42 B1
Nurran, L. = Terewah, L.,
Australia 95 D4
Nurrari Lakes, *Australia* 93 E5
Nurri, *Italy* 42 C2
Nürtingen, *Germany* 25 G5
Nurzec →, *Poland* 31 F9
Nus, *Italy* 40 C4
Nusa Barung, *Indonesia* 63 H15
Nusa Dua, *Indonesia* 63 K18
Nusa Kambangan, *Indonesia* 63 G13
Nusa Tenggara Barat □,
Indonesia 62 F5
Nusa Tenggara Timur □,
Indonesia 63 F6
Nusaybin, *Turkey* 73 D9
Nushki, *Pakistan* 68 E2
Nuuk, *Greenland* 101 B14
Nuwakot, *Nepal* 69 E10
Nuweiba', *Egypt* 70 D2
Nuwerus, *S. Africa* 88 E2
Nuweveldberge, *S. Africa* 88 E3
Nuyts, C., *Australia* 93 F5
Nuyts, Pt., *Australia* 93 G2
Nuyts Arch., *Australia* 95 E1
Nxai Pan △, *Botswana* 88 B3
Nxau-Nxau, *Botswana* 88 B3
Nyaake, *Liberia* 82 E3
Nyabing, *Australia* 93 F2
Nyack, *U.S.A.* 117 E11
Nyagan, *Russia* 52 C7
Nyahanga, *Tanzania* 86 C3
Nyahua, *Tanzania* 86 D3
Nyahururu, *Kenya* 86 B4
Nyainqêntanglha Shan, *China* 60 C4
Nyakanazi, *Tanzania* 86 C3
Nyâkh, *Sudan* 81 E1
Nyâlâ, *Sudan* 81 E1
Nyamandhlovu, *Zimbabwe* ... 87 F2
Nyambiti, *Tanzania* 86 C3
Nyamlell, *Sudan* 81 F2
Nyamwaga, *Tanzania* 86 C3
Nyandekwa, *Tanzania* 86 C3
Nyanding →, *Sudan* 81 F3
Nyandoma, *Russia* 32 B11

Nyanga △, *Zimbabwe* 87 F3
Nyangana, *Namibia* 88 B3
Nyanguge, *Tanzania* 86 C3
Nyankpala, *Ghana* 83 D4
Nyanza, *Rwanda* 86 C2
Nyanza □, *Kenya* 86 C3
Nyanza-Lac, *Burundi* 86 C2
Nyaponges, *Sudan* 81 F3
Nyasa, L., *Africa* 87 E3
Nyasvizh, *Belarus* 33 F4
Nyazura, *Zimbabwe* 87 F3
Nyazwidzi →, *Zimbabwe* 87 G3
Nyborg, *Denmark* 11 J4
Nybro, *Sweden* 11 H9
Nyda, *Russia* 52 C8
Nyeri, *Kenya* 86 C4
Nyerol, *Sudan* 81 F3
Nyhammar, *Sweden* 10 D8
Nyíka △, *Malawi* 87 E3
Nyinahin, *Ghana* 82 D4
Nyíradony, *Hungary* 28 C6
Nyírbátor, *Hungary* 28 C7
Nyíregyháza, *Hungary* 28 C6
Nykarleby = Uusikaarlepyy,
Finland 8 E20
Nykøbing, *Storstrøm, Denmark* 11 K5
Nykøbing, *Vestsjælland, Denmark* 11 J5
Nykøbing, *Viborg, Denmark* .. 11 H2
Nyköping, *Sweden* 11 F11
Nykroppa, *Sweden* 10 E8
Nykvarn, *Sweden* 10 E11
Nyland, *Sweden* 10 A11
Nylstroom = Modimolle, *S. Africa* 89 C4
Nymagee, *Australia* 95 E4
Nymboida →, *Australia* 95 D5
Nymburk, *Czech Rep.* 26 A8
Nynäshamn, *Sweden* 11 F11
Nyngan, *Australia* 95 E4
Nyoma Rap, *India* 69 C8
Nyoman = Nemunas →,
Lithuania 9 J19
Nyon, *Switz.* 25 J2
Nyong →, *Cameroon* 83 E6
Nyons, *France* 21 D9
Nyou, *Burkina Faso* 83 C4
Nýrsko, *Czech Rep.* 26 B6
Nysa, *Poland* 31 H4
Nysa →, *Europe* 24 C10
Nysa Kłodzka →, *Poland* 31 H4
Nysäter, *Sweden* 10 E6
Nyslott = Savonlinna, *Finland* 32 B5
Nyssa, *U.S.A.* 108 E5
Nystad = Uusikaupunki, *Finland* 9 F19
Nysted, *Denmark* 11 K5
Nyunzu, *Dem. Rep. of the Congo* 86 D2
Nyurba, *Russia* 53 C12
Nyzhankovychi, *Ukraine* 31 J9
Nyzhnohirskyy, *Ukraine* 33 K8
Nyzhny Vorota, *Ukraine* 29 B9
Nzébéla, *Guinea* 82 D3
Nzega, *Tanzania* 86 C3
Nzérékoré, *Guinea* 82 D3
Nzeto, *Angola* 84 F2
Nzilo, Chutes de, *Dem. Rep. of
the Congo* 87 E2
N'zo →, *Ivory C.* 82 D3
N'zo →, *Ivory C.* 82 D3
Nzubuka, *Tanzania* 86 C3

O

O Barco, *Spain* 36 C4
O Carballiño, *Spain* 36 C2
O Corgo, *Spain* 36 C3
O Pino, *Spain* 36 C2
O Porriño, *Spain* 36 C2
O-Shima, *Japan* 55 G9
Oa, Mull of, *U.K.* 13 F2
Oacoma, *U.S.A.* 112 D5
Oahe, L., *U.S.A.* 112 C4
Oahe Dam, *U.S.A.* 112 C4
Oahu, *U.S.A.* 106 H16
Oak Harbor, *U.S.A.* 110 B4
Oak Hill, *U.S.A.* 114 G5
Oak Ridge, *U.S.A.* 115 G3
Oak View, *U.S.A.* 111 L7
Oakan-Dake, *Japan* 54 C12
Oakdale, *Calif., U.S.A.* 110 H6
Oakdale, *La., U.S.A.* 113 K8
Oakes, *U.S.A.* 112 B5
Oakesdale, *U.S.A.* 108 C5
Oakey, *Australia* 95 D5
Oakfield, *U.S.A.* 116 C6
Oakham, *U.K.* 15 E7
Oakhurst, *U.S.A.* 110 H7
Oakland, *U.S.A.* 110 H4
Oakley, *Idaho, U.S.A.* 108 E7
Oakley, *Kans., U.S.A.* 112 F4
Oakover →, *Australia* 92 D3
Oakridge, *U.S.A.* 108 E2
Oakville, *Canada* 116 C5
Oakville, *U.S.A.* 110 D3
Oamaru, *N.Z.* 91 L3
Oancea, *Romania* 29 E13
Oasi Faunistica di Vendicari △,
Italy 43 F8
Oasis, *Calif., U.S.A.* 111 M10
Oasis, *Nev., U.S.A.* 110 H9
Oates Land, *Antarctica* 5 C11
Oatlands, *Australia* 95 G4
Oatman, *U.S.A.* 111 K12
Oaxaca, *Mexico* 119 D5
Oaxaca □, *Mexico* 119 D5
Ob →, *Russia* 52 C7
Obala, *Cameroon* 83 E7
Obama, *Japan* 55 G7
Oban, *Nigeria* 83 D6

Oban, *U.K.* 13 E3
Obbia, *Somali Rep.* 75 F4
Obera, *Argentina* 127 B4
Oberammergau, *Germany* 25 H7
Oberasbach, *Germany* 25 F6
Oberbayern □, *Germany* 25 G7
Oberdrauburg, *Austria* 26 E5
Obere Donau △, *Germany* 25 G5
Oberer Bayerischer Wald △,
Germany 25 F8
Oberfranken □, *Germany* 25 E7
Oberhausen, *Germany* 24 D2
Oberkirch, *Germany* 25 G4
Oberlausitz, *Germany* 24 D10
Oberlin, *Kans., U.S.A.* 112 F4
Oberlin, *La., U.S.A.* 113 K8
Oberlin, *Ohio, U.S.A.* 116 E2
Obernai, *France* 19 D14
Oberndorf, *Germany* 25 G4
Oberon, *Australia* 95 E4
Oberösterreich □, *Austria* 26 C7
Oberpfalz □, *Germany* 25 F8
Oberpfälzer Wald, *Germany* .. 25 F8
Oberpfälzer Wald △, *Germany* 25 F8
Oberstdorf, *Germany* 25 H6
Obertyn, *Ukraine* 29 B10
Oberursel, *Germany* 25 E4
Oberwart, *Austria* 27 D9
Obi, *Indonesia* 63 E7
Obiarуku, *Nigeria* 83 D6
Óbidos, *Brazil* 125 D7
Óbidos, *Portugal* 37 F1
Obihiro, *Japan* 54 C11
Obilatu, *Indonesia* 63 E7
Obilnoye, *Russia* 35 G7
Obing, *Germany* 25 G8
Objat, *France* 20 C5
Obluchye, *Russia* 53 E14
Obninsk, *Russia* 32 E9
Obo, *C.A.R.* 86 A2
Obo, Mt., *Uganda* 86 B3
Obock, *Djibouti* 81 E5
Obodivka, *Ukraine* 29 B14
Oborniki, *Poland* 31 F3
Oborniki Śląskie, *Poland* 31 G3
Oboyan, *Russia* 33 G9
Obozerskaya = Obozerskiy,
Russia 52 C5
Obozerskiy, *Russia* 52 C5
Obrenovac, *Serbia & M.* 44 B4
Obrovac, *Croatia* 41 D12
Obruk, *Turkey* 72 C5
Obrzycko, *Poland* 31 F3
Observatory Inlet, *Canada* .. 102 C3
Obshchi Syrt, *Russia* 6 E16
Obskaya Guba, *Russia* 52 C8
Obuasi, *Ghana* 83 D4
Obubra, *Nigeria* 83 D6
Obudu, *Nigeria* 83 D6
Obwalden □, *Switz.* 25 J4
Obzor, *Bulgaria* 45 D11
Ocala, *U.S.A.* 115 L4
Ocampo, *Chihuahua, Mexico* 118 B3
Ocampo, *Tamaulipas, Mexico* 119 C5
Ocaña, *Spain* 36 F7
Ocanomowoc, *U.S.A.* 112 D10
Occidental, Cordillera, *Colombia* 124 C3
Occidental, Grand Erg, *Algeria* 78 B6
Ocean City, *Md., U.S.A.* 114 F8
Ocean City, *N.J., U.S.A.* 114 F8
Ocean City, *Wash., U.S.A.* ... 110 C2
Ocean Falls, *Canada* 102 C3
Ocean I. = Banaba, *Kiribati* .. 96 H8
Ocean Park, *U.S.A.* 110 D2
Oceano, *U.S.A.* 111 K6
Oceanport, *U.S.A.* 117 F10
Oceanside, *U.S.A.* 111 M9
Ochagavía, *Spain* 38 C3
Ochakiv, *Ukraine* 33 J6
Ochamchira, *Georgia* 35 J5
Ochil Hills, *U.K.* 13 E5
Ocho Rios, *Jamaica* .... 120 a
Ochsenfurt, *Germany* 25 F6
Ochsenhausen, *Germany* 25 G5
Ocilla, *U.S.A.* 115 K4
Ockelbo, *Sweden* 10 D10
Ocmulgee →, *U.S.A.* 115 K4
Ocna Mureş, *Romania* 29 D8
Ocna Sibiului, *Romania* 29 E9
Ocnele Mari, *Romania* 29 E9
Ocnița, *Moldova* 29 B12
Oconee →, *U.S.A.* 115 K4
Oconto, *U.S.A.* 114 C2
Oconto Falls, *U.S.A.* 114 C1
Ocosingo, *Mexico* 119 D6
Ocotal, *Nic.* 120 D2
Ocotlán, *Mexico* 118 C4
Ocotlán de Morelos, *Mexico* .. 119 D5
Ocreza →, *Portugal* 37 F3
Oda, *Ghana* 83 D4
Ōda, *Japan* 55 G6
Oda, J., *Sudan* 80 C4
Ódáðahraun, *Iceland* 8 D5
Ódákra, *Sweden* 11 H6
Odate, *Japan* 54 D10
Odawara, *Japan* 55 G9
Odda, *Norway* 9 F12
Odder, *Denmark* 11 J4
Odei →, *Canada* 103 B9
Ödeborg, *Portugal* 37 H2
Ödemiş, *Turkey* 47 C9
Odendaalsrus, *S. Africa* 88 D4
Odensbacken, *Sweden* 10 E9
Odense, *Denmark* 11 J4
Odenwald = Neckartal-
Odenwald △, *Germany* 25 F5
Odenwald, *Germany* 25 F5
Oder →, *Europe* 24 B10
Oder-Havel Kanal, *Germany* .. 24 C10
Oderzo, *Italy* 41 C9

Odesa, *Ukraine* 33 J6
Ödeshög, *Sweden* 11 F8
Odessa = Odesa, *Ukraine* ... 33 J6
Odessa, *Canada* 117 B8
Odessa, *Tex., U.S.A.* 113 K3
Odessa, *Wash., U.S.A.* 108 C4
Odiakwe, *Botswana* 88 C4
Odiel ➤, *Spain* 37 H4
Odienné, *Ivory C.* 82 D3
Odintsovo, *Russia* 32 E9
Odiongan, *Phil.* 61 E4
Odobeşti, *Romania* 29 E12
Odolanów, *Poland* 31 G4
O'Donnell, *U.S.A.* 113 J4
Odorheiu Secuiesc, *Romania* .. 29 D10
Odoyevo, *Russia* 32 F9
Odra = Oder ➤, *Europe* 24 B10
Odra ➤, *Spain* 36 C6
Odžaci, *Serbia & M.* 28 E4
Odžak, *Bos.-H.* 28 E3
Odzi, *Zimbabwe* 89 B5
Odzi ➤, *Zimbabwe* 89 B5
Oebisfelde, *Germany* 24 C6
Oeiras, *Brazil* 125 E10
Oeiras, *Portugal* 37 G1
Oelrichs, *U.S.A.* 112 D3
Oelsnitz, *Germany* 25 E8
Oelwein, *U.S.A.* 112 D9
Oenpelli, *Australia* 92 B5
Oetz, *Austria* 26 D3
Of, *Turkey* 73 B9
Ofanto ➤, *Italy* 43 A9
Offa, *Nigeria* 83 D5
Offaly □, *Ireland* 12 C4
Offenbach, *Germany* 25 E4
Offenburg, *Germany* 25 G3
Officer, The ➤, *Australia* .. 93 E5
Offida, *Italy* 41 F10
Ofidhousa, *Greece* 47 E8
Ofotfjorden, *Norway* 8 B17
Ōfunato, *Japan* 54 E10
Oga, *Japan* 54 E9
Oga-Hantō, *Japan* 54 E9
Ogaden, *Ethiopia* 75 F3
Ōgaki, *Japan* 55 G8
Ogallala, *U.S.A.* 112 E4
Ogasawara Gunto, *Pac. Oc.* .. 96 E6
Ogbomosho, *Nigeria* 83 D5
Ogden, *U.S.A.* 108 F7
Ogdensburg, *U.S.A.* 117 B9
Ogeechee ➤, *U.S.A.* 115 K5
Ogilby, *U.S.A.* 111 N12
Oglio ➤, *Italy* 40 C7
Óglio Nord △, *Italy* 40 C6
Óglio Sud △, *Italy* 40 C7
Ogmore, *Australia* 94 C4
Ognon ➤, *France* 19 E12
Ogoja, *Nigeria* 83 D6
Ogoki, *Canada* 104 B2
Ogoki ➤, *Canada* 104 B2
Ogoki L., *Canada* 104 B2
Ogoki Res., *Canada* 104 B2
Ogooué ➤, *Gabon* 84 E1
Ogosta ➤, *Bulgaria* 44 C7
Ogowe = Ogooué ➤, *Gabon* .. 84 E1
Ogr = Sharafa, *Sudan* 81 E2
Ograźden, *Macedonia* 44 E6
Ogre, *Latvia* 9 H21
Ogrein, *Sudan* 80 D3
Ogulin, *Croatia* 41 C12
Ogun □, *Nigeria* 83 D5
Ogurchinskiy, Ostrov,
    Turkmenistan 71 B7
Oguta, *Nigeria* 83 D6
Ogwashi-Uku, *Nigeria* 83 D6
Ogwe, *Nigeria* 83 E6
Ohai, *N.Z.* 91 L2
Ohakune, *N.Z.* 91 H5
Ohata, *Japan* 54 D10
Ohau, L., *N.Z.* 91 L2
Ohio □, *U.S.A.* 114 F2
Ohio ➤, *U.S.A.* 114 G1
Ohře, *Czech Rep.* 26 A7
Ohre ➤, *Germany* 24 C7
Ohrid, *Macedonia* 44 E4
Ohridsko Jezero, *Macedonia* .. 44 E4
Ohrigstad, *S. Africa* 89 C5
Öhringen, *Germany* 25 F5
Oi Qu, *China* 58 C2
Oiapoque, *Brazil* 125
Oikou, *China* 57 E9
Oil City, *U.S.A.* 116 E5
Oil Springs, *Canada* 116 D2
Oildale, *U.S.A.* 111 K7
Oinousa, *Greece* 47 C8
Oise □, *France* 19 C9
Oise ➤, *France* 19 C9
Oiseaux du Djoudj △, *Senegal* .. 82 B1
Oistins, *Barbados* .... 121 g
Oistins B., *Barbados* .... 121 g
Ōita, *Japan* 55 H5
Ōita □, *Japan* 55 H5
Oiticica, *Brazil* 125 E10
Ojacaliente, *Mexico* 118 C4
Ojai, *U.S.A.* 111 L7
Ojców □, *Poland* 31 H6
Ojinaga, *Mexico* 118 B4
Ojiya, *Japan* 55 F9
Ojo de Liebre △, *Mexico* ... 118 B2
Ojos del Salado, Cerro, *Argentina* .. 126 B2
Oka ➤, *Russia* 34 B7
Okaba, *Indonesia* 63 F9
Okahandja, *Namibia* 88 C2
Okaputa, *Namibia* 88 C2
Okara, *Pakistan* 68 D5
Okaukuejo, *Namibia* 88 B2
Okavango Delta, *Botswana* .. 88 B3

Okavango Swamp = Okavango
    Delta, *Botswana* 88 B3
Okaya, *Japan* 55 F9
Okayama, *Japan* 55 G6
Okayama □, *Japan* 55 G6
Okazaki, *Japan* 55 G8
Oke-Iho, *Nigeria* 83 D5
Okęcie, Warszawa ✈ (WAW),
    Poland 31 F7
Okeechobee, *U.S.A.* 115 M5
Okeechobee, L., *U.S.A.* 115 M5
Okefenokee △, *U.S.A.* 115 K4
Okefenokee Swamp, *U.S.A.* .. 115 K4
Okehampton, *U.K.* 15 G4
Okene, *Nigeria* 83 D6
Oker ➤, *Germany* 24 C6
Okha, *India* 68 H3
Okha, *Russia* 53 D15
Ókhi Óros, *Greece* 46 C6
Okhotsk, *Russia* 53 D15
Okhotsk, Sea of, *Asia* 53 D15
Okhotskiy Perevoz, *Russia* .. 53 C14
Okhtyrka, *Ukraine* 33 G8
Oki-Shotō, *Japan* 55 F6
Okiep, *S. Africa* 88 D2
Okigwi, *Nigeria* 83 D6
Okija, *Nigeria* 83 D6
Okinawa □, *Japan* 55 L4
Okinawa, *N.Z.* 55 L4
Okinawa-Guntō, *Japan* 55 L4
Okinawa-Jima, *Japan* 55 L4
Okino-erabu-Shima, *Japan* .. 55 L4
Okitipupa, *Nigeria* 83 D5
Oklahoma □, *U.S.A.* 113 H6
Oklahoma City, *U.S.A.* 113 H6
Okmulgee, *U.S.A.* 113 H7
Oknitsa = Ocniţa, *Moldova* .. 29 B12
Oko, W. ➤, *Sudan* 80 C4
Okolo, *Uganda* 86 B3
Okolona, *U.S.A.* 113 J10
Okombahe, *Namibia* 88 C2
Okonek, *Poland* 30 E3
Okotoks, *Canada* 102 C6
Okrika, *Nigeria* 83 E6
Oksibil, *Indonesia* 63 E10
Oktabrsk = Oktyabrsk,
    Kazakhstan 52 E6
Oktyabrsk, *Kazakhstan* 52 E6
Oktyabrsk, *Russia* 34 D9
Oktyabrskiy = Aktsyabrski,
    Belarus 33 F5
Oktyabrskiy, *Russia* 35 G5
Oktyabrskoy Revolyutsii, Ostrov,
    Russia 53 B10
Oktyabrskoye = Zhovtneve,
    Ukraine 33 J7
Okulovka, *Russia* 32 C7
Okuru, *N.Z.* 91 K2
Okushiri-Tō, *Japan* 54 C9
Okuta, *Nigeria* 83 D5
Okwa ➤, *Botswana* 88 C3
Ola, *U.S.A.* 113 H8
Ola ➤, *Russia* 53 C16
Ólafsfjörður, *Iceland* 8 C4
Ólafsvík, *Iceland* 8 D2
Olaine, *Latvia* 30 B10
Olancha, *U.S.A.* 111 J8
Olancha Pk., *U.S.A.* 111 J8
Olanchito, *Honduras* 120 C2
Öland, *Sweden* 11 H10
Ölands norra udde, *Sweden* .. 11 G11
Ölands södra udde, *Sweden* .. 11 H10
Olargues, *France* 20 E6
Olary, *Australia* 95 E3
Olascoaga, *Argentina* 126 D3
Olathe, *U.S.A.* 112 F7
Olavarría, *Argentina* 126 D3
Oława, *Poland* 31 H4
Olbernhau, *Germany* 24 E9
Ólbia, *Italy* 42 B2
Ólbia, G. di, *Italy* 42 B2
Olching, *Germany* 25 G7
Olcott, *U.S.A.* 116 C6
Old Bahama Chan. = Bahama,
    Canal Viejo de, *W. Indies* .. 120 B4
Old Baldy Pk. = San Antonio,
    Mt., *U.S.A.* 111 L9
Old Castile = Castilla y Leon □,
    Spain 36 D6
Old Crow, *Canada* 100 B6
Old Dale, *U.S.A.* 111 L11
Old Forge, *N.Y., U.S.A.* ... 117 C10
Old Forge, *Pa., U.S.A.* 117 E9
Old Perlican, *Canada* 105 C9
Old Shinyanga, *Tanzania* ... 86 C3
Old Speck Mt., *U.S.A.* 117 B14
Old Town, *U.S.A.* 115 C11
Old Washington, *U.S.A.* ... 116 F3
Old Wives L., *Canada* 103 C7
Oldbury, *U.K.* 15 F5
Oldcastle, *Ireland* 12 C4
Oldeani, *Tanzania* 86 C4
Oldenburg, *Niedersachsen,
    Germany* 24 B4
Oldenburg, *Schleswig-Holstein,
    Germany* 24 A6
Oldenzaal, *Neths.* 17 B6
Oldham, *U.K.* 14 D5
Oldman ➤, *Canada* 102 D6
Oldmeldrum, *U.K.* 13 D6
Olds, *Canada* 102 C6
Oldziyt, *Mongolia* 56 B5
Olean, *U.S.A.* 116 D6
Olecko, *Poland* 30 D9
Oléggio, *Italy* 40 C5
Oleiros, *Portugal* 36 F3
Oleiros, *Spain* 36 B2
Olekma ➤, *Russia* 53 C13
Olekminsk, *Russia* 53 C13
Oleksandriya, Kirovohrad,
    Ukraine 33 H7
Oleksandriya, *Rivne, Ukraine* .. 33 G4
Oleksandrovka, *Ukraine* 33 H7

Olema, *U.S.A.* 110 G4
Olenek, *Russia* 53 C12
Olenek ➤, *Russia* 53 B13
Olenino, *Russia* 32 D7
Oléron, Î. d', *France* 20 C2
Oleśnica, *Poland* 31 G4
Olesno, *Poland* 31 H5
Olevsk, *Ukraine* 33 G4
Olga, *Russia* 53 E14
Olga, L., *Canada* 104 C4
Olga, Mt., *Australia* 93 E5
Ølgod, *Denmark* 11 J2
Olhão, *Portugal* 37 H3
Olhopil, *Ukraine* 29 B14
Olhovatka, *Russia* 30 D9
Olib, *Croatia* 41 D11
Oliena, *Italy* 42 B2
Oliete, *Spain* 38 D4
Olifants = Elefantes ➤, *Africa* .. 89 C5
Olifants ➤, *Namibia* 88 C2
Olifantshoek, *S. Africa* 88 D3
Ólimbos, *Greece* 47 F9
Ólimbos, Óros, *Greece* 44 F6
Olímpia, *Brazil* 127 A6
Olimpos-Beydaglari △, *Turkey* .. 47 E12
Olinda, *Brazil* 125 E12
Olite, *Spain* 38 C3
Oliva, *Argentina* 126 C3
Oliva, *Spain* 39 G4
Oliva, Punta del, *Spain* 36 B5
Oliva de la Frontera, *Spain* .. 37 G4
Olivares, *Spain* 38 F2
Olivehurst, *U.S.A.* 110 F5
Oliveira de Azeméis, *Portugal* .. 36 E2
Oliveira do Douro, *Portugal* .. 36 D2
Olivenza, *Spain* 37 G3
Oliver, *Canada* 102 D5
Oliver L., *Canada* 103 B8
Olivet, *France* 19 E8
Olivia, *U.S.A.* 112 C7
Olkhovka, *Russia* 34 F7
Olkusz, *Poland* 31 H6
Ollagüe, *Chile* 126 A2
Olmedo, *Spain* 36 D6
Olmeto, *France* 21 G12
Olmos, *Peru* 124 E3
Olney, *Ill., U.S.A.* 114 F1
Olney, *Tex., U.S.A.* 113 J5
Olofström, *Sweden* 11 H8
Oloma, *Cameroon* 83 E7
Olomane ➤, *Canada* 105 B7
Olomouc, *Czech Rep.* 27 B10
Olomoucký □, *Czech Rep.* .. 27 B10
Olonets, *Russia* 32 B7
Olongapo, *Phil.* 61 D4
Olonne-sur-Mer, *France* 20 B2
Oloron, Gave d' ➤, *France* .. 20 E2
Oloron-Ste-Marie, *France* ... 20 E3
Olot, *Spain* 38 C7
Olovo, *Bos.-H.* 28 F3
Olovyannaya, *Russia* 53 D12
Oloy ➤, *Russia* 53 C16
Olsberg, *Germany* 24 D4
Olshammar, *Sweden* 11 F8
Olshanka, *Ukraine* 33 H6
Olshany, *Ukraine* 33 G8
Olsztyn, *Poland* 30 E7
Olsztynek, *Poland* 30 E7
Olt □, *Romania* 29 F9
Olt ➤, *Romania* 29 G9
Olten, *Switz.* 25 H3
Olteniţa, *Romania* 29 F11
Olton, *U.S.A.* 113 H3
Oltu, *Turkey* 73 B9
Oluanpi, *Taiwan* 59 G13
Olula del Rio, *Spain* 39 H2
Olur, *Turkey* 73 B10
Olutanga, *Phil.* 61 H5
Olvega, *Spain* 38 D2
Olvera, *Spain* 37 J5
Olymbos, *Cyprus* 49 D12
Olympia, *Greece* 46 D3
Olympia, *U.S.A.* 110 D4
Olympic △, *U.S.A.* 110 C3
Olympic Dam, *Australia* 95 E2
Olympic Mts., *U.S.A.* 110 C3
Olympus, *Cyprus* 49 E11
Olympus, Mt. = Ólimbos, Óros,
    Greece 44 F6
Olympus, Mt. = Uludağ, *Turkey* .. 45 F13
Olympus, Mt., *U.S.A.* 110 C3
Olyphant, *U.S.A.* 117 E9
Om ➤, *Russia* 52 D8
Om Hajer, *Eritrea* 81 E4
Om Koi, *Thailand* 64 D2
Ōma, *Japan* 54 D10
Ōmachi, *Japan* 55 F8
Ōmae-Zaki, *Japan* 55 G9
Ōmagari, *Japan* 54 E10
Omagh, *U.K.* 12 B4
Omagh □, *U.K.* 12 B4
Omaha, *U.S.A.* 112 E7
Omak, *U.S.A.* 108 B4
Omalos, *Greece* 49 D5
Oman ■, *Asia* 75 C6
Oman, G. of, *Asia* 71 E8
Omaruru, *Namibia* 88 C2
Omaruru ➤, *Namibia* 88 C1
Omate, *Peru* 124 G4
Ombai, Selat, *Indonesia* ... 63 F6
Omboué, *Gabon* 84 E1
Ombrone ➤, *Italy* 40 F8
Omdurmân, *Sudan* 81 D3
Omegna, *Italy* 40 C5
Omemee, *Canada* 116 B6
Omeonga, Dem. Rep. of
    the Congo 86 C1
Ometepe, I. de, *Nic.* 120 D2
Ometepec, *Mexico* 119 D5
Ominato, *Japan* 54 D10
Omineca ➤, *Canada* 102 B4
Omiš, *Croatia* 41 E13
Omišalj, *Croatia* 41 C11

Omitara, *Namibia* 88 C2
Ōmiya, *Japan* 55 G9
Omme Å ➤, *Denmark* 11 J2
Ommen, *Neths.* 17 B6
Ömnögovĭ □, *Mongolia* 56 C3
Omo △, *Ethiopia* 81 F4
Omo ➤, *Ethiopia* 81 F4
Omo Valley, *Ethiopia* 81 F4
Omodeo, L., *Italy* 42 B1
Omodhos, *Cyprus* 49 E11
Omoko, *Nigeria* 83 D6
Omolon ➤, *Russia* 53 C16
Omono-Gawa ➤, *Japan* ... 54 E10
Omsk, *Russia* 52 D8
Omsukchan, *Russia* 53 C16
Ōmu, *Japan* 54 B11
Omul, Vf., *Romania* 29 E10
Omulew ➤, *Poland* 31 E8
Ōmura, *Japan* 55 H4
Omuramba Omatako ➤,
    Namibia 88 B2
Omuramba Ovambo ➤, *Namibia* .. 88 B2
Omurtag, *Bulgaria* 45 C10
Ōmuta, *Japan* 55 H5
Oña, *Spain* 36 C7
Onaga, *U.S.A.* 112 F6
Onalaska, *U.S.A.* 112 D9
Onancock, *U.S.A.* 114 G8
Onang, *Indonesia* 63 E5
Onaping L., *Canada* 104 C3
Oñati, *Spain* 38 B2
Onavas, *Mexico* 118 B3
Onawa, *U.S.A.* 112 D6
Oncócua, *Angola* 88 B1
Onda, *Spain* 38 F4
Ondaejin, *N. Korea* 57 D15
Ondangwa, *Namibia* 88 B2
Ondarroa, *Spain* 38 B2
Ondava ➤, *Slovak Rep.* 27 C14
Ondjiva, *Angola* 88 B2
Ondo, *Nigeria* 83 D5
Ondo □, *Nigeria* 83 D6
Öndörshil, *Mongolia* 56 B5
Öndverðarnes, *Iceland* 8 D1
One Tree, *Australia* 95 E3
Onega, *Russia* 52 C4
Onega ➤, *Russia* 6 C13
Onega, L. = Onezhskoye Ozero,
    Russia 32 B8
Oneida, *U.S.A.* 117 C9
Oneida L., *U.S.A.* 117 C9
O'Neill, *U.S.A.* 112 D5
Onekotan, Ostrov, *Russia* ... 53 E16
Onema, Dem. Rep. of the Congo .. 86 C1
Oneonta, *U.S.A.* 117 D9
Oneşti, *Romania* 29 D11
Onezhskoye Ozero, *Russia* .. 32 B8
Ongarue, *N.Z.* 91 H5
Ongers ➤, *S. Africa* 88 E3
Ongerup, *Australia* 93 F2
Ongjin, *N. Korea* 57 F13
Ongkharak, *Thailand* 64 E3
Ongniud Qi, *China* 57 C10
Ongoka, Dem. Rep. of the Congo .. 86 C1
Ongole, *India* 66 M12
Ongon = Havirga, *Mongolia* .. 56 B7
Oni, *Georgia* 35 J6
Onida, *U.S.A.* 112 C4
Onilahy ➤, *Madag.* 89 C7
Onitsha, *Nigeria* 83 D6
Onoda, *Japan* 55 G5
Onpyŏng-ni, *S. Korea* 57 H14
Ons, I. de, *Spain* 36 C2
Onsala, *Sweden* 11 G6
Onslow, *Australia* 92 D2
Onslow B., *U.S.A.* 115 H7
Ontake-San, *Japan* 55 G8
Ontario, *Calif., U.S.A.* 111 L9
Ontario, *Oreg., U.S.A.* 108 D5
Ontario □, *Canada* 104 B2
Ontario, L., *N. Amer.* 116 C7
Ontinyent, *Spain* 39 G4
Ontonagon, *U.S.A.* 112 B10
Ontur, *Spain* 39 G3
Onyx, *U.S.A.* 111 K8
Oodnadatta, *Australia* 95 D2
Ooldea, *Australia* 93 F5
Oombulgurri, *Australia* 92 C4
Oorindi, *Australia* 94 C3
Oost-Vlaanderen □, *Belgium* .. 17 C3
Oostende, *Belgium* 17 C2
Oosterhout, *Neths.* 17 C4
Oosterschelde ➤, *Neths.* 17 C4
Oosterwolde, *Neths.* 17 B6
Ootacamund = Udagamandalam,
    India 66 P10
Ootsa L., *Canada* 102 C3
Op Luang △, *Thailand* 64 C2
Opaka, *Bulgaria* 45 C10
Opala, Dem. Rep. of the Congo .. 86 C1
Opalenica, *Poland* 31 F3
Opan, *Bulgaria* 45 D9
Opanake, *Sri Lanka* 66 R12
Opasatika, *Canada* 104 C3
Opatija, *Croatia* 41 C11
Opatów, *Poland* 31 H8
Opava, *Czech Rep.* 27 B10
Opelika, *U.S.A.* 115 J3
Opelousas, *U.S.A.* 113 K8
Opémisca, L., *Canada* 104 C5
Opheim, *U.S.A.* 108 B10
Ophthalmia Ra., *Australia* ... 92 D2
Opi, *Nigeria* 83 D6
Opinaca ➤, *Canada* 104 B4
Opinaca, Rés., *Canada* 104 B4
Opinnagau ➤, *Canada* 104 B3
Opiscotéo, L., *Canada* 105 B6
Opobo, *Nigeria* 83 E6
Opochka, *Russia* 32 D5
Opoczno, *Poland* 31 G7
Opol, *Phil.* 61 G6

Opole, *Poland* 31 H4
Opole Lubelskie, *Poland* 31 G8
Opolskie □, *Poland* 31 H5
Oponono L., *Namibia* 88 B2
Oporto = Porto, *Portugal* ... 36 D2
Opotiki, *N.Z.* 91 H6
Opp, *U.S.A.* 115 K2
Oppdal, *Norway* 9 E13
Óppido Mamertina, *Italy* ... 43 D8
Opportunity, *U.S.A.* 108 C5
Oprişor, *Romania* 28 F8
Oprtalj, *Croatia* 41 C10
Opua, *N.Z.* 91 F5
Opunake, *N.Z.* 91 H4
Opuwo, *Namibia* 88 B1
Opuzen, *Croatia* 41 E14
Ora, *Cyprus* 49 E12
Oracle, *U.S.A.* 109 K8
Oradea, *Romania* 28 C6
Öræfajökull, *Iceland* 8 D5
Orahovac, *Serbia & M.* 44 D4
Orahovica, *Croatia* 28 E2
Orai, *India* 69 G8
Oraison, *France* 21 E9
Oral = Zhayyq ➤, *Kazakhstan* .. 52 E6
Oral, *Kazakhstan* 34 E10
Oran, *Algeria* 78 A5
Orange, *Australia* 95 E4
Orange, *France* 21 D8
Orange, *Calif., U.S.A.* 111 M9
Orange, *Mass., U.S.A.* 117 D12
Orange, *Tex., U.S.A.* 113 K8
Orange, *Va., U.S.A.* 114 F6
Orange ➤, *S. Africa* 88 D2
Orange, C., *Brazil* 125 C8
Orange Cove, *U.S.A.* 110 J7
Orange Free State = Free State □,
    S. Africa 88 D4
Orange Grove, *U.S.A.* 113 M6
Orange Walk, *Belize* 119 D7
Orangeburg, *U.S.A.* 115 J5
Orangeville, *Canada* 116 C4
Orango, *Guinea-Biss.* 82 C1
Orani, *Phil.* 61 D4
Oranienburg, *Germany* 24 C9
Oranje = Orange ➤, *S. Africa* .. 88 D2
Oranjemund, *Namibia* 88 D2
Oranjerivier, *S. Africa* 88 D3
Oranjestad, *Aruba* 121 D5
Orapa, *Botswana* 85 J5
Orarak, *Sudan* 81 F3
Oras, *Phil.* 61 E6
Orašje, *Bos.-H.* 28 E3
Orăştie, *Romania* 29 E8
Orava = Slovak Rep. 27 B12
Orava, Vodna nádrž, *Slovak Rep.* .. 27 B12
Oraviţa, *Romania* 28 E6
Orb ➤, *France* 20 E7
Orba ➤, *Italy* 40 D5
Ørbæk, *Denmark* 11 J4
Orbe, *Switz.* 25 J2
Orbec, *France* 18 C7
Orbetello, *Italy* 41 F8
Órbigo ➤, *Spain* 36 C5
Orbisonia, *U.S.A.* 116 F7
Orbost, *Australia* 95 F4
Örbyhus, *Sweden* 10 D11
Orcadas, *Antarctica* 5 C18
Orcas I., *U.S.A.* 110 B4
Orce, *Spain* 39 H2
Orce ➤, *Spain* 39 H2
Orchard City, *U.S.A.* 109 G10
Orchies, *France* 19 B10
Orchila, I., *Venezuela* 121 D6
Orchilla, Pta., *Canary Is.* ... 48 G1
Órcia ➤, *Italy* 41 F8
Orco ➤, *Italy* 40 C4
Orcutt, *U.S.A.* 111 L6
Ord, *U.S.A.* 112 E5
Ord ➤, *Australia* 92 C4
Ord, Mt., *Australia* 92 C4
Ordenes = Ordes, *Spain* 36 B2
Orderville, *U.S.A.* 109 H7
Ordes, *Spain* 36 B2
Ordesa y Monte Perido △, *Spain* .. 38 C4
Ording = St-Peter-Ording,
    Germany 24 A4
Ordos = Mu Us Shamo, *China* .. 56 E5
Ordu, *Turkey* 72 B7
Ordubad, *Azerbaijan* 73 C12
Orduña, *Alava, Spain* 38 C2
Orduña, *Granada, Spain* 37 H7
Ordway, *U.S.A.* 112 F3
Ordzhonikidze, *Ukraine* 33 J8
Ore, Dem. Rep. of the Congo .. 86 B2
Ore Mts. = Erzgebirge, *Germany* .. 24 E8
Orebić, *Croatia* 41 F14
Örebro, *Sweden* 10 E9
Örebro län □, *Sweden* 10 E9
Orecchiella △, *Italy* 40 D7
Oregon, *U.S.A.* 112 D10
Oregon □, *U.S.A.* 108 E3
Oregon City, *U.S.A.* 110 E4
Oregon Dunes △, *U.S.A.* ... 108 E1
Öregrund, *Sweden* 10 D12
Öregrundsgrepen, *Sweden* .. 10 D12
Orekhov = Orikhiv, *Ukraine* .. 33 J8
Orekhovo-Zuyevo, *Russia* ... 32 E10
Orel, *Russia* 33 F9
Orel ➤, *Russia* 33 H8
Orellana, *Spain* 37 F5
Orellana, Canal de, *Spain* ... 37 F5
Orellana, Embalse de, *Spain* .. 37 F5
Orem, *U.S.A.* 108 F8
Ören, *Turkey* 47 D9
Orenburg, *Russia* 52 D6
Örencik, *Turkey* 47 B11
Orense = Ourense, *Spain* 36 C3
Orense □, *Spain* 36 C3
Orepuki, *N.Z.* 91 M1
Orestiás, *Greece* 45 E10
Orestos Pereyra, *Mexico* ... 118 B3

Øresund, Europe 11 J6
Orford Ness, U.K. 15 E9
Organ Pipe Cactus △, U.S.A. 109 K7
Organos, Pta. de los, Canary Is. 48 F2
Organyà, Spain 38 C6
Orgaz, Spain 37 F7
Orgeyev = Orhei, Moldova 29 C13
Orhaneli, Turkey 45 G12
Orhaneli →, Turkey 45 G12
Orhangazi, Turkey 45 F13
Orhei, Moldova 29 C13
Orhon Gol →, Mongolia 60 A5
Óría, Italy 43 B10
Oriental, Cordillera, Colombia 124 B4
Oriental, Grand Erg, Algeria 78 B7
Orientale □, Dem. Rep. of
  the Congo 86 B2
Oriente, Argentina 126 D3
Orihuela, Spain 39 G4
Orihuela del Tremedal, Spain 38 E3
Orikhiv, Ukraine 33 J8
Orikum, Albania 44 F3
Orillia, Canada 116 B5
Orinoco →, Venezuela 124 B6
Orion, Canada 103 D6
Oriskany, U.S.A. 117 C9
Orissa □, India 67 K14
Orissaare, Estonia 9 G20
Oristano, Italy 42 C1
Oristano, G. di, Italy 42 C1
Orizaba, Mexico 119 D5
Orizaba, Pico de, Mexico 119 D5
Orizare, Bulgaria 45 D11
Orjen, Bos.-H. 44 D2
Orjiva, Spain 37 J7
Orkanger, Norway 8 E13
Örkelljunga, Sweden 11 H7
Örken, Sweden 11 G9
Örkény, Hungary 28 C4
Orkla →, Norway 8 E13
Orkney, S. Africa 88 D4
Orkney □, U.K. 13 B5
Orkney Is., U.K. 13 B6
Orland, U.S.A. 110 F4
Orlando, U.S.A. 115 L5
Orlando, C. d', Italy 43 D7
Orléanais, France 19 C8
Orléans, France 19 E8
Orleans, U.S.A. 117 B12
Orléans, Î. d', Canada 105 C5
Orlice →, Czech Rep. 26 A8
Orlivka, Ukraine 29 E13
Orlov, Slovak Rep. 27 B13
Orlov Gay, Russia 34 E9
Orlová, Czech Rep. 27 B11
Orlovat, Serbia & M. 28 E5
Orly, Paris ✈ (ORY), France 19 D9
Ormara, Pakistan 66 G4
Ormea, Italy 40 D4
Ormília, Greece 44 F7
Ormoc, Phil. 61 F6
Ormond, N.Z. 91 H6
Ormond Beach, U.S.A. 115 L5
Ormož, Slovenia 41 B13
Ormskirk, U.K. 14 D5
Ormstown, Canada 117 A11
Ornans, France 19 E13
Orne □, France 18 D7
Orne →, France 18 C6
Orneta, Poland 30 D7
Örnö, Sweden 10 E12
Örnsköldsvik, Sweden 10 A12
Oro →, N. Korea 57 D14
Oro →, Mexico 118 B3
Oro Grande, U.S.A. 111 L9
Oro Valley, U.S.A. 109 K8
Orobie, Alpi, Italy 40 B6
Orobie Bergamasche △, Italy 40 C6
Orobie Valtellinesi △, Italy 40 B6
Orocué, Colombia 124 C4
Orodara, Burkina Faso 82 C4
Orodo, Nigeria 83 D6
Orofino, U.S.A. 108 C5
Orol Dengizi = Aral Sea, Asia 52 E7
Oromiya □, Ethiopia 81 F5
Oromocto, Canada 105 C6
Oron, Nigeria 83 E6
Orono, Canada 116 C6
Orono, U.S.A. 115 C11
Oronsay, U.K. 13 E2
Oropesa, Spain 36 F5
Oroquieta, Phil. 61 G5
Orosei, Italy 42 B2
Orosei, G. di, Italy 42 B2
Orosháza, Hungary 28 D5
Oroszlány, Hungary 28 C3
Orotukan, Russia 53 C16
Oroville, Calif., U.S.A. 110 F5
Oroville, Wash., U.S.A. 108 B4
Oroville, L., U.S.A. 110 F5
Orrefors, Sweden 11 H9
Orroroo, Australia 95 E2
Orrviken, Sweden 10 A8
Orrville, U.S.A. 116 F3
Orsa, Sweden 10 C8
Orsara di Púglia, Italy 43 A8
Orsasjön, Sweden 10 C8
Orsha, Belarus 32 E6
Örsjö, Sweden 11 H9
Orsk, Russia 52 D6
Orșova, Romania 28 F7
Örsted, Denmark 11 H4
Ørsundsbro, Sweden 10 E11
Orta, L. d', Italy 40 C5
Orta Nova, Italy 43 A8
Ortaca, Turkey 47 E10
Ortakent, Turkey 47 D9
Ortaklar, Turkey 47 D9
Ortaköy, Çorum, Turkey 72 B6
Ortaköy, Niğde, Turkey 72 C6
Orte, Italy 41 F9
Ortegal, C., Spain 36 B3

Orthez, France 20 E3
Ortigueira, Spain 36 B3
Orting, U.S.A. 110 C4
Ortisei, Italy 41 B8
Ortles, Italy 40 B7
Ortón →, Bolivia 124 F5
Ortona, Italy 41 F11
Ortonville, U.S.A. 112 C6
Orūmīyeh, Iran 70 B5
Orūmīyeh, Daryācheh-ye, Iran 70 B5
Orune, Italy 42 B2
Oruro, Bolivia 124 G5
Orust, Sweden 11 F5
Oruzgān □, Afghan. 66 C5
Orvault, France 18 E5
Orvieto, Italy 41 F9
Orwell, N.Y., U.S.A. 117 C9
Orwell, Ohio, U.S.A. 116 E4
Orwell →, U.K. 15 F9
Orwigsburg, U.S.A. 117 F8
Oryakhovo, Bulgaria 44 C7
Orynyn, Ukraine 29 B11
Orzinuovi, Italy 40 C6
Orzyc →, Poland 31 F8
Orzysz, Poland 30 E8
Osa →, Poland 30 E5
Osa, Pen. de, Costa Rica 120 E3
Osage, U.S.A. 112 D8
Osage →, U.S.A. 112 F9
Osage City, U.S.A. 112 F7
Ōsaka, Japan 55 G7
Osan, S. Korea 57 F14
Osawatomie, U.S.A. 112 F7
Osborne, U.S.A. 112 F5
Osby, Sweden 11 H7
Osceola, Ark., U.S.A. 113 H10
Osceola, Iowa, U.S.A. 112 E8
Oschatz, Germany 24 D9
Oschersleben, Germany 24 C7
Óschiri, Italy 42 B2
Oscoda, U.S.A. 116 B1
Osečina, Serbia & M. 44 B3
Ösel = Saaremaa, Estonia 9 G20
Osery, Russia 32 E10
Osgoode, Canada 117 A9
Osh, Kyrgyzstan 52 E8
Oshakati, Namibia 85 H3
Oshawa, Canada 116 C6
Oshigambo, Namibia 88 B2
Oshkosh, Nebr., U.S.A. 112 E3
Oshkosh, Wis., U.S.A. 112 C10
Oshmyany = Ashmyany, Belarus 9 J21
Oshnovīyeh, Iran 70 B5
Oshogbo, Nigeria 83 D5
Oshtorīnān, Iran 71 C6
Oshwe, Dem. Rep. of the Congo 84 E3
Osi, Nigeria 83 D6
Osieczna, Poland 31 G3
Osijek, Croatia 28 E3
Ósilo, Italy 42 B1
Ósimo, Italy 41 E10
Osintorf, Belarus 32 E6
Osipovichi = Asipovichy, Belarus 32 F5
Osiyan, India 68 F5
Osizweni, S. Africa 89 D5
Oskaloosa, U.S.A. 112 E8
Oskarshamn, Sweden 11 G10
Oskarström, Sweden 11 H6
Oskélanéo, Canada 104 C4
Öskemen, Kazakhstan 52 E9
Oskol →, Ukraine 33 H9
Oslo, Norway 9 G14
Oslob, Phil. 61 G5
Oslofjorden, Norway 9 G14
Osmanabad, India 66 K10
Osmancık, Turkey 72 B6
Osmaniye, Turkey 70 B3
Osmanlı, Turkey 45 E10
Ösmo, Sweden 10 F11
Osnabrück, Germany 24 C4
Ośno Lubuskie, Poland 31 F1
Osoblaha, Czech Rep. 27 A10
Osogovska Planina, Macedonia 44 D6
Osor, Italy 41 D11
Osorio, Brazil 127 B5
Osorno, Chile 128 E2
Osorno, Spain 36 C6
Osoyoos, Canada 102 D5
Osøyro, Norway 9 F11
Ospika →, Canada 102 B4
Osprey Reef, Australia 94 A4
Oss, Neths. 17 C5
Ossa, Mt., Australia 95 G4
Óssa, Óros, Greece 46 B4
Ossa de Montiel, Spain 39 G2
Ossabaw I., U.S.A. 115 K5
Osse →, France 20 D4
Osse →, Nigeria 83 D6
Ossi, Italy 42 B1
Ossining, U.S.A. 117 E11
Ossipee, U.S.A. 117 C13
Ossokmanuan L., Canada 105 B7
Ossora, Russia 53 D17
Ostashkov, Russia 32 D7
Østavall, Sweden 10 B9
Oste →, Germany 24 B5
Ostend = Oostende, Belgium 17 C2
Österbotten = Pohjanmaa,
  Finland 8 E20
Osterburg, Germany 24 C7
Osterburg, U.S.A. 116 F6
Osterburken, Germany 25 F5
Österbybruk, Sweden 10 D11
Österbymo, Sweden 11 G9
Österdalälven, Sweden 10 C7
Österdalen, Norway 9 F14
Österfärnebo, Sweden 10 D10
Osterforse, Sweden 10 A11
Östergötlands län □, Sweden 11 F9
Osterholz-Scharmbeck, Germany 24 B4
Østerild, Denmark 11 G2

Östermyra = Seinäjoki, Finland 9 E20
Osterode, Germany 24 D6
Östersund, Sweden 10 A8
Östervåla, Sweden 10 D11
Ostfriesische Inseln, Germany 24 B3
Ostfriesland, Germany 24 B3
Östhammar, Sweden 10 D12
Óstia, Lido di, Italy 41 G9
Ostmark, Sweden 10 D6
Östra Husby, Sweden 11 F10
Ostrava, Czech Rep. 27 B11
Ostravský □, Czech Rep. 27 B10
Ostróda, Poland 30 E6
Ostrogozhsk, Russia 33 G10
Ostroh, Ukraine 33 G4
Ostrołęka, Poland 31 E8
Ostrov, Bulgaria 45 C8
Ostrov, Czech Rep. 26 A5
Ostrov, Romania 29 F12
Ostrov, Russia 32 D5
Ostrów Lubelski, Poland 31 G9
Ostrów Mazowiecka, Poland 31 F8
Ostrów Wielkopolski, Poland 31 G4
Ostrowiec-Świętokrzyski, Poland 31 H8
Ostrožac, Bos.-H. 28 G2
Ostrzeszów, Poland 31 G4
Ostseebad Kühlungsborn,
  Germany 24 A7
Osttirol □, Austria 26 E5
Ostuni, Italy 43 B10
Osum →, Albania 44 F4
Osŭm →, Bulgaria 45 C8
Ōsumi-Kaikyō, Japan 55 J5
Ōsumi-Shotō, Japan 55 J5
Osun □, Nigeria 83 D5
Osuna, Spain 37 H5
Oswegatchie →, U.S.A. 117 B9
Oswego, U.S.A. 117 C8
Oswego →, U.S.A. 117 C8
Oswestry, U.K. 14 E4
Święcim, Poland 31 H6
Otaci, Moldova 29 B12
Otago □, N.Z. 91 L2
Otago Harbour, N.Z. 91 L3
Otaheite B., Trin. & Tob. 125 K15
Ōtake, Japan 55 G6
Otaki, N.Z. 91 J5
Otaru, Japan 54 C10
Otaru-Wan = Ishikari-Wan, Japan 54 C10
Otava →, Czech Rep. 26 B7
Otavalo, Ecuador 124 C3
Otavi, Namibia 88 B2
Otchinjau, Angola 88 B1
Otelec, Romania 28 E5
Otelnuk, L., Canada 105 A6
Oțelu Roșu, Romania 28 E7
Otero de Rey = Outeiro de Rei,
  Spain 36 B3
Othello, U.S.A. 108 C4
Othonoí, Greece 46 B1
Óthris, Óros, Greece 46 B4
Oti →, Togo 83 C5
Otjiwarongo, Namibia 88 C2
Otjo, Namibia 88 C2
Otmuchów, Poland 31 H4
Otočac, Croatia 41 D12
Otoineppu, Japan 54 B11
Otok, Croatia 41 E13
Otorohanga, N.Z. 91 H5
Otoskwin →, Canada 104 B2
Otra →, Norway 9 G13
Otradnyy, Russia 34 D10
Otranto, Italy 43 B11
Otranto, C. d', Italy 43 B11
Otranto, Str. of, Italy 43 B11
Otrokovice, Czech Rep. 27 B10
Otse, S. Africa 88 D4
Ōtsu, Japan 55 G7
Ōtsuki, Japan 55 G9
Ottawa = Outaouais →, Canada 104 C5
Ottawa, Canada 117 A9
Ottawa, Ill., U.S.A. 112 E10
Ottawa, Kans., U.S.A. 112 F7
Ottawa Is., Canada 101 C11
Ottélé, Cameroon 83 E7
Ottensheim, Austria 26 C7
Otter Cr. →, U.S.A. 117 B11
Otter L., Canada 103 B8
Otterndorf, Germany 24 B4
Otterup, Denmark 11 J4
Otterville, Canada 116 D4
Ottery St. Mary, U.K. 15 G4
Otto Beit Bridge, Zimbabwe 87 F2
Ottosdal, S. Africa 88 D4
Ottumwa, U.S.A. 112 E8
Otu, Nigeria 83 D5
Otukpa, Nigeria 83 D6
Oturkpo, Nigeria 83 D6
Otway, B., Chile 128 G2
Otway, C., Australia 95 F3
Otwock, Poland 31 F8
Otyniya, Ukraine 29 B9
Ötztaler Ache →, Austria 26 D3
Ötztaler Alpen, Austria 26 E3
Ou →, Laos 64 B4
Ou Neua, Laos 58 F3
Ou-Sammyaku, Japan 54 E10
Ouachita →, U.S.A. 113 K9
Ouachita, L., U.S.A. 113 H8
Ouachita Mts., U.S.A. 113 H7
Ouagadougou, Burkina Faso 83 C4
Ouahigouya, Burkina Faso 82 C4
Ouahran = Oran, Algeria 78 A5
Oualâta, Mauritania 82 B3
Ouallene, Algeria 78 D6
Ouallam, Niger 83 C5
Ouargaye, Burkina Faso 83 C5
Ouargla, Algeria 78 B7
Ouarkoye, Burkina Faso 82 C4
Ouarzazate, Morocco 78 B4

Ouassouas, Mali 83 B5
Ouatagouna, Mali 83 B5
Oubangi →, Dem. Rep. of
  the Congo 84 E3
Ouche →, France 19 E12
Ouddorp, Neths. 17 C3
Oude Rijn →, Neths. 17 B4
Oudeïka, Mali 83 B4
Oudenaarde, Belgium 17 D3
Oudon →, France 18 E6
Oudtshoorn, S. Africa 88 E3
Ouellé, Ivory C. 82 D4
Ouémé →, Benin 83 D5
Ouessa, Burkina Faso 82 C4
Ouessant, Î. d', France 18 D1
Ouesso, Congo 84 D3
Ouest, Pte. de l', Canada 105 C7
Ouezzane, Morocco 78 B4
Ougarou, Burkina Faso 83 C5
Oughterard, Ireland 12 C2
Ouidah, Benin 83 D5
Ouistreham, France 18 C6
Oujda, Morocco 78 B5
Oujeft, Mauritania 82 A2
Oulainen, Finland 8 D21
Ould Yenjé, Mauritania 82 B2
Oullins, France 21 C8
Oulu, Finland 8 D21
Oulujärvi, Finland 8 D22
Oulujoki →, Finland 8 D21
Oulx, Italy 40 C3
Oum Chalouba, Chad 79 E10
Oum Hadjer, Chad 79 F9
Oumé, Ivory C. 82 D3
Ounasjoki →, Finland 8 C21
Ounguati, Namibia 88 C2
Ounianga Sérir, Chad 79 E10
Our →, Lux. 17 E6
Ouranópolis, Greece 44 D8
Ourârene, Niger 83 B6
Ouray, U.S.A. 109 G10
Ourcq →, France 19 C10
Ourense, Spain 36 C3
Ouricuri, Brazil 125 E10
Ourinhos, Brazil 127 A6
Ourique, Portugal 37 H2
Ouro Fino, Brazil 127 A6
Ouro-Ndia, Mali 82 B4
Ouro Prêto, Brazil 127 A7
Oursi, Burkina Faso 83 C4
Ourthe →, Belgium 17 D5
Ouse →, E. Susx., U.K. 15 G8
Ouse →, N. Yorks., U.K. 14 D7
Oust, France 20 F5
Oust →, France 18 E4
Outamba-Kilimi △, S. Leone 82 D2
Outaouais →, Canada 104 C5
Outardes →, Canada 105 C6
Outeiro de Rei, Spain 36 B3
Outer Hebrides, U.K. 13 D1
Outes = Serra de Outes, Spain 36 C2
Outjo, Namibia 88 C2
Outlook, Canada 103 C7
Outokumpu, Finland 8 E23
Outreau, France 19 B8
Ouvèze →, France 21 E8
Ouyen, Australia 95 F3
Ouzouer-le-Marché, France 19 E8
Ovada, Italy 40 D5
Ovalau, Fiji 91 C8
Ovalle, Chile 126 C1
Ovamboland, Namibia 88 B2
Ovar, Portugal 36 E2
Overath, Germany 24 E3
Overflakkee, Neths. 17 C4
Overijssel □, Neths. 17 B6
Overland Park, U.S.A. 112 F7
Overton, U.S.A. 111 J12
Övertorneå, Sweden 8 C20
Överum, Sweden 11 F10
Ovid, U.S.A. 117 D8
Ovidiopol, Ukraine 33 J6
Ovidiu, Romania 29 F13
Oviedo, Spain 36 B5
Oviksfjällen, Sweden 10 A7
Oviši, Latvia 9 H19
Ovoot, Mongolia 56 B7
Övör Hangay □, Mongolia 56 B2
Ovoro, Nigeria 83 D6
Øvre Årdal, Norway 9 F12
Øvre Fryken, Sweden 10 E7
Ovruch, Ukraine 33 G5
Owaka, N.Z. 91 M2
Owambo = Ovamboland,
  Namibia 88 B2
Owasco L., U.S.A. 117 D8
Owase, Japan 55 G8
Owatonna, U.S.A. 112 C8
Owbeh, Afghan. 66 B3
Owego, U.S.A. 117 D8
Owen Falls Dam, Uganda 86 B3
Owen Sound, Canada 116 B4
Owens →, U.S.A. 110 J9
Owens L., U.S.A. 111 J9
Owensboro, U.S.A. 114 G2
Owerri, Nigeria 83 D6
Owl →, Canada 103 B10
Owo, Nigeria 83 D6
Owosso, U.S.A. 114 D3
Owyhee, U.S.A. 108 F5
Owyhee →, U.S.A. 108 E5
Owyhee, L., U.S.A. 108 E5
Ox Mts. = Slieve Gamph, Ireland 12 B3
Oxarfjörður, Iceland 8 C5
Oxbow, Canada 103 D8
Oxelösund, Sweden 11 F11
Oxford, N.Z. 91 K4
Oxford, U.K. 15 F6
Oxford, Mass., U.S.A. 117 D13
Oxford, Miss., U.S.A. 113 H10

Oxford, N.C., U.S.A. 115 G6
Oxford, N.Y., U.S.A. 117 D9
Oxford, Ohio, U.S.A. 114 F3
Oxford L., Canada 103 C9
Oxfordshire □, U.K. 15 F6
Oxía Nísís, Greece 46 C3
Oxie, Sweden 11 J7
Oxílithos, Greece 46 C6
Oxnard, U.S.A. 111 L7
Oxsjövålen, Sweden 10 B7
Oxus = Amudarya →, Uzbekistan 52 E6
Oya, Malaysia 62 D4
Oyama, Japan 55 F9
Oyambre △, Spain 36 B6
Oyem, Gabon 84 D2
Oyen, Canada 103 C6
Oykel →, U.K. 13 D4
Oymyakon, Russia 53 C15
Oyo, Nigeria 83 D5
Oyo □, Nigeria 83 D5
Oyonnax, France 19 F12
Oyster Bay, U.S.A. 117 F11
Ōyūbari, Japan 54 C11
Özalp, Turkey 73 C10
Ozamiz, Phil. 61 G5
Ozark, Ala., U.S.A. 115 K3
Ozark, Ark., U.S.A. 113 H8
Ozark, Mo., U.S.A. 113 G8
Ozark Plateau, U.S.A. 113 G9
Ozarks, L. of the, U.S.A. 112 F8
Ozarów, Poland 31 H8
Ózd, Hungary 28 B5
Ozernoye, Russia 34 E10
Ozero Svityaz, Ukraine 31 G10
Ozersk, Russia 30 D8
Ozette L., U.S.A. 110 B2
Ozieri, Italy 42 B2
Ozimek, Poland 31 H5
Ozinki, Russia 34 E9
Ozona, U.S.A. 113 K4
Ozorków, Poland 31 G6
Ozren, Bos.-H. 28 G3
Ozuluama, Mexico 119 C5
Ozun, Romania 29 E10
Ozurgeti, Georgia 35 K5

P

Pa, Burkina Faso 82 C4
Pa-an, Burma 67 L20
Pa Mong Dam, Thailand 64 D4
Pa Sak →, Thailand 62 B2
Paamiut, Greenland 101 B15
Paar →, Germany 25 G7
Paarl, S. Africa 88 E2
Pab Hills, Pakistan 68 F2
Pabbay, U.K. 13 D1
Pabianice, Poland 31 G6
Pabna, Bangla. 67 G16
Pabo, Uganda 86 B3
Pacaja →, Brazil 125 D8
Pacaraima, Sa., S. Amer. 124 C6
Pacasmayo, Peru 124 E3
Paceco, Italy 42 E5
Pachhar, India 68 G7
Pachino, Italy 43 F8
Pachitea →, Peru 124 E4
Pachmarhi, India 69 H8
Pachpadra, India 66 G8
Pachuca, Mexico 119 C5
Pacific, Canada 102 C3
Pacific-Antarctic Ridge, Pac. Oc. 97 M16
Pacific Grove, U.S.A. 110 J5
Pacific Ocean 97 G14
Pacific Rim △, Canada 102 D4
Pacifica, U.S.A. 110 H4
Pacitan, Indonesia 63 H14
Packwood, U.S.A. 110 D5
Pacov, Czech Rep. 26 B8
Pacy-sur-Eure, France 18 C8
Padaido, Kepulauan, Indonesia 63 E9
Padang, Indonesia 62 E2
Padang Endau, Malaysia 65 L4
Padangpanjang, Indonesia 62 E2
Padangsidempuan, Indonesia 62 D1
Padborg, Denmark 11 K3
Paddle Prairie, Canada 102 B5
Paddockwood, Canada 103 C7
Paderborn, Germany 24 D4
Padeș, Vf., Romania 28 E7
Padina, Romania 29 F12
Padma, India 69 G11
Pádova, Italy 41 C8
Padra, India 68 H5
Padrauna, India 69 F10
Padre I., U.S.A. 113 M6
Padre Island △, U.S.A. 113 M6
Padrón, Spain 36 C2
Padstow, U.K. 15 G3
Padua = Pádova, Italy 41 C8
Paducah, Ky., U.S.A. 114 G1
Paducah, Tex., U.S.A. 113 H4
Padul, Spain 37 H7
Paengnyŏng-do, S. Korea 57 F13
Paeroa, N.Z. 91 G5
Paesana, Italy 40 D4
Pafúri, Mozam. 89 C5
Pag, Croatia 41 D12
Paga, Ghana 83 C4
Pagadian, Phil. 61 H5
Pagai Selatan, Pulau, Indonesia 62 E2
Pagai Utara, Pulau, Indonesia 62 E2
Pagalu = Annobón, Atl. Oc. 77 G4
Pagara, India 69 G9
Pagastikós Kólpos, Greece 46 B5
Pagatan, Indonesia 62 E5
Page, U.S.A. 109 H8
Pagėgiai, Lithuania 30 C8

Pago Pago, *Amer. Samoa*	**91 B13**	Palinuro, C., *Italy*	**43 B8**
Pagosa Springs, *U.S.A.*	**109 H10**	Palioúrion, Ákra, *Greece*	**44 G7**
Pagwa River, *Canada*	**104 B2**	Palisades Reservoir, *U.S.A.*	**108 E8**
Pahala, *U.S.A.*	**106 J17**	Paliseul, *Belgium*	**17 E5**
Pahang →, *Malaysia*	**65 L4**	Palitana, *India*	**68 J4**
Pahiatua, *N.Z.*	**91 J5**	Palizada, *Mexico*	**119 D6**
Pahokee, *U.S.A.*	**115 M5**	Palk Bay, *Asia*	**66 Q11**
Pahrump, *U.S.A.*	**111 J11**	Palk Strait, *Asia*	**66 Q11**
Pahute Mesa, *U.S.A.*	**110 H10**	Palkānah, *Iraq*	**70 C5**
Pai, *Thailand*	**64 C2**	Palkot, *India*	**69 H11**
Paicines, *U.S.A.*	**110 J5**	Pallanza = Verbánia, *Italy*	**40 C5**
Paide, *Estonia*	**9 G21**	Pallarenda, *Australia*	**94 B4**
Paignton, *U.K.*	**15 G4**	Pallasovka, *Russia*	**34 E8**
Paiho, *Taiwan*	**59 F13**	Pallès, Bishti i, *Albania*	**44 E3**
Päijänne, *Finland*	**9 F21**	Pallinup →, *Australia*	**93 F2**
Pailani, *India*	**69 G9**	Pallisa, *Uganda*	**86 B3**
Pailin, *Cambodia*	**64 F4**	Pallu, *India*	**68 E6**
Paimpol, *France*	**18 D3**	Palm Bay, *U.S.A.*	**115 L5**
Painan, *Indonesia*	**62 E2**	Palm Beach, *U.S.A.*	**115 M6**
Painesville, *U.S.A.*	**116 E3**	Palm Coast, *U.S.A.*	**115 L5**
Paint Hills = Wemindji, *Canada*	**104 B4**	Palm Desert, *U.S.A.*	**111 M10**
Paint L., *Canada*	**103 B9**	Palm Is., *Australia*	**94 B4**
Painted Desert, *U.S.A.*	**109 J8**	Palm Springs, *U.S.A.*	**111 M10**
Paintsville, *U.S.A.*	**114 G4**	Palma, *Mozam.*	**87 E5**
País Vasco □, *Spain*	**38 C2**	Palma, B. de, *Spain*	**48 B9**
Paisley, *Canada*	**116 B3**	Palma de Mallorca, *Spain*	**48 B9**
Paisley, *U.K.*	**13 F4**	Palma de Mallorca ✈ (PMI),	
Paisley, *U.S.A.*	**108 E3**	*Spain*	**39 F7**
Paita, *Peru*	**124 E2**	Palma del Río, *Spain*	**37 H5**
Paiva →, *Portugal*	**36 D2**	Palma di Montechiaro, *Italy*	**42 F6**
Paizhou, *China*	**59 B9**	Palma Soriano, *Cuba*	**120 B4**
Pajares, *Spain*	**36 B5**	Palmares, *Brazil*	**125 E11**
Pajares, Puerto de, *Spain*	**36 C5**	Palmarola, *Italy*	**42 B5**
Pajęczno, *Poland*	**31 G5**	Palmas, *Brazil*	**127 B5**
Pak Lay, *Laos*	**64 C3**	Palmas, C., *Liberia*	**82 E3**
Pak Phanang, *Thailand*	**65 H3**	Pálmas, G. di, *Italy*	**42 D1**
Pak Sane, *Laos*	**64 C4**	Palmdale, *U.S.A.*	**111 L8**
Pak Song, *Laos*	**64 E6**	Palmeira das Missões, *Brazil*	**127 B5**
Pak Suong, *Laos*	**58 H4**	Palmeira dos Índios, *Brazil*	**125 E11**
Pakaur, *India*	**69 G12**	Palmela, *Portugal*	**37 G2**
Pakenham, *Canada*	**117 A8**	Palmer, *Antarctica*	**5 C17**
Pákhnes, *Greece*	**49 D6**	Palmer, *U.S.A.*	**100 B5**
Pakhuis, *S. Africa*	**88 E2**	Palmer →, *Australia*	**94 B3**
Pakistan ■, *Asia*	**68 E4**	Palmer Arch., *Antarctica*	**5 C17**
Pakkading, *Laos*	**64 C4**	Palmer Lake, *U.S.A.*	**112 F2**
Pakokku, *Burma*	**67 J19**	Palmer Land, *Antarctica*	**5 D18**
Pakość, *Poland*	**31 F5**	Palmerston, *Australia*	**92 B5**
Pakowki L., *Canada*	**103 D6**	Palmerston, *Canada*	**116 C4**
Pakpattan, *Pakistan*	**68 D5**	Palmerston, *N.Z.*	**91 L3**
Pakrac, *Croatia*	**28 E2**	Palmerston North, *N.Z.*	**91 J5**
Pakruojis, *Lithuania*	**30 C10**	Palmerton, *U.S.A.*	**117 F9**
Paks, *Hungary*	**28 D3**	Palmetto, *U.S.A.*	**115 M4**
Paktīā □, *Afghan.*	**66 C6**	Palmi, *Italy*	**43 D8**
Paktīkā □, *Afghan.*	**66 C6**	Palmira, *Argentina*	**126 C2**
Pakwach, *Uganda*	**86 B3**	Palmira, *Colombia*	**124 C3**
Pakxe, *Laos*	**64 E5**	Palmyra = Tudmur, *Syria*	**70 C3**
Pal Lahara, *India*	**69 J11**	Palmyra, *Mo., U.S.A.*	**112 F9**
Pala, *Chad*	**79 G9**	Palmyra, *N.J., U.S.A.*	**117 F9**
Pala, *Dem. Rep. of the Congo*	**86 D2**	Palmyra, *N.Y., U.S.A.*	**116 C7**
Pala, *U.S.A.*	**111 M9**	Palmyra, *Pa., U.S.A.*	**117 F8**
Palabek, *Uganda*	**86 B3**	Palmyra Is., *Pac. Oc.*	**97 G11**
Palacios, *U.S.A.*	**113 L6**	Palo Alto, *U.S.A.*	**110 H4**
Palafrugell, *Spain*	**38 D8**	Palo Seco, *Trin. & Tob.*	**125 K15**
Palagiano, *Italy*	**43 B10**	Palo Verde, *U.S.A.*	**111 M12**
Palagonía, *Italy*	**43 E7**	Palo Verde △, *Costa Rica*	**120 D2**
Palagruža, *Croatia*	**41 F13**	Paloich, *Sudan*	**81 E3**
Palaiókastron, *Greece*	**49 D8**	Palomar Mt., *U.S.A.*	**111 M10**
Palaiokhóra, *Greece*	**49 D5**	Palompon, *Phil.*	**61 F6**
Pálairos, *Greece*	**46 C2**	Palopo, *Indonesia*	**63 E6**
Palaiseau, *France*	**19 D9**	Palos, C. de, *Spain*	**39 H4**
Palam, *India*	**66 K10**	Palos de la Frontera, *Spain*	**37 H4**
Palamás, *Greece*	**46 B4**	Palos Verdes, *U.S.A.*	**111 M8**
Palamòs, *Spain*	**38 D8**	Palos Verdes, Pt., *U.S.A.*	**111 M8**
Palampur, *India*	**68 C7**	Pålsboda, *Sweden*	**10 E9**
Palamut, *Turkey*	**47 C9**	Palu, *Indonesia*	**63 E5**
Palana, *Australia*	**95 F4**	Palu, *Turkey*	**70 B3**
Palana, *Russia*	**53 D16**	Paluke, *Liberia*	**82 D3**
Palanan, *Phil.*	**61 C5**	Paluzza, *Italy*	**41 B10**
Palanan Pt., *Phil.*	**61 C5**	Palwal, *India*	**68 E7**
Palandri, *Pakistan*	**69 C5**	Pama, *Burkina Faso*	**83 C5**
Palanga, *Lithuania*	**9 J19**	Pama →, *Burkina Faso*	**83 C5**
Palangkaraya, *Indonesia*	**62 E4**	Pamanukan, *Indonesia*	**63 G12**
Palani Hills, *India*	**66 P10**	Pamekasan, *Indonesia*	**63 G15**
Palanpur, *India*	**68 G5**	Pamenang, *Indonesia*	**63 J19**
Palapye, *Botswana*	**88 C4**	Pamiers, *France*	**20 E5**
Palas, *Pakistan*	**69 B5**	Pamir, *Tajikistan*	**52 F8**
Palas de Rei, *Spain*	**36 C3**	Pamlico →, *U.S.A.*	**115 H7**
Palashi, *India*	**69 H13**	Pamlico Sd., *U.S.A.*	**115 H8**
Palasponga, *India*	**69 J11**	Pampa, *U.S.A.*	**113 H4**
Palatka, *Russia*	**53 C16**	Pampa de las Salinas, *Argentina*	**126 C2**
Palatka, *U.S.A.*	**115 L5**	Pampanua, *Indonesia*	**63 E6**
Palau, *Italy*	**42 A2**	Pampas, *Argentina*	**126 D3**
Palau ■, *Pac. Oc.*	**96 G5**	Pampas, *Peru*	**124 F4**
Palauk, *Burma*	**64 F2**	Pamphylia, *Turkey*	**72 D4**
Palawan, *Phil.*	**61 G3**	Pamplona, *Colombia*	**124 B4**
Palayankottai, *India*	**66 Q10**	Pamplona, *Spain*	**38 C3**
Palazzo, Pte., *France*	**21 F12**	Pampoenpoort, *S. Africa*	**88 E3**
Palazzo San Gervásio, *Italy*	**43 B8**	Pamukçu, *Turkey*	**47 B9**
Palazzolo Acréide, *Italy*	**43 E7**	Pamukkale, *Turkey*	**47 D11**
Paldiski, *Estonia*	**9 G21**	Pan de Azúcar △, *Chile*	**126 B1**
Pale, *Bos.-H.*	**28 G3**	Pan Xian, *China*	**58 E5**
Paleleh, *Indonesia*	**63 D6**	Panabo, *Phil.*	**61 H6**
Palembang, *Indonesia*	**62 E2**	Panaca, *U.S.A.*	**109 H6**
Palencia, *Spain*	**36 C6**	Panagyurishte, *Bulgaria*	**45 D8**
Palencia □, *Spain*	**36 C6**	Panaitan, *Indonesia*	**63 G11**
Palenque, *Mexico*	**119 D6**	Panaji, *India*	**66 M8**
Paleokastrítsa, *Greece*	**49 A3**	Panama, *Panama*	**120 E4**
Palermo, *Italy*	**42 D6**	Panama ■, *Cent. Amer.*	**120 E4**
Palermo, *U.S.A.*	**108 G3**	Panamá, *Panama*	**120 E4**
Palermo ✈ (PMO), *Italy*	**42 D6**	Panama Canal, *Panama*	**120 E4**
Palestina, *Chile*	**128 A3**	Panama City, *U.S.A.*	**115 K3**
Palestine, *Asia*	**74 D4**	Panamint Range, *U.S.A.*	**111 J9**
Palestine, *U.S.A.*	**113 K7**	Panamint Springs, *U.S.A.*	**111 J9**
Palestrina, *Italy*	**41 G9**	Panão, *Peru*	**124 E3**
Paletwa, *Burma*	**67 J18**	Panaon I., *Phil.*	**61 F6**
Palghat, *India*	**66 P10**	Panare, *Thailand*	**65 J3**
Palgrave, Mt., *Australia*	**92 D2**	Panarea, *Italy*	**43 D8**
Pali, *India*	**68 G5**	Panaro →, *Italy*	**41 D8**
Palikir, *Micronesia*	**96 G7**	Panay, *Phil.*	**61 F5**
Palinuro, *Italy*	**43 B8**	Panay, G., *Phil.*	**61 B6**
		Pančevo, *Serbia & M.*	**28 F5**

Panch'iao, *Taiwan*	**59 E13**	Paracatu, *Brazil*	**125 G9**
Panciu, *Romania*	**29 E12**	Paracel Is., *S. China Sea*	**62 A4**
Pancorbo, Desfiladero, *Spain*	**36 C2**	Parachilna, *Australia*	**95 E2**
Pâncota, *Romania*	**28 D6**	Parachinar, *Pakistan*	**68 C4**
Panda, *Mozam.*	**89 C5**	Paračin, *Serbia & M.*	**44 C5**
Pandan, *Malaysia*	**65 d**	Paradas, *Spain*	**37 H5**
Pandan, *Antique, Phil.*	**61 F5**	Paradela, *Spain*	**36 C3**
Pandan, *Catanduanes, Phil.*	**61 D6**	Paradhísi, *Greece*	**49 C10**
Pandan, Selat, *Singapore*	**65 d**	Paradip, *India*	**67 J15**
Pandan Tampoi = Tampoi,		Paradise, *Calif., U.S.A.*	**110 F5**
Malaysia	**65 d**	Paradise, *Nev., U.S.A.*	**111 J11**
Pandegelang, *Indonesia*	**63 G12**	Paradise →, *Canada*	**105 B8**
Pandhana, *India*	**68 J7**	Paradise Hill, *Canada*	**103 C7**
Pandharpur, *India*	**66 L9**	Paradise River, *Canada*	**105 B8**
Pando, *Uruguay*	**127 C4**	Paradise Valley, *U.S.A.*	**108 F5**
Pando, L. = Hope, L., *Australia*	**95 D2**	Parado, *Indonesia*	**63 F5**
Pandokrátor, *Greece*	**49 A3**	Paragould, *U.S.A.*	**113 G9**
Pandora, *Costa Rica*	**120 E3**	Paragua →, *Venezuela*	**124 B6**
Pandrup, *Denmark*	**11 G3**	Paraguaçu →, *Brazil*	**125 F11**
Panevéggio-Pale di San		Paraguaçu Paulista, *Brazil*	**127 A5**
Martino △, *Italy*	**41 B8**	Paraguaná, Pen. de, *Venezuela*	**124 A5**
Panevežys, *Lithuania*	**9 J21**	Paraguarí, *Paraguay*	**126 B4**
Panfilov, *Kazakhstan*	**52 E8**	Paraguarí □, *Paraguay*	**126 B4**
Panfilovo, *Russia*	**34 E6**	Paraguay ■, *S. Amer.*	**126 A4**
Pang-Long, *Burma*	**67 H21**	Paraguay →, *Paraguay*	**126 B4**
Pang Sida △, *Thailand*	**64 E4**	Paraíba = João Pessoa, *Brazil*	**125 E12**
Pang-Yang, *Burma*	**67 H21**	Paraíba □, *Brazil*	**125 E11**
Panga, *Dem. Rep. of the Congo*	**86 B2**	Paraíba do Sul →, *Brazil*	**127 A7**
Pangaíon Óros, *Greece*	**45 F8**	Parainen, *Finland*	**9 F20**
Pangalanes, Canal des =		Paraíso, *Mexico*	**119 D6**
Ampangalana, Lakandranon',		Parak, *Iran*	**71 E7**
Madag.	**89 C8**	Parakhino Paddubye, *Russia*	**32 C7**
Pangani, *Tanzania*	**86 D4**	Parakou, *Benin*	**83 D5**
Pangani →, *Tanzania*	**86 D4**	Paralimni, *Cyprus*	**49 D12**
Pangfou = Bengbu, *China*	**57 H9**	Parálion-Astrous, *Greece*	**46 D4**
Pangil, *Dem. Rep. of the Congo*	**86 C2**	Paramaribo, *Suriname*	**125 B7**
Pangkah, Tanjung, *Indonesia*	**63 G15**	Paramithiá, *Greece*	**46 B2**
Pangkajene, *Indonesia*	**63 E5**	Páramos del Batallón y La	
Pangkalanbrandan, *Indonesia*	**62 D1**	Negra △, *Venezuela*	**121 E5**
Pangkalanbuun, *Indonesia*	**62 E4**	Paramushir, Ostrov, *Russia*	**53 D16**
Pangkalpinang, *Indonesia*	**62 E3**	Paran →, *Israel*	**74 E4**
Pangnirtung, *Canada*	**101 B13**	Paraná, *Argentina*	**126 C3**
Pangong Tso, *India*	**68 B8**	Paraná, *Brazil*	**125 F9**
Panguitch, *U.S.A.*	**109 H7**	Paraná □, *Brazil*	**127 A5**
Pangutaran Group, *Phil.*	**61 H4**	Paraná →, *Argentina*	**126 C4**
Panhandle, *U.S.A.*	**113 H4**	Paranã →, *Brazil*	**127 B6**
Pani Mines, *India*	**68 H5**	Paranaíba, *Brazil*	**125 G8**
Pania-Mutombo, *Dem. Rep. of*		Paranaíba →, *Brazil*	**125 H8**
the Congo	**86 D1**	Paranapanema →, *Brazil*	**127 A5**
Panikota I., *India*	**68 J4**	Paranapiacaba, Serra do, *Brazil*	**127 A6**
Panipat, *India*	**68 E7**	Paranas, *Phil.*	**61 F6**
Panjal Range = Pir Panjal Range,		Paranavaí, *Brazil*	**127 A5**
India	**68 C7**	Parang, *Maguindanao, Phil.*	**63 C6**
Panjang, Hon, *Vietnam*	**65 H4**	Parang, *Sulu, Phil.*	**61 J4**
Panjgur, *Pakistan*	**66 F4**	Parângul Mare, Vf., *Romania*	**29 E8**
Panjim = Panaji, *India*	**66 M8**	Paraparaumu, *N.Z.*	**91 J5**
Panjin, *China*	**57 D12**	Parápola, *Greece*	**46 E5**
Panjnad Barrage, *Pakistan*	**66 E7**	Parás, *Mexico*	**118 B5**
Panjnad →, *Pakistan*	**68 E4**	Parasía, *Mad. P., India*	**68 H8**
Panjwai, *Afghan.*	**68 D1**	Paraspóri, Ákra, *Greece*	**47 F9**
Pankshin, *Nigeria*	**83 D6**	Paray-le-Monial, *France*	**19 F11**
Panmunjŏm, *N. Korea*	**57 F14**	Parbati →, *Mad. P., India*	**68 G7**
Panna, *India*	**69 G9**	Parbati →, *Raj., India*	**68 F7**
Panna Hills, *India*	**69 G9**	Parbhani, *India*	**66 K10**
Pannawonica, *Australia*	**92 D2**	Parchim, *Germany*	**24 B7**
Pannga, Tanjung, *Indonesia*	**63 K19**	Parczew, *Poland*	**31 G9**
Pannirtuuq = Pangnirtung,		Pardes Hanna-Karkur, *Israel*	**74 C3**
Canada	**101 B13**	Pardilla, *Spain*	**36 D7**
Pano Akil, *Pakistan*	**68 F3**	Pardo →, *Bahia, Brazil*	**125 G11**
Pano Lefkara, *Cyprus*	**49 E12**	Pardo →, *Mato Grosso, Brazil*	**127 A5**
Pano Panayia, *Cyprus*	**49 E11**	Pardubice, *Czech Rep.*	**26 A8**
Panorama, *Brazil*	**127 A5**	Pardubický □, *Czech Rep.*	**26 B8**
Pánormon, *Greece*	**49 D6**	Pare, *Indonesia*	**63 G15**
Panshan = Panjin, *China*	**57 D12**	Pare Mts., *Tanzania*	**86 C4**
Panshi, *China*	**57 C14**	Parecis, Serra dos, *Brazil*	**124 F7**
Pantanal, *Brazil*	**124 H7**	Paredes de Nava, *Spain*	**36 C6**
Pantanos de Centla △, *Mexico*	**119 D6**	Paren, *Russia*	**53 C17**
Pantar, *Indonesia*	**63 F6**	Parent, *Canada*	**104 C5**
Pante Macassar, *E. Timor*	**63 F6**	Parent, L., *Canada*	**104 C4**
Pante Makasar = Pante Macassar,		Parentis-en-Born, *France*	**20 D2**
E. Timor	**63 F6**	Parepare, *Indonesia*	**63 E5**
Pantelleria, *Italy*	**42 F4**	Parfino, *Russia*	**32 C6**
Pantón, *Spain*	**36 C3**	Párga, *Greece*	**46 B2**
Pánuco, *Mexico*	**119 C5**	Pargas = Parainen, *Finland*	**9 F20**
Panyam, *Nigeria*	**83 D6**	Pargo, Pta. do, *Madeira*	**48 D2**
Panyu, *China*	**59 F9**	Paria, G. de, *Venezuela*	**125 K14**
Panzhihua, *China*	**58 D3**	Pariaguán, *Venezuela*	**124 B6**
Páola, *Italy*	**43 C9**	Paricutín, Cerro, *Mexico*	**118 D4**
Paola, *Malta*	**49 D2**	Parigi, *Indonesia*	**63 E6**
Paola, *U.S.A.*	**112 F7**	Parika, *Guyana*	**124 B7**
Paonia, *U.S.A.*	**109 G10**	Parikkala, *Finland*	**32 B5**
Paoting = Baoding, *China*	**56 E8**	Parima, Serra, *Brazil*	**124 C6**
Paot'ou = Baotou, *China*	**56 D6**	Parinari, *Peru*	**124 D4**
Paoua, *C.A.R.*	**84 C3**	Pariñas, Pta., *S. Amer.*	**122 D2**
Pápa, *Hungary*	**28 C2**	Parincea, *Romania*	**29 D12**
Papa Stour, *U.K.*	**13 A7**	Parintins, *Brazil*	**125 D7**
Papa Westray, *U.K.*	**13 B6**	Pariparit Kyun, *Burma*	**67 M18**
Papagayo →, *Mexico*	**119 D5**	Paris, *Canada*	**116 C4**
Papagayo, G. de, *Costa Rica*	**120 D2**	Paris, *France*	**19 D9**
Papakura, *N.Z.*	**91 G5**	Paris, *Idaho, U.S.A.*	**108 E8**
Papantla, *Mexico*	**119 C5**	Paris, *Ky., U.S.A.*	**114 F3**
Papar, *Malaysia*	**62 C5**	Paris, *Tenn., U.S.A.*	**115 G1**
Paparoa △, *N.Z.*	**91 K3**	Paris, *Tex., U.S.A.*	**113 J7**
Pápas, Ákra, *Greece*	**46 C3**	Paris, Ville de □, *France*	**19 D9**
Papeete, *Tahiti*	**97 J13**	Paris Charles de Gaulle ✈	
Papenburg, *Germany*	**24 B3**	(CDG), *France*	**19 D9**
Paphlagonia, *Turkey*	**72 B5**	Paris Orly ✈ (ORY), *France*	**19 D9**
Paphos, *Cyprus*	**49 E11**	Parish, *U.S.A.*	**117 C8**
Papigochic →, *Mexico*	**118 B3**	Parishville, *U.S.A.*	**117 B10**
Paposo, *Chile*	**126 B1**	Park, *U.S.A.*	**110 B4**
Papoutsa, *Cyprus*	**49 E12**	Park City, *U.S.A.*	**113 G6**
Papua □, *Indonesia*	**63 E9**	Park Falls, *U.S.A.*	**112 C9**
Papua New Guinea ■, *Oceania*	**96 H6**	Park Head, *Canada*	**116 B3**
Papudo, *Chile*	**126 C1**	Park Hills, *U.S.A.*	**113 G9**
Papuk, *Croatia*	**28 E2**	Park Range, *U.S.A.*	**108 G10**
Papun, *Burma*	**67 K20**	Park Rapids, *U.S.A.*	**112 B7**
Papunya, *Australia*	**92 D5**	Park River, *U.S.A.*	**112 A6**
Pará = Belém, *Brazil*	**125 D9**	Park Rynie, *S. Africa*	**89 E5**
Pará □, *Brazil*	**125 D8**	Parkā Bandar, *Iran*	**71 E8**
Paraburdoo, *Australia*	**92 D2**	Parkano, *Finland*	**9 E20**
Paracale, *Phil.*	**61 D5**	Parker, *Pa., U.S.A.*	**116 E5**
		Parker Dam, *U.S.A.*	**111 L12**
		Parkersburg, *U.S.A.*	**114 F5**

Parkes, *Australia*	**95 E4**
Parkfield, *U.S.A.*	**110 K6**
Parkhill, *Canada*	**116 C3**
Parkland, *U.S.A.*	**110 C4**
Parkston, *U.S.A.*	**112 D6**
Parksville, *Canada*	**102 D4**
Parla, *Spain*	**36 E7**
Pârlița, *Moldova*	**29 C12**
Parma, *Italy*	**40 D7**
Parma, *Idaho, U.S.A.*	**108 E5**
Parma, *Ohio, U.S.A.*	**116 E3**
Parma →, *Italy*	**40 D7**
Parnaguá, *Brazil*	**125 F10**
Parnaíba, *Brazil*	**125 D10**
Parnaíba →, *Brazil*	**125 D10**
Parnassós, *Greece*	**46 C4**
Párnis, *Greece*	**46 C5**
Párnitha △, *Greece*	**46 C5**
Párnon Óros, *Greece*	**46 D4**
Pärnu, *Estonia*	**9 G21**
Paroo →, *Australia*	**95 E3**
Páros, *Greece*	**47 D7**
Parowan, *U.S.A.*	**109 H7**
Parpaillon, *France*	**21 D10**
Parral, *Chile*	**126 D1**
Parras, *Mexico*	**118 B4**
Parrett →, *U.K.*	**15 F4**
Parris I., *U.S.A.*	**115 J5**
Parrsboro, *Canada*	**105 C7**
Parry I., *Canada*	**116 A4**
Parry Is., *Canada*	**98 B8**
Parry Sound, *Canada*	**116 A5**
Parsberg, *Germany*	**25 F7**
Parsęta →, *Poland*	**30 D2**
Parsnip →, *Canada*	**102 B4**
Parsons, *U.S.A.*	**113 G7**
Parsons Ra., *Australia*	**94 A3**
Partanna, *Italy*	**42 E5**
Partenio △, *Italy*	**43 B7**
Parthenay, *France*	**18 F6**
Partinico, *Italy*	**42 D6**
Partizánske, *Slovak Rep.*	**27 C11**
Partridge I., *Canada*	**104 A2**
Paru →, *Brazil*	**125 D8**
Parvān □, *Afghan.*	**66 B6**
Parvatipuram, *India*	**67 K13**
Parvatsar, *India*	**68 F6**
Påryd, *Sweden*	**11 H9**
Parys, *S. Africa*	**88 D4**
Pas, Pta. des, *Spain*	**48 C7**
Pas-de-Calais □, *France*	**19 B9**
Pasada, *Spain*	**36 B5**
Pasadena, *Canada*	**105 C8**
Pasadena, *Calif., U.S.A.*	**111 L8**
Pasadena, *Tex., U.S.A.*	**113 L7**
Pasaje →, *Argentina*	**126 B3**
Paşalimanı, *Turkey*	**45 F11**
Pasar, *Indonesia*	**63 J17**
Pasay, *Phil.*	**61 D4**
Pascagoula, *U.S.A.*	**113 K10**
Pascagoula →, *U.S.A.*	**113 K10**
Paşcani, *Romania*	**29 C11**
Pasco, *U.S.A.*	**108 C4**
Pasco, Cerro de, *Peru*	**124 F3**
Pasco I., *Australia*	**92 D2**
Pascoag, *U.S.A.*	**117 E13**
Pascua, I. de, *Chile*	**97 K17**
Pasewalk, *Germany*	**24 B9**
Pasfield L., *Canada*	**103 B7**
Pasha →, *Russia*	**32 B7**
Pasinler, *Turkey*	**73 C9**
Pasir Mas, *Malaysia*	**65 J4**
Pasir Panjang, *Singapore*	**65 d**
Pasir Putih, *Malaysia*	**65 K4**
Pasirian, *Indonesia*	**63 H15**
Pasirkuning, *Indonesia*	**62 E2**
Påskallavik, *Sweden*	**11 G10**
Paskūh, *Iran*	**71 E9**
Pasłęk, *Poland*	**30 D6**
Pasłęka →, *Poland*	**30 D6**
Pasley, C., *Australia*	**93 F3**
Pašman, *Croatia*	**41 E12**
Pasni, *Pakistan*	**66 G3**
Paso Cantinela, *Mexico*	**111 N11**
Paso de Indios, *Argentina*	**128 E3**
Paso de los Libres, *Argentina*	**126 B4**
Paso de los Toros, *Uruguay*	**126 C4**
Paso Robles, *U.S.A.*	**109 J3**
Paspébiac, *Canada*	**105 C6**
Pasrur, *Pakistan*	**68 C6**
Passage West, *Ireland*	**12 E3**
Passaic, *U.S.A.*	**117 F10**
Passero, C., *Italy*	**43 F8**
Passo Fundo, *Brazil*	**127 B5**
Passos, *Brazil*	**125 H9**
Passow, *Germany*	**24 B10**
Passy, *France*	**21 C10**
Pastavy, *Belarus*	**9 J22**
Pastaza →, *Peru*	**124 D3**
Pasto, *Colombia*	**124 C3**
Pastrana, *Spain*	**38 E2**
Pasuruan, *Indonesia*	**63 G15**
Pasym, *Poland*	**30 E7**
Pásztó, *Hungary*	**28 C4**
Patagonia, *Argentina*	**128 F3**
Patagonia, *U.S.A.*	**109 L8**
Patambar, *Iran*	**71 D9**
Patan = Lalitapur, *Nepal*	**69 F11**
Patan, *Gujarat, India*	**66 H8**
Patan, *Maharashtra, India*	**68 H5**
Patani, *Indonesia*	**63 D7**
Pătârlagele, *Romania*	**29 E11**
Pataudi, *India*	**68 E7**
Patchewollock, *Australia*	**95 F3**
Patchogue, *U.S.A.*	**117 F11**
Pate, *Kenya*	**86 C5**
Patea, *N.Z.*	**91 H5**
Pategi, *Nigeria*	**83 D6**
Patensie, *S. Africa*	**88 E3**
Paterna, *Spain*	**39 F4**
Paternion, *Austria*	**26 E6**

Paternò, *Italy* 43 E7
Pateros, *U.S.A.* 108 B4
Paterson, *U.S.A.* 117 F10
Paterson Ra., *Australia* 92 D3
Pathankot, *India* 68 C6
Pathein = Bassein, *Burma* 67 L19
Pathfinder Reservoir, *U.S.A.* .. 108 E10
Pathiu, *Thailand* 65 G2
Pathum Thani, *Thailand* 64 E3
Pati, *Indonesia* 63 G14
Patía →, *Colombia* 124 C3
Patiala, *Punjab, India* 68 D7
Patiala, *Ut. P., India* 69 F8
Patine Kouka, *Senegal* 82 C2
Patitírion, *Greece* 46 B5
Patkai Bum, *India* 67 F19
Pátmos, *Greece* 47 D8
Patna, *India* 69 G11
Patnos, *Turkey* 73 C10
Pato Branco, *Brazil* 127 B5
Patong, Ao, *Thailand* ...... 65 a
Patonga, *Uganda* 86 B3
Patos, *Albania* 44 F3
Patos, *Brazil* 125 E11
Patos, L. dos, *Brazil* 127 C5
Patos, Río de los, *Argentina* .. 126 C2
Patos de Minas, *Brazil* 125 G9
Patquía, *Argentina* 126 C2
Pátrai, *Greece* 46 C3
Pátraikós Kólpos, *Greece* 46 C3
Patras = Pátrai, *Greece* 46 C3
Patrocínio, *Brazil* 125 G9
Pattada, *Italy* 42 B2
Pattani, *Thailand* 65 J3
Pattaya, *Thailand* 62 B2
Patten, *U.S.A.* 115 C11
Patterson, *Calif., U.S.A.* 110 H5
Patterson, *La., U.S.A.* 113 L9
Patterson, Mt., *U.S.A.* 110 G7
Patti, *Punjab, India* 68 D6
Patti, *Ut. P., India* 69 G10
Patti, *Italy* 43 D7
Pattoki, *Pakistan* 68 D5
Patton, *U.S.A.* 116 F6
Patuakhali, *Bangla.* 67 H17
Patuanak, *Canada* 103 B7
Patuca →, *Honduras* 120 C3
Patuca →, *Honduras* 120 C3
Patuca, Punta, *Honduras* .. 120 C3
Pătulele, *Romania* 28 F7
Pátzcuaro, *Mexico* 118 D4
Pau, *France* 20 E3
Pau, Gave de →, *France* 20 E2
Pauillac, *France* 20 C3
Pauk, *Burma* 67 J19
Paul I., *Canada* 105 A7
Paul Smiths, *U.S.A.* 117 B10
Paulatuk, *Canada* 100 B7
Paulhan, *France* 20 E7
Paulistana, *Brazil* 125 E10
Paulo Afonso, *Brazil* 125 E11
Paulpietersburg, *S. Africa* .. 89 D5
Pauls Valley, *U.S.A.* 113 H6
Pauma Valley, *U.S.A.* 111 M10
Pauri, *India* 69 D8
Pāveh, *Iran* 70 C5
Pavelets, *Russia* 32 F10
Pavia, *Italy* 40 C6
Pavilion, *U.S.A.* 116 D6
Pavilly, *France* 18 C7
Pāvilosta, *Latvia* 9 H19
Pavlikeni, *Bulgaria* 45 C9
Pavlodar, *Kazakhstan* 52 D8
Pavlograd = Pavlohrad, *Ukraine* .. 33 H8
Pavlohrad, *Ukraine* 33 H8
Pavlovo, *Russia* 34 C6
Pavlovsk, *Russia* 34 E5
Pavlovskaya, *Russia* 35 G4
Pavlovskiy-Posad, *Russia* .. 32 E10
Pavullo nel Frignano, *Italy* .. 40 D7
Pawai, Pulau, *Singapore* .... 65 d
Pawayan, *India* 69 E9
Pawhuska, *U.S.A.* 113 G6
Pawling, *U.S.A.* 117 E11
Pawnee, *U.S.A.* 113 G6
Pawnee City, *U.S.A.* 112 E6
Pawtucket, *U.S.A.* 117 E13
Paximádhia, *Greece* 49 E6
Paxoí, *Greece* 46 B2
Paxton, *Ill., U.S.A.* 114 E1
Paxton, *Nebr., U.S.A.* 112 E4
Payakumbuh, *Indonesia* 62 E2
Payerne, *Switz.* 25 J2
Payette, *U.S.A.* 108 D5
Paymogo, *Spain* 37 H3
Payne Bay = Kangirsuk, *Canada* 101 B13
Payne L., *Canada* 101 C12
Paynes Find, *Australia* 93 E2
Paynesville, *Liberia* 82 D2
Paynesville, *U.S.A.* 112 C7
Pays de la Loire □, *France* 18 E6
Paysandú, *Uruguay* 126 C4
Payson, *U.S.A.* 109 J8
Paz →, *Guatemala* 120 D1
Paz, B. de la, *Mexico* 118 C2
Pāzanān, *Iran* 71 D6
Pazar, *Turkey* 73 B9
Pazarcık, *Turkey* 72 D7
Pazardzhik, *Bulgaria* 45 D8
Pazarköy, *Turkey* 47 B9
Pazarlar, *Turkey* 47 C11
Pazaryeri, *Turkey* 47 B11
Pazaryolu, *Turkey* 73 B9
Pazin, *Croatia* 41 C10
Pčinja →, *Macedonia* 44 E5
Pe Ell, *U.S.A.* 110 D3
Peabody, *U.S.A.* 117 D14
Peace →, *Canada* 102 B6
Peace Point, *Canada* 102 B6
Peace River, *Canada* 102 B5
Peach Springs, *U.S.A.* 109 J7

Peachland, *Canada* 102 D5
Peachtree City, *U.S.A.* 115 J3
Peak, The = Kinder Scout, *U.K.* . 14 D6
Peak Charles △, *Australia* .. 93 F3
Peak District □, *U.K.* 14 D6
Peak Hill, *N.S.W., Australia* .. 95 E4
Peak Hill, *W. Austral., Australia* . 93 E2
Peak Ra., *Australia* 94 C4
Peake Cr. →, *Australia* 95 D2
Peal de Becerro, *Spain* 37 H7
Peale, Mt., *U.S.A.* 109 G9
Pearblossom, *U.S.A.* 111 L9
Pearl →, *U.S.A.* 113 K10
Pearl City, *U.S.A.* 106 H16
Pearl Harbor, *U.S.A.* 106 H16
Pearl River = Zhu Jiang →, *China* 59 F9
Pearl River, *U.S.A.* 117 E10
Pearsall, *U.S.A.* 113 L5
Peary Land, *Greenland* 4 A6
Pease →, *U.S.A.* 113 H5
Peawanuck, *Canada* 101 C11
Pebane, *Mozam.* 87 F4
Pebas, *Peru* 124 D4
Pebble Beach, *U.S.A.* 110 J5
Peć, *Serbia & M.* 44 D4
Péccioli, *Italy* 40 E7
Pechea, *Romania* 29 E12
Pechenga, *Russia* 52 C4
Pechenizhyn, *Ukraine* 29 B9
Pechiguera, Pta., *Canary Is.* .. 48 F6
Pechnezhskoye Vdkhr., *Ukraine* 33 G9
Pechora, *Russia* 52 C6
Pechora →, *Russia* 52 C6
Pechorskaya Guba, *Russia* .. 52 C6
Pechory, *Russia* 9 H22
Pecica, *Romania* 28 D6
Pecka, *Serbia & M.* 44 B3
Pécora, C., *Italy* 42 C1
Pecos, *U.S.A.* 113 K3
Pecos →, *U.S.A.* 113 L3
Pécs, *Hungary* 28 D3
Pedder, L., *Australia* 95 G4
Peddie, *S. Africa* 89 E4
Pedernales, *Dom. Rep.* 121 C5
Pedies →, *Cyprus* 49 D12
Pedirka, *Australia* 95 D2
Pedra Azul, *Brazil* 125 G10
Pedreguer, *Spain* 39 G5
Pedreiras, *Brazil* 125 D10
Pedro Afonso, *Brazil* 125 E9
Pedro Cays, *Jamaica* 120 C4
Pedro de Valdivia, *Chile* .. 126 A2
Pedro Juan Caballero, *Paraguay* 127 A4
Pedro Muñoz, *Spain* 37 F8
Pedrógão Grande, *Portugal* .. 36 F2
Pee Dee →, *U.S.A.* 115 J6
Peebinga, *Australia* 95 E3
Peebles, *U.K.* 13 F5
Peekskill, *U.S.A.* 117 E11
Peel, *I. of Man* 14 C3
Peel →, *Australia* 95 E5
Peel →, *Canada* 100 B6
Peel Sd., *Canada* 100 A10
Peene →, *Germany* 24 A9
Peera Peera Poolanna L., *Australia* 95 D2
Peerless Lake, *Canada* 102 B6
Peers, *Canada* 102 C5
Pegasus Bay, *N.Z.* 91 K4
Peggau, *Austria* 26 D8
Pegnitz, *Germany* 25 F7
Pegnitz →, *Germany* 25 F6
Pego, *Spain* 39 G4
Pegu, *Burma* 67 L20
Pegu Yoma, *Burma* 67 K20
Pehčevo, *Macedonia* 44 E6
Pehlıvanköy, *Turkey* 45 E10
Pehuajó, *Argentina* 126 D3
Pei Xian = Pizhou, *China* .. 56 G9
Peine, *Chile* 126 A2
Peine, *Germany* 24 C6
Peip'ing = Beijing, *China* .. 56 E9
Peipus, L. = Chudskoye, Ozero, *Russia* 9 G22
Peissenberg, *Germany* 25 H7
Peitz, *Germany* 24 D10
Peixe, *Brazil* 125 F9
Peixe →, *Brazil* 125 H8
Pek →, *Serbia & M.* 44 B5
Pekalongan, *Indonesia* 63 G13
Pekan, *Malaysia* 65 L4
Pekan Nenas, *Malaysia* .... 65 d
Pekanbaru, *Indonesia* 62 D2
Pekang, *Taiwan* 59 F13
Pekin, *U.S.A.* 112 E10
Peking = Beijing, *China* .. 56 E9
Pekutatan, *Indonesia* 63 J17
Péla, *Guinea* 82 D3
Pelabuhan Klang, *Malaysia* .. 65 L3
Pelabuhan Ratu, Teluk, *Indonesia* 63 G12
Pelabuhanratu, *Indonesia* .. 63 G12
Pélagos, *Greece* 46 B6
Pelaihari, *Indonesia* 62 E4
Pelat, Mt., *France* 21 D10
Pełczyce, *Poland* 31 E2
Peleaga, Vf., *Romania* 28 E7
Pelée, Mt., *Martinique* .... 120 c
Pelee, Pt., *Canada* 104 D3
Pelee I., *Canada* 116 E2
Pelekech, *Kenya* 86 B4
Peleng, *Indonesia* 63 E6
Pelentong, *Malaysia* ...... 65 d
Pélézi, *Ivory C.* 82 D3
Pelhřimov, *Czech Rep.* 26 B8
Pelican, *U.S.A.* 102 B1
Pelican L., *Canada* 103 C8
Pelican Narrows, *Canada* .. 103 B8
Pelister △, *Macedonia* 44 F5
Pelješac, *Croatia* 41 F14
Pelkosenniemi, *Finland* 8 C22

Pella, *Greece* 44 F6
Pella, *S. Africa* 88 D2
Pella, *U.S.A.* 112 E8
Pélla □, *Greece* 44 F6
Pello, *Finland* 8 C21
Pellworm, *Germany* 24 A4
Pelly →, *Canada* 100 B6
Pelly Bay, *Canada* 101 B11
Peloponnese = Pelopónnisos □, *Greece* 46 D4
Pelopónnisos □, *Greece* 46 D4
Peloritani, Monti, *Italy* 43 D8
Pelorus Sd., *N.Z.* 91 J4
Pelotas, *Brazil* 127 C5
Pelotas →, *Brazil* 127 B5
Pelovo, *Bulgaria* 45 C8
Pelplin, *Poland* 30 E5
Pelvoux, Massif du, *France* .. 21 D10
Pemalang, *Indonesia* 63 G13
Pemanggil, Pulau, *Malaysia* .. 65 L5
Pematangsiantar, *Indonesia* .. 62 D1
Pemba, *Mozam.* 87 E5
Pemba, *Zambia* 87 F2
Pemba Channel, *Tanzania* .. 86 D4
Pemba I., *Tanzania* 86 D4
Pemberton, *Australia* 93 F2
Pemberton, *Canada* 102 C4
Pembina, *U.S.A.* 112 A6
Pembroke, *Canada* 104 C4
Pembroke, *U.K.* 15 F3
Pembrokeshire □, *U.K.* 15 F3
Pembrokeshire Coast △, *U.K.* 15 F2
Pen-y-Ghent, *U.K.* 14 C5
Peña, Sierra de la, *Spain* .. 38 C4
Peña de Francia, Sierra de la, *Spain* 36 E4
Penafiel, *Portugal* 36 D2
Peñafiel, *Spain* 36 D6
Peñaflor, *Spain* 37 H5
Penal, *Trin. & Tob.* 125 K15
Peñalara, *Spain* 36 E7
Penang = Pinang, *Malaysia* .... 65 c
Penápolis, *Brazil* 127 A6
Peñaranda de Bracamonte, *Spain* 36 E5
Peñarroya, *Spain* 38 E4
Peñarroya-Pueblonuevo, *Spain* . 37 G5
Penarth, *U.K.* 15 F4
Peñas, C. de, *Spain* 36 B5
Penas, G. de, *Chile* 128 F2
Peñas de San Pedro, *Spain* .. 39 G3
Peñas del Chache, *Canary Is.* .. 48 E6
Peñausende, *Spain* 36 D5
Pench'i = Benxi, *China* 57 D12
Pend Oreille →, *U.S.A.* 108 B5
Pend Oreille, L., *U.S.A.* .. 108 C5
Pendálofon, *Greece* 44 F5
Pendembu, *Eastern, S. Leone* .. 82 D2
Pendembu, *Northern, S. Leone* . 82 D2
Pender B., *Australia* 92 C3
Pendik, *Turkey* 45 F13
Pendjari →, *Benin* 83 C5
Pendjari △, *Benin* 83 C5
Pendleton, *U.S.A.* 108 D4
Pendra, *India* 69 H9
Peneda-Gerês △, *Portugal* .. 36 D2
Penedo, *Brazil* 125 F11
Penelokan, *Indonesia* 63 J18
Penetanguishene, *Canada* .. 116 B5
Penfield, *U.S.A.* 116 E6
Pengalengan, *Indonesia* 63 G12
Penge, Kasai-Or., *Dem. Rep. of the Congo* 86 D1
Penge, Sud-Kivu, *Dem. Rep. of the Congo* 86 C2
P'enghu Ch'üntou, *Taiwan* .. 59 F12
Penglai, *China* 57 F11
Pengshan, *China* 58 B4
Pengshui, *China* 58 C7
Penguin, *Australia* 95 G4
Pengxi, *China* 58 B5
Pengze, *China* 59 C11
Penhalonga, *Zimbabwe* 87 F3
Peniche, *Portugal* 37 F1
Penicuik, *U.K.* 13 F5
Penida, Nusa, *Indonesia* .. 63 K18
Peninnes, Alpes = Pennine, Alpi, *Alps* 25 J3
Peninsular Malaysia □, *Malaysia* 65 L4
Peñíscola, *Spain* 38 E5
Penitente, Serra do, *Brazil* .. 125 E9
Penkridge, *U.K.* 14 E5
Penmarch, *France* 18 E2
Penmarch, Pte. de, *France* .. 18 E2
Penn Hills, *U.S.A.* 116 F5
Penn Yan, *U.S.A.* 116 D7
Penna, Punta della, *Italy* .. 41 F11
Pennant, *Canada* 103 C7
Penne, *Italy* 41 F10
Penner →, *India* 66 M12
Pennine, Alpi, *Alps* 25 J3
Pennines, *U.K.* 14 C5
Pennington, *U.S.A.* 110 F5
Pennington →, *Nigeria* 83 E6
Pennino, Mte., *Italy* 41 E9
Pennsburg, *U.S.A.* 117 F9
Pennsylvania □, *U.S.A.* 114 E7
Penny, *Canada* 102 C4
Peno, *Russia* 32 D7
Penobscot →, *U.S.A.* 115 C11
Penobscot B., *U.S.A.* 115 C11
Penola, *Australia* 95 F3
Penong, *Australia* 93 F5
Penonomé, *Panama* 120 E3
Penrith, *Australia* 95 E5
Penrith, *U.K.* 14 C5
Penryn, *U.K.* 15 G2
Pensacola, *U.S.A.* 115 K2
Pensacola Mts., *Antarctica* .. 5 E1
Pense, *Canada* 103 C8
Penshurst, *Australia* 95 F3

Penticton, *Canada* 102 D5
Pentland, *Australia* 94 C4
Pentland Firth, *U.K.* 13 C5
Pentland Hills, *U.K.* 13 F5
Pentland Hills △, *U.K.* 13 F5
Penza, *Russia* 34 D7
Penzance, *U.K.* 15 G2
Penzberg, *Germany* 25 H7
Penzhino, *Russia* 53 C17
Penzhinskaya Guba, *Russia* . 53 C17
Penzhou, *China* 58 B4
Penzlin, *Germany* 24 B9
Peoria, *Ariz., U.S.A.* 109 K7
Peoria, *Ill., U.S.A.* 112 E10
Pepacton Reservoir, *U.S.A.* . 117 D10
Pepani →, *S. Africa* 88 D3
Pepel, *S. Leone* 82 D2
Peqin, *Albania* 44 E3
Pera Hd., *Australia* 94 A3
Perabumulih, *Indonesia* 62 E2
Perak □, *Malaysia* 65 K3
Perakhóra, *Greece* 46 C4
Perales de Alfambra, *Spain* .. 38 E4
Perales del Puerto, *Spain* .. 36 E4
Pérama, *Kérkira, Greece* .. 49 A3
Pérama, *Kríti, Greece* 49 D6
Perancak, *Indonesia* 63 J17
Peräpohjola, *Finland* 8 C22
Perast, *Serbia & M.* 44 D2
Percé, *Canada* 105 C7
Perche, *France* 18 D8
Perche, Collines du →, *France* . 18 D7
Perchtoldsdorf, *Austria* 27 C9
Percival Lakes, *Australia* .. 92 D4
Percy, *France* 18 D5
Percy Is., *Australia* 94 C5
Perdido, Mte., *Spain* 38 C5
Perdu, Mt. = Perdido, Mte., *Spain* 38 C5
Perechyn, *Ukraine* 28 B7
Perehinske, *Ukraine* 29 B9
Pereira, *Colombia* 124 C3
Perelazovskiy, *Russia* 35 F6
Peremyshlyany, *Ukraine* .. 29 B13
Peresecina, *Moldova* 29 C13
Pereslavl-Zalesskiy, *Russia* . 32 D10
Peretu, *Romania* 29 F10
Pereyaslav-Khmelnytskyy, *Ukraine* 33 G6
Pereyma, *Ukraine* 29 B14
Pérez, I., *Mexico* 119 C7
Perg, *Austria* 26 C7
Pergamino, *Argentina* 126 C3
Pergau →, *Malaysia* 65 K3
Pérgine Valsugana, *Italy* .. 41 B8
Pérgola, *Italy* 41 E9
Perham, *U.S.A.* 112 B7
Perhentian, Kepulauan, *Malaysia* 65 K4
Periam, *Romania* 28 D5
Péribonka →, *Canada* 105 C5
Péribonka, L., *Canada* 105 B5
Perico, *Argentina* 126 A2
Pericos, *Mexico* 118 B3
Périers, *France* 18 C5
Périgord, *France* 20 D4
Périgord-Limousin △, *France* . 20 C4
Périgueux, *France* 20 C4
Perijá △, *Venezuela* 121 E5
Perijá, Sierra de, *Colombia* .. 124 B4
Peristéra, *Greece* 46 B5
Peristerona →, *Cyprus* 49 D12
Perito Moreno, *Argentina* .. 128 F2
Perivol = Dragovishtitsa, *Bulgaria* 44 D6
Perkasie, *U.S.A.* 117 F9
Perković, *Croatia* 41 E13
Perlas, Arch. de las, *Panama* . 120 E4
Perlas, Punta de, *Nic.* 120 D3
Perleberg, *Germany* 24 B7
Perlez, *Serbia & M.* 28 E5
Perm, *Russia* 52 D6
Pernambuco = Recife, *Brazil* 125 E12
Pernambuco □, *Brazil* 125 E11
Pernatty Lagoon, *Australia* .. 95 E2
Pernik, *Bulgaria* 44 D7
Peron Is., *Australia* 92 B5
Peron Pen., *Australia* 93 E1
Péronne, *France* 19 C9
Perosa Argentina, *Italy* 40 D4
Perow, *Canada* 102 C3
Perpignan, *France* 20 F6
Perris, *U.S.A.* 111 M9
Perros-Guirec, *France* 18 D3
Perry, *Fla., U.S.A.* 115 K4
Perry, *Ga., U.S.A.* 115 J4
Perry, *Iowa, U.S.A.* 112 E7
Perry, *Okla., U.S.A.* 113 G6
Perryton, *U.S.A.* 113 G4
Perryville, *U.S.A.* 113 G10
Persan, *France* 19 C9
Persberg, *Sweden* 10 E8
Persembe, *Turkey* 72 B7
Persepolis, *Iran* 71 D7
Pershotravensk, *Ukraine* .. 33 G4
Persia = Iran ■, *Asia* 71 C7
Persian Gulf, *Asia* 71 E6
Perstorp, *Sweden* 11 H7
Pertek, *Turkey* 73 C8
Perth, *Australia* 93 F2
Perth, *Canada* 117 B8
Perth, *U.K.* 13 E5
Perth & Kinross □, *U.K.* .. 13 E5
Perth Amboy, *U.S.A.* 117 F10
Perth-Andover, *Canada* 105 C6
Pertuis, *France* 21 E9
Pertusato, C., *France* 21 G13
Peru, *Ind., U.S.A.* 114 E2
Peru, *N.Y., U.S.A.* 117 B11
Peru ■, *S. Amer.* 124 D4
Peru Basin, *Pac. Oc.* 97 J18
Peru-Chile Trench, *Pac. Oc.* . 124 G3
Perúgia, *Italy* 41 E9

Perušić, *Croatia* 41 D12
Pervomaysk, *Russia* 34 C6
Pervomaysk, *Ukraine* 33 H6
Pervouralsk, *Russia* 52 D7
Pésaro, *Italy* 41 E9
Pescadores = P'enghu Ch'üntou, *Taiwan* 59 F12
Pescara, *Italy* 41 F11
Pescara →, *Italy* 41 F11
Peschanokopskoye, *Russia* .. 35 G5
Péscia, *Italy* 40 E7
Pescina, *Italy* 41 F10
Peshawar, *Pakistan* 68 B4
Peshkopi, *Albania* 44 E4
Peshtera, *Bulgaria* 45 D8
Peshtigo, *U.S.A.* 114 C2
Peski, *Russia* 34 E6
Pêso da Régua, *Portugal* .. 36 D3
Pesqueira, *Brazil* 125 E11
Pessac, *France* 20 D3
Pest □, *Hungary* 28 C4
Pestovo, *Russia* 32 C8
Pestravka, *Russia* 34 D9
Péta, *Greece* 46 B3
Petah Tiqwa, *Israel* 74 C3
Petalídhion, *Greece* 46 E3
Petaling Jaya, *Malaysia* .. 65 L3
Petaloudhes, *Greece* 49 C10
Petaluma, *U.S.A.* 110 G4
Pétange, *Lux.* 17 E5
Petaro, *Pakistan* 68 G3
Petatlán, *Mexico* 118 D4
Petauke, *Zambia* 87 E3
Petawawa, *Canada* 104 C4
Petén Itzá, L., *Guatemala* .. 120 C2
Peter I.s Øy, *Antarctica* 5 C16
Peter I., *Br. Virgin Is.* .... 121 e
Peter Pond L., *Canada* 103 B7
Peterbell, *Canada* 104 C3
Peterborough, *Australia* .. 95 E2
Peterborough, *Canada* 116 B6
Peterborough, *U.K.* 15 E7
Peterborough, *U.S.A.* 117 D13
Peterborough □, *U.K.* 15 E7
Peterculter, *U.K.* 13 D6
Peterhead, *U.K.* 13 D7
Peterlee, *U.K.* 14 C6
Petermann Ranges, *Australia* 92 E5
Petersburg, *Alaska, U.S.A.* 100 C6
Petersburg, *Pa., U.S.A.* .. 116 F6
Petersburg, *Va., U.S.A.* .. 114 G7
Petersburg, *W. Va., U.S.A.* 114 F6
Petersfield, *U.K.* 15 F7
Petershagen, *Germany* 24 C4
Petília Policastro, *Italy* 43 C9
Petit-Canal, *Guadeloupe* .. 120 b
Petit Goâve, *Haiti* 121 C5
Petit Jardin, *Canada* 105 C8
Petit Lac Manicouagan, *Canada* . 105 B6
Petit-Mécatina →, *Canada* .. 105 B8
Petit-Mécatina, Î. du, *Canada* . 105 B8
Petit Piton, *St. Lucia* ...... 121 f
Petit-Saguenay, *Canada* .. 105 C5
Petit Saint Bernard, Col du, *Italy* . 21 C10
Petitcodiac, *Canada* 105 C6
Petite Terre, Îles de la, *Guadeloupe* .... 120 b
Petitot →, *Canada* 102 A4
Petitsikapau L., *Canada* .. 105 B6
Petlad, *India* 68 H5
Peto, *Mexico* 119 C7
Petone, *N.Z.* 91 J5
Petorca, *Chile* 126 C1
Petoskey, *U.S.A.* 114 C3
Petra, *Jordan* 74 E4
Petra, *Spain* 48 B10
Petra, Ostrova, *Russia* 4 B13
Petra Velikogo, Zaliv, *Russia* . 54 C6
Petrel = Petrer, *Spain* 39 G4
Petrella, Monte, *Italy* 42 A6
Petrer, *Spain* 39 G4
Petreto-Bicchisano, *France* . 21 G12
Petrich, *Bulgaria* 44 E7
Petrified Forest △, *U.S.A.* . 109 J9
Petrijanec, *Croatia* 41 B13
Petrikov = Pyetrikaw, *Belarus* . 33 F5
Petrila, *Romania* 29 E8
Petrinja, *Croatia* 41 C13
Petrodvorets, *Russia* 32 C5
Petrolândia, *Brazil* 125 E11
Petrolia, *Canada* 116 D2
Petrolina, *Brazil* 125 E10
Petropavl, *Kazakhstan* 52 D7
Petropavlovsk = Petropavl, *Kazakhstan* 52 D7
Petropavlovsk-Kamchatskiy, *Russia* 53 D16
Petropavlovskiy = Akhtubinsk, *Russia* 35 F8
Petrópolis, *Brazil* 127 A7
Petroşani, *Romania* 29 E8
Petrova Gora, *Croatia* 41 C12
Petrovac, *Serbia & M.* 44 B5
Petrovac, *Serbia & M.* 44 D2
Petrovaradin, *Serbia & M.* . 28 E4
Petrovsk, *Russia* 34 D7
Petrovsk-Zabaykalskiy, *Russia* . 53 D11
Petrovskaya, *Russia* 33 K9
Petrozavodsk, *Russia* 32 B8
Petrus Steyn, *S. Africa* .. 89 D4
Petrusburg, *S. Africa* 88 D4
Petzeck, *Austria* 26 E5
Peumo, *Chile* 126 C1
Peur, *N.Z.* 91 J5
Peureulak, *Indonesia* 62 D1
Pevek, *Russia* 53 C18
Peveragno, *Italy* 40 D4
Peyrehorade, *France* 20 E2
Peyruis, *France* 21 D9
Pézenas, *France* 20 E7
Pezinok, *Slovak Rep.* 27 C10
Pfaffenhofen, *Germany* 25 G7

Pfälzerwald △, Germany 25 F5
Pfarrkirchen, Germany 25 G8
Pfeffenhausen, Germany 25 G7
Pforzheim, Germany 25 G4
Pfullendorf, Germany 25 H5
Pfungstadt, Germany 25 F4
Pha Taem △, Thailand 64 E5
Phagwara, India 66 D9
Phaistós, Greece 49 D6
Phala, Botswana 88 C4
Phalera = Phulera, India 68 F6
Phalodi, India 68 F5
Phalsbourg, France 19 D14
Phaluai, Ko, Thailand .... 65 b
Phan, Thailand 64 C2
Phan Rang, Vietnam 65 G7
Phan Ri = Hoa Da, Vietnam ... 65 G7
Phan Thiet, Vietnam 65 G7
Phanae, Greece 47 C7
Phanat Nikhom, Thailand 64 F3
Phangan, Ko, Thailand 65 H3
Phangnga, Thailand 65 H2
Phangnga, Ao, Thailand .... 65 a
Phanom Sarakham, Thailand ... 64 F3
Phaphund, India 69 F8
Pharenda, India 69 F10
Pharr, U.S.A. 113 M5
Phatthalung, Thailand 65 J3
Phayao, Thailand 64 C2
Phelps, U.S.A. 116 D7
Phelps L., Canada 103 B8
Phenix City, U.S.A. 115 J3
Phet Buri, Thailand 64 F2
Phetchabun, Thailand 64 D3
Phetchabun, Thiu Khao, Thailand 64 D3
Phetchaburi = Phet Buri, Thailand 64 F2
Phi Phi, Ko, Thailand 65 J2
Phiafay, Laos 64 E6
Phibun Mangsahan, Thailand .. 64 E5
Phichai, Thailand 64 D3
Phichit, Thailand 64 D3
Philadelphia, Miss., U.S.A. 113 J10
Philadelphia, N.Y., U.S.A. 117 B9
Philadelphia, Pa., U.S.A. 117 G9
Philip, U.S.A. 112 C4
Philippeville, Belgium 17 D4
Philippi, Greece 45 E8
Philippi, U.S.A. 114 F5
Philippi L., Australia 94 C2
Philippine Sea, Pac. Oc. 50 H16
Philippines ■, Asia 61 F5
Philippolis, S. Africa 88 E4
Philippopolis = Plovdiv, Bulgaria 45 D8
Philipsburg, Canada 117 A11
Philipsburg, Mont., U.S.A. 108 C7
Philipsburg, Pa., U.S.A. 116 F6
Philipstown = Daingean, Ireland 12 C4
Philipstown, S. Africa 88 E3
Phillip I., Australia 95 F4
Phillips, U.S.A. 112 C9
Phillipsburg, Kans., U.S.A. ... 112 F5
Phillipsburg, N.J., U.S.A. 117 F9
Philmont, U.S.A. 117 D11
Philomath, U.S.A. 108 D2
Phimai, Thailand 64 E4
Phitsanulok, Thailand 64 D3
Phnom Dangrek, Thailand 62 B2
Phnom Penh, Cambodia 65 G5
Phnum Penh = Phnom Penh,
     Cambodia 65 G5
Phoenicia, U.S.A. 117 D10
Phoenix, Ariz., U.S.A. 109 K7
Phoenix, N.Y., U.S.A. 117 C8
Phoenix Is., Kiribati 96 H10
Phoenixville, U.S.A. 117 F9
Phon, Thailand 64 E4
Phon Tiou, Laos 64 D5
Phong ➜, Thailand 64 D4
Phong Saly, Laos 58 G4
Phong Tho, Vietnam 64 A4
Phonhong, Laos 64 C4
Phonum, Thailand 65 H2
Phosphate Hill, Australia 94 C2
Photharam, Thailand 64 F2
Phra Nakhon Si Ayutthaya,
     Thailand 64 E3
Phra Thong, Ko, Thailand 65 H2
Phrae, Thailand 64 C3
Phrom Phiram, Thailand 64 D3
Phrygia, Turkey 72 C4
Phu Chong-Na Yoi △, Thailand . 64 E5
Phu Dien, Vietnam 64 C5
Phu Hin Rong Kla △, Thailand .. 64 D3
Phu Kradung △, Thailand 64 D3
Phu Loi, Laos 64 B4
Phu Luang △, Thailand 64 D3
Phu Ly, Vietnam 58 G5
Phu Phan △, Thailand 64 D4
Phu Quoc, Dao, Vietnam 65 G4
Phu Tho, Vietnam 58 G5
Phuc Yen, Vietnam 58 G5
Phuket, Thailand .... 65 a
Phuket, Ko, Thailand .... 65 a
Phul, India 68 D6
Phulad, India 68 G5
Phulchari, Bangla. 69 G13
Phulera, India 68 F6
Phulpur, India 69 G10
Phun Phin, Thailand 65 H2
Piacenza, Italy 40 C6
Piai, Tanjung, Malaysia .... 65 d
Pian Cr. ➜, Australia 95 E4
Pian-Upe △, Uganda 86 B3
Piana, France 21 F12
Pianella, Italy 41 F11
Pianosa, Puglia, Italy 41 F12
Pianosa, Toscana, Italy 40 F7
Piapot, Canada 103 D7
Pias, Portugal 37 G3
Piaseczno, Poland 31 F8
Piaski, Poland 31 G9

Piastów, Poland 31 F7
Piatra, Romania 29 G10
Piatra Craiului △, Romania 29 E10
Piatra Neamţ, Romania 29 D11
Piatra Olt, Romania 29 F9
Piauí □, Brazil 125 E10
Piauí ➜, Brazil 125 E10
Piave ➜, Italy 41 C9
Piazza Armerina, Italy 43 E7
Pibor ➜, Sudan 81 F3
Pibor Post, Sudan 81 F3
Picardie □, France 19 C10
Picardie, Plaine de, France 19 C9
Picardy = Picardie □, France 19 C10
Picayune, U.S.A. 113 K10
Picerno, Italy 43 B8
Pichhor, India 69 G8
Pichilemu, Chile 126 C1
Pichor, India 68 G8
Pickerel L., Canada 104 C1
Pickering, U.K. 14 C7
Pickering, Vale of, U.K. 14 C7
Pickle Lake, Canada 104 B1
Pickwick L., U.S.A. 115 H1
Pico Bonito △, Honduras 120 C2
Pico Truncado, Argentina 128 F3
Picos, Brazil 125 E10
Picos de Europa △, Spain 36 B6
Picton, Australia 95 E5
Picton, Canada 116 B7
Picton, N.Z. 91 J5
Pictou, Canada 105 C7
Picture Butte, Canada 102 D6
Pictured Rocks △, U.S.A. 114 B2
Picún Leufú, Argentina 128 D3
Pidbuzh, Ukraine 31 J10
Pidurutalagala, Sri Lanka 66 R12
Piechowice, Poland 31 H2
Piedimonte Matese, Italy 43 A7
Piedmont = Piemonte □, Italy . 40 D5
Piedmont, Ala., U.S.A. 115 J3
Piedmont, S.C., U.S.A. 107 D10
Piedra ➜, Spain 38 D3
Piedrabuena, Spain 37 G6
Piedrahita, Spain 36 E5
Piedralaves, Spain 36 E6
Piedras Blancas, Spain 36 B5
Piedras Negras, Mexico 118 B4
Piekary Śląskie, Poland 31 H5
Pieksämäki, Finland 9 E22
Piemonte □, Italy 40 D5
Pienaarsrivier, S. Africa 89 D4
Pieniężno, Poland 30 D7
Pieniński △, Europe 27 B13
Pieńsk, Poland 31 G2
Piercefield, U.S.A. 117 B10
Pierceland, Canada 103 C7
Piería □, Greece 44 F6
Pierpont, U.S.A. 116 E4
Pierre, U.S.A. 112 C4
Pierre-Buffière, France 20 C5
Pierre-de-Bresse, France 19 F12
Pierrefontaine-les-Varans, France 19 E13
Pierrefort, France 20 D6
Pierrelatte, France 21 D8
Pierreville, Trin. & Tob. 125 K16
Pieštany, Slovak Rep. 27 C10
Piesting ➜, Austria 27 C9
Pieszyce, Poland 31 H3
Piet Retief, S. Africa 89 D5
Pietarsaari, Finland 8 E20
Pietermaritzburg, S. Africa 89 D5
Pietersburg = Polokwane,
     S. Africa 89 C4
Pietragalla, Italy 43 B8
Pietrasanta, Italy 40 E7
Pietroşiţa, Romania 29 E10
Pietrosul, Vf., Maramureş,
     Romania 29 C9
Pietrosul, Vf., Suceava, Romania 29 C10
Pieve di Cadore, Italy 41 B9
Pieve di Teco, Italy 40 D4
Pievepélago, Italy 40 D7
Pigadhítsa, Greece 44 G5
Pigeon L., Canada 116 B6
Piggott, U.S.A. 113 G9
Pigna, Italy 40 E4
Pigüe, Argentina 126 D3
Pihani, India 69 F9
Pihlajavesi, Finland 9 F23
Pijijiapan, Mexico 119 D6
Pikalevo, Russia 32 C8
Pikangikum Berens, Canada ... 103 C10
Pikes Peak, U.S.A. 112 F2
Piketberg, S. Africa 88 E2
Pikeville, U.S.A. 114 G4
Pikou, China 57 E12
Pikwitonei, Canada 103 B9
Piła, Poland 31 E3
Pila, Spain 39 G3
Pilaía, Greece 44 F6
Pilanesberg △, S. Africa 88 D4
Pilani, India 68 E6
Pilar, Paraguay 126 B4
Pilar de la Horadada, Spain ... 39 H4
Pilat △, France 21 C8
Pilawa, Poland 31 G8
Pilaya ➜, Bolivia 124 H6
Pilbara, Australia 92 D2
Pilcomayo ➜, Paraguay 126 B4
Pilgrim's Rest, S. Africa 89 C5
Pilgrimstad, Sweden 10 B9
Pílí, Greece 47 E9
Pilibhit, India 69 E8
Pilica ➜, Poland 31 G8
Pilion, Greece 46 B5
Pilis, Hungary 28 C4
Pilisvörösvár, Hungary 28 C3
Pilkhawa, India 68 E7
Pilliga, Australia 95 E4
Pílos, Greece 46 E3

Pilot Mound, Canada 103 D9
Pilot Point, U.S.A. 113 J6
Pilot Rock, U.S.A. 108 D4
Pilštanj, Slovenia 41 B12
Piltene, Latvia 30 A8
Pilzno, Poland 31 J8
Pima, U.S.A. 109 K9
Pimba, Australia 95 E2
Pimenta Bueno, Brazil 124 F6
Pimentel, Peru 124 E3
Pina de Ebro, Spain 38 D4
Pinamalayan, Phil. 61 E4
Pinang, Malaysia .... 65 c
Pinar, C. des, Spain 48 B10
Pinar del Río, Cuba 120 B3
Pınarbaşı, Çanakkale, Turkey .. 47 B8
Pınarbaşı, Kayseri, Turkey 72 C7
Pınarhisar, Turkey 45 E11
Pinatubo, Mt., Phil. 61 D3
Pincehely, Hungary 28 D3
Pinchang, China 58 B6
Pincher Creek, Canada 102 D6
Pinchi L., Canada 102 C4
Pinckneyville, U.S.A. 112 F10
Pindar, Australia 93 E2
Pindi Gheb, Pakistan 68 C5
Pindiga, Nigeria 83 D7
Pindos △, Greece 46 B3
Pindos Óros, Greece 46 B3
Pindus Mts. = Pindos Óros,
     Greece 46 B3
Pine ➜, B.C., Canada 102 B4
Pine ➜, Sask., Canada 103 B7
Pine, C., Canada 105 C9
Pine Bluff, U.S.A. 113 H9
Pine Bluffs, U.S.A. 112 E2
Pine City, U.S.A. 112 C8
Pine Cr. ➜, U.S.A. 116 E7
Pine Creek, Australia 92 B5
Pine Falls, Canada 103 C9
Pine Flat Res., U.S.A. 110 J7
Pine Grove, U.S.A. 117 F8
Pine Pass, Canada 102 B4
Pine Point, Canada 102 A6
Pine Ridge, U.S.A. 112 D3
Pine River, Canada 103 C8
Pine River, U.S.A. 112 B7
Pine Valley, U.S.A. 111 N10
Pinecrest, U.S.A. 110 G6
Pinedale, Calif., U.S.A. 110 J7
Pinedale, Wyo., U.S.A. 108 E9
Pinega ➜, Russia 52 C5
Pinehill, Australia 94 C4
Pinehouse L., Canada 103 B7
Pineimuta ➜, Canada 104 B1
Pinerolo, Italy 40 D4
Pineto, Italy 41 F11
Pinetop, U.S.A. 109 J9
Pinetown, S. Africa 89 D5
Pineville, U.S.A. 113 K8
Piney, France 19 D11
Ping ➜, Thailand 64 E3
Pingaring, Australia 93 F2
Pingba, China 58 D6
Pingbian, China 58 F4
Pingchuan, China 58 D3
Pingding, China 56 F7
Pingdingshan, China 56 H7
Pingdong, Taiwan 59 F13
Pingdu, China 57 F10
Pingelly, Australia 93 F2
Pingguo, China 58 F6
Pinghe, China 59 E11
Pinghu, China 59 B13
Pingjiang, China 59 C9
Pingle, China 59 E8
Pingli, China 58 A7
Pingliang, China 56 G4
Pinglu, China 56 E7
Pingluo, China 56 E4
Pingnan, Fujian, China 59 D12
Pingnan, Guangxi Zhuangzu,
     China 59 F8
Pingquan, China 57 D10
Pingrup, Australia 93 F2
Pingshan, China 58 C5
Pingtan, China 59 E12
Pingtang, China 58 E6
P'ingtung, Taiwan 59 F13
Pingwu, China 56 H3
Pingxiang, Guangxi Zhuangzu,
     China 58 F6
Pingxiang, Jiangxi, China 59 D9
Pingyao, China 56 F7
Pingyi, China 57 G9
Pingyin, China 56 F9
Pingyuan, Guangdong, China .. 59 E10
Pingyuan, Shandong, China ... 56 F9
Pingyuanjie, China 58 F4
Pinhal, Brazil 127 A6
Pinhal Novo, Portugal 37 G2
Pinheiro, Brazil 125 D9
Pinheiro Machado, Brazil 127 C5
Pinhel, Portugal 36 E3
Pini, Indonesia 62 D1
Piniós ➜, Ilía, Greece 46 D3
Piniós ➜, Tríkkala, Greece 46 B4
Pinjarra, Australia 93 F2
Pink Mountain, Canada 102 B4
Pinkafeld, Austria 27 D9
Pinnacles, U.S.A. 110 J5
Pinnacles △, U.S.A. 110 J5
Pinnaroo, Australia 95 F3
Pinneberg, Germany 24 B5
Pínnes, Ákra, Greece 45 F8
Pinos, Mexico 118 C4
Pinos, Mt., U.S.A. 111 L7
Pinos Pt., U.S.A. 109 H3

Pinos Puente, Spain 37 H7
Pinotepa Nacional, Mexico 119 D5
Pinrang, Indonesia 63 E5
Pins, Pte. aux, Canada 116 D3
Pinsk, Belarus 33 F4
Pintados, Chile 124 H5
Pinyang, China 59 D13
Pinyug, Russia 52 C5
Pioche, U.S.A. 109 H6
Piombino, Italy 40 F7
Piombino, Canale di, Italy 40 F7
Pioner, Ostrov, Russia 53 B10
Pionerskiy, Russia 30 D7
Pionki, Poland 31 G8
Piorini, L., Brazil 124 D6
Piotrków Trybunalski, Poland .. 31 G6
Piove di Sacco, Italy 41 C9
Pip, Iran 71 E9
Pipar, India 68 F5
Pipar Road, India 68 F5
Piparia, Mad. P., India 68 H8
Piparia, Mad. P., India 68 J7
Pipéri, Greece 46 B6
Pipestone, U.S.A. 112 D6
Pipestone ➜, Canada 104 B2
Pipestone Cr. ➜, Canada 103 D8
Piplan, Pakistan 68 C4
Piploda, India 68 H6
Pipmuacan, Rés., Canada 105 C5
Pippingarra, Australia 92 D2
Pipriac, France 18 E5
Piqua, U.S.A. 114 E3
Piquiri ➜, Brazil 127 A5
Pir Panjal Range, India 68 C7
Pir Sohrāb, Iran 71 E9
Pira, Benin 83 D5
Piracicaba, Brazil 127 A6
Piracuruca, Brazil 125 D10
Piraévs = Piraiévs, Greece 46 D5
Piraiévs, Greece 46 D5
Pirajuí, Brazil 127 A6
Piram I., India 68 J5
Piran = Piran, Slovenia 41 C10
Pirané, Argentina 126 B4
Pirano = Piran, Slovenia 41 C10
Pirapora, Brazil 125 G10
Pirawa, India 68 G7
Pirdop, Bulgaria 45 D8
Pírgos, Ilía, Greece 46 D3
Pírgos, Kríti, Greece 47 F7
Pirgovo, Bulgaria 45 C9
Piribebuy, Paraguay 126 B4
Pirimapun, Indonesia 63 F9
Pirin △, Bulgaria 44 E7
Pirin Planina, Bulgaria 44 E7
Pírineos = Pyrénées, Europe .. 20 F4
Piripiri, Brazil 125 D10
Pirmasens, Germany 25 F3
Pirna, Germany 24 E9
Pirot, Serbia & M. 44 C6
Piru, Indonesia 63 E7
Piru, U.S.A. 111 L8
Piryatin = Pyryatyn, Ukraine .. 33 G7
Piryí, Greece 47 C7
Pisa, Italy 40 E7
Pisa ➜, Poland 31 E8
Pisa, Firenze ✈ (PSA), Italy ... 40 E7
Pisagne, Italy 40 C7
Pisagua, Chile 124 G4
Pisarovina, Croatia 41 C12
Pisco, Peru 124 F3
Piscu, Romania 29 E12
Písek, Czech Rep. 26 B7
Pishan, China 60 C2
Pishcha, Ukraine 31 G10
Pīshīn, Iran 71 E9
Pishin, Pakistan 68 D2
Pishin Lora ➜, Pakistan 68 E1
Pising, Indonesia 63 F6
Pismo Beach, U.S.A. 111 K6
Piso, L., Liberia 82 D2
Pissila, Burkina Faso 83 C4
Pissis, Cerro, Argentina 126 B2
Pissos, France 20 D3
Pisticci, Italy 43 B9
Pistóia, Italy 40 E7
Pistol B., Canada 103 A10
Pisuerga ➜, Spain 36 D6
Pisz, Poland 30 E8
Pit ➜, U.S.A. 108 F2
Pita, Guinea 82 C2
Pitarpunga L., Australia 95 E3
Pitcairn I., Pac. Oc. 97 K14
Pitch L., Trin. & Tob. 125 K15
Piteå, Sweden 8 D19
Piteälven ➜, Sweden 8 D19
Piterka, Russia 34 E8
Piteşti, Romania 29 F9
Pithapuram, India 67 L13
Pithara, Australia 93 F2
Pithion, Greece 45 E10
Pithoragarh, India 69 E9
Pithoro, Pakistan 68 G3
Pitigliano, Italy 41 F8
Pitkyaranta, Russia 32 B6
Pitlochry, U.K. 13 E5
Pitsilia, Cyprus 49 E12
Pitt I., Canada 102 C3
Pittsburg, Calif., U.S.A. 110 G5
Pittsburg, Kans., U.S.A. 113 G7
Pittsburg, Tex., U.S.A. 113 J7
Pittsburgh, U.S.A. 116 F5
Pittsfield, Ill., U.S.A. 112 F9
Pittsfield, Mass., U.S.A. 117 D11
Pittsfield, N.H., U.S.A. 117 C13
Pittston, U.S.A. 117 E9

Pittsworth, Australia 95 D5
Pituri ➜, Australia 94 C2
Piura, Peru 124 E2
Piva ➜, Serbia & M. 44 C2
Piwniczna, Poland 31 J7
Pixley, U.S.A. 110 K7
Piyai, Greece 46 B3
Pizarra, Spain 37 J6
Pizhou, China 56 G9
Pizzo, Italy 43 D9
Placentia, Canada 105 C9
Placentia B., Canada 105 C9
Placer, Masbate, Phil. 61 F5
Placer, Surigao N., Phil. 61 G6
Placerville, U.S.A. 110 G6
Placetas, Cuba 120 B4
Plačkovica, Macedonia 44 E5
Plainfield, N.J., U.S.A. 117 F10
Plainfield, Ohio, U.S.A. 116 F3
Plainfield, Vt., U.S.A. 117 B12
Plains, Mont., U.S.A. 108 C6
Plains, Tex., U.S.A. 113 J3
Plainview, Nebr., U.S.A. 112 D6
Plainview, Tex., U.S.A. 113 H4
Plainwell, U.S.A. 114 D3
Plaisance, France 20 E4
Plaistow, U.S.A. 117 D13
Pláka, Greece 47 B7
Pláka, Ákra, Greece 49 D8
Plakenska Planina, Macedonia . 44 E5
Planá, Czech Rep. 26 B5
Plana Cays, Bahamas 121 B5
Planada, U.S.A. 110 H6
Plancoët, France 18 D4
Plandište, Serbia & M. 28 E6
Plano, U.S.A. 113 J6
Plant City, U.S.A. 115 M4
Plaquemine, U.S.A. 113 K9
Plasencia, Spain 36 E4
Plaški, Croatia 41 C12
Plaster City, U.S.A. 111 N11
Plaster Rock, Canada 105 C6
Plastun, Russia 54 B8
Plasy, Czech Rep. 26 B6
Plata, Río de la, S. Amer. 126 C4
Plátani ➜, Italy 42 E6
Plátanos, Greece 49 D5
Plateau □, Nigeria 83 D6
Platí, Ákra, Greece 45 F8
Platte, U.S.A. 112 D5
Platte ➜, Mo., U.S.A. 112 F7
Platte ➜, Nebr., U.S.A. 112 E7
Platteville, U.S.A. 112 D9
Plattling, Germany 25 G8
Plattsburgh, U.S.A. 117 B11
Plattsmouth, U.S.A. 112 E7
Plau, Germany 24 B8
Plauen, Germany 24 E8
Plauer See, Germany 24 B8
Plav, Serbia & M. 44 D3
Plavinas, Latvia 9 H21
Plavnica, Serbia & M. 44 D3
Plavno, Croatia 41 D13
Plavsk, Russia 32 F9
Playa Blanca, Canary Is. 48 F6
Playa Blanca Sur, Canary Is. .. 48 F6
Playa de las Americas, Canary Is. 48 F3
Playa de Mogán, Canary Is. .. 48 G4
Playa del Inglés, Canary Is. ... 48 G4
Playa Esmerelda, Canary Is. .. 48 F5
Playgreen L., Canada 103 C9
Pleasant Bay, Canada 105 C7
Pleasant Hill, U.S.A. 110 H4
Pleasant Mount, U.S.A. 117 E9
Pleasanton, Calif., U.S.A. 110 H5
Pleasanton, Tex., U.S.A. 113 L5
Pleasantville, N.J., U.S.A. 114 F8
Pleasantville, Pa., U.S.A. 116 E5
Pléaux, France 20 C6
Plei Ku, Vietnam 64 F7
Plélan-le-Grand, France 18 D4
Pléneuf-Val-André, France 18 D4
Plenița, Romania 29 F8
Plenty ➜, Australia 94 C2
Plenty, B. of, N.Z. 91 G6
Plentywood, U.S.A. 112 A2
Plérin, France 18 D4
Plessisville, Canada 105 C5
Plestin-les-Grèves, France 18 D3
Pleszew, Poland 31 G4
Pleternica, Croatia 28 E2
Plétipi, L., Canada 105 B5
Pleven, Bulgaria 45 C8
Plevlja, Serbia & M. 44 C3
Plevna, Canada 116 B8
Plitvička Jezera △, Croatia 41 D12
Plješevica, Croatia 41 D12
Ploaghe, Italy 42 B1
Ploče, Croatia 41 E14
Płock, Poland 31 F6
Plöckenpass, Italy 41 B9
Plöckenstein, Germany 25 G9
Ploemeur, France 18 E3
Ploërmel, France 18 E4
Ploieşti, Romania 29 F11
Plomárion, Greece 47 C8
Plombières-les-Bains, France .. 19 E13
Plomin, Croatia 41 C11
Plön, Germany 24 A6
Plonge, Lac la, Canada 103 B7
Płońsk, Poland 31 F7
Plopeni, Romania 29 E10
Plopişului, Munţii, Romania ... 28 C7
Płoty, Poland 30 E2
Plouaret, France 18 D3
Plouay, France 18 E3
Ploučnice ➜, Czech Rep. 26 A7
Ploudalmézeau, France 18 D2
Plouescat, France 18 D2
Plougasnou, France 18 D3
Plougastel-Daoulas, France ... 18 D2

Plouguerneau, *France* 18 D2
Plouha, *France* 18 D4
Plouhinec, *France* 18 E2
Plovdiv, *Bulgaria* 45 D8
Plovdiv □, *Bulgaria* 45 D8
Plum, *U.S.A.* 116 F5
Plum I., *U.S.A.* 117 E12
Plumas, *U.S.A.* 110 F7
Plummer, *U.S.A.* 108 C5
Plumtree, *Zimbabwe* 87 G2
Plungė, *Lithuania* 9 J19
Pluvigner, *France* 18 E3
Plymouth, *Trin. & Tob.* 125 J16
Plymouth, *U.K.* 15 G3
Plymouth, *Calif., U.S.A.* 110 G6
Plymouth, *Ind., U.S.A.* 114 E2
Plymouth, *Mass., U.S.A.* 117 E14
Plymouth, *N.C., U.S.A.* 115 H7
Plymouth, *N.H., U.S.A.* 117 C13
Plymouth, *Pa., U.S.A.* 117 E9
Plymouth, *Wis., U.S.A.* 114 D2
Plympton-Wyoming, *Canada* 116 D2
Plynlimon = Pumlumon Fawr,
U.K. 15 E4
Plyusa, *Russia* 32 C5
Plyusa →, *Russia* 32 C5
Plzeň, *Czech Rep.* 26 B6
Plzeňský □, *Czech Rep.* 26 B6
Pniewy, *Poland* 31 F3
Pô, *Burkina Faso* 83 C4
Pô △, *Burkina Faso* 83 C4
Po →, *Italy* 41 D9
Po, Foci del, *Italy* 41 D9
Po Hai = Bo Hai, *China* 57 E10
Pobé, *Benin* 83 D5
Pobé, *Burkina Faso* 83 C4
Pobeda, *Russia* 53 C15
Pobedy, Pik, *Kyrgyzstan* 52 E8
Pobiedziska, *Poland* 31 F4
Pobla de Segur, *Spain* 38 C5
Pobladura del Valle, *Spain* 36 C5
Pobra de Trives, *Spain* 36 C3
Pocahontas, *Ark., U.S.A.* 113 G9
Pocahontas, *Iowa, U.S.A.* 112 D7
Pocatello, *U.S.A.* 108 E7
Počátky, *Czech Rep.* 26 B8
Pochep, *Russia* 33 F7
Pochinki, *Russia* 34 C7
Pochinok, *Russia* 32 E7
Pöchlarn, *Austria* 26 C8
Pochutla, *Mexico* 119 D5
Pocito Casas, *Mexico* 118 B2
Pocking, *Germany* 25 G9
Pocomoke City, *U.S.A.* 114 F8
Poços de Caldas, *Brazil* 127 A6
Podbořany, *Czech Rep.* 26 A6
Poddębice, *Poland* 31 G5
Poděbrady, *Czech Rep.* 26 A8
Podensac, *France* 20 D3
Podenzano, *Italy* 40 D6
Podgorač, *Croatia* 28 E3
Podgorica, *Serbia & M.* 44 D3
Podgorie, *Albania* 44 F4
Podilska Vysochyna, *Ukraine* ... 29 B13
Podkarpackie □, *Poland* 31 H9
Podkova, *Bulgaria* 45 E9
Podlapača, *Croatia* 41 D12
Podlaskie □, *Poland* 31 E10
Podoleni, *Romania* 29 D11
Podolínec, *Slovak Rep.* 27 B13
Podolsk, *Russia* 32 E9
Podor, *Senegal* 82 B1
Podporozhye, *Russia* 32 B8
Podu Iloaiei, *Romania* 29 C12
Podu Turcului, *Romania* 29 D12
Podujevo, *Serbia & M.* 44 D5
Podyjí △, *Czech Rep.* 26 C8
Poel, *Germany* 24 B6
Pofadder, *S. Africa* 88 D2
Poggiardo, *Italy* 43 B11
Poggibonsi, *Italy* 40 E8
Póggio Mirteto, *Italy* 41 F9
Pogoanele, *Romania* 29 F12
Pogorzela, *Poland* 31 G4
Pogradec, *Albania* 44 F4
Pogranichnyy, *Russia* 54 B5
Poh, *Indonesia* 63 E6
P'ohang, *S. Korea* 57 F15
Pohjanmaa, *Finland* 8 E20
Pohnpei, *Micronesia* 96 G7
Pohorelá, *Slovak Rep.* 27 C13
Pohořelice, *Czech Rep.* 27 C9
Pohorje, *Slovenia* 41 B12
Pohri, *India* 68 G6
Poiana Mare, *Romania* 28 G8
Poiana Ruscăi, Munţii, *Romania* . 28 E7
Poiana Stampei, *Romania* 29 C10
Poinsett, C., *Antarctica* 5 C8
Point Arena, *U.S.A.* 110 G3
Point Baker, *U.S.A.* 102 B2
Point Edward, *Canada* 104 D3
Point Fortin, *Trin. & Tob.* 125 K15
Point Hope, *U.S.A.* 100 B3
Point L., *Canada* 100 B8
Point Lisas, *Trin. & Tob.* 125 K15
Point Pedro, *Sri Lanka* 66 Q12
Point Pelee △, *Canada* 116 E2
Point Pleasant, *N.J., U.S.A.* .. 117 F10
Point Pleasant, *W. Va., U.S.A.* . 114 F4
Point Reyes →, *U.S.A.* 110 G2
Pointe-à-Pitre, *Guadeloupe* .... 120 b
Pointe-au-Pic = La Malbaie,
Canada 105 C5
Pointe-Claire, *Canada* 117 A11
Pointe-Gatineau, *Canada* 117 A9
Pointe-Noire, *Congo* 84 E2
Pointe Noire, *Guadeloupe* ...... 120 b
Poio, *Spain* 36 C2
Poirino, *Italy* 40 D4
Poisonbush Ra., *Australia* 92 D3
Poissonnier Pt., *Australia* 92 C3

Poitiers, *France* 18 F7
Poitou, *France* 20 B3
Poitou-Charentes □, *France* 20 B4
Poix-de-Picardie, *France* 19 C8
Poix-Terron, *France* 19 C11
Pojoaque, *U.S.A.* 109 J11
Pokaran, *India* 66 F7
Pokataroo, *Australia* 95 D4
Pokhara, *Nepal* 69 E10
Pokhvistnevo, *Russia* 34 D11
Poko, *Dem. Rep. of the Congo* .. 86 B2
Poko, *Sudan* 81 F3
Pokrov, *Russia* 32 E10
Pokrovsk, *Russia* 53 C13
Pokrovskoye, *Russia* 33 J10
Pola = Pula, *Croatia* 41 D10
Pola, *Russia* 32 D7
Pola de Allande, *Spain* 36 B4
Pola de Lena, *Spain* 36 B5
Pola de Siero, *Spain* 36 B5
Pola de Somiedo, *Spain* 36 B4
Polacca, *U.S.A.* 109 J8
Polan, *Iran* 71 E9
Pol'ana, *Slovak Rep.* 27 C12
Poland ■, *Europe* 31 G3
Polanica-Zdrój, *Poland* 31 H3
Połaniec, *Poland* 31 H8
Polanów, *Poland* 30 D3
Polar Bear △, *Canada* 104 A2
Polatlı, *Turkey* 72 C5
Polatsk, *Belarus* 32 E5
Polcura, *Chile* 126 D1
Połczyn-Zdrój, *Poland* 30 E3
Poleski △, *Poland* 31 G10
Polessk, *Russia* 9 J19
Polesye = Pripet Marshes, *Europe* 33 F5
Polgar, *Hungary* 28 C6
Pŏlgyo-ri, *S. Korea* 57 G14
Poli, *Cameroon* 83 C7
Poliaigos, *Greece* 46 E6
Policastro, G. di, *Italy* 43 C8
Police, *Poland* 30 E1
Polička, *Czech Rep.* 27 B9
Policoro, *Italy* 43 B9
Polignano a Mare, *Italy* 43 A9
Poligny, *France* 19 F12
Políkhnitas, *Greece* 47 B8
Polillo Is., *Phil.* 61 D4
Polillo Strait, *Phil.* 61 D4
Polis, *Cyprus* 49 D11
Polístena, *Italy* 43 D9
Políyiros, *Greece* 44 F7
Polk, *U.S.A.* 116 E5
Polkowice, *Poland* 31 G3
Polla, *Italy* 43 B8
Pollachi, *India* 66 P10
Pollença, *Spain* 48 B10
Pollença, B. de, *Spain* 48 B10
Póllica, *Italy* 43 B8
Pollino △, *Italy* 43 C9
Pollino, Mte., *Italy* 43 C9
Polna, *Russia* 32 C5
Polnovat, *Russia* 52 C7
Pology, *Ukraine* 33 J9
Polokwane, *S. Africa* 89 C4
Polonne, *Ukraine* 33 G4
Polonnoye = Polonne, *Ukraine* .. 33 G4
Polski Trümbush, *Bulgaria* 45 C9
Polsko Kosovo, *Bulgaria* 45 C9
Polson, *U.S.A.* 108 C6
Poltár, *Slovak Rep.* 27 C12
Poltava, *Ukraine* 33 H8
Põltsamaa, *Estonia* 9 G21
Polunochnoye, *Russia* 52 C7
Põlva, *Estonia* 9 G22
Polyana, *Ukraine* 28 B7
Polynesia, *Pac. Oc.* 97 F11
Polynésie française = French
Polynesia ☑, *Pac. Oc.* 97 K13
Pomarance, *Italy* 40 E7
Pomaro, *Mexico* 118 D4
Pombal, *Portugal* 36 F2
Pómbia, *Greece* 49 E6
Pomene, *Mozam.* 89 C6
Pomeroy, *Ohio, U.S.A.* 114 F4
Pomeroy, *Wash., U.S.A.* 108 C5
Pomézia, *Italy* 42 A5
Pomichna, *Ukraine* 33 H6
Pomona, *Australia* 95 D5
Pomona, *U.S.A.* 111 L9
Pomorie, *Bulgaria* 45 D11
Pomorskie □, *Poland* 30 D5
Pomorskie, Pojezierze, *Poland* . 30 E3
Pomos, *Cyprus* 49 D11
Pomos, C., *Cyprus* 49 D11
Pompano Beach, *U.S.A.* 115 M5
Pompei, *Italy* 43 B7
Pompey, *France* 19 D13
Pompeys Pillar, *U.S.A.* 108 D10
Pompeys Pillar △, *U.S.A.* 108 D10
Pompton Lakes, *U.S.A.* 117 F10
Ponape = Pohnpei, *Micronesia* .. 96 G7
Ponask L., *Canada* 104 B1
Ponca, *U.S.A.* 112 D6
Ponca City, *U.S.A.* 113 G6
Ponce, *Puerto Rico* .... 121 d
Ponchatoula, *U.S.A.* 113 K9
Poncheville, L., *Canada* 104 B4
Pond, *U.S.A.* 111 K7
Pond Inlet, *Canada* 101 A12
Pondicherry, *India* 66 P11
Ponds, I. of, *Canada* 105 B8
Ponferrada, *Spain* 36 C4
Pongo, Wadi →, *Sudan* 81 F2
Pongo, *Indonesia* 63 G14
Poniatowa, *Poland* 31 G9
Poniec, *Poland* 31 G3
Ponikva, *Slovenia* 41 B12
Ponnani, *India* 66 P9
Ponoka, *Canada* 102 C6
Ponorogo, *Indonesia* 63 G14
Pons = Ponts, *Spain* 38 D6

Pons, *France* 20 C3
Ponsul →, *Portugal* 36 F3
Pont-à-Mousson, *France* 19 D13
Pont-Audemer, *France* 18 C7
Pont-Aven, *France* 18 E3
Pont Canavese, *Italy* 40 C4
Pont-d'Ain, *France* 19 F12
Pont-de-Roide, *France* 19 E13
Pont-de-Salars, *France* 20 D6
Pont-de-Veyle, *France* 19 F11
Pont-du-Château, *France* 19 G10
Pont-l'Abbé, *France* 18 E2
Pont-l'Évêque, *France* 18 C7
Pont-St-Esprit, *France* 21 D8
Pont-St-Martin, *Italy* 40 C4
Pont-sur-Yonne, *France* 19 D10
Ponta do Sol, *Madeira* 48 D2
Ponta Grossa, *Brazil* 127 B5
Ponta Pora, *Brazil* 127 A4
Pontacq, *France* 20 E3
Pontailler-sur-Saône, *France* .. 19 E12
Pontarlier, *France* 19 F13
Pontassieve, *Italy* 41 E8
Pontaumur, *France* 20 C6
Pontcharra, *France* 21 C10
Pontchartrain L., *U.S.A.* 113 K10
Pontchâteau, *France* 18 E4
Ponte da Barca, *Portugal* 36 D2
Ponte de Sor, *Portugal* 37 F2
Ponte dell'Olio, *Italy* 40 D6
Ponte di Legno, *Italy* 40 B7
Ponte do Lima, *Portugal* 36 D2
Ponte do Pungué, *Mozam.* 87 F3
Ponte-Leccia, *France* 21 F13
Ponte nelle Alpi, *Italy* 41 B9
Ponte Nova, *Brazil* 127 A7
Ponteareas, *Spain* 36 C2
Pontebba, *Italy* 41 B10
Ponteceso, *Spain* 36 B2
Pontecorvo, *Italy* 42 A6
Pontedeume, *Spain* 36 B2
Ponteix, *Canada* 103 D7
Pontevedra, *Spain* 36 C2
Pontevedra, R. de →, *Spain* 36 C2
Pontevico, *Italy* 40 C7
Pontiac, *Ill., U.S.A.* 112 E10
Pontiac, *Mich., U.S.A.* 114 D4
Pontian Kechil, *Malaysia* ...... 65 d
Pontianak, *Indonesia* 62 E3
Pontine Is. = Ponziane, Ísole, *Italy* 42 B5
Pontine Mts. = Kuzey Anadolu
Dağları, *Turkey* 72 B7
Pontínia, *Italy* 42 A6
Pontivy, *France* 18 D4
Pontoise, *France* 19 C9
Ponton →, *Canada* 102 B5
Pontorson, *France* 18 D5
Pontrémoli, *Italy* 40 D6
Pontrieux, *France* 18 D3
Ponts, *Spain* 38 D6
Pontypool, *Canada* 116 B6
Pontypool, *U.K.* 15 F4
Ponza, *Italy* 42 B5
Ponziane, Ísole, *Italy* 42 B5
Poochera, *Australia* 95 E1
Poole, *U.K.* 15 G6
Poole □, *U.K.* 15 G6
Poona = Pune, *India* 66 K8
Poonamallee, *Australia* 95 E3
Poonamallee △, *Australia* 95 E3
Poopó, L. de, *Bolivia* 124 G5
Popayán, *Colombia* 124 C3
Poperinge, *Belgium* 17 D2
Popilta L., *Australia* 95 E3
Popina, *Bulgaria* 45 B10
Popio L., *Australia* 95 E3
Poplar, *U.S.A.* 112 A2
Poplar →, *Canada* 103 C9
Poplar Bluff, *U.S.A.* 113 G9
Poplarville, *U.S.A.* 113 K10
Popocatépetl, Volcán, *Mexico* .. 119 D5
Popokabaka, *Dem. Rep. of
the Congo* 84 F3
Pópoli, *Italy* 41 F10
Popovača, *Croatia* 41 C13
Popovo, *Bulgaria* 45 C10
Poppberg, *Germany* 25 F7
Poppi, *Italy* 41 E8
Poprad, *Slovak Rep.* 27 B13
Poprad →, *Slovak Rep.* 27 B13
Porali →, *Pakistan* 68 G2
Porbandar, *India* 68 J3
Porcher I., *Canada* 102 C2
Porcuna, *Spain* 37 H6
Porcupine →, *Canada* 103 B8
Porcupine →, *U.S.A.* 100 B5
Porcupine Gorge △, *Australia* .. 94 C3
Pordenone, *Italy* 41 C9
Pordim, *Bulgaria* 45 C8
Poreč, *Croatia* 41 C10
Poretskoye, *Russia* 34 C8
Pori, *Finland* 9 F19
Poríi, *Greece* 46 F5
Porkhov, *Russia* 32 D5
Porlamar, *Venezuela* 124 A6
Porlezza, *Italy* 40 B6
Porma →, *Spain* 36 C5
Pornic, *France* 18 E4
Poronaysk, *Russia* 53 E15
Póros, *Greece* 46 D5
Poroshiri-Dake, *Japan* 54 C11
Poroszló, *Hungary* 28 C5
Poroto Mts., *Tanzania* 87 D3
Porpoise B., *Antarctica* 5 C9
Porquerolles, Î. de, *France* ... 21 F10
Porrentruy, *Switz.* 25 H3
Porreres, *Spain* 48 B10
Porretta, Passo di, *Italy* 40 D7
Porsangen, *Norway* 8 A21

Porsgrunn, *Norway* 9 G13
Port Alberni, *Canada* 102 D4
Port Alfred, *S. Africa* 88 E4
Port Alice, *Canada* 102 C3
Port Allegany, *U.S.A.* 116 E6
Port Allen, *U.S.A.* 113 K9
Port Alma, *Australia* 94 C5
Port Angeles, *U.S.A.* 110 B3
Port Antonio, *Jamaica* .... 120 a
Port Aransas, *U.S.A.* 113 M6
Port Arthur, *Australia* 95 G4
Port Arthur, *U.S.A.* 113 L8
Port au Choix, *Canada* 105 B8
Port au Port B., *Canada* 105 C8
Port-au-Prince, *Haiti* 121 C5
Port Augusta, *Australia* 95 E2
Port Austin, *U.S.A.* 116 B2
Port Bell, *Uganda* 86 B3
Port Bergé Vaovao, *Madag.* 89 B8
Port Blandford, *Canada* 105 C9
Port Bradshaw, *Australia* 94 A2
Port Broughton, *Australia* 95 E2
Port Burwell, *Canada* 116 D4
Port Canning, *India* 69 H13
Port-Cartier, *Canada* 105 B6
Port Chalmers, *N.Z.* 91 L3
Port Charlotte, *U.S.A.* 115 M4
Port Chester, *U.S.A.* 117 F11
Port Clements, *Canada* 102 C2
Port Clinton, *U.S.A.* 114 E4
Port Colborne, *Canada* 116 D5
Port Coquitlam, *Canada* 102 D4
Port Credit, *Canada* 116 C5
Port-Cros →, *France* 21 F10
Port d'Alcúdia, *Spain* 48 B10
Port Dalhousie, *Canada* 116 C5
Port d'Andratx, *Spain* 48 B9
Port Darwin, *Australia* 92 B5
Port Darwin, *Falk. Is.* 128 G5
Port Davey, *Australia* 95 G4
Port-de-Bouc, *France* 21 E8
Port-de-Paix, *Haiti* 121 C5
Port de Pollença, *Spain* 48 B10
Port de Sóller, *Spain* 48 B9
Port Dickson, *Malaysia* 65 L3
Port Douglas, *Australia* 94 B4
Port Dover, *Canada* 116 D4
Port Edward, *Canada* 102 C2
Port Elgin, *Canada* 116 B3
Port Elizabeth, *S. Africa* 88 E4
Port Ellen, *U.K.* 13 F2
Port-en-Bessin-Huppain, *France* . 18 C6
Port Erin, *I. of Man* 14 C3
Port Essington, *Australia* 92 B5
Port Ewen, *U.S.A.* 117 E11
Port Fairy, *Australia* 95 F3
Port Fouâd = Bûr Fuad, *Egypt* .. 80 H8
Port Gamble, *U.S.A.* 110 C4
Port-Gentil, *Gabon* 84 E1
Port Germein, *Australia* 95 E2
Port Gibson, *U.S.A.* 113 K9
Port Glasgow, *U.K.* 13 F4
Port Harcourt, *Nigeria* 83 E6
Port Hardy, *Canada* 102 C3
Port Harrison = Inukjuak, *Canada* 101 C12
Port Hawkesbury, *Canada* 105 C7
Port Hedland, *Australia* 92 D2
Port Henry, *U.S.A.* 117 B11
Port Hood, *Canada* 105 C7
Port Hope, *Canada* 116 C6
Port Hope, *U.S.A.* 116 C2
Port Hope Simpson, *Canada* 105 B8
Port Hueneme, *U.S.A.* 111 L7
Port Huron, *U.S.A.* 116 D2
Port Iliç, *Azerbaijan* 73 C13
Port Jefferson, *U.S.A.* 117 F11
Port Jervis, *U.S.A.* 117 E10
Port-Joinville, *France* 18 F4
Port Katon, *Russia* 33 J10
Port Kelang = Pelabuhan Klang,
Malaysia 65 L3
Port Kenny, *Australia* 95 E1
Port-la-Nouvelle, *France* 20 E7
Port Lairge = Waterford, *Ireland* 12 D4
Port Laoise, *Ireland* 12 C4
Port Lavaca, *U.S.A.* 113 L6
Port Leyden, *U.S.A.* 117 C9
Port Lincoln, *Australia* 95 E2
Port Loko, *S. Leone* 82 D2
Port Louis, *France* 18 E3
Port-Louis, *Guadeloupe* .... 120 b
Port Louis, *Mauritius* 77 H9
Port MacDonnell, *Australia* 95 F3
Port McNeill, *Canada* 102 C3
Port Macquarie, *Australia* 95 E5
Port Maria, *Jamaica* .... 120 a
Port Matilda, *U.S.A.* 116 F6
Port Mellon, *Canada* 102 D4
Port-Menier, *Canada* 105 C7
Port Moody, *Canada* 110 A4
Port Morant, *Jamaica* .... 120 a
Port Moresby, *Papua N. G.* 96 H6
Port Musgrave, *Australia* 94 A3
Port-Navalo, *France* 18 E4
Port Neches, *U.S.A.* 113 L8
Port Nolloth, *S. Africa* 88 D2
Port Nouveau-Québec =
Kangiqsualujjuaq, *Canada* 101 C13
Port of Spain, *Trin. & Tob.* ... 121 D7
Port Orange, *U.S.A.* 115 L5
Port Orchard, *U.S.A.* 110 C4
Port Orford, *U.S.A.* 108 E1
Port Pegasus, *N.Z.* 91 M1
Port Perry, *Canada* 116 B6
Port Phillip B., *Australia* 95 F3
Port Pirie, *Australia* 95 E2
Port Renfrew, *Canada* 102 D4
Port Roper, *Australia* 94 A2
Port Rowan, *Canada* 116 D4

Port Safaga = Bûr Safâga, *Egypt* 70 E2
Port Said = Bûr Sa'îd, *Egypt* .. 80 H8
Port St. Joe, *U.S.A.* 115 L3
Port St. Johns = Umzimvubu,
S. Africa 89 E4
Port-St-Louis-du-Rhône, *France* . 21 E8
Port St. Lucie, *U.S.A.* 115 M5
Port-Ste-Marie, *France* 20 D4
Port Sanilac, *U.S.A.* 116 C2
Port Severn, *Canada* 116 B5
Port Shepstone, *S. Africa* 89 E5
Port Simpson, *Canada* 102 C2
Port Stanley = Stanley, *Falk. Is.* 128 G5
Port Stanley, *Canada* 116 D3
Port Sudan = Bûr Sûdân, *Sudan* . 80 D4
Port Sulphur, *U.S.A.* 113 L10
Port-sur-Saône, *France* 19 E13
Port Talbot, *U.K.* 15 F4
Port Taufiq = Bûr Taufîq, *Egypt* 80 J8
Port Townsend, *U.S.A.* 110 B4
Port-Vendres, *France* 20 F7
Port Vila, *Vanuatu* 96 J8
Port Wakefield, *Australia* 95 E2
Port Washington, *U.S.A.* 114 D2
Portadown, *U.K.* 12 B5
Portaferry, *U.K.* 12 B6
Portage, *Pa., U.S.A.* 116 F6
Portage, *Wis., U.S.A.* 112 D10
Portage la Prairie, *Canada* 103 D9
Portageville, *U.S.A.* 113 G10
Portalegre, *Portugal* 37 F3
Portalegre □, *Portugal* 37 F3
Portales, *U.S.A.* 113 H3
Portarlington, *Ireland* 12 C4
Portbou, *Spain* 38 C8
Portel, *Portugal* 37 G3
Portela, Lisboa ✈ (LIS), *Portugal* 37 G1
Porter L., *N.W.T., Canada* 103 A7
Porter L., *Sask., Canada* 103 B7
Porterville, *S. Africa* 88 E2
Porterville, *U.S.A.* 110 J8
Portes-lès-Valence, *France* 21 D8
Porthcawl, *U.K.* 15 F4
Porthill, *U.S.A.* 108 B5
Porthmadog, *U.K.* 14 E3
Portile de Fier, *Europe* 28 F7
Portimão, *Portugal* 37 H2
Portishead, *U.K.* 15 F5
Portiţei, Gura, *Romania* 29 F14
Portknockie, *U.K.* 13 D6
Portland, *N.S.W., Australia* ... 95 E5
Portland, *Vic., Australia* 95 F3
Portland, *Conn., U.S.A.* 117 E12
Portland, *Maine, U.S.A.* 101 D12
Portland, *Mich., U.S.A.* 114 D3
Portland, *Oreg., U.S.A.* 110 E4
Portland, *Pa., U.S.A.* 117 F9
Portland, *Tex., U.S.A.* 113 M6
Portland ✈ (PDX), *U.S.A.* 110 E4
Portland, I. of, *U.K.* 15 G5
Portland Bight, *Jamaica* .... 120 a
Portland Bill, *U.K.* 15 G5
Portland Canal, *U.S.A.* 102 B2
Portland Pt., *Jamaica* .... 120 a
Portmadoc = Porthmadog, *U.K.* .. 14 E3
Portmore, *Jamaica* .... 120 a
Porto, *France* 21 F12
Porto, *Portugal* 36 D2
Porto □, *Portugal* 36 D2
Porto, G. de, *France* 21 F12
Pôrto Alegre, *Brazil* 127 C5
Porto Azzurro, *Italy* 40 F7
Porto Cristo, *Spain* 48 B10
Pôrto de Móz, *Brazil* 125 D8
Porto Empédocle, *Italy* 42 E6
Pôrto Esperança, *Brazil* 124 G7
Porto Franco, *Brazil* 125 E9
Pórto Lágos, *Greece* 45 E9
Pôrto Mendes, *Brazil* 127 A5
Pôrto Moniz, *Madeira* 48 D2
Pôrto Murtinho, *Brazil* 124 H7
Pôrto Nacional, *Brazil* 125 F9
Porto-Novo, *Benin* 83 D5
Porto Petro, *Spain* 48 B10
Porto San Giórgio, *Italy* 41 E10
Porto Sant'Elpídio, *Italy* 41 E10
Porto Santo, I. de, *Madeira* ... 78 B2
Porto Santo Stéfano, *Italy* 40 F8
Pôrto São José, *Brazil* 127 A5
Pôrto Seguro, *Brazil* 125 G11
Porto Tolle, *Italy* 41 D9
Porto Tórres, *Italy* 42 B1
Pôrto União, *Brazil* 127 B5
Pôrto Válter, *Brazil* 124 E4
Porto-Vecchio, *France* 21 G13
Pôrto Velho, *Brazil* 124 E6
Portobelo, *Panama* 120 E4
Portoferráio, *Italy* 40 F7
Portogruaro, *Italy* 41 C9
Portola, *U.S.A.* 110 F6
Portomaggiore, *Italy* 41 D8
Portoscuso, *Italy* 42 C1
Portovénere, *Italy* 40 D6
Portoviejo, *Ecuador* 124 D2
Portpatrick, *U.K.* 13 G3
Portree, *U.K.* 13 D2
Portrush, *U.K.* 12 A5
Portsmouth, *Dominica* 121 C7
Portsmouth, *U.K.* 15 G6
Portsmouth, *N.H., U.S.A.* 115 D10
Portsmouth, *Ohio, U.S.A.* 114 F4
Portsmouth, *R.I., U.S.A.* 117 E13
Portsmouth, *Va., U.S.A.* 114 G7
Portsoy, *U.K.* 15 G6
Portstewart, *U.K.* 12 A5
Porttipahdan tekojärvi, *Finland* . 8 B22
Portugal ■, *Europe* 36 F3
Portugalete, *Spain* 38 B1

Portumna, Ireland 12 C3
Portville, U.S.A. 116 D6
Porvenir, Chile 128 G2
Porvoo, Finland 9 F21
Porzuna, Spain 37 F6
Posada, Italy 42 B2
Posada →, Italy 42 B2
Posadas, Argentina 127 B4
Posadas, Spain 37 H5
Poschiavo, Switz. 25 J6
Posets, Spain 38 C5
Posht-e Badam, Iran 71 C7
Posídhion, Ákra, Greece 44 G7
Posidium, Greece 47 F9
Poso, Indonesia 63 E6
Posong, S. Korea 57 G14
Posse, Brazil 125 F9
Possession I., Antarctica 5 D11
Pössneck, Germany 24 E7
Possum Kingdom L., U.S.A. 113 J5
Post, U.S.A. 113 J4
Post Falls, U.S.A. 108 C5
Postavy = Pastavy, Belarus 9 J22
Poste-de-la-Baleine =
  Kuujjuarapik, Canada 104 A4
Postmasburg, S. Africa 88 D3
Postojna, Slovenia 41 C11
Poston, U.S.A. 111 M12
Postville, Canada 105 B8
Potamós, Andikíthira, Greece 46 F5
Potamós, Kíthira, Greece 46 E4
Potchefstroom, S. Africa 88 D4
Potcoava, Romania 29 F9
Poteau, U.S.A. 113 H7
Poteet, U.S.A. 113 L5
Potenza, Italy 43 B8
Potenza →, Italy 41 E10
Potenza Picena, Italy 41 E10
Poteriteri, L., N.Z. 91 M1
Potgietersrus = Mokopane,
  S. Africa 89 C4
Poti, Georgia 35 J5
Potiskum, Nigeria 83 C7
Potlogi, Romania 29 F10
Potomac →, U.S.A. 114 G7
Potosí, Bolivia 124 G5
Potosi Mt., U.S.A. 111 K11
Potrerillos, Chile 126 B2
Potsdam, Germany 24 C9
Potsdam, U.S.A. 117 B10
Pottenstein, Germany 25 F7
Pottersville, U.S.A. 117 C11
Pottstown, U.S.A. 117 F9
Pottsville, U.S.A. 117 F8
Pottuvil, Sri Lanka 66 R12
P'otzu, Taiwan 59 F13
Pouancé, France 18 E5
Pouce Coupé, Canada 102 B4
Poughkeepsie, U.S.A. 117 E11
Pouilly-sur-Loire, France 19 E9
Poulaphouca Res., Ireland 12 C5
Poulsbo, U.S.A. 110 C4
Poultney, U.S.A. 117 C11
Poulton-le-Fylde, U.K. 14 D5
Pouso Alegre, Brazil 127 A6
Pout, Senegal 82 C1
Pouthisat, Cambodia 64 F4
Pouzauges, France 18 F6
Pova de Santa Iria, Portugal 37 G1
Považská Bystrica, Slovak Rep. 27 B11
Poverty B., N.Z. 91 H7
Povlen, Serbia & M. 44 B3
Póvoa de Lanhosa, Portugal 36 D2
Póvoa de Varzim, Portugal 36 D2
Povorino, Russia 34 E6
Povungnituk = Puvirnituq,
  Canada 101 B12
Powassan, Canada 104 C4
Poway, U.S.A. 111 N9
Powder →, U.S.A. 112 B2
Powder River, U.S.A. 108 D10
Powell, U.S.A. 108 D9
Powell, L., U.S.A. 109 H8
Powell River, Canada 102 D4
Powers, U.S.A. 114 C2
Powys □, U.K. 15 E4
Poyang Hu, China 59 C11
Poyarkovo, Russia 53 E13
Poysdorf, Austria 27 C9
Poza de la Sal, Spain 36 C7
Poza Rica, Mexico 119 C5
Pozanti, Turkey 72 D6
Požarevac, Serbia & M. 44 B5
Pozazal, Puerto, Spain 36 C6
Požega, Croatia 28 E2
Požega, Serbia & M. 44 C4
Poznań, Poland 31 F3
Poznań ✈ (POZ), Poland 31 F3
Pozo, U.S.A. 111 K6
Pozo Alcón, Spain 37 H8
Pozo Almonte, Chile 124 H5
Pozo Colorado, Paraguay 126 A4
Pozoblanco, Spain 37 G6
Pozzallo, Italy 43 F7
Pozzomaggiore, Italy 42 B1
Pozzuoli, Italy 43 B7
Pra →, Ghana 83 D4
Prabuty, Poland 30 E6
Prača, Bos.-H. 28 G3
Prachatice, Czech Rep. 26 B6
Prachin Buri, Thailand 64 E3
Prachuap Khiri Khan, Thailand 65 G2
Pradelles, France 20 D7
Prades, France 20 F6
Prado, Brazil 125 G11
Prado del Rey, Spain 37 J5
Præstø, Denmark 11 J6
Pragersko, Slovenia 41 B12
Prague = Praha, Czech Rep. 26 A7
Praha, Czech Rep. 26 A7

Praha ✈ (PRG), Czech Rep. 26 A7
Prahecq, France 20 B3
Prahova □, Romania 29 E10
Prahova →, Romania 29 F10
Prahovo, Serbia & M. 44 B6
Praia, C. Verde Is. 77 E1
Pária a Mare, Italy 43 C8
Praid, Romania 29 D10
Prainha, Amazonas, Brazil 124 E6
Prainha, Pará, Brazil 125 D8
Prairie, Australia 94 C3
Prairie City, U.S.A. 108 D4
Prairie Dog Town Fork →,
  U.S.A. 113 H5
Prairie du Chien, U.S.A. 112 D9
Prairies, L. of the, Canada 103 C8
Pramánda, Greece 46 B3
Prampram, Ghana 83 D5
Pran Buri, Thailand 64 F2
Prang, Ghana 83 D4
Prapat, Indonesia 62 D1
Prasonísi, Ákra, Greece 49 D9
Prästmon, Sweden 10 A11
Praszka, Poland 31 G5
Prata, Brazil 125 G9
Pratabpur, India 69 H10
Pratapgarh, Raj., India 68 G6
Pratapgarh, Ut. P., India 69 G9
Pratas Is. = Dongsha Dao, China 59 G11
Prato, Italy 40 E8
Prátola Peligna, Italy 41 F10
Prats-de-Mollo-la-Preste, France 20 F6
Pratt, U.S.A. 113 G5
Prattville, U.S.A. 115 J2
Pravdinsk, Russia 30 D8
Pravdinsk, Russia 34 B6
Pravets, Bulgaria 44 D7
Pravia, Spain 36 B4
Praya, Indonesia 62 F5
Pré-en-Pail, France 18 D6
Precipice △, Australia 95 D5
Precordillera, Argentina 126 C2
Predáppio, Italy 41 D8
Predazzo, Italy 41 B8
Predeal, Romania 29 E10
Predejane, Serbia & M. 44 D6
Preeceville, Canada 103 C8
Preetz, Germany 24 A6
Pregolya →, Russia 30 D7
Pregrada, Croatia 41 B12
Preiļi, Latvia 9 H22
Preko, Croatia 41 D12
Prelog, Croatia 41 B13
Prémery, France 19 E10
Premià de Mar, Spain 38 D7
Premont, U.S.A. 113 M5
Premuda, Croatia 41 D11
Prentice, U.S.A. 112 C9
Prenzlau, Germany 24 B9
Preobrazheniye, Russia 54 C6
Preparis North Channel, Ind. Oc. 67 M18
Preparis South Channel, Ind. Oc. 67 M18
Přerov, Czech Rep. 27 B10
Prescott, Canada 117 B9
Prescott, Ariz., U.S.A. 109 J7
Prescott, Ark., U.S.A. 113 J8
Prescott Valley, U.S.A. 109 J7
Preservation Inlet, N.Z. 91 M1
Preševo, Serbia & M. 44 D5
Presho, U.S.A. 112 D4
Presicce, Italy 43 C11
Presidencia de la Plaza, Argentina 126 B4
Presidencia Roque Saenz Peña,
  Argentina 126 B3
Presidente Epitácio, Brazil 125 H8
Presidente Hayes □, Paraguay 126 A4
Presidente Prudente, Brazil 127 A5
Presidio, Mexico 118 B4
Presidio, U.S.A. 113 L2
Preslav, Bulgaria 45 C10
Preslavska Planina, Bulgaria 45 C10
Prešov, Slovak Rep. 27 B14
Prešovský □, Slovak Rep. 27 B13
Prespa, Bulgaria 45 E8
Préspa △, Greece 44 F5
Prespa, L. = Prespansko Jezero,
  Macedonia 44 F5
Prespansko Jezero, Macedonia 44 F5
Presque I., U.S.A. 116 D4
Presque Isle, U.S.A. 115 B12
Prestatyn, U.K. 14 D4
Prestea, Ghana 82 D4
Presteigne, U.K. 15 E5
Přeštice, Czech Rep. 26 B6
Preston, Canada 116 C4
Preston, U.K. 14 D5
Preston, Idaho, U.S.A. 108 E8
Preston, Minn., U.S.A. 112 D8
Preston, C., Australia 92 D2
Prestonburg, U.S.A. 114 G4
Prestwick, U.K. 13 F4
Pretoria, S. Africa 89 D4
Preuilly-sur-Claise, France 18 F7
Préveza, Greece 46 C2
Préveza □, Greece 46 B2
Prey Veng, Cambodia 65 G5
Priazovskoye, Ukraine 33 J8
Pribilof Is., U.S.A. 100 C2
Priboj, Serbia & M. 44 C3
Příbram, Czech Rep. 26 B7
Price, U.S.A. 108 G8
Price I., Canada 102 C3
Prichard, U.S.A. 115 K1
Priego, Spain 38 E2
Priego de Córdoba, Spain 37 H6
Priekule, Latvia 9 H19
Priekule, Lithuania 30 C8
Prienai, Lithuania 9 J20
Prieska, S. Africa 88 D3
Priest →, U.S.A. 108 B5
Priest L., U.S.A. 108 B5

Priest River, U.S.A. 108 B5
Priest Valley, U.S.A. 110 J6
Prievidza, Slovak Rep. 27 C11
Prignitz, Germany 24 B7
Prijedor, Bos.-H. 41 D13
Prijepolje, Serbia & M. 44 C3
Prikaspiyskaya Nizmennost =
  Caspian Depression, Eurasia 35 G9
Prikro, Ivory C. 82 D4
Prikubanskaya Nizmennost,
  Russia 35 H4
Prilep, Macedonia 44 E5
Priluki = Pryluky, Ukraine 33 G7
Prime Seal I., Australia 95 G4
Primorsk, Russia 30 D6
Primorsk, Russia 32 B5
Primorsko, Bulgaria 45 D11
Primorsko-Akhtarsk, Russia 33 J10
Primorskoye, Ukraine 33 J9
Primrose L., Canada 103 C7
Prince Albert, Canada 103 C7
Prince Albert, S. Africa 88 E3
Prince Albert →, Canada 103 C7
Prince Albert Mts., Antarctica 5 D11
Prince Albert Pen., Canada 100 A8
Prince Albert Sd., Canada 100 A8
Prince Alfred, C., Canada 4 B1
Prince Charles I., Canada 101 B12
Prince Charles Mts., Antarctica 5 D6
Prince Edward I. □, Canada 105 C7
Prince Edward Is., Ind. Oc. 3 G11
Prince Edward Pt., Canada 116 C8
Prince George, Canada 102 C4
Prince of Wales, C., U.S.A. 98 C3
Prince of Wales I., Australia 94 A3
Prince of Wales I., Canada 100 A10
Prince of Wales I., U.S.A. 100 C6
Prince Patrick I., Canada 4 B2
Prince Regent Inlet, Canada 4 B3
Prince Rupert, Canada 102 C2
Princes Town, Trin. & Tob. 125 K15
Princess Charlotte B., Australia 94 A3
Princess May Ranges, Australia 92 C4
Princess Royal I., Canada 102 C3
Princeton, Canada 102 D4
Princeton, Calif., U.S.A. 110 F4
Princeton, Ill., U.S.A. 112 E10
Princeton, Ind., U.S.A. 114 F2
Princeton, Ky., U.S.A. 114 G2
Princeton, Mo., U.S.A. 112 E8
Princeton, N.J., U.S.A. 117 F10
Princeton, W. Va., U.S.A. 114 G5
Principe, I. de, Atl. Oc. 76 F4
Principe da Beira, Brazil 124 F6
Prineville, U.S.A. 108 D3
Prins Harald Kyst, Antarctica 5 D4
Prinsesse Astrid Kyst, Antarctica 5 D3
Prinsesse Ragnhild Kyst,
  Antarctica 5 D4
Prinzapolca, Nic. 120 D3
Prior, C., Spain 36 B2
Priozersk, Russia 32 B6
Pripet = Prypyat →, Europe 33 G6
Pripet Marshes, Europe 33 F5
Pripyat Marshes = Pripet
  Marshes, Europe 33 F5
Pripyats = Prypyat →, Europe 33 G6
Prislop, Pasul, Romania 29 C9
Pristen, Russia 33 G9
Priština, Serbia & M. 44 D5
Pritzwalk, Germany 24 B8
Privas, France 21 D8
Priverno, Italy 42 A6
Privolzhsk, Russia 34 B5
Privolzhskaya Vozvyshennost,
  Russia 34 E7
Privolzhskiy, Russia 34 E8
Privolzhskiy □, Russia 34 B10
Privolzhye, Russia 34 D9
Priyutnoye, Russia 35 G6
Prizren, Serbia & M. 44 D4
Prizzi, Italy 42 E6
Prnjavor, Bos.-H. 28 F2
Probolinggo, Indonesia 63 G15
Prochowice, Poland 31 G3
Proctor, U.S.A. 117 C11
Proddatur, India 66 M11
Prodhromos, Cyprus 49 E11
Proença-a-Nova, Portugal 36 F3
Profítis Ilías, Greece 49 C9
Profondeville, Belgium 17 D4
Progreso, Coahuila, Mexico 118 B4
Progreso, Yucatán, Mexico 119 C7
Prokhladnyy, Russia 35 J7
Prokletije, Albania 44 D3
Prokopyevsk, Russia 52 D9
Prokuplje, Serbia & M. 44 C5
Proletarsk, Russia 35 G5
Proletarskaya = Proletarsk, Russia 35 G5
Prome, Burma 67 K19
Prophet →, Canada 102 B4
Prophet River, Canada 102 B4
Propriá, Brazil 125 F11
Propriano, France 21 G12
Proserpine, Australia 94 J6
Prosna →, Poland 31 F4
Prospect, U.S.A. 117 C9
Prosser, U.S.A. 108 C4
Prostějov, Czech Rep. 27 B10
Prostki, Poland 30 E9
Proston, Australia 95 D5
Proszowice, Poland 31 H7
Próti, Greece 46 D3
Provadiya, Bulgaria 45 C11
Provence, France 21 E9
Provence-Alpes-Côte d'Azur □,
  France 21 D10
Providence, Ky., U.S.A. 114 G2
Providence, R.I., U.S.A. 117 E13
Providence Bay, Canada 104 C3
Providence Mts., U.S.A. 111 K11

Providencia, I. de, Colombia 120 D3
Provideniya, Russia 53 C19
Provins, France 19 D10
Provo, U.S.A. 108 F8
Provost, Canada 103 C6
Prozor, Bos.-H. 28 G2
Prrenjas, Albania 44 E4
Prudhoe Bay, U.S.A. 100 A5
Prudhoe I., Australia 94 C4
Prud'homme, Canada 103 C7
Prudnik, Poland 31 H4
Prüm, Germany 25 E2
Prundu, Romania 29 F11
Prut →, Romania 29 E13
Pruzhany, Belarus 33 F3
Prvić, Croatia 41 D11
Prydz B., Antarctica 5 C6
Pryluky, Ukraine 33 G7
Pryor, U.S.A. 113 G7
Prypyat →, Europe 33 G6
Przasnysz, Poland 31 E7
Przedbórz, Poland 31 G6
Przedecz, Poland 31 F5
Przemków, Poland 31 G2
Przemyśl, Poland 31 J9
Przeworsk, Poland 31 H9
Przewóz, Poland 31 G1
Przhevalsk = Karakol, Kyrgyzstan 52 E8
Przysucha, Poland 31 G7
Psakhná, Greece 46 C5
Psará, Greece 47 C7
Psathoúra, Greece 46 B6
Psel →, Ukraine 33 H7
Pserimos, Greece 47 E9
Psíra, Greece 49 D7
Pskov, Russia 32 D5
Pskovskoye, Ozero, Russia 32 D5
Psunj, Croatia 28 E2
Pteleón, Greece 46 B4
Ptich = Ptsich →, Belarus 33 F5
Ptolemaís, Greece 44 F5
Ptsich →, Belarus 33 F5
Ptuj, Slovenia 41 B12
Ptujska Gora, Slovenia 41 B12
Pu Xian, China 56 F6
Pua, Thailand 64 C3
Puán, Argentina 126 D3
Pu'an, China 58 E5
Puan, S. Korea 57 G14
Pubei, China 58 F7
Pucallpa, Peru 124 E4
Pucheng, China 59 D12
Pucheni, Romania 29 E10
Puchheim, Germany 25 G7
Púchov, Slovak Rep. 27 B11
Pucioasa, Romania 29 E10
Pučišća, Croatia 41 E13
Puck, Poland 30 D5
Pucka, Zatoka, Poland 30 D5
Puçol, Spain 39 F4
Pudasjärvi, Finland 8 D22
Puding, China 58 D5
Pudozh, Russia 32 B9
Puducherri = Pondicherry, India 66 P11
Pudukkottai, India 66 P11
Puebla, Mexico 119 D5
Puebla □, Mexico 119 D5
Puebla de Alcocer, Spain 37 G5
Puebla de Don Fadrique, Spain 39 H2
Puebla de Don Rodrigo, Spain 37 F6
Puebla de Guzmán, Spain 37 H3
Puebla de la Calzada, Spain 37 G4
Puebla de Sanabria, Spain 36 C4
Puebla de Trives = Pobra de
  Trives, Spain 36 C3
Pueblo, U.S.A. 112 F2
Pueblo Hundido, Chile 126 B1
Puelches, Argentina 126 D2
Puelén, Argentina 126 D2
Puente Alto, Chile 126 C1
Puente-Genil, Spain 37 H6
Puente la Reina, Spain 38 C3
Puenteareas = Ponteareas, Spain 36 C2
Puentedeume = Pontedeume,
  Spain 36 B2
Puentes de Garcia Rodriguez =
  As Pontes de García
  Rodríguez, Spain 36 B3
Puerca, Pta., Puerto Rico 121 d
Puerco →, U.S.A. 109 J10
Puerto Aisén, Chile 128 F2
Puerto Ángel, Mexico 119 D5
Puerto Arista, Mexico 119 D6
Puerto Armuelles, Panama 120 E3
Puerto Ayacucho, Venezuela 124 B5
Puerto Barrios, Guatemala 120 C2
Puerto Bermejo, Argentina 126 B4
Puerto Bermúdez, Peru 124 F4
Puerto Bolívar, Ecuador 124 D3
Puerto Cabello, Venezuela 124 A5
Puerto Cabezas, Nic. 120 D3
Puerto Cabo Gracias á Dios, Nic. 120 D3
Puerto Carreño, Colombia 124 B5
Puerto Castilla, Honduras 120 C2
Puerto Chicama, Peru 124 E3
Puerto Coig, Argentina 128 G3
Puerto Cortés, Costa Rica 120 E3
Puerto Cortés, Honduras 120 C2
Puerto Cumarebo, Venezuela 124 A5
Puerto de Alcudia = Port
  d'Alcúdia, Spain 48 B10
Puerto de Cabrera, Spain 48 B9
Puerto de Gran Tarajal,
  Canary Is. 48 F5
Puerto de la Cruz, Canary Is. 48 F3
Puerto de los Angeles △, Mexico 118 C3
Puerto de Mazarrón, Spain 39 H3
Puerto de Pozo Negro, Canary Is. 48 F6

Puerto de Sóller = Port de Sóller,
  Spain 48 B9
Puerto de Somosierra, Spain 36 D7
Puerto del Carmen, Canary Is. 48 F6
Puerto del Rosario, Canary Is. 48 F6
Puerto Deseado, Argentina 128 F3
Puerto Escondido, Mexico 119 D5
Puerto Heath, Bolivia 124 F5
Puerto Inírida, Colombia 124 C5
Puerto Juárez, Mexico 119 C7
Puerto La Cruz, Venezuela 124 A6
Puerto Leguízamo, Colombia 124 D4
Puerto Limón, Colombia 124 C4
Puerto Lobos, Argentina 128 E3
Puerto Lumbreras, Spain 39 H3
Puerto Madryn, Argentina 128 E3
Puerto Maldonado, Peru 124 F5
Puerto Manatí, Cuba 120 B4
Puerto Montt, Chile 128 E2
Puerto Morazán, Nic. 120 D2
Puerto Morelos, Mexico 119 C7
Puerto Natales, Chile 128 G2
Puerto Padre, Cuba 120 B4
Puerto Páez, Venezuela 124 B5
Puerto Peñasco, Mexico 118 A2
Puerto Pinasco, Paraguay 126 A4
Puerto Plata, Dom. Rep. 121 C5
Puerto Pollensa = Port de
  Pollença, Spain 48 B10
Puerto Princesa, Phil. 61 G3
Puerto Quepos, Costa Rica 120 E3
Puerto Real, Spain 37 J4
Puerto Rico, Canary Is. 48 G4
Puerto Rico ☑, W. Indies 121 d
Puerto Rico Trench, Atl. Oc. 121 C6
Puerto San Julián, Argentina 128 F3
Puerto Sastre, Paraguay 126 A4
Puerto Serrano, Spain 37 J5
Puerto Suárez, Bolivia 124 G7
Puerto Vallarta, Mexico 118 C3
Puerto Wilches, Colombia 124 B4
Puertollano, Spain 37 G6
Pueyrredón, L., Argentina 128 F2
Púez Odle △, Italy 41 B8
Puffin I., Ireland 12 E1
Pugachev, Russia 34 D9
Pugal, India 68 E5
Puge, China 58 D4
Puge, Tanzania 86 C3
Puget Sound, U.S.A. 108 C2
Puget-Théniers, France 21 E10
Púglia □, Italy 43 A9
Pugödong, N. Korea 57 C16
Pugu, Tanzania 86 D4
Pügünzī, Iran 71 E8
Pui, Romania 28 E8
Puiești, Romania 29 D12
Puig Major, Spain 48 B9
Puigcerdà, Spain 38 C6
Puigmal, Spain 38 C7
Puigpunyent, Spain 48 B9
Puisaye, Collines de la, France 19 E10
Puiseaux, France 19 D9
Pujehun, S. Leone 82 D2
Pujiang, China 59 C12
Pujols, France 20 D3
Pujon-chŏsuji, N. Korea 57 D14
Pukaki, L., N.Z. 91 L3
Pukapuka, Cook Is. 97 J11
Pukaskwa △, Canada 104 C2
Pukatawagan, Canada 103 B8
Pukchin, N. Korea 57 D13
Pukch'ŏng, N. Korea 57 D15
Pukë, Albania 44 D3
Pukekohe, N.Z. 91 G5
Pukhrayan, India 69 F8
Pukou, China 59 A12
Pula, Croatia 41 D10
Pula, Italy 42 C1
Pulacayo, Bolivia 124 H5
Pulai, Malaysia 65 d
Pulandian, China 57 E11
Pularumpi, Australia 92 B5
Pulaski, N.Y., U.S.A. 117 C8
Pulaski, Tenn., U.S.A. 115 H2
Pulaski, Va., U.S.A. 114 G5
Pulau →, Indonesia 63 F9
Puławy, Poland 31 G8
Pulga, U.S.A. 110 F5
Pulicat L., India 66 N12
Pullman, U.S.A. 108 C5
Pulog, Mt., Phil. 61 C4
Pułtusk, Poland 31 F8
Pülümür, Turkey 73 C8
Pumlumon Fawr, U.K. 15 E4
Puná, I., Ecuador 124 D2
Punakaiki, N.Z. 91 K3
Punakha, Bhutan 67 F16
Punasar, India 68 F5
Punata, Bolivia 124 G5
Punch, India 69 C6
Punch →, Pakistan 68 C5
Punch Maria, S. Africa 89 C5
Pune, India 66 K8
P'ungsan, N. Korea 57 D15
Pungue, Ponte de, Mozam. 87 F3
Puning, China 59 F11
Punjab □, India 68 D7
Punjab □, Pakistan 68 E6
Puno, Peru 124 G4
Punpun →, India 69 G11
Punta, Cerro de, Puerto Rico 121 d
Punta Alta, Argentina 128 D4
Punta Arenas, Chile 128 G2
Punta de Díaz, Chile 126 B1
Punta del Hidalgo, Canary Is. 48 F3
Punta Gorda, Belize 119 D7
Punta Gorda, U.S.A. 115 M5
Punta Prieta, Mexico 118 B2
Punta Prima, Spain 48 B11

Punta Umbria, *Spain* 37 H4
Puntarenas, *Costa Rica* 120 E3
Punto Fijo, *Venezuela* 124 A4
Punxsatawney, *U.S.A.* 116 F6
Pupuan, *Indonesia* 63 J18
Puqi, *China* 59 C9
Puquio, *Peru* 124 F4
Pur →, *Russia* 52 C8
Puracé, Vol., *Colombia* 124 C3
Puračić, *Bos.-H.* 28 F3
Puralia = Puruliya, *India* 69 H12
Puranpur, *India* 69 E9
Purbeck, Isle of, *U.K.* 15 G5
Purcell, *U.S.A.* 113 H6
Purcell Mts., *Canada* 102 D5
Puri, *India* 67 K14
Purmerend, *Neths.* 17 B4
Purnia, *India* 69 G12
Purnululu △, *Australia* 92 C4
Pursat = Pouthisat, *Cambodia* . 64 F4
Purukcahu, *Indonesia* 62 E4
Puruliya, *India* 69 H12
Purus →, *Brazil* 124 D6
Puruvesi, *Finland* 32 B5
Purvis, *U.S.A.* 113 K10
Pūrvomay, *Bulgaria* 45 D9
Purwa, *India* 69 F9
Purwakarta, *Indonesia* 63 G12
Purwodadi, *Indonesia* 63 G14
Purwo, Tanjung, *Indonesia* .. 63 K18
Purwokerto, *Indonesia* 63 G13
Puryŏng, *N. Korea* 57 C15
Pusa, *India* 69 G11
Pusan, *S. Korea* 57 G15
Pushkin, *Russia* 32 C6
Pushkino, *Moskva, Russia* 32 D9
Pushkino, *Saratov, Russia* ... 34 E8
Püspökladány, *Hungary* 28 C6
Pustoshka, *Russia* 32 D5
Puszczykowo, *Poland* 31 F3
Putahow L., *Canada* 103 B8
Putao, *Burma* 67 F20
Putaruru, *N.Z.* 91 H5
Putbus, *Germany* 24 A9
Putian, *China* 59 E12
Putignano, *Italy* 43 B10
Puting, Tanjung, *Indonesia* .. 62 E4
Putlitz, *Germany* 24 B8
Putna, *Romania* 29 C10
Putna →, *Romania* 29 E12
Putnam, *U.S.A.* 117 E13
Putnok, *Hungary* 28 B5
Putorana, Gory, *Russia* 53 C10
Putrajaya, *Malaysia* 65 L3
Puttalam, *Sri Lanka* 66 Q11
Puttgarden, *Germany* 24 A7
Püttlingen, *Germany* 25 F2
Putumayo →, *S. Amer.* 124 D5
Putuo, *China* 59 C14
Putussibau, *Indonesia* 62 D4
Putyla, *Ukraine* 29 B10
Puvirnituq, *Canada* 101 B12
Puy-de-Dôme, *France* 20 C6
Puy-de-Dôme □, *France* 20 C7
Puy-l'Évêque, *France* 20 D5
Puyallup, *U.S.A.* 110 C4
Puyang, *China* 56 G8
Puylaurens, *France* 20 E6
Pūzeh Rīg, *Iran* 71 E8
Puzhaykove, *Ukraine* 29 B14
Pwani □, *Tanzania* 86 D4
Pweto, *Dem. Rep. of the Congo* . 87 D2
Pwllheli, *U.K.* 14 E3
Pyana →, *Russia* 34 C8
Pyapon, *Burma* 67 L19
Pyasina →, *Russia* 53 B9
Pyatigorsk, *Russia* 35 H6
Pyatykhatky, *Ukraine* 33 H7
Pydna, *Greece* 44 F6
Pyè = Prome, *Burma* 67 K19
Pyetrikaw, *Belarus* 33 F5
Pyinmana, *Burma* 67 K20
Pyla, C., *Cyprus* 49 E12
Pymatuning Reservoir, *U.S.A.* . 116 E4
Pyŏktong, *N. Korea* 57 D13
Pyŏnggang, *N. Korea* 57 E14
P'yŏngt'aek, *S. Korea* 57 F14
P'yŏngyang, *N. Korea* 57 E13
Pyote, *U.S.A.* 113 K3
Pyramid L., *U.S.A.* 108 G4
Pyramid Pk., *U.S.A.* 111 J10
Pyramids, *Egypt* 80 J7
Pyrénées, *Europe* 20 F4
Pyrénées △, *France* 20 F3
Pyrénées-Atlantiques □, *France* . 20 E3
Pyrénées-Orientales □, *France* . 20 F6
Pyryatyn, *Ukraine* 33 G7
Pyrzyce, *Poland* 31 E1
Pyskowice, *Poland* 31 H5
Pytalovo, *Russia* 32 D4
Pyu, *Burma* 67 K20
Pyzdry, *Poland* 31 F4

Q

Qaanaaq, *Greenland* 4 B4
Qabirri →, *Azerbaijan* 35 K8
Qachasnek, *S. Africa* 89 E4
Qa'el Jafr, *Jordan* 74 E5
Qa'emābād, *Iran* 71 D9
Qā'emshahr, *Iran* 71 B7
Qagan Nur, *China* 56 C8
Qahar Youyi Zhongqi, *China* .. 56 D7
Qahremānshahr = Bākhtarān,
  Iran 70 C5
Qaidam Pendi, *China* 60 C4
Qajarīyeh, *Iran* 71 D6

Qala, Ras il, *Malta* 49 C1
Qala-i-Jadid = Spīn Büldak,
  Afghan. 68 D2
Qala Point = Qala, Ras il, *Malta* . 49 C1
Qala Viala, *Pakistan* 68 D2
Qala Yangi, *Afghan.* 68 B2
Qal'at al Akhḍar, *Si. Arabia* .. 70 E3
Qal'at Dīzah, *Iraq* 70 B5
Qal'at Şāliḥ, *Iraq* 70 D5
Qal'at Sukkar, *Iraq* 70 D5
Qalyûb, *Egypt* 80 H7
Qamani'tuaq = Baker Lake,
  Canada 100 B10
Qamdo, *China* 58 B1
Qamruddin Karez, *Pakistan* .. 68 D3
Qandahār, *Afghan.* 66 D4
Qandahār □, *Afghan.* 66 D4
Qapān, *Iran* 71 B7
Qapshaghay, *Kazakhstan* 52 E8
Qaqortoq, *Greenland* 101 B6
Qâra, *Egypt* 80 B2
Qara Qash →, *China* 69 B8
Qarabutaq, *Kazakhstan* 52 E7
Qaraçala, *Azerbaijan* 35 L9
Qaraghandy, *Kazakhstan* 52 E8
Qaraghayly, *Kazakhstan* 52 E8
Qārah, *Si. Arabia* 70 D4
Qarataū, *Kazakhstan* 52 E8
Qarataū, *Kazakhstan* 52 E7
Qardho = Gardo, *Somali Rep.* . 75 F4
Qareh →, *Iran* 70 B5
Qareh Tekān, *Iran* 71 B6
Qarqan He →, *China* 60 C3
Qarqaraly, *Kazakhstan* 52 E8
Qarrasa, *Sudan* 81 E3
Qarshi, *Uzbekistan* 52 F7
Qartabā, *Lebanon* 74 A4
Qaryat al Gharab, *Iraq* 70 D5
Qaryat al 'Ulyā, *Si. Arabia* .. 70 E5
Qasr 'Amra, *Jordan* 70 D3
Qaşr-e Qand, *Iran* 71 E9
Qasr Farâfra, *Egypt* 80 B2
Qatanā, *Syria* 74 B5
Qatar ■, *Asia* 71 E6
Qatlish, *Iran* 71 B8
Qattâra, *Egypt* 80 A2
Qattâra, Munkhafed el, *Egypt* . 80 B2
Qattâra Depression = Qattâra,
  Munkhafed el, *Egypt* 80 B2
Qawām al Ḥamzah = Al Ḥamzah,
  Iraq 70 D5
Qāyen, *Iran* 71 C8
Qazaqstan = Kazakhstan ■, *Asia* . 52 E7
Qazimämmäd, *Azerbaijan* 35 K9
Qazvin, *Iran* 71 B6
Qazvin □, *Iran* 71 B6
Qeissan, *Sudan* 81 E3
Qena, *Egypt* 80 B3
Qena, W. →, *Egypt* 80 B3
Qeqertarsuaq, *Greenland* 101 B5
Qeqertarsuaq, *Greenland* 101 B14
Qeshlāq, *Iran* 70 C5
Qeshm, *Iran* 71 E8
Qeys, *Iran* 71 E7
Qezel Owzen →, *Iran* 71 B6
Qezi'ot, *Israel* 74 E3
Qi Xian, *China* 56 G8
Qian Gorlos, *China* 57 B13
Qian Xian, *China* 56 G5
Qiancheng, *China* 58 D7
Qianjiang, *Guangxi Zhuangzu,*
  China 58 F7
Qianjiang, *Hubei, China* 59 B9
Qianjiang, *Sichuan, China* .. 58 C7
Qianshan, *China* 59 B11
Qianwei, *China* 58 C4
Qianxi, *China* 58 D6
Qianyang, *Hunan, China* 59 D8
Qianyang, *Shaanxi, China* ... 56 G4
Qianyang, *Zhejiang, China* .. 59 B12
Qiaojia, *China* 58 D4
Qichun, *China* 59 B10
Qidong, *Hunan, China* 59 D9
Qidong, *Jiangsu, China* 59 B13
Qijiang, *China* 58 C6
Qikiqtarjuaq, *Canada* 101 B13
Qila Safed, *Pakistan* 66 E2
Qila Saifullāh, *Pakistan* 68 D3
Qilian Shan, *China* 60 C4
Qimen, *China* 59 C11
Qin He →, *China* 56 G7
Qin Jiang →, *China* 58 F7
Qin Jiang →, *Guangxi Zhuangzu,*
  China 58 F7
Qin Jiang →, *Jiangxi, China* .. 59 D10
Qin Ling = Qinling Shandi, *China* . 56 H5
Qin'an, *China* 56 G3
Qing Xian, *China* 56 E9
Qingcheng, *China* 57 F9
Qingdao, *China* 57 F11
Qingfeng, *China* 56 G8
Qinghai □, *China* 60 C4
Qinghai Hu, *China* 60 C5
Qinghecheng, *China* 57 D13
Qinghemen, *China* 57 D11
Qingjian, *China* 56 F6
Qingjiang = Huaiyin, *China* .. 57 H10
Qingliu, *China* 59 D11
Qinglong, *China* 58 E5
Qingping, *China* 58 D6
Qingpu, *China* 59 B13
Qingshui, *China* 56 G4
Qingshuihe, *China* 56 E6
Qingtian, *China* 59 C13
Qingtongxia Shuiku, *China* .. 56 F3
Qingxi, *China* 58 D7
Qingxu, *China* 56 F7
Qingyang, *Anhui, China* 59 B11
Qingyang, *Gansu, China* 56 F4
Qingyi Jiang →, *China* 58 C4
Qingyuan, *Guangdong, China* . 59 F9

Qingyuan, *Liaoning, China* .. 57 C13
Qingyuan, *Zhejiang, China* .. 59 D12
Qingyun, *China* 57 F9
Qingzhen, *China* 58 D6
Qinhuangdao, *China* 57 E10
Qinling Shandi, *China* 56 H5
Qinshui, *China* 56 G7
Qinyang = Jiyuan, *China* 56 G7
Qinyuan, *China* 56 F7
Qinzhou, *China* 58 G7
Qionghai, *China* 64 C8
Qionglai, *China* 58 B4
Qionglai Shan, *China* 58 B4
Qiongzhou Haixia, *China* 64 B8
Qiqihar, *China* 53 E13
Qiraîya, W. →, *Egypt* 74 E3
Qiryat Ata, *Israel* 74 C4
Qiryat Gat, *Israel* 74 D3
Qiryat Mal'akhi, *Israel* 74 D3
Qiryat Shemona, *Israel* 74 B4
Qiryat Yam, *Israel* 74 C4
Qishan, *China* 56 G4
Qitai, *China* 60 B3
Qiubei, *China* 58 E5
Qiyang, *China* 59 D8
Qızılağac Körfäzi, *Azerbaijan* . 71 B6
Qojūr, *Iran* 70 B5
Qom, *Iran* 71 C6
Qom □, *Iran* 71 C6
Qomolangma Feng = Everest,
  Mt., *Nepal* 69 E12
Qomsheh, *Iran* 71 D6
Qoraqalpoghistan □, *Uzbekistan* . 52 E6
Qorveh, *Iran* 73 E12
Qostanay, *Kazakhstan* 52 D7
Qotūr, *Iran* 73 C11
Qu Jiang →, *China* 58 B6
Qu Xian, *China* 58 B6
Quabbin Reservoir, *U.S.A.* .. 117 D12
Quairading, *Australia* 93 F2
Quakenbrück, *Germany* 24 C3
Quakertown, *U.S.A.* 117 F9
Qualicum Beach, *Canada* 102 D4
Quambatook, *Australia* 95 F3
Quambone, *Australia* 95 E4
Quamby, *Australia* 94 C3
Quan Long = Ca Mau, *Vietnam* . 65 H5
Quanah, *U.S.A.* 113 H5
Quang Ngai, *Vietnam* 64 E7
Quang Tri, *Vietnam* 64 D6
Quang Yen, *Vietnam* 58 G6
Quannan, *China* 59 E10
Quantock Hills, *U.K.* 15 F4
Quanzhou, *Fujian, China* 59 E12
Quanzhou, *Guangxi Zhuangzu,*
  China 59 E8
Qu'Appelle, *Canada* 103 C8
Quaqtaq, *Canada* 101 B13
Quaraí, *Brazil* 126 C4
Quarré-les-Tombes, *France* .. 19 E11
Quarteira, *Portugal* 37 H2
Quartu Sant'Élena, *Italy* 42 C2
Quartzsite, *U.S.A.* 111 M12
Quatsino Sd., *Canada* 102 C3
Quba, *Azerbaijan* 35 K9
Qūchān, *Iran* 71 B8
Queanbeyan, *Australia* 95 F4
Québec, *Canada* 105 C5
Québec □, *Canada* 105 C6
Quebrada del Condorito △,
  Argentina 126 C3
Quedlinburg, *Germany* 24 D7
Queen Alexandra Ra., *Antarctica* . 5 E11
Queen Charlotte City, *Canada* . 102 C2
Queen Charlotte Is., *Canada* . 102 C2
Queen Charlotte Sd., *Canada* . 102 C3
Queen Charlotte Strait, *Canada* . 102 C3
Queen Elizabeth △, *U.K.* 13 E4
Queen Elizabeth △, *Uganda* .. 86 C3
Queen Elizabeth Is., *Canada* . 98 B10
Queen Mary Land, *Antarctica* . 5 D7
Queen Maud G., *Canada* 100 B9
Queen Maud Land = Dronning
  Maud Land, *Antarctica* .. 5 D3
Queen Maud Mts., *Antarctica* . 5 E13
Queens Chan., *Australia* 92 C4
Queenscliff, *Australia* 95 F3
Queensland □, *Australia* 94 C3
Queenstown, *Australia* 95 G4
Queenstown, *N.Z.* 91 L2
Queenstown, *Singapore* ...... 65 d
Queenstown, *S. Africa* 88 E4
Queets, *U.S.A.* 110 C2
Queguay Grande →, *Uruguay* . 126 C4
Queimadas, *Brazil* 125 F11
Quelimane, *Mozam.* 87 F4
Quellón, *Chile* 128 E2
Quelpart = Cheju do, *S. Korea* . 57 H14
Queluz, *Portugal* 37 G1
Quemado, N. Mex., *U.S.A.* .. 109 J9
Quemado, Tex., *U.S.A.* 113 L4
Quemoy = Chinmen, *Taiwan* .. 59 E13
Quemú-Quemú, *Argentina* .. 126 D3
Quequén, *Argentina* 126 D4
Querétaro, *Mexico* 118 C4
Querétaro □, *Mexico* 118 C5
Querfurt, *Germany* 24 D7
Quérigut, *France* 20 F6
Querqueville, *France* 18 C5
Quesada, *Spain* 37 H7
Queshan, *China* 56 H8
Quesnel, *Canada* 102 C4
Quesnel →, *Canada* 102 C4
Quesnel L., *Canada* 102 C4
Questa, *U.S.A.* 109 H11
Questembert, *France* 18 E4
Quetico △, *Canada* 104 C1
Quetta, *Pakistan* 68 D2
Queyras △, *France* 21 D10
Quezaltenango, *Guatemala* .. 120 D1

Quezon City, *Phil.* 61 D4
Qufār, *Si. Arabia* 70 E4
Qui Nhon, *Vietnam* 64 F7
Quibaxe, *Angola* 84 F2
Quibdo, *Colombia* 124 B3
Quiberon, *France* 18 E3
Quiberon, Presqu'île de, *France* . 18 E3
Quickborn, *Germany* 24 B5
Quiet L., *Canada* 102 A2
Quiindy, *Paraguay* 126 B4
Quila, *Mexico* 118 C3
Quilán, C., *Chile* 128 E2
Quilcene, *U.S.A.* 110 C4
Quilimarí, *Chile* 126 C1
Quilino, *Argentina* 126 C3
Quill Lakes, *Canada* 103 C8
Quillabamba, *Peru* 124 F4
Quillagua, *Chile* 126 A2
Quillaicillo, *Chile* 126 C1
Quillan, *France* 20 F6
Quillota, *Chile* 126 C1
Quilmes, *Argentina* 126 C4
Quilon, *India* 66 Q10
Quilpie, *Australia* 95 D3
Quilpué, *Chile* 126 C1
Quilua, *Mozam.* 87 F4
Quimilí, *Argentina* 126 B3
Quimper, *France* 18 E2
Quimperlé, *France* 18 E3
Quinault →, *U.S.A.* 110 C2
Quincy, *Calif., U.S.A.* 110 F6
Quincy, *Fla., U.S.A.* 115 K3
Quincy, *Ill., U.S.A.* 112 F9
Quincy, *Mass., U.S.A.* 117 D14
Quincy, *Wash., U.S.A.* 108 C4
Quines, *Argentina* 126 C2
Quinga, *Mozam.* 87 F5
Quingey, *France* 19 E12
Quintana de la Serena, *Spain* . 37 G5
Quintana Roo □, *Mexico* 119 D7
Quintanar de la Orden, *Spain* . 37 F7
Quintanar de la Sierra, *Spain* . 38 D2
Quintanar del Rey, *Spain* 39 F3
Quinte West, *Canada* 116 B7
Quintero, *Chile* 126 C1
Quintin, *France* 18 D4
Quinto, *Spain* 38 D4
Quípar →, *Spain* 39 G3
Quirihue, *Chile* 126 D1
Quirindi, *Australia* 95 E5
Quirinópolis, *Brazil* 125 G8
Quiroga, *Spain* 36 C3
Quissac, *France* 21 E8
Quissanga, *Mozam.* 87 E5
Quissico, *Mozam.* 89 C5
Quitilipi, *Argentina* 126 B3
Quitman, *U.S.A.* 115 K4
Quito, *Ecuador* 124 D3
Quixadá, *Brazil* 125 D11
Quixaxe, *Mozam.* 87 F5
Qujing, *China* 58 E4
Qulan, *Kazakhstan* 52 E8
Qul'ân, Jazâ'ir, *Egypt* 70 E2
Qumbu, *S. Africa* 89 E4
Quneitra, *Syria* 74 B4
Qünghirot, *Uzbekistan* 52 E6
Qu'nyido, *China* 58 B2
Quoin I., *Australia* 92 B4
Quoin Pt., *S. Africa* 88 E2
Quorn, *Australia* 95 E2
Qŭqon, *Uzbekistan* 52 E8
Qurein, *Sudan* 81 E3
Qurnat as Sawdā', *Lebanon* .. 74 A5
Qûs, *Egypt* 80 B3
Qusar, *Azerbaijan* 35 K9
Qusaybā', *Si. Arabia* 70 E4
Qusaybah, *Iraq* 70 C4
Quseir, *Egypt* 70 E2
Qüshchī, *Iran* 70 B5
Quthing, *Lesotho* 89 E4
Qūṭīābād, *Iran* 71 C6
Quwo, *China* 56 G6
Quyang, *China* 56 E8
Quynh Nhai, *Vietnam* 64 B4
Quyon, *Canada* 117 A8
Quzhou, *China* 59 C12
Quzi, *China* 56 F4
Qvareli, *Georgia* 35 K7
Qyzylorda, *Kazakhstan* 52 E7

R

Ra, Ko, *Thailand* 65 H2
Raab, *Austria* 26 C6
Raahe, *Finland* 8 D21
Raalte, *Neths.* 17 B6
Raasay, *U.K.* 13 D2
Raasay, Sd. of, *U.K.* 13 D2
Rab, *Croatia* 41 D11
Raba, *Indonesia* 63 F5
Rába →, *Hungary* 28 C2
Raba →, *Poland* 31 H7
Rabaçal →, *Portugal* 36 D3
Rabah, *Nigeria* 83 C6
Rabai, *Kenya* 86 C4
Rabak, *Sudan* 81 E3
Rabastens, *France* 20 E5
Rabastens-de-Bigorre, *France* . 20 E4
Rabat = Victoria, *Malta* 49 C1
Rabat, *Malta* 49 D1
Rabat, *Morocco* 78 B4
Rabaul, *Papua N. G.* 96 H7
Rābigh, *Si. Arabia* 75 C2
Rabka, *Poland* 31 J6
Râbnița, *Moldova* 29 C14
Rābor, *Iran* 71 D8
Rača, *Serbia & M.* 44 B4
Răcăciuni, *Romania* 29 D11

Răcășdia, *Romania* 28 F6
Racconigi, *Italy* 40 D4
Race, C., *Canada* 105 C9
Rach Gia, *Vietnam* 65 G5
Rachid, *Mauritania* 82 B2
Raciąż, *Poland* 31 F7
Racibórz, *Poland* 31 H5
Racichy, *Belarus* 30 E10
Racine, *U.S.A.* 114 D2
Rackerby, *U.S.A.* 110 F5
Radama, Nosy, *Madag.* 89 A8
Radama, Saikanosy, *Madag.* . 89 A8
Radan, *Serbia & M.* 44 D5
Rădăuți, *Romania* 29 C10
Rădăuți-Prut, *Romania* 29 B11
Radbuza →, *Czech Rep.* 26 B6
Radcliff, *U.S.A.* 114 G3
Radeberg, *Germany* 24 D9
Radebeul, *Germany* 24 D9
Radeče, *Slovenia* 41 B12
Radekhiv, *Ukraine* 33 G3
Radekhov = Radekhiv, *Ukraine* . 33 G3
Radenthein, *Austria* 26 E6
Radew →, *Poland* 30 D2
Radford, *U.S.A.* 114 G5
Radhanpur, *India* 68 H4
Radhwa, Jabal, *Si. Arabia* .. 70 E3
Radika →, *Macedonia* 44 E4
Radisson, *Qué., Canada* 104 B4
Radisson, *Sask., Canada* 103 C7
Radium Hot Springs, *Canada* . 102 C5
Radlje ob Dravi, *Slovenia* .. 41 B12
Radnevo, *Bulgaria* 45 D9
Radnice, *Czech Rep.* 26 B6
Radnor Forest, *U.K.* 15 E4
Radolfzell, *Germany* 25 H4
Radom, *Poland* 31 G8
Radom →, *Poland* 31 G8
Radomir, *Bulgaria* 44 D6
Radomka →, *Poland* 31 G8
Radomsko, *Poland* 31 G6
Radomyshl, *Ukraine* 33 G5
Radomyśl Wielki, *Poland* 31 H8
Radoszyce, *Poland* 31 G7
Radoviš, *Macedonia* 44 E6
Radovljica, *Slovenia* 41 B11
Radstadt, *Austria* 26 D6
Radstock, C., *Australia* 95 E1
Răducăneni, *Romania* 29 D12
Raduša, *Macedonia* 44 D5
Radvanichy, *Belarus* 31 F11
Radville, *Canada* 103 D8
Raḍwá, J., *Si. Arabia* 80 C4
Radymno, *Poland* 31 J9
Radzanów, *Poland* 31 F7
Radziejów, *Poland* 31 F5
Radzyń Chełmiński, *Poland* . 30 E5
Radzyń Podlaski, *Poland* 31 G9
Rae, *Canada* 102 A5
Rae Bareli, *India* 69 F9
Rae Isthmus, *Canada* 101 B11
Raeren, *Belgium* 17 D6
Raeside, L., *Australia* 93 E3
Raetihi, *N.Z.* 91 H5
Rafaela, *Argentina* 126 C3
Rafah, *Gaza Strip* 74 D3
Rafai, *C.A.R.* 86 B1
Raffadali, *Italy* 42 E6
Raffili, *Sudan* 81 F2
Rafḥā, *Si. Arabia* 70 D4
Rafsanjān, *Iran* 71 D8
Raft Pt., *Australia* 92 C3
Râga, *Sudan* 81 F2
Raga →, *Sudan* 81 F2
Ragachow, *Belarus* 33 F6
Ragag, *Sudan* 81 E1
Ragama, *Sri Lanka* 66 R11
Ragged, Mt., *Australia* 93 F3
Ragged Pt., *Barbados* ...... 121 g
Raghunathpalli, *India* 69 H11
Raghunathpur, *India* 69 H12
Raglan, *N.Z.* 91 G5
Ragusa, *Italy* 43 F7
Raha, *Indonesia* 63 E6
Rahad, Nahr ed →, *Sudan* 81 E3
Rahaeng = Tak, *Thailand* 64 D2
Rahatgarh, *India* 69 H8
Rahden, *Germany* 24 C4
Raheita, *Eritrea* 81 E5
Rahimyar Khan, *Pakistan* 68 E4
Rāhjerd, *Iran* 71 C6
Rahole △, *Kenya* 86 B4
Rahon, *India* 68 D7
Raichur, *India* 66 L10
Raiganj, *India* 69 G13
Raigarh, *India* 67 J13
Raijua, *Indonesia* 63 F6
Raikot, *India* 68 D6
Railton, *Australia* 95 G4
Rainbow Bridge △, *U.S.A.* .. 109 H8
Rainbow Lake, *Canada* 102 B5
Rainier, *U.S.A.* 110 D4
Rainier, Mt., *U.S.A.* 110 D4
Rainy L., *Canada* 103 D10
Rainy River, *Canada* 103 D10
Raippaluoto, *Finland* 8 E19
Raipur, *India* 67 J12
Ra'is, *Si. Arabia* 80 C4
Raisen, *India* 68 H8
Raisio, *Finland* 9 F20
Raj Nandgaon, *India* 67 J12
Raj Nilgiri, *India* 69 J12
Raja, Ujung, *Indonesia* 62 D1
Raja Ampat, Kepulauan,
  Indonesia 63 E7
Rajahmundry, *India* 67 L12
Rajang →, *Malaysia* 62 D4
Rajanpur, *Pakistan* 68 E4
Rajapalaiyam, *India* 66 Q10
Rajasthan □, *India* 68 F5
Rajasthan Canal = Indira Gandhi
  Canal, *India* 68 F5

Rajauri, *India* 69 C6
Rajgarh, *Mad. P., India* 68 G7
Rajgarh, *Raj., India* 68 F7
Rajgarh, *Raj., India* 68 E6
Rajgir, *India* 69 G11
Rajgród, *Poland* 30 E9
Rajkot, *India* 68 H4
Rajmahal Hills, *India* 69 G12
Rajpipla, *India* 66 J8
Rajpur, *India* 68 H6
Rajpura, *India* 68 D7
Rajshahi, *Bangla.* 67 G16
Rajshahi □, *Bangla.* 69 G13
Rajula, *India* 68 J4
Rakaia, *N.Z.* 91 K4
Rakaia →, *N.Z.* 91 K4
Rakan, Ra's, *Qatar* 71 E6
Rakaposhi, *Pakistan* 69 A6
Rakata, *Indonesia* 62 F3
Rakhiv, *Ukraine* 29 B9
Rakhni, *Pakistan* 68 D3
Rakhni →, *Pakistan* 68 E3
Rakhny-Lisovi, *Ukraine* 29 B13
Rakitnoye, *Russia* 54 B7
Rakitovo, *Bulgaria* 45 E8
Rakiura △, *N.Z.* 91 M1
Rakoniewice, *Poland* 31 F3
Rakops, *Botswana* 88 C3
Rakovica, *Croatia* 41 D12
Rakovník, *Czech Rep.* 26 A6
Rakovski, *Bulgaria* 45 D8
Rakvere, *Estonia* 9 G22
Raleigh, *U.S.A.* 115 H6
Ralja, *Serbia & M.* 44 B4
Ralls, *U.S.A.* 113 J4
Ralston, *U.S.A.* 116 E8
Ram →, *Canada* 102 A4
Rām Allāh, *West Bank* 74 D4
Rama, *Nic.* 120 D3
Ramacca, *Italy* 43 E7
Ramakona, *India* 69 J8
Ramales de la Victoria, *Spain* ... 36 B7
Rāmallāh = Rām Allāh,
    West Bank 74 D4
Raman, *Thailand* 65 J3
Ramanathapuram, *India* 66 Q11
Ramanetaka, B. de, *Madag.* .. 89 A8
Ramanujganj, *India* 69 H10
Ramat Gan, *Israel* 74 C3
Ramatlhabama, *S. Africa* 88 D4
Ramban, *India* 69 C6
Rambervillers, *France* 19 D13
Rambipuji, *Indonesia* 63 H15
Rambouillet, *France* 19 D8
Rame Hd., *Australia* 95 F4
Ramechhap, *Nepal* 69 F12
Ramenskoye, *Russia* 32 E10
Ramganga →, *India* 69 F8
Ramgarh, *Jharkhand, India* .. 69 H11
Ramgarh, *Raj., India* 68 F6
Ramgarh, *Raj., India* 68 F4
Rāmhormoz, *Iran* 71 D6
Ramīān, *Iran* 71 B7
Ramingining, *Australia* 94 A2
Ramla, *Israel* 74 D3
Ramlu, *Eritrea* 81 E5
Ramm = Rum, *Jordan* 74 F4
Ramm, Jabal, *Jordan* 74 F4
Râmna →, *Romania* 29 E12
Ramnad = Ramanathapuram,
    India 66 Q11
Ramnagar, *Jammu & Kashmir,
    India* 69 C6
Ramnagar, *Uttaranchal, India* ... 69 E8
Ramnäs, *Sweden* 10 E10
Râmnicu Sărat, *Romania* 29 E12
Râmnicu Vâlcea, *Romania* ... 29 E9
Ramon, *Russia* 33 G10
Ramona, *U.S.A.* 111 M10
Ramonville-St-Agne, *France* . 20 E5
Ramore, *Canada* 104 C3
Ramos →, *Nigeria* 83 D6
Ramotswa, *Botswana* 88 C4
Rampur, *H.P., India* 68 D7
Rampur, *Mad. P., India* 68 H5
Rampur, *Ut. P., India* 69 E8
Rampur Hat, *India* 69 G12
Rampura, *India* 68 G6
Ramrama Tola, *India* 69 J8
Ramree I., *Burma* 67 K19
Rāmsar, *Iran* 71 B6
Ramsey, *I. of Man* 14 C3
Ramsey, *U.S.A.* 117 E10
Ramsey L., *Canada* 104 C3
Ramsgate, *U.K.* 15 F9
Ramsjö, *Sweden* 10 B9
Ramstein, *Germany* 25 F3
Ramtek, *India* 66 J11
Ramvik, *Sweden* 10 B11
Rana Pratap Sagar Dam, *India* ... 68 G6
Ranaghat, *India* 69 H13
Ranahu, *Pakistan* 68 G3
Ranau, *Malaysia* 62 C5
Rancagua, *Chile* 126 C1
Rance →, *France* 18 D5
Rancheria →, *Canada* 102 A3
Ranchester, *U.S.A.* 108 D10
Ranchi, *India* 69 H11
Rancho Cucamonga, *U.S.A.* .. 111 L9
Randalstown, *U.K.* 12 B5
Randan, *France* 19 F10
Randazzo, *Italy* 43 E7
Randers, *Denmark* 11 H4
Randers Fjord, *Denmark* 11 H4
Randfontein, *S. Africa* 89 D4
Randle, *U.S.A.* 110 D5
Randolph, *Mass., U.S.A.* 117 D13
Randolph, *N.Y., U.S.A.* 116 D6
Randolph, *Utah, U.S.A.* 108 F8
Randolph, *Vt., U.S.A.* 117 C12
Randsburg, *U.S.A.* 111 K9

Rånealven →, *Sweden* 8 D20
Rangae, *Thailand* 65 J3
Ranganu B., *N.Z.* 91 F4
Rangeley, *U.S.A.* 117 B14
Rangeley L., *U.S.A.* 117 B14
Rangely, *U.S.A.* 108 F9
Ranger, *U.S.A.* 113 J5
Rangia, *India* 67 F17
Rangiora, *N.Z.* 91 K4
Rangitaiki →, *N.Z.* 91 G6
Rangitata →, *N.Z.* 91 K3
Rangitoto ke te tonga = D'Urville
    I., *N.Z.* 91 J4
Rangkasbitung, *Indonesia* ... 63 G12
Rangon →, *Burma* 67 L20
Rangoon, *Burma* 67 L20
Rangpur, *Bangla.* 67 G16
Rangsit, *Thailand* 64 F3
Ranibennur, *India* 66 M9
Raniganj, *Ut. P., India* 69 F9
Raniganj, *W. Bengal, India* . 67 H15
Ranikhet, *India* 69 E8
Raniwara, *India* 66 G8
Ranka, *India* 69 H10
Ranken →, *Australia* 94 C2
Rankin, *U.S.A.* 113 K4
Rankin Inlet, *Canada* 100 B10
Rankins Springs, *Australia* . 95 E4
Rankweil, *Austria* 26 D2
Rannoch, L., *U.K.* 13 E4
Rannoch Moor, *U.K.* 13 E4
Ranobe, Helodranon' i, *Madag.* ... 89 C7
Ranohira, *Madag.* 89 C8
Ranomafana, *Toamasina, Madag.* .. 89 B8
Ranomafana, *Toliara, Madag.* . 89 C8
Ranomena, *Madag.* 89 C8
Ranong, *Thailand* 65 H2
Ranotsara Nord, *Madag.* 89 C8
Ränsa, *Iran* 71 C6
Ransiki, *Indonesia* 63 E8
Rantabe, *Madag.* 89 B8
Rantauprapat, *Indonesia* ... 62 D1
Rantemario, *Indonesia* 63 E5
Rantoul, *U.S.A.* 114 E1
Ranum, *Denmark* 11 H3
Ranyah, W. →, *Si. Arabia* .. 80 C5
Raon l'Étape, *France* 19 D13
Raoping, *China* 59 F11
Raoyang, *China* 56 E8
Rap, Ko, *Thailand* .... 65 b
Rapa, *French Polynesia* 97 K13
Rapa Nui = Pascua, I. de, *Chile* . 97 K17
Rapallo, *Italy* 40 D6
Rapar, *India* 68 H4
Rāpch, *Iran* 71 E8
Raper, C., *Canada* 101 B13
Rapid City, *U.S.A.* 112 D3
Rapid River, *U.S.A.* 114 C2
Rapla, *Estonia* 9 G21
Rapti →, *India* 69 F10
Rapu Rapu I., *Phil.* 61 E6
Raqaba ez Zarqa →, *Sudan* . 81 F2
Raquette →, *U.S.A.* 117 B10
Raquette Lake, *U.S.A.* 117 C10
Rarotonga, *Cook Is.* 97 K12
Ra's al 'Ayn, *Syria* 70 B4
Ra's al Khaymah, *U.A.E.* ... 71 E7
Râs el Mâ, *Mali* 82 B4
Râs Ghârib, *Egypt* 80 B3
Râs Mallap, *Egypt* 80 B3
Râs Muhammad △, *Egypt* 80 B3
Rasca, Pta. de la, *Canary Is.* ... 48 G3
Răscani, *Moldova* 29 C12
Raseiniai, *Lithuania* 9 J20
Rashad, *Sudan* 81 E3
Rashîd, *Egypt* 80 H7
Rashîd, Masabb, *Egypt* 80 H7
Rashmi, *India* 68 G6
Rasht, *Iran* 71 B6
Rasi Salai, *Thailand* 64 E5
Raška, *Serbia & M.* 44 C4
Râsnov, *Romania* 29 E10
Rason L., *Australia* 93 E3
Raşova, *Romania* 29 F12
Rasovo, *Bulgaria* 44 C7
Rasra, *India* 69 G10
Rasskazovo, *Russia* 34 D5
Rast, *Romania* 29 G8
Rastatt, *Germany* 25 G4
Rastede, *Germany* 24 B4
Răstoliţa, *Romania* 29 D9
Rasul, *Pakistan* 68 C5
Raszków, *Poland* 31 G4
Rat Buri, *Thailand* 64 F2
Rat Islands, *U.S.A.* 100 C1
Rat L., *Canada* 103 B9
Rätan, *Sweden* 10 B8
Ratangarh, *India* 68 E6
Raţāwī, *Iraq* 70 D5
Rath, *India* 69 G8
Rath Luirc, *Ireland* 12 D3
Rathdrum, *Ireland* 12 D5
Rathenow, *Germany* 24 C8
Rathkeale, *Ireland* 12 D3
Rathlin I., *U.K.* 12 A5
Rathmelton, *Ireland* 12 A4
Ratibor = Racibórz, *Poland* . 31 H5
Rätikon, *Austria* 26 D2
Ratingen, *Germany* 24 D2
Ratlam, *India* 68 H6
Ratnagiri, *India* 66 L8
Ratodero, *Pakistan* 68 F3
Raton, *U.S.A.* 113 G2
Rattaphum, *Thailand* 65 J3
Ratten, *Austria* 26 D8
Rattray Hd., *U.K.* 13 D7
Rättvik, *Sweden* 10 D9
Ratz, Mt., *Canada* 102 B2
Ratzeburg, *Germany* 24 B6

Raub, *Malaysia* 65 L3
Rauch, *Argentina* 126 D4
Raudales de Malpaso, *Mexico* . 119 D6
Raufarhöfn, *Iceland* 8 C6
Raufoss, *Norway* 9 F14
Raukumara Ra., *N.Z.* 91 H6
Rauma, *Finland* 9 F19
Raumo = Rauma, *Finland* 9 F19
Raung, Gunung, *Indonesia* .. 63 J17
Raurkela, *India* 69 H11
Rausu-Dake, *Japan* 54 B12
Rava-Ruska, *Ukraine* 31 C10
Rava Russkaya = Rava-Ruska,
    Ukraine 31 C10
Ravalli, *U.S.A.* 108 C6
Ravānsar, *Iran* 70 C5
Ravanusa, *Italy* 42 E6
Rāvar, *Iran* 71 D8
Ravena, *U.S.A.* 117 D11
Ravenna, *Italy* 41 D9
Ravenna, *Nebr., U.S.A.* 112 E5
Ravenna, *Ohio, U.S.A.* 116 E3
Ravensburg, *Germany* 25 H5
Ravenshoe, *Australia* 94 B4
Ravensthorpe, *Australia* ... 93 F3
Ravenswood, *Australia* 94 C4
Ravenswood, *U.S.A.* 114 F5
Ravi →, *Pakistan* 68 D4
Ravna Gora, *Croatia* 41 C11
Ravna Reka, *Serbia & M.* ... 44 B5
Ravne na Koroškem, *Slovenia* . 41 B11
Rawa Mazowiecka, *Poland* ... 31 G7
Rawalpindi, *Pakistan* 68 C5
Rawāndūz, *Iraq* 70 B5
Rawang, *Malaysia* 65 L3
Rawene, *N.Z.* 91 F4
Rawicz, *Poland* 31 G3
Rawka →, *Poland* 31 F7
Rawlinna, *Australia* 93 F4
Rawlins, *U.S.A.* 108 F10
Rawlinson Ra., *Australia* ... 93 D4
Rawson, *Argentina* 128 E3
Raxaul, *India* 69 F11
Ray, *U.S.A.* 112 A3
Ray, C., *Canada* 105 C8
Raya Ring, Ko, *Thailand* ... 65 a
Rayadurg, *India* 66 M10
Rayagada, *India* 67 K13
Raychikhinsk, *Russia* 53 E13
Rāyen, *Iran* 71 D8
Rayleigh, *U.K.* 15 F8
Raymond, *Canada* 102 D6
Raymond, *Calif., U.S.A.* ... 110 H7
Raymond, *N.H., U.S.A.* 117 C13
Raymond, *Wash., U.S.A.* ... 110 D3
Raymondville, *U.S.A.* 113 M6
Raymore, *Canada* 103 C8
Rayón, *Mexico* 118 B2
Rayong, *Thailand* 64 F3
Rayville, *U.S.A.* 113 J9
Raz, Pte. du, *France* 18 D2
Razan, *Iran* 71 C6
Răzăna, *Serbia & M.* 44 B3
Ražanj, *Serbia & M.* 44 C5
Razāzah, Buḩayrat ar, *Iraq* . 70 C4
Razāzah, L. = Razāzah, Buḩayrat
    ar, *Iraq* 70 C4
Razdelna, *Bulgaria* 45 C11
Razdel'naya = Rozdilna, *Ukraine* . 29 D17
Razdolnoye, *Russia* 54 C5
Razdolnoye, *Ukraine* 33 K7
Razeh, *Iran* 71 C6
Razgrad, *Bulgaria* 45 C10
Razim, Lacul, *Romania* 29 F14
Razlog, *Bulgaria* 44 E7
Razmak, *Pakistan* 68 C3
Ré, Î. de, *France* 20 B2
Reading, *U.K.* 15 F7
Reading, *U.S.A.* 117 F9
Reading □, *U.K.* 15 F7
Realicó, *Argentina* 126 D3
Réalmont, *France* 20 E6
Ream, *Cambodia* 65 G4
Rebais, *France* 19 D10
Rebi, *Indonesia* 63 F8
Rebiana, *Libya* 79 D10
Rebiana, Sahrā', *Libya* 79 D10
Rebun-Tō, *Japan* 54 B10
Recanati, *Italy* 41 E10
Recaş, *Romania* 28 E6
Recco, *Italy* 40 D6
Recherche, Arch. of the, *Australia* . 93 F3
Rechna Doab, *Pakistan* 68 D5
Rechytsa, *Belarus* 33 F6
Recife, *Brazil* 125 E12
Recklinghausen, *Germany* .. 17 C7
Reconquista, *Argentina* 126 B4
Recreo, *Argentina* 126 B2
Recz, *Poland* 31 E2
Red →, *La., U.S.A.* 113 K9
Red →, *N. Dak., U.S.A.* ... 100 C10
Red Bank, *U.S.A.* 117 F10
Red Bay, *Canada* 105 B8
Red Bluff, *U.S.A.* 108 F2
Red Bluff L., *U.S.A.* 113 K3
Red Cliffs, *Australia* 95 E3
Red Cloud, *U.S.A.* 112 E5
Red Creek, *U.S.A.* 117 C8
Red Deer, *Canada* 102 C6
Red Deer →, *Alta., Canada* . 103 C7
Red Deer →, *Man., Canada* . 103 C8
Red Hook, *U.S.A.* 117 E11
Red Indian L., *Canada* 105 C8
Red L., *Canada* 103 C10
Red Lake, *Canada* 103 C10
Red Lake Falls, *U.S.A.* 112 B6
Red Lake Road, *Canada* 103 C10

Red Lodge, *U.S.A.* 108 D9
Red Mountain, *U.S.A.* 111 K9
Red Oak, *U.S.A.* 112 E7
Red Rock, *Canada* 104 C2
Red Rock, L., *U.S.A.* 112 E8
Red Rocks Pt., *Australia* .. 93 F4
Red Sea, *Asia* 75 C2
Red Slate Mt., *U.S.A.* 110 H8
Red Sucker L., *Canada* 104 B1
Red Tower Pass = Turnu Roşu,
    P., *Romania* 29 E9
Red Wing, *U.S.A.* 112 C8
Reda, *Poland* 30 D5
Redang, *Malaysia* 65 K4
Redange, *Lux.* 17 E5
Redcar, *U.K.* 14 C6
Redcar & Cleveland □, *U.K.* . 14 C7
Redcliff, *Canada* 103 C6
Redcliffe, *Australia* 95 D5
Redcliffe, Mt., *Australia* .. 93 E3
Reddersburg, *S. Africa* 88 D4
Redding, *U.S.A.* 108 F2
Redditch, *U.K.* 15 E6
Redfield, *U.S.A.* 112 C5
Redford, *U.S.A.* 117 B11
Redhead, *Trin. & Tob.* 125 K16
Redkino, *Russia* 32 D9
Redlands, *U.S.A.* 111 M9
Redmond, *Oreg., U.S.A.* ... 108 D3
Redmond, *Wash., U.S.A.* ... 110 C4
Redon, *France* 18 E4
Redonda, Antigua & B. 121 C7
Redondela, *Spain* 36 C2
Redondo, *Portugal* 37 G3
Redondo Beach, *U.S.A.* 111 M8
Redruth, *U.K.* 15 G2
Redvers, *Canada* 103 D8
Redwater, *Canada* 102 C6
Redwood, *U.S.A.* 117 B9
Redwood City, *U.S.A.* 110 H4
Redwood Falls, *U.S.A.* 112 C7
Redwood △, *U.S.A.* 108 F1
Ree, L., *Ireland* 12 C3
Reed, L., *Canada* 103 C8
Reed City, *U.S.A.* 114 D3
Reedley, *U.S.A.* 110 J7
Reedsburg, *U.S.A.* 112 D9
Reedsport, *U.S.A.* 108 E1
Reedsville, *U.S.A.* 116 F7
Reefton, *N.Z.* 91 K3
Rees, *Germany* 24 D2
Reese →, *U.S.A.* 108 F5
Refahiye, *Turkey* 73 C8
Reftele, *Sweden* 11 G7
Refugio, *U.S.A.* 113 L6
Rega →, *Poland* 30 D2
Regalbuto, *Italy* 43 E7
Regen, *Germany* 25 G9
Regen →, *Germany* 25 F8
Regensburg, *Germany* 25 F8
Regenstauf, *Germany* 25 F8
Reggâne = Zaouiet Reggâne,
    Algeria 78 C6
Reggello, *Italy* 41 E8
Réggio di Calábria, *Italy* .. 43 D8
Réggio nell'Emília, *Italy* .. 40 D7
Reghin, *Romania* 29 D9
Regina, *Canada* 103 C8
Regina Beach, *Canada* 103 C8
Registro, *Brazil* 127 A6
Reguengos de Monsaraz, *Portugal* . 37 G3
Rehar →, *India* 69 H10
Rehli, *India* 69 H8
Rehoboth, *Namibia* 88 C2
Rehovot, *Israel* 74 D3
Reichenbach, *Germany* 24 E8
Reid, *Australia* 93 F4
Reidsville, *U.S.A.* 115 G6
Reigate, *U.K.* 15 F7
Reillo, *Spain* 38 F3
Reims, *France* 19 C11
Reina Adelaida, Arch., *Chile* . 128 G2
Reina Sofia, Tenerife ✈ (TFS),
    Canary Is. 48 F3
Reinbek, *Germany* 24 B6
Reindeer →, *Canada* 103 B8
Reindeer I., *Canada* 103 C9
Reindeer L., *Canada* 103 B8
Reinga, C., *N.Z.* 91 F4
Reinosa, *Spain* 36 B6
Reitz, *S. Africa* 89 D4
Reivilo, *S. Africa* 88 D3
Rejaf, *Sudan* 81 G3
Rejmyre, *Sweden* 11 F9
Rejowiec Fabryczny, *Poland* . 31 G10
Reka →, *Slovenia* 41 C11
Rekovac, *Serbia & M.* 44 C5
Reliance, *Canada* 103 A7
Rémalard, *France* 18 D7
Remarkable, Mt., *Australia* . 95 E2
Rembang, *Indonesia* 63 G14
Remedios, *Panama* 120 E3
Remeshk, *Iran* 71 E8
Remetea, *Romania* 29 D10
Remich, *Lux.* 17 E6
Remiremont, *France* 19 D13
Remo, *Ethiopia* 81 F5
Remontnoye, *Russia* 35 G6
Remoulins, *France* 21 E8
Remscheid, *Germany* 17 C7
Ren Xian, *China* 56 F8
Rendang, *Indonesia* 63 J18
Rende, *Italy* 43 C9
Rendína, *Greece* 46 B3
Rendsburg, *Germany* 24 A5
Renfrew, *Canada* 117 A8
Renfrewshire □, *U.K.* 13 F4
Rengat, *Indonesia* 62 E2
Rengo, *Chile* 126 C1
Renhua, *China* 59 E9
Renhuai, *China* 58 D6

Reni, *Ukraine* 29 E13
Renk, *Sudan* 81 E3
Renmark, *Australia* 95 E3
Rennell Sd., *Canada* 102 C2
Renner Springs, *Australia* . 94 B1
Rennes, *France* 18 D5
Rennie L., *Canada* 103 A7
Reno, *U.S.A.* 110 F7
Reno →, *Italy* 41 D9
Renovo, *U.S.A.* 116 E7
Renqiu, *China* 56 E9
Rens, *Denmark* 11 K3
Renshou, *China* 58 C5
Rensselaer, *Ind., U.S.A.* .. 114 E2
Rensselaer, *N.Y., U.S.A.* .. 117 D11
Rentería, *Spain* 38 B3
Renton, *U.S.A.* 110 C4
Réo, *Burkina Faso* 82 C4
Reocín, *Spain* 36 B6
Reotipur, *India* 69 G10
Répcelak, *Hungary* 28 C2
Republic, *Mo., U.S.A.* 113 G8
Republic, *Wash., U.S.A.* ... 108 B4
Republican →, *U.S.A.* 112 F6
Repulse B., *Australia* 94 J6
Repulse Bay, *Canada* 101 B11
Requena, *Peru* 124 E4
Requena, *Spain* 39 F3
Réquista, *France* 20 D6
Reşadiye = Datça, *Turkey* .. 47 E9
Reşadiye, *Turkey* 72 B7
Reşadiye Yarımadası, *Turkey* . 47 E9
Resavica, *Serbia & M.* 44 B5
Resen, *Macedonia* 44 E5
Reserve, *U.S.A.* 109 K9
Resht = Rasht, *Iran* 71 B6
Resistencia, *Argentina* 126 B4
Reşiţa, *Romania* 28 E6
Resko, *Poland* 30 E2
Resolution I., *Canada* 101 B13
Resolution I., *N.Z.* 91 L1
Ressano Garcia, *Mozam.* 89 D5
Reston, *Canada* 103 D8
Reszel, *Poland* 30 D8
Retenue, L. de, *Dem. Rep. of
    the Congo* 87 E2
Retezat △, *Romania* 28 E7
Retezat, Munţii, *Romania* .. 28 E8
Retford, *U.K.* 14 D7
Rethel, *France* 19 C11
Rethem, *Germany* 24 C5
Réthímnon, *Greece* 49 D6
Réthímnon □, *Greece* 49 D6
Reti, *Pakistan* 68 E3
Retiche, Alpi, *Switz.* 25 J6
Retiers, *France* 18 E5
Retortillo, *Spain* 36 E4
Retournac, *France* 21 C8
Rétság, *Hungary* 28 C4
Réunion ☑, *Ind. Oc.* 77 J9
Reus, *Spain* 38 D6
Reuterstadt Stavenhagen,
    Germany 24 B8
Reutlingen, *Germany* 25 G5
Reutte, *Austria* 26 D3
Reval = Tallinn, *Estonia* .. 9 G21
Revel, *France* 20 E6
Revelganj, *India* 69 G11
Revelstoke, *Canada* 102 C5
Reventazón, *Peru* 124 E2
Revigny-sur-Ornain, *France* . 19 D11
Revillagigedo, Is. de, *Pac. Oc.* . 118 D2
Revin, *France* 19 C11
Revúca, *Slovak Rep.* 27 C13
Revuè →, *Mozam.* 87 F3
Rewa, *India* 69 G9
Rewari, *India* 68 E7
Rexburg, *U.S.A.* 108 E8
Rey, *Iran* 71 C6
Rey, I. del, *Panama* 120 E4
Rey Malabo, *Eq. Guin.* 83 E6
Reyðarfjörður, *Iceland* 8 D6
Reyes, Pt., *U.S.A.* 110 H3
Reyhanlı, *Turkey* 72 D7
Reykjahlíð, *Iceland* 8 D5
Reykjanes, *Iceland* 8 E2
Reykjavík, *Iceland* 8 D3
Reynolds Ra., *Australia* ... 92 D5
Reynoldsville, *U.S.A.* 116 E6
Reynosa, *Mexico* 119 B5
Rēzekne, *Latvia* 9 H22
Rezina, *Moldova* 29 C13
Rezovo, *Bulgaria* 45 D12
Rezvān, *Iran* 71 E8
Rgotina, *Serbia & M.* 44 B6
Rhamnus, *Greece* 46 C6
Rhayader, *U.K.* 15 E4
Rheda-Wiedenbrück, *Germany* . 24 D4
Rhede, *Germany* 24 D2
Rhein →, *Europe* 17 C6
Rhein-Main-Donau-Kanal,
    Germany 25 F7
Rhein-Ruhr, Düsseldorf ✈
    (DUS), *Germany* 24 D2
Rhein-Taunus △, *Germany* .. 25 E4
Rhein-Westerwald △, *Germany* . 24 E3
Rheinbach, *Germany* 24 E2
Rheine, *Germany* 24 C3
Rheinfelden, *Germany* 25 H3
Rheinhessen-Pfalz □, *Germany* . 25 F3
Rheinland-Pfalz □, *Germany* . 25 E2
Rheinsberg, *Germany* 24 B8
Rhin = Rhein →, *Europe* ... 17 C6
Rhine = Rhein →, *Europe* .. 17 C6
Rhinebeck, *U.S.A.* 117 E11
Rhineland-Palatinate =
    Rhineland-Pfalz □, *Germany* . 25 E2
Rhinelander, *U.S.A.* 112 C10
Rhinns Pt., *U.K.* 13 F2

Rhino Camp, *Uganda* 86 B3
Rhir, Cap, *Morocco* 78 B4
Rho, *Italy* 40 C6
Rhode Island □, *U.S.A.* 117 E13
Rhodes = Ródhos, *Greece* 49 C10
Rhodope Mts. = Rhodopi Planina,
  Bulgaria 45 E8
Rhodopi Planina, *Bulgaria* 45 E8
Rhön, *Germany* 24 E5
Rhondda, *U.K.* 15 F4
Rhondda Cynon Taff □, *U.K.* .. 15 F4
Rhône □, *France* 21 C8
Rhône ➤, *France* 21 E8
Rhône-Alpes □, *France* 21 C9
Rhum, *U.K.* 13 E2
Rhyl, *U.K.* 14 D4
Ri-Aba, *Eq. Guin.* 83 E6
Ria Formosa △, *Portugal* 37 H3
Riachão, *Brazil* 125 E9
Riangnom, *Sudan* 81 F3
Riaño, *Spain* 36 C6
Rians, *France* 21 E9
Riansáres ➤, *Spain* 37 F7
Riasi, *India* 69 C6
Riau □, *Indonesia* 62 D2
Riau, Kepulauan, *Indonesia* .. 62 D2
Riau Arch. = Riau, Kepulauan,
  Indonesia 62 D2
Riaza, *Spain* 36 D7
Riaza ➤, *Spain* 36 D7
Riba de Saelices, *Spain* 38 E2
Riba-Roja de Turia, *Spain* ... 39 F4
Ribadavia, *Spain* 36 C2
Ribadeo, *Spain* 36 B3
Ribadesella, *Spain* 36 B5
Ribado, *Nigeria* 83 D7
Ribao, *Cameroon* 83 D7
Ribas = Ribes de Freser, *Spain* .. 38 C7
Ribas do Rio Pardo, *Brazil* .. 125 H8
Ribauè, *Mozam.* 87 E4
Ribble ➤, *U.K.* 14 D5
Ribe, *Denmark* 11 J2
Ribe Amtskommune □, *Denmark* .. 11 J2
Ribeauvillé, *France* 19 D14
Ribécourt-Dreslincourt, *France* . 19 C9
Ribeira = Santa Uxía, *Spain* .. 36 C2
Ribeira Brava, *Madeira* 48 D2
Ribeirão Prêto, *Brazil* 127 A6
Ribemont, *France* 19 C10
Ribera, *Italy* 42 E6
Ribérac, *France* 20 C4
Riberalta, *Bolivia* 124 F5
Ribes de Freser, *Spain* 38 C7
Ribnica, *Slovenia* 41 C11
Ribnitz-Damgarten, *Germany* .. 24 A8
Riccarton, *N.Z.* 91 K4
Riccia, *Italy* 43 A7
Riccione, *Italy* 41 E9
Rice, *U.S.A.* 111 L12
Rice L., *Canada* 116 B6
Rice Lake, *U.S.A.* 112 C9
Rich, C., *Canada* 116 B4
Richard Toll, *Senegal* 82 B1
Richards Bay, *S. Africa* 89 D5
Richardson ➤, *Canada* 103 B6
Richardson Lakes, *U.S.A.* 114 C10
Richardson Springs, *U.S.A.* .. 110 F5
Riche, C., *Australia* 93 F2
Richelieu, *France* 18 E7
Richey, *U.S.A.* 112 B2
Richfield, *U.S.A.* 109 G8
Richfield Springs, *U.S.A.* ... 117 D10
Richford, *U.S.A.* 117 B12
Richibucto, *Canada* 105 C7
Richland, *Ga., U.S.A.* 115 J3
Richland, *Wash., U.S.A.* 108 C4
Richland Center, *U.S.A.* 112 D9
Richlands, *U.S.A.* 114 G5
Richmond, *Australia* 94 C3
Richmond, *N.Z.* 91 J4
Richmond, *U.K.* 14 C6
Richmond, *Calif., U.S.A.* 110 H4
Richmond, *Ind., U.S.A.* 114 F3
Richmond, *Ky., U.S.A.* 114 G3
Richmond, *Mich., U.S.A.* 116 D2
Richmond, *Mo., U.S.A.* 112 F8
Richmond, *Tex., U.S.A.* 113 L7
Richmond, *Utah, U.S.A.* 108 F8
Richmond, *Va., U.S.A.* 114 G7
Richmond, *Vt., U.S.A.* 117 B12
Richmond Hill, *Canada* 116 C5
Richmond Ra., *Australia* 95 D5
Richtersveld △, *S. Africa* ... 88 D2
Richwood, *U.S.A.* 114 F5
Ricla, *Spain* 38 D3
Ridder = Leninogorsk,
  Kazakhstan 52 D9
Riddlesburg, *U.S.A.* 116 F6
Ridgecrest, *U.S.A.* 111 K9
Ridgefield, *Conn., U.S.A.* ... 117 E11
Ridgefield, *Wash., U.S.A.* ... 110 E4
Ridgeland, *U.S.A.* 115 J5
Ridgetown, *Canada* 116 D3
Ridgewood, *U.S.A.* 117 F10
Ridgway, *U.S.A.* 116 E6
Riding Mountain △, *Canada* ... 103 C9
Ridley, Mt., *Australia* 93 F3
Riebeek-Oos, *S. Africa* 88 E4
Ried, *Austria* 26 C6
Riedlingen, *Germany* 25 G5
Riedstadt, *Germany* 25 F4
Rienza ➤, *Italy* 41 B8
Riesa, *Germany* 24 D9
Riesi, *Italy* 43 E7
Riet ➤, *S. Africa* 88 D3
Rietavas, *Lithuania* 30 C8
Rietbron, *S. Africa* 88 E3
Rietfontein, *Namibia* 88 C3
Rieti, *Italy* 41 F9
Rieupeyroux, *France* 20 D6

Riez, *France* 21 E10
Rif = Er Rif, *Morocco* 78 A5
Riffe L., *U.S.A.* 110 D4
Rifle, *U.S.A.* 108 G10
Rift Valley, *Africa* 76 G7
Rift Valley □, *Kenya* 86 B4
Rīga, *Latvia* 9 H21
Rīga ✈ (RIX), *Latvia* 30 B10
Riga, G. of, *Latvia* 9 H20
Rigacikun, *Nigeria* 83 C6
Rīgān, *Iran* 71 D8
Rīgas Jūras Līcis = Riga, G. of,
  Latvia 9 H20
Rigaud, *Canada* 117 A10
Rigby, *U.S.A.* 108 E8
Rīgestān, *Afghan.* 66 D4
Riggins, *U.S.A.* 108 D5
Rignac, *France* 20 D6
Rigolet, *Canada* 105 B8
Rihand Dam, *India* 69 G10
Riihimäki, *Finland* 9 F21
Riiser-Larsen-halvøya, *Antarctica* . 5 C4
Rijau, *Nigeria* 83 C6
Rijeka, *Croatia* 41 C11
Rijeka Crnojevića, *Serbia & M.* . 44 D3
Rijssen, *Neths.* 17 B6
Rika ➤, *Ukraine* 29 B8
Rike, *Ethiopia* 81 E4
Rikuchū-Kaigan △, *Japan* 54 E11
Rikuzentakada, *Japan* 54 E10
Rila, *Bulgaria* 44 D7
Rila Planina, *Bulgaria* 44 D7
Riley, *U.S.A.* 108 E4
Rima ➤, *Nigeria* 83 C6
Rimah, Wadi ar ➤, *Si. Arabia* . 70 E4
Rimau, Pulau, *Malaysia* ...... 65 c
Rimavská Sobota, *Slovak Rep.* . 27 C13
Rimbey, *Canada* 102 C6
Rimbo, *Sweden* 10 E12
Rimersburg, *U.S.A.* 116 E5
Rimforsa, *Sweden* 11 F9
Rimi, *Nigeria* 83 C6
Rímini, *Italy* 41 D9
Rimouski, *Canada* 105 C6
Rimrock, *U.S.A.* 110 D5
Rinca, *Indonesia* 63 F5
Rincón de la Victoria, *Spain* . 37 J6
Rincón de Romos, *Mexico* 118 C4
Rinconada, *Argentina* 126 A2
Rind ➤, *India* 69 G9
Ringarum, *Sweden* 11 F10
Ringas, *India* 68 F6
Ringe, *Denmark* 11 J4
Ringim, *Nigeria* 83 C6
Ringkøbing, *Denmark* 11 H2
Ringkøbing Amtskommune □,
  Denmark 11 H2
Ringkøbing Fjord, *Denmark* ... 11 H2
Ringsjön, *Sweden* 11 J7
Ringsted, *Denmark* 11 J5
Ringvassøy, *Norway* 8 B18
Ringwood, *U.S.A.* 117 E10
Rinía, *Greece* 47 D7
Rinjani, *Indonesia* 62 F5
Rinteln, *Germany* 24 C5
Río, Punta del, *Spain* 39 J2
Río Branco, *Brazil* 124 E5
Río Branco, *Uruguay* 127 C5
Río Bravo △, *N. Amer.* 118 B4
Río Bravo del Norte ➤, *Mexico* . 119 B5
Rio Brilhante, *Brazil* 127 A5
Río Claro, *Brazil* 127 A6
Río Claro, *Trin. & Tob.* 121 D7
Río Colorado, *Argentina* 128 D4
Río Cuarto, *Argentina* 126 C3
Rio das Pedras, *Mozam.* 89 C6
Rio de Janeiro, *Brazil* 127 A7
Rio de Janeiro □, *Brazil* 127 A7
Rio do Sul, *Brazil* 127 B6
Río Dulce △, *Guatemala* 120 C2
Río Gallegos, *Argentina* 128 G3
Río Grande, *Argentina* 128 G3
Río Grande, *Brazil* 127 C5
Río Grande, *Mexico* 118 C4
Río Grande, *Nic.* 120 D3
Río Grande, *Puerto Rico* ..... 121 d
Río Grande ➤, *U.S.A.* 113 N6
Río Grande City, *U.S.A.* 113 M5
Río Grande de Santiago ➤,
  Mexico 118 C3
Rio Grande do Norte □, *Brazil* . 125 E11
Rio Grande do Sul □, *Brazil* .. 127 C5
Río Hato, *Panama* 120 E3
Río Lagartos, *Mexico* 119 C7
Rio Largo, *Brazil* 125 E11
Rio Maior, *Portugal* 37 F2
Rio Marina, *Italy* 40 F7
Río Mulatos, *Bolivia* 124 G5
Río Muni □, *Eq. Guin.* 84 D2
Rio Negro, *Brazil* 127 B6
Rio Pardo, *Brazil* 127 C5
Río Pilcomayo △, *Argentina* ... 126 B4
Río Platano △, *Honduras* 120 C3
Rio Rancho, *U.S.A.* 109 J10
Río Segundo, *Argentina* 126 C3
Río Tercero, *Argentina* 126 C3
Rio Tinto, *Portugal* 36 D2
Río Verde, *Brazil* 125 G8
Río Verde, *Mexico* 119 C5
Río Vista, *U.S.A.* 110 G5
Ríobamba, *Ecuador* 124 D3
Ríohacha, *Colombia* 124 A4
Riom, *France* 20 C7
Riom-ès-Montagnes, *France* ... 20 C6
Rion-des-Landes, *France* 20 E3
Rionero in Vúlture, *Italy* 43 B8
Rioni ➤, *Georgia* 35 J5
Ríos, *Spain* 36 D3
Ríosucio, *Colombia* 124 B3
Riou L., *Canada* 103 B7
Rioz, *France* 19 E13

Ripatransone, *Italy* 41 F10
Ripley, *Canada* 116 B3
Ripley, *Calif., U.S.A.* 111 M12
Ripley, *N.Y., U.S.A.* 116 D5
Ripley, *Tenn., U.S.A.* 113 H10
Ripley, *W. Va., U.S.A.* 114 F5
Ripoll, *Spain* 38 C7
Ripon, *U.K.* 14 C6
Ripon, *Calif., U.S.A.* 110 H5
Ripon, *Wis., U.S.A.* 114 D1
Riposto, *Italy* 43 E8
Risan, *Serbia & M.* 44 D2
Riscle, *France* 20 E3
Rishã', W. ar ➤, *Si. Arabia* .. 70 E5
Rishiri-Rebun-Sarobetsu △,
  Japan 54 B10
Rishiri-Tō, *Japan* 54 B10
Rishon le Ẕiyyon, *Israel* 74 D3
Risle ➤, *France* 18 C7
Risnjak △, *Croatia* 41 C11
Rison, *U.S.A.* 113 J8
Rita Blanca Cr. ➤, *U.S.A.* ... 113 H3
Riti, *Nigeria* 83 D6
Ritter, Mt., *U.S.A.* 110 H7
Rittman, *U.S.A.* 116 F3
Ritzville, *U.S.A.* 108 C4
Riva del Garda, *Italy* 40 C7
Riva Lígure, *Italy* 40 E4
Rivadavia, *Buenos Aires,*
  Argentina 126 D3
Rivadavia, *Mendoza, Argentina* . 126 C2
Rivadavia, *Salta, Argentina* .. 126 A3
Rivadavia, *Chile* 126 B1
Rivarolo Canavese, *Italy* 40 C4
Rivas, *Nic.* 120 D2
Rive-de-Gier, *France* 21 C8
River Cess, *Liberia* 82 D3
River Jordan, *Canada* 110 B2
Rivera, *Argentina* 126 D3
Rivera, *Uruguay* 127 C4
Riverbank, *U.S.A.* 110 H6
Riverdale, *U.S.A.* 110 J7
Riverhead, *U.S.A.* 117 F12
Riverhurst, *Canada* 103 C7
Rivers □, *Nigeria* 83 E6
Rivers, *Canada* 103 C8
Rivers Inlet, *Canada* 102 C3
Riversdale, *S. Africa* 88 E3
Riverside, *U.S.A.* 111 M9
Riverton, *Australia* 95 E2
Riverton, *Canada* 103 C9
Riverton, *N.Z.* 91 M2
Riverton, *U.S.A.* 108 E9
Riverton Heights, *U.S.A.* 110 C4
Rives, *France* 21 C9
Rivesaltes, *France* 20 F6
Riviera, *U.S.A.* 111 K12
Riviera di Levante, *Italy* 40 D6
Riviera di Ponente, *Italy* 40 D5
Rivière-au-Renard, *Canada* ... 105 C7
Rivière-du-Loup, *Canada* 105 C6
Rivière-Pentecôte, *Canada* ... 105 C6
Rivière-Pilote, *Martinique* .. 120 c
Rivière St-Paul, *Canada* 105 B8
Rivière-Salée, *Martinique* ... 120 c
Rivne, *Ukraine* 29 D14
Rivne, *Ukraine* 33 G4
Rívoli, *Italy* 40 C4
Rivoli B., *Australia* 95 F3
Rixheim, *France* 19 E14
Riyadh = Ar Riyāḍ, *Si. Arabia* . 70 E5
Rize, *Turkey* 73 B9
Rizhao, *China* 57 G10
Rizokarpaso, *Cyprus* 49 D13
Rizzuto, C., *Italy* 43 D10
Rjukan, *Norway* 9 G13
Ro, *Greece* 47 E11
Roa, *Spain* 36 D7
Road Town, *Br. Virgin Is.* ... 121 e
Roag, L., *U.K.* 13 C1
Roan Plateau, *U.S.A.* 108 G9
Roanne, *France* 19 F11
Roanoke, *Ala., U.S.A.* 115 J3
Roanoke, *Va., U.S.A.* 114 G6
Roanoke ➤, *U.S.A.* 115 H7
Roanoke I., *U.S.A.* 115 H8
Roanoke Rapids, *U.S.A.* 115 G7
Roatán, *Honduras* 120 C2
Robât Sang, *Iran* 71 C8
Robāṭkarīm, *Iran* 71 C6
Robāṭkarīm □, *Iran* 71 B6
Robbins I., *Australia* 95 G4
Róbbio, *Italy* 40 C5
Robe ➤, *Australia* 92 D2
Röbel, *Germany* 24 B8
Robert Lee, *U.S.A.* 113 K4
Robertsdale, *U.S.A.* 116 F6
Robertson, *S. Africa* 88 E2
Robertson I., *Antarctica* 5 C18
Robertson Ra., *Australia* 92 D3
Robertsport, *Liberia* 82 D2
Robertstown, *Australia* 95 E2
Roberval, *Canada* 105 C5
Robeson Chan., *N. Amer.* 4 A4
Robesonia, *U.S.A.* 117 F8
Robi, *Ethiopia* 81 F4
Robinson, *U.S.A.* 114 F2
Robinson ➤, *Australia* 94 B2
Robinson Ra., *Australia* 93 E2
Robinvale, *Australia* 95 E3
Robledo, *Spain* 39 G2
Roblin, *Canada* 103 C8
Roboré, *Bolivia* 124 G7
Robson, Mt., *Canada* 102 C5
Robstown, *U.S.A.* 113 M6
Roca, C. da, *Portugal* 37 G1
Roca Partida, I., *Mexico* 118 D2
Rocas, I., *Brazil* 125 D12

Rocca San Casciano, *Italy* ... 41 D8
Roccadáspide, *Italy* 43 B8
Roccastrada, *Italy* 41 F8
Roccella Iónica, *Italy* 43 D9
Rocha, *Uruguay* 127 C5
Rochdale, *U.K.* 14 D5
Rochechouart, *France* 20 C4
Rochefort, *Belgium* 17 D5
Rochefort, *France* 20 C3
Rochefort-en-Terre, *France* .. 18 E4
Rochelle, *U.S.A.* 112 E10
Rocher River, *Canada* 102 A6
Rocheservière, *France* 18 F5
Rochester, *U.K.* 15 F8
Rochester, *Ind., U.S.A.* 114 E2
Rochester, *Minn., U.S.A.* 112 C8
Rochester, *N.H., U.S.A.* 117 C14
Rochester, *N.Y., U.S.A.* 116 C7
Rociu, *Romania* 29 F10
Rock ➤, *Canada* 102 A3
Rock Creek, *U.S.A.* 116 E4
Rock Falls, *U.S.A.* 112 E10
Rock Hill, *U.S.A.* 115 H5
Rock Island, *U.S.A.* 112 E9
Rock Rapids, *U.S.A.* 112 D6
Rock Sound, *Bahamas* 120 B4
Rock Springs, *Mont., U.S.A.* .. 108 C10
Rock Springs, *Wyo., U.S.A.* ... 108 F9
Rock Valley, *U.S.A.* 112 D6
Rockall, *Atl. Oc.* 6 D3
Rockdale, *Tex., U.S.A.* 113 K6
Rockdale, *Wash., U.S.A.* 110 C5
Rockeby = Mungkan Kandju △,
  Australia 94 A3
Rockefeller Plateau, *Antarctica* . 5 E14
Rockford, *U.S.A.* 112 D10
Rockglen, *Canada* 103 D7
Rockhampton, *Australia* 94 C5
Rockingham, *Australia* 93 F2
Rockingham, *U.S.A.* 115 H6
Rockingham B., *Australia* 94 B4
Rocklake, *U.S.A.* 112 A5
Rockland, *Canada* 117 A9
Rockland, *Idaho, U.S.A.* 108 E7
Rockland, *Maine, U.S.A.* 115 C11
Rockland, *Mich., U.S.A.* 112 B10
Rocklin, *U.S.A.* 110 G5
Rockly B., *Trin. & Tob.* 125 J16
Rockmart, *U.S.A.* 115 H3
Rockport, *Mass., U.S.A.* 117 D14
Rockport, *Mo., U.S.A.* 112 E7
Rockport, *Tex., U.S.A.* 113 L6
Rocksprings, *U.S.A.* 113 K4
Rockville, *Conn., U.S.A.* 117 E12
Rockville, *Md., U.S.A.* 114 F7
Rockwall, *U.S.A.* 113 J6
Rockwell City, *U.S.A.* 112 D7
Rockwood, *Canada* 116 C4
Rockwood, *Maine, U.S.A.* 115 C11
Rockwood, *Tenn., U.S.A.* 115 H3
Rocky Ford, *U.S.A.* 112 F3
Rocky Gully, *Australia* 93 F2
Rocky Harbour, *Canada* 105 C8
Rocky Island L., *Canada* 104 C3
Rocky Lane, *Canada* 102 B5
Rocky Mount, *U.S.A.* 115 H7
Rocky Mountain △, *U.S.A.* 108 F11
Rocky Mountain House, *Canada* . 102 C6
Rocky Mts., *N. Amer.* 108 G10
Rocky Point, *Namibia* 88 B2
Rocroi, *France* 19 C11
Rod, *Pakistan* 66 E3
Rødby, *Denmark* 11 K5
Rødbyhavn, *Denmark* 11 K5
Roddickton, *Canada* 105 B8
Rødding, *Denmark* 11 J3
Rødeby, *Sweden* 11 H9
Rødekro, *Denmark* 11 J3
Rodenkirchen, *Germany* 24 B4
Rodez, *France* 20 D6
Rodholívas, *Greece* 44 F7
Rodhópi □, *Greece* 45 E9
Rodhopoú, *Greece* 49 D5
Ródhos, *Greece* 49 C10
Ródhos ✈ (RHO), *Greece* 47 E10
Rodi Gargánico, *Italy* 41 G12
Rodna, *Romania* 29 C9
Rodnei, Munţii, *Romania* 29 C9
Rodney, *Canada* 116 D3
Rodney, C., *N.Z.* 91 G5
Rodniki, *Russia* 34 B5
Rodonit, Kepi i, *Albania* 44 E3
Rodriguez, *Ind. Oc.* 3 E13
Roe ➤, *U.K.* 12 A5
Roebel, *Germany* 24 B8
Roebling, *U.S.A.* 117 F10
Roebourne, *Australia* 92 D2
Roebuck B., *Australia* 92 C3
Roermond, *Neths.* 17 C6
Roes Welcome Sd., *Canada* 101 B11
Roeselare, *Belgium* 17 D3
Rogachev = Ragachow, *Belarus* . 33 F6
Rogagua, L., *Bolivia* 124 F5
Rogaška Slatina, *Slovenia* ... 41 B12
Rogatec, *Slovenia* 41 B12
Rogatica, *Bos.-H.* 28 G4
Rogatyn, *Ukraine* 33 H3
Rogdhia, *Greece* 49 D7
Rogers, *U.S.A.* 113 G7
Rogers City, *U.S.A.* 114 C4
Rogersville, *Canada* 105 C6
Roggan ➤, *Canada* 104 B4
Roggeveldberge, *S. Africa* ... 88 E3
Roggiano Gravina, *Italy* 43 C9
Rogliano, *France* 21 F13
Rogliano, *Italy* 43 C9
Rogoaguado, L., *Bolivia* 124 F5
Rogojampi, *Indonesia* 63 J17
Rogoźno, *Poland* 31 F3
Rogue ➤, *U.S.A.* 108 E1

Rohan, *France* 18 D4
Róhda, *Greece* 49 A3
Rohnert Park, *U.S.A.* 110 G4
Rohri, *Pakistan* 68 F3
Rohri Canal, *Pakistan* 68 F3
Rohtak, *India* 68 E7
Roi Et, *Thailand* 64 D4
Roja, *Latvia* 9 H20
Rojas, *Argentina* 126 C3
Rojiște, *Romania* 29 F8
Rojo, C., *Mexico* 119 C5
Rokan ➤, *Indonesia* 62 D2
Rokel ➤, *S. Leone* 82 D2
Rokiškis, *Lithuania* 9 J21
Rokitno, *Russia* 33 G8
Rokycany, *Czech Rep.* 26 B6
Rolândia, *Brazil* 127 A5
Rolla, *U.S.A.* 113 G9
Rolleston, *Australia* 94 C4
Rollingstone, *Australia* 94 B4
Rom, *Sudan* 81 F3
Rom, *Australia* 95 D4
Roma, *Italy* 41 G9
Roma, *Sweden* 11 G12
Roma, *U.S.A.* 113 M5
Roma Fiumicino ✈ (FCO), *Italy* . 41 G9
Romain C., *U.S.A.* 115 J6
Romaine, *Canada* 105 B7
Romaine ➤, *Canada* 105 B7
Roman, *Bulgaria* 44 C7
Roman, *Romania* 29 D11
Roman-Kosh, Gora, *Ukraine* ... 33 K8
Romanche ➤, *France* 21 C9
Romang, *Indonesia* 63 F7
Români, *Egypt* 74 E1
Romania ■, *Europe* 29 D10
Romanija, Bos.-H. 28 G3
Romano, Cayo, *Cuba* 120 B4
Romans-sur-Isère, *France* 21 C9
Romanshorn, *Switz.* 25 H5
Rombari, *Sudan* 81 G3
Romblon, *Phil.* 61 E5
Rome = Roma, *Italy* 41 G9
Rome, *Ga., U.S.A.* 115 H3
Rome, *N.Y., U.S.A.* 117 C9
Rome, *Pa., U.S.A.* 117 E8
Rometta, *Italy* 43 D8
Romilly-sur-Seine, *France* ... 19 D10
Romney, *U.S.A.* 114 F6
Romney Marsh, *U.K.* 15 F8
Romny, *Ukraine* 33 G7
Rømø, *Denmark* 11 J2
Romodan, *Ukraine* 33 G7
Romodanovo, *Russia* 34 C7
Romont, *Switz.* 25 J2
Romorantin-Lanthenay, *France* . 19 E8
Romsdalen, *Norway* 9 E12
Romsey, *U.K.* 15 G6
Ron, *Vietnam* 64 D6
Rona, *U.K.* 13 D3
Ronan, *U.S.A.* 108 C6
Roncador, Cayos, *Colombia* ... 120 D3
Roncador, Serra do, *Brazil* ... 125 F8
Ronciglione, *Italy* 41 F9
Ronco ➤, *Italy* 41 D9
Ronda, *Spain* 37 J5
Ronda, Serranía de, *Spain* ... 37 J5
Rondane, *Norway* 9 F13
Rondônia □, *Brazil* 124 F6
Rondonópolis, *Brazil* 125 G8
Rong, Koh, *Cambodia* 65 G4
Rong Jiang ➤, *China* 58 E7
Rong Xian, *Guangxi Zhuangzu,*
  China 59 F8
Rong Xian, *Sichuan, China* ... 58 C5
Rong'an, *China* 58 E7
Rongchang, *China* 58 C5
Ronge, L. la, *Canada* 103 B7
Rongjiang, *China* 58 E7
Rongshui, *China* 58 E7
Rønne, *Denmark* 11 J8
Ronne Ice Shelf, *Antarctica* .. 5 D18
Ronneby, *Sweden* 11 H9
Ronnebyån ➤, *Sweden* 11 H9
Rönneshytta, *Sweden* 11 F9
Ronsard, C., *Australia* 93 D1
Ronse, *Belgium* 17 D3
Roodepoort, *S. Africa* 89 D4
Roof Butte, *U.S.A.* 109 H9
Rooiboklaagte ➤, *Namibia* 88 C3
Roorkee, *India* 68 E7
Roosendaal, *Neths.* 17 C4
Roosevelt, *U.S.A.* 108 F8
Roosevelt ➤, *Brazil* 124 E6
Roosevelt, Mt., *Canada* 102 B3
Roosevelt I., *Antarctica* 5 D12
Ropczyce, *Poland* 31 H8
Roper ➤, *Australia* 94 A2
Roper Bar, *Australia* 94 A1
Roque Pérez, *Argentina* 126 D4
Roquefort, *France* 20 D3
Roquemaure, *France* 21 D8
Roquetas de Mar, *Spain* 39 J2
Roquetes, *Spain* 38 E5
Roquevaire, *France* 21 E9
Roraima □, *Brazil* 124 C6
Roraima, Mt., *Venezuela* 124 B6
Røros, *Norway* 9 E14
Rorschach, *Switz.* 25 H5
Rosa, *Zambia* 87 D3
Rosa, L., *Bahamas* 121 B5
Rosa, Monte, *Europe* 40 C4
Rosal de la Frontera, *Spain* .. 37 H3
Rosalia, *U.S.A.* 108 C5
Rosamond, *U.S.A.* 111 L8
Rosans, *France* 21 D9
Rosario, *Argentina* 126 C3
Rosário, *Brazil* 125 D10
Rosario, *Baja Calif., Mexico* . 118 B1
Rosario, *Sinaloa, Mexico* 118 C3
Rosario, *Paraguay* 126 A4

Rosario de la Frontera, *Argentina* 126 B3
Rosario de Lerma, *Argentina* 126 A2
Rosario del Tala, *Argentina* 126 C4
Rosário do Sul, *Brazil* 127 C5
Rosarito, *Mexico* 111 N9
Rosarno, *Italy* 43 D9
Rosas = Roses, *Spain* 38 C8
Roscoe, *U.S.A.* 117 E10
Roscoff, *France* 18 D3
Roscommon, *Ireland* 12 C3
Roscommon □, *Ireland* 12 C3
Roscrea, *Ireland* 12 D4
Rose →, *Australia* 94 A2
Rose Blanche-Harbour Le Cou,
    Canada 105 C8
Rose Pt., *Canada* 102 C2
Rose Valley, *Canada* 103 C8
Roseau, *Dominica* 121 C7
Roseau, *U.S.A.* 112 A7
Rosebery, *Australia* 95 G4
Rosebud, *S. Dak., U.S.A.* 112 D4
Rosebud, *Tex., U.S.A.* 113 K6
Roseburg, *U.S.A.* 108 E2
Rosedale, *U.S.A.* 113 J9
Rosehearty, *U.K.* 13 D6
Roseland, *U.S.A.* 110 G4
Rosemary, *Canada* 102 C6
Rosenberg, *U.S.A.* 113 L7
Rosendaël, *France* 19 A9
Rosenheim, *Germany* 25 H8
Roses, *Spain* 38 C8
Roses, G. de, *Spain* 38 C8
Roseto degli Abruzzi, *Italy* 41 F11
Rosetown, *Canada* 103 C7
Rosetta = Rashîd, *Egypt* 80 H7
Roseville, *Calif., U.S.A.* 110 G5
Roseville, *Mich., U.S.A.* 116 D2
Rosewood, *Australia* 95 D5
Roshkhvār, *Iran* 71 C8
Rosières-en-Santerre, *France* 19 C9
Rosignano Maríttimo, *Italy* 40 E7
Rosignol, *Guyana* 124 B7
Roşiori de Vede, *Romania* 29 F10
Rositsa, *Bulgaria* 45 C11
Rositsa →, *Bulgaria* 45 C9
Roskilde, *Denmark* 11 J6
Roskilde Amtskommune □,
    Denmark 11 J6
Roskovec, *Albania* 44 F3
Roslavl, *Russia* 32 F7
Rosmaninhal, *Portugal* 36 F3
Rosmead, *S. Africa* 88 E4
Røsnæs, *Denmark* 11 J4
Rosolini, *Italy* 43 F7
Rosporden, *France* 18 E3
Ross, *Australia* 95 G4
Ross, *N.Z.* 91 K3
Ross Béthio, *Mauritania* 82 B1
Ross Dependency, *Antarctica* 5 D12
Ross Ice Shelf, *Antarctica* 5 E12
Ross L., *U.S.A.* 108 B3
Ross-on-Wye, *U.K.* 15 F5
Ross River, *Australia* 94 C1
Ross River, *Canada* 102 A2
Ross Sea, *Antarctica* 5 D11
Rossall Pt., *U.K.* 14 D4
Rossan Pt., *Ireland* 12 B3
Rossano, *Italy* 43 C9
Rossburn, *Canada* 103 C8
Rosseau, *Canada* 116 A5
Rosseau, L., *Canada* 116 A5
Rosses, The, *Ireland* 12 A3
Rossignol, L., *Canada* 104 B5
Rossignol L., *Canada* 105 D6
Rossland, *Canada* 102 D5
Rosslare, *Ireland* 12 D5
Rosslare Harbour, *Ireland* 12 D5
Rosslau, *Germany* 24 D8
Rosso, *Mauritania* 82 B1
Rosso, C., *France* 21 F12
Rossosh, *Russia* 33 G10
Røssvatnet, *Norway* 8 D16
Røst, *Norway* 8 C15
Rosthern, *Canada* 103 C7
Rostock, *Germany* 24 A8
Rostov, *Don, Russia* 33 J10
Rostov, *Yaroslavl, Russia* 32 D10
Rostrenen, *France* 18 D3
Roswell, *Ga., U.S.A.* 115 H3
Roswell, *N. Mex., U.S.A.* 113 J2
Rota, *Spain* 37 J4
Rotan, *U.S.A.* 113 J4
Rotenburg, *Hessen, Germany* 24 E5
Rotenburg, *Niedersachsen,*
    Germany 24 B5
Roth, *Germany* 25 F7
Rothaargebirge, *Germany* 24 D4
Rothaargebirge ⌂, *Germany* 24 E4
Rothenburg ob der Tauber,
    Germany 25 F6
Rother →, *U.K.* 15 G8
Rothera, *Antarctica* 5 C17
Rotherham, *U.K.* 14 D6
Rothes, *U.K.* 13 D5
Rothesay, *Canada* 105 C6
Rothesay, *U.K.* 13 F3
Roti, *Indonesia* 63 F6
Rotja, Pta., *Spain* 39 G6
Roto, *Australia* 95 E4
Rotondo, Mte., *France* 21 F13
Rotoroa, L., *N.Z.* 91 J4
Rotorua, *N.Z.* 91 H6
Rotorua, L., *N.Z.* 91 H6
Rott →, *Germany* 25 G9
Rottenburg, *Germany* 25 G4
Rottenmann, *Austria* 26 D7
Rotterdam, *Neths.* 17 C4
Rotterdam, *U.S.A.* 117 D10
Rottne, *Sweden* 11 G8
Rottnest I., *Australia* 93 F2

Rottumeroog, *Neths.* 17 A6
Rottweil, *Germany* 25 G4
Rotuma, *Fiji* 96 J9
Roubaix, *France* 19 B10
Roudnice nad Labem, *Czech Rep.* 26 A7
Rouen, *France* 18 C8
Rouergue, *France* 20 D5
Rouillac, *France* 20 C3
Rouleau, *Canada* 103 C8
Round Mountain, *U.S.A.* 108 G5
Round Mt., *Australia* 95 E5
Round Rock, *U.S.A.* 113 K6
Roundup, *U.S.A.* 108 C9
Rousay, *U.K.* 13 B5
Rouses Point, *U.S.A.* 117 B11
Rouseville, *U.S.A.* 116 E5
Roussillon, *Isère, France* 21 C8
Roussillon, *Pyrénées-Or., France* 20 F6
Rouxville, *S. Africa* 88 E4
Rouyn-Noranda, *Canada* 104 C4
Rovaniemi, *Finland* 8 C21
Rovato, *Italy* 40 C7
Rovenki, *Ukraine* 33 H10
Rovereto, *Italy* 40 C8
Rovigo, *Italy* 41 C8
Rovinj, *Croatia* 41 C10
Rovno = Rivne, *Ukraine* 33 G4
Rovnoye, *Russia* 34 E8
Rovuma = Ruvuma →, *Tanzania* 87 E5
Row'ān, *Iran* 71 C6
Rowena, *Australia* 95 D4
Rowley Shoals, *Australia* 92 C2
Roxa, *Guinea-Biss.* 82 C1
Roxas, *Capiz, Phil.* 61 F5
Roxas, *Isabela, Phil.* 61 C4
Roxas, *Mind. Or., Phil.* 61 E4
Roxboro, *U.S.A.* 115 G6
Roxborough, *Trin. & Tob.* 125 J16
Roxburgh, *N.Z.* 91 L2
Roxbury, *U.S.A.* 116 F7
Roxen, *Sweden* 11 F9
Roy, *Mont., U.S.A.* 108 C9
Roy, *N. Mex., U.S.A.* 113 H2
Roy, *Utah, U.S.A.* 108 F7
Royal Canal, *Ireland* 12 C4
Royal Leamington Spa, *U.K.* 15 E6
Royal Natal ⌂, *S. Africa* 89 D4
Royal Tunbridge Wells, *U.K.* 15 F8
Royale, Isle, *U.S.A.* 112 B10
Royan, *France* 20 C2
Roye, *France* 19 C9
Royston, *U.K.* 15 E7
Rožaj, *Serbia & M.* 44 D4
Różan, *Poland* 31 F8
Rozay-en-Brie, *France* 19 D9
Rozdilna, *Ukraine* 29 D15
Rozhnyativ, *Ukraine* 29 B9
Rozhyshche, *Ukraine* 33 G3
Rožmitál pod Třemšínem,
    Czech Rep. 26 B6
Rožňava, *Slovak Rep.* 27 C13
Rozogi, *Poland* 30 E8
Rozoy-sur-Serre, *France* 19 C11
Roztoczański ⌂, *Poland* 31 H10
Rozzano, *Italy* 40 C6
Rrëshen, *Albania* 44 E3
Rrogozhinë, *Albania* 44 E3
Rtanj, *Serbia & M.* 44 C5
Rtishchevo, *Russia* 34 D6
Rúa = A Rúa, *Spain* 36 C3
Ruacaná, *Namibia* 88 B1
Ruaha △, *Tanzania* 86 D3
Ruahine Ra., *N.Z.* 91 H6
Ruapehu, *N.Z.* 91 H5
Ruapuke I., *N.Z.* 91 M2
Ruâq, W. →, *Egypt* 74 F2
Rub' al Khālī, *Si. Arabia* 75 D4
Rubeho Mts., *Tanzania* 86 D4
Rubezhnoye = Rubizhne, *Ukraine* 33 H10
Rubh a' Mhail, *U.K.* 13 F2
Rubha Hunish, *U.K.* 13 D2
Rubha Robhanais = Lewis, Butt
    of, *U.K.* 13 C2
Rubi, *Spain* 38 D7
Rubicon →, *U.S.A.* 110 G5
Rubicone →, *Italy* 41 D9
Rubino, *Ivory C.* 82 D4
Rubio, *Venezuela* 124 B4
Rubizhne, *Ukraine* 33 H10
Rubondo △, *Tanzania* 86 C3
Ruby L., *U.S.A.* 108 F6
Ruby Mts., *U.S.A.* 108 F6
Rubyvale, *Australia* 94 C4
Rucheng, *China* 59 E9
Ruciane-Nida, *Poland* 30 E8
Rūd Sar, *Iran* 71 B6
Ruda, *Sweden* 11 G10
Ruda Śląska, *Poland* 31 H5
Rudall, *Australia* 95 E2
Rudall →, *Australia* 92 D3
Rudall River △, *Australia* 92 D3
Rüdersdorf, *Germany* 24 C9
Rudewa, *Tanzania* 87 E3
Rudkøbing, *Denmark* 11 K4
Rudky, *Ukraine* 31 J10
Rudna, *Poland* 31 G3
Rudnik, *Bulgaria* 45 D11
Rudnik, *Poland* 31 H9
Rudnik, *Serbia & M.* 44 B4
Rudnya, *Russia* 32 E6
Rudnytsa, *Ukraine* 29 B13
Rudnyy, *Kazakhstan* 52 D7
Rudo, *Bos.-H.* 28 G4
Rudolf, Ostrov, *Russia* 52 A6
Rudolstadt, *Germany* 24 E7
Rudong, *China* 59 A13
Rudozem, *Bulgaria* 45 E8
Rudyard, *U.S.A.* 114 B3
Rue, *France* 19 B8

Ruenya →, *Africa* 87 F3
Rufa'a, *Sudan* 81 E3
Rufiji →, *Tanzania* 86 D4
Rufino, *Argentina* 126 C3
Rufisque, *Senegal* 82 C1
Rufling Pt., *Br. Virgin Is.* 121 e
Rufunsa, *Zambia* 87 F2
Rugao, *China* 59 A13
Rugby, *U.K.* 15 E6
Rugby, *U.S.A.* 112 A5
Rügen, *Germany* 24 A9
Rügen □, *Germany* 24 A9
Rugles, *France* 18 D7
Ruhengeri, *Rwanda* 86 C2
Ruhla, *Germany* 24 E6
Ruhland, *Germany* 24 D9
Ruhnu, *Estonia* 9 H20
Ruhr →, *Germany* 24 D2
Ruhuhu →, *Tanzania* 87 E3
Rui'an, *China* 59 D13
Ruichang, *China* 59 C10
Ruidoso, *U.S.A.* 109 K11
Ruijin, *China* 59 E10
Ruili, *China* 58 E1
Ruivo, Pico, *Madeira* 48 D3
Ruj, *Bulgaria* 44 D6
Rujen, *Macedonia* 44 D6
Rujm Tal'at al Jamā'ah, *Jordan* 74 E4
Ruk, *Pakistan* 68 F3
Rukhla, *Pakistan* 68 C5
Ruki →, *Dem. Rep. of the Congo* 84 E3
Rukwa □, *Tanzania* 86 D3
Rukwa, L., *Tanzania* 86 D3
Rulhieres, C., *Australia* 92 B4
Rum = Rhum, *U.K.* 13 E2
Rum, *Jordan* 74 F4
Rum Cay, *Bahamas* 121 B5
Rum Jungle, *Australia* 92 B5
Ruma, *Serbia & M.* 28 E4
Ruma △, *Kenya* 86 C3
Rumāḥ, *Si. Arabia* 70 E5
Rumania = Romania ■, *Europe* 29 D10
Rumaylah, *Iraq* 70 D5
Rumbek, *Sudan* 81 F2
Rumburk, *Czech Rep.* 26 A7
Rumford, *U.S.A.* 115 C10
Rumia, *Poland* 30 D5
Rumilly, *France* 21 C9
Rumoi, *Japan* 54 C10
Rumonge, *Burundi* 86 C2
Rumson, *U.S.A.* 117 F11
Rumuruti, *Kenya* 86 B4
Runan, *China* 56 H8
Runanga, *N.Z.* 91 K3
Runaway, C., *N.Z.* 91 G6
Runaway Bay, *Jamaica* 120 a
Runcorn, *U.K.* 14 D5
Rundu, *Namibia* 88 B2
Rungwa, *Tanzania* 86 D3
Rungwa →, *Tanzania* 86 D3
Rungwa, *Tanzania* 86 D3
Rungwe, *Tanzania* 87 D3
Rungwe, Mt., *Tanzania* 84 F6
Runka, *Nigeria* 83 C6
Runn, *Sweden* 10 D9
Runton Ra., *Australia* 92 D3
Ruokolahti, *Finland* 32 B5
Ruoqiang, *China* 60 C3
Rupa, *India* 67 F18
Rupar, *India* 68 D7
Rupat, *Indonesia* 62 D2
Rupea, *Romania* 29 D10
Rupen →, *India* 68 H4
Rupert, *U.S.A.* 108 E7
Rupert →, *Canada* 104 B4
Rupert B., *Canada* 104 B4
Rupert House = Waskaganish,
    Canada 104 B4
Rupsa, *India* 69 J12
Rur →, *Germany* 24 D1
Rurrenabaque, *Bolivia* 124 F5
Rus →, *Spain* 39 F2
Rusambo, *Zimbabwe* 87 F3
Rusape, *Zimbabwe* 87 F3
Ruschuk = Ruse, *Bulgaria* 45 C9
Ruse, *Bulgaria* 45 C9
Ruse □, *Bulgaria* 45 C10
Rusenski Lom →, *Bulgaria* 44 C7
Ruşeţu, *Romania* 29 F12
Rush, *Ireland* 12 C5
Rushan, *China* 57 F11
Rushden, *U.K.* 15 E7
Rushmore, Mt., *U.S.A.* 112 D3
Rushville, *Ill., U.S.A.* 112 E9
Rushville, *Ind., U.S.A.* 114 F3
Rushville, *Nebr., U.S.A.* 112 D3
Russas, *Brazil* 125 D11
Russell, *Canada* 103 C8
Russell, *Kans., U.S.A.* 112 F5
Russell, *N.Y., U.S.A.* 117 B9
Russell, *Pa., U.S.A.* 116 E5
Russell Cave △, *U.S.A.* 115 H3
Russell L., *Man., Canada* 103 B8
Russell L., *N.W.T., Canada* 102 A5
Russellkonda, *India* 67 K14
Russellville, *Ala., U.S.A.* 115 H2
Russellville, *Ark., U.S.A.* 113 H8
Russellville, *Ky., U.S.A.* 115 G2
Rüsselsheim, *Germany* 25 F4
Russi, *Italy* 41 D9
Russia ■, *Eurasia* 53 C11
Russian →, *U.S.A.* 110 G3
Russkoye Ustie, *Russia* 4 B15
Rust, *Austria* 27 D9
Rustam Shahr, *Pakistan* 68 F2
Rustavi, *Georgia* 35 K7
Rustenburg, *S. Africa* 88 D4
Ruston, *U.S.A.* 113 J8
Rutana, *Burundi* 86 C3
Rute, *Spain* 37 H6

Ruteng, *Indonesia* 63 F6
Ruth, *U.S.A.* 116 C2
Rutherford, *U.S.A.* 110 G4
Rutland, *U.S.A.* 117 C12
Rutland □, *U.K.* 15 E7
Rutland, *U.S.A.* 113 L5
Rutland Water, *U.K.* 15 E7
Rutledge →, *Canada* 103 A6
Rutledge L., *Canada* 103 A6
Rutqa, W. →, *Syria* 73 E9
Rutshuru, *Dem. Rep. of*
    the Congo 86 C2
Ruvo di Púglia, *Italy* 43 A9
Ruvu, *Tanzania* 86 D4
Ruvu →, *Tanzania* 86 D4
Ruvuba △, *Burundi* 86 C2
Ruvuma □, *Tanzania* 87 E4
Ruvuma →, *Tanzania* 87 E5
Ruwais, *U.A.E.* 71 E7
Ruwenzori, *Africa* 86 B2
Ruwenzori △, *Uganda* 86 B2
Ruya →, *Zimbabwe* 89 B5
Ruyigi, *Burundi* 86 C3
Ruyuan, *China* 59 E9
Ruzayevka, *Russia* 34 C7
Růzhevo Konare, *Bulgaria* 45 D8
Ružomberok, *Slovak Rep.* 27 B12
Ruzyne, Praha ✈ (PRG),
    Czech Rep. 26 A7
Rwanda ■, *Africa* 86 C3
Ryakhovo, *Bulgaria* 45 C10
Ryan, L., *U.K.* 13 G3
Ryazan, *Russia* 32 E10
Ryazhsk, *Russia* 32 F11
Rybache = Rybachye, *Kazakhstan* 52 E9
Rybachiy, *Russia* 30 C7
Rybachye, *Kazakhstan* 52 E9
Rybinsk, *Russia* 32 C10
Rybinskoye Vdkhr., *Russia* 32 C10
Rybnik, *Poland* 31 H5
Rybnitsa = Râbnița, *Moldova* 29 C14
Rybnoye, *Russia* 32 E10
Rychnov nad Kněžnou,
    Czech Rep. 27 A9
Rychwał, *Poland* 31 F5
Rycroft, *Canada* 102 B5
Ryd, *Sweden* 11 H8
Rydaholm, *Sweden* 11 H8
Ryde, *U.K.* 15 G6
Ryderwood, *U.S.A.* 110 D3
Rydzyna, *Poland* 31 G3
Rye, *U.K.* 15 G8
Rye →, *U.K.* 14 C7
Rye Bay, *U.K.* 15 G8
Rye Patch Reservoir, *U.S.A.* 108 F4
Ryegate, *U.S.A.* 108 C9
Ryki, *Poland* 31 G8
Ryley, *Canada* 102 C6
Rylsk, *Russia* 33 G8
Rylstone, *Australia* 95 E4
Rymanów, *Poland* 31 J8
Ryn, *Poland* 30 E8
Ryn Peski, *Kazakhstan* 35 G9
Ryōtsu, *Japan* 54 E9
Rypin, *Poland* 31 E6
Ryssby, *Sweden* 11 H8
Rysy, *Europe* 27 B13
Ryūgasaki, *Japan* 55 G10
Ryūkyū Is. = Ryūkyū-rettō, *Japan* 55 M3
Ryūkyū-rettō, *Japan* 55 M3
Rzepin, *Poland* 31 F1
Rzeszów, *Poland* 31 H8
Rzhev, *Russia* 32 D8

S

Sa, *Thailand* 64 C3
Sa Canal, *Spain* 48 C7
Sa Conillera, *Spain* 48 C7
Sa Dec, *Vietnam* 65 G5
Sa Dragonera, *Spain* 48 B9
Sa Mesquida, *Spain* 48 B11
Sa Pobla, *Spain* 38 F8
Sa Savina, *Spain* 48 C7
Sa'ādatābād, *Fārs, Iran* 71 D7
Sa'ādatābād, *Hormozgān, Iran* 71 D7
Sa'ādatābād, *Kermān, Iran* 71 D7
Saale →, *Germany* 24 D7
Saaler Bodden, *Germany* 24 A8
Saalfeld, *Germany* 24 E7
Saalfelden, *Austria* 26 D5
Saane →, *Switz.* 25 H3
Saanich, *Canada* 110 B3
Saar →, *Europe* 17 E6
Saar-Hunsrück △, *Germany* 25 F2
Saarbrücken, *Germany* 25 F2
Saarburg, *Germany* 25 F2
Saaremaa, *Estonia* 9 G20
Saarijärvi, *Finland* 9 E21
Saariselkä, *Finland* 8 B23
Saarland □, *Germany* 25 F2
Saarlouis, *Germany* 25 F2
Sab 'Abar, *Syria* 70 C3
Saba, *W. Indies* 121 C7
Šabac, *Serbia & M.* 44 B3
Sabadell, *Spain* 38 D7
Sabah □, *Malaysia* 62 C5
Sabak Bernam, *Malaysia* 65 L3
Sabalān, Kūhhā-ye, *Iran* 70 B5
Sabalana, Kepulauan, *Indonesia* 63 F5
Sábana de la Mar, *Dom. Rep.* 121 C6
Sábanalarga, *Colombia* 124 A4
Sabang, *Indonesia* 62 C1
Săbăoani, *Romania* 29 C11
Sabará, *Brazil* 125 G10
Sabarmati →, *India* 68 H5
Sabattis, *U.S.A.* 117 B10
Sabáudia, *Italy* 42 A6
Saberania, *Indonesia* 63 E9

Sabhah, *Libya* 79 C8
Sabi →, *India* 68 E7
Sabidana, J., *Sudan* 80 D4
Sabie, *S. Africa* 89 D5
Sabinal, *Mexico* 118 A3
Sabinal, *U.S.A.* 113 L5
Sabiñánigo, *Spain* 38 C4
Sabinar, Punta del, *Spain* 39 J2
Sabinas, *Mexico* 118 B4
Sabinas →, *Mexico* 118 B4
Sabinas Hidalgo, *Mexico* 118 B4
Sabine →, *U.S.A.* 113 L8
Sabine L., *U.S.A.* 113 L8
Sabine Pass, *U.S.A.* 113 L8
Sabinov, *Slovak Rep.* 27 B14
Sabinsville, *U.S.A.* 116 E7
Sabirabad, *Azerbaijan* 35 K9
Sablayan, *Phil.* 61 E4
Sable, *Canada* 105 A6
Sable, C., *Canada* 105 D6
Sable, C., *U.S.A.* 107 E10
Sable I., *Canada* 105 D8
Sablé-sur-Sarthe, *France* 18 E6
Sabonkafi, *Niger* 83 C6
Sabor →, *Portugal* 36 D3
Sabou, *Burkina Faso* 82 C4
Sabres, *France* 20 D3
Sabrina Coast, *Antarctica* 5 C9
Sabugal, *Portugal* 36 E3
Sabulubbek, *Indonesia* 62 E1
Sabuncu, *Turkey* 47 B12
Sabzevār, *Iran* 71 B8
Sabzvārān, *Iran* 71 D8
Sac City, *U.S.A.* 112 D7
Sacedón, *Spain* 38 E2
Săcele, *Romania* 29 E10
Sachigo →, *Canada* 104 A2
Sachigo, L., *Canada* 104 B1
Sachkhere, *Georgia* 35 J6
Sachsen □, *Germany* 24 E9
Sachsen-Anhalt □, *Germany* 24 D7
Sächsische Schweiz △, *Germany* 24 E10
Sacile, *Italy* 41 C9
Sackets Harbor, *U.S.A.* 117 C8
Sackville, *Canada* 105 C7
Saco, *Maine, U.S.A.* 115 D10
Saco, *Mont., U.S.A.* 108 B10
Sacramento, *U.S.A.* 110 G5
Sacramento →, *U.S.A.* 110 G5
Sacramento Mts., *U.S.A.* 109 K11
Sacramento Valley, *U.S.A.* 110 G5
Sacratif, C., *Spain* 37 J7
Săcueni, *Romania* 28 C7
Sada, *Spain* 36 B2
Sada-Misaki, *Japan* 55 H6
Sádaba, *Spain* 38 C3
Sadabad, *India* 68 F8
Sadani, *Tanzania* 86 D4
Sadao, *Thailand* 65 J3
Sadd el Aali, *Egypt* 80 C3
Saddle Mt., *U.S.A.* 110 E3
Sade, *Nigeria* 83 C7
Sadimi, *Dem. Rep. of the Congo* 87 D1
Sadiola, *Mali* 82 C2
Sa'dīyah, Hawr as, *Iraq* 73 F12
Sado, *Japan* 54 F9
Sado →, *Portugal* 37 G2
Sadon, *Burma* 67 G20
Sadon, *Russia* 35 J6
Sadovoye, *Russia* 35 G7
Sadra, *India* 68 H5
Sadri, *India* 68 G5
Saeby, *Denmark* 11 G4
Saegertown, *U.S.A.* 116 E4
Saelices, *Spain* 38 F2
Safaalan, *Turkey* 45 E12
Safaga, *Egypt* 80 B3
Şafājah, *Si. Arabia* 70 E3
Šafárikovo = Tornal'a,
    Slovak Rep. 27 C13
Säffle, *Sweden* 10 E6
Safford, *U.S.A.* 109 K9
Saffron Walden, *U.K.* 15 E8
Safi, *Morocco* 78 B4
Şafīābād, *Iran* 71 B8
Safid Dasht, *Iran* 71 C6
Safid Kūh, *Afghan.* 66 B3
Safid Rūd →, *Iran* 71 B6
Safipur, *India* 69 F9
Safonovo, *Russia* 32 E7
Safranbolu, *Turkey* 72 B5
Saft Rashîn, *Egypt* 80 J7
Şafwān, *Iraq* 70 D5
Sag Harbor, *U.S.A.* 117 F12
Saga □, *Japan* 55 H5
Saga, *Japan* 55 H5
Sagae, *Japan* 54 E10
Sagala, *Mali* 82 C3
Sagamartha = Everest, Mt., *Nepal* 69 E12
Sagamore, *U.S.A.* 116 F5
Sagar, *Karnataka, India* 66 M9
Sagar, *Mad. P., India* 69 H8
Sagara, L., *Tanzania* 86 D3
Sagay, *Phil.* 61 F5
Saginaw, *U.S.A.* 114 D4
Saginaw →, *U.S.A.* 114 D4
Saginaw B., *U.S.A.* 114 D4
Sagleipie, *Liberia* 82 D3
Saglouc = Salluit, *Canada* 101 B12
Sagŏ-ri, *S. Korea* 57 G14
Sagone, *France* 21 F12
Sagone, G. de, *France* 21 F12
Sagres, *Portugal* 37 J2
Sagua la Grande, *Cuba* 120 B3
Saguache, *U.S.A.* 109 G10
Saguaro △, *U.S.A.* 109 K8
Saguenay →, *Canada* 105 C6
Sagunt, *Spain* 38 F4
Sagunto = Sagunt, *Spain* 38 F4
Sagwara, *India* 68 H6
Sahaba, *Sudan* 80 D3

Sahagún, *Spain* 36 C5
Saham al Jawlān, *Syria* 74 C4
Sahamandrevo, *Madag.* 89 C8
Sahand, Kūh-e, *Iran* 70 B5
Sahara, *Africa* 78 D6
Saharan Atlas = Saharien, Atlas,
  Algeria 78 B6
Saharanpur, *India* 68 E7
Saharien, Atlas, *Algeria* 78 B6
Saharsa, *India* 69 G12
Sahasinaka, *Madag.* 89 C8
Sahaswan, *India* 69 E8
Sahel, *Africa* 78 E5
Sahel, Canal du, *Mali* 82 C3
Sahibganj, *India* 69 G12
Sāḥiliyah, *Iraq* 70 C4
Sahiwal, *Pakistan* 68 D5
Ṣahneh, *Iran* 70 C5
Sahrawi = Western Sahara ■,
  Africa 78 D3
Sahuaripa, *Mexico* 118 B3
Sahuarita, *U.S.A.* 109 L8
Sahuayo, *Mexico* 118 C4
Šahy, *Slovak Rep.* 27 C11
Sai ➤, *India* 69 G10
Sai Buri, *Thailand* 65 J3
Sa'id Bundas, *Sudan* 79 G10
Sa'īdābād = Sīrjān, *Iran* 71 D7
Sa'īdābād, *Iran* 71 B7
Sa'īdīyeh, *Iran* 71 B6
Saidpur, *Bangla.* 67 G16
Saidpur, *India* 69 G10
Saidu, *Pakistan* 69 B5
Saignes, *France* 20 C6
Saigon = Thanh Pho Ho Chi
  Minh, *Vietnam* 65 G6
Saijō, *Japan* 55 H6
Saikai △, *Japan* 55 H4
Saikanosy Masoala, *Madag.* ... 89 B9
Saikhoa Ghat, *India* 67 F19
Saiki, *Japan* 55 H5
Sailana, *India* 68 H6
Saillans, *France* 21 D9
Sailolof, *Indonesia* 63 E8
Saimaa, *Finland* 9 F23
Saimbeyli, *Turkey* 72 D7
Saimen = Saimaa, *Finland* 9 F23
Ṣa'in Dezh, *Iran* 70 B5
St. Abb's Head, *U.K.* 13 F6
St-Affrique, *France* 20 E6
St-Agrève, *France* 21 C8
St-Aignan, *France* 18 E8
St. Alban's, *Canada* 105 C8
St. Albans, *U.K.* 15 F7
St. Albans, Vt., *U.S.A.* 117 B11
St. Albans, W. Va., *U.S.A.* ... 114 F5
St. Alban's Head, *U.K.* 15 G5
St. Albert, *Canada* 102 C6
St-Amand-en-Puisaye, *France* . 19 E10
St-Amand-les-Eaux, *France* ... 19 B10
St-Amand-Montrond, *France* ... 19 F9
St-Amarin, *France* 19 E14
St-Amour, *France* 19 F12
St-André-de-Cubzac, *France* .. 20 D3
St-André-les-Alpes, *France* .. 21 E10
St. Andrew's, *Canada* 105 C8
St. Andrews, *U.K.* 13 E6
St-Anicet, *Canada* 117 A10
St. Anns B., *Canada* 105 C7
St. Ann's Bay, *Jamaica* ...... 120 a
St. Anthony, *Canada* 105 B8
St. Anthony, *U.S.A.* 108 E8
St-Antoine, *Canada* 105 C7
St-Antonin-Noble-Val, *France* . 20 D5
St. Arnaud, *Australia* 95 F3
St-Astier, *France* 20 C4
St-Aubin-du-Cormier, *France* . 18 D5
St-Augustin, *Canada* 105 B8
St-Augustin ➤, *Canada* 105 B8
St. Augustine, *U.S.A.* 115 L5
St-Aulaye, *France* 20 C4
St. Austell, *U.K.* 15 G3
St-Avold, *France* 19 C13
St. Barbe, *Canada* 105 B8
St-Barthélemy, *W. Indies* 121 C7
St-Béat, *France* 20 F4
St. Bees Hd., *U.K.* 14 C4
St. Bees I., *Australia* 94 J7
St-Benoît-du-Sault, *France* .. 20 B5
St-Bonnet-en-Champsaur, *France* 21 D10
St-Brevin-les-Pins, *France* .. 18 E4
St-Brice-en-Coglès, *France* .. 18 D5
St. Bride's, *Canada* 105 C9
St. Brides B., *U.K.* 15 F2
St-Brieuc, *France* 18 D4
St-Calais, *France* 18 E7
St-Cast-le-Guildo, *France* ... 18 D4
St. Catharines, *Canada* 116 C5
St. Catherines I., *U.S.A.* ... 115 K5
St. Catherine's Pt., *U.K.* ... 15 G6
St-Céré, *France* 20 D5
St-Cergue, *Switz.* 25 J2
St-Cernin, *France* 20 C6
St-Chamond, *France* 21 C8
St. Charles, Ill., *U.S.A.* ... 114 E1
St. Charles, Mo., *U.S.A.* 112 F9
St. Charles, Va., *U.S.A.* 114 F7
St-Chély-d'Apcher, *France* ... 20 D7
St-Chinian, *France* 20 E6
St. Christopher-Nevis = St. Kitts
  & Nevis ■, *W. Indies* 121 C7
St-Ciers-sur-Gironde, *France* . 20 C3
St. Clair, Mich., *U.S.A.* 116 D2
St. Clair, Pa., *U.S.A.* 117 F8
St. Clair ➤, *U.S.A.* 116 D2
St. Clair, L., *Canada* 104 D3
St. Clair, L., *U.S.A.* 116 D2
St. Clairsville, *U.S.A.* 116 F4
St-Claud, *France* 20 C4
St. Claude, *Canada* 103 D9
St-Claude, *France* 19 F12

St. Clears, *U.K.* 15 F3
St-Clet, *Canada* 117 A10
St. Cloud, Fla., *U.S.A.* 115 L5
St. Cloud, Minn., *U.S.A.* 112 C7
St. Cricq, C., *Australia* 93 E1
St. Croix, *U.S. Virgin Is.* .. 121 C7
St. Croix ➤, *U.S.A.* 112 C8
St. Croix Falls, *U.S.A.* 112 C8
St-Cyprien, *France* 20 F7
St-Cyr-sur-Mer, *France* 21 E9
St. David's, *Canada* 105 C8
St. David's, *U.K.* 15 F2
St. David's Head, *U.K.* 15 F2
St-Denis, *France* 19 D9
St-Dié, *France* 19 D13
St-Dizier, *France* 19 D11
St-Égrève, *France* 21 C9
St. Elias, Mt., *U.S.A.* 100 B5
St. Elias Mts., *N. Amer.* 102 A1
St-Éloy-les-Mines, *France* ... 19 F9
St-Émilion, *France* 20 D3
St-Étienne, *France* 21 C8
St-Étienne-de-Tinée, *France* . 21 D10
St-Étienne-du-Rouvray, *France* 18 C8
St. Eugène, *Canada* 117 A10
St. Eustatius, *W. Indies* 121 C7
St-Exupery, Lyon ✈ (LYS),
  France 21 C9
St-Fargeau, *France* 19 E10
St-Félicien, *Canada* 104 C5
St-Florent, *France* 21 F13
St-Florent, G. de, *France* ... 21 F13
St-Florent-sur-Cher, *France* . 19 F9
St-Florentin, *France* 19 E10
St-Flour, *France* 20 C7
St. Francis, *Canada* 112 F4
St. Francis ➤, *U.S.A.* 113 H9
St. Francis, C., *S. Africa* .. 88 E3
St. Francisville, *U.S.A.* 113 K9
St-François, L., *Canada* 117 A10
St-Fulgent, *France* 18 F5
St-Gabriel, *Canada* 104 C5
St. Gallen = Sankt Gallen, *Switz.* 25 H5
St-Galmier, *France* 19 G11
St-Gaudens, *France* 20 E4
St-Gaultier, *France* 18 F8
St-Gengoux-le-National, *France* . 19 F11
St-Geniez-d'Olt, *France* 20 D6
St. George, *Australia* 95 D4
St. George, *Canada* 105 C6
St. George, S.C., *U.S.A.* 115 J5
St. George, Utah, *U.S.A.* 109 H7
St. George, C., *Canada* 105 C8
St. George, C., *U.S.A.* 115 L3
St. George Ra., *Australia* ... 92 C4
St. George's, *Canada* 105 C8
St-Georges, *Canada* 105 C5
St. George's, *Grenada* 121 D7
St. George's, *Canada* 105 C8
St. Georges Basin, N.S.W.,
  Australia 95 F5
St. Georges Basin, W. Austral.,
  Australia 92 C4
St. George's Channel, *Europe* . 12 E6
St. Georges Hd., *Australia* .. 95 F5
St-Georges-lès-Baillargeaux,
  France 20 B4
St-Germain-de-Calberte, *France* 20 D7
St-Germain-en-Laye, *France* .. 19 D9
St-Germain-Lembron, *France* .. 20 C7
St-Gervais-d'Auvergne, *France* . 19 F9
St-Gervais-les-Bains, *France* . 21 C10
St-Gildas, Pte. de, *France* .. 18 E4
St-Gilles, *France* 21 E8
St-Girons, Ariège, *France* ... 20 F5
St-Girons, Landes, *France* ... 20 E2
St. Gotthard P. = San Gottardo, P.
  del, *Switz.* 25 J4
St. Helena, Atl. Oc. 76 H3
St. Helena, *U.S.A.* 108 G2
St. Helena, Mt., *U.S.A.* 110 G4
St. Helena B., *S. Africa* 88 E2
St. Helens, *Australia* 95 G4
St. Helens, *U.K.* 14 D5
St. Helens, *U.S.A.* 110 E4
St. Helens, Mt., *U.S.A.* 110 D4
St. Helier, *U.K.* 15 H5
St-Herblain, *France* 18 E5
St-Hilaire-du-Harcouët, *France* 18 D5
St-Hippolyte, *France* 19 E13
St-Hippolyte-du-Fort, *France* . 20 E7
St-Honoré-les-Bains, *France* . 19 F10
St-Hubert, *Belgium* 17 D5
St-Hyacinthe, *Canada* 104 C5
St. Ignace, *U.S.A.* 114 C3
St. Ignace I., *Canada* 104 C2
St. Ignatius, *U.S.A.* 108 C6
St-Imier, *Switz.* 25 H2
St. Ives, Cambs., *U.K.* 15 E7
St. Ives, Corn., *U.K.* 15 G2
St-James, *France* 18 D5
St. James, *U.S.A.* 112 D7
St-Jean, *Canada* 105 B7
St-Jean, L., *Canada* 105 C5
St-Jean-d'Angély, *France* 20 C3
St-Jean-de-Braye, *France* 19 E8
St-Jean-de-Luz, *France* 20 E2
St-Jean-de-Maurienne, *France* . 21 C10
St-Jean-de-Monts, *France* 18 F4
St-Jean-du-Gard, *France* 20 D7
St-Jean-en-Royans, *France* ... 21 C9
St-Jean-Pied-de-Port, *France* . 20 E2
St-Jean-Port-Joli, *Canada* ... 105 C5
St-Jean-sur-Richelieu, *Canada* . 117 A11
St-Jérôme, *Canada* 104 C5
St. John, *Canada* 105 C6
St. John ➤, *Canada* 105 C6
St. John ➤, *Liberia* 82 D2
St. John, C., *Canada* 105 C8
St. John I., *U.S. Virgin Is.* . 121 e

St. John's, Antigua & B. 121 C7
St. John's, *Canada* 105 C9
St. Johns, Ariz., *U.S.A.* 109 J9
St. Johns, Mich., *U.S.A.* 114 D3
St. Johns ➤, *U.S.A.* 115 K5
St. John's Pt., *Ireland* 12 B3
St. Johnsbury, *U.S.A.* 117 B12
St. Johnsville, *U.S.A.* 117 D10
St-Joseph, *Martinique* .... 120 c
St. Joseph, La., *U.S.A.* 113 K9
St. Joseph, Mo., *U.S.A.* 112 F7
St. Joseph ➤, *U.S.A.* 114 D2
St. Joseph, I., *Canada* 104 C3
St. Joseph, L., *Canada* 104 B1
St-Jovite, *Canada* 104 C5
St-Juéry, *France* 20 E6
St-Julien-Chapteuil, *France* . 21 C8
St-Julien-de-Vouvantes, *France* 18 E5
St-Julien-en-Genevois, *France* 19 F13
St-Junien, *France* 20 C4
St-Just-en-Chaussée, *France* . 19 C9
St-Just-en-Chevalet, *France* . 20 C7
St. Kitts & Nevis ■, *W. Indies* . 121 C7
St. Laurent, *Canada* 103 C9
St-Laurent-de-la-Salanque,
  France 20 F6
St-Laurent-du-Pont, *France* .. 21 C9
St-Laurent-en-Grandvaux, *France* 19 F12
St-Laurent-Médoc, *France* 20 C3
St. Lawrence, *Australia* 94 C4
St. Lawrence, *Canada* 105 C8
St. Lawrence ➤, *Canada* 105 C6
St. Lawrence, Gulf of, *Canada* . 105 C7
St. Lawrence I., *U.S.A.* 100 B3
St. Lawrence Islands △, *Canada* . 117 B9
St. Leonard, *Canada* 105 C6
St-Léonard-de-Noblat, *France* . 20 C5
St. Lewis ➤, *Canada* 105 B8
St-Lô, *France* 18 C5
St-Louis, *France* 19 E14
St. Louis, *Guadeloupe* .... 120 b
St. Louis, *Senegal* 82 B1
St. Louis, *U.S.A.* 112 F9
St. Louis ➤, *U.S.A.* 112 B8
St-Loup-sur-Semouse, *France* . 19 E13
St. Lucia ■, *W. Indies* ...... 121 f
St. Lucia, L., *S. Africa* 89 D5
St. Lucia Channel, *W. Indies* . 121 D7
St. Maarten ☑, *W. Indies* 121 C7
St. Magnus B., *U.K.* 13 A7
St-Maixent-l'École, *France* .. 20 B3
St-Malo, *France* 18 D4
St-Malo, G. de, *France* 18 D4
St-Mandrier-sur-Mer, *France* . 21 E9
St-Marc, *Haiti* 121 C5
St-Marcellin, *France* 21 C9
St-Marcouf, Îs., *France* 18 C5
St. Maries, *U.S.A.* 108 C5
St-Martin ☑, *W. Indies* 121 C7
St. Martin, C., *Martinique* .. 120 c
St. Martin, L., *Canada* 103 C9
St-Martin-de-Crau, *France* ... 21 E8
St-Martin-de-Ré, *France* 20 B2
St-Martin-d'Hères, *France* ... 21 C9
St-Martin-Vésubie, *France* ... 21 D11
St. Martins, *Barbados* .... 121 g
St-Martory, *France* 20 E4
St. Mary Pk., *Australia* 95 E2
St. Marys, *Australia* 95 G4
St. Marys, *Canada* 116 C3
St. Mary's, Corn., *U.K.* 15 H1
St. Mary's, Orkney, *U.K.* 13 C6
St. Marys, Ga., *U.S.A.* 115 K5
St. Marys, Pa., *U.S.A.* 116 E6
St. Mary's, C., *Canada* 105 C9
St. Mary's B., *Canada* 105 C9
St. Marys Bay, *Canada* 105 D6
St-Mathieu, Pte., *France* 18 D2
St. Matthew I., *U.S.A.* 100 B3
St-Maurice ➤, *Canada* 104 C5
St. Mawes, *U.K.* 15 G2
St-Maximin-la-Ste-Baume, *France* 21 E9
St-Médard-en-Jalles, *France* . 20 D3
St-Méen-le-Grand, *France* 18 D4
St-Mihiel, *France* 19 D12
St. Moritz, *Switz.* 25 J5
St-Nazaire, *France* 18 E4
St. Neots, *U.K.* 15 E7
St-Nicolas-de-Port, *France* .. 19 D13
St-Niklaas, *Belgium* 17 C4
St-Omer, *France* 19 B9
St-Palais-sur-Mer, *France* ... 20 C2
St-Pamphile, *Canada* 105 C6
St-Pardoux-la-Rivière, *France* . 20 C4
St-Pascal, *Canada* 105 C6
St. Paul, *Canada* 102 C6
St. Paul, *France* 21 D10
St. Paul, Minn., *U.S.A.* 112 C8
St. Paul, Nebr., *U.S.A.* 112 E5
St. Paul ➤, *Canada* 105 B8
St. Paul ➤, *Liberia* 82 D2
St. Paul, I., *Ind. Oc.* 3 F13
St-Paul-de-Fenouillet, *France* . 20 F6
St. Paul I., *Canada* 105 C7
St-Paul-lès-Dax, *France* 20 E2
St-Péray, *France* 21 D8
St. Peter, *U.S.A.* 112 C8
St-Peter-Ording, *Germany* 24 A4
St. Peter Port, *U.K.* 15 H5
St. Peters, N.S., *Canada* 105 C7
St. Peters, P.E.I., *Canada* .. 105 C7
St. Petersburg = Sankt-Peterburg,
  Russia 32 C6
St. Petersburg, *U.S.A.* 115 M4
St-Philbert-de-Grand-Lieu,
  France 18 E5
St-Pie, *Canada* 117 A12
St-Pierre, *Martinique* .... 120 c
St-Pierre, St-P. & M. 105 C8
St-Pierre, L., *Canada* 104 C5
St-Pierre-d'Oléron, *France* .. 20 C2

St-Pierre-en-Port, *France* ... 18 C7
St-Pierre-et-Miquelon ☑,
  N. Amer. 105 C8
St-Pierre-le-Moûtier, *France* . 19 F10
St-Pierre-sur-Dives, *France* . 18 C6
St-Pol-de-Léon, *France* 18 D3
St-Pol-sur-Mer, *France* 19 A9
St-Pol-sur-Ternoise, *France* . 19 B9
St-Pons, *France* 20 E6
St-Pourçain-sur-Sioule, *France* 19 F10
St-Priest, *France* 21 C8
St-Quay-Portrieux, *France* ... 18 D4
St-Quentin, *Canada* 105 C6
St-Quentin, *France* 19 C10
St-Rambert-d'Albon, *France* .. 21 C8
St-Raphaël, *France* 21 E10
St. Regis, *U.S.A.* 108 C6
St-Renan, *France* 18 D2
St-Saëns, *France* 18 C8
St-Savin, *France* 20 B4
St-Savinien, *France* 20 C3
St. Sebastien, Tanjon' i, *Madag.* 89 A8
St-Seine-l'Abbaye, *France* ... 19 E11
St-Sernin-sur-Rance, *France* . 20 E6
St-Sever, *France* 20 E3
St-Siméon, *Canada* 105 C6
St-Sulpice, *France* 20 E5
St-Sulpice-Laurière, *France* . 20 B5
St-Sulpice-les-Feuilles, *France* 20 B5
St-Syprien = St-Cyprien, *France* . 20 F7
St-Thégonnec, *France* 18 D3
St. Thomas, *Canada* 116 D3
St. Thomas I., *U.S. Virgin Is.* 121 e
St-Tite, *Canada* 104 C5
St-Tropez, *France* 21 E10
St-Troud = St. Truiden, *Belgium* 17 D5
St. Truiden, *Belgium* 17 D5
St-Vaast-la-Hougue, *France* .. 18 C5
St-Valery-en-Caux, *France* ... 18 C7
St-Valéry-sur-Somme, *France* . 19 B8
St-Vallier, *France* 19 F11
St-Vallier-de-Thiey, *France* . 21 E10
St-Varent, *France* 18 F6
St-Vaury, *France* 20 B5
St. Vincent, *Italy* 40 C4
St-Vincent, G., *Australia* ... 95 F2
St. Vincent & the Grenadines ■,
  W. Indies 121 D7
St-Vincent-de-Tyrosse, *France* . 20 E2
St. Vincent Passage, *W. Indies* . 121 D7
St-Vith, *Belgium* 17 D6
St-Vivien-de-Médoc, *France* .. 20 C2
St. Walburg, *Canada* 103 C7
St-Yrieix-la-Perche, *France* . 20 C5
Ste-Adresse, *France* 18 C7
Ste-Agathe-des-Monts, *Canada* . 104 C5
Ste-Anne, *Guadeloupe* .... 120 b
Ste-Anne, L., *Canada* 105 B6
Ste-Anne-des-Monts-Tourelle,
  Canada 105 C6
Ste-Croix, *Switz.* 25 J2
Ste-Enimie, *France* 20 D7
Ste-Foy-la-Grande, *France* ... 20 D4
Ste. Genevieve, *U.S.A.* 112 G9
Ste-Hermine, *France* 20 B2
Ste-Livrade-sur-Lot, *France* . 20 D4
Ste-Marguerite ➤, *Canada* 105 B6
Ste-Marie, *Canada* 105 C5
Ste-Marie, *Martinique* .... 120 c
Ste-Marie-aux-Mines, *France* . 19 D14
Ste-Maure-de-Touraine, *France* 18 E7
Ste-Maxime, *France* 21 E10
Ste-Menehould, *France* 19 C11
Ste-Mère-Église, *France* 18 C5
Ste-Rose, *Guadeloupe* .... 120 b
Ste. Rose du Lac, *Canada* 103 C9
Saintes, *France* 20 C3
Saintes, Îs. des, *Guadeloupe* . 120 b
Stes-Maries-de-la-Mer, *France* 21 E8
Saintfield, *U.K.* 12 B6
Saintonge, *France* 20 C3
Saipan, *Pac. Oc.* 96 F6
Sairang, *India* 67 H18
Sairecábur, Cerro, *Bolivia* .. 126 A2
Saitama □, *Japan* 55 F9
Saiteli = Kadınhanı, *Turkey* . 72 C5
Saiţi, *Moldova* 29 D14
Saiyid, *Pakistan* 68 C5
Saja-Besaya △, *Spain* 36 B6
Sajama, *Bolivia* 124 G5
Sajan, *Serbia & M.* 28 E5
Sajó ➤, *Hungary* 28 C6
Sajószentpéter, *Hungary* 28 B5
Sajum, *India* 69 C8
Sak ➤, *S. Africa* 88 E3
Sakaba, *Nigeria* 83 C6
Sakai, *Japan* 55 G7
Sakaide, *Japan* 55 G6
Sakaiminato, *Japan* 55 G6
Sakākah, Si. Arabia 70 D4
Sakakawea, L., *U.S.A.* 112 B4
Sakami ➤, *Canada* 104 B4
Sakami, L., *Canada* 104 B4
Sâkâne, 'Erg i-n, *Mali* 83 A4
Sakania, Dem. Rep. of the Congo 87 E2
Sakaraha, *Madag.* 89 C7
Sakarya, *Turkey* 72 B4
Sakarya ➤, *Turkey* 72 B4
Sakashima-Guntō, *Japan* 55 M2
Sakata, *Japan* 54 E9
Sakchu, N. Korea 57 D13
Sakeny ➤, *Madag.* 89 C8
Sakété, *Benin* 83 D5
Sakha □, *Russia* 53 C13
Sakhalin, *Russia* 53 D15

Sakhalinskiy Zaliv, *Russia* .. 53 D15
Şaki, Azerbaijan 35 K8
Šakiai, *Lithuania* 9 J20
Sakon Nakhon, *Thailand* 64 D5
Sakrand, *Pakistan* 68 F3
Sakri, *India* 69 F12
Sakrivier, S. Africa 88 E3
Sakskøbing, *Denmark* 11 K5
Sakti, *India* 69 H10
Sakuma, *Japan* 55 G8
Sakurai, *Japan* 55 G7
Saky, *Ukraine* 33 K7
Sal ➤, *Russia* 35 G5
Sala, *Eritrea* 81 D4
Šaľa, *Slovak Rep.* 27 C10
Sala, *Sweden* 10 E10
Sala ➤, *Eritrea* 81 D4
Sala Consilina, *Italy* 43 B8
Sala-y-Gómez, *Pac. Oc.* 97 K17
Salaberry-de-Valleyfield, *Canada* 117 A10
Salacgrīva, *Latvia* 30 A11
Salada, L., *Mexico* 109 K6
Saladas, *Argentina* 126 B4
Saladillo, *Argentina* 126 D4
Salado ➤, Buenos Aires,
  Argentina 126 D4
Salado ➤, La Pampa, *Argentina* 128 D3
Salado ➤, Santa Fe, *Argentina* 126 C3
Salado ➤, *Mexico* 113 M5
Salaga, *Ghana* 83 D4
Ṣalāḥ ad Dīn □, *Iraq* 70 C4
Sălaj □, *Romania* 28 C7
Sálakhos, *Greece* 49 C9
Salala, *Liberia* 82 D2
Salala, *Sudan* 80 C4
Salālah, *Oman* 75 D5
Salamanca, *Chile* 126 C1
Salamanca, *Spain* 36 E5
Salamanca, *U.S.A.* 116 D6
Salamanca □, *Spain* 36 E5
Salāmatābād, *Iran* 70 C5
Salamis, *Cyprus* 49 D12
Salamís, *Greece* 46 D5
Salar de Atacama, *Chile* 126 A2
Salar de Uyuni, *Bolivia* 124 H5
Sălard, *Romania* 28 C7
Salas, *Spain* 36 B4
Salas de los Infantes, *Spain* . 36 C7
Salatiga, *Indonesia* 63 G14
Salavat, *Russia* 12 E3
Salawati, *Indonesia* 63 E8
Salaya, *India* 68 H3
Salayar, *Indonesia* 63 F6
Salazar ➤, *Spain* 38 C3
Salbris, *France* 19 E9
Salcia, *Romania* 29 G9
Salcombe, *U.K.* 15 G4
Saldaña, *Spain* 36 C6
Saldanha, S. Africa 88 E2
Saldanha B., S. Africa 88 E2
Saldus, *Latvia* 9 H20
Saldus □, *Latvia* 30 B9
Sale, *Australia* 95 F4
Sale, *Italy* 40 D5
Salé, *Morocco* 78 B4
Sale, *U.K.* 14 D5
Salekhard, *Russia* 52 C7
Salem, *India* 66 P11
Salem, Ill., *U.S.A.* 113 F1
Salem, Ind., *U.S.A.* 114 F2
Salem, Mass., *U.S.A.* 117 D14
Salem, Mo., *U.S.A.* 113 G9
Salem, N.H., *U.S.A.* 117 D13
Salem, N.J., *U.S.A.* 117 F8
Salem, N.Y., *U.S.A.* 117 C11
Salem, Ohio, *U.S.A.* 116 F4
Salem, Oreg., *U.S.A.* 108 D2
Salem, S. Dak., *U.S.A.* 112 D6
Salem, Va., *U.S.A.* 114 G5
Salemi, *Italy* 42 E5
Sälen, *Sweden* 10 C7
Salernes, *France* 21 E10
Salerno, *Italy* 43 B7
Salerno, G. di, *Italy* 43 B7
Salford, *U.K.* 14 D5
Salgir ➤, *Ukraine* 33 K8
Salgótarján, *Hungary* 28 B4
Salgueiro, *Brazil* 125 E11
Salibabu, *Indonesia* 63 D7
Salibea = Salybia, Trin. & Tob. . 125 K15
Salida, *U.S.A.* 106 C4
Salies-de-Béarn, *France* 20 E3
Salihli, *Turkey* 72 C3
Salihorsk, *Belarus* 33 F4
Salima, *Malawi* 85 G6
Salina, *Italy* 43 D7
Salina, Kans., *U.S.A.* 112 F6
Salina, Utah, *U.S.A.* 109 G8
Salina Cruz, *Mexico* 119 D5
Salina di Margherita di Savoia △,
  Italy 43 A9
Salinas, *Brazil* 125 G10
Salinas, *Chile* 126 A2
Salinas, *Ecuador* 124 D2
Salinas, *U.S.A.* 110 J5
Salinas ➤, Guatemala 119 D6
Salinas ➤, *U.S.A.* 110 J5
Salinas, B. de, Nic. 120 D2
Salinas, Pampa de las, *Argentina* 126 C2
Salinas Ambargasta, *Argentina* . 126 B3
Salinas de Hidalgo, *Mexico* .. 118 C4
Salinas Grandes, *Argentina* .. 126 C3
Salinas Pueblo Missions △, *U.S.A.* 109 J10
Saline ➤, Ark., *U.S.A.* 113 J8
Saline ➤, Kans., *U.S.A.* 112 F6
Saline di Trapani e Paceco △,
  Italy 42 E5
Salines, C. de ses, *Spain* ... 48 B10
Salinópolis, *Brazil* 125 D9

Salins-les-Bains, *France* 19 F12
Salir, *Portugal* 37 H2
Salisbury, *U.K.* 15 F6
Salisbury, Md., *U.S.A.* 114 F8
Salisbury, N.C., *U.S.A.* 115 H5
Salisbury I., *Canada* 101 B12
Salisbury Plain, *U.K.* 15 F6
Sălişte, *Romania* 29 E8
Salka, *Nigeria* 83 C5
Şalkhad, *Syria* 74 C5
Salkove, *Ukraine* 29 B14
Salla, *Finland* 8 C23
Sallanches, *France* 21 C10
Sallent, *Spain* 38 D6
Salles, *France* 20 D3
Salles-Curan, *France* 20 D6
Salling, *Denmark* 11 H2
Salliq = Coral Harbour, *Canada* . 101 B11
Sallisaw, *U.S.A.* 113 H7
Sallom Junction, *Sudan* 80 D4
Salluit, *Canada* 101 B12
Salmās, *Iran* 70 B5
Salmerón, *Spain* 38 E2
Salmo, *Canada* 102 D5
Salmon, *U.S.A.* 108 D7
Salmon →, *Canada* 102 C4
Salmon →, *U.S.A.* 108 D5
Salmon Arm, *Canada* 102 C5
Salmon Gums, *Australia* 93 F3
Salmon River Mts., *U.S.A.* ... 108 D6
Salo, *Finland* 9 F20
Salò, *Italy* 40 C7
Salobreña, *Spain* 37 J7
Salome, *U.S.A.* 111 M13
Salon, *India* 69 F9
Salon-de-Provence, *France* 21 E9
Salonica = Thessaloníki, *Greece* . 44 F6
Salonta, *Romania* 28 D6
Salor →, *Spain* 37 F3
Salou, *Spain* 38 D6
Salou, C. de, *Spain* 38 D6
Saloum →, *Senegal* 82 C1
Salpausselkä, *Finland* 9 F22
Salsacate, *Argentina* 126 C2
Salses, *France* 20 F6
Salsk, *Russia* 35 G5
Salso →, *Italy* 42 E6
Salsomaggiore Terme, *Italy* ... 40 D6
Salt, *Spain* 38 D7
Salt →, *Canada* 102 B6
Salt →, *U.S.A.* 109 K7
Salt L., The, *Australia* 95 E3
Salt Lake City, *U.S.A.* 108 F8
Salt Range, *Pakistan* 68 C5
Salta, *Argentina* 126 A2
Salta □, *Argentina* 126 A2
Saltara, *Italy* 41 E9
Saltash, *U.K.* 15 G3
Saltburn by the Sea, *U.K.* 14 C7
Saltcoats, *U.K.* 13 F4
Saltee Is., *Ireland* 12 D5
Saltfjellet, *Norway* 8 C16
Saltfjorden, *Norway* 8 C16
Saltholm, *Denmark* 11 J6
Saltillo, *Mexico* 118 B4
Salto, *Argentina* 126 C3
Salto, *Uruguay* 126 C4
Salto del Guairá, *Paraguay* ... 127 A5
Salton City, *U.S.A.* 111 M11
Salton Sea, *U.S.A.* 111 M11
Saltpond, *Ghana* 83 D4
Saltsburg, *U.S.A.* 116 F5
Saltsjöbaden, *Sweden* 10 E12
Saluda →, *U.S.A.* 115 J5
Salûm, *Egypt* 80 A2
Salûm, Khâlig el, *Egypt* 80 A2
Salur, *India* 67 K13
Saluzzo, *Italy* 40 D4
Salvador, *Brazil* 125 F11
Salvador, *Canada* 103 C7
Salvador, El ■, *Cent. Amer.* ... 120 D2
Salvador, L., *U.S.A.* 113 L9
Salvaterra de Magos, *Portugal* .. 37 F2
Sálvora, I. de, *Spain* 36 C2
Salween →, *Burma* 67 L20
Salyan, *Azerbaijan* 52 F5
Salybia, *Trin. & Tob.* 125 K15
Salza →, *Austria* 26 D7
Salzach →, *Austria* 26 C5
Salzburg, *Austria* 26 D6
Salzburg □, *Austria* 26 D6
Salzgitter, *Germany* 24 C6
Salzkotten, *Germany* 24 D4
Salzwedel, *Germany* 24 C7
Sam, *India* 68 F4
Sam Neua, *Laos* 58 G5
Sam Ngao, *Thailand* 64 D2
Sam Rayburn Reservoir, *U.S.A.* . 113 K7
Sam Son, *Vietnam* 64 C5
Sam Teu, *Laos* 64 C5
Sama de Langreo = Langreo,
  Spain 36 B5
Samagaltay, *Russia* 53 D10
Samales Group, *Phil.* 61 J4
Samâlût, *Egypt* 80 B3
Samana, *India* 68 D7
Samana Cay, *Bahamas* 121 B5
Samanadağı, *Turkey* 72 D6
Samandıra, *Turkey* 45 F13
Samanga, *Tanzania* 87 D4
Samangān □, *Afghan.* 66 B3
Samangwa, *Dem. Rep. of
  the Congo* 86 C1
Samani, *Japan* 54 C11
Samanli Dağları, *Turkey* 45 F13
Samar, *Phil.* 61 F6
Samara, *Russia* 34 D10
Samara →, *Russia* 34 D10
Samara →, *Ukraine* 33 H8
Samaria = Shōmrōn, *West Bank* . 74 C4
Samariá, *Greece* 49 D5

Samaria △, *Greece* 46 F5
Samarinda, *Indonesia* 62 E5
Samarkand = Samarqand,
  Uzbekistan 52 F7
Samarqand, *Uzbekistan* 52 F7
Sāmarrā', *Iraq* 70 C4
Samastipur, *India* 69 G11
Şamaxı, *Azerbaijan* 35 K9
Samba, *Dem. Rep. of the Congo* . 86 C2
Samba, *India* 69 C6
Sambalpur, *India* 67 J14
Sambar, Tanjung, *Indonesia* ... 62 E4
Sambas, *Indonesia* 62 D3
Sambava, *Madag.* 89 A9
Sambawizi, *Zimbabwe* 87 F2
Sambhal, *India* 69 E8
Sambhar, *India* 68 F6
Sambhar L., *India* 68 F6
Sambiase, *Italy* 43 D9
Sambir, *Ukraine* 31 J10
Sambor, *Cambodia* 64 F6
Samborombón, B., *Argentina* .. 126 D4
Sambuca di Sicília, *Italy* 42 E6
Samburu △, *Kenya* 86 B4
Samch'ŏk, S. *Korea* 57 F15
Samch'onp'o, S. *Korea* 57 G15
Same, *Tanzania* 86 C4
Samer, *France* 19 B8
Samfya, *Zambia* 87 E2
Sámi, *Greece* 46 C2
Şämkir, *Azerbaijan* 35 K8
Şamlı, *Turkey* 47 B9
Samnah, Si. *Arabia* 70 E3
Samo Alto, *Chile* 126 C1
Samoa ■, *Pac. Oc.* 91 B13
Samoan Is., *Pac. Oc.* 91 A13
Sambor, *Croatia* 41 C12
Samoëns, *France* 19 F13
Samokov, *Bulgaria* 44 D7
Šamorín, *Slovak Rep.* 27 C10
Samorogouan, *Burkina Faso* ... 82 C4
Sámos, *Greece* 47 D8
Samoš, *Serbia & M.* 28 E5
Samos, *Spain* 36 C3
Sámos □, *Greece* 47 D8
Samothráki = Mathráki, *Greece* . 49 A3
Samothráki, *Greece* 45 F9
Samoylovka, *Russia* 34 E6
Sampa, *Ghana* 82 D4
Sampacho, *Argentina* 126 C3
Sampalan, *Indonesia* 63 K18
Sampang, *Indonesia* 63 G15
Samper de Calanda, *Spain* ... 38 D4
Sampéyre, *Italy* 40 D4
Sampit, *Indonesia* 62 E4
Sampit, Teluk, *Indonesia* 62 E4
Samrong, *Cambodia* 64 E4
Samrong, *Thailand* 64 E3
Samsø, *Denmark* 11 J4
Samsø Bælt, *Denmark* 11 J4
Samsun, *Turkey* 72 B7
Samtredia, *Georgia* 35 J6
Samui, Ko, *Thailand* .... 65 b
Samur →, *Russia* 35 K9
Samurskiy Khrebet, *Russia* ... 35 K8
Samusole, *Dem. Rep. of
  the Congo* 87 E1
Samut Prakan, *Thailand* 64 F3
Samut Songkhram, *Thailand* .. 62 B1
Samwari, *Pakistan* 68 E2
San, *Mali* 82 C4
San →, *Cambodia* 64 F5
San →, *Poland* 31 H8
San Adrián, *Spain* 38 C3
San Adrián, C. de, *Spain* 36 B2
San Agustin, C., *Phil.* 61 H7
San Agustín de Valle Fértil,
  Argentina 126 C2
San Ambrosio, *Pac. Oc.* 97 K20
San Andreas, *U.S.A.* 110 G6
San Andres, *Phil.* 61 E6
San Andrés, I. de, *Caribbean* .. 120 D3
San Andrés del Rabanedo, *Spain* . 36 C5
San Andres Mts., *U.S.A.* 109 K10
San Andrés Tuxtla, *Mexico* ... 119 D5
San Angelo, *U.S.A.* 113 K4
San Anselmo, *U.S.A.* 110 H4
San Antonio, *Belize* 119 D7
San Antonio, *Chile* 126 C1
San Antonio, *Phil.* 61 D4
San Antonio, N. Mex., *U.S.A.* . 109 K10
San Antonio, Tex., *U.S.A.* ... 113 L5
San Antonio →, *U.S.A.* 113 L6
San Antonio, C., *Argentina* ... 126 D4
San Antonio, C. de, *Cuba* 120 B3
San Antonio, C. de, *Spain* 39 G5
San Antonio, Mt., *U.S.A.* 111 L9
San Antonio de los Baños, *Cuba* . 120 B3
San Antonio de los Cobres,
  Argentina 126 A2
San Antonio Oeste, *Argentina* . 128 E4
San Arcángel, *Italy* 43 B9
San Ardo, *U.S.A.* 110 J6
San Agustín, Canary Is. 48 G4
San Augustine, *U.S.A.* 113 K7
San Bartolomé, Canary Is. 48 F6
San Bartolomé de Tirajana,
  Canary Is. 48 G4
San Bartolomeo in Galdo, *Italy* . 43 A8
San Benedetto del Tronto, *Italy* . 41 F10
San Benedetto Po, *Italy* 40 C7
San Benedicto, I., *Mexico* 118 D2
San Benito, *U.S.A.* 113 M6
San Benito →, *U.S.A.* 110 J5
San Benito Mt., *U.S.A.* 110 J6
San Bernardino, *U.S.A.* 111 L9
San Bernardino Mts., *U.S.A.* .. 111 L10
San Bernardino Str., *Phil.* 61 E6
San Bernardo, *Chile* 126 C1
San Bernardo, I. de, *Colombia* . 124 B3
San Blas, *Mexico* 118 B3

San Blas, Arch. de, *Panama* ... 120 E4
San Blas, C., *U.S.A.* 115 L3
San Bonifacio, *Italy* 41 C8
San Borja, *Bolivia* 124 F5
San Buenaventura = Ventura,
  U.S.A. 111 L7
San Buenaventura, *Mexico* ... 118 B4
San Carlos = Sant Carles, *Spain* . 48 B8
San Carlos, *Argentina* 126 C2
San Carlos, *Chile* 126 D1
San Carlos, Baja Calif. S., *Mexico* 118 C2
San Carlos, Coahuila, *Mexico* .. 118 B4
San Carlos, *Nic.* 120 D3
San Carlos, Neg. Occ., *Phil.* ... 61 F5
San Carlos, Pangasinan, *Phil.* .. 61 D4
San Carlos, *Uruguay* 127 C5
San Carlos, *U.S.A.* 109 K8
San Carlos, *Venezuela* 124 B5
San Carlos de Bariloche,
  Argentina 128 E2
San Carlos de Bolívar, *Argentina* 128 D4
San Carlos de la Rápita = Sant
  Carles de la Ràpita, *Spain* ... 38 E5
San Carlos del Zulia, *Venezuela* 124 B4
San Carlos L., *U.S.A.* 109 K8
San Cataldo, *Italy* 42 E6
San Celoni = Sant Celoni, *Spain* . 38 D7
San Clemente, *Chile* 126 D1
San Clemente, *Spain* 39 F2
San Clemente, *U.S.A.* 111 M9
San Clemente I., *U.S.A.* 111 N8
San Cristóbal = Es Migjorn Gran,
  Spain 48 B11
San Cristóbal, *Argentina* 126 C3
San Cristóbal, Dom. Rep. 121 C5
San Cristóbal, *Venezuela* 124 B4
San Cristóbal de la Casas, *Mexico* 119 D6
San Damiano d'Asti, *Italy* 40 D5
San Daniele del Friuli, *Italy* ... 41 B10
San Diego, Calif., *U.S.A.* 111 N9
San Diego, Tex., *U.S.A.* 113 M5
San Diego, C., *Argentina* 128 G3
San Diego de la Unión, *Mexico* . 118 C4
San Diego International ✈
  (SAN), *U.S.A.* 111 N9
San Dimitri, Ras, *Malta* 49 C1
San Dimitri Point = San Dimitri,
  Ras, *Malta* 49 C1
San Donà di Piave, *Italy* 41 C9
San Estanislao, *Paraguay* 126 A4
San Esteban de Gormaz, *Spain* . 38 D1
San Felice Circeo, *Italy* 42 A6
San Felice sul Panaro, *Italy* ... 41 D8
San Felipe, *Chile* 126 C1
San Felipe, *Mexico* 118 A2
San Felipe, *Venezuela* 124 A5
San Felipe →, *U.S.A.* 111 M11
San Félix, *Chile* 126 B1
San Félix, Pac. Oc. 97 K20
San Fernando = Sant Ferran,
  Spain 48 C7
San Fernando, *Chile* 126 C1
San Fernando, Baja Calif., *Mexico* 118 B1
San Fernando, Tamaulipas,
  Mexico 119 C5
San Fernando, La Unión, *Phil.* .. 61 C4
San Fernando, Pampanga, *Phil.* . 61 D4
San Fernando, *Spain* 37 J4
San Fernando, Trin. & Tob. 121 D7
San Fernando, *U.S.A.* 111 L8
San Fernando de Apure,
  Venezuela 124 B5
San Fernando de Atabapo,
  Venezuela 124 C5
San Fernando di Púglia, *Italy* .. 43 A9
San Francisco, *Argentina* 126 C3
San Francisco, *U.S.A.* 110 H4
San Francisco →, *U.S.A.* 109 K9
San Francisco, C. de, *Colombia* . 122 C3
San Francisco, Paso del, S. *Amer.* 126 B2
San Francisco de Macorís,
  Dom. Rep. 121 C5
San Francisco del Monte de Oro,
  Argentina 126 C2
San Francisco del Oro, *Mexico* . 118 B3
San Francisco International ✈
  (SFO), *U.S.A.* 110 H4
San Francisco Javier = Sant
  Francesc de Formentera, *Spain* 48 C7
San Fratello, *Italy* 43 D7
San Gabriel, *Chile* 126 C1
San Gabriel Mts., *U.S.A.* 111 L9
San Gavino Monreale, *Italy* ... 42 C1
San German, Puerto Rico ..... 121 d
San Gimignano, *Italy* 40 E8
San Giórgio di Nogaro, *Italy* .. 41 C10
San Giórgio Iónico, *Italy* 43 B10
San Giovanni Bianco, *Italy* ... 40 C6
San Giovanni in Fiore, *Italy* ... 43 C9
San Giovanni in Persiceto, *Italy* . 41 D8
San Giovanni Rotondo, *Italy* .. 41 G12
San Giovanni Valdarno, *Italy* .. 41 E8
San Giuliano Terme, *Italy* 40 E7
San Gorgonio Mt., *U.S.A.* 111 L10
San Gottardo, P. del, *Switz.* ... 25 J4
San Gregorio, *Uruguay* 127 C4
San Gregorio, *U.S.A.* 110 H4
San Guiseppe Jato, *Italy* 42 E6
San Ignacio, *Belize* 119 D7
San Ignacio, *Bolivia* 124 G6
San Ignacio, *Mexico* 118 B2
San Ignacio, *Paraguay* 120 C2
San Ignacio, *Bolivia* 124 G6
San Ignacio, L., *Mexico* 118 B2
San Ildefonso, C., *Phil.* 61 C5
San Isidro, *Argentina* 126 C4
San Isidro, *Phil.* 61 H7
San Jacinto, *U.S.A.* 111 M10
San Jaime = Sant Jaume, *Spain* . 48 B11
San Javier, Misiones, *Argentina* 127 B5
San Javier, Santa Fe, *Argentina* . 126 C4

San Javier, *Bolivia* 124 G6
San Javier, *Chile* 126 D1
San Javier, *Spain* 39 H4
San Jeronimo Taviche, *Mexico* . 119 D5
San Joaquin, *U.S.A.* 110 J6
San Joaquin →, *U.S.A.* 110 G5
San Joaquin Valley, *U.S.A.* ... 110 J6
San Jon, *U.S.A.* 113 H3
San Jordi = Sant Jordi, *Spain* .. 48 B9
San Jorge, *Argentina* 126 C3
San Jorge, B. de, *Mexico* 118 A2
San Jorge, G., *Argentina* 128 F3
San José = San Josep, *Spain* ... 48 C7
San José, Costa Rica 120 E3
San José, *Guatemala* 120 D1
San José, *Mexico* 118 C2
San Jose, Mind. Occ., *Phil.* ... 61 E4
San Jose, Nueva Ecija, *Phil.* ... 61 D4
San Jose, *U.S.A.* 110 H5
San Jose →, *U.S.A.* 109 J10
San Jose de Buenavista, *Phil.* .. 63 B6
San José de Chiquitos, *Bolivia* . 124 G6
San José de Feliciano, *Argentina* 126 C4
San José de Jáchal, *Argentina* .. 126 C2
San José de Mayo, *Uruguay* ... 126 C4
San José del Guaviare, *Colombia* 124 C4
San Josep, *Spain* 48 C7
San Juan, *Argentina* 126 C2
San Juan, *Mexico* 118 C4
San Juan, *Phil.* 61 F6
San Juan, Puerto Rico .... 121 d
San Juan, Trin. & Tob. 125 K15
San Juan □, *Argentina* 126 C2
San Juan →, *Argentina* 126 C2
San Juan →, *Nic.* 120 D3
San Juan →, *U.S.A.* 109 H8
San Juan Bautista = Sant Joan
  Baptista, *Spain* 48 B8
San Juan Bautista, *Paraguay* .. 126 B4
San Juan Bautista, *Spain* 110 J5
San Juan Bautista Valle Nacional,
  Mexico 119 D5
San Juan Capistrano, *U.S.A.* .. 111 M9
San Juan Cr. →, *U.S.A.* 110 J5
San Juan de Alicante, *Spain* ... 39 G4
San Juan de Guadalupe, *Mexico* 118 C4
San Juan de la Costa, *Mexico* .. 118 C2
San Juan de los Morros,
  Venezuela 124 B5
San Juan del Norte, *Nic.* 120 D3
San Juan del Norte, B. de, *Nic.* . 120 D3
San Juan del Río, *Mexico* 119 C5
San Juan del Sur, *Nic.* 120 D2
San Juan I., *U.S.A.* 110 B3
San Juan Island △, *U.S.A.* ... 110 B4
San Juan Mts., *U.S.A.* 109 H10
San Just, Sierra de, *Spain* 38 E4
San Justo, *Argentina* 126 C3
San Kamphaeng, *Thailand* 64 C2
San Lázaro, C., *Mexico* 118 C2
San Lázaro, Sa., *Mexico* 118 C3
San Leandro, *U.S.A.* 110 H4
San Leonardo de Yagüe, *Spain* . 38 D1
San Lorenzo = Sant Llorenç des
  Cardassar, *Spain* 48 B10
San Lorenzo, *Argentina* 126 C3
San Lorenzo, *Ecuador* 124 C3
San Lorenzo, *Paraguay* 126 B4
San Lorenzo →, *Mexico* 118 C3
San Lorenzo, I., *Mexico* 118 B2
San Lorenzo, Mte., *Argentina* .. 128 F2
San Lorenzo de la Parrilla, *Spain* 38 F2
San Lorenzo de Morunys = Sant
  Llorenç de Morunys, *Spain* .. 38 C6
San Lucas, *Bolivia* 124 H5
San Lucas, Baja Calif. S., *Mexico* 118 C3
San Lucas, Baja Calif. S., *Mexico* 118 B2
San Lucas, *U.S.A.* 110 J5
San Lucas, C., *Mexico* 118 C3
San Lúcido, *Italy* 43 C9
San Luis, *Argentina* 126 C2
San Luis, *Cuba* 120 B3
San Luis, *Guatemala* 120 C2
San Luis, Ariz., *U.S.A.* 109 K6
San Luis, Colo., *U.S.A.* 109 H11
San Luis □, *Argentina* 126 C2
San Luis, Sierra de, *Argentina* . 126 C2
San Luis de la Paz, *Mexico* ... 118 C4
San Luis Obispo, *U.S.A.* 111 K6
San Luis Potosí, *Mexico* 118 C4
San Luis Potosí □, *Mexico* ... 118 C4
San Luis Reservoir, *U.S.A.* ... 110 H5
San Luis Río Colorado, *Mexico* . 118 A2
San Manuel, *U.S.A.* 109 K8
San Marco, C., *Italy* 42 C1
San Marco Argentano, *Italy* ... 43 C9
San Marco in Lámis, *Italy* 41 G12
San Marcos, *Guatemala* 120 D1
San Marcos, *Mexico* 118 B2
San Marcos, Calif., *U.S.A.* ... 111 M9
San Marcos, Tex., *U.S.A.* 113 L6
San Marino, *Italy* 41 E9
San Marino ■, *Europe* 41 E9
San Martín, *Antarctica* 5 C17
San Martín →, *Argentina* 126 C2
San Martín →, *Bolivia* 124 F6
San Martín, L., *Argentina* 128 F2
San Martín de la Vega, *Spain* .. 36 E7
San Martín de los Andes,
  Argentina 128 E2
San Martín de Valdeiglesias,
  Spain 36 E6
San Mateo = Sant Mateu,
  Baleares, *Spain* 48 B7
San Mateo = Sant Mateu,
  Valencia, *Spain* 38 E5
San Mateo, *Phil.* 61 C4
San Mateo, *U.S.A.* 110 H4
San Matías, *Bolivia* 124 G7

San Matías, G., *Argentina* 128 E4
San Miguel = Sant Miguel, *Spain* 48 B7
San Miguel, El Salv. 120 D2
San Miguel, *Panama* 120 E4
San Miguel, *U.S.A.* 110 K6
San Miguel →, *Bolivia* 124 F6
San Miguel de Tucumán,
  Argentina 126 B2
San Miguel del Monte, *Argentina* 126 D4
San Miguel I., *U.S.A.* 111 L6
San Miniato, *Italy* 40 E7
San Nicolás, Canary Is. 48 G4
San Nicolas, *Phil.* 61 B4
San Nicolás de los Arroyas,
  Argentina 126 C3
San Nicolas I., *U.S.A.* 111 M7
San Onofre, *U.S.A.* 111 M9
San Pablo, *Bolivia* 126 A2
San Pablo, *Phil.* 61 D4
San Pablo, *U.S.A.* 110 H4
San Páolo di Civitate, *Italy* ... 41 G12
San Pedro, Buenos Aires,
  Argentina 126 C4
San Pedro, Misiones, *Argentina* 127 B5
San Pedro, *Chile* 126 C1
San Pédro, Ivory C. 82 E3
San Pedro, *Mexico* 118 C2
San Pedro □, *Paraguay* 126 A4
San Pedro →, Chihuahua, *Mexico* 118 B3
San Pedro →, Nayarit, *Mexico* . 118 C3
San Pedro →, *U.S.A.* 109 K8
San Pedro, Pta., *Chile* 126 B1
San Pedro, Sierra de, *Spain* ... 37 F4
San Pedro Channel, *U.S.A.* ... 111 M8
San Pedro de Atacama, *Chile* .. 126 A2
San Pedro de Jujuy, *Argentina* . 126 A3
San Pedro de las Colonias, *Mexico* 118 B4
San Pedro de Macorís, Dom. Rep. 121 C6
San Pedro del Norte, *Nic.* 120 D3
San Pedro del Paraná, *Paraguay* 126 B4
San Pedro del Pinatar, *Spain* .. 39 H4
San Pedro Mártir △, *Mexico* .. 118 A1
San Pedro Mártir, Sierra, *Mexico* 118 A1
San Pedro Mixtepec, *Mexico* .. 119 D5
San Pedro Ocampo = Melchor
  Ocampo, *Mexico* 118 C4
San Pedro Sula, *Honduras* 120 C2
San Pietro, *Italy* 42 C1
San Pietro Vernótico, *Italy* ... 43 B11
San Quintín, *Mexico* 118 A1
San Rafael, *Argentina* 126 C2
San Rafael, Calif., *U.S.A.* 110 H4
San Rafael, N. Mex., *U.S.A.* .. 109 J10
San Rafael Mt., *U.S.A.* 111 L7
San Rafael Mts., *U.S.A.* 111 L7
San Ramón de la Nueva Orán,
  Argentina 126 A3
San Remo, *Italy* 40 E4
San Roque, *Argentina* 126 B4
San Roque, *Spain* 37 J5
San Rosendo, *Chile* 126 D1
San Saba, *U.S.A.* 113 K5
San Salvador, El Salv. 120 D2
San Salvador □, *Spain* 48 B10
San Salvador de Jujuy, *Argentina* 126 A3
San Salvador I., *Bahamas* 121 B5
San Salvo, *Italy* 41 F11
Sebastián = Donostia-San
  Sebastián, *Spain* 38 B3
San Sebastian, Puerto Rico .... 121 d
San Sebastián de la Gomera,
  Canary Is. 48 F2
San Serra = Son Serra, *Spain* .. 48 B10
San Serverino Marche, *Italy* ... 41 E10
San Severo, *Italy* 41 G12
San Simeon, *U.S.A.* 110 K5
San Simon, *U.S.A.* 109 K9
San Stéfano di Cadore, *Italy* .. 41 B9
San Stino di Livenza, *Italy* ... 41 C9
San Telmo = Sant Telm, *Spain* . 48 B9
San Telmo, *Mexico* 118 A1
San Tiburcio, *Mexico* 118 C4
San Valentin, Mte., *Chile* 128 F2
San Vicente de Alcántara, *Spain* 37 F3
San Vicente de la Barquera, *Spain* 36 B6
San Vincente del Raspeig, *Spain* 39 G4
San Vincenzo, *Italy* 40 E7
San Vito, Costa Rica 120 E3
San Vito, *Italy* 42 C2
San Vito, C., *Italy* 42 D5
San Vito al Tagliamento, *Italy* . 41 C9
San Vito Chietino, *Italy* 41 F11
San Vito dei Normanni, *Italy* .. 43 B10
Sana', *Yemen* 75 D3
Sana →, Bos.-H. 41 C13
Sanaba, Burkina Faso 82 C4
Şanâfir, Si. *Arabia* 80 B3
Sanaga →, *Cameroon* 83 E6
Sanaloa, Presa, *Mexico* 118 C3
Sanana, *Indonesia* 63 E7
Sanand, *India* 68 H5
Sanandaj, *Iran* 70 C5
Sanandita, *Bolivia* 126 A3
Sanary-sur-Mer, *France* 21 E9
Sanawad, *India* 68 H7
Sancellas = Sencelles, *Spain* ... 48 B9
Sancergues, *France* 19 E9
Sancerre, *France* 19 E9
Sancerrois, Collines du, *France* . 19 E9
Sanchahe, *China* 57 B14
Sanchahe, *China* 58 D6
Sánchez, Dom. Rep. 121 C6
Sanchor, *India* 68 G4
Sancoins, *France* 19 F9
Sancti Spíritus, *Cuba* 120 B4
Sancy, Puy de, *France* 20 C6
Sand →, S. *Africa* 89 C5
Sand Hills, *U.S.A.* 112 D4
Sand Lakes △, *Canada* 103 B9
Sand Springs, *U.S.A.* 113 G6

Sanda, *Japan* 55 G7
Sandakan, *Malaysia* 62 C5
Sandan = Sambor, *Cambodia* ... 64 F6
Sandanski, *Bulgaria* 44 E7
Sandaré, *Mali* 82 C2
Sandared, *Sweden* 11 G6
Sandarne, *Sweden* 10 C11
Sanday, *U.K.* 13 B6
Sandefjord, *Norway* 9 G14
Sanders, *U.S.A.* 109 J9
Sanderson, *U.S.A.* 113 K3
Sandersville, *U.S.A.* 115 J4
Sandfire Roadhouse, *Australia* .. 92 C3
Sandfly L., *Canada* 103 B7
Sandfontein, *Namibia* 88 C2
Sandhammaren, C., *Sweden* 11 J8
Sandheads, The, *India* 69 J13
Sandía, *Peru* 124 F5
Sandıklı, *Turkey* 47 C12
Sandila, *India* 69 F9
Sandnes, *Norway* 9 G11
Sandnessjøen, *Norway* 8 C15
Sandoa, *Dem. Rep. of the Congo* 84 F4
Sandomierz, *Poland* 31 H8
Sândominic, *Romania* 29 D10
Sandover →, *Australia* 94 C2
Sandoway, *Burma* 67 K19
Sandoy, *Færoe Is.* 8 F9
Sandpoint, *U.S.A.* 108 B5
Sandray, *U.K.* 13 E1
Sandringham, *U.K.* 14 E8
Sandstone, *Australia* 93 E2
Sandu, *China* 58 E6
Sandusky, *Mich., U.S.A.* 116 C2
Sandusky, *Ohio, U.S.A.* 116 E2
Sandvig, *Sweden* 11 J8
Sandviken, *Sweden* 10 D10
Sandwich, C., *Australia* 94 B4
Sandwich B., *Canada* 105 B8
Sandwich B., *Namibia* 88 C1
Sandy, *Oreg., U.S.A.* 110 E4
Sandy, *Pa., U.S.A.* 116 E6
Sandy, *Utah, U.S.A.* 108 F8
Sandy Bay, *Canada* 103 B8
Sandy Bight, *Australia* 93 F3
Sandy C., *Queens., Australia* ... 94 C5
Sandy C., *Tas., Australia* 95 G3
Sandy Cay, *Bahamas* 121 B4
Sandy Cr. →, *U.S.A.* 108 F9
Sandy L., *Canada* 104 B1
Sandy Lake, *Canada* 104 B1
Sandy Valley, *U.S.A.* 111 K11
Sânfjällets △, *Sweden* 10 B7
Sanford, *Fla., U.S.A.* 115 L5
Sanford, *Maine, U.S.A.* 115 D10
Sanford, *N.C., U.S.A.* 115 H6
Sanford →, *Australia* 93 E2
Sanford, Mt., *U.S.A.* 100 B5
Sang-i-Masha, *Afghan.* 68 C2
Sanga, *Mozam.* 87 E4
Sanga →, *Congo* 84 E3
Sangamner, *India* 66 K9
Sanganeb Atoll △, *Sudan* 80 D4
Sangar, *Afghan.* 68 C1
Sangar, *Russia* 53 C13
Sangar Sarai, *Afghan.* 68 B4
Sangaredi, *Guinea* 82 C2
Sangarh →, *Pakistan* 68 D4
Sangasso, *Mali* 82 C3
Sangatte, *France* 19 B8
Sangay, *Ecuador* 124 D3
Sange, *Dem. Rep. of the Congo* 86 D2
Sangeang, *Indonesia* 63 F5
Sanger, *U.S.A.* 110 J7
Sângera, *Moldova* 29 D13
Sangerhausen, *Germany* 24 D7
Sanggan He →, *China* 56 E9
Sanggau, *Indonesia* 62 D4
Sanghar, *Pakistan* 68 F3
Sangihe, Kepulauan, *Indonesia* .. 63 D7
Sangihe, Pulau, *Indonesia* 63 D7
Sangju, *S. Korea* 57 F15
Sangkapura, *Indonesia* 62 F4
Sangkhla, *Thailand* 64 E2
Sangkulirang, *Indonesia* 62 D5
Sangla, *Pakistan* 68 D5
Sangli, *India* 66 L9
Sangmélima, *Cameroon* 83 E7
Sangod, *India* 68 G7
Sangre de Cristo Mts., *U.S.A.* .. 113 G2
Sangre Grande, *Trin. & Tob.* .. 125 K15
Sangro →, *Italy* 41 F11
Sangrur, *India* 68 D6
Sangudo, *Canada* 102 C6
Sangue →, *Brazil* 124 F7
Sangüesa, *Spain* 38 C3
Sangzhi, *China* 59 C8
Sanhala, *Ivory C.* 82 C3
Sanibel, *U.S.A.* 115 M4
Sanikiluaq, *Canada* 101 C12
Sanin-Kaigan △, *Japan* 55 G7
Sanirajak, *Canada* 101 B11
Sanjawi, *Pakistan* 68 D3
Sanje, *Uganda* 86 C3
Sanjiang, *China* 58 E7
Sanjo, *Japan* 54 F9
Sankh →, *India* 69 H11
Sankt Andrä, *Austria* 26 E7
Sankt Augustin, *Germany* 24 E3
Sankt Blasien, *Germany* 25 H4
Sankt Gallen, *Switz.* 25 H5
Sankt Gallen □, *Switz.* 25 H5
Sankt Goar, *Germany* 25 E3
Sankt Ingbert, *Germany* 25 F3
Sankt Johann im Pongau, *Austria* 26 D6
Sankt Johann in Tirol, *Austria* .. 26 D5
Sankt Michel = Mikkeli, *Finland* 9 F22
Sankt-Peterburg, *Russia* 32 C6
Sankt Pölten, *Austria* 26 C8

Sankt Ulrich = Ortisei, *Italy* 41 B8
Sankt Valentin, *Austria* 26 C7
Sankt Veit an der Glan, *Austria* . 26 E7
Sankt Wendel, *Germany* 25 F3
Sankt Wolfgang, *Austria* 26 D6
Sankuru →, *Dem. Rep. of the Congo* 84 E4
Sanliurfa, *Turkey* 70 B3
Sanlúcar de Barrameda, *Spain* .. 37 J4
Sanluri, *Italy* 42 C1
Sânmartin, *Romania* 29 D10
Sanmen, *China* 59 C13
Sanmenxia, *China* 56 G6
Sanming, *China* 59 D11
Sannaspos, *S. Africa* 88 D4
Sannicandro Gargánico, *Italy* .. 41 G12
Sânnicolau Mare, *Romania* 28 D5
Sannieshof, *S. Africa* 88 D4
Sannîn, J., *Lebanon* 74 B4
Sanniquellie, *Liberia* 82 D3
Sannûr, W. →, *Egypt* 80 B3
Sanoe, *Antarctica* 5 D2
Sanok, *Poland* 31 J9
Sanquhar, *U.K.* 13 F5
Sans Souci, *Trin. & Tob.* 125 K16
Sansanding, *Mali* 82 C3
Sansepolcro, *Italy* 41 E9
Sansha, *China* 59 D13
Sanshui, *China* 59 F9
Sanski Most, *Bos.-H.* 41 D13
Sansui, *China* 58 D7
Sant Antoni Abat, *Spain* 48 C7
Sant Boi de Llobregat, *Spain* .. 38 D7
Sant Carles, *Spain* 48 B8
Sant Carles de la Ràpita, *Spain* 38 E5
Sant Celoni, *Spain* 38 D7
Sant Feliu de Guíxols, *Spain* .. 38 D8
Sant Feliu de Llobregat, *Spain* . 38 D7
Sant Ferran, *Spain* 48 C7
Sant Francesc de Formentera, *Spain* 48 C7
Sant Jaume, *Spain* 48 B11
Sant Joan Baptista, *Spain* 48 B8
Sant Jordi, *Ibiza, Spain* 48 C7
Sant Jordi, *Mallorca, Spain* 48 B9
Sant Jordi, G. de, *Spain* 38 E6
Sant Llorenç de Morunys, *Spain* 38 C6
Sant Llorenç del Munt y l'Obac △, *Spain* 38 D3
Sant Llorenç des Cardassar, *Spain* 48 B10
Sant Mateu, *Baleares, Spain* .. 48 B7
Sant Mateu, *Valencia, Spain* .. 38 E5
Sant Miguel, *Spain* 48 B7
Sant Telm, *Spain* 48 B9
Sant' Àgata Militello, *Italy* 43 D7
Santa Agnès, *Spain* 48 B7
Santa Ana, *Bolivia* 124 F5
Santa Ana, *El Salv.* 120 D2
Santa Ana, *Mexico* 118 A2
Santa Ana, *U.S.A.* 111 M9
Sant' Ángelo Lodigiano, *Italy* .. 40 C6
Sant' Antíoco, *Italy* 42 C1
Santa Bárbara, *Chile* 126 D1
Santa Barbara, *Honduras* 120 D2
Santa Bárbara, *Mexico* 118 B3
Santa Bárbara, *Spain* 38 E5
Santa Barbara, *U.S.A.* 111 L7
Santa Bárbara, Mt., *Spain* 39 H2
Santa Barbara Channel, *U.S.A.* . 111 L7
Santa Barbara I., *U.S.A.* 111 M7
Santa Catalina, Gulf of, *U.S.A.* . 111 N9
Santa Catalina, I., *Mexico* 118 B2
Santa Catalina I., *U.S.A.* 111 M8
Santa Catarina □, *Brazil* 127 B6
Santa Catarina, I. de, *Brazil* ... 127 B6
Santa Caterina di Pittinuri, *Italy* . 42 B1
Santa Caterina Villarmosa, *Italy* . 43 E7
Santa Cecília, *Brazil* 127 B5
Santa Clara, *Cuba* 120 B4
Santa Clara, *Calif., U.S.A.* 110 H5
Santa Clara, *Utah, U.S.A.* 109 H7
Santa Clara, El Golfo de, *Mexico* 118 A2
Santa Clara de Olimar, *Uruguay* 127 C5
Santa Clarita, *U.S.A.* 111 L8
Santa Clotilde, *Peru* 124 D4
Santa Coloma de Farners, *Spain* 38 D7
Santa Coloma de Gramenet, *Spain* 38 D7
Santa Comba, *Spain* 36 B2
Santa Croce Camerina, *Italy* ... 43 F7
Santa Croce di Magliano, *Italy* . 41 G11
Santa Cruz, *Argentina* 128 G3
Santa Cruz, *Bolivia* 124 G6
Santa Cruz, *Chile* 126 C1
Santa Cruz, *Costa Rica* 120 D2
Santa Cruz, *Madeira* 48 D3
Santa Cruz, *Phil.* 61 D4
Santa Cruz, *U.S.A.* 110 J4
Santa Cruz □, *Argentina* 128 G3
Santa Cruz de la Palma, *Canary Is.* 48 F2
Santa Cruz de la Palma ✈ (SPC), *Canary Is.* 48 F2
Santa Cruz de Mudela, *Spain* .. 37 G7
Santa Cruz de Tenerife, *Canary Is.* 48 F3
Santa Cruz del Norte, *Cuba* 120 B3
Santa Cruz del Retamar, *Spain* . 36 E6
Santa Cruz del Sur, *Cuba* 120 B4
Santa Cruz do Rio Pardo, *Brazil* 127 A6
Santa Cruz do Sul, *Brazil* 127 B5
Santa Cruz I., *U.S.A.* 111 M7
Santa Cruz Is., *Solomon Is.* 96 J8
Santa Cruz Mts., *Jamaica* ...... 120 a
Santa Domingo, Cay, *Bahamas* . 120 B4
Sant' Egídio alla Vibrata, *Italy* . 41 F10
Santa Elena, *Argentina* 126 C4
Santa Elena, C., *Costa Rica* 120 D2
Sant' Eufémia, G. di, *Italy* 43 D9
Santa Eulàlia des Riu, *Spain* ... 48 C8
Santa Fe, *Argentina* 126 C3

Santa Fe, *Spain* 37 H7
Santa Fe, *U.S.A.* 109 J11
Santa Fé □, *Argentina* 126 C3
Santa Fé do Sul, *Brazil* 125 H8
Santa Filomena, *Brazil* 125 E9
Santa Fiora, *Italy* 41 F8
Santa Gertrudis, *Spain* 48 C7
Santa Giustina, *Italy* 41 B9
Santa Inês, *Brazil* 125 F11
Santa Inés, *Spain* 37 G5
Santa Inés, I., *Chile* 128 G2
Santa Isabel, *Argentina* 126 D2
Santa Isabel, Pico, *Eq. Guin.* .. 83 E6
Santa Isabel do Morro, *Brazil* .. 125 F8
Santa Lucía, *Corrientes, Argentina* 126 B4
Santa Lucía, *San Juan, Argentina* 126 C2
Santa Lucia, *Italy* 39 H4
Santa Lucía, *Uruguay* 126 C4
Santa Lucia Range, *U.S.A.* 110 K5
Santa Magdalena, I., *Mexico* .. 118 C2
Santa Margarita, *Argentina* 126 D3
Santa Margarita, *Spain* 48 B10
Santa Margarita, I., *U.S.A.* 110 K6
Santa Margarita →, *U.S.A.* 111 M9
Santa Margarita, I., *Mexico* 118 C2
Santa Margherita, *Italy* 42 D1
Santa Margherita Lígure, *Italy* .. 40 D6
Santa María, *Argentina* 126 B2
Santa Maria, *Brazil* 127 B5
Santa Maria, *Phil.* 61 C4
Santa Maria, *U.S.A.* 111 L6
Santa María →, *Mexico* 118 A3
Santa Maria, B. de, *Mexico* 118 B3
Santa Maria, C. de, *Portugal* ... 37 J3
Santa Maria Cápua Vétere, *Italy* 43 A7
Santa Maria da Feira, *Portugal* . 36 E2
Santa Maria da Vitória, *Brazil* .. 125 F10
Santa Maria del Camí, *Spain* ... 48 B9
Santa Maria di Léuca, C., *Italy* . 43 C11
Santa María la Real de Nieva, *Spain* 36 D6
Santa Marinella, *Italy* 41 F8
Santa Marta, *Colombia* 124 A4
Santa Marta, Sierra Nevada de, *Colombia* 124 A4
Santa Marta de Tormes, *Spain* .. 36 E5
Santa Marta Grande, C., *Brazil* . 127 B6
Santa Marta Ortigueira, Ría de, *Spain* 36 B3
Santa Maura = Levkás, *Greece* .. 46 C2
Santa Monica, *U.S.A.* 111 M8
Santa Monica Mts. →, *U.S.A.* ... 111 L8
Santa Olalla, *Huelva, Spain* 37 H4
Santa Olalla, *Toledo, Spain* 36 E6
Santa Paula, *U.S.A.* 111 L7
Santa Pola, *Spain* 39 G4
Santa Ponça, *Spain* 48 B9
Santa Rita, *U.S.A.* 109 K10
Santa Rosa, *La Pampa, Argentina* 126 D3
Santa Rosa, *San Luis, Argentina* 126 C2
Santa Rosa, *Brazil* 127 B5
Santa Rosa, *Calif., U.S.A.* 110 G4
Santa Rosa, *N. Mex., U.S.A.* ... 113 H2
Santa Rosa and San Jacinto Mts. △, *U.S.A.* 111 M10
Santa Rosa de Copán, *Honduras* 120 D2
Santa Rosa de Río Primero, *Argentina* 126 C3
Santa Rosa del Sara, *Bolivia* 124 G6
Santa Rosa I., *Calif., U.S.A.* 111 M6
Santa Rosa I., *Fla., U.S.A.* 115 K2
Santa Rosa Range, *U.S.A.* 108 F5
Santa Rosalía, *Mexico* 118 B2
Santa Sylvina, *Argentina* 126 B3
Santa Tecla = Nueva San Salvador, *El Salv.* 120 D2
Santa Teresa, *Argentina* 126 C3
Santa Teresa, *Australia* 94 C1
Santa Teresa, *Mexico* 119 B5
Santa Teresa △, *Uruguay* 127 C5
Santa Teresa di Riva, *Italy* 43 E8
Santa Teresa Gallura, *Italy* 42 A2
Santa Uxía, *Spain* 36 C2
Santa Vitória do Palmar, *Brazil* . 127 C5
Santa Ynez →, *U.S.A.* 111 L6
Santa Ynez Mts. →, *U.S.A.* 111 L6
Santa Ysabel, *U.S.A.* 111 M10
Santadi, *Italy* 42 C1
Santaella, *Spain* 37 H6
Santai, *China* 58 B5
Santana, *Madeira* 48 D3
Sântana, *Romania* 28 D6
Santana, Coxilha de, *Brazil* 127 C4
Santana do Livramento, *Brazil* .. 127 C4
Santander, *Spain* 36 B7
Santander Jiménez, *Mexico* 119 C5
Santanilla, Is., *Honduras* 120 C3
Santanyí, *Spain* 48 B10
Santaquin, *U.S.A.* 108 G8
Santarcángelo di Romagna, *Italy* 41 D9
Santarém, *Brazil* 125 D8
Santarém, *Portugal* 37 F2
Santarém □, *Portugal* 37 F2
Santaren Channel, *W. Indies* ... 120 B4
Santee, *U.S.A.* 115 J6
Santee →, *U.S.A.* 115 J6
Santéramo in Colle, *Italy* 43 B9
Santerno →, *Italy* 41 D8
Santhià, *Italy* 40 C5
Santi-Quaranta = Sarandë, *Albania* 44 G3
Santiago, *Brazil* 127 B5
Santiago, *Canary Is.* 48 F2
Santiago, *Chile* 126 C1
Santiago, *Panama* 120 E3
Santiago, *Phil.* 61 C4
Santiago □, *Chile* 126 C1
Santiago →, *Mexico* 98 G9
Santiago →, *Peru* 124 D3
Santiago, Punta de, *Eq. Guin.* . 83 E6
Santiago de Compostela, *Spain* . 36 C2

Santiago de Cuba, *Cuba* 120 C4
Santiago de los Caballeros, *Dom. Rep.* 121 C5
Santiago del Estero, *Argentina* .. 126 B3
Santiago del Estero □, *Argentina* 126 B3
Santiago del Teide, *Canary Is.* .. 48 F3
Santiago do Cacém, *Portugal* ... 37 G2
Santiago Ixcuintla, *Mexico* 118 C3
Santiago Papasquiaro, *Mexico* .. 118 C3
Santiaguillo, L. de, *Mexico* 118 C4
Santillana, *Spain* 36 B6
Santisteban del Puerto, *Spain* .. 37 G7
Santo Amaro, *Brazil* 125 F11
Santo Anastácio, *Brazil* 127 A5
Santo André, *Brazil* 127 A6
Santo Ângelo, *Brazil* 127 B5
Santo Antônio do Içá, *Brazil* .. 124 D5
Santo Antônio do Leverger, *Brazil* 125 G7
Santo Domingo, *Dom. Rep.* 121 C6
Santo Domingo, *Baja Calif., Mexico* 118 A1
Santo Domingo, *Baja Calif. S., Mexico* 118 B2
Santo Domingo, *Nic.* 120 D3
Santo Domingo de la Calzada, *Spain* 38 C2
Santo Domingo de los Colorados, *Ecuador* 124 D3
Santo Domingo Pueblo, *U.S.A.* . 109 J10
Santo Stéfano di Camastro, *Italy* 43 D7
Santo Tirso, *Portugal* 36 D2
Santo Tomás, *Mexico* 118 A1
Santo Tomás, *Peru* 124 F4
Santo Tomé, *Argentina* 127 B4
Santo Tomé de Guayana = Ciudad Guayana, *Venezuela* .. 124 B6
Santomera, *Spain* 39 G3
Santoña, *Spain* 36 B7
Santoríni = Thíra, *Greece* 47 E7
Santos, *Brazil* 127 A6
Santos, Sierra de los, *Spain* 37 G5
Santos Dumont, *Brazil* 127 A7
Sanur, *Indonesia* 63 K18
Sanwer, *India* 68 H6
Sanxenxo, *Spain* 36 C2
Sanyuan, *China* 56 G5
São Bartolomeu de Messines, *Portugal* 37 H2
São Bernardo do Campo, *Brazil* 127 A6
São Borja, *Brazil* 127 B4
São Brás de Alportel, *Portugal* .. 37 H3
São Carlos, *Brazil* 127 A6
São Cristóvão, *Brazil* 125 F11
São Domingos, *Brazil* 125 F9
São Domingos, *Guinea-Biss.* 82 C1
São Francisco, *Brazil* 125 G10
São Francisco →, *Brazil* 125 F11
São Francisco do Sul, *Brazil* 127 B6
São Gabriel, *Brazil* 127 C5
São Gonçalo, *Brazil* 127 A7
Sao Hill, *Tanzania* 87 D4
São João, *Guinea-Biss.* 82 C1
São João da Boa Vista, *Brazil* .. 127 A6
São João da Madeira, *Portugal* . 36 E2
São João da Pesqueira, *Portugal* 36 D3
São João del Rei, *Brazil* 127 A7
São João do Araguaia, *Brazil* ... 125 E9
São João do Piauí, *Brazil* 125 E10
São Joaquim, *Brazil* 127 B6
São Joaquim △, *Brazil* 127 B6
São José, Pta. de, *Madeira* 48 D3
São José, *Brazil* 127 B5
São José do Norte, *Brazil* 127 C5
São José do Rio Prêto, *Brazil* ... 127 A6
São José dos Campos, *Brazil* ... 127 A6
São Leopoldo, *Brazil* 127 B5
São Lourenço, *Brazil* 127 A6
São Lourenço →, *Brazil* 125 G7
São Lourenço, Pta. de, *Madeira* . 48 D3
São Lourenço do Sul, *Brazil* 127 C5
São Luís, *Brazil* 125 D10
São Luís Gonzaga, *Brazil* 127 B5
São Marcos →, *Brazil* 125 G9
São Marcos, B. de, *Brazil* 125 D10
São Martinho da Cortiça, *Portugal* 36 E2
São Mateus, *Brazil* 125 G11
São Mateus do Sul, *Brazil* 127 B5
São Miguel do Oeste, *Brazil* 127 B5
São Paulo, *Brazil* 127 A6
São Paulo □, *Brazil* 127 A6
São Paulo, I., *Atl. Oc.* 2 D8
São Paulo de Olivença, *Brazil* .. 124 D5
São Pedro do Sul, *Portugal* 36 E2
São Roque, *Madeira* 48 D3
São Roque, C. de, *Brazil* 125 E11
São Sebastião, I. de, *Brazil* 127 A6
São Sebastião do Paraíso, *Brazil* 127 A6
São Teotónio, *Portugal* 37 H2
São Tomé, *São Tomé & Príncipe* 76 F4
São Tomé, C. de, *Brazil* 127 A7
São Tomé & Príncipe ■, *Africa* . 77 F4
São Vicente, *Brazil* 127 A6
São Vicente, *Madeira* 48 D2
São Vicente, C. de, *Portugal* 37 H1
Saona, I., *Dom. Rep.* 121 C6
Saône →, *France* 19 G11
Saône-et-Loire □, *France* 19 F11
Sápai, *Greece* 45 E9
Sápam do, *Thailand* ...... 65 a
Sapanca, *Turkey* 72 B4
Saparua, *Indonesia* 63 E7
Sapele, *Nigeria* 83 D6
Sapelo I., *U.S.A.* 115 K5
Saphane, *Turkey* 47 B11
Sapi △, *Zimbabwe* 87 F2
Sapiéntza, *Greece* 46 E3
Sapo △, *Liberia* 82 D3

Sapone, *Burkina Faso* 83 C4
Saposoa, *Peru* 124 E3
Sapotskina, *Belarus* 30 E10
Sapouy, *Burkina Faso* 83 C4
Sapozhok, *Russia* 34 D5
Sapphire, *Australia* 94 C4
Sappho, *U.S.A.* 110 B2
Sapporo, *Japan* 54 C10
Sapri, *Italy* 43 B8
Sapulpa, *U.S.A.* 113 H6
Saqqez, *Iran* 70 B5
Sar Dasht, *Āzarbāyjān-e Gharbī, Iran* 73 D11
Sar Dasht, *Khuzestān, Iran* 71 C6
Sar-e Pol □, *Afghan.* 66 B4
Sar Gachīneh = Yāsūj, *Iran* 71 D6
Sar Planina, *Macedonia* 44 E4
Sara, *Burkina Faso* 82 C4
Sara, *Phil.* 61 F5
Šara △, *Serbia & M.* 44 D5
Sara Buri = Saraburi, *Thailand* . 64 E3
Sarāb, *Iran* 70 B5
Sarabadi, *Iraq* 70 C5
Saraburi, *Thailand* 64 E3
Saradiya, *India* 68 J4
Saraféré, *Mali* 82 B4
Saragossa = Zaragoza, *Spain* ... 38 D4
Saraguro, *Ecuador* 124 D3
Sarai Naurang, *Pakistan* 68 C4
Saraikela, *India* 69 H11
Saraiu, *Romania* 29 F13
Sarajevo, *Bos.-H.* 28 G3
Sarakhs, *Turkmenistan* 71 B9
Saran, Gunung, *Indonesia* 62 E4
Saranac →, *U.S.A.* 117 B10
Saranac Lake, *U.S.A.* 117 B10
Saranda, *Tanzania* 86 D3
Sarandë, *Albania* 44 G3
Sarandí del Yi, *Uruguay* 127 C4
Sarandí Grande, *Uruguay* 126 C4
Sarangani B., *Phil.* 61 J6
Sarangani Is., *Phil.* 61 J6
Sarangarh, *India* 67 J13
Saransk, *Russia* 34 C7
Sarapul, *Russia* 52 D6
Sarasota, *U.S.A.* 115 M4
Sarata, *Ukraine* 29 D14
Sarata →, *Ukraine* 29 E14
Saratoga, *Calif., U.S.A.* 110 H4
Saratoga, *Wyo., U.S.A.* 108 F10
Saratoga △, *U.S.A.* 117 D11
Saratoga Springs, *U.S.A.* 117 C11
Saratok, *Malaysia* 62 D4
Saratov, *Russia* 34 E7
Sarāvān, *Iran* 71 E9
Saravane, *Laos* 64 E6
Sarawak □, *Malaysia* 62 D4
Saray, *Tekirdağ, Turkey* 45 E11
Saray, *Van, Turkey* 73 C11
Saraya, *Guinea* 82 C2
Saraya, *Senegal* 82 C2
Saraycık, *Turkey* 47 B11
Sarayköy, *Turkey* 47 D10
Saraylar, *Turkey* 45 F11
Sarayönü, *Turkey* 72 C5
Sarbāz, *Iran* 71 E9
Sarbīsheh, *Iran* 71 C8
Sárbogárd, *Hungary* 28 D3
Sarca →, *Italy* 40 C7
Sarcelles, *France* 19 D9
Sarda →, *India* 67 F12
Sardarshahr, *India* 68 E6
Sardegna □, *Italy* 42 B1
Sardhana, *India* 68 E7
Sardina, Pta., *Canary Is.* 48 F4
Sardinia = Sardegna □, *Italy* ... 42 B1
Sardis, *Turkey* 47 C10
Sārdūīyeh = Dar Mazār, *Iran* ... 71 D8
Saren, *Indonesia* 63 J18
S'Arenal, *Spain* 48 B9
Sarentino, *Italy* 41 B8
Saréyamou, *Mali* 82 B4
Sargasso Sea, *Atl. Oc.* 97 D20
Sargodha, *Pakistan* 68 C5
Sarh, *Chad* 79 G9
Sarhala, *Ivory C.* 82 D3
Sārī, *Iran* 71 B7
Sari d'Orcino, *France* 21 F12
Sária, *Greece* 47 F9
Saria, *India* 69 J10
Sariab, *Pakistan* 68 D2
Sarıbeyler, *Turkey* 47 B9
Sarıgöl, *Turkey* 72 C3
Sarikamış, *Turkey* 73 B10
Sarıkaya, *Turkey* 72 C6
Sarikei, *Malaysia* 62 D4
Sarıköy, *Turkey* 45 F11
Sarila, *India* 69 G8
Sarina, *Australia* 94 C4
Sariñena, *Spain* 38 D4
Sarita, *U.S.A.* 113 M6
Sariwŏn, *N. Korea* 57 E13
Sariyar Baraji, *Turkey* 72 B4
Sariyer, *Turkey* 45 E13
Sarju →, *India* 69 F9
Sark, *U.K.* 15 H5
Sarkad, *Hungary* 28 D6
Sarkari Tala, *India* 68 F4
Şarkışla, *Turkey* 72 C7
Şarköy, *Turkey* 45 F11
Sarlat-la-Canéda, *France* 20 D5
Sărmăşag, *Romania* 28 D5
Sărmaşu, *Romania* 29 D9
Sarmi, *Indonesia* 63 E9
Sarmiento, *Argentina* 128 F3
Sarmizegetusa, *Romania* 28 E7
Särna, *Sweden* 10 C7
Sarnano, *Italy* 41 E10
Sarnen, *Switz.* 25 J4
Sarnia, *Canada* 116 D2
Sarno, *Italy* 43 B7

Sarnthein = Sarentino, *Italy* 41 B8
Särö, *Sweden* 11 G5
Sarolangun, *Indonesia* 62 E2
Saronikós Kólpos, *Greece* 46 D5
Saronno, *Italy* 40 C6
Saros Körfezi, *Turkey* 45 F10
Sárospatak, *Hungary* 28 B6
Sarpsborg, *Norway* 9 G14
Sarracín, *Spain* 36 C7
Sarralbe, *France* 19 D14
Sarre = Saar ➤, *Europe* 17 E6
Sarre, *Italy* 40 C4
Sarre-Union, *France* 19 D14
Sarrebourg, *France* 19 D14
Sarreguemines, *France* 19 C14
Sarria, *Spain* 36 C3
Sarrión, *Spain* 38 E4
Sarro, *Mali* 82 C3
Sarstedt, *Germany* 24 C5
Sartène, *France* 21 G12
Sarthe □, *France* 18 D7
Sarthe ➤, *France* 18 E6
Sartilly, *France* 18 D5
Saruhanlı, *Turkey* 47 C9
Saruna ➤, *Pakistan* 68 F2
Sárvár, *Hungary* 28 C1
Sarvar, *India* 68 F6
Sarvestān, *Iran* 71 D7
Särvfjället, *Sweden* 10 B7
Sárvíz ➤, *Hungary* 28 D3
Sary-Tash, *Kyrgyzstan* 52 F8
Sarych, Mys, *Ukraine* 33 K7
Saryshagan, *Kazakhstan* 52 E8
Sarzana, *Italy* 40 D6
Sarzeau, *France* 18 E4
Sasan Gir, *India* 68 J4
Sasaram, *India* 69 G11
Sasebo, *Japan* 55 H4
Saser, *India* 69 B7
Saskatchewan □, *Canada* 103 C7
Saskatchewan ➤, *Canada* 103 C8
Saskatoon, *Canada* 103 C7
Saskylakh, *Russia* 53 B12
Saslaya △, *Nic.* 120 D2
Sasolburg, *S. Africa* 89 D4
Sasovo, *Russia* 34 C5
Sassandra, *Ivory C.* 82 E3
Sassandra ➤, *Ivory C.* 82 E3
Sássari, *Italy* 42 B1
Sassnitz, *Germany* 24 A9
Sasso Marconi, *Italy* 41 D8
Sassocorvaro, *Italy* 41 E9
Sassoferrato, *Italy* 41 E9
Sasstown, *Liberia* 82 E3
Sassuolo, *Italy* 40 D7
Sástago, *Spain* 38 D4
Sasyk, Ozero, *Ukraine* 29 E14
Sata-Misaki, *Japan* 55 J5
Satadougou, *Mali* 82 C2
Satakunda = Satakunta, *Finland* ... 9 F20
Satakunta, *Finland* 9 F20
Satama-Soukoura, *Ivory C.* 82 D4
Satara, *India* 66 L8
Satara, *S. Africa* 89 C5
Satbarwa, *India* 69 H11
Såtenäs, *Sweden* 11 F6
Säter, *Sweden* 10 D9
Satevó, *Mexico* 118 B3
Satilla ➤, *U.S.A.* 115 K5
Satmala Hills, *India* 66 J9
Satna, *India* 69 G9
Šator, *Bos.-H.* 41 D13
Sátoraljaújhely, *Hungary* 28 B6
Satpura Ra., *India* 66 J10
Satrup, *Germany* 24 A5
Satsuna-Shotō, *Japan* 55 K5
Sattahip, *Thailand* 64 F3
Satu Mare, *Romania* 28 C7
Satu Mare □, *Romania* 28 C8
Satui, *Indonesia* 62 E5
Satun, *Thailand* 65 J3
Saturnina ➤, *Brazil* 124 F7
Sauce, *Argentina* 126 C4
Sauceda, *Mexico* 118 B4
Saucillo, *Mexico* 118 B3
Sauda, *Norway* 9 G12
Sauðarkrókur, *Iceland* 8 D4
Saudi Arabia ■, *Asia* 70 B3
Saugeen ➤, *Canada* 116 B3
Saugerties, *U.S.A.* 117 D11
Saugus, *U.S.A.* 111 L8
Saujon, *France* 20 C3
Sauk Centre, *U.S.A.* 112 C7
Sauk Rapids, *U.S.A.* 112 C7
Saulgau, *Germany* 25 G5
Saulieu, *France* 19 E11
Sault, *France* 21 D9
Sault Ste. Marie, *Canada* 104 C3
Sault Ste. Marie, *U.S.A.* 101 D11
Saumlaki, *Indonesia* 63 F8
Saumur, *France* 18 E6
Saunders, C., *N.Z.* 91 L3
Saunders I., *Antarctica* 5 B1
Saunders Point, *Australia* 93 E4
Sauri, *Nigeria* 83 C6
Saurimo, *Angola* 84 F4
Sausalito, *U.S.A.* 110 H4
Sauveterre-de-Béarn, *France* ... 20 E3
Sauzé-Vaussais, *France* 20 B4
Savá, *Honduras* 120 C2
Sava, *Italy* 43 B10
Sava ➤, *Serbia & M.* 28 F5
Savage, *U.S.A.* 112 B2
Savage I. = Niue, *Cook Is.* 97 J11
Savage River, *Australia* 95 G4
Savai'i, *Samoa* 91 A12
Savalou, *Benin* 83 D5
Savane, *Mozam.* 87 F4
Savanna, *U.S.A.* 112 D9

Savanna-la-Mar, *Jamaica* ..... 120 a
Savannah, *Ga., U.S.A.* 115 J5
Savannah, *Mo., U.S.A.* 112 F7
Savannah, *Tenn., U.S.A.* 115 H1
Savannah ➤, *U.S.A.* 115 J5
Savannakhet, *Laos* 64 D5
Savant L., *Canada* 104 B1
Savant Lake, *Canada* 104 B1
Săvârşin, *Romania* 28 D7
Savaştepe, *Turkey* 47 B9
Savé, *Benin* 83 D5
Save ➤, *France* 20 E5
Save ➤, *Mozam.* 89 C5
Sāveh, *Iran* 71 C6
Savelugu, *Ghana* 83 D4
Savenay, *France* 18 E5
Săveni, *Romania* 29 C11
Saverdun, *France* 20 E5
Saverne, *France* 19 D14
Savigliano, *Italy* 40 D4
Savigny-sur-Braye, *France* 18 E7
Sávio ➤, *Italy* 41 D9
Šavnik, *Serbia & M.* 44 D3
Savo, *Finland* 8 E22
Savoie □, *France* 21 C10
Savolax = Savo, *Finland* 8 E22
Savona, *Italy* 40 D5
Savona, *U.S.A.* 116 D7
Savonlinna, *Finland* 32 B5
Savoy = Savoie □, *France* 21 C10
Savsat, *Turkey* 73 B10
Sävsjö, *Sweden* 11 G8
Savur, *Turkey* 70 B4
Sawahlunto, *Indonesia* 62 E2
Sawai, *Indonesia* 63 E7
Sawai Madhopur, *India* 68 G7
Sawang Daen Din, *Thailand* ... 64 D4
Sawankhalok, *Thailand* 64 D2
Sawara, *Japan* 55 G10
Sawatch Range, *U.S.A.* 109 G10
Sawel Mt., *U.K.* 12 B4
Sawi, *Thailand* 65 G2
Sawla, *Ghana* 82 D4
Sawmills, *Zimbabwe* 87 F2
Sawtooth △, *U.S.A.* 108 D6
Sawtooth Range, *U.S.A.* 108 E6
Sawu, *Indonesia* 63 F6
Sawu Sea, *Indonesia* 63 F6
Saxby ➤, *Australia* 94 B3
Saxmundham, *U.K.* 15 E9
Saxony = Sachsen □, *Germany* .. 24 E9
Saxony, Lower =
  Niedersachsen □, *Germany* .. 24 C4
Saxton, *U.S.A.* 116 F6
Say, *Mali* 82 C4
Say, *Niger* 83 C5
Saya, *Nigeria* 83 D5
Sayabec, *Canada* 105 C6
Sayaboury, *Laos* 64 C3
Sayán, *Peru* 124 F3
Sayan, Vostochnyy, *Russia* ... 53 D10
Sayan, Zapadnyy, *Russia* 53 D10
Saydā, *Lebanon* 74 B4
Sayhandulaan = Oldziyt,
  Mongolia 56 B5
Sayḩūt, *Yemen* 75 D5
Saykhin, *Kazakhstan* 35 F8
Saylac = Zeila, *Somali Rep.* ... 75 E3
Saynshand, *Mongolia* 60 B6
Sayre, *Okla., U.S.A.* 113 H5
Sayre, *Pa., U.S.A.* 117 E8
Sayreville, *U.S.A.* 117 F10
Sayula, *Mexico* 118 D4
Sayward, *Canada* 102 C3
Sazanit, *Albania* 44 F3
Sázava ➤, *Czech Rep.* 26 B7
Sazin, *Pakistan* 69 B5
Sazlika ➤, *Bulgaria* 45 E9
Scaër, *France* 18 D3
Scafell Pike, *U.K.* 14 C4
Scalea, *Italy* 43 C8
Scalloway, *U.K.* 13 A7
Scalpay, *U.K.* 13 D3
Scandia, *Canada* 102 C6
Scandiano, *Italy* 40 D7
Scandicci, *Italy* 41 E8
Scandinavia, *Europe* 8 E16
Scansano, *Italy* 41 F8
Scapa Flow, *U.K.* 13 C5
Scappoose, *U.S.A.* 110 E4
Scarámia, Capo, *Italy* 43 F7
Scarba, *U.K.* 13 E3
Scarborough, *Trin. & Tob.* ... 121 D7
Scarborough, *U.K.* 14 C7
Scariff I., *Ireland* 12 E1
Scarp, *U.K.* 13 C1
Scarpe-Escaut △, *France* 19 B10
Scebeli, Wabi ➤, *Somali Rep.* . 75 G3
Ščedro, *Croatia* 41 E13
Schaal See, *Germany* 24 B6
Schaalsee △, *Germany* 24 B6
Schaffhausen, *Switz.* 25 H4
Schagen, *Neths.* 17 B4
Schaghticoke, *U.S.A.* 117 D11
Schärding, *Austria* 26 C6
Scharhörn, *Germany* 24 B4
Scheessel, *Germany* 24 B5
Schefferville, *Canada* 105 B6
Scheibbs, *Austria* 26 C8
Schelde ➤, *Belgium* 17 C4
Schell Creek Ra., *U.S.A.* 108 G6
Schellsburg, *U.S.A.* 116 F6
Schenectady, *U.S.A.* 117 D11
Schenevus, *U.S.A.* 117 D10
Scherfede, *Germany* 24 D5
Schesslitz, *Germany* 25 F7
Schiedam, *Neths.* 17 C4
Schiermonnikoog, *Neths.* 17 A6
Schiltigheim, *France* 19 D14
Schio, *Italy* 41 C8
Schiphol, Amsterdam ✈ (AMS),
  Neths. 17 B4

Schladming, *Austria* 26 D6
Schlanders = Silandro, *Italy* ... 40 B7
Schlei ➤, *Germany* 24 A5
Schleiden, *Germany* 24 E2
Schleiz, *Germany* 24 E7
Schleswig, *Germany* 24 A5
Schleswig-Holstein □, *Germany* . 24 A5
Schlüchtern, *Germany* 25 E5
Schmalkalden, *Germany* 24 E6
Schmölln, *Germany* 24 E8
Schneeberg, *Austria* 26 D8
Schneeberg, *Germany* 24 E8
Schneverdingen, *Germany* 24 B5
Schœlcher, *Martinique* ...... 120 c
Schoharie, *U.S.A.* 117 D10
Schoharie Cr. ➤, *U.S.A.* 117 D10
Scholls, *U.S.A.* 110 E4
Schönberg,
  Mecklenburg-Vorpommern,
  Germany 24 B6
Schönberg, Schleswig-Holstein,
  Germany 24 A6
Schönbuch △, *Germany* 25 G5
Schönebeck, *Germany* 24 C7
Schongau, *Germany* 25 H6
Schöningen, *Germany* 24 C6
Schopfheim, *Germany* 25 H3
Schorndorf, *Germany* 25 G5
Schortens, *Germany* 24 B3
Schouten I., *Australia* 95 G4
Schouten Is. = Supiori, *Indonesia* . 63 E9
Schouwen, *Neths.* 17 C3
Schramberg, *Germany* 25 G4
Schrankogel, *Austria* 26 D4
Schreiber, *Canada* 104 C2
Schrems, *Austria* 26 C8
Schrobenhausen, *Germany* 25 G7
Schroffenstein, *Namibia* 88 D2
Schroon Lake, *U.S.A.* 117 C11
Schruns, *Austria* 26 D2
Schuler, *Canada* 103 C6
Schumacher, *Canada* 104 C3
Schurz, *U.S.A.* 108 G4
Schuyler, *U.S.A.* 112 E6
Schuylerville, *U.S.A.* 117 C11
Schuylkill ➤, *U.S.A.* 117 G9
Schuylkill Haven, *U.S.A.* 117 F8
Schwabach, *Germany* 25 F7
Schwaben □, *Germany* 25 G6
Schwäbisch-Fränkischer Wald △,
  Germany 25 G5
Schwäbisch Gmünd, *Germany* .. 25 G5
Schwäbisch Hall, *Germany* 25 F5
Schwäbische Alb, *Germany* ... 25 G5
Schwabmünchen, *Germany* 25 G6
Schwalmstadt, *Germany* 24 E5
Schwandorf, *Germany* 25 F8
Schwaner, Pegunungan, *Indonesia* 62 E4
Schwanewede, *Germany* 24 B4
Schwarmstedt, *Germany* 24 C5
Schwarzenberg, *Germany* 24 E8
Schwarzrand, *Namibia* 88 D2
Schwarzwald, *Germany* 25 G4
Schwaz, *Austria* 26 D4
Schwechat, *Austria* 27 C9
Schwechat, Wien ✈ (VIA),
  Austria 27 C9
Schwedt, *Germany* 24 B10
Schweinfurt, *Germany* 25 E6
Schweizer-Reneke, *S. Africa* ... 88 D4
Schwenningen = Villingen-
  Schwenningen, *Germany* 25 G4
Schwerin, *Germany* 24 B7
Schweriner See, *Germany* 24 B7
Schwetzingen, *Germany* 25 F4
Schwyz, *Switz.* 25 H4
Schwyz □, *Switz.* 25 H4
Sciacca, *Italy* 42 F6
Scicli, *Italy* 43 F7
Sciliar △, *Italy* 41 B8
Scilla, *Italy* 43 D8
Scilly, Isles of, *U.K.* 15 H1
Ścinawa, *Poland* 31 G3
Scione, *Greece* 44 G7
Scioto ➤, *U.S.A.* 114 F4
Scituate, *U.S.A.* 117 D14
Scobey, *U.S.A.* 112 A2
Scone, *Australia* 95 E5
Scone, *U.K.* 13 E5
Scordia, *Italy* 43 E7
Scoresbysund = Ittoqqortoormiit,
  Greenland 4 B6
Scornicești, *Romania* 29 F9
Scotia, *Calif., U.S.A.* 108 F1
Scotia, *N.Y., U.S.A.* 117 D11
Scotia Sea, *Antarctica* 5 B18
Scotland, *Canada* 116 C4
Scotland □, *U.K.* 13 E5
Scott, *Antarctica* 5 D11
Scott, C., *Australia* 92 B4
Scott City, *U.S.A.* 112 F4
Scott Glacier, *Antarctica* 5 C8
Scott I., *Antarctica* 5 C11
Scott Is., *Canada* 102 C3
Scott L., *Canada* 103 B7
Scott Reef, *Australia* 92 B3
Scottburgh, *S. Africa* 89 E5
Scottdale, *U.S.A.* 116 F5
Scottsbluff, *U.S.A.* 112 E3
Scottsboro, *U.S.A.* 115 H3
Scottsburg, *U.S.A.* 114 F3
Scottsdale, *Australia* 95 G4
Scottsdale, *U.S.A.* 109 K7
Scottsville, *Ky., U.S.A.* 115 G2
Scottsville, *N.Y., U.S.A.* ... 116 C7
Scottville, *U.S.A.* 114 D2
Scranton, *U.S.A.* 117 E9
Scugog, L., *Canada* 116 B6
Sculeni, *Moldova* 29 C12

Scunthorpe, *U.K.* 14 D7
Scuol Schuls, *Switz.* 25 J6
Scutari = Shkodër, *Albania* 44 D3
Scutari = Üsküdar, *Turkey* 45 F13
Seabrook, L., *Australia* 93 F2
Seaford, *U.K.* 15 G8
Seaford, *U.S.A.* 114 F8
Seaforth, *Australia* 94 J6
Seaforth, *Canada* 116 C3
Seaforth, L., *U.K.* 13 D2
Seagraves, *U.S.A.* 113 J3
Seaham, *U.K.* 14 C6
Seal ➤, *Canada* 103 B10
Seal L., *Canada* 105 B7
Sealy, *U.S.A.* 113 L6
Searchlight, *U.S.A.* 111 K12
Searcy, *U.S.A.* 113 H9
Searles L., *U.S.A.* 111 K9
Seascale, *U.K.* 14 C4
Seaside, *Calif., U.S.A.* 110 J5
Seaside, *Oreg., U.S.A.* 110 E3
Seaspray, *Australia* 95 F4
Seattle, *U.S.A.* 110 C4
Seattle-Tacoma International ✈
  (SEA), *U.S.A.* 110 C4
Seaview Ra., *Australia* 94 B4
Sebago L., *U.S.A.* 117 C14
Sebago Lake, *U.S.A.* 117 C14
Sebastián Vizcaíno, B., *Mexico* . 118 B2
Sebastopol = Sevastopol, *Ukraine* 33 K7
Sebastopol, *U.S.A.* 110 G4
Sebba, *Burkina Faso* 83 C5
Sebderat, *Eritrea* 81 D4
Sebele, *Turkey* 72 B4
Seben, *Turkey* 72 B4
Sebeş, *Romania* 29 E8
Sebeşului, Munţii, *Romania* ... 29 E8
Sebewaing, *U.S.A.* 114 D4
Sebezh, *Russia* 32 D5
Sebha = Sabhah, *Libya* 79 C8
Sébi, *Mali* 82 B4
Şebinkarahisar, *Turkey* 73 B8
Sebiş, *Romania* 28 D7
Sebnitz, *Germany* 24 E10
Sebring, *Fla., U.S.A.* 115 M5
Sebring, *Ohio, U.S.A.* 116 F3
Sebringville, *Canada* 116 C3
Sebta = Ceuta, *N. Afr.* 78 A4
Sebuku, *Indonesia* 62 E5
Sebuku, Teluk, *Malaysia* 62 D5
Sečanj, *Serbia & M.* 28 E5
Secchia ➤, *Italy* 40 C8
Sechelt, *Canada* 102 D4
Sechura, Desierto de, *Peru* 124 E2
Seclin, *France* 19 B10
Secondigny, *France* 18 F6
Sečovce, *Slovak Rep.* 27 C14
Secretary I., *N.Z.* 91 L1
Secunderabad, *India* 66 L11
Security-Widefield, *U.S.A.* ... 112 F2
Sedalia, *U.S.A.* 112 F8
Sedan, *France* 19 C11
Sedan, *U.S.A.* 113 G6
Sedano, *Spain* 36 C7
Seddon, *N.Z.* 91 J5
Seddonville, *N.Z.* 91 J4
Sedé Boqér, *Israel* 74 E3
Sedeh, *Fārs, Iran* 71 D7
Sedeh, *Khorāsān, Iran* 71 C8
Séderon, *France* 21 D9
Sederot, *Israel* 74 D3
Sédhiou, *Senegal* 82 C1
Sedico, *Italy* 41 B9
Sedlčany, *Czech Rep.* 26 B7
Sedley, *Canada* 103 C8
Sedona, *U.S.A.* 109 J8
Sedova, Pik, *Russia* 52 B6
Sedro Woolley, *U.S.A.* 110 B4
Šeduva, *Lithuania* 30 C10
Seebad Ahlbeck, *Germany* 24 B10
Seefeld in Tirol, *Austria* 26 D4
Seehausen, *Germany* 24 C7
Seeheim, *Namibia* 88 D2
Seeheim-Jugenheim, *Germany* .. 25 F4
Seeis, *Namibia* 88 C2
Seekoei ➤, *S. Africa* 88 E4
Seeley's Bay, *Canada* 117 B8
Seelow, *Germany* 24 C10
Sées, *France* 18 D7
Seesen, *Germany* 24 D6
Seevetal, *Germany* 24 B6
Seewinkel = Neusiedler See-
  Seewinkel △, *Austria* 27 D9
Sefadu, *S. Leone* 82 D2
Seferihisar, *Turkey* 47 C8
Séfeto, *Mali* 82 C3
Sefwi Bekwai, *Ghana* 82 D4
Segamat, *Malaysia* 65 L4
Şegarcea, *Romania* 29 F8
Ségbana, *Benin* 83 C5
Segbwema, *S. Leone* 82 D2
Segezha, *Russia* ...... 32 ... *(see orig.)*
Seget, *Indonesia* 63 E8
Segonzac, *France* 20 C3
Segorbe, *Spain* 38 F4
Ségou, *Mali* 82 C3
Segovia = Coco ➤, *Cent. Amer.* . 120 D3
Segovia, *Spain* 36 E6
Segovia □, *Spain* 36 E6
Segré, *France* 18 E6
Segre ➤, *Spain* 38 D5
Séguéla, *Ivory C.* 82 D3
Séguénéga, *Burkina Faso* 83 C4
Seguin, *U.S.A.* 113 L6
Segundo ➤, *Argentina* 126 C3
Segura ➤, *Spain* 39 G4
Segura, Sierra de, *Spain* 39 G2
Seh Konj, Küh-e, *Iran* 71 D8
Seh Qal'eh, *Iran* 71 C8

Sehitwa, *Botswana* 88 C3
Sehlabathebe △, *Lesotho* 89 D4
Sehore, *India* 68 H7
Sehwan, *Pakistan* 68 F2
Şeica Mare, *Romania* 29 D9
Seil, *U.K.* 13 E3
Seiland, *Norway* 8 A20
Seilhac, *France* 20 C5
Seiling, *U.S.A.* 113 G5
Seille ➤, *Moselle, France* 19 C13
Seille ➤, *Saône-et-Loire, France* . 19 F11
Sein, Î. de, *France* 18 D2
Seinäjoki, *Finland* 9 E20
Seine ➤, *France* 18 C7
Seine, B. de la, *France* 18 C6
Seine-et-Marne □, *France* 19 D10
Seine-Maritime □, *France* 18 C7
Seine-St-Denis □, *France* 19 D9
Seini, *Romania* 29 C8
Seirijai, *Lithuania* 30 D10
Seistan = Sīstān, *Asia* 71 D9
Seistan, Daryācheh-ye =
  Sīstān, Daryācheh-ye, *Iran* ... 71 D9
Sejerø, *Denmark* 11 J5
Sejerø Bugt, *Denmark* 11 J5
Sejny, *Poland* 30 D10
Seka, *Ethiopia* 81 F4
Sekayu, *Indonesia* 62 E2
Seke, *Tanzania* 86 C3
Sekenke, *Tanzania* 86 C3
Seki, *Turkey* 47 E11
Sekondi-Takoradi, *Ghana* 82 E4
Sekota, *Ethiopia* 81 E4
Seksna, *Russia* 32 C10
Sekudai, *Malaysia* ...... 65 d
Sekuma, *Botswana* 88 C3
Selah, *U.S.A.* 108 C3
Selama, *Malaysia* 65 K3
Selárgius, *Italy* 42 C2
Selaru, *Indonesia* 63 F8
Selatan, Selat, *Malaysia* ..... 65 c
Selb, *Germany* 25 E8
Selby, *U.K.* 14 D6
Selby, *U.S.A.* 112 C4
Selca, *Croatia* 41 E13
Selçuk, *Turkey* 47 D9
Selden, *U.S.A.* 112 F4
Sele ➤, *Italy* 43 B7
Selebi-Pikwe, *Botswana* 89 C4
Selemdzha ➤, *Russia* 53 D13
Selendi, *Manisa, Turkey* 47 C10
Selendi, *Manisa, Turkey* 47 C9
Selenga = Selenge Mörön ➤,
  Asia 60 A5
Selenge Mörön ➤, *Asia* 60 A5
Seleničë, *Albania* 44 F3
Selenter See, *Germany* 24 A6
Sélestat, *France* 19 D14
Seletan, Tanjung, *Indonesia* ... 62 E4
Selevac, *Serbia & M.* 44 B4
Sélibabi, *Mauritania* 82 B2
Seliger, Ozero, *Russia* 32 C7
Seligman, *U.S.A.* 109 J7
Şelim, *Turkey* 73 B10
Selīma, El Wâhât el, *Sudan* ... 80 C2
Selimiye, *Turkey* 47 D9
Selinda Spillway ➤, *Botswana* .. 88 B3
Selinoús, *Greece* 46 D3
Selinsgrove, *U.S.A.* 116 F8
Selizharovo, *Russia* 32 D7
Selkirk, *Canada* 103 C9
Selkirk, *U.K.* 13 F6
Selkirk I. = Horse I., *Canada* ... 103 C9
Selkirk Mts., *Canada* 100 C8
Sellafield, *U.K.* 14 C4
Sellama, *Sudan* 81 E2
Selliá, *Greece* 49 D6
Sellières, *France* 19 F12
Sells, *U.S.A.* 109 L8
Sellye, *Hungary* 28 E2
Selma, *Ala., U.S.A.* 115 J2
Selma, *Calif., U.S.A.* 110 J7
Selma, *N.C., U.S.A.* 115 H6
Selmer, *U.S.A.* 115 H1
Selongey, *France* 19 E12
Selous ➤, *Tanzania* 87 D4
Selowandoma Falls, *Zimbabwe* .. 87 G3
Selpele, *Indonesia* 63 E8
Selsey Bill, *U.K.* 15 G7
Seltso, *Russia* 32 F8
Seltz, *France* 19 D15
Selu, *Indonesia* 63 F8
Sélune ➤, *France* 18 D5
Selva = La Selva del Camp, *Spain* 38 D6
Selva, *Argentina* 126 B3
Selva Lancandona = Montes
  Azules △, *Mexico* 119 D6
Selvas, *Brazil* 124 E5
Selwyn L., *Canada* 103 B8
Selwyn Mts., *Canada* 100 B6
Selwyn Ra., *Australia* 94 C3
Selyatyn, *Ukraine* 29 C10
Seman ➤, *Albania* 44 F3
Semarang, *Indonesia* 63 G14
Sembabule, *Uganda* 86 C3
Sembawang, *Singapore* ...... 65 d
Sembung, *Indonesia* 63 J18
Şemdinli, *Turkey* 73 D11
Sémé, *Senegal* 82 B2
Semeih, *Sudan* 81 E3
Semenanjung Blambangan,
  Indonesia 63 K17
Semenov, *Russia* 34 B7
Semenovka, Chernihiv, *Ukraine* . 33 F7
Semenovka, Kremenchuk,
  Ukraine 33 H7
Semeru, *Indonesia* 63 H15
Semey, *Kazakhstan* 52 D9
Semikarakorskiy, *Russia* 35 G5
Semiluki, *Russia* 33 G10
Seminoe Reservoir, *U.S.A.* ... 108 F10

Seminole, Okla., U.S.A. 113 H6
Seminole, Tex., U.S.A. 113 J3
Seminole Draw ➧, U.S.A. 113 J3
Semipalatinsk = Semey,
   Kazakhstan 52 D9
Semirara Is., Phil. 61 F4
Semitau, Indonesia 62 D4
Semiyarka, Kazakhstan 52 D8
Semiyarskoye = Semiyarka,
   Kazakhstan 52 D8
Semmering P., Austria 26 D8
Semnān, Iran 71 C7
Semnān □, Iran 71 C7
Semporna, Malaysia 63 D5
Semuda, Indonesia 62 E4
Semur-en-Auxois, France 19 E11
Sen ➧, Cambodia 62 B3
Senā, Iran 71 D6
Sena, Mozam. 87 F4
Sena Madureira, Brazil 124 E5
Senador Pompeu, Brazil 125 E11
Senaki, Georgia 35 J6
Senang, Pulau, Singapore ..... 65 d
Senanga, Zambia 85 H4
Senatobia, U.S.A. 113 H10
Sencelles, Spain 48 B9
Sendafa, Ethiopia 81 F4
Sendai, Kagoshima, Japan 55 J5
Sendai, Miyagi, Japan 54 E10
Sendai-Wan, Japan 54 E10
Senden, Bayern, Germany 25 G6
Senden, Nordrhein-Westfalen,
   Germany 24 D3
Sendhwa, India 68 J6
Sene ➧, Ghana 83 D4
Senec, Slovak Rep. 27 C10
Seneca, U.S.A. 115 H4
Seneca Falls, U.S.A. 117 D8
Seneca L., U.S.A. 116 D8
Senecaville L., U.S.A. 116 G3
Senegal ■, W. Afr. 82 C2
Sénégal ➧, W. Afr. 82 B1
Senegambia, Africa 76 E2
Senekal, S. Africa 89 D4
Senftenberg, Germany 24 D10
Senga Hill, Zambia 87 D3
Senge Khambab = Indus ➧,
   Pakistan 68 G2
Sengiley, Russia 34 D9
Sengua ➧, Zimbabwe 87 F2
Senhor-do-Bonfim, Brazil 125 F10
Senica, Slovak Rep. 27 C10
Senigállia, Italy 41 E10
Senio ➧, Italy 41 D9
Senirkent, Turkey 47 C12
Senise, Italy 43 B9
Senj, Croatia 41 D11
Senja, Norway 8 B17
Senkaku-Shotō, Japan 55 L1
Senkuang, Indonesia .... 65 d
Senlis, France 19 C9
Senmonorom, Cambodia 64 F6
Sennâr, Sudan 81 E3
Sennar □, Sudan 81 E3
Senneterre, Canada 104 C4
Senno, Belarus 32 E5
Sénnori, Italy 42 B1
Seno, Laos 64 D5
Senonches, France 18 D8
Senorbì, Italy 42 C2
Senožeče, Slovenia 41 C11
Sens, France 19 D10
Senta, Serbia & M. 28 E5
Sentani, Indonesia 63 E10
Sentery = Lubao, Dem. Rep. of
   the Congo 86 D2
Sentinel, U.S.A. 109 K7
Šentjur, Slovenia 41 B12
Sentosa, Singapore .... 65 d
Senya Beraku, Ghana 83 D4
Seo de Urgel = La Seu d'Urgell,
   Spain 38 C6
Seohara, India 69 E8
Seonath ➧, India 69 J10
Seondha, India 69 F8
Seoni, India 69 H8
Seoni Malwa, India 68 H8
Seoul = Sŏul, S. Korea 57 F14
Sepo-ri, N. Korea 57 E14
Sepīdān, Iran 71 D7
Sępólno Krajeńskie, Poland ... 30 E4
Sepone, Laos 64 D6
Sępopol, Poland 30 D8
Sept-Îles, Canada 105 B6
Septemvri, Bulgaria 45 D8
Sepúlveda, Spain 36 D7
Sequeros, Spain 36 E4
Sequim, U.S.A. 110 B3
Sequoia △, U.S.A. 110 J8
Serafimovich, Russia 34 F6
Seraing, Belgium 17 D5
Serakhis ➧, Cyprus 49 D11
Seram, Indonesia 63 E7
Seram Sea, Indonesia 63 E7
Seranantsara, Madag. 89 B8
Serang, Indonesia 63 G12
Serangoon, Singapore .... 65 d
Serasan, Indonesia 62 D3
Seravezza, Italy 40 E7
Şerbettar, Turkey 45 E10
Serbia ■, Serbia & M. 44 C5
Serbia & Montenegro ■, Europe 44 C4
Şercaia, Romania 29 E10
Serdo, Ethiopia 81 E5
Serdobsk, Russia 34 D7
Sered', Slovak Rep. 27 C10
Seredka, Russia 32 C5
Serednye, Ukraine 29
Şereflikoçhisar, Turkey 72 C5
Seregno, Italy 40 C6
Seremban, Malaysia 65 L3

Serengeti △, Tanzania 86 C3
Serengeti Plain, Tanzania 86 C4
Serenje, Zambia 87 E3
Seret ➧, Ukraine 29 B10
Sereth = Siret ➧, Romania 29 E12
Sergach, Russia 34 C7
Sergen, Turkey 45 E11
Sergino, Russia 52 C7
Sergipe □, Brazil 125 F11
Sergiyev Posad, Russia 32 D10
Seria, Brunei 62 D4
Serian, Malaysia 62 D4
Seriate, Italy 40 C6
Seribu, Kepulauan, Indonesia ... 62 F3
Sérifontaine, France 19 C8
Sérifos, Greece 46 D6
Sérignan, France 20 E7
Sérigny ➧, Canada 105 A6
Serik, Turkey 72 D4
Seringapatam Reef, Australia ... 92 B3
Serinhisar, Turkey 47 D11
Seririt, Indonesia 63 J17
Sermaize-les-Bains, France 19 D11
Sermata, Indonesia 63 F7
Sermersuaq, Greenland 4 B4
Sérmide, Italy 41 D8
Sernovodsk, Russia 34 D10
Sernur, Russia 34 B9
Serock, Poland 31 F8
Serón, Spain 39 H2
Seròs, Spain 38 D5
Serov, Russia 52 D7
Serowe, Botswana 88 C4
Serpa, Portugal 37 H3
Serpeddì, Punta, Italy 42 C2
Serpentara, Italy 42 C2
Serpentine Lakes, Australia ... 93 E4
Serpent's Mouth = Sierpe, Bocas
   de la, Venezuela 125 L15
Serpis ➧, Spain 39 G4
Serpneve, Ukraine 29 D14
Serpukhov, Russia 32 E9
Serra da Estrela ⌂, Portugal ... 36 E3
Serra de Outes, Spain 36 C2
Serra do Navio, Brazil 125 C8
Serra San Bruno, Italy 43 D9
Serradilla, Spain 36 F4
Sérrai, Greece 44 E7
Sérrai □, Greece 44 E7
Serramanna, Italy 42 C1
Serranía San Luís △, Paraguay ... 126 A4
Serras d'Aire e Candeeiros ⌂,
   Portugal 37 F2
Serravalle Scrívia, Italy 40 D5
Serre-Ponçon, L. de, France ... 21 D10
Serres, France 21 D9
Serrezuela, Argentina 126 C2
Serrinha, Brazil 125 F11
Sertã, Portugal 36 F2
Sertanópolis, Brazil 127 A5
Sêrtar, China 58 A3
Serua, Indonesia 63 F8
Serui, Indonesia 63 E9
Serule, Botswana 88 C4
Sérvia, Greece 44 F6
Serzedelo, Portugal 36 D2
Ses Salines, Spain 48 B10
Sese Is., Uganda 86 C3
Sesepe, Indonesia 63 E7
Sesfontein, Namibia 88 B1
Sesheke, Zambia 88 B3
Sésia ➧, Italy 40 C5
Sesimbra, Portugal 37 G1
S'Espalmador, Spain 48 C7
S'Espardell, Spain 48 C7
Sessa Aurunca, Italy 42 A6
S'Estanyol, Spain 48 B9
Sestao, Spain 38 B2
Sesto Calende, Italy 40 C5
Sesto San Giovanni, Italy 40 C6
Sestri Levante, Italy 40 D6
Sestriere, Italy 40 D3
Sestroretsk, Russia 32 B6
Sestrunj, Croatia 41 D11
Sestu, Italy 42 C2
Setana, Japan 54 C9
Sète, France 20 E7
Sete Lagôas, Brazil 125 G10
Sétif, Algeria 78 A7
Seto, Japan 55 G8
Setonaikai, Japan 55 G6
Setonaikai △, Japan 55 G6
Settat, Morocco 78 B4
Séttimo Torinese, Italy 40 C4
Setting L., Canada 103 C9
Settle, U.K. 14 C5
Settlement Pt., Bahamas 115 M6
Settlers, S. Africa 89 C4
Setúbal, Portugal 37 G2
Setúbal □, Portugal 37 G2
Setúbal, B. de, Portugal 37 G2
Seugne ➧, France 20 C3
Seul, Lac, Canada 104 B1
Seurre, France 19 F12
Sevan, Armenia 35 K7
Sevan, Ozero = Sevana Lich,
   Armenia 35 K7
Sevana Lich, Armenia 35 K7
Sevastopol, Ukraine 33 K7
Seven Sisters, Canada 102 C3
Sever ➧, Spain 37 F3
Sévérac-le-Château, France ... 20 D7
Severn ➧, Canada 104 A2
Severn ➧, U.K. 15 F5
Severn L., Canada 104 B1
Severnaya Zemlya, Russia 53 B10
Severo-Kurilsk, Russia 53 D16
Severo-Yenjust, Russia 53 C10
Severo-Zapadny □, Russia 52 C4
Severočeský □, Czech Rep. 26 A7

Severodonetsk = Syeverodonetsk,
   Ukraine 33 H10
Severodvinsk, Russia 52 C4
Severomoravský □, Czech Rep. ... 27 B10
Sevier, U.S.A. 109 G7
Sevier ➧, U.S.A. 109 G7
Sevier Desert, U.S.A. 108 G7
Sevier L., U.S.A. 108 G7
Sevilla, Spain 37 H5
Sevilla □, Spain 37 H5
Seville = Sevilla, Spain 37 H5
Sevlievo, Bulgaria 45 C9
Sevnica, Slovenia 41 B12
Sevsk, Russia 33 F8
Sewa ➧, S. Leone 82 D2
Sewani, India 68 E6
Seward, Alaska, U.S.A. 100 B5
Seward, Nebr., U.S.A. 112 E6
Seward, Pa., U.S.A. 116 F5
Seward Peninsula, U.S.A. 100 B3
Sewell, Chile 126 C1
Sewer, Indonesia 63 F8
Sewickley, U.S.A. 116 F4
Sexsmith, Canada 102 B5
Seychelles ■, Ind. Oc. 50 K9
Seyðisfjörður, Iceland 8 D6
Seydişehir, Turkey 72 D4
Seydvān, Iran 70 B5
Seyhan ➧, Turkey 70 B2
Seyhan Barajı, Turkey 72 D6
Seyitgazi, Turkey 47 B12
Seyitömer, Turkey 47 B11
Seym ➧, Ukraine 33 G7
Seymen, Turkey 45 E11
Seymour, Australia 95 F4
Seymour, S. Africa 89 E4
Seymour, Conn., U.S.A. 117 E11
Seymour, Ind., U.S.A. 114 F3
Seymour, Tex., U.S.A. 113 J5
Seyne, France 21 D10
Seyssel, France 21 C9
Sežana, Slovenia 41 C10
Sézanne, France 19 D10
Sezze, Italy 42 A6
Sfax, Tunisia 79 B8
Sha Xi ➧, China 59 D12
Sha Xian, China 59 D11
Shaanxi □, China 56 G5
Shaba = Katanga □, Dem. Rep. of
   the Congo 86 D2
Shaba ⌂, Kenya 86 B4
Shaballe = Scebeli, Wabi ➧,
   Somali Rep. 75 G3
Shabla, Bulgaria 45 C12
Shabogamo L., Canada 105 B6
Shabunda, Dem. Rep. of
   the Congo 86 C2
Shache, China 60 C2
Shackleton Ice Shelf, Antarctica ... 5 C8
Shackleton Inlet, Antarctica ... 5 E11
Shādegān, Iran 71 D6
Shadi, China 59 D10
Shadi, India 69 C7
Shadrinsk, Russia 52 D7
Shadyside, U.S.A. 116 G4
Shaffa, Nigeria 83 C7
Shafter, U.S.A. 111 K7
Shaftesbury, U.K. 15 F5
Shagamu, Nigeria 83 D5
Shagram, Pakistan 69 A5
Shah Alizai, Pakistan 68 E2
Shah Bunder, Pakistan 68 G2
Shahabad, Punjab, India 68 D7
Shahabad, Raj., India 68 G7
Shahabad, Ut. P., India 69 F8
Shahadpur, Pakistan 68 G3
Shahba, Syria 74 C5
Shahdād, Iran 71 D8
Shahdād, Namakzār-e, Iran ... 71 D8
Shahdadkot, Pakistan 68 F2
Shahdol, India 69 H9
Shahe, China 56 F8
Shahganj, India 69 F10
Shahgarh, India 66 F6
Shahjahanpur, India 69 F8
Shahpur, India 68 H7
Shahpur, Baluchistan, Pakistan ... 68 E3
Shahpur, Punjab, Pakistan 68 C5
Shahpur Chakar, Pakistan 68 G3
Shahpura, Mad. P., India 69 H9
Shahpura, Raj., India 68 G6
Shahr-e Bābak, Iran 71 D7
Shahr-e Kord, Iran 71 C6
Shāhrakht, Iran 71 C9
Shahrig, Pakistan 68 D2
Shahukou, China 56 D7
Shaikhabad, Afghan. 68 B3
Shajapur, India 68 H7
Shakargarh, Pakistan 68 C6
Shakawe, Botswana 88 B3
Shaker Heights, U.S.A. 116 E3
Shakhty, Russia 35 G5
Shakhunya, Russia 34 B8
Shaki, Nigeria 83 D5
Shala, L., Ethiopia 81 F4
Shali, Russia 35 J7
Shallow Lake, Canada 116 B3
Shalqar, Kazakhstan 52 E6
Shalskiy, Russia 32 B8
Shaluli Shan, China 58 B2
Shām, Iran 71 E8

Shām, Bādiyat ash, Asia 70 C3
Shamāl Bahr el Ghazal □, Sudan ... 81 F2
Shamāl Dārfûr □, Sudan 81 E2
Shamāl Kordofân □, Sudan 81 E3
Shamāl Sînî □, Egypt 74 E2
Shamattawa, Canada 104 A1
Shamattawa ➧, Canada 104 A2
Shambe, Sudan 81 F3
Shambe △, Sudan 81 F3
Shambu, Ethiopia 81 F4
Shamil, Iran 71 E8
Shamkhor = Şämkir, Azerbaijan ... 35 K8
Shāmkūh, Iran 71 C8
Shamli, India 68 E7
Shammar, Jabal, Si. Arabia ... 70 E4
Shamo = Gobi, Asia 56 C6
Shamo, L., Ethiopia 81 F4
Shamokin, U.S.A. 117 F8
Shamrock, U.S.A. 113 H4
Shamva, Zimbabwe 87 F3
Shan □, Burma 67 J21
Shan Xian, China 56 G9
Shanan ➧, Ethiopia 81 F5
Shanchengzhen, China 57 C13
Shāndak, Iran 71 D9
Shandon, U.S.A. 110 K6
Shandong □, China 57 G10
Shandong Bandao, China 57 F11
Shang Xian = Shangzhou, China ... 56 H5
Shanga, Nigeria 78 F6
Shangalowe, Dem. Rep. of
   the Congo 87 E2
Shangani, Zimbabwe 89 B4
Shangani ➧, Zimbabwe 87 F2
Shangbancheng, China 57 D10
Shangcheng, China 59 B10
Shangchuan Dao, China 59 G9
Shanggao, China 59 C10
Shanghai, China 59 B13
Shanghai Shi □, China 59 B13
Shanghang, China 59 E11
Shanghe, China 57 F9
Shanglin, China 58 F7
Shangnan, China 56 H6
Shangqiu, China 56 G8
Shangrao, China 59 C11
Shangshui, China 56 H8
Shangsi, China 58 F6
Shangyou, China 59 E10
Shangyu, China 59 B13
Shangzhi, China 57 B14
Shanhetun, China 57 B14
Shani, Nigeria 83 C7
Shanklin, U.K. 15 G6
Shannon, N.Z. 91 J5
Shannon △, Australia 93 F2
Shannon ➧, Ireland 12 D4
Shannon, Mouth of the, Ireland ... 12 D2
Shannon Airport, Ireland 12 D3
Shansi = Shanxi □, China 56 F7
Shantar, Ostrov Bolshoy, Russia ... 53 D14
Shantipur, India 69 H13
Shantou, China 59 F11
Shantung = Shandong □, China ... 57 G10
Shanwei, China 59 F10
Shanxi □, China 56 F7
Shanyang, China 56 H5
Shanyin, China 56 E7
Shaodong, China 59 D8
Shaoguan, China 59 E9
Shaoshan, China 59 D9
Shaowu, China 59 D11
Shaoxing, China 59 C13
Shaoyang, Hunan, China 59 D8
Shaoyang, Hunan, China 59 D8
Shap, U.K. 14 C5
Shapinsay, U.K. 13 B6
Shaqq el Gi'eifer ➧, Sudan ... 81 D2
Shaqra', Si. Arabia 70 E5
Shaqrā', Yemen 75 E4
Sharafa, Sudan 81 E2
Sharafkhāneh, Iran 70 B5
Sharashova, Belarus 31 F11
Sharbot Lake, Canada 117 B8
Sharhorod, Ukraine 29 B13
Shari, Japan 54 C12
Sharjah = Ash Shāriqah, U.A.E. ... 71 E7
Shark B., Australia 93 E1
Shark Bay △, Australia 93 F2
Sharm el Sheikh, Egypt 80 B3
Sharon, Mass., U.S.A. 117 D13
Sharon, Pa., U.S.A. 116 E4
Sharon Springs, Kans., U.S.A. ... 112 F4
Sharon Springs, N.Y., U.S.A. ... 117 D10
Sharp Pt., Australia 94 A3
Sharpe, L., Canada 104 B1
Sharpsville, U.S.A. 116 E4
Sharq el Istiwa'iya □, Sudan ... 81 G3
Sharya, Russia 34 A7
Shasha, Ethiopia 81 F4
Shashemene, Ethiopia 81 F4
Shashi, Botswana 89 C4
Shashi, China 59 B9
Shashi ➧, Africa 87 G2
Shasta, Mt., U.S.A. 108 F2
Shasta L., U.S.A. 108 F2
Shatawi, Sudan 81 E3
Shatsk, Russia 34 C5
Shatsk, Ukraine 31 G10
Shatskyi ⌂, Ukraine 31 G10
Shatt al Arab, Asia 71 D6
Shatura, Russia 32 E10
Shaumyani = Shulaveri, Georgia ... 35 K7
Shaunavon, Canada 103 D7
Shaver, U.S.A. 110 H7
Shaw ➧, Australia 92 D2
Shaw I., Australia 94 J7
Shawanaga, Canada 116 A4
Shawangunk Mts., U.S.A. 117 E10

Shawano, U.S.A. 114 C1
Shawinigan, Canada 104 C5
Shawnee, U.S.A. 113 H6
Shay Gap, Australia 92 D3
Shayang, China 59 B9
Shaybārā, Si. Arabia 70 E3
Shayib el Banat, Gebel, Egypt ... 80 B3
Shaykh, J. ash, Lebanon 74 B4
Shaykh Miskīn, Syria 74 C5
Shaykh Sa'īd, Iraq 70 C5
Shchekino, Russia 32 E9
Shchigry, Russia 33 G9
Shchors, Ukraine 33 G6
Shchuchinsk, Kazakhstan 52 D8
She Xian, Anhui, China 59 C12
She Xian, Hebei, China 56 F7
Shebekino, Russia 33 G9
Shebele = Scebeli, Wabi ➧,
   Somali Rep. 75 G3
Sheboygan, U.S.A. 114 D2
Shebshi Mts., Nigeria 83 D7
Shediac, Canada 105 C7
Sheelin, L., Ireland 12 C4
Sheep Haven, Ireland 12 A4
Sheerness, U.K. 15 F8
Sheet Harbour, Canada 105 D7
Sheffield, U.K. 14 D6
Sheffield, Ala., U.S.A. 115 H2
Sheffield, Mass., U.S.A. 117 D11
Sheffield, Pa., U.S.A. 116 E5
Shehojele, Ethiopia 81 E4
Shehong, China 58 B5
Sheikh Idris, Sudan 81 E3
Sheikhpura, India 69 G11
Shek Hasan, Ethiopia 81 E4
Shekhupura, Pakistan 68 D5
Sheki = Şaki, Azerbaijan 35 K8
Shelburne, N.S., Canada 105 D6
Shelburne, Ont., Canada 116 B4
Shelburne, U.S.A. 117 B11
Shelburne B., Australia 94 A3
Shelburne Falls, U.S.A. 117 D12
Shelby, Mich., U.S.A. 114 D2
Shelby, Miss., U.S.A. 113 J9
Shelby, Mont., U.S.A. 108 B8
Shelby, N.C., U.S.A. 115 H5
Shelby, Ohio, U.S.A. 116 F2
Shelbyville, Ill., U.S.A. 112 F10
Shelbyville, Ind., U.S.A. 114 F3
Shelbyville, Ky., U.S.A. 114 F3
Shelbyville, Tenn., U.S.A. 115 H2
Sheldon, U.S.A. 112 D7
Sheldrake, Canada 105 B7
Shelengo, Khawr ➧, Sudan ... 81 E2
Shelikhova, Zaliv, Russia 53 D16
Shell Lakes, Australia 93 E4
Shellbrook, Canada 103 C7
Shellharbour, Australia 95 E5
Shelon ➧, Russia 32 C6
Shelter I, U.S.A. 117 E12
Shelton, Conn., U.S.A. 117 E11
Shelton, Wash., U.S.A. 110 C3
Shemakha = Şamaxi, Azerbaijan ... 35 K9
Shëmri, Albania 44 D4
Shemsi, Sudan 80 D2
Shen Xian, China 56 F8
Shenandoah, Iowa, U.S.A. 112 E7
Shenandoah, Pa., U.S.A. 117 F8
Shenandoah, Va., U.S.A. 114 F6
Shenandoah △, U.S.A. 114 F6
Shenandoah ➧, U.S.A. 114 F7
Shenchi, China 56 E7
Shendam, Nigeria 83 D6
Shendî, Sudan 81 D3
Shenge, S. Leone 82 D2
Shengfang, China 56 E9
Shëngjergj, Albania 44 E4
Shëngjin, Albania 44 E3
Shengzhou, China 59 C13
Shenjingzi, China 57 B13
Shenmu, China 56 E6
Shennongjia, China 59 B8
Shenqiu, China 56 H8
Shensi = Shaanxi □, China 56 G5
Shenyang, China 57 D12
Shenzhen, China 59 F10
Sheo, India 68 F4
Sheopur Kalan, India 66 G10
Shepetivka, Ukraine 33 G4
Shepetovka = Shepetivka,
   Ukraine 33 G4
Shepparton, Australia 95 F4
Sheppey, I. of, U.K. 15 F8
Shepton Mallet, U.K. 15 F5
Sheqi, China 56 H7
Sher Qila, Pakistan 69 A6
Sherab, Sudan 81 E1
Sherborne, U.K. 15 G5
Sherbro ➧, S. Leone 82 D2
Sherbro I., S. Leone 82 D2
Sherbrooke, N.S., Canada 105 C7
Sherbrooke, Qué., Canada 117 A13
Sherburne, U.S.A. 117 D9
Shereik, Sudan 80 D3
Shergarh, India 68 F5
Sherghati, India 69 G11
Sheridan, Ark., U.S.A. 113 H8
Sheridan, Wyo., U.S.A. 108 D10
Sheringham, U.K. 14 E9
Sherkin I., Ireland 12 E2
Sherkot, India 69 E8
Sherman, U.S.A. 113 J6
Sherpur, India 69 G10
Sherridon, Canada 103 B8
Sherwood Forest, U.K. 14 D6
Sherwood Park, Canada 102 C6
Sheslay ➧, Canada 102 B2
Shethanei L., Canada 103 B9
Shetland □, U.K. 13 A7
Shetland Is., U.K. 13 A7
Shetrunji ➧, India 68 J5

Shevchenkovo, *Ukraine* 29 **E14**
Shewa, *Ethiopia* 81 **F4**
Shewa Gimira, *Ethiopia* 81 **F4**
Sheyenne →, *U.S.A.* 112 **B6**
Shibām, *Yemen* 75 **D4**
Shibata, *Japan* 54 **F9**
Shibecha, *Japan* 54 **C12**
Shibetsu, *Japan* 54 **B11**
Shibîn el Kôm, *Egypt* 80 **H7**
Shibîn el Qanâtir, *Egypt* 80 **H7**
Shibing, *China* 58 **D7**
Shibogama L., *Canada* 104 **B2**
Shibushi, *Japan* 55 **J5**
Shicheng, *China* 59 **D11**
Shickshinny, *U.S.A.* 117 **E8**
Shickshock Mts. = Chic-Chocs, Mts., *Canada* 105 **C6**
Shidao, *China* 57 **F12**
Shidian, *China* 58 **E2**
Shido, *Japan* 55 **G7**
Shiel, L., *U.K.* 13 **E3**
Shield, C., *Australia* 94 **A2**
Shīeli, *Kazakhstan* 52 **E7**
Shifang, *China* 58 **B5**
Shiga ☐, *Japan* 55 **G8**
Shigu, *China* 58 **D2**
Shiguaigou, *China* 56 **D6**
Shihchiachuangi = Shijiazhuang, *China* 56 **E8**
Shihezi, *China* 60 **B3**
Shijak, *Albania* 44 **E3**
Shijiazhuang, *China* 56 **E8**
Shijiu Hu, *China* 59 **B12**
Shikarpur, *India* 68 **E8**
Shikarpur, *Pakistan* 68 **F3**
Shikohabad, *India* 69 **F8**
Shikoku ☐, *Japan* 55 **H6**
Shikoku-Sanchi, *Japan* 55 **H6**
Shikotsu-Ko, *Japan* 54 **C10**
Shikotsu-Tōya △, *Japan* 54 **C10**
Shiliguri, *India* 67 **F16**
Shilka, *Russia* 53 **D12**
Shilka →, *Russia* 53 **D13**
Shillelagh, *Ireland* 12 **D5**
Shillington, *U.S.A.* 117 **F9**
Shillong, *India* 67 **G17**
Shilo, *West Bank* 74 **C4**
Shilong, *China* 59 **F9**
Shilou, *China* 56 **F6**
Shilovo, *Russia* 34 **C5**
Shimabara, *Japan* 55 **H5**
Shimada, *Japan* 55 **G9**
Shimane ☐, *Japan* 55 **G6**
Shimanovsk, *Russia* 53 **D13**
Shimba Hills ⌓, *Kenya* 86 **C4**
Shimen, *China* 59 **C8**
Shimenjie, *China* 59 **C11**
Shimian, *China* 58 **C4**
Shimizu, *Japan* 55 **G9**
Shimodate, *Japan* 55 **F9**
Shimoga, *India* 66 **N9**
Shimoni, *Kenya* 86 **C4**
Shimonoseki, *Japan* 55 **H5**
Shimpuru Rapids, *Namibia* 88 **B2**
Shimsk, *Russia* 32 **C6**
Shin, L., *U.K.* 13 **C4**
Shinan, *China* 58 **F7**
Shinano-Gawa →, *Japan* 55 **F9**
Shināş, *Oman* 71 **E8**
Shīndand, *Afghan.* 66 **C3**
Shinglehouse, *U.S.A.* 116 **E6**
Shingū, *Japan* 55 **H7**
Shingwidzi, *S. Africa* 89 **C5**
Shinjō, *Japan* 54 **E10**
Shinkafe, *Nigeria* 83 **C6**
Shinshār, *Syria* 74 **A5**
Shinyanga, *Tanzania* 86 **C3**
Shinyanga ☐, *Tanzania* 86 **C3**
Shio-no-Misaki, *Japan* 55 **H7**
Shiogama, *Japan* 54 **E10**
Shiojiri, *Japan* 55 **F8**
Shipchenski Prokhod, *Bulgaria* 45 **D9**
Shiping, *China* 58 **F4**
Shippagan, *Canada* 105 **C7**
Shippensburg, *U.S.A.* 116 **F7**
Shippenville, *U.S.A.* 116 **E5**
Shiprock, *U.S.A.* 109 **H9**
Shiqian, *China* 58 **D7**
Shiqma, N. →, *Israel* 74 **D3**
Shiquan, *China* 56 **H5**
Shiquan He = Indus →, *Pakistan* 68 **G2**
Shīr Kūh, *Iran* 71 **D7**
Shiragami-Misaki, *Japan* 54 **D10**
Shirakawa, *Fukushima, Japan* 55 **F10**
Shirakawa, *Gifu, Japan* 55 **F8**
Shirane-San, *Gumma, Japan* 55 **F9**
Shirane-San, *Yamanashi, Japan* 55 **G9**
Shiraoi, *Japan* 54 **C10**
Shīrāz, *Iran* 71 **D7**
Shirbīn, *Egypt* 80 **H7**
Shire →, *Africa* 87 **F4**
Shiretoko-Misaki, *Japan* 54 **B12**
Shirinab →, *Pakistan* 68 **D2**
Shiriya-Zaki, *Japan* 54 **D10**
Shiroishi, *Japan* 54 **F10**
Shīrvān, *Iran* 71 **B8**
Shirwa, L. = Chilwa, L., *Malawi* 87 **F4**
Shishi, *China* 59 **E12**
Shishou, *China* 59 **C9**
Shitai, *China* 59 **B11**
Shivpuri, *India* 68 **G7**
Shixian, *China* 57 **C15**
Shixing, *China* 59 **E10**
Shiyan, *China* 59 **A8**
Shiyata, *Egypt* 80 **B2**
Shizhu, *China* 58 **C7**
Shizong, *China* 58 **E5**
Shizuishan, *China* 56 **E4**
Shizuoka, *Japan* 55 **G9**
Shizuoka ☐, *Japan* 55 **G9**
Shklov = Shklow, *Belarus* 32 **E6**
Shklow, *Belarus* 32 **E6**
Shkodër, *Albania* 44 **D3**
Shkumbini →, *Albania* 44 **E3**
Shmidta, Ostrov, *Russia* 53 **A10**
Shō-Gawa →, *Japan* 55 **F8**
Shoal L., *Canada* 103 **D9**
Shoal Lake, *Canada* 103 **C8**
Shōdo-Shima, *Japan* 55 **G7**
Sholapur = Solapur, *India* 66 **L9**
Shōmrōn, *West Bank* 74 **C4**
Shoreham by Sea, *U.K.* 15 **G7**
Shori →, *Pakistan* 68 **E3**
Shorkot Road, *Pakistan* 68 **D5**
Shoshone, *Calif., U.S.A.* 111 **K10**
Shoshone, *Idaho, U.S.A.* 108 **E6**
Shoshone L., *U.S.A.* 108 **D8**
Shoshone Mts., *U.S.A.* 108 **G5**
Shoshong, *Botswana* 88 **C4**
Shoshoni, *U.S.A.* 108 **E9**
Shostka, *Ukraine* 33 **G7**
Shou Xian, *China* 59 **A11**
Shouchang, *China* 59 **C12**
Shouguang, *China* 57 **F10**
Shouning, *China* 59 **D12**
Shouyang, *China* 56 **F7**
Show Low, *U.S.A.* 109 **J9**
Shpola, *Ukraine* 33 **H6**
Shpykiv, *Ukraine* 29 **B13**
Shreveport, *U.S.A.* 113 **J8**
Shrewsbury, *U.K.* 15 **E5**
Shri Mohangarh, *India* 68 **F4**
Shrirampur, *India* 69 **H13**
Shropshire ☐, *U.K.* 15 **E5**
Shū, *Kazakhstan* 52 **E8**
Shū →, *Kazakhstan* 50 **E10**
Shuangbai, *China* 58 **E3**
Shuangcheng, *China* 57 **B14**
Shuangfeng, *China* 59 **D9**
Shuanggou, *China* 57 **G9**
Shuangjiang, *China* 58 **F2**
Shuangliao, *China* 57 **C12**
Shuangshanzi, *China* 57 **D10**
Shuangyang, *China* 57 **C13**
Shuangyashan, *China* 60 **B8**
Shubra el Kheima, *Egypt* 80 **H7**
Shubra Khit, *Egypt* 80 **H7**
Shucheng, *China* 59 **B11**
Shugozero, *Russia* 32 **C8**
Shuguri Falls, *Tanzania* 87 **D4**
Shuiji, *China* 59 **D12**
Shuiye, *China* 56 **F8**
Shujalpur, *India* 68 **H7**
Shukpa Kunzang, *India* 69 **B8**
Shulan, *China* 57 **B14**
Shulaveri, *Georgia* 35 **K7**
Shule, *China* 60 **C2**
Shumagin Is., *U.S.A.* 100 **C4**
Shumen, *Bulgaria* 45 **C10**
Shumerlya, *Russia* 34 **C8**
Shumikha, *Russia* 52 **D7**
Shunchang, *China* 59 **D11**
Shunde, *China* 59 **F9**
Shungay, *Kazakhstan* 35 **F8**
Shuo Xian = Shuozhou, *China* 56 **E7**
Shuozhou, *China* 56 **E7**
Shūr →, *Fārs, Iran* 71 **D7**
Shūr →, *Kermān, Iran* 71 **D8**
Shūr →, *Yazd, Iran* 71 **D7**
Shūr Āb, *Iran* 71 **C6**
Shūr Gaz, *Iran* 71 **D8**
Shūrāb, *Iran* 71 **C8**
Shūrjestān, *Iran* 71 **D7**
Shurugwi, *Zimbabwe* 87 **F3**
Shūsf, *Iran* 71 **D9**
Shūsh, *Iran* 73 **F13**
Shūshtar, *Iran* 71 **D6**
Shuswap L., *Canada* 102 **C5**
Shuya, *Russia* 34 **B5**
Shuyang, *China* 57 **G10**
Shūzū, *Iran* 71 **D7**
Shwebo, *Burma* 67 **H19**
Shwegu, *Burma* 67 **G20**
Shweli →, *Burma* 67 **H20**
Shymkent, *Kazakhstan* 52 **E7**
Shyok, *India* 69 **B8**
Shyok →, *Pakistan* 69 **B6**
Shyroke, *Ukraine* 28 **B8**
Shyroke, *Ukraine* 29 **E15**
Si Chon, *Thailand* 65 **H2**
Si Kiang = Xi Jiang →, *China* 59 **F9**
Si Lanna △, *Thailand* 64 **C2**
Si-ngan = Xi'an, *China* 56 **G5**
Si Prachan, *Thailand* 64 **E3**
Si Racha, *Thailand* 64 **F3**
Si Xian, *China* 57 **H9**
Siachen Glacier, *Asia* 69 **B7**
Siahaf →, *Pakistan* 68 **E3**
Siahan Range, *Pakistan* 66 **F4**
Siaksriindrapura, *Indonesia* 62 **D2**
Sialkot, *Pakistan* 68 **C6**
Siam = Thailand ■, *Asia* 64 **E4**
Sian = Xi'an, *China* 56 **G5**
Sian Ka'an ⌓, *Mexico* 119 **D7**
Sianów, *Poland* 30 **D3**
Siantan, *Indonesia* 62 **D3**
Sīāreh, *Iran* 71 **D9**
Siargao I., *Phil.* 61 **G7**
Siari, *Pakistan* 69 **B7**
Siasi, *Phil.* 63 **C6**
Siasi I., *Phil.* 61 **J4**
Siátista, *Greece* 44 **F5**
Siau, *Indonesia* 63 **D7**
Šiauliai, *Lithuania* 9 **J20**
Šiauliai ☐, *Lithuania* 30 **C10**
Siazan = Siyäzän, *Azerbaijan* 35 **K9**
Sibâi, Gebel el, *Egypt* 70 **E2**
Sibang, *Indonesia* 63 **K18**
Sibayi, L., *S. Africa* 89 **D5**
Sibdu, *Sudan* 81 **E2**
Šibenik, *Croatia* 41 **E12**
Siberia = Sibirskiy ☐, *Russia* 53 **D10**
Siberia, *Russia* 50 **C13**
Siberut, *Indonesia* 62 **E1**
Sibi, *Pakistan* 68 **E2**
Sibil = Oksibil, *Indonesia* 63 **E10**
Sibiloi △, *Kenya* 86 **B4**
Sibirskiy ☐, *Russia* 53 **D10**
Sibiti, *Congo* 84 **E2**
Sibiu, *Romania* 29 **E9**
Sibiu ☐, *Romania* 29 **E9**
Sibley, *U.S.A.* 112 **D7**
Sibolga, *Indonesia* 62 **D1**
Sibsagar, *India* 67 **F19**
Sibu, *Malaysia* 62 **D4**
Sibuco, *Phil.* 61 **H5**
Sibuguey B., *Phil.* 61 **H5**
Sibut, *C.A.R.* 84 **C3**
Sibutu, *Phil.* 63 **D5**
Sibutu Group, *Phil.* 61 **J3**
Sibutu Passage, *E. Indies* 63 **D5**
Sibuyan I., *Phil.* 61 **E5**
Sibuyan Sea, *Phil.* 61 **E5**
Sic, *Romania* 29 **D8**
Sicamous, *Canada* 102 **C5**
Siccus →, *Australia* 95 **E2**
Sichuan ☐, *China* 58 **B5**
Sichuan Pendi, *China* 58 **B5**
Sicilia, *Italy* 43 **E7**
Sicily = Sicilia, *Italy* 43 **E7**
Sicily, Str. of 42 **E4**
Sicuani, *Peru* 124 **F4**
Šid, *Serbia & M.* 28 **E4**
Sidamo, *Ethiopia* 81 **G4**
Sidaouet, *Niger* 83 **B6**
Sidári, *Greece* 49 **A3**
Siddhapur, *India* 68 **H5**
Siddipet, *India* 66 **K11**
Sidensjö, *Sweden* 10 **A12**
Sidéradougou, *Burkina Faso* 82 **C4**
Siderno, *Italy* 43 **D9**
Sidhauli, *India* 69 **F9**
Sídheros, Ákra, *Greece* 49 **D8**
Sidhi, *India* 69 **G9**
Sidhirókastron, *Greece* 44 **E7**
Sîdi Abd el Rahmân, *Egypt* 80 **A2**
Sîdi Barrâni, *Egypt* 80 **A2**
Sidi-bel-Abbès, *Algeria* 78 **A5**
Sîdi Haneish, *Egypt* 80 **A2**
Sidi Ifni, *Morocco* 78 **C3**
Sîdi Omar, *Egypt* 80 **A1**
Sidlaw Hills, *U.K.* 13 **E5**
Sidley, Mt., *Antarctica* 5 **D14**
Sidmouth, *U.K.* 15 **G4**
Sidmouth, C., *Australia* 94 **A3**
Sidney, *Canada* 102 **D4**
Sidney, *Mont., U.S.A.* 112 **B2**
Sidney, *N.Y., U.S.A.* 117 **D9**
Sidney, *Nebr., U.S.A.* 112 **E3**
Sidney, *Ohio, U.S.A.* 114 **E3**
Sidney Lanier, L., *U.S.A.* 115 **H4**
Sido, *Mali* 82 **C3**
Sidoarjo, *Indonesia* 63 **G15**
Sidon = Saydā, *Lebanon* 74 **B4**
Sidra, G. of = Surt, Khalīj, *Libya* 79 **B9**
Siedlce, *Poland* 31 **F9**
Sieg →, *Germany* 24 **E3**
Siegburg, *Germany* 24 **E3**
Siegen, *Germany* 24 **E4**
Siem Pang, *Cambodia* 64 **E6**
Siem Reap = Siemreab, *Cambodia* 64 **F4**
Siemiatycze, *Poland* 31 **F9**
Siemreab, *Cambodia* 64 **F4**
Siena, *Italy* 41 **E8**
Sieniawa, *Poland* 31 **H9**
Sieradz, *Poland* 31 **G5**
Sieraków, *Poland* 31 **F3**
Sierck-les-Bains, *France* 19 **C13**
Sierning, *Austria* 26 **C7**
Sierpc, *Poland* 31 **F6**
Sierpe, Bocas de la, *Venezuela* 125 **L15**
Sierra Blanca, *U.S.A.* 109 **L11**
Sierra Blanca Peak, *U.S.A.* 109 **K11**
Sierra City, *U.S.A.* 110 **F6**
Sierra Colorada, *Argentina* 128 **E3**
Sierra de Aracena y Picas de Aroche ⌓, *Spain* 37 **H4**
Sierra de Bahoruco △, *Dom. Rep.* 121 **C5**
Sierra de Baza ⌓, *Spain* 39 **H2**
Sierra de Castril ⌓, *Spain* 39 **H2**
Sierra de Espuña ⌓, *Spain* 39 **H3**
Sierra de Grazalema ⌓, *Spain* 37 **J5**
Sierra de Gredos ⌓, *Spain* 36 **E5**
Sierra de Hornachuelos ⌓, *Spain* 37 **H5**
Sierra de Huétor ⌓, *Spain* 37 **H7**
Sierra de La Culata △, *Venezuela* 121 **E5**
Sierra de Lancandón △, *Guatemala* 120 **C1**
Sierra de las Nieves ⌓, *Spain* 37 **J6**
Sierra de las Quijadas △, *Argentina* 126 **C2**
Sierra de María-Los Vélez ⌓, *Spain* 39 **H2**
Sierra de San Luis △, *Venezuela* 121 **D6**
Sierra de Yeguas, *Spain* 37 **H6**
Sierra del São Mamede ⌓, *Portugal* 37 **F3**
Sierra Gorda, *Chile* 126 **A2**
Sierra Leone ■, *W. Afr.* 82 **D2**
Sierra Madre, *Mexico* 119 **D6**
Sierra Mágina ⌓, *Spain* 37 **H7**
Sierra Mojada, *Mexico* 118 **B4**
Sierra Nevada, *Spain* 37 **H7**
Sierra Nevada, *U.S.A.* 110 **H8**
Sierra Nevada ⌓, *Spain* 37 **H7**
Sierra Nevada △, *Venezuela* 121 **E5**
Sierra Nevada de Santa Marta △, *Colombia* 121 **D5**
Sierra Norte de Seville ⌓, *Spain* 37 **H5**
Sierra Subbéticas ⌓, *Spain* 37 **H6**
Sierra Vista, *U.S.A.* 109 **L8**
Sierras de Cardeña y Montoro ⌓, *Spain* 37 **G6**
Sierras de Cazorla, Segura y las Villas ⌓, *Spain* 39 **J2**
Sierraville, *U.S.A.* 110 **F6**
Sierre, *Switz.* 25 **J3**
Sifani, *Ethiopia* 81 **E5**
Sifié, *Ivory C.* 82 **D3**
Sífnos, *Greece* 46 **E6**
Sifton, *Canada* 103 **C8**
Sifton Pass, *Canada* 102 **B3**
Sigean, *France* 20 **E6**
Sighetu-Marmaţiei, *Romania* 29 **C8**
Sighişoara, *Romania* 29 **D9**
Sigli, *Indonesia* 62 **C1**
Siglufjörður, *Iceland* 8 **C4**
Sigmaringen, *Germany* 25 **G5**
Signa, *Italy* 40 **E8**
Signakhi = Tsnori, *Georgia* 35 **K7**
Signal, *U.S.A.* 111 **L13**
Signal de Botrang, *Belgium* 17 **D6**
Signal Pk., *U.S.A.* 111 **M12**
Signy I., *Antarctica* 5 **C18**
Signy-l'Abbaye, *France* 19 **C11**
Sigsig, *Ecuador* 124 **D3**
Sigüenza, *Spain* 38 **D2**
Siguiri, *Guinea* 82 **C3**
Sigulda, *Latvia* 9 **H21**
Sihora, *India* 69 **H9**
Sihui, *China* 59 **F9**
Siikajoki →, *Finland* 8 **D21**
Siilinjärvi, *Finland* 8 **E22**
Siirt, *Turkey* 73 **D9**
Sijarira Ra. = Chizarira, *Zimbabwe* 87 **F2**
Sika, *India* 68 **H3**
Sikani Chief →, *Canada* 102 **B4**
Sikao, *Thailand* 65 **J2**
Sikar, *India* 68 **F6**
Sikasso, *Mali* 82 **C3**
Sikeston, *U.S.A.* 113 **G10**
Sikhote Alin, Khrebet, *Russia* 53 **E14**
Sikhote Alin Ra. = Sikhote Alin, Khrebet, *Russia* 53 **E14**
Sikiá, *Greece* 44 **F7**
Síkinos, *Greece* 47 **E7**
Sikkim ☐, *India* 67 **F16**
Siklós, *Hungary* 28 **E3**
Sil →, *Spain* 36 **C3**
Silacayoapan, *Mexico* 119 **D5**
Šilalė, *Lithuania* 30 **C9**
Silandro, *Italy* 40 **B7**
Silawad, *India* 68 **J6**
Silay, *Phil.* 61 **F5**
Silba, *Croatia* 41 **D11**
Silchar, *India* 67 **G18**
Şile, *Turkey* 45 **E13**
Siler City, *U.S.A.* 115 **H6**
Silgarhi Doti, *Nepal* 69 **E9**
Silghat, *India* 67 **F18**
Sili, *Burkina Faso* 82 **C4**
Silifke, *Turkey* 70 **B2**
Siliguri = Shiliguri, *India* 67 **F16**
Siling Co, *China* 60 **C3**
Silistea Nouă, *Romania* 29 **F10**
Silistra, *Bulgaria* 45 **B11**
Silivri, *Turkey* 45 **E12**
Siljan, *Sweden* 10 **D8**
Siljansnäs, *Sweden* 10 **D8**
Silkeborg, *Denmark* 11 **H3**
Silkwood, *Australia* 94 **B4**
Silla, *Spain* 39 **F4**
Sillajhuay, Cordillera, *Chile* 124 **G5**
Sillamäe, *Estonia* 9 **G22**
Sillé-le-Guillaume, *France* 18 **D6**
Silleda, *Spain* 36 **C2**
Silloth, *U.K.* 14 **C4**
Sílo, *Greece* 45 **E9**
Siloam Springs, *U.S.A.* 113 **G7**
Silopi, *Turkey* 73 **D10**
Silsbee, *U.S.A.* 113 **K7**
Siluko, *Nigeria* 83 **D6**
Šilutė, *Lithuania* 9 **J19**
Silvan, *Turkey* 73 **C9**
Silvani, *India* 69 **H8**
Silver City, *U.S.A.* 109 **K9**
Silver Cr. →, *U.S.A.* 108 **E4**
Silver Creek, *U.S.A.* 116 **D5**
Silver L., *U.S.A.* 110 **G6**
Silver Lake, *Calif., U.S.A.* 111 **K10**
Silver Lake, *Oreg., U.S.A.* 108 **E3**
Silverdalen, *Sweden* 11 **G9**
Silverton, *Colo., U.S.A.* 109 **H10**
Silverton, *Tex., U.S.A.* 113 **H4**
Silves, *Portugal* 37 **H2**
Silvi Marina, *Italy* 41 **F11**
Silvies →, *U.S.A.* 108 **E4**
Silvrettahorn, *Switz.* 40 **B7**
Silwa Bahari, *Egypt* 80 **C3**
Silz, *Austria* 26 **D3**
Simaltala, *India* 69 **G12**
Simanggang = Bandar Sri Aman, *Malaysia* 62 **D4**
Simao, *China* 58 **F3**
Simard, L., *Canada* 104 **C4**
Şīmareh →, *Iran* 73 **F12**
Simav, *Turkey* 47 **B10**
Simav →, *Turkey* 45 **F12**
Simav Dağları, *Turkey* 47 **B10**
Simba, *Tanzania* 86 **C4**
Simbach, *Germany* 25 **G9**
Simbirsk, *Russia* 34 **C9**
Simbo, *Tanzania* 86 **C2**
Simcoe, *Canada* 116 **D4**
Simcoe, L., *Canada* 116 **B5**
Simdega, *India* 69 **H11**
Simeonovgrad, *Bulgaria* 45 **D9**
Simeria, *Romania* 28 **E8**
Simeto →, *Italy* 43 **E8**
Simeulue, *Indonesia* 62 **D1**
Simferopol, *Ukraine* 33 **K8**
Sími, *Greece* 47 **E9**
Simi Valley, *U.S.A.* 111 **L8**
Simien Mts. △, *Ethiopia* 81 **E4**
Simikot, *Nepal* 69 **E9**
Simitli, *Bulgaria* 44 **E7**
Simla, *India* 68 **D7**
Simlångsdalen, *Sweden* 11 **H7**
Şimleu-Silvaniei, *Romania* 28 **C7**
Simmern, *Germany* 25 **F3**
Simmie, *Canada* 103 **D7**
Simmler, *U.S.A.* 111 **K7**
Simnas, *Lithuania* 30 **D10**
Simo älv = Simojoki →, *Finland* 8 **D21**
Simojoki →, *Finland* 8 **D21**
Simojovel, *Mexico* 119 **D6**
Simonette →, *Canada* 102 **B5**
Simonstown, *S. Africa* 88 **E2**
Simontornya, *Hungary* 28 **D3**
Simpang Empat, *Malaysia* 65 **c**
Simplonpass, *Switz.* 25 **J4**
Simplontunnel, *Switz.* 25 **J4**
Simpson Desert, *Australia* 94 **D2**
Simpson Desert △, *Australia* 94 **C2**
Simpson Pen., *Canada* 101 **B11**
Simpungdong, *N. Korea* 57 **D15**
Simrishamn, *Sweden* 11 **J8**
Simsbury, *U.S.A.* 117 **E12**
Simushir, Ostrov, *Russia* 53 **E16**
Sin Cowe I., *S. China Sea* 62 **C4**
Sinabang, *Indonesia* 62 **D1**
Sinadogo, *Somali Rep.* 75 **F4**
Sinai = Es Sînâ', *Egypt* 74 **F3**
Sinai, Mt. = Mûsa, Gebel, *Egypt* 70 **D2**
Sinai Peninsula, *Egypt* 50 **G7**
Sinaia, *Romania* 29 **E10**
Sinaloa ☐, *Mexico* 118 **C3**
Sinaloa de Leyva, *Mexico* 118 **B3**
Sinalunga, *Italy* 41 **E8**
Sinan, *China* 58 **D7**
Sînandrei, *Romania* 28 **E6**
Sinarádhes, *Greece* 49 **A3**
Sincan, *Turkey* 72 **B5**
Sincanlı, *Turkey* 47 **C12**
Sincelejo, *Colombia* 124 **B3**
Sinch'ang, *N. Korea* 57 **D15**
Sinchang-ni, *N. Korea* 57 **E14**
Sinclair, *U.S.A.* 108 **F10**
Sinclair Mills, *Canada* 102 **C4**
Sinclair's B., *U.K.* 13 **C5**
Sinclairville, *U.S.A.* 116 **D5**
Sincorá, Serra do, *Brazil* 125 **F10**
Sind, *Pakistan* 68 **G3**
Sind ☐, *Pakistan* 68 **G3**
Sind →, *Jammu & Kashmir, India* 69 **B6**
Sind →, *Mad. P., India* 69 **F8**
Sind Sagar Doab, *Pakistan* 68 **D4**
Sindal, *Denmark* 11 **G4**
Sindangan, *Phil.* 61 **G5**
Sindangbarang, *Indonesia* 63 **G12**
Sinde, *Zambia* 87 **F2**
Sindelfingen, *Germany* 25 **G4**
Sindh = Sind ☐, *Pakistan* 68 **G3**
Sındırgı, *Turkey* 47 **B10**
Sindou, *Burkina Faso* 82 **C3**
Sindri, *India* 69 **H12**
Sine →, *Senegal* 82 **C1**
Sinegorskiy, *Russia* 35 **G5**
Sinekli, *Turkey* 45 **E12**
Sinelnikovo = Synelnykove, *Ukraine* 33 **H8**
Sinendé, *Benin* 83 **C5**
Sines, *Portugal* 37 **H2**
Sines, C. de, *Portugal* 37 **H2**
Sineu, *Spain* 48 **B10**
Sinfra, *Ivory C.* 82 **D3**
Sing Buri, *Thailand* 64 **E3**
Singa, *Sudan* 81 **E3**
Singapore ■, *Asia* 65 **d**
Singapore, Straits of, *Asia* 65 **d**
Singapore Changi ✕ (SIN), *Singapore* 65 **M4**
Singaraja, *Indonesia* 63 **J18**
Singen, *Germany* 25 **H4**
Singida, *Tanzania* 86 **C3**
Singida ☐, *Tanzania* 86 **D3**
Singitikós Kólpos, *Greece* 44 **F7**
Singkaling Hkamti, *Burma* 67 **G19**
Singkang, *Indonesia* 63 **E6**
Singkawang, *Indonesia* 62 **D3**
Singkep, *Indonesia* 62 **E2**
Singleton, *Australia* 95 **E5**
Singleton, Mt., *N. Terr., Australia* 92 **D5**
Singleton, Mt., *W. Austral., Australia* 93 **E2**
Singö, *Sweden* 10 **D12**
Singoli, *India* 68 **G6**
Singora = Songkhla, *Thailand* 65 **J3**
Singosan, *N. Korea* 57 **E14**
Sinhung, *N. Korea* 57 **D14**
Siniátsikon, Óros, *Greece* 44 **F5**
Siniscóla, *Italy* 42 **B2**
Sinj, *Croatia* 41 **E13**
Sinjai, *Indonesia* 63 **F6**
Sinjajevina, *Serbia & M.* 44 **D3**
Sinjār, *Iraq* 70 **B4**
Sinkat, *Sudan* 80 **D4**
Sinkiang Uighur = Xinjiang Uygur Zizhiqu ☐, *China* 60 **B3**
Sinmak, *N. Korea* 57 **E14**
Sinnai, *Italy* 42 **C2**
Sinnamary, *Fr. Guiana* 125 **B8**
Sinni →, *Italy* 43 **B9**
Sinnuris, *Egypt* 80 **J7**
Sinoie, Lacul, *Romania* 29 **F13**
Sinop, *Turkey* 72 **A6**
Sinor, *India* 68 **J5**
Sinp'o, *N. Korea* 57 **E15**
Sinsheim, *Germany* 25 **F4**
Sinsk, *Russia* 53 **C13**
Sintang, *Indonesia* 62 **D4**
Sinton, *U.S.A.* 113 **L6**
Sintra, *Portugal* 37 **G1**
Sintra-Cascais ⌓, *Portugal* 37 **G1**

Sinŭiju, N. Korea 57 D13
Sinyukha →, Ukraine 33 H6
Sinzig, Germany 24 E3
Sio →, Hungary 28 D3
Siocon, Phil. 61 H5
Siófok, Hungary 28 D3
Sion, Switz. 25 J3
Sion Mills, U.K. 12 B4
Sioux City, U.S.A. 112 D6
Sioux Falls, U.S.A. 112 D6
Sioux Lookout, Canada 104 B1
Sioux Narrows, Canada 103 D10
Sipalay, Phil. 61 G5
Šipan, Croatia 44 D1
Siparia, Trin. & Tob. 125 K15
Sipil Daği △, Turkey 47 C9
Siping, China 57 C13
Sipiwesk L., Canada 103 B9
Siple, Antarctica 5 D7
Šipovo, Bos.-H. 28 F2
Sipra →, India 68 H6
Sipura, Indonesia 62 E1
Siquia →, Nic. 120 D3
Siquijor, Phil. 61 G5
Siquirres, Costa Rica 120 D3
Şīr Abū Nu'ayr, U.A.E. 71 E7
Şīr Banī Yās, U.A.E. 71 E7
Sir Edward Pellew Group,
    Australia 94 B2
Sir Graham Moore Is., Australia 92 B4
Sir James MacBrien, Mt., Canada 100 B7
Sira →, Norway 9 G12
Siracusa, Italy 43 E8
Sirajganj, Bangla. 69 G13
Sirakoro, Mali 82 C3
Şiran, Turkey 73 B8
Sirasso, Ivory C. 82 D3
Sirathu, India 69 G9
Sīrdān, Iran 71 B6
Sirdaryo = Syrdarya →,
    Kazakhstan 52 E7
Sire, Ethiopia 81 F4
Siren, U.S.A. 112 C8
Sirente-Velino △, Italy 41 F10
Sirer, Spain 48 C7
Siret, Romania 29 C11
Siret →, Romania 29 E12
Sirghāyā, Syria 74 B5
Şiria, Romania 28 D6
Sirinath △, Thailand ...... 65 a
Sirino, Mte., Italy 43 B8
Sīrjān, Iran 71 D7
Sirmaur, India 69 G9
Sírna, Greece 47 E8
Şırnak, Turkey 73 D10
Sirohi, India 68 G5
Sironj, India 68 G7
Síros, Greece 46 D6
Sirretta Pk., U.S.A. 111 K8
Sīrrī, Iran 71 E7
Sirsa, India 68 E6
Sirsa →, India 69 F8
Siruela, Spain 37 G5
Sisak, Croatia 41 C13
Sisaket, Thailand 64 E5
Sisante, Spain 39 F2
Sisargas, Is., Spain 36 B2
Sishen, S. Africa 88 D3
Sishui, Henan, China 56 G7
Sishui, Shandong, China 57 G9
Sisipuk L., Canada 103 B8
Sisophon, Cambodia 64 F4
Sisseton, U.S.A. 112 C6
Sissonne, France 19 C10
Sīstān, Asia 71 D9
Sīstān, Daryācheh-ye, Iran .. 71 D9
Sīstān va Balūchestān □, Iran .. 71 E9
Sisteron, France 21 D9
Sisters, U.S.A. 108 D3
Siswa Bazar, India 69 F10
Sitakili, Mali 82 C2
Sitamarhi, India 69 F11
Sitampiky, Madag. 89 B8
Sitapur, India 69 F9
Siteki, Swaziland 89 D5
Sitges, Spain 38 D6
Sithoniá, Greece 44 F7
Sitía, Greece 49 D8
Sitka, U.S.A. 102 B1
Sitoti, Botswana 88 C3
Sitra, Egypt 80 B2
Sittang Myit →, Burma 67 L20
Sittard, Neths. 17 C5
Sittensen, Germany 24 B5
Sittingbourne, U.K. 15 F8
Sittona, Eritrea 81 E4
Sittoung = Sittang Myit →,
    Burma 67 L20
Sittwe, Burma 67 J18
Situbondo, Indonesia 63 G16
Siuna, Nic. 120 D3
Siuri, India 69 H12
Siutghiol, Lacul, Romania .. 29 F13
Sīvand, Iran 71 D7
Sivas, Turkey 70 B3
Sivaslı, Turkey 47 C11
Siverek, Turkey 70 B3
Sivrihisar, Turkey 72 C4
Sīwa, Egypt 80 B2
Sīwa, El Wâhât es, Egypt .. 80 B2
Siwa Oasis = Sīwa, El Wâhât es,
    Egypt 80 B2
Siwalik Range, Nepal 69 F10
Siwan, India 69 F11
Siwana, India 68 G5
Six Cross Roads, Barbados . 121 g
Sixmilebridge, Ireland 12 D3
Sixth Cataract, Sudan 81 D3
Siyâl, Jazā'ir, Egypt 80 C4
Siyäzän, Azerbaijan 35 K9
Siziwang Qi, China 56 D6

Sjælland, Denmark 11 J5
Sjællands Odde, Denmark .. 11 J5
Sjenica, Serbia & M. 44 C3
Sjöbo, Sweden 11 J7
Sjötofta, Sweden 11 G7
Sjötorp, Sweden 11 F8
Sjumen = Shumen, Bulgaria . 45 C10
Sjuntorp, Sweden 11 F6
Skadarsko Jezero, Serbia & M. . 44 D3
Skadovsk, Ukraine 33 J7
Skælskør, Denmark 11 J5
Skærbæk, Denmark 11 J2
Skaftafell, Iceland 8 D5
Skagafjörður, Iceland 8 D4
Skagastølstindane, Norway .. 9 F12
Skagaströnd, Iceland 8 D3
Skagen, Denmark 11 G4
Skagern, Sweden 10 E8
Skagerrak, Denmark 11 G2
Skagit →, U.S.A. 110 B4
Skagway, U.S.A. 100 C6
Skala-Podilska, Ukraine 29 B11
Skala Podolskaya = Skala-
    Podilska, Ukraine 29 B11
Skalat, Ukraine 33 H3
Skalbmierz, Poland 31 H7
Skälderviken, Sweden 11 H6
Skälica, Slovak Rep. 27 C10
Skallingen, Denmark 11 J2
Skalni Dol = Kamenyak, Bulgaria 45 C10
Skanderborg, Denmark 11 H3
Skåne, Sweden 11 J7
Skåne län □, Sweden 11 H7
Skaneateles, U.S.A. 117 D8
Skaneateles L., U.S.A. 117 D8
Skänninge, Sweden 11 F9
Skanör med Falsterbo, Sweden . 11 J6
Skantzoúra, Greece 46 B6
Skara, Sweden 11 F7
Skärblacka, Sweden 11 F9
Skardu, Pakistan 69 B6
Skåre, Sweden 10 E7
Skärhamn, Sweden 11 G5
Skarszewy, Poland 30 D5
Skaryszew, Poland 31 G8
Skarżysko-Kamienna, Poland . 31 G7
Skattkärr, Sweden 10 E7
Skattungbyn, Sweden 10 C8
Skawina, Poland 31 J6
Skebobruk, Sweden 10 E12
Skeena →, Canada 102 C2
Skeena Mts., Canada 102 B3
Skegness, U.K. 14 D8
Skeldon, Guyana 124 B7
Skeleton Coast, Namibia .. 85 H2
Skeleton Coast △, Namibia . 88 C1
Skellefteå, Sweden 8 D19
Skellefteälven →, Sweden .. 8 D19
Skelleftehamn, Sweden 8 D19
Skender Vakuf, Bos.-H. 28 F2
Skerries, The, U.K. 14 D3
Skhidnytsya, Ukraine 31 J10
Skhíza, Greece 46 E3
Skhoinoúsa, Greece 47 E7
Ski, Norway 9 G14
Skíathos, Greece 46 B5
Skibbereen, Ireland 12 E2
Skiddaw, U.K. 14 C4
Skidegate, Canada 102 C2
Skídhra, Greece 44 F6
Skien, Norway 9 G13
Skierniewice, Poland 31 G7
Skíkda, Algeria 78 A7
Skillingaryd, Sweden 11 G8
Skillinge, Sweden 11 J8
Skilloura, Cyprus 49 D12
Skinári, Ákra, Greece 46 D2
Skinnskatteberg, Sweden .. 10 E9
Skipton, U.K. 14 D5
Skiring, C., Senegal 82 C1
Skirmish Pt., Australia 94 A1
Skíropoúla, Greece 46 C6
Skíros, Greece 46 C6
Skivarp, Sweden 11 J7
Skive, Denmark 11 H3
Skjálfandafljót →, Iceland .. 8 D5
Skjálfandi, Iceland 8 C5
Skjern, Denmark 11 J2
Skoczów, Poland 31 J5
Škofja Loka, Slovenia 41 B11
Skoghall, Sweden 10 E7
Skogstorp, Sweden 10 E10
Skoki, Poland 31 F4
Skole, Ukraine 33 H2
Skópelos, Greece 46 B5
Skopí, Greece 49 D8
Skopin, Russia 32 F10
Skopje, Macedonia 44 D5
Skopje ✈ (SKP), Macedonia . 44 E5
Skórcz, Poland 30 D5
Skørping, Denmark 11 H3
Skövde, Sweden 11 F7
Skovorodino, Russia 53 D13
Skowhegan, U.S.A. 115 C11
Skradin, Croatia 41 E12
Skrea, Sweden 11 H6
Skrunda, Latvia 30 B9
Skrwa →, Poland 31 F6
Skukuza, S. Africa 89 D5
Skull, Ireland 12 E2
Skultorp, Sweden 11 F7
Skultuna, Sweden 10 E10
Skunk →, U.S.A. 112 E9
Skuodas, Lithuania 9 H19
Skurup, Sweden 11 J7
Skutskär, Sweden 10 D11
Skvyra, Ukraine 33 H5
Skwierzyna, Poland 31 F2
Skye, U.K. 13 D2
Skykomish, U.S.A. 108 C3
Skyros = Skíros, Greece 46 C6

Skyttorp, Sweden 10 D11
Slade Pt., Australia 94 K7
Slagelse, Denmark 11 J5
Slættaratindur, Faroe Is. .. 8 E9
Slagelse, Denmark 11 J5
Slamet, Indonesia 63 G13
Slaney →, Ireland 12 D5
Slangberge, S. Africa 88 E3
Slano, Croatia 44 D1
Slantsy, Russia 32 C5
Slănic, Romania 29 E10
Slano, Croatia 44 D1
Slantsy, Russia 32 C5
Slaný, Czech Rep. 26 A7
Slate Is., Canada 104 C2
Slatina, Croatia 28 E2
Slatina, Romania 29 F9
Slatina Timiş, Romania 28 E7
Slatington, U.S.A. 117 F9
Slaton, U.S.A. 113 J4
Slave →, Canada 102 A6
Slave Coast, W. Afr. 83 D5
Slave Lake, Canada 102 B6
Slave Pt., Canada 102 A5
Slavgorod, Russia 52 D8
Slavinja, Serbia & M. 44 C6
Slavkov u Brna, Czech Rep. . 27 B9
Slavkovský Les △, Czech Rep. . 26 A5
Slavonia, Europe 28 E2
Slavonski Brod, Croatia 28 E3
Slavsk, Russia 30 C8
Slavska, Ukraine 29 B8
Slavskoye, Russia 30 D7
Slavuta, Ukraine 33 G4
Slavyanka, Russia 54 C5
Slavyanovo, Bulgaria 45 C8
Slavyansk = Slovyansk, Ukraine . 33 H9
Slavyansk-na-Kubani, Russia . 33 K10
Sława, Poland 31 G3
Slawharad, Belarus 32 F6
Sławno, Poland 30 D3
Sławoborze, Poland 30 D2
Sleaford, U.K. 14 D7
Sleaford B., Australia 95 E2
Sleat, Sd. of, U.K. 13 D3
Sleeper Is., Canada 101 C11
Sleeping Bear Dunes △, U.S.A. . 114 C2
Sleepy Eye, U.S.A. 112 C7
Slemon L., Canada 102 A5
Ślesin, Poland 31 F5
Slide Mt., U.S.A. 117 E10
Slidell, U.S.A. 113 K10
Sliema, Malta 49 D2
Slieve Aughty, Ireland 12 C3
Slieve Bloom, Ireland 12 C4
Slieve Donard, U.K. 12 B6
Slieve Gamph, Ireland 12 B3
Slieve Gullion, Ireland 12 B5
Slieve League, Ireland 12 B3
Slieve Mish, Ireland 12 D2
Slievenamon, Ireland 12 D4
Sligeach = Sligo, Ireland .. 12 B3
Sligo, Ireland 12 B3
Sligo, U.S.A. 116 E5
Sligo □, Ireland 12 B3
Sligo B., Ireland 12 B3
Slippery Rock, U.S.A. 116 E4
Slite, Sweden 11 G12
Slīteres, Latvia 30 A9
Sliven, Bulgaria 45 D10
Slivnitsa, Bulgaria 44 D7
Sljeme, Croatia 41 C12
Sloan, U.S.A. 111 K11
Sloansville, U.S.A. 117 D10
Slobidka, Ukraine 29 C14
Slobozia, Argeş, Romania . 29 F10
Slobozia, Ialomiţa, Romania . 29 F12
Slocan, Canada 102 D5
Słomniki, Poland 31 H7
Slonim, Belarus 33 F3
Slough, U.K. 15 F7
Slough □, U.K. 15 F7
Sloughhouse, U.S.A. 110 G5
Slovak Rep. ■, Europe 27 C13
Slovakia = Slovak Rep. ■, Europe 27 C13
Slovakian Ore Mts. = Slovenské
    Rudohorie, Slovak Rep. .. 27 C12
Slovenia ■, Europe 41 C11
Slovenija = Slovenia ■, Europe . 41 C11
Slovenj Gradec, Slovenia .. 41 B12
Slovenska Bistrica, Slovenia . 41 B12
Slovenské Konjice, Slovenia . 41 B12
Slovenské Rudohorie,
    Slovak Rep. 27 C12
Slovenský Raj △, Slovak Rep. . 27 C13
Slovyansk, Ukraine 33 H9
Słowiński □, Poland 30 D4
Słubice, Poland 31 F1
Sluch →, Ukraine 33 G4
Sluis, Neths. 17 C3
Slūnchev Bryag, Bulgaria .. 45 D11
Slunj, Croatia 41 C12
Słupca, Poland 31 F4
Słupia →, Poland 30 D3
Słupsk, Poland 30 D3
Slurry, S. Africa 88 D4
Slutsk, Belarus 33 F4
Slyne Hd., Ireland 12 C1
Slyudyanka, Russia 53 D11
Småland, Sweden 11 G9
Smålandsfarvandet, Denmark . 11 J5
Smålandsstenar, Sweden .. 11 G7
Smalltree L., Canada 103 A8
Smallwood Res., Canada .. 105 B7
Smara, Morocco 78 B4
Smarhon, Belarus 32 E4
Smarje, Slovenia 41 B12
Smartt Syndicate Dam, S. Africa 88 E3
Smartville, U.S.A. 110 F5
Smeaton, Canada 103 C8
Smederevo, Serbia & M. .. 44 B4

Smederevska Palanka,
    Serbia & M. 44 B4
Smedjebacken, Sweden 10 D9
Smela = Smila, Ukraine 33 H6
Smerwick Harbour, Ireland . 12 D1
Smethport, U.S.A. 116 E6
Smidovich, Russia 53 E14
Śmigiel, Poland 31 F3
Smila, Ukraine 33 H6
Smilyan, Bulgaria 45 E8
Smith, Canada 102 B6
Smith Center, U.S.A. 112 F5
Smith River △, U.S.A. 108 F2
Smith Sd., N. Amer. 4 B4
Smithburne →, Australia .. 94 B3
Smithers, Canada 102 C3
Smithfield, S. Africa 89 E4
Smithfield, N.C., U.S.A. .. 115 H6
Smithfield, Utah, U.S.A. .. 108 F8
Smiths Falls, Canada 117 B9
Smithton, Australia 95 G4
Smithville, Canada 116 C5
Smithville, U.S.A. 113 K6
Smoky →, Canada 102 B5
Smoky Bay, Australia 95 E1
Smoky Hill →, U.S.A. 112 F6
Smoky Hills, U.S.A. 112 F5
Smoky Lake, Canada 102 C6
Smøla, Norway 8 E13
Smolensk, Russia 32 E7
Smolikas, Óros, Greece 44 F4
Smolník, Slovak Rep. 27 C13
Smolyan, Bulgaria 45 E8
Smooth Rock Falls, Canada . 104 C3
Smoothstone L., Canada .. 103 C7
Smorgon = Smarhon, Belarus . 32 E4
Smotrych, Ukraine 29 B11
Smotrych →, Ukraine 29 B11
Smulţi, Romania 29 E12
Smyadovo, Bulgaria 45 C11
Smygehamn, Sweden 11 J7
Smyrna = İzmir, Turkey .. 47 C9
Smyrna, U.S.A. 114 F8
Snæfell, Iceland 8 D6
Snaefell, I. of Man 14 C3
Snæfellsjökull, Iceland 8 D2
Snake →, U.S.A. 108 C4
Snake I., Australia 95 F4
Snake Range, U.S.A. 108 G6
Snake River Plain, U.S.A. .. 108 E7
Snasahögarna, Sweden 10 A6
Snåsavatnet, Norway 8 D14
Snedsted, Denmark 11 H2
Sneek, Neths. 17 A5
Sneeuberge, S. Africa 88 E3
Snejbjerg, Denmark 11 H2
Snelling, U.S.A. 110 H6
Snezhnoye, Ukraine 33 J10
Snežnik, Slovenia 41 C11
Sniadowo, Poland 31 E8
Sniardwy, Jezioro, Poland .. 30 E8
Śnieżka, Europe 26 A8
Snigirevka = Snihurivka, Ukraine 33 J7
Snihurivka, Ukraine 33 J7
Snina, Slovak Rep. 27 C15
Snizort, L., U.K. 13 D2
Snøhetta, Norway 9 E13
Snohomish, U.S.A. 110 C4
Snoul, Cambodia 65 F6
Snow Hill, U.S.A. 114 F8
Snow Lake, Canada 103 C8
Snow Mt., Calif., U.S.A. .. 110 F4
Snow Mt., Maine, U.S.A. .. 117 A14
Snow Shoe, U.S.A. 116 E7
Snowbird L., Canada 103 A8
Snowdon, U.K. 14 D3
Snowdonia △, U.K. 14 D4
Snowdrift = Łutselk'e, Canada 103 A6
Snowdrift →, Canada 103 A6
Snowflake, U.S.A. 109 J8
Snowshoe Pk., U.S.A. 108 B6
Snowtown, Australia 95 E2
Snowville, U.S.A. 108 F7
Snowy →, Australia 95 F4
Snowy Mt., U.S.A. 117 C10
Snowy Mts., Australia 95 F4
Snug Corner, Bahamas 121 B5
Snyatyn, Ukraine 29 B10
Snyder, Okla., U.S.A. 113 H5
Snyder, Tex., U.S.A. 113 J4
Soahanina, Madag. 89 B7
Soalala, Madag. 89 B8
Soaloka, Madag. 89 B8
Soamanonga, Madag. 89 C7
Soan →, Pakistan 68 C4
Soanierana-Ivongo, Madag. . 89 B8
Soanindraniny, Madag. 89 B8
Şoarş, Romania 29 E9
Soavina, Madag. 89 C8
Soavinandriana, Madag. .. 89 B8
Sob →, Ukraine 29 B14
Soba, Nigeria 83 C6
Sobat, Nahr →, Sudan 81 F3
Sobdhapur, India 68 H8
Sobinka, Russia 32 E11
Sobótka, Poland 31 H3
Sobra, Croatia 41 F14
Sobradinho, Reprêsa de, Brazil 125 E10
Sobral, Brazil 125 D10
Sobrance, Slovak Rep. 27 C15
Sobreira Formosa, Portugal . 36 F3
Soc Giang, Vietnam 58 F6
Soc Trang, Vietnam 65 H5
Soča →, Europe 26 E6
Sochaczew, Poland 31 F7
Soch'e = Shache, China .. 60 C2
Sochi, Russia 35 J4
Société, Is. de la, French Polynesia 97 J12
Society Is. = Société, Is. de la,
    French Polynesia 97 J12

Socompa, Portezuelo de, Chile . 126 A2
Socorro, N. Mex., U.S.A. .. 109 J10
Socorro, Tex., U.S.A. 109 L10
Socorro, I., Mexico 118 D2
Socotra, Yemen 75 E5
Socovos, Spain 39 G3
Socuéllamos, Spain 39 F2
Soda L., U.S.A. 109 J5
Soda Plains, India 69 B8
Soda Springs, U.S.A. 108 E8
Sodankylä, Finland 8 C22
Soddy-Daisy, U.S.A. 115 H3
Söderala, Sweden 10 C10
Söderåsen △, Sweden 11 H7
Söderbärke, Sweden 10 D9
Söderfors, Sweden 10 D11
Söderhamn, Sweden 10 C11
Söderköping, Sweden 11 F10
Södermanland, Sweden .. 9 G17
Södermanlands län □, Sweden 10 E10
Södertälje, Sweden 10 E11
Sodiri, Sudan 81 E2
Sodo, Ethiopia 81 F4
Södra Dellen, Sweden 10 C10
Södra Finnskoga, Sweden . 10 D6
Södra Sandby, Sweden 11 J7
Södra Ulvön, Sweden 10 B12
Södra Vi, Sweden 11 G9
Sodražica, Slovenia 41 C11
Sodus, U.S.A. 116 C7
Sodwana Bay △, S. Africa .. 89 D5
Soekmekaar, S. Africa 89 C4
Soest, Germany 24 D4
Soest, Neths. 17 B5
Sofádhes, Greece 46 B4
Sofala □, Mozam. 89 B5
Sofara, Mali 82 C4
Sofia = Sofiya, Bulgaria .. 44 D7
Sofia →, Madag. 89 B8
Sofievka, Ukraine 33 H7
Sofikón, Greece 46 D5
Sofiya, Bulgaria 44 D7
Sofiya ✈ (SOF), Bulgaria .. 44 D7
Sôfu-Gan, Japan 55 K10
Sogakofe, Ghana 83 D5
Sogamoso, Colombia 124 B4
Sogār, Iran 71 E8
Sögel, Germany 24 C3
Sogndalsfjøra, Norway 9 F12
Søgne, Norway 9 G12
Sognefjorden, Norway 9 F11
Söğüt, Bilecik, Turkey 47 A12
Söğüt, Burdur, Turkey 47 D11
Söğüt Dağı, Turkey 47 D11
Söğütköy, Turkey 47 E10
Sögwipo, S. Korea 57 H14
Soh, Iran 71 C6
Sohâg, Egypt 80 B3
Sohagpur, India 68 H8
Sŏhori, N. Korea 57 D15
Soignies, Belgium 17 D4
Soin, Burkina Faso 82 C4
Soira, Eritrea 81 E4
Soissons, France 19 C10
Sōja, Japan 55 G6
Sojat, India 68 G5
Sok →, Russia 34 D10
Sokal, Ukraine 33 G3
Söke, Turkey 47 D9
Sokelo, Dem. Rep. of the Congo . 87 D1
Sokhós, Greece 44 F7
Sokhumi, Georgia 35 J5
Soko Banja, Serbia & M. .. 44 C5
Sokodé, Togo 83 D5
Sokol, Russia 32 C11
Sokolac, Bos.-H. 28 G3
Sokółka, Poland 30 E10
Sokolo, Ségou, Mali 82 C3
Sokolo, Sikasso, Mali 82 C3
Sokolov, Czech Rep. 26 A5
Sokołów Małopolski, Poland . 31 H9
Sokołów Podlaski, Poland .. 31 F9
Sokoły, Poland 31 F9
Sokoto, Nigeria 83 C6
Sokoto □, Nigeria 83 C6
Sokoto →, Nigeria 83 C5
Sokyrnytsya, Ukraine 29 B8
Sokyryany, Ukraine 29 B12
Sol Iletsk, Russia 52 D6
Sola →, Poland 31 H6
Solai, Kenya 86 B4
Solan, India 68 D7
Soläns L., U.S.A. 109 J3
Soland, Phil. 61 C4
Solano, Phil. 61 C4
Solapur, India 66 L9
Solca, Romania 29 C10
Solda Gölü, Turkey 47 D11
Soldăneşti, Moldova 29 C13
Soldeu, Andorra 38 C6
Soldotna, U.S.A. 100 B4
Solea, Cyprus 49 D12
Solec Kujawski, Poland .. 31 E5
Soledad, Colombia 124 A4
Soledad, U.S.A. 110 J5
Soledad, Venezuela 124 B6
Solent, The, U.K. 15 G6
Solenzara, France 21 G13
Solesmes, France 19 B10
Solfonn, Norway 9 F12
Solhan, Turkey 70 B4
Solikamsk, Russia 52 D6
Solila, Madag. 89 C8
Solimões = Amazonas →,
    S. Amer. 125 D9
Solin, Croatia 41 E13
Solingen, Germany 24 D3
Sollebrunn, Sweden 11 F6
Sollefteå, Sweden 10 A11

Sollentuna, Sweden 10 E11
Sóller, Spain 48 B9
Sollerön, Sweden 10 D8
Solling, Germany 24 D5
Solling-Vogler △, Germany 24 D5
Solnechnogorsk, Russia 32 D9
Solo →, Indonesia 63 G15
Solofra, Italy 43 B7
Sologne, France 19 E8
Solok, Indonesia 62 E2
Sololá, Guatemala 120 D1
Solomon, N. Fork →, U.S.A. 112 F5
Solomon, S. Fork →, U.S.A. 112 F5
Solomon Is. ■, Pac. Oc. 96 H7
Solon, China 60 B7
Solon Springs, U.S.A. 112 B9
Solor, Indonesia 63 F6
Solotcha, Russia 32 E10
Solothurn, Switz. 25 H3
Solothurn □, Switz. 25 H3
Solotvyn, Ukraine 29 B9
Solsona, Spain 38 C6
Solt, Hungary 28 D4
Šolta, Croatia 41 E13
Solṭānābād, Khorāsān, Iran 71 C8
Solṭānābād, Khorāsān, Iran 71 B8
Soltau, Germany 24 C5
Soltsy, Russia 32 C6
Solunska Glava, Macedonia 44 E5
Solvang, U.S.A. 111 L6
Solvay, U.S.A. 117 C8
Sölvesborg, Sweden 11 H8
Solway Firth, U.K. 14 C4
Solwezi, Zambia 87 E2
Sōma, Japan 54 F10
Soma, Turkey 47 B9
Somabhula, Zimbabwe 89 B4
Somali Pen., Africa 76 F8
Somali Rep. ■, Africa 75 F4
Somalia = Somali Rep. ■, Africa 75 F4
Sombernon, France 19 E11
Sombor, Serbia & M. 28 E4
Sombra, Canada 116 D2
Sombrerete, Mexico 118 C4
Sombrero, Anguilla 121 C7
Şomcuta Mare, Romania 29 C8
Somdari, India 68 G5
Someido △, Spain 36 B4
Somers, U.S.A. 108 B6
Somerset, Ky., U.S.A. 114 G3
Somerset, Mass., U.S.A. 117 E14
Somerset, Pa., U.S.A. 116 F5
Somerset □, U.K. 15 F5
Somerset East, S. Africa 88 E4
Somerset I., Canada 100 A10
Somerset West, S. Africa 88 E2
Somersworth, U.S.A. 117 C14
Somerton, U.S.A. 109 K6
Somerville, U.S.A. 117 F10
Someş →, Romania 28 C7
Someşul Mare →, Romania 29 C8
Somme □, France 19 C9
Somme →, France 19 B8
Somme, B. de la, France 18 B8
Sommen, Jönköping, Sweden .. 11 F8
Sommen, Östergötland, Sweden 11 F9
Sommepy-Tahure, France 19 C11
Sömmerda, Germany 24 D7
Sommesous, France 19 D11
Sommières, France 21 E8
Somnath, India 68 J4
Somogy □, Hungary 28 D2
Somogyszob, Hungary 28 D2
Somoto, Nic. 120 D2
Sompolno, Poland 31 F5
Somport, Puerto de, Spain 38 C4
Son →, India 69 G11
Son Ha, Vietnam 64 E7
Son Hoa, Vietnam 64 F7
Son La, Vietnam 58 G4
Son Serra, Spain 48 B10
Son Servera, Spain 38 F8
Son Tay, Vietnam 58 G5
Soná, Panama 120 E3
Sonamarg, India 69 B6
Sonamukhi, India 69 H12
Sonar →, India 69 G8
Sŏnch'ŏn, N. Korea 57 E13
Sondags →, S. Africa 88 E4
Sóndalo, Italy 40 B7
Sondar, India 69 C6
Sønder Felding, Denmark 11 J2
Sønder Omme, Denmark 11 J2
Sønderborg, Denmark 11 K3
Sønderjyllands Amtskommune □,
   Denmark 11 J3
Sondershausen, Germany 24 D6
Sóndrio, Italy 40 B6
Sone, Mozam. 87 F3
Sonepur, India 67 J13
Song, Nigeria 83 D7
Song, Thailand 64 C3
Song Cau, Vietnam 64 F7
Song Xian, China 56 G7
Songan, Indonesia 63 J18
Songch'ŏn, N. Korea 57 E14
Songea, Tanzania 87 E4
Songeons, France 19 C8
Songhua Hu, China 57 C14
Songhua Jiang →, China 60 B8
Songimvelo △, S. Africa 89 D5
Songjiang, China 59 B13
Songjin, N. Korea 57 D15
Songjŏng-ni, S. Korea 57 G14
Songkan, China 58 C6
Songkhla, Thailand 65 J3
Songming, China 58 E4
Songnim, N. Korea 57 E13
Songo, Mozam. 85 H6
Songo, Sudan 79 G10
Songpan, China 58 A4

Songtao, China 58 C7
Songwe, Dem. Rep. of the Congo 86 C2
Songwe →, Africa 87 D3
Songxi, China 59 D12
Songzi, China 59 B8
Sonhat, India 69 H10
Sonid Youqi, China 56 C7
Sonipat, India 68 E7
Sonkach, India 68 H7
Sonkovo, Russia 32 D9
Sonmiani, Pakistan 68 G2
Sonmiani B., Pakistan 68 G2
Sonnino, Italy 42 A6
Sono →, Brazil 125 E9
Sonoma, U.S.A. 110 G4
Sonora, Calif., U.S.A. 110 H6
Sonora, Tex., U.S.A. 113 K4
Sonora □, Mexico 118 B2
Sonora →, Mexico 118 B2
Sonoran Desert, U.S.A. 111 L12
Sonoyta, Mexico 118 A2
Sonqor, Iran 73 E12
Sonseca, Spain 37 F7
Sonsonate, El Salv. 120 D2
Sonstorp, Sweden 11 F9
Sonthofen, Germany 25 H6
Soochow = Suzhou, China 59 B13
Sooke, Canada 110 B3
Sop Hao, Laos 58 G5
Sop Prap, Thailand 64 D2
Sopelana, Spain 38 B2
Sopi, Indonesia 63 D7
Sopot, Bulgaria 45 D8
Sopot, Poland 30 D5
Sopot, Serbia & M. 44 B4
Sopotnica, Macedonia 44 E5
Sopron, Hungary 28 C1
Sopur, India 69 B6
Sør-Rondane, Antarctica 5 D4
Sora, Italy 41 G10
Sorah, Pakistan 68 F3
Söråker, Sweden 10 B11
Sorano, Italy 41 F8
Soraon, India 69 G9
Sorbas, Spain 39 H2
Sörbygden, Sweden 10 B10
Sore, France 20 D3
Sorel-Tracy, Canada 104 C5
Soresina, Italy 40 C6
Sörforsa, Sweden 10 C10
Sórgono, Italy 42 B2
Sorgues, France 21 D8
Sorgun, Turkey 72 C6
Soria, Spain 38 D2
Soria □, Spain 38 D2
Soriano, Uruguay 126 C4
Soriano nel Cimino, Italy 41 F9
Sorkh, Kuh-e, Iran 71 C8
Sorø, Denmark 11 J5
Soro, Guinea 82 C3
Soroca, Moldova 29 B13
Sorocaba, Brazil 127 A6
Soroki = Soroca, Moldova 29 B13
Sorong, Indonesia 63 E8
Soroní, Greece 49 C10
Soroti, Uganda 86 B3
Sørøya, Norway 8 A20
Sørøysundet, Norway 8 A20
Sorraia →, Portugal 37 G2
Sorrell, Australia 95 G4
Sorrento, Italy 43 B7
Sorsele, Sweden 8 D17
Sörsjön, Sweden 10 C7
Sorso, Italy 42 B1
Sorsogon, Phil. 61 E6
Sortavala, Russia 32 B6
Sortino, Italy 43 E8
Sortland, Norway 8 B16
Sorvizhi, Russia 34 B9
Sos del Rey Católico, Spain .. 38 C3
Sŏsan, S. Korea 57 F14
Soscumica, L., Canada 104 B4
Sösdala, Sweden 11 H7
Sosna →, Russia 33 F10
Sosnovka, Kirov, Russia 34 B10
Sosnovka, Tambov, Russia .. 34 D5
Sosnovyy Bor, Russia 32 C5
Sosnowiec, Poland 31 H6
Sospel, France 21 E11
Sossus Vlei, Namibia 88 C2
Šoštanj, Slovenia 41 B12
Sŏsura, N. Korea 57 C16
Sot →, India 69 F8
Sotkamo, Finland 8 D23
Soto del Barco, Spain 36 B4
Soto la Marina →, Mexico 119 C5
Soto y Amío, Spain 36 C5
Sotrondio, Spain 36 B5
Sotuta, Mexico 119 C7
Souanké, Congo 84 D2
Soubré, Ivory C. 82 D3
Souderton, U.S.A. 117 F9
Soúdha, Greece 49 D6
Soúdhas, Kólpos, Greece 49 D6
Souflíon, Greece 45 E10
Soufrière, Guadeloupe ...... 120 b
Soufrière, St. Lucia .... 121 f
Soufrière Bay, Dominica .... 121 f
Souillac, France 20 D5
Souilly, France 19 C12
Soukhouma, Laos 64 E5
Soul, S. Korea 57 F14
Soulac-sur-Mer, France 20 C2
Soulougou, Burkina Faso 83 C5
Soultz-sous-Forêts, France .. 19 D14
Sound, The = Øresund, Europe .. 11 J6
Sound, The, U.K. 15 G3
Soúnion, Ákra, Greece 46 D6
Sources, Mt. aux, Lesotho .. 89 D4

Soure, Brazil 125 D9
Soure, Portugal 36 E2
Souris, Man., Canada 103 D8
Souris, P.E.I., Canada 105 C7
Souris →, Canada 112 A5
Sourou →, Africa 82 C4
Soúrpi, Greece 46 B4
Sousa, Brazil 125 E11
Sousel, Portugal 37 G3
Sousse, Tunisia 79 A8
Soustons, France 20 E2
Sout →, S. Africa 88 E2
South Africa ■, Africa 88 E3
South America 122 E5
South Atlantic Ocean 2 F8
South Aulatsivik I., Canada .. 105 A7
South Australia □, Australia .. 95 E2
South Ayrshire □, U.K. 13 F4
South Baldy, U.S.A. 109 J10
South Bass I., U.S.A. 116 E2
South Bend, Ind., U.S.A. 114 E2
South Bend, Wash., U.S.A. .. 110 D3
South Boston, U.S.A. 115 G6
South Branch, Canada 105 C8
South Brook, Canada 105 C8
South Carolina □, U.S.A. 115 J5
South Charleston, U.S.A. 114 F5
South China Sea, Asia 62 C4
South Cumberland Is. △,
   Australia 94 J7
South Dakota □, U.S.A. 112 C5
South Deerfield, U.S.A. 117 D12
South Downs, U.K. 15 G7
South East C., Australia 95 G4
South-East Indian Rise, Ind. Oc. 5 B10
South East Is., Australia 93 F3
South Esk →, U.K. 13 E6
South Foreland, U.K. 15 F9
South Fork American →, U.S.A. 110 G3
South Fork Feather →, U.S.A. 110 F5
South Fork Grand →, U.S.A. .. 112 C3
South Fork Republican →,
   U.S.A. 112 E4
South Georgia, Antarctica .. 128 G9
South Gloucestershire □, U.K. 15 F5
South Hadley, U.S.A. 117 D12
South Haven, U.S.A. 114 D2
South Henik L., Canada 103 A9
South Honshu Ridge, Pac. Oc. 96 E6
South Horr, Kenya 86 B4
South I., Kenya 86 B4
South I., N.Z. 91 L3
South Indian Lake, Canada .. 103 B9
South Invercargill, N.Z. 91 M2
South Island △, Kenya 86 B4
South Kitui △, Kenya 86 C4
South Knife →, Canada 103 B10
South Koel →, India 69 H11
South Lake Tahoe, U.S.A. .. 110 G6
South Lanarkshire □, U.K. .. 13 F5
South Loup →, U.S.A. 112 E5
South Luangwa △, Zambia .. 87 E3
South Magnetic Pole, Antarctica 5 C9
South Milwaukee, U.S.A. 114 D2
South Molton, U.K. 15 F4
South Moose L., Canada 103 C8
South Nahanni →, Canada 102 A4
South Natuna Is. = Natuna
   Selatan, Kepulauan, Indonesia 62 D3
South Negril Pt., Jamaica .... 120 a
South Orkney Is., Antarctica .. 5 C18
South Ossetia □, Georgia 35 J7
South Pagai, I. = Pagai Selatan,
   Pulau, Indonesia 62 E2
South Paris, U.S.A. 117 B14
South Pittsburg, U.S.A. 115 H3
South Platte →, U.S.A. 112 E4
South Pole, Antarctica ...... 5 E
South Porcupine, Canada 104 C3
South Portland, U.S.A. 115 D10
South Pt., Barbados .... 121 g
South Pt., U.S.A. 116 B1
South River, Canada 104 C4
South River, U.S.A. 117 F10
South Ronaldsay, U.K. 13 C6
South Sandwich Is., Antarctica 5 B1
South Saskatchewan →, Canada 103 C7
South Seal →, Canada 103 B9
South Shetland Is., Antarctica .. 5 C18
South Shields, U.K. 14 C6
South Sioux City, U.S.A. 112 D6
South Taranaki Bight, N.Z. .. 91 H5
South Thompson →, Canada .. 102 C4
South Twin I., Canada 104 B4
South Tyne →, U.K. 14 C5
South Uist, U.K. 13 D1
South West C., Australia 95 G4
South West C., N.Z. 91 M1
South Williamsport, U.S.A. .. 116 E8
South Yorkshire □, U.K. 14 D6
Southampton, Canada 116 B3
Southampton, U.K. 15 G6
Southampton □, U.K. 15 G6
Southampton, U.S.A. 117 F12
Southampton I., Canada 101 B11
Southaven, U.S.A. 113 H9
Southbank, Canada 102 C3
Southbridge, N.Z. 91 K4
Southbridge, U.S.A. 117 D12
Southend, Canada 103 B8
Southend-on-Sea, U.K. 15 F8
Southend-on-Sea □, U.K. .. 15 F8
Southern = Yedebub Biheroch
   Biheresoboch na Hizboch □,
   Ethiopia 81 F4
Southern = Yuzhnyy □, Russia 35 H5
Southern □, Malawi 87 F4

Southern □, S. Leone 82 D2
Southern □, Zambia 87 F2
Southern Alps, N.Z. 91 K3
Southern Cross, Australia 93 F2
Southern Indian L., Canada .. 103 B9
Southern Ocean, Antarctica .. 5 C6
Southern Pines, U.S.A. 115 H6
Southern Uplands, U.K. 13 F5
Southington, U.S.A. 117 E12
Southland □, N.Z. 91 L1
Southold, U.S.A. 117 E12
Southport, Australia 95 D5
Southport, U.K. 14 D4
Southport, Fla., U.S.A. 115 K3
Southport, N.Y., U.S.A. 116 D8
Southwest △, Australia 95 G4
Southwestern Pacific Basin,
   Pac. Oc. 5 A12
Southwold, U.K. 15 E9
Southwood △, Australia 95 D5
Soutpansberg, S. Africa 89 C4
Souvigny, France 19 F10
Sovata, Romania 29 D10
Soverato, Italy 43 D9
Sovetsk, Kaliningrad, Russia .. 9 J19
Sovetsk, Kirov, Russia 34 B9
Sovetskaya Gavan = Vanino,
   Russia 53 E15
Sovicille, Italy 41 E8
Soweto, S. Africa 89 D4
Sōya-Kaikyō = La Perouse Str.,
   Asia 54 B11
Sōya-Misaki, Japan 54 B10
Soyaux, France 20 C4
Sozh →, Belarus 33 F6
Sozopol, Bulgaria 45 D11
Spa, Belgium 17 D5
Spain ■, Europe 7 H5
Spalding, Australia 95 E2
Spalding, U.K. 14 E7
Spangler, U.S.A. 116 F6
Spanish, Canada 104 C3
Spanish Fork, U.S.A. 108 F8
Spanish Town, Br. Virgin Is. .. 121 e
Spanish Town, Jamaica .... 120 a
Sparks, U.S.A. 110 F7
Sparreholm, Sweden 10 E10
Sparta = Spárti, Greece 46 D4
Sparta, Mich., U.S.A. 114 D3
Sparta, N.J., U.S.A. 117 E10
Sparta, Wis., U.S.A. 112 D9
Spartanburg, U.S.A. 115 H5
Spartansburg, U.S.A. 116 E5
Spárti, Greece 46 D4
Spartivento, C., Calabria, Italy 43 E9
Spartivento, C., Sard., Italy .. 42 D1
Sparwood, Canada 102 D6
Spas-Demensk, Russia 32 E7
Spas-Klepiki, Russia 32 E11
Spassk-Ryazanskiy, Russia .. 32 E11
Spátha, Ákra, Greece 49 D5
Spatsizi →, Canada 102 B3
Spatsizi Plateau Wilderness △,
   Canada 102 B3
Spean →, U.K. 13 E4
Spearfish, U.S.A. 112 C3
Spearman, U.S.A. 113 G4
Speculator, U.S.A. 117 C10
Speia, Moldova 29 D14
Speightstown, Barbados .... 121 g
Speke Gulf, Tanzania 86 C3
Spello, Italy 41 F9
Spence Bay = Taloyoak, Canada 100 B10
Spencer, Idaho, U.S.A. 108 D7
Spencer, Iowa, U.S.A. 112 D7
Spencer, N.Y., U.S.A. 117 D8
Spencer, Nebr., U.S.A. 112 D5
Spencer, C., Australia 95 F2
Spencer B., Namibia 88 D1
Spencer G., Australia 95 E2
Spencerville, Canada 117 B9
Spences Bridge, Canada 102 C4
Spennymoor, U.K. 14 C6
Spenser Mts., N.Z. 91 K4
Spentrup, Denmark 11 H4
Sperkhiós →, Greece 46 C4
Sperrin Mts., U.K. 12 B5
Spessart, Germany 25 F5
Spétsai, Greece 46 D5
Spey →, U.K. 13 D5
Speyer, Germany 25 F4
Spezand, Pakistan 68 E2
Spezzano Albanese, Italy 43 C9
Spiekeroog, Germany 24 B3
Spiez, Switz. 25 J3
Spíli, Greece 49 D6
Spilimbergo, Italy 41 B9
Spin Būldak, Afghan. 68 D2
Spinalónga, Greece 49 D7
Spinazzola, Italy 43 B9
Spineni, Romania 29 F9
Spirit Lake, U.S.A. 110 D4
Spirit River, Canada 102 B5
Spiritwood, Canada 103 C7
Spišská Nová Ves, Slovak Rep. .. 27 C13
Spišské Podhradie, Slovak Rep. .. 27 B13
Spital, Austria 26 D7
Spithead, U.K. 15 G6
Spittal an der Drau, Austria .. 26 E6
Spitzbergen = Svalbard, Arctic 51 B5
Spjelkavik, Norway 9 E12
Split, Croatia 41 E13
Split ✈ (SPU), Croatia 41 E13
Split L., Canada 103 B9
Split Lake, Canada 103 B9
Splitski Kanal, Croatia 41 E13
Splügenpass, Switz. 25 J5
Spofford, U.S.A. 113 L4
Spokane, U.S.A. 108 C5
Spoleto, Italy 41 F9

Spooner, U.S.A. 112 C9
Sporyy Navolok, Mys, Russia .. 52 B7
Sprague, U.S.A. 108 C5
Spratly I., S. China Sea 62 C4
Spratly Is., S. China Sea 62 C4
Spray, U.S.A. 108 D4
Spreča →, Bos.-H. 28 F3
Spree →, Germany 24 C9
Spremberg, Germany 24 D10
Sprengisandur, Iceland 8 D5
Spring City, U.S.A. 117 F9
Spring Creek, U.S.A. 108 F6
Spring Garden, U.S.A. 110 F6
Spring Hall, Barbados ...... 121 g
Spring Hill, U.S.A. 115 L4
Spring Mts., U.S.A. 109 H6
Spring Valley, U.S.A. 111 N10
Springbok, S. Africa 88 D2
Springboro, U.S.A. 116 E4
Springdale, Canada 105 C8
Springdale, U.S.A. 113 G7
Springe, Germany 24 C5
Springer, U.S.A. 113 G2
Springerville, U.S.A. 109 J9
Springfield, Canada 116 D4
Springfield, N.Z. 91 K3
Springfield, Colo., U.S.A. .. 113 G3
Springfield, Ill., U.S.A. 112 F10
Springfield, Mass., U.S.A. .. 117 D12
Springfield, Mo., U.S.A. 113 G8
Springfield, Ohio, U.S.A. .. 114 F4
Springfield, Oreg., U.S.A. .. 108 D2
Springfield, Tenn., U.S.A. .. 115 G2
Springfield, Vt., U.S.A. 117 C12
Springfontein, S. Africa 88 E4
Springhill, Canada 105 C7
Springhill, U.S.A. 113 J8
Springhouse, Canada 102 C4
Springs, S. Africa 89 D4
Springsure, Australia 94 C4
Springvale, U.S.A. 117 C14
Springville, Calif., U.S.A. .. 110 J8
Springville, N.Y., U.S.A. 116 D6
Springville, Utah, U.S.A. .. 108 F8
Springwater, U.S.A. 116 D7
Spruce-Creek, U.S.A. 116 F6
Spruce Knob-Seneca Rocks △,
   U.S.A. 114 F6
Spruce Mt., U.S.A. 117 B12
Spur, U.S.A. 113 J4
Spurn Hd., U.K. 14 D8
Spuž, Serbia & M. 44 D3
Spuzzum, Canada 102 D4
Squam L., U.S.A. 117 C13
Squamish, Canada 102 D4
Square Islands, Canada 105 B8
Squillace, G. di, Italy 43 D9
Squinzano, Italy 43 B11
Squires, Mt., Australia 93 E4
Srbac, Bos.-H. 28 E2
Srbica, Serbia & M. 44 D4
Srbija = Serbia □, Serbia & M. 44 C5
Srbobran, Serbia & M. 28 E4
Sre Ambel, Cambodia 65 G4
Sre Khtum, Cambodia 65 F6
Sre Umbell = Sre Ambel,
   Cambodia 65 G4
Srebrenica, Bos.-H. 28 F4
Sredinny Ra. = Sredinnyy
   Khrebet, Russia 53 D16
Sredinnyy Khrebet, Russia .. 53 D16
Središče, Slovenia 41 B13
Sredna Gora, Bulgaria 45 D8
Srednekolymsk, Russia 53 C16
Sredni Rodopi, Bulgaria 45 E8
Srednogorie, Bulgaria 45 D8
Śrem, Poland 31 F4
Sremska Mitrovica, Serbia & M. .. 28 E4
Sremski Karlovci, Serbia & M. .. 28 E4
Srepok →, Cambodia 64 F6
Sretensk, Russia 53 D12
Sri Lanka ■, Asia 66 R12
Srikakulam, India 67 K13
Srinagar, India 69 B6
Srinagarind Res., Thailand .. 64 E2
Środa Śląska, Poland 31 G3
Środa Wielkopolski, Poland .. 31 F4
Srono, Indonesia 63 J17
Srpska Crnja, Serbia & M. .. 28 E5
Srpski Itebej, Serbia & M. .. 28 E5
Staaten →, Australia 94 B3
Staaten River △, Australia .. 94 B3
Staberhuk, Germany 24 A7
Stade, Germany 24 B5
Stadskanaal, Neths. 17 A6
Stadtallendorf, Germany 24 E5
Stadthagen, Germany 24 C5
Stadtlohn, Germany 24 D2
Stadtroda, Germany 24 E7
Staffa, U.K. 13 E2
Staffanstorp, Sweden 11 J7
Stafford, U.K. 14 E5
Stafford, U.S.A. 113 G5
Stafford Springs, U.S.A. 117 E12
Staffordshire □, U.K. 14 E5
Stagnone, Italy 42 E5
Stagnone di Marsala △, Italy .. 42 E5
Staines, U.K. 15 F7
Stainz, Austria 26 E8
Stakhanov, Ukraine 33 H10
Stalać, Serbia & M. 44 C5
Stalis, Greece 49 D7
Stallarholmen, Sweden 10 E11
Ställdalen, Sweden 10 E8
Stalowa Wola, Poland 31 H9
Stalybridge, U.K. 14 D5
Stamford, Australia 94 C3
Stamford, U.K. 15 E7
Stamford, Conn., U.S.A. 117 E11
Stamford, N.Y., U.S.A. 117 D10

Stamford, Tex., U.S.A. ... 113 J5
Stampriet, Namibia ... 88 C2
Stamps, U.S.A. ... 113 J8
Stančevo = Kalipetrovo, Bulgaria 45 B11
Standerton, S. Africa ... 89 D4
Standish, U.S.A. ... 114 D4
Stanford, S. Africa ... 88 E2
Stanford, U.S.A. ... 108 C8
Stånga, Sweden ... 11 G12
Stanger, S. Africa ... 89 D5
Stängselåsen = Salpausselkä, Finland ... 9 F22
Stanišić, Serbia & M. ... 28 E4
Stanislaus →, U.S.A. ... 110 H5
Stanisławów, Poland ... 31 F8
Stanley, Australia ... 95 G4
Stanley, Falk. Is. ... 128 G5
Stanley, U.K. ... 14 C6
Stanley, Idaho, U.S.A. ... 108 D6
Stanley, N. Dak., U.S.A. ... 112 A3
Stanley, N.Y., U.S.A. ... 116 D7
Stanley Mission, Canada ... 103 B8
Stanovoy Khrebet, Russia ... 53 D13
Stanovoy Ra. = Stanovoy Khrebet, Russia ... 53 D13
Stansmore Ra., Australia ... 92 D4
Stansted, London ✈ (STN), U.K. ... 15 C6
Stanthorpe, Australia ... 95 D5
Stanton, U.S.A. ... 113 J4
Stanwood, U.S.A. ... 110 B4
Staples, U.S.A. ... 112 B7
Stąporków, Poland ... 31 G7
Star City, Canada ... 103 C8
Star Lake, U.S.A. ... 117 B9
Stará Ľubovňa, Slovak Rep. ... 27 B13
Stara Moravica, Serbia & M. ... 28 E4
Stara Pazova, Serbia & M. ... 28 F5
Stara Planina, Bulgaria ... 44 C7
Stara Sil, Ukraine ... 31 J9
Stará Turá, Slovak Rep. ... 27 C10
Stara Ushytsya, Ukraine ... 29 B12
Stara Zagora, Bulgaria ... 45 D9
Starachowice, Poland ... 31 G8
Staraya Russa, Russia ... 32 D6
Starbuck I., Kiribati ... 97 H12
Starchiojd, Romania ... 29 E11
Starcke △, Australia ... 94 A4
Stargard Szczeciński, Poland ... 30 E2
Stari Bar, Serbia & M. ... 44 D3
Stari Trg, Slovenia ... 41 C12
Staritsa, Russia ... 32 D8
Starke, U.S.A. ... 115 L4
Starnberg, Germany ... 25 H7
Starnberger See, Germany ... 25 H7
Starobilsk, Ukraine ... 33 H10
Starodub, Russia ... 33 F7
Starogard Gdański, Poland ... 30 E5
Starokonstantinov = Starokonstyantyniv, Ukraine ... 33 H4
Starokonstyantyniv, Ukraine ... 33 H4
Starokozache, Ukraine ... 29 D14
Starominskaya, Russia ... 33 J10
Staroshcherbinovskaya, Russia ... 33 J10
Start Pt., U.K. ... 15 G4
Stary Sącz, Poland ... 31 J7
Staryy Biryuzyak, Russia ... 35 H8
Staryy Chartoriysk, Ukraine ... 33 G3
Staryy Krym, Ukraine ... 33 K8
Staryy Oskol, Russia ... 33 G9
Staryy Sambir, Ukraine ... 31 J9
Stassfurt, Germany ... 24 D7
Staszów, Poland ... 31 H8
State College, U.S.A. ... 116 F7
Stateline, U.S.A. ... 110 G7
Staten, I. = Estados, I. de Los, Argentina ... 128 G4
Staten I., U.S.A. ... 117 F10
Statesboro, U.S.A. ... 115 J5
Statesville, U.S.A. ... 115 H5
Statia = St. Eustatius, W. Indies 121 C7
Stauffer, U.S.A. ... 111 L7
Staunton, Ill., U.S.A. ... 112 F10
Staunton, Va., U.S.A. ... 114 F6
Stavanger, Norway ... 9 G11
Staveley, N.Z. ... 91 K3
Stavelot, Belgium ... 17 D5
Stavern, Norway ... 9 G14
Stavoren, Neths. ... 17 B5
Stavropol, Russia ... 35 H6
Stavros, Cyprus ... 49 D11
Stavrós, Greece ... 49 D6
Stavrós, Ákra, Greece ... 49 D6
Stavroúpolis, Greece ... 45 E8
Stawell, Australia ... 95 F3
Stawell →, Australia ... 94 C3
Stawiski, Poland ... 30 E9
Stawiszyn, Poland ... 31 G5
Stayner, Canada ... 116 B4
Stayton, U.S.A. ... 108 D2
Steamboat Springs, U.S.A. ... 108 F10
Steblevë, Albania ... 44 E4
Steele, U.S.A. ... 112 B5
Steelton, U.S.A. ... 116 F8
Steen River, Canada ... 102 B5
Steens Mt., U.S.A. ... 108 E4
Steenwijk, Neths. ... 17 B6
Steep Pt., Australia ... 93 E1
Steep Rock, Canada ... 103 C9
Ştefan Vodă, Moldova ... 29 D14
Ştefăneşti, Romania ... 29 C12
Stefanie, = Ethiopia ... 81 G4
Stefanie L. = Chew Bahir, Ethiopia ... 81 G4
Stefansson Bay, Antarctica ... 5 C5
Stege, Denmark ... 11 K6
Ştei, Romania ... 28 D7
Steiermark □, Austria ... 26 D8
Steigerwald, Germany ... 25 F6
Steigerwald △, Germany ... 25 F6
Steilacoom, U.S.A. ... 110 C4
Steilrandberge, Namibia ... 88 B1

Steinbach, Canada ... 103 D9
Steinfurt, Germany ... 24 C3
Steinhausen, Namibia ... 88 C2
Steinheim, Germany ... 24 D5
Steinhuder Meer, Germany ... 24 C5
Steinhuder Meer △, Germany ... 24 C5
Steinkjer, Norway ... 8 D14
Steinkopf, S. Africa ... 88 D2
Stellarton, Canada ... 105 C7
Stellenbosch, S. Africa ... 88 E2
Stelvio, Paso dello, Italy ... 40 B7
Stenay, France ... 19 C12
Stendal, Germany ... 24 C7
Stenhamra, Sweden ... 10 E11
Stenshuvud △, Sweden ... 11 J8
Stenstorp, Sweden ... 11 F7
Stenungsund, Sweden ... 11 F5
Steornabhaigh = Stornoway, U.K. ... 13 C2
Stepanakert = Xankändi, Azerbaijan ... 70 B5
Stepanavan, Armenia ... 35 K7
Stephens Creek, Australia ... 95 E3
Stephens I., Canada ... 102 C2
Stephens L., Canada ... 103 B9
Stephenville, Canada ... 105 C8
Stephenville, U.S.A. ... 113 J5
Stepnica, Poland ... 30 E1
Steppe, Asia ... 50 D9
Stereá Ellas □, Greece ... 46 C4
Sterkstroom, S. Africa ... 88 E4
Sterling, Colo., U.S.A. ... 112 E3
Sterling, Ill., U.S.A. ... 112 E10
Sterling, Kans., U.S.A. ... 112 F5
Sterling City, U.S.A. ... 113 K4
Sterling Heights, U.S.A. ... 114 D4
Sterling Run, U.S.A. ... 116 E6
Sterlitamak, Russia ... 52 D6
Sternberg, Germany ... 24 B7
Šternberk, Czech Rep. ... 27 B10
Stérnes, Greece ... 49 D6
Sterzing = Vipiteno, Italy ... 41 B8
Stettin = Szczecin, Poland ... 30 E1
Stettiner Haff, Germany ... 24 B10
Stettler, Canada ... 102 C6
Steubenville, U.S.A. ... 116 F4
Stevenage, U.K. ... 15 F7
Stevens Point, U.S.A. ... 112 C10
Stevenson, U.S.A. ... 110 E5
Stevenson, The →, Australia ... 95 D2
Stevenson L., Canada ... 103 C9
Stevensville, U.S.A. ... 108 C6
Stewart, Canada ... 102 B3
Stewart, U.S.A. ... 110 F7
Stewart →, Canada ... 100 B6
Stewart, C., Australia ... 94 A1
Stewart, I., Chile ... 128 G2
Stewart I., N.Z. ... 91 M1
Stewarts Point, U.S.A. ... 110 G3
Stewartville, U.S.A. ... 112 D8
Stewiacke, Canada ... 105 C7
Steynsburg, S. Africa ... 88 E4
Steyr, Austria ... 26 C7
Steyr →, Austria ... 26 C7
Steytlerville, S. Africa ... 88 E3
Stia, Italy ... 41 E8
Stigler, U.S.A. ... 113 H7
Stigliano, Italy ... 43 B9
Stigtomta, Sweden ... 11 F10
Stikine →, Canada ... 102 B2
Stilfontein, S. Africa ... 88 D4
Stilís, Greece ... 46 C4
Stillwater, N.Z. ... 91 K3
Stillwater, Minn., U.S.A. ... 112 C8
Stillwater, N.Y., U.S.A. ... 117 D11
Stillwater, Okla., U.S.A. ... 113 G6
Stillwater Range, U.S.A. ... 108 G4
Stillwater Reservoir, U.S.A. ... 117 C9
Stilo, Pta., Italy ... 43 D9
Stilwell, U.S.A. ... 113 H7
Stînga Nistrului □, Moldova ... 29 C14
Ştip, Macedonia ... 44 E6
Stíra, Greece ... 46 C6
Stirling, Canada ... 116 B7
Stirling, U.K. ... 13 E5
Stirling □, U.K. ... 13 E4
Stirling Ra., Australia ... 93 F2
Stirling Range △, Australia ... 93 F2
Stittsville, Canada ... 117 A9
Stjernøya, Norway ... 8 A20
Stjørdalshalsen, Norway ... 8 E14
Stockach, Germany ... 25 H5
Stockaryd, Sweden ... 11 G8
Stockerau, Austria ... 27 C9
Stockholm, Sweden ... 10 E12
Stockholm Arlanda ✈ (ARN), Sweden ... 10 E11
Stockholms län □, Sweden ... 10 E12
Stockport, U.K. ... 14 D5
Stocksbridge, U.K. ... 14 D6
Stockton, Calif., U.S.A. ... 110 H5
Stockton, Kans., U.S.A. ... 112 F5
Stockton, Mo., U.S.A. ... 113 G8
Stockton-on-Tees, U.K. ... 14 C6
Stockton-on-Tees □, U.K. ... 14 C6
Stockton Plateau, U.S.A. ... 113 K3
Stoczek Łukowski, Poland ... 31 G8
Stöde, Sweden ... 10 B10
Stoeng Treng, Cambodia ... 64 F5
Stoer, Pt. of, U.K. ... 13 C3
Stogovo, Macedonia ... 44 E4
Stoholm, Denmark ... 11 H3
Stoke-on-Trent, U.K. ... 14 D5
Stoke-on-Trent □, U.K. ... 14 D5
Stokes △, Australia ... 93 E2
Stokes Pt., Australia ... 95 G3
Stokes Ra., Australia ... 92 C5
Stokksnes, Iceland ... 8 D6
Stokmarknes, Norway ... 8 B16

Stolac, Bos.-H. ... 44 C1
Stolberg, Germany ... 24 E2
Stolbovoy, Ostrov, Russia ... 53 B14
Stolbtsy = Stowbtsy, Belarus ... 32 F4
Stolin, Belarus ... 33 G4
Stolnici, Romania ... 29 F9
Stomión, Greece ... 49 D5
Ston, Croatia ... 41 F14
Stone, U.K. ... 14 E5
Stoneboro, U.S.A. ... 116 E4
Stonehaven, U.K. ... 13 E6
Stonehenge, Australia ... 94 C3
Stonehenge, U.K. ... 15 F6
Stonewall, Canada ... 103 C9
Stony L., Man., Canada ... 103 B9
Stony L., Ont., Canada ... 116 B6
Stony Point, U.S.A. ... 117 E11
Stony Pt., U.S.A. ... 117 C8
Stony Rapids, Canada ... 103 B7
Stony Tunguska = Tunguska, Podkamennaya →, Russia ... 53 C10
Stonyford, U.S.A. ... 110 F4
Stopnica, Poland ... 31 H7
Storá, Sweden ... 10 E9
Storå →, Denmark ... 11 H2
Stora Gla, Sweden ... 10 E6
Stora Le, Sweden ... 10 E5
Stora Lulevatten, Sweden ... 8 C18
Storavan, Sweden ... 8 D18
Stord, Norway ... 9 G11
Store Bælt, Denmark ... 11 J4
Store Heddinge, Denmark ... 11 J6
Store Mosse △, Sweden ... 11 G7
Storebro, Sweden ... 11 G9
Storfors, Sweden ... 10 E8
Storlien, Sweden ... 10 A6
Storm B., Australia ... 95 G4
Storm Lake, U.S.A. ... 112 D7
Stormberge, S. Africa ... 88 E4
Stormsrivier, S. Africa ... 88 E3
Stornoway, U.K. ... 13 C2
Storo, Italy ... 40 C7
Storozhinets = Storozhynets, Ukraine ... 29 B10
Storozhynets, Ukraine ... 29 B10
Storrs, U.S.A. ... 117 E12
Storsjön, Gävleborg, Sweden ... 10 D10
Storsjön, Jämtland, Sweden ... 10 B7
Storsjön, Jämtland, Sweden ... 10 A8
Storstrøms Amtskommune □, Denmark ... 11 J5
Storuman, Sweden ... 8 D17
Storuman, Sweden ... 8 D17
Storvätteshågna, Sweden ... 10 B6
Storvik, Sweden ... 10 D10
Storvreta, Sweden ... 10 E11
Stouffville, Canada ... 116 C5
Stoughton, Canada ... 103 D8
Stour →, Dorset, U.K. ... 15 G6
Stour →, Kent, U.K. ... 15 F9
Stour →, Suffolk, U.K. ... 15 F9
Stourbridge, U.K. ... 15 E5
Stout L., Canada ... 103 C10
Stove Pipe Wells Village, U.S.A. ... 111 J9
Støvring, Denmark ... 11 H3
Stow, U.S.A. ... 116 E3
Stowbtsy, Belarus ... 32 F4
Stowmarket, U.K. ... 15 E9
Strabane, U.K. ... 12 B4
Stracin, Macedonia ... 44 D6
Stradella, Italy ... 40 C6
Strahan, Australia ... 95 G4
Strajitsa, Bulgaria ... 45 C9
Strakonice, Czech Rep. ... 26 B6
Straldzha, Bulgaria ... 45 D10
Stralsund, Germany ... 24 A9
Strand, S. Africa ... 88 E2
Stranda, Møre og Romsdal, Norway ... 9 E12
Stranda, Nord-Trøndelag, Norway ... 8 E14
Strandby, Denmark ... 11 G4
Strangford L., U.K. ... 12 B6
Strängnäs, Sweden ... 10 E11
Stranraer, U.K. ... 13 G3
Strasbourg, Canada ... 103 C8
Strasbourg, France ... 19 D14
Strasburg, Germany ... 24 B9
Strășeni, Moldova ... 29 C13
Strässa, Sweden ... 10 E9
Stratford, Canada ... 116 C4
Stratford, N.Z. ... 91 H5
Stratford, Calif., U.S.A. ... 110 J7
Stratford, Conn., U.S.A. ... 117 E11
Stratford, Tex., U.S.A. ... 113 G3
Stratford-upon-Avon, U.K. ... 15 E6
Strath Spey, U.K. ... 13 D5
Strathalbyn, Australia ... 95 F2
Strathaven, U.K. ... 13 F4
Strathcona △, Canada ... 102 D3
Strathmore, Canada ... 102 C6
Strathmore, U.K. ... 13 E5
Strathmore, U.S.A. ... 110 J7
Strathnaver, Canada ... 102 C4
Strathpeffer, U.K. ... 13 D4
Strathroy, Canada ... 116 D3
Strathy Pt., U.K. ... 13 C4
Strattanville, U.S.A. ... 116 E5
Stratton, U.S.A. ... 117 A14
Stratton Mt., U.S.A. ... 117 C12
Straubing, Germany ... 25 G8
Straumnes, Iceland ... 8 C2
Strausberg, Germany ... 24 C9
Strawberry →, U.S.A. ... 108 F8
Strážnice, Czech Rep. ... 27 C10
Streaky B., Australia ... 95 E1
Streaky Bay, Australia ... 95 E1
Streator, U.S.A. ... 112 E10
Středočeský □, Czech Rep. ... 26 B7
Streetsboro, U.S.A. ... 116 E3
Streetsville, Canada ... 116 C5

Strehaia, Romania ... 29 F8
Strelcha, Bulgaria ... 45 D8
Strelka →, Russia ... 53 D10
Streng →, Cambodia ... 64 F4
Stresa, Italy ... 40 C5
Streymoy, Færoe Is. ... 8 E9
Strezhevoy, Russia ... 52 C8
Stříbro, Czech Rep. ... 26 A6
Strilky, Ukraine ... 31 J9
Strimón →, Greece ... 44 F7
Strimonikós Kólpos, Greece ... 44 F7
Strofádhes, Greece ... 46 D3
Stroma, U.K. ... 13 C5
Stromberg-Heuchelberg △, Germany ... 25 F4
Strómboli, Italy ... 43 D8
Stromeferry, U.K. ... 13 D3
Stromness, U.K. ... 13 C5
Strömsbruk, Sweden ... 10 C11
Stromsburg, U.S.A. ... 112 E6
Strömsnäsbruk, Sweden ... 11 H7
Strömstad, Sweden ... 11 F5
Strömsund, Sweden ... 8 E16
Strongíli, Greece ... 47 E11
Strongsville, U.S.A. ... 116 E3
Stronie Śląskie, Poland ... 31 H3
Stronsay, U.K. ... 13 B6
Stropkov, Slovak Rep. ... 27 B14
Stroud, U.K. ... 15 F5
Stroud Road, Australia ... 95 E5
Stroudsburg, U.S.A. ... 117 F9
Stroumbi, Cyprus ... 49 E11
Struer, Denmark ... 11 H2
Struga, Macedonia ... 44 E4
Strugi Krasnyye, Russia ... 32 C5
Strumica, Macedonia ... 44 E6
Strumica →, Europe ... 44 E7
Strumok, Ukraine ... 29 E14
Struthers, Canada ... 104 C2
Struthers, U.S.A. ... 116 E4
Stryama →, Bulgaria ... 45 D8
Stryker, U.S.A. ... 108 B6
Stryków, Poland ... 31 G6
Stryy, Ukraine ... 33 H2
Strzegom, Poland ... 31 H3
Strzelce Krajeńskie, Poland ... 31 F2
Strzelce Opolskie, Poland ... 31 H5
Strzelecki Cr. →, Australia ... 95 D2
Strzelin, Poland ... 31 H4
Strzelno, Poland ... 31 F5
Strzybnica, Poland ... 31 H5
Strzyżów, Poland ... 31 J8
Stuart, Fla., U.S.A. ... 115 M5
Stuart, Nebr., U.S.A. ... 112 D5
Stuart →, Canada ... 102 C4
Stuart Bluff Ra., Australia ... 92 D5
Stuart L., Canada ... 102 C4
Stuart Ra., Australia ... 95 D1
Stubbekøbing, Denmark ... 11 K6
Stuben, Austria ... 26 D3
Studen Kladenets, Yazovir, Bulgaria ... 45 E9
Studenka, Czech Rep. ... 27 B11
Stugun, Sweden ... 10 A9
Stuhr, Germany ... 24 B4
Stull L., Canada ... 104 B1
Stung Treng = Stoeng Treng, Cambodia ... 64 F5
Stupart →, Canada ... 104 A1
Stupava, Slovak Rep. ... 27 C10
Stupino, Russia ... 32 E10
Sturgeon B., Canada ... 103 C9
Sturgeon Bay, U.S.A. ... 114 C2
Sturgeon Falls, Canada ... 104 C4
Sturgeon L., Alta., Canada ... 102 B5
Sturgeon L., Ont., Canada ... 104 C1
Sturgeon L., Ont., Canada ... 116 B6
Sturgis, Canada ... 103 C8
Sturgis, Mich., U.S.A. ... 114 E3
Sturgis, S. Dak., U.S.A. ... 112 C3
Sturkö, Sweden ... 11 H9
Štúrovo, Slovak Rep. ... 27 D11
Sturt □, Australia ... 95 D3
Sturt Cr. →, Australia ... 92 C4
Sturt Stony Desert, Australia ... 95 D3
Stutterheim, S. Africa ... 88 E4
Stuttgart, Germany ... 25 G5
Stuttgart, U.S.A. ... 113 H9
Stuttgart Echterdingen ✈ (STR), Germany ... 25 G5
Stuyvesant, U.S.A. ... 117 D11
Stykkishólmur, Iceland ... 8 D2
Styria = Steiermark □, Austria ... 26 D8
Styrsö, Sweden ... 11 G5
Su Xian = Suzhou, China ... 56 H9
Suakin, Sudan ... 80 D4
Suan, N. Korea ... 57 E14
Suaqui, Mexico ... 118 B3
Suar, India ... 69 E8
Subang, Indonesia ... 63 G12
Subansiri →, India ... 67 F18
Subarnarekha →, India ... 69 H12
Subayhah, Si. Arabia ... 70 D3
Subcetate, Romania ... 28 E8
Subi, Indonesia ... 62 D3
Subiaco, Italy ... 41 G10
Subotica, Serbia & M. ... 28 D4
Suca, Ethiopia ... 81 F4
Suceava, Romania ... 29 C11
Suceava →, Romania ... 29 C11
Sucha-Bezkidzka, Poland ... 31 J6
Suchań, Poland ... 31 E2
Suchan, Russia ... 54 C6
Suchedniów, Poland ... 31 G7
Suchitoto, El Salv. ... 120 D2
Suchou = Suzhou, China ... 59 B13
Suchowola, Poland ... 30 E10
Suck →, Ireland ... 12 C3

Sucre, Bolivia ... 124 G5
Sućuraj, Croatia ... 41 E14
Sucuriú →, Brazil ... 125 H8
Sud, Pte. du, Canada ... 105 C7
Sud-Kivu □, Dem. Rep. of the Congo ... 86 C2
Sud-Ouest, Pte., Canada ... 105 C7
Suda →, Russia ... 32 C9
Sudak, Ukraine ... 33 K8
Sudan, U.S.A. ... 113 H3
Sudan ■, Africa ... 81 E3
Sudbury, Canada ... 104 C3
Sudbury, U.K. ... 15 E8
Sûdd, Sudan ... 81 F3
Sudeifel = Deutsch-Luxemburgischer △, Germany ... 25 F2
Süderbrarup, Germany ... 24 A5
Süderlügum, Germany ... 24 A4
Süderoogsand, Germany ... 24 A4
Sudeten Mts. = Sudety, Europe ... 27 A9
Sudety, Europe ... 27 A9
Südheide △, Germany ... 24 C6
Suðuroy, Færoe Is. ... 8 F9
Sudi, Tanzania ... 87 E4
Sudirman, Pegunungan, Indonesia ... 63 E9
Sudiţi, Romania ... 29 F12
Sudogda, Russia ... 34 C5
Sudong, Pulau, Singapore ... 65 d
Sudova Vyshnya, Ukraine ... 31 J10
Sudr, Egypt ... 80 B3
Sudzha, Russia ... 33 G8
Sue →, Sudan ... 81 F2
Sueca, Spain ... 39 F4
Sŭedinenie, Bulgaria ... 45 D8
Suemez I., U.S.A. ... 102 B2
Suez = El Suweis, Egypt ... 80 J8
Suez, G. of = Suweis, Khalîg el, Egypt ... 80 J8
Suez Canal = Suweis, Qanâ es, Egypt ... 80 H8
Suffield, Canada ... 102 C6
Suffolk, U.S.A. ... 114 G7
Suffolk □, U.K. ... 15 E9
Şugag, Romania ... 29 E8
Sugargrove, U.S.A. ... 116 E5
Sugarive →, India ... 69 F12
Suğla Gölü, Turkey ... 72 D5
Sugluk = Salluit, Canada ... 101 B12
Suhaia, Lacul, Romania ... 29 G10
Şuḩār, Oman ... 71 E8
Sühbaatar □, Mongolia ... 56 B8
Suhl, Germany ... 24 E6
Şuhut, Turkey ... 47 C12
Sui, Pakistan ... 68 E3
Sui Xian, China ... 56 G8
Suica, Bos.-H. ... 28 G2
Suichang, China ... 59 C12
Suichuan, China ... 59 D10
Suide, China ... 56 F6
Suifenhe, China ... 57 B16
Suihua, China ... 60 B7
Suijiang, China ... 58 C4
Suining, Hunan, China ... 59 D8
Suining, Jiangsu, China ... 57 H9
Suining, Sichuan, China ... 58 B5
Suiping, China ... 56 H7
Suippes, France ... 19 C11
Suir →, Ireland ... 12 D4
Suisun City, U.S.A. ... 110 G4
Suixi, China ... 59 G8
Suiyang, Guizhou, China ... 58 D6
Suiyang, Heilongjiang, China ... 57 B16
Suizhong, China ... 57 D11
Suizhou, China ... 59 B9
Sujangarh, India ... 68 F6
Sukabumi, Indonesia ... 63 G12
Sukadana, Indonesia ... 62 E3
Sukagawa, Japan ... 55 F10
Sukaraja, Indonesia ... 62 E4
Sukawati, Indonesia ... 63 K18
Sukch'ŏn, N. Korea ... 57 E13
Sukhindol, Bulgaria ... 45 C9
Sukhinichi, Russia ... 32 E8
Sukhona →, Russia ... 52 D4
Sukhothai, Thailand ... 64 D2
Sukhumi = Sokhumi, Georgia ... 35 J5
Sukkur, Pakistan ... 68 F3
Sukkur Barrage, Pakistan ... 68 F3
Sukovo, Serbia & M. ... 44 C6
Sukri →, India ... 68 G4
Sukumo, Japan ... 55 H6
Sukunka →, Canada ... 102 B4
Sula →, Ukraine ... 33 H7
Sula, Kepulauan, Indonesia ... 63 E7
Sulaco →, Honduras ... 120 C2
Sulaiman Range, Pakistan ... 68 D3
Sulak →, Russia ... 35 J8
Sülär, Iran ... 71 D6
Sulawesi □, Indonesia ... 63 E6
Sulawesi Sea = Celebes Sea, Indonesia ... 63 D6
Sulawesi Selatan □, Indonesia ... 63 E6
Sulawesi Tengah □, Indonesia ... 63 E6
Sulawesi Tenggara □, Indonesia ... 63 E6
Sulawesi Utara □, Indonesia ... 63 D6
Sulechów, Poland ... 31 F2
Sulęcin, Poland ... 31 F1
Sulejów, Poland ... 31 G6
Sulejówek, Poland ... 31 F8
Süleymanlı, Turkey ... 47 C9
Sulima, S. Leone ... 82 D2
Sulina, Romania ... 29 E14
Sulina, Brațul →, Romania ... 29 E14
Sulingen, Germany ... 24 C4
Suliţa, Romania ... 29 C11
Sulitjelma, Norway ... 8 C17
Sułkowice, Poland ... 31 J6
Sullana, Peru ... 124 D2
Süller, Turkey ... 47 C11
Sullivan, Ill., U.S.A. ... 112 F10

Sullivan, Ind., U.S.A. 114 F2
Sullivan, Mo., U.S.A. 112 F9
Sullivan Bay, Canada 102 C3
Sullivan I. = Lanbi Kyun, Burma 65 G2
Sullom Voe, U.K. 13 A7
Sully-sur-Loire, France 19 E9
Sulmierzyce, Poland 31 G4
Sulmona, Italy 41 F10
Süloğlu, Turkey 45 E10
Sulphur, La., U.S.A. 113 K8
Sulphur, Okla., U.S.A. 113 H6
Sulphur Pt., Canada 102 A6
Sulphur Springs, U.S.A. 113 J7
Sultan, Canada 104 C3
Sultan, U.S.A. 110 C5
Sultan Dağları, Turkey 72 C4
Sultanhisar, Turkey 47 D10
Sultaniça, Turkey 45 F10
Sultaniye, Turkey 45 F12
Sultanpur, Mad. P., India 68 H8
Sultanpur, Punjab, India 68 D6
Sultanpur, Ut. P., India 69 F10
Sulu Arch., Phil. 61 J4
Sulu Sea, E. Indies 61 G4
Sülüklü, Turkey 72 C5
Sulula, Ethiopia 81 F4
Suluova, Turkey 72 B6
Suluq, Libya 79 B10
Sulzbach, Germany 25 F3
Sulzbach-Rosenberg, Germany 25 F7
Sulzberger Ice Shelf, Antarctica 5 E13
Sumalata, Indonesia 63 D6
Sumampa, Argentina 126 B3
Sumatera, Indonesia 62 D2
Sumatera Barat □, Indonesia 62 E2
Sumatera Utara □, Indonesia 62 D1
Sumatra = Sumatera, Indonesia 62 D2
Sumava, Czech Rep. 26 C6
Sumba, Indonesia 63 F5
Sumba, Selat, Indonesia 63 F5
Sumbawa, Indonesia 62 F5
Sumbawa Besar, Indonesia 62 F5
Sumbawanga □, Tanzania 84 F6
Sumbe, Angola 84 G2
Sumbu △, Zambia 87 D3
Sumburgh Hd., U.K. 13 B7
Sumdeo, India 69 D8
Sumdo, China 69 B8
Sumedang, Indonesia 63 G12
Sümeg, Hungary 28 D2
Sumeih, Sudan 81 F2
Sumen = Shumen, Bulgaria 45 C10
Sumenep, Indonesia 63 G15
Sumgait = Sumqayıt, Azerbaijan 35 K9
Summer L., U.S.A. 108 E3
Summerland, Canada 102 D5
Summerside, Canada 105 C7
Summersville, U.S.A. 114 F5
Summerville, Ga., U.S.A. 115 H3
Summerville, S.C., U.S.A. 115 J5
Summit Lake, Canada 102 C4
Summit Peak, U.S.A. 109 H10
Sumner, Iowa, U.S.A. 112 D8
Sumner, Wash., U.S.A. 110 C4
Sumoto, Japan 55 G7
Šumperk, Czech Rep. 27 B9
Sumqayıt, Azerbaijan 35 K9
Sumter, U.S.A. 115 J5
Sumy, Ukraine 33 G8
Sun City, S. Africa 88 D4
Sun City, Ariz., U.S.A. 109 K7
Sun City, Calif., U.S.A. 111 M9
Sun City Center, U.S.A. 115 M4
Sun Lakes, U.S.A. 109 K8
Sun Valley, U.S.A. 108 E6
Sunagawa, Japan 54 C10
Sunan, N. Korea 57 E13
Sunart, L., U.K. 13 E3
Sunburst, U.S.A. 108 B8
Sunbury, Australia 95 F3
Sunbury, U.S.A. 117 F8
Sunchales, Argentina 126 C3
Suncho Corral, Argentina 126 B3
Sunch'ŏn, S. Korea 57 G14
Suncook, U.S.A. 117 C13
Sunda, Selat, Indonesia 62 F3
Sunda Is., Indonesia 96 H2
Sunda Str. = Sunda, Selat, Indonesia 62 F3
Sundance, Canada 103 B10
Sundance, U.S.A. 112 C2
Sundar Nagar, India 68 D7
Sundargarh, India 67 H14
Sundays = Sondags →, S. Africa 88 E4
Sunderland, Canada 116 B5
Sunderland, U.K. 14 C6
Sundown △, Australia 95 D5
Sundre, Canada 102 C6
Sunds, Denmark 11 H3
Sundsvall, Sweden 10 B11
Sundsvallsbukten, Sweden 10 B11
Sung Hei, Vietnam 65 G6
Sungai Acheh, Malaysia 65 c
Sungai Kolok, Thailand 65 J3
Sungai Lembing, Malaysia 65 L4
Sungai Petani, Malaysia 65 K3
Sungaigerong, Indonesia 62 E3
Sungailiat, Indonesia 62 E3
Sungaipenuh, Indonesia 62 E2
Sungari = Songhua Jiang →, China 60 B8
Sunghua Chiang = Songhua Jiang →, China 60 B8
Sungikai, Sudan 81 E2
Sungurlu, Turkey 72 B6
Sunja, Croatia 41 C13
Sunland Park, U.S.A. 109 L10
Sunnansjö, Sweden 10 D8
Sunndalsøra, Norway 9 E13

Sunne, Sweden 10 E7
Sunnemo, Sweden 10 E7
Sunnyside, U.S.A. 108 C3
Sunnyvale, U.S.A. 110 H4
Suntar, Russia 53 C12
Sunyani, Ghana 82 D4
Suomenselkä, Finland 8 E21
Suomussalmi, Finland 8 D23
Suoyarvi, Russia 32 A7
Supai, U.S.A. 109 H7
Supaul, India 69 F12
Superior, Ariz., U.S.A. 109 K8
Superior, Mont., U.S.A. 108 C6
Superior, Nebr., U.S.A. 112 E5
Superior, Wis., U.S.A. 112 B8
Superior, L., N. Amer. 104 C2
Supetar, Croatia 41 E13
Suphan Buri, Thailand 64 E3
Suphan Dağı, Turkey 70 B4
Supiori, Indonesia 63 E9
Supraśl, Poland 31 E10
Supung Shuiku, China 57 D13
Süq Suwayq, Si. Arabia 70 E3
Suqian, China 57 H10
Suquţra = Socotra, Yemen 75 E5
Şūr, Lebanon 74 B4
Şūr, Oman 75 C6
Sur, Pt., U.S.A. 110 J5
Sura →, Russia 34 C8
Surab, Pakistan 68 E2
Surabaja = Surabaya, Indonesia 63 G15
Surabaya, Indonesia 63 G15
Surahammar, Sweden 10 E10
Suraia, Romania 29 E12
Surakarta, Indonesia 63 G14
Surakhany, Azerbaijan 35 K10
Surany, Slovak Rep. 27 C11
Surat, Australia 95 D4
Surat, India 66 J8
Surat Thani, Thailand 65 H2
Suratgarh, India 68 E5
Suraż, Poland 31 F9
Surazh, Belarus 32 K6
Surazh, Russia 33 F7
Surduc, Romania 29 C8
Surduc Pasul, Romania 29 E8
Surdulica, Serbia & M. 44 D6
Surendranagar, India 68 H4
Surf, U.S.A. 111 L6
Surfers Paradise, Australia 95 D5
Surgères, France 20 B3
Surgut, Russia 52 C8
Sùria, Spain 38 D6
Suriapet, India 66 L11
Surigao, Phil. 61 G6
Surigao Strait, Phil. 61 F6
Surin, Thailand 64 E4
Surin Nua, Ko, Thailand 65 H1
Surinam = Suriname ■, S. Amer. 125 C7
Suriname ■, S. Amer. 125 C7
Suriname →, Suriname 125 B7
Sürmaq, Iran 71 D7
Sürmene, Turkey 73 B9
Surovikino, Russia 35 F6
Surrey, Canada 110 A4
Surrey □, U.K. 15 F7
Sursand, India 69 F11
Sursar →, India 69 F12
Sursee, Switz. 25 H4
Sursk, Russia 34 D7
Surskoye, Russia 34 C8
Surt, Libya 79 B9
Surt, Khalīj, Libya 79 B9
Surtanahu, Pakistan 68 F4
Surte, Sweden 11 G6
Surtsey, Iceland 8 E3
Sürüç, Turkey 73 D8
Suruga-Wan, Japan 55 G9
Susa, Italy 40 C4
Sušà →, Denmark 11 J5
Sušac, Croatia 41 F13
Susaki, Croatia 41 D11
Susaki, Japan 55 H6
Süsangerd, Iran 71 D6
Susanville, U.S.A. 108 F3
Susch, Switz. 25 J6
Suşehri, Turkey 73 B8
Sušice, Czech Rep. 26 B6
Susleni, Moldova 29 C13
Susner, India 68 H7
Susong, China 59 B11
Susquehanna, U.S.A. 117 E9
Susquehanna →, U.S.A. 117 G8
Susques, Argentina 126 A2
Sussex, Canada 105 C6
Sussex, U.S.A. 117 E10
Sussex, E. □, U.K. 15 G8
Sussex, W. □, U.K. 15 G7
Sustut →, Canada 102 B3
Susuman, Russia 53 C15
Susunu, Indonesia 63 E8
Susurluk, Turkey 47 B10
Susuz, Turkey 73 B10
Susz, Poland 30 E6
Sütçüler, Turkey 72 D4
Şuţeşti, Romania 29 E12
Sutherland, S. Africa 88 E3
Sutherland, U.K. 13 C4
Sutherland, U.S.A. 112 E4
Sutherland Falls, N.Z. 91 L1
Sutherlin, U.S.A. 108 E2
Suthri, India 68 H3
Sutjeska △, Bos.-H. 28 G3
Sutlej →, Pakistan 68 E4
Sutter, U.S.A. 110 F5
Sutter Creek, U.S.A. 110 G6
Sutton, Canada 117 A12
Sutton, Nebr., U.S.A. 112 E6
Sutton, W. Va., U.S.A. 114 F5

Sutton →, Canada 104 A3
Sutton Coldfield, U.K. 15 E6
Sutton in Ashfield, U.K. 14 D6
Sutton L., Canada 104 B3
Suttor →, Australia 94 C4
Suttsu, Japan 54 C10
Suva, Fiji 91 D8
Suva Gora, Macedonia 44 E5
Suva Planina, Serbia & M. 44 C6
Suva Reka, Serbia & M. 44 D4
Suvorov, Russia 32 E9
Suvorov Is. = Suwarrow Is., Cook Is. 97 J11
Suvorove, Ukraine 29 E13
Suvorovo, Bulgaria 45 C11
Suwałki, Poland 30 D9
Suwana, Indonesia 63 K18
Suwannaphum, Thailand 64 E4
Suwannee →, U.S.A. 115 L4
Suwanose-Jima, Japan 55 K4
Suwarrow Is., Cook Is. 97 J11
Suwayq aş Şuqban, Iraq 70 D5
Suweis, Khalîg el, Egypt 80 J8
Suweis, Qanâ es, Egypt 80 H8
Suwŏn, S. Korea 57 F14
Suzdal, Russia 32 D11
Suzhou, Anhui, China 56 H9
Suzhou, Jiangsu, China 59 B13
Suzu, Japan 55 F8
Suzu-Misaki, Japan 55 F8
Suzuka, Japan 55 G8
Suzzara, Italy 40 D7
Svalbard, Arctic 51 B5
Svalbard Radio = Longyearbyen, Svalbard 4 B8
Svalöv, Sweden 11 J7
Svalyava, Ukraine 28 B7
Svaneke, Denmark 11 J9
Svängsta, Sweden 11 H8
Svansko, Sweden 10 E6
Svappavaara, Sweden 8 C19
Svärdsjö, Sweden 10 D9
Svartå, Sweden 10 E8
Svartisen, Norway 8 C15
Svartvik, Sweden 10 B11
Svatove, Ukraine 33 H10
Svatovo = Svatove, Ukraine 33 H10
Svay Chek, Cambodia 64 F4
Svay Rieng, Cambodia 65 G5
Svealand □, Sweden 10 D9
Svedala, Sweden 11 J7
Sveg, Sweden 10 B8
Svendborg, Denmark 11 J4
Svenljunga, Sweden 11 G7
Svenstavik, Sweden 10 B8
Svenstrup, Denmark 11 H3
Sverdlovsk, Ukraine 33 H10
Sverdrup I., Canada 98 B10
Svetac, Croatia 41 E12
Sveti Nikola, Prokhod, Europe 44 C6
Sveti Nikole, Macedonia 44 E5
Sveti Rok, Croatia 41 D12
Svetlaya, Russia 54 A9
Svetlogorsk = Svyetlahorsk, Belarus 33 F5
Svetlogorsk, Russia 30 D7
Svetlograd, Russia 35 H6
Svetlovodsk = Svitlovodsk, Ukraine 33 H7
Svetlyy, Russia 30 D7
Svidník, Slovak Rep. 27 B14
Svilaja Planina, Croatia 41 E13
Svilajnac, Serbia & M. 44 B5
Svilengrad, Bulgaria 45 E10
Svir →, Russia 32 B7
Sviritsa, Russia 32 B7
Svishtov, Bulgaria 45 C9
Svislach, Belarus 31 E11
Svitava →, Czech Rep. 27 B9
Svitavy, Czech Rep. 27 B9
Svitlovodsk, Ukraine 33 H7
Svobodnyy, Russia 53 D13
Svoge, Bulgaria 44 C7
Svolvær, Norway 8 B16
Svratka →, Czech Rep. 27 B9
Svrljig, Serbia & M. 44 C6
Svyetlahorsk, Belarus 33 F5
Swabian Alps = Schwäbische Alb, Germany 25 G5
Swaffham, U.K. 15 E8
Swainsboro, U.S.A. 115 J4
Swakop →, Namibia 88 C2
Swakopmund, Namibia 88 C1
Swale →, U.K. 14 C6
Swan →, Australia 93 F2
Swan →, Canada 103 C8
Swan Hill, Australia 95 F3
Swan Hills, Canada 102 C5
Swan Is. = Santanilla, Is., Honduras 120 C3
Swan L., Canada 103 C8
Swan Peak, U.S.A. 108 C7
Swan Ra., U.S.A. 108 C7
Swan River, Canada 103 C8
Swanage, U.K. 15 G6
Swansea, Australia 95 G4
Swansea, Canada 116 C5
Swansea, U.K. 15 F3
Swansea □, U.K. 15 F3
Swar →, Pakistan 69 B5
Swartberge, S. Africa 88 E3
Swartmodder, S. Africa 88 D3
Swartnossob →, Namibia 88 C2
Swartruggens, S. Africa 88 D4
Swarzędz, Poland 31 F4
Swastika, Canada 104 C3
Swatow = Shantou, China 59 F11
Swaziland ■, Africa 89 D5
Sweden ■, Europe 9 G16
Swedru, Ghana 83 D4

Sweet Home, U.S.A. 108 D2
Sweetgrass, U.S.A. 108 B8
Sweetwater, Nev., U.S.A. 110 G7
Sweetwater, Tenn., U.S.A. 115 H3
Sweetwater, Tex., U.S.A. 113 J4
Sweetwater →, U.S.A. 108 E10
Swellendam, S. Africa 88 E3
Świder →, Poland 31 F8
Świdnica, Poland 31 H3
Świdnik, Poland 31 G9
Świdwin, Poland 30 E2
Świebodzice, Poland 31 H3
Świebodzin, Poland 31 F2
Świecie, Poland 30 E5
Świerzawa, Poland 31 G2
Świętokrzyski △, Poland 31 H7
Świętokrzyskie □, Poland 31 H7
Świętokrzyskie, Góry, Poland 31 H7
Swift Current, Canada 103 C7
Swift Current →, Canada 103 C7
Swilly, L., Ireland 12 A4
Swindon, U.K. 15 F6
Swindon □, U.K. 15 F6
Swinemünde = Świnoujście, Poland 30 E1
Swinford, Ireland 12 C3
Świnoujście, Poland 30 E1
Switzerland ■, Europe 25 J4
Swords, Ireland 12 C5
Swoyerville, U.S.A. 117 E9
Syasstroy, Russia 32 B7
Sychevka, Russia 32 E8
Syców, Poland 31 G4
Sydenham →, Canada 116 D2
Sydney, Australia 95 E5
Sydney, Canada 105 C7
Sydney L., Canada 103 C10
Sydney Mines, Canada 105 C7
Sydprøven = Alluitsup Paa, Greenland 101 B15
Sydra, G. of = Surt, Khalīj, Libya 79 B9
Syeverodonetsk, Ukraine 33 H10
Syke, Germany 24 C4
Sykesville, U.S.A. 116 E6
Syktyvkar, Russia 52 C6
Sylacauga, U.S.A. 115 J2
Sylarna, Sweden 8 E15
Sylhet, Bangla. 67 G17
Sylhet □, Bangla. 67 G17
Sylt, Germany 24 A4
Sylvan Beach, U.S.A. 117 C9
Sylvan Lake, Canada 102 C6
Sylvania, U.S.A. 115 J5
Sylvester, U.S.A. 115 K4
Sym, Russia 52 C9
Symón, Mexico 118 C4
Synelnykove, Ukraine 33 H8
Synevyr △, Ukraine 29 B8
Synevyrska Polyana, Ukraine 29 B8
Synnott Ra., Australia 92 C4
Synyak, Ukraine 28 B7
Syowa, Antarctica 5 C5
Syracuse, Kans., U.S.A. 113 G4
Syracuse, N.Y., U.S.A. 117 C8
Syracuse, Nebr., U.S.A. 112 E6
Syrdarya →, Kazakhstan 52 E7
Syria ■, Asia 70 C3
Syrian Desert = Shām, Bādiyat ash, Asia 70 C3
Sysslebäck, Sweden 10 D6
Syzran, Russia 34 D9
Szabolcs-Szatmár-Bereg □, Hungary 28 B6
Szadek, Poland 31 G5
Szamocin, Poland 31 E4
Szamos →, Hungary 28 B7
Szamotuły, Poland 31 F3
Száraz →, Hungary 28 D6
Szarvas, Hungary 28 D5
Százhalombatta, Hungary 28 C3
Szczawnica, Poland 31 J7
Szczebrzeszyn, Poland 31 H9
Szczecin, Poland 30 E1
Szczecinek, Poland 30 E3
Szczeciński, Zalew = Stettiner Haff, Germany 24 B10
Szczekociny, Poland 31 H6
Szczucin, Poland 31 H8
Szczuczyn, Poland 30 E9
Szczyrk, Poland 31 J6
Szczytna, Poland 31 H3
Szczytno, Poland 30 E7
Szechuan = Sichuan □, China 58 B5
Szechwan = Sichuan □, China 58 B5
Szécsény, Hungary 28 B4
Szeged, Hungary 28 D5
Szeghalom, Hungary 28 C6
Szegvár, Hungary 28 D5
Székesfehérvár, Hungary 28 C3
Szekszárd, Hungary 28 D3
Szendrő, Hungary 28 B5
Szentendre, Hungary 28 C3
Szentes, Hungary 28 D5
Szentgotthárd, Hungary 28 D1
Szentlőrinc, Hungary 28 D3
Szerencs, Hungary 28 B5
Szigetszentmiklós, Hungary 28 C4
Szigetvár, Hungary 28 D2
Szikszó, Hungary 28 B5
Szklarska Poreba, Poland 31 H2
Szkwa →, Poland 31 E8
Szob, Hungary 28 C3
Szolnok, Hungary 28 C5
Szombathely, Hungary 28 D1
Szprotawa, Poland 31 G2
Sztum, Poland 30 E6
Szubin, Poland 31 E4
Szydłowiec, Poland 31 G7
Szypliszki, Poland 30 D10

T

Ta Khli Khok, Thailand 64 E3
Ta Lai, Vietnam 65 G6
Tab, Hungary 28 D3
Tabacal, Argentina 126 A3
Tabaco, Phil. 61 E5
Tabagné, Ivory C. 82 D4
Ţābah, Si. Arabia 70 E4
Tabanan, Indonesia 63 K18
Tabankort, Niger 83 B5
Ţabas, Khorāsān, Iran 71 C9
Ţabas, Khorāsān, Iran 71 C8
Tabasará, Serranía de, Panama 120 E3
Tabasco □, Mexico 119 D6
Tabāsīn, Iran 71 D8
Tabatinga, Serra da, Brazil 125 F10
Taber, Canada 102 D6
Taberg, Sweden 11 G8
Taberg, U.S.A. 117 C9
Tabla, Niger 83 C5
Tablas de Daimiel △, Spain 37 F7
Tablas I., Phil. 61 E5
Tablas Strait, Phil. 61 E5
Table B., Canada 105 B8
Table B., S. Africa 88 E2
Table Mt., S. Africa 88 E2
Table Rock L., U.S.A. 113 G8
Tabletop, Mt., Australia 94 C4
Tábor, Czech Rep. 26 B7
Tabora, Tanzania 86 D3
Tabora □, Tanzania 86 D3
Tabou, Ivory C. 82 E3
Tabrīz, Iran 70 B5
Tabuaeran, Kiribati 97 G12
Tabuenca, Spain 38 D3
Tabūk, Si. Arabia 70 D3
Taburno-Camposauro △, Italy 43 A7
Täby, Sweden 10 E12
Tacámbaro de Codallos, Mexico 118 D4
Tacheng, China 60 B3
Tach'i, Taiwan 59 E13
Tachia, Taiwan 59 E13
Tach'ing Shan = Daqing Shan, China 56 D6
Tachov, Czech Rep. 26 B5
Tácina →, Italy 43 D9
Tacloban, Phil. 61 F6
Tacna, Peru 124 G4
Tacoma, U.S.A. 110 C4
Tacuarembó, Uruguay 127 C4
Tademaït, Plateau du, Algeria 78 C6
Tadio, L., Ivory C. 82 D3
Tadjoura, Djibouti 81 E5
Tadjoura, Golfe de, Djibouti 81 E5
Tadmor, N.Z. 91 J4
Tadoule L., Canada 103 B9
Tadoussac, Canada 105 C6
Tadrés △, Niger 83 B6
Tadzhikistan = Tajikistan ■, Asia 52 F8
Taechŏn-ni, S. Korea 57 F14
Taegu, S. Korea 57 G15
Taegwan, N. Korea 57 D13
Taejŏn, S. Korea 57 F14
Taen, Ko, Thailand 65 b
Tafalla, Spain 38 C3
Tafar, Sudan 81 F2
Tafelbaai = Table B., S. Africa 88 E2
Tafermaar, Indonesia 63 F8
Tafí Viejo, Argentina 126 B2
Tafīhān, Iran 71 D7
Tafiré, Ivory C. 82 D3
Tafo, Ghana 83 D4
Tafresh, Iran 71 C6
Taft, Iran 71 D7
Taft, Phil. 61 F6
Taft, U.S.A. 111 K7
Taftān, Kūh-e, Iran 71 D9
Taga Dzong, Bhutan 67 F16
Taganrog, Russia 33 J10
Taganrogskiy Zaliv, Russia 33 J10
Tagânt, Mauritania 82 B2
Tagatay, Phil. 61 D4
Tagbilaran, Phil. 61 G5
Tággia, Italy 40 E4
Tagish, Canada 102 A2
Tagish L., Canada 102 A2
Tagliacozzo, Italy 41 F10
Tagliamento →, Italy 41 C10
Táglio di Po, Italy 41 D9
Tago, Phil. 61 G7
Tagomago, Spain 48 B8
Tagourâret, Mauritania 82 B3
Taguatinga, Brazil 125 F10
Tagudin, Phil. 61 C4
Tagum, Phil. 61 H6
Tagus = Tejo →, Europe 37 F2
Tahakopa, N.Z. 91 M2
Tahan, Gunung, Malaysia 65 K4
Tahat, Algeria 78 D7
Täherī, Iran 71 E7
Tahiti, French Polynesia 97 J13
Tahlequah, U.S.A. 113 H7
Tahoe, L., U.S.A. 110 G6
Tahoe City, U.S.A. 110 F6
Tahoka, U.S.A. 113 J4
Tahoua, Niger 83 C6
Tahrūd, Iran 71 D8
Tahsis, Canada 102 D3
Tahta, Egypt 80 B3
Tahtaköprü, Turkey 45 G13
Tahtalı Dağları, Turkey 72 C7
Tahulandang, Indonesia 63 D7
Tahuna, Indonesia 63 D7
Taï, Ivory C. 82 D3
Taï △, Ivory C. 82 D3
Tai Hu, China 59 B12
Tai Rom Yen △, Thailand 65 H2

Tai Shan, China 57 F9
Tai'an, China 57 F9
Taibei = T'aipei, Taiwan 59 E13
Taibique, Canary Is. 48 G2
Taibus Qi, China 56 D8
Taicang, China 59 B13
T'aichung, Taiwan 59 E13
Taieri →, N.Z. 91 M3
Taigu, China 56 F7
Taihang Shan, China 56 G7
Taihape, N.Z. 91 H5
Taihe, Anhui, China 56 H8
Taihe, Jiangxi, China 59 D10
Taihu, China 59 B11
Taijiang, China 58 D7
Taikang, China 56 G8
Tailem Bend, Australia 95 F2
Tailfingen, Germany 25 G5
Tailuko, Taiwan 59 E13
Taimyr Peninsula = Taymyr, Poluostrov, Russia 53 B11
Tain, U.K. 13 D4
T'ainan, Taiwan 59 F13
Taínaron, Ákra, Greece 46 E4
Taining, China 59 D11
T'aipei, Taiwan 59 E13
Taiping, China 59 B12
Taiping, Malaysia 65 K3
Taipingzhen, China 56 H6
Tairbeart = Tarbert, U.K. 13 D2
Taishan, China 59 F9
Taishun, China 59 D12
Taita Hills, Kenya 86 C4
Taitao, Pen. de, Chile 128 F2
T'aitung, Taiwan 59 F13
Taivalkoski, Finland 8 D23
Taiwan ■, Asia 59 F13
Taiwan Strait, Asia 59 E12
Taixing, China 59 A13
Taiyara, Sudan 81 E3
Taïyetos Óros, Greece 46 D4
Taiyiba, Israel 74 C4
Taiyuan, China 56 F7
Taizhong = T'aichung, Taiwan 59 E13
Taizhou, China 59 A12
Taizhou Liedao, China 59 C13
Ta'izz, Yemen 75 E3
Tājābād, Iran 71 D7
Tajikistan ■, Asia 52 F8
Tajima, Japan 55 F9
Tajo = Tejo →, Europe 37 F2
Tajrīsh, Iran 71 C6
Tak, Thailand 64 D2
Takāb, Iran 70 B5
Takachiho, Japan 55 H5
Takachu, Botswana 88 C3
Takada, Japan 55 F9
Takahagi, Japan 55 F10
Takaka, N.Z. 91 J4
Takamatsu, Japan 55 G7
Takaoka, Japan 55 F8
Takapuna, N.Z. 91 G5
Takasaki, Japan 55 F9
Takatsuki, Japan 55 G7
Takaungu, Kenya 86 C4
Takayama, Japan 55 F8
Take-Shima, Japan 55 J5
Takefu, Japan 55 G8
Takengon, Indonesia 62 D1
Takeo, Japan 55 H5
Tåkern, Sweden 11 F8
Takeshima = Tok-do, Asia 55 F5
Tākestān, Iran 71 C6
Taketa, Japan 55 H5
Takev, Cambodia 65 G5
Takh, India 69 C7
Takht-Sulaiman, Pakistan 68 D3
Takikawa, Japan 54 C10
Takla L., Canada 102 B3
Takla Landing, Canada 102 B3
Takla Makan = Taklamakan Shamo, China 60 C3
Taklamakan Shamo, China 60 C3
Taku →, Canada 102 B2
Takua Thung, Thailand .... 65 a
Takum, Nigeria 83 D6
Tal Halāl, Iran 71 D7
Tala, Uruguay 127 C4
Talachyn, Belarus 32 E5
Talacogan, Phil. 61 G6
Talagang, Pakistan 68 C5
Talagante, Chile 126 C1
Talak, Niger 83 B6
Talamanca, Cordillera de, Cent. Amer. 120 E3
Talant, France 19 E11
Talara, Peru 124 D2
Talas, Kyrgyzstan 52 E8
Talas, Turkey 72 C6
Talāta, Egypt 74 E1
Talata Mafara, Nigeria 83 C6
Talaud, Kepulauan, Indonesia 63 D7
Talaud Is. = Talaud, Kepulauan, Indonesia 63 D7
Talavera de la Reina, Spain 36 F6
Talavera la Real, Spain 37 G4
Talayan, Phil. 61 H6
Talayuela, Spain 36 F5
Talbandh, India 69 H12
Talbert, Sillon de, France 18 D3
Talbot, C., Australia 92 B4
Talbragar →, Australia 95 E4
Talca, Chile 126 D1
Talcahuano, Chile 126 D1
Talcher, India 67 J14
Talcho, Niger 83 C5
Taldy Kurgan = Taldyqorghan, Kazakhstan 52 E8
Taldyqorghan, Kazakhstan 52 E8
Tālesh, Iran 71 B6
Tālesh, Kūhhā-ye, Iran 71 B6

Talguharai, Sudan 80 D4
Tali Post, Sudan 81 F3
Taliabu, Indonesia 63 E6
Talibon, Phil. 63 B6
Talibong, Ko, Thailand 65 J2
Talihina, U.S.A. 113 H7
Talisayan, Phil. 61 G6
Taliwang, Indonesia 62 F5
Tall 'Afar, Iraq 70 B4
Tall Kalakh, Syria 74 A5
Talla, Egypt 80 B3
Talladega, U.S.A. 115 J2
Tallahassee, U.S.A. 115 K3
Tallangatta, Australia 95 F4
Tallard, France 21 D10
Tällberg, Sweden 10 D9
Tallering Pk., Australia 93 E2
Talli, Pakistan 68 E3
Tallinn, Estonia 9 G21
Tallmadge, U.S.A. 116 E3
Tallulah, U.S.A. 113 J9
Tălmaciu, Romania 29 E9
Talmont-St-Hilaire, France 20 B2
Talne, Ukraine 33 H6
Talnoye = Talne, Ukraine 33 H6
Talodi, Sudan 81 E3
Talovaya, Russia 34 E5
Taloyoak, Canada 100 B10
Talpa de Allende, Mexico 118 C4
Talparo, Trin. & Tob. 125 K15
Talsi, Latvia 9 H20
Talsi □, Latvia 30 A9
Taltal, Chile 126 B1
Taltson →, Canada 102 A6
Talwood, Australia 95 D4
Talyawalka Cr. →, Australia 95 E3
Tam Ky, Vietnam 64 E7
Tam Quan, Vietnam 64 E7
Tama, U.S.A. 112 E8
Tama △, Ethiopia 81 F4
Tamale, Ghana 83 D4
Taman, Russia 33 K9
Taman Negara △, Malaysia 65 K4
Tamani, Mali 82 C3
Tamano, Japan 55 G6
Tamanrasset, Algeria 78 D7
Tamaqua, U.S.A. 117 F9
Tamar →, U.K. 15 G3
Tamarinda, Spain 48 B10
Tamarite de Litera, Spain 38 D5
Tamashima, Japan 55 G6
Tamási, Hungary 28 D3
Tamaské, Niger 83 C6
Tamaulipas □, Mexico 119 C5
Tamaulipas, Sierra de, Mexico .. 119 C5
Tamazula, Mexico 118 C3
Tamazunchale, Mexico 119 C5
Tamba-Dabatou, Guinea 82 C2
Tambacounda, Senegal 82 C2
Tambelan, Kepulauan, Indonesia .. 62 D3
Tambellup, Australia 93 F2
Tambo, Australia 94 C4
Tambo de Mora, Peru 124 F3
Tambohorano, Madag. 89 B7
Tambora, Indonesia 62 F5
Tambov, Russia 34 D5
Tambre →, Spain 36 C2
Tambuku, Indonesia 63 G15
Tamburâ, Sudan 81 F2
Tâmchekket, Mauritania 82 B2
Tâmega →, Portugal 36 D2
Tamenglong, India 67 G18
Tamgué, Massif du, Guinea 82 C2
Tamiahua, L. de, Mexico 119 C5
Tamil Nadu □, India 66 P10
Tamis →, Serbia & M. 28 F5
Tamluk, India 69 H12
Tammerfors = Tampere, Finland .. 9 F20
Tammisaari, Finland 9 F20
Tämnaren, Sweden 10 D11
Tamo Abu, Pegunungan, Malaysia 62 D5
Tampa, U.S.A. 115 M4
Tampa, Tanjung, Indonesia 63 K19
Tampa B., U.S.A. 115 M4
Tampere, Finland 9 F20
Tampico, Mexico 119 C5
Tampin, Malaysia 65 L4
Tampoi, Malaysia .... 65 d
Tamsweg, Austria 26 D6
Tamu, Burma 67 G19
Tamuja →, Spain 37 F4
Tamworth, Australia 95 E5
Tamworth, Canada 116 B8
Tamworth, U.K. 15 E6
Tamyang, S. Korea 57 G14
Tan An, Vietnam 65 G6
Tan Chau, Vietnam 65 G5
Tan-Tan, Morocco 78 C3
Tana →, Kenya 86 C5
Tana →, Norway 8 A23
Tana, L., Ethiopia 81 E4
Tana River Primate △, Kenya 86 C5
Tanabe, Japan 55 H7
Tanafjorden, Norway 8 A23
Tanahbala, Indonesia 62 E1
Tanahgrogot, Indonesia 62 E5
Tanahjampea, Indonesia 63 F6
Tanahmasa, Indonesia 62 E1
Tanahmerah, Indonesia 63 F10
Tanakpur, India 69 E9
Tanami, Australia 92 C4
Tanami Desert, Australia 92 C5
Tanana →, U.S.A. 100 B4
Tananarive = Antananarivo, Madag. 89 B8
Tánaro →, Italy 40 D5
Tancheng, China 57 G10
Tanch'ŏn, N. Korea 57 D15
Tanda, Ut. P., India 69 F10

Tanda, Ut. P., India 69 E8
Tanda, Ivory C. 82 D4
Tandag, Phil. 61 G7
Tandaia, Tanzania 87 D3
Tăndărei, Romania 29 F12
Tandaué, Angola 88 B2
Tandil, Argentina 126 D4
Tandil, Sa. del, Argentina 126 D4
Tandlianwala, Pakistan 68 D5
Tando Adam, Pakistan 68 G3
Tando Allahyar, Pakistan 68 G3
Tando Bago, Pakistan 68 G3
Tando Mohommed Khan, Pakistan 68 G3
Tandou L., Australia 95 E3
Tandragee, U.K. 12 B5
Tandsjöborg, Sweden 10 C8
Tane-ga-Shima, Japan 55 J5
Tanen Tong Dan = Dawna Ra., Burma 64 D2
Tanew →, Poland 31 H9
Tanezrouft, Algeria 78 D6
Tang, Koh, Cambodia 65 G4
Tang, Ra's-e, Iran 71 E8
Tang Krasang, Cambodia 64 F5
Tanga, Tanzania 86 D4
Tanga □, Tanzania 86 D4
Tanganyika, L., Africa 86 D3
Tangaza, Nigeria 83 C5
Tanger, Morocco 78 A4
Tangerang, Indonesia 63 G12
Tangerhütte, Germany 24 C7
Tangermünde, Germany 24 C7
Tanggu, China 57 E9
Tanggula Shan, China 60 C4
Tanghe, China 56 H7
Tanghla Range = Tanggula Shan, China 60 C4
Tangier = Tanger, Morocco 78 A4
Tangorin, Australia 94 C3
Tangorombohitr'i Makay, Madag. .. 89 C8
Tangshan, China 57 E10
Tangtou, China 57 G10
Tanguiéta, Benin 83 C5
Tangxi, China 59 C12
Tangyan He →, China 58 C7
Tanimbar, Kepulauan, Indonesia .. 63 F8
Tanimbar Is. = Tanimbar, Kepulauan, Indonesia 63 F8
Taninthari = Tenasserim, Burma .. 65 F2
Tanjay, Phil. 61 G5
Tanjong Malim, Malaysia 65 L3
Tanjong Pelepas, Malaysia .... 65 d
Tanjore = Thanjavur, India 66 P11
Tanjung, Indonesia 63 J19
Tanjung, Phil. 62 E5
Tanjung Tokong, Malaysia .... 65 c
Tanjungbalai, Indonesia 62 D1
Tanjungbatu, Indonesia 62 D5
Tanjungkarang Telukbetung, Indonesia 62 F3
Tanjungpandan, Indonesia 62 E3
Tanjungpinang, Indonesia 62 D2
Tanjungredeb, Indonesia 62 D5
Tanjungselor, Indonesia 62 D5
Tank, Pakistan 68 C4
Tankhala, India 68 J5
Tankwa-Karoo △, S. Africa 88 E2
Tännäs, Sweden 10 B6
Tannersville, U.S.A. 117 E9
Tannis Bugt, Denmark 11 G4
Tannu-Ola, Russia 53 D10
Tannum Sands, Australia 94 C5
Tano →, Ghana 82 D4
Tanon Str., Phil. 61 F5
Tanout, Niger 83 C6
Tanshui, Taiwan 59 E13
Tansilla, Burkina Faso 82 C4
Tanta, Egypt 80 H7
Tantoyuca, Mexico 119 C5
Tantung = Dandong, China 57 D13
Tanumshede, Sweden 11 F5
Tanunda, Australia 95 E2
Tanus, France 20 D6
Tanzania ■, Africa 86 D3
Tanzilla →, Canada 102 B2
Tao'an = Taonan, China 57 B12
Tao'er He →, China 57 B13
Taohua Dao, China 59 C14
Taolanaro, Madag. 89 D8
Taole, China 56 E4
Taonan, China 57 B12
Taormina, Italy 43 E8
Taos, U.S.A. 109 H11
Taoudenni, Mali 78 D5
Taoyuan, China 59 C8
T'aoyüan, Taiwan 59 E13
Tapa, Estonia 9 G21
Tapa Shan = Daba Shan, China . 58 B7
Tapachula, Mexico 119 E6
Tapah, Malaysia 65 K3
Tapajós →, Brazil 125 D8
Tapaktuan, Indonesia 62 D1
Tapanahoni →, Suriname 125 C8
Tapanui, N.Z. 91 L2
Tapauá, Brazil 124 E6
Tapauá →, Brazil 124 E6
Tapes, Brazil 127 C5
Tapeta, Liberia 82 D3
Taphan Hin, Thailand 64 D3
Tapi →, India 66 J8
Tapia de Casariego, Spain 36 B4
Tapirapecó, Serra, Venezuela 124 C6
Tapo-Capara △, Venezuela 121 E5
Tapolca, Hungary 28 D2
Tapuae-o-Uenuku, N.Z. 91 K4
Tapul Group, Phil. 61 J4
Tapurucuará, Brazil 124 D5
Taquara, Brazil 127 B5

Taquari →, Brazil 124 G7
Tara, Australia 95 D5
Tara, Canada 116 B3
Tara, Russia 52 D8
Tara, Zambia 87 F2
Tara △, Serbia & M. 44 C3
Tara →, Serbia & M. 44 C2
Taraba □, Nigeria 83 D7
Taraba →, Nigeria 83 D7
Tarābulus, Lebanon 74 A4
Tarābulus, Libya 79 B8
Taraclia, Taraclia, Moldova 29 E13
Taraclia, Tighina, Moldova 29 D14
Taradehi, India 69 H8
Tarajalejo, Canary Is. 48 F5
Tarakan, Indonesia 62 D5
Tarakit, Mt., Kenya 86 B4
Tarama-Jima, Japan 55 M2
Taran, Mys, Russia 9 J18
Taranagar, India 68 E6
Taranaki □, N.Z. 91 H5
Taranaki, Mt., N.Z. 91 H5
Tarancón, Spain 38 E1
Tarangire △, Tanzania 86 C4
Taransay, U.K. 13 D1
Táranto, Italy 43 B10
Táranto, G. di, Italy 43 B10
Tarapacá, Colombia 124 D5
Tarapacá □, Chile 126 A2
Tarapoto, Peru 124 E3
Tarare, France 21 C8
Tararua Ra., N.Z. 91 J5
Tarascon, France 21 E8
Tarascon-sur-Ariège, France 20 F5
Tarashcha, Ukraine 33 H6
Tarauacá, Brazil 124 E4
Tarauacá →, Brazil 124 E4
Taravo →, France 21 G12
Tarawa, Kiribati 96 G9
Tarawera, N.Z. 91 H6
Tarawera, L., N.Z. 91 H6
Taraz, Kazakhstan 52 E8
Tarazona, Spain 38 D3
Tarazona de la Mancha, Spain 39 F3
Tarbagatay, Khrebet, Kazakhstan .. 52 E9
Tarbat Ness, U.K. 13 D5
Tarbela Dam, Pakistan 68 B5
Tarbert, Arg. & Bute, U.K. 13 F3
Tarbert, W. Isles, U.K. 13 D2
Tarbes, France 20 E4
Tarboro, U.S.A. 115 H7
Tărcău, Munţii, Romania 29 D11
Tarcento, Italy 41 B10
Tarcoola, Australia 95 E1
Tarcoon, Australia 95 E4
Tardets-Sorholus, France 20 E3
Tardoire →, France 20 C4
Taree, Australia 95 E5
Tarfa, W. el →, Egypt 80 B3
Tarfaya, Morocco 78 C3
Târgovişte, Romania 29 F10
Târgu Bujor, Romania 29 E12
Târgu Cărbuneşti, Romania 29 F8
Târgu Frumos, Romania 29 C12
Târgu-Jiu, Romania 29 E8
Târgu Lăpuş, Romania 29 C8
Târgu Mureş, Romania 29 D9
Târgu Neamţ, Romania 29 C11
Târgu Ocna, Romania 29 D11
Târgu Secuiesc, Romania 29 E11
Târguşor, Romania 29 F13
Tărhăus, Vf., Romania 29 D11
Ţarif, U.A.E. 71 E7
Tarifa, Spain 37 J5
Tarija, Bolivia 126 A3
Tarija □, Bolivia 126 A3
Tariku →, Indonesia 63 E9
Tarim Basin = Tarim Pendi, China 60 C3
Tarim He →, China 60 C3
Tarim Pendi, China 60 C3
Taritatu →, Indonesia 63 E9
Tarka →, S. Africa 88 E4
Tarkastad, S. Africa 88 E4
Tarkhankut, Mys, Ukraine 33 K7
Tarko Sale, Russia 52 C8
Tarkwa, Ghana 82 D4
Tarlac, Phil. 61 D4
Tarm, Denmark 11 J2
Tarma, Peru 124 F3
Tarn □, France 20 E6
Tarn →, France 20 D5
Tarn-et-Garonne □, France 20 D5
Tarna →, Hungary 28 C4
Târnava Mare →, Romania 29 D8
Târnava Mică →, Romania 29 D8
Târnăveni, Romania 29 D9
Tarnica, Poland 31 J9
Tarnobrzeg, Poland 31 H8
Tarnogród, Poland 31 H9
Tarnos, France 20 E2
Târnova, Moldova 29 B12
Târnova, Romania 28 E6
Tarnów, Poland 31 H8
Tarnowskie Góry, Poland 31 H5
Tärnsjö, Sweden 10 D10
Táro →, Italy 40 C7
Ţārom, Iran 71 D7
Taroom, Australia 95 D4
Taroudannt, Morocco 78 B4
Tarp, Germany 24 A5
Tarpon Springs, U.S.A. 115 L4
Tarquínia, Italy 41 F8
Tarragona, Spain 38 D6
Tarragona □, Spain 38 D6
Tarraleah, Australia 95 G4
Tarrasa = Terrassa, Spain 38 D7
Tarrytown, U.S.A. 117 E11
Tårs, Denmark 11 G4
Ţaqţaq, Iraq 70 C5
Taquara, Brazil 127 B5

Tarsus, Turkey 70 B2
Tartagal, Argentina 126 A3
Tärtär, Azerbaijan 35 K8
Tärtär →, Azerbaijan 35 K8
Tartas, France 20 E3
Tartu, Estonia 9 G22
Ţarţūs, Syria 70 C2
Tarumizu, Japan 55 J5
Tarussa, Russia 32 E9
Tarutao = Ko Tarutao △, Thailand 65 J2
Tarutao, Ko, Thailand 65 J2
Tarutung, Indonesia 62 D1
Tarutyne, Ukraine 29 D14
Tarvísio, Italy 41 B10
Taseko →, Canada 102 C4
Tash-Kömür = Tash-Kömür, Kyrgyzstan 52 E8
Tash-Kumyr = Tash-Kömür, Kyrgyzstan 52 E8
Tashauz = Dashhowuz, Turkmenistan 52 E6
Tashi Chho Dzong = Thimphu, Bhutan 67 F16
Ţashk, Daryācheh-ye, Iran 71 D7
Tashkent = Toshkent, Uzbekistan .. 52 E7
Tashtagol, Russia 52 D9
Tasiilaq, Greenland 4 C6
Tasikmalaya, Indonesia 63 G13
Tåsinge, Denmark 11 J4
Tåsjön, Sweden 8 D16
Taskan, Russia 53 C16
Tasker, Niger 83 C7
Taşköprü, Turkey 72 B6
Taşlâc, Moldova 29 C14
Tasman B., N.Z. 91 J4
Tasman Mts., N.Z. 91 J4
Tasman Pen., Australia 95 G4
Tasman Plateau, S. Ocean 5 A10
Tasman Sea, Pac. Oc. 96 L8
Tasmania □, Australia 95 G4
Tăşnad, Romania 28 C7
Tassili n'Ajjer, Algeria 78 C7
Tassili Tin-Rerhoh, Algeria 83 A5
Tata, Hungary 28 C3
Tata, Morocco 78 C4
Tatabánya, Hungary 28 C3
Tatahouine, Tunisia 79 B8
Tataouine, Tunisia 79 B8
Tatar Republic = Tatarstan □, Russia 34 C10
Tatarbunary, Ukraine 29 E14
Tatarsk, Russia 52 D8
Tatarstan □, Russia 34 C10
Tateyama, Japan 55 G9
Tathlina L., Canada 102 A5
Tathra, Australia 95 F4
Tatinnai L., Canada 103 A9
Tatla L., Canada 102 C4
Tatlısu, Turkey 45 F11
Tatnam, C., Canada 103 B10
Tatra = Tatry, Slovak Rep. 27 B13
Tatranský △, Slovak Rep. 27 B13
Tatry, Slovak Rep. 27 B13
Tatshenshini →, Canada 102 B1
Tatsuno, Japan 55 G7
Tatta, Pakistan 68 G2
Tatuí, Brazil 127 A6
Tatum, U.S.A. 113 J3
Tat'ung = Datong, China 56 D7
Tatvan, Turkey 70 B4
Taubaté, Brazil 127 A6
Tauberbischofsheim, Germany 25 F5
Taucha, Germany 24 D8
Tauern-tunnel, Austria 26 D6
Taufikia, Sudan 81 F3
Taulé, France 18 D3
Taumarunui, N.Z. 91 H5
Taumaturgo, Brazil 124 E4
Taung, S. Africa 88 D3
Taungdwingyi, Burma 67 J19
Taunggyi, Burma 67 J20
Taungup, Burma 67 K19
Taungup Taunggya, Burma 67 K18
Taunsa, Pakistan 68 D4
Taunsa Barrage, Pakistan 68 D4
Taunton, U.K. 15 F4
Taunton, U.S.A. 117 E13
Taunus, Germany 25 E4
Taupo, N.Z. 91 H6
Taupo, L., N.Z. 91 H5
Tauragé, Lithuania 9 J20
Tauragé □, Lithuania 30 C9
Tauranga, N.Z. 91 G6
Tauranga Harb., N.Z. 91 G6
Taureau, Rés., Canada 104 C5
Taurianova, Italy 43 D9
Taurus Mts. = Toros Dağları, Turkey 70 B2
Tauste, Spain 38 D3
Tauz = Tovuz, Azerbaijan 35 K7
Tavas, France 47 D11
Tavastehus = Hämeenlinna, Finland 9 F21
Tavda, Russia 52 D7
Tavda →, Russia 52 D7
Tavernes de la Valldigna, Spain .. 39 F4
Taveta, Tanzania 86 C4
Taveuni, Fiji 91 C9
Taviano, Italy 43 C11
Tavignano →, France 21 F13
Tavira, Portugal 37 H3
Tavistock, Canada 116 C4
Tavistock, U.K. 15 G3
Tavolara, Italy 42 B2
Távora →, Portugal 36 D3
Tavoy, Burma 64 E2
Tavşanlı, Turkey 47 B11
Taw →, U.K. 15 F3
Tawa →, India 69 H8
Tawas City, U.S.A. 114 C4
Tawau, Malaysia 62 D5
Taweisha, Sudan 81 E2

Tawitawi, Phil. 63 B6
Tawu, Taiwan 59 F13
Taxco de Alarcón, Mexico 119 D5
Taxila, Pakistan 68 C5
Tay △, U.K. 13 E5
Tay ➔, U.K. 13 E5
Tay, Firth of, U.K. 13 E5
Tay, L., Australia 93 F3
Tay, L., U.K. 13 E4
Tay Ninh, Vietnam 65 G6
Tayabamba, Peru 124 E3
Tayabas Bay, Phil. 61 E4
Taylakova, Russia 52 D8
Taylakovy = Taylakova, Russia 52 D8
Taylor, Canada 102 B4
Taylor, Nebr., U.S.A. 112 E5
Taylor, Pa., U.S.A. 117 E9
Taylor, Tex., U.S.A. 113 K6
Taylor, Mt., U.S.A. 109 J10
Taylorville, U.S.A. 112 F10
Taymā, Si. Arabia 70 E3
Taymyr, Oz., Russia 53 B11
Taymyr, Poluostrov, Russia 53 B11
Tayport, U.K. 13 E6
Tayrona △, Colombia 121 D5
Tayshet, Russia 53 D10
Taytay, Phil. 61 F3
Tāyyebād, Iran 71 C9
Tāyyebād □, Iran 71 C9
Taz ➔, Russia 52 C8
Taza, Morocco 78 B5
Tāza Khurmātū, Iraq 70 C5
Tazawa-Ko, Japan 54 E10
Tazin, Canada 103 B7
Tazin L., Canada 103 B7
Tazovskiy, Russia 52 C8
Tbilisi, Georgia 35 K7
Tchad = Chad ■, Africa 79 F8
Tchad, L., Chad 79 F8
Tchaourou, Benin 83 D5
Tch'eng-tou = Chengdu, China 58 B5
Tchentlo L., Canada 102 B4
Tchetti, Benin 83 D5
Tchibanga, Gabon 84 E2
Tchien, Liberia 82 D3
Tchin Tabaraden, Niger 83 B6
Tch'ong-k'ing = Chongqing, China 58 C6
Tczew, Poland 30 D5
Te Anau, L., N.Z. 91 L1
Te Aroha, N.Z. 91 G5
Te Awamutu, N.Z. 91 H5
Te Ika a Maui = North I., N.Z. 91 H5
Te Kuiti, N.Z. 91 H5
Te-n-Dghâmcha, Sebkhet, Mauritania 82 B1
Te Puke, N.Z. 91 G6
Te Waewae B., N.Z. 91 M1
Te Wai Pounamu = South I., N.Z. 91 L3
Teaca, Romania 29 D9
Teague, U.S.A. 113 K6
Teano, Italy 43 A7
Teapa, Mexico 119 D6
Teba, Spain 37 J6
Tebakang, Malaysia 62 D4
Teberda, Russia 35 J5
Teberu, Malaysia 65 d
Tébessa, Algeria 78 A7
Tebicuary ➔, Paraguay 126 B4
Tebingtinggi, Riau, Indonesia 62 E2
Tebingtinggi, Sumatera Utara, Indonesia 62 D1
Tebulos, Georgia 35 J7
Tecate, Mexico 111 N10
Tecer Dağları, Turkey 72 C7
Tech ➔, France 20 F7
Techiman, Ghana 82 D4
Techirghiol, Romania 29 F13
Tecka, Argentina 128 E2
Tecomán, Mexico 118 D4
Tecopa, U.S.A. 111 K10
Tecoripa, Mexico 118 B3
Tecuala, Mexico 118 C3
Tecuci, Romania 29 E12
Tecumseh, Canada 116 D2
Tecumseh, Mich., U.S.A. 114 D4
Tecumseh, Okla., U.S.A. 113 H6
Tedzhen = Tejen, Turkmenistan 52 F7
Tees ➔, U.K. 14 C6
Tees B., U.K. 14 C6
Teeswater, Canada 116 C3
Tefé, Brazil 124 D6
Tefenni, Turkey 47 D11
Tegal, Indonesia 63 G13
Tegallalang, Indonesia 63 J18
Tegalsari, Indonesia 63 J17
Tegel, Berlin ✈ (TXL), Germany 24 C9
Tegernsee, Germany 25 H7
Teggiano, Italy 43 B8
Tegid, L. = Bala, L., U.K. 14 E4
Tegina, Nigeria 83 C6
Tegucigalpa, Honduras 120 D2
Teguidda i-n-Tessoum, Niger 83 B6
Tehachapi, U.S.A. 111 K8
Tehachapi Mts., U.S.A. 111 L8
Tehamiyam, Sudan 80 D4
Teheran = Tehrān, Iran 71 C6
Tehilla, Sudan 80 D4
Téhini, Ivory C. 82 D4
Tehoru, Indonesia 63 E7
Tehrān, Iran 71 C6
Tehrān □, Iran 71 C6
Tehri, India 69 D8
Tehuacán, Mexico 119 D5
Tehuantepec, Mexico 119 D5
Tehuantepec, G. de, Mexico 119 D5
Tehuantepec, Istmo de, Mexico 119 D6
Teide, Pico de, Canary Is. 48 F3
Teifi ➔, U.K. 15 E3
Teign ➔, U.K. 15 G4
Teignmouth, U.K. 15 G4

Teiuș, Romania 29 D8
Teixeira Pinto, Guinea-Biss. 82 C1
Tejakula, Indonesia 63 J18
Tejam, India 69 E9
Tejen, Turkmenistan 52 F7
Tejen ➔, Turkmenistan 71 B9
Tejo ➔, Europe 37 F2
Tejon Pass, U.S.A. 111 L8
Tekamah, U.S.A. 112 E6
Tekapo, L., N.Z. 91 K3
Tekax, Mexico 119 C7
Teke, Turkey 45 E13
Tekeli, Kazakhstan 52 E8
Tekeze ➔, Ethiopia 81 E4
Tekija, Serbia & M. 44 B6
Tekirdağ, Turkey 45 F11
Tekirdağ □, Turkey 45 E11
Tekirova, Turkey 47 E12
Tekkali, India 67 K14
Tekke, Turkey 72 B7
Tekman, Turkey 73 C9
Tekoa, U.S.A. 108 C5
Tekong Besar, Pulau, Singapore 65 d
Tel Aviv ✈ (TLV), Israel 74 C3
Tel Aviv-Yafo, Israel 74 C3
Tel Lakhish, Israel 74 D3
Tel Megiddo, Israel 74 C4
Tela, Honduras 120 C2
Telanaipura = Jambi, Indonesia 62 E2
Telašćica △, Croatia 41 E12
Telavi, Georgia 35 J7
Telč, Czech Rep. 26 B8
Telciu, Romania 29 C9
Telde, Canary Is. 48 G4
Telegraph Creek, Canada 102 B2
Telekhany = Tsyelyakhany, Belarus 33 F3
Telemark, Norway 9 G12
Telén, Argentina 126 D2
Telenești, Moldova 29 C13
Teleng, Iran 71 E9
Teleño, Spain 36 C4
Teleorman □, Romania 29 G10
Teleorman ➔, Romania 29 G10
Teles Pires ➔, Brazil 124 E7
Telescope Pk., U.S.A. 111 J9
Teletaye, Mali 83 B5
Telfer Mine, Australia 92 C3
Telford, U.K. 15 E5
Telford and Wrekin □, U.K. 14 E5
Telfs, Austria 26 D4
Télimélé, Guinea 82 C2
Teljo, J., Sudan 81 E2
Telkwa, Canada 102 C3
Tell City, U.S.A. 114 G2
Tellicherry, India 66 P9
Telluride, U.S.A. 109 H10
Teloloapán, Mexico 119 D5
Telpos Iz, Russia 6 C17
Telsen, Argentina 128 E3
Telšiai, Lithuania 9 H20
Telšiai □, Lithuania 30 C9
Teltow, Germany 24 C9
Teluk Anson = Teluk Intan, Malaysia 65 K3
Teluk Bahang, Malaysia 65 c
Teluk Betung = Tanjungkarang Telukbetung, Indonesia 62 F3
Teluk Intan, Malaysia 65 K3
Teluk Kumbar, Malaysia 65 c
Telukbutun, Indonesia 62 D3
Telukdalem, Indonesia 62 D1
Tema, Ghana 83 D5
Temax, Mexico 119 C7
Temba, S. Africa 89 D4
Tembagapura, Indonesia 63 E9
Tembe, Dem. Rep. of the Congo 86 C2
Tembe △, S. Africa 89 D5
Tembleque, Spain 36 F7
Temblor Range, U.S.A. 111 K7
Teme ➔, U.K. 15 E5
Temecula, U.S.A. 111 M9
Temerloh, Malaysia 62 D2
Teminabuan, Indonesia 63 E8
Temir, Kazakhstan 52 E6
Temirtau, Kazakhstan 52 D8
Temirtau, Russia 52 D9
Temiscamie ➔, Canada 105 B5
Témiscaming, Canada 104 C4
Témiscamingue, L., Canada 104 C4
Temnikov, Russia 34 C6
Temo ➔, Italy 42 B1
Temosachic, Mexico 118 B3
Tempe, U.S.A. 109 K8
Témpio Pausánia, Italy 42 B2
Tempiute, U.S.A. 110 H11
Temple, U.S.A. 113 K6
Temple B., Australia 94 A3
Templemore, Ireland 12 D4
Templeton, U.S.A. 110 K6
Templeton ➔, Australia 94 C2
Templin, Germany 24 B9
Tempoal, Mexico 119 C5
Temryuk, Russia 33 K9
Temska ➔, Serbia & M. 44 C6
Temuco, Chile 128 D2
Temuka, N.Z. 91 L3
Tenabo, Mexico 119 C6
Tenaha, U.S.A. 113 K7
Tenakee Springs, U.S.A. 102 B1
Tenali, India 67 L12
Tenancingo, Mexico 119 D5
Tenango, Mexico 119 D5
Tenasserim, Burma 65 F2
Tenasserim □, Burma 64 F2
Tenby, U.K. 15 F3
Tenda, Colle di, France 21 D11
Tendaho, Ethiopia 81 E5
Tende, France 21 D11
Tendelti, Sudan 81 E3
Tendrovskaya Kosa, Ukraine 33 J6

Tendukhera, India 69 H8
Teneguía, Volcanes de, Canary Is. 48 F2
Teneida, Egypt 80 B2
Tenenkou, Mali 82 C4
Ténéré, Niger 83 B7
Tenerife, Canary Is. 48 F3
Tenerife, Pico, Canary Is. 48 G1
Tenerife Norte ✈ (TFN), Canary Is. 48 F3
Tenerife Sur ✈ (TFS), Canary Is. 48 F3
Teng Xian, Guangxi Zhuangzu, China 59 F8
Teng Xian, Shandong, China 57 G9
Tengah, Kepulauan, Indonesia 62 F5
Tengchong, China 58 E2
Tengchowfu = Penglai, China 57 F11
Tenggarong, Indonesia 62 E5
Tenggol, Pulau, Malaysia 65 K4
Tengiz, Ozero, Kazakhstan 52 D7
Tenhult, Sweden 11 G8
Teniente Enciso △, Paraguay 126 A3
Teniente Rodolfo Marsh, Antarctica 5 C18
Tenino, U.S.A. 110 D4
Tenkasi, India 66 Q10
Tenke, Katanga, Dem. Rep. of the Congo 87 E2
Tenke, Katanga, Dem. Rep. of the Congo 87 E2
Tenkodogo, Burkina Faso 83 C4
Tenna ➔, Italy 41 E10
Tennant Creek, Australia 94 B1
Tennessee □, U.S.A. 115 H2
Tennessee ➔, U.S.A. 114 G1
Teno, Pta. de, Canary Is. 48 F3
Tenom, Malaysia 62 C5
Tenosique, Mexico 119 D6
Tenryū-Gawa ➔, Japan 55 G8
Tenterden, U.K. 15 F8
Tenterfield, Australia 95 D5
Teo, Spain 36 C2
Teófilo Otoni, Brazil 125 G10
Tepa, Indonesia 63 F7
Tepalcatepec ➔, Mexico 118 D4
Tepecik, Bursa, Turkey 45 F12
Tepecik, Kütahya, Turkey 47 B11
Tepehuanes, Mexico 118 B3
Tepelenë, Albania 44 F4
Tepetongo, Mexico 118 C4
Tepic, Mexico 118 C4
Teplá, Czech Rep. 26 B5
Teplice, Czech Rep. 26 A6
Teplyk, Ukraine 29 B14
Tepoca, C., Mexico 118 A2
Tequila, Mexico 118 C4
Ter ➔, Spain 38 C8
Ter Apel, Neths. 17 B7
Téra, Niger 83 C5
Tera ➔, Spain 36 D5
Teraina, Kiribati 97 G11
Terakeka, Sudan 81 F3
Téramo, Italy 41 F10
Terang, Australia 95 F3
Terang, Teluk, Indonesia 63 K19
Terazit, Massif de, Niger 83 A6
Tercan, Turkey 73 C9
Tercero ➔, Argentina 126 C3
Terebovlya, Ukraine 33 H3
Teregova, Romania 28 E7
Tereina, Sudan 81 E3
Terek ➔, Russia 35 J8
Terepaima △, Venezuela 121 E6
Tereshka ➔, Russia 34 E8
Teresina, Brazil 125 E10
Terespol, Poland 31 F10
Teresva, Ukraine 29 B8
Terewah, L., Australia 95 D4
Terges ➔, Portugal 37 H3
Tergnier, France 19 C10
Teridgerie Cr. ➔, Australia 95 E4
Terlizzi, Italy 43 A9
Terme, Turkey 72 B7
Termez = Termiz, Uzbekistan 52 F7
Términi Imerese, Italy 42 E6
Términos, L. de, Mexico 119 D6
Termiz, Uzbekistan 52 F7
Térmoli, Italy 41 F12
Ternate, Indonesia 63 D7
Terneuzen, Neths. 17 C3
Terney, Russia 53 E14
Terni, Italy 41 F9
Ternitz, Austria 26 D9
Ternivka, Ukraine 29 B14
Ternopil, Ukraine 33 H3
Ternopol = Ternopil, Ukraine 33 H3
Terowie, Australia 95 E2
Terpní, Greece 44 F7
Terra Bella, U.S.A. 111 K7
Terra Nova △, Canada 105 C9
Terrace, Canada 102 C3
Terrace Bay, Canada 104 C2
Terracina, Italy 42 A6
Terralba, Italy 42 C1
Terrasini, Italy 42 D6
Terrassa, Spain 38 D7
Terrasson-la-Villedieu, France 20 C5
Terre Haute, U.S.A. 114 F2
Terrebonne B., U.S.A. 113 L9
Terrell, U.S.A. 113 J6
Terrenceville, Canada 105 C9
Terry, U.S.A. 112 B2
Terryville, U.S.A. 117 E11
Terschelling, Neths. 17 A5
Tersko-Kumskiy Kanal, Russia 35 H7
Tertenía, Italy 42 C2
Terter = Tärtär ➔, Azerbaijan 35 K8
Teruel, Spain 38 E3
Teruel □, Spain 38 E4
Tervel, Bulgaria 45 C11
Tervola, Finland 8 C21
Teryaweyna L., Australia 95 E3

Tešanj, Bos.-H. 28 F3
Teseney, Eritrea 81 D4
Tesha ➔, Russia 34 C6
Teshio, Japan 54 B10
Teshio-Gawa ➔, Japan 54 B10
Tešica, Serbia & M. 44 C5
Tesiyn Gol ➔, Mongolia 60 A4
Teslić, Bos.-H. 28 F2
Teslin, Canada 102 A2
Teslin ➔, Canada 102 A2
Teslin L., Canada 102 A2
Tessalit, Mali 83 A5
Tessaoua, Niger 83 C6
Tessin, Germany 24 A8
Tessit, Mali 83 B5
Test ➔, U.K. 15 G6
Testa del Gargano, Italy 41 G13
Testigos, Is. Las, Venezuela 121 D7
Tetachuck L., Canada 102 C3
Tetas, Pta., Chile 126 A1
Tete, Mozam. 87 F3
Tete □, Mozam. 87 F3
Teterev ➔, Ukraine 33 G6
Teterow, Germany 24 B8
Teteven, Bulgaria 45 D8
Tethul ➔, Canada 102 A6
Tetiyev, Ukraine 33 H5
Teton ➔, U.S.A. 108 C8
Tétouan, Morocco 78 A4
Tetovo, Macedonia 44 D4
Tetyushi, Russia 34 C9
Teuco ➔, Argentina 126 B3
Teulada, Italy 42 D1
Teulon, Canada 103 C9
Teun, Indonesia 63 F7
Teutoburger Wald, Germany 24 C4
Tevere ➔, Italy 41 F9
Teverya, Israel 74 C4
Teviot ➔, U.K. 13 F6
Tewantin, Australia 95 D5
Tewkesbury, U.K. 15 F5
Texada I., Canada 102 D4
Texarkana, Ark., U.S.A. 113 J8
Texarkana, Tex., U.S.A. 113 J7
Texas, Australia 95 D5
Texas □, U.S.A. 113 K5
Texas City, U.S.A. 113 L7
Texel, Neths. 17 A4
Texline, U.S.A. 113 G3
Texoma, L., U.S.A. 113 J6
Teykovo, Russia 32 D11
Teza ➔, Russia 34 B5
Tezin, Afghan. 68 B3
Teziutlán, Mexico 119 D5
Tezpur, India 67 F18
Tezzeron L., Canada 102 C4
Tha-anne ➔, Canada 103 A10
Tha Deua, Laos 64 D4
Tha Deua, Laos 64 C3
Tha Pla, Thailand 64 D3
Tha Rua, Thailand 64 E3
Tha Sala, Thailand 65 H2
Tha Song Yang, Thailand 64 D1
Thaba Putsoa, Lesotho 89 D4
Thabana Ntlenyana, Lesotho 89 D4
Thabazimbi, S. Africa 89 C4
Thādiq, Si. Arabia 70 E5
Thai Binh, Vietnam 58 G6
Thai Muang, Thailand 65 H2
Thai Nguyen, Vietnam 58 G5
Thailand ■, Asia 64 E4
Thailand, G. of, Asia 65 G3
Thakhek, Laos 64 D5
Thal, Pakistan 68 C4
Thal Desert, Pakistan 68 D4
Thala La = Hkakabo Razi, Burma 67 E20
Thalabarivat, Cambodia 64 F5
Thallon, Australia 95 D4
Thalu, Ko, Thailand 65 b
Thalwil, Switz. 25 H4
Thames, N.Z. 91 G5
Thames ➔, Canada 116 D3
Thames ➔, U.K. 15 F8
Thames ➔, U.S.A. 117 E12
Thames Estuary, U.K. 15 F8
Thamesford, Canada 116 C4
Thamesville, Canada 116 D3
Than, India 68 H4
Than Uyen, Vietnam 64 B4
Thana Gazi, India 68 F7
Thandla, India 68 H6
Thane, India 66 K8
Thanesar, India 68 D7
Thangool, Australia 94 C5
Thanh Hung, Vietnam 65 H5
Thanh Pho Ho Chi Minh, Vietnam 65 G6
Thanh Thuy, Vietnam 64 A5
Thanjavur, India 66 P11
Thann, France 19 E14
Thano Bula Khan, Pakistan 68 G2
Thaolinta L., Canada 103 A9
Thaon-les-Vosges, France 19 D13
Thap Lan △, Thailand 64 E4
Thap Sakae, Thailand 65 G2
Thap Than, Thailand 64 E2
Thar Desert, India 68 F5
Tharad, India 68 G4
Thargomindah, Australia 95 D3
Tharrawaddy, Burma 67 L19
Tharthār, L. = Tharthār, Buḩayrat ath, Iraq 70 C4
Tharthār, W. ath ➔, Iraq 70 C4
Thasopoúla, Greece 45 F8
Thásos, Greece 45 F8
That Khe, Vietnam 58 F6

Thatcher, Ariz., U.S.A. 109 K9
Thatcher, Colo., U.S.A. 113 G2
Thaton, Burma 67 L20
Thau, Bassin de, France 20 E7
Thaungdut, Burma 67 G19
Thayer, U.S.A. 113 G9
Thayetmyo, Burma 67 K19
Thazi, Burma 67 J20
The Bight, Bahamas 121 B4
The Crane, Barbados 121 g
The Dalles, U.S.A. 108 D3
The Great Divide = Great Dividing Ra., Australia 94 C4
The Hague = 's-Gravenhage, Neths. 17 B4
The Pas, Canada 103 C8
The Range, Zimbabwe 87 F3
The Rock, Australia 95 F4
The Settlement, Br. Virgin Is. 121 e
The Woodlands, U.S.A. 113 K7
Thebes = Thívai, Greece 46 C5
Thebes, Egypt 80 B3
Thedford, U.S.A. 112 E4
Theebine, Australia 95 D5
Thekulthili L., Canada 103 A7
Thelon ➔, Canada 103 A8
Thénezay, France 18 F6
Thenon, France 20 C5
Theodore, Australia 94 C5
Theodore, Canada 103 C8
Theodore, U.S.A. 115 K1
Theodore Roosevelt △, U.S.A. 112 B3
Theodore Roosevelt L., U.S.A. 109 K8
Thepha, Thailand 65 J3
Thérain ➔, France 19 C9
Theresa, U.S.A. 117 B9
Thermaïkós Kólpos, Greece 44 F6
Thermí, Greece 47 B8
Thermopolis, U.S.A. 108 E9
Thermopylae P., Greece 46 C4
Thesprotía □, Greece 46 B2
Thessalía □, Greece 46 B4
Thessalon, Canada 104 C3
Thessaloníki, Greece 44 F6
Thessaloníki □, Greece 44 F7
Thessaloníki ✈ (SKG), Greece 44 F7
Thessaloníki, Gulf of = Thermaïkós Kólpos, Greece 44 F6
Thessaly = Thessalía □, Greece 46 B4
Thetford, U.K. 15 E8
Thetford Mines, Canada 105 C5
Theun ➔, Laos 64 C5
Theunissen, S. Africa 88 D4
Thevenard, Australia 95 E1
Thiámis ➔, Greece 46 B2
Thiberville, France 18 C7
Thibodaux, U.S.A. 113 L9
Thicket Portage, Canada 103 B9
Thief River Falls, U.S.A. 112 A6
Thiel Mts., Antarctica 5 E16
Thiene, Italy 41 C8
Thiérache, France 19 C10
Thiers, France 20 C7
Thiès, Senegal 82 C1
Thiesi, Italy 42 B1
Thiet, Sudan 81 F2
Thika, Kenya 86 C4
Thikombia, Fiji 91 B9
Thille-Boubacar, Senegal 82 B1
Thimphu, Bhutan 67 F16
Pingvallavatn, Iceland 8 D3
Thionville, France 19 C13
Thíra, Greece 47 E7
Thirasía, Greece 47 E7
Third Cataract, Sudan 80 D3
Thirsk, U.K. 14 C6
Thiruvananthapuram = Trivandrum, India 66 Q10
Thisted, Denmark 11 H2
Thistle I., Australia 95 F2
Thívai, Greece 46 C5
Thiviers, France 20 C4
Thizy, France 19 F11
Þjórsá ➔, Iceland 8 E3
Thlewiaza ➔, Canada 103 A10
Thmar Puok, Cambodia 64 F4
Tho Vinh, Vietnam 64 C5
Thoa ➔, Canada 103 A7
Thoen, Thailand 64 D2
Thoeng, Thailand 64 C3
Thohoyandou, S. Africa 85 J6
Tholdi, Pakistan 69 B7
Thomas, U.S.A. 113 H5
Thomas, L., Australia 95 D2
Thomaston, U.S.A. 115 J3
Thomasville, Ala., U.S.A. 115 K2
Thomasville, Ga., U.S.A. 115 K4
Thomasville, N.C., U.S.A. 115 H5
Thompson, Canada 103 B9
Thompson, U.S.A. 117 E9
Thompson ➔, Canada 102 C4
Thompson ➔, U.S.A. 112 F8
Thompson Falls, U.S.A. 108 C6
Thompson Pk., U.S.A. 108 F2
Thompson Springs, U.S.A. 109 G9
Thompsontown, U.S.A. 116 F7
Thomson, U.S.A. 115 J4
Thomson ➔, Australia 94 C3
Thônes, France 21 C10
Thong Yang, Thailand 65 b
Thonon-les-Bains, France 19 F13
Thorez, Ukraine 33 H10
Þórisvatn, Iceland 8 D4
Thornaby on Tees, U.K. 14 C6
Thornbury, Canada 116 B4
Thorne, U.K. 14 D7
Thornhill, Canada 102 C3
Thorold, Canada 116 C5
Þórshöfn, Iceland 8 C6
Thouarcé, France 18 E6
Thouars, France 18 F6

Thouet →, France 18 E6
Thouin, C., Australia 92 D2
Thousand Oaks, U.S.A. 111 L8
Thrace, Turkey 45 F10
Thrakikón Pélagos, Greece 45 F8
Three Forks, U.S.A. 108 D8
Three Gorges Dam, China 59 B8
Three Hills, Canada 102 C6
Three Hummock I., Australia 95 G3
Three Pagodas Pass, Asia 64 E2
Three Points, C., Ghana 82 E4
Three Rivers, Calif., U.S.A. 110 J8
Three Rivers, Tex., U.S.A. 113 L5
Three Sisters, U.S.A. 108 D3
Three Springs, Australia 93 E2
Throssell, L., Australia 93 E3
Throssell Ra., Australia 92 D3
Thrushton △, Australia 95 D4
Thuan Hoa, Vietnam 65 H5
Thubun Lakes, Canada 103 A6
Thueyts, France 21 D8
Thuin, Belgium 17 D4
Thuir, France 20 F6
Thule = Qaanaaq, Greenland 4 B4
Thule Air Base = Uummannaq,
  Greenland 4 B5
Thun, Switz. 25 J3
Thunder B., U.S.A. 116 B1
Thunder Bay, Canada 104 C2
Thunersee, Switz. 25 J3
Thung Salaeng Luang △,
  Thailand 64 D3
Thung Song, Thailand 65 H2
Thunkar, Bhutan 67 F17
Thuong Tra, Vietnam 64 D6
Thur →, Switz. 25 H5
Thurgau □, Switz. 25 H5
Thüringen □, Germany 24 D6
Thüringer Wald, Germany 24 E6
Thurles, Ireland 12 D4
Thurn P., Austria 26 D5
Thurrock □, U.K. 15 F8
Thursday I., Australia 94 A3
Thurso, Canada 104 C4
Thurso, U.K. 13 C5
Thurso →, U.K. 13 C5
Thurston I., Antarctica 5 D16
Thury-Harcourt, France 18 D6
Thutade L., Canada 102 B3
Thy, Denmark 11 H2
Thyborøn, Denmark 11 H2
Thyolo, Malawi 87 F4
Ti-n-Amzi →, Niger 83 B5
Ti-n-Barraouene, O. →, Africa 83 B5
Ti-n-Zaouatene, Algeria 83 B5
Ti Tree, Australia 94 C1
Tiadiaye, Senegal 82 C1
Tian Shan, Asia 60 B3
Tianchang, China 59 A12
Tiandeng, China 58 F6
Tiandong, China 58 F6
Tian'e, China 58 E6
Tianhe, China 58 E7
Tianjin, China 57 E9
Tiankoura, Burkina Faso 82 C4
Tianlin, China 58 E6
Tianmen, China 59 B9
Tianquan, China 58 B4
Tianshui, China 56 G3
Tiantai, China 59 C13
Tianyang, China 58 F6
Tianyar, Indonesia 63 J18
Tianzhen, China 56 D8
Tianzhu, China 58 D7
Tianzhuangtai, China 57 D12
Tiaret, Algeria 78 A6
Tiassalé, Ivory C. 82 D4
Tibagi, Brazil 127 A5
Tibagi →, Brazil 127 A5
Tibati, Cameroon 83 D7
Tibe, Ethiopia 81 F4
Tiber = Tevere →, Italy 41 G9
Tiberias = Teverya, Israel 74 C4
Tiberias, L. = Yam Kinneret,
  Israel 74 C4
Tibesti, Chad 79 D9
Tibet = Xizang Zizhiqu □, China 60 C3
Tibet, Plateau of, Asia 50 F12
Tibiao, Phil. 61 F5
Tibiri, Niger 83 C6
Tibleş, Vf., Romania 29 C9
Tibleşului, Munţii, Romania 29 C9
Tibnī, Syria 70 C3
Tibooburra, Australia 95 D3
Tibro, Sweden 11 F8
Tiburón, I., Mexico 118 B2
Ticao I., Phil. 61 E5
Tichît, Mauritania 82 B3
Ticho, Ethiopia 81 F4
Ticino □, Switz. 25 J4
Ticino →, Italy 25 K5
Ticleni, Romania 29 F8
Ticonderoga, U.S.A. 117 C11
Ticul, Mexico 119 C7
Tidaholm, Sweden 11 F7
Tidan, Sweden 11 F8
Tiddim, Burma 67 H18
Tidioute, U.S.A. 116 E5
Tidjikja, Mauritania 82 B2
Tidore, Indonesia 63 D7
Tiébissou, Ivory C. 82 D3
Tiel, Neths. 17 C5
Tiel, Senegal 82 C1
Tieling, China 57 C12
Tielt, Belgium 17 C3
Tien Shan = Tian Shan, Asia 60 B3
Tien-tsin = Tianjin, China 57 E9
Tien Yen, Vietnam 64 B6
T'ienching = Tianjin, China 57 E9
Tienen, Belgium 17 D4
Tiénigbé, Ivory C. 82 D3

Tientsin = Tianjin, China 57 E9
Tieri, Australia 94 C4
Tierp, Sweden 10 D11
Tierra Amarilla, Chile 126 B1
Tierra Amarilla, U.S.A. 109 H10
Tierra Colorada, Mexico 119 D5
Tierra de Barros, Spain 37 G4
Tierra de Campos, Spain 36 C6
Tierra del Fuego, I. Gr. de,
  Argentina 128 G3
Tiétar →, Spain 36 F4
Tietê →, Brazil 127 A5
Tiffin, U.S.A. 114 E4
Tifton, U.S.A. 115 K4
Tifu, Indonesia 63 E7
Tighina, Moldova 29 D14
Tigil, Russia 53 D16
Tignish, Canada 105 C7
Tigray □, Ethiopia 81 E4
Tigre →, Peru 124 D4
Tigre →, Venezuela 124 B6
Tigris = Dijlah, Nahr →, Asia 70 D5
Tigveni, Romania 29 E9
Tigyaing, Burma 67 H20
Tîh, Gebel el, Egypt 80 B3
Tijara, India 68 F7
Tijuana, Mexico 111 N9
Tikal, Guatemala 120 C2
Tikal △, Guatemala 120 C2
Tikamgarh, India 69 G8
Tikaré, Burkina Faso 83 C4
Tikhoretsk, Russia 35 H5
Tikhvin, Russia 32 C7
Tikirarjuaq = Whale Cove,
  Canada 103 A10
Tiko, Cameroon 83 E6
Tikrīt, Iraq 70 C4
Tiksi, Russia 53 B13
Tilamuta, Indonesia 63 D6
Tilburg, Neths. 17 C5
Tilbury, Canada 116 D2
Tilbury, U.K. 15 F8
Tilcara, Argentina 126 A2
Tilden, U.S.A. 112 D6
Tilemses, Niger 83 B5
Tilemsi, Vallée du, Mali 83 B5
Tilhar, India 69 F8
Tilichiki, Russia 53 C17
Tílissos, Greece 49 D7
Till →, U.K. 14 B5
Tillabéri, Niger 83 C5
Tillamook, U.S.A. 108 D2
Tillberga, Sweden 10 E10
Tillia, Niger 83 B5
Tillsonburg, Canada 116 D4
Tillyeria, Cyprus 49 D11
Tilogne, Senegal 82 B2
Tílos, Greece 47 E9
Tilpa, Australia 95 E3
Tilt →, U.K. 13 E5
Tilton, U.S.A. 117 C13
Tiltonsville, U.S.A. 116 F4
Tim, Denmark 11 H2
Timagami, L., Canada 104 C3
Timanfaya △, Canary Is. 48 F6
Timaru, N.Z. 91 L3
Timashevo, Russia 34 D10
Timashevsk, Russia 35 H4
Timau, Kenya 86 B4
Timbákion, Greece 49 D6
Timbedgha, Mauritania 82 B3
Timber Creek, Australia 92 C5
Timber Lake, U.S.A. 112 C4
Timber Mt., U.S.A. 110 H10
Timbo, Guinea 82 C2
Timbo, Liberia 82 D3
Timbuktu = Tombouctou, Mali 82 B4
Timeiaouine, Algeria 83 A5
Timétrine, Mts., Mali 83 B4
Timfi Óros, Greece 46 B2
Timfristós, Óros, Greece 46 C3
Timi, Cyprus 49 E11
Timía, Niger 83 B6
Timimoun, Algeria 78 C6
Timirist, Râs, Mauritania 82 B1
Timiş = Tamiš →, Serbia & M. 28 F5
Timiş □, Romania 28 E6
Timişkaming, L. =
  Témiscamingue, L., Canada 104 C4
Timişoara, Romania 28 E6
Timmersdala, Sweden 11 F7
Timmins, Canada 104 C3
Timok →, Serbia & M. 44 B6
Timor, Asia 63 F7
Timor Leste = East Timor ■, Asia 63 F7
Timor Sea, Ind. Oc. 92 B4
Timrå, Sweden 10 B11
Tin Can Bay, Australia 95 D5
Tin Ethisane, Mali 83 B4
Tin Gornai, Mali 83 B4
Tin Mt., U.S.A. 110 J9
Tina →, S. Africa 89 E4
Tîna, Khalîg el, Egypt 80 A3
Tinaca Pt., Phil. 61 J6
Tinajo, Canary Is. 48 E6
Tinca, Romania 28 D6
Tindal, Australia 92 B5
Tindouf, Algeria 78 C4
Tinée →, France 21 E11
Tineo, Spain 36 B4
Tinfunque △, Paraguay 126 A3
Ting Jiang →, China 59 E11
Tinggi, Pulau, Malaysia 65 L5
Tinglev, Denmark 11 K3
Tingo Maria, Peru 124 E3
Tingrela, Ivory C. 82 C3
Tingsryd, Sweden 11 H9
Tingstäde, Sweden 11 G12
Tinh Bien, Vietnam 65 G5
Tinnevelly = Tirunelveli, India 66 Q10
Tinogasta, Argentina 126 B2

Tínos, Greece 47 D7
Tiñoso, C., Spain 39 H3
Tinpahar, India 69 G12
Tintina, Argentina 126 B3
Tintinara, Australia 95 F3
Tintioulé, Guinea 82 C3
Tinto →, Spain 37 H4
Tioga, N. Dak., U.S.A. 112 A3
Tioga, Pa., U.S.A. 116 E7
Tioman, Pulau, Malaysia 65 L5
Tione di Trento, Italy 40 B7
Tionesta, U.S.A. 116 E5
Tior, Sudan 81 F3
Tipongpani, India 67 F19
Tipperary, Ireland 12 D3
Tipperary □, Ireland 12 D4
Tipton, Calif., U.S.A. 110 J7
Tipton, Iowa, U.S.A. 112 E9
Tipton Mt., U.S.A. 111 K12
Tiptonville, U.S.A. 113 G10
Tīrān, Iran 71 C6
Tīrān, Si. Arabia 80 B3
Tiranë, Albania 44 E3
Tiranë ✈ (TIA), Albania 43 A12
Tirano, Italy 40 B7
Tiraspol, Moldova 29 D14
Tirdout, Mali 83 B4
Tire, Turkey 47 C9
Tirebolu, Turkey 73 B8
Tiree, U.K. 13 E2
Tiree, Passage of, U.K. 13 E2
Tîrgoviște = Târgoviște, Romania 29 F10
Tîrgu-Jiu = Târgu-Jiu, Romania 29 E8
Tîrgu Mureş = Târgu Mureş,
  Romania 29 D9
Tirich Mir, Pakistan 66 A7
Tiriolo, Italy 43 D9
Tiriro, Guinea 82 C3
Tiritiri o te Moana = Southern
  Alps, N.Z. 91 K3
Tírnavos, Greece 46 B4
Tirodi, India 66 J11
Tirol □, Austria 26 D3
Tirschenreuth, Germany 25 F8
Tirso →, Italy 42 C1
Tirstrup, Denmark 11 H4
Tiruchchirappalli, India 66 P11
Tirunelveli, India 66 Q10
Tirupati, India 66 N11
Tiruppur, India 66 P10
Tiruvannamalai, India 66 N11
Tisa, India 68 C7
Tisa →, Serbia & M. 28 E5
Tisdale, Canada 103 C8
Tishomingo, U.S.A. 113 H6
Tisjön, Sweden 10 D7
Tisnaren, Sweden 11 F9
Tišnov, Czech Rep. 27 B9
Tisovec, Slovak Rep. 27 C12
Tisza = Tisa →, Serbia & M. 28 E5
Tiszaföldvár, Hungary 28 D5
Tiszafüred, Hungary 28 C5
Tiszalök, Hungary 28 B6
Tiszavasvári, Hungary 28 C6
Tit-Ary, Russia 53 B13
Titaguas, Spain 38 F3
Titao, Burkina Faso 83 C4
Titel, Serbia & M. 28 E5
Tithwal, Pakistan 69 B5
Titicaca, L., S. Amer. 124 G5
Titiwa, Nigeria 83 C7
Tito, Italy 43 B8
Titova Korenica, Croatia 41 D12
Titu, Romania 29 F10
Titule, Dem. Rep. of the Congo 86 B2
Titusville, Fla., U.S.A. 115 L5
Titusville, Pa., U.S.A. 116 E5
Tivaouane, Senegal 82 C1
Tivat, Serbia & M. 44 D2
Tivedens △, Sweden 11 F8
Tiverton, U.K. 15 G4
Tívoli, Italy 41 G9
Tiyo, Eritrea 81 E5
Tizi-Ouzou, Algeria 78 A6
Tizimín, Mexico 119 C7
Tjæreborg, Denmark 11 J2
Tjällmo, Sweden 11 F9
Tjeggelvas, Sweden 8 C17
Tjeggelvas = Tjeggelvas, Sweden 8 C17
Tjirebon = Cirebon, Indonesia 63 G13
Tjluring, Indonesia 63 J17
Tjörn, Sweden 11 F5
Tkibuli = Tqibuli, Georgia 35 J5
Tkvarcheli = Tqvarcheli, Georgia 35 J5
Tlacotalpan, Mexico 119 D5
Tlahualilo, Mexico 118 B4
Tlaquepaque, Mexico 118 C4
Tlaxcala, Mexico 119 D5
Tlaxcala □, Mexico 119 D5
Tlaxiaco, Mexico 119 D5
Tlemcen, Algeria 78 B5
Tlumach, Ukraine 29 B10
Tłuszcz, Poland 31 F8
Tlyarata, Russia 35 J8
To Bong, Vietnam 64 F7
Toa Payoh, Singapore 65 d
Toad →, Canada 102 B4
Toad River, Canada 102 B3
Toamasina, Madag. 89 B8
Toamasina □, Madag. 89 B8
Toay, Argentina 126 D3
Toba, China 58 B1
Toba, Japan 55 G8
Toba, Danau, Indonesia 62 D1
Toba Kakar, Pakistan 68 D3
Toba Tek Singh, Pakistan 68 D5
Tobago, Trin. & Tob. 121 D7
Tobarra, Spain 39 G3
Tobelo, Indonesia 63 D7
Tobermory, Canada 116 A3

Tobermory, U.K. 13 E2
Tobi, Pac. Oc. 63 D8
Tobin, U.S.A. 110 F5
Tobin, L., Australia 92 D4
Tobin L., Canada 103 C8
Toblach = Dobbiaco, Italy 41 B9
Tobol →, Russia 52 D7
Toboli, Indonesia 63 E6
Tobolsk, Russia 52 D7
Tobor, Senegal 82 C1
Tobruk = Tubruq, Libya 79 B10
Tobyhanna, U.S.A. 117 E9
Tobyl = Tobol →, Russia 52 D7
Tocantinópolis, Brazil 125 E9
Tocantins □, Brazil 125 F9
Tocantins →, Brazil 125 D9
Toccoa, U.S.A. 115 H4
Toce →, Italy 40 C5
Tochi →, Pakistan 68 C4
Tochigi, Japan 55 F9
Tochigi □, Japan 55 F9
Tocina, Spain 37 H5
Töcksfors, Sweden 10 E5
Toco, Trin. & Tob. 125 K16
Toconao, Chile 126 A2
Tocopilla, Chile 126 A1
Tocumwal, Australia 95 F4
Tocuyo →, Venezuela 124 A5
Todd →, Australia 94 C2
Todeli, Indonesia 63 E6
Todenyang, Kenya 86 B4
Todgarh, India 68 G5
Todi, Italy 41 F9
Todos os Santos, B. de, Brazil 125 F11
Todos Santos, Mexico 118 C2
Todtnau, Germany 25 H3
Toe Hd., U.K. 13 D1
Toecé, Burkina Faso 83 C4
Tofield, Canada 102 C6
Tofino, Canada 102 D3
Töfsingdalens △, Sweden 10 B6
Tofua, Tonga 91 D11
Tōgane, Japan 55 G10
Togba, Mauritania 82 B2
Togian, Kepulauan, Indonesia 63 E6
Togliatti, Russia 34 D9
Togo ■, W. Afr. 83 D5
Togtoh, China 56 D6
Tohma →, Turkey 72 C7
Tong Xian, China 56 E9
Tôngâ, Sudan 81 F3
Tonga ■, Pac. Oc. 91 D11
Tonga Trench, Pac. Oc. 96 J10
Tongaat, S. Africa 89 D5
Tong'an, China 59 E12
Tongareva, Cook Is. 97 H12
Tongariro △, N.Z. 91 H5
Tongatapu Group, Tonga 91 E12
Tongbai, China 59 A9
Tongcheng, Anhui, China 59 B11
Tongcheng, Hubei, China 59 C9
Tongchŏn-ni, N. Korea 57 E14
Tongchuan, China 56 G5
Tongdao, China 58 D7
Tongeren, Belgium 17 D5
Tonggu, China 59 C10
Tongguan, China 56 G6
Tonghae, S. Korea 57 F15
Tonghai, China 58 E4
Tonghua, China 57 D13
Tongjiang, China 58 B6
Tongjosŏn Man, N. Korea 57 E15
Tongking, G. of = Tonkin, G. of,
  Asia 60 E5
Tongliang, China 58 C6
Tongliao, China 57 C12
Tongling, China 59 B11
Tonglu, China 59 C12
Tongnae, S. Korea 57 G15
Tongnan = Anyue, China 58 B5
Tongobory, Madag. 89 C7
Tongoy, Chile 126 C1
Tongren, China 58 D7
Tongres = Tongeren, Belgium 17 D5
Tongsa Dzong, Bhutan 67 F17
Tongue, U.K. 13 C4
Tongue →, U.S.A. 112 B2
Tongwei, China 56 G3
Tongxiang, China 59 B13
Tongxin, China 56 F3
Tongyang, N. Korea 57 E14
Tongyu, China 57 B12
Tongzi, China 58 C6
Tonj, Sudan 81 F2
Tonj →, Sudan 81 F2
Tonk, India 68 F6
Tonkawa, U.S.A. 113 G6
Tonkin = Bac Phan, Vietnam 64 B5
Tonkin, G. of, Asia 60 E5
Tonle Sap, Cambodia 64 F4
Tonnay-Charente, France 20 C3
Tonneins, France 20 D4
Tonnerre, France 19 E10
Tönning, Germany 24 A4
Tono, Japan 54 E10
Tonopah, U.S.A. 109 G5
Tonosí, Panama 120 E3
Tons →, Haryana, India 68 D7
Tons →, Ut. P., India 69 F10
Tønsberg, Norway 9 G14
Tonto △, U.S.A. 109 K8
Tonya, Turkey 73 B8
Toobanna, Australia 94 B4
Toodyay, Australia 93 F2
Tooele, U.S.A. 108 F7
Toompine, Australia 95 D3
Toora, Australia 95 F4
Toora-Khem, Russia 53 D10
Toowoomba, Australia 95 D5
Top Springs, Australia 92 C5
Topalu, Romania 29 F13

Topaz, *U.S.A.* ... 110 G7
Topeka, *U.S.A.* ... 112 F7
Topl'a ➛, *Slovak Rep.* ... 27 C14
Topley, *Canada* ... 102 C3
Toplica ➛, *Serbia & M.* ... 44 C5
Topliţa, *Romania* ... 29 D10
Topocalma, Pta., *Chile* ... 126 C1
Topock, *U.S.A.* ... 111 L12
Topola, *Serbia & M.* ... 44 B4
Topolčani, *Macedonia* ... 44 E5
Topol'čany, *Slovak Rep.* ... 27 C11
Topolnitsa ➛, *Bulgaria* ... 45 D8
Topolobampo, *Mexico* ... 118 B3
Topoloveni, *Romania* ... 29 F10
Topolovgrad, *Bulgaria* ... 45 D10
Topolvăţu Mare, *Romania* ... 28 E6
Toppenish, *U.S.A.* ... 108 C3
Topraisar, *Romania* ... 29 F13
Topusko, *Croatia* ... 41 C12
Torà, *Spain* ... 38 D6
Tora Kit, *Sudan* ... 81 E3
Toraka Vestale, *Madag.* ... 89 B7
Torata, *Peru* ... 124 G4
Torbalı, *Turkey* ... 47 C9
Torbat-e Ḥeydārīyeh, *Iran* ... 71 C8
Torbat-e Jām, *Iran* ... 71 C9
Torbay, *Canada* ... 105 C9
Torbay □, *U.K.* ... 15 G4
Torbjörntorp, *Sweden* ... 11 F7
Tordesillas, *Spain* ... 36 D6
Töreboda, *Sweden* ... 11 F8
Torekov, *Sweden* ... 11 H6
Torelló, *Spain* ... 38 C7
Toreno, *Spain* ... 36 C4
Torfaen □, *U.K.* ... 15 F4
Torgau, *Germany* ... 24 D8
Torgelow, *Germany* ... 24 B10
Torhamn, *Sweden* ... 11 H9
Torhout, *Belgium* ... 17 C3
Torhovytsya, *Ukraine* ... 29 B10
Tori, *Ethiopia* ... 81 F3
Tori-Shima, *Japan* ... 55 J10
Torigni-sur-Vire, *France* ... 18 C6
Torija, *Spain* ... 38 E1
Torin, *Mexico* ... 118 B2
Torino, *Italy* ... 40 C4
Torit, *Sudan* ... 81 G3
Torkamān, *Iran* ... 70 B5
Torkovichi, *Russia* ... 32 C6
Tormac, *Romania* ... 28 E6
Tormes ➛, *Spain* ... 36 D4
Tornado Mt., *Canada* ... 102 D6
Tornal'a, *Slovak Rep.* ... 27 C13
Torneå = Tornio, *Finland* ... 8 D21
Torneälven ➛, *Europe* ... 8 D21
Torneträsk, *Sweden* ... 8 B18
Tornio, *Finland* ... 8 D21
Tornionjoki = Torneälven ➛, *Europe* ... 8 D21
Tornquist, *Argentina* ... 126 D3
Toro, *Baleares, Spain* ... 48 B11
Toro, *Zamora, Spain* ... 36 D5
Torö, *Sweden* ... 11 F11
Toro △, *Uganda* ... 86 C3
Toro, Cerro del, *Chile* ... 126 B2
Toro Pk., *U.S.A.* ... 111 M10
Törökszentmiklós, *Hungary* ... 28 C5
Toroníos Kólpos, *Greece* ... 44 F7
Toronto, *Canada* ... 116 C5
Toronto, *U.S.A.* ... 116 F4
Toronto Lester B. Pearson International ✈ (YYZ), *Canada* ... 116 C5
Toropets, *Russia* ... 32 D6
Tororo, *Uganda* ... 86 B3
Toros Dağları, *Turkey* ... 70 B2
Torpa, *India* ... 69 H11
Torquay, *U.K.* ... 15 G4
Torquemada, *Spain* ... 36 C6
Torrance, *U.S.A.* ... 111 M8
Torrão, *Portugal* ... 37 G2
Torre Annunziata, *Italy* ... 43 B7
Torre de Moncorvo, *Portugal* ... 36 D3
Torre del Campo, *Spain* ... 37 H7
Torre del Greco, *Italy* ... 43 B7
Torre del Mar, *Spain* ... 37 J6
Torre-Pacheco, *Spain* ... 39 H4
Torre Péllice, *Italy* ... 40 D4
Torreblanca, *Spain* ... 38 E5
Torrecampo, *Spain* ... 37 G6
Torrecilla en Cameros, *Spain* ... 38 C2
Torredembarra, *Spain* ... 38 D6
Torredonjimeno, *Spain* ... 37 H7
Torrejón de Ardoz, *Spain* ... 36 E7
Torrejoncillo, *Spain* ... 36 F4
Torrelaguna, *Spain* ... 36 E7
Torrelavega, *Spain* ... 36 B6
Torremaggiore, *Italy* ... 41 G12
Torremolinos, *Spain* ... 37 J6
Torrens, L., *Australia* ... 95 E2
Torrens Cr. ➛, *Australia* ... 94 C4
Torrens Creek, *Australia* ... 94 C4
Torrent, *Spain* ... 39 F4
Torrenueva, *Spain* ... 37 G7
Torreón, *Mexico* ... 118 B4
Torreperogil, *Spain* ... 37 G7
Torres, *Brazil* ... 127 B5
Torres, *Mexico* ... 118 B2
Torres Novas, *Portugal* ... 37 F2
Torres Strait, *Australia* ... 96 H6
Torres Vedras, *Portugal* ... 37 F1
Torrevieja, *Spain* ... 39 H4
Torrey, *U.S.A.* ... 109 G8
Torridge ➛, *U.K.* ... 15 G3
Torridon, L., *U.K.* ... 13 D3
Torrijos, *Spain* ... 36 F6
Tørring, *Denmark* ... 11 J3
Torrington, *Conn., U.S.A.* ... 117 E11
Torrington, *Wyo., U.S.A.* ... 112 D2
Torroella de Montgrì, *Spain* ... 38 C8
Torrox, *Spain* ... 37 J7
Torsås, *Sweden* ... 11 H9

Torsby, *Sweden* ... 10 D6
Torshälla, *Sweden* ... 10 E10
Tórshavn, *Færoe Is.* ... 8 E9
Torslanda, *Sweden* ... 11 G5
Torsö, *Sweden* ... 11 F7
Tortola, *Br. Virgin Is.* ... 121 e
Tórtoles de Esgueva, *Spain* ... 36 D6
Tortolì, *Italy* ... 42 C2
Tortona, *Italy* ... 40 D5
Tortorici, *Italy* ... 43 D7
Tortosa, *Spain* ... 38 E5
Tortosa, C., *Spain* ... 38 E5
Tortosendo, *Portugal* ... 36 E3
Tortue, I. de la, *Haiti* ... 121 B5
Tortuguero △, *Costa Rica* ... 120 D3
Tortum, *Turkey* ... 73 B9
Torūd, *Iran* ... 71 C7
Torul, *Turkey* ... 73 B8
Toruń, *Poland* ... 31 E5
Torun, *Ukraine* ... 29 B8
Tory I., *Ireland* ... 12 A3
Torysa ➛, *Slovak Rep.* ... 27 C14
Torzhok, *Russia* ... 32 D8
Torzym, *Poland* ... 31 F2
Tosa, *Japan* ... 55 H6
Tosa-Shimizu, *Japan* ... 55 H6
Tosa-Wan, *Japan* ... 55 H6
Toscana □, *Italy* ... 40 E8
Toscano, Arcipelago, *Italy* ... 40 F7
Toshkent, *Uzbekistan* ... 52 E7
Tosno, *Russia* ... 32 C6
Tossa de Mar, *Spain* ... 38 D7
Tösse, *Sweden* ... 11 F6
Tostado, *Argentina* ... 126 B3
Tostedt, *Germany* ... 24 B5
Tostón, Pta. de, *Canary Is.* ... 48 F5
Tosu, *Japan* ... 55 H5
Tosya, *Turkey* ... 72 B6
Toszek, *Poland* ... 31 H5
Totana, *Spain* ... 39 H3
Totebo, *Sweden* ... 11 G10
Toteng, *Botswana* ... 88 C3
Tôtes, *France* ... 18 C8
Tótkomlós, *Hungary* ... 28 D5
Totma, *Russia* ... 52 C5
Totnes, *U.K.* ... 15 G4
Totness, *Suriname* ... 125 B7
Toto, *Nigeria* ... 83 D6
Totonicapán, *Guatemala* ... 120 D1
Totten Glacier, *Antarctica* ... 5 C8
Tottenham, *Australia* ... 95 E4
Tottenham, *Canada* ... 116 B5
Tottori, *Japan* ... 55 G7
Tottori □, *Japan* ... 55 G7
Touaret, *Niger* ... 83 A6
Touba, *Ivory C.* ... 82 D3
Touba, *Senegal* ... 82 C1
Toubkal, Djebel, *Morocco* ... 78 B4
Toucy, *France* ... 19 E10
Tougan, *Burkina Faso* ... 82 C4
Touggourt, *Algeria* ... 78 B7
Tougouri, *Burkina Faso* ... 83 C4
Tougué, *Guinea* ... 82 C2
Toukoto, *Mali* ... 82 C3
Toul, *France* ... 19 D12
Toulepleu, *Ivory C.* ... 82 D3
Toulon, *France* ... 21 E9
Toulouse, *France* ... 20 E5
Toulouse Blagnac ✈ (TLS), *France* ... 20 E5
Toummo, *Niger* ... 79 D8
Toumodi, *Ivory C.* ... 82 D3
Tounan, *Taiwan* ... 59 F13
Toungo, *Nigeria* ... 83 D7
Toungoo, *Burma* ... 67 K20
Touques ➛, *France* ... 18 C7
Touraine, *France* ... 18 E7
Tourcoing, *France* ... 19 B10
Touriñán, C., *Spain* ... 36 B1
Tournan-en-Brie, *France* ... 19 D9
Tournay, *France* ... 20 E4
Tournon-St-Martin, *France* ... 18 F7
Tournon-sur-Rhône, *France* ... 21 C8
Tournus, *France* ... 19 F11
Tours, *France* ... 18 E7
Toussora, Mt., *C.A.R.* ... 84 C4
Touws ➛, *S. Africa* ... 88 E3
Touwsrivier, *S. Africa* ... 88 E3
Tovarkovskiy, *Russia* ... 32 F10
Tovste, *Ukraine* ... 29 B10
Tovuz, *Azerbaijan* ... 35 K7
Towada, *Japan* ... 54 D10
Towada-Hachimantai △, *Japan* ... 54 D10
Towada-Ko, *Japan* ... 54 D10
Towanda, *U.S.A.* ... 117 E8
Towang, *India* ... 67 F17
Tower, *U.S.A.* ... 112 B8
Towerhill Cr. ➛, *Australia* ... 94 C3
Towner, *U.S.A.* ... 112 A4
Townsend, *U.S.A.* ... 108 C8
Townshend I., *Australia* ... 94 C5
Townsville, *Australia* ... 94 B4
Towraghondi, *Afghan.* ... 66 B3
Towson, *U.S.A.* ... 114 F7
Towuti, Danau, *Indonesia* ... 63 E6
Toya-Ko, *Japan* ... 54 C10
Toyama, *Japan* ... 55 F8
Toyama □, *Japan* ... 55 F8
Toyama-Wan, *Japan* ... 55 F8
Toyapakeh, *Indonesia* ... 63 K18
Toyohashi, *Japan* ... 55 G8
Toyokawa, *Japan* ... 55 G8
Toyonaka, *Japan* ... 55 G7
Toyooka, *Japan* ... 55 G7
Toyota, *Japan* ... 55 G8
Tozeur, *Tunisia* ... 78 B7
Tozkhurmato, *Iraq* ... 70 C5
Tqibuli, *Georgia* ... 35 J6
Tqvarcheli, *Georgia* ... 35 J5
Trá Li = Tralee, *Ireland* ... 12 D2

Tra On, *Vietnam* ... 65 H5
Trabancos ➛, *Spain* ... 36 D5
Traben-Trarbach, *Germany* ... 25 F3
Trabzon, *Turkey* ... 73 B8
Tracadie-Sheila, *Canada* ... 105 C7
Tracy, *Calif., U.S.A.* ... 110 H5
Tracy, *Minn., U.S.A.* ... 112 C7
Tradate, *Italy* ... 40 C5
Trade Town, *Liberia* ... 82 D3
Trafalgar, C., *Spain* ... 37 J4
Traian, Brăila, *Romania* ... 29 E12
Traian, Tulcea, *Romania* ... 29 E13
Trail, *Canada* ... 102 D5
Trainor L., *Canada* ... 102 A4
Tralee, *Ireland* ... 12 D2
Tralee B., *Ireland* ... 12 D2
Tramore, *Ireland* ... 12 D4
Tramore B., *Ireland* ... 12 D4
Tran Ninh, Cao Nguyen, *Laos* ... 64 C4
Tranås, *Sweden* ... 11 F8
Tranbjerg, *Denmark* ... 11 H4
Trancas, *Argentina* ... 126 B2
Trancoso, *Portugal* ... 36 E3
Tranebjerg, *Denmark* ... 11 J4
Tranemo, *Sweden* ... 11 G7
Trang, *Thailand* ... 65 J2
Trangahy, *Madag.* ... 89 B7
Trangan, *Indonesia* ... 63 F8
Trangie, *Australia* ... 95 E4
Trångsviken, *Sweden* ... 10 A7
Trani, *Italy* ... 43 A9
Tranoroa, *Madag.* ... 89 C8
Tranqueras, *Uruguay* ... 127 C4
Transantarctic Mts., *Antarctica* ... 5 E12
Transilvania, *Romania* ... 29 D9
Transilvanian Alps = Carpaţii Meridionali, *Romania* ... 29 E9
Transnistria = Stînga Nistrului □, *Moldova* ... 29 C14
Transtrand, *Sweden* ... 10 C7
Transtrandsfjällen, *Sweden* ... 10 C6
Transylvania = Transilvania, *Romania* ... 29 D9
Trápani, *Italy* ... 42 D5
Trapper Pk., *U.S.A.* ... 108 D6
Traralgon, *Australia* ... 95 F4
Trarza, *Mauritania* ... 82 B2
Trasacco, *Italy* ... 41 G10
Trăscău, Munţii, *Romania* ... 29 D8
Trasimeno, L., *Italy* ... 41 E9
Träslövsläge, *Sweden* ... 11 G6
Trasvase Tajo-Segura, Canal de, *Spain* ... 38 E2
Trat, *Thailand* ... 65 F4
Tratani ➛, *Pakistan* ... 68 E3
Traun, *Austria* ... 26 C7
Traunreut, *Germany* ... 25 H8
Traunsee, *Germany* ... 26 D6
Traunstein, *Germany* ... 25 H8
Traveller's L., *Australia* ... 95 E3
Travemünde, *Germany* ... 24 B6
Travers, Mt., *N.Z.* ... 91 K4
Traverse City, *U.S.A.* ... 114 C3
Travis, L., *U.S.A.* ... 113 K5
Travnik, *Bos.-H.* ... 28 F7
Trbovlje, *Slovenia* ... 41 B12
Trébbia ➛, *Italy* ... 40 C6
Trebel ➛, *Germany* ... 24 B9
Trébeurden, *France* ... 18 D3
Trebević △, *Bos.-H.* ... 28 G3
Třebíč, *Czech Rep.* ... 26 B8
Trebinje, *Bos.-H.* ... 44 D2
Trebisacce, *Italy* ... 43 C9
Trebišnjica ➛, *Bos.-H.* ... 44 D2
Trebišov, *Slovak Rep.* ... 27 C14
Trebižat ➛, *Bos.-H.* ... 41 E14
Trebnje, *Slovenia* ... 41 C12
Třeboň, *Czech Rep.* ... 26 B7
Trebonne, *Australia* ... 94 B4
Třeboňsko △, *Czech Rep.* ... 26 B7
Trebujena, *Spain* ... 37 J4
Trecate, *Italy* ... 40 C5
Tregaron, *U.K.* ... 15 E4
Tregnago, *Italy* ... 41 C8
Tregrosse Is., *Australia* ... 94 B5
Tréguier, *France* ... 18 D3
Trégunc, *France* ... 18 E3
Treherne, *Canada* ... 103 D9
Tréia, *Italy* ... 41 E10
Treignac, *France* ... 20 C5
Treinta y Tres, *Uruguay* ... 127 C5
Treis-karden, *Germany* ... 25 E3
Treklyano, *Bulgaria* ... 44 D6
Trelawney, *Zimbabwe* ... 89 B5
Trélazé, *France* ... 18 E6
Trélissac, *France* ... 20 C4
Trelew, *Argentina* ... 128 E3
Trelleborg, *Sweden* ... 11 J7
Tremadog Bay, *U.K.* ... 14 E3
Trémiti, *Italy* ... 41 F12
Tremonton, *U.S.A.* ... 108 F7
Tremp, *Spain* ... 38 C5
Trenche ➛, *Canada* ... 104 C5
Trenčiansky □, *Slovak Rep.* ... 27 C11
Trenčín, *Slovak Rep.* ... 27 C11
Trenggalek, *Indonesia* ... 63 H14
Trenque Lauquen, *Argentina* ... 126 D3
Trent ➛, *Canada* ... 116 B7
Trent ➛, *U.K.* ... 14 D7
Trentino-Alto Adige □, *Italy* ... 41 B8
Trento, *Italy* ... 40 B8
Trenton = Quinte West, *Canada* ... 116 B7
Trenton, *Mo., U.S.A.* ... 112 E8
Trenton, *N.J., U.S.A.* ... 117 F10
Trenton, *Nebr., U.S.A.* ... 112 E4
Trepassey, *Canada* ... 105 C9
Trepuzzi, *Italy* ... 43 B11
Três Arroyos, *Argentina* ... 126 D3
Três Corações, *Brazil* ... 127 A6
Três Lagoas, *Brazil* ... 125 H8

Tres Lomas, *Argentina* ... 126 D3
Tres Marías, Islas, *Mexico* ... 118 C3
Tres Montes, C., *Chile* ... 128 F1
Tres Pinos, *U.S.A.* ... 110 J5
Três Pontas, *Brazil* ... 127 A6
Tres Puentes, *Chile* ... 126 B1
Tres Puntas, C., *Argentina* ... 128 F3
Três Rios, *Brazil* ... 127 A7
Tres Valles, *Mexico* ... 119 D5
Tresco, *U.K.* ... 15 H1
Treska ➛, *Macedonia* ... 44 E5
Treskavica, Bos.-H. ... 28 G3
Trespaderne, *Spain* ... 36 C7
Tresticklan △, *Sweden* ... 11 F5
Trets, *France* ... 21 E9
Treuchtlingen, *Germany* ... 25 G6
Treuenbrietzen, *Germany* ... 24 C8
Trevi, *Italy* ... 41 F9
Trevíglio, *Italy* ... 40 C6
Trevínca, Peña, *Spain* ... 36 C4
Treviso, *Italy* ... 41 C9
Trévoux, *France* ... 21 C8
Treysa, *Germany* ... 24 E5
Trgovište, *Serbia & M.* ... 44 D6
Triabunna, *Australia* ... 95 G4
Triánda, *Greece* ... 49 C10
Triangle, *Zimbabwe* ... 89 C5
Triaucourt-en-Argonne, *France* ... 19 D12
Tribal Areas □, *Pakistan* ... 68 C4
Tribsees, *Germany* ... 24 A8
Tribulation, C., *Australia* ... 94 B4
Tribune, *U.S.A.* ... 112 F4
Tricárico, *Italy* ... 43 B9
Tricase, *Italy* ... 43 C11
Trichinopoly = Tiruchchirappalli, *India* ... 66 P11
Trichur, *India* ... 66 P10
Trida, *Australia* ... 95 E4
Trier, *Germany* ... 25 F2
Trieste, *Italy* ... 41 C10
Trieste, G. di, *Italy* ... 41 C10
Trigno ➛, *Italy* ... 41 F11
Triggiano, *Italy* ... 43 A9
Triglav, *Slovenia* ... 41 B10
Triglavski △, *Slovenia* ... 41 B10
Trigueros, *Spain* ... 37 H4
Tríkeri, *Greece* ... 46 B5
Trikhonís, Límni, *Greece* ... 46 C3
Tríkkala, *Greece* ... 46 B3
Tríkkala □, *Greece* ... 46 B3
Trikomo, *Cyprus* ... 49 D12
Trikora, Puncak, *Indonesia* ... 63 E9
Trilj, *Croatia* ... 41 E13
Trillo, *Spain* ... 38 E2
Trim, *Ireland* ... 12 C5
Trincomalee, *Sri Lanka* ... 66 Q12
Trindade, *Brazil* ... 125 G9
Trindade, I., *Atl. Oc.* ... 2 F8
Třinec, *Czech Rep.* ... 27 B11
Trinidad, *Bolivia* ... 124 F6
Trinidad, *Cuba* ... 120 B4
Trinidad, *Trin. & Tob.* ... 121 D7
Trinidad, *Uruguay* ... 126 C4
Trinidad, *U.S.A.* ... 113 G2
Trinidad ➛, *Mexico* ... 119 D5
Trinidad & Tobago ■, *W. Indies* ... 121 D7
Trinitápoli, *Italy* ... 43 A9
Trinity, *Canada* ... 105 C9
Trinity, *U.S.A.* ... 113 K7
Trinity ➛, *Calif., U.S.A.* ... 108 F2
Trinity ➛, *Tex., U.S.A.* ... 113 L7
Trinity B., *Canada* ... 105 C9
Trinity Hills, *Trin. & Tob.* ... 125 K15
Trinity Is., *U.S.A.* ... 100 C4
Trinity Range, *U.S.A.* ... 108 F4
Trinkitat, *Sudan* ... 80 D4
Trino, *Italy* ... 40 C5
Trinway, *U.S.A.* ... 116 F2
Trionto, C., *Italy* ... 43 C9
Triora, *Italy* ... 40 D4
Tripoli = Tarābulus, *Lebanon* ... 74 A4
Tripoli = Tarābulus, *Libya* ... 79 B8
Trípolis, *Greece* ... 46 D4
Tripolitania, N. Afr. ... 79 B8
Tripura □, *India* ... 67 H18
Tripylos, *Cyprus* ... 49 E11
Trischen, *Germany* ... 24 A4
Tristan da Cunha, *Atl. Oc.* ... 77 K2
Trisul, *India* ... 69 D8
Trivandrum, *India* ... 66 Q10
Trivento, *Italy* ... 41 G11
Trnava, *Slovak Rep.* ... 27 C10
Trnavský □, *Slovak Rep.* ... 27 C10
Troarn, *France* ... 18 C6
Trochu, *Canada* ... 102 C6
Trodely I., *Canada* ... 104 B4
Troezen, *Greece* ... 46 D5
Trogir, *Croatia* ... 41 E13
Troglav, *Croatia* ... 41 E13
Tróia, *Italy* ... 43 A8
Troilus, L., *Canada* ... 104 B5
Troina, *Italy* ... 43 E7
Trois-Pistoles, *Canada* ... 105 C6
Trois-Rivières, *Canada* ... 104 C5
Trois-Rivières, *Guadeloupe* ... 120 b
Troisdorf, *Germany* ... 24 E3
Troitsk, *Russia* ... 52 D7
Troitsko Pechorsk, *Russia* ... 52 C6
Troitskoye, *Russia* ... 35 G7
Trölladyngja, *Iceland* ... 8 D5
Trollhättan, *Sweden* ... 11 F6
Trollheimen, *Norway* ... 8 E13
Trombetas ➛, *Brazil* ... 125 D7
Tromsø, *Norway* ... 8 B18
Tronador, Mte., *Argentina* ... 128 E2
Trøndelag, *Norway* ... 8 D14
Trondheim, *Norway* ... 8 E14
Trondheimsfjorden, *Norway* ... 8 E14
Trönninge, *Sweden* ... 11 H6
Tronto ➛, *Italy* ... 41 F10

Troodos, *Cyprus* ... 49 E11
Troon, *U.K.* ... 13 F4
Tropea, *Italy* ... 43 D8
Tropic, *U.S.A.* ... 109 H7
Tropojë, *Albania* ... 44 D4
Trosa, *Sweden* ... 11 F11
Trostan, *U.K.* ... 12 A5
Trostberg, *Germany* ... 25 G8
Trostyanets, *Ukraine* ... 29 B14
Trostyanets, *Ukraine* ... 29 G8
Trou Gras Pt., *St. Lucia* ... 121 f
Trout ➛, *Canada* ... 102 A5
Trout L., *N.W.T., Canada* ... 102 A4
Trout L., *Ont., Canada* ... 103 C10
Trout Lake, *Canada* ... 102 B6
Trout Lake, *U.S.A.* ... 110 E5
Trout River, *Canada* ... 105 C8
Trout Run, *U.S.A.* ... 116 E7
Trouville-sur-Mer, *France* ... 18 C7
Trowbridge, *U.K.* ... 15 F5
Troy, *Turkey* ... 47 B8
Troy, *Ala., U.S.A.* ... 115 K3
Troy, *Kans., U.S.A.* ... 112 F7
Troy, *Mo., U.S.A.* ... 112 F9
Troy, *Mont., U.S.A.* ... 108 B6
Troy, *N.Y., U.S.A.* ... 117 D11
Troy, *Ohio, U.S.A.* ... 114 E3
Troy, *Pa., U.S.A.* ... 117 E8
Troyan, *Bulgaria* ... 45 D8
Troyes, *France* ... 19 D11
Trpanj, *Croatia* ... 41 E14
Trstenik, *Serbia & M.* ... 44 C5
Trubchevsk, *Russia* ... 33 F7
Truchas Peak, *U.S.A.* ... 113 H2
Trucial States = United Arab Emirates ■, *Asia* ... 71 F7
Truckee, *U.S.A.* ... 110 F6
Trudfront, *Russia* ... 35 H8
Trudovoye, *Russia* ... 54 C6
Trujillo, *Honduras* ... 120 C2
Trujillo, *Peru* ... 124 E3
Trujillo, *Spain* ... 37 F5
Trujillo, *U.S.A.* ... 113 H2
Trujillo, *Venezuela* ... 124 B4
Truk, *Micronesia* ... 96 G7
Trumann, *U.S.A.* ... 113 H9
Trumansburg, *U.S.A.* ... 117 D8
Trumbull, Mt., *U.S.A.* ... 109 H7
Trün, *Bulgaria* ... 44 D6
Trun, *France* ... 18 D7
Trundle, *Australia* ... 95 E4
Trung-Phan = Annam, *Vietnam* ... 64 E7
Truro, *Canada* ... 105 C7
Truro, *U.K.* ... 15 G2
Truskavets, *Ukraine* ... 33 H2
Trŭstenik, *Bulgaria* ... 45 C8
Trustrup, *Denmark* ... 11 H4
Trutch, *Canada* ... 102 B4
Truth or Consequences, *U.S.A.* ... 109 K10
Trutnov, *Czech Rep.* ... 26 A8
Truxton, *U.S.A.* ... 117 D8
Truyère ➛, *France* ... 20 D6
Tryavna, *Bulgaria* ... 45 D9
Tryonville, *U.S.A.* ... 116 E5
Trzcianka, *Poland* ... 31 E3
Trzciel, *Poland* ... 31 F2
Trzcińsko Zdrój, *Poland* ... 31 F1
Trzebiatów, *Poland* ... 30 D2
Trzebiez, *Poland* ... 30 E1
Trzebnica, *Poland* ... 31 G4
Trzemeszno, *Poland* ... 31 F4
Tržič, *Croatia* ... 41 B11
Tsagan Aman, *Russia* ... 35 G8
Tsamandás, *Greece* ... 46 B2
Tsandi, *Namibia* ... 88 B1
Tsaratanana, *Madag.* ... 89 B8
Tsaratanana △, *Madag.* ... 89 A8
Tsaratanana, Mt. de = Maromokotro, *Madag.* ... 89 A8
Tsarevo, *Bulgaria* ... 45 D9
Tsaritsáni, *Greece* ... 46 B4
Tsau, *Botswana* ... 88 C3
Tsavo East △, *Kenya* ... 86 C4
Tsavo West △, *Kenya* ... 86 C4
Tsebrykove, *Ukraine* ... 33 J6
Tsentralnyy □, *Russia* ... 34 D4
Tses, *Namibia* ... 88 D2
Tsetserleg, *Mongolia* ... 60 B5
Tsévié, *Togo* ... 83 D5
Tshabong, *Botswana* ... 88 D3
Tshane, *Botswana* ... 88 C3
Tshela, *Dem. Rep. of the Congo* ... 84 E2
Tshesebe, *Botswana* ... 89 C4
Tshibeke, *Dem. Rep. of the Congo* ... 86 C2
Tshibinda, *Dem. Rep. of the Congo* ... 86 C2
Tshikapa, *Dem. Rep. of the Congo* ... 84 F4
Tshilenge, *Dem. Rep. of the Congo* ... 86 D1
Tshinsenda, *Dem. Rep. of the Congo* ... 87 E2
Tshofa, *Dem. Rep. of the Congo* ... 86 D2
Tshwane = Pretoria, *S. Africa* ... 89 D4
Tshwane, *Botswana* ... 88 C3
Tsigara, *Botswana* ... 88 C4
Tsihombe, *Madag.* ... 89 D8
Tsiigehtchic, *Canada* ... 100 B6
Tsimlyansk, *Russia* ... 35 G6
Tsimlyansk Res. = Tsimlyanskoye Vdkhr., *Russia* ... 35 F6
Tsimlyanskoye Vdkhr., *Russia* ... 35 F6
Tsinan = Jinan, *China* ... 56 F9
Tsineng, *S. Africa* ... 88 D3
Tsínga, *Greece* ... 45 E8
Tsinghai = Qinghai □, *China* ... 60 C4
Tsingtao = Qingdao, *China* ... 57 F11
Tsingy de Bemaraha △, *Madag.* ... 89 B8
Tsingy de Namoraka △, *Madag.* ... 89 B8
Tsinjoarivo, *Madag.* ... 89 B8
Tsinjomitondraka, *Madag.* ... 89 B8
Tsiroanomandidy, *Madag.* ... 89 B8
Tsiteli-Tsqaro, *Georgia* ... 35 K8

Tsitondroina, *Madag.* 89 C8
Tsitsikamma △, *S. Africa* 88 E3
Tsivilsk, *Russia* 34 C8
Tsivory, *Madag.* 89 C8
Tskhinvali, *Georgia* 35 J7
Tsna ➤, *Russia* 34 C6
Tsnori, *Georgia* 35 K7
Tso Moriri, L., *India* 69 C8
Tsobis, *Namibia* 88 B2
Tsodilo Hill, *Botswana* 88 B3
Tsogttsetsiy = Baruunsuu,
  Mongolia 56 C3
Tsolo, *S. Africa* 89 E4
Tsomo, *S. Africa* 89 E4
Tsu, *Japan* 55 G8
Tsu L., *Canada* 102 A6
Tsuchiura, *Japan* 55 F10
Tsuen Wan, *China* 59 F10
Tsugaru-Kaikyō, *Japan* 54 D10
Tsumeb, *Namibia* 88 B2
Tsumis, *Namibia* 88 C2
Tsuruga, *Japan* 55 G8
Tsurugi-San, *Japan* 55 H7
Tsuruoka, *Japan* 54 E9
Tsushima, *Gifu, Japan* 55 G8
Tsushima, *Nagasaki, Japan* .. 55 G4
Tsuyama, *Japan* 55 G7
Tsvetkovo, *Ukraine* 33 H6
Tsyelyakhany, *Belarus* 33 F3
Tua ➤, *Portugal* 36 D3
Tual, *Indonesia* 63 F8
Tuam, *Ireland* 12 C3
Tuamotu Arch. = Tuamotu Is.,
  French Polynesia 97 J13
Tuamotu Is., *French Polynesia* 97 J13
Tuamotu Ridge, *Pac. Oc.* 97 K14
Tuanfeng, *China* 59 B10
Tuanxi, *China* 58 D6
Tuao, *Phil.* 61 C4
Tuapse, *Russia* 35 H4
Tuas, *Singapore* .... 65 d
Tuatapere, *N.Z.* 91 M1
Tuba City, *U.S.A.* 109 H8
Tuban, *Indonesia* 63 G15
Tubani, *Botswana* 88 C3
Tubarão, *Brazil* 127 B6
Tūbās, *West Bank* 74 C4
Tubas ➤, *Namibia* 88 C2
Tübingen, *Germany* 25 G5
Tubruq, *Libya* 79 B10
Tubuai Is., *French Polynesia* . 97 K13
Tuc Trung, *Vietnam* 65 G6
Tucacas, *Venezuela* 124 A5
T'uch'ang, *Taiwan* 59 E13
Tuchodi ➤, *Canada* 102 B4
Tuchola, *Poland* 30 E4
Tuchów, *Poland* 31 J8
Tuckanarra, *Australia* 93 E2
Tucson, *U.S.A.* 109 K8
Tucumán □, *Argentina* 126 B2
Tucumcari, *U.S.A.* 113 H3
Tucupita, *Venezuela* 124 B6
Tucuruí, *Brazil* 125 D9
Tucuruí, Reprêsa de, *Brazil* . 125 D9
Tuczno, *Poland* 31 E3
Tudela, *Spain* 38 C3
Tudmur, *Syria* 70 C3
Tudor, L., *Canada* 105 A6
Tudora, *Romania* 29 C11
Tuella ➤, *Portugal* 36 D3
Tugela ➤, *S. Africa* 89 D5
Tuguegarao, *Phil.* 61 C4
Tugur, *Russia* 53 D14
Tui, *Spain* 36 C2
Tuineje, *Canary Is.* 48 F5
Tukangbesi, Kepulauan,
  Indonesia 63 F6
Tukarak I., *Canada* 104 A4
Tukayyid, *Iraq* 70 D5
Tûkh, *Egypt* 80 H7
Tukhlya, *Ukraine* 29 B8
Tukkae, Ao, *Thailand* .... 65 a
Tukobo, *Ghana* 82 D4
Tuktoyaktuk, *Canada* 100 B6
Tukums, *Latvia* 9 H20
Tukums □, *Latvia* 30 B10
Tukuyu, *Tanzania* 87 D3
Tula, *Hidalgo, Mexico* 119 C5
Tula, *Tamaulipas, Mexico* ... 119 C5
Tula, *Nigeria* 83 D7
Tula, *Russia* 32 E9
Tulancingo, *Mexico* 119 C5
Tulare, *Serbia & M.* 44 D5
Tulare, *U.S.A.* 110 J7
Tulare Lake Bed, *U.S.A.* 110 K7
Tularosa, *U.S.A.* 109 K10
Tulbagh, *S. Africa* 88 E2
Tulcán, *Ecuador* 124 C3
Tulcea, *Romania* 29 E13
Tulcea □, *Romania* 29 E13
Tulchyn, *Ukraine* 29 B13
Tūleh, *Iran* 71 C7
Tulemalu L., *Canada* 103 A9
Tulghes, *Romania* 29 D10
Tuli, *Zimbabwe* 87 G2
Tulia, *U.S.A.* 113 H4
Tuliszków, *Poland* 31 F5
Tulita, *Canada* 100 B7
Tūlkarm, *West Bank* 74 C4
Tulla, *Ireland* 12 D3
Tullahoma, *U.S.A.* 115 H2
Tullamore, *Australia* 95 E4
Tullamore, *Ireland* 12 C4
Tulle, *France* 20 C5
Tulln, *Austria* 26 C9
Tullow, *Ireland* 12 D5
Tullus, *Sudan* 81 E1
Tully, *Australia* 94 B4
Tully, *U.S.A.* 117 D8
Tulnici, *Romania* 29 E11
Tulovo, *Bulgaria* 45 D9

Tulsa, *U.S.A.* 113 G7
Tulsequah, *Canada* 102 B2
Tulu Milki, *Ethiopia* 81 F4
Tulu Welel, *Ethiopia* 81 F3
Tulua, *Colombia* 124 C3
Tulucești, *Romania* 29 E13
Tulun, *Russia* 53 D11
Tulungagung, *Indonesia* 63 H14
Tuma ➤, *Russia* 32 E11
Tuma ➤, *Nic.* 120 D3
Tumaco, *Colombia* 124 C3
Tumacacori △, *U.S.A.* 109 L8
Tumatumari, *Guyana* 124 B7
Tumba, *Sweden* 10 E11
Tumba, L., *Dem. Rep. of
  the Congo* 84 E3
Tumbarumba, *Australia* 95 F4
Tumbaya, *Argentina* 126 A2
Tumbes, *Peru* 124 D2
Tumbur, *Sudan* 81 G3
Tumbwe, *Dem. Rep. of the Congo* 87 E2
Tumby Bay, *Australia* 95 E2
Tumd Youqi, *China* 56 D6
Tumen, *China* 57 C15
Tumen Jiang ➤, *China* 57 C16
Tumeremo, *Venezuela* 124 B6
Tumkur, *India* 66 N10
Tump, *Pakistan* 66 F3
Tumpat, *Malaysia* 65 J4
Tumu, *Ghana* 82 C4
Tumucumaque, Serra, *Brazil* 125 C8
Tumut, *Australia* 95 F4
Tumwater, *U.S.A.* 110 C4
Tuna, *India* 68 H4
Tunadal, *Sweden* 10 B11
Tunapuna, *Trin. & Tob.* 125 K15
Tunas de Zaza, *Cuba* 120 B4
Tunbridge Wells = Royal
  Tunbridge Wells, *U.K.* 15 F8
Tunçbilek, *Turkey* 47 B11
Tunceli, *Turkey* 73 C8
Tuncurry, *Australia* 95 E5
Tundla, *India* 68 F8
Tundubai, *Sudan* 80 D2
Tunduru, *Tanzania* 87 E4
Tundzha ➤, *Bulgaria* 45 E10
Tungabhadra ➤, *India* 66 M11
Tungaru, *Sudan* 81 E3
Tungla, *Nic.* 120 D3
Tungsha Tao = Dongsha Dao,
  China 59 G11
Tungshih, *Taiwan* 59 E13
Tungsten, *Canada* 102 A3
Tunguska, Nizhnyaya ➤, *Russia* 53 C9
Tunguska, Podkamennaya ➤,
  Russia 53 C10
Tunica, *U.S.A.* 113 H9
Tunis, *Tunisia* 78 A7
Tunis ✈ (TUN), *Tunisia* ... 42 F3
Tunisia ■, *Africa* 78 B6
Tunja, *Colombia* 124 B4
Tunkhannock, *U.S.A.* 117 E9
Tunliu, *China* 56 F7
Tunnel Creek △, *Australia* . 92 C4
Tunnsjøen, *Norway* 8 D15
Tunø, *Denmark* 11 J4
Tunungayualok I., *Canada* .. 105 A7
Tunuyán, *Argentina* 126 C2
Tunuyán ➤, *Argentina* 126 C2
Tuo Jiang ➤, *China* 58 C5
Tuolumne, *U.S.A.* 110 H6
Tuolumne ➤, *U.S.A.* 110 H5
Tūp Āghāj, *Iran* 70 B5
Tupã, *Brazil* 127 A5
Tupelo, *U.S.A.* 115 H1
Tupik, *Russia* 32 E7
Tupinambaranas, *Brazil* 124 D7
Tupiza, *Bolivia* 126 A2
Tupižnica, *Serbia & M.* 44 C6
Tupman, *U.S.A.* 111 K7
Tupper, *Canada* 102 B4
Tupper Lake, *U.S.A.* 117 B10
Tupungato, Cerro, *S. Amer.* 126 C2
Tuquan, *China* 57 B11
Túquerres, *Colombia* 124 C3
Tura, *Russia* 53 C11
Turabah, *Ḥā'il, Si. Arabia* . 70 D4
Turabah, *Makkah, Si. Arabia* 80 C5
Tūrān, *Iran* 71 C8
Turan, *Russia* 53 D10
Turayf, *Si. Arabia* 70 D3
Turbacz, *Poland* 31 J7
Turbe, *Bos.-H.* 28 F2
Turčianske Teplice, *Slovak Rep.* 27 C11
Turcoaia, *Romania* 29 E13
Turda, *Romania* 29 D8
Turek, *Poland* 31 F5
Turen, *Venezuela* 124 B5
Turfan = Turpan, *China* 60 B3
Turfan Basin = Turpan Hami,
  China 50 E12
Turfan Depression = Turpan
  Hami, *China* 50 E12
Turgeon ➤, *Canada* 104 C4
Tŭrgovishte, *Bulgaria* 45 C10
Turgut, *Turkey* 47 D10
Turgutlu, *Turkey* 47 C9
Turgwe ➤, *Zimbabwe* 89 C5
Turhal, *Turkey* 72 B7
Turia ➤, *Spain* 39 F4
Turiaçu, *Brazil* 125 D9
Turiaçu ➤, *Brazil* 125 D9
Turiec ➤, *Slovak Rep.* 27 B11
Turin = Torino, *Italy* 40 C4
Turka, *Russia* 31 J10
Turkana, L., *Africa* 86 B4
Türkeli, *Turkey* 45 F11
Turkestan = Türkistan,
  Kazakhstan 52 E7
Túrkeve, *Hungary* 28 C5
Turkey ■, *Eurasia* 72 C7

Turkey Creek, *Australia* 92 C4
Turki, *Russia* 34 D6
Türkistan, *Kazakhstan* 52 E7
Turkmenbashi, *Turkmenistan* 52 E6
Turkmenistan ■, *Asia* 52 F6
Türkmenli, *Turkey* 47 B8
Türkoğlu, *Turkey* 72 D7
Turks & Caicos Is. ☑, *W. Indies* 121 B5
Turks Island Passage, *W. Indies* 121 B5
Turku, *Finland* 9 F20
Turkwel ➤, *Kenya* 86 B4
Turlock, *U.S.A.* 110 H6
Turnagain ➤, *Canada* 102 B3
Turnagain, C., *N.Z.* 91 J6
Turneffe Is., *Belize* 119 D7
Turner, *U.S.A.* 108 B9
Turner Pt., *Australia* 94 A1
Turner Valley, *Canada* 102 C6
Turners Falls, *U.S.A.* 117 D12
Turnhout, *Belgium* 17 C4
Türnitz, *Austria* 26 D8
Turnor L., *Canada* 103 B7
Turnov, *Czech Rep.* 26 A8
Tŭrnovo = Veliko Tŭrnovo,
  Bulgaria 45 C9
Turnu Măgurele, *Romania* .. 29 G9
Turnu Roșu, P., *Romania* ... 29 E9
Turobin, *Poland* 31 H9
Turpan, *China* 60 B3
Turpan Hami, *China* 50 E12
Turrës, Kala e, *Albania* 44 E3
Turriff, *U.K.* 13 D6
Tursāq, *Iraq* 70 C5
Tursi, *Italy* 43 B9
Turtle Head I., *Australia* ... 94 A3
Turtle Is., *S. Leone* 82 D2
Turtle L., *Canada* 103 C7
Turtle Lake, *U.S.A.* 112 B4
Turtleford, *Canada* 103 C7
Turuépano △, *Venezuela* ... 121 D7
Turukhansk, *Russia* 53 C9
Turzovka, *Slovak Rep.* 27 B11
Tuscaloosa, *U.S.A.* 115 J2
Tuscánia, *Italy* 41 F8
Tuscany = Toscana □, *Italy* 40 E8
Tuscarawas ➤, *U.S.A.* 116 F3
Tuscarora Mt., *U.S.A.* 116 F7
Tuscola, *Ill., U.S.A.* 114 F1
Tuscola, *Tex., U.S.A.* 113 J5
Tuscumbia, *U.S.A.* 115 H2
Tuskegee, *U.S.A.* 115 J3
Tustin, *U.S.A.* 111 M9
Tuszyn, *Poland* 31 G6
Tutak, *Turkey* 73 C10
Tutayev, *Russia* 32 D10
Tuticorin, *India* 66 Q11
Tutin, *Serbia & M.* 44 D4
Tutóia, *Brazil* 125 D10
Tutong, *Brunei* 62 D4
Tutova ➤, *Romania* 29 D12
Tutrakan, *Bulgaria* 45 B10
Tuttle Creek L., *U.S.A.* 112 F6
Tuttlingen, *Germany* 25 H4
Tutuala, *E. Timor* 63 F7
Tutuila, *Amer. Samoa* 91 B13
Tutume, *Botswana* 85 J5
Tutun, *Egypt* 80 J7
Tututepec, *Mexico* 119 D5
Tuva □, *Russia* 53 D10
Tuvalu ■, *Pac. Oc.* 96 H9
Tuxer Alpen, *Austria* 26 D4
Tuxpan, *Mexico* 119 C5
Tuxtla Gutiérrez, *Mexico* ... 119 D6
Tuy = Tui, *Spain* 36 C2
Tuy An, *Vietnam* 64 F7
Tuy Duc, *Vietnam* 65 F6
Tuy Hoa, *Vietnam* 64 F7
Tuy Phong, *Vietnam* 65 G7
Tuya L., *Canada* 102 B2
Tuyen Hoa, *Vietnam* 64 D6
Tuyen Quang, *Vietnam* 58 G5
Tūysarkān, *Iran* 71 C6
Tuz Gölü, *Turkey* 72 C5
Ṭūz Khurmātū = Tozkhurmato,
  Iraq 70 C5
Tuzi, *Serbia & M.* 44 D3
Tuzigoot △, *U.S.A.* 109 J7
Tuzla, *Bos.-H.* 28 F3
Tuzlov ➤, *Russia* 33 J10
Tuzluca, *Turkey* 73 B10
Tuzly, *Ukraine* 29 E15
Tvååker, *Sweden* 11 G6
Tvardița, *Moldova* 29 D13
Tver, *Russia* 32 D8
Tvrdošín, *Slovak Rep.* 27 B12
Tvrdošovce, *Slovak Rep.* ... 27 C11
Tvŭrditsa, *Bulgaria* 45 D9
Twain, *U.S.A.* 110 E5
Twain Harte, *U.S.A.* 110 G6
Twardogóra, *Poland* 31 G4
Tweed, *Canada* 116 B7
Tweed ➤, *U.K.* 13 F6
Tweed Heads, *Australia* 95 D5
Tweedsmuir, *Canada* 102 C3
Twentynine Palms, *U.S.A.* .. 111 L10
Twillingate, *Canada* 105 C9
Twin Bridges, *U.S.A.* 108 D7
Twin Falls, *Canada* 105 B7
Twin Falls, *U.S.A.* 108 E6
Twin Valley, *U.S.A.* 112 B6
Twinsburg, *U.S.A.* 116 E3
Twisp, *U.S.A.* 108 B4
Twistringen, *Germany* 24 C4
Twitchell Reservoir, *U.S.A.* . 111 L6
Two Harbors, *U.S.A.* 112 B9
Two Hills, *Canada* 102 C6
Two Rivers, *U.S.A.* 114 C2
Two Rocks, *Australia* 93 F2
Twofold B., *Australia* 95 F4
Tyachiv, *Ukraine* 33 H2
Tychy, *Poland* 31 H5
Tyczyn, *Poland* 31 J9

Tykocin, *Poland* 31 E9
Tyler, *Minn., U.S.A.* 112 C6
Tyler, *Tex., U.S.A.* 113 J7
Tyligul ➤, *Ukraine* 33 J6
Tymanivka, *Ukraine* 29 B13
Týn nad Vltavou, *Czech Rep.* 26 B7
Tynda, *Russia* 53 D13
Tyndall, *U.S.A.* 112 D6
Tyne ➤, *U.K.* 14 C6
Tyne & Wear □, *U.K.* 14 B6
Týnec nad Sázavou, *Czech Rep.* 26 B7
Tynemouth, *U.K.* 14 B6
Tyre = Sūr, *Lebanon* 74 B4
Tyresta □, *Sweden* 10 E12
Tyrifjorden, *Norway* 9 F14
Tyringe, *Sweden* 11 H7
Tyrnyauz, *Russia* 35 J6
Tyrol = Tirol □, *Austria* ... 26 D3
Tyrone, *U.S.A.* 116 F6
Tyrone □, *U.K.* 12 B4
Tyrrell ➤, *Australia* 95 F3
Tyrrell, L., *Australia* 95 F3
Tyrrell L., *Canada* 103 A7
Tyrrhenian Sea, *Medit. S.* .. 6 G8
Tysfjorden, *Norway* 8 B17
Tysmenytsya, *Ukraine* 29 B9
Tystberga, *Sweden* 11 F11
Tytuvėnai, *Lithuania* 30 C10
Tyub Karagan, Mys, *Kazakhstan* 35 H10
Tyuleni, Ostrova, *Kazakhstan* 35 H10
Tyuleniy, *Russia* 35 H8
Tyuleniy, Mys, *Azerbaijan* .. 35 K10
Tyumen, *Russia* 52 D7
Tywi ➤, *U.K.* 15 F3
Tywyn, *U.K.* 15 E3
Tzaneen, *S. Africa* 89 C5
Tzermiádhes, *Greece* 49 D7
Tzoumérka, Óros, *Greece* ... 46 B3
Tzukong = Zigong, *China* ... 58 C5

U

U Taphao, *Thailand* 64 F3
U.S.A. = United States of
  America ■, *N. Amer.* 106 C7
U.S. Virgin Is. ☑, *W. Indies* 121 e
Uatumã ➤, *Brazil* 124 D7
Uaupés, *Brazil* 124 D5
Uaupés ➤, *Brazil* 124 C5
Uaxactún, *Guatemala* 120 C2
Ub, *Serbia & M.* 44 B4
Ubá, *Brazil* 127 A7
Uba, *Nigeria* 83 C7
Ubaitaba, *Brazil* 125 F11
Ubangi = Oubangi ➤, *Dem. Rep.
  of the Congo* 84 E3
Ubauro, *Pakistan* 68 E3
Ubaye ➤, *France* 21 D10
Ubayyiḍ, W. al ➤, *Iraq* ... 70 C4
Ube, *Japan* 55 H5
Úbeda, *Spain* 37 G7
Uberaba, *Brazil* 125 G9
Uberlândia, *Brazil* 125 G9
Überlingen, *Germany* 25 H5
Ubiaja, *Nigeria* 83 D6
Ubin, Pulau, *Singapore* .... 65 d
Ubolratna Res., *Thailand* ... 64 D4
Ubombo, *S. Africa* 89 D5
Ubon Ratchathani, *Thailand* . 64 E5
Ubondo, *Dem. Rep. of the Congo* 86 C2
Ubort ➤, *Belarus* 33 F5
Ubrique, *Spain* 37 J5
Ubud, *Indonesia* 63 J18
Ubundu, *Dem. Rep. of the Congo* 86 C2
Ucayali ➤, *Peru* 124 D4
Uchab, *Namibia* 88 B2
Uchiura-Wan, *Japan* 54 C10
Uchquduq, *Uzbekistan* 52 E7
Uchte, *Germany* 24 C4
Uchur ➤, *Russia* 53 D14
Uckermark, *Germany* 24 B9
Ucluelet, *Canada* 102 D3
Uda ➤, *Russia* 53 D14
Udagamandalam, *India* 66 P10
Udainagar, *India* 68 H7
Udaipur, *India* 68 G5
Udaipur Garhi, *Nepal* 69 F12
Udala, *India* 69 J12
Udbina, *Croatia* 41 D12
Uddeholm, *Sweden* 10 D7
Uddevalla, *Sweden* 11 F5
Uddjaure, *Sweden* 8 D17
Uden, *Neths.* 17 C5
Udgir, *India* 66 K10
Udhampur, *India* 69 C6
Udi, *Nigeria* 83 D6
Údine, *Italy* 41 B10
Udmurtia □, *Russia* 52 D6
Udon Thani, *Thailand* 64 D4
Udupi, *India* 66 N9
Udvoy Balkan, *Bulgaria* 45 D10
Udzungwa △, *Tanzania* 86 D4
Udzungwa Range, *Tanzania* . 87 D4
Ueckermünde, *Germany* 24 B10
Ueda, *Japan* 55 F9
Uedineniya, Os., *Russia* ... 4 B12
Uele ➤, *Dem. Rep. of the Congo* 84 D4
Uelen, *Russia* 53 C19
Uelzen, *Germany* 24 C6
Uetze, *Germany* 24 C6
Ufa, *Russia* 52 D6
Ufa ➤, *Russia* 34 D10
Uffenheim, *Germany* 25 F6
Ugab ➤, *Namibia* 88 C1
Ugalla ➤, *Tanzania* 86 D3
Ugalla River △, *Tanzania* .. 86 D3
Uganda ■, *Africa* 86 B3
Ugento, *Italy* 43 C11

Ugep, *Nigeria* 83 D6
Ughelli, *Nigeria* 83 D6
Ugie, *S. Africa* 89 E4
Ugíjar, *Spain* 37 J7
Ugine, *France* 21 C10
Uglegorsk, *Russia* 53 E15
Uglich, *Russia* 32 D10
Ugljan, *Croatia* 41 D12
Ugljane, *Croatia* 41 E13
Ugra ➤, *Russia* 32 E9
Uğurchin, *Bulgaria* 45 C8
Uh ➤, *Slovak Rep.* 27 C15
Uherské Hradiště, *Czech Rep.* 27 B10
Uherský Brod, *Czech Rep.* .. 27 B10
Úhlava ➤, *Czech Rep.* 26 B6
Uhlenhorst, *Namibia* 88 C2
Uhniv, *Ukraine* 31 H10
Uhrichsville, *U.S.A.* 116 F3
Uibhist a Deas = South Uist, *U.K.* 13 D1
Uibhist a Tuath = North Uist,
  U.K. 13 D1
Uig, *U.K.* 13 D2
Uíge, *Angola* 84 F2
Uijŏngbu, *S. Korea* 57 F14
Ŭiju, *N. Korea* 57 D13
Uinta Mts., *U.S.A.* 108 F8
Uis, *Namibia* 88 C1
Uitenhage, *S. Africa* 88 E4
Uithuizen, *Neths.* 17 A6
Ujazd, *Poland* 31 H5
Újfehértó, *Hungary* 28 C6
Ujh ➤, *India* 68 C6
Ujhani, *India* 69 F8
Uji-guntō, *Japan* 55 J4
Ujjain, *India* 68 H6
Ujście, *Poland* 31 E3
Újszász, *Hungary* 28 C5
Ujung Pandang, *Indonesia* . 63 F5
Uka, *Russia* 53 D17
Ukara I., *Tanzania* 86 C3
Uke-Shima, *Japan* 55 K4
Ukerewe I., *Tanzania* 86 C3
Ukholovo, *Russia* 34 D5
Ukhrul, *India* 67 G19
Ukhta, *Russia* 52 C6
Ukiah, *U.S.A.* 110 F3
Ukmergė, *Lithuania* 9 J21
Ukraine ■, *Europe* 33 H7
Ukwi, *Botswana* 88 C3
Ulaan-Uul, *Mongolia* 56 B6
Ulaanbaatar, *Mongolia* 53 E11
Ulaangom, *Mongolia* 60 A4
Ulaanjirem, *Mongolia* 56 B3
Ulamba, *Dem. Rep. of the Congo* 87 D1
Ulan Bator = Ulaanbaatar,
  Mongolia 53 E11
Ulan Erge, *Russia* 35 G7
Ulan Khol, *Russia* 35 H8
Ulan Ude, *Russia* 53 D11
Ulanów, *Poland* 31 H9
Ulaș, *Sivas, Turkey* 72 C7
Ulaş, *Tekirdağ, Turkey* 45 E11
Ulaya, *Morogoro, Tanzania* . 86 D4
Ulaya, *Tabora, Tanzania* ... 86 C3
Ulcinj, *Serbia & M.* 44 E3
Ulco, *S. Africa* 88 D3
Ule älv = Oulujoki ➤, *Finland* 8 D21
Ule träsk = Oulujärvi, *Finland* 8 D22
Uleåborg = Oulu, *Finland* .. 8 D21
Ulefoss, *Norway* 9 G13
Ülëz, *Albania* 44 E3
Ulfborg, *Denmark* 11 H2
Ulhasnagar, *India* 66 K8
Uliastay, *Mongolia* 60 B4
Uljma, *Serbia & M.* 28 E6
Ulla ➤, *Spain* 36 C2
Ulladulla, *Australia* 95 F5
Ullapool, *U.K.* 13 D3
Ullared, *Sweden* 11 G6
Ulldecona, *Spain* 38 E5
Ullswater, *U.K.* 14 C5
Ullŭng-do, *S. Korea* 55 F5
Ulm, *Germany* 25 G5
Ulmarra, *Australia* 95 D5
Ulmeni, *Buzău, Romania* ... 29 E11
Ulmeni, *Maramureș, Romania* 29 C8
Ulonguè, *Mozam.* 87 E3
Ulricehamn, *Sweden* 11 G7
Ulrika, *Sweden* 11 F9
Ulsan, *S. Korea* 57 G15
Ulsta, *U.K.* 13 A7
Ulster □, *U.K.* 12 B5
Ulstrem, *Bulgaria* 45 D10
Ulubat Gölü, *Turkey* 45 F12
Ulubey, *Turkey* 47 C11
Uluborlu, *Turkey* 47 C12
Uluçinar, *Turkey* 72 D6
Uludağ, *Turkey* 45 F13
Uludağ △, *Turkey* 45 F13
Uludere, *Turkey* 73 D10
Uluguru Mts., *Tanzania* 86 D4
Ulukışla, *Turkey* 72 D6
Ulungur He ➤, *China* 60 B3
Uluru = Ayers Rock, *Australia* 93 E5
Uluru-Kata Tjuta △, *Australia* 93 E5
Ulutau, *Kazakhstan* 52 E7
Uluwatu, *Indonesia* 63 K18
Ulva, *U.K.* 13 E2
Ulverston, *U.K.* 14 C4
Ulverstone, *Australia* 95 G4
Ulya, *Russia* 53 D15
Ulyanovo, *Russia* 30 D9
Ulyanovsk = Simbirsk, *Russia* 34 D9
Ulyasutay = Uliastay, *Mongolia* 60 B4
Ulysses, *U.S.A.* 113 G4
Umag, *Croatia* 41 C10
Umala, *Bolivia* 124 G5
Uman, *Ukraine* 33 H6
Umaria, *India* 67 H12
Umarkot, *Pakistan* 66 G6
Umarpada, *India* 68 J5

Umatilla, *U.S.A.* 108 D4
Umbagog L., *U.S.A.* 117 B13
Umbakumba, *Australia* ... 94 A2
Umbértide, *Italy* 41 E9
Umbrella Mts., *N.Z.* 91 L2
Umbria □, *Italy* 41 F9
Umeå, *Sweden* 8 E19
Umeälven →, *Sweden* ... 8 E19
Umera, *Indonesia* 63 E7
Umfolozi □, *S. Africa* ... 89 D5
Umfuli →, *Zimbabwe* ... 87 F2
Umfurudzi △, *Zimbabwe* . 87 F3
Umgusa, *Zimbabwe* 87 F2
Umim Urūmah, *Si. Arabia* . 80 B4
Umka, *Serbia & M.* 44 B4
Umkomaas, *S. Africa* ... 89 E5
Umlazi, *S. Africa* 85 L6
Umm ad Daraj, J., *Jordan* . 74 C4
Umm al Qaywayn, *U.A.E.* . 71 E7
Umm al Qittayn, *Jordan* . 74 C5
Umm Arda, *Sudan* 81 D3
Umm Bāb, *Qatar* 71 E6
Umm Badr, *Sudan* 81 E2
Umm Baiyud, *Sudan* 81 E3
Umm Bel, *Sudan* 81 E2
Umm Birkah, *Si. Arabia* .. 80 B4
Umm Boim, *Sudan* 81 E2
Umm Dam, *Sudan* 81 E3
Umm Debi, *Sudan* 81 E3
Umm Dubban, *Sudan* ... 81 D3
Umm Durman = Omdurmân,
    Sudan 81 D3
Umm el Fahm, *Israel* ... 74 C4
Umm Gafala, *Sudan* 81 E2
Umm Gimala, *Sudan* 81 E2
Umm Inderaba, *Sudan* ... 80 D3
Umm Keddada, *Sudan* ... 81 E2
Umm Koweika, *Sudan* ... 81 E3
Umm Lajj, *Si. Arabia* ... 70 E3
Umm Merwa, *Sudan* 80 D3
Umm Qantur, *Sudan* 81 E3
Umm Qurein, *Sudan* 81 F2
Umm Ruwaba, *Sudan* ... 81 E3
Umm Saiyala, *Sudan* ... 81 E3
Umm Shanga, *Sudan* 81 E2
Umm Shutur, *Sudan* 81 F3
Umm Sidr, *Sudan* 81 E2
Umm Zehetir, *Egypt* ... 80 J8
Umnak I., *U.S.A.* 100 C3
Umniati →, *Zimbabwe* ... 87 F2
Umpqua →, *U.S.A.* 108 E1
Umreth, *India* 68 H5
Umtata, *S. Africa* 89 E4
Umvukwe Ra., *Zimbabwe* . 87 F3
Umzimvubu →, *S. Africa* . 89 E4
Umzingwane →, *Zimbabwe* 87 G2
Umzinto, *S. Africa* 89 E5
Una →, *India* 68 J4
Una →, *Bos.-H.* 41 D13
Unac →, *Bos.-H.* 41 D13
Unadilla, *U.S.A.* 117 D9
Unalakleet, *U.S.A.* 100 B3
Unalaska, *U.S.A.* 100 C3
Unalaska I., *U.S.A.* 100 C3
'Unayzah, *Si. Arabia* ... 70 E4
'Unayzah, J., *Asia* 70 C3
Uncastillo, *Spain* 38 C3
Uncía, *Bolivia* 124 G5
Uncompahgre Peak, *U.S.A.* 109 G10
Uncompahgre Plateau, *U.S.A.* 109 G9
Undara Volcanic △, *Australia* 94 B3
Unden, *Sweden* 11 F8
Underbool, *Australia* ... 95 F3
Undersaker, *Sweden* 10 A7
Unecha, *Russia* 33 F7
Ungarie, *Australia* 95 E4
Ungarra, *Australia* 95 E2
Ungava, Pén. d', *Canada* . 101 C12
Ungava B., *Canada* 101 C13
Ungeny = Ungheni, *Moldova* 29 C12
Unggi, *N. Korea* 57 C16
Ungheni, *Moldova* 29 C12
Unguala →, *Ethiopia* ... 81 F5
Ungwana B., *Kenya* 86 C5
Ungwatiri, *Sudan* 81 D4
Uni, *Russia* 34 B10
União da Vitória, *Brazil* . 127 B5
Uničov, *Czech Rep.* ... 27 B10
Uniejów, *Poland* 31 G5
Unije, *Croatia* 41 D11
Unimak I., *U.S.A.* 100 C3
Union, *Miss., U.S.A.* ... 113 J10
Union, *Mo., U.S.A.* 112 F9
Union, *S.C., U.S.A.* 115 H5
Union City, *Calif., U.S.A.* 110 H4
Union City, *N.J., U.S.A.* . 117 F10
Union City, *Pa., U.S.A.* . 116 E5
Union City, *Tenn., U.S.A.* 113 G10
Union Gap, *U.S.A.* 108 C3
Union Springs, *U.S.A.* ... 115 J3
Uniondale, *S. Africa* ... 88 E3
Uniontown, *U.S.A.* 114 F6
Unionville, *U.S.A.* 112 E8
Unirea, *Romania* 29 F12
United Arab Emirates ■, *Asia* 71 F7
United Kingdom ■, *Europe* 7 E5
United States of America ■,
    N. Amer. 106 C7
Unity, *Canada* 103 C7
Universales, Mtes., *Spain* . 38 E3
University Park, *U.S.A.* . 109 K10
Unjha, *India* 68 H5
Unna, *Germany* 24 D3
Unnao, *India* 69 F9
Uno, Ilha, *Guinea-Biss.* . 82 C1
Unsengedsi →, *Zimbabwe* 87 F3
Unst, *U.K.* 13 A8
Unstrut →, *Germany* 24 D7

Unterfranken □, *Germany* 25 F5
Unterschleissheim, *Germany* .. 25 G7
Unuk →, *Canada* 102 B2
Ünye, *Turkey* 72 B7
Unzen-Amakusa △, *Japan* .. 55 H5
Unzha, *Russia* 34 A7
Unzha →, *Russia* 34 A6
Uozu, *Japan* 55 F8
Upata, *Venezuela* 124 B6
Upemba △, *Dem. Rep. of
    the Congo* 87 D2
Upemba, L., *Dem. Rep. of
    the Congo* 87 D2
Upernavik, *Greenland* ... 4 B5
Upington, *S. Africa* 88 D3
Upleta, *India* 68 J4
'Upolu, *Samoa* 91 A13
Upper □, *Ghana* 83 C4
Upper Alkali L., *U.S.A.* . 108 F3
Upper Arrow L., *Canada* . 102 C5
Upper Foster L., *Canada* . 103 B7
Upper Hutt, *N.Z.* 91 J5
Upper Klamath L., *U.S.A.* 108 E3
Upper Lake, *U.S.A.* 110 F4
Upper Manzanilla, *Trin. & Tob.* 125 K15
Upper Missouri River Breaks △,
    U.S.A. 108 C9
Upper Musquodoboit, *Canada* 105 C7
Upper Red L., *U.S.A.* ... 112 A7
Upper Sandusky, *U.S.A.* . 114 E4
Upper Volta = Burkina Faso ■,
    Africa 82 C4
Upphärad, *Sweden* 11 F6
Uppland, *Sweden* 10 D12
Upplands-Väsby, *Sweden* . 10 E11
Uppsala, *Sweden* 10 E11
Uppsala län □, *Sweden* ... 10 D11
Upshi, *India* 69 C7
Upstart, C., *Australia* ... 94 B4
Upton, *U.S.A.* 112 C2
Uqsuqtuuq = Gjoa Haven,
    Canada 100 B10
Ur, *Iraq* 70 D5
Urad Qianqi, *China* 56 D5
Urakawa, *Japan* 54 C11
Ural = Uralskiy □, *Russia* 52 C7
Ural = Zhayyq →, *Kazakhstan* 52 E6
Ural, *Australia* 95 E4
Ural Mts. = Uralskie Gory,
    Eurasia 52 D6
Uralla, *Australia* 95 E5
Uralsk = Oral, *Kazakhstan* 34 E10
Uralskie Gory, *Eurasia* ... 52 D6
Uralskiy □, *Russia* 52 C7
Urambo, *Tanzania* 86 D3
Urandangi, *Australia* ... 94 C2
Uranium City, *Canada* ... 103 B7
Uraricoera →, *Brazil* ... 124 C6
Urawa, *Japan* 55 G9
Uray, *Russia* 52 C7
'Uray'irah, *Si. Arabia* ... 71 E6
Urbana, *Ill., U.S.A.* 114 E1
Urbana, *Ohio, U.S.A.* ... 114 E4
Urbánia, *Italy* 41 E9
Urbel →, *Spain* 36 C7
Urbino, *Italy* 41 E9
Urbión, Picos de, *Spain* . 38 C2
Urcos, *Peru* 124 F4
Urdinarrain, *Argentina* . 126 C4
Urdos, *France* 20 F3
Urdzhar, *Kazakhstan* ... 52 E9
Ure →, *U.K.* 14 C6
Uren, *Russia* 34 B7
Ures, *Mexico* 118 B2
Urewera △, *N.Z.* 91 H6
Urfa = Sanliurfa, *Turkey* . 70 B3
Urganch, *Uzbekistan* ... 52 E7
Urgench = Urganch, *Uzbekistan* 52 E7
Ürgüp, *Turkey* 70 B2
Uri, *India* 69 B6
Uri □, *Switz.* 25 J4
Uribia, *Colombia* 124 A4
Uricani, *Romania* 28 E8
Uriondo, *Bolivia* 126 A3
Urique, *Mexico* 118 B3
Urique →, *Mexico* 118 B3
Urk, *Neths.* 17 B5
Urkiola □, *Spain* 38 B3
Urla, *Turkey* 47 C8
Urlaţi, *Romania* 29 F11
Uroševac, *Serbia & M.* . 44 D5
Uroyan, Montanas de,
    Puerto Rico .... 121 d
Urshult, *Sweden* 11 H8
Uruaçu, *Brazil* 125 F9
Uruapan, *Mexico* 118 D4
Urubamba →, *Peru* 124 F4
Uruçara, *Brazil* 124 D7
Uruçuí, *Brazil* 125 E10
Uruguai →, *Brazil* 127 B5
Uruguaiana, *Brazil* 126 B4
Uruguay ■, *S. Amer.* ... 126 C4
Uruguay →, *S. Amer.* ... 126 C4
Urumchi = Ürümqi, *China* 52 E9
Ürümqi, *China* 52 E9
Urup →, *Russia* 35 H5
Urup, Ostrov, *Russia* ... 53 E16
Uryupinsk, *Russia* 34 E5
Urzhum, *Russia* 34 B9
Urziceni, *Romania* 29 F11
Usa →, *Russia* 52 C6
Uşak, *Turkey* 47 C11
Uşak □, *Turkey* 47 C11
Usakos, *Namibia* 88 C2
Ušće, *Serbia & M.* 44 C4
Usedom, *Germany* 24 B10
Usedom △, *Germany* ... 24 B10
Useless Loop, *Australia* . 93 E1
'Usfān, *Si. Arabia* 80 C4
Ush-Tobe, *Kazakhstan* ... 52 E8

Ushakova, Ostrov, *Russia* . 4 A12
Ushakovo, *Russia* 30 D7
Ushant = Ouessant, Î. d', *France* 18 D1
Ushashi, *Tanzania* 86 C3
Ushat, *Sudan* 81 F2
Ushibuka, *Japan* 55 H5
Ushuaia, *Argentina* 128 G3
Ushumun, *Russia* 53 D13
Ushytsya →, *Ukraine* ... 29 B12
Usk, *Canada* 102 C3
Usk →, *U.K.* 15 F5
Uska, *India* 69 F10
Üsküdar, *Turkey* 45 F13
Uslar, *Germany* 24 D5
Usman, *Russia* 33 F10
Usoke, *Tanzania* 86 D3
Usoro, *Nigeria* 83 D6
Uspallata, P. de, *Argentina* 126 C2
Uspenskiy, *Kazakhstan* . 52 E8
Ussel, *France* 20 C6
Usson-du-Poitou, *France* . 20 B4
Ussuri →, *Asia* 54 A7
Ussuriysk, *Russia* 53 E14
Ussurka, *Russia* 54 B6
Ust-Bolsheretsk, *Russia* . 53 D16
Ust-Buzulukskaya, *Russia* . 34 E6
Ust-Chaun, *Russia* 53 C18
Ust-Chorna, *Ukraine* ... 29 B8
Ust-Donetskiy, *Russia* ... 35 G5
Ust-Ilimsk, *Russia* 53 D11
Ust-Ishim, *Russia* 52 D8
Ust-Kamchatsk, *Russia* . 53 D17
Ust-Kamenogorsk = Öskemen,
    Kazakhstan 52 E9
Ust-Khayryuzovo, *Russia* . 53 D16
Ust-Kut, *Russia* 53 D11
Ust-Kuyga, *Russia* 53 B14
Ust-Labinsk, *Russia* ... 35 H4
Ust-Luga, *Russia* 32 C5
Ust-Maya, *Russia* 53 C14
Ust-Mil, *Russia* 53 D14
Ust-Nera, *Russia* 53 C15
Ust-Nyukzha, *Russia* ... 53 D13
Ust-Olenek, *Russia* 53 B12
Ust-Omchug, *Russia* ... 53 C15
Ust-Port, *Russia* 52 C9
Ust-Tsilma, *Russia* 52 C6
Ust Urt = Ustyurt Plateau, *Asia* . 52 E6
Ustaritz, *France* 20 E2
Ústecký □, *Czech Rep.* . 26 A7
Uster, *Switz.* 25 H4
Ústí nad Labem, *Czech Rep.* 26 A7
Ústí nad Orlicí, *Czech Rep.* . 27 B9
Ústica, *Italy* 42 D6
Ustinov = Izhevsk, *Russia* . 52 D6
Ustka, *Poland* 30 D3
Ustroń, *Poland* 31 J5
Ustrzyki Dolne, *Poland* . 31 J9
Ustyluh, *Ukraine* 31 H11
Ustyurt Plateau, *Asia* ... 52 E6
Ustyuzhna, *Russia* 32 C9
Usu, *China* 60 B3
Usuki, *Japan* 55 H5
Usulután, *El Salv.* 120 D2
Usumacinta →, *Mexico* . 119 D6
Usumbura = Bujumbura, *Burundi* 86 C2
Usure, *Tanzania* 86 C3
Usutuo →, *Mozam.* 89 D5
Uta, *Indonesia* 63 E9
Utah □, *U.S.A.* 108 G8
Utah L., *U.S.A.* 108 F8
Utansjö, *Sweden* 10 B11
Utara, Selat, *Malaysia* ... 65 c
Utarni, *India* 68 F4
Utatlan, *Guatemala* 120 C1
Ute Creek →, *U.S.A.* ... 113 H3
Utebo, *Spain* 38 D3
Utena, *Lithuania* 9 J21
Utete, *Tanzania* 86 D4
Uthai Thani, *Thailand* ... 64 E3
Uthal, *Pakistan* 68 G2
Utiariti, *Brazil* 124 F7
Utica, *N.Y., U.S.A.* 117 C9
Utica, *Ohio, U.S.A.* 116 F2
Utiel, *Spain* 39 F3
Utikuma L., *Canada* ... 102 B5
Utö, *Sweden* 10 F12
Utopia, *Australia* 94 C1
Utraula, *India* 69 F10
Utrecht, *Neths.* 17 B5
Utrecht, *S. Africa* 89 D5
Utrecht □, *Neths.* 17 B5
Utrera, *Spain* 37 H5
Utsjoki →, *Finland* 8 B22
Utsunomiya, *Japan* 55 F9
Uttar Pradesh □, *India* . 69 F9
Uttaradit, *Thailand* 64 D3
Uttaranchal □, *India* ... 69 D8
Uttoxeter, *U.K.* 14 E6
Utuado, *Puerto Rico* ... 121 d
Uummannaq, *Greenland* . 4 B4
Uummannaq, *Greenland* . 4 B5
Uummannarsuaq = Nunap Isua,
    Greenland 101 C15
Uusikaarlepyy, *Finland* . 8 E20
Uusikaupunki, *Finland* ... 9 F19
Uva, *Russia* 34 B11
Uvac →, *Serbia & M.* ... 44 C3
Uvalde, *U.S.A.* 113 L5
Uvarovo, *Russia* 34 E6
Uvinza, *Tanzania* 86 D3
Uvira, *Dem. Rep. of the Congo* 86 C2
Uvs Nuur, *Mongolia* ... 60 A4
'Uwairidh, Harrat al, *Si. Arabia* . 70 E3
Uwajima, *Japan* 55 H6
Uwanda △, *Tanzania* ... 86 D3
Uweinat, Jebel, *Sudan* ... 80 C1
Uxbridge, *Canada* 116 B5

Uxin Qi, *China* 56 E5
Uxmal, *Mexico* 119 C7
Üydzin, *Mongolia* 56 B4
Uyo, *Nigeria* 83 D6
Üyük Tepe, *Turkey* 47 D9
Uyûn Mûsa, *Egypt* 74 F1
Uyuni, *Bolivia* 124 H5
Uzbekistan ■, *Asia* 52 E7
Uzen, Bolshoi →, *Kazakhstan* 35 F9
Uzen, Mal →, *Kazakhstan* . 35 F9
Uzerche, *France* 20 C5
Uzès, *France* 21 D8
Uzh →, *Ukraine* 33 G6
Uzhgorod = Uzhhorod, *Ukraine* . 28 B7
Uzhhorod, *Ukraine* 28 B7
Uzhok, *Ukraine* 28 B7
Užice, *Serbia & M.* 44 C3
Uzlovaya, *Russia* 32 F10
Üzümlü, *Turkey* 47 E11
Uzunköprü, *Turkey* 45 E10
Uzunkuyu, *Turkey* 47 C8

V

Vaal →, *S. Africa* 88 D3
Vaal Dam, *S. Africa* 89 D4
Vaalbos △, *S. Africa* ... 88 D3
Vaalwater, *S. Africa* ... 89 C4
Vaasa, *Finland* 8 E19
Vabre, *France* 20 E6
Vác, *Hungary* 28 C4
Vacaria, *Brazil* 127 B5
Vacaville, *U.S.A.* 110 G5
Vaccarès, Étang de, *France* . 21 E8
Vach = Vakh →, *Russia* . 52 C8
Vache, Î. à, *Haiti* 121 C5
Väckelsång, *Sweden* ... 11 H8
Väddö, *Sweden* 10 D12
Väderstad, *Sweden* 11 F8
Vadnagar, *India* 68 H5
Vado Lígure, *Italy* 40 D5
Vadodara, *India* 68 H5
Vadsø, *Norway* 8 A23
Vadstena, *Sweden* 11 F8
Vaduz, *Liech.* 25 H5
Værøy, *Norway* 8 C15
Vágar, *Færoe Is.* 8 E9
Vaggeryd, *Sweden* 11 G8
Vagney, *France* 19 D13
Vagnhärad, *Sweden* 11 F11
Vagos, *Portugal* 36 E2
Vågsfjorden, *Norway* ... 8 B17
Váh →, *Slovak Rep.* 27 D11
Vahsel B., *Antarctica* ... 5 D1
Váí, *Greece* 49 D8
Vaigach, *Russia* 52 B6
Vaiges, *France* 18 D6
Vaihingen, *Germany* ... 25 G4
Vail, *U.S.A.* 106 C5
Vailly-sur-Aisne, *France* . 19 C10
Vaisali →, *India* 69 F8
Vaison-la-Romaine, *France* . 21 D9
Vakarel, *Bulgaria* 44 D7
Vakfıkebir, *Turkey* 73 B8
Vakh →, *Russia* 52 C8
Vakhtan, *Russia* 34 B8
Vál, *Hungary* 28 C3
Val-de-Marne □, *France* . 19 D9
Val-d'Isère, *France* 21 C10
Val-d'Oise □, *France* ... 19 C9
Val-d'Or, *Canada* 104 C4
Val Grande △, *Italy* 40 B5
Val Marie, *Canada* 103 D7
Val Thorens, *France* 21 C10
Valaam, *Russia* 32 B6
Valadares, *Portugal* 36 D2
Valahia, *Romania* 29 F9
Valais □, *Switz.* 25 J3
Valais, Alpes du, *Switz.* . 25 J3
Valandovo, *Macedonia* ... 44 E6
Valašské Meziříčí, *Czech Rep.* . 27 B10
Valáxa, *Greece* 46 C6
Vålberg, *Sweden* 10 E7
Valbo, *Sweden* 10 D10
Valbondione, *Italy* 40 B7
Vâlcani, *Romania* 28 D5
Vâlcea □, *Romania* 29 F9
Valcheta, *Argentina* ... 128 E3
Valdagno, *Italy* 41 C8
Valdahon, *France* 19 E13
Valdai Hills = Valdayskaya
    Vozvyshennost, *Russia* . 32 D7
Valday, *Russia* 32 D7
Valdayskaya Vozvyshennost,
    Russia 32 D7
Valdeazogues →, *Spain* . 37 G6
Valdecañas, Embalse de, *Spain* . 36 F5
Valdemarsvik, *Sweden* ... 11 F10
Valdemoro, *Spain* 36 E7
Valdepeñas, *Spain* 37 G7
Valderaduey →, *Spain* ... 36 D5
Valderrobres, *Spain* 38 E5
Valdés, Pen., *Argentina* . 128 E4
Valdez, *U.S.A.* 100 B5
Valdivia, *Chile* 128 D2
Valdobbiádene, *Italy* ... 41 C8
Valdosta, *U.S.A.* 115 K4
Valdoviño, *Spain* 36 B2
Valdres, *Norway* 9 F13
Vale, *Georgia* 35 K6
Vale, *U.S.A.* 108 E5
Valea lui Mihai, *Romania* . 28 C7
Valea Mărului, *Romania* . 29 E12
Valemount, *Canada* 102 C5
Valença, *Brazil* 125 F11

Valença, *Portugal* 36 C2
Valença do Piauí, *Brazil* . 125 E10
Valençay, *France* 19 E8
Valence, *France* 21 D8
Valence d'Agen, *France* . 20 D4
Valencia, *Spain* 39 F4
Valencia, *Trin. & Tob.* ... 125 K15
Valencia, *Venezuela* 124 A5
Valencia □, *Spain* 39 F4
Valencia ✈ (VLC), *Spain* . 39 F4
Valencia de Alcántara, *Spain* . 37 F3
Valencia de Don Juan, *Spain* . 36 C5
Valencia I., *Ireland* 12 E1
Valenciennes, *France* ... 19 B10
Văleni, *Romania* 29 F9
Vălenii de Munte, *Romania* . 29 E11
Valensole, *France* 21 E9
Valentigney, *France* 19 E13
Valentim, Sa. do, *Brazil* . 125 E10
Valentin, *Russia* 54 C7
Valentine, *U.S.A.* 113 K2
Valenza, *Italy* 40 C5
Valera, *Venezuela* 124 B4
Valga, *Estonia* 9 H22
Valguarnera Caropepe, *Italy* . 43 E7
Valier, *U.S.A.* 108 B7
Valinco, G. de, *France* ... 21 G12
Valjevo, *Serbia & M.* ... 44 B3
Valka, *Latvia* 9 H21
Valkeakoski, *Finland* ... 9 F20
Valkenswaard, *Neths.* ... 17 C5
Vall de Uxó = La Vall d'Uixó,
    Spain 38 F4
Valla, *Sweden* 10 E10
Valladolid, *Mexico* 119 C7
Valladolid, *Spain* 36 D6
Valladolid □, *Spain* 36 D6
Vallata, *Italy* 43 A8
Valldemossa, *Spain* 48 B9
Valle d'Aosta □, *Italy* ... 40 C4
Valle de Arán, *Spain* ... 38 C5
Valle de la Pascua, *Venezuela* . 124 B5
Valle de las Palmas, *Mexico* . 111 N10
Valle de Santiago, *Mexico* . 118 C4
Valle de Suchil, *Mexico* . 118 C4
Valle de Zaragoza, *Mexico* . 118 B3
Valle del Ticino △, *Italy* . 40 C6
Valle Fértil, Sierra del, *Argentina* . 126 C2
Valle Gran Rey, *Canary Is.* . 48 F2
Valle Hermoso, *Mexico* . 119 B5
Valledupar, *Colombia* ... 124 A4
Vallehermoso, *Canary Is.* . 48 F2
Vallejo, *U.S.A.* 110 G4
Vallenar, *Chile* 126 B1
Valletuna, *Sweden* 10 E12
Valleraugue, *France* 20 D7
Vallet, *France* 18 E5
Valletta, *Malta* 49 D2
Valley Center, *U.S.A.* ... 111 M9
Valley City, *U.S.A.* 112 B6
Valley Falls, *Oreg., U.S.A.* . 108 E3
Valley Falls, *R.I., U.S.A.* . 117 E13
Valley of the Kings, *Egypt* . 80 B3
Valley Springs, *U.S.A.* ... 110 G6
Valley View, *U.S.A.* 117 F8
Valley Wells, *U.S.A.* ... 111 K11
Valleyview, *Canada* 102 B5
Valli di Comácchio, *Italy* . 41 D9
Vallimanca, Arroyo, *Argentina* . 126 D4
Vallo della Lucánia, *Italy* . 43 B8
Vallon-Pont-d'Arc, *France* . 21 D8
Vallorbe, *Switz.* 25 J2
Valls, *Spain* 38 D6
Valmaseda = Balmaseda, *Spain* . 38 B1
Valmiera, *Latvia* 9 H21
Valnera, *Spain* 36 B7
Valognes, *France* 18 C5
Valona = Vlorë, *Albania* . 44 F3
Valongo, *Portugal* 36 D2
Valozhyn, *Belarus* 32 E4
Valpaços, *Portugal* 36 D3
Valparaíso, *Chile* 126 C1
Valparaíso, *Mexico* 118 C4
Valparaiso, *U.S.A.* 114 E2
Valparaíso □, *Chile* 126 C1
Valpovo, *Croatia* 28 E3
Valréas, *France* 21 D9
Vals, *Switz.* 25 J5
Vals →, *S. Africa* 88 D4
Vals, Tanjung, *Indonesia* . 63 F9
Vals-les-Bains, *France* ... 21 D8
Valsad, *India* 66 J8
Valtellina, *Italy* 40 B6
Valuyki, *Russia* 33 G10
Valverde, *Canary Is.* ... 48 G2
Valverde del Camino, *Spain* . 37 H4
Valverde del Fresno, *Spain* . 36 E4
Vama, *Romania* 29 C10
Vamdrup, *Denmark* 11 J3
Våmhus, *Sweden* 10 C8
Vammala, *Finland* 9 F20
Vámos, *Greece* 49 D6
Van, *Turkey* 70 B4
Van, L. = Van Gölü, *Turkey* . 70 B4
Van Alstyne, *U.S.A.* 113 J6
Van Blommestein Meer,
    Suriname 125 C7
Van Buren, *Canada* 105 C6
Van Buren, *Ark., U.S.A.* . 113 H7
Van Buren, *Maine, U.S.A.* . 115 B11
Van Buren, *Mo., U.S.A.* . 113 G9
Van Canh, *Vietnam* 64 F7
Van Diemen, C., *N. Terr.,
    Australia* 92 B5
Van Diemen, C., *Queens.,
    Australia* 94 B2
Van Diemen G., *Australia* . 92 B5
Van Gölü, *Turkey* 70 B4
Van Horn, *U.S.A.* 113 K2

Van Ninh, *Vietnam* 64 F7
Van Rees, Pegunungan, *Indonesia* 63 E9
Van Wert, *U.S.A.* 114 E3
Van Yen, *Vietnam* 58 G5
Vanadzor, *Armenia* 35 K7
Vanavara, *Russia* 53 C11
Vancouver, *Canada* 102 D4
Vancouver, *U.S.A.* 110 E4
Vancouver, C., *Australia* 93 G2
Vancouver I., *Canada* 102 D3
Vancouver International ✈
  (YVR), *U.S.A.* 110 A3
Vanda = Vantaa, *Finland* 9 F21
Vandalia, *Ill., U.S.A.* 112 F10
Vandalia, *Mo., U.S.A.* 112 F9
Vandenburg, *U.S.A.* 111 L6
Vanderbijlpark, *S. Africa* 89 D4
Vandergrift, *U.S.A.* 116 F5
Vanderhoof, *Canada* 102 C4
Vanderkloof Dam, *S. Africa* ... 88 E3
Vanderlin I., *Australia* 94 B2
Vänern, *Sweden* 11 F7
Vänersborg, *Sweden* 11 F6
Vang Vieng, *Laos* 64 C4
Vanga, *Kenya* 86 C4
Vangaindrano, *Madag.* 89 C8
Vanguard, *Canada* 103 D7
Vanino, *Russia* 53 E15
Vânju Mare, *Romania* 28 F7
Vanna, *Norway* 8 A18
Vännäs, *Sweden* 8 E18
Vannes, *France* 18 E4
Vanoise, Massif de la, *France* .. 21 C10
Vanrhynsdorp, *S. Africa* 88 E2
Vansittart B., *Australia* 92 B4
Vansbro, *Sweden* 10 D8
Vantaa, *Finland* 9 F21
Vanua Balavu, *Fiji* 91 C9
Vanua Levu, *Fiji* 91 C8
Vanuatu ■, *Pac. Oc.* 96 J8
Vanwyksvlei, *S. Africa* 88 E3
Vanzylsrus, *S. Africa* 88 D3
Vapnyarka, *Ukraine* 29 B13
Var □, *France* 21 E10
Var ➤, *France* 21 E11
Vara, *Sweden* 11 F6
Varades, *France* 18 E5
Varáita ➤, *Italy* 40 D4
Varallo, *Italy* 40 C5
Varāmīn, *India* 71 C6
Varāmīn □, *Iran* 71 B6
Varanasi, *India* 69 G10
Varangerfjorden, *Norway* 8 A23
Varangerhalvøya, *Norway* 8 A23
Varano, Lago di, *Italy* 41 G12
Varaždin, *Croatia* 41 B13
Varazze, *Italy* 40 D5
Varberg, *Sweden* 11 G6
Vardak □, *Afghan.* 66 B6
Vardar = Axiós ➤, *Greece* ... 44 F6
Varde, *Denmark* 11 J2
Varde Å ➤, *Denmark* 11 J2
Vardø, *Norway* 8 A24
Varel, *Germany* 24 B4
Varella, Mui, *Vietnam* 64 F7
Varéna, *Lithuania* 9 J21
Varennes-sur-Allier, *France* ... 19 F10
Varennes-Vauzelles, *France* ... 19 E10
Vareš, *Bos.-H.* 28 F3
Varese, *Italy* 40 C5
Vărfurile, *Romania* 28 D7
Vårgårda, *Sweden* 11 F6
Varginha, *Brazil* 127 A6
Vargön, *Sweden* 11 F6
Varillas, *Chile* 126 A1
Varkaus, *Finland* 9 E22
Värmdölandet, *Sweden* 10 E12
Värmeln, *Sweden* 10 E6
Värmlands län □, *Sweden* 10 E6
Värmlandsbro, *Sweden* 10 E7
Varna, *Bulgaria* 45 C11
Varna □, *Bulgaria* 45 C11
Värnamo, *Sweden* 11 G8
Varnsdorf, *Czech Rep.* 26 A7
Várpalota, *Hungary* 28 C3
Vars, *Canada* 117 A9
Vars, *France* 21 D10
Varto, *Turkey* 73 C9
Varvarin, *Serbia & M.* 44 C5
Varysburg, *U.S.A.* 116 D6
Varzaneh, *Iran* 71 C7
Varzi, *Italy* 40 D6
Varzo, *Italy* 40 B5
Varzy, *France* 19 E10
Vas □, *Hungary* 28 C1
Vasa = Vaasa, *Finland* 8 E19
Vasa Barris ➤, *Brazil* 125 F11
Vascão ➤, *Portugal* 37 H3
Vașcău, *Romania* 28 D7
Vascongadas = País Vasco □,
  Spain 38 C2
Vashkivtsi, *Ukraine* 29 B10
Vasht = Khāsh, *Iran* 66 E2
Vasilevichi, *Belarus* 33 F5
Vasilikón, *Greece* 46 C5
Vasilkov = Vasylkiv, *Ukraine* ... 33 G6
Vaslui, *Romania* 29 D12
Vaslui □, *Romania* 29 D12
V:;sman, *Sweden* 10 D9
Vassar, *Canada* 103 D9
Vassar, *U.S.A.* 114 D4
Västerås, *Sweden* 10 E10
Västerbotten, *Sweden* 8 D18
Västerdalälven ➤, *Sweden* ... 10 D8
Västergötland, *Sweden* 11 F7
Västerhaninge, *Sweden* 10 E12
Västervik, *Sweden* 11 G10
Västmanland, *Sweden* 9 G16
Västmanlands län □, *Sweden* . 10 E10
Vasto, *Italy* 41 F11

Västra Götalands Län □, *Sweden* 11 F6
Vasvár, *Hungary* 28 C1
Vasylivka, *Ukraine* 29 E13
Vasylkiv, *Ukraine* 33 G6
Vatan, *France* 19 E8
Vatersay, *U.K.* 13 E1
Váthia, *Greece* 46 E4
Vatican City ■, *Europe* 41 G9
Vaticano, C., *Italy* 43 D8
Vatili, *Cyprus* 49 D12
Vatin, *Serbia & M.* 28 E6
Vatnajökull, *Iceland* 8 D5
Vatoa, *Fiji* 91 D9
Vatólakkos, *Greece* 49 D5
Vatoloha, *Madag.* 89 B8
Vatomandry, *Madag.* 89 B8
Vatra-Dornei, *Romania* 29 C10
Vatrak ➤, *India* 68 H5
Vättern, *Sweden* 11 F8
Vaucluse □, *France* 21 E9
Vaucouleurs, *France* 19 D12
Vaud □, *Switz.* 25 J2
Vaudreuil-Dorion, *Canada* ... 117 A10
Vaughn, *Mont., U.S.A.* 108 C8
Vaughn, *N. Mex., U.S.A.* 109 J11
Vaujours L., *Canada* 104 A5
Vaupés = Uaupés ➤, *Brazil* .. 124 C5
Vaupes □, *Colombia* 124 C4
Vauvert, *France* 21 E8
Vauxhall, *Canada* 102 C6
Vav, *India* 68 G4
Vavatenina, *Madag.* 89 B8
Vava'u, *Tonga* 91 D12
Vavoua, *Ivory C.* 82 D3
Vawkavysk, *Belarus* 33 F3
Vaxholm, *Sweden* 10 E12
Växjö, *Sweden* 11 H8
Växtorp, *Sweden* 11 H7
Vaygach, Ostrov, *Russia* 52 C6
Váyia, *Greece* 46 C5
Váyia, Ákra, *Greece* 49 C10
Veaikevárri = Svappavaara,
  Sweden 8 C19
Vechelde, *Germany* 24 C6
Vechta, *Germany* 24 C4
Vechte ➤, *Neths.* 17 B6
Vecsés, *Hungary* 28 C4
Veddige, *Sweden* 11 G6
Vedea ➤, *Romania* 29 G10
Vedia, *Argentina* 126 C3
Vedrette di Ries-Aurina △, *Italy* 41 B9
Vedum, *Sweden* 11 F7
Veendam, *Neths.* 17 A6
Veenendaal, *Neths.* 17 B5
Vefsna ➤, *Norway* 8 D15
Vega, *Norway* 8 D14
Vega, *U.S.A.* 113 H3
Vega Baja, *Puerto Rico* ...... 121 d
Vegadeo, *Spain* 36 B3
Vegorrítis, Límni, *Greece* 44 F5
Vegreville, *Canada* 102 C6
Veinge, *Sweden* 11 H7
Veisiejai, *Lithuania* 30 D10
Vejbystrand, *Sweden* 11 H6
Vejen, *Denmark* 11 J3
Vejer de la Frontera, *Spain* ... 37 J5
Vejle, *Denmark* 11 J3
Vejle Amtskommune □,
  Denmark 11 J3
Vejle Fjord, *Denmark* 11 J3
Vela Luka, *Croatia* 41 F13
Velas, C., *Costa Rica* 120 D2
Velasco, Sierra de, *Argentina* . 126 B2
Velay, Mts. du, *France* 20 D7
Velbert, *Germany* 24 D3
Velddrif, *S. Africa* 88 E2
Velebit △, *Croatia* 41 D12
Velebit Planina, *Croatia* 41 D12
Velebitski Kanal, *Croatia* 41 D11
Veleka ➤, *Bulgaria* 45 D11
Velenci-tó, *Hungary* 28 C3
Velenje, *Slovenia* 41 B12
Veles, *Macedonia* 44 E5
Velestínon, *Greece* 46 B4
Vélez-Málaga, *Spain* 37 J6
Vélez Rubio, *Spain* 39 H2
Velhas ➤, *Brazil* 125 G10
Velika, *Croatia* 28 E2
Velika Gorica, *Croatia* 41 C13
Velika Kapela, *Croatia* 41 C12
Velika Kladuša, *Bos.-H.* 41 C12
Velika Kruša, *Serbia & M.* ... 44 D4
Velika Morava ➤, *Serbia & M.* 44 B5
Velika Plana, *Serbia & M.* ... 44 B5
Velikaya ➤, *Russia* 32 D5
Velikaya Kema, *Russia* 54 B8
Velikaya Lepetikha, *Ukraine* . 33 J7
Veliké Kapušany, *Slovak Rep.* . 27 C15
Velike Lašče, *Slovenia* 41 C11
Veliki Jastrebac, *Serbia & M.* . 44 C5
Veliki Kanal, *Serbia & M.* ... 28 E4
Veliki Popović, *Serbia & M.* .. 44 B5
Velikiye Luki, *Russia* 32 D6
Veliko Gradište, *Serbia & M.* . 44 B5
Veliko Tŭrnovo, *Bulgaria* 45 C9
Velikonda Range, *India* 66 M11
Vélingara, Kolda, *Senegal* 82 C2
Vélingara, Louga, *Senegal* 82 B2
Velingrad, *Bulgaria* 44 D7
Velino, Mte., *Italy* 41 F10
Velizh, *Russia* 32 E6
Veľké Karlovice, *Czech Rep.* .. 27 B11
Veľké Meziřičí, *Czech Rep.* ... 26 B9
Veľký Javorník, *Slovak Rep.* .. 27 B11
Veľký Krtíš, *Slovak Rep.* 27 C12
Veľký Meder, *Slovak Rep.* 27 D10
Veľký Tribeč, *Slovak Rep.* 27 C11
Velletri, *Italy* 42 A5
Vellinge, *Sweden* 11 J6
Vellmar, *Germany* 24 D5
Vellore, *India* 66 N11

Velsk, *Russia* 32 B11
Velten, *Germany* 24 C9
Veluwezoom △, *Neths.* 17 B6
Velva, *U.S.A.* 112 A4
Velvendós, *Greece* 44 F6
Velyka Mykhaylivka, *Ukraine* . 29 C14
Velyki Luchky, *Ukraine* 28 B7
Velykyy Bereznyy, *Ukraine* ... 28 B7
Velykyy Bychkiv, *Ukraine* 29 C9
Vemb, *Denmark* 11 H2
Vemdalen, *Sweden* 10 B7
Ven, *Sweden* 11 J6
Venado Tuerto, *Argentina* ... 126 C3
Venafro, *Italy* 43 A7
Venarey-les-Laumes, *France* .. 19 E11
Venaría, *Italy* 40 C4
Vendas Novas, *Portugal* 37 G2
Vendée □, *France* 18 F5
Vendée ➤, *France* 18 F5
Vendéen, Bocage, *France* 20 B2
Vendeuvre-sur-Barse, *France* . 19 D11
Vendôme, *France* 18 E8
Vendrell = El Vendrell, *Spain* . 38 D6
Vendsyssel, *Denmark* 11 G4
Vendychany, *Ukraine* 29 B12
Venelles, *France* 21 E9
Véneta, L., *Italy* 41 C9
Véneto □, *Italy* 41 C9
Venev, *Russia* 32 E10
Venézia, *Italy* 41 C9
Venézia, G. di, *Italy* 41 C10
Venezuela ■, *S. Amer.* 124 B5
Venezuela, G. de, *Venezuela* .. 124 A4
Vengurla, *India* 66 M8
Venice = Venézia, *Italy* 41 C9
Venice, *U.S.A.* 115 M4
Vénissieux, *France* 21 C8
Venjan, *Sweden* 10 D8
Venjansjön, *Sweden* 10 D8
Venkatapuram, *India* 67 K12
Venlo, *Neths.* 17 C6
Vennesla, *Norway* 9 G12
Venosa, *Italy* 43 B8
Venray, *Neths.* 17 C6
Venta, *Lithuania* 30 B9
Venta ➤, *Latvia* 30 A8
Venta de Baños, *Spain* 36 D6
Venta de Cardeña = Cardeña,
  Spain 37 G6
Ventana, Punta de la, *Mexico* . 118 C3
Ventana, Sa. de la, *Argentina* . 126 D3
Ventersburg, *S. Africa* 88 D4
Venterstad, *S. Africa* 88 E4
Ventimíglia, *Italy* 40 E4
Ventnor, *U.K.* 15 G6
Ventoténe, *Italy* 42 B6
Ventoux, Mt., *France* 21 D9
Ventspils, *Latvia* 9 H19
Ventspils □, *Latvia* 30 A8
Ventuari ➤, *Venezuela* 124 C5
Ventucopa, *U.S.A.* 111 L7
Ventura, *U.S.A.* 111 L7
Venus B., *Australia* 95 F4
Vera, *Argentina* 126 B3
Vera, *Spain* 39 H3
Veracruz, *Mexico* 119 D5
Veracruz □, *Mexico* 119 D5
Veraval, *India* 68 J4
Verbánia, *Italy* 40 C5
Verbicaro, *Italy* 43 C8
Verbier, *Switz.* 25 J3
Vercelli, *Italy* 40 C5
Verchovchevo, *Ukraine* 33 H8
Vercors △, *France* 21 D9
Verdalsøra, *Norway* 8 E14
Verde ➤, *Argentina* 128 E3
Verde ➤, *Goiás, Brazil* 125 G8
Verde ➤, *Mato Grosso do Sul,
  Brazil* 125 H8
Verde ➤, *Chihuahua, Mexico* . 118 B3
Verde ➤, *Oaxaca, Mexico* ... 119 D5
Verde ➤, *Veracruz, Mexico* .. 118 C4
Verde ➤, *Paraguay* 126 A4
Verde ➤, *U.S.A.* 106 D4
Verde, Cay, *Bahamas* 120 B4
Verde Island Pass, *Phil.* 61 E4
Verden, *Germany* 24 C5
Verdhikoúsa, *Greece* 46 B3
Verdi, *U.S.A.* 110 F7
Verdon △, *France* 21 E10
Verdon ➤, *France* 21 E9
Verdun, *France* 19 C12
Verdun-sur-le-Doubs, *France* . 19 F12
Vereeniging, *S. Africa* 89 D4
Verga, C., *Guinea* 82 C2
Vergara, *Uruguay* 127 C5
Vergato, *Italy* 40 D8
Vergemont Cr. ➤, *Australia* . 94 C3
Vergennes, *U.S.A.* 117 B11
Vergt, *France* 20 C4
Verín, *Spain* 36 D3
Verkhnedvinsk =
  Vyerkhnyadzvinsk, *Belarus* . 32 E4
Verkhnevilyuysk, *Russia* 53 C13
Verkhniy Baskunchak, *Russia* . 35 F8
Verkhovye, *Russia* 33 F9
Verkhoyansk, *Russia* 53 C14
Verkhoyansk Ra. =
  Verkhoyanskiy Khrebet, *Russia* 53 C13
Verkhoyanskiy Khrebet, *Russia* 53 C13
Verlímnion, *France* 19 E10
Vermenton, *France* 19 E10
Vermilion, *Canada* 103 C6
Vermilion, *U.S.A.* 116 E2
Vermilion ➤, *Canada* 103 C6
Vermilion, B., *U.S.A.* 113 L9
Vermilion Bay, *Canada* 103 D10
Vermilion L., *U.S.A.* 112 B8
Vermillion, *U.S.A.* 112 D6
Vermillion ➤, *Canada* 104 C5

Vermont □, *U.S.A.* 117 C12
Vermosh, *Albania* 44 D3
Vernadsky, *Antarctica* 5 C17
Vernal, *U.S.A.* 108 F9
Vernalis, *U.S.A.* 110 H5
Vernazza, *Italy* 40 D6
Verner, *Canada* 104 C3
Verneuil-sur-Avre, *France* 18 D7
Verneukpan, S. Africa* 88 E3
Vernier, *Switz.* 25 J2
Vernon, *Canada* 102 C5
Vernon, *France* 18 C8
Vernon, *U.S.A.* 113 H5
Vernonia, *U.S.A.* 110 E3
Vernouillet, *France* 18 D8
Vero Beach, *U.S.A.* 115 M5
Véroia, *Greece* 44 F6
Véroli, *Italy* 41 G10
Verona, *Canada* 117 B8
Verona, *Italy* 40 C7
Verona, *U.S.A.* 112 D10
Verrès, *Italy* 40 C4
Versailles, *France* 19 D9
Versmold, *Germany* 24 C4
Vert, C., *Senegal* 82 C1
Vertou, *France* 18 E5
Vertus, *France* 19 D11
Verulam, S. Africa* 89 D5
Verviers, *Belgium* 17 D5
Vervins, *France* 19 C10
Veržej, *Slovenia* 41 B13
Verzy, *France* 19 C11
Vescovato, *France* 21 F13
Veselí nad Lužnicí, *Czech Rep.* 26 B7
Veselie, *Bulgaria* 45 D11
Veselovskoye Vdkhr., *Russia* .. 35 G5
Veshenskaya, *Russia* 34 F5
Vesle ➤, *France* 19 C10
Vesoul, *France* 19 E13
Vessigebro, *Sweden* 11 H6
Vesterålen, *Norway* 8 B16
Vestfjorden, *Norway* 8 C15
Vestmannaeyjar, *Iceland* 8 E3
Vestsjællands Amtskommune □,
  Denmark 11 J5
Vestspitsbergen, *Svalbard* 4 B8
Vestvågøy, *Norway* 8 B15
Vesuvio, *Italy* 43 B7
Vesuvius, Mt. = Vesuvio, *Italy* 43 B7
Vesyegonsk, *Russia* 32 C9
Veszprém, *Hungary* 28 C2
Veszprém □, *Hungary* 28 C2
Vésztő, *Hungary* 28 D6
Vetlanda, *Sweden* 11 G9
Vetluga, *Russia* 34 B7
Vetlugu ➤, *Russia* 34 B8
Vetluzhskiy, *Kostroma, Russia* . 34 A7
Vetluzhskiy, *Nizhniy Novgorod,
  Russia* 34 B7
Vetovo, *Bulgaria* 45 C10
Vetralla, *Italy* 41 F9
Vetren, *Bulgaria* 45 D8
Vettore, Mte., *Italy* 41 F10
Veurne, *Belgium* 17 C2
Veveno ➤, *Sudan* 81 F3
Vevey, *Switz.* 25 J2
Vévi, *Greece* 44 F5
Veynes, *France* 21 D9
Veys, *Iran* 71 D6
Vézelay, *France* 19 E10
Vézelise, *France* 19 D13
Vézère ➤, *France* 20 D4
Vezhen, *Bulgaria* 45 D8
Vezzani, *France* 21 F13
Vi Thanh, *Vietnam* 65 H5
Viacha, *Bolivia* 124 G5
Viadana, *Italy* 40 D7
Viamão, *Brazil* 127 C5
Viana, *Brazil* 125 D10
Viana, *Spain* 38 C2
Viana do Alentejo, *Portugal* .. 37 G3
Viana do Bolo, *Spain* 36 C3
Viana do Castelo, *Portugal* ... 36 D2
Viana do Castelo □, *Portugal* . 36 D2
Vianden, *Lux.* 17 E6
Viangchan = Vientiane, *Laos* . 64 D4
Vianópolis, *Brazil* 125 G9
Viar ➤, *Spain* 37 H5
Viaréggio, *Italy* 40 E7
Viaur ➤, *France* 20 D5
Vibble, *Sweden* 11 G12
Vibo Valéntia, *Italy* 43 D9
Viborg, *Denmark* 11 H3
Viborg Amtskommune □,
  Denmark 11 H3
Vibraye, *France* 18 D7
Vic, *Spain* 38 D7
Vic, Étang de, *France* 20 E7
Vic-en-Bigorre, *France* 20 E4
Vic-Fezensac, *France* 20 E4
Vic-le-Comte, *France* 19 G10
Vic-sur-Cère, *France* 20 D6
Vícar, *Spain* 39 J2
Vicenza, *Italy* 41 C8
Vich = Vic, *Spain* 38 D7
Vichada ➤, *Colombia* 124 C5
Vichuga, *Russia* 34 B5
Vichy, *France* 19 F10
Vicksburg, *Ariz., U.S.A.* 111 M13
Vicksburg, *Miss., U.S.A.* 113 J9
Vico, *France* 21 F12
Vico, L. di, *Italy* 41 F9
Vico del Gargano, *Italy* 41 G12
Vicovu de Sus, *Romania* 29 C10
Victor, *India* 68 J4
Victor Harbor, *Australia* 95 F2
Victoria, *Argentina* 126 C3
Victoria, *Canada* 102 D4
Victoria, *Chile* 128 D2

Victoria, *Guinea* 82 C2
Victoria, *Malta* 49 C1
Victoria, *Phil.* 61 D4
Victoria, *Romania* 29 E9
Victoria, *Kans., U.S.A.* 112 F5
Victoria, *Tex., U.S.A.* 113 L6
Victoria □, *Australia* 95 F3
Victoria ➤, *Australia* 92 C4
Victoria, Grand L., *Canada* ... 104 C4
Victoria, L., *Africa* 86 C3
Victoria, L., *Australia* 95 E3
Victoria, Mt., *Burma* 67 J18
Victoria Beach, *Canada* 103 C9
Victoria de Durango = Durango,
  Mexico 118 C4
Victoria de las Tunas, *Cuba* .. 120 B4
Victoria Falls, *Zimbabwe* 87 F2
Victoria Harbour, *Canada* 116 B5
Victoria I., *Canada* 100 A8
Victoria L., *Canada* 105 C8
Victoria Ld., *Antarctica* 5 D11
Victoria Nile ➤, *Uganda* 86 B3
Victoria River, *Australia* 92 C5
Victoria Str., *Canada* 100 B9
Victoria West, S. Africa* 88 E3
Victorias, *Phil.* 61 F5
Victoriaville, *Canada* 105 C5
Victorica, *Argentina* 126 D2
Victorville, *U.S.A.* 111 L9
Vicuña, *Chile* 126 C1
Vicuña Mackenna, *Argentina* . 126 C3
Vidal, *U.S.A.* 111 L12
Vidal Junction, *U.S.A.* 111 L12
Vidalia, *U.S.A.* 115 J4
Vidamlya, *Belarus* 31 F10
Vidauban, *France* 21 E10
Videbæk, *Denmark* 11 H2
Videle, *Romania* 29 F10
Vídho, *Greece* 49 A3
Vidigueira, *Portugal* 37 G3
Vidin, *Bulgaria* 44 C6
Vidisha, *India* 68 H7
Vidra, *Romania* 29 E11
Viduša, *Bos.-H.* 44 D2
Vidzy, *Belarus* 9 J22
Viechtach, *Germany* 25 F8
Viedma, *Argentina* 128 E4
Viedma, L., *Argentina* 128 F2
Vieira do Minho, *Portugal* ... 36 D2
Vielha, *Spain* 38 C5
Viella = Vielha, *Spain* 38 C5
Vielsalm, *Belgium* 17 D5
Vienenburg, *Germany* 24 D6
Vieng Pou Kha, *Laos* 58 G3
Vienna = Wien, *Austria* 27 C9
Vienna, *Ill., U.S.A.* 113 G10
Vienna, *Mo., U.S.A.* 112 F9
Vienne, *France* 21 C8
Vienne □, *France* 20 B4
Vienne ➤, *France* 18 E7
Vientiane, *Laos* 64 D4
Vientos, Paso de los, *Caribbean* 121 C5
Vieques, Isla de, *Puerto Rico* . 121 d
Vierge Pt., *St. Lucia* .... 121 f
Viernheim, *Germany* 25 F4
Viersen, *Germany* 24 D2
Vierwaldstättersee, *Switz.* ... 25 J4
Vierzon, *France* 19 E9
Vieste, *Italy* 41 G13
Vietnam ■, *Asia* 64 C6
Vieux-Boucau-les-Bains, *France* 20 E2
Vieux Fort, *St. Lucia* .... 121 f
Vif, *France* 21 C9
Vigan, *Phil.* 58 G13
Vigévano, *Italy* 40 C5
Vigia, *Brazil* 125 D9
Vigía Chico, *Mexico* 119 D7
Víglas, Ákra, *Greece* 49 D9
Vignemalle, *France* 20 F3
Vigneulles-lès-Hattonchâtel,
  France 19 D12
Vignola, *Italy* 40 D8
Vigo, *Spain* 36 C2
Vigo, Ría de, *Spain* 36 C2
Vigsø Bugt, *Denmark* 11 G2
Vihiers, *France* 18 E6
Vihowa, *Pakistan* 68 D4
Vihowa ➤, *Pakistan* 68 D4
Vijayawada, *India* 67 L12
Vijosë ➤, *Albania* 44 F3
Vík, *Iceland* 8 E4
Vika, *Sweden* 10 D8
Vikarbyn, *Sweden* 10 D9
Vikeke = Viqueque, *E. Timor* . 63 F7
Viken, *Skåne, Sweden* 11 H6
Viken, *Västra Götaland, Sweden* 11 F8
Viking, *Canada* 102 C6
Vikmanshyttan, *Sweden* 10 D9
Vikna, *Norway* 8 D14
Vikos-Aoos △, *Greece* 46 B2
Vila da Maganja, *Mozam.* 87 F4
Vila de Rei, *Portugal* 36 F2
Vila do Bispo, *Portugal* 37 H2
Vila do Conde, *Portugal* 36 D2
Vila Franca de Xira, *Portugal* . 37 G2
Vila Gamito, *Mozam.* 87 E3
Vila Gomes da Costa, *Mozam.* 89 C5
Vila Machado, *Mozam.* 87 F3
Vila Mouzinho, *Mozam.* 87 E3
Vila Nova de Famalicão, *Portugal* 36 D2
Vila Nova de Fos Côa, *Portugal* 36 D3
Vila Nova de Gaia, *Portugal* .. 36 D2
Vila Nova de Ourém, *Portugal* 37 F2
Vila Pouca de Aguiar, *Portugal* 36 D3
Vila Real, *Portugal* 36 D3
Vila Real □, *Portugal* 36 D3
Vila-real de los Infantes, *Spain* 38 F4
Vila Real de Santo António,
  Portugal 37 H3
Vila Vasco da Gama, *Mozam.* . 87 E3
Vila Velha, *Brazil* 127 A7

Vila Viçosa, *Portugal* 37 G3
Vilafranca del Maestrat, *Spain* .. 38 E4
Vilafranca del Penedès, *Spain* .. 38 D6
Vilagarcía de Arousa, *Spain* 36 C2
Vilaine →, *France* 18 E4
Vilanandro, Tanjona, *Madag.* ... 89 B7
Vilanculos, *Mozam.* 89 C6
Vilanova de Castelló, *Spain* 39 F4
Vilanova i la Geltrú, *Spain* 38 D6
Vilar Formosa, *Portugal* 36 E4
Vilaseca, *Spain* 38 D6
Vilaseca-Salou = Vilaseca, *Spain* 38 D6
Vilbjerg, *Denmark* 11 H2
Vilcheka, Zemlya, *Russia* 4 A11
Vilches, *Spain* 37 G7
Vileyka, *Belarus* 32 E4
Vilhelmina, *Sweden* 8 D17
Vilhena, *Brazil* 124 F6
Viliya = Neris →, *Lithuania* 9 J21
Viljandi, *Estonia* 9 G21
Vilkaviškis, *Lithuania* 30 D10
Vilkija, *Lithuania* 30 C10
Vilkitskogo, Proliv, *Russia* 53 B11
Vilkovo = Vylkove, *Ukraine* 29 E14
Villa Abecia, *Bolivia* 126 A2
Villa Ahumada, *Mexico* 118 A3
Villa Ana, *Argentina* 126 B4
Villa Ángela, *Argentina* 126 B3
Villa Bella, *Bolivia* 124 F5
Villa Cañás, *Argentina* 126 C3
Villa Colón, *Argentina* 126 C2
Villa Constitución, *Argentina* ... 126 C3
Villa de María, *Argentina* 126 B3
Villa del Rio, *Spain* 37 H6
Villa Dolores, *Argentina* 126 C2
Villa Frontera, *Mexico* 118 B4
Villa Guillermina, *Argentina* 126 B4
Villa Hayes, *Paraguay* 126 B4
Villa Iris, *Argentina* 126 D3
Villa Juárez, *Mexico* 118 B4
Villa María, *Argentina* 126 C3
Villa Mazán, *Argentina* 126 B2
Villa Minozzo, *Italy* 40 D7
Villa Montes, *Bolivia* 126 A3
Villa Ocampo, *Argentina* 126 B4
Villa Ocampo, *Mexico* 118 B3
Villa Ojo de Agua, *Argentina* ... 126 B3
Villa San Giovanni, *Italy* 43 D8
Villa San José, *Argentina* 126 C4
Villa San Martín, *Argentina* 126 B3
Villa Santina, *Italy* 41 B9
Villa Unión, *Mexico* 118 C3
Villablino, *Spain* 36 C4
Villacarlos, *Spain* 48 B11
Villacarriedo, *Spain* 36 B7
Villacarrillo, *Spain* 37 G7
Villacastín, *Spain* 36 E6
Villach, *Austria* 26 E6
Villacidro, *Italy* 42 C1
Villada, *Spain* 36 C6
Villadiego, *Spain* 36 C6
Villadóssola, *Italy* 40 B5
Villafeliche, *Spain* 38 D3
Villafranca, *Spain* 38 C3
Villafranca de los Barros, *Spain* . 37 G4
Villafranca de los Caballeros,
  Baleares, Spain 48 B10
Villafranca de los Caballeros,
  Toledo, Spain 37 F7
Villafranca del Cid = Vilafranca
  del Maestrat, *Spain* 38 E4
Villafranca del Panadés =
  Vilafranca del Penedès, *Spain* 38 D6
Villafranca di Verona, *Italy* 40 C7
Villafranca Tirrena, *Italy* 43 D8
Villagrán, *Mexico* 119 C5
Villaguay, *Argentina* 126 C4
Villaharta, *Spain* 37 G6
Villahermosa, *Mexico* 119 D6
Villahermosa, *Spain* 39 G2
Villaines-la-Juhel, *France* 18 D6
Villajoyosa, *Spain* 39 G4
Villalba, *Spain* 36 B3
Villalba de Guardo, *Spain* 36 C6
Villalón de Campos, *Spain* 36 C5
Villalpando, *Spain* 36 D5
Villaluenga, *Spain* 36 E7
Villamañán, *Spain* 36 C5
Villamartín, *Spain* 37 J5
Villamayor de Santiago, *Spain* .. 38 F2
Villamblard, *France* 20 C4
Villanova Monteleone, *Italy* 42 B1
Villanueva, *U.S.A.* 113 H2
Villanueva de Castellón =
  Vilanova de Castelló, *Spain* .. 39 F4
Villanueva de Córdoba, *Spain* .. 37 G6
Villanueva de la Fuente, *Spain* .. 39 G2
Villanueva de la Serena, *Spain* . 37 G5
Villanueva de la Sierra, *Spain* .. 36 E4
Villanueva de los Castillejos,
  Spain 37 H3
Villanueva de los Infantes, *Spain* 39 G2
Villanueva del Arzobispo, *Spain* 39 G3
Villanueva del Fresno, *Spain* ... 37 G3
Villanueva y Geltrú = Vilanova i
  la Geltrú, *Spain* 38 D6
Villaputzu, *Italy* 42 C2
Villaquilambre, *Spain* 36 C5
Villar del Arzobispo, *Spain* 38 F4
Villar del Rey, *Spain* 37 F4
Villard-de-Lans, *France* 21 C9
Villarramiel, *Spain* 36 C6
Villarreal = Vila-real de los
  Infantes, *Spain* 38 F4
Villarrica, *Chile* 128 D2
Villarrica, *Paraguay* 126 B4
Villarrobledo, *Spain* 39 F2
Villarroya de la Sierra, *Spain* .. 38 D3
Villarrubia de los Ojos, *Spain* .. 37 F7
Villars-les-Dombes, *France* 19 F12
Villasayas, *Spain* 38 D2

Villaseca de los Gamitos =
  Villaseco de los Gamitos, *Spain* 36 D4
Villaseco de los Gamitos, *Spain* . 36 D4
Villasimíus, *Italy* 42 C2
Villastar, *Spain* 38 E3
Villatobas, *Spain* 36 F7
Villavicencio, *Argentina* 126 C2
Villavicencio, *Colombia* 124 C4
Villaviciosa, *Spain* 36 B5
Villazón, *Bolivia* 126 A2
Ville-Marie, *Canada* 104 C4
Ville Platte, *U.S.A.* 113 K8
Villedieu-les-Poêles, *France* 18 D5
Villefort, *France* 20 D7
Villefranche-de-Lauragais, *France* 20 E5
Villefranche-de-Rouergue, *France* 20 D6
Villefranche-du-Périgord, *France* 20 D5
Villefranche-sur-Saône, *France* . 21 C8
Villel, *Spain* 38 E3
Villemur-sur-Tarn, *France* 20 E5
Villena, *Spain* 39 G4
Villenauxe-la-Grande, *France* ... 19 D10
Villenave-d'Ornon, *France* 20 D3
Villeneuve-d'Ascq, *France* 19 B10
Villeneuve-l'Archevêque, *France* 19 D10
Villeneuve-lès-Avignon, *France* . 21 E8
Villeneuve-sur-Allier, *France* ... 19 F10
Villeneuve-sur-Lot, *France* 20 D4
Villeneuve-sur-Yonne, *France* ... 19 D10
Villeréal, *France* 20 D4
Villers-Bocage, *France* 18 C6
Villers-Cotterêts, *France* 19 C10
Villers-sur-Mer, *France* 18 C6
Villersexel, *France* 19 E13
Villerupt, *France* 19 C12
Villeurbanne, *France* 21 C8
Villiers, *S. Africa* 89 D4
Villingen-Schwenningen,
  Germany 25 G4
Villmanstrand = Lappeenranta,
  Finland 9 F23
Vilna, *Canada* 102 C6
Vilnius, *Lithuania* 9 J21
Vils, *Austria* 26 D3
Vils →, *Bayern, Germany* 25 G9
Vils →, *Bayern, Germany* 25 F7
Vilsbiburg, *Germany* 25 G8
Vilshofen, *Germany* 25 G9
Vilusi, *Serbia & M.* 44 D2
Vilvoorde, *Belgium* 17 D4
Vilyuy →, *Russia* 53 C13
Vilyuysk, *Russia* 53 C13
Vimianzo, *Spain* 36 B1
Vimioso, *Portugal* 36 D4
Vimmerby, *Sweden* 11 G9
Vimoutiers, *France* 18 D7
Vimperk, *Czech Rep.* 26 B6
Viña del Mar, *Chile* 126 C1
Vinarós, *Spain* 38 E5
Vincennes, *U.S.A.* 114 F2
Vincent, *U.S.A.* 111 L8
Vinchina, *Argentina* 126 B2
Vindelälven →, *Sweden* 8 E18
Vindeln, *Sweden* 8 D18
Vinderup, *Denmark* 11 H2
Vindhya Ra., *India* 68 H7
Vineland, *U.S.A.* 114 F8
Vineuil, *France* 18
Vinga, *Romania* 28 D6
Vingåker, *Sweden* 10 E9
Vinh, *Vietnam* 64 C5
Vinh Linh, *Vietnam* 64 D6
Vinh Long, *Vietnam* 65 G5
Vinh Yen, *Vietnam* 58 G5
Vinhais, *Portugal* 36 D3
Vinica, *Croatia* 41 B13
Vinica, *Macedonia* 44 E6
Vinica, *Slovenia* 41 C12
Vinita, *U.S.A.* 113 G7
Vinkovci, *Croatia* 28 E3
Vinnitsa = Vinnytsya, *Ukraine* . 33 H5
Vinnytsya, *Ukraine* 33 H5
Vinslöv, *Sweden* 11 H7
Vinson Massif, *Antarctica* 5 D16
Vintjärn, *Sweden* 10 D10
Vinton, Calif., *U.S.A.* 110 F6
Vinton, Iowa, *U.S.A.* 112 D8
Vinton, La., *U.S.A.* 113 K8
Vințu de Jos, *Romania* 29 D8
Viöl, *Germany* 24 A5
Viqueque, *E. Timor* 63 F7
Vir, *Croatia* 41 D12
Virachey, *Cambodia* 64 F6
Virachey Δ, *Cambodia* 64 E6
Virago Sd., *Canada* 102 C2
Viramgam, *India* 68 H5
Viranşehir, *Turkey* 70 B3
Virawah, *Pakistan* 68 G4
Virbalis, *Lithuania* 30 D9
Virden, *Canada* 103 D8
Vire, *France* 18 D6
Vire →, *France* 18 C5
Vírgenes, C., *Argentina* 128 G3
Virgin →, *U.S.A.* 109 H6
Virgin Gorda, *Br. Virgin Is.* ... 121 e
Virgin Is. (British) ☑, *W. Indies* 121 e
Virgin Is. (U.S.) ☑, *W. Indies* . 121 e
Virgin Islands Δ, *U.S. Virgin Is.* 121 C7
Virginia, *S. Africa* 88 D4
Virginia, *U.S.A.* 112 B8
Virginia ☐, *U.S.A.* 114 G7
Virginia Beach, *U.S.A.* 114 G8
Virginia City, Mont., *U.S.A.* .. 108 D8
Virginia City, Nev., *U.S.A.* ... 110 F7
Virginia Falls, *Canada* 102 A3
Virginiatown, *Canada* 104 C4
Virje, *Croatia* 41 B13
Viroqua, *U.S.A.* 112 D9
Virovitica, *Croatia* 28 E2

Virpazar, *Serbia & M.* 44 D3
Virpur, *India* 68 J4
Virserum, *Sweden* 11 G9
Virton, *Belgium* 17 E5
Virudunagar, *India* 66 Q10
Virunga Δ, *Dem. Rep. of*
  the Congo 86 B2
Vis, *Croatia* 41 E13
Visalia, *U.S.A.* 110 J7
Visayan Sea, *Phil.* 61 F5
Visby, *Sweden* 11 G12
Viscount Melville Sd., *Canada* . 98 B9
Visé, *Belgium* 17 D5
Višegrad, *Bos.-H.* 44 C3
Viseu, *Brazil* 125 D9
Viseu, *Portugal* 36 E3
Viseu ☐, *Portugal* 36 E3
Vişeu de Sus, *Romania* 29 C9
Vishakhapatnam, *India* 67 L13
Vişina, *Romania* 29 G9
Vişineşti, *Moldova* 29 D13
Visingsö, *Sweden* 11 F8
Viskafors, *Sweden* 11 G6
Viskan →, *Sweden* 11 G6
Viški Kanal, *Croatia* 41 E13
Vislanda, *Sweden* 11 H8
Visnagar, *India* 68 H5
Višnja Gora, *Slovenia* 41 C11
Viso, Mte., *Italy* 40 D4
Viso del Marqués, *Spain* 37 G7
Visoko, *Bos.-H.* 28 G3
Visokoi I., *Antarctica* 5 B1
Visp, *Switz.* 25 J3
Vissefjärda, *Sweden* 11 H9
Visselhövede, *Germany* 24 C5
Vissenbjerg, *Denmark* 11 J4
Vista, *U.S.A.* 111 M9
Vistonikos, Ormos = Vistonís,
  Límni, *Greece* 45 E9
Vistonís, Límni, *Greece* 45 E9
Vistula = Wisła →, *Poland* 30 D5
Vit →, *Bulgaria* 45 C8
Vitanje, *Slovenia* 41 B12
Vitebsk = Vitsyebsk, *Belarus* .. 32 E6
Viterbo, *Italy* 41 F9
Vitez, *Bos.-H.* 28 F2
Viti Levu, *Fiji* 91 C7
Vitigudino, *Spain* 36 D4
Vitim, *Russia* 53 D12
Vitim →, *Russia* 53 D12
Vitina, *Bos.-H.* 41 E14
Vitina, *Greece* 46 D4
Vítkov, *Czech Rep.* 27 B10
Vitória, *Brazil* 125 H10
Vitória da Conquista, *Brazil* ... 125 F10
Vitória de São Antão, *Brazil* .. 125 E11
Vitoria-Gasteiz, *Spain* 38 C2
Vitosha Δ, *Bulgaria* 44 D7
Vitré, *France* 18 D5
Vitry-le-François, *France* 19 D11
Vitry-sur-Seine, *France* 19 D9
Vitsand, *Sweden* 10 D7
Vitsi, Óros, *Greece* 44 F5
Vitsyebsk, *Belarus* 32 E6
Vittangi, *Sweden* 11 H7
Vitteaux, *France* 19 E11
Vittel, *France* 19 D12
Vittória, *Italy* 43 F7
Vittório Véneto, *Italy* 41 C9
Vittsjö, *Sweden* 11 H7
Viveiro, *Spain* 36 B3
Vivian, *U.S.A.* 113 J8
Viviers, *France* 21 D8
Vivonne, *France* 20 B4
Vizcaíno, Desierto de, *Mexico* . 118 B2
Vizcaíno, Sierra, *Mexico* 118 B2
Vizcaya ☐, *Spain* 38 B2
Vize, *Turkey* 45 E11
Vizianagaram, *India* 67 K13
Vizille, *France* 21 C9
Viziñada, *Croatia* 41 C10
Viziru, *Romania* 29 E12
Vizzini, *Italy* 43 E7
Vlaardingen, *Neths.* 17 C4
Vlădeasa, Vf., *Romania* 28 D7
Vladičin Han, *Serbia & M.* 44 D6
Vladikavkaz, *Russia* 35 J7
Vladimir, *Russia* 32 D11
Vladimir Volynskiy = Volodymyr-
  Volynskyy, *Ukraine* 33 G3
Vladimirci, *Serbia & M.* 44 B3
Vladimirovac, *Serbia & M.* 28 E5
Vladimirovka, *Russia* 35 F8
Vladimirovo, *Bulgaria* 44 C7
Vladimorka, *Kazakhstan* 34 E10
Vladislavovka, *Ukraine* 33 K8
Vladivostok, *Russia* 53 E14
Vlăhița, *Romania* 29 D10
Vlakhiótis, *Greece* 46 E4
Vlasenica, *Bos.-H.* 28 F3
Vlašić, *Bos.-H.* 28 F2

Vohibinany, *Madag.* 89 B8
Vohilava, *Madag.* 89 C8
Vohimarina = Iharana, *Madag.* . 89 A9
Vohimena, Tanjon' i, *Madag.* .. 89 D8
Vohipeno, *Madag.* 89 C8
Voi, *Kenya* 86 C4
Void-Vacon, *France* 19 D12
Voinești, Iași, *Romania* 29 C12
Voinești, Prahova, *Romania* ... 29 E10
Voiótía ☐, *Greece* 46 C5
Voiron, *France* 21 C9
Voisey B., *Canada* 105 A7
Voitsberg, *Austria* 26 D8
Vojens, *Denmark* 11 J3
Vojmsjön, *Sweden* 8 D17
Vojnić, *Croatia* 41 C12
Vojnik, *Italy* 41 B12
Vojvodina ☐, *Serbia & M.* 28 E5
Volary, *Czech Rep.* 26 C6
Volborg, *U.S.A.* 112 C2
Volcán de Colima Δ, *Mexico* .. 118 D4
Volcano Is. = Kazan-Rettō,
  Pac. Oc. 96 E6
Volcans, *Rwanda* 86 C2
Volcans d'Auvergne ☐, *France* . 20 C6
Volchansk = Vovchansk, *Ukraine* 33 G9
Volchya →, *Ukraine* 33 H8
Volda, *Norway* 9 E12
Volga →, *Privolzhskiy ☐, Russia* 34 B10
Volga, *Russia* 32 C10
Volga →, *Russia* 35 G9
Volga Hts. = Privolzhskaya
  Vozvyshennost, *Russia* 34 E7
Volgo-Baltiyskiy Kanal, *Russia* . 32 B9
Volgo-Donskoy Kanal, *Russia* . 35 F7
Volgodonsk, *Russia* 35 G6
Volgograd, *Russia* 35 F7
Volgogradskoye Vdkhr., *Russia* . 34 E8
Volgorechensk, *Russia* 34 B5
Volímai, *Greece* 46 D2
Volintiri, *Moldova* 29 D14
Volissós, *Greece* 47 C7
Volkach, *Germany* 25 F6
Völkermarkt, *Austria* 26 E7
Volkhov, *Russia* 32 C7
Volkhov →, *Russia* 32 B7
Völklingen, *Germany* 25 F2
Volkovysk = Vawkavysk, *Belarus* 33 F3
Volksrust, *S. Africa* 89 D4
Volnansk, *Ukraine* 33 H8
Volnovakha, *Ukraine* 33 J9
Volochanka, *Russia* 53 B10
Volodarsk, *Russia* 34 B6
Volodymyr-Volynskyy, *Ukraine* . 33 G3
Vologda, *Russia* 32 C10
Volokolamsk, *Russia* 32 D8
Volokonovka, *Russia* 33 G9
Vólos, *Greece* 46 B4
Volosovo, *Russia* 32 C5
Volovets, *Ukraine* 29 B8
Volovo, *Russia* 32 F10
Volozhin = Valozhyn, *Belarus* .. 32 E4
Volsk, *Russia* 34 D8
Volta ☐, *Ghana* 83 D5
Volta →, *Ghana* 83 D5
Volta, L., *Ghana* 83 D5
Volta Blanche = White Volta →,
  Ghana 83 D4
Volta Redonda, *Brazil* 127 A7
Voltaire, C., *Australia* 92 B4
Volterra, *Italy* 40 E7
Voltri, *Italy* 40 D5
Volturno →, *Italy* 42 A6
Vólvi, L., *Greece* 44 F7
Volyně, *Czech Rep.* 26 B6
Volzhsk, *Russia* 34 C9
Volzhskiy, *Russia* 35 F7
Vondrozo, *Madag.* 89 C8
Vónitsa, *Greece* 46 C2
Vopnafjörður, *Iceland* 8 D6
Vorarlberg ☐, *Austria* 26 D2
Vóras Óros, *Greece* 44 F5
Vorbasse, *Denmark* 11 J3
Vorchdorf, *Austria* 26 C6
Vorderrhein →, *Switz.* 25 J5
Vordingborg, *Denmark* 11 J5
Vorë, *Albania* 44 E3
Voreio Aigaío = Vórios
  Aiyaíon ☐, *Greece* 47 C7
Voreppe, *France* 21 C9
Vóriai Sporádhes, *Greece* 46 B5
Vórios Aiyaíon ☐, *Greece* 47 C7
Vórios Evvoïkos Kólpos, *Greece* 46 C5
Vorkuta, *Russia* 52 C7
Vormsi, *Estonia* 9 G20
Vóroi, *Greece* 49 F6
Vorona →, *Russia* 34 E6
Voronezh, *Russia* 33 G10
Voronezh, *Ukraine* 33 G7
Voronezh →, *Russia* 33 G10
Vorontsovo-Aleksandrovskoye =
  Zelenokumsk, *Russia* 35 H6
Vorpommersche
  Boddenlandschaft Δ, *Germany* 24 A8
Vorskla →, *Ukraine* 33 H8
Võrts Järv, *Estonia* 9 G22
Võru, *Estonia* 9 H22

Vouzela, *Portugal* 36 E2
Vouziers, *France* 19 C11
Vovchansk, *Ukraine* 33 G9
Vowchyn, *Belarus* 31 F10
Voyageurs ☐, *U.S.A.* 112 A8
Vozhe, Ozero, *Russia* 32 B10
Vozhega, *Russia* 32 B11
Voznesensk, *Ukraine* 33 J6
Voznesenye, *Russia* 32 B8
Vrå, *Denmark* 11 G3
Vráble, *Slovak Rep.* 27 C11
Vračevšnica, *Serbia & M.* 44 B4
Vrakhnéíka, *Greece* 46 C3
Vrancea ☐, *Romania* 29 E11
Vrancei, Munții, *Romania* 29 E11
Vrangelya, Ostrov, *Russia* 53 B19
Vranica, *Bos.-H.* 28 G2
Vranje, *Serbia & M.* 44 D5
Vranjska Banja, *Serbia & M.* .. 44 D6
Vranov nad Topl'ou, *Slovak Rep.* 27 C14
Vransko, *Slovenia* 41 B11
Vransko Jezero, *Croatia* 41 E12
Vrapčište, *Macedonia* 44 E4
Vratsa, *Bulgaria* 44 C7
Vrbas, *Serbia & M.* 28 E4
Vrbas →, *Bos.-H.* 28 E2
Vrbnik, *Croatia* 41 C11
Vrbovec, *Croatia* 41 C13
Vrbovsko, *Croatia* 41 C12
Vrchlabí, *Czech Rep.* 26 A8
Vrede, *S. Africa* 89 D4
Vredefort, *S. Africa* 88 D4
Vreden, *Germany* 24 C2
Vredenburg, *S. Africa* 88 E2
Vredendal, *S. Africa* 88 E2
Vretstorp, *Sweden* 10 E8
Vrgorac, *Croatia* 41 E14
Vrhnika, *Slovenia* 41 C11
Vríði, *Ivory C.* 82 D4
Vrigstad, *Sweden* 11 G8
Vrindavan, *India* 68 F7
Vríses, *Greece* 49 D6
Vrnograč, *Bos.-H.* 41 C12
Vrondádhes, *Greece* 47 C8
Vrpolje, *Croatia* 28 E3
Vršac, *Serbia & M.* 28 E6
Vrsacki Kanal, *Serbia & M.* ... 28 E5
Vrútky, *Slovak Rep.* 27 B11
Vryburg, *S. Africa* 88 D3
Vryheid, *S. Africa* 89 D5
Vsetín, *Czech Rep.* 27 B11
Vu Liet, *Vietnam* 64 C5
Vúcha →, *Bulgaria* 45 D8
Vučitrn, *Serbia & M.* 44 D4
Vukovar, *Croatia* 28 E3
Vulcan, *Canada* 102 C6
Vulcan, *Romania* 29 E8
Vulcanești, *Moldova* 29 E13
Vulcano, *Italy* 43 D7
Vâlchedruma, *Bulgaria* 44 C7
Vulkaneshty = Vulcanești,
  Moldova 29 E13
Vunduzi →, *Mozam.* 87 F3
Vung Tau, *Vietnam* 65 G6
Vûrbitsa, *Bulgaria* 45 D10
Vurshets, *Bulgaria* 44 C7
Vutcani, *Romania* 29 D12
Vuya, *Sudan* 81 F2
Vuzlove, *Ukraine* 28 B7
Vwaza Δ, *Malawi* 87 E3
Vyartsilya, *Russia* 32 A6
Vyatka = Kirov, *Russia* 52 D5
Vyatka →, *Russia* 34 C10
Vyatskiye Polyany, *Russia* 34 B10
Vyazemskiy, *Russia* 53 E14
Vyazma, *Russia* 32 E8
Vyazniki, *Russia* 34 B6
Vyborg, *Russia* 32 B5
Vychegda →, *Russia* 52 C5
Vychodné Beskydy, *Europe* ... 27 B15
Vyerkhnyadzvinsk, *Belarus* 32 E4
Vyhoda, *Ukraine* 29 B8
Vyksa, *Russia* 34 C6
Vylkove, *Ukraine* 29 E14
Vylok, *Ukraine* 28 B7
Vynohradiv, *Ukraine* 28 B8
Vyrnwy, L., *U.K.* 14 E4
Vyshkiv, *Ukraine* 29 B8
Vyshkove, *Ukraine* 28 B8
Vyshniy Volochek, *Russia* 32 D8
Vyshza = imeni 26 Bakinskikh
  Komissarov, *Turkmenistan* .. 71 B7
Vyškov, *Czech Rep.* 27 B9
Vysokaye, *Belarus* 31 F10
Vysoké Mýto, *Czech Rep.* 27 B9
Vysokovsk, *Russia* 32 D9
Vyšší Brod, *Czech Rep.* 26 C7
Vytegra, *Russia* 32 B9
Vyzhnytsya, *Ukraine* 29 B10
Vyzhnytsya Δ, *Ukraine* 29 B10

W

W du Benin Δ, *Benin* 83 C5
W du Burkina Faso Δ,
  Burkina Faso 83 C4
W du Niger Δ, *Niger* 83 C5
W.A.C. Bennett Dam, *Canada* . 102 B4
Wa, *Ghana* 82 C4
Waal →, *Neths.* 17 C5
Waalwijk, *Neths.* 17 C5
Waat, *Sudan* 81 F3
Wabakimi Δ, *Canada* 104 B2
Wabana, *Canada* 105 C9
Wabasca →, *Canada* 102 B5
Wabasca-Desmarais, *Canada* .. 102 B6
Wabash, *U.S.A.* 114 E3
Wabash →, *U.S.A.* 114 G1

Wabi →, Ethiopia	81	F5
Wabigoon L., Canada	103	D10
Wabowden, Canada	103	C9
Wąbrzeźno, Poland	31	E5
Wabu Hu, China	59	A11
Wabuk Pt., Canada	104	A2
Wabush, Canada	105	B6
Wąchock, Poland	31	G8
Wächtersbach, Germany	25	E5
Waco, U.S.A.	113	K6
Waconichi, L., Canada	104	B5
Wad Ban Naqa, Sudan	81	D3
Wad Banda, Sudan	81	E2
Wad el Haddad, Sudan	81	E3
Wad en Nau, Sudan	81	E3
Wad Hamid, Sudan	81	D3
Wad Medanî, Sudan	81	E3
Wad Thana, Pakistan	68	F2
Wadai, Africa	76	E5
Wadayama, Japan	55	G7
Waddeneilanden, Neths.	17	A5
Waddenzee, Neths.	17	A5
Waddi, Chappal, Nigeria	83	D7
Waddington, U.K.	117	B9
Waddington, Mt., Canada	102	C3
Waddy Pt., Australia	95	C5
Wadebridge, U.K.	15	G3
Wadena, Canada	103	C8
Wadena, U.S.A.	112	B7
Wädenswil, Switz.	25	H4
Wadern, Germany	25	F2
Wadeye, Australia	92	B4
Wadhams, Canada	102	C3
Wâdî as Sîr, Jordan	74	D4
Wadi Gemâl, Egypt	80	C4
Wadi Halfa, Sudan	80	C3
Wadi Rum △, Jordan	74	F4
Wadian, China	59	A9
Wadlew, Poland	31	G6
Wadowice, Poland	31	J6
Wadsworth, Nev., U.S.A.	108	G4
Wadsworth, Ohio, U.S.A.	116	E3
Waegwan, S. Korea	57	G15
Wafangdian, China	57	E11
Wafrah, Si. Arabia	70	D5
Wageningen, Neths.	17	C5
Wager B., Canada	101	B11
Wagga Wagga, Australia	95	F4
Waghete, Indonesia	63	E9
Wagin, Australia	93	F2
Wagner, U.S.A.	112	D5
Wagon Mound, U.S.A.	113	G2
Wagoner, U.S.A.	113	H7
Wagrowiec, Poland	31	F4
Wah, Pakistan	68	C5
Wahai, Indonesia	63	E7
Wahiawa, U.S.A.	106	H15
Wâḩid, Egypt	74	E1
Wahnai, Afghan.	68	C1
Wahni, Ethiopia	81	E4
Wahoo, U.S.A.	112	E6
Wahpeton, U.S.A.	112	B6
Waiau →, N.Z.	91	K4
Waibeem, Indonesia	63	E8
Waiblingen, Germany	25	G5
Waidhofen an der Thaya, Austria	26	C8
Waidhofen an der Ybbs, Austria	26	D7
Waigeo, Indonesia	63	E8
Waihi, N.Z.	91	G5
Waihou →, N.Z.	91	G5
Waika, Dem. Rep. of the Congo	86	C2
Waikabubak, Indonesia	63	F5
Waikaremoana, L., N.Z.	91	H6
Waikari, N.Z.	91	K4
Waikato →, N.Z.	91	G5
Waikerie, Australia	95	E3
Waikokopu, N.Z.	91	H6
Waikouaiti, N.Z.	91	L3
Wailuku, U.S.A.	106	H16
Waimakariri →, N.Z.	91	K4
Waimate, N.Z.	91	L3
Wainganga →, India	66	K11
Waingapu, Indonesia	63	F6
Waini →, Guyana	124	B7
Wainwright, Canada	103	C6
Waiouru, N.Z.	91	H5
Waipara, N.Z.	91	K4
Waipawa, N.Z.	91	H6
Waipiro, N.Z.	91	H7
Waipoua Forest, N.Z.	91	F4
Waipu, N.Z.	91	F5
Waipukurau, N.Z.	91	J6
Wairakei, N.Z.	91	H6
Wairarapa, L., N.Z.	91	J5
Wairoa, N.Z.	91	H6
Waitaki →, N.Z.	91	L3
Waitangi, N.Z.	91	F5
Waitara, N.Z.	91	H5
Waitomo Caves, N.Z.	91	H5
Waitsburg, U.S.A.	108	C5
Waiuku, N.Z.	91	G5
Wajima, Japan	55	F8
Wajir, Kenya	86	B5
Waka, Ethiopia	81	F4
Wakasa, Japan	55	G7
Wakasa-Wan, Japan	55	G7
Wakatipu, L., N.Z.	91	L2
Wakaw, Canada	103	C7
Wakayama, Japan	55	G7
Wakayama □, Japan	55	H7
Wake Forest, U.S.A.	115	H6
Wake I., Pac. Oc.	96	F8
WaKeeney, U.S.A.	112	F5
Wakefield, Jamaica	120	a
Wakefield, N.Z.	91	J4
Wakefield, U.K.	14	D6
Wakefield, Mass., U.S.A.	117	D13
Wakefield, Mich., U.S.A.	112	B10
Wakkanai, Japan	54	B10
Wakkerstroom, S. Africa	89	D5
Wakool, Australia	95	F3
Wakool →, Australia	95	F3

Wakre, Indonesia	63	E8
Wakuach, L., Canada	105	A6
Walamba, Zambia	87	E2
Wałbrzych, Poland	31	H3
Walbury Hill, U.K.	15	F6
Walcha, Australia	95	E5
Walcheren, Neths.	17	C3
Walcott, U.S.A.	108	F10
Waldbröl, Germany	24	E3
Waldeck, Germany	24	D5
Walden, Colo., U.S.A.	108	F10
Walden, N.Y., U.S.A.	117	E10
Waldkirch, Germany	25	G3
Waldkirchen, Germany	25	G9
Waldkraiburg, Germany	25	G8
Waldport, U.S.A.	108	D1
Waldron, U.S.A.	113	H7
Waldviertel, Austria	26	C8
Walebing, Australia	93	F2
Walembele, Ghana	82	C4
Walensee, Switz.	25	H5
Wales □, U.K.	15	E3
Walewale, Ghana	83	C4
Walgett, Australia	95	E4
Walgreen Coast, Antarctica	5	D15
Walker, U.S.A.	112	B7
Walker, L., Canada	105	B6
Walker L., Canada	103	C9
Walker L., U.S.A.	108	G4
Walkerston, Australia	94	K7
Walkerton, Canada	116	B3
Wall, U.S.A.	112	D3
Walla Walla, U.S.A.	108	C4
Wallace, Idaho, U.S.A.	108	C6
Wallace, N.C., U.S.A.	115	H7
Wallaceburg, Canada	116	D2
Wallachia = Valahia, Romania	29	F9
Wallal, Australia	95	D4
Wallam Cr. →, Australia	95	D4
Wallambin, L., Australia	93	F2
Wallangarra, Australia	95	D5
Wallaroo, Australia	95	E2
Walldürn, Germany	25	F5
Wallenhorst, Germany	24	C4
Wallenpaupack, L., U.S.A.	117	E9
Wallingford, U.S.A.	117	E12
Wallis & Futuna, Is., Pac. Oc.	96	J11
Wallowa, U.S.A.	108	D5
Wallowa Mts., U.S.A.	108	D5
Walls, U.K.	13	A7
Walls of Jerusalem △, Australia	95	G4
Wallula, U.S.A.	108	C4
Wallumbilla, Australia	95	D4
Walmsley, L., Canada	103	A7
Walney, I. of, U.K.	14	C4
Walnut Canyon △, U.S.A.	109	J8
Walnut Creek, U.S.A.	110	H4
Walnut Ridge, U.S.A.	113	G9
Walpole, Australia	93	F2
Walpole, U.S.A.	117	D13
Wals, Austria	26	D5
Walsall, U.K.	15	E6
Walsenburg, U.S.A.	113	G2
Walsh, U.S.A.	113	G3
Walsh →, Australia	94	B3
Walsrode, Germany	24	C5
Walterboro, U.S.A.	115	J5
Walters, U.S.A.	113	H5
Waltershausen, Germany	24	E6
Waltham, U.S.A.	117	D13
Waltman, U.S.A.	108	E10
Walton, U.S.A.	117	D9
Walton-on-the-Naze, U.K.	15	F9
Walvis Bay, Namibia	88	C1
Walvisbaai = Walvis Bay, Namibia	88	C1
Wamba, Dem. Rep. of the Congo	86	B2
Wamba, Kenya	86	B4
Wamba, Nigeria	83	D6
Wamego, U.S.A.	112	F6
Wamena, Indonesia	63	E9
Wamsutter, U.S.A.	108	F9
Wamulan, Indonesia	63	E7
Wan Xian, China	56	E8
Wana, Pakistan	68	C3
Wanaaring, Australia	95	D3
Wanaka, N.Z.	91	L2
Wanaka, L., N.Z.	91	L2
Wan'an, China	59	D10
Wanapitei L., Canada	104	C3
Wandel Sea = McKinley Sea, Arctic	4	A7
Wandérama, Ivory C.	82	D4
Wanderer, Zimbabwe	87	F3
Wandhari, Pakistan	68	F2
Wanding, China	58	E2
Wandoan, Australia	95	D4
Wanfu, China	57	D12
Wang →, Thailand	64	D2
Wang Kai, Sudan	81	F2
Wang Noi, Thailand	64	E3
Wang Saphung, Thailand	64	D3
Wang Thong, Thailand	64	D3
Wanga, Dem. Rep. of the Congo	86	B2
Wangal, Indonesia	63	F8
Wanganella, Australia	95	F3
Wanganui, N.Z.	91	H5
Wangaratta, Australia	95	F4
Wangary, Australia	95	E2
Wangcang, China	58	A6
Wangcheng, China	59	C9
Wangdu, China	56	E8
Wangen, Germany	25	H5
Wangerooge, Germany	24	B3
Wangiwangi, Indonesia	63	F6
Wangjiang, China	59	B11
Wangmo, China	58	E6
Wangolodougou, Ivory C.	82	D3
Wangqing, China	57	C15
Wankaner, India	68	H4

Wanless, Canada	103	C8
Wanneroo, Australia	93	F2
Wannian, China	59	C11
Wanning, China	64	C8
Wanon Niwat, Thailand	64	D4
Wanquan, China	56	D8
Wanrong, China	56	G6
Wanshan, China	58	D7
Wanshengchang, China	58	C6
Wantage, U.K.	15	F6
Wanxian, China	58	B7
Wanyuan, China	58	A7
Wanzai, China	59	C10
Wapakoneta, U.S.A.	114	E3
Wapato, U.S.A.	108	C3
Wapawekka L., Canada	103	C8
Wapikopa L., Canada	104	B2
Wapiti →, Canada	102	B5
Wappingers Falls, U.S.A.	117	E11
Wapsipinicon →, U.S.A.	112	E9
Wapusk △, Canada	103	B10
Warab □, Sudan	81	F2
Warangal, India	66	L11
Waraseoni, India	69	J9
Waratah, Australia	95	G4
Waratah B., Australia	95	F4
Warburg, Germany	24	D5
Warburton, Vic., Australia	95	F4
Warburton, W. Austral., Australia	93	E4
Warburton, The →, Australia	95	D2
Warburton Ra., Australia	93	E4
Ward, N.Z.	91	J5
Ward →, Australia	95	D4
Ward Mt., U.S.A.	110	H8
Warden, S. Africa	89	D4
Wardha, India	66	J11
Wardha →, India	66	K11
Ware, Canada	102	B3
Ware, U.K.	15	F8
Ware, U.S.A.	117	D12
Waregem, Belgium	17	D3
Wareham, U.S.A.	117	E14
Waremme, Belgium	17	D5
Waren, Germany	24	B8
Warendorf, Germany	24	D4
Warialda, Australia	95	D5
Wariap, Indonesia	63	E8
Warin Chamrap, Thailand	64	E5
Warka, Poland	31	G8
Warkopi, Indonesia	63	E8
Warm Springs, U.S.A.	109	G5
Warman, Canada	103	C7
Warmbad = Bela Bela, S. Africa	89	C4
Warmbad, Namibia	88	D2
Warmińsko-Mazurskie □, Poland	30	D8
Warminster, U.K.	15	F5
Warminster, U.S.A.	117	F9
Warnemünde, Germany	24	A8
Warner Mts., U.S.A.	108	F3
Warner Robins, U.S.A.	115	J4
Warnow →, Germany	24	A8
Waroona, Australia	93	F2
Warracknabeal, Australia	95	F3
Warragul, Australia	95	F4
Warrego →, Australia	95	E4
Warrego Ra., Australia	94	C4
Warren, Australia	95	E4
Warren, Ark., U.S.A.	113	J8
Warren, Mich., U.S.A.	114	D4
Warren, Minn., U.S.A.	112	A6
Warren, Ohio, U.S.A.	116	E4
Warren, Pa., U.S.A.	116	E5
Warrenpoint, U.K.	12	B5
Warrensburg, Mo., U.S.A.	112	F8
Warrensburg, N.Y., U.S.A.	117	C11
Warrenton, S. Africa	88	D3
Warrenton, U.S.A.	110	D3
Warri, Nigeria	83	D6
Warrina, Australia	95	D2
Warrington, U.K.	14	D5
Warrington, U.S.A.	115	K2
Warrington □, U.K.	14	D5
Warrnambool, Australia	95	F3
Warroad, U.S.A.	112	A7
Warruwi, Australia	94	A1
Warsa, Indonesia	63	E9
Warsak Dam, Pakistan	68	B4
Warsaw = Warszawa, Poland	31	F8
Warsaw, Ind., U.S.A.	114	E3
Warsaw, N.Y., U.S.A.	116	D6
Warsaw, Ohio, U.S.A.	116	F3
Warstein, Germany	24	D4
Warszawa, Poland	31	F8
Warszawa ✈ (WAW), Poland	31	F7
Warta, Poland	31	G5
Warta →, Poland	31	F1
Warthe = Warta →, Poland	31	F1
Waru, Indonesia	63	E8
Warwick, Australia	95	D5
Warwick, U.K.	15	E6
Warwick, N.Y., U.S.A.	117	E10
Warwick, R.I., U.S.A.	117	E13
Warwickshire □, U.K.	15	E6
Wasaga Beach, Canada	116	B4
Wasagaming, Canada	103	C9
Wasatch Ra., U.S.A.	108	F8
Wasbank, S. Africa	89	D5
Wasco, Calif., U.S.A.	111	K7
Wasco, Oreg., U.S.A.	108	D3
Wase, Nigeria	83	D6
Waseca, U.S.A.	112	C8
Wasekamio L., Canada	103	B7
Wash, The, U.K.	14	E8
Washago, Canada	116	B5
Washburn, N. Dak., U.S.A.	112	B4
Washburn, Wis., U.S.A.	112	B9
Washim, India	66	J10
Washington, U.K.	14	C6
Washington, D.C., U.S.A.	114	F7
Washington, Ga., U.S.A.	115	J4
Washington, Ind., U.S.A.	114	F2
Washington, Iowa, U.S.A.	112	E9

Washington, Mo., U.S.A.	112	F9
Washington, N.C., U.S.A.	115	H7
Washington, N.J., U.S.A.	117	F10
Washington, Pa., U.S.A.	116	F4
Washington, Utah, U.S.A.	109	H7
Washington □, U.S.A.	108	C3
Washington, Mt., U.S.A.	117	B13
Washington Court House, U.S.A.	114	F4
Washington I., U.S.A.	114	C2
Washougal, U.S.A.	110	E4
Washpool △, Australia	95	D5
Wasian, Indonesia	63	E8
Wasilków, Poland	31	E10
Wasilla, U.S.A.	100	B5
Wasior, Indonesia	63	E8
Wāsiṭ □, Iraq	70	C5
Waskaganish, Canada	104	B4
Waskaiowaka, L., Canada	103	B9
Waskesiu Lake, Canada	103	C7
Wasserburg, Germany	25	G8
Wasserkuppe, Germany	24	E5
Wassy, France	19	D11
Waswanipi, Canada	104	C4
Waswanipi, L., Canada	104	C4
Watampone, Indonesia	63	E6
Watamu, Kenya	86	C5
Watarrka △, Australia	92	D5
Water Park Pt., Australia	94	C5
Water Valley, U.S.A.	113	H10
Waterberg Plateau △, Namibia	88	C2
Waterberge, S. Africa	89	C4
Waterbury, Conn., U.S.A.	117	E11
Waterbury, Vt., U.S.A.	117	B12
Waterbury L., Canada	103	B8
Waterdown, Canada	116	C5
Waterford, Ireland	12	D4
Waterford, Calif., U.S.A.	110	H6
Waterford, Pa., U.S.A.	116	E5
Waterford □, Ireland	12	D4
Waterford Harbour, Ireland	12	D5
Waterhen L., Canada	103	C9
Waterloo, Belgium	17	D4
Waterloo, Ont., Canada	116	C4
Waterloo, Qué., Canada	117	A12
Waterloo, S. Leone	82	D2
Waterloo, Ill., U.S.A.	112	F9
Waterloo, Iowa, U.S.A.	112	D8
Waterloo, N.Y., U.S.A.	116	D8
Watersmeet, U.S.A.	112	B10
Watertown, Conn., U.S.A.	117	E11
Watertown, N.Y., U.S.A.	117	C9
Watertown, S. Dak., U.S.A.	112	C6
Watertown, Wis., U.S.A.	112	D10
Waterval-Boven, S. Africa	89	D5
Waterville, Canada	117	A13
Waterville, Maine, U.S.A.	115	C11
Waterville, N.Y., U.S.A.	117	D9
Waterville, Pa., U.S.A.	116	E7
Waterville, Wash., U.S.A.	108	C3
Watervliet, U.S.A.	117	D11
Wates, Indonesia	63	G14
Watford, Canada	116	D3
Watford, U.K.	15	F7
Watford City, U.S.A.	112	B3
Wathaman →, Canada	103	B8
Wathaman L., Canada	103	B8
Watheroo, Australia	93	F2
Watheroo △, Australia	93	F2
Wating, China	56	G4
Watkins Glen, U.S.A.	116	D8
Watling I. = San Salvador I., Bahamas	121	B5
Watonga, U.S.A.	113	H5
Watrous, Canada	103	C7
Watrous, U.S.A.	113	H2
Watsa, Dem. Rep. of the Congo	86	B2
Watseka, U.S.A.	114	E2
Watson, Australia	93	F5
Watson, Canada	103	C8
Watson Lake, Canada	102	A3
Watsontown, U.S.A.	116	E8
Watsonville, U.S.A.	110	J5
Wattiwarriganna Cr. →, Australia	95	D2
Wattwil, Switz.	25	H5
Watuata = Batuata, Indonesia	63	F6
Watubela, Kepulauan, Indonesia	63	E8
Watubela Is. = Watubela, Kepulauan, Indonesia	63	E8
Wau = Wâw, Sudan	81	F2
Waubamik, Canada	116	A4
Waubay, U.S.A.	112	C6
Wauchope, N.S.W., Australia	95	E5
Wauchope, N. Terr., Australia	94	C1
Wauchula, U.S.A.	115	M5
Waukarlycarly, L., Australia	92	D3
Waukegan, U.S.A.	114	D2
Waukesha, U.S.A.	114	D1
Waukon, U.S.A.	112	D9
Waupaca, U.S.A.	112	C10
Waupun, U.S.A.	112	D10
Waurika, U.S.A.	113	H6
Wausau, U.S.A.	112	C10
Wautoma, U.S.A.	112	C10
Wauwatosa, U.S.A.	114	D2
Waveney →, U.K.	15	E9
Waverley, N.Z.	91	H5
Waverly, Iowa, U.S.A.	112	D8
Waverly, N.Y., U.S.A.	117	E8
Wavre, Belgium	17	D4
Wâw, Sudan	81	F2
Wāw al Kabīr, Libya	79	C9
Wawa, Nigeria	83	D5
Wawa, Sudan	104	C3
Wawanesa, Canada	103	D9
Wawona, U.S.A.	110	H7
Waxahachie, U.S.A.	113	J6
Way, L., Australia	93	E3
Waycross, U.S.A.	115	K4
Wayi, Sudan	81	F3

Wayland, U.S.A.	116	D7
Wayne, Nebr., U.S.A.	112	D6
Wayne, W. Va., U.S.A.	114	F4
Waynesboro, Ga., U.S.A.	115	J4
Waynesboro, Miss., U.S.A.	115	K1
Waynesboro, Pa., U.S.A.	114	F7
Waynesboro, Va., U.S.A.	114	F6
Waynesburg, U.S.A.	114	F5
Waynesville, U.S.A.	115	H4
Waynoka, U.S.A.	113	G5
Wazirabad, Pakistan	68	C6
Wda →, Poland	30	E5
We, Indonesia	62	C1
Weald, The, U.K.	15	F8
Wear →, U.K.	14	C6
Weatherford, Okla., U.S.A.	113	H5
Weatherford, Tex., U.S.A.	113	J6
Weaverville, U.S.A.	108	F2
Webb City, U.S.A.	113	G7
Webequie, Canada	104	B2
Webo = Nyaake, Liberia	82	E3
Webster, Mass., U.S.A.	117	D13
Webster, N.Y., U.S.A.	116	C7
Webster, S. Dak., U.S.A.	112	C6
Webster City, U.S.A.	112	D8
Webster Springs, U.S.A.	114	F5
Weda, Indonesia	63	D7
Weda, Teluk, Indonesia	63	D7
Weddell I., Falk. Is.	128	G4
Weddell Sea, Antarctica	5	D1
Wedderburn, Australia	95	F3
Wedel, Germany	24	B5
Wedemark, Germany	24	C5
Wedgeport, Canada	105	D6
Wedza, Zimbabwe	87	F3
Wee Waa, Australia	95	E4
Weed, U.S.A.	108	F2
Weed Heights, U.S.A.	110	G7
Weedsport, U.S.A.	117	C8
Weedville, U.S.A.	116	E6
Weenen, S. Africa	89	D5
Weener, Germany	24	B3
Weert, Neths.	17	C5
Węgierska-Górka, Poland	31	J6
Węgliniec, Poland	31	G2
Węgorzewo, Poland	30	D8
Węgorzyno, Poland	30	E2
Węgrów, Poland	31	F9
Wehda □, Sudan	81	F3
Wei He →, Hebei, China	56	F8
Wei He →, Shaanxi, China	56	G6
Weichang, China	57	D9
Weichuan, China	56	G7
Weida, Germany	24	E8
Weiden, Germany	25	F8
Weifang, China	57	F10
Weihai, China	57	F12
Weil, Germany	25	H3
Weilburg, Germany	24	E4
Weilheim, Germany	25	H7
Weimar, Germany	24	E7
Weinan, China	56	G5
Weingarten, Germany	25	F4
Weinheim, Germany	25	F4
Weining, China	58	D5
Weipa, Australia	94	A3
Weir →, Australia	95	D4
Weir →, Canada	103	B10
Weir River, Canada	103	B10
Weirton, U.S.A.	116	F4
Weiser, U.S.A.	108	D5
Weishan, Shandong, China	57	G9
Weishan, Yunnan, China	58	E3
Weissenburg, Germany	25	F6
Weissenfels, Germany	24	D7
Weisswasser, Germany	24	D10
Wéitra, Austria	26	C7
Weixi, China	58	D2
Weixin, China	58	D5
Weiyuan, China	56	G3
Weiz, Austria	26	D8
Weizhou Dao, China	58	G7
Wejherowo, Poland	30	D5
Wekusko L., Canada	103	C9
Welch, U.S.A.	114	G5
Weldya, Ethiopia	81	E4
Welega, Ethiopia	81	F3
Welford △, Australia	94	D3
Welkite, Ethiopia	81	F4
Welkom, S. Africa	88	D4
Welland, Canada	116	D5
Welland →, U.K.	15	E7
Wellesley Is., Australia	94	B2
Wellingborough, U.K.	15	E7
Wellington, Australia	95	E4
Wellington, Canada	116	C7
Wellington, N.Z.	91	J5
Wellington, S. Africa	88	E2
Wellington, Somst., U.K.	15	G4
Wellington, Telford & Wrekin, U.K.	15	E5
Wellington, Colo., U.S.A.	112	E2
Wellington, Kans., U.S.A.	113	G6
Wellington, Nev., U.S.A.	110	G7
Wellington, Ohio, U.S.A.	116	E2
Wellington, Tex., U.S.A.	113	H4
Wellington, I., Chile	128	F2
Wellington, L., Australia	95	F4
Wells, U.K.	15	F5
Wells, Maine, U.S.A.	117	C14
Wells, N.Y., U.S.A.	117	C10
Wells, Nev., U.S.A.	108	F6
Wells, L., Australia	93	E3
Wells, Mt., Australia	92	C4
Wells Gray △, Canada	102	C4
Wells-next-the-Sea, U.K.	14	E8
Wells River, U.S.A.	117	B12
Wellsboro, U.S.A.	116	E7
Wellsburg, U.S.A.	116	F4
Wellsville, N.Y., U.S.A.	116	D7
Wellsville, Ohio, U.S.A.	116	F4
Wellsville, Utah, U.S.A.	108	F8

Wellton, *U.S.A.* 109 K6
Welmel, Wabi →, *Ethiopia* 81 F5
Welo, *Ethiopia* 81 E4
Wels, *Austria* 26 C7
Welshpool, *U.K.* 15 E4
Welwyn Garden City, *U.K.* 15 F7
Wem, *U.K.* 14 E5
Wembere →, *Tanzania* 86 C3
Wemindji, *Canada* 104 B4
Wen Xian, *China* 56 G7
Wenatchee, *U.S.A.* 108 C3
Wenchang, *China* 64 C8
Wencheng, *China* 59 D13
Wenchi, *Ghana* 82 D4
Wenchow = Wenzhou, *China* 59 D13
Wenchuan, *China* 58 B4
Wenden, *U.S.A.* 111 M13
Wendeng, *China* 57 F12
Wendesi, *Indonesia* 63 E8
Wendo, *Ethiopia* 81 F4
Wendover, *U.S.A.* 108 F6
Weng'an, *China* 58 D6
Wengcheng, *China* 59 E9
Wengyuan, *China* 59 E10
Wenjiang, *China* 58 B4
Wenling, *China* 59 C13
Wenlock →, *Australia* 94 A3
Wenshan, *China* 58 F5
Wenshang, *China* 56 G9
Wenshui, *China* 56 F7
Wensleydale, *U.K.* 14 C6
Wensu, *China* 60 B3
Wensum →, *U.K.* 14 E8
Wentworth, *Australia* 95 E3
Wentzel L., *Canada* 102 B6
Wenut, *Indonesia* 63 E8
Wenxi, *China* 56 G6
Wenxian, *China* 56 H3
Wenzhou, *China* 59 D13
Weott, *U.S.A.* 108 F2
Wepener, *S. Africa* 88 D4
Werda, *Botswana* 88 D3
Werdau, *Germany* 24 E8
Werder, *Germany* 24 C8
Werdohl, *Germany* 24 D3
Wereilu, *Ethiopia* 81 E4
Weri, *Indonesia* 63 E8
Werneck, *Germany* 25 F6
Wernigerode, *Germany* 24 D6
Werra →, *Germany* 24 D5
Werribee, *Australia* 95 E3
Werris Creek, *Australia* 95 E5
Wertach →, *Germany* 25 G6
Wertheim, *Germany* 25 F5
Wertingen, *Germany* 25 G6
Wesel, *Germany* 24 D2
Weser →, *Germany* 24 B4
Weser-Ems □, *Germany* 24 C3
Weserbergland, *Germany* 24 C5
Weserbergland Schaumburg
  Hameln △, *Germany* 24 C5
Wesiri, *Indonesia* 63 F7
Weslemkoon L., *Canada* 116 A7
Wesleyville, *Canada* 116 D4
Wessel, C., *Australia* 94 A2
Wessel Is., *Australia* 94 A2
Wesselburen, *Germany* 24 A4
Wessington Springs, *U.S.A.* 112 C5
West, *U.S.A.* 113 K6
West →, *U.S.A.* 117 D12
West Antarctica, *Antarctica* 5 D15
West Baines →, *Australia* 92 C4
West Bank ⊠, *Asia* 74 C4
West Bend, *U.S.A.* 114 D1
West Bengal □, *India* 69 H13
West Berkshire □, *U.K.* 15 F6
West Beskids = Západné
  Beskydy, *Europe* 27 B12
West Branch, *U.S.A.* 114 C3
West Branch Susquehanna →,
  U.S.A. 117 F8
West Bromwich, *U.K.* 15 E6
West Burra, *U.K.* 13 A7
West Canada Cr. →, *U.S.A.* 117 C10
West Cape Howe, *Australia* 93 G2
West Chazy, *U.S.A.* 117 B11
West Chester, *U.S.A.* 117 G9
West Coast □, *Namibia* 88 C1
West Coast △, *S. Africa* 88 E2
West Columbia, *U.S.A.* 113 L7
West Covina, *U.S.A.* 111 L9
West Des Moines, *U.S.A.* 112 E8
West Dunbartonshire □, *U.K.* 13 F4
West End, *Bahamas* 120 A4
West Falkland, *Falk. Is.* 128 G5
West Fargo, *U.S.A.* 112 B6
West Farmington, *U.S.A.* 116 E4
West Fjord = Vestfjorden,
  Norway 8 C15
West Fork Trinity →, *U.S.A.* 113 J6
West Frankfort, *U.S.A.* 112 G10
West Hartford, *U.S.A.* 117 E12
West Haven, *U.S.A.* 117 E12
West Hazleton, *U.S.A.* 117 F9
West Helena, *U.S.A.* 113 H9
West Hurley, *U.S.A.* 117 E10
West Ice Shelf, *Antarctica* 5 C7
West Indies, *Cent. Amer.* 121 D7
West Jordan, *U.S.A.* 108 F8
West Lorne, *Canada* 116 D3
West Lothian □, *U.K.* 13 F5
West Lunga →, *Zambia* 87 E1
West MacDonnell △, *Australia* 92 D5
West Memphis, *U.S.A.* 113 H9
West Midlands □, *U.K.* 15 E6
West Mifflin, *U.S.A.* 116 F5
West Milton, *U.S.A.* 116 E8
West Monroe, *U.S.A.* 113 J8
West Newton, *U.S.A.* 116 F5
West Nicholson, *Zimbabwe* 87 G2
West Palm Beach, *U.S.A.* 115 M5
West Plains, *U.S.A.* 113 G9

West Point, *N.Y., U.S.A.* 117 E11
West Point, *Nebr., U.S.A.* 112 E6
West Point, *Va., U.S.A.* 114 G7
West Pt. = Ouest, Pte. de l',
  Canada 105 C7
West Pt., *Australia* 95 F2
West Road →, *Canada* 102 C4
West Rutland, *U.S.A.* 117 C11
West Schelde =
  Westerschelde →, *Neths.* 17 C3
West Seneca, *U.S.A.* 116 D6
West Siberian Plain, *Russia* 50 C11
West Sussex □, *U.K.* 15 G7
West-Terschelling, *Neths.* 17 A5
West Valley City, *U.S.A.* 108 F8
West Virginia □, *U.S.A.* 114 F5
West-Vlaanderen □, *Belgium* 17 D2
West Walker →, *U.S.A.* 110 G7
West Wyalong, *Australia* 95 E4
West Yellowstone, *U.S.A.* 108 D8
West Yorkshire □, *U.K.* 14 D6
Westall, Pt., *Australia* 95 E1
Westbrook, *U.S.A.* 115 D10
Westbury, *Australia* 95 G4
Westby, *U.S.A.* 112 A2
Westend, *U.S.A.* 111 K9
Westerland, *Germany* 9 J13
Westerly, *U.S.A.* 117 E13
Western □, *Ghana* 82 D4
Western □, *Kenya* 86 B3
Western □, *S. Leone* 82 D2
Western □, *Zambia* 87 F1
Western Australia □, *Australia* 93 E2
Western Cape □, *S. Africa* 88 E3
Western Dvina = Daugava →,
  Latvia 9 H21
Western Ghats, *India* 66 N9
Western Isles □, *U.K.* 13 D1
Western Sahara ■, *Africa* 78 D3
Western Samoa = Samoa ■,
  Pac. Oc. 91 B13
Westernport, *U.S.A.* 114 F6
Westerschelde →, *Neths.* 17 C3
Westerstede, *Germany* 24 B3
Westerwald, *Germany* 24 E3
Westfield, *Mass., U.S.A.* 117 D12
Westfield, *N.Y., U.S.A.* 116 D5
Westfield, *Pa., U.S.A.* 116 E7
Westhill, *U.K.* 13 D6
Westhope, *U.S.A.* 112 A4
Westland △, *N.Z.* 91 K2
Westland Bight, *N.Z.* 91 K3
Westlock, *Canada* 102 C6
Westmar, *Australia* 95 D4
Westmeath □, *Ireland* 12 C4
Westminster, *U.S.A.* 114 F7
Westmont, *U.S.A.* 116 F6
Westmoreland, *Barbados* 121 g
Westmorland, *U.S.A.* 111 M11
Weston, *Oreg., U.S.A.* 108 D4
Weston, *W. Va., U.S.A.* 114 F5
Weston I., *Canada* 104 B4
Weston-super-Mare, *U.K.* 15 F5
Westover, *U.S.A.* 116 F6
Westport, *Canada* 117 B8
Westport, *Ireland* 12 C2
Westport, *N.Z.* 91 J3
Westport, *N.Y., U.S.A.* 117 B11
Westport, *Oreg., U.S.A.* 110 D3
Westport, *Wash., U.S.A.* 110 D2
Westray, *Canada* 103 C8
Westray, *U.K.* 13 B5
Westree, *Canada* 104 C3
Westville, *U.S.A.* 110 F6
Westwood, *U.S.A.* 108 F3
Wetar, *Indonesia* 63 F7
Wetaskiwin, *Canada* 102 C6
Wete, *Tanzania* 84 F7
Wetherby, *U.K.* 14 D6
Wethersfield, *U.S.A.* 117 E12
Wetteren, *Belgium* 17 D3
Wetzlar, *Germany* 24 E4
Wewoka, *U.S.A.* 113 H6
Wexford, *Ireland* 12 D5
Wexford □, *Ireland* 12 D5
Wexford Harbour, *Ireland* 12 D5
Weyburn, *Canada* 103 D8
Weyer Markt, *Austria* 26 D7
Weyhe, *Germany* 24 C4
Weyib →, *Ethiopia* 81 F5
Weymouth, *Canada* 105 D6
Weymouth, *U.K.* 15 G5
Weymouth, *U.S.A.* 117 D14
Weymouth, C., *Australia* 94 A3
Wha Ti, *Canada* 100 B8
Whakaari = White I., *N.Z.* 91 G6
Whakatane, *N.Z.* 91 G6
Whale →, *Canada* 105 A6
Whale Cove, *Canada* 103 A10
Whales, B. of, *Antarctica* 5 D12
Whalsay, *U.K.* 13 A8
Whangamata, *N.Z.* 91 G5
Whangamomona, *N.Z.* 91 H5
Whanganui △, *N.Z.* 91 H5
Whangarei, *N.Z.* 91 F5
Whangarei Harb., *N.Z.* 91 F5
Wharfe →, *U.K.* 14 D6
Wharfedale, *U.K.* 14 C5
Wharton, *N.J., U.S.A.* 117 F10
Wharton, *Pa., U.S.A.* 116 E6
Wharton, *Tex., U.S.A.* 113 L6
Wheatland, *Calif., U.S.A.* 110 F5
Wheatland, *Wyo., U.S.A.* 112 D2
Wheatley, *Canada* 116 D2
Wheaton, *Md., U.S.A.* 114 F7
Wheaton, *Minn., U.S.A.* 112 C6
Wheelbarrow Pk., *U.S.A.* 110 H10
Wheeler, *Oreg., U.S.A.* 108 D2
Wheeler, *Tex., U.S.A.* 113 H4
Wheeler →, *Canada* 105 A6
Wheeler L., *U.S.A.* 115 H2
Wheeler Pk., *N. Mex., U.S.A.* 109 H11

Wheeler Pk., *Nev., U.S.A.* 109 G6
Wheeler Ridge, *U.S.A.* 111 L8
Wheeling, *U.S.A.* 116 F4
Whernside, *U.K.* 14 C5
Whiskey Jack L., *Canada* 103 B8
Whiskeytown-Shasta-Trinity △,
  U.S.A. 108 F2
Whistleduck Cr. →, *Australia* 94 C2
Whistler, *Canada* 102 C4
Whitby, *Canada* 116 C6
Whitby, *U.K.* 14 C7
White →, *Ark., U.S.A.* 113 J9
White →, *Ind., U.S.A.* 114 F2
White →, *S. Dak., U.S.A.* 112 D5
White →, *Tex., U.S.A.* 113 J4
White →, *Utah, U.S.A.* 108 F9
White →, *Vt., U.S.A.* 117 C12
White →, *Wash., U.S.A.* 110 C4
White, L., *Australia* 92 D4
White B., *Canada* 105 C8
White Bird, *U.S.A.* 108 D5
White Butte, *U.S.A.* 112 B3
White City, *U.S.A.* 108 E2
White Cliffs, *Australia* 95 E3
White Hall, *U.S.A.* 112 F9
White Haven, *U.S.A.* 117 E9
White Horse, Vale of, *U.K.* 15 F6
White I., *N.Z.* 91 G6
White L., *Canada* 117 A8
White L., *U.S.A.* 113 L8
White Mountain Peak, *U.S.A.* 109 G4
White Mts., *Calif., U.S.A.* 110 H8
White Mts., *N.H., U.S.A.* 117 B13
White Mts. △, *Australia* 94 C4
White Nile = Nîl el Abyaḍ →,
  Sudan 81 D3
White Nile Dam = Khazzân Jabal
  al Awliyâ, *Sudan* 81 D3
White Otter L., *Canada* 104 C1
White Pass, *U.S.A.* 110 D5
White Plains, *U.S.A.* 117 E11
White River, *Canada* 104 C2
White River, *S. Africa* 89 D5
White River, *U.S.A.* 112 D4
White Rock, *Canada* 110 A4
White Russia = Belarus ■,
  Europe 32 F4
White Sands, *U.S.A.* 109 K10
White Sea = Beloye More, *Russia* 52 C4
White Sulphur Springs, *Mont.,
  U.S.A.* 108 C8
White Sulphur Springs, *W. Va.,
  U.S.A.* 114 G5
White Swan, *U.S.A.* 110 D6
White Volta →, *Ghana* 83 D4
Whitecliffs, *N.Z.* 91 K3
Whitecourt, *Canada* 102 C5
Whiteface Mt., *U.S.A.* 117 B11
Whitefield, *U.S.A.* 117 B13
Whitefish, *U.S.A.* 108 B6
Whitefish L., *Canada* 103 A7
Whitefish Point, *U.S.A.* 114 B3
Whitegull, L. = Goélands, L. aux,
  Canada 105 A7
Whitehall, *Mich., U.S.A.* 114 D2
Whitehall, *Mont., U.S.A.* 108 D7
Whitehall, *N.Y., U.S.A.* 117 C11
Whitehall, *Wis., U.S.A.* 112 C9
Whitehaven, *U.K.* 14 C4
Whitehorse, *Canada* 102 A1
Whitemark, *Australia* 95 G4
Whiteplains, *Liberia* 82 D2
Whiteriver, *U.S.A.* 109 K9
Whitesand →, *Canada* 102 A5
Whitesands, *S. Africa* 88 E3
Whitesboro, *N.Y., U.S.A.* 117 C9
Whitesboro, *Tex., U.S.A.* 113 J6
Whiteshell □, *Canada* 103 D9
Whitesville, *U.S.A.* 116 D7
Whiteville, *U.S.A.* 115 H6
Whitewater, *U.S.A.* 114 D1
Whitewater Baldy, *U.S.A.* 109 K9
Whitewater L., *Canada* 104 B2
Whitewood, *Australia* 94 C3
Whitewood, *Canada* 103 C8
Whithorn, *U.K.* 13 G4
Whitianga, *N.Z.* 91 G5
Whitman, *U.S.A.* 117 D14
Whitney, *Canada* 116 A6
Whitney, Mt., *U.S.A.* 110 J8
Whitney Point, *U.S.A.* 117 D9
Whitstable, *U.K.* 15 F9
Whitsunday I., *Australia* 94 J7
Whitsunday Islands △, *Australia* 94 J7
Whitsunday Passage, *Australia* 94 J6
Whittier, *U.S.A.* 111 M8
Whittlesea, *Australia* 95 F4
Wholdaia L., *Canada* 103 A8
Whyalla, *Australia* 95 E2
Wiang Kosai △, *Thailand* 64 D2
Wiarton, *Canada* 116 B3
Wiawso, *Ghana* 82 D4
Wiay, *U.K.* 13 D1
Wiązów, *Poland* 31 H4
Wibaux, *U.S.A.* 112 B2
Wichian Buri, *Thailand* 64 E3
Wichita, *U.S.A.* 113 G6
Wichita Falls, *U.S.A.* 113 J5
Wick, *U.K.* 13 C5
Wicked Pt., *Canada* 116 C7
Wickenburg, *U.S.A.* 109 K7
Wickepin, *Australia* 93 F2
Wickham, *Australia* 92 D2
Wickham, C., *Australia* 95 F3
Wickliffe, *U.S.A.* 116 E3
Wicklow, *Ireland* 12 D5
Wicklow □, *Ireland* 12 D5
Wicklow Hd., *Ireland* 12 D6
Wicklow Mts. △, *Ireland* 12 C5
Widawa →, *Poland* 31 G5
Widawka →, *Poland* 31 G5

Widgeegoara Cr. →, *Australia* 95 D4
Widgiemooltha, *Australia* 93 F3
Widnes, *U.K.* 14 D5
Więcbork, *Poland* 31 E4
Wiehengebirge = Nördlicher
  Teutoburger Wald-
  Wiehengebirge △, *Germany* 24 C4
Wiehl, *Germany* 24 E3
Wiek, *Germany* 24 A9
Wielbark, *Poland* 30 E7
Wieleń, *Poland* 31 F3
Wieliczka, *Poland* 31 J7
Wielkopolski △, *Poland* 31 F3
Wielkopolskie □, *Poland* 31 F4
Wieluń, *Poland* 31 G5
Wien, *Austria* 27 C9
Wien ✈ (VIA), *Austria* 27 C9
Wiener Neustadt, *Austria* 27 D9
Wieprz →, *Poland* 31 G8
Wieprza →, *Poland* 30 D3
Wieruszów, *Poland* 31 G5
Wiesbaden, *Germany* 25 E4
Wiesental, *Germany* 25 F4
Wiesloch, *Germany* 25 F4
Wiesmoor, *Germany* 24 B3
Wieżyca, *Poland* 30 D5
Wigan, *U.K.* 14 D5
Wiggins, *Colo., U.S.A.* 112 E2
Wiggins, *Miss., U.S.A.* 113 K10
Wight, I. of □, *U.K.* 15 G6
Wigierski △, *Poland* 30 D10
Wigry, Jezioro, *Poland* 30 D10
Wigston, *U.K.* 15 E6
Wigton, *U.K.* 14 C4
Wigtown, *U.K.* 13 G4
Wigtown B., *U.K.* 13 G4
Wil, *Switz.* 25 H5
Wilamowice, *Poland* 31 J6
Wilber, *U.S.A.* 112 E6
Wilberforce, *Canada* 116 A6
Wilberforce, C., *Australia* 94 A2
Wilburton, *U.S.A.* 113 H7
Wilcannia, *Australia* 95 E3
Wilcox, *U.S.A.* 116 E6
Wildbad, *Germany* 25 G4
Wildeshausen, *Germany* 24 C4
Wildeshauser Geest △, *Germany* 24 C4
Wildon, *Austria* 26 E8
Wildrose, *U.S.A.* 111 J9
Wildspitze, *Austria* 26 E3
Wilga →, *Poland* 31 G8
Wilge →, *S. Africa* 89 D4
Wilhelm II Coast, *Antarctica* 5 C7
Wilhelmsburg, *Austria* 26 C8
Wilhelmshaven, *Germany* 24 B4
Wilhelmstal, *Namibia* 88 C2
Wilkes-Barre, *U.S.A.* 117 E9
Wilkes Land, *Antarctica* 5 D9
Wilkie, *Canada* 103 C7
Wilkinsburg, *U.S.A.* 116 F5
Wilkinson Lakes, *Australia* 93 E5
Willandra Creek →, *Australia* 95 E4
Willapa B., *U.S.A.* 108 C2
Willapa Hills, *U.S.A.* 110 D3
Willard, *N.Y., U.S.A.* 116 D8
Willard, *Ohio, U.S.A.* 116 E2
Willcox, *U.S.A.* 109 K9
Willemstad, *Neth. Ant.* 121 D6
Willet, *U.S.A.* 117 D9
William →, *Canada* 103 B7
William 'Bill' Dannelly Res.,
  U.S.A. 115 J2
William Creek, *Australia* 95 D2
Williams, *Australia* 93 F2
Williams, *Ariz., U.S.A.* 109 J7
Williams, *Calif., U.S.A.* 110 F4
Williams Harbour, *Canada* 105 B8
Williams Lake, *Canada* 102 C4
Williamsburg, *Ky., U.S.A.* 115 G3
Williamsburg, *Pa., U.S.A.* 116 F6
Williamsburg, *Va., U.S.A.* 114 G7
Williamson, *N.Y., U.S.A.* 116 C7
Williamson, *W. Va., U.S.A.* 114 G4
Williamsport, *U.S.A.* 116 E7
Williamston, *U.S.A.* 115 H7
Williamstown, *Australia* 95 F3
Williamstown, *Ky., U.S.A.* 114 F3
Williamstown, *Mass., U.S.A.* 117 D11
Williamstown, *N.Y., U.S.A.* 117 C9
Willimantic, *U.S.A.* 117 E12
Willingboro, *U.S.A.* 114 E8
Williston, *S. Africa* 88 E3
Williston, *Fla., U.S.A.* 115 L4
Williston, *N. Dak., U.S.A.* 112 A3
Williston L., *Canada* 102 B4
Willits, *U.S.A.* 108 G2
Willmar, *U.S.A.* 112 C7
Willmore Wilderness △, *Canada* 102 C5
Willoughby, *U.S.A.* 116 E3
Willow Bunch, *Canada* 103 D7
Willow L. →, *Canada* 102 A5
Willow Wall, The, *China* 57 C12
Willowick, *U.S.A.* 116 E3
Willowlake →, *Canada* 102 A4
Willowmore, *S. Africa* 88 E3
Willows, *U.S.A.* 110 F4
Willowvale = Gatyana, *S. Africa* 89 E4
Wills, L., *Australia* 92 D4
Wills Cr. →, *Australia* 94 C3
Willsboro, *U.S.A.* 117 B11
Willunga, *Australia* 95 F2
Wilmette, *U.S.A.* 114 D2
Wilmington, *Australia* 95 E2
Wilmington, *Del., U.S.A.* 114 F8
Wilmington, *N.C., U.S.A.* 115 H7
Wilmington, *Ohio, U.S.A.* 114 F4
Wilmington, *Vt., U.S.A.* 117 D12
Wilmslow, *U.K.* 14 D5
Wilpena Cr. →, *Australia* 95 E2
Wilsall, *U.S.A.* 108 D8
Wilson, *N.C., U.S.A.* 115 H7

Wilson, *N.Y., U.S.A.* 116 C6
Wilson, *Pa., U.S.A.* 117 F9
Wilson →, *Australia* 92 C4
Wilson Bluff, *Australia* 93 F4
Wilson Inlet, *Australia* 93 G2
Wilsons Promontory, *Australia* 95 F4
Wilster, *Germany* 24 B5
Wilton, *U.S.A.* 112 B4
Wilton →, *Australia* 94 A1
Wiltshire □, *U.K.* 15 F6
Wiltz, *Lux.* 17 E5
Wiluna, *Australia* 93 E3
Wimborne Minster, *U.K.* 15 G6
Wimereux, *France* 19 B8
Wimmera →, *Australia* 95 F3
Winam G., *Kenya* 86 C3
Winburg, *S. Africa* 88 D4
Winchendon, *U.S.A.* 117 D12
Winchester, *U.K.* 15 F6
Winchester, *Conn., U.S.A.* 117 E11
Winchester, *Idaho, U.S.A.* 108 C5
Winchester, *Ind., U.S.A.* 114 E3
Winchester, *Ky., U.S.A.* 114 G3
Winchester, *N.H., U.S.A.* 117 D12
Winchester, *Nev., U.S.A.* 111 J11
Winchester, *Tenn., U.S.A.* 115 H2
Winchester, *Va., U.S.A.* 114 F6
Wind →, *U.S.A.* 108 E9
Wind Cave △, *U.S.A.* 112 D3
Wind River Range, *U.S.A.* 108 E9
Windau = Ventspils, *Latvia* 9 H19
Windber, *U.S.A.* 116 F6
Windermere, *U.K.* 14 C5
Windhoek, *Namibia* 88 C2
Windischgarsten, *Austria* 26 D7
Windom, *U.S.A.* 112 D7
Windorah, *Australia* 94 D3
Window Rock, *U.S.A.* 109 J9
Windrush →, *U.K.* 15 F6
Windsor, *Australia* 95 E5
Windsor, *N.S., Canada* 105 D7
Windsor, *Ont., Canada* 116 D2
Windsor, *U.K.* 15 F7
Windsor, *Colo., U.S.A.* 112 E2
Windsor, *Conn., U.S.A.* 117 E12
Windsor, *Mo., U.S.A.* 112 F8
Windsor, *N.Y., U.S.A.* 117 D9
Windsor, *Vt., U.S.A.* 117 C12
Windsor & Maidenhead □, *U.K.* 15 F7
Windsorton, *S. Africa* 88 D3
Windward Is., *W. Indies* 121 D7
Windward Passage = Vientos,
  Paso de los, *Caribbean* 121 C5
Winefred L., *Canada* 103 B6
Winejok, *Sudan* 81 F2
Winfield, *U.S.A.* 113 G6
Wingate Mts., *Australia* 92 B5
Wingham, *Australia* 95 E5
Wingham, *Canada* 116 C3
Winisk, *Canada* 104 A2
Winisk →, *Canada* 104 A2
Winisk L., *Canada* 104 B2
Wink, *U.S.A.* 113 K3
Winkler, *Canada* 103 D9
Winklern, *Austria* 26 E5
Winlock, *U.S.A.* 110 D4
Winneba, *Ghana* 83 D4
Winnebago, L., *U.S.A.* 114 D1
Winnecke Cr. →, *Australia* 92 C5
Winnemucca, *U.S.A.* 108 F5
Winnemucca L., *U.S.A.* 108 F4
Winnett, *U.S.A.* 108 C9
Winnfield, *U.S.A.* 113 K8
Winnibigoshish, L., *U.S.A.* 112 B7
Winnipeg, *Canada* 103 D9
Winnipeg →, *Canada* 103 C9
Winnipeg, L., *Canada* 103 C9
Winnipeg Beach, *Canada* 103 C9
Winnipegosis, *Canada* 103 C9
Winnipegosis L., *Canada* 103 C9
Winnipesaukee, L., *U.S.A.* 117 C13
Winnisquam L., *U.S.A.* 117 C13
Winnsboro, *La., U.S.A.* 113 J9
Winnsboro, *S.C., U.S.A.* 115 H5
Winnsboro, *Tex., U.S.A.* 113 J7
Winokapau, L., *Canada* 105 B7
Winona, *Minn., U.S.A.* 112 C9
Winona, *Miss., U.S.A.* 113 J10
Winooski, *U.S.A.* 117 B11
Winooski →, *U.S.A.* 117 B11
Winschoten, *Neths.* 17 A7
Winsen, *Germany* 24 B6
Winsford, *U.K.* 14 D5
Winslow, *Ariz., U.S.A.* 109 J8
Winslow, *Wash., U.S.A.* 110 C4
Winsted, *U.S.A.* 117 E11
Winston-Salem, *U.S.A.* 115 G5
Winter Garden, *U.S.A.* 115 L5
Winter Haven, *U.S.A.* 115 M5
Winter Park, *U.S.A.* 115 L5
Winterberg, *Germany* 24 D4
Winterhaven, *U.S.A.* 111 N12
Winters, *U.S.A.* 110 G5
Wintersville, *U.S.A.* 116 F4
Winterswijk, *Neths.* 17 C6
Winterthur, *Switz.* 25 H4
Winthrop, *U.S.A.* 108 B3
Winton, *Australia* 94 C3
Winton, *N.Z.* 91 M2
Wipper →, *Germany* 24 D7
Wirrulla, *Australia* 95 E1
Wisbech, *U.K.* 15 E8
Wisconsin □, *U.S.A.* 112 C10
Wisconsin →, *U.S.A.* 112 D9
Wisconsin Rapids, *U.S.A.* 112 C10
Wisdom, *U.S.A.* 108 D7
Wishaw, *U.K.* 13 F5
Wisła, *Poland* 31 J5
Wisła →, *Poland* 30 D5
Wisłok →, *Poland* 31 H9

Wisłoka →, *Poland* ... 31 H8
Wismar, *Germany* ... 24 B7
Wisner, *U.S.A.* ... 112 E6
Wissant, *France* ... 19 B8
Wissembourg, *France* ... 19 C14
Wisznice, *Poland* ... 31 G10
Witbank, *S. Africa* ... 89 D4
Witdraai, *S. Africa* ... 88 D3
Witham, *U.K.* ... 15 F8
Witham →, *U.K.* ... 14 E7
Withernsea, *U.K.* ... 14 D8
Witjira △, *Australia* ... 95 D2
Witkowo, *Poland* ... 31 F4
Witney, *U.K.* ... 15 F6
Witnica, *Poland* ... 31 F1
Witnossob →, *Namibia* ... 88 D3
Wittdün, *Germany* ... 24 A4
Witten, *Germany* ... 24 D3
Wittenberge, *Germany* ... 24 B7
Wittenburg, *Germany* ... 24 B7
Wittenheim, *France* ... 19 E14
Wittenoom, *Australia* ... 92 D2
Wittingen, *Germany* ... 24 C6
Wittlich, *Germany* ... 25 F2
Wittmund, *Germany* ... 24 B3
Wittow, *Germany* ... 24 A9
Wittstock, *Germany* ... 24 B8
Witvlei, *Namibia* ... 88 C2
Witzenhausen, *Germany* ... 24 D5
Wkra →, *Poland* ... 31 F7
Władysławowo, *Poland* ... 30 D5
Wleń, *Poland* ... 31 G2
Wlingi, *Indonesia* ... 63 H15
Włocławek, *Poland* ... 31 F6
Włodawa, *Poland* ... 31 G10
Włoszczowa, *Poland* ... 31 H6
Woburn, *U.S.A.* ... 117 D13
Wodian, *China* ... 56 H7
Wodonga = Albury-Wodonga, *Australia* ... 95 F4
Wodzisław Śląski, *Poland* ... 31 H5
Wœrth, *France* ... 19 D14
Woinbogoin, *China* ... 58 A2
Woippy, *France* ... 19 C13
Wojcieszow, *Poland* ... 31 H2
Wokam, *Indonesia* ... 63 F8
Woking, *U.K.* ... 15 F7
Wokingham, *U.K.* ... 15 F7
Wokingham □, *U.K.* ... 15 F7
Wolbrom, *Poland* ... 31 H6
Wołczyn, *Poland* ... 31 G5
Woldegk, *Germany* ... 24 B9
Wolf →, *Canada* ... 102 A2
Wolf Creek, *U.S.A.* ... 108 C7
Wolf L., *Canada* ... 102 A2
Wolf Point, *U.S.A.* ... 112 A2
Wolfe I., *Canada* ... 117 B8
Wolfeboro, *U.S.A.* ... 117 C13
Wolfen, *Germany* ... 24 D8
Wolfenbüttel, *Germany* ... 24 C6
Wolfratshausen, *Germany* ... 25 H7
Wolfsberg, *Austria* ... 26 E7
Wolfsburg, *Germany* ... 24 C6
Wolgast, *Germany* ... 24 A9
Wolhusen, *Switz.* ... 25 H4
Wolin, *Poland* ... 30 E1
Woliński △, *Poland* ... 30 E1
Wollaston, Is., *Chile* ... 128 H3
Wollaston L., *Canada* ... 103 B8
Wollaston Lake, *Canada* ... 103 B8
Wollaston Pen., *Canada* ... 100 B8
Wollongong, *Australia* ... 95 E5
Wolmaransstad, *S. Africa* ... 88 D4
Wolmirstedt, *Germany* ... 24 C7
Wołomin, *Poland* ... 31 F8
Wołów, *Poland* ... 31 G3
Wolseley, *S. Africa* ... 88 E2
Wolsey, *U.S.A.* ... 112 C5
Wolstenholme, C., *Canada* ... 98 C12
Wolsztyn, *Poland* ... 31 F3
Wolvega, *Neths.* ... 17 B6
Wolverhampton, *U.K.* ... 15 E5
Wondai, *Australia* ... 95 D5
Wongalarroo L., *Australia* ... 95 E3
Wongan Hills, *Australia* ... 93 F2
Wŏnju, *S. Korea* ... 57 F14
Wonosari, *Indonesia* ... 63 G14
Wonosobo, *Indonesia* ... 63 G13
Wonowon, *Canada* ... 102 B4
Wŏnsan, *N. Korea* ... 57 E14
Wonthaggi, *Australia* ... 95 F4
Wood Buffalo △, *Canada* ... 102 B6
Wood Is., *Australia* ... 92 C3
Wood L., *Canada* ... 103 B8
Woodah I., *Australia* ... 94 A2
Woodbourne, *U.S.A.* ... 117 E10
Woodbridge, *Canada* ... 116 C5
Woodbridge, *U.K.* ... 15 E9
Woodburn, *U.S.A.* ... 108 D2
Woodenbong, *Australia* ... 95 D5
Woodend, *Australia* ... 95 F3
Woodford, *Australia* ... 95 D5
Woodfords, *U.S.A.* ... 110 G7
Woodlake, *U.S.A.* ... 110 J7
Woodland, Calif., *U.S.A.* ... 110 G5
Woodland, Maine, *U.S.A.* ... 115 C12
Woodland, Pa., *U.S.A.* ... 116 F6
Woodland, Wash., *U.S.A.* ... 110 E4
Woodland Caribou △, *Canada* ... 103 C10
Woodlands, *Singapore* ... 65 d
Woodridge, *Canada* ... 103 D9
Woodroffe, Mt., *Australia* ... 93 E5
Woods, L., *Australia* ... 94 B1
Woods, L. of the, *Canada* ... 103 D10
Woodstock, *Australia* ... 94 B4
Woodstock, N.B., *Canada* ... 105 C6
Woodstock, Ont., *Canada* ... 116 C4
Woodstock, *U.K.* ... 15 F6
Woodstock, Ill., *U.S.A.* ... 112 D10
Woodstock, Vt., *U.S.A.* ... 117 C12
Woodsville, *U.S.A.* ... 117 B13
Woodville, *N.Z.* ... 91 J5

Woodville, Miss., *U.S.A.* ... 113 K9
Woodville, Tex., *U.S.A.* ... 113 K7
Woodward, *U.S.A.* ... 113 G5
Woody, *U.S.A.* ... 111 K8
Woody →, *Canada* ... 103 C8
Woolacombe, *U.K.* ... 15 F3
Woolamai, C., *Australia* ... 95 F4
Wooler, *U.K.* ... 14 B5
Woolgoolga, *Australia* ... 95 E5
Woomera, *Australia* ... 95 E2
Woonsocket, R.I., *U.S.A.* ... 117 E13
Woonsocket, S. Dak., *U.S.A.* ... 112 C5
Wooramel →, *Australia* ... 93 E1
Wooramel Roadhouse, *Australia* ... 93 E1
Wooster, *U.S.A.* ... 116 F3
Worcester, S. Africa ... 88 E2
Worcester, *U.K.* ... 15 E5
Worcester, Mass., *U.S.A.* ... 117 D13
Worcester, N.Y., *U.S.A.* ... 117 D10
Worcestershire □, *U.K.* ... 15 E5
Wörgl, *Austria* ... 26 D5
Workington, *U.K.* ... 14 C4
Worksop, *U.K.* ... 14 D6
Workum, *Neths.* ... 17 B5
Worland, *U.S.A.* ... 108 D10
Wormhout, *France* ... 19 B9
Worms, *Germany* ... 25 F4
Worsley, *Canada* ... 102 B5
Wortham, *U.S.A.* ... 113 K6
Worms, *Germany* ... 24 A4
Wörther See, *Austria* ... 26 E7
Worthing, *Barbados* ... 121 g
Worthing, *U.K.* ... 15 G7
Worthington, Minn., *U.S.A.* ... 112 D7
Worthington, Pa., *U.S.A.* ... 116 F5
Wosi, *Indonesia* ... 63 E7
Wou-han = Wuhan, *China* ... 59 B10
Wousi = Wuxi, *China* ... 59 B13
Wowoni, *Indonesia* ... 63 E6
Wrangel I. = Vrangelya, Ostrov, *Russia* ... 53 B19
Wrangell, *U.S.A.* ... 102 B2
Wrangell Mts., *U.S.A.* ... 100 B5
Wrath, C., *U.K.* ... 13 C3
Wray, *U.S.A.* ... 112 E3
Wrekin, The, *U.K.* ... 15 E5
Wrens, *U.S.A.* ... 115 J4
Wrexham, *U.K.* ... 14 D4
Wrexham □, *U.K.* ... 14 D5
Wriezen, *Germany* ... 24 C10
Wright = Paranas, *Phil.* ... 61 F6
Wright, *U.S.A.* ... 112 D2
Wright Pt., *Canada* ... 116 C3
Wrightson, Mt., *U.S.A.* ... 109 L8
Wrightwood, *U.S.A.* ... 111 L9
Wrigley, *Canada* ... 100 B7
Wrocław, *Poland* ... 31 G4
Wronki, *Poland* ... 31 F3
Września, *Poland* ... 31 F4
Wschowa, *Poland* ... 31 G3
Wu Jiang →, *China* ... 58 C6
Wu'an, *China* ... 56 F8
Wubin, *Australia* ... 93 F2
Wubu, *China* ... 56 F6
Wuchang, *China* ... 57 B14
Wucheng, *China* ... 56 F9
Wuchuan, Guangdong, *China* ... 59 G8
Wuchuan, Guizhou, *China* ... 58 C7
Wuchuan, Nei Monggol Zizhiqu, *China* ... 56 D6
Wudi, *China* ... 57 F9
Wuding, *China* ... 58 E4
Wuding He →, *China* ... 56 F6
Wudinna, *Australia* ... 95 E2
Wudu, *China* ... 56 H3
Wufeng, *China* ... 59 B8
Wugang, *China* ... 59 D8
Wugong Shan, *China* ... 59 D9
Wuhan, *China* ... 59 B10
Wuhe, *China* ... 57 H9
Wuhsi = Wuxi, *China* ... 59 B13
Wuhu, *China* ... 59 B12
Wujiang, *China* ... 59 B13
Wukari, *Nigeria* ... 83 D6
Wulajie, *China* ... 57 B14
Wulanbulang, *China* ... 56 D6
Wular L., *India* ... 69 B6
Wulehe, *Ghana* ... 83 D5
Wulian, *China* ... 57 G10
Wuliang Shan, *China* ... 58 E3
Wuliaru, *Indonesia* ... 63 F8
Wuling Shan, *China* ... 58 C7
Wulong, *China* ... 58 C6
Wulumuchi = Ürümqi, *China* ... 52 B3
Wum, *Cameroon* ... 83 D7
Wuming, *China* ... 58 F7
Wun Rog, *Sudan* ... 81 F2
Wuning, *China* ... 59 C10
Wunnummin L., *Canada* ... 104 B2
Wunsiedel, *Germany* ... 25 E8
Wunstorf, *Germany* ... 24 C5
Wuntho, *Burma* ... 67 H19
Wupatki △, *U.S.A.* ... 109 J8
Wuping, *China* ... 59 E11
Wuppertal, *Germany* ... 24 D3
Wuppertal, S. Africa ... 88 E2
Wuqing, *China* ... 57 E9
Wurtsboro, *U.S.A.* ... 117 E10
Würzburg, *Germany* ... 25 F5
Wurzen, *Germany* ... 24 D8
Wushan, *China* ... 56 G3
Wushishi, *Nigeria* ... 83 D6
Wusuli Jiang = Ussuri →, *Asia* ... 54 A7
Wutach →, *Germany* ... 25 H4
Wutai, *China* ... 56 F7
Wuting = Huimin, *China* ... 57 F9
Wutong, *China* ... 59 E8
Wutonghaolai, *China* ... 57 C11
Wutongqiao, *China* ... 58 C4
Wuwei, Anhui, *China* ... 59 B11
Wuwei, Gansu, *China* ... 60 C5
Wuxi, Jiangsu, *China* ... 59 B13

Wuxi, Sichuan, *China* ... 58 B7
Wuxiang, *China* ... 56 F7
Wuxuan, *China* ... 58 F7
Wuxue, *China* ... 59 C10
Wuyang, *China* ... 56 H7
Wuyi, Hebei, *China* ... 56 F8
Wuyi, Zhejiang, *China* ... 59 C12
Wuyi Shan, *China* ... 59 D11
Wuyishan, *China* ... 59 D12
Wuyo, *Nigeria* ... 83 C7
Wuyuan, Jiangxi, *China* ... 59 C11
Wuyuan, Nei Monggol Zizhiqu, *China* ... 56 D5
Wuzhai, *China* ... 56 E6
Wuzhi Shan, *China* ... 64 C7
Wuzhong, *China* ... 56 E4
Wuzhou, *China* ... 59 F8
Wyaaba Cr. →, *Australia* ... 94 B3
Wyalkatchem, *Australia* ... 93 F2
Wyalusing, *U.S.A.* ... 117 E8
Wyandotte, *U.S.A.* ... 114 D4
Wyandra, *Australia* ... 95 D4
Wyangala, L., *Australia* ... 95 E4
Wyara, L., *Australia* ... 95 D3
Wycheproof, *Australia* ... 95 F3
Wye →, *U.K.* ... 15 F5
Wyemandoo, *Australia* ... 93 E2
Wyk, *Germany* ... 24 A4
Wymondham, *U.K.* ... 15 E9
Wymore, *U.S.A.* ... 112 E6
Wyndham, *Australia* ... 92 C4
Wyndham, *N.Z.* ... 91 M2
Wynne, *U.S.A.* ... 113 H9
Wynyard, *Australia* ... 95 G4
Wynyard, *Canada* ... 103 C8
Wyola L., *Australia* ... 93 E5
Wyoming = Plympton-Wyoming, *Canada* ... 116 D2
Wyoming □, *U.S.A.* ... 108 E10
Wyomissing, *U.S.A.* ... 117 F9
Wyong, *Australia* ... 95 E5
Wyrzysk, *Poland* ... 31 E4
Wyśmierzyce, *Poland* ... 31 G7
Wysoka, *Poland* ... 31 E4
Wysokie, *Poland* ... 31 H9
Wysokie Mazowieckie, *Poland* ... 31 F8
Wyszków, *Poland* ... 31 F8
Wyszogród, *Poland* ... 31 F7
Wytheville, *U.S.A.* ... 114 G5
Wyżyna Małopolska, *Poland* ... 31 H7

X

Xaafuun, *Somali Rep.* ... 75 E5
Xaçmaz, *Azerbaijan* ... 35 K9
Xai-Xai, *Mozam.* ... 89 D5
Xainza, *China* ... 60 C3
Xalapa, *Mexico* ... 119 D5
Xangongo, *Angola* ... 88 B2
Xankändi, *Azerbaijan* ... 70 B5
Xanlar, *Azerbaijan* ... 35 K8
Xanten, *Germany* ... 24 D2
Xánthi, *Greece* ... 45 E8
Xánthi □, *Greece* ... 45 E8
Xanthos, *Turkey* ... 47 E11
Xanxerê, *Brazil* ... 127 B5
Xapuri, *Brazil* ... 124 F5
Xar Moron He →, *China* ... 57 C11
Xarrë, *Albania* ... 44 G4
Xátiva, *Spain* ... 39 G4
Xau, L., *Botswana* ... 88 C3
Xavantina, *Brazil* ... 127 A5
Xenia, *U.S.A.* ... 114 F4
Xeropotamos →, *Cyprus* ... 49 E11
Xertigny, *France* ... 19 D13
Xhora, S. Africa ... 89 E4
Xhumo, *Botswana* ... 88 C3
Xi Jiang →, *China* ... 59 F9
Xi Xian, Henan, *China* ... 59 A10
Xi Xian, Shanxi, *China* ... 56 F6
Xia Xian, *China* ... 56 G6
Xiachengzi, *China* ... 57 B16
Xiachuan Dao, *China* ... 59 G9
Xiaguan, *China* ... 60 D5
Xiajiang, *China* ... 59 D10
Xiajin, *China* ... 56 F9
Xiamen, *China* ... 59 E12
Xi'an, *China* ... 56 G5
Xian Xian, *China* ... 56 E9
Xianfeng, *China* ... 58 C7
Xiang Jiang →, *China* ... 59 C9
Xiangcheng, Henan, *China* ... 56 H8
Xiangcheng, Henan, *China* ... 56 H7
Xiangcheng, Sichuan, *China* ... 58 C2
Xiangfan, *China* ... 59 A9
Xianggang = Hong Kong □, *China* ... 59 F10
Xianghuang Qi, *China* ... 56 C7
Xiangning, *China* ... 56 G6
Xiangquan, *China* ... 56 F7
Xiangquan He = Sutlej →, *Pakistan* ... 68 E4
Xiangshan, *China* ... 59 C13
Xiangshui, *China* ... 57 G10
Xiangtan, *China* ... 59 D9
Xiangxiang, *China* ... 59 D9
Xiangyin, *China* ... 59 C9
Xiangyun, *China* ... 58 E3
Xiangzhou, *China* ... 58 F7
Xianju, *China* ... 59 C13
Xianning, *China* ... 59 C10
Xianshui He →, *China* ... 58 B3
Xiantao, *China* ... 59 B9
Xianyang, *China* ... 56 G5
Xianyou, *China* ... 59 E12
Xiao Hinggan Ling, *China* ... 60 B7
Xiao Xian, *China* ... 56 G9

Xiaofeng, *China* ... 59 B12
Xiaogan, *China* ... 59 B9
Xiaojin, *China* ... 58 B4
Xiaolan, *China* ... 59 F9
Xiaoshan, *China* ... 59 B13
Xiaoyi, *China* ... 56 F6
Xiapu, *China* ... 59 D12
Xichang, *China* ... 58 D4
Xichong, *China* ... 58 B5
Xichou, *China* ... 58 E5
Xichuan, *China* ... 56 H6
Xide, *China* ... 58 C4
Xiemahe, *China* ... 59 B8
Xieng Khouang, *Laos* ... 64 C4
Xifei He →, *China* ... 56 H9
Xifeng, Gansu, *China* ... 56 G4
Xifeng, Guizhou, *China* ... 58 D6
Xifeng, Liaoning, *China* ... 57 C13
Xifengzhen = Xifeng, *China* ... 56 G4
Xigazê, *China* ... 60 D3
Xihe, *China* ... 56 G3
Xihua, *China* ... 56 H8
Xilaganí, *Greece* ... 45 F9
Xiliao He →, *China* ... 57 C12
Xilin, *China* ... 58 E5
Xilókastron, *Greece* ... 46 C4
Ximana, *Mozam.* ... 87 F3
Xime, Guinea-Biss. ... 82 C2
Ximeng, *China* ... 58 F2
Xin Jiang →, *China* ... 59 C11
Xin Xian = Xinzhou, *China* ... 56 E7
Xinavane, *Mozam.* ... 89 D5
Xinbin, *China* ... 57 D13
Xincai, *China* ... 59 A10
Xinchang, *China* ... 59 C13
Xincheng, Guangxi Zhuangzu, *China* ... 58 E7
Xincheng, Jiangxi, *China* ... 59 D10
Xindu, *China* ... 58 B5
Xinfeng, Guangdong, *China* ... 59 E10
Xinfeng, Jiangxi, *China* ... 59 D11
Xinfeng, Jiangxi, *China* ... 59 E10
Xinfengjiang Skuiku, *China* ... 59 F10
Xing Xian, *China* ... 56 E6
Xing'an, Guangxi Zhuangzu, *China* ... 59 E8
Xingan, Jiangxi, *China* ... 59 D10
Xingcheng, *China* ... 57 D11
Xingguo, *China* ... 59 D10
Xinghe, *China* ... 56 D7
Xinghua, *China* ... 57 H10
Xinghua Wan, *China* ... 59 E12
Xinglong, *China* ... 57 D9
Xingning, *China* ... 59 E10
Xingping, *China* ... 56 G5
Xingren, *China* ... 58 E5
Xingshan, *China* ... 59 B8
Xingtai, *China* ... 56 F8
Xingu →, *Brazil* ... 125 D8
Xingwen, *China* ... 58 C5
Xingyang, *China* ... 56 G7
Xinhe, *China* ... 56 F8
Xinhua, *China* ... 59 D8
Xinhuang, *China* ... 58 D7
Xinhui, *China* ... 59 F9
Xining, *China* ... 60 C5
Xinjian, *China* ... 59 C10
Xinjiang, *China* ... 56 G6
Xinjiang Uygur Zizhiqu □, *China* ... 60 B3
Xinjie, *China* ... 58 D3
Xinjin = Pulandian, *China* ... 57 E11
Xinjin, *China* ... 58 B4
Xinkai He →, *China* ... 57 C12
Xinle, *China* ... 56 E8
Xinlitun, *China* ... 57 D12
Xinlong, *China* ... 58 B3
Xinmin, *China* ... 57 D12
Xinning, *China* ... 59 D8
Xinping, *China* ... 58 E3
Xinshao, *China* ... 59 D8
Xintai, *China* ... 57 G9
Xintian, *China* ... 59 E9
Xinxian, *China* ... 59 B10
Xinxiang, *China* ... 56 G7
Xinxing, *China* ... 59 F9
Xinyang, *China* ... 59 A10
Xinye, *China* ... 59 A9
Xinyi, *China* ... 59 F8
Xinyu, *China* ... 59 D10
Xinzhan, *China* ... 57 C14
Xinzheng, *China* ... 56 G7
Xinzhou, Hubei, *China* ... 59 B10
Xinzhou, Shanxi, *China* ... 56 E7
Xinzo de Limia, *Spain* ... 36 C3
Xiongyuecheng, *China* ... 57 D12
Xiping, Henan, *China* ... 56 H8
Xiping, Henan, *China* ... 56 H6
Xiping, Zhejiang, *China* ... 59 C12
Xique-Xique, *Brazil* ... 125 F10
Xisha Qundao = Paracel Is., S. China Sea ... 62 A4
Xishui, Guizhou, *China* ... 58 C6
Xishui, Hubei, *China* ... 59 B10
Xitole, Guinea-Biss. ... 82 C2
Xiu Shui →, *China* ... 59 C10
Xiuning, *China* ... 59 C12
Xiuren, *China* ... 59 E8
Xiushan, *China* ... 58 C7
Xiushui, *China* ... 59 C10
Xiuwen, *China* ... 58 D6
Xiuyan, *China* ... 57 D12
Xixabangma Feng, *China* ... 67 E14
Xixia, *China* ... 56 H6
Xixiang, *China* ... 56 H4
Xiyang, *China* ... 56 F7
Xizang Zizhiqu □, *China* ... 60 C3
Xlendi, *Malta* ... 49 C1
Xochob, *Mexico* ... 119 D7
Xu Jiang →, *China* ... 59 D11
Xuan Loc, *Vietnam* ... 65 G6

Xuan'en, *China* ... 58 C7
Xuanhan, *China* ... 58 B6
Xuanhua, *China* ... 56 D8
Xuanwei, *China* ... 58 C5
Xuanzhou, *China* ... 59 B12
Xuchang, *China* ... 56 G7
Xudat, *Azerbaijan* ... 35 K9
Xuefeng Shan, *China* ... 59 D8
Xuejiaping, *China* ... 59 B8
Xun Jiang →, *China* ... 59 F8
Xun Xian, *China* ... 56 G8
Xundian, *China* ... 58 E4
Xunwu, *China* ... 59 E10
Xunyang, *China* ... 56 H5
Xunyi, *China* ... 56 G5
Xupu, *China* ... 59 D8
Xúquer →, *Spain* ... 39 F4
Xushui, *China* ... 56 E8
Xuwen, *China* ... 59 G8
Xuyen Moc, *Vietnam* ... 65 G6
Xuyong, *China* ... 58 C5
Xuzhou, *China* ... 57 G9
Xylophagou, *Cyprus* ... 49 E12

Y

Ya Xian, *China* ... 64 C7
Yaamba, *Australia* ... 94 C5
Ya'an, *China* ... 58 C4
Yaapeet, *Australia* ... 95 F3
Yabassi, *Cameroon* ... 83 E6
Yabelo, *Ethiopia* ... 81 G4
Yabelo ○, *Ethiopia* ... 81 F4
Yablanitsa, *Bulgaria* ... 45 C8
Yablonovy Ra. = Yablonovyy Khrebet, *Russia* ... 53 D12
Yablonovyy Khrebet, *Russia* ... 53 D12
Yabluniv, *Ukraine* ... 29 B9
Yablunytsya, *Ukraine* ... 29 B9
Yabrai Shan, *China* ... 56 E2
Yabrūd, *Syria* ... 74 B5
Yabucoa, *Puerto Rico* ... 121 d
Yacambú △, *Venezuela* ... 121 E6
Yacheng, *China* ... 64 C7
Yacuiba, *Bolivia* ... 126 A3
Yacuma →, *Bolivia* ... 124 F5
Yadgir, *India* ... 66 L10
Yadkin →, *U.S.A.* ... 115 H5
Yadrin, *Russia* ... 34 C8
Yaeyama-Rettō, *Japan* ... 55 M1
Yagaba, *Ghana* ... 83 C4
Yağcılar, *Turkey* ... 47 B10
Yagodnoye, *Russia* ... 53 C15
Yahila, Dem. Rep. of the Congo ... 86 B1
Yahk, *Canada* ... 102 D5
Yahotyn, *Ukraine* ... 33 G6
Yahuma, Dem. Rep. of the Congo ... 84 D4
Yahyalı, *Turkey* ... 72 C6
Yaita, *Japan* ... 55 F9
Yaiza, Canary Is. ... 48 F6
Yajiang, *China* ... 58 B3
Yajua, *Nigeria* ... 83 C7
Yakima, *U.S.A.* ... 108 C3
Yakima →, *U.S.A.* ... 108 C3
Yako, Burkina Faso ... 82 C4
Yakobi I., *U.S.A.* ... 102 B1
Yakoruda, *Bulgaria* ... 44 D7
Yakovlevka, *Russia* ... 54 B6
Yaku-Shima, *Japan* ... 55 J5
Yakumo, *Japan* ... 54 C10
Yakutat, *U.S.A.* ... 100 C6
Yakutia = Sakha □, *Russia* ... 53 C13
Yakutsk, *Russia* ... 53 C13
Yala, *Thailand* ... 65 J3
Yalboroo, *Australia* ... 94 J6
Yale, *U.S.A.* ... 116 C2
Yalgoo, *Australia* ... 93 E2
Yalgorup △, *Australia* ... 93 D2
Yalinga, C.A.R. ... 84 C4
Yalleroi, *Australia* ... 94 C4
Yalobusha →, *U.S.A.* ... 113 J9
Yalong Jiang →, *China* ... 58 D3
Yalova, *Turkey* ... 45 F13
Yalpuh, Ozero, *Ukraine* ... 29 E13
Yalta, *Ukraine* ... 33 K8
Yalu Jiang →, *China* ... 57 E13
Yalvaç, *Turkey* ... 72 C4
Yam Ha Melah = Dead Sea, *Asia* ... 74 D4
Yam Kinneret, *Israel* ... 74 C4
Yamada, *Japan* ... 55 H5
Yamagata, *Japan* ... 54 E10
Yamagata □, *Japan* ... 54 E10
Yamaguchi, *Japan* ... 55 G5
Yamaguchi □, *Japan* ... 55 G5
Yamal, Poluostrov, *Russia* ... 52 B8
Yamal Pen. = Yamal, Poluostrov, *Russia* ... 52 B8
Yamanashi □, *Japan* ... 55 G9
Yamanie Falls △, *Australia* ... 94 B4
Yamba, *Australia* ... 95 D5
Yambarran Ra., *Australia* ... 92 C5
Yambéring, *Guinea* ... 82 C2
Yâmbiô, *Sudan* ... 81 G2
Yambol, *Bulgaria* ... 45 D10
Yamdena, *Indonesia* ... 63 F8
Yame, *Japan* ... 55 H5
Yamethin, *Burma* ... 67 J20
Yamma-Yamma, L., *Australia* ... 95 D3
Yamoussoukro, Ivory C. ... 82 D3
Yampa →, *U.S.A.* ... 108 F9
Yampi Sd., *Australia* ... 92 C3
Yampil, *Moldova* ... 33 H5
Yampol = Yampil, *Moldova* ... 33 H5
Yamrat, *Nigeria* ... 83 C6
Yamrukchal = Botev, *Bulgaria* ... 45 D8
Yamuna →, *India* ... 69 G9
Yamunanagar, *India* ... 68 D7

Yamzho Yumco, China 60 D4
Yan, Nigeria 83 C7
Yana →, Russia 53 B14
Yanagawa, Japan 55 H5
Yanai, Japan 55 H6
Yan'an, China 56 F5
Yanbian, China 58 D3
Yanbu 'al Baḥr, Si. Arabia 70 F3
Yanchang, China 56 F6
Yancheng, Henan, China 56 H8
Yancheng, Jiangsu, China 57 H11
Yanchep Beach, Australia 93 F2
Yanchi, China 56 F4
Yanchuan, China 56 F6
Yanco Cr. →, Australia 95 F4
Yandicoogina, Australia 92 D2
Yandoon, Burma 67 L19
Yanfeng, China 58 E3
Yanfolila, Mali 82 C3
Yang Xian, China 56 H4
Yang-Yang, Senegal 82 B1
Yangambi, Dem. Rep. of the Congo 86 B1
Yangbi, China 58 E2
Yangcheng, China 56 G7
Yangch'ü = Taiyuan, China 56 F7
Yangchun, China 59 F8
Yanggao, China 56 D7
Yanggu, China 56 F8
Yangjiang, China 59 G8
Yangliuqing, China 57 E9
Yangon = Rangoon, Burma 67 L20
Yangping, China 59 B8
Yangpingguan, China 56 H4
Yangquan, China 56 F7
Yangshan, China 59 E9
Yangshuo, China 59 E8
Yangtse = Chang Jiang →, China 59 B13
Yangtze Kiang = Chang Jiang →, China 59 B13
Yangudi Rassa △, Ethiopia 81 E5
Yangxin, China 59 C10
Yangyang, S. Korea 57 E15
Yangyuan, China 56 D8
Yangzhong, China 59 A12
Yangzhou, China 59 A12
Yanhe, China 58 C7
Yanji, China 57 C15
Yanjin, China 58 C5
Yanjing, China 58 C2
Yankari △, Nigeria 83 D7
Yankton, U.S.A. 112 D6
Yanonge, Dem. Rep. of the Congo 86 B1
Yanqi, China 60 B3
Yanqing, China 56 D8
Yanshan, Hebei, China 57 E9
Yanshan, Jiangxi, China 59 C11
Yanshan, Yunnan, China 58 F5
Yanshou, China 57 B15
Yantabulla, Australia 95 D4
Yantai, China 57 F11
Yantarnyy, Russia 30 D6
Yanting, China 58 B5
Yantra →, Bulgaria 45 C9
Yanwa, China 58 D2
Yanyuan, China 58 D3
Yanzhou, China 56 G9
Yao Noi, Ko, Thailand 65 a
Yao Xian, China 56 G5
Yao Yai, Ko, Thailand 65 a
Yao'an, China 58 E3
Yaodu, China 58 A5
Yaoundé, Cameroon 83 E7
Yaowan, China 57 G10
Yap, Pac. Oc. 96 G5
Yapen, Indonesia 63 E9
Yapen, Selat, Indonesia 63 E9
Yapero, Indonesia 63 E9
Yappar →, Australia 94 B3
Yaqui →, Mexico 118 B2
Yar-Sale, Russia 52 C8
Yaraka, Australia 94 C3
Yaransk, Russia 34 B8
Yarbasan, Turkey 47 C10
Yare →, U.K. 15 E9
Yaremcha, Ukraine 29 B9
Yarensk, Russia 52 C5
Yarfa, Si. Arabia 80 C4
Yarí →, Colombia 124 D4
Yarkand = Shache, China 60 C2
Yarker, Canada 117 B8
Yarkhun →, Pakistan 69 A5
Yarlung Ziangbo Jiang = Brahmaputra →, Asia 69 H13
Yarmouth, Canada 105 D6
Yarmūk →, Syria 74 C4
Yaroslavl, Russia 32 D10
Yarqa, W. →, Egypt 74 F2
Yarra Yarra Lakes, Australia 93 E2
Yarram, Australia 95 F4
Yarraman, Australia 95 D5
Yarras, Australia 95 E5
Yartsevo, Sib., Russia 53 C10
Yartsevo, Smolensk, Russia 32 E7
Yarumal, Colombia 124 B3
Yasawa Group, Fiji 91 C7
Yaselda, Belarus 33 F4
Yasen, Ukraine 29 B9
Yashi, Nigeria 83 C6
Yashikera, Nigeria 83 D5
Yashkul, Russia 35 G7
Yasin, Pakistan 69 A5
Yasinovataya, Ukraine 33 H9
Yasinski, L., Canada 104 B4
Yasinya, Ukraine 29 B9
Yasothon, Thailand 64 E5
Yass, Australia 95 E4
Yāsūj, Iran 71 D6
Yataǧan, Turkey 47 D10
Yatakala, Niger 83 C5
Yates Center, U.S.A. 113 G7

Yathkyed L., Canada 103 A9
Yatsushiro, Japan 55 H5
Yatta Plateau, Kenya 86 C4
Yauco, Puerto Rico 121 d
Yavari →, Peru 124 D4
Yávaros, Mexico 118 B3
Yavatmal, India 66 J11
Yavne, Israel 74 D3
Yavoriv, Ukraine 31 J10
Yavorov = Yavoriv, Ukraine 31 J10
Yavuzeli, Turkey 72 D7
Yawatahama, Japan 55 H6
Yawri B., S. Leone 82 D2
Yaxi, China 58 D6
Yazd, Iran 71 D7
Yazd □, Iran 71 D7
Yazd-e Khvāst, Iran 71 D7
Yazıköy, Turkey 47 E9
Yazman, Pakistan 68 E4
Yazoo →, U.S.A. 113 J9
Yazoo City, U.S.A. 113 J9
Ybbs, Austria 26 C8
Ybycuí, Paraguay 126 B4
Ybytyruzú △, Paraguay 127 B4
Yding Skovhøj, Denmark 11 J3
Ye, Burma 64 E1
Ye Xian, China 56 H7
Yebyu, Burma 64 E2
Yechŏn, S. Korea 57 F15
Yecla, Spain 39 G3
Yécora, Mexico 118 B3
Yedebub Biheroch Bihereseboch na Hizboch □, Ethiopia 81 F4
Yedintsy = Edineţ, Moldova 29 B12
Yedseram →, Nigeria 83 C7
Yefremov, Russia 32 F10
Yeghegnadzor, Armenia 73 C11
Yegorlyk →, Russia 35 G5
Yegorlykskaya, Russia 35 G5
Yegoryevsk, Russia 32 E10
Yegros, Paraguay 126 B4
Yehbuah, Indonesia 63 J17
Yehuda, Midbar, Israel 74 D4
Yei, Sudan 81 G3
Yei, Nahr →, Sudan 81 F3
Yejmiadzin, Armenia 35 K7
Yekaterinburg, Russia 52 D7
Yelabuga, Russia 34 C11
Yelan, Russia 34 E6
Yelarbon, Australia 95 D5
Yelatma, Russia 34 C5
Yelets, Russia 33 F10
Yélimané, Mali 82 B2
Yelizavetgrad = Kirovohrad, Ukraine 33 H7
Yell, U.K. 13 A7
Yell Sd., U.K. 13 A7
Yellow Sea, China 57 G12
Yellowhead Pass, Canada 102 C5
Yellowknife, Canada 102 A6
Yellowknife →, Canada 102 A6
Yellowstone △, U.S.A. 108 D9
Yellowstone →, U.S.A. 112 B3
Yellowstone L., U.S.A. 108 D8
Yelnya, Russia 32 E7
Yelsk, Belarus 33 G5
Yelwa, Nigeria 83 C5
Yemen ■, Asia 75 E3
Yen Bai, Vietnam 58 G5
Yenagoa, Nigeria 83 E6
Yenakiyeve, Ukraine 33 H10
Yenakiyevo = Yenakiyeve, Ukraine 33 H10
Yenangyaung, Burma 67 J19
Yenbo = Yanbu 'al Baḥr, Si. Arabia 70 F3
Yenda, Australia 95 E4
Yende Millimou, Guinea 82 D2
Yendéré, Burkina Faso 82 C4
Yendi, Ghana 83 D4
Yéni, Niger 83 C5
Yenice, Ankara, Turkey 72 C5
Yenice, Aydın, Turkey 47 D10
Yenice, Çanakkale, Turkey 47 B9
Yenice, Edirne, Turkey 45 F10
Yenice →, Turkey 72 D6
Yenifoça, Turkey 47 C8
Yenihisar, Turkey 47 D9
Yeniköy, Bursa, Turkey 45 F13
Yeniköy, Çanakkale, Turkey 47 B8
Yeniköy, Kütahya, Turkey 47 C11
Yenipazar, Turkey 47 D10
Yenisaía, Greece 45 E8
Yenişehir, Turkey 45 F13
Yenisey →, Russia 52 B9
Yeniseysk, Russia 53 D10
Yeniseyskiy Zaliv, Russia 52 B9
Yennádhi, Greece 49 C9
Yenne, France 21 C9
Yenotayevka, Russia 35 G8
Yenyuka, Russia 53 D13
Yeo →, U.K. 15 G5
Yeo, L., Australia 93 E3
Yeo I., Canada 116 A3
Yeola, India 66 J9
Yeoryioúpolis, Greece 49 D6
Yeovil, U.K. 15 G5
Yepes, Spain 36 F7
Yeppoon, Australia 94 C5
Yeráki, Greece 46 D4
Yerbent, Turkmenistan 52 F6
Yerbogachen, Russia 53 C11
Yerevan, Armenia 35 K7
Yerington, U.S.A. 108 G4
Yerkesik, Turkey 47 D10
Yerköy, Turkey 72 C6
Yermak, Kazakhstan 52 D8
Yermo, U.S.A. 111 L10
Yeropol, Russia 53 C17
Yeropótamos →, Greece 49 D6
Yeroskipos, Cyprus 49 E11

Yershov, Russia 34 E9
Yerushalayim = Jerusalem, Israel 74 D4
Yerville, France 18 C7
Yes Tor, U.K. 15 G4
Yesan, S. Korea 57 F14
Yeşilhisar, Turkey 72 C6
Yeşilırmak →, Turkey 72 B7
Yeşilkent, Turkey 72 D7
Yeşilköy, Turkey 45 F12
Yeşilova, Turkey 47 D11
Yeşilyurt, Manisa, Turkey 47 C10
Yeşilyurt, Muğla, Turkey 47 D10
Yesnogorsk, Russia 32 E9
Yessentuki, Russia 35 H6
Yessey, Russia 53 C11
Yeste, Spain 39 G2
Yetman, Australia 95 D5
Yeu, Î. d', France 18 F4
Yevlakh = Yevlax, Azerbaijan 35 K8
Yevlax, Azerbaijan 35 K8
Yevpatoriya, Ukraine 33 K7
Yeya →, Russia 33 J10
Yeysk, Russia 33 J10
Yezd = Yazd, Iran 71 D7
Yezerishche, Belarus 32 E5
Yhati, Paraguay 126 B4
Yhú, Paraguay 127 B4
Yi →, Uruguay 126 C4
Yi 'Allaq, G., Egypt 74 E2
Yi He →, China 57 G10
Yi Xian, Hebei, China 59 C11
Yi Xian, Liaoning, China 57 D11
Yialí, Greece 47 E9
Yialiás →, Cyprus 49 D12
Yi'allaq, G., Egypt 80 A3
Yialousa, Cyprus 49 D13
Yiáltra, Greece 46 C4
Yianisádhes, Greece 49 D8
Yiannitsa, Greece 44 F6
Yibin, China 58 C5
Yichang, China 59 B8
Yicheng, Henan, China 59 B9
Yicheng, Shanxi, China 56 G6
Yichuan, China 56 F6
Yichun, Heilongjiang, China 60 B7
Yichun, Jiangxi, China 59 D10
Yidu, China 57 F10
Yidun, China 58 B2
Yifag, Ethiopia 81 E4
Yifeng, China 59 C10
Yihuang, China 59 D11
Yijun, China 56 G5
Yıldız Dağları, Turkey 45 E11
Yiliang, Yunnan, China 58 D5
Yiliang, Yunnan, China 58 D4
Yilong, China 58 B6
Yimen, China 58 E4
Yimianpo, China 57 B15
Yinchuan, China 56 E4
Yindarlgooda, L., Australia 93 F3
Ying He →, China 56 H9
Ying Xian, China 56 E7
Yingcheng, China 59 B9
Yingde, China 59 E9
Yingjiang, China 58 E1
Yingjing, China 58 C4
Yingkou, China 57 D12
Yingshan, Henan, China 59 B9
Yingshan, Hubei, China 59 B10
Yingshan, Sichuan, China 58 B6
Yingshang, China 59 A11
Yingtan, China 59 C11
Yining, China 52 E9
Yinjiang, China 58 C7
Yinmabin, Burma 67 H19
Yirba Muda, Ethiopia 81 F4
Yirga Alem, Ethiopia 81 F4
Yirol, Sudan 81 F3
Yirrkala, Australia 94 A2
Yishan, China 58 E7
Yishui, China 57 G10
Yishun, Singapore 65 d
Yitong, China 57 C13
Yiwu, China 59 C13
Yixing, China 59 B12
Yiyang, Henan, China 56 G7
Yiyang, Hunan, China 59 C9
Yiyang, Jiangxi, China 59 C11
Yizhang, China 59 E9
Yizheng, China 59 A12
Yli-Kitka, Finland 8 C23
Ylitornio, Finland 8 C20
Ylivieska, Finland 8 D21
Yngaren, Sweden 11 F10
Yoakum, U.S.A. 113 L6
Yob →, Eritrea 81 D4
Yobe □, Nigeria 83 C7
Yog Pt., Phil. 63 B6
Yogan, Togo 83 D5
Yoğuntaş, Turkey 45 E11
Yogyakarta, Indonesia 63 G14
Yogyakarta □, Indonesia 63 G14
Yoho △, Canada 102 C5
Yojoa, L. de, Honduras 120 D2
Yŏju, S. Korea 57 F14
Yok Don △, Vietnam 64 F6
Yokadouma, Cameroon 84 D2
Yoko, Cameroon 83 D7
Yokkaichi, Japan 55 G8
Yokohama, Japan 55 G9
Yokosuka, Japan 55 G9
Yokote, Japan 54 E10
Yola, Nigeria 83 D7
Yolaina, Cordillera de, Nic. 120 D3

Yoloten, Turkmenistan 71 B9
Yom →, Thailand 62 A2
Yonago, Japan 55 G6
Yonaguni-Jima, Japan 55 M1
Yŏnan, N. Korea 57 F14
Yonezawa, Japan 54 F10
Yong Peng, Malaysia 65 L4
Yong Sata, Thailand 65 J2
Yongamp'o, N. Korea 57 E13
Yong'an, China 59 E11
Yongcheng, China 56 H9
Yongchuan, China 58 C5
Yongchun, China 59 E12
Yongde, China 58 E2
Yongdeng, China 56 F2
Yongding, China 59 E11
Yŏngdŏk, S. Korea 57 F15
Yŏngdŭngpo, S. Korea 57 F14
Yongfeng, China 59 D10
Yongfu, China 58 E7
Yonghe, China 56 F6
Yŏnghŭng, N. Korea 57 E14
Yongji, China 56 G6
Yongjia, China 59 C13
Yongkang, Yunnan, China 58 E2
Yongkang, Zhejiang, China 59 C13
Yongnian, China 56 F8
Yongning, Guangxi Zhuangzu, China 58 F7
Yongning, Ningxia Huizu, China 56 E4
Yongping, China 58 E2
Yongqing, China 56 E9
Yongren, China 58 D3
Yongshan, China 58 C4
Yongsheng, China 58 D3
Yongshun, China 58 C7
Yongtai, China 59 E12
Yŏngwŏl, S. Korea 57 F15
Yongxin = Jinggangshan, China 59 D10
Yongxing, China 59 D9
Yongxiu, China 59 C10
Yongzhou, China 59 D8
Yonibana, S. Leone 82 D2
Yonkers, U.S.A. 117 F11
Yonne □, France 19 E10
Yonne →, France 19 D9
York, Australia 93 F2
York, U.K. 14 D6
York, Ala., U.S.A. 113 J10
York, Nebr., U.S.A. 112 E6
York, Pa., U.S.A. 114 F7
York, C., Australia 94 A3
York, City of □, U.K. 14 D6
York, Kap, Greenland 4 B4
York, Vale of, U.K. 14 C6
York Haven, U.S.A. 116 F8
York Sd., Australia 92 C4
Yorke Pen., Australia 95 E2
Yorkshire Dales △, U.K. 14 C5
Yorkshire Wolds, U.K. 14 C7
Yorkton, Canada 103 C8
Yorkville, U.S.A. 110 G3
Yoro, Honduras 120 C2
Yoron-Jima, Japan 55 L4
Yorosso, Mali 82 C4
Yos Sudarso, Pulau = Dolak, Pulau, Indonesia 63 F9
Yosemite △, U.S.A. 110 H7
Yosemite Village, U.S.A. 110 H7
Yoshino-Kumano △, Japan 55 H8
Yoshkar Ola, Russia 34 B8
Yŏsu, S. Korea 57 G14
Yotvata, Israel 74 F4
You Jiang →, China 58 F6
You Xian, China 59 D9
Youbou, Canada 110 B2
Youghal, Ireland 12 E4
Youghal B., Ireland 12 E4
Youkounkoun, Guinea 82 C2
Young, Australia 95 E4
Young, Canada 103 C7
Young, Uruguay 126 C4
Younghusband, L., Australia 95 E2
Younghusband Pen., Australia 95 F2
Youngstown, Canada 103 C6
Youngstown, N.Y., U.S.A. 116 C5
Youngstown, Ohio, U.S.A. 116 E4
Youngsville, U.S.A. 116 E5
Youngwood, U.S.A. 116 F5
Youxi, China 59 D12
Youyang, China 58 C7
Youyu, China 56 D7
Yozgat, Turkey 72 C6
Ypacaraí △, Paraguay 126 B4
Ypané →, Paraguay 126 A4
Yport, France 18 C7
Ypres = Ieper, Belgium 17 D2
Yreka, U.S.A. 108 F2
Yssingeaux, France 21 C8
Ystad, Sweden 11 J7
Ysyk-Köl, Kyrgyzstan 52 E8
Ythan →, U.K. 13 D7
Ytterhogdal, Sweden 10 B8
Ytyk-Kyuyel, Russia 53 C14
Yu Jiang →, China 58 F7
Yu Shan, Taiwan 59 F13
Yu Xian = Yuzhou, China 56 G7
Yu Xian, Hebei, China 56 E8
Yu Xian, Shanxi, China 56 E7
Yuan Jiang →, Hunan, China 59 C8
Yuan Jiang →, Yunnan, China 58 F4
Yuan'an, China 59 B8
Yuanjiang, Hunan, China 59 C9
Yuanjiang, Yunnan, China 58 F4
Yüanli, Taiwan 59 E13
Yüanlin, Taiwan 59 F13
Yuanling, China 59 C8
Yuanmou, China 58 E3
Yuanqu, China 56 G6
Yuanyang, Henan, China 56 G7

Yuanyang, Yunnan, China 58 F4
Yuba →, U.S.A. 110 F5
Yuba City, U.S.A. 110 F5
Yūbari, Japan 54 C10
Yubdo, Ethiopia 81 F4
Yübetsu, Japan 54 B11
Yubo, Sudan 81 F2
Yucatán □, Mexico 119 C7
Yucatán, Canal de, Caribbean 120 B2
Yucatán, Península de, Mexico 98 H11
Yucatan Basin, Cent. Amer. 98 H11
Yucatan Channel = Yucatán, Canal de, Caribbean 120 B2
Yucca, U.S.A. 111 L12
Yucca Valley, U.S.A. 111 L10
Yucheng, China 56 F9
Yuci, China 56 F7
Yudu, China 59 E10
Yuechi, China 58 B6
Yuendumu, Australia 92 D5
Yueqing, China 59 C13
Yueqing Wan, China 59 D13
Yuexi, Anhui, China 59 B11
Yuexi, Sichuan, China 58 C4
Yueyang, China 59 C9
Yugan, China 59 C11
Yugoslavia = Serbia & Montenegro ■, Europe 44 C4
Yuhuan, China 59 C13
Yühuan Dao, China 59 C13
Yujiang, China 59 C11
Yukhnov, Russia 32 E8
Yukon →, U.S.A. 100 B3
Yukon Territory □, Canada 100 B6
Yüksekova, Turkey 73 D11
Yukta, Russia 53 C11
Yukuhashi, Japan 55 H5
Yulara, Australia 93 E5
Yule →, Australia 92 D2
Yuleba, Australia 95 D4
Yuli, Nigeria 83 D7
Yuli, Taiwan 59 F13
Yulin, Guangxi Zhuangzu, China 59 F8
Yülin, Hainan, China 65 C7
Yulin, Shaanxi, China 56 E5
Yuma, Ariz., U.S.A. 111 N12
Yuma, Colo., U.S.A. 112 E3
Yuma, B. de, Dom. Rep. 121 C6
Yumbe, Uganda 86 B3
Yumbi, Dem. Rep. of the Congo 86 C2
Yumen, China 60 C4
Yumurtalık, Turkey 72 D6
Yun Gui Gaoyuan, China 58 E3
Yun Ho →, China 57 E9
Yun Ling, China 58 D2
Yun Xian, Hubei, China 59 A8
Yun Xian, Yunnan, China 58 E3
Yuna, Australia 93 E2
Yunak, Turkey 72 C4
Yunan, China 59 F8
Yuncheng, Henan, China 56 G8
Yuncheng, Shanxi, China 56 G6
Yunfu, China 59 F9
Yungas, Bolivia 124 G5
Yungay, Chile 126 D1
Yunhe, China 59 C12
Yunkai Dashan, China 59 F8
Yunlin, Taiwan 59 F13
Yunlong, China 58 E2
Yunmeng, China 59 B9
Yunnan □, China 58 E4
Yunquera de Henares, Spain 38 E1
Yunt Dağı, Turkey 47 C9
Yunta, Australia 95 E2
Yunxi, China 58 H6
Yunxiao, China 59 F11
Yuping, China 58 D7
Yupyongdong, N. Korea 57 D15
Yuqing, China 58 D6
Yuraygir △, Australia 95 D5
Yurga, Russia 52 D9
Yurimaguas, Peru 124 E3
Yurkiyka, Ukraine 29 B13
Yurubí △, Venezuela 121 D6
Yuryev-Polskiy, Russia 32 D10
Yuryevets, Russia 34 B6
Yuscarán, Honduras 120 D2
Yūsef, Bahr →, Egypt 80 B3
Yushan, China 59 C12
Yushanzhen, China 58 C7
Yushe, China 56 F7
Yushu, Jilin, China 57 B14
Yushu, Qinghai, China 60 C4
Yusufeli, Turkey 73 B9
Yutai, China 56 G9
Yutian, China 57 E9
Yuxarı Qarabağ = Nagorno-Karabakh □, Azerbaijan 70 B5
Yuxi, China 58 E4
Yuyao, China 59 B13
Yuzawa, Japan 54 E10
Yuzha, Russia 34 B6
Yuzhno-Sakhalinsk, Russia 53 E15
Yuzhnyy □, Russia 35 H5
Yuzhou, China 56 G7
Yvelines □, France 19 D8
Yverdon-les-Bains, Switz. 25 J2
Yvetot, France 18 C7
Yzeure, France 19 F10

Z

Zaanstad, Neths. 17 B4
Zāb al Kabīr →, Iraq 70 C4
Zāb aş Şaghīr →, Iraq 70 C4
Žabalj, Serbia & M. 28 E5
Žabari, Serbia & M. 44 B5
Zabarjad, Egypt 80 C4

Zabaykalsk, *Russia* 53 E12
Zabki, *Poland* 31 F8
Ząbkowice Śląskie, *Poland* ... 31 H3
Žabljak, *Serbia & M.* 44 C3
Zabłudów, *Poland* 31 F9
Žabno, *Poland* 31 H7
Zābol, *Iran* 71 D9
Zābol □, *Afghan.* 66 D5
Zābolī, *Iran* 71 E9
Zabolotiv, *Ukraine* 29 B10
Zabolottya, *Ukraine* 31 G11
Zabré, *Burkina Faso* 83 C4
Zábřeh, *Czech Rep.* 27 B9
Zabrze, *Poland* 31 H5
Zabuzhzhya, *Ukraine* 31 G10
Zabzuga, *Ghana* 83 D5
Zacapa, *Guatemala* 120 D2
Zacapu, *Mexico* 118 D4
Zacatecas, *Mexico* 118 C4
Zacatecas □, *Mexico* 118 C4
Zacatecoluca, *El Salv.* 120 D2
Zachary, *U.S.A.* 113 K9
Zachodnio-Pomorskie □, *Poland* 30 E2
Zacoalco, *Mexico* 118 C4
Zacualtipán, *Mexico* 119 C5
Zadar, *Croatia* 41 D12
Zadawa, *Nigeria* 83 C7
Zadetkyi Kyun, *Burma* 65 G2
Zadonsk, *Russia* 33 F10
Zafarqand, *Iran* 71 C7
Zafora, *Greece* 47 E8
Zafra, *Spain* 37 G4
Zagań, *Poland* 31 G2
Zagaoua, *Chad* 79 E10
Žagarė, *Lithuania* 30 B10
Zagazig, *Egypt* 80 H7
Zāgheh, *Iran* 71 C6
Zaglivérion, *Greece* 44 F7
Zagnanado, *Benin* 83 D5
Zagorá, *Greece* 46 B5
Zagorje, *Slovenia* 41 B11
Zagórów, *Poland* 31 F4
Zagórz, *Poland* 31 J9
Zagreb, *Croatia* 41 C12
Zagreb ✈ (ZAG), *Croatia* 41 C13
Zāgros, Kūhhā-ye, *Iran* 71 C6
Zagros Mts. = Zāgros, Kūhhā-ye,
    Iran 71 C6
Žagubica, *Serbia & M.* 44 B5
Zaguinaso, *Ivory C.* 82 C3
Zagyva →, *Hungary* 28 C5
Zahamena △, *Madag.* 89 B8
Zāhedān, *Fārs, Iran* 71 D7
Zāhedān, *Sīstān va Balūchestān,
    Iran* 71 D9
Zahlah, *Lebanon* 74 B4
Zahna, *Germany* 24 D8
Záhony, *Hungary* 28 B7
Zainsk, *Russia* 34 C11
Zaïre = Congo →, *Africa* 84 F2
Zaječar, *Serbia & M.* 44 C6
Zaka, *Zimbabwe* 89 C5
Zakamensk, *Russia* 53 D11
Zakarpatska □, *Ukraine* 29 B8
Zakataly = Zaqatala, *Azerbaijan* 35 K8
Zakháro, *Greece* 46 D3
Zakhodnaya Dzvina =
    Daugava →, *Latvia* 9 H21
Zākhū, *Iraq* 70 B4
Zákinthos, *Greece* 46 D2
Zákinthos □, *Greece* 46 D2
Zakopane, *Poland* 31 J6
Zakroczym, *Poland* 31 F7
Zákros, *Greece* 49 D8
Zala, *Ethiopia* 81 F4
Zala □, *Hungary* 28 D1
Zala →, *Hungary* 28 D2
Zalaegerszeg, *Hungary* 28 D1
Zalakomár, *Hungary* 28 D2
Zalalövö, *Hungary* 28 D1
Zalamea de la Serena, *Spain* .. 37 G5
Zalamea la Real, *Spain* 37 H4
Zalău, *Romania* 28 C8
Žalec, *Slovenia* 41 B12
Zaleshchiki = Zalishchyky,
    Ukraine 29 B10
Zalesye, *Russia* 30 D8
Zalew Wiślany, *Poland* 30 D6
Zalewo, *Poland* 30 E6
Zalingei, *Sudan* 79 F10
Zalishchyky, *Ukraine* 29 B10
Zama L., *Canada* 102 B5
Zambeke, *Dem. Rep. of
    the Congo* 86 B2
Zambeze →, *Africa* 87 F4
Zambezi = Zambeze →, *Africa* 87 F4
Zambezi, *Zambia* 85 G4
Zambezi △, *Zimbabwe* 87 F2
Zambézia □, *Mozam.* 87 F4
Zambia ■, *Africa* 87 F2
Zamboanga, *Phil.* 61 H5
Zambrów, *Poland* 31 F9
Zametchino, *Russia* 34 D6
Zamfara □, *Nigeria* 83 C6
Zamfara →, *Nigeria* 83 C5
Zamora, *Mexico* 118 D4
Zamora, *Spain* 36 D5
Zamora □, *Spain* 36 D5
Zamość, *Poland* 31 H10
Zamtang, *China* 58 A3
Zan, *Ghana* 83 D4
Záncara →, *Spain* 39 F1
Zandvoort, *Neths.* 17 B4
Zanesville, *U.S.A.* 116 G2
Zangābād, *Iran* 70 B5
Zangue →, *Mozam.* 87 F4
Zanjān, *Iran* 71 B6
Zanjān □, *Iran* 71 B6
Zanjān →, *Iran* 71 B6
Zannone, *Italy* 42 B6
Zante = Zákinthos, *Greece* ... 46 D2

Zanthus, *Australia* 93 F3
Zanzibar, *Tanzania* 86 D4
Zaouiet El-Kala = Bordj Omar
    Driss, *Algeria* 78 C7
Zaouiet Reggâne, *Algeria* 78 C6
Zaoyang, *China* 59 A9
Zaozhuang, *China* 57 G9
Zap Suyu = Zāb al Kabīr →, *Iraq* 70 C4
Zapadna Morava →, *Serbia & M.* 44 C5
Zapadnaya Dvina = Daugava →,
    Latvia 9 H21
Zapadnaya Dvina, *Russia* 32 D7
Západné Beskydy, *Europe* 27 B12
Zapadni Rodopi, *Bulgaria* 44 E7
Zapadočeský □, *Czech Rep.* .. 26 B6
Zapala, *Argentina* 128 D2
Zapaleri, Cerro, *Bolivia* 126 A2
Zapata, *U.S.A.* 113 M5
Zapatón →, *Spain* 37 F4
Zaporizhzhya, *Ukraine* 33 J8
Zaporozhye = Zaporizhzhya,
    Ukraine 33 J8
Zaqatala, *Azerbaijan* 35 K8
Zara, *Turkey* 70 B3
Zaragoza, *Coahuila, Mexico* .. 118 B4
Zaragoza, *Nuevo León, Mexico* 119 C5
Zaragoza, *Spain* 38 D4
Zaragoza □, *Spain* 38 D4
Zarand, *Kermān, Iran* 71 D8
Zarand, *Markazī, Iran* 71 C6
Zărandului, Munţii, *Romania* . 28 D7
Zaranj, *Afghan.* 66 D2
Zarasai, *Lithuania* 9 J22
Zárate, *Argentina* 126 C4
Zarautz, *Spain* 38 B2
Zaraysk, *Russia* 32 E10
Zard, Kūh-e, *Iran* 71 C6
Zāreh, *Iran* 71 C6
Zari, *Nigeria* 83 C7
Zaria, *Nigeria* 83 C6
Žarki, *Poland* 31 H6
Zárkon, *Greece* 46 B4
Zarneh, *Iran* 71 C6
Zărneşti, *Romania* 29 E10
Zarós, *Greece* 49 D6
Żarów, *Poland* 31 H3
Zarqā', Nahr az →, *Jordan* ... 74 C4
Zarrīn, *Iran* 71 C7
Zaruma, *Ecuador* 124 D3
Zary, *Poland* 31 G2
Zarza de Granadilla, *Spain* ... 36 E4
Zarzis, *Tunisia* 79 B8
Zas, *Spain* 36 B2
Zaskar →, *India* 69 B7
Zaskar Mts., *India* 69 C7
Zastavna, *Ukraine* 29 B10
Zastron, *S. Africa* 88 E4
Žatec, *Czech Rep.* 26 A6
Zaterechnyy, *Russia* 35 H7
Zator, *Poland* 31 J6
Zatyshshya, *Ukraine* 29 C14
Zavala, *Bos.-H.* 44 D1
Zavāreh, *Iran* 71 C7
Zave, *Zimbabwe* 89 B4
Zavetnoye, *Russia* 35 G6
Zavidovići, *Bos.-H.* 28 F3
Zavitinsk, *Russia* 53 D13
Zavodovski, I., *Antarctica* ... 5 B1
Zavolzhsk, *Russia* 34 B6
Zavolzhye, *Russia* 34 B6
Zawadzkie, *Poland* 31 H5
Zawichost, *Poland* 31 H8
Zawidów, *Poland* 31 G2
Zawiercie, *Poland* 31 H6
Zāwiyat al Bayḍā = Al Bayḍā,
    Libya 79 B10
Zāwyet Shammâs, *Egypt* 80 A2
Zāwyet Um el Rakham, *Egypt* . 80 A2
Zâwyet Ungeîla, *Egypt* 80 A2
Zāyā, *Iraq* 70 C5
Zāyandeh →, *Iran* 71 C7
Zaysan, *Kazakhstan* 52 E9
Zaysan, Oz., *Kazakhstan* 52 E9
Zayü, *China* 58 C1
Zazafotsy, *Madag.* 89 C8
Zázrivá, *Slovak Rep.* 27 B12
Zbarazh, *Ukraine* 33 H3
Zbąszyń, *Poland* 31 F2
Zbąszynek, *Poland* 31 F2
Zblewo, *Poland* 30 E5
Zbruch →, *Ukraine* 29 B11
Žďár nad Sázavou, *Czech Rep.* 26 B8
Zdolbuniv, *Ukraine* 33 G4
Ždrelo, *Serbia & M.* 44 B5
Zduńska Wola, *Poland* 31 G5
Zduny, *Poland* 31 G4
Zeballos, *Canada* 102 D3
Zebediela, *S. Africa* 89 C4
Zebila, *Ghana* 83 C4
Zeebrugge, *Belgium* 17 C3
Zeehan, *Australia* 95 G4
Zeeland □, *Neths.* 17 C3
Zeerust, *S. Africa* 88 D4
Zefat, *Israel* 74 C4
Zege, *Ethiopia* 81 E4
Zeggerene, Iracher, *Mali* 83 B5
Zégoua, *Mali* 82 C3
Zehdenick, *Germany* 24 C9
Zeil, Mt., *Australia* 92 D5
Zeila, *Somali Rep.* 75 E3
Zeist, *Neths.* 17 B5
Zeitz, *Germany* 24 D8
Zelechów, *Poland* 31 G8
Zelena, *Russia* 29 B9
Zelengora, *Bos.-H.* 44 C2
Zelenodolsk, *Russia* 34 C9
Zelenogorsk, *Russia* 32 B5
Zelenograd, *Russia* 32 D9
Zelenogradsk, *Russia* 9 J19
Zelenokumsk, *Russia* 35 H6
Železná Ruda, *Czech Rep.* 26 B6
Železnik, *Serbia & M.* 44 B4

Zelienople, *U.S.A.* 116 F4
Želiezovce, *Slovak Rep.* 27 C11
Zelina, *Croatia* 41 C13
Zell, *Baden-W., Germany* 25 H3
Zell, *Rhld.-Pfz., Germany* 25 E3
Zell am See, *Austria* 26 D5
Zella-Mehlis, *Germany* 24 E6
Zeltweg, *Austria* 26 D7
Zelów, *Poland* 31 G6
Žemaitijos △, *Lithuania* 30 B8
Zémio, *C.A.R.* 86 A2
Zempléni-hegység, *Hungary* .. 28 B6
Zemplínska šírava, *Slovak Rep.* 27 C15
Zempoala, *Mexico* 119 D5
Zemun, *Serbia & M.* 44 B4
Zengbé, *Cameroon* 83 D7
Zengcheng, *China* 59 F9
Zenica, *Bos.-H.* 28 F2
Zepče, *Bos.-H.* 28 F3
Zeraf, Bahr ez →, *Sudan* 81 F3
Zerbst, *Germany* 24 D8
Zerków, *Poland* 31 F4
Zermatt, *Switz.* 25 J3
Zernez, *Switz.* 25 J6
Zernograd, *Russia* 35 G5
Zerqan, *Albania* 44 E4
Zestaponi, *Georgia* 35 J6
Zetel, *Germany* 24 B3
Zeulenroda, *Germany* 24 E7
Zeven, *Germany* 24 B5
Zevenaar, *Neths.* 17 C6
Zévio, *Italy* 40 C8
Zeya, *Russia* 53 D13
Zeya →, *Russia* 53 D13
Zeytinbaǧi, *Turkey* 45 F12
Zeytindaǧ, *Turkey* 47 C9
Zgharta, *Lebanon* 74 A4
Zgierz, *Poland* 31 G6
Zgorzelec, *Poland* 31 G2
Zguriţa, *Moldova* 29 B13
Zhabinka, *Belarus* 31 F11
Zhabokrych, *Ukraine* 29 B13
Zhailma, *Kazakhstan* 52 D7
Zhambyl = Taraz, *Kazakhstan* 52 E8
Zhangaly, *Kazakhstan* 35 G10
Zhangaqazaly, *Kazakhstan* ... 52 E7
Zhangbei, *China* 56 D8
Zhangguangcai Ling, *China* .. 57 B15
Zhangjiakou, *China* 56 D8
Zhangping, *China* 59 E11
Zhangpu, *China* 59 E11
Zhangshu, *China* 59 C10
Zhangwu, *China* 57 C12
Zhangye, *China* 60 C5
Zhangzhou, *China* 59 E11
Zhanhua, *China* 57 F10
Zhanjiang, *China* 59 G8
Zhannetty, Ostrov, *Russia* ... 53 B16
Zhanyi, *China* 58 E4
Zhanyu, *China* 57 B12
Zhao Xian, *China* 56 F8
Zhao'an, *China* 59 F11
Zhaocheng, *China* 56 F6
Zhaojue, *China* 58 C4
Zhaoping, *China* 59 E8
Zhaoqing, *China* 59 F9
Zhaotong, *China* 58 D4
Zhaoyuan, *Heilongjiang, China* 57 B13
Zhaoyuan, *Shandong, China* . 57 F11
Zharkovsky, *Russia* 32 E7
Zhashkiv, *Ukraine* 33 H6
Zhashui, *China* 56 H5
Zhayyq →, *Kazakhstan* 52 E6
Zhdanov = Mariupol, *Ukraine* 33 J9
Zhecheng, *China* 56 G8
Zhegao, *China* 59 B11
Zhejiang □, *China* 59 C13
Zheleznodorozhnyy, *Russia* .. 30 D8
Zheleznogorsk, *Russia* 33 F8
Zheleznogorsk-Ilimskiy, *Russia* 53 D11
Zheltyye Vody = Zhovti Vody,
    Ukraine 33 H7
Zhen'an, *China* 56 H5
Zhenba, *China* 58 A6
Zhenfeng, *China* 58 E5
Zheng'an, *China* 58 C6
Zhengding, *China* 56 E8
Zhenghe, *China* 59 D12
Zhengyang, *China* 59 A10
Zhengyangguan, *China* 59 A11
Zhengzhou, *China* 56 G7
Zhenhai, *China* 59 C13
Zhenjiang, *China* 59 A12
Zhenkang, *China* 58 F2
Zhenlai, *China* 57 B12
Zhenning, *China* 58 D5
Zhenping, *Henan, China* 56 H7
Zhenping, *Shaanxi, China* ... 58 B7
Zhenxiong, *China* 58 D5
Zhenyuan, *Gansu, China* 56 G4
Zhenyuan, *Guizhou, China* .. 58 D7
Zherdevka, *Russia* 34 E5
Zherebkove, *Ukraine* 29 C14
Zherong, *China* 59 D12
Zhetiqara, *Kazakhstan* 52 D7
Zhezqazghan, *Kazakhstan* ... 52 E7
Zhicheng, *China* 59 B8
Zhidan, *China* 56 F5
Zhigansk, *Russia* 53 C13
Zhigulevsk, *Russia* 34 D9
Zhijiang, *Hubei, China* 59 B8
Zhijiang, *Hunan, China* 58 D7
Zhijin, *China* 58 D5
Zhilino, *Russia* 30 D8
Zhirnovsk, *Russia* 34 E7
Zhitomir = Zhytomyr, *Ukraine* 33 G5
Zhizdra, *Russia* 32 F8
Zhlobin, *Belarus* 33 F6
Zhmerinka = Zhmerynka,
    Ukraine 33 H5
Zhmerynka, *Ukraine* 33 H5

Zhob, *Pakistan* 68 D3
Zhob →, *Pakistan* 68 C3
Zhodino = Zhodzina, *Belarus* 32 E5
Zhodzina, *Belarus* 32 E5
Zhokhova, Ostrov, *Russia* ... 53 B16
Zhongdian, *China* 58 D2
Zhongdong, *China* 58 F6
Zhongdu, *China* 58 E7
Zhongning, *China* 56 F3
Zhongshan, *Guangdong, China* 59 F9
Zhongshan, *Guangxi Zhuangzu,
    China* 59 E8
Zhongtiao Shan, *China* 56 G6
Zhongwei, *China* 56 F3
Zhongxiang, *China* 59 B9
Zhongyang, *China* 56 F6
Zhoran y, *Ukraine* 31 G10
Zhoucun, *China* 57 F9
Zhouning, *China* 59 D12
Zhoushan, *China* 59 B14
Zhoushan Dao, *China* 59 C14
Zhouzhi, *China* 56 G5
Zhovti Vody, *Ukraine* 33 H7
Zhovtneve, *Ukraine* 33 J7
Zhovtneve, *Ukraine* 33 J7
Zhovtnevoye = Zhovtneve,
    Ukraine 33 J7
Zhu Jiang →, *China* 59 F9
Zhuanghe, *China* 57 E12
Zhucheng, *China* 57 G10
Zhugqu, *China* 56 H3
Zhuhai, *China* 59 F9
Zhuji, *China* 59 C13
Zhukova, *Russia* 32 F7
Zhumadian, *China* 56 H8
Zhuo Xian = Zhuozhou, *China* 56 E8
Zhuolu, *China* 56 D8
Zhuozhou, *China* 56 E8
Zhuozi, *China* 56 D7
Zhushan, *China* 59 A8
Zhuxi, *China* 58 A7
Zhuzhou, *China* 59 D9
Zhvanets, *Ukraine* 29 B11
Zhytomyr, *Ukraine* 33 G5
Zi Shui →, *China* 59 C9
Žiār nad Hronom, *Slovak Rep.* 27 C11
Ziārān, *Iran* 71 B6
Ziarat, *Pakistan* 68 D2
Zibo, *China* 57 F10
Zichang, *China* 56 F5
Zidarovo, *Bulgaria* 45 D11
Zidi = Wandhari, *Pakistan* ... 68 F2
Zięþice, *Poland* 31 H4
Zielona Góra, *Poland* 31 G2
Zierikzee, *Neths.* 17 C3
Ziesar, *Germany* 24 C8
Zifta, *Egypt* 80 H7
Zigey, *Chad* 79 F9
Zigong, *China* 58 C5
Ziguinchor, *Senegal* 82 C1
Zihuatanejo, *Mexico* 118 D4
Zijin, *China* 59 F10
Zile, *Turkey* 72 B6
Žilina, *Slovak Rep.* 27 B11
Žilinský □, *Slovak Rep.* 27 B12
Zillah, *Libya* 79 C9
Zillertaler Alpen, *Austria* 26 D4
Zima, *Russia* 53 D11
Zimapán, *Mexico* 119 C5
Zimba, *Zambia* 87 F2
Zimbabwe, *Zimbabwe* 87 G3
Zimbabwe ■, *Africa* 87 F3
Zimi, *S. Leone* 82 D2
Zimnicea, *Romania* 29 G10
Zimovniki, *Russia* 35 G6
Zinave □, *Mozam.* 89 C5
Zinder, *Niger* 83 C6
Zinga, *Tanzania* 87 D4
Zingaro △, *Italy* 42 D5
Zingst, *Germany* 24 A8
Ziniaré, *Burkina Faso* 83 C4
Zinnowitz, *Germany* 24 A9
Zion △, *U.S.A.* 109 H7
Zirbitzkogel, *Austria* 26 D7
Zirc, *Hungary* 28 C2
Žiri, *Slovenia* 41 B11
Žirje, *Croatia* 41 E12
Zirl, *Austria* 26 D4
Zirndorf, *Germany* 25 F6
Ziros, *Greece* 49 D8
Zirreh, Gowd-e, *Afghan.* 66 E3
Zisterdorf, *Austria* 27 C9
Zitácuaro, *Mexico* 118 D4
Žitava →, *Slovak Rep.* 27 C11
Žitište, *Serbia & M.* 28 E5
Zitong, *China* 58 B5
Zítsa, *Greece* 46 B2
Zittau, *Germany* 24 E10
Zitundo, *Mozam.* 89 D5
Živinice, *Bos.-H.* 28 F3
Ziwa Magharibi = Kagera □,
    Tanzania 86 C3
Ziway, L., *Ethiopia* 81 F4
Zixi, *China* 59 D11
Zixing, *China* 59 E9
Ziyang, *Shaanxi, China* 56 H5
Ziyang, *Sichuan, China* 58 B5
Ziyuan, *China* 59 D8
Ziyun, *China* 58 E6
Zizhong, *China* 58 C5
Zlarin, *Croatia* 41 E12
Zlatar, *Croatia* 41 B13
Zlatar, *Serbia & M.* 44 C3
Zlataritsa, *Bulgaria* 45 C9
Zlaté Moravce, *Slovak Rep.* .. 27 C11
Zlatibor, *Serbia & M.* 44 C3
Zlatitsa, *Bulgaria* 45 D8
Zlatna Panega, *Bulgaria* 45 C8
Zlatni Pyasŭtsi, *Bulgaria* 45 C12
Zlatograd, *Bulgaria* 45 E9

Zlatoust, *Russia* 52 D6
Zletovo, *Macedonia* 44 E6
Zlín, *Czech Rep.* 27 B10
Zlínský □, *Czech Rep.* 27 B10
Złocieniec, *Poland* 30 E3
Złoczew, *Poland* 31 G5
Zlot, *Serbia & M.* 44 B5
Złotoryja, *Poland* 31 G2
Złotów, *Poland* 30 E4
Zmeinogorsk, *Kazakhstan* ... 52 D9
Zmigród, *Poland* 31 G3
Zmiyev, *Ukraine* 33 H9
Znamenka = Znamyanka,
    Ukraine 33 H7
Znamensk, *Russia* 30 D8
Znamyanka, *Ukraine* 33 H7
Żnin, *Poland* 31 F4
Znojmo, *Czech Rep.* 26 C9
Zobeyrī, *Iran* 70 C5
Zobia, *Dem. Rep. of the Congo* 86 B2
Zoetermeer, *Neths.* 17 B4
Zogang, *China* 58 C1
Zogno, *Italy* 40 C6
Zogqên, *China* 58 A2
Zolochev = Zolochiv, *Ukraine* 33 H3
Zolochiv, *Ukraine* 33 H3
Zolotonosha, *Ukraine* 33 H7
Zolotyy Potik, *Ukraine* 29 B10
Zomba, *Malawi* 87 F4
Zongo, *Dem. Rep. of the Congo* 84 D3
Zonguldak, *Turkey* 72 B4
Zonqor Pt., *Malta* 49 D2
Zonza, *France* 21 G13
Zorgo, *Burkina Faso* 83 C4
Zorita, *Spain* 37 F5
Zorleni, *Romania* 29 D12
Zornitsa, *Bulgaria* 45 D10
Zorritos, *Peru* 124 D2
Zory, *Poland* 31 H5
Zorzor, *Liberia* 82 D3
Zossen, *Germany* 24 C9
Zou Xiang, *China* 56 G9
Zouan-Hounien, *Ivory C.* 82 D3
Zouar, *Chad* 79 D9
Zouérate = Zouîrât, *Mauritania* 78 D3
Zouîrât, *Mauritania* 78 D3
Zourika, *Niger* 83 B6
Zourma, *Burkina Faso* 83 C4
Zoutkamp, *Neths.* 17 A6
Zrenjanin, *Serbia & M.* 28 E5
Zuarungu, *Ghana* 83 C4
Zuba, *Nigeria* 83 D6
Zubayr, *Yemen* 81 D5
Zubtsov, *Russia* 32 D8
Zuénoula, *Ivory C.* 82 D3
Zuera, *Spain* 38 D4
Žufār, *Oman* 75 D5
Zug, *Switz.* 25 H4
Zugersee, *Switz.* 25 H4
Zugspitze, *Germany* 25 H6
Zuid-Holland □, *Neths.* 17 C4
Zuidbeveland, *Neths.* 17 C3
Zuidhorn, *Neths.* 17 A6
Zújar, *Spain* 37 H8
Zújar →, *Spain* 37 G5
Zukowo, *Poland* 30 D5
Zula, *Eritrea* 81 D4
Zülpich, *Germany* 24 E2
Zumaia, *Spain* 38 B2
Zumárraga, *Spain* 38 B2
Zumbo, *Mozam.* 87 F3
Zummo, *Nigeria* 83 D7
Zumpango, *Mexico* 119 D5
Zungeru, *Nigeria* 83 D6
Zunhua, *China* 57 D9
Zuni, *U.S.A.* 109 J9
Zunyi, *China* 58 D6
Zuozhou, *China* 58 F6
Zuozhou, *China* 58 F6
Zuoz, *Switz.* 25 J6
Zuo Jiang →, *China* 58 F6
Županja, *Croatia* 28 E3
Žur, *Serbia & M.* 44 D4
Zurbātiyah, *Iraq* 70 C5
Zürich, *Switz.* 25 H4
Zürich □, *Switz.* 25 H4
Zürichsee, *Switz.* 25 H4
Zuromin, *Poland* 31 E6
Žut, *Croatia* 41 E12
Zutphen, *Neths.* 17 B6
Zuurberg △, *S. Africa* 88 E4
Zuwārah, *Libya* 79 B8
Žužan, *Iran* 71 C8
Žužemberk, *Slovenia* 41 C11
Zvenigorodka = Zvenyhorodka,
    Ukraine 33 H6
Zvenyhorodka, *Ukraine* 33 H6
Zverinogolovskoye, *Russia* .. 52 D7
Zvezdets, *Bulgaria* 45 D11
Zvishavane, *Zimbabwe* 87 G3
Zvolen, *Slovak Rep.* 27 C12
Zvonce, *Serbia & M.* 44 D6
Zvornik, *Bos.-H.* 28 F4
Zwedru = Tchien, *Liberia* ... 82 D3
Zweibrücken, *Germany* 25 F3
Zwelitsha, *S. Africa* 85 L5
Zwenkau, *Germany* 24 D8
Zwettl, *Austria* 26 C8
Zwickau, *Germany* 24 E8
Zwierzyniec, *Poland* 31 H9
Zwiesel, *Germany* 25 F9
Zwoleń, *Poland* 31 G8
Zwolle, *Neths.* 17 B6
Zwolle, *U.S.A.* 113 K8
Zychlin, *Poland* 31 F6
Żyrardów, *Poland* 31 F7
Zyryan = Zyryanka,
    Kazakhstan 52 E9
Zyryanka, *Russia* 53 C16
Zyryanovsk = Zyryan,
    Kazakhstan 52 E9
Żywiec, *Poland* 31 J6
Zyyi, *Cyprus* 49 E12

KEY TO EUROPEAN MAP PAGES

Large scale maps
(>1:2 500 000)

Medium scale maps
(1:2 800 000 – 1:9 900 000)

Small scale maps
(<1:10 000 000)

8 ICELAND

Arctic Circle

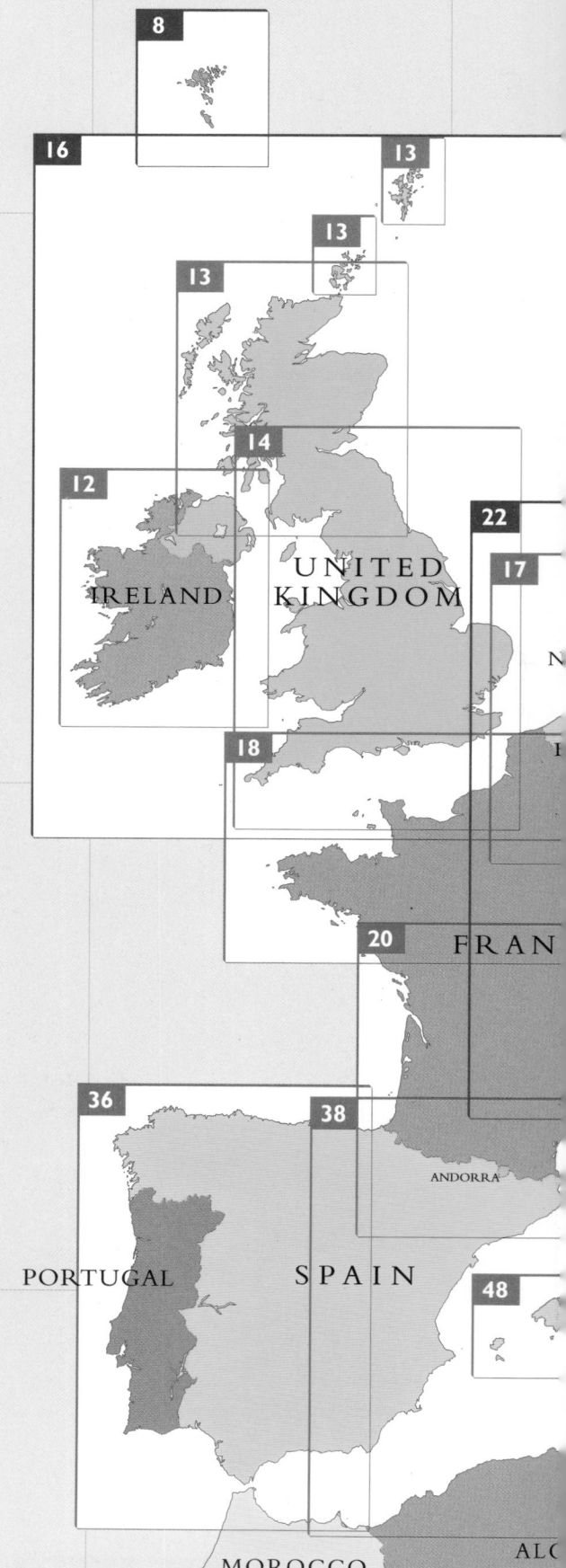

WORLD COUNTRY INDEX

Country	Page	Country	Page	Country	Page
Afghanistan	66	**G**ermany	24–25	**P**akistan	66, 68
Albania	44	Ghana	82–83	Panama	120
Algeria	78	Greece	44–47	Papua New Guinea	96
Angola	84–85	Greenland	4	Paraguay	126–127
Argentina	126, 128	Guadeloupe	120	Peru	124
Armenia	73	Guatemala	120	Philippines	61
Australia	92–95	Guinea	82	Poland	30–31
Austria	26–27	Guinea-Bissau	82	Portugal	36–37
Azerbaijan	73	Guyana	124	Puerto Rico	121
Bahamas	120–121	**H**aiti	121	**Q**atar	71
Bahrain	71	Honduras	120		
Bangladesh	67	Hungary	28	**R**omania	28–29
Barbados	121			Russia	32–35, 52–53
Belarus	32–33	**I**celand	8	Rwanda	86
Belgium	17	India	66–69		
Belize	120	Indonesia	62–63	**S**t. Lucia	121
Benin	83	Iran	70–71, 73	Samoa	91
Bhutan	67	Iraq	70–71, 73	Saudi Arabia	70–71, 75
Bolivia	124	Irish Republic	12	Scotland	13
Bosnia-Herzegovina	41, 44	Israel	74	Senegal	82
Botswana	88	Italy	40–43	Serbia and Montenegro	28, 44
Brazil	124–125, 127	Ivory Coast	82	Sierra Leone	82
Brunei	62			Singapore	65
Bulgaria	44–45	**J**amaica	120	Slovak Republic	27
Burkina Faso	82–83	Japan	54–55	Slovenia	41
Burma (Myanmar)	67	Jordan	74	Solomon Is.	96
Burundi	86			Somali Republic	75
		Kazakhstan	52	South Africa	88–89
Cambodia	64–65	Kenya	86	Spain	36–39
Canary Is.	48	Korea, North	57	Sri Lanka	66
Cameroon	83, 84	Korea, South	57	Sudan	80–81
Canada	100–105	Kuwait	70–71	Suriname	124–125
Central African Republic	84	Kyrgyzstan	52	Swaziland	89
Chad	79			Sweden	8–9
Chile	126–127, 128	**L**aos	64	Switzerland	25
China	56–60	Latvia	32	Syria	70, 72–73
Colombia	124	Lebanon	74		
Congo	84	Lesotho	89	**T**aiwan	59
Congo, Dem. Rep.		Liberia	82	Tajikistan	52
of the	84–85, 86–87	Libya	79	Tanzania	86–87
Costa Rica	120	Lithuania	32	Thailand	64–65
Croatia	41	Luxembourg	17	Togo	83
Cuba	120–121			Tonga	91
Cyprus	49	**M**acedonia	44	Trinidad and Tobago	125
Czech Republic	26–27	Madagascar	89	Tunisia	78–79
		Malawi	87	Turkey	72–73
Denmark	11	Malaysia	62–63, 65	Turkmenistan	52
Djibouti	81	Mali	78, 82–83		
Dominican Republic	121	Malta	49	**U**ganda	86
		Martinique	120	Ukraine	33
East Timor	63	Mauritania	78, 82	United Arab Emirates	75
Ecuador	124	Mexico	118–119	United Kingdom	12–16
Egypt	80	Moldova	29	USA	106–117
El Salvador	120	Mongolia	60	Uruguay	126–127
England	14–15	Morocco	78	Uzbekistan	52
Equatorial Guinea	84	Mozambique	87, 89		
Eritrea	80–81			**V**anuatu	96
Estonia	32	**N**amibia	88	Venezuela	124
Ethiopia	75, 81	Nepal	69	Vietnam	64–65
		Netherlands	17		
Fiji	91	New Zealand	91	**W**ales	14–15
Finland	8–9	Nicaragua	120		
France	18–21	Niger	78–79, 83	**Y**emen	75
French Guiana	125	Nigeria	83		
		Northern Ireland	12	**Z**ambia	85, 87
Gabon	84	Norway	8–9	Zimbabwe	87
Gambia	82				
Georgia	35	**O**man	75		

8

16 **13**

13

13

14

12 IRELAND

UNITED KINGDOM

22

17 N

18

20 FRAN

36 **38**

ANDORRA

PORTUGAL SPAIN **48**

MOROCCO AL